NEWSGATHERING AND THE LAW

Second Edition

C. Thomas Dienes
Lee Levine
Robert C. Lind

LEXIS® LAW PUBLISHING
Charlottesville, Virginia

COPYRIGHT © 1999
BY
MATTHEW BENDER & COMPANY, INC.

COPYRIGHT © 1997
BY
MICHIE
A Division of Reed Elsevier Inc.

Library of Congress Catalog Card No. 99-67232
ISBN 0-327-04972-3

All rights reserved.

DEDICATIONS

From C.T.D. to his wife Peggy.

From L.L. to his family, Shelley, Sara and Hilary.

From R.C.L. to his parents, Lorraine and Spencer Swanson; and Paul Nussbaum, a country lawyer.

TABLE OF CONTENTS

	Page
About the Authors	xxi
Preface to the Second Edition	xxiiii
Acknowledgments for the First Edition	xxv

Chapter 1

INTRODUCTION

§ 1-1. The Principle of Freedom of Expression 1
§ 1-2. The Rationale of Preference 5
    § 1-2(a). The Marketplace Model 5
    § 1-2(b). The Democratic Model 7
    § 1-2(c). The Liberty Model 8
§ 1-3. The Right to Acquire Information and the Right to Know 9
§ 1-4. Freedom of the Press 11
    § 1-4(a). The Press Clause 11
    § 1-4(b). Press as Agent or Surrogate 13
§ 1-5. Newsgathering and the Right of Access 14

Chapter 2

ACCESS TO JUDICIAL PROCEEDINGS: THE CONSTITUTIONAL FOUNDATIONS

§ 2-1. The Constitutional Law of Fair Trial/Free Press 17
    § 2-1(a). Background 17
    § 2-1(b). The *Sheppard* Mandate 20
    § 2-1(c). Criminal Sanctions Against the Media 23
    § 2-1(d). Restraining Publication 27
§ 2-2. The Constitutional Right of Access in the Supreme Court 35
    § 2-2(a). Perspectives on the Constitutional Right of Access 35
    § 2-2(b). *Gannett Co. v. DePasquale* 37
    § 2-2(c). *Richmond Newspapers, Inc. v. Virginia* 43
    § 2-2(d). *Globe Newspaper Co. v. Superior Court* 48
    § 2-2(e). *Press-Enterprise Co. v. Superior Court (Press-Enterprise I)* 52
    § 2-2(f). *Press-Enterprise Co. v. Superior Court (Press-Enterprise II)* 55
    § 2-2(g). *El Vocero de Puerto Rico v. Puerto Rico* 58
    § 2-2(h). The Supreme Court Doctrine 59
§ 2-3. Procedural Requirements 62
§ 2-4. Justice Department Guidelines 68

TABLE OF CONTENTS

Chapter 3

ACCESS TO JUDICIAL PROCEEDINGS: THE LOWER COURTS

Page

§ 3-1. Criminal Proceedings 71
   § 3-1(a). Pretrial Proceedings — In General 71
      § 3-1(a)(1). Bail and Detention Hearings 81
      § 3-1(a)(2). Preliminary Hearings 84
      § 3-1(a)(3). Grand Jury Proceedings 88
      § 3-1(a)(4). Suppression Hearings 94
      § 3-1(a)(5). Competency Hearings 100
      § 3-1(a)(6). Plea Hearings 102
   § 3-1(b). Voir Dire Proceedings 104
   § 3-1(c). Criminal Trial Proceedings 109
   § 3-1(d). Post-Trial Proceedings 116
   § 3-1(e). Military Courts 120
§ 3-2. Civil Proceedings 122
   § 3-2(a). Establishing the Access Right 122
   § 3-2(b). Privacy Interests 128
   § 3-2(c). Trade Secrets 131
   § 3-2(d). Settlement Proceedings 133
   § 3-2(e). Depositions 134
§ 3-3. Juvenile Proceedings 136
   § 3-3(a). Juvenile Delinquency 136
   § 3-3(b). Abuse, Neglect, Dependency, and Custody Proceedings 149

Chapter 4

CAMERAS IN THE COURTROOM

§ 4-1. Supreme Court Precedent 157
§ 4-2. Federal Court Proceedings 163
   § 4-2(a). Constitutional Challenges and Waiver 163
   § 4-2(b). Changing the Rules 168
§ 4-3. State Court Proceedings 170

Chapter 5

ACCESS TO JUDICIAL RECORDS: CRIMINAL PROCEEDINGS

§ 5-1. Sources of the Access Right 179
§ 5-2. Records of Criminal Proceedings 186

TABLE OF CONTENTS

	Page
§ 5-2(a). Pretrial Records — In General	186
§ 5-2(a)(1). Wiretap Records	192
§ 5-2(a)(2). Search Warrants	195
§ 5-2(a)(3). Grand Jury Records	200
§ 5-2(a)(4). Information and Indictment	210
§ 5-2(a)(5). Discovery Documents	212
§ 5-2(a)(6). Preliminary Hearings	215
§ 5-2(a)(7). Suppression Hearing Records	218
§ 5-2(a)(8). Bail and Detention Records	220
§ 5-2(a)(9). Plea Agreements	222
§ 5-2(b). Trial Records	224
§ 5-2(c). Jury Records	234
§ 5-2(d). Post-Trial Records	240
§ 5-2(e). Criminal Justice Act Vouchers	245
§ 5-2(f). Military Courts	249

Chapter 6

ACCESS TO JUDICIAL RECORDS: CIVIL PROCEEDINGS

§ 6-1. Records in Civil Proceedings	251
§ 6-1(a). Discovery Materials	251
§ 6-1(a)(1). Background	251
§ 6-1(a)(2). *Seattle Times Co. v. Rhinehart*	256
§ 6-1(a)(3). Unfiled Discovery Materials	258
§ 6-1(a)(4). Filed Discovery Materials	261
§ 6-1(a)(5). Competing Interests	266
§ 6-1(a)(6). Law Reform	272
§ 6-1(b). Settlement Agreements	274
§ 6-1(c). Court Files	282
§ 6-1(c)(1). Pretrial Motions, Records, and Pleadings	286
§ 6-1(c)(2). Transcripts of Judicial Proceedings	290
§ 6-1(d). Other Civil Court Records	292
§ 6-2. Juvenile Records	294
§ 6-2(a). Transcripts and Records of Delinquency Proceedings	294
§ 6-2(b). Other Juvenile Records	297

Chapter 7

ACCESS TO PARTICIPANTS IN THE JUDICIAL PROCESS

§ 7-1. Participants in the Judicial Process Generally	299
§ 7-2. Attorneys	311

TABLE OF CONTENTS

Page

§ 7-3. Jurors 318
§ 7-4. Checkbook Journalism..326

Chapter 8

ACCESS TO PUBLIC PLACES AND EVENTS

§ 8-1. Prisons and Prisoners..331
§ 8-2. Executions..340
§ 8-3. Disaster, Accident and Crime Scenes.......................................345
§ 8-4. Voters and Polling Places 348
§ 8-5. Military Operations...351

Chapter 9

ACCESS TO THE EXECUTIVE AND LEGISLATIVE BRANCHES

§ 9-1. Constitutional Overview...358
§ 9-2. Nonstatutory Access to Executive Events 360
  § 9-2(a). Issuance of Press Credentials 362
  § 9-2(b). Discriminatory Access 363
§ 9-3. Non-Statutory Access to Legislative Proceedings...................366
§ 9-4. Non-Statutory Access to Administrative Proceedings.............368
§ 9-5. Statutory Access to Federal Government Meetings.................369
  § 9-5(a). Government in the Sunshine Act......................................369
    § 9-5(a)(1). Introduction 369
    § 9-5(a)(2). Agencies Subject to the Act.....................................370
    § 9-5(a)(3). Definition of "Meeting"..372
    § 9-5(a)(4). Notice of Meetings 373
    § 9-5(a)(5). Access to Meetings 374
    § 9-5(a)(6). Access to Meeting Transcripts and Tapes 374
    § 9-5(a)(7). Procedures to Close Meetings.................................375
    § 9-5(a)(8). Exemptions 376
      § 9-5(a)(8)(A). Exemption 1: National Security 377
      § 9-5(a)(8)(B). Exemption 2: Internal Agency Personnel Rules............377
      § 9-5(a)(8)(C). Exemption 3: Disclosure Prohibited by Other Federal Statutes..378
      § 9-5(a)(8)(D). Exemption 4: Trade Secrets and Confidential Commercial Information 378
      § 9-5(a)(8)(E). Exemption 5: Accusation of a Crime or Formal Censure...378
      § 9-5(a)(8)(F). Exemption 6: Personal Privacy 379

TABLE OF CONTENTS

Page

§ 9-5(a)(8)(G). Exemption 7: Law Enforcement Investigations 379
§ 9-5(a)(8)(H). Exemption 8: Financial Institutions 380
§ 9-5(a)(8)(I). Exemption 9: Premature Disclosure of Information 380
§ 9-5(a)(8)(J). Exemption 10: Agency Participation in Civil Actions
    or Proceedings 381
§ 9-5(a)(9). Challenges to Closed Meetings 382
§ 9-5(a)(9)(A). Challenges Prior to Commencement of the Meeting 382
§ 9-5(a)(9)(B). Post-Meeting Challenges 383
§ 9-5(b). Federal Advisory Committee Act 383
§ 9-5(b)(1). Introduction 383
§ 9-5(b)(2). Definition of "Advisory Committee" 384
§ 9-5(b)(3). Meetings 388
§ 9-5(b)(4). Notice of Meetings 388
§ 9-5(b)(5). Procedures to Close Meetings 389
§ 9-5(b)(6). Public Access to Meetings 390
§ 9-5(b)(7). Challenges to Closed Meetings 390
§ 9-6. Statutory Access to Meetings of State and Local Government 391
§ 9-6(a). Introduction 391
§ 9-6(b). Entities Subject to Open Meeting Laws 392
§ 9-6(c). Meetings Subject to Open Meeting Laws 395
§ 9-6(d). Notice Requirements 397
§ 9-6(e). Access to Meetings 400
§ 9-6(f). Access to Minutes, Transcripts, and Tapes 402
§ 9-6(g). Procedures 403
§ 9-6(h). Exemptions 404
§ 9-6(h)(1). Personnel Matters 405
§ 9-6(h)(2). Disclosure Prohibited by Other Laws 405
§ 9-6(h)(3). Confidential Financial and Commercial Information 406
§ 9-6(h)(4). Invasion of Personal Privacy or Injury to Reputation 407
§ 9-6(h)(5). Law Enforcement and Public Safety Matters 407
§ 9-6(h)(6). Civil Litigation Matters 408
§ 9-6(i). Categories of Meetings 408
§ 9-6(i)(1). Personnel Matters 408
§ 9-6(i)(1)(A). Interviews for Employment 408
§ 9-6(i)(1)(B). Performance Reviews 409
§ 9-6(i)(1)(C). Disciplinary Matters 410
§ 9-6(i)(1)(D). Employer-Employee Negotiations and Collective
    Bargaining 410
§ 9-6(i)(2). Probation and Parole Boards 411
§ 9-6(i)(3). Medical or Psychiatric Matters 411
§ 9-6(i)(4). Student Information 412

TABLE OF CONTENTS

	Page
§ 9-6(i)(5). Matters Involving Public Assistance	412
§ 9-6(i)(6). Professional Licensing and Disciplinary Proceedings	412
§ 9-6(j). Challenges to Improperly Noticed or Closed Meetings	413

Chapter 10

ACCESS TO FEDERAL GOVERNMENT RECORDS

§ 10-1. Introduction	417
§ 10-2. The Freedom of Information Act	418
§ 10-2(a). Introduction	418
§ 10-2(b). Obtaining Information	419
§ 10-2(b)(1). Records	419
§ 10-2(b)(2). Organizations	421
§ 10-2(b)(3). Procedures	422
§ 10-2(b)(4). Limitations on Agency Response Time	424
§ 10-2(b)(5). Fees	425
§ 10-2(c). Exemptions	426
§ 10-2(c)(1). Introduction	426
§ 10-2(c)(2). Exemption 1: National Security	427
§ 10-2(c)(3). Exemption 2: Internal Agency Personnel Rules	432
§ 10-2(c)(4). Exemption 3: Disclosure Forbidden by Other Federal Statutes	433
§ 10-2(c)(5). Exemption 4: Trade Secrets and Confidential Commercial Information	435
§ 10-2(c)(6). Exemption 5: Internal Agency Memoranda and Policy Discussions	437
§ 10-2(c)(7). Exemption 6: Personal Privacy	440
§ 10-2(c)(8). Exemption 7: Law Enforcement Investigations	443
§ 10-2(c)(8)(A). Exemption 7(A)	445
§ 10-2(c)(8)(B). Exemption 7(B)	445
§ 10-2(c)(8)(C). Exemption 7(C)	446
§ 10-2(c)(8)(D). Exemption 7(D)	447
§ 10-2(c)(8)(E). Exemption 7(E)	448
§ 10-2(c)(8)(F). Exemption 7(F)	449
§ 10-2(c)(9). Exemption 8: Financial Institutions	449
§ 10-2(c)(10). Exemption 9: Oil and Gas Wells	450
§ 10-2(d). Exclusions	451
§ 10-2(d)(1). Exclusion (c)(1)	451
§ 10-2(d)(2). Exclusion (c)(2)	452
§ 10-2(d)(3). Exclusion (c)(3)	452
§ 10-2(e). Segregation of Exempt Material	453

TABLE OF CONTENTS

Page

§ 10-2(f). Reverse FOIA Suits 453
§ 10-2(g). Administrative Appeals 454
§ 10-2(h). Litigation 455
§ 10-3. Access to Records Under the Federal Advisory Committee Act 459
  § 10-3(a). Introduction 459
  § 10-3(b). Records 459
  § 10-3(c). Procedures 459

Chapter 11

ACCESS TO STATE GOVERNMENT RECORDS

§ 11-1. Introduction 462
§ 11-2. Records 464
§ 11-3. Organizations 467
  § 11-3(a). Executive Branch 467
  § 11-3(b). Legislative Branch 468
  § 11-3(c). Judicial Branch 469
  § 11-3(d). Advisory Committees 469
  § 11-3(e). Nongovernmental Organizations 469
§ 11-4. Procedures 470
§ 11-5. Exemptions from Disclosure 473
  § 11-5(a). Statutory Exemptions 473
    § 11-5(a)(1). Internal Agency Personnel Rules and Practices 474
    § 11-5(a)(2). Disclosures Forbidden by Other Statutes 475
    § 11-5(a)(3). Trade Secrets and Certain Financial Information 475
    § 11-5(a)(4). Inter-Agency and Intra-Agency Memoranda 476
    § 11-5(a)(5). Disclosures Constituting an Unwarranted Invasion of
       Privacy 478
    § 11-5(a)(6). Law Enforcement Records 480
    § 11-5(a)(7). Financial Institution Records 481
    § 11-5(a)(8). Geological Information Relating to Oil and Gas Wells 482
  § 11-5(b). Other Statutory Exemptions 483
  § 11-5(c). Common Law Exemptions 483
  § 11-5(d). Waiver of Exemptions 484
§ 11-6. Segregation of Exempt Material 485
§ 11-7. Categories of Records 486
  § 11-7(a). Personnel Records 486
    § 11-7(a)(1). Applications for Employment 487
    § 11-7(a)(2). Salary Information 488
    § 11-7(a)(3). Disciplinary Records 488
    § 11-7(a)(4). Records of Labor Negotiations 489

TABLE OF CONTENTS

	Page
§ 11-7(a)(5). Promotional Examinations	490
§ 11-7(b). Police Records	491
§ 11-7(b)(1). Arrest and Incident Reports	491
§ 11-7(b)(2). Police Blotter	493
§ 11-7(b)(3). Investigatory Records	493
§ 11-7(b)(3)(A). Active Files	493
§ 11-7(b)(3)(B). Closed Files	495
§ 11-7(b)(4). Rap Sheets and Other Compilations of Criminal Histories	495
§ 11-7(b)(5). Victim Information	496
§ 11-7(b)(6). Confessions	497
§ 11-7(b)(7). Confidential Informants	497
§ 11-7(b)(8). 911 Tapes	497
§ 11-7(b)(9). Police Investigatory Techniques	498
§ 11-7(b)(10). Accident Reports	498
§ 11-7(c). Probation and Parole Reports	499
§ 11-7(d). Coroner Reports, Autopsy Reports, and Photographs	499
§ 11-7(e). Medical Records	500
§ 11-7(f). Financial Information	501
§ 11-7(f)(1). Business Records	501
§ 11-7(f)(2). Financial Data	502
§ 11-7(f)(3). Bank Records	503
§ 11-7(f)(4). Contract Proposals and Bids	504
§ 11-7(f)(5). Real Estate Appraisals	505
§ 11-7(f)(6). Audits of Public Offices	506
§ 11-7(g). Educational Records	506
§ 11-7(h). Election Records	507
§ 11-7(i). Trade Secrets and Proprietary Information	508
§ 11-7(j). Vital Statistics	508
§ 11-7(k). Motor Vehicle Records	509
§ 11-7(*l*). Public Utility Records	512
§ 11-7(m). Litigation Records	513
§ 11-8. Administrative Appeals	515
§ 11-9. Litigation	516

Chapter 12

NEWSGATHERING IN NONGOVERNMENTAL PLACES

§ 12-1. Introduction	519
§ 12-2. Public Places	520
§ 12-2(a). The Public Street	520

TABLE OF CONTENTS

Page

§ 12-2(b). Public View 529
§ 12-3. Crime and Disaster Scenes 533
§ 12-4. Private Property 538
    § 12-4(a). The Home 538
    § 12-4(b). Public Institutions 554
    § 12-4(c). Private Businesses 556
        § 12-4(c)(1). Restaurants and Bars..557
        § 12-4(c)(2). Public Areas Generally 559
        § 12-4(c)(3). Private Areas Generally 563
§ 12-5. Accompanying Authorized Individuals 578
§ 12-6. Consent: Special Issues..583
    § 12-6(a). Children and the Mentally Impaired............................583
    § 12-6(b). Inmates 585

Chapter 13

THE MEANS OF NEWSGATHERING

§ 13-1. Introduction..590
§ 13-2. Misrepresentation and Impersonation..................................591
    § 13-2(a). Misrepresentation in Newsgathering...........................591
    § 13-2(b). Impersonation in Newsgathering 594
§ 13-3. Theft, Conversion, Stolen Documents and Criminal Conduct 602
    § 13-3(a). Constitutional Overview...602
    § 13-3(b). Civil Liability 610
    § 13-3(c). Criminal Liability 617
        § 13-3(c)(1). Criminal Trespass 619
        § 13-3(c)(2). Criminal Harassment 621
        § 13-3(c)(3). Disorderly Conduct...624
        § 13-3(c)(4). Impersonation of a Public Official........................626
        § 13-3(c)(5). Theft of Government Property..............................627
        § 13-3(c)(6). Mail Fraud 629
        § 13-3(c)(7). Wire Fraud...630
        § 13-3(c)(8). Receiving Purloined Documents or Other Property 632
            § 13-3(c)(8)(A). Receipt of Stolen Property 632
            § 13-3(c)(8)(B). Interstate Transportation of Stolen Property 634
        § 13-3(c)(9). Federal Government Secrets and Espionage Statutes...........635
            § 13-3(c)(9)(A). The Pentagon Papers Case 637
            § 13-3(c)(9)(B). Subsequent cases 638
§ 13-4. Sources and Interview Subjects 642
    § 13-4(a). Breach of Contract and Promissory Estoppel..............643

TABLE OF CONTENTS

	Page
§ 13-4(a)(1). Judicial Pronouncements Prior to *Cohen v. Cowles Media*	644
§ 13-4(a)(1)(A). The Defamation and Privacy Context	644
§ 13-4(a)(1)(B). The National Security Context	647
§ 13-4(a)(2). *Cohen v. Cowles Media Co.*	649
§ 13-4(a)(2)(A). The Trial Court Proceedings	651
§ 13-4(a)(2)(B). The Minnesota Appellate Courts — Round 1	652
§ 13-4(a)(2)(C). The Supreme Court	654
§ 13-4(a)(2)(D). The Minnesota Appellate Courts — Round 2	657
§ 13-4(a)(3). *Cohen*-Inspired and Related Causes of Action	658
§ 13-4(a)(3)(A). The New York and Minnesota Experiences	658
§ 13-4(a)(3)(A)(i). The New York Cases	658
§ 13-4(a)(3)(A)(ii). *Ruzicka v. Conde Nast Publications*	661
§ 13-4(a)(3)(B). Other Post-*Cohen* Cases	665
§ 13-4(a)(4). Paying for News	668
§ 13-4(b). The Ambush Interview	668
§ 13-4(c). Interference with Contract	671
§ 13-5. Stake Outs	675
§ 13-6. Communications in the Newsgathering Process	678
§ 13-7. Audio Recording	680
§ 13-7(a). Federal Law	680
§ 13-7(a)(1). Fourth Amendment Considerations	680
§ 13-7(a)(2). Federal Statutes	682
§ 13-7(a)(2)(A). Federal Wiretap Act	682
§ 13-7(a)(2)(A)(i). Prohibited Conduct	682
§ 13-7(a)(2)(A)(ii). Restricted Equipment	688
§ 13-7(a)(2)(A)(iii). The Qualified One-Party Consent Exception	689
§ 13-7(a)(2)(A)(iv). Sanctions and Remedies	691
§ 13-7(a)(2)(B). Federal Communications Act	692
§ 13-7(a)(2)(C). Federal Communications Commission Regulations	693
§ 13-7(b). State Law	694
§ 13-7(b)(1). Introduction	694
§ 13-7(b)(2). Consensual Monitoring Jurisdictions	696
§ 13-7(b)(3). All-Party Consent Jurisdictions	697
§ 13-7(b)(4). Exceptions	699
§ 13-7(b)(4)(A). Inadvertent Interceptions of Communications	699
§ 13-7(b)(4)(B). Communications in Public Places	699
§ 13-7(b)(4)(C). Communications on Business Premises	701
§ 13-7(b)(4)(D). Unprotected Subject Matter	702
§ 13-7(b)(4)(E). Use of Unrestricted Equipment	702
§ 13-7(b)(4)(F). Law Enforcement Monitoring	703

TABLE OF CONTENTS

Page

§ 13-7(b)(4)(G). Monitoring of Emergency Communications 704
§ 13-7(b)(5). Sanctions and Remedies 704
§ 13-7(c). Common Law 704
§ 13-8. Hidden Cameras 710
§ 13-9. Unauthorized Access to Computer Systems 717
§ 13-9(a). Federal Law 717
§ 13-9(b). State Law 717

Chapter 14

EVOLUTION OF THE JOURNALISTS' PRIVILEGE

§ 14-1. The Privilege at Early Common Law 720
§ 14-2. The Constitutional Privilege: The Early Cases 722
§ 14-3. *Branzburg v. Hayes*: The Consolidated Cases 726
§ 14-4. *Branzburg v. Hayes* 729
§ 14-4(a). The Opinion of the Court 730
§ 14-4(b). Justice Powell's Concurring Opinion 735
§ 14-4(c). Justice Stewart's Dissenting Opinion 736
§ 14-5. *Branzburg* in The Supreme Court 738
§ 14-5(a). The Prison Access Cases 739
§ 14-5(b). The Privilege Cases 741
§ 14-5(c). The Incidental Restraint Cases 746
§ 14-5(d). The Court Closure Cases 749
§ 14-5(e). The *McIntyre* Decision 751
§ 14-5(f). The Chambers Opinions 753
§ 14-6. *Branzburg* in The Lower Courts 757
§ 14-6(a). The Second Circuit Approach 757
§ 14-6(b). The Sixth Circuit Approach 763

Chapter 15

STATE SHIELD LAWS AND FEDERAL CODIFICATIONS

§ 15-1. Introduction 768
§ 15-2. State Shield Laws 771
§ 15-2(a). Constitutionality 771
§ 15-2(b). Recipients of Protection 772
§ 15-2(b)(1). Definitional Issues 772
§ 15-2(b)(2). Standing Issues 775
§ 15-2(c). Proceedings Covered 776
§ 15-2(c)(1). Criminal Proceedings 777
§ 15-2(c)(2). Civil Proceedings 782

TABLE OF CONTENTS

	Page
§ 15-2(c)(2)(A). Third-Party Proceedings	782
§ 15-2(c)(2)(B). The Press as a Party	784
§ 15-2(c)(2)(C). Non-Judicial Proceedings	789
§ 15-2(d). Scope of Protection	790
§ 15-2(d)(1). Sources of Information	790
§ 15-2(d)(2). Confidential Information	793
§ 15-2(d)(3). Nonconfidential Information	794
§ 15-2(d)(3)(A). Nonconfidential Sources	794
§ 15-2(d)(3)(B). Eyewitness Testimony	795
§ 15-2(d)(3)(C). Unpublished Information	797
§ 15-2(d)(3)(D). Editorial Process Materials	800
§ 15-2(d)(3)(E). Published Information	801
§ 15-2(e). Contours of the Privilege	802
§ 15-2(e)(1). Absolute Privilege	802
§ 15-2(e)(2). Qualified Privilege	804
§ 15-2(e)(2)(A). Relevance Requirements	806
§ 15-2(e)(2)(B). Exhaustion Requirements	807
§ 15-2(e)(2)(C). Other Requirements	809
§ 15-2(f). Privilege v. Immunity	810
§ 15-2(g). Penalties for Non-Disclosure	812
§ 15-2(h). Waiver	813
§ 15-2(i). Procedural Requirements	817
§ 15-2(i)(1). Procedures Generally	817
§ 15-2(i)(2). In Camera Review	818
§ 15-2(i)(3). Appellate Review	820
§ 15-2(i)(4). Special Broadcast Rules	821
§ 15-2(i)(5). Other Requirements	822
§ 15-2(j). Choice of Law	822
§ 15-3. Federal Codifications	825
§ 15-3(a). Search Warrants	825
§ 15-3(b). Justice Department and Administrative Regulations	829
§ 15-3(c). Federal Rules of Procedure	832

Chapter 16

THE CONSTITUTIONAL AND COMMON LAW PRIVILEGES

§ 16-1. Introduction	837
§ 16-2. The Constitutional Privilege	838
§ 16-2(a). Judicial Acceptance	838
§ 16-2(a)(1). Federal Courts	838
§ 16-2(a)(2). State Courts	843

TABLE OF CONTENTS

	Page
§ 16-2(b). Recipients of Protection	847
§ 16-2(b)(1). Definitional Issues	847
§ 16-2(b)(2). Standing Issues	852
§ 16-2(c). Nature of the Proceedings	853
§ 16-2(c)(1). Criminal Proceedings	853
§ 16-2(c)(2). Civil Proceedings	862
§ 16-2(c)(2)(A). Third-Party Proceedings	863
§ 16-2(c)(2)(B). The Press as a Party	866
§ 16-2(d). Scope of Protection	872
§ 16-2(d)(1). Sources of Information	872
§ 16-2(d)(2). Other Confidential Information	877
§ 16-2(d)(3). Nonconfidential Information	877
§ 16-2(d)(3)(A). Nonconfidential Sources	880
§ 16-2(d)(3)(B). Eyewitness Testimony	881
§ 16-2(d)(3)(C). Unpublished Information	883
§ 16-2(d)(3)(D). Published Information	891
§ 16-2(e). Contours of the Privilege	892
§ 16-2(e)(1). Generally	892
§ 16-2(e)(2). Relevance Requirements	896
§ 16-2(e)(3). Exhaustion Requirements	900
§ 16-2(e)(4). Other Requirements	906
§ 16-2(f). Penalties for Non-Disclosure	908
§ 16-2(g). Waiver	911
§ 16-2(h). Procedural Requirements	912
§ 16-2(h)(1). In Camera Review	914
§ 16-2(h)(2). Appellate Review	917
§ 16-2(i). Choice of Law	921
§ 16-2(j). Avoiding the Privilege	923
§ 16-2(j)(1). Third Party Subpoenas	923
§ 16-2(j)(2). Non-Traditional Subpoenas	925
§ 16-3. Common Law Privilege	926
Appendix A — Federal Statutes	929
Freedom of Information Act	929
Government in the Sunshine Act	938
Federal Wiretap Act	942
Privacy Protection Act of 1980	950
Appendix B — State Statutes	955
Part One: Newsperson Shield Laws	955
Alabama	955
Alaska	955

TABLE OF CONTENTS

	Page
Arizona	957
Arkansas	958
California	958
Colorado	959
Delaware	963
District of Columbia	965
Florida	966
Georgia	967
Illinois	967
Indiana	969
Kentucky	970
Louisiana	970
Maryland	974
Michigan	975
Minnesota	975
Montana	977
Nebraska	978
Nevada	979
New Jersey	979
New Mexico	984
New York	987
North Carolina	989
North Dakota	990
Ohio	990
Oklahoma	991
Oregon	992
Pennsylvania	993
Rhode Island	993
South Carolina	994
Tennessee	995
Part Two: Wiretap and Eavesdropping Laws (selected provisions)	996
Alabama	996
Alaska	997
Arizona	1000
Arkansas	1002
California	1003
Colorado	1006
Connecticut	1010
Delaware	1011
District of Columbia	1013

xviii

TABLE OF CONTENTS

	Page
Florida	1015
Georgia	1018
Hawaii	1020
Idaho	1024
Illinois	1025
Indiana	1027
Iowa	1029
Kansas	1031
Kentucky	1031
Louisiana	1032
Maine	1035
Maryland	1037
Massachusetts	1040
Michigan	1044
Minnesota	1045
Mississippi	1052
Missouri	1053
Montana	1055
Nebraska	1056
Nevada	1061
New Jersey	1063
New Mexico	1067
New York	1068
North Carolina	1070
North Dakota	1074
Ohio	1075
Oklahoma	1080
Oregon	1082
Pennsylvania	1084
Rhode Island	1088
South Carolina	1090
South Dakota	1090
Tennessee	1092
Texas	1095
Utah	1096
Vermont	1097
Virginia	1097
Washington	1101
West Virginia	1102
Wisconsin	1105
Wyoming	1108

TABLE OF CONTENTS

	Page
Table of Cases	1111
Table of Statutes	1213
Index	1257

ABOUT THE AUTHORS

C. Thomas Dienes is the Patricia Roberts Harris Research Professor of Law at George Washington University Law School. He is a legal consultant to *U.S. News and World Report*, where he served as General Counsel in 1998, and also to *Atlantic Monthly* and *Fast Company* magazines. He has authored or co-authored nine books and numerous articles on constitutional and communications law. He earned his J.D. and Ph.D. from Northwestern University.

Lee Levine is an Adjunct Professor of Law at the Georgetown University Law Center and a member of the Washington, D.C. law firm of Levine Sullivan & Koch, L.L.P. He has represented media clients in libel, newsgathering, invasion of privacy, and related First Amendment cases for two decades. He is a former chair of the American Bar Association's Forum on Communications Law and is recognized in *The Best Lawyers in America* as a leading expert in media law. He earned his law degree from The Yale Law School.

Robert C. Lind is a Professor of Law at Southwestern University School of Law. He has authored or co-authored five books and numerous articles on media, intellectual property, entertainment, museum and art law. He earned his J.D. and L.L.M. from George Washington University.

ABOUT THE AUTHORS

G. Thomas Dienes is the Patricia Roberts Harris Research Professor of Law at George Washington University Law School. He was legal Consultant to the News and Now Report, where it served as General Counsel in 1998 and also to Atlantic Monthly and Esq. Company magazines. He has authored or co-authored nine books and numerous articles on constitutional and communications law. He earned his J.D. and Ph.D. from Northwestern University.

Lee Levine is an Adjunct Professor of Law at the Georgetown University Law Center and a member of the Washington, D.C. law firm of Levine Sullivan & Koch, LLP. He has represented media clients in First Amendment cases in the law of privacy, and litigated First Amendment cases for two decades. He is a former chair of the American Bar Association's Forum on Communications Law and is recognized in the Legal 500 (USA) and as a leading American media lawyer. He earned his law degree from The Yale Law School.

Robert C. Lind is a Professor of Law at Southwestern University School of Law. He has authored or co-authored five books and numerous articles in the law of intellectual property, entertainment, museum and art law. He earned his J.D. and LL.M. from George Washington University.

PREFACE TO THE SECOND EDITION

When we completed the manuscript of the First Edition of *Newsgathering and the Law* in the Summer of 1996, we contemplated that, if developments in the law warranted the effort, we would prepare a Second Edition five years after its initial publication. Even we, who conceived the notion that the law of newsgathering had become sufficiently discrete and important to warrant its own treatise, did not anticipate the explosion of legal developments over the last three years that has virtually mandated preparation of a Second Edition at this time.

The evolution of legal doctrine distilled in this edition is, of course, ongoing. Thus, while the Second Edition reflects the important changes in the law of newsgathering through the Summer of 1999 — from the Supreme Court's pronouncements in *Wilson v. Layne*[1] and *Hanlon v. Berger*,[2] to the California Supreme Court's extraordinary output of decisions over the last year,[3] to the virtual creation of a body of precedent addressing news media liability for violation of federal and state wiretapping statutes,[4] to the Second Circuit's reconsideration of the journalists' privilege in *Gonzales v. National Broadcasting Co.*[5] — there will undoubtedly be additional watersheds in the not-too-distant future. Most significantly, this volume was completed before the United States Court of Appeals for the Fourth Circuit had spoken to the media's liability for fraud, misrepresentation and trespass in newsgathering in *Food Lion, Inc. v. Capital Cities/ABC Inc.*[6]

Nevertheless, we believe that this volume — like its predecessor — will prove to be a comprehensive resource for lawyers and journalists seeking to understand this increasingly complex and dynamic area of the law. In addition to those we specifically acknowledged in the First Edition, we are also indebted to Seth Berlin, Michael Blaha, Jay Ward Brown, Susanna Lowy, and Mark Rotenstreich. Finally, we could not have completed this project without the dedicated and (mostly) cheerful assistance of our colleagues at Levine Sullivan & Koch, L.L.P.,

---

1. 119 S. Ct. 1692 (1999).
2. 119 S. Ct. 1706 (1999) (per curiam).
3. See, e.g., Sanders v. American Broadcasting Cos., 978 P.2d 67 (Cal. 1999) (intrusion and eavesdropping claims arising from hidden camera investigation); Shulman v. Group W Prods., Inc., 955 P.2d 469 (Cal. 1998) (intrusion and eavesdropping claims arising from media ride along with emergency rescue helicopter crew); In re NBC Subsidiary (NBC-TV), Inc. v. Superior Ct., 980 P.2d 337 (Cal. 1999) (access to civil trials); Daily Journal Corp. v. Superior Ct., 979 P.2d 982 (Cal. 1999) (access to grand jury records).
4. See, e.g., Boehner v. McDermott, 1999 U.S. App. LEXIS 23135 (D.C. Cir. Sept. 24, 1999); Peavy v. New Times, Inc., 976 F. Supp. 532 (N.D. Tex. 1997); Ferrara v. Detroit Free Press, Inc., 26 MEDIA L. REP. (BNA) 2355 (E.D. Mich. 1998); Oliver v. WFAA-TV, Inc., 37 F. Supp. 2d 495 (N.D. Tex. 1998).
5. 1998 U.S. App. LEXIS 38583 (2d Cir. Aug. 27, 1999).
6. 951 F. Supp. 1224 (M.D.N.C. 1996); 951 F. Supp. 1217 (M.D.N.C. 1996).

PREFACE

the George Washington University Law School, and the Southwestern University School of Law. The Second Edition literally owes its existence to the research expertise of Audrey Billingsley, Natalie Eckart, Brian Granville, Marianna Horton, Joy Ilano, Jennifer Karmonick, Kerwin Miller, Jay Orlandi, Helen Quan, Merav Shefler, Sonja Sonnenburg, Brad Thornton, and Gary Zernich, as well as the incomparable support of Caretta Anderson, Sandra Burch, Virginia Fenner, Amanda Hammond, Kathy Hussmann, Angela Shearer, Patricia Snowden, and Sharon Wester. We are grateful to you all.

ACKNOWLEDGMENTS FOR THE FIRST EDITION

There really is no way to capture in a few sentences the contribution of those who have assisted me in completing my share of this book. Without the assistance of Dean Jack Friendenthal, the administration, the library staff (especially Leslie Lee), and the students of the George Washington University Law School, the research and writing effort would have been far more difficult, if not impossible. Special thanks are due to my research assistants and those student volunteers who gave so generously of their time and skills: Loren P. Ambinder, Kevin M. Goldberg, John M. Kloosterman, Mark M. Kodama, Michael A. Poltnick, John T. Ruskusky and John T. Ryan. My colleagues on the faculty, especially Jerome A. Barron, have always provided a rich source of ideas, commentary and helpful criticism.

Fred Drasner, President and Chief Executive Officer, and Gail Lione, General Counsel, of *U.S. News and World Report*, provided unique opportunities for me to pursue the study of communications law as both an academic and in the world of practice. And my collaboration with Lee Levine and Bob Lind has provided a constant source of stimulation bridging the law school experience and legal practice.

I especially want to acknowledge and express my appreciation to my secretary Angela Shearer, who devoted countless hours, even on weekends and holidays, to assist in the successful completion of this book. Thanks also to the other members of the secretarial staff at the law school, especially Winifred Hercules and Cynthia Webb-Manly, who pitched in to help and to Beverly Calvert, Office Manager, who always sought to accommodate my endless requests for assistance.

Finally, and most important, I want to express my gratitude to my family. To my daughter Kimberly, for sharing her vacation home from college with my book. And especially to my wife, Peggy. As the book consumed increasing hours of my time and energies and good humor, her love and support became more essential. My dedication of my contribution to this book to her is small payment for her patience and encouragement during its writing.

C. Thomas Dienes

This book is, for me, the product of lessons learned during the twenty odd years I have devoted to studying and practicing media law. It has been my hope, from the outset, to combine my affection for the First Amendment with an appreciation for the practical realities of the litigation process that surrounds it. Whether or not this book has successfully accomplished that task, I am personally indebted to the many colleagues, friends, and family who have enabled me to make the effort.

ACKNOWLEDGMENTS

First, and foremost, is my family. My wife and daughters have made do without their husband and father for large parts of many weekends over the last two years. For the most part, they have done so with good grace, humor and affection. For that, I dedicate my share of this work to them.

Next, there are my colleagues, with whom I have had the privilege of working over much of the last two decades, and whose guidance and wisdom are hopefully reflected in these pages, I am grateful to them all, but especially to my partners and friends Michael Sullivan, Jim Grossberg, Celeste Phillips, and Betsy Koch. I am also indebted to the media law bar, an unusually generous and talented group of lawyers. A special expression of gratitude is due to my particular heroes among that distinguished group — Cam DeVore, Victor Kovner, and Bob Sack — and to my friends Stuart Pierson, Kelli Sager, and Dan Waggoner.

Of course, there would be no experience to draw upon without the cases and controversies, and those are the product of a wonderful group of clients, each of whom it has been my honor to represent. I am grateful to all of them.

In its initial stages, this book benefited greatly from the work of John Zucker and from my previous collaborations with Monica Langley. It could not have been written without the help of a small army of summer associates at Ross, Dixon & Masback and research assistants at the George Washington University Law School. All of them, but especially Jennifer Mathis, Craig Canetti and Jonathan Burke, have my gratitude. I am especially grateful as well to Tom Dienes for the privilege of collaborating with him on this and other projects, and to Bob Lind for his masterful work on this project. Finally, this book literally could not have been written without the assistance of my secretary Steve Parker, who has my sincere thanks for a job well done.

Lee Levine

Special thanks go to my student research assistants Charles Steenveld, Todd Whiteley, Tim Griggs, Irena Kopelev, Wendy Jaffe and Peter Cole, without whose tremendous efforts this book would not have been completed. I especially offer my heartfelt appreciation and love to my significant other, Ellen R. Hurley, Esq., who not only contributed to the federal meeting law materials, but made numerous personal sacrifices that ensured the completion of this project. Her good humor, intelligence and companionship have provided me with a constant source of fulfillment and inspiration. I also thank Tom Dienes and Lee Levine for providing me with the opportunity to collaborate with them on this book.

One of the benefits of working in academia is the ability to work with gifted colleagues. Three of my faculty colleagues, Michael Frost, James Kushner and Marin Scordato, were of particular help with the preparation of this book. The outstanding assistance provided by the Southwestern University School of Law

ACKNOWLEDGMENTS

library staff, Director Linda Whisman, Sharrel Gerlach, Dennis Ladd, David McFadden, Carole Weiner, LeVont Crockett and Tom Hall, made the daunting task of completing this work possible. The efforts of Director Jeannie Nicholson and Martha Fink of the Southwestern University Faculty Support Center, as well as Julia Mason, made the production of this book more efficient and reduced logistical difficulties endemic to such a project.

Lastly, I would like to thank Dean Leigh Taylor, Associate Dean Catherine Carpenter, Assistant Dean Doreen Heyer and the Trustees of Southwestern University School of Law for their financial and scheduling support of this project.

Robert C. Lind

ACKNOWLEDGMENTS

library staff, Director Linda Whitman, Sheryl Gerety, Dennis Laird, David Meredith, Carole Wells, LeVon Crocker, and Lou Hall met the daunting task of completing this work. Assia, The Director of Oregon Institute Foundation and Marti Peck of the Southwestern University Faculty Support Center, as well as Julia Nguyen made the production of this manuscript efficient and eased typical difficulties endemic to such a project.

Lastly, I would like to thank Dean Leigh Taylor, Associate Dean Catherine Carpenter, Assistant Dean Doreen Heyer and the Trustees of Southwestern University School of Law for their financial and scholarly support of all my projects.

Robert C. Lind

Chapter 1

INTRODUCTION: FASHIONING THE NEWSGATHERING RIGHT

§ 1-1. The Principle of Freedom of Expression.
§ 1-2. The Rationale of Preference.
   § 1-2(a). The Marketplace Model.
   § 1-2(b). The Democratic Model.
   § 1-2(c). The Liberty Model.
§ 1-3. The Right to Acquire Information and the Right to Know.
§ 1-4. Freedom of the Press.
   § 1-4(a). The Press Clause.
   § 1-4(b). Press as Agent or Surrogate.
§ 1-5. Newsgathering and the Right of Access.

§ 1-1. The Principle of Freedom of Expression.

Courts and commentators often speak of a "principle of freedom of speech" or of "freedom of expression."[1] The principle is variously stated, but generally provides that when "the freedom of speech" protected by the Constitution is significantly burdened, more than mere rationality is to be demanded of government as justification and more rigorous forms of judicial review are to be employed.[2] If a law regulates speech on the basis of its content (i.e., its viewpoint or subject matter),[3] the law is presumptively invalid.[4] In such cases, the

---

1. See, e.g., F. SCHAUER, FREE SPEECH: A PHILOSOPHICAL ENQUIRY (1982) (analysis of the philosophical foundations supporting an independent principle of freedom of speech). For general discussions of the doctrines and rules flowing from the principle of freedom of speech, see J. BARRON & C.T. DIENES, FIRST AMENDMENT LAW IN A NUTSHELL (1993); J. NOWAK & R. ROTUNDA, CONSTITUTIONAL LAW ch. 16 (5th ed. 1995); 2 R. SMOLLA, SMOLLA AND NIMMER ON FREEDOM OF SPEECH: A TREATISE ON THE THEORY OF THE FIRST AMENDMENT (1996); L. TRIBE, AMERICAN CONSTITUTIONAL LAW ch. 12 (2d ed. 1988).

2. See BARRON & DIENES, *supra* note 1, at ch. 2; SMOLLA, *supra* note 1, at §§ 2.61-2.67.

3. See Consolidated Edison Co. v. Public Serv. Comm'n, 447 U.S. 530, 537 (1980) (the "First amendment's hostility to content-based regulation extends . . . to prohibition of public discussion of an entire topic"); Boos v. Barry, 485 U.S. 312, 313 (1988) (an entire category of speech — signs or displays critical of foreign governments — may not be prohibited). The Supreme Court has held that "illicit legislative intent is not the *sine qua non* of a violation of the First Amendment." Minneapolis Star & Tribune Co. v. Minnesota Comm'r of Revenue, 460 U.S. 575, 592 (1983); see Turner Broadcasting Sys., Inc. v. FCC, 512 U.S. 622, 641-43 (1994); Simon & Schuster, Inc. v. New York State Crime Victims Bd., 502 U.S. 105, 117 (1991). Viewpoint regulation and subject matter regulation are subsets of content-based regulation. See BARRON & DIENES, *supra* note 1, at 33-39; SMOLLA, *supra* note 1, at ch. 3.

4. See, e.g., Turner Broadcasting Sys., Inc. v. FCC, 512 U.S. 622, 641 (1994) ("the First Amendment, subject only to narrow and well understood exceptions, does not countenance governmental control over the content of messages expressed by private individuals"); Simon & Schuster, Inc. v. New York State Crime Victims Bd., 502 U.S. 105, 115 (1991) ("A statute is

courts are to apply strict scrutiny — i.e., the government must demonstrate that the law is necessary to serve a compelling interest.[5] If the government undertakes content-neutral regulation of speech, the law should be narrowly tailored to further significant or substantial government interests, and alternative means of effective communication must remain available.[6] Clarity and precision of regulation are required when First Amendment freedoms are otherwise placed at risk.[7] Prior restraints on protected expression carry an especially heavy burden of

---

presumptively inconsistent with the First Amendment if it imposes a financial burden on speakers because of the content of their speech."). In *Police Department of Chicago v. Mosley*, 408 U.S. 92, 95 (1975), for example, the Supreme Court held unconstitutional a statute proscribing picketing other than labor picketing and asserted that "above all else the first amendment means that government has no power to restrict expression because of its message, its ideas, its subject matter, or its content."

    5. See, e.g., Reno v. ACLU, 521 U.S. 844, 868, 879 (1997) (The Communications Decency Act "is a content-based blanket restriction on speech," subject to the "most stringent review of its provisions" and "[t]he breadth of this content–based restriction of speech imposes an especially heavy burden on the Government to explain why a less restrictive provision would not be as effective as the CDA"); Turner Broadcasting Sys., Inc. v. FCC, 512 U.S. at 642 ("the most exacting scrutiny"); Burson v. Freeman, 504 U.S. 191, 200 (1992); Simon & Schuster, Inc. v. New York State Crime Victims Bd., 502 U.S. at 117; Arkansas Writers' Project, Inc. v. Ragland, 481 U.S. 221, 231 (1987). See generally Williams, *Content Discrimination and the First Amendment*, 139 U. PA. L. REV. 615 (1991); Stone, *Restrictions of Speech Because of Its Content: The Peculiar Case of Subject Matter Restrictions*, 46 U. CHI. L. REV. 81 (1978).

    6. See United States v. O'Brien, 391 U.S. 367, 377 (1968) (content-neutral regulation will be upheld if "it furthers an important or substantial government interest; if the governmental interest is unrelated to the suppression of free expression; and if the incidental restriction on alleged First Amendment freedoms is no greater than is essential to the furtherance of that interest."); see also Turner Broadcasting Sys., Inc. v. FCC, 512 U.S. at 642, 662; International Soc'y for Krishna Consciousness, Inc. v. Lee, 505 U.S. 672 (1992) (neutral regulation of soliciting at airports held constitutional); United States v. Grace, 461 U.S. 171 (1983) (total ban on leafletting on sidewalks adjoining the United States Supreme Court held unconstitutional); Heffron v. International Soc'y for Krishna Consciousness, 452 U.S. 640 (1981) (state fair rule limiting sale or distribution of materials to fixed locations held to be reasonable time, place and manner regulation). See generally SMOLLA, *supra* note 1, at ch. 9; Stone, *Content-Neutral Restrictions*, 54 U. CHI. L. REV. 46 (1987).

    7. The First Amendment's demand for clarity and precision of regulation is reflected in the doctrines of vagueness and overbreadth. See Reno v. ACLU, 521 U.S. 844, 874 (1997) ("We are persuaded that the [Communications Decency Act] lacks the precision that the First Amendment requires when a statute regulates the content of speech."); City of Lakewood v. Plain Dealer Publ'g Co., 486 U.S. 750, 759 (1988) ("[A] facial challenge lies whenever a licensing law gives a governmental official or agency substantial power to discriminate based on the content or viewpoint of speech by suppressing disfavored speech or disliked speakers."); Los Angeles City Council v. Taxpayers for Vincent, 466 U.S. 789, 801 (1984) (there "must be a realistic danger that the statute itself will significantly compromise recognized First Amendment protection of parties not before the Court for it to be challenged on overbreadth grounds"); Board of Airport Comm'rs v. Jews for Jesus, Inc., 482 U.S. 569, 574 (1987) (law prohibiting all First Amendment activities within the central terminal area of airport is overbroad since it "reaches the universe of expressive activity"); Secretary of State of Maryland v. Joseph H. Munson Co., 467 U.S. 947 (1984) (25% limitation on administrative expenses for fundraising by charities held overbroad); New York v.

justification, and exacting procedural requirements must also be satisfied before such restraints may constitutionally be imposed.[8]

These doctrinal rules, grounded in the principle of freedom of expression, reflect the vital importance of this freedom to the American legal and political system. Yet, the doctrine is replete with limitations, caveats, and uncertainties. For example, determining whether a regulation is content-based or content-neutral can be challenging.[9] If expression takes place in a "public forum," the Supreme Court has held that doctrines governing content-based and content-neutral regulation apply.[10] However, if the expression takes place in a "non-public forum," the preferences accorded First Amendment values are substantially abandoned and a deferential standard of review is adopted, which requires only that the government act rationally, and not take sides (i.e., no viewpoint

---

Ferber, 458 U.S. 747 (1982) (child pornography law held not to be substantially overbroad); Broadrick v. Oklahoma, 413 U.S. 601 (1973) (state law prohibiting various political activities by public employees held not to be substantially overbroad); Coates v. Cincinnati, 402 U.S. 611 (1971) (law prohibiting three or more persons from congregating on street corners and behaving in an "annoying" manner to passersby held vague and overbroad). A law must be drawn with sufficient clarity as to inform persons of common intelligence and law enforcement agencies what conduct is proscribed. See, e.g., Smith v. Goguen, 415 U.S. 566 (1974) (flag misuse statute held unconstitutionally vague). See generally BARRON & DIENES, *supra* note 1, at 39-47; SMOLLA, *supra* note 1, at ch. 6.

8. See Chap. 2-1(d) *infra*.

9. See Turner Broadcasting Sys., Inc. v. FCC, 512 U.S. at 642 ("Deciding whether a particular regulation is content-based or content-neutral is not always a simple task."); Chemerinsky, *The First Amendment: When The Government Must Make Content-Based Choices*, 42 CLEV. ST. L. REV. 199, 204-07 (1994) (noting that content-based choices are sometimes inevitable); Redish, *The Content Distinction in First Amendment Analysis*, 34 STAN. L. REV. 113 (1981) (discussing the theoretical bases for the content-based/content-neutral distinction); Stephan, *The First Amendment and Content Discrimination*, 68 VA. L. REV. 203 (1982) (analyzing the development and application of the broad content-neutrality rule); Stone, *Content Regulation and the First Amendment*, 25 WM. & MARY L. REV. 189 (1983) (discussing difficulty of defining the distinction between content-based and content-neutral regulation).

10. Public forum analysis is frequently applied to regulation of expression that takes place on public property. In that context, the Supreme Court has indicated that it is first necessary to define the nature of the forum. A *traditional* public forum is public property that has historically been recognized as open for expressive activity, including streets, parks, and sidewalks. Government may not close a traditional public forum to all First Amendment activity. A *limited* or *designated* public forum is public property that, expressly or by implication, the government indicates an intent to open for public expression. See International Soc'y for Krishna Consciousness, Inc. v. Lee, 505 U.S. 672 (1992) (airports are nonpublic fora); Heffron v. International Soc'y for Krishna Consciousness, Inc., 452 U.S. 640 (1981) (state fair ground is a public forum). See generally BARRON & DIENES, *supra* note 1, at ch. 9; SMOLLA, *supra* note 1, at ch. 8; BeVier, *Rehabilitating Public Forum Doctrine: In Defense of Categories*, 1992 SUP. CT. REV. 79; Dienes, *The Trashing of the Public Forum: Problems in First Amendment Analysis*, 55 GEO. WASH. L. REV. 109 (1986); Post, *Between Governance and Management: The History and Theory of the Public Forum*, 34 UCLA L. REV. 1713 (1987).

discrimination).[11] Further, the First Amendment applies only to expression that is held to fit within "the freedom of speech." If a particular species of expression is deemed to fall in a category of "lower value" speech, such as obscenity or commercial speech, strict scrutiny is again abandoned in favor of less speech-protective modes of judicial review.[12]

The principle of freedom of expression is subject to still another important caveat. The Supreme Court has also fashioned exceptions for "special contexts" or "restricted environments," where ordinary speech-protective rules are simply not applied or are applied in a materially altered or greatly diminished form. Within these exceptions — involving the military,[13] government employees,[14] prisons,[15] and children in schools[16] — certain interests are deemed so critical as to alter the substantive law. In these exceptions, the Court has effectively abandoned presumptions designed to protect free speech values in favor of a deferential approach that frequently amounts to a general requirement of rationality.

---

11. See, e.g., Arkansas Educ. Television Comm'n v. Forbes, 523 U.S. 666 (1998) (candidate debate sponsored by public television broadcaster held to be a nonpublic forum from which the broadcaster could exclude a candidate based on a reasonable, viewpoint-neutral exercise of discretion); Cornelius v. NAACP Legal Defense & Educ. Fund, Inc., 473 U.S. 788 (1985) (exclusion of political advocacy groups from participation in federally sponsored charitable fund drive among government employees upheld, but remanded for consideration of viewpoint discrimination).

12. See New York v. Ferber, 458 U.S. 747 (1982) (child pornography); Central Hudson Gas & Elec. Corp. v. Public Serv. Comm'n, 447 U.S. 557 (1980) (false and misleading commercial speech not protected; diminished protection for truthful commercial speech); Miller v. California, 413 U.S. 15 (1973) (obscenity); Gooding v. Wilson, 405 U.S. 518 (1972) (fighting words); New York Times Co. v. Sullivan, 376 U.S. 254 (1964) (defamatory speech published with actual malice). But see R.A.V. v. City of St. Paul, 505 U.S. 377 (1992) (even within categories of no-value or low-value speech, First Amendment restrictions apply, with some exceptions, when government discriminates on the basis of content). See generally Shaman, *The Theory of Low-Value Speech*, 48 SMU L. REV. 297 (1995).

13. See Chap. 8-5 *infra*.

14. See Rankin v. McPherson, 483 U.S. 378 (1987) (discharge of clerical employee for remark "If they go for him again, I hope they get him," made following an attempt on President's life, held improper); Connick v. Myers, 461 U.S. 138 (1983) (courts balance the competing interests only when the employee's speech involves a matter of public concern); Pickering v. Board of Educ., 391 U.S. 563 (1968) (employee's interest in expression balanced against government's interest in efficiency in performance of government's business).

15. See Chap. 8-1 *infra*.

16. See Hazelwood Sch. Dist. v. Kuhlmeier, 484 U.S. 260 (1988) (student publications reasonably related to legitimate pedagogical concerns of school, a nonpublic forum, may be censored); Bethel Sch. Dist. v. Fraser, 478 U.S. 675 (1986) (school discipline of high school student for delivering lewd and offensive speech in school assembly upheld). But see Tinker v. Des Moines Indep. Community Sch. Dist., 393 U.S. 503, 509 (1969) (school may not prohibit wearing of black armband as symbolic expression absent proof such conduct would "materially and substantially interfere with the requirements of appropriate discipline in the operation of the school").

§ 1-2. The Rationale of Preference.

What is the rationale for the special protection accorded freedom of expression? While a host of theories have been offered, three appear to have had enduring value: the marketplace, the democratic, and the liberty models.

§ 1-2(a). The Marketplace Model.

The marketplace model of free expression is memorialized in Justice Holmes' famous assertion "that the best test of truth is the power of the thought to get itself accepted in the competition of the market."[17] In fact, this model is the oldest of the rationales explaining the principle of free expression, derived initially from Milton's *Areopagitica*:

> And though all the winds of doctrine were let loose to play upon the earth so truth be in the field, we do injuriously by licensing and prohibiting to misdoubt her strength. Let her and Falsehood grapple; who ever knew truth put to the worse in a free and open encounter?[18]

John Stuart Mill similarly urged the values of the marketplace. If a suppressed idea or opinion is right, Mill argued, society loses the opportunity "of exchanging error for truth."[19] On the other hand, even if the suppressed view is false, society loses "what is almost as great a benefit, the clearer perception and livelier impression of truth, produced by its collision with error."[20]

These romantic renditions of the marketplace model assume the existence of objective, discoverable truth. Perhaps it is possible to speak of truth in the sense of scientific "fact." Galileo espoused what we today might be willing to deem "truth."[21] But, it is not as easy to speak of "truth" in relation to political opinion and debate in the context of normative statements about the virtues of capitalism, democracy, or communism.

---

17. Abrams v. United States, 250 U.S. 616, 630 (1919) (Holmes, J., dissenting). But see A. BICKEL, THE MORALITY OF CONSENT 71 (1975) ("[W]e have lived through too much to believe it."); Ingber, *The Marketplace of Ideas: A Legitimizing Myth*, 1984 DUKE L.J. 1 (1984) (criticizing marketplace model).
18. J. MILTON, AREOPAGITICA, A SPEECH FOR THE LIBERTY OF UNLICENSED PRINTING TO THE PARLIAMENT OF ENGLAND 51-52 (1644).
19. Mill, *On Liberty*, in ESSENTIAL WORKS OF JOHN STUART MILL 269 (M. Lerner ed. 1961).
20. *Id.*
21. Professor Baker attacks the classic marketplace model's emphasis on the search for truth, asserting that "truth is not objective." Baker, *Scope of the First Amendment Freedom of Speech*, 25 UCLA L. REV. 964, 974 (1978). Similarly, Judge Bork has asserted that "[t]ruth is what the majority thinks it is at any given moment precisely because the majority is permitted to govern and to redefine its values constantly." Bork, *Neutral Principles and Some First Amendment Problems*, 47 IND. L.J. 1, 30 (1971).

Even if one accepts the existence of an objective order of knowable truth or, perhaps, a less demanding substitute such as a "best policy choice," it is not at all clear that uninhibited debate is the means to achieve it. The marketplace model assumes that, somehow, truth will eventually emerge triumphant and falsity will be overcome. In short, it assumes a process of rational choice. If the marketplace behaves irrationally, however, unfettered expression may itself be risky. Further, speech can produce serious harm. For example, it is argued that racist speech or pornography can cause serious harm to racial minorities and women. The speech itself may be an exercise of power or subordination.[22] But, even if one doubts that free expression will produce truth or the best policy or, indeed, believes that it will cause harm, the fact remains that suppression of ideas, beliefs, opinion, or information may nevertheless impair efficacious public policy or individual choice. Ideas or information never spoken or heard cannot be considered, accepted or rejected. It would appear that individual decisions and public policy selection can become rational only if the alternatives are known. The possibility and desirability of at least limited rational public policy making and individual decisionmaking would appear to require supporting those values that promise to enhance rational choice. Thus, the marketplace model may not yield objective truth, but it may well be a more desirable platform for policy formation and personal decisionmaking than the suppression of opinions or ideas believed to be false or deemed to be potentially harmful.[23]

Still other critics of the marketplace model argue that it is malfunctioning; that the communications marketplace is dominated by wealthy, powerful interests.[24] These "failure of the marketplace" theorists argue that when the marketplace falters, government regulation is appropriate to correct it. But this notion directly challenges the central focus of the First Amendment as a limit on government.[25]

---

22. See, e.g., C. MACKINNON, ONLY WORDS 30-31 (1993) (arguing that "speech acts" can do harm and that "so-called speech can be an exercise of power which constructs the social reality in which people live"). But see Baker, *Of Course, More Than Words*, 61 U. CHI. L. REV. 1181 (1994) (challenging Professor MacKinnon's thesis using the liberty model, emphasizing individual freedom of choice).

23. See Marshall, *In Defense of the Search for Truth as a First Amendment Value*, 30 GA. L. REV. 1 (1995) (arguing that the process of searching for truth furthers personal and democratic values).

24. See, e.g., Barron, *Access to the Press — A New First Amendment Right*, 80 HARV. L. REV. 1641 (1967) (arguing for a public right of access to the media); Fiss, *Why the State?*, 100 HARV. L. REV. 781, 788 (1987) ("The state is to act as the much-needed countervailing power, to counteract the skew of public debate attributable to the market and thus preserve the essential conditions of democracy.").

25. See Powe, *Scholarship and Markets*, 56 GEO. WASH. L. REV. 172, 182-84 (1987).

§ 1-2(b). The Democratic Model.

"We the people of the United States, in order to form a more perfect Union. . . ."[26] With these words, popular sovereignty became the premise of the second theory supporting freedom of expression, at least in the United States — the democratic model. Political power resides ultimately in the people and flows from them. Governments derive their just powers from the consent of the governed and public officials are both guardians of a public trust and answerable to the people themselves. If "we the people" are to exercise properly our role in a democratic society, we must be free to express our ideas and opinions and must be able to obtain information to enhance the likelihood that our opinions and our decisions are informed. As Alexander Meiklejohn put it, the "principle of the freedom of speech springs from the necessities of the program of self-government. . . . It is a deduction from the basic American agreement that public issues shall be decided by universal suffrage."[27]

Both a right to speak and a right to hear are implicated by the democratic model. Through expression, citizens participate in self-government. They communicate their needs and demands, they praise and criticize their delegated governors. Through expression, citizens receive the ideas, the opinions, the data, that make their participation in democratic government meaningful.[28]

In addition, if a democratic society is to yield rational policy choices, the democratic model holds that provision must be made for hearing all views, even those of the dissident. The tyranny of the majority must be avoided because, when the majority uses its power to suppress dissenting views, the polity loses a vital attribute of democracy — the ability of the citizen-governor to make informed political choices. Thus, we have committed ourselves to this principle of a democratic form of government that tolerates, even celebrates, dissent.[29]

---

26. U.S. CONST., preamble.

27. A. MEIKLEJOHN, FREE SPEECH AND ITS RELATION TO SELF-GOVERNMENT 26-27 (1948). Accord, Bork, *supra* note 21, at 29. The Supreme Court has said that "'speech concerning public affairs is more than self-expression; it is the essence of self-government.'" Red Lion Broadcasting Co. v. FCC, 395 U.S. 367, 390 (1969) (citation omitted). See New York Times Co. v. Sullivan, 376 U.S. 254, 273 (1964); Kalven, *The* New York Times *Case: A Note on "the Central Meaning of the First Amendment,"* 1964 SUP. CT. REV. 191.

Closely related to the democratic model is the "checking value" identified by Blasi, *The Checking Value in First Amendment Theory*, 1977 AM. B. FOUND. RES. J. 521. Professor Blasi distinguished his approach from that of Meiklejohn: "[T]he role of the ordinary citizen is not so much to contribute on a continuing basis to the formation of public policy as to retain a veto power to be employed when the decisions of officials pass certain bounds." *Id.* at 542.

28. See Board of Educ. v. Pico, 457 U.S. 853, 867 (1982) (plurality opinion) ("the right to receive ideas is a necessary predicate to the *recipient's* meaningful exercise of his own rights of speech, press, and political freedom") (emphasis in original).

29. See S. SHIFFRIN, THE FIRST AMENDMENT, DEMOCRACY AND ROMANCE (1990).

But, as in the marketplace model, there are those who find the basis for government regulation in the failings of the democratic model. It is argued that, if the First Amendment is designed to promote deliberative democracy, current constitutional doctrine protects both more and less speech than it should. In place of a laissez-faire marketplace model, it is argued that government regulation to promote democratic deliberation is desirable.[30] Still, the fact remains that "[f]reedom of speech is based in large part on a distrust of the ability of government to make the necessary distinctions . . . and a somewhat deeper distrust of governmental power in a more general sense."[31]

§ 1-2(c). The Liberty Model.

In *On Liberty*, Mill wrote that "[h]uman nature is not a machine to be built after a model, and set to do exactly the work prescribed for it, but a tree, which requires to grow and develop itself on all sides."[32] To be human is to develop and nurture those capabilities within us. In *Whitney v. California*,[33] Justice Brandeis drew on this theme: "Those who won our independence believed that the final end of the state was to make men free to develop their faculties; and that in its government the deliberative forces should prevail over the arbitrary. They valued liberty both as an end and as a means."[34]

The liberty model, therefore, explains the freedom of expression as an essential component of a process of individual self-realization. Through expression, each person is empowered to test her ideas, opinions, and beliefs — to grow as an individual. Speech is valued not simply in instrumental terms of how it serves society. Rather, speech has an intrinsic worth.[35]

In the final analysis, the values undergirding the principle of freedom of expression are interrelated, reflecting the role of expression in the lives of people, their government and their society. These interrelated values provide the foundation for the freedom of expression and have demanded judicial scrutiny of government regulation that threatens that freedom.

---

30. See, e.g., Sunstein, *Free Speech Now*, 59 U. CHI. L. REV. 255, 315-16 (1942). See generally C. SUNSTEIN, DEMOCRACY AND THE PROBLEM OF FREE SPEECH (1993).

31. SCHAUER, *supra* note 1, at 86. See Post, *Meiklejohn's Mistake: Individual Autonomy and the Reform of Public Discourse*, 64 COLO. L. REV. 1109 (1993) (warning of the danger of state censorship of public discourse).

32. Mill, *supra* note 19, at 308.

33. 274 U.S. 357 (1927).

34. *Id.* at 375-76 (Brandeis, J., concurring).

35. See L. BOLLINGER, THE TOLERANT SOCIETY (1986); Murchison, *Speech and the Self-Realization Value*, 33 HARV. C.R-C.L. L. REV. 443 (1998); Redish, *The Value of Free Speech*, 130 U. PA. L. REV. 591 (1982).

§ 1-3. The Right to Acquire Information and the Right to Know.

The law and philosophy of free expression has focused largely on the freedom to communicate. There is, however, another dimension to the exercise of that freedom of equal importance — the right of the public to receive information and ideas and, perhaps, the right to know.[36] As Madison put it, "a popular government, without popular information, or the means of acquiring it, is but a prologue to a farce or a tragedy; or, perhaps both."[37]

If public debate is to be meaningful, it must not only be free, it must also be informed.[38] If the values supporting the principle of free expression are to be realized, the public must have the freedom to acquire information. Justice Brennan, concurring in *Lamont v. Postmaster General,* observed that "the right to receive publications is . . . a fundamental right. The dissemination of ideas can accomplish nothing if otherwise willing addressees are not free to receive and consider them. It would be a barren marketplace of ideas that had only sellers and no buyers."[39]

To the extent that the First Amendment is functionally designed to promote self-realization, the acquisition of information, to enable each person to identify and evaluate competing choices, is vital.[40] If the model undergirding free expression is based on the democratic ideal, the importance of a right to acquire information is even more pronounced. Meiklejohn saw the public's right to obtain information as essential to his democratic model of the First Amendment.[41] If the citizen is to perform her role in democratic society, she must have

---

36. See generally, Symposium, *The First Amendment and the Right to Know*, 1976 WASH. U.L.Q. 1; Note, *What Ever Happened to "The Right to Know"? Access to Government Controlled Information Since* Richmond Newspapers, 73 VA. L. REV. 1111 (1987); Note, *The First Amendment Right to Gather State-Held Information*, 89 YALE L. J. 923 (1980); Note, *The Rights of the Public and the Press to Gather Information*, 87 HARV. L. REV. 1505 (1974); Note, *The Right to Know in First Amendment Analysis*, 57 TEX. L. REV. 505 (1979).

37. Letter from J. Madison to W.T. Barry (Aug. 4, 1822), *reprinted in* 9 WRITINGS OF JAMES MADISON 103 (S. Hunt ed. 1910).

38. See Saxbe v. Washington Post Co., 417 U.S. 843, 862-63 (1974) (Powell, J., dissenting) ("[P]ublic debate must not only be unfettered; it must also be informed. For that reason this Court has repeatedly stated that First Amendment concerns encompass the receipt of information and ideas as well as the right of free expression.") (citations omitted).

39. 381 U.S. 301, 308 (1965) (Brennan, J., concurring).

40. See Emerson, *Towards a General Theory of the First Amendment*, 72 YALE L.J. 877, 880 (1963) (from the value of speech to further self-realization, "there follows the right of the individual to access to knowledge. . . . To cut off the search for truth . . . is thus to elevate society and the state to a despotic command and to reduce the individual to the arbitrary control of others").

41. A. MEIKLEJOHN, POLITICAL FREEDOM: THE CONSTITUTIONAL POWERS OF THE PEOPLE 26 (1960) ("Just so far as, at any point, the citizens who are to decide an issue are denied acquaintance with information or opinions or doubt or disbelief or criticism which is relevant to that issue, just so far the result must be ill-considered, ill-balanced planning for the public good. It is the

the information necessary to evaluate governmental policies. If citizens are to monitor the activities of government and hold their chosen governors accountable, they must have access to information relevant to government institutions and the performance of public officials.[42] As Justice Stevens explained, "[w]ithout some protection for the acquisition of information about the operation of public institutions such as prisons by the public at large, the process of self-governance contemplated by the Framers would be stripped of its substance."[43]

The courts have recognized the need to protect the public's ability to acquire information. The Supreme Court has, with some frequency, articulated a First Amendment-based right to receive information. In *Grosjean v. American Press Co.*,[44] the Court held unconstitutional a tax on publications, a so-called "tax on knowledge,"[45] because it recognized that an "informed public opinion is the most potent of all restraints on misgovernment."[46] A tax on newspapers "limit[s] the circulation of information to which the public is entitled by virtue of the constitutional guarantees."[47] In *Lamont v. Postmaster General*,[48] the Court rejected — in the name of the First Amendment — restrictions on the public's ability to receive publications through the mails. And in *Stanley v. Georgia*, the Court confirmed that "[i]t is now well established that the Constitution protects the right to receive information and ideas."[49]

---

mutilation of the thinking process for the community against which the First Amendment to the Constitution is directed.").

42. See New York Times Co. v. Sullivan, 376 U.S. 254, 282 (1964) (emphasizing the role of the "citizen-critic" of government — "it is as much his duty to criticize as it is the [public] official's duty to administer"); Lewis, *A Public Right to Know About Public Institutions: The First Amendment as a Sword*, 1980 SUP. CT. REV. 1.

43. Houchins v. KQED, Inc., 438 U.S. 1, 32 (1978) (Stevens, J., dissenting).

44. 297 U.S. 233 (1936).

45. *Id.* at 246.

46. *Id.* at 250.

47. *Id.* The tax at issue in *Grosjean* went "to the heart of the natural right of the members of an organized society, united for their common good, to impart and acquire information in their common interest." *Id.* at 243.

48. 381 U.S. 301 (1965).

49. 394 U.S. 557, 564 (1969). See First Nat'l Bank of Boston v. Bellotti, 435 U.S. 765, 783 (1978) ("[T]he First Amendment goes beyond protection of the press and the self-expression of individuals to prohibit government from limiting the stock of information from which members of the public may draw."); Kleindienst v. Mandel, 408 U.S. 753, 762 (1972) ("In a variety of contexts this Court has referred to a First Amendment right to 'receive information and ideas.'") (citation omitted); Red Lion Broadcasting Co. v. FCC, 395 U.S. 367, 390 (1969) ("It is the right of the viewers and listeners, not the right of the broadcasters, that is paramount here."); Martin v. City of Struthers, 319 U.S. 141, 143 (1943) ("[The First Amendment] embraces the right to distribute literature and necessarily protects the right to receive it."); Montana ex rel. Missoulian v. Montana Twenty-First Judicial Dist. Ct., 933 P.2d 829, 839 (Mont. 1997) ("[T]he First Amendment protects not just speech itself but the entire process of communication, including the exchange of ideas and information between speaker and listener. Although the United States Constitution, unlike the Montana Constitution, does not specifically guarantee a 'right to know,' a right to receive infor-

This right to receive information, like all First Amendment-based rights, is not absolute. As the Court explained in *Zemel v. Rusk*: "[t]he right to speak and publish does not carry with it the unrestrained right to gather information. . . . There are few restrictions on action which could not be elevated by ingenious argument in the garb of decreased data flow."[50] Nor has it been established that the right to receive information necessarily carries with it an affirmative constitutional obligation of government to provide it. The First Amendment, it has been said, requires only that government not fetter the process of acquiring information; it does not impose a constitutional duty on government to make information publicly available. Thus, the beguiling phrase "the right to know" straddles the often fine line between governmental restriction on the right to receive information, which the freedom of expression principle typically will not tolerate, and an affirmative right to compel government to disclose that which it would prefer to hold in confidence, a right that has not traditionally been held to be secured by the First Amendment.[51] Throughout this volume, we explore this ever-shifting line and its consequences for the law of newsgathering.

§ 1-4. Freedom of the Press.

§ 1-4(a). The Press Clause.

The First Amendment guarantees both freedom of speech and of the press. A question that has captured the attention of commentators,[52] though not especially the Supreme Court, is whether the First Amendment's press clause adds anything to its guarantee of "freedom of speech." Textually, courts are generally reluctant

---

mation has been recognized under First Amendment principles."); see also Griswold v. Connecticut, 381 U.S. 479, 482 (1965) ("The right to freedom of speech and press includes . . . the right to receive, the right to read . . . and freedom of inquiry. . . .").

50. 381 U.S. 1, 16-17 (1965). See Kleindienst v. Mandel, 408 U.S. 753 (1972) (rejecting First Amendment right to hear foreign lecturer denied a visa).

51. See L. POWE, THE FOURTH ESTATE AND THE CONSTITUTION: FREEDOM OF THE PRESS IN AMERICA 133-59 (1991); BeVier, *An Informed Public, an Informing Press: The Search for a Constitutional Principle*, 68 CAL. L. REV. 482, 517 (1980) (concluding "that a judicially enforceable right to know would be inconsistent with the democratic processes envisioned by the Constitution and thus could not be justified by a First Amendment principle whose office is to vindicate those processes"); O'Brien, *The First Amendment and the Public's "Right to Know,"* 7 HASTINGS CONST. L.Q. 579 (1980) (rejecting a First Amendment right to know).

52. See generally Abrams, *The Press Is Different: Reflections on Justice Stewart and the Autonomous Press*, 7 HOFSTRA L. REV. 563 (1979); Anderson, *The Origins of the Press Clause*, 30 UCLA L. REV. 455 (1983); Bezanson, *The New Free Press Guarantee*, 63 VA. L. REV. 731 (1977); Lange, *The Speech and Press Clauses*, 23 UCLA L. REV. 77 (1975); Lewis, *A Preferred Position for Journalism?*, 7 HOFSTRA L. REV. 595 (1979); Nimmer, *Introduction — Is Freedom of the Press a Redundancy: What Does it Add to Freedom of Speech?*, 26 HASTINGS L.J. 639 (1975); Van Alstyne, *The Hazards to the Press of Claiming a "Preferred Position,"* 28 HASTINGS L.J. 761 (1977).

to treat any constitutional language as meaningless. Looking to history, commentators disagree about the Framers' intent.[53]

Justice Stewart argued that the press clause has independent force; it recognizes the press as the Fourth Estate. "The primary purpose of the constitutional guarantee of a free press was [to] create a fourth institution outside the Government as an additional check on the three rival branches."[54] For Justice Stewart, the press clause was intended by the Framers to be a separate structural provision of the Constitution. The press, he noted, is the only private business afforded institutional protection under the Constitution so that it can act as a check on the abuse of governmental power.[55] If the press is to perform this checking function, it must enjoy a unique institutional autonomy from government regulation.[56]

But, even in Justice Stewart's formulation, the press clause does not afford the news media privileged access to governmental information. The public's interest in receiving information is served only indirectly, Justice Stewart asserted. "There is no constitutional right to have access to particular government information, or to require openness from the bureaucracy.... The Constitution itself is neither a Freedom of Information Act nor an Official Secrets Act."[57]

These views help explain Justice Stewart's opinions for the Court in *Pell v. Procunier*,[58] and *Saxbe v. Washington Post Co.*,[59] rejecting an affirmative First Amendment-based right of access to prisons. At least as construed by Justice Stewart, the press in these cases sought special rights of access not available to the public generally. By the same token, Justice Stewart's emphasis on the institutional autonomy of the press has also found expression in his influential dissenting opinion in *Branzburg v. Hayes*,[60] which has become the foundation for the constitutional journalists' privilege.

---

53. Compare Anderson, *supra* note 52, at 487 ("[T]he press clause has its own origins, separate and distinct from the other first amendment rights. Freedom of the press was neither equated with nor viewed as a derivative of freedom of speech.") with L. LEVY, LEGACY OF SUPPRESSION 174 (1960) ("[M]ost writers ... who employed the terms 'freedom of speech' with great frequency, used it synonymously with freedom of the press."). See also First Nat'l Bank of Boston v. Bellotti, 435 U.S. 765, 798 (1978) (Burger, C.J., concurring) ("First, although certainty on this point is not possible, the history of the clause does not suggest that the [Framers] contemplated a 'special' or 'institutional' privilege.").

54. Stewart, *"Or of the Press,"* 26 HASTINGS L.J. 631, 634 (1975).

55. *Id.* at 633-34.

56. *Id.* at 634.

57. *Id.* at 636.

58. 417 U.S. 817 (1974). See Chap. 8-1 *infra*.

59. 417 U.S. 843 (1974). See Chap. 8-1 *infra*.

60. 408 U.S. 665, 725 (1972) (Stewart, J., dissenting). See Chap. 14 *infra*.

§ 1-4(b). Press as Agent or Surrogate.

In significant part, the press enjoys First Amendment protection as the agent or surrogate of the public when performing its informing and checking functions. Justice Powell, dissenting in *Saxbe v. Washington Post Co.*, characterized this informing role:

> No individual can obtain for himself the information needed for the intelligent discharge of his political responsibilities. For most citizens, the prospect of personal familiarity with newsworthy events is hopelessly unrealistic. In seeking out the news the press therefore acts as an agent of the public at large. It is the means by which the people receive that free flow of information and ideas essential to intelligent self-government. . . . The underlying right is the right of the public generally. The press is the necessary representative of the public's interest in this context and the instrumentality which effects the public's right.[61]

Similarly, when recognizing a First Amendment-based right of access to criminal trials in *Richmond Newspapers, Inc. v. Virginia*, Chief Justice Burger acknowledged the public's reliance on the media for information about what goes on at trials.[62] The press serves as "the eyes and ears of the public," allowing the public to see and understand how the public's business is conducted.[63]

The press as agent or surrogate also serves the public function of holding government officials accountable for their conduct of the public's business. In *Mills v. Alabama*, the Court discussed the press's role in public affairs: "[t]he press serves and was designated to serve as a powerful antidote to any abuses of power by governmental officials and as a constitutionally chosen means for keeping officials responsible to all the people whom they were selected to

---

[61]. 417 U.S. 843, 863-64 (1974) (Powell, J., dissenting).

[62]. 448 U.S. 555, 577 n.12 (1980). See *id.* at 586 n.2 (Brennan, J., concurring) ("As a practical matter . . . the institutional press is the likely, and fitting, chief beneficiary of a right of access because it serves as the 'agent' of interested citizens.").

[63]. *Id.* at 572-73 (Burger, C.J., announcing judgment). In *Richmond Newspapers, Inc.*, 448 U.S. at 572-73, Chief Justice Burger noted the role of the press in bringing the public into the courtroom: "Instead of acquiring information about trials by firsthand observation or by word of mouth from those who attended, people now acquire it chiefly through the print and electronic media. In a sense, this validates the media claim of functioning as surrogates for the public." See also Houchins v. KQED, Inc., 438 U.S. 1, 8 (1978) ("Beyond question, the role of the media is important; acting as the 'eyes and ears' of the public, they can be a powerful and constructive force, contributing to remedial action in the conduct of public business. They have served that function since the beginning of the Republic, but like all other components of our society, media representatives are subject to limits.").

serve."[64] This is the checking function of the press. It has been argued that, in modern society, citizens generally lack the will or capacity to check government abuse, that only the media has the resources and ability to restrain government and preserve accountability.[65] Anthony Lewis has noted the relationship between the media's meaningful exercise of this checking function and constitutional support for the media's quest for information:

> If big government is to be effectively criticized and controlled, it will take more than the exhortations of an orator. It will take the countervailing force of big newspapers and broadcast networks and public-interest groups and lobbying organizations of all kinds. And they cannot succeed without information. In our society information is power. Officials struggle to control it, and in that struggle the citizen-critic needs constitutional support.[66]

§ 1-5. Newsgathering and the Right of Access.

If the press is to perform its informing and checking functions, it must be free to publish and to obtain information affecting matters of public concern. The constitutional freedom of the press to publish is well established. The freedom of the press to gather the news, free of excessive governmental interference, and its ability to obtain access to government institutions and to information in the hands of government are, however, less certain.[67]

Justice Brennan attempted to explain this dichotomy by reference to two First Amendment models.[68] The first, the *free speech* model, posits that "the primary purpose of the First Amendment is more or less absolutely to prohibit any interference with freedom of expression."[69] Under this model, the press, like all of us, is free to express its views. At least for Justice Brennan, the First Amendment mandates a near absolute protection for such speech.

The second, the *structural* model, seeks to protect "the structure of communications necessary for the existence of our democracy."[70] When the press circulates information that promotes meaningful public discussion, it performs "communicative functions required by our democratic beliefs" and is protected

---

64. 384 U.S. 214, 219 (1966). See Saxbe v. Washington Post Co., 417 U.S. at 864 (Powell, J., dissenting) ("The press is the necessary representative of the public's interest in this context and the instrumentality which effects the public's right.").

65. See generally Blasi, *supra* note 27.

66. Lewis, *supra* note 42, at 25.

67. See Dyk, *Newsgathering, Press Access, and the First Amendment*, 44 STAN. L. REV. 927, 928 (1992) ("Notably, however, the Court has not been as generous in the area of newsgathering. . . . [T]he Court has yet to explicitly afford special protections to the newsgathering process.").

68. *Address by William J. Brennan, Jr.*, 32 RUTGERS L. REV. 173 (1979).

69. *Id.* at 176.

70. *Id.*

by the First Amendment.[71] Under this model, the press enjoys constitutional protection for activities necessary to gather and disseminate the news. But the potential reach of this structural right requires "a court to weigh the effects" of a regulation burdening newsgathering "against the social interests which are served by the imposition of such regulation."[72] According to Justice Brennan, interest-balancing replaces the near-absolutism of the free speech model in this context, and the First Amendment protection afforded newsgathering activities is not as great as that accorded publication itself.

Justice Brennan articulated this structural model in his concurring opinion in *Richmond Newspapers, Inc. v. Virginia*,[73] and in his opinion for the Court in *Globe Newspaper Co. v. Superior Court*,[74] which together established a First Amendment-based right of access to criminal trials. In *Richmond Newspapers, Inc.*, noting that structural protection for newsgathering is "theoretically endless," he proposed "helpful principles," based on history and function, which are designed to confine access rights within sensible bounds.[75]

In any event, the Supreme Court has plainly accepted that the First Amendment extends to at least some newsgathering activities. In *Branzburg v. Hayes*, Justice White, writing for the Court, acknowledged that "news gathering is not without its First Amendment protections,"[76] and Justice Stewart, in dissent, emphasized that "[n]ews must not be unnecessarily cut off at its source, for without freedom to acquire information the right to publish would be impermissibly compromised. Accordingly, a right to gather news, *of some dimension*, must exist."[77]

The dimensions of the newsgathering right are, nevertheless, decidedly uncertain. In *Branzburg*, Justice White stressed that generally applicable laws are not rendered unconstitutional as applied to the press simply because they incidentally burden its ability to gather news.[78] In *Cohen v. Cowles Media Co.*,[79] the Court again embraced this maxim, which has been repeated in numerous cases involving civil and criminal liability arising from newsgathering activities.[80] And yet, the First Amendment does extend its protection to newsgathering, as the numerous judicial decisions enforcing the journalists' privilege attest.[81] Moreover, constitutional considerations have been held relevant in scrutinizing

---

71. *Id.* at 177.
72. *Id.*
73. 448 U.S. 555, 584-98 (1980) (Brennan, J., concurring). See Chap. 2-2(c) *infra*.
74. 457 U.S. 596 (1982). See Chap. 2-2(d) *infra*.
75. 448 U.S. at 588-89 (Brennan, J., concurring).
76. 408 U.S. 665, 707 (1972). See Chap. 14 *infra*.
77. 408 U.S. at 728 (Stewart, J., dissenting) (emphasis added).
78. 408 U.S. at 682-83.
79. 501 U.S. 663, 669-70 (1991).
80. See Chap. 14-5(c) *infra*.
81. See Chaps. 14-16 *infra*.

the efficacy of civil and criminal laws when applied to newsgathering activities.[82]

In *Richmond Newspapers, Inc. v. Virginia*,[83] the Supreme Court broke new ground. In a "watershed decision,"[84] the Court held, for the first time, that the press and public have a First Amendment-based right of access to criminal trials. Today, as the chapters that follow demonstrate, this right of access has spread to criminal and civil proceedings generally and lower courts continue to explore the boundaries of the access right, as well as the contours of constitutional protection for the newsgathering process generally.

---

82. See Chaps. 12-13 *infra*.
83. 448 U.S. 555 (1980). See Chap. 2-2(c) *infra*.
84. 448 U.S. at 582-83 (Stevens, J., concurring).

Chapter 2

ACCESS TO JUDICIAL PROCEEDINGS: THE CONSTITUTIONAL FOUNDATIONS

§ 2-1. The Constitutional Law of Fair Trial/Free Press.
    § 2-1(a). Background.
    § 2-1(b). The *Sheppard* Mandate.
    § 2-1(c). Criminal Sanctions Against the Media.
    § 2-1(d). Restraining Publication.
§ 2-2. The Constitutional Right of Access in the Supreme Court.
    § 2-2(a). Perspectives on the Constitutional Right of Access.
    § 2-2(b). *Gannett Co. v. DePasquale*.
    § 2-2(c). *Richmond Newspapers, Inc. v. Virginia*.
    § 2-2(d). *Globe Newspaper Co. v. Superior Court*.
    § 2-2(e). *Press-Enterprise Co. v. Superior Court (Press-Enterprise I)*.
    § 2-2(f). *Press-Enterprise Co. v. Superior Court (Press-Enterprise II)*.
    § 2-2(g). *El Vocero de Puerto Rico v. Puerto Rico*.
    § 2-2(h). The Supreme Court Doctrine.
§ 2-3. Procedural Requirements.
§ 2-4. Justice Department Guidelines.

§ 2-1. The Constitutional Law of Fair Trial/Free Press.

§ 2-1(a). Background.

The First Amendment-based right of access to judicial proceedings was born in the wake of what has been commonly described as the "fair trial/free press" debate.[1] The Constitution guarantees to persons charged with crime that they will be tried by an "impartial jury" in a fair proceeding.[2] But press coverage of significant criminal trials in an age of mass media arguably places our ability to deliver on this constitutional promise in jeopardy. And, in an effort to fulfill the

---

1. Much of the material in the text is based on J. BARRON & C. T. DIENES, HANDBOOK OF FREE SPEECH AND FREE PRESS ch. 9 (1979). See also Symposium, *The Right to a Fair Trial,* 1998 U. CHI. LEGAL F. 1; Colloquy, *Impact of the Media on Criminal Trials,* 4 SW. J.L. & TRADE AM. 1 (1997); Liotti, *Closing the Courtroom Door to the Public: Whose Rights are Violated?,* 63 BROOK. L. REV. 501 (1997).

2. The Sixth Amendment to the Constitution guarantees "trial, by an impartial jury" in federal criminal prosecutions. See U.S. CONST. amend. VI. Because trial by an impartial jury is "fundamental to the American scheme of justice," Duncan v. Louisiana, 391 U.S. 145, 149 (1968), this right is also guaranteed in state criminal proceedings as part of the liberty interest protected by the Fourteenth Amendment's Due Process Clause. *Id.* Federal criminal prosecutions are also subject to the Due Process Clause of the Fifth Amendment and to the supervisory power of the Supreme Court. See Rosales-Lopez v. United States, 451 U.S. 182 (1981). See also In re Application of Dow Jones & Co., 842 F.2d 603, 609 (2d Cir.), *cert. denied,* 488 U.S. 946 (1988); Johnson v. Mississippi, 476 So. 2d 1195, 1209 (Miss. 1985) ("A fair trial is, after all, the reason we have our system of justice.").

promise of due process, there is a danger of employing rules and regulations that are inconsistent with the First Amendment.

It has been argued that media coverage of a trial can create a courtroom atmosphere at odds with the calm, deliberative proceedings envisioned in the guarantee of a fair trial. The circus-like trial of Bruno Hauptmann for the kidnapping and murder of the Lindbergh baby is a classic example of the potential danger of uncontrolled media coverage.[3] Some have argued that the very presence of reporters and cameras in the courtroom is inconsistent with the order and decorum contemplated by due process.[4]

Another perceived threat to due process is the potential prejudicial impact of media reporting of pretrial and trial proceedings. Sensational criminal cases such as those involving cult leader Charles Manson,[5] the mass murderer Richard Speck,[6] or more recently, the trials of William Kennedy Smith,[7] O.J. Simpson,[8] and Theodore Kaczynski (the Unabomber)[9] and the Oklahoma City bombing trials of Timothy McVeigh and Terry Nichols,[10] periodically raise the issue of

---

3. See New Jersey v. Hauptmann, 180 A. 809 (N.J.), *cert. denied*, 296 U.S. 649 (1935). See also Reimer, *Television Coverage of Trials: Constitutional Protection Against Absolute Denial of Access in the Absence of a Compelling Interest*, 30 VILL. L. REV. 1267, 1269 (1985); Stephen, *Prejudicial Publicity Surrounding a Criminal Trial: What A Trial Court Can Do to Ensure a Fair Trial in the Face of a Media Circus*, 26 SUFFOLK U. L. REV. 1063, 1068-69 (1992).

4. See Estes v. Texas, 381 U.S. 532, 540 (1965) (telecasts of a hearing and trial "inherently prevented a sober search for truth"). In *Estes*, the Supreme Court asserted that "the atmosphere essential to the preservation of a fair trial — the most fundamental of all freedoms — must be maintained at all costs." *Id.* Since *Estes*, however, courts have concluded that cameras in the courtroom are not inherently prejudicial. See, e.g., Chandler v. Florida, 449 U.S. 560 (1981); Diehl v. Virginia, 384 S.E.2d 801 (1989), *vacated*, 390 S.E.2d 550 (Va. 1990); West Virginia v. Hanna, 378 S.E.2d 640 (W. Va. 1987). See generally Harris, *The Appearance of Justice: Court TV, Conventional Television, and Public Understanding of the Criminal Justice System*, 35 ARIZ. L. REV. 785 (1993); Chap. 4 *infra*.

5. People v. Manson, 139 Cal. Rptr. 275 (Ct. App. 1977), *cert. denied*, 435 U.S. 953 (1978). See also Stephen, *supra* note 3, at 1076-78.

6. People v. Speck, 242 N.E.2d 208 (Ill. 1965), *vacated in part*, 403 U.S. 946 (1971).

7. See Harris, *supra* note 4, at 801; Stephen, *supra* note 3.

8. See Sager, *First Amendment Issues in the O.J. Simpson Trial*, 12 COMM. LAW. 3 (Winter 1995); Schuyler, *The Simpson Spins: Through the Looking Glass With O.J. and a Host of Legal Critics*, CAL. LAW., Sept. 1994, at 5.

9. Kaczynski pleaded guilty to the Unabomber crimes and was sentenced to life imprisonment without the possibility of parole. The media successfully sought access to the psychiatric report establishing Kaczynski's competency to stand trial. See United States v. Kaczynski, 154 F.3d 930 (9th Cir. 1998).

10. McVeigh was convicted on eleven counts, including first-degree murder, stemming from the bombing of the Alfred E. Murrah Federal Building in Oklahoma City, which resulted in the deaths of 168 people. The Eighth Circuit rejected his contention that pretrial publicity unfairly prejudiced his right to a fair trial. See United States v. McVeigh, 153 F.3d 1166 (10th Cir. 1998), *cert. denied*, 119 S. Ct. 1148 (1999). Nichols was convicted of conspiring to use a weapon of mass destruction and eight counts of involuntary manslaughter for his role in the bombing. United States v. Nichols,

reconciling the guarantees of an impartial judge and jury with press freedom. Due process contemplates that a defendant be tried on the evidence admitted in court, not on the basis of outside influences.[11] If a jury is exposed to press accounts of inadmissible evidence, such as a confession, prior criminal record, illegally seized evidence or hearsay, it may become difficult to fulfill the constitutional promise of fair proceedings.

Of course, very few criminal cases attract significant media attention.[12] Further, if media coverage does influence the outcome of a trial, an appellate court can reverse a conviction for prejudice — actual[13] or inherent.[14] But the

---

169 F.3d 1255 (10th Cir. 1999). See also Jones & Hillerman, *McVeigh, McJustice, McMedia*, 1998 U. CHI. LEGAL F. 53 (defense counsel's analysis of fair trial and access issues in the *McVeigh* case); Walton, *From O.J. to Tim McVeigh and Beyond: The Supreme Court's Totality of the Circumstances Test as Ringmaster in the Expanding Media Circus*, 75 DENV. U. L. REV. 549 (1998).

11. In *Patterson v. Colorado*, 205 U.S. 454, 462 (1907), Justice Holmes stated that, in our criminal justice system, "conclusions to be reached in a case will be induced only by evidence and argument in open courts and not by any outside influence, whether of private talk or public print." Justice Black echoed this sentiment in *Bridges v. California*, 314 U.S. 252, 281 (1941): "Legal trials are not like elections, to be won through the use of the meeting hall, the radio, and the newspaper."

12. In a study of 63,000 criminal appeals in state criminal cases between 1976 and 1980, only 368 involved a claim of prejudicial publicity. In these 368 appeals, reversals based on the publicity were ordered in only 18 cases, or five percent. Spencer, *The So-Called Problem of Prejudicial Publicity Is a Red Herring*, 2 COMM. LAW. 11 (1984). The evidence concerning the effect of publicity on jurors is far from conclusive. See Levine & Grossberg, *The Myth of Pretrial Publicity*, WASH. JOURNALISM REV., Oct. 1986. Further, even if it were established that publicity can cause prejudice, there would still be a question whether a particular jury was biased. See generally Ogloff & Vidmar, *The Impact of Pretrial Publicity on Jurors*, 18 LAW & HUM. BEHAV. 507 (1994); Dreschsel, *An Alternative View of Media-Judiciary Relations: What the Non-Legal Evidence Suggests About the Fair-Trial-Free Press Issue*, 18 HOFSTRA L. REV. 1 (1989).

13. Actual prejudice requires a showing of the publicity's actual effects on jurors. See Irwin v. Dowd, 366 U.S. 717 (1961). In *Irwin*, extensive media coverage publicized Irwin's arrest, confession to six murders and 24 burglaries, his lineup identification, his unsuccessful plea bargaining, and the prosecutor's promise to secure a death sentence for the "confessed slayer of six." Ninety percent of the 370 prospective jurors had some established conviction regarding Irwin's guilt. Eight of the 12 selected jurors believed Irwin was guilty, although they claimed they could reach a judgment based solely on the evidence. In *Patton v. Yount*, 467 U.S. 1025, 1029 (1984), 124 of 126 potential jurors had heard of the case through the media and eight of 14 jurors seated had at one time formed an opinion as to the defendant's guilt, yet no bias was presumed. See generally Flynn, *Prejudicial Publicity in Criminal Trials: Bringing* Sheppard v. Maxwell *Into the Nineties*, 27 NEW ENG. L. REV. 857 (1993).

14. See Rideau v. Louisiana, 373 U.S. 723 (1963). In *Rideau*, the Supreme Court noted that, as a result of telecast of Rideau's interrogation, a community of 150,000 "had been exposed repeatedly and in depth to the spectacle of Rideau personally confessing in detail to the crimes with which he was later to be charged." *Id.* at 726. Requests for a change of venue were denied. These circumstances were sufficient to establish inherent prejudice — i.e., there was no need to prove jurors were in fact prejudiced. The Court concluded that, after three days of rebroadcasting the confession, any proceeding "could be but a hollow formality." *Id.*

relationship between publicity and prejudice is far from clear — jury exposure to publicity is not alone sufficient to establish prejudice.[15] And, reversal of a conviction because of prejudice is a serious and costly response to the problem.

Judicial efforts to prevent prejudice generally fall under two headings. First, the trial court can employ a variety of traditional techniques that only indirectly affect the ability of the press to attend and report on a criminal proceeding, such as sequestration of a jury, continuance, or change of venue. While such indirect devices may burden newsgathering, their impact is generally incidental and limited, leaving a variety of alternatives open to journalists. More problematic is the imposition of direct restraints on the press such as gag orders, the closure of proceedings to the media, and post-publication sanctions. The use of such restraints has proved difficult to square with the First Amendment.

§ 2-1(b). The *Sheppard* Mandate.

The Supreme Court's effort to reconcile the competing demands of the First and Sixth Amendments began, for all practical purposes, in *Sheppard v. Maxwell*.[16] In 1954, Dr. Sam Sheppard was charged with the bludgeoning death of his pregnant wife. While the doctor proclaimed his innocence, he was subjected to "massive" and "pervasive"[17] prejudicial publicity both before and

---

15. In *Irwin v. Dowd*, for example, the Court indicated that a juror is qualified "if the juror can lay aside his impression or opinion and render a verdict based on the evidence presented in court." 366 U.S. at 723. However, jurors' assurances are not dispositive and the defendant may prove that a juror is, in fact, biased. In *Murphy v. Florida*, 421 U.S. 794 (1975), although there was extensive publicity concerning the saga of "Murph the Surf," the Court held it was insufficient to establish actual or inherent prejudice. News reports tended to be factual and not inflammatory. Media coverage dissipated prior to trial. Only 20 of the 78 persons questioned for the jury had been excused. "The voir dire in this case indicates no such hostility in his trial as to suggest a partiality that could not be laid aside." *Id.* at 800.

In *DeLisle v. Rivers*, 161 F.3d 370 (6th Cir. 1998), the Sixth Circuit held that bias of the jurors could not be presumed from their knowledge of DeLisle's suppressed alleged confession in the murder of his four children and attempted murder of his wife. The court examined precedent in which the Supreme Court determined that bias could be presumed and found that "these cases are so wholly distant from the one before us that we are compelled to conclude that DeLisle's claim fails." *Id.* at 383. The court observed that press coverage of the case had substantially diminished in the four months between press access to audio and video tapes of the defendant's statements to the police and the time of trial, and the media coverage was not of the virulent sort that would cause a presumption of bias. See *id.* at 385-86. The Sixth Circuit rejected the argument that confessions are "unlike any other piece of information" in causing prejudice, noting that the Supreme Court's holdings "foreclose the argument that jurors who read that [a] defendant had confessed to the murder ... should be disqualified as a matter of law." *Id.* at 386. The court found that nothing in the record suggests "extraordinary or utterly corrupting circumstances that give us reason to impute partiality to jurors who explicitly and firmly state their lack of bias." *Id.* at 386.

16. 384 U.S. 333 (1966).

17. *Id.* at 353.

during his trial.[18] Much of the "evidence" printed or broadcast was never admitted in court. During the nine-week trial, a "carnival atmosphere"[19] prevailed — "[t]he fact is that bedlam reigned at the courthouse during the trial and newsmen took over practically the entire courtroom, hounding most of the participants in the trial, especially Sheppard."[20] In spite of this potential for prejudice, the trial judge limited his involvement to "suggestions" and "requests" that the jury avoid outside influences and Sheppard was denied a change of venue.[21] The jury was not sequestered until the case was submitted and, even then, jurors had uncontrolled access to telephones.[22] Defense requests that the trial judge question the jurors about their exposure to prejudicial press coverage were denied.[23] Sheppard was convicted of second-degree murder.

After Sheppard had spent a decade in prison, his conviction was reversed. Citing the massive publicity, the lack of "judicial serenity and calm,"[24] and the trial judge's failure to take preventive action, the Supreme Court held that "the totality of circumstances"[25] established inherent prejudice requiring reversal.[26] Justice Clark, writing for the Court, recognized that this was an unsatisfying response to the problem: "reversals are but palliatives; the cure lies in those remedial measures that will prevent the prejudice at its inception. The courts must take such steps by rule and regulation that will protect their process from prejudicial outside influences."[27] At the same time, Justice Clark recognized the value of a free press to the administration of justice:

> A responsible press has always been regarded as the handmaiden of effective judicial administration, especially in the criminal field. Its function in this regard is documented by an impressive record of service over several centuries. The press does not simply publish information about trials but guards against the miscarriage of justice by subjecting the police, prosecutors, and judicial processes to extensive public scrutiny and criticism.[28]

---

18. See *id.* at 356-57. Writing for the Court, Justice Clark noted that there was no doubt "that this deluge of publicity reached at least some of the jury." *Id.* at 357. All jurors selected, with one exception, had read something about the case in the newspapers. See *id.* at 354 n.9.
19. *Id.* at 358.
20. *Id.* at 355.
21. *Id.*
22. See *id.* at 352-53.
23. See *id.* at 357.
24. *Id.* at 355.
25. *Id.* at 352.
26. See *id.* at 363 ("Since the state trial judge did not fulfill his duty to protect Sheppard from the inherently prejudicial publicity which saturated the community and to control disruptive influences in the courtroom, we must reverse the denial of the habeas petition.").
27. *Id.*
28. *Id.* at 350.

The Court indicated that the trial judge's fundamental error lay in his belief that he lacked the power to control prejudice because he could not restrict prejudicial news accounts. In the Court's view, the trial judge had ignored a variety of procedures short of direct sanctions against the media that "would have been sufficient to guarantee Sheppard a fair trial."[29] Thus, the Court in *Sheppard* placed responsibility for taking preventive action squarely on the trial judge and outlined a variety of available procedures.

The "carnival atmosphere could easily have been avoided since the courtroom and courthouse premises are subject to the control of the court,"[30] Justice Clark asserted. And, he explained, there were a variety of techniques available to the trial judge to limit the prejudicial effects of publicity: express warnings to the jury to avoid outside influences; sequestration of witnesses and jurors; a continuance until the threat abated; warnings to and proscription of extrajudicial statements by trial participants; a change of venue to a locale not so permeated with publicity; and, if these measures failed, a new trial.[31] To this list could be added judicial involvement in voir dire to ascertain whether a prospective juror was truly impartial.[32]

---

29. *Id.* at 358.

30. *Id.* While Justice Clark did not endorse closing the courtroom, he did note that "the judge should have adopted stricter rules governing the use of the courtroom by newsmen." *Id.* The contempt power is the trial court's primary tool for dealing with offensive conduct in the courtroom. See generally R. GOLDFARB, THE CONTEMPT POWER (1971).

31. 384 U.S. at 357-63. Such devices are not, however, free from risk. A change of venue might violate the defendant's Sixth Amendment right to be tried before a "jury of the State and district wherein the crime shall have been committed." U.S. CONST. amend. VI. Delay produced by continuances could conflict with the defendant's Sixth Amendment right to a "speedy and public trial." *Id.* The effectiveness of jury warnings and instructions may, in a given case, be suspect. The impact of sequestration on jurors' lives and attitudes suggests it is not a remedy to be invoked lightly. See Minow & Cate, *Who Is an Impartial Juror in an Age of Mass Media?*, 40 AM. U. L. REV. 631, 654 (1991). Compare Stabile, *Free Press-Fair Trial: Can They Be Reconciled in a Highly Publicized Criminal Case?*, 79 GEO. L.J. 337, 343 (1990) ("In most highly publicized criminal cases, these less drastic alternatives will be insufficient to safeguard the fair trial rights of the defendant."), with Stephen, *supra* note 3, at 1075-78 (discussing cases in which combinations of these methods were employed successfully to combat pretrial publicity). On the use of sequestration, see Strauss, *Sequestration*, 24 AM. J. CRIM. L. 63 (1996).

32. In *Patton v. Yount*, 467 U.S. 1025, 1038 (1984), the Court said of voir dire: "It is fair to assume that the method we have relied on since the beginning, e.g., *United States v. Burr*, usually identifies bias." Indeed, in *Hitchcock v. Florida*, 578 So. 2d 685 (Fla. 1990), *cert. denied*, 502 U.S. 912 (1991), *vacated*, 505 U.S. 1215 (1992), the use of voir dire during the resentencing phase of a death penalty case was sufficient to ascertain partiality by jurors who were aware, through pretrial publicity, of the death penalty to which the defendant previously had been sentenced. Nevertheless, critics argue that voir dire often excludes the more intelligent and informed, and raises serious questions concerning whether it is effective in identifying prejudiced jurors. See Minow & Cate, *supra* note 31, at 650-54; Walton, *supra* note 10 (suggesting that extensive questioning during voir dire may be constitutionally mandated to deal with possible nationwide jury bias and consequent risk to the defendant's fair trial rights in extremely high profile cases).

Finally, in *Sheppard*, Justice Clark warned that, "[g]iven the pervasiveness of modern communications and the difficulty of effacing prejudicial publicity from the minds of the jurors, the trial courts must take strong measures to ensure that the balance is never weighted against the accused."[33] Since the Court determined that indirect preventives would have protected Sheppard's due process rights, however, it was unnecessary to address "what sanctions might be available against a recalcitrant press."[34] Still, the Court's firm mandate that trial judges take action to protect the accused from prejudicial publicity was read by many as an instruction to take action, when necessary, against the press.

§ 2-1(c). Criminal Sanctions Against the Media.

In the United Kingdom, courts regularly seek to control prejudicial publicity in pending cases through the issuance of contempt citations.[35] In the United States, however, such direct restraints on the press will almost always be held to be unconstitutional. In a series of cases, the Supreme Court has erected significant constitutional barriers to their use.[36]

In *Bridges v. California*,[37] Harry Bridges, president of a Longshoreman's Union, had been held in common law contempt for criticizing a judge's decision in a suit against his union and threatening strikes. In a companion case, the *Los Angeles Times* was held in contempt for publishing editorials held to constitute an effort to influence the outcome of judicial proceedings.[38] Reversing both contempt citations, the Supreme Court held that the First Amendment marked a break with the English common law of contempt.[39] Citations for out-of-court publications could be justified only by a "clear and present danger" that there was an "extremely high" degree of imminence of an "extremely serious" substantive evil.[40]

---

33. 384 U.S. at 362.
34. *Id.* at 358.
35. See Gillmor, *Free Press and Fair Trial in English Law*, 22 WASH. & LEE L. REV. 17 (1965); 17 AM. JUR. 2d *Contempt* § 124; 40 A.L.R.3d 1205, §§ 2-3.
36. See generally Schmidt, *Nebraska Press Association: An Expansion of Freedom and Contraction of Theory*, 29 STAN. L. REV. 431, 433-36 (1977); Isaacson, *Fair Trial and Free Press: An Opportunity for Coexistence*, 29 STAN. L. REV. 516, 572-73 (1977).

18 U.S.C. § 401(1) limits the use of the contempt power in federal courts to misconduct "in [the judge's] presence or so near thereto as to obstruct the administration of justice." In *Nye v. United States*, 313 U.S. 33 (1941), the Supreme Court held that the phrase "so near thereto" reflects a geographical limitation to contempt "within" or proximate to the courtroom.

37. 314 U.S. 252 (1941). See Isaacson, *supra* note 36, at 572.
38. The *Times* had published an editorial commenting that a trial judge would make a "serious mistake" if he granted probation in the criminal trial of two union workers. See 314 U.S. at 272.
39. See *id.* at 265.
40. *Id.* at 263. See also Garland v. Georgia, 325 S.E.2d 131, 133 (Ga. 1985); In re Hinds, 449 A.2d 483, 491 (N.J. 1982) (both discussing out-of-court expression by attorneys).

Writing for the Court, Justice Black held that the state's interest in promoting respect for the judiciary was insufficient to overcome the "prized American privilege to speak one's mind, although not always with perfect good taste, on all public institutions."[41] While the state interest in the fair administration of justice was more compelling, the Court concluded that the record did not present the requisite clear and present danger of harm. A mind of "reasonable fortitude," such as would be expected of a judge, would not, in the Court's view, be easily pressured by adverse publicity.[42]

The principle established in *Bridges* has governed the Court's response to subsequent cases of allegedly prejudicial press coverage. In *Pennekamp v. Florida*,[43] a unanimous Court reversed the criminal contempt convictions of two editors who, based on mistaken information, had criticized the judicial use of perceived technicalities to free criminals. The Court concluded that "the danger . . . to fair judicial administration has not the clearness and immediacy necessary to close the door of permissible public comment. When that door is closed, it closes all doors behind it."[44]

In *Craig v. Harney*,[45] which arose in the context of caustic press commentary about a lay judge's refusal to accept a jury's decision, the court noted that judges must not be unnerved by "the winds of public opinion,"[46] which will typically pose no "imminent and serious threat to the ability of the court to give fair consideration" to litigants.[47] Fifteen years after *Bridges*, in *Wood v. Georgia*,[48] the Court reaffirmed its continuing applicability. Lower courts had held that a sheriff's criticism of instructions to a grand jury did present a clear and present danger to the administration of justice. But the Supreme Court examined the record and found nothing to indicate "the serious degree of harm to the administration of law necessary to justify exercise of the contempt power."[49] Rather,

---

41. 314 U.S. at 270-71. See also In re Hinds, 449 A.2d at 488 ("The Constitution unquestionably guarantees the right of citizens to criticize public officials, including judges.").

42. 314 U.S. at 278.

43. 328 U.S. 331 (1946). See also Schmidt, *supra* note 36, at 433-36.

44. 328 U.S. at 350. In assessing the competing interests, the Court asserted that "freedom of public comment should weigh heavily against a possible tendency to influence pending cases. Freedom of discussion should be given the widest range compatible with the essential requirement of the fair and orderly administration of justice." *Id.* at 347.

45. 331 U.S. 367 (1947). In *Craig*, while a motion for a new trial was pending in a civil case, the newspaper castigated the judge for taking "arbitrary action" and labeled his rulings a "travesty." *Id.* at 369-70.

46. *Id.* at 376; see *id.* ("Judges are supposed to be men of fortitude, able to thrive in a hardy climate."). But see *id.* at 392 (Frankfurter, J., dissenting) ("Even a conscientious judge . . . may find himself in a dilemma when subjected to a barrage pressing a particular result in a case immediately before him.").

47. *Id.* at 378.

48. 370 U.S. 375 (1962).

49. *Id.* at 392.

the Court found the type of political expression that the First Amendment was designed to protect.[50]

More recently, the First Amendment's antipathy to criminal sanctions directed at publications commenting on the operation of government institutions has driven a series of decisions by the Supreme Court commencing with *Landmark Communications, Inc. v. Virginia*.[51] In that case, a Virginia statute made it a crime for a newspaper to publish confidential material relating to judicial disciplinary proceedings. When the *Virginian-Pilot* accurately reported that an identified judge was under investigation, its corporate owner was charged with violating the statute and convicted of a misdemeanor. The Virginia Supreme Court upheld the conviction on the ground that confidentiality was necessary to protect the reputation of the judge under investigation, to maintain confidence in the judiciary, and to encourage the filing of complaints and the participation of witnesses in disciplinary proceedings.[52]

The Supreme Court reversed. Writing for the Court, Chief Justice Burger emphasized that "the publication Virginia seeks to punish under its statute lies near the core of the First Amendment, and the Commonwealth's interests advanced by the imposition of criminal sanctions are insufficient to justify the actual and potential encroachments on freedom of speech and the press which follow therefrom."[53] The Court did not question that confidentiality served the asserted state interests, but concluded that they did not justify use of criminal sanctions.[54] *Bridges* and its progeny, the Court noted, also establish that press commentary on pending cases generally does not constitute a clear and present

---

50. See *id.* at 388. See generally Schmidt, *supra* note 36, at 433-36; 17 AM. JUR. 2d *Contempt* §§ 120-28; 40 A.L.R. 3d 1205, §§ 2-3.

51. 435 U.S. 829 (1978). See generally Kept, *Reconciling the Need for Confidentiality in Judicial Discipline Proceedings with the First Amendment: A Justification Based Analysis*, 7 GEO. J. LEGAL ETHICS 959, 970-72 (1994).

52. See 435 U.S. at 833; see also Del Papa v. Steffen, 915 P.2d 245 (Nev. 1996) (orders appointing special master to investigate media leaks regarding judicial disciplinary inquiry invalid). In *Del Papa*, the Nevada Supreme Court held that neither a judge's interest in confidentiality nor potential harm to the judiciary from publicizing frivolous complaints constitutes a compelling interest "that override[s] the constitutionally protected rights of freedom of speech and press and access to the courts in a case of the highest public concern." *Id.* at 249. See also Del Papa v. Steffen, 920 P.2d 489, 490 (Nev. 1996), *cert. denied*, 519 U.S. 1109 (1997) ("[T]he court must get on with its regular business and not conduct unconstitutional investigations.").

53. 435 U.S at 838. Cf. Worrell Newspapers of Indiana, Inc. v. Westhafer, 739 F.2d 1219, 1224 (7th Cir. 1984), *aff'd*, 469 U.S. 1200 (1985) (publication of facts surrounding the indictment of an arson suspect was near the core of the First Amendment and state's interest in preventing flight before capture was not sufficient to outweigh public interest in publication).

54. See 435 U.S. at 842. See also Marin Indep. Journal v. Municipal Ct., 16 Cal. Rptr. 2d 550, 555 (Ct. App. 1993) (while photographs may not be published if obtained in an unlawful manner, nothing in the First Amendment prevents the publication of lawfully obtained information).

danger to the administration of justice.[55] Further, what risk there was could be eliminated by internal safeguards designed to protect legitimate confidentiality interests.[56]

Then, in *Smith v. Daily Mail Publishing Co.*,[57] the Court held that a West Virginia statute making it a crime for a newspaper to publish the name of a youth charged as a juvenile offender without prior judicial approval was unconstitutional. The reporting at issue had revealed the identity of a fourteen-year-old suspected of shooting and killing a classmate.[58] While the newspaper claimed that the requirement that it seek court approval before publishing created a prior restraint, the Court found it unnecessary to reach that issue because another basic constitutional principle was deemed to be controlling: "[I]f a newspaper lawfully obtains truthful information about a matter of public significance then state officials may not constitutionally punish publication of the information, absent a need to further a state interest of the highest order."[59] In the Court's view, a "free

---

55. See 435 U.S. at 844. See also Worrell Newspapers of Indiana, Inc. v. Westhafer, 739 F.2d 1219 (7th Cir. 1984), *aff'd*, 469 U.S. 1200 (1985) (finding no evidence of a clear and present danger that indictees who hear about their indictments in the news might flee so as to require a statute punishing any person by criminal contempt for truthfully publishing the name of an individual against whom a sealed information or indictment has been filed).

56. See 435 U.S. at 841. See also In re a Minor, 537 N.E.2d 292, 301 (Ill. 1989) ("It serves no purpose to shut the barn door when the horse has already fled."). Justice Stewart concurred in *Landmark* because Virginia had

> extended its law to punish a newspaper, and that it cannot constitutionally do. If the constitutional protection of a free press means anything, it means that government cannot take it upon itself to decide what a newspaper may and may not publish. Though government may deny access to information and punish its theft, government may not prohibit or punish the publication of that information once it falls into the hands of the press, unless the need for secrecy is manifestly overwhelming.

435 U.S. at 849 (Stewart, J., concurring).

57. 443 U.S. 97 (1979). See generally Giampetruzzi, *Raped Once, But Violated Twice: Constitutional Protection of a Rape Victim's Privacy*, 66 ST. JOHN'S L. REV. 151, 163-65 (1993); Haughtnout, *Publishing Rape Victim Identification in the Media: Is It Constitutional?*, 23 U. TOLEDO L. REV. 735 (1992).

58. See 443 U.S. at 99-100.

59. *Id.* at 103. See The Florida Star v. B.J.F., 491 U.S. 524 (1989) (reversing an award of civil damages based on negligence per se for publishing a rape victim's name contrary to a state statute requiring confidentiality); Cox Broadcasting Corp. v. Cohn, 420 U.S. 469 (1975) (rejecting civil liability for publishing a rape victim's name in violation of a state statute where the name was obtained from government records open to the public); Oklahoma Publ'g Co. v. District Ct., 430 U.S. 308 (1977) (reversing injunction prohibiting publication of a juvenile defendant's name and picture where the information was obtained at an open hearing of the juvenile court). See generally Denno, *The Privacy Rights of Rape Victims in the Media and Law: Perspectives on Disclosing Rape Victims' Names*, 61 FORDHAM L. REV. 1113 (1993); Giampetruzzi, *supra* note 57; Haughtnout, *supra* note 57.

press cannot be made to rely solely upon the sufferance of government to supply it with information."[60]

Thus, in *Smith*, the Court concluded that the state's interest in preserving the anonymity of juvenile offenders was not sufficient to justify a criminal sanction against the press.[61] Indeed, the statute's failure to regulate media other than newspapers meant that it could not accomplish its intended purpose in any event.[62] Finally, there was inadequate evidence that criminal penalties were "necessary" to protect confidentiality,[63] at least where there was no claim of invasion of privacy or prejudicial pretrial publicity.[64] Taken together, the *Bridges* and the *Landmark* lines of cases establish the principle that criminal sanctions can be used against a free press only if there is an imminent danger to the fair trial rights of a defendant or if the government demonstrates that such a sanction is necessary to further an interest of the highest order. While protecting the Sixth Amendment rights of an accused is a compelling interest, the First Amendment severely limits the government's ability to invoke criminal sanctions against the press as a means of furthering that interest.

§ 2-1(d). Restraining Publication.

The Supreme Court's decision in *Sheppard* generated a rash of trial court orders designed to curb prejudicial publicity. While the Court's opinion in *Sheppard* had, on its face, endorsed only restraining orders preventing extrajudicial commentary by trial participants, many of the restraints that followed were

---

60. 443 U.S. at 105. See also First Nat'l Bank of Boston v. Bellotti, 435 U.S. 765, 783 (1978) ("The First Amendment goes beyond protection of the press and self-expression of individuals to prohibit government from limiting the stock of information from which members of the public may draw.").

61. See 443 U.S. at 104-05. See also Colorado v. Denver Publ'g Co., 597 P.2d 1038 (Colo. 1979) (holding statute imposing criminal sanctions for publishing, without leave of court, information identifying persons appearing as witnesses in juvenile proceedings unconstitutionally overbroad); Florida v. Globe Communications Corp., 648 So. 2d 110 (Fla. 1994) (holding statute mandating criminal sanctions for identifying the victim of a sexual offense in any instrument of mass communication unconstitutionally overbroad and underinclusive); Jeffries v. Mississippi, 724 So. 2d 897 (Miss. 1998) (reversing criminal contempt conviction of newspaper reporter who, in violation of court order, reported juvenile record discussed in open court because the reporter was not accorded the necessary procedural safeguards for such a contempt charge and because the order was an invalid prior restraint).

62. See 443 U.S. at 105. See also Florida v. Globe Communications Corp., 622 So. 2d 1066, 1073 (Fla. App. 1993), *aff'd*, 684 So. 2d 110 (Fla. 1994) (holding that because the media, including many British tabloids, had already published the victim's name in a highly publicized rape trial, barring the American press from doing so would be largely fruitless).

63. See 443 U.S. at 105.

64. See *id.* at 105. See also In re a Minor, 537 N.E.2d at 301 (government's vague reference to "certain threats" that had been circulating in the community does not demonstrate sufficient potential for harm to prohibit publication of minor's name in murder trial).

"gag orders" — as they are described by the press — prohibiting *media* publications about particular subjects, e.g., a criminal defendant's confession.

The Supreme Court addressed the validity of such orders in *Nebraska Press Association v. Stuart*.[65] In 1975, Irwin Charles Simants was arrested for the murder of six members of the Henry Kellie family in a small Nebraska town. Three days after the arrest, Simants' attorney and the prosecutor jointly sought a county court order restraining "matters that may or may not be publicly reported or disclosed to the public;" the court issued a restraining order restricting coverage of the trial and requiring the press to observe otherwise voluntary Nebraska bar-press guidelines for reporting on criminal cases.[66]

Simants was bound over to the district court, which issued an order prohibiting media publication on designated subjects until the jury was impaneled. The district court found the restraint necessary because "there is a clear and present danger that pretrial publicity could impinge upon the defendant's right to a fair trial."[67] The Nebraska Supreme Court affirmed, after balancing "the heavy presumption against [the] constitutional validity" of an order restraining publication against the importance of the defendant's right to an impartial jury.[68] The court did, however, modify the order, limiting it to three subjects: (1) confessions or admissions made by the defendants to law enforcement officers, (2) confessions or admissions made to third parties, excepting the press, and (3) other facts "strongly implicative" of the accused.[69]

The United States Supreme Court unanimously reversed. Chief Justice Burger, for the Court, described the prior restraint at issue as "one of the most extraordinary remedies known to our jurisprudence."[70] Such an order, the Court

---

65. 427 U.S. 539 (1976). See generally Stabile, *supra* note 31, at 341-43; Peterson, *A First Amendment-Sixth Amendment Dilemma: Manuel Noriega Pushes the American Judicial System to the Outer Limits of the First Amendment*, 25 J. MARSHALL L. REV. 563, 576-81 (1992); Symposium, *Nebraska Press Association v. Stuart*, 29 STAN. L. REV. 383 (1977).

66. 427 U.S. at 542. Such guidelines are voluntary agreements entered into between the state bar and the institutional press. They typically describe what subjects are and are not appropriate for news coverage. The Nebraska Guidelines established a bar-press committee to resolve specific problems as they emerged. See Ezzard, *Confidentiality in Civil Proceedings: Public Access vs. Litigant's Privacy*, 22 COLO. L. 2237, 2240 (1993) (discussing various state guidelines); Chafetz, *Fair Trial and Free Press — Washington Conditions Media Access to the Courtroom*, 57 WASH. L. REV. 759 (1982) (discussing Federated Publications, Inc. v. Swedberg, 633 P.2d 74 (Wash. 1981), *cert. denied*, 456 U.S. 984 (1982), which conditioned media access to trial upon voluntary adherence to guidelines).

67. 427 U.S. at 543.

68. *Id.* at 545.

69. *Id.*

70. *Id.* at 562. "Any system of prior restraint of expression comes to [the Court] bearing a heavy presumption against its constitutionality." Bantam Books, Inc. v. Sullivan, 372 U.S. 58, 70 (1963). The government, therefore, "carries a heavy burden of justification for the imposition of such a restraint." Organization for a Better Austin v. Keefe, 402 U.S. 415, 419 (1971). "Prior restraints, if

asserted, is "the most serious and the least tolerable infringement on First Amendment rights,"[71] because while the threat of sanctions after publication chills speech, "prior restraint 'freezes' it at least for a time."[72] Given the importance of a free press to effective judicial administration, the Court held that "the protection against prior restraint should have particular force as applied to reporting of criminal proceedings."[73] In the Court's view, even when the order at issue only delays publication, "the element of time is not unimportant if press coverage is to fulfill its traditional function of bringing news to the public promptly."[74]

To determine if the "presumption" against the validity of the prior restraint had been overcome, the Court invoked a variant of the clear and present danger doctrine — whether the gravity of the evil, discounted by its improbability, justifies such a limitation on the freedom of expression as is necessary to avoid the danger.[75] Thus, the Court explained, the trial judge in the first instance must examine the evidence to determine: "(a) the nature and extent of pretrial news coverage; (b) whether other measures would be likely to mitigate the effects of unrestrained pretrial publicity; and (c) how effectively a restraining order would operate to prevent the threatened danger."[76]

While the Court in *Nebraska Press Association* did not announce an absolute prohibition on prior restraints in the Sixth Amendment context, its application of the clear and present danger standard suggests as much.[77] First, Chief Justice

---

permissible at all, are permissible only in the most extraordinary of circumstances." United States v. DeLorean, 729 F.2d 1174, 1183 (9th Cir. 1990). See Fort Wayne Journal-Gazette v. Baker, 788 F. Supp. 379, 384 (N.D. Ind. 1992). See generally Scordato, *Distinction Without a Difference: A Reappraisal of the Doctrine of Prior Restraint*, 68 N.C. L. REV. 1 (1989).

71. 427 U.S. at 559.
72. *Id*. (citing A. BICKEL, THE MORALITY OF CONSENT 61 (1975)).
73. 427 U.S. at 559.
74. *Id*. at 561. In *Elrod v. Burns*, 427 U.S. 347, 373-74 (1976), the Court indicated that "the loss of First Amendment freedoms for even minimal periods of time unquestionably constitutes irreparable injury." This principle was reaffirmed by Justice Blackmun who, sitting as Circuit Justice, granted a stay against an injunction that prohibited a television network from broadcasting videotape footage shot inside a meat packing plant with an undercover camera. CBS Inc. v. Davis, 114 S. Ct. 912, 914 (1994) (Blackmun, J., in chambers) (citing Nebraska Press Ass'n v. Stuart, 423 U.S. 1327, 1329 (1976)) ("Where . . . a direct prior restraint is imposed upon the reporting of news by the media, each passing day may constitute a separate and cognizable infringement of the First Amendment.").
75. See 427 U.S. at 562 (citing Dennis v. United States, 183 F.2d 201, 212 (2d Cir. 1950), *aff'd*, 341 U.S. 494 (1951)). This "gravity of the evil" formulation is generally considered a watered-down version of the clear and present danger test fashioned by Justices Holmes and Brandeis. See Schmidt, *supra* note 36, at 459-60 (criticizing use of *Dennis* formulation). See also Stabile, *supra* note 31, at 349-52 (discussing cases invoking the clear and present danger test).
76. 427 U.S. at 562.
77. Professor Tribe has suggested that *Nebraska Press Association* "announced a virtual bar to prior restraints on reporting of news about crime." L. TRIBE, AMERICAN CONSTITUTIONAL LAW 858-

Burger acknowledged that the trial judge had reasonably concluded that there would be intense and pervasive publicity that *could* impinge on the defendant's right to a fair trial. Nevertheless, any conclusion that this publicity *would* prejudice prospective jurors "was of necessity speculative, dealing as he was with factors unknown and unknowable."[78] Second, the record did not establish "that alternatives to a prior restraint . . . would not have sufficiently mitigated the adverse effects of pretrial publicity so as to make prior restraint unnecessary."[79] Indeed, the trial judge had not examined the "probable efficacy" of alternative measures such as those identified in *Sheppard* and had not made findings, supported by competent evidence, of their inadequacy. The Court observed that "pretrial publicity, even if pervasive and concentrated, cannot be regarded as leading automatically and in every kind of criminal case to an unfair trial."[80] Third, the Court could not conclude that a prior restraint would serve its intended purpose.[81] Given the territorial jurisdiction of the issuing court, its order could not deal meaningfully with nationwide publicity.[82] Moreover, a trial court could not reasonably be expected to draft a narrow order, restricting as little expression as possible, when it could only speculate about the information that might be reported and whether it would undermine the jury's impartiality.[83]

The Court also noted the problems of vagueness and overbreadth inherent in such restraining orders. A prior restraint must be drawn with specificity and clarity regarding who is to be restrained, the subjects that cannot be publicized, and the duration of the restraint.[84] To the extent that the order at issue in *Nebraska Press Association* prohibited reporting about evidence introduced at an open hearing, the Court concluded, it was an overbroad intrusion on freedom of expression.[85] Accordingly, the order's prohibition on publishing facts "strongly

---

59 (2d ed. 1988). See also Garner, *Billionaire Boys' Club: Billionaires by Crime*, 10 LOY. L.A. ENT. L.J. 573, 588-94 (1990) (advocating a per se rule against prior restraints); Peterson, *supra* note 65, at 580-81 (there were "fifteen years of confidence" conferred on the media by *Nebraska Press Association* and since that time "no prior restraint on a publication has ever survived the scrutiny of the *Nebraska Press* test"); Prettyman, Nebraska Press Association v. Stuart: *Have We Seen the Last of Prior Restraints on the Reporting of Judicial Proceedings?*, 20 ST. LOUIS U. L.J. 654, 659 (1976); Swartz, *Trial Participant Speech Restrictions: Gagging First Amendment Rights*, 90 COLUM. L. REV. 1411, 1421 n.63 (1990).

78. 427 U.S. at 563.
79. *Id.* at 569.
80. *Id.* at 565.
81. See *id.* at 568.
82. See *id.* at 565-67.
83. *Id.* at 568.
84. *Id.*
85. See *id.*

implicative" of Simant's guilt was too vague and too broad to survive First Amendment scrutiny.[86]

Nevertheless, the Court was unwilling in *Nebraska Press Association* to "rule out the possibility of showing the kind of threat to fair trial rights that would possess the requisite degree of certainty to justify restraint."[87] A majority of the justices, however, indicated their inclination towards adopting such a *per se* rule.[88] Justices Brennan, Stewart, and Marshall, concurring in the judgment, would have held "that resort to prior restraints on the freedom of the press is a constitutionally impermissible method" for enforcing the right to a fair trial.[89] Justice White, in a separate concurring opinion, expressed "grave doubt . . . whether orders with respect to the press such as were entered in this case would ever be justifiable."[90] Justice Stevens, who also joined the Court's opinion, acknowledged the force of Justice Brennan's argument and wrote separately that, if he were ever required to face the issue squarely, he might well conclude that the First Amendment requires an absolute ban.[91]

The Court's failure to adopt a *per se* rule in *Nebraska Press Association* has not been without consequence for the news media. As a result, parties to litigation of all kinds continue to seek restraining orders requiring litigation and trial judges continue to issue the occasional order necessitating appeal and delay in publishing news and information. In one case, a federal district court restrained a CNN telecast of tape recordings, made by the government, of conversations between imprisoned former Panamanian General Manuel Antonio Noriega and his attorneys.[92] The cable television network challenged a court order that it produce the tapes for *in camera* review to determine if they involved privileged material or if their public dissemination would deny Noriega his right to a fair

---

86. See *id*. See also Times Publ'g Co. v. Florida, 632 So. 2d 1072, 1075 (Fla. App. 1994) (invalidating trial court order that media could not disseminate "any identifying information concerning any potential, excused, or sitting juror, obtained or learned about through court proceedings"); In re Johnson, 632 A.2d 539, 541 (N.J. App. 1993) (nondisclosure order covering any identifying facts or information about minor murder defendant was overly broad). But see Howard Publications, Inc. v. Lake Michigan Charters, Ltd., 658 N.E.2d 582, 583 (Ind. 1995) (denying newspaper's petition to transfer case in which protective orders were issued enjoining publication of information disclosed during discovery).

87. 427 U.S. at 569-70.

88. The American Bar Association Standards for Fair Trial and Free Press provide for such an absolute prohibition on the grounds that *Nebraska Press Association* was deemed to have articulated virtually a *per se* rule and that Justice Brennan's concurrence was "persuasive." ABA STANDARDS FOR CRIMINAL JUSTICE, FAIR TRIAL AND FREE PRESS 29-31 (2d ed. 1980).

89. 427 U.S. at 572 (Brennan, J., concurring).

90. See *id*. at 570 (White, J., concurring). Justice White added that, if subsequent cases similarly rejected analogous prior restraints, "we should at some point announce a more general rule and avoid the interminable litigation that our failure to do so would necessarily entail." *Id*. at 571.

91. See *id*. at 617 (Stevens, J., concurring).

92. See United States v. Noriega, 917 F.2d 1543 (11th Cir.), *cert. denied*, 498 U.S. 976 (1990).

trial. While CNN sought expedited appellate review, arguing the restraint violated *Nebraska Press Association*, it aired one of the tapes, which it believed did not contain conversations governed by the trial court's order.[93] The Eleventh Circuit, however, affirmed both the restraining order and the trial court's ruling that CNN deliver the tapes for *in camera* review.[94] The Supreme Court denied CNN's application for a stay and its petition for a writ of certiorari.[95] Subsequently, after CNN produced the tapes to the trial judge as ordered, the district court vacated the restraining order, twenty days after it was issued. In further proceedings, CNN was found guilty of criminal contempt for violating the initial order through its telecast of one of the tapes.[96]

Cases such as *Noriega*, however, appear to be aberrations.[97] Although there have been an increasing number of prior restraints issued by trial courts (a

---

93. *Id.* at 1546.

94. See *id.* For a critical discussion of the *Noriega* case, see R. SMOLLA, FREE SPEECH IN AN OPEN SOCIETY ch. 9 (1992); Waggoner, CNN v. Noriega: *Gagging the Messenger*, 8 COMM. LAW. 3 (Summer 1990).

95. United States v. Noriega, 917 F.2d 1543 (11th Cir.), *cert. denied*, 498 U.S. 976 (1990).

96. See United States v. Cable News Network Inc., 865 F. Supp. 1549 (S.D. Fla. 1994):

> The thin but bright line between anarchy and order — the delicate balance which ultimately is the vital protection of the individual and the public generally — is the respect which litigants and the public have for the law and the orders issued by the courts. Defiance of court orders and, even more so, public display of such defiance cannot be justified or permitted.

Id. at 1564. The trial court sentenced CNN to pay a fine of $85,000 to reimburse the judiciary for the costs of appointing a special prosecutor to represent its interests in the contempt proceedings. In addition, CNN agreed to telecast the following statement:

> On further consideration, CNN realizes that it was in error in defying the order of the court and publishing the Noriega tape while appealing the court's order. We do now and always have recognized that our justice system cannot long survive if litigants take it upon themselves to determine which judgments or orders of court they will or will not follow. Ours is a nation of laws under which the very freedoms we espouse can be preserved only if those laws are observed. In the event unfavorable judgments are rendered, the right of appeal is provided. This is the course on which we should have relied. We regret that we did not.

97. But see In re State Record Co., 504 S.E.2d 592 (S.C. 1998), *cert. denied*, 119 S. Ct. 1355 (1999), in which the South Carolina Supreme Court upheld a prior restraint on a television station's dissemination of the contents of a surreptitiously videotaped, privileged communication between a murder defendant and his attorney. Applying *Nebraska Press Association*, the court found that "the remedial measures employed by the trial court here were necessary to guarantee [the defendant's] right to a fair trial. Moreover, the order imposed by the trial court was as narrowly tailored, both in scope and duration, as was possible under the circumstances." *Id.* at 596. The court found that there was "sufficient evidence in the record from which to conclude [that] the pretrial publicity had the potential to impair [the defendant's] right to a fair trial." *Id.* In addition, the court recognized that it is "simply untenable to suggest that other measures would not, in any case, be 'likely to mitigate' the effects of pretrial publicity." *Id.* The court refused, however, to read this prong so as to foreclose the possibility of prior restraint, believing that the Supreme Court could not have intended such a result because "it would have imposed an absolute ban on prior restraints." *Id.* Rather, the court decided that *Nebraska Press Association* "must be viewed in its

§ 2-1(d)   CONSTITUTIONAL FOUNDATIONS   § 2-1(d)

phenomenon that appeared to precede *Noriega*), such orders are typically and promptly reversed on appeal.[98] At least for the present, the barrier to the use of prior restraint remains where the Court in *Nebraska Press Association* put it — "the guarantees of freedom of expression are not an absolute prohibition under all circumstances, but the barriers to prior restraint remain high and the presumption against its use continues intact."[99]

---

entirety, with a view toward ensuring a defendant's fundamental right to a fair trial, and not merely with an eye toward 'mitigating the effects' of pre-trial publicity." *Id.* at 597. Under this interpretation, the court found that the "limited prior restraint imposed here was necessary to avoid the potential prejudice to [the defendant] as would ensue from disclosure of the videotape." *Id.* Finally, the court found that "[u]ndoubtedly, the prior restraint prevented prospective jurors from learning the contents of the privileged communication contained in the videotape . . . prevent[ing] the threatened danger to [the defendant's] right to a fair trial," because only local media sources had the videotape and all were restrained from disclosing its contents. *Id.* at 596. Justice Toal, while believing "that the *Nebraska Press* test should be revisited by the Supreme Court," nevertheless was "compelled to dissent under the current state of the law." *Id.* at 600 (Toal, J., dissenting).

98. See, e.g., Procter & Gamble Co. v. Bankers Trust Co., 78 F.3d 219 (6th Cir. 1996); CBS Inc. v. Davis, 510 U.S. 1315 (1994) (Blackmun, J., in chambers); In re Lifetime Cable, 17 MEDIA L. REP. (BNA) 1648 (D.C. Cir.), *cert. denied*, 498 U.S. 847 (1990); In re Charlotte Observer, 921 F.2d 47 (4th Cir. 1990); In re King World Productions, Inc., 898 F.2d 56 (6th Cir. 1990); McClatchy Newspapers, Inc. v. Fresno County Super. Ct., 19 MEDIA L. REP. (BNA) 1555 (Cal. App. 1991); Connecticut v. Kelly, 695 A.2d 1, 4 (Conn. App. 1997); Rockdale Citizen Publ'g Co. v. Georgia, 463 S.E.2d 864 (Ga. 1995); Austin Daily Herald v. Mork, 507 N.W.2d 854 (Minn. App. 1993); Montana ex rel. Missoulian v. Montana Twenty-First Judicial Dist. Ct., 933 P.2d 829, 840, 842 (Mont. 1997); Wittek v. Cirigliano, 576 N.Y.S.2d 527 (App. Div. 1991); Ohio ex rel. Cincinnati Post v. Court of C.P., 570 N.E.2d 1101 (Ohio 1991); San Antonio Express-News v. Roman, 861 S.W.2d 265 (Tex. App. 1993). See generally Peterson, *supra* note 65, at 580 nn.126-28; Resnick, *Noriega Fallout: Noriega Case Muddles Prior Restraint Law*, NAT'L L.J., Nov. 26, 1990, at 3. Of these cases, in addition to *In re State Record Co.*, 504 S.E.2d 592 (S.C. 1998), *cert. denied*, 119 S. Ct. 1355 (1999), see note 97 *supra*, only one was upheld on appeal, i.e., *Austin Daily Herald v. Mork*, in which the trial judge allowed reporters to attend a closed session of a trial for sexual misconduct as long as they did not publish the names of or information about the victims of the crimes. See 507 N.W.2d at 856. See also George W. Prescott Publ'g Co. v. Stoughton Div., Dist. Ct., 701 N.E.2d 307, 309 (Mass. 1998) (vacating trial court's order restricting media access to certain juvenile records and proceedings as an unlawful prior restraint, noting "[t]he right of the press [to report] could not be abridged in the absence of detailed findings of fact clearly establishing and supporting the criteria" set forth in *Nebraska Press Association*).

99. 427 U.S. at 570. In *Jeffries v. Mississippi*, 724 So. 2d 897, 900 (Miss. 1998), the court, in reversing a trial court order holding a reporter in contempt, stated that "when information has been obtained legally from a public proceeding or document, the United States Supreme Court and appellate courts around the country have consistently rejected any restraint on its publication." See also FTC v. Freecom Communications, Inc., 966 F. Supp. 1066, 1069-70 (D. Utah 1997) (denying defendant's motion for protective order preventing FTC from issuing press releases on ground that deleterious effect on the defendant's businesses does not justify prior restraint); Ohio ex rel. News Herald v. Ottawa County Ct. of C.P., 671 N.E.2d 5, 8 (Ohio 1996) (holding "patently unconstitutional" a gag order preventing nonparty media from publishing material concerning open proceeding in juvenile court until juvenile is transferred to be tried as adult); Charter Behavioral Health Sys. LLC v. CBS Inc., No. 3-99-CV-150-MU (W.D.N.C. Apr. 21, 1999) (declining to

Indeed, in an influential post-*Noriega* decision, the Sixth Circuit provided strong reaffirmation of the rule against prior restraints in *Procter & Gamble Co. v. Bankers Trust Co.*[100] Upon application by the parties in a civil action, the district court had issued an *ex parte* temporary restraining order preventing *Business Week* magazine from publishing material placed under seal by stipulation of the parties.[101] After the magazine unsuccessfully sought emergency appellate review,[102] the district court conducted a hearing that focused on how the documents at issue had been obtained.[103] Following the hearing, the district court purported permanently to enjoin *Business Week* from publishing the specific materials in its possession, which it concluded had been "unlawfully" obtained. Nevertheless the court simultaneously purported to hold that the parties in the civil action had failed to demonstrate a "substantial government interest" requiring that the documents remain confidential, so they were released to the public, including *Business Week*.[104]

Reversing this "classic case of a prior restraint,"[105] the Sixth Circuit concluded that the planned publication did not pose "such a grave threat to a critical government interest or to a constitutional right" to justify any of the trial court's restraining orders.[106] The permanent injunction, the court held, "was patently

---

enjoin hidden camera investigation of psychiatric hospital chain because "the Supreme Court has elevated press powers to a point that prior restraint is all but impossible even where, as in this case, it appears that the press may well have set out to and committed a federal crime"); Zamora v. Adams, 25 MEDIA L. REP. (BNA) 1638 (Tex. Dist. 1997) (rejecting defendant's pretrial motion in criminal proceeding for injunction seeking to prevent airing of made-for-television movie about her pending case).

100. 78 F.3d 219 (6th Cir. 1996). See generally Kirtley, *Vanity and Vexation: Shifting the Focus to Media Conduct*, 4 WM. & MARY BILL OF RTS. J. 1069, 1089-96 (1996); O'Neil, *Tainted Sources: First Amendment Rights and Journalistic Wrongs*, 4 WM. & MARY BILL OF RTS. J. 1005, 1007-08, 1018-22 (1996); Comment, *Protective Orders, Property Interests and Prior Restraints: Can the Courts Prevent Media Nonparties From Publishing Court-Protected Discovery Materials?*, 144 U. PA. L. REV. 2463 (1996) (arguing that protective orders may be enforced by enjoining media publication in limited circumstances to protect private property interest in information).

101. See Chap. 6-1(a)(1) *infra* (discussing district court's use of stipulated protective order, which authorized the parties, rather than the court, to determine if good cause for sealing materials or modifying a protective order existed).

102. The Sixth Circuit dismissed the emergency appeal on the ground that a temporary restraining order is not an appealable final order. Justice Stevens denied an emergency stay in order to allow a hearing in the trial court to determine the potentially relevant facts. See 78 F.3d at 222; McGraw-Hill Cos. v. Procter & Gamble Co., 515 U.S. 1309 (1995) (Stevens, J., in chambers).

103. Although the Sixth Circuit indicated that such inquiries might be appropriate in a contempt proceeding, they were "not appropriate bases for issuing a prior restraint." 78 F.3d at 225. But see 515 U.S. at 1310 (Stevens, J., in chambers) ("the manner in which [*Business Week*] came into possession of the information it seeks to publish may have a bearing on its right to do so").

104. 78 F.3d at 223.

105. *Id.* at 225.

106. *Id.* at 225 (citing CBS Inc. v. Davis, 510 U.S. 1315, 1317 (1994) (Blackmun, J., in chambers).

invalid and should never have been entered."[107] Nor was the temporary restraining order justified to preserve the status quo; indeed, in the First Amendment context, the court explained, such relief is "severely limited."[108] Under such circumstances, "the hurdle" that must be cleared to secure injunctive relief, even of short duration, is "substantially higher: publication must threaten an interest more fundamental than the First Amendment itself."[109]

§ 2-2. The Constitutional Right of Access in the Supreme Court.

§ 2-2(a). Perspectives on the Constitutional Right of Access.

In the wake of the Supreme Court's restrictions on the imposition of criminal sanctions in the news media context, and its virtually *per se* rule against prior restraints on publication, trial judges turned to closure orders as an alternative vehicle for avoiding potentially prejudicial publicity. If the press and public were denied access to prejudicial information, the theory went, there would be less danger of detrimental publicity. When coupled with restraining orders barring extrajudicial commentary by trial participants, closure orders were conceived as a potent weapon against prejudicial publicity.

At common law, however, in both England and in the United States, criminal and civil trials were generally open.[110] State constitutions and statutes contain provisions guaranteeing public trials,[111] and the Sixth Amendment explicitly guarantees a public trial as well.[112]

---

107. 78 F.3d at 225.
108. *Id.* at 226.
109. *Id.* (citing Carroll v. Princess Anne, 393 U.S. 175, 180 (1968)). See In re Providence Journal Co., 820 F.2d 1342, 1351 (1st Cir. 1986), *cert. dismissed*, 485 U.S. 693 (1988) (restraining order "issued prior to a full and fair hearing . . . faces an even heavier presumption of invalidity").
110. An extensive history of the common law history of public access to judicial proceedings is provided by Justice Blackmun, concurring in part and dissenting in part, in *Gannett Co. v. DePasquale*, 443 U.S. 368, 410-39 (1979), Chief Justice Burger's opinion announcing the Court's judgment in *Richmond Newspapers, Inc. v. Virginia*, 448 U.S. 555, 563-75 (1980), and Justice Brennan's opinion, concurring in the judgment in *Richmond Newspapers, Inc.*, 448 U.S. at 589-93. Indeed, in *In re Oliver*, 333 U.S. 257, 266 (1948), the Court noted that it had been "unable to find a single instance of a criminal trial conducted in camera in any federal, state, or municipal court during the history of this country." See generally Radin, *The Right to a Public Trial*, 6 TEMP. L.Q. 381 (1932).
111. See Gannett Co. v. DePasquale, 443 U.S. at 414 n.3 (Blackmun, J., dissenting) (citing 45 state constitutional provisions that guarantee a right to a public trial). In his separate opinion in *Gannett Co.*, Justice Blackmun noted that the Due Process Clause of the New Hampshire Constitution had been held to guarantee public trials and that Maryland, by judicial decision, and New York, by statute, required open trials as well. Only Massachusetts and Nevada appeared to lack a guarantee of public trial. See *id.* at 429-32 nn.10-11.
112. U.S. CONST. amend. VI ("In all criminal prosecutions, the accused shall enjoy the right to a speedy and public trial. . . ."). See also 21A AM. JUR. 2d *Criminal Law* § 666 et seq. (discussing

By the same token, nothing in the First Amendment expressly guarantees a right of access to any governmental proceedings, including those of the judiciary.[113] Indeed, the Court has rejected a First Amendment-based right of access to some government institutions such as prisons.[114] The Sixth Amendment, on its face, references the right of "the accused" to a public trial, but does not mention the public or the press.[115] Nor does the fact that open trials were recognized at common law necessarily mean that there is a comparable constitutional right, especially since changes in mass communication at least arguably create an enhanced potential for harmful publicity. Finally, even if there is a constitutional right of public access to criminal trials, it does not automatically follow that the First Amendment guarantees access to other judicial proceedings where openness was not so well-established at common law.[116]

Nevertheless, in the dizzying span of less than a decade from 1980 to 1986, the Supreme Court established a First Amendment-based right of public access to criminal trials and other judicial proceedings.[117] As a result, there has been an explosion of case law recognizing a qualified right of access grounded in the First Amendment, which spans an expanding array of judicial proceedings.[118]

The fashioning of a First Amendment-based right of public access to judicial proceedings has generally involved application of a two-part inquiry designed to determine if the press and public enjoy a presumptive right to be present. First, there is the *historical* inquiry: "whether the place and process have historically been open to the press and general public."[119] Second, there is the *functional* inquiry: "whether public access plays a significant positive role in the function-

---

criminal defendant's right to a public trial); F. HELLER, THE SIXTH AMENDMENT TO THE CONSTITUTION OF THE UNITED STATES 17-18 (1951) (chronicling rise of the public trial right in colonial America that led to adoption of Sixth Amendment).

113. See generally BeVier, *Like Mackerel in the Moonlight: Some Reflections on Richmond Newspapers*, 10 HOFSTRA L. REV. 311, 312 n.8 (1982); Hayes, *What Ever Happened to "The Right to Know"?: Access to Government-Controlled Information Since Richmond Newspapers*, 73 VA. L. REV. 1111 (1987); Litt, *"Citizen-Soldiers" or Anonymous Justice: Reconciling the Sixth Amendment Right of the Accused, the First Amendment Right of the Media and the Privacy Right of Jurors*, 25 COLUM. J. L. & SOC. PROBS. 371, 377 (1992).

114. Chap. 8-1 *infra*; BeVier, *supra* note 113, at 322 (distinguishing *Richmond Newspapers, Inc.* from prison access cases).

115 See generally Liotti, *Closing the Courtroom Door to the Public: Whose Rights Are Violated?*, 63 BROOK. L. REV. 501 (1997) (discussing the differences in policy and purpose of the First and Sixth Amendments in access cases and arguing for a bright line test to determine whether access is mandated).

116. See Chap. 2-2(h) *infra*.

117. See Chap. 2-2(b)-(g) *infra*.

118. See Chap. 3 *infra*.

119. Press-Enter. Co. v. Superior Ct., 478 U.S. 1, 8 (1986) (*Press-Enterprise II*). Many commentators have criticized the Court's reliance on history. See BeVier, *supra* note 113, at 325-28; Hayes, *supra* note 113, at 1130-34; Wood, *Re-Examining the Access Doctrine*, 11 COMM. LAW. 3, 3-6 (Winter 1994). See generally Chap. 2-2(h) *infra*.

ing of the particular process in question."[120] This judicial emphasis on tradition and function mirrors the methodology traditionally employed in constitutional due process analysis.[121]

The Supreme Court's recognition of a First Amendment-based right of public access to a particular category of judicial proceeding establishes a presumption that it should be open. It remains possible, however, that the interests supporting closure will override the First Amendment claim. Nevertheless, a party seeking closure assumes a heavy burden. In one case, involving access to testimony at a criminal trial, the Court required that closure be shown to be necessary to further a compelling interest.[122] Moreover, in cases involving access to voir dire and preliminary hearings in criminal cases, the Court has held that the right of access "may be overcome only by an overriding interest based on findings that closure is essential to preserve higher values and is narrowly tailored to serve that interest."[123] In addition, trial judges considering closure motions must now conduct hearings. If closure is to be ordered, the judge must make specific findings, on the record, justifying her decision to exclude the press and public.[124]

§ 2-2(b). *Gannett Co. v. DePasquale.*

The constitutional right of public access to judicial proceedings had something of a difficult birth. In *Gannett Co. v. DePasquale*,[125] the Court first considered "whether members of the public have an independent constitutional right to insist upon access to a pretrial judicial proceeding, even though the accused, the prosecutor, and the trial judge all have agreed to the closure of the proceeding in order to assure a fair trial."[126] The defendants, who pled not guilty

---

120. 478 U.S. at 8. The Court's functional analysis has also been scrutinized. See generally Hayes, *supra* note 113, at 1134-36; Weakland, *Confusion in the Courthouse: The Legacy of the Gannett and Richmond Newspapers Public Right of Access Cases*, 59 S. CAL. L. REV. 603, 611-18 (1986); Wood, *supra* note 119, at 6; Chap. 2-2(h) *infra*.

121. To determine if a claimed interest is a fundamental personal right protected as part of the liberty guaranteed by the Due Process Clause, the Supreme Court has typically examined whether the interest is "implicit in the concept of ordered liberty," Palko v. Connecticut, 302 U.S. 319 (1937), and is "deeply rooted in this Nation's history and tradition," Moore v. City of East Cleveland, 431 U.S. 494 (1977). See also Washington v. Glucksberg, 521 U.S. 702 (1997); Bowers v. Hardwick, 478 U.S. 186 (1986); Griswold v. Connecticut, 381 U.S. 479 (1965).

122. See Globe Newspaper Co. v. Superior Ct, 457 U.S. 596, 606-07 (1982). See generally Chap. 2-2(d) *infra*.

123. *Press-Enterprise II*, 478 U.S. 1, 13-14 (1986) (preliminary hearings); Press-Enter. Co. v. Superior Ct., 464 U.S. 501, 510 (1984) (*Press-Enterprise I*) (voir dire). See generally Wood, *supra* note 119, at 3; Chap. 2-2(e) & (f) *infra*.

124. See *Press Enterprise II*, 478 U.S. at 15; *Press-Enterprise I*, 464 U.S. at 570. See generally Wood, *supra* note 119; Weakland, *supra* note 120, at 625-32; Chap. 2-3 *infra*.

125. 443 U.S. 368 (1979). See generally Weakland, *supra* note 120, at 606-09; Litt, *supra* note 113, at 382-85; *The Supreme Court, 1978 Term*, 93 HARV. L. REV. 62, 62-72 (1979).

126. 443 U.S. at 370-71.

to charges of murder, robbery, and larceny, moved to close a suppression hearing on the ground that the unabated buildup of adverse publicity had jeopardized their right to a fair trial.[127] The prosecutor did not oppose the motion and a reporter, who was present in the courtroom, did not object. Judge DePasquale granted the motion and conducted the closed hearing.[128] The next day, the reporter's newspaper moved to set aside the order and the trial judge, after conducting a hearing, held that an open court would create a "reasonable probability of prejudice" to the defendants' fair trial rights that outweighed any constitutional right of access otherwise afforded the press and public.[129] Although an intermediate appellate court reversed Judge DePasquale's decision,[130] the New York Court of Appeals upheld the closure order[131] and the United States Supreme Court affirmed.[132]

Justice Stewart, writing for the Court, began by noting that "[c]losure of pretrial proceedings is often one of the most effective methods that a trial judge can employ to attempt to insure that the fairness of a trial will not be jeopardized by the dissemination of [prejudicial] information throughout the community

---

127. See *id.* at 375.
128. See *id.*
129. *Id.* at 376.
130. The appellate division held that the closure order violated the public's vital interest in open proceedings and constituted an unconstitutional prior restraint. See *id.* The Supreme Court rejected application of the prior restraint doctrine in this context: "The proper inquiry . . . is whether the petitioner was denied any constitutional right of access." *Id.* at 393 n.25. See *id.* at 411 (Blackmun, J., dissenting); 93 HARV. L. REV., *supra* note 125, at 68 n.49 ("As an initial matter, it is clear that closure of judicial proceedings cannot be characterized as a prior restraint. As both Justice Powell, 443 U.S. at 399, and Justice Blackmun, *id.* at 411, pointed out, a prior restraint occurs only when the state controls dissemination of information already known to the parties restrained."). This distinction has been criticized. See Weakland, *supra* note 120, at 605 n.19 ("[T]he distinction between prior restraints and restricting access to proceedings is not valid."). See generally Chap. 2-1(d) *supra*.
131. The Court of Appeals held that, under New York law, "[c]riminal trials are presumptively open to the public, including the press," but that this presumption was overcome by the danger of prejudice to the defendant's right to a fair trial. 443 U.S. at 376-77.
132. Justice Stewart's opinion for the Court was joined by Chief Justice Burger and Justices Powell, Rehnquist, and Stevens. The Chief Justice and Justices Powell and Rehnquist also wrote concurring opinions. Justice Blackmun, joined by Justices Brennan, Marshall, and White, concurred in part and dissented in part. Their concurrence was limited to the determination that the case was not moot, even though the trial was over, since it involved an issue "capable of repetition, yet evading review." See generally B. SCHWARTZ, FREEDOM OF THE PRESS 34-38 (1992); Litt, *supra* note 113, at 384 ("The Court, however, was sharply divided, issuing five opinions, which offered three separate standards to be employed in balancing the Sixth and First Amendment rights at stake."); Weakland, *supra* note 120, at 610 ("The Supreme Court's decisionmaking process in the post-*Richmond Newspapers* access cases was complicated by the unusual number of opinions published in both *Gannett* and *Richmond Newspapers* and the expansive language used in those opinions. The *Gannett* Court issued five separate opinions and presented three different standards for balancing the constitutional interests involved.").

before the trial itself has even begun."[133] But, he also recognized the common law tradition of public trials and its value to society:

> There can be no blinking the fact that there is a strong societal interest in public trials. Openness in court proceedings may improve the quality of testimony, induce unknown witnesses to come forward with relevant testimony, cause all trial participants to perform their duties more conscientiously, and generally give the public an opportunity to observe the judicial system.[134]

In the last analysis, however, the court bottomed its decision on the fact that the text of the Sixth Amendment vests the right to a public trial exclusively in the accused: "The Constitution nowhere mentions any right of access to a criminal trial on the part of the public; its guarantee ... is personal to the accused."[135] The public, the Court concluded, has no correlative right to insist on a public proceeding just as the defendant has no affirmative right "to compel a private trial."[136] History established only "a common-law rule of open civil and criminal proceedings."[137] In the context of a suppression hearing especially, Justice Stewart noted, there was "no persuasive evidence that at common law members of the public had any right to attend pretrial proceedings; indeed, there is substantial evidence to the contrary."[138]

---

133. 443 U.S. at 379.
134. *Id.* at 383.
135. *Id.* at 379-80. See Estes v. Texas, 381 U.S. 532, 588 (1965) (Harlan, J., concurring) ("thus the right of 'public trial' is not one belonging to the public but one belonging to the accused, and inhering in the institutional process by which justice is administered"); In re Oliver, 333 U.S. 257, 270 n.25 (1948) (quoting T. COOLEY, CONSTITUTIONAL LIMITATIONS 647 (8th ed. 1927)) ("The requirement of a public trial is for the benefit of the accused."); Radin, *supra* note 110, at 382 (a public right to a public trial "cannot be derived from the Constitution because the Constitution certainly does not mention a public trial as the privilege of the public, but expressly as that of the accused").
136. 443 U.S. at 382. See Singer v. United States, 380 U.S. 24, 35 (1965) ("[Defendant] has no absolute right to compel a public trial."); Detroit Free Press, Inc. v. Recorder's Ct. Judge, 294 N.W.2d 827 (Mich. 1980) (rejecting Sixth Amendment right of defendant to require closed trial).
137. 443 U.S at 384. See *id.* at 386 n.15 ("[i]f the existence of a common-law rule were the test for whether there is a Sixth Amendment public right to a public trial, there would be such a right in civil as well as criminal cases"). The Court noted that "many of the advantages of public criminal trials are equally applicable in the civil trial context." *Id.* Indeed, "in some civil cases the public interest in access, and the salutary effect of publicity may be as strong as, or stronger than, in most criminal cases." *Id.* See Chap. 3-2 *infra*.
138. 443 U.S. at 387. See *id.* at 389, 390 ("Under English common law, the public had no right to attend pretrial proceedings. Closed pretrial proceedings have been a familiar part of the judicial landscape in this country as well."). Nevertheless, the Court used historical analysis in extending the First Amendment-based right of public access to pretrial proceedings in *Press-Enterprise II*, discussed in Chap. 2-2(f) *infra*. See also 93 HARV. L. REV., *supra* note 125, at 66-67 ("[T]he majority's argument that the sixth amendment does not give the public a right of access to judicial

While *Gannett Co.* is rightly treated as a Sixth Amendment case, the Court at least suggested the relevance of the First Amendment. Justice Stewart found it unnecessary to decide whether a First Amendment-based right would ever be recognized since, even assuming such a right existed, the trial court had given it "all appropriate deference."[139] Even though the press had not objected when closure was ordered, it was given an opportunity to be heard. Judge DePasquale had balanced the competing interests, concluding that the defendant's fair trial rights "outweighed" the First Amendment. Moreover, there was only a "temporary" denial of access since a transcript of the hearing was made available.[140] Thus, although the Court in *Gannett Co.* asserted that it was not deciding the First Amendment issue, the standard it endorsed appeared to afford minimal protection to First Amendment interests.

The actual import of *Gannett Co. v. DePasquale*, however, was, at the time, the subject of much confusion. Chief Justice Burger, concurring, stressed that the Court had not addressed access to criminal *trials*, but only *pretrial* hearings.[141] Indeed, while Justice Stewart's opinion for the Court often spoke of "trials," the case itself involved only a pretrial hearing. On the other hand, *Gannett Co.* appeared to contemplate a per se rule, which treated the Sixth Amendment as a *personal* right of the accused.[142] It is only when the accused objects to a motion for closure of the criminal trial (or of a pretrial proceeding) that the Sixth Amendment guarantee of a public trial appeared, in the wake of *Gannett Co.*, to become effective.[143]

---

proceedings is convincing. Since the text of the amendment guarantees a public trial to the accused alone, recognition of a public right can be justified only with difficulty, particularly since such a right might work to the detriment of the accused.").

139. 443 U.S. at 392.

140. *Id.* at 393.

141. See *id.* at 394 (Burger, C.J., concurring). In a post-decision interview, the Chief Justice again indicated that "the opinion referred to pretrial proceedings only." N.Y. Times, Aug. 9, 1979, at A17, col. 1. In *Gannett Co.*, he asserted that "to make public the evidence developed in a motion to suppress evidence . . . would, so long as the exclusionary rule is not modified, introduce a new dimension to the problem of conducting fair trials." 443 U.S. at 396 (Burger, C.J., concurring). But see Chap. 3-1(a)(4) *infra* (discussing extension of right of public access to pretrial suppression hearings).

142. See Borow & Kruth, *Closed Preliminary Hearings*, 55 CALIF. ST, B.J. 18, 23 (1980) ("Despite the public disclaimers . . . , the majority holding appears to embrace the right of access to trials as well as pretrial hearings.").

143. In *Waller v. Georgia*, 467 U.S. 39 (1984), the Court expressly extended the defendant's Sixth Amendment right to a public trial to pretrial suppression hearings. Waller objected to closure of a seven-day suppression hearing ordered by the trial court. The Supreme Court held that a party seeking closure, over an accused's objection, must "advance an overriding interest that is likely to be prejudiced, [and establish that] the closure [is] no broader than necessary to protect that interest," and the trial court must both consider alternatives to closure and make appropriate findings. *Id.* at 48. For a discussion of *Waller*, see generally Weakland, *supra* note 120, at 614-18.

Justice Powell, concurring, would have held that the press enjoys a First and Fourteenth Amendment right to be present at pretrial suppression hearings.[144] Stressing "the importance of the public's having accurate information concerning the operation of the criminal justice system,"[145] Justice Powell observed that "suppression hearings often are as important as the trial which may follow."[146] Under the First Amendment, he wrote, the press acts as the "agent of the public at large"[147] and, if present when closure is ordered, must be afforded an opportunity to be heard.[148] But Justice Powell, unlike his dissenting colleagues, was unwilling to apply a stringent standard of judicial review and override the determination of the trial judge.[149]

Justice Rehnquist, concurring, contended that the Court had, without qualification, rejected *any* Sixth Amendment right of the public to attend criminal trial or pretrial proceedings.[150] Further, he argued that there is no First Amendment-based right of access and no constitutionally mandated procedures that trial courts must follow before ordering closure.[151]

The four dissenting justices, in an opinion by Justice Blackmun, argued that the Court's rejection of a public right of access under the Sixth Amendment ignored "important interests of the public and the press (as a part of that public)" and lacked support in the intent or history of the Sixth Amendment.[152] For Justice Blackmun, "the tradition of our system of criminal justice is that a trial is a 'public event' and '[w]hat transpires in the court room is public property,'"[153] such that secret proceedings are inconsistent with that tradition.[154] The public

---

144. Justice Powell specifically noted that he agreed with the constitutional position of the four dissenting justices "that there are limitations and that they require the careful attention of trial courts before closure can be ordered." 443 U.S. at 398 n.2 (Powell, J., concurring).
145. *Id.*
146. *Id.* at 397 n.1.
147. *Id.* at 398.
148. See *id.* at 401.
149. See *id.* at 399-403. Justice Powell suggested that the substantive standard applied by Judge DePasquale "was essentially correct" and deferred to his judgment given his proximity to the surrounding circumstances. *Id.* at 403.
150. See *id.* at 403-04 (Rehnquist, J., concurring).
151. See *id.* at 404 ("Despite the Court's seeming reservation of the question whether the First Amendment guarantees the public a right of access to pretrial proceedings, it is clear that this Court repeatedly has held that there is no First Amendment right of access in the public or the press to judicial or other governmental proceedings."). Noting the procedural regimen articulated by Justice Powell, Justice Rehnquist argued that the majority had embraced the contrary position that "the lower courts are under no constitutional constraint either to accept or reject those procedures. . . . [S]o far as the Constitution is concerned, the question is for them, not us, to resolve." *Id.* at 405-06.
152. *Id.* at 407 (Blackmun, J., dissenting).
153. *Id.* at 412 (quoting Craig v. Harney, 331 U.S. 367 (1947)).
154. See 443 U.S. at 412. ("[T]he requirement that a trial of a criminal case be public embodies our belief that secret judicial proceedings would be a menace to liberty.").

trial guarantee of the Sixth Amendment, embodied in the concept of due process, ensures that all participants in the criminal justice system are subject to public scrutiny when they conduct the public's business.[155] Even if the defendant waives his right to a public trial, Justice Blackmun contended, that fact alone is not determinative of the public's right of access.[156] Accordingly, in Justice Blackmun's view, the states ought to be prohibited from excluding the public from a proceeding "without affording full and fair consideration to the public's interest in maintaining an open proceeding."[157] And,

> because of the critical importance of suppression hearings to our system of criminal justice — as well as because of the close similarity in form of a suppression hearing to a full trial — for purposes of the Sixth Amendment public trial provision, the pretrial suppression hearing at issue in this case must be considered part of the trial.[158]

The four dissenting justices did agree that the Sixth Amendment creates only a presumption of openness, but argued that any exception must be "narrowly drawn."[159] An accused who seeks closure must establish "that it is strictly and inescapably necessary in order to protect the fair-trial guarantee."[160]

Because they viewed the Sixth Amendment as dispositive, the dissenters never addressed the issue of a First Amendment-based right of public access. Justice Powell had embraced a First Amendment-based right, but concluded that it had been honored. Justice Rehnquist, who was one of the four concurring justices, rejected any notion of a First Amendment-based right of public access. And, of course, the case involved closure of pretrial proceedings, not the trial itself. *Gannett Co. v. DePasquale*, therefore, left the First Amendment issue demonstrably unsettled.

As a result, *Gannett Co.* was perceived by trial judges as an endorsement of closure as a mechanism to avoid prejudicial publicity. There were reportedly almost 300 motions to close criminal proceedings in the year following *Gannett*

---

155. See *id*.
156. See *id*. at 418.
157. *Id*. at 433.
158. *Id*. at 436-37. Justice Blackmun did not, however, claim that there was a common law tradition of open pretrial proceedings. Rather, he stressed the unique character of the modern suppression hearing. See *id*. at 437.
159. *Id*. at 440.
160. *Id*. Justice Blackmun cited a number of factors that must be considered, essentially mirroring those articulated in *Nebraska Press Association*. See Chap. 2-1(d) *supra*. Nevertheless, Justice Blackmun also purported to reject adoption of the *Nebraska Press Association* standards as defining the Sixth Amendment right. See 443 U.S. at 447 (Blackmun, J., dissenting).

§ 2-2(c)

Co. — over half of which were granted.[161] Apparently of the view that *Gannett Co.* had been misunderstood, a number of the justices made rare extrajudicial statements about the case, which only heightened the uncertainty.[162] Clearly, the question of a public right of access was still on the table.

§ 2-2(c). *Richmond Newspapers, Inc. v. Virginia.*

An opportunity to reconsider the issues raised in *Gannett Co.* came the following term in *Richmond Newspapers, Inc. v. Virginia.*[163] In that case, seven of the eight participating justices agreed that the public and press enjoy a First Amendment-based right to attend criminal trials, although none of the seven separate opinions commanded a majority.[164] Nevertheless, Justice Stevens was undoubtedly correct when he wrote that *Richmond Newspapers, Inc.* "is a watershed case. Until today the Court has accorded virtually absolute protection to the dissemination of information or ideas, but never before has it squarely held that the acquisition of newsworthy matter is entitled to any constitutional protection whatsoever."[165]

---

161. See L. POWE, THE FOURTH ESTATE AND THE CONSTITUTION 192 (1991). See also Litt, *supra* note 113, at 381 ("[The *Gannett Co.* Court] clearly tipped toward protecting the rights of the accused, marking a low point for the media's right of access to criminal trial proceedings.").

162. See W. FRANCIS, MASS MEDIA LAW AND REGULATION 330 (6th ed. 1994). On the confusion generated by *Gannett Co.*, see Justice Blackmun's concurring opinion in *Richmond Newspapers, Inc. v. Virginia*, 448 U.S. 555, 602 nn.1-2 (1980) (Blackmun, J., concurring).

163. 448 U.S. 555 (1980). See generally BeVier, *supra* note 113; Fenner & Koley, *Access to Judicial Proceedings: To Richmond Newspapers and Beyond*, 16 HARV. C.R.-C.L. L. REV. 415 (1981); *The Supreme Court, 1979 Term*, 94 HARV. L. REV. 75, 149-59 (1980).

164. Chief Justice Burger announced the judgment of the Court in an opinion joined by Justices White and Stevens, both of whom wrote separate concurring opinions. Justice Brennan's opinion concurring in the judgment was joined by Justice Marshall. Justices Stewart and Blackmun filed separate opinions concurring in the judgment as well. Justice Rehnquist filed a dissenting opinion. Justice Powell did not participate. Once again, the Court's inability to speak with one voice was heavily criticized. See Litt, *supra* note 113, at 385 ("Like the *DePasquale* decision, it was marked by a multiplicity of opinions and a lack of clarity about its holding."); Weakland, *supra* note 113, at 610 ("*Richmond Newspapers* contained seven separate opinions, with no one opinion joined by more than three Justices."); BeVier, *supra* note 113, at 313 ("Such a cacophony of judicial voice alone implies both the absence of a consensus and the presence of considerable individual intransigence among members of the court concerning the access question.").

165. 448 U.S. at 582 (Stevens, J., concurring); see *id.* at 583 ("Today . . . for the first time, the Court unequivocally holds that an arbitrary interference with access to important information is an abridgment of the freedoms of speech and the press protected by the First Amendment."). This statement has been read in varying ways. Compare BeVier, *supra* note 113, at 311-12 ("Justice Stevens' statement may be neither a fair reading of the holding nor an accurate accounting of the noses of his brethren.") with ABA STANDARDS FOR CRIMINAL JUSTICE, *supra* note 88, § 8-3.2 at 25 (2d ed. 1980) ("*Richmond Newspapers* was therefore quite a turnaround for the Court. Not only did it recognize a First Amendment-based right of access to the judicial branch but it did so by embracing the broadly political implications of a structural right to know.").

The case commenced when the defendant John Stevenson, who was on trial on the same murder charge for the fourth time, moved that his trial be closed to the public. Neither the prosecutor nor the two reporters who were present objected.[166] The trial judge, citing a state statute authorizing exclusion of persons in the interests of fair trial, granted the motion.[167] Later the same day, the local press sought to vacate the order but, citing his concern that the presence of the public might distract the jury and the need to protect the defendant's rights, the trial judge declined.[168] The defendant was subsequently acquitted in a closed trial and the Virginia Supreme Court dismissed the newspapers' appeal.[169] The United States Supreme Court reversed.

Justice Burger's opinion announcing the Court's judgment emphasized the historical importance of the public trial both in the United States and in England. The presumption of openness was "no quirk of history [but] an indispensable attribute of an Anglo-American trial."[170] According to the Chief Justice, openness improves the functioning of a trial,[171] has therapeutic value by "providing an outlet for community concern, hostility and emotion,"[172] and educates and enhances public acceptance that justice is being done.[173] "From this unbroken, uncontradicted history, supported by reasons as valid today as in centuries past," the Chief Justice asserted that the Court was "bound to conclude that a presumption of openness inheres in the very nature of a criminal trial under our system of justice."[174]

The Chief Justice's emphasis on this historical tradition of openness has been the subject of significant controversy. After all, a history of open criminal trials was held insufficient in *Gannett Co.* to establish a Sixth Amendment-based right of access, even when supported by consideration of the value of openness in the

---

166. See 448 U.S. at 560.
167. See *id.*
168. See *id.* at 561.
169. The Virginia Supreme Court denied the press' petitions for a writ of mandamus, prohibition, and leave to appeal. While the United States Supreme Court held that appeal was inappropriate, certiorari was granted. See *id.* at 562-63. Since the dispute was "capable of repetition, yet evading review," the case was not moot. *Id.* at 563.
170. *Id.* at 569; see *id.* at 564 ("What is significant for present purposes is that throughout its evolution, the trial has been open to all who care to observe.").
171. See *id.* at 516 (openness discourages perjury, the misconduct of participants and biased decisions). See 6 J. WIGMORE, EVIDENCE § 1834, at 435-42 (McNaughton rev. ed. 1961) (discussing reasons for traditional openness of trials).
172. See 448 U.S. at 571. See also 6 WIGMORE, *supra* note 171, at 435-42.
173. See 448 U.S. at 572-73 ("When a criminal trial is conducted in the open, there is at least an opportunity both for understanding the system in general and its workings in a particular case."). See also 6 WIGMORE, *supra* note 171, at 435-42.
174. 448 U.S. at 573.

criminal justice system.[175] Moreover, not all legal traditions and historical practices enjoy constitutional protection.[176] In short, it is not immediately obvious why a tradition of openness is relevant to First Amendment analysis.

One answer, however, lies in the constitutional values that undergird the First Amendment. While the Constitution contains no express right of public access to criminal trials, Chief Justice Burger argued that such a right is implicit in the First Amendment, which is designed to ensure a meaningful freedom to communicate on matters relating to the functioning of government.[177] For the freedoms of speech and press to serve their intended purpose, the Chief Justice suggested, the public must enjoy a "freedom to listen," including a "right of access" in appropriate circumstances.[178] Chief Justice Burger found additional support for an implied, First Amendment-based right of access to criminal trials in the right of assembly and the legal doctrine of the "public forum."[179] A trial has histori-

---

175. Professor BeVier contends that "[i]n ascribing doctrinal significance to history in *Richmond Newspapers*, . . . Chief Justice Burger's opinion does not explicate how he determined that the common law rule of open proceedings was incorporated in — rather than 'rejected or left undisturbed by' — the first amendment. Nor does the opinion acknowledge the need that Justice Stewart discerned in *Gannett* to 'distinguish between what the Constitution permits and what it requires.'" BeVier, *supra* note 113, at 321. See also Cohen, *Access to Pretrial Documents Under the First Amendment*, 84 COLUM. L. REV. 1813, 1824 (1984) ("The earlier decision is a strong statement of the criminal defendant's rights and expectations; it is not a refutation of the press or public's right of access in all circumstances. *Gannett* and *Richmond Newspapers* are contradictory only in the same way that the first and sixth amendments can be contradictory — they represent constitutional values whose occasional competition requires careful examination and balancing.").

176. See Hayes, *supra* note 113, at 1132 ("Another major problem with the history prong is that there is no logical link between the history factor and the first amendment rationale underlying the right of access."); Wood, *supra* note 119, at 4 ("there was far less concern about the effect of pretrial publicity 200 years ago and little or no cause for concern about the juror's privacy interests."). As Judge Wood has noted, "[u]nless we also examine whether *our* circumstances and *our* values should prompt us to maintain the tradition, we risk making the wrong decision on access and of erring either on the side of openness or of closure." *Id.*

177. 448 U.S. at 575 (Burger, C.J., announcing judgment). See generally Fenner & Koley, *supra* note 163, at 422 n.35 (discussing the Chief Justice's opinion); Hayes, *supra* note 113, at 1116 ("The Chief Justice, however, did not rely solely on this political argument to justify the right of access. He also invoked what Justice Blackmun called a 'veritable potpourri' of constitutional guarantees.").

178. 448 U.S. at 576-77 (Burger, C.J., announcing judgment) ("The explicit, guaranteed rights to speak and to publish concerning what takes place at a trial would lose much meaning if access to observe the trial could, as it was here, be foreclosed arbitrarily."). Justice Stevens' separate concurring opinion similarly emphasized the press and public's "rights of access to information about the operation of their government, including the Judicial Branch." *Id.* at 584 (Stevens, J., concurring in judgment).

179. *Id.* at 578 (Burger, C.J., announcing judgment) ("[A] trial courtroom also is a public place where the people generally — and representatives of the media — have a right to be present, and where their presence historically has been thought to enhance the integrity and quality of what takes place.") Justice Stewart similarly relied on public forum analysis to support the access right: "Even more than city streets, sidewalks, and parks as areas of traditional First Amendment activity,

cally been a place where the public gathers to do the public's business. A right to attend criminal trials is implicit in the First Amendment, the Chief Justice indicated, for without such a right, "which people have exercised for centuries, important aspects of freedom of speech and 'of the press could be eviscerated.'"[180]

Having found a presumptive right of access, the Chief Justice considered those circumstances that might justify closure. "Absent an overriding interest articulated in findings," he determined, "the trial of a criminal case must be open to the public."[181] The trial judge in *Richmond Newspapers, Inc.*, however, had made no findings to support closure, had failed to consider any alternatives, and did not even consider competing First Amendment rights. Accordingly, in the Chief Justice's view, reversal was required.[182]

Justices White[183] and Blackmun[184] wrote concurring opinions to reaffirm their belief that the Sixth Amendment guarantee of a public trial also established a right of public access to criminal trial and pretrial proceedings. Justice Stewart, the author of *Gannett Co.*, citing the tradition of open trials, embraced a First Amendment-based right of access to "civil as well as criminal" trials.[185] Only Justice Rehnquist dissented.[186]

---

a trial courtroom is a place where representatives of the press and the public are not only free to be, but where their presence serves to assure the integrity of what goes on." *Id.* at 599-600 (Stewart, J., concurring). See also ABA STANDARDS FOR CRIMINAL JUSTICE, *supra* note 88, § 8-3.2, at 26 ("Therefore, the *Richmond* right of access now accomplishes with respect to the judiciary much of what the Sunshine Act and the Freedom of Information Act together provide for the legislative and executive branches."); 94 HARV. L. REV., *supra* note 163, at 155 ("*Richmond Newspapers* suggests a revival of the dormant principal of minimum access. But for the fact that it involved plaintiffs who sought access to a forum not to express but rather to inform themselves, the case implicated precisely the same concerns that gave rise to the original public forum doctrine.").

180. 448 U.S. at 580 (Burger, C.J., announcing judgment) (quoting Branzburg v. Hayes, 408 U.S. 665, 681 (1972)).

181. 448 U.S. at 581 (Burger, C.J., announcing judgment). A judge may impose "reasonable" limitations on access to a trial, "including preferential seating for media representatives." *Id.* at 581 n.18.

182. See *id.* at 580-81.

183. See *id.* at 581-82 (White, J., concurring).

184. See *id.* at 601-04 (Blackmun, J., concurring). While Justice Blackmun found the First Amendment analysis "troublesome," *id.* at 603, he was "driven to conclude, as a secondary position, that the First Amendment must provide some measure of protection for public access to trial." *Id.* at 604.

185. *Id.* at 599 (Stewart, J., concurring) ("With us, a trial is by every definition a proceeding open to the press and the public."). Justice Stewart noted that "[t]he right to speak implies a freedom to listen," *id.* at 599 n.2 (citing Kleindienst v. Mandel, 408 U.S. 753 (1972)), and "[t]he right to publish implies a freedom to gather information," 448 U.S. at 599 n.2 (citing Branzburg v. Hayes, 408 U.S. 665 (1972)).

186. See 448 U.S. at 604-06 (Rehnquist, J., dissenting). Justice Rehnquist criticized the concentration of excessive authority in the Supreme Court and emphasized the need for a "healthy pluralism" in our federal system. *Id.* at 606.

Justice Brennan, concurring, provided an alternative approach. Chief Justice Burger, invoking common law tradition, had argued for recognition of a right of public access to give meaning to the express guarantees of the First Amendment. Justice Brennan, in contrast, linked the right of public access to the *structural* role of the First Amendment "in securing and fostering our republican system of government."[187] Implicit in this structural model is the public's ability to gather information, because "valuable public debate — as well as other civic behavior — must be informed."[188] A right of public access is thus derived from the very structure of our self-government. By the same token, although freedom of expression is, "with only rare and stringent exceptions," absolutely protected from government suppression, Justice Brennan emphasized that "the First Amendment has not been viewed by the Court in all settings as providing an equally categorical assurance of the correlative freedom of access to information."[189] Accordingly, while newsgathering is protected by the First Amendment, access to information can be regulated based on "the nature of the information and countervailing interests in security or confidentiality."[190]

Justice Brennan recognized that his structural analysis for extending First Amendment protection to newsgathering is "theoretically endless."[191] He proposed, therefore, employing two "helpful principles" in evaluating access claims. "First, the case for a right of access has special force when drawn from an enduring and vital tradition of public entree to particular proceedings or information."[192] Attention to *tradition* is appropriate because "the Constitution carries the gloss of history" and because "a tradition of accessibility implies the favorable judgment of experience."[193] Second, Justice Brennan urged that analysis of access claims address a *functional* question — "whether access to a particular government process is important in terms of that very process."[194] As the discussion that follows confirms, this two-part inquiry has since dominated judicial analysis of the right of public access.

In *Richmond Newspapers, Inc.*, Justice Brennan applied his analysis to the context of criminal trials. First, he noted, as had the Chief Justice, that "[t]radi-

---

187. *Id*. at 587 (Brennan, J., concurring). See Chap. 1-5 *supra*.

188. 448 U.S. at 587-88 (Brennan, J., concurring); see *id*. at 587-88 ("The structural model links the First Amendment to that process of communication necessary for a democracy to survive, and thus entails solicitude not only for communication itself, but also for the indispensable conditions of meaningful communication.").

189. *Id*. at 585. See Brennan, *The Supreme Court and the Meiklejohn Interpretation of the First Amendment*, 79 HARV. L. REV. 1 (1965).

190. 448 U.S. at 586 (Brennan, J., concurring).

191. *Id*. at 588. See Zemel v. Rusk, 381 U.S. 1 (1965) ("[t]here are few restrictions on action which could not be clothed by ingenious argument in the garb of decreased data flow.").

192. 448 U.S. at 589 (Brennan, J., concurring).

193. *Id*.

194. *Id*.

tion, contemporaneous state practice and this Court's own decisions manifest a common understanding that '[a] trial is a public event. What transpires in the court room is public property.'"[195] Second, he determined that openness advances several objectives of the trial system, including "a fair and accurate adjudication of guilt or innocence."[196] In addition, an open proceeding serves to assure the citizenry "that procedural rights are respected, and that justice is afforded equally."[197] A public trial also "acts as an important check, akin in purpose to the other checks and balances that infuse our system of government"[198] and "[p]ublicizing trial proceedings aids accurate factfinding" as well.[199] Finally, Justice Brennan found it unnecessary to determine what countervailing interests might override this First Amendment right, since the Virginia statute at issue unconstitutionally vested unfettered discretion in the trial judge.[200]

While the Court was fragmented in *Richmond Newspapers, Inc.*, the case clearly established a First Amendment-based right of access to at least some judicial proceedings — it is therefore truly a "watershed case." Shortly after the decision, the Justice Department issued guidelines indicating that the government has a "general overriding affirmative duty" to oppose trial closures unless it "is plainly essential to the interests of justice."[201] Nevertheless, *Richmond Newspapers, Inc.* does not establish a constitutional Sunshine Law or a Freedom of Information Act. It provides a rationale for a constitutional right of access, but does not purport to decide finally when the right attaches or the nature of the competing interests that will justify closure. The scope of the public access right and the appropriate standards of judicial review, therefore, remained unsettled after *Richmond Newspapers, Inc.*

§ 2-2(d). *Globe Newspaper Co. v. Superior Court.*

The First Amendment-based right of public access to criminal trials first recognized in *Richmond Newspapers, Inc.* was reaffirmed by the full Court in *Globe Newspaper Co. v. Superior Court*.[202] The Court, in an opinion by Justice

---

195. *Id.* at 593 (quoting Craig v. Harney, 331 U.S. 367, 374 (1947)). Public trials are supported by "virtually immemorial custom" manifested in an "abiding adherence to the principle of open trials." 448 U.S. at 589 (Brennan, J., concurring).
196. *Id.*
197. *Id.* at 595 ("Closed trials breed suspicion of prejudice and arbitrariness, which in turn spawns disrespect for law.").
198. *Id.* at 596.
199. *Id.*
200. See *id.* at 598.
201. See Chap. 2-4 *infra*. See generally ABA STANDARDS FOR CRIMINAL JUSTICE, *supra* note 88, § 8-3.2, at 26 (closure of trials is permitted only in the most extreme circumstances).
202. 457 U.S. 596 (1982).

Brennan, invalidated a state statute requiring exclusion of the press and the public during the testimony of minor victims of designated sexual offenses.

The defendant in the underlying case had been charged with the rape of three minors. When the *Boston Globe* objected to closure of the courtroom during hearings on preliminary motions, the trial judge, citing the statute, ordered the exclusion of the press and public for the duration of the trial.[203] The defendant and the prosecutor, purporting to act on behalf of the minor victims, waived any objection to a public proceeding.[204] Nine months after the trial, the Massachusetts Supreme Judicial Court dismissed the newspaper's appeal. While that court agreed that the statute did not require exclusion of the public and press from the entire trial, it concluded that closure during the victim's testimony was appropriate.[205] On remand after *Richmond Newspapers, Inc.*, the Supreme Judicial Court reaffirmed its holding that such a limited mandatory exclusion is constitutional, citing an historical exception to public trials in cases involving sexual assaults[206] and the need for a mandatory rule to protect legitimate state interests.[207]

The United States Supreme Court, after disposing of a mootness challenge,[208] held that the statute's mandatory-closure rule violates the First Amendment. Writing for the Court, Justice Brennan again cited the structural values that undergird the First Amendment as supporting a presumptive right of public access "to ensure that this constitutionally protected 'discussion of governmental affairs' is an informed one."[209] According to the Court, the value of public access to criminal trials is confirmed by history[210] and by the role of openness in "the functioning of the judicial process and the government as a whole."[211] In response to Massachusetts's argument that trials involving minor sex victims

---

203. See *id*. at 598-99.
204. See *id*. at 599.
205. See *id*. at 600.
206. See *id*. at 601-02 ("In cases involving sexual assaults, portions of trials have been closed to some segments of the public, even when the victim was an adult.").
207. See *id*. at 602.
208. The Court held that the controversy was "capable of repetition, yet evading review." *Id*. at 602-03. Justice Stevens, however, dissented on the ground that the statute, construed to apply only to the testimony of minor victims of sexual assaults, had never been applied in a live controversy. He concluded that the Court's comments about the First Amendment were "advisory, hypothetical, and, at best, premature." *Id*. at 623 (Stevens, J., dissenting).
209. *Id*. at 604-05 (citation omitted); see *id*. ("Underlying the First Amendment right of access to criminal trials is the common understanding that 'a major purpose of the Amendment was to protect the free discussion of governmental affairs,' by offering such protection, the First Amendment serves to ensure that the individual citizen can effectively participate in and contribute to our republican system of self-government.") (citation omitted); Weakland, *supra* note 120, at 612.
210. See 457 U.S. at 605.
211. *Id*. at 606; see *id*. ("In sum, the institutional value of the open criminal trial is recognized in both logic and experience.").

have historically been closed to the public, Justice Brennan cautioned that closure of any category of judicial proceeding must be assessed in the context of the facts of each particular case. In *Globe Newspaper Co.*, the Court concluded, the State was simply arguing that its interests justified closure during the testimony of minor victims of sexual assaults, a judgment that must be made on a case-by-case, not a categorical, basis.[212]

Thus having established a presumptive right of access, Justice Brennan turned to determining whether the mandatory closure rule "is necessitated by a compelling governmental interest, and is narrowly tailored to serve that interest."[213] Massachusetts asserted two interests to justify its rule: (1) the protection of minor victims of sex crimes from trauma and embarrassment, and (2) encouraging minor victims to come forward and testify in a truthful and credible manner.[214]

The Court concluded that the former interest — protecting the minor victim — is compelling, but does not justify a *mandatory* closure rule. The rule "cannot be viewed as a narrowly tailored means of accommodating the State's asserted interest: that the interest could be served just as well by requiring the trial court to determine on a case-by-case basis whether the State's legitimate concern for the well-being of the minor victim necessitates closure."[215] In addition, Justice Brennan questioned whether the latter interest — encouraging testimony — was sufficiently compelling since "that same interest could be relied on to support an array of mandatory closure rules designed to encourage victims to come forward."[216] Moreover, "logic and common sense" did not support the argument,

---

212. *Id.* at 605 n.13 ("Whether the First Amendment right of access to criminal trials can be restricted in the context of any particular criminal trial, such as a murder trial (the setting for the dispute in *Richmond Newspapers*) or a rape trial, depends not on the historical openness of that type of criminal trial but rather on the state interests assertedly supporting the restriction.").

213. *Id.* at 607. Justice Brennan explained that such strict scrutiny is required where the government seeks closure to prevent public access to information. *Id.* at 606. But cf. *id.* at 607 n.17 (limitations on the access right that resemble time, place and manner restrictions would not be subject to strict scrutiny).

214. *Id.* at 607. See 6 WIGMORE, *supra* note 171, at 445 n.2 ("By statute in most states [closures] are expressly sanctioned, either in general terms or for *special classes of cases,* such as divorce, rape and the like, or for *special classes of persons,* such as minors.").

215. 457 U.S. at 609. Justice Brennan noted that the trial judge should consider circumstances such as the victim's age, psychological maturity and understanding, the nature of the crime, the desires of the victim, and the interests of parents and relatives. *Id.* at 608. In that regard, he asserted that, in the underlying case, the names of the victims were already a matter of public record and they may well have been willing to have the press and public present during their testimony. *Id.* The Court also recognized that, since the victims would be testifying even in a closed proceeding, any injury must be "incremental" and attributable solely to the presence of the public and press. *Id.* at 607 n.19.

216. *Id.* at 610.

since the press would still have access to a transcript of the testimony and other news sources if it wished to publicize the victim's testimony.[217]

Chief Justice Burger dissented. Joined by Justice Rehnquist, the Chief Justice argued that the Court had ignored the historical practice of excluding the public from sexual assault cases, especially those involving minor victims.[218] There was no "history of openness" of the kind that had provided the foundation for the presumption of public access articulated in *Richmond Newspapers, Inc.*[219] The Chief Justice also asserted that the strict scrutiny employed by the Court was inappropriate given the incidental character of the burden on newsgathering arising from a closed proceeding; Massachusetts did not deny the press access to information concerning what took place at trial; and transcripts and other sources of information remained available.[220] Accordingly, the Chief Justice concluded that a reasonableness test would be more appropriate: "[o]ur obligation in the case is to balance the competing interests."[221]

Not surprisingly, the Chief Justice's balancing of the competing interests, pursuant to a "reasonableness" standard, differed markedly from that of the Court. Citing studies demonstrating the traumatic effect of court proceedings on minor rape victims, the Chief Justice concluded that a mandatory closure rule "rationally serves" the government's asserted interest.[222] "The legislature did not act irrationally in deciding not to leave the closure determination to the idiosyncracies of individual judges subject to the pressures available to the media."[223]

The Chief Justice's disagreement notwithstanding, *Globe Newspaper Co.* both reaffirmed the validity of a First Amendment-based right of public access to criminal trials and broke new ground by embracing strict scrutiny as the appropriate standard of judicial review for orders closing criminal trials. In another sense, however, the decision is a limited response to a limited problem. No state other than Massachusetts had adopted a mandatory rule requiring closure in connection with the testimony of minor victims of sexual assault. Moreover, the Court took pains to emphasize that "the First Amendment does not necessarily stand as a bar to the exclusion from the courtroom of the press

---

217. *Id.* at 609-10.
218. See *id.* at 614 (Burger, C.J., dissenting).
219. *Id.*
220. See *id.* at 615. But cf. Richmond Newspapers, Inc. v. Virginia, 448 U.S. at 579 n.22 (Brennan, J., concurring) ("In advancing these purposes, the availability of a trial transcript is no substitute for a public presence at the trial itself. As any experienced appellate judge can attest, the 'cold' record is a very imperfect reproduction of events that transpire in the courtroom."). See also In re Iowa Freedom of Info. Council, 724 F.2d 658 (8th Cir. 1983).
221. 457 U.S. at 616 (Burger, C.J., dissenting).
222. *Id.* at 617.
223. *Id.* at 618. Similarly, the Chief Justice opined that the rule was a "rational response" to the problem of under-reporting sex crimes. *Id.* at 617.

and general public during the testimony of minor sex-offense victims."[224] Only a mandatory rule, which by definition is not supported by an individualized determination that closure is necessary to further overriding state interests under specific circumstances, fails to pass constitutional muster.

§ 2-2(e). *Press-Enterprise Co. v. Superior Court (Press-Enterprise I).*

In *Press-Enterprise Co. v. Superior Court (Press-Enterprise I)*,[225] decided two years after *Globe Newspaper Co.*, the Court considered "whether the guarantees of open public proceedings in criminal trials cover proceedings for the voir dire examination of potential jurors."[226] Prior to the trial of a defendant charged with the rape and murder of a teenage girl, the *Riverside Press-Enterprise* affirmatively moved the trial judge to hold voir dire proceedings in open court. The trial judge nevertheless closed all but three days of the six-week voir dire proceeding.[227] After the jury was impaneled, and again after the defendant was convicted and sentenced to death, the *Press-Enterprise* unsuccessfully sought release of a transcript of the voir dire. The trial judge denied both motions, reasoning that confidentiality was needed to protect the privacy of jurors.[228] The orders closing the voir dire and prohibiting release of its transcript were left standing by the California appellate courts.[229] The Supreme Court unanimously reversed.

Writing for the Court, Chief Justice Burger emphasized, as he had in *Richmond Newspapers, Inc.*, an historical tradition of openness. "[S]ince the development of trial by jury, the process of selection of jurors has presumptively been a public process with exceptions only for good cause shown."[230] By the

---

224. *Id.* at 611 n.27. A number of states have enacted rules that authorize a trial judge, in his or her discretion, to close criminal sex-offense trials during the testimony of minor victims. See *id.* at 608 n.22. See generally 6 WIGMORE, *supra* note 171, § 1835, at 445 (listing cases dealing with closure of courts for the protection of minors); 75 AM. JUR. 2d *Trial* § 207, at 433 ("An exception to the public's right to attend court proceedings exists in cases in which the demands of individual privacy clearly outweigh the merits of public disclosure.").
225. 464 U.S. 501 (1984).
226. *Id.* at 503.
227. See *id.* at 503-04.
228. See *id.* at 504. After the jury had been impaneled, counsel for the defendant and the prosecutor both opposed release of the transcript. The trial judge agreed that the jurors' right to privacy and the defendant's fair trial rights should prevail over the "right of the people to know." *Id.* After the trial, the judge acknowledged that much of the voir dire involved "dull and boring" information. Nevertheless, he denied the motion because "some of the jurors had some special experiences in sensitive areas that do not appear to be appropriate for public discussion." *Id.*
229. See *id.* at 504-05.
230. *Id.* at 505. See *id.* at 507 ("If we accept this account it appears that beginning in the sixteenth century, jurors were selected in public."). But see Wood, *supra* note 119, at 4 ("[T]he Court barely acknowledged the dramatic differences between jury selection now and jury selection during the historical period the Court examined and it did not ask whether those differences should prompt us to deviate today from a practice that was deemed appropriate 200 years ago.").

time the Bill of Rights was adopted, "[p]ublic jury selection thus was the common practice in America."[231] Openness in proceedings such as voir dire, the Chief Justice explained, promotes fairness and the appearance of fairness and has therapeutic value — "public proceedings vindicate the concerns of the victims and the community in knowing that offenders are being brought to account for their criminal conduct by jurors fairly and openly selected."[232] While the Chief Justice never directly characterized voir dire as part of the trial itself, as the newspaper had urged, the Court expressly extended the presumption of openness to the selection of jurors.[233]

While closure of voir dire proceedings is not absolutely precluded, Chief Justice Burger indicated that exclusion of the public from such judicial proceedings must be "rare and only for cause shown that outweighs the value of openness."[234] Rather than reiterate the strict scrutiny formulation articulated by Justice Brennan in *Globe Newspaper Co.*, however, the Chief Justice asserted that "[t]he presumption of openness may be overcome only by an overriding interest based on findings that closure is essential to preserve higher values and is narrowly tailored to serve that interest."[235]

The trial court in *Press-Enterprise I* had held that two different interests required closure: the defendant's right to a fair trial and the privacy rights of prospective jurors. Chief Justice Burger acknowledged that both these interests could be compelling.[236] But, in the case at issue, there were no lower court findings establishing that these concerns justified such a prolonged closure and the trial court had apparently failed to consider alternatives to closure at all.[237] Given these failings, the Court concluded, closure could not be constitutionally justified.[238]

While this holding was sufficient to dispose of the case, the Chief Justice went on to instruct trial judges concerning how to respond to the issue of juror privacy. He acknowledged that, "in some circumstances," a prospective juror

---

231. 464 U.S. at 508.
232. *Id.* at 509.
233. See also *id.* at 516 (Stevens, J., concurring) ("[T]he distinction between trials and other official proceedings is not necessarily dispositive, or even important, in evaluating the First Amendment issues.").
234. *Id.* at 509.
235. *Id.* at 510. In addition, the Court emphasized that the trial judge must articulate the interest justifying closure and provide "findings specific enough that a reviewing court can determine whether the closure order was properly entered." *Id.* See Litt, *supra* note 113, at 387 ("In so holding, the Court moved even closer to the position urged by Justice Blackmun's dissent in *DePasquale*. Although the decision in *Richmond Newspapers* also required an 'overriding interest based on findings' in order to justify closure, in *Press Enterprise I* the Court further required that the trial court's remedy be 'narrowly tailored.'").
236. See 464 U.S. at 510-11.
237. See *id.*
238. See *id.*

may have a compelling privacy interest in not disclosing information in open court.[239] In such cases, the trial judge should inform prospective jurors that they may "request an opportunity to present the problem to the judge *in camera* but with counsel present and on the record."[240] Even when this "limited closure" is appropriate, the judge should protect constitutional values "by making a transcript of the closed proceedings available within a reasonable time, if the judge determines that disclosure can be accomplished while safeguarding the juror's valid privacy interests."[241]

Justice Stevens, concurring separately, stressed that the public right of access to voir dire is grounded, not in the relation of that proceeding to the criminal trial, but in an assessment of the First Amendment value of openness: "Our system of self-government assumes the existence of an informed citizenry."[242] Public voir dire proceedings, in Justice Stevens' view, improve public understanding and allow critical public examination of the process.[243] While the privacy interests of jurors might justify some limitation on public access, in the case at issue, the trial judge had "applied an impermissibly broad rule of secrecy."[244] Justice Marshall, concurring in the judgment, adopted the strict scrutiny formulation initially advanced in *Globe Newspaper Co.*[245] "Only in the most extraordinary circumstances," Justice Marshall suggested, "can the substance of a juror's response to questioning at voir dire be permanently excluded from the salutary scrutiny of the public and the press."[246]

---

239. Confidentiality may be compelling "when interrogation touches on deeply personal matters that a person has legitimate reasons for keeping out of the public domain." *Id.* at 511. In such cases, the privacy interests of the juror "must be balanced against the historic values we have discussed and the need for openness of the process." *Id.* at 512.

Justice Blackmun, concurring, emphasized that the Court had not held that a prospective juror has a constitutional right of privacy to refuse to answer questions. He also expressed concern that recognition of such a right might needlessly complicate voir dire. See *id.* at 514-15 (Blackmun, J., concurring). A juror's privacy interest, Justice Blackmun argued, "can be fully protected through the interests of the defendant and the State in encouraging his full cooperation." *Id.* at 516. Judge Wood has argued that no burden to request privacy should be placed on jurors during the voir dire process, because they are often afraid to come forward and request a private examination. See Wood, *supra* note 119, at 7.

240. 464 U.S. at 512.

241. *Id.* Privacy may still require that portions of the closed proceeding be sealed or that the prospective juror's name be redacted. See *id.*

242. *Id.* at 518 n.4 (Stevens, J., concurring).

243. See *id.* at 518.

244. *Id.* at 520.

245. See *id.* (Marshall, J., concurring) ("[P]rior to issuing a closure order, a trial court should be obliged to show that the order in question constitutes the least restrictive means available for protecting compelling state interests.").

246. *Id.* at 520-21.

§ 2-2(f). *Press-Enterprise Co. v. Superior Court (Press-Enterprise II)*.

Given the linkage of voir dire to the criminal trial, *Press-Enterprise I* did not firmly establish that a right of public access extends to pretrial proceedings. Thus, the confusion generated by the Court's rejection in *Gannett Co. v. DePasquale* of a right of public access to pretrial proceedings persisted. To unsettle matters further, in *Waller v. Georgia*, the Court had extended the defendant's Sixth Amendment right to a public trial to a suppression hearing and at least implied that public access to pretrial proceedings would be constitutionally protected by the First Amendment.[247] In *Press-Enterprise Co. v. Superior Court (Press-Enterprise II)*, decided two years after its namesake,[248] the Court finally addressed squarely "whether [the press] has a First Amendment right of access to the transcript of a *preliminary hearing* growing out of a criminal prosecution."[249]

Robert Diaz, a nurse charged with murdering twelve patients by administering lethal drugs, moved to close his preliminary hearing. Relying on a state statute authorizing closure only when necessary to protect the defendant's right to a fair trial, a magistrate granted the unopposed motion.[250] Following a forty-one day preliminary hearing, which consisted primarily of evidence concerning the defendant's guilt, the *Press-Enterprise* sought a transcript of the hearing. The

---

247. In *Waller v. Georgia*, 467 U.S. 39 (1984), the defendant objected to the prosecution's efforts to close a suppression hearing. The government feared that publicity would render some of the information inadmissible at trial and would compromise the privacy interests of some persons who would not be brought to trial. See *id.* at 42. The seven-day hearing was closed even though only 2½ hours involved intercepted information. *Id.* The Supreme Court, applying the First Amendment-derived standard of review articulated in *Press-Enterprise I*, held that closure of the entire hearing violated the defendant's Sixth Amendment right to a public trial. *Id.* at 46.

Justice Powell, writing for the Court in *Waller*, cited the First Amendment cases and concluded, "there can be little doubt that the explicit Sixth Amendment right of the accused is no less protective of a public trial than the First Amendment right of the press and public." *Id.* The Court therefore held "that under the Sixth Amendment any closure of a suppression hearing over the objections of the accused must meet the tests set out in *Press-Enterprise* and its predecessors." *Id.* at 47.

248. 478 U.S. 1 (1986).
249. *Id.* at 3 (emphasis added).
250. See *id.* The California statute provided that preliminary hearings must be open unless "exclusion of the public is necessary in order to protect the defendant's right to a fair and impartial trial." *Id.* at 3-4. The magistrate determined that the case had attracted national publicity and that the media might report only one side if they had access to the hearing. *Id.* Prior to 1982, the statute had afforded the defendant an unqualified right to close the preliminary hearing. The California Supreme Court had upheld that law against First Amendment challenge, see San Jose Mercury-News v. Municipal Ct., 638 P.2d 655 (Cal. 1982), although the California legislature subsequently amended the statute, see 478 U.S. at 4 n.1.

magistrate denied the motion and sealed the record.[251] On appeal, the California Supreme Court held that there is no First Amendment-based right of access to preliminary hearings and that, under the statute, access could constitutionally be denied if the defendant established a "reasonable likelihood of substantial prejudice."[252]

Chief Justice Burger, again writing for the Court, premised its decision reversing the California courts on the First Amendment,[253] and emphasized that the relevant inquiry is not whether the proceeding is labeled a "trial" or "pretrial" proceeding. Rather, the Court determined, the First Amendment requires that the constitutional inquiry focus solely on two "considerations" — i.e., "whether the place and process have historically been open to the press and general public" and "whether public access plays a significant positive role in the functioning of the particular process in question."[254] With respect to the historical inquiry, the Court determined that "there has been a tradition of accessibility to preliminary hearings of the type conducted in California."[255] But, as Justice Stevens stressed in dissent, the historical record of open preliminary hearings is far less uniform and compelling than that supporting a right of public access to criminal trials.[256] States have, in fact, followed different rules regarding access to preliminary hearings, although the trend has clearly been towards openness.[257] Nevertheless, Chief Justice Burger invoked Justice Brennan's argu-

---

251. The trial court acknowledged that the information contained in the transcript was primarily factual but found "a reasonable likelihood that release of all or any part of the transcripts might prejudice defendant's right to a fair and impartial trial." 478 U.S. at 5.

252. *Id*. at 5-6.

253. But see *id*. at 7 ("The right to an open public trial is a shared right of the accused and the public, the common concern being the assurance of fairness.").

254. *Id*. at 8.

255. *Id*. at 10. But see Wood, *supra* note 119, at 6 ("Because history is often equivocal, courts tend either to rely more heavily on analogy to proceedings whose history *is* clear or to find in history whatever is needed to justify the result. An example of the latter is found in the Supreme Court's opinions in *Press Enterprise II*, the decision according an access right to preliminary hearings as they are conducted in California.").

256. See 478 U.S. at 24 (Stevens, J., dissenting). See also Gannett Co. v. DePasquale, 443 U.S. at 387-89 (absence of a common law right of public access to pretrial proceedings); Geis, *Preliminary Hearings and the Press*, 8 UCLA L. REV. 397 (1961).

257. For example, the original Field Code of Criminal Procedure, adopted by many jurisdictions, provides that preliminary hearings will be closed at the request of the accused. Dissenting in *Press-Enterprise II*, Justice Stevens cited this diversity of rules as "merely a reflection of our federal system, which demands tolerance for a spectrum of state procedures dealing with a common problem of law enforcement." 478 U.S. at 24 (Stevens, J., dissenting). Justice Stevens stressed that the fact that California is in a shrinking minority of states that permit closure where there is a "reasonable likelihood" of prejudice does not render its rule unconstitutional. *Id*. See *id*. at 22 ("[I]t is uncontroverted that a common law right of access did not inhere in preliminary proceedings at the time the First Amendment was adopted, and that the Framers and ratifiers of that provision could not have intended such proceedings to remain open.").

ment that a history of openness provides "the favorable judgment of experience,"[258] and the Court therefore relied on the "near uniform practice" of state and federal courts to open preliminary hearings as reflecting the "favorable judgment of experience."[259]

Turning to the second inquiry, the Court determined that "California preliminary hearings are sufficiently like a trial" to support the conclusion that access is required for the proper functioning of the criminal justice system.[260] The broad scope of the preliminary hearing, at least in California, indicated that it "is often the final and most important step in the criminal proceeding."[261] Indeed, in the Court's view, the absence of the jury as a safeguard at this critical proceeding makes public access especially important to provide a check on governmental abuse and to ensure that the system is functioning properly.[262]

Having concluded that a First Amendment-based right of access applies to preliminary hearings "of the type conducted in California," the Court in *Press-Enterprise II* examined whether "specific, on the record findings [were] made demonstrating that 'closure is essential to preserve higher values and is narrowly tailored to serve that interest.'"[263] When the competing interest is a criminal defendant's right to a fair trial, Chief Justice Burger explained, the trial judge must make specific findings establishing, "first, there is a substantial probability that the defendant's right to a fair trial will be prejudiced by publicity that closure would prevent and, second, reasonable alternatives to closure cannot adequately protect the defendant's fair trial rights."[264]

---

258. *Id*. at 8 (opinion of the Court).
259. See *id*. at 10. The Court provided extensive case citation to support its claim that "[t]he vast majority of States considering the issue have concluded that the same tradition of accessibility that applies to criminal trials applies to preliminary proceedings." *Id*. at 10 n.3. While several states did authorize closure, the Chief Justice explained that even they make proceedings presumptively open. See *id*. at 11.
260. *Id*. at 12.
261. *Id*. The Chief Justice did acknowledge that, unlike a criminal trial, the preliminary hearing cannot result in conviction and is held before a judicial officer without a jury. See *id*.
262. See *id*. at 12-13. Justice Stevens argued that the Court's analysis proved too much. The functional rationale invoked by the Chief Justice would apply equally to grand jury proceedings, he observed, which are often conducted in secret, as well as to civil proceedings. See *id*. at 25-26 (Stevens, J., dissenting). A grand jury proceeding may well be as much the "final step" in a criminal proceeding and the "sole occasion" for public scrutiny as is a preliminary hearing: "[W]hat emerges is the reality that the California preliminary hearing is functionally identical to the traditional grand jury." *Id*. at 26. Accordingly, Justice Stevens concluded that, "[d]espite the Court's valiant attempt to limit the logic of its holding, the *ratio decidendi* of today's decision knows no bounds." *Id*. at 28.
263. *Id*. at 13-14 (citation omitted). The Chief Justice also cited to the strict scrutiny standard, articulated in *Globe Newspaper Co.*, using a "see also" signal. See *id*.
264. *Id*. at 14. It does not appear that any preliminary hearings have successfully been closed under this standard since *Press-Enterprise II*. See People v. Davis, 22 MEDIA L. REP. (BNA) 2465,

The Chief Justice concluded that the California statute's "reasonable likelihood" test imposed "a lesser burden on the defendant than the substantial probability test which . . . is called for by the First Amendment."[265] Further, the trial judge had failed to consider whether alternatives to complete closure of the hearing would have protected the defendant's fair trial rights. Closure of an entire forty-one day hearing appeared unlikely to satisfy the requirement that restrictions on public access be narrowly tailored.[266]

Justice Stevens dissented in *Press Enterprise II* even though he had supported the right of public access in *Richmond Newspapers, Inc.* and *Press-Enterprise I*. He had even championed constitutional protection for newsgathering in other contexts.[267] Indeed, in *Press-Enterprise II*, he reaffirmed his view "that a proper construction of the First Amendment embraces a right of access to information about the conduct of public affairs."[268]

For Justice Stevens, however, First Amendment-based newsgathering rights are narrower than the right to publish.[269] Rather than two-part tests and a standard of review mirroring or approximating strict scrutiny, Justice Stevens would employ a more generalized balancing test, which assesses both the information sought and the competing interests asserted. In some cases, Justice Stevens concluded, the accused's right to a fair trial if he were bound over for trial, and his reputational interest if he were not, will provide a "substantial reason" for delaying release of a transcript of the preliminary hearing "for at least the short time before trial."[270]

§ 2-2(g). *El Vocero de Puerto Rico v. Puerto Rico*.

Press-Enterprise II's frequent references to preliminary hearings "of the type conducted in California" raised questions concerning the scope of its holding.[271] The Supreme Court's decision in *El Vocero de Puerto Rico v. Puerto Rico*,[272] however, suggests that few, if any, preliminary hearings will fall outside the ambit of the First Amendment. In that case, Puerto Rico sought to distinguish its rule closing preliminary hearings unless the defendant requested otherwise by

---

2466 (Cal. Mun. 1994). But see People v. Rollins, 24 MEDIA L. REP. (BNA) 2569 (Cal. Super. 1996) (closing hearings on motions in limine involving admissibility of evidence).
265. 478 U.S. at 14.
266. See *id.* at 15.
267. See, e.g., Houchins v. KQED, Inc., 438 U.S. 1, 31-32 (1978) (Stevens, J., dissenting). See Chap. 8-1 *infra*.
268. 478 U.S. at 18 (Stevens, J., dissenting).
269. See *id.* at 20.
270. *Id.* at 29.
271. Indeed, Justice Stevens noted that the Court's opinion invoked the "comforting phrase," referring to preliminary hearings "as they are conducted in California," eight times. *Id.* at 25.
272. 508 U.S. 147 (1993) (*per curiam*).

arguing that its preliminary hearing is different from those conducted in California.[273] Nevertheless, the Supreme Court unanimously found the distinctions "insubstantial" and that the functional similarity of the preliminary hearing in Puerto Rico to a criminal trial required public access.[274]

Puerto Rico also sought to rely upon "the unique history and traditions of the Commonwealth" to justify its practice of closing preliminary hearings.[275] The Supreme Court, however, held that "the 'experience' test of *Globe Newspaper* does not look to the particular practice of any one jurisdiction, but instead 'to the experience in that *type* or *kind* of hearing throughout the United States."[276] It is the "established and widespread tradition of open preliminary hearings among the States" that controls.[277]

§ 2-2(h). The Supreme Court Doctrine.

Richmond Newspapers, Inc. and its progeny establish that the First Amendment affords a right of public access to criminal trials and to at least some pretrial criminal proceedings.[278] Supreme Court precedent also indicates that the determination of whether there is a right of public access to other proceedings is governed by a two-part inquiry based on historical experience and functional values.[279]

But what if there is little or no tradition of openness? Should this preclude recognition of a First Amendment-based right of access? Tradition can be a static concept, whereas the criminal justice system and the needs of a democratic society constantly change. Mass communication has altered the free press-fair trial equation from early common law.[280] Experience may provide a useful

---

273. Puerto Rico relied specifically on its markedly different rules regarding the burden of proof, the parties' access to evidence, and the ability of a prosecutor to present the matter *de novo* to a higher court. See *id.* at 149 n.2.

274. *Id.* at 149. While the Puerto Rico Supreme Court had upheld the closure rule, the First Circuit had held it unconstitutional under *Press-Enterprise II.* See Rivera-Puig v. Garcia-Rosario, 983 F.2d 311 (1st Cir. 1992).

275. 508 U.S. at 150. The Puerto Rico Supreme Court had reasoned that the Commonwealth's traditions "display a special concern for the honor and reputation of the citizenry" and that the small size and dense population of the island created special problems in protecting criminal defendants from prejudicial publicity. *Id.*

276. *Id.* at 150 (citations omitted).

277. *Id.* at 150-51.

278. See ABA STANDARDS FOR CRIMINAL JUSTICE, *supra* note 88, § 8-3.2(a), at 21 ("In any criminal case, all judicial proceedings and related documents and exhibits, and any record made thereof, not otherwise required to remain confidential should be accessible to the public, except as provided in section (b).") The ABA standard establishes a qualified right of access in all judicial proceedings. The commentaries note that the standard is designed to provide "a single, comprehensive rule of access," which is premised on a "structural" theory. *Id.* at 28.

279. See Chap. 2-2(c) *supra*.

280. See Wood, *supra* note 119, at 5:

guidepost in some cases, to be sure, but its utility as a hard-and-fast requirement is problematic. How long must public access exist for there to be a tradition of openness? How widespread must a tradition of public access to a particular proceeding be before openness is blessed by the judgment of experience? In other contexts, Justice Brennan has noted that tradition is "malleable" and that "reasonable people can disagree about the content of a particular tradition."[281] And the disputes in *Press-Enterprise II* and *El Vocero* over just what constitutes the relevant experience would seem to demonstrate the ambiguity of the standard. If what the courts seek from history and tradition is the judgment of experience on the values served and costs incurred in the name of openness in the particular proceeding, it would seem that there really is no threshold requirement. The teaching of history is no doubt relevant information in evaluating an access claim, but the absence of a tradition of openness, standing alone, would not appear to be dispositive.

The functional component of the *Press-Enterprise II* standard also presents difficulties. As formulated, it does not focus on the value of openness to self-government or to citizenship. At least on its face, it looks largely to the value of access to the functioning of the proceeding in question. But even if public access has some arguably negative impact on a particular species of proceeding, that fact may be outweighed by the importance of public access to self-government. The functional inquiry, at least as articulated in *Press-Enterprise II*, threatens to distract the judicial inquiry from its principal focus — the public interest in information concerning governmental affairs.

For some, the problem with the functional prong of the two-part test is that it appears to be boundless; it dictates public access in almost all cases.[282] For example, Justice Stevens, dissenting in *Press-Enterprise II,* contended that the

---

> Despite language in the decisional law about suppression and other pretrial hearings providing the only court appearance for most criminal defendants, the plain fact is that most criminal cases go straight from indictment or information to plea — with no motion to suppress, no suppression hearing, and no other type of pretrial hearing. It is at the charge and plea bargaining stages that most criminal cases are disposed of and, thus, where most of the workings of justice occur for most criminal defendants. And, in today's federal system, with the new statutory, mandatory minimum practices, and the sentencing guidelines, it is often at the charging stage — where the prosecutor alone has the ultimate say — that a defendant's fate is sealed because it is at that stage that the parameters of the sentence are set.

See also Hayes, *supra* note 113, at 1132 ("The size and power of many governmental institutions, particularly administrative agencies, have increased greatly in this century. As their power has increased, so has the public's need for access to information on their activities.").

281. Michael H. v. Gerald D., 491 U.S. 110, 137 (1989). See also Hayes, *supra* note 113, at 1130 ("Should courts look at the process' own brief 'history,' analogize to older functionally similar processes, or simply declare that because there is no long tradition, there is also no right of access?").

282. See generally Wood, *supra* note 119, at 6; Weakland, *supra* note 120, at 620-21; Hayes, *supra* note 113, at 1134-36.

Court's functional analysis recognizing a right of public access to preliminary hearings would be equally applicable to civil and to grand jury proceedings.[283]

Once a right of public access is established, the proceeding in question is presumptively open. A trial judge must make specific, on-the-record findings establishing that closure is justified.[284] In *Globe Newspapers Co.*, in the context of criminal trials, the Court employed strict scrutiny — i.e., closure must be necessary to serve compelling interests, and less burdensome alternatives to closure must be considered.[285] In the *Press-Enterprise* cases, however, the Court opted for another formulation — closure must be "essential to preserve higher values and . . . narrowly tailored to serve that interest."[286] Whether these standards are in fact different remains unclear. Certainly, the Court's application of the standards articulated in the *Press-Enterprise* cases was as demanding as any inquiry premised on strict scrutiny.[287]

Justice Stevens has offered a different approach to resolving access cases. Instead of a two-part test to determine if a public access right exists followed by heightened judicial scrutiny in assessing the interests supporting closure, he has argued for ad hoc balancing.[288] Considerations favoring public access would be balanced against the interests supporting closure. While balancing offers greater flexibility than the formulaic approaches applied in *Globe Newspaper Co.* and the *Press-Enterprise* cases, it is subjective and open-ended. The balancing of interests depends very much on the personal values of the individual judge. There are no presumptions reflecting the importance of either the First Amendment interests or the values burdened by public access.

Finally, Supreme Court precedent has traditionally treated the First Amendment rights of the public and the press as interchangeable. While arguments have been made for a broader right of press access, at least in some cases,[289] the Supreme Court has not drawn distinctions between the access rights of the public and those of the news media.

---

283. See Chap. 2-2(f) *supra*.

284. See 75 AM. JUR. 2d *Trial* § 208, at 434 ("Findings justifying closure of a hearing must be made before closure takes place.").

285. See Chap. 2-2 (d) *supra*.

286. See Chap. 2-2 (e) & (f) *supra*.

287. See ABA STANDARDS FOR CRIMINAL JUSTICE, *supra* note 88, § 8-3.2(b) (1), at 21 (requiring findings that "(A) unrestricted access would pose a substantial probability of harm to the fairness of the trial or other overriding interest which substantially outweighs the defendant's right to a public trial; (B) the proposed order will effectively prevent the aforesaid harm; and (C) there is no less restrictive alternative reasonably available to prevent the aforesaid harm."). The commentary indicates that "[t]his is essentially the standard promulgated by the Supreme Court, although there is no single or composite statement of it in any of the court opinions." *Id.* at 29.

288. See Chap. 2-2 (f) *supra*. For a critique and application of this balancing test, see Hayes, *supra* note 113, at 1126-29, 1136-42.

289. See, e.g., Dyk, *Newsgathering, Press, Access, and the First Amendment*, 44 STAN. L. REV. 927 (1992).

§ 2-3. Procedural Requirements.

In his concurring opinion in *Gannett Co. v. DePasquale*, Justice Powell noted that "[i]f the constitutional right of the press and public to access is to have substance, representatives of these groups must be given an opportunity to be heard on the question of their exclusion."[290] In fact, those subject to exclusion must generally be afforded some opportunity to object and to state their reasons for opposing closure.[291] If a reporter is present in the courtroom when a closure motion is made, he or she may object and request a delay until counsel can be summoned. If the closed proceeding has already taken place, the press can seek a hearing by moving for access to sealed transcripts.[292] The hearing requirement is generally treated as a flexible one contemplating a reasonable opportunity to be

---

290. 443 U.S. at 401 (Powell, J., concurring). The Court repeated this admonition in *Globe Newspaper Co.*, 457 U.S. at 609 n.25. Justice Powell would limit this opportunity to those present in the courtroom when the motion for closure is made, "for the alternative would require substantial delays in trial and pretrial proceedings while notice was given to the public." 443 U.S. at 401. The four dissenting justices in *Gannett Co.* indicated that "any person removed from a court should be given a reasonable opportunity to state his objections prior to the order taking effect." 443 U.S. at 445-46 (Blackmun, J., dissenting). Justice Rehnquist, concurring in *Gannett Co.*, 443 U.S. at 405, rejected the suggestion that the First Amendment was "some sort of constitutional 'sunshine law' that requires notice, an opportunity to be heard, and substantial reasons before a governmental proceeding may be closed to the public and press." See also United States v. Valenti, 987 F.2d 708, 713 (11th Cir. 1993) (right to notice and hearing limited to those present when the motion for closure is made).

291. See, e.g., Phoenix Newspapers, Inc. v. United States Dist. Ct., 156 F.3d 940, 949 (9th Cir. 1998) ("If a court contemplates sealing a document or transcript, it must provide sufficient notice to the public and press to afford them the opportunity to object or offer alternatives."); United States v. Raffoul, 826 F.2d 218, 222 (3d Cir. 1987) ("notice and an opportunity for a hearing appropriate to the nature of the case"); United States v. Brooklier, 685 F.2d 1162, 1167-68 (9th Cir. 1982); Sacramento Bee v. United States Dist. Ct., 656 F.2d 477, 482 (9th Cir. 1981); Ex parte Birmingham News Co., 624 So. 2d 1117, 1133 (Ala. Crim. App. 1993) ("the minimum due process requirements" of appropriate notice and hearing); Louisiana v. Womack, 551 So. 2d 855, 858 (La. App.1989) ("Due process requires that some reasonable notice of a hearing affecting the closure of pretrial criminal proceedings and an opportunity to oppose closure must be given to the public before closure may be ordered."); In re Gannett River States Publ'g Corp., 630 So. 2d 351, 352 (Miss. 1994) ("A preclosure hearing must be conducted in which the press is allowed to intervene and argue against closure."); In re Glens Falls Newspapers, Inc., 614 N.Y.S.2d 628, 629 (App. Div. 1994) ("Petitioner should have been given an opportunity, through counsel, to appear and be heard in opposition to closure."); Note, *A First Amendment Right of Access to Affidavits in Support of Search Warrants*, 90 COLUM. L. REV. 2216, 2244 (1990).

292. See United States v. Raffoul, 826 F.2d 218, 224 (3d Cir. 1987) ("In balancing the competing interests here, we hold first that the public and press who are excluded from a criminal trial have a right to a hearing at a reasonable time regarding access to the transcripts."). *Raffoul* has been cited in support of applying the hearing requirement to situations in which the pretrial proceeding was not closed, but transcripts were sealed. See United States v. Antar, 38 F.3d 1348, 1362 (3d Cir. 1994).

heard.[293] The closure hearing is not intended to be self-defeating; there may be rare occasions where it is necessary to exclude the public and press from the closure hearing and to seal the transcript where the constitutionally required findings of overriding need for closure are met.[294]

While Justice Powell would have limited the opportunity to be heard to those present in the courtroom who contemporaneously object, many courts have required public notice prior to closure. This does not mean individual, personal notice to the press or any particular segment of the public.[295] Nevertheless, a motion seeking closure generally must be docketed in advance of the time it is considered, unless it would unreasonably delay the underlying proceedings.[296]

---

293. See United States v. Raffoul, 826 F.2d at 225 ("a brief hearing consistent with the interests of justice"); In re Globe Newspaper Co., 729 F.2d 47 (1st Cir. 1984) (describing a one-hour hearing after a one-and-one-half hour recess as a sufficient hearing); In re Herald Co. (Klepfer), 734 F.2d 93, 102 (2d Cir. 1984) (requirements "must remain sufficiently flexible to accommodate the exigencies of the litigation process and avoid unwarranted delays.").

294. See ABA STANDARDS FOR CRIMINAL JUSTICE, *supra* note 88, § 8-3.2(b) (2), at 21-22:

> A proceeding to determine whether a closure order should issue may itself be closed only upon a prima facie showing of the findings required. . . . In making the determination as to whether such a prima facie showing exists, the court should not require public disclosure of or access to the matter which is the subject of the closure proceeding itself and the court should accept submissions under seal, in camera or in any other manner designed to permit a party to make a prima facie showing without public disclosure of such matter.

See also Globe Newspaper Co. v. Superior Ct., 457 U.S. 596, 609 n.25 (1982); In re Storer Communications, Inc., 828 F.2d 330, 335 (6th Cir. 1987) (allowing *in camera* consideration of information in closure hearing); Ex parte Birmingham News Co., 624 So. 2d at 1135.

295. United States v. Raffoul, 826 F.2d at 225; United States v. Criden, 675 F.2d 550, 559 (3d Cir. 1982) (individual notice would be "unwarranted and impractical in the context of the administration of criminal litigation"). But, "when the district court has been made aware of the desire of specific members of the public to be present, reasonable steps to afford them an opportunity to submit their views should be taken before closure." In re Knight Publ'g Co., 743 F.2d 231, 234 (4th Cir. 1984). See United States v. Brooklier, 685 F.2d 1162, 1168 (9th Cir. 1982) ("[I]n determining what steps are reasonable, a court should avoid any that might result in material delay in the underlying proceedings.").

296. The *ABA Standards for Criminal Justice* require "reasonable notice" prior to closure; the requirement "is meant to be flexible" and contemplates "public notice that is adequate to the circumstances." ABA STANDARDS FOR CRIMINAL JUSTICE, *supra* note 88, § 8-3.2(6)(1), at 31. See United States v. Criden, 675 F.2d at 559-60 ("Public notice in a legal publication was no more effective than docketing."); Ex parte Birmingham News Co., 624 So. 2d at 1134 ("Docketing of the motion is sufficient to provide notice to the press or public of the impending hearing."); Baltimore Sun Co. v. Colbert, 593 A.2d 224, 229 (Md. 1991) ("[F]or the public to be able to assert this right in a meaningful fashion, the motion must be docketed in advance of the time of the hearing to provide notice to afford an opportunity to oppose the closure motion, as well as to present alternatives to closure."); In re Gannett River States Publ'g Corp., 630 So. 2d 351, 352 (Miss. 1994) ("Any request for an intent to exercise closure either by a party or the court must be filed and docketed with the clerk's office a minimum of 24 hours before any hearing."). But see Miami Herald Publ'g Co. v. Lewis, 426 So. 2d 1, 8 (Fla. 1982) (holding that notice must be given to at

For example, some federal courts have required that there be notice in the public docket, "normally on the day that the pertinent event occurs."[297] Where prior notice is impractical, notice should be given in the courtroom that closure is being considered and opportunity should be afforded to oppose it.[298]

To close a proceeding to which the First Amendment-based right of access extends, the trial court must make specific findings on the record that justify closure. For example, *Press-Enterprise II* requires record findings that "closure is essential to preserve higher values and is narrowly tailored to serve that interest."[299] These findings must be sufficiently specific to allow meaningful appellate review.[300]

---

least one member of the local media); Richmond Newspapers, Inc. v. Virginia, 281 S.E.2d 915, 924 n.9 (Va. 1981).

297. See United States v. Cojab, 996 F.2d 1404, 1408 (2d Cir. 1993) (error to conduct closure hearing without public notice); United States v. Raffoul, 826 F.2d at 225 ("We will ... require public notice in the form of immediate docketing of all closure motions."); In re Washington Post Co., 807 F.2d 383, 390 (4th Cir. 1986) (pretrial motions must be "docketed reasonably in advance of their disposition so as to give the public and press an opportunity to intervene and present their objections to the Court"); In re Herald Co. (Klepfer), 734 F.2d 93, 102 (2d Cir. 1984) ("Some form of public notice should be given — since it is important, perhaps especially so, to afford an opportunity to challenge courtroom closure accomplished in the absence of spectators. The fact that no member of the public was sufficiently interested to attend a particular court session does not mean that there is lacking a significant public interest in later seeking access. . . ."); United States v. Brooklier, 685 F.2d at 1168 ("reasonable steps should be taken to afford such persons an opportunity to submit their views to the court before exclusion is to be accomplished"); United States v. Criden, 675 F.2d at 558-59 ("We hold that . . . motions for closure of such hearings must be posted on the docket to give notice to the public. . . . We believe that due process requires some notice to the public before a trial court may close a pretrial criminal hearing.").

298. See Baltimore Sun Co. v. Colbert, 593 A.2d at 229. In *United States v. Raffoul*, 826 F.2d at 220, the Third Circuit held "that a closure motion made out of the public's hearing, e.g., during a conference in chambers, must be renewed in open court before disposition." See Ex parte Birmingham News Co., 624 So. 2d at 1134 ("interested members of the press and public must be permitted a hearing within a reasonable time in order to move for access to sealed transcripts of a closed hearing"); Note, Publicker Industries v. Cohen: *Public Access to Civil Proceedings and a Corporation's Right to Privacy*, 80 Nw. U.L. REV. 1319, 1332-33 (1986).

299. 478 U.S. at 13-14. See United States v. Antar, 38 F.3d 1348, 1359 (3d Cir. 1994) ("[L]imitations imposed are both necessary to and effective in protecting the interest."); United States v. Cojab, 996 F.2d 1404, 1408 (2d Cir. 1993); United States v. Haller, 837 F.2d 84, 87 (2d Cir. 1988); In re New York Times Co., 828 F.2d 110, 116 (2d Cir. 1987); In re Knight Publ'g Co., 743 F.2d 231, 234 (4th Cir. 1984) (court "must state its reasons on the record, supported by specific findings").

300. See 464 U.S. at 510 ("findings specific enough that a reviewing court can determine whether the closure order was properly entered"). But the findings need not be so specific as to disclose matter that is constitutionally subject to closure and the findings themselves may be placed under seal in appropriate, albeit rare, circumstances. See In re Washington Post Co., 807 F.2d 383, 391 (4th Cir. 1986). The requirement of specific findings, however, is not solely for the benefit of the reviewing court on appeal. It "exists, most fundamentally, to assure careful analysis by the

§ 2-3　　　　　　　　　　CONSTITUTIONAL FOUNDATIONS　　　　　　　　　§ 2-3

These three requirements — notice, hearing and record findings — are often cited as essential procedural prerequisites to closure.[301] In *In re Washington Post Co.*,[302] the Government argued that an exception from these requirements should be made for national security, especially where the lives of American agents and their foreign informants are involved. The Fourth Circuit declined to make such a broad exception: "A blind acceptance by the courts of the government's insistence on the need for secrecy, without notice to others, without argument, and without a statement of reasons, would impermissibly compromise the independence of the judiciary and open the door to possible abuse. Accordingly, we hold that the procedural requirements . . . are fully applicable in the context of closure motions based on threats to national security."[303] In criminal cases, the press may attempt to intervene[304] for the limited purpose of objecting to the closure order. If successful, the press will typically be able to have a closure order reviewed on appeal.[305] The closure order typically is considered a final

---

district court before any limitation is imposed, because reversal cannot fully vindicate First Amendment rights." United States v. Antar, 38 F.3d at 1362.

301. State law can also provide a basis for imposing such procedural requirements. See, e.g., In re Gannett River States Publ'g Corp., 27 MEDIA L. REP. (BNA) 1096 (Miss. 1998) (reaffirming that a court must have compelling reasons for closing the courtroom during the exercise of peremptory challenges and that the court must follow notice and hearing procedures before doing so); Allied Daily Newspapers of Washington v. Eikenberry, 848 P.2d 1258, 1260-62 (Wash. 1993) (holding that statute prohibiting disclosure of identity of child victims of sexual assault to the public or press during judicial proceedings or in court documents violated state constitution's right of open access to judicial proceedings because case-by-case determination is constitutionally required). In practice, however, such procedural requirements can be burdensome. See Comment, *First Amendment Right of Access to Pretrial Proceedings in Criminal Cases*, 32 EMORY L.J. 619, 685-86 (1993).

302. 807 F.2d 383, 392 (4th Cir. 1986).

303. *Id.*

304. In *In re Associated Press*, 162 F.3d 503 (7th Cir. 1998), the Seventh Circuit overruled the trial court's refusal to allow the press to intervene to oppose an order to conduct the videotaping of defense witness Governor James Edgar's testimony *in camera* in a case alleging a scheme to defraud the Illinois Department of Public Aid. See *id.* at 508. In order to assure immediate and contemporaneous access where appropriate, the court concluded, those who oppose the suppression of material should be allowed to intervene. See *id.* at 506. Although the district court did address the press's First Amendment-based right of access to the testimony, the Seventh Circuit declined to reach the issue of whether "a failure to permit intervention can be considered harmless if the position of the petitioner has been fully considered by the court," because the press's right of access "was not explored as fully as it should have been." *Id.* at 508-09. Other courts, however, have held that such a failure can be considered harmless error. See *id.* at 508-09 & n.7 (citing United States v. Preate, 91 F.3d 10, 12 n.1 (3d Cir. 1996); In re Grand Jury Proceedings (Freeman), 708 F.2d 1571, 1575 (11th Cir. 1983)).

305. See, e.g., In re Subpoena to Testify Before Grand Jury Directed to Custodian of Records, 864 F.2d 1559, 1561 (11th Cir. 1989) ("[I]ntervenors have standing to appeal the scope of order even though they are not parties to the action."); In re Tribune Co. (Sierra), 784 F.2d 1518, 1520 (11th Cir. 1986) (holding that the press has standing to intervene in actions to which it is otherwise not a party in order to petition for access to court proceedings and records); Vermont v. Schaefer, 599 A.2d 337, 341 (Vt. 1991), *cert. denied*, 502 U.S. 1077 (1992) (press may directly intervene and

order and is appealable by virtue of the collateral order doctrine.[306] If the press is treated as a nonparty, appellate courts differ as to whether the press's representative has standing to challenge a closure order by appeal.[307] Some courts have refused to hear such appeals and have required the press to seek review by petitioning for an extraordinary writ.[308] Other courts permit appeal by a non-

---

appeal); see also In re Motion of Atlanta Journal-Constitution, 502 S.E.2d 720 (Ga. 1998) (denying press member's "original action" seeking review of a lower court order sealing court records in a suit seeking to establish paternity, noting that a party seeking such review must make an interlocutory appeal for the court to exercise jurisdiction).

306. See Cohen v. Beneficial Indus. Loan Corp., 337 U.S. 541 (1949). The critical factors are that the order (1) is a final disposition by the district court; (2) is collateral to the rights asserted in the main action; (3) entails a risk of irreparable injury; and (4) involves a serious and unsettled question of law. See United States v. Cojab, 996 F.2d 1404, 1406 (2d Cir. 1993) (holding that a closure order meets all of the *Cohen* requirements); In re Subpoena to Testify, 864 F.2d at 1561; United States v. Haller, 837 F.2d 84 (2d Cir. 1988); United States v. Chagra, 701 F.2d 354, 358 (5th Cir. 1983). But see Pennsylvania v. Sartin, 708 A.2d 121, 123 (Pa. Super. 1998) (holding that an order that only partially unsealed a redacted transcript of *in camera* recusal hearing and accompanying materials was not appealable under the collateral order rule because the right of access is not "too important to be denied immediate review" and is not in danger of being "irreparably lost if review is postponed").

307. See generally Rendleman, *Free Press-Fair Trial: Restrictive Orders After* Nebraska Press, 67 KY. L.J. 867, 879-88 (1979); Annotation, *Standing of Media Representatives or Organizations to Seek Review of, or to Intervene to Oppose, Order Closing Criminal Proceedings to Public*, 74 A.L.R.4th 476.

308. In *United States v. McVeigh*, 119 F.3d 806, 809-11 (10th Cir. 1997), *cert. denied*, 118 S. Ct. 1110 (1998), the Tenth Circuit held that "mandamus is the proper vehicle for the press to utilize in challenging bar orders directed towards trial participants when the press itself was not a party to the bar order" and further "that mandamus is the proper vehicle for reviewing court orders sealing or redacting court documents in criminal proceedings." *Id.* at 810. The court purported to align itself with the First, Fourth, Eighth and Ninth Circuits in this regard, and noted that the Second, Third, Fifth, Sixth, Seventh and Eleventh Circuits allow appeal under the collateral order doctrine. See *id.* The court then treated the asserted appeal as a petition for a writ of mandamus, applying five considerations:

> (1) whether the petitioner seeking the writ has no other adequate means to secure the relief desired;
> (2) whether the petitioning party will be damaged or prejudiced in a way not correctable on appeal;
> (3) whether the district court's order constitutes an abuse of discretion;
> (4) whether the court's order represents an often repeated error and manifests persistent disregard of federal rules; and,
> (5) whether the district court's order raises new and important problems or legal issues of first impression.

Id. at 810. See also, e.g., Oregonian Publ'g Co. v. United States Dist. Ct., 920 F.2d 1462, 1468 (9th Cir. 1990); United States v. Brooklier, 685 F.2d at 1165-66; Sacramento Bee v. United States Dist. Ct., 656 F.2d 477 (9th Cir. 1981), *cert. denied*, 456 U.S. 983 (1982); CBS Inc. v. Young, 522 F.2d 234, 237 (6th Cir. 1975); Cable News v. Superior Ct., 1994 WL 315850, at *2 n.3 (D. Guam 1994) ("mandamus is the appropriate vehicle for challenging [a closure] order"). The Fourth Circuit treats an appeal as a petition for writ of mandamus if the requirements for securing a writ are

Deputy Attorney General or a supervising Associate Attorney General.[317] There are specific exceptions when the guidelines do not apply.[318] The records of closed proceedings are to be reviewed regularly and, if sealing is not warranted, an appropriate motion for unsealing is to be made.[319]

---

317. *Id.*
318. See *id.* § 50.9(e). These include national security cases, *in camera* inspection of documents, grand jury proceedings or proceedings ancillary thereto, bench conferences or proceedings in chambers, or proceedings for the protection of child victims or witnesses. See *id.*
319. See *id.* § 50.9(f).

Chapter 3

ACCESS TO JUDICIAL PROCEEDINGS: THE LOWER COURTS

§ 3-1. Criminal Proceedings.
    § 3-1(a). Pretrial Proceedings — In General.
        § 3-1(a)(1). Bail and Detention Hearings.
        § 3-1(a)(2). Preliminary Hearings.
        § 3-1(a)(3). Grand Jury Proceedings.
        § 3-1(a)(4). Suppression Hearings.
        § 3-1(a)(5). Competency Hearings.
        § 3-1(a)(6). Plea Hearings.
    § 3-1(b). Voir Dire Proceedings.
    § 3-1(c). Criminal Trial Proceedings.
    § 3-1(d). Post-Trial Proceedings.
    § 3-1(e). Military Courts.
§ 3-2. Civil Proceedings.
    § 3-2(a). Establishing the Access Right.
    § 3-2(b). Privacy Interests.
    § 3-2(c). Trade Secrets.
    § 3-2(d). Settlement Proceedings.
    § 3-2(e). Depositions.
§ 3-3. Juvenile Proceedings.
    § 3-3(a). Juvenile Delinquency.
    § 3-3(b). Abuse, Neglect, Dependency, and Custody Proceedings.

§ 3-1. Criminal Proceedings.

§ 3-1(a). Pretrial Proceedings — In General.

While the Supreme Court in *Press-Enterprise II* established a First Amendment-based right of public access to at least some pretrial criminal proceedings,[1]

---

1. Even before *Press-Enterprise II*, 478 U.S. 1 (1986), a number of lower courts had recognized a First Amendment-based right of access to pretrial criminal proceedings. See, e.g., United States v. Chagra, 701 F.2d 354 (5th Cir. 1983) (bail reduction hearings); United States v. Brooklier, 685 F.2d 1162, 1167 (9th Cir. 1982) (considering voir dire to be part of the trial, the court held that "public access to the process will heighten public respect for that system"); United States v. Criden, 675 F.2d 550, 555 (3d Cir. 1982) ("the relative importance of pretrial procedure to that of trial has grown immensely in the last two hundred years").

Many state courts have recognized a right of public access to pretrial criminal proceedings based on their own constitutions or statutes. See, e.g., New Jersey v. Williams, 459 A.2d 641, 650 (N.J. 1983) (finding that New Jersey constitution provides a right of public access to pretrial criminal proceedings); Ohio ex rel. The Repository v. Unger, 504 N.E.2d 37, 40 (Ohio 1986) ("[W]e see no reason under the Ohio Constitution to differentiate between the public's right to attend pretrial proceedings and its right to attend trials."); West Virginia ex rel. Herald Mail Co. v. Hamilton, 267 S.E.2d 544, 547 (W. Va. 1980) (relying on West Virginia's constitution).

Twenty-five states have a constitutional provision expressly requiring open courts. See, e.g., ALA. CONST. art. I, § 13; COLO. CONST. art. II, § 6; CONN. CONST. art. I, § 10; DEL. CONST. art. I, § 9; FLA. CONST. art. I, § 4; IDAHO CONST. art. I, § 18; IND. CONST. art. I, § 12; KY. CONST. § 14;

the Court suggested that the public and press may not enjoy a right of access to all pretrial proceedings, most notably, grand jury proceedings.[2] In the wake of *Press-Enterprise II*, lower courts have applied its analysis to a variety of pretrial proceedings in criminal cases. As a result, they have extended the First Amendment-based right of access to preliminary hearings, suppression hearings, bail and detention hearings, competency hearings, and plea hearings.[3] Today, almost all pretrial proceedings are presumptively open.

In *Ex parte Consolidated Publishing Co.*,[4] for example, the Alabama Supreme Court considered a trial court order closing all pretrial hearings until the jury was selected.[5] Citing frequently to *Press-Enterprise II*, the court focused on the historical tradition of access to pretrial proceedings. While noting that "the near uniform practice in the federal and state court systems has been to conduct pretrial criminal proceedings in open court,"[6] the court acknowledged that not all pretrial proceedings have a tradition of public access. Nevertheless, like the Supreme Court in *Press Enterprise II*, the Alabama Supreme Court stressed that pretrial proceedings "'are often critical, sometimes dispositive, to the outcome in a criminal prosecution.'"[7] Given the importance of such proceedings, the court determined that a lack of tradition should not be determinative of the constitutional issue. Rather, in cases in which an historical tradition of public access is lacking, courts should focus on a functional analysis, i.e., "on the importance of the hearings to the case."[8]

LA. CONST. art. I, § 6; MISS. CONST. art. III, § 24; MO. CONST. art. I, § 35; MONT. CONST. art. III, § 6; NEB. CONST. art. I, § 13; N.C. CONST. art. I, § 35; N.D. CONST. art. I, § 22; OHIO CONST. art. I, § 16; OKLA. CONST. art. II, § 6; OR. CONST. art. I, § 16; PA. CONST. art. I, § 11; S.D. CONST. art. VI, § 20; TENN. CONST. art. I, § 17; TEX. CONST. art. I, § 13; UTAH CONST. art. I, § 11; W. VA. CONST. art. III, § 17; WYO. CONST. art. I, § 8.

2. See 478 U.S. at 8-9 ("Although many governmental processes operate best under public scrutiny, it takes little imagination to recognize that there are some kinds of government operations that would be totally frustrated if conducted openly."); *id.* at 9 ("the proper functioning of our grand jury system depends upon the secrecy of grand jury proceedings") (citing Douglas Oil Co. v. Petrol Stops Northwest, 441 U.S. 211, 218 (1979)). See Chap. 3-1(a)(3) *infra* (grand jury proceedings).

3. See Chap. 3-1(a)(1), (2), (4)-(6) *infra*.

4. 601 So. 2d 423 (Ala.), *cert. denied*, 506 U.S. 1024 (1992).

5. The order was entered on the motion of a defendant who had secured a new trial after being convicted of kidnapping, rape, and murder and sentenced to death. The trial court found that there had been "massive publicity," press publication of often inadmissible evidence, a "substantial probability" of prejudice to defendant's fair trial rights without closure, no reasonable less restrictive alternatives available, and a "substantial probability" that closure would lead to a fair trial. *Id.* at 425. In its order, the trial court stressed the "unique and compelling facts and circumstances" requiring closure and its respect for public access rights generally. *Id.*

6. *Id.* at 429 (citing New Jersey v. Williams, 459 A.2d 641, 649 (N.J. 1983)).

7. 601 So. 2d at 430 (quoting Minneapolis Star & Tribune Co. v. Kammeyer, 341 N.W.2d 550, 555 (Minn. 1983)).

8. 601 So. 2d at 429.

The Alabama Supreme Court recognized the special danger of prejudice from pretrial publicity but emphasized the value of public access to the functioning of pretrial hearings.[9] Public and press scrutiny, the court concluded, further the efficiency, competence and fairness of the criminal justice system and promote public support for the system generally.[10] Given the extensive role now played by pretrial proceedings in criminal prosecution, rejection of a right of public access would necessarily mean that a substantial portion of the work of the criminal courts would occur "'behind closed doors.'"[11] This inquiry into experience and function, mandated by the First Amendment, as well as analogous precedent interpreting several state constitutions,[12] led the Alabama Supreme Court to hold both "that the qualified First Amendment right of access to criminal proceedings described in *Press-Enterprise II* applies to pretrial hearings,"[13] and that the trial court's closure order did not satisfy the demanding *Press-Enterprise II* standard.[14]

Similarly, in *Application of National Broadcasting Co.*,[15] the Sixth Circuit considered whether the First Amendment extended a right of access to documents and proceedings with respect to motions to disqualify a judge in the wake of alleged attorney conflicts of interest.[16] Applying *Press-Enterprise II*'s test of

---

9. In particular, the court recognized the greater potential for prejudice from publicity at the pretrial stage, resulting in part from the absence of safeguards such as sequestration, which are available at trial. *Id.* at 430 (citing Minneapolis Star & Tribune Co. v. Kammeyer, 341 N.W.2d 550, 556 (Minn. 1983); Ashland Publ'g Co. v. Asbury, 612 S.W.2d 749, 752 (Ky. App. 1980)).

10. 601 So. 2d at 430 (quoting Gannett Pac. Corp. v. Richardson, 580 P.2d 49, 54-55 (Haw. 1978); New Jersey v. Williams, 459 A.2d 641, 648-49 (N.J. 1983), and citing Richmond Newspapers, Inc. v. Virginia, 281 S.E.2d 915 (Va. 1981); Arkansas Television Co. v. Tedder, 662 S.W.2d 174 (Ark. 1983)).

As one court has noted, access to pretrial proceedings permits them to be "evaluated by individuals who are informed about the issues. . . . Pretrial access to information helps the public better understand judicial proceedings and public confidence in the judicial system as a whole can be enhanced." In re Consumers Power Co. Sec. Litig., 109 F.R.D. 45, 54 (E.D. Mich. 1985).

11. 601 So. 2d at 432 (quoting Westchester Rockland Newspapers, Inc. v. Leggett, 399 N.E.2d 518, 523 (N.Y. 1979)). See Buzbee v. Journal Newspapers, Inc., 465 A.2d 426, 433 (Md. 1983) (pretrial proceedings are "the only proceedings had in the great mass of criminal cases").

12. See, e.g., Iowa Freedom of Info. Council v. Wifvat, 328 N.W.2d 920, 923-24 (Iowa 1983); Ashland Publ'g Co. v. Asbury, 612 S.W.2d 749, 751-53 (Ky. App. 1980); Great Falls Tribune v. District Ct., 608 P.2d 116, 120 (Mont. 1980); New Jersey v. Williams, 459 A.2d 641, 650 (N.J. 1983); Kearns-Tribune Corp. v. Lewis, 685 P.2d 515, 521-22 (Utah 1984); Richmond Newspapers, Inc. v. Virginia, 281 S.E.2d 915, 922 (Va. 1981).

13. 601 So. 2d at 433.

14. The court held that the editorial comments and publicity surrounding the case were insufficient to establish a substantial probability of prejudice. Moreover, the broad order closing "all" pretrial proceedings and the court file was neither "narrowly tailored" nor necessary to protect the defendant's right to a fair trial. *Id.* at 434.

15. 828 F.2d 340 (6th Cir. 1987).

16. The motions seeking closure arose in the context of the prosecution of Jackie Presser, the president of the teamsters union, and two other union officials. Defendants' attorneys moved to

function and experience, the court of appeals vacated the closure order and recognized a First Amendment-based right of access in both contexts.[17]

First, the court determined that disqualification proceedings have typically been conducted in open court and traditionally have not been sealed. A survey of Sixth Circuit disqualification cases between 1924 and 1984 did not reveal any closures or sealing of records. Writing for the court, Chief Judge Lively concluded that "there is clearly a tradition of accessibility to disqualification proceedings."[18] As for the functional inquiry, the court recognized that public access serves a significant and positive role in disqualification proceedings: "The background, experience, and associations of the judge are important factors in any trial. When a judge's impartiality is questioned, it strengthens the judicial process for the public to be informed of how the issue is approached and decided."[19]

Turning to proceedings relating to motions seeking an inquiry into attorney conflicts of interest, Judge Lively again concluded that an open hearing "is the traditional method of conducting such inquiries."[20] With only one exception, prior decisions applying Federal Rule of Criminal Procedure 44(c), which governs joint representation, gave no indication that such proceedings are to be closed.[21] While the court acknowledged that such motion hearings are not "like a trial," it reasoned that they do call for factual determinations and the application of legal principles that can have a significant bearing on all subsequent pro-

---

disqualify District Judge Ann Aldrich because of past conflicts between the judge, Presser, and Presser's attorneys, and requested that proceedings in connection with the motion be held *in camera* and that briefing be submitted under seal. *Id.* at 341-42. At the same time, the Justice Department filed a motion seeking an inquiry concerning conflicts of interest of the attorneys for the three defendants, which they moved to seal as well because of the asserted threat of prejudicial publicity. *Id.*

Following an open hearing on NBC's efforts to obtain access to documents relating to both motions, the district court ordered that all documents remain under seal and that the transcript be made available only after the trial, when "the danger of prejudice will have passed." *Id.* Rejecting NBC's motion to reconsider, the district court concluded that the network had failed to satisfy the "two-pronged test" set forth in *Press-Enterprise II* and that there was a "substantial probability" of prejudice from publicity generated by the two motions as well as no reasonable alternatives to closure. *Id.*

17. See *id.* at 343-44. The court of appeals applied the collateral order doctrine to establish its jurisdiction to review the interlocutory orders. See *id.* at 343. It described the question before it as "the right of the public and representatives of the 'the media' to have access to documents filed in a district court at the preliminary stages of a criminal prosecution." *Id.*

18. *Id.* at 344.

19. *Id.* at 345 (citing United States v. Chagra, 701 F.2d 354, 363 (5th Cir. 1983)).

20. 828 F.2d at 345.

21. See *id.* The exception was *United States v. Foster*, 469 F.2d 1 (1st Cir. 1972), in which the First Circuit suggested that, in "unusual circumstances," closure of such proceedings may be required to avoid prejudicial disclosures. See 828 F.2d at 345.

ceedings in the case, especially the trial.[22] From a functional perspective, therefore, the court concluded that such proceedings "meet and satisfy the requirements of a qualified First Amendment right of access."[23] Like the Alabama Supreme Court in *Consolidated Publishing Co.*, the Sixth Circuit proceeded to hold that the district court's findings did not justify closure under the standards articulated in *Press-Enterprise II*.[24]

Decisions like *Consolidated Publishing Co.* and *National Broadcasting Co.*, rendered by state and federal courts respectively, illustrate the ease with which lower courts have applied the two-part test articulated by the Supreme Court in *Press-Enterprise II* to find a First Amendment-based right of access to a variety of pretrial proceedings in criminal cases. All of these decisions, however, recognize that even when the First Amendment does provide a right of access to the pretrial proceeding at issue, it establishes only presumptive openness. First, reasonable "time, place and manner" regulations may still be imposed.[25] Second, narrowly tailored closure orders can be justified by overriding interests; closure may be necessary "to preserve higher values."[26] Interests held to be "overriding," thereby justifying closure of pretrial proceedings in some cases, include the protection of parties or witnesses from violence,[27] safeguarding ongoing law enforcement investigations,[28] protecting the identity of undercover police

---

22. 828 F.2d at 345.
23. *Id.*
24. See *id.* at 345-46. The court of appeals characterized the district court's order as based on conclusions, rather than "specific findings" demonstrating a substantial probability of prejudice and the absence of reasonable alternatives. *Id.* at 346.
25. See, e.g., Herring v. Meachum, 11 F.3d 374, 379-80 (2d Cir. 1993), *cert. denied*, 511 U.S. 1059 (1994) (affirming trial judge's order to lock courtroom doors during reading of the jury charge to keep out a large group of people, which would have distracted the jury); United States v. Hastings, 695 F.2d 1278, 1282 (11th Cir.), *cert. denied*, 461 U.S. 931 (1983) (applying FED. R. CRIM. P. 53, which bars cameras in the courtroom as a legitimate restriction on First Amendment-based access rights, because the rule "merely impose[s] a restriction on the manner of the media's news gathering activities," it does not bar the media from any portion of the trial); Tsokalas v. Purtill, 756 F. Supp. 89, 94 (D. Conn. 1991) (upholding an order prohibiting the publication of an artist's sketch as a legitimate time, place, and manner restriction because the order did not prohibit access or publication of anything observed).
26. *Press-Enterprise II*, 478 U.S. at 14; *Press-Enterprise I*, 464 U.S. at 510.
27. See, e.g., United States v. Farmer, 32 F.3d 369, 372 (8th Cir. 1994) (allowing partial closure of trial when victim feared defendant and his family). But see Seattle Times Co. v. Ishikawa, 640 P.2d 716, 725 (Wash. 1982) (Dolliver, J., concurring) ("It is not the business of the courts through pretrial secrecy orders to provide 'protection' for witness or parties. . . . If the unavoidable circumstances are indeed such that a witness or a party to an action must be protected, then this must be accomplished by appropriate police action and not by the closure of the court.").
28. See, e.g., In re Tribune Co. (Sierra), 784 F.2d 1518, 1522-23 (11th Cir. 1986) (allowing denial of access to transcripts of bench conferences because they contained references to an ongoing investigation and closure of voir dire to preserve secrecy of the investigation); In re Herald Co. (Klepfer), 734 F.2d 93, 100 (2d Cir. 1984) (recognizing that ongoing undercover operations are a legitimate reason to close suppression hearing).

officers or informants,[29] preserving the secrecy of grand jury information,[30] maintaining the attorney-client privilege,[31] protecting the privacy interests of jurors[32] and the psychic well-being of juveniles,[33] and, of course, vindicating a criminal defendant's right to a fair trial.[34]

In *United States v. Cojab*,[35] for example, Marcus Cojab was prosecuted in a drug-related murder. The trial judge had held a closed pretrial hearing in his robing room without notice or hearing and had sealed the transcript of that proceeding without making any findings. The Second Circuit, hearing the case on expedited appeal, accepted that "it is now established that a qualified right of access applies not only to public trials, but also to pretrial hearings, such as the one before us in the instant case."[36] Nevertheless, applying *Press-Enterprise II*,

---

29. See, e.g., United States v. De Los Santos, 810 F.2d 1326, 1334 (5th Cir.), *cert. denied*, 484 U.S. 978 (1987) (upholding closure of a suppression hearing to protect the identity of an informant); People v. C.M., 614 N.Y.S.2d 491, 495 (Sup. Ct. 1994) (allowing closure of testimony of police informant for protection of his identity). But see People v. Cordero, 541 N.Y.S.2d 417 (App. Div.), *aff'd*, 551 N.E.2d 103 (N.Y. 1989) (holding that representation that the witness is undercover officer is not enough alone for closure; more specific findings are necessary).

30. See, e.g., United States v. Haller, 837 F.2d 84, 88 (2d Cir. 1988) ("[P]reservation of grand jury secrecy and the sensitivity of an ongoing criminal investigation were 'higher values' justifying sealing."); Ex parte Birmingham News Co., 624 So. 2d 1117, 1128 (Ala. Crim. App. 1993) (allowing for closure of pretrial materials to protect grand jury secrecy).

31. See, e.g., Ex parte Birmingham News Co., 624 So. 2d at 1130 ("It is clear that the attorney-client privilege may serve as a 'higher interest' sufficient to justify closure or sealing of records."); see also In re Continental Illinois Sec. Litig., 732 F.2d 1302, 1315 (7th Cir. 1984) ("[t]he public interest in preservation of the attorney-client privilege . . . is a significant factor to be weighed.").

32. See, e.g., In re Tribune Co. (Sierra), 784 F.2d 1518, 1522-23 (11th Cir. 1986) (allowing closure of voir dire to protect juror's privacy interest).

33. See, e.g., New Jersey Div. of Youth & Family Servs. v. J.B., 576 A.2d 261, 269 (N.J. 1990) ("court must balance public's right of access to judicial proceedings against the state's interest in protecting children from . . . possible detrimental effects"). But see Ex parte The Island Packet, 417 S.E.2d 575, 578 (S.C. 1992) ("lessening a defendant's 'anxiety,' even a juvenile's, does not promote a higher value than protection of the public's constitutional right of access"). See also Chap. 3-3 *infra*.

34. See, e.g., People v. Rollins, 24 MEDIA L. REP. (BNA) 2569 (Cal. Super. 1996) (closing hearings on motions in limine involving the foundation or admissibility of evidence); Southeastern Newspapers Corp. v. Georgia, 454 S.E.2d 452 (Ga. 1995) (affirming an order closing all pretrial evidentiary proceedings in a capital murder case based on "clear and convincing" proof of a "clear and present danger" to defendants' fair trial rights from extensive and prejudicial publicity).

35. 996 F.2d 1404 (2d Cir. 1993).

36. *Id*. at 1407 (citing United States v. Haller, 837 F.2d 84, 86-87 (2d Cir. 1988); In re Herald Co. (Klepfer), 734 F.2d 93, 99 (2d Cir. 1984)). The court noted that "under the common law there was no right to attend pretrial hearings." 966 F.2d at 1407. Nevertheless, it cited *Press-Enterprise I* and *II* as providing "compelling functional reasons for assuring openness of criminal proceedings, both trial and pretrial," including "the victim's and the community's interest in seeing that offenders are brought to account, and the public's interest in knowing that fair standards are followed in the conduct of such proceedings and that variance from established norms will come to light." *Id*.

the court concluded "that this is the rare case requiring closure for reasons overriding the constitutional rule of openness."[37] The court of appeals did not disclose those overriding reasons that apparently justified closure on the facts of the case, averting generally to the defendant's right to a fair trial, the government interest in ongoing investigations and protecting the lives or safety of its agents, and the need to maintain the secrecy of grand jury proceedings.[38] In addition, it embraced, without explanation, the district court's conclusion that there were no less burdensome alternatives available.[39]

The court in *Cojab* did find procedural error in the trial court's initial failure to afford notice on the public docket, to make findings in support of its order, and to conduct the hearing on the press's motion in open court.[40] Thus, the Second Circuit vacated the original closure order but concluded that it had been superseded by the trial court's subsequent ruling, issued following a hearing on the press's motion that was preceded by notice and accompanied by sealed findings.[41] The latter order denying press access to the proceedings was affirmed.

In most cases involving pretrial proceedings, however, it is unlikely that the demanding standards endorsed in *Press-Enterprise II* will be satisfied.[42] Even if an overriding interest is implicated, courts have recognized that it will not justify closure unless the order is also shown to be "necessary" and "narrowly tailored," such that there are no less restrictive means of protecting the "overriding" interest.

Thus, although protection of a defendant's right to a fair trial is an overriding and "compelling" interest,[43] to justify closure of a pretrial proceeding, it must be shown that there is a substantial probability of prejudice that closure might avoid, that there are no reasonable alternatives to closure, and that the contem-

---

37. 996 F.2d at 1408.

38. See *id*. The court characterized the interests sought to be protected as "compelling." *Id*. at 1409.

39. See *id*. The court also noted that the burden on the public's right of access was not permanent, since the closure order was of limited duration and the press's motion to unseal the transcript remained pending. *Id*.

40. See *id*. at 1408 ("The public must be afforded notice in the public docket, 'normally on the day the pertinent event occurs.'") (quoting In re Herald Co. (Klepfer), 734 F.2d at 102).

41. See 996 F.2d at 1408.

42. The Ninth Circuit has held that closure of suppression hearings must be "strictly and inescapably necessary in order to protect the fair-trial guarantee." United States v. Brooklier, 685 F.2d 1162, 1167 (9th Cir. 1982) (quoting Gannett Co. v. DePasquale, 443 U.S. at 440 (Blackmun, J., dissenting)). The Fifth Circuit requires that, to close a pretrial bail hearing, there must be a "likely" prejudice to the protected interest, alternatives to closure cannot "adequately" protect the interest, and closure must be shown to "probably be effective." United States v. Chagra, 701 F.2d 354, 365 (5th Cir. 1983).

43. *Press-Enterprise II*, 478 U.S. at 9; see *Press-Enterprise I*, 464 U.S. at 511-12.

plated closure order is narrowly tailored.[44] Even if the case involves extensive publicity indicating a potential for prejudice, courts have generally found that the alternative measures catalogued in *Sheppard v. Maxwell*[45] provide adequate safeguards. Extensive voir dire, a continuance, or a change of venue are typically cited as sufficient protective devices at the pretrial stage of criminal proceedings.[46] Further, concern for prejudicial publicity will seldom justify the closure of all pretrial proceedings.[47] Partial closure, in the form of *in camera* sessions for the disclosure of particularly sensitive information, or even closure of a discrete portion of a proceeding, typically provide less burdensome alternatives as well.[48]

In *In re Charlotte Observer*,[49] for example, a magistrate issued an order sealing documents and closing a hearing on a change of venue motion. The magistrate had justified closure because of a perceived danger of prejudicial publicity.[50] The Fourth Circuit applied the *Press-Enterprise II* standards and

---

44. 478 U.S. at 14. See United States v. Chagra, 701 F.2d at 365 (findings that absent closure of a pretrial bail hearing, a likelihood of prejudice would exist to defendant's fair trial rights, that no alternatives to closure could adequately protect that interest, and that closure would "probably be effective"); Connecticut v. Kelly, 695 A.2d 1, 4 (Conn. App. 1997) (vacating trial court's *sua sponte* order closing a hearing on defendant's motion to dismiss, since trial court must do more than enter "conclusory assertion[s] that publicity might deprive the defendant of a fair trial"); Rockdale Citizen Publ'g Co. v. Georgia, 468 S.E.2d 764 (Ga. 1996) (reversing order closing pretrial evidentiary hearings absent evidence of a "clear and present danger" that defendant would not receive fair trial in different venue); Rockdale Citizen Publ'g Co. v. Georgia, 463 S.E.2d 864, 868 (Ga. 1995) (vacating trial court order closing pretrial proceedings because trial court's conclusory statements that it had considered alternatives were insufficient to justify closure); Baltimore Sun Co. v. Colbert, 593 A.2d 224 (Md. 1991) (holding that trial court failed to make the required findings to justify a broad order closing a pretrial hearing on defendant's motion to enforce the terms of a plea bargain agreement in a capital murder case); New York v. Arroyo, 675 N.Y.S.2d 272, 276 (County Ct. 1998) (denying defendants' motion to close court proceedings on various pretrial motions since "[t]he public interest in this case has not been overridden by the defendants' speculative assertions that publicity of routine pre-trial hearings may prejudice the jury").

45. 384 U.S. 333, 357-63 (1966).

46. See, e.g., Baltimore Sun Co. v. Colbert, 593 A.2d at 230; New Jersey v. Williams, 459 A.2d 641, 654 (N.J. 1983).

47. See, e.g., Baltimore Sun Co. v. Colbert, 593 A.2d at 230-31. Thus, a Michigan statute interpreted to mandate closure, upon the request of counsel, a victim, or the defendant in various sexual assault prosecutions, has been held unconstitutional on its face. See Booth Newspapers v. Twelfth Dist. Ct. Judge, 432 N.W.2d 400 (Mich. App. 1988).

48. See Minot Daily News v. Holum, 380 N.W.2d 347, 351 (N.D. 1986) ("The paramount concern is that closure be tailored to the circumstances of the perceived risk to a fair trial."); United States v. Chagra, 701 F.2d at 365 (allowing closure of one proceeding).

49. 882 F.2d 850 (4th Cir. 1989).

50. See *id.* at 853. The underlying criminal action involved multiple charges of mail and wire fraud against defendants arising from their affiliation with the PTL religious organization. When the defendants moved for a change of venue because of prejudicial publicity, the magistrate on his own motion closed the hearing and sealed the record. *Id.* After a hearing at the request of media

reversed. It accepted the magistrate's premise that there had been "pervasive, sensational, [and] inflammatory" publicity,[51] but nevertheless questioned whether, given the information already in the public domain, additional news coverage would result in a substantial probability of prejudice.[52] Moreover, the court of appeals rejected the trial court's conclusion that closure could prevent such prejudice — "the 'republication' genie was out of the bottle" such that "any press barrage and frenzy occasioned by an open hearing would be as nothing to the firestorms of purely speculative 'republication' that would occur if press access to the hearing is denied."[53]

In addition, the Fourth Circuit stressed the availability of voir dire to guard against the alleged dangers of pretrial publicity. Citing other highly publicized cases in which defendants had been acquitted[54] or there had been no showing of meaningful prejudice, the court observed that: "[i]ncreasingly the courts are expressing confidence that *voir dire* can serve in almost all cases as a reliable protection against juror bias however induced."[55] Finally, the court of appeals criticized the magistrate's conclusion that the closure order was narrowly tailored because the transcript would be available once the jury was selected, involving only a "minimal delay" in providing the public with knowledge of the proceeding.[56] The trial judge's conclusion, the court held, unduly minimized, "if it does not entirely overlook, the value of 'openness' itself, a value which is threatened whenever immediate access to ongoing proceedings is denied, whatever provision is made for later public disclosure."[57]

Protecting a victim of sexual abuse, especially a minor, from emotional trauma has also been held to constitute a compelling, overriding interest that may

---

intervenors, the magistrate reaffirmed his order, concluding "that republication of the prejudicial publicity would eviscerate the effectiveness of any order the court made on the motion." *Id.*

51. *Id.* at 854.

52. See *id.*; see also Connecticut v. Kelly, 695 A.2d 1, 4 (Conn. App. 1997) (vacating trial court's *sua sponte* order closing hearing on defendant's motion to dismiss and holding that closure "is especially questionable in light of the extensive prior publicity concerning the defendant and the charges against him"); Whitehurst v. Kavanaugh, 636 N.Y.S.2d 591, 593 (Sup. Ct. 1995), *aff'd*, 640 N.Y.S.2d 345 (App. Div. 1996) (given extensive publicity, petitioner had not made a compelling showing of substantial probability of prejudice in proceeding to enforce a cooperation agreement).

53. 882 F.2d at 854.

54. See Columbia Broadcasting Sys., Inc., v. United States Dist. Ct., 729 F.2d 1174 (9th Cir. 1983) (John DeLorean); In re National Broadcasting Co., 635 F.2d 945 (2d Cir. 1980) (Myers).

55. 882 F.2d at 856. But cf. Ex parte Lexington County, 442 S.E.2d 589 (S.C. 1994) (ordering closure of ex parte hearing on appointed defense counsel's request for investigative and expert services for indigent defendant facing the death penalty based on "substantial probability" of prejudice and no reasonable alternatives).

56. See 882 F.2d at 856.

57. *Id.*

justify closure of a pretrial proceeding in a criminal case.[58] Once again, however, lower courts have declined to permit closure of all such proceedings involving minors, even at the pretrial stage.[59] Instead, the courts have applied the standards articulated in *Press-Enterprise II* and have, even when those standards are satisfied, ordered limited closure of only those portions of pretrial hearings in which the overriding interest is implicated.[60]

In some cases involving pretrial proceedings, courts have attempted to rely on the subsequent availability of a transcript of the proceeding as justification for its closure. Some courts have held that such orders are "narrowly tailored" as required by *Press-Enterprise II*.[61] Other courts, however, have rejected this analysis,[62] asserting that a transcript is not an effective substitute for experiencing and reporting on the actual pretrial proceeding.[63]

The availability of a transcript has also been deemed relevant in fashioning remedies in the wake of a closure order. If the pretrial proceeding has already occurred by the time the press received notice, for example, the only meaningful remedy is an order that a transcript be made publicly available and that the record be unsealed.[64]

---

58. See, e.g., In re Closure of Preliminary Examination, 505 N.W.2d 24, 26 (Mich. App. 1993) (holding that protection of the psychological well-being of a victim of sexual assault could justify partial closure of a preliminary examination as long as the order is narrowly tailored); New Hampshire v. Guajardo, 605 A.2d 217, 219-20 (N.H. 1992) (holding that state has compelling interest in protecting minor victims of sexual assault).

59. See, e.g., People v. Holveck, 565 N.E.2d 919, 927 (Ill. 1990) (holding that an interest in making testifying as palatable as possible for a minor victim of sexual assault could justify closing the courtroom to public without direct interest, but not to the media); New Hampshire v. Weber, 624 A.2d 967, 969 (N.H. 1993) (holding that the interest in protecting the psychological well-being of a minor victim of sexual assault "does not, however, justify a rule requiring closure of the courtroom in all such cases").

60. See, e.g., In re Closure of Preliminary Examination, 505 N.W.2d 24, 26 (Mich. App. 1993) (holding that closure of testimony in a preliminary examination could have been constitutional if order was narrowly tailored).

61. See In re Charlotte Observer, 882 F.2d at 850 (trial judge ordered transcripts of proceeding to be made available in order to "narrowly tailor" closure order).

62. See Florida v. Kozma, 22 MEDIA L. REP. (BNA) 1539, 1542 (Fla. Cir. 1994) ("News delayed is news denied.").

63. See United States v. Antar, 38 F.3d 1348, 1360 n.13 (3d Cir. 1994) ("We emphasize, however, that documentary access is not a substitute for concurrent access .... Thus, where a right of access exists, a court may not deny access to a live proceeding solely on the grounds that a transcript may later be made available. Such a transcript would not fully implement the right of access because some information, concerning demeanor, non-verbal responses, and the like, is necessarily lost in the translation of a live proceeding to a cold transcript.").

64. In *Ex parte Birmingham News Co.*, 624 So. 2d 1117 (Ala. Crim. App. 1993), which arose from the prosecution of then-Alabama governor Guy Hunt, the trial judge conducted closed pretrial proceedings in his chambers. The Alabama Court of Criminal Appeals held that the trial court had violated the First Amendment and ordered access to the transcript and court files, unless the trial court, after notice and hearing, made specific findings justifying closure. See *id.* at 1134-35. The

§ 3-1(a)(1). Bail and Detention Hearings.

Like many pretrial proceedings, there is no tradition of public access to bail or detention hearings.[65] While bail was often set in open court at the defendant's initial appearance before a magistrate at common law, bail proceedings have generally been informal and conducted in a variety of open and closed settings.[66] Nevertheless, courts have generally recognized a qualified First Amendment-based right of access to bail or detention proceedings.[67] In so doing, they have stressed functional considerations and the increasing public importance of bail proceedings, illustrated by the Federal Bail Reform Acts of 1966 and 1984.[68]

While bail reform legislation had long stressed the importance of the prompt release of persons from custody, political debate has increasingly focused on instances of additional crimes committed by persons who are released from custody pending trial on previous charges.[69] Public concern with crimes committed by such persons has rendered the bail or detention determination a matter of significant public interest. As the Fifth Circuit held in *United States v.*

---

trial court held hearings, released most of the transcript and sealed records, but denied access to approximately 120 pages of the 1,084-page transcript. See *id.*

Following the filing of a petition for writ of mandamus by the press, the appellate court engaged in a detailed review of those portions of the transcript that remained sealed and ordered a significant portion released. See *id.* Nevertheless, it upheld that portion of the closure order denying access in order to protect the names of grand jury witnesses, as well as the secrecy of grand jury proceedings, as "narrowly tailored" to preserve "higher interests." *Id.* at 1227-28, 1130.

65. See United States v. Chagra, 701 F.2d 354, 362-63 (5th Cir. 1983) ("[b]ond reduction hearings do not have a similar history" of public access as trials themselves, but "[a]ccess to bail reduction hearings ... should not be foreclosed because these proceedings lack the history of openness relied on by the *Richmond Newspapers* court"); Seattle Times Co. v. United States Dist. Ct., 845 F.2d 1513, 1516 (9th Cir. 1988) ("Pretrial detention proceedings do not share with criminal trials an unbroken history of public access.").

66. See United States v. Chagra, 701 F.2d at 363.

67. See Seattle Times Co. v. United States Dist. Ct., 845 F.2d 1513, 1517 (9th Cir. 1988); In re Globe Newspaper Co., 729 F.2d 47, 52 (1st Cir. 1984); United States v. Chagra, 701 F.2d at 364; United States v. Edwards, 430 A.2d 1321, 1344 (D.C. 1981), *cert. denied*, 455 U.S. 1022 (1982). In *Ex parte First Charleston Corp.*, 495 S.E.2d 423, 424 (S.C. 1998), noting that a "presumption of openness applied to preliminary pre-trial hearings," the court vacated a trial judge's *sua sponte* closure of a bond hearing because he had failed to make specific findings of fact as required by *Press-Enterprise II*. The court also noted that the record did not support a finding of substantial probability of prejudice because "extensive details" had already been disclosed to the press and the trial judge could have used voir dire to identify any prejudice from press coverage. *Id.*

68. Bail Reform Act of 1966, as amended, 18 U.S.C. §§ 3141-3156. The 1984 Act made "dangerousness" an independent ground for detention and rejected much of the previous informality that had characterized federal bail proceedings. See generally W.R. LaFave & J.H. Israel, Criminal Procedure ch. 12 (2d ed. 1992).

69. See United States v. Salerno, 481 U.S. 739, 747 (1987) (indicating that the 1984 Bail Reform Act was enacted as a response to public concern over crimes committed by released persons); Seattle Times Co. v. United States Dist. Ct., 845 F.2d at 1516 ("Public interest in the conditions of pretrial release is understandably great because the community is directly affected.").

Chagra,[70] "[p]retrial release proceedings require decisions that attract significant public interest, and invite legitimate and healthy public scrutiny."[71] The First Circuit in *In re Globe Newspaper Co.*[72] similarly noted that the decision to release an accused who subsequently flees may effectively end a criminal proceeding and the decision to detain deprives a citizen who has not been convicted of his liberty — "[i]n either case, the bail decision is one of major importance to the administration of justice, and openness will help to assure the public that the decision is properly reached."[73]

While the courts have extended the right of public access to bail and detention proceedings, closure has been approved in a surprising number of cases, especially when potentially inadmissible electronic surveillance evidence is involved. In such cases, closure is supported not only by the defendant's Sixth Amendment rights but also by the Fourth Amendment prohibition against illegal searches and the policy concerns underlying federal wiretap legislation.[74]

In *In re Globe Newspaper Co.*,[75] for example, a magistrate closed portions of the bail proceedings and sealed transcripts and some documents relating to

---

70. 701 F.2d 354 (5th Cir. 1983).

71. *Id.* at 363. In *Chagra*, the court noted that the First Amendment-based right of access is founded on the societal interest in public awareness, understanding and confidence in the judicial system, on its value as a check on judicial conduct, and on enhancing the performance of the parties and the judiciary: "These interests are as affected by proceedings to determine conditions of pretrial release as they are by other judicial proceedings." *Id.* See In re Globe Newspaper Co., 729 F.2d 47, 52 (1st Cir. 1984) ("The same policy concerns that the Supreme Court identified when it found that the public has a First Amendment right of access to criminal trials — the need for a public educated in the workings of the criminal justice system and for a justice system subjected to the scrutiny of the public — operate in pretrial proceedings."); Seattle Times Co. v. United States Dist. Ct., 845 F.2d at 1516 ("We agree with the First and Third [sic] Circuits that pretrial release proceedings implicate the related policy concerns of a public educated in the workings of the justice system and a system [being] subjected to healthy public scrutiny."); Fenner & Koley, *Access to Judicial Proceedings: To* Richmond Newspapers *and Beyond*, 16 HARV. C.R.-C.L. L. REV. 415, 436 n.109 (1981).

72. 729 F.2d 47 (1st Cir. 1984).

73. *Id.* at 52. See, e.g., Delaware v. Shipley, 497 A.2d 1052, 1055 n.6 (Del. Super. 1985); United States v. Edwards, 430 A.2d 1321, 1344 (D.C. 1981), *cert. denied*, 455 U.S. 1022 (1982) ("The principles that support a right of access to trials apply with equal force to pretrial proceedings."); Indiana ex rel. Post-Tribune Publ'g Co. v. Porter Super. Ct., 412 N.E.2d 748, 751 (Ind. 1980) (holding that the Indiana Constitution guarantees a right of access to pretrial bail proceedings); New Jersey v. Williams, 459 A.2d 641, 647-48 (N.J. 1983) (holding that open pretrial hearings, including bail hearings, serve societal interests).

74. See Omnibus Crime Control and Safe Streets Act of 1968, Title III, 18 U.S.C. §§ 2510-2520. See generally LAFAVE & ISRAEL, *supra* note 68, at ch. 4; United States v. Gotti, 753 F. Supp. 443, 447 (E.D.N.Y. 1990) (while simply citing Title III concerns is not enough to overcome First Amendment-based right of access, "a careful reading of the government's evidentiary proffer of Title III excerpts" led to the conclusion that the need for closure outweighed the right of access).

75. 729 F.2d 47 (1st Cir. 1984). A magistrate, fearing prejudicial pretrial publicity, concluded that "considerations of defendants' Sixth Amendment right to a fair trial, when considered in

evidence intercepted by electronic surveillance. The district court affirmed, noting that the defendants had not yet had the opportunity to test the legality of the electronic surveillance. While the First Circuit recognized a First Amendment-based right of access to the bail hearing,[76] it held that "the privacy and fair trial interests of the defendants outweigh the public's interest in having access to the bail proceedings."[77]

Judge Coffin, writing for the court, emphasized that "the protection of privacy was an overriding concern" of Congress in enacting Title III.[78] The wiretap law strictly regulates the disclosure of intercepted communications in an effort to protect the privacy of individuals and to deter unlawful searches. "It is clear then, that if an electronic surveillance has been shown to be unlawful, Title III prevents its fruits from being disclosed to the public, and both Title III and the Fourth Amendment forbid the use of its fruits as evidence in any court proceeding."[79] In that regard, Judge Coffin concluded that the fact that officers may testify at a bail hearing regarding intercepted materials has nothing to do with whether closure of the hearing is appropriate; "[i]n a highly publicized case such as this one, the premature publication of damaging communications that are later determined to have been unlawfully obtained and so not admissible in evidence might make fair trial impossible, at least in the venue defendant would ordinarily prefer."[80]

Finally, the court concluded that closure of the bail hearing at issue was appropriate even under the strictest standard for closure articulated by the Supreme Court.[81] There was, according to Judge Coffin, a "substantial probability of irreparable damage" from disclosure of Title III material *before* defendants had an opportunity to seek suppression. Moreover, "since disclosure itself is the injury to be avoided," other means of protecting the defendant's privacy were unavailable and there was a "substantial probability" that closure would be

---

combination with defendants' [privacy] rights under the provisions of Title III, unequivocally outweigh the public's right of access to the overheard conversations at this time." *Id.* at 49-50 (emphasis in original).

76. See *id.* at 51-52. The Court found the right of access despite the lack of a history of openness, citing "societal interests." *Id.*

77. *Id.* at 49.

78. *Id.* at 53 (citing Gelbard v. United States, 408 U.S. 41, 48 (1972)).

79. 729 F.2d at 54. Indeed, disclosure of unauthorized wiretaps may be subject to criminal and civil penalties. See 18 U.S.C. §§ 2511(1), 2520. Fruits of an unauthorized wiretap may not be received into evidence in any judicial proceeding. See *id.* § 2515. Moreover, as the First Circuit has noted, "the invasion of privacy is not over when the interception occurs, but is compounded by disclosure." Providence Journal Co. v. FBI, 602 F.2d 1010, 1013 (1st Cir. 1979).

80. 729 F.2d at 55.

81. See *id.* at 57.

effective.[82] The court also concluded that the First Amendment interest weighed less heavily in this context because of the lack of a tradition of access to bail proceedings and the fact that the public would have access to the sealed materials at a later time.[83]

While *Globe Newspaper Co.* was decided prior to the *Press-Enterprise* cases, later decisions have shown a similar deference to the concerns embodied in Title III. The potential for disclosure of illegally seized communications continues to weigh heavily in assessing the need for closure of bail proceedings.[84] Nevertheless, courts have decidedly not adopted a per se rule; closure may still be unconstitutional even where Title III material is at issue.[85] Further, absent Title III interests, the fair trial rights of a defendant have fared less well when measured against the First Amendment rights of the press and public.[86]

§ 3-1(a)(2). Preliminary Hearings.

In most jurisdictions, a preliminary hearing, preliminary examination or probable cause hearing provides, in the same manner as grand jury review, "a screening of the decision to charge by a neutral body. In the preliminary hearing, that neutral body is the magistrate who must determine whether, on the evidence presented, there is probable cause to believe that the defendant committed the crime charged."[87] Since the proceeding is devoted to determining if the prosecu-

---

82. *Id.* at 59; see *id.* ("We can scarcely imagine a stronger case for closure than the one now before us, in which the defendants are accused of participation in organized crime, the pretrial publicity is intense, and the material to which the press seeks access is extremely prejudicial.").

83. See *id.*

84. See, e.g., United States v. Martin, 684 F. Supp. 341, 343 (D. Mass. 1988) (applying *Press-Enterprise II* standards, the court denied access to portions of detention hearings where Title III materials were discussed); United States v. Gotti, 753 F. Supp. 443, 446 (E.D.N.Y. 1990) ("Applying the 'substantial probability' standard [of *Press-Enterprise II*] to this case [involving Title III materials in a RICO prosecution] drives me to conclude that the bail proceedings should be closed to the press and the public.").

85. See In re New York Times Co., 828 F.2d 110, 115-16 (2d Cir. 1987), *cert. denied*, 485 U.S. 977 (1988) ("[W]here a qualified First Amendment right of access exists, it is not enough simply to cite Title III. Obviously, a statute cannot override a constitutional right."); United States v. White, 855 F. Supp. 13 (D. Mass. 1994) (media provided access to transcript of wiretap evidence introduced at a suppression hearing after defendant pled guilty).

86. See Seattle Times Co. v. United States Dist. Ct., 845 F.2d 1513 (9th Cir. 1988) (court ordered release of four documents, filed under seal in a pretrial detention hearing, finding that there was no substantial probability of irreparable damage to defendant's fair trial rights); Williams v. Stafford, 589 P.2d 322, 325 (Wyo. 1979) (closure required finding of "clear and present danger to the fairness of trial" and the absence of reasonable alternatives).

87. LaFave & Israel, *supra* note 68, at 24. In most states, the defendant may waive the preliminary hearing and prosecutors may bypass it entirely in many jurisdictions. When conducted, the preliminary hearing often becomes a means of discovery for the defense. The prosecution presents its evidence establishing probable cause; the defense, in most cases, limits itself to cross-examination of the prosecution witnesses. See generally *id.* at ch. 14.

tion has demonstrated probable cause, the evidence is generally one-sided. Defendants, therefore, often fear that press coverage of the proceeding will be unbalanced as well, including material that will not be admissible at trial. As a result, defendants have occasionally perceived the need to seek closure of the hearing to prevent prejudicial publicity.

Nevertheless, in *Press Enterprise II*[88] and *El Vocero de Puerto Rico*,[89] the Supreme Court recognized a qualified First Amendment-based right of access to preliminary hearings. While the Court in *Press-Enterprise II* employed language that might have limited the right to the trial-like preliminary hearings held in California,[90] *El Vocero* and subsequent lower court decisions have effectively rejected any such limitation. They emphasize that preliminary examination proceedings are adjudicative and are often critical in the determination of guilt or innocence. A finding of no probable cause usually, but not always, ends the criminal proceeding. In most cases, a finding of probable cause leads to a guilty plea.[91] As in *Press-Enterprise II*, preliminary hearings across the country generally "are sufficiently like a [criminal] trial" so that "public access ... is essential to the proper functioning of the ... criminal justice process."[92] Accordingly, a federal trial judge in *Rivera Puig v. Garcia Rosario*[93] applied the Supreme Court's reasoning in *Press-Enterprise II* to a preliminary hearing held in Puerto Rico:

> First of all, the preliminary hearing held in Puerto Rico has many of the same characteristics as those conducted in California. The hearings are held before a detached neutral magistrate; both prosecutor and defense counsel

---

88. See Chap. 2-2(f) *supra*.

89. See Chap. 2-2(g) *supra*.

90. See Chap. 2-2(f)-(g) *supra*. In *Press-Enterprise II*, 478 U.S. at 12, the Court noted that, while the prosecutor could bypass the preliminary hearing and go directly to the grand jury, the accused had "an absolute right" to a preliminary hearing before a neutral magistrate. Some states do not recognize such a right. At the California hearing, "[t]he accused has the right to appear personally ... to be represented by counsel, to cross-examine hostile witnesses, to present exculpatory evidence, and to exclude illegally obtained evidence." *Id.* If probable cause is found, the accused is bound over for trial. In some states, the accused may not suppress evidence at the preliminary hearing stage. See, e.g., Des Moines Register & Tribune Co. v. Iowa Dist. Ct., 426 N.W.2d 142, 147 (Iowa 1988); Capital Newspapers Div. of Hearst Corp. v. Lee, 530 N.Y.S.2d 872 (App. Div. 1988).

91. See *Press Enterprise II*, 478 U.S. at 12.

92. *Id.* at 12. See, e.g., Cowles Publ'g Co. v. Magistrate Ct., 800 P.2d 640, 645 (Idaho 1990) ("The process in conducting preliminary hearings in Idaho is likewise sufficiently like a trial to generally justify public access."); Kearns-Tribune Corp. v. Lewis, 685 P.2d 515, 521 (Utah 1984) ("[T]he preliminary hearing is more like a trial ... than the grand jury proceeding.... Thus, the fact that the grand jury proceeding is traditionally closed provides no support for the argument that a preliminary hearing should also be closed. An accused who has the procedural safeguards afforded in his preliminary hearing has less need of closure to safeguard his rights.").

93. 785 F. Supp. 278 (D.P.R.), *aff'd*, 983 F.2d 311 (1st Cir. 1992).

are present; evidence may be presented by both sides, including exculpatory evidence by the accused; witnesses are heard and can be cross-examined; and based on the evidence, the magistrate will either hold the accused over for trial or exonerate and set him or her free. It is clear that the magistrate is performing an adjudicative function in the preliminary hearing and, like California, this hearing may be the only formal judicial proceeding, both in the cases where the accused pleads guilty and in those cases where no probable cause is found.[94]

Much the same could be said of preliminary hearings in any jurisdiction.[95] No jurisdiction, even those following the Field Code that permitted a defendant to close the proceeding, has rejected a right of public access to preliminary hearings after *Press-Enterprise II*, either as a matter of state or federal constitutional law.[96]

The right of public access to preliminary hearings is, however, qualified. As the Supreme Court explained in *Press-Enterprise II*, an order closing preliminary hearings remains constitutional if the court makes "specific, on the record findings," which demonstrate that "closure is essential to preserve higher values and is narrowly tailored to serve that interest."[97] If closure of a preliminary hearing is premised on the need to protect the right of the defendant to a fair trial, the court must make specific record findings that there is a "substantial

---

94. *Id.* at 289. On appeal, the First Circuit listed sixteen similarities shared by the preliminary hearing in Puerto Rico and California, concluding that there "is no substantial difference between the Puerto Rico and the California preliminary hearings with respect to basic scope or purpose, importance of the proceeding within the judicial setting, or legal context within the criminal process. Distinguishing between these two proceedings is an attempt to distinguish the 'indistinguishable.'" 983 F.2d 311, 324 (1st Cir. 1992).

95. "[T]he vast majority of states have concluded that the same tradition of accessibility that applies to criminal trials applies to preliminary hearings." W. FREEDMAN, PRESS AND MEDIA ACCESS TO THE CRIMINAL COURTROOM 3 (1988). See, e.g., Cowles Publ'g Co. v. Magistrate Ct., 800 P.2d 640, 646 (Idaho 1990) ("Since preliminary hearings are presumptively open and considering that openness of preliminary hearings plays a significant positive role in our society, we hold that in Idaho a qualified first amendment right of public access attaches to preliminary hearings."); Des Moines Register & Tribune Co. v. District Ct., 426 N.W.2d 142, 147 (Iowa 1988) ("We hold that both elements of the *Press-Enterprise II* test are satisfied and that a qualified right of public access attaches to preliminary hearings as they are conducted in Iowa.").

96. See, e.g., Gannett Pac. Corp. v. Richardson, 580 P.2d 49, 55-57 (Haw. 1978) (recognizing a qualified right of access to preliminary hearings because of "the policy of open and public administration of justice"); Minot Daily News v. Holum, 380 N.W.2d 347, 350 (N.D. 1986) (public access to preliminary examination and right to notice and to be heard on closure upheld "as a matter of strong judicial policy"); Kearns-Tribune Corp. v. Lewis, 685 P.2d 515, 522 (Utah 1984) (holding that Utah Constitution mandates a qualified right of access to preliminary hearings). But cf. In re Detention of D.A.H., 924 P.2d 49 (Wash. App. 1996) (holding that probable cause hearing under sexually violent predator act is presumptively closed because of privacy considerations and different rules of evidence).

97. 478 U.S. at 13-14.

probability" of prejudice from publicity concerning the type of information that will be presented at the preliminary examination, prejudice that closure would serve to prevent.[98] In ordering closure, some courts have emphasized the one-sided character of the evidence likely to be developed at the probable cause proceeding or that some information presented at the preliminary hearing will be inadmissible at trial.[99] The trial court must also consider "reasonable alternatives to closure" and make specific findings that they would not adequately protect the defendant's rights.[100] Finally, the closure order must be narrowly limited to furthering the defendant's interest in receiving a fair trial.[101] Given these required record findings, it is not surprising that the threat of prejudicial publicity generally fails to overcome the presumptive right of access to preliminary hearings.[102]

---

98. See, e.g., Gannett Co. v. Falvey, 582 N.Y.S.2d 580, 580 (App. Div. 1992) (affirming closure order in highly publicized murder and conspiracy case, based on findings that "there was a substantial probability that, if the information . . . [were] reported to the public, it would be virtually impossible to select a jury that would not be affected by the publicity generated"); Capital Newspapers Div. of Hearst Corp. v. Lee, 530 N.Y.S.2d 872, 875 (App. Div. 1988) (to meet the substantial probability standard, proponent of closure must do more than present vague evidence of prejudice which amounts to no more than a "hypothetical risk of prejudice").

99. See, e.g., Gannett Co. v. Falvey, 582 N.Y.S.2d 580 (App. Div. 1992); Minot Daily News v. Holum, 380 N.W.2d 347 (N.D. 1986) (closure order based on prejudicial publicity arising from prosecution use of inadmissible evidence vacated where trial judge failed to make specific findings on inadequacy of alternatives to closure). But see North Dakota v. Ash, 22 MEDIA L. REP. (BNA) 1607 (N.D. County Ct. 1993) (rejecting closure where there would not be any inadmissible evidence used at the preliminary hearing).

100. See, e.g., Gannett Co. v. Falvey, 582 N.Y.S.2d 580 (App. Div. 1992); Capital Newspapers Div. of Hearst Corp. v. Lee, 530 N.Y.S.2d 872, 875 (App. Div. 1988).

101. See, e.g., Booth Newspapers, Inc. v. Twelfth Dist. Ct. Judge, 432 N.W.2d 400, 404 (Mich. App. 1988) (noting that sensitive part of hearing could have been held in chambers).

102. See People v. Martin, 22 MEDIA L. REP. (BNA) 2312 (Cal. Mun. 1994) ("the Supreme Court . . . has set forth a fairly consistent rule which . . . strongly favors the certainty of the public's right of access over the defendant's fair trial rights and it has formulated a burden of proof which is extremely high on the defense"); Davis v. Municipal Ct., 22 MEDIA L. REP. (BNA) 2466 (Cal. Super. 1994); Booth Newspapers, Inc. v. Twelfth Dist. Ct. Judge, 432 N.W.2d 400 (Mich. App. 1988) (reversing closure order (1) that, because transcript would be made public when accused was arraigned, would not prevent pretrial prejudicial publicity, (2) where voir dire was a reasonable alternative, and (3) where only discrete portions of the hearing could properly have been held *in camera*); Capital Newspapers Div. of Hearst Corp. v. Lee, 530 N.Y.S.2d 872, 875 (App. Div. 1988) (holding that closure order was improper where judge failed to make specific findings required by *Press-Enterprise II*). In *Billings Gazette v. Justice Court*, 771 F. Supp. 1062 (D. Mont. 1987), *Des Moines Register & Tribune Co. v. District Court*, 426 N.W.2d 142 (Iowa 1988), and *Booth Newspapers, Inc. v. Twelfth District Court Judge*, 432 N.W.2d 400 (Mich. App. 1988), courts held that statutes modeled on the Field Code, which require closure of a preliminary hearing at the request of the defendant, violate the First Amendment. But see Cowles Publ'g Co. v. Magistrate Ct., 800 P.2d 640, 647 (Idaho 1990) (court upheld a similar statute by reading it to permit closure only if the requirements of *Press-Enterprise II* are satisfied).

Fair trial rights are not the only interest that can overcome the presumption of public access to preliminary hearings. Other "higher values" have been held to justify "narrowly tailored" closure orders.[103] In any case, however, the interest justifying closure must be clearly articulated with record findings sufficient to permit appellate review, and the basic fact remains that the demanding showing necessary to overcome the rule of presumptive access means that virtually all preliminary hearings will be conducted in open court.[104]

§ 3-1(a)(3). Grand Jury Proceedings.

No right of public access to grand jury proceedings has been recognized. The rule of grand jury secrecy precludes, in most cases, the disclosure of matters occurring before a grand jury, particularly while the grand jury is in session. A more contested issue is the right of public access to ancillary proceedings in which grand jury information may be relevant. In such cases, a court must typically apply the *Press-Enterprise II*[105] analysis to determine whether a qualified right of access attaches to the proceeding, creating a presumption of openness. The court must then determine whether grand jury secrecy presents an overriding interest that requires closing the proceeding to the public.

Grand jury proceedings have historically been conducted in secret.[106] Only prosecuting attorneys, witnesses, interpreters, a court reporter and jurors may typically be present during grand jury proceedings.[107] In the federal system and in most states, courts are required to close hearings on matters affecting a grand jury proceeding "to the extent necessary to prevent disclosure of matters

---

103. In *In re Closure of Preliminary Examination*, 505 N.W.2d 24 (Mich. App. 1993), for example, the trial judge in a sexual assault case closed the preliminary examination to protect the victim's emotional well-being. The appellate court reversed, finding abuse of discretion in failing to tailor the order narrowly by closing the courtroom only during specific portions of the proceeding. See *id.* at 26.

104. See, e.g., Cowles Publ'g Co. v. Magistrate Ct., 800 P.2d 640, 647 (Idaho 1990) ("Only under unusually compelling circumstances should preliminary hearings be closed, and when closed the magistrate must comply with the requirements of *Press-Enterprise II*. . . .").

105. See Chap. 2-2(f) *supra*.

106. See Illinois v. Abbott & Assoc., Inc., 460 U.S. 557, 572 (1983) (secrecy of grand jury proceedings is "deeply rooted in our traditions"); Kadish, *Behind the Locked Door of an American Grand Jury: Its History, Its Secrecy, and its Process*, 24 FLA. ST. U.L. REV. 1, 12-22 (1996). Since the 17th century, grand jury proceedings have been closed to the public. See Douglas Oil Co. v. Petrol Stops Northwest, 441 U.S. 211, 218-19 n.9 (1979); Caulkins, *Grand Jury Secrecy*, 63 MICH. L. REV. 455, 456-58 (1965). It has also been argued that grand jury secrecy is based on the Fifth Amendment right of the individual to be free from unfounded prosecutions. See Kadish, *supra*, at 21.

107. See, e.g., FED. R. CRIM. P. 6(d); CAL. PENAL CODE § 939.

occurring before a grand jury."[108] Those involved in a grand jury proceeding are generally prohibited from disclosing matters occurring before the grand jury.[109] A knowing violation of the grand jury secrecy rules may be punished as a contempt of court.[110] This "General Rule of Secrecy" continues after a grand jury has ended its activities.[111] Some states, however, permit public sessions of a grand jury where the subject matter of the investigation affects the general welfare.[112]

Witnesses are one category of grand jury participant normally not constrained by grand jury secrecy. As a general rule, witnesses who testify before a grand jury are not prevented from disclosing the contents of that testimony,[113] unless it

---

108. FED. R. CRIM. P. 6(e)(5). See In re Subpoena to Testify Before Grand Jury, 864 F.2d 1559, 1563 (11th Cir. 1989) (although criminal proceedings are presumptively open, grand jury proceedings are presumptively closed).

109. See, e.g., FED. R. CRIM. P. 6(e)(2). An Independent Counsel, as an attorney for the government, is subject to the secrecy requirements of Rule 6(e)(2). See In re Sealed Case, 151 F.3d 1059, 1062 n.2 (D.C. Cir. 1998); In re North, 16 F.3d 1234, 1245 (D.C. Cir. 1994). The Federal Rules of Criminal Procedure provide for several exceptions to the rule of grand jury secrecy that allow disclosures to government attorneys and personnel, or by a court, for limited purposes. See FED. R. CRIM. P. 6(e)(3). Many states have similar grand jury secrecy provisions. See, e.g., FLA. STAT. § 905.24.

110. See FED. R. CRIM. P. 6(e)(2). Early cases held that the publication of a newspaper article that divulged information from a grand jury investigation constituted an obstruction of justice for which the newspaper could be cited for contempt. See, e.g., United States v. Providence Tribune Co., 241 F. 524, 528 (D.R.I. 1917). The codification of the grand jury secrecy rule in the Federal Rules of Criminal Procedure is applicable only to those identified in the statute, which does not include the media. See United States v. Lovecchio, 561 F. Supp. 221, 229 (M.D. Pa. 1983).

111. See Illinois v. Abbott & Assocs., Inc., 460 U.S. 557, 566 n.11 (1983) ("Even after the conclusion of a particular grand jury's investigation, continued secrecy protects the reputations of the innocent and safeguards witnesses from possible retaliation. In addition, stringent protection of the secrecy of completed grand jury investigations may be necessary to encourage persons to testify fully and freely before future grand juries.").

112. See, e.g., CAL. PENAL CODE § 939.1 (grand jury may be directed to conduct its investigation in public session where it involves alleged corruption, misfeasance, or malfeasance in office or dereliction of duty of public officials or employees).

113. "Witnesses before all federal grand juries . . . have been free since 1946 to disclose what transpired during their presence in the grand jury room." In re Russo, 53 F.R.D. 564, 570 (C.D. Cal. 1971). See In re Eisenberg, 654 F.2d 1107 (5th Cir. 1981); In re Investigation Before April 1975 Grand Jury, 531 F.2d 600 (D.C. Cir. 1976); In re Grand Jury Investigation, 748 F. Supp. 1188 (E.D. Mich. 1990); In re Vescovo Special Grand Jury, 473 F. Supp. 1335, 1336 (C.D. Cal. 1979) ("Witnesses may be interviewed after their appearance and repeat what they said before the grand jury or relate any knowledge they have on the subject of the inquiry); In re Alvarez, 351 F. Supp. 1089 (S.D. Cal. 1972); In re Grand Jury Summoned Oct. 12, 1970, 321 F. Supp. 238, 240 (N.D. Ohio 1970). The majority of states permit witnesses to disclose the contents of their testimony before the grand jury. See Butterworth v. Smith, 494 U.S. 624, 634-35 (1990). Some states purport to impose an obligation of secrecy on grand jury witnesses. See, e.g., FLA. STAT. § 905.27. These statutes have been held to violate the First Amendment to the extent that they prohibit a grand jury witness from disclosing her own testimony after the term of the grand jury has

is determined that secrecy is necessary to protect the investigative function of the grand jury.[114] As a result, witnesses before a grand jury may generally disclose whatever they wish to the media.[115]

On occasion, grand jury information is inadvertently disclosed in open court, or disseminated by the government to the public. In such situations, courts have held that the media cannot be enjoined from publishing it.[116] A court may, however, order the government to cease disseminating the information.[117]

In the federal system, Rule 6(e) of the Federal Rules of Criminal Procedure preserves grand jury secrecy by providing for the confidentiality of all matters occurring before the grand jury.[118] Such matters have been held to encompass not only what has occurred and what is occurring before the grand jury, but also what is likely to occur,[119] including the identities of witnesses,[120] and the strategy or direction of the investigation.[121]

The Supreme Court has indicated that the public and the press do not enjoy a right of access to grand jury proceedings.[122] Lower court decisions, applying the function and experience test of *Press-Enterprise II*,[123] have determined that

---

ended. See Butterworth v. Smith, 494 U.S. 624 (1990) (reporter permitted to disclose own grand jury testimony after the grand jury's term had ended).

114. See In re Grand Jury Subpoena (Doe No. 4 v. Doe No. 1), 103 F.3d 234, 240 (2d Cir. 1996); In re Subpoena to Testify Before Grand Jury, 864 F.2d 1559, 1563-64 (11th Cir. 1989); In re Grand Jury Subpoena Duces Tecum, 797 F.2d 676, 681 (8th Cir.), *cert. dismissed*, 479 U.S. 1013 (1986) (imposing secrecy obligation on grand jury witness on showing of compelling necessity); In re Swearingen Aviation Corp., 486 F. Supp. 9 (D. Md. 1979); In re Grand Jury Summoned Oct. 12, 1970, 321 F. Supp. 238, 240 (N.D. Ohio 1970).

115. See United States v. Lovecchio, 561 F. Supp. 221, 229 (M.D. Pa. 1983); In re Russo, 53 F.R.D. 564, 572 (C.D. Cal. 1971) ("the witness may voluntarily disclose the substance of his testimony to whomever he chooses — his attorney, an associate, the person under investigation, or the news media.").

116. In re Charlotte Observer, 921 F.2d 47, 50 (4th Cir. 1990). See United States v. Smith, 123 F.3d 140, 155 (3d Cir. 1997).

117. See United States v. Smith, 123 F.3d 140, 154-55 (3d Cir. 1997).

118. See In re North, 16 F.3d 1234, 1242 (D.C. Cir. 1994) (Federal Rules of Criminal Procedure embody the ancient principle of grand jury secrecy); United States v. Smith, 992 F. Supp. 743, 751 (D.N.J. 1998).

119. See In re Dow Jones & Co., 142 F.3d 496, 500 (D.C. Cir. 1998); In re Grand Jury Investigation, 610 F.2d 202, 216-17 (5th Cir. 1980).

120. See In re Dow Jones & Co., 142 F.3d at 505; In re Grand Jury Proceedings, 914 F.2d 1372, 1374 (9th Cir. 1990); In re Grand Jury Investigation, 610 F.2d 202, 216-17 (5th Cir. 1980).

121. See In re Dow Jones & Co., 142 F.3d at 505.

122. See *Press-Enterprise II*, 478 U.S. at 9 ("the proper functioning of our grand jury system depends upon the secrecy of grand jury proceedings"); Branzburg v. Hayes, 408 U.S. 665, 684 (1972) ("Despite the fact that news gathering may be hampered, the press is regularly excluded from grand jury proceedings. . . ."). See also In re Subpoena to Testify Before Grand Jury, 864 F.2d 1559, 1562 (11th Cir. 1989); Krause v. Rhodes, 535 F. Supp. 338, 348 (N.D. Ohio 1979), *aff'd*, 671 F.2d 212 (6th Cir. 1982).

123. 478 U.S. 1 (1986). See Chap. 2-2(f) *supra*.

grand jury proceedings are not subject to a First Amendment-based right of access.[124] Similarly, courts have declined to recognize a common law right of access to grand jury proceedings or hearings that involve grand jury matters.[125]

When analyzing the function prong of the *Press-Enterprise II* test, the courts have found that preserving the secrecy of grand jury information is an overriding interest sufficient to justify closure.[126] In so holding, the courts have emphasized the historical interests in favor of grand jury secrecy:

> (1) To prevent the escape of those whose indictment may be contemplated; (2) to insure the utmost freedom to the grand jury in its deliberations, and to prevent persons subject to indictment or their friends from importuning the grand jurors; (3) to prevent subornation of perjury or tampering with the witnesses who may testify before the grand jury and later appear at the trial of those indicted by it; (4) to encourage free and untrammeled disclosures by persons who have information with respect to the commission of crimes; (5) to protect an innocent accused who is exonerated from disclosure of the fact that he has been under investigation, and from the expense of standing trial where there was no probability of guilt.[127]

A more recent concern has been public access to ancillary proceedings such as hearings regarding whether the government violated grand jury secrecy,[128] the disclosure of electronic surveillance,[129] motions to quash grand jury subpoenas,[130] motions to compel testimony,[131] and motions seeking immunity from prosecution,[132] where information concerning a grand jury proceeding is relevant and may be disclosed.

---

124. See, e.g., United States v. Smith, 123 F.3d 140, 148 (3d Cir. 1997); In re Subpoena to Testify Before Grand Jury, 864 F.2d 1559, 1561-62 (11th Cir. 1989). Other courts have made the determination that there is no right of access to grand jury proceedings without consulting *Press-Enterprise II*. See, e.g., In re Dow Jones & Co., 142 F.3d 496 (D.C. Cir. 1998).

125. See In re Dow Jones & Co., 142 F.3d at 504 (any common law right of access to such proceedings has been supplanted by Rule 6(e)(5) of the Federal Rules of Criminal Procedure); United States v. Smith, 123 F.3d at 156.

126. See, e.g., United States v. Haller, 837 F.2d 84, 88 (2d Cir. 1988) ("[P]reservation of grand jury secrecy and the sensitivity of ongoing criminal investigation were "higher values" justifying sealing."); Ex parte Birmingham News Co., 624 So. 2d 1117, 1128 (Ala. Crim. App. 1993).

127. United States v. Procter & Gamble Co., 356 U.S. 677, 682 n.6 (1958). See McClatchy Newspapers v. Superior Ct., 751 P.2d 1329, 1334-35 (Cal. 1988).

128. See, e.g., In re Sealed Case, 151 F.3d 1059 (D.C. Cir. 1998); In re Dow Jones & Co., 142 F.3d 496 (D.C. Cir. 1998); United States v. Smith, 123 F.3d 140 (3d Cir. 1997).

129. See, e.g., In re Grand Jury Subpoena (Doe No. 4 v. Doe No. 1), 103 F.3d 234 (2d Cir. 1996).

130. See, e.g., In re Dow Jones & Co., 142 F.3d at 502; In re Grand Jury Subpoena (Doe No. 4 v. Doe No. 1), 103 F.3d at 238; In re Grand Jury Empaneled March 8, 1983, 579 F. Supp. 189, 192 (E.D. Tenn. 1984).

131. See, e.g., In re Dow Jones & Co., 142 F.3d at 502.

132. See, e.g., In re Grand Jury Subpoena (Doe No. 4 v. Doe No. 1), 103 F.3d at 238.

Such ancillary proceedings may be open to the public where it can be determined that no grand jury material will be discussed.[133] Pursuant to Rule 6(e), courts hearing matters affecting a grand jury proceeding may close the ancillary proceeding to the extent necessary to prevent the disclosure of matters occurring before the grand jury.[134]

> [C]ertain hearings which would reveal matters which have previously occurred before a grand jury or are likely to occur before a grand jury with respect to a pending or on-going investigation must be conducted *in camera* in whole or in part in order to prevent public disclosure of such secret information.[135]

In the Second Circuit, for example, once a proceeding is found to fall within the statutory dictates of Rule 6(e), a rebuttable presumption of secrecy attaches to it.[136] This presumption can be overcome if those seeking disclosure make a showing of a particularized need by proving "that the material they seek is needed to avoid a possible injustice in another judicial proceeding, that the need for disclosure is greater than the need for continued secrecy, and that their request is structured to cover only material so needed."[137] Even when such a particularized need is demonstrated, courts do not generally open hearings to the press while the grand jury investigation remains ongoing.[138]

Some courts have subjected media requests for access to ancillary proceedings to the *Press-Enterprise II* test.[139] Pursuant to that analysis, the court must

---

133. See In re Dow Jones & Co., 142 F.3d at 502 (public access to an ancillary proceeding can be allowed under Federal Rule of Criminal Procedure 6(e)(5) where the subject of the proceeding removes the danger of disclosure or the proceedings are structured to prevent disclosure without disruption or delay).

134. See FED. R. CRIM. P. 6(e)(5) ("the court shall order a hearing on matters affecting a grand jury proceeding to be closed to the extent necessary to prevent disclosure of matters occurring before a grand jury."); In re Dow Jones & Co., 142 F.3d at 501; United States v. Smith, 123 F.3d 140, 149-50 (3d Cir. 1997). A proceeding "affects" a grand jury investigation if it would reveal matters actually or potentially occurring before the grand jury. In re Grand Jury Subpoena (Doe No. 4 v. Doe No. 1), 103 F.3d at 238. "The determination of whether a particular matter is related to a matter occurring before a grand jury is one that depends entirely upon a fact-specific inquiry and the district court's judgment." *Id.* at 239. This statutory ability to close the ancillary proceeding is "[s]ubject to any right to an open hearing in contempt proceedings." FED. R. CRIM. P. 6(e)(5).

135. In re Grand Jury Subpoena (Doe No. 4 v. Doe No. 1), 103 F.3d at 237-38 (quoting Advisory Committee Notes to 1983 Amendment to Federal Rule of Criminal Procedure 6).

136. See *id.* at 239.

137. Douglas Oil Co. v. Petrol Stops Northwest, 441 U.S. 211, 222 (1979).

138. See In re Grand Jury Subpoena (Doe No. 4 v. Doe No. 1), 103 F.3d at 240.

139. See Chap. 2-2(f) *supra*. Where such a hearing is a civil proceeding, an initial consideration is whether the First Amendment provides the press with a right of access to such a proceeding. See In re Grand Jury Subpoena (Doe No. 4 v. Doe No. 1), 103 F.3d at 241-42. Courts disagree as to whether the nature of a proceeding to enforce the secrecy mandate of Rule 6(e)(2) is civil or criminal. Some courts take the view that the proceeding is civil in nature. See, e.g., Barry v. United

determine whether a qualified right of access attaches to the ancillary proceeding at issue. Where it is determined that the ancillary proceeding will involve the disclosure of matters occurring before a grand jury that is still in session, any presumption of access is typically deemed overcome by the government's interest in maintaining the secrecy of the grand jury process.[140] Once the grand jury investigation has terminated, the need for secrecy is diminished and public access may be more readily permitted.[141]

Although closure is to be narrowly tailored to serve the overriding interest in grand jury secrecy, courts have not been receptive to media requests that a bifurcated hearing be held during which the media and public are afforded access to nonsecret aspects of the hearing and excused during the discussion of grand jury matters, finding that such an approach would be cumbersome, impractical, and inefficient.[142] Nor have the courts been responsive to media arguments that more narrow alternatives to closure should be adopted, such as keeping the identities of grand jury witnesses secret.[143]

The events that led to President Clinton's impeachment involved multiple grand jury investigations and eventually resulted in the disclosure to the House

---

States, 865 F.2d 1317 (D.C. Cir. 1989); United States v. Eisenberg, 711 F.2d 959 (11th Cir. 1983); In re Grand Jury Investigation, 610 F.2d 202 (5th Cir. 1980). Other courts interpret the Rule as providing for both civil or criminal contempt. See, e.g., Finn v. Shiller, 72 F.3d 1182 (4th Cir. 1996). Yet others limit the Rule to providing only for criminal contempt. See, e.g., In re Grand Jury Investigation, 748 F. Supp. 1188 (E.D. Mich. 1990).

140. See, e.g., In re Grand Jury Subpoena (Doe No. 4 v. Doe No. 1), 103 F.3d at 242 ("Even if the presumption of openness attaches to that qualified right, however, it is overcome in the grand jury context by the overriding interest in secrecy.").

141. See, e.g., id. at 242-43.

142. See, e.g., In re Dow Jones & Co., 142 F.3d at 501-02 ("[N]either the press nor any member of the public has a First Amendment right to demand that the Chief Judge conduct open ancillary hearings in a way that would not reveal grand jury matters."); United States v. Smith, 123 F.3d at 153 ("The newspapers would, in essence, have the district court conduct a 'revolving door' hearing to which the media would be let in and then excluded from time to time (or minute to minute) depending on whether grand jury material (or putative grand jury material) was under consideration. But courts cannot conduct their business that way, and we will not tie the hands of the district court in this fashion."). It has been noted that appellate court proceedings may be more easily structured to protect grand jury secrecy than trial court proceedings. See In re Dow Jones & Co., 142 F.3d at 502.

143. See, e.g., In re Grand Jury Subpoena (Doe No. 4 v. Doe No. 1), 103 F.3d at 243 ("[M]ore narrow solutions do not adequately account for all of the factors that make up the need for grand jury secrecy, including the protection of the grand jurors themselves and the possibility of alerting the actual target of the investigation."). This is particularly the case while a grand jury investigation remains ongoing. See In re Subpoena to Testify Before Grand Jury, 864 F.2d 1559, 1564 (11th Cir. 1989) (court is not compelled to take the least restrictive means available to protect the secrecy of the grand jury proceedings during the pendency of those proceedings); Blalock v. United States, 844 F.2d 1546, 1550 n.5 (11th Cir. 1988) ("The courts' concern for grand jury secrecy and for the grand jury's law enforcement function is generally greatest during the investigative phase of grand jury proceedings.").

of Representatives by Independent Counsel Kenneth Starr of grand jury testimony contained in his report. In an unprecedented action, the House of Representatives then disclosed the grand jury material to the public via the Internet. Although no legal challenge was made regarding these disclosures, earlier litigation concerned the access that should be afforded to ancillary proceedings arising from the grand jury investigations and the invocation of various privileges by presidential aides.

In *In re Dow Jones & Co.*,[144] the D.C. Circuit considered challenges to closed hearings with respect to ancillary motions concerning the grand jury testimony of these aides. Confronted with a broad claim of access by members of the press, the court confirmed that there is no right of access to grand jury proceedings.[145] It noted that this rule is in accord with the general protection of grand jury secrecy afforded by Federal Rule of Criminal Procedure 6(e) and, in particular, Rule 6(e)(5). The press, however, contended that a right of access of some dimension ought to attach to ancillary proceedings concerning disputes about executive privilege.[146] Although cognizant that assertions of executive privilege are matters of intense public interest, the court nevertheless concluded that even these proceedings properly could be held in secret.[147]

§ 3-1(a)(4). Suppression Hearings.

The Supreme Court has not expressly held that there is a First Amendment-based right of access to pretrial suppression hearings.[148] In *Gannett Co. v. DePasquale*,[149] the Court held that the Sixth Amendment does not afford the public a right of access to suppression hearings. The Court noted that "there exists no persuasive evidence that at common law members of the public had any right to attend" such pretrial proceedings; "indeed, there is substantial evidence to the contrary."[150] In fact, the suppression hearing was unknown at early

---

144. 142 F.3d 496, 503 (D.C. Cir. 1998).
145. See *id.* at 499.
146. See *id.* at 503 (citing In re Subpoena to Nixon, 360 F. Supp. 1 (D.D.C. 1973)).
147. See 142 F.3d at 503.
148. While some states follow a "contemporaneous objection rule," allowing the defendant to object to illegally seized evidence at trial, when the prosecution seeks to introduce it, most require that such objections be made in the form of a pretrial motion to suppress the evidence. The admissibility of a confession or other evidence may often prove determinative of the outcome of a criminal proceeding. See LAFAVE & ISRAEL, *supra* note 68, at 500-01.
149. 443 U.S. 368 (1979).
150. *Id.* at 387. Chief Justice Burger, concurring in *Gannett Co.*, emphasized the lack of any common law tradition of public access to pretrial, as opposed to trial, proceedings. See *id.* at 394-97 (Burger, C.J., concurring); *id.* at 396 ("To make public the evidence developed in a motion to suppress evidence, would, so long as the exclusionary rule is not modified, introduce a new dimension to the problem of conducting fair trials.").

common law; it is largely a modern product of constitutional criminal procedure.[151]

Nevertheless, the absence of a common law history of public access to suppression hearings has not proven determinative of the First Amendment-based right of access. The modern suppression hearing was born of the desire to have an early, pretrial determination of the admissibility of evidence under the more demanding constitutional standards unknown at common law including, most particularly, the exclusionary rule.[152] Changes in constitutional law and criminal procedure have, therefore, brought forth a new form of judicial proceeding. Accordingly, courts have held that the First Amendment inquiry should turn not on history and tradition, but on "logic" or "function," on the value of public access to the effectiveness of the proceeding and to the ability of citizens to supervise their government. It is this functional inquiry that has provided the foundation for extending the First Amendment-based right of access to the suppression hearing.[153]

As the Supreme Court itself noted in *Waller v. Georgia*,[154] "suppression hearings are often as important as the trial itself."[155] The suppression hearing may well determine the outcome of the criminal prosecution. A decision that evidence is admissible will often be followed by a guilty plea. A decision that evidence is constitutionally defective often precludes further prosecution.[156] The

---

151. See *id.* at 437 (Blackmun, J., dissenting) ("the modern suppression hearing, unknown at common law, is a type of objection to evidence such as took place at common law, and as takes place today in the case of non-constitutional objections, in open court during trial").

152. See LAFAVE & ISRAEL, *supra* note 68, at 500.

153. See United States v. Criden, 675 F.2d 550, 555 (3d Cir. 1982) ("We do not think that historical analysis is relevant in determining whether there is a first amendment right of access to pretrial criminal proceedings.... [T]here was no counterpart at common law to the modern suppression hearing. And it is clear that the relative importance of pretrial procedure to that of trial has grown immensely in the last two hundred years."); see also United States v. Brooklier, 685 F.2d 1162, 1170 (9th Cir. 1982) (rejecting historical inquiry as determinative).

154. 467 U.S. 39 (1983).

155. *Id.* at 46 (citations omitted); see Gannett Co. v. DePasquale, 443 U.S. at 397 n.1 (Powell, J., concurring) ("In our criminal justice system as it has developed, suppression hearings often are as important as the trial which may follow.... In view of the special significance of a suppression hearing, the public's interest in this proceeding often is comparable to its interest in the trial itself.").

156. Justice Blackmun, dissenting in *Gannett Co.*, argued that "the suppression hearing often is the only judicial proceeding of substantial importance that takes place during a criminal prosecution." 443 U.S. at 434 (Blackmun, J., dissenting). As Justice Blackmun noted:

[T]he pretrial suppression hearing often is critical, and it may be decisive, in the prosecution of a criminal case. If the defendant prevails, he will have dealt the prosecution's case a serious, perhaps fatal, blow; the proceeding often then will be dismissed or negotiated on terms favorable to the defense. If the prosecution successfully resists the motion to suppress, the defendant may have little hope of success at trial (especially where a confession is in issue), with the result that the likelihood of a guilty plea is substantially increased.

Court in *Waller* also noted that pretrial suppression hearings are adversary, fact-finding proceedings analogous in form to criminal trials.[157] Finally, the Court in *Waller* stressed the importance of public access to the suppression hearing: "A challenge to the seizure of evidence frequently attacks the conduct of police and prosecutor . . . . '[S]trong pressures are naturally at work on the prosecution's witnesses to justify the propriety of their conduct in obtaining' the evidence. The public in general also has a strong interest in exposing substantial allegations of police misconduct to the salutary effects of public scrutiny."[158] Access to the suppression hearing therefore permits the public to scrutinize the work of law enforcement officials and hold them accountable. For these reasons, Justice Blackmun, dissenting in *Gannett Co.*, similarly concluded that, "unlike almost any other proceeding apart from the trial itself, the suppression hearing implicates all the policies that require that the trial be public."[159]

Even before *Press-Enterprise II* extended the right of public access to some pretrial proceedings, several federal circuits had concluded "that the First Amendment extends some degree of public access to a pretrial suppression hearing."[160] Vacating an order closing a suppression hearing in *United States v. Criden*,[161] the Third Circuit concluded that the constitutional values articulated by the Supreme Court in *Richmond Newspapers, Inc.* apply with equal force to pretrial suppression hearings. Because such a hearing "often is the most critical stage of a criminal proceeding,"[162] the court determined that "[t]he public's vital interest in evaluating the public officials who work in the criminal justice system cannot be fully vindicated unless the public and press can attend pretrial hearings. Otherwise, much of the work of prosecutors and trial judges may go unscrutinized."[163]

Id.

157. The Court observed that, in both proceedings, the outcome frequently depends on resolving factual disputes. To this end, "witnesses are sworn and testify, and of course, counsel argue their positions." Waller v. Georgia, 467 U.S. at 47. Justice Blackmun, dissenting in *Gannett Co.*, similarly observed that "the suppression hearing resembles and relates to the full trial in almost every particular." 443 U.S. at 434 (Blackmun, J., dissenting).

158. 467 U.S. at 47 (quoting United States ex rel. Bennett v. Rundle, 419 F.2d 599, 605 (3d Cir. 1969)).

159. 443 U.S. at 436 (Blackmun, J., dissenting).

160. In re Herald Co. (Klepfer), 734 F.2d 93, 99 (2d Cir. 1984) (citing United States v. Criden, 675 F.2d 550, 557 (3d Cir. 1982); United States v. Brooklier, 685 F.2d 1162, 1169-71 (9th Cir. 1982)).

161. 675 F.2d at 556.

162. *Id.* Decisions made at a suppression hearing "often determine whether the defendant or the Government wants to proceed to trial. In many cases, the pretrial hearing is the only adversary proceeding the accused will have in resolving his case." *Id.* at 557.

163. *Id.* Suppression hearings often involve objections to the propriety of police conduct. "Because such conduct frequently occurs outside the public view, beneficial public scrutiny may never take place if not at the hearing itself." *Id.* See also New York v. Arroyo, 675 N.Y.S.2d 272,

Similarly, in *United States v. Brooklier*,[164] the Ninth Circuit rejected an effort to close a suppression hearing convened to determine the admissibility of evidence based on alleged misconduct by FBI agents. The court held that "'[a]llegations of this kind, although they may prove to be unfounded, are of importance to the public as well as the defendant.'"[165] And in *In re Herald Co. (Klepfer)*,[166] the Second Circuit held that the district court had failed to make adequate findings to justify closure of a suppression hearing on the ground that "[i]t makes little sense to recognize a right of public access to criminal courts and then limit that right to the trial phase of a criminal proceeding, something that occurs in only a small fraction of criminal cases. There is a significant benefit to be gained from public observation of many aspects of a criminal proceeding, including pretrial suppression hearings that may have a decisive effect upon the outcome of a prosecution."[167]

While some early cases did reject a First Amendment-based right of access to suppression hearings,[168] *Press-Enterprise II* and *Waller* appear to have settled the issue.[169] Once again, however, the constitutional right is qualified and the presumption of openness can be overcome. In the context of the suppression hearing, the most significant competing interest asserted is the defendant's right to a fair trial, where closure is directed to preventing evidence that is suppressed from being publicly disclosed and influencing potential jurors. As the New York Court of Appeals has put it: "We recognize that suppression hearings pose a

---

276 (County Ct. 1998) (granting public access to suppression hearing in capital case because defendants failed to show a substantial probability that their rights to a fair trial would be prejudiced by publicity and because citizens "have an obligation to be aware of every stage of such capital proceedings to assure that the system, whereby a person found guilty of a capital crime may pay with his or her life, affords that person the fair and impartial administration of justice through the entire proceeding").

164. 685 F.2d 1162 (9th Cir. 1982).

165. *Id.* at 1171 (quoting Gannett Co. v. DePasquale, 443 U.S. at 435 (Blackmun, J., dissenting)). In *Brooklier*, the suppression hearing began prior to trial but concluded during the trial itself. The court of appeals noted that there was unquestionably a right of public access to suppression hearings held during trial and that "[i]t would elevate form over substance to deny access to an identical proceeding because it began prior to trial." 685 F.2d at 1171. The court added that this circumstance "illustrates the impracticability of attaching dispositive significance to the distinction between trial and pretrial proceedings for the purpose of determining the applicability of the first amendment." *Id.* at 1170.

166. 734 F.2d 93 (2d Cir. 1984).

167. *Id.* at 98.

168. See, e.g., Connecticut v. Burak, 431 A.2d 1246, 1248 (Conn. Super. 1981).

169. See, e.g., Johnson Newspaper Corp. v. Morton, 862 F.2d 25 (2d Cir. 1988) (recognizing that *Press-Enterprise II* standards must be satisfied to justify closure of a pretrial suppression hearing); Ohio v. Nobles, 21 MEDIA L. REP. (BNA) 1501 (Ohio C.P. 1993), *aff'd*, 665 N.E.2d 1137 (Ohio App. 1995) (suppression hearings are presumptively open); New Jersey v. Williams, 459 A.2d 641, 649 (N.J. 1983) (recognizing that practice of open pretrial proceedings, such as suppression hearings, has been "near uniform").

peculiar risk in that adverse pretrial publicity could inflame public opinion and taint potential jurors by exposing them to inadmissible but highly prejudicial evidence."[170] Nevertheless, a substantial majority of the recent cases appear to have employed the demanding *Press-Enterprise II* standards, which has resulted in very few decisions holding that closure is constitutionally permissible.[171]

A residue of judicial uncertainty concerning the appropriate standards governing closure of suppression hearings is reflected in the Vermont Supreme Court's decision in *Vermont v. Schaefer*.[172] Upon the request of Schaefer, who was charged with second-degree murder, the trial court had sealed an affidavit of probable cause. Citing evidence of potentially prejudicial publicity, the court found that the defendant had "demonstrated by clear necessity" that sealing was required to protect his right to a fair trial and that alternatives to secrecy would be ineffective.[173] The trial court then closed the suppression hearing, held to determine whether statements made by the defendant to the police should be

---

170. Associated Press v. Bell, 510 N.E.2d 313, 315 (N.Y. 1987). Similarly, in *Westchester Rockland Newspapers, Inc. v. Leggett*, 399 N.E.2d 518, 523 (N.Y. 1979), the same court explained:

> If these hearings were open to the public and the press in a well-publicized case, it is most likely that the substance of the evidence would be disclosed to the community from which the jurors would be drawn, even though the court may ultimately rule that the evidence should not be submitted to the jury at trial. This would not only destroy the purpose for which the hearing was held, but would, perversely, have the very opposite effect of that intended and desired. Instead of shielding the jurors from evidence they should not hear, the public airing at the pretrial suppression hearing would serve to broadcast the evidence to most, if not all potential jurors.

171. For example, in *In re Greenville News Co.*, 505 S.E.2d 340 (S.C. 1998), a case in which the death penalty was sought, the court relied on *Ex parte First Charleston Corp.*, 495 S.E.2d 423 (S.C. 1998), applied *Press-Enterprise II*, and vacated a trial court's order closing a hearing to determine the voluntariness of a confession, where there were no facts supporting the trial court ruling that closure was necessary and alternatives would be ineffective in protecting the defendant's right to a fair trial. And in *New York v. Arroyo*, 675 N.Y.S.2d 272, 276 (County Ct. 1998), the court granted public access to a suppression hearing in a capital case because the defendants failed to show a substantial probability that their rights to a fair trial would be prejudiced by publicity and because citizens "have an obligation to be aware of every stage of such capital proceedings to assure that the system, whereby a person found guilty of a capital crime may pay with his or her life, affords that person the fair and impartial administration of justice through the entire proceedings." See also, e.g., Johnson Newspaper Corp. v. Morton, 862 F.2d 25 (2d Cir. 1988) (*Press Enterprise II* standard applies to orders closing suppression hearings); People v. McIntosh, 26 MEDIA L. REP. (BNA) 1891 (N.Y. County Ct. 1997); People v. Franklin, 22 MEDIA L. REP. (BNA) 1255 (N.Y. Crim. 1993); North Carolina v. Demery, 22 MEDIA L. REP. (BNA) 2383 (N.C. Super. 1994); Ohio v. Nobles, 21 MEDIA L. REP. (BNA) 1501 (Ohio C.P. 1993); Pennsylvania v. Bercaw, 20 MEDIA L. REP. (BNA) 1518 (Pa. C.P. 1992); People v. Rowe, 18 MEDIA L. REP. (BNA) 1980 (N.Y. County Ct. 1991).

172. 599 A.2d 337 (Vt. 1991), *cert. denied*, 502 U.S. 1077 (1992).

173. *Id.*

admitted at trial, in order to prevent disclosure of information contained in the sealed affidavit.

The Vermont Supreme Court initially held that its own precedent had established "that the press, and public have a qualified right of access to pretrial suppression hearings and affidavits of probable cause, which must be balanced with defendant's Sixth Amendment right to a fair trial."[174] The court in *Schaefer* then held that the *Press-Enterprise II* standard applied: "[E]very court that has found a qualified First Amendment right to attend a particular pretrial event has also found that closure of the event to the public can be done only where the *Press-Enterprise II* standard has been met."[175] Applying the *Press-Enterprise II* standard, the appellate court reversed the sealing and closure orders on the ground that the trial judge had failed to consider alternatives to sealing and closure, even if there was a danger of prejudice.[176]

Chief Justice Allen concurred in the result but not in the court's invocation of *Press-Enterprise II*. Emphasizing the potential prejudice that may result from disclosure of matters that are ultimately suppressed, he argued for a less demanding rule that asks "whether a fair trial for the defendant is likely to be jeopardized by publicity."[177]

Justice Peck, in a caustic dissent, accused the court of an "inexcusable obeisance to the media on one hand and, on the other, [a] relative indifference to the extreme uncertainty confronting a defendant."[178] He asserted that the burden imposed on the defendant to prove prejudice was impossible to satisfy[179] and,

---

174. *Id.* at 341-42 (citing Vermont v. Tallman, 537 A.2d 422, 427 (Vt. 1987); Greenwood v. Wolchik, 544 A.2d 1156 (Vt. 1988)).

175. 599 A.2d at 343 (citing Associated Press v. Bell, 510 N.E.2d 313, 316-17 (N.Y. 1987); Ohio ex rel. The Repository v. Unger, 504 N.E.2d 37, 40 (Ohio 1986)).

176. See 599 A. 2d at 345. ("As a basic principle, voir dire is the normal and preferred method of combating any effects of pretrial publicity.... We cannot conclude that the potential publicity in this case, especially if combined with a change of venue, would rise to the level where voir dire would be ineffective."). The trial court's reasoning that voir dire would be ineffective because potential jurors are not always candid or might not remember news accounts until the jury was impaneled, the appellate court concluded, "amounts to a total rejection of the use of voir dire to avoid impaneling prejudiced jurors." *Id.* See *id.* at 343-44 ("If the information were suppressed, it would be critical that potential jurors not know of the information," even though the murder "arose in a relatively small town" and there had already been widespread publicity indicating the defendant had murdered other young women).

177. *Id.* at 348-49 (Allen, C.J., concurring).

178. *Id.* at 349-50 (Peck, J., dissenting).

179. See *id.* at 352:

I say that the burden of proof placed on defendants by the majority, to establish prejudice, is all but impossible to satisfy, and is now made even more difficult by the standards and guidelines established today by majority fiat. This is for the very simple reason that no one is psychic, no one can predict with absolute certainty, before the fact, what will or will not prejudice the fair-trial right of a defendant.

like Chief Justice Allen, questioned the effectiveness of alternatives to closure. Accordingly, Judge Peck urged that priority be given to the defendant's Sixth Amendment right and that the burden be placed on the press to prove that publication would not prejudice the accused.[180]

§ 3-1(a)(5). Competency Hearings.

The First Amendment-based right of public access has also been litigated in the context of competency hearings. Competency to stand trial should not be confused with the insanity defense, which focuses on the defendant's state of mind at the time of the crime. Competency determinations focus on the defendant's mental condition at the time of trial: i.e., whether the defendant is able to understand the charges against her and to participate in her own defense.[181]

The New York Court of Appeals issued an early, influential decision recognizing a right of public access to competency hearings in *Westchester Rockland Newspapers, Inc. v. Leggett*.[182] Adopting a functional approach, the court nevertheless relied on state law rather than the First Amendment as the basis for the access right.[183] The court reasoned that access to competency hearings protects the accused from "secret inquisitional techniques" and promotes the public interest in a full and impartial enforcement of the law, thereby promoting public trust in the judicial process.[184] Public attendance at a competency hearing would not generally involve a risk of prejudicial pretrial publicity threatening the defendant's right to a fair trial, the court determined, because the focus is not on responsibility for the crime, but rather on the defendant's present mental capacity to stand trial.[185] Further, the court emphasized that a record showing of "a strong likelihood" that evidence admitted in the competency hearing would prejudice the defendant's trial or involve sordid matters could justify closure in a given case.[186]

---

180. *Id.* at 353.
181. The constitutional requirement that the accused be competent to stand trial was fashioned by the Supreme Court in *Dusky v. United States*, 362 U.S. 402 (1960). In *Dusky*, the Court held that, before an accused can stand trial, the trial judge must determine whether he has "sufficient present ability to consult with his lawyer with a reasonable degree of rational understanding and whether he has a rational as well as factual understanding of the proceedings against him." *Id.* The test is codified at 18 U.S.C. § 4241(a).
182. 399 N.E.2d 518 (N.Y. 1979). At the request of the defendant in a multiple rape case, the court closed the entire competency hearing and denied access to the transcript. *Id.*
183. See *id.* at 525.
184. *Id.* at 522.
185. See *id.* at 524 (recognizing that an open hearing would not be prejudicial because a different standard exists for making an insanity defense). See *Miami Herald Publ'g Co. v. Chappell*, 403 So. 2d 1342, 1345 (Fla. App. 1981) ("It is . . . unlikely that testimony jeopardizing a defendant's right to a fair trial would be elicited [at a competency hearing].").
186. 399 N.E.2d at 525.

Other cases involving competency hearings, reflecting the developing First Amendment jurisprudence after *Gannett Co. v. DePasquale*,[187] manifest a less cautious approach.[188] Emphasizing the functional values of openness in establishing a First Amendment-based right of access, these courts employ more demanding standards for closure. In *Louisiana v. Eaton*,[189] for example, the court characterized a competency hearing as a "critical stage of the prosecution," which "requires decisions by the court that attract significant public interest and invite legitimate and healthy public scrutiny."[190] Thus, a defendant seeking closure of a competency hearing, the court held, must demonstrate not only a likelihood of prejudice but also the inadequacy of alternatives and the efficacy of closure in protecting the asserted right to a fair trial.[191] Applying these standards, the court in *Eaton* held that the trial judge had erred in closing the hearing and denying access to its transcript.[192]

In *Miami Herald Publishing Co. v. Chappell*,[193] the court also began from the premise that "the same reasoning that requires open trials mandates open competency proceedings."[194] Competency hearings are a critical stage of the proceedings, since they may "eliminate the need for a trial, either as a result of dismissal of the charges or by rulings made at the hearing which destroy a party's chances of success at trial."[195] Accordingly, the court concluded that the trial judge had erred in failing to consider whether "(1) closure is necessary to prevent a serious and imminent threat to the administration of justice, (2) no less restrictive alternative is available, and (3) closure will in fact achieve the court's purpose."[196]

---

187. 443 U.S. 368 (1979).

188. See, e.g., Society of Prof'l Journalists v. Bullock, 743 P.2d 1166, 1178 (Utah 1987) ("pretrial competency proceedings in criminal cases may be closed only upon a showing that access raises a realistic likelihood of prejudice to the defendant's right to a fair trial"). But see *Press-Enterprise II*, 478 U.S. at 14 (Supreme Court noted that "the 'reasonable likelihood' test places a lesser burden on the defendant than the 'substantial probability' test which we held is called for by the First Amendment.").

189. 483 So. 2d 651 (La. App. 1986).

190. *Id.* at 658.

191. See *id.* at 660.

192. See *id.* at 662. The court specifically rejected the defendant's argument that the jury would be unable to distinguish between the issues of insanity and mental capacity to stand trial. See *id.* at 661. In any case, the fact that the defendant was found competent to proceed was a matter of public record, which the public would learn. See *id.* at 661, 662.

193. 403 So. 2d 1342 (Fla. App. 1981).

194. *Id.* at 1344. See In re Times-World Corp., 488 S.E.2d 677, 682 (Va. App. 1997) (Because criminal competency hearings pass "these tests of tradition and logic, *Press-Enterprise II*, 478 U.S. at 9, we hold that both the First Amendment and Article I, § 12 of the Virginia Constitution grant the media a qualified right to attend these proceedings.").

195. 403 So. 2d at 1345.

196. *Id.* See In re Times-World Corp., 488 S.E.2d at 682 (Since First Amendment-based right of access attaches to a criminal competency hearing, access can only be denied by showing "a

§ 3-1(a)(6). Plea Hearings.

While there is apparently no case recognizing a constitutional right of access to plea negotiations, courts have found a qualified First Amendment-based right of access to the judicial proceeding at which a plea is entered.[197] In *In re Washington Post Co.*,[198] for example, the Fourth Circuit endorsed a press claim of access to a plea hearing and sealed transcript allegedly involving information the disclosure of which would endanger national security. The defendant, a Ghanaian national, had been indicted for espionage. Ghana and the United States entered into an agreement involving a plea by defendant of nolo contendere, the suspension of his sentence, and an exchange of prisoners by the governments.[199] The parties jointly moved to have the plea and sentencing hearings and supporting affidavits kept secret. The matter was not docketed, closed hearings were held, and the pleadings, transcript, and supporting documents were sealed.[200]

The court of appeals initially addressed whether the First Amendment-based right of access applied to plea and sentencing hearings at all. The proceeding, the court asserted, was arguably the functional equivalent of a trial: "Because the taking of a guilty plea serves as a substitute for trial, it may reasonably be treated in the same manner as a trial for First Amendment purposes."[201] Even if the proceedings were not deemed to be a "trial," however, the court held that "they are surely as much an integral part of a criminal prosecution as are [other pretrial proceedings] which have been held to be subject to the public's First Amendment right of access."[202] Further, while plea hearings "do not have the same long tradition" of public access as sentencing hearings, the court noted, "they are

---

'compelling governmental interest' and the denial must be 'narrowly tailored to serve that interest.'") (citation omitted).

197. See, e.g., United States v. Danovaro, 877 F.2d 583, 589 (7th Cir. 1989); United States v. Haller, 837 F.2d 84, 86 (2d Cir. 1988); In re Washington Post Co., 807 F.2d 383, 388-89 (4th Cir. 1986). These cases also recognize a First Amendment-based right of access to plea agreements and related documents. See Washington Post Co. v. Robinson, 935 F.2d 282, 288 (D.C. Cir. 1991); Oregonian Publ'g Co. v. United States Dist. Ct., 920 F.2d 1462, 1465-66 (9th Cir. 1990), cert. denied, 501 U.S. 1210 (1991); United States v. Kooistra, 796 F.2d 1390, 1391 (11th Cir. 1986); United States v. Northrop Corp., 746 F. Supp. 1002, 1003-04 (C.D. Cal. 1990). See also Baltimore Sun Co. v. Colbert, 593 A.2d 224 (Md. 1991) (First Amendment-based right of access to hearing on motion to enforce a plea bargain agreement). See generally Chap. 5-2(a)(9) *infra*.

198. 807 F.2d 383 (4th Cir. 1986).
199. *Id.* at 386.
200. *Id.*
201. *Id.* at 389. See United States v. Danovaro, 877 F.2d at 589 ("Guilty pleas share . . . some of the attributes of trials.").
202. 807 F.2d at 389. In *United States v. Haller*, 837 F.2d 84, 87 (2d Cir. 1988), the court noted that "the taking of a plea is the most common form of adjudication of criminal litigation," accounting for over three-fourths of criminal convictions.

typically held in open court."[203] Moreover, the court concluded that "[p]ublic access serves the important function of discouraging either the prosecutor or the court from engaging in arbitrary or wrongful conduct."[204]

Having concluded that the First Amendment contemplates a right of access to plea hearings, the court considered whether "closure is essential to preserve higher values and is narrowly tailored to serve that interest,"[205] and whether the procedural requirements of notice, hearing and specific findings had been satisfied.[206] In that regard, the court rejected the government's efforts to create an exception from established access law in "national security" cases. While recognizing the risk that disclosure could endanger lives, the court was "equally troubled by the notion that the judiciary should abdicate its decisionmaking responsibility to the executive branch whenever national security concerns are present."[207] Thus, the Fourth Circuit concluded both that the trial court had failed to provide the requisite notice and hearing to the press and that the closure order, premised solely on citation to the Classified Information Procedures Act, did not excuse the need for a constitutional inquiry.[208]

Other courts recognizing a First Amendment-based right of access to plea hearings and plea agreements have similarly held that the procedural requirements of notice, hearing and specific findings must be satisfied.[209] The courts have also grappled with the findings that will justify a closure order in plea proceedings. Applying *Press-Enterprise II* standards, closure has been upheld to protect the secrecy of grand jury proceedings and ongoing criminal investiga-

---

203. 807 F.2d at 389. See United States v. Haller, 837 F.2d at 86 ("Plea hearings have typically been open to the public...."); Oregonian Publ'g Co. v. United States Dist. Ct., 920 F.2d at 1465 ("plea agreements have typically been open to the public. Nothing has been provided to suggest historical practice is to the contrary"); Washington Post Co. v. Robinson, 935 F.2d at 288 ("plea agreements have traditionally been open to the public").

204. 807 F.2d at 389; see *id.* ("[t]he presence of the public operates to check any temptation that might be felt by either the prosecutor or the court to obtain a guilty plea by coercion or trick, or to seek or impose an arbitrary or disproportionate sentence").

205. *Id.* at 390 (citing *Press-Enterprise I*, 464 U.S. at 510).

206. See 807 F.2d at 390 (citing In re Knight Publ'g Co., 743 F.2d 231 (4th Cir. 1984)). See generally Chap. 2-3 *supra*.

207. 807 F.2d at 391. The court noted the danger that repressive government action could too easily be cloaked under the "spectre of a threat to 'national security.'" *Id.*

208. See *id.* The Classified Information Procedures Act, 18 U.S.C. §§ 1-16 (1994), is designed to deal with "graymail," the threat by a defendant to reveal classified information during a criminal trial. It was "simply irrelevant," the Fourth Circuit held, to the issue of access. 807 F.2d at 393.

209. See, e.g., Washington Post Co. v. Robinson, 935 F.2d at 289, 292 ("the necessary procedures were not followed and the justifications advanced by the government were not adequately demonstrated"); United States v. Haller, 837 F.2d at 84, 87 (initial closure order vacated "because it did not comply with the procedural and substantive requirements of the first amendment").

tions.[210] In one case, however, the court held that denial of access to a plea agreement was not supported by adequate findings that disclosure posed a risk of harm to the defendant and his family.[211] Similarly, another court held that closure of plea proceedings and sealing of the transcript in a highly publicized racial killing was not supported by findings establishing the need for closure to protect the defendant's rights to a fair trial.[212]

§ 3-1(b). Voir Dire Proceedings.

In *Press-Enterprise I*, the Supreme Court recognized a First Amendment-based right of access to voir dire proceedings. The Court indicated that the constitutional presumption of openness could be overcome "only be an overriding interest based on findings that closure is essential to preserve higher values and is narrowly tailored to serve that interest."[213] In some circumstances, the Court noted, the need to protect the privacy of a prospective juror could constitute an overriding interest.[214] To minimize the risk of unnecessary closure, a prospective juror must make an "affirmative request" to disclose her privacy concerns *in camera*. The trial judge must then determine if the privacy interest outweighs the public interest in access.[215] Even when such limited closure is appropriate, a transcript of the closed proceeding must be made available within a reasonable time, with portions redacted where necessary.[216]

In *Cable News Network, Inc. v. United States*,[217] the trial court, concerned with the sensitive nature of some prospective juror responses to a questionnaire, closed voir dire proceedings and left it to the discretion of each juror whether he or she would be questioned *in camera* or in open court. Citing *Press-Enterprise I*, the D.C. Circuit summarily reversed. While the trial court had made no

---

210. See United States v. Haller, 837 F.2d at 87-89; United States v. Northrop Corp., 746 F. Supp. 1002 (C.D. Cal. 1990) (granting access to plea agreement, redacted to protect ongoing grand jury proceedings).

211. See Oregonian Publ'g Co. v. United States Dist. Ct., 920 F.2d at 1467.

212. See New York Times Co. v. Demakos, 529 N.Y.S.2d 97, 101 (App. Div. 1988) ("despite the extensive publicity which preceded the first Howard Beach trial, [the judge] was able to empanel a fair and impartial jury after conducting a thorough voir dire process").

213. 464 U.S. at 510. See Chap. 2-2(e) *supra*. Even prior to *Press-Enterprise I*, several courts had recognized a right of access to voir dire proceedings. See United States v. Brooklier, 685 F.2d 1162 (9th Cir. 1982); United States ex rel. Pulitzer Publ'g Co., 635 F.2d 676 (8th Cir. 1980). See generally Annotation, *Exclusion of Public and Media From Voir Dire Examination of Prospective Jurors in State Criminal Cases*, 16 A.L.R. 5th 152 (1994).

214. See 464 U.S. at 511 (a prospective juror's interest in privacy becomes compelling "when interrogation touches on deeply personal matters that [a] person has legitimate reasons for keeping out of the public domain").

215. *Id.* at 511-12.

216. See *id.* at 512.

217. 824 F.2d 1046 (D.C. Cir.), *cert. denied*, 484 U.S. 914 (1987). Only five of the approximately 30 prospective jurors volunteered to be questioned in open court. *Id.*

findings that individual privacy concerns were sufficiently compelling to outweigh the values of openness, the court of appeals held that *"Press-Enterprise* is to the contrary; it requires the trial court to determine whether a juror's request is 'legitimate.'"[218] In addition, the trial judge had failed to consider alternatives to closure, such as conducting voir dire in open court and responding to individual privacy claims as appropriate, on a case-by-case basis.[219]

Similarly, in *In re Dallas Morning News*,[220] closure of the individual questioning of the venire because of *anticipated* privacy concerns was held to be inconsistent with *Press-Enterprise I*. Nevertheless, the Fifth Circuit indicated that a potential juror's affirmative request need not be made in open court; voir dire may be closed for the limited purpose of explaining the nature of the questions and informing jurors of the possibility of requesting that questioning be held *in camera*. The Fifth Circuit emphasized, however, that the court must make an individualized determination that a given juror's privacy interest is sufficiently significant "to justify the extraordinary measure of the closed proceeding."[221]

In *Press-Enterprise I*, the Court also held that "the right of an accused to fundamental fairness in the jury selection process is a compelling interest."[222] Still, the Court asserted, there must be specific findings that an open proceeding threatens this interest and that alternatives to closure would be ineffective. In *United States v. Peters*,[223] the trial judge closed an ongoing voir dire proceeding in a well-publicized drug case because news coverage had already focused on the examination of potential jurors. In vacating the closure order, the Seventh Circuit held that, "[b]ecause the district court failed to question potential jurors as to their awareness of media coverage of the voir dire, or engage in any other inquiry to support its conclusion that the 'integrity of the process' was infected," the trial court had "failed to establish a 'threat' to the interest in an impartial

---

218. *Id.* at 1048-49. Absent such individualized findings, the court noted, an appellate court cannot conclude that closure is warranted. See *id.*
219. *Id.*
220. 916 F.2d 205 (5th Cir. 1990).
221. *Id.* at 206. The same methodology was adopted by the Rhode Island Supreme Court in *Providence Journal Co. v. Superior Court*, 593 A.2d 446 (R.I. 1991), where closure of individual voir dire was held to violate the right of access because there were no facts in the record demonstrating that an open proceeding would prejudice significant privacy interests. The trial court's concerns were "speculative" and there was no "compelling governmental interest" justifying closure. *Id.* at 449. The court also stressed the need for trial judges to consider alternatives to closure and to assure that any closure orders are "narrowly-tailored." *Id.* at 450. See also Houston Chronicle Publ'g Co. v. Crapitto, 907 S.W.2d 99, 106 (Tex. App. 1995) (holding that trial judge "abused her discretion because she failed to sufficiently articulate findings with required specificity, and thus, her order excluding the media violated the First Amendment").
222. 464 U.S. at 510.
223. 754 F.2d 753 (7th Cir. 1985).

jury."[224] Employing the standards articulated in *Press-Enterprise I*, the court of appeals held that the trial judge had "failed to consider fully on the record other alternatives to closure, or to narrowly tailor its closure order."[225]

The trial court in *Ukiah Daily Journal v. Superior Court*,[226] in an effort to protect the impartiality of the jury in a death penalty case, closed the so-called *Witherspoon*-related voir dire.[227] In granting a newspaper's petition for a writ of mandamus, the appellate court concluded that *Witherspoon* required only that death-qualifying voir dire be conducted outside of the presence of other venirepersons; it did not, however, contemplate closure of the proceeding to the public.[228] Moreover, the trial judge had made no findings that ongoing press coverage would influence potential jurors' attitudes about the death penalty. Specifically, there were no findings that a public voir dire would make jurors less candid in their responses.[229] More generally, the court was skeptical of the need for closure to ensure candid responses: "[I]f this general theory of potential prejudice were accepted as sufficient for closure, all testimony could be taken in secret."[230]

By the same token, closure of voir dire based on the need to protect the defendant's right to a fair trial has, on occasion, been upheld. Shortly after *Press-Enterprise I*, for example, the Fourth Circuit affirmed a decision permitting closure of the voir dire in a highly publicized case involving the murder of civil rights marchers by Nazis and Klansmen,[231] although the court of appeals referred to the case as "nearly unique."[232] In *In re South Carolina Press Asso-*

---

224. *Id.* at 761.
225. *Id.* The Seventh Circuit noted that, while sequestration had been rejected, the trial judge could have given frequent admonitions to the panel to avoid the press and questioned the venire to assure that his instructions were followed. See *id.* at 761-62.
226. 211 Cal. Rptr. 673 (Ct. App. 1985).
227. See *id.* Under *Witherspoon v. Illinois*, 391 U.S. 510 (1968), a jury may be "death-qualified" — i.e., qualified to consider imposition of the death penalty — by removing those who indicate in voir dire that they are unequivocally opposed to capital punishment.
228. See 211 Cal. Rptr. at 674-76. See also *Press-Enterprise I*, 464 U.S. at 511 n.11 (California precedent did not require closure of *Witherspoon* voir dire).
229. See 211 Cal. Rptr. at 675.
230. *Id.* (quoting United States v. Brooklier, 685 F.2d 1162, 1169 (9th Cir. 1982)). The court also noted that the availability of a transcript of the closed proceeding "is no substitute for the right to attend a criminal trial." 211 Cal. Rptr. at 676 n.2. See also Kansas v. Aikens, 932 P.2d 408 (Kan. 1997) (affirming trial court denial of defendant's motion for individually sequestered voir dire).
231. In re Greensboro News Co., 727 F.2d 1320 (4th Cir.), *cert. denied*, 469 U.S. 829 (1984). A panel of 1500 potential jurors had been assembled. The court stressed the need to ensure frank and forthcoming responses from potential jurors in order to protect defendants' fair trial rights and the failure of the press to identify any meaningful alternative to closure. See *id.* at 1322-23.
232. *Id.* at 1328 n.4. The court of appeals characterized the district court's closure order as having "identified one of the few acceptable exceptions to a virtually unanimous rule [favoring First Amendment rights]." *Id.* at 1324. In *United States v. Peters*, 754 F.2d at 760, the Seventh

ciation,[233] the same court held that the closed voir dire in the criminal prosecutions of state legislators charged with extortion satisfied the constitutional standards set forth in *Press-Enterprise* cases. Potential jurors in the case had been sent a questionnaire promising confidentiality and closure of the voir dire had been based on findings that the step was necessary to secure candid responses and thereby detect juror bias.[234]

The Fourth Circuit embraced the analytical premise that "[f]ull and frank answers from potential jurors, when they are questioned on voir dire are essential to the process of selecting" a fair and impartial jury.[235] In the court's view, "[f]ear of publicity that might be given to the answers of venirepersons during voir dire may so inhibit or chill truthful response that an accused is denied the fair trial to which he is entitled under the Fourteenth Amendment."[236] Moreover, the court concluded that closure would be effective, since it would insulate potential jurors from the answers of their colleagues and allow them to answer free of "worry about what the public's opinion of those responses might be."[237] Finally, the Fourth Circuit held that "under the very unusual circumstances of these cases, no reasonable alternatives to closure will adequately protect the fair trial rights of the accused."[238]

The Second Circuit employed a similar rationale in *United States v. King*.[239] Charged with wire fraud, boxing promoter Don King had successfully moved to limit press access to voir dire proceedings. The district court found "(1) 'that candor on the part of the prospective jurors is of particularly great importance in this case,' and (2) 'that, absent a degree of juror privacy, such candor is likely to be restricted.'"[240] These findings were based on the controversy surrounding King and the extensive publicity (mostly negative) about him.[241] The trial judge concluded that the fear of publicity might "so inhibit and chill truthful responses" in voir dire as to deny the accused a fair trial.[242] After rejecting various alternatives to closure,[243] the trial court denied access to the completed voir dire

---

Circuit indicated that the Fourth Circuit's decision had limited "persuasive force," adding that it "sheds little light on the application of the *Press-Enterprise* test."

233. 946 F.2d 1037 (4th Cir. 1991).
234. The questionnaire and voir dire were said to involve "highly personal, sensitive" questions concerning racial prejudice and attitudes towards elected officials. *Id*. at 1038 n.2.
235. *Id*. at 1043.
236. *Id*.
237. *Id*. at 1044 (quoting In re Greensboro News Co., 727 F.2d 1320, 1326 (4th Cir. 1984)).
238. 946 F.2d at 1044.
239. 140 F.3d 76 (2d Cir. 1998) (*King II*). The media had unsuccessfully attempted to secure transcripts of voir dire from an earlier trial of the defendant which had ended in a mistrial. See United States v. King, 911 F. Supp. 113 (S.D.N.Y. 1995) (*King I*).
240. 140 F.3d at 79 (citations omitted).
241. See 140 F.3d at 79-80.
242. *Id*. at 80 (quoting In re South Carolina Press Ass'n, 946 F.2d at 1043).
243. See *id*. at 80. The use of individual questioning of jurors to determine the need for closure,

questionnaire and transcripts of follow up questioning until the jury was impaneled. There was no general voir dire in open court.[244]

The court of appeals, in an opinion by Judge Newman, narrowly construed the procedures set forth in *Press-Enterprise I*: "The Court there outlined one course for a trial judge to follow when confronted with one problem — the risk of juror embarrassment about disclosing highly personal matters."[245] Even though *Press-Enterprise I* had noted the risk to juror candor, the court found little attention to the problem in the Supreme Court's discussion.[246] In the present case, in contrast, the trial court had made explicit findings and imposed narrow limitations only after considering and rejecting alternatives. While accepting the presumption in favor of open proceedings,[247] the Second Circuit concluded that "this is that unusual case where the fairness of a trial, or at least the voir dire phase, that is usually promoted by public access is seriously at risk of being impaired unless some modest limitation on access is imposed."[248]

Judge Cabranes, dissenting, argued that the district court order was "neither justified by the circumstances of this case nor narrowly tailored to avoid trenching upon the public's First Amendment interest in an open trial."[249] The controversy surrounding Don King, according to Judge Cabranes, did not distinguish the case: "Were mere notoriety to be deemed a sufficient basis for courtroom closure, the broad presumption of openness established by the Supreme Court in *Press Enterprise I* would soon lose all force."[250]

These decisions, however, appear to be somewhat anomalous, reflecting a more tolerant view toward closure than *Press-Enterprise I* contemplates. In these cases, the courts credited a relationship between publicity and potential juror prejudice that most other cases have rejected. Moreover, they appear to assume

---

suggested in *Press-Enterprise I*, was rejected since raising the issue in the presence of the press might nevertheless chill the witness' response. See United States v. King, 26 MEDIA L. REP. (BNA) 1464, 1470 (S.D.N.Y.), *aff'd*, 140 F.3d 76 (2d Cir. 1998). The Second Circuit agreed:

> It is one thing to oblige jurors to state in public that they prefer a closed door session to identify sensitive matters elicited by a questionnaire. It is quite a different matter to expect them to acknowledge in public that their own candor will be inhibited by questioning in public.

140 F.3d at 82. Anonymity was also rejected by the trial court as unworkable because of the presence of the press and the concern that it "might well convey a sense of danger entirely inappropriate to the present case." *Id.*

244. See 140 F.3d at 80.
245. *Id.* at 81.
246. See *id.* at 82.
247. See *id.* at 84 (citing Ayala v. Speckard, 131 F.3d 62, 70 (2d Cir. 1997)).
248. 140 F.3d at 83.
249. *Id.* at 84 (Cabranes, J., dissenting).
250. *Id.* at 84-85. See *id.* at 85 ("Indeed, it is precisely in those cases involving controversial or notorious defendants that the public — and its media proxies — are likely to take an interest in criminal proceedings.").

that closure will promote candid responses from potential jurors, whereas most other courts have concluded that public access ensures the quality of testimony and the proper functioning of the judicial process. Finally, the context in which these cases arose would appear to suggest the importance of public access to all phases of the proceedings, including jury selection.

Press-Enterprise I has promoted a general right of public access to voir dire. While *in camera* proceedings are occasionally employed to protect significant privacy interests, blanket closure of such proceedings remains rare. Similarly, fair trial concerns arising from publicity have seldom justified wholesale closure of voir dire.[251] While a trial judge may adopt reasonable administrative means of preserving order in her court, exclusion of the public and press because of administrative concerns over space and distractions are unlikely to satisfy the "overriding interest" and "narrowly-tailored means" requirements of *Press-Enterprise I*.[252] Finally, the failure of courts ordering closure of voir dire to satisfy procedural requirements such as notice, hearing, and specific fact-finding justifying closure has been held to constitute error of constitutional dimension.[253]

§ 3-1(c). Criminal Trial Proceedings.

In *Richmond Newspapers, Inc.*[254] and *Globe Newspaper Co.*,[255] the Supreme Court recognized a First Amendment-based right of access to criminal trials. With few exceptions, such as bench or "in chambers" conferences,[256] the closure

---

251. See, e.g., Memphis Publ'g Co. v. Burnett, 871 S.W.2d 359 (Ark. 1994) ("The trial court was in error in excluding the public and Memphis Publishing from voir dire in this trial.").

252. See Williams v. Florida, 736 So. 2d 699 (Fla. App. 1999) (holding that it was plain error for trial court to refuse to allow any members of public, including defendant's family, to attend voir dire); In re Closure of Jury Voir Dire, 516 N.W.2d 514 (Mich. App. 1994) ("It is clear that any number of simple solutions might have been considered to accommodate legitimate concerns of the press with regard to the right of access to the jury selection process."); In re Times-World Corp., 373 S.E.2d 474, 478 (Va. App. 1988) (inconvenience to the court does not "rise to the level of an 'overriding interest' that outweighs the first amendment right of public access").

253. See, e.g., In re Gannett River States Publ'g Corp., 630 So. 2d 351, 353 (Miss. 1994) (trial court failed to provide "procedural safeguards," including notice and preclosure hearing, which "are a condition precedent to closure;" there were "no factual findings supporting the trial court's decision" to conduct individual sequestered voir dire outside courtroom).

254. See Chap. 2-2(c) *supra*.

255. See Chap 2-2(d) *supra*.

256. See Globe Newspaper Co. v. Superior Ct., 457 U.S. at 609 n.25 (limitation on access based on court's discretion "is consistent with the traditional authority of trial judges to conduct *in camera* conferences"); Richmond Newspapers, Inc. v. Virginia, 448 U.S. at 597 n.23 (Brennan, J., concurring) ("[W]hen engaging in interchanges at the bench, the trial judge is not required to allow public or press intrusion upon the huddle. Nor does this opinion intimate that judges are restricted in their ability to conduct conferences in chambers, inasmuch as such conferences are distinct from trial proceedings."); United States v. Valenti, 987 F.2d 708, 714 (11th Cir. 1993) ("we find no

of trial proceedings is presumptively unconstitutional.[257] In *Globe Newspaper Co.*, the Court required that the party seeking closure demonstrate that it is necessary to serve a compelling state interest, and the closure order must be narrowly tailored to serve that interest.[258] While subsequent decisions have occasionally articulated different formulations, the demand for record findings setting forth a need for closure to serve overriding interests has persisted.

In *Globe Newspaper Co.*, the Court acknowledged that psychological harm to a minor victim of sexual assault can constitute a sufficiently compelling interest to justify closure during her testimony.[259] Subsequently, in *Massachusetts v. Martin*,[260] the Massachusetts Supreme Judicial Court disapproved the closure, over the defendant's objections, of the trial testimony of a thirteen-year-old rape victim. The trial judge ordered closure "[i]n view of the nature of the allegations here and the desire" of the alleged victim.[261] The appellate court concluded that the closure order was narrowly drawn, since it lasted only for the duration of the complainant's testimony, did not exclude the defendant's close relatives and

---

error in the district court's exercise of its traditional authority to conduct closed bench conferences"); United States v. Edwards, 823 F.2d 111, 117 (5th Cir. 1987), *cert. denied*, 485 U.S. 934 (1988) ("[F]or first amendment purposes, no presumption of openness attaches to proceedings involving the midtrial questioning of jurors."); United States v. Gurney, 558 F.2d 1202, 1210 (5th Cir. 1977), *cert. denied*, 435 U.S. 968 (1978) ("Bench conferences between judge and counsel outside of public hearing are an established practice . . . and protection of their privacy is generally within the court's discretion. . . . [S]uch conferences are an integral part of the internal management of a trial, and screening them from access by the press is well within a trial judge's broad discretion."); United States v. Moody, 746 F. Supp. 1090, 1093 (M.D. Ga. 1990) ("[t]he press has no First Amendment right of access to communications between counsel and the court which take place at the bench or in chambers"). However, if the conference involves evidentiary matters that are integral to the trial or pretrial proceeding, the First Amendment-based right of access may apply. See United States v. Smith, 787 F.2d 111, 115 (3d Cir. 1986) (holding common law right of access attaches to transcripts of sidebar or chambers conferences in which evidentiary matters are adjudicated).

257. In *United States v. McVeigh*, 106 F.3d 325, 335-36 (10th Cir. 1996), the court rejected a First Amendment-based right of access to criminal proceedings by victim-impact witnesses. As a result of the trial court's order, a victim observing the trial might be excluded from giving impact testimony. The Tenth Circuit held that the "structural interests" served by a right of public access did not require "the personal attendance of any particular individual." *Id.* at 336. The trial court order had not "deprived the public at large direct or indirect access to the trial process." *Id.*

258. 457 U.S. at 607.

259. See *id.* at 607-08 ("[I]t is clear that the circumstances of the particular case may affect the significance of the interest."). The Court indicated that the trial judge must consider the age, maturity, and desires of the complainant, the nature of the alleged crime, and the interests of the complainant's parents and relatives. See *id.* The focus must be on the "incremental injury suffered by testifying in the presence of the press and the general public." *Id.* at 607 n.19.

260. 629 N.E.2d 297 (Mass. 1994).

261. *Id.* at 300 n.4. The statute had been interpreted to require a finding of psychological harm or trauma to the minor witness. See *id.* at 302.

§ 3-1(c)   ACCESS TO JUDICIAL PROCEEDINGS: THE LOWER COURTS   § 3-1(c)

friends,[262] and there were no reasonable alternatives to closure.[263] Nevertheless, the trial court's findings were deficient because no compelling interest requiring closure was demonstrated with respect to this particular witness. While the Commonwealth had alleged that the minor experienced difficulty discussing the sexual assault, and that "it would be overwhelming for her to properly testify," these prosecutorial assertions were deemed insufficient and the trial judge had made no particularized findings to facilitate meaningful appellate review.[264] In future cases, the Supreme Judicial Court indicated:

> Counsel may present the following types of evidence to support a finding of a risk of harm: expert psychological evidence; testimony of the complainant; testimony of a victim-witness advocate who is familiar with the witness; or the testimony of a parent, guardian, or other family member. This list, of course, is not exhaustive, and the judge's personal observations of the witness may also be valuable.[265]

In an effort to reconcile the privacy interest of a minor with the First Amendment interest in public access, some courts have afforded conditional access during the testimony of minor victims of sexual assault. In *Austin Daily Herald v. Mork*,[266] for example, the trial judge allowed press representatives, but not the public, access to testimony of juvenile victims regarding their past records, provided that the press agreed not to reveal the names of the minors or information regarding the juvenile records of the minor victims and witnesses. While expressing concern over the "selective access" contemplated by the trial court order, a Minnesota appellate court rejected the suggestion that the restriction constituted an invalid prior restraint.[267] The trial judge had made specific findings that closure was necessary to serve a compelling interest, safeguarding the physical and psychological welfare of minor victims.[268] Indeed, the trial judge had focused on the incremental harm to the minors that would result from allowing their testimony to be given in open court and had made specific

---

262. See *id.* at 302, 303 (citing Massachusetts v. Marshall, 253 N.E.2d 333 (Mass. 1969)).
263. See 629 N.E. 2d at 302.
264. See *id.* at 302-03 ("assertions of counsel are insufficient to support an order for closure"). See also People v. Garrett, 637 N.E.2d 615, 617 (Ill. App. 1994) ("The record reveals that the court did not give due consideration to the complainant's psychological maturity and understanding. . . . Moreover, the court did not inquire as to why or to what degree the complainant felt uncomfortable at the presence of defendant's parents.").
265. 629 N.E.2d at 302.
266. 507 N.W.2d 854 (Minn. App. 1993).
267. *Id.* at 856-57. See *id.* at 857 ("By permitting some reporting while prohibiting other reporting, the trial court in effect parcels out news to the press and the public.").
268. See *id.* at 857 ("If the record does not include findings that closure is necessary to protect the witnesses, a restrictive order is invalid.").

findings that the juveniles would suffer embarrassment and fright and would be traumatized further if required to testify in a public forum.[269]

In *United States v. Jacobson*,[270] the government sought to close a trial during the testimony of eleven persons who were parents of children allegedly fathered by the defendant doctor when he artificially inseminated women patients with his own sperm. The trial court acknowledged "that keeping secret the true identity of the parents and their children is necessitated by the compelling and overriding governmental interest in the psychological health and welfare of the children involved in this matter,"[271] but nevertheless concluded that closure of the courtroom was not a narrowly tailored means to achieve that end. In the court's view, the government failed to meet its burden of showing the inadequacy of alternatives to closure, such as the use of pseudonyms, careful preparation and questioning of the parent witnesses to avoid disclosure, the exclusion of sketch artists, and redacting of all identifying judicial records.[272]

The threat of physical harm can also provide a compelling interest justifying closure when other alternatives are found inadequate. Thus, in *United States v. Raffoul*,[273] the Third Circuit characterized the threat of death to defendant's family from portions of his trial testimony as "the best example one could imagine of an overriding interest."[274] In addition, the court questioned the adequacy of alternatives to closure in protecting defendant's family from harm.[275] Nevertheless, the court held that the trial judge had failed to provide timely notice of the proposed closure and an opportunity to be heard,[276] so it

---

269. See *id*. See also People v. Leggans, 625 N.E.2d 1133, 1137 (Ill. App. 1993) (exclusion of the public during minor victim's testimony held not to violate the defendant's Sixth Amendment right to a public trial even though trial judge failed to make a "formal declaration of the reasons for closing the courtroom" because the record indicated need to protect minor victims).
270. 785 F. Supp. 563 (E.D. Va. 1992).
271. *Id*. at 568.
272. See *id*. at 568-69.
273. 826 F.2d 218 (3d Cir. 1987). The defendant, claiming duress in defense to a charge of importing heroin, refused to identify persons in Lebanon responsible for drug trafficking because of fear for his family. See *id*. at 221.
274. *Id*. at 226.
275. See *id*.
276. See *id*. at 226:

> In summary, the procedure to be followed in cases where a closure motion is made during a criminal trial in progress is as follows: All motions for closure should be docketed immediately. Motions for closure that are made outside the public's hearing shall also be renewed in open court before being acted upon and the courtroom shall not be closed except upon the court's order. The trial proceedings shall be interrupted to allow those actually present and objecting to removal to be heard before a closure order is entered. Interested persons must be granted a hearing within a reasonable time upon motion for access to sealed transcripts of the closed proceeding. Before closing the courtroom, the court must consider alternatives to closure and state on the record its reasons for rejecting them.

remanded the case for a hearing to determine if the transcript of the closed proceeding should be unsealed.[277]

Protecting the safety of an undercover agent can also constitute a compelling interest. But, in *People v. Martinez*,[278] the New York Court of Appeals, applying the *Press-Enterprise I* standard,[279] held that closing the trial during an undercover officer's testimony violated the defendant's Sixth Amendment right to a public trial set forth in *Waller v. Georgia*.[280] The court asserted that closure requires particularized findings of danger. Where, as in the case before the court, closure was justified by little more than the officer's own assertion that he feared for his safety, the requisite showing had not been made.[281] Nevertheless, in a companion case, *People v. Pearson*,[282] a particularized factual showing justifying closure was made. In *Pearson*, the officer was shown to be engaged in an ongoing undercover investigation in a particular area near the courthouse such that testimony in open court might "blow" her cover and endanger her life.[283] While the trial court had not considered certain possible alternatives to closure, in light of the referenced record findings, the court held that this omission did not rise to the level of reversible error.[284]

The Second Circuit, in contrast, initially rejected the position of the New York state courts on the need for trial courts *sua sponte* to consider alternatives

---

277. See *id.* at 226-27. In *Williams v. Indiana*, 690 N.E.2d 162 (Ind. 1997), the Indiana Supreme Court criticized requirements imposed by a trial judge that spectators walk through metal detectors and provide identification prior to entering the courtroom, "[b]ecause the court did not provide the reasons for its decision to authorize the procedures, and because the record does not clearly substantiate the need for these additional precautions." *Id.* at 170. The court cited *Globe Newspaper Co.*, 457 U.S. at 596, for the proposition that even a slight burden such as identification may hinder the public's willingness to attend an open trial and diminish the free flow of ideas, but held that the trial court's requirements did not constitute reversible error because the public was not excluded from the courtroom. See 690 N.E.2d at 169-70.

278. 624 N.E.2d 1027 (N.Y. 1993).

279. 464 U.S. 501 (1984).

280. 467 U.S. 39 (1984). See Note, *Closing the Courtroom for Undercover Police Witnesses: New York Must Adopt a Consistent Standard*, 4 J.L. & POL'Y 659, 717 (1996) (urging adoption of *Waller v. Georgia* standard).

281. 624 N.E.2d at 1031. The court noted that there was no reference to associates of the defendant or targets of investigation likely to be present at the trial or threats that had been received. "Indeed, no link was made, or even attempted, between the officer's fear for his safety throughout the Bronx area and open-court testimony in his buy-and-bust case." *Id.* A new trial was ordered. See *id.* at 1032.

282. 624 N.E.2d 1027 (N.Y. 1993).

283. *Id.* at 1029, 1031. See People v. C.M., 614 N.Y.S.2d 491 (Sup. Ct. 1994); People v. Hinton, 286 N.E.2d 265, 267 (N.Y. 1972), *cert. denied*, 410 U.S. 911 (1973) (affirming closure "to shield the identity of the witness from the public and to preserve not only (his) her future usefulness but also (his) her life").

284. 624 N.E.2d at 1031-32. The court suggested that admittance to the courtroom might have been controlled or the undercover officer could have testified from behind a screen. *Id.*

to closure. In *Ayala v. Speckard*,[285] the Second Circuit reaffirmed an earlier holding that the defendant's Sixth Amendment rights were violated by closure of his trial during the testimony of an undercover police officer to whom he allegedly sold crack cocaine. While the safety of law enforcement personnel and the government's interest in minimizing the risk to undercover agents constituted "overriding" interests, the Second Circuit held that the trial court had failed to consider alternatives to closure. "Because the First Amendment requires consideration of less restrictive alternatives even absent a suggestion of such alternatives, and because the Sixth Amendment is at least as protective of the public trial as the First Amendment, the Sixth Amendment also does not require the party seeking to keep the courtroom open to suggest alternatives to full closure."[286]

Subsequently, the state courts either distinguished or rejected the view of the federal courts in *Ayala* that alternatives be considered.[287] Different panels of the Second Circuit, while often critical of *Ayala I*, apparently felt bound to adhere to it.[288] In another *Ayala* appeal,[289] the Second Circuit, in an *en banc* review of three unrelated cases,[290] responded to the different approaches of the federal courts and the New York state courts on the issue of excluding the press and public during the testimony of an undercover police officer. The court concluded that, in all three cases, "the prosecution sufficiently justified the courtroom closure, and that a trial judge, having already considered closure during the testimony of one witness as an alternative to complete closure, is not required to

---

285. 102 F.2d 649 (2d Cir. 1996) (*Ayala I*).
286. *Id.* at 653.
287. See People v. Ayala, 685 N.E.2d 492 (N.Y.), *cert. denied*, 118 S. Ct. 574 (1997) (upholding closure order where it had been shown that open-court testimony by undercover officer would jeopardize his safety and effectiveness and trial court implicitly determined that no lesser alternative to closure would be effective); People v. Rivera, 654 N.Y.S.2d 771 (App. Div. 1997) (closure warranted even under *Ayala* guidelines); People v. Ford, 654 N.Y.S.2d 2 (App. Div. 1997) (rejecting *Ayala* in upholding closure); People v. Brown, 653 N.Y.S.2d 544 (App. Div. 1997) (same); People v. Pepe, 653 N.Y.S.2d 101 (App. Div. 1997) (same).
288. See Okonkwo v. Lacy, 104 F.3d 21, 26 (2d Cir. 1997) ("[I]t is incumbent upon trial judges to consider reasonable alternatives before closing the courtroom."); Pearson v. James, 105 F.3d 828 (2d Cir. 1997) (two judges concurred to indicate their disagreement with *Ayala*).
289. Ayala v. Speckard, 131 F.3d 62 (2d Cir. 1997), *cert. denied*, 118 S. Ct. 2380 (1998) (en banc). Seven judges joined Judge Newman's opinion for the court. Two judges concurred in the judgment but declined to reach the merits since the proposed rule was "new" and could not be applied on collateral review. Three judges dissented, arguing that *Waller* requires a trial judge *sua sponte* to consider alternatives to closure. See *id.* at 75 (Parker, J., dissenting).
290. See Ayala v. Speckard, 102 F.3d 649 (2d Cir. 1996); Okonkwo v. Lacy, 104 F.3d 21 (2d Cir. 1997); Pearson v. James, 105 F.3d 828 (2d Cir. 1997).

consider *sua sponte* further alternatives to closure but has to consider only further alternatives suggested by the parties."[291]

Judge Newman, writing for the court, invoked substantive standards drawn from both the Sixth and the First Amendments.[292] Whether an interest is sufficiently "overriding" to support closure is to be determined in light of the degree of closure requested.[293] In each of the three cases, the trial judge properly determined that the "extremely substantial interest" in the continued effectiveness of an undercover officer would be "seriously prejudiced" by requiring testimony in open court.[294]

The *Ayala* court avoided the broad question of whether a trial judge is constitutionally required to consider alternatives *sua sponte* before ordering complete closure.[295] The cases before the Court involved only partial closure during the testimony of a single witness and the judge's failure *sua sponte* to consider alternatives to such partial closure. Since a transcript was available, and no alternatives were suggested by the parties, the court held that applicable constitutional standards had been satisfied, at least in the absence of a blanket closure order.[296] The Second Circuit's opinion appears to bring the federal rule closer to the approach taken by New York's state courts.[297]

---

291. *Ayala*, at 64; see *id.* at 71 ("Whether or not a *sua sponte* obligation exists to consider alternatives to complete closure, we see nothing in the First Amendment cases or in *Waller* to indicate that once a trial judge has determined that limited closure is warranted as an alternative to complete closure, the judge must *sua sponte* consider further alternatives to the alternative deemed appropriate. At that point, it becomes the obligation of the party objecting to the trial court's proposal to urge consideration of any further alternatives that might avoid the need for even a limited closure.").

292. See *id.* at 69 ("The explicit Sixth Amendment right of the accused is complemented by an implicit, 'qualified' First Amendment right of the press and the public of access to a criminal trial.").

293. See *id.* at 70 ("We believe the sensible course is for the trial judge to recognize that open trials are strongly favored, to require persuasive evidence of serious risk to an important interest in ordering any closure, and to realize that the more extensive is the closure requested, the greater must be the gravity of the required interest and the likelihood of risk to that interest.").

294. *Id.* at 72.

295. See *id.* at 70 ("Some, but not all, members of the majority are of the view that *Waller* appears to indicate that alternatives to complete closure are what the Court required trial judges to consider *sua sponte* when First Amendment closure standards are applied in the Sixth Amendment context.").

296. See *id.* at 72-73. The court noted that alternatives such as disguising the officer or using screens posed substantial risks to the defendant's fair trial rights. See *id.* at 71-72.

297. See also Mason v. Schriver, 14 F. Supp. 2d 321, 324-25 (S.D.N.Y. 1998) (after en banc decision in *Ayala*, court granted a writ of habeas corpus based on defendant's Sixth Amendment right to a public trial, which challenged closure of the courtroom during the testimony of two undercover detectives responsible for defendant's arrest, because the trial judge failed to make specific record findings to support closure). On the New York and Second Circuit cases closing courtrooms during undercover testimony, see Jonakait, *Secret Testimony and Public Trials in New York*, 42 N.Y.L. SCH. L. REV. 407 (1998) ("the courts have not been correctly balancing the proper

As these cases demonstrate, even when the interest asserted in support of closing a trial is compelling or overriding in the abstract, the critical issue is whether there is a need for closure in the particular context. That issue ultimately reduces itself to a fact-intensive assessment, including consideration of the availability of alternatives to closure. Thus, although the Supreme Court has stated that "[n]o right ranks higher than the right of the accused to a fair trial,"[298] to justify closure of trial proceedings on that basis, there must be specific findings that there is a "substantial probability that the defendant's right to a fair trial will be prejudiced by publicity that closure would prevent" and that reasonable alternatives to closure would be inadequate to ensure a fair trial.[299] At the trial stage of criminal proceedings, where the jury has been chosen and sequestration is an available alternative to closure, this standard is extremely difficult to satisfy.[300] Indeed, closure orders of *pretrial* proceedings are often argued to be "narrowly tailored" because the order is limited in duration to the time until the jury is selected and sequestered, when the danger of prejudicial publicity is perceived as less serious.[301]

§ 3-1(d). Post-Trial Proceedings.

The First Amendment-based right of public access extends as well to post-trial criminal proceedings. In *United States v. Simone*,[302] a trial court granted a motion by Robert Simone who had been convicted of racketeering and extortion for an *in camera* examination into alleged jury misconduct during his trial. The court of appeals, however, held "that the First Amendment right of access attaches to post-trial hearings to investigate jury misconduct."[303]

---

interests in determining whether closures are appropriate"); Note, *Closing the Court Room for the Testimony of Undercover Officers: The En Banc Rehearing in* Ayala v. Speckard, Okonkwo v. Lacy *and* Pearson v. James, 31 CONN. L. REV. 243 (1998).

298. *Press-Enterprise I*, 464 U.S. at 508. See generally Chap 2-1 *supra*.

299. *Press-Enterprise II*, 478 U.S. at 14.

300. See In re Daily Item, 456 A.2d 580, 589 (Pa. Super. 1983) (Beck, J., concurring) ("Since an already assembled jury can, if necessary, be sequestered to prevent prejudicial publicity, there is minimal need to request closure of the trial itself.").

301. See, e.g., Poughkeepsie Newspapers, Inc. v. Rosenblatt, 459 N.Y.S.2d 857, 859 (App. Div. 1983), *aff'd* 463 N.E.2d 1222 (N.Y. 1984) (permitting closure of evidentiary hearing, in part, because the judge "did not exclude the public from the trial itself, but only from a brief hearing to determine the admissibility of certain evidence.").

302. 14 F.3d 833 (3d Cir. 1994). In a case in which allegations of jury improprieties had been widely publicized, the trial court justified closure because "the presence of the press in the proceedings will be coercive and will interfere with the expressions of candor of the jurors." *Id.* at 836. In the trial court's view, only the government and defense had an interest in the proceeding; "[t]he public has no outcome interest." *Id.*

303. *Id.* at 840. See Ex parte Greenville News, 482 S.E.2d 556, 558 (S.C. 1997) (holding that presumption of openness applies to post-trial hearings on alleged juror misconduct and requiring

The Third Circuit acknowledged that trial judges have traditionally enjoyed broad discretion in dealing with jury misconduct and that most post-trial proceedings concerning jury misbehavior had been conducted *in camera*.[304] Nevertheless, in his opinion for the court, Judge Roth asserted that traditional recognition of trial court discretion did not negate a First Amendment-based right of access,[305] especially in the absence of an established tradition of closed proceedings.[306] In short, the court concluded, inquiry into "experience" provided limited guidance.[307]

Examining the value of public access to the functioning of post-trial proceedings generally, the court could "see no reason to suspect that post-trial proceedings as a general category are any different with respect to the First Amendment right of access than the other components of a criminal trial."[308] Thus, the court found that all of the societal interests served by public access identified in *Richmond Newspapers, Inc.* are fully applicable to a post-trial inquiry into jury misconduct:

> [P]ublic access to such proceedings helps provide the public with the assurance that the system is fair to all concerned. Furthermore, cases in which there are allegations of jury misconduct probably also tend to be those cases in which the public is more likely to be suspicious of other corrupt practices. Opening the judicial process to public scrutiny discourages such practices and assures the public of the integrity of the participants in the system. Finally, public access to such proceedings will in many cases discourage perjury. Members of the public who might be able to contradict the perjured testimony of jurors will not be

---

release of transcript of closed hearing and unsealing of record with redaction of jurors' names and identifying information).

304. See *id.* at 838.

305. See *id.* ("Thus the mere existence of discretion does not, without more, mean that that discretion is not subject to the First Amendment right of access.").

306. See *id.* ("Given the overwhelming historical support for access in other phases of the criminal process, we are reluctant to presume that the opposite rule applies in this case in the absence of a distinct tradition to the contrary.").

307. See *id.* at 840 ("Though experience provides little guidance, logic counsels that access to these proceedings will in general have a positive effect."). See also Note, *Behind the Gray Door:* Williams, *Secrecy, and the Federal Grand Jury*, 69 N.Y.U. L. REV. 563, 613 (1994).

308. 14 F.3d at 839. The court quoted from the opinion of then-Judge Kennedy in *CBS Inc. v. United States District Court*, 765 F.2d 823, 825 (9th Cir. 1985), that there is "no principled basis for affording greater confidentiality to post-trial documents and proceedings than is given to pre-trial matters." See 14 F.3d at 839.

able to learn of the perjury unless the public and press are given access to these proceedings.[309]

The *Simone* court also considered whether the closure order was narrowly tailored and essential to serve an overriding interest.[310] Such an inquiry demanded an "independent consideration of the district court's order and the factual findings inferred from the evidence before it."[311] The court's independent review led it to reject the trial court's generic concern with assuring the veracity of juror testimony. There was no empirical support for claiming that closure promoted more truthful testimony and "it proved too much in that it could be used in favor of almost any limitation on access."[312] Similarly, the trial court's concern that jurors might inadvertently reveal information about their deliberative process could be dealt with by precise instructions.[313] Thus, even if there were an overriding interest, the trial court had failed to provide adequate findings to demonstrate that closure was necessary.[314]

Sentencing hearings have also been held to be presumptively open to the public under the First Amendment. In *In re Washington Post Co.*,[315] the Fourth Circuit characterized sentencing hearings as a part of the criminal trial process

---

309. 14 F.3d at 839. But cf. United States v. Edwards, 823 F.2d 111 (5th Cir. 1987), *cert. denied*, 485 U.S. 934 (1988) (approving closure of midtrial voir dire of jury amidst allegation of juror misconduct).

310. See *id.* at 840.

311. *Id.* at 837. The court engaged in a review "substantially broader than that for abuse of discretion." *Id.* While emphasis on independent appellate review of the record is a vital ingredient of the determination of actual malice in defamation cases, courts seldom emphasize it in the access context. Given the First Amendment issues involved, however, such independent appellate review would appear appropriate. See generally Dienes, *Appellate Review of Actual Malice*, 10 COMM. LAW 3 (Spring 1992); Dienes & Levine, *Implied Libel, Defamatory Meaning and State of Mind: The Promise of* New York Times v. Sullivan, 78 IOWA L. REV. 237, 259-63 (1993).

312. 14 F.3d at 840. See Chap. 2-2(d) *supra*.

313. See 14 F.3d at 840.

314. See *id*. The fact that a transcript would be made available after the closed hearing was viewed by the court as irrelevant and as unduly minimizing the value of openness itself. See *id.* at 841 (quoting In re Charlotte Observer, 882 F.2d 850, 856 (4th Cir. 1989)). "Furthermore, a transcript is not the equivalent of presence at proceedings; it does not reflect the numerous verbal and nonverbal cues that aid in the interpretation of meaning." 14 F.3d at 841 (citing Publicker Indus., Inc. v. Cohen, 733 F.2d 1059, 1072 (3d Cir. 1984); In re Iowa Freedom of Info. Council, 724 F.2d 658, 662-63 (8th Cir. 1983)). See also Times Publishing Co. v. Florida, 718 So. 2d 1246 (Fla. App. 1998) (reversing order closing post-conviction proceedings because the trial judge made no record findings to justify closure).

315. 807 F.2d 383 (4th Cir. 1986). See also Miami Herald Publ'g Co. v. Florida, 363 So. 2d 603, 605 (Fla. App. 1978) ("We first hold that the public's right to be informed continues beyond the trial itself and also applies to sentencing proceedings.").

— "It clearly amounts to the culmination of the trial."[316] Even apart from its relation to the criminal trial, sentencing hearings are as integral a part of the criminal prosecution as other proceedings to which the First Amendment-based right of access had been extended.[317]

Historical and functional considerations were also cited in *In re Washington Post Co.* to support extending the access right. As for tradition, "sentencings have historically been open to the public."[318] Turning to function, the court reasoned that "public access serves the important function of discouraging either the prosecutor or the court from engaging in arbitrary or wrongful conduct."[319] Citing similar historical and functional considerations, the Ninth Circuit could also "find no principled basis for affording greater confidentiality to post-trial documents and proceedings," such as sentencing, "than is given to pretrial matters."[320]

Like other criminal proceedings, however, the sentencing hearing is only presumptively open. A showing of a substantial probability that a compelling interest will be impaired absent closure and that no reasonable alternatives are available can justify a narrow closure order.[321] While embarrassment or exposure of the defendant's family to details of his crime would almost certainly fail this test, a showing that public access would endanger a person's life or an ongoing criminal investigation may be sufficient to justify closure in a given case.[322] In one sentence reduction hearing, the court held that the need for public under-

---

316. 807 F.2d at 389. See Palm Beach Newspapers, Inc. v. Cook, 434 So. 2d 355, 358 (Fla. App. 1983) ("sentencing is a part of the criminal trial process of which the public has the right to be informed").

317. See 807 F.2d at 389.

318. *Id.* See United States v. Byrd, 812 F. Supp. 76, 78 (D.S.C. 1993) ("sentencing has traditionally been an open part of the criminal process").

319. See 807 F.2d at 389.

320. CBS Inc. v. United States Dist. Ct., 765 F.2d 823, 824 (9th Cir. 1985) (historical and functional considerations "apply with as much force to post conviction proceedings as to the trial itself").

321. See In re Washington Post Co., 807 F.2d at 392. Some Florida courts have applied a standard for closure resembling the clear and present danger test. In addition to requiring findings that closure would be effective and that no reasonable alternatives would suffice, these courts have demanded findings that "[c]losure is necessary to prevent a serious and imminent threat to the administration of justice." Palm Beach Newspapers, Inc. v. Cook, 434 So. 2d at 357; see Miami Herald Publ'g Co. v. Florida, 363 So. 2d at 606.

322. See Miami Herald Publ'g Co. v. Florida, 363 So. 2d at 606 (citing "cogent and compelling reasons indicating imminent peril to the safety of witnesses"). In *Palm Beach Newspapers, Inc. v. Cook*, 434 So. 2d at 358-60, the court discussed the type of evidence required to support closure, such as testimony demonstrating work with law enforcement over time, corroboration by law enforcement personal, testimony on how lives would be endangered by public access and about witnesses reluctant to testify because of their fear.

standing of the corrections process overrode the law enforcement interest claimed to justify the sealing of post-trial documents.[323]

The First Amendment-based right of access has similarly been applied to other post-trial proceedings.[324] In each such instance, a similar fact-intensive examination under a heightened standard of judicial scrutiny has been undertaken to determine if closure is justified. In such contexts as well, procedural requirements of notice, hearing, and specific record findings have also been required.[325]

§ 3-1(e). Military Courts.

A qualified First Amendment-based right of public access applies to trials by courts-martial.[326] The Manual for Courts-Martial provides that "courts-martial shall be open to the public."[327] Such openness "reduces the chance of arbitrary

---

323. See CBS Inc. v. United States Dist. Ct., 765 F.2d at 826 ("The penal structure is the least visible, least understood, least effective part of the justice system, and each such failure is consequent from the others. Public examination, study, and comment is essential if the corrections process is to improve. Those objectives are disserved if the government conceals its position on so critical a matter as the modification of a felony sentence in a celebrated case.").

324. See, e.g., Newman v. Graddick, 696 F.2d 796, 801-02 (11th Cir. 1983) (indicating that the First Amendment-based right of access applies to post-trial proceedings in civil suits that "pertain to the release or incarceration of prisoners and conditions of their confinement."); Globe Newspaper Co. v. Massachusetts, 556 N.E.2d 356, 360 (Mass. 1990) (applying the First Amendment-based right of access to post-verdict questioning of jurors); Mankato Free Press v. Dempsey, 581 N.W.2d 311, 312 (Minn. 1998) (requiring lower court to open remainder of hearing and to furnish media with transcripts of already-completed portion of hearing to determine whether jurors were aware that defendant was wearing a leg restraint during his murder trial and whether that awareness deprived him of his right to a fair trial, because the trial court record was insufficient to support closure under *Press-Enterprise I*); Montana ex rel. Great Falls Tribune Co v. Montana Eighth Judicial Dist. Ct., 777 P.2d 345, 346 (Mont. 1989) (probation revocation hearings); Gannett Co. v. Mark, 387 N.Y.S.2d 336, 338-39 (App. Div. 1976) (motions to set aside guilty verdict); Houston Chronicle Publ'g Co. v. McMaster, 598 S.W.2d 864, 867 (Tex. Crim. App. 1980) (post-conviction habeas corpus hearings). But see United States v. Smith, 123 F.3d 140, 150 (3d Cir. 1997) (holding there is no First Amendment-based or common law right of access to hearing on whether government had violated FED. R. CRIM. P. 6(e) in publicly disclosing a presentencing memorandum containing grand jury materials).

325. See, e.g., In re Washington Post Co., 807 F.2d at 390-92 (procedural requirements not complied with); Palm Beach Newspapers, Inc. v. Cook, 434 So. 2d at 359 (holding that "the notice and hearings on the motion to prohibit public access was procedurally defective" but that continued sealing of the record was substantively justified); Miami Herald Publ'g Co. v. Florida, 363 So. 2d at 606-07 (error to hold access hearing after closed proceedings but sealing record was justified; remanded to determine if closure order could now be modified).

326. See United States v. Scott, 48 M.J. 663, 665 (Army Crim. App. 1998) ("This [constitutional] right of public access to criminal trials applies with equal validity to trials by courts martial.").

327. Rule for Courts-Martial 806(a).

or capricious decision and enhances public confidence in the court-martial process."[328]

The United States Army Court of Criminal Appeals held, in *United States v. Anderson*,[329] that "absent national security concerns or other adequate justification clearly set forth on the record, trials in the United States military justice system are to be open to the public."[330] The military courts have held that maintaining public confidence in the courts-martial[331] and promoting accurate fact-finding require that military courts be presumptively open.[332] While the trial judge in *Anderson* abused her discretion by closing the court-martial without providing record justification, the court held there was no prejudice to the defendant that required relief.[333]

---

328. *Id.* at 806(b), discussion.

329. 46 M.J. 728 (Army Crim. App. 1997).

330. *Id.* at 729. See United States v. Hood, ARMY 9401841 (Army Crim. App. Feb. 20, 1996) (unpublished), *petition denied*, 45 M.J. 15 (1996) (published in Appendix to *Anderson*) (courts-martial are open to public and can be closed only if *Press-Enterprise* standards are met); San Antonio Express-News v. Morrow, 44 M.J. 706 (Air Force Crim. App. 1996) (while holding that Article 32 pretrial investigations are "presumptively public," court rejected use of mandamus to reverse decision closing pretrial hearing in highly publicized murder trial).

In *ABC, Inc. v. Powell*, 47 M.J. 363 (C.A.A.F. 1997), the Court of Appeals for the Armed Forces granted a writ of mandamus and reversed an order closing an Article 32 hearing on charges against Sgt. Major of the Army Gene C. McKinney for various sexual offenses and obstruction of justice. The military accused has a Sixth Amendment right to an open Article 32 hearing: "absent 'cause shown that outweighs the value of openness'" there is a right to a public proceeding. *Id.* at 365. Further, "when an accused is entitled to a public hearing, the press enjoys the same right and has standing to complain if access is denied." *Id.* Citing *Globe Newspaper Co. v. Superior Court*, 457 U.S. 596 (1982), the court held that the entire proceeding had been closed "for unsubstantiated reasons." 47 M.J. at 367. The privacy interests of alleged victims and the desire to prevent court members from being tainted by outside influences were "insufficient." *Id.* Only "compelling circumstances" would justify a limit on public access. *Id.*

331. See United States v. Travers, 25 M.J. 61, 62 (C.M.A. 1987) ("[W]e believe that public confidence in matters of military justice would quickly erode if courts-martial were arbitrarily closed to the public."); United States v. Hood, *published as appendix to* United States v. Anderson, 46 M.J. 728 (Army Crim. App. 1997), at 731 ("Public scrutiny of the courts-martial 'reduces the chance of arbitrary or capricious decisions and enhances confidence in the court-martial process.'").

332. United States v. Anderson, 46 M.J. at 729 ("One aspect of the nature of an open trial forum is to ensure that testimony is subjected to public scrutiny and is thus more likely to be truthful or to be exposed as fraudulent.").

333. See *id.* See generally Kulish, *The Public's Right of Access to Pretrial Proceedings Versus the Accused's Right to a Fair Trial*, ARMY LAW., Sept. 1998, at 1 (arguing that in determining access questions in military justice proceedings, "the courts should adopt a more evenly weighted balancing test than the prevailing standards").

§ 3-2. Civil Proceedings.

§ 3-2(a). Establishing the Access Right.

The Federal Rules of Civil Procedure provide for open civil trials.[334] State legislation and court rules generally call for open civil trials as well.[335] The Supreme Court has not addressed directly whether there is a First Amendment-based right of access to civil proceedings.[336]

Individual justices have, however, indicated that historical considerations support such access rights. For example, in *Richmond Newspapers, Inc.*, Chief Justice Burger observed that "[w]hether the public has a right to attend trials of civil cases is a question not raised by this case, but we note that historically both civil and criminal trials have been presumptively open."[337] The Supreme Court's functional analysis would also appear to support extension of the First Amendment-based right of access to at least some civil proceedings.[338] While civil

---

334. See FED. R. CIV. P. 77(b) ("All trials upon the merits shall be conducted in open court and so far as convenient in a regular court room. . . ."); FED. R. CIV. P. 43(a) (providing that "the testimony of witnesses be taken orally in open court").

335. The common law has been held to provide the basis for a right of public access to civil proceedings. See, e.g., Sentinel Star Co. v. Edwards, 387 So. 2d 367, 374 (Fla. App. 1980) ("The press and public had a common law right of access to the [civil post-trial] hearing [concerning possible juror misconduct]."). State constitutions can also provide the basis for challenging closed proceedings. See, e.g., DTH Publ'g Corp. v. University of North Carolina at Chapel Hill, 496 S.E.2d 8, 13-15 (N.C. App. 1998) (affirming district court decision that university's undergraduate court that handles disciplinary matters is not a court under the open courts provision of the state constitution). But see Virmani v. Presbyterian Health Servs. Corp., 515 S.E.2d 675 (N.C. 1999) (holding that open courts provision of state constitution does not create right of access to civil hearing where confidential medical peer review committee records and materials were discussed).

336. See DTH Publ'g Corp. v. University of North Carolina at Chapel Hill, 496 S.E.2d 8, 16 (N.C. App. 1998) ("The United States Supreme Court has held that the First Amendment provides the public with a presumptive right to attend certain criminal proceedings but the Court has not yet decided whether this right extends to civil proceedings . . . . We have also not found any cases in which either the United States Supreme Court or a North Carolina Appellate Court has held that state university student court disciplinary proceedings, like those at issue here, are presumptively open to the public under the First Amendment.").

337. 448 U.S. at 580 n.17 (Burger, C.J., announcing judgment). In *Gannett Co. v. DePasquale*, 443 U.S. at 384, the Court also noted that history demonstrates "the existence of a common-law rule of open civil and criminal proceedings" and concluded that "there is no principled basis upon which a public right of access to judicial proceedings can be limited to criminal cases if the scope of the right is defined by the common law rather than the text and structure of the Constitution," *id.* at 386 n.15.

338. See 443 U.S. at 387 ("[M]any of the advantages of criminal trials are equally applicable in the civil trial context. . . . [I]n some civil cases, the public interest in access, and the salutary effect of publicity, may be as strong as or stronger than in most criminal cases."). Justice Stewart, the author of the Court's opinion in *Gannett Co.*, later asserted that "[t]he First and Fourteenth Amendments clearly give the press and the public a right of access to trials themselves, civil as well as criminal." Richmond Newspapers, Inc. v. Virginia, 448 U.S. at 599 (Stewart, J., concurring). Justice Stevens, dissenting in *Press-Enterprise II*, 478 U.S. at 27, argued that, "the logic of the

proceedings are often thought of as private disputes, many arise in the context of claims of invidious discrimination, public protest, operations of public institutions, and other issues of significant public concern. Even in purely private disputes, the public has an interest in how controversies are resolved in its courts and in the consequences of the litigation for society at large.[339] Indeed, it has been asserted that "[n]o court has expressly concluded that the first amendment does not guarantee some form of access to civil trials."[340]

In *Newman v. Graddick*,[341] decided shortly after *Richmond Newspapers, Inc.* and *Globe Newspaper Co.*, the Eleventh Circuit did not expressly extend the access right to civil proceedings, but the constitutional implications of its opinion suggested as much. The trial court had closed various proceedings in a class action involving unconstitutional overcrowding of Alabama prisons. The court of appeals, however, could find no difference between the value of public access in this litigation and the public interest in access to criminal proceedings. "We need not here decide that the presumption of openness applies to all civil trials. All we decide is that civil trials which pertain to the release or incarceration of prisoners and the conditions of their confinement are presumptively open to the press and the public."[342] Nor was the rationale for public access limited to the trial. Given the importance of pre-trial and post-trial proceedings to the outcome of the case, the court reasoned, "it would seem to defeat the purpose to provide access to the trial, but not to the enforcement proceedings."[343] Thus, the *Graddick* court invoked a "presumption of access" and applied the strict scrutiny test of *Globe Newspaper Co.* to the civil proceedings at issue.[344] The trial judge had made no specific findings justifying closure; there had been no "hearing

---

Court's access right extends beyond the confines of the criminal justice system to encompass proceedings held on the civil side of the docket."

339. See, e.g., Fenner & Koley, *Access to Judicial Proceedings: To* Richmond Newspapers *and Beyond*, 16 HARV. C.R.-C.L. L. REV. 415, 430-32 (1979); Comment, *The First Amendment Right of Access to Civil Trials After* Globe Newspaper Co. v. Superior Court, 51 U. CHI. L. REV. 286 (1984); Comment, *All Courts Shall Be Open: The Public's Right to View Judicial Proceedings and Records,* 52 TEMP. L.Q. 311, 320-33 (1979); Note, *Trial Secrecy and the First Amendment Right of Public Access to Judicial Proceedings,* 91 HARV. L. REV. 1899, 1921-23 (1978).

340. Mokhiber v. Davis, 537 A.2d 1100, 1107 (D.C. 1988).

341. 696 F.2d 796 (11th Cir. 1983).

342. *Id.* at 801.

343. *Id.*; see Hutchinson v. Luddy, 581 A.2d 578, 582 (Pa. Super. 1990) ("[t]he prevailing trend appears to indicate that pretrial proceedings are also subject to the presumption in favor of public access").

344. 696 F.2d at 802 (citing Globe Newspaper Co. v. Superior Ct., 457 U.S. 596 (1982)) ("[I]t must be shown that the denial is necessitated by a compelling governmental interest, and is narrowly tailored to that interest. . . . Less intrusive alternatives must be considered.").

after proper notice."[345] Accordingly, the trial court's order was constitutionally invalid.

The next year, in *Publicker Industries, Inc. v. Cohen*,[346] the Third Circuit expressly held that "the First Amendment does secure a right of access to civil proceedings."[347] The case arose from a trial court order closing a motions hearing in a corporate proxy battle.[348] The court of appeals determined that civil proceedings had traditionally been open to the public at common law,[349] and that functional considerations similarly supported a right of public access "inherent in the nature of our democratic form of government."[350] Thus, the court concluded:

> [P]ublic access to civil trials "enhances the quality and safeguards the integrity of the factfinding process." It "fosters an appearance of fairness," and heightens "public respect for the judicial process." It "permits the public to participate in and serve as a check upon the judicial process — an essential component in our structure of self-government." Public access to civil trials, no less than criminal trials, plays an important role in the participation and the free discussion of governmental affairs.[351]

Having established a qualified right of public access to civil proceedings, the Third Circuit considered the standards governing closure. Citing *Globe Newspaper Co.*, the court held that "[t]o limit the public's access to civil trials there

---

345. 696 F.2d at 802; see Wilson v. American Motors Corp., 759 F.2d 1568 (11th Cir. 1985) (employing a stringent standard of review without expressly recognizing a First Amendment-based right).

346. 733 F.2d 1059 (3d Cir. 1984).

347. *Id.* at 1061.

348. See *id.* at 1061-65; see also Note, Publicker Industries v. Cohen: *Public Access to Civil Proceedings and a Corporate Right to Privacy*, 80 Nw. U.L. REV. 1319 (1986); Note, *Restricting the First Amendment Right of Access to Civil Hearing and Transcripts* — Publicker Industries, Inc. v. Cohen, 58 TEMP. L.Q. 159 (1985).

349. See 733 F.2d at 1068-69.

350. *Id.* at 1069; see also Cook v. First Morris Bank, 719 A.2d 724, 728 (N.J. Super. 1998) (in granting an application by Court TV to televise a civil proceeding, the court noted: "Nothing is more inimical to the values of a democracy than secrecy in any part of government, and the judiciary is an important part of government[.] . . . The concerns of litigants must give way to the policy of openness in the judicial system, in our democratic tradition as enshrined in the United States Constitution.").

351. 733 F.2d at 1070. Similarly, the Sixth Circuit in *Brown & Williamson Tobacco Corp. v. FTC*, 710 F.2d 1165, 1178 (6th Cir. 1983), *cert. denied*, 465 U.S. 1100 (1984), concluded that "[t]he Supreme Court's analysis of the justifications for access to the criminal courtroom apply as well to the civil trial." The court explained that, "in either the civil or the criminal courtroom, secrecy insulates the participants, masking impropriety, obscuring incompetence and concealing corruption. . . . Openness in the courtroom discourages perjury and may result in witnesses coming forward with new information regardless of the type of the proceeding." *Id.* at 1179.

must be a showing that the denial serves an important governmental interest and that there is no less restrictive way to serve that governmental interest."[352] Procedurally, the court of appeals held, a trial judge must make record findings sufficiently specific to ensure meaningful appellate review.[353]

In *Publicker Industries, Inc.,* the trial court feared that an open hearing would reveal the very information claimed to be confidential before the court could determine if it should be publicly available. In such circumstances, the Third Circuit held, the trial judge should typically hold an *in camera* hearing, with counsel present and on the record. If the court then finds the interest supporting closure insufficient, a transcript should be made public.[354] Thus, while the trial court had properly excluded the public from that part of the hearing addressing whether certain information should be kept confidential, closure of the entire proceeding was not justified.[355] And although the Third Circuit did not decide whether the trial judge should have required public disclosure, the court indicated that neither the movant's economic interests nor corporate management's desire to avoid embarrassment could overcome the presumption of access.[356]

Graddick and *Publicker Industries, Inc.* were shortly followed by other federal[357] and state[358] cases recognizing a First Amendment-based right of access

---

352. 733 F.2d at 1070 (citing Globe Newspaper Co. v. Superior Ct., 457 U.S. 596 (1982)).
353. See 733 F.2d at 1070.
354. See *id.* at 1071-72.
355. See *id.* at 1072.
356. See *id.* at 1074; see also Brown & Williamson Tobacco Corp. v. FTC, 710 F.2d at 1179 ("Simply showing that the information would harm the company's reputation is not sufficient to overcome the strong common law presumption in favor of public access to court proceedings and records."); Maryland v. Cottman Transmission Sys., Inc., 542 A.2d 859, 864 (Md. Spec. App. 1988) ("Possible harm to a corporate reputation does not serve to surmount the strong presumption in favor of public access to court proceedings and records. . . . Injury to corporate or personal reputation is an inherent risk in almost every civil suit.").
357. See, e.g., Simmons v. Conger, 86 F.3d 1080 (11th Cir. 1996) (holding that district court abused its discretion in enjoining state court judges from excluding public from divorce trials absent judicial determination that public interest in a particular trial is outweighed by specifically identified and compelling interest); United States v. A.D., 28 F.3d 1353, 1356 (3d Cir. 1994) ("The First Amendment provides a right of public access in both civil and criminal cases."); Westmoreland v. CBS Inc., 752 F.2d 16, 23 (2d Cir.), *cert. denied,* 472 U.S. 1017 (1985) ("We agree with the Third Circuit in *Publicker Industries* . . . that the First Amendment does secure to the public and to the press a right of access to civil proceedings. . . ."); Doe v. Santa Fe Indep. Sch. Dist., 933 F. Supp. 647, 650 (S.D. Tex. 1996) ("This Court, in light of the Fifth Circuit's reasoning . . . and the holdings reached by other circuit courts, concludes that the right of the public to attend civil trials is grounded in the First Amendment as well as the common law.").
358. See Hutchinson v. Luddy, 581 A.2d 578, 581 (Pa. Super. 1990) (in civil action arising from alleged sexual abuse by a priest, the court stated: "In Pennsylvania, the common law, the first amendment to the United States Constitution, and the Pennsylvania Constitution all support the principle of openness."); Maryland v. Cottman Transmission Sys., Inc., 542 A.2d 859, 862-63 (Md. Spec. App. 1988) (recognizing a "presumption of openness" in a civil action by the Attorney

to civil cases. In *NBC Subsidiary (NBC-TV), Inc. v. Superior Court*,[359] for example, the California Supreme Court expressly held that there is a First Amendment-based right of public access to civil trials. In the course of determining that the trial court had failed to comply with the requirements of the California open court statute[360] when it closed portions of a civil trial held outside the jury's presence, the unanimous Court interpreted the statute in light of "relevant constitutional principles, relating to public access to court proceedings, that more recently have been articulated by the United States Supreme Court."[361]

Chief Justice George, writing for the court, reviewed the Supreme Court and lower court precedent.[362] Although the Supreme Court has never explicitly extended its First Amendment-based holdings to civil cases, the court concluded that "there is no reason to doubt that, in general, the First Amendment right of access applies to civil proceedings as well as to criminal proceedings."[363] While the public is not formally a party in civil proceedings, the court explained, it "has an interest, in all civil cases, in observing and assessing the performance of its public judicial system, and that interest strongly supports a general right of access in ordinary civil cases."[364] Indeed, the court noted, the "utilitarian values supporting public criminal trials and proceedings apply with at least equal force

---

General involving consumer fraud, the court held that the "policy considerations buttressing the public common law and First Amendment access rights apply equally to civil and criminal actions"); Virmani v. Presbyterian Health Servs. Corp., 515 S.E.2d 675, 697 (N.C. 1999) (assuming that First Amendment-based right of access applies in civil cases, but concluding that "the compelling public interest in protecting the confidentiality of the medical peer review process outweighs the right of access"). But cf. DTH Publ'g Corp. v. University of North Carolina at Chapel Hill, 496 S.E.2d 8 (N.C. App. 1998) (rejecting student newspaper's contention that closure of school disciplinary proceedings of the student undergraduate court violates First Amendment).

359. 980 P.2d 337 (Cal. 1999).

360. See CAL. CIV. PROC. CODE § 124 ("Except as provided in Section 214 of the Family Code or any other provision of law, the sitting of every court shall be public"). The court held that the trial judge's "closure order improperly denied the public and the press access to these proceedings, in violation of Section 124." 980 P.2d at 340.

361. 980 P.2d at 347. Finding the language and history of Section 124 unclear, the court concluded that "it is necessary and appropriate to consider the constitutional issue set out in our initial order granting review." *Id.*

362. See *id.* at 358 ("Although the high court opinions in *Richmond Newspapers, Globe, Press-Enterprise I* and *Press-Enterprise II* all arose in the criminal context, the reasoning of these decisions suggests that the First Amendment right of access extends beyond the context of criminal proceedings and encompasses civil proceedings as well. . . . Indeed, every lower court opinion of which we are aware that has addressed the issue of First Amendment access to civil trials and proceedings has reached the conclusion that the constitutional right of access applies as well as to criminal trials.").

363. *Id.* at 359.

364. *Id.* at 360.

in the context of ordinary civil trials and proceedings."[365] The Chief Justice specifically rejected the contention that providing a transcript at the conclusion of a civil trial is an acceptable alternative to contemporaneous access, concluding that

> [i]n light of the high court case law and its progeny . . . in general, the First Amendment provides a right of access to ordinary civil trials and proceedings, constitutional standards governing closure of trial proceedings apply in the civil setting, and section 124 must, accordingly, be interpreted in a manner compatible with those standards.[366]

The court similarly dismissed the suggestion that the right of access is confined to proceedings where the jury is present.[367] Instead, the court adopted the prevailing constitutional standards for closure.[368]

And, while acknowledging that fair trial concerns can provide an overriding interest justifying closure, the California Supreme Court emphasized that the trial judge had made no finding of probable prejudice justifying its "blanket and sweeping" order closing the courtroom during all nonjury proceedings.[369] The order "was not narrowly tailored" and "there were less restrictive means" available to protect fair trial rights, including on the record, frequent and specific admonitions and instructions, as well as careful voir dire.[370] Ultimately, the court concluded:

> The need to comply with the requirements of the First Amendment right of access may impose some burdens on trial courts. But courts can and should minimize such inconveniences by proposing to close proceedings only in the rarest of circumstances, as explained above. Accordingly, the burden imposed by requiring trial courts to give notice of a closure hearing and make the constitutionally required findings, and the ensuing burden imposed by permitting review of closure orders by extraordinary writ, will not unduly encumber our trial or appellate courts.[371]

As the California Supreme Court explained, the constitutional right of access to civil proceedings is not absolute. The following sections discuss a variety of

---

365. *Id.*

366. See *id.* at 361.

367. See *id.* The court also rejected the argument that "substantive chambers proceedings are categorically not part of the trial process, and are not subject to the First Amendment right of access." *Id.* at 363.

368. See *id.* at 361. ("[I]t is clear today that substantive courtroom proceedings in ordinary civil cases are 'presumptively open' and that Section 124 must be interpreted to preclude closure of proceedings that satisfy the high court's historical traditional/utility considerations . . . .").

369. *Id.* at 368–69.

370. *Id.* at 369.

371. *Id.* at 371.

§ 3-2(b) NEWSGATHERING AND THE LAW § 3-2(b)

interests that on occasion have been held to override the access right, permitting closure of specific civil proceedings.[372] None of these interests yield a per se rule of closure; they all contemplate a particularized determination based on the facts of a given case — a determination subject to a First Amendment-based presumption of openness.

§ 3-2(b). Privacy Interests.

Protecting personal privacy is a recurrent theme in cases arising from the closure of civil proceedings, especially cases involving divorce and minors. The Supreme Court, in *Globe Newspaper Co.* and *Press-Enterprise I*, while rejecting mandatory closure rules, indicated that privacy can constitute an overriding interest sufficient to justify closure.[373] Moreover, privacy is often an interest protected by state constitutions as well as by statutes limiting public access to civil proceedings involving juveniles, adoption, custody, paternity, divorce, and civil commitment.[374]

---

372. In *Barron v. Florida Freedom Newspapers, Inc.*, 531 So. 2d 113, 118 (Fla. 1988), for example, the court identified several interests that might, in certain circumstances, override "a strong presumption of openness" in civil proceedings:

[C]losure of court proceedings or records should occur only when necessary (a) to comply with established public policy set forth in the constitution, statutes, rules or case law; (b) to protect trade secrets; (c) to protect a compelling governmental interest [e.g., national security; confidential information]; (d) to obtain evidence to properly determine legal issues in a case; (e) to avoid substantial injury to innocent third parties [e.g. to protect young witnesses from offensive testimony; to protect children in divorce]; or (f) to avoid substantial injury to a party by disclosure of matters protected by a common law or privacy right not generally inherent in the specific type of civil proceeding sought to be closed.

373. See Chaps. 2-2(d) & (e) *supra*.

374. See Barron v. Florida Freedom Newspapers, Inc., 531 So. 2d 113, 119 (Fla. 1988); see also Chap. 3-3 *infra*; Note, *The First Amendment Right of Access to Civil Trials After* Globe Newspaper Co. v. Superior Court, 51 U. CHI. L. REV. 286, 311 (1984) ("Some states, out of concern for these privacy interests and in an effort to preserve public morals, have provided by statute or judicial decision that public access to divorce proceedings may be denied. The majority of courts have rejected this view."). For examples of state laws limiting access to divorce proceedings, see, e.g., IDAHO R. CIV. P. 77 (B); N.Y. JUD. L. § 4; UTAH CODE ANN. §§ 78-74. See In re Marriage of Lechowick, 77 Cal. Rptr. 2d 395, 401 (Ct. App. 1998) (interpreting state statute authorizing closure of family court proceedings as pertaining only "to the trial of one or more particular 'issue[s] of fact' [which must] be justified by a showing of particularized need by the moving party"); Wilkinson v. Wiegand, 1997 Conn. Super. LEXIS 1699 (Conn. Super. June 17, 1997) (in litigation following dissolution of marriage, involving financial issues and matters relating to child custody, court found no "overriding interest" in children's privacy and safety that justified closing proceeding and sealing court files).

In *Vermont v. Koch*, 730 A.2d 577 (Vt. 1999), the Vermont Supreme Court reversed orders closing hearings and sealing documents related to the revocation of a nonhospitalization order of a criminal defendant. See *id.* at 579. The court based its decision to reverse on statutory grounds and declined to address First Amendment arguments. See *id.* at 579-80. In *In re Detention of D.A.H.*,

In *Barron v. Florida Freedom Newspapers, Inc.*,[375] the Florida Supreme Court rejected the argument that motions seeking closure of divorce proceedings must be given special consideration, since such proceedings are essentially private. Instead, the court held that divorce actions must be treated like other civil proceedings,[376] i.e., a "public event" to which "the well-established common law right of access to court proceedings and records" applies.[377] "Since a strong presumption of openness exists for all court proceedings,"[378] the court concluded, it follows that "a closure order must be drawn with particularity and narrowly applied."[379] Before ordering closure, the Florida Supreme Court held, a trial judge must determine "that no reasonable alternative is available to accomplish the desired results."[380]

Similarly, in *Doe v. Museum of Science & History*,[381] the court relied on *Barron* when plaintiffs, victims of sexual abuse, sought to exclude the public from the trial of their civil damages action. In denying the closure motion, the court stressed the court's articulation of a presumption of access in *Barron*: "In serving the right of each citizen to be informed, judicial openness, of which the press is an instrument, sustains public confidence in the judiciary and thus serves

---

924 P.2d 49, 53 (Wash. App. 1996), in contrast, the court rejected a presumption of openness of a probable cause hearing for civil commitment of a convicted sex offender. The appellate court concluded that "[c]losure of the probable cause hearing does not unduly interfere with the public's right of access to the justice system or the freedom of the press, and it serves a number of valid interests, including protection of whatever privacy interest D.A.H. might have, at least on a preliminary basis." *Id.* In the subsequent civil commitment proceeding itself, however, the lower court invoked the First Amendment and the state constitution to forbid closure, to order the unsealing of the record, and to require public access to transcripts of earlier proceedings held in closed court. See In re Detention of Hendrickson, 25 MEDIA L. REP. (BNA) 1543, 1544 (Wash. Super. 1996) ("[T]his court is of the view that, probable cause being found to proceed in a case for involuntary civil commitment of the respondent, the privacy interests of the respondent are outweighed by the public's legitimate concerns in the trial on the merits.").

375. 531 So. 2d 113 (Fla. 1988).
376. See *id.* at 119.
377. *Id.* at 116. The court's acceptance of a common law right of access to civil proceedings was grounded in its perception that "openness is basic to our form of government. Public trials are essential to the judicial system's credibility in a free society." *Id.*; see *id.*:

> [Access] plays an important part as security for testimonial trustworthiness.... Subjectively, a wholesome effect is produced, analogous to that secured for witnesses upon all the officers of the court, in particular, upon judge, jury and counsel.... Persons ... should have the opportunity of learning whether they are [affected].... The educative effect of public attendance is a material advantage.

378. *Id.* at 118; see Huberner, *Rights of Privacy in Open Courts—Do They Exist?*, 2 EMERGING ISSUES OF ST. CONST. L. 189, 198 (1989).
379. 531 So. 2d at 117.
380. *Id.* at 118.
381. 22 MEDIA L. REP. (BNA) 2497 (Fla. Cir. 1994).

the ultimate value of popular sovereignty."[382] While the case admittedly involved sensitive, intimate, and embarrassing private facts, in a system of public trials, the court concluded, litigants who institute civil actions must "abandon qualms about disclosure of private facts."[383] Further, the court observed, since litigation has an inherent tendency to invade privacy, "a litigant has no reasonable expectation of privacy in the subject matter of a case."[384]

While these Florida cases invoked a right of access based in the common law, their concern for public access and the standards for closure are as demanding as those employed in access cases decided on the basis of the First Amendment. In contrast, in *Webster Groves School District v. Pulitzer Publishing Co.*,[385] the court emphasized privacy interests over the right of access in the context of a school district's efforts to enjoin a handicapped student, who had threatened fellow students with a gun, from attending public school pending exhaustion of administrative remedies. The Eighth Circuit found it unnecessary to decide whether there was a First Amendment-based right of access to civil proceedings since exclusion of the public would have been appropriate under any qualified right of access.[386] Legislatures and the judiciary have adopted a variety of measures, the court noted, that "all reflect a strong public policy favoring the special protection of minors and their privacy where sensitive and possibly stigmatizing matters are concerned."[387] To safeguard the confidentiality of such information, the court held, it is "appropriate to restrict access to the courtroom and the court file."[388]

The court observed that the evidence included sensitive matters such as the testimony of minors and of psychologists and psychiatrists about the student's mental status and handicap. For the Eighth Circuit, this showing was sufficient

---

382. *Id.* at 2499.
383. *Id.* at 2501.
384. *Id.*
385. 898 F.2d 1371 (8th Cir. 1990).
386. See *id.* at 1374-75. The court held that closure would be justified even under the most stringent standards because the case involved a handicapped child and testimony regarding his disability. See *id.*; see also Doe v. Santa Fe Indep. Sch. Dist., 933 F. Supp. 647 (S.D. Tex. 1996) (allowing trial to be closed to extent necessary to protect minor plaintiffs threatened with violence and social ostracism in establishment clause case but refusing to close proceeding to protect adult plaintiffs).
387. 898 F.2d at 1375. The court specifically noted the Family Educational Rights and Privacy Act (FERPA), 20 U.S.C. § 1232g(b) (1988); 34 C.F.R. § 99.30 (1988), which protects against release of certain information concerning students. See generally Chap. 3-3 *infra*.
388. 898 F.2d at 1375. See New Jersey ex rel. K.P., 709 A.2d 315 (N.J. Super. 1997) (granting standing to the victim in a juvenile delinquency case to oppose press access on a showing of a substantial likelihood of specific harm from Post Traumatic Stress Disorder if access were ordered).

to justify closure, even absent consideration of alternatives or any requirement for narrow tailoring of the closure order.[389]

§ 3-2(c). Trade Secrets.

The fact that public access might harm economic interests or damage the reputation of corporate management will generally not justify exclusion of the public and press from a civil proceeding.[390] Nevertheless, if the party seeking closure is able to demonstrate that disclosure of "trade secrets" or competitive harm from disclosure of confidential business information is threatened, some courts have ordered closure.[391]

In *In re Iowa Freedom of Information Council,* the Eighth Circuit reviewed a closure order in a civil contempt proceeding against a lawyer for violating a protective order.[392] The court noted that, historically, civil proceedings were "presumptively open,"[393] and that functional considerations dictated access in civil proceedings generally: "[T]he presence of the public and press at civil proceedings will enhance and safeguard the quality of the fact-finding process, just as it does in criminal trials."[394] Thus, the court concluded, "the protection of the First Amendment extends to proceedings for contempt, a hybrid containing both civil and criminal characteristics."[395]

Procedurally, the Eighth Circuit held, the access right requires a trial court to "allow objecting parties a reasonable opportunity to state their objections."[396] But, in the trade secrets context, the requirement of prior findings must be modified because trade secrets "are a peculiar kind of property," the "only

---

389. See 898 F.2d at 1376. The court also concluded that there was no reasonable alternative to sealing the court file. Redaction was "virtually impossible" since the record was replete with personal information concerning the student. *Id.* at 1377.

390. See Chap. 3-2(a) *supra.*

391. See generally Chap. 6-1(a)(5) *infra* (citing cases granting access to judicial records containing business information). But see Bone, *A New Look at Trade Secret Law: Doctrine in Search of Justification,* 86 CAL. L. REV. 241 (1998) (critically examining policy justifications for trade secret law and arguing that courts should independently base any liability for breach of secrecy safeguards on contract law).

392. 724 F.2d 658 (8th Cir. 1983). The lawyer was charged with selling trade secrets obtained in discovery in violation of a protective order. While the contempt proceeding was initially held in open court, the corporate plaintiff successfully moved to close the hearings because the testimony involved trade secrets. Most of the transcript of the hearings was later released to the public. See *id.* at 661.

393. *Id.*

394. *Id.* While acknowledging that the public interest in the integrity of the fact-gathering process is greater in criminal proceedings, the court nevertheless concluded that "the public has a great interest in the fairness of civil proceedings" as well. *Id.*

395. *Id.*

396. *Id.*

value" of which "consists in their being kept private."[397] In such cases, limited *in camera* proceedings are required to determine if trade secrets are involved and to assess the consequences of disclosure.

In the Eighth Circuit's view, "trade secrets were in fact involved" in the case before it, and "substantial damage to property rights in these secrets would have occurred had the hearing not been closed."[398] There was, moreover, "no reasonable alternative . . . to closure, sufficient to protect these property rights."[399] This conclusion also justified the continued sealing of portions of the hearing transcript and certain exhibits.[400] By the same token, the court emphasized that the presence of trade secrets will not always justify closure and that if the material at issue "had some substantial relation to an important governmental or political question, an entirely different question would be presented, and we might be required to embark on the weighing process urged on us by petitioners."[401]

As *In re Iowa Freedom of Information Council* indicates, if trade secrets are actually at stake, closure *may* well be ordered. Other courts, however, have emphasized that the presence of trade secrets does not justify broad, sweeping closure orders. In *Pepsico, Inc. v. Redmond*,[402] for example, Judge Easterbrook rejected efforts to seal an opinion either in its entirety or in part because of its discussion of trade secrets. Judicial proceedings are "presumptively in the public domain," the Seventh Circuit emphasized, even when trade secrets are involved.[403] "Holding trade secrets in confidence is one thing, holding entire judicial proceedings in confidence quite another. Opinions are not the litigants' property. They belong to the public, which underwrites the judicial system that produces them."[404]

---

397. *Id.* at 662. The district court had denied the press's request that its counsel be allowed to participate in the *in camera* hearing. No objection to this refusal was pursued on appeal. See *id.* at 660, 662. See *id.* at 664 ("[T]rade secrets partake of the nature of property, the value of which is completely destroyed by disclosure. Where only private commercial interests or damage are involved, we think the law justifies the steps taken by the District Court to avoid the destruction of these property rights.").

398. *Id.* at 661. But see Littlejohn v. Bic Corp., 851 F.2d 673 (3d Cir. 1988) (holding that the contention that documents contained trade secrets was without merit).

399. 724 F.2d at 661.
400. See *id.* at 664.
401. *Id.* at 661.
402. 46 F.3d 29 (7th Cir. 1995).
403. *Id.* at 31 (citing In re Continental Ill. Sec. Litig., 732 F.2d 1302 (7th Cir. 1984); Grove Fresh Distribs. Inc. v. Everfresh Juice Co., 24 F.3d 893 (7th Cir. 1994)); see Sports Management News, Inc. v. Nachtigal, 921 P.2d 1304 (Or. 1996) (holding that Oregon Trade Secrets Act, OR. REV. STAT. § 646.469, which authorizes court to prohibit parties to civil litigation from disclosing putative trade secrets, violates Oregon Constitution).

404. 46 F.3d at 31.

§ 3-2(d). Settlement Proceedings.

There is a strong public policy in favor of settlements and there is a prevailing belief that privacy is often essential to securing agreement of the parties. Public access is, therefore, often viewed as an impediment to successful negotiation. It is not surprising, then, that claims of public access to settlement conferences and similar proceedings in civil litigation have fared poorly.

The summary jury trial is a modern device employed to encourage the settlement of civil disputes.[405] In *Cincinnati Gas & Electric Co. v. General Electric Co.*,[406] the Sixth Circuit held that "the public has no First Amendment right of access to the summary jury trial."[407] Since the technique is of recent vintage, there was no historic right of access to the proceeding. In any event, the court noted, "[s]ettlement techniques have historically been closed to the press and the public."[408] The fact that summary jury trials are structurally similar to civil jury trials, which have historically been open, was of little relevance, the court noted, because of the "manifold differences" between them.[409] Most important, while the settlement technique might have an important effect on the outcome of the litigation, and even though the parties may have been required to participate in the summary trial, nothing is finally adjudicated by virtue of the proceeding.[410]

From a functional perspective, the media argued in *Cincinnati Gas & Electric Co.* that the strong public interest in the subject matter of the litigation — nuclear power and utility rates — required public access. But the court emphasized the dysfunctional nature of public access in the context of settlement proceedings, where confidentially is of concern to the parties. There is no "right to know," the court concluded, that requires public access to settlement negotiations.[411]

---

405. See Lambros, *The Summary Jury Trial, A Report to the Judicial Conference of the United States,* 103 F.R.D. 461, 465 (1984).

406. 854 F.2d 900 (6th Cir. 1988), *cert. denied*, 489 U.S. 1033 (1989); see In re Cincinnati Enquirer, 94 F.3d 198, 199 (6th Cir. 1996), *cert. denied*, 520 U.S. 1104 (1997) (holding that the First Amendment does not require access to summary jury trial and district court did not err in ordering closure because summary jury trials are settlement proceedings, which are historically closed proceedings).

407. 854 F.2d at 905.

408. *Id.* at 903 (citing Palmieri v. New York, 779 F.2d 861, 865 (2d Cir. 1985)) ("[s]ecrecy of settlement terms . . . is a well-established American litigation practice").

409. 854 F.2d at 904. For example, the court asserted, summary jury trials involve abbreviated arguments, informal verdicts, and presentation of evidence (which might be inadmissible at an actual trial) in a descriptive summary to mock jurors. See *id.*

410. See *id.* at 905. ("[I]t is the presence of the exercise of the courts' coercive powers that is the touchstone of the recognized right to access, not the presence of a procedure that might lead the parties to voluntarily terminate the litigation.").

411. *Id.* at 904. In *United States v. Town of Moreau*, 979 F. Supp. 129 (N.D.N.Y. 1997), the court applied the calibrated presumption approach of *United States v. Amodeo*, 71 F.3d 1044 (2d

Similarly, a federal district court denied media access to a status conference of attorneys of record in asbestos litigation designed to assist in creating a national policy for handling such cases. In *In re Asbestos Products Liability Litigation*,[412] the court analogized the conference to settlement techniques that "have historically been private and closed to the press and public."[413] Functionally, the court concluded that media access would impair open and frank discussion because, if "preliminary negotiating positions are required to be publicly disclosed they will be divorced from reality, waste time with needless posturing and hamper the parties' efforts to successfully conclude an amicable settlement to their dispute."[414]

In a class action instituted on behalf of abused and neglected children against the Illinois Department of Children and Family Services, the court denied public access to status conferences relating to the enforcement of a consent decree. In *B.H. v. Ryder*,[415] the court rejected the "public interest" as the touchstone for a right of access. Rather, it found that "[t]he hallmark of a proceeding traditionally open to the public is that the proceeding is one in which the court will adjudicate a party's substantive rights."[416] While the press and public were afforded access to the adjudicatory proceedings leading to the decree, privacy was deemed critical to the success of the in-chambers settlement conferences that produced it. The court concluded confidentiality was similarly vital to the decree's enforcement.[417]

§ 3-2(e). Depositions.

In *Seattle Times Co. v. Rhinehart*,[418] the Supreme Court held that "[p]retrial depositions and interrogatories are not public components of a civil trial. Such proceedings were not open to the public at common law and, in general, they are

---

Cir. 1995), in rejecting a request for public access to settlement conferences. After concluding that no First Amendment-based right applied, the court found the common law presumption of public access to be "very low indeed, if not nonexistent." *Id.* at 135. "Settlement conferences are not now and never have been part of the public process of litigation." *Id.* at 134. Any slight presumption, moreover, was outweighed by "the strong public policy which encourages the settlement of cases through a negotiated compromise." *Id.* at 136.

412. 19 MEDIA L. REP. (BNA) 1220 (E.D. Pa. 1991).
413. *Id.* at 1221.
414. *Id.*
415. 856 F. Supp. 1285 (N.D. Ill. 1994).
416. *Id.* at 1292.
417. See *id.* at 1290 ("[S]ome of the most essential purposes of private conferences with the court could not be accomplished in an open session with the public and press in attendance.").
418. 467 U.S. 20 (1984); see Chap. 6-1(a)(2) *infra*.

conducted in private as a matter of general practice."[419] This observation reflects the general approach of lower courts, which have typically rejected claims for public access to depositions in civil cases.[420] For example, in *Amato v. Richmond*,[421] the court denied a newspaper's efforts to gain access to depositions in a civil rights action against the city police department. The court concluded that public policy and concerns for judicial economy "'strongly militate' against allowing the media to attend the depositions."[422]

There are, however, exceptions. In *Avirgan v. Hull*,[423] the court held that "good cause" had not been shown for issuance of a protective order to exclude the press from a civil deposition. And, in *Estate of Rosenbaum v. New York City*,[424] the court ordered that four pool reporters could attend depositions of the Mayor and former police commissioner of New York City, defendants in a civil action. Opposing press access, the defendants argued that it would turn the proceedings into a media event. Nevertheless, the court applied a "good cause" standard and stressed the strong "public interest" in the litigation. Since the defendants were "public figures" who knew how to deal with reporters, there was no serious danger "that the Court's primary interest here, promoting the integrity of this deposition and the ultimate fairness of the trial," would be sacrificed by allowing a limited number of reporters to attend.[425]

More recently, in *United States v. Microsoft Corp.*,[426] the D.C. Circuit affirmed a district court ruling that granted public access to all "depositions taken in the antitrust lawsuit against Microsoft Corp.," subject to "protections for

---

419. 467 U.S. at 33; see In re Reporters Comm. for Freedom of the Press, 773 F.2d 1325, 1338 (D.C. Cir. 1985) ("It can thus hardly be said that there was a tradition, or is even now a general practice, of public access to pretrial depositions.").

420. See, e.g., Times Newspapers, Ltd. v. McDonnell Douglas Corp., 387 F. Supp. 189, 197 (C.D. Cal. 1974) (holding that newspaper was not entitled to have reporters present at all depositions because depositions "are not a judicial trial, nor a part of a trial, but a proceeding preliminary to a trial"). But see Kimberlin v. Quinlan, 145 F.R.D. 1, 2 (D.D.C. 1992) (allowing press access to depositions); 15 U.S.C. § 30 (requiring that depositions in Sherman Act cases brought in equity by the United States be open to public "as freely as trials").

421. 157 F.R.D. 26 (E.D. Va. 1994).

422. *Id.* at 27 (quoting Kimberlin v. Quinlan, 145 F.R.D. at 2) ("Allowing the media to attend every deposition in any case of public interest would significantly hinder the discovery process and burden the courts with increased litigation over discovery issues."). The court in *Amato* did emphasize that, after the depositions were completed and filed with the court, the rights of the public and the press to inspect the documents would be governed by different standards. See 157 F.R.D. at 27. See also Chap. 6-1(a)(4) *infra*.

423. 118 F.R.D. 252 (D.D.C. 1987); see Chap. 6-1(a)(1) *infra* ("good cause" standard for protective orders). In *Avirgan*, the court found "in this unique case, that, while the attendance of the press at a deposition is certainly an unorthodox practice, to prohibit it in advance of a good cause showing would be an improper balancing of the interests." 118 F.R.D. at 256.

424. 21 MEDIA L. REP. (BNA) 1987 (E.D.N.Y. 1993).

425. *Id.* at 1990.

426. 165 F.3d 952 (D.C. Cir. 1999).

trade secrets and confidential business information" pursuant to the Publicity in Taking Evidence Act of 1913, which provides for public access to depositions taken for use "in any suit in equity brought by the United States" under the Sherman Act.[427] First, as a matter of statutory construction, the court held that "a deposition taken in pretrial discovery in an antitrust case brought by the Government seeking injunctive relief" falls within the plain meaning of the term "deposition" as used in the Act.[428] Then, the court concluded that the Act had not been superseded by Federal Rule of Civil Procedure 26(c), which authorizes a district court to grant confidentiality orders to protect a party from "undue burden" upon a showing of "good cause."[429] Rather, the court characterized Section 30 as "one of the interests to be weighed" in assessing Microsoft's need for a protective order pursuant to Rule 26, thereby avoiding a statutory conflict that would require supersession.[430] The court held that the "good cause" standard "is a flexible one that requires an individualized balancing of the many interests that may be present in a particular case," including the interest advanced by Section 30.[431]

§ 3-3. Juvenile Proceedings.

§ 3-3(a). Juvenile Delinquency.

The juvenile justice system was originally designed to provide juveniles with a significantly different treatment than that afforded adults accused of crime. Treatment and rehabilitation, rather than punishment, were the objectives of government intervention in the case of a juvenile. Individualized handling, procedural informality, and confidentiality were to be hallmarks of the system. Unfortunately, the reality of juvenile justice often departs markedly from the rehabilitative ideal.[432] Frequently, juvenile justice mirrors the experience of the

---

427. *Id.* at 953 (citing 15 U.S.C. § 30).
428. *Id.* at 959.
429. *Id.*
430. *Id.*
431. *Id.* at 960.
432. See generally In re Gault, 387 U.S. 1, 14-19, 25-27 (1967). On the rehabilitative ideal and the problems of the juvenile justice system, see generally *Juvenile Courts: Access to Justice, Hearings Before the Subcomm. on Juvenile Justice of the Senate Comm. on the Judiciary*, 102d CONG., 2d SESS. (1992) [*Access to Justice*]; R. MOONKIN & D. WEISBERG, CHILD, FAMILY AND STATE pt. 7 (3d ed. 1995), CHILD, PARENT & STATE § 11 (S.R. Humm ed., 1994); Cohen, *Reconciling Media Access with Confidentiality for the Individual in Juvenile Court*, 20 SANTA CLARA L. REV. 405, 405-10 (1980); Geis, *Publicity and Juvenile Court Proceedings*, 30 ROCKY MTN. L. REV. 101, 103-07 (1958); Jonas, *Press Access to the Juvenile Courtroom: Juvenile Anonymity and the First Amendment*, 17 COLUM. J.L. & SOC. PROBS. 287, 288-97 (1982). For a state-by-state guide on access to juvenile courts, see generally REPORTERS COMMITTEE FOR FREEDOM OF THE PRESS, ACCESS TO JUVENILE COURTS (Spring 1999).

adult criminal offender.[433] Nevertheless, juvenile court proceedings are not criminal proceedings. Supreme Court precedent extending a First Amendment-based right of access to criminal pretrial and trial proceedings may not, therefore, be directly applicable to juvenile delinquency matters.[434]

Given the juvenile justice system's overriding concern with protecting the juvenile offender, it is not surprising that claims for a First Amendment-based right of access to delinquency proceedings generally have been unsuccessful. Public scrutiny has traditionally been considered inconsistent with the rehabilitative ideal — "confidentiality is essential to the goal of rehabilitation, which is in turn the major purpose of the separate juvenile justice system."[435] The juvenile, most courts have concluded, is to be protected from the stigma and emotional trauma that can accompany publicity: "The only issue in a juvenile proceeding is the care, needs and protection of the minor and his rehabilitation and restoration to useful citizenship."[436] Nor have historical considerations been

---

433. Criticism of the juvenile justice system provided the predicate for extending due process protections to the juvenile in *Kent v. United States*, 383 U.S. 541 (1966), and in *In re Gault*, 387 U.S. 1 (1967).

434. See United States v. A.D., 28 F.3d 1353 (3d Cir. 1994) ("[P]roceedings to determine whether a juvenile is a delinquent are not generally regarded as criminal proceedings."); New Jersey ex rel. K.P., 709 A.2d 315, 322 (N.J. Super. 1997) (noting that "the United States Supreme Court and the Supreme Court of New Jersey have yet to decide whether this [First Amendment] right extends to juvenile proceedings"); In re J.S., 438 A.2d 1125, 1127 (Vt. 1981) ("[J]uvenile proceedings are not criminal prosecutions, a fact which makes at least some of the First Amendment purposes served by open criminal trials inapplicable.").

435. Wisconsin ex rel. Herget v. Waukesha County Cir. Ct., 267 N.W.2d 309, 316 (Wis. 1978); see San Bernardino County Dep't of Soc. Servs. v. Superior Ct., 283 Cal. Rptr. 332, 339 (Ct. App. 1991) ("Private hearings . . . traditionally have been considered an important tool in the juvenile court system, both in terms of eliminating or reducing any stigma which might attach and, more broadly, in assisting in the rehabilitative process."); New Jersey ex rel. K.P., 709 A.2d 315, 325 (N.J. Super. 1997) ("Juvenile proceedings are still viewed as closed family court matters which are more rehabilitative than adversarial[.] . . . The juvenile justice system is obligated to protect the best interests of juveniles. That obligation extends to both a juvenile defendant and a juvenile victim."). See generally Laubenstein, *Media Access to Juvenile Justice: Should Freedom of the Press Be Limited to Promote Rehabilitation of Youthful Offenders?*, 68 TEMP. L. REV. 1897 (1995) (arguing that juvenile proceedings should be presumptively closed).

436. In re J.S., 438 A.2d 1125, 1127 (Vt. 1981); see *id.* at 1129:

> Confidential proceedings protect the delinquent from the stigma of conduct which may be outgrown and avoids the possibility that the adult is penalized for what he used to be, or worse yet, the possibility that the stigma becomes self-perpetuating, thereby making change and growth impossible. Publication of a delinquent's name may handicap his prospects for adjustment into society, for acceptance by the public, or it may cause him to lose employment opportunities. Public proceedings could so embarrass the youth's family members that they withhold their support in rehabilitative efforts.

See also Bishop v. Craft-Jones, 2 F. Supp. 2d 1317, 1318 (D. Or. 1998) ("The purpose of cloaking juvenile proceedings with privacy is to spare youths the baggage of public stigma as the court, their parents, and state officials work with them to overcome whatever problems invoked the jurisdiction

deemed to support recognition of First Amendment-based access rights.[437] As Justice Rehnquist, concurring in *Smith v. Daily Mail Publ'g Co.*, asserted: "It is a hallmark of our juvenile justice system in the United States that virtually from its inception at the end of the last century its proceedings have been conducted outside of the public's full gaze and the youths brought before our juvenile courts have been shielded from publicity."[438]

The argument for a First Amendment-based right of access to juvenile proceedings, therefore, relies heavily on functional considerations. Juvenile delinquency proceedings are, in many respects, analogous to criminal cases. Given the harm to the community flowing from serious juvenile crime, the public has a strong interest in the workings of the juvenile justice system.[439] Public access serves both an educational and policymaking function — it is important that public understanding of how the system works be enhanced in order to improve its operation.[440] Just as the Supreme Court determined that it

---

of the juvenile court."); New Jersey ex rel. K.P., 709 A.2d 315, 317, 327-28 (N.J. Super. 1997) (denying press access under statute based on a showing of a "substantial likelihood of specific harm to the juvenile(s) involved," which was evidenced by expert witness testimony that press coverage would subject the juvenile victim of sexual assault to "further set backs in her recovery" and aggravate her chronic Post Traumatic Stress Disorder).

437. See, e.g., Florida Publ'g Co. v. Morgan, 322 S.E.2d 233, 238 (Ga. 1984) ("We are unable to conclude that there is an historically-based constitutional presumption of openness applicable to juvenile court proceedings."); Associated Press v. Bradshaw, 410 N.W.2d 577, 578 (S.D. 1987) ("There is no absolute right of access to juvenile hearings, which have been traditionally closed."); In re N.H.B., 769 P.2d 844, 849 (Utah App. 1989) ("[t]he presumption of openness applied in criminal trials under the first amendment does not extend to juvenile proceedings."); In re J.S., 438 A.2d 1125, 1127 (Vt. 1981) ("Far from a tradition of openness, juvenile proceedings are almost invariably closed.").

438. 443 U.S. 97, 107 (1979) (Rehnquist, J., concurring).

439. In amending California law to open juvenile proceedings involving serious crimes, a legislative committee explained the bill was designed "to make minors more fully responsible for their crimes, to make juvenile judges more accountable to the public, and to increase public understanding of the juvenile justice system." Tribune Newspapers W. Inc. v. Superior Ct., 218 Cal. Rptr. 505, 508 (Ct. App. 1986); see Ohio v. Evans, 26 MEDIA L. REP. (BNA) 1735, 1736 (Ohio C.P. 1997) (stating that the "public interest is accentuated when an alleged delinquent is subject to a pending motion to transfer jurisdiction for prosecution as an adult"); Brelsford & Silvers, *Juvenile Courts: Part I, The Battle for Access*, 12 COMM. LAW. 7 (Summer 1994) ("As juveniles increasingly commit violent crime, these [rehabilitative] goals have been replaced by society's desire for accountability and punishment.").

440. See In re N.H., 626 N.E.2d 697, 703 (Ohio C.P. 1992) ("[T]he public does have an interest in access to delinquency proceedings which corresponds to the public's interest in criminal matters."); San Bernardino County Dep't of Soc. Servs. v. Superior Ct., 283 Cal. Rptr. at 341 ("The public's ability to understand how the system operates and, in turn, its ability to make informed decisions regarding the need for positive changes to the system will be enhanced by allowing access to the proceedings."); Dalton, *At the Crossroads of* Richmond *and* Gault: *Addressing Media Access to Juvenile Proceedings Through a Functional Analysis*, 28 SETON HALL L. REV. 1155, 1229 (1998) ("Having become a sprawling network of courts and post-adjudicative

was necessary to extend procedural safeguards to juvenile proceedings in order to protect the juvenile, so public scrutiny can help to prevent abuse by judges, prosecutors, probation officers, and other public officials.[441] Such scrutiny is especially important because there is no jury in the juvenile courts.[442]

While the functional values of public access are surely applicable in the juvenile context, the courts have generally held that they are trumped by historical considerations and the interests in preserving confidentiality and protecting the juvenile from trauma and stigma. While commentators often argue for a First Amendment-based access right,[443] courts have thus far been unwilling to extend the constitutional guarantee to juvenile proceedings.[444]

Every state and the federal government have enacted legislation limiting public access to juvenile proceedings.[445] Some statutes appear to create a mandatory rule of exclusion.[446] Others appear to provide for press access, but purport to

---

institutions, ... the juvenile justice system is in dire need of the kind of thoughtful, reasoned reform that can only come from an open — and informed — debate.").

441. See THE AMERICAN BAR ASSOCIATION–INSTITUTE OF JUDICIAL ADMINISTRATION, JUVENILE JUSTICE STANDARDS, Summ. § 2.4 (1990) ("Visibility and accountability of decision making should replace closed proceedings and unrestrained official discretion."). In explaining this "basic principle," the ABA noted that "closed hearings and unregulated procedures have resulted in arbitrary decision making and unjustifiable disparity in outcomes." *Id.* at § 1.3.

442. See McKeiver v. Pennsylvania, 403 U.S. 528 (1971).

443. See, e.g., Brelsford & Silvers, *supra* note 439; Dalton, *supra* note 440; Geis, *supra* note 432; Note, *The Public Right of Access to Juvenile Delinquency Hearings*, 81 MICH. L. REV. 1540 (1983). The National Council of Juvenile and Family Court Judges has declared:

> Traditional notions of secrecy and confidentiality should be re-examined and relaxed to promote public confidence in the court's work. The public has a right to know how courts deal with children and families. The court should be open to the media, interested professionals, and students and, when appropriate, the public, in order to hold itself accountable, educate others, and encourage greater community participation.

NATIONAL COUNCIL OF JUVENILE & FAMILY COURT JUDGES, CHILDREN AND FAMILY FIRST: A MANDATE FOR AMERICA'S COURTS 3 (1995).

444. See, e.g., In re N.H.B., 769 P.2d 844, 849 (Utah App. 1989) ("[T]he presumption of openness applied in criminal trials under the First Amendment does not extend to juvenile proceedings."); Edward A. Sherman Publ'g Co. v. Goldberg, 443 A.2d 1252, 1258 (R.I. 1982) ("The right of access in criminal trials ... does not apply to juvenile proceedings. ... The interests of the juvenile ... are most often best served by anonymity and confidentiality."); In re J.S., 438 A.2d 1125, 1127 (Vt. 1981) ("[J]uvenile proceedings are not criminal prosecutions, a fact which makes at least some of the First Amendment purposes served by open criminal trials inapplicable.").

445. See Smith v. Daily Mail Publ'g Co., 443 U.S. 97, 105 (1979); United States v. Three Juveniles, 61 F.3d 86, 89 n.3 (1st Cir. 1995), *cert. denied*, 517 U.S. 1166 (1996); Laubenstein, *supra* note 435, at 1908-13; REPORTERS COMMITTEE FOR FREEDOM OF THE PRESS, *supra* note 432; Dalton, *supra* note 440, at 1205 (suggesting "pro-access trends").

446. See, e.g., N.H. REV. STAT. ANN. § 169-C:14; VT. STAT. ANN. tit. 33, § 651(c).

include limitations on publication.[447] Most of these laws limit access to those having a "direct" or "proper" interest in the proceedings, which often provides a basis for press (but not necessarily public) access.[448] Finally, increasing public concern over youth violence has provided impetus for adoption of statutory provisions that provide for public access in proceedings involving certain serious offenses.[449]

United States v. A.D.[450] illustrates how the constitutional and statutory lines of authority can intersect. A.D. and T.Y. were charged with gang-related armed robbery. The juveniles and the government moved to close detention hearings under the Federal Juvenile Delinquency Act.[451] After hearing press objections, the magistrate granted the motion, accepting the government's argument that the Act mandates closed proceedings and records.

The Third Circuit, in an opinion by Judge Stapleton, reversed, but avoided the press's constitutional challenge to a "mandatory" rule by interpreting the Act to permit judicial discretion to allow access. "[W]e start with the proposition that the task of statutory interpretation we face implicates First Amendment values and that the government's construction of the Act raises a substantial constitutional question."[452] The court acknowledged that there was no "centuries-old tradition of openness" of juvenile proceedings, "which are a relatively recent creation."[453] Further, statutes limiting public access reflect "the special sensitivity of information regarding juveniles and the impact that dissemination of such information may have on the youths involved."[454] Nevertheless, the court con-

---

447. See, e.g., ALA. CODE § 12-15-65; D.C. CODE ANN. § 16-2316(e); GA. CODE ANN. § 15-11-28(c); 705 ILL. COMP. STAT. 405/1-6; N.J. JUV. & DOM. REL. CT. R. 5:9-2(a); N.M. STAT. ANN. § 32A-2-16(B); N.Y. FAM. CT. ACT § 741(b); N.Y. FAM. CT. R. 205.4(a); WIS. STAT. § 938.299(1)(a). Many such restraints on publication are constitutionally suspect under the prior restraint doctrine. See Brelsford & Silvers, *supra* note 439, at 8-9.

448. See, e.g., CONN. GEN. STAT. § 46b-122; DEL. R. FAM. CT. CRIM. P. 24; HAW. REV. STAT. § 571-41; IDAHO CODE § 16-1608(b), 20-519; LA. CODE JUV. PROC. ANN. art. 407; MASS. GEN. LAWS ANN. ch. 119, § 65; MINN. STAT. § 260.155(c); MISS. CODE ANN. § 43-21-203(6); NEV. REV. STAT. § 62.193(1); N.D. CENT. CODE § 27-20-24(5); OR. REV. STAT. § 419B.310(1); 42 PA. CONS. STAT. ANN. § 6336(d); VA. CODE ANN. § 16.1-302; WASH. REV. CODE § 13.34.110; W. VA. CODE § 49-5-2; WYO. STAT. ANN. § 14-6-224(b).

449. See, e.g., CAL. WELF. & INST. CODE § 676(a) (requiring open delinquency hearings if any of 28 violent crimes is involved); LA. CODE JUV. PROC. ANN. art. 407; S.D. CODIFIED LAWS § 26-7A-36. See generally P. TORBET, NATIONAL CENTER FOR JUVENILE JUSTICE, STATE RESPONSES TO SERIOUS AND VIOLENT JUVENILE CRIME (1996).

450. 28 F.3d 1353 (3d Cir. 1994).

451. 18 U.S.C. §§ 5031-5042. Sections 5032 and 5038 of the Act contain most of the statute's provisions concerning confidentiality.

452. 28 F.3d at 1356.

453. *Id.* at 1358.

454. *Id.* at 1357; see *id.* at 1361 ("We, like the government, recognize the need to avoid embarrassing and humiliating juveniles, to obtain evidence about delicate matters, and not to affect the rehabilitation of juveniles adversely.").

cluded that detention and delinquency proceedings "are closely analogous to criminal proceedings, and all the public interests in criminal proceedings ... seem present and equally cogent here."[455]

Most important, the court found it difficult to reconcile a mandatory rule of closure with the Supreme Court's analysis in *Globe Newspaper Co.*, which had rejected a mandatory closure rule governing the trial testimony of minor victims.[456] In *Globe Newspaper Co.*, particularized determinations, made on a case-by-case basis, were required to reconcile the First Amendment interests with those of the victim.[457] Similarly, in the absence of an "unambiguous directive to the contrary," the Third Circuit was unwilling "to attribute to Congress an intention to deprive district courts of discretion to strike on a case-by-case basis the balance between the interests protected by the First Amendment and competing privacy interests."[458]

Nevertheless, the court recognized that its analogy to *Globe Newspaper Co.* was inexact, since there the Supreme Court sought to reconcile a First Amendment-based right of access with the interests of minor victims. In rejecting a mandatory rule, the Supreme Court had employed strict scrutiny to determine if the minor's interest in privacy justified closure. In *A.D.*, in contrast, the trial court had declined to extend the constitutional access right to juvenile proceedings at all. At bottom, therefore, the court in *A.D.* reasoned that First Amendment interests *are* implicated in delinquency proceedings and that statutory rules regarding closure must be interpreted consistently with those functional values.[459]

Even if federal law does not mandate closure, the facts of the particular case may justify exclusion of the public from delinquency proceedings under the Juvenile Delinquency Act. In *United States v. Three Juveniles*,[460] a federal district court initially interpreted the Act to mandate closure of such hearings in order to protect the juvenile's anonymity and concluded that a mandatory rule

---

455. *Id.* at 1358.
456. See 457 U.S. 596 (1982); Chap. 2-2(d) *supra*.
457. See 28 F.3d at 1358. ("[*Globe*] does suggest that an across the board ban on access to juvenile proceedings under the Act would pose a substantial constitutional question."). The court conceded that it could not say "that the countervailing interests that would be served by denying public access to proceedings under the Act are any more compelling than those that the Supreme Court acknowledged were being served by the challenged statute in *Globe*." *Id.* at 1350.
458. *Id.* at 1359.
459. For analogous examples of statutory interpretation that avoids the constitutional difficulties posed by a mandatory rule, see In re N.H.B., 769 P.2d 844, 852 (Utah App. 1989) ("Although we have held that a presumption of closure in juvenile court proceedings is constitutionally permissible, the presumption is not irrebuttable, because of the constitutional considerations previously discussed."); In re Brown, 18 MEDIA L. REP. (BNA) 1460, 1461 (Fla. County Ct. 1990) (stating that a statute requiring closure of custody hearings would not "pass constitutional tests" if construed to preclude judicial discretion).
460. 862 F. Supp. 651 (D. Mass. 1994), *aff'd*, 61 F.3d 86 (1st Cir. 1995), *cert. denied*, 517 U.S. 1166 (1996).

was constitutional.[461] In any event, the district court also held that, even if it had discretion to open proceedings under the Act or if there were a qualified constitutional right of access, it would still order closure. Specifically, the court noted the potential for rehabilitation of the juvenile offenders, the need to protect the confidentiality of juveniles not charged, the juveniles' opposition to opening the proceedings, the lack of any alternative means of protecting against disclosure of their identities, and the court's ability to protect the public interest by releasing transcripts of the proceedings.[462] Closure was, therefore, "necessitated by a compelling governmental interest."[463]

Although the First Circuit affirmed,[464] it pointedly rejected the district court's approach and held that the Federal Juvenile Delinquency Act does not mandate across-the-board closure of juvenile proceedings. Measures designed to protect confidentiality, the court emphasized, are to be evaluated on a case-by-case basis.[465] Like the Third Circuit in *United States v. A.D.*, the First Circuit accepted that "[t]he Act implicates First Amendment concerns, and thus must be interpreted with the Supreme Court's jurisprudence in mind."[466] Accordingly, the court of appeals proceeded to consider the implications of *Globe Newspapers Co.*: "Assuming *arguendo* that the First Amendment right of public access does apply to some degree to juvenile proceedings, we agree that while *Globe* is not directly applicable here, the Court's reasoning in that case strongly suggests that the district court's preferred [mandatory] reading of the Act raises some serious First Amendment concerns."[467] Nevertheless, the court described the assumption that the First Amendment applies to juvenile proceedings as "highly dubious,"[468]

---

461. The district court relied on 18 U.S.C. § 5038(e), which requires that there be no disclosure of the name or the picture of any juvenile in a delinquency proceeding — "Closure appears to be the only way to protect the juvenile's anonymity." 862 F. Supp. at 655-56. But see United States v. A.D., 28 F.3d at 1360 (noting that § 5038(e) would be "an indirect and unlikely way for Congress to stipulate that all hearings under the Act will be closed to the public"). The Third Circuit concluded that "section 5038(e), then, like the rest of the Act, provides no evidence of a congressional mandate to close all juvenile hearings and seal all records." *Id.* at 1361.
462. See 862 F. Supp. at 657.
463. *Id.* The district court accepted that "it is undeniable that the public's scrutiny of a proceeding under the Act would 'enhance[ ] quality and safeguard[ ] the integrity of the factfinding process.'" *Id.* (citation omitted) Nevertheless, "after weighing the interest of the juveniles in confidentiality, and in rehabilitation, against the interests of the public, particularly the victims, to open hearings, the court concludes that closure is necessitated by a compelling governmental interest." *Id.* at 657-58.
464. United States v. Three Juveniles, 61 F.3d 86 (1st Cir. 1995), *cert. denied*, 517 U.S. 1166 (1996).
465. See *id.* at 92.
466. *Id.* at 88.
467. *Id.* at 90.
468. *Id.* at 90 n.4. In this regard, the court noted "the long, entrenched, and well-founded" tradition of confidentiality regarding juvenile proceedings, and the compelling rehabilitative

and questioned whether the stringent First Amendment standards applied in adult criminal cases should be invoked in the juvenile context,[469] where the exercise of judicial discretion in favor of closure "is not an exception to some general rule of openness, but the norm."[470] Even if strict scrutiny were the rule, the appellate court concluded, it was satisfied in the case at issue in the wake of the district court's analysis and specific findings.[471]

As these cases suggest, the constitutionality of a mandatory closure rule in the juvenile context is at best uncertain. In *In re J.S.*,[472] the Vermont Supreme Court interpreted its state law to impose a mandatory closure rule in juvenile court proceedings,[473] and rejected the lower court holding that the statute thereby violated the First Amendment: "Neither the Vermont nor the United States Constitution . . . provides a right of public access which overrides the compelling interests served by our juvenile confidentiality shield laws."[474] On the other hand, the Georgia Supreme Court in *Florida Publishing Co. v. Morgan*,[475] held that constitutional considerations require that the presumption that hearings in juvenile court be closed to the public and the press cannot be conclusive. "The public and/or press must be given an opportunity to show that the state's or juveniles' interest in a closed hearing is not 'overriding' or 'compelling.'"[476] In *Morgan*, however, the Georgia Supreme Court placed the burden squarely on the public or press to justify a claim of access; the court did not question that the legislature could constitutionally establish a rebuttable presumption of closure.[477]

Most state statutes governing access to juvenile proceedings begin by excluding the public, but provide exceptions for those with a special interest. In this manner, they implement a rule of statutory discretion.[478] The California

---

purposes behind this tradition. *Id.* (citing In re Sealed Case (Juvenile Transfer), 893 F.2d 363, 367 (D.C. Cir. 1990)).
469. See 61 F.3d at 93.
470. *Id.* at 92.
471. See *id.* ("the juveniles' own assessment of their interest is a highly reliable indicator of whether they will be irreparably stigmatized by open proceedings").
472. 438 A.2d 1125 (Vt. 1981).
473. See *id.* at 1131 ("The juvenile shield law does not give the court below discretion to make the proceedings public."). This holding was limited to proceedings already in juvenile court. Proceedings prior to transfer are presumptively open, given the need to accommodate the First Amendment and the delinquent's confidentiality interests. See In re K.F., 559 A.2d 663 (Vt. 1989). See also Ex parte Island Packet, 417 S.E.2d 575 (S.C. 1992) (applying *Press-Enterprise II* to a juvenile's detention and transfer hearing).
474. 438 A.2d at 1129.
475. 322 S.E.2d 233 (Ga. 1984).
476. *Id.* at 238.
477. See *id.*
478. In *In re Presha*, 677 A.2d 806 (N.J. Super. 1996), for example, the court interpreted the New Jersey statute to create a presumption of public access upon application by the media, which generally may be defeated by the juvenile establishing that access would pose a "substantial

statute, for example, closes juvenile hearings to the public generally but creates an exception for those with "a direct and legitimate interest in the particular case or the work of the court."[479] In *Brian W. v. Superior Court*,[480] a seventeen-year-old juvenile, charged with kidnapping and murder, sought to close his fitness hearing, arguing that the law should be narrowly construed to preserve confidentiality. Instead, the California Supreme Court found in the exception a legislative purpose to permit press access as a matter of judicial discretion.[481] The effects of publicity on juveniles, the court concluded, could be ameliorated by other means for preventing disclosure of the juvenile's identity.[482] The juvenile had also failed to establish, in the court's judgment, a "reasonable likelihood" that publicity would impair his interest in a fair trial, given the large number of jurors available for jury service and the alternative safeguards available.[483]

---

likelihood of specific harm." *Id*. at 808. The juvenile's assertion of a generalized harm of increased trauma to him and his family, however, is not sufficient to rebut the statutory presumption of access. See *id*. at 810. In *New Jersey ex rel. K.P.*, 709 A.2d 315, 318 (N.J Super. 1997), therefore, the court held that the juvenile defendants had not met the statutory standard for denial of press access to the proceedings by claiming generally embarrassment and harm to their rehabilitation. See *id*. However, the court also held that a *victim* has standing to oppose a petition by the press to open the juvenile proceeding. See *id*. at 326. "It is inconsistent to find a direct intention [in N.J.S.A. § 2A:4A-60(i)] to grant victims the right to be heard prior to imposing a disposition and simultaneously finding it was the legislature's intent to specifically exclude the victim when deciding whether or not to close a juvenile proceeding." 709 A.2d at 321. The court found support for this conclusion in the New Jersey Constitution's Victims' Rights Amendment, which provides that "[a] victim of a crime shall be treated with fairness, compassion and respect by the criminal justice system." *Id*. (citing N.J. CONST., art. I, § 22). In addition, the court noted that "the New Jersey Constitution explicitly provides victims of crimes with more rights than the Federal Constitution," and that the right to be treated with fairness and respect is "fundamental and . . . meant to serve as a floor and not a ceiling." 709 A.2d at 324. See Ohio v. Evans, 26 MEDIA L. REP. (BNA) 1735, 1736 (Ohio C.P. 1997) ("The proceedings in juvenile court are not presumed to be open or closed; rather, in each case the court must weigh competing interests for and against public access."). But see Kearns-Tribune Corp. v. Hornak, 917 P.2d 79 (Utah App. 1996) (holding that the public does not have a direct interest in juvenile proceedings and court has no discretion to order public or press access).

479. CAL. WELF. & INST. CODE § 676(a). The minor or her family may also request that the hearing be open. See *id*.

480. 574 P.2d 788 (Cal. 1978).

481. See *id*. at 791 ("We conclude that in vesting the judge with discretion to admit to juvenile court proceedings persons having a 'direct and legitimate interest in the particular case or the work of the court' it was the purpose of the legislature to allow press attendance at juvenile hearings."). The report of the legislative commission that drafted section 676 in 1961 states: "We believe the press can assist juvenile courts in becoming more effective instruments of social rehabilitation by providing the public with greater knowledge of juvenile court processes, procedures, and unmet needs. We, therefore, urge juvenile courts to actively encourage greater participation by the press." *Id*. at 790-91.

482. *Id*. at 791.

483. See *id*. at 792. The court assumed that the "reasonable likelihood" standard, more favorable to the juvenile than the demanding "clear and present danger" test, is most appropriately

In some cases interpreting discretionary state statutes, the courts have been influenced by constitutional standards. For example, in *Associated Press v. Bradshaw*,[484] the South Dakota Supreme Court held that a juvenile judge was "clearly erroneous and abused his discretion" in closing all hearings in a juvenile proceeding. The appellate court required the juvenile judge to make specific findings demonstrating that "closure is essential to preserve higher values" and specified that its "order must be narrowly tailored to serve that interest."[485] Since no evidence at all had been presented to justify closure, the court granted a writ of mandamus affording press access to the proceeding.[486] But, in 1991, the South Dakota legislature responded to *Bradshaw* by revising its law to provide that "all juvenile court hearings are closed unless the court finds compelling reasons to provide otherwise." [487] In *In re M.C.*,[488] therefore, the court held that the *Bradshaw* "balancing test no longer applies as the legislature has abrogated the presumption of open juvenile hearings." The constitutionality of the new law requiring presumptive closure in order to preserve juvenile confidentiality and promote rehabilitation had not been challenged.[489]

---

applied to the closure of juvenile proceedings. See *id.* at 792 n.7. As a result, the court concluded "that when past media coverage relating to a case has been neither excessive nor sensational and the jury pool in the jurisdiction is large, a court does not err in refusing to bar press representatives from a juvenile fitness hearing. Adequate safeguards are available, should they be necessary, to protect the defendant's right if he is certified to adult court." *Id.* at 793. *Brian W.* was decided prior to the United States Supreme Court decisions in the *Press-Enterprise* cases. See Chap. 2-2(e) & (f) *supra*.

484. 410 N.W.2d 577 (S.D. 1987). The court held that S.D. CODIFIED LAWS § 26-8-32 "provides only a permissive standard. The juvenile court judge may allow the press into closed juvenile proceedings, but he is not required to do so." 410 N.W.2d at 579.

485. *Id.* See *id.* at 580:

In the future, before ordering closure, a trial court should consider (1) the nature and extent of press coverage, including the circulation and geographic distribution; (2) whether the coverage prior to the closure hearing has been excessive or sensational; (3) whether the minor's name has been released to the public; (4) whether there are alternative measures to closure; and (5) whether the proceedings closed to the public and press will be temporary. This list of factors is not intended to be exclusive. Once evidence regarding these factors has been elicited, the competing interests of the confidentiality and anonymity of a juvenile court proceeding must be balanced against the Media's rights under the First Amendment.

486. See *id.* In *In re Hughes County Action*, 452 N.W.2d 128 (S.D. 1990), the court, applying *Associated Press v. Bradshaw*, upheld closure of the adjudicatory portion of a juvenile proceeding. Given the "widespread and pervasive" and "excessive and sensational" media coverage of the rape case, the court concluded, "[i]t is clear that the State has a strong interest in preserving the confidentiality of juvenile proceedings." *Id.* at 131-32. The fact that the name of one of the juveniles had become public, in the court's view, did not negate this interest. See *id.* at 132. The interest of the minor victim also had to be considered. See *id.* at 130.

487. S.D. CODIFIED LAWS § 26-7A-36.
488. 527 N.W.2d 290, 292 (S.D. 1995).
489. See *id.* at 291.

Even when a discretionary statutory rule is applicable, there is no assurance that constitutional access standards will be employed in interpreting whether the press has a "direct" interest or whether public access is in the best interests of the child. Absent Supreme Court guidance, it is unlikely that any particular formulation of rules for closure of juvenile proceedings generally, or of particular types of juvenile proceedings, will develop.[490]

A number of jurisdictions, reacting to increased violent crime among juveniles, have amended their laws to expand public and press access.[491] For example, following *Brian W.*, California amended its law to require that "members of the public shall be admitted, on the same basis as they may be admitted to trials in a court of criminal jurisdiction," to juvenile hearings involving designated violent crimes.[492] In *Tribune Newspapers West, Inc. v. Superior Court*,[493] the court concluded that the amendment was designed "to provide additional public access to fitness hearings [which] is both in accord with the traditional

---

490. Granting public access to a probable cause hearing and parts of an "amenability" or fitness hearing, for example, an Ohio juvenile court in *In re N.H.*, 626 N.E.2d 697 (Ohio County Ct. 1992), interpreting a discretionary statute, held that closure would not be an effective and efficient means of protecting the child. *Id.* at 704, 705. But, in *In re D.R.*, 624 N.E.2d 1120 (Ohio County Ct. 1993), the court held that closure can be ordered based on a finding that there is (1) a reasonable and substantial basis for believing that public access could harm the child or endanger the fairness of the proceedings and (2) the potential for harm outweighs the benefits of public access. See *id.* at 1122, 1124. See In re T.R., 556 N.E.2d 439 (Ohio 1990); Ohio v. Evans, 26 MEDIA L. REP. (BNA) 1735 (Ohio C.P. 1997) (granting newspaper access to probable cause hearing for juveniles, because the public's interest outweighs confidentiality concerns, but not permitting any photographs of juveniles or their families during the proceedings). In *Tennessee v. The Tennessean*, 902 S.W.2d 911 (Tenn. 1995), the court applied "balancing" standards reflecting constitutional considerations. On remand, the trial court again ordered closure but, in *Tennessee v. James*, 1996 WL 22631 (Tenn. 1996), the Tennessee Supreme Court again ordered the proceedings open. See generally Dienes, *Access to Juvenile Proceedings*, 14 COMM. LAW. 7 (Winter 1996). See also Washington v. Loukaitis, 918 P.2d 535 (Wash. App. 1996) (trial court abused discretion in closing declination hearing without making specific findings concerning how open hearing would prejudice fair trial rights). In *Loukaitis*, which adjudicated a claim of access to a transfer proceeding, the court did not invoke a First Amendment-based rule of presumptive access directly, but employed "balancing" standards that appeared to reflect constitutional considerations. Thus, the court held that the party seeking closure bears the burden of establishing "particularized prejudice" that would "override the public's compelling interest in open proceedings." *Id.* at 914. In addition, the court required that closure orders, supported by "adequate written findings," must not be "broader than necessary" to protect the competing interest and that the presiding judge "must consider alternatives to closure." *Id.*

491. See Note, *Removing Confidentiality Protections and the "Get Tough" Rhetoric: What Has Gone Wrong with the Juvenile Justice System?*, 18 B.C. THIRD WORLD L.J. 105, 115 (1998) ("Between 1992 and 1995, ten states opened juvenile proceedings to the public. Twenty-eight states now allow some access to juvenile records. In all, forty states now permit the release of a juvenile's name, a picture of the juvenile, or both, to the media or general public under certain conditions.").

492. CAL. WELF. & INST. CODE § 676(a).
493. 218 Cal. Rptr. 505 (Ct. App. 1985).

openness of judicial proceedings and a response to public concern about the increase in criminal activity among young people."[494] But neither *Tribune Newspapers West, Inc.* nor subsequent California cases have employed First Amendment-based standards in the juvenile context.[495]

New York amended its law in 1978 to provide that its rule of closure would not apply to juveniles charged with felonies.[496] In *Capital Newspapers v. Moynihan*,[497] the New York Court of Appeals held that sentencing proceedings for youthful offenders under this provision "are presumptively open to the public and the press,"[498] and cannot be closed simply because juveniles are involved. But, the Court left to another day whether constitutional standards apply in determining if the presumption is overcome.[499]

In *New Group Boston, Inc. v. Massachusetts*,[500] the Massachusetts Supreme Judicial Court held that, as a result of a 1990 statutory amendment, in delin-

---

494. *Id.* at 508. See KGTV Channel 10 v. Superior Ct., 32 Cal. Rptr. 2d 181, 182 (Ct. App. 1994) ("Murder is one of the serious offenses which opens the door to a public hearing. The media has a statutory right to attend the hearing and a constitutional right to say what transpires.").

495. In *Tribune Newspapers West, Inc.*, the court held that fitness hearings could be closed if "a minor can establish a reasonable likelihood of substantial prejudice to the right to receive a fair and impartial trial." 218 Cal. Rptr. at 510; see Cheyenne K. v. Superior Ct., 256 Cal. Rptr. 68, 70 (Ct. App. 1989) (applying the *Tribune Newspapers West, Inc.* standard to juvenile competency hearings); KGTV Channel 10 v. Superior Ct., 32 Cal. Rptr. 2d at 188 (indicating that closure of juvenile proceedings is permitted if there is a reasonable likelihood of substantial prejudice). But see *Press-Enterprise II*, 478 U.S. at 14 (rejecting the reasonable likelihood test); Chap. 2-2(f) *supra*.

496. N.Y. CRIM. PROC. LAW § 720.15(3). The Family Court Act, section 741(b), authorizes exclusion of the general public, but makes an exception for those having "a direct interest in the case." *Id.* § 741(b).

497. 519 N.E.2d 825 (N.Y. 1988).

498. *Id.* at 830.

499. See *id.* ("Because the presumption of openness was not overcome, the cases before us are resolved under the statutes without reaching constitutional issues."); see In re Thomas Chase, 446 N.Y.S.2d 1000, 1009 (Fam. Ct. 1982) (holding juvenile in delinquency proceeding failed to overcome the "presumption of openness of the trial"). The family court allowed two members of the press to be seated inconspicuously in the rear of the room (no audio-visual coverage) in the hearing on charges that Malcolm Shabazz set a fire resulting in the death of his grandmother Betty Shabazz, the widow of Malcolm X. See In re Application for News Media Coverage in the Matter of M.S., 662 N.Y.S.2d 207 (Fam. Ct. 1997). The court found that the First Amendment, as well as state law, "strongly favor public access to court proceedings and the presumption of openness." *Id.* at 210. In interpreting family court rules on access, "[j]udicial discretion must be exercised against a strong presumption of openness." *Id.* at 209. Moreover, the court held that "public as represented by the press, has a right to know that the court is meeting its responsibility towards the community." *Id.* Citing the value of openness and applying constitutional standards, the court found that the juvenile had failed to establish "an overriding interest establishing that closure is essential to preserve higher values." *Id.* at 210. See Daily Gazette Co. v. Harrigan, 618 N.Y.S.2d 469 (App. Div. 1994) (granting public and press access to a sentencing hearing of a youth offender charged with a felony).

500. 568 N.E.2d 600 (Mass. 1991).

quency hearings involving children charged with murder,[501] it "is reasonably clear that the legislature intended generally that a judge not exclude the public from [the] hearing."[502] The legislature could rationally conclude that the public interest in such a serious crime "warrants opening the courtroom to all proceedings."[503] While the court did not adopt a standard for closure, it did hold that "the presumption is that the courtroom will be open."[504]

Finally, some state statutes and courts have granted public access to delinquency proceedings conditioned on press agreement not to publish certain information. It has been argued that placing such a condition on public access is an abuse of statutory discretion.[505] The media has also asserted that the condition operates as a prior restraint on publication. If the restraint extends to publication of material lawfully derived from sources other than the juvenile proceedings, such a restriction is especially troublesome.[506]

---

501. MASS. GEN. LAWS ch. 119, § 65 was amended by adding the words "except when the child is charged with murder in the first or second degree," preceding a requirement that a judge in a juvenile session "shall exclude the general public from the room, admitting only such persons as may have a direct interest in the case."

502. 568 N.E.2d at 601. The trial judge had allowed the public access to delinquency proceedings involving five juveniles charged with murder, aggravated rape, and armed robbery. *Id.* at 602-03.

503. *Id.* at 603.

504. *Id.* at 604. See Ohio ex rel. News Herald v. Ottawa County Ct. of C.P., 671 N.E.2d 5, 8 (Ohio 1996) (holding "patently unconstitutional" gag order preventing nonparty media from publishing material concerning open proceeding in juvenile court until juvenile is transferred to be tried as adult).

505. See Brelsford & Silvers, *supra* note 439, at 9.

506. See Chap. 2-1(d) *supra*. The Supreme Court has held that the press has a First Amendment right to publish truthful material lawfully obtained absent extraordinary circumstances. See Smith v. Daily Mail Publ'g Co., 443 U.S. 97 (1979); Chap. 2-1(c) *supra*. Examples of the use of the prior restraint doctrine against conditional access orders in delinquency cases include *Edward A. Sherman Publishing Co. v. Goldberg*, 443 A.2d 1252, 1257 (R.I. 1982) ("That portion of the order conditioning petitioners' attendance upon their agreeing in advance not to publish the name of the juvenile is impermissibly overbroad, as well as an unconstitutional prior restraint on the press.").

In *George W. Prescott Publishing Co. v. Stoughton Division, District Court*, 701 N.E.2d 307 (Mass. 1998), the court reversed as "an unlawful prior restraint on the press" a lower court order allowing press access to the juvenile session proceeding, but which prohibited the press from photographing or from publishing the names or addresses of any child who engaged in delinquent conduct or who testified during the trial of adults charged with contributing to the delinquency of minors. *Id.* at 309. The court held that the trial judge failed to satisfy the standard "that any order seeking to enjoin speech must be based on detailed findings of fact that (a) identify a compelling interest that the restraint will serve and (b) demonstrate that no reasonable, less restrictive alternative to the order is available." *Id.* (citing Care & Protection of Edith, 659 N.E.2d 1174 (Mass. 1996)). See Ohio ex rel. News Herald v. Ottawa County Ct. of C.P., 671 N.E.2d 5, 8 (Ohio 1996) (holding "patently unconstitutional" gag order preventing nonparty media from publishing material concerning open proceeding in juvenile court until juvenile is transferred to be tried as adult).

In *In re J.D.C.*,[507] the District of Columbia Court of Appeals applied a statute and court rule affording the juvenile judge discretion to admit the media on condition that they not identify the child or members of his family. The juvenile judge had granted a child's motion to close the proceedings to the *Wall Street Journal*, which had previously published his name, but denied it as to other media.[508] The court of appeals held that all of the media should be excluded because "there is no reasonable assurance that J.D.C.'s anonymity can be adequately protected in the event of press coverage of further proceedings in the case."[509] Thus, the court concluded that "fidelity to the scheme requires us to hold that the [minor's] right to anonymity trumps the media's interest in attending and reporting on proceedings in a specific juvenile case."[510] The prior restraint doctrine was not implicated by the statute and rule, the court held, because the restraint was limited to information obtained through the judicial proceeding: "A prior restraint occurs when the state attempts to prohibit the publication of material already in the possession of the media."[511] The constitutionality of these conditional restraints is discussed further in the section that follows.

§ 3-3(b). Abuse, Neglect, Dependency, and Custody Proceedings.

The law of public access to abuse, neglect, dependency and custody matters in juvenile court has developed in a manner similar to the law surrounding access to juvenile delinquency proceedings.[512] In this context as well, courts have hesitated to extend a First Amendment-based right of access or to recognize the applicability of state open court laws.[513] Rather, access issues largely involve

---

507. 594 A.2d 70 (D.C. 1991) (applying D.C. CODE ANN. § 16-2316(e) and D.C. SUPER. CT. JUV. R. 53).

508. While the court indicated that the *Journal* had pledged to abide by the condition, the newspaper obtained the minor's identity from other sources and did not violate its agreement. See In re J.D.C., 594 A.2d at 72.

509. *Id.*

510. *Id.* at 77. See *id.* at 75 ("[I]f there is no reasonable assurance that the admission of the press will be consistent with the protection of juvenile respondent's anonymity, then exclusion may be the only alternative which will not compromise the legislature's paramount aim.").

511. *Id.* at 74 n.6.

512. See generally Brelsford & Myers, *Juvenile Courts: Part II, The Value of Access*, 12 COMM. LAW. 14 (Fall 1994); Sokol, *Trying Dependency Cases in Public: A First Amendment Inquiry*, 45 UCLA L. REV. 881, 918, 926 (1998) (arguing for a presumption of openness for dependency hearings because public access would enhance "the reliability of judicial fact finding," establish "procedural regularity," and lead to "greater public trust in the institutions charged with protecting children"). The discussion that follows will generally refer to neglect, abuse, dependency, or custody proceedings collectively as "dependency" proceedings.

513. See, e.g., In re Reuben R., 641 N.Y.S.2d 621 (Sup. Ct. 1996) (holding that in abuse and neglect proceeding involving parents charged with murdering six-year-old child, family court erred in opening proceedings to the public in "light of the extraordinarily sensitive and personal nature of

statutory interpretation. Statutes that mandate or rebuttably presume closure may be interpreted flexibly in the name of the First Amendment.[514]

The Florida Supreme Court, following the decision in *Barron v. Florida Freedom Newspapers, Inc.*,[515] has recognized that "family law proceedings must be cloaked with a presumption of openness."[516] Some statutes create a presumption of public and/or press access. For example, in 1997, New York revised its rules to provide that "the public, including the news media, shall have access" to the Family Court.[517] Closure is allowed "only if the judge presiding ... determines, on a case-by-case [basis,] using supporting evidence, that such exclusion

---

the information that will be addressed ... coupled with the strong evidence presented that publication of this information would be harmful to the [surviving] children and the impossibility of protecting the children's right to privacy due to the previous disclosure of the children's identities"); In re Katherine B., 596 N.Y.S.2d 847, 851 (App. Div. 1993) (rejecting a media claim of constitutional right of access to child protective proceedings that "have historically been closed in New York State"); see also P.B. v. C.C., 647 N.Y.S.2d 732 (App. Div. 1996) (reversing decision opening portions of custody hearing in case involving child actor); In re Marcovitz Children, 22 MEDIA L. REP. (BNA) 1031 (N.Y. County Ct. 1992) (citing *Katherine B.* but allowing a single media representative to be present at the neglect hearing to take hand written notes). But see Anonymous v. Anonymous, 550 N.Y.S.2d 704, 705 (App. Div. 1990) ("Public access to court proceedings is strongly favored, both as a matter of constitutional law and as matter of statutory imperative.").

In *New Jersey Division of Youth & Family Services v. J.B.*, 576 A.2d 261, 266-67 (N.J. 1990), the court appeared to embrace a First Amendment-based right of access to a custody hearing. "There is an expectation based in history and the first amendment, and embodied in our court rules, see R.1:2-1, that civil trials and proceedings will be open to the public." *Id.* at 269. But, the court added, the "compelling state interest in protecting victims of child abuse from the embarrassment of testifying in an open courtroom, with the attendant possibility of media coverage, justifies a presumption that [proceedings] will be closed to the public." *Id.* The court noted that it would be "an unusual case in which a factual context that poses no danger of trauma or embarrassment to the child coincides with the general public's interest in following the proceeding." *Id.* However, the court determined that the proceedings at bar constituted such "a rare situation" and the court, therefore, affirmed an order granting press access to a preliminary neglect hearing. *Id.* at 270.

514. See In re Nogues, 22 MEDIA L. REP. (BNA) 1932 (Fla. County Ct. 1994) (interpreting Florida's mandatory rule to require notice and a hearing to determine whether "compelling government interests exist which would justify closure"); see also In re Brown, 18 MEDIA L. REP. (BNA) 1460, 1461 (Fla. County Ct. 1990) ("This court believes that the court has discretion as to when media will have access to dependency proceedings but that discretion is not unlimited."); New Jersey Div. of Youth & Family Servs. v. J.B., 576 A.2d at 269 ("The presumption of closure does not, however, equate with a mandatory rule. Members of the public, including the press, must be free to make application to the trial court to be permitted to attend [juvenile] proceedings.").

515. See Chap. 3-2(b) *supra*.

516. See Amendments to the Florida Family Law Rules of Procedure, 723 So. 2d 208, 209 (Fla. 1998).

517. N.Y. UNIF. R. FAM. CT., § 205.4(a). The section begins "The Family Court is open to the public." See generally Burton, *Reflections on Open Family Courts: The First 100 Days*, N.Y. L.J., Dec. 31, 1997 ("Since the adoption of this rule, there has not been a case on record where the public has been barred from Family Court.").

is warranted in that case," based on specified factors guiding judicial discretion.[518] Most statutes, however, vest broad discretion in the courts. The same diversity of standards governing the exercise of that discretion that exists in the delinquency context is evident in dependency cases as well.

Nevertheless, there are differences between these two classes of juvenile proceedings. In *In re T.R.*,[519] the Ohio Supreme Court asserted that "[t]he need for confidentiality is even more compelling in the case of a child who is abused, neglected, or dependent."[520] Such a proceeding, the court noted, does not involve an alleged delinquent but an innocent victim — thus, government can often demonstrate a compelling interest in protecting the minor victim from psychological harm and in protecting the minor's privacy interests.[521] Further, while delinquency proceedings are in many ways analogous to criminal cases, especially when older juveniles are charged with serious crimes, the same cannot be said of dependency proceedings.[522] And, the court in *In re T.R.* continued, public access would threaten the effectiveness of laws designed to protect the confidential records of juvenile courts and child services agencies.[523]

These and similar considerations led the court in *In re T.R.* to "hold that there is no qualified right of public access to juvenile court proceedings to determine if a child is abused, neglected or dependent, or to determine custody of a minor

---

518. N.Y. UNIF. R. FAM. CT. § 205.4(b). Findings must be made prior to ordering exclusion. Among the factors governing the court's exercise of its discretion are "the nature of the proceeding, the privacy interests of individuals before the court, and the need for protection of the litigants, in particular, children, from harm," and the unavailability or inappropriateness of "less restrictive alternatives to exclusion." *Id.* § 205.4(b)(3)(4). The Family Court in *In re Application for News Media Coverage in the Matter of M.S.*, 662 N.Y.S.2d 207, 210 (Fam. Ct. 1997), noted concern for "revictimization" in child protective proceedings as a basis for distinguishing access issues in such cases from those that arise in the context of delinquency proceedings. See Chap. 3-3(a) *supra*.

519. 556 N.E.2d 439 (Ohio), *cert. denied*, 498 U.S. 958 (1990). The case involved a consolidated custody and dependency proceeding relating to Baby Tessa, a child born to a surrogate mother.

520. *Id.* at 449.

521. See *id.*; see also In re a Minor, 595 N.E.2d 1052, 1057 (Ill. 1992) ("The dissent does not recognize the significant fact that *victims of child abuse* should not be treated in the same manner as *juvenile criminal offenders*.") (emphasis added); see also Sanchez, *Barring the Media from the Courtroom in Child Abuse Cases: Who Should Prevail?*, 46 BUFF. L. REV. 217 (1998) ("To avoid further trauma to children, courts, at a minimum, must be given and must use their power to exclude all the media during at least the child victim-witness's testimony.").

522. See In re T.R., 556 N.E.2d at 449. In *San Bernardino County Department of Social Services v. Superior Court*, 283 Cal. Rptr. 332, 341 (Ct. App. 1991), the court acknowledged that "[b]ecause juvenile proceedings, in particular dependency proceedings, are civil in nature and intended to be rehabilitative instead of punitive, admittedly there is less concern of unjust convictions against which public access might serve as a check."

523. 556 N.E.2d at 449.

child."[524] In this regard, the Ohio Supreme Court noted that juvenile courts did not exist at common law, function differently than courts of general jurisdiction, and "are usually private."[525] The court did acknowledge the public interest in juvenile proceedings and that "[p]ublic access to the juvenile court process can promote informed public involvement in government and enhance public confidence in the judicial process."[526] Nevertheless, the court concluded that "it seems clear that public access to such proceedings does not necessarily play a positive role in the juvenile court process."[527]

Applying the state's discretionary statute, the Ohio Supreme Court held that abuse, neglect, dependency, and custody proceedings "are neither presumptively open nor presumptively closed" to the press and public.[528] Accordingly, it rejected the "overriding interest" test of *Press-Enterprise I* and other standards weighted in favor of access.[529] Proceedings may be closed, after an evidentiary hearing, based on findings that "(1) there exists a reasonable and substantial basis for believing public access could harm the child or endanger the fairness of the proceeding, and (2) the potential for harm outweighs the benefits of public access."[530]

It has been argued that the Ohio Supreme Court in *Ohio ex rel. Dispatch Printing Co. v. Lias*,[531] implicitly overruled *In re T.R.* and recognized a constitutional right of access to juvenile proceedings.[532] *Lias* places far greater emphasis on values of public access than its predecessor, concluding that "the rationale underlying the public right of access in criminal trials pertain, with minor exceptions to juvenile court proceedings."[533] While the court in *Lias* reiterated the standard fashioned in *T.R.*, it added a requirement that there be "no reason-

---

524. *Id.* at 450. The court further held that the open courts provision of the Ohio Constitution created no greater access rights than the First Amendment. See *id.* at 448.

525. *Id.* at 448-49; see Florida Publ'g Co. v. Morgan, 322 S.E.2d 233, 238 (Ga. 1984) ("[I]n their relatively brief history, it would appear that juvenile proceedings have been closed to the public. Therefore we are unable to conclude that there is any historically-based constitutional presumption of openness applicable to juvenile court proceedings.").

526. In re T.R., 556 N.E.2d at 450. The court also noted the value of public access to check governmental abuses: "As with all operations of government, the public has an interest in scrutinizing the workings of the juvenile court." *Id.* (citing In re N.H.B., 769 P.2d 844, 849 (Utah App. 1989)).

527. 556 N.E.2d at 449.
528. *Id.* at 451.
529. See *id.* at 450-51.
530. *Id.* at 451.
531. 628 N.E.2d 1368 (Ohio 1994).
532. See Brelsford & Myers, *supra* note 512, at 18.
533. 628 N.E.2d at 1372.

able alternatives to closure."[534] And, the court "reaffirmed" a requirement that closure orders be "narrowly tailored" to protect the child's welfare and not unduly burden "the public's right of access."[535] At bottom, however, *Lias* is a case of statutory interpretation, purporting to apply, not overrule, *In re T.R.* A majority of the court that concurred in *Lias*, a unanimous decision, had also joined in *In re T.R.* And, a subsequent decision observes that "[n]othing in *Lias* suggests that the holding in *In re T.R.* was modified or overruled."[536] Nevertheless, *Lias* certainly employs constitutional values and some constitutional standards in reviewing a juvenile court's exercise of statutory discretion.

In *San Bernardino County Department of Social Services v. Superior Court*,[537] a California appellate court concluded that "[p]ublic access may improve juvenile court practice and serve many, if not all of the societal values first recognized in the context of a criminal trial."[538] Whereas the court in *In re T.R.* questioned the functional value of public access to juvenile proceedings, the California court emphasized that open proceedings can improve fact-finding in dependency proceedings by discouraging perjury and encouraging other witnesses to come forward.[539] Moreover, the court noted that "[p]ublic access does serve as a check against governmental abuse or misuse of power which might result in unnecessary and unjust interference with these important liberties."[540] Noting the community outrage that often arises from cases of child abuse and neglect, the court asserted that "[p]ublic access to juvenile proceedings can serve 'an important prophylactic purpose, providing an outlet for community concern, hostility, and emotion.'"[541] Open proceedings, the court added, also serve an educational function, improving public understanding of the operation of the system and its ability to make informed decisions regarding the need for reform.[542]

Nevertheless, the court held that "the First Amendment right of access does not extend to juvenile dependency proceedings."[543] In part, this conclusion flowed from the court's uncertainty in assessing the potential harm to the minor

---

534. *Id*. at 1372; see New Jersey Div. of Youth & Family Servs. v. J.B., 576 A.2d 261, 267 (N.J. 1990) ("The societal and institutional values served by open access to criminal proceedings are also implicated in civil proceedings.").
535. 628 N.E.2d at 1373.
536. In re Joanne M., 659 N.E.2d 864, 867 (Ohio App. 1995).
537. 283 Cal. Rptr. 332 (Ct. App. 1991).
538. *Id*. at 341; see *id*. at 342 ("[W]e believe that public access can play 'a significant positive role in the functioning' of juvenile court dependency proceedings.").
539. See *id*. at 342.
540. *Id*.
541. *Id*. (citation omitted).
542. See *id*.
543. *Id*. at 343.

from public access.[544] "With the welfare of minors at stake, we are reluctant to impose the strict standard for closure required for a First Amendment right unless compelled to do so by the United States Supreme Court."[545] Rather than adopt a constitutional standard, therefore, the court asked whether "there is a reasonable likelihood that such access will be harmful to the child's or children's best interest in this case."[546]

The question of conditional access has also arisen in the context of dependency proceedings. For example, in *In re Minor*,[547] the Illinois Supreme Court held that a juvenile court could constitutionally require the press to pledge not to reveal the identity of the child victims of physical and sexual abuse as a condition of access to dependency proceedings.[548] The court distinguished its earlier decision holding that a state statute protecting the juvenile's identity by conditioning press access could not be constitutionally applied on two grounds. First, the juvenile in the earlier case was involved in a delinquency matter, whereas the case at issue involved innocent victims of abuse. Second, in the case before it, the newspaper "discovered the identities of the minor victims only through their presence at the closed juvenile proceedings concerning those minors."[549] In the earlier case, the newspaper had learned the minor's identity through routine reportorial techniques.

---

544. See *id.*; see also *id.* at 341:

> In our view, there can be little doubt that the embarrassment, emotional trauma and additional stress placed on the minor by public proceedings and the publicity engendered by public proceedings may well interfere with the rehabilitation and reunification of the family. Further, the parents of a dependent child face a potential social stigma from public proceedings which would further interfere with rehabilitation and reunification.

545. *Id.* at 343.

546. *Id.* at 345. The court deemed the constitutional standard "possibly too constraining in the juvenile court setting and constitutionally unnecessary." *Id.* It did not decide whether express findings would be required or who would bear the burden of proof. See *id.* at 345 n.11.

547. 595 N.E.2d 1052 (Ill. 1992).

548. 705 ILL. COMP. STAT. 405/1-5(6), excepts the news media from exclusion of the public from juvenile proceedings but allows the court, for the minor's "protection and for good cause shown, [to] prohibit any person or agency present in court from further disclosing a minor's identity." See Geraghty & Raphael, *Reporter's Privilege and Juvenile Anonymity: Two Confidentiality Policies on a Collision Course*, 16 LOY. U. CHI. L.J. 43, 72-80 (1984).

549. In re a Minor, 595 N.E.2d at 1055 (distinguishing In re a Minor, 537 N.E.2d 292 (Ill. 1989)). A California Court of Appeal in *San Bernardino County Department of Social Services v. Superior Court,* 283 Cal. Rptr. at 344 (citations omitted), rejected the lower court's order conditioning access, finding that it restricted publication of information obtained outside the courtroom:

> The juvenile court clearly was without the power to restrict the press's right to investigate and publish information which it has lawfully obtained. The judiciary cannot prohibit the publication of a juvenile's name and picture when that information has been lawfully obtained by the media. Here the court, through its conditions, attempted to prohibit the publication of information without regard to how the press obtained the information. If the infor-

In the court's view, the government has a "compelling interest" as *parens patriae* since public disclosure of the victims' identities "could cause continuing emotional trauma to these unfortunate children and impede the lengthy and difficult healing process which they must endure."[550] Further, the court held that the minor victims had a compelling interest in nondisclosure — their state constitutional right to be free from governmental invasions of privacy.[551] Thus, the court concluded that "[u]nder the facts of the case, there is no compelling need for free and unfettered disclosure of the minor victims' identities."[552] The press was free to report everything about the proceeding but the victims' identities and, the court concluded, it had no right to publish information obtained only by attending a juvenile proceeding closed to the public. Unlike *Oklahoma Publishing Co. v. District Court*,[553] the case before the court involved closed proceedings, the minors' identities had never been publicity revealed, and they were innocent victims.[554] *Smith v. Daily Mail Publishing Co.*[555] was similarly distinguished as involving a juvenile offender whose identity was "obtained through routine reporting techniques."[556]

Absent Supreme Court pronouncement, it is unlikely that many lower courts will fashion a First Amendment-based right of access to juvenile proceedings. The tradition of confidentiality and closure is apparently too strong. But some courts do appear willing to consider a rule of presumptive access and to invoke First Amendment-inspired balancing standards in interpreting and applying state law.[557]

---

mation was or is lawfully obtained, it is beyond the juvenile court's power to so restrain the press.

See Baltimore Sun Co. v. Maryland, 667 A.2d 166, 169 (Md. 1995) ("[W]hile a court can place reasonable restrictions on the media's use of information obtained in a confidential judicial proceeding, it cannot limit the media's publication of information which it legitimately collected from other sources, and cannot condition access to the juvenile proceeding upon the media's publication of material specified by the court."); Note, *The Maryland Survey: 1995-1996, Recent Decisions: The Maryland Court of Appeals*, 56 MD. L. REV. 656 (1997) (critiquing the *Baltimore Sun* holding that media could attend juvenile proceedings but could not publish information so acquired).

550. In re a Minor, 595 N.E.2d at 1056; see *id.* ("We find that the danger of public disclosure and the probability of irreparable adverse effects which such disclosure would entail to be compelling state interests at stake in the case.").

551. See *id.*
552. *Id.*
553. 430 U.S. 308 (1977). See Chap. 2-1(d) *supra*.
554. See 595 N.E.2d at 1057.
555. 443 U.S. 97 (1979). See Chap. 2-1(c) *supra*.
556. 595 N.E.2d at 1057.
557. See Tennessee v. James, 902 S.W.2d 911 (Tenn. 1995) (although not directly invoking a First Amendment-based rule of presumptive access, court employed "balancing" standards that reflect constitutional consideration); Tennessee v. James, 1996 WL 22631 (Tenn. 1996) (same).

Chapter 4

CAMERAS IN THE COURTROOM

§ 4-1. Supreme Court Precedent.
§ 4-2. Federal Court Proceedings.
  § 4-2(a). Constitutional Challenges and Waiver.
  § 4-2(b). Changing the Rules.
§ 4-3. State Court Proceedings.

§ 4-1. Supreme Court Precedent.

The advent of *Court TV* and sensational trials such as the O.J. Simpson case serve to illustrate the considerable public interest in television coverage of judicial proceedings.[1] Years earlier, negative public reaction to the assertedly circus-like media coverage of the trial of Bruno Hauptmann[2] had produced an unfavorable reaction to the practice of courtroom photography[3] and an outpouring of state restrictions. By the mid-1960s, the Federal Rules of Criminal Procedure prohibited televised coverage of criminal proceedings.[4]

---

1. See generally Harris, *The Appearance of Justice: Court TV, Conventional Television, and Public Understanding of the Criminal Justice System*, 35 ARIZ. L. REV. 785 (1993); Lind, *Defender of the Faith in the Midst of the Simpson Circus*, 24 SW. U. L. REV. 1215 (1995); Roberts, *An Empirical and Normative Analysis of the Impact of Televised Courtroom Proceedings*, 51 SMU L. REV. 621 (1998); Sager & Frederiksen, *Televising the Judicial Branch: In Furtherance of the Public's First Amendment Rights*, 69 S. CAL. L. REV. 1519 (1996); Comment, *Lights, Camera, Trial: Pursuit of Justice or the Emmy?*, 27 SETON HALL L. REV. 1542 (1997). Compare Burcham, *High-Profile Trials: Can Government Sell the "Right" to Broadcast the Proceedings?*, 3 UCLA ENT. L. REV. 169, 218 (1996) ("The First Amendment ... prohibits government from seeking to leverage public desire to observe public court proceedings into additional revenue.") with Easton, *Whose Life Is It Anyway?: A Proposal to Redistribute Some of the Economic Benefits of Cameras in the Courtroom from Broadcasters to Crime Victims*, 49 S.C. L. REV. 1 (1997) (arguing that fees should be imposed for broadcast rights to criminal trials and the proceeds used to compensate victims).

2. See New Jersey v. Hauptmann, 180 A. 809 (N.J.), *cert. denied*, 296 U.S. 649 (1935); Anderson, *Democracy and the Demystification of Courts: An Essay*, 14 REV. LITIG. 627, 627-31 (1995).

3. See, e.g., 62 A.B.A. REP. 1134-35 (1937). Canon 35 of the ABA CANONS OF JUDICIAL ETHICS, as amended in 1952 to include broadcasting, 77 A.B.A. REP. 610-11 (1952), provided: "Proceedings in court should be conducted with fitting dignity and decorum. The taking of photographs in the court room, during sessions of the court or recesses between sessions, and the broadcasting or televising of court proceedings are calculated to detract from the essential dignity of the proceedings, distract the witness in giving testimony, degrade the court, and create misconceptions with respect thereto in the mind of the public and should not be permitted." The *Code of Judicial Conduct*, which replaced the Canons from 1972 until the 1980s, also adopted a ban, with limited exceptions, on broadcasting in Canon 3A(7). For the early history of these rules, see *Estes v. Texas*, 381 U.S. 532, 596-601 (1965) (Harlan, J., concurring).

4. See, e.g., People v. Munday, 117 N.E. 286, 300 (Ill. 1917) (rejecting courtroom photography, "since it was not in keeping with the dignity a court should maintain, or with the proper and orderly conduct of its business"). The argument that cameras in the courtroom are inconsistent with the

The Supreme Court entered the debate in *Estes v. Texas*,[5] which arose in the context of the highly publicized prosecution of financier Billy Sol Estes, a former aide to President Lyndon Johnson. Photographic and broadcast coverage of the pretrial proceedings had caused considerable disruption[6] and the trial judge imposed significant restrictions on media coverage of the trial itself.[7] Nevertheless, the Supreme Court held that Estes' right to a fair trial had been infringed by the media presence in the courtroom.

Justice Clark, writing for the Court, acknowledged that the public has a right to be informed of what occurs in its courts, but concluded that the First Amendment requires only that the press, including the television press, be able to attend and report what occurs in open court. In the courtroom, Justice Clark asserted, the news media has no First Amendment rights beyond those of the public. Banning cameras is not discriminatory against the broadcast media because, like the print media and the public, it remains free to attend and report on the proceeding.[8] The press' exercise of its own First Amendment rights "must necessarily be subject to the maintenance of absolute fairness in the judicial process."[9] In finding that Estes had been denied a fair trial, the Court did not rely on record evidence of actual prejudice; rather, it concluded that the use of cameras in the courtroom "involves such a probability that prejudice will result that it is deemed inherently lacking in due process."[10]

In that regard, the Court identified four sources of potential prejudice from the presence of cameras — the jury, the independent witnesses, the trial judge, and

---

"dignity and decorum" of the courts has been a leading theme. In *Ex parte Strum*, 136 A. 312 (Md. Spec. App. 1927), for example, a Maryland court invoked its contempt powers to punish photographers and editors for violating the "decorum of the court" by taking photographs of a murder trial. See Dyer & Hauserman, *Electronic Coverage of the Courts: Exceptions to Exposure*, 75 GEO. L.J. 1633, 1634 (1987).

5. 381 U.S. 532 (1965).

6. See *id.* at 536. More than a dozen cameramen reportedly moved around the courtroom during the proceedings. Wires crossed the courtroom and microphones were fixed on the judge, the jury, and counsel. After viewing filmed footage of these hearings, Justice Clark asserted that they "clearly illustrate that the picture presented was not one of that judicial serenity and calm to which petitioner was entitled." *Id.*

7. See *id.* at 537-38. During trial, recording equipment and cameras were placed in a booth at the rear of the courtroom. Live broadcast coverage was limited to the prosecution's opening and closing statements and the return of the jury verdict. Most coverage was through film, without sound, used as a backdrop to news commentary. See *id.* at 536-37.

8. See *id.* at 541-42. But see *id.* at 540 ("When the advances in these arts permit reporting by printing press or by television without their present hazards to a fair trial we will have another case."). Similarly, Chief Justice Warren, in a concurring opinion, observed that "[s]o long as the television industry, like other communications media, is free to send representatives to trials and to report on those trials to its viewers, there is no abridgement of the freedom of the press." *Id.* at 584 (Warren, C.J., concurring).

9. *Id.* at 539.

10. *Id.* at 542-43.

the defendant. Of greatest significance to the Court was the potential impact of cameras on the jury. Jurors in a televised trial, the Court suggested, will know that friends and neighbors are watching.[11] Further, cameras, even when camouflaged, can distract a juror's attention — "[i]t is the awareness of the fact of telecasting that is felt by the juror throughout the trial."[12] Similarly, witnesses might be intimidated, might play to the camera, or might be unable to testify.[13] Moreover, the court asserted, televising trials imposes additional management responsibilities on judges and subjects them to unnecessary pressure — "Judges are human beings also and are subject to the same psychological reactions as laymen."[14] Finally, for the defendant, the Court indicated, the presence of cameras is "a form of mental — if not physical — harassment, resembling a police lineup or the third degree."[15]

Chief Justice Warren, joined by Justices Douglas and Goldberg, appeared even more critical of cameras in the courtroom and more dogmatic in the view "that the televising of criminal trials is inherently a denial of due process."[16] According to the Chief Justice, three propositions could not be disputed:

> (1) that the televising of trials diverts the trial from its proper purpose in that it has an inevitable impact on all the trial participants; (2) that it gives the public the wrong impression about the purpose of trials, thereby detracting from the dignity of court proceedings and lessening the reliability of trials; and (3) that it singles out certain defendants and subjects them to trials under prejudicial conditions not experienced by others.[17]

The Chief Justice asserted that, even when trial participants do not deliberately play to the television audience, subconsciously "all trial participants act differently in the presence of television cameras."[18] In addition, the Chief Justice

---

11. See *id.* at 545.

12. *Id.* at 546; see also Comment, *supra* note 1, at 1562-63 ("[T]he camera may also impact jurors indirectly by affecting the duration of a trial, the length of which directly affects jurors' attitudes, or motivate attorney grandstanding behavior that may influence jurors as well.").

13. See 381 U.S. at 547; see Comment, *supra* note 1, at 1564 ("At a minimum, it must be acknowledged that the impact of the camera is 'incalculable,' potentially causing witnesses to overdramatize or re-shape their testimony.").

14. 381 U.S. at 548; see Comment, *supra* note 1, at 1559 ("[C]ertain judges may, even subconsciously, base their decision whether to allow camera access on personal desires for fame and notoriety. Other judges may feel pressure to succumb to media and public pleas to view the trial on television and allow camera access although they are aware of the complications the camera may add to an already notorious trial.").

15. 381 U.S. at 549.

16. *Id.* at 565 (Warren, C.J., concurring).

17. *Id.*

18. *Id.* at 570; see *id.* at 569-70 ("The present record provides ample support for scholars who have claimed that awareness that a trial is being televised to a vast, but unseen audience, is bound

warned, "[t]he televising of trials would cause the public to equate the trial process with the forms of entertainment regularly seen on television and with the commercial objectives of the television industry."[19] Finally, he argued that it would be the sensational case that would draw media coverage of the courtroom, focusing public attention on those persons who already experience the greatest difficulty in securing a fair trial.[20]

The four dissenting justices in *Estes* rejected any absolute constitutional prohibition on cameras in the courtroom.[21] Although no First Amendment claim had been made, the dissenters cautioned against "imposing any per se rule which, in the light of future technology, might serve to stifle or abridge true First Amendment rights."[22] As nothing in the record indicated that Estes had suffered actual prejudice, Justice Stewart asserted that hypothetical adverse effects of camera coverage should not be sufficient to reverse a conviction.

While Justice Clark's and Chief Justice Warren's opinions in *Estes* plainly embrace a per se prohibition against telecasting criminal trials, there did not appear to be a majority of the Court in support of such a rule. Justice Harlan, who provided the fifth vote in *Estes*, limited his concurrence to the facts of the case, which he described as involving the televising of "a notorious criminal trial."[23] While rejecting any First Amendment-based right to televise trials,[24] and labeling the arguments for television access to the courtroom "peculiarly unpersuasive,"[25] Justice Harlan expressed concern that the Court not prevent

---

to increase nervousness and tension, cause an increased concern about appearances, and bring to the surface latent opportunism that the traditional dignity of the courtroom would discourage.").

19. *Id.* at 571.

20. See *id.* at 576-77.

21. See *id.* at 601-02 (Stewart, J., dissenting). Justices Black, Brennan, and White dissented as well and joined Justice Stewart's opinion.

22. *Id.* at 604; see *id.* at 614-15 ("The suggestion that there are limits upon the public's right to know what goes on in the courts causes me deep concern. The idea of imposing upon any medium of communications the burden of justifying its presence is contrary to where I had always thought the presumption must be in the area of First Amendment freedoms.").

23. *Id.* at 587 (Harlan, J., concurring). Although Justice Harlan concurred in Justice Clark's opinion, he did so subject "to the reservations and only to the extent indicated in this opinion." *Id.* at 590.

24. See *id.* at 589 ("The rights to print and speak, over television as elsewhere, do not embody an independent right to bring the mechanical facilities of the broadcasting and printing industries into the courtroom.").

25. *Id.* at 594-95. Responding to the argument that cameras in the courtroom can educate the public, Justice Harlan feared that it would be curiosity about the participants that would attract viewers. "Indeed, it would be naive not to suppose that it would be largely such factors that would qualify for commercial television 'billing,' and it is precisely that kind of case where the risks of permitting television coverage of the proceedings are at their greatest." *Id.* at 595. Justice Harlan also questioned the value of television in promoting accurate factfinding and diligent jurors, judges, and lawyers. "Once openness is . . . assured, the addition of masses of spectators would, I venture to say, detract rather than add to the reliability of the process." *Id.*; see also Comment,

"the States from pursuing a novel course of procedural experimentation."[26]

In his dissenting opinion, Justice Stewart read the Court's majority as having in fact adopted a per se ban.[27] But, Justice Brennan, in a separate dissent, contended that "only four of the five Justices voting to reverse rest on the proposition that televised criminal trials are constitutionally infirm, whatever the circumstances. . . . [T]oday's decision is not a blanket constitutional prohibition against the televising of state criminal trials."[28]

In the mid-1970s, several states began to experiment with televising court proceedings, but *Estes* created substantial doubt concerning the constitutionality of such programs.[29] In *Chandler v. Florida*,[30] the Supreme Court removed the uncertainty by rejecting the assertion that televising criminal trials is inherently prejudicial. Two Miami policemen, convicted of burglary, claimed that the Florida Supreme Court's rule authorizing cameras in the courtroom during their trial, without their consent, denied them due process.[31]

The Supreme Court, in an opinion by Chief Justice Burger, emphasized both advancements in broadcast technology and more traditional notions of federalism. *Estes* was not to be read, according to the Court, "as an absolute ban on state experimentation with an evolving technology, which, in terms of modes of

---

supra note 1, at 1567-68 ("The educational value of televised proceedings is undermined, however, because public perception is formed by watching courtroom drama that is arguably atypical. And even if the broadcast is truly indicative of conventional courtroom proceedings, commentary by the newscasters coupled with questionable camera focus may actually skew the accuracy of the broadcast.").

26. 381 U.S. at 587.

27. See *id.* at 614-15 (Stewart, J., dissenting); see also *id.* at 615 (White, J., dissenting) ("I agree with Mr. Justice Stewart that a finding of constitutional prejudice on this record entails erecting a flat ban on the use of cameras in the courtroom and believe that it is premature to promulgate such a broad constitutional principle at the present time.").

28. *Id.* at 617 (Brennan, J., dissenting).

29. In 1978, the Conference of State Chief Justices voted 44 to 1 to allow the highest court of each state to promulgate standards regulating radio, television, and photographic coverage of court proceedings. By October 1980, 19 states permitted televising trials and appellate proceedings, three permitted trial coverage only, and three others allowed only telecasting of appellate proceedings. Nevertheless, in 1979, the American Bar Association rejected the recommendation of two of its committees that would have allowed judges to permit cameras. See Chandler v. Florida, 449 U.S. 560, 564-65 (1981).

30. 449 U.S. 560 (1981). Florida initially required consent of the parties, which was seldom given. The Florida Supreme Court, after an extensive study including surveys of attorneys, judges, witnesses, and court personnel and a review of the experience of other states, determined that more was to be gained than lost by authorizing controlled telecasting. See *id.* at 564-66 (citing In re Petition of Post-Newsweek Stations, Fla., Inc., 370 So. 2d 764, 780 (Fla. 1979)).

31. Under the Florida program, only one camera in a fixed location and one technician were permitted. Only two minutes and 55 seconds of the trial, presenting only the prosecution's evidence, were ever broadcast. See 449 U.S. at 566-68.

mass communication, was in its relative infancy in 1964, and is, even now, in a state of continuing change."[32]

Nor was an absolute ban required by the potential for prejudice.[33] While studies exploring the impact of television on trial participants were limited and debatable, the Court found no empirical evidence that justified a per se rule. Technological change had diminished many of the concerns expressed in *Estes*,[34] the Court concluded, and safeguards had been built into the state experimental programs. Under these circumstances, the Court held that federalism dictated that states be allowed to continue to experiment.[35] *Chandler*'s rejection of a per se rule, however, did not mean that televising trials never violates due process. A criminal defendant, the Court emphasized, can still show an adverse impact on the jury or on trial participants in his case sufficient to establish a denial of due process.[36]

Chandler, therefore, embraced an essentially permissive position towards cameras in the courtroom. This same approach is now reflected in the American Bar Association's Standards for Criminal Justice.[37] Thus, the debate over cam-

---

32. *Id.* at 573-74.

33. See *id.* at 575 ("The risk of juror prejudice in some cases does not justify an absolute ban on news coverage of trials by printed media; so also the risk of such prejudice does not warrant an absolute constitutional ban on all broadcast coverage.").

34. See *id.* at 576-77.

35. See *id.* at 580 (quoting New State Ice Co. v. Liebmann, 285 U.S. 262, 311 (1932) (Brandeis, J., dissenting)) ("It is one of the happy incidents of the federal system that a single courageous State may, if its citizens choose, serve as a laboratory; and try novel social and economic experiments without risk to the rest of the country.").

36. See *id.* at 581. But see Missouri v. Simmons, 944 S.W.2d 165, 179 (Mo.), *cert. denied*, 118 S. Ct. 376 (1997) (holding that defendant failed to produce evidence that electronic media coverage "had an adverse impact on the trial participants sufficient to constitute a denial of due process"); South Carolina v. Byram, 485 S.E.2d 360, 366 (S.C. 1997) (holding that while the trial judge erred in deciding that he lacked discretion to exclude television without excluding other media, there was no evidence that defendant was prejudiced by having television cameras in courtroom during sentencing); Deatherage v. State Examining Bd., 932 P.2d 1267, 1272 (Wash. App.), *rev'd on other grounds*, 948 P.2d 828 (Wash. 1997) (holding that use of cameras and recording equipment at administrative hearing on disciplinary charges against psychologist resulting in license suspension does not deny due process absent proof of actual prejudice).

37. Following *Chandler*, the ABA in 1981 revised Canon 3A(7) of the *Code of Judicial Conduct* to permit cameras in the courtroom. In 1991, the ABA repealed Canon 3A(7), but retained a fair trial–free press standard adopted in 1981, which mirrors the revised Canon. Standard 8-3.8 of the *ABA Standards for Criminal Justice, Fair Trial and Free Press* provides:

> A judge should prohibit broadcasting, televising, recording, or photographing in courtrooms and areas immediately adjacent thereto during sessions of court, or recesses between sessions, except that under rules prescribed by a supervising appellate court or other appropriate authority, a judge may authorize broadcasting, televising, recording and photographing of judicial proceedings in courtrooms and areas immediately adjacent thereto consistent with the right to a fair trial and subject to express conditions, limitations, and guidelines which allow such coverage in a manner that will be unobtrusive, will not distract or otherwise ad-

eras in the courtroom has now shifted from the Supreme Court to the federal and state legislatures, courts, and judicial conferences. The per se approach adopted in *Estes* continues to be influential in the federal forum, but some assaults on that citadel have been made. In the states, the argument for television access has been far more successful, with 47 states now authorizing at least some form of courtroom photography, recording, or telecasting.

§ 4-2. Federal Court Proceedings.

§ 4-2(a). Constitutional Challenges and Waiver.

Since 1946, Federal Rule of Criminal Procedure 53 has expressly prohibited cameras in federal criminal proceedings.[38] In 1972, the Judicial Conference adopted a prohibition against "broadcasting, televising, recording, or taking photographs in the courtroom and areas immediately adjacent thereto," applicable to both criminal and civil proceedings.[39]

In *United States v. Hastings*,[40] the Eleventh Circuit rejected First and Sixth Amendment challenges to Rule 53 and to a corresponding local rule.[41] Although

---

versely affect witnesses or other trial participants, and will not otherwise interfere with the administration of justice.

38. FED. R. CRIM. P. 53 provides that, "taking of photographs in the court room during the progress of judicial proceedings or radio broadcasting of judicial proceedings from the court room shall not be permitted by the court." Although Rule 53 does not expressly prohibit television broadcasting, it is generally understood to include the electronic media. See United States v. Hastings, 695 F.2d 1278, 1279 n.5 (11th Cir.), *cert. denied*, 461 U.S. 931 (1983).

In response to the change of venue of the Oklahoma City bombing trial, Congress authorized closed circuit televising of trials to crime victims where the trial is moved more than 350 miles and out-of-state. See 42 U.S.C. § 10608(a) (1996) ("[I]n order to permit victims of crime to watch criminal trial proceedings . . . the court shall order closed circuit television of the proceeding . . . for viewing by such persons the court determines have a compelling interest in doing so and are otherwise unable to do so by reason of the inconvenience and expense caused by the change of venue."); see also United States v. McVeigh, 931 F. Supp. 753, 755 (D. Colo. 1996) (Court discontinued the sale of audio tapes of court proceedings from the Oklahoma City bombing case and refused to permit an audio feed of court proceedings, which would have allowed the media to create its own recordings.).

39. CODE OF JUDICIAL CONDUCT FOR UNITED STATES COURTS, Canon 3A(7) (1972).

40. 695 F.2d 1278 (11th Cir.), *cert. denied,* 461 U.S. 931 (1983); see Conway v. United States, 852 F.2d 187 (6th Cir.), *cert. denied,* 488 U.S. 943 (1988); United States v. Edwards, 785 F.2d 1293 (5th Cir. 1986); United States v. Kerley, 753 F.2d 617 (7th Cir. 1985); see also United States v. Yonkers Bd. of Educ., 587 F. Supp. 51 (S.D.N.Y.), *aff'd*, 747 F.2d 111 (2d Cir. 1984) (rejecting a constitutional challenge to local rule prohibiting use of tape-recording devices); Frank, *Cameras in the Courtroom: A First Amendment Right of Access*, 9 HASTINGS COMM. & ENT. L.J. 749, 765-67 (1987).

41. The defendant, Judge Alcee Hastings, moved to have his trial for accepting bribes televised, relying on his Sixth Amendment right to a public trial. The media intervened and, citing the First Amendment, sought an order authorizing camera coverage of the trial. The trial court, believing itself bound by Rule 53, denied both motions. See 695 F.2d at 1280.

Chandler had rejected a per se rule prohibiting cameras, the court of appeals asserted that, "just because television coverage is not constitutionally prohibited does not mean that television coverage is constitutionally mandated."[42] Nor did cases establishing a right of public access to criminal trials establish a right to televise because "[t]he right of access therein was the right to attend."[43] So long as journalists remain free to attend, listen, and report on the trial, the court concluded, their and the public's right of access to the proceeding is not infringed by operation of Rule 53.[44]

While the court in *Hastings* did recognize that Rule 53 restricts public access and newsgathering activities, it analogized the ban on cameras to a "time, place, and manner" restriction. Such a regulation, the court noted, is constitutional if it is "reasonable," promotes a "significant governmental interest," and does not "unwarrantedly abridge" the freedom of expression.[45] Applying this standard, the court of appeals concluded that trial judges have a significant interest "in preserving order and decorum in the courtroom" and an "institutional interest in procedures designed to increase the accuracy of the essential truth-seeking function of the trial."[46] While the court acknowledged the value of media coverage of courtroom proceedings, it could find no significant additional benefit from televising trials beyond those resulting from public access generally.[47] In addition, relying on *Estes*, the court noted the difficulty of determining the impact of television on trial participants and concluded:

> Promulgation of the current rules in a legislative-type manner is more appropriate than a case-by-case approach in light of the difficulty of detecting the adverse impact of media coverage, and in view of the minimal or nonexistent infringement on First Amendment concerns. Finally, judicial efficiency and economy are served by a per se rule.[48]

---

42. *Id.* But see Sager & Frederiksen, *supra* note 1, at 1549 ("[A]bsent a showing in a given case that televised coverage will demonstrably prejudice the parties or interfere with the conduct of justice, televised coverage should be permitted as a matter of constitutional right.").

43. 695 F.2d at 1280.

44. See *id.* at 1280-81 (citing Nixon v. Warner Comm., Inc., 435 U.S. 589, 608-09 (1978); Belo Broadcasting Corp. v. Clark, 654 F.2d 423, 426-27 (5th Cir. 1981)).

45. 695 F.2d at 1282.

46. *Id.* at 1283.

47. See *id.* at 1283:

> The key factor affecting public confidence [in the fairness of the criminal justice system] is the fact that trials are open and subject to public scrutiny, i.e., that trials are not secret. We can foresee no additional measure of confidence that might emanate merely from the different manner of media access. . . . Similarly, we do not conceive that the requested manner of access would enhance either the function of public trials as a check on judicial abuses, or the truth-finding role.

48. *Id.* at 1284.

The constitutionality of the federal ban on televising *civil* proceedings was similarly upheld in *Westmoreland v. CBS Inc.*[49] The case presented perhaps the paradigm First Amendment claim to televise civil proceedings. Both sides were willing to permit CNN to record and televise a libel trial of significant public importance. Then-trial judge Leval had catalogued powerful considerations that led him to conclude that CNN's petition seeking a waiver of the rules banning cameras "should be granted."[50] Judge Leval argued that the experience of 41 states had shown "that under appropriate rules preserving the court's control over the use of cameras, live filming and telecasting need not interfere in any significant degree with fair and orderly administration of justice."[51] In addition, Judge Leval noted that CNN was prepared to comply with guidelines governing courtroom telecasting used by many states.[52]

According to Judge Leval, "people should have the opportunity to see how the courts function," but they are too busy and judicial proceedings too time consuming for open access to provide that opportunity,[53] which could be achieved through televised proceedings. Moreover, Judge Leval contended that "it is very much in the interest of the federal judiciary to admit the camera into its proceedings,"[54] especially because the comparatively low public esteem in which the federal judiciary is held may be attributable to a lack of public familiarity with court proceedings. For these reasons, Judge Leval deemed "the eventual entry of the camera into the federal courtroom inevitable,"[55] but "in spite of its merit" denied CNN's petition for a waiver of the ban on the ground that the rules of the Judicial Conference and of his own court left him no choice.[56]

The Second Circuit, in an opinion by Judge Oakes, also rejected CNN's petition. Like the Eleventh Circuit in *Hastings*, Judge Oakes reasoned that, although there is a public right to attend criminal and civil trials, "[n]o case . . . has held that the public has a right to televised trials."[57] Until a First Amendment-based right is recognized, the Second Circuit concluded, "television cover-

---

49. 752 F.2d 16 (2d Cir.), *cert. denied,* 472 U.S. 1017 (1985); see Frank, *supra* note 40, at 767-72.

50. 596 F. Supp. 1166, 1169 (S.D.N.Y. 1984). The court of appeals summarized Judge Leval's views at 752 F.2d at 18 n.3.

51. 596 F. Supp. at 1168; see *id.* at 1167 ("It appears that filming can be done without the slightest obstruction of dignified, orderly court procedure.").

52. See *id.*

53. *Id.* at 1168-69.

54. *Id.* at 1168-69. But see Anderson, *supra* note 2, at 643.

55. 596 F. Supp. at 1169.

56. *Id.*

57. 752 F.2d at 22; see *id.* at 23 ("[T]hese [access] cases articulate a right to attend trials, not a right to view them on a television screen.").

age of federal trials is a right created by the consent of the judiciary, which has always had control over the courtrooms."[58]

Judge Winter concurred in the result but, unlike Judge Oakes, took the position that, "[s]ince live television is one of the many ways in which information [to the public about judicial proceedings] may be conveyed, the First Amendment is implicated in a request to televise."[59] Nevertheless, he concluded, like the Eleventh Circuit in *Hastings*, that a television ban is a legitimate "time, place, and manner" restriction.[60] Accordingly, Judge Winter also rejected a requirement of case-by-case balancing of the competing interests in the face of the Judicial Conference's "reasonable belief that the potentially undesirable effects of television cannot be detected, or detected in a timely fashion, on a case-by-case basis."[61]

Other federal judges have expressed frustrations similar to those of Judge Leval at being bound by an absolute prohibition on cameras in their courts. For example, in *Lac Courte Oreilles Band v. Wisconsin*,[62] a federal district judge considered herself compelled to deny the motion of numerous media entities seeking an order that would permit them to photograph and televise proceedings in her court. Judge Crabb agreed "that televising the proceedings in the manner they propose would be beneficial for the public and the judicial system" and expressed her view that the presence of cameras "would not interfere with the court proceedings."[63] Wisconsin had televised trials for ten years in its state courts, thereby demonstrating that photographing proceedings "does not impair the fair and orderly administration of justice."[64] Nevertheless, "as strongly as [she] may disagree with the Judicial Conference's position on this question," Judge Crabb held that she was "not free to disregard it."[65]

---

58. *Id.* at 24.
59. *Id.* (Winter, J., concurring).
60. *Id.*
61. *Id.* at 26.
62. 17 MEDIA L. REP. (BNA) 1381 (W.D. Wis. 1990).
63. *Id.* at 1382; see *id.* (summarizing arguments of movants):

> [T]his litigation will have substantial and far-reaching consequences for the entire state, affecting directly or indirectly, millions of people with interests in northern Wisconsin; that broadcast coverage would provide the only meaningful access to the trial for the public, because as a practical matter many of them are unable to attend because of the time requirements, the distance, and the limited size of the courtroom; that broadcast coverage of the trial would foster public understanding of the issues in this case and the conduct of the parties, their counsel and the judicial system; and that the public is entitled to an opportunity to witness and better understand this unique debate and the peaceful resolution of a conflict of profound importance.

64. *Id.*
65. *Id.* at 1383. Although Judge Crabb asserted that she would likely violate no law if she were to order a temporary suspension of the rules governing cameras, she would "be violating the

However, in *Marisol A. v. Giuliani*,[66] another federal district court concluded that the policy of the Judicial Conference does not overrule or supplant local court rules.[67] Thus, the local general rule affording the court discretion over camera coverage of proceedings "empowers the court to grant written permission to televise a civil proceeding and the court should consider the Conference policy only as a persuasive factor in the exercise of that power."[68]

Again, in *Katzman v. Victoria's Secret Catalogues*,[69] the same court, relying on *Marisol*, concluded that "[w]hile the recent action of the Judicial Conference [rejecting televising] is persuasive, this court is not required to defer to it."[70] Finding that the "plain language" of the local rule vested discretion to permit televising of proceedings in each individual judge, the court held that *Court TV* should be authorized to televise.[71] The court noted that experiments conducted between 1979 and 1994 had established that "a silent, unobtrusive in-court camera can increase public access to the courtroom without interfering with the fair administration of justice."[72] Indeed, the court concluded that these changes "have demonstrated that the stated objections can readily be addressed and should no longer stand as a bar to a presumptive First Amendment right of the press to televise as well as publish court proceedings, and of the public to view those proceedings on television."[73]

---

general understanding that federal judges operate subject to the supervisory authority of the Judicial Conference." *Id.*

66. 929 F. Supp. 660 (S.D.N.Y. 1996).

67. See *id.* at 661 (citing 28 U.S.C. §§ 331, 2071(c)).

68. 929 F. Supp. at 661. After balancing the interests, the court "determined that the public interest would be served by allowing televising," noting the "profound social, political, and legal issues raised by the instant case," the willingness of Court TV to televise the day's argument "gavel to gavel," and the absence of witnesses. *Id.* The court refused to accept the public's inability to grasp the issues as a basis for denying access, especially given the presence of commentators. See *id.*

69. 923 F. Supp. 580 (S.D.N.Y. 1996).

70. *Id.* at 584; see Chap. 4-2(b) *infra* (discussing Judicial Conference actions on cameras in the courtroom).

71. The court dismissed arguments based on attorney grandstanding, the dangers of selective televising, the potential for jury prejudice, and the lack of public interest in the dispute at bar. See 923 F. Supp. at 587-88.

72. *Id.* at 586. The court cited three studies in New York determining that cameras did not impair the fairness of the proceedings and "have enhanced public education." *Id.*

73. *Id.* at 589; see Hamilton v. Accu-Tek, 942 F. Supp. 136, 137-38 (E.D.N.Y. 1996) (applying local rule to permit television broadcast of motions hearing absent any objection because "in general, the public should be permitted and encouraged to observe the operation of its courts in the most convenient manner possible, so long as there is no interference with the due process, the dignity of litigants, jurors and witnesses, or with other appropriate aspects of the administration of justice").

§ 4-2(b). Changing the Rules.

The alternative to constitutional litigation or waiver of applicable court rules has been concerted efforts to change the rules themselves. As early as 1983, the Judicial Conference appointed an ad hoc committee to consider media requests to authorize the televising of civil proceedings. That committee, however, recommended that the ban be retained.[74] Following other unsuccessful media efforts, the Judicial Conference in September 1990 agreed to conduct a study of televising civil proceedings in six district courts and two courts of appeal.[75]

The pilot program was conducted from July 1991 through December 1994. Guidelines required reasonable advance notice of the request to televise a proceeding, prohibited photographing of jurors in and around the courtroom, permitted only one television and one still camera in trial courts (two cameras were allowed in New York), and authorized two television cameras and one still camera in appellate courts. The trial judge retained discretion to refuse, terminate, or limit coverage.[76]

At the study's conclusion, the research project staff and the Conference's Committee on Court Administration and Case Management recommended that the Judicial Conference authorize the nationwide use of cameras in civil proceedings. The recommendation was based on the results of the study:

> The converging results from each of our inquiries suggest that members of the electronic media generally complied with program guidelines and that their presence did not disrupt court proceedings, affect participants in the proceedings, or interfere with the administration of justice. To the extent decisions about expanding access would rest on these considerations, our results support expansion.[77]

---

74. See Dyk & McDowell, Further Comments of News Organizations Concerning Possible Revisions to Canon 3A(7), Submitted to the Judicial Conference Ad Hoc Committee on Cameras in the Courtroom (Apr. 9, 1990).

75. See FEDERAL JUDICIAL CENTER, ELECTRONIC MEDIA COVERAGE OF FEDERAL PROCEEDINGS 3-4 (1994) [hereinafter FEDERAL CENTER STUDY]. See generally Note, *Cameras and the Need for Unrestricted Electronic Media Access to Federal Courtrooms*, 69 S. CAL. L. REV. 827 (1996).

76. FEDERAL CENTER STUDY, *supra* note 75, at 5. The text of the Guidelines is set forth in an Appendix to the Report. See *id*. at 47-49. Section 1(c) of the Guidelines vests broad discretion in the presiding judge:

> A presiding judicial officer may refuse, limit, or terminate media coverage of an entire case, portions thereof, or testimony of particular witnesses, in the interests of justice to protect the rights of the parties, witnesses, and the dignity of the court; to assure the orderly conduct of the proceedings; or for any other reason considered necessary or appropriate by the presiding judicial officer.

See generally Weiner, *The Courtroom Camera*, 21 LITIG. 1 (Winter 1995); Vradenburg & Zucker, *New Focus on Cameras in Federal Courtrooms*, 8 COMM. LAW. 18 (Fall 1990).

77. FEDERAL CENTER STUDY, *supra* note 75, at 43.

During the study period, the news media sought to televise 257 cases; 82 percent of the applications were granted. Responding to surveys, judges and attorneys reported observing minimal or no effects of cameras on participants, courtroom decorum, or the administration of justice.[78] "Nearly all judges thought that educating the public about how the federal courts work was the greatest potential benefit of coverage, and most thought this benefit could be more fully realized with electronic media rather than traditional media."[79]

On September 20, 1994, the Judicial Conference voted by a 2-to-1 margin, without explanation, to reject its committee's recommendation. No formal reason for the decision was made public. A committee recommendation to end the federal ban on televising criminal trials was also rejected.[80] A number of factors that may have influenced the Conference have been suggested. For example, the study relied on survey data concerning the *perceived effects* of cameras on trial participants rather than on scientific studies of *actual* effects.[81] The perceived negative impact of cameras on trial participants, although minimal, also reportedly raised concern.[82] Further, content analysis of actual broadcast coverage indicated that recorded courtroom footage was most typically used as background for reporters' narrations and did little to inform viewers about the legal process itself.[83]

Efforts to persuade the Judicial Conference to reconsider its rejection of cameras have been unavailing. As of this writing, the federal ban on cameras in civil and criminal trials continues, although appellate courts have once again

---

78. See *id.* at 7; FEDERAL JUDICIAL CENTER, ELECTRONIC MEDIA COVERAGE OF COURTROOM PROCEEDINGS: EFFECTS ON WITNESSES AND JURORS (Jan. 18, 1994). The state studies often included televising criminal trials as well. See Chap. 4-3 *infra*.

79. FEDERAL CENTER STUDY, *supra* note 75, at 24.

80. See Reske, *No More Cameras in Federal Courts,* 80 A.B.A.J. 28 (Nov. 1994) N.Y. Times, Sept. 21, 1994, at A18. It had been argued that "the role of the electronic press in our modern first amendment regime is qualitatively and quantitatively greater than that of the print media. Television exerts a pervasive influence in our society by reason of both its broad reach and its ability to stimulate our eyes and ears simultaneously. Moreover, electronic media can transmit events as they occur, providing an unbroken path from the message source to the viewer." Frank, *supra* note 75, at 774-75.

81. See FEDERAL CENTER STUDY, *supra* note 75, at 8 (discussing difficulties of measuring actual effects); *Federal Judges' Group Rejects Cameras in Court*, News Notes, 22 MEDIA L. REP. (BNA) (Sept. 27, 1994) ("No independent study of distractions or harm in federal civil proceedings was undertaken, [public affairs officer for the Administrative Office of the U.S. Courts] Sellers stated.").

82. See News Notes, 22 MEDIA L. REP. (BNA) (Sept. 27, 1994).

83. See FEDERAL CENTER STUDY, *supra* note 75, at 24 ("The potential disadvantage of electronic media coverage most frequently mentioned by judges was the possibility of distorting or misrepresenting what goes on in court, although generally they did not feel this problem had occurred under the program."); In re Permitting of Media Coverage for an Indefinite Period, 539 A.2d 976, 977 (R.I. 1988) ("We suggest that a forty-five second fragment of a judicial proceeding accompanied by a still or moving image scarcely contributes to such public understanding.").

been authorized to experiment. Some appellate courts have in fact begun permitting camera coverage of their proceedings.[84] The Supreme Court, however, continues to ban cameras from its proceedings.[85]

§ 4-3. State Court Proceedings.

As of 1999, 47 states allowed cameras in the courtroom in some judicial proceedings,[86] but there are significant differences among them.[87] In seven states, coverage of certain proceedings is permitted on an experimental basis; permanent coverage rules have been adopted covering some proceedings in 45 states.[88] In most states, both trial and appellate proceedings are televised but, in four states, only appellate courts admit cameras.[89] In most jurisdictions, both civil and

---

84. The Second and Ninth Circuits authorize coverage. The First, Fourth, Fifth, Seventh, Tenth, and Eleventh Circuits have rejected television. The other circuits have not yet spoken to the issue.

85. See Pincus, Note, *Demystifying the Least Understood Branch: Opening the Supreme Court to Broadcast Media,* 71 TEX. L. REV. 1053 (1993).

86. See generally Dyer & Hauserman, *supra* note 4. For recent developments in the states, see Reporters Committee for Freedom of the Press, *Camera Access to Courts Gains Favor in More States, Feels Friction from Some State Judges,* THE NEWS MEDIA & THE LAW 32-34 (Winter 1995).

87. See NATIONAL CENTER FOR STATE COURTS, SUMMARY OF TV CAMERAS IN THE STATE COURTS (1998); RADIO-TELEVISION NEWS DIRECTORS ASS'N, NEWS MEDIA COVERAGE OF JUDICIAL PROCEEDINGS WITH CAMERA AND MICROPHONES: A SURVEY OF THE STATES (summary) (1998) [hereinafter RTNDA]. The RTNDA annual loose-leaf publication provides a state-by-state discussion of the guidelines governing television, broadcasting, recording, and still photography coverage of judicial proceedings. *Id.* As of January 1999, only Mississippi, New York, South Dakota, and the District of Columbia ban camera coverage of all judicial proceedings. *Id.* See also Dyer & Hauserman, *supra* note 4, at 1635-39 nn.12-13; Mississippi Comm'n on Judicial Performance v. Emmanuel, 688 So. 2d 222 (Miss. 1996) (affirming fine on judge for violations of the Code of Judicial Conduct, including allowing cameras in courtroom); Associated Press v. Bost, 656 So. 2d 113, 114 (Miss. 1995) (upholding the constitutionality of Mississippi Code of Judicial Conduct Canon 3(A)(7) prohibiting cameras in courtrooms except in a few specific circumstances until the state has "thoroughly researched the benefits and ramifications" of allowing electronic media access to judicial proceedings).

88. Delaware, Idaho, Indiana, Minnesota, Nebraska, and Pennsylvania have experimental projects in progress in some courts. Idaho, Minnesota, and Nebraska also have permanent rules governing media coverage of some courts. See RTNDA, *supra* note 87, at (i), (ii), (iii). Experimental coverage also extends to New Jersey municipal courts. See NATIONAL CENTER FOR STATE COURTS, *supra* note 87.

89. Only appellate coverage is permitted in Delaware, Illinois, Indiana, and Louisiana. Nebraska allows only audio coverage in trial courts. Pennsylvania permits camera coverage only of civil trial courts. Maryland and Texas allow only appellate coverage of criminal proceedings. Utah permits televising, broadcasting, and recording of appellate proceedings, but only still photography of trial court proceedings. See RTNDA, *supra* note 87, at (i), (ii), (iii); Dyer & Hauserman, *supra* note 4, at 1647-48.

criminal proceedings may be televised but, in a minority of states, television coverage is limited to civil proceedings.[90]

Apart from differences concerning the type of proceeding that may be televised, the states maintain a variety of limitations restricting the use of cameras.[91] Some jurisdictions require the consent of certain participants to televise proceedings in which they are involved.[92] Several states have promulgated rules regulating the photographing or filming of certain participants such

---

90. Pennsylvania allows television coverage only of civil non-jury trials. Maryland and Texas permit coverage of civil trial court and appellate proceedings, but only criminal appellate proceedings. Delaware's experiment with cameras covers appellate proceedings on civil and criminal matters, but only civil trials. See RTNDA, *supra* note 87, at (i), (ii), (iii); NATIONAL CENTER FOR STATE COURTS, *supra* note 87. Maine allows coverage of civil trials but limits coverage of criminal matters to arraignments, sentencings and other non-testimonial proceedings. See RTNDA, *supra* note 87.

91. See generally Comment, *supra* note 1. In *Cook v. First Morris Bank*, 719 A.2d 724 (N.J. Super. 1998), however, the court noted that, if the media "has the right to broadcast a trial . . . as a surrogate for the public's right of access," the First Amendment "prohibit[s] courts from dictating to the media when it may broadcast, just as courts may not tell newspapers when they may publish." *Id*. at 726-27. Such interference with "journalistic judgment about how best to serve the needs of its audience" would require "compelling circumstances." *Id*. at 727.

92. The consent of the defendant in criminal proceedings is required in Alabama, Arkansas, Minnesota, and Oklahoma. The prosecutor must consent to criminal trial coverage in Alabama, Arkansas, Minnesota, and Tennessee. Consent of all parties is required in Alabama, Arkansas (coverage ceases with objection by any party/attorney), Maryland (civil trial cases), Minnesota (trials), and Texas. See RTNDA, *supra* note 87, at (i), (ii), (iii). Some states require consent of the parties to coverage of particular categories of proceedings or permit a party to object to coverage, including courts in Alaska, Iowa, and Tennessee. See *id*. Counsel's consent is required in some civil proceedings and in appeals in Alabama, Arkansas, Maryland (civil trials), Tennessee, and Texas. See *id*.; Dyer & Hauserman, *supra* note 4, at 1650-94; Frank, *supra* note 40, at 801-02. In Iowa and Alaska, courts require the consent of victims in sexual offense and sexual abuse cases before allowing coverage. In Ohio, victims and witnesses have the right to object to televised proceedings. See RTNDA, *supra* note 87.

Florida originally required the consent of the parties but found that such a rule almost always precluded coverage. As a result, the requirement met with "total failure" and was abandoned. See In re Petition of Post-Newsweek Stations, Fla., Inc., 370 So. 2d 764, 766 (Fla. 1979). Arkansas concluded a consent requirement might be "too burdensome" and amended its local rules to authorize parties to object to camera coverage instead. In re Modification of the Code of Judicial Conduct Relating to Broadcasting and Photographing Ct. Proceedings, 628 S.W.2d 573 (Ark. 1982). But see Montoya v. Texas, 1998 Tex. App. LEXIS 7377 (Tex. App. Nov. 25, 1998) (unpublished opinion) (stating that Texas court rules "no longer require consent by the parties to broadcast court proceedings"); Cook v. First Morris Bank, 719 A.2d 724, 727 (N.J. Super. 1998) (granting an application by *Court TV* to televise an employment termination case alleging pregnancy discrimination over the objections of defendant employer claiming reputational injury, noting that New Jersey Court guidelines provide "permission for coverage shall not be conditioned upon obtaining consent of any party"); see also Duff v. Basilica of St. John, 26 MEDIA L. REP. (BNA) 1156, 1157 (Iowa Dist. 1997) (noting that, although the media needs the consent of victims/witnesses to film their testimony in a criminal sexual abuse trial, "no such consent . . . in a civil case alleging sexual abuse is necessary").

as jurors and specified witnesses.[93] Televised proceedings involving some subject matters, such as adoption, divorce, guardianship or custody, juvenile proceedings, sexual assaults, or trade secrets, have been proscribed as well.[94] Some jurisdictions have rules, similar to those employed in the federal pilot program, which regulate the number and kinds of cameras and recording equipment and their placement in the courtroom.[95]

States generally require notice to the court and/or its consent in order to televise proceedings.[96] In all jurisdictions, the presiding judge retains broad discretion to reject or limit coverage in particular cases.[97] Some jurisdictions afford the judge absolute discretion. For example, the Rhode Island guidelines provide that the "trial justice may in his or her sole discretion prohibit the video recording, broadcasting, and/or photographing of a participant with a film, videotape, or still camera on the trial justice's own motion or on the request of a participant in a court proceeding."[98]

---

93. Many states allow certain witnesses, including police informants, minors, witnesses who are in danger, and specified law enforcement personnel, to object to camera coverage. See generally RTNDA, *supra* note 87. In Hawaii (certain cases), Kansas, Missouri, North Carolina (certain cases), Ohio, Oregon, and Pennsylvania, witnesses have the right to object to coverage. In Michigan and New Mexico, judges can prohibit the filming of witnesses on a case-by-case basis, using their own discretion. See *id.* The Center for State Courts' summary indicates that in Maine, Maryland, and Utah, witnesses have the right to object to coverage as well. See NATIONAL CENTER FOR STATE COURTS, *supra* note 87. Coverage of jurors is prohibited in 17 states and limited in 16 others. See RTNDA, *supra* note 87; Dyer & Hauserman, *supra* note 4, at 1648-56; Frank, *supra* note 40, at 802. But see Sunbeam Television Corp. v. Florida, 723 So. 2d 275, 278 (Fla. App. 1998) ("The pre-trial publicity problems associated with high profile criminal cases, like the problems of jury intimidation and bribery, are not new, and were undoubtedly considered by the [Florida] Supreme Court in the exhaustive study which led to its decision in *Post-Newsweek Stations*. No special treatment was formulated for prospective or seated jurors.").

94. Such restrictions apply, in whole or in part, in Alabama, Arizona (adoption/juvenile proceedings), Arkansas, Colorado, Connecticut (trade secret and "family" cases), Hawaii, Idaho, Maine, Maryland, Massachusetts, Minnesota, Missouri, Nebraska, New Jersey (sexual penetration cases), North Carolina, Oregon, Pennsylvania, Rhode Island, Virginia (sex offense cases), and Wisconsin. See RTNDA, *supra* note 87, at (i)-(iii).

95. These rules and others reviewed in the text are discussed in Dyk, Supplemental Information on State Rules Governing Camera Coverage of Judicial Proceedings, Submitted to the Judicial Conference Ad Hoc Committee on Cameras in the Courtroom (May 25, 1990).

96. States with no notice or consent requirement include Arkansas, Florida, Georgia (no consent required by Supreme Court), Hawaii (appellate), Idaho (appellate), Nebraska, North Carolina, Oregon (appellate), Rhode Island, Utah (still photography), Vermont, Virginia, and Wyoming (appellate). See RTNDA, *supra* note 87, at (i)-(iii). The rules requiring notice may specify "reasonable" notice or prescribe a particular duration from one to 20 days. See *id.*

97. States that permit the presiding judge to exercise broad discretion in granting media access include California, Colorado, Georgia, Idaho, Kentucky, Montana, Nevada, New Hampshire, North Dakota, Rhode Island (certain cases), South Carolina, Tennessee, Washington, West Virginia, Wisconsin, and Wyoming. See generally RTNDA, *supra* note 87.

98. Amended Guidelines 11, *quoted in* In re Permitting of Media Coverage for an Indefinite Period, 539 A.2d 976, 979 (R.I. 1988). The Guidelines specifically provide that "there shall be no

§ 4-3 CAMERAS IN THE COURTROOM § 4-3

Other guidelines provide vague standards vesting broad discretion in the trial judge to balance the competing interests on a case-by-case basis.[99] Such standards have been interpreted to prohibit excessive restrictions on television coverage unsupported by findings.[100] Florida essentially provides a rebuttable

---

review." See 539 A.2d at 978 ("We therefore authorize the trial justice, in his or her sole and unreviewable discretion, to determine whether the media as defined in our guidelines may have access to the courtroom during any trial or other judicial proceeding.").

99. See, e.g., South Carolina v. Byram, 485 S.E.2d 360, 366 (S.C. 1997) (finding that although the trial judge erred in holding that he lacked discretion to exclude television media without excluding other media, there was no evidence defendant was prejudiced by having television cameras in courtroom during sentencing); In re Petition of Arkansas Bar Ass'n, 609 S.W.2d 28, 30 (Ark. 1980) ("A judge may authorize broadcasting . . . [if] the participants will not be distracted nor will the dignity of the proceedings be impaired."); Multimedia WMAZ, Inc. v. Georgia, 353 S.E.2d 173, 174 (Ga. 1987) ("We hold that Rule 22 requires the presiding judge to make his own independent determination as to whether or not electronic media trial coverage is 'within the requirements of due process of law' and can be 'done without detracting from the dignity and decorum of the court.'"); Tennessee v. Pike, 1997 Tenn. Crim. App. LEXIS 1186 (Tenn. Crim. App. Nov. 26, 1997)) (unpublished opinion) (holding trial court did not err in denying defendant's motion to bar media coverage of pretrial proceedings by applying Tennessee Supreme Court Rule 30, which creates a presumption of access to trial proceedings subject to the discretion of the trial judge to "(i) control the conduct of the proceedings before the court, (ii) maintain decorum and prevent distraction; (iii) guarantee the safety of any party, witness, or juror; and (iv) ensure the fair and impartial administration of justice"). While Utah had promulgated vague judicial guidelines, they have been superseded by statute. See In re Guidelines for Experimental Use of Cameras in Utah S. Ct., 911 P.2d 978 (Utah 1995).

100. See Hearst Corp. v. Justices of Super. Ct., 24 MEDIA L. REP. (BNA) 1478, 1480 (Mass. 1996) (vacating trial court order prohibiting electronic media coverage other than of the closing, opening, and sentencing in favor of permitting coverage during all phases of the criminal proceeding); South Carolina v. Hill, 501 S.E.2d 122, 126-27 (S.C.), *cert. denied*, 119 S. Ct. 597 (1998) (upholding trial judge's refusal to discontinue media filming during jury selection in the absence of findings of a "disruptive atmosphere" or proof that jurors were intimidated by the media, rather than simply concerned with the general lack of privacy during *voir dire*); Tennessee v. Pike, 1997 Tenn. Crim. App. LEXIS 1186 (Tenn. Crim. App. Nov. 26, 1997) (unpublished opinion) (holding a general unsubstantiated concern that pretrial media coverage would "make jury selection difficult and would deprive the defendant of a fair trial" by affecting witness testimony and disrupting the proceedings insufficient); Tennessee v. Cooper, 1998 Tenn. Crim. App. LEXIS 923 (Tenn. Crim. App. Sept. 9, 1998) (rejecting defendant's claim that because the jury was not sequestered "the trial court erred in allowing television coverage of the trial" or in failing to suppress a video of activity during a jury-out period because the defendant did not show "either actual impropriety or any prejudice," and offered no independent proof that the tapes at issue were actually broadcast, emphasizing the trial judge had given proper rehabilitative jury instructions and had questioned jurors during the proceedings); see also Montoya v. Texas, 1998 Tex. App. LEXIS 7377 (Tex. App. Nov. 25, 1998) (unpublished opinion) (upholding trial court's refusal to ban cameras in the courtroom despite parties' joint request to prevent cameras at the proceedings in the absence of any evidence that the "presence of cameras . . . affected appellant's substantial rights"); Detroit Free Press v. 36th Dist. Judge, 24 MEDIA L. REP. (BNA) 1886 (Mich. App. 1996) (holding that trial judge's general and non-particularized policy of excluding photographic coverage violated clear legal duty under Administrative Order 1989-1, allowing electronic media coverage, but finding only that the order denying any trial court discretion was overly broad); Massachusetts v.

presumption of camera coverage by authorizing the "presiding judge" to exclude "electronic media coverage of a particular participant only upon a finding that such coverage will have a substantial effect upon the particular individual which would be qualitatively different from the effect on members of the public in general and such effect will be qualitatively different from coverage by other types of media."[101]

New York had an experimental audiovisual coverage of trials which ended on June 30, 1997.[102] New York's court rules set forth a series of factors to be considered by the trial judge in exercising her discretion. The judge was to examine the type of case involved; whether coverage would interfere with the fair administration of justice, the advancement of a fair trial, or the rights of the

---

Salvi, 24 MEDIA L. REP. (BNA) 1734, 1736 (Mass. Super. 1996) (finding that electronic coverage of trial of defendant charged with shootings at abortion clinic posed "a substantial likelihood" of harm to defendant, witnesses, surviving victims, families of murdered victims, and defendant's right to a fair trial, but taking of photographs did not).

101. In re Petition of Post-Newsweek Stations, Fla., Inc., 370 So. 2d at 779; see Sunbeam Television Corp. v. Florida, 723 So. 2d 275, 277 (Fla. App. 1998) (applying this standard and finding trial judge's "general concerns" that "unknown people may approach the jurors at restaurants, the market, church [or] synagogue" were insufficient to justify a prohibition on video photography of prospective and seated jurors); WFTV, Inc. v. Florida, 704 So. 2d 188, 190 (Fla. App. 1997) (vacating trial court *sua sponte* order prohibiting video and still camera operators from photographing prospective or seated jurors in the courtroom during a criminal trial by characterizing jurors as trial participants, and as such, finding the trial court may not restrict coverage without: (1) "substantial effect" findings and (2) a "noticed evidentiary hearing at which media representatives have a fair opportunity to be heard").

Similarly, in *Duff v. Basilica of Saint John*, 26 MEDIA L. REP. (BNA) 1156 (Iowa Dist. 1997), the court upheld a presumption of media access unless the judge finds "coverage would materially interfere with the rights of the parties to a fair trial." *Id.* at 1157 (citing IOWA CODE OF JUDICIAL CONDUCT Canon 3(B)(2)(b)). Because the plaintiff, alleging sexual abuse by a parish priest 25 years earlier, was willing to allow print media coverage during the proceedings and still photographers could photograph the plaintiff, the court found that he had not met his burden of identifying any additional interference that would be caused by expanded television media coverage. See *id.* at 1158. "When [plaintiff] elected this forum he by necessity made his dispute public and knew or should have known that some members of the public would follow the case either in person or through the media." *Id.* at 1157. The court also found that defendant could not meet its burden of proving television coverage would adversely affect jury selection in two similar pending cases, because the broadcast would not air in the jurisdiction and additional safeguards existed to "make certain that only fair and impartial jurors are selected for the subsequent trials." *Id.* See also KMOV-TV v. Kirksey, 26 MEDIA L. REP. (BNA) 2435 (Mo. Cir. 1998) (enjoining police board from prohibiting media's video recording of a police officer's disciplinary proceeding because the discriminatory closure of the proceeding to video media was "premised only on speculation and conjecture" and was not a reasonable restriction of the use of video); Tennessee v. Pike, 1997 Tenn. Crim. App. LEXIS 1186 (Tenn. Crim. App. Nov. 26, 1997) (holding Tennessee Supreme Court Rule 30 "presumptively entitles the media to in-court camera coverage" and "any finding that such coverage should be denied . . . must be supported by substantial evidence" of a lack of fairness to the parties or disruption in the courtroom).

102. News Notes, 23 MEDIA L. REP. (BNA) (Feb. 14, 1995).

parties; whether coverage might undermine orders excluding witnesses from the courtroom; possible interference with law enforcement; whether lewd or scandalous matters are involved; objections of the participants; the physical structure of the courtroom and potential disruption from media equipment; whether coverage was barred by other law; and especially whether a participant was a child.[103] Plainly, such considerations afforded the trial judge significant leeway in deciding whether to admit cameras. But, even though a state commission recommended permanent authorization of cameras in the courtroom, the experiment ended in 1997.[104] New York presently bans camera coverage of all judicial proceedings.

Following the televised O.J. Simpson criminal trial, California enacted new rules limiting film and electronic media coverage, which became effective January 1, 1997.[105] California now prohibits media coverage of jury selection, jurors or spectators, bench conferences, and conversations between counsel and between attorneys and clients or witnesses.[106] Judges are to consider eighteen factors, including the importance of maintaining public trust and confidence in the judicial system, the importance of promoting public access, the consent of the parties, the nature of the case, privacy rights of participants, effects on minor participants, potential impact on jury selection and ongoing law enforcement, and the security and dignity of the court.[107] A judge is not required to make findings or to render a statement of decision.[108]

---

103. N.Y. R. CT., RULES OF THE CHIEF ADMINISTRATOR § 131.4(c). See, e.g., New York v. Georgia M., 22 MEDIA L. REP. (BNA) 2252 (N.Y. Fam. Ct. 1994) (rejecting, after applying referenced criteria, application to provide audio-visual coverage of a dispositional hearing involving a 15-year-old defendant in a murder case, but granting petition to install a small camera, in a stationary position, to record a victim impact statement by the victim's widow).

104. See NEW YORK STATE COMM. TO REVIEW AUDIO-VISUAL COVERAGE OF COURT PROCEEDINGS, AN OPEN COURTROOM: CAMERAS IN NEW YORK COURTS xx (1997) ("Cameras should be permitted in New York State courts on a permanent basis with all of the safeguards of current law for parties, prospective witnesses, jurors, crime victims, and other trial participants."). See *New York's Darkened Courts*, N.Y. Times, Sept. 8, 1997, § A, at 18. See also Reynolds v. Guiliani, 27 MEDIA L. REP. (BNA) 1383, 1384 (S.D.N.Y. 1999) (denying *ex parte* application seeking permission to videotape and televise courtroom proceedings based on the likely "conspicuous and unduly distracting" presence of an inexperienced cameraman on witnesses and counsel, compounded by the "spatial constraints" of the courtroom).

105. See CAL. R. CT. 980; News Notes, 24 MEDIA L. REP. (BNA) (June 15, 1996).

106. CAL. R. CT. 980(e)(6).

107. *Id.* at 980(e)(3).

108. *Id.* at 980(e)(4). In *WALB-TV, Inc. v. Gibson*, 501 S.E.2d 281 (Ga. 1998), the court upheld in part and reversed in part an order denying a television station's request to install audio and visual recording equipment in the courtroom to broadcast the separate trials of co-defendants charged with murder. The court applied new guidelines adopted to guide the exercise of discretion by trial courts, including "the consent of the parties, the impact on the administration of the court, the impact on due process, and whether the access would 'detract from the ends of justice.'" *Id.* at 822. In so doing, the court upheld a denial of a request for electronic coverage of the first

Most jurisdictions that have permanent rules permitting cameras initially sponsored experimental projects, which provided valuable findings about the potentially harmful effects of electronic coverage. The Florida Supreme Court challenged the claim that television coverage of trial proceedings is harmful by noting that such "assertions are but assumptions unsupported by any evidence. No respondent has been able to point to any instance during the pilot program period where these fears were substantiated. Such evidence as exists would appear to refute the assumptions."[109] The 1990 Federal Judicial Center pilot project cited a dozen state studies in support of its recommendation to permit cameras in the federal courts — "[t]he studies report that the majority of jurors and witnesses who experience electronic media coverage do not report negative consequences or concerns. These findings are consistent with what judges and lawyers in the pilot courts observed about jurors and witnesses in those courts."[110]

In any case, the potential negative effects of cameras in the courtroom must be weighed against the value of electronic coverage.[111] Critics of cameras in the courtroom pose the question: if the public and press are given access to the proceeding and are free to report what they see and hear, why is television coverage necessary? In a very real sense, however, electronic media coverage makes more meaningful and enhances the values of public access recognized by the Supreme Court.[112] The public relies on television as a source of informa-

---

defendant's trial because both trials would be sufficiently similar in content that broadcasting the proceedings "could create a tainted jury pool for the second trial." *Id.* at 823. However, that same rationale could not support a denial of coverage of the second trial; the Georgia Supreme Court held it would have no effect on the defendant's due process rights because the jury would already be seated when coverage began. See *id.*

109. In re Petition of Post-Newsweek Stations, Fla., Inc., 370 So. 2d at 775-76; see In re Petition of Ark. Bar Ass'n, 609 S.W.2d 28, 29 (Ark. 1980) ("The workings of the court should be known to the public and it is our judgment that the media have reached that stage of electronic sophistication that they can, in most cases, photograph and record trial proceedings without disruption and without prejudice to the rights of the parties."); South Carolina v. Byram, 485 S.E.2d 360, 366 (S.C. 1997) (finding that while the trial judge erred in holding that he lacked discretion to exclude television media without excluding other media, there was no evidence defendant was prejudiced by having television cameras in courtroom during sentencing).

110. FEDERAL CENTER STUDY, *supra* note 75, at 38.

111. See generally In re Petition of Post-Newsweek Stations, Fla., Inc., 370 So. 2d at 779 ("While we do not accept all of the claims made by proponents . . . we are persuaded that on balance there is more to be gained than lost by permitting electronic coverage of judicial proceedings subject to standards for such coverage."); Frank, *supra* note 40, at 795-98.

112. See Chap. 2-2 *supra*; see Hamilton v. Accu-Tek, 942 F. Supp. 136, 138 (E.D.N.Y. 1996) ("Actually seeing and hearing court proceedings, combined with the commentary of informed members of the press and academia, provides a powerful device for monitoring the courts."); see generally Harding, *Cameras and the Need for Unrestricted Electronic Media Access to Federal Courtrooms,* 69 S. CAL. L. REV. 827, 828 (1996) ("Restrictions on electronic media access are entirely unnecessary because the benefits of unrestricted access far outweigh any risks."). But see

tion.[113] Millions of television viewers can observe a single trial, rather than the few spectators in a courtroom. Just as a transcript is no substitute for access to the proceedings, so print media reporting is no substitute for electronic coverage. In state judicial proceedings, therefore, the per se rule of exclusion has largely been abandoned in favor of case-by-case assessment of the competing interests. In making such an assessment, the presiding judge possesses broad discretion. Although there is no constitutional presumption of openness to weight the scales, the First Amendment values served by audiovisual coverage of judicial proceedings and the generally speculative nature of the perceived harms — especially as technology continues to develop — suggest that claims for televised coverage of judicial proceedings will continue to be the subject of litigation.

Sloviter, *If Courts Are Open, Must Cameras Follow?*, 26 HOFSTRA L. REV. 873, 887-88 (1998) ("[T]here is no reason to assume that the televised proceedings will not be primarily of the sensational, notorious, or shocking portions of a trial that may fail to give the public the well-balanced look into litigation that is really necessary to understand how the judicial system operates.").

113. For an argument that "the print media adequately satisfied the public's right to know," see Lassiter, *TV or Not TV — That Is the Question*, 86 J. CRIM. L. & CRIMINOLOGY 928, 1001 (1996) ("[B]ecause the eye of the press is one-to-one and face-to-face, it is less invasive and disruptive than the unblinking eye of the camera. The constitutional balance between the virtue and abuse of publicity weighs in favor of the [print] press.").

Chapter 5

ACCESS TO JUDICIAL RECORDS: CRIMINAL PROCEEDINGS

§ 5-1. Sources of the Access Right.
§ 5-2. Records of Criminal Proceedings.
   § 5-2(a). Pretrial Records — In General.
      § 5-2(a)(1). Wiretap Records.
      § 5-2(a)(2). Search Warrants.
      § 5-2(a)(3). Grand Jury Records.
      § 5-2(a)(4). Information and Indictment.
      § 5-2(a)(5). Discovery Documents.
      § 5-2(a)(6). Preliminary Hearings.
      § 5-2(a)(7). Suppression Hearing Records.
      § 5-2(a)(8). Bail and Detention Records.
      § 5-2(a)(9). Plea Agreements.
   § 5-2(b). Trial Records.
   § 5-2(c). Jury Records.
   § 5-2(d). Post-Trial Records.
   § 5-2(e). Criminal Justice Act Vouchers.
   § 5-2(f). Military Courts.

§ 5-1. Sources of the Access Right.

Supreme Court precedent has provided the impetus for recognition and expansion of a First Amendment-based right of access to judicial proceedings. There has, however, been no comparable Supreme Court decision firmly establishing a First Amendment-based right of access to judicial records. Nevertheless, *Richmond Newspapers, Inc. v. Virginia* and its progeny do provide useful precedent for extending access rights to judicial records. In *Press-Enterprise Co. v. Superior Court (Press-Enterprise I)*, for example, the Court held that the First Amendment required access to the transcript of a voir dire proceeding.[1] The constitutional right to an open proceeding included a right of access to the judicial record created during voir dire. Further, the Court suggested that the Constitution might require access to a transcript, even when parts of a judicial proceeding had been properly closed.[2] And, in *Press-Enterprise Co. v. Superior Court (Press-Enterprise II)*, the Court recognized a First Amendment-based right to a transcript of a preliminary hearing.[3] While these are the only Supreme Court decisions extending First Amendment-based access rights to

---

1. 464 U.S. 501 (1984). See Chap. 2-2(e) *supra* (discussing *Press-Enterprise I*).
2. See 464 U.S. at 512 ("When limited closure is ordered, the constitutional values sought to be protected by holding open proceedings may be satisfied later by making a transcript . . . available within a reasonable time, if the judge determines that disclosure can be accomplished while safeguarding the juror's valid privacy interests.").
3. 478 U.S. 1 (1986). See Chap. 2-2(f) *supra*.

judicial records, lower courts have fashioned an impressive body of constitutional law on the subject. Still, much of the law of access to judicial records and documents has been built on federal and state statutes, court rules, state constitutions and, especially, the common law.[4]

Beyond the *Press-Enterprise* cases, the Supreme Court has addressed the issue of a First Amendment-based right of access to judicial records only indirectly. In *Nixon v. Warner Communications, Inc.*,[5] for example, the Court considered the news media's request to copy, broadcast, and sell tapes that had been admitted into evidence in the trial of former Attorney General John Mitchell.[6] Although transcripts of the recordings had been disseminated widely, the press argued that the actual conversations, replete with nuance and inflection, should be heard by the public as well. President Nixon objected, and, after two trial judges disagreed about whether the recordings were subject to a common law right of access, the D.C. Circuit ordered that they be made public.[7]

The Supreme Court reversed. In an opinion by Justice Powell, the Court assumed, *arguendo*, that a common law right to inspect and copy judicial records and documents extended to the tapes.[8] Nevertheless, Justice Powell emphasized, the common law right is not absolute. The adjudication of claims that judicial records should be kept under seal are committed to the discretion of the trial

---

4. While the federal Freedom of Information Act does not apply to judicial records, many state statutes do establish access rights. Other statutes may restrict public access, especially in sensitive areas involving family law, juveniles, and trade secrets. See generally REPORTERS COMMITTEE FOR FREEDOM OF THE PRESS, JUDICIAL RECORDS: A GUIDE TO ACCESS IN STATE AND FEDERAL COURTS (Summer 1990); Steinfeld & Bertsche, *Recent Developments in the Law of Access — 1998*, in 3 COMM. LAW — 1998, at 53 (PLI 1998); Paul & Ovelman, *Access*, in 3 COMM. LAW — 1998, §§ 3, 5 (PLI 1998).

5. 435 U.S. 589 (1978).

6. Tape recordings of presidential conversations had been subpoenaed by the Watergate Special Prosecutor. Twenty-two hours of taped conversations, played at the public trial, were admitted into evidence. See *id.* at 594.

7. See United States v. Mitchell, 551 F.2d 1252 (D.C. Cir. 1976), *rev'd sub nom.* Nixon v. Warner Communications Inc., 435 U.S. 589 (1978). Judge Gesell, who presided at Attorney General Mitchell's trial, warned against "overcommercialization of the evidence," but nonetheless recognized a common law right of access. See 435 U.S. at 595. The parties, however, failed to submit satisfactory proposals for the release of the tapes before the trial ended, so the issue was transferred to Judge Sirica. Denying the petition for access, Judge Sirica emphasized the danger to the defendants' rights on appeal and asserted that release of the transcripts had already satisfied the public's "right to know." *Id.* The Court of Appeals, in contrast, held that the common law right of access was not defeated by speculative assertions of prejudice. See *id.* at 596.

8. 435 U.S. at 599. All parties acknowledged the common law right. Indeed, Justice Powell asserted that it is "clear" that American courts recognize a right to inspect documents generated in the course of judicial proceedings. His opinion rejected English precedent in which access turned on proprietary interests. In the United States, the right is premised on "the citizen's desire to keep a watchful eye on the workings of public agencies, . . . and in a newspaper publisher's intention to publish information concerning the operation of government." *Id.* at 598.

court.[9] In the case at issue, Justice Powell observed, the balance was close.[10] It did, however, tip against access because Congress, in the Presidential Recordings Act, had already provided an administrative procedure for release of the recordings to the public.[11]

In so holding, the Court in *Nixon v. Warner Communications, Inc.* rejected the press' argument that the First Amendment mandates access to the recordings themselves. Justice Powell emphasized that the public and press had been provided access to the tapes when they were played in court, had ongoing access to the transcripts, and remained free to report on their contents.[12] Neither the public nor the press was entitled to physical access to the tapes; under such circumstances, the Court held, "[t]he First Amendment generally grants the press no right to information about a trial superior to that of the general public."[13]

The Court's acceptance in *Nixon* of a common law right of access to judicial records has had continuing force in adjudicating such cases. While common law balancing is typically not perceived to be as exacting as constitutional review, the common law right has widely been construed to create a presumption of access that often rivals the standards courts traditionally apply in the First Amendment context.[14]

---

9. See *id.* at 599.

10. In arguing against access, President Nixon asserted his proprietary interest in the tapes, his right to privacy, and executive privilege. He also suggested that it would be "unseemly" for a court to facilitate commercialization of evidence. *Id.* at 600-02. By the same token, the Court recognized that, "[o]n the respondent's side of the scales is the incremental gain in public understanding of an immensely important historical occurrence that arguably would flow from the release of aural copies of these tapes, a gain said not to be inconsequential despite the already widespread dissemination of printed transcripts," as well as "the presumption — however gauged — in favor of public access to judicial records." *Id.* at 602.

11. See *id.* at 606 (citing Presidential Recordings and Materials Preservation Act, 44 U.S.C. § 2107). Justices White and Brennan, dissenting in part, would have ordered the district court to deliver the tapes to the Administrator of General Services pursuant to the Act. See 435 U.S. at 611-12 (White, J., dissenting). Justices Marshall and Stevens, dissenting, would have permitted public access. Justice Marshall relied on the common law right which, he suggested, found support in the Act as well. See *id.* at 612-13 (Marshall, J., dissenting). Justice Stevens stressed the trial court's (i.e., Judge Gesell's) discretion — "[o]nly an egregious abuse of discretion should merit reversal." *Id.* at 614 (Stevens, J., dissenting).

12. See *id.* at 609; see also People v. McLoughlin, 473 N.Y.S.2d 904, 906 (Sup. Ct. 1983), *aff'd*, 479 N.Y.S.2d 30 (App. Div. 1984) (rejecting a First Amendment challenge to a law requiring sealing of records of criminal proceedings because "[t]he proceedings below were open to the public and the press; a representative of The Times, if so inclined, could have attended and reported that which transpired").

13. 435 U.S. at 609. See People v. McLoughlin, 473 N.Y.S.2d at 906 ("Since [the statute] does not deny the press access to sources of information available to members of the general public, it does not curtail First Amendment freedoms.").

14. See, e.g., United States v. McVeigh, 119 F.3d 806, 811 (10th Cir. 1997) ("judicial documents are presumptively available to the public, but may be sealed if the right to access is outweighed by the interest favoring nondisclosure"); United States v. Edwards, 672 F.2d 1289,

In *United States v. Amodeo*,[15] the Second Circuit determined that the common law presumption of access varies with the role that the material at issue plays in the adjudicative proceeding and with its value to the public in monitoring the work of the courts. Information subject to presumptive access spans a continuum "from matters that directly affect an adjudication to matters that come within a court's purview solely to insure their irrelevance."[16] In the Second Circuit, an especially strong presumption of access attaches to documents consulted in determining the substantive rights of litigants, a core judicial function that the public can and should scrutinize.[17] Where, however, the records at issue play a peripheral role in the exercise of the judicial function, the presumption loses much of its force.[18] All along the continuum, the Second Circuit observed, the presumption's vitality is largely a function of tradition. Thus, the court noted, if the documents at issue are typically maintained in the public court file, the presumption is greater than if such material is traditionally maintained under

---

1294 (7th Cir. 1982) ("there is a strong presumption in support of the common law right to inspect and copy judicial records"); United States v. Salemme, 985 F. Supp. 193, 195 (D. Mass. 1997) ("The presumption of public access to judicial [records] . . . is an essential feature of democratic control and accountability.").

In *Providence Journal Co. v. Rodgers*, 711 A.2d 1131 (R.I. 1998), the Rhode Island Supreme Court reasoned that *Nixon v. Warner Communications, Inc.* imposed a balancing test "identical to that performed in the case of governmental curtailment of a constitutional right." *Id.* at 1136. The court interpreted a state statute providing for the confidentiality of "all court records" concerning child victims of molestation and sexual assaults to require a balance between "protecting the identity of an innocent child who has been victimized by a sex offender" and "safeguarding the public's interest in the fairness of criminal prosecutions." *Id.* at 1136-37. The court established a "dual filing system" for child sexual assault cases. *Id.* at 1138. In effect, a party submitting documents that identify a victim "shall submit two versions" — one redacted for the public, and one unaltered for the confidential court records. *Id.* During proceedings, a "public file," containing the charging documents, with the victim's identity redacted, but not including victim-specific documents otherwise made confidential by state law or policy (e.g., school records, medical records), would be maintained and made available to the public. *Id.* Unredacted, victim-specific information would be contained in a "confidential court file," which would serve to protect child victims from further "stigmatization and embarrassment." *Id.*

15. 71 F.3d 1044 (2d Cir. 1995).

16. *Id.* at 1049. The Seventh Circuit cited *Amodeo* with approval in *United States v. Andreas*, 150 F.3d 766, 768 (7th Cir. 1998).

17. See 71 F.3d at 1049; see also United States v. Vazquez, 31 F. Supp. 2d 85, 88-91 (D. Conn. 1998) (applying *Amodeo* and holding that the government could not overcome the "especially strong" common law presumption of access to videotapes filmed outside a clinic and later used as evidence in defendant's trial for allegedly violating the Freedom of Access to Clinic Entrances Act); Marisol A. v. Giuliani, 26 MEDIA L. REP. (BNA) 1151, 1153-54 (S.D.N.Y. 1997) (recognizing "strong" presumption of access to report prepared pursuant to court order because it is likely to play important role in court's exercise of its Article III function and because parties and subject matter of litigation are of public interest).

18. See 71 F.3d at 1050.

§ 5-1   ACCESS TO JUDICIAL RECORDS: CRIMINAL PROCEEDINGS   § 5-1

seal.[19] Whether the calibrated presumption employed by the court in *Amodeo* will find favor in other jurisdictions remains to be determined.[20]

In the years since *Nixon*, especially following the Supreme Court's subsequent decisions in *Richmond Newspapers, Inc.* and its progeny,[21] many lower courts have interpreted those cases as creating a First Amendment-based right of access to judicial records in criminal proceedings as well. In *Globe Newspaper Co. v. Pokaski*, for example, the First Circuit sustained a constitutional challenge to a Massachusetts statute that authorized the sealing of court records of criminal cases that had not resulted in conviction.[22] Under the statute, when a defendant was found not guilty, the grand jury failed to indict, or the court found no probable cause, the entire record was automatically sealed. Where the case ended with a *nolle prosequi* or other dismissal of the charges, the law provided that the record would be sealed if the court found that "substantial justice would best be served" by doing so.[23]

Basing its holding squarely on the First Amendment, the First Circuit emphasized "that without access to documents the public often would not have a 'full understanding' of the proceeding and therefore would not always be in a position to serve as an effective check on the system."[24] Thus, the court in *Pokaski* employed the two-part test of tradition and function articulated in *Press-Enterprise II*.[25] The First Circuit pointed to the use made by the Constitution's Framers and by the first Congress of records of secret criminal proceedings in deliberations leading to the Bill of Rights[26] and, more importantly from its perspective, to the very same functional values that motivated the Supreme Court

---

19. See *id.*

20. The Eighth Circuit has rejected a strong presumption of access in favor of deference to the discretion exercised by the trial court. See Webster Groves Sch. Dist. v. Pulitzer Publ'g Co., 898 F.2d 1371, 1376 (8th Cir. 1990); United States v. Webbe, 791 F.2d 103, 106 (8th Cir. 1986); see also United States v. Salemme, 985 F. Supp. 193 (D. Mass. 1997) (employing *Amodeo* calibrated presumption of access to require that public interest in access to defendant's motion to dismiss and related submissions "on which the court will act" be "outweighed by legitimate countervailing interests").

21. See Chap. 2-2 *supra*.

22. 868 F.2d 497 (1st Cir. 1989). But see United States v. McVeigh, 119 F.3d 806, 812 (10th Cir. 1997) ("There is not yet any definitive Supreme Court ruling on whether there is a [First Amendment] constitutional right [in addition to the common law right] of access to court documents and, if so, the scope of such right.").

23. 868 F.2d at 510-11.

24. *Id.* at 502 (citing In re Globe Newspaper Co., 729 F.2d 47, 52 (1st Cir. 1984); In re New York Times Co., 828 F.2d 110, 114 (2d Cir. 1987), *cert. denied*, 485 U.S. 777 (1988); In re Washington Post Co., 807 F.2d 383, 390 (4th Cir. 1986); United States v. Smith, 776 F.2d 1104, 1111 (3d Cir. 1985); United States v. Peters, 754 F.2d 753, 763 (7th Cir. 1985); Associated Press v. United States Dist. Ct., 705 F.2d 1143, 1145 (9th Cir. 1983)).

25. See 478 U.S. at 13-14.

26. See 868 F.2d at 503.

in *Richmond Newspapers, Inc.* That the statute contemplated criminal proceedings would have been completed when the records became sealed did not, the First Circuit concluded, denigrate the value of public access since "the present prospect of future access is a felt presence, just as the prospect of appellate review is for the lawyers and judge in the trial of a case."[27] Accordingly, the court held, "[i]f the press is to fulfill its function of surrogate, it surely cannot be restricted to report on only those judicial proceedings that it has sufficient personnel to cover contemporaneously."[28]

Significantly, the court in *Pokaski* rejected the suggestion that *Nixon* precluded application of the First Amendment to the records of completed judicial proceedings that had themselves been held in open court. "In light of *Richmond Newspapers*, decided two years later, we cannot read *Warner Communications* as laying down a general rule for all criminal cases that once the substance of testimony and evidence has been exposed to public view, there is no right of access to visual and aural means of preserving it."[29] Such a rule, the court reasoned, would preclude meaningful public inspection of the numerous records and documents to which it did not have realistic access during the proceedings.[30]

Applying a First Amendment-based right of access, the First Circuit held that the statute could not survive the strict scrutiny mandated by *Press-Enterprise II* and *Globe Newspaper Co. v. Superior Court*.[31] Although the court recognized that the statute's automatic sealing provisions constituted an effective means of furthering the government's compelling interest in protecting the privacy of vindicated former criminal defendants,[32] it was not, by any measure, the least restrictive means of doing so.[33] The state could accomplish as much, the court concluded, by requiring the defendant to move to seal the record at the conclusion of the proceedings.[34] Access to judicial records is constitutionally required, the court asserted, unless the trial court makes "specific, on the record findings" that sealing is necessary to achieve a compelling interest.[35]

---

27. *Id.* at 503-04.
28. *Id.* at 504.
29. *Id.*
30. See *id.*
31. See *id.* at 505. The court reasoned that *Press-Enterprise II* imposed the same rigorous burden on the government as the strict scrutiny articulated in *Globe Newspaper Co. v. Superior Court. Id.* at 505 n.15. See Chap. 2-2(d) & (f) *supra*.
32. See 868 F.2d at 506. The asserted privacy interest included the avoidance of both embarrassment and humiliation, on the one hand, and professional and economic hardship on the other. See *id.* at 505-06.
33. See *id.* at 507.
34. See *id.*
35. *Id.* at 510 (citing *Press-Enterprise II*, 478 U.S. at 13-14). The court reached a different result with respect to statutory provisions authorizing the automatic sealing of cases that conclude at the grand jury stage. "[T]he First Amendment attaches only to those records connected with proceedings about which the public has a right to know." *Id.* at 509. Since the public has no right

The First Amendment analysis fashioned in *Pokaski* has been held equally applicable in other cases involving access to judicial records where the underlying proceeding is open to the public,[36] as well as in cases concerning access to the transcripts of closed proceedings.[37] Indeed, the American Bar Association has promulgated standards that incorporate the teaching of *Richmond Newspapers, Inc.* by articulating a right of public access to "all judicial proceedings and related documents and exhibits, and any record made thereof," subject to specific, narrowly defined circumstances that may justify sealing.[38] The standard

---

of access to grand jury proceedings, the court held it has no First Amendment-based right to the records of such a proceeding. See *id.* See also In re Associated Press, 162 F.3d 503 (7th Cir. 1998) (requiring the trial court to articulate its reasons for sealing various documents and to provide a description of the documents in order to permit meaningful judicial review of the decision to seal them).

36. In *Globe Newspaper Co. v. Fenton*, 819 F. Supp. 89 (D. Mass. 1993), the court applied *Pokaski* in holding that the Massachusetts Criminal Offender Records Information System (CORI) violates the First Amendment. CORI denied public access to alphabetic indices of parties in closed criminal cases, which indices are maintained by trial court clerks. "The indices thus are a key to effective public access to court activity. And the importance of public access to the proper functioning of our judicial system cannot be overstated." *Id.* at 94. To be sure, the court noted, denial of access to the indices is an effective means of vindicating the privacy, rehabilitation, and reintegration interests of the defendant, *id.* at 96-98, but "[d]enying access to the most effective means for accessing records in all closed criminal cases can hardly be considered a policy narrowly tailored to advance the Commonwealth's interests in a few such cases . . . . The Commonwealth is obligated, before a record of a determination of a criminal case may be kept from the public, to require a judicial finding on an adequate record that, with respect to the individual defendant, the documents should be kept confidential because of compelling state interests." *Id.* at 98-99.

37. If a criminal proceeding has been properly closed and documents sealed, transcripts of the closed proceedings must be released to the public once the danger of prejudice has passed. See United States v. Corces, 1997 U.S. Dist. LEXIS 11139 (M.D. Fla. 1997) (media motions to unseal various documents after conviction and appeals in racketeering case granted for some documents but denied for others); United States v. Fierer, 26 MEDIA L. REP. (BNA) 1090 (N.D. Ga. 1997) (following conclusion of case, various documents unsealed but others, involving confidential medical records of a non-party and notes of *in camera* proceeding, remained under seal because of "compelling higher interest").

38. ABA STANDARDS FOR CRIMINAL JUSTICE, FAIR TRIAL AND FREE PRESS 8-3.2, 21 (1991). Standard 8-3.2 provides, in pertinent part:

(a) In any criminal case, all judicial proceedings and related documents and exhibits, and any record made thereof, not otherwise required to remain confidential, should be accessible to the public, except as provided in section (b).

(b)(1) A court may issue a closure order to deny access to the public to specified portions of a judicial proceeding or related document or exhibit only after reasonable notice of and an opportunity to be heard on such proposed order has been provided to the parties and the public and the court thereafter enters findings that:

(A) unrestricted access would pose a substantial probability of harm to the fairness of the trial or other overriding interest which substantially outweighs the defendant's right to a public trial;

(B) the proposed order will effectively prevent the aforesaid harm; and

is expressly intended to conform to the Supreme Court's recognition in *Richmond Newspapers, Inc.* of a First Amendment-based right of access premised on the "structural design of the Constitution to guarantee a self-informed citizenry."[39]

§ 5-2. Records of Criminal Proceedings.

§ 5-2(a). Pretrial Records — In General.

With few exceptions, the courts have recognized a qualified First Amendment-based right of access to pretrial proceedings in criminal cases and have applied a rigorous standard to justify closure.[40] It is not surprising, then, that judges typically reject efforts to seal pretrial records in those same cases. As the Ninth Circuit observed in *Associated Press v. United States District Court*,[41] "[t]here is no reason to distinguish between pretrial proceedings [which are presumptively open] and the documents filed in regard to them."[42]

In *Associated Press*, a trial judge issued a pretrial order automatically sealing all documents filed with the court in a highly publicized prosecution.[43] On appeal, the Ninth Circuit unequivocally held "that the public and press have a first amendment right of access to pretrial documents in general."[44] Judge Reinhardt, writing for the court, reasoned that "[t]here can be little dispute that the press and public have historically had a common law right of access to most

---

(C) there is no less restrictive alternative reasonably available to prevent the aforesaid harm.

(2) A proceeding to determine whether a closure order should issue may itself be closed only upon a prima facie showing of the findings required by Section b(1). In making the determination as to whether such a prima facie showing exists, the court should not require public disclosure of or access to the matter which is the subject of the closure proceeding itself and the court should accept submissions under seal, in camera, or in any other manner designed to permit a party to make a prima facie showing without public disclosure of said matter.

Id.

39. *Id.* at 23.
40. See Chap. 3-1(a) *supra*.
41. 705 F.2d 1143 (9th Cir. 1983).
42. *Id.* at 1145. See generally Tennessee v. Drake, 701 S.W.2d 604, 608 (Tenn. 1985) (finding that the court must provide a transcript of hearing on a motion for closure of pre-trial proceedings and of any subsequent pre-trial or trial proceedings at the earliest time consistent with the preservation of interests warranting closure); Note, *Access to Pretrial Documents Under the First Amendment*, 84 COLUM. L. REV. 1813 (1984).
43. In the midst of the pretrial proceedings, the trial judge, *sua sponte*, without notice, hearing, or findings, sealed all future filings in the case. Subsequently, citing defendant's Sixth Amendment rights, the judge affirmed the blanket sealing order but modified it to provide for notice to the news media. See 705 F.2d at 1144-45.
44. *Id.* at 1145.

§ 5-2(a)　　ACCESS TO JUDICIAL RECORDS: CRIMINAL PROCEEDINGS　　§ 5-2(a)

pretrial documents . . . though not to some, such as transcripts of grand jury proceedings."[45] In addition, the court explained, "pretrial documents . . . are often important to a full understanding of the way in which 'the judicial process and the government as a whole' are functioning."[46]

Given the First Amendment-based presumption of access, therefore, a party seeking to seal documents in a criminal case must establish that secrecy "'is strictly and inescapably necessary in order to protect the fair trial guarantee.'"[47] More particularly, the Ninth Circuit held, "sufficiently specific findings on a document-by-document basis" must satisfy a three-part test.[48] There must be findings establishing a "substantial probability" of irreparable harm to defendant's fair trial rights,[49] "no less drastic alternative available,"[50] and a substantial probability that the closure order would be effective in preventing harm.[51] None of these three requirements, the court determined, were satisfied in the context of the case at bar.[52] Indeed, the court was especially critical of blanket sealing

---

45. *Id.* (citing United States v. Brooklier, 685 F.2d 1162 (9th Cir. 1982)).
46. 705 F.2d at 1145 (citation omitted).
47. *Id.* (quoting United States v. Brooklier, 685 F.2d at 1167). See United States v. Nix, 976 F. Supp. 417 (S.D. Miss. 1997) (recognizing presumption of access to court files but sealing motion to dismiss, motion to sever and accompanying exhibits in conspiracy to commit murder case); *id.* at 420 ("[I]n striking the balance between the defendants' right to a fair trial and the right of the public to have access to those motions and exhibits attached thereto, the balance must be struck in this specific instance by leaving the motions sealed . . . only as long as necessary to protect the rights of the criminally accused here."); United States v. Porter, 988 F. Supp. 519, 526 (M.D. Pa. 1997) (following conviction, court unsealed motions and orders relating to defendant's *in forma pauperis* defense, holding that documents filed with the court are part of the litigation, not in anticipation of litigation, and are not attorney work product).
48. 705 F.2d at 1147.
49. *Id.* at 1146; see also United States v. Porter, 988 F. Supp. 519, 527 (M.D. Pa. 1997) (following conviction, court unsealed motions and orders relating to defendant's *in forma pauperis* defense, rejecting argument that this discriminates against indigent defendants, since "the rights appurtenant to the right to counsel are more limited when counsel is appointed, and practical considerations further limit the confidentiality of the relationship when counsel is appointed").
50. 705 F.2d at 1146.
51. See *id.* ("Given the extensive publicity that is occurring even while the orders are outstanding, we doubt that the limitation on publicity accomplished by the closure orders would have any significant effect on DeLorean's right to a fair trial."). To justify sealing records, according to the Ninth Circuit, the lower court must find: "(1) a substantial probability that irreparable damage to defendant's fair trial right will result . . . (2) a substantial probability that alternatives to sealing will not adequately protect his right to a fair trial . . . and (3) a substantial probability that sealing will be effective in protecting against the perceived harm." *Id.*
52. See *id.*; see also In re Charlotte Observer, 882 F.2d 850 (4th Cir. 1989) (court recognized a First Amendment-based right of access to documents filed in connection with a motion for change of venue); United States v. Cojab, 996 F.2d 1404, 1405 (2d Cir. 1993) ("[T]he power . . . to seal the records of [criminal] proceedings is one to be very seldom exercised, and even then only with the greatest caution, under urgent circumstances, and for very clear and apparent reasons."). In *United States v. Salemme*, 985 F. Supp. 193 (D. Mass. 1997), the court denied the government's request to delay unsealing a motion to dismiss and attached documents until the government had an

orders, which "impermissibly reverse the 'presumption of openness' that characterizes criminal proceedings 'under our system of justice.'"[53]

Associated Press is illustrative of a wealth of precedent applying the First Amendment-based right of access to pretrial filings in criminal cases.[54] Other courts have invoked the First Amendment in this manner to invalidate orders sealing court records in proceedings where parties seek to disqualify a judge,[55]

---

opportunity to file a response. "To find temporary impoundment justified merely on the ground that the public record is at the moment incomplete would generally erode the presumption in favor of public access to judicial documents." *Id.* at 196. The court concluded that the defendants' submissions are "presumed to be matters of public record" and the government had failed to overcome the presumption of access. *Id.* at 197.

53. 705 F.2d at 1147 (citing Richmond Newspapers, Inc. v. Virginia, 448 U.S. 555, 573 (1980)). But see United States v. Nix, 976 F. Supp. 417, 421 (S.D. Miss. 1997) (motions to dismiss indictment and to sever, and accompanying exhibits, sealed without public notice, would remain sealed since public access would prejudice defendants' fair trial rights and compromise safety and well being of potential witnesses).

In *United States v. Andreas*, 150 F.3d 766 (7th Cir. 1998), the court avoided the difficult issue of reconciling confidentiality concerns with the right of access to pretrial documents. The press sought access to certain sealed papers and materials related to the prosecution of Andreas, an officer of the Archer Daniels Midland Company, and others indicted on charges of price fixing in violation of the Sherman Act. On appeal from the district court's refusal to modify the protective order sealing the documents, the press argued that the "material, even if initially properly filed under seal, becomes public documents when a district court reviews and relies on such documents in making public pre-trial rulings in a criminal case." *Id.* at 768. The Seventh Circuit stated that it was "not unsympathetic to the merits of the newspapers' argument, which has had some acceptance in the courts of appeals." *Id.* (citing United States v. Amodeo, 71 F.3d 1044, 1048-50 (2d Cir. 1995)); see Chap. 5-1 *supra*. The court held, however, that the newspapers had waived this argument because it "differs in kind from the argument that they raised in the district court — which was merely that all judicial documents are presumptively accessible, unless there are reasons that they should be confidential." *Id.* at 769.

54. See, e.g., United States v. Salemme, 985 F. Supp. 193, 195 (D. Mass. 1997) ("The presumption of public access is particularly strong concerning 'pretrial documents . . . containing allegations . . . of government misconduct, [because access to them is] often important to a full understanding of the way in which the judicial process and the government as a whole are functioning.'") (citation omitted); United States v. Porter, 988 F. Supp. 519, 527 (M.D. Pa. 1997) (following conviction, court unsealed various motions and orders relating to defendant's Fed. R. Crim. P. 17(b) *in forma pauperis* defense; the court concluded that "the right to public access outweighs any interest on the part of Porter to having the record remain sealed"). See also United States v. Andreas, 150 F.3d 766, 768-69 (7th Cir. 1998) (holding that newspaper waived argument that it was entitled to access to sealed materials relied upon by district court in making pretrial rulings).

55. See In re Storer Communications, Inc., 828 F.2d 330, 336 (6th Cir. 1987) (materials filed relating to recusal motion, with the exception of a grand jury transcript, "are subject to a qualified right to access"); In re Application of NBC, Inc., 828 F.2d 340, 344 (6th Cir. 1987) ("when a judge is disqualified as the result of an affidavit of bias, there is a record, and we believe the public is entitled to access").

§ 5-2(a) ACCESS TO JUDICIAL RECORDS: CRIMINAL PROCEEDINGS § 5-2(a)

proceedings examining the alleged conflicts of interest of attorneys,[56] proceedings seeking the disqualification of defense counsel,[57] hearings regarding access to privately owned interview tapes,[58] and competency hearings.[59]

In *United States v. Kaczynski*, the Ninth Circuit applied the common law right of access to judicial proceedings and upheld a district court order granting public and media access to a redacted copy of a report assessing the defendant's competency.[60] Kaczynski, accused of being the "Unabomber," was charged with a number of bombings that resulted in multiple deaths and injuries. After the jury was selected, he requested to proceed *pro se* because he opposed his counsel's plan to present a mental illness defense.[61] This raised the court's concern about Kaczynski's competence to stand trial, and the district judge ordered a psychiatric exam and report.[62] The psychiatrist concluded that Kaczynski was fit to stand trial and, based on the report, defense counsel stipulated that no hearing on the issue was required; the government agreed and the report was filed under seal.[63] The district court then made its own determination that Kaczynski was competent to stand trial, and denied his motion to represent himself because it was untimely.[64] Kaczynski pled guilty two days later.[65] The media, asserting both a

---

56. See In re Application of NBC, Inc., 828 F.2d at 345 (holding that "there is a qualified right of access to the materials").
57. See United States v. Castellano, 610 F. Supp. 1151, 1167-68 (S.D.N.Y. 1985) (court denied motion to seal two opinions relating to disqualification of defense counsel since the mere possibility of prejudicial publicity is insufficient to satisfy First Amendment standards).
58. See United States v. Brooklier, 685 F.2d 1162, 1172-73 (9th Cir. 1982).
59. See Miami Herald Publ'g Co. v. Chappell, 403 So. 2d 1342 (Fla. App. 1981) (First Amendment violated when trial court closed competency hearings and denied public access to tapes of testimony); Louisiana v. Eaton, 483 So. 2d 651 (La. App. 1986) (newspaper had a right to a transcript of a competency hearing improperly closed under First Amendment and state constitution); Express News Corp. v. MacRae, 787 S.W.2d 451, 452 (Tex. Crim. App. 1990) (holding that, under the First Amendment, there is a "presumption that judicial records will be open to inspection by the press and the public" and holding that the presumption had not been overcome); Society of Prof'l Journalists v. Bullock, 743 P.2d 1166, 1177-80 (Utah 1987); In re Times-World Corp., 488 S.E.2d 677, 684 (Va. App. 1997) ("we hold that the First Amendment of the United States Constitution and Article I, § 12 of the Virginia Constitution grant a qualified right of access to criminal competency hearings and documents admitted into evidence therein"). See also People v. Parkison, 25 MEDIA L. REP. (BNA) 2503 (Cal. Super. 1997) (report of court-appointed psychiatrist following defendant's plea of not guilty by reason of insanity is part of public record absent privilege or "a statutory right of privacy"). But see Detroit News, Inc. v. Recorder's Ct. Judge, 514 N.W.2d 148, 150 (Mich. 1994) (since competency reports not admitted into evidence have traditionally been treated as confidential in Michigan, "there is no right of access to the competency report prepared pursuant to the defendant's request for a competency hearing").
60. 154 F.3d 930 (9th Cir. 1998).
61. See *id.* at 931.
62. *Id.*
63. See *id.*
64. See *id.*
65. See *id.*

First Amendment and common law right of access, moved to unseal the psychiatric competency report. Kaczynski opposed the motion, asserting his and his family's privacy interests, and the government took no position. After a hearing, the district court redacted a portion of the report and ordered that the redacted version be unsealed and disclosed to the public.[66]

Because the district court based its decision solely on a common law right of access, the Ninth Circuit affirmed on this ground, and did not consider whether there is a First Amendment-based right to such records.[67] Recognizing "the public's and media's common law right to inspect and copy judicial records,"[68] the Ninth Circuit concluded that the trial court did not abuse its discretion.[69] The court explained that, to gain access, the press must first "make a threshold showing of a legitimate need for disclosure. Once that showing has been made, the court must balance the media's asserted need against any asserted reasons for confidentiality."[70] The Ninth Circuit concluded that the media had made the requisite showing, establishing that disclosure of the report would "serve the ends of justice by informing the public about the court's competency determination and Kaczynski's motivation for committing the Unabomber crimes."[71] In addition, the Ninth Circuit determined that the district court had properly redacted those portions of the report that implicated Kaczynski's privacy interest but had little connection to his competency or to his motivation.[72]

In *United States v. McVeigh*,[73] the Tenth Circuit affirmed the trial judge's orders sealing one defendant's motion to suppress evidence, which had been released only in redacted form, and accompanying exhibits, as well as another defendant's motion for severance, which was similarly made public only in redacted form. The court assumed, without deciding, that access to judicial records is governed by the constitutional standards articulated in *Press-Enterprise II*.[74] Nevertheless, it concluded that the right of access "does not extend to the *evidence actually ruled inadmissible* in such a hearing" because "[n]either tradition nor logic supports public access to inadmissible evidence."[75] In addition, the court held that the trial judge had properly vindicated the compelling interest of assuring candor by counsel in placing portions of the several motions under seal: "[G]ranting general access to such documents would

---

66. See *id.*
67. See *id.* at 932.
68. *Id.* at 931 (citing Valley Broadcasting Co. v. United States Dist. Ct., 798 F.2d 1289, 1293 (9th Cir. 1986); United States v. Schlette, 842 F.2d 1574 (9th Cir. 1988)).
69. 154 F.3d at 932.
70. *Id.* at 931 (citing United States v. Schlette, 842 F.2d at 1581).
71. 154 F.3d at 931.
72. See *id.* at 932.
73. 119 F.3d 806 (10th Cir. 1997), *cert. denied*, 118 S. Ct. 1110 (1998) (per curiam).
74. *Id.* at 812.
75. *Id.* at 813.

§ 5-2(a) ACCESS TO JUDICIAL RECORDS: CRIMINAL PROCEEDINGS § 5-2(a)

create a Hobson's choice between the need to obtain severance and the need to protect the client's interest in avoiding prejudicial pre-trial publicity."[76] Finally, the court held that the district judge's orders were supported by adequate findings and narrowly tailored to further the compelling interests at stake.[77]

Access to pretrial records and documents in criminal cases has also been based on the common law or state constitutional requirements. For example, one court found a right of access to written transcripts of tape recordings played during open pretrial proceedings in the common law as well as in First Amendment precedent.[78] Similarly, the Washington Supreme Court has held that closure of a hearing on a motion to dismiss and sealing of its record violated the state constitution without resort to federal law.[79] Whatever the source of the access right, however, courts at all levels have emphasized that it is qualified and that judicial records may be sealed in appropriate cases.[80]

---

76. *Id.* at 814.

77. *Id.* at 815.

78. See New Jersey v. Grecco, 455 A.2d 485, 487 (N.J. Super. 1982) (common law right to inspect public documents "should take into account modern copying techniques, and the use of such techniques, where reasonable, is a part of the right to access").

79. See Seattle Times Co. v. Ishikawa, 640 P.2d 716, 722-23 (Wash. 1982) (trial judge failed to "explicitly outline the nature of the interests protected," provide adequate "factual findings," make findings "why reasonable alternatives would have been ineffective," and "narrowly tailor the protective restriction on access to suit the specific needs of this case"). In reversing a trial court order requiring that all evidentiary material filed with the court be placed under seal, the Montana Supreme Court in *Montana ex rel. Missoulian v. Montana Twenty-First Judicial District Court*, 933 P.2d 829, 835 (Mont. 1997), relied on a state statute requiring a clear and present danger to a defendant's right to a fair trial and an absence of reasonable alternatives to disclosure. See MONT. CODE ANN. § 46-11-701. But cf. Federated Publications, Inc. v. Kurtz, 615 P.2d 440 (Wash. 1980) (pretrial order sealing the file of a closed suppression hearing because of fair trial concerns satisfied state constitutional requirements).

80. See, e.g., United States v. McVeigh, 918 F. Supp. 1452 (W.D. Okla. 1996). In *McVeigh*, various news organizations sought to unseal documents in the criminal prosecutions arising from the bombing of a federal building in Oklahoma City. The court determined that access issues arising in the case would be adjudicated by reference to a series of questions drawn from *Press-Enterprise II*:

> Does the matter involve activity within the tradition of free public access to information concerning criminal prosecutions? Will public access play a significant positive role in the activity and in the functioning of the process? Is there a *substantial probability* that some recognized interest of higher value than public access to information will be prejudiced or affected adversely by the disclosure? Does the need for protection of that interest override the qualified First Amendment right of access? Is the closure by the court essential to protect that interest, considering all reasonable alternatives? This same analysis will also be used in considering any future motions to seal.

Id. at 1464. Applying this standard, the court in *McVeigh* considered a request for public access to documents disclosing amounts paid to appointed counsel and other services provided to the defense. See *id.* Distinguishing those documents directly related to the process of adjudication from those that are not, the court denied access until after final judgment. See *id.* at 1467. But see United

§ 5-2(a)(1). Wiretap Records.

Title III of the Federal Omnibus Crime Control and Safe Streets Act of 1968 typically governs electronic surveillance and the subsequent use of the information obtained.[81] Although, with limited exceptions, Title III does not provide for public access to wiretap materials, courts have recognized that "[w]here a qualified First Amendment right of access exists, it is not enough simply to cite Title III. Obviously a statute cannot override a constitutional right."[82]

Indeed, nothing in Title III expressly precludes public access to legally obtained wiretap materials.[83] Nevertheless, to protect individual privacy,[84] intercepted communications are sealed pursuant to Title III and wiretap applications and orders are to be disclosed only for good cause.[85] On its face, the statute provides only that law enforcement officials may disclose and use wiretap information in their operations and that such information may be disclosed by other persons in giving testimony.[86]

In *United States v. Dorfman*,[87] the Seventh Circuit held that these Title III provisions permitting limited disclosure imply "that what is not permitted is forbidden."[88] Even when disclosures are made during testimony in an *in camera* proceeding, the court held, a trial judge is not thereby authorized to release them to the public.[89] The only way such material may be made public, the Seventh Circuit explained, is by being admitted into evidence in a public proceeding.[90] Other courts similarly have cited Title III in rejecting efforts to unseal orders and

---

States v. Ellis, 90 F.3d 447, 450-51 (11th Cir. 1996) (holding that transcript of *in camera* hearing regarding defendants' motion for appointment of counsel, including details of payment to retained counsel, should be unsealed because it does not infringe the attorney-client privilege or otherwise prejudice defendant).

81. See 18 U.S.C. §§ 2510-2520.
82. In re New York Times Co., 828 F.2d 110, 115 (2d Cir. 1987).
83. 18 U.S.C. §§ 2512, 2518 (9) & (10)(a) prohibit disclosure of materials seized in violation of Title III.
84. See S. REP. NO. 90-1097, at 66-67 (1968). See generally Gelbard v. United States, 408 U.S. 41, 46-49 (1972) (discussing the importance of privacy under Title III).
85. See 18 U.S.C. § 2515. See also In re Globe Newspaper Co., 729 F.2d 47, 54 (1st Cir. 1984) ("if an electronic surveillance has been shown to be unlawful, Title III prevents its fruits from being disclosed to the public").
86. See 18 U.S.C. § 2517(1-3); see also Wisconsin v. Gilmore, 535 N.W.2d 21, 23 (Wis. App. 1995), aff'd, 549 N.W.2d 401 (Wis. 1996) (court permitted prosecutor to quote communications, intercepted under a state wiretapping law, in a criminal complaint).
87. 690 F.2d 1230 (7th Cir. 1982).
88. See *id.* at 1232.
89. See *id.* at 1233.
90. *Id.* at 1234 ("[Title III] put no limits on the public disclosure of lawfully obtained wiretap evidence through public testimony in legal proceedings; but neither did it authorize wiretap evidence not made public in this manner to be made public another way without the consent of the people whose phone conversations were intercepted.").

applications for electronic surveillance. The public interest in access to such materials is generally "not enough in itself to justify a finding of good cause under the statute."[91]

Nevertheless, most courts have rejected any per se rule closing proceedings or sealing records where Title III materials are involved, even where the legality of the wiretap has not yet been determined. In *In re Globe Newspaper Co.*,[92] for example, the First Circuit declined "to create a *per se* rule that a proceeding must always be closed if it involves Title III material whose legality has not been tested," emphasizing that the "court may find in some cases that the Title III material is not sufficiently private to warrant protection, or sufficiently prejudicial to endanger the defendant's fair trial right."[93] By the same token, the court held that, while there is a First Amendment-based right of access to the bail hearing at issue,[94] the privacy and fair trial rights of the defendants outweighed the public's interest in access.[95]

In *In re New York Times Co.*,[96] the Second Circuit held that there is a qualified, First Amendment-based right of access "to written documents, submitted in connection with judicial proceedings that themselves implicate the right of access,"[97] including documents containing Title III materials.[98] Nevertheless, the court accepted that, in applying *Press-Enterprise II* standards for closure, privacy interests of defendants and innocent third parties should "weigh heavily."[99] Other courts have similarly weighed the public's access rights against the privacy interests protected by Title III.[100]

---

91. In re Kansas City Star, 666 F.2d 1168, 1177 n.12 (8th Cir. 1981). See In re Interception of Wire & Oral Communications (Kattar), 682 F. Supp. 669, 673 (D.N.H. 1988); United States v. Ferle, 563 F. Supp. 252, 253 (D.R.I. 1983).
92. 729 F.2d 47 (1st Cir. 1984).
93. *Id.* at 58. But see Pennsylvania v. Frattarola, 485 A.2d 1147, 1151 (Pa. Super. 1984) ("There can be no disclosure of intercepted communications until a court has ruled that the interception was lawful.") (citing United States v. Cianfrani, 573 F.2d 835 (3d Cir. 1978)).
94. 729 F.2d at 51-52.
95. *Id.* at 49. See United States v. Martin, 684 F. Supp. 341 (D. Mass. 1988) (denying access to portions of a detention hearing in which audio tapes and a transcript were discussed). In *Martin*, however, the court did grant access to certain wiretap materials; see also United States v. White, 855 F. Supp. 13, 17 (D. Mass. 1994) ("the First Amendment right of access does extend to documents containing Title III material introduced in pretrial criminal proceedings").
96. 828 F.2d 110 (2d Cir. 1987).
97. *Id.* at 114.
98. See *id.* at 115-16.
99. *Id.* at 116. The Second Circuit remanded for more specific findings. On appeal after remand, the Second Circuit held that redaction was warranted, even where it leaves the disclosed documents "almost meaningless," if "important Title III privacy interests cannot otherwise be protected." In re New York Times Co., 834 F.2d 1152, 1154 (2d Cir. 1987), *cert. denied*, 485 U.S. 977 (1988).
100. See, e.g., In re Grand Jury Subpoena, 103 F.3d 234, 241-43 (2d Cir. 1996) (closure of proceeding and sealing of documents relating to motion of victim of allegedly illegal electronic surveillance to compel disclosure of such surveillance does not violate First Amendment); Certain

When wiretap materials are admitted into evidence or such information is otherwise disclosed in a public proceeding, courts typically hold that Title III does not bar public access to the relevant documents and records.[101] Similarly, when wiretap information is otherwise included in a public record — e.g., a search warrant application to which the public has access[102] — most, but not all, courts have held that Title III does not itself preclude public scrutiny.[103]

Interested Individuals v. Pulitzer Publ'g Co., 895 F.2d 460, 466-67 (8th Cir.), *cert. denied*, 498 U.S. 880 (1990); United States v. Gerena, 869 F.2d 82, 85 (2d Cir. 1989) ("the district court must balance the public's right of access against the privacy and fair trial interests of defendants, witnesses and third parties"); United States v. Gotti, 771 F. Supp. 567 (E.D.N.Y. 1991) (Title III materials unsealed following denial of motion to suppress since fair trial concerns were of less weight and because of public declarations calling court's integrity into question); see also Providence Journal Co. v. FBI, 602 F.2d 1010, 1011-14 (1st Cir. 1979), *cert. denied*, 444 U.S. 1071 (1980) (denying media access to electronic surveillance obtained in violation of intervenor's Fourth Amendment rights, prior to enactment of Title III, because release would constitute invasion of privacy).

101. See, e.g., United States v. Rosenthal, 763 F.2d 1291, 1294 (11th Cir. 1985) ("Thus, we hold that Title III creates no independent bar to the public's right of access to judicial materials with respect to wiretap materials legally intercepted and admitted into evidence pursuant to the statute."); United States v. Dorfman, 690 F.2d 1230 (7th Cir. 1982) (quoting United States v. Edwards, 672 F.2d 1289, 1290 (7th Cir. 1982)) (Title III imposes no independent restriction on the dissemination of information that enters the public domain in manner deemed permissible under the statute); United States v. Cianfrani, 573 F.2d 835, 855-61 (3d Cir. 1978) (granting public access to transcripts of Title III material introduced at suppression hearing where the materials lawfully obtained, and where danger of prejudice to the defendant was minimal because no trial would follow); Kuhn v. City of Detroit, 610 F. Supp. 364, 369 (E.D. Mich. 1984) (court allowed plaintiffs in an antitrust action to subpoena electronic surveillance material disclosed in a related criminal prosecution because under Title III, "[o]nce the material has been revealed . . . the purpose of Section 2517(3) ceases and the requirements of that section no longer govern"); see also United States v. Masselli, 638 F. Supp. 206, 208-13 (S.D.N.Y. 1986) (court refused to hold prosecutor in contempt for disclosing transcripts of Title III materials in a motion for severance, and to the press at the time the motion was filed, where a judicial order prohibiting disclosure mirrored the language of Title III and authorized public disclosure of transcripts "in any proceeding").

102. See, e.g., In re Newsday, Inc., 895 F.2d 74, 79 (2d Cir.), *cert. denied*, 496 U.S. 931 (1990) ("The presence of material derived from intercepted communications in the warrant application does not change its status as a public document subject to a common law right of access, although the fact that the application contains such material may require careful review by a judge before the papers are unsealed.").

103. See Certain Interested Individuals v. Pulitzer Publ'g Co., 895 F.2d 460, 465 (8th Cir.), *cert. denied*, 498 U.S. 880 (1990) ("We do not agree that once wiretap information is used in search warrant affidavits, it is no longer subject to Title III's restrictions on use and disclosure."); see also In re Search Warrant for Secretarial Area Outside Office of Gunn, 855 F.2d 569, 570, 574-75 (8th Cir. 1988) (recognizing qualified, First Amendment-based right of access to documents filed in connection with search warrant applications, but denying access to those documents where the government had a compelling interest in keeping them sealed because of an on-going investigation, and the documents contained verbatim excerpts of telephone conversations obtained through court-authorized electronic surveillance).

§ 5-2(a)(2). Search Warrants.

In the late 1980s, the federal government launched Operation Ill-Wind, a major investigation of fraud and bribery in the defense contracting industry. Prosecutors applied for a host of search warrants nationwide. When the media sought access to sealed search warrant applications, several federal courts were presented with an opportunity to opine on the relevance of a First Amendment-based right of access to search warrant materials.[104]

In *Times Mirror Co. v. United States*,[105] the Ninth Circuit held "that members of the public have no right of access to search warrant materials while a pre-indictment investigation is under way."[106] The court found "no historical tradition of open search warrant proceedings and materials,"[107] and the secret nature of the process, which is similar to closed grand jury proceedings, is facilitated by *ex parte* applications and *in camera* review.[108] Although the court acknowledged that "legitimate" public interests are served by access to search warrant materials, they were outweighed by the potential damage to the law enforcement process and the privacy interests of those identified in such materials.[109] Accordingly, the Ninth Circuit was unwilling to put the government to "the considerable burden of responding on a case-by-case basis to actions . . . brought during the middle of an ongoing investigation."[110]

---

104. See generally Note, *An Ill Wind Blows: Restricting the Public's Right of Access to Search Warrant Affidavits*, 74 MINN. L. REV. 661 (1990); Note, *A First Amendment Right of Access to Affidavits in Support of Search Warrants*, 90 COLUM. L. REV. 2216 (1990).

105. 873 F.2d 1210 (9th Cir. 1989).

106. *Id.* at 1211.

107. *Id.* at 1214; see also In re Two Sealed Search Warrants, 710 A.2d 202, 208, 209-10 (Del. Super. 1997) (rejecting First Amendment right of access to pre-indictment search warrants sealed for 90 days, noting that cases reveal that there is as much historical basis for closure as disclosure, and hence, no strong national tradition exists, and that the present case fits none of the six considerations identified in *Richmond Newspapers*); Wisconsin v. Cummings, 546 N.W.2d 406 (Wis. 1996) (denying access to search warrants and supporting materials).

108. 873 F.2d at 1214. But see In re Newsday, Inc., 895 F.2d 74, 79 (2d Cir.), *cert. denied*, 496 U.S. 931 (1990) ("the fact that search warrants are commonly filed under seal until the warrant is executed does not change their status as public documents").

109. 873 F.2d at 1215-16. Accord In re Four Search Warrants, 945 F. Supp. 1563, 1567 (N.D. Ga. 1996) (no First Amendment-based right of access to sealed search warrant affidavits used to obtain search warrants of suspect's residence, truck, storage unit and hair samples in connection with bombing at Centennial Olympic Park).

110. 873 F.2d at 1217 n.8. The same considerations led the court to reject extending the common law right of access to search warrant materials — "the ends of justice would be frustrated, not served, if the public were allowed access to warrant materials in the midst of a preindictment investigation into suspected criminal activity." *Id.* at 1219. Federal Rule of Criminal Procedure 41(g), which provides for filing of warrants with the court clerk, the Ninth Circuit determined, merely facilitates the efficient and orderly maintenance of warrant materials. It does not make the material a "judicial record" subject to public access. *Id.* at 1220. In *United States v. Certain Real Property*, 977 F. Supp. 833, 835 (E.D. Mich. 1997), the court "adopted the reasoning of the

Other courts, however, have recognized a First Amendment-based right of public access to search warrant materials. In *In re Search Warrant for Secretarial Area Outside Office of Thomas Gunn*,[111] the Eighth Circuit held "that the qualified first amendment right of public access extends to the documents filed in support of search warrants and that the documents may [only] be sealed if the district court specifically finds that sealing is necessary to protect a compelling government interest and that less restrictive alternatives are impracticable."[112] Unlike the Ninth Circuit in *Times Mirror Co.*, which focused on the traditional secrecy of warrant proceedings, the Eighth Circuit in *Gunn* emphasized that, historically, the *documents* themselves are routinely filed in the court record without seal.[113] Moreover, the Eighth Circuit concluded that public access "is important to the public's understanding of the function and operation of the judicial process and the criminal justice system and may operate as a curb on prosecutorial or judicial misconduct."[114] Thus, while the court in *Times Mirror Co.* emphasized the warrant's role in the criminal *investigation*, the court in *Gunn* focused on the warrant process as "an integral part of a criminal *prosecution*."[115]

Despite the presence of a First Amendment-based right, however, the Eighth Circuit concluded that restricting public access to the documents at issue was necessitated by the government's compelling interest in the integrity of the ongoing investigation. There was a "substantial probability," the court found, that Operation Ill-Wind would be "severely compromised" if the sealed documents were released.[116] The district court, moreover, had correctly concluded

---

Second, Fourth and Ninth Circuits and declined to extend the first amendment right of public access to search warrants and the affidavits supporting them." The court found that "[p]ublic access would not play a significant role in the ongoing criminal investigation but could impede or even halt the process." *Id.* In *In re Search Warrants in Connection with Investigation of Columbus/HCA Health Care Corp.*, 971 F. Supp. 251 (W.D. Tex. 1997), the court similarly denied a motion to unseal affidavits and other materials supporting search warrants.

111. 855 F.2d 569 (8th Cir. 1988).

112. *Id.* at 575; see In re Search Warrants Issued on June 11, 1988, for the Premises of Three Bldgs. at UNISYS, Inc., 710 F. Supp. 701, 704 (D. Minn. 1989) (holding that a qualified, First Amendment-based right of access applies to search warrant documents which can only be overcome by a narrowly tailored restriction aimed at vindicating a compelling governmental interest).

113. 855 F.2d at 573.

114. *Id.*

115. *Id.* (emphasis added). See Newspapers of New England, Inc. v. Clerk-Magistrate, 531 N.E.2d 1261, 1265 (Mass. 1988), *cert. denied*, 490 U.S. 1066 (1989) ("The affidavit in question has no integral relationship with any particular pretrial proceedings to which the public enjoys a First Amendment right of access.").

116. 855 F.2d at 574.

that line-by-line redaction was not practicable.[117] Accordingly, the documents remained sealed.[118]

A third judicial approach has extended the common law right of access to search warrant materials. In *In re Baltimore Sun Co. (Goetz)*,[119] the Fourth Circuit held that search warrant affidavits are judicial records subject to a qualified common law right of public access, even prior to indictment.[120] The court emphasized that a warrant is obtained from judicial officers, is filed with the district court, and is subject to judicial review, all of which led to the conclusion that "affidavits for search warrants are judicial records."[121]

For purposes of the common law right, the court noted, the question of access "is committed to the sound discretion of the judicial officer who issued the warrants" and is reviewed under an "abuse of discretion" standard.[122] Neverthe-

---

117. See *id.*
118. The court did hold that the district court erred in sealing the relevant docket sheets. See *id.* at 574. See Certain Interested Individuals v. Pulitzer Publ'g Co., 895 F.2d 460, 467 (8th Cir.), *cert. denied*, 498 U.S. 880 (1990) (balancing privacy interest of unindicted persons identified in warrants against the right of access and concluding that "pre-indictment status of the government's criminal investigation tips the balance decisively in favor of the privacy interests and against disclosure of even the redacted version of the search warrant affidavits at this time").
119. 886 F.2d 60 (4th Cir. 1989).
120. See *id.* at 62 ("Although the press and public do not have a first amendment right of access, they have a qualified common law right of access."). See In re Application & Affidavit for a Search Warrant (Hughes), 923 F.2d 324, 326 (4th Cir.), *cert. denied*, 505 U.S. 944 (1991) (press has "a common law right of access to affidavits supporting search warrants, although not a First Amendment right of access"); In re Search Warrants, 26 MEDIA L. REP. (BNA) 2564 (M.D.N.C. 1998) (adopting magistrate judge's order unsealing affidavit filed in support of search warrant, citing *Goetz*). See also In re Search of Flower Aviation of Kansas, Inc., 789 F. Supp. 366 (D. Kan. 1992) (adopting *Goetz*); PG Publ'g Co. v. Pennsylvania, 614 A.2d 1106, 1108 (Pa. 1992) (recognizing common law right of access to search warrant materials).
121. 886 F.2d at 64. See In re Newsday, Inc., 895 F.2d at 79 ("there is a common law right to inspect what is commanded thus to be filed"); Newspapers of New England, Inc. v. Clerk-Magistrate, 531 N.E.2d at 1263 ("On filing with the court the affidavit is a public document both under the statute [governing filing of warrants] and the common law.").
122. 886 F.2d at 65. In *In re Four Search Warrants*, 945 F. Supp. 1563, 1567 (N.D. Ga. 1996), the court held that a common law right of access attached to the affidavits submitted in support of an application to obtain search warrants in the Centennial Olympic Park bombing investigation. In so holding, the court asserted that a trial judge must balance the presumptive right of access against competing interests. "Among the factors to be considered by the court when balancing the interests are whether the records are sought for improper purposes, 'whether access is likely to promote public understanding of historically significant events, and whether the press has already been permitted substantial access to the contents of the records.'" *Id.* at 1568 (quoting Newman v. Graddick, 696 F.2d 796, 803 (11th Cir. 1983)). The court determined that the "unique" circumstances of the case were sufficient reason to permit access to redacted documents, circumstances which included the facts that (1) the media was seeking only information already released to the subject of the warrants; (2) the criminal investigation with respect to the subject of the warrants had ended; (3) much of the information contained in the affidavits had already been made public, apparently through government leaks; (4) the public had an interest in understanding the legal process and

less, the Fourth Circuit also relied on constitutional precedent and adopted procedures and standards of review derived from the First Amendment in the search warrant context. According to the court, notice is to be given by docketing the order sealing the documents,[123] the district court must make findings specific enough to allow meaningful appellate review,[124] and access may be denied only when sealing is "essential to preserve higher values and is narrowly tailored to serve that interest" and less burdensome alternatives are unavailable.[125] Because these procedures were not followed by the trial court, the orders at issue were vacated.[126]

Whether under the First Amendment, the common law, or state constitutional or statutory authority, most courts have now recognized a right of public access to search warrant materials. But, the fact that a right of public access is extended to search warrants provides no assurance that disclosure will be ordered. Even when a presumption in favor of public access is accepted, the right remains qualified.[127] Thus, for example, the need for secrecy in an ongoing investigation may well warrant sealing.[128] Concern for the privacy

---

preserving the integrity of the fact-finding process; and (5) the subject of the warrants — Richard Jewell — had an interest in vindicating his reputation and ability to gain employment in his chosen field. 945 F. Supp. at 1568-69. By the same token, the court noted "that the truly compelling interest in this case is the identification and prosecution of the actual perpetrator," and therefore ordered the redaction of any information in the affidavits that reflected investigative methods, details of the crime, and the names of witnesses not yet released to the public. *Id.* at 1570. See also In re Macon Tel. Publ'g Co., 900 F. Supp. 489 (M.D. Ga. 1995) (common law right did not require access to sealed search warrants and supporting affidavits); In re Office Suites for World & Islam Studies Enter., 925 F. Supp. 738 (M.D. Fla. 1996).

123. See 886 F.2d at 65 (citing In re Washington Post Co., 807 F.2d 383 (4th Cir. 1986)). But see In re Two Sealed Search Warrants, 710 A.2d 202, 213 (Del. Super. 1997) (holding that intervening newspapers do not have a right to notice before court issues order sealing pre-indictment search warrants because the issuance and sealing of a search warrant involves an ex parte action not involving open hearings that would afford an opportunity to challenge the warrant's authorization).

124. See 886 F.2d at 65 (citing *Press-Enterprise I*, 464 U.S. at 510; In re Washington Post Co., 807 F.2d at 389-90; In re Knight Publ'g Co., 743 F.2d 231, 235 (4th Cir. 1984)).

125. See 886 F.2d at 65-66 (citing *Press-Enterprise I*, 464 U.S. at 510; In re Washington Post Co., 807 F.2d at 390; In re Knight Publ'g Co., 743 F.2d at 235).

126. See 886 F.2d at 65; see also Houston Chronicle Publ'g Co. v. Woods, 949 S.W.2d 492 (Tex. App. 1997) (writ of mandamus ordering judge to set aside order denying access to affidavits in support of arrest warrant and search warrants).

127. See In re Application & Affidavit for a Search Warrant (Hughes), 923 F.2d at 329; Newspapers of New England Inc. v. Clerk-Magistrate, 531 N.E.2d at 1263-64 ("Through this balancing process, 'a judge must determine whether "good cause" to order impoundment exists' and must tailor the scope of the impoundment order so that it does not exceed the need for impoundment.") (citation omitted).

128. See, e.g., In re Kaczynski, 24 MEDIA L. REP. (BNA) 1700, 1702 (D. Mont. 1996) (finding substantial likelihood that the government's investigation of suspected Unabomber would be compromised by premature release of investigation data); In re Search Warrants Issued on June 11,

interests[129] or safety[130] of persons named in warrant materials, or persons identified in wiretap transcripts submitted in support of a warrant application, may necessitate redaction.[131] Fair trial concerns have also been weighed against

---

1988, for the Premises of Three Bldgs. at UNISYS, Inc., 710 F. Supp. 701, 704 (D. Minn. 1989) ("[The government] has shown that public disclosure of these portions of the record would significantly compromise its ongoing investigation."). But see In re Search Warrants, 26 MEDIA L. REP. (BNA) 2564 (M.D.N.C. 1998) (unsealing an affidavit filed in support of a search warrant in a case in which the government failed to make a specific showing that unsealing the affidavit would jeopardize its ongoing investigation).

129. See, e.g., In re New York Times Co., 834 F.2d at 1153-54 (privacy interests of third parties named in warrant material); In re Search of 1993 Jeep Grand Cherokee, 958 F. Supp. 205 (D. Del. 1996) (no First Amendment-based right of access to pre-indictment warrants and common law right is overcome by privacy interests in ongoing investigation); In re Kaczynski, 24 MEDIA L. REP. (BNA) at 1702 ("Privacy interests could be significantly impaired."); In re Buffalo News, 969 F. Supp. 869 (W.D.N.Y. 1997) (warrant to search premises of father and sister of Timothy McVeigh, and related filings, unsealed after government withdrew its objections, except for titles to books and father's description of his children's beliefs contained in attached affidavit; United States v. Thomas, 25 MEDIA L. REP. (BNA) 2116, 2118 (E.D. Pa. 1997) (granting intervening newspaper's motion to unseal and for access to search warrant in case involving murder of parents by two teenagers who allegedly had visited white supremacist organization); In re Two Sealed Search Warrants, 710 A.2d 202, 211-12 (Del. Super. 1997) (holding that the common law presumption of openness extending to pre-indictment search warrants and supporting documents as judicial records is overcome by possibility of compromising the integrity of an ongoing criminal investigation and the danger of infringing on the privacy interests of several individuals who may not be suspects). But see In re Search Warrants, 26 MEDIA L. REP. (BNA) 1127 (Colo. County Ct. 1997) (ordering that search warrants, search warrant affidavits and returns, and other documents filed with the court in connection with the death of JonBenet Ramsey be unsealed because privacy interests had been diminished by the publication of information on investigation and by the child's parents' statements to the media; ordering the redaction of certain descriptive information in the search warrants still important to the ongoing investigation and ordering that certain affidavits remain sealed). In a ruling affirmed by the district court, the magistrate judge in *Jeep Grand Cherokee* unsealed the warrants, supporting affidavits and returns in redacted form, holding that the common law right of public access prevailed over any remaining privacy concerns. See In re Search of 1993 Jeep Grand Cherokee, 958 F. Supp. 205 (D. Del. 1996).

130. See In re Search Warrants, 26 MEDIA L. REP. (BNA) 2564 (M.D.N.C. 1998) (unsealing an affidavit filed in support of a search warrant in a case in which there was no evidence to support the government's assertion that the confidential informant named in the affidavit would be retaliated against by the officer under investigation because the officer was reassigned to administrative duties and because the government failed to show that the officer had violent tendencies).

131. In *In re Newsday, Inc.*, 895 F.2d at 78, the Second Circuit initially held that "Title III does not forbid public access to the warrant application." But, the court went on to hold that the trial judge had properly balanced the public's access rights and the privacy interests of the wiretap target and innocent third parties in releasing a redacted affidavit. See *id.* See also United States v. Shenberg, 791 F. Supp. 292, 294 (S.D. Fla. 1991) (requiring redaction of search warrant affidavits of wiretap materials because of privacy interests protected by Title III); In re Search Warrants Issued on June 11, 1988, 710 F. Supp. at 705 ("Where redaction is required to protect privacy interests, it must be narrowly tailored to allow as much disclosure as is feasible. . . . The court finds that the privacy rights of certain individuals implicated in the sealed documents are of a compelling

public access rights in this context.[132]

§ 5-2(a)(3). Grand Jury Records.

The limitations placed on public access to grand jury and ancillary proceedings[133] are also placed on the materials that accompany those proceedings. Unless specifically permitted by statute, material submitted to or generated by a grand jury is generally held to be secret. A more contested issue is the right of public access to material submitted in or generated by an ancillary proceeding in which grand jury information may be relevant. In such cases, the court must determine whether a common law or First Amendment-based right of access to court records attaches to the proceeding, creating a presumption of openness.[134] The court must then determine whether grand jury secrecy or other concerns present an overriding interest that requires sealing of the relevant materials of record.

Since the 17th century, the records of grand jury proceedings have been closed to the public.[135] In the federal system and in most states, courts have denied access to grand jury records on the ground that granting such access might frustrate the functioning of the grand jury system.[136] In the federal system,

---

nature adequate to overcome the first amendment right of public access."); Connecticut v. Clein, 1996 Conn. Super. LEXIS 1292 (Conn. Super. 1996).

132. See, e.g., In re Application & Affidavit for a Search Warrant (Hughes), 923 F.2d at 328-29 ("We are not disposed to overturn the district court's conclusion that release of the paragraph will not deprive Hughes of a fair trial and we emphasize also the importance of the common law right of access to judicial documents related to the criminal justice system.").

In *In re Kaczynski*, 24 MEDIA L. REP. (BNA) 1700, 1702 (D. Mont. 1996), the court held that, even if the Ninth Circuit were to accept a First Amendment-based or common law right of public access, it would nevertheless preclude access to the search warrant documents involving the Unabomber suspect:

> I find that the government's need for secrecy in its pre-indictment investigation outweighs the public desire for access to the search warrant materials prior to conclusion of the criminal investigation or indictment by a grand jury. Based upon these considerations, I find that disclosure would not serve the ends of justice and that the higher values outlined above preempt any public right of access at this juncture. Sealing of the search warrant documents is narrowly tailored to these ends, and I can think of no reasonable alternative short of sealing the documents that will protect both the integrity of the investigation and the privacy interests of the Defendant and witnesses.

133. See Chap. 3-1(a)(3) *supra*.
134. See Chap. 5-1 *supra*.
135. See Douglas Oil Co. v. Petrol Stops Northwest, 441 U.S. 211, 218-19 n.9 (1979); In re Grand Jury Proceedings, 942 F.2d 1195, 1198 (7th Cir. 1991); Birmingham News Co. v. Hunt, 624 So. 2d 1117, 1124 (Ala. Crim. App. 1993); Caulkins, *Grand Jury Secrecy*, 63 MICH. L. REV. 455, 456-58 (1965). See generally Note, *Behind the Gray Door: Williams, Secrecy, and the Federal Grand Jury*, 69 N.Y.U. L. REV. 563 (1994).
136. See, e.g., In re Donovan, 801 F.2d 409, 410 (D.C. Cir. 1986). The reasons underlying grand jury secrecy include:

§ 5-2(a)(3)   ACCESS TO JUDICIAL RECORDS: CRIMINAL PROCEEDINGS   § 5-2(a)(3)

Rule 6(e) of the Federal Rules of Criminal Procedure preserves grand jury secrecy by providing for the confidentiality of all matters occurring before the grand jury.[137] A knowing violation of the grand jury secrecy rule may be punished as a contempt of court.[138] Under the rule, indictments returned by a grand jury may be kept secret at the direction of the federal magistrate judge to whom the indictment is returned.[139] Records, orders and subpoenas relating to

---

(1) To prevent the escape of those whose indictment may be contemplated; (2) to insure the utmost freedom to the grand jury in its deliberations, and to prevent persons subject to indictment or their friends from importuning the grand jurors; (3) to prevent subornation of perjury or tampering with the witnesses who may testify before grand jury and later appear at the trial of those indicted by it; (4) to encourage free and untrammeled disclosures by persons who have information with respect to the commission of crimes; (5) to protect an innocent accused who is exonerated from disclosure of the fact that he has been under investigation, and from the expense of standing trial where there was no probability of guilt.

United States v. Procter & Gamble Co., 356 U.S. 677, 682 n.6 (1958). See In re Biaggi, 478 F.2d 489, 491-92 (2d Cir. 1973); McClatchy Newspapers v. Superior Ct., 751 P.2d 1329, 1332-33 (Cal. 1988); Ohio ex rel. Beacon Journal Publ'g Co. v. Waters, 617 N.E.2d 1110 (Ohio 1993).

137. See In re North, 16 F.3d 1234, 1242 (D.C. Cir. 1994) (Federal Rules of Criminal Procedure embody the ancient principle of grand jury secrecy); Martin v. Consultants & Adm'rs, Inc., 966 F.2d 1078, 1097 (7th Cir. 1992) (FBI reports are not to be released "where they are closely related to the grand jury's investigation itself and where disclosure would reveal the identities of targets and other witnesses."); In re Grand Jury Proceedings, 851 F.2d 860, 866 (6th Cir. 1988) (general rule is "that confidential documentary information not otherwise public obtained by the grand jury via coercive means is presumed to be 'matters occurring before the grand jury'"); United States v. Smith, 992 F. Supp. 743, 751 (D.N.J. 1998); WBZ-TV4 v. District Attorney, 562 N.E.2d 817, 821 (Mass. 1990) (not every document placed before a grand jury is automatically exempt from disclosure, but videotape of lineup especially prepared for grand jury should remain secret). Disclosure of information that is produced by a criminal investigation which parallels, but is independent of, a grand jury investigation is not a violation of grand jury secrecy because it is not a matter occurring before the grand jury. See In re Grand Jury Subpoena (Under Seal), 920 F.2d 235, 241-43 (4th Cir. 1990); Anaya v. United States, 815 F.2d 1373, 1379-80 (10th Cir. 1987); In re Grand Jury Matter (Catania), 682 F.2d 61, 64-65 (3d Cir. 1982). A "target letter" sent by a United States Attorney to a subject of a grand jury investigation that does not reveal grand jury information does not emanate from the grand jury and, therefore, is not a matter "occurring before the grand jury." United States v. Smith, 787 F.2d 111, 115 (3d Cir. 1986) ("target letter" appears to be an expression of the opinion of the United States Attorney); see also In re Grand Jury Investigation, 610 F.2d 202, 217 (5th Cir. 1980). A draft indictment that did not reveal any grand jury information falls outside Rule 6(e). See In re Grand Jury Matter (Catania), 682 F.2d 61, 64 n.4 (3d Cir. 1982). A request for a list of unindicted co-conspirators, denominated a "bill of particulars," that merely facilitates voluntary discovery is not a court document the public and press are entitled to view. See United States v. Anderson, 799 F.2d 1438, 1442 (11th Cir. 1986), cert. denied, 480 U.S. 931 (1987). See generally Comment, *FRCP 6(e) and the Disclosure of Documents Reviewed by a Grand Jury*, 57 U. CHI. L. REV. 221 (1990).

138. See FED. R. CRIM. P. 6(e)(2).

139. See FED. R. CRIM. P. 6(e)(4) ("The federal magistrate judge to whom an indictment is returned may direct that the indictment be kept secret until the defendant is in custody or has been released pending trial. Thereupon the clerk shall seal the indictment and no person shall disclose

grand jury proceedings must be sealed and remain secret so long as necessary to prevent disclosure of matters occurring before the grand jury.[140]

Rule 6(e) does not provide for complete secrecy. It does not apply to grand jury witnesses, or others not identified in the rule, such as members of the media, who may be in receipt of such records.[141] A witness called to testify before a grand jury is generally free to disclose the documentary evidence the witness has been compelled to provide to the grand jury.[142] Courts disagree about whether a grand jury witness is entitled to a transcript of her own grand jury testimony, or whether she must establish a particularized need for the materials before any disclosure will be permitted.[143]

In addition, Rule 6(e) sets forth several exceptions to the rule of secrecy.[144] Disclosure may be made by a court in connection with a judicial proceeding[145] and in certain circumstances to defendants,[146] government attorneys,[147] specified government personnel[148] or other federal grand juries.[149] A private party,[150] or

---

the return of the indictment except when necessary for the issuance and execution of a warrant or summons.").

140. See FED. R. CRIM. P. 6(e)(6) ("Records, orders and subpoenas relating to grand jury proceedings shall be kept under seal to the extent and for such time as is necessary to prevent disclosure of matters occurring before a grand jury.").

141. Rule 6(e) identifies those on whom an obligation of secrecy is imposed:

A grand juror, an interpreter, a stenographer, an operator of a recording device, a typist who transcribes recorded testimony, an attorney for the government, or any person to whom disclosure is made under paragraph (3)(A)(ii) of this subdivision shall not disclose matters occurring before the grand jury, except as otherwise provided for in these rules. No obligation of secrecy may be imposed on any person except in accordance with this rule. . . .

FED. R. CRIM. P. 6(e)(2). The codification of the grand jury secrecy rule in the Federal Rules of Criminal Procedure is applicable only to those identified in the statute, which does not include the media. See United States v. Lovecchio, 561 F. Supp. 221, 229 (M.D. Pa. 1983).

142. See In re Vescovo Special Grand Jury, 473 F. Supp. 1335, 1336 (C.D. Cal. 1979).

143. Compare In re Russo, 53 F.R.D. 564, 573 (C.D. Cal. 1971) ("It has generally been held that the defendant is entitled as a matter of right to a copy of his own testimony before the grand jury, unless the government affirmatively establishes a substantial reason why it should be withheld.") with Davis v. United States, 641 A.2d 484, 491-92 (D.C. 1994) (particularized need standard applies to witness' pretrial request for a transcript of her own grand jury testimony).

144. See FED. R. CRIM. P. 6(e)(3)(C); Fund for Constitutional Gov't v. National Archives & Records Serv., 656 F.2d 856, 868 (D.C. Cir. 1981).

145. Grand jury material that is relevant to guilt or sentence determination may be disclosed at a hearing to accept a guilty plea. See United States v. Manglitz, 773 F.2d 1463 (4th Cir. 1985).

146. See FED. R. CRIM. P. 6(e)(3)(C)(ii).

147. See FED. R. CRIM. P. 6(e)(3)(A)(i).

148. See FED. R. CRIM. P. 6(e)(3)(A)(ii). Disclosure may be made to "such government personnel (including personnel of a state or subdivision of a state) as are deemed necessary by an attorney for the government to assist an attorney for the government in the performance of such attorney's duty to enforce federal criminal law." Id.

149. See FED. R. CRIM. P. 6(e)(3)(C)(iii).

150. See Douglas Oil Co. v. Petrol Stops Northwest, 441 U.S. 211, 223 (1979) (civil antitrust

§ 5-2(a)(3)   ACCESS TO JUDICIAL RECORDS: CRIMINAL PROCEEDINGS   § 5-2(a)(3)

the government,[151] seeking disclosure pursuant to a Rule 6(e) exception bears the burden of demonstrating a "particularized need" for the materials.[152] The assessment of whether a particularized need has been established involves a flexible balancing of the need for secrecy against the need for disclosure.[153] Once a party makes the required showing, the court must weigh that particularized need against public interests served by safeguarding the confidentiality of grand jury proceedings.[154] Where disclosure of information is ordered, it must be limited to that which satisfies the claimed particularized need.[155] Where criminal proceed-

---

plaintiffs seeking disclosure of grand jury transcript must demonstrate that the need for disclosure outweighs the public interest in secrecy of grand jury materials through use of a three-pronged test); In re Grand Jury Testimony, 832 F.2d 60, 63-64 (5th Cir. 1987); Cullen v. Margiotta, 811 F.2d 698, 715, 716 (2d Cir.), *cert. denied*, 483 U.S. 1021 (1987); United States v. Alexander, 428 A.2d 42, 53-54 (D.C. 1981) (particularized need is established where the parties seeking disclosure "show that the material they seek is needed to avoid a possible injustice in another judicial proceeding, that the need for disclosure is greater than the need for continued secrecy, and that their request is structured to cover only material so needed.").

151. See, e.g., United States v. Sells Eng'g, Inc., 463 U.S. 418, 442-44 (1983); In re Grand Jury Investigation of Cerro Maravilla Events, 783 F.2d 20, 21 (1st Cir. 1986) (per curiam); In re Grand Jury Proceedings (Kluger), 827 F.2d 868, 874 (2d Cir. 1987); United States v. Walczak, 783 F.2d 852, 857 (9th Cir. 1986). See generally Hughes, *Administrative Subpoenas and the Grand Jury: Converging Streams of Criminal and Civil Compulsory Process*, 47 VAND. L. REV. 573 (1994). A document in the possession of a grand jury may be disclosed without a showing of particularized need if the use of the document is unrelated to the substance of the grand jury proceedings. See In re Subpoena to Testify Before Grand Jury, 864 F.2d 1559, 1564 (11th Cir. 1989); In re Grand Jury Investigation (New Jersey State Comm'n), 630 F.2d 996, 1000-01 (3d Cir. 1980), *cert. denied*, 449 U.S. 1081 (1981).

152. See United States v. John Doe, Inc. I, 481 U.S. 102, 104, 111-12 (1987). The Supreme Court has enunciated a three-part test to determine whether a "particularized need" has been demonstrated: parties seeking disclosure "must show that the material they seek is needed to avoid a possible injustice in another judicial proceeding, that the need for disclosure is greater than the need for continued secrecy, and that their request is structured to cover only material so needed." Douglas Oil Co. v. Petrol Stops Northwest, 441 U.S. 211, 222 (1979). See In re Special Grand Jury 89-2, 143 F.3d 565, 569-71 (10th Cir. 1998) ("Almost uniformly, the federal courts have interpreted the requirement of particularized need literally, and rejected a blanket approach to the determination."). This test continues to apply when the grand jury has concluded its operations. See 441 U.S. at 222.

153. See United States v. John Doe, Inc. I, 481 U.S. at 104; see also Butterworth v. Smith, 494 U.S. 624, 632-33 (1990); United States v. Sells Eng'g, Inc., 463 U.S. 418, 443, 445 (1983); Illinois v. Abbott & Assoc., Inc., 460 U.S. 557, 567-68 n.15 (1983).

154. See Douglas Oil Co. v. Petrol Stops Northwest, 441 U.S. at 219; In re Special Grand Jury 89-2, 143 F.3d 565, 571 (10th Cir. 1998). Individuals who were investigated, but not indicted, have been found to have an increased interest in limiting disclosure of grand jury material. See 143 F.3d at 572.

155. See In re Special Grand Jury 89-2, 143 F.3d at 572; In re Grand Jury Matter (Catania), 682 F.2d 61, 66 (3d Cir. 1982).

ings are concluded and the grand jury disbanded, the public interests in secrecy are reduced, but not eliminated.[156]

Some federal courts have also adopted a non-statutory "special circumstances" exception to grand jury secrecy[157] that is based on the inherent power of a court to supervise a grand jury[158] and to interpret the appropriate scope of grand jury secrecy.[159] Access pursuant to this non-statutory exception requires the demonstration of a "special circumstance,"[160] a more stringent test than the showing of "particularized need" that would be required if the request for disclosure were made pursuant to an enumerated exception under Rule 6(e).[161] Grand jury materials that involve matters of public interest[162] or great historical

---

156. See In re Special Grand Jury 89-2, 143 F.3d at 571 (focus of public interest shifts from the immediate effects of disclosure on a particular grand jury to the possible effect of disclosure on the functioning of future grand juries).

157. The "special circumstances" exception was first articulated by the Second Circuit in *In re Biaggi*, 478 F.2d 489 (2d Cir. 1973) ("special circumstances" could warrant disclosure of grand jury materials outside the confines of Rule 6(e)). In *Biaggi*, the court found that such an exception is permitted as an exercise in sound judicial discretion following an especially careful analysis of whether the purposes underlying the presumption of grand jury secrecy would be undermined by disclosure, taking into consideration the specific facts of the case. The court determined that "special circumstances" existed because information about the grand jury proceeding had been leaked, both the government and the witness had requested disclosure and the grand jury minutes could be redacted to protect the privacy of third parties. See *id*. at 490-94.

158. See In re Petition of Craig, 131 F.3d 99, 103 (2d Cir. 1997).

159. Historically and statutorily, courts have been granted discretion in ordering the release of grand jury material. See FED. R. CRIM. P. 6(e)(3)(C) ("If the court orders disclosure of matters occurring before the grand jury, the disclosure shall be made in such manner, at such time, and under such conditions as the court may direct."); Douglas Oil Co. v. Petrol Stops Northwest, 441 U.S. 211, 223 (1979) ("[A] court called upon to determine whether grand jury transcripts should be released necessarily is infused with substantial discretion.").

160. See In re Petition of Craig, 131 F.3d 99, 106 (2d Cir. 1997):

> Mindful that there is no talismanic formula or rigid set of prerequisites, we offer the following non-exhaustive list of factors that a trial court might want to consider when confronted with these highly discretionary and fact-sensitive "special circumstances" motions: (i) the identity of the party seeking disclosure; (ii) whether the defendant to the grand jury proceeding or the government opposes the disclosure; (iii) why disclosure is being sought in the particular case; (iv) what specific information is being sought for disclosure; (v) how long ago the grand jury proceedings took place; (vi) the current status of the principals of the grand jury proceedings and that of their families; (vii) the extent to which the desired material — either permissibly or impermissibly — has been previously made public; (viii) whether witnesses to the grand jury proceedings who might be affected by disclosure are still alive; and (ix) the additional need for maintaining secrecy in the particular case in question.

161. See *id*. at 105-06 & n.10.

162. See, e.g., In re Biaggi, 478 F.2d 489 (2d Cir. 1973) (court permitted disclosure of grand jury testimony of mayoral candidate after issue arose as to whether candidate had invoked the Fifth Amendment before the grand jury).

significance[163] have been released under this exception.[164] Courts also have the discretion to permit the disclosure of grand jury material where what was once Rule 6(e) material is no longer secret because it has been made public during a subsequent criminal trial[165] or has been reported by the news media.[166]

Some state statutes permit a broader release of grand jury material for purposes such as using grand jury witness testimony to compare it to the testimony of the witness at trial,[167] delivery of the transcripts of grand jury testimony to an indicted defendant,[168] release of the transcripts of grand jury testimony to the public following an indictment of a defendant[169] and disclosing grand jury evidentiary materials to a succeeding grand jury.[170] State courts have also permitted the disclosure of otherwise secret grand jury materials when required in the public interest, in the protection of private rights, or in the furtherance of justice.[171]

Where grand jury material has been inadvertently disclosed in open court, or disseminated by the government to the public, the media cannot be enjoined

---

163. See, e.g., In re Petition of Craig, 131 F.3d at 105 (there is nothing that prohibits historical interest, on its own, from justifying release of grand jury material in an appropriate case, though merely asserting a public or historical interest in grand jury materials will not suffice); In re Petition of Am. Historical Assoc., 49 F. Supp. 2d 274 (S.D.N.Y. 1999) (release ordered of portions of transcripts of two grand juries investigating Alger Hiss that concerned four significant historical issues).

164. The exception has also been termed the "historical-interest exception." See In re Grand Jury Investigation, 580 N.E.2d 868, 875 (Ohio C.P. 1991) (under the historical-interest exception, "grand jury proceedings have been opened to the public in a long-completed case of historical interest, or in a recent case involving matters of unique, statewide, historical interest.").

165. See In re Grand Jury Proceedings, 800 F.2d 1293, 1303 (4th Cir. 1986).

166. See In re North, 16 F.3d 1234, 1245 (D.C. Cir. 1994) (court found it impossible to remove leaked material from the news media and cram it back into grand jury secrecy). "There must come a time, however, when information is sufficiently widely known that it has lost its character as Rule 6(e) material. The purpose in Rule 6(e) is to preserve secrecy. Information widely known is not secret." *Id.* See also In re Capital Cities/ABC, Inc.'s Application for Access to Sealed Transcripts, 913 F.2d 89, 98 (3d Cir. 1990).

167. See, e.g., CAL. PENAL CODE § 924.2; Oregon v. Hartfield, 624 P.2d 588, 593 (Or. 1981).

168. See, e.g., CAL. PENAL CODE § 938.1. But see Davis v. United States, 641 A.2d 484, 489 (D.C. 1994) (criminal defendant's access to grand jury testimony is limited to defendant's own testimony).

169. See, e.g., CAL. PENAL CODE § 938.1(b); Press-Enter. v. Superior Ct., 27 Cal. Rptr. 2d 708, 710 (Ct. App. 1994). Where transcripts of grand jury proceedings are delivered to a defendant in a criminal trial, they may be sealed during the criminal trial to avoid prejudicing the defendant's right to a fair trial, but are to be unsealed after the trial. See Craemer v. Superior Ct., 71 Cal. Rptr. 193 (Ct. App. 1968).

170. See, e.g., CAL. PENAL CODE § 924.4.

171. See Florida v. Tillett, 111 So. 2d 716, 723 (Fla. App. 1959); Mannon v. Frick, 295 S.W.2d 158 (Mont. 1956).

from publishing the information.[172] A court may, however, order the government to cease disseminating the material.[173] Whether a reporter can be required to divulge the identity of her source is dependent on the balance struck between the reporter's First Amendment interest in newsgathering and the governmental interest in preserving grand jury secrecy.[174]

Challenges to the secrecy given to grand jury materials based on claims that a right of public access has been created by the federal Freedom of Information Act,[175] or by state public records legislation[176] have been unsuccessful. Challenges based on a common law right of access to judicial records have similarly failed,[177]

---

172. See United States v. Smith, 123 F.3d 140, 154-55 (3d Cir. 1997); In re Capital Cities/ABC, Inc.'s Application for Access to Sealed Transcripts, 913 F.2d 89 (3d Cir. 1990); Hays v. Marano, 493 N.Y.S.2d 904 (App. Div. 1985).

173. See United States v. Sells Eng'g, Inc., 463 U.S. 418, 422 n.6 (1983); United States v. Smith, 123 F.3d at 154-55 (government ordered to remove its sentencing memorandum from Internet web page maintained by United States Attorney's Office); In re Polypropylene Carpet Antitrust Litig., 181 F.R.D. 680, 693 (N.D. Ga. 1998) (if grand jury materials are improperly disclosed to the public, grand jury participants identified in Rule 6(e)(2) are not permitted to make further disclosures of the materials unless approved by court).

Federal Rule of Criminal Procedure 6(e)(2), which codifies the grand jury secrecy rule, does not apply to the press. See Worrell Newspapers of Indiana, Inc. v. Westhafer, 739 F.2d 1219, 1223 (7th Cir. 1984), aff'd, 469 U.S. 1200 (1985) ("[T]he secrecy provision in Rule 6(e) applies, by its terms, only to individuals who are privy to the information contained in a sealed document by virtue of their positions in the criminal justice system."); In re Polypropylene Carpet Antitrust Litig., 181 F.R.D. at 693. In addition, any such prohibition would violate the First Amendment. See Landmark Communications, Inc. v. Virginia, 435 U.S. 829, 844-45 (1978); Worrell Newspapers of Indiana, Inc. v. Westhafer, 739 F.2d at 1225 ("[W]hen the press, by whatever means, obtains the information contained in a court-sealed document, a state cannot prohibit the publication of the information without violating the First Amendment.").

174. See Chap. 16-2(c)(1) *infra*. But see Daily Journal Corp. v. Superior Ct., 979 P.2d 982, 991-92 (Cal. 1999) (reduced privacy interests of grand jury targets or witnesses where no indictment issues do not warrant release of grand jury records).

175. See, e.g., Fund for Constitutional Gov't v. National Archives & Records Serv., 656 F.2d 856, 867-70 (D.C. Cir. 1981) (grand jury information within the scope of Federal Rule of Criminal Procedure 6(e) is exempt from FOIA disclosure).

176. See McClatchy Newspapers v. Superior Ct., 751 P.2d 1329, 1341 (Cal. 1988) (grand jury's nature as a judicial entity and the important public interests requiring its institutional secrecy exempt it from Public Records Act); Pigman v. Evansville Press, 537 N.E.2d 547 (Ind. App. 1989) (grand jury subpoenas exempted from Public Records Act); Hewitt v. Webster, 118 So. 2d 688, 693-94 (La. App. 1960) (law respecting grand jury secrecy takes precedence over the Public Records Act); Ohio ex rel. Beacon Journal Publ'g Co. v. Waters, 617 N.E.2d 1110 (Ohio 1993) (grand jury secrecy rule within state law exemption to public records law).

177. See In re Dow Jones & Co., Inc., 142 F.3d 496, 504 (D.C. Cir. 1998) (any common law right of access to grand jury materials has been supplanted by Rule 6(e)(6) of the Federal Rules of Criminal Procedure); United States v. Smith, 123 F.3d 140, 155-56 (3d Cir. 1997) ("Unlike judicial records to which a presumption of access attaches when filed with a court, grand jury materials have historically been inaccessible to the press and the general public, and are therefore not judicial records in the same sense."); Associated Press v. United States Dist. Ct., 705 F.2d 1143, 1145 (9th Cir. 1983) (no common law right of access to transcripts of grand jury proceed-

§ 5-2(a)(3) ACCESS TO JUDICIAL RECORDS: CRIMINAL PROCEEDINGS § 5-2(a)(3)

as have claims of a constitutional right of access to grand jury materials.[178]

A more recent concern has been public access to materials submitted as part of a proceeding ancillary to the grand jury, such as related criminal proceedings,[179] hearings regarding whether the government violated grand jury secrecy,[180] motions to quash a grand jury subpoena,[181] *qui tam* actions,[182] and plea hearings[183] where information concerning a grand jury proceeding is relevant and may be disclosed. Courts have reached different conclusions regarding claims of a common law right of access to grand jury materials submitted in connection with such ancillary proceedings. Some courts have found that any common law right of access to such materials has been supplanted by Rule 6(e)(6).[184] Others have held that the common law may require access to some grand jury materials.[185]

Courts have been more consistent when analyzing First Amendment-based access claims, subjecting such requests to the standards for closure derived from *Press-Enterprise II*.[186] Pursuant to that analysis, the trial court must determine

---

ings); Daily Journal Corp. v. Superior Ct., 979 P.2d 982, 991-92 (Cal. 1999) (rejecting claim that common law right of access warrants access to grand jury records once investigation is complete).

178. See *Press-Enterprise II*, 478 U.S. 1 (1986) (public access frustrates the grand jury function); Times-Mirror Co. v. United States, 873 F.2d 1210, 1213 (9th Cir. 1989) ("traditionally, . . . grand jury proceedings have been kept secret though they are judicial proceedings closely related to the criminal fact finding process"); People v. Superior Ct. (1973 Grand Jury), 531 P.2d 761 (Cal. 1975); Daily Journal Corp. v. Superior Ct., 979 P.2d 982, 991-92 (Cal. 1999) (rejecting claim that common law right of access warrants access to grand jury records once investigation is complete).

179. See, e.g., In re Capital Cities/ABC, Inc.'s Application for Access to Sealed Transcripts, 913 F.2d 89 (3d Cir. 1990); United States v. Smith, 776 F.2d 1104 (3d Cir. 1985); United States v. Gurney, 558 F.2d 1202 (5th Cir. 1977); People v. Private Sanitation Indus. Ass'n, 519 N.Y.S.2d 106 (County Ct. 1987) (presentence memorandum).

180. See, e.g., In re Sealed Case, 151 F.3d 1059 (D.C. Cir. 1998); In re Dow Jones & Co., 142 F.3d 496 (D.C. Cir. 1998); United States v. Smith, 123 F.3d 140 (3d Cir. 1997).

181. See, e.g., In re Dow Jones & Co., 142 F.3d 496 (D.C. Cir. 1998); In re Grand Jury Subpoena (Doe No. 4 v. Doe No. 1), 103 F.3d 234, 238 (2d Cir. 1996); In re Grand Jury Empaneled March 8, 1983, 579 F. Supp. 189, 192 (E.D. Tenn. 1984) (motions, responses to motions, and briefs which tend to reveal the substance of grand jury subpoenas ordered sealed); Birmingham News Co. v. Hunt, 624 So. 2d 1117, 1124 (Ala. Crim. App. 1993).

182. See, e.g., In re Special Grand Jury 89-2, 143 F.3d 565 (10th Cir. 1998).

183. See, e.g., United States v. Northrop Corp., 746 F. Supp. 1002 (C.D. Cal. 1990).

184. See, e.g., In re Dow Jones & Co., 142 F.3d 496, 504 (D.C. Cir. 1998).

185. See, e.g., United States v. Smith, 776 F.2d 1104, 1113 (3d Cir. 1985).

186. See United States v. Northrop Corp., 746 F. Supp. 1002, 1003 (C.D. Cal. 1990); Birmingham News Co. v. Hunt, 624 So. 2d 1117, 1124 (Ala. Crim. App. 1993); Chap. 2-2(f) *supra*. Where such a hearing is a civil proceeding, an initial consideration is whether the First Amendment provides the press with a right of access to the underlying proceeding. See In re Grand Jury Subpoena (Doe No. 4 v. Doe No. 1), 103 F.3d 234, 241-42 (2d Cir. 1996). Courts disagree as to whether the nature of a proceeding to enforce the secrecy mandate of Rule 6(e)(2) is civil or criminal. Some courts take the view that the proceeding is civil in nature. See, e.g., Barry v. United States, 865 F.2d 1317 (D.C. Cir. 1989); United States v. Eisenberg, 711 F.2d 959 (11th Cir. 1983);

whether a qualified right of access attaches to the ancillary proceeding at issue. This determination involves the consideration of two complementary concerns: whether the materials submitted as part of the ancillary proceeding at issue have historically been open to the press and public,[187] and whether public access plays a significant positive role in the functioning of the particular process in question.[188] If a qualified right of access attaches to the ancillary proceeding, it creates a rebuttable presumption that the materials submitted in connection with that proceeding are to be open to the press and public.[189] This presumption of openness may be overcome "only by an overriding interest based on findings that closure is essential to preserve higher values and is narrowly tailored to serve that interest."[190]

The protection of grand jury secrecy has been deemed an important interest.[191] Where it can be determined that no grand jury material will be disclosed, records submitted in the ancillary proceeding may be made available to the public and to

---

In re Grand Jury Investigation (Lance v. Dep't of Justice), 610 F.2d 202 (5th Cir. 1980). Others interpret the Rule as providing for both civil and criminal contempt. See, e.g., Finn v. Shiller, 72 F.3d 1182 (4th Cir. 1996). Yet others limit the Rule to providing only a criminal contempt remedy. See, e.g., In re Grand Jury Investigation (90-3-2), 748 F. Supp. 1188 (E.D. Mich. 1990).

187. Some courts have found that there is no long-standing tradition of public access to materials submitted as part of an ancillary proceeding relating to a grand jury investigation. See, e.g., In re Dow Jones & Co., 142 F.3d 496, 502-03 (D.C. Cir. 1998) (transcript of hearings and transcripts relating to President Clinton's motion to show cause why Office of the Independent Counsel should not be found in contempt for allegedly leaking grand jury material to the press). Other courts have found that the public has historically been granted access to certain categories of documents. See, e.g., In re Capital Cities/ABC, Inc.'s Application for Access to Sealed Transcripts, 913 F.2d 89 (3d Cir. 1990) (bill of particulars should be viewed within the historical tradition of public access to all charging documents absent an overriding need for secrecy).

188. See, e.g., In re Grand Jury Subpoena (Doe No. 4 v. Doe No. 1), 103 F.3d 234, 242 (2d Cir. 1996) (public scrutiny of allegations of illegal electronic surveillance by law enforcement serves as a check on potential governmental abuse).

189. See California v. Steiner, 26 MEDIA L. REP. (BNA) 1575, 1576 (Cal. Super. 1998).

190. *Press-Enterprise II*, 478 U.S. at 9. See United States v. Northrop Corp., 746 F. Supp. 1002, 1003 (C.D. Cal. 1990). Where the interest claimed is prejudice to defendants' fair trial rights, defendants must demonstrate that the size of the potential jury pool and the nature and extent of the publicity are such that publicizing the contents of the entire grand jury transcript would prejudice the entire jury pool so that twelve unbiased jurors could not be found. See Press-Enter. v. Superior Ct., 27 Cal. Rptr. 2d 708, 711 (Ct. App. 1994). Where the interest claimed is an individual's privacy or reputation, the weight given to the interest varies with the severity of the risk of harm. See, e.g., United States v. Smith, 776 F.2d 1104, 1113-14 (3d Cir. 1985) (access denied to sealed portion of bill of particulars containing list of unindicted co-conspirators because disclosure created a grave risk of serious injury to innocent third parties); Birmingham News Co. v. Hunt, 624 So. 2d 1117, 1128 (Ala. Crim. App. 1993) (sealing of grand jury materials containing identity of unindicted witnesses was narrowly tailored to preserve the higher interests of maintaining grand jury secrecy and protecting investigation); WBZ-TV4 v. District Attorney, 562 N.E.2d 817, 820-21 (Mass. 1990) (unindicted individual has right to be free from the additional notoriety and disgrace that could attend publication of other details of grand jury's investigation).

191. See Butterworth v. Smith, 494 U.S. 624 (1990).

the media.[192] Where the ancillary proceeding will involve the disclosure of matters occurring before a grand jury that is still in session, the presumption of openness is typically deemed to be overcome by the government's interest in maintaining the secrecy of the grand jury process.[193] Once the grand jury investigation has terminated, the need for secrecy is diminished and public access may be more readily permitted.[194] Where it is uncertain whether material is related to a grand jury proceeding, the court may examine the material *in camera*.[195] Material knowingly disclosed in open court must be made available to the public.[196]

Although the sealing of records is to be narrowly tailored to serve the overriding interest identified, some courts have not been receptive to requests that district judges be required to redact material submitted for the ancillary proceeding that is related to a grand jury proceeding, finding that such an approach would be cumbersome, impractical, and inefficient.[197] Others demand that reasonable alternatives to sealing must be considered.[198] Some courts are willing to

---

192. See In re Dow Jones & Co., 142 F.3d 496, 501 n.8 (D.C. Cir. 1998).

193. See, e.g., In re Grand Jury Subpoena (Doe No. 4 v. Doe No. 1), 103 F.3d 234, 242 (2d Cir. 1996) ("Even if the presumption of openness attaches to that qualified right, however, it is overcome in the grand jury context by the overriding interest in secrecy."); United States v. Haller, 837 F.2d 84, 88 (2d Cir. 1988) ("preservation of grand jury secrecy and the sensitivity of an ongoing criminal investigation may serve as 'higher values' justifying sealing").

194. See Douglas Oil Co. v. Petrol Stops Northwest, 441 U.S. 211, 223 (1979) ("[A]s the considerations justifying secrecy become less relevant, a party asserting a need for grand jury transcripts will have a lesser burden in showing justification."); In re Grand Jury Subpoena (Doe No. 4 v. Doe No. 1), 103 F.3d 234, 242-43 (2d Cir. 1996); California v. Steiner, 26 MEDIA L. REP. (BNA) 1575, 1576 (Cal. Super. 1998). The California Supreme Court has held that courts do not have the authority to release transcripts of a grand jury proceeding terminated by a settlement prior to the deliberations of the grand jury. See Daily Journal Corp. v. Superior Ct., 979 P.2d 982, 991-92 (Cal. 1999).

195. See In re Grand Jury, 103 F.3d 1140, 1145 (3d Cir.), *cert. denied*, 520 U.S. 1253 (1997) ("Ex parte *in camera* hearings have been held proper in order to preserve the ongoing interest in grand jury secrecy); United States v. Smith, 123 F.3d 140, 151 (3d Cir. 1997). A court's failure to conduct an in camera review of requested grand jury transcripts has been held to constitute an abuse of discretion. See In re Special Grand Jury 89-2, 143 F.3d 565, 572 (10th Cir. 1998).

196. See, e.g., United States v. Gurney, 558 F.2d 1202, 1210 (5th Cir. 1977), *cert. denied*, 435 U.S. 968 (1978).

197. See, e.g., United States v. Smith, 123 F.3d 140, 153-54 (3d Cir. 1997); In re North, 16 F.3d 1234, 1242 (D.C. Cir. 1994) ("The intermingling of grand jury material with the rest of the [Independent Counsel] Report is more like leaven in a loaf of bread. It cannot be separated out. Release is an up-or-down vote: redaction is simply not possible."). But see In re Sealed Case, 26 MEDIA L. REP. (BNA) 1319 (D.C. Cir. 1997) (court ordered redaction of court orders and briefs filed by the parties in litigation arising out of grand jury subpoenas).

198. The California Supreme Court has recognized that there are a "panoply of measures" available to protect defendants' fair trial rights short of sealing judicial records. See Brian W. v. Superior Ct., 574 P.2d 788, 792 (Cal. 1978) (these measures include granting a change of venue,

provide access to redacted material after the completion of the ancillary proceeding[199] or when continued secrecy is no longer necessary to prevent disclosure of matters occurring before the grand jury.[200]

§ 5-2(a)(4). Information and Indictment.

Courts have typically recognized a right of access, grounded in the First Amendment, state statutes, or the common law, to information contained in or attached to indictments, criminal complaints,[201] pleadings,[202] and bills of particulars.[203] Federal courts have suggested that access in these contexts may be a function of the nature of the particular information sought, rather than on the document in which it is contained.

In *United States v. Smith*,[204] for example, two newspapers sought access to the names of unindicted coconspirators referred to in an indictment alleging a scheme to obtain state contracts through bribery of public officials.[205] The Third

---

postponing trial until the effect of pretrial publicity subsides, conducting a searching voir dire, giving clear and emphatic instructions to the jury, and sequestering its members).

199. See, e.g., In re Dow Jones & Co., 142 F.3d 496, 500-01, 506 (D.C. Cir. 1998) (appellate court approved of trial judge's decision to deny public access to entire unredacted transcript of hearing on President Clinton's motion to show cause against independent counsel for alleged violations of grand jury secrecy, but indicated request by the press for a redacted version of the transcript would be granted).

200. See, e.g., *id.* at 500-01, 506 (President Clinton's motion to show cause against independent counsel for alleged violations of grand jury secrecy unsealed after court determined it was no longer necessary to prevent disclosure of matters occurring before the grand jury). Courts have been admonished for delegating the redacting to attorneys. See In re Special Grand Jury 89-2, 143 F.3d 565, 572-73 (10th Cir. 1998).

201. See In re Kansas City Star Co., 143 F.R.D. 223, 227 (W.D. Mo. 1992) (holding that defendant's Sixth Amendment right to fair trial outweighed a newspaper's common law right of access to an affidavit filed under seal in support of complaint for murder and assault); Northwest Publications, Inc. v. Anderson, 259 N.W.2d 254 (Minn. 1977) (finding Minnesota statutory right of access to murder complaint and files sealed from public inspection under MINN. STAT. § 15.17); People v. Hodges, 657 N.Y.S.2d 857 (Sup. Ct. 1997) (press has common law and First Amendment-based right of access to a nonconfidential Voluntary Disclosure Form containing copy of defendant's handwritten and signed confession voluntarily filed with court at arraignment). Orange County Publications v. Sawyer, 14 MEDIA L. REP. (BNA) 1766, 1767 (N.Y. Sup. Ct. 1987) (granting access to felony complaint filed against defendant who may have been eligible for "youthful offender" status, but had not yet been so adjudicated).

202. See In re Sealed Case, 20 MEDIA L. REP. (BNA) 2231, 2231-32 (D.D.C. 1993) (granting newspaper right of access to pleadings filed by congressman in connection with a grand jury proceeding).

203. See In re New York Times Co., 9 MEDIA L. REP. (BNA) 2077, 2077-80 (N.D. Ga. 1983) (right of access to bills of particulars as public documents); see also United States v. Anderson, 799 F.2d 1438 (11th Cir. 1986), *cert. denied*, 480 U.S. 931 (1987); United States v. Smith, 776 F.2d 1104 (3d Cir. 1985).

204. 776 F.2d 1104 (3d Cir. 1985).

205. See *id.* at 1105-07.

Circuit recognized both First Amendment-based and common law rights of access to such information because it is "more properly regarded as a supplement[ ] to the indictment than as the equivalent of civil discovery."[206] As the court explained, "[h]istorically and functionally, the bill of particulars is closely related to the indictment."[207] And, while Federal Rule of Criminal Procedure 16 authorizes discovery to be furnished to the defendant,[208] Rule 7(f) provides independent authorization for courts to "'direct the filing of a bill of particulars.'"[209] Thus, the court concluded that "the institutional value of public indictments is recognized in both logic and experience" and that the "historic tradition of public access to the charging document in a criminal case reflects the importance of its role in the criminal process and the public's interest in knowing its contents."[210] Nevertheless, the court declined to require the government to release the names of unindicted coconspirators contained in the bill of particulars in those instances where their privacy rights, coupled with the possibility for serious injury to their reputations, outweighed the value of public access.[211]

In *United States v. Anderson*,[212] the Eleventh Circuit denied a newspaper's petition for access to a bill of particulars filed by the government in a criminal case.[213] Following the indictment of thirty defendants on charges arising from the alleged bribery of local officials, most of the defendants filed motions for a bill of particulars identifying certain unnamed and unindicted participants in the bribery referenced in the indictment.[214] A magistrate granted the motions and the government thereupon filed a bill of particulars and notice of possible similar acts under seal.[215]

Rejecting the newspapers' application for access to these documents, the Eleventh Circuit characterized the defense motion for pretrial notice of similar

---

206. *Id.* at 1111.
207. *Id.*
208. See Chap. 5-2(a)(5) *infra*.
209. 776 F.2d at 1111 (quoting FED. R. CRIM. P. 7(f)).
210. *Id.* at 1112; see *id.* at 1112 (quoting *Press-Enterprise I*, 464 U.S. at 510):

> Since access to bills of particulars is protected by the First Amendment, as well as the common law right of access to the judicial process, we need not reach the issue of whether the standard for overcoming the common law "strong presumption" of access is the same as the standard for overriding First Amendment protection. Since a First Amendment right of access is involved, the trial court ensealment of the list of names can be sustained only if it "is necessitated by a compelling government interest, and is narrowly tailored to serve that interest."

211. 776 F.2d at 1112-14.
212. 799 F.2d 1438 (11th Cir. 1986), *cert. denied*, 480 U.S. 931 (1987).
213. See *id.* at 1439-42.
214. See *id.* at 1439. Some of the defendants also filed motions seeking pretrial notice of the government's intention to use "similar act" evidence under FED. R. EVID. 404(b). See 799 F.2d at 1439.
215. See 799 F.2d at 1439.

acts evidence as akin to a request for voluntary discovery,[216] which is "neither a public process nor typically a matter of public record."[217] Similarly, the court found that the purpose of the bill of particulars is to inform the defendant of the charges against him, to minimize surprise at trial, and to enable the defendant to plead double jeopardy should he be prosecuted again upon the same charge.[218] "[P]roperly viewed," the court concluded, a bill of particulars "supplements an indictment by providing the defendant with information necessary for trial preparation. Generalized discovery, however, is not an appropriate function of a bill of particulars and is not a proper purpose in seeking the bill."[219] The court expressly rejected the invitation of the Third Circuit, in *Smith*, to view bills of particulars as supplements to indictment rather than as akin to pretrial discovery.[220]

§ 5-2(a)(5). Discovery Documents.

Rule 16 of the Federal Rules of Criminal Procedure provides for pre-trial disclosure of evidence by the government and by the defendant in criminal proceedings. Although the rule does not specifically address disclosure of discovery materials to third parties, it does authorize courts to limit discovery on a "sufficient showing."[221] Many states, in turn, have modeled their criminal discovery rules on Rule 16.[222]

Courts have generally recognized a right of public access to the fruits of the discovery process contemplated by Rule 16 and its state law analogues.[223] Some

---

216. See *id.* ("Simply because the Government filed the notice in compliance with a court order does not make the notice information something other than voluntary discovery.").
217. *Id.* at 1441.
218. See *id.*
219. *Id.* (citing United States v. Colson, 662 F.2d 1389, 1391 (11th Cir. 1981)).
220. See 799 F.2d at 1442 n.4; see *id.* at 1442 ("A request for a list of 'unindicted co-conspirators,' so called, is a discovery request that is not a matter of public record and cannot be made a matter of public record simply by attaching to it the label 'bill of particulars.'").
221. FED. R. CRIM. P. 16(d).
222. See Chap. 5-1 *supra*.
223. See, e.g., Florida v. Bennett, 19 MEDIA L. REP. (BNA) 1383 (Fla. Cir. 1991) (defendant charged with arson and murder not entitled to *in camera* inspection and sealing of notices where notices were public judicial records and case did not present extensive and prejudicial pretrial publicity to justify sealing); Alvarez v. Gersten, 450 So. 2d 861 (Fla. App. 1983) (denying petition from lower court order refusing to seal pretrial discovery but allowing petitioner to reapply to trial court for a determination, after *in camera* inspection, whether his right to fair trial would be jeopardized by release of pretrial discovery materials); Sentinel Star Co. v. Booth, 372 So. 2d 100, 101-02 (Fla. App. 1979) (remanding order sealing discovery depositions and statement of defendant in criminal case where press did not have adequate notice of sealing and was not given adequate opportunity to be heard); Tallahassee Democrat, Inc. v. Willis, 370 So. 2d 867, 870-71 (Fla. App. 1979) (although defendant's right to a fair trial may require sealing pretrial discovery depositions, blanket administrative order invalid); News-Press Publ'g Co. v. Florida, 345 So. 2d

§ 5-2(a)(5) ACCESS TO JUDICIAL RECORDS: CRIMINAL PROCEEDINGS § 5-2(a)(5)

courts have held the right of access to be grounded in the First Amendment,[224] while others have indicated that it flows from the common law[225] or statutory

---

865, 866-68 (Fla. App. 1977) (remanding order sealing discovery documents but noting that there must exist compelling reasons to seal the depositions and that desire to protect the victim's family from the details of the crime would not suffice); Rhode Island v. Cianci, 496 A.2d 139, 141-47 (R.I. 1985) (request for access to pretrial discovery materials remanded for determination of adequacy of protective order based upon balancing of defendant's right to fair trial and right of the press to have access to criminal proceedings). But see In re Associated Press, 162 F.3d 503 (7th Cir. 1998) (videotaped testimony of Illinois Governor merely a deposition of potential witness until played to jury, rather than trial testimony, and as such, was not within scope of access right); In re Gannett News Serv., 772 F.2d 113, 114-16 (5th Cir. 1985) (news media not entitled to have evidence in criminal prosecution unsealed and filed in public record where the material was filed solely in connection with and in response to defendants' motion in limine); United States v. Gangi, 1998 U.S. Dist. LEXIS 6308, at * 6-7 (S.D.N.Y. May 4, 1998) (finding no presumption of public access to prosecution memorandum containing government's legal theories, analysis of evidence, and names of third parties where memorandum had been inadvertently publicly filed and widely distributed, because mere filing did not convert it into a judicial document and because it constitutes confidential attorney work product); United States v. Tomison, 969 F. Supp. 587 (E.D. Cal. 1997) (sealing motion for pretrial production of documents and exhibits thereto not precluded by right of public access to pretrial proceedings); In re Application of New York 1 News & CBS Inc., 22 MEDIA L. REP. (BNA) 1406 (S.D.N.Y. 1994) (barring disclosure of pretrial discovery materials in criminal prosecution of Omar Ahmad Abdel Rahman because disclosure would have impact on jury selection, ongoing prosecution, grand jury investigation, and integrity of judicial system); United States v. Rahman, 22 MEDIA L. REP. (BNA) 1063 (S.D.N.Y. 1993) (defendant's Sixth Amendment right to fair trial and integrity of judicial system justify restrictions on access to transcripts reflecting conversations recorded pursuant to wiretap by a government informant); Florida Freedom Newspapers v. McCrary, 497 So. 2d 652, 653-56 (Fla. App. 1986) (balancing right of access to pretrial transcribed statements taken by the state and furnished to the defendants in discovery against the defendant's right to fair trial); Post-Newsweek Stations, Fla., Inc. v. Florida, 474 So. 2d 344 (Fla. App. 1985) (finding no constitutional, substantive, or procedural right to attend pretrial discovery depositions in criminal cases, though holding "does not preclude the public and media from inspecting such depositions when same are filed in the court file").

224. See, e.g., Florida v. Black, 24 MEDIA L. REP. (BNA) 2117, 2118 (Fla. Cir. 1996); Louisiana v. Widenhouse, 556 So. 2d 187, 189-90 (La. App. 1990) (newspaper had First Amendment-based right of access to discovery record in murder prosecution); see also Note, *The First Amendment and Confidentiality Orders Since Seattle Times v. Rhinehart*, 13 AM. J. TRIAL ADVOC. 681 (1989). But see Florida Freedom Newspapers, Inc. v. McCrary, 520 So. 2d 32, 36 (Fla. 1988) (no First Amendment-based right of access to pretrial discovery material); Palm Beach Newspapers, Inc. v. Burk, 504 So. 2d 378, 382-84 (Fla.), *cert. denied*, 484 U.S. 954 (1987) (no right of access under the First Amendment, the Florida Public Records Law, or the Florida Rules of Criminal Procedure to unfiled criminal depositions or copies of the depositions, but noting that, once a transcribed deposition is filed with the court, it is open to public inspection); Ohio ex rel. WHIO-TV-7 v. Lowe, 673 N.E.2d 1360, 1364 (Ohio 1997) ("information that a criminal prosecutor has disclosed to the defendant for discovery purposes ... is not thereby subject to release as a 'public record'").

225. See, e.g., United States v. Anderson, 799 F.2d 1438, 1441-42 (11th Cir. 1986), *cert. denied*, 480 U.S. 931 (1987) (discovery documents historically were not available to the public and were not considered judicial records); United States v. Smith, 602 F. Supp. 388, 397-98 (M.D. Pa.), *aff'd*, 726 F.2d 1104 (3d Cir. 1985) (finding a common law, but not a First Amendment-

§ 5-2(a)(5)　　　　　　　NEWSGATHERING AND THE LAW　　　　　　§ 5-2(a)(5)

enactment.[226]

Public access is typically required when pretrial discovery materials have already been filed with the court or introduced into evidence in a criminal proceeding.[227] Where the materials have not been placed in the public court file

---

based, right of access to document containing the names of unindicted coconspirators but holding that government had shown "good cause" to maintain secrecy). But see United States v. Vazquez, 31 F. Supp. 2d 85, 91-92 (D. Conn. 1998) (holding that although there is no First Amendment-based or common law presumption of access to videotapes exchanged during discovery but not admitted into evidence at trial, plaintiffs did not meet their burden of demonstrating that the tapes should remain under seal); Palm Beach Newspapers, Inc. v. Burk, 471 So. 2d 571, 572, 578 (Fla. App. 1985), aff'd, 504 So. 2d 378 (Fla.), cert. denied, 484 U.S. 954 (1987); In re Worrell Enters., 419 S.E.2d 271, 274-78 (Va. App. 1992) (no common law or First Amendment-based right of access to pretrial criminal discovery documents not yet filed with court).

226. See Post-Newsweek Stations, Fla., Inc. v. Doe, 612 So. 2d 549, 551-53 (Fla. 1992) (both Florida Public Records Act and common law require balancing the privacy rights of third parties against the public interest in government scrutiny); WESH Television, Inc. v. Freeman, 691 So. 2d 532, 534 (Fla. App. 1997) (vacating protective order denying access to audio and video tapes delivered to defendant because "the media, in its role as a public surrogate, must be given notice of the hearing as well as an opportunity to be heard on the question of closure"); Wolfinger v. Sentinel Communications Co., 538 So. 2d 1276, 1278 (Fla. App. 1989) (recognizing qualified statutory right of public access to pretrial discovery material); Bludworth v. Palm Beach Newspapers, Inc., 476 So. 2d 775 (Fla. App. 1985) (state's attorney required to furnish to news media all information provided to defense counsel in a criminal investigation under the Florida Public Records Act); Memphis Publ'g Co. v. Holt, 710 S.W.2d 513, 515-18 (Tenn. 1986) (granting media access to information in closed investigative file of police department where materials were public records under Tennessee statute); see also Davis, *Access to Discovery Records in Criminal Trials: Public Justice and Public Records*, 6 U. FLA. J.L. & PUB. POL'Y 297 (1994). But see City of Miami v. Metropolitan Dade County, 745 F. Supp. 683, 686-87 (S.D. Fla. 1990) (news organization not entitled to inspect and copy photographs pertaining to federal criminal prosecution under Florida Public Records Act); Piedmont v. Winston-Salem, 434 S.E.2d 176, 177-78 (N.C. 1993) (statute providing for criminal discovery, rather than statute providing for discovery of public records, governed attempt by newspaper to access communications recorded by police department in criminal investigation); News & Observer Publ'g Co. v. North Carolina ex rel. Starling, 322 S.E.2d 133, 137-40 (N.C. 1984) (discovery in criminal cases governed by statute).

227. In *In re Associated Press*, 162 F.3d 503 (7th Cir. 1998), the court held that access to videotaped testimony was properly denied until played to a jury. Illinois Governor James Edgar was called as a defense witness in a case alleging a scheme to defraud the Illinois Department of Public Aid. Because the Governor's schedule and the illness of a juror made arranging his court appearance difficult, the parties and the court agreed that his testimony should be taken by video deposition. Over the objection of the press, the videotaping of his testimony was conducted *in camera* and then sealed until played for the jury in open court. See *id.* at 505-06. The Seventh Circuit held that, until the testimony was played to the jury, it was merely a deposition of a potential witness, properly taken under FED. R. CIV. P. 15(g), rather than trial testimony. As such, it was discovered but not-yet-admitted evidence and thus was not within the scope of the access right. See *id.* at 513. See also Chap. 5-2(b) (denial of access to videotape of President Clinton's deposition in *United States v. McDougal*, 103 F.3d 651 (8th Cir. 1996), cert. denied, 118 S. Ct. 49 (1997)). But see United States v. Gangi, 1998 U.S. Dist. LEXIS 6308 (S.D.N.Y. May 4, 1998) (finding no presumption of public access to prosecution memorandum containing government's legal theories and analysis of evidence, where memorandum had been inadvertently publicly filed or otherwise in the public record, however, courts have been reluctant to authorize access. In *United States v. Wolfson*,[228] for example, the Second Circuit explained that, where a defendant himself was not entitled to discovery of certain documents, the public had no right of access to it under either the First Amendment or the common law.[229] Wolfson had been convicted of a violation of federal securities laws in 1967.[230] Years later, he sought to discover those portions of his broker's testimony against him that the government had originally withheld.[231] The Second Circuit found neither a "tradition of accessibility" nor that "public access 'plays a particularly significant positive role in the actual functioning'" of the pretrial discovery aspect of the criminal justice process.[232] Similarly, in *United States v. Poindexter*, a federal district court held that, although the press would be entitled to a videotaped deposition of former President Reagan in the prosecution of former National Security Advisor John Poindexter, its release was properly delayed until the tape was played at trial.[233] Release of the tapes so close to trial would likely "complicate the process of jury selection."[234] The court, however, held that the public was entitled to stenographic transcripts of the deposition testimony.[235]

§ 5-2(a)(6). Preliminary Hearings.

In *Press Enterprise II*[236] and *El Vocero de Puerto Rico*,[237] the Supreme Court recognized a qualified, First Amendment-based right of access to preliminary

---

and widely distributed, because mere filing did not convert it into a judicial document).

228. 55 F.3d 58 (2d Cir.), *cert. denied*, 516 U.S. 990 (1995).
229. See *id.* at 60-61.
230. See *id.* at 58-59.
231. See *id.* at 59.
232. *Id.* at 60 (quoting *Press-Enterprise II*, 478 U.S. at 10-11). See United States v. Salemme, 985 F. Supp. 197 (D. Mass. 1997) ("[U]nless and until documents and information disclosed in discovery prove to be relevant to a decision that this court must make and the court determines that countervailing considerations do not justify confidentiality, such documents and information will remain subject to the ... protective order."); see also United States v. Gangi, 1998 U.S. Dist. LEXIS 6308, at *7-8 (S.D.N.Y. May 4, 1998) (assuming *arguendo* that prosecution memorandum containing government's legal theories and analysis of evidence that was inadvertently publicly filed is a judicial document, the court found that there was no traditional right of public access to confidential attorney work product because it is not usually made part of the record introduced at trial or relied upon by the courts in deciding substantive issues and there is little public interest in access to it).
233. 732 F. Supp. 170 (D.D.C. 1990). In *United States v. McDougal*, 940 F. Supp. 224 (E.D. Ark.), *aff'd*, 103 F.3d 651 (8th Cir. 1996), *cert. denied*, 118 S. Ct. 49 (1997), the press was unsuccessful in its efforts to secure a copy of President Clinton's deposition in a criminal prosecution prior to trial. See Chap. 5-2(b) *infra* (access to videotape at trial).
234. 732 F. Supp. at 172.
235. See *id.* at 171-73.
236. See Chap. 2-2(f) *supra*.
237. See Chap. 2-2(g) *supra*.

hearings. Subsequent decisions have similarly held that a presumption of openness attaches to probable cause hearings.[238] For the same reasons, it is generally acknowledged that, "[a]lthough *Press-Enterprise II* involved in-court proceedings rather than documents, the factors the Court considered there are equally applicable to documents."[239]

In *Utah v. Archuleta*,[240] for example, the press sought to secure access to pretrial documents "associated with the presumptively open preliminary hearing"[241] and to exhibits, including tangible physical evidence, admitted into evidence at that proceeding. The court held that "there is a First Amendment presumptive right of access to documents filed in connection with a criminal preliminary hearing."[242] It recognized that "the general practice in Utah and the common law both reveal that there is a tradition of accessibility to such documents,"[243] and concluded that there was "no reason to distinguish generally between access to a preliminary hearing and the documents filed in relation to

---

238. See Chap. 3-1(a)(2) *supra*.

239. Greenwood v. Wolchik, 544 A.2d 1156, 1158 (Vt. 1988); see *id.* ("The press and the public have a qualified right of access to affidavits of probable cause, which must be balanced with the defendant's Sixth Amendment right to a fair trial."); see also Ex parte Birmingham News Co. 624 So. 2d 1117, 1128-33 (Ala. Crim. App. 1993) (granting in part news media's request for access to transcripts of a preliminary hearing in criminal prosecution of governor); Cowles Publ'g Co. v. Magistrate Ct., 800 P.2d 640, 648 (Idaho 1990) (issuing writ of mandate requiring magistrate to make findings as to whether a substantial probability exists that the defendant's right to a fair trial will be prejudiced by release of transcripts to hearing); Louisiana v. Fletcher, 537 So. 2d 805 (La. App. 1989) (reversing trial court's denial of public access to transcript of testimony given by minors at preliminary hearing in sexual abuse case on First Amendment grounds); Vermont v. Schaefer, 599 A.2d 337, 342 (Vt.), *cert. denied*, 502 U.S. 1077 (1991) (finding that First Amendment creates a qualified right of access to affidavits of probable cause). See also Kearns-Tribune Corp. v. Lewis, 685 P.2d 515, 524 (Utah 1984) (finding that, if any portion of a preliminary proceeding is closed to the public, a transcript of the proceeding should be made available at the earliest time). But see Herald Co. v. Mariani, 487 N.Y.S.2d 413, 415 (App. Div. 1985), *aff'd*, 490 N.E.2d 539 (N.Y. 1986) (holding that, once a rape case was removed to Family Court, only the Family Court possessed jurisdiction and discretion to allow the news media access to the preliminary hearing transcript); Wyoming ex rel. Feeney v. District Ct., 607 P.2d 1259, 1266 (Wyo. 1980) (finding that public and media access to pre-trial proceedings is at the discretion of trial court).

240. 857 P.2d 234 (Utah 1993).

241. *Id.* at 237; see also Society of Prof'l Journalists v. Bullock, 743 P.2d 1166, 1177 (Utah 1987).

242. 857 P.2d at 239. But see Honolulu Advertiser, Inc. v. Takao, 580 P.2d 58, 61 (Haw. 1978) ("The First Amendment does not protect against whatever incidental burdens the . . . order [denying access to the transcript of the preliminary hearing] might have placed upon the [paper's] news gathering capabilities."); Johnson Newspaper Corp. v. Hamblin, 499 N.Y.S.2d 341 (Sup. Ct. 1986) (prohibiting press access to probable cause affidavits filed at arraignment and at preliminary hearing).

243. 857 P.2d at 238. See Pennsylvania v. Frattarola, 485 A.2d 1147, 1150, 1152 (Pa. Super. 1984) (finding right of access to the transcript of a closed preliminary hearing after all the charges against the named defendant have been dismissed, but declining to disclose those portions referring to tape recordings of intercepted communications).

that hearing."[244] Access, in the court's view, promoted the same societal needs in both contexts:

> Disclosing documents used by courts in reaching a decision in a preliminary hearing will discourage decisions based on improper means and will promote conscientious performance by the officials involved in the criminal justice system. Therefore, providing a presumptive right of access to documents filed in connection with preliminary hearings can play a significant positive role in the functioning of that process.[245]

Nevertheless, the court in *Archuleta* upheld that portion of the order barring public access to the documents, on the ground that the potential harm to the defendant's fair trial rights outweighed the public interest in access.[246] It also affirmed that portion of the trial court's order prohibiting access to the hearing exhibits, in this instance finding no First Amendment-based right of access at all. There was, the court concluded, no history of the public being authorized to handle or copy exhibits, "especially at the preliminary hearing."[247] Further, authorizing the public to inspect the evidence "would severely disrupt the efficient performance of justice and create obvious problems concerning the court's and the state's mandate to adequately preserve the integrity of the evidence."[248]

---

244. 857 P.2d at 238.
245. *Id.* at 238-39. The court also found authority for this access right in the state constitution and in the common law. See *id.* at 240-41.
246. See *id.* at 239 ("The record and the court's findings reveal that the documents contain inadmissible and possibly inaccurate information, publication of which would not serve defendant's interest in receiving a fair trial. Given the documents' inflammatory and speculative nature, we believe that a substantial probability exists that alternatives to closure would not have adequately protected defendants' right to a fair trial."). The court noted that the trial judge had heard "extensive testimony concerning the horrific circumstances of the case and the potential for prejudice." *Id.* at 240. See also Reilly v. McKnight, 439 N.Y.S.2d 727, 728-29 (App. Div.), *aff'd*, 430 N.E.2d 922 (N.Y. 1981). In *Reilly*, a New York trial court found that public disclosure of the transcript of a preliminary hearing, along with copies of the exhibits introduced at that hearing, would jeopardize the right of the defendant to receive a fair trial. See *id.* at 729. The court concluded that the transcript and exhibits were to be released only when the respondent was no longer in jeopardy from the criminal charges. See *id.*
247. 857 P.2d at 241.
248. *Id.* at 241-42 ("[p]roviding public access to the exhibits requested would not serve the administration of justice and . . . could very well jeopardize defendant's rights to a fair trial."); see also Cromer v. Superior Ct., 167 Cal. Rptr. 671 (Ct. App. 1980) (order denying defendant's motion to prevent disclosure of her confession placed in evidence at the preliminary examination reversed given the substantial probability of irreparable damage to fair trial rights); Honolulu Advertiser, Inc. v. Takao, 580 P.2d 58 (Haw. 1978) (upholding trial judge's exercise of discretion in sealing and preventing the dissemination of transcript of open preliminary hearing); Pennsylvania v. Freeman, 25 MEDIA L. REP. (BNA) 1225 (Pa. C.P. 1996) (common law presumption of access does not attach to audio and videotapes introduced at preliminary hearing or to notes of testimony transcribed by private company).

§ 5-2(a)(7). Suppression Hearing Records.

Although the Supreme Court has not spoken to the issue, lower courts have generally embraced a First Amendment-based right of access to suppression hearings and to transcripts and other materials relating to such hearings.[249] Other courts have reached the same result by reference to state law.[250]

Documents generated in the context of suppression hearings often contain information from court-ordered wiretaps. In *In re New York Times Co.*,[251] the Second Circuit considered the issue of public access to papers filed under seal as part of a motion to suppress electronic surveillance evidence. The court looked to the First Amendment-based right of access to suppression hearings as the basis for extending that right to associated materials. A First Amendment-based right of access, the court concluded, applies to documents "submitted in connection with judicial proceedings that themselves implicate the right of access," such as a suppression hearing.[252] Though the court expressed concern that criminal defendants may be unwilling to file pretrial motions if the supporting materials could be made public and that public access could jeopardize privacy rights reflected in Title III of the Omnibus Crime Control and Safe Streets Act, it noted that these interests do not denigrate the right of access, but rather "should

---

[249]. See Chap. 3-1(a)(4) *supra*. See also People v. McIntosh, 26 MEDIA L. REP. (BNA) 1891, 1893 (N.Y. County Ct. 1997) (denying defendant's motion to seal all court documents and transcripts related to suppression hearings until a jury is selected, citing First Amendment and state law, because "the defendant has failed to demonstrate a substantial probability that [his] right to a fair trial would be prejudiced by publicity that closure would prevent, or that reasonable alternatives to closure cannot adequately protect the defendant's fair trial rights," and because much of the information that the defendant sought to shield has already been made public). But, in *United States v. McVeigh*, 119 F.3d 806, 813 (10th Cir. 1997) (per curiam), the court held that the First Amendment-based right of public access does not extend "to the evidence actually ruled inadmissible" in suppression hearings, concluding that "[n]either tradition nor logic supports public access to inadmissible evidence."

[250]. See, e.g., Herald Ass'n v. Ellison, 419 A.2d 323, 326-27 (Vt. 1980) (order sealing transcript of suppression hearing, where defendant pled guilty and had been sentenced, vacated on basis of state's policy of public judicial proceedings); Federated Publications, Inc. v. Kurtz, 615 P.2d 440 (Wash. 1980) (order temporarily sealing file of closed suppression hearing did not violate state constitution given risk of prejudice to defendant's fair trial rights).

[251]. 828 F.2d 110 (2d Cir. 1987), *cert. denied*, 485 U.S. 977 (1988).

[252]. *Id.* at 114; see *id.* ("We agree that a qualified First Amendment right of access extends to such documents.") (citing In re Washington Post Co., 807 F.2d 383, 390 (4th Cir. 1986); Associated Press v. United States Dist. Ct., 705 F.2d 1143, 1145 (9th Cir. 1983)). Similarly, the Ninth Circuit, in *United States v. Brooklier*, 685 F.2d 1162, 1172 (9th Cir. 1982), held that "denial of [a] motion to release the transcripts was itself a denial of the right of access protected by the first amendment. It must be tested by the same standard and must satisfy the same procedural prerequisites as the initial closure." See Iowa Freedom of Info. Council v. Wifvat, 328 N.W.2d 920 (Iowa 1983) (trial court erred in closing a pretrial suppression hearing and sealing the transcript until completion of trial).

weigh heavily in a court's balancing equation."[253] In the case before it, the Second Circuit held, the lower court's findings were not sufficiently specific to satisfy the demanding requirements set forth in *Press-Enterprise II*.[254] As subsequent proceedings in the case demonstrate, however, if the interests favoring secrecy are sufficiently compelling, redaction of the documents at issue may be appropriate even if it renders the disclosed materials "almost meaningless."[255]

In *United States v. White*,[256] a federal district court granted a newspaper's request for access to the transcript of a conversation intercepted pursuant to Title III, which had been introduced in evidence at a suppression hearing. The district court began from the premise that "[t]he public has a qualified First Amendment right of access to hearings on motions to suppress and documents on which suppression decisions are based."[257] While fair trial and privacy interests might preclude access in some cases, the court held, specific record findings must demonstrate that sealing the documents at issue is "essential to preserve higher values and is narrowly tailored to serve that interest."[258]

The court in *White* distinguished *In re Globe Newspaper Co.*,[259] where the First Circuit, while recognizing a right of access to bail hearings and related documents, had denied access to certain wiretap materials. In *White*, the defendant whose conversation was intercepted had not sought to suppress the wiretap evidence or to oppose access.[260] Further, the court held that the public had a significant interest in the proceedings and there was no showing of intense pretrial publicity; indeed, none of the objecting defendants had participated in

---

253. 828 F.2d at 114-16; see *id*. at 115 ("Obviously, a statute cannot override a constitutional right.").

254. See *id*. at 116; see also United States v. Brooklier, 685 F.2d 1162, 1173 (9th Cir. 1982) (district court erred in declining to release transcript of hearing on motion to suppress evidence, absent, "[a]t the least, a statement of the reasons for rejecting . . . possible alternatives to complete denial of the motion for access to the transcripts — disclosure accompanied by admonitory instructions to the jury, for example, or a voluntary agreement by the media to limit publicity").

255. See In re New York Times Co., 834 F.2d 1152, 1154 (2d Cir. 1987), *cert. denied*, 485 U.S. 977 (1988) ("Redaction is permissible . . . even if redaction will render 'almost meaningless' the documents to be disclosed, if the district judge finds that important Title III privacy interests cannot otherwise be protected and such privacy interests outweigh the public's interest in access.").

256. 855 F. Supp. 13 (D. Mass. 1994).

257. *Id*. at 15 (citing In re New York Times Co., 828 F.2d 110, 114 (2d Cir. 1987), *cert. denied*, 485 U.S. 977 (1988)). See In re Globe Newspaper Co., 729 F.2d 47, 52 (1st Cir. 1984); United States v. Criden, 675 F.2d 550, 557 (3d Cir. 1982).

258. 855 F. Supp. at 16 (quoting *Press-Enterprise I*, 464 U.S. at 510). If fair trial rights are asserted, it must be shown that there is a "substantial probability" of prejudice "that closure would prevent" and that reasonable alternatives to closure are inadequate. 855 F. Supp. at 16 (quoting *Press-Enterprise II*, 478 U.S. at 14).

259. 729 F.2d 47 (1st Cir. 1984).

260. 855 F. Supp. at 17-18.

the intercepted conversations or had any legitimate expectations of privacy in them.[261]

The common law right of public access to judicial records has also been invoked to secure documents relating to suppression hearings. For example, when videotapes are admitted into evidence at an open suppression hearing, they have been held to become judicial records subject to the common law right.[262] While some courts have extended the common law right to tapes played in an open hearing even when not admitted into evidence,[263] others limit the right of access to evidentiary records.[264] Some courts, while embracing a common law right to view tapes and to secure access to transcripts of them, have been reluctant to authorize copying and broadcast of the tapes themselves.[265]

§ 5-2(a)(8). Bail and Detention Records.

Even in the absence of a perceived tradition of openness in bail and detention proceedings, lower courts have generally recognized a qualified, First Amendment-based right of access to them.[266] The same functional considerations that undergird such access rights have given rise as well to a qualified right of access to the records of such proceedings. In *Seattle Times Co. v. United States District Court*,[267] for example, the Ninth Circuit ordered that the public be afforded access to four documents filed under seal in a pretrial detention hearing. The court held "that the press and public have a right of access to pretrial release proceedings and documents filed therein,"[268] in order to nurture "a public edu-

---

261. See *id.*

262. See People v. Glogowski, 517 N.Y.S.2d 403, 405 (County Ct. 1987) ("The federal and state case law on this subject is unanimous in holding that any exhibit received at a hearing or trial becomes part of the public record and as such is accessible to the media and public.").

263. See, e.g., New Jersey v. Grecco, 455 A.2d 485, 486 (N.J. Super. 1982) (order denying press access to transcripts of tape recordings played, but not admitted as evidence, at suppression hearing, was error "[i]n light of both New Jersey common law and recent federal and Supreme Court decisions under the First Amendment.").

264. See, e.g., United States v. Beckham, 789 F.2d 401, 411 (6th Cir. 1986) (limiting common law right of access to public records to tapes admitted into evidence); United States v. Duran, 884 F. Supp. 526 (D.D.C. 1995) (holding that resolution of motion seeking access to letter written by defendant charged with shooting at White House be stayed until resolution of defendant's own motion on the subject); In re WFMJ Broadcasting Co., 566 F. Supp. 1036, 1040 (N.D. Ohio 1983).

265. See People v. Glogowski, 517 N.Y.S.2d 403, 406 (County Ct. 1987) ("Since the request of the media to copy is essentially a request to duplicate information already made available to the public and the media, the trial court has more discretion in balancing the defendant's right to a fair trial against the media's right to copy.").

266. See Chap. 3-1(a)(1) *supra*.

267. 845 F.2d 1513 (9th Cir. 1988).

268. *Id.* at 1517; see *id.* at 1516 ("We begin with the presumption that the public and press have a right of access to criminal proceedings and documents."); In re Globe Newspaper Co., 729 F.2d 47, 52 (1st Cir. 1984) ("the public has a First Amendment right of access to pretrial proceedings

cated in the workings of the justice system and a system subjected to healthy public scrutiny."[269] While the crime at issue — implanting cyanide in over-the-counter drugs — was "dramatic and violent," the Ninth Circuit concluded that Seattle was a large city with a large pool of potential jurors, the documents were not inflammatory or prejudicial, and disclosure would occur two months before the jury would be impaneled.[270] Thus, especially since there had been no showing that alternatives to sealing would be inadequate, the defendants had not demonstrated a substantial probability of irreparable harm to their rights to a fair trial.[271]

In *United States v. Saunders*,[272] the court reversed a magistrate's order denying a media request to copy videotapes introduced into evidence at a bond hearing in a drug case: "[O]nce a tape has been admitted into evidence and played in open court, the common law and the first amendment establish the right of those interested to inspect and copy the tape."[273] The fact that the press had already published and broadcast sketches based on the tape did not diminish its right to inspect and copy the recording, which "was the most accurate account of the conduct which led to the Defendant's arrest."[274] Applying *Globe Newspaper Co. v. Superior Court*,[275] the court held that denial of press access to the tapes was not necessary to ensure a fair trial.[276]

The district court in *United States v. Miller*[277] relied on the common law in granting media access to tapes played in open court at a bail reduction hearing

---

setting and modifying bail, and to the documents on which the bail decisions are based"); United States v. Martin, 684 F. Supp. 341, 344 (D. Mass. 1988) ("the public has a First Amendment right to view those portions of the DEA agent's affidavit relied upon in pretrial detention decisions").

269. 845 F.2d at 1516 (citing In re Globe Newspaper Co., 729 F.2d at 51-52).
270. *Id.* at 1517-18.
271. See *id.* at 1518.
272. 611 F. Supp. 45 (S.D. Fla. 1985).
273. *Id.* at 47 (citing United States v. Miller, 579 F. Supp. 862 (S.D. Fla. 1984)); see also United States v. Martin, 746 F.2d 964 (3d Cir. 1984); In re Nat'l Broadcasting Co. (Jenrette), 653 F.2d 609 (D.C. Cir. 1981); In re Nat'l Broadcasting Co. (Myers), 635 F.2d 945, 952 (2d Cir. 1980); United States v. Lacayo, 572 F. Supp. 1222 (S.D. Fla. 1983); In re WFMJ Broadcasting Co., 566 F. Supp. 1036 (N.D. Ohio 1983); United States v. Mouzin, 559 F. Supp. 463 (C.D. Cal. 1983); United States v. Hastings, 9 MEDIA L. REP. (BNA) 1488 (S.D. Fla. 1983); In re CBS Inc., 540 F. Supp. 769 (N.D. Ill. 1982); United States v. Pageau, 535 F. Supp. 1031 (N.D.N.Y. 1982); United States v. Maddox, 7 MEDIA L. REP. (BNA) 2600 (S.D. Fla. 1982); United States v. Carpentier, 526 F. Supp. 292 (E.D.N.Y. 1981).
274. 611 F. Supp. at 48.
275. See *id.* (citing Globe Newspaper Co. v. Superior Ct., 457 U.S. at 606-07) ("it must be shown that the denial is necessitated by a compelling governmental interest, and is narrowly tailored to serve that interest").
276. See 611 F. Supp. at 50. The alleged risk to defendant's fair trial rights was deemed "speculative." *Id.* at 48. Nor had the defendants demonstrated that alternatives such as careful voir dire and cautionary instructions could not protect their fair trial rights just as well. See *id.* at 49.
277. 579 F. Supp. 862 (S.D. Fla. 1984).

and admitted into evidence.[278] On the other hand, the court held there is no First Amendment-based right of access to tapes neither introduced in evidence nor played in open court, even when they are discussed in an affidavit admitted into evidence at the bail hearing.[279]

§ 5-2(a)(9). Plea Agreements.

While plea negotiations are generally conducted in secret, lower courts have recognized a qualified, First Amendment-based right of access to those judicial proceedings at which the plea is entered.[280] Courts have similarly recognized a First Amendment-based right of access to the plea agreements themselves and to related documents.[281] And plea agreements, at least when they play a role in the adjudicatory process, are generally deemed to be judicial records subject to a common law privilege.

In *Washington Post Co. v. Robinson*,[282] a newspaper sought access to a sealed plea agreement and related documents in the prosecution of a key figure in the investigation of District of Columbia Mayor Marion Barry for cocaine possession. The D.C. Circuit held "that plea agreements have traditionally been open to the public, and public access to them 'enhances both the basic fairness of the criminal [proceeding] and the appearance of fairness so essential to public confidence in the system.'"[283] Accordingly, the court concluded, there is a First

---

278. See *id.* at 864 ("The introduction of the hearing tapes into evidence makes them part of the public judicial record in this action, and therefore subject to inspection and copying under the well-recognized common law right of access to judicial records.") (citations omitted).

279. See *id.* at 866.

280. See Chap. 3-1(a)(6) *supra*.

281. See generally Annotation, *Right of Access to Federal District Court Guilty Plea Proceedings or Records Pertaining to Entry or Acceptance of Guilty Plea in Criminal Prosecution*, 118 A.L.R. FED. 621, 634-35 (1994). But see Florida v. D.H.W., 686 So. 2d 1331, 1336 (Fla. 1996) (rejecting "an automatic constitutional test for court-ordered sealing" of ten-year old records involving a *nolo contendere* plea; "the policy of public access to old records must be weighed against the long-standing public policy of providing a second chance to criminal defendants who have not been adjudicated guilty" and "a court must examine the constitutionality of a requested sealing order if a specific constitutional issue is raised in a particular proceeding").

282. 935 F.2d 282 (D.C. Cir. 1991).

283. *Id.* at 288 (citing Oregonian Publ'g Co. v. United States Dist. Ct., 920 F.2d 1462, 1465 (9th Cir. 1990); United States v. Haller, 837 F.2d 84, 86 (2d Cir. 1988); In re Washington Post Co., 807 F.2d 383, 390 (4th Cir. 1986)). In *United States v. El-Sayegh*, 131 F.3d 158 (D.C. Cir. 1997), however, the D.C. Circuit held that a proposed plea agreement submitted under seal to the court before the plea is offered solely to allow the court to rule on a motion to seal is not a judicial record subject to the common law right of access. Since the defendant withdrew his plea and the government dismissed the indictment, the district court erred in denying defendant's motion to withdraw the agreement from the court's docket. *Id.* at 163. The plea agreement, the court concluded, had played no adjudicatory role except for proceedings relating to its disclosure and therefore was not a judicial record. See *id.* at 163 ("Public access to unconsummated plea agreements cannot be squared with the confidentiality required for candid negotiations.").

Amendment-based right of access to them.[284]

Moreover, the court determined that, unlike the more lenient standard under the common law,[285] the *constitutional* presumption of access could be overcome "only by an overriding interest based on findings that closure is essential to preserve higher values and is narrowly tailored to serve that interest."[286] The court concluded that the government had not demonstrated "a compelling interest to justify sealing the plea agreement,"[287] which would only confirm what was already public knowledge — that the key witness was cooperating with the government.[288]

In *Oregonian Publishing Co. v. United States District Court*,[289] the Ninth Circuit similarly recognized a First Amendment-based right of access to plea agreements and related documents.[290] Not only had "plea agreements . . . typically been open to the public,"[291] the court asserted, but given that most criminal convictions rest on guilty pleas, denying access to plea agreements

---

284. See 935 F.2d at 288; see also United States v. Ansaldo N. Am., Inc. 26 MEDIA L. REP. (BNA) 1285 (S.D.N.Y. 1997) (unsealing plea agreement based on First Amendment-based right of access, but holding that the higher values of privacy of persons named in the plea agreement and the need to protect information in the agreement relevant to an ongoing grand jury investigation required that the plea agreement be redacted).

285. See 935 F.2d at 288 n.7. Indeed, the court reached the constitutional issue in the first instance "because of the different and heightened protections of access that the first amendment provides over common law rights." *Id.*

286. *Id.* at 288 (quoting *Press-Enterprise I*, 464 U.S. at 510).

287. *Id.* at 292. But see United States v. Ansaldo N. Am., Inc., 26 MEDIA L. REP. (BNA) 1285, 1286 (S.D.N.Y. 1997) (ordering a redacted version of a plea agreement to be released to media because of fears that a full version would compromise an ongoing grand jury investigation and would inhibit the cooperation of named persons or damage the reputation of innocent parties; the court noted that ongoing criminal investigations and person's privacy interests were both recognized "higher values" that may limit the qualified right of access).

288. See 935 F.2d at 291-92; see *id.* at 290:

> Under the first amendment, plea agreements are presumptively open to the public and the press. Absent extraordinary cause, the public may be denied access to them only after notice on the public docket has been given of a motion to seal, so that interested parties have an opportunity to be heard, and after specific findings are made on the record that sealing the plea agreement is essential to preserve an overriding compelling interest and is narrowly tailored to serve that interest.

289. 920 F.2d 1462 (9th Cir. 1990), *cert. denied*, 501 U.S. 1210 (1991).

290. See *id.* at 1466 ("the press and the public have a qualified right of access to plea agreements and related documents under the first amendment"). The case involved the guilty plea of a high school student charged with various federal drug and firearm offenses. The defendant's plea agreement, supporting memoranda, and parts of the court's opinion were sealed. See *id.* at 1463-64.

291. *Id.* at 1465. But, in *United States v. El-Sayegh*, 131 F.3d 158 (D.C. Cir. 1997), the court of appeals held that a proposed plea agreement, submitted as an exhibit to a motion to seal, is not subject to the public's right of access under the First Amendment or the common law. The defendant had withdrawn the plea and the indictment had been dismissed by the government.

"would effectively block the public's access to a significant segment of our criminal justice system."[292] Moreover, the court squarely placed the burden of proof on the party seeking to seal such records.[293] In the case before it, the Ninth Circuit concluded the defendant had failed to make a showing sufficient to warrant closure.[294]

§ 5-2(b). Trial Records.

In *Nixon v. Warner Communications, Inc.*, the Supreme Court acknowledged that the common law right to inspect and copy judicial records and documents admitted into evidence extended to copying the Watergate tapes for broadcast.[295] While the Court, writing before *Richmond Newspapers, Inc.*, did not embrace a First Amendment-based right of access,[296] its endorsement of the common law presumption, grounded in the public's need for information in controlling government, has had an enduring influence. As a result, the law governing access to trial records has been cast largely in terms of the common law. State courts have similarly embraced the common law right of access to trial records and documents.[297]

---

292. 920 F.2d at 1465.
293. See *id.* at 1467 ("Where the first amendment supplies the right of access, the party seeking access has the benefit of the presumption that disclosure should be made; the burden is upon the proponent of closure to justify a closure order.").
294. See *id.*
295. See Chap. 5-1 *supra*. See generally Whelan, *Copying and Broadcasting Video and Audio Tape Evidence: A Threat to Fair Trial Rights*, 50 FORDHAM L. REV. 551, 581 (1982) ("When the records are video and audio tapes introduced into evidence at trial, the presumption in favor of release should not apply.").
296. See also United States v. Webbe, 791 F.2d 103, 105 (8th Cir. 1986); United States v. Shenberg, 817 F. Supp. 118, 119 (S.D. Fla. 1993); Group W Television, Inc. v. Maryland, 626 A.2d 1032, 1035 (Md. Spec. App. 1993); In re Globe Newspaper Co., 729 F.2d 47 (1st Cir. 1984); Associated Press v. District Ct., 705 F.2d 1143 (9th Cir. 1983); United States v. Posner, 594 F. Supp. 930, 935 (S.D. Fla. 1984) ("this Court finds that the press has a First Amendment right of access to the tax returns that were admitted into evidence at Scharrer's trial and this right of access can only be overcome by a compelling interest, narrowly drawn"). But see United States v. Beckham, 789 F.2d 401, 415 (6th Cir. 1986) (Contie, J., dissenting).
297. In *KNSD Channels 7/39 v. Superior Court of San Diego County*, 74 Cal. Rptr. 2d 595, 597-98 (Ct. App. 1998), for example, the court granted a media motion to copy and broadcast an audiotape played at trial. The court cited the common law right of access to judicial records and held that "absent a showing that providing access would create a significant risk of impairment of the integrity of the evidence, the court must make evidence previously presented to a jury in open court reasonably available to the public." See also NBC, Inc. v. Santa Clara County Super. Ct., 27 MEDIA L. REP. (BNA) 1160 (Cal. Super. 1998) (holding that there is a presumptive right of access to copy a videotape admitted into evidence in a criminal trial, and that providing access "will serve important public interests, including promoting openness and understanding of judicial proceedings, and disseminating information about a criminal trial and verdict engendering substantial community concern and debate"); Louisiana v. Mart, 697 So. 2d 1055 (La. App. 1997) (in civil

§ 5-2(b) ACCESS TO JUDICIAL RECORDS: CRIMINAL PROCEEDINGS § 5-2(b)

Although the Court in *Nixon* left the force of the common law right uncertain,[298] a relatively strong presumption of access emerged from a series of appellate court decisions a decade later, which arose from a government "sting" operation dubbed "Abscam."[299] In *In re National Broadcasting Co. (Myers)*,[300] for example, the court held that "there is a presumption in favor of public inspection and copying of any item entered into evidence at the public session of a trial."[301] Once the information has been made known to the public and press, the Second Circuit explained, only "the most extraordinary circumstances" could justify denying those not in attendance the opportunity to see and hear the evidence through copying.[302] While transcripts of the videotapes at issue had provided the press with the words spoken by the participants in secretly recorded conversations between the defendant and government agents posing as businessmen, the public had "a legitimate and important interest" in seeing and hearing the recorded evidence.[303] The fact that one trial was still in progress, and that

---

proceeding concerning disposition of property, court held that videotape of assault on school bus that resulted in juvenile pleading guilty, admitted into evidence, is public record; the burden is on party seeking to prevent disclosure to prove that "withholding of a public record is justified"). But see Times-News Publ'g Co. v. North Carolina, 476 S.E.2d 450, 453 (N.C. App. 1996) (lower court erred by invoking North Carolina Public Records Act in ordering district attorney to provide news organization access to previously admitted trial exhibits that were to be used in preparation for retrial because materials were exempt from disclosure under that statute).

298. The Court held that it was unnecessary "to delineate precisely the contours of the common law right," 435 U.S. at 599, but noted that whether particular documents should be sealed is a question left to "the sound discretion of the trial court," *id*. The Court referred to "the presumption — however gauged — in favor of public access to judicial records." *Id*. at 602.

299. In Abscam, law enforcement officials posing as Middle Eastern businessmen offered bribes to secure favors from governmental officials. Members of Congress were videotaped apparently accepting bribes to sponsor private bills or to influence executive actions.

300. 635 F.2d 945 (2d Cir. 1980).

301. *Id*. at 952.

302. *Id*. ("When physical evidence is in a form that permits inspection and copying without any significant risk of impairing the integrity of the evidence or interfering with the orderly conduct of the trial, only the most compelling circumstances should prevent contemporaneous public access to it."); see also United States v. Vazquez, 31 F. Supp. 2d 85, 88-91 (D. Conn. 1998) (holding that the government could not overcome the "especially strong" common law presumption of access to videotapes filmed outside a clinic and later used as evidence in defendant's trial for allegedly violating the Freedom of Access to Clinic Entrances Act because there is no constitutional or common law right of privacy to protect the identity of women on the public street outside an abortion clinic, and any harm to the government's efforts to enforce the Act was speculative); KNSD Channels 7/39 v. Superior Ct. of San Diego County, 74 Cal. Rptr. 2d 595, 597-98 (Ct. App. 1998) (granting media motion to copy and broadcast audiotape played at trial, holding that "absent a showing that providing access would create a significant risk of impairment of the integrity of the evidence, the court must make evidence previously presented to a jury in open court reasonably available to the public").

303. 635 F.2d at 952. The court noted that the public had an interest in being afforded this opportunity "contemporaneously" with the introduction of the evidence, "when public attention is

other Abscam defendants awaited subsequent trials did not overcome the "strong presumption" favoring access.[304]

A "strong presumption" favoring access to real evidence admitted at trial was affirmed in other Abscam cases, *In re National Broadcasting Co. (Jenrette)*[305] and *In re National Broadcasting Co. (Criden).*[306] In *Jenrette*, the trial court's denial of access to videotapes admitted in evidence in open court was held to be an abuse of discretion.[307] The D.C. Circuit stressed the "strong case"[308] for access given the public interest in the material[309] and the "speculative" nature of claims of "potential prejudice" arising from a possible retrial.[310]

In *Criden*, the Third Circuit reversed a trial court's denial of a media application to copy Abscam videotapes for rebroadcast.[311] The court emphasized "that there is a strong presumption that material introduced at trial should be made reasonably accessible in a manner suitable for copying and broader dissemination."[312] Especially given the context of the Abscam litigation, there was a "legi-

---

alerted to the ongoing trial." *Id.*

304. *Id.* The jury in *Myers* had already seen the tapes and had been told to avoid exposure to news reports. In subsequent cases involving other defendants, the Second Circuit noted, careful voir dire examination could avoid a tainted jury. See *id.* at 953.

305. 653 F.2d 609 (D.C. Cir 1981).

306. 648 F.2d 814 (3d Cir. 1981).

307. See 653 F.2d at 620. In *Jenrette*, the D.C. Circuit indicated that a trial judge's discretion is not open-ended. Rather, the district court must weigh the competing interests, affording appropriate weight to the "'precious'" and "'fundamental'" common law right. *Id.* at 613. Access may be denied only if "'justice so requires.'" *Id.* (quoting United States v. Mitchell, 551 F.2d 1252, 1260, 1261 (D.C. Cir. 1976), *rev'd on other grounds sub nom.* Nixon v. Warner Communications, Inc., 435 U.S. 589 (1978)). The fact that the case involved "issues of major public importance," the court noted, gave added weight to the presumption of access. 653 F.2d at 621.

308. *Id.* at 614.

309. *Id.*

310. *Id.* at 616; see *id.* at 618 ("We thus adhere to our holding in *Mitchell* that the interest in avoiding the risk of potential prejudice at a hypothetical second trial is seldom of sufficient weight to justify denying access to judicial records which have been displayed in open court.") (citing United States v. Mitchell, 551 F.2d at 1261).

311. See 648 F.2d at 829 ("[W]e conclude that the trial court accorded too little weight to the strong common law presumption of access and to the educational and informational benefit which the public would derive from broadcast of evidence introduced at a trial which raised significant issues of public interest. Similarly, the court accorded too much weight to concerns which we believe either are irrelevant or capable of resolution in some manner short of denial of the application.").

312. *Id.* at 823. The court in *Criden* relied on *Richmond Newspapers, Inc.*, reasoning that "the public forum values emphasized in that case can be fully vindicated only if the opportunity for personal observation is extended to persons other than those few who can manage to attend the trial in person." *Id.* at 822. See also Louisiana v. Mart, 697 So. 2d 1055 (La. App. 1997) (since there is right of public access to videotape of beating on school bus under Public Records Act, judge's order that television station possessing copy of tape could not make and disseminate copies invalid). But see Pennsylvania v. Freeman, 25 MEDIA L. REP. (BNA) 1225 (Pa. C.P. 1996)

timate public interest in the proceedings far beyond the usual criminal case."[313] While the court declined to consider the applicability of the First Amendment, it cited favorably to *Richmond Newspapers, Inc.*, concluding "that some of the same policy considerations identified as supporting open trials may be considered when the issue involves the common law right of access to trial materials."[314]

Unlike the trial court, the Third Circuit viewed the rebroadcast of the videotape evidence to large audiences not as a threat, but as contributing to the public's understanding of trial proceedings. Like the Second Circuit in *Jenrette*, the Third Circuit deemed danger of prejudice at a potential retrial "hypothetical" and best handled through voir dire at any subsequent proceeding.[315] Moreover, the court held, copying videotapes for broadcast could not properly be analogized to broadcasting actual trials, which is prohibited in federal courts.[316] Nevertheless, the court emphasized that the trial judge could properly "deny copying for rebroadcast of evidence which may inflict unnecessary and intensified pain on third persons who the court reasonably finds are entitled to such protection,"[317] although even this legitimate concern could be ameliorated by excision of the offending material rather than by foreclosing access.[318]

(rejecting common law presumption of access to audio and video tapes introduced at preliminary hearing).

313. 648 F.2d at 822.

314. *Id.* at 820; see *id.* at 822-23 ("[B]roader dissemination would serve the same values of 'community catharsis,' observation of the criminal trial process, and public awareness served by the open trial guarantee .... [W]hen the common law right of access is buttressed by the significant interest of the public in observation, participation, and comment on the trial events, we believe that the existence of a presumption of release is undeniable."); see also NBC, Inc. v. Santa Clara County Super. Ct., 27 MEDIA L. REP. (BNA) 1160 (Cal. Super. 1998) (providing access to copy a videotape admitted into evidence in a criminal trial "will serve important public interests, including promoting openness and understanding of judicial proceedings, and disseminating information about a criminal trial and verdict engendering substantial community concern and debate").

315. 648 F.2d at 826-28.

316. See *id.* at 828-29. The court reasoned that the federal ban on cameras in the courtroom, see Chap. 4-2 *supra*, is based on the effects of cameras in the courtroom on the trial itself. This, the court explained, cannot be a relevant factor when the material sought for copying is merely videotape of a preexisting event, since the participants on the tape cannot posture or otherwise change their behavior to play before a television audience. See *id.* at 829.

317. *Id.* at 829; see also Louisiana v. Mart, 697 So. 2d 1055, 1060 (La. App. 1997) (privacy interests of minors pictured in videotaped school bus beating do not justify sealing of videotape; to preclude access to public records, "the custodian or individual claiming the privacy right must prove that there is a reasonable expectation of privacy against disclosure of the information").

318. See 648 F.2d at 829. On remand, the trial court ordered removal of all references to any third party, requiring deletion of some 20% of the taped conversations. In *In re National Broadcasting Co.*, 681 F.2d 919 (3d Cir. 1982), the Third Circuit again reversed. Few of the deleted references "rise to the level of 'intensified pain,' as distinguished from mere embarrassment, which would warrant deletion from the tapes themselves particularly because the transcripts of these conversations are already public information." *Id.* at 922.

The expansive view of the common law right of access adopted in the Abscam cases reflects the majority position in the federal[319] and state courts.[320] But, even within this generally consistent line of authority, there are distinctions. Some courts view the *Myers* standard of "compelling circumstances" as creating a heavy burden favoring access, comparable to that imposed by the First Amendment.[321] *Jenrette* and *Criden*, in contrast, have been construed to provide a somewhat less-demanding "strong presumption" of access to trial records, which is deemed to be more consistent with the common law right and its focus on whether the trial judge had abused her discretion.[322] Since the latter cases relied greatly on *Myers* and emphasized the similarity of the policies underlying the constitutional and common law rights, the distinction is questionable. In any case, the "strong presumption" formulation, with its demand for findings of fact rather than speculation and conjecture,[323] is typically — but not always —

---

319. See, e.g., Valley Broadcasting Co. v. United States Dist. Ct., 798 F.2d 1289, 1294 (9th Cir. 1986) ("such factors as promoting the public's understanding of the judicial process and of significant public events justify creating a 'strong presumption' in favor of copying access"); United States v. Smith, 787 F.2d 111, 115 (3d Cir. 1986) (party opposing disclosure of transcripts of sidebar conferences failed to satisfy *Criden* standards); United States v. Guzzino, 766 F.2d 302, 304 (7th Cir. 1985) ("[t]here is a strong presumption in favor of the common law right of access"); In re Video-Indiana, Inc. (Edwards), 672 F.2d 1289, 1294 (7th Cir. 1982) ("[W]e hold that there is a strong presumption in support of the common law right to inspect and copy judicial records."); United States v. Vazquez, 31 F. Supp. 2d 85, 88 (D. Conn. 1998) (evidence relied on by the court in determining whether the defendant violated the criminal law "must be afforded the strongest presumption of access"); In re CBS, Inc. (Shannon), 540 F. Supp. 769 (N.D. Ill. 1982) ("there exists a strong presumption in favor of public access to judicial records.").

320. See, e.g., KNSD Channels 7/39 v. Superior Ct. of San Diego County, 74 Cal. Rptr. 2d 595, 597-98 (Ct. App. 1998) (granting media motion for access for copying and broadcasting of an audiotape played at trial, the court recognized a common law right of access to judicial records and held that "absent a showing that providing access would create a significant risk of impairment of the integrity of the evidence, the court must make evidence previously presented to the jury in open court reasonably available to the public").

321. See Valley Broadcasting Co. v. United States Dist. Ct., 798 F.2d at 1293-94; In re Video-Indiana, Inc. (Edwards), 672 F.2d at 1293-94.

322. See, e.g., In re Video-Indiana, Inc. (Edwards), 672 F.2d at 1294 ("Thus, while we are unwilling to go as far as the Second Circuit's statement that only exceptional circumstances will justify non-access, we hold there is a strong presumption in support of the common law right to inspect and copy judicial records."). The court in *Valley Broadcasting Co.* characterized the "strong presumption" approach as a majority "middle ground stance" between *Myers* and *Belo Broadcasting Corp. v. Clark*, 654 F.2d 423 (5th Cir. 1981), which the court construed as "adopting a general balancing test that characterizes the public's right of access as typically subordinate to a defendant's competing fair trial rights." 798 F.2d at 1293.

323. See Valley Broadcasting Co. v. United States Dist. Ct., 798 F.2d at 1295 ("While we recognize the added danger of jury taint arising from the transmission of the tapes themselves may vary from case to case, we reemphasize that the district court must articulate the factual bias for the danger without relying on hypothesis or conjecture."); In re Video-Indiana, Inc. (Edwards), 672 F.2d at 1294 ("Where there is a clash between the common law right of access and a defendant's constitutional right to a fair trial, a court may deny access, but only on the basis of articulable facts sufficient to require access to evidence admitted at trial.[324] Claims that access would impose administrative inconvenience have been met by a showing of the availability of unobtrusive procedures for copying that do not endanger the original exhibits.[325] The harm to fair trial rights in a possible retrial or in future trials of others is typically characterized as, at best, incremental, given the exposure of the evidence in open court and is, almost by definition, speculative.[326]

There is, however, a minority approach, articulated most forcefully in cases arising from another FBI sting operation dubbed "Brilab," which concerned alleged bribery in the award of state-employee insurance contracts in Texas. In *Belo Broadcasting Corp. v. Clark*,[327] the Fifth Circuit rejected First Amendment and common law-based claims of access to audiotapes admitted in evidence at trial. Judge Gee, writing for the court, disposed of the First Amendment claim on the authority of *Nixon v. Warner Communications Inc.*, noting that in "copying" cases the media already had "untrammeled access" to what transpired in open court.[328] While the court assumed *arguendo* that the common law right of access

---

known to the court, not on the basis of unsupported hypothesis or conjecture."); see also United States v. Andreas, 1998 U.S. Dist. LEXIS 11347 at *14 (N.D. Ill. July 16, 1998) (citing *Edwards* in granting media's motion for access to those portions of audio and video tapes admitted into evidence and played to the jury and to any transcripts admitted into evidence, because defendants failed to demonstrate that their release "would cause a definite and articulable harm").

324. See, e.g., Valley Broadcasting Co. v. United States Dist. Ct., 798 F.2d at 1294 ("We concluded that the reasons asserted by the district court were inadequate . . . to overcome the strong presumption in favor of copying access."); Smith v. United States Dist. Ct., 956 F.2d 647, 650 (7th Cir. 1992) (holding fact that memorandum had not been admitted into evidence was not enough to overcome strong presumption of access); United States v. Schlette, 842 F.2d 1574, 1584 (9th Cir. 1988) (holding that arguments for the confidentiality of pre-sentence reports failed to overcome presumption); In re CBS, Inc. (Salerno), 828 F.2d 958, 961 (2d Cir. 1987) ("we believe that the circumstances [illness of witness and privacy concerns] relied upon by the district court . . . do not overcome that presumption"). Courts invoking the "strong presumption" have, however, denied access as well. See, e.g., In re Video-Indiana, Inc. (Edwards), 672 F.2d at 1295-96 (district court did not abuse its discretion in denying access).

325. See Valley Broadcasting Co. v. United States Dist. Ct., 798 F.2d at 1295 ("In light of these procedures, the district court should have given little, if any, weight to its administrative burdens in this case.").

326. See *id.* at 1295-96; KNSD Channels 7/39 v. Superior Ct. of San Diego County, 74 Cal. Rptr. 2d 595, 597 (Ct. App. 1998) ("[W]here the evidence to which access is sought has already been presented to the jury, a defendant's interest in preventing access to it [to avoid prejudicial publicity and ensure a fair trial] is diminished, if not ameliorated altogether"); see also In re Video-Indiana, Inc. (Edwards), 672 F.2d at 1294. But see Times-News Publ'g Co. v. North Carolina, 476 S.E.2d 450 (N.C. App. 1996) (physical evidence used as exhibits in murder trial and returned to district attorney for reinvestigation and retrial held exempt from disclosure under state public records act).

327. 654 F.2d 423 (5th Cir. 1981).

328. See *id.* at 427 ("Members of the press were allowed to listen as the tapes were played in court; transcripts were prepared and distributed for their use; reporters and broadcasters were free

to judicial records extended to tape recordings, Judge Gee focused on whether the trial judge had abused his discretion.[329] The court rejected the "overpowering presumption in favor of access" developed in the Abscam cases.[330] The majority position, Judge Gee argued, reflects standards "more appropriate for protection of constitutional than of common law rights."[331] The focus of appellate review, the Fifth Circuit reasoned, should be on whether the trial court, in exercising its supervising power over its records and files, had "good reasons" to deny access.[332]

The trial judge's concern for the defendant's right to a fair proceeding, Judge Gee asserted, was reasonable. Since the defendant had been indicted, the possibility of a future trial was not "hypothetical."[333] Moreover, the court emphasized that appellate judges are in a poor position to assess the potential prejudice from a public broadcast.[334] Reliance on alternative measures, such as voir dire, would require the appellate court "to direct the trial judge in the practical management and operation of his courtroom," a course which should be pursued only in extreme circumstances.[335] Finally, the court distinguished Supreme Court precedent favoring alternative devices over denial of access as grounded in the First Amendment.[336]

The deference to trial court discretion reflected in *Belo Broadcasting Corp.* has been manifested by some other federal courts as well.[337] Indeed, some courts,

---

to report this information as they wished. All that was denied them was the right to play these tapes over the air waves; that the Constitution does not require.").

329. See *id*. at 429-31.
330. *Id*. at 434.
331. *Id*.
332. *Id*.
333. *Id*. at 431.
334. See *id*:

> A forecast of future difficulty is by definition uncertain, but equally uncertain is the rejection of the forecast. Speculative dismissal by an appellate court of a trial judge's admittedly uncertain but quite reasonable prognostication only compounds the problem. The informed and considered judgment of the trial judge should prevail in any choice between such equally speculative results. It is better to err, if err we must, on the side of generosity in the protection of a defendant's right to a fair trial before an impartial jury.

335. *Id*. at 432.
336. See *id*. ("That the balance is heavily weighted in favor of protective measures other than absolute closure of the trial to press or public, or of prior restraints on publication of information, does not mean that the same balance prevails when less compelling rights are asserted by the press.").
337. See, e.g., United States v. Schlette, 842 F.2d 1574, 1576-77 (9th Cir. 1988) ("abuse of discretion" standard); United States v. Webbe, 791 F.2d 103, 107 (8th Cir. 1986) (adopting the approach in *Belo Broadcasting Corp.*, the court held that "the decision as to access is properly handled on an ad hoc basis by the district judge, who is in the best position to recognize and weigh the appropriate factors on both sides of the issue"); United States v. Beckham, 789 F.2d 401 (6th Cir. 1986) ("[W]hen the right to make copies of tapes played in open court is essentially a request

§ 5-2(b)   ACCESS TO JUDICIAL RECORDS: CRIMINAL PROCEEDINGS   § 5-2(b)

citing the importance of protecting a defendant's right to a fair trial, have permitted public release of videotapes only after the jury has delivered its verdict.[338] Nevertheless, this narrow view of the common law right of access appears to remain a distinctly minority position.

While the Abscam and Brilab cases focused on public access to videotape evidence admitted in open court, the right of public access also extends to other judicial records surrounding the criminal trial.[339] In *In re Philadelphia Newspapers, Inc. (Martin)*,[340] the Third Circuit explained that the "common law right of access is not limited to evidence, but rather encompasses all 'judicial records and documents.'"[341] The strong presumption in favor of public access has been held applicable to transcripts not admitted in evidence of tape recordings, which had been admitted.[342] Other courts, however, have declined to extend the common law right to nonevidentiary materials on the ground that they are not "public records."[343] The common law right has been extended to a videotaped deposition

---

for a duplicate of information already made available to the public and the media, then the district court has far more discretion in balancing the factors.").

338. See, e.g., United States v. Shenberg, 817 F. Supp. 118 (S.D. Fla. 1993); United States v. Eaves, 685 F. Supp. 1243 (N.D. Ga. 1988); see also In re Pac. & S. Co., 361 S.E.2d 159 (Ga. 1987) (affirming order denying press access to videotaped evidence played in open court until appeal process is completed); Group W Television, Inc. v. Maryland, 626 A.2d 1032 (Md. Spec. App. 1993) (affirming court order releasing videotapes when fair trial considerations are no longer present).

339. See, e.g., United States v. Peters, 754 F.2d 753, 763 (7th Cir. 1985) (discriminatory order barring reporter from access to trial exhibits held to be an abuse of discretion); United States v. Camacho, 22 MEDIA L. REP. (BNA) 1845 (S.D. Fla. 1994) (ordering release of photographs previously admitted into evidence, on retrial, citing presumption of access); United States v. Posner, 594 F. Supp. 930 (S.D. Fla. 1984) (First Amendment-based right of access to tax return).

340. 746 F.2d 964 (3d Cir. 1984).

341. *Id.* at 968. The access right has been held to extend to "'transcripts, evidence, pleadings and other materials submitted by litigants.'" *Id.* (quoting Comment, *All Courts Shall Be Open: The Public's Right to View Judicial Proceedings*, 52 TEMPLE L.Q. 311, 337-38 (1979)).

342. See 746 F.2d at 968-69; see also United States v. Raffoul, 826 F.2d 218, 226-27 (3d Cir. 1987) (order denying access to transcript reversed and case remanded to determine "whether prejudice to the defendant or the state or injury to third parties is likely to result if the court unseals the transcript of the closed courtroom proceedings"); United States v. Brooklier, 685 F.2d 1162, 1172 (9th Cir. 1982) ("the denial of the motion to release the transcript was in itself a denial of the right of access protected by the first amendment"); Connecticut v. Ross, 543 A.2d 284 (Conn. 1988) (finding a public right of access to transcript of criminal trial).

343. See, e.g., United States v. McKnight, 771 F.2d 388, 391 (8th Cir. 1985), *cert. denied*, 475 U.S. 1014 (1986) ("Generally, pre-sentence reports are considered as confidential reports to the court and are not considered public records . . . ."); United States v. Andreas, 1998 U.S. Dist. LEXIS 11347 (N.D. Ill. July 16, 1998) (denying access to transcripts of audio and video tapes where the tapes but not the transcripts had been admitted into evidence, and denying access to portions of audio and video tapes not admitted into evidence); Baltimore Sun v. Thanos, 607 A.2d 565, 573 (Md. Spec. App. 1992) (holding that non-admitted pre-sentence reports are not public records, so no common law right of access attaches).

of a witness admitted into evidence in a criminal case,[344] although there is contrary authority.[345] While no right of access has been recognized to bench conferences at trial,[346] there may be a right to a transcript of such proceedings.[347] Finally, several courts have held that Title III of the federal Omnibus Crime Control and Safe Streets Act of 1968 "creates no independent bar to the public's right of access to judicial materials with respect to wiretap materials legally intercepted and admitted into evidence pursuant to the statute."[348]

In *United States v. McDougal*,[349] the Eighth Circuit held that the common law right of access was not infringed by a trial court's refusal to grant the press physical access to an edited videotape of President Clinton's testimony played at trial in open court. Even though only the transcript of the testimony had been admitted as evidence, the media had argued that the videotape was played at the trial and therefore was a judicial record subject to the common law right.[350] But, the court distinguished cases in which videotapes recorded the primary conduct of witnesses or parties and were admitted into evidence. The videotape at issue in *McDougal*, in contrast, recorded witness testimony. The press, the court concluded, had no "cognizable common law claim . . . because the videotape is not a judicial record to which the common law right of public access attaches."[351]

---

344. See In re CBS Inc. (Salerno), 828 F.2d 958 (2d Cir. 1987).

345. See In re ABC, Inc. (Hinckley), 537 F. Supp. 1168 (D.D.C. 1982) ("the video recording [of witness Jodie Foster] is not encompassed by the common law right of access to judicial records and the broadcasters, therefore, have no right to copy and broadcast the recording").

346. See Richmond Newspapers, Inc. v. Virginia, 448 U.S. at 598 n.23 (Brennan, J., concurring); Rovinsky v. McKaskle, 722 F.2d 197, 201 (5th Cir. 1984); United States v. Gurney, 558 F.2d 1202, 1210 (5th Cir. 1977), *cert. denied*, 435 U.S. 968 (1978).

347. See, e.g., United States v. Smith, 787 F.2d 111, 115 (3d Cir. 1986) ("We hold, therefore, that the common law right of access to judicial records . . . is fully applicable to transcripts of sidebar or chambers conferences in criminal cases at which evidentiary or other substantive rulings have been made."). But see In re Tribune Co. (Sierra), 784 F.2d 1518 (11th Cir. 1986) (affirming order barring access to transcripts of bench conference involving on-going criminal investigations and grand jury matters).

348. United States v. Rosenthal, 763 F.2d 1291, 1293 (11th Cir. 1985). See United States v. Dorfman, 690 F.2d 1230 (7th Cir. 1982); United States v. White, 855 F. Supp. 13 (D. Mass. 1994).

349. 103 F.3d 651 (8th Cir. 1996), *cert. denied*, 118 S. Ct. 49 (1997). See Note, *Access to President Clinton's Videotaped Testimony Denied: The Eighth Circuit Addresses the Common Law and Constitutional Rights of Access to Judicial Records in* United States v. McDougal, 31 CREIGHTON L. REV. 571 (1998) (arguing that the court erred in holding that videotaped deposition testimony is not a judicial record, in its determination of the weight accorded the common law presumption favoring access, and in holding that the denial of access was justified).

350. See *id.* at 655 (quoting Brief for the Appellants, at 13) ("'[T]he defendants should not be permitted to circumvent the common law and constitutional rights of access by marking only the transcript of the videotaped deposition. . . . Effectively, the videotape was introduced into evidence by being played in open court.'").

351. *Id.* at 657. The court did not rely on the fact that the tape was not itself admitted into evidence. *Id.* at 656. Indeed, the court observed that "[e]ven if the defendants had moved for the

The Eighth Circuit went on to assert that, even if the videotape were a judicial record subject to the common law right, it would hold that the trial judge had not abused his discretion in denying access.[352] The court rejected a strong presumption of access grounded in the common law,[353] and embraced instead a rule of deference to the trial judge's determination,[354] based on its concern that the tape itself would be used for commercial or partisan political purposes.[355] Finally, the court noted that there had never been compelled live testimony by a president in court or compelled dissemination of recorded testimony.[356] Thus, despite the obviously strong public interest in President Clinton's testimony, the court characterized the public's interest in physical access to the tapes as marginal because the testimony had been made available in open court and transcripts had been widely disseminated.[357] In this regard, the Eighth Circuit also declined to recognize a First Amendment-based right of access, noting that "members of the public, including the press, were given access to the information contained in the videotape. Therefore, appellants received all the information to which they were entitled under the First Amendment."[358]

State law can also provide the basis for public access to trial records. For example, in *Providence Journal Co. v. Rodgers*,[359] the Rhode Island Supreme Court held that the lower court's interpretation of a state statute intended to protect the identity of child molestation victims did not justify sealing the entire

---

admission of the videotape into evidence, the videotape itself would not necessarily have become a judicial record subject to public review." *Id.* at 652.

352. See *id.* at 659.

353. See *id.* at 657-58 (citing United States v. Webbe, 791 F.2d 103 (8th Cir. 1986); Webster Groves Sch. Dist. v. Pulitzer Publ'g Co., 898 F.2d 1371 (8th Cir. 1990)); see also Chap. 6-2(b) *infra*.

354. See 103 F.3d at 657-58.

355. See *id.* at 658 ("We agree, as a matter of public policy, that courts should avoid becoming the instrumentalities of commercial or other private pursuits.").

356. See *id.*

357. *Id.* While the court in *United States v. Poindexter*, 732 F. Supp. 170 (D.D.C. 1990), indicated that it intended to release the videotape of former President Reagan's testimony after its use at trial, the Eighth Circuit concluded that this comment was dicta. See 103 F.3d at 658.

358. 103 F.3d at 659. In *In re Associated Press*, 162 F.3d 503 (7th Cir. 1998), the Seventh Circuit held that access to videotaped testimony was properly denied until played to a jury. Illinois Governor James Edgar was called as a defense witness in a case alleging a scheme to defraud the Illinois Department of Public Aid. Because the Governor's schedule and the illness of a juror made arranging his court appearance difficult, the parties and the court agreed that his testimony should be taken by video deposition. *Id.* at 505-06. Over the objection of the press, his testimony was taken *in camera* and then sealed until played for the jury in open court. *Id.* The Seventh Circuit held that, until the testimony was played to the jury, it was merely a deposition of a potential witness, properly taken under FED. R. CIV. P. 15(g), rather than trial testimony, and as such, was not within the scope of the access right. See *id.* at 513.

359. 711 A.2d 1131 (R.I. 1998).

court record in such cases.[360] Invoking the common law right of public access to trial records, the court employed a somewhat different standard than that used by the federal courts. Any limitation of public access to criminal case records or documents in criminal proceedings, the court held, requires a balancing of the respective interests of the parties and the public. The Rhode Island Supreme Court required that any limitation "(1) must be narrowly tailored to serve the interests sought to be protected, (2) must be the only reasonable alternative, (3) must permit access to those parts of the record not deemed sensitive, and (4) must be accompanied by the trial justice's specific findings explaining the necessity for the order."[361] After balancing the interests of the child victim "with safeguarding the public's interest in the fairness of criminal prosecutions,"[362] the court required that a dual filing system be established for future cases. In one file, complete and unredacted records are to be kept confidential. The other file, containing files from which the names and identifying information of the victims have been redacted and victim-specific documents have been removed, is to be made available to the public.[363]

§ 5-2(c). Jury Records.

In *Press-Enterprise I*,[364] the Supreme Court held that the public and press enjoy a First Amendment-based right of access to the transcript of a voir dire proceeding improperly closed to the press and public. In *United States v. Antar*,[365] the government invited the court to limit *Press-Enterprise I* to transcripts of voir dire proceedings that had themselves been closed.[366] The Third

---

360. *Id.* at 1134-35; see also Louisiana v. Mart, 697 So. 2d 1055 (La. App. 1997) (in civil proceeding concerning disposition of property, court held that videotape of assault on school bus that resulted in juvenile pleading guilty, admitted into evidence, is public record; the burden is on party seeking to prevent disclosure to prove that "withholding of a public record is justified"). But see Times-News Publ'g Co. v. North Carolina, 476 S.E.2d 450, 453 (N.C. App. 1996) (lower court erred by invoking North Carolina Public Records Act in ordering district attorney to provide news organization access to previously admitted trial exhibits that were to be used in preparation for retrial because materials were exempt from disclosure under that statute).

361. 711 A.2d at 1136 (quoting Rhode Island v. Cianci, 496 A.2d 139, 144 (R.I. 1985)). See Providence Journal Co. v. Cresto, 716 A.2d 726 (R.I. 1998) (holding that in determining the appropriateness of a protective order issued in a criminal case, the reviewing court must first review the *in camera* record of the trial court to determine if the court followed the standards set forth in *Cianci*).

362. 711 A.2d at 1137.

363. See *id.* at 1138. In pending cases, creation of a public file is to be determined on a motion by the party seeking access. See *id.* at 1139.

364. 464 U.S. 501 (1984). See Chap. 2-2(e) *supra*.

365. 38 F.3d 1348 (3d Cir. 1994). The defendants, founders of the well-known consumer electronics firm "Crazy Eddie's," were charged with, *inter alia*, securities fraud.

366. While voir dire proceedings in *Antar* were open, the press had complied with the trial judge's request to leave the courtroom to provide additional seating. The press' absence prevented

Circuit, in an opinion by Judge Roth, declined the invitation, holding that "the right to access to voir dire examinations encompasses equally the live proceedings and the transcripts which document those proceedings."[367] Relying on the First Amendment, Judge Roth determined that meaningful public access, in the sense of securing information about what occurred in court, is served not only by witnessing a proceeding, "but also by learning about it through a secondary source."[368] Affording media access to the transcript of judicial proceedings permits broad dissemination, the court held, "for what exists of the right of access if it extends only to those who can squeeze through the [courthouse] door?"[369] Accordingly, Judge Roth wrote, "at the most basic level, the transcript at issue is a public judicial document, covered by a presumptive right of access."[370]

Applying the constitutional standard derived from *Press-Enterprise II*, the court in *Antar* also held that the order sealing the transcript "violated procedural and substantive aspects of the press's right of access to the voir dire transcript," which were not cured by its subsequent release.[371] The trial court "did not satisfy its burden of placing findings on the record which clearly established that closure was necessary to protect an overriding interest."[372] While the need to protect the confidentiality of jury deliberations might compel some limitation on access, the court conceded, "threats to that process must be actual and specific,

---

reporters from learning the jurors' identities. When the Associated Press wrote the court requesting the jurors' names and their addresses, the court, without hearing or findings, sealed the transcript of the voir dire and other portions of the public record identifying the jurors. Following the defendants' conviction, the AP sought to intervene and obtain access. While the court permitted intervention and held a hearing, the transcript remained sealed for five months. When the records were unsealed, the trial judge, citing "the compelling societal and governmental interest in maintaining the secrecy of the jury deliberative process and protecting jurors from harassment, judgment and/or punishment after rendering a verdict," imposed restrictions on the press's ability to seek information from the jurors. *Id.* at 1351-55. See Chap. 7-3 *infra*.

367. 38 F.3d at 1359. See *id.* at 1351 ("We hold . . . that the presumptive right of access applied to the voir dire proceedings as they were recorded in the trial transcript.").

368. *Id.* at 1360 ("documentary access is not a substitute for concurrent access, and vice versa"). See United States v. Simone, 14 F.3d 833, 842 (3d Cir. 1994); United States v. Smith, 787 F.2d 111, 114-15 (3d Cir. 1986).

369. 38 F.3d at 1360 (citing In re Nat'l Broadcasting Co. (Criden), 648 F.2d 814, 822 (3d Cir. 1981)) ("the public forum values emphasized [in *Richmond Newspapers, Inc.*] can be fully vindicated only if the opportunity for personal observation is extended to persons other than those few who can manage to attend the trial in person").

370. 38 F.3d at 1360 (quoting Anderson v. Cryovac, Inc., 805 F.2d 1, 13 (1st Cir. 1986)) ("The common law presumption that the public may inspect judicial records has been the foundation on which the courts have based the first amendment right of access to judicial proceedings.").

371. 38 F.3d at 1352. See *id.* at 1362 (citing United States v. Raffoul, 826 F.2d 218 (3d Cir. 1987)).

372. 38 F.3d at 1361.

not conclusory and generic," and the limitation imposed must be the least restrictive means available.[373]

The trial court in *Antar* had sealed the transcript of voir dire proceedings to prevent the media from ascertaining the identity of jurors. A number of other cases have considered media efforts to gather the names and addresses of jurors in criminal cases or to secure access to voir dire questionnaires.[374] In *In re Baltimore Sun Co.*,[375] the Fourth Circuit recognized a common law right of access to the names and addresses of jurors and alternates, which attaches once the jury is chosen.[376] At this stage of the proceeding, the court reasoned, such information becomes part of the public record.[377] The court expressly declined to base its decision on the First Amendment,[378] but it was obviously influenced by *Press-Enterprise II*. Historically, at the outset of the jury system, "everybody knew everybody on the jury."[379] Moreover, the court held, an anonymous jury poses too great a "risk of loss of confidence of the public in the judicial process."[380]

The First Circuit, in *In re Globe Newspaper Co. (Hurley)*,[381] also invoked First Amendment considerations in interpreting a local court rule to create a right of access to jurors' names and addresses unless the trial judge identifies specific, valid reasons necessitating confidentiality. The local rule authorized trial judges to keep juror names confidential "in any case where the interests of justice so

---

373. *Id.* at 1363; see also In re Dallas Morning News Co., 916 F.2d 205, 206 (5th Cir. 1990) (holding that the First Amendment-based right of access precludes court from closing voir dire based only on expectations that jurors might not be truthful and open due to privacy concerns). But see United States v. Jackson, 969 F. Supp. 881, 882 (S.D.N.Y. 1997) (sealing, *sua sponte*, record of in-chambers conference with juror leading to her dismissal for health reasons, and noting "that the sealing is necessary to protect the juror's privacy in light of the intense media attention this case has received" and "that releasing the transcripts would have a chilling effect on the candor of other jurors in this and other high-publicity cases in disclosing health problems or other concerns that might make it difficult for them to continue acting as jurors [which] could seriously undermine the defendants' Sixth Amendment right to a fair trial").

374. See Chap. 7-3 *infra*. See generally Raskopf, *A First Amendment Right of Access to a Juror's Identity: Toward a Fuller Understanding of the Jury's Deliberative Process*, 17 PEPP. L. REV. 357 (1990).

375. 841 F.2d 74 (4th Cir. 1988).

376. See *id.* at 75.

377. See *id.* Prior to selection of the jury, the court held, such information is protected by 28 U.S.C. § 1867(f). See 841 F.2d at 75.

378. See 841 F.2d at 75 n.4 ("We see no need to and do not base our decision on the First Amendment."). While the court acknowledged that *United States v. Gurney*, 558 F.2d 1202 (5th Cir. 1977), *cert. denied*, 435 U.S. 968 (1978), had rejected a claim of press access to juror names, it noted that *Gurney* was decided prior to *Press-Enterprise II*. See 841 F.2d at 76.

379. 841 F.2d at 75.

380. *Id.* at 76.

381. 920 F.2d 88 (1st Cir. 1990).

require."[382] While some federal courts had interpreted the language of the analogous federal statute, and its local counterparts, to require that jurors' names be kept confidential,[383] the court in *Hurley* read the language to allow juror names to be made public after summons and appearance. Thereafter, impoundment of juror names required a specific determination that the interests of justice demanded secrecy.[384] Thus, the federal statute and the local district court rule were interpreted to create a "presumption of public access to petit jury lists."[385]

The court found support for this broad statutory construction in the policy of avoiding the First Amendment issues that would arise in the wake of a narrow interpretation favoring secrecy.[386] While there is no constitutional right of access to jury deliberations, the court reasoned, "many of the purposes which open justice serves are equally served by access to the identities of jurors."[387] Specifically, the First Circuit argued that access to juror identities "allows the public to verify the impartiality of key participants in the administration of justice, and thereby ensures fairness, the appearance of fairness and public confidence in that system."[388]

Exceptional circumstances, such as a credible threat of jury tampering, a risk to the personal safety of individual jurors, and other harms to the administration of justice could, the court noted, justify sealing records containing jurors' identities.[389] Nevertheless, a juror's preference for personal privacy was not sufficient to overcome the presumption of access:[390]

> Jurors may be citizen soldiers, but they are soldiers nonetheless, and like soldiers of any sort, they may be asked to perform distasteful duties. Their participation in publicized trials may sometimes force them into the lime-

---

382. D. MASS. PLAN FOR RANDOM SELECTION OF JURORS § 10(c). The federal counterpart is 28 U.S.C. § 1863(b)(7).

383. See 920 F.2d at 92 n.5.

384. See *id.* at 92-93. See Minnesota v. Swart, 20 MEDIA L. REP. (BNA) 1703 (Minn. App. 1992) (local rule interpreted to prevent trial court from sealing records containing identities of jurors).

385. 920 F.2d at 92.

386. See *id.* at 93.

387. *Id.* at 94.

388. *Id.* See also In re Disclosure of Juror Names & Addresses, 592 N.W.2d 798, 808 (Mich. App. 1999) (holding that, absent a right of access to jurors' identities, "in an extreme case, a court could, with unlimited discretion, totally conceal the identity of jurors and thus create the impression of a secret process that *Press-Enterprise I* and *II* caution against").

389. See 920 F.2d at 97. See also United States v. Giraldi, 858 F. Supp. 85 (S.D. Tex. 1994) (restricting access to jurors in drug case by allowing the media to contact only those jurors who indicated to the court their willingness to be interviewed, because of presumed danger to jurors from drug ring).

390. See 920 F.2d at 97-98 ("While anonymity is acceptable in the exceptional case where there is a particular need for it, the prospect of criminal justice being routinely meted out by unknown persons does not comport with democratic values of accountability and openness.").

light against their wishes. We cannot accept the mere generalized privacy concerns of jurors, no matter how sincerely felt, as a sufficient reason for withholding their identities under the interests-of-justice standard.[391]

Since no particularized findings were made by the lower court which reasonably justified a sealing order, the court held that the jurors' names and addresses must be made available to the press and public.[392]

While the courts in *Antar* and *In re Globe Newspaper Co. (Hurley)* invoked constitutional values but otherwise appeared to avoid grounding the access right they recognized in the First Amendment, some courts have taken that next step. In *United States v. Doherty*,[393] for example, the court held that, "under the First Amendment, the public has a general right, at some reasonable time after a verdict is delivered, to the names and addresses of the jurors discharging this important public trust."[394] Although the historical record was "scant," the court concluded that "the public's right of access to jurors after the verdict is returned is historically protected."[395] In any event, the court held:

> It is important for the public to receive information about the operation of the administration of justice, including information about the actual people who do render justice in the truest sense of the word. Access to such information not only serves the cause of justice generally by providing an independent, non-governmental verification of the utter impartiality of the process involved in selecting jurors and shielding them from improper influences, it also serves to enhance the operation of the jury system itself

---

391. *Id.* at 98.
392. See *id.*
393. 675 F. Supp. 719 (D. Mass. 1987).
394. *Id.* at 723. See In re Indianapolis Newspapers Inc., 837 F. Supp. 956 (S.D. Ind. 1992) ("In order to accommodate the petitioner's request for disclosure of this information, and in light of the need to balance all the competing interests, the court finds that disclosure should occur. The decision is premised on the fact that one week has passed since the jury returned its verdict."). In *United States v. Espy*, 31 F. Supp. 2d 1 (D.D.C. 1998), the court sealed the names of jurors for seven days after the acquittal of the former Secretary of Agriculture for offenses arising from allegations that he accepted illegal gratuities while in office. Although the jurors indicated to the court that they neither wished to speak to nor have their names disclosed to the media, the court concluded that keeping the jurors' names sealed for seven days was the best way to balance the jurors' privacy interests and the press's First Amendment right of access to criminal proceedings. See *id.* at 1-2 ("Many of the purposes served by open access to criminal proceedings are also served by recognizing the interest and putative right of the press to have access to the names of jurors following a verdict.") The court reasoned that the "limitation on the interests of the press is narrowly tailored in time and scope and will not ultimately thwart the purposes served by providing open access to criminal proceedings. *Id.* at 2. See also In re Disclosure of Juror Names & Addresses, 592 N.W.2d 798, 808 (Mich. App. 1999) (recognizing First Amendment-based right of access to juror names and addresses).
395. 675 F. Supp. at 722.

by educating the public as to their own duties and obligations should they be called for jury service.[396]

California courts have also held that "the public access mandate of *Press-Enterprise* applies to voir dire questionnaires as well as to oral questioning."[397] These courts have concluded that, once the individual juror is called to the jury box for voir dire, the questionnaire, with some exceptions, becomes part of the voir dire and the First Amendment mandates access.[398] To overcome the constitutional presumption of access, the California courts hold, specific record findings are required.[399] Prospective jurors are therefore to be told in advance that their written responses are not confidential and that they have a right to request an *in camera* hearing if they believe public disclosure will cause them embarrassment or other harm.[400]

In *Phoenix Newspapers Inc. v. United States District Court*,[401] the Ninth Circuit held that the trial judge had erred in denying the public post-trial access to the transcripts of hearings conducted during jury deliberations in the criminal trial of John Symington, the then-sitting governor of Arizona.[402] The hearings were held to investigate reports by Symington's secretary and two jurors that they had received threatening telephone calls.[403] The trial judge had not only closed the proceedings and sealed the transcripts, "but requested the two jurors not to respond to the open court inquiry to all jurors about contact by anyone outside the jury."[404] This, the Ninth Circuit concluded, "resulted in the creation of a trial record at variance with the true facts . . . [a] particularly unfortunate [consequence] when the salient issue is jury tampering in the criminal trial of a public official."[405] According to the Ninth Circuit, the trial judge failed both to meet the procedural requirements of providing "sufficient notice to the public

---

396. *Id.* at 723.
397. Lesher Communications, Inc. v. Superior Ct., 274 Cal. Rptr. 154, 156 (Ct. App. 1990). See Copley Press, Inc. v. Superior Ct., 278 Cal. Rptr. 443, 447-48 (Ct. App. 1991).
398. Lesher Communications, Inc. v. Superior Ct., 274 Cal. Rptr at 156 ("The questionnaire is a part of the voir dire itself."). In *Copley Press, Inc. v. Superior Court*, 278 Cal. Rptr. at 450-51, the court held that certain information, relevant to the qualification and management of the jury, such as telephone numbers, social security number, and driver's license number, is not properly part of the voir dire and need not be disclosed. In addition, *Lesher* holds that there is no constitutional right of access to questionnaires completed by venirepersons who have not been called to the jury box. Such persons play no part in the voir dire and the court could envision "no legitimate public interest in disclosure of these questionnaires." 274 Cal. Rptr. at 157.
399. See Copley Press, Inc. v. Superior Ct., 278 Cal. Rptr. at 448.
400. *Id.* at 449-50, 451. See *id.* at 450 ("the venirepersons shall be expressly informed that questionnaires are public records").
401. 156 F.3d 940 (9th Cir. 1998).
402. See *id.* at 943.
403. See *id.*
404. *Id.* at 949-50.
405. *Id.* at 951.

and press to afford them the opportunity to object" before sealing the transcripts, and to satisfy "the First Amendment's substantive requirements."[406] Although the jurors' security "was in fact a compelling interest," the court of appeals concluded that "every fact present in the record" indicated that they were not in danger.[407] Moreover, the trial court had made no specific findings that alternatives to closure were inadequate.[408] For the Ninth Circuit, these "procedural and substantive safeguards . . . are not mere punctilios, to be observed when convenient. They provide the essential, indeed only, means by which the public's voice can be heard."[409]

Not all courts, however, have embraced claims of access to jury records. In *United States v. Edwards*,[410] the Fifth Circuit recognized a "limited" First Amendment right to a transcript of a closed, mid-trial inquiry into jury misconduct, but only if access were delayed until a reasonable time after the jury verdict.[411] And, the court found no error in the trial judge's redaction of the transcript to eliminate the jurors' names, citing the interest in safeguarding them from "unwarranted embarrassment."[412] In *Newsday, Inc. v. Sise*,[413] the New York Court of Appeals upheld a trial judge's declination to disclose the names and addresses of jurors who failed to reach a verdict in a murder trial. The Delaware Supreme Court similarly rejected a constitutional right of access to juror names in *Gannett Co. v. Delaware*.[414] In that court's view, "[a]nnouncement of jurors' names in court promotes neither the fairness nor the perception of fairness, when the parties are provided with the jurors' names and all proceedings are open to the public."[415]

§ 5-2(d). Post-Trial Records.

There has been general recognition of a First Amendment-based or common law right of public access to the records of post-trial proceedings.[416] The Ninth

---

406. *Id.* at 949-50.
407. *Id.* at 950.
408. See *id.* at 950-51.
409. *Id.* at 951.
410. 823 F.2d 111 (5th Cir. 1987), *cert. denied*, 485 U.S. 934 (1988).
411. See *id.* at 119.
412. *Id.* at 120; see *id.* ("The usefulness of releasing jurors' names appears to us highly questionable. The transcripts will reveal the substance and significance of the issues"). See also United States v. Gurney, 558 F.2d 1202, 1210 (5th Cir. 1977), *cert. denied*, 435 U.S. 965 (1978) (upholding trial court's refusal to reveal jurors' names even though they had been called out in open court during voir dire).
413. 518 N.E.2d 930 (N.Y. 1987), *cert. denied*, 486 U.S. 1056 (1988).
414. 571 A.2d 735 (Del. 1989).
415. *Id.* at 751. But see *id.* at 751 (Walsh, J., dissenting).
416. See Chap. 3-1(d) *supra*; United States v. Gonzalez, 927 F. Supp. 768 (D. Del. 1996) (holding that press has First Amendment-based right of access to documents concerning allegedly

§ 5-2(d)   ACCESS TO JUDICIAL RECORDS: CRIMINAL PROCEEDINGS   § 5-2(d)

Circuit, in *CBS Inc. v. United States District Court*,[417] "could find no principled basis for affording greater confidentiality to post-trial documents and proceedings than to pretrial matters."[418] Applying the *Press-Enterprise* standards, the court held that the government interests in protecting information regarding confidential witnesses and criminal investigations did not "override the presumption of openness that is at the foundation of our judicial system."[419]

Similarly, the Vermont Supreme Court has recognized a First Amendment-based right of access to a psychosexual evaluation submitted by a defendant.[420] The court concluded that "a presumption of openness prevails and that documents submitted by the parties in sentencing hearings are subject to a qualified right of inspection by the public."[421] This qualified right could be overcome only by specific factual findings establishing a substantial probability that, absent closure, a compelling interest would be harmed.[422]

"sloppy work" by Bureau of Alcohol, Tobacco and Firearms chemist); United States v. Carpentier, 526 F. Supp. 292, 294-95 (E.D.N.Y. 1981) ("the public has a strong First Amendment claim to access to evidence admitted in a public sentencing hearing"); Phoenix Newspapers, Inc. v. Superior Ct., 680 P.2d 166, 171 (Ariz. App. 1983) ("[t]he right to keep confidential that information received during in camera hearings must give way to the constitutional requirements of openness when 'the danger of prejudice has dissipated'"); Sarasota Herald Tribune v. Holtzendorf, 507 So. 2d 667 (Fla. App. 1987) ("While a judge may impose whatever legal sentence he chooses, if such a sentence is based on a tangible proceeding or document, it is within the public domain unless privileged."); Ex parte Greenville News, 482 S.E.2d 556, 558 (S.C. 1997) (First Amendment-based presumption of access applies to post-trial hearings on alleged juror misconduct and requires release of transcript of closed hearing and unsealing of record with redaction of jurors' names and identifying information).

417. 765 F.2d 823 (9th Cir. 1985).
418. *Id.* at 825. The court reasoned that the primary historical and functional justifications for access rights in criminal proceedings "apply with as much force to post-conviction proceedings as to the trial itself." *Id.* The "presumption that the public and the press have a right of access to criminal proceedings and documents filed therein," based on the First Amendment and the common law, was therefore applied to both post-conviction proceedings and documents. See also Vermont v. Densmore, 624 A.2d 1138, 1142-43 (Vt. 1993) (importance of public access to sentencing to assure fairness and to enhance public understanding).
419. 765 F.2d at 825. See Mankato Free Press v. Dempsey, 581 N.W.2d 311, 312 (Minn. 1998) (requiring lower court to open remainder of hearing and to furnish media with transcripts of already-completed portion of hearing to determine whether jurors were aware that defendant was wearing a leg restraint during his murder trial and whether that awareness deprived him of his right to a fair trial, because the trial court record was insufficient to support closure under *Press-Enterprise I*).
420. See Vermont v. Densmore, 624 A.2d 1138 (Vt. 1993).
421. *Id.* at 1141; see *id.* at 1142 ("We hold, therefore, that a qualified First Amendment right of public access attaches to documents submitted by the parties in sentencing proceedings.").
422. See *id.* at 1142-43. See also United States v. Smith, 123 F.3d 140, 143-44 (3d Cir. 1997) ("We conclude that grand jury secrets might be disclosed by the briefs and hearing [regarding possible government misconduct in publicly disclosing a presentencing memorandum] to which the newspapers seek access, and conclude that the district court acted properly in ensuring that such material remains confidential while it makes its determination whether that material is in fact secret

Judicial willingness to provide access to sentencing documents does not, however, appear to extend to presentence reports. Courts ordering unsealing of sentencing documents often specifically distinguish presentence reports.[423] The Federal Rules of Criminal Procedure expressly provide for limited access to such reports[424] and many states place similar statutory restrictions on their disclosure.[425] In *United States v. Corbitt*,[426] moreover, the court expressly rejected any First Amendment-based right of access to presentence reports,[427] regardless of whether the public has a constitutional right of access to sentencing hearings themselves.[428] Not only was it "clear that presentence reports have traditionally been confidential,"[429] the Seventh Circuit concluded, but their disclosure "would constitute a positive hindrance to the probation office's performance of its

---

grand jury material."); United States v. Smith, 992 F. Supp. 743, 749 (D.N.J. 1998) (the court should determine "whether there exists a compelling need for disclosure [of a sentencing memorandum] or whether disclosure will serve the ends of justice").

423. See, e.g., CBS, Inc. v. United States Dist. Ct., 765 F.2d at 826 ("Our opinion is not to be read to disapprove the practice of keeping presentence reports confidential."); Sarasota Herald Tribune v. Holtzendorf, 507 So. 2d 667, 668 (Fla. App. 1987) ("[w]e see no reason to extend the confidentiality afforded presentence investigation reports to materials, although of a similar nature, that are not part of the report."); Vermont v. Densmore, 624 A.2d at 1142 ("This opinion should not be read to remove the privilege attached to presentence reports, . . . an issue that is not before us."). In *United States v. Preate*, 927 F. Supp. 163 (M.D. Pa. 1996), the district court summarily rejected a publisher's contention that a portion of a presentence report should be opened to the public. "It is established beyond reasonable argument that presentence reports, in their entirety, are confidential and that there is a strong presumption against disclosing such reports to third parties." *Id.* at 165. Nevertheless, although the court extended this presumption of confidentiality to "proceedings whose purpose is to examine the soundness and sufficiency of the presentence report prior to sentencing," it held there was a "compelling need for disclosure to meet the ends of justice." *Id.* at 166, 168. See also United States v. Preate, 91 F.3d 10 (3d Cir. 1996) (not an abuse of discretion for trial court to refuse media request to continue sentencing hearing pending resolution of media's appeal of trial court's refusal to release transcript of in-chambers conference discussing presentence report).

424. See FED. R. CRIM. P. 32(c)(4) (allowing for *in camera* summary of information to be used in making sentencing determination); United States v. Smith, 123 F.3d 140, 150 (3d Cir. 1997) (no First Amendment-based or common law right of access to briefs or hearing on whether government had violated Fed. R. Crim. P. 6(e) in publicly disclosing presentencing memorandum containing grand jury materials); see also United States v. Smith, 992 F. Supp. 743, 749 (D.N.J. 1998) (holding that Assistant U.S. Attorney violated Fed. R. Crim. P. 32(b) by publishing sentencing memorandum without first obtaining leave of court in "a flagrant attempt to circumvent the clearly established confidentiality provisions of Rule 32," requiring a compelling need for disclosure and striking the memo as a sanction).

425. See, e.g., VT. R. CRIM. P. 32(c)(5); N.Y. CRIM. PROC. LAW § 390.50; see also Vermont v. LaBounty, 702 A.2d 82 (Vt. 1997) (public's First Amendment-based right of access does not attach to presentence investigation reports).

426. 879 F.2d 224 (7th Cir. 1989).
427. See *id.* at 229.
428. See *id.* at 228-29.
429. *Id.* at 229.

obligation to provide the sentencing court with a comprehensive analysis of the defendant's character."[430] Sealing the reports is justified, the court reasoned, by the privacy interest of the defendant, his family, and the crime victim, the judicial interest in full disclosure of information relevant to sentencing, and the government's interest in the secrecy of information relating to ongoing criminal investigations and information derived from grand jury proceedings.[431]

Given the confidential, intimate nature of a typical presentence report,[432] the court held, the party seeking disclosure must make a specific showing of need.[433] "Only where a compelling, particularized need for disclosure is shown should the district court disclose the report; even then, however, the court should limit disclosure to those portions of the report which are directly relevant to the demonstrated need."[434]

Even in the context of presentence reports, however, some courts have adopted an approach more hospitable to public access.[435] In *United States v. Schlette*,[436] the Ninth Circuit acknowledged that most courts had established a

---

430. *Id.*
431. See *id.* at 229-34.
432. The court analogized the presentence investigation "to psychiatric or spiritual counseling," distinguishing it from "the public, adversarial cast of the trial of the guilt phase of a criminal proceeding." *Id.* at 237.
433. See *id.* at 238.
434. *Id.* at 239. See United States v. McKnight, 771 F.2d 388, 390 (8th Cir. 1985), *cert. denied*, 475 U.S. 1014 (1986) ("Generally, pre-sentence reports are considered as confidential reports to the court and are not considered public records except to the extent that they or portions of them are placed on the court records or authorized for disclosure to serve the interests of justice."); United States v. Charmer Indus., 711 F.2d 1164, 1176 (2d Cir. 1983) ("the court should not release a presentence report to a third person unless that person has shown a compelling need for disclosure to meet the ends of justice"); United States v. Boesky, 674 F. Supp. 1128, 1130 (S.D.N.Y. 1987) ("American Lawyer has not met its burden of establishing a particularized need for the material contained in the presentence report. . . . [D]isclosure of the report or any part of it is neither required nor justified to meet the ends of justice."); Hancock Bros. v. Jones, 293 F. Supp. 1229, 1233 (N.D. Cal. 1968) ("a presentence report should not be disclosed to third parties unless lifting confidentiality is required to meet the ends of justice"); see also Copley Press, Inc. v. Administrative Office of Cts., 648 N.E.2d 324 (Ill. App. 1995) (denying access to documents in Pretrial Services Agency).
435. In *Mitchell v. Superior Court*, 690 P.2d 51, 54 (Ariz. 1984), the Arizona Supreme Court held that a secrecy order was void "to the extent that it enacts a general rule keeping all presentence reports confidential even after sentencing." The court indicated that "[t]he burden of showing the probability that specific, material harm will result from disclosure, thus justifying an exception to the usual rule of full disclosure is on the party that seeks non-disclosure rather than on the party that seeks access." *Id.* Similarly, in *People v. Private Sanitation Industry Ass'n*, 519 N.Y.S.2d 106 (County Ct. 1987), the court interpreted a New York law providing for the confidentiality of presentence reports or memoranda narrowly: "A pre-sentence memorandum is part of a court proceeding . . . . Once the information is used at trial or pre-sentence proceedings, it becomes subject to First Amendment rights." *Id.* at 110.
436. 842 F.2d 1574 (9th Cir. 1988).

strong presumption favoring the confidentiality of presentence reports.[437] Nevertheless, the court asserted, most of the concerns expressed have "been proven empirically false" and disclosure has, in fact, "brought greater objectivity to the sentencing process."[438] Even so, the court acknowledged that presentence reports should not be routinely released and that the party seeking access must make a threshold showing that disclosure will serve the ends of justice.[439] Ultimately, in the Ninth's Circuit's view, the courts must balance the asserted need for access against the reasons supporting confidentiality.[440]

The press has also been denied access to documents filed in support of motions to reduce sentences. In *United States v. Milken*,[441] the defendant, who pled guilty to securities and tax fraud and market manipulation, sought a reduction in his sentence based on his post-sentence cooperation with the government in its ongoing investigations, including the investigation of his former employer.[442] Milken moved to seal an affidavit and portions of his memorandum in support of the motion, and the government joined in the motion to seal.[443] The district court recognized that there is a qualified right of public access to motion papers in criminal proceedings, but nevertheless sealed material relating to the defendant's family's medical records because of their strong privacy interest as well as information the disclosure of which would jeopardize the government's ongoing and future investigations.[444] Because orders sealing documents must be "tailored to the circumstances of the individual case" and "the trial judge must consider alternatives to closure," the court limited the information to be held

---

437. See *id.* at 1579.

438. *Id.* at 1580 (citing Fennell & Hall, *Due Process at Sentencing: An Empirical and Legal Analysis of the Disclosure of Presentence Reports in Federal Courts*, 93 HARV. L. REV. 1613 (1980)). Similarly, in the context of a Freedom of Information Act request for a presentence report in *Berry v. Department of Justice*, 733 F.2d 1343 (9th Cir. 1984), the court rejected the argument that disclosure would chill sources of information and decrease the accuracy of reports: "[T]his contention has been raised for decades; and has now been disproved, both analytically and empirically." *Id.* at 1355.

439. 842 F.2d at 1580-81.

440. *Id.* at 1581; see also United States v. Smith, 123 F.3d 140, 143 (3d Cir. 1997) ("[E]ven though the proceedings [and briefs] at issue before the district court concern alleged government misconduct and hence public access to them would serve important functions, there is no presumptive First Amendment or common law right of access to them if secret grand jury material would be disclosed by that access."); United States v. Preate, 927 F. Supp. 163, 168 (M.D. Pa. 1996) (in sentencing of former state attorney general guilty of mail fraud, court granted access to transcript of in-chambers conference and government's *in camera* offer of proof; "[h]aving weighed the limited interest in confidentiality in this case against the substantial desirability of third-party access, the court concludes that there is a compelling need for disclosure to meet the needs of justice").

441. 780 F. Supp. 123 (S.D.N.Y. 1991).

442. See *id.* at 124-25.

443. See *id.* at 124.

444. See *id.* at 126-27.

confidential to those passages about which the government could establish that unsealing in fact posed a risk to the criminal investigations.[445]

The Eleventh Circuit considered the right of access to the transcript of an *in camera* hearing on a defendant's motion for leave to appeal in forma pauperis in *United States v. Ellis*.[446] The defendant, who had been represented throughout his trial by retained counsel, moved pursuant to the Criminal Justice Act to be represented by appointed counsel on appeal. Following Eleventh Circuit rules, the magistrate judge held an *in camera* hearing to review the financial circumstances of the applicant and his fee arrangement with retained counsel.[447] When a newspaper sought disclosure of the transcript, the magistrate ordered it unsealed. On appeal, the Eleventh Circuit agreed, holding that there is a "First Amendment right of access to information about the fees and costs paid to and costs incurred and services rendered by retained counsel."[448]

§ 5-2(e). Criminal Justice Act Vouchers.

Access to the billing and other records of court appointed counsel, experts and investigators is provided by relevant statutes, though disputes arise as to the timing of the release of the information and the type of information that is to be disclosed. Post-trial disclosure of the total amount of fees and expenses paid to court-appointed defense counsel is easier to obtain than information regarding interim fees and expenses or detailed backup documentation. Claims of a common law right of access to such records have had varied success. There is no judicial consensus as to whether a First Amendment-based right of access attaches to such material.

Attorneys appointed by the courts to represent indigent defendants in criminal cases are paid with public funds. In the federal system, since 1964, such payment is made pursuant to the Criminal Justice Act.[449] The CJA specifies the hourly rate of payment for legal representation, compensation for investigative, expert or other services, and the payment of expenses. Permission for the defense to engage the services of non-attorneys is generally sought in an ex parte applica-

---

445. *Id.* at 127.
446. 90 F.3d 447 (11th Cir. 1996), *cert. denied*, 519 U.S. 1118 (1997).
447. *Id.* at 449.
448. *Id.* at 450-51; see also United States v. Porter, 988 F. Supp. 519, 526 (M.D. Pa. 1997) (following conviction, court unsealed documents relating to defendant's *in forma pauperis* status, stating that "the public has a right to know both that the attorney for which it is paying is performing the task for which funds are expended and that the defendant is being given a fair trial by the court").
449. 18 U.S.C. § 3006A.

tion and determined in an ex parte proceeding.[450] Motions, orders and transcripts relating to the appointment of non-attorneys are generally placed under seal.[451] The Act requires that claims for payment be submitted on prescribed forms that require information as to the type of service performed, as well as an itemization of the time expended, services rendered and expenses incurred. Backup documentation, including detailed time sheets and receipts for expenses incurred, must accompany these forms.[452] The forms are generally submitted at the end of trial, though a court may grant an attorney's request for interim billing, particularly in capital cases.[453]

In 1998, the Act was amended to provide for the public disclosure of the information contained in the forms. As a general rule, the amounts paid for services are to be made available to the public upon the court's approval of payment.[454] If payment is made while the proceeding is in its pre-trial stage or is in progress, the court is to redact any detailed information from the payment voucher and release to the public the amounts approved for payment.[455] After the completion of the trial, the court is to make an unredacted copy of the expense voucher available to the public, unless it determines that the defendant's interests require limited disclosure.[456]

Litigation has focused on whether statutory access rights to CJA vouchers include materials related to the appointment and compensation of counsel, non-attorneys, and backup documentation submitted with the vouchers. In *United States v. Gonzales*,[457] a newspaper requested the disclosure of all CJA-related documents, motions, orders, and hearing transcripts related to the retention and compensation of services by non-attorneys. The Tenth Circuit found that such information is presumptively sealed under the CJA statutory scheme.[458] The

---

450. See *id.* § 3006A(e). In death penalty cases, hearings regarding the engagement of services of non-attorneys are not to be held ex parte "unless a proper showing is made concerning the need for confidentiality." 21 U.S.C. § 848(q)(9).

451. See United States v. Gonzales, 150 F.3d 1246, 1252 (10th Cir. 1998), *cert. denied*, 119 S. Ct. 918 (1999).

452. See 18 U.S.C. § 3006A(d)(5).

453. See United States v. Gonzales, 150 F.3d at 1251.

454. See 18 U.S.C. § 3006A(d)(4)(A).

455. See *id.* § 3006A(d)(4)(B). See also United States v. Gonzales, 150 F.3d at 1266-76 (vouchers may contain information that could reveal trial strategy).

456. See 18 U.S.C. § 3006A(d)(4)(C)-(E). Where there are multiple defendants, the disclosure is to take place after the sentencing of all the defendants. See United States v. Gonzales, 150 F.3d at 1264. The interests of the defendant that may require the disclosure to be limited to a redacted voucher, even after trial, include "Fifth and Sixth Amendment rights, the attorney-client privilege, the work product privilege, safety of any person, and any other interest justice may require." *Id.* at 1263 n.21.

457. 150 F.3d 1246, 1251 (10th Cir. 1998), *cert. denied*, 119 S. Ct. 918 (1999).

458. See *id.* at 1264-65. The court reasoned that such information, even though released at the end of the trial, could be used by the government to investigate and bring new charges against a

court also held that the district court had abused its discretion when it ordered the post-trial release of materials related to the appointment and compensation of counsel and backup documentation submitted with the vouchers.[459]

Claims that the billing and other records of court-appointed counsel, experts and investigators must be released under the common law right of access to judicial records have been rejected by some courts.[460] These courts have held that the Criminal Justice Act and similar state statutes have preempted any common law right of access.[461] The Tenth Circuit has also found that CJA materials are administrative documents, not judicial documents, to which the common law right of access does not apply.[462]

Courts are in disagreement as to whether there is a constitutional right of access to CJA-related material such as payment vouchers, billing and other records of court appointed counsel, experts and investigators. The press has argued that the amount and nature of the charges court-appointed defense counsel submits are of public concern due to the public's interest in the administration of justice and the use of tax dollars to pay the charges.[463] Cases in which the *Press-Enterprise II* test has been applied to determine whether there is a right of access to such material have reached differing conclusions.

In *United States v. Suarez*,[464] the Second Circuit considered whether there is a constitutional right of access to CJA vouchers, without any backup documentation.[465] Deciding the case prior to the CJA amendments that codified a right to such material, the court determined that, under *Press-Enterprise II*, the public has a qualified, First Amendment-based right of access to CJA vouchers after

---

defendant or other individuals. As a result, the threat of ultimate disclosure would decrease the amount of information provided by the defense in the application to engage the services of non-attorneys, thereby impeding the court's ability to decide correctly whether and how much assistance to afford the defendant. See *id.* at 1259.

459. The court found that disclosure may unduly intrude on the privacy interests of defendants and innocent persons who had been interviewed or investigated, may physically endanger witnesses and non-witnesses, may implicate the defendants' Fifth Amendment rights, and would reveal information protected by the attorney-client privilege and the attorney work-product doctrine. See *id.* at 1265-66.

460. See *id.* at 1263. But see United States v. McVeigh, 918 F. Supp. 1452, 1464 (W.D. Okla. 1996) (common law principle of openness and qualified, First Amendment-based right of access conflated in *Press-Enterprise II* standard).

461. See United States v. Gonzales, 150 F.3d at 1263; Lanphere & Urbaniak v. Colorado, 21 F.3d 1508, 1511 (10th Cir. 1994) (common law right of access to criminal justice records supplanted by state statute).

462. See United States v. Gonzales, 150 F.3d at 1263.

463. See *id.* at 1254; United States v. Suarez, 880 F.2d 626, 630 (2d Cir. 1989).

464. 880 F.2d 626, 630 (2d Cir. 1989).

465. The newspaper in *Suarez* sought only the "barebones data" of who was paid, how much and for what general services. See *id.* at 631.

payment has been approved.[466] The court noted that, due to the relatively recent enactment of the Criminal Justice Act, there has been no long tradition of accessibility to CJA forms; even so, the court held that this lack of tradition did "not detract from the public's strong interest in how its funds are being spent in the administration of criminal justice and what amounts of public funds are paid to particular private attorneys or firms."[467] The Second Circuit also found that the public's right of access must be weighed against any harm to privacy interests, attorney-client privilege or work-product protection that could arise from disclosure of the vouchers.[468] In the event that disclosure would result in such harm, the court of appeals held that the trial court retains discretion to either delay the release of the material or to redact the necessary information from the vouchers before disclosure.

The issue of public access to attorney fees and expense claims was also addressed by the Tennessee Court of Criminal Appeals in *Knoxville News-Sentinel v. Huskey*.[469] In that case, a newspaper sought access to sealed fee and expense documents relating to public monies expended in the defense of an indigent criminal defendant on trial for capital murder. The trial court ordered the release of the summary cover sheets of attorney fee and expense claims that set forth the total fees and expenses paid to defense counsel. In addition, the court ordered the release of documents reflecting the total amounts paid out for the services of expert witnesses and the amounts paid to any specific expert who had offered evidence on the record in the case.[470] The trial court further ordered that the detailed time records and expense reports submitted by defense counsel and defense experts were to remain sealed until the defendant's case concluded.[471] The appellate court, basing its analysis on *Suarez*, upheld the trial court's release of the "barebones" summary of information.[472]

The district court in *United States v. McVeigh*[473] disagreed with the Second Circuit decision in *Suarez* regarding the disclosure of CJA vouchers. In *Mc-*

---

466. See *id*. at 631.
467. *Id*.
468. See *id*. at 631-33.
469. 982 S.W.2d 359 (Tenn. Crim. App. 1998).
470. See *id*. at 360-61.
471. See *id*. at 361.
472. See *id*. at 363. Subsequently, the newspaper obtained a copy of the detailed time records of the defendant's court-appointed counsel. See Tennessee v. Huskey, 1999 Tenn. Crim. App. LEXIS 76, at *7-8 (Tenn. Crim. App. Jan. 29, 1999). The trial court entered an order enjoining the newspaper from publishing or disseminating the records. Nevertheless, the newspaper, believing the order was invalid on its face, published an article that utilized some of the information. On appeal, the Tennessee Court of Criminal Appeals held that, because the records at issue had not been included in the appellate record, it was unable to review the constitutionality of the prior restraint on its merits and dismissed the appeal as improvidently granted. See *id*. at *24-25.
473. 918 F. Supp. 1452 (W.D. Okla. 1996).

Veigh, the media had requested disclosure of the amounts paid to appointed counsel and others providing services to the defendants accused of the Oklahoma City bombing. The district court distinguished *Suarez* on the grounds that it was not a death penalty case, did not have the "heightened sensitivity" of the *McVeigh* case, and had allowed disclosure of CJA vouchers after jury selection.[474] The court emphasized that the CJA forms were not directly related to the process of adjudication and, therefore, were "not within the strong presumption of open access to proceedings in court."[475]

In *United States v. Ellis*,[476] the Eleventh Circuit considered whether a newspaper must be granted access to the transcript of an *in camera* hearing on the defendant's application for the appointment of counsel under the CJA. The defendant, a former sheriff convicted of drug trafficking and obstruction of justice, had been represented by retained counsel during the trial and sought appointed counsel for his appeal. The defendant opposed the newspaper's motion for access to the transcript on the grounds that disclosure would infringe his Fifth Amendment rights, violate his right of financial privacy, and invade his retained counsel's privacy interest in the fee agreement.[477] Relying on the Second Circuit's analysis in *Suarez*, the Eleventh Circuit found that the newspaper had a qualified constitutional right of access to the transcript.[478] The court further determined that the transcript revealed no privileged information that would overcome the presumption of openness.[479]

§ 5-2(f). Military Courts.

In *United States v. Scott*,[480] the U.S. Army Court of Criminal Appeals recognized a qualified, First Amendment-based right of access to documents admitted into evidence at a pretrial proceedings open to the public.[481] The military judge presiding over the court-martial had made no findings of facts to support his conclusion that several persons had privacy interests that justified sealing a stipulation of facts.[482] However, while the trial judge abused his discretion in sealing the record, the "error affecting the public interest in no way

---

474. See *id.* at 1465.
475. *Id.* at 1464.
476. 90 F.3d 447 (11th Cir. 1996), *cert. denied*, 519 U.S. 1118 (1997).
477. See *id.* at 449-50.
478. *Id.* at 450.
479. See *id.* at 450-51.
480. 48 M.J. 663 (Army Crim. App. 1998). After Scott pled guilty to attempted murder of a soldier and carnal knowledge of a 15-year-old high school student, the trial court sealed the stipulation of facts in order to protect the privacy interests of the minor. See *id.* at 666-67.
481. See *id.* at 666.
482. See *id.*

harmed the substantial rights of the appellant."[483] The finding of guilt and the sentence were therefore affirmed.[484]

---

483. *Id.* at 667.
484. See *id.*

Chapter 6

ACCESS TO JUDICIAL RECORDS: CIVIL PROCEEDINGS

§ 6-1. Records in Civil Proceedings.
    § 6-1(a). Discovery Materials.
        § 6-1(a)(1). Background.
        § 6-1(a)(2). *Seattle Times Co. v. Rhinehart*.
        § 6-1(a)(3). Unfiled Discovery Materials.
        § 6-1(a)(4). Filed Discovery Materials.
        § 6-1(a)(5). Competing Interests.
        § 6-1(a)(6). Law Reform.
    § 6-1(b). Settlement Agreements.
    § 6-1(c). Court Files.
        § 6-1(c)(1). Pretrial Motions, Records, and Pleadings.
        § 6-1(c)(2). Transcripts of Judicial Proceedings.
    § 6-1(d). Other Civil Court Records.
§ 6-2. Juvenile Records.
    § 6-2(a). Transcripts and Records of Delinquency Proceedings.
    § 6-2(b). Other Juvenile Records.

§ 6-1. Records in Civil Proceedings.

§ 6-1(a). Discovery Materials.

§ 6-1(a)(1). Background.

Civil litigation, even when the government is not itself a party, often affects the public interest.[1] Such litigation can, and does, establish legal rules governing social policy from medical malpractice and environmental hazards to dangerous products, toxic pollution, and other issues that impact the public health and safety. Thus, although civil litigation is often styled as a dispute between private parties, the controversies such parties seek to resolve through the courts more than occasionally assume a public dimension.[2] It is not surprising, therefore, that the press and public have had incentive to seek access to the records generated in the course of such proceedings, or that the litigants themselves have taken steps to secure the court's assistance in keeping such records from public view.[3]

---

    1. See, e.g., Wilson v. Science Applications Int'l Corp., 60 Cal. Rptr. 2d 883, 884 (Ct. App. 1997) ("[W]e hold that after entry of an order sealing all or part of the record in a civil proceeding, members of the public, who are not members of the proceeding at the time the order was entered, may challenge the continued need for the order."). See generally Walsh & Weiser, *Public Courts, Private Justice: Court Secrecy Masks Safety Issues*, WASH. POST., Oct. 23, 1988, at A1.
    2. See generally Chayes, *The Role of the Judge in Public Law Litigation*, 89 HARV. L. REV. 1281 (1976); Fiss, *The Supreme Court, 1978 Term — Foreword: The Forms of Justice*, 93 HARV. L. REV. 1 (1979).
    3. See, e.g., SOCIETY OF PROFESSIONAL JOURNALISTS AND AMERICAN TRIAL LAWYERS' ASS'N, KEEPING SECRETS: JUSTICE ON TRIAL, REPORT OF THE CONFERENCE ON COURTROOM SECRECY (1990); Corboy, *Court Secrecy: The Closed Circle and the Public Interest*, 3 MD. J. CONTEMP.

Indeed, confidentiality, privacy, and national security interests may well be implicated by civil litigation. Cases involving divorce, family life, juveniles, trade secrets, and other proprietary information have all generated confidentiality claims. It has been argued that "[c]onsensual secrecy pervades virtually every phase of modern civil litigation."[4] The proponents of protective orders securing the confidentiality of discovery materials typically argue that the public interest is furthered by assuring the effective resolution of civil litigation, which might be impaired by harmful disclosures, especially since much of the information generated in discovery proves irrelevant to the litigation and is never admitted in evidence.[5] For this reason, Rule 26(c) of the Federal Rules of Civil Procedure authorizes courts to issue protective orders to maintain the confidentiality of discovery materials upon a showing of "good cause."[6]

As a practical matter, however, the discovery process often operates independently of meaningful judicial supervision and, as a result, many courts have

---

LEGAL ISSUES 1 (1991); Dore, *Secrecy by Consent: The Use and Limits of Confidentiality in the Pursuit of Settlement*, 74 NOTRE DAME L. REV. 283, 300 (1999) (discussing current controversy between "the propriety of confidentiality and the need for public access to civil litigation"); Morrison, *Protective Orders, Plaintiffs, Defendants and the Public Interest in Disclosure: Where Does the Balance Lie?*, 24 U. RICH. L. REV. 109 (1989).

4. Dore, *supra* note 3, at 285.

5. See Marcus, *The Discovery Confidentiality Controversy*, 1991 U. ILL. L. REV. 457, 459 ("[D]espite the clamor for change by statute or rule revision, it appears that current legal doctrine is well adapted to handling the actual problems, and that radical changes would be risky."); Miller, *Confidentiality, Protective Orders and Public Access to the Courts*, 105 HARV. L. REV. 427, 432 (1991) ("A presumption of public access alters the system itself in a way that might undermine its primary goal of providing citizens an effective truth seeking procedure for resolving their disputes without impairing their other rights."). See generally Comment, *Protective Orders, Property Interests and Prior Restraints: Can the Courts Prevent Media Nonparties From Publishing Court-Protected Discovery Materials?*, 144 U. PA. L. REV. 2463 (1996) (arguing that protective orders may be enforced by enjoining media publication in limited circumstances to protect property interest in information).

6. FED. R. CIV. P. 26(c). See generally F. HARE, J. GILBERT & W. REMINE, CONFIDENTIALITY ORDERS (1988); 8 C. WRIGHT, A. MILLER & R. MARCUS, FEDERAL PRACTICE AND PROCEDURE, §§ 2035-2044, at 474-584 (1994). FED. R. CIV. P. 1 provides that the rules are to be construed "to secure the just, speedy and inexpensive determination of every action." See Miller, *supra* note 5, at 446 (asserting the value of protective orders as "effective tools of pretrial management" and as "a tool particularly well-adapted to minimize discovery abuse"); see also Eastman Kodak Co. v. Worden, 25 MEDIA L. REP. (BNA) 1485, 1486-87 (W.D.N.Y. 1996) (holding a consent order modifying protective order in trade secrets case to unseal certain documents requires: (1) plaintiff filing redacted copies of affidavits and related exhibits to delete only proprietary, confidential or trade secret information; (2) parties to have a good faith basis to request sealing; (3) parties to place duplicate copy of submissions in public file; (4) notification of nonparty newspaper's attorney if sealing is sought; and (5) permission for newspaper's attorney to view unredacted documents in order to determine whether it wishes to challenge sealing).

§ 6-1(a)(1)   ACCESS TO JUDICIAL RECORDS: CIVIL PROCEEDINGS   § 6-1(a)(1)

effectively delegated to the parties the power to undertake discovery in secret.[7] Confidentiality agreements and protective orders, generated by the parties and entered by the court, have become familiar devices in the context of discovery and settlement in civil cases.[8] Broad confidentiality agreements and "umbrella" or "stipulated" protective orders typically empower one party to designate discovery materials as confidential, subject to the other party's motion to unseal them.[9] Even when a plaintiff may have some incentive to disclose discovery materials publicly (e.g., to counsel in similar litigation or to the press), the availability of a favorable settlement conditioned on confidentiality may prove

---

7. In *Procter & Gamble Co. v. Bankers Trust Co.*, 78 F.3d 219, 227 (6th Cir. 1996), the Sixth Circuit, speaking through Chief Judge Merritt, was especially critical of the district court's failure to fulfill its own responsibility under Rule 26(c):

> The District Court cannot abdicate its responsibility to oversee the discovery process and to determine whether filings should be made available to the public. It certainly should not turn this function over to the parties, as it did here, allowing them to modify the terms of a court order without even seeking the consent of the court. The protective order in this case allows the parties to control public access to court papers, and it should be vacated or substantially changed.

Thus, the court held, the protective order at issue, entered at the request of the parties, was invalid since, pursuant to its terms, "the parties were allowed to adjudicate their own case based upon their own self-interest." *Id.*

8. See *Pansy v. Borough of Stroudsburg*, 23 F.3d 772, 785 (3d Cir. 1994) ("Disturbingly, some courts routinely sign orders which contain confidentiality clauses without considering the propriety of such orders, or the countervailing public interests which are sacrificed by the orders."); see also *Procter & Gamble Co. v. Bankers Trust Co.*, 78 F.3d 219, 223-24 (6th Cir. 1996) ("The increasing, routine use of protective orders in the courts only assures that challenges of this type will continue."); *City of Hartford v. Chase*, 942 F.2d 130, 137-38 (2d Cir. 1991) (Pratt, J., concurring):

> [A] troubling tendency accompanies the increasing frequency and scope of confidentiality agreements that are ordered by the court. These agreements are reached by private parties and often involve materials and information that is never even presented to the court. With the signature of a federal judge, however, they are converted into a powerful means of maintaining and enforcing secrecy. Once signed, a confidentiality order, which has converted a private agreement into an order of a court, requires the court to use its contempt power to enforce the private agreement. . . . [B]ecause they often involve information not in the control of the court, and may . . . implicate public concerns, confidentiality orders, when not subject to proper supervision, have a great potential for abuse. For this reason, judges should review such agreements carefully and skeptically before signing them.

9. See *Zenith Radio Corp. v. Matsushita Elec. Indus. Co.*, 529 F. Supp. 866, 889 (E.D. Pa. 1981) (court was not aware "of any case in the past half-dozen years of even a modicum of complexity where an umbrella protective order . . . has not been agreed to by the parties and approved by the court").

irresistible.[10] And, it is the rare judge who questions the terms of an agreement between the parties ending the litigation.[11]

In the wake of this phenomenon, the rules of several courts have been amended, sunshine legislation has been widely proposed and sometimes enacted,[12] and congressional hearings on court secrecy have been held.[13] A number of courts have invoked a presumption of public access to the documents generated in civil litigation, grounded in the common law or in the First Amendment.[14] With increasing frequency, intervenors from the press and public have sought to modify secrecy orders.[15] Some courts have required a showing of "extraordinary circumstances or compelling need" to modify an existing secrecy order,[16] while others have rejected such a rule, reasoning that the entry or modification of a protective order is always a matter within the court's discre-

---

10. See, e.g., Reed v. Zizka, 1998 Conn. Super. LEXIS 1522, at *1 (Conn. Super. May 29, 1998) ("[T]he parties stipulated that 'the court file . . . be sealed from the public for a period of six weeks . . . to facilitate settlement of the lawsuit.'").

11. See *Panel-Confidentiality Orders: Parties' Protection Versus Public Access*, 134 F.R.D. 387 (D.C. Cir. 1990) (discussing protective orders and the problems they pose for judges).

12. See Chap. 6-1(a)(6) *infra*. See generally Dore, *supra* note 3, at 300 (discussing current controversy between "the propriety of confidentiality and the need for public access to civil litigation").

13. See *Court Secrecy, Examining the Use of Secrecy and Confidentiality of Documents by Courts in Civil Litigation, 1990: Hearing Before the Subcomm. on Cts. & Admin. Pract. of the Sen. Comm. on the Judiciary*, 101st Cong. (1990).

14. See, e.g., Greater Miami Baseball Club Ltd. Partnership v. Selig, 955 F. Supp. 37, 40 (S.D.N.Y. 1997) (holding that deposition transcripts and exhibits made part of trial record "are presumptively matters to which the public is entitled to access"). See generally Chap. 6-1(a)(4), 6-1(b)-(d) *infra*.

15. Intervention is the primary means by which the press has challenged confidentiality orders in civil litigation. See, e.g., Pansy v. Borough of Stroudsburg, 23 F.3d at 777 (citing cases); In re Coordinated Pretrial Proceedings in Petroleum Prods. Antitrust Litig., 101 F.R.D. 34, 36-39 (C.D. Cal. 1984). Other third parties have also been granted leave to intervene, at least when they have some interest in the materials at issue. See Greater Miami Baseball Club Ltd. Partnership v. Selig, 955 F. Supp. at 44-45. Some courts have suggested, however, that, at least where discovery materials would not be independently accessible, third-party intervenors have no standing to challenge a protective order. See Oklahoma Hosp. Ass'n v. Oklahoma Publ'g Co., 748 F.2d 1421, 1445-46 (10th Cir. 1984), *cert. denied*, 473 U.S. 905 (1985); Booth Newspapers, Inc. v. Midland Circuit Judge, 377 N.W.2d 868, 870 (Mich. App. 1985), *cert. denied*, 479 U.S. 1031 (1987).

16. See, e.g., In re Agent Orange Prod. Liab. Litig., 821 F.2d 139, 147 (2d Cir.), *cert. denied*, 484 U.S. 953 (1987); Palmieri v. New York, 779 F.2d 861 (2d Cir. 1985); Martindell v. International Tel. & Tel. Corp., 594 F.2d 291 (2d Cir. 1979); cf. United States v. Kentucky Util. Co., 927 F.2d 252, 255 (6th Cir. 1991). But see United Nuclear Corp. v. Cranford Ins. Co., 905 F.2d 1424, 1428 n.1 (10th Cir. 1990), *cert. denied*, 498 U.S. 1073 (1991); Westchester Radiological v. Blue Cross/Blue Shield, 138 F.R.D. 33, 36 (S.D.N.Y. 1991). See generally Note, *Third Party Modification of Protective Orders Under Rule 26(c)*, 94 MICH. L. REV. 854 (1995).

tion.[17] In any case, the movement for enhanced public access to civil records has plainly made advances.

In *Hammock v. Hoffmann-LaRoche, Inc.*,[18] for example, Public Citizen, as intervenor, unsuccessfully sought access to documents filed with the trial court under a protective order by a drug manufacturer sued by parents of children born with birth defects.[19] Relying on the common law right of access to judicial records, the New Jersey Supreme Court held that "[t]here is a presumption of public access to documents and materials filed with a court in connection with civil litigation."[20] The court looked beyond the interests of the parties and attorneys, to the "profound public interest" at stake when matters of health, safety, and consumer fraud are placed at issue in civil litigation.[21] Under such circumstances, "as a matter of public policy there must be careful scrutiny prior to sealing records and documents filed with a court in a high public interest case. That heightened interest requires that trial courts be more circumspect when deciding whether to seal or unseal records used in litigation."[22]

To implement this presumption of access, the court fashioned a "reasonableness" standard for measuring "good cause."[23] First, the presumption does not apply to discovery motions filed with the court.[24] Second, it does apply to pretrial, nondiscovery motions, whether preliminary or dispositive, and the materials filed in support or opposition to such a motion.[25] Third, the presumption attaches to such materials "regardless of whether the trial court relied on them in reaching its decision on the merits."[26] Fourth, the presumption applies regardless of the disposition of the nondiscovery motion and, fifth, "a flexible

---

17. See, e.g., Pansy v. Borough of Stroudsburg, 23 F.3d at 789-90; Beckman Indus. v. International Ins. Co., 966 F.2d 470, 475 (9th Cir.), *cert. denied*, 506 U.S. 868 (1992); Public Citizen v. Liggett Group, Inc., 858 F.2d 775, 790 (1st Cir. 1988), *cert. denied*, 488 U.S. 1030 (1989); SEC v. Stratton Oakmont, Inc., 24 MEDIA L. REP. (BNA) 2179 (D.D.C. 1996); see also Wolhar v. General Motors Corp., 712 A.2d 464 (Del. Super. 1997) (stating that modification of confidentiality order involves same balancing test, except court should consider reliance by original parties on order); Mokhiber v. Davis, 537 A.2d 1100, 1116-17 (D.C. 1988).

18. 662 A.2d 546 (N.J. 1995). See *New Jersey, Louisiana Continue National Trend Against Court Secrecy*, CIV. JUST. DIG., Fall 1995, at 1.

19. The trial court had based its good cause determination on a finding that many of the documents contained trade secrets, confidential and proprietary information, and material involving nonparties protected by the physician-patient privilege. 662 A.2d at 549. The order was amended to prevent plaintiff's counsel from consulting with attorneys in other jurisdictions prosecuting similar litigation. *Id.*

20. *Id.* at 556.
21. *Id.* at 558.
22. *Id.*
23. *Id.* at 556.
24. See *id.*
25. *Id.*
26. *Id.* at 559.

balancing process adaptable to different circumstances must be conducted to determine whether the need for secrecy substantially outweighs the presumption of access."[27] Sixth, "the person who seeks to overcome the strong presumption of access must establish by a preponderance of the evidence that the interest in secrecy outweighs the presumption."[28] Seventh, the party resisting disclosure must demonstrate a need for secrecy and, eighth, the court must examine each document individually and "make factual findings with regard to why the presumption of public access has been overcome."[29] All of these rules, the court explained, are illustrative of the "national trend . . . away from sealing documents and materials filed with a court."[30]

§ 6-1(a)(2). *Seattle Times Co. v. Rhinehart.*

Prior to 1984, a number of federal courts had held that the First Amendment restricts a court's ability to prevent a party from disseminating to the public material it receives through civil discovery.[31] In *Seattle Times Co. v. Rhinehart*,[32] however, the Supreme Court rejected the claim that parties to civil litigation have a First Amendment-based right to disseminate, prior to trial, information received solely through the discovery process.

The *Seattle Times* had published allegedly defamatory articles about the Aquarian Foundation and its spiritual leader, Keith Rhinehart. During the pretrial discovery phase of his defamation suit, Rhinehart refused to disclose certain financial information to the newspaper, including the identities of the Foundation's donors and a list of its members. When the *Times* moved to compel discovery of these items, Rhinehart sought a protective order prohibiting the newspaper from disseminating to the public any information it gained through discovery.[33]

The trial court, acting pursuant to discovery rules modeled on the Federal Rules of Civil Procedure, issued an order compelling Rhinehart to produce the requested information.[34] Nevertheless, pursuant to the state's version of Rule

---

27. *Id.*
28. *Id.*
29. *Id.* at 559; see *id.* ("The need for secrecy must be demonstrated with specificity as to each document.").
30. *Id.*
31. See, e.g., In re San Juan Star Co., 662 F.2d 108, 116 (1st Cir. 1981) (holding that Rule 26(c)'s "good cause" standard should be read with a "heightened sensitivity" to the First Amendment); In re Halkin, 598 F.2d 176 (D.C. Cir. 1979) ("First Amendment rights attach to materials made available through the discovery process."); Reliance Ins. Co. v. Barron's, 428 F. Supp. 200 (S.D.N.Y. 1977) (holding that a protective order was an unconstitutional prior restraint).
32. 467 U.S. 20 (1984). See generally Post, *The Management of Speech: Discretion and Rights*, 1984 SUP. CT. REV. 169.
33. See 467 U.S. at 25.
34. See *id.*

26(c), the court also issued a protective order prohibiting the newspaper from publishing, disseminating, or using the information in any way except to litigate the case.[35] The order did not, however, apply to information gained by means other than the discovery process.[36]

In the Supreme Court, Justice Powell framed the critical issue as "whether a litigant's freedom comprehends the right to disseminate information that he has obtained pursuant to a court order that both granted him access to that information and placed restraints on the way in which the information might be used."[37] The Court acknowledged that the information at issue was "protected speech," and that the public had an interest in learning more about Rhinehart. Nevertheless, Justice Powell observed, "[i]t does not necessarily follow . . . that a litigant has an unrestrained right to disseminate information that has been obtained through pretrial discovery."[38]

When a party seeks documents or other information in civil litigation, the Court concluded, a protective order "is not the kind of classic prior restraint that requires exacting First Amendment scrutiny. . . . Such a protective order prevents a party from disseminating only that information obtained through use of the discovery process. Thus, the party may disseminate the identical information covered by the protective order as long as the information is gained through means independent of the Court's processes."[39] Accordingly, the Court held, the applicable constitutional standard assesses whether the

> practice in question [furthers] an important or substantial governmental interest unrelated to the suppression of expression" and whether "the limitation of First Amendment freedom [is] no greater than is necessary or essential to the protection of the particular governmental interest involved.[40]

Applying this standard, Justice Powell noted that the impairment of First Amendment rights caused by a protective order is not as great as restraints on the dissemination of information in other contexts. The rules authorizing discovery are a matter of "legislative grace," since "[a] litigant has no First Amendment right of access to information made available only for purposes of trying his suit."[41] As a result, Justice Powell concluded, "pretrial depositions and interrogatories are not public components of a civil trial. . . . Restraints placed on

---

35. *Id.*
36. See *id.* at 26.
37. *Id.* at 32.
38. *Id.*
39. *Id.* at 33-34. But cf. Cooper Hosp. Univ. Med. Center v. Sullivan, 183 F.R.D. 135, 138 (D.N.J. 1998) (denying protective order as a form of prior restraint that would prohibit defendants from disseminating information to the public about the documents used in the proceedings even if that information were obtained outside the discovery process).
40. 467 U.S. at 32 (quoting Procunier v. Martinez, 416 U.S. 396 (1974)).
41. 467 U.S. at 32.

discovered, but not yet admitted, information are not a restriction on a traditionally public source of information."[42] In addition, the Court determined that Rule 26(c) furthers a substantial government interest unrelated to the suppression of expression. Discovery rules enable parties to obtain relevant information necessary to the preparation, settlement, or trial of a case.[43] By the same token, Justice Powell noted, they may be abused if litigants employ the discovery process and obtain and disseminate information harmful to the reputation and injurious to the privacy of litigants or third parties. "The prevention of the abuse that can attend the coerced production of information under a state's discovery rule is sufficient justification for the authorization of protective orders."[44] Moreover, the Court concluded, the trial judge "is in the best position to weigh fairly the competing needs and interests of parties affected by discovery. The unique character of the discovery process requires that the trial court have substantial latitude to fashion protective orders."[45]

§ 6-1(a)(3). Unfiled Discovery Materials.

In *Seattle Times Co.*, the Supreme Court rejected the claim that litigants have a First Amendment-based right to disclose materials obtained through civil discovery. Subsequent courts have concluded that this holding similarly forecloses a third party right of access to discovery materials,[46] though several courts have held that First Amendment considerations remain relevant.

---

42. *Id.* at 33.
43. See *id.* at 34-35.
44. *Id.* at 35-36.
45. *Id.* at 36.
46. In *Mokhiber v. Davis*, 537 A.2d 1100, 1111 (D.C. 1988), for example, the court held that "there is no public right of access under the first amendment, let alone at common law, to discovery materials as such." First, the court determined, "there exists no common law tradition of access to discovery materials as such." *Id.* at 1110. Second, the court concluded, "a general right to see discovery materials not only would fail to serve the purposes underlying the right of access to judicial proceedings but also would undermine the discovery process itself." *Id.* at 1111. See In re Alexander Grant & Co. Litig., 820 F.2d 352, 355 (11th Cir. 1987) (rejecting common law and First Amendment-based right of access); In re Reporters Comm. for Freedom of the Press, 773 F.2d 1325 (D.C. Cir. 1985) (rejecting First Amendment-based right of access to discovery documents prior to trial). In *United States v. $9,041,598.68*, 976 F. Supp. 654 (S.D. Tex. 1997), a civil forfeiture action, the court rejected a newspaper's request for access to sealed depositions of confidential informants. The court noted that "a deposition is not a proceeding that historically has been open to the public," and, if "access were to be mandated, the civil discovery process might actually be made more complicated and burdensome than it already is." *Id.* at 657-58. See Coalition Against Police Abuse v. Superior Ct., 216 Cal. Rptr. 614, 621 (Ct. App. 1985); Reed v. Zizka, 1998 Conn. Super. LEXIS 1522, at *9 (Conn. Super. May 29, 1998) (holding discovery is not a public component of a civil trial, so a "request to limit dissemination of discovery materials does not implicate the First Amendment"). See generally Comment, *The First Amendment and Pretrial Discovery Hearings: When Should the Public and Press Have Access?*, 36 UCLA L. REV. 609, 622-23 (1989).

In *Cipollone v. Liggett Group, Inc.*,[47] for example, the Third Circuit held that *Seattle Times Co.* prohibits a court "considering a protective order from concerning itself with first amendment considerations."[48] The court in *Cipollone* reasoned that, since the First Amendment was not implicated by the protective order, a heightened level of appellate review was inappropriate and the "clearly erroneous" standard applied.[49] In *Anderson v. Cryovac, Inc.*,[50] however, the First Circuit declined to follow *Cipollone*. While the court acknowledged that *Seattle Times Co.* had rejected strict scrutiny of protective orders, "the first amendment is still a presence in the review process. Protective discovery orders are subject to first amendment scrutiny, but that scrutiny must be made within the framework of Rule 26(c)'s requirement of good cause."[51] Nevertheless, the court held that protection of the defendant's right to a fair trial supplied the necessary "good cause" to justify the protective order at issue.[52]

Apart from the First Amendment, courts have generally recognized a common law right of access to judicial records and documents.[53] Unfiled discovery materials, however, are generally not considered "judicial records" and, as a result, no common law right — with its presumption of access — has been held to attach to unfiled discovery materials.[54] On the other hand, public and press

---

47. 785 F.2d 1108 (3d Cir. 1986), *cert. denied*, 484 U.S. 976 (1987). The plaintiffs sought damages from tobacco companies for failure to warn of the dangers of cigarette smoking. The defendants secured a blanket protective order from a federal magistrate, which was substantially modified by the district court. See *id.* at 1110.

48. *Id.* at 1119; see Worrell Newspapers of Indiana, Inc. v. Westhafer, 739 F.2d 1219, 1223-24 n.4 (7th Cir. 1984), *aff'd*, 469 U.S. 1200 (1985); Tavoulareas v. Washington Post Co., 737 F.2d 1170, 1172-73 (D.C. Cir. 1984) (en banc); see also Campbell, *The Protective Order in Products Liability Litigation: Safeguard or Misnomer?*, 31 B.C. L. REV. 771, 797-802 (1990).

49. 785 F.2d at 1120.

50. 805 F.2d 1 (1st Cir. 1986). The case arose from alleged contamination of a water supply by discharge of toxic chemicals. A blanket protective order covering three years of discovery had been issued. See *id.* at 3.

51. *Id.* at 7; see United States v. Microsoft Corp, 165 F.3d 952, 959-60 (D.C. Cir. 1999) ("As we understand [*Seattle Times*], the good cause standard of Rule 26(c) comports with the First Amendment not fortuitously but precisely because it takes into account all relevant interests, including those protected by the First Amendment"); Public Citizen v. Liggett Group, Inc., 858 F.2d 775, 780 (1st Cir. 1988), *cert. denied*, 488 U.S. 1030 (1989) ("Indeed, the Supreme Court has noted that parties have general first amendment freedoms with regard to information gained through discovery and that, absent a valid court order to the contrary, they are entitled to disseminate the information as they see fit. . . .").

52. See 805 F.2d at 12.

53. See Chap. 5-1 *supra* (discussing Nixon v. Warner Communications, Inc., 435 U.S. 589 (1978)).

54. See generally Campbell, *supra* note 48, at 803-04. Chief Justice Burger, concurring in *Gannett Co. v. DePasquale*, 443 U.S. 368, 396 (1979), noted that, "during the last 40 years in which the pretrial processes have been enormously expanded, it has never occurred to anyone, as far as I am aware, that a pretrial deposition or pretrial interrogatories were other than wholly private to the litigants." See Public Citizen v. Liggett Group, Inc., 858 F.2d at 788 (noting that the

efforts to obtain access to unfiled discovery materials pursuant to the Federal Rules of Civil Procedure have proven successful. In *In re Agent Orange Product Liability Litigation*,[55] the Second Circuit recognized a presumptive right of access to discovery materials based on Rules 26(c) and 5(d). The court reasoned that Rule 26(c)'s requirement that a party seeking a protective order demonstrate good cause establishes a corollary principle that, if good cause is not established, the material is not judicially protected and is open to the public.[56] Accordingly, the court concluded, a party seeking access can claim "a statutory right of access to the discovery materials in question."[57]

In addition, the requirement of good cause embodied in Rule 26(c) has operated to limit the use of broad protective orders. To establish good cause, the party seeking a protective order bears the burden of making a particularized

---

common law right to inspect discovery materials "has been largely foreclosed by the Supreme Court's decision in *Seattle Times Co. v. Rhinehart*"); In re Reporters Comm. for Freedom of the Press, 773 F.2d 1325 (D.C. Cir. 1985) (rejecting First Amendment-based right of access to depositions and discovery materials); Ferrara v. Detroit Free Press, Inc., 1997 U.S. Dist. LEXIS 22624, at *4 (E.D. Mich. Dec. 30, 1997) (upholding plaintiff's protective order against defendant's motion to reconsider, and stating defendant is not permitted to file "protected" documents [deposition testimony] in support of a summary judgment motion "thus making them public," thereby assuring that the "defendant not use the discovery process . . . for a non-litigation purpose"); West Virginia v. Moore, 902 F. Supp. 715 (S.D. W. Va. 1995) (concluding that depositions not filed with court are not "judicial documents" subject to right of public access); Mokhiber v. Davis, 537 A.2d 1100 (D.C. 1988) ("No court of record has extended the public right of access to pretrial depositions, interrogatories, and documents gained through discovery."); Kurtzman v. Hankin, 714 A.2d 450, 453 (Pa. Super. 1998) (permitting trial court order sealing discovery materials to stand because, "while there is a presumptive right of access to pleadings and proceedings, there is no presumptive right to discovery materials"); see also Jones v. Clinton, 12 F. Supp. 2d 931, 935, 938 (E.D. Ark. 1998) (denying motion to unseal videotapes of President's deposition in part because it was "not on file with the court" and did not constitute a judicial record to which a common law right of access attaches). But see Marisol A. v. Giuliani, 26 MEDIA L. REP. (BNA) 1151, 1153 (S.D.N.Y. 1997) (holding a report, submitted to but not filed with court, is a "judicial document" since it was ordered prepared by the court and "is likely to play a significant role in the determination of the litigants' substantive rights").

55. 821 F.2d 139 (2d Cir.), *cert. denied*, 484 U.S. 953 (1987).

56. See *id.* at 145; see also EEOC v. National Children's Center, Inc., 98 F.3d 1406, 1411 (D.C. Cir. 1996) (requiring district court on remand to "make a finding of whether 'good cause' exists for restricting" access to deposition transcripts); Tavoulareas v. Washington Post Co., 724 F.2d 1010, 1015 (D.C. Cir. 1984) ("A statutory presumption of openness for discovery materials, even those not used at trial, derives from the Federal Rules of Civil Procedure.").

57. 821 F.2d at 146; see Tavoulareas v. Washington Post Co., 724 F.2d at 1015 ("Simply stated, the Federal Rules of Civil Procedure and the Advisory Committee notes indicate that discovery proceedings are presumptively open unless otherwise ordered by the court."); see also United States v. Microsoft Corp., 165 F.3d 952, 954 (D.C. Cir. 1999) (granting public access to records and transcripts of all depositions taken in the antitrust lawsuit against Microsoft Corp., based on the Publicity in Taking Evidence Act of 1913, 15 U.S.C. § 30, which mandates public access to depositions taken for use "in any suit in equity brought by the United States under sections 1 to 7 [Title 15, U.S.C.]").

factual showing of *serious* potential harm and may not rely on conclusory statements or conjecture.[58] Under an umbrella order, in contrast, parties are often permitted to stipulate the confidentiality of broad categories of discovery material. Third parties, including consumer groups and the press, have been permitted to intervene in civil litigation to require that "good cause" for such orders be demonstrated.[59]

§ 6-1(a)(4). Filed Discovery Materials.

When discovery materials are filed in support of some requested judicial action, there is a much greater likelihood that the courts will recognize a presumptive right of public access. Many courts treat such materials as "judicial records" subject to a common law right of the public to inspect and copy them.[60] Indeed, some courts have even recognized a First Amendment-based right of access to such documents.[61] However, others have held that the document must in fact be consulted in adjudicating substantive legal rights in order to be considered a judicial record to which a presumption of public access attaches.[62] Further, the nature of the proceeding can affect the contours of the access right.

---

58. See H. HARE, J. GILBERT & W. REMINE, *supra* note 6, at 114 (citations omitted); see generally C. WRIGHT, A. MILLER & R. MARCUS, *supra* note 6, § 2035, at 264-66; Dore, *supra* note 3, at 371-83.

59. See, e.g., Public Citizen v. Liggett Group, Inc., 858 F.2d at 783-84; United States v. Criden, 675 F.2d 550, 552 n.2 (3d Cir. 1982); Savitt v. Vacco, 1996 U.S. Dist. LEXIS 16875 (N.D.N.Y. Nov. 8, 1996); Mokhiber v. Davis, 537 A.2d at 1113-15; Ballard v. Herzke, 924 S.W.2d 652 (Tenn. 1996).

60. See, e.g., FTC v. Standard Fin. Management Corp., 830 F.2d 404, 409 (1st Cir. 1987) ("[W]e rule that relevant documents which are submitted to, and accepted by, a court of competent jurisdiction in the course of adjudicatory proceedings, become documents to which the presumption of public access applies."); Zenith Radio Corp. v. Matsushita Elec. Indus. Co., 529 F. Supp. 866, 897 (E.D. Pa. 1981) (holding right of access attaches to materials filed with court); Pratt & Whitney Canada, Inc. v. United States, 14 Cl. Ct. 268, 273 (1988) ("The right of access applies to materials submitted to the court in civil adjudicatory proceedings."). See also Marisol A. v. Giuliani, 26 MEDIA L. REP. (BNA) 1151 (S.D.N.Y. 1997) (holding report, submitted to but not filed with court, is "judicial document" since it was ordered prepared by the court and "is likely to play a significant role in the determination of the litigants' substantive rights"); see generally Dore, *supra* note 3, at 371-83.

61. See, e.g., In re Continental Ill. Sec. Litig., 732 F.2d 1302, 1308, 1309 n.11 (7th Cir. 1984) (weighing First Amendment against confidentiality interests in determining whether to disclose a special litigation report filed with the court); Brown & Williamson Tobacco Corp. v. FTC, 710 F.2d 1165, 1177 (6th Cir. 1983), *cert. denied*, 465 U.S. 1110 (1984) (holding that the First Amendment and common law limit court's discretion to seal documents filed by FTC).

62. See, e.g., In re Policy Management Sys. Corp., 67 F.3d 296, 23 MEDIA L. REP. (BNA) 2486, 2489-90 (4th Cir. 1995); United States v. Amodeo, 44 F.3d 141, 145 (2d Cir. 1995); Anderson v. Cryovac, Inc., 805 F.2d 1, 12 (1st Cir. 1986); In re Perrigo Co., 128 F.3d 430, 440 (6th Cir. 1997) (noting that, if and when district court relies on report in rendering decision in stockholder's derivative action, it would become "judicial record").

Although there is contrary authority,[63] the filing of documents in support of motions associated with discovery has, standing alone, generally been held insufficient to create a right of access.[64] Nevertheless, discovered materials filed in proceedings that determine substantive legal claims generally trigger a presumptive right of access.[65]

When a discovered document is filed with the court accompanying a request for judicial action, the Third Circuit has held, the filing of "a document gives rise to a presumptive right of access"[66] because at that juncture the contents of the document are no longer simply a private matter.[67] Thus, the Third Circuit has concluded, settlement agreements and supporting documents filed with the court constitute public records subject to a presumptive right of access,[68] while those settlement agreements not so filed have been held to fall outside the presumption.[69] For the same reason, while trial exhibits are typically treated as judicial records to which a presumptive right of access attaches, when the litigation has ended and the documents have been returned to the party resisting disclosure, courts have held that they are no longer judicial records subject to a right of public access.[70]

Other federal circuits have rejected the Third Circuit's approach. In the Fourth Circuit, for example, "a document must play a relevant and useful role in the adjudication process in order for the common law right of public access to

---

63. See Mokhiber v. Davis, 537 A.2d at 1111 ("[T]he presumptive public right of access does apply to motions filed with the court concerning discovery, to evidence submitted with such motions including materials produced during discovery and to the court's dispositions, if any.").

64. See Anderson v. Cryovac, Inc., 805 F.2d at 13 ("History and logic lead us to conclude that there is no presumptive first amendment public right of access to documents submitted to a court in connection with discovery motions. Instead, the same good cause standard is to be applied that must be met for protective order in general."); see also United States v. $9,041,598.68, 976 F. Supp. 654 (S.D. Tex. 1997) (finding no public right of access to sealed deposition of confidential government informant who did not testify).

65. See Chap. 6-1(a)(1) *supra*.

66. Leucadia, Inc. v. Applied Extrusion Techs., Inc., 998 F.2d 157, 161-62 (3d Cir. 1993) ("Other courts have also recognized a principle that the filing of a document gives rise to a presumptive right of access."); see Republic of Philippines v. Westinghouse Elec. Corp., 949 F.2d 653, 660-62 (3d Cir. 1991) (finding papers filed in connection with motion for summary judgment are subject to presumptive right of access).

67. See In re Johnson, 598 N.E.2d 406, 410 (Ill. App. 1992) ("Once documents are filed with the court, they lose their private nature and become part of the court file and 'public components' of the judicial proceeding to which the right of access attaches.").

68. See Bank of Am. Nat'l Trust & Sav. Ass'n v. Hotel Rittenhouse Assocs., 800 F.2d 339, 344-45 (3d Cir. 1986).

69. See Pansy v. Borough of Stroudsburg, 23 F.3d at 781 (holding that because a confidential settlement agreement was not filed with, interpreted by, or enforced by the district court, it is not a judicial record "and the right of access doctrine cannot be a basis for the Newspaper to obtain access to the Agreement"); Enprotech Corp. v. Renda, 983 F.2d 17 (3d Cir. 1993).

70. See Littlejohn v. BIC Corp., 851 F.2d 673, 683 (3d Cir. 1988).

attach."[71] Similarly, the Second Circuit has held that a document must be "relevant to the performance of the judicial function and useful in the judicial process" to give rise to the presumptive right of access.[72] And, the First Circuit has adopted the same position, based on its conclusion that "courts have not extended [the common law access right] beyond materials on which the court relies in determining the litigants' substantive rights."[73]

The nature of the judicial proceeding in which discovery documents are submitted has also been deemed relevant in determining if a presumptive right of access attaches. Courts generally accept "that 'there is a strong presumption that material introduced into evidence at trial should be made' available for public access."[74] Thus, the right of access typically has been held to attach to deposition testimony admitted in evidence at trial and to other discovery material made part of the official record.[75] In *Poliquin v. Garden Way, Inc.*,[76] for example, the First Circuit vacated a trial court order issued following settlement, which prohibited disclosure of discovery materials that had been admitted in evidence at trial. The court held "that only the most compelling showing can justify post-trial restriction on disclosure of testimony or documents actually introduced at trial."[77] Judge Boudin, writing for the court, noted that the ordinary showing of good cause to prevent disclosure "cannot alone justify protecting such material

---

71. In re Policy Management Sys. Corp., 67 F.3d 296, 23 MEDIA L. REP. (BNA) 2486, 2489-90 (4th Cir. 1995) (citing United States v. Amodeo, 44 F.3d 141, 145 (2d Cir. 1995)); see also United States v. El-Sayegh, 131 F.3d 158, 163 (D.C. Cir. 1997) (holding that a proposed plea agreement filed solely for the purpose of having it sealed is not a judicial record and, citing civil precedent, stating: "We thus hold that what makes a document a judicial record and subjects it to the common law right of access is the role it plays in the adjudicatory process.").

72. United States v. Amodeo, 44 F.3d 141, 145 (2d Cir. 1995).

73. Anderson v. Cryovac, Inc., 805 F.2d at 13; see FTC v. Standard Fin. Management Corp., 830 F.2d 404, 410 (1st Cir. 1987); Wilk v. American Med. Ass'n, 635 F.2d 1295, 1299 n.7 (7th Cir. 1980) ("If the purpose of the common law right of access is to check judicial abuses then that right should only extend to materials upon which a judicial decision is based.") (citations omitted); see also Zenith Radio Corp. v. Matsushita Elec. Indus. Co., 529 F. Supp. 866, 901 (E.D. Pa. 1981) (holding that the right of access attaches to documents relied upon in judicial decision making, even if they have not been filed).

74. Littlejohn v. BIC Corp., 851 F.2d 673, 678 (3d Cir. 1988) (citing In re Nat'l Broadcasting Co. (Criden), 648 F.2d 814, 823 (3d Cir. 1981)); see Seattle Times Co. v. Rhinehart, 467 U.S. at 33.

75. Littlejohn v. BIC Corp., 851 F.2d at 683; see Greater Miami Baseball Club Ltd. Partnership v. Selig, 955 F. Supp. 37, 40 (S.D.N.Y. 1997) (holding deposition transcripts and exhibits made part of the trial record "are presumptively matters to which the public is entitled to access"); Burkes v. Klausner, 24 MEDIA L. REP. (BNA) 2276 (Wis. Cir. 1996).

76. 989 F.2d 527 (1st Cir. 1993). In *Poliquin*, the plaintiffs sought to disclose to the public discovery information regarding other accidents caused by defendant's product, which had been admitted in evidence. The trial court issued an order sealing all testimony and arguments made during trial that related to matters covered by a pretrial umbrella protective order. See *id.* at 530.

77. *Id.* at 533.

after it has been introduced at trial."[78] Once the material is introduced in evidence, it moves from being "presumptively private" to being "presumptively public."[79]

In *Rushford v. New Yorker Magazine*,[80] the Fourth Circuit determined that the same principle applies to documents attached as exhibits to a motion for summary judgment. The court began from the premise that, "[o]nce the documents are made part of a dispositive motion, such as a summary judgment motion, they lose their status as being 'raw fruits of discovery.'"[81] Since a summary judgment motion "adjudicates substantive rights and serves as a substitute for trial,"[82] the court concluded, documents filed in support of such a motion are subject to a presumption of public access under "the more rigorous First Amendment standard."[83] Accordingly, the court held, public access may be limited only on a showing "that the denial serves an important governmental interest and that there is no less restrictive way to serve that governmental interest."[84]

Other courts have applied the common law presumption of access to discovery documents filed in connection with a summary judgment motion.[85] The fact

---

78. *Id.*
79. *Id.*
80. 846 F.2d 249 (4th Cir. 1988).
81. *Id.* at 252 (quoting In re Agent Orange Prod. Liab. Litig., 98 F.R.D. 539, 544-45 (E.D.N.Y. 1983)). Such a motion puts the discovery materials "on a wholly different footing." 846 F.2d at 252. The Fourth Circuit subsequently held that the common law access right attaches only "when a court uses [discovery materials] in determining litigants' substantive rights." In re Policy Management Sys. Corp., 67 F.3d 296, 23 MEDIA L. REP. (BNA) 2486, 2490 (4th Cir. 1995); see In re Brand Name Prescription Drug Antitrust Litig., 1996 U.S. Dist. LEXIS 9838 (N.D. Ill. July 9, 1996).
82. 846 F.2d at 252.
83. *Id.*; see Stone v. University of Maryland Med. Sys. Corp., 948 F.2d 128, 131 (4th Cir. 1991) (recognizing First Amendment-based right of access to discoverable records of medical review proceedings which "have been filed with and considered by a court in connection with a dispositive motion like a motion for a summary judgment").
84. 846 F.2d at 252 (citing Globe Newspaper Co. v. Superior Ct., 457 U.S. 596, 606-07 (1982); see Publicker Indus. v. Cohen, 733 F.2d 1059, 1070 (3d Cir. 1984). The court also held that there must be public notice of the potential sealing, an opportunity for interested parties to be heard and, if closure is ordered, specific record findings, including stating reasons for rejecting alternatives to closure. See 846 F.2d at 253-54 (citing In re Knight Publ'g Co., 743 F.2d 231 (4th Cir. 1984)).
85. See, e.g., Grove Fresh Distribs. Inc. v. Everfresh Juice Co., 24 F.3d 893, 895 (7th Cir. 1994). On remand, the trial court cited the need to prevent disclosure of confidential material and adverse publicity, and the appellate court upheld the sealing of the case and issuance of the protective order. See also Grove Fresh Distribs. Inc. v. Everfresh Juice Co., 1998 U.S. App. LEXIS 1836 (7th Cir. Nov. 19, 1997); Joy v. North, 692 F.2d 880 (2d Cir. 1982), *cert. denied*, 460 U.S. 1051 (1983) ("documents used by the parties moving for, or opposing, summary judgment should not remain under seal absent the most compelling reasons"); In re Savitt/Adler Litig., 1997 WL 797511, at *2 (N.D.N.Y. Dec. 23, 1997), *modified*, 26 MEDIA L. REP. (BNA) 1882 (N.D.N.Y. 1998) (reaffirming the common law presumption of access to summary judgment documents established in *Joy v. North*, and requiring compelling reasons for the nondisclosure of materials used in

that the summary judgment motion fails, these courts have held, does not extinguish the access right because, as the court in *Republic of Philippines v. Westinghouse Electric Corp.*[86] noted, such a motion still "shaped the scope and substance of the litigation and put the litigants squarely on a path toward trial."[87] Similarly, a common law presumption of access has been recognized to a report, admitted into evidence, and relied on by the court in deciding a motion to terminate a shareholder derivative suit.[88]

In *In re Policy Management Systems Corp.*,[89] however, the Fourth Circuit rejected a presumptive right of access to discovery documents filed in support of a motion to dismiss. Unlike the summary judgment motion at issue in *Rushford*, the court noted, a motion to dismiss tests only the facial validity of the complaint and materials other than the pleadings are generally not relevant.[90] "Because [discovery] documents are not considered by the court, they do not serve as a substitute for a trial and are more akin to discovery materials."[91] The court concluded that, since the documents "do not play any role in the adjudicative process," they do not lose their status as discovery materials "and are therefore not subject to the First Amendment guarantee of access."[92] In addition, the court rejected a common law right of access to such documents on similar grounds: "Because the documents played no role in the court's adjudication of the motion to dismiss, we hold that the documents did not achieve the status of judicial documents to which the common law presumption of public access attaches."[93]

In one especially high-profile case, the district court in Paula Jones' sexual harassment action against President Clinton entered a confidentiality order with the consent of all parties limiting disclosure of discovery information and sealing filings dealing with discovery.[94] Media efforts to rescind the order failed,

---

arguing summary judgment motions). In *Ferrara v. Detroit Free Press, Inc.*, 1997 U.S. Dist. LEXIS 22624 (E.D. Mich. Dec. 30, 1997), the court denied defendant's motion to reconsider plaintiff's protective order to seal deposition testimony, stating defendant should "take the deposition and then determine whether or not, in presenting its defense, it believes that reference to the deposition in a motion for summary judgment is necessary." *Id.* at *4. Then, "defendant can supply the Court with an in camera copy of the deposition and inform the Court, *in camera*, what portions of the deposition it believes are necessary." *Id.*

86. 949 F.2d 653 (3d Cir. 1991).
87. *Id.* at 660.
88. See In re Continental Ill. Sec. Litig., 732 F.2d 1302, 1310 (7th Cir. 1984) ("We therefore find that all of the policies favoring public scrutiny of judicial decision-making apply to this case. Further, the presumption of access normally involves a right of contemporaneous access . . . .").
89. 67 F.3d 296, 23 MEDIA L. REP. (BNA) 2486 (4th Cir. 1995).
90. See *id.* at 2489.
91. *Id.*
92. *Id.*
93. *Id.* at 2490.
94. See Jones v. Clinton, 12 F. Supp. 2d 931, 932 (E.D. Ark. 1998).

primarily because of the court's expressed interest in ensuring a fair trial and protecting "the privacy interests of third-party witnesses."[95] After the media intervenors filed notice of appeal, but before the Eighth Circuit issued a decision, the district court granted the President's motion for summary judgment and dismissed the case.[96] Consequently, the Eighth Circuit dismissed the media appeal but remanded for the district court to consider whether the confidentiality order should be lifted.[97] "Because a significant part of the record relating to discovery has, in one form or another, been made public," and no trial in which "prejudicial pretrial publicity" threatened fairness was imminent, the district court largely vacated its confidentiality order.[98] But, the court kept its order in force with respect to the identities of "any Jane Does that may be revealed in the record," given the compelling privacy interests asserted by such witnesses, as well as videotapes of all depositions related to the suit.[99]

In response to the President's motion to reconsider, the court adopted a two-part test to determine whether discovery-related materials should be made publicly available: public access could neither "impact upon the parties' rights to a fair trial" nor "adversely affect the privacy interests of any Jane Does."[100] The court emphasized the absence of any common law presumption of access to the videotaped deposition, which it deemed not to be a judicial record, and asserted "a strong judicial tradition of proscribing public access to recordings of testimony given by a sitting President."[101] The transcripts of all depositions, redacted to protect Jane Does, were thereafter released.[102]

§ 6-1(a)(5). Competing Interests.

Even if a court rejects a presumptive right of public access to the fruits of civil discovery, *good cause* must nonetheless support the issuance and maintenance of a protective order. The party seeking such an order is typically required to provide a particular and specific demonstration of need for protection.[103] In

---

95. *Id.* at 933.
96. See Jones v. Clinton, 990 F. Supp. 657 (E.D. Ark. 1998).
97. See Jones v. Clinton, 138 F.3d 758 (8th Cir. 1998).
98. 12 F. Supp. 2d at 934-35.
99. *Id.*
100. *Id.*
101. *Id.* at 938 (quoting United States v. McDougal, 103 F.3d 651, 656-59 (8th Cir. 1996), *cert. denied*, 118 S. Ct. 49 (1997)).
102. 12 F. Supp. 2d at 938.
103. See Cipollone v. Liggett Group, Inc., 785 F.2d at 1121 ("[T]he party seeking the protective order must show good cause by demonstrating a particular need for protection. Broad allegations of harm, unsubstantiated by specific examples or unarticulated reasoning do not satisfy the rule 26(c) test."); Publicker Indus. v. Cohen, 733 F.2d 1059, 1071 (3d Cir. 1984) ("Good cause is established on a showing that disclosure will work a clearly defined and serious injury to the party seeking closure. The injury must be shown with specificity."); see also 8 C. WRIGHT, A. MILLER, & R.

assessing "good cause," courts will typically engage in interest balancing.[104] If a *common law* right of access attaches, the presumption of access will apply and weight the scales against the claim for confidentiality.[105] In *Nixon v. Warner Communications, Inc.*, the Supreme Court referenced the requirement of balancing, "however gauged."[106] The Second Circuit, in *United States v. Amodeo*, held that the strength of the presumption varies depending on the role played by the material at issue in the adjudicative process and its value to the public in moni-

---

MARCUS, *supra* note 5, § 2035, at 483-86. In *Wiggins v. Burge*, 173 F.R.D. 226, 228 (N.D. Ill. 1997) (quoting Jepson, Inc. v. Makita Elec. Works, Ltd., 30 F.3d 854, 858 (7th Cir. 1996) (quoting Public Citizen v. Liggett Group, Inc., 858 F.2d at 789)), a case involving allegations of torture at the hands of police, the court held that "even if the parties [voluntarily] agree that a protective order should be entered, they still have 'the burden of showing that good cause exists for the issuance of that order.'" Although the case was settled before trial, the court ruled that, notwithstanding a written agreement by the parties, discovery materials would not be sealed because a voluntary confidentiality agreement is not the same as a court finding of "good cause," and the party seeking that protection had not satisfied the burden of showing "good cause." See 30 F.3d 858.

104. See, e.g., Courier-Journal v. Marshall, 828 F.2d 361, 367 (6th Cir. 1987) (denying public access after balancing "the very limited right of access the press has to the presumptively nonpublic fruits of civil discovery" against the economic and social retribution threatened if lists of KKK members were disclosed); Wiggins v. Burge, 173 F.R.D. at 229 ("In deciding whether good cause exists, the district court must balance the interests involved: the harm to the party seeking the protective order and the importance of disclosure to the public."); In re Savitt/Adler Litig., 1997 WL 797511, at *3 (N.D.N.Y. Dec. 23, 1997), *modified*, 26 MEDIA L. REP. (BNA) 1882 (N.D.N.Y. 1998) (documents filed in support of a motion for summary judgment generally enjoy "a strong presumption of access," but information concerning the identity of public employees involved in employment actions that would not play a role in the court's Article III functions enjoys only a "relatively weak" presumption of access); Cooper Hosp. Univ. Med. Center v. Sullivan, 183 F.R.D. 135, 143 (D.N.J. 1998) ("In exercising its discretion, a District Court must balance a movant's interests in shielding the information from discovery against countervailing public interests."); United States v. $9,041,598.68, 976 F. Supp. 654, 658-59 (S.D. Tex. 1997) (finding sufficient "good cause" exists for protective order preventing access to deposition of government's confidential informant who did not testify in civil forfeiture action, given legitimate concern for safety of informants and progress of government's ongoing criminal investigation).

In *County Council v. SHL Systemhouse Corp.*, 182 F.R.D. 161, 162 (E.D. Pa. 1998) (citing Glenmede Trust Co. v. Thompson, 56 F.3d 476, 483 (3d Cir. 1995)), the court enumerated several factors to be considered "to determine whether good cause has been shown," including: "1) whether disclosure will violate any privacy interests; 2) whether the information is being sought for a legitimate purpose or for an improper purpose; 3) whether disclosure of the information will cause a party embarrassment; 4) whether confidentiality is being sought over information important to public health and safety; 5) whether the sharing of information among litigants will promote fairness and efficiency; 6) whether a party benefiting from the order of confidentiality is a public entity or official; and 7) whether the case involves issues important to the public."

105. See, e.g., Bank of Am. Nat'l Trust & Sav. Ass'n v. Hotel Rittenhouse Assocs., 800 F.2d 339, 344 (3d Cir. 1986) (noting "the strong common law presumption of access must be balanced against the factors militating against access"); Johnson v. Greater Southeast Community Hosp. Corp., 951 F.2d 1268, 1277 n.14 (D.C. Cir. 1991).

106. 435 U.S. at 602; see Chap. 5-1 *supra*.

§ 6-1(a)(5) NEWSGATHERING AND THE LAW § 6-1(a)(5)

toring the courts.[107] But, if a *First Amendment-based* right of access attaches, an even more demanding standard will typically be applied.[108] All these approaches, however, involve some degree of interest balancing.

Several competing interests have been arrayed against the right of public access.[109] Rule 26(c) expressly indicates that the need to protect trade secrets and

---

107. 71 F.3d 1044, 1049 (2d Cir. 1995); see In re Savitt/Adler Litig., 1997 WL 797511, at *3 (N.D.N.Y. Dec. 23, 1997), *modified*, 26 MEDIA L. REP. (BNA) 1882 (N.D.N.Y. 1998) (applying *Amodeo*, the court held that documents filed in connection with a motion for summary judgment generally enjoy "a strong presumption of access," but noting that information in the documents concerning the identity of public employees involved in employment actions that would not play a role in the court's Article III functions would enjoy only a "relatively weak" presumption of access); In re NASDAQ Market-Makers Antitrust Litig., 164 F.R.D. 346 (S.D.N.Y. 1996).

108. See, e.g., In re Continental Ill. Sec. Litig., 732 F.2d 1302, 1314 (7th Cir. 1984) (holding that First Amendment concerns should not be taken lightly and can only be overridden by "exceptional circumstances" requiring confidentiality). In *In re Savitt/Adler Litigation*, 1997 WL 797511, at *4 (N.D.N.Y. Dec. 23, 1997), *modified*, 26 MEDIA L. REP. (BNA) 1882 (N.D.N.Y. 1998), the court noted that neither the Second Circuit nor the Supreme Court has recognized a First Amendment-based right of access to documents filed in civil cases. Assuming that such a First Amendment-based right to submissions made in connection with a summary judgment motion exists, the court applied a balancing test similar to that employed to adjudicate claims of access to documents filed in support of *criminal* pretrial suppression motions. See *id*. at *3-4 (documents can be sealed "if specific, on the record findings established that closure is essential to preserve higher values and is narrowly tailored to serve that interest"). The documents in question were made publicly available but with names and identifying information redacted to protect the privacy interests of third parties. See *id*. at *3. But see Anderson v. Cryovac, Inc., 805 F.2d 1, 6 (1st Cir. 1986) (holding that, though First Amendment considerations apply, strict or heightened scrutiny is not the applicable standard).

109. See F. HARE, J. GILBERT & W. REMINE, *supra* note 6, at 115 n.8 (ranking the competing interests: "(1) national security; (2) constitutional rights; (3) trade secrets; (4) adverse publicity; (5) and annoyance"); Miller, *supra* note 5, at 463-97 (examining the values served by confidentiality and the potential harm of presumptive public access); note 104, *supra*.

In *Barron v. Florida Freedom Newspapers, Inc.*, 531 So. 2d 113, 118 (Fla. 1988), the Florida Supreme Court identified several interests that might, under particular circumstances, outweigh the right of public access:

> (a) to comply with established public policy set forth in the constitution, statutes, rules, or case law; (b) to protect trade secrets; (c) to protect a compelling governmental interest [e.g., national security; confidential informants]; (d) to obtain evidence to properly determine legal issues in a case; (e) to avoid substantial injury to innocent third parties [e.g., to protect young witnesses from offensive testimony; to protect children in a divorce]; or (f) to avoid substantial injury to a party by disclosure of matters protected by common law or privacy right not generally inherent in the specific type of civil proceeding sought to be closed.

And, in *Holland v. Eads*, 614 So. 2d 1012, 1016 (Ala. 1993), the Alabama Supreme Court required written findings that the party seeking to seal records had proven, by clear and convincing evidence, that the information: "(1) constitutes a trade secret or other confidential commercial research or information; (2) is a matter of national security; (3) promotes scandal or defamation; 4) pertains to wholly private family matters, such as divorce, child custody, or adoption; (5) poses a serious threat of harassment, exploitation, physical intrusion, or other particularized harm to the

proprietary information from disclosure may justify a protective order of some dimension.[110] Courts have regularly entered protective orders to safeguard a party's legitimate trade secrets from public disclosure.[111] Some courts have held, however, that "non-trade secret but confidential business information is not entitled to the same level of protection from disclosure as trade secret protection."[112] Moreover, the burden of proof is on the party seeking the protective

---

parties to the action; or (6) poses the potential for harm to third persons not parties to the litigation."

110. See FED. R. CIV. P. 26(c) ("[U]pon motion by a party or by the person from whom discovery is sought, ... and for good cause shown, the court ... may make any order which justice requires ... (7) that a trade secret or other confidential research, development or commercial information not be revealed or be revealed only in a designated way."); see also Kamyr A.B. v. Kamyr, Inc., 20 MEDIA L. REP. (BNA) 1969 (N.D.N.Y. 1992) (upholding trial court's finding of good cause and issuance of a protective order based on evidence that disclosure of sensitive proprietary materials would have a "detrimental effect" on parties' market positions). But see Musicom Int'l, Inc. v. Serubo, 22 MEDIA L. REP. (BNA) 2507 (E.D. Pa. 1994) (holding parties' stipulation to the need for a protective order "failed to show with specificity that disclosure would cause a defined and serious injury" and was insufficient to establish good cause). Cf. Oregon ex rel. Sports Management News, Inc. v. Nachtigal, 921 P.2d 1304 (Or. 1996) (holding the injunction provisions of Oregon Trade Secret Act violate state constitution). See generally Comment, *supra* note 5 (arguing that protective orders may be enforced by enjoining publication in limited circumstances to protect property interest in information).

111. See Nixon v. Warner Communications, Inc., 435 U.S. at 598 (stating "[c]ourts have refused to permit their files to serve as ... sources of business information that might harm a litigant's competitive standing"); Carpenter v. United States, 484 U.S. 19, 26 (1987) (stating that "[c]onfidential information ... is a species of property to which the corporation has the exclusive right and benefit"); Leucadia, Inc. v. Applied Extrusion Techs., Inc., 998 F.2d 157, 166 (3d Cir. 1993) ("Documents containing trade secrets or other confidential business information may be protected from disclosure."); Republic of Philippines v. Westinghouse Elec. Corp., 949 F.2d at 663 ("The potential effects of the disclosure of business information that might harm the litigant's competitive standing may in some cases meet the burden of [keeping] the judicial record under seal."); County Council v. SHL Systemhouse Corp., 182 F.R.D. 163-64 (E.D. Pa. 1998) (entering confidentiality order to protect "technical equipment specifications not publicly available ... and non-public personnel and recruiting files" upon defendant corporation's showing that it would suffer a "grave competitive disadvantage" if the information were disclosed); Wolhar v. General Motors Corp., 712 A.2d 464 (Del. Super. 1997) (holding that a report designated "confidential" or "proprietary" by company detailing litigation problems arising from seat back failures in vehicles was subject to protective order agreed to by parties). See generally Adolph, *Trade Secrets: An Update on the Impact of State and Federal Efforts to Broaden the Public Right of Access to Court Records,* 23 AM. INTELL. PROP. L. ASS'N L.Q. 161 (1995); Eckstein, *Can Products Liability Cases Be Secret?*, 20 LITIG. 22 (Spring 1994); but see Bone, *A New Look at Trade Secret Law: Doctrine in Search of Justification,* 86 CAL. L. REV. 241 (1998) (critically examining policy justifications for trade secret law and arguing that courts should independently base any liability for breach of secrecy safeguards on contract law).

112. Littlejohn v. BIC Corp., 851 F.2d 673, 685 (3d Cir. 1988). In *Littlejohn,* the court held that the district court did not abuse its discretion in holding that the presumption of public access outweighed a litigant's interest in the continued confidentiality of exhibits and deposition testimony admitted in evidence. See *id.* But see In re Orion Pictures Corp., 21 F.3d 24, 27 (2d Cir.

order.[113]

Rule 26(c) also indicates that protective orders may be entered to protect a party "from annoyance, embarrassment, oppression, or undue burden or expense."[114] Courts are often reluctant to find good cause or to override a right of access based on generalized corporate interests in reputation or potential embarrassment. In *Cipollone v. Liggett Group, Inc.*,[115] a products liability suit against tobacco companies, the Third Circuit asserted that "an applicant for a protective order whose chief concern is embarrassment must demonstrate that the embarrassment will be particularly serious."[116] Instead, the court required a showing of competitive or financial harm. As the court indicated in a subsequent case, *Glenmede Trust Co. v. Thompson*:[117] a "[g]eneral allegation of injury to reputation and client relationships or embarrassment that may result from dissemination of privileged documents is insufficient to justify endorsement of an umbrella confidentiality order."[118]

1994) (holding "good cause" is not required to issue a sealing order pursuant to Bankruptcy Code § 107(b), which authorizes court to protect "confidential" and "commercial" information).

113. See Cipollone v. Liggett Group, Inc., 785 F.2d at 1121; Leucadia, Inc. v. Applied Extrusion Techs., Inc., 998 F.2d at 166-67 (holding that the district court erred in placing burden on challenger to provide "a sufficient reason to discover the documents under seal"); County Council v. SHL Sys. Corp., 182 F.R.D. 161, 163 (E.D. Pa. 1998) (holding that defendant corporation which provided 911 services for county did not meet its "burden of demonstrating the need for protection" against disclosure of information regarding its profits and profit margin, costs, pricing, staffing analyses, and project management plans and techniques, when balanced against plaintiff County's argument that "911 services are at the heart of public health and safety" and the citizens of the county, who are paying for the services, have a "right to know").

114. FED. R. CIV. P. 26(c). See generally F. HARE, J. GILBERT & W. REMINE, *supra* note 6, at 135-37.

115. 785 F.2d 1108 (3d Cir. 1986), *cert. denied*, 484 U.S. 976 (1987).

116. *Id.* at 1121; see Brown & Williamson Tobacco Corp. v. FTC, 710 F.2d 1165, 1179 (6th Cir. 1983), *cert. denied*, 465 U.S. 1100 (1984); Joy v. North, 692 F.2d 880, 894 (2d Cir. 1982), *cert. denied*, 460 U.S. 1051 (1983) (holding that claims of reputational injury fell "woefully short" of justifying nondisclosure); But see Reed v. Zizka, 1998 Conn. Super. LEXIS 1522, at *9-10 (Conn. Super. May 29, 1998) (granting a protective order to prohibit "public disclosure of discovery materials" in a damages action against a church arising from charges of sexual abuse against a priest, emphasizing the inflammatory nature of the allegations, considerations of defendants' "reasonable privacy interest," potential "injury to [defendants'] professional standing," and the minimal interference the order would have on plaintiffs' ability to prepare their cases).

117. 56 F.3d 476 (3d Cir. 1995).

118. *Id.* at 484. See Cooper Hosp. Univ. Med. Center v. Sullivan, 183 F.R.D. 135, 143-45 (D.N.J. 1998) (holding "broad allegations of possible harm" resulting from the disclosure of particular documents to the public failed to meet the "requisite level of specificity" and were insufficient to demonstrate "good cause" for a protective order); Marisol A. v. Giuliani, 26 MEDIA L. REP. (BNA) 1151, 1154-55 (S.D.N.Y. 1997) (holding possible negative publicity, prejudice and misunderstanding resulting from disclosure of report subject to strong presumption of access is insufficient to justify protective order).

§ 6-1(a)(5) ACCESS TO JUDICIAL RECORDS: CIVIL PROCEEDINGS § 6-1(a)(5)

Privacy interests are not specifically mentioned in Rule 26(c). But, in *Seattle Times Co. v. Rhinehart*, the Supreme Court noted that protection of privacy is "implicit in the broad purpose and language" of the rule.[119] Other interests have been urged in support of protective orders as well.[120] The mere presence of a competing interest, of course, only begins the inquiry. The court must still determine if, under the circumstances of the case, it warrants subordinating the right of access. In *Davis v. East Baton Rouge Parish School District*,[121] for example, a school board argued that a confidentiality order was necessary to allow it to formulate a desegregation plan. But, the Fifth Circuit concluded, the sweeping order entered by the district court, even if it would arguably facilitate formulation of a plan, "intrudes severely upon the news agencies' First Amendment right to gather the news and receive speech and it is not justified by protection of any countervailing governmental interest or individual rights."[122] Similarly, in *Republic of Philippines v. Westinghouse Electric Corp.*,[123] the

---

119. 467 U.S. at 35 n.21; see In re Am. Tobacco Co., 880 F.2d 1520, 1530 (2d Cir. 1989) (protecting privacy interest of patients involved in research); In re Alexander Grant & Co. Litig., 820 F.2d 352, 355 (11th Cir. 1987) ("[P]rivate litigants have protectable privacy interests in confidential information disclosed through discovery."); Jones v. Clinton, 12 F. Supp. 2d 931, 934-35 (E.D. Ark. 1998) (finding that the protection of privacy interests involving the identities of possible Jane Does is good cause under Federal Rule 26(c) to maintain an order sealing discovery filings in a civil suit against President Clinton); In re Savitt/Adler Litig., 1997 WL 797511, at *3 (N.D.N.Y. Dec. 23, 1997), *modified*, 26 MEDIA L. REP. (BNA) 1882 (N.D.N.Y. 1998) (balancing the privacy interests of "innocent third parties" against the common law presumption of access, the court determined that the employment histories of public employees and their references are "traditionally considered private," and that redaction of names and identifying details would serve such privacy interests while permitting the public and press to assess the basis for the court's ruling on the summary judgment motion).

120. See, e.g., Littlejohn v. BIC Corp., 851 F.2d 673, 685 (3d Cir. 1988) (preservation of corporate reputation); Courier-Journal v. Marshall, 828 F.2d 361, 367 (6th Cir. 1987) (protection of associational privacy rights of non-parties); In re Continental Ill. Sec. Litig., 732 F.2d 1302, 1313 (7th Cir. 1984) (interests in attorney-client privilege, work product immunity, and effective functioning of special litigation committee); In re Am. Continental Corp. Litig., 18 MEDIA L. REP. (BNA) 2303 (D. Ariz. 1991) (administrative burdens and an impeding of progress of case towards trial); Jochims v. Isuzu Motors, Ltd., 151 F.R.D. 338, 342 (S.D. Iowa 1993) (interest in the efficiency of the discovery process and the "efficient administration of justice").

121. 78 F.3d 920, 923 (5th Cir. 1996).

122. *Id.* at 929; see Wiggins v. Burge, 173 F.R.D. 226, 230 (N.D. Ill. 1997) ("The defendants have not shown that the privacy interest of the police officers, the alleged chilling effect to internal investigations and the possibility of false allegations outweigh the significant public interest in the disclosure of these documents. The public has a right to know whether allegations of police torture are appropriately investigated and resolved by the City of Chicago."). But see Marcus v. St. Tammany Parish Sch. Bd., 1997 U.S. Dist. LEXIS 8380 (E.D. La. 1997) (holding that a protective order is not a prior restraint and is "narrowly drafted, only deeming confidential the parties' sexual and medical histories" since it "protects a compelling interest, here the parties' privacy interest in not having their sexual or medical histories promulgated in open court and in the press").

123. 949 F.2d 653 (3d Cir. 1991).

public's interest in learning about alleged bribes paid by a major American corporation to a foreign leader was deemed to be of sufficient public interest to override the corporate claim of serious competitive harm.

§ 6-1(a)(6). Law Reform.

Between 1985 and 1995, twenty-one legal restrictions on the use of sealing orders in civil litigation were adopted by sixteen states.[124] One of the earliest and most sweeping reforms was Texas Rule of Civil Procedure 76a, adopted by the Texas Supreme Court in 1990.[125] The Rule declares that "court records . . . are presumed to be open to the general public."[126] A movant seeking to seal court records must establish, by a preponderance of the evidence, "(a) a specific, serious and substantial interest which clearly outweighs: (1) this presumption of openness; (2) any probable adverse effect that sealing will have upon the general public health or safety; [and that] (b) no less restrictive means than sealing records will adequately and effectively protect the specific interest asserted."[127] This presumptive right of access is enhanced by a broad definition of "court records," which extends to unfiled discovery materials "concerning matters that have a probable adverse effect upon the general public health or safety."[128]

In addition, the Rule's substantive protections are enhanced by procedural safeguards. The party seeking a sealing order must file a written motion, schedule a public hearing, and post a public notice.[129] Nonparties to the litigation

---

124. Roscoe Pound Foundation, *New Jersey, Louisiana Continue National Trend Against Court Secrecy*, 2 CIV. JUST. DIG. 1, 2 (1995). See, e.g., Hammock v. Hoffmann-LaRoche, Inc., 662 A.2d 546, 559 (N.J. 1995). See generally Dore, *supra* note 3, at 309-16; Roscoe Pound Foundation, *Overview of State Anti-Secrecy Measures*, 2 CIV. JUST. DIG. 5 (1995); Basinski, *"Sunshine" Laws Bar Secret Settlement*, NAT'L L.J., March 24, 1997, at B10; Rosen, *Confidentiality Agreements Become Increasingly Elusive*, NAT'L L.J., July 20, 1998, at B7.

125. See generally Doggett & Muchetti, *Public Access to Public Courts: Discouraging Secrecy in the Public Interest*, 69 TEX. L. REV. 643 (1991).

126. TEX. R. CIV. P. 76a(1).

127. *Id*. See Upjohn Co. v. Freeman, 906 S.W.2d 92, 95 (Tex. App. 1995) (finding right of access to unfiled discovery documents that "have a probable adverse effect upon the general public health or safety").

128. TEX. R. CIV. P. 76a(2)(c). An exception is made for discovery involving "bona fide trade secrets or other intangible property rights." *Id.* "Civil records" is defined, with listed exceptions, to include "all documents of any nature filed in connection with any matter before any civil court." TEX. R. CIV. P. 76a(2)(a). Nonfiled settlement agreements concerning matters having a probable adverse effect on the general public health or safety are also subject to the access right. See TEX. R. CIV. P. 76a(2)(b); see also General Tire, Inc. v. Kepple, 970 S.W.2d 520 (Tex. 1998) (holding that court erred in determining that unfiled discovery documents were "court records" under Rule 76a, and in allowing intervenors access to these documents before a determination that they constituted "court records").

129. See TEX. R. CIV. P. 76a(3), 76(a)(4).

are afforded a right to intervene.[130] Sealing orders must be written, providing specific justification for sealing and specifying its duration.[131]

Shortly after promulgation of the Texas rule, Florida enacted a Sunshine in Litigation Act directed against secrecy involving "public hazards" dangerous to health or safety.[132] Orders sealing court files in cases involving such hazards are restricted and agreements to conceal such dangers are unenforceable.[133] The public and the news media (i.e., any "substantially affected person") are authorized to enforce the access rights created by the Act.[134] Louisiana has adopted legislation modeled on the Florida statute, which is designed to provide public access to analogous information, "unless such information or material is a trade secret or other confidential research, development or commercial information."[135]

Less sweeping legislation has been enacted in Arkansas,[136] Connecticut,[137] Kentucky,[138] Nevada,[139] North Carolina,[140] Oregon,[141] Virginia,[142] and Washington.[143] Court rules have been revised to limit the permissible scope of secrecy in

---

130. See TEX. R. CIV. P. 76a(3); TEX. R. CIV. P. 76a(7) (recognizing a right to intervene "at any time before or after judgment to seal or unseal court records").

131. See TEX. R. CIV. P. 76a(6).

132. See FLA. STAT. § 69.081.

133. See id. § 69.081(4).

134. See id. § 69.081(6).

135. LA. CODE CIV. PROC. ANN. art. 1426(D).

136. ARK. CODE ANN. §§ 25-18-401–25-18-403 limit the ability of state officials to conceal settlement agreements. Section 16-55-122 invalidates any provision of a settlement agreement that restricts disclosure of environmental hazards.

137. CONN. SUPER. CT. R. 11-20 requires public access unless the court determines a protective order "is necessary to preserve an interest which is determined to override the public's interest . . . in viewing such materials." See Sabanosh v. Durant, 1997 WL 804871, at *1 (Conn. Super. Dec. 17, 1997) (holding that rule creates a "strong presumption against allowing the sealing of files").

138. KY. REV. STAT. ANN. § 224.10-210 provides for access to executive branch information useful in enforcing pollution control laws.

139. NEV. REV. STAT. § 41.0385 makes information concerning tort claims against state agencies and local governments a "public record."

140. N.C. GEN. STAT. § 132-1.3 limits the ability of state officials to enter into confidential settlement agreements.

141. OR. REV. STAT. § 30.402 provides enhanced access to certain settlement agreements.

142. VA. CODE ANN. § 8.01-420.01 permits attorneys to share discovered information in personal injury or wrongful death actions with court permission if the receiving attorneys agree to be bound by protective orders.

143. WASH. REV. CODE § 4.24.601 is a more limited version of the Florida legislation. A 1994 statute requires that courts issue confidentiality orders only after determining that it is in the public interest to do so. See id. § 4.24.611.

San Diego[144] and San Francisco[145] counties in California, and also in Delaware,[146] Georgia,[147] Idaho,[148] Michigan,[149] New Jersey,[150] and New York.[151]

Proposed revisions to Federal Rule of Civil Procedure 26(c) have produced ongoing controversy.[152] On one front, Senator Herbert Kohl has introduced legislation designed to require courts deciding motions for protective orders to consider public health and safety interests.[153] On another, the Judicial Conference has considered proposals that would authorize judges to issue protective orders on request of the parties, absent "good cause," unless a *party* objects.[154] Another proposal identifies factors to be considered by a judge in reviewing a request by a litigant or third party for access, including reliance by the parties on the existing order and any risk to public health and safety.[155]

§ 6-1(b). Settlement Agreements.

When parties settle a civil case, it is common practice to include a confidentiality provision in the settlement agreement. Indeed, the willingness of one party to settle is often conditioned upon the acceptance of such a commitment to secrecy. The confidentiality provision may cover the settlement agreement itself

---

144. SAN DIEGO COUNTY SUPER. CT. R., Div. II, Rule 6.9 establishes a policy disfavoring confidentiality agreements and protective orders. A protective order is authorized only if there is a recognized right to secrecy, disclosure would cause harm, and the order is in the public interest.

145. SAN FRANCISCO COUNTY SUPER. CT. R. 6.10 disfavors protective orders.

146. DEL. SUPER. CT. CIV. PROC. R. 5(g) and DEL. CHANCERY CT. R. 5(g) establish a presumption in favor of public access. See Wolhar v. General Motors Corp., 712 A.2d 464, 466 (Del. Super. 1997) (holding that a court can modify a protective order if it finds that disclosure will not prejudice the original parties' rights).

147. GA. UNIF. SUP. CT. R. 21 establishes that court records are public and requires finding that privacy interests outweigh the public interest in access before secrecy may be imposed.

148. IDAHO CT. ADMIN. R. 32 identifies the following countervailing interests that will justify nondisclosure: embarrassing facts, potentially libelous material, economic harm, and individual safety.

149. MICH. CT. R. 8.105D, based on the New York and Texas rules, makes court records presumptively open.

150. N.J. CT. R. 1:2-1 & 4:10-3 were interpreted to establish a broad presumption of access in *Hammock v. Hoffmann-LaRoche, Inc.*, 662 A.2d 546, 546 (N.J. 1995).

151. N.Y. COMP. CODES R. & REGS. tit. 22, § 216 defines "good cause" for sealing court files as part of a settlement to require judicial consideration of the interests of the public as well as of the parties.

152. See generally Dore, *supra* note 3, at 339-44; Vangelisti, *Proposed Amendment to Federal Rule of Civil Procedure 26(c) Concerning Protective Orders: A Critical Analysis of What It Means and How It Operates*, 48 BAYLOR L. REV. 163 (1996).

153. See Dore, *supra* note 3, at 311; *Open-Documents Bill Wins Support*, Legal Times, July 4, 1994, at 16; *Senator Takes Aim at Secret Court Settlements*, LEGAL TIMES, May 2, 1994, at 1.

154. See News Notes, *Revised Protective Order Rule Would Allow Stipulations*, 23 MEDIA L. REP. (BNA), Aug. 1, 1995; *Secrecy Dispute Heats Up*, LEGAL TIMES, Feb. 26, 1996, at 6.

155. See, e.g., *Secrecy Dispute Heats Up*, LEGAL TIMES, Feb. 26, 1996, at 6.

as well as other documents, records, and information connected with the litigation. The parties may well file the settlement agreement with the court and seek a court order sealing the file or prohibiting public disclosure of information contained in it. The confidentiality order may place the entire court file in the litigation under a seal.[156] A court order opens the door to invocation of the court's contempt power, rather than merely an action for breach of contract, to enforce the confidentiality agreement. "[T]he widespread and increasing use of confidentiality orders by district courts to facilitate settlements and the consequential sacrifice of public access to the information deemed confidential by such orders" have, not surprisingly, become the subject of litigation themselves.[157]

In *Bank of America National Trust & Savings Association v. Hotel Rittenhouse Associates*,[158] the Third Circuit concluded that the parties' use of the courts to enforce the terms of a settlement agreement altered the ordinary presumption of secrecy inherent in such agreements. "Having undertaken to utilize the judicial process to interpret the settlement and to enforce it, the parties are no longer entitled to invoke the confidentiality ordinarily accorded settlement agreements. Once a settlement is filed in the district court, it becomes a judicial record, and subject to the access accorded such records."[159] Public access to filed

---

156. See Luban, *Settlements and the Erosion of the Public Realm*, 83 GEO. L.J. 2619 (1995) (criticizing the secrecy of settlements); Note, *Sealed v. Sealed: A Public Court System Going Secretly Private*, 6 J.L. & POL'Y, 381, 382 (1990) ("Unfortunately, the incidence of secrecy in the judicial process appears to be on the rise, particularly in the complex litigation area. Equally disturbing is the trend for a party to condition any pretrial settlement on the court's granting a total sealing order covering all materials in the court's possession.").

157. Pansy v. Borough of Stroudsburg, 23 F.3d 772, 775 (3d Cir. 1994); see *id.* at 785-86 ("Because defendants request orders of confidentiality as a condition of settlement, courts are willing to grant these requests in an effort to facilitate settlement without sufficiently inquiring into the potential public interest in obtaining information concerning the settlement agreement."); Brown v. Advantage Eng'g Inc., 960 F.2d 1013, 1017 (11th Cir. 1992) (Edmondson, J., dissenting) ("Allowing private parties in civil litigation in federal court to seal the terms of their settlements and other parts of pretrial records significantly promotes voluntary settlements in some cases."); see also Zielke v. Wagner, 684 N.E.2d 1095 (Ill. App. 1997) ("[W]here a protective order is challenged on appeal as an unconstitutional 'prior restraint,' [the standard of review is] abuse of discretion such that the court acted arbitrarily without employment of conscientious judgment and ignored principles of law so that substantial prejudice resulted."). See generally Dore, *supra* note 3, at 384-401.

158. 800 F.2d 339 (3d Cir. 1986).

159. *Id.* at 345; see *id.* at 343 ("[A] motion or a settlement agreement filed with the court is a public component of a civil trial.... It follows ... that the common law presumption of access applies to motions filed in court proceedings and to the settlement agreement ... which [the parties] filed and submitted to the district court for approval."). In *Copley Press, Inc. v. Superior Court*, 74 Cal. Rptr. 2d 69, 74 (Ct. App. 1998), the court quoted from *Estate of Hearst*, 136 Cal. Rptr. 821, 824 (Ct. App. 1977): "'[W]hen individuals employ the public powers of state courts to accomplish private ends ... they do so in full knowledge of the possibly disadvantageous circumstance that the documents and records filed ... will be open to public inspection.'" The

settlement agreements, the court concluded, promotes "informed discussion of governmental affairs" by educating the public, providing it with a "perception of fairness" of the judicial system, and by serving as "a check on the integrity of the judicial process."[160]

As a result, the Third Circuit in *Hotel Rittenhouse Associates* recognized a "strong presumption of access"[161] to such settlement agreements. While acknowledging "the strong public interest in encouraging settlement of private litigation,"[162] the court concluded that "the generalized interest in encouraging settlements does not rise to the level of interests that we have recognized may outweigh the public's common law right of access."[163]

---

court unsealed court records disclosing the amount of a settlement paid to a student who had been sexually assaulted, because the student and the school district had "sought judicial approval and protection" for the settlement, and the interposition of an insurance carrier "[did] not make the claim private and the District counsel approved the settlement." 74 Cal. Rptr. 2d at 74. See Brown v. Advantage Eng'g, Inc., 960 F.2d 1013, 1016 (11th Cir. 1992) ("Once a matter is brought before a court for resolution, it is no longer solely the parties' case, but also the public's case."). But see Savannah College of Art & Design v. School of Visual Arts, Inc., 515 S.E.2d 370, 371 (Ga. 1999) (trial court abused its discretion in unsealing filed settlement documents since presumption of access created by court rule may be overcome by showing that "'the harm otherwise resulting to the privacy of a person in interest clearly outweighs the public interest'") (citation omitted); Dore, *supra* note 3, at 401 ("Even court-sponsored or filed settlements carry little to no presumption of public access. A court can and should, however, exert significant discretion when asked to convert a confidentiality agreement into a court order.").

160. 800 F.2d at 345 (citing United States v. Smith, 787 F.2d 111, 114 (3d Cir. 1986); Wilson v. American Motors Corp., 759 F.2d 1568, 1571 (11th Cir. 1985)); see Copley Press, Inc. v. Superior Ct., 74 Cal. Rptr. 2d at 72 ("Public policy requires public records and documents to be available for public inspection to prevent secrecy in public affairs.... [T]he public has a legitimate interest in knowing how public funds are spent and how claims (formal or informal) against public entities are settled.").

161. 800 F.2d at 346. "In *Criden I*, we held the strong common law presumption of access must be balanced against the factors militating against access.... The burden is on the party who seeks to overcome the presumption of access to show that the interest in secrecy outweighs the presumption." *Id.* at 344 (citing In re Nat'l Broadcasting Co. (Criden), 648 F.2d 814, 818 (3d Cir. 1981); United States v. Criden, 681 F.2d 919, 921 (3d Cir. 1982)); see Copley Press, Inc. v. Superior Ct., 74 Cal. Rptr. 2d at 72-73 ("Court records are available to the public in general, including news reporters, unless a specific exception makes specific records nonpublic.... The burden rests on the party seeking to deny public access to court records to establish compelling reasons why and to what extent the records should be made private.").

162. 800 F.2d at 344.

163. *Id.* at 346; see Arkansas Best Corp. v. General Elec. Capital Corp., 878 S.W.2d 708, 712 (Ark. 1994) ("We agree ... that mere encouragement of settlement is not a sufficient basis to overcome the public's right of access."); Anderson v. Home Ins. Co., 924 P.2d 1123, 1127 (Colo. App. 1996); In re Estate of Zimmer, 442 N.W.2d 578, 584 (Wis. App. 1989); see also Copley Press, Inc. v. Superior Ct., 74 Cal. Rptr. 2d at 74 (unsealing court records indicating the amount of a settlement between a school district insurer and a student who had been sexually assaulted, stating, "[t]he fact of a damage award, whatever size, is not in itself a private fact deserving protection, and secrecy in public education is not in the public interest"). But see United States v.

If a settlement agreement has not been filed with the court, it is significantly less likely that public access will be ordered. In *Pansy v. Borough of Stroudsburg*,[164] the Third Circuit distinguished its holding in *Hotel Rittenhouse Associates* because the settlement agreement to which access was sought had not been filed with, interpreted by, or enforced by the trial court. Hence, it was not a "judicial record" subject to a right of public access.[165] Nor did the fact that the trial court had entered a confidentiality order governing the settlement agreement, and had reviewed it in that context, convert it into a judicial record.[166] The court declined to follow the First Circuit, which had held that a document becomes a judicial record if the court consults it, even if it does not become part of the court file.[167]

Rejection of the claim of access to the settlement agreement did not, however, end the matter in *Pansy*. The newspapers had also sought to vacate the confidentiality order itself. That issue, the Third Circuit concluded, is independent of whether the settlement agreement is subject to a right of access.[168] While courts do have inherent power to enter confidentiality orders governing material not in the court file, the court of appeals explained, such action may not be taken

---

Glens Falls Newspapers Inc., 160 F.3d 853, 856 (2d Cir. 1998) ("fostering settlement is an important Article III function of the federal district courts," and particularly where a case is "complex and expensive, and resolution . . . will benefit the public, the public has a strong interest in the settlement," which includes "giving the parties ample opportunity to settle the case").

164. 23 F.3d 772 (3d Cir. 1994). The case involved a civil rights suit filed by a former police chief. After settlement, newspapers moved to intervene and to reconsider, vacate, or modify a confidentiality order issued pursuant to the settlement agreement. The district court denied intervention and, in the alternative, rejected the access claim. See *id.* at 776. The court of appeals held that the newspapers had standing to challenge protective and confidentiality orders and permitted intervention as timely even following settlement. See *id.* at 777-79.

165. See *id.* at 781 (citing Enprotech Corp. v. Renda, 983 F.2d 17, 20-21 (3d Cir. 1993)); see also United States v. Glens Falls Newspapers Inc., 160 F.3d 853, 856 (2d Cir. 1998) ("[O]pening settlement negotiations in this case prior to the crafting of a tentative agreement would not be in the public interest, nor required by the Constitution or laws.").

166. See 23 F.3d at 782-83. According to the Third Circuit, the trial court did not — and could not, since the agreement was not filed — order the parties to abide by its terms. See *id.* at 782. See also Holmes v. Elias, 27 MEDIA L. REP. (BNA) 1031, 1032 (E.D. Pa. 1998) ("Judicial records are records that are filed with the court, placed under seal, interpreted by the court or enforced by the court. Confidentiality orders over the terms of the agreement alone, are not interpretation or enforcement by the court.").

167. See 23 F.3d at 782-83 (rejecting FTC v. Standard Fin. Management Corp., 830 F.2d 404, 409 (1st Cir. 1987)) ("relevant documents which are submitted to, and accepted by, a court of competent jurisdiction in the course of adjudicatory proceedings, become documents to which the presumption of access applies"). In *Pansy*, the lower court had only "briefly perused and returned to the parties" the settlement agreement. 23 F.3d at 783.

168. See 23 F.3d at 784-85; see also Holmes v. Elias, 27 MEDIA L. REP. (BNA) 1031, 1032 (E.D. Pa. 1998) (applying the *Pansy* test to define judicial records and vacating the order of confidentiality on judicial documents, but denying access to the settlement agreement and release which had never been made part of the court record).

arbitrarily.[169] "Disturbingly, some courts routinely sign orders which contain confidentiality clauses without considering the propriety of such orders, or the countervailing public interests which are sacrificed by the orders."[170]

Applying, the "good cause" standard,[171] the Third Circuit reasoned that in determining whether to *modify* an existing secrecy order, the reliance of the parties on the extant order is relevant, but not conclusive.[172] When parties to a settlement agreement rely on a confidentiality order, the court noted, they do so with knowledge that it is subject to modification.[173] The court rejected the Second Circuit's holding that a confidentiality order can be modified only if warranted by "extraordinary circumstances or compelling needs" as "too stringent" — "[t]he party seeking to modify the order of confidentiality must come forward with a reason to modify the order. Once that is done, the court should then balance the interests, including the reliance by the original parties to the order, to determine whether good cause still exists for the order."[174] Moreover, in the context of litigation involving the government, the court added an additional factor, which materially enhances the likelihood of access in such cases:

> To provide some measure of uniformity and predictability of outcome in this important area, we hold that where it is likely that information is accessible under a relevant freedom of information law, a strong presumption exists against granting or maintaining an order of confidentiality whose

---

169. See 23 F.3d at 785 (quoting City of Hartford v. Chase, 942 F.2d 130, 136 (2d Cir. 1991)) ("We do not . . . give parties carte blanche either to seal documents related to a settlement agreement or to withhold documents they deem so 'related.' Rather, the trial court — not the parties themselves — should scrutinize every such agreement involving the sealing of court papers and [determine] what, if any, of them are to be sealed, and it is only after very careful, particularized review by the court that a Confidentiality Order may be executed."); see also United States v. Glens Falls Newspapers Inc., 160 F.3d 853, 856 (2d Cir. 1998) (citing City of Hartford v. Chase, 942 F.2d at 135; In re Baldwin-United Corp., 770 F.2d 328, 337-38 (2d Cir. 1985)) (recognizing that a trial judge has inherent power to "prevent access to settlement negotiations when necessary to encourage the amicable resolution of disputes" and to "aid in crafting a settlement by enjoining the interference of others").

170. 23 F.3d at 785.

171. See *id.* ("[P]rotective orders over discovery materials and orders of confidentiality over matters relating to other stages of litigation have comparable features and raise similar public policy concerns. All such orders are intended to offer litigants a measure of privacy, while balancing against this privacy interest the public's right to obtain information concerning judicial proceedings."); Holmes v. Elias, 27 MEDIA L. REP. (BNA) 1031, 1032 (E.D. Pa. 1998) (rejecting a confidentiality order imposed on a settlement in a case involving a student and a teacher by balancing public and private interests to determine "good cause," and concluding that the suit involved "matters of legitimate public concern" and that the defendant teacher failed to prove "a clearly defined serious injury will follow disclosure").

172. See 23 F.3d at 788.

173. See *id.* at 790.

174. *Id.*

scope would prevent disclosure of that information pursuant to the relevant freedom of information law. In the good cause balancing test, this strong presumption tilts the scales heavily against entering or maintaining an order of confidentiality.[175]

In *United States v. Glens Falls Newspapers Inc.*,[176] the Second Circuit applied criteria proffered in *United States v. Amodeo*[177] to determine the propriety of a newspaper's motion to intervene solely to vacate a consent order that provided for confidentiality of draft settlement documents. The court's two-part test examined the "weight of the presumption of public access" and "countervailing factors to be balanced against the presumption of access."[178] First, the court found no presumption of public access to draft settlement documents.[179] Next, the court emphasized the significance of maintaining an opportunity for "frank discussion" and found that "settlement negotiations in this case would be chilled to the point of ineffectiveness if draft materials were to be made public."[180] Accordingly, the court held the presumption of access was "negligible to nonexistent" and denied the motion to intervene.[181]

In *In re Ford Motor Co. Bronco II Products Liability Litigation*,[182] a federal court ordered Ford Motor Company to produce the original complaints and settlement agreements in all personal injury litigation involving a particular vehicle. Thereafter, the court considered hundreds of prior settlements in determining the adequacy of the proposed settlement in the then-pending liti-

---

175. *Id.* at 791. The *Pansy* court explained its "strong presumption" in this context:

[W]e believe that a strong presumption against entering or maintaining confidentiality orders strikes the appropriate balance by recognizing the enduring beliefs underlying freedom of information laws: that an informed public is desirable, that access to information prevents governmental abuse and helps secure freedom, and that, ultimately, government must answer to its citizens. Neither the interests of parties in settling cases, nor the interests of the federal courts in cleaning their dockets, can be said to outweigh the important values manifested by freedom of information laws.

Id. at 792; see Marcus v. St. Tammany Parish Sch. Bd., 1997 U.S. Dist. LEXIS 8380 (E.D. La. 1997) (finding media is entitled to a transcript of settlement agreement since parties' reliance on confidentiality of transcript as a basis for sealing was rejected in *Pansy* and *Rittenhouse*); Mullins v. City of Griffin, 886 F. Supp. 21 (N.D. Ga. 1995) (following *Pansy*'s rejection of confidentiality order based on terms of settlement).
176. 160 F.3d 853, 856 (2d Cir. 1998).
177. 71 F.3d 1044 (2d Cir. 1995).
178. 160 F.3d at 857-58.
179. See *id.* at 857.
180. *Id.* at 857-58.
181. *Id.* at 858.
182. 1995 U.S. Dist. LEXIS 8298 (E.D. La. June 9, 1995) (*Ford III*); see In re Ford Motor Co. Bronco II Prods. Liab. Litig., 1995 U.S. Dist. LEXIS 5672 (E.D. La. Apr. 12, 1995) (*Ford II*); In re Ford Motor Co. Bronco II Prods. Liab. Litig., 1995 U.S. Dist. LEXIS 15867 (E.D. La. Oct. 28, 1994) (*Ford I*).

gation.[183] Since the documents had been consulted by the court, it denied Ford's motion for a protective order covering the prior settlement agreements pursuant to Rule 26(c)'s "good cause" standard.[184]

Because of the courts' apparent preference for Rule 26(c) and the common law presumption of access to settlement agreements reflected in the "good cause" standard, only a few reported decisions have grounded a right of access in the First Amendment itself.[185] Indeed, although some courts have found a right of access to settlement agreements in their state public records laws,[186] it is the common law that has produced an impressive body of case law recognizing a right of access to settlement agreements, whether in the context of challenges to issuance of a protective order as part of a settlement agreement in the first instance, or in a subsequent motion to modify such an order.[187] Under this

---

183. See *Ford II*, 1995 U.S. Dist. LEXIS 5672, at *3 (citing FTC v. Standard Fin. Management Corp., 830 F.2d 404, 409 (1st Cir. 1987); SEC v. Van Waeyenberghe, 990 F.2d 845, 848 (5th Cir. 1993)); see also *Ford III*, 1995 U.S. Dist. LEXIS 8298, at *2.

184. In *Ford II*, 1995 U.S. Dist. LEXIS 5672, at *8, the court held "that the public's interest in access to the settlement agreements outweighs the interest of Ford." In *Ford III*, 1995 U.S. Dist. LEXIS 8298, at *8-10, the court held that Ford had failed to provide "direct evidence" of harm from public access, but did limit disclosure to those prior settlement agreements actually consulted by the judge.

185. See, e.g., Society of Prof'l Journalists v. Briggs, 675 F. Supp. 1308, 1310-11 (D. Utah 1987) (holding access to settlement agreements involving public entities which are "public documents" that implicate First Amendment); In re Johnson, 461 N.W.2d 767, 768-69 (S.D. 1990) (stating that affidavit filed by attorney consenting to disbarment and acknowledging truth of accusations against him is judicial record subject to public access under both common law and First Amendment); Fidelity Fin. Servs. v. Hicks, 642 N.E.2d 759, 762-63 (Ill. App. 1994) (finding that settlement agreements filed with Illinois courts are subject to both a common law and First Amendment-based right of access); In re Marriage of Johnson, 598 N.E.2d 406, 411 (Ill. App. 1992) (holding that under either common law or constitutional analysis, lower court abused its discretion in denying access to settlement agreement).

186. See, e.g., Anderson v. Home Ins. Co., 924 P.2d 1123, 1126 (Colo. App. 1996) (noting that Colorado Open Records Act creates presumption of access which can be overridden only if party seeking to limit public disclosure demonstrates that party's privacy rights outweigh public interest in openness of court files); Lakeland Ledger Publ'g Co. v. Prison Health Servs. Inc., 718 So. 2d 204 (Fla. Cir. 1997) (granting summary judgment in favor of a newspaper seeking access to a settlement agreement between the widow of a deceased inmate, the sheriff's office, and the corporation that provides health care for the prison facility because the corporation was acting on behalf of the sheriff's office and is therefore covered by Florida's Public Records Law); Tribune Co. v. Hardee Mem. Hosp., 19 MEDIA L. REP. (BNA) 1318, 1318-19 (Fla. Cir. 1991) (holding Florida Public Records Act requires public hospital to disclose settlement agreement); City of Helen v. White County News, 25 MEDIA L. REP. (BNA) 1123 (Ga. Super. 1996) (holding nondisclosure provisions of settlement agreement void as against public policy embodied in state open records act); In re Estate of Zimmer, 442 N.W.2d 578, 582 (Wis. App. 1989) (stating open records law and other similar statutes create "presumption that the public has a right to inspect the settlement agreements").

187. See, e.g., Hagestad v. Tragesser, 49 F.3d 1430, 1434 (9th Cir. 1995); SEC v. Van Waeyenberghe, 990 F.2d 845, 847-49 (5th Cir. 1993) ("Once a settlement is filed in district court it

§ 6-1(b)   ACCESS TO JUDICIAL RECORDS: CIVIL PROCEEDINGS   § 6-1(b)

approach, courts have applied the "good cause" standard embodied in Rule 26(c) and analogous state rules of procedure to determine whether the press and the public must be afforded access to settlement agreements.[188]

---

becomes a judicial record. The presumption in favor of the public's common law right of access to court records therefore applies to settlement agreements that are filed and submitted to the district court for approval."); Brown v. Advantage Eng'g, Inc., 960 F.2d 1013, 1014-16 (11th Cir. 1992) ("Absent a showing of extraordinary circumstances set forth by the district court in the record . . . the court file must remain accessible to the public."); Goodman v. Fuller, 960 F.2d 149 (6th Cir. 1992) (unpublished); Oregonian Publ'g Co. v. United States Dist. Ct., 19 MEDIA L. REP. (BNA) 1704 (9th Cir. 1991); United Nuclear Corp. v. Cranford Ins. Co., 905 F.2d 1424, 1427-29 (10th Cir. 1990), *cert. denied*, 498 U.S. 1073 (1991); EEOC v. Erection Co., 900 F.2d 168, 169 (9th Cir. 1990); United States v. Oregon, 19 MEDIA L. REP. (BNA) 1506, 1507-09 (D. Or. 1991); Arkansas Best Corp. v. General Elec. Capital Corp., 878 S.W.2d 708, 711-13 (Ark. 1994); In re Analytical Sys., 83 B.R. 833 (N.D. Ga. 1987); In re Marriage of Purcell, 879 P.2d 468, 469 (Colo. App. 1994); Miami Herald Publ'g Co. v. Collazo, 329 So. 2d 333, 336-39 (Fla. App. 1997); In re Marriage of Johnson, 598 N.E.2d 406, 410 (Ill. App. 1992) ("We hold the right of access extends to the documents filed with the court, including the settlement agreement in the dissolution case."); Des Moines Sch. Dist. v. Des Moines Register & Tribune Co., 487 N.W. 2d 666, 669-70 (Iowa 1992); Providence Journal Co. v. Clerk of Family Ct., 643 A.2d 210, 211 (R.I. 1994); Schnell v. Farmers Ins. Exch., 23 MEDIA L. REP. (BNA) 1542, 1543-44 (Wis. Cir. 1994); C.L. v. Edson, 409 N.W.2d 417, 423 (Wis. App. 1987) ("The parties have failed to show that the public's interest in encouraging settlements overcomes the strong presumption favoring disclosure of court documents."); see also Glenmede Trust Co. v. Thompson, 56 F.3d 476, 482-86 (3d Cir. 1995) (refusing to issue umbrella protective order covering documents disclosed in discovery pursuant to confidentiality agreement between a law firm and its client where the "good cause" standard was not satisfied); Pepsico, Inc. v. Redmond, 46 F.3d 29, 30-31 (7th Cir. 1995) (refusing to permit a lower court's written opinion to be included in information sealed as part of a confidentiality agreement between the parties).

In *United States v. Town of Moreau*, 979 F. Supp. 129 (N.D.N.Y. 1997), *aff'd sub nom.* United States v. Glens Falls Newspapers Inc., 160 F.3d 853 (2d Cir. 1998), the court rejected both a First Amendment-based and common law right of access to settlement proposals or settlement conference statements. The documents, the court found, were not judicial records and played a negligible role in the court's performance of its Article III duties. But the court did emphasize that "[a]n entirely different question would be presented if the parties sought an order sealing the final consent decree and its related settlement documents." 979 F. Supp. at 136-37; see also United States v. Glens Falls Newspapers Inc., 160 F.3d 853, 858 (2d Cir. 1998) (quoting City of Hartford v. Chase, 942 F.2d 130, 135-36 (2d Cir. 1991)) ("We have previously recognized that settlement documents in draft form are not part of the public record of a federal case . . . and that the district court's power to seal documents 'takes precedence over FOIA rules that would otherwise allow those documents to be disclosed.'").

188. See, e.g., Doe v. Shapiro, 852 F. Supp. 1256, 1257 (E.D. Pa. 1994) (after balancing public interest against the interests of the parties to a settlement agreement neither disclosed to, nor filed with, the court in an action by an attorney who contended he was discharged from his job because he had AIDS, the court determined it appropriate to place defendant's pre-settlement motion for summary judgment under seal); Short v. Western Elec. Co., 566 F. Supp. 932, 934 (D.N.J. 1982) (refusing to unseal discovery documents in libel action after balancing interests); H.S. Gere & Sons v. Frey, 509 N.E.2d 271, 274-75 (Mass. 1987) (refusing to grant relief from judicial impoundment of discovery information and other information in settlement agreement because the information was "not generally public information"); Minneapolis Star & Tribune Co. v. Schumacher, 392

§ 6-1(c). Court Files.

Parties to civil litigation often negotiate agreements designed to prevent disclosure of *any* materials relating to the proceedings. While courts have been surprisingly willing to issue such blanket orders governing the fruits of discovery, they have been reluctant to place a judicial imprimatur on agreements that purport to seal the entire court file.[189] In most cases, courts have concluded that "good cause" does not support such a sweeping secrecy order or

---

N.W.2d 197, 206 (Minn. 1986) ("The historical and philosophical privacy of settlement documents, along with the relevant facts and circumstances in this case, demonstrate that the privacy interests asserted by the litigants were strong enough to justify restricting access."). See also Savannah College of Art & Design v. School of Visual Arts, Inc., 515 S.E.2d 370, 371 (Ga. 1999) (trial court abused its discretion by unsealing filed settlement documents since "'the harm otherwise resulting to the privacy of a person in interest clearly outweighs the public interest'"); Empire Blue Cross & Blue Shield v. Janet Greeson's A Place for Us, Inc., 62 F.3d 1217, 1221 (9th Cir. 1995) (holding motion to intervene for purposes of modifying protective orders over settlement agreement untimely given danger of jeopardizing settlement); Enprotech Corp. v. Renda, 983 F.2d 17, 19-20 (3d Cir. 1993) (stating that a settlement agreement was not a court record subject to public disclosure under public access doctrine unless and until the court orders parties to comply with its terms, even where district court retains jurisdiction over the agreement); Banco Popular de Puerto Rico v. Greenblatt, 964 F.2d 1227, 1230-34 (1st Cir. 1992) (holding motion to intervene to modify protective order issued in connection with confidentiality agreement between the parties was not timely); Wagar v. United States Dep't of Justice, 846 F.2d 1040, 1045-47 (6th Cir. 1988) (upholding order of district court directing the Department of Justice to destroy documents obtained in discovery prior to settlement agreement between the parties in an underlying antitrust action); Minnesota v. Hennepin County, 505 N.W.2d 294, 295-97 (Minn. 1993) (holding the court has inherent power to order public bodies into closed settlement conferences despite Open Meeting Law, but finding that trial court did not appropriately close conferences where not all parties were present and conferences occurred after trial); Crain Communications, Inc. v. Hughes, 539 N.E.2d 1099, 1099-1100 (N.Y. 1989); Courier-Journal & Louisville Times Co. v. Peers, 747 S.W.2d 125, 126-30 (Ky. 1988); Doe v. Roe, 495 A.2d 1235, 1237-38 (Me. 1985).

189. See, e.g., Marcus v. St. Tammany Parish Sch. Bd., 1997 U.S. Dist. LEXIS 8380 (E.D. La. 1997) (holding that blanket confidentiality order covering entire court record which did not satisfy strict scrutiny or the less demanding "reasonable likelihood" of prejudice standard is unconstitutional regardless of whether it constitutes a prior restraint); Stamy v. Packer, 138 F.R.D. 412, 418 (D.N.J. 1990) (refusing to seal the entire court file in action by patient against Princeton University and university psychologist alleging medical malpractice arising from alleged homosexual relationship between patient and psychologist, absent a showing that court records were being used for an improper purpose such as "'to gratify spite or provide public scandal'") (quoting Nixon v. Warner Communications, Inc., 435 U.S. 589, 598 (1978)). But see In re Knoxville News-Sentinel Co., 723 F.2d 470, 473-78 (6th Cir. 1983) (permitting bank, in a lawsuit between bank and FDIC, to remove two documents containing the names of bank customers from court file prior to making file public); Los Angeles Times v. County of Los Angeles, 956 F. Supp. 1530, 1531 (C.D. Cal. 1996) (granting summary judgment to defendant and holding that Information Access Provider, an automated civil case management system, "is not the type of court record to which [media] have a First Amendment right of access").

that the common law presumption of public access has not otherwise been overcome.

In *Glenmede Trust Co. v. Thompson*,[190] for example, the Third Circuit invoked the demanding "good cause" standards fashioned in *Pansy v. Borough of Stroudsburg*[191] to affirm a district court's denial of a motion seeking a protective order to enforce a broad confidentiality agreement restricting public disclosure of documents generated in litigation. The court rejected the parties' reliance on generalized notions of injury to reputation, harm to a law firm's relationship with its professional clientele, or embarrassment as sufficient to constitute good cause.[192] Moreover, the court emphasized, there must be a showing that "a defined and serious injury will result from open proceedings."[193]

Similarly, in *Hagestad v. Tragesser*,[194] the Ninth Circuit held that a district court abused its discretion when it granted a litigant's motion to seal the entire court file in a civil action in which he was a defendant.[195] Invoking the common law's "strong presumption in favor of access," the court concluded that "the district court must base [such a] decision on a compelling reason and articulate the factual basis for its ruling, without relying on hypothesis or conjecture."[196]

---

190. 56 F.3d 476 (3d Cir. 1995).
191. 23 F.3d 772 (3d Cir. 1994); see Chap. 6-1(b) *supra*. The court identified a variety of considerations relevant in assessing "good cause":

> 1) whether disclosure will violate any privacy interests; 2) whether the information is being sought for a legitimate purpose or for an improper purpose; 3) whether disclosure of the information will cause a party embarrassment; 4) whether confidentiality is being sought over information important to public heath and safety; 5) whether the sharing of information among litigants will promote fairness and efficiency; 6) whether a party benefiting from the order of confidentiality is a public entity or official; and 7) whether the case involves issues important to the public.

56 F.3d at 483 (citing Pansy v. Borough of Stroudsburg, 23 F.3d at 787-91).
192. See 56 F.3d at 484.
193. *Id.* at 485.
194. 49 F.3d 1430 (9th Cir. 1995).
195. The underlying civil action, in which plaintiff alleged that Tragesser had sexual relations with her for seven years during which she was a minor, had been settled. Later, the State Bar, which was conducting a disciplinary investigation of Tragesser, issued a subpoena *duces tecum* to Hagestad. Tragesser moved to enforce the settlement agreement, quash the subpoena, and seal the record. The State Bar intervened, seeking to compel production of testimony and copies of the pleadings. See *id.* at 1430-34.
196. *Id.* at 1434 (citing Valley Broadcasting Co. v. United States Dist. Ct., 798 F.2d 1289, 1295 (9th Cir. 1986)). In *Grove Fresh Distributors, Inc. v. Everfresh Juice Co.*, 24 F.3d 893, 894, 897-99 (7th Cir. 1994), the Seventh Circuit required a district court to specify the basis for its decision to seal a court file. On remand, the trial court cited the need to prevent disclosure of confidential material and adverse publicity and the appellate court upheld issuance of the protective order. Grove Fresh Distribs. Inc. v. Everfresh Juice Co., 134 F.3d 374 (7th Cir. 1998). See Goodman v. Fuller, 960 F.2d 149 (6th Cir. 1992) ("Nondisclosure cannot be justified solely on the basis of a sweeping order agreed to by the litigants, but otherwise unexplained, sealing the entire record of a

The Sixth Circuit has held that reliance on a protective order by the parties does not, standing alone, justify continued sealing of a court file in the face of subsequent objection by third parties. In *Brown & Williamson Tobacco Corp. v. FTC*,[197] the court vacated an order sealing the entire record pursuant to a prior confidentiality agreement entered by the parties. "Under the First Amendment and the common law ... the district court erred by failing to state findings or conclusions which justify nondisclosure to the public."[198] The court concluded that there was no danger of disclosing legitimate trade secrets and emphasized the strong public interest in the actions of the FTC and the courts in tobacco-related litigation.[199] Similarly, the Eleventh Circuit in *Brown v. Advantage Engineering, Inc.*[200] held that sealing the entire court record is not justified merely because the parties assert that such confidentiality is an integral part of a negotiated settlement.[201] The court again relied on the "strong common law presumption in favor of access"[202] and concluded that "[a]bsent a showing of extraordinary circumstances set forth by the district court in the record ... the court must remain accessible to the public."[203]

---

concluded case."); EEOC v. Erection Co., 900 F.2d 168, 169 (9th Cir. 1990); Stone v. University of Md. Med. Sys. Corp., 855 F.2d 178, 180-81 (4th Cir. 1988) (remanding case and requiring that lower court give public notice of the request to seal and a reasonable opportunity to oppose it, consider reasonable alternatives to sealing, and state reasons for its decision). But see Siedle v. Putnam Inv., Inc., 147 F.3d 7, 11-12 (1st Cir. 1998) (reversing the district court's order summarily unsealing filings in an action brought by a lawyer against his former client as an abuse of discretion in the absence of "evidence that the district court identified and balanced the interests at stake," or that the court scrutinized the documents to determine whether they were otherwise subject to the attorney-client privilege, stating "Putnam's unrebutted prima facie showing that the attorney-client privilege applies entitles it to protection").

197. 710 F.2d 1165 (6th Cir. 1983), *cert. denied*, 465 U.S. 1100 (1984).

198. *Id.* at 1176; see *id.* at 1177 ("[T]he First Amendment and the common law do limit judicial discretion."). The Sixth Circuit relied on First Amendment principles undergirding the constitutional right of access which, it held, "apply as well to the determination of whether to permit access to information in court documents because court records often provide important, sometimes the only, bases for explanations for a court's decision." *Id.*

199. See *id.* at 1180-81.

200. 960 F.2d 1013 (11th Cir. 1992).

201. See *id.* at 1016 ("It is immaterial whether the sealing of the record is an integral part of a negotiated settlement between the parties even if the settlement comes with the court's active encouragement.").

202. *Id.* at 1015; see Stapp v. Overnite Transp. Co., 1998 U.S. Dist. LEXIS 6412, at *3 (D. Kan. Apr. 9, 1998) (denying a joint motion to seal the court record following settlement and holding that the claim that access to pleadings would negatively affect the parties' employment relationship was not sufficiently specific or severe enough to override the "strong presumption" created by the common law right to access since, by proceeding to trial, the parties had "placed their dispute in the public forum").

203. 960 F.2d at 1016; see Wilson v. American Motors Corp., 759 F.2d 1568, 1571 (11th Cir. 1985) (rejecting sealing of court file absent showing that denial of access "is necessitated by a compelling governmental interest, and is narrowly tailored to ... that interest") (quoting Globe

§ 6-1(c)　　　ACCESS TO JUDICIAL RECORDS: CIVIL PROCEEDINGS　　　§ 6-1(c)

State courts have also demonstrated a pronounced reluctance to seal an entire court file.[204] In *Barron v. Florida Freedom Newspapers, Inc.*, the Florida

---

Newspaper Co. v. Superior Ct., 457 U.S. 596, 606-07 (1982)); see also United Nuclear Corp. v. Cranford Ins. Co., 905 F.2d 1424, 1428 (10th Cir. 1990), *cert. denied*, 498 U.S. 1073 (1991) (holding that, where third party seeks modification of protective order, modification can be denied "only where it would tangibly prejudice substantial rights"). In *Siedle v. Putnam Investments, Inc.*, 147 F.3d 7 (1st Cir. 1998), however, the court held that the district court's rescission of a sealing order, without determining whether any of the information contained in the filings was otherwise protected by attorney-client privilege, was an abuse of discretion.

204. The court in *In re Marriage of Lechowick*, 77 Cal. Rptr. 2d 395, 398, 400 (Ct. App. 1998), reversed a trial court order closing marital dissolution proceedings and sealing the entire court record. The court construed CAL. FAM. CODE § 214, which states that a court may, "when it considers it necessary in the interests of justice and the persons involved, direct the trial of any issue of fact joined in a proceeding under this code to be private," to grant a judge discretion to close family court proceedings. However, the court of appeal emphasized that the statute does not authorize sealing entire court files unless they are themselves the fruits of the closed proceedings. See *id*. Generally, court files, including Family Court files, are open. See Hearst v. Estate of Hearst, 27 MEDIA L. REP. (BNA) 1223, 1224 (Cal. App. 1998) (unsealing appellate record in a civil testamentary case because movant could not show that trust beneficiaries would be placed in "serious danger of loss of life or property" as a result of disclosure, but maintaining seal over the names and addresses of the trustees because of a lack of objection by either party).

In *Reed v. Zizka*, 1998 Conn. Super. LEXIS 1522 (Conn. Super. May 28, 1998), the court denied a motion to continue an order sealing the court file and found "a priest's right to maintain a good reputation" did not override the public's First Amendment right to access, particularly because the defendant did not present any specific evidence that "unsealing the file . . . will have an adverse impact on the defendant's reputation." *Id*. at *4, *9. Absent a finding that it is necessary to "preserve an interest which is determined to override the public's interest in . . . viewing such materials," the court asserted, it will deny a motion to seal a file from pretrial disclosure. *Id*. at *3-4. See Goldberg v. Johnson, 485 So. 2d 1386, 1388-90 (Fla. App. 1986), *cert. denied*, 498 U.S. 1073 (1991) (reversing order sealing court file under common law standard requiring that sealing must be "necessary to prevent a serious and imminent threat to the administration of justice"); George W. Prescott Publ'g Co. v. Register of Probate, 479 N.E.2d 658, 662-65 (Mass. 1985) (reversing impoundment of records of divorce proceeding of public official under a "good cause" standard because of public's interest in conduct of a public official while in office); Lutz v. Lutz, 20 MEDIA L. REP. (BNA) 2029, 2029-32 (Mich. Cir. 1992) (vacating order suppressing court file in divorce action on Michigan statutory, common law, and First Amendment grounds); Providence Journal Co. v. Clerk of Family Ct., 643 A.2d 210, 211 (R.I. 1994) ("[b]asically, all court documents are public"); see also Courier-Journal & Louisville Times Co. v. Peers, 747 S.W.2d 125 (Ky. 1988) (holding trial court must conduct a hearing before sealing court file). But see Wilkinson v. Wiegand, 1997 Conn. Super. LEXIS 1699 (Conn. Super. June 17, 1997) (in litigation following dissolution of marriage, involving financial issues and matters relating to child custody, court found no "overriding interest" in children's privacy and safety justifying closing proceeding and sealing court files); In re du Pont, 25 MEDIA L. REP. (BNA) 2436 (Del. Ch. 1997) (citing "Delaware's long-standing policy of restricting public access to guardianship files," court denied newspaper's motion to intervene and for access to guardianship file of John E. du Pont, heir to the du Pont fortune, who was held to be criminally incompetent after killing Olympic wrestler David Schultz): see also Wilson v. Science Applications Int'l Corp., 60 Cal. Rptr. 2d 883 (Ct. App. 1997) (remanding case because trial judge failed to rule on newspaper's motion to unseal court file,

Supreme Court invoked the common law presumption of access to court records in rejecting a trial judge's order sealing a substantial portion of the court file in a marital dissolution proceeding.[205] "[A] strong presumption of openness exists for all court proceedings," the court held.[206] "A trial is a public event, and the filed records of court proceedings are public records available for public examination."[207] Accordingly, the court concluded, sealing orders must be drawn "with particularity and narrowly applied,"[208] and the court must make an express determination that there is no alternative to closure.[209]

§ 6-1(c)(1). Pretrial Motions, Records, and Pleadings.

As has been noted, documents filed in support of a dispositive motion in civil litigation, such as a motion for summary judgment, are generally held to con-

---

thereby preventing newspaper from meeting its burden of demonstrating new or changed circumstances that would warrant access).
   205. 531 So. 2d 113 (Fla. 1988).
   206. *Id.* at 118.
   207. *Id.* The court held that a civil proceeding is subject "to the well established common law right of access to court proceedings and records." *Id.* at 116. Marital dissolution cases are subject to the same presumption of access applicable to other civil proceedings, see *id.* at 114, and a "heavy burden" of proof is placed on the party seeking closure, *id.* at 118-19. The fact that the proceedings involved divorce did not erase the presumption of openness. See *id.* at 119; In re Marriage of Lechowick, 77 Cal. Rptr. 2d 395, 400 (Ct. App. 1998) ("[C]ourt files in family law cases should be treated no differently than the court files in any other cases for purposes of considering the propriety of granting a motion to seal any of those files."). But see Virmani v. Presbyterian Health Servs. Corp., 515 S.E.2d 675 (N.C. 1999) (holding open courts provision of state constitution provides public and press with constitutional right of access to confidential medical peer review committee records and materials attached to complaint, but not to materials submitted to trial judge during motions hearing but not filed).
   208. 531 So. 2d at 117; see Hearst v. Estate of Hearst, 27 MEDIA L. REP. (BNA) 1223, 1224 (Cal. Ct. App. 1998) (indicating that, although there is a presumption of "maximum public access" to judicial records, courts may restrict access to "portions of court records on a temporary basis" in exceptional circumstances, such as a showing that an individual would be placed in "serious danger of loss of life or property," but finding that evidence of threats to the Hearst family made 22 years ago were not sufficient to prove imminent danger); In re du Pont, 25 MEDIA L. REP. (BNA) 2436 (Del. Ch. 1997) (holding that sealing files of guardianship proceeding did not violate the public's rights, since the order provides media access to the transcript of the hearing and to the court's ruling and is therefore narrowly tailored to protect legitimate privacy interests).
   209. See 531 So. 2d at 118; see also Shenandoah Publ'g House, Inc. v. Fanning, 368 S.E.2d 253, 258-59 (Va. 1988) ("We further believe that, to overcome that presumption, the moving party must bear the burden of establishing an interest so compelling that it cannot be protected reasonably by some measure other than a protective order, . . . and that any such order must be drafted in the manner least restrictive of the public's interest."). But see In re du Pont, 25 MEDIA L. REP. (BNA) 2436 (Del. Ch. 1997) (characterizing rule placing burden of proof for showing good cause for sealing civil court file on party seeking order as "a prudential one, not a constitutional mandate").

stitute public records subject to the common law presumption of access.[210] Courts typically reason that the policies favoring access, most notably public scrutiny of the judicial process, apply most fully in the context of dispositive motions.[211] If the motion is successful, the proceeding may end, without any public trial. Whether the motion succeeds or fails, substantive rights are adjudicated.[212]

In *Leucadia, Inc. v. Applied Extrusion Technologies, Inc.*,[213] the Third Circuit articulated "a presumptive right of public access to pretrial motions of a nondiscovery nature, whether preliminary or dispositive, and the material filed in connection therewith."[214] The court grounded this "pervasive common law right"[215] in the many cases establishing that the *filing* of a document gives rise to

---

210. See Chap. 6-1(a)(4) *supra*; Rushford v. New Yorker Magazine, 846 F.2d 249, 253 (4th Cir. 1988) ("We believe that the more rigorous First Amendment standard should also apply to documents filed in connection with a summary judgment motion in a civil case."); Joy v. North, 692 F.2d 880, 893-97 (2d Cir.), *cert. denied*, 460 U.S. 1051 (1982) (vacating protective order sealing a report filed with a summary judgment motion in a shareholder's derivative action and stating that "documents used by parties moving for, or opposing, summary judgment should not remain under seal absent the most compelling reasons"); see also Stone v. University of Md. Med. Sys. Corp., 948 F.2d 128, 129-31 (4th Cir. 1991) (reversing order sealing records attached to summary judgment motion); Cianci v. New Times Publ'g Co., 88 F.R.D. 562, 564-65 (S.D.N.Y. 1980) (vacating protective order, under either common law or First Amendment, to allow for public access to discovery materials filed in connection with defendants' unsuccessful motion to dismiss); Hammock v. Hoffmann-LaRoche, Inc., 662 A.2d 546, 558-61 (N.J. 1995) (reversing and remanding order sealing documents submitted in connection with summary judgment motion and stating that "the presumption of public access attaches to pretrial non-discovery motions whether preliminary or dispositive, and the materials, briefs, and documents 'filed' with the court in support of, or in opposition to, such motions"); Atlanta Journal v. Long, 369 S.E.2d 755, 757-60 (Ga. 1988) (finding that "the privacy interests of the appellees in the pre-judgment records of this civil suit do not clearly outweigh the public interest in open access to those records").
211. See In re Continental Ill. Sec. Litig., 732 F.2d 1302, 1304 (7th Cir. 1984); In re Coordinated Pretrial Proceedings in Petroleum Prods. Antitrust Litig., 101 F.R.D. 34, 38-39 (C.D. Cal. 1984). But see In re Reporters Comm. for Freedom of the Press, 773 F.2d 1325, 1325-26, 1340 (D.C. Cir. 1985) (Scalia, J.) (finding no right of access to discovery materials consulted by court in connection with summary judgment motion under the First Amendment or common law).
212. See Rushford v. New Yorker Magazine, 846 F.2d 249, 252 (4th Cir. 1988); see also Republic of Philippines v. Westinghouse Elec. Corp., 949 F.2d 653, 660 (3d Cir. 1991) (finding that even if the motion failed, it "shaped the scope and substance of the litigation and put the litigants squarely on a path toward trial").
213. 998 F.2d 157 (3d Cir. 1993). In *Leucadia, Inc.*, the trial judge issued a blanket protective order covering discovery materials produced in the case. The parties subsequently filed various motions under seal. The trial court made references to some of these materials in adjudicating the motions. Subsequently, the case was settled and the settlement agreement was filed under seal. See *id.* at 161-64.
214. *Id.* at 164.
215. *Id.* at 161.

the presumption of access.[216] While the Third Circuit acknowledged that even the "strong common law presumption of access" must be balanced against the asserted interest in protecting trade secrets and sensitive business information, it held that the trial court had improperly placed the burden of proof on the party seeking access.[217]

By the same token, courts have occasionally held that the balance should be tipped in favor of placing pretrial motions themselves under seal. In *Doe v. Shapiro*,[218] for example, a federal trial court agreed to seal the defendant's motion for summary judgment, which had been filed before the parties reached a settlement. The underlying case concerned a claim for wrongful discharge by an attorney suffering from AIDS. The court focused on the "genuine privacy issues involved" as legitimate grounds for sealing the motion itself.[219] Another court,[220]

---

216. See *id.* (citing Republic of the Philippines v. Westinghouse Elec. Corp., 949 F.2d 653, 660-62 (3d Cir. 1991)); see also Littlejohn v. BIC Corp., 851 F.2d 673, 678-80 (3d Cir. 1988) (transcript of civil trial and filed exhibits); FTC v. Standard Fin. Management Corp., 830 F.2d 404, 409 (1st Cir. 1987) (stating that "documents which are submitted to, and accepted by, a court of competent jurisdiction in the course of adjudicatory proceedings become documents to which the presumption of public access applies"); Bank of Am. Nat'l Trust & Sav. Ass'n v. Hotel Rittenhouse Assocs., 800 F.2d 339, 343-46 (3d Cir. 1986) (settlement-related materials); Publicker Indus. v. Cohen, 733 F.2d 1059, 1066-67 (3d Cir. 1984) (transcripts of preliminary hearing); Crystal Grower's Corp. v. Dobbins, 616 F.2d 458, 460-61 (10th Cir. 1980) (right of access attaches to docketing statement, joint appendix, and briefs filed in court of appeals); Pratt & Whitney Canada, Inc. v. United States, 14 Cl. Ct. 268, 273 (1988) (right of access attaches to "pleadings, orders, notices, exhibits and transcripts filed"); In re Agent Orange Prods. Liab. Litig., 98 F.R.D. 539, 544-45 (E.D.N.Y. 1983) (right of access attaches to documents filed with district court); In re Johnson, 598 N.E.2d 406, 410 (Ill. App. 1992) ("Once documents are filed with the court, they lose their private nature and become part of the court file and 'public components' of the judicial proceedings to which the right of access attaches."); Wilson v. American Motors Corp., 759 F.2d 1568, 1569, 1571 (11th Cir. 1985) (access right attaches to "pleadings, docket entries, orders, affidavits or depositions duly filed, and transcripts or court reporters' notes of hearings or trial proceedings"); Mokhiber v. Davis, 537 A.2d 1100, 1117 (D.C. 1988) (reversing order sealing papers submitted to the court for decision based on common law access right).

217. 998 F.2d at 165.

218. 852 F. Supp. 1256 (E.D. Pa. 1994). The court in *In re Savitt/Adler Litigation*, 1997 WL 797511 (N.D.N.Y. Dec. 23, 1997), *modified*, 26 MEDIA L. REP. (BNA) 1882 (N.D.N.Y. 1998), applying a common law and First Amendment-based presumption, granted press access to documents filed in support of summary judgment after redacting "names and identifying details" to protect the "strong privacy interests" of nonparties. *Id.* at *3. The court found the minimal redaction was largely unrelated to the public interest and permitted the public and press to assess both the basis for the court's decision on the summary judgment motion and whether the defendant politically discriminated in employment practices. See *id.* at *4.

219. 852 F. Supp. at 1257; see *id.* ("To disclose to the public the contents of the defendants' summary judgment motion, which relied in large part on a legal theory that involved digging up details of the plaintiff's personal life, would subject a critically ill individual to unnecessary embarrassment and, perhaps, revelation of his persona.").

220. See In re Coordinated Pretrial Proceedings in Petroleum Prods. Antitrust Litig., 101 F.R.D. 34 (C.D. Cal. 1984).

however, in the context of a consolidated antitrust action, vacated a protective order covering, *inter alia*, a summary judgment motion on the ground that the "significant public concern" surrounding an alleged conspiracy among oil companies to control prices outweighed the parties' interest in secrecy.[221]

The presumption of access has been held to extend beyond motions and the exhibits thereto, to reach a host of pretrial pleadings and other filings.[222] In one case,[223] the Fourth Circuit affirmed the district court's refusal to permit the complaint in a quit claim action to be placed under seal because the government's involvement in the case made the public interest plain, and the reputational harm claimed by the defendant contractor was speculative.[224] Similarly, in *Hutchinson v. Luddy*,[225] another appellate court held that the trial judge did not abuse his discretion when he denied a motion to seal the pleadings in a civil action arising from alleged sexual misconduct by a priest. The court concluded that the "presumption that the public may inspect and copy judicial records extends to pleadings,"[226] under both the common law and the First Amendment.[227]

---

221. *Id.* at 38-39.
222. See Willie Nelson Music Co. v. Commissioner, 12 MEDIA L. REP. (BNA) 1657 (U.S. Tax Ct. 1985) (refusing to seal pleadings, depositions, exhibits, and filings up until time of trial); W.B. v. R.K., 18 MEDIA L. REP. (BNA) 2207 (Minn. Dist. 1991); Shenandoah Publ'g House, Inc. v. Fanning, 368 S.E.2d 253, 258-62 (Va. 1988) (reversing and remanding order sealing pleading, exhibits, and motions filed by parties, but affirming lower court order insofar as there was good cause to seal data assembled during pretrial discovery); Bilder v. Township of Delavan, 334 N.W.2d 252, 255, 260-63 (Wis. 1983) (holding that once exhibits were annexed to petition for writ of prohibition and mandamus in a civil action, they became court records subject to public access); Charlottesville Newspapers, Inc. v. Berry, 206 S.E.2d 267, 267-68 (Va. 1974) (reversing order sealing pleadings and files in a civil action). But see M.P. v. Schwartz, 853 F. Supp. 164, 166-69 (D. Md. 1994) (finding no public access to complaint and attachments to complaint in civil rights action by minor who sustained physical and emotional abuse while in the custody of the county department of social services); Times Herald Printing Co. v. Jones, 717 S.W.2d 933, 936-40 (Tex. App. 1986) (affirming protective order sealing orders, opinions, and nondiscovery pleadings), *vacated*, 730 S.W.2d 648, 649 (Tex. 1987) (holding that lower court had no jurisdiction to decide issue because intervenor newspaper was not a party).
223. See Under Seal v. Under Seal, 27 F.3d 564, 22 MEDIA L. REP. (BNA) 1922 (4th Cir. 1994) (unpublished opinion).
224. See *id.*
225. 581 A.2d 578 (Pa. Super. 1990).
226. *Id.* at 582-83; see Stapp v. Overnite Transp. Co., 1998 U.S. Dist. LEXIS 6412, at *2-3 (D. Kan. April 10, 1998) (denying joint motion to seal the court record following settlement and holding that the claim of the parties that the pleadings "contain allegations of a private nature that may negatively impact the parties' continuing employment relationship" did not override the public's common law right of access which involves "a strong presumption in favor of access").
227. See 581 A.2d at 582-83 ("In Pennsylvania, the common law, the First Amendment to the United States Constitution, and the Pennsylvania Constitution, all support the principle of openness."). In *Kurtzman v. Hankin*, 714 A.2d 450 (Pa. Super. 1998), the court reversed a trial judge's order sealing records as an abuse of discretion, because the judge "failed to use the proper

§ 6-1(c)(2). Transcripts of Judicial Proceedings.

When a civil judicial proceeding is open to the public, it is generally accepted that there is a common law right of access to the transcript of that proceeding.[228] And, typically, when a civil judicial proceeding is improperly closed, there is a qualified right of public access to the transcript of that proceeding.[229] Even when such proceedings have been properly closed, but the rationale for secrecy no longer applies, courts have recognized a qualified right of access to a transcript. These principles generally apply whether the proceeding at issue is a pretrial hearing or the trial itself.

In *Publicker Industries, Inc. v. Cohen*,[230] for example, a district court closed a pretrial hearing held to consider a motion for a preliminary injunction and sealed

---

legal standards or articulate its reasons for closure of the pleadings and judicial proceedings," under either the First Amendment or the common law. *Id.* at 453; see also Does I-III v. Archdiocese of Santa Fe, Inc., 924 P.2d 273, 279 (N.M. App. 1996) (holding that the press has standing to seek access to nonparty deposition).

228. See, e.g., Littlejohn v. BIC Corp., 851 F.2d 673, 678 (3d Cir. 1988); In re Continental Ill. Sec. Litig., 732 F.2d 1302, 1309-13 (7th Cir. 1984); Black v. United States, 24 Cl. Ct. 461, 465 (1991) (noting embarrassment would not suffice to overcome common law right of public access to transcript); Pratt & Whitney Canada v. United States, 15 MEDIA L. REP. (BNA) 1033, 1037-42 (Cl. Ct. 1988) (holding that the common law right of access to pleadings, documents, transcripts, and other records in patent infringement action was not outweighed by parties' privacy interests); In re Johnson, 598 N.E.2d 406, 409-12 (Ill. App. 1992) ("[m]atters publicly testified to (when a transcript of proceedings is or can be made available) and other matters filed with the court become thereby the business of our public system of justice"); Coopersmith v. Gold, 594 N.Y.S.2d 521, 526-30 (Sup. Ct. 1992) (releasing transcript of oral argument and decision); see also In re Coordinated Pretrial Proceedings in Petroleum Prods. Antitrust Litig., 101 F.R.D. 34, 43-45 (C.D. Cal. 1984) (finding a broad common law presumption of access to civil proceedings); Zenith Radio Corp. v. Matsushita Elec. Indus. Co., 529 F. Supp. 866, 895, 903 (E.D. Pa. 1981) (recognizing a presumption of public access to records of civil proceedings and transcripts of open court proceedings); Minneapolis Star & Tribune Co. v. Schumacher, 392 N.W.2d 197, 203, 209 (Minn. 1986) (holding a denial of access to settlement documents and transcripts relating to wrongful death actions not abuse of discretion).

229. See, e.g., United States v. A.D., 28 F.3d 1353, 1360-62 (3d Cir. 1994) (reversing order sealing juvenile delinquency proceeding and record of proceedings under the Juvenile Delinquency Act, the First Amendment, and the common law presumption of public access); Publicker Indus. v. Cohen, 733 F.2d 1059 (3d Cir. 1984); Doe v. Walker, 15 MEDIA L. REP. (BNA) 1333, 1334-36 (Fla. Cir. 1988) (finding a lower court erred in excluding press from in-chambers conference call and holding that a transcript of proceeding should be released); Maryland v. Cottman Transmission Sys., 542 A.2d 859, 863-65 (Md. Spec. App. 1988) (noting harm to corporate reputation does not suffice to overcome strong presumption of public access to court proceedings and records). But see In re Iowa Freedom of Info. Council, 724 F.2d 658, 661-64 (8th Cir. 1983) (refusing to issue a writ of mandamus where transcript under seal in a contempt hearing contained trade secrets, even though the trial court may have erred by failing to provide the media notice to permit objection to closure of hearing); Standard & Poor's Corp. v. Commodity Exch., Inc., 541 F. Supp. 1273, 1277-78 (S.D.N.Y. 1982) (refusing to unseal transcript of record of closed session of civil suit where transcript contained trade secrets).

230. 733 F.2d 1059 (3d Cir. 1984).

portions of the hearing transcript. The Third Circuit reversed, holding that both aspects of the order violated the common law and First Amendment-based rights of access.[231] The trial court had abused its discretion because it "failed to articulate overriding interests based on specific findings showing that the sealing of the transcripts [is] essential to articulated interests of Publicker and because [it] failed to consider less restrictive means to keep this information from the public."[232]

Beyond the transcript, courts have recognized that the presumptive right of access extends as well to materials admitted in evidence in a civil evidentiary proceeding, whether pretrial or trial.[233] As the Seventh Circuit has explained, "judicial records include transcripts of proceedings, everything in the record, including items not admitted into evidence."[234] In another case, *In re Continental Illinois Securities Litigation*,[235] the Seventh Circuit asserted that a First Amendment-based "presumption of access applies to the hearings held and evidence introduced" in a civil action.[236] The fact that the matters admitted in evidence had previously been the subject of a protective order issued in the case did not exempt them from the presumption of access, even if the parties had relied on the order's ongoing efficacy.[237] Once the material had become known to the public and press present in the courtroom when it was admitted as evidence, only "the most extraordinary circumstances" would justify denying access to those not physically present in the courtroom.[238]

---

231. See *id.* at 1061.
232. *Id.* at 1074.
233. See, e.g., Brown v. Advantage Eng'g, Inc., 960 F.2d 1013 (11th Cir. 1992); Wilson v. American Motors Corp., 759 F.2d 1568, 1570, 1571 (11th Cir. 1985) ("There is no question that a common law right of access exists as to civil proceedings."). But see Virmani v. Presbyterian Health Servs. Corp., 515 S.E.2d 675 (N.C. 1999) (holding that the open courts provision of state constitution provides public and press with constitutional right of access to confidential medical peer review committee records attached to complaint, but not to material submitted to trial judge during hearing but not filed).
234. Smith v. United States Dist. Ct., 956 F.2d 647, 650 (7th Cir. 1992) (citing United States v. Martin, 746 F.2d 964, 968 (3d Cir. 1984)).
235. 732 F.2d 1302 (7th Cir. 1984).
236. *Id.* at 1309; see also Pepsico, Inc. v. Redmond, 46 F.3d 29, 31 (7th Cir. 1995) ("This circuit has insisted, moreover, that the judicial proceedings held, and evidence taken, on the way to a final decision also are presumptively in the public domain.").
237. See In re Continental Ill. Sec. Litig., 732 F.2d at 1310-13. But see Jochims v. Isuzu Motors, Ltd., 151 F.R.D. 338 (S.D. Iowa 1993) (denying access to documents introduced in evidence at trial that were subject to a protective order specifically providing for continued confidentiality); Livingston v. Isuzu Motors, Ltd., 910 F. Supp. 1473 (D. Mont. 1995) (holding that trial exhibits, subject to protective order and returned to party producing them, retain confidential status).
238. 732 F.2d at 1313 (citing United States v. Myers, 635 F.2d 945, 952 (2d Cir. 1980)); see also Joy v. North, 692 F.2d 880, 893 (2d Cir.), *cert. denied*, 460 U.S. 1051 (1982) (without public disclosure, "confidence in the administration of justice would be severely weakened").

Similarly, in *Littlejohn v. BIC Corp.*,[239] the Third Circuit began from the premise that "'there is a strong presumption that materials introduced into evidence at trial should be made' available for public access."[240] The court reasoned that, in civil cases, the common law right of access "promotes public confidence in the judicial system by enhancing testimonial trustworthiness and the quality of the justice dispensed by the court."[241] Accordingly, the court held, deposition testimony read into evidence and trial exhibits became *judicial records* subject to the presumptive right of access.[242] The fact that such material had originally been produced or generated pursuant to a blanket protective order did not defeat the presumption.[243] By the same token, the Third Circuit concluded, trial exhibits that had been restored to their owner after the case had ended, and which would have been destroyed by the court clerk had they been kept in its possession, were no longer public records subject to the common law right.[244]

§ 6-1(d). Other Civil Court Records.

In *United States v. Amodeo*,[245] the Second Circuit considered a newspaper's efforts to secure access to a sealed investigative report filed by a court officer appointed under a consent decree to investigate alleged union-related corruption. Part of the report discussed a law firm that had represented the union and, more particularly, one of its partners, who was then Deputy Chief of Staff to President Clinton. In *Amodeo I*, the court held that, since the report was relevant to and had played a role in the judicial proceeding, it had become a judicial record subject to the common law presumption of access.[246] In balancing the interests, the Second Circuit determined, the district court had properly considered the desire of the court officer to protect the confidential identity of cooperating witnesses and others, as well as confidential law enforcement information and the law firm's interest in privacy.[247] On remand, the district court ordered the release of a redacted version of the report, but without certain redactions proposed by the law firm.[248]

---

239. 851 F.2d 673 (3d Cir. 1988).
240. *Id.* at 678 (citing In re Nat'l Broadcasting Co. (Criden), 648 F.2d 814, 823 (3d Cir. 1981)).
241. *Id.*
242. See *id.* at 683.
243. See *id.* at 680-81.
244. See *id.* at 681-83.
245. 44 F.3d 141 (2d Cir. 1995) (*Amodeo I*); United States v. Amodeo, 71 F.3d 1044 (2d Cir. 1995) (*Amodeo II*).
246. See 44 F.3d at 145-46.
247. See *id.* at 147-48.
248. See 71 F.3d at 1047.

In *Amodeo II*, the Second Circuit characterized the report as lying "on the periphery of the adjudicative process,"[249] entitled to only a "weak" presumption of access.[250] Moreover, although the law firm had waived any work product protection by producing the material at issue for the court officer, it retained a privacy interest in the information contained in it.[251] In addition, portions of the report were based on hearsay and could well contain misinformation.[252] Accordingly, the Second Circuit concluded, unsealing this portion of the report would place the law firm "in the unfair position of choosing between suffering the accusations in silence or revealing redacted information," and the trial court had therefore abused its discretion in releasing that portion of the report to the public at all.[253]

In *Pepsico Inc. v. Redmond*, the Seventh Circuit vacated a trial court order sealing its own opinion on the ground that "[o]pinions are not the litigant's property. They belong to the public, which underwrites the judicial system that produces them."[254] For similar reasons, the Seventh Circuit has also held that a memorandum addressed to the court clerk and read in open court constituted a judicial record subject to the common law right of access.[255] The Eleventh Circuit has held that appellate briefs, a joint appendix, docketing statement, and a memorandum opinion issued by the trial court constitute records of the appellate court subject to a presumptive right of access, although the court concluded that this material should remain under seal for five years because significant countervailing interests overcame the presumption of access.[256] "Minute books" of a court clerk showing the daily activities of judges, including gifts they accepted, have been held to be subject to a presumptive right of access,[257] as has a master list of qualified jurors indicating their names and addresses,[258] and advisory opinions issued by a committee on judicial ethics.[259]

---

249. *Id.* at 1051. There was no requirement that the court officer file such reports; they were apparently filed only to demonstrate she had fulfilled her duties under the consent decree. See *id.*

250. See *id.* at 1052. Compare Marisol A. v. Giuliani, 26 MEDIA L. REP. (BNA) 1151, 1153-54 (S.D.N.Y. 1997) (recognizing "strong" presumption of access to report prepared pursuant to court order because it was likely to play an important role in court's performance of its Article III function and because both the parties and subject matter of litigation were of public interest).

251. See 71 F.3d at 1047.

252. See *id.*

253. *Id.* at 1052-53.

254. 46 F.3d 29, 31 (7th Cir. 1995).

255. See Smith v. United States Dist. Ct., 956 F.2d 647, 649-50 (7th Cir. 1992).

256. See Crystal Grower's Corp. v. Dobbins, 616 F.2d 458 (10th Cir. 1980) (sealing documents alleged to be subject to attorney-client privilege or work product doctrine).

257. See Copley Press, Inc. v. San Diego County Super. Ct., 7 Cal. Rptr. 2d 841 (Ct. App. 1992).

258. See Pantos v. City & County of San Francisco, 198 Cal. Rptr. 489 (Ct. App. 1984).

259. See In re Access to Certain Records of Rhode Island Advisory Comm. on Code of Judicial Conduct, 637 A.2d 1063 (R.I. 1994).

And, the D.C. Circuit has held that the independent counsel's final report on the Iran-Contra investigation was subject to public access under federal law.[260]

While confidential information concerning physicians' salaries contained in a brief was properly subject to a protective order, the Seventh Circuit has determined that the material should have been redacted and the remainder of the document placed in the public record.[261] But a federal court sitting in California has held that an automated civil case management system, the Information Access Provider, did not constitute "the type of 'court record' or 'court document' to which the public has a First Amendment right of access."[262]

In *In re Symington*,[263] the court considered whether the press could intervene in bankruptcy proceedings to seek dissolution of a protective order covering confidential financial records. After permitting intervention, the court held that the press and public are entitled to attend Rule 2004 examinations (bankruptcy proceedings) because such examinations have historically been public proceedings and because public access can play a significant role in the bankruptcy process.[264] Open proceedings, the court concluded, are likely to make witnesses more forthcoming and assure "that witnesses [are] treated fairly and equitably."[265] In addition, the court held that "the news media has a right to view the fruits of a document production pursuant to Rule 2004 (bankruptcy proceedings), [since] 'the overriding public interest' in learning the facts about criminal misconduct allegedly committed by a debtor while currently serving as the Governor of Arizona constitutes such 'extraordinary circumstances' that outweigh the interest of the debtor and his mother in preserving the confidentiality of her personal financial records."[266]

§ 6-2. Juvenile Records.

§ 6-2(a). Transcripts and Records of Delinquency Proceedings.

Juvenile court records, like juvenile proceedings, are typically closed to the press and public.[267] Nevertheless, as with so many traditional rules mandating secrecy, there are an increasing number of exceptions to this general proposi-

---

260. See In re North, 16 F.3d 1234 (D.C. Cir. 1994); see also SEC v. Stratton Oakmont, Inc., 24 MEDIA L. REP. (BNA) 2179 (D.C. Cir. 1996) (unsealing findings of independent consultant in SEC action).
261. See Methodist Hosp., Inc. v. Sullivan, 91 F.3d 1026, 1031-32 (7th Cir. 1996).
262. Los Angeles Times v. County of Los Angeles, 956 F. Supp. 1530, 1540 (C.D. Cal. 1996).
263. 209 B.R. 678, 681 (D. Md. 1997).
264. See *id.*
265. *Id.* at 694.
266. *Id.* at 681-82.
267. See REPORTERS COMMITTEE FOR FREEDOM OF THE PRESS, ACCESS TO JUVENILE COURTS, Fall 1995, at 2.

tion.[268] As more courts and states have opened juvenile proceedings to the press and public,[269] the transcripts and records of such proceedings have also been made available for public inspection.[270]

All states have laws regulating juvenile proceedings,[271] many of which allow for access in some circumstances,[272] especially in cases involving violent crimes.[273] Some state laws that generally forbid public access to juvenile court records expressly provide exceptions when the proceedings are open or the

---

268. In *Bishop v. Craft-Jones*, 2 F. Supp. 2d 1317 (D. Or. 1998), a civil action alleging assault by a police officer against parents of minors who counterclaimed for civil rights violations, the court permitted limited discovery of juvenile court records. The court noted that "no public inspection of the record of a juvenile proceeding is allowed but the record is open to inspection by the child . . . parent, guardian . . . and their attorneys." *Id.* at 1318. In the case at issue, however, the juveniles waived the confidentiality of their juvenile records by obtaining portions of the materials for use in an independent civil lawsuit, in which they would then be "testifying in a public forum about the same matters" addressed in the private forum, leaving no benefit to closure. *Id.* at 1319. Juveniles "should not be allowed to use [the confidentiality statute] as a tool to obtain materials for use in an independent civil lawsuit, while at the same time invoking the statute as a shield to deny the opposing parties a level playing field." *Id.* at 1318.

269. See, e.g., United States v. A.D., 28 F.3d 1353 (3d Cir. 1994) (reversing order closing a delinquency proceeding); see generally Chap. 3-3(a) *supra*; REPORTERS COMMITTEE FOR FREEDOM OF THE PRESS, *supra* note 267, at 2 (noting that change in the goal of juvenile justice system from rehabilitation to retribution has led to more states opening juvenile proceedings); Dienes, *Access to Juvenile Proceedings*, 14 COMM. LAW. 7, 8 (Winter 1996) (noting that increase in violent crimes committed by juveniles has led more states to amend laws in favor of access to juvenile proceedings); Symposium, *Future of the Juvenile Court*, 88 J. CRIM. L. & CRIMINOLOGY 1 (1997).

270. Nearly 30 states permit the names of juvenile offenders to be released, at least in some circumstances. See Szymanski, NATIONAL CENTER FOR JUVENILE JUSTICE, RELEASING JUVENILE DELINQUENT NAMES TO MEDIA — STATUTES ANALYSIS: 1993 UPDATE 1-17. See generally Martin, *Open the Doors: A Judicial Call to End Confidentiality in Delinquency Proceedings*, 21 NEW ENG. J. CRIM. & CIV. CONFINEMENT 393, 404-06 (1995).

271. See Torbet et al., NATIONAL CENTER FOR JUVENILE JUSTICE, STATE RESPONSES TO SERIOUS AND VIOLENT JUVENILE CRIME 36 (1996); REPORTERS COMMITTEE FOR FREEDOM OF THE PRESS, *supra* note 267.

272. See, e.g., WIS. STAT. § 938.396, amended by 1997-1998 Wis. Legis. Serv. Act 27 § 5275(g)-(m), Act 35 § 567-68 (establishing several exceptions to presumption of confidentiality of juvenile records, including requiring police and juvenile courts to open certain records for inspection and preventing them from considering rehabilitation and other interests of the juvenile as a basis for closure); In re Lewis, 25 MEDIA L. REP. (BNA) 2179, 2180, 2182 (Fla. Cir. 1997) (holding that while the statute provides that juvenile court records are not public records, it allows inspection by interested persons, which is to be interpreted "with due consideration given to the First Amendment"). See also Dienes, *supra* note 269, at 7.

273. See In re Lewis, 25 MEDIA L. REP. (BNA) 2179, 2181-82 (Fla. Cir. 1997) (while confidentiality provisions of statute were intended to protect juvenile's identity, through recent statutory access rights "the Legislature has determined that the public must be informed of serious juvenile crimes" and "[a]s the conduct becomes more serious or repetitive, the interest of the child in preserving his or her privacy yields in favor of disclosure"). See Chap. 3-3(a) *supra*; Brelsford & Silvers, *Juvenile Courts: Part I, The Battle for Access*, 12 COMM. LAW. 7, 8 (Summer 1994); Dienes, *supra* note 269, at 7.

public's interest outweighs the need for confidentiality.[274] And, even in the absence of a statutory exception, where the press and public gain access to specific juvenile proceedings, the argument is increasingly made that the transcripts and records of those proceedings should be available to the press and public as well.[275] In *Ohio ex rel. Scripps Howard Broadcasting Co. v. Cuyahoga County Court of Common Pleas*,[276] for example, the Ohio Supreme Court permitted the media to purchase the transcript of a contempt proceeding held in juvenile court, despite a juvenile court rule prohibiting public access to such a record. The court reasoned that the juvenile court's order denying access to the transcript "impinged on the public's constitutional right of access."[277] In *Ex parte The Island Packet*,[278] the South Carolina Supreme Court held that transcripts of a closed hearing, conducted to determine if the underlying case should be transferred out of juvenile court, should be made available to the public because the family court had improperly closed the transfer hearing.[279] The court concluded that the "request for a transcript implicates the same first amendment rights that protect the public's access to the actual proceeding."[280] Some states, however, have been reluctant to open juvenile records as readily as juvenile proceedings. In Florida, juvenile proceedings can only be closed by court order,[281] whereas court files may only be inspected pursuant to a specific order.[282] In *News Group Boston, Inc. v. Massachusetts*,[283] the Massachusetts Supreme Judicial Court concluded that a statutory requirement of open juvenile

---

274. See, e.g., ARK. CODE ANN. § 9-27-309 (providing an exception to the sealing of all juvenile records for cases involving juveniles who could have been tried as adults); CAL. WELFARE & INST. CODE § 389 (juvenile may not request sealing if he has been convicted of a felony or misdemeanor involving moral turpitude); GA. CODE ANN. § 15-11-58 (affording access to records if public has a statutory right of access to the proceeding itself); ME. REV. STAT. ANN. tit. 15, § 3308 (if the hearing is open to the general public, "the record of the hearing . . . [is] open to public inspection" as well).

275. See Garsh & Albano, *In the Matter of John Doe Grand Jury, 410 Mass. 596 (1991), News Group Boston, Inc. v. Commonwealth, 407 Mass. 879 (1990)*, 36 BOSTON B.J. 5, 7 (1992).

276. 652 N.E.2d 179 (Ohio 1995).

277. *Id.* at 182 (citing United States v. Antar, 38 F.3d 1348, 1359-61 (3d Cir. 1994)). Cf. Ohio ex rel. News Herald v. Ottawa County Ct., 671 N.E.2d 5 (Ohio 1996) (finding mandamus an appropriate vehicle for newspaper to seek access to juvenile records).

278. 417 S.E.2d 575 (S.C. 1992).

279. See *id.* at 577.

280. *Id*; see In re Richmond Newspapers, Inc., 16 MEDIA L. REP. (BNA) 1049, 1052 (Va. App. 1988) ("The factors that mandate free access to court hearings apply with equal force to public review of records.").

281. FLA. STAT. § 985.205.

282. See *id.* § 985.05 ("[O]fficial records required by this part are not open to inspection by the public, but may be inspected only upon order of the court by persons deemed by the court to have a proper interest therein . . . .").

283. 568 N.E.2d 600, 604 (Mass. 1991). See generally Garsh & Albano, *supra* note 275.

proceedings does not necessarily extend to the record of those proceedings.[284] "To the extent that information is presented in written form," the court held, "we would expect that the statutory requirement of opening juvenile courtrooms to the public when murder charges are involved would not override the exercise of a well-articulated judicial judgment to impound particular records, reports, or documents."[285]

Other states, in contrast, have opened records of juvenile proceedings even when the hearings themselves have remained closed. In Kansas, for example, a juvenile's file is open to the public if he was at least fourteen years old at the time of the offense,[286] although the proceedings are only open if the juvenile is at least sixteen.[287] In Tennessee, petitions and orders in cases of violent offenses committed by a juvenile at least fourteen years old are open to the public,[288] which can nevertheless be excluded from such a proceeding.[289]

§ 6-2(b). Other Juvenile Records.

In *In re Richmond Newspapers, Inc.*,[290] a Virginia appellate court interpreted two state statutes,[291] which purported to seal the records of all children committed to the Department of Corrections[292] and other children whether delinquent or dependent, to provide at least a limited right of public access.[293] Indeed, the court held that only safeguarding the interest of the juvenile in rehabilitation could outweigh the right of access.[294] In the case before it, in which the juvenile who was the subject of the records at issue had died, the court concluded that damage to his family and to the deceased child could not justify maintaining the juvenile's record under seal.[295]

In *Webster Groves School District v. Pulitzer Publishing Co.*,[296] in contrast, the Eighth Circuit affirmed a district court order sealing the record and a memorandum order denying a motion for a preliminary injunction in a juvenile proceeding. The motion sought to enjoin a handicapped fourteen-year-old, who

---

284. See 568 N.E.2d at 604.
285. *Id.*
286. See KAN. STAT. ANN. § 38-1607.
287. See *id.* § 38-1652.
288. See TENN. CODE ANN. § 37-1-153.
289. See *id.* § 37-1-124(d).
290. 16 MEDIA L. REP. (BNA) 1049 (Va. Cir. 1988).
291. See VA. CODE ANN. §§ 16.1-300, 16.1-305.
292. See *id.* § 16.1-300.
293. See *id.* § 16.1-305.
294. See 16 MEDIA L. REP. (BNA) at 1053.
295. See *id.* (holding that the interest of the family and child of a juvenile is no different than that of a family or child of an adult offender and, therefore, does not outweigh the public's right of access).
296. 898 F.2d 1371 (8th Cir. 1990).

threatened classmates with a loaded gun, from attending school pending an administrative review. The Eighth Circuit rejected a presumption of access, concluding that "[w]hether we apply a constitutional standard or a common law standard, the result is the same: Pulitzer's interest in access to the records is outweighed by [the minor's] privacy interest and the state's interest in protecting minors from the public dissemination of hurtful information."[297]

In granting release of most records and files in a child abuse case, the court in *In re Buentipo*[298] noted that, given the incidence of child abuse in society and the public's misinformation and misunderstanding regarding the child abuse and neglect system, the public has a legitimate right "to have sufficient information to make informed and educated opinions regarding the child abuse and neglect process."[299] In evaluating the rights of the juvenile victim, the court emphasized that his best interests would not be affected by a limited disclosure of the court files.[300] Although the parents and siblings had "inherent privacy rights," those rights had largely been extinguished by extensive media coverage.[301] Further, the identifying information of any siblings would be redacted prior to disclosure, to protect their privacy.[302] "The Court does not believe that disclosure of these records will 'chill' families from cooperating with Child Protective Services" or "unfairly prejudice" the mother's right to a fair trial.[303]

---

297. *Id.* at 1377.
298. 26 MEDIA L. REP. (BNA) 1888 (Haw. Fam. Ct. 1997).
299. *Id.* at 1890 (noting "the public's right to know, the public's right to be educated, and the public's right to have sufficient information").
300. See *id.*
301. *Id.*
302. See *id.*
303. *Id.*

Chapter 7

ACCESS TO PARTICIPANTS IN THE JUDICIAL PROCESS

§ 7-1. Participants in the Judicial Process Generally.
§ 7-2. Attorneys.
§ 7-3. Jurors.
§ 7-4. Checkbook Journalism.

§ 7-1. Participants in the Judicial Process Generally.

In *Sheppard v. Maxwell*,[1] the Supreme Court, albeit in *dicta*, appeared to endorse restraints on trial participants as a means of preventing prejudice to a defendant's right to a fair trial. Such restrictions, the Court suggested, were preferable to reversing a conviction. "The courts must take such steps by rule and regulation that will protect their processes from prejudicial outside influences. Neither prosecutor, counsel for defense, the accused, witnesses, court staff nor enforcement officers coming under the jurisdiction of the court should be free to frustrate its function."[2] After *Nebraska Press Association v. Stuart*,[3] moreover, the use of gag orders directed at the news media has largely been eliminated. As a result, courts have increasingly employed restrictive orders directed to trial participants generally and invoked standing court rules for the discipline of counsel and law enforcement personnel to control pretrial publicity.[4] Backed by the contempt power and other potential sanctions, trial courts can

---

1. 384 U.S. 333 (1966). See Chap. 2-1(b) *supra*.

2. 384 U.S. at 362-63. See *id*. at 359-60 ("[T]he court should have made some effort to control the release of leads, information, and gossip to the press by police officers, witnesses, and the counsel for both sides. . . . [I]t is obvious that the judge should have further sought to alleviate this problem by imposing control over the statements made to the news media by counsel, witnesses, and especially the Coroner and police officers.").

3. 427 U.S. 539 (1976). See Chap. 2-1(d) *supra*. The Court in *Nebraska Press Association* did not directly consider the validity of gag orders on trial participants. It did, however, indicate that prohibiting extrajudicial commentary by trial participants is less restrictive of First Amendment freedoms than a prior restraint on the press itself. See 427 U.S. at 554-55. Justice Brennan, concurring, cited the *Sheppard* Court's apparent endorsement of restraints on trial participants as an example of a less onerous alternative to gag orders directed at the media. See *id*. at 601 (Brennan, J., concurring) ("judges may stem much of the flow of prejudicial publicity at its source, before it is obtained by representatives of the press"). See also Gentile v. State Bar, 501 U.S. 1030, 1072 (1991) (in *Sheppard*, "[w]e expressly contemplated that the speech of those participating before the courts could be limited").

4. See, e.g., Koch v. Koch Indus., Inc., 6 F. Supp. 2d 1185, 1189 (D. Kan. 1998) (rejecting media's overbreadth challenge to issuance of a restrictive order preventing any party from contacting prospective jurors, making "extrajudicial statements to the news media," or placing advertisements or commercials connected to the case in any medium until the jury pool was selected, because the order was a direct response to requests of both parties, it was based on a balancing of the interests, and it was a proper means of safeguarding the state's compelling interest in a fair and impartial verdict); United States v. Hill, 893 F. Supp. 1039 (N.D. Fla. 1994) (concluding that an

impose such restraints and thereby choke off important sources of information. Such orders, therefore, plainly burden both the newsgathering activities of the press and the freedom of expression of participants in the judicial process. It is not surprising, therefore, that these so-called "gag orders" have been challenged by the press as well as by those subject to them according to their terms.[5]

Despite some early decisions holding that the news media lacks Article III standing to challenge a restraining order directed at trial participants,[6] courts today typically hold that the press may intervene and raise objections. In *CBS Inc. v. Young*,[7] for example, the trial court had entered an order restraining all parties, their relatives, close friends, and associates from discussing a civil action

---

order restraining trial participants was justified, since a gag order on the media would be unconstitutional). See generally Chemerinsky, *Silence Is Not Golden: Protecting Lawyer Speech Under the First Amendment*, 47 EMORY L.J. 859 (1998); Swartz, *Trial Participant Speech Restrictions: Gagging First Amendment Rights*, 90 COLUM. L. REV. 1411 (1990); Weinreb, *Speaking Out Outside the Courtroom*, 47 EMORY L.J. 889 (1998); Symposium, *The Sound of Silence: Reflections on the Use of the Gag Order*, 17 LOY. L.A. ENT. L.J. 629 (1997); Comment, *Gag Orders and the Ultimate Sanction*, 18 LOY. L.A. ENT. L.J. 305 (1998); Comment, *The Impartial Jury and Media Overload: Rethinking Attorney Speech Regulations in the 1990s*, 16 N. ILL. U. L. REV. 483 (1996); Note, *Looking for Fair Trials in the Information Age: The Need for More Stringent Gag Orders Against Trial Participants*, 30 U.S.F. L. REV. 95 (1995); Note, *Free Press-Fair Trial: Can They Be Reconciled in a Highly Publicized Criminal Case?*, 79 GEO. L.J. 337 (1990); Note, *Prior Restraint by Any Other Name: The Judicial Response to Media Challenges to Gag Orders Directed at Trial Participants*, 88 MICH. L. REV. 1171 (1990).

5. See generally J. BARRON & C.T. DIENES, HANDBOOK OF FREE SPEECH AND FREE PRESS § 9-8 (1979). The press has also sought to obtain access to criminal defendants in custody who express a willingness to be interviewed. See United States v. Fort, 14 MEDIA L. REP. (BNA) 1942 (N.D. Ill. 1987); Ohio v. Barker, 23 MEDIA L. REP. (BNA) 1124 (Ohio C.P. 1994). Cf. Abu-Jamal v. Price, 23 MEDIA L. REP. (BNA) 2406 (W.D. Pa. 1995) (media may file amicus brief in civil suit by inmate based on refusal to allow interviews). On the gag order restricting public statements by trial participants in the O.J. Simpson civil case, see Hoffman, *The Gag Order in the O.J. Simpson Civil Action: Lessons to Be Learned?*, 17 LOY. L.A. ENT. L.J. 333, 351-52 (1997) ("The judicial consideration of the gag order issues in the Simpson case proceedings revealed the erosion of First Amendment standards in this area in the past decade."); Mirell, *Gag Orders and the Attorney Discipline Rules: Why Not Base the Former on the Latter?*, 17 LOY. L.A. ENT. L.J. 353 (1997) (attorney discipline rules should not be basis for crafting judicial gag orders).

6. In *Central South Carolina Chapter v. Martin*, 431 F. Supp. 1182 (D.S.C.), aff'd, 556 F.2d 706 (4th Cir. 1977), cert. denied, 434 U.S. 1022 (1978), the district court held that the press lacked standing to challenge a gag order that applied only to trial participants on the ground that the press had not alleged any interest different from that of citizens generally. *Id.* at 1185. Moreover, even if the order were vacated, the court asserted, "it is merely speculation that the trial participants would voluntarily disclose such information" to the press. *Id.* at 1187-88. Curiously, the court also concluded that the media claim was not in the "zone of interests" protected by the First Amendment. *Id.* at 1187. While the Fourth Circuit affirmed on the merits, it rejected the trial court's standing analysis: "We do not regard as wholly speculative the relationship between the district court's order and the plaintiffs' difficulties in seeking to perform their reportorial function." 556 F.2d at 708.

7. 522 F.2d 234 (6th Cir. 1975).

§ 7-1   ACCESS TO PARTICIPANTS IN THE JUDICIAL PROCESS   § 7-1

arising from the deaths of several students at Kent State University with the news media or the public. The Sixth Circuit afforded mandamus relief to the network,[8] noting that it was "not persuaded by the argument that petitioner lacks standing because it is not a party to the civil litigation. The fact remains that its ability to gather the news concerning the trial is directly impaired or curtailed. The protected right to publish the news would be of little value in the absence of sources from which to obtain it."[9]

The Sixth Circuit in *Young* characterized the order as "an extreme example of a prior restraint," which could not satisfy the First Amendment unless it was necessary to obviate serious and imminent threats to the fairness and integrity of the trial.[10] Newspaper coverage of the case prior to the order's entry, the court observed, had been "innocuous" and the jury had been impaneled with little difficulty. Accordingly "[t]he presumption against the constitutional validity of the order" had not been overcome and it was "constitutionally impermissible."[11] Indeed, the Sixth Circuit concluded, the order constituted a "prior direct restraint upon freedom of expression of trial participants"[12] and burdened the newsgathering rights of the press itself.[13] The court did not discuss whether the press had standing to litigate the free speech rights of the nonparty trial participants, apparently not considering the issue to be significant.[14]

In *Radio & Television News Association v. United States District Court*,[15] however, the standing of the press in this context proved to be determinative. The case arose when a group of news organizations sought a writ of mandamus to compel the trial court to vacate an order restraining defense counsel from making extrajudicial statements to the press.[16] The petitioners asserted that the order constituted an unconstitutional prior restraint on their ability to gather

---

8. The court held that it had jurisdiction under the All Writs Act, 28 U.S.C. § 1651. See 522 F.2d at 237.

9. 522 F.2d at 237-38 (media, though not a specific target of the order, was "effectively cut off from any access whatever to important sources of information about the trial").

10. *Id.* at 240 (citing Chase v. Robson, 435 F.2d 1059 (7th Cir. 1970)).

11. 522 F.2d at 240-41. The order was also held to be overbroad "as to subject matter or content of any prohibited discussions. According to its literal terms, no discussions whatsoever about the case are permitted by the persons upon whom the ban is placed whether prejudicial or innocuous, whether subjective or objective, whether reportorial or interpretive." *Id.*

12. *Id.* at 239.

13. See *id.* ("Although the news media are not directly enjoined from discussing the case, it is apparent that significant and meaningful sources of information concerning the case are effectively removed from them and their representatives. To that extent their protected right to obtain information concerning the trial is curtailed and impaired.") (citing Branzburg v. Hayes, 408 U.S. 665 (1972)).

14. See Swartz, *supra* note 4, at 1413 n.20.

15. 781 F.2d 1443 (9th Cir. 1986).

16. See *id.* at 1443.

news.[17] The Ninth Circuit held that the press had demonstrated a sufficient stake to establish Article III standing "to raise freedom of the press concerns under the first amendment."[18] Nevertheless, the court also held that "[t]he RTNA lacks standing to assert the free speech constitutional rights of the nonparty trial counsel in challenging this order."[19] The third-party standing doctrine, which prohibits a litigant from raising the legal rights of a party not before the court, precluded the news organizations from asserting the free speech rights of the trial participants.[20]

Having thus limited the issue to the rights of the press to gather news, the court held that "the media's collateral interest in interviewing trial participants is outside the scope of protection offered by the first amendment."[21] The press' own rights had not been infringed, the court concluded, since the order's "impact on the media is significantly different from situations where the media is denied access to a criminal trial or is restricted in disseminating any information it obtains."[22] The press remained free to attend the trial and report its observations, the court reasoned, and it was also "free to direct questions at trial counsel. Trial counsel simply may not be free to answer."[23]

Moreover, since the press' First Amendment rights had only been incidentally or indirectly burdened, the court asserted, the prior restraint doctrine was inapposite.[24] Thus, the court concluded that it "need only 'examine whether the restrictions imposed are reasonable and whether the interests [of the government] override the very limited incidental effects of the [order] on First Amendment rights.'"[25] Applying this "limited" standard of review, the Ninth Circuit affirmed the district court's holding that a restraint on extrajudicial statements by trial counsel was reasonably related to the legitimate purpose of limiting prejudicial publicity.[26]

---

17. See *id.* at 1445.
18. *Id.* at 1445-46; *see id.* (order "impairs the media's ability to gather news by effectively denying the media access to trial counsel, a concrete personal interest").
19. *Id.* at 1448.
20. See also In re Dow Jones & Co., 842 F.2d 603, 609 (2d Cir.), *cert. denied*, 488 U.S. 946 (1988) ("nothing prevented the restrained parties in the present litigation from challenging the July 10 order"); J. BARRON & C.T. DIENES, CONSTITUTIONAL LAW IN A NUTSHELL 48-50 (4th ed. 1999); J. NOWAK & R. ROTUNDA, CONSTITUTIONAL LAW § 2.12(f)(4) (5th ed. 1995); L. TRIBE, AMERICAN CONSTITUTIONAL LAW § 3-19 (2d ed. 1988).
21. 781 F.2d at 1447.
22. *Id.* at 1446.
23. *Id*; see *id.* at 1446 n.3 ("[T]he 'right to gather information' does not include a constitutional 'right' to understand what has been gathered.").
24. See *id.* at 1447.
25. *Id.* (quoting KPNX Broadcasting Co. v. Maricopa County Super. Ct., 678 P.2d 431, 441 (Ariz. 1984)).
26. See 781 F.2d at 1447-48.

The Second Circuit adopted a similar analysis in *In re Dow Jones & Co.*,[27] in which it affirmed a gag order on parties and attorneys, issued at the request of defense counsel.[28] The court held that the press had standing to assert a First Amendment right to receive information and ideas.[29] It could not, however, assert the defendants' free speech rights "when defendants refuse to challenge that infringement themselves."[30] In addition, like the Ninth Circuit, the court rejected the news organizations' claim that the gag order constituted "a classic prior restraint on the press."[31] There was, the court explained, "a substantial difference between a restraining order directed against the press — a form of censorship which the First Amendment sought to abolish from these shores — and the order here directed solely against trial participants and challenged only by the press. The distinction is critical."[32] Thus, while the Second Circuit acknowledged that the restraining order has "an effect similar to that of a prior restraint" in limiting the flow of news and information, "the order is not directed at the news agencies and . . . they cannot therefore be hauled into court for violating its terms."[33]

The court emphasized, however, that even an indirect effect on press freedoms must be justified under the First Amendment.[34] Indeed, such an order will survive constitutional scrutiny only when there is a "reasonable likelihood" that

---

27. 842 F.2d 603 (2d Cir.), *cert. denied*, 488 U.S. 946 (1988).
28. See *id.* at 605.
29. See *id.* at 607 ("A First Amendment challenge by the news agencies as recipients of information must certainly be permitted when the restrained speech, as here, concerns allegations of corruption by public officials in obtaining federal contracts.").
30. *Id.* at 609. See Koch v. Koch Indus., Inc., 6 F. Supp. 2d 1185, 1190 & n.8 (D. Kan. 1998) (media has no standing to challenge order precluding extrajudicial statements by parties, counsel, and witnesses in a civil case in which the order was entered at the parties' request and the court found that no party objected to the order).
31. 842 F.2d at 608. See also Montana ex rel. Missoulian v. Montana Twenty-First Judicial Dist. Ct., 933 P.2d 829, 839 (Mont. 1997) (stating that "prior restraint analysis is dependent upon the status of the party bringing the challenge" and "[w]hile an order restraining the trial participants from communicating with the press may be a prior restraint upon the participants as communicators, it is not a prior restraint upon the press").
32. *Id.*
33. *Id.*; see *id.* at 609 ("[w]hen the exercise of free press rights actually tramples upon Sixth Amendment rights, the former must nonetheless yield to the latter"); United States v. Davis, 904 F. Supp. 564 (E.D. La. 1995) (partial gag order on trial participants not prior restraint); South Bend Tribune v. Elkhart Circuit Ct., 691 N.E.2d 200, 202 (Ind. App. 1998) (affirming gag order on participants in murder trial).
34. See 842 F.2d at 609 ("To conclude that this is not a case of prior restraint of the press is not to say that the restraining order need not be justified. On the contrary, it must be. The impact of the subject order implicates press freedom, even though it does so indirectly."); United States v. Davis, 904 F. Supp. 564 (E.D. La. 1995).

pretrial publicity will prejudice a fair trial[35] and that other less restrictive remedies had been unsuccessfully explored.[36]

The Eleventh Circuit as well appears to draw a constitutionally significant distinction between gag orders on trial participants challenged by the media and those challenged by the participants themselves. In *News-Journal Corp. v. Foxman*,[37] a newspaper challenged a trial judge's order prohibiting extrajudicial statements by counsel, witnesses, defendants, court personnel, and law enforcement officers in a sensational murder-for-hire case. The court concluded that the press' "First Amendment rights did not extend to interviews of the trial participants, when such interviews and subsequent reporting had evidenced to [the trial judge] the potential inability of impaneling an impartial jury."[38] Moreover, counsel had encouraged and agreed to the restrictions in order to combat "sensationalized" reporting.[39] Ultimately, however, the Eleventh Circuit affirmed the trial court's order under the abstention doctrine, since the newspaper had an adequate state forum in which to present its claim and had failed to show specific irreparable injury as a result of the restrictive order, "which was not directed to the press, but to the trial participants."[40]

---

35. 842 F.2d at 610. See S.D.N.Y. CRIM. R. 7(a); South Bend Tribune v. Elkhart Circuit Ct., 691 N.E.2d 200 (Ind. App. 1998) (noting trial court's consideration of alternatives to a gag order on trial participants, upholding the use of the reasonable likelihood test, and finding that no abuse of discretion occurred in court's entry of gag order); but see Montana ex rel. Missoulian v. Montana Twenty-First Judicial Dist. Ct., 933 P.2d 829, 841 (Mont. 1997) (holding that, although gag order restricting trial participants is not prior restraint, "reasonableness" is "too lenient a standard to protect the right to know" under state constitution and "heightened scrutiny" must be applied).

36. See In re Dow Jones & Co., 842 F. 2d at 611 (noting that "each [precaution] must be explored and ultimately rejected — individually and in combination — as a remedy before a restraining order is entered"); see also In re New York Times Co., 878 F.2d 67 (2d Cir. 1989) (holding that, absent finding that prejudice could result from statements made to press by counsel, or even that any statements were likely to be made, gag order was unconstitutional); Connecticut Magazine v. Moraghan, 676 F. Supp. 38 (D. Conn. 1987) (holding that gag order was an unconstitutional prior restraint because there was no evidence that the state court judge had considered less restrictive alternatives); New York Times Co. v. Rothwax, 533 N.Y.S.2d 73 (App. Div. 1988) (holding that, absent factual findings of necessity for prior restraints on counsel and employees, gag order was unconstitutional); National Broadcasting Co. v. Cooperman, 501 N.Y.S.2d 405 (App. Div. 1986).

37. 939 F.2d 1499 (11th Cir. 1991).

38. *Id.* at 1515. The Eleventh Circuit noted that the district court had conducted a hearing before entering the order, and had concluded that there were no less restrictive means of safeguarding the defendant's Sixth Amendment rights. See *id.* See also In re Subpoena to Testify Before Grand Jury, 864 F.2d 1559, 1564 (11th Cir. 1989) (affirming a similar order).

39. 939 F.2d at 1515 ("[i]n this case, the sensationalized reporting of extrajudicial statements by trial participants clearly created a strong probability of prejudicing the prosecution of the defendants").

40. *Id.* at 1516.

Although the full Supreme Court has not had occasion to address the issue, Chief Justice Rehnquist, sitting as Circuit Justice in *KPNX Broadcasting Co. v. Superior Court*,[41] declined to stay enforcement of a gag order directed at trial participants in a criminal case. The order at issue required that all court personnel, counsel, witnesses, and jurors refrain from speaking directly with the media concerning a highly publicized murder trial involving organized crime and established a court-appointed liaison to provide a "unified and singular source for the media concerning these proceedings."[42] Justice Rehnquist noted that the trial court "had evaluated the press's First Amendment rights against the defendant's Sixth Amendment rights to a fair trial . . . [and] found that the least restrictive course of conduct was to restrict the participants' outside contact with the press."[43] Citing the aforementioned language from *Sheppard*, Justice Rehnquist stated that "[t]he mere potential for confusion if unregulated communication between trial participants and the press at a heavily covered trial were permitted is enough to warrant a measure such as the trial judge took in this case."[44]

When gag orders against trial participants are challenged by the participants themselves, rather than by the press alone, courts have required a qualitatively heightened level of constitutional scrutiny. In an early case, *Chase v. Robson*,[45] for example, the Seventh Circuit held that there must be a serious and imminent threat to the administration of justice to justify such a restraint. Moreover, the Supreme Court has held that where a trial participant has lawfully obtained truthful information about a matter of public significance, its subsequent dissemination to the public cannot be punished absent the demonstrated need to further a state interest of the highest order.[46] Nevertheless, while the issue remains unsettled, most courts appear to have concluded that such restraints on trial participants do not constitute presumptively invalid prior restraints for purposes of the First Amendment.[47]

---

41. 459 U.S. 1302 (1982) (Rehnquist, J., in chambers).
42. *Id.* at 1303.
43. *Id.* at 1304.
44. *Id.* at 1307; see *id.* ("Continuation of this proscription against communication to hours and places where the court is not in session appears to me to be warranted under the above-quoted language from *Sheppard*.") (citing Sheppard v. Maxwell, 384 U.S. 333 (1966)); see also KPNX Broadcasting v. Maricopa County Super. Ct., 678 P.2d 431, (Ariz. 1984) (press has no First Amendment-based right of access to materials unavailable to the public).
45. 435 F.2d 1059, 1061 (7th Cir. 1970).
46. See, e.g., Butterworth v. Smith, 494 U.S. 624, 632 (1990) (grand jury witness cannot be prevented from disclosing information he possessed prior to his appearance); see also The Florida Star v. B.J.F., 491 U.S. 524 (1989); Smith v. Daily Mail Publ'g Co., 443 U.S. 97 (1979); Chap. 2-1(c) *supra*.
47. Compare M. FRANKLIN & D. ANDERSON, MASS MEDIA LAW 96 (4th ed. 1990) ("Although they *are* prior restraints on the speech of [trial] participants, they generally are not scrutinized with the same rigor as prior restraints against the media . . . . Such restraints have been upheld . . . upon

In another early case, *United States v. Tijerina*,[48] a trial court entered a gag order at the suggestion of defense counsel. Thereafter, the defendant violated the order when he made comments at a convention about the trial.[49] The Tenth Circuit upheld the order's constitutionality, concluding that "[t]he Supreme Court has never said that a clear and present danger to a right of fair trial must exist before a trial court can forbid extrajudicial statements about the trial."[50] Stressing the responsibilities of the trial judge to control trial participants under *Sheppard*, the court held that a "reasonable likelihood" of harm to the integrity of the trial was sufficient to justify such an order.[51]

Similarly, in *Chicago Council of Lawyers v. Bauer*,[52] the Seventh Circuit declined to invoke the prior restraint doctrine to gauge the constitutionality of standing "no-comment" rules that limited commentary by attorneys about pending litigation. Although the court invalidated the rules as constitutionally overbroad,[53] they were not prior restraints because, unlike gag orders, their validity could be tested at the time of their enforcement.[54] Still, the court recognized that the "rules do have some of the inherent features of 'prior restraints' which have caused the judiciary to review them with particular care."[55] Thus, the court recognized that, even though a heavy presumption against the rule's validity was inappropriate, it required close scrutiny.[56]

---

a showing of a 'reasonable likelihood' that the extrajudicial statements would prejudice the defendant's right to a fair trial."), with D. GILLMORE, ET AL., MASS COMMUNICATION LAW 446 (5th ed. 1990) ("the courts have looked favorably on challenges from persons subject to restrictive no-comment orders, often opting for a prior restraint analysis").

48. 412 F.2d 661 (10th Cir.), *cert. denied*, 396 U.S. 990 (1969).

49. See *id*. at 665. The defendant boasted that he told witnesses what to do and charged that the judge was misusing the law. See *id*. at 665-66.

50. *Id*. at 666.

51. *Id*. at 667 ("The order against extrajudicial statements was designed to maintain the atmosphere essential to the preservation of fair trial, 'the most fundamental of all freedoms.' Both the defendants and the public have the right to expect that justice will be done. The defendants have the protection of the order and the responsibility to obey it.").

52. 522 F.2d 242 (7th Cir. 1975), *cert. denied*, 427 U.S. 912 (1976).

53. See *id*. at 249.

54. See *id*. at 248 (citing In re Oliver, 452 F.2d 111 (7th Cir. 1971)). See also Hirschkop v. Snead, 594 F.2d 356, 370 (4th Cir. 1979) (holding that an analogous provision of the Virginia Code of Professional Responsibility was not a prior restraint, and its reasonable likelihood standard was not overbroad).

55. 522 F.2d at 249.

56. See *id*.; see also Montana ex rel. Missoulian v. Montana Twenty-First Judicial Dist. Ct., 933 P.2d 829, 841 (Mont. 1997) (holding that, although gag order restricting trial participants is not a prior restraint, "heightened scrutiny" applies, requiring hearing, consideration of reasonable alternatives, narrow tailoring and specific findings of substantial probability of prejudice to defendant's fair trial rights).

It is, however, arguable that *Nebraska Press Association v. Stuart*,[57] decided after all of the foregoing cases, has altered the appropriate constitutional analysis. In *Levine v. United States District Court*,[58] for example, the court interpreted *Nebraska Press Association* as requiring that a district court order restricting attorneys in a criminal case from communicating with the media regarding the merits of the case be subject to a heavy presumption of invalidity. Although the Ninth Circuit acknowledged that a narrow restraining order could serve as an appropriate remedy for excessive trial publicity in the case, the order at issue was overbroad.[59] Nevertheless, the court held that the record supported the district court's finding that comments by defense counsel concerning the merits of the case did pose a serious and imminent threat to the administration of justice.[60] The Ninth Circuit also noted that the district court had considered various alternatives to the order, and that they were "either ineffective or counter-productive."[61] Accordingly, the court of appeals directed the trial judge to narrow the scope of the order and specify the subject matter of the prohibited statements.[62]

Prior restraint analysis was similarly employed following *Nebraska Press Association* by the Sixth Circuit in *United States v. Ford*,[63] in which a Congressman sought to set aside a broad gag order entered by the district court in a criminal prosecution against him.[64] The government argued, on the authority of *Sheppard*, that the less demanding "reasonable likelihood" standard should apply. In the wake of *Nebraska Press Association*, however, the court saw "no legitimate reasons for a lower threshold standard for individuals, including defendants, seeking to express themselves outside of the court than for the press."[65] Indeed, the court noted, the more demanding standard was especially

---

57. 427 U.S. 539 (1976). See Chap. 2-1(d) *supra*.
58. 764 F.2d 590, 595 (9th Cir. 1985), *cert. denied*, 476 U.S. 1158 (1986).
59. See *id*. at 599 ("It is apparent that many statements that bear 'upon the merits to be resolved by the jury' present no danger to the administration of justice.").
60. See *id*. at 598.
61. *Id*. at 600.
62. See *id*. at 599.
63. 830 F.2d 596 (6th Cir. 1987).
64. See *id*. at 598. The order prohibited any extrajudicial statement that a "reasonable person would expect to be disseminated by the means of public communication." *Id*. It contained exceptions for speech on the floor of the House and in committees, as well as statements by the Congressman that he was not guilty. See *id*.
65. *Id*. See also Stanfield v. Florida Dep't of Children & Families, 698 So. 2d 321, 323 (Fla. App. 1997) (holding gag order on trial participants, which prevented disclosure of information about case involving termination of parental rights, unconstitutional because "court cannot prohibit citizens from exercising their First Amendment right to publicly discuss knowledge that they have gained independent of court documents even though the information may mirror the information contained in court documents").

appropriate given the political context of the case.[66] The appellate court held that the order was not supported by findings establishing a serious and imminent threat, it was not narrowly tailored, and there had been inadequate consideration of less restrictive alternatives.[67]

But, in *In re Russell*,[68] the Fourth Circuit affirmed a gag order on potential trial witnesses under the "reasonable likelihood" standard, even after *Nebraska Press Association*. The trial court had issued an order prohibiting potential witnesses in a murder trial of Nazis and KKK members from discussing their proposed testimony with the press. Petitioners, the potential witnesses themselves, argued that the order was an unconstitutional prior restraint, that the district judge did not conduct an "evidentiary" hearing before entering it or articulate specific findings, and that the order was unconstitutionally overbroad and vague.[69] Nevertheless, the Fourth Circuit concluded that:

> [t]he tremendous publicity attending this trial, the potentially inflammatory and highly prejudicial statements that could reasonably be expected from petitioners (and had indeed been openly forecast by their counsel in proceedings before the trial judge), and the relative ineffectiveness of the considered alternatives dictated the 'strong measure' of suppressing the speech of potential witnesses to ensure a fair trial.[70]

The courts have, on the whole, applied similar constitutional analysis to gag orders entered in *civil* proceedings, although the differences between them have

---

66. See 830 F.2d at 600 ("It is the public to whom the First Amendment guarantees reasonable access to criminal proceedings. And it is individuals, not the government, to whom First Amendment interests attach. To the extent that publicity is a disadvantage for the government, the government must tolerate it. The government is our servant, not our master.").

67. See *id.*

68. 726 F.2d 1007 (4th Cir.), *cert. denied*, 469 U.S. 837 (1984).

69. 726 F.2d at 1008.

70. *Id.* at 1010. In *Pedini v. Bowles*, 940 F. Supp. 1020, 1025 (N.D. Tex. 1996), which arose in the context of the drug-use trial of a prominent professional football player, the court noted "a surprising dearth of authority involving constitutional challenges to restrictive orders directed to witnesses in criminal cases." The court upheld a contempt citation issued to Pedini, a key witness, who allegedly violated a gag order by selling a tape recording to a tabloid television program. *Id.* at 102-25. According to the court, it was "difficult to envision how the respondent [judge] could have conducted a more thorough investigation or crafted a more specific and detailed order." *Id.* at 1024. See also People v. Schmitz, 24 Media L. Rep. (BNA) 2535 (Mich. App. 1996) (appellate court vacated order forbidding persons other than attorneys from speaking with witnesses until after verdict and barring media coverage in courtroom, finding it "overly broad and impermissibly restrict[ing] First Amendment rights without a showing of a reasonable likelihood of prejudice to a fair trial"); Strauss, *From Witness to Riches: The Constitutionality of Restricting Witness Speech*, 38 Ariz. L. Rev. 291 (1996).

been noted.[71] In *Bailey v. Systems Innovation, Inc.*,[72] for example, a Pennsylvania public official and Commonwealth employees, defendants in a civil action, asked the Third Circuit to invalidate a trial court order barring extrajudicial statements by the litigants and counsel. The court of appeals agreed that the order constituted an unconstitutional prior restraint under *Nebraska Press Association*.[73] Similarly, in *East Baton Rouge Parish School Board v. Capital City Press*,[74] the Fifth Circuit vacated an order[75] prohibiting the members of a school board, its attorneys, employees, and agents from discussing "any aspect of any drafts of desegregation plans" with anyone other than the parties to the litigation.[76]

Noting the judicial uncertainty concerning whether the prior restraint doctrine applied to media challenges to gag orders on trial participants,[77] the Fifth Circuit simply avoided the issue because, "even assuming that the order is not a prior

---

71. See Hirschkop v. Snead, 594 F.2d 356, 373 (4th Cir. 1979) (criminal and civil proceedings differ in the more protracted character of civil litigation, its broader discovery rules, their overall complexity and the priority given criminal trials on a court's docket); Chicago Council of Lawyers v. Bauer, 522 F.2d at 257-58 (employing a hierarchical analysis suggesting that criminal trials involve greater fair trial concerns than civil trials); Ruggieri v. Johns-Manville Prods. Corp., 503 F. Supp. 1036, 1040 (D.R.I. 1980) (holding that rule adopting "serious and imminent threat" standard for pending criminal cases and "reasonable likelihood" test for civil cases made no sense).

72. 852 F.2d 93 (3d Cir. 1988).

73. See *id.* at 98; *id.* at 100 ("Comparison of this case to other cases further convinces us that no prior restraint is justified on the facts presented here."). The court acknowledged that extrajudicial comments by public officials can disrupt civil proceedings and cause economic harm. Nevertheless, citing *Wood v. Georgia*, 370 U.S. 375, 388 (1962), the court held:

> *Wood* teaches us that a public official has the right and, we add, sometimes the duty, to address issues of public concern within his or her domain. While often these concerns are the focus of a civil trial, the public official's ability and resources to command press conferences and issue press releases that could potentially interfere with a fair trial do not justify imposing restrictions on that official's speech unless there is a clear threat to the seventh amendment right.

852 F.2d at 100. See also Sherrill v. Amerada Hess Corp., 504 S.E.2d 802, 808 (N.C. App. 1998) (reversing order prohibiting any party or counsel in civil environmental pollution case "from communicating with 'any media representative or other person or entity,' not a party to the proceeding 'concerning' the claims until the suit was resolved" because the order was a presumptively unconstitutional prior restraint, there was no evidence in the record to support the trial court's finding that such communication would be "detrimental to the fair and impartial administration of justice," and the trial court failed to make findings regarding less restrictive alternatives).

74. 78 F.3d 920 (5th Cir. 1996).

75. See *id.* at 920. The case arose out of what had become a 40-year struggle to desegregate the public schools of Baton Rouge, Louisiana. In early 1996, the new school board had indicated its willingness to formulate a plan that would end the litigation. See *id.* at 922-23.

76. *Id.* at 923. The order had been entered without a formal motion, and without written or oral findings. See *id.*

77. See *id.* at 928 ("Whether we should analyze the confidentiality order as a prior restraint in determining the First Amendment rights of the news agencies — the potential recipients of the restrained speech — is unclear.").

restraint, its effect on the news agencies' First Amendment rights must still be justified."[78] Moreover, since "this was not a criminal trial, nor a civil jury trial," the court asserted "[t]here is no possibility that publicity will prejudice potential jurors."[79] Although the school board argued that the confidentiality order was necessary to facilitate formulation of an effective desegregation plan, the Fifth Circuit concluded that the order itself played no meaningful role in desegregating the school system.[80]

As the cases discussed in this section demonstrate, there is continuing confusion regarding both the applicability of the prior restraint doctrine to gag orders imposed on participants in the judicial process, even when the challenge is mounted by those litigation participants themselves. And, the confusion is heightened when the media, rather than trial participants, challenge such an order.[81] Not surprisingly, the state courts have indicated similar uncertainty.[82]

---

78. *Id.* (citing In re Dow Jones & Co., 842 F.2d at 609). See Grossnickle v. Grossnickle, 935 S.W.2d 830 (Tex. App. 1996) (finding that gag order in divorce proceeding violated both federal and state constitutions).

79. 78 F.3d at 929.

80. See *id.* at 929 & n.8.

81. See In re Dow Jones & Co. v. Simon, 488 U.S. 946 (1988) (White, J., dissenting from denial of certiorari).

82. See, e.g., Florida ex rel. Miami Herald Publ'g Co. v. McIntosh, 340 So. 2d 904 (Fla. 1977) (gag order on trial participants an abuse of discretion when jury is sequestered); Florida v. Eyrich, 22 MEDIA L. REP. (BNA) 1863 (Fla. Cir. 1993) (denying defendant's request for gag order on trial participants because defendant had not shown substantial likelihood of prejudicial statements); Georgia v. Williams, 7 MEDIA L. REP. (BNA) 1852 (Ga. Super. 1981); Kemner v. Monsanto Co., 492 N.E.2d 1327 (Ill. 1986) (reversing a gag order as unconstitutionally vague and overbroad); In re J.S., 640 N.E.2d 1379 (Ill. App. 1994) (upholding order to protect privacy interest of child victim); James v. Hines, 1998 WL 720735, at *4 (Ky. App. Oct. 16, 1998) (prohibiting enforcement of order enjoining murder victims' families, as prospective witnesses, from making extrajudicial statements because the order was a "presumptively void" prior restraint and the trial court failed to find that there was a reasonable likelihood of material prejudice [to the defendant's fair trial rights], did not consider less restrictive methods of eliminating the prejudice, and "did not limit the scope of its injunction"); In re Hattiesburg Am., 26 MEDIA L. REP. (BNA) 2183, 2184 (Miss. 1998) (reversing, as a violation of the First Amendment, the trial court's order prohibiting all parties and attorneys in a civil case from communicating with the media because the movant did not "advance [with specificity] an overriding interest that is likely to be prejudiced" and because there is no record that the court considered any less restrictive means to protect the defendant against "potentially prejudicial publicity"); Mississippi Publishers Corp. v. Circuit Ct., 12 MEDIA L. REP. (BNA) 1342 (Miss. 1985) (upholding order restraining comment on defendant's criminal record); Sherrill v. Amerada Hess Corp., 504 S.E.2d 802, 808 (N.C. App. 1998) (reversing gag order on any communication "concerning" the claims in the suit as a presumptively unconstitutional prior restraint because there was no evidence in the record to support the trial court's finding that such communication would be "detrimental to the fair and impartial administration of justice" and the trial court failed to make findings regarding less restrictive alternatives); In re T.R., 556 N.E.2d 439 (Ohio), *cert. denied*, 498 U.S. 958 (1990); Ohio ex rel. E.W. Scripps Co. v. Stillwell, 10 MEDIA L. REP. (BNA) 1380 (Ohio App. 1993) (gag order on trial participants was not prior

§ 7-2. Attorneys.

It has been argued that the imposition of gag orders is particularly appropriate with respect to counsel in pending litigation. Proponents of such restraints claim that lawyers, as officers of the court, have a fiduciary responsibility not to make public disclosures that are likely to result in prejudice or an unfair trial. In addition, it is argued, lawyers have access to unique, often confidential information by virtue of their participation in the judicial process.[83] Indeed, in *Sheppard v. Maxwell*, the Supreme Court observed that "collaboration between counsel and the press as to information affecting the fairness of trial is not only subject to regulation, but is highly censurable and worthy of disciplinary measures."[84] By the same token, counsel for a criminal defendant often feels compelled to respond to public statements made by prosecutors and other law enforcement personnel, while police and prosecutors believe it is often necessary to report to the public about the progress of high-profile investigations and prosecutions. In that regard, these very lawyers' familiarity with the legal process as well as their role in the administration of justice render their ability to speak publicly of critical importance.[85]

Following *Sheppard*, the imposition of gag orders on attorneys gained increasing favor. In 1968, the American Bar Association responded to *Sheppard* (and to the report of the Warren Commission on publicity accompanying the arrest of Lee Harvey Oswald for the assassination of President Kennedy) by adopting DR 7-107. The Rule prohibited pretrial statements in criminal proceedings and, during trial, barred statements "reasonably likely to interfere with a fair trial."[86]

In *Nebraska Press Association*, the Supreme Court's invocation of the clear and present danger doctrine in the context of gag orders, albeit on press publication, raised serious questions concerning the constitutionality of the reasonable likelihood standard in connection with expression by counsel. Nevertheless,

---

restraint, but limitation on media's right to gather news); Davenport v. Garcia, 834 S.W.2d 4 (Tex. 1992) (invalidating gag order under Texas Constitution).

83. See note 4 *supra*.

84. 384 U.S. at 363.

85. See generally Berkowitz-Caballero, *In the Aftermath of* Gentile: *Reconsidering the Efficiency of Trial Publicity Rules*, 68 N.Y.U. L. REV. 494 (1993); Chemerinsky, *supra* note 4; Comment, *ABA Rule 3.6 and California Rule 5-120: A Flawed Approach to the Problem of Trial Publicity*, 43 UCLA L. REV. 1321 (1996).

86. ABA CODE OF PROFESSIONAL RESPONSIBILITY, DR 7-107 (1968). The reasonable likelihood standard had been proposed by the Reardon Committee. ABA ADVISORY COMM. ON FAIR TRIAL AND FREE PRESS, STANDARDS RELATING TO FAIR TRIAL AND FREE PRESS STANDARD 1-1 (1968). See Comment, *supra* note 85, at 1335 ("the language of the reasonable likelihood standard seemed to imply that lawyers could be disciplined for statements that posed a more hypothetical risk, with no requirements of innocence, or proof of actual harm."). Almost all states adopted DR-7-107.

Chief Justice Burger referenced *Sheppard*'s endorsement of such restraints,[87] and Justice Brennan, in his concurring opinion, observed that "attorneys have a fiduciary responsibility not to engage in public debate that will redound to the detriment of the accused or that will obstruct the fair administration of justice. It is very doubtful that the court would not have the power to control release of information by these individuals in appropriate cases and to impose suitable limitations on those whose transgression could result in disciplinary proceedings."[88] Ultimately, however, in the wake of *Nebraska Press Association*, the ABA amended its Fair Trial-Free Press Standards to endorse the more demanding "clear and present danger requirement."[89]

Then, in 1983, the ABA introduced the Model Rules of Professional Conduct. Rule 3.6 of the Model Rules, which serves as the blueprint on these matters in most states,[90] was divided into three sections. The first prohibited extrajudicial statements that a reasonable person would expect to be disseminated by means of public communication and which "a lawyer knows or reasonably should know" will have a "substantial likelihood of materially prejudicing an adjudicative proceeding."[91] The second part, borrowing language from DR 7-107, catalogued statements that are likely to be prejudicial in a civil matter tried by a jury or a criminal matter or other proceeding that could result in incarceration.[92] The third part provided a "safe harbor," by setting forth a litany of statements that can be made, in the absence of elaboration, with impunity.[93]

Nevada adopted Rule 3.6, making its regulations part of its own Rule 177. In *Gentile v. State Bar*,[94] the Supreme Court considered the constitutionality of Rule 177. Dominic Gentile, hours after the indictment of his client, called a press conference to deliver a prepared statement and answer questions. Because he believed he was obliged to respond to adverse media coverage about his client, Gentile had determined the night before to hold his first news conference and had planned his remarks in light of Nevada Rule 177. His comments asserted his

---

87. See Nebraska Press Ass'n v. Stuart, 427 U.S. 539, 552-54 (1976); see also Chicago Council of Lawyers v. Bauer, 522 F.2d 242 (7th Cir. 1975), *cert. denied*, 427 U.S. 912 (1976) (holding reasonable likelihood standard unconstitutional).
88. Nebraska Press Ass'n v. Stuart, 427 U.S. at 601 (Brennan, J., concurring) (citing In re Sawyer, 360 U.S. 622 (1959)).
89. ABA STANDARDS FOR CRIMINAL JUSTICE, FAIR TRIAL AND FREE PRESS § 8-1.1 (2d ed. 1980). Five states and the District of Columbia embrace some version of the clear and present danger formulation. See Comment, *supra* note 85, at 1337 n.54.
90. ABA MODEL RULE OF PROFESSIONAL CONDUCT 3.6 (1983). See Comment, *supra* note 85, at 1337-38. Thirty-two states continue to employ the 1983 version of Rule 3.6(a) verbatim, or virtually verbatim. *Id.* at 1337 n.54.
91. ABA MODEL RULE OF PROFESSIONAL CONDUCT 3.6(a).
92. See *id.* at Rule 3.6(b).
93. *Id.* at Rule 3.6(c).
94. 501 U.S. 1030 (1991).

client's innocence, the probability that it was a police officer who was responsible for the crime, and that Gentile's client was a scapegoat for a corrupt police department. The trial was held six months later and his client was acquitted.[95] Thereafter, the Nevada State Bar instituted disciplinary proceedings against Gentile under Rule 177. Following a hearing, Gentile was found to have violated the Rule and received a private reprimand.[96]

The Supreme Court, in an opinion by Justice Kennedy for a five-justice majority, held that the safe harbor portion of the rule was unconstitutionally vague. Gentile, the Court concluded, had been misled. The rule provided him with no basis to determine if his statements in defense of his client were in fact "safe."[97] But, a different alignment of the Court, in an opinion by Chief Justice Rehnquist, again on behalf of five justices, held "that the 'substantial likelihood of material prejudice' standard applied by Nevada and most other states satisfies the First Amendment."[98] The standard "constitute[d] a constitutionally permissible balance between First Amendment rights of attorneys and the State interest in fair trials."[99] In each case, Justice O'Connor provided the determinative fifth vote to form a majority.[100]

Addressing the "substantial likelihood" test, a majority of the Court began from the premise that a state may regulate speech by an attorney in a pending case more readily than it may regulate the press.[101] Lawyers "are key participants

---

95. There did not appear to be any difficulty arising from Gentile's statements in impaneling a jury. "Indeed, not a single member of the jury venire indicated any recollection of Gentile or his press conference." *Id.* at 1047. See Comment, *supra* note 85, at 1340.

96. See 501 U.S. at 1047-48.

97. See *id.* at 1048-51. The safe harbor provision, on its face, stated that "notwithstanding the prohibition," a lawyer may state "without elaboration the general nature of the claim or defense." This aspect of the rule "misled [Gentile] into thinking that he could give his press conference without fear of discipline." *Id.* at 1048. Justice Kennedy noted that Gentile had spent several hours researching the provision before holding the press conference and "on numerous occasions declined to answer reporters' questions seeking more detailed comments." *Id.* at 1049. In *Pennsylvania v. Lambert*, 723 A.2d 684 (Pa. 1998), however, the Pennsylvania Supreme Court upheld identical "safe harbor" language in Pennsylvania's rule. The court held that the Pennsylvania provision provides "clear guidance to attorneys . . . regarding what may permissibly be said," and "the general nature of [the rule] does not mandate a finding that it is so inherently imprecise that discriminatory enforcement is a real possibility." *Id.* at 694-95.

98. *Id.* at 1063. Justice Kennedy, in contrast, asserted that the case "does not call into question the constitutionality of other states' prohibitions upon an attorney's speech." *Id.* at 1034 (opinion of Kennedy, J.). The Chief Justice disagreed, noting that Gentile had challenged Rule 177 as unconstitutional on its face as well as in its application. See *id.* at 1070 n.4 (opinion of Rehnquist, C.J.).

99. *Id.* at 1075.

100. See *id.* at 1081-82 (O'Connor, J. concurring).

101. *Id.* at 1074 (opinion of Rehnquist, C.J.) ("the speech of lawyers representing clients in pending cases may be regarded under a less demanding standard than established in *Nebraska Press Ass'n v. Stuart* and the cases which preceded it"); *id.* at 1081 (O'Connor, J., concurring) ("a

in the criminal justice system, and the State may demand some adherence to the precepts of that system in regulating their speech as well as their conduct."[102] Moreover, because "lawyers have special access to information through discovery and client communications, their extrajudicial comments pose a threat to the fairness of a pending proceeding since lawyers' statements are likely to be received as especially authoritative."[103] Accordingly, the Chief Justice concluded that the substantial likelihood standard was narrowly tailored to meet its objectives[104] because it applies only to expression "substantially likely to have a materially prejudicial effect; it is neutral as to points of view, applying to all attorneys participating in a pending case; and it merely postpones attorney comments until after the trial."[105] Rejecting Gentile's overbreadth argument, the Court concluded that "Rule 177 is not broader than necessary to protect the State's interest" because it "applies only to lawyers involved in the pending case at issue, and even those lawyers involved in pending cases can make extrajudicial statements as long as such statements do not present a substantial risk of material prejudice to an adjudicative proceeding."[106] Finally, the Court determined that, because the clear and present danger standard was inapplicable, Nevada was not required to show actual prejudice to the judicial proceeding flowing from the specific statements at issue.[107]

Justice Kennedy, in this context writing for four justices, rejected the majority's analysis.[108] The majority, Justice Kennedy wrote, overstated the danger to the fair administration of justice from extrajudicial statements by trial counsel.[109] The danger of prejudice was especially inapplicable to extrajudicial commentary by defense counsel.[110] In Justice Kennedy's view, the Nevada rule operates to create an uneven playing field for defendants: "The police, the prosecution, other

---

State may regulate speech by lawyers representing clients in pending cases more readily than it may regulate the press.").

102. *Id.* at 1074 (opinion of Rehnquist, C.J.); see *id.* at 1081-82 (O'Connor, J., concurring) ("Lawyers are officers of the court and, as such, may legitimately be subject to ethical precepts that keep them from engaging in what might otherwise be constitutionally protected speech.").

103. *Id.* at 1074 (opinion of Rehnquist, C.J.); see also In re Hinds, 449 A.2d 483, 496 (N.J. 1982) (statements by attorneys of record relating to a case "are likely to be considered knowledgeable, reliable and true" because of their unique access to information).

104. See 501 U.S. at 1074.

105. *Id.* at 1076.

106. *Id.* at 1076-77.

107. See *id.* at 1081.

108. See *id.* at 1054 (opinion of Kennedy, J.).

109. See *id.* at 1054-55 ("Only the occasional case presents a danger of prejudice from pretrial publicity. Empirical research suggests that in the few instances when jurors have been exposed to extensive and prejudicial publicity, they are able to disregard it and base their verdict upon the evidence presented in court.").

110. See *id.* at 1055 (stating that "not a single example [exists] when a defense attorney has managed by public statements to prejudice the prosecution of the State's case").

government officials . . . hold innumerable avenues for the dissemination of adverse information . . . [but] a defendant cannot speak without fear of prejudicing himself and prejudicing his defense. . . ."[111]

Justice Kennedy recognized that some limits on trial counsel are appropriate since "a court can require an attorney's cooperation to an extent not possible of nonparticipants."[112] Nevertheless, he added, "the Rule which punished petitioner's statements represents a limitation of First Amendment freedoms greater than is necessary or essential to the protection of the particular government interest, and does not protect against a danger of the necessary gravity, imminence, or likelihood."[113] Gentile's case, Justice Kennedy asserted, involved "pure speech in the political forum" laying "at the very center of the First Amendment"[114] because it concerned allegations of police corruption.[115] Thus, conceding that some limitations on the extrajudicial comments of trial counsel are constitutionally sound, "[t]he record does not support the conclusion that petitioner knew or reasonably should have known his remarks created a substantial likelihood of material prejudice, if the Rule's terms are given any meaningful content."[116]

It has been said that *Gentile* provides more of an outline than an answer to the question of what standards restricting attorney speech are constitutionally acceptable.[117] In August 1994, the ABA approved revisions to Model Rule 3.6. The new rule removes the list of presumptively prejudicial statements and purports to clarify the safe harbor provision held unconstitutional in *Gentile*.[118] It retains the "substantial likelihood of material prejudice" standard approved by the Supreme Court in *Gentile*.[119]

---

111. *Id.* at 1056.
112. *Id.* at 1057.
113. *Id.* at 1057-58.
114. *Id.* at 1034.
115. See *id.* at 1035-36.
116. *Id.* at 1037-38; see *id.* at 1048 ("There is no support for the conclusion that petitioner's statements created a likelihood of material prejudice, or indeed of any harm of sufficient magnitude or imminence to support a punishment for speech.").
117. See Brown, *The Worsening Problem of Trial Publicity: Is "New" Model Rule 3.6 Solution or Surrender?*, 29 IND. L. REV. 379, 381 (1995); Cole & Zacharias, *The Agony of Victory and the Ethics of Lawyer Speech*, 69 CAL. L. REV. 1627, 1678 (1996); Coyle & Strassen, *Split Rulings on Lawyer Speech Puzzle Many*, Nat'l L.J., July 8, 1991, at 1, 5 ("[*Gentile*] left him and other lawyers to wade carefully through the still-murky waters of what a lawyer can say publicly about his client and his case. . . ."); DeBendicts, *Gentile's Unanswered Questions: Drafters Struggle to Rewrite Ethics Rule on Lawyer's Out-of-Court Statements*, 79 A.B.A. J., Apr. 1993, at 28 ("'One sort of understands [*Gentile*] for about five minutes and then it fades away.'").
118. See MODEL RULES OF PROFESSIONAL CONDUCT RULE 3.6 (1994).
119. See *id.* at Rule 3.6(a). Subsection (a) applies to "a lawyer who is participating or has participated in the investigation or litigation of a matter." Rule 3.6(d) extends the restraint to lawyers associated in the firm or government agency. According to the new Rule 3.6(a), the

In the wake of *Gentile*, courts have continued to grapple with the issue. In *United States v. Salameh*,[120] for example, the defendants in the World Trade Center bombing case appealed an order, entered without notice or opportunity for argument, that barred counsel from publicly discussing any aspect of the case.[121] The Second Circuit acknowledged that, after *Gentile*, attorney speech can be subjected to greater limitations than the speech of other citizens or the press.[122] Nevertheless, it held that such restrictions can be "no broader than necessary to protect the integrity of the judicial system and the defendant's right to a fair trial."[123] The court concluded, therefore, that the order at issue was "an overly broad prior restraint of [counsel's] rights under the First Amendment to the Constitution,"[124] especially because "[t]he record does not support a conclusion that no reasonable alternatives to a blanket prohibition exist."[125]

In *United States v. Cutler*,[126] Cutler, attorney for reputed underworld figure John Gotti, challenged an order holding him in criminal contempt after repeated media appearances made in defiance of court orders that he comply with Local Rule 7, which embodied the "reasonable likelihood" standard. Cutler argued that the Rule and orders were unconstitutional and that his conviction was not supported by sufficient evidence under the First Amendment.[127] The Second Circuit, however, held that Cutler was procedurally barred from challenging the constitutionality of the orders because he "could have, and should have, sought modification of the orders in district court, challenged them on a direct appeal, or sought a writ of mandamus or declaratory relief. Having failed utterly to make any good faith effort to undertake even one of these steps, he cannot now challenge the orders' validity."[128] The court further concluded that "the record amply supports findings that the orders were specific, and that Cutler's com-

---

prejudice must be to "an adjudicative proceeding in the matter." Rule 3.8(g) restricts the extrajudicial statements of prosecutors.

120. 992 F.2d 445 (2d Cir. 1993).

121. *Id*. at 446 ("The next time I pick up the paper and see a quotation from any of you, you had best be prepared to have some money. The first time will be $200. Thereafter, the fines will be squared.").

122. See *id*. at 447.

123. *Id*.

124. *Id*. at 446; see *id*. ("An order that prohibits the utterance or publication of particular information or commentary imposes a 'prior restraint' on speech.").

125. *Id*.; see New York Times Co. v. Rothwax, 533 N.Y.S.2d 73 (App. Div. 1988) (vacating gag order on counsel because of inadequate factual findings); National Broadcasting Co. v. Cooperman, 501 N.Y.S.2d 405 (App. Div. 1986) (order prohibiting counsel from speaking with media violated First Amendment due to failure to demonstrate necessity for the restraint); Ohio ex rel. Nat'l Broadcasting Co. v. Court of C.P., 556 N.E.2d 1120 (Ohio 1990) (striking down gag order as applied to counsel because no specific findings were made).

126. 58 F.3d 825 (2d Cir. 1995).

127. See *id*. at 832.

128. *Id*. at 833.

ments were reasonably likely to prejudice prospective jurors and were willfully made with the intent of prejudicing prospective jurors."[129] Affirming the contempt conviction, the Second Circuit asserted that, "[g]iven the more lenient 'reasonable likelihood' standard here, we do not doubt that a majority of the *Gentile* Court would find that Cutler violated the orders."[130]

In *United States v. McVeigh*,[131] the Oklahoma City bombing case, the district court rejected the efforts of the media and of the defendant to vacate or modify a judicially imposed ban on extrajudicial statements by attorneys and support personnel. Citing *Gentile*, the court concluded: "[t]his case calls for a blanket bar on out of court comments because no lesser restriction would adequately protect against a substantial likelihood of prejudicing the proceedings."[132]

After Timothy McVeigh and Terry Nichols were convicted for their roles in the bombing, but while their appeals were still pending, the trial court, upon motion of the government, rescinded some of the restrictions in order to allow federal cooperation with Oklahoma prosecutors and an Oklahoma grand jury investigating the bombing, although it retained restrictions on disclosure of materials and information provided by the defendants through reciprocal discovery. The Tenth Circuit affirmed the order,[133] finding that the trial court made "a very careful and deliberate examination of the issues involved," and that the possible harm that leaks to the press would cause to the defendants' fair trial rights if new trials were granted was speculative.[134] The court also dismissed the argument that the disclosures would "impugn the secrecy of the federal grand jury" because the Federal Rules of Criminal Procedure allow for disclosure of such information to state officials for the purpose of enforcing state criminal law.[135]

Gentile held that court rules based on Model Rule 3.6, embodying a standard of substantial likelihood of material prejudice, pass constitutional muster. State

---

129. *Id.* at 838.

130. *Id.* at 837. In *In re Morrissey*, 168 F.3d 134 (4th Cir. 1999), the Fourth Circuit upheld the contempt conviction of an attorney who violated local rules prohibiting extrajudicial statements having a "reasonable likelihood" of prejudice. See *id.* at 138. The court held that the rule was constitutional on its face and as applied. See *id.* at 141. The standard was "both narrow and necessary" to protect fair trial rights, *id.* at 140, and was narrowly tailored because it was limited to statements identified by the Court in *Sheppard* as most likely to be prejudicial. See *id.* Finally, the Court concluded, the order had been constitutionally applied since Morrissey's public statements questioned the credibility of a key prosecution witness, cast doubt on the strength of the government's case and was likely to influence the outcome of the trial. See *id.*

131. 964 F. Supp. 313 (D. Colo. 1997).

132. *Id.* at 316. The court rejected defendant McVeigh's request to create a limited exception to allow him to reply publicly to extrajudicial comments to which he could not respond in court. See *id.*

133. See United States v. McVeigh, 157 F.3d 809, 811-12 (10th Cir. 1998).

134. *Id.* at 814.

135. *Id.* (citing FED. R. CRIM. P. 6(e)(3)(C)(iv)).

law, however, may still require a more demanding standard to curb extrajudicial statements by trial counsel. In *Twohig v. Blackmer*,[136] attorney Ray Twohig sought to vacate an order prohibiting all trial participants from communicating with the media about the third trial of one of his clients.[137] Twohig claimed that the gag order impermissibly restricted his rights under the New Mexico Constitution and a recently amended court rule governing trial publicity, which embodied the clear and present danger test.[138] The New Mexico Supreme Court canvassed the available case law, comparing the cases upholding[139] and those invalidating[140] gag orders, and concluded that, in New Mexico, such an order must be based on a clear and present danger to the administration of justice.[141] The order at issue, it held, failed to satisfy that rigorous standard.[142]

§ 7-3. Jurors.

It has generally been accepted that jury deliberations should be secret, so that jurors are able to express their opinions freely. If jurors knew that their discussions and votes would be open to subsequent scrutiny, it is argued, they might be inhibited such that candor would be lost. The integrity of the process might be impaired and the fair trial rights of the criminal defendant prejudiced.[143] On the

---

136. 918 P.2d 332 (N.M. 1996).

137. See *id.* at 333. The court described the amount of publicity surrounding the trial as "unprecedented." *Id.* In response to allegations of racism (Twohig's client, the defendant, was Native American) and public statements by the prosecutor, Twohig had written an article in *The Albuquerque Journal* and had appeared on several radio talk shows, answering questions about the law and evidence in the first two trials. See *id.* at 334.

138. See *id.* at 333. The local rule stated that "[a] lawyer shall not make any extrajudicial . . . statement in a criminal proceeding that may be tried by a jury that the lawyer knows or reasonably should know . . . creates a clear and present danger of prejudicing the proceeding." *Id.* at 335. The rule had been amended following *Gentile*. See *id.* at 337.

139. See Levine v. United States Dist. Ct., 764 F.2d 590 (9th Cir. 1985), *cert. denied*, 476 U.S. 1158 (1986); In re Russell, 726 F.2d 1007 (4th Cir.), *cert. denied*, 469 U.S. 837 (1984); In re San Juan Star Co., 662 F.2d 108 (1st Cir. 1981); United States v. Tijerina, 412 F.2d 661 (10th Cir.), *cert. denied*, 396 U.S. 990 (1969); Florida Freedom Newspapers, Inc. v. McCrary, 520 So. 2d 32 (Fla. 1988).

140. See Chase v. Robson, 435 F.2d 1059 (7th Cir. 1970); Breiner v. Takao, 835 P.2d 637 (Haw. 1992); Kemner v. Monsanto Co., 492 N.E.2d 1327 (Ill. 1986).

141. See 918 P.2d at 335.

142. See *id.* at 341.

143. It has also been suggested that jurors may be reluctant to serve in future cases if they fear their comments will be passed on by other jurors, and that public knowledge of the reasoning behind a verdict may undermine respect for the process. See Goldstein, *Jury Secrecy and the Media: The Problem of Post-Verdict Interviews*, 1993 U. ILL. L. REV. 295, 297 (1993) ("if the media continues to reveal the contents of jury deliberations, there is a genuine risk that the authority of jury verdicts will decline — and that the jury will be less able to perform its constitutional role of restraining an arbitrary government"); Note, *Public Disclosure of Jury*

other hand, permitting former jurors to discuss the nature of their experience publicly, to explain the reasons for their decision in the case, and to reassure the community that the outcome was fair and proper may serve a host of salutary purposes.[144]

In *United States v. Sherman*,[145] following the verdict in a criminal case, the trial judge instructed jurors not to discuss the case further with anyone and ordered everyone, including the press, to stay away from the jurors. The Ninth Circuit held that precluding the press from approaching jurors in this manner constituted an unconstitutional restraint on newsgathering.[146] And, since the order was a prior restraint, there was "a heavy presumption against its constitutional validity."[147] The government, the Ninth Circuit concluded, had failed to demonstrate the requisite "clear and present danger or a serious and imminent threat to a protected competing interest."[148] Since the trial was over, the

---

Deliberations, 96 HARV. L. REV. 889, 890 (1983) ("juries may be intimidated into rendering certain verdicts by the specter of subsequent pressures").

144. See Press Enter. Co. v. Superior Ct., 464 U.S. 501, 509 (1984) (emphasizing need to "vindicate the concerns of the victims and the community in knowing that offenders are being brought to account for their criminal conduct by jurors fairly and openly selected"); United States v. Espy, 31 F. Supp. 2d 1, 2 (D.D.C. 1998) (recognizing that many of the interests served by open access to criminal proceedings are also served by the right of the press to have access to the names of jurors after a verdict has been rendered); United States v. Doherty, 675 F. Supp. 719, 723 (D. Mass. 1987) (discussing reasons for allowing post-trial interviews, including providing "for an independent non-governmental verification of the impartiality of the jury deliberation process"). See generally Marder, *Deliberations and Disclosures: A Study of Post-Verdict Interviews of Jurors*, 83 IOWA L. REV. 467, 545 (1997) (empirical study of press-juror interactions finding that "courts can and should give guidance to jurors with respect to post-verdict interviews with the press"); Nunn, *When Juries Meet the Press: Rethinking the Jury's Representative Function in Highly Publicized Cases*, 22 HASTINGS CONST. L.Q. 405 (1995); Weinstein, *Protecting a Juror's Right to Privacy: Constitutional Constraints and Policy Options*, 70 TEMP. L. REV. 1, 33 (1997) ("While there are strong arguments in favor of denying access, any statutory reform barring the release of juror identities will be built on an uncertain constitutional foundation."); Comment, *Post-Verdict Interviews: The Key to Understanding the Decision Behind the Verdict*, 30 J. MARSHALL L. REV. 507, 532 (1997) ("[C]ourts should find that the press has a guaranteed First Amendment right of access to jurors after a verdict," but names and addresses should be impounded for ten days to inform jurors of their rights to refuse interviews.").

145. 581 F.2d 1358 (9th Cir. 1978).

146. See *id.* at 1361 (citing Branzburg v. Hayes, 408 U.S. 665, 681 (1972)); Contra Costa Newspapers Inc. v. Superior Ct., 72 Cal. Rptr. 2d 69, 72-73 (Ct. App. 1998) (holding that "the trial court's order restricting press contact with former jurors was without jurisdiction and was impermissibly overbroad" and that the overbroad order violated the First Amendment because: (1) it was a prior restraint, (2) there was no showing of a compelling need for nondisclosure, and (3) the California Code of Civil Procedure "does not purport to allow the court to prohibit discharged jurors from discussing a case if they choose to do so").

147. 581 F.2d at 1361.

148. *Id.* (citing Wood v. Georgia, 370 U.S. 375 (1962)).

defendants' fair trial rights were not prejudiced,[149] concerns over the ability of the jurors interviewed to serve on future juries could be met by less restrictive alternatives,[150] and there was no evidence of actual harassment of jurors.[151] Even though no juror was required to respond to press inquiries, the Ninth Circuit held, the trial court erred in preventing the media from making the inquiries.[152]

In *In re Express-News Corp.*,[153] the Fifth Circuit similarly invoked both a First Amendment-based right to gather news[154] and the constitutional right of the public to receive information from former jurors. "Government imposed secrecy denies the free flow of information and ideas not only to the press but also to the public,"[155] the court observed, and "[t]he public has no less a right under the first amendment to receive information about the operation of the nation's courts than it has to know how other governmental agencies work and to receive other ideas and information."[156]

According to the Fifth Circuit, the press' right to seek juror interviews could be overcome only by a showing that any such restraint is "narrowly tailored to prevent a substantial threat to the administration of justice."[157] The order at issue, which purported to forbid *any* person from interviewing jurors, was "unlimited in time and in scope, applying equally to jurors willing and anxious to speak and to jurors desiring privacy, forbidding both courteous as well as uncivil communications, and foreclosing questions about a juror's general reactions as well as specific questions about other jurors' votes that might, under at least some circumstances, be inappropriate."[158]

---

149. 581 F.2d at 1361 ("[t]hose cases dealing with the so-called 'free press-fair trial' issue are not applicable here").

150. See *id.* ("If a juror's impartiality were to be questioned because the jurors had spoken to the media that could be discovered on future voir dire and the juror excused.").

151. See *id.* ("The jurors as individuals, perhaps, may not regard media interviews as harassing. If harassment should occur, the court might properly then act to correct the actual intrusion suffered, but this order is too broad.").

152. See *id.* at 1361-62.

153. 695 F.2d 807 (5th Cir. 1982).

154. See *id.* at 808 ("The first amendment's broad shield for freedom of speech and of the press is not limited to the right to talk and to print. The value of these rights would be circumscribed were those who wish to disseminate information denied access to it, for freedom to speak is of little value if there is nothing to say.").

155. *Id.* at 809.

156. *Id.*

157. *Id.* at 810.

158. *Id.*; see Ohio ex rel. Beacon Journal Publ'g Co. v. McMonagle, 8 MEDIA L. REP. (BNA) 1927 (Ohio App. 1982) (holding that the trial court cannot require jurors to remain silent); see also Dove Audio v. Lungren, 1995 WL 432631 (C.D. Cal. June 14, 1995) (enjoining statute that prohibits jurors from receiving more than $50 in order to discuss the case for 90 days after trial has ended). See Chap. 7-4 *infra*.

In *Journal Publishing Co. v. Mechem*,[159] the Tenth Circuit also relied on the prior restraint doctrine to invalidate a court order instructing jurors not to discuss their verdict.[160] Such a restraint on news coverage of a trial could be justified, the court held, only by a "clear and imminent danger to the administration of justice"[161] or a showing that "the restraint is necessitated by a compelling governmental interest."[162] In addition, any such order must be narrowly tailored and the court must consider reasonable, less restrictive alternatives.[163]

Narrower orders regulating press interviews with former jurors have, however, survived constitutional scrutiny. In *United States v. Harrelson*,[164] for example, the press unsuccessfully challenged (1) restrictions on "repeated requests for interviews" after a juror had expressed a desire not to be interviewed and (2) a prohibition on inquiries concerning how specific jurors, other than the juror being interviewed, had voted. The court concluded that the ban on "repeated requests" was sufficiently definite to overcome a vagueness challenge[165] and was a constitutional means of protecting jurors' privacy and their right to be free from harassment.[166] Moreover, the court held, the restrictions on the content of the interviews — i.e., the prohibition on discussing other jurors' votes — were justified to protect the secrecy of jury deliberations. "[M]embers of the press, in common with all others, are free to report whatever takes place in

---

159. 801 F.2d 1233 (10th Cir. 1986).

160. See *id*. at 1236 ("[W]hile a court may broadly proscribe attorney and party contact with former jurors, it does not have the same freedom to restrict press interviews with former jurors."); see also Contra Costa Newspapers, Inc. v. Superior Ct., 72 Cal. Rptr. 2d 69, 72 (Ct. App. 1998) ("[A]ny inhibitions against news coverage of a trial carry a heavy presumption of an unconstitutional prior restraint . . . . In the absence of particularized findings reasonably justifying nondisclosure [using strict scrutiny], federal courts have required that juror names and addresses must be made public after the trial has terminated.") (citing In re Globe Newspaper Co. (Hurley), 920 F.2d 88, 98 (1st Cir. 1990)); see also Haeberle v. Texas Int'l Airlines, 739 F.2d 1019 (5th Cir. 1984) (distinguishing between press interviews of jurors and attorney interviews designed to "satisfy curiosity" and improve advocacy techniques).

161. 801 F.2d at 1236 (citing CBS Inc. v. Young, 522 F.2d 234, 240 (6th Cir. 1975)).

162. 801 F.2d at 1236.

163. See *id*.; Contra Costa Newspapers Inc. v. Superior Ct., 72 Cal. Rptr. 2d 69, 72-73 (Ct. App. 1998) (holding that "the trial court's order restricting press contact with former jurors was without jurisdiction and was impermissibly overbroad" and that the overbroad order violated the First Amendment because: (1) it was a prior restraint, (2) there was no showing of a compelling need, and (3) the California Code of Civil Procedure "does not purport to allow the court to prohibit discharged jurors from discussing a case if they choose to do so").

164. 713 F.2d 1114 (5th Cir. 1983), *cert. denied*, 465 U.S. 1041 (1984).

165. See *id*. at 1118 ("Mathematical certainty is not necessary; what is forbidden is wheedling and importuning. And even this is only partly forbidden; the juror is fair game until he expresses his desire not to be interviewed in such a manner that the would-be interviewer knows of that desire.").

166. See *id*. ("Common sense tells us that a juror who has once indicated a desire to be let alone and to put the matter of his jury service behind him by declining to be interviewed regarding it is unlikely to change his mind; and if he does, he is always free to initiate an interview.").

open court but [they] enjoy no special, First Amendment right of access to matters not available to the public at large."[167]

In *United States v. Cleveland*,[168] the court invoked *Harrelson* and purported to distinguish *In re Express-News Corp*. Following a trial on racketeering and other charges involving alleged efforts to influence state gambling legislation,[169] the trial judge, without a hearing or factual findings, issued an order that "absent a special order by me, no juror may be interviewed by anyone concerning the deliberations of the jury."[170]

The Fifth Circuit held that the order was "sufficiently narrow to satisfy the requirement of *Express-News*,"[171] since (1) it applied only to jurors, not relatives, friends or associates; (2) it applied only to "deliberations," not the verdict itself; and (3) the absence of a termination date in the order was not conclusive.[172] Although the order applied broadly to interviews in all contexts, the sheer volume of media coverage "justifies the imposition of the order entered in this case without regard to the willingness of the jurors to be interviewed or the civility of the reporters seeking to conduct interviews."[173] The media's concerns about vagueness — i.e., that jurors could construe "deliberations" to include their own reactions to the proceedings — was rejected as well; according to the Fifth Circuit, the order was intended to be limited to actual discussions in the jury room; jurors could still be interviewed concerning their general reactions and could speak out "on their own initiative."[174] The appellate court stressed that the strict standard articulated in *Express-News* must be tempered, as in *Harrelson*, by recognition that the press enjoys no special rights of access beyond those of the public.[175]

In *United States v. Antar*,[176] a trial court had sealed the transcript of open voir dire proceedings and other court records to prevent disclosure of jurors' identities to the media. The court also suggested that the press would be required to overcome a presumption that any communication with jurors should be

---

167. *Id.* (citing United States v. Gurney, 558 F.2d 1202 (5th Cir. 1977), *cert. denied*, 435 U.S. 968 (1978)).

168. 128 F.3d 267 (5th Cir. 1997), *cert. denied*, 523 U.S. 1075 (1998).

169. Two defendants, including a state senator, were acquitted of all charges. Four defendants, including another state senator, were convicted on some counts and acquitted on others. See *id.* at 269.

170. *Id.* The judge also informed the jurors that they were under no obligation to speak to anyone and that lawyers and the parties could not question them without his consent. See *id.*

171. *Id.*; see *id.* at 270 ("We hold that the term 'jury deliberations' is sufficiently definite to convey the idea the district court intended and does not realistically threaten First Amendment protected communication. That is all the law requires.").

172. *Id.* at 269.

173. *Id.*

174. *Id.*; see *id.* ("A juror who wishes to do so may make a statement.").

175. See *id.*

176. 38 F.3d 1348 (3d Cir. 1994). See Chap. 5-2(c) *supra*.

restricted in order to protect jury deliberations.[177] According to the trial court, a press claim of access to jurors after they concluded deliberations constitutes an "assertion of a right to invade the secret deliberations of the jury rooms."[178] Accordingly, the trial court imposed four restrictions on post-trial press interviews: (1) No juror was obligated to talk with the press; (2) repeated requests for interviews were prohibited; (3) all questioning must cease once a juror expresses a desire to conclude an interview; and (4) inquiries concerning the specific votes, statements, or other comments of any juror other than the one being interviewed were prohibited.[179]

On appeal, the Third Circuit considered each of these restrictions separately. It affirmed the trial court's holding that no juror was obligated to speak to the press.[180] Reminding the jurors of their right not to speak to the press and counseling them against discussing the deliberations, the Third Circuit concluded, constitutes a reasonable means of accommodating the competing interests. But, the court rejected the restrictions on repeated requests for interviews and the termination of interviews by jurors since there were "no specific findings by the trial court that harassment had occurred or was intended."[181] Such preventive measures could not be justified by the possibility the press might become overzealous. In marked contrast to *Harrelson*, the Third Circuit held that the trial court must articulate findings identifying an existing or threatened basis for any such restrictions.[182] Further, the trial court must consider less restrictive means of protecting jurors, e.g., providing a neutral area for press interviews or assuring jurors that the court is available to shield them from harassment.[183] The Third Circuit affirmed the final prohibition, a restriction on revealing the "specific votes, statements, opinions or other comments" of other jurors, but observed that it was "troubled" by the lack of any explanation why it was neces-

---

177. See 38 F.3d at 1352 ("You have a laboring oar with me to show me ... what, if any, prevailing news gathering or First Amendment arguments are sufficient to overcome the very sacred nature of a jury's deliberation.").

178. *Id*. at 1354; see *id*. at 1352 (quoting district court) ("All of a sudden, the minute they finish their job, you send them outside and the press can go asking them about their feelings about the case? How did you vote in the case? This sensationalism has got to stop some place. We have to get back to our system of justice.... There is something radically wrong if we're trying cases in the press.").

179. See *id*. at 1355.

180. See *id*. at 1364.

181. *Id*. at 1364.

182. See *id*.

183. See *id*. at 1364. ("[W]e conclude that restrictions on post-trial interviews must reflect an impending threat of jury harassment rather than a generalized misgiving about the wisdom of such interviews."). In fact, the court noted that the press had suggested, from the outset, that it would interview those jurors who were willing after the verdict in a separate room at the courthouse so as to allow the trial judge to supervise and to minimize any potential for disturbing the jurors at their homes. *Id*. at 1363.

sary in the case at issue,[184] since such restrictions should be imposed only rarely.[185]

With the exception of *Harrelson* and *Cleveland*, therefore, the federal courts have been skeptical of claims that post trial interviews per se will impair the deliberative integrity of the petit jury. Narrower restrictions, however, especially when based on articulated findings on the record, have been upheld in federal[186] and state[187] courts. In the case of grand jurors, additional restrictions have been held appropriate as well.[188]

---

184. *Id.* at 1364.

185. See *id.* Several courts, however, have placed broad restraints on jurors designed to prevent disclosure of the votes or deliberations of other jurors. These courts cite their concern that jurors who think that fellow jurors will reveal their opinions and deliberations to the press may not be entirely open or honest. See, e.g., United States v. Harrelson, 713 F.2d at 1118 (no abuse of discretion to preclude questions about the votes of jurors other than the party being interviewed); Sentinel Communications Co. v. Watson, 615 So. 2d 768 (Fla. App. 1993) (concluding that news media have a right to interview jurors after trial, but restrictions on interviews that involve the verdict or the jury's deliberations are permissible).

186. In *United States v. Espy*, 31 F. Supp. 2d 1 (D.D.C. 1998), the court sealed the names of jurors for seven days after the acquittal of the former Secretary of Agriculture for offenses arising from allegations that he accepted illegal gratuities while in office. Although the jurors indicated to the court that they neither wished to speak to nor have their names disclosed to the media, the court concluded that keeping the jurors' names sealed for seven days was the best way to balance the jurors' privacy interests and the press' right of access to criminal proceedings. See *id.* at 1-2. The court reasoned that its "limitation on the interests of the press is narrowly tailored in time and scope and will not ultimately thwart the purposes served by providing open access to criminal proceedings." *Id.* at 2. The delay would also afford jurors a respite after a two-month trial and time to reflect on what they would like to discuss with the press. *Id.* See also Sullivan v. National Football League, 839 F. Supp. 6 (D. Mass. 1993) (allowing access 10 days after verdict is returned and order is received by jurors); United States v. Franklin, 546 F. Supp. 1133, 1145 (N.D. Ind. 1982) (prohibiting media from interviewing jurors on the premises of courthouse and declaring that any conduct by member of the media constituting harassment "would be handled appropriately by the court"); Raskopf, *A First Amendment Right of Access to a Juror's Identity: Towards a Fuller Understanding of the Jury's Deliberative Process*, 17 PEPP. L. REV. 357 (1990). But cf. In re Memphis Publ'g Co., 887 F.2d 646 (6th Cir. 1989) (if ambiguous statement made to jury by court that they not talk about the case was a post-trial gag order, it would be unconstitutional).

187. See, e.g., In re Stone, 703 P.2d 1319 (Colo. App. 1985) (affirming contempt judgment against reporters for contacting prospective jurors under order not to discuss case); In re Disclosure of Juror Names & Addresses, 592 N.W.2d 798 (Mich. App. 1999) (holding that press has First Amendment-based right of access to names and addresses of jurors after verdict); In re Detroit Free Press, 11 MEDIA L. REP. (BNA) 1368 (Mich. App. 1985) (vacating order gagging discharged jurors in case scheduled for retrial); Tasin v. SIFCO Indus., 553 N.E.2d 257 (Ohio 1990) (upholding local rule that bars contact with jurors except by leave of court). But see Ohio ex rel. Cincinnati Post v. Court of C.P., 570 N.E.2d 1101 (Ohio 1991) (holding post verdict order prohibiting juror communication overbroad).

188. See, e.g., In re Subpoena to Testify Before Grand Jury, 864 F.2d 1559 (11th Cir. 1989) (stating that public has no right to a hearing on access to grand jury proceedings); In re Multi-county Grand Jury Proceedings, 847 P.2d 812 (Okla. Crim. App. 1993) (holding that media has no First Amendment-based right of access to hearings before grand jury's presiding judge regarding

The use of anonymous juries has raised additional issues of press and public access. Some courts have permitted juries in selected cases, typically involving concerns over juror safety, to be selected anonymously, followed by immediate sequestration.[189] Occasionally, however, anonymous juries have been empaneled for the express purpose of shielding them from the media. As one court put it: "[a]nonymity and sequestration measures will serve the . . . purpose of ensuring that the jurors are not exposed to members of the media or to publicity about the trial."[190] Appellate courts have generally taken a dim view of this latter practice. In *United States v. Ross*, the Eleventh Circuit emphasized that "the empanelment of an anonymous jury is a drastic measure, one which should be undertaken only in limited and carefully defined circumstances."[191] Nevertheless, at least one state has adopted a statute sealing juror identification information absent a showing of good cause[192] and the device has been employed when the case for anonymity appears at best tenuous.[193]

In the Oklahoma City bombing trial of Timothy McVeigh, the trial court took a variety of steps to insulate the jury from the public, including the use of juror numbers and the scrambling of those numbers to prevent juror identification.

---

grand jury witness immunity). Still, it has been argued that "the mere fact that a proceeding relates in some way to a grand jury does not justify conducting it behind closed doors." Sager, *First Amendment Issues in the O.J. Simpson Trial*, 12 COMM. LAW. 3, 4 (Winter 1995). See Butterworth v. Smith, 494 U.S. 624 (1990) (holding that Florida statute, which prohibits grand jury witness from disclosing his own grand jury testimony, violates First Amendment). See generally Note, *Grand Jury Secrecy v. The First Amendment: A Case for Press Interviews of Grand Jurors*, 23 VAL. U. L. REV. 559, 560 (1989) ("the secrecy surrounding grand jury proceedings . . . has curtailed the press' ability to carry out its watchdog function").

189. See King, *Nameless Justice: The Case for the Routine Use of Anonymous Juries in Criminal Trials*, 49 VAND. L. REV. 123, 124 (1996) ("By alleviating jurors' fear, anonymity can enhance the participation of citizens in jury service, the reliability of the voir dire process, the quality of jury deliberations, and the fairness of criminal verdicts."); Weinstein, *Protecting a Juror's Right to Privacy: Constitutional Constraints and Policy Options*, 70 TEMP. L. REV. 1 (1997) (examining alternatives for protecting juror privacy such as anonymous juries and the elimination of peremptory challenges). Two California courts reportedly have allowed anonymity upon request, with one judge stating that, during the year he used anonymous juries, only a half dozen of the 2,800 jurors in his court chose to have their names made public. See King, *supra*, at 133, 159 n.44. See also Note, *Minnesota's First Anonymous Jury*, 22 WM. MITCHELL L. REV. 133, 147 (1996) (discussing Minnesota v. Bowles, 530 N.W.2d 521 (1995), *cert. denied*, 516 U.S. 1162 (1996)).

190. United States v. Edmond, 730 F. Supp. 1144, 1148 (D.D.C. 1990), *aff'd sub nom*. United States v. Childress, 58 F.3d 693 (D.C. Cir. 1995), *cert. denied*, 516 U.S. 1098 (1996). See King, *supra* note 189, at 129 ("Jurors are beginning to express their concerns about being pursued by the media as well.").

191. 33 F.3d 1507, 1519 (11th Cir. 1994), *cert. denied*, 515 U.S. 1132 (1995).

192. See TEX. CRIM. P. CODE ANN. § 35.29. California has passed similar legislation. See CAL. CIV. PROC. CODE § 237. See generally King, *supra* note 189, at 132, 159 n.44.

193. See, e.g., Minnesota v. Bowles, 530 N.W.2d 521, 531 (Minn. 1995), *cert. denied*, 516 U.S. 1162 (1996) ("The jurors could have reasonably concluded that were they to acquit Bowles, they or their families would be vulnerable to harassment from the public.").

The court also erected a screen for the asserted purpose of preventing closed-circuit video cameras from distracting jurors. The screen served the collateral purpose of blocking the view of the press and public during voir dire.[194] All challenges for cause were heard in the judge's chambers and the transcript of voir dire held in open court was released only when jury selection was completed.[195]

§ 7-4. Checkbook Journalism.

Courts have also had occasion to consider another aspect of press access to participants in the judicial process, i.e., the phenomenon of "checkbook journalism."[196] Indeed, in the wake of extensive publicity surrounding payments made to witnesses and jurors in exchange for interviews in the prosecution of football hero O.J. Simpson in connection with the murder of two people, including his former wife, the California legislature enacted legislation designed to prohibit the practice.

While the California Penal Code already had provisions governing jury tampering, it was amended in 1995 to make it a misdemeanor to offer payment in excess of $50 to a juror or his/her agent for supplying information concerning the proceeding for ninety days after the jury was discharged. A similar penalty was imposed on a juror accepting or agreeing to accept such a payment.[197] In *Dove Audio, Inc. v. Lungren*,[198] these provisions were held unconstitutional as applied to a dismissed juror and their enforcement was permanently enjoined.

---

194. See Official Trial Transcript, United States v. McVeigh, 97-X-29, April 26, 1997, at 1997 WL 202233. See generally Ross, *Oklahoma Bombing Trial Judge Imposes Cloak of Secrecy*, NAT'L L.J., April 28, 1997, at A11. The identities of the jurors were also withheld from the public in the Unabomber case. See United States v. Kaczynski, No. CRS-96-259 GEB (E.D. Cal. 1997).

195. See 1997 WL 202233.

196. See generally Olson, *Checkbook Journalism and the First Amendment*, 13 COMM. LAW. 7 (Spring 1995); Strauss, *From Witness to Riches: The Constitutionality of Restricting Witness Speech*, 38 ARIZ. L. REV. 291, 329 (1996) (arguing that "even purchased speech deserves — and receives — protection under the Constitution"); Vassiles, *Checkbook Journalism: It May Involve Free Speech Interests but It Is Not Free; Can Witnesses Be Prohibited from Selling Their Stories to the Media Under the First Amendment?*, 56 OHIO ST. L.J. 1619 (1995); Comment, *Checkbook Journalism, Free Speech, and Fair Trials*, 143 U. PA. L. REV. 1739 (1995); Note, *Balancing "Checkbook Journalism": A Balance Between the First and Sixth Amendments in High Profile Criminal Cases*, 4 WM. & MARY BILL RTS. J. 671 (1995); Note, *Banning the Sale of Witness Testimony: A First Amendment Challenge to California Penal Code Section 132.5*, 75 B.U. L. REV. 1135 (1995).

197. See CAL. PENAL CODE § 116.5.

198. 1995 WL 432631 (C.D. Cal. June 14, 1995). Michael Knox, a dismissed juror in the O.J. Simpson case, wished to enter into a book contract with Dove Audio. California indicated it would prosecute Knox and the prospective publisher if they entered into such an agreement. See *id.*

The court in *Dove Audio, Inc.* held that the statute was a content-based restriction on speech.[199] Like the legislation invalidated by the Supreme Court in *Simon & Schuster, Inc. v. New York State Crime Victims Board*,[200] the law discriminated on the basis of the subject matter of the speech and the restraint was imposed only on expressive activity. As Justice O'Connor wrote for the Court in *Simon & Schuster, Inc.*, "[a] statute is presumptively inconsistent with the First Amendment if it imposes a financial burden on speakers because of the content of their speech."[201] Indeed, the court in *Dove Audio, Inc.* went one step further, holding that the jury tampering provision was a content-based *prior restraint*.[202] Applying strict scrutiny, the court acknowledged that protecting the integrity and impartiality of jury deliberations is a compelling governmental interest, but held that the legislation was not "necessary" to serve that interest.[203] The state could cite no evidence that the prospect of financial gain at the conclusion of jury service, as a result of providing information, has ever compromised a trial.[204]

California also amended its criminal and civil codes to prohibit prospective witnesses from receiving compensation in exchange for providing the public with information about the case.[205] Again, the O.J. Simpson trial served as the impetus for the legislation, after a potential witness was allegedly not called to testify because she had agreed to "sell" her "story" to the media.[206]

California Penal Code Section 132.5 applied to payments to anyone who witnesses an event or occurrence that he knows, or reasonably should know, is a crime; or to any person who has personal knowledge of facts that he knows, or reasonably should know, may require that the person be called as a witness.[207]

---

199. See *id.* at *2.
200. 502 U.S. 105 (1991). The New York law at issue in *Simon & Schuster, Inc.* provided that income received by an accused or convicted criminal derived from publications dealing with his crime be deposited in a victims' compensation fund. See *id.*
201. *Id.* at 123.
202. See 1995 WL 432631 at *2.
203. *Id.*
204. See *id.* at *1.
205. See CAL. PENAL CODE § 132.5; CAL. CIV. CODE § 1669.7.
206. Jill Shively, who allegedly saw Simpson in his Ford Bronco rushing from the crime scene the night of the murders, received $5,000 from *Hard Copy*, a tabloid television program, and $2,600 from *The Star*, a tabloid newspaper. See Olson, *supra* note 196, at 7 n.3. The prosecution, however, did call Jose Camacho and Allen Wattenburg, an employee and a part owner of a Los Angeles cutlery store respectively, who testified that Mr. Simpson had visited their store and bought a 15-inch knife. They had sold the rights to their "stories" for $12,500 to the *National Enquirer*. After failing in their attempts to dismiss Camacho, the defense impeached his testimony by stressing the payment he had received. See generally Curriden, *Tabloid Tales Hindering Prosecution*, A.B.A. J., Dec. 1994, at 16; *Effluence for Affluence . . . A Scorecard*, MEDIA & THE LAW, Aug. 1994, at 43 (summary of publicized payments).
207. See CAL. PENAL CODE § 132.5(b-c).

Violation was punishable by a fine of up to three times the payment received or six months in jail.[208] The statute did not apply if the information was provided without a fee,[209] or if one year had passed from the date of the prohibited act, unless prosecution had already commenced, in which case the ban remained in force until final judgment.[210] Further, the law provided exceptions for lawful compensation paid to expert witnesses, investigators, and agents by a prosecutor.[211] Section 1669.7 was added to the Civil Code to invalidate contracts made in violation of section 132.5 and provisions were made for the state to institute civil proceedings to enjoin their performance.[212]

In *California First Amendment Coalition v. Lungren*,[213] a federal court entered a permanent injunction prohibiting enforcement of the statutes on the ground that they violated both the First Amendment and the California Constitution.[214] As in *Dove Audio, Inc.*, the court held that the laws were content-based and subject to strict scrutiny because they "target only speech relative to crimes."[215] The fact that the laws were viewpoint-neutral and aimed at protecting the integrity of the criminal justice system did not mean, the court emphasized, that they were content-neutral.[216]

In the court's view, the statutes constituted a prior restraint on speech "at the core of protected expression."[217] Applying strict scrutiny, the court dismissed the state's asserted interest in preventing erosion of public confidence in the courts "not sufficiently compelling" to justify such "wholesale burdens on speech."[218] And, while the governmental interest in ensuring fair trials and maintaining witness credibility was admittedly compelling, these laws were not narrowly tailored to serve those goals and less restrictive alternative means of doing so were available.[219] In addition, the court held, the statutes were overbroad, restricting speech even if there were no trial, criminalizing all compensation no matter how small, and regulating all information, even if undisputed or bearing no relevance to a criminal prosecution.[220] The time limits did not save the

---

208. See *id.* § 132.5(d)-(e).
209. See *id.* § 132.5(a) ("This section is not intended to prevent any person from disseminating any information or opinion.").
210. See *id.* § 132.5(f).
211. See *id.* § 132.5(g).
212. CAL. CIV. CODE § 1669.7.
213. 1995 WL 482066 (N.D. Cal. Aug. 10, 1995).
214. See *id.* at *1. See also CAL. CONST. art. I, § 2(a).
215. 1995 WL 482066 at *4.
216. See *id.*
217. *Id.* at *5.
218. *Id.*
219. See *id.* at *6 (citing statutes criminalizing perjury, CAL. PENAL CODE § 118, subordination of perjury, CAL. PENAL CODE § 127, the bribing of witnesses, CAL. PENAL CODE § 138 and cross-examination, CAL. EVID. CODE § 761).
220. See 1995 WL 482066 at *8.

legislation either, since "'[t]he loss of First Amendment freedoms,' for even minimal periods of time, unquestionably constitutes irreparable injury."[221]

---

221. *Id.* (quoting Elrod v. Burns, 427 U.S. 347, 362 (1976)). See Bridges v. California, 314 U.S. 252, 269 (1941) ("An endless series of moratoria, even if very short, could hardly be dismissed as an insignificant abridgement of freedom of expression.").

Other states have considered legislation aimed at regulating "checkbook" journalism. See, e.g., 1995 ILL. S.B. 344; 1995 OHIO H.B. 41; 1994 MASS. S.B. 878; N.J. STAT. ANN. § 2C:29-8.1; N.Y. PENAL LAW § 215.28.

Chapter 8

ACCESS TO PUBLIC PLACES AND EVENTS

§ 8-1. Prisons and Prisoners.
§ 8-2. Executions.
§ 8-3. Disaster, Accident and Crime Scenes.
§ 8-4. Voters and Polling Places.
§ 8-5. Military Operations.

§ 8-1. Prisons and Prisoners.

The public has an obvious interest in access to the workings of the prison system.[1] Prison uprisings and the numerous prisoner petitions filed in federal court alleging violations of prisoners' fundamental rights attest to the need for understanding and monitoring how prisons operate. Yet, prisons are security institutions often treated as nonpublic fora and hence not subject to ordinary First Amendment standards.[2] It is not surprising, therefore, that the courts have not generally been receptive to a First Amendment-based right of access to prison facilities.

The issue of media access to the prisons first came to the Supreme Court in companion cases in 1974. In *Pell v. Procunier*,[3] the Court heard challenges by prisoners and the press to California regulations prohibiting media interviews with specific inmates. In *Saxbe v. Washington Post Co.*,[4] the Court confronted a press challenge to similar federal regulations.

Rejecting the prisoners' challenge, the Court in *Pell* stressed the availability of alternative means of communication. While a prisoner does not forfeit his First Amendment rights entirely, the Court acknowledged, the prison environ-

---

[1]. Much of the discussion that follows is based on J. BARRON & C.T. DIENES, HANDBOOK OF FREE SPEECH AND FREE PRESS §§ 8:12, 8:13 (1979). See REPORTERS COMMITTEE FOR FREEDOM OF THE PRESS, ACCESS TO PLACES 4-5 (Fall 1997); Paul & Ovelman, *Access*, in 3 COMM. L. 1998, at 157, 431-33 (PLI 1998); Steinfield & Bertsche, *Recent Developments in the Law of Access — 1997*, in 3 COMM. L. 1998, at 36-37, 53 (PLI 1998).

[2]. See, e.g., Thornburgh v. Abbott, 490 U.S. 401 (1989) (holding that restrictions on prisoners receiving certain publications were facially valid); O'Lone v. Estate of Shabazz, 482 U.S. 342, 349 (1987) ("[T]o ensure that courts afford appropriate deference to prison officials, we have determined that prison regulations alleged to infringe constitutional rights are judged under a 'reasonableness' test less restrictive than that ordinarily applied to alleged infringements of fundamental constitutional rights."); Turner v. Safley, 482 U.S. 78, 89 (1987) ("When a prison regulation impinges on inmates' constitutional rights, the regulation is valid if it is reasonably related to legitimate penological interests.").

[3]. 417 U.S. 817 (1974).

[4]. 417 U.S. 843 (1974). *Saxbe* and *Pell* are discussed in Comment, *Prisons and the Right of the Press to Gather Information: A Review of* Pell v. Procunier *and* Saxbe v. Washington Post, 43 U. CIN. L. REV. 913 (1974); Note, *The Public's Right to Know:* Pell v. Procunier *and* Saxbe v. Washington Post, 2 HASTINGS CONST. L.Q. 829 (1975).

ment, with its peculiar security considerations, contemplates some restriction on the access enjoyed by outsiders.[5] Such restrictions, Justice Stewart concluded on behalf of the Court, were not based on the content of any specific communication, but rather constituted reasonable time, place, and manner regulation:[6]

> When ... the question involves the entry of people into the prisons for face-to-face communication with inmates, it is obvious that institutional considerations, such as security and related administrative problems, as well as the accepted and legitimate policy objectives of the corrections system itself, require that some limitation be placed on such visitations. So long as reasonable and effective means of communication remain open and no discrimination in terms of content is involved, we believe that, in drawing such lines, prison officials must be accorded latitude.[7]

Applying this standard in *Pell*, the Court held that reasonable alternatives were available and that the prohibition of one means of information gathering was constitutionally permissible. Communication by mail and visitation with members of the inmate's family, the clergy, the inmate's attorney, and his friends still provided an inmate with avenues of communication to the outside world.[8] Accordingly, the Court concluded that, insofar as the California regulation merely limited the particular forms of public communication available to prison inmates, it was not an excessive restriction on their First Amendment rights. "So long as this restriction operates in a neutral fashion, without regard to the content of the expression, it falls within the 'appropriate rules and regulations' to which 'prisoners necessarily are subject,' and does not abridge any First Amendment freedoms retained by prison inmates."[9]

Nor were the media's First Amendment rights violated by the California restriction on prisoner interviews. In *Pell*, the press had argued that the First Amendment protected its right to interview any prisoner willing to speak to reporters, in the absence of a particularized determination that a given interview presented a clear and present danger to some substantial interest.[10] While the Court had suggested in *Branzburg v. Hayes*[11] that the burden on newsgathering from the compelled disclosure of confidential sources was uncertain, the press argued in *Pell* that the governmental interference with newsgathering embodied

---

5. Since imprisonment necessarily brings about a withdrawal or limitation of rights and privileges, "a prison inmate retains those First Amendment rights that are not inconsistent with his status as a prisoner or with the legitimate penological objectives of the corrections system." 417 U.S. at 822.
6. See *id.* at 826-827, 828.
7. *Id.* at 826 (quoting Cruz v. Beto, 405 U.S. 319, 321 (1972)).
8. See 417 U.S. at 828.
9. *Id.* (quoting 405 U.S. at 321).
10. 417 U.S. at 830.
11. 408 U.S. 665 (1972).

in the California regulation was both consequential and certain.[12] Further, the press asserted that no substantial government interest justified denial of press access to designated prison inmates.[13] The Court, however, disagreed.

Justice Stewart's opinion for the Court in *Pell* proceeds from the premise that the press was seeking a unique right of access beyond that available to the general public. In that regard, the Court stressed those means of communication with inmates that were available to press and public alike.[14] Tours were conducted for interested citizens. Journalists could visit prisons and interview any prisoner they might encounter. Further, a journalist could request an interview with prisoners selected at random or sit in on group meetings with prisoners. "In short, members of the press enjoy access to California prisons that is not available to other members of the public."[15]

Thus, the Court determined that the issue before it was whether the First Amendment could be invoked to confer upon the press a special right of access — the right to interview designated inmates — not available to the general public. The Court rejected any "constitutional right of access to prisons or their inmates beyond that afforded the general public."[16] The regulation at issue, the Court held, in no sense restricted press access to sources of information available to the general public. As a result, it did not violate the First Amendment. "The Constitution does not . . . require government to accord the press special access to information not shared by members of the public generally."[17]

In *Saxbe*, which the Court viewed as largely indistinguishable from *Pell*,[18] the federal government also argued that concentrated press attention on particular inmates had transformed them into virtual public figures, creating severe problems of discipline for prison authorities. A selective policy of denying interviews where they might lead to disciplinary problems, which had been suggested by the lower courts, had proven unworkable.[19] Nevertheless, while Justice Stewart noted the rationale underlying the prison policy, he rejected any balancing of interests because access to prisons "is generally limited," and the federal regulations had not placed the press in a worse position than the public generally.[20]

---

12. See 417 U.S. at 830-31.
13. See *id.*
14. See *id.* at 830-34.
15. *Id.*
16. *Id.* at 834; see *id.* (government has no "affirmative duty to make available to journalists sources of information not available to members of the public generally"); Branzburg v. Hayes, 408 U.S. 665, 684 (1972) ("[T]he First Amendment does not guarantee the press a constitutional right of special access to information not available to the public generally.").
17. 417 U.S. at 834.
18. See 417 U.S. at 849-50.
19. See *id.*
20. *Id.* at 849.

Justice Powell, joined by Justices Brennan and Marshall, dissented, stressing the unique value of face-to-face interviews for acquiring information about prison conditions and the inadequacy of alternative modes of communication.[21] The district court had found, as a fact, "that the absolute interview ban precludes accurate and effective reporting on prison conditions and inmate grievances."[22] It had also concluded that alternative forms of communication were insufficient to compensate for the loss of meaningful information occasioned by the prohibition on personal interviews.[23] Only personal interviews permitted immediate follow-up questions, Justice Powell argued, because they enable a reporter to pursue a particular line of inquiry to a fully investigated conclusion.[24]

But, it was the majority's treatment of the constitutional status of the press claim to prison access that particularly drew Justice Powell's fire. While he agreed that the press does not enjoy any special right of access beyond that afforded the general public,[25] the majority opinions in both *Pell* and *Saxbe* appeared to him to go further: "From all that appears in the Court's opinion, one would think that any governmental restriction on access to information, no matter how severe, would be constitutionally acceptable to the majority so long as it does not single out the media for special disabilities not applicable to the public at large."[26] Even such a nondiscriminatory policy, Justice Powell asserted, "may so undermine the function of the First Amendment that it is both appropriate and necessary to require the government to justify such regulations in terms more compelling than discretionary authority and administrative convenience."[27] For Justice Powell, special press access is sometimes required by the First Amendment:

---

21. See *id.* at 850-75 (Powell, J., dissenting). Justice Powell's dissenting opinion in *Saxbe* also applied to the portion of the *Pell* majority opinion addressing the rights of the press. Justice Powell joined the Court's opinion in *Pell* insofar as it dealt with the rights of the prisoners themselves, an issue not present in *Saxbe*. See *id.* at 835. Justices Douglas, Brennan, and Marshall dissented from the Court's resolution of the prisoners' rights issues in *Pell* as well. See *id.* at 836-42 (Douglas, J., dissenting).

22. *Id.* at 854 (Powell, J., dissenting).

23. See *id.* at 854-55:

> Random conversations during supervised tours of prison facilities are also no substitute for personal interviews with designated inmates. The conversations allowed by the Policy Statement are restricted in both duration and permissible subject matter. If a reporter is investigating a particular incident, the opportunity to converse with inmates who were not present is of little consequence. Moreover, the conversations associated with guided tours are often held in the presence of several inmates, a factor likely to result in distortion of the information obtained.

24. See *id.*
25. See *id.* at 857.
26. *Id.*
27. *Id.* at 860.

An informed public depends on accurate and effective reporting by the news media. No individual can obtain for himself the information needed for the intelligent discharge of his political responsibilities. For most citizens the prospect of personal familiarity with newsworthy events is hopelessly unrealistic. In seeking out the news the press therefore acts as an agent of the public at large. It is the means by which the people receive that free flow of information and ideas essential to intelligent self-government. By enabling the public to assert meaningful control over the political process, the press performs a crucial function in effecting the societal purpose of the First Amendment.[28]

Balancing the competing interests, Justice Powell concluded that, although an *absolute* ban on press interviews with inmates was unnecessary, prison authorities could adopt a policy that would not intrude so substantially on First Amendment rights.[29] Although case-by-case evaluation of each interview request was not constitutionally mandated, Justice Powell asserted that the First Amendment did require the government to devise its own policy that reflected "the public's legitimate interest in a free flow of information and ideas" about prisons.[30]

The majority in *Pell* and *Saxbe* squarely rejected any special right of access for the media beyond that possessed by the public. Nevertheless, the Court's emphasis on effective alternative avenues of communication with prison inmates could be read as limiting even that portion of the holdings. Thus, although there may be no right of press access to specific prisoners where there are alternative means of investigating conditions in the prison, the balance might be struck differently in the absence of effective alternative means of gathering information about prison conditions.

Pell and *Saxbe*, therefore, left open two critical questions with respect to prison access. First, to what extent could prison authorities deny access to the prisons to the public generally, including the press? Second, assuming that some effective access for the general public is provided by prison authorities, could media representatives nevertheless claim that prison regulations uniquely denied

---

28. *Id.* at 863; see *id.* at 864 ("The Bureau's absolute prohibition of prisoner-press interviews negates the ability of the press to discharge that function and thereby substantially impairs the right of the people to a free flow of information and ideas on the conduct of their Government. The underlying right is the right of the public generally. The press is the necessary representative of the public's interest in this context and the instrumentality which effects the public's right.").

29. See *id.* at 864-70 ("First, the regulation or practice in question must further an important or substantial governmental interest unrelated to the suppression of expression. . . . Second, the limitation of First Amendment freedoms must be no greater than is necessary or essential to the protection of the particular governmental interest involved.") (quoting Procunier v. Martinez, 416 U.S. 396, 413 (1974)).

30. 417 U.S. at 872.

them effective access? The Court undertook to respond to these questions in *Houchins v. KQED, Inc.*,[31] but the fragmentation among the justices did little to eliminate the uncertainty and confusion generated by the *Pell* and *Saxbe* decisions.

In *Houchins*, the NAACP and press representatives alleged the public generally was denied effective access to the county jail in Santa Rita, California.[32] At the time suit was filed, there was no formal policy regarding public access to the prison. Shortly thereafter, the prison began conducting six public tours every month to some parts of the prison. The tours did not, however, include "Little Greystone," a part of the jail that had received particular notoriety as the site of rapes, beatings, and intolerable physical conditions.[33] No cameras or tape recorders were permitted on the tour. Inmates were generally removed from public view and could not be interviewed.[34]

The Supreme Court could not muster a majority opinion, especially since only seven justices participated in the case. The Chief Justice, in an opinion joined by Justices White and Rehnquist, announced the Court's judgment affirming the prison's restrictive access policy.[35] Justice Stewart, concurring only in the judgment, filed a separate opinion.[36] Chief Justice Burger's opinion returned to the principles articulated in *Pell v. Procunier* and *Saxbe v. Washington Post Co.* — i.e., the press has no special right of access "different from or greater than that accorded the public generally."[37] The Chief Justice found nothing in the Constitution that "*compels* the government to provide the media with information or access to it on demand."[38] In short, the right to acquire information did not imply any obligation on the part of government or private parties to supply it.[39] The case for a special privilege of access, "a right which is not essential to guarantee the freedom to communicate or publish,"[40] had been rejected in *Pell* and *Saxbe*, and the Chief Justice saw no need to decide *Houchins* differently. In addition, the Chief Justice purported to reject as well any suggestion "that the *public* and the media have a First Amendment right to government information regarding the conditions of jails and their inmates and presumably all other public facilities such as hospitals and mental institutions."[41]

---

31. 438 U.S. 1 (1978).
32. See *id.* at 6.
33. See *id.* at 7.
34. See *id.* at 8.
35. See *id.* at 12-16 (Burger, C.J., announcing judgment).
36. See *id.* at 16 (Stewart, J., concurring).
37. *Id.* at 15.
38. *Id.* at 9 (emphasis in original).
39. See *id.* at 11.
40. *Id.* at 12.
41. *Id.* at 14 (emphasis added). Chief Justice Burger's opinion on this point is, nevertheless, far from clear since it appears to vacillate between several lines of analysis simultaneously. See *id.* at

Throughout his opinion, the Chief Justice emphasized the propriety of broad judicial deference to the political branches in deciding the extent to which public institutions should be open to the press or public. "Whether the government should open penal institutions in the manner sought by respondents is a question of policy which a legislative body might appropriately resolve one way or the other."[42] Accordingly, the Chief Justice asserted:

> [T]he choice as to the most effective and appropriate method is a policy decision to be resolved by legislative decision. We must not confuse what is "good," "desirable," or "expedient," with what is constitutionally commanded by the First Amendment. To do so is to trivialize constitutional adjudication.[43]

In addition, the Chief Justice concluded, there were no judicially manageable standards for implementing a constitutional duty to disclose information, and there were alternative means available for informing the public.[44]

Concurring in the result, Justice Stewart appeared to part company with the Chief Justice's aversion to media access to prisons. Justice Stewart did, however, reject an affirmative constitutional right of access to information under government control when the government has decided to maintain secrecy:

> The First and Fourteenth Amendments do not guarantee the public a right of access to information generated or controlled by government, nor do they guarantee the press any basic right of access superior to that of the public generally. The Constitution does no more than assure the public and the press equal access once government has opened its doors.[45]

When the government has "opened its doors," however, Justice Stewart emphasized that the concept of "equal access" between the press and public does not necessarily mean identical treatment.[46] Thus, what is reasonable access for the public may not constitute reasonable access for the media. "In short, terms of

---

12 ("The right to *receive* ideas and information is not the issue in this case . . . The issue is a claim [of a] special privilege of access. . . .").

42. *Id.* at 12.

43. *Id.* at 12-13; see *id.* at 14 ("Because the Constitution affords no guidelines, absent statutory standards, hundreds of judges would, under the Court of Appeals' approach, be at large to fashion *ad hoc* standards, in individual cases, according to their own ideas of what seems 'desirable' or 'expedient.'").

44. See *id.* at 12-13. Among the means identified by the Chief Justice were citizen task forces, grand juries, and legislative investigations. See *id.* One perceived advantage of these methods of informing the public about prison conditions was that they were publicly accountable should they attempt to conceal information. However, "[n]o comparable pressures are available to anyone to compel publication by the media of what they might prefer not to make known." *Id.* at 14.

45. *Id.* at 16 (Stewart, J., concurring).

46. See *id.* ("The concept of equal access must be accorded more flexibility in order to accommodate the practical distinction between the press and the general public.").

access that are reasonably imposed on individual members of the public may, if they impede effective reporting without sufficient justification, be unreasonable as applied to journalists who are there to convey to the general public what the visitors see."[47]

The prison regulations at issue in *Houchins*, according to Justice Stewart, did not afford the press *effective access* to areas of the prison otherwise open to the public. Nevertheless, by ordering prison officials to permit reporters into the "Little Greystone" facility and to interview randomly encountered inmates, the district court had afforded the press a right of access to sources of information beyond that available to the public. The district court's order was, therefore, too broad, although properly framed relief granting the press the ability to use cameras was, in Justice Stewart's view, required by the Constitution.[48]

In dissent, Justice Stevens asserted, on behalf of three justices, that the public cannot constitutionally be excluded from all meaningful access to public facilities such as prisons.[49] *Pell*, in his view, never suggested "that a nondiscriminatory policy of excluding entirely both the public and the press from access to information about prison conditions would avoid constitutional scrutiny."[50] Indeed, the Court in *Pell* had emphasized that the press and the public already possessed the means to acquire information about the prison and its inmates under existing prison regulations. Thus, Justice Stevens contended that the prison's policy could not survive constitutional scrutiny because the public has a right to be informed about prison conditions and hence a right of access to prisons themselves:

> The preservation of a full and free flow of information to the general public has long been recognized as a core objective of the First Amendment to the Constitution. It is for this reason that the First Amendment protects not only the dissemination but also the receipt of information and ideas.[51]

The Supreme Court has not revisited the question of public and press access to prisons since *Houchins*. Accordingly, that decision, along with *Pell* and *Saxbe,* continues to control the disposition of prison access cases in the lower courts.[52] For example, one court rejected a prisoner's First Amendment-based

---

47. *Id.* at 17; see *id.* ("A person touring Santa Rita jail can grasp its reality with his own eyes and ears. But if a television reporter is to convey the jail's sights and sounds to those who cannot personally visit the place, he must use cameras and sound equipment.").

48. See *id.* at 18-19.

49. *Id.* at 27-28 (Stevens, J., dissenting).

50. *Id.*

51. *Id.* at 30.

52. See, e.g., Jersawitz v. Hanberry, 783 F.2d 1532 (11th Cir.), *cert. denied*, 479 U.S. 883 (1986) (upholding regulation at Atlanta federal prison permitting only representatives of FCC-licensed media principally employed as newsgatherers to interview inmates for broadcast); Sidebottom v. Schiriro, 927 F. Supp. 1221 (E.D. Mo. 1996) (rejecting claim that ban on taking

claim when prison officials denied a television producer an opportunity to conduct a face-to-face interview with him because he was free to communicate through the mail and by telephone.[53] Similarly, another court upheld the decision of a prison director to deny a television journalist access to a prison for the purpose of videotaping a polygraph examination of a prisoner; the court concluded that alternative means of communication remained available to the prisoner and that corrections officials were entitled to judicial deference.[54] Moreover, courts have held that unauthorized communications between a prisoner and a journalist within the prison may be punished.[55] Finally, in the wake of the Supreme Court decisions in the *Pell-Saxbe-Houchins* line of cases, several states have implemented or at least considered more restrictive rules regarding press access to inmates.[56]

---

video camera into prison is unconstitutional); Phoenix Newspapers, Inc. v. Department of Corrections, 934 P.2d 801, 806 (Ariz. App. 1997) (affirming dismissal of claim that state correctional policy unconstitutionally discriminates against media by denying prison visitation privileges enjoyed by other designated classes of persons since "limitations on persons permitted entry to prisons are rationally related to the State's interest in public safety and prison order"); Mann v. State's Attorney, 468 A.2d 124 (Md. Spec. App. 1983) (upholding Maryland law allowing counsel for defendant found incompetent to stand trial and committed to maximum security facility for treatment of criminally insane to deny media interviews on his behalf); see also Buffalo Broadcasting Co. v. New York Dep't of Correctional Servs., 578 N.Y.S.2d 928 (App. Div. 1992) (finding state freedom of information laws require disclosure of state-made videotapes depicting conditions at Attica prison to local broadcasting company, subject to redactions on grounds of privacy and danger to officers' personal safety).

The right of access to incarcerated defendants awaiting trial may be broader. See, e.g., United States v. Fort, 14 MEDIA L. REP. (BNA) 1942 (N.D. Ill. 1987) (holding prison warden may not deny media access to incarcerated defendants awaiting criminal trial who desire to be interviewed, despite defense counsel's opposition); Ohio v. Barker, 23 MEDIA L. REP. (BNA) 1124 (Ohio C.P. 1994) (holding, without reaching constitutional issue, that television station may interview criminal defendant in custody who has consented, regardless of defense counsel's objection); see also Abu-Jamal v. Price, 23 MEDIA L. REP. (BNA) 2406 (W.D. Pa. 1995) (holding press groups may file amicus brief in death row inmate's suit challenging prison's refusal to permit media interviews).

53. See Johnson v. Stephan, 6 F.3d 691 (10th Cir. 1993).

54. See Arney v. Director, Kansas State Penitentiary, 671 P.2d 559 (Kan. 1983); see also Cunningham v. Oregon Dep't of Corrections, 166 F.3d 342 (9th Cir. 1998) (unpublished disposition) (granting summary judgment in favor of defendant Department of Corrections, stating that the denial of prisoner's "request to be interviewed on camera was within the ODOC's unfettered discretion").

55. See Florida v. Olson, 586 So. 2d 1239 (Fla. App. 1991).

56. See, e.g., *State Prisons Clamp Down on Prisoner Interviews*, THE NEWS MEDIA & THE LAW, Spring 1996, at 5 (describing prison access developments in California, Illinois, Indiana, and Virginia). Denial of access has, however, often been challenged successfully under state law. See, e.g., Times Publ'g Co. v. Florida Dep't of Corrections, 375 So. 2d 307 (Fla. App. 1979) (invalidating a rule as it applied to media interviews with prisoners whose execution warrants were outstanding as lacking sufficient emergency justification). For a discussion of media access to prisons on the state level, see Davis, *Access to Prisons: Officials Increasingly Limit Contact*

§ 8-2. Executions.

In 1994, television talk show host Phil Donahue and death row inmate David Lawson sought permission to videotape Lawson's execution by lethal gas for inclusion in a documentary broadcast. Lawson said he desired that his death serve as an educational vehicle to prevent others from following his lifestyle and that it contribute to the death penalty debate.[57] The prison warden denied the application and the North Carolina Supreme Court, relying on the Supreme Court's prison access cases, held that there was no First Amendment or state constitutional right to videotape the execution.[58] The Fourth Circuit denied review since the constitutional issue had been litigated in the state court to final judgment on the merits.[59] Two concurring judges, however, would have held that, in any event, the First Amendment had not been violated.[60]

Prior to the 1830s, public executions were common in England and in the United States. In response to the movement to abolish the death penalty, however, states began to adopt statutes restricting access to executions.[61] Today, a small number of states permit access only to those persons selected by the condemned or to persons acting in an official capacity.[62] Seventeen states designate a given number of witnesses who may attend; most include the condemned's relatives and friends.[63] A third category of statutes authorizes media

---

Between Inmates and the Press, THE QUILL, May 1998, at 19; see also *Cameras in Prisons; What's Going On?*, VIRGINIAN-PILOT, Apr. 7, 1998, at B10.

57. Lawson designated Donahue and James Arnold, an award-winning cameraman, as individuals authorized to attend his execution. He also requested that his execution be videotaped. See Lawson v. Dixon, 25 F.3d 1040 (4th Cir. 1994).

58. See Lawson v. Dixon, 446 S.E.2d 799 (N.C. 1994).

59. Lawson v. Dixon, 25 F.3d 1040, 22 MEDIA L. REP. (BNA) 1839, 1840 (4th Cir. 1994).

60. See *id.* at 1844-45 (Widener, J., concurring).

61. See generally Bessler, *Televised Executions and the Constitution: Recognizing a First Amendment Right of Access to State Executions*, 45 FED. COMM. L.J. 355, 359-67 (1993); Richards & Easter, *Televising Executions: The High-Tech Alternative to Public Hangings*, 40 UCLA L. REV. 381, 383-86 (1992).

62. See, e.g., IND. CODE § 35-38-6-6; OR. REV. STAT. § 137.473; TEX. CRIM. P. CODE ANN. § 43.20; WYO. STAT. ANN. § 7-13-908.

63. See, e.g., ARIZ. REV. STAT. § 13-705 (Director shall invite "at least twelve reputable citizens of his selection"); ARK. CODE ANN. § 16-90-502(d)(2) ("At the execution there shall be present . . . a number of respectable citizens numbering not fewer than six (6) nor more than twelve (12)."); CAL. PENAL CODE § 3605 (Warden must invite "at least 12 reputable citizens, to be selected by him"); COLO. REV. STAT. § 16-11-404 ("such witnesses as the executive director . . . in his or her discretion deems desirable, not to exceed 18 persons" may attend execution); 725 ILL. COMP. STAT. 5/119-5(d) (execution "shall be conducted in the presence of 6 witnesses who shall certify the execution of the sentence"); LA. REV. STAT. ANN. § 15:570 ("[n]ot less than five nor more than seven other witnesses" shall be present); MASS. GEN. LAWS ch. 279, § 65 ("[w]ith the approval of the superintendent, not more than three other persons" may witness execution); MO. REV. STAT. § 546.740 (chief administrative officer of the correctional facility shall invite "at least eight reputable citizens, to be selected by him"); MONT. CODE ANN. § 46-19-103(6) ("warden must allow

§ 8-2 ACCESS TO PUBLIC PLACES AND EVENTS § 8-2

access.[64] No state expressly authorizes audiotaping or videotaping executions, and many states specifically prohibit the practice.[65] Federal prison regulations provide that up to ten representatives of the press, selected by the warden, may be present at an execution; recordings are not permitted.[66]

In *Garrett v. Estelle*,[67] the Fifth Circuit reviewed a Texas policy permitting print media coverage of the execution chamber as part of a pool or through closed circuit coverage, but prohibiting any audio or film recording of the event.[68] Garrett, a television news reporter who was denied permission to film

---

the execution to be observed by 12 witnesses"); NEB. REV. STAT. § 29-2534 ("[s]uch other persons, not exceeding six in number, as the warden may designate"); NEV. REV. STAT. § 176.355 (director of the department of prisons shall invite "not less than six nor more than nine reputable citizens"); N.H. REV. STAT. ANN. § 630:6 ("[T]he sheriff of the county in which the person was convicted . . . may admit other reputable citizens not exceeding 12" to the execution.); N.M. STAT. ANN. § 31-14-15 (warden must invite "at least twelve reputable citizens, to be selected by him"); N.C. GEN. STAT. § 15-190 ("Four respectable citizens, two members of the victim's family, the counsel and any relatives . . . may be present if they so desire"); TEX. CRIM. P. CODE ANN. § 43.20 (804) ("[A]ny of the relatives or friends of the condemned person . . . not exceeding five in number, shall be admitted."); VA. CODE ANN. § 53.1-234 ("At the execution there shall be present . . . at least six citizens who shall not be employees of the Department.").

64. See, e.g., ALA. CODE § 15-18-83(a)(6) ("Such newspaper reporters as may be admitted by the warden. . . ."); CONN. GEN. STAT. § 54-100 ("The number of newsmedia representatives present shall be nine . . . ."); FLA. STAT. § 922.11(2) ("Representatives of news media may be present under rules approved by the Secretary of Corrections."); FLA. ADMIN. CODE ANN. r. 33-15.001; KY. REV. STAT. ANN. § 431.250 ("[n]ine (9) representatives of the news media"); MISS. CODE ANN. § 99-19-55(2) ("[b]ona fide members of the press, not to exceed eight (8) in number"); N.J. STAT. ANN. § 2C:49-7(c) ("The commissioner shall permit eight representatives of the news media to be present at the execution. . . ."); OHIO REV. CODE ANN. § 2949.25 ("The director shall authorize at least one representative of a newspaper, at least one representative of a television station, and at least one representative of a radio station to be present at the execution. . . ."); OHIO ADMIN. CODE § 5120-9-54; OKLA. STAT. tit. 22, § 1015 ("[R]eporters from recognized members of the news media will be admitted upon proper identification, application, and approval of the warden."); PA. CONS. STAT. tit. 42, § 9711(1) ("[n]ot more than six duly accredited representatives of the news media" shall witness an execution); S.C. CODE ANN. § 24-3-550 ("[a] group of not more than three representatives of the South Carolina media. . . ."); S.D. CODIFIED LAWS § 23A-27A-34 ("[a]t least one member of the news media to be selected by the warden"); TENN. CODE ANN. § 40-23-116 ("A total of seven (7) members of the print, radio and television news media . . . shall make available coverage . . . to other news media members not selected to attend."); UTAH CODE ANN. § 77-19-11(4) ("[n]ine members of the press and broadcast news media . . . provided that [they] . . . serve as a pool for other members of the news media as a condition of attendance"); WASH. REV. CODE § 10.95.185 ("[T]he superintendent shall designate the total number of individuals who will be allowed to attend . . . [including] media representatives.").

65. See, e.g., FLA. ADMIN. CODE ANN. r. 33-15.002; KY. REV. STAT. ANN. § 431.250; MISS. CODE ANN. § 99-19-55(2); OHIO ADMIN. CODE § 5120-9-54(B); S.C. CODE ANN. § 24-3-550; TENN. CODE ANN. § 40-23-116; UTAH CODE ANN. § 77-19-11(4)(a).

66. Implementation of Death Sentences in Federal Cases, 28 C.F.R. § 26.4 (1995).

67. 556 F.2d 1274 (5th Cir. 1977), *cert. denied*, 438 U.S. 914 (1978).

68. The district court had issued a preliminary injunction and declared unconstitutional a statutory provision read to prohibit press attendance at executions and press access to interview

Texas' first execution in twelve years and to film interviews with death row inmates, sought declaratory and injunctive relief. While the district court found that the policy violated the First Amendment,[69] the Fifth Circuit reversed.

Asserting a right to gather the news, Garrett sought to restrict *Pell* and *Saxbe* to prison regulations that prohibit singling out specific inmates for interviews. The Fifth Circuit rejected such a narrow reading, concluding instead that the cases stand for the proposition that "the press has no greater right of access to information than does the public at large; and that the first amendment does not require government to make available to the press information not available to the public."[70] Applying that principle, the court held "that the first amendment does not invalidate nondiscriminatory prison access regulations."[71] Under the Texas policy, both the public and the press had access to the execution; neither could use recording devices.[72] "Despite the unavailability of film of the actual execution the public can be fully informed; the free flow of ideas and information need not be inhibited."[73]

In *KQED, Inc. v. Vasquez*,[74] a federal district court rejected a public broadcasting station's claim that it enjoyed a First Amendment-based right to videotape California's first execution in over twenty years for use in a documentary film about capital punishment. The court upheld the government's restriction on filming by citing the interest of prison personnel in concealing their identities, the risk to prison security from the use of heavy recording equipment, and the potential for severe prisoner reaction.[75] At the same time, however, the court prohibited any effort to exclude the press or to prevent the use of papers and

---

death row inmates. Texas did not appeal from this portion of the district court judgment. See *id*. at 1277.

69. See Garrett v. Estelle, 424 F. Supp. 468 (N.D. Tex.), *rev'd*, 556 F.2d 1274 (5th Cir. 1977), *cert. denied*, 438 U.S. 914 (1978).

70. 556 F.2d at 1278.

71. *Id*.

72. The press enjoyed "the broadest kind of access, extending, as in *Pell* and *Saxbe*, well beyond that afforded the public generally." *Id*. at 1279.

73. *Id*. at 1278. The Fifth Circuit also rejected the district court's efforts to distinguish *Pell* and *Saxbe* by stressing the public importance of the death penalty compared to the day-to-day operations of a prison: "While we agree that the death penalty is a matter of wide public interest, we disagree that the protections of the First Amendment depend upon the notoriety of the issue." *Id*. at 1279. But see Halquist v. Department of Corrections, 783 P.2d 1065, 1067 (Wash. 1989) ("[C]ommon experience suggests that a videotape of an execution is information that is qualitatively different from a mere verbal report about an execution."); Note, *First Amendment Analysis of State Regulations Prohibiting the Filming of Prisoner Executions*, 60 GEO. WASH. L. REV. 1042, 1049-50 (1992) ("The *Garrett* court did not address the question of whether the public had a general constitutional right of access to executions. Rather, it assumed that no such right existed, and concluded that the press had no special right of access over that of the public.").

74. 1991 U.S. Dist. LEXIS 1971 (N.D. Cal. 1991). See generally Richards & Easter, *supra* note 61, at 389-91.

75. See 1991 U.S. Dist. LEXIS at *8-10.

pencils[76] — "the press has a right of access to whatever the public has a right to, but it has no special right of access and no right that's not available to the public generally."[77]

The decisions in *Garrett* and *Vasquez* indicate that discrimination in access to executions against the media or denial of public access entirely are both constitutionally suspect. Indeed, blanket denial of access rights would raise serious questions of content-based regulation with its requirement of heightened judicial scrutiny. It is probable that such a prohibition could not be justified as a content-neutral time, place, or manner regulation, but would rather be held to reflect a concern with stimulating negative public reaction to the death penalty itself. Discrimination against the media similarly could not be reasonably explained as a neutral regulation reflecting prison security or other administrative concerns.[78] Moreover, where a state does have a history of authorizing witnesses to attend executions, media representatives, as well as the public, would appear to have a right to view the entire event.

Since states generally do not discriminate against the media and do typically provide for some public access,[79] there is no significant judicial authority establishing such rights of public access. Nevertheless, in *Kearns-Tribune v. Utah Board of Corrections*,[80] a federal district court, relying on *Pell* and *Saxbe*, upheld application of a statute to exclude the press from an execution. The court held that the statute, which did allow the person to be executed to select five "persons, relatives or friends" to attend, rationally served prison interests in institutional discipline and security as well as the condemned man's privacy interests.[81] Whether a statute authorizing only a few friends and relatives to

---

76. See *id.* at *1, *12.

77. *Id.* at *5-6; see San Francisco Examiner v. Vasquez, 20 MEDIA L. REP. (BNA) 1328 (Cal. Super. 1992) (ordering prison authorities to include a reporter from the *San Francisco Examiner* in the press pool because it is an afternoon newspaper capable of providing same day coverage of an execution).

78. See Note, *supra* note 73, at 1071 ("There is evidence that the concerns that publicity would result in the abolition of the death penalty still exist today, and may in fact be the driving force behind the regulations on filming. Thus, the statutes appear to be motivated at least in part by a content-based purpose."); Bessler, *supra* note 61, at 404 ("The asserted justifications for private execution statutes clearly indicate that such regulations are 'content-based'.... Because these alleged concerns relate *in toto* to the communicative impact of televised broadcasts, private execution laws are obviously concerned with the regulation of the content of speech.").

79. A Washington statute, WASH. REV. CODE § 10.95.180, does appear to provide for private executions. IDAHO CODE § 19-2716 does not address who can attend an execution, and DEL. CODE ANN. tit. 11, § 4209(f) authorizes the sentencing court to determine the conditions of access.

80. 2 MEDIA L. REP. (BNA) 1353 (D. Utah 1977); see also Holden v. Minnesota, 137 U.S. 483, 491 (1890) ("[T]he exclusion altogether of reporters or representatives of newspapers.... [is a] regulation[] which the legislature ... for the public good could legally prescribe in respect to executions....").

81. See 2 MEDIA L. REP. (BNA) at 1354.

attend an execution as witnesses provides "public access" is undetermined, but as the Supreme Court's prison access cases suggest, the palpable judicial deference accorded prison authorities in managing these institutions has resulted in significant practical limitations on public and press rights of access.[82]

In *California First Amendment Coalition v. Calderon*,[83] the Ninth Circuit reversed an injunction granted by a federal district court which had held that the First Amendment required California prison officials to allow witnesses to view executions by lethal injection "from the time the inmate is secured to the gurney until just after the pronouncement of death."[84] The appellate court held that the First Amendment rights of the public and the press would not be violated by restrictions limiting viewing of the procedure from just after the insertion of intravenous tubes until the pronouncement of death.[85] Although emphasizing that it was not holding that the public and press do not have First Amendment rights to view executions,[86] the Ninth Circuit indicated that any such right is "severely limited."[87] Restricting its holding to the facts of the case, the court concluded that the state allowed "for some access and observations," while minimizing "the exposure of the members of the execution team to the media or other witnesses, out of a concern for staff safety and institutional security."[88] The court remanded the case to determine whether the plaintiff could present "substantial evidence" that such restrictions on access represent an exaggerated response to the articulated security and safety concerns.[89]

---

82. See generally Note, *The Executioner's Song: Is There a Right to Listen?*, 69 VA. L. REV. 373 (1983) (arguing against a constitutional right of access to executions, but favoring statutory right of access as a matter of policy).
83. 150 F.3d 976 (9th Cir. 1998) (reversing 956 F. Supp. 883 (N.D. Cal. 1997)).
84. 150 F.3d at 976.
85. See *id.* at 982.
86. See *id.*
87. *Id.*
88. *Id.*
89. *Id.* at 983. The court stressed Warden Calderon's claims that the limitations were "directly related" to security and safety concerns, and deferred to his expert judgment. *Id.* (quoting Pell v. Procunier, 417 U.S. at 827). In *Oregon Newspaper Publishers Association v. Department of Corrections*, 966 P.2d 819 (Or. App. 1998), the court upheld Department of Corrections rules preventing "all witnesses from viewing the inmate until after the inmate is strapped down and the intravenous catheter ... has been inserted." *Id.* at 821 (citing OR. ADMIN. R. 291-024-0065, R. 291-024-0070, R. 291-024-0080). Petitioners challenged the regulations on the ground that they violated Article I, sections 8 and 10 of the Oregon Constitution and the First and Fourteenth Amendments. See 966 P.2d at 820. The court noted that the public has no "unqualified right of access to penal institutions under the First Amendment," *id.* at 825, and deferred to Oregon's Department of Corrections policy to "insure the safety of those involved in the administration of executions," *id.* at 826.

§ 8-3. Disaster, Accident and Crime Scenes.

When an airplane goes down or a train crashes, it can be expected that reporters and cameras will soon be on the scene. The Supreme Court has not ruled directly on the issue of media access to sites of disasters and accidents, although its decisions concerning access in other contexts have influenced lower courts confronting the issue. In *Branzburg v. Hayes*,[90] Justice White offered a general observation frequently repeated by lower courts: "Newsmen have no constitutional right of access to the scenes of crime or disaster when the general public is excluded. . . ."[91] While this dicta purports to reject unique rights of access for the media, it does not provide meaningful parameters for adjudicating public, or press, access claims. Moreover, as Justice Stewart recognized in *Houchins v. KQED, Inc.*, reasonable access for the media may implicate considerations not relevant or applicable to the public at large.[92]

Generally, the public and the press both enjoy a right of access to a public forum.[93] This includes access both to traditional public fora (e.g., parks, streets, sidewalks) and to dedicated public fora (i.e., places that generally have been made available for public use by government). There is, however, no generally recognized right of access to nonpublic fora, even if governmental activities vital to the citizenry take place there. And, even access to a public forum is subject to content-neutral, reasonable time, place, and manner regulation. Thus, the real question in this context is, as a practical matter, what kind of media access is reasonable at a disaster or accident site. Not surprisingly, the answer depends on the circumstances surrounding a given case.

In *City of Oak Creek v. King*,[94] the Wisconsin Supreme Court upheld the disorderly conduct conviction of a reporter for refusing to leave the scene of an airplane crash.[95] The sheriff's department had secured the site, a nonpublic restricted area of a county-owned airport, and had established a road block as the sole means of access to the site for emergency vehicles. Three members of a television camera crew that drove through the roadblock agreed to leave the restricted area, but a fourth jumped a fence and began taking pictures from a hill.[96] He refused to leave the restricted area and was arrested. Less than thirty

---

90. 408 U.S. 665 (1972).
91. *Id.* at 684-85.
92. See Chap. 8-1 *supra* (discussing Houchins v. KQED, Inc., 438 U.S. 1, 17 (1978) (Stewart J., concurring)).
93. See Chap. 1-1 *supra*.
94. 436 N.W.2d 285 (Wis. 1989).
95. The court held that the reporter's conduct was disorderly within the meaning of the state statute since it involved a "repeated refusal" to obey a "reasonable order in a situation in which crowd control was a major concern, combined with [a] continued penetration into a nonpublic restricted area in the presence of the general public." *Id.* at 289-90.
96. See *id.*

minutes later, pursuant to a media guide for airport emergencies, the airport director held a briefing for the press and took representatives to the crash site for photographs.[97]

The Wisconsin Supreme Court acknowledged that "under the first amendment, the [reporter] has an undoubted right to gather news from any source by means within the law."[98] But, the court rejected any "constitutional right of special access to information not available to the public generally."[99] Noting that the government certainly might grant preferences to the media voluntarily,[100] the court held that a reporter nonetheless "does not have a First Amendment right of access, solely because he is a news gatherer, to the scene of this airplane crash when the general public has been reasonably excluded."[101]

In contrast, a federal district court in *Connell v. Town of Hudson*[102] acknowledged a news photographer's First Amendment right to be present at the scene of an automobile accident. While the right is undoubtedly not absolute, the court held that "those who gather news 'have a constitutional right not to be interfered with' by the police so long as they 'do not unreasonably obstruct or interfere with the defendant's official investigations of physical evidence or gain access to any place from which the general public is prohibited for essential safety purposes.'"[103] In *Connell*, the photographer had followed all police instructions reasonably designed to prevent interference with emergency activities.[104] Thus, while the town sought to justify its interference with the photographer as an effort to protect the victim's privacy and the sensibilities of her family, the court rejected this "paternalistic view of police authority."[105]

The failure of government to offer a persuasive justification for denying press access was also decisive in the air crash context in *Westinghouse Broadcasting Corp. v. National Transportation Safety Board*.[106] The court held that an administrative regulation restricting media access to a crash site at Boston's Logan Airport to one hour per day unreasonably interfered with "the constitutional right of the [media] to obtain news about the salvaging of [the] aircraft, . . . the search for missing persons . . . and in all other respects to photograph, if

---

97. See *id.* at 292.

98. *Id.* at 293.

99. *Id.* at 291.

100. See *id.* at 292-93 ("[T]here is a difference between an institution allowing news gatherers priority of access on its own accord, in a setting in which the institution may closely control and monitor access, and this court mandating access in an emergency situation.").

101. *Id.*

102. 733 F. Supp. 465 (D.N.H. 1990).

103. *Id.* at 469 (quoting Channel 10, Inc. v. Gunnarson, 337 F. Supp. 634, 638 (D. Minn. 1972)).

104. See 733 F. Supp. at 470.

105. *Id.* at 471.

106. 8 MEDIA L. REP. (BNA) 1177 (D. Mass. 1982).

they wish to, what is going on at the scene."[107] In the court's view, any privilege of access to governmental information is subject to a degree of restraint dictated by the nature of the information and countervailing interests in security and confidentiality.[108] Nevertheless, in the case at bar, there was no adequate alternative means to provide the public with an appreciation of what occurred at the crash site.[109] Accordingly, the court found no reason to preclude media access to the site, and ordered that it be opened to reporters.[110]

Access to disaster and accident sites is often governed by preexisting rules and regulations. Two states, California and Ohio, recognize a special statutory right of press access to emergency and disaster sites. California authorizes state officials to close disaster areas to the general public where there is a threat to public health or safety. Nevertheless, the statute further provides that "[n]othing in this section shall prevent a duly authorized representative of any news service, newspaper, or radio or television station or network from entering the areas closed pursuant to this section."[111] Similarly, the Ohio statute provides that "[n]othing in this section shall be construed to limit access or deny information to any news media representative in the lawful exercise of his duties."[112]

In *Leiserson v. City of San Diego*,[113] the court indicated that the California statute "represents the Legislature's considered judgment that members of the news media must be afforded special access to disaster sites in order that they may properly perform their function of informing the public."[114] It followed, therefore, that "press representatives must be given unrestricted access to disaster sites unless police personnel at the scene reasonably determine that such unrestricted access will interfere with emergency operations."[115] Restrictions on media access are permitted only to the extent necessary to prevent actual interference with emergency operations, and press representatives must be accommodated with whatever limited access can be afforded without such interference.[116]

---

107. *Id.* at 1184.
108. See *id.* at 1183.
109. See *id.* at 1182.
110. See *id.* at 1185.
111. CAL. PENAL CODE § 409.5(a),(d).
112. OHIO REV. CODE ANN. § 2917.13(B). See also ALASKA STAT. § 26.23.200(1) ("Nothing in [the Alaska Disaster Act] interferes with or allows interference with dissemination of news or comment on public affairs . . . ."). But see MICH. COMP. LAWS § 750.160a (prohibiting public and media from photographing "a decedent located in a human grave," which includes "a decedent who died in an accident or disaster").
113. 229 Cal. Rptr. 22 (Ct. App. 1986).
114. *Id.* at 29.
115. *Id.*
116. See *id.*

The court in *Leiserson* upheld a reporter's disorderly conduct conviction, however, because the officers investigating the air disaster reasonably believed that foul play may have been involved in the crash,[117] which justified the photographer's exclusion from the site as the scene of a possible crime. Crime scenes, the court acknowledged, "have traditionally been subject to exclusion orders which apply to the press as well as the general public."[118] The *Leiserson* case illustrates that even where the press is afforded access to a greater extent than the public generally, authorities at the scene retain some discretion to curtail access where law enforcement may be threatened by the media's presence.

The Justice Department has issued guidelines for media access to Department operations in which "prosecutors are authorized to request that the news media leave an area if the media's presence puts the operation or the safety of officers 'in jeopardy.'"[119] Indeed, many law enforcement and investigative agencies have established guidelines for media access, including regulations that balance the public's interest in obtaining timely and accurate information with the government's interest in public safety.[120] Such rules may limit access to those bearing designated credentials and may limit who qualifies to receive them.[121] Media familiarity with such regulations, and participation in their formulation, have generally ensured that newsgatherers have secured reasonable access.

§ 8-4. Voters and Polling Places.

Modern data collection and broadcast technology have made it possible for the news media to predict accurately who will win an election before the polls have even closed. For many, election information is important news that the media should have a right to gather and report to the public as quickly as possible. By the same token, journalists' interviews with citizens at polling places involves freedom of speech at the core of the First Amendment — political speech about the electoral process. Others argue, however, that such

---

117. See *id.* at 50-53.
118. *Id.* at 52.
119. *Justice Department to Deny Access, Information In Wake of Waco Raid*, THE NEWS MEDIA & THE LAW, Fall 1994, at 22.
120. See THE NEWS MEDIA & THE LAW, Spring 1998, at 19 ("Portland police and local television stations agreed . . . to guidelines restricting news media's helicopter coverage of police activity in hostage situations or any incidents involving barricaded armed assailants.").
121. See, e.g., Mintz v. Director, Dep't of Motor Vehicles, 691 F.2d 507 (9th Cir. 1982), *cert. denied*, 460 U.S. 1071 (1983) (affirming denial of special press license plates to photographer not "regularly employed or engaged" as news gatherer); Watson v. Cronin, 384 F. Supp. 652 (D. Colo. 1974) (upholding denial of press pass to person with criminal record); Los Angeles Free Press, Inc. v. City of Los Angeles, 88 Cal. Rptr. 605 (Ct. App. 1970), *cert. denied*, 401 U.S. 982 (1971) (affirming denial of press pass to publisher of weekly newspaper not regularly covering current accidents or crimes).

"exit polling" interferes with the electoral process, influencing undecided voters and discouraging citizens from voting at all.[122]

The Supreme Court has not directly addressed the constitutionality of government regulation of media exit polling.[123] But, in *Burson v. Freeman*,[124] the Court upheld a Tennessee law prohibiting solicitation of votes and display and distribution of campaign material within one hundred feet of a polling place. Justice Blackmun, in a plurality opinion, acknowledged that the law regulated core political speech at a quintessential public forum, triggering strict judicial scrutiny.[125] Nevertheless, he concluded that this was one of those "rare cases" where strict scrutiny was satisfied[126] because the "widespread and time-tested consensus" of limiting access to the areas around polling places demonstrated that "some restricted zone is necessary in order to serve the States' compelling interest in preventing voter intimidation and election fraud."[127] Thus, the plurality concluded, "[g]iven the conflict between these two rights, we hold that requiring solicitors to stand 100 feet from the entrances to polling places does not constitute an unconstitutional compromise."[128]

Burson certainly does not mean that states are free to outlaw exit polling. It establishes only that some limited regulation of First Amendment freedoms is permissible when necessary to protect fundamental voting rights. And, there is serious doubt that the damage to the franchise from media interviewing of voters or exit polling is as significant or as well-grounded empirically as the concerns

---

122. See generally REPORTERS COMMITTEE FOR FREEDOM OF THE PRESS, *supra* note 1, at 3; Fischer, *Network "Early Calls" of Elections: An Analysis of the Legality of Proposals to Keep the Voting Process from Becoming an Academic Exercise*, 14 SW. U.L. REV. 427 (1984); Note, *Exit Polls and the First Amendment*, 98 HARV. L. REV. 1927 (1985); Note, *Curtailment of Early Election Predictions: Can We Predict the Outcome?*, 36 U. FLA. L. REV. 489 (1984).

123. In *Mills v. Alabama*, 384 U.S. 214 (1966), the Court held that a statute making it a crime to publish editorials on election day discussing particular candidates violated the First Amendment. The Court noted, however, that the holding "in no way involve[d] the extent of a State's power to regulate conduct in and around the polls in order to maintain peace, order and decorum there." *Id.* at 218.

124. 504 U.S. 191 (1992).

125. See *id.* at 196-97 (plurality opinion of Blackmun, J.) ("Whether individuals may exercise their free speech rights near polling places depends entirely on whether their speech is related to a political campaign.") Justice Scalia, concurring in the judgment, argued that the environs of a polling place are not a public forum, and that the law was a reasonable viewpoint-neutral regulation. See *id.* at 214 (Scalia, J., concurring).

126. See *id.* at 198 ("As a facially content-based restriction on political speech in a public forum, [the law] must be subjected to exacting scrutiny. . . .").

127. *Id.* at 206; see *id.* at 197-98 (discussing governmental interest in allowing citizens to vote freely without confusion and undue influence and in preserving the integrity of the electoral process).

128. *Id.* at 211. Whether the boundary could be somewhat tightened was not deemed to be an issue of "constitutional dimension" because alternative boundaries provided a "difference only in degree, not a less restrictive alternative in kind." *Id.* at 210.

that influenced the *Burson* plurality. Indeed, responding to the claim that the Tennessee law was underinclusive since it did not include other forms of solicitation or exit polling, the plurality observed that "there is simply no evidence that political candidates have used other forms of solicitation or exit polling to commit such electoral abuses."[129]

The lower courts that have considered the constitutionality of restrictions on exit polling within designated distances of polling places have uniformly invalidated such legislation.[130] In *Daily Herald Co. v. Munro*,[131] for example, the Ninth Circuit held unconstitutional a Washington law prohibiting exit polling within 300 feet of polling places. The court began from the premise that both the First Amendment right to discuss governmental affairs, including candidates for public office, and the press' right to gather news are burdened by such regulation.[132] The environs of polling places are traditional public fora "open to the public for expressive purposes, including random interviews by reporters, and encompass streets and sidewalks."[133] The statute was content-based "because it regulate[d] a specific subject matter, the discussion of voting, and a certain category of speakers, exit pollsters."[134] Such laws, the court held, are presumptively invalid and are subject to strict scrutiny.[135]

While the Ninth Circuit acknowledged that states have a compelling interest in preserving peace, order, and decorum at polling places, as well as protecting the integrity of their electoral processes, the statute at issue was not narrowly tailored to advance these interests. It unnecessarily extended to nondisruptive exit polling, and there were less restrictive alternatives available for furthering the aforementioned governmental interests.[136] The Ninth Circuit also concluded

---

129. *Id.* at 207.

130. See Daily Herald Co. v. Munro, 838 F.2d 380 (9th Cir. 1988); National Broadcasting Co. v. Colburg, 699 F. Supp. 241 (D. Mont. 1988); National Broadcasting Co. v. Cleland, 697 F. Supp. 1204 (N.D. Ga. 1988); CBS Inc. v. Smith, 681 F. Supp. 794 (S.D. Fla. 1988); Firestone v. News-Press Publ'g Co., 538 So. 2d 457 (Fla. 1989).

131. 838 F.2d 380 (9th Cir. 1988).

132. See *id.* at 384 ("Exit polling is thus speech that is protected, on several levels, by the First Amendment.").

133. *Id.* at 384; see also CBS, Inc. v. Smith, 681 F. Supp. at 803-04 (holding statute overbroad because it reached "public streets, sidewalks, and parks"); Firestone v. News-Press Publ'g Co., 538 So. 2d at 459 (finding statute overbroad in reaching "traditional public forums for free expression").

134. 838 F.2d at 385 (citations omitted).

135. See *id.*

136. See *id.* (citing alternatives such as reducing the size of the restricted area, requiring the media to explain that the poll is completely voluntary, requiring polling places to have separate entrances and exits, or limiting access to the polling room). Several other courts considering similar statutes found no disruption caused by exit polling to justify the zones of media exclusion. See National Broadcasting Co. v. Cleland, 697 F. Supp. at 1211-12 ("The State produced no first hand evidence that any voter had ever decided not to vote because of the existence of exit polls, or that

that the statute was unconstitutional because "at least one" of its purposes "was to prevent broadcasting early returns."[137] In that regard, Judge Reinhardt, concurring, argued "that the Washington statute restricts the media's right of access to information crucial to the political process and, for that reason, also violates the principles embodied in the First Amendment."[138] For him, the First Amendment is not simply a limitation on governmental authority: "The state has an affirmative duty to protect the media's right of access to information crucial to the societal process of political deliberation."[139]

§ 8-5. Military Operations.

The military context is a unique environment in which the ordinary principles of First Amendment law are simply not applicable. As the Supreme Court stated in *Goldman v. Weinberger*,[140] "[o]ur review of military regulations challenged on First Amendment grounds is far more deferential than constitutional review of similar laws or regulations designed for civilian society."[141] In light of the special military mission, courts regularly exercise deference in reviewing First Amendment challenges to military regulations.

An example is judicial treatment of claims of a First Amendment-based right of access to military bases. "Military bases generally are not public fora,"[142] and

---

such a result was in any way a real danger."); CBS Inc. v. Smith, 681 F. Supp. at 901 ("[N]o evidence has been presented that exit polls or other voter interviews by journalists in any way have disrupted any polling place in this state."); Firestone v. News-Press Publ'g Co., 538 So. 2d at 459 ("The state's unsubstantiated concern of potential disturbance is not sufficient to overcome the chilling effect on first amendment rights."); see also National Broadcasting Co. v. Colburg, 699 F. Supp. at 242 (finding statute "fails [the least-restrictive means] test and instead is seemingly a broadside attack upon significant, traditional, and cherished first amendment freedoms").

137. 838 F.2d at 387.

138. *Id.* at 389 (Reinhardt, J., concurring). See also CBS, Inc. v. Smith, 681 F. Supp. at 803 ("Without the ability to collect information, viewpoints, and opinions from voters, the right to report and publish political news would be left with little means of fulfillment.").

139. 838 F.2d at 389.

140. 475 U.S. 503 (1986) (rejecting free exercise challenge to an air force regulation prohibiting the wearing of headgear indoors, as applied to an Orthodox Jew and ordained rabbi wearing his yarmulke in accordance with his religion).

141. *Id.* at 507; see *id.* at 506 ("The Court has noted that the military is, by necessity, a specialized society. . . ."); Bryant v. Secretary of the Army, 862 F. Supp. 574, 579 (D.D.C. 1994) ("There is a more limited role for judicial review of military regulations challenged on First Amendment grounds than there would otherwise be in a civilian context"); see generally Dienes, *When the First Amendment Is Not Preferred: The Military and Other "Special Contexts,"* 56 U. CIN. L. REV. 779 (1988).

142. United States v. Albertini, 472 U.S. 675, 686 (1985) (holding the First Amendment does not protect defendant who has been barred from reentry on a military base from illegally reentering the base during open house); see *id.* at 684 ("A military base . . . is ordinarily not a public forum for First Amendment purposes even if it's open to the public."); see also United States v. Corrigan, 144 F.3d 763, 767 (11th Cir. 1998) (upholding lower court's conviction of political demonstrators

the fact that the public is permitted to visit such bases does not make them public fora.[143] Since military bases are not public fora, government can and does discriminate against speakers based on the content of their messages, so long as it does not do so because of viewpoint and the regulation is otherwise reasonable in light of the purposes of the base.[144]

As a result, in *J.B. Pictures, Inc. v. Department of Defense*,[145] the D.C. Circuit upheld the exclusion of the media from Dover Air Force Base during the arrival of the bodies of soldiers killed in Operation Desert Storm. The media claimed that this change in military policy constituted impermissible viewpoint discrimination[146] — an effort to control the visual images of caskets of dead soldiers arriving home. The court, however, reasoned that if this theory of discrimination were accepted, "virtually any restriction on access to government facilities including the restrictions in *Saxbe* and *Pell* — would be vulnerable to challenge on grounds of 'viewpoint discrimination.'"[147]

In addition, the court in *J.B. Pictures, Inc.* held that the First Amendment does not create access rights to government property or activities simply because it

---

for criminal trespass, stating military bases are nonpublic fora, and as such, government can regulate speech "as long as the regulations are reasonable and are content-neutral"). The Court in *Albertini* also noted "the historically unquestioned power of a commanding officer to exclude civilians from the area of his command." 472 U.S. at 687 (quoting Cafeteria Workers v. McElroy, 367 U.S. 886, 893 (1961)). See United States v. LaValley, 957 F.2d 1309, 1314 (6th Cir.), *cert. denied*, 506 U.S. 972 (1992); Brown v. Palmer, 944 F.2d 732 (10th Cir. 1991); Persons for Free Speech at SAC v. United States Air Force, 675 F.2d 1010 (8th Cir.), *cert. denied*, 459 U.S. 1092 (1982).

143. See Greer v. Spock, 424 U.S. 828, 836 (1976) (holding that there is "no generalized constitutional right to make political speeches or distribute leaflets" at a military base).

144. See, e.g., *id.* at 839 (holding that facially valid regulation was a "considered" policy "objectively and even handedly applied" in avoiding partisan political entanglements); see also Brown v. Palmer, 944 F.2d 732, 734 (10th Cir. 1991) ("The Supreme Court has made it abundantly clear that the government may selectively preclude discussion of certain general topics while nevertheless inviting the public onto its premises to participate in speech on a variety of other topics."). In *Albertini*, the Court held that the regulation was a reasonable, content-neutral measure, only incidentally burdening speech. See 472 U.S. at 688.

145. 86 F.3d 236 (D.C. Cir. 1996) (affirming 21 MEDIA L. REP. (BNA) 1564 (D.D.C. 1993)). See Note, *Operation Media Control: The Military's Assault on the First Amendment Right to Access*, 65 GEO. WASH. L. REV. 735, 741 (1997) ("With this decision, the D.C. Circuit definitively placed the right of access to military property and events into the category of areas in which the press has no qualified right of access greater than that given to the general public."); Note, *Is There a Right to View the Dead at Dover? J.B. Pictures v. Department of Defense: Limits on the Media's Right to Gather Information*, 4 VILL. SPORTS & ENT. L.J. 387, 414 (1997) ("[T]he D.C. Circuit failed to address J.B. Pictures' free speech argument and therefore arbitrarily dismissed J.B. Pictures' contention that the Department of Defense restriction created a biased viewpoint.").

146. The public and press had previously been admitted to the base for ceremonies honoring the dead. The new policy was initiated shortly before the start of Operation Desert Storm. See 86 F.3d at 238.

147. *Id.* at 240; see *supra* Chap. 8-1 (discussing *Saxbe* and *Pell*).

will facilitate newsgathering.[148] The court noted that there was no tradition of access to military bases and the burden on newsgathering was "relatively modest."[149] The government's interest in reducing the hardship and protecting the privacy of the families of the dead was deemed sufficient to justify any burden on newsgathering.[150]

Analogous reasoning has governed press access to the field of military operations.[151] Prior to the 1980s, the press enjoyed relatively broad rights of access to the battlefield. Indeed, media reporting from Vietnam was extensive and is generally acknowledged to have played an important role in developing antiwar sentiment. In the 1983 invasion of Grenada, however, the press was denied access until the fighting was essentially over. Even then, reporters enjoyed only limited access and were accompanied by military escorts, who allegedly sought to inhibit newsgathering. An official government study of the episode concluded that "it is essential that the U.S. news media cover U.S. military operations to the maximum degree possible consistent with mission security and the safety of U.S. forces."[152] The study endorsed the use of reporter pools, as a substitute for wider press access, but "only for the minimum time possible" during the initial stages of combat.[153]

Nevertheless, in the subsequent United States invasion of Panama, the pool of reporters arrived five hours late and were kept from observing combat until it was virtually over. Thereafter, another review panel recommended greater media access but, in Operation Desert Storm, the institutional press claimed that military restrictions "made it impossible for reporters and photographers to tell

---

148. See 86 F.3d at 238.
149. *Id.* at 240.
150. See *id.* at 240-41.
151. See generally GANNETT FOUNDATION, THE MEDIA AT WAR: THE PRESS AND THE PERSIAN GULF CONFLICT (1991); R. SMOLLA, FREE SPEECH IN AN OPEN SOCIETY 303-20 (1992); O'Neil, *The Media and the Military: The Persian Gulf War and Beyond*, 1 J. NAT'L SECURITY L. 1 (1997); Jacobs, *Assessing the Constitutionality of Press Restrictions in the Persian Gulf War*, 44 STAN. L. REV. 675 (1992); Smith, *From the Front Lines to the Front Page: Media Access to War in the Persian Gulf and Beyond*, 26 COLUM. J.L. & SOC. PROBS. 291 (1993); Comment, *The Persian Gulf War and the Press: Is There a Constitutional Right of Access to Military Operations?*, 87 NW. U.L. REV. 287 (1992); Note, *War and the First Amendment: A Call for Legislation to Protect a Press Right of Access to Military Operations*, 35 COLUM. J. TRANSNAT'L L. 131, 173 (1997) ("Absent congressional or judicial intervention, the government remains free to impose restrictions upon the press that extend beyond the limits of legitimate national security concerns, with no effective system of review."); see also Nation Magazine v. Department of Defense, 762 F. Supp. 1558, 1563-65 (S.D.N.Y. 1991).
152. CHAIRMAN OF THE JOINT CHIEFS OF STAFF MEDIA-MILITARY RELATIONS PANEL 3 (1984).
153. *Id.* The pool was to be the largest practicable and pooling was to be used for the minimum time necessary "before 'full coverage' is feasible." *Id.*

the public the full story of the war in a timely fashion."[154] Thus, new regulations were promulgated in 1992, again reaffirming the value of open and independent reporting of military operations.[155]

Media efforts to challenge restrictions on press access to military operations have been unsuccessful. Such actions have floundered on the threshold requirements governing the use of the judicial power. For example, in *Nation Magazine v. United States Department of Defense*,[156] news organizations challenged Department of Defense regulations governing media access to military operations under the First Amendment.[157] In addition, a wire service, which had been excluded from the pool, alleged unconstitutional discrimination, arguing that the regulations violated the First Amendment on their face and as applied.[158]

The court held that the plaintiffs possessed the requisite Article III standing since the media "alleged, in both their access and discrimination claims, injury to interests which lie at the core of the First and Fifth Amendment."[159] The wire service excluded from the pools plainly suffered injury in fact caused by the challenged regulations. The more difficult justiciability issue, the court observed, was mootness. An earlier case challenging the exclusion of the press from the initial stages of the Grenada intervention, *Flynt v. Weinberger*,[160] had been dismissed on this basis. In *Nation Magazine*, the Persian Gulf War was over, but the court nevertheless accepted that, "as a general matter," the issue was "capable of repetition, yet evading review."[161] But, the court emphasized, this did not end the inquiry as to whether, as a prudential matter, it *should* decide the case on its

---

154. REPORT OF 17 NEWS EXECUTIVES TO SECRETARY RICHARD CHENEY, COVERING THE PERSIAN GULF WAR, June 14, 1991, discussed in Comment, *supra* note 151.

155. Department of Defense, Proposed Rules: Eligibility Criteria for News Media Membership in the DoD National Media Pool, 57 Fed. Reg. 43645, 43646, § 202.4 (Sept. 22, 1992) ("It is a DoD policy that while open and independent reporting shall be the principal means of coverage of U.S. military operations, under some mission requirements, pools may provide the only feasible means of early access to a military operation. In such situations unless national security considerations require otherwise, the DoD will activate the national Media Pool to allow a representative group of journalists access to DoD activities.").

156. 762 F. Supp. 1558 (S.D.N.Y. 1991).

157. The court characterized the "fundamental claim" as being that "the press has a First Amendment right to unlimited access to a foreign arena in which American military forces are engaged." *Id*. at 1561. The media did not challenge restrictions on what pool members could publish.

158. See *id*.

159. *Id*. at 1566. The court also held that the case did not present a nonjusticiable political question. See *id*. at 1567.

160. 762 F.2d 134 (D.C. Cir. 1985). Since the Grenada intervention was over, the court concluded, the request for injunctive relief was moot and, since the media request for declaratory relief related only to the press ban on Grenada, it was also moot. *Id*. at 135.

161. 762 F. Supp. at 1569.

merits.[162] To that question, the court responded by holding that the case was not justiciable.[163] The claims involved significant and novel constitutional doctrines and the regulations were under review by the government for possible revision. In the court's view, the access claims, and particularly the equal access claims, were "not sufficiently in focus at this time to meet the . . . requirement that the underlying constitutional issues [be presented] in a clear-cut and concrete form.'"[164]

The court did, however, examine preliminarily the potentially determinative constitutional issues. It noted that, while the press has no right of access to nonpublic fora and limitations could properly be placed on access to government-controlled institutions such as prisons and military bases,[165] in *Richmond Newspapers, Inc. v. Virginia* and its progeny, the Supreme Court had emphasized the "importance of an informed American citizenry."[166] If the rationale of these decisions were followed in the military context, the court suggested, the press could not be completely excluded from military operations; there would have to be "at least some minimal right of access to view and report about major events that affect the functioning of government, including, for example, an overt military operation."[167] Moreover, by historically allowing some access to the press, the court indicated, the government had created a limited public forum.[168] In such a forum, the court intimated, the government cannot arbitrarily discriminate in affording access to information.[169]

---

162. See *id.* at 1562 ("The second, more delicate and troublesome mootness inquiry is whether, in an action such as this, where plaintiffs seek both declaratory and injunctive relief, the court should in its discretion exercise such power to adjudicate the merits of the dispute.").

163. See *id.* at 1571 ("In determining whether to exercise its power to hear plaintiff's claim for declaratory relief, the Court must evaluate each of the underlying claims in the context of existing First and Fifth Amendment doctrine to consider if the issues at this time are presented in a 'clear-cut and concrete form.'") (quoting Rescue Army v. Municipal Ct. of Los Angeles, 331 U.S. 549, 584 (1947)).

164. 762 F. Supp. at 1575; see *id.* at 1562 ("We conclude that such power should not be exercised in this case. We base this conclusion primarily on the abstract nature of the important issues now before the court.").

165. See *id.* at 1571.

166. *Id.* at 1572 (citing Richmond Newspapers, Inc. v. Virginia, 448 U.S. 555, 575 (1980)); see 762 F. Supp. at 1572 ("Given the broad grounds invoked in these holdings, the affirmative right to gather news, ideas and information is certainly strengthened by these cases. By protecting the press, the flow of information to the public is preserved.").

167. 762 F. Supp. at 1572.

168. See *id.* at 1573 ("By opening the door, albeit in a limited manner, the government created a place for expressive activity.").

169. See *id.* (citing Sherrill v. Knight, 569 F.2d 124, 129 (D.C. Cir. 1977)).

Chapter 9

ACCESS TO THE EXECUTIVE AND LEGISLATIVE BRANCHES

§ 9-1. Constitutional Overview.
§ 9-2. Nonstatutory Access to Executive Events.
    § 9-2(a). Issuance of Press Credentials.
    § 9-2(b). Discriminatory Access.
§ 9-3. Non-Statutory Access to Legislative Proceedings.
§ 9-4. Non-Statutory Access to Administrative Proceedings.
§ 9-5. Statutory Access to Federal Government Meetings.
    § 9-5(a). Government in the Sunshine Act.
        § 9-5(a)(1). Introduction.
        § 9-5(a)(2). Agencies Subject to the Act.
        § 9-5(a)(3). Definition of "Meeting."
        § 9-5(a)(4). Notice of Meetings.
        § 9-5(a)(5). Access to Meetings.
        § 9-5(a)(6). Access to Meeting Transcripts and Tapes.
        § 9-5(a)(7). Procedures to Close Meetings.
        § 9-5(a)(8). Exemptions.
            § 9-5(a)(8)(A). Exemption 1: National Security.
            § 9-5(a)(8)(B). Exemption 2: Internal Agency Personnel Rules.
            § 9-5(a)(8)(C). Exemption 3: Disclosure Prohibited by Other Federal Statutes.
            § 9-5(a)(8)(D). Exemption 4: Trade Secrets and Confidential Commercial Information.
            § 9-5(a)(8)(E). Exemption 5: Accusation of a Crime or Formal Censure.
            § 9-5(a)(8)(F). Exemption 6: Personal Privacy.
            § 9-5(a)(8)(G). Exemption 7: Law Enforcement Investigations.
            § 9-5(a)(8)(H). Exemption 8: Financial Institutions.
            § 9-5(a)(8)(I). Exemption 9: Premature Disclosure of Information.
            § 9-5(a)(8)(J). Exemption 10: Agency Participation in Civil Actions or Proceedings.
        § 9-5(a)(9). Challenges to Closed Meetings.
            § 9-5(a)(9)(A). Challenges Prior to Commencement of the Meeting.
            § 9-5(a)(9)(B). Post-Meeting Challenges.
    § 9-5(b). Federal Advisory Committee Act.
        § 9-5(b)(1). Introduction.
        § 9-5(b)(2). Definition of "Advisory Committee."
        § 9-5(b)(3). Meetings.
        § 9-5(b)(4). Notice of Meetings.
        § 9-5(b)(5). Procedures to Close Meetings.
        § 9-5(b)(6). Public Access to Meetings.
        § 9-5(b)(7). Challenges to Closed Meetings.
§ 9-6. Statutory Access to Meetings of State and Local Government.
    § 9-6(a). Introduction.
    § 9-6(b). Entities Subject to Open Meeting Laws.
    § 9-6(c). Meetings Subject to Open Meeting Laws.
    § 9-6(d). Notice Requirements.
    § 9-6(e). Access to Meetings.
    § 9-6(f). Access to Minutes, Transcripts, and Tapes.
    § 9-6(g). Procedures.

§ 9-6(h). Exemptions.
   § 9-6(h)(1). Personnel Matters.
   § 9-6(h)(2). Disclosure Prohibited by Other Laws.
   § 9-6(h)(3). Confidential Financial and Commercial Information.
   § 9-6(h)(4). Invasion of Personal Privacy or Injury to Reputation.
   § 9-6(h)(5). Law Enforcement and Public Safety Matters.
   § 9-6(h)(6). Civil Litigation Matters.
§ 9-6(i). Categories of Meetings.
   § 9-6(i)(1). Personnel Matters.
      § 9-6(i)(1)(A). Interviews for Employment.
      § 9-6(i)(1)(B). Performance Reviews.
      § 9-6(i)(1)(C). Disciplinary Matters.
      § 9-6(i)(1)(D). Employer-Employee Negotiations and Collective Bargaining.
   § 9-6(i)(2). Probation and Parole Boards.
   § 9-6(i)(3). Medical or Psychiatric Matters.
   § 9-6(i)(4). Student Information.
   § 9-6(i)(5). Matters Involving Public Assistance.
   § 9-6(i)(6). Professional Licensing and Disciplinary Proceedings.
§ 9-6(j). Challenges to Improperly Noticed or Closed Meetings.

§ 9-1. Constitutional Overview.

Based on the Supreme Court's decisions establishing a First Amendment-based right of access to various judicial proceedings[1] and a limited right of access to other public institutions,[2] courts have recognized a qualified, constitutional right of access to the executive and legislative branches of government. These courts have adopted the Supreme Court's two-tiered standard set forth in the *Press-Enterprise Co.* decisions[3] to determine whether there is a constitutionally protected right of access to executive, legislative, and administrative proceedings.[4] The standard assesses two factors: (1) "whether the place and process have historically been open to the press and general public," and (2) "whether public access plays a significant positive role in the functioning of the particular process in question."[5]

Should a court determine that a right of access exists, it proceeds to balance that right against any countervailing governmental interests:

> [T]his Court finds that the rights guaranteed and protected by the First Amendment include a right of access to news or information concerning

---

1. See Chap. 2 *supra.*
2. See Chap. 8 *supra.*
3. See Press-Enter. Co. v. Superior Ct., 464 U.S. 501 (1984) (*Press-Enterprise I*); Press-Enter. Co. v. Superior Ct., 478 U.S. 1 (1986) (*Press-Enterprise II*).
4. See, e.g., Cable News Network, Inc. v. American Broadcasting Cos., 518 F. Supp. 1238 (N.D. Ga. 1981); Johnson Newspaper Corp. v. Melino, 563 N.Y.S.2d 380 (App. Div. 1990).
5. *Press-Enterprise II*, 478 U.S. at 8. But see Cuban Am. Bar Ass'n, Inc. v. Christopher, 43 F.3d 1412, 1430 (11th Cir. 1995) (government has no constitutional duty to disclose information).

the operations and activities of government. This right is held by both the general public and the press, with the press acting as a representative or agent of the public as well as on its own behalf. Without such a right, the goals and purposes of the First Amendment would be meaningless. However, such a right of access is qualified, rather than absolute, and is subject to limiting considerations such as confidentiality, security, orderly process, spatial limitation, and doubtless many others.[6]

In addition, where a constitutionally protected right of access has been recognized, courts have been responsive as well to the equal protection rights of journalists and have prohibited government discrimination between journalists, between media organizations, and between the electronic and print media.[7]

Although many states view their own constitutions as providing no greater access to government information and meetings than does the federal constitution,[8] the constitutions of four states, New Hampshire,[9] North Dakota,[10] Louisiana,[11] and Montana,[12] contain explicit provisions concerning the right of the public to know about information in the possession of governmental agencies or to attend government meetings. New Hampshire's constitution permits no "unreasonable restrictions" on the public's right of access to proceedings and records.[13] The constitutions of North Dakota and Louisiana require that meetings be open to the public, except as otherwise provided by law.[14] In practice, these constitutional provisions have caused courts interpreting state open records or

---

6. Cable News Network, Inc. v. American Broadcasting Cos., 518 F. Supp. 1238, 1244 (N.D. Ga. 1981).

7. See Chap. 9-2(b) *infra*.

8. See, e.g., Johnson Newspaper Corp. v. Melino, 564 N.E.2d 1046, 1049 (N.Y. 1990).

9. See N.H. CONST. part I, art. 8 ("All power residing originally in, and being derived from, the people, all the magistrates and officers of government are their substitutes and agents, and at all times accountable to them. Government, therefore, should be open, accessible, accountable and responsive. To that end, the public's right of access to governmental proceedings and records shall not be unreasonably restricted.").

10. See N.D. CONST. art. XI, § 5 ("Unless otherwise provided by law, all records of public or governmental bodies, boards, bureaus, commissions, or agencies of the state or any political subdivision of the state, or organizations or agencies supported in whole or in part by public funds, or expending public funds, shall be public records, open and accessible for inspection during reasonable office hours.").

11. See LA. CONST. art. XII, § 3 ("No person shall be denied the right to observe the deliberations of public bodies and examine public documents, except in cases established by law.").

12. See MONT. CONST. art. II, § 9 ("No person shall be deprived of the right to examine documents or to observe the deliberations of all public bodies or agencies of state government and its subdivisions, except in cases in which the demand of individual privacy clearly exceeds the merits of public disclosure.").

13. N.H. CONST. part I, art. 8.

14. See N.D. CONST. art. XI, § 5; LA. CONST. art. XII, § 3. North Dakota's constitution also mandates public access to all records except as otherwise provided by law. See N.D. CONST. art. XI, § 6.

open meeting laws to construe their statutory exemptions and exclusions narrowly.[15]

The courts of Montana, however, have interpreted its constitution to provide more substantive access rights. The Montana constitution declares that the public has a right to know about governmental matters and provides for public access to all meetings except where "the demand of individual privacy clearly exceeds the merits of public disclosure."[16] This provision has led the Montana Supreme Court to invalidate statutory exemptions for litigation and collective bargaining strategy meetings contained in Montana's open meeting legislation.[17] In balancing the benefit to the public from disclosure and the privacy interest of the individual, as required by the state constitution, Montana courts generally have held the stronger interest to be that of the public and have required access.[18]

§ 9-2. Nonstatutory Access to Executive Events.

Traditionally, the press has been afforded access to the President, governors, and mayors as well as to representatives of their administrations. Courts have typically held that the First Amendment guarantees a right of access to events involving these public officials, limited by the type of event, security concerns, and spatial limitations.

In *Cable News Network, Inc. v. American Broadcasting Cos.*,[19] television networks sought to enjoin the White House Press Secretary from excluding all

---

15. See, e.g., Orford Teachers Ass'n v. Watson, 427 A.2d 21 (N.H. 1981); Amoco Prod. Co. v. Landry, 426 So. 2d 220, 223 (La. App. 1982); Adams County Record v. Greater North Dakota Ass'n, 529 N.W.2d 830, 832-33 (N.D. 1995).

16. MONT. CONST. art. II, § 9. See Great Falls Tribune Co. v. Day, 959 P.2d 508 (Mont. 1998) (state committee appointed by Department of Corrections to evaluate proposals for construction of private prison must conduct its meetings in public and provide public access to its records). The Montana Supreme Court has determined that a person has a constitutionally protected privacy interest when the person involved has a subjective or actual expectation of privacy and society is willing to recognize that expectation as reasonable. See Missoulian v. Board of Regents, 675 P.2d 962, 967 (Mont. 1984).

17. See Associated Press v. Board of Pub. Educ., 804 P.2d 376, 379 (Mont. 1991) (litigation strategy exemption held unconstitutional); Great Falls Tribune Co. v. Great Falls Pub. Schs., 841 P.2d 502 (Mont. 1992) (collective bargaining strategy meeting exemption held unconstitutional).

18. See Great Falls Tribune Co. v. Day, 959 P.2d 508 (Mont. 1998) (public had right to observe the deliberations of Department of Corrections committee established to screen proposals for construction of private prison); Citizens to Recall Mayor James Whitlock v. Whitlock, 844 P.2d 74 (Mont. 1992) (investigative report concerning alleged sexual harassment by mayor must be made public); Great Falls Tribune Co. v. Cascade County Sheriff, 775 P.2d 1267 (Mont. 1989) (identity of law enforcement officers subject to internal discipline ordered disclosed).

19. 518 F. Supp. 1238 (N.D. Ga. 1981).

television recording of "limited coverage"[20] White House events. Such events are typically covered by a designated "pool" of media representatives who are obliged to share their observations with those not included in the "pool."[21] The Press Secretary had requested television media representatives to make their own selections as to membership in the pool, but they could not reach a consensus. As a result, the Press Secretary announced press pool assignments only for the print media.[22]

The district court, relying on *Richmond Newspapers, Inc. v. Virginia*,[23] initially determined that there has been a history of press access to presidential events: "It is undisputed that there is a history of pool coverage of presidential activities going back through several past Administrations in which television news representatives took part."[24] Thus, the court concluded, "[i]n this sense there is an 'enduring and vital tradition of public entree' (through the press as agents) to the presidential activities covered by press pools."[25] In addition, the court determined that such access serves a strong public purpose. Indeed, the court noted, such coverage "is important to the President," since "public awareness and understanding of the President's behavior facilitates his effectiveness as President. Such public insight is also necessary for a determination by the public of the adequacy of the President's performance."[26]

Having determined that the television media enjoyed a limited right of access to White House pool coverage, the court proceeded to weigh the constitutional interest served by such newsgathering activity against the governmental interest in restrained access.[27] Although the court acknowledged that, pursuant to the Press Secretary's determination, the public continued to receive pertinent information about the President through the print media, it concluded that the public had a significant interest in continued *television* coverage, the absence of which

---

20. A White House event was considered to be a "limited coverage" event when space limitations or other consideration required the Office of the Press Secretary to limit the number of media representatives permitted to attend. *Id.* at 1239.

21. See *id.* See also WPIX, Inc. v. League of Women Voters, 595 F. Supp. 1484, 1489 (S.D.N.Y. 1984).

22. See 518 F. Supp. at 1240.

23. 448 U.S. 555 (1980).

24. 518 F. Supp. at 1244 (citations omitted). But cf. JB Pictures, Inc. v. Department of Defense, 86 F.3d 236, 240 (D.C. Cir. 1996) (past media access to Dover Air Force Base ceremonies honoring deceased military personnel did not create a tradition of openness of military bases).

25. 518 F. Supp. at 1244.

26. *Id.*

27. See *id.* at 1242-43 (quoting Zemel v. Rusk, 381 U.S. 1, 17 (1965)) ("'For example, the prohibition of unauthorized entry into the White House diminishes the citizen's opportunities to gather information he might find relevant to his opinion of the way the country is being run, but that does not make entry into the White House a First Amendment right. The right to speak and publish does not carry with it the unrestricted right to gather information.'").

adversely affected the citizenry and the manner in which it obtained news concerning the President.[28]

By the same token, the court was at a loss to discern a meaningful governmental interest served by the Press Secretary's policy of total exclusion of television media from limited coverage of White House events. In the court's view, any reduction in the Press Office's administrative tasks as a result of the policy was insignificant. Accordingly, the court held the policy violated the First Amendment-based right of access.[29]

§ 9-2(a). Issuance of Press Credentials.

Representatives of the media are provided with press credentials, often in the form of a press card or press pass, in order to obtain access to events and places to which the general public is not invited or permitted. The issuance of a press card identifies the journalist "as a responsible individual engaged in the important task of bringing a newsworthy event to the attention of the public at large."[30] Such credentials, however, have not afforded journalists the freedom to wander wherever they may choose. Indeed, courts have suggested that media representatives possessing "credentials" remain obligated to comply with the reasonable directions of the issuing agency.[31]

In addition, the courts have indicated, the issuing agency need not enunciate narrow and specifically drawn standards for issuance of press passes.[32] Never-

---

28. See 518 F. Supp. at 1245:

[I]t cannot be denied that television news coverage plays an increasingly prominent part in informing the public at large of the workings of government. Many citizens likely rely on television as their sole source of news. Further, visual impressions can and sometimes do add a material dimension to one's impression of particular news events. Television film coverage of the news provides a comprehensive visual element and an immediacy, or simultaneous aspect, not found in print media. Finally, the importance of conveying the fullest information possible increases as the importance of the particular news event or news setting increases. To most Americans, presidential activities rank higher in importance than those of any other public official.

29. See *id.* at 1245. But see Combined Communications Corp. v. Finesilver, 672 F.2d 818 (10th Cir. 1982) (television cameras not permitted in jury room where court-ordered redistricting negotiations held).

30. New Jersey v. Lashinsky, 404 A.2d 1121, 1135 (N.J. 1979) (Pashman, J., dissenting).

31. See *id.* at 1130 (opinion of the court) ("In our view, a photographer, . . . enjoying the respectability of a State Police press card, would realize that a refusal to obey an officer's reasonable order to withdraw from the immediate scene of an accident under emergency conditions, based on objective and obvious facts, comes within the disorderly persons statute."). The court noted, however, the "special role performed by the press. An officer should, if made aware of the identity and status of an individual as a newsperson engaged in gathering news, be mindful that such an individual has a legitimate and proper reason to be where he is and, if possible, this important interest should be accommodated." *Id.* at 1127-28.

32. See Sherrill v. Knight, 569 F.2d 124, 130 (D.C. Cir. 1977) ("[T]he governmental interest

theless, the criteria for press pass issuance may neither be arbitrary nor content-based,[33] and the criteria must typically be published or otherwise made publicly known.[34] Most courts require a showing of a compelling governmental interest supporting a refusal to grant a press pass.[35] Others, however, find it sufficient that the issuing agency articulate a reasonable basis for its determination.[36] The issuing agency is typically required to provide journalists with notice of the factual bases for denial of press credentials, an opportunity for the applicant to respond, and a final written statement of the reasons supporting denial.[37]

§ 9-2(b). Discriminatory Access.

The First Amendment-based right of access has generally been held to protect against different treatment between and among members of the media by government officials. In *Southwestern Newspapers Corp. v. Curtis*,[38] for example, a newspaper publisher sought to enjoin a district attorney from enforcing a rule that required the publisher's reporters to make appointments for access to official news sources, but did not require appointments by other journalists. The publisher alleged that the discriminatory restriction placed on its reporters was in retaliation for its publication of articles critical of the district attorney and its refusal to retract the statements as he requested. The Texas Court of Civil Appeals held that the discriminatory actions of the district

---

here does not lend itself to detailed articulation of narrow and specific standards or precise identification of all the factors which may be taken into account in applying this standard. It is enough that the Secret Service be guided solely by the principle of whether the applicant presents a potential source of physical danger to the President and/or his immediate family so serious as to justify his exclusion.").

33. See *id.* at 129; Borreca v. Fasi, 369 F. Supp. 906 (D. Haw. 1974); Quad-City Community News Serv. v. Jebens, 334 F. Supp. 8 (S.D. Iowa 1971).

34. See Sherrill v. Knight, 569 F.2d at 130. Subsequent to the *Sherrill* decision, the Secret Service published standards for the issuance of a White House press pass. See 31 C.F.R. § 409.1.

35. See, e.g., Sherrill v. Knight, 569 F.2d at 130 ("Given these important first amendment rights implicated by refusal to grant White House press passes to bona fide Washington journalists, such refusal must be based on a compelling governmental interest.").

36. See Watson v. Cronin, 384 F. Supp. 652, 658 (D. Colo. 1974); Los Angeles Free Press, Inc. v. City of Los Angeles, 88 Cal. Rptr. 605 (Ct. App. 1970), *cert. denied*, 401 U.S. 982 (1971). Courts have determined what constitutes a sufficient basis for the denial of press credentials in a variety of contexts. See, e.g., Sherrill v. Knight, 569 F.2d 124, 130 (D.C. Cir. 1977) ("Clearly, protection of the President is a compelling, 'even an overwhelming,' interest."); Stevens v. New York Racing Ass'n, 665 F. Supp. 164 (E.D.N.Y. 1987) (New York Racing Association had a legitimate interest in preventing conduct that annoys patrons and participants or disrupts racing events); Watson v. Cronin, 384 F. Supp. 652 (D. Colo. 1974) (applicant had a conviction for forgery and was pending trial for robbery); Haggerty v. Bloomington Bd. Pub. Safety, 474 N.E.2d 114 (Ind. App. 1985) (freelance writers excluded from executive session of public safety board as not "bona fide" members of the press, determined by reference to Indiana press shield statute).

37. See Sherrill v. Knight, 569 F.2d at 130-31.

38. 584 S.W.2d 362 (Tex. App. 1979).

attorney violated the publisher's First Amendment-based right of access and the Fourteenth Amendment's right to equal protection:[39]

> While public officials need not furnish information, other than public records, to any news agency, a public official may not constitutionally deny to one media access that is enjoyed by other media, because one media is entitled to the same right of access as any other. Moreover and in the absence of some compelling government interest to the contrary, all representatives of news organizations must not only be given equal access, but within reasonable limits, access with equal convenience to official news sources.[40]

Courts have also found constitutional violations where an official, absent a compelling governmental interest,[41] attempts to ostracize a particular journalist or journalistic organization.[42] However, courts recognize that it would be

---

39. See *id.* at 364. See also Quad-City Community News Serv. v. Jebens, 334 F. Supp. 8 (S.D. Iowa 1971) (police department's denial of access by "underground newspaper" to police department records, but allowing access to another newspaper, constituted denial of equal protection).

40. Southwestern Newspapers Corp. v. Curtis, 584 S.W.2d at 364-65 (citation omitted). See Wisconsin Freedom of Info. Council v. Hill, 7 MEDIA L. REP. (BNA) 2061 (Wis. Cir. 1981) (public has right to receive audiovisual account of inquest).

41. But see Los Angeles Free Press, Inc. v. City of Los Angeles, 88 Cal. Rptr. 605, 609 (Ct. App. 1970), *cert. denied*, 401 U.S. 982 (1971) (city policy of issuing press passes only to media that regularly covered police and fire news constituted a reasonable basis for classification imposed).

42. See Times-Picayune Publ'g Corp. v. Lee, 15 MEDIA L. REP. (BNA) 1713, 1719-20 (E.D. La. 1988) (citations omitted):

> Promoting the accuracy or objectivity of news reporting is not a compelling governmental interest that justifies content-based discrimination against a news organization. Especially is this so when the government official enforcing the discrimination is himself the subject of the news reporting which he purportedly wishes to purify of inaccuracy. In such circumstances, the official's discriminatory actions seek to promote an interest with which the government may not concern itself at all — control by an official of what is said and written about him. This is the essence of censorship forbidden by the First Amendment and so abhorred by the founding fathers.

See also El Dia, Inc. v. Rossello, 165 F.3d 106, 109 (1st Cir. 1999) ("[U]sing government funds to punish political speech by members of the press and to attempt to coerce commentary favorable to the government would run afoul of the First Amendment."); North Mississippi Communications, Inc. v. Jones, 792 F.2d 1330, 1337 (5th Cir. 1986) (government's withdrawal of advertisements from newspaper in retaliation for critical editorials and news violates the First Amendment); American Broadcasting Cos. v. Cuomo, 570 F.2d 1080, 1083 (2d Cir. 1977); McBride v. Village of Michiana, 100 F.3d 457 (6th Cir. 1996); Stevens v. New York Racing Ass'n, 665 F. Supp. 164 (E.D.N.Y. 1987); Westinghouse Broadcasting Co. v. Dukakis, 409 F. Supp. 895 (D. Mass. 1976) (city council could not exclude non-union camera crews of television station embroiled in labor dispute from council meetings and press conferences); Borreca v. Fasi, 369 F. Supp. 906 (D. Haw. 1974) (mayor's directive to staff to exclude reporter from general news conference violated First Amendment right of reasonable access to news).

§ 9-2(b) ACCESS TO EXECUTIVE AND LEGISLATIVE BRANCHES § 9-2(b)

impossible to treat every journalist with absolute equality,[43] and have acknowledged that public officials cannot be expected to forego all discretion in granting press access to interviews or briefings.[44] When differential treatment comes at

---

The Fourth Circuit, however, has held that a reporter's constitutional right of equal or nondiscriminatory access to government information that need not otherwise be made available to the public has not been clearly established. See Snyder v. Ringgold, 26 MEDIA L. REP. (BNA) 1249 (4th Cir.), *cert. denied*, 119 S. Ct. 50 (1998) (unpublished decision). The court found that the reporter's claimed right of equal access would improperly confer a privileged First Amendment status on the press that exceeds the protection afforded ordinary citizens. "[P]laintiff's asserted right would require that, in each and every circumstance where the government made news available, it would have to give access to that information to everyone on equal terms. The broad rule for which plaintiff contends thus appears untenable. In any event, the contours of any such right would be difficult to delineate, and certainly cannot be discerned through a straightforward and obvious application of existing First Amendment principles." *Id.* at 1252. The court also determined that the government is permitted to make content-based distinctions between reporters in granting access to governmental information. "Indeed, the government can certainly control the content of its own speech in ways it could never regulate or control the content of private speech. Arguably, by analogy, the government should be able to choose to limit its audience in a way it could not choose to limit the audience available to private speakers." *Id.* at 1253.

43. See Southwestern Newspapers Corp. v. Curtis, 584 S.W.2d at 368.

44. See Sherrill v. Knight, 569 F.2d 124, 129 (D.C. Cir. 1977) ("It would certainly be unreasonable to suggest that because the President allows interviews with some bona fide journalists, he must give this opportunity to all."). In *JB Pictures, Inc. v. Department of Defense*, 86 F.3d 236 (D.C. Cir. 1996), the court rejected the media's argument that denial of access to Dover Air Force Base was an unconstitutional "viewpoint discrimination" because it effectively precluded the dissemination of visual images of caskets of deceased soldiers. The court held that acceptance of the media's argument would

> represent a complete transformation of the law's permissive treatment of restrictions on access to government operations not historically open to the public. It is a commonplace, for example, that holders of high political office showcase their roles in popular initiatives with signing ceremonies, announcements and news conferences, often with carefully selected backdrops, while performing acts less likely to be acclaimed in venues from which the public and press are excluded. Acceptance of plaintiffs' theory would have the courts grant tickets to all these events, absent a special government justification for each differential in access.

Id. at 240 (citations omitted).

In *Snyder v. Ringgold,* 26 MEDIA L. REP. (BNA) 1249 (4th Cir.), *cert. denied*, 119 S. Ct. 50 (1998) (unpublished decision), the Fourth Circuit rejected a reporter's civil rights claim based in part on the refusal of a public affairs official of the Baltimore City Police Department to grant her interviews with department personnel. "[T]he broad [equal protection] rule for which plaintiff argues would presumably preclude the common and widely accepted practice among politicians of granting an exclusive interview to a particular reporter. And, it would preclude the equally widespread practice of public officials declining to speak to reporters whom they view as untrustworthy because the reporters have previously violated a promise of confidentiality or otherwise distorted their comments. Additionally, even if the right was somehow limited to situations in which access is provided to a broad spectrum of reporters, the plaintiff's rule would still presumably preclude the White House's practice of allowing only certain reporters to attend White House press conferences, even though space constraints make it impractical to open up the conference to all media organizations." *Id.* at 1252. By the same token, the adoption by government agencies of

the hand, not of public officials, but of private parties, the courts have held that the First Amendment is implicated only when those private parties are engaged in state action.[45]

Although their right of access is constitutionally protected, journalists are typically required to comply with reasonable time, place, or manner restrictions that may be imposed due to space limitations, security concerns, or other logistical difficulties.[46] Often, such restrictions necessitate that a pool of media representatives be designated to attend and to report back to those not included. Such pool arrangements, when performed on a rotating basis, have been held to constitute reasonable accommodations that do not unduly infringe on the access rights protected by the First or Fourteenth Amendments.[47]

§ 9-3. Non-Statutory Access to Legislative Proceedings.

The Constitution does not explicitly require Congress to open its sessions, meetings or hearings to the public or to the press. In fact, it provides that the House of Representatives and the Senate may each determine the rules of its

---

press policies that forbid employees from speaking with the media without first obtaining permission have been held to violate the First Amendment rights of government employees to speak about matters of public concern. See Harman v. City of New York, 140 F.3d 111 (2d Cir. 1998) (governmental interests of protecting confidentiality and promoting efficiency of social service agencies held insufficient to support press policies forbidding employees from speaking with the media regarding any policies or activities of the agency without first obtaining permission from the agency's media relations department). But see McBride v. Village of Michiana, 26 MEDIA L. REP. (BNA) 1833, 1840 (W.D. Mich. 1998) (instructions to village employees not to speak to reporter in retaliation for her critical reporting constituted protected counterspeech).

45. See National Broadcasting Co. v. Communications Workers of Am., 860 F.2d 1022 (11th Cir. 1988) (political convention held in city-leased convention center was not state action); Fulani v. League of Women Voters Educ. Fund, 684 F. Supp. 1185 (S.D.N.Y. 1988), aff'd, 882 F.2d 621 (2d Cir. 1989); National Broadcasting Co. v. Association of State Democratic Chairs, 14 MEDIA L. REP. (BNA) 1383 (N.D. Ohio 1987) (caucus of potential presidential candidates held in public facility was state action); WPIX, Inc. v. League of Women Voters, 595 F. Supp. 1484, 1489 (S.D.N.Y. 1984) (presidential and vice-presidential candidate debates arranged by League of Women Voters found to be state action).

46. See, e.g., Combined Communications Corp. v. Finesilver, 672 F.2d 818 (10th Cir. 1982); Los Angeles Free Press, Inc. v. City of Los Angeles, 88 Cal. Rptr. 605, 610 (Ct. App. 1970), cert. denied, 401 U.S. 982 (1971).

47. See WPIX, Inc. v. League of Women Voters, 595 F. Supp. 1484, 1489 (S.D.N.Y. 1984) ("Pooling has apparently become a commonplace practice. The vast number of media organizations interested in covering significant public events, and the need for security on many such occasions, make pooling a practical device for permitting press coverage in situations where unregulated access would otherwise permit total exclusion."); Cable News Network, Inc. v. American Broadcasting Cos., 518 F. Supp. 1238, 1239-40 (N.D. Ga. 1981). But see Note, *Pool Coverage, Press Access, and Presidential Debates: What's Wrong with This Picture?*, 9 CARDOZO L. REV. 1371 (1988).

proceedings.[48] Both houses of Congress have established press galleries, the management of which is governed by regulations promulgated by Congress.[49] The press galleries are administered by press associations that issue credentials to members. The final authority on applications for press credentials is lodged in the Speaker of the House of Representatives and the Senate Committee on Rules and Administration.[50]

The constitutions of some states require that legislative sessions be open to the public.[51] Most state constitutions, however, provide for a qualified guarantee of public access, requiring that the legislature be open to the public except in circumstances requiring secrecy,[52] when meetings are held in executive session,[53] or on a vote of the members to close.[54]

Efforts to exclude journalists from legislative proceedings[55] or to regulate access other than on the basis of time, place, or manner restrictions, have been held unconstitutional.[56] Due to the separation of powers doctrine, some courts have declared themselves unable to adjudicate these access claims.[57] Courts have nevertheless enforced access rights to local government meetings.[58] Even a con-

---

48. U.S. CONST. art. I, § 5, cl. 2.

49. The purpose of the regulations "is to assure that the . . . Press Galleries, within space limitation, will be used by bona fide reporters who will not abuse the privilege of accreditation by importuning Members on behalf of private interests or causes to which lobbying or advocacy groups are committed. The manner of assuring independence of those accredited from such groups or interests is for the Congress to determine as a matter of constitutional power." Consumers Union v. Periodical Correspondents' Ass'n, 515 F.2d 1341, 1347 (D.C. Cir. 1975).

50. See id. at 1343-44.

51. See, e.g., IDAHO CONST. art. 3, § 12; MONT. CONST. art. V, § 10; N.M. CONST. art. IV, § 12; N.D. CONST. art. IV, § 14; OR. CONST. art. IV, § 14.

52. See, e.g., ALA. CONST. art. IV, § 57; COLO. CONST. art. V, § 14; CONN. CONST. art. III, § 16; DEL. CONST. art. II, § 11; IND. CONST. art. IV, § 13; MD. CONST. art. III, § 21; MICH. CONST. art. IV, § 20; MINN. CONST. art. IV, § 14; MISS. CONST. art. IV, § 58; MO. CONST. art. III, § 20; NEB. CONST. art. III, § 11; N.H. CONST. part 2, art. VIII; N.Y. CONST. art. III, § 10; OHIO CONST. art. II, § 13; S.C. CONST. art. III, § 23; S.D. CONST. art. III, § 15; TENN. CONST. art. II, § 22; VT. CONST. ch. II, § 8; WASH. CONST. art. II, § 11; WIS. CONST. art. IV, § 10; WYO. CONST. art. III, § 14.

53. See, e.g., NEV. CONST. art. IV, § 15; TEX. CONST. art. III, § 16; UTAH CONST. art. VI, § 15.

54. See, e.g., CAL. CONST. art. IV, § 7(c); GA. CONST. art. III, § 4, ¶ 11; ILL. CONST. art. IV, § 5(c).

55. See Kovach v. Maddux, 238 F. Supp. 835 (M.D. Tenn. 1965).

56. See Lewis v. Baxley, 368 F. Supp. 768 (M.D. Ala. 1973) (limiting access to journalists who had submitted financial interest questionnaires held unconstitutional); Opinion of Justices to the Senate, 392 N.E.2d 849 (Mass. 1979) (requiring financial interest forms of reporters held unconstitutional).

57. See Consumers Union v. Periodical Correspondents' Ass'n, 515 F.2d 1341 (D.C. Cir. 1975), cert. denied, 423 U.S. 1051 (1976); Moffit v. Willis, 459 So. 2d 1018 (Fla. 1984).

58. See WJW-TV v. City of Cleveland, 686 F. Supp. 177 (N.D. Ohio 1988), vacated as moot, 878 F.2d 906 (6th Cir.), cert. denied, 493 U.S. 819 (1989) (First Amendment-based right of access to city council meeting); Atlantic City Convention Center Auth. v. South Jersey Publ'g Co., 637 A.2d 1261 (N.J. 1994) (common law right of access to audio tapes of authority's closed executive

stitutional right of access, however, does not necessarily authorize the use of cameras or other devices.[59]

§ 9-4. Non-Statutory Access to Administrative Proceedings.

Courts have also invoked the *Press-Enterprise* analysis[60] to determine whether journalists have a constitutional right of access to various administrative proceedings. The history of access to the particular type of proceeding at issue and the personal interests of the parties involved in them often dictate the result in such cases. Generally, however, proceedings that are fact-finding in nature tend to be subject to a qualified right of access,[61] particularly where there is a strong public interest in the matter at issue.[62] Other proceedings to which the public generally has been afforded access include meetings of university governing boards,[63] unemployment compensation hearings,[64] coroner's inquests,[65] and the meetings of judicial nominating commissions.[66]

Disciplinary hearings and records, however, have generally been held, absent a statute, not to be subject to a right of access,[67] though some jurisdictions may

---

sessions). See generally Note, *Mr. Smith Comes Home: The Constitutional Presumption of Openness in Local Legislative Meetings*, 40 CASE W. RES. L. REV. 227 (1990).

59. See Combined Communications Corp. v. Finesilver, 672 F.2d 818 (10th Cir. 1982) (television camera access to settlement negotiations between governor and members of legislature denied); Johnson v. Adams, 629 F. Supp. 1563 (E.D. Tex. 1986) (videotaping of county board meetings denied); Sigma Delta Chi v. Speaker, Maryland House of Delegates, 310 A.2d 156 (Md. 1973) (use of tape recorders on floor of General Assembly denied).

60. See *Press-Enterprise II*, 478 U.S. at 8; Chap. 2-2(f) *supra*.

61. See Society of Prof'l Journalists v. Secretary of Labor, 616 F. Supp. 569 (D. Utah 1985), *appeal dismissed*, 832 F.2d 1180 (10th Cir. 1987).

62. See *id*. at 576 (the sorrow, grief, and confusion felt by the community after a mine fire, as well as the issue of whether the Mine Safety and Health Administration "properly does its job," were held to be significant public interest factors in granting access to hearings).

63. In California and Michigan, the state constitution requires that meetings of the governing boards of state universities be open to the public. See CAL. CONST. art. IX § 9(g) (Board of Regents meetings open to the public except as provided by statute); MICH. CONST. art. VIII, § 4 (formal sessions of university governing boards open).

64. See Herald Co. v. Weisenberg, 452 N.E.2d 1190 (N.Y. 1983).

65. See, e.g., Courier-Journal v. Gash, 9 MEDIA L. REP. (BNA) 1735 (Ky. Cir. 1983) (coroner's inquest is "a public function . . . in all essential aspects at least equivalent to a judicial proceeding").

66. Under the Florida constitution, meetings of the Judicial Nominating Commission are to be open to the public except during its deliberations. See FLA. CONST. art. V, § 11(d). But see Nero v. Hyland, 386 A.2d 846 (N.J. 1978) (no access to records of investigation of nominee to lottery commission).

67. See, e.g., Nelson v. Boundary County, 706 P.2d 94 (Idaho App. 1985) (employee pretermination hearing); Marion County Sheriff's Merit Bd. v. People Broadcasting Corp., 547 N.E.2d 235 (Ind. 1989) (disciplinary charges brought against sheriff's deputy); Johnson Newspaper Corp. v. Melino, 564 N.E.2d 1046 (N.Y. 1990) (professional disciplinary hearing, such as that brought against dentist, had no tradition of being open to the public). See generally Landmark

require access if there is a recommendation that disciplinary action be taken.[68] First Amendment-based claims of public access have also been rejected in the context of licensing proceedings,[69] death certificates,[70] and other public records.[71]

§ 9-5. Statutory Access to Federal Government Meetings.

The right of the public and press to attend meetings of governmental bodies is largely the result of state constitutional provisions[72] and open meeting statutes of relatively recent vintage.[73] The federal government has provided for public access to its meetings in the Government in the Sunshine Act[74] and the Federal Advisory Committee Act.[75] Each state has enacted similar legislation opening the meetings of at least some of its governmental bodies to the public.[76]

§ 9-5(a). Government in the Sunshine Act.

§ 9-5(a)(1). Introduction.

The Government in the Sunshine Act[77] provides for public access to the decisionmaking process of federal agencies. An adjunct to the Freedom of Infor-

---

Communications, Inc. v. Virginia, 435 U.S. 829, 835-36 (1978) (discussing advantages of confidentiality in judicial disciplinary proceedings); Comment, *A First Amendment Right of Access to Judicial Disciplinary Proceedings*, 132 U. PA. L. REV. 1163 (1984). But see Daily Gazette Co. v. Committee on Legal Ethics, 326 S.E.2d 705 (W. Va. 1984) (attorney disciplinary proceeding).

68. See First Amendment Coalition v. Judicial Inquiry & Review Bd., 784 F.2d 467 (3d Cir. 1986) (board's hearing was analogized to closed grand jury proceedings, but its recommendation of disciplinary action was analogized to a public indictment); Whitehead v. Nevada Comm'n on Judicial Discipline, 893 P.2d 866, 893-97 (Nev. 1995) (court assumed, but did not decide, the existence of a constitutional right of access to judicial disciplinary proceedings at some stage); Daily Gazette Co. v. West Va. Bd. of Med., 352 S.E.2d 66 (W. Va. 1986) (right of access to physician disciplinary proceeding exists after state board of medicine determines there is probable cause to proceed).

69. See, e.g., WBZ-TV4 v. Executive Office of Labor, 610 N.E.2d 923 (Mass. 1993).

70. See, e.g., Birmingham News Co. v. Roper, 4 MEDIA L. REP. (BNA) 1075 (N.D. Ala. 1978); Yeste v. Miami Herald Publ'g Co., 451 So. 2d 491 (Fla. App. 1984).

71. See, e.g., Calder v. IRS, 890 F.2d 781 (5th Cir. 1989) (IRS records); Register Div. of Freedom Newspapers v. County of Orange, 205 Cal. Rptr. 92 (Ct. App. 1984) (settlement records); News & Observer Publ'g Co. v. North Carolina, 322 S.E.2d 133 (N.C. 1984) (state police records).

72. See Chaps. 9-1 & 9-3 *supra*.

73. See generally Deering, *Closing the Door on the Public's Right to Know: Alabama's Open Meetings Law After* Dunn v. Alabama State University Board of Trustees, 28 CUMB. L. REV. 361, 364-67 (1997-98).

74. See Chap. 9-5(a) *infra*.

75. See Chap. 9-5(b) *infra*.

76. See Chap. 9-6 *infra*.

77. Pub. L. 94-409, 90 Stat. 1241, codified at 5 U.S.C. § 552b.

mation Act,[78] which provides access to documents, Congress enacted the Sunshine Act to permit the public to observe the federal government in action.[79]

The Sunshine Act is the last of four statutes passed by Congress from 1966 through 1976 in response to concerns about "secret government" and the concomitant lack of accountability of administrative bodies.[80] To this end, the Act declares that "the public is entitled to the fullest practicable information regarding the decisionmaking processes of the Federal Government."[81] It is the general policy of the Act that federal agencies should "conduct their meetings in open rather than behind closed doors,"[82] while also protecting the ability of the "Government to carry on its responsibilities."[83]

§ 9-5(a)(2). Agencies Subject to the Act.

Not all federal agencies fall within the scope of the Sunshine Act.[84] An "agency," as defined by the Act, is a federal agency subject to the Freedom of

---

78. See 5 U.S.C. § 552; Chap. 10-2 *infra*.

79. See S. REP. NO. 94-354, at 5, *reprinted in Government-in-the-Sunshine Source Book: Legislative History, Texts, and Other Documents*, Comms. on Gov't Ops., 94th Cong., 2d Sess. (1976) (hereafter "*Sunshine Source Book*"):

> Documents disclosed under the FOIA represent a record of what has already transpired. Yet, up to now the public has not had a full opportunity to learn how or why government official[s] make the important policy decisions which they do. All too often the meetings at which such decisions are made are closed to the public. Interested persons must content themselves with elementary minutes, or background papers tangentially related to the official agenda. Formal statements in support of agency action are frequently too brief, or too general, to fully explain the Commission's reasoning, or the compromises that were made. As a result, the public may not understand the reasons an agency has acted in a certain way, or even what exactly it has decided to do. By requiring important decisions to be made openly, this bill will create better understanding of agency decisions.

80. The other statutes are the Freedom of Information Act, 5 U.S.C. § 552, see Chap. 10-2 *infra*; the Federal Advisory Committee Act, 5 U.S.C. App. II §§ 1-15, see Chaps. 9-5(b) & 10-3 *infra*; and the Privacy Act, 5 U.S.C. § 552a. The Sunshine Act was modeled after the Florida Sunshine Act, FLA. STAT. § 286.011. The Act was also passed in response to a growing concern that regulated industries had more access to government than did the public. See P. STRAUSS, AN INTRODUCTION TO ADMINISTRATIVE JUSTICE IN THE UNITED STATES 200 (1989).

81. 5 U.S.C. § 552b (Declaration of Policy).

82. See S. REP. NO. 94-354, at 1 (1975).

83. 5 U.S.C. § 552b (Declaration of Policy). The increased access to meetings does not translate, however, into an increase in the public's participation in them. S. REP. NO. 94-354, at 1-2 (1975); J. O'REILLY, FEDERAL INFORMATION DISCLOSURE § 23.04 (1998). See generally Bensch, *Seventeen Years Later: Has Government Let the Sun Shine In?*, 61 GEO. WASH. L. REV. 1475 (1993).

84. See, e.g., Rushforth v. Council of Econ. Advisors, 762 F.2d 1038, 1044 (D.C. Cir. 1985) (Council of Economic Advisors whose sole function is to advise and assist the President is not an agency because it is not a collegial body); Public Citizen Health Research Group v. HEW, 668 F.2d 537 (D.C. Cir. 1981) (medical foundation acting under contract with HEW to serve as professional

Information Act[85] that is headed by a collegial body of two or more members who have been appointed by the President with the advice and consent of the Senate.[86] Agencies such as the Postal Service and Amtrak have been deemed to fall within the Act's definition, even though their day-to-day management is committed to the authority of a single individual.[87] Advisory Committees, which are governed by the Federal Advisory Committee Act,[88] are not subject to the Sunshine Act.[89] The distinction between an "agency" and an advisory committee under the Sunshine Act, however, is not clear.[90]

---

standards review organization is not an agency); Hunt v. NRC, 611 F.2d 332, 335 (10th Cir. 1979), *cert. denied*, 445 U.S. 906 (1988) (Atomic Safety and Licensing Board is not an agency because "members of such a Board are not appointed by the President but by the Nuclear Regulatory Commission"); Symons v. Chrysler Corp. Loan Guar. Bd., 670 F.2d 238 (D.C. Cir. 1981) (Chrysler Corporation Loan Guarantee Board is not an agency because none of its members were appointed to positions on the Board by the President, rather Board members serve ex officio by virtue of their appointment to other high government offices).

85. An agency not subject to the Freedom of Information Act ("FOIA") is not subject to the Sunshine Act because "the Sunshine Act expressly incorporates the FOIA definition of agency." Rushforth v. Council of Econ. Advisors, 762 F.2d at 1043.

86. See 5 U.S.C. § 552b(a) ("[T]he term 'agency' means any agency, as defined in section 552(e) of this title, headed by a collegial body composed of two or more individual members, a majority of whom are appointed to such position by the President with the advice and consent of the Senate, and any subdivision thereof authorized to act on behalf of the agency."); Nichols v. Reno, 931 F. Supp. 748, 753 (D. Colo. 1996) (Sunshine Act is not applicable to Department of Justice, the authority of which is vested in a single individual, the Attorney General). Section 552(e), redesignated section 552(f) by Act of Oct. 27, 1986, Pub. L. 99-570, § 1802, 1986 U.S.C.C.A.N. 3207, 3207-49, provides the definition of "agency" for FOIA. The Sunshine Act's definition of agency is narrower than that of other laws. O'REILLY, *supra* note 83, at § 23.02. It applies to approximately 50 agencies, including all major regulatory agencies. Note, *Facilitating Government Decision Making: Distinguishing Between Meetings and Nonmeetings Under the Federal Sunshine Act*, 66 TEX. L. REV. 1195, 1199 (1988).

87. See S. CONF. REP. NO. 94-1178, at 10 (1976), *reprinted in* 1976 U.S.C.C.A.N. 2246.

88. See Chap. 10-3(b) *infra*.

89. By its terms, advisory committees are excluded from the Sunshine Act, which applies only to agencies that have ultimate decisional power and "any subdivision thereof authorized to act on behalf of the agency." 5 U.S.C. § 552b(a). Nevertheless, in the rare instance where an advisory body, such as the Postal Service Board of Governors, has oversight and decisional power, they too qualify as "agencies." See, e.g., Time, Inc. v. Postal Serv., 667 F.2d 329 (2d Cir. 1981). The Defense Nuclear Facilities Safety Board, the duties of which include review, evaluation, investigations, and recommendations to the Secretary of Energy concerning the military application of nuclear energy, has been held to be an agency under the Sunshine Act even though it has no authority to enforce its recommendations. Energy Research Found. v. Defense Nuclear Facilities Safety Bd., 917 F.2d 581, 582 (D.C. Cir. 1990).

90. See, e.g., Time, Inc. v. Postal Serv., 667 F.2d 329 (2d Cir. 1981). An advisory committee will generally not be considered an agency "unless, in rare cases they are empowered to oversee the actions of an operating officer of the agency." O'REILLY, *supra* note 83, at § 23.02 & n.29.

A subdivision of a collegial body is subject to the Act if it is authorized to make decisions on behalf of the agency.[91] An interagency meeting may be subject to the Act if a majority of the members from one agency is in attendance.[92]

§ 9-5(a)(3). Definition of "Meeting."

A meeting of an agency occurs when a quorum of its members[93] deliberate to conduct agency business.[94] It is the deliberation of the requisite number of members, not the taking of formal agency action, that determines whether there has been a meeting.[95] A meeting may include lunches or telephone conference calls, if the members confer with the intent or the result that agency business is discussed.[96] A meeting does not occur when members meet only to schedule a future session.[97] Members have circumvented the Act, however, by sequential

---

91. See H.R. REP. NO. 94-880 at 7 (1976), *reprinted in* 1976 U.S.C.C.A.N. 2188-80 ("Panels, or regional boards of an agency, are covered if authorized to act on behalf of the agency, even if the action is not final in nature. Thus, panels or boards authorized to submit recommendations, or to conduct hearings on behalf of the agency are required to comply with the provisions of section 552b."). See also Hunt v. NRC, 611 F.2d 332, 336 (10th Cir. 1979), *cert. denied*, 445 U.S. 906 (1980) ("[T]he term 'any subdivision thereof' can only mean subdivision of a collegial body.").

92. See FCC v. ITT World Communications, 466 U.S. 463, 465-66 (1984) (quorum of subcommittee of the Federal Communications Commission in attendance at an international conference held to be an agency subject to the Sunshine Act with regard to "matters that are within that subdivision's formally delegated authority to take official action for the agency").

93. A "member" is defined as "an individual who belongs to a collegial body heading an agency." 5 U.S.C. § 552b(a)(3).

94. A "meeting" is defined by the Act as "the deliberations of at least the number of individual agency members required to take action on behalf of the agency where such deliberations determine or result in the joint conduct or disposition of official agency business." 5 U.S.C. § 552b(a)(2). The Supreme Court has determined that the participation of a quorum of the Telecommunications Committee of the FCC in consultative process sessions with foreign counterparts regarding implementation of policy decisions was not a meeting. "Congress did not intend the Sunshine Act to encompass such discussions." FCC v. ITT World Communications, 466 U.S. 463, 472 (1984).

95. See S. REP. NO. 94-354, at 18, *reprinted in Sunshine Source Book* at 214 ("The definition of meetings includes the conduct, as well as the disposition, of official agency matters. It is not sufficient for the purposes of open government to merely have the public witness agency votes. The meetings opened by Section 201(a) are not intended to be merely reruns staged for the public after the agency members have discussed the issue in private and predetermined their views. The whole decision-making process, not merely its results, must be exposed to public scrutiny.").

96. See Pacific Legal Found. v. Council on Envtl. Quality, 636 F.2d 1259, 1266 (D.C. Cir. 1980) (section "does not require an agency to hold meetings in order to function . . . [b]ut where the deliberations and discussions among agency members in fact 'determine or result in joint conduct or disposition of official agency business' they are meetings . . . no matter how the agency may characterize them for internal purposes").

97. See Washington Ass'n for Television & Children v. FCC, 665 F.2d 1264, 1272 (D.C. Cir. 1981).

notational voting[98] rather than gathering for a formal vote.[99] A session conducted by employees, not by members of the collegial governing body, is not a "meeting" within the terms of the statute.[100]

§ 9-5(a)(4). Notice of Meetings.

The Sunshine Act requires agencies to provide fair notice in advance of their meetings. An agency must announce, at least one week prior to a meeting, its subject matter, time, place, and whether or not the meeting is open to the public.[101] The notice must also provide the name of the official designated by the agency to respond to requests for information.[102] The Act permits shorter advance notice only where a "majority of the members of the agency determines by a recorded vote that agency business requires that such meeting be called at an earlier date."[103] Such shortened advance notice must, however, be given "at the earliest practicable time,"[104] and must be published in the Federal Register.[105]

An agency can change the time or place of a meeting only if the "agency publicly announces such change at the earliest practicable time."[106] The subject matter of the meeting, or whether the meeting will be opened or closed, can be altered only by a recorded majority vote that the "agency business so requires"

---

98. See Railroad Comm'n of Texas v. United States, 765 F.2d 221, 230 (D.C. Cir. 1985) ("Notational voting is a management device whereby the several members of a multi-member agency or commission vote individually and separately, as opposed to a vote at a meeting of the members of the agency.").

99. See Common Cause v. NRC, 674 F.2d 921, 935 n.42 (D.C. Cir. 1982) ("The Sunshine Act does not, however, prevent agencies from making decisions by sequential, notational voting rather than by gathering at a meeting for deliberations and decision. Therefore, an agency might make its budget decisions by circulating staff memoranda and voting by notation . . . ."); Republic Airlines v. CAB, 756 F.2d 1304, 1319 (10th Cir. 1995) (discussions between Board members and its staff as well as receiving memoranda prior to an adjudicating meeting did not violate the Act because "[s]ection 552b was not intended to prevent Board members from receiving advice of staff or to prevent the exchange of views between two Board members off-the-record"); Pacific Legal Found. v. Council on Envtl. Quality, 636 F.2d at 1266 ("The Sunshine Act does not require an agency to hold meetings in order to function . . . Congress intended to permit agencies to consider and act on agency business by circulating written proposals for sequential approval by individual agency members without formal meetings."). See also Railroad Comm'n of Texas v. United States, 765 F.2d 221, 230 (D.C. Cir. 1985) ("The Sunshine Act does not require that meetings be held in order to conduct agency business; rather, that statute requires only that, if meetings are held, they be open to the public. . . ."); Communications Sys. v. FCC, 595 F.2d 797 (D.C. 1978).

100. See Hunt v. NRC, 611 F.2d at 336; O'REILLY, *supra* note 83, at § 23.02 & n.27.
101. 5 U.S.C. § 552b(e)(1).
102. *Id.* § 552b(e)(1).
103. *Id.*
104. *Id.* § 552b(e)(2).
105. *Id.* § 552b(e)(3).
106. *Id.* § 552b(e)(2).

and that "no earlier announcement was possible."[107] The agency must publicly announce the change and the vote at the "earliest practicable time."[108]

§ 9-5(a)(5). Access to Meetings.

The Sunshine Act provides that, except for meetings specifically exempted, "every portion of every meeting of an agency shall be open to public observation,"[109] regardless of whether the public has asked to attend.[110] Unless the meeting is a public hearing, the public has only the "right to attend the meetings, to listen and to observe the proceedings."[111] The Sunshine Act provides only that the meeting "shall be open to public observation."[112] The rules and regulations of each agency determine whether the public may participate in or record[113] its meetings.[114]

§ 9-5(a)(6). Access to Meeting Transcripts and Tapes.

The Sunshine Act requires agencies to maintain a complete transcript or an electronic recording of meetings closed pursuant to one of the ten statutory exemptions set forth in the Act.[115] When meetings are closed pursuant to the financial institutions[116] or adjudicatory proceedings[117] exemptions, the agency may maintain minutes of the meeting, rather than a transcript or electronic recording.[118] The minutes must "fully and accurately describe all matters discussed" and "provide a full and accurate summary of any actions taken" includ-

---

107. *Id.*
108. *Id.* Agencies subject to the Sunshine Act are required to promulgate regulations implementing the Act. See, e.g., United Postal Serv., 39 C.F.R. §§ 7.1-7.8 (1993).
109. 5 U.S.C. § 552b(b). See Pacific Legal Found. v. Council on Envtl. Quality, 636 F.2d 1259, 1265 (D.C. Cir. 1980) (language of Act's open meeting requirement is "sweeping, unqualified and mandatory").
110. See Pan Am. World Airways, Inc. v. CAB, 684 F.2d 31, 35 (D.C. Cir. 1982).
111. H.R. REP. NO. 94-854, at 19 (1975).
112. 5 U.S.C. § 552b(b).
113. See O'REILLY, *supra* note 83, at § 23.04 ("An agency should permit unobtrusive recordings but need not permit full photo coverage if this would disrupt the meeting.").
114. See, e.g., We The People, Inc. v. NRC, 746 F. Supp. 213, 217 (D.D.C. 1990) (First Amendment challenge to banning political posters and bumper stickers at a public meeting of the Nuclear Regulatory Commission was unsuccessful because agency's regulations interpret the Sunshine Act as prohibiting right to participate in public meetings).
115. 5 U.S.C. § 552b(f)(1). See Chap. 9-5(a)(8) *infra*.
116. 5 U.S.C. § 552b(c)(8) & (9)(A). See Chaps. 9-5(a)(8)(H)-(I) *infra*.
117. 5 U.S.C. § 552b(c)(10). See Chap. 9-5(a)(8)(J) *infra*.
118. 5 U.S.C. § 552b(f)(1) ("The agency shall maintain a complete transcript or electronic recording adequate to record fully the proceedings of each meeting, or portion of a meeting, closed to the public, except that in the case of a meeting, or portion of meeting, closed to the public pursuant to paragraph (8), (9)(A), or (10) of subdivision (c), the agency shall maintain either such a transcript or recording, or a set of minutes.").

ing a "description of each of the views expressed on any item."[119] In addition, the minutes must identify all "documents considered in connection with any action."[120] The Act requires the agency to maintain the verbatim copy of each transcript, a complete set of minutes, and a complete copy of each electronic recording of a meeting closed to the public for at least two years.[121]

The Act also requires the agency to make the transcript, electronic recording, or minutes of the closed meeting promptly available "in a place easily accessible to the public."[122] The public may obtain a copy of any such recording unless its content falls within one of the ten statutory exemptions.[123]

§ 9-5(a)(7). Procedures to Close Meetings.

The Sunshine Act permits an agency to close a meeting under specified circumstances. To do so, a majority of its members must vote for closure,[124] with no proxies permitted.[125] Within one day of voting to close a meeting, the agency must publicly provide a written explanation of its decision,[126] along with a list of all persons expected to attend and their affiliation.[127] Even after an unsuccessful vote to close a meeting, the agency must make a record of each member's vote publicly available.[128]

In addition, the General Counsel or chief legal officer of the agency must publicly certify that the meeting was properly closed to the public and state each relevant exemption relied on to close the meeting.[129] Where discussions of exempt subjects do not occupy the entire meeting, the remainder must be held in

---

119. *Id.*
120. *Id.*
121. *Id.* § 552b(f)(2) ("The agency shall maintain a complete verbatim copy of the transcript, a complete copy of the minutes, or a complete electronic recording of each meeting, or portion of a meeting closed to the public for a period of at least two years after such meeting, or until one year after the conclusion of any agency proceeding with respect to which the meeting or portion was held, whichever occurs later.").
122. *Id.*
123. *Id.* § 552b(k).
124. *Id.* § 552b(d)(1) ("A single vote may be taken with respect to a series of meetings, a portion or portions of which are proposed to be closed . . . so long as each meeting in such series involves the same particular matters and is scheduled to be held no more than thirty days after the initial meeting in such series.").
125. *Id.*
126. *Id.* § 552b(d)(3).
127. *Id.*
128. *Id.*
129. *Id.* § 552b(f)(1).

open session.[130] Moreover, unless exempted,[131] the agency must record any meeting that is closed.[132]

Any person whose interests may be directly affected by a matter addressed during a meeting may require the agency to close that portion of the session if the matter to be discussed relates to personal privacy, a criminal accusation, or law enforcement information.[133] Expedited procedures for closure are available to an agency which determines that the meeting will address specified exemptions relating to highly sensitive matters.[134] To invoke an expedited procedure under these circumstances, the agency must have promulgated appropriate regulations and must publicly announce the subject matter, time, and place of the meeting.[135] Finally, those regulations must require that the agency provide the public with the vote of each member with respect to closure.[136]

§ 9-5(a)(8). Exemptions.

Although the Sunshine Act establishes a general presumption that agency meetings should be held in public,[137] the open meeting requirement does not apply "when the agency properly determines that a portion or portions of its meeting will disclose or is likely to disclose information which falls within one of the ten exemptions under the Act."[138] The courts have construed these exemptions narrowly,[139] and the agency bears the burden of demonstrating that the meeting falls within a specific exemption.[140] Where an agency discusses both exempt and non-exempt matters at a given meeting, it must segregate exempt

---

130. See Common Cause v. NRC, 674 F.2d 921, 929 (D.C. Cir. 1982).
131. 5 U.S.C. § 552b(f)(1).
132. *Id.* § 552b(f)(2). See Chap. 9-5(a)(6) *supra*.
133. See 5 U.S.C. § 552b(d)(2).
134. *Id.* § 552b(c)(4), (8)-(10).
135. *Id.* § 552b(d)(4).
136. *Id.*
137. See Common Cause v. NRC, 674 F.2d 921, 928-29 (D.C. Cir. 1982).
138. 5 U.S.C. § 552b(c). Seven of these exemptions are patterned after FOIA Exemptions 1-4 and 6-8. These seven exemptions are largely interpreted the same as the analogous FOIA exemptions. See H.R. REP. No. 94-880 (part 1), at 9-13, *reprinted in* 1976 U.S.C.C.A.N. 2190-95, *Sunshine Source Book* at 520-24; H.R. REP. No. 94-880 (part 2), at 15, *reprinted in* 1976 U.S.C.C.A.N. 2213, 2224-25, *Sunshine Source Book* at 554, 565; S. CONF. REP. NO. 94-1178, at 14-15, *reprinted in* 1976 U.S.C.C.A.N. 2249-51, *Sunshine Source Book* at 796-97; see also S. REP. NO. 94-354, at 20-27, *reprinted in Sunshine Source Book* at 215-22. This is true at least with respect to case law interpreting FOIA prior to its amendment in 1986. "Once the case law of the 1986 FOIA language develops, a court in a Sunshine Act case will cease to follow that case law because the 1974, not the 1986, version of FOIA is to be the benchmark." O'REILLY, *supra* note 83, at § 23.06. The Sunshine Act has no parallel to FOIA's exemption of discovery privileges (Exemption 5) or geological data (Exemption 9).
139. See, e.g., Common Cause v. NRC, 674 F.2d at 932.
140. See *id.* at 929; S. REP. No. 94-354 (1975).

from non-exempt discussions and open the latter portions of the session to the public.[141]

Even though one of the ten statutory exemptions may apply to the subject matter of a meeting, it must nonetheless be held in open session if the agency determines that the public interest so dictates.[142] Accordingly, before closing a meeting, an agency must determine both (1) whether the matter or matters to be discussed are "likely to disclose" information subject to the exemption,[143] and (2) whether the public interest requires that the meeting be open nonetheless.[144]

§ 9-5(a)(8)(A). Exemption 1: National Security.

The first exemption to the Sunshine Act[145] is patterned after Exemption 1 to FOIA.[146] Information that may be withheld under the FOIA exemption may allow an agency to close a meeting or portion of a meeting where the same information is likely to be discussed or disclosed.

§ 9-5(a)(8)(B). Exemption 2: Internal Agency Personnel Rules.

The second exemption to the Sunshine Act[147] is patterned after FOIA Exemption 2.[148] It is designed to exclude from the open meeting requirement routine matters of only internal significance and of no interest to the public.[149] Where the public has an interest, such as agency budget discussions relating to personnel cutbacks or performance, the meeting must remain open.[150]

---

141. See Common Cause v. NRC, 674 F.2d at 936 n.46 ("Even if a portion of a budget meeting may be lawfully closed because that part of the discussion is protected by a specific exemption, the Commission may not close the entire meeting. Congress declared that meetings should be opened to the fullest extent possible. We therefore reject the Commission's contention that the Sunshine Act does not require an agency to segregate exempt discussions into a closed portion of its meeting.") (citations omitted).

142. See 5 U.S.C. § 552b(c).

143. S. CONF. REP. NO. 94-1178, at 15 (1976) ("'[L]ikely to disclose' means it is more likely than not that a discussion will involve these areas").

144. See 5 U.S.C. § 552b(c).

145. See *id.* § 552b(c)(1) ("[M]atters that are (A) specifically authorized under criteria established by an executive order to be kept secret in the interest of national defense or foreign policy and (B) in fact properly classified pursuant to such Executive order.").

146. See Chap. 10-2(c)(2) *infra*.

147. See 5 U.S.C. § 552b(c)(2) ("relate solely to the internal personnel rules and practices of an agency").

148. See Chap. 10-2(c)(3) *infra*.

149. The dearth of case law concerning Exemption 2 of the Sunshine Act has created a heavy reliance on decisions interpreting Exemption 2 of FOIA. See Wilkinson v. Legal Servs. Corp., 865 F. Supp. 891, 895 (D.D.C. 1994), *rev'd on other grounds*, 80 F.3d 535 (D.C. Cir.), *cert. denied*, 519 U.S. 927 (1996); Common Cause v. NRC, 674 F.2d at 937.

150. See Common Cause v. NRC, 674 F.2d at 938.

§ 9-5(a)(8)(C). Exemption 3: Disclosure Prohibited by Other Federal Statutes.

The third exemption to the Sunshine Act[151] is patterned after FOIA Exemption 3.[152] It is intended to permit meetings to be held in closed session when the information to be discussed is prohibited from disclosure by other federal statutes. In *Natural Resource Defense Council, Inc. v. Defense Nuclear Facilities Safety Board*,[153] the D.C. Circuit held that the Sunshine Act does not require public access to meetings of the Defense Nuclear Facilities Safety Board, which involve deliberations on recommendations that, pursuant to statute,[154] could not be made publicly available until after being received by the Secretary of Energy or the President.[155]

§ 9-5(a)(8)(D). Exemption 4: Trade Secrets and Confidential Commercial Information.

The fourth exemption to the Sunshine Act[156] is patterned after FOIA Exemption 4.[157] It protects the commercial interests of those who have provided information to the government against disclosure of that information at a public meeting of an agency. Because the Sunshine Act has not specifically exempted geological and geophysical information concerning wells, as has FOIA,[158] those who have disclosed such information to the government will likely look to this exemption for protection in the context of agency meetings.

§ 9-5(a)(8)(E). Exemption 5: Accusation of a Crime or Formal Censure.

The fifth exemption to the Sunshine Act[159] has no parallel under FOIA.[160] It applies only when the discussion to be held at a meeting relates to a specific

---

151. See 5 U.S.C. § 552b(c)(3) ("[M]atters specifically exempted from disclosure by statute (other than section 552 of this title), provided that such statute (A) requires that the matters be withheld from the public in such a manner as to leave no discretion on the issue, or (B) establishes particular criteria for withholding or refers to particular types of matters to be withheld.").

152. See Chap. 10-2(c)(4) *infra*.

153. 969 F.2d 1248, 1252 (D.C. Cir. 1992), *cert. denied*, 508 U.S. 906 (1993).

154. 42 U.S.C. §§ 2286-2286i.

155. See Natural Resources Defense Council, Inc. v. Defense Nuclear Facilities Safety Bd., 969 F.2d at 1252.

156. See 5 U.S.C. § 552b(c)(4) ("trade secrets and commercial or financial information obtained from a person and privileged or confidential").

157. See Chap. 10-2(c)(5) *infra*.

158. See Chap. 10-2(c)(10) *infra*.

159. See 5 U.S.C. § 552b(c)(5) ("involve accusing any person of a crime, or formally censuring any person").

160. See Chap. 10(c) *infra*.

person. If a possible criminal violation is at issue, the discussion must relate to a specific crime and the agency must be considering possible action of a formal nature against the person in question.[161]

§ 9-5(a)(8)(F). Exemption 6: Personal Privacy.

The sixth exemption to the Sunshine Act[162] is patterned after FOIA Exemption 6.[163] It protects the privacy interests of those who may be the subject of discussions at an agency meeting. Unlike the parallel exemption under FOIA, the Sunshine Act Exemption 6 is not limited to information contained in personnel, medical, and similar files. Exemption 6 will not, however, shelter from public discussion the substandard performance of government officials.[164] In *Common Cause v. Nuclear Regulatory Commission*, the Nuclear Regulatory Commission sought to close a budgetary meeting to protect discussions regarding a particular manager's qualifications, characteristics, and professional competence in connection with a budget request he had made.[165] The D.C. Circuit, which held that the meeting could not properly be closed on that ground, emphasized the narrow scope of Exemption 6:

> Exemption 6 applies to information of a personal nature, including discussions of a person's health, drinking habits, or financial circumstances. It provides greater protection to private individuals, including applicants for federal grants and officials of regulated private companies, and to low-level government employees, than to government officials with executive responsibilities.[166]

§ 9-5(a)(8)(G). Exemption 7: Law Enforcement Investigations.

The seventh exemption to the Sunshine Act[167] is patterned after FOIA Ex-

---

161. H.R. REP. No. 94-880 (part 1) at 10, *reprinted in* 1976 U.S.C.C.A.N. 2191-92, *Sunshine Source Book* at 521; see also S. REP. No. 94-354, at 22, *reprinted in Sunshine Source Book* at 217.

162. See 5 U.S.C. § 552b(c)(6) ("information of a personal nature where disclosure would constitute a clearly unwarranted invasion of personal privacy").

163. See Chap. 10-2(c)(7) *infra*.

164. See Common Cause v. NRC, 674 F.2d at 938.

165. See *id.* at 938.

166. *Id.*

167. See 5 U.S.C. § 552b(c)(7):

> [I]nvestigatory records compiled for law enforcement purposes, or information which if written would be contained in such records, but only to the extent that the production of such records or information would (A) interfere with enforcement proceedings, (B) deprive a person of a right to a fair trial or an impartial adjudication, (C) constitute an unwarranted invasion of personal privacy, (D) disclose the identity of a confidential source and, in the case of a record compiled by a criminal law enforcement authority in the course of a criminal investigation, or by an agency conducting lawful national security intelligence investigation,

emption 7, the so-called law enforcement exemption.[168] It is designed to protect from untimely disclosure in an agency meeting open to the public information that would jeopardize criminal or civil investigations or cause harm to individuals who aid law enforcement.

§ 9-5(a)(8)(H). Exemption 8: Financial Institutions.

The eighth exemption to the Sunshine Act[169] is patterned after FOIA Exemption 8.[170] The exemption seeks to prevent the undermining of public confidence in individual financial institutions or the federal banking system by the disclosure of sensitive financial information at public meetings of relevant agencies.[171]

§ 9-5(a)(8)(I). Exemption 9: Premature Disclosure of Information.

The ninth exemption to the Sunshine Act[172] is divided into two subparts. Exemption 9(A) applies to premature disclosures by agencies that regulate currencies, securities, commodities, or financial institutions, where the disclosure would be likely to (i) lead to "significant financial speculation," or (ii) "significantly endanger the financial stability of any financial institution."[173] Exemption 9(B) may be invoked by any agency covered by the Sunshine Act. It authorizes the agency to close a meeting or portion of a meeting where the disclosure of information to be discussed is likely to "significantly frustrate implementation

---

confidential information furnished only by the confidential source, (E) disclose investigative techniques and procedures, or (F) endanger the life or physical safety of law enforcement personnel.

168. See Chap. 10-2(c)(8) *infra*.
169. See 5 U.S.C. § 552b(c)(8) ("information contained in or related to examination, operating, or condition reports prepared by, on behalf of, or for the use of an agency responsible for the regulation or supervision of financial institutions").
170. See Chap. 10-2(c)(9) *infra*.
171. Exemption 8 has also been held to protect from disclosure certain information concerning securities. See Mermelstein v. SEC, 629 F. Supp. 672, 674 (D.D.C. 1986).
172. See 5 U.S.C. § 552b(c)(9):

[I]nformation the premature disclosure of which would — (A) in the case of an agency which regulates currencies, securities, commodities, or financial institutions, be likely to (i) lead to significant financial speculation in currencies, securities, or commodities, or (ii) significantly endanger the stability of any financial institution; or (B) in the case of any agency, be likely to significantly frustrate implementation of a proposed agency action, except that subparagraph (B) shall not apply in any instance where the agency has already disclosed to the public the content or nature of its proposed action, or where the agency is required by law to make such disclosure on its own initiative prior to taking final agency action on such proposal.

173. *Id.* § 552b(c)(9)(A).

of a proposed agency action."[174] Courts have interpreted this exemption to apply only to those discussions that "would permit either financial gain at government expense or circumvention of agency regulation."[175] The exemption does not apply where the agency has already intentionally disclosed to the public the content or nature of its proposed action.[176]

§ 9-5(a)(8)(J). Exemption 10: Agency Participation in Civil Actions or Proceedings.

Exemption 10 to the Sunshine Act[177] also has no counterpart under FOIA. It applies to information regarding an agency's issuance of subpoenas or its participation in a civil action or proceeding,[178] policy discussions that are incidental to a determination of litigation strategy,[179] discussions concerning

---

174. *Id.* § 552b(c)(9)(B). Courts have found this exemption "difficult to interpret and, perhaps, more perplexing to apply" because of the deliberate exclusion from the Sunshine Act of an exemption for predecisional deliberations, and the potential for Exemption 9(B), if not narrowly construed, to be misused as an equivalent to Exemption 5 of FOIA. See Wilkinson v. Legal Servs. Corp., 865 F. Supp. 891, 895 (D.D.C. 1994), *rev'd on other grounds*, 80 F.3d 535 (D.C. Cir.), *cert. denied*, 519 U.S. 927 (1996). See generally O'Reilly & Berg, *Stealth Caused by Sunshine: How Sunshine Act Interpretation Results in Less Information for the Public About the Decision Making Process of the International Trade Commission*, 36 HARV. INT'L L.J. 425 (1995).

175. Common Cause v. NRC, 674 F.2d at 934. See O'REILLY, *supra* note 83, at § 23.07 ("Frustration of proposed action occurs when persons to be subject to the action can avoid or evade it, and courts will probably defer to agency claims of potential frustration when agencies are operating in their sphere of delegated expertise").

176. See Common Cause v. NRC, 674 F.2d at 936. An unauthorized "leak" of information, however, would not necessarily render Exemption 9(B) inapplicable. See S. CONF. REP. NO. 94-1178 at 15, *reprinted in* 1976 U.S.C.C.A.N. 2250-51, *Sunshine Source Book* at 797. Providing information to an advisory committee will generally not be considered a disclosure to the public, despite the fact that advisory committees necessarily include at least one public member, thereby allowing an agency both to claim Exemption 9(b) and utilize an advisory committee. See Marblestone, *The Relationship Between the Government in the Sunshine Act and the Federal Advisory Committee Act*, 36 FED. B.J. 65, 75 (1977).

177. See 5 U.S.C. § 552b(c)(10) ("specifically concern the agency's issuance of a subpoena, or the agency's participation in a civil action or proceeding, an action in a foreign court or international tribunal, or an arbitration, or the initiation, conduct, or disposition by the agency of a particular case of formal agency adjudication pursuant to the procedures in section 554 of this title or otherwise involving a determination on the record after the opportunity for a hearing").

178. It has been argued that the inclusion of the term "otherwise" in this exemption is an invitation for flexibility in its application beyond adjudication to hybrid proceedings that include both elements of rulemaking and adjudication. See O'Reilly & Berg, *supra* note 174, at 440-41.

179. See Clark-Cowlitz Joint Operating Agency v. FERC, 798 F.2d 499, 503 (D.C. Cir. 1986). Transcripts and minutes of meetings in which litigation strategy has been discussed may be withheld even though the litigation has ended. See *id.* at 503.

whether to initiate or participate in adjudicatory proceedings,[180] and to any meetings that are the subject of, or subject to, formal agency adjudication, even though they may be outside the formal adjudicatory process.[181]

§ 9-5(a)(9). Challenges to Closed Meetings.

§ 9-5(a)(9)(A). Challenges Prior to Commencement of the Meeting.

When an agency provides the requisite statutory notice of its intention to hold a closed meeting, suit may be instituted in federal district court by any person to enjoin the closure.[182] The complaint must allege that the agency intends to close the meeting.[183] The burden of proof is on the agency to show that closing the meeting would be proper.[184] Courts employ a foreseeability standard such that the agency must demonstrate that it is "more likely than not that exempt matters would be discussed at the closed portion or portions of the meeting."[185] Reason-

---

180. See, e.g., Wilkinson v. Legal Servs. Corp., 865 F. Supp. 891 (D.D.C. 1994), *rev'd on other grounds*, 80 F.3d 535 (D.C. Cir.), *cert. denied*, 519 U.S. 927 (1996); A.G. Becker, Inc. v. Board of Governors, 502 F. Supp. 378 (D.D.C. 1980).

181. See, e.g., Shurberg Broadcasting of Hartford, Inc. v. FCC, 617 F. Supp. 825, 830 (D.D.C. 1985); Philadelphia Newspapers, Inc. v. NRC, 727 F.2d 1195, 1199-1202 (D.C. Cir. 1984). It has been held that Congress' intent "was that when a statute required an agency to act as would a court, its deliberations should be protected from disclosure as a court's would be." Time, Inc. v. United States Postal Serv., 667 F.2d 329, 334 (2d Cir. 1981). Utilizing this rationale, one court held that the FTC, when deciding whether a specific corporation had engaged in deceptive trade practices, could rely on Exemption 10 to deny public access to the meeting. See Amrep Corp. v. FTC, 768 F.2d 1171, 1179 (10th Cir. 1985), *cert. denied*, 475 U.S. 1034 (1986).

182. See 5 U.S.C. § 552b(h)(1):

> This district court of the United States shall have jurisdiction to enforce the requirements of subsections (b) through (f) of this section by declaratory judgment, injunctive relief or other relief as may be appropriate. Such action may be brought by any person against an agency prior to, or within sixty days after, the meeting of which the violation of this section arises.

Venue is limited to the district in which the meeting was or is to be held, where the agency is headquartered or in the District of Columbia "to prevent 'duplicative lawsuits spread across the country covering the same agency meeting or meetings.'" Johnson v. NRC, 766 F.2d 1182, 1188 (7th Cir. 1985) (citation omitted).

183. See Johnston v. NRC, 766 F.2d at 1188; O'REILLY, *supra* note 83, at § 23.04 (to establish a prima facie case, the plaintiff need only show that she made a request to attend, the agency announced its intent to close the meeting, and that the agency meeting is subject to the Act). Though the Act itself is silent as to the prima facie elements of such challenges, its legislative intent appears to favor an exhaustion of remedies in the form of informal communications between the requestor or her attorney and the agency before bringing suit. *Id.* § 23.04 n.61 (citing to S. CONF. REP. NO. 94-1178, at 22 (1975)).

184. See 5 U.S.C. § 552b(h)(1) ("The burden is on the defendant to sustain his action."). See also Common Cause v. NRC, 674 F.2d at 929 ("Once a person has challenged an agency's decision to close a meeting, the agency bears the burden of proof.").

185. Common Cause v. NRC, 674 F.2d at 929 n.19.

able attorneys fees and other litigation costs may be awarded to a prevailing plaintiff challenging the closure of a meeting.[186]

§ 9-5(a)(9)(B). Post-Meeting Challenges.

Any person may file suit against an agency for equitable relief pursuant to the Sunshine Act within sixty days after a closed meeting has been held.[187] "The agency bears the burden of proof in defense of the closure and must reply to the Complaint in an expedited matter."[188] In a post-meeting case, the court must base its decision on the discussions that actually occurred.[189]

Equitable relief may include an injunction against future violations and an order that the agency make available to the public transcripts, recordings, or minutes of the relevant meeting.[190] Attorneys fees and other litigation costs reasonably incurred may be awarded to the plaintiff if she "substantially prevails."[191] Such fees and costs are available to the defendant only on a showing that the action was brought for "frivolous or dilatory purposes."[192]

§ 9-5(b). Federal Advisory Committee Act.

§ 9-5(b)(1). Introduction.

The federal government has relied on the assistance of advisory committees since its inception.[193] Business leaders, academics, scientists, and citizens of all types have assisted government planning and programs. In 1972, in response to a growing concern about the creation of a "shadow government" made up of an ever-increasing number of advisory committees that were unaccountable to the public, Congress enacted the Federal Advisory Committee Act ("FACA").[194]

---

186. 5 U.S.C. § 552b(i). See Chap. 9-5(a)(9)(B) *infra*; Sisk, *A Primer on Awards of Attorney's Fees Against the Federal Government*, 25 ARIZ. ST. L.J. 733, 776 (1993).

187. Such actions must be instituted within 60 days after the meeting "except that if public announcement of such meeting is not initially provided by the agency in accordance with the requirement of this section, such action may be instituted pursuant to the section at any time prior to sixty days after any public announcement of such meeting." 5 U.S.C. § 552b(h)(1).

188. *Id.* § 552b(h)(1).

189. See Common Cause v. NRC, 674 F.2d at 929 n.19.

190. See 5 U.S.C. § 552b(h)(1).

191. *Id.* § 552b(h)(2)(i). See generally Sisk, *supra* note 186, at 776.

192. *Id.* § 552b(h)(2)(i). It has been argued that the inclusion of an attorneys fee provision leads to frivolous litigation concerning the Sunshine Act and is more burdensome than beneficial. See O'REILLY, *supra* note 83, at § 23.04.

193. See Markham, *The Federal Advisory Committee Act*, 35 U. PITT. L. REV. 557, 557 (1974); Cardozo, *The Federal Advisory Committee Act in Operation*, 33 ADMIN. L. REV. 1, 1-2 (1981).

194. See Pub. L. No. 92-463, 86 Stat. 770 (1972); 5 U.S.C. App. II §§ 1-15. The Act became effective January 4, 1973. 5 U.S.C. App. II § 15. See generally CONGRESSIONAL RESEARCH SERVICE, 95th Cong., 2d Sess., FEDERAL ADVISORY COMMITTEE ACT: SOURCE BOOK: LEGISLATIVE HISTORY, TEXTS, AND OTHER DOCUMENTS (Comm. Print 1978) [hereinafter "*FACA Source Book*"].

By enacting FACA, Congress acknowledged that these groups "are frequently a useful and beneficial means of furnishing expert advice, ideas, and diverse opinions" to executive agencies.[195] It recognized, however, that it is necessary to control their creation, operation, and accountability.[196] "The lack of public scrutiny of the activities of advisory committees was found to pose the danger that subjective influences not in the public interest could be exerted on the federal decision-makers."[197]

§ 9-5(b)(2). Definition of "Advisory Committee."

What constitutes an advisory committee is not fully explained by the statute.[198] An advisory committee is subject to FACA if it has been "established" by

---

The General Services Administration is responsible for promulgating regulations governing advisory committees subject to FACA. See 41 C.F.R. §§ 101-6.1001 to 101-6.1035. See generally Chap. 9-5(b) *supra*.

195. 5 U.S.C. App. II § 2(a).
196. In enacting FACA, Congress declared that:

(1) the need for many existing advisory committees has not been adequately reviewed;
(2) new advisory committees should be established only when they are determined to be essential and their number should be kept to the minimum necessary;
(3) advisory committees should be terminated when they are no longer carrying out the purposes for which they were established;
(4) standards and uniform procedures should govern the establishment, operation, administration, and duration of advisory committees;
(5) the Congress and the public should be kept informed with respect to the number, purpose, membership, activities, and cost of advisory committees; and
(6) the function of advisory committees should be advisory only, and all matters under their consideration should be determined, in accordance with law, by the official, agency, or officer involved.

5 U.S.C. App. II § 2(b). See Public Citizen v. Department of Justice, 491 U.S. 440, 459 (1989) ("FACA's principal purpose was to enhance the public accountability of advisory committees established by the Executive Branch and to reduce wasteful expenditures on them."); National Anti-Hunger Coalition v. Executive Comm. of President's Private Sector Survey on Cost Control, 711 F.2d 1071, 1072 (D.C. Cir. 1983) (purpose of FACA to "control the advisory committee process and to open to public scrutiny the manner in which government agencies obtain advice from private individuals"). See generally Bybee, *Advising the President: Separation of Powers and the Federal Advisory Committee Act*, 104 YALE L.J. 51 (1994).

197. S. REP. NO. 92-1098, at 6 (1972).
198. See Animal Legal Defense Fund, Inc. v. Shalala, 104 F.3d 424 (D.C. Cir.), *cert. denied*, 522 U.S. 949 (1997); Aluminum Co. of Am. v. National Marine Fisheries Serv., 92 F.3d 902 (9th Cir. 1996). Although FACA requires that advisory committee membership be "fairly balanced," 5 U.S.C. App. II § 5(b)(2), it has been suggested that this provision is not justiciable. See Sanchez v. Pena, 17 F. Supp. 2d 1235, 1238 (D.N.M. 1998). Accord Public Citizen v. National Advisory Comm. on Microbiological Criteria for Foods, 886 F.2d 419, 426-30 (D.C. Cir. 1989) (Silberman, J., concurring). See generally Croley, *Practical Guidance on the Applicability of the Federal Advisory Committee Act*, 10 ADMIN. L.J. AM. U. 111 (1996); Comment, *The Federal Advisory*

statute, the President, or an agency, or "utilized" by the President or one or more agencies to obtain advice or recommendations.[199] Much of the litigation regarding FACA has focused on whether a particular group was "established" or "utilized" within the meaning of the Act.

Under FACA, an advisory committee can be "established" only by an agency, a statute, or the President.[200] To be established by an agency, a committee must be "formed" by the agency,[201] after the head of that agency has made a formal determination that the advisory committee is "essential to the conduct of agency business" and "in the public interest."[202] To be established by statute, an advisory committee must be a direct creation of Congress,[203] which directs or authorizes its establishment.[204] "The term 'established' does not include committees which merely can be said to owe their existence to legislation. A measure of more direct congressional creation must be shown before a committee is found to have been 'established by statute' for purposes of the F.A.C.A."[205] To be established by the President, an advisory committee must be created by an Executive

---

Committee Act: Balanced Representation and Open Meetings in Conflict with Dispute Resolution, 11 OHIO ST. J. ON DISP. RESOL. 489 (1996).

199. 5 U.S.C. § 3(2). The term "advisory committee" is defined under FACA as:

> any committee, board, commission, council, conference, panel, task force, or other similar group, or any subcommittees or other subgroup thereof . . . which is —
>
> (A) established by statute or reorganization plan, or
> (B) established or utilized by the President, or
> (C) established or utilized by one or more agencies, in the interest of obtaining advice or recommendations for the President or one or more agencies or officers of the Federal Government . . . .

200. See 5 U.S.C. App. II §§ 3(2) & 9(a). See Washington Legal Found. v. United States Sentencing Comm'n, 21 MEDIA L. REP. (BNA) 2110 (D.D.C. 1993) (U.S. Sentencing Commission's advisory group on environmental sanctions held not subject to FACA because Commission not an agency).

201. California Forestry Ass'n v. United States Forest Serv., 102 F.3d 609 (D.C. Cir. 1996) (steering committee and research panel established by Forest Service to advise it on California spotted owl held subject to FACA even though its study was also submitted to Congress); Food Chem. News, Inc. v. Young, 900 F.2d 328, 332 (D.C. Cir.), *cert. denied*, 498 U.S. 846 (1990); 41 C.F.R. § 101-6.1005(d).

202. 41 C.F.R. § 101-6.1002(a). See *id.* § 101-6.1015(a)(1). The head of the agency must also publish a timely notice in the Federal Register, *id.* § 101-6.1015(a), file the committee's charter with Congress, the Library of Congress, and the General Services Administration, *id.* § 101-6.1013(a), and follow the numerous additional requirements set forth in 41 C.F.R. § 101-6.1009.

203. See Lombardo v. Handler, 397 F. Supp. 792, 796 (D.D.C. 1975), *aff'd*, 546 F.2d 1043 (D.C. Cir. 1976), *cert. denied*, 431 U.S. 932 (1977).

204. See 41 C.F.R. § 101-6.1015(a) & (b). Once created, the charter of the advisory committee is to be filed in the same manner as a committee established by an agency. See *id.* § 101-6.1013(a) & (b).

205. Lombardo v. Handler, 397 F. Supp. at 796.

Order.[206] The appointed chairperson of the advisory committee is responsible for ensuring that the committee complies with FACA's procedural requirements.[207]

Under FACA, an advisory committee that has not been established by an agency, Congress, or the President is subject to the Act if it is "utilized" by the President or one or more agencies.[208] The implementing regulations define an advisory committee as "utilized" when it is adopted "as a preferred source from which to obtain advice or recommendations on a specific issue or policy . . . in the same manner as . . . from an established advisory committee."[209] To come within the "utilized" advisory committee category, the committee must be primarily advisory in nature[210] and the advice provided must concern an identified governmental policy.[211]

---

206. See 41 C.F.R. § 101-6.1005.
207. *Id.* §§ 101-6.1011, 101-6.1013(c).
208. 5 U.S.C. App. II § 3(2).
209. 41 C.F.R. § 101-6.1003. See People for Ethical Treatment of Animals, Inc. v. Barshefsky, 925 F. Supp. 844, 848-49 (D.D.C. 1996) (working group composed of experts from various countries seeking to develop international humane trapping standards not subject to FACA as it is not managed or controlled by the United States Trade Representative); Huron Envtl. Activist League v. EPA, 917 F. Supp. 34, 40-41 (D.D.C. 1996) (group of cement industry representatives that submitted proposal for regulation of cement kiln dust not federal advisory committee because it was not established at prompting of EPA, nor was it utilized by EPA, which lacked management control over group).
210. See Judicial Watch, Inc. v. Clinton, 76 F.3d 1232, 1233 (D.C. Cir. 1996) (main purpose of Presidential Legal Expense Trust Fund was the collecting and managing of funds, and it was not primarily advisory in nature); Public Citizen v. Committee on the Bicentennial of the U.S. Const., 622 F. Supp. 753, 758 (D.D.C. 1985) (Commission's duties were primarily operational, therefore not utilized as an advisory committee).
211. See Judicial Watch, Inc. v. Clinton, 76 F.3d at 1234 ("The term 'policy' implies choice; advice on an identified government policy is necessarily advice which favors one of alternative positions or courses of action. The function of a group giving such advice is thus to aid the decision makers in choosing the direction of government behavior."); Sofamor Danek Group, Inc. v. Gaus, 61 F.3d 929, 934 (D.C. Cir. 1995), *cert. denied*, 516 U.S. 1112 (1996) (panel of experts and consumers convened to develop clinical practice guideline on treatment of lower back pain created to provide advice to private health care practitioners, not federal government); Food Chem. News, Inc. v. Young, 900 F.2d 328, 332 (D.C. Cir.), *cert. denied*, 498 U.S. 846 (1990) (group of experts assembled by private contractor not an advisory committee where panel established and utilized by organization, not FDA); National Nutritional Foods Ass'n v. Califano, 603 F.2d 327, 336 (2d Cir. 1979) (group providing advice on how to regulate substance is utilized as advisory committee); Nader v. Baroody, 396 F. Supp. 1231 (D.D.C. 1975) (constituent and interest groups meeting at White House not utilized as advisory committees where meetings were random in nature, informal, and not conducted for obtaining advice on specific subjects indicated in advance); Food Chem. News, Inc. v. Davis, 378 F. Supp. 1048 (D.D.C. 1974) (agency's informal meetings with consumer and distilled spirits industry representative in connection with drafting proposed ingredient labeling restrictions subject to FACA); Chung, *Federal Advisory Committee Act*, 65 GEO. WASH. L. REV. 786 (1997).

In *Public Citizen v. Department of Justice*,[212] the Supreme Court was asked to determine whether the American Bar Association's Standing Committee on the Federal Judiciary was "utilized" as an advisory committee when it evaluated nominees for federal judgeships. The Court found the term "utilize" a "wooly verb" that should not be given the "almost unfettered breadth of a dictionary reading."[213] In the Court's view, "although its reach is extensive, we cannot believe that it was intended to cover every formal and informal consultation between the President or an Executive agency and a group rendering advice."[214]

Accordingly, the Court found that the regulatory definition of a "utilized" advisory committee "appears too sweeping to be read without qualification."[215] As a result, the Court analyzed how the Committee was formed and held that the term "utilized" advisory committee encompassed "groups formed indirectly by quasi-public organizations . . . 'for' public agencies as well as 'by' such agencies themselves."[216] The Court determined that the Committee did not fall within the term "utilized" advisory committee.[217] Subsequent decisions concerning FACA have continued to invoke this more stringent standard.[218]

FACA expressly exempts from the Act the Advisory Commission on Intergovernmental Relations, the Commission on Government Procurement, and "any committee which is composed wholly of full-time officers or employees of the Federal Government."[219] FACA regulations also identify a number of advisory

---

212. 491 U.S. 440 (1989).
213. *Id.* at 453.
214. *Id.*
215. *Id.* at 463 n.12.
216. *Id.* at 462. See Food Chem. News, Inc. v. Young, 900 F.2d 328, 332 (D.C. Cir.), *cert. denied*, 498 U.S. 846 (1990) (FACA limited to groups organized by or closely tied to federal government, enjoying quasi-public status).
217. Public Citizen v. Department of Justice, 491 U.S. at 453; see *id.* at 460 ("There is no indication . . . that a purely private group like the ABA Committee that was not formed by the Executive, accepted no public funds, and assisted the Executive in performing a constitutionally specified task committed to the Executive was . . . the type of advisory entity that legislation was urgently needed to address.").
218. See, e.g., American Soc'y of Dermatology v. Shalala, 962 F. Supp. 144, 147 (D.C. Cir. 1996), *aff'd*, 116 F.3d 941 (1997) (American Medical Association committees recommending revision of Medicare fee schedule were not utilized by agency that did not have actual management or control of the committees); Animal Legal Defense Fund v. Shalala, 104 F.3d 424 (D.C. Cir.), *cert. denied*, 522 U.S. 949 (1997); Washington Legal Found. v. United States Sentencing Comm'n, 17 F.3d 1446, 1450 (D.C. Cir. 1994) ("utilized . . . is a stringent standard, denoting something along the lines of actual management or control of the advisory committee").
219. 5 U.S.C. App. II § 3(2)(C)(i)-(iii). See Association of Am. Physicians & Surgeons v. Clinton, 997 F.2d 898, 905 (D.C. Cir. 1993) (President's spouse is a de facto officer or employee of federal government, such that President's Task Force on National Health Care Reform, made up of several cabinet members and presidential advisors, and chaired by Hillary Rodham Clinton, was exempted from FACA); Abrams, *The First Lady: Federal Employee or Citizen-Representative Under FACA?*, 62 GEO. WASH. L. REV. 855 (1994).

meetings or groups not covered by the Act.[220] Also exempt are advisory committees established by an Act of Congress that Congress has specifically excepted from FACA,[221] and any advisory committee established or utilized by the Central Intelligence Agency or the Federal Reserve System.[222]

§ 9-5(b)(3). Meetings.

In addition to public access to advisory committee records,[223] FACA mandates public access to the meetings of federally created advisory committees. Access to meetings under the Act is designed to ensure effective scrutiny of the work of advisory committees in an effort to safeguard the public interest.[224] Congress rejected the argument that opening the meetings of advisory committees to the public would inhibit debate and the frank expression of views.[225]

§ 9-5(b)(4). Notice of Meetings.

Each meeting of an advisory committee "shall be open to the public,"[226] unless it is closed in accordance with the exemptions set forth in the Sunshine Act.[227] An officer or employee of the federal government must be designated to chair or attend each advisory committee meeting.[228] This official must approve the agenda and no meeting may be held without that person's advance approval.[229] FACA regulations require that notice of advisory committee meetings

---

220. See 41 C.F.R. § 101-6.1004.
221. See 5 U.S.C. App. II § 4(a).
222. See *id.* § 4(b).
223. See Chap. 10-3 *infra*.
224. See H.R. REP. NO. 92-1017 (1972); Nader v. Dunlop, 370 F. Supp. 177, 178 (D.D.C. 1973).
225. Gates v. Schlesinger, 366 F. Supp. 797, 799-80 (D.D.C. 1973) ("Argument that public participation and disclosure would inhibit debate and the frank expression of views was heard and rejected by Congress."). See Vandegrift & Rosenblat, *The Federal Advisory Committee Act: Its Impact on Informal Contacts with the Staffs of Administrative Agencies*, 41 BUS. LAW. 1281 (1986); Lynch, *The Federal Advisory Committee Act: An Obstacle to Ecosystem Management*, 71 WASH. L. REV. 431 (1996). But see Association of Am. Physicians & Surgeons v. Clinton, 997 F.2d 898, 909 (D.C. Cir. 1993) (application of FACA to Task Force that reports directly to the President might represent an unconstitutional intrusion on the presidential communications privilege).
226. See 5 U.S.C. App. II § 10(a)(1).
227. *Id.* § 10(d). See Chap. 9-5(a)(8) *supra*; Marblestone, *The Relationship Between the Government in the Sunshine Act and the Federal Advisory Committee Act*, 36 FED. B. J. 65 (1977).
228. See 5 U.S.C. App. II § 10(e).
229. See *id.* § 10(f). An advisory committee cannot be compelled to convene a meeting in derogation of this provision. See Dabney v. Reagan, 559 F. Supp. 861, 865 (S.D.N.Y. 1982). An agency official has no duty to adjourn a meeting of an advisory committee to prevent unauthorized committee actions. See Claybrook v. Slater, 111 F.3d 904 (D.C. Cir. 1997).

be published in the Federal Register fifteen days prior to the meeting.[230] In exceptional circumstances, less than fifteen days notice may be provided, so long as the reasons for doing so are set forth in the Federal Register.[231]

§ 9-5(b)(5). Procedures to Close Meetings.

Each advisory committee meeting must be open to the public except when the President, or the head of the agency to which the advisory committee reports, determines that the meeting or a portion of it should be closed pursuant to one of the enumerated exemptions under the Sunshine Act.[232] To close all or part of a meeting, the advisory committee must submit a request to the agency head or, in the case of an independent presidential advisory committee, to the administrator, setting forth the specific Sunshine Act exemption that justifies closure.[233] The request must be submitted in sufficient time to enable the agency head or administrator to make a determination prior to publication of the notice of meeting.[234] If the agency head or administrator agrees that the request is consistent with the provisions of the Sunshine Act and FACA,[235] that determination must be in writing and set forth the specific reasons for closure.[236] A copy of that

---

230. See 41 C.F.R. § 101-6.1015(b)(1). Notice must include the name of the advisory committee; the time, date, place, and purpose of the meeting; a summary of the agenda; and a statement as to whether all or part of the meeting will be closed. *Id.* The President has authority to dispense with notification of a meeting for reasons of national security. See 5 U.S.C. App. II § 10(a)(2).

231. See 41 C.F.R. § 101-6.1015(b)(2).

232. See 5 U.S.C. App. II § 10(d). Prior to the passage of the Sunshine Act, FACA incorporated the FOIA exemptions. See Pub. L. 92-463, 86 Stat. 775, § 10(d) (1972). During this period, advisory committees would typically assert the deliberative process privilege (FOIA Exemption 5, 5 U.S.C. § 552(b)(5)), as a basis to close meetings. See, e.g., Nader v. Dunlop, 370 F. Supp. 177 (D.D.C. 1973); Gates v. Schlesinger, 366 F. Supp. 797 (D.D.C. 1973); Aviation Consumer Action Project v. Washburn, 535 F.2d 101 (D.C. Cir. 1976). When Congress passed the Sunshine Act, it amended FACA to incorporate the Sunshine Act exemptions, which do not include the deliberative process privilege. 5 U.S.C. § 552b, Pub. L. 94-409, 90 Stat. 1247, § 5(c) (1976). As a result, advisory committees can no longer rely on that privilege to close meetings to the public. See Public Citizen v. Barshefsky, 939 F. Supp. 31 (D.C. Cir. 1996) (United States Trade Representative's authority to close advisory committee meetings to public based on Trade Act rather than the Sunshine Act); S. CONF. REP. NO. 94-1178, at 26 (1976), *reprinted in* 1976 U.S.C.C.A.N. 2183, 2262, *Sunshine Source Book* at 808; Note, *Do You Feel the Sunshine? Government in the Sunshine Act: Its Objectives, Goals, and Effect on the FCC and You*, 49 FED. COMM. L.J. 473 (1997).

233. See 41 C.F.R. § 101-6.1023(a).

234. *Id.*

235. *Id.* § 101-6.1023(c).

236. See 5 U.S.C. App. II § 10(d); 41 C.F.R. § 101-6.1023(d). The reasons must be specific. See, e.g., Nader v. Dunlop, 370 F. Supp. 177 (D.D.C. 1973) (successful challenge to closure of meetings of advisory committee to Cost of Living Council where conclusory rather than specific reasons were offered to support closing meetings).

determination must be made available to the public upon request.[237] The agency has the burden of proof as to whether an exemption is properly asserted.[238]

§ 9-5(b)(6). Public Access to Meetings.

FACA provides that "[i]nterested persons shall be permitted to attend, appear before, or file statements with any advisory committee, subject to . . . reasonable rules or regulations."[239] Pursuant to regulations promulgated to implement FACA, the agency head or chairperson of the advisory committee must ensure that the meeting is held at a reasonable time and place reasonably accessible to the public; the meeting room size is sufficient to accommodate advisory committee members, staff, and interested members of the public; any member of the public desiring to do so is permitted to file a written statement with the advisory committee; and any member of the public may speak at the advisory committee meeting if the agency's guidelines permit.[240] Although FACA's statutory language specifically contemplates that an interested person may "appear before" an advisory committee,[241] and Congress rejected the argument that public participation would compromise the advisory process,[242] one court has interpreted the Act to preclude public participation at advisory committee meetings.[243]

§ 9-5(b)(7). Challenges to Closed Meetings.

Unlike the Sunshine Act, FACA does not explicitly provide for a cause of action to remedy a violation of the statute.[244] Courts, however, have recognized a private right of action under FACA.[245] Any person, according to those courts recognizing a private right of action, has standing to challenge the denial of

---

237. See 41 C.F.R. § 101-6.1023(d). Each advisory committee must issue an annual report that provides a summary of its activities, including any closure of its meetings, and that informs the public of the actions it has taken. See 5 U.S.C. App. II § 10(d).

238. See Public Citizen v. National Econ. Comm., 703 F. Supp. 113, 117, 119 (D.D.C. 1989); Nader v. Dunlop, 370 F. Supp. at 177, 179; Gates v. Schlesinger, 366 F. Supp. at 799.

239. 5 U.S.C. App. II § 10(a)(3).

240. See 41 C.F.R. § 101-6.1021.

241. 5 U.S.C. § 10(a)(3).

242. See H.R. REP. NO. 92-1017 (1972); Nader v. Dunlop, 370 F. Supp. at 178.

243. See Gates v. Schlesinger, 366 F. Supp. at 801 (meeting of Defense Advisory Committee on Women in the Services was required to be open; plaintiffs could observe but could not participate; "[p]laintiffs have not pointed out, however, any statutory language creating a right of public participation in advisory committees, and the Court can find none").

244. See Natural Resources Defense Council v. Pena, 147 F.3d 1012 (D.C. Cir. 1998).

245. See Washington Legal Found. v. American Bar Ass'n, 648 F. Supp. 1353, 1361 (D.D.C. 1986).

access to advisory committee meetings.[246] The agency to whom the advisory committee reports may be sued if the committee violates the Act.[247] Plaintiffs may seek declaratory and injunctive relief,[248] as well as reasonable attorneys fees and costs.[249]

§ 9-6. Statutory Access to Meetings of State and Local Government.

§ 9-6(a). Introduction.

Like their federal counterparts, state open meetings laws permit the public to view its government at work.[250] These laws generally require governmental meetings to be open to the public unless designated subject matter permits the governmental body to meet in an executive session from which the public is excluded.[251] Through these statutes, members of the public are afforded an opportunity to observe the operations of state and local governments, as well as to participate in their governance.[252] In addition, such legislation has provided

---

246. See Public Citizen v. Department of Justice, 491 U.S. 440, 450-51 (1989); HLI Lordship Indus. v. Committee for Purchase from the Blind & Other Severely Handicapped, 615 F. Supp. 970 (E.D. Va. 1985), *rev'd on other grounds*, 791 F.2d 1136 (4th Cir. 1986); National Anti-Hunger Coalition v. Executive Comm. of President's Private Sector Survey on Cost Control, 557 F. Supp. 524 (D.D.C.), *aff'd*, 711 F.2d 1071 (D.C. Cir. 1983); Center for Auto Safety v. Tiemann, 414 F. Supp. 215 (D.D.C. 1976), *remanded on other grounds*, 580 F.2d 689 (D.C. Cir. 1978). But see Mulqueeny v. National Comm'n on the Observance of Int'l Women's Year, 549 F.2d 1115 (7th Cir. 1975).

247. See Public Citizen v. Department of Justice, 491 U.S. 440 (1989). A private entity that is not established, appointed, or financed by the government may not be sued for violation of FACA. See Washington Legal Found. v. American Bar Ass'n, 648 F. Supp. 1353, 1361 (D.D.C. 1986).

248. See, e.g., Natural Resources Defense Council v. Pena, 147 F.3d 1012 (D.C. Cir. 1998); California Forestry Ass'n v. U.S. Forest Serv., 102 F.3d 609 (D.C. Cir. 1996); National Anti-Hunger Coalition v. President's Private Sector Survey on Cost Control, 566 F. Supp. at 1516-17; Public Citizen v. National Econ. Comm., 703 F. Supp. at 120.

249. FACA does not explicitly provide for attorneys fees or costs. Fees may, however, be recoverable under the Equal Access to Justice Act. See 28 U.S.C. § 2412(d). See also Association of Am. Physicians & Surgeons, Inc. v. Clinton, 989 F. Supp. 8 (D.D.C. 1997).

250. All 50 states and the District of Columbia have adopted some form of open meetings law. See Deering, *supra* note 73, at 362-76 (1997-98); Davis, *Sunshine Laws and Judicial Discretion: A Proposal for Reform of State Sunshine Law Enforcement Provisions*, 28 URB. LAW. 41, 42 (1996); Pupillo, *The Changing Weather Forecast: Government in the Sunshine in the 1990's — An Analysis of State Sunshine Laws*, 71 WASH. U. L.Q. 1165 (1993).

251. See Chap. 9-6(h) *infra*.

252. "[Open governmental meetings] should be a marketplace of ideas, so that the governmental agency may have sufficient input from the citizens who are going to be affected by the subsequent action of the municipality." Palm Beach v. Gradison, 296 So. 2d 473, 475 (Fla. 1974). See Cohan v. City of Thousand Oaks, 35 Cal. Rptr. 2d 782, 786 (Ct. App. 1994) ("The [Open Meeting] Act thus serves to facilitate public participation in all phases of local government decisionmaking and to curb misuse of the democratic process by secret legislation of public bodies.").

journalists access to a great deal of information about state and local government.[253]

§ 9-6(b). Entities Subject to Open Meeting Laws.

State open meeting laws typically include all levels of governmental bodies within their scope, including state, regional, county, and local entities.[254] Although jurisdictions may vary as to the particular types of governmental entities that are subject to open meeting laws, most state statutes include agencies,[255] commissions,[256] boards,[257] committees,[258] and public educational

---

253. See Board of Trustees v. Cox Enters., 679 S.W.2d 86 (Tex. App. 1984), aff'd, 706 S.W.2d 956 (Tex. 1986) (legislature intended for Open Meetings Act to grant standing to news media without showing of special interest apart from that of general public). See generally A. SCHWING, OPEN MEETING LAWS (1994); REPORTERS COMMITTEE FOR FREEDOM OF THE PRESS, TAPPING OFFICIALS' SECRETS (1997).

254. Some statutes treat state-wide entities separately from local bodies. See, e.g., CAL. GOV'T CODE §§ 11120-11132 (state bodies); CAL. GOV'T CODE §§ 54950-54962 (local bodies); MASS. GEN. LAWS ch. 30A, § 11A-11A1/2 (state bodies); MASS. GEN. LAWS ch. 34, § 9F-9G (county bodies); MASS. GEN. LAWS ch. 39, § 23A-23B (local bodies); Pine v. McGreavy, 687 A.2d 1244 (R.I. 1997) (financial town meeting is not "public body" subject to Open Meetings Act).

255. See, e.g., ALASKA STAT. § 44.62.310(a); ARK. CODE ANN. § 25-19-103(2); COLO. REV. STAT. § 24-6-402(1)(d); FLA. STAT. § 286.0105; HAW. REV. STAT. § 92-2(1); IND. CODE § 5-14-1.5-2(a)(1); ME. REV. STAT. ANN. tit. 1, § 402(2)(B); MONT. CODE ANN. § 2-3-203(1); N.H. REV. STAT. ANN. § 91-A:1-a; N.M. STAT. ANN. § 10-15-1(B); N.D. CENT. CODE § 44-04-19; R.I. GEN. LAWS § 42-46-2(b); TEX. REV. CIV. STAT. ANN. art. 6252-17, § 1(c); VA. CODE ANN. § 2.1-341; WIS. STAT. § 19.82(1).

256. See, e.g., ARK. CODE ANN. § 25-19-103(2); CAL. GOV'T CODE § 11121; COLO. REV. STAT. § 24-6-402(1)(d); KAN. STAT. ANN. § 75-4318(a); OKLA. STAT. tit. 25, § 304(1); PA. STAT. ANN. tit. 65, § 273; S.D. CODIFIED LAWS § 1-25-1; WASH. REV. CODE § 42.30.020(1); Southwestern Bell Tel. Co. v. State Corp. Comm'n, 629 P.2d 1174, 1185 (Kan. App. 1981); Wisconsin v. Swanson, 284 N.W.2d 655 (Wis. 1979).

257. See, e.g., ARIZ. REV. STAT. § 38-431(5); CAL. GOV'T CODE §§ 11121, 54951, 54952; FLA. STAT. §§ 286.0105, 286.011(1); MINN. STAT. § 471.705.1; OHIO REV. CODE ANN. § 121.22(B)(1); R.I. GEN. LAWS § 42-46-2(b); VA. CODE ANN. § 2.1-341; International Longshoremen's & Warehousemen's Union v. Los Angeles Export Terminal, Inc., 81 Cal. Rptr. 2d 456, 461 (Ct. App. 1999) (board of directors of private corporation appointed to operate coal export facility is legislative body within meaning of open meeting law); Wolf v. Zoning Bd. of Adjustment, 192 A.2d 305, 308 (N.J. Super. 1963); Sanders v. Benton, 579 P.2d 815 (Okla. 1978) (board of correction); Independent State Store Union v. Pennsylvania Liquor Control Bd., 432 A.2d 1375 (Pa. 1981).

258. See, e.g., CAL. GOV'T CODE § 54952(b); HAW. REV. STAT. § 92-2(1) (any "committee of the State or its political subdivisions which is created by constitution, statute, rule, or executive order, to have supervision, control, jurisdiction or advisory power over specific matters and which is required to conduct meetings and take official action"); MASS. GEN. LAWS ch. 39, § 23A; LA. REV. STAT. ANN. tit. 42, § 4.2(A)(2); Herald Co. v. Bay City, 577 N.W.2d 696, 701 (Mich. App. 1998) (search committee for position of fire chief subject to open meeting law). There is no consensus as to whether advisory committees are subject to state open meeting laws. Some states have specifically included such committees, see, e.g., ARIZ. REV. STAT. § 38-431(4); CAL. GOV'T CODE § 11121.8; N.H. REV. STAT. ANN. § 91-A:1-a; Newspapers of New Hampshire, Inc. v. City of

institutions.[259] In some jurisdictions, only those bodies created by constitution, statute, ordinance, or executive order are subject to the open meeting law.[260] The open meeting laws of most states, however, are broadly inclusive.[261] For example, New Mexico's law governs "any public body except the legislature and the courts."[262] Other states more specifically address the various bodies subject to open meeting requirements.[263]

In states with open meeting laws that only vaguely define their scope, or in situations where the public body in question does not clearly fall within the statutory language, courts have identified several factors to be consulted in determining whether an open meeting law is applicable. Among the factors favoring an open meetings requirement are (1) whether the public body exercises traditional governmental powers,[264] (2) whether the public body has policymaking authority,[265] (3) whether public officials compose the public

---

Concord, 13 MEDIA L. REP. (BNA) 1685 (N.H. Super. 1986), while others have excluded them by applying their open meeting laws only to "governing" bodies, see Andrews v. Independent Sch. Dist. No. 29, 737 P.2d 929, 931 (Okla. 1987).

259. See, e.g., ALASKA STAT. § 44.62.310(a); CAL. EDUC. CODE § 92030; MICH. COMP. LAWS §§ 390.20, 390.645, 390.715; MO. ANN. STAT. § 610.010(2); OKLA. STAT. tit. 25, § 304(1); WASH. REV. CODE § 42.30.020(1); Regents of Univ. of California v. Superior Ct., 976 P.2d 808 (Cal. 1999); Marston v. Gainesville Sun Publ'g Co., 341 So. 2d 783, 784 (Fla. App. 1976); People ex rel. Byron v. Board of Trustees, 412 N.E.2d 1188 (Ill. App. 1980); A.S. Abell Publ'g Co. v. Board of Regents, 514 A.2d 25, 27 (Md. App. 1986); Knight Publ'g Co. v. University of South Carolina, 367 S.E.2d 20 (S.C. 1988). See Cleveland, *The Costs and Benefits of Openness: Sunshine Laws and Higher Education*, 12 J.C. & U.L. 127 (1985); Shurtz, *The University in the Sunshine: Application of the Open Meetings Laws in the University Setting*, 5 J.L. & EDUC. 453 (1976).

260. See, e.g., CAL. GOV'T CODE § 11121; IOWA CODE § 21.2(1)(a); KY. REV. STAT. ANN. § 61.805(2); MD. CODE ANN., STATE GOV'T § 10-502(h); MO. ANN. STAT. § 610.010(2); NEB. REV. STAT. § 84-1409(1); WASH. REV. CODE § 42030.020(1)(a); WIS. STAT. § 19.82(1).

261. See, e.g., ARIZ. REV. STAT. § 38-431(5); ARK. CODE ANN. § 25-19-103(2); CAL. GOV'T CODE § 11127; COLO. REV. STAT. § 24-6-402(1)(d); CONN. GEN. STAT. ANN. § 1-18a(a); 5 ILL. COMP. STAT. 120/1.02; N.H. REV. STAT. ANN. § 91-A:1-a; OHIO REV. CODE ANN. § 121.22(B)(1); OKLA. STAT. tit. 25, § 304(1); VA. CODE ANN. § 2.1-341.

262. N.M. STAT. ANN. § 10-15-1(A).

263. See, e.g., ALASKA STAT. § 44.62.310(a):

All meetings of a legislative body, of a board of regents, or of an administrative body, board, commission, committee, subcommittee, authority, council, agency, or other organization, including subordinate units of the above groups, of the state or any of its political subdivisions, including but not limited to municipalities, boroughs, school boards, and all other boards, agencies, assemblies, councils, departments, divisions, bureaus, commissions or organizations, advisory or otherwise, of the state or local government supported in whole or in part by public money or authorized to spend public money.

264. See Connelly v. School Comm. of Hanover, 565 N.E.2d 449, 451 n.8 (Mass. 1991); Ohio ex rel. Toledo Blade Co. v. Economic Opportunity Planning Ass'n, 582 N.E.2d 59, 65 (Ohio C.P. 1990).

265. See Sovereign v. Dunn, 498 N.W.2d 62, 67 (Minn. App. 1993).

body,[266] (4) whether a constitutional provision, statute, ordinance, or executive order formally created the public body,[267] (5) how long the public body has been or will be in existence,[268] (6) whether public funds support the public body,[269] and (7) whether another statute requires the public body to hold open meetings.[270]

Many open meeting laws exempt from their coverage judicial[271] and legislative[272] bodies, as well as political parties.[273] Private organizations are generally

---

266. See, e.g., CAL. GOV'T CODE § 54952(b); MO. REV. STAT. § 610.010(2); Spillis Candela & Partners, Inc. v. Centrust Sav. Bank, 535 So. 2d 694 (Fla. App. 1988); Godheim v. City of Tampa, 426 So. 2d 1084, 1088 (Fla. App. 1983); Daily Gazette Co. v. North Colonie Bd. of Educ., 412 N.Y.S.2d 494, 495 (App. Div. 1979); Sanders v. Benton, 579 P.2d 815 (Okla. 1978).

267. See Farron v. City of San Francisco, 265 Cal. Rptr. 317, 319 n.2 (Ct. App. 1989) (task force not subject to open meeting law because it had not been created by charter, ordinance, resolution, or similar formal action); Lexington Herald-Leader Co. v. University of Kentucky Presidential Search Comm., 732 S.W.2d 884 (Ky. 1987) (presidential search committee appointed by formal action of university board of trustees was public agency subject to open meetings law); Ristau v. Casey, 647 A.2d 642 (Pa. Commw. 1994) (judicial nominating commission not an agency subject to open meeting law because it was not created by statute).

268. See Goodson Todman Enters. v. Town Bd. of Milan, 542 N.Y.S.2d 373, 374 (App. Div. 1989) (meetings of committee created to advise town board about contemplated zoning ordinance changes not required to hold open meetings in part because "committee's members do not hold fixed terms"). See also N.H. Op. Att'y Gen. No. 86-134 (1986) (temporary committee of engineers created solely to negotiate contracts for one project is not required to hold open meetings).

269. See, e.g., ALASKA STAT. § 44.62.310(a); Kansas ex rel. Murray v. Palmgren, 646 P.2d 1091, 1100 (Kan.), *appeal dismissed*, 459 U.S. 1081 (1982); Carl v. Board of Regents, 577 P.2d 912 (Okla. 1978).

270. See ARIZ. REV. STAT. § 15-721F(2) ("all meetings of committees authorized for the purpose of textbook review and selection" are to be open as required in Arizona's open meeting laws); WIS. STAT. § 19.82(1) ("a non-profit corporation operating the Olympic ice training center" must hold open meetings pursuant to Wisconsin's open meeting laws).

271. See, e.g., ARIZ. REV. STAT. § 38-431.08(A)(1); CAL. GOV'T CODE § 11121(a); KY. REV. STAT. ANN. § 61.810(1)(j); LA. REV. STAT. ANN. § 42:6.1(B); MASS. GEN. LAWS ch. 30A, § 11A; NEV. REV. STAT. § 241.030(3)(a); N.J. STAT. ANN. § 10:4-8(a); N.M. STAT. ANN. § 10-15-1(A); N.Y. PUB. OFF. LAW § 108(1); R.I. GEN. LAWS § 42-46-5(c); VT. STAT. ANN. tit. 1, § 312(e); WASH. REV. CODE § 42.30.020(1)(a); Fathers Are Parents Too, Inc. v. Hunstein, 415 S.E.2d 322, 323 (Ga. App. 1992) ("The legislature did not intend for the [Open Meeting] Act to apply to the judicial branch of government."). Several courts have interpreted exemptions for judicial proceedings as including administrative agencies performing quasi-judicial functions. See, e.g., Arizona Press Club, Inc. v. Arizona Bd. of Tax Appeals, 558 P.2d 697 (Ariz. 1976); Monson v. Oklahoma ex rel. Oklahoma Corp. Comm'n, 673 P.2d 839 (Okla. 1983); Roberts v. City of Cranston Zoning Bd., 448 A.2d 779 (R.I. 1982). But see City of Flagstaff v. Bleeker, 600 P.2d 49, 50-51 (Ariz. App. 1979) (Arizona has limited its exemption to proceedings of courts); Occidental Chem. Co. v. Mayo, 351 So. 2d 336 (Fla. 1977) (Public Service Commission not exempt from Sunshine Law even though some of its functions are quasi-judicial).

272. See, e.g., COLO. REV. STAT. § 24-6-402(6); DEL. CODE ANN. tit. 29, § 10002(a); 5 ILL. COMP. STAT. 120/1.02; MISS. CODE ANN. § 25-41-7(4)(e); MONT. CODE ANN. § 2-3-102(1)(a); NEV. REV. STAT. § 241.015(3); WYO. STAT. ANN. § 16-4-402(a)(ii). Many state constitutions provide for public access to legislative sessions. See Pupillo, *supra* note 250, at 1167 n.18 (34 state constitutions require open meetings of the state legislature); Chap. 9-3 *supra*.

273. See, e.g., N.J. STAT. ANN. § 10:4-8(a); N.Y. PUB. OFF. LAW § 108(2); R.I. GEN. LAWS

excluded from coverage,[274] except when receiving public funds[275] or, in some states, when providing governmental services.[276]

§ 9-6(c). Meetings Subject to Open Meeting Laws.

What constitutes a "meeting" for purposes of an open meeting law varies from state to state.[277] The most limited definition of "meeting" is found in those laws that confine the term to the "official" convening of a public body.[278] Other states define "meeting" as a prearranged gathering of members of a public body for the purpose of deliberating on public business or taking official action.[279]

Neither of these definitions accounts for the "spontaneous" meetings of members of the public body or their private encounters. Some jurisdictions, however, specifically include within the definition of "meeting" unplanned or unofficial gatherings at which public business is discussed.[280] Other jurisdictions merely exclude this sort of meeting from the scope of the open meeting law,[281] or

---

§ 42-46-2(b); UTAH CODE ANN. § 52-4-2(2); Malone v. Meekins, 650 P.2d 351, 359 (Alaska 1982); People ex rel. Difanis v. Barr, 414 N.E.2d 731 (Ill. 1980); Oneonta Star v. County of Schoharie, 492 N.Y.S.2d 145 (App. Div. 1985). But see Cole v. Colorado, 673 P.2d 345, 348-49 (Colo. 1983) (legislative caucus is de facto policy-making body subject to state open meeting law). See generally Whelan, *New York's Open Meetings Law: Revision of the Political Caucus Exemption and Its Implications for Local Government*, 60 BROOK. L. REV. 1483 (1995).

274. See, e.g., McCoy Restaurants, Inc. v. City of Orlando, 392 So. 2d 252 (Fla. 1980); Perlongo v. Iron River Co-operative TV Antenna Corp., 332 N.W.2d 502 (Mich. App. 1983); Southern Minnesota Mun. Power Agency, 578 N.W.2d 362 (Minn. 1998) (statutorily created municipal power agency deemed a private corporation not subject to open meeting law).

275. See, e.g., ARK. CODE ANN. § 25-19-103(2); KAN. STAT. ANN. § 75-4318(a); MONT. CODE ANN. § 2-3-203(1); N.D. CENT. CODE § 44-04-19; OKLA. STAT. tit. 25, § 304(1); VA. CODE ANN. § 2.1-341; Rehabilitation Hosp. Serv. Corp. v. Delta-Hills Health Sys. Agency, Inc., 687 S.W.2d 840 (Ark. 1985); Seghers v. Community Advancement, Inc., 357 So. 2d 626 (La. App. 1978).

276. See, e.g., IOWA CODE §§ 21.2, 21.11; Wisconsin ex rel. Journal/Sentinel, Inc. v. Pleva, 456 N.W.2d 359 (Wis. 1990).

277. See generally SCHWING, *supra* note 253, at § 6.6.

278. See, e.g., N.Y. PUB. OFF. LAW § 102(1).

279. See, e.g., KAN. STAT. ANN. § 75-4317a; OHIO REV. CODE ANN. § 121.22(B)(2); PA. STAT. ANN. tit. 65, § 273; VA. CODE ANN. § 2.1-341; Kansas ex rel. Stephan v. Board of County Comm'rs, 770 P.2d 455, 457 (Kan. 1989).

280. The Florida Attorney General has discouraged luncheon meetings due to the potential for violation of the open meeting law if attending members of a public board discuss matters on which government action could foreseeably be taken. See Fla. Op. Att'y Gen. No. 71-159 (1971); Sacramento Newspaper Guild v. Sacramento County Bd. of Supervisors, 69 Cal. Rptr. 480, 487 (Ct. App. 1968) (informality of luncheon attended by city council members not determinative factor, but rather whether public business was discussed).

281. See, e.g., COLO. REV. STAT. § 24-6-402(2)(e) ("This [open meetings law] does not apply to any chance meeting or social gathering at which discussion of public business is not the central purpose."); CONN. GEN. STAT. § 1-18a(b); HAW. REV. STAT. § 92-5(b); MD. CODE ANN., STATE GOV'T § 10-503(a)(2); MASS. GEN. LAWS ch. 30A, § 11A1/2; MO. REV. STAT. § 610.010(3).

exempt the gathering unless matters within the public body's authority are discussed.[282]

Another approach, followed by a majority of states, is to define a "meeting" as any gathering at which a quorum[283] of the public body is present and at which public business is discussed.[284] A further refinement, adopted by Wyoming, defines "meeting" as any occasion on which a public body takes "action."[285]

Members of public bodies have experimented with various configurations and devices in an effort to circumvent open meeting laws. A popular method is the "serial communication," a succession of private communications between individual members in person, by letter, via telephone, or through the use of electronic mail.[286] These actions, however, have generally been determined to violate open meeting laws,[287] particularly when the activity appears designed to circumvent

---

282. See, e.g., Cal. Gov't Code § 54952.2(c)(5) ("Nothing in this section shall impose the requirements of this chapter upon . . . [t]he attendance of a majority of the members of a legislative body at a purely social or ceremonial occasion, provided that a majority of the members do not discuss among themselves business of a specific nature that is within the subject matter jurisdiction of the legislative body of the local agency"); Ga. Code Ann. § 50-14-1(a)(2); Ky. Rev. Stat. Ann. § 61.810(1); N.J. Stat. Ann. § 10:4-8(b); Tex. Rev. Civ. Stat. Ann. art. 6252-17, § 1(a).

283. "One of the principal dividing lines in many open meeting acts is whether a meeting regulated by the act is limited to a gathering of at least a quorum of the members of the public entity or extends to apply to gatherings of fewer than the number required to make a quorum. A quorum is the number of members who must be present for an organized body to act." SCHWING, *supra* note 253, at 244.

284. See, e.g., ARIZ. REV. STAT. § 38-431(3); KY. REV. STAT. ANN. § 61.810(1); N.C. GEN. STAT. § 143-318.10(d); VT. STAT. ANN. tit. 1, § 310(2); McComas v. Board of Educ., 475 S.E.2d 280 (W. Va. 1996) (Gathering of four of five school board members to ask questions of superintendent on day before noticed meeting of school board to decide issue of school closings constituted a meeting within meaning of the Open Government Proceedings Act.). Many of these states have also placed prohibitions on meetings involving less than a quorum to prevent circumvention of the open meeting law. See, e.g., HAW. REV. STAT. § 92-5(b); IOWA CODE § 21.2(2); MD. CODE ANN., STATE GOV'T § 10-503(a)(2); NEB. REV. STAT. § 84-1410(4); S.C. CODE ANN. § 30-4-70(b).

285. WYO. STAT. ANN. § 16-4-402(a); see Emery v. City of Rawlins, 596 P.2d 675, 679-80 (Wyo. 1979).

286. See, e.g., Regents of Univ. of California v. Superior Ct., 976 P.2d 808 (Cal. 1999); Del Papa v. Board of Regents, 956 P.2d 770 (Nev. 1998).

287. See, e.g., CAL. GOV'T CODE § 54952.2; HAW. REV. STAT. § 92-5(b); KAN. STAT. ANN. § 75-4317(a); KY. REV. STAT. ANN. § 61.810(2); Okla. Stat. tit. 25, § 306; TENN. CODE ANN. § 8-44-102(d); City Council v. Cooper, 358 So. 2d 440 (Ala. 1978); Stockton Newspapers, Inc. v. Members of Redevelopment Agency, 214 Cal. Rptr. 561 (Ct. App. 1985); Blackford ex rel. Cherokee Junior High Sch. PTA v. School Bd., 375 So. 2d 578 (Fla. App. 1979); Booth Newspapers, Inc. v. Wyoming City Council, 425 N.W.2d 695, 701 (Mich. App. 1988) ("To accept the city council's suggestion that a public body can avoid the OMA by deliberately dividing itself into groups of less than a quorum and still deliberate on public policy would circumvent the legislative principles as well as the overall objective of the OMA to promote openness and accountability in government."); Trustees v. Mississippi Publishers Corp., 478 So. 2d 269 (Miss. 1985); Board of Trustees v. Board of County Comm'rs, 606 P.2d 1069 (Mont. 1980); Del Papa v. Board of Regents, 956 P.2d 770, 778 (Nev. 1998) ("[W]e hold that a quorum of a public body

the statute at issue. The same result has been reached in the context of gatherings labeled seminars, retreats, or work sessions,[288] as well as so-called "pre-meeting" meetings.[289]

§ 9-6(d). Notice Requirements.

Notice of the date, time, and location of a meeting is a vital element of open meeting laws. Pursuant to most statutes, notice is to be reasonably calculated to afford actual notice to the general public. Many state open meeting laws set forth the substance of the notice requirements. Failure to satisfy such requirements may be penalized, particularly when the failure to give proper notice is perceived as bad faith on the part of the public body.[290]

Most state open meeting laws do not identify the person required to provide notice of a meeting. Because giving notice is a ministerial function, courts usually recognize notice provided by anyone acting on behalf of the public

---

using serial electronic communication to deliberate toward a decision or to make a decision on any matter over which the public body has supervision, control, jurisdiction or advisory power violates the Open Meeting Law."); Hitt v. Mabry, 687 S.W.2d 791 (Tex. App. 1985).

288. See, e.g., R.I. GEN. LAWS § 42-46-2(a); Sacramento Newspaper Guild v. Sacramento County Bd. of Supervisors, 69 Cal. Rptr. 480 (Ct. App. 1968); Bagby v. School Dist., 528 P.2d 1299 (Colo. 1974); Journal Publ'g Co. of Rockville, Inc. v. Town of Enfield, 373 A.2d 193 (Conn. Super. 1974); Pearson v. Board of Health, 525 N.E.2d 400 (Mass. 1988); St. Cloud Newspapers, Inc. v. District 742 Community Schs., 332 N.W.2d 1 (Minn. 1983); Binghamton Press Co. v. Board of Educ., 412 N.Y.S.2d 492 (App. Div. 1979); Neese v. Paris Special Sch. Dist., 813 S.W.2d 432 (Tenn. App. 1990); Wisconsin v. Swanson, 284 N.W.2d 655 (Wis. 1979).

289. See, e.g., Sacramento Newspaper Guild v. Sacramento County Bd. of Supervisors, 69 Cal. Rptr. 480 (Ct. App. 1968); Bagby v. School Dist., 528 P.2d 1299 (Colo. 1974); Simon v. City of Auburn, 519 N.E.2d 205 (Ind. App. 1988); Louisiana v. Guidry, 364 So. 2d 589 (La. 1978); Wisconsin ex rel. Newspapers, Inc. v. Showers, 398 N.W.2d 154 (Wis. 1987). But see Bundren v. Peters, 732 F. Supp. 1486 (E.D. Tenn. 1989) (pre-meeting meetings not a violation where public business not deliberated or decided); Emery v. City of Rawlins, 596 P.2d 675 (Wyo. 1979) (preliminary gathering not a violation where there was no collective decision, commitment, or promise).

290. Thus, in *National Independent Business Alliance v. City of Beverly Hills*, 180 Cal. Rptr. 59, 64 (Ct. App. 1982), a California appellate court held that an ordinance was void due to violation of the statutory requirement that no ordinance be enacted within five days of its introduction. See Davis v. East Baton Rouge Parish Sch. Bd., 78 F.3d 920 (5th Cir. 1995) (district court abused its discretion by ordering school board to meet in private session, without notice, to draw up desegregation plan). However, in *Bowen v. New York Commission of Correction*, 484 N.Y.S.2d 210 (App. Div. 1984), where a meeting was scheduled less than a week in advance and notice was given almost immediately after scheduling, a New York appellate court held that the notice was reasonable and satisfied the statutory requirement.

body.[291] Some states, however, require the presiding officer of the public body to give notice.[292] Others require that the governing body or staff do so.[293]

There is no universally accepted notice period. Specific notice periods set by statute range from twenty-four hours to ten days in advance of the meeting.[294] A number of states merely require that the public body provide "reasonable notice."[295] Other states permit the public body to set the length of notice required for its regular meetings.[296]

When the meeting is scheduled in response to unforeseen, special circumstances, a different notice requirement will usually attach. Special meetings are typically "set at a special time or place to address a particular subject matter or meetings scheduled by the public body after its regular schedule of meetings has been established."[297] The timing of notice of such a special meeting is usually more flexible,[298] though the notice must disclose the topic of the meeting. Such meetings are, however, limited to the topic specified in the notice.[299]

---

291. See, e.g., Ky. Op. Att'y Gen. No. 84-250 (1984) (presiding officer or majority of public body calling special meeting may delegate duty to clerk); Carter v. City of Nashua, 308 A.2d 847, 852 (N.H. 1973) (counsel may post and provide notice for public entity).

292. See, e.g., KAN. STAT. ANN. § 75-4318(c); MASS. GEN. LAWS ch. 30A, § 11A 1/2; MASS. GEN. LAWS ch. 34, § 9G; MASS. GEN. LAWS ch. 39, § 23B; N.D. CENT. CODE § 44-04-20; Wis. Op. Att'y Gen. No. 37-77 (1977) (chief presiding officer or designee).

293. See, e.g., HAW. REV. STAT. § 92-7; OR. REV. STAT. § 192.640(1).

294. See ARIZ. REV. STAT. § 38-431.02(C) (24 hours); CAL. GOV'T CODE § 11125(a) (10 days); CONN. GEN. STAT. § 1-21(a) (24 hours); NEV. REV. STAT. § 241.020(2) (three working days); N.Y. PUB. OFF. LAW § 104(1) (72 hours); W. VA. CODE § 6-9A-3 (five days).

295. See, e.g., ALASKA STAT. § 44.6310(e); IOWA CODE § 21.4(1); MD. CODE ANN., STATE GOV'T § 10-506(a); MO. REV. STAT. § 610.020; NEB. REV. STAT. § 84-1411(1); N.M. STAT. ANN. § 10-15-1(D); OR. REV. STAT. § 192.640(1); Tunley v. Municipality of Anchorage Sch. Dist., 631 P.2d 67 (Alaska 1980); KCOB/KLVN, Inc. v. Jasper County Bd. of Supervisors, 473 N.W.2d 171 (Iowa 1991); City of College Park v. Cotter, 525 A.2d 1059 (Md. 1987); Pokorny v. City of Schuyler, 275 N.W.2d 281 (Neb. 1979); New Mexico Mun. League, Inc. v. New Mexico Envtl. Impact Bd., 539 P.2d 221 (N.M. App. 1975).

296. See, e.g., CONN. GEN. STAT. § 1-21f; KY. REV. STAT. ANN. § 61.920 (public agencies shall provide for schedule of meetings "convenient to the public"); OHIO REV. CODE ANN. § 121.22(F); WASH. REV. CODE § 42.30.070.

297. SCHWING, supra note 253, at 168. See, e.g., IDAHO CODE § 67-2341(6)(b); Barile v. City Comptroller, 288 N.Y.S.2d 191 (Sup. Ct. 1968).

298. See, e.g., ARIZ. REV. STAT. § 38-431.02(C) (24 hours); CAL. GOV'T CODE § 54956 (24 hours); COLO. REV. STAT. § 24-6-402(c) (24 hours); GA. CODE ANN. § 50-14-1(d) (24 hours); MASS. GEN. LAWS ch. 30A, § 11A1/2 (48 hours); MICH. COMP. LAWS § 15.265(4) (18 hours); MISS. CODE ANN. § 25-41-13(1) (one hour); PA. STAT. ANN. tit. 65, § 279(a) (24 hours); WIS. STAT. § 19.84(3) (two hours); Yarbrough v. Young, 462 So. 2d 515 (Fla. App. 1985) (reasonable notice required); News & Observer Publ'g Co. v. Interim Bd. of Educ., 223 S.E.2d 580 (N.C. App. 1976) (one hour telephone notice insufficient).

299. See, e.g., CAL. GOV'T CODE § 54956; CONN. GEN. STAT. § 1-21(a); IDAHO CODE § 67-2341(6)(b); IND. CODE § 36-2-2-8; OKLA. STAT. tit. 25, § 311(A)(11).

The least restrictive of the notice requirements is required for emergency meetings. These meetings can be held, with little or no notice, and may be treated as a special meeting.[300] Since emergency meetings require little or no notice, they provide fertile ground for abuse. States have addressed this concern by banning executive sessions during emergency meetings,[301] or requiring that any action taken at an emergency meeting be reconsidered and acted upon at an open public meeting within a fixed period of time.[302]

Open meeting laws often require that the notice be posted in a location where the public and journalists have access to it. Possible locations may include the scheduled meeting place, a place selected by the public body, or a place established by statute.[303] Because a posting cannot realistically serve as notice to a large population within a relatively short period of time, there is often a publication requirement as well.[304] The open meeting law may require that the notice be printed in a "newspaper of general circulation" within the locale where the meeting is to be held,[305] and it may permit notice to be given in other media as well. New Mexico requires that notice be given to broadcast stations licensed by the FCC,[306] and Michigan allows for posting public notices on cable television.[307] Several states require public bodies to supply notice of meetings to interested persons and journalists who request such information.[308] Some open

---

300. See, e.g., ARK. CODE ANN. § 25-19-106(b)(2); DEL. CODE ANN. tit. 29, § 10004(e)(1); IDAHO CODE § 67-2343(2); MONT. CODE ANN. § 2-3-112(1); PA. STAT. ANN. tit. 65, § 279(a); WASH. REV. CODE § 42.30.070.

301. See, e.g., CAL. GOV'T CODE § 54956.5.

302. See, e.g., WYO. STAT. ANN. § 16-4-404(d).

303. See, e.g., 5 ILL. COMP. STAT. 120/2.02(b) ("Public notice shall be given by posting a copy of the notice at the principal office of the body holding the meeting or, if no such office exists, at the building in which the meeting is to be held."). Texas specifies different locations for postings by various bodies, including state, city, and county bodies, school districts, and water districts. TEX. REV. CIV. STAT. ANN. art. 6252-17, § 3A.

304. But see City of New Carrollton v. Rogers, 410 A.2d 1070, 1077 (Md. 1980) (posting of notice of city council workshop meetings on city hall bulletin board deemed sufficient notice in light of earlier published notice that council would use such method of notification).

305. See, e.g., GA. CODE ANN. § 50-14-1(d); HAW. REV. STAT. § 92-41; MONT. CODE ANN. § 2-3-104(4); N.J. STAT. ANN. § 10:4-8(d); PA. STAT. ANN. tit. 65, § 273; UTAH CODE ANN. § 52-4-6(3); Moore v. Alaska, 553 P.2d 8, 21 (Alaska 1976); Albia Publ'g Co. v. Klobnak, 434 N.W.2d 636 (Iowa 1989).

306. See N.M. STAT. ANN. § 10-15-1(C).

307. See MICH. COMP. LAWS § 15.264(b).

308. See, e.g., MICH. COMP. LAWS § 15.266(1):

> Upon the written request of an individual, organization, firm, or corporation, and upon the requesting party's payment of a yearly fee of not more than the reasonable estimated cost for printing and postage of such notices, a public body shall send the requesting party by first class mail a copy of any notice required to be posted pursuant to sections 5(2) to (5).

See also CAL. GOV'T CODE § 11125(e).

meeting laws specifically provide for notice to be given to the news media.[309] If notice is given in accordance with applicable law, failure of any specific person to receive it does not typically form a basis for invalidation of an action taken at the meeting.[310]

§ 9-6(e). Access to Meetings.

The typical open meeting law requires that sessions of public bodies subject to the law be open to the public,[311] unless the public body is meeting in a closed "executive session" that is permitted by the law under certain circumstances.[312] The language of the California statute is typical: "All meetings of a state body shall be open and public and all persons shall be permitted to attend any meeting of a state body except as otherwise provided in this article."[313]

Most states leave to the discretion of the public body whether to allow members of the public to address it during its meetings.[314] Others specifically provide for the public's right to address certain bodies under specified circumstances.[315] Some authorities have interpreted open meeting laws as prohibiting such public participation.[316] A number of states allow the use of cameras and recording devices to record open meetings, subject to reasonable regulation by the public body.[317] Michigan, for example, recognizes that the right of a person

---

309. See, e.g., N.Y. PUB. OFF. LAW § 104(1) & (2). See also White v. Battaglia, 434 N.Y.S.2d 537 (App. Div. 1980) (notice posted on bulletin board without any notice to the media was not reasonable and was patently inadequate for meeting called on 3½ hours' notice).

310. See CAL. GOV'T CODE § 54954.1; 5 ILL. COMP. STAT. 120/2.04 ("Failure of any news medium to receive a notice provided for by this Act shall not invalidate any meeting provided notice was in fact given in accordance with this Act.").

311. See, e.g., ALA. CODE § 13A-14-2; CAL. GOV'T CODE §§ 11123, 11132, 54953, 54962; IND. CODE § 5-14-1.5-3(a); KAN. STAT. ANN. tit. 42, § 5(A); ME. REV. STAT. ANN. tit. 1, § 403; MO. REV. STAT. §§ 610.011(2), 610.015; NEV. REV. STAT. § 241.020(1); N.Y. PUB. OFF. LAW § 103(a); OHIO REV. CODE ANN. § 121.22(C); S.C. CODE ANN. § 30-4-60; TENN. CODE ANN. § 8-44-102(a); VA. CODE. ANN. § 2.1-343.

312. See Chap. 9-6(h) *infra*.

313. CAL. GOV'T CODE § 11123.

314. See, e.g., MASS. GEN. LAWS ch. 39, § 23C; NEB. REV. STAT. § 84-1412(2).

315. See, e.g., CAL. GOV'T CODE § 54954.3(a); MONT. CODE ANN. § 2-3-101; NEB. REV. STAT. § 84-1411(2); VT. STAT. ANN. tit. 1, § 312(h); WYO. STAT. ANN. § 16-4-403(b); White v. City of Norwalk, 900 F.2d 1421 (9th Cir. 1990) (applying California law); Eudaly v. City of Colleyville, 642 S.W.2d 75 (Tex. App. 1982).

316. See, e.g., Wood v. Marston, 442 So. 2d 934 (Fla. 1983); Yaro v. Board of Appeals, 410 N.E.2d 725 (Mass. App. 1980); Hinds County Bd. of Supervisors v. Common Cause of Mississippi, 551 So. 2d 107 (Miss. 1989) ("A citizen spectator or news reporter is not a participant. He has no right to intrude or interfere in any manner with the discussion, deliberation or decision-making process.").

317. See, e.g., CAL. GOV'T CODE §§ 6090, 6091, 54953.5; CONN. GEN. STAT. § 1-21a(a); GA. CODE ANN. § 50-14-1(c); HAW. REV. STAT. § 92-9(c); IOWA CODE § 21.7; KAN. STAT. ANN. § 75-4318(e); KY. REV. STAT. ANN. § 61.840; LA. REV. STAT. ANN. tit. 42, § 8(A), (B); MD. CODE ANN.,

to attend a meeting of a public body includes the right to tape-record, to videotape, to broadcast live on radio, and to telecast live on television the proceedings of a public body at a public meeting. The exercise of this right shall not be dependent upon the prior approval of the public body. However, a public body may establish reasonable rules and regulations in order to minimize the possibility of disrupting the meeting.[318]

The rules promulgated by the public body may address noise levels, available space, lighting, the obstruction of views, and other considerations designed to diminish disruption of the proceedings.[319] A few states permit only audio taping.[320] Where the open meeting law does not address the issue of recording, the courts have tended to interpret the relevant statute to permit it.[321] Some courts, however, have authorized the complete exclusion of recording devices.[322]

STATE GOV'T § 10-507(b); MASS. GEN. LAWS ch. 30A, § 11A1/2, ch. 39, § 23B; MICH. COMP. LAWS § 15.263(1); NEB. REV. STAT. § 84-1412(1)(2); NEV. REV. STAT. § 241.035(3); N.H. REV. STAT. ANN. § 91-A:2II; OKLA. STAT. tit. 25, § 312(C); PA. STAT. ANN. tit. 65, § 281; S.C. CODE ANN. § 30-4-90(c); UTAH CODE ANN. § 52-4-7; VA. CODE ANN. § 2.1-343; WIS. STAT. § 19.90; Peloquin v. Arsenault, 616 N.Y.S.2d 716 (Sup. Ct. 1994) (ban on all cameras and camcorders violates open meetings law); People v. Ystueta, 418 N.Y.S.2d 508 (Dist. Ct. 1979); Oklahoma v. Patton, 837 P.2d 483 (Okla. 1992); Hain v. Board of Sch. Directors, 641 A.2d 661, 663-64 (Pa. Commw. 1994). See generally Helm, *Hain v. Board of School Directors of Reading School District: Videotaping Meetings and the Sunshine Act*, 4 WIDENER J. PUB. L. 803 (1995).

318. MICH. COMP. LAWS § 15.263(1).

319. See, e.g., CAL. GOV'T CODE § 54953.6; MONT. CODE ANN. § 2-3-211; N.M. STAT. ANN. § 10-15-1(A); Westinghouse Broadcasting Co. v. Dukakis, 409 F. Supp. 895 (D. Mass. 1976).

320. See, e.g., HAW. REV. STAT. § 92-9(c).

321. See, e.g., Nevens v. City of Chino, 44 Cal. Rptr. 50 (Ct. App. 1965); Berry v. Peoples Broadcasting Corp., 547 N.E.2d 231 (Ind. 1989) (sound recordings may not be prohibited from public meetings); Sudol v. Borough of North Arlington, 348 A.2d 216 (N.J. Super. 1975); Mitchell v. Board of Educ., 493 N.Y.S.2d 826 (App. Div. 1985); Belcher v. Mansi, 569 F. Supp. 379 (D.R.I. 1983). State constitutions have been interpreted as providing a right to record public meetings, see, e.g., Maurice River Township Bd. of Educ. v. Maurice River Township Teachers Ass'n, 475 A. 2d 59 (N.J. Super. 1984), but not the United States Constitution, see, e.g., Johnson v. Adams, 629 F. Supp. 1563 (E.D. Tex. 1986); Pierce v. School Comm., 322 F. Supp. 957 (D. Mass. 1971).

322. See Blackston v. Alabama, 30 F.3d 117, 120 (11th Cir. 1994) (ban on tape recording a public meeting must be content-neutral); Thompson v. City of Clio, 765 F. Supp. 1066, 1081 (M.D. Ala. 1991) (Alabama Open Meetings Law grants only the right to be present at public meetings, not the right to record); Combined Communications Corp. v. Finesilver, 672 F.2d 818, 821 (10th Cir. 1982) (television broadcast coverage of settlement negotiations of congressional redistricting lawsuit was denied due to the fact that "the spirit of the open meeting law was not violated because reporters from the media were permitted to attend"); Gorman v. University of Rhode Island, 646 F. Supp. 799 (D.R.I. 1986), *modified*, 837 F.2d 7 (1st Cir. 1988); Sigma Delta Chi v. Speaker, Md. House of Delegates, 310 A.2d 156 (Md. 1973).

§ 9-6(f). Access to Minutes, Transcripts, and Tapes.

Generally, open meeting laws require that minutes be taken of all regular, special, and emergency sessions of a public body.[323] Minutes must typically contain a description of the topics discussed during the meeting and any action taken.[324] Most statutes also require minutes of executive sessions, though in less detail than those of an open meeting.[325]

Minutes usually must be made available to the public within a "reasonable"[326] or specified[327] period of time,[328] although some statutes are silent on the issue.[329] Recordings or transcripts of a meeting made by the governmental body may be available to the public pursuant to the state's public records law,[330] or the open

---

323. See, e.g., COLO. REV. STAT. § 24-6-402(2)(d).

324. See MICH. COMP. LAWS § 15.269(1); MONT. CODE ANN. § 2-3-212(2)(c); NEV. STAT. ANN. § 10:4-14; UTAH CODE ANN. § 52-4-7; VT. STAT. ANN. tit. 1, § 312(b); Hokanson v. High Sch. Dist., 589 P.2d 907 (Ariz. 1978).

325. See, e.g., COLO. REV. STAT. § 24-6-402(2)(d). See Orford Teachers Ass'n v. Watson, 427 A.2d 21 (N.H. 1981); Wm. J. Kline & Sons Inc. v. County of Hamilton, 663 N.Y.S.2d 339, 341 (App. Div. 1997) ("Only in the event that action is taken by a formal vote at an executive session do both FOIL and the Open Meetings Law require a public record of the manner in which each Board member voted.").

326. See, e.g., IDAHO CODE § 67-2344(1); IND. CODE § 5-14-1.5-4(c); LA. REV. STAT. ANN. tit. 42, § 7.1(B); MISS. CODE ANN. § 25-41-11; NEV. REV. STAT. § 241.035(2); OR. REV. STAT. § 192.650(1); W. VA. CODE § 6-9A-5.

327. See, e.g., ARIZ. REV. STAT. § 38-431.01(D) (three working days); CONN. GEN. STAT. § 1-21(a); 5 ILL. COMP. STAT. 120/2.06(b) (seven days); NEB. REV. STAT. § 84-1413(5) (10 working days); N.H. REV. STAT. ANN. § 91-A:2II (144 hours); N.Y. PUB. OFF. LAW § 106(3) (two weeks); R.I. GEN. LAWS § 42-46-7(b) (35 days); VT. STAT. ANN. tit. 1, § 312(b) (five days).

328. Other states require that minutes promptly be made available to the public. See, e.g., COLO. REV. STAT. § 24-6-402(2)(d); FLA. STAT. § 286.011(2); ME. REV. STAT. ANN. tit. 1, § 403; N.J. STAT. ANN. § 10:4-14; OHIO REV. CODE ANN. § 121.22(C); TENN. CODE ANN. § 8-44-104(a); WASH. REV. CODE § 42.32.030.

329. See SCHWING, *supra* note 253, at 205.

330. See, e.g., CAL. GOV'T CODE § 11125.1; MD. CODE ANN., STATE GOV'T § 10-509(d); MISS. CODE ANN. §§ 25-6-1 to 25-61-17; NEV. REV. STAT. § 241.035; N.C. GEN. STAT. § 143-318.10(e); Orford Teachers Ass'n v. Watson, 427 A.2d 21 (N.H. 1981); Cline v. Board of Trustees, 351 N.Y.S.2d 81 (Sup. Ct. 1973), *aff'd mem.*, 357 N.Y.S.2d 1022 (App. Div. 1974); News & Observer Publ'g Co. v. Poole, 412 S.E.2d 7 (N.C. 1992); Cooper v. Bales, 233 S.E.2d 306 (S.C. 1977); Shackelford v. City of Abilene, 585 S.W.2d 665 (Tex. 1979); Veltri v. Charleston Urban Renewal Auth., 363 S.E.2d 746 (W. Va. 1987); Oshkosh Northwestern Co. v. Oshkosh Library Bd., 373 N.W.2d 459 (Wis. App. 1985); Laramie River Conservation Council v. Dinger, 567 P.2d 731 (Wyo. 1977). But see Wm. J. Kline & Sons, Inc. v. County of Hamilton, 663 N.Y.S.2d 339, 341 (App. Div. 1997) (records of lawfully closed executive and emergency sessions held to be exempt from disclosure under Freedom of Information Law: "[i]t makes little sense to permit governmental bodies to meet in private under clearly defined circumstances only to subsequently allow the minutes of those private meetings to be publicly accessed under FOIL"). Private recordings made by a member of a public body for personal use need not be made available to the public. See Brent v. Paquette, 567 A.2d 976 (N.H. 1989).

meeting law itself.[331]

§ 9-6(g). Procedures.

State open meeting laws typically have "executive session" provisions that authorize closing certain meetings to the public and to the press.[332] These provisions specify the circumstances and conditions under which a meeting that is open to the public may be recessed to an executive session.[333] An executive session is generally described as a meeting or part of a meeting that is "closed to any persons for deliberation on certain matters,"[334] or from which the public is excluded.[335] A public body may call for an executive session when there is a need to exclude the public from the discussion of matters that fall within one of the statutory exemptions to the open meeting law.[336]

An executive session typically may not be initiated by a public body outside the context of an open meeting.[337] Before the public body may retire to an executive session, most statutes provide that it must first meet in public and announce the statutory justification for the executive session, the subjects to be discussed in the session, as well as the time and place the open meeting will resume.[338] A formal motion to recess to an executive session must typically be made, seconded, and passed.[339] Discussion during the executive session must be

---

331. See, e.g., CAL. GOV'T CODE §§ 54953.5(b), 54960(b); N.H. REV. STAT. ANN. § 91-A:4II. There is generally no requirement that the sessions of public agencies be recorded. See Keddie v. Rutgers Univ., 689 A.2d 702, 708 (N.J. 1997).

332. See, e.g., ARK. CODE ANN. § 25-19-106(c); CAL. GOV'T CODE §§ 11126, 54956; COLO. REV. STAT. § 24-6-402(3); IDAHO CODE § 67-2345(1); 5 ILL. COMP. STAT. 120/2; IOWA CODE § 21.5; KAN. STAT. ANN. § 75-4319(a); MD. CODE ANN., STATE GOV'T § 10-508; MINN. STAT. § 471.705.1(d); MO. REV. STAT. § 610.021; NEV. REV. STAT. § 241.030; N.J. STAT. ANN. § 10:4-12; N.Y. PUB. OFF. LAW § 105; OHIO REV. CODE ANN. § 121.22(G); PA. STAT. ANN. tit. 65, §§ 277, 278; VA. CODE ANN. § 2.1-344; WASH. REV. CODE § 42.30.110.

333. See, e.g., KY. REV. STAT. ANN. § 61.815.

334. IDAHO CODE § 67-2341(3).

335. See Sanders v. City of Fort Smith, 473 S.W.2d 182, 183 (Ark. 1971); Thomas v. Board of Trustees, 215 N.E.2d 434, 436 (Ohio App. 1966).

336. See Chap. 9-6(h) *infra*.

337. See N.C. GEN. STAT. § 143-318.11(c); but see Ghiglione v. School Comm., 378 N.E.2d 984 (Mass. 1978).

338. See, e.g., CAL. GOV'T CODE §§ 54954.5, 54957.7; CONN. GEN. STAT. § 1-21-(a); KAN. STAT. ANN. § 75-4319(a); KY. REV. STAT. ANN. § 61.815(1); MASS. GEN. LAWS ch. 30A, § 11A1/2; MD. CODE ANN., STATE GOV'T § 10-509(d); PA. STAT. ANN. tit. 65, § 278(b); R.I. GEN. LAWS § 42-46-4; TEX. REV. CIV. STAT. ANN. art. 6252-17, § 2(a); Floyd County Bd. of Educ. v. Ratliff, 955 S.W.2d 921, 924 (Ky. 1997); Gerstein v. Superintendent Search Screening Comm., 541 N.E.2d 984 (Mass. 1989); Houman v. Mayor & Council, 382 A.2d 413 (N.J. Super. 1977); Daily Gazette Co. v. Town of Cobleskill, 444 N.Y.S.2d 44 (Sup. Ct. 1981); Herald Publ'g Co. v. Barnwell, 351 S.E.2d 878 (S.C. App. 1986).

339. See ARIZ. REV. STAT. § 38-431.03A; GA. CODE ANN. § 50-14-4; IDAHO CODE § 67-2345(1); MICH. COMP. LAWS § 15.267; N.Y. PUB. OFF. LAWS § 105(1); VT. STAT. ANN. tit. 1,

limited to the specific subjects identified as the basis for the motion to recess.[340] Additional topics, not identified in the motion to recess, may not be discussed during the executive session, even though they may be properly exempted from discussion in an open meeting as well.[341] States generally prohibit public bodies from taking any substantive action while in executive session; such action is to be taken when the open meeting resumes.[342]

§ 9-6(h). Exemptions.

Statutory exemptions provide the basis for public bodies to recess from an open meeting to an executive session. Each exemption reflects a legislative determination that the exempted matter is entitled to greater weight than the public interest in open meetings. Such exemptions are typically construed strictly.[343] Information that is exempted from disclosure under a state's open records statute is generally exempted from public discussion under the state's open meeting law as well.[344] Although the scope and application of the exemptions vary from state to state, most jurisdictions have exempted certain subject matters from the requirement that they be discussed in an open meeting. The fact that a particular subject may fall within a recognized exemption does not, however, *require* the public body to deal with it in executive session. The public

---

§ 313(a); KCOB/KLVN, Inc. v. Jasper County Bd. of Supervisors, 473 N.W.2d 171 (Iowa 1991); Norris v. Monroe City Sch. Bd., 580 So. 2d 425 (La. App. 1991); Caldwell v. Lambrou, 391 A.2d 590 (N.J. Super. 1978).

340. See ALASKA STAT. § 44.62.310(b); CAL. GOV'T CODE §§ 11126.3(b), 54957.7; COLO. REV. STAT. § 24-6-402(3)(a), (4); 5 ILL. COMP. STAT. 120/2a; KY. REV. STAT. ANN. § 61.815(4); MD. CODE ANN., STATE GOV'T § 10-509(d); MO. REV. STAT. § 610.022(3); N.M. STAT. ANN. § 10-15-1(I); R.I. GEN. LAWS § 42-46-4; WIS. STAT. § 19.85(1); Marsh v. Richmond Newspapers, Inc., 288 S.E.2d 415 (Va. 1982); Wisconsin ex rel. Schaeve v. Van Lare, 370 N.W.2d 271 (Wis. App. 1985).

341. See, e.g., IOWA CODE § 21.5(2); NEB. REV. STAT. § 84-1410(3); N.H. REV. STAT. ANN. § 91-A:3I(c); S.D. CODIFIED LAWS § 1-25-2; Kloepfer v. Commissioner of Educ., 440 N.Y.S.2d 785 (App. Div. 1981), *aff'd mem.*, 436 N.E.2d 1334 (N.Y. 1982). But see Marsh v. Richmond Newspapers, Inc., 288 S.E.2d 415, 421 (Va. 1982) (assuming without deciding that exempted matters may be discussed even though not stated in motion to recess).

342. See, e.g., ARIZ. REV. STAT. § 38-431.03(D); DEL. CODE ANN. tit. 29, § 10004(c); FLA. STAT. § 286.011(1); 5 ILL. COMP. STAT. 120/2(c); N.M. STAT. ANN. § 10-15-1(A); OHIO REV. CODE ANN. § 121.22(H); W. VA. CODE § 6-9A-4; Rose v. Freedom of Info. Comm'n, 602 A.2d 1019 (Conn. 1992); Houman v. Mayor & Council, 382 A.2d 413 (N.J. Super. 1977).

343. See Board Pub. Instruction v. Doran, 224 So. 2d 693, 699 (Fla. 1969); Spradlin v. Fulton, 982 S.W.2d 255, 259 (Mo. 1998).

344. See COLO. REV. STAT. § 24-6-402(4)(g); DEL. CODE ANN. tit. 29, § 10004(b)(6); IND. CODE § 5-14-1.5-6.1(b)(1), (6); MO. REV. STAT. § 610.021(14); Capeletti Bros. v. Department of Transp., 499 So. 2d 855 (Fla. App. 1986); Wm. J. Kline & Sons, Inc. v. County of Hamilton, 663 N.Y.S.2d 339 (App. Div. 1997).

body is generally given the discretion to discuss the matter in an open meeting if it chooses to do so.[345]

§ 9-6(h)(1). Personnel Matters.

One of the most often cited bases for recessing to executive session is the discussion of personnel matters relating to specific public employees and other identified persons.[346] Most open meeting laws contain a personnel exception that is intended to protect employees from public embarrassment and to permit free and candid discussions of personnel matters by public bodies.[347] Not all personnel matters are, however, exempted. Where the personnel issue does not raise privacy concerns, it generally is required to be discussed in an open meeting. Public employees, particularly those in management positions, are not accorded the same level of privacy protection by open meeting laws as are employees in the private sector.[348]

§ 9-6(h)(2). Disclosure Prohibited by Other Laws.

Most state open meeting laws contain exemptions for the discussion of information required by some other law to remain confidential. The strength and scope of such exceptions vary among the states. Some jurisdictions exempt from the requirement of public discussion only those statutes that expressly require certain matters to be kept confidential.[349] Most other jurisdictions employ a broader standard, requiring that matters be discussed in an open meeting unless "otherwise provided by law"[350] or "except as otherwise provided" by the open

---

345. See, e.g., 5 ILL. COMP. STAT. 120/2a; IOWA CODE § 21.5(5); NEB. REV. STAT. § 84-1410(4); NEV. REV. STAT. § 241.030(3); PA. STAT. ANN. tit. 65, § 277(c); Miglionico v. Birmingham News Co., 378 So. 2d 677 (Ala. 1979); Berry County Sheriff's Merit Bd. v. Peoples Broadcasting Corp., 547 N.E.2d 231 (Ind. 1989); Kurlander v. Sch. Comm., 451 N.E.2d 138 (Mass. App. 1983).

346. See Hudson v. School Dist., 578 S.W.2d 301, 307 (Mo. App. 1979) ("the problem of closing personnel matters is recognized in nearly all jurisdictions which have passed open meetings legislation") (citation omitted).

347. See San Diego Union v. City Council, 196 Cal. Rptr. 45 (Ct. App. 1983).

348. "By accepting public employment an individual steps from the category of a purely private citizen to that of a public citizen. And in that transition he must of necessity subordinate his private rights to the extent that they may compete or conflict with the superior right of the public to achieve honest and efficient government." Lehrhaupt v. Flynn, 356 A.2d 35, 42 (N.J. Super. 1976), aff'd, 383 A.2d 428 (N.J. 1978). See Redding v. Brady, 606 P.2d 1193, 1196-97 (Utah 1980) (right of press or public to publish gross salaries of college employees outweighs employee privacy rights).

349. See, e.g., ALASKA STAT. § 44.62.310(c)(3).

350. See, e.g., ARK. CODE ANN. § 25-19-106(a); GA. CODE ANN. § 50-14-1(b); KY. REV. STAT. ANN. § 61.800; MO. REV. STAT. § 610.011(2).

meeting law.[351] In addition to incorporating the dictates of other state statutes, this exemption also recognizes confidentiality provisions contained in the state constitution, as well as in federal statutes and regulations.[352]

§ 9-6(h)(3). Confidential Financial and Commercial Information.

Many statutes provide exemptions from their open meeting requirements designed to afford privacy protection to those who have disclosed financial or commercial information to the government. Moreover, in most states, information that has been gathered or used by the government is also exempted from the requirement that it be discussed in a public meeting if to do so would cause financial injury.[353] This exemption is particularly relevant to public bodies that supervise financial institutions.[354] Many states similarly protect, in varying degrees, trade secrets and other sensitive business information.[355] Some states will permit the closure of meetings at which real estate transactions, confidential contracts, contract negotiations or strategic plans are discussed.[356]

---

351. See, e.g., ALASKA STAT. § 44.62.310(a); CAL. GOV'T CODE §§ 11123, 54953(a); IDAHO CODE § 67-2342(1); IND. CODE § 5-14-1.5-3(a); MASS. GEN. LAWS ch. 30A, § 11A1/2; N.H. REV. STAT. ANN. § 91-A:3I(a); N.C. GEN. STAT. § 143-318.10(a); VT. STAT. ANN. tit. 1, § 313; WASH. REV. CODE § 42.30.130. Such statutory language prevents the public body from using its own rules as the basis for closing its meetings. See SCHWING, *supra* note 253, § 7.98.

352. See, e.g., COLO. REV. STAT. § 24-6-402(4)(c); FLA. STAT. § 286.011(1); MICH. COMP. LAWS § 15.263; NEB. REV. STAT. § 84-1408; N.J. STAT. ANN. § 10:4-12(b)(1); OHIO REV. CODE ANN. § 121.22(G)(5); TENN. CODE ANN. § 8-44-102(a). Some states exempt matters the discussion of which could lead to the loss of federal funding. See, e.g., N.J. STAT. ANN. § 10:4-12(b)(2); N.C. GEN. STAT. § 143-318.11(a)(12).

353. See, e.g., ALASKA STAT. § 44.62.310(c)(1); CAL. GOV'T CODE § 11126(I); COLO. REV. STAT. § 24-6-402(4)(a); MISS. CODE ANN. § 25-41-7(4)(g); N.M. STAT. ANN. § 10-15-1(H)(6); N.Y. PUB. OFF. LAW § 105(1)(h); OR. REV. STAT. § 192.660(1)(j); VA. CODE ANN. § 2.1-344(A)(6); W. VA. CODE § 6-9A-4(9); WIS. STAT. § 19.85(1)(e).

354. See OKLA. STAT. tit. 25, § 307(C); N.J. STAT. ANN. § 10:4-12(b)(5); VA. CODE ANN. § 2.1-344(A)(14); WASH. REV. CODE § 42.30.110(1)(k). Some states specifically except from open meeting laws those public bodies that supervise financial institutions. See, e.g., MASS. GEN. LAWS ch. 30A, § 11A; OR. REV. STAT. § 192.690(1); TEX. REV. CIV. STAT. ANN. art. 6252-17, § 2(q).

355. See, e.g., CONN. GEN. STAT. §§ 1-18a(e)(5), 1-19(b)(5); KAN. STAT. ANN. § 75-4319(b)(4); S.C. CODE ANN. § 30-4-40(a)(1). See generally Samuels & Johnson, *The Uniform Trade Secrets Act: The State's Response*, 24 CREIGHTON L. REV. 49 (1990).

356. See, e.g., MO. REV. STAT. § 610.021(2) (real estate transaction exception); Spradlin v. Fulton, 982 S.W.2d 255, 259 (Mo. 1998) (to close meeting under real estate transaction exception the meeting must relate directly to "the leasing, purchase, or sale of real estate by a public governmental body," which must demonstrate that "public knowledge of the transaction might adversely affect the legal consideration therefor"). But see Halifax Hosp. Med. Center v. News-Journal Corp., 724 So. 2d 567 (Fla. 1999) (strategic plans exemption to Florida's public disclosure law held unconstitutional due to failure to define "strategic plans" or "critical and confidential information").

§ 9-6(h)(4). Invasion of Personal Privacy or Injury to Reputation.

Protection of an individual's interest in personal privacy is recognized by some form of open meeting exemption in every state.[357] Some open meeting laws follow the federal government's provision in the Sunshine Act, which exempts from the open meeting requirement the disclosure of "information of a personal nature where disclosure would constitute a clearly unwarranted invasion of personal privacy."[358] Several states authorize the use of executive sessions when a person's reputation is at risk.[359] These provisions often protect discussions of a person's character, conduct, competence, or health from mandatory discussion in open meetings.[360]

§ 9-6(h)(5). Law Enforcement and Public Safety Matters.

The protection granted to law enforcement materials under state open records laws is typically duplicated in its open meeting legislation.[361] Such an exemption seeks to protect crime victims, ongoing investigations, the identity of confidential informants, and certain police tactics and techniques from mandatory discussion in open meetings.[362] Information concerning public health and safety may also fall within such an exemption.[363]

---

357. See, e.g., CONN. GEN. STAT. §§ 1-18a(e)(5), 1-19(b)(2); MONT. CODE ANN. § 2-3-203(3); N.J. STAT. ANN. § 10:4-7; VA. CODE ANN. § 2.1-344(A)(4).

358. 5 U.S.C. § 552b(c)(6). See Chap. 9-5(a)(8)(F) *supra*.

359. See, e.g., ALASKA STAT. § 44.62.310(c)(2); MD. CODE ANN., STATE GOV'T § 10-508(a)(2); MASS. GEN. LAWS ch. 30A, § 11A1/2(1), ch. 34, § 9G, ch. 39, § 23B(1); Miglionico v. Birmingham News Co., 378 So. 2d 677 (Ala. 1979). New Hampshire's open meeting law, for example, provides for executive sessions concerning "[m]atters which, if discussed in public, would likely affect adversely the reputation of any person, other than a member of the body or agency itself, unless such person requests an open meeting." N.H. REV. STAT. ANN. § 91-A:3II(c).

360. "We believe that the legislature intended . . . to permit executive sessions whenever there is a discussion of one's general reputation, i.e., the estimate the public places on a person, his reputation, good or bad, and the personal attributes of an individual. It might also include such personal traits as honesty, loyalty, integrity, reliability, and other such characteristics, good or bad, which make up one's individual personality." Miglionico v. Birmingham News Co., 378 So. 2d 677, 681 (Ala. 1979).

361. See Chap. 11-5(a)(6) *infra*.

362. See COLO. REV. STAT. § 24-6-402(3)(a)(IV), (4)(d); CONN. GEN. STAT. §§ 1-18a(e)(3), (e)(5), 1-19(b)(3); HAW. REV. STAT. § 92-5(a)(5), (6); IOWA CODE § 21.5(1)(g), (h); N.Y. PUB. OFF. LAW § 105(1)(a)-(c); VA. CODE ANN. § 2.1-344(A)(17), (20), (21).

363. See CAL. GOV'T CODE § 11126(y); DEL. CODE ANN. tit. 29, § 10004(b)(11); LA. REV. STAT. ANN. tit. 42, §§ 6.1(A)(5), 6.2(A)(6); MD. CODE ANN., STATE GOV'T § 10-508(a)(10); MONT. CODE ANN. § 2-3-112(1).

§ 9-6(h)(6). Civil Litigation Matters.

Many states exempt from the reach of their open meetings legislation communications between a public body and its attorney, paralleling the attorney-client privilege recognized by most open records laws.[364] The exemption is designed to protect the public body's consultations with its attorney, not a discussion of legal issues between members of the body.[365] Some jurisdictions limit the reach of such an exemption to matters concerning litigation in which the public body is already engaged or which it anticipates.[366]

§ 9-6(i). Categories of Meetings.

The broadly defined exemptions found in public meeting laws have been applied to a wide assortment of issues. A public body's determination whether to address an issue in an open meeting or in closed executive session often depends on the application of one or more statutory exemptions.

§ 9-6(i)(1). Personnel Matters.

§ 9-6(i)(1)(A). Interviews for Employment.

Some states take the position that an employment interview is not a "meeting" and not subject to open meeting laws.[367] Generally, interviews conducted by staff are held to be beyond the reach of open meeting laws.[368] Other states, however,

---

364. See, e.g., ARIZ. REV. STAT. § 38-431.03(A)(3), (4); COLO. REV. STAT. § 24-6-402(3)(a)(II); KAN. STAT. ANN. § 75-4319(b)(2); KY REV. STAT. § ANN. 61.810(1)(C); MINN. STAT. § 471.705.1d(e); MO. REV. STAT. § 610.021(1); N.J. STAT. ANN. § 10:4-12(b)(7); N.C. GEN. STAT. § 143-318.11(a)(5); Zorc v. Vero Beach, 722 So. 2d 891, 897 (Fla. App. 1998) ("only those persons listed in the statutory exemption, i.e., the entity, the entity's attorney, the chief administrative officer of the entity and the court reporter, are authorized to attend closed attorney-client sessions"). See Chaps. 10-2(c)(6) & 11-5(a)(4) *infra*.

365. See COLO. REV. STAT. § 24-6-402(3)(a)(II), (4)(b); DEL. CODE ANN. tit. 29, § 10004(b)(12); HAW. REV. STAT. § 92-5(a)(4); VA. CODE ANN. § 2.1-344(A)(7); City of Prescott v. Town of Chino Valley, 803 P.2d 891 (Ariz. 1990).

366. See, e.g., CONN. GEN. STAT. § 1-18a(e)(5); FLA. STAT. § 286.011(8) (pending litigation); 5 ILL. COMP. STAT. 120/2(c)(11); IND. CODE § 5-14-1.5-6.1(b)(2); IOWA CODE § 21.5(1)(c); MICH. COMP. LAWS § 15.268(e); NEB. REV. STAT. § 84-1410(1)(a); N.M. STAT. ANN. § 10-15-1(H)(7); N.Y. PUB. OFF. LAW § 105(1)(d); OHIO REV. CODE ANN. § 121.22(G)(3); S.D. CODIFIED LAWS § 1-25-2(3); UTAH CODE ANN. § 52-4-5(2); WASH. REV. CODE § 42.30.110(1)(I); WYO. STAT. ANN. § 16-4-405(a)(iii); Dunn v. Alabama State Univ. Bd. of Trustees, 628 So. 2d 519 (Ala. 1993), *overruled on other grounds*, Watkins v. Board of Trustees of Alabama State Univ., 703 So. 2d 335 (Ala. 1997) (exemption applies only to litigation matters in which the public body is a named party).

367. See Ky. Op. Att'y Gen. No. 91-144 (1991); Va. Op. Att'y Gen. (July 12, 1985).

368. See COLO. REV. STAT. § 24-6-402(1)(a), (d); People ex rel. Cooper v. Carlson, 328 N.E.2d 675 (Ill. App. 1975); Indiana State Bd. of Health v. Journal-Gazette Co., 608 N.E.2d 989 (Ind. App.), *aff'd*, 619 N.E.2d 272 (Ind. 1993).

require that interviews take place in the open,[369] but may permit discussion of character, competence, or health in executive session.[370] The initial meetings of search committees may be held in executive session in some states,[371] but discussions regarding the "short list" of applicants is likely a matter for an open meeting.[372] In most states, offers of employment and salary discussions may occur in executive session,[373] but the final vote must take place in an open meeting.[374]

§ 9-6(i)(1)(B). Performance Reviews.

Meetings to consider the job performance of a specific person may typically take place in executive session,[375] particularly when so requested by the person being reviewed.[376] The individual may have a right to prior notice of any such meeting[377] and may request that the matter be addressed in public session.[378] In

---

369. See, e.g., MICH. COMP. LAWS § 15.268(f) ("all interviews by a public body for employment or appointment to a public office shall be held in an open meeting pursuant to this act"); Herald Co. v. Bay City, 577 N.W.2d 696, 701 (Mich. App. 1998) (interviews of candidates for position of fire chief must be open to the public); Channel 10, Inc. v. Independent Sch. Dist., 215 N.W.2d 814, 825 (Minn. 1974).

370. See, e.g., WASH. REV. CODE § 4230.110(1)(h); Dale v. Birmingham News Co., 452 So. 2d 1321 (Ala. 1984); Brown v. East Baton Rouge Parish Sch. Bd., 405 So. 2d 1148 (La. App. 1981).

371. See, e.g., IND. CODE § 5-14-1.5-6.1(9); MASS. GEN. LAWS ch. 39, § 23B; Gerstein v. Superintendent Search Screening Comm., 541 N.E.2d 984 (Mass. 1989).

372. See Gerstein v. Superintendent Search Screening Comm., 541 N.E.2d 984 (Mass. 1989) (applicants on short list are identified by name, therefore no privacy considerations require an executive session); Attorney Gen. v. School Comm., 375 N.E.2d 1188 (Mass. 1978).

373. See OR. REV. STAT. § 192.660(1)(a); People v. Board of Educ., 353 N.E.2d 147, 150 (Ill. App. 1976); Port Townsend Publ'g Co. v. Brown, 567 P.2d 664, 666 (Wash. App. 1977).

374. See, e.g., N.C. GEN. STAT. § 143-318.11(a)(8); WASH. REV. CODE § 4230.110(1)(g).

375. See CAL. GOV'T CODE § 54957; CONN. GEN. STAT. § 1-18a(e)(1); IDAHO CODE § 67-2345(1)(b); LA. REV. STAT. ANN. § 42:6.1(A)(1); San Diego Union v. City Council, 196 Cal. Rptr. 45 (Ct. App. 1983); Missoulian v. Board of Regents, 675 P.2d 962 (Mont. 1984).

376. See DEL. CODE ANN. tit. 29, § 10004(b)(1), (8), (9); N.M. STAT. ANN. § 10-15-1(H)(2); Cozzolino v. City of Fontana, 289 P.2d 248 (Cal. App. 1955); Tribune Co. v. School Bd., 367 So. 2d 627 (Fla. 1979); Easton Area Joint Sewer Auth. v. Morning Call, Inc., 581 A.2d 684, 687 (Pa. Commw. 1990).

377. See CAL. GOV'T CODE §§ 11126(a), 54957; LA. REV. STAT. ANN. § 42:6.1(A)(1); University of Alaska v. Geistauts, 666 P.2d 424, 429 (Alaska 1983); Fischer v. Los Angeles Unified Sch. Dist., 82 Cal. Rptr. 2d 452, 456 (Ct. App. 1999) (notice required only when hearing deals with specific complaints or charges against employee, not when hearing is to consider continued employment of employee); Wisconsin ex rel. Schaeve v. Van Lare, 370 N.W.2d 271, 275 (Wis. App. 1985). But see Cooner v. Board of Educ., 663 P.2d 1002, 1007-08 (Ariz. App. 1982). A meeting to review evaluation methods must be open to the public. See Schmiedicke v. Clare Sch. Bd., 577 N.W.2d 706 (Mich. App. 1998).

378. See ALASKA STAT. § 44.62.310(c)(2). But see Ramsey v. City of Sand Point, 936 P.2d 126, 134 (Alaska 1997) (police chief's decision not to appear at public meeting called to discuss his

contrast to public employees, the job performance evaluation of a senior government official may have to take place in a public meeting.[379]

§ 9-6(i)(1)(C). Disciplinary Matters.

Disciplinary matters or termination proceedings regarding a specific person are often excluded from the open meeting requirement to protect the individual's privacy.[380] The person may have a right to prior notice of the meeting,[381] and his request that the matter be addressed in open session will usually be honored.[382] The ultimate action taken by the public body regarding the matter generally must occur in an open meeting.[383] A closed executive session is typically not appropriate where the privacy interests of an individual are not at risk, and only the general personnel policies of the public body are under review.[384]

§ 9-6(i)(1)(D). Employer-Employee Negotiations and Collective Bargaining.

Meetings concerning labor negotiations between the public employer and its employees are one of the most often exempted categories of meetings.[385] Some

---

removal constituted a waiver of his right to request that the issue be discussed publicly); Furtado v. Sierra Community College, 80 Cal. Rptr. 2d 589 (Ct. App. 1998) (employee has right to have complaints or charges heard in open session, but not other personnel matters).

379. See, e.g., IND. CODE § 5-14-1.5-6.1(4), (8) & (9).

380. See, e.g., CAL. GOV'T CODE § 11126(a); IDAHO CODE § 67-2345(1)(b); KY. REV. STAT. ANN. § 61.810(1)(f); TEX. REV. CIV. STAT. ANN. art. 6252-17, § 2(g); VA. CODE ANN. § 2.1-344(A)(1); Blair v. City of Winchester, 743 S.W.2d 28, 31 (Ky. App. 1987); Nasrallah v. Missouri State Bd. of Chiropractic Exm'rs, 1996 Mo. App. LEXIS 1994 (Mo. App. Nov. 26, 1996).

381. See Cleveland Bd. of Educ. v. Loudermill, 470 U.S. 532, 546 (1985); Bollinger v. San Diego Civil Serv. Comm'n, 84 Cal. Rptr. 2d 27, 31 (Ct. App. 1999) (notice not required when sole purpose of meeting is to deliberate whether complaints or charges justify disciplinary action and is not evidentiary in nature); Johnson v. Nash, 608 A.2d 200, 202 (N.H. 1992).

382. See, e.g., CAL. GOV'T Code § 54957 (public employee must be given 24-hour written notice of employee's right to have an open session when local legislative body hears specific complaints or charges brought against the employee by another person or employee); KY. REV. STAT. ANN. § 61.810(1)(f); N.H. REV. STAT. ANN. § 91-A:3II; S.C. CODE ANN. § 30-4-70(a)(1).

383. See MINN. STAT. § 471.705.1d(c); Commercial Printing Co. v. Rush, 549 S.W.2d 790, 795 (Ark. 1977) ("once a decision has been made in executive session that discipline or other action is needed, all further acts of the board should be public"); Librach v. Cooper, 778 S.W.2d 351, 355 (Mo. App. 1989). But see WIS. STAT. § 19.85(1)(b) (formal action may be taken in executive session).

384. See KY. REV. STAT. ANN. § 61.810(1)(f) ("This exception shall not be interpreted to permit discussion of general personnel matters in secret."); Hudson v. School Dist., 578 S.W.2d 301, 308 (Mo. App. 1979).

385. See generally McClintock, *Impact of "Sunshine" or "Open Meeting" Laws: In Washington and Other States Are Public Sector Negotiation Sessions Open or Closed to the Public?*, 15 GONZ. L. REV. 65 (1979); Summers, *Public Sector Bargaining: Problems of Governmental*

states afford a blanket exemption to all employer-employee grievance meetings, negotiations and strategy discussions of the public body.[386] Other states exempt only the strategy meetings of the public body,[387] or only collective bargaining sessions between the public body and employee representatives,[388] or grievance meetings.[389]

§ 9-6(i)(2). Probation and Parole Boards.

Open meeting laws typically either exclude meetings of probation and parole boards from the scope of coverage or permit such boards to deliberate in executive session.[390] The statute may, however, require that hearings and final votes take place in an open meeting.[391]

§ 9-6(i)(3). Medical or Psychiatric Matters.

Open meeting laws generally permit public bodies to discuss the medical or psychiatric history of identifiable persons in executive session.[392] Some states

---

Decisionmaking, 44 U. CIN. L. REV. 669 (1975); Comment, *Public Sector Collective Bargaining and Sunshine Laws — A Needless Conflict*, 18 WM. & MARY L. REV. 159 (1976).

386. See, e.g., 5 ILL. COMP. STAT. 120/2(c)(2); KAN. STAT. ANN. § 75-4319(b)(3); LA. REV. STAT. ANN. tit. 42, §§ 6.1(A)(2), 6.2(A)(3); ME. REV. STAT. ANN. tit. 1, § 405(6)(D); MD. CODE ANN., STATE GOV'T § 10-508(a)(9); N.J. STAT. ANN. § 10:4-12(b)(4); OR. REV. STAT. § 192.660(3) & (4) (labor negotiations may be conducted in executive session, though representatives of the news media may attend and may be prohibited from disclosing specified information); WASH. REV. CODE § 42.30.140(4)(a); Jefferson County Bd. of Educ. v. Courier-Journal, 551 S.W.2d 25 (Ky. App. 1977); Talbot v. Concord Union Sch. Dist., 323 A.2d 912 (N.H. 1974); County of Saratoga v. Newman, 476 N.Y.S.2d 1020 (Sup. Ct. 1984).

387. See, e.g., DEL. CODE ANN. tit. 29, § 10004(b)(4); NEB. REV. STAT. § 84-1410(1(a); TENN. CODE ANN. § 8-44-201; UTAH CODE ANN. § 52-4-5(1).

388. See, e.g., HAW. REV. STAT. § 92-5(a)(3); KY. REV. STAT. ANN. § 61.810(1)(e); R.I. GEN. LAWS § 42-46-5(a)(2). See Southwestern Oregon Publ'g Co., v. Southwestern Oregon Community College Dist., 559 P.2d 1289, 1291 (Or. App. 1977) (open meeting law does not apply to negotiations conducted by a retained negotiator).

389. See Waterbury Teachers Ass'n v. Freedom of Info. Comm'n, 694 A.2d 1241 (Conn. 1997) (evidentiary portions of grievance hearings not excluded from open meeting requirement, though portion of hearings involving negotiations regarding remedies or settlements are exempted).

390. See, e.g., ALASKA STAT. § 44.62.310(d); DEL. CODE ANN. tit. 29, § 10004(h)(5); MISS. CODE ANN. § 25-41-3(a); N.H. REV. STAT. ANN. § 91-A:5; N.J. STAT. ANN. § 10:4-8(a); OR. REV. STAT. § 192.690.

391. See, e.g., COLO. REV. STAT. § 24-6-402(3)(c); IDAHO CODE § 67-2345(1)(g).

392. See CONN. GEN. STAT. §§ 1-18a(e)(5), 1-19(b)(2); GA. CODE ANN. § 50-14-3(5); 5 ILL. COMP. STAT. 120/2(A)(f); MINN. STAT. § 471.705.1d(b)(3); MO. REV. STAT. § 610.021(5), (7), (8), (11), (12), (15); MONT. CODE ANN. §§ 50-16-501 et seq., 50-16-601 et seq.; NEV. REV. STAT. § 241.030(1); N.C. GEN. STAT. § 143-318.11(a)(7); UTAH CODE ANN. § 52-4-5(1)(a); WIS. STAT. § 19.85(1)(f).

permit a public hearing if one is requested by the person who is the subject of the discussion.[393]

§ 9-6(i)(4). Student Information.

Although open meeting laws require that educational policy and budgetary matters be discussed in open meetings, information relating to identified students may often be considered in executive session.[394] Many open meeting laws specifically provide for executive sessions to deal with student disciplinary proceedings,[395] or apply an exemption protective of reputation that permits executive sessions.[396] Some states have a specific exemption for meetings involving the placement of students,[397] though students, parents, or guardians are usually entitled to request that the meeting or hearing be opened to the public.[398]

§ 9-6(i)(5). Matters Involving Public Assistance.

Discussion by a public body of general issues and policies concerning public assistance programs must typically be held in open meetings. The body is, however, usually permitted to recess to executive session when the discussion focuses on identifiable individuals.[399]

§ 9-6(i)(6). Professional Licensing and Disciplinary Proceedings.

States generally regulate the licensing of professionals and determine public access to such proceedings in specific statutes.[400] Some states, however, address these proceedings in their open meeting laws by authorizing the licensing body

---

393. See, e.g., KAN. STAT. ANN. § 75-4319(b)(5); W. VA. CODE § 6-9A-4(5).
394. See COLO. REV. STAT. § 24-6-402(4)(h); CONN. GEN. STAT. §§ 1-18a(e)(5), 1-19(b)(11); KY. REV. STAT. ANN. § 61.810(6).
395. See, e.g., ARK. CODE ANN. § 6-18-507(c); IDAHO CODE § 67-2345(1)(b); 5 ILL. COMP. STAT. 120/2(B)(3); IND. CODE § 20-8.1-5-10; IOWA CODE § 21.5; Me. REV. STAT. ANN. tit. 1, § 405(6)(B); MO. REV. STAT. § 610.021(6); N.C. GEN. STAT. § 143-318.11(a)(10); S.D. CODIFIED LAWS § 1-25-2(2); VT. STAT. ANN. tit. 1, § 313(a)(7); WYO. STAT. ANN. § 16-4-405(a)(xi); Schumacher v. Lisbon Sch. Bd., 582 N.W.2d 183, 185-86 (Iowa 1998) (student has right to have hearing on proposed suspension held in open session); Armstead v. Lima City Bd. of Educ., 600 N.E.2d 1085 (Ohio App. 1991).
396. See, e.g., Pierce v. School Comm., 322 F. Supp. 957, 961 (D. Mass. 1971).
397. See, e.g., DEL. CODE tit. 29, § 10004(b)(7), (9); FLA. STAT. § 230.23(4)(m); 5 ILL. COMP. STAT. 120/2(B)(3); IND. CODE § 5-14-1.5-6.1(b)(7); N.C. GEN. STAT. § 143-318.11(a)(10); OKLA. STAT. tit. 25, § 307(B)(5).
398. See, e.g., CAL. EDUC. CODE §§ 48912(b) & (c), 48918; IOWA CODE § 21.5(1)(e); KAN. STAT. ANN. § 75-4319(b)(5); N.M. STAT. ANN. § 10-15-1(H)(4); W. VA. CODE § 6-9A-4(3).
399. See MICH. COMP. LAWS § 15.263(11); MINN. STAT. § 471.705.1d(b)(3).
400. See, e.g., CAL. BUS. & PROF. CODE § 827; CAL. HEALTH & SAFETY CODE § 32155.

to discuss personal information regarding such individuals in executive session.[401]

Many states require that disciplinary proceedings occur in a public meeting.[402] A few states permit the licensing body to deliberate in executive session, but require that all other aspects of the proceeding be held in an open meeting.[403] Some states treat disciplinary proceedings as quasi-judicial proceedings not subject to open meeting laws.[404] Others require that such proceedings take place in executive session, unless the licensee requests a public meeting.[405]

§ 9-6(j). Challenges to Improperly Noticed or Closed Meetings.

Several states permit "any person" or any "citizen of the state" to bring an action alleging the improper notice or closing of a meeting of a public body subject to an open meeting law.[406] In these states, journalists have standing to challenge unlawfully held meetings.[407] In several other states, the open meeting law is enforced by the attorney general or a district attorney.[408]

Except in jurisdictions that provide only for imposition of criminal penalties for violation of an open meeting law,[409] available remedies include injunc-

---

401. See, e.g., CONN. GEN. STAT. §§ 1-18a(e)(5), 1-19(b)(8); N.C. GEN. STAT. § 143-318.18(6); OHIO REV. CODE ANN. § 121.22(D); WASH. REV. CODE § 42.30.140(1). But see DEL. CODE ANN. tit. 29, § 10004(b)(1) (executive sessions prohibited).

402. See Christiansen v. Missouri State Bd. of Accountancy, 764 S.W.2d 943, 950 (Mo. App. 1988).

403. See, e.g., N.J. STAT. ANN. § 10:4-12(b)(9); N.M. STAT. ANN. § 10-15-1(H)(1). See Della Serra v. Borough of Mountainside, 481 A.2d 547, 551 (N.J. Super. 1984).

404. See, e.g., W. VA. CODE § 6-9A-2(4).

405. See, e.g., IOWA CODE § 21.5(1)(d); OHIO REV. CODE ANN. § 121.22(G)(1); WIS. STAT. § 19.85(1)(b).

406. See, e.g., FLA. STAT. § 286.011(2); KAN. STAT. ANN. § 75-4320(a); ME. REV. STAT. ANN. tit. 1, § 409(2); MINN. STAT. § 471.705.2; NEB. REV. STAT. § 84-1414(3); S.C. CODE ANN. § 30-4-100(a); TENN. CODE ANN. § 8-44-106(a); VA. CODE § 2.1-346; WIS. STAT. § 19.97; N.M. STAT. ANN. § 10-15-3(C).

407. See TEX. REV. CIV. STAT. ANN. art. 6252-17, § 3; Miglionico v. Birmingham News Co., 378 So. 2d 677 (Ala. 1979); Common Council v. Peru Daily Tribune, Inc., 440 N.E.2d 726 (Ind. App. 1982); Channel 10, Inc. v. Independent Sch. Dist., 215 N.W.2d 814 (Minn. 1974); Kansas City Star Co. v. Shields, 771 S.W.2d 101 (Mo. App. 1989); Barker v. City of Portland, 767 P.2d 460 (Or. App. 1989); Press-Enter., Inc. v. Benton Area School Dist., 604 A.2d 1221 (Pa. Commw. 1992); Board of Trustees v. Cox Enters., 679 S.W.2d 86 (Tex. App. 1984), aff'd in part, 706 S.W.2d 956 (Tex. 1986).

408. See, e.g., ARIZ. REV. STAT. § 38-431.07(A); IDAHO CODE § 67-2347(3); KY. REV. STAT. ANN. §§ 61.846, 61.848; MASS. GEN. LAWS ch. 34, § 9G; MICH. COMP. LAWS §§ 15.270, 15.271; NEB. REV. STAT. § 84-1414(2); N.M. STAT. ANN. § 10-15-3(B); UTAH CODE ANN. § 52-4-9(1). See generally Smoot & Clothier, *Open Meetings Profile: The Prosecutor's View*, 20 WASHBURN L.J. 241 (1981).

409. See, e.g., ARK. CODE ANN. § 25-19-104; CAL. GOV'T Code § 11130.7; MICH. COMP. LAWS § 15.272; MONT. CODE ANN. § 45-7-401; OKLA. STAT. tit. 25, § 314; PA. STAT. ANN. tit. 65, § 284;

tions,[410] declaratory relief,[411] civil penalties[412] or removal.[413] Some states permit open meeting law violations to be cured by subsequent open meetings.[414] In other states, the open meeting law may void actions taken at a session not held in compliance with the open meeting law.[415] Under many open meeting laws,

---

S.C. CODE ANN. § 30-4-110; S.D. CODIFIED LAWS § 1-25-1; WIS. STAT. § 19.96; Griswold v. Mt. Diablo Unified Sch. Dist., 134 Cal. Rptr. 3 (Ct. App. 1976) (acts of legislative body in violation of open meeting law are not invalid, they merely subject the member of the body to criminal penalties); Tovar v. Texas, 949 S.W.2d 370 (Tex. Crim. App. 1997), aff'd, 978 S.W.2d 584 (Tex. Crim. App. 1998) (affirmed conviction of former president of school board for violating Open Meetings Act by calling and participating in closed meeting, even though official was unaware of the illegality).

410. See IND. CODE § 5-14-1.5-7(a); N.Y. PUB. OFF. LAW § 107(1); Miglionico v. Birmingham News Co., 378 So. 2d 677 (Ala. 1979); Sacramento Newspaper Guild v. Sacramento County Bd. of Supervisors, 69 Cal. Rptr. 480 (Ct. App. 1968); Sentinel Communications Co. v. School Bd., 20 MEDIA L. REP. 1103 (Fla. Cir. 1992); Lewiston Daily Sun, Inc. v. City of Auburn, 544 A.2d 335 (Me. 1988); Detroit News, Inc. v. City of Detroit, 460 N.W.2d 312 (Mich. App. 1990); Kansas City Star Co. v. Lewellen, 15 MEDIA L. REP. 2345 (Mo. Cir. 1988).

411. See CAL. GOV'T CODE §§ 11130, 11130.3; MD. CODE ANN., STATE GOV'T § 10-510(d)(3); N.Y. PUB. OFF. LAW § 107(1); PA. STAT. ANN. tit. 65, § 285; Arkansas Gazette Co. v. Pickens, 522 S.W.2d 350 (Ark. 1975); Regents of Univ. of California v. Superior Ct., 976 P.2d 808 (Cal. 1999) (right to commence action to stop or prevent violations of open meeting law extends only to present and future actions and violations, not past ones); Hain v. Board of Sch. Dirs., 641 A.2d 661, 662-63 (Pa. Commw. 1994).

412. See IDAHO CODE § 67-2347(2); IOWA CODE § 21.6(3)(a); KAN. STAT. ANN. § 75-4320(a); LA. REV. STAT. ANN. tit. 42, § 13; ME. REV. STAT. ANN. tit. 1, § 410; MINN. STAT. § 471.705.2; MO. REV. STAT. § 610.027.3 (member of public governmental body who purposely violates open meetings law may be subject to civil fine of not more than five hundred dollars); N.J. STAT. ANN. § 10:4-17; OHIO REV. CODE ANN. § 121.22(I)(2); WASH. REV. CODE § 42.30.120(1); WIS. STAT. § 19.96.

413. See, e.g., ARIZ. REV. STAT. § 38-431.07(A); HAW. REV. STAT. § 92-13; IOWA CODE § 21.6(3)(d); MINN. STAT. § 471.705.2; OHIO REV. CODE ANN. § 121.22(I)(4).

414. See Tolar v. School Bd. of Liberty County, 398 So. 2d 427, 429 (Fla. 1981); Zorc v. Vero Beach, 722 So. 2d 891, 903 (Fla. App. 1998).

415. See ALASKA STAT. § 44.62.310(f); CAL. GOV'T CODE §§ 54960.1, 54960.5; COLO. REV. STAT. § 24-6-402(8); FLA. STAT. ANN. § 286.011(1); GA. CODE ANN. § 50-14-1(b); ME. REV. STAT. ANN. tit. 1, § 409(2); NEV. REV. STAT. § 241.036; N.M. STAT. ANN. § 10-15-3(A); R.I. GEN. LAWS § 42-46-8(d); WYO. STAT. § 16-4-403(a); Regents of Univ. of California v. Superior Ct., 976 P.2d 808 (Cal. 1999) (suit to make state body's action null and void must be commenced within 30 days from the date the action was taken); Zorc v. Vero Beach, 722 So. 2d 891, 902 (Fla. App. 1998) ("The principle that a Sunshine Law violation renders void a resulting official action does not depend on a finding of intent to violate the law or resulting prejudice. Once the violation is established, prejudice is presumed."); Kennedy v. Powell, 401 So. 2d 453, 457 (La. App. 1981) (suit to make public body's action null and void must be commenced within 60 days from the date the action was taken); McComas v. Board of Educ., 475 S.E.2d 280 (W. Va. 1996) (court relied upon factors of seriousness of violation, intent, and possible effects, in affirming decision to void school board's vote taken at noticed meeting following unlawful private meeting).

attorneys fees[416] and costs[417] are available.

---

416. See CAL. GOV'T CODE §§ 11130.5, 54960.5; MD. CODE ANN., STATE GOV'T § 10-510(d); MINN. STAT. § 471.705.1; MO. REV. STAT. § 610.027.3; N.Y. PUB. OFF. LAW § 107(2); UTAH CODE ANN. § 52-4-9; International Longshoremen's & Warehousemen's Union v. Los Angeles Export Terminal, Inc., 81 Cal. Rptr. 2d 456, 466 (Ct. App. 1999); City Council v. Reno Newspapers, Inc., 784 P.2d 974 (Nev. 1989); Bradshaw v. Shaw, 360 A.2d 123 (N.H. 1976). But see Schumacher v. Lisbon Sch. Bd., 582 N.W.2d 183, 186-87 (Iowa 1998).

417. See ARK. CODE ANN. § 25-19-107(d); CAL. GOV'T CODE §§ 11130.5, 54960.5; CONN. GEN. STAT. § 1-21i; FLA. STAT. § 286.011(7); IOWA CODE § 21.6(3); KAN. STAT. ANN. § 75-4320(c); MD. CODE ANN., STATE GOV'T § 10-510(d)(5); MO. REV. STAT. § 610.027.3; MONT. CODE ANN. § 2-3-221; N.Y. PUB. OFF. LAW § 107(2); OHIO REV. CODE ANN. § 121.22(I)(2): WIS. STAT. § 19.97.

Chapter 10
ACCESS TO FEDERAL GOVERNMENT RECORDS

§ 10-1. Introduction.
§ 10-2. The Freedom of Information Act.
    § 10-2(a). Introduction.
    § 10-2(b). Obtaining Information.
        § 10-2(b)(1). Records.
        § 10-2(b)(2). Organizations.
        § 10-2(b)(3). Procedures.
        § 10-2(b)(4). Limitations on Agency Response Time.
        § 10-2(b)(5). Fees.
    § 10-2(c). Exemptions.
        § 10-2(c)(1). Introduction.
        § 10-2(c)(2). Exemption 1: National Security.
        § 10-2(c)(3). Exemption 2: Internal Agency Personnel Rules.
        § 10-2(c)(4). Exemption 3: Disclosure Forbidden by Other Federal Statutes.
        § 10-2(c)(5). Exemption 4: Trade Secrets and Confidential Commercial Information.
        § 10-2(c)(6). Exemption 5: Internal Agency Memoranda and Policy Discussions.
        § 10-2(c)(7). Exemption 6: Personal Privacy.
        § 10-2(c)(8). Exemption 7: Law Enforcement Investigations.
            § 10-2(c)(8)(A). Exemption 7(A).
            § 10-2(c)(8)(B). Exemption 7(B).
            § 10-2(c)(8)(C). Exemption 7(C).
            § 10-2(c)(8)(D). Exemption 7(D).
            § 10-2(c)(8)(E). Exemption 7(E).
            § 10-2(c)(8)(F). Exemption 7(F).
        § 10-2(c)(9). Exemption 8: Financial Institutions.
        § 10-2(c)(10). Exemption 9: Oil and Gas Wells.
    § 10-2(d). Exclusions.
        § 10-2(d)(1). Exclusion (c)(1).
        § 10-2(d)(2). Exclusion (c)(2).
        § 10-2(d)(3). Exclusion (c)(3).
    § 10-2(e). Segregation of Exempt Material.
    § 10-2(f). Reverse FOIA Suits.
    § 10-2(g). Administrative Appeals.
    § 10-2(h). Litigation.
§ 10-3. The Federal Advisory Committee Act.
    § 10-3(a). Introduction.
    § 10-3(b). Records.
    § 10-3(c). Procedures.

§ 10-1. Introduction.

Federal, state, and local governments collect and generate an enormous amount of information about their operations, about important issues of public concern, about foreign governments and peoples, and about their own citizens. Perhaps because of the sheer volume of material over which the government exercises dominion, and no doubt because of the press' fundamental role in reporting on governmental affairs, journalists look to government-generated and collected information as their principal source of newsgathering. For generations, the press' ability to obtain such information was limited to reliance on government handouts and the guile and resourcefulness of individual journalists in cultivating sources within the government. Passage of the federal Freedom of Information Act ("FOIA") in 1966, however, provided journalists with a legally enforceable right to secure broad categories of information in the government's control. Indeed, the Act made all records of the federal government presumptively open to public inspection.

Although some states had opened their records to the public on a limited basis prior to 1966, the passage of FOIA created the impetus for state and local governments to expand their existing open records laws or to enact legislation granting public access to government records in the manner of the federal statute. These laws, which are discussed in Chapter 11, have become important sources of information as well. In this chapter, we focus on FOIA and related federal legislation as well as the rich body of precedent they have spawned.

§ 10-2. The Freedom of Information Act.

§ 10-2(a). Introduction.

The Freedom of Information Act establishes a statutory right of public access to federal government information. The Act is designed to ensure openness and accountability by providing citizens with the means to understand and evaluate the workings of their government.[1] Although its application has been inconsistent,[2] the Act's basic philosophy remains that government records are presumed to be available for public scrutiny because open government is better government.[3]

---

1. See Chrysler Corp. v. Brown, 441 U.S. 281, 290 n.10 (1979) (quoting H.R. REP. NO. 89-497, at 12 (1966)) ("A democratic society requires an informed, intelligent electorate, and the intelligence of the electorate varies as the quantity and quality of its information varies."); NLRB v. Robbins Tire & Rubber Co., 437 U.S. 214, 242 (1978) ("The basic purpose of FOIA is to ensure an informed citizenry, vital to the functioning of a democratic society, needed to check against corruption and to hold the governors accountable to the governed.").

2. The Clinton administration, for example, replaced a policy in force in the Reagan and Bush administrations which had required withholding information under the Act whenever a substantial legal basis existed for doing so. See Church of Scientology Int'l v. Department of Justice, 30 F.3d 224, 227 (1st Cir. 1994) (finding that disclosure of 75 pages directly resulted from Clinton administration policy). In the Clinton administration, agencies are not to invoke a FOIA exemption unless the disclosure will result in a "foreseeable harm." See Memorandum for Heads of Departments and Agencies from Attorney General Janet Reno, Oct. 4, 1993, *reprinted in* J. FRANKLIN & R. BOUCHARD, GUIDEBOOK TO THE FREEDOM OF INFORMATION AND PRIVACY ACTS App. D5 (1998).

3. See Department of Air Force v. Rose, 425 U.S. 352, 361 (1976) ("disclosure, not secrecy, is the dominant objective of the Act"); Maricopa Audubon Soc'y v. United States Forest Serv., 108

§ 10-2(b). Obtaining Information.

§ 10-2(b)(1). Records.

FOIA requires public access to all "records" created or obtained by an agency governed by the Act[4] that are under the agency's control at the time of the FOIA request.[5] Records created solely for personal convenience, such as personal calendars and telephone message slips, are not subject to the Act.[6]

F.3d 1082, 1085 (9th Cir. 1997) ("The Freedom of Information Act . . . mandates a policy of broad disclosure of government documents."). The voluminous litigation generated by FOIA is itself the subject of a number of treatises, several of which are cited in the discussion that follows. The reader is referred to those sources for a more comprehensive treatment of the FOIA case law and relevant agency regulations. What follows is an overview of the Act, including the scope of information it covers, its procedural requirements, and the statutory exemptions from its disclosure requirements.

4. The Act applies to "agencies" within the executive branch of the federal government, including the Executive Office of the President and independent regulatory agencies. It does not apply to state and local governments, the courts, Congress, or private persons. 1 FRANKLIN & BOUCHARD, *supra* note 2, at § 1.03.

5. For requested materials to qualify as "agency records," two requirements must be satisfied: (1) an agency must either create or obtain the requested materials, and (2) the agency must be in control of the requested materials at the time the FOIA request is made. See Department of Justice v. Tax Analysts, 492 U.S. 136, 144-45 (1989); Grand Central Partnership, Inc. v. Cuomo, 166 F.3d 473, 479 (2d Cir. 1999). Courts will inquire as to whether the information was created, controlled, used, relied upon, or filed by the agency. See Wolfe v. Department of Health & Human Servs., 711 F.2d 1077 (D.C. Cir. 1983); Note, *A Control Test for Determining "Agency Record" Status Under the Freedom of Information Act*, 85 COLUM. L. REV. 611 (1985). The burden is on the agency to demonstrate that the materials sought are not agency records. See Department of Justice v. Tax Analysts, 492 U.S. 136, 142 n.3 (1989). The Act itself does not define the term "record," RCA Global Communications, Inc. v. FCC, 524 F. Supp. 579, 582 (D. Del. 1981), and the mere physical presence of materials within an agency is not determinative, see Kissinger v. Reporters Comm. for Freedom of the Press, 445 U.S. 136, 157 (1980); Wolfe v. Department of Health & Human Servs., 711 F.2d 1077 (D.C. Cir. 1983). See also Bureau of Nat'l Affairs, Inc. v. Department of Justice, 742 F.2d 1484, 1486 (D.C. Cir. 1984) (materials belonging to an individual, that may be disposed of at his discretion, are not agency records); Goland v. CIA, 607 F.2d 339, 345 (D.C. Cir. 1978), *cert. denied*, 445 U.S. 927 (1980) (congressional hearing transcript in agency's possession not an "agency record" because Congress did not intend to relinquish control of document). An agency must consider granting or denying a records request for documents in its possession that were created by a different agency, particularly if referring the FOIA request to the creating agency would significantly impair the requester's ability to obtain the records or receive them in a timely manner. See Peralta v. United States Attorney's Office, 136 F.3d 169, 175 (D.C. Cir. 1998).

6. See Gallant v. NLRB, 26 F.3d 168, 171 (D.C. Cir. 1994) (personal papers that may relate to an employee's work, but which the individual does not rely on to perform her duties, are not agency records); Bureau of Nat'l Affairs, Inc. v. Department of Justice, 742 F.2d 1484, 1492-93 (D.C. Cir. 1984) (factors used to determine whether document is an "agency record" or employee's personal record include: i) circumstances that led to creation of the document; ii) purpose for which document was created; iii) document's actual use; and iv) maintenance of document); *id.* (telephone slips and appointment calendars not agency records); Kissinger v. Reporters Comm. for Freedom of the Press, 445 U.S. 136 (1980) (telephone logs and other personal records and

The term "records" is broadly defined to include all types of reproducible[7] documentary information, including papers, letters, reports,[8] manuals,[9] computer files,[10] photographs,[11] films,[12] and sound recordings.[13] The fact that requested information may be available from another source does not affect an agency's obligation to produce a record pursuant to the Act.[14]

---

memorabilia of National Security Adviser to President Nixon did not become a State Department agency record when he became Secretary of State); Spannaus v. Department of Justice, 942 F. Supp. 656, 658 (D.D.C. 1996) (personal files of former United States Attorney beyond reach of FOIA).

7. Physical objects that cannot be reproduced are generally not considered "records" under the Act. See, e.g., Nichols v. United States, 325 F. Supp. 130, 135 (D. Kan. 1971), *aff'd on other grounds*, 460 F.2d 671 (10th Cir.), *cert. denied*, 409 U.S. 966 (1972) (guns, bullets, and other physical objects are not records).

8. See Soucie v. David, 448 F.2d 1067, 1075-76 (D.C. Cir. 1971).

9. See 5 U.S.C. § 552(a)(2)(C) ("Each agency shall make available to the public information as follows: . . . administrative staff manuals and instructions to staff that affect a member of the public; unless the materials are promptly published and copies offered for sale.").

10. See Burka v. Department of Health & Human Servs., 87 F.3d 508, 519 (D.C. Cir. 1996) (computer data tapes are "agency records" for purposes of FOIA); Yeager v. DEA, 678 F.2d 315, 321 (D.C. Cir. 1982); Long v. IRS, 596 F.2d 362, 364-65 (9th Cir. 1979), *cert. denied*, 446 U.S. 917 (1980) (computer tapes can be agency records). Issues concerning the Act's application to computer/electronic records are, however, still emerging. See Tax Analysts v. Department of Justice, 913 F. Supp. 599 (D.D.C. 1996), *aff'd*, 107 F.3d 923 (D.C. Cir.), *cert. denied*, 522 U.S. 931 (1997) (electronic legal research database licensed to agency did not qualify as an agency record); Brooks, *Adventures in Cyber-Space: Computer Technology and the Arkansas Freedom of Information Act*, 17 U. ARK. LITTLE ROCK L.J. 417 (1995); Bunker et al., *Access to Government-Held Information in the Computer Age: Applying Legal Doctrine to Emerging Technology*, 20 FLA. ST. U. L. REV. 543 (1993); Grodsky, *The Freedom of Information Act in the Electronic Age: The Statute Is Not User Friendly*, 31 JURIMETRICS J. 17 (1990); Sorokin, *The Computerization of Government Information Under the FOIA and the Depository Library Program*, 24 COLUM. J.L. & SOC. PROBS. 267 (1991).

11. See Weisberg v. Department of Justice, 631 F.2d 824, 827-28 (D.C. Cir. 1980) (privately created copyrighted photographs of the Martin Luther King assassination scene in possession of FBI deemed "agency records" subject to FOIA). Copyright considerations caused the court of appeals to remand the *Weisberg* case to the district court to seek joinder of the copyright owner, which had not objected to a viewing of the photographs, but objected to any copying of them. See *id.* at 825-26. See generally Kidwell, *Open Records Laws and Copyright*, 1989 WIS. L. REV. 1021; Perritt, *Sources of Rights to Access Public Information*, 4 WM. & MARY BILL OF RTS. J. 179 (1995) (analyzing tension between public records acts and intellectual property law); Note, *The Applicability of the Freedom of Information Act's Disclosure Requirements to Intellectual Property*, 57 NOTRE DAME L. REV. 561 (1982).

12. See, e.g., Save the Dolphins v. Department of Commerce, 404 F. Supp. 407, 411 (N.D. Cal. 1975).

13. See Forsham v. Harris, 445 U.S. 169, 183 (1980). The Electronic Freedom of Information Act Amendments of 1996 have further broadened the definition of "records" specifically to include electronic media. 5 U.S.C. § 552(f)(2).

14. See Department of Justice v. Tax Analysts, 492 U.S. 136, 155 (1989) (rejecting claim that agencies should be able to factor in public availability when deciding if disclosure is proper).

The Electronic Freedom of Information Act Amendments of 1996[15] amended FOIA in an effort to improve public access to agency records and information in the wake of the increased use of digital technology. Under the amendments, agencies are instructed to make available previously released records that are likely to be requested by others[16] and to create a general index of such records.[17] In addition, all records created on or after November 1, 1996 are to be made available electronically,[18] and each agency is to make reasonable efforts to maintain its records in reproducible forms or formats.[19] Records are now to be provided in any form or format requested if the record is readily reproducible by the agency in that manner.[20]

§ 10-2(b)(2). Organizations.

The definition of "agency"[21] under FOIA includes executive branch agencies,[22] as well as the Executive Office of the President,[23] independent regulatory agencies and commissions,[24] government controlled corporations,[25] and presidential commissions. Many governmental organizations are not subject to FOIA,

---

15. Pub. L. No. 104-231, 110 Stat. 3048 (1996). See generally, Comment, *Revising the Freedom of Information Act for the Information Age: The Electronic Freedom of Information Act*, 14 J. MARSHALL J. COMPUTER & INFO. L. 817 (1996).

16. See 5 U.S.C. § 552(a)(2)(D).

17. See *id.* § 552(a)(2)(E) (to be made available via computer telecommunications by December 31, 1999).

18. *Id.* § 552(a)(2).

19. *Id.* § 552(a)(3)(B).

20. See *id.*

21. See *id.* § 552(f):

> For purposes of this section, the term "agency" as defined in section 551(1) of this title includes any executive department, military department, Government corporation, Government controlled corporation, or other establishment in the executive branch of the Government (including the Executive Office of the President), or any independent regulatory agency.

22. Executive agencies include the departments of Defense, Interior, State, Treasury, and Justice, including the FBI, the INS, and the Bureau of Prisons. FOIA incorporates and expands the Administrative Procedure Act's definition of agency. Recognized characteristics of an "agency" are "establishment in the executive branch," and "substantial independent authority," such as, but not limited to, rule making and adjudication authority. Armstrong v. Executive Office of the President, 877 F. Supp. 690, 700-01 (D.D.C. 1995), *aff'd in part*, 90 F.3d 553, 558 (D.C. Cir. 1996), *cert. denied*, 520 U.S. 1239 (1997). See also Meyer v. Bush, 981 F.2d 1288, 1292 (D.C. Cir. 1993).

23. See, e.g., 5 C.F.R. §§ 1303.1-1303.70 (1992) (Office of Management and Budget).

24. See, e.g., Dobronski v. FCC, 17 F.3d 275 (9th Cir. 1994) (Federal Communications Commission); 16 C.F.R. §§ 1015.1-1015.20 (1992) (Consumer Product Safety Commission); 16 C.F.R. §§ 4.8-4.11 (1992) (Federal Trade Commission).

25. See, e.g., Rocap v. Indiek, 539 F.2d 174, 177 (D.C. Cir. 1976) (finding Federal Home Loan Mortgage Corporation to be a "Government controlled corporation").

most notably Congress,[26] the courts[27] and state agencies.[28] The Act also excludes the President, the personal staff of the President and those whose sole function is to advise and assist the President.[29] Courts have held that entities, autonomous of the government, such as a President-elect's transition operation or private recipients of agency grants, are not agencies for purposes of the Act.[30]

§ 10-2(b)(3). Procedures.

"[A]ny person" may utilize FOIA[31] to request "agency records."[32] The Supreme Court has shunned restrictions on standing under FOIA, finding that the

---

26. See, e.g., Mayo v. United States Gov't Printing Office, 9 F.3d 1450, 1451 (9th Cir. 1994); Dow Jones & Co. v. Department of Justice, 917 F.2d 571, 574 (D.C. Cir. 1990); Goland v. CIA, 607 F.2d 339, 348 (D.C. Cir. 1978), *cert. denied*, 445 U.S. 927 (1980).

27. See, e.g., Warth v. Department of Justice, 595 F.2d 521, 523 (9th Cir. 1979). See also Andrade v. United States Sentencing Comm'n, 989 F.2d 308, 309-10 (9th Cir. 1993).

28 See Grand Central Partnership, Inc. v. Cuomo, 166 F.3d 473, 484 (2d Cir. 1999); Philip Morris, Inc. v. Harshbarger, 122 F.3d 58, 83 (1st Cir. 1997); Day v. Shalala, 23 F.3d 1052, 1064 (6th Cir. 1994); St. Michael's Convalescent Hosp. v. California, 643 F.2d 1369, 1373 (9th Cir. 1981); Johnson v. Wells, 566 F.2d 1016, 1018 (5th Cir. 1978).

29. See H.R. REP. NO. 93-1380, at 14-15 (1974); S. REP. NO. 93-1200, at 15 (1974). See Clinton v. Association of Am. Physicians & Surgeons, 997 F.2d 898, 910 (D.C. Cir. 1993); see also Meyer v. Bush, 981 F.2d 1288, 1293 (D.C. Cir. 1993). The records of the President and Vice President are regulated by The Presidential Records Act, 44 U.S.C. §§ 2201-2207. "The term 'Presidential records' means documentary materials, or any reasonably segregable portion thereof, created or received by the President, his immediate staff, or a unit or individual of the Executive Office of the President whose function is to advise and assist the President...." *Id.* § 2201. Under the Act, a president's records are to be made publicly available five years after he leaves office. Certain information, such as that dealing with national defense, is to be made available no later than 12 years after the end of a president's term. See Armstrong v. Executive Office of the President, 90 F.3d 553, 556 (D.C. Cir. 1996), *cert. denied*, 520 U.S. 1239 (1997); Katz v. National Archives & Records Admin., 68 F.3d 1438 (D.C. Cir. 1995) (autopsy x-rays and photographs of President Kennedy's body are personal presidential papers not subject to FOIA). The National Security Council has been held not to be an agency subject to FOIA. "[T]he NSC is more like 'the President's immediate personal staff' than it is like an agency exercising authority, independent of the President." Armstrong v. Executive Office of the President, 90 F.3d at 567.

30. See Illinois Inst. for Continuing Legal Educ. v. Department of Labor, 545 F. Supp. 1229, 1232 (N.D. Ill. 1982); Dong v. Smithsonian Inst., 125 F.3d 877, 878-79 (D.C. Cir. 1997) (Smithsonian Institution is neither an "establishment in the executive branch" nor a "government controlled corporation" and therefore is not an agency under FOIA). State entities are not agencies under FOIA. See Beard v. Department of Justice, 917 F. Supp. 61, 63 (D.D.C. 1996) (Metropolitan Police Department of the District of Columbia is not an agency under FOIA).

31. 5 U.S.C. § 552(a)(3).

32. Department of Justice v. Tax Analysts, 492 U.S. 136, 142 (1989) (citing Kissinger v. Reporters Comm. for Freedom of the Press, 445 U.S. 136, 150 (1980)); 5 U.S.C. § 552(a)(4)(B). See Military Audit Project v. Casey, 656 F.2d 724, 730-31 n.11 (D.C. Cir. 1981) (military attaché at Soviet embassy would have same standing as United States citizen to request records from CIA or FBI).

identity of the requester,[33] the purpose of the request,[34] and the requester's alternative access to the information [35] are all generally irrelevant.

Records are often made available pursuant to an informal oral request made of the agency's public information, press, or freedom of information ("FOI") officer. If an informal approach is not successful, a formal written request places the agency under a legal duty to act.[36] The Act requires that the written request be "made in accordance with published rules . . . and procedures,"[37] and that the records sought be reasonably described by the person making the request.[38] Courts have repeatedly recognized that "broad, sweeping requests lacking specificity are not permissible." [39] Agencies are required to make a reasonable search for the requested records, and they are not to be chary in their interpreta-

---

33. See Department of Justice v. Reporters Comm. for Freedom of the Press, 489 U.S. 749, 771-72 (1989).

34. See *id*. See also Department of Defense v. FLRA, 510 U.S. 487, 496 (1994); NLRB v. Sears, Roebuck & Co., 421 U.S. 132, 149 (1975) ("Congress clearly intended the FOIA to give any member of the public as much right to disclosure as one with a special interest" in a particular document); North v. Walsh, 881 F.2d 1088, 1096 (D.C. Cir. 1989); Forsham v. Califano, 587 F.2d 1128, 1134 (D.C. Cir. 1978) (factors such as need or public interest have no bearing on requester's right of access under FOIA, but may influence an agency's order of processing FOIA requests). See generally Tomlinson, *Use of the Freedom of Information Act for Discovery Purposes*, 43 MD. L. REV. 119 (1984).

35. See EPA v. Mink, 410 U.S. 73, 92 (1973) ("need" is not relevant). But see Triestman v. Department of Justice, 878 F. Supp. 667, 671 (S.D.N.Y. 1995) (seeking disclosure of documents readily available in public record is abusive and dissipation of agency and judicial resources).

36. "Any written request for records . . . shall be deemed to be a request for records pursuant to the Freedom of Information Act. . . . An oral request for records will not be considered a request for records pursuant to the Freedom of Information Act. Responses to oral requests shall be made as promptly as resources and time restraints permit." 16 C.F.R. § 1015.3 (1992) (Consumer Product Safety Commission regulation). See Wood, *You Should See Your IRS File: Access to IRS Information — What Are a Taxpayer's Rights?*, 21 ST. MARY'S L.J. 325, 336 (1989).

37. 5 U.S.C. § 552(a)(3)(B). See, e.g., McDonnell v. United States, 4 F.3d 1227, 1236-37 (3d Cir. 1993) (one who does not follow agency regulations has not made a formal request for documents within meaning of FOIA); Television Wisconsin, Inc. v. NLRB, 410 F. Supp. 999, 1001 (W.D. Wis. 1976) (failure to request records through agency's executive secretary, as required by published rules).

38. See 5 U.S.C. § 552(a)(3)(A). See also H.R. REP. NO. 93-876, at 6 (1974) (description is sufficient "if it enabled a professional employee of the agency who was familiar with the subject area of the request to locate the record with a reasonable amount of effort"); 28 C.F.R. § 16.3(b) (Department of Justice requires that requests not "be unreasonably burdensome or disruptive of Department operations").

39. See Marks v. Department of Justice, 578 F.2d 261, 263 (9th Cir. 1978). See also Ruotolo v. Department of Transp., 53 F.3d 4, 9 (2d Cir. 1995); American Fed'n of Gov't Employees v. Department of Commerce, 632 F. Supp. 1272, 1278 (D.D.C. 1986), *aff'd*, 907 F.2d 203 (D.C. Cir. 1990) (request for "[e]very chronological office file and correspondence file, internal and external, for every branch office" found unreasonable).

tions of FOIA requests.[40] An agency "must be careful not to read [a] request so strictly that the requester is denied information the agency well knows exists in its files, albeit in a different form from that anticipated by the requester."[41]

§ 10-2(b)(4). Limitations on Agency Response Time.

Under the Act, an agency has twenty days to respond to a FOIA request.[42] As a practical matter, however, agencies frequently extend the time for response. Delays caused by voluminous requests, insufficient funding, or backlogs are generally handled by a "first-in, first-out" approach.[43] The Act provides that an

---

40. See Campbell v. Department of Justice, 164 F.3d 20, 28 (D.C. Cir. 1998) ("[T]he court evaluates the reasonableness of an agency's search based on what the agency knew at its conclusion rather than what the agency speculated at its inception."); Nation Magazine v. United States Customs Serv., 71 F.3d 885, 890 (D.C. Cir. 1995) (response to FOIA request for information "pertaining to" Ross Perot's offers to aid Customs Service's drug interdiction efforts must include any relevant files not indexed under Perot's name); Citizens Comm'n on Human Rights v. FDA, 45 F.3d 1325, 1328 (9th Cir. 1995) (declaration that 140 hours reviewing files in eight offices was sufficiently detailed to prove reasonableness of effort); SafeCard Servs., Inc. v. SEC, 926 F.2d 1197, 1201 (D.C. Cir. 1991) (adequacy of agency's search is determined by whether the search was reasonably calculated to discover the requested documents, not whether it actually uncovered every document extant); Meeropol v. Meese, 790 F.2d 942, 956 (D.C. Cir. 1986) ("[A] search need not be perfect, only adequate, and adequacy is measured by the reasonableness of the effort in light of the specific request.").

As a result of the Electronic Freedom of Information Act Amendments of 1996, an agency is now required to make reasonable efforts to search for records in electronic form or format, except when such efforts would significantly interfere with the operation of the agency's automated information system. See 5 U.S.C. § 552(a)(3)(C).

41. Hemenway v. Hughes, 601 F. Supp. 1002, 1005 (D.D.C. 1985). See Campbell v. Department of Justice, 164 F.3d 20, 28 (D.C. Cir. 1998) (agency cannot limit its search to only one record system if there are others that are likely to turn up the information requested). But see Kowalczyk v. Department of Justice, 73 F.3d 386, 389 (D.C. Cir. 1996) (FBI is not obliged to look beyond four corners of FOIA request for leads to location of responsive documents).

42. See 5 U.S.C. § 552(a)(6)(A)(i); Sinrod, *Freedom of Information Act Response Deadlines: Bridging the Gap Between Legislative Intent and Economic Reality*, 43 AM. U. L. REV. 325 (1994). See also Oglesby v. Department of Army, 920 F.2d 57, 61 (D.C. Cir. 1990). Responses must include a grant or denial of the request, the reasons therefor, and notice of a right to administrative appeal. See *id.* at 65; see 5 U.S.C. § 552(a)(6)(A). The deadlines may be extended for 10 days, upon written notice to the requester, under "unusual circumstances," or indefinitely under "exceptional circumstances." *Id.* § 552(a)(6)(B), (C).

43. See Open America v. Watergate Special Prosecution Force, 547 F.2d 605, 614-16 (D.C. Cir. 1976); Rabin v. Department of State, 980 F. Supp. 116, 122 (E.D.N.Y. 1997) (State Department departs from its strict "first in, first out" policy only when an individual's life, safety or substantial due process rights would be jeopardized by a failure to respond to a request immediately); Freeman v. Department of Justice, 822 F. Supp. 1064, 1067 (S.D.N.Y. 1993); Dacosta v. Department of Justice, 782 F. Supp. 147 (D.D.C. 1992). See generally Sinrod, *Improving Access to Government Information in an Era of Budgetary Constraints*, 27 URB. LAW. 105, 110-11 (1995). The Electronic Freedom of Information Act Amendments of 1996 permit agencies to adopt a multi-track system of processing requests for records that allows an agency to treat easily handled requests separately

agency may extend the time for response, in the event of "unusual circumstances,"[44] by providing written notice to the requester of those circumstances and the date on which a determination to comply is expected to be dispatched.[45]

§ 10-2(b)(5). Fees.

Fees under the Act are assessed according to the identity of the requester and the intended use of the requested information.[46] There are three levels of fees. The first governs records requested for commercial use.[47] The second level applies to records requested for noncommercial use by an educational or noncommercial scientific institution, or a representative of the news media.[48] The

---

from more time consuming requests. See 5 U.S.C. § 552(a)(6)(D). Agencies are now required to promulgate regulations providing for the expedited processing of requests for records for which there is a demonstrated "compelling need." The term "compelling need" is defined as a situation where the failure to obtain the requested records on an expedited basis could reasonably be expected to pose an imminent threat to the life or physical safety of an individual, or "with respect to a request made by a person primarily engaged in disseminating information, urgency to inform the public concerning actual or alleged Federal government activity." *Id.* § 552(a)(6)(E).

44. Three specific situations are deemed "unusual circumstances" under FOIA:

> (i) the need to search for and collect the requested records from field facilities or other establishments that are separate from the office processing the request;
>
> (ii) the need to search for, collect, and appropriately examine a voluminous amount of separate and distinct records which are demanded in a single request; or
>
> (iii) the need for consultation, which shall be conducted with all practicable speed, with another agency having a substantial interest in the determination of the request or among two or more components of the agency having substantial subject-matter interest therein.

Id. § 552(a)(6)(B). The Electronic Freedom of Information Act Amendments of 1996 provide for agency notification to the requester if the request cannot be processed in the allotted time. The requester is then provided with an opportunity to limit the scope of the request so that it may be processed within the statutory time limit or an opportunity to arrange with the agency an alternative time frame. A requester's refusal to cooperate with the agency is a factor in determining whether exceptional circumstances exist. *Id.* § 552(a)(6)(B)(ii).

45. See *id.* § 552(a)(6)(B)(i).

46. See *id.* § 552(a)(4)(ii); Office of Management & Budget, Uniform Freedom of Information Act Fee Schedule and Guidelines, 52 Fed. Reg. 10,011 (1987) ("OMB Fee Sched."), *reprinted in* FRANKLIN & BOUCHARD, *supra* note 2, App. E.

47. See 5 U.S.C. § 552(a)(4)(A)(ii)(I). Charges are made for the direct costs of document search, duplication, and review. *Id.* See McClellan Ecological Seepage Situation v. Carlucci, 835 F.2d 1282, 1285 (9th Cir. 1987) (commercial use of information relates to commerce, trade, or profit). See also OMB Fee Sched. § 6(g), 52 Fed. Reg. 10,018 (1987).

48. See 5 U.S.C. § 552(a)(4)(A)(ii)(II). Charges are limited to document duplication costs. The term "a representative of the news media" has been defined as "a person or entity that gathers information of potential interest to a segment of the public, uses its editorial skills to turn the raw materials into a distinct work, and distributes that work to an audience." National Sec. Archive v. Department of Defense, 880 F.2d 1381, 1387 (D.C. Cir. 1989), *cert. denied*, 494 U.S. 1029 (1990). A request from such a news media representative is not considered a commercial use. See *id.* at 1387-88. The term may include a foreign news service, see Southam News v. INS, 674 F. Supp.

third level governs all other requests for agency records.[49] An agency is permitted to require payment of fees after processing the request and duplicating the relevant records, but prior to release of the records.[50] FOIA also provides for a total or partial reduction of fees when disclosure is in the public interest and is not primarily for the commercial use of the requester.[51]

§ 10-2(c). Exemptions.

§ 10-2(c)(1). Introduction.

FOIA contains nine discretionary exemptions, which constitute the grist of most litigation under the Act. The government carries the burden of demonstrating a record's exempted status in such cases.[52] Such exemptions are narrowly construed by the courts.[53] All of the FOIA exemptions, except for Exemption 3 which contemplates that disclosure is forbidden by another federal statute, are discretionary. Thus, information may be withheld by the government pursuant to one or more exemptions, but it is not required to do so.[54]

881, 892 (D.D.C. 1987), as well as freelance journalists who can demonstrate a realistic expectation that the information will be disseminated by a news organization, see OMB Fee Sched. § 6(j), 52 Fed. Reg. 10,018 (1987).

49. See 5 U.S.C. § 552(a)(4)(A)(ii)(III). Such requesters must pay reasonable charges for document search and duplication. "Direct costs" for special services, e.g., certifying records or express mail, may also be charged. OMB Fee Sched. § 7(e), 52 Fed. Reg. 10,018 (1987).

50. See Strout v. United States Parole Comm'n, 842 F. Supp. 948, 951 (E.D. Mich.), aff'd, 40 F.3d 136, 139 (6th Cir. 1994).

51. See Campbell v. Department of Justice, 164 F.3d 20, 35-36 (D.C. Cir. 1998) ("The fact that a bona fide scholar profits from his scholarly endeavors is insufficient to render his actions "primarily . . . commercial" for purposes of calculating a fee waiver, as Congress did not intend for scholars (or journalists and public interest groups) to forego compensation when acting within the scope of their professional roles."). Factors considered to determine whether disclosure is in the public interest are promulgated by the agency. The factors employed by the Department of Defense, for example, are: (1) whether operations or activities of the government are the subject of the request; (2) the records' informative value; (3) enhanced public understanding resulting from disclosure; and (4) the significance of the disclosure's contribution to public information. See McClellan Ecological Seepage Situation v. Carlucci, 835 F.2d 1282, 1286 (9th Cir. 1987). See also Ettlinger v. FBI, 596 F. Supp. 867, 874 (D. Mass. 1984) (Justice Department factors).

52. See Department of State v. Ray, 502 U.S. 164, 173 (1991); John Doe Agency v. John Doe Corp., 493 U.S. 146, 152 (1989); Department of Justice v. Reporters Comm. for Freedom of the Press, 489 U.S. 749, 755 (1989); Department of Air Force v. Rose, 425 U.S. 352, 361 (1976).

53. See Department of Air Force v. Rose, 425 U.S. 352, 361 (1976); Kamman v. IRS, 56 F.3d 46, 48 (9th Cir. 1995).

54. See 5 U.S.C. § 552(b)(3)(A). See also Crumpton v. Stone, 59 F.3d 1400, 1404 (D.C. Cir. 1995).

§ 10-2(c)(2). Exemption 1: National Security.

Exemption 1 authorizes an agency to withhold information that is "(A) specifically authorized under the criteria established by an Executive order to be kept secret in the interest of national defense or foreign policy and (B) [is] in fact properly classified pursuant to such Executive order."[55] Historically, the federal government, through various classification systems, has withheld information from the public in the name of national security or foreign affairs.[56] By explicitly codifying this tradition in Exemption 1, FOIA places the power and discretion to classify and keep documents unavailable to the public squarely in the hands of the executive branch.

President Clinton implemented the current classification system in Executive Order No. 12,958, which became effective in 1995.[57] The classification system applies to and includes any information owned by, in the possession of, or created by the government, a scheme similar in its breadth to FOIA itself.[58] The three tiers created by the system are "top secret," "secret," and "confidential."[59] The "top secret" designation is reserved for information that, if disclosed, "reasonably could be expected to cause exceptionally grave damage to the

---

55. 5 U.S.C. § 552(b)(1). See generally Baez v. Department of Justice, 647 F.2d 1328, 1331-37 (D.C. Cir. 1980).

56. See generally S. DYCUS ET AL., NATIONAL SECURITY LAW (1990); Note, *Keeping Secrets: Congress, the Courts, and National Security Information*, 103 HARV. L. REV. 906 (1990).

57. Exec. Order No. 12,958, §§ 1.1-6.2, 3 C.F.R. § 333 (1996). The immediate predecessor to Executive Order No. 12,958 was President Reagan's Executive Order No. 12,356. See Exec. Order No. 12,356, §§ 1.1-6.2, 3 C.F.R. §§ 166-178 (1982). The Reagan classification system was criticized as unnecessarily tipping the scales towards secrecy. See, e.g., H.R. REP. NO. 97-731 (1982). Indeed, President Reagan's Executive Order expressly called for the classification of documents when the need for classification was doubtful, and the over-classification of documents when the necessary level of classification was in doubt, at least until further review was undertaken. See Exec. Order No. 12,356 § 1.1(c), 3 C.F.R. § 167 (1982). The Executive Order that preceded President Reagan's Order had been implemented by President Carter. See Exec. Order No. 12,065, 3 C.F.R. § 190 (1979). Though both Orders utilized a three-tiered classification scheme employing similar standards, they fundamentally differed in their approach to document classification. The approach taken by President Carter's Executive Order was to under-classify or not classify documents when there was doubt as to the need for classification, thus making them available for public inspection. See Exec. Order No. 12,065 § 1-1, 3 C.F.R. § 191 (1978). The Clinton Executive Order adopts the less restrictive approach that was taken by President Carter not to classify documents when there is "significant doubt about the need to classify information." Exec. Order No. 12,958 § 1.2(b). See Summers v. Department of Justice, 140 F.3d 1077, 1082 (D.C. Cir. 1998) ("The newer order, Executive Order No. 12,958, differs considerably from its predecessor, Executive Order No. 12,356. Significantly, the newer order is less restrictive, reflecting what it refers to as 'dramatic changes' in national security concerns in the late 1980's following the United States' victory in the Cold War.").

58. See Exec. Order No. 12,958 § 6.1(c), 3 C.F.R. § 333 (1996).

59. *Id.* § 1.3.

national security."[60] The "Secret" designation is applied to information, "the unauthorized disclosure of which reasonably could be expected to cause serious damage to the national security."[61] The lowest level of classification, "confidential," is to be used for information the disclosure of which could "reasonably be expected to cause damage to the national security."[62] Once a record has been classified, it is given appropriate markings identifying its classification level, the identity of the original classification authority, the agency and office of origin, a concise reason for classification, and declassification instructions.[63] Unless a waiver is obtained, each portion of each document is to be separately classified.[64] In situations where only a small portion of an otherwise unclassified document warrants protection, use of a classified addendum is required.[65]

The Executive Order expressly identifies several categories of classified information, including, but not limited to: military plans, weapons, or operations; the vulnerabilities of military plans, weapons, or operations; foreign relations or foreign government information; scientific or technological information; confidential sources and intelligence activities.[66] The mere fact that information falls within one of the referenced categories does not automatically result in its classification. For information to be classified, four conditions must be met:

(1) the information must be classified by an "original classification authority"; (2) the information must be "under the control of" the government; (3) the information must fall within one of the authorized withholding categories under this order; and (4) the original classification authority must "determine[ ] that the unauthorized disclosure of the information reasonably could be expected to result in damage to the national security" and must be "able to identify or describe the damage."[67]

The Executive Order specifically prohibits certain information from classification.[68] It also restricts an agency's ability to classify a record after the receipt

---

60. *Id.* § 1.3(a)(1).
61. *Id.* § 1.3(a)(2).
62. *Id.* § 1.3(a)(3).
63. See *id.* § 1.7(a).
64. *Id.* § 1.7(c).
65. *Id.* § 1.7(g).
66. See *id.* § 1.5.
67. Weatherhead v. United States, 157 F.3d 735, 738 (9th Cir. 1998) (quoting Exec. Order No. 12,958 § 1.2(a)).
68. Information cannot be classified in order to conceal violations of law, inefficiency, or administrative error; prevent embarrassment to a person, organization, or agency; restrain competition; or prevent or delay the release of information that does not require protection in the interest of national security. Exec. Order No. 12,958 § 1.8(a). In addition, "[b]asic scientific research information" not clearly related to the national security may not be classified. *Id.* § 1.8(b).

of a FOIA request[69] and strictly prohibits the reclassification of information after it has been declassified and released to the public under proper authority.[70]

Only officials and agencies specified in the Executive Order may classify records.[71] As a general rule, classification authority exists in the President as well as in designated agency heads and officials.[72] Each agency that handles potentially classifiable material must designate an official with the authority to classify.[73]

Executive Order No. 12,958 instituted a new system for declassification and classification review. For information classified under the new Executive Order, most documents are to be declassified after ten years.[74] Any information classified under an earlier order is to be automatically declassified after twenty-five years[75] unless exempted by an agency head for certain specified reasons.[76] Under Executive Order No. 12,958, classification review has been liberalized. Authorized holders of information "are encouraged and expected to challenge the classification status" of information the person believes to be improperly classified.[77]

Pursuant to the Executive Order, each agency is required to conduct a program for the systematic declassification review of historically valuable records exempted from automatic declassification.[78] The United States archivist is required to conduct a systematic declassification review of material accessioned into the National Archives.[79] The agencies and the archivist are required to conduct a mandatory review of classifications when requested, provided the request adequately specifies the document to be reviewed.[80] All documents that are originated by the incumbent President; the incumbent President's White House Staff; committees, commissions, or boards appointed by the incumbent

---

69. See *id.* § 1.8(d).

70. See *id.* § 1.8(c).

71. See *id.* § 1.4. Guidelines concerning the identification and marking requirements of the new Executive Order have been issued by the Information Security Oversight Office. See 60 Fed. Reg. 53,492, 53,494-97 (1995).

72. Exec. Order No. 12,958 § 1.4(a)(1).

73. *Id.* § 5.6. Additionally, a party designated with a particular level of classification authority may grant to another official a lower level of classification authority, with the caveat that only the minimum number of delegations of authority required to implement Order No. 12,958 shall be permitted. *Id.* § 1.4(c). Any and all granting of authority to classify must be in writing. *Id.* § 1.4(c)(4).

74. *Id.* § 1.6.

75. *Id.* § 3.4.

76. *Id.* § 3.4(b) (information such as identity of confidential human source, or that would assist in development of weapons of mass destruction, may be exempted from automatic declassification).

77. *Id.* § 1.9.

78. *Id.* § 3.5(a).

79. *Id.* § 3.3(b).

80. See *id.* § 3.6.

President; or other entities within the Executive Office of the President that solely advise and assist the incumbent President are exempt from this mandatory review requirement.[81]

The Executive Order provides protection against possible abuses from the improper classification of records through the establishment of the Information Security Oversight Office.[82] The Office assists in the proper implementation of the Executive Order, reviews agency actions under it, takes action in response to complaints,[83] and levies sanctions against violators.[84]

An Interagency Security Classification Appeals Panel has been established by the Executive Order to adjudicate appeals by authorized holders of information who have filed classification challenges, to determine appeals by persons or entities who have filed requests for mandatory declassification review, and to approve, deny, or amend agency exemptions from automatic declassification.[85] The Panel consists of senior representatives appointed by the Secretaries of State and Defense, the Attorney General, the Director of Central Intelligence, the Archivist of the United States and the Assistant to the President for National Security Affairs.[86] In addition, the new Executive Order establishes an Information Security Policy Advisory Council, comprised of seven private-sector experts appointed by the President, who are to advise the President and other officials on national security classification policy.[87]

When a requested record has been properly classified, it is difficult to contest an agency's withholding of the record pursuant to Exemption 1. Mere classification has been typically sufficient to deny public access.[88] Although courts review Exemption 1 claims *de novo*, judicial inquiry has been effectively limited to whether the information was "properly classified" by the executive branch.[89]

---

81. *Id.* § 3.6(b).
82. See *id.* § 5.3. The Director of the Office is an executive official subject to presidential appointment. *Id.* § 5.3(a).
83. *Id.* § 5.3(1)-(9).
84. *Id.* § 5.7.
85. *Id.* § 5.4(b).
86. *Id.* § 5.4(a).
87. See *id.* § 5.5.
88. See Note, *supra* note 56, at 909 (classification is not reviewed against a judicial standard, but rather against the current classification scheme, and courts have consistently deferred to executive agencies classification decisions). The role of the court is to determine that the documents are of the type listed in the government's affidavit, that they have been classified, and that there is a logical nexus between the information and the claimed exemption. Stein v. Department of Justice, 662 F.2d 1245, 1254 (7th Cir. 1981). The agency's burden is limited to a showing that it followed proper classification procedures and that its affidavit logically places the document within the claimed exemption. Hayden v. National Sec. Agency/Central Sec. Serv., 608 F.2d 1381, 1387 (D.C. Cir. 1979), *cert. denied*, 446 U.S. 937 (1980).
89. 5 U.S.C. § 552(a)(4)(B); see EPA v. Mink, 410 U.S. 73, 81-83 (1973). See generally Deyling, *Judicial Deference and De Novo Review in Litigation Over National Security Information*

This approach flows from the premise that courts do not possess "the expertise necessary to second guess such agency opinions in the typical national security FOIA case."[90]

A prominent example of this judicial reticence is *Environmental Protection Agency v. Mink*,[91] in which members of Congress brought suit under FOIA to compel the Environmental Protection Agency ("EPA") to disclose information concerning underground nuclear testing. The Supreme Court upheld the agency's reliance on Exemption 1. Rather than second guess the classification of a document, the Court held "the test was to be simply whether the President has determined by Executive Order that particular documents are to be kept secret."[92] The Court reasoned that, once the EPA had shown that the documents were properly classified, the agency had met its burden since any attempt "to subject the soundness of executive security classifications to judicial review" was "wholly untenable."[93]

Such judicial deference to the executive branch has endured.[94] Courts tend to accord an agency's affidavit explaining the classification determination "substantial weight."[95] Thus, while *in camera* review is available at the court's discretion,[96] the agency's classification determination is often accepted on the sole basis of "reasonably detailed" affidavits.[97] Though the agency has the

---

Under the Freedom of Information Act, 37 VILL. L. REV. 67 (1992). President Clinton's Executive Order No. 12,958 removed the presumption contained in President Reagan's Executive Order No. 12,356 § 1.3(c) that information concerning foreign governments, intelligence techniques or sources, or the identity of confidential foreign sources, is damaging to national security. As a result, courts now may scrutinize the required governmental proof that the disclosure of the information reasonably could be expected to result in damage to the national security. See, e.g., Weatherhead v. United States, 157 F.3d 735 (9th Cir. 1998).

90. Halperin v. CIA, 629 F.2d 144, 148 (D.C. Cir. 1980). See also Stein v. Department of Justice, 662 F.2d 1245, 1254 (7th Cir. 1981) ("The court is in no position to second guess either the agency's determination of the need for classification or the agency's prediction of harm should release be permitted.").

91. 410 U.S. 73 (1973).

92. *Id.* at 82.

93. *Id.* at 84.

94. See Stein v. Department of Justice, 662 F.2d 1245, 1254 (7th Cir. 1981); Military Audit Project v. Casey, 656 F.2d 724, 738 (D.C. Cir. 1981); Hayden v. National Sec. Agency, 608 F.2d 1381, 1386 (D.C. Cir. 1979).

95. Ray v. Turner, 587 F.2d 1187 (D.C. Cir. 1978) (citing S. REP. NO. 93-1200, at 12 (1974), *reprinted in* 1974 U.S.C.C.A.N. 6290). See Campbell v. Department of Justice, 164 F.3d 20, 30 (D.C. Cir. 1998).

96. See 587 F.2d at 1195. See also Weatherhead v. United States, 157 F.3d 735, 739 (9th Cir. 1998) (*in camera* review is a last resort).

97. See Campbell v. Department of Justice, 164 F.3d 20, 30 (D.C. Cir. 1998) ("[T]he affidavits must show, with reasonable specificity, why the documents fall within the exemption. The affidavits will not suffice if the agency's claims are conclusory, merely reciting statutory standards, or if they are too vague or sweeping."). See also Miller v. Casey, 730 F.2d 773, 776 n.19 (D.C. Cir. 1984); Baez v. Department of Justice, 647 F.2d 1328, 1335 (D.C. Cir. 1980); Lesar v. Department

burden of persuasion, those requesting documents typically do not have access to the information necessary to rebut a preliminary agency showing.[98]

§ 10-2(c)(3). Exemption 2: Internal Agency Personnel Rules.

Exemption 2 excludes from FOIA's mandatory disclosure requirements those records that are "related solely to the internal personnel rules and practices of an agency."[99] The purpose of this exemption is to "relieve agencies of the burden of assembling and maintaining for public inspection matter in which the public could not reasonably be expected to have an interest."[100] Under Exemption 2, records addressing routine matters of only internal significance, such as informant or violator identifier codes, file codes, and administrative markings, are exempt from disclosure on the ground that the public is unlikely to have a legitimate interest in them.[101]

In *Crooker v. Bureau of Alcohol, Tobacco & Firearms*,[102] the D.C. Circuit held that, if requested material is "predominantly internal" and disclosure risks circumvention of agency regulations, then it is exempt, even though the public may have an interest in the information.[103] The court drew a distinction between information related to regulating the public and information aimed at regulating agency personnel. Information related to the former, such as prosecutorial guide-

---

of Justice, 636 F.2d 472, 481 (D.C. Cir. 1980); Ray v. Turner, 587 F.2d 1187, 1194-95 (D.C. Cir. 1978).

98. See Military Audit Project v. Casey, 656 F.2d 724, 749-50 (D.C. Cir. 1981) (holding discovery inappropriate).

99. 5 U.S.C. § 552(b)(2).

100. Department of Air Force v. Rose, 425 U.S. 352, 369-70 (1976); see also Vaughn v. Rosen, 523 F.2d 1136, 1140-43 (D.C. Cir. 1975). Predominantly internal documents that deal with trivial administrative matters are protected by the so-called "low 2" exemption. Schiller v. NLRB, 964 F.2d 1205, 1207 (D.C. Cir. 1992); J. O'REILLY, FEDERAL INFORMATION DISCLOSURE § 12.03 (2d ed. 1995 & Supp. 1998).

101. See, e.g., Massey v. FBI, 3 F.3d 620 (2d Cir. 1993); Lesar v. Department of Justice, 636 F.2d 472, 485-86 (D.C. Cir. 1980); Nix v. United States, 572 F.2d 998, 1005 (4th Cir. 1978); Maroscia v. Levi, 569 F.2d 1000, 1002 (7th Cir. 1977). Predominantly internal documents the disclosure of which would risk circumvention of agency statutes and regulations are protected by the so-called "high 2" exemption. Schiller v. NLRB, 964 F.2d 1205, 1207 (D.C. Cir. 1992); see J. O'REILLY, *supra* note 100, at § 12.04.

102. 670 F.2d 1051 (D.C. Cir. 1981) (en banc). Other courts have also dealt with this issue. See, e.g., Delome Publ'g Co. v. National Oceanic & Atmospheric Admin., 917 F. Supp. 867, 875 (D. Me. 1996); Hanson Bros. Meat Packing Co. v. Department of Agric., 640 F. Supp. 402, 405 (D. Pa. 1986). See generally LITIGATION UNDER THE FEDERAL OPEN GOVERNMENT LAWS 54 (A. Adler ed., 20th ed. 1997) [hereinafter LITIGATION].

103. 670 F.2d at 1074. *Crooker* constitutes a repudiation of the D.C. Circuit's earlier construction of Exemption 2 in *Jordan v. Department of Justice*, 591 F.2d 753 (D.C. Cir. 1978) (en banc). See 670 F.2d at 1056. See also Founding Church of Scientology v. Smith, 721 F.2d 828, 830 (D.C. Cir. 1983).

lines, must be disclosed on the basis that FOIA forbids "secret law."[104] However, information aimed at regulating agency personnel, such as a manual on surveillance techniques or other "instructions" to agency personnel, are considered "predominantly internal," even though some members of the public might have an interest in them, and therefore exempt if disclosure might result in the circumvention of agency law.[105]

§ 10-2(c)(4). Exemption 3: Disclosure Forbidden by Other Federal Statutes.

Under Exemption 3, matters that are "specifically exempted from disclosure by statute, (other than section 552(b) of this title) provided that such statute (A) requires that the matters be withheld from the public in such a manner as to leave no discretion on the issue, or (B) establishes particular criteria for withholding or refers to particular types of matters to be withheld,"[106] need not be disclosed pursuant to a FOIA request. Exemption 3 is known as the "Catch-All" exemption and is the only exemption in the Act that may be mandatory.

Exemption 3 attempts to reconcile FOIA with other statutes that often contain broad exemptions from disclosure.[107] Statutes meeting the requirements of Exemption 3 may require or permit the withholding of information requested under FOIA,[108] while other statutes are held to be partially superseded by FOIA's affirmative disclosure requirements.[109] Courts have been asked to determine

---

104. 670 F.2d at 1075. See Audubon Soc'y v. United States Forest Serv., 104 F.3d 1201, 1204 (10th Cir. 1997) (maps depicting location of Mexican spotted owl used by Forest Service to protect owl pursuant to Endangered Species Act did not "relate" to personnel practices of Service and were thus not exempt from disclosure).

105. 670 F.2d at 1075. See Wilder v. Commissioner of Internal Revenue, 601 F. Supp. 241, 243 (N.D. Ala. 1984) (exempting information which would reveal when a tax code violator will not be pursued); Fiumara v. Higgins, 572 F. Supp. 1093, 1102 (D.N.H. 1983) (exempting identification numbers for Treasury Enforcement Communications System). See also National Treasury Employees Union v. United States Customs Serv., 802 F.2d 525, 528-29 (D.C. Cir. 1986) (finding promotion guidelines exempt from disclosure on grounds that some employees might be provided an unfair advantage); Kaganove v. EPA, 856 F.2d 884, 889 (7th Cir. 1988), *cert. denied*, 488 U.S. 1011 (1989); Dirksen v. Department of Health & Human Servs., 803 F.2d 1456 (9th Cir. 1986).

106. 5 U.S.C. § 552(b)(3).

107. See H.R. REP. NO. 89-1497, at 10 (1966).

108. See, e.g., Iglesias v. CIA, 525 F. Supp. 547, 556-57 (D.D.C. 1981) (withholding of grand jury materials under Federal Rule of Criminal Procedure 6(e)); Irons & Sears v. Dann, 606 F.2d 1215, 1220 (D.C. Cir. 1979), *cert. denied*, 444 U.S. 1075 (1980) (withholding of patent applications under Patent Act). See also O'REILLY, *supra* note 100, at § 9.11, 1S-105.

109. See, e.g., CIA v. Sims, 471 U.S. 159, 167 (1984) (determining whether National Security Act of 1947 constituted a statutory exemption from disclosure); FAA v. Robertson, 422 U.S. 255 (1974) (determining whether information must be disclosed under FOIA when the Federal Aviation

whether a host of other statutes fall within Exemption 3.[110]

For an agency to rely on Exemption 3, it must demonstrate that the nondisclosure statute at issue falls within the exemption, and that the material to be withheld is covered by it.[111] To fall within Exemption 3, the statute must be the result of a positive enactment by Congress[112] and must specifically exempt matters from disclosure.[113] Once this threshold requirement has been satisfied, the agency must demonstrate as well that the statute falls within either subpart (A) or (B) of the Exemption. To satisfy subpart (A), the statute must require information to be withheld without agency discretion.[114] In the alternative, the agency may prove that the statute falls under subpart (B) because it provides specific criteria for withholding information,[115] or because it refers to particular

---

Act of 1958 permitted withholding); CNA Fin. Corp. v. Donovan, 830 F.2d 1132, 1141 (D.C. Cir. 1987), *cert. denied*, 495 U.S. 977 (1988).

110. See Hunt v. CIA, 981 F.2d 1116, 1121 (9th Cir. 1992) (CIA Information Act provided a blanket exemption from FOIA requirements for most CIA operational files in order "to relieve the Central Intelligence Agency from an unproductive Freedom of Information Act (FOIA) requirement to search and review certain CIA operational files."). See generally LITIGATION, *supra* note 102, at 67-75 (comprehensive citation to cases and statutes). Trade secret legislation and the federal Privacy Act have been litigated frequently under Exemption 3. The D.C. Circuit, for example, does not consider statutes protecting trade secrets to fall within Exemption 3. See CNA Fin. Corp. v. Brown, 830 F.2d 1132, 1137-41 (D.C. Cir. 1987), *cert. denied*, 485 U.S. 977 (1988). But see Chrysler Corp. v. Brown, 441 U.S. 281, 319 n.49 (1979) (leaving issue open). The Privacy Act, by its own terms, may not override the FOIA. See Department of Justice v. Provensano, 469 U.S. 14, 15 (1989). Congress, through section 2(c) of the Central Intelligence Information Act, amended the Privacy Act, Pub. L. 98-477, 98 Stat. 2209, to forbid the use of the Privacy Act's specific exemptions to override a FOIA request.

111. See CIA v. Sims, 471 U.S. at 167; Minier v. CIA, 88 F.3d 796, 801 (9th Cir. 1996).

112. See CIA v. Sims, 471 U.S. at 167 (finding that "Congress had chartered the Agency with the responsibility"); Founding Church of Scientology v. Bell, 603 F.2d 945, 952 (D.C. Cir. 1979) (Federal Rule of Civil Procedure 26(c) held not an Exemption 3 statute because the rule was promulgated by the Supreme Court, and was not "affirmatively adopted by the legislature"); Fund for Constitutional Gov't v. National Archives & Records Serv., 656 F.2d 856, 867 (D.C. Cir. 1981) (Federal Rule of Criminal Procedure 6(e) found to be an Exemption 3 statute, because it was "positively enacted" by Congress).

113. See Cal-Almond, Inc. v. Department of Agric., 960 F.2d 105, 108 (9th Cir. 1992).

114. See 5 U.S.C. § 552(b)(3)(A). See also Essential Info., Inc. v. United States Info. Agency, 134 F.3d 1165, 1166-67 (D.C. Cir. 1998) (USIA prohibited from disseminating information or distributing program material within the United States by the Smith-Mundt Act); American Centennial Ins. Co. v. EEOC, 722 F. Supp. 180, 183 (D.N.J. 1989) (sections of Title VII of the 1964 Civil Rights Act meet the requirements for mandatory withholding under Exemption 3).

115. See 5 U.S.C. § 552(b)(3)(B). See also Consumer Prod. Safety Comm'n v. GTE Sylvania, Inc., 447 U.S. 102, 122 (1980) (part of the Consumer Product Safety Act provided criteria for withholding sufficient for Exemption 3(B)).

matters to be exempt from disclosure.[116] Statutes purporting to vest unbridled discretion in agency officials do not fall within Exemption 3.[117]

§ 10-2(c)(5). Exemption 4: Trade Secrets and Confidential Commercial Information.

Exemption 4 protects "trade secrets and commercial or financial information obtained from a person and privileged or confidential" from mandatory disclosure.[118] The Exemption is intended to encourage people to contribute useful information to government officials, to ensure access by government policymakers to commercial and financial data, and to protect those persons who contribute such information.[119]

A dispute regarding the meaning of "trade secrets" under the Act has resulted in competing definitions of the term. The *Restatement of Torts*, with which many courts are comfortable,[120] broadly defines a trade secret as "any formula, pattern, device or compilation of information which is used in one's business, and which gives him an advantage over competitors who do not know it or use it."[121] More recently, some courts have rejected the *Restatement* approach as incompatible with FOIA's mandate of liberal access and have replaced it with a more narrow definition of trade secret.[122]

In addition to exempting trade secrets from mandatory disclosure, Exemption 4 also permits an agency to withhold certain commercial or financial information. For this type of information to be exempt from disclosure, the agency must

---

116. 5 U.S.C. § 552(b)(3)(B). See, e.g., Mudge Rose Guthrie Alexander & Ferdon v. United States Int'l Trade Comm'n, 846 F.2d 1527, 1530 (D.C. Cir. 1988) (section 777 of the Tariff Act deemed to refer to particular types of information for withholding as required by Exemption 3(B)).

117. See CIA v. Sims, 471 U.S. at 173-74 (directive to protect the identities of "intelligence sources" held not too broad a grant of discretion); Association of Retired R.R. Workers v. United States Retirement Bd., 830 F.2d 331, 333 (D.C. Cir. 1987).

118. 5 U.S.C. § 552(b)(4).

119. See National Parks & Conservation Ass'n v. Morton, 498 F.2d 765, 767-69 (D.C. Cir. 1974).

120. See Union Oil Co. v. FPC, 542 F.2d 1036, 1044 (9th Cir. 1976); St. Paul's Benevolent Educ. & Missionary Inst. v. United States, 506 F. Supp. 822, 830 (N.D. Ga. 1980).

121. RESTATEMENT OF TORTS § 757 & cmt. b (1939).

122. See Public Citizen Health Research Group v. FDA, 704 F.2d 1280, 1288 (D.C. Cir. 1983) (defining trade secret as "a secret, commercially valuable plan, formula, process, or device that is used for the making, preparing, compounding, or processing of trade commodities and that can be said to be the end product of either innovation or substantial effort").

demonstrate that it constitutes commercial or financial information,[123] obtained from a person,[124] which is confidential or privileged.[125]

Although the first two requirements are often undisputed, it is more difficult to satisfy the third by making a showing of confidentiality or privilege. When disclosure has been compelled in the face of this requirement, the courts have typically applied an objective test of privilege,[126] i.e., the information at issue is deemed confidential if its disclosure is likely to "impair the Government's ability to obtain necessary information in the future" or to "cause substantial harm to the competitive position of the person from whom the information was obtained."[127] Some courts have deemed information to be confidential if its disclosure is likely to affect program effectiveness adversely.[128] Different interests, however, are implicated when the information is voluntarily submitted to an

---

123. Commercial or financial information means "all financial information, despite the apparent commercial focus of the exemption." Washington Post Co. v. Department of Health & Human Servs., 690 F.2d 252, 266 (D.C. Cir. 1982) (personal financial information is included).

124. The term "person" includes virtually any entity except the United States government. See, e.g., Grumman Aircraft Eng'g Corp. v. Renegotiation Bd., 425 F.2d 578, 582 (D.C. Cir. 1970); Consumers Union v. Veterans Admin., 301 F. Supp. 796, 803 (S.D.N.Y. 1969).

125. See Frazee v. United States Forest Serv., 97 F.3d 367, 372 (9th Cir. 1996) (proposals for permit promised confidentiality, but successful proposal becomes public record on granting of permit); National Parks & Conservation Ass'n v. Morton, 498 F.2d 765, 766 (D.C. Cir. 1974).

126. See Critical Mass Energy Project v. NRC, 975 F.2d 871, 880 (D.C. Cir. 1992), *cert. denied*, 507 U.S. 984 (1993) (en banc). It is not considered dispositive that the information would customarily be disclosed to the public by the person submitting it, or that an agency had promised that the information would not be released. See National Parks & Conservation Ass'n v. Morton, 498 F.2d at 767; Washington Post Co. v. Department of Health & Human Servs., 690 F.2d 252, 268 (D.C. Cir. 1982).

127. National Parks & Conservation Ass'n v. Morton, 498 F.2d at 770; see National Parks & Conservation Ass'n v. Kleppe, 547 F.2d 673, 679 (D.C. Cir. 1976); United Tech. Corp. v. FAA, 102 F.3d 688 (2d Cir. 1996) (public disclosure of third parties' design drawings submitted to FAA would cause substantial harm, even if requesting manufacturer of aircraft engines had knowledge of information); Acumenics Research & Tech. v. Department of Justice, 843 F.2d 800 (4th Cir. 1988) (unit prices of government contractor not protected); Gulf & W. Indus. v. United States, 615 F.2d 527, 530 (D.C. Cir. 1979) (profit rate, actual loss data, general expense rates withheld as disclosure would allow competitors to undercut submitter's future bids); Continental Oil Co. v. FPC, 519 F.2d 31 (5th Cir. 1975), *cert. denied*, 425 U.S. 971 (1976) (information relating to intrastate sales of natural gas company protected); Sterling Drug, Inc. v. FTC, 450 F.2d 698 (D.C. Cir. 1971) (sales and profit data compiled over a 10-year period); Northwest Coalition for Alternatives to Pesticides v. Browner, 941 F. Supp. 197, 202 (D.D.C. 1996) (where information sought to be disclosed is available to requester through "reverse engineering," test is "whether the release of the requested information, given its commercial value to competitors and the cost of acquiring it through other means, will cause substantial competitive harm to the business that submitted it").

128. 9 to 5 Org. for Women Office Workers v. Board of Governors of Fed. Reserve Sys., 721 F.2d 1 (1st Cir. 1983). The D.C. Circuit has adopted the First Circuit's approach. See Critical Mass Energy Project v. NRC, 975 F.2d 871, 879 (D.C. Cir. 1992), *cert. denied*, 507 U.S. 984 (1993) (en banc).

agency.[129] Such information is typically deemed confidential unless it is "customarily disclosed to the public by the submitter."[130]

§ 10-2(c)(6). Exemption 5: Internal Agency Memoranda and Policy Discussions.

Exemption 5 protects from mandatory disclosure "inter-agency or intra-agency memorandums or letters which would not be available by law to a party other than an agency in litigation with the agency."[131] This exemption has been construed to apply to documents that are normally privileged in the context of civil discovery,[132] pursuant to both statutory and common law privileges.[133] The three most frequently invoked privileges incorporated into Exemption 5 are the deliberative process privilege,[134] the attorney work-product privilege, and the attorney-client privilege.[135]

---

129. See Critical Mass Energy Project v. NRC, 975 F.2d at 879. See generally Taylor, *The Critical Mass Decision: A Dangerous Blow to Exemption Four Litigation*, 2 COMM. L. CONSPECTUS 133 (1994); Rainey, *Freedom of Information Act: Stare Decisis and Statutory Interpretation: An Argument for Complete Overruling of the National Parks Test*, 61 GEO. WASH. L. REV. 1430 (1993).

130. Critical Mass Energy Project v. NRC, 975 F.2d at 879-80; see *id.* ("presumption is that [the government's] interests will be threatened by disclosure as the persons whose confidences have been betrayed will, in all likelihood, refuse further cooperation").

131. 5 U.S.C. § 552(b)(5).

132. See NLRB v. Sears, Roebuck & Co., 421 U.S. 132, 149 (1975); FTC v. Grolier Inc., 462 U.S. 19, 26 (1983); Martin v. Office of Special Counsel, 819 F.2d 1181, 1184 (D.C. Cir. 1987); H.R. REP. NO. 89-1497, at 10 (1966); S. REP. NO. 89-813, at 29 (1965); S. REP. NO. 88-1219, at 6-7, 13-14 (1964).

133. See United States v. Weber Aircraft Corp., 465 U.S. 792, 800 (1984); Department of Justice v. Julian, 486 U.S. 1, 13 (1988); Badhwar v. Department of Air Force, 829 F.2d 182, 184 (D.C. Cir. 1987).

134. This privilege is referred to as "executive privilege" by some courts. See NLRB v. Sears, Roebuck & Co., 421 U.S. 132, 149 (1975); City of Virginia Beach v. Department of Commerce, 995 F.2d 1247, 1251 (4th Cir. 1993).

135. Other privileges include the air-crash privilege and the government commercial information privilege. The air-crash privilege was established to encourage witnesses to speak freely to safety investigators. See United States v. Weber Aircraft Corp., 465 U.S. 792 (1984) (air-crash privilege incorporated into Exemption 5); Comment, *The Freedom of Information Act in Air Crash Discovery: Friend or Foe?*, 52 J. AIR L. 479 (1986). The government commercial information privilege protects pre-contractual commercial information generated by the government and ceases to exist at the completion of the contracting process. See Federal Open Market Comm. v. Merrill, 443 U.S. 340, 355-60 (1979). Additionally, a privilege has been recognized for appraisal information and reports which, if disclosed, could harm the bargaining position of the government regarding the purchase, sale, or condemnation of property. See generally Hoover v. Department of Interior, 611 F.2d 1132, 1141-42 (5th Cir. 1980); Government Land Bank v. GSA, 671 F.2d 663, 665-66 (1st Cir. 1982). See Reish, *Protection of Government-Generated Evaluative Estimates Under Exemption 5 of the Freedom of Information Act*, 29 A.F.L. REV. 201 (1988); Belazis, *The Government's Commercial Information Privilege: Technical Information and the FOIA's*

The initial determination to be made by courts applying Exemption 5 is whether the information is contained in "inter-agency or intra-agency memorandums or letters."[136] This phrase has been construed to include not only documents generated by an agency, but "any agency document that is part of the deliberative process,"[137] including documents created outside an agency.[138] Once this threshold requirement is met, the information will be exempt if a privilege applies.

The deliberative process privilege is the most commonly invoked under Exemption 5. The primary interest protected by the privilege is the prevention of "injury to the quality of agency decisions,"[139] which is accomplished by safeguarding the agency's deliberative process.[140] The privilege is concerned with the "give and take" of the deliberative process and tends to protect "[r]ecommendations, draft documents, proposals, suggestions, and other subjective documents which reflect the personal opinions of the writer rather than the policy of the agency."[141]

In order for a record to fall within the deliberative process privilege, an agency must prove that the communication is both predecisional[142] and delibera-

---

Exemption 5, 33 ADMIN. L. REV. 415 (1981) (privilege might apply to any technical data generated by the government used in products sold domestically and abroad).

136. Federal Open Market Comm. v. Merrill, 443 U.S. 340, 352 (1979).

137. Ryan v. Department of Justice, 617 F.2d 781, 790 (D.C. Cir. 1980).

138. See Soucie v. David, 448 F.2d 1067, 1078 (D.C. Cir. 1971); Durns v. Bureau of Prisons, 804 F.2d 701, 704 (D.C. Cir. 1986); Hoover v. Department of Interior, 611 F.2d 1132, 1138 (5th Cir. 1980). But see Dow Jones & Co. v. Department of Justice, 917 F.2d 571, 575 (D.C. Cir. 1990) (agency records transmitted to Congress for use in congressional inquiry held not "inter-agency" records). A minority of courts have found that documents generated by nonagency personnel are not protected by Exemption 5. See, e.g., Thurner Heat Treating Corp. v. NLRB, 839 F.2d 1256, 1259-60 (7th Cir. 1988); Van Bourg, Allen, Weinberg & Roger v. NLRB, 751 F.2d 982, 985 (9th Cir. 1985); Poss v. NLRB, 654 F.2d 659, 659 (10th Cir. 1977).

139. NLRB v. Sears, Roebuck & Co., 421 U.S. 132, 151 (1975). Harms that the privilege is intended to avert include: (1) the loss of straightforward, candid discussions within an agency, which are crucial to the quality of agency decisions; (2) the deterioration of the integrity of agency decisions; and (3) public confusion as to an agency's intentions, which would result from premature disclosure. Jordan v. Department of Justice, 591 F.2d 753, 772-74 (D.C. Cir. 1978) (en banc); see Petroleum Info. Corp. v. Department of Interior, 976 F.2d 1429, 1433 n.5 (D.C. Cir. 1992).

140. See National Wildlife Fed'n v. United States Forest Serv., 861 F.2d 1114, 1119 (9th Cir. 1988); Schell v. Department of Health & Human Servs., 843 F.2d 933, 940 (6th Cir. 1988); Wolfe v. Department of Health & Human Servs., 839 F.2d 768, 775 (D.C. Cir. 1988) (en banc).

141. Coastal States Gas Corp. v. Department of Energy, 617 F.2d 854, 866 (D.C. Cir. 1980). See generally Seal, *The Future of the Freedom of Information Act's Deliberative Process Exemption*, 71 DENV. U. L. REV. 719 (1994).

142. See Coastal States Gas Corp. v. Department of Energy, 617 F.2d at 866; Providence Journal Co. v. Department of Army, 981 F.2d 552, 557 (1st Cir. 1992); Hopkins v. HUD, 929 F.2d 81, 84 (2d Cir. 1991) (document is predecisional when it is prepared in order to assist an agency decisionmaker in arriving at his decision). Predecisional documents are protected unless an agency

tive.[143] The privilege does not protect post-decisional documents or final opinions,[144] because such undisclosed records, in the courts' view, would constitute "secret law."[145] Purely factual material must generally be segregated from the exempt portions of records and disclosed, on the theory that facts, unlike opinions, do not reveal the deliberative process.[146]

The attorney work-product privilege is also incorporated into Exemption 5.[147] The policy underlying the privilege, which applies to documents prepared by an attorney in contemplation of litigation, is the protection of the integrity of the adversarial system.[148] An agency may withhold a record, pursuant to the privilege, if it was prepared by, or at the request of, an attorney in anticipation of

---

has "*expressly*" adopted the document as the basis of its decision, in which case the document loses its protected status. See NLRB v. Sears, Roebuck & Co., 421 U.S. at 161 (emphasis in original). See generally Kadlubak, *The Federal Presentence Investigation Report: Postsentence Disclosure Under the Freedom of Information Act*, 40 ADMIN. L. REV. 79 (1988).

143. See Coastal States Gas Corp. v. Department of Energy, 617 F.2d at 866; Providence Journal Co. v. Department of Army, 981 F.2d 552, 559 (1st Cir. 1992); Hopkins v. HUD, 929 F.2d 81, 84 (2d Cir. 1991) (document is deliberative when it is actually related to the process by which policies are formulated).

144. NLRB v. Sears, Roebuck & Co., 421 U.S. at 151-52. See also S. REP. NO. 88-1219, at 6-7 (1964) ("final agency determinations or legal and policy matters which affect the public" are to be made available to the public).

145. Coastal States Gas Corp. v. Department of Energy, 617 F.2d at 866. Some courts have limited the final opinion rule to matters of formal adjudication, holding that documents describing the disposition of informal, routine agency matters need not be disclosed. See, e.g., Skelton v. United States Postal Serv., 678 F.2d 35, 39-42 (5th Cir. 1982).

146. See EPA v. Mink, 410 U.S. at 89. See also S. REP. NO. 88-1219, at 6-7, 13-14 (1964) (factual material must be made available to the public). Segregable facts are, however, not beyond the privilege if the quality of decisions, or the deliberative process itself, would be threatened by disclosure. See, e.g., Mapother v. Department of Justice, 3 F.3d 1533, 1537-40 (D.C. Cir. 1993); Wolfe v. Department of Health & Human Servs., 839 F.2d 768, 774 (D.C. Cir. 1988) (en banc). If facts are selected or summarized in a way that reflects the deliberative process, then the facts may be exempt under the privilege. See Mapother v. Department of Justice, 3 F.3d at 1540 (factual material concerning suspected war criminal Kurt Waldheim need not be disclosed because it was "assembled through an exercise of judgment"). This fact/opinion distinction is likely to arise with increasing frequency in cases addressing access to computer databanks created from paper files. See Seal, *The Future of the Freedom of Information Act's Deliberative Process Exemption and Disclosure of Computerized Records After Petroleum Information Corp. v. United States Department of Labor*, 71 DENV. U. L. REV. 719 (1994).

147. See FTC v. Grolier, Inc., 462 U.S. 19 (1983). The privilege is codified in FED. R. CIV. P. 26(b)(3).

148. See FTC v. Grolier, Inc., 462 U.S. 19, 25-28 (1983). *Hickman v. Taylor*, 329 U.S. 495 (1947), is the leading case articulating the policies that undergird the attorney work-product privilege. In *Hickman*, the Supreme Court held that the adversarial system depends on a lawyer's ability to develop legal theories, process factual information, and devise trial tactics without unnecessary interference. See 329 U.S. at 509-10.

litigation, or an articulable claim likely to lead to litigation.[149] The status of the litigation does not affect application of the privilege.[150] Thus, information produced in anticipation of litigation may be protected even if that litigation has ended.[151]

Finally, the attorney-client privilege, which is also incorporated in Exemption 5, protects confidential communications between attorney and client relating to a legal matter for which the client has sought professional advice.[152] For purposes of FOIA, the client is the agency.[153] The attorney-client privilege is available to protect all such confidential communications between lawyer and client and is not limited to the litigation context, as is the attorney work-product privilege.[154]

§ 10-2(c)(7). Exemption 6: Personal Privacy.

Exemption 6 to FOIA's mandatory disclosure requirement authorizes an agency to withhold information in "personnel and medical files and similar files the disclosure of which would constitute a clearly unwarranted invasion of personal privacy."[155] The exemption is designed to protect certain privacy interests of persons identified in government records. At the threshold, the exemption contemplates that the requested record constitutes a personnel, medical, or similar file. The Supreme Court has interpreted the term "similar file" as a file containing information that "applies to a particular individual."[156]

---

149. FTC v. Grolier, Inc., 462 U.S. at 25; Coastal States Gas Corp. v. Department of Energy, 617 F.2d 854, 865 (D.C. Cir. 1980).

150. See FTC v. Grolier, Inc., 462 U.S. at 28.

151. See In re Murphy, 560 F.2d 326, 334 (8th Cir. 1977). Post-decisional documents not protected under the deliberative process exemption may, therefore, be exempt from disclosure pursuant to the attorney work-product doctrine. See Federal Open Market Comm. v. Merrill, 443 U.S. 340, 360 n.23 (1979); NLRB v. Sears, Roebuck & Co., 421 U.S. 132, 159-61 (1975).

152. See Mead Data Cent., Inc. v. Department of Air Force, 566 F.2d 242, 252 (D.C. Cir. 1977).

153. See Coastal States Gas Corp. v. Department of Energy, 617 F.2d at 862-64.

154. See Upjohn Co. v. United States, 449 U.S. 383, 395-96 (1981).

155. 5 U.S.C. § 552(b)(6).

156. Department of State v. Washington Post Co., 456 U.S. 595, 602 (1982). The individual may be either the author or subject of a file. See New York Times Co. v. NASA, 920 F.2d 1002, 1007-08 (D.C. Cir. 1990) (en banc). The information may be "lexical" or "nonlexical." Id. at 1005 (tape recording containing the sound and inflection of the last words of the crew of the space shuttle Challenger held to be a protected file). Nevertheless, the information must pertain to an identifiable specific individual, not to a large group. See, e.g., Arieff v. Department of Navy, 712 F.2d 1462, 1467-68 (D.C. Cir. 1983). Where deletion of the individual's name from the record makes identification impossible, Exemption 6 does not apply. See Department of State v. Ray, 502 U.S. 164, 178 (1991); Citizens for Envtl. Quality v. Department of Agric., 602 F. Supp. 534, 538-39 (D.D.C. 1984).

Once the requested record is deemed to be subject to Exemption 6, an agency and, if necessary, a court, must determine if the information contained in it implicates a protected privacy interest that would be threatened by disclosure.[157] Courts have been particularly concerned for the privacy interests of individuals regarding the disclosure of names and addresses,[158] particularly in connection with financial information[159] and where such information may be used for solicitation purposes.[160] If a protected privacy interest exists,[161] it is assessed and weighed against the public interest in disclosure[162] to ascertain whether an "unwarranted invasion of personal privacy" would result if the record were disclosed.[163]

---

157. See Department of Air Force v. Rose, 425 U.S. 352, 372 (1976); Fund for Constitutional Gov't v. National Archives & Records Serv., 656 F.2d 856, 862 (D.C. Cir. 1981). Corporations and other business associations generally have no privacy interests. See, e.g., Sims v. CIA, 642 F.2d 562, 572 n.47 (D.C. Cir. 1980); Ivanhoe Citrus Ass'n v. Handley, 612 F. Supp. 1560, 1567 (D.D.C. 1985). An individual who has business dealings with the government is afforded no privacy in matters concerning "business judgments and relationships." McCutchen v. Department of Health & Human Servs., 30 F.3d 183, 187-88 (D.C. Cir. 1994). The majority of courts hold that the privacy of deceased persons is extinguished at death, "[h]owever, particularly sensitive, often graphic, personal details about the circumstances surrounding an individual's death may be withheld where necessary to protect the privacy interests of surviving family members." FRANKLIN & BOUCHARD, *supra* note 2, § 1.09[3].

158. See FLRA v. Department of Defense, 977 F.2d 545 (11th Cir. 1992); FLRA v. Department of Veterans Affairs, 958 F.2d 503, 510 (2d Cir. 1992) (names and addresses of federal employees contained in computer databases).

159. See Painting & Drywall Work Preservation Fund, Inc. v. HUD, 936 F.2d 1300, 1302-03 (D.C. Cir. 1991) (wage data); National Ass'n of Retired Fed. Employees v. Horner, 879 F.2d 873, 875-76 (D.C. Cir. 1989), *cert. denied*, 494 U.S. 1078 (1990) (annuitant status).

160. See O'Kane v. United States Customs Serv., 169 F.3d 1308, 1310 (11th Cir. 1999) (attorney solicitation); Painting & Drywall Work Preservation Fund, Inc. v. HUD, 936 F.2d 1300, 1303 (D.C. Cir. 1991); National Ass'n of Retired Fed. Employees v. Horner, 879 F.2d 873, 875-76 (D.C. Cir. 1989), *cert. denied*, 494 U.S. 1078 (1990).

161. If no privacy interest is found, there is no Exemption 6 protection. See Ripskis v. HUD, 746 F.2d 1, 3 (D.C. Cir. 1984).

162. See *id.* at 3. By the same token, if there is no public interest in the information, it will not be disclosed. See National Ass'n of Retired Fed. Employees v. Horner, 879 F.2d 873, 879 (D.C. Cir. 1989), *cert. denied*, 494 U.S. 1078 (1990); International Bhd. of Elec. Workers Local No. 5 v. HUD, 852 F.2d 87, 89 (3d Cir. 1988). Any interest an individual may have in the release of the information requested by a third person must be analyzed. See Lepelletier v. FDIC, 164 F.3d 37, 48 (D.C. Cir. 1999).

163. See, e.g., Department of Navy v. FLRA, 840 F.2d 1131 (3d Cir.), *cert. dismissed*, 488 U.S. 881 (1988) (court permitted disclosure of employee names and addresses to unions because employee interest in privacy was outweighed by the public interest in collective bargaining); but see IBEW, Local 3 v. NLRB, 845 F.2d 1177, 1181 (2d Cir. 1988) (union and employer lists containing employees' names, addresses, birth dates, social security numbers, sex and marital status, union membership, wages and tax information held exempt because disclosure would constitute clearly unwarranted invasion of personal privacy); FLRA v. Department of Treasury, 884 F.2d 1446, 1456 (D.C. Cir. 1989), *cert. denied*, 493 U.S. 1055 (1990) (disclosure of employee

The privacy interests implicated by the information need not be intimate or embarrassing,[164] but there must be a reasonable expectation of privacy[165] and a substantial probability that disclosure will invade that privacy.[166] The requester has the burden of establishing that disclosure would shed light on the federal agency's performance of its statutory duties or otherwise would let citizens know "what their government is up to."[167] Because Exemption 6 applies only to "clearly unwarranted" invasions of privacy, the scale is weighted in favor of disclosure,[168] though courts have been somewhat more protective of personal information that would cause the identified individual emotional distress or embarrassment.[169]

---

names and addresses not required because the public interest in collective bargaining was not within FOIA's central purpose of opening government activity to public scrutiny). See generally Note, *Collective Bargaining in the Federal Public Sector: Disclosing Employee Names and Addresses Under Exemption 6 of the Freedom of Information Act*, 89 MICH. L. REV. 980 (1991); Note, *Applying the Freedom of Information Act's Privacy Exemption to Requests for Lists of Names and Addresses*, 58 FORDHAM L. REV. 1033 (1990).

164. Department of State v. Washington Post Co., 456 U.S. 595, 600 (1982); National Ass'n of Retired Fed. Employees v. Horner, 879 F.2d 873, 875 (D.C. Cir. 1989), *cert. denied*, 494 U.S. 1078 (1990).

165. See National W. Life Ins. Co. v. United States, 512 F. Supp. 454, 461 (N.D. Tex. 1980); Core v. United States Postal Serv., 730 F.2d 946, 948 (4th Cir. 1984).

166. The threat to privacy must be real, not speculative. See Department of Air Force v. Rose, 425 U.S. at 380 n.19; Arieff v. Department of Navy, 712 F.2d 1462, 1467-68 (D.C. Cir. 1983). Moreover, the threat may be attributable not only to the disclosure, but also to its secondary effects. See National Ass'n of Retired Fed. Employees v. Horner, 879 F.2d at 878.

167. Department of Justice v. Reporters Comm. for Freedom of the Press, 489 U.S. 749, 773 (1989); Department of Defense v. FLRA, 510 U.S. 487 (1994). The Supreme Court has stressed that FOIA was enacted to serve the public's interest concerning the operation or activities of the federal government. See, e.g., Department of Justice v. Reporters Comm. for Freedom of the Press, 489 U.S. 749, 775 (1989); Department of State v. Ray, 502 U.S. 164 (1991). See also Andrews v. Department of Justice, 769 F. Supp. 314, 316-17 (E.D. Mo. 1991); Lepelletier v. FDIC, 164 F.3d 37, 47 (D.C. Cir. 1999) (no clearly discernible public interest in releasing names associated with unclaimed deposits held by FDIC, "because such a release would not inform the public of what the FDIC is 'up to.'"). Information that reveals agency abuse or details official behavior creates a formidable public interest. See Department of Air Force v. Rose, 425 U.S. at 367.

It has been argued that, in passing the Electronic Freedom of Information Act Amendments of 1996, Pub. L. 104-231, Oct. 2, 1996, 110 Stat. 3048, Congress intended to curb the overuse of the privacy exemptions to FOIA caused by the Supreme Court's limiting the public's interest in *United States Department of Justice v. Reporters Committee for Freedom of the Press*, by finding that the purpose of FOIA was to allow access to government records "for any public or private purpose." *Id.* § 2(A)(1). The courts, however, have interpreted the amendments as merely clarifying that electronic records are subject to FOIA and not as narrowing FOIA's privacy exclusions. See O'Kane v. United States Customs Serv., 169 F.3d 1308, 1310 (11th Cir. 1999).

168. See Ripskis v. HUD, 746 F.2d 1, 3 (D.C. Cir. 1984).

169. See, e.g., Department of State v. Ray, 502 U.S. at 164, 175-77 (physical harm faced by Haitians forced to return to Haiti); Department of Justice v. Reporters Comm. for Freedom of the Press, 489 U.S. 749, 780 (1989) (rap sheets); McDonnell v. United States, 4 F.3d 1227, 1254 (3d

§ 10-2(c)(8). Exemption 7: Law Enforcement Investigations.

Exemption 7 to FOIA protects

> records or information compiled for law enforcement purposes, but only to the extent that the production of such law enforcement records or information (A) could reasonably be expected to interfere with enforcement proceedings, (B) would deprive a person of a right to a fair trial or an impartial adjudication, (C) could reasonably be expected to constitute an unwarranted invasion of personal privacy, (D) could reasonably be expected to disclose the identity of a confidential source, including state, local, or foreign agency or authority or any private institution which furnished information on a confidential basis, and, in the case of a record or information compiled by criminal law enforcement authority in the course of a criminal investigation, or by an agency conducting a lawful national security intelligence investigation, information furnished by a confidential source, (E) would disclose techniques and procedures for law enforcement investigations or prosecutions, or would disclose guidelines for law enforcement investigations or prosecutions if such disclosure could reasonably be expected to risk circumvention of the law, or (F) could reasonably be expected to endanger the life or physical safety of any individual.[170]

The purpose of Exemption 7 is to protect from untimely disclosure documents that would jeopardize criminal or civil investigations or cause harm to individuals who assist law enforcement. To invoke the exemption, an agency must first demonstrate that the requested information was contained in "records or information compiled for law enforcement purposes." If so, the agency must also demonstrate that disclosure would threaten one of the six types of foreseeable harms enumerated in the Exemption.[171]

A record or information is deemed "compiled for law enforcement purposes" if it was initially obtained or generated for such a purpose,[172] or was originally

---

Cir. 1993) (medical condition); Norwood v. FAA, 993 F.2d 570, 575 (6th Cir. 1993) (social security number); Ripskis v. HUD, 746 F.2d 1, 3 (D.C. Cir. 1984) (performance evaluation); Harbolt v. Department of State, 616 F.2d 772, 774 (5th Cir.), cert. denied, 449 U.S. 856 (1980) (United States citizens in foreign prisons); Church of Scientology v. Department of Army, 611 F.2d 738, 747 (9th Cir. 1979) (religious affiliation); Rural Hous. Alliance v. Department of Agric., 498 F.2d 73, 77 (D.C. Cir. 1974) (wide range of potentially embarrassing disclosures); Hemenway v. Hughes, 601 F. Supp. 1002, 1006 (D.D.C. 1985) (citizenship data).

170. 5 U.S.C. § 552(b)(7).

171. See generally Note, *Threshold Requirements for the FBI Under Exemption 7 of the Freedom of Information Act*, 86 MICH. L. REV. 620 (1987).

172. Information originally compiled for a law enforcement purpose, but later reproduced or summarized in a non-law enforcement record, can fall within the exemption. See FBI v. Abramson, 456 U.S. 615, 631-32 (1982). An internal investigation in which an agency, acting as the employer, simply supervises its own employees, does not constitute information compiled for law enforce-

gathered for another purpose, but compiled for law enforcement purposes prior to the agency's invocation of the exemption.[173] For purposes of the exemption, "law enforcement" can include criminal, civil, and administrative matters,[174] as well as state, local, and foreign law.[175] There must, however, be a nexus between the requested record and a proper law enforcement purpose.[176] Once an agency establishes that the requested record was "compiled for law enforcement purposes," it must further demonstrate that disclosure of the record threatens to result in one of the harms set out in subdivisions (A)-(F).

---

ment purposes. See Stern v. FBI, 737 F.2d 84, 89 (D.C. Cir. 1984). On the other hand, an agency's investigation of its own employees is for "law enforcement purposes" if it focuses directly on a specific alleged illegal act by a particular identified official. See Kimberlin v. Department of Justice, 139 F.3d 944, 947 (D.C. Cir. 1998).

173. Documents originally compiled for a non-law enforcement purpose, such as an audit, but later transferred for use in a law enforcement proceeding, such as an investigation into fraud, are considered as having been "compiled for a law enforcement purpose." See John Doe Agency v. John Doe Corp., 493 U.S. 146, 153 (1989). See also KTVY-TV v. United States, 919 F.2d 1465, 1469 (10th Cir. 1990). Congress originally required records to be "investigatory" to fall within Exemption 7. The statute was amended in 1986, however, to delete the "investigatory" requirement. See Pub. L. No. 99-570, § 1802, 100 Stat. 3207, 3207-48 (1986). See Hopkinson v. Shillinger, 866 F.2d 1185, 1222 n.27 (10th Cir. 1989), *cert. denied*, 497 U.S. 1010 (1990). Thus, pre-1986 cases concerning the threshold test should be consulted with some caution.

174. See, e.g., McDonnell v. United States, 4 F.3d 1227, 1255 (3d Cir. 1993) (FBI investigation of criminal allegations); Cappabianca v. Commissioner, 847 F. Supp. 1558, 1565 (M.D. Fla. 1994) (investigation into acts that could result in criminal or civil sanctions); Kay v. FCC, 867 F. Supp. 11 (D.D.C. 1994) (complaints against licensees).

175. See, e.g., Rojem v. Department of Justice, 775 F. Supp. 6, 10 (D.D.C. 1991) (material provided to FBI by state law enforcement agency); Wojtczak v. Department of Justice, 548 F. Supp. 143, 146-48 (E.D. Pa. 1982) ("Exemption 7 applies to all law enforcement records, federal, state, or local, that lie within the possession of the federal government."); Benis v. Department of State, 801 F.2d 1386, 1388 (D.C. Cir. 1986) (no distinction between foreign and domestic enforcement purposes).

176. See Campbell v. Department of Justice, 164 F.3d 20, 32 (D.C. Cir. 1998). Agencies with mixed law enforcement and administrative functions are usually required to demonstrate that the requested records involve the enforcement of a statute or regulation within their authority. See Church of Scientology Int'l v. IRS, 995 F.2d 916, 919 (9th Cir. 1993); Birch v. United States Postal Serv., 803 F.2d 1206, 1210-11 (D.C. Cir. 1986). Agencies whose principal function is criminal law enforcement are generally accorded at least some deference. See Pratt v. Webster, 673 F.2d 408, 416-21 (D.C. Cir. 1982). Some circuits have adopted a per se rule that presumptively qualifies all investigative records of such agencies for protection under the Exemption. See, e.g., Ferguson v. FBI, 957 F.2d 1059, 1070 (2d Cir. 1992); Jones v. FBI, 41 F.3d 238, 246 (6th Cir. 1994). The law enforcement purpose, however, must be legitimate. See Rosenfeld v. Department of Justice, 57 F.3d 803, 808 (9th Cir. 1995), *cert. denied*, 116 U.S. 833 (1996).

§ 10-2(c)(8)(A). Exemption 7(A).

Exemption 7(A) authorizes the withholding of records that "could reasonably be expected to interfere with enforcement proceedings."[177] This exemption, drafted to protect the "government's case in court,"[178] excuses from mandatory disclosure information which, if made public, might have an adverse effect on a present or pending law enforcement proceeding.[179] To invoke Exemption 7(A), an agency must first demonstrate that a relevant law enforcement proceeding is pending or in the offing.[180] The agency must then show that release of the requested record could reasonably be expected to cause some articulable harm to that proceeding.[181] The harm resulting from the disclosure need not be established on a document-by-document basis. An agency can argue for categorical exemption, rather than specifically demonstrating the consequences of disclosure of each requested document.[182] The burden, however, rests with the agency to categorize information into functional groups and to demonstrate that disclosure of each category would characteristically result in harm to the government's case.[183]

§ 10-2(c)(8)(B). Exemption 7(B).

Exemption 7(B) authorizes the withholding of records that "would deprive a person of a right to a fair trial or an impartial adjudication."[184] This exemption is designed to prevent prejudicial pretrial publicity that *would* impair a trial or

---

177. 5 U.S.C. § 552(b)(7)(A).
178. NLRB v. Robbins Tire & Rubber Co., 437 U.S. 214, 224 (1978).
179. See *id.* at 236.
180. See Marzen v. Department of Health & Human Servs., 632 F. Supp. 785, 805 (N.D. Ill. 1985), *aff'd*, 825 F.2d 1148 (7th Cir. 1987). After the conclusion or abandonment of proceedings, Exemption 7(A) will no longer protect the information sought. See Barney v. IRS, 618 F.2d 1268, 1273-74 (8th Cir. 1980).
181. See Miller v. Department of Agric., 13 F.3d 260, 263 (8th Cir. 1993). Attorney General Reno has required specific reference to the harms upon which agencies base their determinations. Memorandum for Heads of Departments and Agencies from Attorney General Janet Reno, Oct. 4, 1993, *reprinted in* 2 FRANKLIN & BOUCHARD, *supra* note 2, at App. D5.
182. See NLRB v. Robbins Tire & Rubber Co., 437 U.S. 214, 236 (1978); Department of Justice v. Reporters Comm. for Freedom of the Press, 489 U.S. 749, 776-80 (1989).
183. See NLRB v. Robbins Tire & Rubber Co., 437 U.S. at 236; Curran v. Department of Justice, 813 F.2d 473 (D.C. Cir. 1987) (discussing functionality requirement of categories). The Supreme Court has reasoned that subsection 7(A) references "enforcement proceedings" in the plural and, therefore, generic determinations of harm are not contrary to the statute. See NLRB v. Robbins Rubber & Tire Co., 437 U.S. at 223-24. For example, in *NLRB v. Robbins Tire & Rubber Co.*, the Court held that, in unfair labor practice proceedings, witness statements are presumptively exempt prior to actual hearings due to their unique potential for witness intimidation. See *id.* at 241. See generally LITIGATION, *supra* note 102, at 166-68 (noting application of principle to EEOC, INS, IRS, and FTC proceedings, and to labor audits).
184. 5 U.S.C. § 552(b)(7)(B).

adjudication,[185] and applies when an agency demonstrates "(1) that a trial or adjudication is pending or truly imminent; and (2) that it is more probable than not that disclosure of the material sought would seriously interfere with the fairness of those proceedings."[186]

§ 10-2(c)(8)(C). Exemption 7(C).

Exemption 7(C) authorizes the withholding of records that "could reasonably be expected to constitute an unwarranted invasion of personal privacy,"[187] thereby affording agencies a greater latitude in protecting privacy interests in the law enforcement context than is provided by Exemption 6. Accordingly, Exemption 7(C) provides protection against the disclosure of information that "could reasonably be expected" to constitute an unwarranted invasion of privacy, a less stringent standard than Exemption 6's protection against the disclosure of information that "would" constitute a "clearly unwarranted" invasion of privacy.[188]

Application of Exemption 7(C) involves a balancing of privacy concerns and the public's interest in disclosure similar to that required by Exemption 6.[189] Where the information is contained in law enforcement records, however, a heightened privacy interest of those identified in such records is typically acknowledged.[190] As a result, the identities of law enforcement officials,[191]

---

185. The use of the term "would" as opposed to "could reasonably be expected" in the statute indicates that Congress contemplated a high threshold. See Washington Post Co. v. Department of Justice, 863 F.2d 96 (D.C. Cir. 1988).

186. *Id.* at 102 (plea of nolo contendere in a criminal proceeding and a mere assertion of a pending civil proceeding by a non-governmental agency did not satisfy the requirement that the proceeding be imminent).

187. 5 U.S.C. § 552(b)(7)(C).

188. See *id.* § 552(b)(6).

189. See Chap. 10-2(c)(7) *supra*.

190. "It is generally recognized that the mention of an individual's name in a law enforcement file carries a stigmatizing connotation . . . . Although there may be a public interest in the release of this information, as long as the individuals mentioned are alive, their privacy interest is paramount to the public interest in disclosure." Branch v. FBI, 658 F. Supp. 204, 209 (D.D.C. 1987). Although the death of a person on whose behalf exemption 7(C) is invoked diminishes the privacy interests to be balanced, see Campbell v. Department of Justice, 164 F.3d 20, 33-34 (D.C. Cir. 1998) ("the deceased by definition cannot personally suffer the privacy-related injuries that may plague the living"), after the Supreme Court's decision in *Swidler & Berlin v. United States*, 118 S. Ct. 2081, 2086 (1998) (attorney-client privilege survives the death of the client, who "may be concerned about reputation, civil liability, or possible harm to friends or family"), a court must take into account the fact that certain reputational interests and family related privacy expectations may survive death.

191. See Jones v. FBI, 41 F.3d 238, 246 (6th Cir. 1994); Baez v. Department of Justice, 647 F.2d 1328, 1339 (D.C. Cir. 1980).

informants,[192] interviewees,[193] and witnesses[194] as well as information in "rap sheets"[195] have been deemed exempt from disclosure in specific cases.[196]

§ 10-2(c)(8)(D). Exemption 7(D).

Exemption 7(D) authorizes the withholding of records that

> could reasonably be expected to disclose the identity of a confidential source, including state, local, or foreign agency or authority or any private institution which furnished information on a confidential basis, and, in the case of a record or information compiled by criminal law enforcement authority in the course of a criminal investigation, or by an agency conducting a lawful national security intelligence investigation, information furnished by a confidential source.[197]

This exemption, in an effort to encourage persons to furnish information for use in law enforcement investigations,[198] protects the identities of confidential law enforcement sources and, under certain circumstances, the information they have provided as well.

Exemption 7(D) protects the identity of those who provide information to government agencies in confidence,[199] as well as information that would "tend to reveal" the source's identity.[200] The term "source" has been interpreted to include a variety of individuals and organizations,[201] although to fall within the

---

192. See Epps v. Department of Justice, 801 F. Supp. 787, 793 (D.D.C. 1992), *modified*, 995 F.2d 305 (D.C. Cir. 1993); Nadler v. Department of Justice, 955 F.2d 1479, 1490 (11th Cir. 1992).

193. See KTVY-TV v. United States, 919 F.2d 1465, 1469 (10th Cir. 1990).

194. See Farese v. Department of Justice, 683 F. Supp. 273, 275 (D.D.C. 1987); Friedman v. FBI, 605 F. Supp. 306, 321 (N.D. Ga. 1981).

195. See Department of Justice v. Reporters Comm. for Freedom of the Press, 489 U.S. 749, 774-75 (1989).

196. The D.C. Circuit, for example, categorically excludes the disclosure of names and addresses of private individuals compiled for law enforcement purposes *unless* disclosure is necessary to uncover illegal agency activity. See SafeCard Servs., Inc. v. SEC, 926 F.2d 1197, 1206 (D.C. Cir. 1991). But see Detroit Free Press, Inc. v. Department of Justice, 73 F.3d 93, 97-98 (6th Cir. 1996) (mug shots of criminal defendants subject to disclosure under FOIA where identities have already been divulged and they have already appeared in court); Lurie v. Department of Army, 970 F. Supp. 19, 40 (D.D.C. 1997) (substantial interest in AIDS research and testing outweighs privacy interests of military medical researcher who played significant role in funding AIDS research).

197. 5 U.S.C. § 552(b)(7)(D).

198. See Department of Justice v. Landano, 508 U.S. 165, 170-72 (1993).

199. See Computer Prof'ls for Social Responsibility v. United States Secret Serv., 72 F.3d 897, 905 (D.C. Cir. 1996); Cuccaro v. Secretary of Labor, 770 F.2d 355, 360 (3d Cir. 1985).

200. See Pollard v. FBI, 705 F.2d 1151, 1155 (9th Cir. 1983); Williams v. FBI, 822 F. Supp. 808, 812 (D.D.C. 1993), *aff'd*, 76 F.3d 1244 (D.C. Cir. 1994); Church of Scientology v. IRS, 816 F. Supp. 1138 (W.D. Tex. 1993); Doe v. Department of Justice, 790 F. Supp. 17 (D.D.C. 1992).

201. See United Techs. Corp. v. NLRB, 777 F.2d 90, 93-94 (2d Cir. 1985) (employees supplying information regarding their employers); Ferguson v. FBI, 957 F.2d 1059, 1068 (2d Cir. 1992)

exemption, the source must have provided the information in confidence.[202] Whether the source's information was communicated in confidence is determined on a case-by-case basis.[203] The source may have acted in response to an express promise of confidentiality[204] or an implied assurance that her identity would remain secret.[205] Where the source has furnished information to law enforcement authorities in the course of a criminal[206] or national security intelligence investigation,[207] that information, in addition to the identity of the source, may be withheld from disclosure.[208]

§ 10-2(c)(8)(E). Exemption 7(E).

Exemption 7(E) authorizes the withholding of records that "would disclose techniques and procedures for law enforcement investigations or prosecutions, or would disclose guidelines for law enforcement investigations or prosecutions if such disclosure could reasonably be expected to risk circumvention of the law."[209] The exemption applies to investigative techniques and procedures not generally known to the public, and to investigation or prosecution guidelines the disclosure of which would risk circumvention of the law.

(non-federal law enforcement agencies); Founding Church of Scientology of Washington, D.C. v. Levi, 579 F. Supp. 1060, 1063 (D.D.C. 1982), aff'd, 721 F.2d 828 (D.C. Cir. 1983) (commercial institutions).

202. See Shaw v. FBI, 749 F.2d 58, 61 (D.C. Cir. 1984); Irons v. FBI, 880 F.2d 1446, 1447-48 (1st Cir. 1989).

203. See Department of Justice v. Landano, 508 U.S. 165, 165 (1993).

204. See id. at 172 (quoting S. REP. NO. 93-1200, at 13 (1974)); Oliva v. Department of Justice, 996 F.2d 1475, 1476 (2d Cir. 1993).

205. In *Department of Justice v. Landano*, 508 U.S. 165, 179-80 (1993), the Supreme Court focused on two factors in determining whether there has been an implied assurance of confidentiality — the nature of the crime and the source's relationship to it. See Steinberg v. Department of Justice, 23 F.3d 548, 549 (D.C. Cir. 1994); McDonnell v. United States, 4 F.3d 1227, 1260 (3d Cir. 1993); Massey v. FBI, 3 F.3d 620, 623 (2d Cir. 1993). The Supreme Court has noted that there may be "generic circumstances" in which implied confidentiality may be inferred, such as where the informant is a witness to a gang-related murder or where the informant is paid by the government for her information. See 508 U.S. at 179. Courts may look to the risks an informant might face were her identity disclosed, such as retaliation, reprisal or harassment, in inferring implied confidentiality. See Grand Central Partnership, Inc. v. Cuomo, 166 F.3d 473, 487-88 (2d Cir. 1999) (retaliation need not be in the form of physical violence, but may constitute workplace harassment, demotions, job transfers or loss of employment).

206. See Shaw v. FBI, 749 F.2d at 63-65; Harvey v. Department of Justice, 747 F. Supp. 29, 38 (D.D.C. 1990); Hopkinson v. Shillinger, 866 F.2d 1185, 1222 (10th Cir. 1989), cert. denied, 497 U.S. 1010 (1990); Gordon v. Thornberg, 790 F. Supp. 374, 377-78 (D.R.I. 1992); Payne v. Department of Justice, 722 F. Supp. 229, 231 (E.D. Pa. 1989), aff'd, 904 F.2d 695 (3d Cir. 1990).

207. See Pratt v. Webster, 673 F.2d 408, 420-21 (D.C. Cir. 1982).

208. See Providence Journal Co. v. Department of Army, 981 F.2d 552, 566 (1st Cir. 1992).

209. 5 U.S.C. § 552(b)(7)(E).

For a requested record within the category of law enforcement techniques and procedures to be withheld, the technique or procedure must not be well known to the public.[210] Routine techniques, such as fingerprinting, ballistics tests, wiretapping, and photographing, are outside the scope of Exemption 7(E).[211] A guideline for law enforcement investigations or prosecutions[212] may be withheld if its disclosure "could reasonably be expected to risk circumvention of the law."[213]

§ 10-2(c)(8)(F). Exemption 7(F).

Exemption 7(F) authorizes the withholding of records that "could reasonably be expected to endanger the life or physical safety of any individual."[214] It is designed to protect the physical safety of individuals by exempting from mandatory disclosure information which, if made public, would endanger a specific person's life or physical safety. The principal recipients of this protection are law enforcement agents,[215] though the exemption permits the withholding of information to protect the physical well-being of others threatened with such harm as well.[216]

§ 10-2(c)(9). Exemption 8: Financial Institutions.

Exemption 8 protects from mandatory disclosure information "contained in or related to examination, operating, or condition reports prepared by, on behalf of, or for the use of an agency responsible for the regulation or supervision of financial institutions."[217] The purpose of the exemption is to prevent the undermining of public confidence in individual financial institutions or the federal

---

210. See S. REP. NO. 98-221, at 25 (1983) (citing H.R. REP. NO. 93-1380, at 12 (1974)). Thus, an agency must show that the technique it is seeking to keep secret is not already well known to the public or otherwise commonly used. See Albuquerque Publ'g Co. v. Department of Justice, 726 F. Supp. 851, 858 (D.D.C. 1989); Jaffe v. CIA, 573 F. Supp. 377, 387 (D.D.C. 1983).
211. See Albuquerque Publ'g Co. v. Department of Justice, 726 F. Supp. 851, 858 (D.D.C. 1989); Jaffe v. CIA, 573 F. Supp. 377, 387 (D.D.C. 1983).
212. See 5 U.S.C. § 552(b)(7)(E).
213. *Id.*
214. *Id.* § 552(b)(7)(F). Previously, Exemption 7(F) was more narrow, covering information that "would endanger" only "law enforcement personnel." 5 U.S.C. § 552(b)(7)(F) (1976). The expansion of this exemption in 1986 to its current language allows for claims of exemption for information potentially harmful to informants, the families of enforcement personnel, and various other parties not encompassed by the previous Exemption. O'REILLY, *supra* note 100, § 17-12.
215. See Albuquerque Publ'g Co. v. Department of Justice, 726 F. Supp. at 858.
216. See O'REILLY, *supra* note 100, § 17.12; see also Kimberlin v. Department of Treasury, 774 F.2d 204, 208 (7th Cir. 1985). Exemption 7(F) does not protect against boycotts, harassment, or other less concrete threats related to past actions. See Irons v. FBI, 880 F.2d 1446 (1st Cir. 1989); O'REILLY, *supra* note 100, § 17.12.
217. 5 U.S.C. § 552(b)(8). See generally Schotland, *Re-examining the Freedom of Information Act's Exemption 8: Does It Give an Unduly "Full Service" Exemption for Bank Examination Reports and Related Material?*, 9 ADMIN. L.J. AM. U. 43 (1995).

banking system by the disclosure of sensitive financial reports or audits and to promote cooperation and communication between employees of financial institutions and examiners.[218]

Courts have construed the term "financial institutions" to include banks, trust companies, investment bankers, banking associations,[219] and securities exchanges.[220] Information subject to Exemption 8 has also been construed to include "all records, regardless of the source, of a bank's financial condition and operations."[221] Unlike other FOIA exemptions, courts have generally not required agencies to segregate and disclose the unprotected portions of otherwise exempt documents pursuant to Exemption 8.[222] There is, moreover, no requirement that the withholding agency be specifically responsible for the "financial institution," so long as it is generally charged with supervision of "financial institutions."[223]

§ 10-2(c)(10). Exemption 9: Oil and Gas Wells.

Exemption 9 allows for the withholding of "geological and geophysical information and data, including maps, concerning wells."[224] The exemption is intended to protect companies that have filed such data with federal agencies from speculators seeking information about the location of oil and gas wells, and other technical or scientific matters.[225] Exemption 9 is the least utilized FOIA exemption. When it is invoked, it is often in conjunction with Exemption 4, the trade secrets exemption.[226]

---

218. See H. REP. NO. 89-1497, at 11 (1966); Consumers Union v. Heimann, 589 F.2d 531, 534 (D.C. Cir. 1978) (disclosure of frank evaluations of investigated banks could cause unwarranted runs on those banks).

219. See M.A. Schapiro & Co. v. SEC, 339 F. Supp. 467, 470 (D.D.C. 1972).

220. See Mermelstein v. SEC, 629 F. Supp. 672 (D.D.C. 1986) (finding securities exchange to be covered). But see M.A. Schapiro & Co. v. SEC, 339 F. Supp. at 470 (SEC documents concerning investigation of New York Stock Exchange not exempt under Exemption 8).

221. McCullough v. FDIC, 1 GOV'T DISCLOSURE SERV. (P-H) ¶ 80,194 at 80,495 (D.C. Cir. 1980). Documents held to fall within the exemption include bank examinations reports and related documents, as well as operating or condition reports. See Gregory v. FDIC, 631 F.2d 896, 898 (D.C. Cir. 1980).

222. See Atkinson v. FDIC, 1 GOV'T DISCLOSURE SERV. (P-H) ¶ 80,034, at 80,103 (D.D.C. 1980).

223. See Public Citizen v. Farm Credit Ass'n, 938 F.2d 290, 293 (D.C. Cir. 1991).

224. 5 U.S.C. § 552(b)(9).

225. See Black Hills Alliance v. United States Forest Serv., 603 F. Supp. 117, 122 (D.S.D. 1984); H. REP. NO. 89-1497, at 11 (1966).

226. See National Broadcasting Co. v. SBA, 836 F. Supp. 121, 124 n.2 (S.D.N.Y. 1993); Pennzoil Co. v. FPC, 534 F.2d 627 (5th Cir. 1976).

§ 10-2(d). Exclusions.

The Freedom of Information Reform Act of 1986 created three record "exclusions" intended to provide greater protection for certain sensitive law enforcement matters.[227] Unlike the invocation of an exemption, these three specialized exclusions authorize an agency to treat the records as if they do not exist, on the theory that they are explicitly outside of the scope of FOIA. As a result, an agency responding to a request for a record falling within one of these exclusions may state that it possesses no records responsive to the FOIA request.[228]

§ 10-2(d)(1). Exclusion (c)(1).

Exclusion (c)(1)[229] supplements the protection provided to law enforcement investigations or proceedings by Exemption 7(A).[230] It responds to the perceived danger that a response to a FOIA request, invoking Exemption 7(A), may inadvertently inform the subject of an investigation of its very existence. Accordingly, the exclusion authorizes an agency to shield the existence of records concerning ongoing investigations or proceedings from FOIA requesters.

To qualify for Exclusion (c)(1), the records at issue must be subject to complete withholding under Exemption 7(A).[231] Further, the "investigation or proceeding" in question must involve "a possible violation of criminal law."[232]

---

227. See 5 U.S.C. § 552(c)(1), (c)(2), (c)(3).

228. Following *Phillippi v. CIA*, 546 F.2d 1009 (D.C. Cir. 1976), a procedure commonly known as "Glomarization" has been available to agencies, allowing them to answer a FOIA request by refusing to confirm or deny the existence of the records sought when to do otherwise could cause a particular harm contemplated by the FOIA exemption itself. But utilizing a "Glomar" response is inadequate to protect against the harm caused by the very invocation of a specific exemption when a very broad request for information is received. "It is precisely because 'Glomarization' inadequately protects against the particular harms in question that the more delicate exclusion mechanism, which affords a higher level of protection, sometimes must be employed." Attorney General's Memorandum on the Amendments to the Freedom of Information Act, at 26 (Dec. 1987); see FRANKLIN & BOUCHARD, *supra* note 2, at 1-336 n.6. See generally Gotanda, *Glomar Denials Under FOIA: A Problematic Privilege and a Proposed Alternative Procedure of Review*, 56 U. PITT. L. REV. 165 (1994); Aitchison, Comment, *Reining in the Glomar Response: Reducing CIA Abuse of the Freedom of Information Act*, 27 U.C. DAVIS L. REV. 219 (1993). The ability of an agency to issue a "Glomar response" has been codified in Exec. Order No. 12,958 § 3.7(a), 3 C.F.R. 333 (1996).

229. See 5 U.S.C. § 552(c)(1).

230. See Chap. 10-2(c)(8)(A) *supra*.

231. See 5 U.S.C. § 552(c)(1).

232. *Id.* § 552(c)(1)(A). Records related to a civil law enforcement matter do not fall within Exclusion (c)(1). The language does not specify that the investigation actually must be performed by a law enforcement agency, only that it possibly involves a crime, leaving the door open for other agency investigations where a crime has potentially been committed. See Attorney General's Memorandum on the 1986 Amendments to the Freedom of Information Act, at 20 (Dec. 1987).

In addition, an agency must have "reason to believe . . . the subject of the investigation or proceeding is not aware of its pendency."[233] Finally, it must be shown that disclosure of the mere existence of the records at issue "could reasonably be expected to interfere with enforcement proceedings."[234] The Exclusion may be invoked "during only such time" as such circumstances persist.[235]

§ 10-2(d)(2). Exclusion (c)(2).

Exclusion (c)(2) protects against the potential identification of confidential informants.[236] This exclusion was created to remedy the situation whereby invoking Exemption 7(D)[237] would likely provide the requester with information that a record exists, thereby identifying the informant about whom the information had been requested.[238] Thus, the exclusion applies only to "informant records maintained by a criminal law enforcement agency under an informant's name or personal identifier."[239] Under the exclusion, an agency would have "no obligation to acknowledge the existence of such records in response to such request."[240] The exclusion does not apply, or no longer applies, when the person's status as an informant has otherwise been officially confirmed.[241]

§ 10-2(d)(3). Exclusion (c)(3).

Exclusion (c)(3) is narrow in scope, in that it is limited to records maintained by a single agency, the FBI,[242] and to records of a specific type — i.e., "pertaining to foreign intelligence or counterintelligence, or international terrorism," the existence of which is classified pursuant to Exemption 1.[243] This supplement to Exemption 1 was deemed necessary because of congressional concern that invocation of Exemption 1 in response to a targeted FOIA request could inform the requester of the existence of records, thereby threatening the safety and security of the United States. Exclusion (c)(3), as with the other exclusions,

---

233. 5 U.S.C. § 552(c)(1)(B)(i).
234. *Id.* § 552(c)(1)(B)(ii).
235. *Id.* § 552(c)(1).
236. See *id.* § 552(c)(2).
237. See Chap. 10-2(c)(8)(D) *supra*.
238. See Attorney General's Memorandum on the 1986 Amendments to the Freedom of Information Act, at 23-24 (Dec. 1987).
239. 5 U.S.C. § 552(c)(2).
240. S. REP. NO. 98-221, at 25 (1983).
241. See 5 U.S.C. § 552(c)(2).
242. The Attorney General contemplated the existence of records in other agencies derived from FBI records that are no less in need of this type of protection and recommended that other agencies and the FBI jointly consider the sensitivity of such documents so that anomalous treatment of the information does not result. See Attorney General's Memorandum on the 1986 Amendments to the Freedom of Information Act, at 25 n.45 (Dec. 1987).
243. 5 U.S.C. § 552(c)(3). See Chap. 10-2(c)(2) *supra*.

contains a temporal limitation, permitting exclusion only so long as the existence of the record remains classified.[244]

§ 10-2(e). Segregation of Exempt Material.

FOIA also places a burden of reasonable segregation of information on agencies,[245] preventing entire documents from being withheld on the basis of discrete exempt portions.[246] "Any reasonably segregable portion of a record shall be provided to any person requesting such record after deletion of the portions which are exempt under this subsection."[247] An entire record may be withheld if the nonexempt material is "inextricably intertwined" with exempt material,[248] or if a line-by-line review of the record to segregate a relatively small amount of nonexempt material would impose an inordinate burden on the agency.[249]

§ 10-2(f). Reverse FOIA Suits.

Although the stated purpose of FOIA is to open government operations to citizen review, one of its side effects has been to give business competitors access to commercial information.[250] One tool to offset this phenomenon and to protect commercial information from government disclosure to competitors is the so-called "reverse FOIA" action brought to enjoin an agency to withhold specific records pursuant to applicable FOIA exemptions.

The Supreme Court recognized the viability of the reverse FOIA action in *Chrysler Corp. v. Brown*.[251] In that case, Chrysler had challenged an agency regulation that required disclosure of previously submitted "exempt" information.[252] Chrysler argued that Exemption 4 and the Federal Trade Secrets Act[253]

---

244. See 5 U.S.C. § 552(c)(3).
245. See *id.* § 552(b).
246. See Kimberlin v. Department of Justice, 139 F.3d 944, 949 (D.C. Cir. 1998) (to withhold an entire file pursuant to Exemption 7(C), government must show that disclosure of any part of the file could reasonably be expected to constitute an unwarranted invasion of personal privacy); Yeager v. DEA, 678 F.2d 315, 323 (D.C. Cir. 1982).
247. 5 U.S.C. § 552(b).
248. Neufeld v. IRS, 646 F.2d 661, 663 (D.C. Cir. 1981); see Krikorian v. Department of State, 984 F.2d 461, 466 (D.C. Cir. 1993).
249. See, e.g., Lead Indus. Ass'n v. OSHA, 610 F.2d 70, 86 (2d Cir. 1979); Doherty v. Department of Justice, 775 F.2d 49, 52 (2d Cir. 1985).
250. One critic for change has commented that FOIA was "subsidizing Swedish ball bearing makers . . . and French aviation firms," at the expense of American companies. O'Reilly, *Regaining a Confidence: Protection of Business Confidential Data Through Reform of the Freedom of Information Act*, 34 ADMIN. L. REV. 263, 264 (1982).
251. 441 U.S. 281 (1979).
252. *Id.* at 287. See Peacock, *Developments Under the Freedom of Information Act — 1980*, 1981 DUKE L.J. 338, 363.
253. 18 U.S.C. § 1905.

barred disclosure of the information and that any disclosure would constitute an abuse of discretion.[254] The Court rejected Chrysler's argument regarding Exemption 4 on the ground that FOIA's exemptions are discretionary.[255] In addition, it was unwilling to imply a private right of action under a criminal statute such as the Trade Secrets Act.[256] Nevertheless, the Court reasoned that Chrysler had standing to bring suit to review an agency's decision to disclose requested records under section 10(a) of the Administrative Procedure Act ("APA"),[257] as a person "adversely affected or aggrieved by agency action."[258] As a result, Chrysler could challenge the agency's action as an abuse of discretion if it violated the Trade Secrets Act,[259] because such an action would "not be in accordance with law" or would be "arbitrary and capricious" within the meaning of the APA.[260]

§ 10-2(g). Administrative Appeals.

Each agency subject to FOIA is required to publish regulations concerning access to its records, including its administrative appeal procedures.[261] A requester's failure to follow these regulations may be deemed a failure properly to exhaust administrative remedies.[262] Thus, a requester must typically file an administrative appeal, seeking reversal of an initial agency denial of a FOIA request, before filing suit in court.[263] When a request has been wholly or partially

---

254. See 441 U.S. at 287.
255. See *id.* at 292 ("FOIA by itself protects the submitter's interest in confidentiality only to the extent that this interest is endorsed by the agency collecting this information").
256. See *id.* at 316. The Trade Secrets Act is a criminal statute. See Westinghouse Elec. Corp. v. Schlesinger, 542 F.2d 1190, 1203-4 (4th Cir. 1976), *cert. denied*, 431 U.S. 924 (1977).
257. 5 U.S.C. §§ 701-706. See Environmental Tech., Inc. v. EPA, 822 F. Supp. 1226, 1228 (E.D. Va. 1993).
258. 441 U.S. at 317.
259. *Id.* at 318. Typically, reverse-FOIA suits involve the Trade Secrets Act. See *id.*; GTE Sylvania, Inc. v. Consumers Union, 445 U.S. 375 (1980); National Org. for Women v. Department of Health & Human Servs., 736 F.2d 727 (D.C. Cir. 1984). Since the Trade Secrets Act bars disclosure of certain information unless "authorized by law," the issue becomes whether an agency's mandatory disclosure regulation for information falling within Exemption 4 or other exemptions had the "force and effect of law" through adherence to APA rulemaking procedures. See Chrysler Corp. v. Brown, 441 U.S. at 301.
260. Typically, the reviewing court will be limited to the agency's record when determining whether the applicable standard has been breached. See National Org. for Women v. Department of Health & Human Servs., 736 F.2d at 736-37 (finding *de novo* provisions under APA are narrow in scope). See also Camp v. Pitts, 411 U.S. 138, 141-42 (1973); Citizens to Preserve Overton Park, Inc. v. Volpe, 401 U.S. 402, 415 (1971); Nick, *De Novo Review in Reverse Freedom of Information Act Suits*, 50 OHIO ST. L.J. 1307 (1989).
261. See 5 U.S.C. § 552(a)(3), (4)(A).
262. See Muhammad v. United States Bureau of Prisons, 789 F. Supp. 449, 450 (D.D.C. 1992).
263. See, e.g., Oglesby v. Department of Army, 920 F.2d 57, 61-62 (D.C. Cir. 1990) (exhaustion of remedies required).

denied within twenty days as required by the statute,[264] an administrative appeal is usually accomplished by making a written submission to the head of the agency or other designated official.[265] The administrative appeal must be decided within twenty working days.[266] If an agency response to the FOIA request has not been made within twenty days, the requester is deemed to have constructively exhausted her administrative remedies and may file suit without pursuing an administrative appeal.[267] If, however, an agency has been late in its response to the FOIA request, but has responded before the requester has filed suit, an administrative appeal should be pursued prior to litigation.[268]

§ 10-2(h). Litigation.

As a last resort,[269] a person challenging an agency decision under FOIA may seek redress in a federal district court, which will consider the matter *de novo*,[270] and which has exclusive jurisdiction[271] to compel disclosure of "agency records"

---

264. 5 U.S.C. § 552(a)(6)(A)(i).
265. "The appeal shall be in writing and should include a copy of the original request and a copy of the response of the Deputy Executive Director for Planning and Information, if any." 16 C.F.R. § 4.11 (1992) (Federal Trade Commission regulation). See 5 U.S.C. § 552 (a)(6)(A)(i); Taylor v. Appleton, 30 F.3d 1365, 1368 (11th Cir. 1994).
266. 5 U.S.C. § 552(a)(6)(A)(ii).
267. See *id.*; Pollack v. Department of Justice, 49 F.3d 115, 118 (4th Cir. 1995) (when agency fails to comply in timely fashion with proper FOIA request, it may not insist on exhaustion of administrative remedies).
268. See 5 U.S.C. § 552(a)(6)(A)(ii); Pollack v. Department of Justice, 49 F.3d at 118 (when agency fails to comply in timely fashion with proper FOIA request, it may not insist on exhaustion of administrative remedies, unless agency responds to request before suit is filed).
269. "Freedom of Information Act cases are peculiarly difficult." Miscavige v. IRS, 2 F.3d 366, 367 (11th Cir. 1993). The Department of Justice has adopted the following policy regarding the defense of FOIA lawsuits:

> The Department will no longer defend an agency's withholding of information merely because there is a "substantial legal basis" for doing so. Rather, in determining whether or not to defend a nondisclosure decision, we will apply a presumption of disclosure. . . . In short, it shall be the policy of the Department of Justice to defend the assertion of a FOIA exemption only in those cases where the agency reasonably foresees that disclosure would be harmful to an interest protected by that exemption.

Memorandum for Heads of Departments and Agencies from Attorney General Janet Reno, Oct. 4, 1993, *reprinted in* 1 FRANKLIN & BOUCHARD, *supra* note 2, at App. D5. See *id.* at 1-389 & n.2.
270. See 5 U.S.C. § 552(a)(4)(B). In contrast, reverse FOIA actions only receive an "examination of the record compiled" on appeal. CNA Fin. Corp. v. Donovan, 830 F.2d 1132, 1162 (D.C. Cir. 1987).
271. See 5 U.S.C. § 552(a)(4)(B):

> On complaint, the district court of the United States in the district in which the complainant resides, or has his principal place of business, or in which the agency records are situated, or in the District of Columbia, has jurisdiction to enjoin the agency from withholding agency

§ 10-2(h) NEWSGATHERING AND THE LAW § 10-2(h)

that are "improperly withheld."[272] An agency may be given additional time to complete its review of the requested records if it can show that exceptional circumstances exist and that the agency is exercising due diligence in responding to the request.[273] The court may compel an administrative investigation of agency personnel who mishandle FOIA requests.[274] The plaintiff may challenge the agency's reliance on or application of particular exemptions, as well as the adequacy of the agency's search for the requested records.[275]

To aid the district courts, FOIA affords them specific authority to conduct *in camera* inspection of agency files.[276] *In camera* review is discretionary[277] and a court will generally not engage in such a review where the agency has supplied

---

records and to order the production of any agency records improperly withheld from the complainant.

272. *Id.* § 552(a)(4)(B); see Kissinger v. Reporters Comm. for Freedom of the Press, 445 U.S. 136, 150 (1980).

273. See 5 U.S.C. § 552(a)(6)(C); Rabin v. Department of State, 980 F. Supp. 116, 123 (E.D.N.Y. 1997).

274. See 5 U.S.C. § 552(a)(4)(F):

Whenever the court orders the production of any agency records improperly withheld from the complainant and assesses against the United States reasonable attorney fees and other litigation costs, and the court additionally issues a written finding that the circumstances surrounding the withholding raise questions whether agency personnel acted arbitrarily or capriciously with respect to the withholding, the Special Counsel shall promptly initiate a proceeding to determine whether disciplinary action is warranted against the officer or employee who was primarily responsible for the withholding. The Special Counsel, after investigation and consideration of the evidence submitted, shall submit his findings and recommendations to the administrative authority of the agency concerned and shall send copies of the findings and recommendations to the officer or employee or his representative. The administrative authority shall take the corrective action that the Special Counsel recommends.

See generally, Note, *Revitalizing the Sanctions Provision of the Freedom of Information Act Amendments of 1974*, 84 GEO. L.J. 617 (1996).

275. The agency has a duty to conduct a "reasonable" search for responsive records. See, e.g., In re Wade, 969 F.2d 241, 249 n.11 (7th Cir. 1992); Oglesby v. Department of Army, 920 F.2d 57, 68 (D.C. Cir. 1990). In a FOIA action, the agency must prove that "each document that falls within the class requested either has been produced, is unidentifiable, or is wholly exempt from the Act's inspection requirements." Miller v. Department of State, 779 F.2d 1378, 1383 (8th Cir. 1985).

276. 5 U.S.C. § 552(a)(4)(B). See Carter v. Department of Commerce, 830 F.2d 388, 392 (D.C. Cir. 1987) (quoting Ray v. Turner, 587 F.2d 1187, 1195 (D.C. Cir. 1978)).

277. A district court may opt for *in camera* review when it believes it will be necessary to make a reasonable *de novo* determination of the exempt status of the information requested. See NLRB v. Robbins Tire & Rubber Co., 437 U.S. 214, 224 (1978); Quinon v. FBI, 86 F.3d 1222, 1230 (D.C. Cir. 1996) (discretionary factors that weigh in favor of *in camera* review include number of records at issue, whether focus of dispute centers on content of documents at issue, and whether agency has proposed an *in camera* inspection); Center for Auto Safety v. EPA, 731 F.2d 16, 21 (D.C. Cir. 1984); Church of Scientology Int'l v. Department of Justice, 30 F.3d 224, 233 (1st Cir. 1994).

sufficiently detailed affidavits,[278] though a failure to perform an *in camera* review can constitute an abuse of discretion.[279] Courts tend to require agencies to submit detailed affidavits, describing the requested material and explaining the basis for non-disclosure.[280] Known as *Vaughn* indexes,[281] they enable judges to bypass *in camera* review of what may be thousands of documents, or ease the burden of *in camera* review, since the affidavits are to be cross-referenced to the actual documents requested.[282] To neutralize the imbalance caused by the requester's difficulty in ascertaining the facts being litigated, the *Vaughn* index is typically made available to the opposing party.[283]

FOIA also permits the district court to award reasonable attorney fees, as well as litigation costs, to a successful plaintiff.[284] For the plaintiff to be awarded attorney fees, the action must be brought by an attorney,[285] the plaintiff must be

---

278. See Carter v. Department of Commerce, 830 F.2d at 392; Krikorian v. Department of State, 984 F.2d 461, 467 (D.C. Cir. 1993).
279. See Center for Auto Safety v. EPA, 731 F.2d at 21-22.
280. See, e.g., Founding Church of Scientology v. Bell, 603 F.2d 945, 947 (D.C. Cir. 1979); Vaughn v. Rosen, 484 F.2d 820, 826-28 (D.C. Cir. 1973), *cert. denied*, 415 U.S. 977 (1974).
281. The requirement that agencies prepare such indexes was fashioned by the D.C. Circuit in *Vaughn v. Rosen*, 484 F.2d 820, 826 (D.C. Cir. 1973), *cert. denied*, 415 U.S. 977 (1974).
282. See *id.*; McNamara v. Department of Justice, 949 F. Supp. 478, 484 (W.D. Tex. 1996) (*Vaughn* index is to contain description sufficient to enable court to reach its own conclusion as to what is in record, without compromising its secrecy).
283. See Schiller v. NLRB, 964 F.2d 1205, 1209 (D.C. Cir. 1992) (citations omitted):

> The purpose of a Vaughn index is to permit adequate adversary testing of the agency's claimed right to an exemption, and those who contest denials of FOIA requests — who are, necessarily, at a disadvantage because they have not seen the withheld documents — can generally prevail only by showing that the agency's Vaughn index does not justify withholding information under the exemptions invoked.

See also Davin v. Department of Justice, 60 F.3d 1043, 1050 (3d Cir. 1995) (hallmark test of sufficiency of *Vaughn* index is "that the requester and the trial judge be able to derive from the index a clear explanation of why each document or portion of a document withheld is putatively exempt from disclosure"); Keys v. Department of Justice, 830 F.2d 337, 349 (D.C. Cir. 1987); Lykins v. Department of Justice, 725 F.2d 1455, 1463 (D.C. Cir. 1984); Founding Church of Scientology v. Bell, 603 F.2d at 947; Vaughn v. Rosen, 484 F.2d at 826.
284. See 5 U.S.C. § 552(a)(4)(E). See generally Sisk, *A Primer on Awards of Attorney's Fees Against the Federal Government*, 25 ARIZ. ST. L.J. 733, 772 (1993).
285. The majority of courts have refused to award attorney fees to pro se, non-attorney litigants. See, e.g., Benavides v. Bureau of Prisons, 993 F.2d 257, 259 (D.C. Cir.), *cert. denied*, 510 U.S. 996 (1993) ("absent congressional intent . . . the word 'attorney,' when used in the context of a fee-shifting statute, does not encompass a lay-person proceeding on his own behalf"). There is considerable doubt whether pro se attorney litigants will be granted such awards. See Kay v. Ehrler, 499 U.S. 432, 436 (1991) (court rejected claim that pro se attorney litigants were eligible for fees in 42 U.S.C. § 1988 civil rights actions); Ray v. Department of Justice, 856 F. Supp. 1576, 1581 (1994), *aff'd*, 87 F.3d 1250 (11th Cir. 1996) (not awarding attorney fees to pro se attorney litigant on basis of *Kay*); SEC v. Kaufman, 835 F. Supp. 157 (S.D.N.Y. 1993); Manos v. Department of Air Force, 829 F. Supp. 1191 (N.D. Cal. 1993). See also Aronson v. HUD, 866 F.2d 1, 4-6

eligible for the award by having "substantially prevailed" in the litigation,[286] and the court must find that the plaintiff is entitled to an award.[287] The court will award "reasonable"[288] attorneys fees if these requirements are met.[289] Litigation

---

(1st Cir. 1989) (pre-*Kay* case not awarding attorney fees to pro se attorney litigant); Falcone v. IRS, 714 F.2d 646, 648 (6th Cir. 1983), *cert. denied*, 466 U.S. 908 (1984). But see Cazalas v. Department of Justice, 709 F.2d 1051, 1055-57 (5th Cir. 1983), *cert. denied*, 469 U.S. 1207 (1985).

286. 5 U.S.C. § 552(a)(4)(E). To be eligible for attorney fees, one must have "substantially prevailed," which means the filing of the litigation must have been "reasonably necessary," and have had a "substantial causative effect" on the resulting disclosure. See, e.g., Weisberg v. Department of Justice, 848 F.2d 1265, 1268 (D.C. Cir. 1988); Chesapeake Bay Found. v. Department of Agric., 11 F.3d 211, 216 (D.C. Cir. 1993), *cert. denied*, 513 U.S. 927 (1994); Miller v. Department of State, 779 F.2d 1378, 1389 (8th Cir. 1985); Church of Scientology v. United States Postal Serv., 700 F.2d 486, 489 (9th Cir. 1983); Lovell v. Alderete, 630 F.2d 428, 432 (5th Cir. 1980); Vermont Low Income Advocacy Council, Inc. v. Usery, 546 F.2d 509, 513 (2d Cir. 1976).

287. Determination of entitlement is left to the discretion of the court. See, e.g., Chesapeake Bay Found. v. Department of Agric., 11 F.3d 211, 216 (D.C. Cir. 1993), *cert. denied*, 513 U.S. 927 (1994); Miller v. Department of State, 779 F.2d 1378, 1389 (8th Cir. 1985); Church of Scientology v. United States Postal Serv., 700 F.2d 486, 492 (9th Cir. 1983). Most courts consult four factors in adjudicating a plaintiff's fee request: (1) the benefit to the public; (2) commercial benefit; (3) the nature of the complainant's interest; and (4) whether the government had a reasonable basis in law to withhold the record. S. REP. NO. 93-854, at 19 (1974). The "public benefit" guideline has led courts to award fees when disclosure disseminates useful information to the public, such as material to be used in a television documentary on the Rosenberg espionage case. See Goldstein v. Levi, 415 F. Supp. 303, 305 (D.D.C. 1976). The press and public interest groups are commonly associated with the "public benefit" factor. See Detroit Free Press v. Department of Justice, 73 F.3d 93, 98 (6th Cir. 1996) (affirmed award of attorney fees partly on ground that, although newspaper would reap some commercial benefit from its access to mug shots, "news interests should not be considered commercial interests," and fees are generally awarded where "the complainant's interest in the information sought was scholarly or journalistic or public interest oriented"); Blue v. Bureau of Prisons, 570 F.2d 529, 533 (5th Cir. 1988); Nationwide Bldg. Maintenance v. Sampson, 559 F.2d 704, 712 (D.C. Cir. 1976); Matlack, Inc. v. EPA, 868 F. Supp. 627 (D. Del. 1994).

288. 5 U.S.C. § 552(a)(4)(E). See Anderson v. Secretary of Health & Human Servs., 80 F.3d 1500, 1504 (10th Cir. 1996).

289. An attorney may be denied a fee award if he makes an outrageous request, or fails to keep time records. See National Ass'n of Concerned Vets v. Secretary of Defense, 675 F.2d 1319, 1331 n.19 (D.C. Cir. 1982); Jordan v. Department of Justice, 691 F.2d 514, 518-19 (D.C. Cir. 1982); Brown v. Stackler, 612 F.2d 1057, 1059 (7th Cir. 1980). See also Anderson v. Secretary of Health & Human Servs., 80 F.3d 1500, 1505 (10th Cir. 1996) (district court acted properly in denying attorneys fees for period of litigation during which plaintiff was seeking information primarily for state court litigation in which she was a party). Calculation of attorneys fees are initially based upon the "lodestar": the number of hours a lawyer should get credit for multiplied by a reasonable rate of pay. See, e.g., Copeland v. Marshall, 641 F.2d 880, 889 (D.C. Cir. 1980) (en banc); McDonnell v. United States, 870 F. Supp. 576, 586 (D.N.J. 1994). See generally Hensley v. Eckerhart, 461 U.S. 424 (1983) (creation of the initial standard). Other factors that may raise or lower the award are the quality of the representation, the degree of success, and the contingent nature of the fee. See, e.g., Long v. IRS, 932 F.2d 1309, 1314 (9th Cir. 1991); McDonnell v. United States, 870 F. Supp. at 587.

costs, fixed by statute,[290] are available to any plaintiff who has "substantially prevailed" in the litigation.[291]

§ 10-3. Access to Records Under the Federal Advisory Committee Act.

§ 10-3(a). Introduction.

In addition to public access to advisory committee meetings,[292] the Federal Advisory Committee Act, commonly known as FACA, mandates public access to the records of federally created advisory committees.

§ 10-3(b). Records.

Under FACA, the "records, reports, transcripts, minutes, appendices, working papers, drafts, studies, agenda, or other documents which were made available to or prepared for or by each advisory committee" must be made available for public inspection and copying, subject to FOIA exemptions.[293] Detailed minutes of any meeting of the advisory committee must be taken and must include a record of the persons present, a complete and accurate description of matters discussed and conclusions reached, and copies of all reports received, issued, or approved by the committee. The minutes must be made available to the public.[294]

§ 10-3(c). Procedures.

Records subject to FACA must be made available to the public, without a FOIA request,[295] "at a single location in the offices of the advisory committee or the agency to which the advisory committee reports,"[296] before or on the date of the advisory committee meeting for which those materials were prepared.[297]

---

290. See 28 U.S.C. § 1920.

291. 5 U.S.C. § 552(a)(4)(E). In addition, upon a finding that the circumstances surrounding the withholding of agency records raises questions as to whether agency personnel acted arbitrarily or capriciously, a special counsel is to investigate whether disciplinary action is warranted against the officer or employee primarily responsible. See 5 U.S.C. § 552(a)(4)(F). Such action is extremely rare. See Note, *supra* note 274, at 617.

292. See Chap. 9-5 *supra*.

293. 5 U.S.C. App. II § 10(b). See Chap. 10-2(c) *supra*.

294. See 5 U.S.C. App. II § 10(c); 41 C.F.R. § 101-6.1025.

295. The agency responsible for the advisory committee may require a FOIA request for advisory committee records for which an exemption from disclosure is claimed. See Food Chem. News, Inc. v. Department of Health & Human Servs., 980 F.2d 1468 (D.C. Cir. 1992).

296. 5 U.S.C. App. II § 10(b).

297. See Food Chem. News, Inc. v. Department of Health & Human Servs., 980 F.2d 1468, 1472 (D.C. Cir. 1992) ("In order for 'interested parties to present their views,' and for the public to 'be informed with respect to the subject matter,' it is essential that, whenever practicable, parties have access to the relevant materials before or at the meeting at which the materials are used and discussed. Opening the meetings to the public would be meaningless if the public could not follow

Copies of transcripts of advisory committee meetings must be made available to the public at the actual cost of duplication.[298] Copies of each report made by an advisory committee and, where appropriate, background papers prepared by consultants, must be filed with the Library of Congress to be made available for public inspection and use.[299]

A FOIA request may be required for those materials the advisory committee claims to be exempt from public disclosure. In such a case, the agency responsible for the advisory committee must follow the applicable FOIA procedures and exemptions.[300] In the event such a request is denied, any person has standing to challenge that denial in a judicial proceeding.[301] A court may enjoin the use of records created by an advisory committee that failed to comply with the requirements of FACA.[302]

---

the substance of the discussions."). Executive agencies are responsible for establishing "uniform administrative guidelines and management controls" for advisory committees, which include designating an advisory management officer who, among other responsibilities, must "assemble and maintain reports, records, and other papers" of advisory committees. 5 U.S.C. App. II § 8.

298. See 5 U.S.C. App. II § 11(a).

299. See *id.* § 13.

300. See *id.* § 8(b)(3); Food Chem. News, Inc. v. Advisory Comm. on Food & Drug Admin., 760 F. Supp. 220, 222 (D.D.C. 1991), *aff'd as clarified sub nom.* Food Chem. News, Inc. v. Department of Health & Human Servs., 980 F.2d 1468 (D.C. Cir. 1992) ("In practical terms, some mechanism is needed to route requests for advisory committee documents through the sponsoring agency to give it a chance in the first instance to apply FOIA exemptions through the administrative process."). See also Meyerhoff v. EPA, 958 F.2d 1498, 1503 (9th Cir. 1992) (nondisclosure of financial statements of members of advisory committee of EPA pursuant to FOIA Exemption 3).

301. See Public Citizen v. Department of Justice, 491 U.S. 440, 450-51 (1989).

302. See Alabama-Tombigbee Rivers Coalition v. Department of Interior, 26 F.3d 1103, 1107 (11th Cir. 1994) ("We find injunctive relief as the only vehicle that carries the sufficient remedial effect to ensure future compliance with FACA's clear requirements. Anything less would be tantamount to nothing."); Comment, *Alabama-Tombigbee Rivers Coalition v. Department of Interior: Giving Sabers to a "Toothless Tiger," The Federal Advisory Committee Act*, 26 ENVTL. L. 393 (1996).

Chapter 11

ACCESS TO STATE GOVERNMENT RECORDS

§ 11-1. Introduction.
§ 11-2. Records.
§ 11-3. Organizations.
  § 11-3(a). Executive Branch.
  § 11-3(b). Legislative Branch.
  § 11-3(c). Judicial Branch.
  § 11-3(d). Advisory Committees.
  § 11-3(e). Nongovernmental Organizations.
§ 11-4. Procedures.
§ 11-5. Exemptions from Disclosure.
  § 11-5(a). Statutory Exemptions.
    § 11-5(a)(1). Internal Agency Personnel Rules and Practices.
    § 11-5(a)(2). Disclosures Forbidden by Other Statutes.
    § 11-5(a)(3). Trade Secrets and Certain Financial Information.
    § 11-5(a)(4). Inter-Agency and Intra-Agency Memoranda.
    § 11-5(a)(5). Disclosures Constituting an Unwarranted Invasion of Privacy.
    § 11-5(a)(6). Law Enforcement Records.
    § 11-5(a)(7). Financial Institution Records.
    § 11-5(a)(8). Geological Information Relating to Oil and Gas Wells.
  § 11-5(b). Other Statutory Exemptions.
  § 11-5(c). Common Law Exemptions.
  § 11-5(d). Waiver of Exemptions.
§ 11-6. Segregation of Exempt Material.
§ 11-7. Categories of Records.
  § 11-7(a). Personnel Records.
    § 11-7(a)(1). Applications for Employment.
    § 11-7(a)(2). Salary Information.
    § 11-7(a)(3). Disciplinary Records.
    § 11-7(a)(4). Records of Labor Negotiations.
    § 11-7(a)(5). Promotional Examinations.
  § 11-7(b). Police Records.
    § 11-7(b)(1). Arrest and Incident Reports.
    § 11-7(b)(2). Police Blotter.
    § 11-7(b)(3). Investigatory Records.
      § 11-7(b)(3)(A). Active Files.
      § 11-7(b)(3)(B). Closed Files.
    § 11-7(b)(4). Rap Sheets and Other Compilations of Criminal Histories.
    § 11-7(b)(5). Victim Information.
    § 11-7(b)(6). Confessions.
    § 11-7(b)(7). Confidential Informants.
    § 11-7(b)(8). 911 Tapes.
    § 11-7(b)(9). Police Investigatory Techniques.
    § 11-7(b)(10). Accident Reports.
  § 11-7(c). Probation and Parole Reports.
  § 11-7(d). Coroner Reports, Autopsy Reports, and Photographs.
  § 11-7(e). Medical Records.

§ 11-7(f). Financial Information.
  § 11-7(f)(1). Business Records.
  § 11-7(f)(2). Financial Data.
  § 11-7(f)(3). Bank Records.
  § 11-7(f)(4). Contract Proposals and Bids.
  § 11-7(f)(5). Real Estate Appraisals.
  § 11-7(f)(6). Audits of Public Offices.
§ 11-7(g). Educational Records.
§ 11-7(h). Election Records.
§ 11-7(i). Trade Secrets and Proprietary Information.
§ 11-7(j). Vital Statistics.
§ 11-7(k). Motor Vehicle Records.
§ 11-7(*l*). Public Utility Records.
§ 11-7(m). Litigation Records.
§ 11-8. Administrative Appeals.
§ 11-9. Litigation.

§ 11-1. Introduction.

The enactment of the federal Freedom of Information Act ("FOIA") prompted many states to codify their laws granting access to state and local government records as well. Currently, all fifty states and the District of Columbia have enacted legislation providing some form of public access to governmental records.[1] These laws generally provide the public, including the press,[2] with a broad right of access to public records to facilitate a better understanding of governmental activities, while protecting the legitimate interests of government and the privacy rights of individual citizens.[3]

---

1. See generally Nowadzky, *A Comparative Analysis of Public Record Statutes*, 28 URB. LAW. 65 (1996); UNIF. INFO. PRAC. CODE, 13 U.L.A. 277 (1986).
2. State courts have largely rejected any suggestion that journalists be afforded greater rights of access under these statutes than is accorded the general public. See In re Hearst Estate, 136 Cal. Rptr. 821 (Ct. App. 1977); McLaughlin v. Philadelphia Newspapers, Inc., 348 A.2d 376 (Pa. 1975). See also Houston Chronicle Publ'g Co. v. City of Houston, 531 S.W.2d 177 (Tex. App. 1975); City of St. Matthews v. Voice of St. Matthews, 519 S.W.2d 811 (Ky. 1974).
3. "The policy of open records statutes is to maximize accountability through maximum public dissemination of information about the actions of government agencies." J. O'REILLY, FEDERAL INFORMATION DISCLOSURE § 27.03 (2d ed. 1995); Ohio ex rel. WHIO-TV-7 v. Lowe, 673 N.E.2d 1360, 1364 (Ohio 1997) ("[T]he purpose of Ohio's Public Records Act . . . is to expose government activity to public scrutiny, which is absolutely essential to the proper working of a democracy."). This lofty goal, however, may not be at the heart of those requesting records. The most likely requester of state records is one engaged in litigation with the agency, or a person defending against a government prosecution or regulatory proceeding. O'REILLY, *supra*, at § 27.05. See generally Note, *Freedom of Information Statutes: The Unfulfilled Legacy*, 48 FED. COMM. L.J. 371 (1996). State open records statutes are also employed by attorneys in civil litigation to obtain information that may not be available under traditional discovery rules. See Watkins, *Using the Freedom of Information Act as a Discovery Device*, 1994 ARK. L. NOTES 59.

State open records laws attempt to balance the public's interest in learning what government is doing, the interest of individual citizens in keeping their affairs private, and the government's interest in effective operations. It is this inherent tension that shapes the policies and exemptions common to most open records laws.

As under FOIA,[4] the general rule under state law is that government records will be deemed to be open to the public unless specifically exempted, creating a general presumption in favor of access.[5] In addition, it is typically the government's burden to prove that a record is exempted,[6] and the courts have, on the whole, narrowly construed exemptions authorizing the withholding of records.[7]

Because the federal FOIA preceded most state open records laws, many states have chosen to model their open records laws directly after FOIA and look to federal case law for guidance in statutory interpretation.[8] Other states have consulted FOIA more generally as a rough blueprint for the creation of their open records laws.[9] In either case, a general understanding of FOIA will be helpful in interpreting state open records laws.[10]

---

4. 5 U.S.C. § 552. See Chap. 10-1 *supra*.

5. New York's Freedom of Information Law, for example, asserts as its statement of policy that "the public, individually and collectively and represented by the press, should have access to the records of government." N.Y. PUB. OFF. LAW § 84. See CAL. GOV'T CODE § 6253(a) (requiring disclosure of all records not falling within a statutory exception); 5 ILL. COMP. STAT. 140/3; N.Y. PUB. OFF. LAW § 87(2); Chambers v. Birmingham News Co., 552 So. 2d 854 (Ala. 1989); Cook v. Craig, 127 Cal. Rptr. 712 (Ct. App. 1976); Wilson v. Freedom of Info. Comm'n, 435 A.2d 353 (Conn. 1980); American Broadcasting Cos. v. Siebert, 442 N.Y.S.2d 855 (Sup. Ct. 1981).

6. See, e.g., Cooper v. Department of Lottery, 640 N.E.2d 1299, 1302 (Ill. App., 1994); Globe Newspaper Co. v. Police Comm'r, 648 N.E.2d 419, 424 (Mass., 1995); Vallejos v. California Highway Patrol, 152 Cal. Rptr. 846 (Ct. App. 1979); National Broadcasting Co. v. Cleveland, 526 N.E.2d 786 (Ohio 1988) (burden of proof on agency to establish applicability of exemption).

7. See, e.g., Union Leader Corp. v. New Hampshire Hous. Fin. Auth., 705 A.2d 725 (N.H. 1997); Cooper v. Department of Lottery, 640 N.E.2d 1299, 1302 (Ill. App., 1994); Cook v. Craig, 127 Cal. Rptr. 712 (Ct. App. 1976); Amoco Prod. Co. v. Landry, 426 So. 2d 220 (La. App. 1982); Pooler v. Nyquist, 392 N.Y.S.2d 948 (Sup. Ct. 1976); Petty v. Wurst, 550 N.E.2d 214 (Ohio App. 1989); Laborers Int'l Union v. City of Aberdeen, 642 P.2d 418 (Wash. App. 1982).

8. See, e.g., Campbell v. Town of Machias, 661 A.2d 1133, 1136 (Me. 1995); Newark Morning Ledger Co. v. Saginaw County Sheriff, 514 N.W.2d 214 (Mich. App. 1994) (decisions interpreting federal Freedom of Information Act provide starting point for analysis); Faulk v. State's Attorney for Harford County, 474 A.2d 880, 887 (Md. 1984) (cases interpreting FOIA will be persuasive authority in interpreting Maryland's Public Information Act); Black Panther Party v. Kehoe, 117 Cal. Rptr. 106 (Ct. App. 1974) (California's public records act is modeled after FOIA and California courts will look to federal case law for guidance). Cf. Williams v. Superior Ct., 19 Cal. Rptr. 2d 882, 892-93 (Ct. App. 1993) (California Public Records Act should not be interpreted as including federal FOIA provisions that CPRA does not contain).

9. See Globe Newspaper Co. v. Boston Retirement Bd., 446 N.E.2d 1051 (Mass. 1983) (Massachusetts' open records law is patterned only generally after FOIA).

10. See Chap. 10 *supra*.

§ 11-2. Records.

The initial step in determining what information is available pursuant to a public records law is ascertaining whether such information is contained in a "record" subject to the statute. The presumption of access that underlies these laws has resulted in most states defining the term "record" broadly so as to make as many documents available to the public as possible. The Illinois Freedom of Information Act's definition is representative of many state laws. It includes:

> all records, reports, forms, writings, letters, memoranda, books, papers, maps, photographs, microfilms, cards, tapes, recordings, electronic data processing records, recorded information and all other documentary materials, regardless of physical form or characteristics, having been prepared, or having been or being used, received, possessed or under the control of any public body.[11]

Other jurisdictions include, within the reach of their legislation, all records kept by the government, whether legislatively required or not.[12] Some jurisdictions limit the scope of "record" to those mandated to be created, received, or retained by state law.[13] These latter states appear to constitute a distinct minority, however; most jurisdictions prefer a broader definition similar to the one offered by Ohio, which encompasses any record kept by or in a public office.[14]

---

11. 5 ILL. COMP. STAT. 140/2(c). See also KY. REV. STAT. ANN. § 61.870(2) (Kentucky Open Records Act broadly defines "records"); Ohio ex rel. Cincinnati Enquirer v. Hamilton County, 662 N.E.2d 334, 336 (Ohio 1996).

12. Massachusetts clarifies this point in its law by specifically opening all records to the public, whether required to be kept by another statute or not. See MASS. GEN. LAWS ch. 4, § 7.

13. See Affiliated Constr. Trades Found. v. Regional Jail & Correctional Facility Auth., 490 S.E.2d 708 (W. Va. 1997) (copies of certified payrolls from jail authority are not public records because they were not prepared, owned, retained, or controlled by jail authority). The North Carolina Public Records Law applies to only those records "made or received pursuant to law or ordinance," which appears to include only those records that are required to be created or received by government. See N.C. GEN. STAT. § 132-1. New Jersey case law specifically states that records not required to be kept are outside of the scope of its act. Collins v. Camden County Dep't of Health, 491 A.2d 66 (N.J. Super. 1984); Keddie v. Rutgers Univ., 689 A.2d 702, 707 (N.J. 1997) ("Right-to-Know Law's definition of a public record is narrow and is to be strictly construed"); Atlantic City Convention Ctr. Auth. v. South Jersey Publ'g Co., 637 A.2d 1261, 1264 (N.J. 1994) (audio recordings made in course of public meeting for purpose of assisting in preparation of official minutes did not constitute a record under public records act, but came within common law definition of "public record").

14. See OHIO REV. CODE ANN. § 149.43(A) (public record includes any record kept by any public office); Ohio ex rel. Findlay Publ'g Co. v. Hancock County Bd. of Comm'rs, 684 N.E.2d 1222, 1225 (Ohio 1997) (settlement agreement of lawsuit in which public office is a party is a public record). But see Ohio ex rel. Wilson-Simmons v. Lake County Sherriff's Dep't, 693 N.E.2d 789, 792-93 (Ohio 1998) (e-mail consisting of racist slurs against government employee by individual co-workers is not a public record because it does not serve to document the organiza-

Records that are open for inspection under a public records law are generally deemed to be available for copying as well by nearly every jurisdiction that has addressed the issue.[15] With the emergence of computer technology, the form in which the copy will be provided is of increasing importance.[16] The broad definition of "records" that is endorsed by most states includes the vast amount of information now stored in computers.[17] Most statutes, expressly or by implication, endorse the sentiment expressed in the North Carolina Public Records Law that information is available "regardless of physical form or characteristics."[18]

The ability of the public to access electronic records has increased. Most states recognize that the receipt of information in computer-ready form plainly makes it more useful and accessible.[19] Indeed, disclosure in digital form becomes increasingly significant as technology continues to create greater flexibility in the use of data if it is available electronically. Some states, however, have placed a greater emphasis on the information sought than the usefulness of the medium in which it is stored.[20] A few other states have either declined to require that

---

tion, functions, policies, decisions, procedures, operations, or other activities of the sheriff's department).

15. See, e.g., 5 ILL. COMP. STAT. 140/3; MASS. GEN. LAWS ch. 66, § 10(a); N.Y. PUB. OFF. LAW § 87(2) (no limitation on copying any record available for inspection).

16. See generally Petersen & Roberts, *Access to Electronic Public Records*, 22 FLA. ST. U.L. REV. 443 (1994); Note, *A Double-Barrelled Assault: How Technology and Judicial Interpretations Threaten Public Access to Law Enforcement Records*, 48 FED. COMM. L.J. 341 (1996).

17. See, e.g., ARK. CODE ANN. § 25-27-102(5); FLA. STAT. § 119.011(1); GA. CODE ANN. § 50-18-70(a); HAW. REV. STAT. § 92F-3; IDAHO CODE § 9-337; 5 ILL. COMP. STAT. 140/2(c); KY. REV. STAT. ANN. § 61.870(2); LA. REV. STAT. ANN. § 44:1; ME. REV. STAT. ANN. tit. 1, § 402(3); MD. CODE ANN., STATE GOV'T § 10-611; MICH. COMP. LAWS § 15.232(2)(e); MO. REV. STAT. § 610.010(6); N.Y. PUB. OFF. LAW § 86(4); TENN. CODE ANN. § 10-7-301(6); TEX. GOV'T CODE ANN. § 552.002; WIS. STAT. § 19.32(2). See Birmingham News Co. v. Peevy, 21 MEDIA L. REP. (BNA) 2125 (Ala. Cir. 1993). But see COLO. REV. STAT. § 24-72-202(7) (public record does not include computer software). See generally Sanders, *Arizona's Public Records Laws and the Technology Age: Applying "Paper" Laws to Computer Records*, 37 ARIZ. L. REV. 931 (1995); see also Brooks, *Adventures in Cyberspace: Computer Technology and the Arkansas Freedom of Information Act*, 17 U. ARK. LITTLE ROCK L.J. 417 (1995).

18. N.C. GEN. STAT. § 132-1. See, e.g., ALASKA STAT. §§ 09.25.120, 09.25.220(3); CAL. GOV'T CODE § 6252; DEL. CODE ANN. Tit 29, § 10002(d); 5 ILL. COMP. STAT. 140/2(c)-(d); IOWA CODE § 22.1; KAN. STAT. ANN. § 45-217(f)(1); KY. REV. STAT. ANN. § 61.870(2); MASS. GEN. LAWS ch. 4, § 7, cl. 26; MINN. STAT. § 13.01, Subd. 7; MISS. CODE ANN. § 25-61-3(b); MONT. CODE ANN. § 2-6-202(1); NEB. REV. STAT. § 84-712.01(1).

19. See ALASKA STAT. § 09.25.115(a)(h); VA. CODE ANN. § 2.1-342(A)(4), ¶ 4 (electronic data records must be reasonably accessible at reasonable cost). Florida, for example, has expressly allowed for remote access by the public to government databases. See FLA. STAT. § 119.085. But see CAL. GOV'T CODE § 6256 ("computer data shall be provided in a form determined by the agency)).

20. See Margoulis v. City of Cleveland, 584 N.E.2d 665 (Ohio 1992) (court required that only a printout of computer data be provided absent a showing that such a copy would be insufficient, on

material be provided in computerized form or have placed limitations on accessing such material.[21] Such limited access to computerized information undermines the process that open records laws seek to achieve and is increasingly rare.

Most states have opted to provide access to information recorded on digital media by copying the information in the same medium if requested, so long as the request for computerized information is not overly burdensome to the government. Those requesting such information are thereby afforded the same ease of access to data as is the government itself.[22]

The general availability of information contained in computer files does not, however, carry over to the software utilized by governmental agencies.[23] Such treatment of software, the courts have generally concluded, results from the fact that the purpose of public records laws is to provide public access to information, not to technology.[24] Indeed, the proprietary rights of the government or third party providers of computer software may be protected by intellectual property laws[25] or by a statutory exemption that protects trade secrets from man-

---

the ground that only the message, but not the exact medium, need be copied unless the medium enhances the message); Blaylock v. Staley, 732 S.W.2d 152 (Ark. 1987) (paper printout provided adequate access to public record).

21. See N.J. STAT. ANN. § 47:1A-2.1 (public access limited to hard copies of computerized records); Tax Data Corp. v. Hutt, 826 P.2d 353, 355 (Colo. App. 1991).

22. See, e.g., AFSCME v. County of Cook, 555 N.E.2d 361 (Ill. 1990) (if a computer copy of data is requested it must be supplied unless exemption applies). See also Farrell v. City of Detroit, 530 N.W.2d 105 (Mich. App. 1995) (reversing decision against newspaper reporter who had requested information in computer form).

23. See IND. CODE § 5-14-3-4(b)(11); IOWA CODE § 22.3(A); A & T Consultants, Inc. v. Sharp, 904 S.W.2d 668, 680 (Tex. 1995) (source code and documentation geared to a specific computer program is not subject to disclosure); Mich. Op. Att'y Gen. No. 5593 (1979) (software developed by or in the possession of the government is not an available public record).

24. This theory is also reflected in statutory exemptions and exclusions, see, e.g., CAL. GOV'T CODE § 6254.9(a-e); 5 ILL. COMP. STAT. 140/7(1)(p), as well as the fact that state and local governments may be required to honor distribution limitations included in software licensing agreements, see FLA. STAT. § 119.07(3)(o); Fla. Op. Att'y Gen. No. 90-104 (1990) (voting software obtained under a licensing agreement prohibiting disclosure that is deemed a trade secret is exempt from disclosure); Fla. Op. Att'y Gen. No. 90-102 (1990) (copyrighted software that is licensed to a county agency may be made available only for inspection purposes, as reproduction would violate copyright laws).

25. State and local governments may own the copyright in computer software they have developed. See, e.g., IOWA CODE § 22.3A(3); MINN. STAT. § 13.03, Subd. 5; MONT. CODE ANN. § 2-6-110(1); N.D. CENT. CODE § 44-04-18.5 (exempts software for which state agencies have acquired a copyright). See Gellman, *Twin Evils: Government Copyright and Copyright-like Controls over Government Information*, 45 SYRACUSE L. REV. 999, 1027 (1995) ("[S]tate copyright claims are routinely made for some categories of state data and states employ copyright like other copyright owners."). But see MISS. CODE ANN. § 25-61-10 (use of proprietary software not to restrict public access).

datory access.[26] Some states have created an express statutory exception for software,[27] while others have chosen to exclude software from their definition of "record."[28]

Although open records laws do provide access to a great deal of information in the possession of the government, they do not contemplate the creation of a new record to comply with a request.[29] Governments have not been required to create a computerized database that is more convenient to the person making the request.[30] Rather, information is typically required to be made available to the public in the same form as it is then available to the government entity in possession of it.[31]

§ 11-3. Organizations.

§ 11-3(a). Executive Branch.

With few exceptions, the records that are created and maintained by the executive branch of a state or local government are open to the public, pursuant to either an express statutory provision,[32] a broad general definition of those government organizations that are subject to the public records law,[33] or case

---

26. See Chap. 11-5(a)(3) *infra*; IDAHO CODE § 9-340(2); Brown v. Iowa Legislative Council, 490 N.W.2d 551 (Iowa 1992) (computer data held to be trade secret of vendor not made available to the public).

27. For example, Florida's statute expressly excludes "data processing software obtained by an agency under a licensing agreement which prohibits its disclosure and which software is a trade secret . . . and agency-produced data processing software which is sensitive." FLA. STAT. § 119.07(3)(o). See, e.g., CAL. GOV'T CODE § 6254.9; IDAHO CODE § 9-340(16); IOWA CODE § 45-221(16); MO. REV. STAT. § 610.021(10).

28. See, e.g., ALASKA STAT. § 09.25.220(3); IDAHO CODE § 9-340(16) (express exemption for purchased or created software); MICH. COMP. LAWS § 15.232(2)(e).

29. See KY. REV. STAT. ANN. § 61.874(2) (agency is not required to make electronic copies of records available only in hard copy); MICH. COMP. LAWS § 15.233(3); N.Y. PUB. OFF. LAW § 89(3) (public entities not required to create records, summaries, or compilations not already kept by the government); Affiliated Constr. Trades Found. v. Regional Jail & Correctional Facility Auth., 490 S.E.2d 708, 711 (W. Va. 1997); A & T Consultants, Inc. v. Sharp, 904 S.W.2d 668, 676 (Tex. 1995) (Open Records Act does not require government entity to prepare or assemble new information in response to request).

30. See, e.g., HAW. REV. STAT. § 92F-11(c); NEB. REV. STAT. § 84-712.01(2); Barry v. Seigle, 422 So. 2d 63 (Fla. App. 1982) (use of supplied software left to discretion of custodian of records).

31. See, e.g., CONN. GEN. STAT. § 1-19(a); IND. CODE § 5-14-3-2; MISS. CODE ANN. § 25-61-10; White v. Regan, 575 N.Y.S.2d 375 (App. Div. 1991) (agency not required to rearrange its filing system to respond to request for public information).

32. See, e.g., FLA. STAT. § 119.14(2) (1991) (law expressly states that executive records are open).

33. See, e.g., 5 ILL. COMP. STAT. 140/2(a) (including executive branch in its definition of "public body" to which act applies); CAL. GOV'T CODE § 6252(a) (broad general definition encompasses executive branch); TEX. GOV'T CODE § 552.003(a)(1); Holmes v. Morales, 924 S.W.2d 920, 922 (Tex. 1996); Capital Newspapers Div. of Hearst Corp. v. Whalen, 505 N.E.2d

law.[34] Most state open records statutes include agencies, commissions, boards, committees and public educational institutions.[35] Some jurisdictions have further clarified the issue by prohibiting a claim of executive privilege to protect such records from mandatory public access.[36] A few jurisdictions specifically exclude certain executive offices or officials from the reach of their open records laws.[37]

§ 11-3(b). Legislative Branch.

Access to the records of state and local legislative bodies varies greatly among open records laws, but is typically much less prevalent in the context of the records created by the legislature and its bureaucracy.[38] Some jurisdictions do afford a statutory right of access to legislative records, although they permit the legislature to limit the degree or type of access,[39] or place statutory restrictions on the disclosure of select categories of records.[40] Other jurisdictions do not permit access to legislative records at all,[41] or prohibit access to the records of the state legislature while granting access to the records created by other legislative bodies.[42] Some state records laws are silent on the issue.[43]

---

932 (N.Y. 1987) (statute affords access to all of mayor's papers, whether related to government decisionmaking or not).

34. See, e.g., Lodge v. Knowlton, 391 A.2d 893, 894 (N.H. 1978) (court held "all State executive branch agencies and departments were meant to be and are included" in its public records act).

35. See Citizens for Alternatives to Animal Labs, Inc. v. Board of Trustees, 703 N.E.2d 1218 (N.Y. 1998).

36. See, e.g., Babets v. Secretary of Executive Office, 526 N.E.2d 1261 (Mass. 1988). But see New England Coalition for Energy Efficiency & Env't v. Office of Governor, 670 A.2d 815 (Vt. 1995) (common law executive privilege protects high-ranking aide's memoranda containing policy and legal advice to governor).

37. See, e.g., MICH. COMP. LAWS § 15.232(b)(i) (open records laws do not include "the governor or lieutenant governor, the executive office of the governor or lieutenant governor, or employees thereof").

38. See 5 ILL. COMP. STAT. 140/2(a); KY. REV. STAT. ANN. § 61.870(1); MICH. COMP. LAWS § 15.232(b)(ii) (excludes General Assembly or caucuses or committees thereof from public records law).

39. Florida, for example, grants access to its legislature unless the legislature itself creates a rule to the contrary. See Fla. Op. Att'y Gen. 75-282 (1975). See also MISS. CODE ANN. § 25-61-17.

40. Illinois limits access to certain documents utilized by its General Assembly in promulgating legislation. 5 ILL. COMP. STAT. 140/7(1)(f). See also HAW. REV. STAT. § 92F-13(5) (records of legislature subject to disclosure except for draft working papers and the files of individual members).

41. See MASS. GEN. LAWS ch. 66, § 18; Westinghouse Broadcasting Corp. v. Sergeant-at-Arms of Gen. Ct., 375 N.E.2d 1205 (Mass. 1978).

42. See DEL. CODE ANN. tit. 29, § 10002(a).

43. See CAL. GOV'T CODE § 6252(a).

§ 11-3(c). Judicial Branch.

Although documents filed with a court are generally accessible to the public,[44] most state open records laws do not afford a right of access,[45] or only very limited access, to records created by its judiciary.[46] One significant exception is California, where the open records statute does not include its courts, but case law has generally held that judicial records, except grand jury documents, are open to the public.[47]

§ 11-3(d). Advisory Committees.

The records of advisory committees or boards created pursuant to law are generally available for inspection or copying pursuant to state open records laws.[48] Some states, however, afford access to the records of such entities only if they are established and controlled by a government agency.[49]

§ 11-3(e). Nongovernmental Organizations.

A nongovernmental organization may also be required to afford public access to its records under certain circumstances, such as when it is acting on behalf of

---

44. See Chaps. 5-6 *supra*.

45. New York and Massachusetts do not include the judiciary within their definition of agencies to which their public records acts apply. See N.Y. PUB. OFF. LAW §§ 86(1), (3); MASS. GEN. LAWS ch. 4, § 7, cl. 26; MASS. REGS. CODE tit. 950, § 32.03. Michigan expressly excludes the courts from its public records law. MICH. COMP. LAWS § 15.232(b)(v). See also Copley Press, Inc. v. Administrative Office of Cts., 648 N.E.2d 324 (Ill. App. 1995) (records of pretrial services agency, deemed an "arm of the court," were exempt from open records law).

46. See Denoux v. Bertel, 682 So. 2d 300 (La. App. 1996) (indigent defender program, funded by the judiciary, is a "public body" subject to the public records law).

47. See In re Hearst Estate, 136 Cal. Rptr. 821, 823 (Ct. App. 1977) (court records open); McClatchy Newspapers v. Superior Ct., 245 Cal. Rptr. 774, 787 (Cal. 1988) (public interest requires secrecy of grand jury documents).

48. See MISS. CODE ANN. § 25-61-3 (any committee, board, commission, or agency created "by the Constitution or by law, executive order, ordinance, or resolution" is subject to the Mississippi open records statute); N.J. STAT. ANN. § 47:1A-2; Observer Publ'g Co. v. Poole, 412 S.E.2d 7, 12-13 (N.C. 1992) (North Carolina Public Records Act mandated the release of draft reports and minutes generated from closed meetings of state commission); Comment, *You Can't Always Get What You Want: A Look at North Carolina's Public Records Law*, 72 N.C.L. REV. 1527, 1560 (1994).

49. See, e.g., CAL. GOV'T CODE § 6252(a) (nongovernment group that is board or commission of agency of government will have open records); DEL. CODE ANN. tit. 29, § 10002(a)(3) (board is required to make records available to public if it is charged with power to advise, investigate, or make reports for government); KY. REV. STAT. ANN. § 61.870(1)(j) (access available if board "established, created, and controlled" by public agency); N.Y. PUB. OFF. LAW § 86(3) (includes board or committee performing government function).

a government agency,[50] receives public funds,[51] or is subject to public audit.[52] In general, however, state open records laws do not apply if the organization is not a public agency.[53]

§ 11-4. Procedures.

Most open records laws mandate broad public access to government records by "any person."[54] Some states broadly define "person" to include corporations, partnerships, associations, and other entities.[55] Although some jurisdictions re-

---

50. See FLA. STAT. § 119.011(2); Stanfield v. Salvation Army, 695 So. 2d 501 (Fla. App. 1997) (by providing misdemeanor probation services for county, Salvation Army deemed agency subject to public records law); Buffalo News v. Buffalo Enter. Dev. Corp., 578 N.Y.S.2d 945 (App. Div. 1991).

51. See KY. REV. STAT. ANN. § 61.870(1)(h) ("any body" receiving at least 25% of its funds spent in Kentucky from state will have open records); MICH. COMP. LAWS § 15.232(b)(iv) (provides for open records law to apply to any organization primarily funded by a state or local agency); KAN. STAT. ANN. § 45-217(e)(1); OKLA. STAT. tit. 51, § 24A.3.2 (bodies "supported in whole or in part by public funds or entrusted with the expenditure of public funds" covered by the statute); Ohio ex rel. Strothers v. Wertheim, 684 N.E.2d 1239 (Ohio 1997) (county ombudsman office, a private nonprofit corporation established to assist citizens in resolving complaints against county government, was supported by public funds and was, therefore, subject to disclosure requirements of Public Records Act). But see Adams County Record v. Greater North Dakota Ass'n, 564 N.W.2d 304 (N.D. 1997) (state received sufficient benefits from magazine published by private nonprofit organization receiving public funds that state's provision of funds did not constitute support rendering organization subject to open records law); Bello v. South Shore Hosp., 429 N.E.2d 1011 (Mass. 1981) (receipt of public funds does not alone render private entity public).

52. See Indianapolis Convention & Visitors Ass'n v. Indianapolis Newspapers, Inc., 577 N.E.2d 208 (Ind. App. 1991) (private organization, a travel and tourism bureau, became public when it was subject to audit by Indiana Board of Accountants).

53. See Kneeland v. National Collegiate Athletic Ass'n, 850 F.2d 224 (5th Cir. 1988); Affiliated Constr. Trades Found. v. Regional Jail & Correctional Facility Auth., 490 S.E.2d 708, 712-14 (W. Va. 1997) (payroll records prepared, created and maintained by private subcontractor, copies of which have not been obtained by contracting public body, are not public records); News & Sun-Sentinel Co. v. Schwab, Twitty & Hanser Architect Group, 596 So. 2d 1029 (Fla. 1992) (private contractor supplying services to agency not subject to state public records law). See generally Note, *Attempting to Keep the Tablets Undisclosed: Susceptibility of Private Entities to the Texas Open Records Act*, 41 BAYLOR L. REV. 203 (1989); Note, *Detectives Following the Wrong Clues: Identification of Private Entities Subject to Florida's Public Records Law*, 22 STETSON L. REV. 785 (1993).

54. See FLA. STAT. § 119.01(a); KY. REV. STAT. ANN. § 61.872; MASS. GEN. LAWS ch. 66, § 10(a); N.Y. PUB. OFF. LAW § 89(3); OHIO REV. CODE ANN. § 149.43(B).

55. See FLA. STAT. § 1.01(3) (person includes "individuals, children, firms, associations, joint ventures, partnerships, estates, trusts, business trusts, syndicates, fiduciaries, corporations, and all other groups or combinations"); KY. REV. STAT. ANN. § 446.010(26) ("'person' may extend to and be applied to bodies-politic and corporate societies, communities, the public generally, individuals, partnerships and joint stock companies"); MICH. COMP. LAWS § 15.233(1) ("person" may be "an individual, corporation, partnership, firm, organization, or association").

quire that the requester be a citizen of the state,[56] most allow a request to come from anyone.[57] The purpose for which the requested information is sought is generally deemed irrelevant.[58] Some states, however, treat information requested for a "commercial purpose" differently, authorizing the agency to charge a fee based on the fair market value for any such information supplied.[59]

Although oral requests for records may be permitted,[60] the better practice is to make a request in writing. In most cases, an administrative review or an appeal of an agency denial of a request can only commence upon declination of a written request.[61] As a practical matter, a written request is more likely to be understood by the agency in the first instance, and may be required in certain states.[62]

Requests to inspect a public record are typically to be made to the party with custody of the record sought.[63] Under most public records laws, the definition of a "custodian" is broad, framed in terms of "the chief administrative officer or any other officer or employee of a public agency who is responsible for the maintenance, care and keeping of public records, regardless of whether such records are in his actual custody and control."[64] A request should identify or reasonably describe the record to which access is sought.[65] In some cases, an

---

56. See DEL. CODE ANN. tit. 29, § 10003; MO. REV. STAT. § 109.80; PA. STAT. ANN. tit. 65, § 66.2; Keddie v. Rutgers Univ., 689 A.2d 702, 706 (N.J. 1997).

57. See Fla. Op. Att'y Gen. No. 75-175 (1975) (state employee is a "person" within the meaning of the Florida Public Records Law and possesses right of access to public records for personal inspection without supervisor's authorization).

58. See Los Angeles Police Dep't v. Superior Ct., 135 Cal. Rptr. 575 (Ct. App. 1977); Leham v. San Francisco, 145 Cal. Rptr. 493 (Ct. App. 1978); State Employees Ass'n v. Department of Management & Budget, 404 N.W.2d 606 (Mich. 1987); Capital Newspapers Div. of Hearst Corp. v. Burns, 496 N.E.2d 665 (N.Y. 1986) (purpose for request or intended use of information deemed irrelevant); Ohio ex rel. Fant v. Enright, 610 N.E.2d 997 (Ohio 1993).

59. See, e.g., ARIZ. REV. STAT. § 39-121.03(A) & (D). The Arizona Attorney General has asserted that reporters engaged in newsgathering do not fall within the "commercial purpose" definition. Ariz. Op. Att'y Gen. No. I86-90 (1986).

60. See CAL. GOV'T CODE § 6257 (allows for "any request" for copy of records); MASS. REGS. CODE tit. 950, § 32.05(3); MICH. COMP. LAWS § 15.235(1) (requester "may make an oral or written request" for records).

61. See MASS. GEN. LAWS ch. 66, § 10(b); MICH. COMP. LAWS § 15.240(2) (both requiring written confirmation of a refused oral request prior to commencement of action).

62. See, e.g., KY. REV. STAT. ANN. § 61.872(2) (requiring written requests for access to information); MD. CODE ANN., STATE GOV'T § 10-614(a); N.Y. PUB. OFF. LAW § 89.3.

63. See, e.g., FLA. STAT. § 119.07(1)(a); KY. REV. STAT. ANN. § 61.872(2); MD. CODE ANN., STATE GOV'T § 10-614.

64. KY. REV. STAT. ANN. § 61.870(3).

65. See CAL. GOV'T CODE § 6257 (request must describe reasonably an identifiable record); MICH. COMP. LAWS § 15.233(1) (request must be sufficient to allow official to find record); N.Y. PUB. OFF. LAW § 89(3) (requires reasonable description); Florida ex rel. Cummer v. Pace, 159 So. 679 (Fla. 1935) (requester need not specify book or account; request need only be sufficient to identify information).

unreasonably vague request is grounds for nondisclosure, unless the record has actually been located by the agency.[66]

The time by which government agencies must respond to record requests varies from jurisdiction to jurisdiction. Most states allow between five and ten days for an agency to respond to a request.[67] If additional time is needed to process a request, many open records laws will grant an agency an extension of time in which to respond, provided the requester is notified of the delay.[68]

Fees are generally charged for reasonable copying costs, but not for the right to inspect the records or the labor required to locate them.[69] Many states leave the decision to require a fee and the amount of the fee to the agency that receives the request. Some jurisdictions have established a schedule of stated maximum fees for copied material.[70] In those rare cases when a requester is charged for an agency's administrative time in processing a request, the fee will generally be calculated at the hourly wage of the lowest paid employee in the agency, or by reference to a similar calculation.[71] Courts have held that such fees must not be so high as to be tantamount to a denial of access.[72]

---

66. See Capital Newspapers Div. of Hearst Corp. v. Burns, 496 N.E.2d 665 (N.Y. 1986) (location of requested documents means request was reasonable); Konigsberg v. Coughlin, 501 N.E.2d 1 (N.Y. 1986) (agency not required to seek additional information to locate records); Ohio ex rel. Zauderer v. Joseph, 577 N.E.2d 444 (Ohio App. 1989).

67. See, e.g., CAL. GOV'T CODE § 6256 (10-day response time); MASS. GEN. LAWS ch. 66, § 10(b) (10-day response time); MICH. COMP. LAWS § 15.235(2) (five-day response time); N.Y. PUB. OFF. LAW § 89(3) (five-day response time). Other states require as few as three or as many as 30 days for a response. See KY. REV. STAT. ANN. § 61.880(1) (three days to respond); MD. CODE ANN., STATE GOV'T § 10-614(b)(1) (30 days to respond). Florida requires an agency to respond within a "reasonable" time, while North Carolina and Alabama are silent on the subject. See ALA. CODE § 36-12-40; N.C. GEN. STAT. §§ 132-1 to 132-9; Tribune Co. v. Cannella, 458 So. 2d 1075 (Fla. 1984), *appeal dismissed*, 471 U.S. 1096 (1985). Hawaii does not impose a response time. See Hawaii Org. of Police Officers v. Society of Prof'l Journalists, 927 P.2d 386, 400 (Haw. 1996) (Uniform Information Practices Act does not impose deadlines on agency's response to records requests).

68. See CAL. GOV'T CODE § 6256.1; 116 ILL. COMP. STAT. 203(d); MICH. COMP. LAWS § 15-235(2).

69. See CAL. GOV'T CODE § 6257 (copies available after payment of direct costs of copying; no payment required for administrative time involved); 5 ILL. COMP. STAT. 140/6(a) (fees to exclude the cost of searching for and reviewing records); N.Y. PUB. OFF. LAW § 89(3) (fee is payable only when agency is ready to give requester copies of records).

70. See, e.g., DEL. CODE ANN. tit. 29, § 10112(b)(5) (agency determines fees charged for copying); MASS. REGS. CODE tit. 950, § 32.05(6) (fee may be required prior to copying); FLA. STAT. § 119.07(1)(a) (a $.15 maximum charge imposed per copy); 5 ILL. COMP. STAT. 140/6(b) (fees calculated by agency to reimburse actual cost to copy); N.Y. PUB. OFF. LAW §§ 87(1)(b)(iii) & 87(1)(h) (fees set by agency, but maximum fee set by statute at $.25 per copy and the actual cost of producing other records).

71. See, e.g., MICH. COMP. LAWS § 15.234(3).

72. See Home News Publ'g Co. v. New Jersey, 570 A.2d 1267 (N.J. Super. 1990).

Public records laws often allow for the waiver of fees. The most common fee waiver is dependent upon whether furnishing the copies will primarily benefit the general public.[73] Factors that have been applied when a journalist has sought such a fee waiver include the public benefit derived from the disclosure and the chilling effect withholding the information would have on the freedom of the press.[74]

§ 11-5. Exemptions from Disclosure.

Each jurisdiction allows for the exemption of at least some records from the otherwise mandatory public access established by its open records law. Many of these exemptions are expressly included in the jurisdiction's open records law. Additional records may be excluded pursuant to other statutes[75] or, in some jurisdictions, by common law.[76]

§ 11-5(a). Statutory Exemptions.

Every public records act includes a list of exempted records that are not required to be made available to the public. These exemptions are strictly construed pursuant to the legislative policy of presumptive disclosure.[77] The burden of proving that a record is exempt falls on the agency seeking to invoke the

---

73. See 5 ILL. COMP. STAT. 140/6(b); MICH. COMP. LAWS § 15.234(1). One Michigan court has held that a requester's personal records do not benefit the general public, and are therefore not eligible for a fee waiver. See Kearney v. Department of Mental Health, 425 N.W.2d 161 (Mich. App. 1988).
74. See Mayor of Baltimore v. Burke, 506 A.2d 683, 688 (Md. Spec. App. 1985).
75. See § 11-5(b) *infra*.
76. See § 11-5(c) *infra*.
77. See, e.g., MASS. GEN. LAWS ch. 66, § 10(c); N.Y. PUB. OFF. LAW § 87(2) (exemptions are specific); Progressive Animal Welfare Soc'y v. University of Washington, 884 P.2d 592, 597 (Wash. 1994); Legislative Joint Auditing Comm. v. Woosley, 722 S.W.2d 581, 583 (Ark. 1987); Delaware Solid Waste Auth. v. News Journal Co., 480 A.2d 628, 631 (Del. 1984); Hardaway Co. v. Rives, 422 S.E.2d 854, 857 (Ga. 1992); Hechler v. Casey, 333 S.E.2d 799, 810 (W. Va. 1985). Statutory exemptions are generally deemed to be specific and may not be broadly construed by an agency. See News-Press Publ'g Co. v. Gadd, 388 So. 2d 276 (Fla. App. 1980) (records subject to disclosure unless specifically exempt, and not subject to balancing test). The "specific" versus "general" distinction has shaped much of the case law interpreting such statutory exemptions. In *Troutt Brothers v. Emison*, 841 S.W.2d 604 (Ark. 1992), the Arkansas Supreme Court held that, because of statutory language employing the term "specifically," a statute requiring confidentiality of a juvenile's identity applied only when he or she was the subject of a judicial proceeding. Thus, until a charge is actually brought against the juvenile, there exists a window during which her name could be obtained through the state's open records law, even if the juvenile is in custody or suspected of a crime. *Id*. at 606-07. In a less literal approach, the New York Court of Appeals has interpreted "specifically exempted" to require only "clear legislative intent." Washington Post Co. v. New York State Ins. Dep't, 463 N.E.2d 604, 607 (N.Y. 1984).

exemption.[78] The agency often has the burden of describing the records withheld and of justifying the decision not to disclose them.[79] Many jurisdictions view statutory exemptions as permissive rather than mandatory.[80] In such jurisdictions, agencies are permitted to disclose records even though they may fall within a statutory exemption.

Those states that have modeled their public records acts after FOIA have adopted exemptions similar to those set forth in the federal legislation.[81] The courts of these states often look to the language and purpose of the comparable federal exemption and relevant federal case law when interpreting the state law exemption.[82] At times, however, the federal case law has been found lacking or has not been followed.[83] Some of the FOIA exemptions, such as the exemption for classified national defense and foreign policy matters,[84] have limited applicability to state and local governments. Most of the other FOIA exemptions, however, have been deemed relevant.

§ 11-5(a)(1). Internal Agency Personnel Rules and Practices.

Many open records acts fail to address specifically the type of information that is exempt from mandatory disclosure pursuant to Exemption 2 of the federal FOIA.[85] California and Illinois, however, have both expressly exempted such internal agency rules and practices from disclosure.[86]

---

78. See Bougas v. Chief of Police of Lexington, 354 N.E.2d 872, 876 (Mass. 1976); Vallejos v. California Highway Patrol, 152 Cal. Rptr. 846, 849 (Ct. App. 1979).

79. See, e.g., Evening News Ass'n v. City of Troy, 339 N.W.2d 421, 431-32 (Mich. 1983); Fink v. Lefkowitz, 393 N.E.2d 463, 465 (N.Y. 1979) (agency "is required to articulate particularized and specific justification and, if necessary, submit the requested materials to the court for *in camera* inspection, to exempt its records from disclosure").

80. See, e.g., MICH. COMP. LAWS § 15.243; N.Y. PUB. OFF. LAW § 87(2) ("agency may deny access"); 1979-80 Op. Mich. Att'y Gen. 468, 469 (1979).

81. See, e.g., Black Panther Party v. Kehoe, 117 Cal. Rptr. 106, 110 (Ct. App. 1974) (California's Public Records Act modeled after FOIA); Faulk v. State's Attorney for Harford County, 474 A.2d 880, 887 (Md. 1984) (language and historical development of Maryland's law enforcement exemption found to be nearly identical to that of FOIA Exemption 7(A)).

82. See, e.g., American Civil Liberties Union Found. v. Deukmejian, 651 P.2d 822 (Cal. 1982); Roulette v. Department of Cent. Management Servs., 490 N.E.2d 60, 64 (Ill. App. 1986).

83. The West Virginia Supreme Court has, for example, noted that its statute's privacy exemption, while facially similar to its federal counterpart, mandates different burdens of persuasion. See Child Protection Group v. Cline, 350 S.E.2d 541, 545 (W. Va. 1986). See also Wisconsin Family Counseling Servs. v. Wisconsin, 291 N.W.2d 631, 633 (Wis. App. 1980); Newberry Publ'g Co. v. Newberry County Comm'n, 417 S.E.2d 870, 872 n.4 (S.C. 1992); Globe Newspaper Co. v. Boston Retirement Bd., 446 N.E.2d 1051, 1055 (Mass. 1983).

84. 5 U.S.C. § 552(b)(1) (1988). See Chap. 10-2(c)(2) *supra*.

85. See 5 U.S.C. § 552(b)(2); Chap. 10-2(c)(3) *supra*.

86. See CAL. GOV'T CODE § 6254(p); 5 ILL. COMP. STAT. 140/7(w).

§ 11-5(a)(2). Disclosures Forbidden by Other Statutes.

Most states have "specifically or by necessary implication"[87] exempted from mandatory disclosure records the release of which is prohibited by other state or federal legislation.[88] New York courts, interpreting this exemption to New York's Freedom of Information Law, have held that to fall within the exemption a statute need not expressly forbid disclosure, though it must contain a "clear legislative intent to establish and preserve that confidentiality that one resisting a FOIL disclosure claims as protection."[89]

§ 11-5(a)(3). Trade Secrets and Certain Financial Information.

While some open records laws fail to address the issue directly,[90] many protect trade secrets from mandatory disclosure.[91] Some states, such as Illinois, specifically exempt "[t]rade secrets and commercial or financial information obtained from a person or business where such . . . secrets . . . are proprietary, privileged or confidential, or where disclosure of such . . . secrets . . . may cause competitive harm."[92] The open records laws of other jurisdictions do not provide such a definition[93] and rely instead on judicial articulation of what constitutes an exempt trade secret.[94]

---

87. MASS. GEN. LAWS ch. 4, § 7, cl. 26(a).
88. See, e.g., 5 ILL. COMP. STAT. 140/7(1)(a); OHIO REV. CODE ANN. § 149.43(A)(1); Doe v. Board of Regents, 452 S.E.2d 776 (Ga. App. 1994) (state statute exempts disclosure of name and identity of rape victim even though same documents are subject to disclosure under Public Records Act); Morris v. Martin, 434 N.E.2d 1079 (N.Y. 1982) (exemption cannot be based on city administrative code); Ohio ex rel. Lippitt v. Kovacic, 591 N.E.2d 422 (Ohio App. 1991) (FBI arrest record "rap sheets").
89. Capital Newspapers Div. of Hearst Corp. v. Burns, 496 N.E.2d 665, 668 (N.Y. 1986).
90. See, e.g., ALA. CODE § 36-12-40; KAN. STAT. ANN. § 45-221; MONT. CODE ANN. § 2-6-101; OKLA. STAT. tit. 51, § 24A.1.
91. See, e.g., 5 ILL. COMP. STAT. 140/7(1)(g); MICH. COMP. LAWS § 15.243(g); W. VA. CODE § 29B-1-4(1). See Masonite Corp. v. County of Mendocino Air Quality Management Dist., 49 Cal. Rptr. 2d 639, 651-52 (Ct. App. 1996) (voluntary disclosure of information without trade secret designation constitutes valid waiver of trade secret protection); Valco Cincinnati v. N & D Machining Serv., 492 N.E.2d 814 (Ohio 1986); Ohio ex rel. Allright Parking v. Cleveland, 591 N.E.2d 708 (Ohio 1992) (building and financial plans for commercial development project deemed trade secret); Washington Post Co. v. Minority Bus. Opportunity Comm'n, 560 A.2d 517, 522 (D.C. 1989) ("salutary legislation enacted in the public interest is not to be converted into a vehicle for commercial espionage"); Alberghini v. Tizes, 328 N.Y.S.2d 272 (Sup. Ct. 1972).
92. 5 ILL. COMP. STAT. 140/7(1)(g). See also OR. REV. STAT. § 192.501(2); W. VA. CODE § 29B-1-4.
93. See, e.g., MISS. CODE ANN. § 25-61-9(4); WASH REV. CODE § 42.17.310(1)(h). See Caldwell & Gregory, Inc. v. University of S. Mississippi, 716 So. 2d 1120, 1122 (Miss. App. 1998) (court not bound by definition of trade secrets found in the Uniform Trade Secrets Act when interpreting the Mississippi Public Records Act exemption).
94. The Washington Supreme Court, for example, has defined its exemption to prevent the appropriation of "valuable intellectual property for private gain," and exempted from mandatory

The release of records containing commercial information not considered a trade secret will often be required, unless economic harm[95] or an interest in confidentiality[96] can be demonstrated by the party objecting to such disclosure. The courts of some jurisdictions have taken into account the public interest in ordering access to commercial information that may otherwise be exempt.[97]

§ 11-5(a)(4). Inter-Agency and Intra-Agency Memoranda.

Several state open records laws exempt from mandatory disclosure preliminary drafts of records and information consulted in preparing agency records.[98] Like the deliberative process privilege under the federal FOIA,[99] the exemption is intended to facilitate "frank and uninhibited discussions during [an agency's]

---

disclosure information that could reveal research theories. See Progressive Animal Welfare Soc'y v. University of Washington, 884 P.2d 592, 599 (Wash. 1994).

95. See, e.g., ARK. CODE ANN. § 25-19-105(b)(9)(A) ("files which, if disclosed, would give advantage to competitors or bidders"); D.C. CODE ANN. § 1-1524(a)(1); IOWA CODE § 22.7(6) (exempts reports that "would give advantage to competitors and serve no public purpose"); N.Y. PUB. OFF. LAW § 87(2)(d) (exempts records that are maintained for the regulation of "a commercial enterprise and which if disclosed would cause substantial injury to the competitive position of the subject enterprise"); Arkansas Dep't of Fin. & Admin. v. Pharmacy Ass'n, Inc., 970 S.W.2d 217, 220 (Ark. 1998) (competitive-advantage exception to disclosure under Arkansas Freedom of Information Act protects documents in state's possession if release would result in competitive harm to person who supplied them); AT&T Communications of West Virginia v. Public Serv. Comm'n, 423 S.E.2d 859, 862 (W. Va. 1992).

96. In *Cooper v. Department of Lottery*, 640 N.E.2d 1299, 1303-04 (Ill. App. 1994), an Illinois appellate court held that an advertising plan developed for a state lottery agency was not exempt from the state's public records law because: (1) there was no agreement contemplating confidentiality; (2) the state lottery agency had a monopoly and therefore had no competitors; (3) disclosure would not inflict competitive harm on the submitter; (4) the submitter of the plan did not have a proprietary interest in it; and (5) no evidence was submitted indicating that disclosure would damage future efforts by the agency to obtain similar information. See generally Samuels, *Protecting Confidential Business Information Supplied to State Governments: Exempting Trade Secrets from State Open Records Laws*, 27 AM. BUS. L.J. 467 (1989).

97. See Union Leader Corp. v. New Hampshire Housing Fin. Auth., 705 A.2d 725, 734 (N.H. 1997); Griffin v. S.W. Devanney & Co., 775 P.2d 555, 562 (Colo. 1989). But cf. 5 ILL. COMP. STAT. 140/7(1)(g); N.Y. PUB. OFF. LAW § 87(2)(d).

98. See CAL. GOV'T CODE § 6254(a), (d)(3); N.Y. PUB. OFF. LAW § 87(2)(g); WIS. STAT. § 19.32(2); Daily Gazette Co. v. West Virginia Dev. Office, 482 S.E.2d 180, 190 (W. Va. 1996) (no exemption for written communications between agency and private persons where such communications did not contain advice, opinions or recommendations to agency from outside consultants or experts obtained during agency's deliberative, decisionmaking process); Bryant v. Mars, 830 S.W.2d 869 (Ark. 1992) ("working papers" exemption applies to staff members and private consultants as well as to officeholders); Kheel v. Ravitch, 464 N.E.2d 118 (N.Y. 1984).

99. See Chap. 10-2(c)(6) *supra*.

decision making process."[100] Florida has created a limited exemption for drafts and notes used in the preparation of records, an approach taken by many other states as well.[101] California explicitly provides an exemption for "[p]reliminary drafts, notes, or interagency or intra-agency memoranda that are not retained by the public agency in the ordinary course of business."[102] Massachusetts makes intra- and interagency memoranda concerning the development of new policies exempt until such time as the policy has been determined.[103] Illinois also excludes from disclosure drafts of documents in which policies and opinions are formulated, at least until such documents are "publicly cited and identified by the head of the public body."[104] Michigan, in contrast, requires that the agency seeking to avoid disclosure apply a balancing test that weighs the benefit of the free exchange of information to the agency against the harm to the public interest resulting from secrecy.[105] As in the case law interpreting Exemption 5 to the federal FOIA, state open records laws generally do not regard factual materials and final decisions as subject to such an exemption.[106]

Also in conformity with federal law,[107] nearly every state has incorporated the attorney-client and attorney work-product privileges to exempt records containing such privileged material from mandatory disclosure.[108] Some jurisdictions, however, recognize the exemption only in matters relating directly to litigation.[109] Other jurisdictions treat the privilege as creating an absolute exemption

---

100. Hearst Corp. v. Hoppe, 580 P.2d 246, 251 (Wash. 1978). See Times Mirror Co. v. Superior Ct., 813 P.2d 240 (Cal. 1991) (disclosure of appointment calendar would improperly intrude on Governor's ability to select sources of input on critical issues).

101. See, e.g., MICH. COMP. LAWS § 15.243(1)(n); Shevin v. Byron, Harless, Schaffer, Reid & Assocs., 379 So. 2d 633 (Fla. 1980).

102. CAL. GOV'T CODE § 6254(a).

103. See MASS. GEN. LAWS ch. 4, § 7, cl. 26(d); Babets v. Secretary of Executive Office, 526 N.E.2d 1261 (Mass. 1988).

104. 5 ILL. COMP. STAT. 140/7(1)(f).

105. See MICH. COMP. LAWS § 15.243(1)(n); Herald Co. v. Ann Arbor Pub. Schs., 568 N.W.2d 411, 415 (Mich. App. 1997) (significant public interest in disclosing memorandum containing public observations of teacher convicted of carrying concealed weapon not clearly outweighed by public interest in encouraging frank communications within public body).

106. See MICH. COMP. LAWS § 15.243(1)(n) (excludes factual material in intra- or inter-agency correspondence).

107. See Chap. 10-2(c)(6) *supra*.

108. See Shew v. Freedom of Info. Comm'n, 714 A.2d 664, 670 (Conn. 1998); Texaco, Inc. v. Louisiana Land & Exploration Co., 805 F. Supp. 385 (M.D. La. 1992). Arkansas's statute does not provide an exemption for material protected by the attorney-client privilege. See City of Fayetteville v. Edmark, 801 S.W.2d 275 (Ark. 1990); Scott v. Smith, 728 S.W.2d 515 (Ark. 1987). Arkansas relies on the theory that the attorney-client privilege is only applicable to court proceedings, and therefore cannot be applied to create an exception to its Freedom of Information Act. See McCambridge v. City of Little Rock, 766 S.W.2d 909 (Ark. 1989).

109. See, e.g., Lane City Sch. Dist. v. Parks, 637 P.2d 1383, 1385 (Or. App. 1981). Settlement agreements that conclude litigation may not be exempt. See Register Div. of Freedom Newspapers,

in all circumstances.[110] Such exemptions may be stated expressly in the open records statute,[111] created through statutory provisions relating generally to litigation,[112] or incorporated through other provisions of the law.[113] Although most jurisdictions exempt the work-product of any attorney advising a public body,[114] some jurisdictions limit the exemption to work-product created by certain categories of attorneys.[115] While at least one state specifically mandates that its open records act does not alter the privileges, duties, or rights of attorneys simply because they work for the state,[116] another has held that the privilege may be waived at the discretion of the public agency receiving the legal services and, even if not waived, the records automatically become public after three years.[117]

§ 11-5(a)(5). Disclosures Constituting an Unwarranted Invasion of Privacy.

The federal courts, in interpreting Exemption 6 to FOIA, have adopted a balancing test to determine when files should be kept from public view in order to protect the privacy interests of persons identified in them.[118] Courts interpreting state open records laws have largely followed this approach as well.[119]

Inc. v. County of Orange, 205 Cal. Rptr. 92 (Ct. App. 1984); News & Observer Publ'g Co. v. Wake County Hosp. Sys., 284 S.E.2d 542 (N.C. App. 1981); Ohio ex rel. Kinsley v. Berea Bd. of Educ., 582 N.E.2d 653 (Ohio App. 1990); Daily Gazette Co. v. Withrow, 350 S.E.2d 738 (W. Va. 1986).

110. See, e.g., Roberts v. City of Palmdale, 853 P.2d 496, 501 (Cal. 1993) (no pending litigation requirement is needed); George v. Record Custodian, 485 N.W.2d 460, 464 (Wis. App. 1992).

111. See, e.g., 5 ILL. COMP. STAT. 140/7(1)(n) ("[c]ommunications between a public body and an attorney . . . representing such public body that would not be subject to discovery in litigation"); N.C. GEN. STAT. § 132-1.1 ("attorney-client relationship"); TENN. CODE ANN. § 10-7-504(a)(5)(A)(iii) ("work product"). The Illinois Act exempts "materials prepared or compiled by or for a public body in anticipation of a criminal, civil or administrative proceeding upon the request of an attorney advising the public body," and is representative of other state statutes. 5 ILL. COMP. STAT. 140/7(1)(n). See also IOWA CODE § 22.7(4).

112. See, e.g., OHIO REV. CODE § 149.43(A)(1)(g) ("trial preparation records"); OR. REV. STAT. § 192.501(1) ("pertaining to litigation").

113. See, e.g., CAL. GOV'T CODE § 6254(b); Roberts v. City of Palmdale, 853 P.2d 496 (Cal. 1993); Denver Post Corp. v. University of Colorado, 739 P.2d 874, 880 (Colo. App. 1987).

114. See, e.g., 5 ILL. COMP. STAT. 140/7(1)(n).

115. See Bryant v. Mars, 830 S.W.2d 869, 871-72 (Ark. 1992) (applicable exemption includes staff of attorney general); Memphis Publ'g Co. v. City of Memphis, 871 S.W.2d 681, 688 (Tenn. 1994) (legislature had not exempted the work-product of municipal and county attorneys).

116. See MINN. STAT. § 13.30.

117. See N.C. GEN. STAT. § 132-1.1.

118. See Chap. 10-2(c)(7) *supra*.

119. See City of Dubuque v. Telegraph Herald, Inc., 297 N.W.2d 523, 526 (Iowa 1980); Young v. Rice, 826 S.W.2d 252, 255 (Ark. 1992); Board of Pardons v. Freedom of Info. Comm., 563 A.2d 314 (Conn. App. 1989); Pawtucket Teachers Alliance v. Brady, 556 A.2d 556, 559 (R.I. 1989).

The privacy exemptions of state open records laws, however, vary. Some jurisdictions have expressed the privacy exemption in broad but general terms.[120] Others limit the exemption to specific categories of records.[121] A few jurisdictions attempt to identify the parameters of the exemption through the use of specific, but non-exhaustive, examples of what constitutes an "unwarranted invasion" of privacy.[122]

Many courts balance the competing interests implicated by the privacy exemption.[123] The threshold issue in these cases is typically whether the information is sufficiently private to deserve protection in the first instance.[124] The importance of privacy protection is then weighed against the benefits derived from public disclosure.[125] Although the factors consulted differ, most jurisdictions evaluate:

(1) whether disclosure would result in an invasion of privacy and, if so, the extent of the invasion;
(2) the public interest in disclosure;
(3) the availability of the information from other sources;
(4) whether the information was provided to government with a legitimate expectation of confidentiality; and
(5) whether limited relief is practicable.[126]

---

120. See, e.g., D.C. CODE ANN. § 1-1524(a)(2) (exemption excludes "information of a personal nature where the public disclosure thereof would constitute a clearly unwarranted invasion of personal privacy").

121. See, e.g., IDAHO CODE § 9-340(11).

122. See, e.g., 5 ILL. COMP. STAT. 140/7(1)(b)(i-v); IDAHO CODE § 9-340(36) (nonexhaustive list of examples of personnel information excluded from disclosure includes information regarding sex, race, marital status, birth date, home address and telephone number, applications, testing and scoring materials, grievances, correspondence and performance evaluations). Compare City of Monmouth v. Galesburg Printing & Publ'g Co., 494 N.E.2d 896, 899 (Ill. App. 1986) (protection from disclosure for all victims of crimes would violate First Amendment) with Copely Press, Inc. v. City of Springfield, 493 N.E.2d 127, 128 (Ill. App. 1986) (exemption from disclosure for certain licensing information recognized, and First Amendment deemed inapplicable).

123. See, e.g., Perkins v. Freedom of Info. Comm'n, 635 A.2d 783, 791 (Conn. 1993) ("the invasion of personal privacy exception precludes disclosure . . . only when the information sought by the request does not pertain to legitimate matters of public concern and is highly offensive to a reasonable person"); Kentucky Bd. of Exmrs. v. Courier-Journal, 826 S.W.2d 324, 328 (Ky. 1992).

124. See Herald Co. v. Ann Arbor Pub. Schs., 568 N.W.2d 411, 414 (Mich. App. 1997) ("In determining whether the information withheld is of a 'personal nature,' 'the customs, mores, or ordinary views of the community' must be taken into account."); Vandiver v. Star-Telegram, Inc., 756 S.W.2d 103, 106 (Tex. App. 1988).

125. See Brouillet v. Cowles Publ'g Co., 791 P.2d 526 (Wash. 1990).

126. See Child Protection Group v. Cline, 350 S.E.2d 541, 543-45 (W. Va. 1986) (balancing test used to determine whether an "unreasonable invasion of privacy" would result from release of a school bus driver's medical records); CBS Inc. v. Partee, 556 N.E.2d 648, 654 (Ill. App. 1990) (consulting similar factors).

In *Kentucky Board of Examiners v. Courier-Journal*,[127] a newspaper sought access to a complaint alleging sexual misconduct filed against a psychologist. Applying its own version of the foregoing balancing test, the Kentucky Supreme Court first determined that the information requested was of a "personal nature."[128] It proceeded to strike the balance in favor of the patient's privacy interest because disclosure of the details of the case would have constituted a serious invasion of her privacy.[129] Because the psychologist had been punished to the furthest extent possible and the formal complaints against her, as well as the Board of Examiner's final order, had been disclosed to the public, the court found that the public interest had already been effectively served.[130]

§ 11-5(a)(6). Law Enforcement Records.

States following the federal FOIA model tend to provide the same level of protection from mandatory disclosure to law enforcement records as FOIA[131] and the federal courts.[132] Some jurisdictions identify specific harms to which such an exemption may apply,[133] while others have codified a more general exemption encompassing information compiled for law enforcement purposes.[134] Several states, recognizing a potential benefit to the public in the release of law enforcement information, as well as the potential harm to individuals and the agencies involved flowing from disclosure, have adopted a balancing approach.[135] Factors to be considered in striking an appropriate balance typically include:

---

127. 826 S.W.2d 324 (Ky. 1992). See also Woznicki v. Erickson, 549 N.W.2d 699 (Wis. 1996) (court must balance the interest of the public and the private individual when determining whether a record, not specifically exempt under statute, is exempt due to privacy interest); Kestenbaum v. Michigan State Univ., 294 N.W.2d 228 (Mich. App. 1980), *aff'd by equally divided court*, 327 N.W.2d 783 (Mich. 1982) (applications of balancing tests to interpret privacy exemptions); Lyon v. Dunne, 580 N.Y.S.2d 803 (App. Div. 1992).
128. 826 S.W.2d at 328-29.
129. See *id.* at 327-29.
130. See *id.* at 325, 328.
131. See Chap. 10-2(c)(8) *supra*.
132. See CAL. GOV'T CODE § 6254(f); N.Y. PUB. OFF. LAW § 87(2)(e); Herald Co. v. City of Kalamazoo, 581 N.W.2d 295 (Mich. App. 1997) (Michigan has imposed a more restrictive standard on the law enforcement exemption than federal FOIA); Campbell v. Town of Machias, 661 A.2d 1133, 1135-36 (Me. 1995); Evening News Ass'n v. City of Troy, 339 N.W.2d 421, 428 (Mich. 1983) (applied federal law to interpret "interfere with law enforcement proceeding"). See generally Note, *supra* note 16, at 341.
133. See, e.g., D.C. CODE ANN. § 1-1524(a)(3); MD. CODE ANN., STATE GOV'T, § 10-618(f)(2); KY. REV. STAT. ANN. § 17-150(2); CONN. GEN. STAT. § 1-19(b)(3); 5 ILL. COMP. STAT. 140/7(1)(c).
134. See, e.g., ARK. CODE ANN. § 12-12-211; DEL. CODE ANN. tit. 29, § 10002(d); TEX. GOV'T CODE ANN. § 552.108; W. VA. CODE § 29B-1-4(4).
135. See, e.g., CONN. GEN. STAT. § 1-19(b)(3); D.C. CODE ANN. § 1-1524(a)(3); S.C. CODE ANN. § 30-4-40(3); 5 ILL. COMP. STAT. 140/7(1)(c); N.Y. PUB. OFF. LAW § 87(2)(e); MICH. COMP. LAWS § 15.243(1)(t).

(1) potential identification of a confidential informant;
(2) revelation of police investigative techniques;
(3) interference with ongoing investigations or judicial proceedings; and
(4) disclosure of the identities of law enforcement officers.[136]

California, however, flatly prohibits the disclosure of records containing certain categories of law enforcement information, including investigatory and security files, while other information, such as the identity of persons arrested or parties otherwise involved in incidents, can be made public, provided it does not endanger an investigation or anyone involved in it.[137] Nevertheless, California courts have held that investigations conducted by law enforcement personnel, but not for the purpose of furthering specific law enforcement proceedings, do not fall within the exemption.[138] Still other jurisdictions provide a blanket exemption for all records "related to the detection and investigation of crime."[139]

The Arizona Supreme Court, sitting in one of the few states in which the public records law is silent on the subject,[140] has exempted from disclosure investigation reports made in active and on-going criminal prosecutions and in the possession of the prosecuting attorney.[141] The District of Columbia, where the statutory law enforcement exemption closely follows that of the federal FOIA,[142] exempts investigatory records that pertain to specific investigations and focus upon specific parties and certain acts.[143]

§ 11-5(a)(7). Financial Institution Records.

Various states have adopted provisions similar to the federal FOIA's financial institutions exemption.[144] Some states explicitly exempt bank examination

---

136. See D.C. CODE ANN. § 1-1524(a)(3); N.Y. PUB. OFF. LAW § 87(2)(e); MICH. COMP. LAW § 15-243(1)(f).

137. See CAL. GOV'T CODE § 6254(f); Rivero v. Superior Ct., 63 Cal. Rptr. 2d 213 (Ct. App. 1997) (compelled disclosure of closed criminal investigation file pursuant to city ordinance would obstruct investigatory function of district attorney's office in violation of state statute).

138. See Register Div. of Freedom Newspapers, Inc. v. County of Orange, 205 Cal. Rptr. 92, 98 (Ct. App. 1984).

139. DEL. CODE ANN. tit. 29, § 10002(d)(3). But see Ohio ex rel. Gannett Satellite Info. Network v. Petro, 685 N.E.2d 1223, 1229 (Ohio 1997) ("Records which are unquestionably non-exempt do not become exempt simply because they are placed in a prosecutor's file or . . . are the subject of grand jury subpoenas.").

140. See generally ARIZ. REV. STAT. §§ 39-121, 39-122. See also IDAHO CODE § 9-340; MONT. CODE ANN. §§ 2-6-101 to 2-6-103 (act silent as to law enforcement records).

141. See Cox Arizona Publications, Inc. v. Collins, 852 P.2d 1194 (Ariz. 1993).

142. See D.C. CODE ANN. § 1-1524(a)(3).

143. See Barry v. Washington Post Co., 529 A.2d 319 (D.C. 1987).

144. See Chap. 10-2(c)(9) *supra*.

records from their statutes.[145] North Carolina also exempts information that is reported to the Administrator of Credit Unions, including audit and examination records.[146] Delaware's open records law includes a provision exempting records containing information concerning investigations of financial institutions for civil purposes,[147] which may encompass bank examination records as well.[148] In New York, a bank may request that submitted records be kept confidential pursuant to an exemption that extends to records "submitted . . . by a commercial enterprise . . . which if disclosed would cause substantial injury to the competitive position of the subject enterprise."[149]

§ 11-5(a)(8). Geological Information Relating to Oil and Gas Wells.

Geological information is, in some instances, exempt from disclosure under state open records laws, as it is under the federal statute.[150] Maryland and Kentucky categorize such information as exempted trade secrets.[151]

Many states deem geological information submitted by a private entity to the state pursuant to statute to be confidential[152] or exempt from public disclosure,[153] at least for a limited period of time.[154] In some states, a company must request that such reports remain confidential in order to avoid public disclosure.[155]

Many states maintain state geological departments which, among other duties, produce reports relating to oil and gas and mineral resources in the state.[156] Many of these agencies have a statutory duty to issue public reports, statistics, maps, or other information regarding geological findings.[157] In some states, geological agencies release geological reports as a matter of discretion in light of

---

145. See, e.g., ALA. CODE § 5-3A-11 (examination records maintained and created by superintendent of banks are exempt); CAL. GOV'T CODE § 6254(d); 5 ILL. COMP. STAT. 140/7(1)(x). Florida exempts such information so long as the institution involved is the subject of an active investigation by the state's Department of Banking and Finance. See FLA. STAT. § 494.0012(3)-(5).

146. See N.C. GEN. STAT. § 54-109.105.

147. See DEL. CODE ANN. tit. 29, § 10002(d)(3).

148. See News-Journal Co. v. Billingsley, 1980 Del. Ch. LEXIS 553 (Del. Ch. Oct. 7, 1980) (files of investigations of engineers not open to public).

149. N.Y. PUB. OFF. LAW § 87(2)(d).

150. See, e.g., ALASKA STAT. § 38.06.060; CAL. GOV'T CODE § 6254(e); MD. CODE ANN., STATE GOV'T § 10-617(d); N.C. GEN. STAT. § 89E-14(c). See generally Chap. 10-2(c)(10) *supra*.

151. See MD. CODE ANN., STATE GOV'T § 10-617(d); KY. REV. STAT. ANN. § 61.878(1)(c).

152. See, e.g., VT. STAT. ANN. tit. 29 § 542.

153. See, e.g., W. VA. CODE § 11-1C-14.

154. See, e.g., TEX. GOV'T CODE ANN. § 552.113; ALASKA STAT. § 31.05.035.

155. See, e.g., OR. REV. STAT. § 469.090.

156. See, e.g., FLA. STAT. § 377.075; MO. REV. STAT. § 256.050; ARIZ. REV. STAT. § 27-152.01; DEL. CODE ANN. tit. 7, § 5505.

157. See, e.g., FLA. STAT. § 377.075; ARIZ. REV. STAT. § 27-152.01.

their perception of the public interest.[158] Under some statutes, a mineral, oil, or gas company may request that certain information compiled by a state geological agency remain confidential.[159]

§ 11-5(b). Other Statutory Exemptions.

In most jurisdictions, statutory exemptions from the requirement of disclosure are specifically set forth in the state's open records statute.[160] Virtually every state has, however, codified through separate legislation other exemptions that specifically prohibit the disclosure of certain categories of information,[161] including privacy statutes that limit the dissemination of personal data from government files,[162] as well as legislation protecting from disclosure the circulation records of public libraries,[163] the rental records of video stores[164] and information that is contained in an application to carry a concealed firearm.[165] In some jurisdictions, various exemptions are scattered throughout other statutes, rendering knowledge of all potentially relevant exemptions difficult.[166]

§ 11-5(c). Common Law Exemptions.

Most jurisdictions do not recognize nonstatutory exemptions beyond those codified in their public records statute.[167] Prior to the promulgation of existing

---

158. See, e.g., ARK. CODE ANN. § 55-301; WYO. STAT. ANN. § 9-2-803; MO. REV. STAT. § 256.050; MISS. CODE ANN. § 53-5-11; DEL. CODE ANN. tit. 7, § 5505.

159. See, e.g., VT. STAT. ANN. tit. 10, § 101.

160. See, e.g., 5 ILL. COMP. STAT. 140/7 (exemptions specifically enumerated).

161. See CAL. CIV. CODE § 1899.5(d) (exempts notices of intent to preserve an interest in property from Public Records Act); COLO. REV. STAT. § 24-72-204(1)(a); W. VA. CODE § 29B-1-4(5). States often have trade secret statutes that may prevent disclosure. See Progressive Animal Welfare Soc'y v. University of Washington, 884 P.2d 592, 603 (Wash. 1994).

162. See, e.g., IOWA CODE § 749B; MINN. STAT. § 15.162.

163. See, e.g., CAL. GOV'T CODE § 6267 (circulation records of libraries funded at least partially by public monies are exempt); DEL. CODE ANN. tit. 29, § 10002(d)(12) (public library records that reveal identity of user and materials used are exempt); MD. CODE ANN., STATE GOV'T, § 10-616(a).

164. In response to 18 U.S.C. § 2710, which prohibits the disclosure of customer's personal information by video stores to third parties, several states have enacted similar statutory provisions, making such disclosures misdemeanors. See, e.g., CAL. CIV. CODE § 1799.3(a); CONN. GEN. STAT. § 53-450(a); IOWA CODE § 727.11(1); MD. CODE ANN. art. 27, § 583; MASS. GEN. LAWS ch. 93, § 106(2); MICH. COMP. LAWS §§ 445.1712–445.1714; MINN. STAT. § 325I.02, subd. 1; N.H. REV. STAT. ANN. § 351-A:1(I); N.Y. GEN. BUS. LAW §§ 671-674; R.I. GEN. LAWS § 11-18-32(a).

165. See CAL. GOV'T CODE § 6254(u); MASS. GEN. LAWS ch. 66, § 10(c).

166. See FLA. STAT. § 119.01-16 (200-600 exemptions scattered throughout other laws and bills).

167. "The public policy concerning government disclosure is fixed by the Freedom of Information Law; the common-law interest privilege cannot protect from disclosure materials which that law requires to be disclosed." Doolan v. BOCES, 398 N.E.2d 533, 537 (N.Y. 1979). See, e.g., Miami Herald Publ'g Co. v. City of N. Miami, 452 So. 2d 572 (Fla. App. 1984); Ohio ex rel.

public records statutes and ordinances, however, several states recognized a species of common law privilege or exception that authorized an agency to refuse public access to its records. In applying such a privilege, the agency was empowered to balance the benefit that would be obtained by the requester if access was permitted, against the burden the request placed on the agency.[168] This common law privilege has survived in a few states through express incorporation into the jurisdiction's public records statute.[169] New Jersey courts continue to apply a common law exemption by balancing the government's need for confidentiality against the competing interests of the requesting party in each case.[170]

§ 11-5(d). Waiver of Exemptions.

A government entity that has custody of public records waives its right to rely on exemptions once it has disclosed them to the public.[171] The fact that the

---

MADD v. Gosser, 485 N.E.2d 706 (Ohio 1985) (both holding that only express statutory exemptions will be recognized). More often than not, inclusion of terms such as "provided by law" or "specifically provided by law" have precluded the creation of additional common law exemptions. See Laman v. McCord, 432 S.W.2d 753, 756 (Ark. 1968) ("specifically provided by law"); Wait v. Florida Power & Light Co., 372 So. 2d 420, 424, (Fla. 1979) ("provided by law"); Industrial Found. of South v. Texas Indus. Accounting Bd., 540 S.W.2d 668, 681 (Tex. 1976), *cert. denied*, 430 U.S. 931 (1977).

168. See, e.g., Stone v. Consolidated Publ'g Co., 404 So. 2d 678, 681 (Ala. 1981) (common law balancing test).

169. See, e.g., DEL. CODE ANN. tit. 29, § 10002(d)(6) (open records law exempts "any records specifically exempted from public disclosure by statute or common law"). Both Michigan and California continue to authorize an agency to refuse access to otherwise available records by balancing the benefit to the requester against the burden on the agency, a test similar to that invoked at common law. See CAL. GOV'T CODE § 6255; MICH. COMP. LAWS § 15.233(2). See also American Civil Liberties Union Found. v. Deukmejian, 651 P.2d 822 (Cal. 1982); Cashel v. Regents of Univ. of Mich., 367 N.W.2d 841 (Mich. App. 1982). Colorado's public records act contains a general public interest exemption that contemplates analogous balancing. See Civil Serv. Comm'n v. Pinder, 812 P.2d 645, 648 (Colo. 1991) ("substantial injury to the public interest"). See also MD. CODE ANN., STATE GOV'T § 10-618(a) (discretionary exemption if disclosure is counter to public interest); S.C. CODE ANN. §§ 1-20, 30-4-10 (excludes from disclosure "records concerning which it is shown that the public interest is best served by not disclosing them to the public").

170. See Keddie v. Rutgers Univ., 689 A.2d 702, 709 (N.J. 1997) ("A common-law record is one that is made by a public official in the exercise of his or her public function, either because the record was required or directed by law to be made or kept, or because it was filed in a public office."); Loigman v. Kimmelman, 505 A.2d 958 (N.J. 1986); McClain v. College Hosp., 492 A.2d 991 (N.J. 1985); Irval Realty, Inc. v. Board of Pub. Util. Comm'rs, 294 A.2d 425 (N.J. 1972).

171. See CAL. GOV'T CODE § 6254.5 ("[W]henever a state or local agency discloses a public record which is otherwise exempt from this chapter, to any member of the public, this disclosure shall constitute a waiver of the exemptions specified in Sections 6254, 6254.7, or other similar provisions of law."); Ohio ex rel. Gannett Satellite Info. Network v. Petro, 685 N.E.2d 1223, 1227-28 (Ohio 1997).

records have been the subject of publicity does not constitute a waiver of the government's right to assert exemptions.[172] An unauthorized disclosure of a record ordinarily does not operate as a waiver of the exemptions otherwise provided by the state public records act.[173]

§ 11-6. Segregation of Exempt Material.

Following the practice under the federal FOIA,[174] most jurisdictions require the segregation of exempt from non-exempt information whenever possible, thereby maximizing the amount of non-exempt material made available to the public.[175] Accordingly, when information falls within one of the exempt categories, the entire record in which the exempted material is found does not also become unavailable for inspection or copying. Many states make the segregation of exempted material mandatory and require that the remainder of the record be made available to the public.[176] Other states have chosen to make segregation permissive rather than mandatory.[177] Some states superimpose a reasonableness standard on the requirement of segregation and apply a balancing test to determine if the burden of segregation outweighs the public interest in disclosure.[178]

---

172. See Ohio ex rel. WLWT-TV5 v. Leis, 673 N.E.2d 1365, 1369-70 (Ohio 1997); Ohio ex rel. Master v. Cleveland, 667 N.E.2d 974, 976 (Ohio 1996) (uncharged-suspect exception applicable even where person's status as suspect has been previously disclosed by media reports).

173. See, e.g., Mitzner v. Sobol, 570 N.Y.S.2d 402, 404 (Sup. Ct. 1991). The unauthorized disclosure of a designated trade secret by a public agency will not be deemed a waiver of the trade secret exemption. See Masonite Corp. v. County of Mendocino Air Quality Management Dist., 49 Cal. Rptr. 2d 639, 649-52 (Ct. App. 1996) (information disclosed to public agency properly designated as trade secret must be protected; however, voluntary disclosure of information without trade secret designation constitutes valid waiver of trade secret protection).

174. See Chap. 10-2(e) *supra*.

175. See, e.g., CAL. GOV'T CODE § 6257; KY. REV. STAT. ANN. § 61.878(4); UTAH CODE § 63-2-307; MD. CODE ANN., STATE GOV'T § 10-610. See Herald Co. v. Ann Arbor Pub. Schs., 568 N.W.2d 411, 415 (Mich. App. 1997) ("FOIA imposes a duty to segregate, to the extent practicable, exempt material from disclosable nonexempt material"); Nichols v. Gamso, 315 N.E.2d 770 (N.Y. 1974). See generally Comment, *Administrative Law: Deletion of Confidential Information from Official Public Records*, 22 WASHBURN L.J. 364 (1983); Chap. 10-2(e) *supra*.

176. See, e.g., 5 ILL. COMP. STAT. 140/8 (exempt records containing non-exempt material must be separated by agency and non-exempt material made available); KY. REV. STAT. ANN. § 61.878(4); MICH. COMP. LAWS § 15.244(1) (agency "shall" separate and make non-exempt material available).

177. See, e.g., MASS. GEN. LAWS ch. 66, § 10(a) (non-exempt portions of records should be produced if segregable).

178. See, e.g., CAL. GOV'T CODE § 6257 ("[a]ny reasonably segregable portion of a record shall be provided to any person requesting such record after deletion of the portions which are exempt by law"); American Civil Liberties Union Found. v. Deukmejian, 651 P.2d 822 (Cal. 1982) (public interest not served by requiring segregation of police index cards due to burden and reduction in usefulness of segregated information). When seeking information in California, it is apparently the duty of the requester to request redacted files when access to the entire record has been refused. See

§ 11-7. Categories of Records.

§ 11-7(a). Personnel Records.

State open records laws have reached a variety of different results in their treatment of personnel records,[179] primarily because the myriad exemptions reflected in each state's law may affect such information, including privacy exemptions,[180] internal personnel practices,[181] and even law enforcement exemptions.[182] Some states exempt from disclosure "evaluative" records found in a personnel file,[183] while others are specially protective of the privacy of public employees.[184]

Northern California Police Practices Project v. Craig, 153 Cal. Rptr. 173 (Ct. App. 1979). Ohio, though its statute is silent on the issue, has created a similar test through case law, which exempts otherwise public information if it is so interwoven with exempt material that redaction is impracticable. See Ohio ex rel. Polovischak v. Mayfield, 552 N.E.2d 635 (Ohio 1990); Ohio ex rel. Thompson Newspapers, Inc. v. Martin, 546 N.E.2d 939 (Ohio 1989).

179. Compare Fincher v. Georgia, 497 S.E.2d 632 (Ga. App. 1998) (no blanket exclusion exempting personnel records from disclosure) and Alaska Wildlife Alliance v. Rue, 948 P.2d 976 (Alaska 1997) (time sheets indicating hours worked were non-exempt public records), with Woznicki v. Erickson, 531 N.W.2d 465 (Wis. App. 1995) (decision allowing district attorney to release personnel and telephone records violated public policy against disclosure of public employee personnel records).

180. See Chap. 11-5(a)(5) *supra*; Ericson v. University of Alaska, 23 MEDIA L. REP. (BNA) 1724 (Alaska Super. 1994) (personnel file subject to public inspection to extent contents do not deal with "personal, intimate, or otherwise private life" of employee).

181. See Chap. 11-5(a)(1) *supra*.

182. See MICH. COMP. LAWS § 243(1)(t)(ix) (personnel records of law enforcement agencies exempt unless disclosure benefit outweighs interest in nondisclosure); New York Times Co. v. Superior Ct., 60 Cal. Rptr. 2d 410 (Ct. App. 1997) (statutes protecting confidentiality of peace officer's personnel records do not exempt officer's name from disclosure).

183. See, e.g., Board of Regents v. Atlanta Journal, 378 S.E.2d 305 (Ga. 1989); Pawtucket Teachers Alliance v. Brady, 556 A.2d 556, 559 (R.I. 1989). But see Obiajulu v. City of Rochester, 625 N.Y.S.2d 779 (App. Div. 1995) (disclosure of performance evaluations and appraisals, after deletion of identifying details, does not constitute invasion of privacy); Municipality of Anchorage v. Anchorage Daily News, 794 P.2d 584 (Alaska 1990) (performance evaluation report subject to disclosure).

184. See, e.g., IOWA CODE § 68A.7(11); N.Y. PUB. OFF. LAW § 89(2)(b)(I); Ohio ex rel. Beacon Journal Publ'g Co. v. City of Akron, 640 N.E.2d 164, 166 (Ohio 1994) (social security numbers of city employees excluded from mandatory disclosure under Public Records Act because disclosure would violate federal constitutional right to privacy); Young v. Rice, 826 S.W.2d 252 (Ark. 1992) (disclosure of evaluation portion of lieutenant examination would constitute an unwarranted invasion of personal privacy). Rhode Island's Access to Public Records Act presumptively exempts from disclosure any personnel records that even identify an individual employee, with few exceptions. See R.I. GEN. LAWS § 38-2-2(d)(1). Courts in Colorado, which also exempts most personnel file information from mandatory disclosure under its public records statute, have held that the placement in a personnel file of otherwise nonexempt material will not protect the information from disclosure. See Denver Publ'g Co. v. University of Colorado, 812 P.2d 682 (Colo. App. 1990). But see Hackworth v. Board of Educ., 447 S.E.2d 78 (Ga. App. 1994) (personnel records not exempted); Pottle v. School Comm. of Braintree, 482 N.E.2d 813, 817

§ 11-7(a)(1). Applications for Employment.

State open records laws generally do not treat employment applications directly. Factual information furnished by an applicant is, therefore, likely to be made public,[185] unless to do so would constitute an unwarranted invasion of privacy.[186] Polygraph tests used in hiring decisions[187] and personnel background reports[188] have been deemed public records subject to disclosure as well.

(Mass. 1985) ("Public employees, by virtue of their public employment, have diminished expectations of privacy.").

185. See, e.g., Mothers on the Move, Inc. v. Messer, 652 N.Y.S.2d 773 (App. Div. 1997) (names of candidates and names of members of interviewing committee not exempt from disclosure); Capital City Press v. East Baton Rouge Parish, 696 So. 2d 562 (La. 1997) (applications for public employment are public records not subject to any specific exemption); Federated Publications, Inc. v. Boise City, 915 P.2d 21 (Idaho 1996) (résumés of city council applicants must be disclosed); Ohio ex rel. Gannett Satellite Info. Network v. Shirley, 678 N.E.2d 557, 560 (Ohio 1997) (documents provided by applicants for city safety director's position, including résumés and supporting documentation, are public records subject to disclosure); Bangor Publ'g Co. v. Bangor, 544 A.2d 733 (Me. 1988); New Mexico ex rel. Blanchard v. City Comm'rs of Clovis, 750 P.2d 469 (N.M. App. 1988) (applications of persons seeking public employment must be disclosed); City of Kenai v. Kenai Peninsula Newspapers, 642 P.2d 1316, 1324 (Alaska 1982) (résumés and applications of applicants for employment involving substantial discretion and decisionmaking authority must be made public); Dubuque v. Telegraph Herald, Inc., 297 N.W.2d 523, 527 (Iowa 1980) (employment applications not exempt from disclosure). But see Lambert v. Judicial Nominating Council, 681 N.E.2d 285, 288 (Mass. 1997) ("Personal Data Questionnaire" completed by candidates for judicial appointment and submitted to governor through Nominating Council are essentially the Governor's records on judicial appointments, not subject to disclosure); Wings v. Dunlap, 527 N.W.2d 407 (Iowa App. 1994) (employment applications are confidential records for which disclosure is not required); LaRocca v. Board of Educ., 602 N.Y.S.2d 1009 (App. Div. 1993) (employment record exception applies to all material considered part of an employment record, including employment applications).

186. See Chap. 11-5(a)(5) *supra*; Kureczka v. FOIC, 636 A.2d 777 (Conn. 1994) (personal information masked before employment application disclosed); Providence Journal Co. v. Sundlun, 616 A.2d 1131, 1136 (R.I. 1992) (personal information contained in employee's personnel file, as well as any record that identifies specific employee, is exempt from disclosure). But see Capital City Press v. East Baton Rouge Parish Metro. Council, 696 So. 2d 562, 565-66 (La. 1997) (balancing test not appropriate to determine whether names and résumés of applicants for position of director of metropolitan airport authority must be disclosed in light of legislative decision not to provide exception for employment applications in public records law). Illinois, however, does exempt applications for employment from mandatory disclosure. See 5 ILL. COMP. STAT. 140/7(1)(b)(ii) & (iii). Florida specifically exempts the addresses, telephone numbers, and identification of the family of law enforcement personnel. See FLA. STAT. § 119.07(3)(K). An Arizona court has held that the records of more than 250 people who were merely employment prospects, including some who were unaware they were being considered, need not be disclosed pursuant to that state's open records act. See Arizona Bd. of Regents v. Phoenix Newspapers, Inc., 806 P.2d 348 (Ariz. 1991). The court did require that the names and résumés of the 17 people seriously considered for the position and who interviewed with the agency be made public. *Id.*

187. See Ohio ex rel. Lorain Journal Co. v. Lorain, 621 N.E.2d 894 (Ohio App. 1993).

188. See Ohio ex rel. Multimedia, Inc. v. Snowden, 647 N.E.2d 1374 (Ohio 1995); Doe v. Superior Ct., 721 P.2d 617, 625 (Alaska 1986) (unsolicited letters regarding applicant for

§ 11-7(a)(2). Salary Information.

Salary information concerning public employees is generally deemed available for public inspection,[189] unless it falls within the privacy exemption recognized in most states.[190] Portions of payroll records regarding deductions for investments and deferred compensation have been withheld in the name of employee privacy.[191]

§ 11-7(a)(3). Disciplinary Records.

The disciplinary records of public employees are generally open to the public pursuant to state statutes, on the ground that the job performance of public employees is a matter of legitimate concern.[192] Access to such records may,

---

appointment to public post are subject to disclosure). But see City of Westminster v. Dogan Constr. Co., 930 P.2d 585 (Colo. 1997) (city engineer's notes taken during telephone survey of contractor's references were exempt as "letters of reference concerning employment").

189. See, e.g., CAL. GOV'T CODE § 6254.8; N.Y. PUB. OFF. LAW § 87(3)(b); R.I. GEN. LAWS § 38-2-2(d)(1); Ky. Op. Att'y Gen. Nos. 78-231 (1978), 76-717 (1976), 92-ORD-1088 (1992); Tacoma Pub. Library v. Woessner, 951 P.2d 357 (Wash. App. 1998) (names, salaries, fringe benefits, vacation and sick leave pay without identification numbers is subject to disclosure); Freedom Newspapers Inc. v. Tollefson, 961 P.2d 1150 (Colo. App. 1998) (severance payments received not exempt because not part of employee's personnel file); Missouri ex rel. Missouri Local Gov't Retirement Sys. v. Bill, 935 S.W.2d 659, 664-65 (Mo. App. 1996) (names of government employees who received refunds of their contributions to retirement plan not exempt from disclosure); Braun v. Taft, 201 Cal. Rptr. 654 (Ct. App. 1984); Ohio ex rel. Petty v. Whalen, 549 N.E.2d 167 (Ohio App. 1989); Hastings & Sons Publ'g Co. v. City Treasurer of Lynn, 375 N.E.2d 299 (Mass. 1978); Doolan v. BOCES, 398 N.E.2d 533 (N.Y. 1979); Buffalo News v. Buffalo Mun. Hous. Auth., 558 N.Y.S.2d 364 (App. Div. 1990).

190. See Chap. 11-5(a)(5) *supra.*

191. See Blankenship v. City of Hoover, 590 So. 2d 245, 250 (Ala. 1991) (information contained in W2 forms, pertaining to income deferral, retirement, and tax withholding is more personal than public); Ohio ex rel. Jones v. Myers, 581 N.E.2d 629 (Ohio C.P. 1991). But see Zubeck v. El Paso County Retirement Plan, 961 P.2d 597 (Colo. App. 1998) (documents relating to retirement plan, including real estate contracts and leases for rental property owned by plan, are not exempt from disclosure); Pulitzer Publ'g Co. v. Missouri State Employees' Retirement Sys., 927 S.W.2d 477 (Mo. App. 1996) (pension benefits are not exempt from disclosure).

192. See Fincher v. Georgia, 497 S.E.2d 632 (Ga. App. 1998) (investigatory report into alleged sexual harassment by public official was public record subject to disclosure); Hawaii Org. of Police Officers v. Society of Prof'l Journalists, 927 P.2d 386, 408 (Haw. 1996) (information that must be disclosed under public records act regarding public employee's employment-related misconduct and resulting discipline is not "highly personal and intimate information"); New York 1 News v. Office of President of Borough of Staten Island, 631 N.Y.S.2d 479 (App. Div. 1995) (findings regarding investigation of employee for racial insensitivity not exempt from disclosure); Citizens to Recall Mayor Whitlock v. Whitlock, 844 P.2d 74 (Mont. 1992) (mayor did not have "reasonable expectation of privacy" in preventing disclosure of report regarding investigation of his alleged misconduct); Demers v. City of Minneapolis, 468 N.W.2d 71 (Minn. 1991) (names of complainants to internal affairs units of police departments are public data); Barton v. Shupe, 525 N.E.2d 812 (Ohio 1988) (report involving investigation of alleged wrongdoing by former chief of police

however, be denied if disclosure would constitute an unwarranted invasion of privacy,[193] or if the records are relevant to a pending disciplinary proceeding.[194] In some jurisdictions, such records are presumptively exempt, particularly those that concern police officers.[195]

§ 11-7(a)(4). Records of Labor Negotiations.

The records surrounding labor negotiations are, when they are treated in open records legislation at all, generally deemed exempt from mandatory disclosure.[196] In one case concerning the requested disclosure of a salary report designed to assist school districts in their collective bargaining negotiations with their public employee unions, a New York court applied a statutory exemption permitting the agency to withhold any record the disclosure of which would impair collective

---

held to be public record subject to disclosure); Ky. Op. Att'y Gen. No. 92-ORD-1515 (1992) ("This Office has repeatedly recognized that 'disciplinary action taken against a public employee is a matter related to his job performance and a matter about which the public has a right to know.'"). But see MO. REV. STAT. § 610.021(3) (records relating to disciplining employees of governmental body may be withheld). See also Oklahoma State Bd. of Med. Licensure & Supervision v. Migliaccio, 917 P.2d 483 (Okla. App. 1996) (records of state medical board subject to open records act; records of dismissed disciplinary proceeding open to public).

193. See, e.g., Beckham v. Board of Educ., 873 S.W.2d 575 (Ky. 1994) (employees have standing to challenge release of disciplinary records on grounds that they contain personal information release of which would constitute unwarranted invasion of personal privacy); News-Journal Co. v. Billingsley, 1980 Del. Ch. LEXIS 553 (Del. Ch. Nov. 20, 1980).

194. See, e.g., Wolfskill v. Henderson, 823 S.W.2d 112, 114 (Mo. App. 1991) (investigative files dealing with disciplinary matters withheld); Union Leader Corp. v. Fenniman, 620 A.2d 1039, 1040 (N.H. 1993) (records of internal investigation of police officer "pertain[ ] to internal personnel practices" because they document procedures leading to internal personnel discipline and are exempt from disclosure); Mich. Op. Att'y Gen. No. 5500 (1979); Mass. Op. Att'y Gen. No. 166 (1977).

195. See, e.g., CAL. EVID. CODE §§ 1043-1047; Lyon v. Dunne, 580 N.Y.S.2d 803 (App. Div. 1992) (denying access to complaints and reprimands of police). But see Daily Gazette Co. v. Schenectady, 673 N.Y.S.2d 783 (App. Div. 1998) (records of disciplinary actions taken against police officers for their off-duty actions not exempt from disclosure); Hawaii Org. of Police Officers v. Society of Prof'l Journalists, 927 P.2d 386 (Haw. 1996) (information concerning public employees' employment-related misconduct and resulting discipline is not highly personal and intimate, and must be disclosed pursuant to Hawaii Uniform Information Practices Act); Federated Publications, Inc. v. Boise City, 915 P.2d 21, 24 (Idaho 1996) (administrative review of shooting incident was not personnel record and could be disclosed); City of Columbia v. ACLU of South Carolina, 475 S.E.2d 747 (S.C. 1996) (rejecting claim that internal police department investigation per se exempt from disclosure).

196. See, e.g., DEL. CODE ANN. tit. 29, § 10002(d)(8); 5 ILL. COMP. STAT. 140/7(1)(q); N.Y. PUB. OFF. LAW § 87(2)(c); N.C. GEN. STAT. § 95-36; City of Las Cruces v. Public Employee Labor Relations Bd., 917 P.2d 451, 454 (N.M. 1996) (public employee's privacy interest in his personal position regarding union representation requires protecting representation petitions from public disclosure). But see City of Gainesville v. Florida ex rel. Int'l Ass'n of Fire Fighters, 298 So. 2d 478 (Fla. App. 1974) (budgets affected by labor negotiations are not exempt).

bargaining negotiations on the ground that "[t]o compel disclosure would impinge upon the participating school boards' predecisional and negotiating process, and . . . would only serve an inequitable one-sided negotiating ploy, rather than the furnishing of information intended to be included within the purposes of the Freedom of Information Law."[197]

§ 11-7(a)(5). Promotional Examinations.

Several interests are implicated in the disclosure of information concerning promotional examinations. The citizenry has a legitimate interest in the credibility of the promotional process of its public servants, particularly in the grading accuracy of these types of examinations.[198] Countervailing interests, however, are also present. Initially, the examinations themselves may be exempt from disclosure due to the need to protect the integrity of the examination process[199] or because they are proprietary.[200] Additionally, the privacy of those taking the examinations may be implicated by the disclosure of their scores.[201]

Courts attempt to provide the public with sufficient information to evaluate the means of promotion of its civil servants while exempting from disclosure personal information concerning the candidates.[202] As a result, grading scales and anonymous raw scores may be released. Evaluation forms and final test scores have been made available to the public after information that would identify the candidate has been deleted and the list of scores scrambled so as to prevent the identification of the score of any particular person.[203]

---

197. Trauernicht v. Board of Coop. Educ. Serv., 407 N.Y.S.2d 398, 399 (Sup. Ct. 1978). See Traverse City Record Eagle v. Traverse City Area Pub. Schs., 459 N.W.2d 284 (Mich. App. 1990) (tentative collective bargaining agreement exempt from disclosure because premature disclosure would have negative impact on negotiation process).

198. DeLaMater v. Marion Civil Serv. Comm., 554 N.W.2d 875, 880 (Iowa 1996).

199. See IOWA CODE § 22.7(19) (confidential examination exemption).

200. See College Entrance Examination Bd. v. Pataki, 889 F. Supp. 554 (N.D.N.Y. 1995) (disclosure provisions of New York's Standardized Testing Act infringed copyrights in standardized tests).

201. See Ruberti, Girvin & Ferlazzo v. New York State Div. of State Police, 641 N.Y.S.2d 411 (App. Div. 1996) (scores achieved by police officers on promotional examinations were not subject to inspection or review); Young v. Rice, 826 S.W.2d 252, 255 (Ark. 1992).

202. See DeLaMater v. Marion Civil Serv. Comm., 554 N.W.2d 875, 880 (Iowa 1996) ("It should not matter to the public which candidate had a particular score; what matters is that the score was properly calculated."). But see Rainey v. Levitt, 525 N.Y.S.2d 551, 553 (Sup. Ct. 1988) (names of unsuccessful candidates had already been made public, so court saw no "meaningful distinction" between releasing names of those candidates and disclosing their test scores).

203. See, e.g., DeLaMater v. Marion Civil Serv. Comm., 554 N.W.2d 875, 881-82 (Iowa 1996); Ohio ex rel. Cater v. City of N. Olmsted, 631 N.E.2d 1048 (Ohio 1994) (civil service aptitude test scores released); Young v. Rice, 826 S.W.2d 252, 255 (Ark. 1992).

§ 11-7(b). Police Records.

Law enforcement records are generally exempt from the mandatory public access requirements of most state open records laws, on the ground that disclosure threatens to hamper investigations or enforcement proceedings, reveal sensitive investigative techniques, expose sources, interfere with a defendant's right to a fair trial, invade personal privacy, or threaten personal safety.[204] In addition, records regarding juvenile offenders are typically deemed confidential.[205] Nevertheless, certain records used by and in the possession of law enforcement agencies are subject to mandatory disclosure pursuant to most statutory schemes, including the files of closed cases or cases that are otherwise no longer pending.[206]

§ 11-7(b)(1). Arrest and Incident Reports.

Contemporaneous arrest reports,[207] mug shots[208] and booking information regarding an alleged criminal offender are generally open for public inspection

---

204. See OHIO REV. CODE ANN. § 149.43(A)(2)(a) (exempts from release any confidential law enforcement investigatory record that would create high probability of disclosure of identity of suspect who has not been charged with offense to which record pertains); Ohio ex rel. Master v. Cleveland, 667 N.E.2d 974, 977 (Ohio 1996) (purposes of uncharged suspect exception include avoiding subjecting uncharged suspects to additional adverse publicity and preventing compromising subsequent efforts to reopen and solve inactive cases); South Coast Newspapers, Inc. v. City of Oceanside, 206 Cal. Rptr. 527 (Ct. App. 1984); City of Santa Rosa v. Press Democrat, 232 Cal. Rptr. 445 (Ct. App. 1986) (law enforcement agency faced with request for investigatory records has burden of establishing that disclosure would interfere with law enforcement, threaten a fair trial, invade a person's privacy, disclose sensitive information or sources or investigative techniques, or endanger the life of law enforcement personnel); DeZimm v. Connelie, 479 N.Y.S.2d 871 (App. Div. 1984), aff'd, 476 N.E.2d 646 (N.Y. 1985).

205. See Ogden Newspapers, Inc. v. City of Williamstown, 453 S.E.2d 631, 637 (W. Va. 1994) ("Because of the sensitive nature of crimes involving juveniles and the central role confidentiality plays in a juvenile's rehabilitation, the scale generally tips in favor of confidentiality rather than disclosure of juvenile law enforcement records.").

206. See DEL. CODE ANN. tit. 29, § 10002(d)(3); FLA. STAT. § 119.07(3)(d); Ohio ex rel. Steckman v. Jackson, 639 N.E.2d 83 (Ohio 1994) (routine incident reports not exempt).

207. An arrest report or arrest record consists of notations of an arrest, detention, indictment, the filing of an information or formal criminal charge against a person by a law enforcement agency. See, e.g., N.M. STAT. ANN. § 29-10-3. It usually includes the full name, address, and physical characteristics of the arrested person, as well as the time and date of arrest and general information regarding the charge. See, e.g., CAL. GOV'T CODE § 6254(f).

208. Booking photographs or mug shots are photographs taken pursuant to "booking" an arrested individual. Mug shots are usually available to the public, see N.M. STAT. ANN. § 29-10-7 (Arrest Record Information Act); MINN. STAT. § 13.82(17); NEB. REV. STAT. § 29-3521(1), and generally are not considered confidential in nature. See People v. McCloud, 194 Cal. Rptr. 75 (Ct. App. 1983) (mug shots not part of confidential criminal summary history and are routinely made available to press and public); Detroit Free Press, Inc. v. Oakland County Sheriff, 418 N.W.2d 124

in several states.[209] Incident reports are also generally deemed public records subject to disclosure,[210] subject to applicable exemptions in the relevant statute.[211] Some courts have applied a balancing test weighing the public's right to know about police and criminal activity in the community against the government's interest in preserving the secrecy of its records and have allowed partial access to information contained in incident reports.[212]

In California, an agency is required to release information concerning the person arrested, as well as general information regarding the incident. Under the California Public Records Act:

> state and local law enforcement agencies shall make public the following information . . . (1) The full name, current address, and occupation of every individual arrested by the agency, the individual's physical description including date of birth, color of eyes and hair, sex, height and weight, the

---

(Mich. App. 1987) (mug shot of person awaiting trial did not contain information of a personal nature and was subject to disclosure).

209. See, e.g., FLA. STAT. § 119.011(3)(c)(2); 5 ILL. COMP. STAT. 140/7(1)(d)(I) (chronological arrest records are open); IOWA CODE § 22.7(9); MO. REV. STAT. § 610.100.2; R.I. GEN. LAWS § 38-2-2(d)(4). See Ohio ex rel. Outlet Communications, Inc. v. Lancaster Police Dep't, 528 N.E.2d 175 (Ohio 1988). But see ARK. CODE ANN. § 9-27-352 (records of arrest or detention of juvenile generally exempt from disclosure); DEL. CODE ANN. tit. 29, § 10002(d)(4) (arrest records exempt, except those of requester); HAW. REV. STAT. § 831.1 (prohibits dissemination of arrest record not followed by valid conviction); Union Leader Corp. v. City of Nashua, 686 A.2d 310 (N.H. 1996) (disclosure depends on balancing interest of community in disclosure with individual's privacy interest and law enforcement interests); Gifford v. FOIC, 631 A.2d 252 (Conn. 1993) (arrest reports not required to be disclosed to public during pendency of prosecution); Sullivan v. City of Pittsburgh, 561 A.2d 863, 865 (Pa. Commw. 1989) (records of police investigations, even those that are completed, are excluded from definition of "public record" under state "Right-to-Know Act").

210. Incident reports include information such as details of the offense committed, the time and location of the incident, the identity of the complainant, the premises and property involved, any identification or description of witnesses, and additional information such as the weather, and the names of the investigating officers. Houston Chronicle Publ'g Co. v. City of Houston, 531 S.W.2d 177, 179 (Tex. App. 1975). See Ogden Newspapers, Inc. v. City of Williamstown, 453 S.E.2d 631, 634 (W. Va. 1994) (the police are conducting "the public's business" when they respond to reported incidents of crime); Hengel v. City of Pine Bluff, 821 S.W.2d 761 (Ark. 1991); Asbury Park Press, Inc. v. Borough of Seaside Heights, 586 A.2d 870 (N.J. Super. 1990); Louisiana v. McDaniel, 504 So. 2d 160 (La. 1987); South Coast Newspapers, Inc. v. City of Oceanside, 206 Cal. Rptr. 527 (Ct. App. 1984).

211. See, e.g., Ogden Newspapers, Inc. v. City of Williamstown, 453 S.E.2d 631, 639 (W. Va. 1994) (incident report released with names of juveniles redacted due to confidentiality accorded to juvenile records); Houston Chronicle Publ'g Co. v. City of Houston, 531 S.W.2d 177, 187 (Tex. App. 1975) (law enforcement records exception).

212. See, e.g., Ogden Newspapers, Inc. v. City of Williamstown, 453 S.E.2d 631, 636 (W. Va. 1994); Donrey of Nevada v. Bradshaw, 798 P.2d 144 (Nev. 1990) (balancing of interests required the disclosure of entire police investigation report to newspapers); Houston Chronicle Publ'g Co. v. City of Houston, 531 S.W.2d 177, 186 (Tex. App. 1975).

time and date of arrest, the time and date of booking, the location of the arrest, the factual circumstances surrounding the arrest, the amount of bail set, the time and manner of release or the location where the individual is currently being held, and all charges the individual is being held upon, including any outstanding warrants from other jurisdictions and parole or probation holds.[213]

§ 11-7(b)(2). Police Blotter.

The information contained in a police blotter, or in a chronologically maintained arrest log that generally contains no investigative information,[214] is open to the public pursuant to most state statutory schemes.[215]

§ 11-7(b)(3). Investigatory Records.

Concern for the integrity of current or imminent criminal proceedings often limits the availability of investigatory records.[216] The open records laws of some states expressly distinguish active from closed investigatory records, authorizing access only to the latter.[217] Most states, however, do not so categorize their investigatory records, but rely instead on a more general exemption from mandatory disclosure of information that would "interfere with pending or actually and reasonably contemplated enforcement proceedings conducted by any law enforcement or correctional agency."[218]

§ 11-7(b)(3)(A). Active Files.

Many state open records laws define an "active file" as one that "is related to an ongoing investigation which is continuing with a reasonable, good faith

---

213. CAL. GOV'T CODE § 6254(f)(1); see also N.C. GEN. STAT. § 132-1.4(c)(1)-(3).
214. See Sheehan v. City of Binghamton, 398 N.Y.S.2d 905, 906 (App. Div. 1977).
215. See, e.g., 5 ILL. COMP. STAT. 140/7(1)(d)(I); MASS. GEN. LAWS ch. 41, § 98F; OKLA. STAT. tit. 51, § 24A.8. See Hengel v. City of Pine Bluff, 821 S.W.2d 761 (Ark. 1991); Pennsylvania v. Mines, 680 A.2d 1227 (Pa. Commw. 1996); Newspapers, Inc. v. Breier, 279 N.W.2d 179 (Wis. 1979); Houston Chronicle Publ'g Co. v. City of Houston, 531 S.W.2d 177 (Tex. App. 1975) (police blotter, "showup sheet," and arrest sheet were public records available to press and public). But see Post-Tribune v. Police Dep't, 643 N.E.2d 307 (Ind. 1994) (to protect victim's privacy, exact location of sex crime need not be disclosed).
216. See Cowles Publ'g Co. v. City of Spokane, 849 P.2d 1271 (Wash. App. 1993) (police reports about police dog contact with public not an investigative report and not exempt from disclosure).
217. See, e.g., FLA. STAT. § 119.07(3)(d); KY. REV. STAT. ANN. § 61.878(1)(g); WASH. REV. CODE § 42.17.310(1)(d).
218. 5 ILL. COMP. STAT. 140/7(1)(c)(I). See KAN. STAT. ANN. § 45-221(a)(10); ME. REV. STAT. ANN. tit. 16, § 614(1)(A); MICH. COMP. LAWS § 15.243(1)(b); OHIO REV. CODE ANN. § 149.43(A)(2).

anticipation of securing an arrest or prosecution in the foreseeable future."[219] Records of such an "active and ongoing" investigation are almost always exempt from mandatory disclosure.[220] In Michigan, which does not distinguish between active or closed files,[221] a court must determine that disclosure "would" interfere with law enforcement for its statutory exemption to apply.[222] In Arkansas, where the statutory exemption applies only to ongoing investigations, an investigatory file that has been closed with respect to one suspect, but remains open as to others, is exempt from disclosure.[223]

In *Times-News Publishing Co. v. North Carolina*,[224] a news organization made a request under the North Carolina Public Records Act for access to the physical exhibits introduced as evidence in a murder trial.[225] The exhibits had been returned to the district attorney's office to be used in the reinvestigation of the case and in preparation for the defendant's retrial. The Court of Appeals held that, under these circumstances, the exhibits once again became "records of criminal investigations" specifically exempted from disclosure under the Act.[226]

---

219. FLA. STAT. § 119.011(3)(d)(2). See ME. REV. STAT. ANN. tit. 16, § 614(1)(A) (records may not be disseminated if there is "reasonable possibility" that public release or inspection of records would interfere with law enforcement proceedings); Turner v. North Charleston Police Dep't, 351 S.E.2d 583 (S.C. App. 1984); OHIO REV. CODE ANN. § 149.43(A)(2)(c) (law enforcement investigatory records are exempt where release "would create a high probability of disclosure of . . . specific investigatory work product"); Ohio ex rel. Gannett Satellite Info. Network v. Petro, 685 N.E.2d 1223, 1228-29 (Ohio 1997) (doubtful that disclosure of audit working papers would create high probability of disclosure of investigatory work product).

220. See, e.g., N.J. STAT. ANN. § 47:1A-3; FLA. STAT. § 119.07(3)(d); KY. REV. STAT. ANN. § 61.878(1)(g). See Wells v. Sarasota Herald Tribune Co., 546 So. 2d 1105 (Fla. App. 1989); Appman v. Worthington, 746 S.W.2d 165 (Tenn. 1987); Stone v. Consolidated Publ'g Co., 404 So. 2d 678, 681 (Ala. 1981); Ashley v. Public Disclosure Comm'n, 560 P.2d 1156 (Wash. App. 1977). But see Nichols v. Bennett, 544 N.W.2d 428 (Wis. 1996) (copies of open records requests sent to district attorney were not per se exempt from disclosure solely because they were placed in a prosecutorial file since it "is the nature of the documents and not their location which determines their status"); City of Fayetteville v. Rose, 743 S.W.2d 817 (Ark. 1988) (exemption limited to "undisclosed" investigations; records subject to disclosure after indictments returned).

221. See MICH. COMP. LAWS § 15.243(1)(b).

222. Payne v. Grand Rapids Police Chief, 443 N.W.2d 481, 484 (Mich. App. 1988); see Evening News Ass'n v. City of Troy, 339 N.W.2d 421, 436 (Mich. 1983) (identities of two officers involved in a killing not exempt).

223. See Martin v. Musteen, 799 S.W.2d 540, 542 (Ark. 1990).

224. 476 S.E.2d 450 (N.C. App. 1996).

225. The evidence included the murder weapon, blood scrapings, crime scene photographs, fingerprints and clothing worn by the victims at the time of their deaths. See *id.* at 451.

226. *Id.* at 453. See New York News, Inc. v. Office of Special State Prosecutor, 544 N.Y.S.2d 151 (App. Div. 1989) (access to investigative materials denied due to possibility that investigation may be reopened).

§ 11-7(b)(3)(B). Closed Files.

In most states, once investigatory "operations are concluded, the need for secrecy is no longer present"[227] and public disclosure of relevant records, with the exception of the identities of confidential informants,[228] is required.[229] Notable exceptions include Texas, where the state Supreme Court has determined that the state's Open Records Act exemption for law enforcement records that deal with the detection, investigation, or prosecution of crime does not distinguish between "open" and "closed" cases,[230] New York, where case law has held that the conclusion of an investigation does not automatically open a file to the public,[231] and Wisconsin, which balances the benefit of closed-file disclosure against the potential harms.[232]

§ 11-7(b)(4). Rap Sheets and Other Compilations of Criminal Histories.

Whether a rap sheet or other compilation of criminal history is accessible under a public records law varies from jurisdiction to jurisdiction.[233] Most tend to follow the approach taken under the federal FOIA that the disclosure of criminal history records is generally not permitted because it would constitute an unwarranted invasion of privacy.[234] Some states permit the disclosure of these

---

227. Louisiana v. Campbell, 566 So. 2d 1038, 1043 (La. App. 1990).

228. See Mayfair Chrysler Plymouth, Inc. v. Baldarotta, 453 N.W.2d 922, 925 (Wis. App. 1990); Bougas v. Chief of Police of Lexington, 354 N.E.2d 872 (Mass. 1976) (materials relating to an inactive investigation may require confidentiality in order to convince citizens that they may safely confide in law enforcement officials).

229. See, e.g., MINN. STAT. § 13.82(5); McCambridge v. City of Little Rock, 766 S.W.2d 909 (Ark. 1989); In re Quinn, 517 N.W.2d 895 (Minn. 1994) (newspapers granted access to police files regarding closed investigation concerning alleged rape by professional hockey players). But see Holmes v. Morales, 924 S.W.2d 920, 924 (Tex. 1996) (no distinction between "open" and "closed" cases); Ohio ex rel. McGee v. Ohio State Bd. of Psychiatry, 550 N.E.2d 945 (Ohio 1990) (investigatory records remain confidential even if agency declines to prosecute); Ohio ex rel. Thompson Newspapers, Inc. v. Martin, 546 N.E.2d 939 (Ohio 1989). After conviction, some courts treat the case as no longer active. See Downs v. Austin, 522 So. 2d 931, 934 (Fla. App. 1988); Parker v. Lee, 378 S.E.2d 677 (Ga. 1989). But see Bougas v. Chief of Police, 354 N.E.2d 872 (Mass. 1976) (mere completion of investigation not sufficient to override continuing confidentiality concerns).

230. See Holmes v. Morales, 924 S.W.2d 920, 923 (Tex. 1996).

231. See Williams v. Superior Ct., 852 P.2d 377, 381 (Cal. 1993) (exemption for investigatory files does not terminate with conclusion of investigation); Moore v. Santucci, 543 N.Y.S.2d 103 (App. Div. 1989) (use of investigation material in open court waives confidentiality).

232. See Wisconsin ex rel. Richards v. Foust, 477 N.W.2d 608 (Wis. 1991).

233. See, e.g., Fla. Op. Att'y Gen. No. 77-125 (1977) (criminal history compilations are available to the public).

234. See Chap. 10-2(c)(8)(C) *supra*; ARK. CODE ANN. §§ 12-12-211, 12-12-1003(e); CAL. PENAL CODE § 13300; IOWA CODE § 692.19; 5 ILL. COMP. STAT. 140/7(1)(d) (defining and

records,[235] while at least one jurisdiction conditions disclosure on whether a criminal prosecution is reasonably anticipated.[236]

§ 11-7(b)(5). Victim Information.

Several states flatly exempt from disclosure information pertaining to the victims of crime.[237] Those that do authorize access to some information regarding crime victims will generally not permit disclosure in the case of victims of sexual crimes or abuse.[238] Information concerning a victim's relatives may not, however, be exempt from disclosure.[239]

---

exempting "criminal history record information"); S.D. CODIFIED LAWS § 22-22-40; VA. CODE ANN. § 15.1-135.1. See, e.g., Ohio ex rel. Multimedia, Inc. v. Snowden, 647 N.E.2d 1374 (Ohio 1995). But see NEV. REV. STAT. § 179A.100(5)(I) (records closed to public but must be disclosed to "reporter for the electronic or printed media in his professional capacity for communication to the public").

235. See COLO. REV. STAT. § 24-72-303; NEB. REV. STAT. § 29-3520; GA. CODE ANN. §§ 35-3-34, 35-3-35; Note, *The Exaltation of Privacy Doctrines over Public Information Law*, 45 DUKE L.J. 1249, 1293 (1996) ("In 1995, the Georgia legislature . . . [decided] for itself that certain compilations of criminal information 'rap sheets' were exactly the kind of information the public ought to have."). See also Blum, *Disclosing the Identities of Juvenile Felons: Introducing Accountability to Juvenile Justice*, 27 LOY. U. CHI. L.J. 349, 377-78 (1996) ("[S]tates like Kentucky, Maryland, and Nevada permit judges to disclose juvenile identities to persons or entities who show good cause or a legitimate interest in viewing the juvenile's records.").

236. See La. Op. Att'y Gen. No. 77-1370 (1977). But see Ellerbe v. Andrews, 623 So. 2d 41 (La. App. 1993) (party's rap sheet obtained from state's centralized computer database cannot be disclosed in civil case).

237. See, e.g., ALASKA STAT. §§ 12.61.100 to 12.61.150; FLA. STAT. § 119.07(3)(z); 5 ILL. COMP. STAT. 140/7(1)(b)(v). See generally Note, *Michigan's Freedom of Information Act and Personal Privacy: A Divergence from the Federal Freedom of Information Act as to Privacy Interests of Deceased Persons and Their Families*, 69 U. DET. L. REV. 599 (1992).

238. See ALA. CODE § 26-14-8(c); ARK. CODE ANN. §§ 5-28-213, 12-12-506; IND. CODE § 5-14-3-5(c)(3)(B); CAL. GOV'T CODE § 6254(f)(2); MASS. GEN. LAWS ch. 41, § 97D; UTAH CODE ANN. §§ 63-2-103(12)(a)(ii), 63-2-301(2)(g), 63-2-302(2)(d). See Doe v. Board of Regents, 452 S.E.2d 776 (Ga. App. 1994); Post-Tribune v. Police Dep't, 643 N.E.2d 307, 309 (Ind. 1994) (police department's statutory obligation to disclose "location" of rapes satisfied by providing "the most specific location which reasonably protects the privacy of the victim"). See also MO. REV. STAT. § 610.100.3 (law enforcement agencies permitted to withhold records if they contain information that is reasonably likely to pose clear and present danger to safety of any victim). Other states deem victim information generally to be available to the public. See N.C. GEN. STAT. § 132-1.4(c)(6); Pinkava v. Corrigan, 581 N.E.2d 1181 (Ohio 1990).

239. See Ohio ex rel. Johnson v. City of Cleveland, 603 N.E.2d 1011 (Ohio 1992) (identities and addresses of victim's relatives will be disclosed unless law enforcement agency proves disclosure has potential to cause harm). But see Pennington v. Washtenaw County Sheriff, 336 N.W.2d 828 (Mich. App. 1983) (names of complainant's parents, their address and telephone number exempt from disclosure as unwarranted invasion of personal privacy).

§ 11-7(b)(6). Confessions.

Confessions are generally not available for inspection or copying because they are either contained within exempt investigatory files,[240] or because their disclosure would interfere with adjudication of a pending case.[241] A confession may, however, be made public when the investigation or adjudication is concluded.[242]

§ 11-7(b)(7). Confidential Informants.

The identities of confidential informants are generally not available pursuant to state open records laws because of concerns for their personal safety and the potential harm that may be caused to ongoing investigations.[243]

§ 11-7(b)(8). 911 Tapes.

The contents of 911 telephone calls are generally available to the public pursuant to open records legislation,[244] unless the information contained therein is otherwise exempt,[245] such as when it is part of an open investigatory file.[246] Tapes of police radio communications have generally been made available as well.[247]

---

240. See, e.g., DEL. CODE ANN. tit. 29, § 10002(d)(3)-(4); ME. REV. STAT. ANN. tit. 16, §§ 611-622.

241. See FLA. STAT. § 119.07(m)(1); LA. REV. STAT. ANN. § 44:3.A(1).

242. See FLA. STAT. § 119.07(m)(1); LA. REV. STAT. ANN. § 44:3.A(1).

243. See ALASKA STAT. § 09.25.120(6)(D), (E); CAL. GOV'T CODE § 6254(f); GA. CODE ANN. § 50-18-72(a)(3); N.Y. PUB. OFF. LAW § 87(2)(e)(iii); N.C. GEN. STAT. § 132-1.4(b); R.I. GEN. LAWS § 38-2-2(16); University of Conn. v. Freedom of Info. Comm'n, 585 A.2d 690 (Conn. 1991); Pretash v. City of Leadville, 715 P.2d 1272 (Colo. App. 1985); Salcines v. Tampa Television, 454 So. 2d 639 (Fla. App. 1984); Suttleworth v. City of Camden, 610 A.2d 985 (N.J. Super. 1992); Houston Chronicle Publ'g Co. v. City of Houston, 531 S.W.2d 177, 187 (Tex. App. 1975).

244. See, e.g., CAL. GOV'T CODE § 6254(f); N.C. GEN. STAT. § 132-1.4(c)(4); Ohio ex rel. Cincinnati Enquirer v. Hamilton County, 662 N.E.2d 334 (Ohio 1996). But see R.I. GEN. LAWS § 39-21.1-17 (all telephone calls and tapes shall remain confidential); MO. REV. STAT. § 610.150 (not accessible to general public).

245. See Tull v. Brown, 494 S.E.2d 855 (Va. 1988) (911 tape is a "noncriminal incidents report" that is exempt from disclosure under Virginia Freedom of Information Act).

246. See Chap. 11-7(b)(2) supra; FLA. STAT. § 119; LA. REV. STAT. ANN. § 44:3; WASH. REV. CODE § 42.17.310(1)(d). The Texas Attorney General has mandated that 911 tapes fall within the definition of public records under the Texas statute. See Tex. Op. Att'y Gen. No. ORD 519 (1989).

247. See N.C. GEN. STAT. § 132-1.4(c)(5); Buffalo Broadcasting Co. v. City of Buffalo, 511 N.Y.S.2d 759 (App. Div. 1987); Ohio ex rel. Multimedia Inc. v. Whalen, 549 N.E.2d 167 (Ohio 1990); Tex. Op. Att'y Gen. No. ORD-394 (1983).

§ 11-7(b)(9). Police Investigatory Techniques.

Public access to records detailing police investigatory techniques is typically dependent upon whether the techniques involved are deemed to be "routine."[248] Nonroutine techniques — generally those dealing with surveillance procedures[249] or analogous methods[250] — are exempt from compelled disclosure because of the potential harm to law enforcement officers or to current or future investigations. Routine techniques, in contrast, are "those generally used and known,"[251] and therefore lack the potentially damaging effects associated with the disclosure of nonroutine methods.[252]

§ 11-7(b)(10). Accident Reports.

Accident reports are generally open to the public pursuant to most state records laws, provided that an unwarranted invasion of privacy would not result from disclosure.[253] Information generally permitted or required to be disclosed includes: the names and addresses of persons involved in and witnesses to the incident; descriptions of any property involved; the date, time, and location of the incident; diagrams; statements of the parties; and statements of witnesses.[254]

---

248. See, e.g., CONN. GEN. STAT. § 1-19(b)(3) (investigatory techniques "not otherwise known to the general public" are exempt); 5 ILL. COMP. STAT. 140/7(1)(c)(v); N.Y. PUB. OFF. LAW § 87(2)(3)(iv) (criminal investigative techniques or procedures exempt, unless routine); OHIO REV. CODE ANN. § 149.43(A)(2)(c) (non-routine investigative techniques exempt); S.C. CODE ANN. § 30-4-40(a)(3) (exempts investigative techniques not known outside government); UTAH CODE ANN. § 63-2-304(8)(e) (exempts investigative techniques not known outside government). Some states generally exempt investigatory techniques. See, e.g., ALASKA STAT. § 09.25.120(6); CAL. GOV'T CODE § 6254(f); IOWA CODE § 21.5(1)(g) & (h); LA. REV. STAT. ANN. § 44:3.A(3); MINN. STAT. § 13.82(16).

249. See FLA. STAT. § 119.07(3)(f); DeZimm v. Connelie, 476 N.E.2d 646 (N.Y. 1985) (access denied to administrative manual containing procedures for electronic surveillance and monitoring devices).

250. See N.Y. PUB. OFF. LAW § 87(2)(e)(iv); Burtis v. New York Police Dep't, 659 N.Y.S.2d 875 (App. Div. 1997) (placement of telephone traps cannot be characterized as "routine" criminal investigation techniques or procedures).

251. 5 ILL. COMP. STAT. 140/7(1)(c)(v).

252. See Fink v. Lefkowitz, 393 N.E.2d 463, 466 (N.Y. 1979) (in determining whether investigative technique is routine, consider whether violators could use information to evade agency personnel or their avenues of inquiry); Moore v. Santucci, 543 N.Y.S.2d 103, 106 (App. Div. 1989) (ballistic and fingerprinting tests are routine).

253. See, e.g., 5 ILL. COMP. STAT. 140/7(1)(b) (accident reports available unless clearly unwarranted personal privacy invasion); Wisconsin ex rel. Young v. Shaw, 477 N.W.2d 340 (Wis. App. 1991) (motor vehicle accident reports subject to public inspection); Scott v. Records Access Officer, 480 N.E.2d 1071 (N.Y. 1985) (access to accident reports with names and addresses deleted).

254. See, e.g., CAL. GOV'T CODE § 6254(f); Shannon v. Hansen, 469 N.W.2d 412, 415 (Iowa 1991) (statements made by witnesses to peace officers investigating motor vehicle accident are public records). But see Hawk Eye v. Jackson, 521 N.W.2d 750 (Iowa 1994) (communication

§ 11-7(c). Probation and Parole Reports.

Though there exists little uniformity regarding the accessibility of parole and probation records under the various state statutory schemes, a majority of jurisdictions have apparently declined to afford access to such information.[255] There is a growing movement among the states to require convicted sex offenders to register with local law enforcement authorities and for these registrations to be made available to the public.[256]

§ 11-7(d). Coroner Reports, Autopsy Reports, and Photographs.

Jurisdictions are divided on the issue of public access to coroner and autopsy reports. Some states deny access to such material.[257] Other states permit access,[258] but not without some exceptions.[259] To the extent that an autopsy or

---

contained in investigative report that was made to peace officer in official confidence may be exempt from disclosure).

255. See, e.g., CAL. GOV'T CODE § 6254(f) (parole information closed); 5 ILL. COMP. STAT. 140/7(1)(d) (rehabilitation and release information closed); FLA. STAT. § 945.10(1) (Department of Corrections granted authority to create its own rules regarding file confidentiality); MASS. GEN. LAWS ch. 276, § 100; MINN. STAT. § 559.125; WYO. STAT. ANN. § 7-13-409; Collins v. New York State Div. of Parole, 674 N.Y.S.2d 145, 145-46 (App. Div. 1998); Senk v. Board of Pardons, 521 A.2d 532 (Pa. Commw. 1987) (files of state Board of Pardons not public records). See also Konigsberg v. Coughlin, 501 N.E.2d 1 (N.Y. 1986) (inmate given access to own files).

256. See, e.g., IND. CODE § 5-2-12-11; LA. REV. STAT. ANN. §§ 540-544; N.J. REV. STAT. § 2C:7-6; OR. REV. STAT. §§ 586-589. Similar provisions are included in the Federal Violent Crime Control and Law Enforcement Act of 1994, Pub. L. No. 103-322, 108 Stat. 1796 (codified at 42 U.S.C. § 14071). The constitutionality of these statutes has been challenged. See, e.g., Russell v. Gregoire, 124 F.3d 1079 (9th Cir. 1997) (Washington's community notification statute held constitutional); Artway v. Attorney Gen., 81 F.3d 1235 (3d Cir. 1996) (registration aspects of law held constitutional). See generally Schopf, *"Megan's Law": Community Notification and the Constitution*, 29 COLUM. J.L. & SOC. PROBS. 117 (1995).

257. Mitchell v. Borakove, 639 N.Y.S.2d 791, 792 (App. Div. 1996) (New York City Charter prohibits disclosure of autopsy records); Diaz v. Lukash, 624 N.E.2d 156, 158 (N.Y. 1993) (district attorney and close relatives of decedent may obtain autopsy report as of right, but other persons who "may be affected in a civil or criminal action" or anyone with a "substantial interest" in the autopsy report may be afforded access only with judicial approval); Globe Newspaper Co. v. Chief Med. Exmr., 533 N.E.2d 1356 (Mass. 1989) (autopsy report held to be medical record and exempt); Herald Co. v. Murray, 524 N.Y.S. 2d 949 (App. Div. 1988) (autopsy report and motor vehicle blood test result held not to be subject to disclosure); Galvin v. FOIC, 518 A.2d 64 (Conn. 1986) (autopsy reports exempt from disclosure); Dayton Newspapers v. Rauch, 465 N.E.2d 458 (Ohio 1984) (autopsy report held not subject to disclosure).

258. See Williams v. City of Mineola, 575 So. 2d 683 (Fla. App. 1991) (autopsy report and photos are public records); San Francisco Examiner v. Plummer, 19 MEDIA L. REP. (BNA) 1319 (Cal. Super. 1991) (autopsy reports of bridge collapse victims to be released); Kilgore v. R.W. Page Corp., 385 S.E.2d 406 (Ga. 1989) (coroner's reports not exempt); Denver Publ'g Co. v. Dreyfus, 520 P.2d 104 (Colo. 1974) (autopsy reports are public records open to inspection).

259. See, e.g., WASH. REV. CODE § 68.50.300 (coroner records may be withheld for 48 hours or until next-of-kin notified); Star Publ'g Co. v. Parks, 875 P.2d 837, 838 (Ariz. App. 1993) (autopsy

coroner's report is relevant to an ongoing law enforcement investigation, it will generally be exempted from mandatory disclosure.[260] Although surviving family members may have privacy interests, an individual's privacy rights generally end at death. As a result, the right of privacy tends not to exempt coroner's records from disclosure.[261] Nor do the requests of the victim's relatives to withhold suicide records alter their public nature.[262] And, while some jurisdictions permit the disclosure of autopsy photographs,[263] such access is not always required.[264]

§ 11-7(e). Medical Records.

Medical records are nearly universally exempt from disclosure, either by special statute,[265] case law,[266] or statutory exemption from a state's public

---

reports are public records that are to be disclosed, pending notification of relatives, unless disclosure creates "specific risks with respect to a specific disclosure"); Freedom Newspapers, Inc. v. Bowerman, 739 P.2d 881 (Colo. App. 1987) (autopsy report may be exempted from disclosure if it would do "substantial injury to the public interest").

260. See Chap. 11-5(a)(6) *supra*; News-Press & Gazette Co. v. Cathcart, 974 S.W.2d 576, 580 (Mo. App. 1998) (autopsy report prepared by county medical examiner exempted from disclosure); Meyer v. ABC, Inc., 25 MEDIA L. REP. (BNA) 1605 (Colo. Dist.), *petition granted*, 25 MEDIA L. REP. (BNA) 224 (Colo. Dist. 1997) (autopsy report exempt from disclosure for 90 days on grounds that disclosure would do "substantial injury" to public interest in unimpeded criminal investigation); In re Meyer, 25 MEDIA L. REP. (BNA) 2244 (Colo. Dist. 1997) (autopsy report ordered disclosed with descriptive information redacted); Althaus v. Evansville Courier Co., 615 N.E.2d 441 (Ind. App. 1993) (autopsy report exempt from disclosure as investigatory record); Journal/Sentinel, Inc. v. Aagerup, 429 N.W.2d 772, 776 (Wis. App. 1988) (autopsy records containing undisclosed clues in unresolved homicide cases are exempt from disclosure); Ohio ex rel. Dayton Newspapers, Inc. v. Rauch, 465 N.E.2d 458 (Ohio 1984).

261. See e.g., Ohio ex rel. Findlay Publ'g Co. v. Schroeder, 669 N.E.2d 835, 838 (Ohio 1996); Swickard v. Wayne County Med. Exmr., 475 N.W.2d 304 (Mich. 1991) (disclosure of autopsy report and toxicology test results would not amount to "clearly unwarranted invasion of privacy" of deceased or his family).

262. See Ohio ex rel. Findlay Publ'g Co. v. Schoede, 669 N.E.2d at 838.

263. See, e.g., Williams v. City of Mineola, 575 So. 2d 683 (Fla. App. 1991) (autopsy and photos are public records).

264. See, e.g., CAL. CIV. PROC. CODE § 129 (prohibits release of photographs, or copies thereof, including instant photos and videotape, taken by coroner of a deceased party, except for use in a criminal proceeding pertaining to the death or if a court determines that good cause supports public disclosure).

265. See, e.g., CAL. CIV. CODE § 56-10 ("No provider of health care shall disclose medical information regarding a patient of the provider without first obtaining an authorization...."); MASS. GEN. LAWS ch. 111, § 70E(b) (patient has right to confidentiality of records); *Id.* ch. 111, § 70 (treatment records are only available to patients to whom they pertain and are expressly outside scope of public records law).

266. Where medical records are not clearly exempted in the open records laws, courts have generally not required disclosure. See, e.g., Mitchell v. Greenburg, 640 So. 2d 1367 (La. App. 1994) (juvenile rape attempt victim's medical records excepted from disclosure); Horne v. Patton, 287 So. 2d 824, 829-30 (Ala. 1973) (patient records exempt from disclosure due to physician-patient privilege); Hagin v. Department of Motor Vehicles, 588 N.E.2d 750 (N.Y. 1992)

records law.[267] Medical examinations required for employment promotions are usually exempt from disclosure as well.[268]

§ 11-7(f). Financial Information.

Many categories of financial records maintained by a state have been declared exempt from mandatory public access by statute, due to the perceived potential abuse of such information by requesters.[269]

§ 11-7(f)(1). Business Records.

Business records are typically available to the public pursuant to state law,[270] barring an applicable exemption, such as palpable harm to the corporation the

---

(information in driver's license application regarding disabilities exempt as medical history); Houghton v. Franscell, 870 P.2d 1050, 1054-55 (Wyo. 1994) (hospital records exempt from disclosure); Guy Gannett Publ'g Co. v. University of Maine, 555 A.2d 470 (Me. 1989) ("medical information of any kind" contained in public employee personnel records is exempt); Short v. Board of Managers, 442 N.E.2d 1235 (N.Y. 1982) (Public Health Laws and Social Services Laws support denial of access to medical records, with no segregation of exempt material required); Montana Human Rights Div. v. City of Billings, 649 P.2d 1283, 1287 (Mont. 1982) (medical and chemical or alcohol dependency problems contained in employment records are to remain private if employee subjectively expected the information would remain private and if that expectation is reasonable).

267. See, e.g., 5 ILL. COMP. STAT. 140/7(aa), (b)(I); CAL. GOV'T CODE § 6254(c); N.Y. PUB. OFF. LAW § 89(2)(b)(ii); MICH. COMP. LAWS § 15.243(1)(m) (Michigan FOIA exempts "[m]edical, counseling, or psychological facts or evaluations concerning an individual if the individual's identity would be revealed by a disclosure of those facts or evaluation."); New York Times Co. v. New York State Dep't of Health, 660 N.Y.S.2d 810, 814 (Sup. Ct. 1997) (medical information that is traceable to and/or closely connected with particular individual, such as patient's name, address, social security number, medicaid number, medicare number, medical record number, admit number, patient identification number and room number, exempt from disclosure, though physician identifiers may be disclosed). See also Robinson v. Merritt, 375 S.E.2d 204 (W. Va. 1988) (Worker's Compensation Committee records revealing types of injuries sustained withheld under medical file exemption to state Freedom of Information Act).

268. See, e.g., FLA. STAT. § 119.07(3)(c); Dickerson v. Hayes, 543 So. 2d 836 (Fla. App. 1989).

269. See, e.g., ALA. CODE § 40-1-33 (tax documentation and information gathered for assessment of taxes); CAL. GOV'T CODE § 6254(i) & (n) (tax information and statements of net worth in connection with application for license or permit); FLA. STAT. §§ 112.21(1), 112.215(7) (information concerning participants in tax-sheltered annuities); MD. CODE ANN., STATE GOV'T § 10-617(f); OHIO REV. CODE ANN. §§ 5703.21, 718.07 (tax information).

270. See Freedom Newspapers, Inc. v. Denver & Rio Grande W. R.R., 731 P.2d 740 (Colo. App. 1986) (business record in custody of state agency relevant to receipt or expenditure of public funds is public record); San Gabriel Valley Tribune v. Superior Ct., 192 Cal. Rptr. 415 (Ct. App. 1983) (business records are open if used as basis for public decisionmaking).

records of which are to be disclosed,[271] or impairment of the government's future ability to gain necessary information.[272]

§ 11-7(f)(2). Financial Data.

Tax files[273] and personal financial statements[274] are generally deemed to be exempt from mandatory public access requirements imposed by state open records laws.[275] Although California requires the disclosure of financial information that is the basis for public decisionmaking,[276] other jurisdictions have concluded that "commercial or financial information voluntarily provided to an agency for use in developing governmental policy and upon a promise of con-

---

271. See generally D.C. CODE ANN. § 1-1524(a)(1) (business records exempt to extent that disclosure would result in substantial harm to competitive position of person from whom information obtained); 5 ILL. COMP. STAT. 140/7(1)(g), (h), (i), (k), (p) & (r) (records exempt if competitive harm would result from disclosure); N.Y. PUB. OFF. LAW § 87(2)(d) (agency may only deny access if information is a trade secret or if disclosure would cause substantial injury to an enterprise subject to regulation).

272. See International Bhd. of Elec. Workers Local 68 v. Denver Metro. Major League Baseball Stadium Dist., 880 P.2d 160, 166 (Colo. App. 1994).

273. See CAL. GOV'T CODE § 6254(i); COLO. REV. STAT. § 39-21-113(4)(a); CONN. GEN. STAT. § 1-19(b)(10); VA. CODE ANN. § 2.1-342(B)(3); W. VA. CODE § 11-10-5(d); Tartan Oil Corp. v. New York Dep't of Tax. & Fin., 668 N.Y.S.2d 76, 78 (App. Div. 1998); Bowers v. Shelton, 453 S.E.2d 741, 745 (Ga. 1995) (criminal investigative file regarding taxpayer consisted of confidential tax information which was not subject to disclosure); A & T Consultants, Inc. v. Sharp, 904 S.W.2d 668, 676 (Tex. 1995) (Tax Code prevents disclosure of data "obtained" or "derived" from taxpayer); Daily Gazette Co. v. Caryl, 380 S.E.2d 209 (W. Va. 1989). But see Wallace v. Guzman, 687 So. 2d 1351, 1353 (Fla. App. 1997) (housing authority's application that included tax records from authority's members not exempt from public disclosure); Wiggins v. McDevitt, 473 A.2d 420 (Me. 1984) (sheriff's tax return containing fee and mileage charges related to public business and therefore not exempt).

274. See Ohio ex rel. Plain Dealer v. Ohio Dep't of Ins., 687 N.E.2d 661, 675 (Ohio 1997); Sublette County Rural Health Care Dist. v. Miley, 942 P.2d 1101 (Wyo. 1997) (required financial reports of physicians submitted to health care agency under contracts governing their operation of clinic exempt); Bowers v. Shelton, 453 S.E.2d 741, 744 (Ga. 1995) (personal financial documents contained in criminal investigation file exempt); Marina Management Serv. v. Kentucky Cabinet for Tourism, 906 S.W.2d 318, 319 (Ky. 1995) (financial reports of privately owned corporation submitted to a public agency pursuant to a license agreement with the state for use in closed meetings were classified as confidential). But see Zubeck v. El Paso County Retirement Plan, 961 P.2d 597, 600 (Colo. App. 1998) (financial information generated by Retirement Plan Board itself not exempt); Union Leader Corp. v. New Hampshire Hous. Fin. Auth., 705 A.2d 725, 737 (N.H. 1997) (financial information not exempt because public interest in disclosure greater than developers' interest in keeping information confidential).

275. See CAL. GOV'T CODE § 6254(n); Ashley v. Washington State Pub. Disclosure Comm'n, 560 P.2d 1156 (Wash. App. 1977).

276. See San Gabriel Valley Tribune v. Superior Ct., 192 Cal. Rptr. 415 (Ct. App. 1983).

fidentiality will be exempt."[277] Financial information submitted by a private entity in an application to a government agency or in the process of its contractual dealings with the government are usually not subject to disclosure.[278] Candidates for elected office, public officers and government employees may be required to file financial information that may be disclosed to the public.[279]

§ 11-7(f)(3). Bank Records.

Pursuant to state banking laws, state banking agencies or departments maintain various bank records. Such bank records may include auditing and investigatory files as well as applications and supporting documentation filed under bank charter laws. Bank records in government possession are often exempt from disclosure pursuant to a specific exemption contained in a state's open records act[280] or the nondisclosure provisions of a state's banking laws,[281] or laws

---

277. MASS. GEN. LAWS ch. 4, § 7, cl. 26(g). See DEL. CODE ANN. § 29-10002(d)(2); HIP of New Jersey v. New Jersey Dep't of Banking & Ins., 707 A.2d 1044, 1051 (N.J. Super. 1998) (financial information "required by law" was not voluntarily submitted and therefore not exempt).

278. See KAN. STAT. ANN. § 45-221(17) (student financial aid application information is exempt from public disclosure); OKLA. STAT. tit. 51, § 24A.10 (pursuant to Open Records Act, state department of commerce may hold as confidential financial proposals and financial statement submitted by private person or entity seeking economic advice); People ex rel. Better Broadcasting Council, Inc. v. Keane, 309 N.E.2d 362 (Ill. App. 1974) (financial records filed with city by applicant for cable television franchise not public records and not subject to public disclosure). But see OHIO REV. CODE ANN. § 149.431 (non-profit organizations' financial statements submitted to government agency pursuant to state service contract law are deemed public records); Lewis v. Spurney, 456 So. 2d 206 (La. App. 1984) (pursuant to public records law, newspaper entitled to examine financial records of world's fair corporation because the corporation had received public money).

279. See GA. CODE ANN. § 21-5-50 (financial disclosure statements submitted to government agency by candidates for various elected offices are deemed public records and are subject to inspection and copying by the public); MD. CODE ANN., STATE GOV'T § 15-823 (financial disclosure statements of certain government officers are subject to public inspection); N.J. STAT. ANN. § 19:44B-2 (financial disclosure statements submitted by candidates for certain state-wide offices are deemed public records and are subject to public disclosure); WASH. REV. CODE § 42.17.440 (financial disclosure statements made pursuant to state campaign law are subject to public inspection and copying); Wallace v. Guzman, 687 So. 2d 1351 (Fla. App. 1997) (financial statements and tax records of members of county housing authority, and financial records of their spouses, which were submitted to state agency with application for state-chartered savings bank, are subject to public disclosure and inspection).

280. See, e.g., CAL. GOV'T CODE § 6254(d); IDAHO CODE § 9-340(11) & (21); LA. REV. STAT. ANN. § 44:4(4); VT. STAT. ANN. tit. 1, § 317 (information and records provided to Department of Banking in connection with resolving dispute are exempt from public inspection).

281. See, e.g., FLA. STAT. § 655.057 (active investigatory records maintained by state banking department are not subject to public disclosure); TEX. REV. CIV. STAT. ANN. art. 350, § 20; KAN. STAT. ANN. § 9-1712 ("All information the state bank commissioner generates in making an investigation or examination of a state bank or trust company shall be confidential information."); MISS. CODE ANN. § 81-14-167 (audit and investigatory records and account information of savings

governing a state treasury.[282] Some jurisdictions designate certain bank files as public records, subject to disclosure.[283] Other jurisdictions provide for disclosure of banking information under certain limited conditions,[284] often times giving the state's banking commissioner or department head discretion to decide whether certain bank records should be disclosed in the public interest.[285] New York, for example, has held that bank records gathered pursuant to a government investigation are exempt from disclosure unless the Superintendent of Banking determines that the public benefit of disclosure outweighs the potential harm.[286]

§ 11-7(f)(4). Contract Proposals and Bids.

Contract proposals or bids generally remain confidential until the contract has been awarded.[287] As a result, it is believed, potential abuse of the information by

---

banks are considered confidential and shall not be disclosed, if the records are confidential under federal law); MO. REV. STAT. § 369.099(2); Ottoway Newspapers v. Appeals Ct., 362 N.E.2d 1189 (Mass. 1977) (Commissioner of Banks statutorily relieved of any duty to disclose reports pertaining to bank operations to newspaper).

282. See, e.g., GA. CODE ANN. § 50-5A-11 (bank records of local government investment pool and bank account numbers and records under the control of Georgia's Office of the Treasury and Fiscal Services are not public records and are not subject to public inspection). Cf. OR. REV. STAT. § 295.018 (financial institutions named in records received or compiled by Oregon State Treasurer are exempt unless the public interest requires disclosure).

283. See, e.g., OKLA. STAT. tit. 6, § 208 (certain bank records, such as applications for state bank charters and supporting documentation, with the exception of personal financial records of individual applicants, are designated public records and are subject to inspection upon request).

284. See, e.g., 5 ILL. COMP. STAT. 140/7(1)(x) (exempts information contained in or related to reports prepared for a public body which regulates financial institutions or insurance companies, unless disclosure is required by state law).

285. See KAN. STAT. ANN. § 9-1712 (although information gathered by state bank commissioner pursuant to an investigation is considered confidential, commissioner has limited discretion to release such confidential information); OKLA. STAT. tit. 6, § 2027 (certain credit union records maintained by State Banking Department, which are not designated as public records, may be disclosed when "good cause exists" under discretion of the bank commissioner); IDAHO CODE § 26-1112 (Idaho Department of Finance may disclose information about a "problem bank" if it is "necessary or advisable" for the "good of the public," in the discretion of department director); GA. CODE ANN. § 7-1-70 (Georgia Department of Banking may provide public access to certain banking records if, in discretion of banking commissioner, records do not contain "sensitive information" and if disclosure would be in public interest).

286. See N.Y. BANKING LAW § 36(10). See also Carbondale Township v. Murray, 440 A.2d 1273 (Pa. Commw. 1982) (township's canceled checks held to be public records under state's Right to Know Law); Ohio ex rel. Plain Dealer Publ'g Co. v. Lesak, 457 N.E.2d 821 (Ohio 1984) (court ordered disclosure of certain records in bank account that were kept by public school athletic director in violation of state law).

287. See, e.g., FLA. STAT. § 119.07(3)(o) (sealed contract to remain closed until opened by agency); IDAHO CODE § 9-340(7) (contracts, proposals and bids become open records after contract is awarded); IND. CODE §§ 4-13.4-2-7, 4-13.4-5-2(b) (bids subject to public inspection after they are opened); N.Y. PUB. OFF. LAW § 87(2)(c) (agency may deny access if disclosure would impair

competing bidders is prevented.[288] Michigan's law, for example, requires that such documents be withheld from the public until the "opening of the bids or proposals, or if a public opening is not to be conducted, until the time for the receipt of bids or proposals has expired."[289]

§ 11-7(f)(5). Real Estate Appraisals.

When a state agency seeks to purchase real estate, it typically generates appraisals and other documents relating to anticipated or ongoing negotiations that lead to the transaction itself. Such documents will generally remain unavailable to the public until the contingent sale does or does not occur.[290] Maryland, however, limits its real estate exemption by authorizing public access to an appraisal undertaken by the owner of the property involved.[291] Massachusetts extends its exemption until litigation surrounding the transaction is complete or the statute of limitations for litigation relating to the transaction has run.[292] Michigan requires that, in the event an agreement is not reached, the information remains exempt from disclosure for three years.[293]

---

contract awards); Freedom Newspapers, Inc. v. Denver & Rio Grande W. R.R., 731 P.2d 740 (Colo. App. 1986) (contracts made by any government agency involving expenditure of public funds are open to public inspection); Nicita v. City of Detroit, 487 N.W.2d 814, 819 (Mich. App. 1992) (exemption for bids applies only to competitive bidding process).

288. See 5 ILL. COMP. STAT. 140/7(1)(h).

289. MICH. COMP. LAWS § 15.243(1)(k).

290. See, e.g., ARK. CODE ANN. § 25-19-105(b)(9)(A) (exempts files which, if disclosed, would give advantage to competitors or bidders); CAL. GOV'T CODE §§ 6254(h), 54956.8; CONN. GEN. STAT. § 1-19(b)(7); FLA. STAT. § 119.07(3)(a) (no right of inspection where agency seeks to acquire land until after such acquisition); GA. CODE ANN. § 50-18-72(a)(6); KY. REV. STAT. ANN. § 61.878(1)(f); R.I. GEN. LAWS § 38-2-2(4)(N). But see City of Chester v. Getek, 572 A.2d 1319 (Pa. Commw. 1990) (real estate appraisals constitute "public records" subject to disclosure under Right-to-Know Act). Records containing information regarding the sale or lease of public land are generally open to the public. See ALA. CODE § 9-15-78.

291. See MD. CODE ANN., STATE GOV'T § 10-618(e). See also WYO. STAT. ANN. § 16-4-203((b)(iv) (contents of the appraisal shall be available to the owner of the property or the property interest at any time); COLO. REV. STAT. § 24-72-204(2)(a)(IV) (contents of appraisal shall be available to owner of the property involved in condemnation proceeding).

292. See MASS. GEN. LAWS ch. 4, § 7, cl. 26(I)(2) & (3). See also Black v. Georgia Dep't of Transp., 417 S.E.2d 655 (Ga. 1992).

293. See MICH. COMP. LAWS § 15.243(1)(k)(ii) (appraisal documents closed for three years unless litigation has not yet terminated). See also WASH. REV. CODE § 42.17.310(g) (in no event shall disclosure be denied for more than three years after appraisal).

§ 11-7(f)(6). Audits of Public Offices.

In general, audits of public offices, as well as drafts and other papers relating to such audits, are viewed as public records that are subject to disclosure.[294] Such information is subject to disclosure even where the audit was performed by a private entity on behalf of a public office.[295] The disclosure of records that are in active use by an auditor may be delayed.[296]

§ 11-7(g). Educational Records.

The availability of educational records under state public records laws varies greatly. Some states generally keep such records closed to the public, with only a few exceptions,[297] such as university records that pertain to the expenditure of government funds.[298] Other states have chosen to make state-funded universities or colleges generally subject to their open records laws,[299] though federal law

---

294. See, e.g., Bedingfield v. Birmingham News Co., 595 So. 2d 1379 (Ala. 1992); Ohio ex rel. Gannett Satellite Info. Network v. Petro, 685 N.E.2d 1223, 1227 (Ohio 1997). But see TEX. GOV'T CODE ANN. § 522.116 (audit working paper of state auditor exempt from disclosure).

295. See, e.g., Swaney v. Tilford, 898 S.W.2d 462 (Ark. 1995) (working papers of private auditors hired by state deemed public records); Ohio ex rel. Mazzaro v. Ferguson, 550 N.E.2d 464 (Ohio 1990) (city audit begun by state auditor and completed by private independent auditor deemed public record).

296. See, e.g., LA. REV. STAT. ANN. § 44:33(B) (if, at time of application, public record is deemed in active use, the custodian shall fix day and hour within three days for its disclosure); Ferguson v. Stephens, 623 So. 2d 711 (La. App. 1993).

297. See, e.g., CAL. EDUC. CODE § 49076 ("[a] school district is not authorized to permit access to pupil records to any person without written parental consent or under judicial order"); FLA. STAT. § 228.093(3)(d) (each student has right of privacy in his or her own records). See also Gibson v. Illinois State Bd. of Educ., 683 N.E.2d 894 (Ill. App. 1997) (names and addresses of all freshmen admitted or all students admitted are not personal information and is outside exemption); Florida State Univ. v. Hatton, 672 So. 2d 576 (Fla. App. 1996) (disciplinary investigation records containing identifying information about students held exempt); Ohio ex rel. Miami Student v. Miami Univ., 680 N.E.2d 956 (Ohio), cert. denied, 522 U.S. 1022 (1997) (records of student disciplinary proceedings deemed not education records and subject to disclosure because they did not contain education-related information such as grades or other academic data and were unrelated to financial aid or academic performance); Wisconsin ex rel. Blum v. Board of Educ., 565 N.W.2d 140, 143 (Wis. App. 1997) (interim grades are pupil records exempted from disclosure). But see Lieber v. Board of Trustees, 680 N.E.2d 374, 378 (Ill. 1997) (request for names and addresses of individuals accepted to attend university, but not yet enrolled, held outside exemption protecting personal information maintained with respect to students or other individuals receiving educational services from public body); Oregon County R-IV Sch. Dist. v. LeMon, 739 S.W.2d 553 (Mo. App. 1987) (school district required to release names, addresses and telephone numbers of all its students).

298. See DEL. CODE ANN. tit. 29, § 10002(g).

299. See, e.g., 5 ILL. COMP. STAT. 140/2(a) (state universities, colleges, and school districts fall within definition of "public body" for purpose of open records statute); MICH. COMP. LAWS § 15.232(b)(iii) (school districts are "public bodies" and subject to Freedom of Information Act); Red & Black Publ'g Co. v. Board of Regents, 427 S.E.2d 257 (Ga. 1993); Booth Newspapers, Inc.

potentially restricts the ability to access student files through such legislation.[300] Records of student disciplinary proceedings generally may be made available to the public.[301]

§ 11-7(h). Election Records.

Election records and results are universally made available under open records laws,[302] though certain related materials may be exempt from mandatory disclosure[303] and other materials may not be made available for copying.[304] Due to the sheer number of available documents, the costs of copying some election records, such as voter registration lists, may be high.[305]

---

v. University of Michigan Bd. of Regents, 507 N.W.2d 422 (Mich. 1993); Davis, *Scaling the Ivory Tower: State Public Records Laws and Presidential Searches*, 21 J.C. & U.L. 353 (1994) (state courts have ruled that a public university meets the definition of "state agency" under states' respective public-records laws).

300. See 20 U.S.C. § 1232g-i (school receiving federal funds may not disclose certain information about their students that is "personally identifiable" without written consent of the parents, or the student, if over 18 years of age); Red & Black Publ'g Co. v. Board of Regents, 427 S.E.2d 257, 261 (Ga. 1993) (release of records of student organization court dealing with hazing charges against social fraternities not prohibited by federal law); Kirwan v. Diamondback, 721 A.2d 196 (Md. 1998). See generally Daggett, *Bucking Up* Buckley I: *Making the Federal Student Records Statute Work*, 46 CATH. U. L. REV. 617 (1997).

301. See Ohio ex rel. Miami Student v. Miami Univ., 680 N.E.2d 956 (Ohio 1997) (records of student disciplinary proceedings are not exempt as education records).

302. See, e.g., CAL. ELEC. CODE §§ 606, 17120, 17122; 62 Md. Op. Att'y Gen. No. 396 (1977); Donrey Media Group v. Ikeda, 959 F. Supp. 1280 (D. Haw. 1996) (statute that permitted political parties access to voter registration records while denying access to press violates equal protection); Blaylock v. Staley, 732 S.W.2d 152 (Ark. 1987) (voter registration lists open to public); Rentz v. City of Moultrie, 203 S.E.2d 216 (Ga. 1974) (special election petition is public record). But see Milton v. Hayes, 770 P.2d 14 (Okla. 1989) (access to election material determined exclusively by Election Code). See also Libertarian Party of Indiana v. Board of Voter Registration, 778 F. Supp. 1458 (S.D. Ind. 1991) (statute permitting major political parties access to computer tape of voter registration lists and denying same access to non-major political parties violates First Amendment and equal protection).

303. See, e.g., FLA. STAT. § 106.25(5) (complaints filed with election governing board exempt); Laudig v. Board of Voter Registration, 585 N.E.2d 700 (Ind. App. 1992) (board of voter registration not required to disseminate voter registration lists).

304. See, e.g., FLA. STAT. § 98.211 (public may examine, but not copy, voter registration books).

305. See Phoenix Newspapers v. Arizona, 927 P.2d 340 (Ariz. App. 1996) (court upheld statutory charge of $.10 per voter for a registration list, though political organizations were provided list without cost).

§ 11-7(i). Trade Secrets and Proprietary Information.

Most states exempt trade secrets from disclosure under their open records statutes.[306] In addition, in many states, agencies may withhold information, such as lists of names and addresses, that will be used for mailing lists and other commercial purposes.[307] Some states, however, permit access to such information.[308]

§ 11-7(j). Vital Statistics.

Records containing vital statistics, such as birth and death certificates, are generally not available for public inspection.[309] Adoption records, due to their

---

[306]. See Chap. 11-5(a)(3) *supra*; CAL. GOV'T CODE §§ 6254.7(d), 6254.15; COLO. REV. STAT. §§ 8-1-115, 25-8-405; CONN. GEN. STAT. § 1-19(b)(5); D.C. CODE ANN. § 1-1524(a)(1); FLA. STAT. § 199.07(3)(q); IDAHO CODE § 9-340(4)(a)(i) & (ii); IND. CODE § 5-14-3-4(a)(4); MICH. COMP. LAWS § 15.243(g); N.C. GEN. STAT. § 132-1.2(1) & (4); S.C. CODE ANN. § 30-4-40(1); TEX. GOV'T CODE ANN. § 552.110.

[307]. See, e.g., KAN. STAT. ANN. § 21-3914; N.Y. PUB. OFF. LAW § 89(2)(b)(iii); WASH. REV. CODE § 42.17.260(5); US W. Communications, Inc. v. Office of Consumer Advocate, 498 N.W.2d 711, 714 (Iowa 1993); Empire Realty Corp. v. New York State Div. of Lottery, 657 N.Y.S.2d 504 (App. Div. 1997) (request by company that makes lump-sum payments for lottery prize winnings for list of names and cities of lottery winners, but not their addresses, did not fall within commercial exemption). See Person-Wolinsky Assocs. v. Nyquist, 377 N.Y.S.2d 897 (Sup. Ct. 1975); McMullan v. Wohlgemuth, 308 A.2d 888 (Pa.), *appeal dismissed*, 415 U.S. 970 (1973); Note, *Out of the Sunshine and into the Shadows: Six Years of Misinterpretation of the Personal Privacy Exemption of the Kentucky Open Records Act*, 71 KY. L.J. 853 (1982-83); Note, *Confidentiality and Dissemination of Personal Information: An Examination of State Laws Governing Data Protection*, 41 EMORY L. REV. 1185 (1992). A governmental entity may also attempt to prevent private persons from using a public records act to appropriate potentially valuable intellectual property for private gain. See WASH. REV. CODE § 42.17.301(1)(h) (excludes from disclosure certain valuable formulae, designs, drawings and research data); Progressive Animal Welfare Soc'y v. University of Washington, 884 P.2d 592, 599 (Wash. 1994) (Public Records Act protects recently acquired intellectual property from being converted to private gain).

[308]. See, e.g., Dalton v. Idaho Dairy Prods. Comm'n, 684 P.2d 983 (Idaho 1984); Ohio ex rel. Milo's Beauty Supply Co. v. Ohio Bd. of Cosmetology, 361 N.E.2d 444 (Ohio 1977); MacEwan v. Holm, 359 P.2d 413 (Or. 1961); Hathaway v. Joint Sch. Dist. No. 1, 342 N.W.2d 682 (Wis. 1984).

[309]. See, e.g., DEL. CODE ANN. tit. 16, § 3110, tit. 29, § 10002(d)(6); FLA. STAT. §§ 382.025(2)(a), 63.162(2); OKLA. STAT. tit. 63, § 1-323(a); Katz v. Scott, 653 N.Y.S.2d 346, 347 (App. Div. 1997) (records relating to death as to which there was "indication of criminality" excluded from public inspection); Barvick v. Cisneros, 941 F. Supp. 1015 (D. Kan. 1996) (information such as place of birth and date of marriage falls within the privacy exception of Freedom of Information Act); Ohio ex rel. Findlay Publ'g Co. v. Schroeder, 669 N.E.2d 835 (Ohio 1996) (death records are public records); Arkansas Dep't of Health v. Westark Christian Action Council, 910 S.W.2d 199 (Ark. 1995) (reports of aborted pregnancies exempt from disclosure); Eugene Cervi & Co. v. Russell, 519 P.2d 1189 (Colo. 1974) (vital statistics records not subject to Open Records Act); Yeste v. Miami Herald Publ'g Co., 451 So. 2d 491 (Fla. App. 1984) (medical certification of cause of death in death certificate held confidential); Home News v. New Jersey Dep't of Health, 677 A.2d 195 (N.J. 1996) (newspaper's interest in obtaining cause of death out-

§ 11-7(k) ACCESS TO STATE GOVERNMENT RECORDS § 11-7(k)

perceived sensitive and confidential nature, are often specifically exempted from disclosure.[310] Disclosure of social security numbers is prohibited by federal law.[311] As a result, state records containing social security numbers may not be disclosed.[312] States vary as to the disclosure of marriage certificates.[313]

§ 11-7(k). Motor Vehicle Records.

Motor vehicle documents such as driver's license applications, driver's licenses, vehicle titles, vehicle licenses and driver's records are generally considered public records that must be disclosed pursuant to state public records laws.[314] The public has traditionally been accorded full access to motor vehicle information.[315] As a general rule, the names and addresses contained in motor vehicle records have been released.[316] Personal information falling within statutory exemptions or limitations has typically been redacted from the requested record.[317] Information relating to medical history, age, height or social security number has often been deemed an unwarranted invasion of personal privacy and removed from the document before its release.[318] Due to purported

---

weighed public interest in confidentiality where no sensitive medical condition was implicated); Scottsdale Unified Sch. Dist. No. 48 v. KPNX Broadcasting Co., 955 P.2d 534 (Ariz. 1998) (disclosure of teachers' birth dates properly withheld from media because privacy interest of teachers outweighed public interest in disclosure).

310. See, e.g., DEL. CODE ANN. tit. 29, § 10002(d)(3); OHIO REV. CODE ANN. § 149.43(A)(1)(d). See generally Lum, *Privacy v. Secrecy: The Open Adoption Records Movement and Its Impact on Hawaii*, 15 U. HAW. L. REV. 483 (1993); Weiss, *Ohio House Bill 419: Increased Openness in Adoption Records Law*, 45 CLEV. ST. L. REV. 101 (1997).

311. See 42 U.S.C. § 405.

312. See Tribune-Review Publ'g Co. v. Allegheny County Hous. Auth., 662 A.2d 677, 683 (Pa. Commw. 1995).

313. See, e.g., ALA. CODE § 22-9A-21(e) (nonrestricted public record); ARK. CODE ANN. §§ 20-18-102, 20-18-304 (exempt from disclosure); FLA. STAT. § 382.025(4) (copies may be obtained by any person); IOWA CODE § 144.43; NEV. REV. STAT. § 122.040(6) (open record); S.D. CODIFIED LAWS § 34-25-1 (open record); Gannett Co. v. City Clerk's Office, 596 N.Y.S.2d 968 (Sup. Ct.), *aff'd*, 604 N.Y.S.2d 848 (App. Div. 1993) (disclosure of names of marriage license application to journalistic organization is invasion of personal privacy).

314. See, e.g., Robert v. Mississippi Republican Party, 465 So. 2d 1050 (Miss. 1985); Hanig v. Department of Motor Vehicles, 588 N.E.2d 750, 753 (N.Y. 1992); Ohio ex rel. Patterson v. Ayers, 171 N.E.2d 508, 509 (Ohio 1960).

315. See, e.g., Direct Mail Serv., Inc. v. Registrar of Motor Vehicles, 5 N.E.2d 545 (Mass. 1937); Robert v. Mississippi Republican Party, 465 So. 2d 1050, 1051 (Miss. 1985); Stewart v. Maybury, 3 P.2d 138, 139 (Wash. 1931).

316. See, e.g., Perkey v. Department of Motor Vehicles, 721 P.2d 50, 54 (1986); Doe v. Registrar of Motor Vehicles, 528 N.E.2d 880, 882 (Mass. App. 1988).

317. See, e.g., Department of Highway Safety & Motor Vehicles v. Krejci Co., 570 So. 2d 1322, 1323 (Fla. App. 1990) (driver's license photographic records are exempt from public inspection).

318. See, e.g., Doe v. Registrar of Motor Vehicles, 528 N.E.2d 880 (Mass. App. 1988); Hanig v. Department of Motor Vehicles, 588 N.E.2d 750, 753 (N.Y. 1992).

abuses of information obtained from motor vehicle records, however, some states restricted the dissemination of such information to specified recipients.[319]

These perceived abuses also caused Congress to pass the Driver's Privacy Protection Act ("DPPA") in 1997.[320] The DPPA makes it unlawful for a state department of motor vehicles to "knowingly disclose or otherwise make available to any person or entity personal information[321] about any individual obtained by the department in connection with a motor vehicle record."[322] The Act permits the disclosure of such information for limited purposes such as government functions, law enforcement, safety and product notifications.[323] State departments of motor vehicles are permitted to disclose personal information for other purposes only if the department has provided "clear and conspicuous" notice on its documents that such information may be disclosed, with an opportunity for individuals to prohibit such disclosures.[324] The state also has the ability to rent or sell such information in bulk for purposes of surveys, marketing and solicitations, but only if individuals are provided an opportunity to prohibit the use of their own information.[325] The Act restricts the manner in which third parties are permitted to use, sell or otherwise re-disclose personal information obtained pursuant to the DPPA's exceptions.[326]

Any state department of motor vehicles "that has a policy or practice of substantial noncompliance" with the Act is subject to a fine of up to $5,000 a day for each day of substantial noncompliance.[327] Persons who knowingly violate the Act are subject to criminal fines.[328] An individual whose personal information has been used in violation of the Act is entitled to bring a civil action against the person who knowingly obtained, disclosed or used the

---

319. See CAL. VEH. CODE § 1808.21. Virginia was also prompted to pass similar legislation. See VA. CODE ANN. § 46.2-208.

320. See 18 U.S.C. §§ 2721-2725. See generally Watkins, *The Driver's Privacy Protection Act: Congress Makes a Wrong Turn*, 49 S.C. L. REV. 983 (1998).

321. Personal information is defined by the Act as "information that identifies an individual, including an individual's photograph, social security number, driver identification number, name, address (but not the 5-digit zip code), telephone number, and medical or disability information, but does not include information on vehicular accidents, driving violations, and driver's status." 18 U.S.C. § 2725(3).

322. *Id* § 2721(a). "Motor vehicle record" is defined as "any record that pertains to a motor vehicle operator's permit, motor vehicle title, motor vehicle registration, or identification card issued by a department of motor vehicles." *Id.* § 2725(1).

323. See *id.* § 2721(b).
324. *Id.* § 2721(b)(11).
325. See *id.* § 2721(b)(12).
326. See *id.* § 2721(c).
327. *Id.* § 2723(b).
328. See *id.* § 2723(a).

information.[329] The remedies established by the Act include a minimum of $2,500 in actual damages, punitive damages, attorneys fees and costs.[330]

A majority of states have complied with the Act by providing drivers with the ability to request that the state's department of motor vehicles keep their personal information confidential.[331] Other states have made such information exempt from disclosure.[332] A few states have excused journalists from these restrictions.[333] Some states have additionally increased the privacy protection of drivers by curtailing the sale of personal information contained in drivers, vehicle or title lists for commercial solicitation purposes.[334] Others have continued to seek the revenue derived from the sale of such records.[335]

The constitutionality of the DPPA has been challenged primarily on the grounds that the Act unlawfully requires states to create and maintain a system to enforce an unfunded federal mandate in violation of the Tenth Amendment's protection of state sovereignty and the Eleventh Amendment's prohibition of suits against states or their officials. The four federal courts of appeal that have addressed these suits have been evenly divided on the issue of whether the DPPA is constitutional.[336]

Only one appellate decision has addressed the First Amendment issues involved in the DPPA litigation. In *Travis v. Reno*,[337] the original plaintiffs argued that the DPPA violated the First Amendment by limiting their access to

---

329. See *id.* § 2724(a). A civil action against a state or its department of motor vehicles is not authorized by the Act because its definition of "person" excludes "a State or agency thereof." *Id.* § 2725(2).

330. See *id.* § 2724(b).

331. See, e.g., ALASKA STAT. § 28.10.505(e); COLO. REV. STAT. § 24-72-204(3.5); CONN. GEN. STAT. § 14-10; IND. CODE §§ 9-14-3.5-1 to 9-14-3.5-15; IOWA CODE § 321.11; ME. REV. STAT. ANN. tit. 29-A, §§ 255-256, 2102; MD. CODE ANN., STATE GOV'T § 10-616(p); N.D. CENT. CODE § 39-33-05(12); OHIO REV. CODE ANN. § 4501.27; S.C. CODE ANN. § 56-3-540; TENN. CODE ANN. §§ 55-25-101 to 55-25-112; TEX. TRANSP. CODE ANN. §§ 731.001-731.009; W. VA. CODE §§ 17A-2A-1 to 17A-2A-14.

332. See, e.g., ARIZ. REV. STAT. § 28-450; CAL. VEH. CODE §§ 1808.21-1808.47; DEL. CODE ANN. tit. 21, § 305; GA. CODE ANN. § 40-5-2; KAN. STAT. ANN. § 74-2012; NEV. REV. STAT. § 481.063; N.H. REV. STAT. ANN. § 260:14; N.M. STAT. ANN. § 66-2-7.1; OKLA. STAT. tit. 51, § 24A.5; VA. CODE ANN. § 46.2-208.

333. See, e.g., COLO. REV. STAT. § 24-72-204(3.5)(d); NEV. REV. STAT. § 481.063(5)(h).

334. See, e.g., R.L. Polk & Co. v. Ryan, 694 N.E.2d 1027 (Ill. App. 1998); 21 Ill. Reg. 466 (1997).

335. See Travis v. Reno, 163 F.3d 1000, 1002 (7th Cir. 1998) (state of Wisconsin annually derives approximately $8 million from the sale of its motor vehicle licensing records for use in creating mailing lists).

336. See Pryor v. Reno, 171 F.3d 1281 (11th Cir. 1999) (DPPA is unconstitutional); Travis v. Reno, 163 F.3d 1000 (7th Cir. 1998) (DPPA is constitutional); Oklahoma v. United States, 161 F.3d 1266 (10th Cir. 1998) (DPPA is constitutional); Condon v. Reno, 155 F.3d 453 (4th Cir. 1998), *cert. granted*, 119 S. Ct. 1753 (1999) (DPPA is unconstitutional).

337. 163 F.3d 1000 (7th Cir. 1998).

information in public records. The Seventh Circuit held that the Act did not violate the First Amendment on its face, finding that there is no constitutional right of access to particular government information.[338] As to whether a First Amendment-based claim that a particular record should be deemed constitutionally exempt from the Act would be successful, the Seventh Circuit stated that such a challenge could be brought only after a request for the record has been made by a person entitled to assert a constitutional claim and, if access is denied, that person sues the custodian who could have disclosed it.[339]

§ 11-7(*l*). Public Utility Records.

Some states make the records of public utilities, such as telephone records, generally unavailable to the public,[340] while others require that such records be available for public inspection.[341] Several states, including Illinois, have adopted specific exemptions concerning the records of public utilities,[342] and still others, such as California, apply general exemptions to such records and have withheld them from disclosure through case law.[343]

---

338. See *id.* at 1007 (citing Houchins v. KQED, Inc., 438 U.S. 1, 14 (1978)).
339. 163 F.3d at 1007.
340. See KAN. STAT. ANN. § 45-221(a)(26); VA. CODE ANN. § 2.1-342(B)(29); In re Maxfield, 945 P.2d 196 (Wash. 1997) (consumer's electric consumption records constitutionally protected from disclosure); Hunerjager v. Dixie Elec. Membership Corp., 434 So. 2d 590, 591 (La. App. 1983) (financial records of electric service-providing cooperative held not open); Kan. Op. Att'y Gen. No. 85-175 (1985) ("[A]s the electric cooperatives . . . are not legislative or administrative bodies or agencies of the state, or political and taxing subdivisions thereof, and do not receive public funds, they are not subject to the Kansas Open Meetings Act.").
341. See Tennesssean v. Electric Power Bd. of Nashville, 979 S.W.2d 297 (Tenn. 1998) (city electric utility was required to disclose to newspaper its customers' names, addresses, and telephone numbers); Concerned Ratepayers Ass'n v. Public Utility Dist. No. 1, 960 P.2d 466 (Wash. App. 1998); City of Springfield v. Events Publ'g Co., 951 S.W.2d 366, 372 (Mo. App. 1997) (city required to reveal requested names and addresses of all new utility customers except residential customers who requested confidentiality); Woznicki v. Erickson, 549 N.W.2d 699, 701-02 (Wis. 1996) (telephone records not exempt from open records law when held by district attorney); Detroit News, Inc. v. City of Detroit, 516 N.W.2d 151 (Mich. App. 1994) (mayor's telephone records to and from his office and residence held public records); PG Publ'g Co. v. County of Washington, 638 A.2d 422 (Pa. Commw. 1994) (county official's itemized cellular telephone bills subject to disclosure, so long as officials were able to redact items involved in investigation); Fla. Op. Att'y Gen. No. 74-35 (1974) (records of publicly owned and operated utilities are open, unless otherwise exempt). But see FLA. STAT. § 119.07(3)(w) (customer lists given to the government by telecommunications companies exempt).
342. See 5 ILL. COMP. STAT. 140/7(y) (exempts information restricted under 1921 Public Utilities Act); WASH. REV. CODE § 42.17.310(1)(v) (public utility customer addresses and telephone numbers may be withheld).
343. See Rogers v. City of Burbank, 23 Cal. Rptr. 2d 412 (Ct. App. 1993) (reimbursed telephone records of Burbank City Council members exempt from disclosure under deliberative process exemption).

§ 11-7(m). Litigation Records.

Records concerning litigation involving public entities are generally deemed to be subject to disclosure.[344] Such disclosure may be required even though the requesting party is also involved in litigation with the public entity.[345] Possession of records by a private party, such as an attorney hired by the public entity's insurance carrier, does not relieve the entity from its duties arising under a public records act.[346] Records that are the subject of a protective order are generally exempt from disclosure required by a public records act, so long as the court order is in force.[347] Other records generated by government entities or their attorneys concerning current or potential litigation may be exempt from disclosure as well.[348]

---

344. See, e.g., Poway v. Superior Ct., 73 Cal. Rptr. 2d 777 (Ct. App. 1998) (claims form filed in lawsuit against public entity not exempt from disclosure under Public Records Act); City of Los Angeles v. Superior Ct., 49 Cal. Rptr. 2d 35, 37 (Ct. App. 1996) (depositions generated in concluded litigation arising out of claims against city are subject to disclosure pursuant to Public Records Act); News Observer Publ'g Co. v. Wake County Hosp. Sys., 284 S.E.2d 542, 549-50 (N.C. App. 1981) (records concerning settlement of civil actions by nonprofit hospital held to be public records that must be disclosed); Ohio ex rel. Findlay Publ'g Co. v. Hancock County Bd. of Comm'rs, 684 N.E.2d 1222, 1224 (Ohio 1997) (settlement agreement in which public office is a party is public record); Daily Gazette Co. v. Withrow, 350 S.E.2d 738, 743 (W. Va. 1986) (settlement document in which one party is a public body, involving an act or omission in its official capacity, is public record).

345. See Central Michigan Univ. Supervisory-Tech. Ass'n, MEA/NEA v. Board of Trustees of Cent. Michigan Univ., 567 N.W.2d 696, 697 (Mich. App. 1997) ("The fact that discovery is available as a result of pending litigation between the parties does not exempt a public body from complying with the public records law."). But see Roberts v. City of Palmdale, 20 Cal. Rptr. 2d 330, 334 (Cal. 1993) (pending litigation exemption of Public Records Act "was primarily designed to prevent a litigant opposing the government from using the [Public] Records Act's disclosure provisions to accomplish earlier or greater access to records pertaining to pending litigation or tort claims than would otherwise be allowed under the rules of discovery").

346. See Ohio ex rel. Findlay Publ'g Co. v. Hancock County Bd. of Comm'rs, 684 N.E.2d 1222, 1225 (Ohio 1997) ("Government entities cannot conceal public records by delegating a public duty to a private entity."); Daily Gazette Co. v. Withrow, 350 S.E.2d 738, 744-45 (W. Va. 1986).

347. Ballard v. Herzke, 924 S.W.2d 652, 662 (Tenn. 1996).

348. See, e.g., CONN. GEN. STAT. § 1-19(b)(4) (disclosure is not required where document pertains "to strategy and negotiations with respect to pending claims or pending litigation to which the public agency is a party until such litigation or claim has been finally adjudicated or otherwise settled"); MO. REV. STAT. § 610.021(1) (authorizes withholding of records related to "[l]egal actions, causes of action or litigation involving a public governmental body and any confidential or privileged communications between a public governmental body or its representatives and its attorneys"); City of Stamford v. Freedom of Info. Comm'n, 696 A.2d 321 (Conn. 1997); Keddie v. Rutgers Univ., 689 A.2d 702, 708 (N.J. 1996) (under state Right to Know Law, attorney's bills and internally generated legal billing documents are not public records subject to disclosure because the law does not require that they "be made, maintained or kept on file"); Times-News Publ'g Co. v. North Carolina, 476 S.E.2d 450, 453 (N.C. App. 1996) (exhibits transmitted to district attorney's

Settlement agreements, even those containing confidentiality provisions,[349] are generally deemed public records subject to disclosure.[350] Courts have recognized that the public has an interest in knowing whether charges of official misconduct against a public official or employee have been tacitly admitted, as well as an interest in assessing the financial impact on the public of a settlement paid either with public funds or with insurance proceeds generated by publicly financed insurance premiums.[351] This public interest has typically been held to outweigh whatever privacy interests may be implicated by disclosure.[352] Where the settle-

---

office were exempt from disclosure despite the fact that at one point they were public records when in the hands of clerk of court).

[349]. See Ohio ex rel. Findlay Publ'g Co. v. Hancock County Bd. of Comm'rs, 684 N.E.2d 1222, 1225 (Ohio 1997) ("A public entity cannot enter into enforceable promises of confidentiality regarding public records."); Daily Gazette Co. v. Withrow, 350 S.E.2d 738, 746 (W. Va. 1986).

[350]. See IOWA CODE § 22.13; Register Div. of Freedom Newspapers, Inc. v. County of Orange, 205 Cal. Rptr. 92, 96 (Ct. App. 1984) (documents relating to settlement of private personal injury claim with public funds are subject to public inspection and disclosure); Pierce v. St. Vrain Valley Sch. Dist., 944 P.2d 646, 650 (Colo. App. 1997) (permitting enforcement of confidentiality provision in settlement agreement between school district and former superintendent "would be tantamount to allowing a public entity to create by contract a new exception to the disclosure requirements of the Open Records Act"); Dutton v. Guste, 395 So. 2d 683, 685 (La. 1981) (settlement agreements, which are not obtained or prepared in anticipation of litigation or in preparation for trial but in attempt to conclude litigation, are not exempt from disclosure); Librach v. Cooper, 778 S.W.2d 351, 354-55 (Mo. App. 1989) (settlement that was not a communication between school board and its attorneys was unlikely to reveal board's thought processes and would not unduly infringe on employee's legitimate privacy interests, ordered disclosed); Toth v. Disciplinary Bd., 562 N.W.2d 744, 749 (N.D. 1997) (open records law cannot be circumvented by confidentiality clause in settlement agreement); Yakima Newspapers, Inc. v. City of Yakima, 890 P.2d 544, 547 (Wash. App. 1995) (jurisdictions have uniformly held that settlement agreements are public records). But cf. Tuft v. City of St. Louis, 936 S.W.2d 113, 118 (Mo. App. 1997) ("Settlements have long been a favorite of the law and an agreement not to disclose the terms of the settlement is often an important factor in achieving a settlement in the first place.... [W]e discern no legislative intent to deprive governmental bodies of the same valuable settlement techniques available to and prized by other litigants, which include agreements to maintain confidentiality with respect to the terms of settlement.").

[351]. See, e.g., Morning Call, Inc. v. Lower Saucon Township, 627 A.2d 297 (Pa. Commw. 1993) (settlement agreement between public entity and private person is public record subject to disclosure when the settlement is paid with public money, even though funds were not paid directly to private party but through insurance carrier); Miami Herald Publ'g Co. v. Collazo, 329 So. 2d 333, 338 (Fla. App. 1976); Des Moines Indep. Community Sch. Dist. Pub. Records v. Des Moines Register & Tribune Co., 487 N.W.2d 666, 669 (Iowa 1992) ("[T]he outstanding characteristic of the settlement agreement was the fact that public funds were being paid to settle a private dispute."); Daily Gazette Co. v. Withrow, 350 S.E.2d 738, 743 (W. Va. 1986).

[352]. See, e.g., Anonymous v. Board of Educ., 616 N.Y.S.2d 867, 870-71 (Sup. Ct. 1994) (teacher had no reasonable expectation of privacy regarding settlement agreement placed in his personnel file where agreement contains teacher's admission of misconduct); Yakima Newspapers, Inc. v. City of Yakima, 890 P.2d 544, 548-49 (Wash. App. 1995) ("The fact a public body may not be able to keep the specific terms of a settlement agreement confidential does not have such a chilling effect on future settlements so as to affect the efficient administration of government.

ment is relevant to pending or potential litigation, however, access has been denied on the basis of attorney-client or attorney work-product privilege.[353]

§ 11-8. Administrative Appeals.

Every state open records law establishes an appellate procedure when a request has either been denied expressly by an agency or when the agency has delayed its response for a period exceeding the statutory limit.[354] A few jurisdictions tolerate some delay to permit an agency to obtain an advisory opinion regarding the requested record.[355]

Once an agency has denied a request, an administrative appeal of the decision may be required.[356] The low cost and relative speed of such an appeal make it a favored alternative to litigation. Several states, however, make no mention of an administrative appeal process in their open records laws.[357] Those states that

---

Indeed, if a public agency's settlement agreement cannot withstand public scrutiny, it may be flawed in the first place."); Lexington-Fayette Urban County Gov't v. Lexington Herald-Leader Co., 941 S.W.2d 469, 472 (W. Va. 1997). But see LaRocca v. Board of Educ., 602 N.Y.S.2d 1009, 1011 (Sup. Ct. 1993) (settlement agreement disposing of disciplinary charges against school principal without finding of guilt deemed employment record, disclosure of which would constitute unwarranted invasion of privacy).

353. See Tuft v. City of St. Louis, 936 S.W.2d 113, 117-18 (Mo. App. 1997) (settlement document that is clearly related to substantially likely potential litigation may be withheld from disclosure).

354. See MASS. GEN. LAWS ch. 66, § 10(b) (no response within 10-day statutory period constitutes constructive denial); Campbell v. Town of Machias, 661 A.2d 1133, 1135 (Me. 1995) ("A governmental body cannot moot a claim of violation of the [Freedom of Access] Act by making disclosure long after the original request."); De Corse v. City of Buffalo, 659 N.Y.S.2d 604 (App. Div. 1997) (City's failure to respond in timely manner to plaintiff's Freedom of Information Law request is deemed denial triggering petitioner's right to appeal); Tribune Co. v. Cannella, 458 So. 2d 1075 (Fla. 1984), *appeal dismissed*, 471 U.S. 1096 (1985) (unreasonable delay in responding to request deemed denial for purposes of further action).

355. See, e.g., TEX. GOV'T CODE ANN. §§ 552.301(a), 552.302; WYO. STAT. ANN. § 9-692.1 (agency may seek court's determination of document's status as public record); Buffalo News, Inc. v. Buffalo Enter. Dev. Corp., 644 N.E.2d 277 (N.Y. 1994); John P. v. Whalen, 429 N.E.2d 117 (N.Y. 1981).

356. New York, however, has determined that failure to pursue an administrative appeal will preclude a later lawsuit in most circumstances. See N.Y. PUB. OFF. LAW § 89(4)(a). See also City of Kingston v. Surles, 582 N.Y.S.2d 844 (App. Div. 1992); New York News Inc. v. Grinker, 537 N.Y.S.2d 770 (Sup. Ct. 1989) (failure to appeal denial administratively was excused because agency's public statements showed that appeal would be futile); Kurland v. McLaughlin, 505 N.Y.S.2d 967 (App. Div. 1986) (subsequent relief denied due to failure to exhaust administrative appeals); Johnson Newspaper Corp. v. Stainkamp, 463 N.Y.S.2d 122 (App. Div. 1983), *aff'd*, 463 N.E.2d 613 (N.Y. 1984).

357. See, e.g., ALA. CODE § 36-12-40; FLA. STAT. §§ 119.01-119.16; MICH. COMP. LAWS §§ 15.231-15.246.

have established an administrative appeal procedure have generally made it optional, rather than a bar to immediate litigation.[358]

§ 11-9. Litigation.

At times, the commencement of a judicial proceeding will be the sole avenue to pursue a realistic remedy for a denied public record request. Standing to initiate suit is typically granted to any party who has been denied access.[359] Although some statutes allow the commencement of suit in the place where the plaintiff resides,[360] more typically the suit is brought in the county where the office denying access is located.[361] Many states require that such suits "take precedence on the docket over all other causes and shall be assigned for hearing and trial at the earliest practicable date."[362]

An agency must generally support its denial of access with specific justification, not conclusory statements.[363] It is typically not sufficient justification that disclosure may embarrass government officials[364] or that the requested records are available from another source.[365] Similarly to litigation under the federal FOIA,[366] state courts may order an *in camera* review of materials that have not been disclosed.[367]

The most often used and readily available remedy in open records suits is the writ of mandamus or other injunctive order compelling disclosure by the agency

---

358. See, e.g., KY. REV. STAT. ANN. § 61.880(2) (permitting, but not requiring, administrative appeal); MD. CODE ANN., STATE GOV'T § 10-622; Campbell v. Town of Machias, 661 A.2d 1133, 1135 n. 3 (Me. 1995).

359. See 5 ILL. COMP. STAT. 140/11(a); KY. REV. STAT. ANN. § 61.882(1); N.Y. PUB. OFF. LAW § 89(4)(b).

360. See, e.g., 5 ILL. COMP. STAT. 140/11(b).

361. See CAL. GOV'T CODE § 6259; KY. REV. STAT. ANN. § 61.882(1); MD. CODE ANN., STATE GOV'T § 10-623(a)(1).

362. KY. REV. STAT. ANN. § 61-882(4). See also CAL. GOV'T CODE § 6258 ("earliest possible time"); FLA. STAT. § 19.11(1); 5 ILL. COMP. STAT. 140/11(h) (granting priority on dockets to open records law suits).

363. See Cranford v. Montgomery County, 481 A.2d 221 (Md. 1984); Farbman & Sons v. New York City Health & Hosp. Corp., 464 N.E.2d 437 (N.Y. 1984).

364. See Braun v. Taft, 201 Cal. Rptr. 654 (Ct. App. 1984); Laramie River Conservation Council v. Dinger, 567 P.2d 731 (Wyo. 1977).

365. See Wiggins v. McDevitt, 473 A.2d 420 (Me. 1984).

366. See Chap. 10-2(h) *supra*.

367. See Ohio ex rel. Clark v. Toledo, 584 N.E.2d 662 (Ohio 1992); Yakima Newspapers, Inc. v. City of Yakima, 890 P.2d 544, 549-50 (Wash. App. 1995) (decision determining whether *in camera* review of documents is necessary is reviewed only for abuse of discretion).

that has refused access.[368] California's statute affords courts the power to grant an *ex parte* order requiring disclosure immediately upon filing of a petition.[369]

Generally, compensatory or punitive damage awards are not available to a successful plaintiff. In the rare case, some form of bad faith in the government's refusal to release a record may result in a damages award.[370] Although some states mandate that attorneys fees be paid to a successful plaintiff,[371] many leave the awarding of fees to the discretion of the court.[372] Other states make an award of attorneys fees conditional upon explicit criteria set forth in their statutes.[373] The determination of reasonable attorneys fees generally parallels the analysis under the federal FOIA.[374] In some states, criminal actions may be instituted for a failure to disclose a nonexempt record.[375]

If an appeal is permitted following a trial court's denial of access to records, the normal appellate process typically applies.[376] Notable exceptions are Maryland, which offers an expedited appeals process,[377] and California, which

---

368. See CAL. GOV'T CODE § 6258; FLA. STAT. § 119.12(2); MD. CODE ANN., STATE GOV'T § 10-623(b)(3); Florida Soc'y of Newspaper Editors v. Florida Pub. Serv. Comm'n, 543 So. 2d 1262 (Fla. App. 1989).

369. See CAL. GOV'T CODE § 6259(a).

370. See, e.g., MD. CODE ANN., STATE GOV'T § 10-623(d) (punitive damages awarded for knowing refusal without basis); MICH. COMP. LAWS § 15.240(5) ($500 punitive damage award is available when a request is refused "capriciously or arbitrarily"); LA. REV. STAT. ANN. § 44:35(E) (custodian is personally liable for actual damages resulting from capricious or arbitrary failure to respond to public record request and for civil penalties not to exceed $100 per day where custodian is found to have unreasonably or arbitrarily failed to respond to request); WIS. STAT. § 19.37(3).

371. See CAL. GOV'T CODE § 6259(d) (court shall award attorneys fees to successful movant); LA. REV. STAT. ANN. § 44:35(D) (prevailing plaintiff shall be awarded reasonable attorneys fees and other costs of litigation, but such fees are at discretion of court where plaintiff prevails only in part); City of Springfield v. Events Publ'g Co., 951 S.W.2d 366, 374 (Mo. App. 1997) (opposing party's attorneys fees are to be paid when public governmental body brings declaratory judgment action regarding state Sunshine Law); Beth v. Garamendi, 283 Cal. Rptr. 829 (Ct. App. 1991).

372. See DEL. CODE ANN. tit. 29, § 10005(d) (court "may" grant attorneys fees to victorious plaintiff); MD. CODE ANN., STATE GOV'T § 10-623(f) (court has discretion to grant fees where plaintiff has "substantially prevailed"); Ohio ex rel. McGowan v. Cuyahoga Metro. Hous. Auth., 678 N.E.2d 1388 (Ohio 1997) (attorneys fees not awarded to pro se litigants); Ohio ex rel. Olander v. French, 680 N.E.2d 962, 964 (Ohio 1997) ("In granting or denying attorney fees, the court should consider the reasonableness of the government's failure to comply with the public records request and the degree to which the public will benefit from release of the records in question.").

373. See N.Y. PUB. OFF. LAW § 89(4) (grants attorneys fees to substantially prevailing litigant if the record is of significant public interest and agency lacked reasonable legal ground for refusing request).

374. See Kline & Sons v. Fallows, 478 N.Y.S.2d 524 (Sup. Ct. 1984); Chap. 10-2(h)(1) *supra*.

375. See, e.g., NEB. REV. STAT. § 84-712.09; TEX. GOV'T CODE ANN. § 552.353; Moore v. Collins, 897 S.W.2d 496 (Tex. App. 1995).

376. See Wait v. Florida Power & Light Co., 372 So. 2d 420 (Fla. 1979); Munroe v. Braatz, 549 N.W.2d 451, 453 (Wis. App. 1996).

377. See MD. CODE ANN., STATE GOV'T § 10-623(c).

has eliminated any right of appeal and substituted a discretionary writ procedure.[378]

---

[378] See also CAL. GOV'T CODE § 6259; Times Mirror Co. v. Superior Ct., 813 P.2d 240 (Cal. 1991) (interpreted 1990 amendment to statute to require appellate review on merits).

Chapter 12

NEWSGATHERING IN NONGOVERNMENTAL PLACES

§ 12-1. Introduction.
§ 12-2. Public Places.
  § 12-2(a). The Public Street.
  § 12-2(b). Public View.
§ 12-3. Crime and Disaster Scenes.
§ 12-4. Private Property.
  § 12-4(a). The Home.
  § 12-4(b). Public Institutions.
  § 12-4(c). Private Businesses.
    § 12-4(c)(1). Restaurants and Bars.
    § 12-4(c)(2). Public Areas Generally.
    § 12-4(c)(3). Private Areas Generally.
§ 12-5. Accompanying Authorized Individuals.
§ 12-6. Consent: Special Issues.
  § 12-6(a). Children and the Mentally Impaired.
  § 12-6(b). Inmates.

§ 12-1. Introduction.

Gathering the news from governmental sources or in governmental facilities has, as we have seen, spawned precedent, both common law and constitutional, delineating the press' and the public's right of access to such information and places.[1] In nongovernmental contexts, by contrast, the law has concerned itself largely with the news media's liability for its newsgathering activities and methods. In this chapter, we address those liability issues that relate most directly to the places in which the press gathers news and information. In the chapter that follows, we consider the media's potential liability for the manner in which it gathers the news.

From the outset, the courts have recognized that seeking out and reporting the news on government property implicates, albeit to varying degrees, a First Amendment-based interest in access to information. Newsgathering in nongovernmental venues, however, has largely given rise to a body of law rich in common law and statutory complexity, but decidedly underdeveloped in constitutional doctrine. Thus, in the following sections, we examine the common law and statutory aspects of newsgathering in places such as crime scenes, homes and private businesses, and places of public accommodation, as well as the nascent constitutional law that currently surrounds this jurisprudence.[2] In addi-

---

1. See Chap. 2 – Chap. 11 *supra*.
2. The discussion in this chapter is organized to reflect primarily the places in which the news media gathers information. The chapter that follows, in contrast, considers — largely by newsgathering technique — the manner in which news and information is collected. In both chapters, the

tion, we examine the unique issues raised when the press accompanies authorized individuals — such as law enforcement authorities — into otherwise private places, as well the role of consent in validating otherwise actionable press conduct in a variety of locations.

§ 12-2. Public Places.

§ 12-2(a). The Public Street.

The common law has long recognized that newsgathering from the public streets is, in the vast majority of circumstances, nonactionable. Even in the non-media context, the courts have declined to afford a cause of action to those who have been followed and observed in public.[3] The general view has been that, at least to the extent that such surveillance takes place "in the open on public thoroughfares" where the plaintiff's activities "could be observed by passers-by," the plaintiff "has exposed herself to public observation and therefore is not entitled to the same degree of privacy that she would enjoy within the confines of her own home."[4]

For the news media, this rule has typically not been altered by its use of cameras or video recording devices on the public streets.[5] Thus, in *Jackson v.*

---

various legal theories pursuant to which legislatures and the courts have evaluated journalistic conduct are addressed in these specific contexts. Many, though by no means all, of these legal theories have developed in the context of the common law (and occasional legislative codification) of invasion of privacy. In this regard, it should be noted that several American jurisdictions — including Indiana, Minnesota, New York, North Carolina, North Dakota, Texas, Virginia, and Wisconsin — have declined to recognize at least some causes of action typically denominated as a sub-species of the law of invasion of privacy. See, e.g., Doe v. Methodist Hosp., 690 N.E.2d 281 (Ind. 1997) (declining to recognize tort of public disclosure of private facts); Lake v. Walmart Stores, Inc., 582 N.W.2d 231 (Minn. 1998) (no cause of action for false light invasion of privacy); Arrington v. New York Times Co., 434 N.E.2d 1319 (N.Y. 1982), *cert. denied*, 459 U.S. 1146 (1983); Dunn v. Town of Emerald Isle, 722 F. Supp. 1309, 1314 (M.D.N.C. 1989), *aff'd*, 918 F.2d 955 (4th Cir. 1990) ("North Carolina has rejected . . . the 'false light' branch and the publication of private facts branch" of the invasion of privacy tort); City of Grand Forks v. Grand Forks Herald, 307 N.W.2d 572, 578 n.3 (N.D. 1981) ("Whether or not the tort of invasion of privacy exists under North Dakota law has not been determined."); Falwell v. Penthouse Int'l, 521 F. Supp. 1204, 1210 (W.D. Va. 1981) ("Virginia has never recognized a common law cause of action for invasion of privacy."); Cain v. Hearst Corp., 878 S.W.2d 577, 578 (Tex. 1994) (declining to recognize false light invasion of privacy tort); Zinda v. Louisiana Pacific Corp., 440 N.W.2d 548, 555 (Wis. 1989) (finding no cause of action for false light).

3. See, e.g., Forster v. Manchester, 189 A.2d 147 (Pa. 1963).

4. *Id.* at 150. See also RESTATEMENT (SECOND) OF TORTS § 652D, cmt. b (publication of a picture taken on a public street not an invasion of privacy).

5. See McClurg, *Bringing Privacy Law Out of the Closet: A Tort Theory of Liability for Intrusions in Public Places*, 73 N.C. L. REV. 989, 991-92 (1995) ("tort law currently provides little protection from intrusive videotaping, photography, or surveillance, so long as the activity occurs in a public place").

Playboy Enterprises, Inc.,[6] a federal district court dismissed plaintiffs' invasion of privacy claim, which was based on *Playboy* magazine's publication of a photograph depicting them on a public sidewalk with a female police officer who was kneeling on a sidewalk in an apparent attempt to help them fix a bicycle. Even though the photograph accompanied an article that also contained partially nude photos of the police officer, the court held that there had been no actionable intrusion because "the photograph of which plaintiffs complain clearly shows that [the] policewoman and plaintiffs were on a city sidewalk in plain view of the public eye."[7]

Similarly, in *Aisenson v. American Broadcasting Cos.*,[8] a California appellate court rejected the contention that the filming of the plaintiff, a judge, as he walked from his home to his car constituted an actionable invasion of privacy by intrusion. The court concluded that, "[i]n light of appellant's voluntary accession to a position of public trust, the social interest in allowing videotaped depictions of him, and the fact that appellant was photographed only while in public view," there was no invasion of his privacy as a matter of law.[9] Specifically, the court determined that the plaintiff's car and driveway, where he was filmed, "was in full public view from the street at the time he was videotaped," a fact that was not diminished by plaintiff's contention that "he could not be seen from the photographer's location unless an enhanced lens was being used."[10]

Other courts have reached essentially the same result. In *Cape Publications, Inc. v. Bridges*,[11] for example, a newspaper photographed the plaintiff as she emerged naked on to the street from her home, where she had been held hostage by her husband, holding only a dish towel to conceal her nudity. The court of appeals reversed a jury verdict in favor of the plaintiff on theories of invasion of privacy and intentional infliction of emotional distress, holding that the law "seems settled that where one becomes an actor in an occurrence of public interest, it is not an invasion of . . . privacy to publish her photograph with an account of such occurrence."[12] For analogous reasons, in *Arrington v. New York*

---

6. 574 F. Supp. 10, 11 (S.D. Ohio 1983).

7. *Id.* at 13 (citing RESTATEMENT (SECOND) OF TORTS § 652B, cmt. c). The tort of "intrusion," as defined in the RESTATEMENT (SECOND) OF TORTS, contemplates that "[o]ne who intentionally intrudes, physically or otherwise, upon the solitude or seclusion of another or his private affairs or concerns, is subject to liability to the other for invasion of his privacy, if the intrusion would be highly offensive to a reasonable person." RESTATEMENT (SECOND) OF TORTS § 652B. See also Miller v. National Broadcasting Co., 232 Cal. Rptr. 668 (Ct. App. 1986).

8. 269 Cal. Rptr. 379, 387 (Ct. App. 1990).

9. *Id.* at 388.

10. *Id.*

11. 423 So.2d 426 (Fla. App. 1982), *cert. denied*, 464 U.S. 893 (1983).

12. *Id.* at 427. See also Dempsey v. National Enquirer, Inc., 702 F. Supp. 927, 931 (D. Me. 1988) (no intrusion where reporter photographed and attempted to interview plaintiff "on a public thoroughfare").

Times Co.,[13] the New York Court of Appeals held that plaintiff, a businessman photographed on a public street, could not maintain a statutory or common law privacy claim against a magazine that published his photograph to illustrate an article about the "expanding black middle/professional class."[14]

The right of government to interfere with newsgathering on the public streets is severely limited as well. In *Fordyce v. City of Seattle*,[15] for example, the Ninth Circuit held that police officers could potentially be held liable, under federal statutory law,[16] for interfering with a journalist's ability to videotape a public protest march. Fordyce, who claimed to have been recording the event for broadcast on a public access cable television channel, was arrested for violating a state privacy statute,[17] after he recorded both "the activities of the police officers assigned to work the event" and "some sidewalk bystanders against their wishes."[18] He spent one night in jail and, after the charges against him were dismissed on motion of the prosecuting attorney, he initiated his own action for damages. The Ninth Circuit reversed the district court's grant of summary judgment for the defendants in part, holding that there were genuine issues of material fact "regarding whether Fordyce was assaulted and battered by a Seattle police officer in an attempt to prevent or dissuade him from exercising his First Amendment right to film matters of public interest."[19]

The same protections appear to govern, albeit less emphatically, the recording of conversations on the public streets in the course of newsgathering. In *Brooks*

---

13. 434 N.E.2d 1319 (N.Y. 1982), *cert. denied*, 459 U.S. 1146 (1983).

14. *Id.* at 1320. The court held both that New York does not recognize a cause of action for common law invasion of privacy and that the state's statutory cause of action is limited to uses of a plaintiff's likeness for "purely commercial" purposes. See *id.* at 1323 (citing N.Y. CIV. RIGHTS LAW §§ 50, 51) ("an inability to vindicate a personal predilection for greater privacy may be part of the price every person must be prepared to pay for a society in which information and opinion flow freely"). Nevertheless, the court declined to dismiss similar statutory claims against the photographer and the agency that employed him, at least at the pleadings stage, on the ground that each of them were "operating independently of the publisher" and arguably "'commercialized the photograph' in 'furtherance of [his] trade.'" 434 N.E.2d at 1323 (quoting Holmes v. Underwood & Underwood, 233 N.Y.S. 153 (App. Div. 1929)). For a critical look at the *Arrington* decision, see Richards, *Arrington v. New York Times Company: A Missed Opportunity to Recognize a Constitutional Right to Privacy of Personality*, 26 HOW. L.J. 1579, 1583 (1983) (considering the foundations for a constitutional right to privacy).

15. 55 F.3d 436 (9th Cir.), *judgment entered*, 907 F. Supp. 1446 (W.D. Wash. 1995).

16. See 42 U.S.C. § 1983.

17. 55 F.3d at 438 (citing WASH. REV. CODE § 9.73.030). The statute prohibits recording of private conversations without the consent of all participants. See Chap. 13-7(b) (discussing the application of such legislation to newsgathering activities).

18. 55 F.3d at 438.

19. *Id.* at 439.

v. American Broadcasting Cos.,[20] for example, the plaintiff alleged that a television reporter, accompanied by a crew carrying cameras and recording equipment, confronted him on a public street and, cameras rolling, began "to barrage" him with questions about his connections to a local judge. Among other causes of action, the plaintiff alleged that the use of cameras to record his statements constituted a violation of the federal wiretapping statute.[21] The trial court, affirmed by the Sixth Circuit, rejected the claim.

Initially, the court recognized that, although the "conversation did take place on a public street, there are questions as to whether Brooks knew the conversation was being recorded."[22] Thus, while the court professed "serious doubts as to whether Brooks could have had an expectation of total privacy," it nevertheless concluded that he may have had "a reasonable expectation of non-interception."[23] By the same token, however, the court recognized that, to recover under the federal statute, the plaintiff must prove that "interception of the oral communication was for the purpose of committing criminal or tortious act[s]."[24] In *Brooks*, the plaintiff alleged that the necessary illegal act resulted from defendants' violation of regulations issued by the Federal Communications Commission, which prohibit the use of certain recording devices "for the purpose of overhearing or recording the private conversations of others unless such use is authorized by all of the parties engaging in the conversation."[25] The trial court rejected this contention, holding that the "[e]mphasized language requires the conversation in question to be private and the court has already noted that the . . . conversation took place in public on an Akron street."[26] Thus, the court concluded, if a conversation takes place on a public street, it cannot properly be considered "private," even if there is a legitimate expectation that the conversation will not be surreptitiously intercepted.

Some courts have, however, recognized limitations governing the scope of newsgathering on the public streets. In the oft-cited case of *Galella v. Onassis*,[27]

---

20. 737 F. Supp. 431, 433 (N.D. Ohio 1990), *aff'd in part*, 932 F.2d 495 (6th Cir. 1991), *aff'd*, 999 F.2d 167 (6th Cir. 1993), *cert. denied*, 510 U.S. 1014 (1993).

21. See *id.* at 434 (citing 18 U.S.C. § 2510). See also Chap. 13-7(a)(2)(A) *infra* (discussing federal wiretapping statute and related case law).

22. 737 F. Supp. at 436.

23. *Id.*

24. *Id.* at 437 (citing 18 U.S.C. § 2511(2)(d)). See Boddie v. American Broadcasting Cos., 881 F.2d 267 (6th Cir. 1989), *cert. denied*, 493 U.S. 1028 (1990).

25. 47 C.F.R. § 2.701(a), *quoted in* Brooks v. American Broadcasting Cos., 737 F. Supp. at 437.

26. 737 F. Supp. at 437. But see Dickerson v. Raphael, 27 MEDIA L. REP. (BNA) 2215, 2216 (Mich. 1999) (holding that plaintiff, surreptitiously recorded in public park by her children, entitled to new trial under the Michigan eavesdropping statute, MICH. COMP. LAWS § 28.807, where children arranged to have recorded conversation simultaneously transmitted to television crew).

27. 487 F.2d 986 (2d Cir. 1973).

the Second Circuit roundly condemned a freelance photographer's effort to seek First Amendment protection for his campaign to photograph Jacqueline Kennedy Onassis and her children. Indeed, the court not only rejected Galella's own claim against three secret service agents for false arrest, malicious prosecution and interference with trade, it affirmed — albeit with some modification — the trial court's entry of an injunction restricting his ability to approach Mrs. Onassis and her children on the public streets.

Galella was a self-styled "paparazzo," a species of photographer who "make themselves as visible to the public and obnoxious to their photographic subjects as possible to aid in the advertisement and wide sale of their works."[28] In his pursuit of the Kennedy family, the trial court found that Galella:

> took pictures of John Kennedy riding his bicycle in Central Park across the way from his home. He jumped out into the boy's path, causing the [secret service] agents concern for John's safety .... Galella on other occasions interrupted Caroline at tennis, and invaded the children's private schools. At one time, he came uncomfortably close in a power boat to Mrs. Onassis swimming. He often jumped and postured around while taking pictures of her party notably at a theater opening but also on numerous other occasions. He followed a practice of bribing apartment house, restaurant and nightclub doormen as well as romancing a family servant to keep him advised of the movements of the family.[29]

At the request of Mrs. Onassis and the federal government, the trial court enjoined Galella from "harassing, alarming, startling, tormenting, [or] touching" Mrs. Onassis or her children and "from blocking their movements in the public places and thoroughfares, invading their immediate zone of privacy by means of physical movements, gestures or with photographic equipment and from performing any act reasonably calculated to place the lives and safety" of the family "in jeopardy."[30] After Galella violated that order, the trial court expanded it to require that he come no closer than within 100 yards of the family apartment or the children's school, 75 yards of the children themselves, and 50 yards of Mrs. Onassis.[31]

On appeal, the Second Circuit conceded that Mrs. Onassis was a public figure and "thus subject to news coverage."[32] Nevertheless, the court concluded that Galella's "action went far beyond the reasonable bounds of news gathering."[33] The court rejected Galella's assertion that there is "a wall of immunity protecting

---

28. *Id.* at 992.
29. *Id.*
30. *Id.* at 992-93.
31. *Id.*
32. *Id.* at 995.
33. *Id.*

newsmen from any liability for their conduct while gathering news," holding that "[c]rimes and torts committed in news gathering are not protected."[34]

Nevertheless, the Second Circuit also held that the trial court's injunction with respect to Mrs. Onassis was "broader than required to protect the defendant."[35] While the court of appeals agreed that "[r]elief must be tailored to protect Mrs. Onassis from the 'paparazzo' attack which distinguishes Galella's behavior from that of other photographers," it concluded that it could not "unnecessarily infringe on reasonable efforts to 'cover'" her.[36] Thus, the court modified the injunction to prohibit only:

> (1) any approach within twenty-five (25) feet of defendant or any touching of the person of the defendant . . .; (2) any blocking of her movement in public places and thoroughfares; (3) any act foreseeably or reasonably calculated to place the life and safety of defendant in jeopardy; and (4) any conduct which would reasonably be foreseen to harass, alarm or frighten the defendant.[37]

Relying on *Galella*, one federal district court enjoined a camera crew for the so-called "tabloid" television series *Inside Edition* from filming or audio recording the plaintiffs, two executives with a large health care company, and their children from public locations.[38] Defendants' activities had included photographing the plaintiffs' homes from a nearby driveway, following the plaintiffs and their children to work and school on public roads, and filming and attempting to record their conversations from a boat — with sophisticated microphones — while they visited the home of other family members.[39] The court enjoined the defendants from "engaging in conduct, with or without the use of cameras and sound equipment," which "invades" the privacy of plaintiffs or their children, "including but not limited to actions of: harassing, hounding, following, intruding, frightening, terrorizing or ambushing" them.[40]

Although the court confirmed that "[i]mplicit in the right to publish is the right to gather the news,"[41] it asserted that the First Amendment's framers

---

34. *Id.* (citing Branzburg v. Hayes, 408 U.S. 665 (1972); Dietemann v. Time, Inc., 449 F.2d 245 (9th Cir. 1971)).
35. 487 F.2d at 998.
36. *Id.*
37. *Id.*
38. See Wolfson v. Lewis, 924 F. Supp. 1413 (E.D. Pa. 1996). The complaint alleged causes of action sounding in "tortious stalking, harassment, trespass, intrusions upon seclusion and invasion of privacy." *Id.* at 1415-16.
39. See *id.* at 1422-31.
40. *Id.* at 1435.
41. *Id.* 1417 (citing Branzburg v. Hayes, 408 U.S. 665, 681 (1972) ("[W]ithout some protection for seeking out the news, freedom of the press could be eviscerated."); Houchins v. KQED, Inc., 438 U.S. 1, 11 (1978) (there is an "undoubted right to gather news 'from any source by means

"could not have imagined the existence of a television in most homes and the sophisticated tools available to T.V. journalists," including "cameras with powerful zoom lenses, video camcorders that simultaneously record pictures and sound," and "directional microphones with the capacity to pick up sound sixty yards away."[42] In the court's view, the "use of sophisticated video and recording equipment by T.V. journalists has increased the threat that a person's right to privacy may be violated" and the "television market for scandal and sensationalism has encouraged T.V. journalists to engage in forms of newsgathering that may bring about a clash between the right to privacy and freedom of the press."[43]

Under such circumstances, the court divined an exception to the general rule that the tort of intrusion "generally does not apply to matters which occur in a public place or a place otherwise open to the public eye."[44] Citing *Galella*, the court held that conduct amounting "to a persistent course of hounding, harassment and unreasonable surveillance, even if conducted in a public or 'semipublic' place, may nevertheless rise to the level of invasion of privacy."[45] According to the court, the defendants' conduct, even though it all took place on public streets and waterways, satisfied this standard because, "[a]s a result of the videotaping and recording with the 'shotgun mike',"[46] the plaintiffs had become "prisoners" in their own home, unable to take their "children out to play in the back yard."[47]

Following *Wolfson*, both California's legislature and its highest court addressed analogous contentions that technological innovation warrants recalibration of the scope of legally protected privacy in the media context, even in otherwise public places. In *Shulman v. Group W. Productions, Inc.*,[48] the plaintiffs were the unfortunate victims of an auto accident on an interstate highway that left one of them, Mrs. Shulman, a paraplegic. Both plaintiffs were videotaped by

---

within the law'") (citation omitted); Smith v. Daily Mail Publ'g Co., 443 U.S. 97, 103 (1979) ("a free press cannot be made to rely solely upon the sufferance of government to supply it with information" and can lawfully obtain information using "routine newspaper reporting techniques")).

42. 924 F. Supp. at 1416.

43. *Id.* at 1418.

44. *Id.* at 1419 (citing RESTATEMENT (SECOND) OF TORTS § 652, cmt. c) ("Nor is there liability for observing [plaintiff] or even taking his photograph, while he is walking on the public highway, since he is not then in seclusion, and his appearance is public and open to the public eye.").

45. 924 F. Supp. at 1420 (citing Galella v. Onassis, 487 F.2d 986 (2d Cir. 1973)). See also RESTATEMENT (SECOND) OF TORTS § 652B, cmt. d (intrusion may arise from a "course of hounding the plaintiff").

46. The court found the use of the "shot gun mike" to constitute an especially "serious intrusion." 924 F. Supp. at 1431; *see id.* ("Aiming the 'shotgun mike' at the ... family home was a significant part of the harassing course of conduct, ... which greatly intruded upon the solitude and privacy" of plaintiffs, even though they were never recorded.).

47. *Id.* at 1433.

48. 955 P.2d 469 (Cal. 1998).

the television program "On Scene: Emergency Response" as Mrs. Shulman was extricated from the car by "the jaws of life."[49] Through a wireless microphone worn by the emergency paramedic that attended to her at the accident scene, Mrs. Shulman could be heard communicating with the nurse and asserting, among other things, that "I just want to die."[50] Neither of the plaintiffs' full names was mentioned in the broadcast account of the rescue and neither of their faces was shown.[51]

A divided California Supreme Court held that summary judgment had properly been granted against both plaintiffs with respect to their tort claim for the "publication of private facts," but that a portion of their "intrusion" cause of action could proceed to trial.[52] In rejecting the plaintiffs' private facts claim, the court proceeded from the premise that the broadcast's subject matter — *i.e.*, "automobile accidents" and the "rescue and medical treatment of accident victims" — is one of "legitimate public concern."[53] Moreover, the court concluded that "the broadcast video depicting Ruth [Shulman's] injured physical state (which was not luridly shown) and audio showing her disorientation and despair were substantially relevant to the segment's newsworthy subject matter."[54] The broadcast did not, therefore, "constitute a 'morbid and sensational prying into private lives for its own sake,'" but rather bore a "logical nexus" to a newsworthy subject.[55] Accordingly, the court held, it could not "create liability under the private facts tort," because, *inter alia*, "the publication of truthful, lawfully obtained material of legitimate public concern is constitutionally privileged."[56]

The common law and constitutional doctrines that precluded plaintiffs' private facts claim did not, however, render the defendant similarly immune from potential liability for the tort of intrusion. Thus, although a majority of the court held that the "mere presence" of a video camera "at the accident scene and the filming of the events occurring there cannot be deemed either a physical or sensory intrusion on plaintiffs' seclusion,"[57] the same majority concluded that a reasonable jury could find "highly offensive," and thus actionable as intrusion, the use of a wireless microphone to record Mrs. Shulman's conversations at the

---

49. *Id.* at 475.
50. *Id.* at 476.
51. *Id.*
52. *Id.* at 477. The portion of the Court's decision addressing the plaintiffs' intrusion claim arising from the video and audio taping of Mrs. Shulman as she was transported in the rescue helicopter to the hospital is addressed in Chap. 12-4(b) *infra*.
53. 955 P.2d at 488.
54. *Id.*
55. *Id.* at 484, 488 (quoting RESTATEMENT (SECOND) OF TORTS § 652D, cmt. h).
56. 955 P.2d at 487.
57. *Id.* See also Sanders v. American Broadcasting Cos., 978 P.2d 67, 71 (Cal. 1999) (intrusion claim cannot be maintained "when the plaintiff has merely been observed, or even photographed or recorded, in a public place").

accident scene with the paramedic.[58] Specifically, the court indicated that there remained a factual dispute concerning whether Mrs. Shulman's comments could be overheard by others at the scene and that, if the jury found that — absent the microphone — her words would have been heard only by the paramedic, it would be justified in concluding both that (a) Mrs. Shulman had a reasonable expectation of privacy in those discussions and (b) recording them without her knowledge was "highly offensive" and therefore actionable.[59]

The court's holding in *Shulman* reflects its effort to reconcile the tension it perceived between the intrusion tort and the First Amendment. In that regard, the controlling opinion in *Shulman* concluded, on the authority of *Cohen v. Cowles Media Co.*,[60] that the intrusion tort — a neutral law of general application — is subject to First Amendment scrutiny only if, in the context of a given case, its application would place an "impermissibly severe burden on the press."[61] That circumstance, the court explained, did not obtain in *Shulman* because "the conduct of journalism does not depend, as a general matter, on the use of secret devices to record private conversations."[62]

By the same token, the court emphasized that a media defendant's "motive — to gather usable material for a potentially relevant story" — can be critical in determining whether its conduct is "highly offensive" for purposes of intrusion liability.[63] Accordingly, it explained that "information collecting techniques that may be highly offensive when done for socially unprotected reasons — for purposes of harassment, blackmail or prurient curiosity, for example — may not be offensive to a reasonable person when employed by journalists in pursuit of a socially or politically important story."[64] Indeed, although "the mere fact that the intruder was in pursuit of a 'story' does not . . . generally justify an otherwise offensive intrusion," the court noted, the use of "routine reporting techniques," such as the mere posing of questions, "could rarely, if ever, be deemed an actionable intrusion."[65]

---

58. 955 P.2d at 494.

59. *Id.* See also Sanders v. American Broadcasting Cos., 978 P.2d 67, 71 (Cal. 1999) ("our analysis of the issues in *Shulman* suggested . . . that mass media videotaping may constitute an intrusion even when the events and communications recorded were visible and audible to some limited set of observers at the time they occurred"); *id.* at 72 (in *Shulman*, court "implied the plaintiff patient could have a reasonable expectation of privacy in her communications even if some of them may have been overheard by those involved in the rescue, but not by the general public").

60. 501 U.S. 663, 669 (1991).

61. 955 P.2d at 495, 497.

62. *Id.* at 495.

63. *Id.* at 494.

64. *Id.* at 493.

65. *Id.* at 495. When initially released, the controlling opinion in *Shulman*, written on behalf of a plurality of the justices by Justice Werdegar, suggested that the use of a wireless microphone to record "confidential" communications may also be actionable under section 632 of the California

Less than three months after the California Supreme Court announced its decision in *Shulman*, the California legislature enacted a new statutory cause of action against photographers for invasion of privacy.[66] Under the statute, described by some of its proponents as "anti-paparazzi" legislation in the aftermath of the death of Diana, Princess of Wales, a person who trespasses "in order to physically invade the privacy of the plaintiff with the intent to capture any type of visual image, sound recording, or other physical impression of the plaintiff engaging in a personal or familial activity [where] the physical invasion occurs in a manner that is offensive to a reasonable person" is liable for the resulting invasion of privacy.[67] If the defendant uses enhanced audio or video devices to obtain physical impressions that could not have been obtained otherwise without trespassing, the defendant is liable for "constructive trespass."[68] In addition, any person who induces or causes another to violate the statute is liable for damages resulting from the violation.[69] Similar legislation has been introduced in Congress.[70]

§ 12-2(b). Public View.

The right to engage in newsgathering activities on the public streets has typically been held to extend to those matters that take place on private property but can nevertheless be observed or heard from public places. In *Wehling v.*

Penal Code, the state's eavesdropping statute, if Mrs. Shulman reasonably believed her conversations with the paramedic would not be overheard by third parties. 18 Cal. 4th at 233-35 & n.15. In a subsequently issued "Modification of Opinion," however, the Court deleted footnote 15 of the original plurality opinion and replaced it with an explicit advisory that it had not yet "had occasion to decide whether a communication may be deemed confidential under Penal Code section 632 . . . when a party reasonably expects and desires that the conversation itself will not be directly overheard by a non-participant" or otherwise recorded, "but does not reasonably expect that the contents of the communication will remain confidential to the parties." 955 P.2d at 492 n.15 (citing Coulter v. Bank of Am., 33 Cal. Rptr. 2d 766, 770-71 (Ct. App. 1994); O'Laskey v. Sortino, 273 Cal. Rptr. 674, 677-78 (Ct. App. 1990); Deteresa v. American Broadcasting Cos., 121 F.3d 460, 463-64 (9th Cir. 1997), *cert. denied*, 118 S. Ct. 1840 (1998)). See Chap. 13-7 *infra* (discussing issues arising under eavesdropping statute). Cf. Sanders v. American Broadcasting Cos., 978 P.2d 67, 72 (Cal. 1999) (*Shulman* "suggests that a person may reasonably expect privacy against the electronic recording of a communication, even though he or she had no reasonable expectation as to confidentiality of the communication's content").

66. See CAL. CIV. CODE § 1708.8.
67. *Id.* § 1708.8(a).
68. *Id.* § 1708.8(b).
69. *Id.* § 1708.8(d).
70. See, e.g., Protection for Personal Intrusion Act, H.R. 2448, 105th Cong. § 1 (1997) (introduced by Rep. Bono), Privacy Protection Act of 1998, H.R. 3224, 105th Cong. (1998) (sponsored by Rep. Gallegly); Personal Privacy Protection Act, S. 1203, 105th Cong. (1998) (sponsored by Sens. Feinstein and Hatch); Personal Privacy Protection Act, H.R. 97, 106th Cong. (1999) (sponsored by Reps. Conyers and McCollum).

Columbia Broadcasting System,[71] for example, the Fifth Circuit affirmed dismissal of an invasion of privacy claim based on a television program's videotaping of the exterior of plaintiff's residence. The broadcast, the court concluded, "'provided the public with nothing more than could have been seen from a public street.'"[72] Other courts have similarly held that plaintiffs may not maintain claims against the news media based on the videotaping of the interior of a pharmacy through a window from the street outside,[73] or the photographing of the exterior of the plaintiffs' home from an adjoining road.[74] As one court observed, "no right of privacy attaches to material in the public view."[75]

---

71. 721 F.2d 506 (5th Cir. 1983).
72. *Id.* at 509 (quoting district court).
73. See Mark v. King Broadcasting Co., 618 P.2d 512 (Wash. App. 1980), *aff'd*, 635 P.2d 1081 (Wash. 1981), *cert. denied*, 457 U.S. 1124 (1982). In *Mark*, the videotape of the pharmacy "included shots of the exterior and interior as seen through the front window while the pharmacy was closed. The view of the interior included a view of an individual talking on the telephone." *Id.* at 519. The Washington Supreme Court rejected plaintiff's claim for invasion of privacy by intrusion on the ground that "the place from which the film was shot was open to the public and thus any passerby could have viewed the scene recorded by the camera." 635 P.2d at 1095. See also Solomon v. National Enquirer Inc., 24 MEDIA L. REP. (BNA) 2269, 2272 (D. Md. 1996) (plaintiff failed to state claim for invasion of privacy by publication of private facts where "there is no allegation that the photographer did anything other than take a photo of Plaintiff standing in her window from outside of Plaintiff's home").
74. See Jaubert v. Crowley Post-Signal, Inc., 375 So. 2d 1386 (La. 1979). In *Jaubert*, a local newspaper photographed the plaintiffs' home and published the photo under the caption: "One of Crowley's stately homes, a bit weatherworn and unkempt, stands in the shadow of a spreading oak." *Id.* at 1387. The Louisiana Supreme Court reversed a jury verdict in favor of the plaintiffs on their claim for invasion of privacy by intrusion, holding that "[b]ecause the situation or activity which is intruded upon must be private, an invasion does not occur when an individual takes a photograph of a public sight which anyone is free to see." *Id.* at 1388.
75. *Id.* at 1391; see *id.* ("It is clear from the record that the [plaintiffs'] home was plainly visible from the public street, and the passersby were presented with a view of the property which was identical to that published by the defendant."); Shulman v. Group W Prods., Inc., 59 Cal. Rptr. 2d 434 (Ct. App. 1996), *aff'd in part*, 955 P.2d 469 (Cal. 1998); Marcus Garvey Charter Sch. v. Washington Times Corp., 27 MEDIA L. REP. (BNA) 1225, 1229-30 (D.C. Super. 1998) ("Taking a photograph of an individual in a public place does not subject the photographer to liability for invasion of privacy by intrusion."); Muratore v. M/S Scotia Prince, 656 F. Supp. 471, 482-83 (D. Me. 1987), *modified on other grounds*, 845 F.2d 347 (1st Cir. 1988) (claim of cruise ship passenger photographed by ship photographer over her objection rejected because allegedly offensive conduct occurred in public area of ship). See also Deteresa v. American Broadcasting Co., 121 F.3d 460, 466 (9th Cir. 1997), *cert. denied*, 118 S. Ct. 1840 (1998) (where plaintiff "does not dispute that she was videotaped in public view by a cameraperson in a public place, . . . the intrusion was not sufficiently offensive to state a common law intrusion into seclusion privacy claim"); Early v. Toledo Blade, No. 90-3434, slip op. at 27, 31 (Ohio C.P. July 9, 1997), *aff'd*, 26 MEDIA L. REP. (BNA) 2569 (Ohio App. 1998) (plaintiffs could not base invasion of privacy claims on reporting of events that took place in public bars). But see Wolfson v. Lewis, 924 F. Supp. 1413 (E.D. Pa. 1996) (holding that video and audio recording of plaintiffs' home from public street constitutes actionable intrusion; discussed at Chap. 13-4(b) *infra*).

Indeed, the concept of "public view" typically extends beyond the street to other places in which the public is traditionally welcome. Thus, in *Gill v. Hearst Publishing Co.*,[76] the California Supreme Court held early on that the common law, especially when considered in conjunction with "the constitutional guaranties of freedom of expression," precludes a cause of action premised on the act of recording — in this case by photograph — what can be observed by any member of the public. In *Gill*, the plaintiffs, who owned a confectionery and ice cream concession at Los Angeles' Farmers Market, were photographed there "in a romantic pose, the young man having one arm about the young woman."[77] The California Supreme Court held that the plaintiffs, by operating a concession at the "'worldfamed' Farmers Market, had voluntarily exposed themselves to public gaze in a pose open to the view of any persons who might be near or at their place of business."[78] The photograph, therefore, "merely permitted other members of the public, who were not at plaintiffs' place of business at the time it was taken, to see them as they had voluntarily exhibited themselves."[79] Other courts have applied the "public view" standard to preclude claims by a man photographed exiting from a portable toilet on a college campus,[80] a couple photographed standing at the check-in counter at an airport,[81] a man approached by a journalist "several times at public gatherings,"[82] a man lined up at a public building to collect unemployment benefits,[83] and a man photographed with "the front zipper of his trousers completely opened" while he mugged for photographers from the stands at a professional football game.[84]

---

76. 253 P.2d 441, 444 (Cal. 1953).
77. *Id.*
78. *Id.*
79. *Id.*
80. See Livingston v. Kentucky Post, 14 MEDIA L. REP. (BNA) 2076, 2077 (Ky. Cir. 1987) (since "plaintiff was simply stepping out of a Port-O-Let toilet," and his "action could easily be seen by anyone walking by," the act of "merely photographing the plaintiff ... cannot be categorized as an unreasonable intrusion").
81. See Fogel v. Forbes, Inc., 500 F. Supp. 1081 (E.D. Pa. 1980).
82. Lee v. The Columbian, Inc., 826 P.2d 217, 220 (Wash. App. 1991).
83. See Cefalu v. Globe Newspaper Co., 391 N.E.2d 935 (Mass. App. 1979), *cert. denied*, 444 U.S. 1060 (1980). In *Cefalu*, a *Boston Globe* photographer took pictures of the plaintiff, while he stood on line at the Hurley Building in Boston to act as a translator for a friend who was picking up a check. *Id.* at 937. A photograph depicting the plaintiff was published twice in the newspaper in connection with articles concerning unemployment. *Id.* The appellate court rejected plaintiff's privacy-based claims, holding that a person's appearance "in a public place necessarily involves doffing the cloak of privacy." *Id.* at 939 (citing Themo v. New England Newspaper Publ'g Co., 27 N.E.2d 753, 755 (Mass. 1940) (holding that persons on public streets have no right to preclude newspapers from photographing them)).
84. See Neff v. Time, Inc., 406 F. Supp. 858, 859 (W.D. Pa. 1976). In *Neff*, the plaintiff's photograph, taken with his consent (although he presumably was unaware of the condition of his trousers), was published to accompany an article in *Sports Illustrated* magazine about fans of the

Some otherwise "public" places, however, have been held to fall outside the "plain view" doctrine, at least on occasion. In *Y.G. v. Jewish Hospital*,[85] for example, a Missouri appellate court held that plaintiffs, a married couple who had participated in an *in vitro* fertilization program at a hospital, could maintain a claim for invasion of privacy when they were photographed at a hospital "party" for participants in the program, to which the news media was invited. "The mere fact that an event takes place where others are present," the court concluded, "does not waive the right to privacy."[86] Attendance at such a gathering does not "constitute an appearance in a public place" sufficient to vitiate the privacy surrounding "matters of procreation and sexual relations as well as medical treatment."[87] For similar reasons, another court held plaintiffs stated a claim for intrusion against uninvited news photographers who attended a private party, held "on an open hill at some distance from any passersby," and took pictures of plaintiffs' "unwedding" ceremony.[88]

Pittsburgh Steelers football team. Relying on both common law and constitutional doctrines, the court rejected plaintiff's various theories of invasion of privacy:

> Neff's picture was taken in a public place with his knowledge and with his encouragement; he was catapulted into the news by his own actions; nothing was falsified; a photograph taken at a public event which everyone present could see, with the knowledge and implied consent of the subject, is not a matter concerning a private fact. A factually accurate public disclosure is not tortious when connected with a newsworthy event even though offensive to ordinary sensibilities. The constitutional privilege protects all truthful publications relevant to matters of public interest.

Id. at 861 (citing, *inter alia*, Samuel v. Curtis Publ'g Co., 122 F. Supp. 327 (N.D. Cal. 1954) ("plaintiff attempting to dissuade woman hanging on bridge from committing suicide"); Themo v. New England Newspaper Publ'g Co., 27 N.E.2d 753 (Mass. 1940) (police station); Murray v. New York Magazine Co., 267 N.E.2d 256 (N.Y. 1971) (parade); Humiston v. Universal Film Mfg. Co., 178 N.Y.S. 752 (App. Div. 1919) (street)). See also Gautier v. Pro-Football, Inc., 107 N.E.2d 485, 489 (N.Y. 1952) ("One traveling upon the public highway may expect to be televised, but only as an incidental part of the general scene. So, one attending a public event such as a professional football game may expect to be televised in the status in which he attends."); Marcus Garvey Charter Sch. v. Washington Times Corp., 27 MEDIA L. REP. (BNA) 1225 (D.C. Super. 1998) (public school).

85. 795 S.W.2d 488 (Mo. App. 1990).
86. *Id.* at 502.
87. *Id.* at 500, 503. See also Green v. Chicago Tribune Co., 675 N.E.2d 249, 256 (Ill. App. 1996) (plaintiff stated claim for intentional infliction of emotional distress and for publication of private facts where newspaper photographed homicide victim in hospital and quoted statements made by victim's mother in private hospital room).
88. See Rafferty v. Hartford Courant Co., 416 A.2d 1215, 1216 (Conn. Super. 1980) (citing RESTATEMENT (SECOND) OF TORTS § 652B) ("The plaintiffs' affidavits make it clear that they thought their behavior was to be viewed privately. It is well known that acts which are privately funny may in public appear bizarre and weird because they are not viewed through a warming lens of friendship.").

§ 12-3. Crime and Disaster Scenes.

With some significant limitations, the freedom to gather news in public places, without fear of tort liability, has extended to crime and disaster scenes and to those who find themselves present at such locations. Thus, in *Williams v. KCMO Broadcasting*,[89] a Missouri appellate court affirmed the entry of summary judgment in favor of a television station that had filmed plaintiff's arrest in a public parking lot. The plaintiff, a high school senior, had been falsely arrested with several of his friends in the corridor of the county courthouse, paraded by police officers through an outdoor parking lot "with their hands above their heads," and "searched with their hands against a police vehicle."[90] The court concluded that the television station, which showed the film on its evening newscast, had not invaded the plaintiff's privacy because the "general privilege of giving publicity to matters of general public interest applies even though the individual publicized may have been drawn out of his seclusion and become involved in a noteworthy event involuntarily and against his will and over his protest."[91]

In addition, the court relied on "authority that reporting events which take place in public cannot give rise to a cause of action for invasion of privacy" because "the events are public to start with and the news report merely informed the listening or reading audience of matters which the public was free to observe."[92] Other courts have similarly held that the news media is not liable for photographing or videotaping even falsely accused criminal suspects when they are "handcuffed" and "paraded in front of the invited media," who are "permitted to film and photograph the event" on public streets, in police stations, or in courthouses.[93]

---

89. 472 S.W.2d 1 (Mo. App. 1971).
90. *Id.* at 2.
91. *Id.* at 4.
92. *Id.* at 6. See Penwell v. Taft Broadcasting Co., 469 N.E.2d 1025, 1028 (Ohio App. 1984) ("persons who are so unfortunate as to be present at the scene of a crime are regarded as properly subject to the public interest and publishers are permitted to '. . . satisfy the curiosity of the public as to its heroes, leaders, villains and victims . . . .'") (citation omitted).
93. Haynik v. Zimlich, 508 N.E.2d 195, 201 (Ohio C.P. 1986) (summary judgment granted on invasion of privacy claims because liability "does not exist where the defendant merely observes, films, or records a person in a public place, such as a courthouse or a police station"); see Penwell v. Taft Broadcasting Co., 469 N.E.2d 1025, 1027-28 (Ohio App. 1984) (summary judgment in favor of television station affirmed on invasion of privacy claim arising from videotaping of plaintiff, an "innocent bystander," who was "frisked, handcuffed and removed" from a bar following a police "bust"; "[t]he videotape footage was an accurate portrayal of the events of the evening as they related to the appellant's arrest"); RESTATEMENT (SECOND) OF TORTS § 652D, cmt. f (persons present at crime scenes are properly subject to the public interest and publishers may "satisfy the curiosity of the public as to its heroes, leaders, villains and victims"). But see Lauro v. City of New York, 39 F. Supp. 2d 351 (S.D.N.Y. 1999) (seizure of plaintiff for purposes of "perp walk" violated Fourth Amendment and subjected law enforcement officers to liability under 42 U.S.C.

The news media's right to enter upon crime scenes and disaster sites has, in contrast, been somewhat limited when a law enforcement investigation or other official activity remains in progress. The unique issues raised when the news media accompanies law enforcement or other public officials to gain access to such locations is addressed below.[94] Even in the absence of such express permission, however, courts have grappled with the issue of the news media's liability for gathering information in these venues.

In many circumstances the press' access to crime and disaster scenes is, as a practical matter, unfettered by public officials. In such cases, the courts have looked to the established traditions of newsgathering to determine whether the press conduct at issue is actionable. In the leading case of *Florida Publishing Co. v. Fletcher*,[95] for example, the press accompanied firefighters and a large group of onlookers inside a home that had been ravaged by fire. The press "entered through the open door; there was no objection to their entry; they entered quietly and peaceably; they did no damage to the property; and their entry was for the purpose of their news coverage" of the fire and the death of a young woman who had been alone in the house.[96] While there, news photographers captured on film the "silhouette" left on the floor after the victim's body had been removed.[97]

The Florida Supreme Court dismissed claims for trespass, invasion of privacy, and intentional infliction of emotional distress brought by the victim's family. The evidence before the trial judge on summary judgment was, the appellate court held, undisputed that "it was common usage, custom and practice for news media to enter private premises and homes *under the circumstances present here.*"[98] The Florida Supreme Court credited affidavits, submitted by the news media defendants, which demonstrated that:

> it has been a long-standing custom and practice throughout the country for representatives of the news media to enter upon private property where a disaster of great public interest has occurred — entering in a peaceful manner, without causing any physical damage, and at the invitation of the officers who are investigating the calamity.[99]

---

§ 1983). The court in *Lauro* did not consider the potential liability of the broadcaster that filmed the perp walk, but noted that a claim against the network "would not be far-fetched in this case given that Fox 5 News appears to have encouraged, and participated in, the perp walk conducted by" the detective and given the unlikelihood "that the police would have undertaken the [perp walk] absent the participation, encouragement, and aid of the press." 39 F. Supp. 2d at 365 n.11.

94. See Chap. 12-5 *infra*.
95. 340 So. 2d 914 (Fla. 1976), *cert. denied*, 431 U.S. 930 (1977).
96. *Id.* at 915.
97. *Id.* at 915-16.
98. *Id.* at 918 (emphasis in original).
99. *Id.* (quoting dissenting opinion of McCord, J. in appellate court).

As a result, the court held that there had been an "implied consent by custom and usage" to what otherwise might have been actionable trespass by the news media.[100] Although such consent would "vanish if one were informed not to enter at that time by the owner or possessor or by their direction," in the *Fletcher* case itself, "there was not only no objection to the entry, . . . *there was an invitation to enter by the officers investigating the fire*."[101] Entry by the news media under such circumstances, the court concluded, "has been accepted by the general public since it is a widespread practice of long-standing."[102]

In *Prahl v. Brosamle*,[103] in contrast, a Wisconsin appellate court considered a television news crew's liability for trespass by entering plaintiff's property, the scene of an active law enforcement operation, without permission. Police had arrived at plaintiff's property, a six-acre lot facing a public road, after receiving information that shots had been fired at four boys who were bicycling in the area; while there, the police surrounded and ultimately charged plaintiff's residence, which was on the property as well, and arrested him. A television photographer accompanied law enforcement authorities to the building, "positioned himself in the entrance-way or vestibule, and filmed officers" confiscating guns and interviewing plaintiff.[104] The photographer "did not request or receive" the plaintiff's permission to enter his property and "'[n]o trespassing' signs were located at points on the boundaries of the premises," although there was no evidence that the photographer was aware of them.[105]

---

100. *Id.*
101. *Id.* (emphasis in original).
102. *Id.* at 919-20; see Barger v. Courier-Journal, 20 MEDIA L. REP. (BNA) 1189, 1193 (Ky. App. 1991) (photograph of mass murder victim on company premises not actionable because "there is no allegation" that news photographer "lacked permission to enter the areas in which the crime occurred" and "news media personnel are customarily permitted access to such scenes whenever they involve events of great public concern"); Jacova v. Southern Radio & Television Co., 83 So. 2d 34 (Fla. 1955) (plaintiff who had been present at a cigar store during a police raid could not maintain action against news media for photographing him there because "he was in a public place and present at a scene where news was in the making"). But see Shulman v. Group W Prods., Inc., 955 P.2d 469, 490 (Cal. 1998) ("Although the attendance of reporters and photographers at the scene of an accident is to be expected, we are aware of no law or custom permitting the press to ride in ambulances or enter hospital rooms during treatment without the patient's consent."); Green Valley Sch., Inc. v. Cowles Florida Broadcasting, Inc., 327 So. 2d 810, 819 (Fla. App. 1976) (rejecting appeal to "common usage and custom" where television crew accompanied law enforcement officers when they staged a midnight raid on a private boarding school, entering the sleeping quarters of the children living there without prior warning); Lauro v. City of New York, 39 F. Supp. 2d 351 (S.D.N.Y. 1999) (city and public officials not immune from liability for custom of conducting "perp walks" for media).
103. 295 N.W.2d 768 (Wis. App. 1980).
104. *Id.* at 773.
105. *Id.*

Among other claims,[106] plaintiff sought recovery against the photographer for trespass, but the trial court dismissed the cause of action at the conclusion of trial.[107] The Wisconsin Court of Appeal ordered a new trial, however, rejecting the photographer's reliance on *Fletcher*.[108] While the court acknowledged that it is "well known that news representatives want to enter a private building after or even during a newsworthy event within the building," it concluded that such "knowledge is no basis for an implied consent."[109] In the absence of the kind of factual record established in *Fletcher*, the court concluded that:

> Few private persons anticipate . . . that an unplanned newsworthy event will occur on their property. An advance objection to entry under remotely possible circumstances need not be made, and it is unreasonable to require an objection after entry under distracting circumstances, especially when the identity of the intruder is unknown.[110]

The court concluded, therefore, that "custom and usage have not been shown in fact or law to confer an implied consent upon news representatives to enter a building under the circumstances presented by this case."[111] Finally, the court rejected the photographer's assertion of a First Amendment-based privilege, asserting that "'[n]ewsmen have no constitutional right of access to the scenes of crime or disaster when the general public is excluded.'"[112]

In another case, a federal district court held that — despite the absence of roadblocks or any other effort by law enforcement officers to secure the scene of an imminent raid by armed officers — the news media could be held liable for negligently entering the area and allegedly provoking a violent confrontation between the officers and the targets of the raid. In *Risenhoover v. England*,[113] several agents of the federal Bureau of Alcohol, Tobacco and Firearms ("ATF"),

---

106. The court's consideration of plaintiff's claim against the photographer pursuant to 42 U.S.C. § 1983 is considered in Chap. 12-5 *infra*.

107. The court looked to the RESTATEMENT (SECOND) OF TORTS § 158, for the common law rule of liability for trespass:

> One is subject to liability to another for trespass, irrespective of whether he thereby causes harm to any legally protected interest of the other, if he intentionally:
>
> (a) enters land in the possession of the other, or causes a thing or a third person to do so.

See also *id.*, cmt. e (conduct which would otherwise constitute a trespass is privileged by consent of the possessor or by law); Reeves v. Fox Television Network, 983 F. Supp. 703, 714 (N.D. Ohio 1997) ("Plaintiff's consent bars plaintiff's claims for trespass or intrusion.").

108. See 295 N.W.2d at 779-80.
109. *Id.* at 780.
110. *Id.*
111. *Id.*
112. *Id.* (quoting Le Mistral, Inc. v. Columbia Broadcasting Sys., 402 N.Y.S.2d 815 (App. Div. 1978)).
113. 936 F. Supp. 392 (W.D. Tex. 1996).

who were injured in a raid on the compound inhabited by members of the Branch Davidian religious sect, as well as the families of agents who lost their lives in the raid, survived a motion for summary judgment filed by a newspaper and television station with respect to the agents' negligence claims against them. Employees of both the newspaper and the station had entered the area surrounding the compound, where they could allegedly be seen by the Davidians, after they had received a tip that a government raid was imminent.

The district court held that the First Amendment did not bar the agents' negligence claims[114] and that the defendants were constrained by a common law "duty not to interfere with a law enforcement officer during the course of his responsibilities."[115] In the court's view, the defendants

> appreciated the risk of compromising the secrecy of the raid, and the likelihood that agents would be injured if that secrecy were compromised. They were aware that a raid was going to be conducted, and that the timing of the raid would not be disclosed. ATF had consistently refused to confirm a time or date for the raid to the newspaper. Nor did ATF promise to inform any of the media to allow them to observe the raid. Knowing of the violent nature of the Davidians, and the ATF's desire for secrecy, it was entirely foreseeable that a breach of that secrecy would increase the danger attendant upon serving the warrants upon the Davidians. The members of the media recognized that the officers could be harmed if secrecy were not maintained.[116]

Under these circumstances, the court reasoned that the "social utility of newsgathering in general" was not "at issue," but only whether the "actions of the Defendants in failing to exercise some degree of caution to avoid warning the Davidians of the impending raid outweigh[ed] the risk that compromising the secrecy of the operation would result in death and injury to a number of law enforcement officers."[117] In the court's view, "demanding that the press act responsibly in such a unique situation will not 'chill' First Amendment rights, no more so than demanding that any individual citizen act responsibly. Nor will it interfere with normal, run-of-the-mill press investigations."[118]

---

114. The court's First Amendment analysis is discussed at Chap. 13-5 *infra*.
115. 936 F. Supp. at 407.
116. *Id.*
117. *Id.* at 408.
118. *Id.*

§ 12-4. Private Property.

§ 12-4(a). The Home.

Courts have been especially hostile to efforts by the news media to gather news in a private home. Surreptitious or otherwise unauthorized entry by the press into a private home has been condemned under theories of Fourth Amendment liability, invasion of privacy, trespass and, occasionally, intentional infliction of emotional distress. In *Wilson v. Layne*,[119] the Supreme Court held that law enforcement officers violated the Fourth Amendment when, "[w]hile executing an arrest warrant in a private home," they "invite[ ] representatives of the media to accompany them."[120] Although the Court unanimously condemned "such a 'media ride along'" in the context of a private home, it held that the officers who had issued the invitation were entitled to "the defense of qualified immunity" because "the state of the law was not clearly established at the time the search" at issue took place in 1992.[121] And, in a companion case captioned *Hanlon v. Berger*, the justices declined to address the news media's own liability under the Fourth Amendment for accepting an invitation to accompany law enforcement officers executing a search warrant.[122]

The arrest warrant before the Court in *Wilson* was issued pursuant to "Operation Gunsmoke," a national fugitive apprehension program authorized by the Attorney General, in which U.S. Marshals collaborated with local law enforcement officers to apprehend "dangerous criminals."[123] Pursuant to a warrant issued for the arrest of Dominic Wilson, who had violated his probation on previous felony charges, federal and state law enforcement officers entered the home of Wilson's parents "[i]n the early morning hours" accompanied by a reporter and a photographer from the *Washington Post*.[124] Dominic Wilson was not in the house but his father, "dressed only in a pair of briefs, ran into the living room to investigate" when he heard unknown persons there.[125] The five officers assembled in the Wilson living room and, believing Mr. Wilson "to be an angry Dominic Wilson, . . . quickly subdued him on the floor."[126] Mrs.

---

119. 119 S. Ct. 1692 (1999).
120. *Id.* at 1695.
121. *Id.*
122. See 119 S. Ct. 1706, 1707 (1999), *vacating* Berger v. Hanlon, 129 F.3d 505 (9th Cir. 1997); see also Berger v. Cable News Network, Inc., 119 S. Ct. 403 (1999) (denying petition for writ of *certiorari* by Cable News Network); Berger v. Hanlon, 1999 U.S. App. LEXIS 20262, *2-3 (9th Cir. Aug. 27, 1999) (reaffirming prior decision holding that CNN could properly be held liable for Fourth Amendment violation and is not entitled to qualified immunity). The media's liability for Fourth Amendment violations generally is discussed in Chap. 12-5 *infra*.
123. 119 S. Ct. at 1695.
124. *Id.*
125. *Id.* at 1696.
126. *Id.*

Wilson then entered the room, wearing only a nightgown, during which time the *Post* photographer took numerous pictures, none of which were published in the newspaper.[127]

Although the Court, in an opinion by Chief Justice Rehnquist, recognized that the officers entered the home pursuant to a lawfully issued warrant, it held that "it does not necessarily follow that they were entitled to bring a newspaper reporter and a photographer with them."[128] The "presence of the reporters," the Court concluded, "was not related to the objectives of the authorized intrusion" and therefore could not be squared with the "centuries-old principle of respect for the privacy of the home" embodied in the Fourth Amendment.[129] Thus, although the Court acknowledged that "[i]t may well be that media ride-alongs further the law enforcement objectives of the police in a general sense," by serving to publicize "the government's efforts to combat crime and facilitate accurate reporting on law enforcement activities," it held that such "generalized 'law enforcement objectives'" are themselves insufficient "to trump the Fourth Amendment."[130]

In addition, the Court concluded that the possibility that media scrutiny of an arrest "could serve in some situations to minimize police abuses and protect suspects" or "to protect the safety of the officers" was similarly insufficient to justify the presence of reporters and photographers in a private home.[131] According to the Chief Justice:

---

127. *Id.*

128. *Id.* at 1697 (citing Horton v. California, 496 U.S. 128, 140 (1990); Arizona v. Hicks, 480 U.S. 321, 325 (1987)).

129. 119 S. Ct. at 1697 (quoting Semayne's Case, 77 Eng. Rep. 194, 5 Co. Rep. 91a, 91b, 195 (K.B. 1604) ("'the house of every one is to him as his castle and fortress, as well for his defense against injury and violence, as for his repose'"); 4 W. BLACKSTONE, COMMENTARIES ON THE LAWS OF ENGLAND 223 (1765-1769) ("'the law of England has so particular and tender a regard for the immunity of a man's house, that it stiles it his castle, and will never suffer it to be violated with impunity'")).

130. 119 S. Ct at 1698. In this regard, the Court broadly acknowledged "language in our opinions interpreting the First Amendment which points to the importance of 'the press' in informing the general public about the administration of criminal justice," and asserted that "[n]o one could gainsay the truth of these observations, or the importance of the First Amendment in protecting press freedom from abridgment by the government." *Id.* (citing Cox Broadcasting Corp. v. Cohn, 420 U.S. 469, 491-92 (1975); Richmond Newspapers, Inc. v. Virginia, 448 U.S. 555, 572-73 (1980)). Nevertheless, the Court concluded:

> Surely the possibility of good public relations for the police is simply not enough, standing alone, to justify the ride-along intrusion into a private home. And even the need for accurate reporting on police issues in general bears no direct relation to the constitutional justification for the police intrusion into a home in order to execute a felony arrest warrant.

119 S. Ct. at 1698.

131. *Id.* at 1699.

The Washington Post reporters in the Wilsons' home were working on a story for their own purposes. They were not present for the purpose of protecting the officers, much less the Wilsons. A private photographer was acting for private purposes, as evidenced in part by the fact that the newspaper and not the police retained the photographs. Thus, although the presence of third parties during the execution of a warrant may in some circumstances be constitutionally permissible, . . . the presence of *these* third parties was not.[132]

Over a lone dissent by Justice Stevens, however, the Court proceeded to hold that the officers were immune from Fourth Amendment liability. The officers had not been "unreasonable" in inviting the press to accompany them into the Wilsons' home, the Court held, because "[a]ccurate media coverage of police activities serves an important public purpose, and it is not obvious from the general principles of the Fourth Amendment that the conduct of the officers in this case violated the Amendment."[133] Justice Stevens, in contrast, would have held that "the homeowner's right to protection against this type of trespass was clearly and long established" at the time of the entry into the Wilsons' home.[134]

In *Hanlon v. Berger*,[135] decided the same day as *Wilson*, the Court — in a brief, *per curiam* order — vacated a decision of the Ninth Circuit that had held officers of the United States Fish and Wildlife Service liable under the Fourth Amendment for inviting Cable News Network ("CNN") photographers and reporters to accompany them as they searched the 75,000 acre ranch of Paul and Erma Berger for evidence of "the taking of wildlife in violation of federal laws."[136] The Court concluded that the Bergers' claims that the "'CNN media crew . . . accompanied and observed the officers, and the media crew recorded the officers' conduct in executing the warrant'" both "alleged a Fourth Amendment violation" as articulated in *Wilson* and were insufficient to overcome the officers' defense of qualified immunity.[137]

---

132. *Id.* (emphasis in original).
133. *Id.* at 1700.
134. *Id.* at 1701 (Stevens, J., dissenting in part); see *id.* ("That the Court today speaks with a single voice on the merits of the constitutional question is0 unusual and certainly lends support to the notion that the question is indeed 'open and shut.'").
135. 119 S. Ct. 1706 (1999) (vacating 129 F.3d 505 (9th Cir. 1997)).
136. 119 S. Ct. at 1706.
137. *Id.* (quoting Brief for Petitioners at 5). On remand from the Supreme Court, the Ninth Circuit reinstated that portion of its earlier decision holding that there had been a Fourth Amendment violation, see Berger v. Hanlon, 129 F.3d 505, 514-15 (9th Cir. 1997), on the ground that the "Supreme Court affirmed our holding that a violation of the Fourth Amendment occurred in this case" and CNN is "not entitled to assert qualified immunity as a defense," Berger v. Hanlon, 1999 U.S. App. LEXIS 20262, *2-3 (9th Cir. Aug. 27, 1999) (citing Wyatt v. Cole, 504 U.S. 158, 168-69 (1992); Kimes v. Stone, 84 F.3d 1121, 1128 (9th Cir. 1996)). The Ninth Circuit's assessment of the scope of the Supreme Court's holding would, however, appear to be overstated, since the

The Supreme Court's decisions in *Wilson* and *Hanlon* leave unresolved the news media's own liability for Fourth Amendment violations under analogous circumstances. Its holding that the officers in both cases were entitled to qualified immunity casts at least some doubt on the efficacy of prior decisions that had reached the opposite conclusion while suggesting as well that the news media may be liable in damages when it accompanies law enforcement personnel into a private home. In one such influential case, *United States v. Sanusi*, the news media's conduct first drew the district court's attention when, in the context of the criminal prosecution of Babatunde Ayeni for credit card fraud, CBS moved the court to quash a subpoena issued by Ayeni, which sought outtakes of videotape its camera crew had shot inside the Ayeni home.[138] The CBS crew had accompanied Secret Service agents there when they executed a search warrant.

The district court denied the motion to quash, in significant part,[139] on the ground that CBS's and the government's conduct in securing the information precluded assertion of the reporters' privilege.[140] In so holding, the court, which had viewed the videotape outtakes in chambers, described in graphic terms the "window into the ordinarily unseen and sometimes highly violative events attending the execution of a search warrant in a private person's home."[141] According to the court, the videotape revealed that the CBS crew arrived shortly after Secret Service agents first entered the apartment, finding only Ayeni's wife and young child there. "Clearly having been caught unawares by the service of process," the videotape depicted Mrs. Ayeni

> wearing a dressing gown. Virtually the instant she sees the group she says, "Please don't take my picture." She then asks, "Why do you want to take a picture?" Her words and the tone in which they are spoken make clear that she assumes the camera crew is an unauthorized participant in the search. As the crew enters the apartment, she retreats into the living room, demanding three times in succession that her picture not be taken. She then covers her face with a magazine and directs defendant's child, who is now sitting beside her on a couch, not to look at the camera.[142]

In addition, the videotape indicated that the "agent apparently in charge wears a wireless microphone for the benefit of the CBS crew" and is shown, among other

---

Supreme Court purported to hold only that the plaintiffs had "alleged a Fourth Amendment violation" of the kind identified in *Wilson*, 119 S. Ct. at 106, not that "a violation of the Fourth Amendment" had in fact "occurred in this case," 1999 U.S. App. LEXIS 20262, at *2.

138. 813 F. Supp. 149 (E.D.N.Y. 1992).
139. See Chap. 16-2(e)(4) *infra* (discussing case in context of reporters' privilege).
140. United States v. Sanusi, 813 F. Supp. at 160.
141. *Id.* at 152.
142. *Id.*

things, interrogating Mrs. Ayeni about her husband's whereabouts. When she "sees the camera again," she is filmed as she "covers her face with a magazine saying she does not want to comment."[143]

Rejecting CBS's assertion of the constitutional reporters' privilege, the district court concluded that, "[w]hile the First Amendment provides the press with a shield from government censorship, the press may not use this protection to justify otherwise illegal actions."[144] Thus, the court concluded that the reporters' privilege "operates weakly, if at all, in this case":

> CBS entered defendant's home without the consent of defendant or his family. As a participant in the execution of a search warrant, it did so, in effect under color of official right. The tape reveals that defendant's wife believed the camera crew to be a part of the team executing the warrant. CBS's argument that she impliedly consented to the crew's presence by failing to ask it to leave is fanciful. The reasonable person confronted by a phalanx of Secret Service agents, including a camera crew that failed to identify itself or request permission to be present, would not entertain the notion that she had an option to exclude the camera's eye and the reporter's recorder. That the woman had the presence of mind to request not to be photographed was, under the circumstances, remarkable.[145]

More significantly, at least for present purposes, the court observed that the Ayenis "do not seek damages from CBS at this time" and that the court "could not, in any event, entertain such a request for relief in a criminal case."[146] Nevertheless, the court opined, albeit in *dicta*, that "CBS both trespassed upon defendant's home and engaged in conduct, with the connivance of the government, directly contrary to Fourth Amendment principles."[147] The First Amendment, the court asserted, "is a shield not a sword. Even a reporter must accept limits on how far upon another person's privacy he or she may intrude."[148]

In the wake of these comments, the Ayenis not surprisingly instituted a civil action against CBS and the Secret Service agents, alleging violation of their rights under the Fourth Amendment.[149] The same federal district court, affirmed

---

143. *Id.* at 152.
144. *Id.* at 155.
145. *Id.* at 160.
146. *Id.*
147. *Id.*; See *id.* ("Sanctity of the home is certainly one of our oldest and most deeply felt constitutional rights. Accordingly, the Fourth Amendment has been interpreted to require a judicial warrant for the search of a person's home. . . .").
148. *Id.* The court also cited, with approval, the decision of a New York trial court in *Anderson v. WROC-TV*, 441 N.Y.S.2d 220 (Sup. Ct. 1981), which is discussed at note 172 *infra*.
149. See Ayeni v. CBS Inc., 848 F. Supp. 362 (E.D.N.Y.) *aff'd*, 35 F.3d 680 (2d Cir. 1994), *cert. denied*, 514 U.S. 1062 (1995); Chap. 12-5 *infra* (discussing liability under Fourth Amendment).

in significant part by the Second Circuit, rejected the Secret Service agents' assertion of qualified immunity and, in the district court, CBS's effort to claim such immunity derivatively.[150] As Chief Judge Newman bluntly summarized his court's view, a "private home is not a soundstage for law enforcement theatricals."[151]

The news media's efforts to gather information from private homes is also the subject of the Ninth Circuit's seminal decision in *Dietemann v. Time, Inc.*[152] There, the plaintiff, who "was engaged in the practice of healing with clay, minerals, and herbs," allegedly maintained something of a "medical" practice in

---

150. 848 F. Supp. at 365-68. See Ayeni v. Mottola, 35 F.3d 680, 684 (2d Cir. 1994), *cert. denied*, 514 U.S. 1062 (1995) (citing Bivens v. Six Unknown Named Agents, 403 U.S. 388 (1971) and quoting Soares v. Connecticut, 8 F.3d 917, 920 (2d Cir. 1993)); see also Robinson v. City of Denver, Civ. No. 94 N 0771 (D. Colo. Feb. 26, 1999) (rejecting city and county law enforcement officers' assertions of immunity from tort liability and Fourth Amendment claims where they invited media into private home to film execution of arrest warrant, and where at time of arrest they knew or should have known that plaintiff did not consent to entry and that their conduct was unreasonable under Fourth Amendment). Prior to adjudication of the appeal, CBS had reached a separate settlement with the Ayenis, so the Second Circuit did not consider the district court's ruling with respect to the network's claim of derivative immunity. 35 F.3d at 684 n.2. See Chap. 12-5 *infra* (discussing district court's ruling concerning press liability under Fourth Amendment).

151. Ayeni v. Mottola, 35 F.3d at 685 (footnote omitted). Accord Parker v. Clarke, 905 F. Supp. 638, 644 (E.D. Mo. 1995), *aff'd in part sub nom.* Parker v. Boyer, 93 F.3d 445 (8th Cir. 1996), *cert. denied*, 117 S. Ct. 1081 (1997) (applying *Ayeni* to defeat claim of qualified immunity by law enforcement officials to support entry of summary judgment against them); Robinson v. City of Denver, Civ. No. 94 N 0771, slip op. at 14 (D. Colo. Feb. 26, 1999) ("Given the sanctity of the home in Fourth Amendment jurisprudence, police facilitation of media coverage of an individual's arrest in his house is a highly intrusive government entry into a private home. In fact, the filming and photographing of the arrest and the subsequent broadcast of the film and publication of the pictures strikes this court as the epitome of intrusiveness in modern society.") (citing *Ayeni*); Green Valley Sch., Inc. v. Cowles Florida Broadcasting, Inc., 327 So. 2d 810, 819 (Fla. App. 1976) ("To uphold appellees' assertion that their entry upon appellants' property at the time, manner, and circumstances as reflected in this record was as a *matter of law* sanctioned by 'the request of and with the consent of the State Attorney' and within the 'common usage and custom in Florida' could well bring to the citizenry of this state the hobnail boot of a Nazi stormtrooper equipped with glaring lights invading a couple's bedroom at midnight with the wife hovering in her nightgown in an attempt to shield herself from the scanning TV camera."). See also Nichols v. Hendrix, 27 MEDIA L. REP. (BNA) 1503 (N.D. Ga. 1999) (declining to exercise supplemental jurisdiction over trespass and defamation claims after finding that television station was not acting under color of state law and therefore not liable for Fourth Amendment violation, where media defendant accompanied law enforcement officers and filmed execution of raid of plaintiffs' home); Swate v. Taylor, 12 F. Supp. 2d 591 (S.D. Tex. 1998) (DEA agent who brought news crew with her to film search and seizure of methadone from private clinics exceeded scope of warrant). Cf. United States v. Appelquist, 145 F.3d 976, 979 (8th Cir. 1998) (no Fourth Amendment violation where police invited media into private home "only after the police completed the warrant search").

152. 449 F.2d 245 (9th Cir. 1971). But see Metter v. Los Angeles Examiner, 95 P.2d 491 (Cal. App. 1939) (directed verdict granted to defendant newspaper where plaintiff, the surviving spouse of woman who committed suicide, could not prove that defendant broke into family home and took photograph later published in newspaper).

his home.[153] Two reporters for *Life* magazine, in cooperation with the Los Angeles District Attorney, visited plaintiff's residence and used a ruse to gain entrance to his den. While there, one of the reporters photographed plaintiff with a hidden camera without his consent while he "examined" the other reporter, and their conversation was recorded by a hidden microphone and transmitted to law enforcement and public health officials outside.[154]

The Ninth Circuit affirmed the trial court's award of $1,000 to plaintiff on his intrusion claim, asserting that "we have little difficulty in concluding that clandestine photography of the plaintiff in his den and the recordation and transmission of his conversation without his consent resulting in emotional distress warrants recovery for invasion of privacy."[155] In so holding, the court was particularly troubled by the fact that the defendants' reporters had gained entry to the home by subterfuge and had photographed and tape recorded plaintiff surreptitiously:

> Plaintiff's den was a sphere from which he could reasonably expect to exclude eavesdropping newsmen. He invited two of defendant's employees to the den. One who invites another to his home or office takes a risk that the visitor may repeat all he hears and observes when he leaves. But he does not and should not be required to take the risk that what is heard and seen will be transmitted by photograph or recording, or in our modern world, in full living color and hi-fi to the public at large or to any segment of it that the visitor may select.[156]

The Court also rejected the defendant's claim that the First Amendment "immunizes" its newsgathering activity in these circumstances.[157] Although it "agree[d] that newsgathering is an integral part of news dissemination," the Ninth Circuit "strongly disagree[d]" that "hidden mechanical contrivances are 'indispensable tools' of newsgathering."[158] In a frequently quoted passage, the court noted that:

---

153. 449 F.2d at 246.
154. *Id.*
155. *Id.* at 245, 248. See Dietemann v. Time, Inc., 284 F. Supp. 925 (C.D. Cal. 1968), *aff'd*, 449 F.2d 245 (9th Cir. 1971). The Ninth Circuit also affirmed the district court's conclusion that plaintiff's home was not a place of business "open to the public." 449 F.2d at 247; see *id.* ("'The plaintiff was administering his so-called treatments to people who visited him. He was not a medical man of any type. He did not advertise. He did not have a phone. He did have a lock on his gate. To obtain entrance it was necessary to ring a bell.'") (quoting district court).
156. 449 F.2d at 248-49; see *id.* (decrying "'the increasing capability of . . . electronic devices with their capacity to destroy an individual's anonymity, to intrude upon his most intimate activities, and expose his most personal characteristics to public gaze'") (quoting Briscoe v. Reader's Digest Ass'n, 483 P.2d 34, 37 (Cal. 1971)).
157. 449 F.2d at 245.
158. *Id.*

Investigative reporting is an ancient art; its successful practice long antecedes the invention of miniature cameras and electronic devices. The First Amendment has never been construed to accord newsmen immunity from torts or crimes committed during the course of newsgathering. The First Amendment is not a license to trespass, to steal, or to intrude by electronic means into the precincts of another's home or office.[159]

Even in the absence of surreptitious conduct, several courts have held that unauthorized newsgathering within a private home can form the basis of civil liability. In *Miller v. National Broadcasting Co.*,[160] for example, a television camera crew entered an apartment, without the consent of the occupants, a married couple, to film fire department paramedics called to the home to administer to the husband who had suffered a heart attack in his bedroom. Although the crew entered the apartment with the consent of the Fire Department personnel they accompanied,[161] a California Court of Appeal held the absence of the occupants' consent crucial in adjudicating the trespass claim brought by the wife of the stricken man, who later died:

> "The essence of the cause of action for trespass is an 'unauthorized entry' onto the land of another. Such invasions are characterized as intentional torts, regardless of the actor's motivation. Where there is a consensual entry, there is no tort, because lack of consent is an element of the [cause of action]. . . ."[162]

In addition, the court held that the defendants' benign intention to gather news was of no consequence in adjudicating the trespass claim: "the trespass was intentional in the sense that the law understands and uses that word: the defendants intended to cross the threshold of the Miller home."[163] The damages recoverable for a trespass of this nature are, the court added, limited to the "direct consequences of any conduct engaged in while trespassing," but may

---

159. *Id.* See *id.* at 250 ("No interest protected by the First Amendment is adversely affected by permitting damages for intrusion to be enhanced by the fact of later publication of the information that the publisher improperly acquired.").

160. 232 Cal. Rptr. 668 (Ct. App. 1986).

161. See *id.* at 683 ("One seeking emergency medical attention does not thereby 'open the door' for persons without any clearly identifiable and justifiable official reason who may wish to enter the premises where the medical aid is being administered.").

162. *Id.* at 677 (quoting 4 B. WITKIN, SUMMARY OF CALIFORNIA LAW § 351, at 2612 (8th ed. 1974) and citing Civic W. Corp. v. Zila Indus., Inc. 135 Cal. Rptr. 915 (Ct. App. 1977)).

163. 232 Cal. Rptr. at 677. See W. PROSSER & W. KEETON, THE LAW OF TORTS § 13, at 73-74 (5th ed. 1984) ("The intent required as a basis for liability as a trespasser is simply an intent to be at the place on the land where the trespass allegedly occurred. . . . The defendant is liable for an intentional entry although he has acted in good faith, under the mistaken belief, however reasonable, that he is committing no wrong.").

include "emotional distress neither accompanied by a physical injury to the person or to the land."[164]

The court of appeal in *Miller* further held that the defendants could be found liable for an actionable invasion of privacy by intrusion. Applying the *Restatement*'s articulation of the tort,[165] the court determined that defendants' unauthorized entry into a private home could be considered "highly offensive," as required to state a claim for intrusion:

> [E]ven today most individuals not acting in some clearly identified official capacity do not go into private homes without the consent of those living there; not only do widely held notions of decency preclude it, but most individuals understand that to do so is either a tort, a crime, or both.[166]

In addition, the court in *Miller* held that the plaintiff might recover as well on her claim for intentional infliction of emotional distress.[167] It was sufficient, the court concluded, if a jury could reasonably find that the defendants had acted in "reckless disregard" of the consequences of their actions and, although there was

---

164. Miller v. National Broadcasting Co., 232 Cal. Rptr. at 677. Accord Prahl v. Brosamle, 295 N.W.2d 768, 781 (Wis. App. 1980) ("[c]ompensatory and punitive damages have been held recoverable from news representatives for trespass" and "include nonphysical harm subsequent to the trespass"); see also Le Mistral, Inc. v. Columbia Broadcasting Sys., 402 N.Y.S.2d 815 (App. Div. 1978); Belluomo v. KAKE TV & Radio, Inc., 596 P.2d 832 (Kan. App. 1979). In *Prahl*, the court recognized the potential difficulty of "[e]stablishing the effect of publication of the tortiously acquired information at trial, as contrasted to the effect of publication of information lawfully acquired by" the news media. 295 N.W.2d at 782. Accordingly, the court cautioned that:

> It is only the film and information obtained during the trespass which were tortiously acquired. The damages recoverable from publication, insofar as mental distress is claimed, are further subject to the rule that, "In intentional torts, substantial other damages in addition to damages for emotional distress are required."

Id. (citation omitted).
165. See RESTATEMENT (SECOND) OF TORTS § 652B.
166. 232 Cal. Rptr. at 678-79. The court also concluded that the damages recoverable in the wake of an actionable intrusion are somewhat broader than those available in trespass:

> The elements of emotional distress damages, i.e., anxiety, embarrassment, humiliation, shame, depression, feelings of powerlessness, anguish, etc. would ... be subject of legitimate inquiry by a jury ..., taking into account *all* of the consequences and events which flowed from the actionable wrong.

Id. (citing Fairfield v. American Photocopy Equip. Co., 291 P.2d 194 (Cal. App. 1955)).
167. See 232 Cal. Rptr. at 681 (quoting Cervantes v. J.C. Penney Co., 595 P.2d 975 (Cal. 1979); Davidson v. City of Westminster, 649 P.2d 894 (Cal. 1982)):

> The elements of a prima facie case for the tort of intentional infliction of emotional distress [are]: "(1) extreme and outrageous conduct by the defendant with the intention of causing, or reckless disregard [for] the probability of causing, emotional distress; (2) the plaintiff's suffering severe or extreme emotional distress; and (3) actual and proximate causation of the emotional distress by the defendant's outrageous conduct."

no evidence that the camera crew "had any specific malicious or evil purpose," the fact that it "devoted little or no thought whatsoever to its obvious transgression" could constitute, "in this context, 'reckless disregard.'"[168] Moreover, the court of appeal determined that a reasonable jury might consider the defendants' conduct to be "outrageous," as required to sustain a cause of action for intentional infliction of emotional distress.[169]

Finally, the court in *Miller* concluded that the First Amendment would not, under the circumstances presented, immunize defendants' otherwise tortious conduct from liability. Although the court recognized that "[n]ewsgathering, as well as news dissemination, may be within the protective ambit of the First Amendment,"[170] it held that "the obligation not to make unauthorized entry into the private premises of individuals like the Millers does not place an impermis-

---

168. 232 Cal. Rptr. at 682.

169. *Id.* This conclusion was bolstered by the fact that defendants had, according to the plaintiff and her daughter, ignored their "subsequent protestations" and "broadcast to the world . . . the last moments of her dying husband's life." *Id.* Nevertheless, the court rejected analogous claims asserted by the plaintiff's daughter, who was not present in the home at the time of the defendants' unauthorized entry but viewed the filmed footage of her father on television. *Id.* at 682-83.

Relying on *Miller*, another California appellate court reached an analogous conclusion with respect to a cause of action for intentional infliction of emotional distress in *KOVR-TV Inc. v. Superior Court*, 37 Cal. Rptr. 2d 431 (Ct. App. 1995). In *KOVR*, a television reporter and camera crew came to plaintiffs' residence and, with cameras rolling, asked the young children (ages 11, 7 and 5) who answered the door whether they were aware that the children who lived next door had been murdered by their mother. *Id.* at 432. The videotape of the encounter, according to the court of appeal, "reveals an uninvited, intrusive encounter by adult strangers with children of tender years not in a public place but in their homes." *Id.* at 434. Thus, the court concluded that "[e]ven if defendant was innocently gathering news when he initiated the interview, it is a reasonable inference that when he discovered the minors were friends of the [deceased] children but unaware of their demise, he abruptly informed them 'the mom has killed the two little kids and herself,' in the hope it would elicit an emotional reaction that would be 'newsworthy,' e.g., suitable to redeem a promise of 'film at eleven.'" *Id.* at 435. As a result, even though defendants did not broadcast the interview:

> a jury could find that a television reporter who attempts deliberately to manipulate the emotions of young children for some perceived journalistic advantage has engaged in conduct "so outrageous in character, and so extreme in degree, as to go beyond all possible bounds of decency."

Id. (citation omitted). See also Marich v. QRZ Media, Inc., 86 Cal. Rptr. 2d 406, 419 (Ct. App. 1999) (holding that parents of drug overdose victim stated claim for intrusion arising from videotape of police telephone call notifying them of son's death; "a call to a parent to advise of the untimely death of a child is a very personal and potentially agonizing situation").

170. 232 Cal. Rptr. at 684 (citing Branzburg v. Hayes, 408 U.S. 665, 681 (1972); Cox Broadcasting Corp. v. Cohn, 420 U.S. 469 (1975); Nicholson v. McClatchy Newspapers, 223 Cal. Rptr. 58 (Ct. App. 1986)).

sible burden on newsgatherers, nor is it likely to have a chilling effect on the exercise of First Amendment rights."[171]

The court's analysis in *Miller* has been replicated, in substantial part, by courts in other jurisdictions as well.[172] Thus, for example, in *Berger v. Hanlon*,[173] the Ninth Circuit, in opinions issued both before and after the Supreme Court addressed the Fourth Amendment issue raised in that case,[174] similarly held that CNN was not entitled to summary judgment on plaintiffs' claims of trespass and intentional infliction of emotional distress arising from the network's conduct in accompanying law enforcement officers when they executed a search warrant on

---

171. 232 Cal. Rptr. at 685 (citing Dietemann v. Time, Inc., 449 F.2d 245, 249 (9th Cir. 1971)). See also KOVR-TV Inc. v. Superior Ct., 37 Cal. Rptr. 2d 431, 436 (Ct. App. 1995) (where "defendant sought to elicit an emotional reaction from . . . minors for the voyeuristic titillation" of its "viewing audience, this is shameless exploitation" and "not the gathering of news which the public has a right to know"); Nimmer, *The Right to Speak from Times to Time: First Amendment Theory Applied to Libel and Misapplied to Privacy*, 56 CAL. L. REV. 935, 957 (1968) ("Intrusion does not raise First Amendment difficulties since its perpetration does not involve speech or other expression. It occurs by virtue of the physical or mechanical observation of the private affairs of another, and not by the publication of such observations.").

172. See, e.g., Anderson v. WROC-TV, 441 N.Y.S.2d 220 (Sup. Ct. 1981); Copeland v. Hubbard Broadcasting, Inc., 526 N.W.2d 402 (Minn. App. 1995). In *Copeland*, the defendant television station sent one of its employees, who posed as a "student," to accompany a veterinarian admitted into plaintiffs' home to treat their pets. *Id.* at 404. While there, the "student" videotaped the veterinarian's practice methods, which became the basis of an investigative report about local veterinarians broadcast by the station. *Id.* The court of appeals reversed a summary judgment in defendant's favor on the plaintiffs' trespass claim, holding that, even though the "student" had secured plaintiffs' permission to enter the home, "an entrant may become a trespasser by moving beyond the possessor's invitation or permission." *Id.* The defendant's use of "secret cameras," the court concluded, constituted the kind of "wrongful conduct following an authorized entry [that] can result in trespass." *Id.* at 405 (citing Miller v. National Broadcasting Co., 232 Cal. Rptr. 668 (Ct. App. 1986); Anderson v. WROC-TV, 441 N.Y.S.2d 220 (Sup. Ct. 1981); Ayeni v. CBS Inc., 848 F. Supp. 362, 368 (E.D.N.Y.), *aff'd*, 35 F.3d 680 (2d Cir. 1994), *cert. denied*, 514 U.S. 1062 (1995)).

In *Anderson*, an investigator employed by a local Humane Society invited representatives of several television stations to accompany him while he executed a search warrant that entitled him "to enter plaintiffs' house and seize any animals 'found to be in a confined, crowded or unhealthy condition or in unhealthy or unsanitary surroundings or . . . not properly cared for or without sustenance, food and drink.'" 441 N.Y.S.2d at 222. According to the plaintiffs' complaint, the television crews entered her home despite her instructions that they not do so. *Id.* The court granted plaintiffs' motion to dismiss those affirmative defenses alleging that "the public's right of access to information of public interest made [the defendants'] conduct reasonable, that the entry was constitutionally protected, and that based upon custom and usage and the social necessity of the need to assure access to information in matters of public interest, defendants had the implied consent of the plaintiffs, . . . and that the entry was nontrespassory and privileged because it was made to observe and record a genuinely newsworthy event which made the plaintiff's premises open to the public by custom and usage." *Id.* at 222-23.

173. 1999 U.S. App. LEXIS 20262, *2-3 (9th Cir. Aug. 27, 1999) (9th Cir. 1999) (*aff'g* 129 F.3d 505 (9th Cir. 1997)).

174. See Chap. 12-4(a) n.37 *supra* & Chap. 12-5 *infra*.

their ranch. According to these courts, "[n]ewsgathering does not create a license to trespass or to intrude by electronic means into the precincts of another's home."[175]

Other courts, however, have held the news media's presence at or entry into a private residence nonactionable in a variety of circumstances. In *Magenis v. Fisher Broadcasting, Inc.*,[176] for example, an Oregon appellate court affirmed a jury verdict in favor of a television station that "accompanied police officers, who were executing a warrant to search plaintiffs' residence, and filmed the raid with video cameras." The plaintiffs had grounded their claim in invasion of

---

175. Copeland v. Hubbard Broadcasting, Inc., 526 N.W.2d 402, 405 (Minn. App. 1995). Declining to follow the Florida Supreme Court's decision in *Florida Publishing Co. v. Fletcher*, 340 So. 2d 914 (Fla. 1976), *cert. denied*, 431 U.S. 930 (1977), the court in *Anderson v. WROC-TV* similarly held that the "gathering of news and the means by which it is obtained does not authorize, whether under the First Amendment or otherwise, the right to enter into a private home by an implied invitation arising out of a self-created custom and practice. This is a bootstrap argument which does not eliminate the trespassory conduct of the defendants in this case." 441 N.Y.S.2d at 223. Thus, although the court conceded that "consent may be implied from custom, usage or conduct," it held that such consent "may not be extended by inference to justify the unlicensed entry of others." *Id.* The news media, the court observed, does "not stand in any favored position with respect to newsgathering activity" and therefore has "no special First Amendment immunity or special privilege to invade the rights and liberties of others." *Id.* at 223-24. The court further rejected the suggestion that it balance "the degree of intrusion sought to be justified" against "the newsworthiness of the story" at issue on the ground that such a "test . . . is too vague and subjective to counter-balance the predominant interest served in protecting the rights of individuals in a free society against invasion of their privacy or their home." *Id.* at 224.

In *Cliff v. Narragansett Television, L.P.*, 688 A.2d 805 (R.I. 1996), the Rhode Island Supreme Court held that plaintiff, the surviving spouse of a man who had committed suicide in his home, stated a cause of action for wrongful death against a television station and its reporter. The deceased had secluded himself in the family home, precipitating a significant police presence outside the house and efforts by law enforcement authorities to dissuade the man from taking his own life. During this time, the reporter telephoned the man in the home, recorded their conversation, and told him that it would be played on the evening news. The man took his own life minutes after the interview was broadcast and, when police entered the home, the television was tuned to defendants' station. The court held that the plaintiff had stated a claim for common law negligence which, in the case of third party responsibility for suicide, is governed by the so-called "uncontrollable impulse" rule. *Id.* at 808 (quoting Tate v. Canonica, 5 Cal. Rptr. 28, 40 (Ct. App. 1960) ("'if the negligent wrong causes mental illness which results in an uncontrollable impulse to commit suicide, then the wrongdoer may be held liable for the death'")). Moreover, the court concluded that the First Amendment did not preclude a finding of liability because, "not withstanding First Amendment constitutional protections, everyone, including the press, should be answerable for unprivileged negligent actions that proximately result in suicide." 688 A.2d at 811 (citing Branzburg v. Hayes, 408 U.S. 665, 683 (1972)). The court did, however, hold that plaintiff had failed to state a claim for intentional infliction of emotional distress or for common law invasion of privacy. See 688 A.2d at 812, 814 ("Certainly, no one can question the newsworthiness of the sad but public incident. Only one telephone call during the publicity-charged incident was made by the reporter, and that simple telephone call was insufficient to sustain an invasion of privacy claim.").

176. 798 P.2d 1106, 1107 (Or. App. 1990).

§ 12-4(a) NEWSGATHERING AND THE LAW § 12-4(a)

privacy, not trespass, and the court determined that, to sustain the former claim, it is "not sufficient that [plaintiffs] prove that defendants entered their property without permission."[177] According to the court, a jury reasonably "could find other factors relevant to whether the defendant's conduct was 'highly offensive,' including the extent of the intrusion, the context, conduct and circumstances surrounding the intrusion, the defendant's motives, the setting into which defendants intruded and the plaintiff's expectation of privacy."[178]

Still other courts have held that a cause of action for intrusion or trespass cannot be premised simply on the fact that a journalist or photographer came to plaintiff's residence to request an interview or a picture,[179] that a journalist entered an apartment with the tenant's permission in a suit by the building owner,[180] that magazine photographers entered plaintiff's home without her knowledge but with the permission of the house's architect and plaintiff's fourteen-year-old daughter,[181] that a newspaper published an article based on information secured by two electric company officials who entered a motel to read electric

---

177. *Id.* at 1110 See *id.* ("In determining whether the defendant's conduct was tortious, the fact that it constituted an unlawful trespass is only one factor to be considered.").

178. *Id.* (citing Miller v. National Broadcasting Co., 232 Cal. Rptr. at 678).

179. See Dempsey v. National Enquirer, Inc., 702 F. Supp. 927, 931 (D. Me. 1988) (allegation that defendant came to plaintiff's "house and continued to press for an interview even after plaintiff refused" does not constitute actionable intrusion because "[t]here is no assertion that the . . . reporter went beyond the front door of the plaintiff's house"); cf. Cape Publications, Inc. v. Bridges, 423 So.2d 426 (Fla. App. 1982) (rejecting claims of intrusion, trespass, and invasion of privacy where news photographers, standing outside plaintiff's home, took her picture emerging from the house partially nude after being held hostage by her husband).

180. See Lal v. CBS Inc., 551 F. Supp. 356 (E.D. Pa. 1982), *aff'd*, 726 F.2d 97 (3d Cir. 1984). In *Lal*, plaintiff sought recovery in trespass when a television news crew entered an apartment he owned, with the occupant's permission, to investigate conditions there. 551 F. Supp. at 358. The district court granted, and the Third Circuit affirmed, summary judgment for the defendants on the ground that "an owner who is not in possession cannot maintain an action for trespass absent an injury to his reversion" interest, and the news crew "had the right to rely on" the tenant's "apparent right to possession" in securing permission to enter. *Id.* at 96. Accord 726 F.2d at 100 ("lessor of improved land who is out of possession of the property cannot maintain an action for trespass absent some injury to the lessor's reversionary interest" and "the consent of the person in possession of the property to the entry onto the premises is a complete defense to a trespass claim").

181. See Rawls v. Conde Nast Publications, Inc., 446 F.2d 313 (5th Cir. 1971), *cert. denied*, 404 U.S. 1038 (1972). In *Rawls*, *Vogue* magazine sent a photographer, a model, and an editor into plaintiff's home, when she was not present, after securing the permission of plaintiff's daughter through the architect who designed the house. *Id.* at 314. Although plaintiff objected to the group's presence when she returned home, she acquiesced in their request to complete their work before departing. *Id.* at 314-15. The Fifth Circuit affirmed a jury verdict in defendant's favor on plaintiff's intrusion claim because, "at the time of the alleged invasion the plaintiff made no meaningful effort to protect her privacy or demonstrated no visible emotional distress, but rather acquiesced in the continued presence of the defendant's employees in her home." *Id.* at 317.

meters,[182] that a journalist entered plaintiffs' home and took photographs of their young children, who had suffocated to death after being locked in a refrigerator,[183] or that a television crew entered the apartment of an elderly man who "suffered frequent lapses of memory" and had allegedly "become disoriented and confused."[184]

The actionability of newsgathering within a private home often turns on the propriety of the media's presence there in the company of law enforcement officials. When its occupants are not present, and the home becomes a venue for official activity, courts have wrestled with the relevance of tradition and custom in authorizing public officials to consent to the news media's presence.[185] In that context, the Florida Supreme Court's decision in *Florida Publishing Co. v. Fletcher*[186] has sparked extensive judicial debate concerning the relevance to a common law cause of action against the news media of "consent," actual or implied, arising from a public official's agreement to permit journalists to accompany them, or otherwise enter on to private property. In *Fletcher*, where

---

182. See McCraig v. Talladega Publ'g Co., 544 So. 2d 875, 879 (Ala. 1989) ("by accepting electrical services ... as members of [a] cooperative," plaintiffs, "by implication, accepted the policies" of the cooperative "and thereby granted the Co-op's agents and representatives a right of access for the limited purpose of inspecting and servicing the Co-op's equipment").

183. See Costlow v. Cusimano, 311 N.Y.S.2d 92, 93 (App. Div. 1970). In *Costlow*, the plaintiffs sought damages, under a variety of theories, because "by reason of the publication and exhibition" of the photographs of their deceased children, they "became sick, nervous, unable to eat, suffered severe mental anguish and emotional distress," and were "required to obtain medical and psychiatric care." *Id.* On appeal, the court held that "[a]lthough a cause of action for trespass could be established" based on defendant's unauthorized entry on to plaintiffs' property "unless that entry was justified by his status as a radio station employee investigating the death of two children," the complaint had failed "to allege damages proper to a trespass action":

> There is no support for plaintiffs' argument that damages for injury to reputation and for emotional disturbance are recoverable on the alleged facts as the natural consequence of the trespass. A trespasser may be subject to liability for physical harm done while on the land, irrespective of whether his conduct would be subject to liability were he not a trespasser. . . . However, since the tort of trespass is designed to protect interests in possession of property, damages for trespass are limited to consequences flowing from the interference with possession and not for separable acts more properly allocated under other categories of liability.

Id. at 97 (citing RESTATEMENT (SECOND) OF TORTS § 162).

184. Rand v. National Broadcasting Co., N.Y. L.J. April 19, 1989, at 22 (N.Y. Sup. Ct. 1989). In *Rand*, a New York trial court granted a television station's motion for summary judgment on claims instituted by plaintiff's conservator for invasion of privacy and trespass based on the defendant's entry into his apartment and videotaping it in a state of "most extreme disarray," with his permission. *Id.* The privacy claims were dismissed because of the limited nature of such a cause of action under N.Y. CIV. RIGHTS LAW §§ 50-51; the court rejected the trespass claim because there was "no evidence that the defendants' entry was without permission." *Id.*

185. See, e.g., Florida Publ'g Co. v. Fletcher, 340 So. 2d 914 (Fla. 1976), *cert. denied,* 431 U.S. 930 (1997); Prahl v. Brosamle, 295 N.W.2d 768 (Wis. App. 1980); Robinson v. City of Denver, Civ. No. 94 N 0771 (D. Colo. Feb. 26, 1999). This issue is discussed at Chap. 12-3 *supra*.

186. 340 So. 2d 914 (Fla. 1976). See Chap. 12-3 *supra* (discussing *Fletcher*).

the Fire Marshal and a police official "invited the news media to accompany them" into plaintiffs' fire-damaged home, as was "their standard practice," the Florida Supreme Court concluded that there had been no trespass because it was the "common custom, usage and practice for news media to enter private premises and homes" under such circumstances.[187] When residents are in the home, however, courts have focused instead on the degree to which they are aware of, and consent to, the news media's presence.[188]

In *Baugh v. CBS Inc.*,[189] for example, a CBS News crew accompanied a Mobile Crisis Intervention Team to plaintiff's residence, where she had just been beaten by her husband. Plaintiff testified that police officers who had come to her home in response to her 911 call identified both the CBS crew and the

---

187. 340 So. 2d at 915, 918. See Wood v. Fort Dodge Messenger, 13 MEDIA L. REP. (BNA) 1610, 1614 (Iowa Dist. 1986) (where television reporters "check[ed] in with Sheriff's office" before entering plaintiff's farm and Sheriff subsequently "ratified their acts and expressed no criticism," such "[c]onsent is a complete defense to any claim of trespass").

188. See generally Green Valley Sch., Inc. v. Cowles Florida Broadcasting, Inc., 327 So. 2d 810, 819 (Fla. App. 1976) (where camera crew accompanied public officials on raid of private boarding school, court rejected contention that news media's "entry upon appellant's property . . . was as a matter of law sanctioned by 'the request of and with the consent of the State Attorney' and within the 'common usage and custom of Florida'"); Prahl v. Brosamle, 295 N.W.2d 768, 780 (Wis. App. 1980) (distinguishing *Fletcher* and finding no implied consent "as a matter of law," on the ground that, when defendant journalist entered plaintiff's property at the time of police investigation of gun shots there, "[n]o official requested [his] assistance in the investigation" and defendant did "not rely upon record evidence of custom of the type described in *Fletcher*"); Belluomo v. KAKE TV & Radio, Inc., 596 P.2d 832, 844 (Kan. App. 1979) (where film crew accompanied government food inspectors into restaurant kitchen, "there was no consent" for it to enter the area "[i]f the purported consent was fraudulently induced"); Anderson v. WROC-TV, 441 N.Y.S.2d 220, 223 (Sup. Ct. 1981) (where news media accompanied Humane Society investigator in executing a warrant at plaintiff's home, court rejected *Fletcher* analysis on ground that the "gathering of news and the means by which it is obtained does not authorize, whether under the First Amendment or otherwise, the right to enter into a private home by an implied invitation arising out of a self-created custom and practice"); Miller v. National Broadcasting Co., 232 Cal. Rptr. 668, 683 (Ct. App. 1986) (where film crew accompanied paramedics into plaintiff's bedroom, court held that "[o]ne seeking emergency medical attention does not thereby 'open the door' for persons without any clearly identifiable and justifiable official reason who may wish to enter the premises where the medical aid is being administered"); Berger v. Hanlon, 129 F.3d 505, 517 (9th Cir. 1997), *vacated*, 119 S. Ct. 1706 (1999), *aff'd*, 1999 U.S. App. LEXIS 20262, *2-3 (9th Cir. Aug. 27, 1999) (distinguishing *Fletcher* on its facts, involving "'a disaster of great public interest' and a 'calamity,'" and rejecting implied consent argument where plaintiff "consented to [the law enforcement officer's] initial entry into the home . . . [but] never consented to the entry of the [concealed] media-owned microphone that [the agent] wore"); Robinson v. City of Denver, Civ. No. 94 N 0771, slip op. at 3 (D. Colo. Feb. 26, 1999) (plaintiff did not consent to entry of media defendants into his home, and "demanded that they leave"); cf. Reeves v. Fox Television Network, 983 F. Supp. 703, 712 (N.D. Ohio 1997) (granting summary judgment to defendants on trespass and intrusion claims where "plaintiff voluntarily permitted the camera crew to enter his home with the police and videotape what occurred").

189. 828 F. Supp. 745 (N.D. Cal. 1993).

crisis team as "from the D.A.'s office. They are here to help you."[190] Moreover, she testified that, when she asked what the camera was for, she was told "they were doing a segment . . . for the District Attorney's Office."[191] At no time, according to plaintiff, did the crew identify themselves as affiliated with the news media.

The court rejected plaintiff's claims for misappropriation of likeness,[192] trespass, and intrusion.[193] With respect to the latter cause of action, the court reasoned that "no trespass can be found if actual consent to entry was given," even though there may be a valid trespass claim "where the defendant exceeds the scope of the consent."[194] The court concluded that the CBS crew "acted within the scope of [plaintiff's] consent while they were on the premises," since she knew that they were videotaping her home; "[i]f they exceeded the scope" of plaintiff's consent, "they did so by broadcasting the videotape, an act which occurred after they left [her] property and which cannot support a trespass claim."[195] Even in "a case where consent was fraudulently induced, but consent was nonetheless given, plaintiff has no claim for trespass."[196] Similarly, the court rejected plaintiff's intrusion claim, on the ground that "consent is an absolute defense, even if improperly induced."[197] The court did, however, permit plaintiff to pursue claims for fraud, publication of private facts,[198] and intentional infliction of emotional distress. With respect to the latter, the court, citing *Miller*,

---

190. *Id.* at 751.

191. *Id.*

192. See *id.* at 753-54 (misappropriation claim codified in CAL. CIV. CODE § 3344(a) does not apply to bona fide "news accounts").

193. The court did, however, decline to embrace defendant's suggestion that the Uniform Single Publication Act barred plaintiff's claims. See CAL. CIV. CODE § 3425.3 ("No person shall have more than one cause of action for damages for libel or slander or invasion of privacy or any other tort founded upon any single publication"). While the Act "bars any claims based on the *broadcast* of Plaintiffs' story," the court held that it only affected plaintiff's claims for intrusion and trespass "to the extent they rely on the actual broadcast." 828 F. Supp. at 756. "The claims remain viable, however, to the extent they rely on a tortious *physical* intrusion into Plaintiffs' home." *Id.* (emphasis in original).

194. *Id.* at 756.

195. *Id.* at 756-57.

196. *Id.* at 757. The court distinguished the holding in *Miller v. National Broadcasting Co.*, 232 Cal. Rptr. 668 (Ct. App. 1986), on the ground that, in *Miller*, "no member of the camera crew attempted to obtain plaintiff's consent; they simply barged in with the paramedics." 828 F. Supp. at 757; see *id.* ("*Miller* does not stand for the proposition that consent must be knowing.").

197. 828 F. Supp. at 757.

198. This claim, however, appears to have been based on the subsequent broadcast concerning plaintiff and not on the defendant's newsgathering. See *id.* at 755 ("While the court finds the issue of domestic violence . . . to be newsworthy, the Court is not yet convinced that Plaintiffs' personal involvement in an incident of domestic violence is newsworthy as a matter of law.").

held that it could not "say that Defendants' behavior was not outrageous as a matter of law."[199]

§ 12-4(b). Public Institutions.

Civil actions against the media have also been adjudicated in the context of efforts to gather news and information in mental health facilities,[200] alcohol treatment centers,[201] private psychiatric facilities,[202] institutions for the care of dependent and neglected children,[203] hospitals and related health care facili-

---

199. *Id.* at 758 (citing Miller v. National Broadcasting Co., 232 Cal. Rptr. 668 (Ct. App. 1986)).
200. See, e.g., Commonwealth v. Wiseman, 249 N.E.2d 610 (Mass. 1969) *cert. denied*, 398 U.S. 960 (1970); Cullen v. Grove Press, Inc., 276 F. Supp. 727 (S.D.N.Y. 1967). In *Wiseman*, the Massachusetts Supreme Judicial Court enjoined most distribution of the film "Titicut Follies," which contained scenes filmed at the Massachusetts Correctional Institution at Bridgewater "to which insane persons . . . and defective delinquents may be committed." 249 N.E.2d at 612. The film included scenes of "mentally incompetent patients . . . in the nude . . . [and] in the most personal and private situations." *Id.* at 613. The court concluded that the film's

> massive, unrestrained invasion of the intimate lives of these State patients may be prevented by properly framed injunctive relief. The Commonwealth has standing and a duty to protect reasonably, and in a manner consistent with other public interests the inmates from any invasions of their privacy substantially greater than those inevitably arising from the very fact of confinement.

Id. at 615. In *Cullen*, however, another case arising out of the same film, a federal court in New York declined to enjoin its distribution, recognizing that the "conditions in public institutions such as Bridgewater for the care of the criminally insane, including the physical facilities, conduct of employees, and the type of treatment administered to inmates, are matters which are of great interest to the public generally. Such public interest is both legitimate and healthy." 276 F. Supp. at 728-29.
201. See W.C.H. of Waverly, Missouri., Inc. v. Meredith Corp., 13 MEDIA L. REP. (BNA) 1648 (W.D. Mo. 1986) (no claim for intrusion resulting from television station's undercover investigation at alcoholic treatment center, but court recognized potential validity of claims for fraud, violation of federal eavesdropping statute, and for negligence).
202. See, e.g., Howell v. New York Post Co., 612 N.E.2d 699 (N.Y. 1993) (*aff'g* 581 N.Y.S.2d 330 (App. Div. 1992)) (photographs of plaintiff taken on the grounds of private psychiatric facility not actionable as invasion of privacy or intentional infliction of emotional distress); Charter Behavioral Health Sys. v. CBS Inc., No. 3:99-CV-150-MV (W.D.N.C. Apr. 21, 1999) (declining to enjoin broadcast of hidden camera investigation in private psychiatric hospital).
203. See Quinn v. Johnson, 381 N.Y.S.2d 875 (App. Div. 1976). In *Quinn*, two New York courts declined to enjoin the televising of a news report about conditions at St. Michael's Home, a state-licensed institution for the care and treatment of dependent and neglected children, including videotape shot inside the facility. Even though the appellate court was not "persuaded" that the videotape's "sole or even its chief object is to provide information which could lead to a correction of the conditions it claims exist," it nevertheless concluded that "nothing appears on the videotape which, in our opinion, warrants a prior restraint upon its exhibition." *Id.* at 878 (citing Organization for a Better Austin v. Keefe, 402 U.S. 415 (1971)). See also Special Force Ministries v. WCCO Television, 584 N.W.2d 789 (Minn. App. 1998) (plaintiff residents, outpatients, and operators of facility for mentally retarded stated claims for trespass and fraud against television station and reporter who had volunteered at facility and used hidden camera to record events there).

ties,[204] child day care centers,[205] and schools.[206] In *W.C.H. of Waverly, Missouri, Inc. v. Meredith Corp.*,[207] for example, a television station employee posed as a potential patient at an alcohol and drug abuse rehabilitation center to gain entrance to the facility. Although the court held that a corporate plaintiff could not maintain a cause of action for intrusion,[208] it nevertheless permitted the plaintiff to pursue claims for, *inter alia*, fraud and negligence.[209] The First Amendment did not "shield" the station from liability for claims that "involve challenges to defendant's alleged tortious actions, not to the content of its stories or its right to investigate and air such stories."[210]

In *Howell v. New York Post Co.*,[211] however, the New York Court of Appeals held that plaintiff, a patient at Four Winds Hospital, a private psychiatric facility, could not maintain claims for invasion of privacy or intentional infliction of emotional distress against a newspaper that took her photograph on the facility's private grounds. The plaintiff was photographed walking with Hedda Nussbaum, who had been the subject of significant press attention when her six-year-old

---

204. See, e.g., Green v. Chicago Tribune Co., 675 N.E.2d 249, 256 (Ill. App. 1996) (plaintiff stated claim for intentional infliction of emotional distress and for publication of private facts where newspaper photographed homicide victim in hospital and quoted statements made by victim's mother in private hospital room); Shulman v. Group W Prods., Inc., 955 P.2d 469, 490 (Cal. 1998) ("we are aware of no law or custom permitting the press to ride in ambulances or enter hospital rooms during treatment without the patient's consent").

205. See, e.g., Willis v. Griffin Television, L.L.C., Case No. 91,812 (Okla. App. Mar. 5, 1999) (plaintiffs stated claims for defamation and false light invasion of privacy, but not for trespass, misappropriation of likeness violative of right to privacy, fraudulent misrepresentation, illegal interception of communications, negligent supervision, or unfair trade practices, against television station that produced series of investigative reports based on hidden camera investigation of local child day-care centers).

206. See, e.g., Green Valley Sch., Inc. v. Cowles Florida Broadcasting, Inc., 327 So. 2d 810 (Fla. App. 1976). In *Green Valley School*, a television news crew accompanied 50 law enforcement officers on a raid of a private boarding school — including unannounced entry into the students' sleeping quarters at night — and aired a report that yielded a suit by the school alleging, among other things, a claim for trespass. *Id.* at 812. A Florida appellate court rejected the defendants' assertion that the trespass claim was barred by the consent of the State's Attorney to accompany officers as they executed a search warrant. *Id.* at 819 ("In this jurisdiction, a law enforcement officer is not *as a matter of law* endowed with the right or authority to invite people of his choosing to invade private property and participate in a midnight raid of the premises."). See also Marcus Garvey Charter Sch. v. Washington Times Corp., 27 MEDIA L. REP. (BNA) 1225 (D.C. Super. 1998) (court was "unwilling to hold that the taking of photographs when pursuing a news story in a public school is highly offensive to a reasonable person" so as to warrant claim for intrusion against newspaper).

207. 13 MEDIA L. REP. (BNA) 1648 (W.D. Mo. 1986).

208. See *id.* at 1650 ("we decline to extend this privacy action to allow recovery for corporations") (citing Barr v. Arco Chem. Corp., 529 F. Supp. 1275, 1282 (S.D. Tex. 1982)).

209. 13 MEDIA L. REP. (BNA) at 1650.

210. *Id.* at 1651.

211. 612 N.E.2d 699 (N.Y. 1993).

"adoptive" daughter died as the result of child abuse.[212] The photograph was published along with a news report about Ms. Nussbaum. The court professed its "reluctan[ce] to intrude upon reasonable editorial judgments in determining whether there is a real relationship between an article and photograph," and accordingly held that plaintiff could not maintain a claim for invasion of privacy.[213] Similarly, the court held that, although "newsgathering methods may be tortious,"[214] the conduct at issue — *i.e.*, "a trespass onto Four Winds' grounds — does not remotely approach the required standard" to maintain a claim for intentional infliction of emotional distress.[215]

In *Shulman v. Group W. Productions, Inc.*,[216] the California Supreme Court held that the plaintiffs, who were airlifted from the scene of an auto accident in which they were severely injured to a nearby hospital in a rescue helicopter, had stated a cause of action for intrusion against a television camera operator who accompanied plaintiffs, without their knowledge or consent, to the hospital. The Court concluded that "a triable issue exists as to whether both plaintiffs had an objectively reasonable expectation of privacy in the interior of the rescue helicopter" because, although the "attendance of reporters and photographers at the scene of an accident is to be expected," there is "no law or custom permitting the press to ride in ambulances or enter hospital rooms during treatment without the patient's consent."[217] In addition, the Court held that a jury could properly find that such filming was "highly offensive to a reasonable person."[218]

§ 12-4(c). Private Businesses.

The news media's efforts to gather information on the premises of private businesses have given rise to a variety of legal challenges. As the following discussion illustrates, the press has generally — though not universally — avoided liability when gathering news on the premises of private business establishments that nevertheless welcome the public. The courts have, however, afforded less protection to newsgathering that occurs in otherwise private areas of a business open to the public, especially when the conduct at issue involves

---

212. *Id.* at 700.
213. *Id.* at 704 (citing Finger v. Omni Publications, Int'l, 566 N.E.2d 141 (N.Y. 1990)).
214. 612 N.E.2d at 705 (citing Galella v. Onassis, 487 F.2d 986, 995 (2d Cir. 1973)).
215. 612 N.E.2d at 705; see *id.* (successful claim would require showing of "such atrocious, indecent and utterly despicable conduct as to meet the rigorous requirements of an intentional infliction of emotional distress claim").
216. 955 P.2d 469 (Cal. 1998).
217. *Id.* at 490.
218. *Id.* at 494.

elements of misrepresentation or surreptitious methods of collecting information.[219]

§ 12-4(c)(1). Restaurants and Bars.

Many privately owned businesses are nevertheless open to the public. Restaurants and bars routinely welcome members of the public and, in fact, solicit their patronage. Journalists are traditionally afforded the same freedom to enter such places, without risking liability, as their fellow citizens, regardless of their purpose in doing so. Thus, under most circumstances, courts have declined to sustain causes of action asserted against the news media for gathering information in the public areas of bars and restaurants.[220] As one federal court concluded, a "reporter's presence ... in a restaurant open to the public cannot constitute intrusion upon the seclusion of another."[221]

By the same token, some courts have recognized limitations on the news media's ability to gather information in restaurants and bars. In *Stressman v. American Black Hawk Broadcasting Co.*,[222] for example, the plaintiff was filmed by a television station while she was dining in a restaurant despite her express objection. The Iowa Supreme Court reversed the trial judge's decision granting the station's motion to dismiss, on the ground that, even if the restaurant was open to the public, "it is not inconceivable" that plaintiff "was seated in the sort of private dining room offered by many restaurants. To film a person in a private

---

219. The latter subject is treated extensively in Chap. 13 *infra*. This chapter focuses instead on the location in which the press seeks to gather information for publication or broadcast, regardless of the method of newsgathering involved.

220. See, e.g., Penwell v. Taft Broadcasting Co., 469 N.E.2d 1025 (Ohio App. 1984) (videotape footage of plaintiff's arrest at a bar); Gill v. Hearst Publ'g Co., 253 P.2d 441, 444 (Cal. 1953) (photograph of plaintiffs taken at ice cream concession at Farmers' Market); Dempsey v. National Enquirer, Inc., 702 F. Supp. 927 (D. Me. 1988) (reporter followed plaintiff to a restaurant and requested an interview). In *Penwell*, for example, the plaintiff was an "innocent bystander" in a drug raid on a local tavern, where a television news crew videotaped his erroneous arrest and subsequent removal from the bar. 469 N.E.2d at 1027. The Ohio Court of Appeals affirmed summary judgment for the television station on plaintiff's privacy-based claim that his "arrest in a public bar and his removal from the bar ... were private affairs." *Id.* See also Early v. Toledo Blade, No. 90-3434, slip op. at 27, 31 (Ohio C.P. July 8, 1997), *aff'd*, 26 MEDIA L. REP. (BNA) 2569 (Ohio App. 1998) (plaintiffs could not base invasion of privacy claims on reporting of events that took place at public bars).

221. Dempsey v. National Enquirer, Inc., 702 F. Supp. at 931; see *id.* ("Since taking a photograph of the plaintiff in a public place cannot constitute an invasion of privacy based on intrusion ..., it is obvious that an *attempt* to take a photograph cannot create liability. Although these contacts may well have been annoying, they cannot reasonably be seen as highly offensive.") (citing RESTATEMENT (SECOND) OF TORTS § 652B, cmt. c); Wilkins v. National Broadcasting Co., 84 Cal. Rptr. 2d 329, 336 (Ct. App. 1999) (affirming dismissal of intrusion claim brought by salesmen surreptitiously videotaped in an "outdoor patio area of a public restaurant," a location that was "within close proximity of other tables" and "not secluded").

222. 416 N.W.2d 685 (Iowa 1987).

dining room might conceivably be a highly offensive intrusion upon that person's seclusion."[223]

In *Le Mistral, Inc. v. Columbia Broadcasting System*,[224] a New York appellate court affirmed a jury verdict in favor of a restaurant on a cause of action sounding in trespass against a television station. The evidence at trial indicated that the station's camera crew and reporter:

> entered the restaurant at approximately 2:00 p.m. with the camera working ("rolling"), which necessitated the utilization of bright lights for filming purposes. After entering the premises in this fashion, Ms. Rich [the reporter] and the camera crew were commanded to leave by plaintiff's president. It appears that these CBS employees were on the premises for a period of time during which the camera continued to roll.[225]

Although the appellate court did not expressly address the elements of plaintiff's common law trespass claim,[226] it affirmatively rejected defendant's constitutional defense on the ground that "the First Amendment is not a shibboleth before which all other rights must succumb."[227]

Finally, the news media has not been immune from liability when gathering information in those portions of otherwise public restaurants that are not open to the public at large. In *Belluomo v. KAKE TV & Radio, Inc.*,[228] for example,

---

223. *Id.* at 687. The court in *Stressman* further suggested that, even if the plaintiff had been seated in a purely public portion of the restaurant, "[t]here are some matters about a person that should not be exhibited to the public because they could prove embarrassing to an ordinary person of reasonable sensitivity." *Id.* at 688.

224. 402 N.Y.S.2d 815 (App. Div. 1978).

225. *Id.* at 816. The trial judge observed that:

> From the evidence the jury was entitled to conclude that . . . the defendant's employees burst into plaintiff's restaurant in noisy and obtrusive fashion and following the loud commands of the reporter, Rich, to photograph the patrons dining, turned their lights and camera upon the dining room. Consternation, the jury was informed, followed. Patrons waiting to be seated left the restaurant. Others who had finished eating, left without waiting for their checks. Still others hid their faces behind napkins or table cloths or hid themselves beneath tables.

Id.

226. The trial court had rejected the defendant's effort to "justify her crew's entry into the restaurant by calling it . . . a 'place of public accommodation'" on the ground that "they did not seek to avail themselves of the plaintiff's 'accommodation'; they had no intention of purchasing food or drink." *Id.* at 817.

227. *Id.* at 817 (citing Dietemann v. Time, Inc., 449 F.2d 245, 249 (9th Cir. 1971); Galella v. Onassis, 487 F.2d 986, 995-96 (2d Cir. 1973)). The appellate court did, however, hold that the defendant was entitled to a new trial on the issue of punitive damages (the jury had awarded them in the amount of $250,000) so that it could submit evidence concerning "its motive" for entering the restaurant with "cameras rolling." 402 N.Y.S.2d at 818.

228. 596 P.2d 832, 836 (Kan. App. 1979).

television reporters accompanied a government inspector to Doc's Steak House, where they used a "silent" camera to record "conditions in the food handling, preparation and serving areas of the restaurant." The reporters had identified themselves and secured a signed release from the restaurant's co-owner, which he purported to revoke in writing the following day.[229] Although the Kansas Court of Appeals affirmed a jury verdict in favor of the defendants on the restaurant's claims of fraud, misrepresentation and trespass, it nevertheless proceeded to address "various issues extraneous to those necessary to our decision."[230] Among other matters, the court rejected the defendants' reliance on the signed release, asserting both that "gratuitous consent to the use of one's name and portrait is revocable at any time" and that, if "the purported consent was fraudulently induced, there was no consent" in the first place.[231] In addition, the court concluded that the defendants were not entitled to "absolute protection under the First Amendment," suggesting that such protection is available only when a plaintiff seeks damages for injury to reputation.[232] Thus, the court purported to "hold that a party is entitled to recover compensatory damages for injury resulting from publication of information acquired by tortious conduct" and "punitive damages if the tortious conduct constitutes fraud or a willful, wanton or malicious invasion of the injured party's rights."[233]

§ 12-4(c)(2). Public Areas Generally.

Perhaps the most thoughtful and comprehensive judicial consideration of the media's liability for newsgathering in those portions of otherwise private businesses that are open to the public is the Seventh Circuit's decision in *Desnick v. American Broadcasting Cos.*[234] The case arose from a television network's alleged trespass and other tortious conduct in gathering information at the Desnick Eye Center, a chain of large ophthalmic clinics. According to the complaint, Dr. Desnick — the proprietor of the clinics — "permitted an ABC crew to videotape the Desnick Eye Center's main premises in Chicago, to film a cataract operation 'live,' and to interview doctors, technicians, and patients" after being assured by the producer that the planned broadcast "would not involve 'ambush' interviews or 'undercover' surveillance, and that it would be

---

229. *Id.*
230. *Id.* at 836.
231. *Id.* at 836, 844.
232. *Id.* at 838; see *id.* at 840 ("The theory upon which plaintiffs' claim was submitted to the jury was tortious conduct, trespass, in defendant's news gathering, not defamatory falsehood.").
233. *Id.* at 842.
234. 44 F.3d 1345 (7th Cir. 1995). See also Desnick v. Capital Cities/ABC Inc., 851 F. Supp. 303 (N.D. Ill. 1994), *aff'd in part sub nom.* Desnick v. American Broadcasting Cos., 44 F.3d 1345 (7th Cir. 1995).

'fair and balanced.'"[235] In fact, however, the plaintiff alleged that, "[u]nbeknownst" to him, the producer "had dispatched persons equipped with concealed cameras to offices of the Desnick Eye Center" where, posing "as patients, these persons — seven in all — requested eye examinations" and "secretly videotaped" ophthalmologists "examining these 'test patients.'"[236]

In all, the plaintiffs asserted four distinct claims arising from "the methods that the defendants used to create the broadcast segment" — (1) trespass "in insinuating the test patients" into plaintiffs' offices, (2) invasion of privacy, (3) violation of state and federal statutes governing electronic surveillance, and (4) fraud "by gaining access to the Chicago office by means of a false promise that they would present a 'fair and balanced' picture of the Center's operations and would not use 'ambush' interviews or undercover surveillance."[237] The court of appeals affirmed the trial judge's decision granting the defendants' motion to dismiss with respect to all four claims.

Although the court recognized the general rule that to "enter upon another's land without consent is a trespass," it noted that the rule's "force" has been "diluted somewhat by concepts of privilege and of implied consent."[238] Even so, the court observed, "there is no journalists' privilege to trespass,"[239] and "there can be no implied consent in any nonfictitious sense of the term when express consent is procured by a misrepresentation or misleading omission."[240] The law, however, has demonstrated a "willingness to give effect to consent procured by fraud" when there is no resulting "invasion . . . of any of the specific interests that the tort of trespass seeks to protect."[241] By gaining entry "into the plaintiffs'

---

235. 44 F.3d at 1348.
236. *Id.*
237. *Id.* at 1351. The court's decision with respect to the wiretapping and fraud claims are discussed in Chap. 13-2(b) *infra.*
238. 44 F.3d at 1351.
239. *Id.* (citing Prahl v. Brosamle, 295 N.W.2d 768, 780-81 (Wis. App. 1980); Le Mistral, Inc. v. Columbia Broadcasting Sys., 402 N.Y.S.2d 815 (App. Div. 1978)).
240. 44 F.3d at 1351; see *id.* ("The Desnick Eye Center would not have agreed to the entry of the test patients into its offices had it known they wanted eye examinations only in order to gather material for a television expose of the Center and that they were going to make secret videotapes of the examinations.").
241. *Id.* at 1352. See also Medical Lab. Management Consultants v. American Broadcasting Cos., 30 F. Supp. 2d 1182, 1204 (D. Ariz. 1998) (dismissing trespass claim, even though plaintiffs "did not consent to the use of the cameras concealed in Mr. Cooke's wig used to take pictures of the Medical Lab property," because "[a]ny damages caused by the publication of the videotaped meeting were not proximately caused by the trespass and Plaintiffs do not claim to have incurred any other damages as a result of the trespass"); Willis v. Griffin Television, L.L.C., Case No. 91,812, slip op. at 14 (Okla. App. Mar. 5, 1999) (affirming dismissal of trespass claims, despite reporters' misrepresentations, where plaintiffs "clearly consented to the challenged entry [and] alleged no injury to any interest in the property which a trespass claim protects"); Borger, *New Whines in Old Bottles, Taking Newsgathering Torts Off the Food Lion Shelf,* 34 TORT & INS. L.J.

premises by misrepresenting their purposes (more precisely by a misleading omission to disclose their purposes)," the defendants had not interfered with the plaintiffs' "ownership or possession of land."[242] Thus, because the defendants "entered offices that were open to anyone expressing a desire for ophthalmic services and videotaped physicians engaged in professional, not personal, communications with strangers," without disrupting the offices' activities, the court held that there could be no cause of action for trespass as a matter of law.[243]

In addition, the court concluded that the foregoing reasoning "largely disposes of" plaintiffs' privacy claims as well.[244] The arguably implicated privacy torts — intrusion and publication of private facts — require the invasion of "legitimately private activities" and "intimate personal facts" respectively.[245] Since "no intimate personal facts concerning the two individual plaintiffs," the doctors who were videotaped without their knowledge, were revealed, and "the only conversations that were recorded were" with defendants' representatives, neither privacy claim could survive a motion to dismiss.[246]

61, 71 (1998) ("The lawful use of information . . . creates no independent liability, and should not retroactively create liability for trespass.").

242. 44 F.3d at 1353.

243. *Id.* at 1352. Accord Baugh v. CBS Inc., 828 F. Supp. 745 (N.D. Cal. 1993); Miller v. National Broadcasting Co., 232 Cal. Rptr. 668 (Ct. App. 1986). The district court, in reaching the same conclusion, relied on *Baugh* and *Miller* and rejected the contrary reasoning of the Kansas Court of Appeals in *Belluomo v. KAKE TV & Radio*, 596 P.2d 832 (Kan. App. 1979). See 851 F. Supp. at 306. In addition, the district court distinguished the Wisconsin Supreme Court's decision in *Prahl v. Brosamle*, 295 N.W.2d 768 (Wis. App. 1980), because "[i]nstrumental to the *Prahl* court's holding" that plaintiff could maintain a trespass claim "was the reporter's failure to request or receive plaintiff's permission to enter the premises." 851 F. Supp. at 306. But see Shiffman v. Empire Blue Cross & Blue Shield, 681 N.Y.S.2d 511, 511 (App. Div. 1998) (affirming denial of motion to dismiss trespass claim predicated on fraudulently obtained consent, despite absence of allegations that defendant interfered with possession or caused injury to property, on ground that "consent obtained by misrepresentation or fraud is invalid [and] nominal damage is always presumed from a trespass"); Special Force Ministries v. WCCO Television, 584 N.W.2d 789, 793 (Minn. App. 1998) ("trespass requires only an unlawful entry upon another's rightful possession; whether a defendant's conduct while on the premises proximately caused the plaintiff's injuries is a fact issue for the jury").

244. 44 F.3d at 1353.

245. *Id.*

246. *Id.* (citing Thomas v. Pearl, 998 F.2d 447, 452 (7th Cir. 1993), *cert. denied*, 510 U.S. 1043 (1994)); see Medical Lab. Management Consultants v. American Broadcasting Cos., 30 F. Supp. 2d 1182, 1189 (D. Ariz. 1998) (dismissing intrusion claim where defendant used false pretenses to gain entrance to plaintiff's laboratory and secretly videotaped conversation, because plaintiff could "claim no reasonable expectation of privacy in the location or contents of the conversation"). Cf. Willis v. Griffin Television, L.L.C., Case No. 91,812 (Okla. App. Mar. 5, 1999) (adopting *Desnick* analysis and dismissing fraud and trespass claims arising from hidden camera investigation and subsequent news reports).

Finally, the court spoke to the relevance of the First Amendment in the context of "claims concerning the making of the program segment, as distinct from the content of the segment itself."[247] "Today's 'tabloid' style investigative television reportage, conducted by networks desperate for viewers in an increasingly competitive television market," the court asserted, though "it is often shrill, one-sided, and offensive, and sometimes defamatory," is nevertheless "entitled to all the safeguards with which the Supreme Court has surrounded liability for defamation. And it is entitled to them regardless of the name of the tort" and "regardless of whether the tort suit is aimed at the content of the broadcast or the production of the broadcast."[248] Thus, the court concluded that:

> [i]f the broadcast itself does not contain actionable defamation, and no established rights are invaded in the process of creating it (for the media have no general immunity from tort or contract liability, . . .), then the target has no legal remedy even if the investigatory tactics used by the network are surreptitious, confrontational, unscrupulous, and ungentlemanly.[249]

Prior to *Desnick*, other courts had reached often conflicting conclusions regarding the news media's right to gather news in the public areas of private businesses. As a result, while some plaintiffs have been unsuccessful in pressing causes of action arising from such newsgathering activities, including the taking

---

247. 44 F.3d at 1355.
248. *Id.* (citing Hustler Magazine, Inc. v. Falwell, 485 U.S. 46 (1988)); see Medical Lab. Management Consultants v. American Broadcasting Cos., 30 F. Supp. 2d 1182, 1192 (D. Ariz. 1998) ("Because the alleged injury stems from a news broadcast, this Court must ensure that the First Amendment's requirements for constitutionally protected speech have been met.").
249. 44 F.3d at 1355 (citing Cohen v. Cowles Media Co., 501 U.S. 663, 669-70 (1991); Le Mistral, Inc. v. Columbia Broadcasting Sys., 402 N.Y.S.2d 815 (App. Div. 1978)). See also Russell v. American Broadcasting Cos., 23 MEDIA L. REP. (BNA) 2428 (N.D. Ill. 1995); Frome v. Renner, 26 MEDIA L. REP. (BNA) 1956, 1958 (C.D. Cal. 1997) (where defendant posed as patient in order to gain access to doctor's office and services, and plaintiff failed to show that misrepresentation affected doctor-patient relationship, "[t]he fact that Renner later criticized Plaintiff's methods on national television does not somehow convert this relationship into an action for fraud"); Marcus Garvey Charter Sch. v. Washington Times Corp., 27 MEDIA L. REP. (BNA) 1225 (D.C. Super. 1998) (discussed in Chap. 12-4(b) *supra*). In *Russell*, which was decided shortly after *Desnick*, the court considered claims arising from an analogous broadcast, by the same defendant, about sanitation problems in the commercial fish industry. 23 MEDIA L. REP. (BNA) at 2429. In the course of the broadcast, an ABC employee secured a job at a small, retail grocery at which the plaintiff was manager. The defendant's employee wore a hidden camera and microphone and recorded conversations in which the plaintiff instructed her "always to tell customers that the fish is 'today fresh,'" and told her that "fish too old to be sold as 'fresh' can still be cooked and then sold." *Id.* The district court, relying on *Desnick*, rejected plaintiff's intrusion claim. See 23 MEDIA L. REP. (BNA) at 2434 ("[P]laintiff alleges that defendants secretly recorded a conversation she willingly had with a co-worker at her place of business. This is hardly 'offensive prying into the private domain of another.'"). See also 26 MEDIA L. REP. (BNA) 1012 (N.D. Ill. 1997) (dismissing plaintiff's defamation and invasion of privacy claims).

of plaintiff's photograph as he stood next to a wall in a cigar store,[250] other courts have found liability in analogous circumstances.[251]

§ 12-4(c)(3). Private Areas Generally.

Once beyond those places to which the public is traditionally welcome, the media's liability for gathering information tends to vary largely with the means by which it has gained access to a restricted area, or the methods it employs to gather news while there. The resulting common law and constitutional issues were first considered at any length in *Dietemann v. Time, Inc.*[252] There, where the news media gained entry — under false pretenses — to a portion of plaintiff's home that he used to "engage[] in the practice of healing with clay, minerals, and herbs,"[253] the Ninth Circuit concluded that plaintiff's "den was a sphere from which he could reasonably expect to exclude eavesdropping newsmen."[254] Thus, the court held that, although "[o]ne who invites another to his home or office takes a risk that the visitor may not be what he seems, and that the visitor may repeat all he hears and observes when he leaves," the plaintiff in *Dietemann*, who was apparently viewed by the court as part homeowner and part business proprietor, "does not and should not be required to take the risk that what is heard and seen will be transmitted by photograph or recording, or in our modern world, in full living color and hi-fi to the public at large."[255]

In many ways, *Dietemann* has become the starting point for subsequent judicial consideration of these issues, despite the fact that it arose in the context of what might charitably be described as newsgathering in a "home office." Thus, in *Prahl v. Brosamle*,[256] a Wisconsin appellate court applied the reasoning of *Dietemann* to a trespass claim arising from the news media's uninvited entry

---

250. See, e.g., Jacova v. Southern Radio & Television Co., 83 So.2d 34, 40 (Fla. 1955) ("the showing of plaintiff's picture on the telecast in the manner in which it appeared was not an unreasonable or unwarranted invasion of privacy, as a matter of law").

251. See Daily Times Democrat v. Graham, 162 So.2d 474, 477-78 (Ala. 1964) (court rejects argument that because plaintiff's "picture was taken at the time she was a part of a public scene," its publication could not "be deemed an invasion of privacy," because to "hold that one who is involuntarily and instantaneously enmeshed in an embarrassing pose forfeits her right to privacy merely because she happened at the moment to be part of a public scene would be illogical, wrong, and unjust").

252. 449 F.2d 245 (9th Cir. 1971). See Chap. 12-2(a) *supra*. Outside the news media context, courts have also indicated that the tort of intrusion contemplates consideration of the location in which the allegedly tortious conduct takes place. See, e.g., Harkey v. Abate, 346 N.W.2d 74, 76 (Mich. App. 1983) ("Clearly, plaintiff and her daughter in this case had a right to privacy in the public restroom in question" and "the installation of the hidden viewing devices alone constitutes an interference with that privacy which a reasonable person would find highly offensive.").

253. 449 F.2d at 245.
254. *Id.* at 249.
255. *Id.*
256. 295 N.W.2d 768 (Wis. App. 1980).

on to plaintiff's property, which doubled as his home and his private research laboratory, following the firing of gun shots there.[257] The court rejected the contention that Brosamle, a broadcast journalist, was not a trespasser, asserting specifically that "the research corporation" may bring a trespass action for "entry of its laboratory."[258] In addition, the court concluded that an "implied consent to enter the land of another for business or informational purposes creates a privilege to enter only for that purpose."[259] Finally, the court relied on *Dietemann* to reject the defendants' argument "that they should be accorded a privilege to trespass stemming from the first amendment."[260]

Several courts have, however, retreated from a broad reading of *Dietemann*'s analysis of the First Amendment interest in newsgathering. In the prior restraint context, for example, Justice Blackmun — sitting as circuit justice — stayed enforcement of a preliminary injunction designed to prevent CBS from broadcasting a news report containing footage obtained inside a meat packing plant.[261] The footage was obtained "through the cooperation of" an employee of the company "who voluntarily agreed to wear undercover camera equipment during his shift."[262] The plaintiff had obtained preliminary injunctive relief on theories of trespass, breach of the duty of loyalty, and violation of the Uniform Trade Secrets Act.[263] The trial court concluded that "because the videotape 'was

---

257. The news media's entry on to Dr. Prahl's property was undertaken in the company of a police SWAT team that surrounded and then entered his home/laboratory after the gun shots. See *id.* at 772-74.

258. *Id.* at 778. The court's analysis of the trespass claim is discussed in Chap. 12-4(a) *supra*.

259. 295 N.W.2d at 780; see *id.* ("Brosamle did not enter Dr. Prahl's land to do business with the plaintiffs or to obtain permission to gather news on the land or in the building."); Special Force Ministries v. WCCO Television, 584 N.W.2d 789, 792 (Minn. App. 1998) ("While respondents initially welcomed Johnson onto their property, if she exceeded the scope of her consent by secretly videotaping their activities, her continuing presence became unpermitted and unlawful.").

260. *Id.* at 780-81 (citing Dietemann v. Time, Inc., 449 F.2d 245, 249 (9th Cir. 1971)). Relying on *Belluomo v. KAKE TV & Radio, Inc.*, 596 P.2d 832 (Kan. App. 1979), and echoing the Ninth Circuit's analysis in *Dietemann*, the court in *Prahl* also held that the defendants' potential liability for trespass extended "to include nonphysical harm subsequent to the trespass." 295 N.W.2d at 781 (citing RESTATEMENT (SECOND) OF TORTS § 162, at 291-92). "To allow only nominal damages under the circumstances presented here," the court held, "would permit the trespasser to enjoy the benefits of his tort without fully compensating a plaintiff for his loss." 295 N.W.2d at 781-82. Nevertheless, the court acknowledged that "[e]stablishing the effect of publication of the tortiously acquired information at the trial, as contrasted to the effect of publication of information lawfully acquired by Brosamle, may be difficult." *Id.* at 782. Thus, the court emphasized that it "is only the film and information obtained during the trespass which were tortiously acquired" and which may form the basis of damages "recoverable from publication, insofar as mental distress is claimed." *Id.*

261. See CBS Inc. v. Davis, 114 S. Ct. 912 (1994).

262. *Id.* at 913.

263. *Id.* (citing S.D. CODIFIED LAWS § 37-29-1 *et seq.*).

obtained by CBS, at the very least, through calculated misdeeds,' . . . conventional First Amendment prior restraint doctrine was inapplicable."[264]

Justice Blackmun rejected that notion, pointing out that, even in the *Pentagon Papers* case,[265] the Supreme Court had "refused to suppress publication of papers stolen from the Pentagon by a third party."[266] Thus, Justice Blackmun concluded that, even assuming newsgathering activity could give rise to civil or criminal liability "in the First Amendment context," there was no basis to conclude in the case before it either that CBS had engaged in "criminal activity" or that, in that event, a prior restraint would be "the appropriate sanction."[267]

Indeed, in the civil damages context as well, several courts have calibrated the First Amendment interests in newsgathering more finely than the Ninth Circuit in *Dietemann*. In *Allen v. Combined Communications Corp.*,[268] for example, the plaintiffs, who owned and operated a livery stable, brought a trespass action against a local television station. Although the court's opinion is less than clear on the point, the station apparently trespassed on plaintiffs' property in the course of gathering information for subsequent broadcast. The court concluded that, while trespass "is a tort which is uncomplicated by notions of scienter or fault,"[269] such "notions" must be modified in the newsgathering context because, as the Ninth Circuit recognized in *Dietemann*, "newsgathering is an integral part of news dissemination."[270] Accordingly, the court rejected "such pieties" as the *Dietemann* court's pronouncement that "'[t]he First Amendment is not a license to trespass,'" as well as "the tendency of courts to distinguish between newsgathering and news publication."[271] Instead, the court considered the ongoing viability of a bright line distinction between "news dissemination" and "newsgathering" in the context of modern mass media:

> We are sure that "pure speech" is protected; we are not so sure about other activities of the news reporter. We visualize the reporter conducting the interview with pen and pad in hand and then later at the typewriter composing the story. The distinction regarding the quality of constitutional protection to be accorded follows just as easily and, we assume, just as obviously. But does it? When confronted with the application of modern technology to the news business, the distinctions in the duties of reporters quickly blur and disappear, and the distinctions in constitutional rule become just as old fashioned as the brash reporter wearing baggy pants, food

---

264. 114 S. Ct. at 914 (quoting trial court).
265. New York Times Co. v. United States, 403 U.S. 713 (1971).
266. 114 S. Ct. at 914.
267. *Id.*
268. 7 MEDIA L. REP. (BNA) 2417 (Colo. Dist. 1981).
269. *Id.* at 2418.
270. *Id.* at 2419 (citing 449 F.2d at 249).
271. 7 MEDIA L. REP. (BNA) at 2419.

spotted tie and 1940's hat with his press card tucked in the band. In an age of instant communication who is to say whether a television reporter standing in a field reporting his/her story by means of one of those video devices called a "mini cam" or "insta cam" or "live action cam" is at that moment gathering the news or disseminating it?[272]

Ultimately, the court suggested, the "role of the news media as primary purveyor of news of general interest to society" requires recognition of some First Amendment-based right "to acquire the news beyond that of the general public."[273] In the context of news media liability for trespass in the course of gathering information, the court recognized both the "need to avoid media self censorship and thereby preserve an unimpeded flow of information to the public" and the "legitimate state interest in preserving to individuals their long-established right to undisturbed possession of their property," an interest that is "more compelling where compensation is sought for damages in fact suffered as a result of the tort."[274] To reconcile the competing interests, the court in *Allen* asserted:

> The work of the modern reporter is most realistically viewed as a continuum, consisting of components (i.e., finding the story, researching the story, composing it for delivery to the public and publication or broadcast) which may or may not occur simultaneously depending on the nature of the story, the nature of the medium and the choice of the reporter and his/her editors. In this context, a chilling effect on speech could occur whenever there is a substantial risk of liability for activities necessary to acquisition of the story.[275]

So viewed, the court held that a trespass claim against the media for newsgathering activity can only be maintained, consistent with the First Amendment, where (1) "the reporter knew that he/she was committing a trespass or committed the trespass in reckless disregard of that fact" or (2) the plaintiff "suffered damages as a result of the trespass."[276]

---

272. *Id.*
273. *Id.* at 2420 (citing Note, *The Right of the Public and Press to Gather Information*, 87 HARV. L. REV. 1505 (1974)). For a related view, see Note, *Press Passes and Trespasses: Newsgathering on Private Property*, 84 COLUM. L. REV. 1298, 1299 (1984) (proposing greater judicial recognition of the news media's "first amendment interest in gathering news on private property" based upon the media's role in checking governmental abuses of power and in informing the public).
274. 7 MEDIA L. REP. (BNA) at 2420.
275. *Id.*
276. *Id.*

The Second Circuit similarly placed some distance between itself and *Dietemann* in *Machleder v. Diaz*,[277] which arose from a broadcast news report about the dumping of toxic chemicals at a site in New Jersey. A television film crew entered the private property of a company that operated from an adjacent building and, cameras rolling, sought to interview the owner. A jury awarded the owner $1,250,000 in compensatory and punitive damages on his claim for false light invasion of privacy, after the trial court granted summary judgment to the defendants on, *inter alia*, the plaintiff's causes of action for intrusion and trespass.[278] The false light claim focused upon the defendants' conduct in entering and filming a so-called "ambush interview" on plaintiff's property.[279] The film crew apparently gained access to the building when, after approaching the facility itself, the reporter, Diaz, was directed there by plaintiff's son, the plant manager.[280] When the crew came upon the plaintiff,

> with audio and video cameras rolling — [the reporter] asked him if he knew anything about the chemical barrels dumped next to his building. Machleder replied that he did not want to be filmed for television and began to move away. Diaz and his crew followed. Machleder became agitated, shouted "get that damn camera out of here . . . . I don't want, I don't need, I don't need any publicity." When Machleder reached the door to his office he said to Diaz, "We don't . . . we didn't dump 'em"; Diaz asked, "Who did?" and Machleder responded, "You call the Housing Department. They have all the information."[281]

---

277. 801 F.2d 46 (2d Cir. 1986), *cert. denied*, 479 U.S. 1088 (1987).
278. *Id.* at 49, 59. See Machleder v. Diaz, 538 F. Supp. 1364 (S.D.N.Y. 1982). With respect to the intrusion claim, the district court held that, because plaintiff "was accosted and filmed in a semi-public area, and he was visible to the public eye," even the reporter's "aggressive and possibly abrasive" questioning "does not constitute unabated hounding of the plaintiff" sufficient to render defendants "liable for intruding upon plaintiff's seclusion." *Id.* at 1374. With respect to the trespass claim, the district court concluded that:

> Defendants' entrance onto plaintiffs' property was not forcible and there were no signs warning visitors to keep off the property. It is uncontroverted that Bruce Machleder met the defendants and instructed them to proceed to the building's office. . . . His actions implied his consent to the defendants' remaining on the lot. . . . This implied consent to be on plaintiff's property precludes liability for trespass.

Id. at 1375.
279. The Second Circuit explained that an "[a]mbush interview is a derogatory descriptive term for a controversial investigative reporting technique in which a reporter and his news crew intercept an 'unsuspecting newsworthy subject on the street and [bombard] him with incriminating accusations ostensibly framed as questions.'" 801 F.2d at 49 (quoting Note, *The Ambush Interview: A False Light Invasion of Privacy?*, 34 CASE W. RES. L. REV. 72, 72 (1983)). This newsgathering "technique" is considered further in Chap. 13-4(b) *infra*.
280. 801 F.2d at 50.
281. *Id.* at 50.

A portion of the tape of this episode was included in a news report broadcast that evening.

The court of appeals concluded that the trial court should have granted the defendants' motion for judgment n.o.v. on the false light claim because, among other reasons, no reasonable juror could have concluded that the resulting broadcast's depiction of plaintiff was "highly offensive."[282] That element of the false light tort, the court held, must be construed "narrowly" in order to "avoid a head-on collision with First Amendment rights."[283] The Second Circuit further affirmed the district court's entry of summary judgment for the defendants on the trespass claim on the ground that the crew had entered the building "peacefully; there were no signs warning them to keep off the property," and no one affiliated with the company asked them to leave.[284] Even if the plaintiff's son had not directed the crew to the front office, the court concluded, it would have been a "licensee" and not a "trespasser" because, although the plaintiff "expressed anger at being filmed and questioned, this did not negate consent."[285]

In *People for the Ethical Treatment of Animals v. Berosini*,[286] the Nevada Supreme Court reversed a $4.2 million verdict entered against an animal rights advocacy group — PETA — in favor of Berosini, a Las Vegas entertainer who allegedly abused the animals with which he performed on stage, based on theories of invasion of privacy and defamation. The relevant privacy claims arose from PETA's efforts to gather information about Berosini "back stage" at the Stardust Hotel by videotaping him and the animals prior to their performance.

The court rejected Berosini's contention that PETA's taping activity, which took place without his knowledge or consent, constituted an actionable invasion of privacy by intrusion.[287] Although its analysis does not purport to be premised on the First Amendment, the court's parsing of the elements of the intrusion tort

---

282. *Id.* at 58.
283. *Id.* The court cited a number of examples of cases supporting its conclusion that "the alleged portrayal of Irving Machleder as intemperate and evasive fails to meet" the "highly offensive standard." *Id.* (citing Time, Inc. v. Hill, 385 U.S. 374, 378 (1967) (false portrayal of family held hostage, depicting violence and verbal sexual insult); Douglass v. Hustler Magazine, Inc., 769 F.2d 1128 (7th Cir. 1985), *cert. denied*, 457 U.S. 1094 (1986) (unauthorized use of model's nude photograph falsely portrayed her as a lesbian); Virgil v. Sports Illustrated, 424 F. Supp. 1286, 1289 (S.D. Cal. 1976) (portrayal of plaintiff as participating in gang fights and eating insects); Arrington v. New York Times Co., 434 N.E.2d 1319 (N.Y. 1982), *cert. denied*, 459 U.S. 1146 (1983) (unauthorized use of private individual's photograph to illustrate "'materialistic, status-conscious'" black middle class)).
284. 801 F.2d at 59 (citing Martin v. Struthers, 319 U.S. 141, 147 (1943) ("[t]raditionally, American law punishes persons who enter onto the property of another after having been warned by the owner to keep off")).
285. 801 F.2d at 59 (citing RESTATEMENT (SECOND) OF TORTS § 332, cmt. b).
286. 895 P.2d 1269 (Nev. 1995).
287. *Id.* at 1279.

appears to reflect a perceived need to limit the tort's reach to avoid such constitutional issues. Thus, the court concluded that, in order "to have an interest in seclusion or solitude which the law will protect, a plaintiff must show that he or she had an actual expectation of seclusion or solitude and that that expectation was objectively reasonable."[288] The "focus" of this aspect of Berosini's intrusion claim, the court indicated, was his assertion that the PETA photographer had "trespassed onto the Stardust Hotel with a video camera" and "unlawfully filmed" him without his knowledge or consent.[289] The court considered it of "no relevance" to the intrusion tort whether the photographer trespassed onto the hotel or whether he "'unlawfully' filmed Berosini, unless at the time he was violating a justifiable expectation of privacy on Berosini's part."[290] With respect to the latter, the court indicated that Berosini's expectation of backstage privacy had not been intruded upon:

> The supposed intruder . . . was in a real sense just "standing there." By observing Berosini through the eye of his video camera, he was merely doing what other backstage personnel were also permissibly doing. The camera did not interfere in any way with Berosini's pre-act animal discipline or his claimed interest in being "secured from the other cast members and people before [he] went on stage." Having testified that he would have done the same thing if people were standing there, he can hardly complain about a camera "standing there."[291]

In addition, the court concluded that the presence of PETA's camera backstage was not "*highly* offensive to a reasonable person," pursuant to an analysis analogous to that embraced in the false light context by the Second Circuit in *Machleder* and the California Court of Appeal in *Miller v. National Broadcasting Co.*[292] Thus, in determining whether PETA's conduct was sufficiently

---

288. *Id.* (citing 2 F. HARPER & F. JAMES, THE LAW OF TORTS § 9.6, at 636 (2d ed. 1986) ("The extent to which seclusion can be protected is severely limited by the protection that must be accorded to the freedom of action and expression of those who threaten the seclusion of others.")).
289. 895 P.2d at 1280.
290. *Id.*
291. *Id.* In addition, the court indicated that, even assuming that the photographer did intrude on Berosini's "*expected* seclusion," it was unlikely that such an expectation would be "objectively reasonable":

> It is probably not reasonable for a well known, headliner entertainer to expect that his picture will not be taken backstage at his place of performance, even when it is a violation of company rules. Furthermore, we note that there is, generally speaking, a reduced objective expectation of privacy in the workplace.

Id. at 1281 n.20 (citing Baggs v. Eagle-Picher Indus., 957 F.2d 268 (6th Cir. 1992), *cert. denied*, 506 U.S. 975 (1992); Yarbray v. Southern Bell Tel. & Tel. Co., 409 S.E.2d 835 (Ga. 1991)).
292. 895 P.2d at 1281 (citing Miller v. National Broadcasting Co., 232 Cal. Rptr. 668, 678 (Ct. App. 1986) ("While what is 'highly offensive to a reasonable person' suggests a standard upon

offensive as a matter of law to ground an intrusion claim, the Nevada Supreme Court looked to "'the degree of intrusion, the context, conduct and circumstances surrounding the intrusion as well as the intruder's motives and objectives, the setting into which he intrudes, and the expectations of those whose privacy is invaded.'"[293] Applying these factors, the court rejected Berosini's claim based on the "nonintrusive nature of the taping process," the questionably "private" context in which the taping occurred,[294] and the fact that PETA's purpose "was not to eavesdrop or to invade into a realm that Berosini claimed for personal seclusion" but rather to memorialize "on tape" what others "could readily perceive."[295]

The California Supreme Court considered the viability of an intrusion claim in the context of non-public areas of a workplace in *Sanders v. American Broadcasting Cos.*[296] There, Lescht, an ABC reporter, obtained employment as a "telepsychic" with the Psychic Marketing Group ("PMG"). She wore a miniature camera hidden in her hat while she interacted with her fellow employees, including the plaintiff, Sanders, who also worked for the company giving "readings" to persons who telephoned PMG's 900 number.[297] The "telepsychics" all worked together in a common area, consisting "of a large room with rows of cubicles, about 100 total, in which the psychics took their calls. Each cubicle was enclosed on three sides by five-foot high partitions."[298] Although "the door to the PMG facility was unlocked during business hours," the company "prohibited access to the office by nonemployees without specific permission."[299]

While she sat at her desk in her own cubicle, Lescht "could easily overhear conversations conducted in surrounding cubicles or in the aisles near her cubi-

---

which a jury would properly be instructed, there is a preliminary determination of 'offensiveness' which must be made by the court in discerning the existence of a cause of action for intrusion.")).

293. 895 P.2d at 1282 (quoting Miller v. National Broadcasting Co., 232 Cal. Rptr. at 679).

294. See 895 P.2d at 1282 ("We must remember that the videotaping did not take place in a private bedroom, . . . or in a hospital room, . . . or in a restroom, . . . or in a young ladies' dressing room, . . . or in any other place traditionally associated with a legitimate expectation of privacy.") (citing Miller v. National Broadcasting Co., 232 Cal. Rptr. at 668 (bedroom); Bethiaume's Estate v. Pratt, 365 A.2d 792 (Me. 1976) (hospital room); Harkey v. Abate, 346 N.W.2d 74 (Mich. App. 1983) (restroom); Doe by Doe v. B.P.S. Guard Servs., Inc., 945 F.2d 1422 (8th Cir. 1991) (dressing room)).

295. 895 P.2d at 1282. See also Medical Lab. Management Consultants v. American Broadcasting Co., 931 F. Supp. 1487 (D. Ariz. 1996) (dismissing invasion of privacy and intentional infliction of emotional distress claims arising from hidden camera investigation of lab conducting pap smear testing); Medical Lab. Management Consultants v. American Broadcasting Cos., 30 F. Supp. 2d 1182, 1186 (D. Ariz. 1998) (dismissing intrusion, fraud, interference with contractual relations, trespass, eavesdropping, and punitive damage claims arising from same investigation).

296. 978 P.2d 67 (Cal. 1999).

297. *Id.* at 69-70.

298. *Id.* at 69.

299. *Id.*

cle"; in fact, she not only "talked with some of the other psychics in the phone room," she "secretly videotaped" those conversations, including two with the plaintiff:

> During the first conversation, Sanders and, after a period, a third employee, were standing in the aisle just outside Lescht's cubicle. They talked in moderate tones of voice, and a fourth employee, passing by, joined in the conversation at one point. Sanders conceded there was a "possibility" the psychic in the next cubicle beyond Lescht could have overheard the first conversation if he tried, although in Sanders's view that was very unlikely because he had no reason to eavesdrop. The second conversation, which took place with both Lescht and Sanders seated in Sanders's cubicle, was conducted in relatively soft voices and was interrupted once by Sanders's receiving a customer call and once by a passing coworker's offer of a snack. During this second, longer conversation, Sanders discussed his personal aspirations and beliefs and gave Lescht a psychic reading.[300]

A short excerpt from the second conversation was included in an ABC broadcast about the telepsychic industry.[301] Thereafter, Sanders and several other workers secretly videotaped by Lescht asserted civil claims against Lescht and ABC. Sanders' claims relating to the broadcast itself were dismissed prior to trial, but two causes of action arising from the videotaping — a claim for violation of the California eavesdropping statute and a common law intrusion claim — were tried to a jury in a bifurcated proceeding.[302] The jury initially rejected Sanders' statutory claim on the ground that Lescht's conversations with the plaintiff were "conduced 'in circumstances in which the parties to the communication may reasonably have expected that the communications may have been overheard.'"[303] The trial court nevertheless permitted the jury to proceed to hear Sanders' intrusion claim, which it characterized in this context as a "'subtort with regard to invasion of privacy by photography,'"[304] and the jury there-

---

300. *Id.* at 70.
301. *Id.* at 70 n.1.
302. *Id.* (citing CAL. PENAL CODE § 632). The jury also considered the claims of another plaintiff, a second employee videotaped by Lescht, who died during its deliberations. See Kersis v. American Broadcasting Cos., 1999 U.S. App. LEXIS 15222 (9th Cir. June 8, 1999). Subsequently, the deceased plaintiff's parents instituted a wrongful death action against the same defendants based on their alleged participation in the "descending spiral of tragedies" that led to his death. *Id.* The Ninth Circuit affirmed a district court's dismissal of the wrongful death action. *Id.* Other civil actions, raising similar claims on behalf of other videotaped employees, were dismissed, albeit on the authority of the California Court of Appeal's subsequently reversed decision in *Sanders*. See Sussman v. American Broadcasting Cos., 971 F. Supp. 432 (C.D. Cal. 1997), *aff'd*, 1999 U.S. App. LEXIS 19646 (9th Cir. Aug. 18, 1999).
303. 978 P.2d at 70 (quoting special verdict). See Chap. 13-7(b)(4)(c) *infra* (discussing California eavesdropping statute).
304. 978 P.2d at 70 (citing Dietemann v. Time, Inc:, 449 F.2d 245 (9th Cir. 1971)).

after found the defendants liable, awarding compensatory and punitive damages.[305]

The court of appeal initially reversed on the ground that the jury's finding with respect to the statutory claim demonstrated that "Sanders lacked an objectively reasonable expectation of privacy" in his conversations with Lescht, a determination that served to preclude his intrusion claim as well.[306] The California Supreme Court, however, disagreed, holding squarely that "the fact a workplace interaction might be witnessed by others on the premises" does not "necessarily defeat[ ], for purposes of tort law, any reasonable expectation of privacy the participants have against covert videotaping by a journalist."[307] According to Justice Werdegar's opinion for a unanimous court:

> In an office or other workplace to which the general public does not have unfettered access, employees may enjoy a limited, but legitimate, expectation that their conversations and other interactions will not be secretly videotaped by undercover television reporters, even though those conversations may not have been completely private from the participants' coworkers.[308]

By the same token, the court asserted that it did not intend to "hold or imply that investigative journalists necessarily commit a tort by secretly recording events and conversations in offices, stores or other workplaces."[309] Rather, the court emphasized, whether "a reasonable expectation of privacy is violated by such recording depends on the exact nature of the conduct and all the surrounding circumstances," and liability for intrusion requires as well a determination

---

305. 978 P.2d at 70. In addition, the trial judge awarded some $600,000 in attorneys fees, a ruling not addressed by the California Supreme Court. See also Kersis v. Capital Cities/ABC, Inc., 22 MEDIA L. REP. (BNA) 2321 (Cal. Super. 1994) (denying defendants' motion for summary judgment).

306. See Sanders v. American Broadcasting Cos., 60 Cal. Rptr. 2d 595, 596 (Ct. App. 1997), rev'd, 978 P.2d 67 (Cal. 1999).

307. 978 P.2d at 69. See id. at 78:

> The evidence and argument indicating that the Sanders-Lscht conversations could be overheard related only to possible overhearing by coworkers. There was no evidence the public was invited into the PMG Los Angeles office, or that the office was visited by the press or other public observers on a routine basis or was ordinarily subject to videotaped surveillance by the mass media. . . . In light of this evidence and argument, the jury's finding cannot reasonably be construed to negate *all* reasonable expectations of privacy by plaintiff in his interactions with Lescht.

308. Id. at 69.

309. Id. See id. ("We hold only that, where the other elements of the intrusion tort are proven, the cause of action is not defeated as a matter of law simply because the events or conversations upon which the defendant allegedly intruded were not completely private from all other eyes and ears.").

that "the invasion be highly offensive to a reasonable person, considering, among other factors, the motive of the alleged intruder."[310]

The court's analysis in *Sanders* is, therefore, noteworthy on two scores. First, the unanimous holding specifically rejected the contention that "an expectation of privacy, in order to be reasonable for purposes of the intrusion tort, must be of *absolute* or *complete* privacy."[311] Instead, the court held, in substantial reliance on the Ninth Circuit's decision in *Dietemann v. Time, Inc.* and on its own decision in *Shulman v. Group W Productions, Inc.*, "a person may reasonably expect privacy against electronic recording of a communication, even though he or she had no reasonable expectation as to confidentiality of the communication's contents."[312] Accordingly, "in the workplace, as elsewhere, the reasonableness of a person's expectation of visual and aural privacy depends not only on who might have been able to observe the subject interaction, but on the identity of the claimed intruder and the means of intrusion."[313] Put differently, the court determined that "a person who lacks a reasonable expectation of complete privacy in a conversation, because it could be seen and overheard by coworkers (but not the general public), may nevertheless have a claim for invasion of privacy by intrusion based on a television reporter's videotaping of that conversation":

> [P]rivacy, for purposes of the intrusion tort, is not a binary, all-or-nothing characteristic. There are degrees and nuances to societal recognition of our expectations of privacy: the fact the privacy one expects in a given setting is not complete or absolute does not render the expectation unreasonable as a matter of law. Although the intrusion tort is often defined in terms of "seclusion," . . . the seclusion referred to need not be absolute.[314]

---

310. *Id.* (citing Shulman v. Group W Prods., Inc., 955 P.2d 469, 489-90 (Cal. 1998); Miller v. National Broadcasting Co., 232 Cal. Rptr. 668, 679 (Ct. App. 1986)).

311. 978 P. 2d at 71 (citing Shulman v. Group W Prods., Inc. 955 P.2d at 490-91).

312. 978 P.2d at 72 (citing Dietemann v. Time, Inc., 449 F.2d 245 (9th Cir. 1971)); see also 978 P.2d at 72 (quoting Shulman v. Group W Prods., Inc., 955 P.2d at 492; Ribas v. Clark, 696 P.2d 637, 670 (Cal. 1985)) ("'While one who imparts private information risks the betrayal of his confidence by the other party, a substantial distinction has been recognized between the second-hand repetition of the contents of a conversation and its simultaneous dissemination to an unannounced second auditor, whether that auditor be a person or a mechanical device'"; the latter "'denies the speaker an important aspect of privacy of communication — the right to control the nature and the extent of the firsthand dissemination of his statements'").

313. 978 P.2d at 77.

314. *Id.* at 72 (quoting RESTATEMENT (SECOND) OF TORTS § 652B) (other citations omitted). See also 978 P.2d at 79 (rejecting defendants' claim that jury had been erroneously instructed because the trial court deleted reference to "solitude or seclusion" from its description of the elements of the intrusion tort since those terms are "not a unique or essential label for a reasonable expectation of privacy"). The California Supreme Court also distinguished the Seventh Circuit's decision in *Desnick v. American Broadcasting Cos.*, 44 F.3d 1345 (7th Cir. 1995), on the ground that it had

Second, the court rejected "'a doctrine of *per se* workplace privacy'" that would, according to the defendants, "'place a dangerous chill on the press' investigation of abusive activities in open work areas, implicating substantial First Amendment concerns.'"[315] The court emphasized that where a "workplace is regularly open to entry or observation by the public or press, or the interaction that was the subject of the alleged intrusion was between proprietor (or employee) and customer, any expectation of privacy against press recording is less likely to be deemed reasonable."[316] Moreover, relying again on its previous decision in *Shulman,* the court authorized a media entity defending against an intrusion claim "to attempt[ ] to show, in order to negate the offensiveness element of the intrusion tort, that the claimed intrusion, even if it infringed on a reasonable expectation of privacy, was 'justified by the legitimate motive of gathering the news.'"[317] In addition, the court took pains to explain that it was not adjudicating any "possible First Amendment defenses" that might be available, since "no constitutional issue was decided by the lower courts or presented here for our review."[318]

In *Food Lion, Inc. v. Capital Cities/ABC, Inc.*,[319] however, a federal district court did consider the interplay of the First Amendment and a host of common law and statutory causes of action arising from the use of hidden cameras in the nonpublic areas of a business. As in *Sanders,* in *Food Lion,* cameras were "worn" by network personnel who had assumed false identities to secure employment at plaintiff's supermarkets and thereby gain entry to its food preparation facilities not otherwise available to the public. The plaintiff asserted causes of action ranging from tort claims for intentional misrepresentation, deceit, fraud, negligent supervision, trespass, and breach of fiduciary duty, to civil conspiracy, violation of federal wiretapping statutes, unfair and deceptive trade practices and violations of the Racketeer Influenced and Corrupt Organizations Act ("RICO").[320] A jury awarded plaintiff approximately $1,500 in compensa-

---

"characterized the doctor-patient relationship" at issue there "as one between a service provider and a customer and therefore viewed these parties' conversations in the medical office as essentially public conversations between strangers." 978 P.2d at 76-77. In *Sanders,* in contrast, the Court concluded that it was "concerned . . . with interactions between coworkers rather than between a proprietor and customer." *Id.* at 77.

315. 978 P.2d at 77 (quoting defendants).
316. *Id.*
317. *Id.* (quoting Shulman v. Group W Prods., Inc., 955 P.2d at 493). See also 978 P.2d at 76 n.4 (distinguishing Russell v. American Broadcasting Cos., 23 MEDIA L. REP. (BNA) 2428 (N.D. Ill. 1995); Medical Lab. Management Consultants v. American Broadcasting Cos., 30 F. Supp. 2d 1182 (D. Ariz. 1998), on ground that those courts effectively determined that intrusions at issue were not "highly offensive in light of the importance of the investigation's subject").
318. 978 P.2d at 77.
319. 887 F. Supp. 811 (M.D.N.C. 1995).
320. 18 U.S.C. § 1961 et seq.

tory damages and $5.5 million in punitive damages on plaintiff's claims for trespass, fraud and breach of fiduciary duty, although the trial court ultimately reduced the punitive damage award to $315,000.[321]

The district court denied defendants' motion to dismiss the trespass claim on the ground that it correctly pled the elements of such a cause of action under North Carolina law: "'(1) that the plaintiff was either actually or constructively in possession of the land; (2) that the defendant made an unauthorized and therefore an unlawful entry on the land; and (3) that the plaintiff suffered damage by the trespass.'"[322] In so doing, the court — affirming a magistrate's decision — rejected the defendants' suggestion that the trespass claim was, in fact, a "thinly disguised" claim of intrusion "based upon an alleged privacy interest that is not legally cognizable," on the ground that defendants had no power to "rewrite" plaintiff's complaint.[323] Moreover, the court concluded that, even if plaintiff was held to have consented to defendants' entry on to its property (albeit under the misimpression that they were plaintiff's, not defendants', employees), "consent to enter upon real property can be negated by a subsequent wrongful act in excess or in abuse of the authority to enter."[324] Thus, if plaintiff were to succeed on its fraud claim, the court asserted, it "could constitute wrongful conduct which could negate any consent to enter" given by the plaintiff.[325]

---

321. See Food Lion Inc. v. Capital Cities/ABC, Inc., 984 F. Supp. 923, 937-38 (M.D.N.C. 1997). The court's treatment of those several causes of action arising from the manner in which the defendants gathered information, including its dismissal of the RICO claim and its decision permitting the fraud and breach of fiduciary duty claims to proceed to trial, are considered in Chapter 13 *infra*.

322. Food Lion, Inc. v. Capital Cities/ABC Inc., 951 F. Supp. 1217, 1221 (M.D.N.C. 1996) (quoting Matthews v. Forrest, 69 S.E.2d 553, 555 (N.C. 1952)).

323. Food Lion, Inc. v. Capital Cities/ABC Inc., No. 6:92 CV900592, slip op. at 15-16 (M.D.N.C. 1994) (recommendation of magistrate judge).

324. 887 F. Supp. at 820 (citing Blackwood v. Cates, 297 N.C. 163, 166 (1979)). See 951 F. Supp. at 1223 ("A reasonable jury could find that Food Lion would never have employed [ABC operatives] if it had known their true identities and purposes for entering Food Lion property."). The court distinguished the Seventh Circuit's apparently contrary decision in *Desnick v. American Broadcasting Cos.*, 44 F.3d 1345, 1351 (7th Cir. 1995), see Chap. 12-4(c)(2) *supra*, noting that "even the Desnick court did not say that misrepresentation could never operate to negate consent." 951 F. Supp. at 1222 (citing 44 F.3d at 1352). *Desnick*, the court in *Food Lion* asserted, involved entry into "offices that were open to anyone expressing a desire for ophthalmic services," 951 F. Supp. at 1222, while the ABC employees in *Food Lion* "were, through their ruse, allowed to enter parts of the stores not generally open to the public," *id*. See also Special Force Ministries v. WCCO Television, 584 N.W.2d 789, 794 (Minn. App. 1998) (permitting trespass and fraud claims, even though no damages attributable to misrepresentation were shown, because, "[h]ad Special Force known Johnson worked for WCCO, it would not have given Johnson the volunteer position and placed her in a position of trust").

325. 887 F. Supp. at 820. In this regard, the court held, even if "consent is properly given and the consent is not negated," an authorized entry can become a trespass if the ABC employees

Nevertheless, the district court indicated that the damages recoverable on all of plaintiff's claims, including its trespass claim, were severely limited by the First Amendment and by the common law. Specifically, the court suggested that the plaintiff could not, consistent with the First Amendment, recover damages for injury to its reputation, pursuant to any of its causes of action, even though they all arise from "laws of general applicability which do not 'target or single out the press'" for adverse treatment.[326] Thus, although the court asserted that the network, "as a member of the press, has no special immunity from the application of laws" such as the tort of trespass, "the fact that Food Lion's claims are not barred by the First Amendment does not mean that Food Lion may recover all of the damages that it has allegedly suffered."[327]

The *Food Lion* court recognized that the plaintiff did not claim "that any of the alleged unlawfully obtained and published information was false" — rather,

---

thereafter "exceeded the scope of the consent authorized by Food Lion." 951 F. Supp. at 1223. See *id*. at 1172 (citing Copeland v. Hubbard Broadcasting, Inc., 526 N.W.2d 402 (Minn. App. 1995)) ("As the *Copeland* court noted, '[w]hether a possessor of land has given consent for entry is, when disputed, a factual issue.'"). See also Special Force Ministries v. WCCO Television, 584 N.W.2d 789, 794 (Minn. App. 1998) (same); Shiffman v. Empire Blue Cross & Blue Shield, 681 N.Y.S.2d 511, 512 (App. Div. 1998) ("affirmative defenses based upon consent and implied consent to enter the premises were legally insufficient since consent obtained by misrepresentation or fraud is invalid") (citing RESTATEMENT (SECOND) OF TORTS § 330, cmt. g).

326. 887 F. Supp at 822 (quoting Cohen v. Cowles Media Co., 501 U.S. 663 (1991)).

327. 887 F. Supp. at 822. Following the jury's verdict, the *Food Lion* court issued another written opinion grounding its decision with respect to broadcast damages in the alternative ground of the plaintiff's inability to prove common law causation. See Food Lion, Inc. v. Capital Cities/ABC, Inc., 964 F. Supp. 956, 963 (M.D.N.C. 1997) (While defendants' "tortious activities may have enabled access to store areas in which the public was not allowed . . . it was the food handling practices themselves — not the method by which they were recorded or published — which caused the loss of consumer confidence," which in turn proximately caused lost profits and sales.); Frome v. Renner, 26 MEDIA L. REP. (BNA) 1956, 1958 (C.D. Cal. 1997) (plaintiff could not recover on fraud, interference with contractual relations, or trespass claims for damages to business based on nondefamatory broadcast that "merely served as a forum through which the public could learn about Plaintiff's medical practices"); Medical Lab. Management Consultants v. American Broadcasting Cos., 30 F. Supp. 2d 1182, 1198 (D. Ariz. 1998) (declining to reach First Amendment issue addressed in *Food Lion* but holding that where "the most damaging portion of the broadcast resulted, not from the hidden camera interview . . . but from Medical Lab's own performance on the slides, . . . any damages flowing from the broadcast's portrayal of the results of those slides must be disregarded"). See also Shiffman v. Empire Blue Cross & Blue Shield, 681 N.Y.S.2d 511, 512 (App. Div. 1998) ("Although plaintiff failed to allege any actual damage to his possessory interest by reason of the reporter's unlawful, yet non-disruptive, entry into his private medical office, nominal damage is always presumed from a trespass," but punitive damages "are not recoverable inasmuch as there is no evidence the complained of trespass was motivated by malice"). But see Special Force Ministries v. WCCO Television, 584 N.W.2d 789, 791, 793-94 (Minn. App. 1998) (rejecting defendant's contention that plaintiff could not prove damages properly attributable to alleged misrepresentations); Shulman v. Group W Prods., Inc., 955 P.2d 469, 496 n.18 (Cal. 1998) (declining to dismiss intrusion claim for failure to allege damages unrelated to broadcast).

it asserted that "ABC's alleged wrongful actions in obtaining information about Food Lion are sufficient to allow Food Lion to recover both reputational and non-reputational damages regardless of whether the information published by ABC was true or false."[328] The plaintiff's theory failed, the court indicated, because it both misread the Supreme Court's decision in *Cohen v. Cowles Media Co.*,[329] and ignored the Court's decision in *Hustler Magazine, Inc. v. Falwell*.[330] In *Cohen*, the Supreme Court "was mindful of the *type* of damages that the plaintiff sought to recover," emphasizing that the plaintiff there was not "'attempting to use a promissory estoppel cause of action to avoid the strict requirements for establishing a libel or defamation claim'" or "'seeking damages for injury to his reputation or his state of mind.'"[331] Thus, while *Cohen* indicates that a plaintiff can recover damages, consistent with the First Amendment, "for non-reputational or non-state of mind injuries," it cannot "use a generally applicable law to recover for injury to reputation or state of mind while avoiding the requirements of a defamation claim (requiring proof of falsity and actual malice)."[332] This, the court continued, is the lesson of *Hustler*, where the Supreme Court determined that the "First Amendment barred the plaintiff from recovering damages under the generally applicable law of intentional infliction of emotional distress."[333]

Accordingly, the court in *Food Lion* held that, to the extent "that Food Lion's damages are reputational in nature, the Supreme Court's decision in *Hustler* prevents recovery."[334] Simply put, the plaintiff could not "'recover damages for injury to its reputation (the publication damages that are characteristic of defamation actions) while avoiding the First Amendment requirements of showing falsity and actual malice.'"[335]

The court did, however, permit *Food Lion* to recover punitive damages, which the jury returned in the amount of $5.5 million.[336] In that regard, although the court had refused to permit defendants to show the broadcast that resulted from

---

328. 887 F. Supp. at 822.
329. 501 U.S. 663 (1991).
330. 485 U.S. 46 (1988).
331. 887 F. Supp. at 822 (quoting 501 U.S. at 671).
332. 887 F. Supp. at 823. Cf. Aequitron Medical, Inc. v. CBS Inc., 964 F. Supp. 704, 710 (S.D.N.Y. 1997) (dismissing tortious interference with prospective business advantage claim based on allegedly defamatory statements where plaintiff failed to satisfy "special rules" of defamation, including showing falsity and constitutional malice).
333. 887 F. Supp. at 823 (citing Hustler Magazine, Inc. v. Falwell, 485 U.S. at 47-48). Indeed, in *Cohen* itself, the Supreme Court distinguished *Falwell*, "where we held that the constitutional libel standards apply to a claim alleging that the publication of a parody was a state-law tort of intentional infliction of emotional distress." Cohen v. Cowles Media Co., 501 U.S. at 671.
334. 887 F. Supp. at 823.
335. *Id.* (quoting Magistrate Judge's Recommendation at 30-31).
336. See Singer, *Food, Lies and Videotape*, AM. LAW., April 1997, at 57.

the undercover reporting at issue to the jury in either the liability or damages phases of the trial, on the ground that the broadcast itself was irrelevant to the claims of trespass, fraud, and breach of fiduciary duty,[337] the trial judge did allow plaintiff, during the separate, punitive damages phase of the trial, to attempt to demonstrate a connection between the network's use of hidden cameras generally and its corporate profits.[338]

§ 12-5. Accompanying Authorized Individuals.

In the companion cases of *Hanlon v. Berger*[339] and *Wilson v. Layne*,[340] the Supreme Court declined to address whether the news media could be held liable, either under 42 U.S.C. § 1983 or directly under the Fourth Amendment, when reporters and photographers accompany law enforcement on to otherwise private property.[341] The Court denied CNN's separate petition for a writ of *certiorari* in *Hanlon*, which squarely raised the issue,[342] but also vacated the Ninth Circuit's judgment, which had embodied its holding that CNN could be liable under the Fourth Amendment as a "governmental actor."[343]

In *Hanlon v. Berger*, a CNN camera crew accompanied federal and state officials as they executed a search warrant on plaintiffs' ranch. The Ninth Circuit, in addition to holding that the search violated the Fourth Amendment and that the officers were not entitled to qualified immunity (the latter conclusion was subsequently rejected by the Supreme Court),[344] held as well that CNN could be held liable for the Fourth Amendment violation as a "government actor."[345] Noting the "planning, cooperation and assistance"[346] that law enforcement officers lent to the media, the court found that "[t]his was no ordinary search. It was jointly planned by law enforcement officers and the media. This search stands out as one that at all times was intended to serve a major purpose other than law enforcement."[347] Applying a "joint action test," the court reversed the trial judge's finding that the media did not act under color of law, holding

---

337. *Id.* at 61.
338. *Id.* at 63. See *id.* at 64 (quoting jury charge) ("For purposes of your deliberations, the broadcast must be assumed to be true and you may not consider any effect the broadcast may have had upon the viewing public or upon Food Lion's sales or profits in considering punitive damages. The only fact pertaining to the broadcast which may be considered is whether the broadcast made a profit for ABC and what that profit was.").
339. 119 S. Ct. 1706 (1999) (per curiam).
340. 119 S. Ct. 1692 (1999).
341. See Chap. 12-4(a) *supra* (discussing Supreme Court decisions).
342. 119 S. Ct. 403 (1998).
343. 129 F.3d 505, 512 (9th Cir. 1997), *vacated*, 119 S. Ct. 1706 (1999) (per curiam).
344. 129 F.3d at 507.
345. *Id.* at 508.
346. Berger v. Hanlon, 129 F.3d at 512.
347. *Id.* at 510.

that "the 'inextricable' involvement of the media with both the planning and execution of this search, the government's active involvement with the media's newsgathering activities, and the mutually-derived benefits, is more than enough to make the media government actors."[348] On remand from the Supreme Court, the Ninth Circuit reaffirmed its earlier view of the Fourth Amendment and also indicated that the "media defendants," unlike the federal agents, "are not entitled to assert qualified immunity as a defense."[349]

The Ninth Circuit had at least presaged this view of the media's liability for constitutional torts nearly three decades earlier in *Dietemann*.[350] There, the magazine journalists coordinated their activities with law enforcement officers, some of whom waited in a nearby truck while the journalists entered the home with a hidden camera and microphone.[351] The magazine had apparently entered into an arrangement with the local District Attorney's office, pursuant to which the former "would obtain pictures and information for use as evidence," as well as for publication.[352] The trial court concluded, among other things, that the magazine's activities in this regard "constituted an invasion of plaintiffs' right of privacy guaranteed by the Constitution," which would "entitle him to relief" pursuant to 42 U.S.C. § 1983.[353] In the trial court's view, both the law enforcement authorities and the journalists "as their agents were subject to the restric-

---

348. *Id.* at 515. See also Bezanson, *Means and Ends and Food Lion: The Tension Between Exemption and Independence in Newsgathering by the Press*, 47 EMORY L.J. 895, 913 (1998) (arguing that a finding that CNN had "constitutional immunity for newsgathering would have freed [CNN] . . . to conspire with the government [which] would have placed the press in a vastly increased position of dependence on government for leads, for information, and for the facilities of privacy invasion . . . or trespass or harassment, fraud, and deception"). In *Wilson v. Layne*, 119 S. Ct. 1692 (1999), the companion case to *Hanlon v. Berger*, the plaintiffs did not assert claims against the *Washington Post*, its reporter or its photographer, so the Supreme Court did not have occasion to address directly the "governmental action" issue that was before the Ninth Circuit in *Berger*. Writing for the Court in *Wilson*, however, Chief Justice Rehnquist did make several observations about the nature of the relationship between the news media and law enforcement in that case that would appear to cast doubt on the continued efficacy of the Ninth Circuit's reasoning in *Hanlon*:

> The Washington Post reporters in the Wilsons' home were working on a story for their own purposes. They were not present for the purpose of protecting the officers, much less the Wilsons. A private photographer was acting for private purposes, as evidenced in part by the fact that the newspaper and not the police retained the photographs.

Id. at 1699. In *Hanlon*, the principal evidence of "inextricable involvement" between CNN and law enforcement authorities was their express agreement that CNN would retain editorial control with respect to use of all video footage. See 129 F.3d at 512.

349. Berger v. Hanlon, 1999 U.S. App. LEXIS 20262, *2-3 (9th Cir. Aug. 27, 1999) (citing Wyatt v. Cole, 504 U.S. 158, 168-69 (1992); Kimes v. Stone, 84 F.3d 1121, 1128 (9th Cir. 1996)).
350. 449 F.2d 245 (9th Cir. 1971).
351. *Id.* at 246.
352. *Id.*
353. *Id.* at 247.

tions of the Fourth Amendment, particularly where they were acting in concert."[354]

The Ninth Circuit did not reach the issue, posited on appeal as whether "the defendant's employees acted as special agents of the police and, if so, did their acts violate the First, Fourth and Fourteenth Amendments, . . . thereby subjecting defendant to liability under the Civil Rights Act?," holding that plaintiff had otherwise sustained his common law claims.[355] In a separate opinion, however, Judge Carter suggested that, by entering an agreement with the police, the magazine and its employees had become its agents, and that "California would recognize a cause of action for intrusion" against the magazine for the activities of its "employees as agents of the police."[356]

Several courts have addressed the question left unresolved in *Dietemann* and by the Supreme Court in *Berger* — *i.e.*, the news media's liability under the federal civil rights laws or under the Fourth Amendment itself as alleged "agents" of the public officials who permit them access to otherwise private locations. In *Prahl v. Brosamle*,[357] for example, a Wisconsin appellate court concluded both that a journalist who followed police officers onto plaintiff's property did not act "under color of state law" and that the plaintiff could not identify a constitutional right of privacy that had been violated by the reporter's conduct.[358]

---

354. Dietemann v. Time, Inc., 284 F. Supp. 925, 931-32 (C.D. Cal. 1968), *aff'd*, 449 F.2d 245 (9th Cir. 1971) (citing York v. Story, 324 F.2d 450, 456 (9th Cir. 1963), *cert. denied*, 376 U.S. 939 (1964) (plaintiff who went to police station to make complaint was photographed in the nude and her photograph was circulated among police officers; court held that plaintiff stated claim under 42 U.S.C. § 1983 because "such acts constituted an arbitrary intrusion upon the security of her privacy")).

355. 449 F.2d at 247. The court did note, however, that "[w]ere it necessary to reach the Civil Rights Act questions, we would be obliged to explore the relationship between the defendant's employees and the police for the purpose of ascertaining the existence of the 'color of law' element of the Act." *Id.*

356. *Id.* at 251-52 (Carter, J., dissenting). In Judge Carter's view:

> Here, Time, through its publication *Life*, realizing it could not unilaterally invade Dietemann's house and privacy, sought the protection of cooperation with state officials. The officials, recognizing their duty not to publicly expose the results of police investigations, accepted the services of Life. Each thereby achieved jointly that which neither could have achieved separately.

Id. at 252. See also Lauro v. City of New York, 39 F. Supp. 2d 351 (S.D.N.Y. 1999). In *Lauro*, a federal district court held that the city and its detective were not immune from liability under 42 U.S.C. § 1983 for conducting a "perp walk" for the media in front of the precinct. While the court did not address media liability for the constitutional violation, it suggested that the assembled photographers might be found to be state actors, given "the participation, encouragement, and aid" they rendered to the police. *Id.* at 365 n.11.

357. 295 N.W.2d 768 (Wis. App. 1980).

358. *Id.* at 774 (citing Paul v. Davis, 424 U.S. 693 (1976)). Accord Scheetz v. Morning Call, Inc., 946 F.2d 202, 206 (3d Cir. 1991), *cert. denied*, 502 U.S. 1095 (1992) (no cause of action

In *Parker v. Clarke*,[359] plaintiffs, a mother and her sixteen-year old daughter, instituted an action pursuant to 42 U.S.C. § 1983 against various public officials and a television station, alleging, *inter alia*, that the station had become a "state actor" for purposes of the statute when it accompanied law enforcement officials to plaintiffs' residence and filmed the execution of a search warrant there. The camera crew had "entered the house behind the police through the unlocked front door. Two weapons and several substances believed to be cocaine, in both rock and powder forms, were seized during the search."[360] The crew was not "given any instructions or directions by any police officers, and were not advised by them of any limitations on their location, conduct or filming."[361]

Under the circumstances, the Eighth Circuit concluded, as a matter of law, that the station was not a "state actor" for purposes of 42 U.S.C. § 1983. The station, the court noted, "acted independently of the police in deciding to enter the house and videotape the events there."[362] In addition, neither the station "nor the police assisted the other in the performance of their separate and respective tasks."[363] Rather, the record indicated that the camera crew, in the words of the district court:

> had been allowed to "ride along" with Mobile Reserve Unit officers during their shift, and that when, in the course of that shift, a determination was made to execute this particular search warrant, the KSDK personnel came along. The passivity of this circumstance demonstrates the absence of any affirmative agreement between KSDK and the police concerning the particular conduct of KSDK which plaintiffs now challenge.[364]

---

under 42 U.S.C. § 1983 when news media obtained copy of allegedly private police report because plaintiffs "did not have a constitutionally protected privacy interest in the information they divulged in the police report"); Moncrief v. Hanton, 10 MEDIA L. REP. (BNA) 1620 (N.D. Ohio 1984) (no cause of action under 42 U.S.C. § 1983 where news media accompanied police officers in executing a search warrant in their home).

359. 905 F. Supp. 638 (E.D. Mo. 1995), *aff'd in part*, 93 F.3d 445 (8th Cir. 1996), *cert. denied*, 117 S. Ct. 1081 (1997).

360. *Id.* at 641.

361. *Id.*

362. 93 F.3d at 448. Thus, the court held that the state action requirement was not satisfied by a showing that "the deprivation" was "caused by the exercise of some right or privilege created by the State or by a rule of conduct imposed by the State or by a person for whom the State is responsible." *Id.* (citing Lugar v. Edmondson Oil Co., 457 U.S. 922, 936-37 (1982)).

363. 93 F.3d at 448.

364. 905 F. Supp. at 641; *see id.* ("The entirely distinct purposes of the two groups bolster this conclusion .... The KSDK personnel were present for the purpose of gathering news and preparing a report for broadcast. The police were engaged in the conduct of law enforcement activity. The police did not participate in the filming of the objects and events in the house, the KSDK personnel did not participate in the execution of the search.") (footnote omitted). See also United States v. Appelquist, 145 F.3d 976, 979 (8th Cir. 1998) (denying motion to suppress evi-

Similarly, in *Nichols v. Hendrix*,[365] a case decided after the Ninth Circuit's ruling in *Hanlon*, a federal district court rejected a claim that media defendants were state actors for purposes of 42 U.S.C. § 1983 when they accompanied law enforcement officers executing a raid on plaintiffs' house. Even if the television station crew was present at the express invitation of the sheriff and served no law enforcement purpose, the court found that plaintiffs "fail[ ] to allege those 'rare circumstances' in which a private party constitutes a state actor."[366] Noting the absence of a formal agreement or conspiracy between the media defendants and police, and the absence of allegations that the media defendants and police aided each other in their respective newsgathering and law enforcement tasks, the court held that "[t]he fact that the media defendants were invited to accompany the officers and to film the raid is not enough to turn the defendants into state actors."[367]

In *Ayeni v. CBS Inc.*,[368] however, another federal district court indicated that the news media may be properly held liable, directly under the Fourth Amendment, when it accompanies public officials conducting an unreasonable search or seizure. The plaintiffs, whose home was searched, pursuant to a warrant, by federal law enforcement authorities accompanied by a CBS camera crew, instituted an action under the Fourth Amendment against the network and the responsible public officials. The court concluded, in denying the defendants' motion for summary judgment, both that a "prima facie gross violation of plaintiffs' clear constitutional rights" had been pleaded against the government officials and that "a private broadcaster cannot cloak itself in immunity of a government official under the facts of this case."[369] The news media defendants, the court held:

> had no greater right than that of a thief to be in the home, to "capture" the scene of the search on film and to remove the photographic record. The images, though created by the camera, are a part of the household; they could not be removed without permission or official right.[370]

Noting that CBS claimed "no First Amendment right to be present," the court held that "as a private corporation," it was not "on the pleadings, entitled to qualified immunity."[371]

---

dence seized in "a valid and completed search" where media entered home "only after the police completed the warrant search").

365. 27 MEDIA L. REP. (BNA) 1503 (N.D. Ga. 1999).
366. *Id.* at 1505.
367. *Id.*
368. 848 F. Supp. 362 (E.D.N.Y. 1994).
369. *Id.* at 364.
370. *Id.* at 368.
371. *Id.* CBS settled with the plaintiffs during the pendency of the government official's ultimately unsuccessful interlocutory appeal of the immunity issue, see Ayeni v. Mottola, 35 F.3d

§ 12-6. Consent: Special Issues.

As the preceding sections indicate, newsgathering in places not generally open to the public is often accomplished by securing the assistance and/or consent of persons with the practical ability to provide access. By the same token, the law recognizes consent as a legal defense to most tort claims arising in the newsgathering process, including trespass and intrusion.[372] The legal efficacy of such consent can, however, be problematic in certain circumstances, such as when the person purporting to provide it is a child or is mentally impaired, or when the plaintiff is incarcerated or otherwise institutionalized.

§ 12-6(a). Children and the Mentally Impaired.

Courts have always exhibited a special and heightened level of concern for children caught up in the newsgathering process.[373] In the typical case, therefore, children have been held incapable of providing meaningful consent to newsgathering activity. In *KOVR-TV Inc. v. Superior Court*,[374] for example, a California appellate court affirmed a trial judge's denial of a television station's motion to dismiss tort claims against it made on behalf of children who had been filmed and interviewed at the front door to their home without their parents' knowledge. During the interview, the children were informed, for the first time, that their

---

680, 686 n.3 (2d Cir. 1994), *cert. denied*, 514 U.S. 1062 (1995), a decision effectively called into question in *Wilson v. Layne*, 119 S. Ct. 1692 (1999). See also Hagler v. Philadelphia Newspapers, Inc., 24 MEDIA L. REP. (BNA) 2332 (E.D. Pa. 1996) (adopting *Ayeni* analysis in context of reporters who accompanied police on raid of plaintiff's apartment); Swate v. Taylor, 12 F. Supp. 2d 591, 596 (S.D. Tex. 1998) ("If the DEA decided it should as a function of the public's business film its search to protect itself against claims of vandalism or brutality, it could have done that. What it did, however, was turn the clinics into resources for television shows.").

372. See Chap. 12-3 *supra* (citing cases).

373. See, e.g., Galella v. Onassis, 487 F.2d 986 (2d Cir. 1973) (affirming entry of injunction prohibiting photographer from approaching children of President Kennedy); Green Valley Sch., Inc. v. Cowles Florida Broadcasting, Inc., 327 So. 2d 810 (Fla. App. 1976) (reversing summary judgment for television station that had entered dormitory rooms of children during police raid on private school); Weber v. Multimedia Entertainment, Inc., 26 MEDIA L. REP. (BNA) 1376 (S.D.N.Y. 1998) (denying defendants' motion to dismiss invasion of privacy claim because material issue of fact as to validity of consent remained, where fifteen-year-old plaintiff featured on talk show alleged that defendants knowingly induced her to forge mother's signature on form consenting to plaintiff's appearance on program); Ayeni v. CBS Inc., 848 F. Supp. 362 (E.D.N.Y. 1994) (rejecting immunity claim by television crew that accompanied law enforcement agents executing search warrant in home where small child present); cf. Y.G. v. Jewish Hosp., 795 S.W.2d 488 (Mo. App. 1990) (reinstating claim for invasion of privacy brought by couple pregnant with triplets, who were participating in *in vitro* fertilization program at hospital and were photographed without their consent). But cf. Morgan v. Celender, 780 F. Supp. 307, 311 (W.D. Pa. 1992) (dismissing fraudulent misrepresentation claim brought on behalf of children whose photograph was taken by newspaper in absence of evidence that it "ever made any promise" to them).

374. 37 Cal. Rptr. 2d 431 (Ct. App. 1995).

friends had been murdered by their own mother. The court concluded that the children, "ages, 5, 7 and 11, were manifestly of tender years," there were "no adults in the home and the minors were obviously too young either to consent to an intrusion by strangers into a private residence or to exercise any control over strangers who appeared there."[375] In the court's view, "a jury could find that a television reporter who attempts deliberately to manipulate the emotions of young children for some perceived journalistic advantage has engaged in conduct 'so outrageous in character, and so extreme in degree, as to go beyond all bounds of decency.'"[376]

Similarly, in *Commonwealth v. Wiseman*,[377] the Massachusetts Supreme Judicial Court enjoined most showing of the documentary film *Titicut Follies*, which depicted the treatment of patients at a state correctional institution, including pictures of "of mentally incompetent patients ... in the nude ... [and] in the most personal and private situations."[378] Although the filmmaker had received permission to film the patients from the institution's administrator, the court concluded that some of the inmates were "incompetent to understand a release" and that the film was, therefore, "a collective, indecent intrusion into the most private aspects of the lives of these unfortunate persons."[379]

---

375. *Id.* at 434.

376. *Id.* at 435 (quoting RESTATEMENT (SECOND) OF TORTS § 46, cmt. d). Cf. Quinn v. Johnson, 381 N.Y.S.2d 875, 877 (App. Div. 1976) (denying motion to enjoin broadcast concerning conditions in institution for treatment of neglected children, but noting that children, who were "minors and wards of the State," might have other remedies since "it is questionable that they could or did validly consent to the intrusion upon their privacy"); Foretich v. Lifetime Cable, 777 F. Supp. 47 (D.D.C. 1991) (holding that disputed issues of material fact precluded summary judgment for television network that broadcast videotape of minor child received from her mother). But see Prescott v. Newsday, Inc., 541 N.Y.S.2d 501, 503 (App. Div. 1989) (dismissing suit brought by 17-year-old claiming that school district had wrongfully permitted newspaper onto school premises because the district had no "duty to protect students from the publication of a newspaper article"); Howell v. Tribune Entertainment Co., 106 F.3d 215, 221 (7th Cir. 1997) (affirming dismissal of invasion of privacy action brought by sixteen-year-old whose stepmother read aloud portions of plaintiff's confidential, juvenile police record for taped broadcast in which they voluntarily appeared together; "We need not decide at what age a child is sufficiently mature to waive her right of privacy, but 16 is old enough when no circumstances of deception or overreaching or limited competence are shown .... [T]here is no principle in the law that by staging an event at which one person is likely to defame or invade the privacy of the other, the media become complicit in the defamation or the invasion of privacy.").

377. 249 N.E.2d 610 (Mass. 1969).

378. *Id.* at 613.

379. *Id.* at 615. But see Cullen v. Grove Press, Inc., 276 F. Supp. 727 (S.D.N.Y. 1967) (declining to enjoin same film at behest of correctional officers on ground that First Amendment prohibited injunctive relief).

Nevertheless, in *Delan v. CBS Inc.*,[380] a New York appellate court affirmed dismissal of a suit by a mentally disabled patient at Creedmoor Psychiatric Center who objected to the use of film taken of him and used in a documentary about "the effects of, and alternatives to, institutionalization in mental hospitals."[381] In *Delan*, the institution's director had granted permission to film and had secured the patient's written consent following a "therapeutic community meeting" and a determination that he had "the capacity to make a reasoned decision as to whether . . . to consent to participate in the program."[382] The court concluded that the film "dealt with a matter of legitimate public interest, i.e., the deinstitutionalization of mental patients and their placement in an outpatient program designed to benefit both themselves and society as a whole."[383] Accordingly, the court held that the plaintiff could not state a claim for invasion of his privacy because "there existed a legitimate connection between the theme of the telecast and the use of plaintiff's person in a brief scene," rendering the "validity of the written consent . . . irrelevant."[384]

§ 12-6(b). Inmates.

For obviously different reasons, inmates at correctional facilities have limited freedom to prevent unwanted intrusions into their daily lives, including intrusions by the news media. Several courts have held that prisoners retain at least some ability to safeguard their privacy, although that right is subject to significant restrictions. Thus, in *Smith v. Fairman*,[385] the court denied a prison official's motion for summary judgment in an inmate's suit arising from the prison's alleged grant of permission to a television crew to film him without his consent while incarcerated. "Even if those portions of the film containing the plaintiff's image were removed in the editing process" and never shown to the public, the court held, "the initial filming of the plaintiff would nonetheless constitute a violation of plaintiff's legitimate expectation of privacy."[386] Simi-

---

380. 458 N.Y.S.2d 608 (App. Div. 1983).
381. *Id.* at 611.
382. *Id.* at 612.
383. *Id.* at 613.
384. *Id.* at 614. See Howell v. New York Post Co., 612 N.E.2d 699, 704-05 (N.Y. 1993) (patient at private psychiatric hospital could not state claim against newspaper for photographing her while walking on hospital grounds since photograph involved matter of public concern and trespass not sufficiently outrageous to support claim for intention infliction of emotional distress). Cf. Totten v. Time, Inc., 14 MEDIA L. REP. (BNA) 1027 (Mass. Super. 1987), *rev'd on other grounds*, 532 N.E.2d 1211 (Mass. 1989) (holding that plaintiff's "mental disorder" did not serve to toll statute of limitations governing her claims against magazine that photographed her while she was a patient at state hospital).
385. 98 F.R.D. 445 (C.D. Ill. 1982).
386. *Id.* at 450.

larly, in *Huskey v. National Broadcasting Co.*,[387] the court denied a television station's motion to dismiss a suit brought by a prisoner who had been photographed in a prison "exercise cage," without his consent, wearing only gym shorts. The court held that "the mere fact that a person can be seen by others does not mean that the person cannot legally be 'secluded,'" and that, although "prisoners may become understandably inured to the gaze of staff and other prisoners," they may "at the same time feel justifiably secured from the outside world (at least in certain areas not normally visited by outsiders)."[388]

In *Holman v. Central Arkansas Broadcasting Co.*,[389] however, the Eighth Circuit affirmed dismissal of a civil rights action brought against police officers and a television station by a local attorney who was incarcerated following his arrest for driving while intoxicated. The officers had apparently permitted a television reporter to enter the jail and tape record the plaintiff, without his knowledge, while he was "hitting and banging on his cell door," and "hollering and cursing from the time of his arrest until his release" the following morning.[390] The court concluded that these "boisterous complaints" were not made "with the expectation of privacy or confidentiality" and the reporter "could not be prevented from reporting the statements he could so easily overhear."[391]

Similarly in *Cox Communications, Inc. v. Lowe*,[392] a Georgia appellate court entered summary judgment for a television station on an inmate's privacy claim arising from a videotape of him walking in the prison yard. The tape was shot by a television station cameraman, positioned outside the prison fence in a parking lot, for inclusion in a news report about the improper use of prison labor. The court concluded that the presence of the camera was "not unlawful," because the public had access to the lot, the "scene depicted in the videotape was visible from a public place," and plaintiff "was photographed while he was in "open public view."[393] In addition, the court held that, because the news report addressed a matter of public concern, plaintiff had no claim for invasion of privacy

---

387. 632 F. Supp. 1282 (N.D. Ill. 1986).

388. *Id.* at 1288. The court in *Huskey* further held that broadcast of the footage taken of plaintiff could be enjoined consistent with the First Amendment, which it held "offers no protection to those who publish private or defamatory matter." *Id.* at 1295.

389. 610 F.2d 542 (8th Cir. 1979).

390. *Id.* at 543.

391. *Id.* at 564. Accord, Huskey v. Dallas Chronicle, Inc., 13 MEDIA L. REP. (BNA) 1057 (D. Or. 1986) (dismissing and finding "frivolous" civil rights and privacy claim made by prisoner who was photographed by newspaper during booking procedure inside county jail); Jones/Seymour v. LeFebvre, 19 MEDIA L. REP. (BNA) 2064, 2065 (E.D. Pa.), *aff'd*, 961 F.2d 1567 (3d Cir. 1992) (dismissing civil rights action brought by inmate who was allegedly filmed without his consent because such conduct does not violate any constitutional right of privacy); Jenkins v. Winchester Star, 8 MEDIA L. REP. (BNA) 1403 (W.D. Va. 1981).

392. 328 S.E.2d 394 (Ga. App.), *cert. denied*, 474 U.S. 92 (1985).

393. *Id.* at 385.

even though he only "incidentally became involved in the publicity concerning an occurrence of public interest due to his incarceration in a correctional facility which was part of the focus of an official investigation of alleged wrongdoing."[394]

---

394. *Id.* at 386.

Chapter 13

THE MEANS OF NEWSGATHERING

§ 13-1. Introduction.
§ 13-2. Misrepresentation and Impersonation.
    § 13-2(a). Misrepresentation in Newsgathering.
    § 13-2(b). Impersonation in Newsgathering.
§ 13-3. Theft, Conversion, Stolen Documents and Criminal Conduct.
    § 13-3(a). Constitutional Overview.
    § 13-3(b). Civil Liability.
    § 13-3(c). Criminal Liability.
        § 13-3(c)(1). Criminal Trespass.
        § 13-3(c)(2). Criminal Harassment.
        § 13-3(c)(3). Disorderly Conduct.
        § 13-3(c)(4). Impersonation of a Public Official.
        § 13-3(c)(5). Theft of Government Property.
        § 13-3(c)(6). Mail Fraud.
        § 13-3(c)(7). Wire Fraud.
        § 13-3(c)(8). Receiving Purloined Documents or Other Property.
            § 13-3(c)(8)(A). Receipt of Stolen Property.
            § 13-3(c)(8)(B). Interstate Transportation of Stolen Property.
        § 13-3(c)(9). Federal Government Secrets and Espionage Statutes.
            § 13-3(c)(9)(A). The Pentagon Papers Case.
            § 13-3(c)(9)(B). Subsequent cases.
§ 13-4. Sources and Interview Subjects.
    § 13-4(a). Breach of Contract and Promissory Estoppel.
        § 13-4(a)(1). Judicial Pronouncements Prior to *Cohen v. Cowles Media*.
            § 13-4(a)(1)(A). The Defamation and Privacy Context.
            § 13-4(a)(1)(B). The National Security Context.
        § 13-4(a)(2). *Cohen v. Cowles Media Co*.
            § 13-4(a)(2)(A). The Trial Court Proceedings.
            § 13-4(a)(2)(B). The Minnesota Appellate Courts — Round 1.
            § 13-4(a)(2)(C). The Supreme Court.
            § 13-4(a)(2)(D). The Minnesota Appellate Courts — Round 2.
        § 13-4(a)(3). *Cohen*-Inspired and Related Causes of Action.
            § 13-4(a)(3)(A). The New York and Minnesota Experiences.
                § 13-4(a)(3)(A)(i). The New York Cases.
                § 13-4(a)(3)(A)(ii). *Ruzicka v. Conde Nast Publications*.
            § 13-4(a)(3)(B). Other Post-*Cohen* Cases.
        § 13-4(a)(4). Paying for News.
    § 13-4(b). The Ambush Interview.
    § 13-4(c). Interference with Contract.
§ 13-5. Stake Outs.
§ 13-6. Communications in the Newsgathering Process.
§ 13-7. Audio Recording.
    § 13-7(a). Federal Law.
        § 13-7(a)(1). Fourth Amendment Considerations.
        § 13-7(a)(2). Federal Statutes.

§ 13-7(a)(2)(A). Federal Wiretap Act.
§ 13-7(a)(2)(A)(i). Prohibited Conduct.
§ 13-7(a)(2)(A)(ii). Restricted Equipment.
§ 13-7(a)(2)(A)(iii). The Qualified One-Party Consent Exception.
§ 13-7(a)(2)(A)(iv). Sanctions and Remedies.
§ 13-7(a)(2)(B). Federal Communications Act.
§ 13-7(a)(2)(C). Federal Communications Commission Regulations.
§ 13-7(b). State Law.
§ 13-7(b)(1). Introduction.
§ 13-7(b)(2). Consensual Monitoring Jurisdictions.
§ 13-7(b)(3). All-Party Consent Jurisdictions.
§ 13-7(b)(4). Exceptions.
§ 13-7(b)(4)(A). Inadvertent Interception of Communications.
§ 13-7(b)(4)(B). Communications in Public Places.
§ 13-7(b)(4)(C). Communications on Business Premises.
§ 13-7(b)(4)(D). Unprotected Subject Matter.
§ 13-7(b)(4)(E). Use of Unrestricted Equipment.
§ 13-7(b)(4)(F). Law Enforcement Monitoring.
§ 13-7(b)(4)(G). Monitoring of Emergency Communications.
§ 13-7(b)(5). Sanctions and Remedies.
§ 13-7(c). Common Law.
§ 13-8. Hidden Cameras.
§ 13-9. Unauthorized Access to Computer Systems.
§ 13-9(a). Federal Law.
§ 13-9(b). State Law.

§ 13-1. Introduction.

Any journalist will confirm that ingenuity, if not creativity, has always been essential to effective newsgathering. The institutional press has depended on the skill of its reporters in gaining access to places they are not welcome, securing documents not meant for public consumption, and unlocking the secrets of those who make the news. This chapter examines the law that has evolved to cabin, at least to some extent, this aspect of the journalistic enterprise, as well as the First Amendment doctrine that has, in turn, served to limit the reach of that jurisprudence.

Inevitably, the law surrounding the means of newsgathering has reflected the ever increasing sophistication of the technology employed in that cause. As the pencil and notepad have given way to the telephone, the tape recorder, the video camera and, more recently, the hidden "hatcam"[1] and the computer, the law has been called upon — with increasing frequency — to place limitations on the means and methods of newsgathering. Legislatures and common law courts alike have, on occasion, responded to such calls in a variety of settings, leading to

---

1. Sanders v. American Broadcasting Cos., 978 P.2d 67 (Cal. 1999) (journalist equipped with hidden camera mounted in hat).

further judicial explication of the role of the First Amendment in safeguarding the newsgathering process.

This chapter begins with a review of the legal standing of familiar tools of the journalistic trade — the use of trickery and impersonation to secure the news, the act of securing confidential documents, the coaxing and persuasion of reluctant sources to come forward, and libel in the newsgathering process. It concludes with an examination of the role of technology in the development of that law — that is, the tape recording of telephone conversations, the use of electronic eavesdropping devices, the phenomenon of hidden video cameras, and newsgathering in the computer age.

§ 13-2. Misrepresentation and Impersonation.

§ 13-2(a). Misrepresentation in Newsgathering.

Journalists of all stripes have, with some frequency, been less than candid with the persons from whom they seek to gather the news. In *Desnick v. American Broadcasting Cos.*,[2] for example, the plaintiff alleged that a television network, for the purpose of securing an interview with him, falsely represented that the planned broadcast "would not involve 'ambush' interviews or 'undercover' surveillance, and that it would be 'fair and balanced.'"[3] The Seventh Circuit rejected plaintiff's claim, which sounded largely in fraud, because it concluded that "promissory fraud is actionable only if it either is particularly egregious or, what may amount to the same thing, is embedded in a larger pattern of deceptions or enticements that reasonably induces reliance and against which the law ought to provide a remedy."[4] Measured against this standard, Chief Judge Posner concluded that the plaintiff had failed to state a claim:

> Investigative journalists well known for ruthlessness promise to wear kid gloves. They break their promise, as any person of normal sophistication would expect. If that is "fraud," it is the kind against which potential victims can easily arm themselves by maintaining a minimum of skepticism about journalistic goals and methods.[5]

---

2. 44 F.3d 1345 (7th Cir. 1995).
3. *Id.* at 1348.
4. *Id.* at 1354. Cf. Deteresa v. American Broadcasting Co., 121 F.3d 460, 467-68 (9th Cir. 1997), *cert. denied*, 118 S. Ct. 1840 (1999) (affirming summary judgment for defendants on fraud and conspiracy to commit fraud claims for surreptitious video and audio taping of conversation with plaintiff: "[E]ven if the audiotaping and videotaping were wrongful under tort principles or a statute, [defendant] is not liable for failing to disclose its intention to commit those wrongful acts.").
5. 44 F.3d at 1354.

Indeed, a finding of fraud would be particularly inappropriate, the court concluded, where the "only scheme" alleged by the plaintiff was one "to expose publicly any bad practices that the investigative team discovered."[6]

Similarly, in *Ramirez v. Time, Inc.*,[7] the plaintiff alleged that a magazine reporter had used a "ruse" by leaving a false message on plaintiff's answering machine for the purpose of inducing her to provide information. Rejecting plaintiff's fraud claim, the court concluded that she had failed to allege any legally cognizable injury flowing from the reporter's misrepresentation; other than meeting with the reporter, the court held, "plaintiff fails to allege that she did anything whatsoever in reliance upon his alleged misrepresentation."[8]

In *WDIA Corp. v. McGraw-Hill, Inc.*,[9] in contrast, a federal district court, following a bench trial, entered judgment for fraud and breach of contract against the publishers of *Business Week* magazine arising from misrepresentations made by one of its reporters in seeking information from plaintiff, a credit reporting agency. The reporter had falsely represented to the plaintiff, both in a formal application to subscribe to its services and in oral statements, that his company sought to use the information in conducting background checks on prospective employees.[10] In fact, *Business Week* was conducting an investigation of lax procedures in the credit-reporting industry, specifically the unauthorized

---

6. *Id.* See also Homsy v. King World Entertainment, Inc., 1997 Tex. App. LEXIS 761 (Tex. App. Feb. 6, 1997) (granting summary judgment to defendant on fraud claim brought by man who consented to on camera interview based on misrepresentation that interviewer was a potential investor in employer's products); Morgan v. Celender, 780 F. Supp. 307 (W.D. Pa. 1992). In *Morgan*, plaintiff alleged that a reporter had made false representations to her for the purpose of inducing her to allow her children to be photographed. See *id.* at 309 (reporter "fraudulently promised that no names would be used in the publication involving a silhouette picture" and plaintiff "consented to the picture on this basis"). The court rejected plaintiff's claim for intentional misrepresentation on the ground that "[a] promise to do something in the future" — in this case, a promise not to publish the childrens' names or unconcealed photograph — "which promise is not kept, is not fraud." *Id.* at 311. See Chap. 13-4(a)(3)(B) *infra* (discussing *Morgan* and other breach of promise cases). Compare Borger, *New Whines in Old Bottles: Taking Newsgathering Torts Off the Food Lion Shelf,* 34 TORT & INS. L.J. 61, 76 (1998) (hidden camera or recording subjects' "only interest in not being recorded without their knowledge is to maintain 'plausible deniability,' which they cannot do in the face of videotape of their actual words. That is not an interest that courts should protect.") with Logan, *Masked Media: Judges, Juries, and the Law of Surreptitious Newsgathering,* 83 IOWA L. REV. 161, 198 (1997) (lying "is especially pernicious when done by representatives of those institutions [such as the media] in whom people place their trust"). See also Veilleux v. National Broadcasting Co., 8 F. Supp. 2d 23 (D. Me. 1998) (dismissing fraud and negligent misrepresentation claims asserted by plaintiff who suffered no pecuniary loss, but permitting same claims to proceed where asserted by plaintiffs who justifiably relied on promises of future performance and sustained pecuniary harm as a result).

7. 12 MEDIA L. REP. (BNA) 2230 (N.Y. Sup. Ct. 1986).
8. *Id.* at 2231.
9. 34 F. Supp. 2d 612, 616-23 (S.D. Ohio 1998).
10. *Id.* at 614-15.

disclosure of personal credit information to subscribers. *Business Week* thereafter used the plaintiff's service to obtain improperly the credit history of, *inter alia*, then-Vice President Dan Quayle.[11]

The court concluded both that the plaintiff had "an enforceable right to insist" that the defendants honor their written agreement to use the credit information provided to them for proper purposes and that, by entering into the agreement "knowing they had no permissible purpose" for the information, they "fraudulently induced WDIA to provide credit information to them."[12] Such "[w]illful or wanton misconduct on the part of a party to a contract," the court held, "can result in tort liability."[13]

In addition, the court rejected the defendants' contention that their conduct was protected from civil liability by the First Amendment. Citing *Cohen v. Cowles Media Co.*[14] and *Smith v. Daily Mail Publishing Co.*,[15] the court explained that, while the "press is privileged to publish truthful information lawfully obtained," the enforcement against the news media of "[g]enerally applicable laws do[es] not offend the First Amendment" whenever doing so "has an incidental effect on news gathering."[16] Specifically, the court concluded that "the application of the generally applicable laws regarding fraud and contract do not offend the First Amendment," and the defendants were therefore properly held liable in damages for both breach of contract and fraud.[17]

Nevertheless, the court also held that the plaintiff could recover only $7,500 in damages, which represented the costs it incurred to travel to Chicago to explain what had happened to the major credit reporting services from which it obtained its information.[18] The plaintiff was precluded from recovering damages caused by the subsequent "publication of the truthful article" as opposed to "the breach of contract or fraud," and could not recover punitive damages because the defendants' conduct, though "willful," was neither motivated by "malice or ill will" nor "particularly gross or egregious."[19] According to the court, "[d]efen-

---

11. *Id.* at 615.
12. *Id.* at 623-24.
13. *Id.* at 623.
14. 501 U.S. 663 (1991).
15. 443 U.S. 97 (1979).
16. 34 F. Supp. 2d at 624.
17. *Id.* (citing Boddie v. American Broadcasting Cos., 881 F.2d 267, 271 (6th Cir. 1989)); see 34 F. Supp. 2d at 624 ("[D]efendants are not immunized for their wrongful behavior simply because it was undertaken in the name of newsgathering. The defendants intentionally engaged in fraud which induced W.D.I.A. to permit access to credit information."). Prior to trial, the court had dismissed plaintiff's civil claims for violation of Ohio's RICO statute and for wire and mail fraud. See W.D.I.A. Corp. v. McGraw-Hill, Inc., No. C-1-93-448 (W.D. Ohio Apr. 4, 1995).
18. See 34 F. Supp. 2d at 627.
19. *Id.* at 622, 627 (citing OHIO REV. CODE ANN. § 315.21(c)(3); Logsdon v. Graham Ford Co., 376 N.E.2d 1333, 1336 n.2 (Ohio 1978)).

dants' test of the credit reporting system does not support an award of punitive damage in this case because it served to inform Congress and the general public about a matter of vital public interest and was done in such a way to protect the identity of W.D.I.A. and the rights of the consumers."[20]

Plaintiffs have been largely unsuccessful in maintaining causes of action for intrusion arising from misrepresentations in the newsgathering process, at least in the absence of conduct that can be said to invade a plaintiff's reasonable expectation of privacy.[21] In *Rifkin v. Esquire Publishing Inc.*,[22] for example, the plaintiff alleged that a magazine reporter had contacted his ex-wife and another person, and falsely told them that he was plaintiff's friend and had already interviewed him for the planned article. The court concluded that, even "liberally understood," the plaintiff had not stated an actionable claim for intrusion because the reporter "in no way (physically or otherwise) intruded upon plaintiff's solitude or seclusion."[23] In the court's view, "[l]iability for intrusion upon one's physical solitude or seclusion exists only if the intrusion goes beyond the limits of decency," and therefore the magazine's "attempts to gather information about plaintiff from third parties or to elicit the assistance of third parties in contacting plaintiff, even if pursued using subterfuge and fraud, cannot constitute an intrusion upon *plaintiff's* solitude or seclusion."[24] Similarly, in *Ault v. Hustler Magazine, Inc.*,[25] the plaintiff claimed that a magazine was liable for intrusion because it attempted to gain credit information about her by using a fictitious name. The district court held that such allegations, even if true, failed to state a claim because the method employed was not, apparently as a matter of law, "unreasonable."[26]

§ 13-2(b). Impersonation in Newsgathering.

The assumption of false identities by journalists in the course of gathering the news has given rise to a number of civil actions, raising a host of alternative

---

20. 34 F. Supp. 2d at 628. See *id.* ("'Testers' serve an important role in determining whether a statute intended to safeguard the rights of individuals is properly protecting those rights" and testers "need not be an arm of the governmental agency charged with the law's enforcement.") (citing United States v. Centennial Builders, Inc., 747 F.2d 678, 683 (11th Cir. 1984); Grant v. Smith, 574 F.2d 252, 254 n.3 (5th Cir. 1978); Northside Realty Assocs. v. United States, 605 F.2d 1348, 1354-55 (5th Cir. 1979)). The court also noted that defendants had promised to embrace "an enlightened philosophy that they will never again engage in similar conduct and will always publish the truth." 34 F. Supp. 2d at 628.
21. See Chap. 12-4 *supra*.
22. 8 MEDIA L. REP. (BNA) 1384 (C.D. Cal. 1982).
23. *Id.* at 1386.
24. *Id.*
25. 13 MEDIA L. REP. (BNA) 2232 (D. Or. 1987), *aff'd*, 860 F.2d 877 (9th Cir. 1988).
26. *Id.* at 2234.

theories of liability. In *Dietemann v. Time, Inc.*,[27] the defendant magazine's reporters gained access to plaintiff's home by falsely representing that they had been sent by "a friend" to secure medical treatment. Although the Ninth Circuit focused its analysis primarily on the reporters' subsequent surreptitious recording of conversations while in plaintiff's home,[28] it sustained plaintiff's intrusion claim in part on its generic observation that "there is no First Amendment interest in protecting news media from calculated misdeeds."[29]

In the years following *Dietemann*, courts have had numerous opportunities to consider the assumption of false identities by journalists. Most of these cases arise when journalists, equipped with hidden recording devices and cameras, falsify their names and credentials to gain entrance to plaintiff's businesses. The leading case is *Desnick v. American Broadcasting Cos.*,[30] in which the Seventh Circuit addressed the First Amendment's relevance to the law surrounding this newsgathering technique.

In *Desnick*, employees of the defendant television network, posing as patients and equipped with concealed cameras, requested eye examinations at several of plaintiffs' eye clinics.[31] The plaintiffs contended that, in so doing, the defendant "committed a trespass" and "invaded the right of privacy of the Center and its doctors at those offices."[32] Recognizing that "[t]o enter upon another's land without consent is a trespass," Chief Judge Posner further acknowledged that "there can be no implied consent in any nonfictitious sense of the term when express consent is procured by a misrepresentation or a misleading omission."[33] Nevertheless, the court concluded that "[t]here was no invasion in the present case of any of the specific interests that the tort of trespass seeks to protect:"

> [D]efendants' test patients gained entry into the plaintiffs' premises by misrepresenting their purposes (more precisely by a misleading omission to disclose those purposes). But the entry was not invasive in the sense of infringing the kind of interest of the plaintiffs that the law of trespass protects; it was not an interference with the ownership or possession of land.[34]

Beyond the specific application of the law surrounding each of plaintiff's common law claims, the court in *Desnick* made "[o]ne further point about the

---

27. 449 F.2d 245 (9th Cir. 1971).
28. See Chap.12-4(a) *supra*.
29. 449 F.2d at 250.
30. 44 F.3d 1345 (7th Cir. 1995).
31. *Id.* at 1348.
32. *Id.* at 1351.
33. *Id.*
34. *Id.* at 1353. Accord Willis v. Griffin Television, L.L.C., Case No. 91,812 (Okla. App. Mar. 5, 1999). The court in *Desnick* reached the same conclusion with respect to plaintiffs' privacy claim, holding that — the defendants' misrepresentations notwithstanding — "no intimate personal facts concerning the two individual plaintiffs . . . were revealed." 44 F.3d at 1353.

claims concerning the making of the program segment, as distinct from the content of the segment itself."[35] In somewhat stark contrast with the views expressed by the Ninth Circuit in *Dietemann*, the Seventh Circuit opined that, although "[t]oday's 'tabloid' style investigative television reportage" is undertaken "by networks desperate for viewers in an increasingly competitive television market," and is often "shrill, one-sided, and offensive," it is nevertheless "entitled to all the safeguards with which the Supreme Court has surrounded liability for defamation."[36] Moreover, such constitutional protections remain in force "regardless of the name of the tort," and "regardless of whether the tort suit is aimed at the content of the broadcast or the production of the broadcast."[37] Thus, the court held:

> If the broadcast itself does not contain actionable defamation, and no established rights are invaded in the process of creating it (for the media have no general immunity from tort or contract liability) . . . , then the target has no legal remedy even if the investigative tactics used by the network are surreptitious, confrontational, unscrupulous, and ungentlemanly.[38]

The Sixth Circuit employed analogous constitutional reasoning, albeit in the context of a prior restraint, in *In re King World Productions, Inc.*[39] There, a producer for a syndicated television magazine program, "claiming to be a patient, surreptitiously videotaped" the plaintiff.[40] Alleging, *inter alia*, that the defendants "committed fraud by misrepresenting their purpose in visiting" his office, plaintiff secured a temporary restraining order preventing defendants from broadcasting the video footage filmed there.[41] Echoing the Ninth Circuit in *Dietemann*, the district court held that "'the First Amendment is just not interested in protecting the news media from calculated misdeeds.'"[42] The Sixth Circuit, however, disagreed:

> Without a doubt, the district court's temporary restraining order constitutes a prior restraint of the use of the video footage. . . . Protection of the right to information that appeals to the public at large and which is disseminated by the media is the cornerstone of the free press clause of the first amendment. No matter how inappropriate the acquisition, or its correctness, the

---

35. 44 F.3d at 1355.
36. *Id.*
37. *Id.* (citing Hustler Magazine, Inc. v. Falwell, 485 U.S. 46 (1988)).
38. 44 F.3d at 1355.
39. 898 F.2d 56 (6th Cir. 1990).
40. *Id.* at 57-58.
41. *Id.* at 58.
42. *Id.* at 59 (quoting district court).

right to disseminate that information is what the Constitution intended to protect.[43]

Thus, although the court emphasized that its grant of mandamus relief was "not intended to constitute an approval of the surreptitious means used to gather this information," it concluded that it could not "nibble away at first amendment rights" by entering an injunction.[44]

Other courts have disposed of analogous claims without reaching the constitutional issue. In *Baugh v. CBS Inc.*,[45] for example, the plaintiff alleged trespass and intrusion causes of action arising from a television camera crew's alleged misrepresentation, in order to gain access to plaintiff's home, that it was affiliated with the district attorneys' office. Although plaintiff conceded that she consented to the entry of the camera crew into her home and their videotaping her discussions there, she alleged that "she did so only because she was led to believe that the crew was making the film for the District Attorney's office and that it would not be used commercially."[46] The court, however, concluded that — despite defendants' alleged misrepresentation of their true identity — they "acted within the scope" of plaintiff's consent "while they were on the premises," and only arguably exceeded it "by broadcasting the videotape" subsequently, a consequence that "cannot support a trespass claim."[47] In addition, the court held that, under California law, even in "a case where consent was fraudulently induced, but consent was nonetheless given, plaintiff has no claim for trespass," but must look instead to the fairly rigorous burdens imposed by the law of fraud or intentional misrepresentation.[48] The same reasoning, the court added, disposed of plaintiffs' intrusion claim.[49]

---

43. *Id.* at 59.
44. *Id.* at 60. See Charter Behavioral Health Sys. v. CBS Inc., No. 3:99-CV-150-MU (W.D.N.C. Apr. 21, 1999) (declining to enjoin broadcast of fruits of investigation of psychiatric hospital where licensed social worker, wearing hidden camera, secured employment at facility and videotaped treatment of patients).
45. 828 F. Supp. 745 (N.D. Cal. 1993).
46. *Id.* at 756.
47. *Id.* at 756-57. Accord Willis v. Griffin Television, L.L.C., Case No. 91,812 (Okla. App. Mar. 5, 1999).
48. 828 F. Supp. at 757. But see Shiffman v. Empire Blue Cross & Blue Shield, 681 N.Y.S.2d 511, 511 (App. Div. 1998) (affirmative defenses based upon consent and implied consent to enter premises were legally insufficient to defeat civil trespass claim "since consent obtained by misrepresentation or fraud is invalid").
49. 828 F. Supp. at 757 ("as with any intentional tort, consent is an absolute defense, even if improperly induced"). But see Copeland v. Hubbard Broadcasting, Inc., 526 N.W.2d 402, 404 (Minn. App. 1995) (distinguishing *Baugh* and holding that, where television station employee posed as student and accompanied veterinarian to plaintiffs' home, trespass claim survived summary judgment because "an entrant may become a trespasser by moving beyond the possessor's invitation or permission"); Special Force Ministries v. WCCO Television, 584 N.W.2d 789, 792-93 (Minn. App. 1998) (denying defense motion for summary judgment on trespass and fraud claims

A California appellate court rejected a fraud claim arising from journalists' alleged misrepresentation of their identities in *Wilkins v. National Broadcasting Co.*[50] There, two reporters using hidden cameras arranged to meet with plaintiffs, salesmen for a telephone services company, ostensibly as potential investors. The reporters falsely claimed that they were married and did not disclose that they were journalists working on a story about the plaintiffs' industry.[51] The court of appeal held that the plaintiffs were "unable to prove they relied to their detriment" on any affirmative misrepresentations by the reporters, since "they were not induced to provide any information" about their company because of any such representations.[52] Moreover, the court concluded that the plaintiffs and the reporters did not share any pre-existing or other relationship that would have imposed upon the latter "a duty to disclose the use of hidden cameras."[53]

In *W.C.H. of Waverly v. Meredith Corp.*,[54] in contrast, an employee of defendant television station posed as a patient and secured admission to plaintiff's alcohol and drug rehabilitation center. While there, the station employee "purported to be an alcoholic," brandished a knife, and "behaved in an abusive manner."[55] The court denied defendant's motion for summary judgment on plaintiff's fraud claim, holding that the above-referenced facts — if credited by a jury — would support a verdict for plaintiff. Moreover, the court rejected defendant's claim of "qualified privilege under the First Amendment," on the ground that any such privilege applies only to "*communications* made in the public interest."[56] In contrast, the court reasoned, "the claims to be tried in this case involve challenges to defendant's alleged tortious actions, not to the content of its stories or its right to investigate and air such stories."[57]

---

where television station employee misrepresented that she was unemployed in order to gain access as volunteer to care facility for mentally retarded persons) (relying on *Copeland*).

50. 84 Cal. Rptr. 2d 329 (Ct. App. 1999).
51. *Id.* at 337-38.
52. *Id.* at 338.
53. *Id.* at 339 (citing Deteresa v. American Broadcasting Cos., 121 F.3d 460 (9th Cir. 1997), *cert. denied*, 118 S. Ct. 1840 (1998); LiMandri v. Judkins, 60 Cal. Rptr. 2d 539 (Ct. App. 1997)).
54. 13 MEDIA L. REP. (BNA) 1648 (W.D. Mo. 1986).
55. *Id.* at 1649.
56. *Id.* at 1651.
57. *Id.* Accord Copeland v. Hubbard Broadcasting, Inc., 526 N.W.2d 402, 405 (Minn. App. 1995) ("Newsgathering does not create a license to trespass or intrude by electronic means into the precincts of another's home or office") (citing Dietemann v. Time, Inc., 449 F.2d 245, 249 (9th Cir. 1971)); Special Force Ministries v. WCCO Television, 584 N.W.2d 789, 793 (Minn. App. 1998) ("There is no inherent conflict or tension with the First Amendment in holding media representatives liable for the torts of fraud or trespass; neither the courts nor the legislature has given such representatives carte blanche to commit such torts in their pursuit of videotape."). But see Medical Lab. Management Consultants v. American Broadcasting Cos., 931 F. Supp. 1487 (D. Ariz. 1996) (dismissing intentional infliction of emotional distress claim arising from analogous

Another federal court considered a number of alternative causes of action in the context of assumed identities in *Food Lion, Inc. v. Capital Cities/ABC, Inc.*[58] There, the television network had undertaken elaborate efforts to equip certain of its employees with false identities, pursuant to which they obtained employment at supermarkets operated by the plaintiff. Specifically, according to plaintiff's complaint, the defendants "create[d] false identities and backgrounds, complete with supporting documentation," and including false "references for the background checks that Food Lion would conduct in reviewing applications for employment."[59] Defendants completed the Food Lion application using "false name[s], false background[s], false employment history, and false reasons for seeking work in a Food Lion store."[60]

Food Lion asserted a number of alternative causes of action, including tort claims of fraud, negligent supervision, trespass, breach of fiduciary duty, and statutory claims for violations of federal wiretapping laws,[61] and violation of the federal Racketeer Influenced and Corrupt Organizations Act ("RICO").[62] The court declined to dismiss plaintiff's claims for common law fraud and trespass, which defendants had attacked largely on the ground that they allegedly constituted "thinly-disguised claim[s] for 'intrusion.'"[63] The defendants could not, in the court's view, "'rewrite' Food Lion's complaint," which properly alleged both that they had "concealed their identities while applying for employment," and that Food Lion would not have hired them "if it had known their true identities."[64]

Ultimately, the court permitted plaintiff's claims for fraud, trespass, and breach of fiduciary duty to proceed to trial, where the jury rendered a verdict against the defendants for approximately $1,500 in compensatory damages and

---

circumstances); Medical Lab. Management Consultants v. American Broadcasting Cos., 30 F. Supp. 2d 1182 (D. Ariz. 1998) (granting summary judgment for defendants on fraud, trespass, intrusion and interference with contractual relations claims arising from analogous circumstances); Frome v. Renner, 26 MEDIA L. REP. (BNA) 1956, 1958 (C.D. Cal. 1997) (dismissing fraud claim where plaintiff failed to show damages proximately caused by misrepresentations rather than by publication, and where "use of a false identity did not affect the basic nature of [defendants'] relationship with Plaintiff").

58. 887 F. Supp. 811 (M.D.N.C. 1995) (adopting, in part, No. 6:92CV00592 (M.D.N.C. Apr. 26, 1994) (recommendation of magistrate judge)); see Food Lion, Inc. v. Capital Cities/ABC, Inc., 951 F. Supp. 1217 (M.D.N.C. 1996) (denying motion for summary judgment).

59. 887 F. Supp. at 814.

60. *Id.* at 815.

61. See Chap. 13-8 *infra*.

62. See 18 U.S.C. § 1961 et seq.

63. Food Lion, Inc. v. Capital Cities/ABC Inc., No. 6:92CV00592, slip op. at 15, 16 (M.D.N.C. Apr. 26, 1994) (magistrate's recommendation).

64. *Id.*

$5.5 million in punitive damages.[65] In denying defendants' motion for summary judgment, the court concluded that applicable state law recognized "a duty of loyalty in the employment context which is not confined to maintaining employer confidences."[66] Since an "employee has a duty to use her efforts, while working, for the service of her employer," the court held, the "potential violation of that duty here lies" in ABC undercover investigators "being employed by Food Lion and ABC at the same time."[67] Similarly, the court held that the plaintiff was entitled to go to trial on its fraud claim which, under applicable law, required a showing of: "'(1) false representation or concealment of a material fact; (2) reasonably calculated to deceive; (3) made with intent to deceive; (4) which does in fact deceive; (5) resulting in damage to the injured party.'"[68] According to the court, those elements were potentially satisfied based on evidence that ABC personnel "misrepresented themselves and their backgrounds, accepted jobs with Food Lion when they were actually employed by ABC, and had goals in those positions far different from those normally associated with the jobs."[69]

---

65. Food Lion, Inc. v. Capital Cities/ABC, Inc., 951 F. Supp. 1224 (M.D.N.C. 1996). The trial court subsequently reduced the punitive damages award to $315,000. See Food Lion, Inc. v. Capital Cities/ABC, Inc., 984 F. Supp. 923 (M.D.N.C. 1997) (denying motion for summary judgment); Singer, *Food, Lies and Videotape*, AM. LAW., April 1997, at 57 (describing trial). The court's rulings with respect to the trespass claims are addressed in Chap. 12-(c)(3) *supra*.

66. 951 F. Supp. at 1229 (citing McKnight v. Simpson's Beauty Supply, Inc., 358 S.E.2d 107, 109 (N.C. App. 1987); Lowndes Prods., Inc. v. Brower, 191 S.E.2d 761, 767 (S.C. 1972)).

67. 951 F. Supp. at 1229. See *id*. ("A reasonable jury could find that, because of [the ABC producers'] affiliation with and allegiance to ABC, they did not adequately perform their duties while working with Food Lion."). See also Food Lion, Inc. v. Capital Cities/ABC, Inc., 946 F. Supp. 420 (M.D.N.C. 1996) (dismissing copyright action filed by Food Lion seeking a declaration that it owned the copyright in the undercover videotapes made by ABC personnel while they were employed in Food Lion stores).

68. 951 F. Supp. at 1219 (quoting Myers & Chapman, Inc. v. Thomas G. Evans, Inc., 374 S.E.2d 385, 391 (N.C. 1988)). The court also rejected defendants' motion for summary judgment with respect to plaintiff's claim under the North Carolina Unfair Trade Practices Act, N.C. GEN. STAT. § 75-1, which was premised as well on plaintiff's allegations of fraudulent conduct. See 951 F. Supp. at 1232 ("Defendant ABC is a business and the production of stories for its news magazine show *PrimeTime Live* is one aspect of that business.").

69. 951 F. Supp. at 1220. The court in *Food Lion* also rebuffed the defendants' claim of attorney-client privilege in connection with discovery aimed at their consultations with their lawyers in advance of the broadcast. See Food Lion, Inc. v. Capital Cities/ABC, Inc., No. 6:92-CV-00592 (M.D.N.C. Aug. 22, 1994) (magistrate's order enforced by district court). Those discussions "took place while ABC was in the process of establishing false identities" for two of its employees "who were to apply for employment with Food Lion for the purpose of obtaining information about Food Lion's sanitation and labor practices." *Id*. slip op. at 2. To overcome the defendants' assertion of privilege, the court held, "Food Lion must present a *prima facie* case that ABC employees consulted with the attorneys in order to facilitate or further their intended frauds," *i.e.*, the assumption of false identities to gain unauthorized access to Food Lion facilities. *Id*. at 4. In that regard, the court concluded that "allegations of attorney involvement in the undercover operations" were

The court did, however, dismiss plaintiff's RICO claim, which Food Lion attempted to premise on predicate acts arising from "schemes to defraud" it and "other targets of investigations" for the "common purpose of gaining information through fraudulent means."[70] In the court's view, Food Lion's claim "depends on the key assumption that undercover reporting necessarily entails criminal conduct which would qualify as a predicate act such as mail or wire fraud," an assumption the court was unwilling to indulge.[71] In addition, the court declined to hold that a "series of predicate acts occurring over a six month span and directed at one victim," *i.e.*, Food Lion, could support a RICO claim, thereby preventing "the transformation of an ordinary fraud case into a federal RICO claim."[72]

By the same token, the court rejected defendants' assertion that the First Amendment barred all of plaintiff's claims, though it held that Food Lion could not constitutionally "use its remaining claims to recover damages for injury to its reputation."[73] Steering a course between the Supreme Court's decisions in *Cohen v. Cowles Media Co.*[74] and *Hustler Magazine v. Falwell*,[75] the district court in *Food Lion* recognized that:

> In this case, Food Lion has alleged that ABC has committed fraud, trespass, and other wrongful acts. Like promissory estoppel, the laws governing this

---

"sufficient to state a *prima facie* case that ABC attorneys were consulted in furtherance of a fraud, that fraud being the creation of 'false identities' for ABC employees who would seek 'employment' with Food Lion." *Id.* at 5.

An analogous argument was, however, rejected by another federal district court in *Medical Laboratories Management Consultants v. American Broadcasting Cos.*, 30 F. Supp. 2d 1182, 1207 (D. Ariz. 1998). Because "the law regarding liability for newsgathering activities involving undercover reporting is far from settled," that court concluded, "it is not plausible that Defendants 'knew or should have known' that they would be liable for fraud. In fact, there is every indication that Defendants, recognizing the uncertainty in the law, sought the advice of staff counsel to assist in designing the undercover operation so that it would conform with the law." *Id.* Accordingly, the court held, plaintiffs could not carry their burden of proving that "Defendants' communications with ABC counsel were conducted with the *express purpose* of promoting intended or continuing criminal or fraudulent activity." *Id.*

70. Food Lion, Inc. v. Capital Cities/ABC, Inc., 887 F. Supp. at 817.
71. *Id.* at 819. See also Medical Lab. Management Consultants v. American Broadcasting Cos., 30 F. Supp. 2d 1182, 1205 (D. Ariz. 1998) (granting summary judgment for defendants on federal eavesdropping claim under 18 U.S.C. § 2511(d), where "Plaintiffs have offered no convincing evidence or arguments explaining why Defendants would have any reason to record the meeting with [Plaintiff] other than to gain information and video footage for their broadcast").
72. 887 F. Supp. at 820. Accord Word of Faith World Outreach Center Church, Inc. v. Sawyer, 90 F.3d 118, 123 (5th Cir. 1996) (citing Food Lion, Inc. v. Capital Cities/ABC Inc., 887 F. Supp. at 819-20).
73. 887 F. Supp. at 821 (citing Cohen v. Cowles Media Co., 501 U.S. 663 (1991); Hustler Magazine, Inc. v. Falwell, 485 U.S. 46 (1988)).
74. 501 U.S. 663 (1991).
75. 485 U.S. 46 (1988).

behavior are laws of general applicability which do not "target or single out the press." . . . However, the fact that Food Lion's claims are not barred by the First Amendment does not mean that Food Lion may recover all of the damages it has allegedly suffered. . . . [T]he First Amendment bars Food Lion from recovering publication damages for injury to its reputation. . . .[76]

§ 13-3. Theft, Conversion, Stolen Documents and Criminal Conduct.

§ 13-3(a). Constitutional Overview.

Documents are the stuff of newsgathering. Journalists routinely ask for and receive documents of all kinds from their most trusted sources, including governmental agencies, businesses, and other individuals and entities. Occasionally, however, the manner in which the press has come into possession of documents and other tangible things has provoked litigation, both civil and criminal.[77]

The Supreme Court has never confronted directly the press' liability, if any, in such circumstances. It has, however, had isolated opportunities to speak to the issue, albeit in *dicta* and separate opinions. In *New York Times Co. v. United*

---

76. Food Lion, Inc. v. Capital Cities/ABC, Inc., 887 F. Supp. at 822 (citations omitted). See also *id.* 822-23 (citing Cohen v. Cowles Media Co., 501 U.S. 663 (1991); Hustler Magazine, Inc. v. Falwell, 485 U.S. 46 (1988)):

> [I]t appears that in determining that the First Amendment does not prohibit a plaintiff from recovery for a defendant's violation of a generally applicable law, the *Cohen* Court was mindful of the *type* of damages that the plaintiff sought to recover. Where a plaintiff sought recovery for non-reputational or non-state of mind injuries, the *Cohen* Court indicated that such a plaintiff could recover these damages without offending the First Amendment. Where, however, a plaintiff seeks to use a generally applicable law to recover for injury to reputation or state of mind while avoiding the requirements of a defamation claim (requiring proof of falsity and actual malice), the *Cohen* holding does not appear to be applicable. To the extent that Food Lion is attempting to recover reputational damages without establishing the requirements of a defamation claim, this case more closely resembles *Hustler*.

Based on this finding, the court declined to permit the jury to see the actual broadcast at any stage of the tripartite trial — liability, compensatory damages, or punitive damages. See Singer, *supra* note 65, at 58. Accord Food Lion, Inc. v. Capital Cities/ABC, Inc., 984 F. Supp. 923, 929 (M.D.N.C. 1997) (application of torts of trespass, breach of duty of loyalty, and fraud to media defendants, and non-publication punitive damages imposed on such defendants, do not violate First Amendment). See also W.D.I.A. Corp. v. McGraw-Hill, Inc., 34 F. Supp. 2d 612, 622, 627 (S.D. Ohio 1998). But see Special Force Ministries v. WCCO Television, 584 N.W.2d 789, 795 (Minn. App. 1998) (permitting recovery of broadcast damages in connection with fraud and trespass claims). See generally Chap 12-4(c) *supra*.

77. See generally Wade, *The Tort Liability of Investigative Reporters*, 37 VAND. L. REV. 301 (1984); Note, *Intrusion and the Investigative Reporter*, TEX. L. REV. 433 (1992). The press' invocation of affirmative rights of access to information — constitutional, statutory, and common law — is treated elsewhere in this volume. See Chaps. 5-6, 10-11 *supra*.

States,[78] the Court rebuffed the government's efforts to secure a prior restraint prohibiting publication of the contents of documents, which "were purloined from the Government's possession" and which the newspaper defendants received "with knowledge that they had been feloniously acquired."[79] Nevertheless, several members of the Court indicated, without deciding, that the newspapers might be subject to post-publication criminal prosecution under federal espionage laws.[80]

The full Court touched on the issue, also in the context of a prior restraint, in *Oklahoma Publishing Co. v. District Court*.[81] There, the Court invalidated a state court injunction that prohibited the news media from publishing the name or photograph of a juvenile. The court had permitted the press to attend a hearing in the juvenile's case, despite the fact that state law required the proceedings be closed to the public. Subsequently, after the judge attempted to prevent publication by issuing an injunction, the Supreme Court reversed, holding that once such truthful information is "publicly revealed" or otherwise "in the public domain," its further dissemination could not be constitutionally restrained.[82]

---

78. 403 U.S. 713 (1971).
79. *Id.* at 754 (Harlan, J., dissenting).
80. See, e.g., *id.* at 733 (White, J., concurring); *id.* at 730 (Stewart, J., concurring); *id.* at 748 (Marshall, J., concurring). The issue of press liability under federal espionage laws is treated at Chap. 13-3(c)(8) *infra*. In *CBS Inc. v. Davis*, 114 S. Ct. 912 (1994) (Blackmun, J., in chambers), Justice Blackmun stayed a prior restraint entered by a trial judge, holding that even "calculated misdeeds" by the press in obtaining information are not sufficient to justify a prior restraint:

> Nor is the prior restraint doctrine inapplicable because the videotape was obtained through the "calculated misdeeds" of CBS. In *New York Times Co.*, the Court refused to suppress publication of papers stolen from the Pentagon by a third party. Subsequent civil or criminal proceedings, rather than prior restraints, ordinarily are the appropriate sanction for calculated defamation or other misdeeds.

Id. at 914. Justice Blackmun further noted that, "[e]ven if criminal activity . . . could justify an exception to the prior restraint doctrine in some circumstances," there was no "clear evidence of criminal activity" in the case before him that would justify injunctive relief. *Id.*
81. 430 U.S. 308 (1977).
82. *Id.* at 311. In *McGraw-Hill Cos., Inc. v. Procter & Gamble Co.*, 116 S. Ct. 6 (1995) (Stevens, J., in chambers), Justice Stevens declined, largely on jurisdictional grounds, to vacate a prior restraint that had been entered against *Business Week* magazine. Subsequent proceedings in the litigation, which illuminated the relevant facts, are discussed *infra*. In its early submission to Justice Stevens, however, the magazine explained that "the documents whose contents it wants to publish were attachments to a motion" in civil litigation, which motion "'was not filed under seal'" and contained "'no indication anywhere on the motion itself that any of the described attachments were being filed under seal.'" *Id.* at 6 (quoting motion for stay). Justice Stevens interpreted this representation as an indication "that petitioner's agents obtained knowledge of the contents of the attachments either (1) without any notice that they were filed under seal, or (2) under the legitimate belief that their filing in court without any effort to preserve their confidentiality had the effect of placing their contents in the public domain." *Id.* Moreover, Justice Stevens construed petitioner's assertion as an "acknowledge[ment]" that the manner in which petitioner came into possession of

In the context of subsequent punishment, the Court has similarly been reluctant to impose liability premised on the manner in which a journalist has acquired information for publication or broadcast. The starting point for the Court's consideration of such issues appears to be its decision in *Cox Broadcasting Corp. v. Cohn*.[83] There, a television station broadcast the name of a rape victim, in violation of Georgia law.[84] A reporter for the station "learned the name of the victim from an examination of the indictments which were made available for his inspection in the courtroom."[85] The Supreme Court rejected the Georgia Supreme Court's conclusion that the victim's family could maintain a cause of action for invasion of privacy, construing the relevant constitutional issue to be "whether the State may impose sanctions on the accurate publication of the name of a rape victim obtained from public records — more specifically, from judicial records which are maintained in connection with a public prosecution and which themselves are open to public inspection."[86]

Having so framed the issue, the Court emphasized that "[g]reat responsibility" is placed on the press "to report fully and accurately the proceedings of government, and official records" and that, accordingly, "documents open to the public are the basic data of governmental operations."[87] As a result, the Court pronounced itself

> reluctant to embark on a course that would make public records generally available to the media but forbid their publication if offensive to the sensibilities of the supposed reasonable man. Such a rule would make it very difficult for the media to inform citizens about the public business and yet stay within the law. The rule would invite timidity and self-censorship and very likely lead to the suppression of many items that would otherwise be published and that should be made available to the public.[88]

It is the role of the "political institutions," the Court concluded, to "weigh the interests in privacy with the interests of the public to know and of the press to

---

the information it seeks to publish may have a bearing on its right to do so." *Id.* Accordingly, given that the parties to the underlying litigation had disputed the magazine's rendition of the operative facts, Justice Stevens concluded that the "wiser course is to give the District Court an opportunity to find the relevant facts, and to allow both that Court and the Court of Appeals to consider the merits of the First Amendment issue before it is addressed in this Court." *Id.*

83. 420 U.S. 469 (1975).
84. See GA. CODE ANN. § 26-9901 (1972).
85. 420 U.S. at 472.
86. *Id.* at 490.
87. *Id.* at 492. See also *id.* at 494 ("'there is no liability for the examination of a public record concerning the plaintiff, or of documents which the plaintiff is required to keep and make available for public inspection'") (quoting RESTATEMENT (SECOND) OF TORTS § 652B, cmt. c (tentative draft)).
88. 420 U.S. at 496.

publish" and thereby determine what information to place on the public record in the first place.[89] Once that decision is made, however, and "true information is disclosed in public court documents open to public inspection, the press cannot be sanctioned for publishing it."[90]

In *Landmark Communications, Inc. v. Virginia*,[91] the Court considered the constitutional propriety of a statute authorizing the imposition of criminal sanctions against a newspaper "for divulging information regarding proceedings before a state judicial review commission which is authorized to hear complaints as to judges' disability or misconduct, when such proceedings are declared confidential by the State Constitution and statutes."[92] The article at issue, on which the criminal prosecution was based, identified a state judge whose conduct was being investigated by the commission.

The Court determined that the "narrow and limited question" before it was whether the First Amendment "permits the criminal punishment of third persons who are strangers to the inquiry, including the news media, for divulging or publishing truthful information regarding confidential proceedings" of the commission, and not "the possible applicability of the statute to one who secures the information by illegal means and thereafter divulges it."[93] Similarly, the Court declined to address the "broader question" left unanswered in *Cox*, i.e., "whether the publication of truthful information withheld by law from the public domain" is constitutionally immune from subsequent sanction — holding only that Virginia had failed to identify a sufficiently important interest to override the First Amendment's preference for robust reporting about public officials and the judicial process.[94]

Landmark and *Cox* form the cornerstone of the Court's decision in *Smith v. Daily Mail Publishing Co.*,[95] in which it held that a West Virginia statute, making it a crime to publish the identity of an alleged juvenile offender, violated

---

89. *Id.*

90. *Id.* See also Hogan v. Hearst Corp., 945 S.W.2d 246, 252 (Tex. App. 1997) ("If the government has failed to police itself in releasing information, the imposition of damages [on the press] for its subsequent publication is not narrowly tailored to the state's interest."); Early v. The Toledo Blade, 26 MEDIA L. REP. (BNA) 2569, 2594 (Ohio App. 1998) ("the United States Supreme Court has made it clear that once the government makes public the names of victims of crimes, 'reliance must rest upon the judgment of those who decide what to publish or broadcast'") (quoting Cox Broadcasting Corp. v. Cohn, 420 U.S. at 496).

91. 435 U.S. 829 (1978).

92. *Id.* at 830 (citing VA. CODE ANN. § 2.1-37.13 (1973)).

93. 435 U.S. at 837.

94. *Id.* at 841; see *id.* ("[N]either the Commonwealth's interest in protecting the reputation of its judges, nor its interest in maintaining the institutional integrity of its courts is sufficient to justify the subsequent punishment of speech at issue here, even on the assumption that criminal sanctions do in fact enhance the guarantee of confidentiality.").

95. 443 U.S. 97 (1979).

the First Amendment.[96] The newspaper defendants in the case had each ascertained the juvenile's identity "by monitoring routinely the police band radio frequency" and "by asking various witnesses, the police, and an assistant prosecuting attorney" who were present at the crime scene for the information.[97] In what appeared to be a considerably broader pronouncement than it had been prepared to make in either *Cox* or *Landmark*, the Court asserted that those decisions "suggest strongly" that

> if a newspaper lawfully obtains truthful information about a matter of public significance then state officials may not constitutionally punish publication of the information, absent a need to further a state interest of the highest order. These cases involved situations where the government itself provided or made possible press access to the information. That factor is not controlling. Here respondents relied on routine newspaper reporting techniques to ascertain the identity of the alleged assailant. A free press cannot be made to rely solely upon the sufferance of government to supply it with information.[98]

The Supreme Court's most recent guidance is found in *The Florida Star v. B.J.F.*,[99] in which it again held that a rape victim could not recover damages from a newspaper that had published her name in violation of state law.[100] Unlike in *Cox*, the newspaper in *The Florida Star* did not obtain the victim's name from a public court file; rather, in apparent violation of the statute, the local Sheriff's Department had placed an incident report revealing the victim's name in its press room, where the newspaper retrieved it.[101] The Court thus decided the case based on the principle, "articulated in *Daily Mail*," that "if a newspaper lawfully obtains truthful information about a matter of public significance then state officials may not constitutionally punish publication of the information, absent a need to further a state interest of the highest order."[102]

---

96. See W. VA. CODE § 49-7-3.
97. 443 U.S. at 99.
98. *Id.* at 104 (citing Houchins v. KQED, Inc., 438 U.S. 1 (1978); Branzburg v. Hayes, 408 U.S. 665 (1972)).
99. 491 U.S. 524 (1989).
100. See FLA. STAT. ch. 794.03 (1987).
101. 491 U.S. at 527.
102. Smith v. Daily Mail Publ'g Co., 443 U.S. at 103, *quoted in* The Florida Star v. B.J.F., 491 U.S. at 533. See also Early v. The Toledo Blade, 26 MEDIA L. REP. (BNA) 2569, 2594 (Ohio App. 1998) (quoting The Florida Star v. B.J.F., 491 U.S. at 538); Boehner v. McDermott, 1999 U.S. App. LEXIS 23135, *49-55 (D.C. Cir. Sept. 24, 1999) (Ginsburg, J., concurring) (asserting that Congressman who knowingly received recording made in violation of federal and Florida wiretap statutes had participated in "illegal" activity that rendered strict scrutiny under *The Florida Star* inapplicable).

In so doing, however, the Court took pains to emphasize that the "*Daily Mail* formulation only protects the publication of information which a newspaper has 'lawfully obtained.'"[103] In *dicta*, moreover, the Court indicated that,

> [t]o the extent sensitive information rests in private hands, the government may under some circumstances forbid its nonconsensual acquisition, thereby bringing outside of the *Daily Mail* principle the publication of any information so acquired. To the extent sensitive information is in the government's custody, it has even greater power to forestall or mitigate the injury caused by its release. The government may classify certain information, establish and enforce procedures ensuring its redacted release, and extend a damages remedy against the government or its officials where the government's mishandling of sensitive information leads to its dissemination.[104]

Moreover, the Court asserted that the "*Daily Mail* principle does not settle the issue whether, in cases where information has been acquired *unlawfully* by a newspaper or by a source, government may ever punish not only the unlawful acquisition, but the ensuing publication as well," an issue it also declined to address it in *The Florida Star*.[105]

Nevertheless, the Court did conclude in *The Florida Star* that information is not "unlawfully" acquired by the press when it is generally made available by public officials, albeit in apparent violation of state law. "A contrary rule," the

---

103. 491 U.S. at 534 (quoting Smith v. Daily Mail Publ'g Co., 443 U.S. at 103). In *Doe v. Star Telegram, Inc.*, 915 S.W.2d 471 (Tex. 1995), the Texas Supreme Court reversed a court of appeals decision remanding a case to determine whether the information at issue had been lawfully obtained and instead affirmed the trial court's summary judgment for the defendants without reaching the issue. See *id.* at 474 (plaintiff could not recover on public disclosure of private facts claim where defendants disproved "that the articles in question, considered in their full context, disclosed embarrassing private facts which were not of legitimate public concern").

104. 491 U.S. at 534. Cf. Hogan v. Hearst Corp., 945 S.W.2d 246, 251, 252 (Tex. App. 1997) (while not opining as to whether newspaper "*should* exercise its right to publish the names of persons arrested for lewd conduct," court dismissed invasion of privacy, intentional infliction of emotional distress, and wrongful death claims against media defendants for publication of information lawfully obtained from public records).

105. 491 U.S. at 536 n.8. As the Court in *The Florida Star* went on to note, the "issue was raised but not definitively resolved in *New York Times Co. v. United States*, 403 U.S. 713 (1971), and reserved in *Landmark Communications, [Inc. v. Virginia,]* 435 U.S. at 837." 491 U.S. at 536 n.8. See Boehner v. McDermott, 1999 U.S. App. LEXIS 23135, *28-29 (D.C. Cir. Sept. 24, 1999) (opinion of Randolph, J.) (asserting that footnote 8 in *The Florida Star* indicates that the case does not "determine" whether a newspaper has a "First Amendment right to publish" where "a 'source' breaks into an office, steals documents, gives them to a newspaper and the newspaper, knowing the documents were stolen, publishes them in violation of a state or federal law"). Oliver v. WFAA-TV, Inc., 37 F. Supp. 2d 495 (N.D. Tex. 1998) (holding that First Amendment prohibits imposition of liability upon media defendants for knowing acquisition and publication of illegally obtained, truthful information about matter of public concern, as long as defendants did not participate in illegal activity).

Court held, "depriving protection to those who rely on the government's implied representations of the lawfulness of dissemination, would force upon the media the onerous obligation of sifting through government press releases, reports, and pronouncements to prune out material arguably unlawful for publication."[106] Indeed, "the fact that state officials are not required to disclose such reports does not make it unlawful for a newspaper to receive them when furnished by the government."[107]

The concept of "unlawful acquisition" has, however, not been easily applied in the lower courts, a phenomenon illustrated by *Procter & Gamble Co. v. Bankers Trust Co.*[108] In that case, a reporter for *Business Week* magazine obtained from a confidential source a motion and the exhibits thereto, the latter of which had been filed in a federal civil action under seal. The source turned out to be a lawyer at a firm representing one of the parties, who was not working on the case. He apparently did not know that the exhibits had been filed under seal when he secured a copy of the motion from a colleague and gave it to the reporter. For her part, the reporter was also unaware that the exhibits were filed under seal when she requested a copy from her source, although other *Business Week* journalists working on the story arguably did.[109]

The exhibits had been sealed pursuant to a "broad stipulated protective order" that the trial court had entered, at the parties' request, "as part of the discovery process."[110] The order empowered the "parties and not the court" to decide whether "particular documents" would be deemed confidential and filed under seal.[111] When the parties learned that *Business Week* planned to publish an article based on the sealed exhibits, they secured from the district court an *ex parte* order prohibiting publication without the court's consent.[112]

---

106. 491 U.S. at 536.
107. *Id.* at 536. See also *id.* at 538 (quoting Smith v. Daily Mail Publ'g Co., 443 U.S. at 103):

That appellant gained access to the information in question through a government news release makes it especially likely that, if liability were to be imposed, self-censorship would result. Reliance on a news release is a paradigmatically "routine newspaper reporting techniqu[e]." The government's issuance of such a release, without qualification, can only convey to recipients that the government considered dissemination lawful, and indeed expected the recipients to disseminate the information further.

Accord Cape Publications, Inc. v. Hitchner, 549 So. 2d 1374, 1375 (Fla.), *appeal dismissed*, 493 U.S. 929 (1989) (after *The Florida Star*, Florida Supreme Court held that a newspaper cannot be held liable, on a private facts theory, for "publishing lawfully obtained, confidential child abuse information in a story on a related child abuse trial").

108. 78 F.3d 219 (6th Cir. 1996).
109. *Id.* at 222-23.
110. *Id.* at 221.
111. *Id.*
112. *Id.* at 222-23.

The magazine's initial efforts to vacate the order, in the court of appeals and through emergency application to the Supreme Court,[113] proved unsuccessful and the district court thereafter convened an evidentiary hearing "to determine how the documents had been obtained and whether the injunction should remain in place."[114] Indeed, the district court took the position that "the manner in which *Business Week* came into possession of the protected discovery information has an important bearing on its right to publish it."[115] Thus, after two days of evidentiary hearings, the district judge concluded that the magazine had "unlawfully obtained court-protected confidential information and that, accordingly, it may not use and publish such information."[116]

According to the district court, the "uncontroverted testimony" presented at the hearing "made it clear" that *Business Week* "knew that these documents were sealed and unavailable while it actively attempted and eventually succeeded in procuring them."[117] This conclusion appears to have been drawn largely from the court's finding that, although there was no evidence that the reporter who actually received the documents was aware of the sealing order, another reporter knew they were under seal and nevertheless persisted in his efforts to secure them from the court itself.[118] Accordingly, the district court concluded that it could not "permit *Business Week* to snub its nose at court orders" because the "integrity of a court and the entire judicial system requires that its orders be acknowledged and obeyed."[119]

The Sixth Circuit reversed. Although its ruling was based largely on the First Amendment's "heavy presumption" against prior restraints, the Court of Appeals felt constrained to "clear up the considerable confusion generated by the proceedings below."[120] Specifically, the Sixth Circuit chastised the district court for "holding hearings on issues that bore no relation to the right of *Business*

---

113. See Procter & Gamble Co. v. Bankers Trust Co., 23 MEDIA L. REP. (BNA) 2535 (6th Cir. 1995); McGraw-Hill Cos. v. Procter & Gamble Co., 116 S. Ct. 6 (1995) (Stevens, J., in chambers).
114. Procter & Gamble Co. v. Bankers Trust Co., 78 F. 3d 219, 222-23 (6th Cir. 1996).
115. Procter & Gamble Co. v. Bankers Trust Co., 900 F. Supp. 186, 188 (S.D. Ohio 1995) (citing McGraw-Hill Cos. v. Procter & Gamble Co., 116 S. Ct. at 6 (Stevens, J., in chambers)).
116. Procter & Gamble Co. v. Bankers Trust Co., 900 F. Supp. 193, 196 (S.D. Ohio 1995). At the same time it purported to issue a permanent injunction prohibiting publication, however, the district court "lifted the bar of the protective order," which it asserted rendered the exhibits in question "publicly available." *Id.* As a result, *Business Week* published information contained in the previously sealed exhibits but pursued its appeal of the district court's injunction and prior orders. Cf. Ashcraft v. Conoco, Inc., 26 MEDIA L. REP. (BNA) 1620 (E.D.N.C. 1998) (holding reporter and newspaper with actual knowledge of valid confidentiality order liable for civil contempt for violating express terms of order).
117. 900 F. Supp. at 188-89.
118. *Id.* at 188-89.
119. *Id.* at 193.
120. Procter & Gamble Co. v. Bankers Trust Co., 78 F.3d 219, 225 (6th Cir. 1996).

Week to disseminate the information in its possession."[121] Indeed, it held that "how *Business Week* obtained the documents and whether or not its personnel had been aware that they were sealed" do not constitute "appropriate bases for issuing a prior restraint."[122]

§ 13-3(b). Civil Liability.

Analogous reasoning has been applied by other courts adjudicating claims for civil damages against the news media based on its receipt of documents and the information gleaned from them. In *Lence v. Hagadone Investment Co.*,[123] for example, the Montana Supreme Court confronted a false light invasion of privacy and negligence claim brought by an attorney, who was the subject of a confidential investigation by the court's Commission on Practice, against a reporter who published confidential information about the proceeding. The complainant, in violation of the confidentiality rules governing such proceedings,

---

121. *Id.*

122. *Id.* In this regard, the Sixth Circuit's decision is consistent with its prior holding in *In re King World Productions, Inc.*, 898 F.2d 56 (6th Cir. 1990). There, the producer of a television program, claiming to be a patient, surreptitiously videotaped the plaintiff. The district court granted a temporary injunction prohibiting broadcast of the videotape, because the defendants had allegedly secured the footage in violation of 18 U.S.C. § 2511. See 898 F.2d at 59. The Sixth Circuit reversed in *King World* as well, holding that:

> Here, the district court essentially ruled that a carefully pled violation of § 2511 trumped the defendants' first amendment right to broadcast their surreptitiously obtained video footage.... While § 2511 proscribes certain conduct, it in no way provides for a prior restraint of the press in the their exercise of first amendment rights even if the press's conduct clearly violates § 2511.

Id. In *King World*, moreover, the court emphasized that "[n]o matter how inappropriate the acquisition, or its correctness, the right to disseminate that information is what the Constitution intended to protect." *Id.* See also Worrell Newspapers of Indiana, Inc, v. Westhafer, 739 F.2d 1219, 1225 (7th Cir. 1984), *aff'd*, 469 U.S. 1200 (1985) ("Indisputably, courts may seal informations as well as other documents. However, when the press, by whatever means, obtains the information contained in a court sealed document, a state cannot prohibit the publication of the information without violating the First Amendment."); Food Lion, Inc. v. Capital Cities/ABC, Inc., 20 MEDIA L. REP. (BNA) 2263, 2264 (M.D.N.C. 1992) (allegations that ABC "secured the material in question unlawfully and by defrauding Food Lion," although "accepted for argument as true, are not sufficient to raise a serious issue that prior restraint could be ordered by this Court consistent with established First Amendment principles"). But see Ex parte State Record Co., 504 S.E.2d 592, 599 (S.C. 1998) (upholding prior restraint against dissemination of surreptitiously recorded videotape of privileged conversation between accused and his attorney in death penalty case; "[i]f [the accused]'s Sixth Amendment rights were insufficient to justify imposition of the prior restraint in this case, we can think of *no* situation in which a prior restraint would ever be justified") (emphasis in original); Marin Indep. Journal v. Municipal Ct., 16 Cal. Rptr. 2d 550 (Ct. App. 1993); Howard Publications, Inc. v. Lake Michigan Charters, Ltd., 649 N.E.2d 129 (Ind. App. 1995).

123. 853 P.2d 1230 (Mont. 1993).

approached a reporter and gave her a copy of the complaint.[124] Relying on *Smith*, *Landmark* and *The Florida Star*, the court rejected the attorney's claim.[125] Indeed, the court noted that, although the complainant violated the court's rules when he approached the reporter, the reporter "committed no wrong in receiving the information."[126]

Similarly, in *Larson v. Philadelphia Newspapers, Inc.*,[127] the court held that plaintiff, a state Supreme Court judge, could not maintain a cause of action against a newspaper premised on its alleged violation of court rules and state statutory and constitutional provisions governing the confidentiality of judicial disciplinary proceedings.[128] The court concluded that the plaintiff's claims could not be sustained "without running afoul of *Landmark*," noting that "the imposition of monetary damages (civil sanction) can be just as inimical to and an encroachment of one's First Amendment guarantees as criminal sanctions."[129]

Nevertheless, the court afforded plaintiff leave to replead his common law intrusion claim, holding that although his conclusory allegation that the newspaper had obtained the information at issue "illegally" was insufficient to sustain a cause of action, "illegal conduct in the securement" of the confidential documents, if properly alleged, would support a claim that "'reasonable' person[s] would be offended by such a course of conduct aimed at exposing personal information to the public."[130] In this regard, the court drew a constitutionally

---

124. *Id.* at 1233.
125. *Id.* at 1236.
126. *Id.* at 1238.
127. 543 A.2d 1181 (Pa. Super. 1988).
128. See *id.* at 1183 (citing PA. CONST. art. V, § 18(h); 42 PA. CONS. STAT. § 3334; PA. S. CT. R. 20).
129. 543 A.2d at 1185-86 (citing Landmark Communications, Inc. v. Virginia, 435 U.S. 829 (1978)).

The Pennsylvania Supreme Court adopted a similar view in *Boettger v. Loverro*, 587 A.2d 712 (Pa. 1991), after its contrary conclusion was vacated and remanded by the United State Supreme Court for reconsideration in light of *The Florida Star*. See *id.* at 713 (citing Boettger v. Loverro, 555 A.2d 1234 (Pa. 1989), *vacated*, 493 U.S. 885 (1989)). In *Boettger*, a reporter copied from a court file information contained in the transcript of a wiretapped conversation, which had been accidentally placed there in violation of state law. 587 A.2d at 714. In light of *The Florida Star*, the court concluded that, "when the assistant district attorney filed a copy of the transcript with the Clerk of Courts, . . . it went in the public domain, irrespective of whether or not the action of the assistant district attorney was inadvertent." *Id.* at 718. See also The Florida Star v. B.J.F., 491 U.S. 524, 551 n.4 (1989) (White, J., dissenting) (suggesting that prior decision of Pennsylvania Supreme Court "was erroneous" in light of *The Florida Star*).

130. 543 A.2d at 1188 (citing RESTATEMENT (SECOND) OF TORTS § 652B). See 543 A.2d at 1187 (quoting Associated Press v. NLRB, 301 U.S. 103, 132-33 (1937); Galella v. Onassis, 487 F.2d 986, 995-96 (2d Cir. 1973)):

> [An] attribution of "illegality" would appear to negate, at first blush, the use of proper methodology in the gathering of information which would render immune from suit the news media. This is in accord with the precept that a "publisher of a newspaper has no special

significant distinction between mere violation of state law governing the confidentiality of proceedings and records, on the one hand, and "the use of subterfuge in obtaining the information which goes beyond the acceptable bounds of newsgathering techniques," on the other.[131]

Although few other courts have equated use of "subterfuge" of this kind in the newsgathering process with "illegality," other courts have attempted to draw the line, however elusive it may be, between routine newsgathering on the one hand and illegal conduct on the other. In *Nicholson v. McClatchy Newspapers*,[132] for example, a newspaper published the confidential fact that the California Commission on Judicial Nominee Evaluation had found that plaintiff was not qualified for judicial appointment. Although the court purported to agree with plaintiff that "illegal conduct by a reporter is not privileged simply because the ultimate purpose is to obtain information to publish," it nevertheless concluded that "the First Amendment protects the ordinary news gathering techniques of reporters and those techniques cannot be stripped of their constitutional shield by calling them tortious."[133] Thus, the court held that:

> [w]hile reporters are not privileged to commit crimes and independent torts in gathering the news, and the press has no special constitutional right of access to information, "newsgathering is not without its First Amendment protections." ... The First Amendment therefore bars interference with this traditional function of a free press in seeking out information by asking questions.... Consequently, the news gathering component of the freedom of the press — the right to seek out information — is privileged at least to the extent it involves "routine" ... reporting techniques.... Such techniques, of course, include asking persons questions, including those with confidential or restricted information.[134]

---

immunity from the application of general laws, [since he] has no special privilege to invade the rights and liabilities of others." ... Stated differently, "[c]rimes and torts committed in news gathering are not protected[, and this] is no threat to a free press in requiring its agents to act within the law."

131. 543 A.2d at 1187 (citing Nicholson v. McClatchy Newspapers, 223 Cal. Rptr. 58 (Ct. App. 1986)).

132. 223 Cal. Rptr. 58, 59 (Ct. App. 1986).

133. *Id.* See also Mayes v. Lin Television of Texas, Inc., 27 MEDIA L. REP. (BNA) 1214 (N.D. Tex. 1998) (granting summary judgment for defendants on federal wiretap and state privacy claims where defendants lacked knowledge of challenged audiotape's illegality).

134. 223 Cal. Rptr. at 63-64 (quoting Branzburg v. Hayes, 408 U.S. 665, 681, 707 (1972); Smith v. Daily Mail Publ'g Co., 443 U.S. 97, 103 (1979)). See also Ashcraft v. Conoco, Inc., 26 MEDIA L. REP. (BNA) 1620, 1624 (E.D.N.C. 1998) (by-line writer's reported efforts to induce party to violate confidentiality order could not give rise to civil contempt since writer's conduct "contravened no express terms of that order [and] [f]undamental principles of the First Amendment unequivocally shelter legitimate news-gathering techniques"). Cf. Anti-Defamation League v. Superior Ct., 79 Cal. Rptr. 2d 597 (Ct. App. 1998) (holding that journalists are not immune from

§ 13-3(b)   THE MEANS OF NEWSGATHERING   § 13-3(b)

Similarly, in *Reuber v. Food Chemical News, Inc.*,[135] the Fourth Circuit held that there could be no liability for intrusion where the media defendant "played no role in leaking the letter" that formed the basis of its story, and which it had been provided by a source "in violation of government policy." The court noted that the result might have been different if the defendant had "unlawfully obtained" the letter through some "positive act."[136] The source's illegal conduct, the court explained, "does not mean" that the reporter "unlawfully obtained" the document.[137]

Even before the Supreme Court spoke to the issue from a constitutional perspective in the line of cases stretching from *Cox Broadcasting Corp.* through *The Florida Star*, many courts had reached the same result through application of the common law. The leading case appears to be *Pearson v. Dodd*,[138] in which the District of Columbia Circuit declined to hold columnists Drew Pearson and Jack Anderson liable for their receipt of copies of documents stolen from the offices of Senator Thomas Dodd. Anderson, who received the documents in

---

liability under CAL. CIV. CODE § 1798.53, which limits government entities' right to disclose personal information about individuals and provides cause of action against any individual who intentionally discloses such information, where journalists obtain, use, and disseminate such information about nonpublic figures in manner and for purpose "unrelated to conventional journalism," e.g., for private disclosure to foreign governments).

135. 925 F.2d 703 (4th Cir.), *cert. denied*, 501 U.S. 1212 (1991).

136. *Id.* at 719

137. *Id.* See also Bilney v. Evening Star Newspaper Co., 406 A.2d 652, 656 (Md. Spec. App. 1979) (no intrusion claim where newspaper secured confidential student transcripts from confidential source because "the information, though perhaps emanating *ultimately* from confidential University records, was not obtained by any personal act of invasion or intrusion" by the newspaper); Scheetz v. Morning Call, Inc., 747 F. Supp. 1515, 1526 (E.D. Pa. 1990), *aff'd*, 946 F.2d 202 (3d Cir. 1991) (rejecting claim that press unlawfully received confidential police report through conspiracy with unnamed police sources, in violation of 42 U.S.C. § 1983, on ground that reporter who simply copies information contained in report "would not be a receiver of stolen goods"); Oliver v. WFAA-TV, Inc., 37 F. Supp. 2d 516-17 (N.D. Tex. 1998) (media defendants not liable for intrusion or federal or state wiretap claims where they knowingly accepted information obtained by third parties in violation of wiretap laws); Peavy v. New Times, Inc., 976 F. Supp. 532 (N.D. Tex. 1997) (media defendants not liable under Federal Wiretap Act, 18 U.S.C. § 2511, for publication of "truthful information taken from a transcript of a public school board meeting, even though the media defendants may have known that this public information had been illegally obtained by someone else"); Early v. The Toledo Blade, No. 90-3434, slip op. at 13 (Ohio C.P. July 8, 1997), *aff'd*, 26 MEDIA L. REP. (BNA) 2569 (Ohio App. 1998) ("[I]f the material published by the Blade about these plaintiffs was exempted from [the state's public disclosure statute], then it was the government body's legal duty to redact such items. The Blade, on the other hand, had no legal duty to refrain from publishing such information."); but cf. Boehner v. McDermott, 1999 U.S. App. LEXIS 23135, *49-55 (D.C. Cir. Sept. 24, 1999) (Ginsburg, J., concurring) (asserting that knowing receipt by Congressman of tape of illegally recorded cellular telephone conversation constituted involvement in "illegal transaction" that rendered inappropriate strict scrutiny under the First Amendment of civil claims asserted pursuant to federal and state wiretap statutes).

138. 410 F.2d 701 (D.C. Cir. 1970).

question, was "aware of the manner in which the copies had been obtained," but did not participate in or otherwise authorize their theft.[139] Under these circumstances, the court held that, although a "person approached by an eavesdropper with an offer to share in the information gathered though the eavesdropping would perhaps play the nobler part should he spurn the offer and shut his ears," it "would place too great a strain on human weakness to hold one liable in damages who merely succumbs to temptation and listens."[140]

In addition, the court rejected the Senator's argument that the columnists were liable for the tort of "conversion" — *i.e.*, "the substantive tort theory which underlay the ancient common law form of trover" pursuant to which a plaintiff "alleged that he had lost a chattel which he rightfully possessed, and that the defendant had found it and converted it to his own use."[141] The court noted that liability for conversion cannot be premised on "intermeddling" that "falls short of the complete or very substantial deprivation of possessory rights in the property."[142] Thus, the court concluded that Pearson and Anderson had "committed no conversion of the physical documents taken from" Senator Dodd's offices, because they were "removed from the files at night, photocopied, and returned to the files undamaged before office operations resumed in the morning."[143]

---

139. *Id.* at 704-05.

140. *Id.* at 705. See also O'Connell v. CBS Inc., 782 F.2d 1414, 1420 (7th Cir. 1986) (no liability for intrusion where plaintiff's secretary removed documents from his desk and gave them to defendants absent "'evidence in the record that CBS in any way 'induced' the alleged intrusion"); Harris v. Easton Publ'g Co., 483 A.2d 1377, 1384 (Pa. Super. 1984) (no liability for intrusion where newspaper received "unsolicited" information at issue from a governmental agency); Lee v. Penthouse Int'l Ltd., 25 MEDIA L. REP. (BNA) 1651, 1657 (C.D. Cal. 1997) (defendant's publication of previously published photos allegedly stolen from plaintiffs' home by unknown person not actionable as intrusion); Howell v. Tribune Entertainment Co., 106 F.3d 215, 221 (7th Cir. 1997) (broadcaster not liable under Wisconsin privacy statute for airing program in which plaintiff's stepmother read from plaintiff's confidential juvenile police record; "It is one thing to impose liability on the press for invading someone's privacy, and another to impose liability on it for failing to prevent or take steps to rectify an invasion of privacy by another.... That kind of vicarious liability would put quite a damper on the media's taste for public controversy, in rather clear violation of the free speech clause of the First Amendment.").

141. 410 F.2d at 706.

142. *Id.*

143. *Id.* In addition, the court asserted that, to the extent that plaintiff's claim was premised on the documents' value "above and beyond that springing from their physical possession," it was equally without merit because he complained "not of the misappropriation of property bought or created by him, but of the exposure of information either (1) injurious to his reputation or (2) revelatory of matters which he has a right to keep to himself." *Id.* at 707-08. These claims, the court concluded, are properly addressed "at law by suit for libel and invasion of privacy respectively, where defendants' liability for those torts can be established under the limitations created by common law and by the Constitution." *Id.* at 708.

The conversion theory first expounded by Senator Dodd in *Pearson* has been asserted as well in subsequent cases.[144] In *Ault v. Hustler Magazine, Inc.*,[145] the Ninth Circuit rejected a conversion claim asserted by a plaintiff whose photograph, taken of her for other purposes, found its way into the hands of a magazine because "[c]onversion requires the intentional exercise of dominion and control over a chattel" and, although the photograph was arguably a chattel, "it was the property of the photographer," not of the plaintiff depicted in it.[146] Similarly, in *Berger v. Cable News Network*,[147] the court dismissed a conversion claim premised on a television network's entry on to plaintiffs' ranch, where they allegedly "seized and appropriated both statements and private images" of the plaintiffs, "their premises, and possessions."[148] The court held that "the use of photographed or videotaped images and sound recordings does not give rise to a cause of action for conversion" because, even if the tapes could be viewed as chattel, "it is the chattel of the defendants."[149]

In *FMC Corp. v. Capital Cities/ABC, Inc.*,[150] however, the Seventh Circuit upheld a conversion claim against the news media, at least in part. In that case, ABC had secured documents discussing the pricing policies of FMC Corp., the manufacturer of the Bradley Fighting Vehicle for the Department of Defense.[151] The documents were displayed in the course of a broadcast news report. FMC sued for conversion, alleging that the documents and all copies of them were missing from company files, and demanding their return.[152] The Seventh Circuit determined that, although FMC had stated a cause of action for conversion that required ABC to return the originals of the documents (if it had them) or copies (if it did not have the originals), the First Amendment required that ABC be

---

144. Even before *Pearson*, in *Metter v. Los Angeles Examiner*, 95 P.2d 491 (Cal. App. 1939), a California appellate court considered the claim of a plaintiff who alleged that his deceased wife's photograph, which had been published in the newspaper, was unlawfully converted from his home by its employees. The court rejected the plaintiff's conversion theory because, it held, the record was "barren of any evidence to prove either that the [newspaper] or its agents had entered" his home "or even had possession of the missing photograph." *Id.* at 494.

145. 860 F.2d 877, 883 (9th Cir. 1988).

146. *Id.* at 883.

147. 24 MEDIA L. REP. (BNA) 1757 (D. Mont. 1996), *aff'd in relevant part sub nom.* Berger v. Hanlon, 129 F.3d 505 (9th Cir. 1997), *vacated on other grounds*, 119 S. Ct. 1706 (1999).

148. *Id.* at 1760.

149. *Id.* at 1761 (citing Ault v. Hustler Magazine, Inc., 860 F.2d 877, 883 (9th Cir. 1988); Zacchini v. Scripps-Howard Broadcasting Co., 351 N.E.2d 454, 457 (Ohio 1976), *rev'd on other grounds*, 433 U.S. 562 (1977) (one's image is not converted by being photographed); Ippolito v. Lennon, 542 N.Y.S.2d 3, 6 (App. Div. 1989) (any possible interest by musician in his performance contained on video and sound recording is intangible and not actionable as conversion)).

150. 915 F.2d 300 (7th Cir. 1990).

151. *Id.* at 301.

152. *Id.*

permitted to retain copies of the documents and that it suffer no additional liability for having possessed the originals or the only copies.[153]

As construed by the Seventh Circuit, the tort of conversion "in most states" contemplates "'a distinct act of dominion wrongfully exerted over another's property in denial of or inconsistent with his title or rights therein, . . . without the owner's consent and without lawful justification.'"[154] Thus, the court concluded that, if "ABC has the originals, they must be returned to FMC for it is axiomatic that property known to belong to another must be returned."[155] Moreover, because "neither FMC, the district court, nor this court had or has any way of knowing exactly what documents ABC possesses," the Seventh Circuit concluded that "the burden should be on ABC, and not FMC, to come forward with evidence that it does not have the originals of the documents pilfered from FMC's files."[156]

In addition, although the court of appeals acknowledged that "'the receipt of copies of documents, rather than the documents themselves, should not ordinarily give rise to a claim for conversion,'" a different result obtains where, as in the case before it, FMC did "not have a copy of the documents known to be in the possession of the alleged converter, ABC."[157] Because the "gravamen of the tort of conversion is the *deprivation* of the possession or use of one's property," the court held that, where the "alleged converter has the originals *or* the only known copies of the originals, the retention of such property — to the exclusion of the owner — constitutes conversion."[158] Indeed, the Seventh Circuit emphasized that ABC's innocent receipt of the materials — *i.e.*, it did not participate in or solicit their theft — was immaterial to a conversion claim: "it is not the intent to steal or pilfer property that matters, but rather 'an intent to exercise a dominion or control over the goods which is in fact inconsistent with the plaintiff's rights.'"[159]

---

153. See *id.* at 303-05.

154. *Id.* at 303 (quoting Moore v. Regents of Univ. of California, 249 Cal. Rptr. 494, 503 (Ct. App. 1988)).

155. 915 F.2d at 303.

156. *Id.* The court added that, because it was "mindful of the First Amendment issues attending such a demonstration," it would "leave it to the district court, and to the parties, to determine what form ABC's proof may take," including the possibility that the district court might undertake an *in camera* inspection of the documents in ABC's possession. *Id.* Moreover, the court indicated that, if FMC were willing to accept copies of the documents, ABC would not be required to "submit" to *in camera* review at all. *Id.*

157. *Id.* at 303-04 (quoting district court).

158. *Id.* at 304 (quoting W. PROSSER & W. KEETON, PROSSER & KEETON ON THE LAW OF TORTS § 15, at 102 (5th ed. 1984) ("The gist of the conversion is the *interference* with *control* of the property.") (emphasis in original)).

159. 915 F.2d at 304 (quoting PROSSER & KEETON, *supra* note 158, § 15, at 92). The court also suggested that, even if possession of the only copies, rather than the original documents, did not

Finally, however, the court emphasized that the First Amendment requires that ABC remain "free to retain copies of any of FMC's documents in its possession" and "to disseminate any information contained in them."[160] In addition, the court held that ABC could "in no way be[] punished for the dissemination of FMC's information" and could legitimately "make copies of documents" it is required to return.[161]

§ 13-3(c). Criminal Liability.

The media has not been granted an exemption from criminal laws applicable to the general public.[162] In *Branzburg v. Hayes*,[163] the Supreme Court noted:

> It would be frivolous to assert—and no one does in these cases—that the First Amendment, in the interest of securing news or otherwise, confers a license on either the reporter or his news source to violate valid criminal laws. Although stealing documents or wiretapping could provide newsworthy information, neither reporter nor source is immune from conviction for such conduct, whatever the impact on the flow of news.[164]

Thus, the courts have generally not been receptive to claims that the First Amendment shields from criminal liability those who are undertaking news-

---

give rise to a claim, "FMC would have a valid claim for conversion on the grounds that ABC is essentially depriving FMC of the *use* of its own business information." 915 F.2d at 304.

160. *Id.* at 305.

161. *Id.* Moreover, the court emphasized that, if "ABC can legitimately show that, by returning copies of FMC's documents, it will be in danger of revealing its sources, ABC should be allowed to furnish FMC with its information in some way that will protect its sources." *Id.* at 306 n.4.

162. See, e.g., New York v. Ferber, 458 U.S. 747, 761-62 (1982) (quoting Giboney v. Empire Storage & Ice Co., 336 U.S. 490, 498 (1949) ("'It rarely has been suggested that the constitutional freedom for speech . . . extends its immunity to speech or writing used as an integral part of conduct in violation of a valid criminal statute.'"); United States v. Varani, 435 F.2d 758, 762 (6th Cir. 1970); New Jersey v. Cantor, 534 A.2d 83, 86 (N.J. Super. 1987) ("The First Amendment has never been construed to provide immunity from either tortious or criminal conduct committed in the course of newsgathering"); United States v. Matthews, 11 F. Supp. 2d 656, 664 (D. Md. 1998) (rejecting reporter's invocation of newsgathering privilege as defense to receiving and transporting child pornography over the Internet in violation of 18 U.S.C. § 2252, where "[i]t is Defendant's actions which contribute to the very problem that he wanted to investigate"); Utah v. Krueger, 975 P.2d 489, 498 (Utah App. 1999) (reporter and photographer who allegedly suggested that students chew tobacco on camera to provide video images for story not protected by First Amendment from liability for contributing to delinquency of minors; "representatives of the press may not encourage crime so that they may record it and report on it, and then claim that the prosecution amounts to an attempt by the government to restrain or abridge the freedom of the press").

163. 408 U.S. 665, 691 (1972).

164. *Id.* at 691.

gathering activities, simply because they are engaged in that salutary pursuit,[165] and have frequently asserted that "the First Amendment does not countenance that kind of end run around criminal law."[166] In *United States v. Matthews*,[167] for example, a freelance journalist was indicted for receiving and transmitting child pornography over the Internet in violation of the federal child pornography statute.[168] Matthews, who asserted that he posed as a trader in child pornography in order to conduct research for an article, moved to dismiss the complaint on the ground that it was unconstitutional as applied to a journalist's newsgathering activities. The district court recognized that newsgathering is protected by the First Amendment, but found it equally well-settled that the First Amendment does not exempt the press from generally applicable criminal laws.[169] In addition, the court concluded that Matthews' interest in gaining knowledge about child pornography on the Internet was "insignificant compared to the government's interest in preventing the exploitation of children."[170] It therefore denied Matthews' motion to dismiss and forbade him from arguing to the jury that it may find him not guilty if it were to conclude that his acts were committed in the course of newsgathering.[171]

The *Matthews* decision reflects the law's antipathy to media claims that journalists are somehow exempt from the operation of otherwise generally appli-

---

165. See, e.g., Galella v. Onassis, 487 F.2d 986, 995-96 (2d Cir. 1973) ("Crimes and torts committed in news gathering are not protected.... There is no threat to a free press in requiring its agents to act within the law."); Dietemann v. Time, Inc., 449 F.2d 245, 249 (9th Cir. 1971) ("The First Amendment has never been construed to accord newsmen immunity from torts or crimes committed during the course of newsgathering. The First Amendment is not a license to trespass, to steal, or to intrude by electronic means into the precincts of another's home or office."); United States v. Sanders, 17 F. Supp. 2d 141, 144 (E.D.N.Y. 1998) ("[T]he press may not use First Amendment protection to justify otherwise illegal actions."); United States v. Matthews, 11 F. Supp. 2d 656, 664 (D. Md. 1998) ("the law is clear that a press pass is not a license to break the law"); Utah v. Krueger, 975 P.2d 489, 498 (Utah App. 1999) ("While the First Amendment protects newsgathering activities, it does not, in the interest of securing news, give the press license to violate criminal laws."). See generally Burton, *Where Are All the Angry Journalists? The Use of Criminal Statutes and Tactics to Limit Newsgathering*, 16 COMM. LAW. 19 (Summer 1998).

166. United States v. Riggs, 743 F. Supp. 556, 561 (N.D. Ill. 1990), *aff'd*, 967 F.2d 561 (7th Cir. 1992).

167. 11 F. Supp. 2d 656 (D. Md. 1998).

168. 18 U.S.C. § 2252.

169. See 11 F. Supp. 2d at 662.

170. *Id.* at 664; see *id.* ("While the Court is hesitant to give news gathering tips, the Court agrees with the government that other, legal avenues of investigation are available. For example, a reporter could study the number of prosecutions brought by the government and examine the public records in those cases. A reporter could develop sources, including victims of child pornography and people already convicted of violations. Finally, a reporter could examine reports to public interest groups that track incidents of child pornography distribution.").

171. See *id.* at 665. Matthews subsequently pled guilty and was sentenced to 18 months in prison.

cable criminal laws by virtue of the First Amendment. As a practical matter, however, special protection has been provided to the media, in a number of contexts, when its newsgathering activities have become the subject of criminal prosecution.[172]

§ 13-3(c)(1). Criminal Trespass.

On occasion, journalists will enter the private property of another, or government property, without authorization, either in search of a story or while accompanying those involved in an event that entails a trespass on the property of another. The invocation of criminal trespass statutes in these circumstances has received less attention in reported cases than potential civil liability.[173] Some criminal trespass convictions have nevertheless been sustained based on judicial findings that any First Amendment-based right of access to gather news is outweighed by the governmental interest in protecting property rights and in maintaining law and order.

In *Stahl v. Oklahoma*,[174] for example, several journalists were convicted of criminal trespass for accompanying a group of protestors who entered Black Fox Station, the site of a proposed nuclear power generating plant owned by a utility company. The protestors sought to express their opposition to the proposed nuclear facility. Although the grounds of Black Fox were closed to the press and public, a designated public viewing area had been created near the center of the site. The defendant journalists, however, had entered the property with the protestors, rather than use the authorized vantage point of the public viewing area.[175]

On appeal, the journalists argued they lacked the necessary criminal intent because they entered the property to gather news, not to violate the rights of a landowner. The court, however, held that the criminal trespass statute that

---

172. Some courts, for example, tend to analyze the legal requirements of a crime with exactitude, arguably with hypertechnical precision, when a journalist engaged in newsgathering is charged with a crime. See, e.g., People v. Berliner, 3 MEDIA L. REP. (BNA) 1942 (N.Y. Sup. Ct. 1978) (information charging reporter and photographers with criminal trespass for entering the apartment of alleged "Son of Sam" killer dismissed because it failed to allege that entry was made without consent of owner or tenant).

173. See Chap. 12-2(b) *supra*.

174. 665 P.2d 839 (Okla. Crim. App.), *cert. denied,* 464 U.S. 1069 (1983).

175. The trial court had found that the "ignoble" intent of the utility company was to place limitations on the press in order to restrict news reporting regarding the protest. Oklahoma v. Bernstein, 5 MEDIA L. REP. (BNA) 2313, 2323 (Okla. Dist. 1980), *aff'd sub nom.* Stahl v. Oklahoma, 665 P.2d 839 (Okla. Crim. App.), *cert. denied*, 464 U.S. 1069 (1983).

formed the basis of their conviction[176] did not require an intent to violate the law, merely a willingness to enter land after being forbidden to do so by its owner.[177]

More significantly, the journalists argued that, absent a sufficient countervailing state interest, they had a constitutional right to enter Black Fox and accompany the protesters in order to cover the event adequately. The appellate court, however, concluded that the "First Amendment does not shield newspersons from liability for torts and crimes committed in the course of newsgathering."[178] In an analysis that appeared to be premised less on the propriety of civil liability than whether the press had an affirmative First Amendment-based right of access to the facility, the court assumed, without deciding, that the utility company, whose employees assisted in the arrest of the journalists, was engaged in state action.[179] Nevertheless, the court asserted that a governmental entity is empowered to regulate property under its control,[180] that Black Fox was not a traditional public forum subject only to reasonable time, place and manner restrictions, and that "the First Amendment does not guarantee the press a constitutional right of special access not available to the public generally."[181]

Based on this somewhat inapposite reasoning, the court's majority rejected a First Amendment-based defense to the trespass claim.[182] In dissent, however, Judge Brett, applying the Oklahoma Constitution,[183] proposed a balancing test to determine when the rights of the press to reasonable access to gather news may be restrained by the enforcement of a criminal trespass statute: "[A]ny press access claim to government information is subject to a degree of restraint dictated by the kind of forum, the nature of the information sought and the countervailing governmental interests."[184]

---

176. OKLA. STAT. tit. 21, § 1835(a).
177. 665 P.2d at 840. The gravamen of the criminal trespass offense is typically the failure to halt or leave after being requested to do so by the owner or occupant of the property. *Id.* at 845 (Brett, J., dissenting).
178. *Id.* at 841.
179. *Id.*
180. See *id.* at 842 (quoting United States Postal Serv. v. Council of Greenburgh Civic Ass'ns, 453 U.S. 114, 129-30 (1981)) ("[T]he First Amendment does not guarantee access to property simply because it is owned or controlled by the government. In *Greer v. Spock*, 424 U.S. 828 (1976), the court cited approvingly from its earlier opinion in *Adderly v. Florida*, 385 U.S. 39 (1966), wherein it explained that 'The State, no less than a private owner of property, has power to preserve the property under its control for the use to which it is lawfully dedicated.' 424 U.S. 828, 836.").
181. 665 P.2d at 842.
182. *Id.*
183. OKLA. CONST. art. II, § 22.
184. 665 P.2d at 846 (Brett, J., dissenting). Judge Brett asserted that Black Fox had a quasi-public character, that a determination of the protest's newsworthiness was beyond the proper scope of judicial review, that the defendants posed no harm to property interests, and that the limitations

Another court reached a similar result in *New Mexico v. McCormack*,[185] in which it affirmed a free-lance journalist's conviction for criminal trespass after he crossed a police barricade while covering a demonstration at a nuclear waste disposal site. The court rejected the journalist's argument that he lacked the requisite intent, finding that he had purposely entered the area after he had been warned not to cross the barricade.[186]

The journalist also contended that his conviction offended the First Amendment by impermissibly abridging his right to gather news. Relying on the Supreme Court's decision in *Richmond Newspapers, Inc. v. Virginia*,[187] the journalist argued that, although the site was legitimately closed to the public, the First Amendment requires that members of the press be given special access to areas controlled by the government to ensure the free flow of information to the public. The court, however, held that unlike criminal trials, nuclear waste disposal sites have not historically been open to the public,[188] and that "the defendant, as a member of the press, had no greater right than the public generally to cross the barricade."[189]

§ 13-3(c)(2). Criminal Harassment.

Persistent journalists may pursue a story so diligently that a source will seek redress in the criminal law of harassment. From the few reported decisions, it appears that courts will not sustain such prosecutions, at least where the journalist is engaged in routine newsgathering activity.

In *Galella v. Onassis*,[190] the Second Circuit affirmed and modified an injunction against a photographer, in part because his actions violated New York's criminal harassment statute, which makes it a crime to follow another in a public place, to inflict physical contact, or to engage in any annoying conduct without legitimate cause, with the intent to harass that person.[191] The court did not analyze the possible culpability of journalists under the statute outside the unusual facts of the *Galella* case, which are discussed elsewhere in this volume.[192] In most cases, it would appear safe to assume that newsgathering activities by

---

placed on press coverage were for the illegitimate purpose of controlling the news. As a result, Judge Brett concluded that defendants' convictions violated the First Amendment. *Id.* at 845-49.

185. 682 P.2d 742 (N.M. App. 1984).
186. *Id.* at 744-45.
187. 448 U.S. 555, 575-76 (1980) ("'[T]he First Amendment goes beyond protection of the press and the self-expression of individuals to prohibit government from limiting the stock of information from which members of the public may draw.'") (citation omitted).
188. 682 P.2d at 747.
189. *Id.*
190. 487 F.2d 986 (2d Cir. 1973). See Chap. 12-2(a) *supra*.
191. 487 F.2d at 994 n.11 (citing N.Y. PENAL LAW § 240.25 (McKinney 1967)).
192. See Chap.12-2(a) *supra*.

journalists would constitute a "legitimate cause" exempted from such a harassment statute. The *Galella* case is a reminder, however, that extreme conduct may be actionable, even in the newsgathering context.

In another civil action, a plaintiff alleged a violation of a state telephone harassment statute by a newspaper and several of its journalists for a series of articles written about him and the local legal poker industry.[193] The plaintiff complained that three telephone calls to his unlisted home number and ten calls to his law office over a period of seven months constituted a violation of Washington's telephone harassment statute.[194] The calls were made by a reporter in an effort to obtain the plaintiff's views and comments regarding various newsworthy events in which he was involved.[195] The trial court prohibited enforcement of the telephone harassment statute in the newsgathering context, holding that, "[b]ecause the conduct complained of consists of routine newsgathering activities, . . . liability based upon these causes of action would constitute an unwarranted interference in the newsgathering process" in violation of the federal and state constitutions.[196]

Since 1991, every state has enacted so-called "stalking" legislation. Such legislation is intended to provide protection against those who repeatedly follow or harass another person.[197] Because stalking takes many forms, the criminalized activity is defined broadly. California's statute, which was the first to be enacted and has been a model for other states, provides: "Any person who willfully, maliciously, and repeatedly follows or harasses another person and who makes a credible threat with the intent to place that person in reasonable fear for his or her safety, or the safety of his or her immediate family, is guilty of the crime of stalking."[198] "Harasses" is defined in the statute as "a knowing and wilful course of conduct directed at a specific person that seriously alarms, annoys, torments, or terrorizes the person, and that serves no legitimate purpose."[199]

---

193. See Lee v. The Columbian, 16 MEDIA L. REP. (BNA) 1261 (Wash. Super. 1989), *aff'd*, 826 P.2d 217 (Wash. App. 1991).
194. WASH. REV. CODE § 9.61.230.
195. 16 MEDIA L. REP. (BNA) at 1264.
196. *Id.* But see Hone v. Cortland City Sch. Dist., 985 F. Supp. 262 (N.D.N.Y. 1997) (First Amendment did not prevent public school from barring male sports reporter from school grounds after reporter made repeated attempts to initiate unwanted and bothersome personal contacts with female coaches).
197. See generally Diacovo, *California's Anti-Stalking Statute: Deterrent or False Sense of Security?*, 24 SW. U.L. REV. 389 (1995); Note, *A National Survey of Stalking Laws: A Legislative Trend Comes to the Aid of Domestic Violence Victims and Others*, 27 SUFFOLK U.L. REV. 67 (1993).
198. CAL. PENAL CODE § 646.9(a).
199. *Id.* § 646.9(e).

To date, there have been no reported cases of a journalist convicted under a stalking statute,[200] though the actions of some journalists have come close to falling within the activities proscribed by such statutes.[201] Several states have expressly excluded the press from the reach of their stalking statutes or have excluded all lawful business activity.[202]

---

200. A Minnesota district court declined to apply that state's anti-stalking statute, MINN. STAT. §§ 609.748-609.749, to prevent a reporter from attempting to interview a source. See Marshall v. Egan, No. C1-94-13844 (Minn. Dist. July 7, 1994); see also TORTS AND INSURANCE PRACTICE SECTION, AMERICAN BAR ASSOCIATION, NEWSLETTER OF MEDIA LAW AND DEFAMATION TORTS COMMITTEE, Winter 1996, at 20 (hereinafter cited as "TIPS"). The statute authorizes temporary and permanent injunctive relief to prevent "harassment," defined as "repeated, intrusive, or unwanted acts, words, or gestures that are intended to adversely affect the safety, security, or privacy of another, regardless of the relationship between the actor and the intended target." MINN. STAT. § 609.748.

Initially, a district judge signed an *ex parte* form order that purported to find "reasonable grounds" to believe the reporter had harassed plaintiff by "making visits and telephone calls . . . after being told to stay away." TIPS, at 21. The Minnesota Court of Appeal vacated that order on procedural grounds, though it also noted that "no explanation has been offered for the issuance of an *ex parte* order restricting constitutionally protected newsgathering activity." Marshall v. Egan, No. C6-94-1390 (Minn. App. July 1, 1994). The case returned to the district court where, after an evidentiary hearing, the court found that, while the reporter "had engaged in repeated and unwanted words and acts," there had been "no attempt to adversely affect Marshall's safety, security or privacy." TIPS, at 23. Accordingly, the court concluded that the conduct at issue did not amount to an invasion of privacy, since "'it was all done in a public area.'" *Id.* (quoting court). Finally, the court held:

> The U.S. Supreme Court has made it very clear that we courts and legislatures cannot do anything by way of ordinances or rulings by injunction to in any way prevent people from asking other people questions.

Id. (citing Madsen v. Women's Health Center, Inc., 512 U.S. 1277 (1994)).

201. See, e.g., Hone v. Cortland City Sch. Dist., 985 F. Supp. 262 (N.D.N.Y. 1997) (male sports writer accused of repeated attempts to initiate unwanted and bothersome personal contacts with female coaches at public secondary school); Koehler, *Journalistic Stalking*, 5 DEPAUL-LCA J. ART & ENT. L. 240 (1995) (describing conduct of television commentator who, unhappy with decision written by Illinois Supreme Court justice, urged viewers to call the justice at home while displaying the justice's home phone number on the screen). See generally Bjerregaard, *Stalking and the First Amendment: A Constitutional Analysis of State Stalking Laws*, 32 CRIM. L. BULL. 307, 307-11 (1996).

202. See, e.g., GA. CODE ANN. § 16-5-92; MINN. STAT. § 609.749 (excludes lawful commercial purposes); MONT. CODE ANN. § 45-5 (excludes exercise of freedom of speech and press); NEV. REV. STAT. § 200(5)(b)(2) (excludes reporters, photographers, or employees of press, radio or television acting in professional capacity gathering information); TENN. CODE ANN. § 39-17-315(c) (lawful business activity excluded). See Washington v. Lee, 957 P.2d 741 (Wash. 1998) (stalking statute not void for vagueness, nor unconstitutionally overbroad). In the wake of Princess Diana's death, several federal and state laws were proposed that would have imposed criminal penalties on journalists who persistently follow or chase a person who has a reasonable expectation of privacy. See Kirtley, *Freedom of the Press: An Inalienable Right or a Privilege to Be Earned?*, 9 U. FLA. J.L. & PUB. POL'Y 209, 209-10 (1998); Lidsky, *Prying, Spying, and Lying: Intrusive Newsgathering and What the Law Should Do About It*, 73 TUL. L. REV. 173, 183 (1998). An argument raised

§ 13-3(c)(3). Disorderly Conduct.

Journalists often find themselves at the scene of a newsworthy event along with law enforcement personnel.[203] On occasion, a conflict develops between law enforcement's perception of what is necessary to protect public safety and a journalist's perceived need to gather the news, leading to criminal charges of disorderly conduct against the journalist.

An early case addressing such a prosecution is *New Jersey v. Lashinsky*,[204] in which the conviction of a press photographer as a disorderly person was affirmed by the New Jersey Supreme Court. The photographer entered the scene of a fatal automobile accident, where he took several pictures. Twenty minutes later, a state trooper arrived, was told one passenger was alive, noticed gas leaking from the automobile, and ordered the numerous onlookers to withdraw from the area. The photographer refused, showing his press card to the trooper. When the trooper repeated his order, the photographer engaged him in a heated argument, which led to the photographer's arrest on charges of violating New Jersey's disorderly person statute.[205]

The photographer argued that his conduct did not violate the statute because he had neither the intent to interfere with the officer nor physically interfered with his movements. The court, however, held that the statute does not require such specific intent, nor actual physical interference, but that "each case calls for an assessment of defendant's actions in light of all the surrounding circumstances," including the activity giving rise to a policeman's order, the reasonableness of that order itself, and the defendant's reaction to it.[206] In the court's view, a person may not "be arrested for disorderly conduct solely because the arresting officer capriciously or in bad faith finds behavior annoying or distracting. To trigger the application of the statute, conduct must be truly obstructive."[207] The court concluded that the photographer's presence in close proximity to the automobile made the trooper's job more difficult in light of the problems of crowd control, the threat of fire, the needs of the surviving victim and the presence of valuable personal property. Accordingly, the court held that the trooper's "order to Lashinsky to withdraw was clearly reasonable. Lashinsky's dogged and willful refusal to obey that order was palpably unreasonable."[208] In

---

against the adoption of such legislation is that those proposing such new laws were "seemingly oblivious to the panoply of statutes that already prohibit stalking, harassment, trespassing, and similar crimes." Kirtley, *supra*, at 209. No new legislation has in fact been enacted.

203. See Chap. 12-5 *supra*.
204. 404 A.2d 1121 (N.J. 1979).
205. See N.J. STAT. ANN. § 2A:170-29(2)(b) ("Any person who in any place, public or private . . . obstructs, molests or interferes with any person lawfully therein . . . is a disorderly person.").
206. 404 A.2d at 1126.
207. *Id.*
208. *Id.* at 1127.

addition, the court rejected the photographer's contention that the disorderly person statute was unconstitutionally vague and overbroad as applied to newsgathering, holding that the statute adequately communicated its essential prohibition of conduct that constitutes an interference with a police officer.[209]

The Wisconsin Supreme Court reached a similar result in *City of Oak Creek v. King*,[210] affirming the conviction of a reporter who repeatedly refused to leave a restricted area near an airplane crash site. The court concluded that the reporter's conduct came within the "catchall" clause of the state's disorderly conduct statute, which proscribes "otherwise disorderly conduct."[211] Although the court recognized that neither the refusal to obey a police command nor a journalist's mere presence, absent any conduct that tends to cause or provoke a disturbance, would constitute disorderly conduct, it concluded that the arresting officer's concern for crowd control, "combined with [the reporter's] continued penetration into a nonpublic restricted area in the presence of the general public,"[212] had the requisite tendency to cause disruption. Given the presence of the public and other members of the media, the reporter's repeated refusal to obey the officer's order was deemed to be conduct of a type that tends to cause or provoke a disturbance, in violation of the statute.[213]

---

209. *Id.* at 1130. In dissent, Judge Pashman argued that the majority failed to give proper weight to the photographer's status as a newsperson and should have found that the trooper acted unreasonably by requesting that the photographer leave the accident scene. *Id.* at 1134 (Pashman, J., dissenting) ("[T]he majority has ruled that a newsman acts illegally if he stands up for his rights and refuses to accede to an arbitrary, and hence unlawful, request."). In Judge Pashman's view, "the [photographer's] actions constitute the precise type of conduct in which any media photographer must engage if he is to adequately report a news event. To characterize such conduct as an unreasonable interference with police activities is equivalent to a holding that the police may remove a newsman from the scene of an accident merely because that newsman is competently performing his job. As such, the 'special access rights' of the press to which the majority pays lip service are rendered meaningless." *Id.* at 1131 (Pashman, J., dissenting).

Also in dissent, Judge Clifford argued that, no matter how extraordinary a nuisance the photographer made of himself, his conduct is unlawful only if the disorderly conduct statute is given a narrowing construction that requires a showing of actual physical interference or an intent to interfere with the police officer. *Id.* at 1136-37 (Clifford, J., dissenting) (citing Colten v. Kentucky, 407 U.S. 104 (1972); Shuttlesworth v. City of Birmingham, 382 U.S. 87 (1965)).

210. 436 N.W.2d 285 (Wis. 1989).

211. *Id.* at 288-90. The reporter was convicted of a violation of City of Oak Creek Municipal Ordinance § 9:947:01, adopting WIS. STAT. § 974.01, which provided:

> Whoever, in a public or private place, engages in violent, abusive, indecent, profane, boisterous, unreasonably loud or otherwise disorderly conduct under circumstances in which the conduct tends to cause or provoke a disturbance is guilty of a Class B misdemeanor.

212. 436 N.W.2d at 289-90.

213. *Id.* at 290. But see *id.* at 295 (Abrahamson, J., dissenting) (arguing that any concern that reporter's presence could have interfered with rescue efforts or may have placed reporter in personal danger was speculative and that a number of other journalists were inside police boundary without being challenged).

The court also rejected the reporter's claim that the statute was unconstitutionally vague, on the ground that its "catchall" clause proscribing "otherwise disorderly conduct" was reasonably explicit.[214] "The statute does not imply that all conduct which tends to annoy another is disorderly conduct," the court asserted; rather, the "design of the disorderly conduct statute is to proscribe substantial intrusions which offend the normal sensibilities of average persons or which constitute significantly abusive or disturbing demeanor in the eyes of reasonable persons."[215] Thus, the court concluded that "persons of common intelligence would realize that repeated refusals to obey a police officer's reasonable order in a situation in which crowd control was a major concern, combined with continued penetration into a nonpublic restricted area in the presence of the general public, is conduct which . . . [has] a tendency to disrupt good order and to provoke a disturbance."[216]

In *Pennsylvania v. Chini*,[217] in contrast, a reporter and a photographer stood in the middle of a street observing the aftermath of an automobile collision involving a police vehicle. The reporter refused to move from the street after being instructed to do so by a police officer and threatened to have the officer arrested for harassment. Instead, the officer charged the reporter with disorderly conduct.[218] Although the court viewed the reporter's conduct as unprofessional and arrogant,[219] it did not, in the court's judgment, create a hazardous condition. Accordingly, it did not constitute a statutory offense.[220]

§ 13-3(c)(4). Impersonation of a Public Official.

The assumption of false identities by journalists in the course of gathering the news may not only give rise to civil actions[221] but may also provide the basis for a criminal prosecution if the impersonation violates a penal code provision. In

---

214. *Id.* at 290.
215. *Id.* at 291.
216. *Id.*
217. 18 MEDIA L. REP. (BNA) 1335 (Pa. C.P. 1990).
218. See 18 PA. CONS. STAT. § 5503(a)(4):

(a) Offense defined. — A person is guilty of disorderly conduct if, with intent to cause public inconvenience, annoyance or alarm, or recklessly creating a risk thereof, he:

(4) creates a hazardous or physically offensive condition by any act which serves no legitimate purpose of the actor.

219. See 18 MEDIA L. REP. (BNA) at 1336 ("The court is unaware that freedom of the press has ever been thoughtfully interpreted by the professional press to serve as a cloak for arrogant public conduct, and a lever to pry loose the patience of officers charged with assuring the good order of the community at its frontline points of stress.").
220. *Id.* at 1336.
221. See Chapter 13-2 (b) *supra*.

New Jersey v. Cantor,[222] a reporter was convicted of impersonating a public official.[223] The reporter had identified herself as an official from the county morgue when interviewing the mother of a homicide victim.[224]

On appeal, the reporter argued that the statute at issue must be interpreted to avoid infringing upon the constitutional protections that shelter newsgathering activity from governmental intrusion. The court, utilizing the reasonableness test enunciated in *New Jersey v. Lashinsky*,[225] found that the defendant's status as a newsperson did not protect her from the application of criminal laws forbidding the false impersonation of a public official, particularly when the deceit was practiced upon a vulnerable person.[226] "While defendant has attempted to wrap herself in the constitutional cloak of press freedom, the rights of the press do not exist in a vacuum,"[227] the court explained, "[a] presssperson has no special immunity from the application of general laws and no special privilege to invade the rights and liberties of others."[228] The court also noted that the statute had no requirement that the defendant be motivated by personal gain, "although the enhancement of her professional reputation for the 'scoop' might lend some aura of individual aggrandizement to this offense."[229]

§ 13-3(c)(5). Theft of Government Property.

It is rare that a member of the press is charged with the theft of government property.[230] More often, a reporter's source, typically a government employee or former employee, will face prosecution for taking, without authorization, and supplying to the press documents or other material from a government installation. Nevertheless, a journalist who acts in concert with such a source, or who solicits him to misappropriate classified documents, is not immune from criminal prosecution.

The federal larceny statute, for example, renders criminally liable any person who "converts to his use or the use of another, or without authority, sells, conveys or disposes of any . . . thing of value of the United States . . . or [w]ho-

---

222. 534 A.2d 83 (N.J. Super. 1987).
223. Under New Jersey's disorderly persons statute, a person commits such an offense "if he falsely pretends to hold a position in the public service with purpose to induce another to submit to such pretended official authority or otherwise to act in reliance upon that pretense." N.J. STAT. ANN. § 2C:28-8.
224. 534 A.2d at 84.
225. 404 A.2d 1121, 1126 (N.J. 1979) ("[A] balancing of competing values is required in order to assess the reasonableness of a criminal statute or governmental sanction as applied to a member of the press engaged in his profession."). See Chap. 13-3(c)(3) *supra*.
226. 534 A.2d at 86.
227. *Id.* at 85.
228. *Id.*
229. *Id.* at 86.
230. See note 165 *supra* (citing cases).

ever receives ... the same with intent to convert it to his use or gain."[231] Where theft has been made of tangible government property, the courts have upheld convictions under this statute, even when the theft was made in order to provide the property to the press for dissemination to the public.[232]

The courts have had greater difficulty where the "property" taken constitutes intangible information.[233] In *Carpenter v. United States*,[234] albeit in a somewhat different context, the Supreme Court held that intangible confidential business information constitutes property that may be the subject of a criminal prosecution.[235] Also of potential concern is 18 U.S.C. § 2071(a), a federal statute that prohibits the unauthorized, willful removal of records filed with any United

---

231. See 18 U.S.C. § 641:

> Whoever embezzles, steals, purloins, or knowingly converts to his use or the use of another, or without authority, sells, conveys or disposes of any record, voucher, money, or thing of value of the United States or of any department or agency thereof, or any property made or being made under contract for the United States, or any department or agency thereof; or
>
> Whoever receives, conceals, or retains the same with intent to convert it to his use or gain, knowing it to have been embezzled, stolen, purloined or converted—
>
> Shall be fined under this title or imprisoned not more than ten years, or both; but if the value of such property does not exceed the sum of $100, he shall be fined under this title or imprisoned not more than one year, or both.
>
> The word "value" means face, par, or market value, or cost price, either wholesale or retail, whichever is greater.

232. "The mere fact that one has stolen a document in order that he may deliver it to the press, whether for money or for other personal gain, will not immunize him from responsibility for his criminal act. To use the first amendment for such a purpose would be to convert the first amendment into a warrant for thievery.... [T]he First Amendment may not be used for such a sordid purpose ... to enable the governmental employee to excuse his act of theft...." United States v. Morison, 844 F.2d 1057, 1077 (4th Cir.), *cert. denied*, 488 U.S. 908 (1988).

233. For example, Anthony Russo and Daniel Ellsberg were indicted under 18 U.S.C. § 641 for depriving the United States of the exclusive possession of the information contained in the Pentagon Papers by making and distributing copies of the documents. The case was dismissed due to governmental misconduct. See Nimmer, *National Security Secrets v. Free Speech: The Issues Left Undecided in the Ellsberg Case*, 26 STAN. L. REV. 311 (1974).

234. 484 U.S. 19 (1987).

235. *Id.* at 25-26. Although *Carpenter* addressed violations of securities laws, aiding and abetting, federal mail and wire fraud statutes, and conspiracy, the Court's analysis has been applied to the federal theft of government property statute. See, e.g., United States v. McAusland, 979 F.2d 970 (4th Cir. 1992), *cert. denied*, 507 U.S. 1003 (1993) (disclosure of procurement information); United States v. Fowler, 932 F.2d 306 (4th Cir. 1991) (Department of Defense classified documents); United States v. Morison, 844 F.2d 1057, 1077 (4th Cir.), *cert. denied*, 488 U.S. 908 (1988). See also United States v. Jeter, 775 F.2d 670 (6th Cir.), *cert. denied*, 475 U.S. 1142 (1985) (carbon sheets of typed grand jury documents); United States v. Girard, 601 F.2d 69 (2d Cir.), *cert. denied*, 444 U.S. 871 (1979) (sale of names of Drug Enforcement Agency informants deemed property under the statute); United States v. DiGilio, 538 F.2d 972 (3d Cir.), *cert. denied*, 429 U.S. 1038 (1976) (photocopies of FBI files).

States court or public office.[236] Unlike the federal larceny statute, however, the reach of 18 U.S.C. § 2071(a) has been limited to tangible items and does not proscribe mere photocopying of documents.[237]

§ 13-3(c)(6). Mail Fraud.

The federal mail fraud statute prohibits the use of the mails as part of a scheme to defraud or to deprive another of money or property by means of false or fraudulent pretenses, representations, or promises.[238] In *Carpenter v. United States*,[239] a reporter for the *Wall Street Journal* was convicted under the mail fraud statute for defrauding the publication of its exclusive right to use confidential information. The journalist, Foster Winans, wrote a daily "Heard on the Street" column that discussed stock information. Winans allegedly entered into a scheme with stockbrokers pursuant to which he disclosed information to them

---

236. See 18 U.S.C. § 2071(a):

> Whoever willfully and unlawfully conceals, removes, mutilates, obliterates, or destroys, or attempts to do so, or, with intent to do so takes and carries away any record, proceeding, map, book, paper, document, or other thing, filed or deposited with any clerk or officer of any court of the United States, or in any public office, or with any judicial or public officer of the United States, shall be fined under this title or imprisoned not more than three years, or both.

237. See United States v. Rosner, 352 F. Supp. 915, 919 (S.D.N.Y. 1972) (construing 18 U.S.C. § 2071(a)). See also United States v. Sanders, 17 F. Supp. 2d 141 (E.D.N.Y. 1998) (rejecting claim that First Amendment protects freelance journalist from liability under 49 U.S.C. § 1155(b), which applies to any "person who knowingly and without authority removes, conceals, or withholds a part of a civil aircraft involved in an accident," when he secured fabric from seat on TWA Flight 800, which crashed in 1996).

238. See 18 U.S.C. § 1341:

> Whoever, having devised or intending to devise any scheme or artifice to defraud, or for obtaining money or property by means of false or fraudulent pretenses, representations, or promises. . . . places in any post office or authorized depository for mail matter, any matter or thing whatever to be sent or delivered by the Postal Service, or deposits or causes to be deposited any matter or thing whatever to be sent or delivered by any private or commercial interstate carrier, or takes or receives therefrom, any such matter or thing . . . shall be fined under this title or imprisoned not more than five years, or both. If the violation affects a financial institution, such person shall be fined not more than $1,000,000 or imprisoned not more than 30 years, or both.

See generally Carpenter v. United States, 484 U.S. 19, 27 (1987). The Supreme Court limited the scope of the statute to frauds involving money or property in *McNally v. United States*, 483 U.S. 350, 359 (1987). In 1988, Congress enacted 18 U.S.C. § 1346, which broadened the scope of the mail and wire fraud statutes to protect "any person's right to the honest services of another, including the right of the public to the honest services of public officials." 134 CONG. REC. S17360-02 (Nov. 10, 1988). See United States v. Wang, 898 F. Supp. 758, 761 (D. Colo. 1995). See generally Moohr, *Mail Fraud and the Intangible Rights Doctrine: Someone to Watch Over Us*, 31 HARV. J. LEGIS. 153 (1994).

239. 484 U.S. 19 (1987).

regarding the contents of his column, which they used, prior to publication, to purchase and sell various stocks. Winans purportedly exchanged the information for a share of the investor's profits.[240] Although there was no evidence that the *Journal* suffered a monetary loss as a result of these activities, the Supreme Court affirmed Winans' conviction, holding that the *Journal*'s confidential business information was property protected by the mail fraud statute,[241] and the newspaper was defrauded of its right to exclusive use of the information. The use of the mails to send the *Journal* to its customers, ensuring the circulation of the "Heard on the Street" columns, was deemed an essential part of the scheme.[242]

§ 13-3(c)(7). Wire Fraud.

Criminal wire fraud involves the use of telephone, telegraph, radio or television in a scheme to defraud another of property.[243] The federal wire fraud statute has been interpreted in a manner similar to the mail fraud statute.[244] A journalist who provides prepublication information derived from newsgathering to an unauthorized recipient through the use of wire or broadcast media may, therefore, be susceptible to prosecution.[245]

---

240. See generally R. WINANS, TRADING SECRETS: SEDUCTION AND SCANDAL AT THE WALL STREET JOURNAL (1984).

241. See 484 U.S. at 26-27 ("Petitioners cannot successfully contend . . . that a scheme to defraud requires a monetary loss, such as giving the information to a competitor; it is sufficient that the Journal has been deprived of its right to exclusive use of the information, for exclusivity is an important aspect of confidential business information and most private property for that matter.").

242. *Id.* at 28. See United States v. Thaw, 353 F.2d 581, 584 (4th Cir. 1965) (placing advertisements with fraudulent information in newspapers with mailing privileges constituted use of the mails for purposes of 18 U.S.C. § 1341).

243. 18 U.S.C. § 1343:

> Whoever, having devised or intending to devise any scheme or artifice to defraud, or for obtaining money or property by means of false or fraudulent pretenses, representations, or promises, transmits or causes to be transmitted by means of wire, radio, or television communication in interstate or foreign commerce, any writings, signs, signals, pictures, or sounds for the purpose of executing such scheme or artifice, shall be fined under this title or imprisoned not more than five years, or both. If the violation affects a financial institution, such person shall be fined not more than $1,000,000 or imprisoned not more than 30 years, or both.

244. See Carpenter v. United States, 484 U.S. 19, 25 n.6 (1987).

245. The reporter in *Carpenter v. United States*, 484 U.S. 19 (1987), was also convicted of violating the wire fraud statute. The conviction was based upon the use of telephone wires to print and send the *Wall Street Journal* to customers. *Id.* at 28. See also Food Lion, Inc. v. Capital Cities/ABC Inc., 887 F. Supp. 811, 819 (M.D.N.C. 1995):

> Food Lion's conclusion [that defendant violated the federal RICO statute, 18 U.S.C. § 1961] depends on the key assumption that undercover reporting necessarily entails criminal conduct which would qualify as a predicate act such as mail or wire fraud. However, the use of a

The wire fraud statute has also been invoked in the relatively new arena of computer communications, where a single computer operator is capable of publishing information to thousands, if not millions, of potential recipients via telephone lines. The increased worldwide access to the Internet has greatly reduced the relevance of any distinction between a mass media publisher and an individual communication in this context. In addition, information obtained through unauthorized access to government or private sources may arguably be disseminated via electronic bulletin boards, on-line discussion groups or on the Internet.

In *United States v. Riggs*,[246] for example, two computer hackers were indicted under the wire fraud statute as a result of the publication of a stolen computer text file in an issue of PHRACK, a computer hacker newsletter. One hacker gained unauthorized access to a telephone company computer, downloaded a computer file containing confidential information describing the computerized control of emergency 911 services, and uploaded the file to a bulletin board. The second hacker then obtained the file from the bulletin board, edited it to conceal its source, uploaded the edited version to the bulletin board, and published the text from the edited file in his regularly published newsletter.

Both hackers were indicted for using telephone lines in furtherance of a scheme to steal and disseminate the valuable proprietary information contained in the computer file. The hacker who published PHRACK argued that criminalizing his publication of the text file in the newsletter was an unconstitutional abridgement of his First Amendment rights that could be sustained only on a showing of "the highest form of governmental interest."[247] The court distinguished the publisher's reliance on *Smith v. Daily Mail Publishing Co.*[248] and *Landmark Communications, Inc. v. Virginia*[249] on the ground that those cases — and the standard they articulated — apply only in the context of lawfully obtained information.[250]

The defendant next argued that the text file he published "is plainly of interest to any member of the public concerned with the operation of the system through which he can reach 'police, fire, and/or ambulance services.'"[251] The court

---

hidden camera in no way requires the use of the mails or of wire communications. This Court declines to equate the use of hidden cameras and microphones with mail and wire fraud.

See generally Chap. 12-2(c)(3) *supra*.

246. 743 F. Supp. 556 (N.D. Ill. 1990), *aff'd*, 967 F.2d 561 (7th Cir. 1992).
247. *Id.* at 559 (citing Smith v. Daily Mail Publ'g Co., 443 U.S. 97 (1979); Landmark Communications, Inc. v. Virginia, 435 U.S. 829 (1978)).
248. 443 U.S. 97 (1979).
249. 435 U.S. 829 (1978).
250. 743 F. Supp. at 559.
251. *Id.* at 560.

nevertheless refused to excuse his violation of the wiretap statute "simply because he provided the public with interesting information"[252] and declined to permit the First Amendment to "act as a shield to preclude the prosecution of that individual simply because his criminal conduct involves speech."[253]

Finally, the court rejected one defendant's attack on his indictment for wire fraud arising from his transmission of his newsletter via telephone lines. Rather than containing illicitly obtained computer files, these issues included no more than information and tutorials regarding the "art" of computer hacking. The defendant argued that his mere advocacy of illegal activity constituted protected speech under *Brandenburg v. Ohio*.[254] The court, however, responded that these additional issues of PHRACK were actionable as an essential part of the scheme to defraud the telephone company, "since the aim of the communications was ostensibly to encourage others to illicitly obtain confidential, computer-stored information."[255] In this manner, the court adopted the curious reasoning that the defendant's involvement in the theft of the computer file rendered the First Amendment inapplicable to his subsequent publications concerning computer hacking: "[T]he *Brandenburg* test cannot be reasonably applied to violations of the mail fraud or wire fraud statutes, which usually 'involve long-term, slowly-developing wrongs, not "imminent lawless action."'"[256]

§ 13-3(c)(8). Receiving Purloined Documents or Other Property.

Journalists routinely find themselves in the possession of files, documents, recordings or other materials that have been delivered to them by third parties. The provenance of these materials may or may not be known. Their receipt, however, raises the unresolved issue of whether a journalist can be criminally liable for the receipt of purloined documents.

§ 13-3(c)(8)(A). Receipt of Stolen Property.

The leading case regarding the press' receipt of stolen property is *People v. Kunkin*.[257] In that case, the California Supreme Court reversed the conviction of a newspaper publisher and reporter for their possession of a stolen government

---

252. *Id.*
253. *Id.* See *id.* at 561 ("Interpreting the First Amendment as shielding Neidorf from criminal liability would open a gaping hole in criminal law; individuals could violate criminal laws with impunity simply by engaging in criminal activities which involve speech-related activity. The First Amendment does not countenance that kind of end run around criminal law.").
254. 395 U.S. 444 (1969). The defendant argued that the newsletter articles were not directed at producing imminent lawless action, nor were they likely to produce or incite such action. 743 F. Supp. at 562.
255. 743 F. Supp. at 562.
256. *Id.* at 562 (quoting United States v. Rowlee, 899 F.2d 1275, 1280 (2d Cir. 1990)).
257. 507 P.2d 1392 (Cal. 1973).

document[258] under a California statute criminalizing the receipt of stolen property.[259] The statute was interpreted to require three elements for conviction: "(1) the property was received, concealed, or withheld by the accused; (2) such property had been obtained by theft or extortion; and (3) the accused knew that the property had been so obtained."[260]

The California Supreme Court assumed that the roster was property, concluded that it had been stolen, and that it had been "received" within the meaning of the statute. The convictions were reversed, however, because the court found that "there was no substantial evidence to support the jury's finding that the defendant knew the roster was stolen."[261] In so holding, the court declined to provide a broader, First Amendment-based protection from prosecution under the statute for journalists who receive "leaked" documents.[262] Moreover, as a result of *Kunkin*, the California legislature enacted a statute specifically prohibiting the malicious dissemination, disclosure and publication of private information regarding a law enforcement officer.[263]

Among the issues left unresolved by *Kunkin* is whether a copy of a government document can be deemed "property" for purposes of a criminal statute aimed at stolen "property." The issue was the subject of considerable attention by the court of appeal in the *Kunkin* case,[264] where the majority held that the

---

258. The document was a copy of a personnel roster that listed the names, addresses and telephone numbers of state undercover narcotics agents. The roster had been taken from the office of the California Attorney General by a mail clerk. The clerk gave the copy to a reporter for *The Free Press*, a Los Angeles newspaper. The roster was published by the newspaper and was accompanied by an article titled "There Should Be No Secret Police: Know Your Local Nark." *Id.* at 1394.

259. See CAL. PENAL CODE § 496:

> Every person who buys or receives any property which has been stolen or which has been obtained in any manner constituting theft or extortion, knowing the property to be so stolen or obtained, or who conceals, withholds or aids in concealing or withholding any such property from the owner, knowing the property to be so stolen or obtained, is punishable by imprisonment. . . .

260. 507 P.2d at 1395.

261. *Id.* at 1399.

262. One commentator has suggested that the court's failure to address the First Amendment issues raised in *Kunkin* constituted a lost opportunity to provide protection to journalists who publish the results of laudable investigations that are often aided by leaks from inside government. See Sobel, *Government Documents as "Stolen Property": Reflections on the "Free Press" Case*, 49 L.A. B.J. 291, 294-96 (June 1973). See also Boehner v. McDermott, 1999 U.S. App. LEXIS 23135, *29 (D.C. Cir. Sept. 24, 1999) (opinion of Randolph, J.) (suggesting, without deciding, that a newspaper that received and published documents, knowing they were stolen, would not be protected by the First Amendment standard articulated by the Supreme Court in *The Florida Star v. B.J.F.*, 491 U.S. 524, 533 (1989)).

263. See CAL. PENAL CODE § 146e(a). A violation of the statute that results in bodily injury is deemed a felony. *Id.* § 146e(b).

264. People v. Kunkin, 100 Cal. Rptr. 845 (Ct. App. 1972), *rev'd on other grounds*, 507 P.2d 1392 (Cal. 1973).

roster constituted property because it had value as paper, as a useful item, and as a tangible compilation of information.[265] As such, the court held, it was similar to material, such as stolen telephone subscription lists,[266] stolen geophysical maps[267] and a stolen description of a manufacturing process[268] that had been held to be property under the California statute criminalizing the receipt of stolen property or the federal statute prohibiting the transportation of stolen goods in interstate commerce.[269]

Justice Roth, however, dissented from the court of appeal's decision, arguing that the roster, which he characterized as intangible government information having no commercial value, could not properly be considered property.[270] In *Carpenter v. United States*,[271] the Supreme Court held that the intangible nature of such information did not preclude a conviction under the federal mail and wire fraud statutes.[272] The *Carpenter* decision, however, did not address whether information must have commercial value to fall within these penal statutes.[273]

§ 13-3(c)(8)(B). Interstate Transportation of Stolen Property.

A person who has received a document or other material that is known to be stolen or accessed without authorization, and who travels across state boundaries with the document or disseminates it over telephone lines, may be charged with violation of federal law prohibiting interstate transportation of stolen property.[274]

---

265. 100 Cal. Rptr. at 850-51.
266. See, e.g., People v. Dolbeer, 29 Cal. Rptr. 573 (Ct. App. 1963); People v. Parker, 31 Cal. Rptr. 716 (Ct. App. 1963).
267. See, e.g., United States v. Seagraves, 265 F.2d 876 (3d Cir. 1959); United States v. Lester, 282 F.2d 750 (3d Cir.), *cert. denied,* 364 U.S. 937 (1960).
268. See, e.g., United States v. Bottone, 365 F.2d 389 (2d Cir.), *cert. denied,* 385 U.S. 974 (1966).
269. See, e.g., 18 U.S.C. § 2314.
270. 100 Cal. Rptr. at 863-66 (Roth, J., dissenting). In this regard, Justice Roth cited *In re Vericker*, 446 F.2d 244 (2d Cir. 1971), a case involving FBI documents, as authority for the proposition that documents that have no commercial value are not considered property under the federal transportation of stolen goods statute. 100 Cal. Rptr. at 864-65 (Roth, J., dissenting).
271. 484 U.S. 19 (1987).
272. *Id.* at 25-26.
273. In *Carpenter,* the Court referred to the information contained in unpublished *Wall Street Journal* columns as confidential business information, something the Court appeared to conclude had intrinsic value. *Id.* at 26-27. As a result, *Carpenter* is consistent with the view that information, to be deemed stolen property, must have commercial value. In the civil context, however, the Court has held that the unauthorized use of confidential government information may be actionable even absent a showing of commercial value. See Snepp v. United States, 444 U.S. 507 (1980). Although *Snepp* was premised on a breach of contract, the existence of the contract requiring prepublication review was not necessarily essential to the Court's analysis. See *id.* at 515 n.11 ("[E]ven in the absence of a written contract, an employee has a fiduciary obligation to protect confidential information obtained during the course of his employment.").
274. See 18 U.S.C. § 2314:

Proprietary business information contained in copies of documents,[275] computer files[276] or maps[277] has been held to constitute "goods, wares, or merchandise" within the meaning of the statute.[278]

The statute requires that the requisite transportation be made knowing the goods were "stolen, converted or taken by fraud."[279] A person who merely receives such documents, albeit knowing they have been taken across state lines without authorization, may also be in violation of federal law, at least as written. The courts, however, have not had occasion to adjudicate the significant constitutional issues that undoubtedly would be raised in the wake of any such prosecution.[280]

§ 13-3(c)(9). Federal Government Secrets and Espionage Statutes.

The United States Code does not contain a general statute that purports to punish the unauthorized disclosure of classified information. Instead, Congress

---

> Whoever transports, transmits, or transfers in interstate or foreign commerce any goods, wares, merchandise, securities or money, of the value of $5,000 or more, knowing the same to have been stolen, converted or taken by fraud . . . [s]hall be fined under this title or imprisoned not more than ten years, or both.

In one reported case, a defendant charged with violation of § 2314 and other federal crimes unsuccessfully raised a First Amendment defense based on his status as the publisher of a newsletter. See United States v. Riggs, 743 F. Supp. 556 (N.D. Ill. 1990), aff'd, 967 F.2d 561 (7th Cir. 1992).

275. See, e.g., United States v. Greenwald, 479 F.2d 320, 322 (6th Cir.), *cert. denied*, 414 U.S. 854 (1973) (documents containing valuable chemical formulae); United States v. Bottone, 365 F.2d 389, 393 (2d Cir.), *cert. denied*, 385 U.S. 974 (1966) (documents describing a manufacturing process of patented drugs); but cf. In re Vericker, 446 F.2d 244, 248 (2d Cir. 1971) (FBI documents are not the ordinary subject of sale and, therefore, do not constitute "goods, wares, or merchandise").

276. See, e.g., United States v. Riggs, 739 F. Supp. 414, 420 (N.D. Ill. 1990), *aff'd*, 967 F.2d 561 (7th Cir. 1992) (computer text file describing the computerized control and maintenance of emergency 911 services). But see United States v. Brown, 925 F.2d 1301, 1308 (10th Cir. 1991).

277. See, e.g., United States v. Lester, 282 F.2d 750, 754-55 (3d Cir.), *cert. denied*, 364 U.S. 937 (1960) (copies of geophysical maps identifying oil deposits).

278. See United States v. Riggs, 739 F. Supp. 414, 423 (N.D. Ill. 1990), *aff'd*, 967 F.2d 561 (7th Cir. 1992) ("The owner of confidential proprietary business information . . . possesses something which has clearly been recognized as an item of property."). Information that is not deemed valuable proprietary business information, but is protected only by copyright law, will not fall within § 2314. See Dowling v. United States, 473 U.S. 207 (1985).

279. 18 U.S.C. § 2314.

280. See 18 U.S.C. § 2315:

> Whoever receives, possesses, conceals, stores, barters, sells, or disposes of any goods, wares, or merchandise, securities, or money of the value of $5,000 or more . . . which have crossed a State or United States boundary after being stolen, unlawfully converted, or taken, knowing the same to have been stolen, unlawfully converted, or taken. . . . shall be fined under this title or imprisoned not more than ten years, or both.

has enacted a patchwork of legislation that seeks to protect the military and strategic secrets of the United States. This legislation, most of which is enacted in the form of espionage and censorship laws,[281] collectively makes it a crime to receive, disclose, communicate, withhold, or publish certain information, documents, photographs or drawings. These statutes, rarely the basis for prosecution, traditionally have been used only to prosecute those charged with ordinary espionage.[282] Whether journalists could be convicted under current law, or even under more narrowly drafted statutes, has been much debated, but remains unresolved.[283] In *New York Times Co. v. United States*,[284] such statutes formed the basis of threatened prosecution against the newspapers publishing the Pentagon Papers. In *United States v. Morison*,[285] the Fourth Circuit affirmed the conviction of a government employee who had leaked national defense information to a publisher.

---

281. See 18 U.S.C. § 793 (prohibits the gathering or transmitting of certain defense information); 18 U.S.C. § 794 (prohibits the gathering or delivering of certain defense information to aid a foreign nation); 18 U.S.C. § 795 (prohibits the making of graphic representations of certain vital defense installations); 18 U.S.C. § 796 (prohibits the use of aircraft to photograph vital defense installations); 18 U.S.C. § 797 (prohibits the unauthorized sale of graphic representations of vital defense installations); 18 U.S.C. § 798 (prohibits the disclosure of classified information); 18 U.S.C. § 799 (prohibits violation of NASA regulations). Other statutory provisions that prohibit and punish the dissemination of national security information include: 42 U.S.C. §§ 2161-2166 (prohibits the communication of information deemed to be "Restricted Data" by the Energy Research and Development Administration; 42 U.S.C. §§ 2274-2277 (prohibits the acquisition of documents incorporating "Restricted Data"); 50 U.S.C. § 421(a) & (b) (prohibits the intentional disclosure of the identity of a covert agent); 50 U.S.C. § 783(b) (prohibits the communication of classified material to an agent of any foreign government); 50 U.S.C. App. § 781 (prohibits making a graphic representation of military equipment). The unauthorized disclosure of nondefense information may also be prohibited. See, e.g., 18 U.S.C. § 952 (prohibits disclosure of any matter transmitted in the diplomatic code of a foreign country).

282. See United States v. Hung, 629 F.2d 908 (4th Cir.), *cert. denied*, 454 U.S. 1144 (1980); United States v. Kampiles, 609 F.2d 1233 (7th Cir.), *cert. denied*, 446 U.S. 954 (1979); United States v. Boyce, 594 F.2d 1246 (9th Cir.), *cert. denied*, 444 U.S. 855 (1979).

283. See P. SCHRAG, TEST OF LOYALTY: DANIEL ELLSBERG AND THE RITUALS OF SECRET GOVERNMENT (1974); S. UNGAR, THE PAPERS & THE PAPERS (1972); Abrams et al., *The First Amendment and National Security*, 43 U. MIAMI L. REV. 61 (1988); Edgar & Schmidt, *The Espionage Statutes and Publication of Defense Information*, 73 COLUM. L. REV. 929 (1973); Koffler & Gershman, *The New Seditious Libel*, 69 CORNELL L. REV. 816, 830-40 (1984) (interpreting the Espionage Act as a contemporary doctrine of seditious libel); Lewis, *National Security: Muting the 'Vital Criticism,'* 34 UCLA L. REV. 1687 (1987); Nimmer, *supra* note 233; Ballou & McSlarrow, *Plugging the Leak: The Case for a Legislative Resolution of the Conflict Between the Demands of Secrecy and the Need for an Open Government*, 71 VA. L. REV. 801 (1985); Topol, *United States v. Morison: A Threat to the First Amendment Right to Publish National Security Information*, 43 S.C. L. REV. 591 (1992).

284. 403 U.S. 713 (1971).

285. 844 F.2d 1057 (4th Cir.), *cert. denied*, 488 U.S. 908 (1988).

§ 13-3(c)(9)(A). The Pentagon Papers Case.

In 1970, two employees of the Rand Corporation, Daniel Ellsberg and Anthony Russo, delivered portions of a 47-volume "top secret" Department of Defense study to the *New York Times*, the *Washington Post* and Arkansas Senator William Fulbright. The document, officially titled the "History of U.S. Decision-Making Process on Vietnam Policy," is now known as the Pentagon Papers. The day following the publication of a portion of its contents, the United States sought to enjoin further publication by both newspapers. In the *Washington Post* case,[286] the district court denied the government's request for a preliminary injunction, in part on the ground that criminal sanctions are the government's only remedy for the publication of classified information.[287] On appeal from the district court's order, a panel of the D.C. Circuit reversed and directed the district court to hold a hearing. In so doing, the court of appeals emphasized the existence of exceptions to the rule against injunctions to prevent crimes in cases where an important public interest, pursuant to statutes such as the espionage laws, is threatened with irreparable harm.[288] In a subsequent appeal after remand, the court of appeals affirmed the district court's denial of the government's motion for an injunction.[289]

In the *New York Times* case,[290] the district court denied the government's request for an injunction, in part because it found no reasonable likelihood of the government successfully proving a violation of the relevant espionage statute.[291] The district court held that it was doubtful the government could prove, as an essential element of the offense, that the *Times* had a willful belief that the information to be published "could be used to the injury of the United States or to the advantage of any foreign nation."[292] On appeal, the Second Circuit ordered that the case be remanded for further *in camera* proceedings.[293] Two days later, the Supreme Court granted *certiorari*.

While a majority of the Supreme Court held in *New York Times Co. v. United States*[294] that it was improper to enjoin the publication of the Pentagon

---

286. See United States v. Washington Post Co., 446 F.2d 1322 (D.C. Cir.), *aff'd after remand*, 446 F.2d 1327 (D.C. Cir.), *aff'd*, 403 U.S. 713 (1971).
287. 446 F.2d at 1323.
288. *Id.* at 1324 ("Section 1(b) of the Internal Security Act of 1950 indicates that the criminal sanctions which the Act provides for dissemination of classified information are not to be construed as establishing military or civilian censorship. 64 Stat. 987; see 18 U.S.C. § 793 (1964).").
289. United States v. Washington Post Co., 446 F.2d 1327 (D.C. Cir. 1971).
290. See United States v. New York Times Co., 328 F. Supp. 324 (S.D.N.Y.), *remanded*, 444 F.2d 544 (2d Cir.), *rev'd*, 403 U.S. 713 (1971).
291. See 18 U.S.C. § 793.
292. 328 F. Supp. at 330.
293. 444 F.2d 544 (2d Cir.), *rev'd*, 403 U.S. 713 (1971) (en banc).
294. 403 U.S. 713 (1971) (consolidating for decision United States v. Washington Post Co., 446 F.2d 1327 (D.C. Cir. 1971)). See Oakes, *The Doctrine of Prior Restraint Since the Pentagon*

Papers,[295] six of the justices entertained the possibility of criminal prosecution of the newspapers,[296] even though the government had not argued for equitable relief under a criminal statute.[297] Indeed, no criminal prosecutions were instituted against either newspaper or against any other publisher of the Pentagon Papers.[298]

§ 13-3(c)(9)(B). Subsequent cases.

Although no criminal prosecution was ever undertaken against the newspapers for their receipt or publication of the Pentagon Papers, subsequent cases have

---

Papers, 15 U. MICH. J.L. REF. 497 (1982); Sims, *Triangulating the Boundaries of Pentagon Papers*, 2 WM. & MARY BILL OF RTS. J., 341 (1993); Redish, *The Proper Role of the Prior Restraint Doctrine in First Amendment Theory*, 70 VA. L. REV. 53 (1984).

295. See Chap. 13-3(a) *supra*.

296. See 403 U.S. at 727, 729 (Stewart, J., concurring) ("Undoubtedly Congress has the power to enact specific and appropriate criminal laws to protect government property and preserve government secrets. Congress has passed such laws, and several of them are of very colorable relevance to the apparent circumstances of these cases. And if a criminal prosecution is instituted, it will be the responsibility of the courts to decide the applicability of the criminal law under which the charge is brought."); *id.* at 730, 740 (White, J., concurring) ("[Congress] has not, however, authorized the injunctive remedy against threatened publication. It has apparently been satisfied to rely on criminal sanctions and their deterrent effect on the responsible as well as the irresponsible press. I am not, of course, saying that either of these newspapers has yet committed a crime or that either would commit a crime if it published all the material now in its possession. That matter must await resolution in the context of a criminal proceeding if one is instituted by the United States."); *id.* at 740, 744 (Marshall, J., concurring) ("Of course, at this stage this Court could not and cannot determine whether there has been a violation of a particular statute or decide the constitutionality of any statute."); *id.* at 747, 751 (Burger, C.J., dissenting) ("To me it is hardly believable that a newspaper long regarded as a great institution in American life would fail to perform one of the basic and simple duties of every citizen with respect to the discovery or possession of stolen property or secret government documents. That duty, I had thought—perhaps naively—was to report forthwith, to responsible public officers. This duty rests on taxi drivers, Justices, and the *New York Times*."); *id.* at 752, 754 (Harlan, J., dissenting) (Justice Blackmun joined in this dissent). See generally Edgar & Schmidt, *Curtiss-Wright Comes Home: Executive Power and National Security Secrecy*, 21 HARV. C.R.-C.L.L. REV. 349, 361 (1986) (majority of the Court had "volunteered readings of the espionage statutes in relation to hypothetical criminal proceedings against the publishers, reporters and information sources involved, even though such questions had not been briefed, were dreadfully difficult, and were quite unnecessary to a ruling about the injunction").

297. See 403 U.S. at 721 n.2 (Douglas, J., concurring) ("These documents contain data concerning the communications system of the United States, the publication of which is made a crime. But the criminal sanction is not urged by the United States as the basis of equity power."); *id.* at 744 (Marshall, J., concurring) ("The Solicitor General does not even mention in his brief whether the Government considers that there is probable cause to believe a crime has been committed or whether there is a conspiracy to commit future crimes.").

298. See generally D. RUDENSTINE, THE DAY THE PRESSES STOPPED: A HISTORY OF THE PENTAGON PAPERS CASE (1996); Glendon, *The Pentagon Papers — Victory for a Free Press*, 19 CARDOZO L. REV. 1295 (1998).

been brought against the sources of leaked national defense materials. Daniel Ellsberg and Anthony Russo, who provided the Pentagon Papers to the press, were prosecuted under the Espionage Act.[299] The case was dismissed, however, due to governmental misconduct.[300]

In *United States v. Morison*,[301] an employee of the Naval Intelligence Support Center provided classified information regarding explosions at Soviet military bases and reconnaissance satellite photographs to the editor-in-chief of *Jane's Defence Weekly*, a publication specializing in military information. The defendant allegedly provided the information in an attempt to curry favor with the editor, in the hopes of securing full-time employment with *Jane's*.[302]

In his defense, Morison argued that the espionage statutes apply only to "classic spying and espionage activity," not leaks to the press.[303] Although the court found that 18 U.S.C. § 794 was intended to combat acts of "classic spying," the provisions the defendant had been convicted of violating, sections 793(d) and (e) of title 18, were not so limited and made actionable the delivery of national defense information "to a person not entitled to receive it," such as the editor of a newspaper: "The language of the two statutes includes no limitation to spies or to 'an agent of a foreign government,' either as to the transmitter or the transmittee of the information, and they declare no exemption in favor of one who leaks to the press. It covers 'anyone.'"[304] Moreover, the court asserted that it "is not necessary to read into sections 793(d) and (e) an exception for national defense secret materials given the press, in order to sustain the constitutionality of such statutes."[305]

The defendant also unsuccessfully argued that the statutes are unconstitutionally vague[306] and overbroad.[307] In this regard, the court addressed several issues that had been raised by the defendant and by commentators regarding basic elements of the espionage statutes at issue and their applicability to leaks of classified information to the press. First, the court approved the definition of

---

299. See United States v. Russo, No. 9373-(WMB)-(1) (filed Dec. 29, 1971), *dismissed* (C.D. Cal. May 11, 1973).

300. Nimmer, *supra* note 233, at 311; SCHRAG, *supra* note 283, at 329-51.

301. 844 F.2d 1057 (4th Cir.), *cert. denied*, 488 U.S. 908 (1988).

302. *Id.* at 1060-61.

303. *Id.* at 1063.

304. *Id.* See Rabban, *The Emergence of Modern First Amendment Doctrine*, 50 U. CHI. L. REV. 1205, 1218 (1983).

305. 844 F.2d at 1070.

306. The vagueness argument was premised on the statutory phrases "relating to the national defense," "willfully" and "entitled to receive." *Id.* at 1073, 1075-76.

307. The court held that any concern that the term "national defense" is overbroad was negated by the district court's jury instruction that confined it to matters "which 'directly or may reasonably be connected with the defense of the United States,' the disclosure of which 'would be potentially damaging to the United States or might be useful to an enemy of the United States' and which had been 'closely held' by the government and was 'not available to the general public.'" *Id.* at 1076.

"national defense" formulated by the trial court,[308] and deemed the term not to be unconstitutionally vague in light of the requirement that the prohibited activity be proven to have been willful.[309]

Second, the court addressed the espionage statute's scienter requirement. Section 793(e) requires that the communication or retention of national defense information be willful. This scienter requirement had been previously addressed by the Supreme Court in *Hartzel v. United States*,[310] where it reversed the conviction, under the Espionage Act, of the author of three pamphlets during World War II.[311] A majority of the Court interpreted the statutory use of the word "willfully" as requiring proof of a specific intent to cause insubordination or disloyalty in the armed forces or to obstruct the recruiting and enlistment service.[312] In *Hartzel*, the court held that the defendant's purpose was to propagate his ideas, not to influence military personnel or individuals of draft age.[313] Although the court in *Morison* distinguished *Hartzel* as a "pure speech" case, rather than one "in the shadow of the First Amendment" as it characterized the *Morison* case, the Fourth Circuit found that the district court had properly followed the dictates of *Hartzel* by construing the statutory term "willfully" to require "that the prohibited act be done deliberately and with a specific purpose to do that which was proscribed."[314]

Lastly, the court in *Morison* considered section 793(e)'s requirement that the national defense information be communicated "to any person not entitled to receive it" or retained by one who fails to deliver it to a United States officer or employee "entitled to receive it." Morison argued that the phrase "entitled to receive" was unconstitutionally vague. The court of appeals, however, held that the statute is clarified by the government's classification system and that the phrase "entitled to receive" was well understood by the defendant, who had agreed in writing to abide by it.[315]

---

308. See *id.* at 1071 ("[T]he term national defense, includes all matters that directly or may reasonably be connected with the defense of the United States against any of its enemies.").

309. *Id.* at 1071-72. The combination of the national defense definition and the willfulness requirement had been held to defeat a claim that the statute was unconstitutionally vague in *United States v. Truong Dinh Hung*, 629 F.2d 908, 919 (4th Cir. 1981), *cert. denied*, 454 U.S. 1144 (1982).

310. 322 U.S. 680 (1944).

311. In the pamphlets, the defendant had attacked the President and America's wartime allies and urged a German victory. *Id.* at 683.

312. *Id.* at 686 ("That word, when viewed in the context of a highly penal statute restricting freedom of expression, must be taken to mean deliberately and with a specific purpose to do the acts proscribed by Congress.").

313. *Id.* at 688.

314. 844 F.2d at 1073.

315. *Id.* at 1074-75. Accord United States v. Truong Dinh Hung, 629 F.2d 908, 919 n.10 (4th Cir. 1981), *cert. denied*, 454 U.S. 1144 (1982); United States v. Girard, 601 F.2d 69 (2d Cir.), *cert. denied*, 444 U.S. 871 (1979); McGehee v. Casey, 718 F.2d 1137, 1143-44 (D.C. Cir. 1983).

Jane's apparently was not implicated in any violation of the espionage statutes[316] in part because Morison had cropped the words "Top Secret" and "Warning Notice: Intelligence Sources or Methods Involved" from the borders of the photographs before submitting them to the publication. Morison had previously submitted material to *Jane's* with the permission of the Navy, subject to his agreement that he would not supply classified information, so it was apparently not unusual for *Jane's* to receive similar information from him. *Jane's* also cooperated with the investigation and returned the original photographs to the Navy, which then discovered Morison's fingerprints on one of the photographs. The court did not, therefore, view the case as involving issues of press freedom or First Amendment rights.[317]

In a concurring opinion, Judge Wilkinson directly addressed the concerns raised by a number of news media organizations as *amici curiae*. "I do not think the First Amendment interests here are insignificant. Criminal restraints on the disclosure of information threaten the ability of the press to scrutinize and report on government activity. There exists the tendency, even in a constitutional democracy, for government to withhold reports of disquieting developments and to manage news in a fashion most favorable to itself."[318] Although he refused to view the words "national security" as determinative in the balance to be struck between the need for security and the free flow of information,[319] Judge Wilkinson also declined to engage in "aggressive balancing" pursuant to which the governmental interest served by restraints on the press is weighed against the interest in unhindered newsgathering.[320]

In Judge Wilkinson's view, in cases involving national security, the judiciary is required to grant deference to the political branches and sustain restrictions

---

316. In a concurring opinion, Judge Wilkinson emphasized that the prosecution in *Morison* was "not an attempt to apply the espionage statute to the press for either the receipt or publication of classified materials," 844 F.2d at 1085, and opined that press organizations were not "and probably could not be, prosecuted under the espionage statute." United States v. Morison, 844 F.2d at 1081 (4th Cir. 1988) (Wilkinson, J., concurring).

317. See *id.* at 1067 ("Freedom of the press issues arise only when the enforcement of governmental secrecy impacts the press itself.") (citing Henkin, *The Right to Know and the Duty to Withhold: The Case of the Pentagon Papers*, 120 U. PA. L. REV. 271, 277 (1971)). Both concurring opinions, however, emphasized the seriousness of the First Amendment issues raised by Morison. See 844 F.2d at 1081 (Wilkinson, J., concurring); *id.* at 1085 (Phillips, J., concurring).

318. 844 F.2d at 1081 (Wilkinson, J., concurring).

319. *Id.* at 1081 ("The First Amendment interest in informed popular debate does not simply vanish at the invocation of the words 'national security.' National security is public security, not government security from informed criticism.").

320. Judge Wilkinson asserted that the courts had only adopted such an "aggressive" balancing approach in cases involving access to judicial proceedings, see Richmond Newspapers, Inc v. Virginia, 448 U.S. 555 (1980), the search of newspaper offices, Zurcher v. Stanford Daily, 436 U.S. 547 (1978), and disclosure of press sources to grand juries, see Branzburg v. Hayes, 408 U.S. 665 (1971). *Morison*, 844 F.2d at 1081 (Wilkinson, J., concurring).

that would be impermissible in other contexts because (1) courts lack the expertise needed to evaluate national security concerns;[321] (2) the executive and legislative branches have been constitutionally empowered to conduct foreign affairs; and (3) serious repercussions could result from the actions of even a single person.[322] Although Judge Wilkinson expressed concern that application of the espionage statutes to those who leak information to the press could result in shielding corruption, scandal and incompetence in the defense establishment from scrutiny, he suggested that larger forces would ultimately protect the free flow of information. "Even if juries could ever be found that would convict those who truly expose governmental waste and misconduct, the political firestorm that would follow prosecution of one who exposed an administration's own ineptitude would make such prosecutions a rare and unrealistic prospect."[323]

§ 13-4. Sources and Interview Subjects.

Perhaps the most common "sources" of news are the people who participate in making it. Indeed, in the journalistic and popular vernacular, a "source" is a person who provides information for ultimate dissemination by the press to the public. The journalist/source relationship, though typically no more complicated than a routine telephone interview, can become an intricate and complicated affair, one that can and has yielded legal consequences. Other issues surrounding the interaction between reporters and their sources are discussed elsewhere in this volume,[324] including the reporters' privilege. Here, we address potential liability arising from those methods of newsgathering directed uniquely at securing information from sources.

---

321. See 844 F.2d at 1082-83 (Wilkinson, J., concurring) ("Evaluation of the government's interest ... would require the judiciary to draw conclusions about the operation of the most sophisticated electronic systems and the potential effects of their disclosure. . . . Judges can understand the operation of a subpoena more readily than that of a satellite.").

322. See *id.* at 1083:

> [T]he judicial role must be a deferential one because the alternative would be grave. To reverse Morison's conviction on the general ground that it chills press access would be tantamount to a judicial declaration that the government may never use criminal penalties to secure the confidentiality of intelligence information. Rather than enhancing the operation of democracy, as Morison suggests, this course would install every government worker with access to classified information as a veritable satrap. Vital decisions and expensive programs set into motion by elected representatives would be subject to summary derailment at the pleasure of one disgruntled employee.

323. *Id.* at 1084 (Wilkinson, J., concurring).
324. See Chaps. 14-16 *infra*.

§ 13-4(a). Breach of Contract and Promissory Estoppel.

Journalists and their sources interact in a seemingly endless variety of ways, spawning relationships as distinct from each other as are the articles, broadcasts, and media through which the fruits of those relationships are ultimately disseminated. Often times, a journalist's relationship with a source will appear to assume at least some of the trappings of a business arrangement pursuant to which two parties, each wanting something that the other has, will discuss and ultimately arrive at the terms of a deal.

The journalist, of course, wants information. The agenda of the source, on the other hand, can span a broad spectrum. Sources have been known to demand payment in exchange for their information, and some purveyors of news and information regularly enter into such bargains.[325] Many sources, especially those with whom journalists have regular contact, also want the information they possess disseminated publicly, but in a manner acceptable to them. Accordingly, these sources may demand anonymity, may insist that certain of the information they provide remain unpublished, or may impose conditions on the timing of the dissemination itself. These sophisticated, arguably "professional" sources of news often develop with their journalistic counterparts a complex set of ground rules — implicit and explicit — that set the terms and conditions of their dealings.[326]

---

325. The O.J. Simpson murder trial, for example, was a financial bonanza for many of its potential witnesses. California legislators, in response to perceived credibility problems, passed a series of laws to prevent potential witnesses from being paid for interviews. Enforcement of these statutes has been permanently enjoined. See California First Amendment Coalition v. Lungren, 1995 U.S. Dist. LEXIS 11655 (N.D. Cal. Aug. 9, 1995). See Chap. 13-4(a)(4) *infra*.

326. It has been suggested, for example, that the "confidential interactions between journalist and public official have become so institutionalized that they now manifest the attributes of a business transaction." Langley & Levine, *Branzburg Revisited: Confidential Sources and First Amendment Values*, 57 GEO. WASH. L. REV. 13, 30 (1988). In that regard, there is evidence that

> the confidential transfer of information from governmental official to journalist is increasingly the product of sophisticated negotiations. Governmental officials seek to protect their identities by receiving extremely vague attribution for the information they are otherwise unwilling to provide, while journalists prefer to reveal their sources of information as precisely as possible. As a result, extensive bargaining typically occurs as to the measure of anonymity governing the exchange, and elaborate ground rules are negotiated by the parties. Journalists and public officials alike have become conversant in a transactional vocabulary, featuring precisely defined terms such as "background," "off-the-record," and "not-for-attribution," each of which signifies a decidedly different undertaking by the journalist as to the scope of confidentiality promised to the source.

Id. at 30-31 (citations omitted). See J. WOODRUFF, "THIS IS JUDY WOODRUFF AT THE WHITE HOUSE" 105 (1982); W. GREIDER, THE EDUCATION OF DAVID STOCKMAN AND OTHER AMERICANS xvii (1982); E. ABEL, LEAKING: WHO DOES IT? WHO BENEFITS? AT WHAT COSTS? 39 (1987); S HESS, THE WASHINGTON REPORTERS 19 (1981); M.L. STEIN, SHAPING THE NEWS: HOW THE MEDIA FUNCTION IN TODAY'S WORLD 171-72 (1974); D. BRODER, BEHIND THE FRONT PAGE 347 (1987).

Another category of source, however, is both unsophisticated and uncertain about the entire enterprise. Such a source often has no desire or incentive to provide information to a journalist and would just as soon be left alone. In such circumstances, the journalist may find that proposing conditions upon her own newsgathering and publication activities is the best available method of securing any information at all. Thus, a journalist may propose a variety of incentives to the reluctant source, from a promise of confidentiality to a representation that certain details of the source's "story" will not be revealed.

Throughout most of the history of American law, the relationship between journalist and source was a matter of little interest. As the following chapters demonstrate, the law was occasionally called upon to protect a journalist from a third party's efforts to compel the disclosure of information obtained in confidence.[327] Before 1987, however, only a handful of courts had been asked to address the law governing the direct relationship between reporter and source and the Supreme Court had only touched on it tangentially in the largely *sui generis* context of national security. In that year, however, a state trial court in Minnesota issued the first of what has become a handful of judicial decisions, including a pronouncement by the United States Supreme Court in *Cohen v. Cowles Media Co.*[328] Following the multiple decisions in *Cohen*, courts across the nation have been asked to wrestle with the constitutional and common law implications of a journalist's breach of a promise allegedly made to a source in the course of gathering the news.

§ 13-4(a)(1). Judicial Pronouncements Prior to *Cohen v. Cowles Media*.

§ 13-4(a)(1)(A). The Defamation and Privacy Context.

Early judicial consideration of the legal consequences of promises made in the newsgathering process typically arose in the context of cases alleging chiefly claims for defamation or invasion of privacy. In *Cullen v. Grove Press, Inc.*,[329] for example, the court considered a claim for invasion of privacy arising from a widely advertised and disseminated documentary film entitled "Titicut Follies," which depicted — among other things — scenes of naked inmates being subjected to "skin searches" by corrections officers employed at the Massachusetts Correctional Institution in South Bridgewater, Massachusetts ("Bridgewater"). The filmmaker had secured access to the Bridgewater facility, according to the plaintiff corrections officers, after having "assured plaintiffs that the filming of 'skin searches' of inmates would reveal only the inmates' upper extremities and that the film would be used and displayed only for the purpose of education

---

327. See Chaps. 14-16 *infra*.
328. 501 U.S. 663 (1991).
329. 276 F. Supp. 727 (S.D.N.Y. 1967).

in connection with the care of the criminally insane."[330] The case came before the court in the context of plaintiffs' request for a preliminary injunction.

The court rejected the claim, which was pled as a cause of action for invasion of privacy arising under New York statutory law,[331] on the ground that plaintiffs had "offered no proof that the filmed events and activities are false or distorted."[332] As a result, even if plaintiffs' allegations regarding the filmmaker's "assurances" were true, the film would nevertheless fall "within the protection of the First Amendment."[333] The court, however, added that its decision did not "constitute an adjudication of rights of non-parties, such as individual inmates claiming violation of their own personal rights or state officials suing for breach of contract, if any, with respect to conditions for exhibition of the film."[334]

That litigation — instituted by the Commonwealth of Massachusetts in the name of the inmates — resulted in an eighteen-day trial and a decision by a trial judge and the Massachusetts Supreme Judicial Court enjoining broad commercial distribution of the film.[335] Although the appellate court chastised state officials for not having reduced their agreement with the filmmaker "to writing," which "risked the misunderstandings possible in oral discussions," it found that he had "represented in writing that only pictures of inmates 'legally competent to sign releases' would be used and that the 'question of competency would . . . be determined by the Superintendent and his staff.'"[336] In addition, the court credited testimony that "some of the sixty-two inmates identified as shown in the film were incompetent to understand a release and, on the basis of a stipulation, that releases were obtained only from eleven or twelve of the numerous inmates depicted."[337] Beyond the filmmaker's "failure . . . to comply with the contractual condition," the court concluded that the film itself constituted "a collective, indecent intrusion into the most private aspects of the lives of these unfortunate persons."[338] Taken together, the court concluded, these considerations "amply justify granting injunctive relief."[339]

---

330. *Id.* at 729.
331. See N.Y. CIV. RIGHTS LAW § 51.
332. 276 F. Supp. at 730 (citing Time, Inc. v. Hill, 385 U.S. 374 (1967)).
333. 276 F. Supp. at 731.
334. *Id.*
335. See Massachusetts v. Wiseman, 249 N.E.2d 610 (Mass. 1969).
336. *Id.* at 615.
337. *Id.*
338. *Id.*
339. *Id.* at 616. The court distinguished *Cullen v. Grove Press, Inc.*, 276 F. Supp. 727 (S.D.N.Y. 1967), on the grounds that (1) the plaintiffs there "did not represent the inmates as the Commonwealth (as *parens patriae*) does," and (2) the *Cullen* court's "interpretation" of *Time, Inc. v. Hill*, 385 U.S. 374 (1967), was too "broad." 249 N.E.2d at 616.

In *Bindrim v. Mitchell*,[340] a California Court of Appeal affirmed a trial court's decision striking a $12,000 damage award made by a jury on a breach of contract contention against an author. The plaintiff, a clinical psychologist, conducted a form of group therapy known as the "Nude Marathon." He required all participants in such sessions to execute a written agreement specifying that they "'will not take photographs, write articles, or in any manner disclose who has attended the workshop or what has transpired.'"[341] The defendant, a well known author, signed the contract and "reassured plaintiff . . . she would not write about the session."[342] Shortly thereafter, defendant signed a book contract and published a novel about, among other things, a "Nude Marathon."

A jury found in the plaintiff's favor with respect to the contract cause of action and defamation claim. Although the court of appeal affirmed the judgment with respect to the defamation claim — based on its conclusion that the author deliberately falsified her accounts of what she had witnessed at the actual sessions — it affirmed the trial court's decision striking the jury's damage award on the contract claim. In that regard, it held that there is "no authority that a professional person can, by contract or otherwise, prevent one of his patients from reporting the treatment that patient received."[343] Accordingly, defendant "was free to report what went on. The limits to her right to report were those involved in the libel counts. Plaintiff has no separate cause of action for the mere reporting."[344]

Shortly before the first published opinion in *Cohen*, another federal court considered a claim — pled chiefly as a cause of action for invasion of privacy — arising from conditions placed on the news media's access to a correctional facility. In *Huskey v. National Broadcasting Co.*,[345] a prisoner incarcerated at the Marion, Illinois United States Penitentiary ("Marion") alleged both that the defendant television network filmed him "without his consent — a common-law invasion of privacy" and "breached its contract" with Marion's warden "to abide by federal regulations prohibiting nonconsensual photography of inmates."[346]

---

340. 155 Cal. Rptr. 29 (Ct. App. 1979).
341. *Id.* at 33.
342. *Id.*
343. *Id.* at 41.
344. *Id.*
345. 632 F. Supp. 1282 (N.D. Ill. 1986).
346. *Id.* at 1285. Plaintiff alleged that he was a "third-party beneficiary" of the contract, which he claimed arose by virtue of 28 C.F.R. § 540.62(b):

> An inmate has the right not to be photographed and not to have his or her voice recorded by the media. A visiting representative of the media is required to obtain written permission from an inmate before photographing or recording the voice of an inmate participating in authorized programs and activities.

See 632 F. Supp. at 1292.

The district court denied defendant's motion to dismiss with respect to both claims. First, the court rejected the network's claim that the regulations did not invest plaintiff with a private right of action to enforce its terms. "Whether or not Huskey could sue NBC directly under the regulations," the court held, "NBC allegedly contracted to abide by them."[347] Second, the court concluded that, because "NBC makes no claim it got Huskey's written permission or any permission at all, . . . it clearly did not live up to its agreement."[348] Third, the court rejected the contention that allowing plaintiff to proceed on both his privacy and contract claims was "duplicative;" rather, it held that, while plaintiff "might lose on the tort claim," he might nevertheless "prevail on the contractual claim, which is not subject to tort defenses."[349] Finally, the court opined that plaintiff could be awarded damages "for mental suffering caused by the wanton or reckless breach of a contract to render a performance of such character that the promisor had reason to know when the contract was made that a breach would cause such suffering."[350]

§ 13-4(a)(1)(B). The National Security Context.

Prior to *Cohen v. Cowles Media Co.*,[351] the Supreme Court considered agreements made in the context of newsgathering only once, in *Snepp v. United States*.[352] That case, as well as an analogous action in which the Court denied

---

347. *Id.* at 1292 n.14.
348. *Id.* at 1292.
349. *Id.* In that regard, the court hypothesized the case of "an obvious public figure" who "would not be able to sue for invasion of privacy where the private facts revealed were in the legitimate sphere of public curiosity." *Id.* at 1292 n.15. That plaintiff, the court indicated, "would have a valid breach of contract claim" if he could prove that "a newspaper had contracted" with him "not to print the information." *Id.*
350. *Id.* at 1293. In addition to the judicial decisions discussed in this section, at least two other cases — which did not result in published opinions — addressed analogous claims in the years preceding *Cohen v. Cowles Media Co.*, 501 U.S. 663 (1991). In *Fries v. National Broadcasting Co.*, a California trial court ruled that a complaint, filed by a source alleging that a journalist breached an oral promise not to reveal the source's identity, stated a cause of action for breach of contract. The source, a police officer, had made statements to the journalist concerning alleged improper behavior by an assistant chief of police. The case eventually settled following a hung jury and the commencement of a second trial. See Langley & Levine, *Broken Promises*, COLUM. JOURNALISM REV., July/Aug. 1988, at 24.

In *MacDonald v. McGinniss*, another California jury was unable to reach a verdict in a civil action instituted by Jeffrey MacDonald, a convicted murderer, against Joe McGinniss, the author of *Fatal Vision*, a book about the crime. The case, in which MacDonald claimed that the author had both defrauded him and breached a written contract pursuant to which McGinniss was afforded exclusive access to his subject, was thereafter settled. The trial is chronicled in J. MALCOLM, THE JOURNALIST AND THE MURDERER (1990).
351. 501 U.S. 663 (1991).
352. 444 U.S. 507 (1980).

certiorari,³⁵³ assessed the efficacy of a contract entered into by employees of the Central Intelligence Agency ("CIA"), pursuant to which they promised both not to reveal classified information to the public and "to submit all writings about the agency," even those created after the cessation of employment, "for prepublication review" by the CIA.³⁵⁴

In *United States v. Marchetti*,³⁵⁵ Marchetti, a former CIA employee, claimed that his "First Amendment rights foreclose any prior restraint upon him in carrying out his purpose to write and publish what he pleases about the Agency and its operations."³⁵⁶ The district court, relying on "a secrecy agreement signed by Marchetti when he became an employee of the Agency and on a secrecy oath signed by Marchetti when he resigned from the Agency," ordered him to "submit to the Agency thirty days in advance of the release to any person or corporation, any writing, fictional or non-fictional, relating to the Agency or to intelligence."³⁵⁷ In addition, the district court entered an injunction prohibiting Marchetti from publishing "any writing relating to the Agency or to intelligence without prior authorization from the Director of Central Intelligence."³⁵⁸

The court of appeals concluded that the contract was "constitutional and otherwise reasonable and lawful."³⁵⁹ It added, however, that the "First Amendment limits the extent to which the United States, contractually or otherwise, may impose secrecy requirements upon its employees and enforce them through a system of prior censorship."³⁶⁰ According to the court, any such contractual agreement in restraint of publication may not extend to information "unclassified or officially disclosed;" only "secret information touching upon the national defense and the conduct of foreign affairs, acquired by Marchetti while in a position of trust and confidence" could properly be the subject of a contractual obligation to refrain from publication.³⁶¹ The court, therefore, indicated that it

---

353. See United States v. Marchetti, 466 F.2d 1309 (4th Cir), *cert. denied*, 409 U.S. 1063 (1972).
354. Snepp v. United States, 444 U.S. 507, 507 (1980).
355. 466 F.2d 1309 (4th Cir.), *cert. denied*, 409 U.S. 1063 (1972).
356. *Id.* at 1311.
357. *Id.*
358. *Id.*
359. *Id.*
360. *Id.* at 1313.
361. *Id.* In affirming the portion of the agreement requiring Marchetti to submit materials he wished to publish for prior review by the Agency, the court of appeals relied on *Maas v. United States*, 371 F.2d 348 (D.C. Cir. 1966). In *Maas*, the Justice Department successfully enjoined publication of a book version of the so-called "Valachi papers," written by Valachi while he was in prison and edited for publication by Maas. Valachi had signed a "Memorandum of Understanding," based on regulations promulgated pursuant to 18 U.S.C. §§ 4001, 4002, which required the prior approval of any publication by a federal prisoner "if it deals with the life history or the criminal career of the writer." But see Simon & Schuster, Inc. v. New York State Crime Victims Bd., 502

"would decline enforcement of the secrecy oath . . . to the extent that it purports to prevent disclosure of unclassified information, for, to that extent, the oath would be in contravention" of the First Amendment.[362]

In *Snepp*, the Supreme Court affirmed a judgment enforcing the secrecy agreement that Snepp had signed with the Agency, and reversed a court of appeals decision prohibiting the CIA from imposing a constructive trust on all profits derived by Snepp for publications that had not been submitted for prior approval.[363] In a *per curiam* opinion decided solely on cross-petitions for *certiorari*, the Court rejected Snepp's claim that the "agreement is unenforceable as a prior restraint on protected speech."[364] According to the Court, "even in the absence of an express agreement, . . . the CIA could have acted to protect substantial government interests in imposing reasonable restrictions on employee activities that in other contexts might be protected by the First Amendment," because of the government's "compelling interest in protecting both the secrecy of information important to our national security and the appearance of confidentiality so essential to the effective operation of our foreign intelligence service."[365]

§ 13-4(a)(2). *Cohen v. Cowles Media Co.*

The *Cohen* litigation arose in the fall of 1983 when Dan Cohen, the director of public relations for an advertising agency and an activist in the Independent Republican Party, was asked by other party loyalists to contact various journalists with newly discovered information about the Democratic-Farmer-Labor Party's candidate for lieutenant governor in the approaching election.[366] Cohen thereafter contacted four reporters representing the two daily newspapers in the

---

U.S. 105 (1991) (invalidating statute requiring certain convicted persons to forfeit proceeds from sale of publications about their crimes).

In *Marchetti*, the court also recognized some constitutional limitations on the enforcement of the Agency's contractual right to undertake prepublication review. Specifically, the court held that the Agency must complete any such review "promptly" and Marchetti "would be entitled to judicial review of any action by the CIA disapproving publication." 466 F.2d at 1317.

362. 466 F.2d at 1317.
363. Snepp v. United States, 444 U.S. 507 (1980).
364. *Id.* at 509 n.3.
365. *Id.* In dissent, Justice Stevens — joined by Justices Brennan and Marshall — suggested that it was "noteworthy that the Court does not disagree with the Fourth Circuit's view in *Marchetti* . . . that a CIA employee has a First Amendment right to publish unclassified information." *Id.* at 521 n.11 (Stevens, J., dissenting). Moreover, Justice Stevens indicated that any effort by the CIA to secure the contractual right to restrain the publication of such information "would have great difficulty" surviving constitutional scrutiny. *Id.* at 522.
366. The information consisted of court documents indicating that the candidate had, years earlier, been arrested for unlawful assembly and convicted of petty theft. The unlawful assembly charge was subsequently dropped and the conviction was vacated. See Cohen v. Cowles Media Co., 445 N.W.2d 248, 252 (Minn. App. 1989) (subsequent history omitted).

Minneapolis-St. Paul area, a television station, and the Associated Press. He told them all, in substance, that he had:

> some documents which may or may not relate to a candidate in the upcoming election, and if you will give me a promise of confidentiality, that is that I will be treated as an anonymous source, that my name will not appear in any material in connection with this, and that you will also agree that you're not going to pursue with me a question of who my source is, then I will furnish you with the documents.[367]

All four reporters agreed to Cohen's conditions and were therefore provided by him with the documents. At the Minneapolis *Star Tribune*, a different reporter was assigned to verify the authenticity of the documents and independently confirmed through court records that they had been obtained by a political ally of Cohen and then provided to him. Thereafter, the newspaper unsuccessfully asked Cohen to release it from its promise of confidentiality. The *Star Tribune* decided to publish Cohen's name in a front-page article that reported both the contents of the documents and the fact that he, a supporter of the opposing candidate, had provided them to the press. The article was published over the objection of the reporter who had made the promise, which was not mentioned by the newspaper.

The other newspaper independently came to the same conclusion and published an article revealing Cohen's name and his role in providing the documents as well. Neither newspaper had ever before abrogated a promise of confidentiality to a news source.[368] In contrast, the Associated Press honored its promise of confidentiality to Cohen by simply stating that the documents "were slipped to reporters." The television station also honored its promise, by deciding not to broadcast the story at all.

---

367. *Id.*

368. The Minnesota Supreme Court described the newspapers' decisionmaking process as follows:

> The decision to identify Cohen in the stories was the subject of vigorous debate within the editorial staffs of the two newspapers. Some staff members argued that the reporter's promise of confidentiality should be honored at all costs. Some contended that the ... incidents were not newsworthy and did not warrant publishing, and, in any case, if the story was published, it would be enough to identify the source as a source close to the Whitney campaign. Other editors argued that not only was the ... story newsworthy but so was the identification of Cohen as the source; that to attribute the story to a veiled source would be misleading and cast suspicion on others; and that the ... story was already spreading throughout the news media community and was discoverable from other sources not bound by confidentiality. ... [S]ome of its editors feared if the newspaper did not print the ... story, other news media would, leaving the Star Tribune vulnerable to a charge it was protecting the ticket it favored [editorially].

Cohen v. Cowles Media Co., 457 N.W.2d 199, 201 (Minn. 1990) (subsequent history omitted).

Following publication of the newspaper articles, Cohen was questioned by his employer and was either "fired or otherwise forced to resign as a result of the story."[369] Subsequently, he commenced a civil action against both newspapers, alleging breach of contract and misrepresentation.

§ 13-4(a)(2)(A). The Trial Court Proceedings.

Both newspapers initially moved for summary judgment, motions which were denied in all respects by the trial court.[370] With respect to the misrepresentation claim, the court held that "repudiation of a promise soon after it is made with no intervening change in the circumstances constitutes evidence of an intention not to perform," rendering the issue of the newspapers' intent one "properly reserved for the trier of fact."[371] The court also rejected the defendants' contention that "to require the newspaper to perform its agreement would somehow operate to censor the news in violation of the First Amendment[]."[372] According to the trial court, the First Amendment does not "operate to excuse news organizations from the consequences of a decision to publish when that decision involved the breach of a valid contract."[373]

The case was thereafter tried to a jury which, following a two-week trial, returned a verdict in Cohen's favor. The jury awarded Cohen $200,000 in compensatory and $500,000 in punitive damages. The trial court denied the newspapers' motion for judgment n.o.v. and for a new trial, rejecting their assertion that the First Amendment "shield[s] them from the consequences of breach of contract or violation of the general tort laws."[374] First, the court held that it was "not persuaded that the relationship between reporter and source is anything other than commercial."[375] Second, the court rejected the contention that permitting breach of contract claims in the newsgathering context would give potential plaintiffs an incentive to "make unfounded accusations" and would "play havoc with the newsgathering process;" in the court's view, "any restric-

---

369. 445 N.W.2d at 254.
370. Cohen v. Cowles Media Co., 14 MEDIA L. REP. (BNA) 1460 (Minn. Dist. 1987) (subsequent history omitted).
371. *Id.* at 1463.
372. *Id.* at 1464.
373. *Id.* The trial court rejected the newspapers' reliance on Supreme Court decisions that, it noted, "involve instances where information was obtained by lawful means." *Id.* (citing New York Times Co. v. Sullivan, 376 U.S. 254 (1964); Smith v. Daily Mail Publ'g Co., 435 U.S. 829 (1978); Cox Broadcasting Corp. v. Cohn, 420 U.S. 469 (1975)). Instead, the court relied on those cases suggesting that "'[t]he publisher of a newspaper had no special immunity from the application of general laws.'" 14 MEDIA L. REP. (BNA) at 1464 (quoting Branzburg v. Hayes, 408 U.S. 665, 683 (1972) and citing Dietemann v. Time, Inc., 449 F.2d 245, 250 (9th Cir. 1971); Galella v. Onassis, 487 F.2d 986, 995-96 (2d Cir. 1973)).
374. Cohen v. Cowles Media Co., 15 MEDIA L. REP. (BNA) 2288, 2290 (Minn. Dist. 1988).
375. *Id.* at 2290.

tions reporters may place upon themselves with regard to source anonymity are undertaken voluntarily and in exchange for the valuable consideration of 'getting the scoop.'"[376] Finally, the court held that "no First Amendment interest exists in protecting news media from 'calculated misdeeds,'" including "the knowing and willful breach of a legally sufficient contract."[377]

§ 13-4(a)(2)(B). The Minnesota Appellate Courts — Round 1.

The Minnesota Court of Appeals affirmed the trial court in part and reversed in part.[378] The court of appeals rejected the newspapers' contention that the First Amendment barred either of Cohen's claims. First, the court held that "there is no state action present in this case to trigger first amendment scrutiny" because the "neutral application of state laws is not state action."[379] Second, even assuming that state action was present, the court concluded that any "burden on first amendment rights is justified" in order to "achieve an overriding governmental interest" in "protecting the expectations of a person who freely enters into a contract in reliance on the court's power to remedy any damage he or she might suffer should the other party fail to perform."[380] Relying on state law and on the Supreme Court's decision in *Snepp v. United States*,[381] the court of appeals found "the protection of contractual rights to be a sufficient governmental interest to outweigh first amendment rights."[382] Third, the court held that the newspapers had "effectively waived any first amendment rights they may have had to publish Cohen's name" by entering into an agreement with him that they would not do so.[383]

---

376. *Id.*
377. *Id.* at 2291. Accordingly, as it had in the context of defendants' motion for summary judgment, the court concluded that the First Amendment "should not be construed to immunize news organizations from the application" of general laws for activity undertaken "'during the course of newsgathering.'" *Id.* (quoting Dietemann v. Time, Inc., 449 F.2d 245, 249 (9th Cir. 1971)).
378. Cohen v. Cowles Media Co., 445 N.W.2d 248 (Minn. App. 1989) (subsequent history omitted).
379. *Id.* at 254. The court of appeals distinguished *Shelley v. Kraemer*, 334 U.S. 1 (1948), on the ground that the trial court in *Cohen* had not engaged in "'active intervention' at the request of third parties," and *New York Times Co. v. Sullivan*, 376 U.S. 254 (1954), because while "[d]efamation law inherently limits the content of speech," the law of contracts does "not sanction the words or conduct themselves, but rather the failure to honor a promise." 445 N.W.2d at 255-56.
380. 445 N.W.2d at 256-57. As had the trial court, the court of appeals noted that "the first amendment does not invalidate the application of civil or criminal laws to members of the press despite the burden on press freedom which their application may impose." *Id.* at 256 (citing Branzburg v. Hayes, 408 U.S. 665 (1972); Galella v. Onassis, 487 F.2d 986 (2d Cir. 1973)).
381. 444 U.S. 507 (1980); see Chap. 13-4(a)(1)(B) *supra*.
382. 445 N.W.2d at 257 (citing Huskey v. National Broadcasting Co., 632 F. Supp. 1282 (N.D. Ill. 1986)).
383. 445 N.W.2d at 258.

The court of appeals did, however, reverse the trial court's judgment with respect to the misrepresentation claim and the resulting award of punitive damages. In so doing, the court held, as a matter of state law, that "[s]imply because a party in the future fails to perform does not mean that there was any misrepresentation at the time the contract was made."[384] The newspapers remained liable for the $200,000 in "nonpunitive damages," which "were awarded to compensate Cohen for the loss of his job."[385]

The Minnesota Supreme Court affirmed the court of appeals' dismissal of the misrepresentation claim, but reversed with respect to the cause of action for breach of contract.[386] The court held that the newspapers' promises to Cohen were "not enforceable, neither as a breach of contract claim nor, in this case, under promissory estoppel."[387] According to the court, Minnesota law "does not create a contract where the parties intended none."[388] Moreover, the court concluded that "in the special milieu of media newsgathering," a journalist and his source do not "ordinarily believe they are engaged in making a legally binding contract."[389] Not only are they "not thinking in terms of offers and acceptances in any commercial or business sense," but they "understand that the reporter's promise of anonymity is given as a moral commitment," one which "alone will not support a contract."[390] Thus, the court concluded, "contract law seems here an ill fit for a promise of news source confidentiality."[391]

In the wake of its decision that a "confidentiality promise is not a legally binding contract," the court undertook to determine whether the promise was nevertheless enforceable under the "doctrine of promissory estoppel," which holds that "a promise expected or reasonably expected to induce definite action by the promisee that does induce action is binding if injustice can be avoided only by enforcing the promise."[392] Although the court found that the first two requirements of the doctrine were satisfied in the case of a reporter's promise of confidentiality to a source, it determined that the "injustice" to Cohen in losing his job was outweighed by the newspapers' "contention that any state-imposed

---

384. *Id.* at 260.
385. *Id.* Judge Crippen dissented from that portion of the court of appeals' decision affirming the award for breach of contract. In his view, "what has happened here involves the exercise of the coercive power of the state to punish the choice of the private press to publish. Making the problem still more critical, this sanction occurs for printing a true story on the purely political behavior of a public figure." *Id.* at 262 (Crippen, J., dissenting in part).
386. Cohen v. Cowles Media Co., 457 N.W.2d 199 (Minn. 1990) (subsequent history omitted).
387. *Id.* at 200.
388. *Id.* at 203 (citing Line v. Ronkainen, 37 N.W.2d 237, 239 (Minn. 1949)).
389. 457 N.W.2d at 203.
390. *Id.* (citing Cruickshank v. Ellis, 226 N.W.2d 192 (Minn. 1929)).
391. 457 N.W.2d at 203.
392. *Id.* Cohen had not pled a promissory estoppel claim and the jury had not considered such a cause of action. *Id.* at 204 n.5.

sanction in this case violates their constitutional rights of a free press and free speech."[393]

In this regard, the court rejected the court of appeals' conclusion that there was no state action. Relying on *New York Times Co. v. Sullivan*, the court concluded that "a state may not apply a state rule of law to impose impermissible restrictions on the federal constitutional freedoms of speech and press."[394] Accordingly, the court determined that it had no choice but to consider the applicability of the Constitution.[395] Under the circumstances of the case before it, the court held that the "critical" factor was that the "promise of anonymity arises in the classic First Amendment context of the quintessential public debate in our democratic society, namely, a political source involved in a political campaign":

> The potentiality for civil damages for promises made in this context chills public debate, a debate which Cohen willingly entered albeit hoping to do so on his own terms. In this context, and considering the nature of the political story involved, it seems to us that the law best leaves the parties here to their trust in each other.[396]

Thus, the court concluded, "in this case enforcement of the promise of confidentiality under a promissory estoppel theory would violate defendants' First Amendment right."[397]

§ 13-4(a)(2)(C). The Supreme Court.

The Supreme Court granted *certiorari* to consider "whether the First Amendment prohibits a plaintiff from recovering damages, under state promissory estoppel law, for a newspaper's breach of a promise of confidentiality given to a plaintiff in exchange for information."[398] The Court, by a one-vote majority,

---

393. *Id.* at 204.
394. *Id.* at 204 n.6 (quoting New York Times Co. v. Sullivan, 376 U.S. 254, 265 (1964)); see 457 N.W.2d at 204 n.6 ("The test is not the form which the state action takes — such as in this case, breach of contract or promissory estoppel — but, 'whatever the form, whether such power has in fact been exercised.'").
395. 457 S.W.2d at 205.
396. *Id.*
397. *Id.* The court added that there "may be instances where a confidential source would be entitled to a remedy such as promissory estoppel, when the state's interest in enforcing the promise to the source outweighs First Amendment considerations, but this is not such a case." *Id.*
Justices Yetka and Kelly dissented. See *id.* at 205 (Yetka, J., dissenting) ("the news media should be compelled to keep their promises like anyone else"); *id.* at 207 (Kelley, J., dissenting) (criticizing "the perfidy of these defendants, the liability for which they now seek to escape by trying to crawl under the aegis of the First Amendment, which, in my opinion, has nothing to do with the case").
398. Cohen v. Cowles Media Co., 501 U.S. 663, 665 (1991). Before reaching the merits, the Court rejected the newspapers' contention that the Minnesota Supreme Court's decision "rests entirely on the interpretation of state law." *Id.* at 667. According to the Supreme Court, "that the

concluded that "it does not," and remanded the case for application of the promissory estoppel doctrine under state law.[399]

Initially, the Court held that a "private cause of action for promissory estoppel involves 'state action' within the meaning of the Fourteenth Amendment such that the protections of the First Amendment are triggered."[400] As in *New York Times Co. v. Sullivan*, "the application of state rules of law in state courts in a manner alleged to restrict First Amendment freedoms constitutes 'state action.'"[401] The "legal obligations" created by the state-law doctrine of promissory estoppel "would be enforced through the official power of the Minnesota courts," which is "enough to constitute 'state action.'"[402]

Next, Justice White, writing for the five-justice majority, rejected the newspapers' contention that the case was controlled by precedent establishing that, "if a newspaper lawfully obtains truthful information about a matter of public significance then state officials may not constitutionally punish publication of the information, absent a need to further a state interest of the highest order."[403] Rather, the Court looked to "the equally well-established line of decisions holding that generally applicable laws do not offend the First Amendment simply because their enforcement against the press has incidental effects on its ability to gather and report the news."[404] The cases cited by the newspapers were distinguished because they all required that, to receive constitutional protection, "the truthful information sought to be published must have been lawfully obtained."[405] Moreover, in cases like *Smith v. Daily Mail Publishing Co.*,[406] "the State itself defined the content of publications that would trigger liability," whereas the Minnesota law of promissory estoppel "simply requires those

---

Minnesota Supreme Court rested its holding on federal law could not be made more clear than by its conclusion that 'in this case enforcement of the promise of confidentiality under a promissory estoppel theory would violate defendants' First Amendment rights.'" *Id.* (quoting 457 S.W.2d at 205).

399. 501 U.S. at 665. See *id.* at 672 ("The Minnesota Supreme Court's incorrect conclusion that the First Amendment barred Cohen's claim may well have truncated its consideration of whether a promissory estoppel claim had otherwise been established under Minnesota law and whether Cohen's jury verdict could be upheld on a promissory estoppel basis.").

400. *Id.*

401. *Id.* (citing New York Times Co. v. Sullivan, 376 U.S. 254, 265 (1964); NAACP v. Claiborne Hardware Co., 458 U.S. 886, 916 n.51 (1982); Philadelphia Newspapers, Inc. v. Hepps, 475 U.S. 767, 777 (1986)).

402. 501 U.S. at 668.

403. Smith v. Daily Mail Publ'g Co., 443 U.S. 97, 103 (1979). See also The Florida Star v. B.J.F., 491 U.S. 524 (1989); Landmark Communications, Inc. v. Virginia, 435 U.S. 829 (1978).

404. 501 U.S. at 669 (citing Branzburg v. Hayes, 408 U.S. 665 (1972); Zacchini v. Scripps-Howard Broadcasting Co., 433 U.S. 562 (1977)).

405. 501 U.S. at 669 ("The press may not with impunity break and enter an office or dwelling to gather news.").

406. 443 U.S. 97 (1979).

making promises to keep them" and thereby empowers the "parties themselves, as in this case, [to] determine the scope of their legal obligations and any restrictions which may be placed on the publication of truthful information."[407]

Thus, the Court proceeded to determine that "the Minnesota doctrine of promissory estoppel is a law of general applicability," which does not "target or single out the press."[408] Accordingly, even assuming *arguendo* that "permitting Cohen to maintain a cause of action for promissory estoppel will inhibit truthful reporting because news organizations will have legal incentives not to disclose a confidential source's identity even when that person's identity is itself newsworthy," that result "is no more than the incidental, and constitutionally insignificant, consequence of applying to the press a generally applicable law that requires those who make certain kinds of promises to keep them."[409]

In a dissenting opinion, Justice Blackmun, joined by Justices Marshall and Souter, asserted that use of a claim of promissory estoppel "to penalize the reporting of truthful information regarding a political campaign" violates the First Amendment.[410] Justice Blackmun disputed the majority's reliance on the constitutionality of "generally applicable laws" that have "incidental effects on the ability to gather and report the news" — the Minnesota Supreme Court, he noted, had not "create[d] any exception to or immunity from the laws of that State for members of the press" and the protection it afforded the press "would be equally available to non-media defendants."[411] Rather, Justice Blackmun asserted, relying on *Hustler Magazine, Inc. v. Falwell*,[412] "the doctrine of promissory estoppel in this case cannot be said to have a merely 'incidental' burden on speech; the publication of important political speech *is* the claimed

---

407. 501 U.S. at 671.
408. *Id.*
409. *Id.* at 672.
410. *Id.* at 676 (Blackmun, J., dissenting). See *id.* at 676 n.4 ("we have long held that the imposition of civil liability based on protected expression constitutes 'punishment' of speech for First Amendment purposes") (citing Pittsburgh Press Co. v. Pittsburgh Comm'n on Human Relations, 413 U.S. 376, 386 (1973); New York Times Co. v. Sullivan, 376 U.S. 254, 279-80 (1964); Gertz v. Robert Welch, Inc., 418 U.S. 323, 340 (1974)). For the majority, Justice White responded that Justice Blackmun's contention was "not strictly accurate because compensatory damages are not a form of punishment, as were the criminal sanctions at issue in" *Smith v. Daily Mail Publ'g Co.*, 443 U.S. 97 (1979). 501 U.S. at 670 (opinion of the Court). According to Justice White, the "payment of compensatory damages in this case is constitutionally indistinguishable from a generous bonus paid to a confidential news source." *Id.*
411. *Id.* at 673 (Blackmun, J., dissenting).
412. 485 U.S. 46 (1988). In *Falwell*, the Court concluded that "public figures and public officials may not recover for the tort of intentional infliction of emotional distress by reason of publications such as the one here at issue without showing in addition that the publication contains a false statement of fact which was made with 'actual malice.'" *Id.* at 56.

violation."[413] Thus, he would have concluded that, "as in *Hustler*, the law may not be enforced to punish the expression of truthful information or opinion."[414]

In a separate dissenting opinion, Justice Souter, joined by Justices Blackmun, Marshall, and O'Connor, asserted that even "general laws" may "entail effects on the content of speech," and may be found constitutional only when such effects "'have been justified by subordinating valid governmental interests, a prerequisite to constitutionality which has necessarily involved a weighing of the governmental interest involved.'"[415] According to Justice Souter, because "the fact of Cohen's identity expanded the universe of information relevant to the choice faced by Minnesota voters in that State's 1982 gubernatorial election," its publication was "of the sort quintessentially subject to strict First Amendment protection."[416] Thus, on the facts of *Cohen*, he would strike the balance in favor of the newspapers, although, in other cases, where "the injured party is a private individual, whose identity is of less public concern," liability "might not be constitutionally prohibited."[417]

§ 13-4(a)(2)(D). The Minnesota Appellate Courts — Round 2.

On remand, the Minnesota Supreme Court held that the jury's verdict in favor of Cohen was "sustainable on the theory of promissory estoppel" and affirmed the jury's award of $200,000 in damages.[418] The court rejected the newspapers' claims that either the State Constitution or state law generally should bar judicial enforcement of a journalist's promise of confidentiality to a news source. "Courts should not invalidate enforceable promises except in the clearest of cases," the court concluded, holding that "the newsworthiness of Cohen's identity" had not "achieved a level of such grave importance as to require invalidation of the anonymity promise on grounds of public policy."[419] Thus, although the court conceded that "neither side in this case holds the higher moral ground,"

---

413. 501 U.S. at 675 (Blackmun, J., dissenting).

414. *Id.* at 675-76. Justice White rejected the contention that Cohen had attempted "to use a promissory estoppel cause of action to avoid the strict requirements for establishing a libel or defamation claim," as in *Hustler*. *Id.* at 671 (opinion of the Court). According to Justice White, *Hustler* was inapplicable because Cohen was "not seeking damages for injury to his reputation or his state of mind," but merely damages "for a breach of a promise that caused him to lose his job and lowered his earning capacity." *Id.*

415. *Id.* at 677 (Souter, J., dissenting) (quoting Konigsberg v. State Bar of California, 366 U.S. 36, 51 (1961)).

416. 501 U.S. at 678 (Souter, J., dissenting).

417. *Id.* Justice Souter also indicated that, in some cases, "the circumstances of acquisition" might be relevant as well, "although they may go only to what balances against, and not to diminish, the First Amendment value of any particular piece of information." *Id.*

418. Cohen v. Cowles Media Co., 479 N.W.2d 387, 388 (Minn. 1992).

419. *Id.* at 391.

the harm that Cohen sustained as a result of the newspapers' failure to honor their promise "requires a remedy here to avoid an injustice."[420]

§ 13-4(a)(3). *Cohen*-Inspired and Related Causes of Action.

From the trial court's initial decision denying the defendants' motion for summary judgment in 1987, through the Minnesota Supreme Court's decision affirming a $200,000 judgment in the plaintiff's favor, *Cohen v. Cowles Media Co.*[421] spawned a number of lawsuits based on similar theories of liability. Moreover, as *Cohen* itself worked its way through the trial and appellate courts, with constantly shifting results, these other cases often reflected the transient nature of the *Cohen* jurisprudence of the moment. Since the Supreme Court spoke to at least some of the relevant First Amendment issues in *Cohen*,[422] however, judicial consideration of cases alleging a breach of promise in the newsgathering process has begun to stabilize.

§ 13-4(a)(3)(A). The New York and Minnesota Experiences.

During the long pendency of the *Cohen* litigation, state courts in New York and federal courts applying the law of Minnesota were called upon to address similar causes of action grounded in alleged breaches of promise made by journalists in the newsgathering process.[423] Not unexpectedly, courts within each jurisdiction reached varying and often conflicting conclusions.

§ 13-4(a)(3)(A)(i). The New York Cases.

In *Virelli v. Goodson-Todman Enterprises*,[424] a New York appellate court rejected a claim by several plaintiffs who complained that a newspaper reporter had "breached an agreement not to disclose their identities" and to permit one of them "to review the article prior to publication."[425] The plaintiffs, who asserted causes of action for invasion of privacy, intentional infliction of emotional distress and common law negligence, contended that the article, which discussed "the societal scourge of drug abuse," contained "identifiable portrayals of plaintiffs, . . . as a result of which they were readily identified, humiliated in the

---

420. *Id.* at 392.
421. 479 N.W.2d 387 (Minn. 1992).
422. 501 U.S. 663 (1991).
423. Commentators have joined the debate as well. See, e.g., Note, *Promises and the Press: First Amendment Limitations on News Source Recovery for Breach of a Confidentiality Agreement*, 73 MINN. L. REV. 1553 (1989); Vickery, *Breach of Confidence: An Emerging Tort*, 82 COLUM. L. REV. 1426 (1982).
424. 536 N.Y.S.2d 571 (App. Div. 1989).
425. *Id.* at 573.

community and exposed to public ridicule."[426] The court rejected the privacy claim because New York law bars that statutory cause of action where the publication at issue concerns "newsworthy events or matters of public interest."[427] For the same reason, it held that the plaintiffs could not plead the kind of "outrageous, extreme behavior required" to substantiate a claim of intentional infliction.[428]

The court premised its dismissal of the negligence claim on alternative grounds. First, it noted that the damages alleged by the plaintiffs — *i.e.*, "injuries to reputation" — are the "traditional province of defamation tort law."[429] Under such circumstances, the court concluded, "ordinary negligence is a constitutionally insufficient basis upon which to impose liability."[430] Second, it concluded that state constitutional law precludes a negligence-based claim, requiring instead a showing that a publisher "acted in a *grossly irresponsible manner* without due consideration for the standards of information gathering and dissemination ordinarily followed by responsible parties."[431] Since the plaintiffs had not alleged, "even in conclusory fashion, that this heightened standard of fault was violated," dismissal of their negligence claim was affirmed.[432]

In *Doe v. American Broadcasting Cos.*,[433] the plaintiffs, two rape victims and one of their boyfriends, asserted claims for breach of contract and negligent and intentional infliction of emotional distress against a television station. According

---

426. *Id.*
427. *Id.* at 575 (quoting Stephano v. News Group Publications, Inc., 474 N.E.2d 580 (N.Y. 1984)); see N.Y. CIV. RIGHTS LAW §§ 50, 51.
428. 536 N.Y.S.2d at 575.
429. *Id.*
430. *Id.* The court based its analysis on *New York Times Co. v. Sullivan*, 376 U.S. 254, 270 (1964), and concluded that the constitutional safeguards developed by the Supreme Court in the defamation context should be applied "to shield freedom of expression from *any* effort by the State to recognize and enforce other competing interests in the form of granting civil damages recovery." 536 N.Y.S.2d at 576 (citing Time, Inc. v. Hill, 385 U.S. 374 (1967); Hustler Magazine, Inc. v. Falwell, 485 U.S. 46 (1988); Smith v. Daily Mail Publ'g Co., 443 U.S. 97 (1979)). In addition, the court relied on Judge Mansfield's decision in *Cullen v. Grove Press, Inc.*, 276 F. Supp. 727, 729 (S.D.N.Y. 1967). See 536 N.Y.S.2d at 576. Subsequently, of course, the Supreme Court rejected the defendants' reliance on this line of authority in *Cohen*, 501 U.S. at 669. Nevertheless, it is at least arguable that the *Virelli* court's analysis — in a case, unlike *Cohen*, where the *only* alleged damages are in the form of injury to reputation — reflects an appropriate application of *Sullivan*, *Falwell*, *Smith*, and *Hill*. See Food Lion, Inc. v. Capital Cities/ABC, Inc., 887 F. Supp. 811, 822-23 (M.D.N.C. 1995) (holding non-reputational damages can be recovered for claims of "fraud, trespass, and other wrongful acts," but reputational damages may only be awarded under constitutional defamation standards); Francione, *Experimentation and the Marketplace Theory of the First Amendment*, 136 U. PA. L. REV. 417 (1987).
431. 536 N.Y.S.2d at 576 (quoting Chapadeau v. Utica Observer-Dispatch, 341 N.E.2d 569 (N.Y. 1975)) (emphasis added).
432. 536 N.Y.S.2d at 576-77.
433. 543 N.Y.S.2d 455 (App. Div. 1989).

to the complaint, the plaintiffs, who were interviewed by the station in connection with a news report about rape victims, "received repeated assurances from defendants that neither their faces nor their voices would be recognizable."[434] In several subsequent broadcasts, the plaintiffs alleged, they were "recognizable to those who knew them and there appeared to be no attempt to disguise their voices."[435]

The trial court denied defendants' motion for summary judgment with respect to all three causes of action, and the appellate division affirmed that decision as it applied to the contract and negligent infliction claims. Nevertheless, the court of appeals dismissed the intentional infliction claim on the ground that the defendants' alleged conduct "did not constitute the intentional, deliberate and outrageous conduct necessary" to sustain that cause of action.[436]

Shortly after the Supreme Court's decision in *Cohen*, a New York trial court, over a constitutional challenge by a newspaper publisher, permitted a doctor and a hospital to pursue claims against the newspaper arising from its alleged failure to comply with a promise that an HIV-positive patient would not be recognizable in a published photograph. In *Anderson v. Strong Memorial Hospital*,[437] the estate of the then-deceased patient had been awarded $35,000 in an action against the doctor and hospital for breach of the doctor-patient privilege arising from their furnishing a photograph of the patient to the newspaper. The doctor and hospital commenced a third-party action against the newspaper, alleging negligence, negligent misrepresentation, breach of contract, and culpably causing the breach of the doctor-patient privilege.[438]

According to the third-party complaint, the patient's photograph had been taken by the newspaper — in connection with a story about the hospital's Infectious Disease Unit — "upon the express assurance" that the patient "would not be recognizable."[439] Nevertheless, when the story was subsequently published, the patient was allegedly "recognized by members of his family and friends."[440] The court denied the newspaper's motion for summary judgment on the ground that, in the wake of the Supreme Court's decision in *Cohen*, "any

---

434. *Id.* at 456 (Rosenberger, J., dissenting).

435. *Id.* According to the separate opinion of one dissenting justice, in advertising for the program and in the first of several broadcasts, one plaintiff's "outline, shape and facial features were clear enough to identify her to those who knew her. Her voice was 'an absolute, instantaneous, positive identification.'" *Id.* After this plaintiff complained, and the defendants "assured the plaintiffs that they would be unidentifiable in future broadcasts," the complaint alleged, they were in fact "recognizable to those who knew them and there appeared to be no attempt to disguise their voices in subsequent broadcasts." *Id.*

436. *Id.* (opinion of Court).
437. 573 N.Y.S.2d 828 (Sup. Ct. 1991).
438. *Id.* at 829.
439. *Id.* at 829-30.
440. *Id.* at 830.

extended discussion" of the newspaper's "obligation to honor a promise solemnly made, and its liability for dishonoring that promise, would appear to be unnecessary," at least as a matter of federal law.[441] Moreover, in light of the conflict it perceived between the appellate decisions in *Virelli* and *Doe*, the court concluded that

> even under a broader state law analysis, there is no reasonable policy basis to invoke the free speech protection of our State Constitution . . . in the circumstances of this case. There is no strong public interest in knowing the identity of someone who is HIV positive or suffering from AIDS. There is no free speech interest which the state must recognize in revealing the identity of such a person.[442]

Thus, the court distinguished *Virelli* and held, based on *Cohen*, that the "Federal and State Constitutions insulate the press from government action or coercion, not from agreements voluntarily entered into."[443] When such agreements are breached, the court concluded, "state laws of general application come into play, rather than the defamation standard of 'gross irresponsibility.'"[444]

§ 13-4(a)(3)(A)(ii). *Ruzicka v. Conde Nast Publications.*

Shortly after *Cohen* began its journey through the Minnesota state courts, another plaintiff undertook to prosecute similar claims in the federal courts of that state.[445] In 1981, plaintiff Jill Ruzicka had sued her psychiatrist and charged him with improper sexual conduct during therapy sessions. In addition, she sued the Minnesota Board of Medical Examiners for its alleged failure to supervise the psychiatrist properly.[446] Both cases were the subject of several press reports in 1981 and 1982, which revealed the plaintiff's identity. Plaintiff thereafter attended law school and became a practicing attorney. She was appointed to the Minnesota Task Force on Sexual Exploitation — which proposed model legis-

---

441. *Id.*
442. *Id.* at 831.
443. *Id.* at 832.
444. *Id.* at 832. In reaching this conclusion, the court relied on *Cohen*, *Huskey v. National Broadcasting Co.*, 632 F. Supp. 1282 (N.D. Ill. 1986), and *Snepp v. United States*, 444 U.S. 507 (1980). See 573 N.Y.S.2d at 832. The court also rejected the newspaper's contention that, because the patient — as depicted in the photograph — "was not recognizable by the reporter and photographer," the promise was unenforceable. *Id.* Nor was the court moved by the newspaper's suggestion that either the patient or the doctor "'could have required a much more particular agreement as to the parameters of the photo'" or insisted "on pre-publication review" of it; the "burden of carrying out its promise of anonymity," the court held, fell on the newspaper and "may not be so facilely shifted." *Id.*
445. See Ruzicka v. Conde Nast Publications, Inc., 999 F.2d 1319 (8th Cir. 1993).
446. See Ruzicka v. Conde Nast Publications, Inc., 733 F. Supp. 1289, 1291 (D. Minn. 1990) (subsequent history omitted).

lation on the subject — in 1984, testified before a committee of the Minnesota State Senate that same year, and spoke at a national conference on the subject of sexual exploitation by therapists in 1986, all of which were reported in the press.[447]

In 1987, a reporter under contract to *Glamour* magazine sought to interview plaintiff for an article on the subject of "patient-therapist sex." According to plaintiff, she claims to have told the reporter, at the outset, "that she was willing to be interviewed 'only if I not be identified or identifiable.'"[448] The reporter, however, asserted that plaintiff "'wanted some kind of masking,' but 'was very casual about it.'"[449] It was undisputed that the plaintiff did not specify what information would threaten her anonymity, except to insist that the magazine not report "some problems she had had at one of her previous jobs."[450]

The information provided by plaintiff — excluding any discussion about her previous job — became a central focus of the article. In it, the plaintiff's name was changed to "Jill Lundquist." The article reported that Ms. Lundquist attended law school after her suit against her psychiatrist was settled, "that she is now a Minneapolis attorney and that she served on a state task force which helped draft a statute."[451] Plaintiff could not point to anyone who identified her as a result of the article, except for two former therapists who "had extensive prior knowledge of plaintiff's history of abuse."[452] Nevertheless, she alleged that the article's reference to "her service on the state task force makes her absolutely identifiable . . . because the task force's report lists the participants and she was the only woman."[453] Accordingly, she filed a complaint alleging six separate causes of action, including breach of contract, fraudulent misrepresentation, and unjust enrichment.

At the time that the defendants' motion for summary judgment came before the district court, the Minnesota Court of Appeals had just issued its decision affirming the jury's breach of contract verdict for the plaintiff in *Cohen*.[454] Nevertheless, the district court granted summary judgment for the defendants, holding that, although *Cohen* controlled as a matter of state law, it was "obligated to make an independent determination as to the effect of the United States

---

447. *Id.* Some of these articles identified plaintiff by name and others did not. *Id.*
448. *Id.*
449. *Id.*
450. *Id.*
451. *Id.* at 1292.
452. *Id.*
453. Ruzicka v. Conde Nast Publications, Inc., 939 F.2d 578, 580 (8th Cir. 1991) (subsequent history omitted).
454. See Cohen v. Cowles Media Co., 445 N.W.2d 248 (Minn. App. 1989).

Constitution."[455] In reaching that decision, the district court distinguished *Cohen* on the ground that the promise at issue in *Ruzicka* was, at best, an ambiguous undertaking to make the plaintiff "unidentifiable," not an express promise to refrain from publishing a source's identity: "at a minimum, the Constitution requires plaintiffs in contract actions to enforce a reporter-source agreement to prove specific, unambiguous terms and to provide clear and convincing proof that the agreement was breached."[456]

In the wake of the Supreme Court's decision in *Cohen*, the Eighth Circuit reversed in part and remanded to the district court for further proceedings.[457] The court concluded that it, like the Supreme Court, was bound by the Minnesota Supreme Court's decision in *Cohen* to the extent it declined to recognize, as a matter of state law, a "cause of action for breach of contract" when news organizations breach promises of confidentiality.[458] By the same token, it followed the Supreme Court's lead and remanded the case to the district court for consideration of whether Ruzicka could maintain a cause of action for promissory estoppel.[459]

On remand, the district court again granted summary judgment for the defendants, even in the face of the Minnesota Supreme Court's ultimate affirmance of Cohen's recovery on a promissory estoppel theory.[460] The court determined that, although its initial decision granting defendants' summary judgment motion "occurred in the context of plaintiff's breach of contract claim," its concern regarding "the ambiguities inherent in a promise of nonidentifiability applies with equal force to the question of whether the promise extended to plaintiff was sufficiently clear and definite to support her claim of promissory

---

455. 733 F. Supp. at 1294. The court did rely on the court of appeal's decision in *Cohen* in granting the motion for summary judgment with respect to the claim for fraudulent misrepresentation. See *id.* at 1301 (citing Cohen v. Cowles Media Co., 445 N.W.2d at 359).

456. 733 F. Supp. at 1299. See *id.* at 1300-01 ("The Court holds that where an agreement between a reporter and a source requires that the source not be made identifiable, with no further particulars or specific facts about what information would identify the source to the relevant audience, the agreement is too ambiguous to be enforced."). The district court granted summary judgment with respect to the unjust enrichment claim on the ground that, "[i]n cases involving allegations of wrongful publication, a publisher is not held to have received a benefit merely because it referred to plaintiff in a magazine that was published for profit." *Id.* at 1301.

457. Ruzicka v. Conde Nast Publications, Inc., 939 F.2d 578 (8th Cir. 1991). See generally Koepke, *Reporters Privilege; Shield or Sword?*, 42 FED. COMM. L.J. 277 (1990).

458. 939 F.2d at 580 (citing Cohen v. Cowles Media Co., 457 N.W.2d 199 (Minn. 1990), *rev'd*, 501 U.S. 663 (1991)).

459. 939 F.2d at 579. The court of appeals did, however, affirm the district court's decision dismissing all of the plaintiff's remaining claims, including her claim for unjust enrichment. See *id.* at 583 n.8.

460. See Ruzicka v. Conde Nast Publications, Inc., 794 F. Supp. 303 (D. Minn. 1992) (distinguishing Cohen v. Cowles Media Co., 479 N.W.2d 387 (Minn. 1992)) (subsequent history omitted).

estoppel."[461] Moreover, the court reiterated that the case before it was "substantially different from *Cohen* because neither the promise nor the breach is clear" and the defendants in *Cohen* "made a conscious and calculated decision to violate an unambiguous promise not to name the plaintiff."[462] Thus, the court concluded, "[f]ar from preventing an injustice, enforcing such an ambiguous promise could create injustice by placing on editors and reporters the impossible burden of guessing at what steps such a promise requires."[463]

On appeal, the Eighth Circuit once again reversed and remanded "for a plenary trial."[464] The court of appeals found the promise at issue in *Ruzicka* to be "sufficiently specific and distinct" to satisfy the Minnesota law of promissory estoppel.[465] Indeed, the court concluded that, when "the promise was made not to identify the plaintiff, the plain meaning of the promise was that [defendants] . . . would mask the identity of the plaintiff in such a way that a reasonable reader could not identify Jill Ruzicka by factual description."[466] Thus, although Ruzicka could not "base a breach of promise claim on facts she consensually disclosed and approved for publication," she could enforce the promise as it applies to identifying information obtained from other sources.[467] Finally, the court concluded that enforcement of a promise of nonidentifiability would not work an injustice sufficient to preclude application of the law of promissory estoppel:

> Here, Ruzicka agreed to the interview only upon the assurance that she would not be identified. She had revealed . . . matters of utmost privacy relating to familial incest which had never before been revealed. . . . Moreover, enforcement of the promise would not be unjust to the media defendant. When the press feels disclosure of the identity of a confidential source is valuable to the story and thus disregards its promise, the payment of compensatory damages is . . . simply "a cost of acquiring newsworthy material to be published at a profit."[468]

---

461. 794 F. Supp. at 308.
462. *Id.* at 311.
463. *Id.*
464. Ruzicka v. Conde Nast Publications, Inc., 999 F.2d 1319, 1320 (8th Cir. 1993).
465. *Id.* at 1321.
466. *Id.*
467. *Id.* at 1322. The court analogized to the "issues of identification in defamation and libel contexts," which it asserted "is a question for the jury to be determined from the story as a whole." *Id.* (citing Pring v. Penthouse Int'l, Ltd., 695 F.2d 438, 439 (10th Cir. 1982), *cert. denied*, 462 U.S. 1132 (1983)). The court's assumption in this regard, however, is open to debate. See, e.g., New York Times Co. v. Sullivan, 376 U.S. 254, 269 (1964); Gintert v. Howard Publications, Inc., 565 F. Supp. 829, 837 (N.D. Ind. 1983); Michigan United Conservation Club v. CBS News, 485 F. Supp. 893, 900 (W.D. Mich. 1980); Levine, *Judge and Jury in the Law of Defamation; Putting the Horse Behind the Cart*, 35 AM. U.L. REV. 3 (1985).
468. 999 F.2d at 1323 (quoting Cohen v. Cowles Media Co., 501 U.S. at 670).

§ 13-4(a)(3)(B).   Other *Post-Cohen* Cases.

Since the Supreme Court's decision in *Cohen*, several other lower courts have also had occasion to address breach of promise claims in the newsgathering context. In *O'Connell v. Housatonic Valley Publishing Co.*,[469] a Connecticut trial court granted a newspaper's motion for summary judgment in a suit by a plaintiff who claimed that "while she received no specific assurances of anonymity, she believed that because anonymity was specifically requested, such would be granted."[470] The court held that *Cohen* does not apply when the claim is not for breach of a promise and the alleged damages are solely for injury to plaintiff's "state of mind;" in that circumstance, there "is no reason to believe that the First Amendment provides less protection when the claim is negligent infliction of emotional distress" than it did, in *Hustler Magazine, Inc. v. Falwell*,[471] when the plaintiff alleged an intentional infliction.[472]

In *Morgan v. Celender*,[473] the plaintiff asserted causes of action of invasion of privacy, fraudulent misrepresentation, and intentional infliction of emotional distress, on her own behalf and on behalf of her child, arising from a newspaper's alleged breach of its promise not to publish their names and to photograph them only in silhouette. In fact, the newspaper published, on page one, a photograph of plaintiff and her daughter bearing the caption "Heather Morgan, a victim of sexual abuse, talks with her mother, Diane."[474]

On defendants' motion for a directed verdict at trial, the court rejected the privacy and intentional infliction claims on the ground that the photograph was taken in a public place, the plaintiffs' names were available in public court records, and the judicial proceedings in which they were involved constituted a matter of public concern.[475] In addition, the court granted a directed verdict with respect to the fraudulent misrepresentation claim because, under Pennsylvania law, "a promise to do something in the future (such as keeping information confidential) which promise is not kept, is not fraud."[476]

In *Wildmon v. Berwick Universal Pictures*,[477] a federal court rejected the Reverend Donald Wildmon's effort to enjoin distribution, in the United States,

---

469. 1991 Conn. Super. LEXIS 2749 (1991).
470. *Id.* at *3.
471. 485 U.S. 46 (1988). See Food Lion, Inc. v. Capital Cities/ABC, Inc., 887 F. Supp. 811, 823 (M.D.N.C. 1995) (differentiating claim for breach of promise in *Cohen* from intentional infliction of emotional distress claim in *Hustler*).
472. 1991 Conn. Super. LEXIS 2749, at *4.
473. 780 F. Supp. 307 (W.D. Pa. 1992).
474. *Id.* at 309.
475. *Id.* The court held that the publication of such truthful information, even if "obtained illegally, unethically or deceptively by the reporter," is protected by the First Amendment. *Id.* (citing The Florida Star v. B.J.F., 491 U.S. 524 (1989)).
476. 780 F. Supp. at 311.
477. 803 F. Supp. 1167 (N.D. Miss.), *aff'd*, 979 F.2d 209 (5th Cir. 1992).

of a motion picture in which he was interviewed on camera. Wildmon claimed that he had entered into a contract with the filmmaker, pursuant to which he was afforded the right to limit such distribution, and that the agreement had been breached by showings of the film in the United States despite his objections. The court concluded that the "most reasonable interpretation" of the agreement, construed as a whole, was that "Wildmon did not have control over distribution of the entire film."[478] In so holding, the court observed that, following the Supreme Court's decision in *Cohen*, "Wildmon's rights under his contract are not diminished simply because the defendants are producers and distributors or because they made a film to be shown to the public."[479] By the same token, the court noted that "*Cohen* does not relieve a drafter of the responsibility of making the contract clear" and, therefore, "unless the contracting parties have clearly promised to limit the flow of information as they did with the confidentiality agreement in *Cohen*, an ambiguous contract should be read in a way that allows viewership and encourages debate."[480]

In *Multimedia WMAZ, Inc. v. Kubach*,[481] however, a Georgia appellate court affirmed a $500,000 jury verdict in favor of plaintiff, an AIDS patient, who had appeared on a television program broadcast by defendant after being promised that his face would be electronically "digitized" so that he could not be recognized. The evidence at trial indicated that, because the level of digitization was inadequate for the first seven seconds of the broadcast, plaintiff was in fact recognizable during that interval.[482] After the broadcast, according to the plaintiff's evidence, he became withdrawn, depressed, "almost suicidal," and "refused to leave his home for fear of being recognized."[483]

Although the plaintiff's cause of action sounded in invasion of privacy, the court of appeals cited *Cohen* in rejecting the defendants' contention that, because the disclosure of plaintiff's identity "occurred during a broadcast on a matter of public concern," he could not state such a claim under Georgia tort law.[484] In the court's view, the "identities of those suffering from AIDS are generally *not* a matter of public interest," especially when the defendant "was only in the position to disclose plaintiff's identity as an AIDS patient because of its promise to plaintiff that there would be no such disclosure."[485]

---

478. *Id.* at 1177.
479. *Id.* at 1177-78 (citing Cohen v. Cowles Media Co., 501 U.S. 663 (1991)).
480. 803 F. Supp. at 1178.
481. 443 S.E.2d 491 (Ga. App. 1994).
482. *Id.* at 493.
483. *Id.*
484. *Id.* at 494 (citing Ramsey v. Georgia Gazette Publ'g Co., 297 S.E.2d 94 (Ga. App. 1982)).
485. 443 S.E.2d at 495 (citing Cohen v. Cowles Media Co., 501 U.S. 663 (1991)). Four of the court's nine members dissented and one concurred specially. See 443 S.E.2d at 496.

Similarly, in *Doe v. Univision Television Group, Inc.*,[486] a Florida appellate court reversed a trial judge's dismissal of claims for invasion of privacy, breach of contract, and promissory estoppel brought by a plaintiff who had agreed to be interviewed for a television broadcast about the risks associated with low-cost plastic surgery in Costa Rica. Plaintiff, who was badly scarred as a result of such surgery, was allegedly promised that her face and voice would be disguised. In fact, she contended, her voice was not disguised at all and she was recognized by friends and family. While the court of appeals affirmed dismissal of her negligent infliction of emotional distress claim as duplicative of the invasion of privacy cause of action,[487] it permitted plaintiff to plead her contract and promissory estoppel claims in the alternative,[488] noting that, "while the topic of the broadcast was of legitimate public concern, the plaintiff's identity was not."[489]

Finally, in *Veilleux v. National Broadcasting Co.*,[490] a jury awarded plaintiff damages after finding the television network liable for negligent and fraudulent misrepresentation. The broadcast at issue reported safety problems in the long-distance trucking industry and featured extensive coverage of the plaintiff, a truck driver. The jury found that NBC had induced plaintiff's participation by agreeing to "ground rules,"[491] including "the explicit and repeated promises ... that the story would be a positive one."[492] On summary judgment, the trial court had dismissed plaintiff's intentional infliction of emotional distress claims because defendant's conduct was not so outrageous that it could be said to exceed the bounds of decency or to justify an implication of common law malice.[493] Nevertheless, the court noted that "a duty of reasonable care could arise from Defendants' alleged assurances designed to coerce the Plaintiffs' participation in their project."[494] According to the court, "[i]f imposing a duty of care on media representatives inhibits truthful reporting, as Defendants claim, 'it is no more than the incidental, and constitutionally insignificant, consequence of applying to the press a generally applicable law' that requires those who make certain kinds of representations to use reasonable care in doing so."[495]

---

486. 717 So. 2d 63 (Fla. App. 1998).
487. See *id.* at 65.
488. *Id.*
489. *Id.*
490. 8 F. Supp. 2d 23 (D. Me. 1998).
491. *Id.* at 30.
492. *Id.* at 31.
493. *Id.* at 41-42.
494. *Id.* at 41.
495. *Id.* at 41 n.9 (quoting Cohen v. Cowles Media Co., 501 U.S. at 671-72). See also W.D.I.A. Corp. v. McGraw-Hill, Inc., 34 F. Supp. 2d 612, 622-27 (S.D. Ohio 1998) (magazine liable for breach of written contract to use information obtained from credit agency only for proper purpose).

§ 13-4(a)(4). Paying for News.

Journalists, especially those employed by so-called newspaper and television "tabloids," sometimes pay sources for an interview or for information.[496] When the paid source is a potential witness in a criminal trial, the source's credibility as a witness is potentially called into question.[497] In the wake of the O.J. Simpson murder trial, where several potential witnesses sold their stories to tabloid journalists, the California legislature passed two laws to prohibit potential witnesses in criminal trials from receiving compensation for interviews.[498] The legislature reasoned that, by diminishing the credibility of witnesses, the practice of paying interviewees deprived criminal defendants of a fair trial.[499]

The statutes, however, were promptly challenged in federal court by the California First Amendment Coalition[500] as violative of the First Amendment.[501] The district court issued a permanent injunction against enforcement of the statutes, concluding that they "impose a prior restraint on speech," and the speech targeted by the statutes "is at the core of protected expression."[502]

§ 13-4(b). The Ambush Interview.

Sources have, on rare occasions, instituted litigation against the news media after having been subjected to what they characterize as "ambush interviews." According to the Second Circuit, an "[a]mbush interview is a derogatory descriptive term for a controversial investigative reporting technique in which a reporter and his news crew intercept an 'unsuspecting newsworthy subject on the street and [bombard] him with incriminating accusations ostensibly framed as

---

496. One potential witness in the O.J. Simpson case was paid $5,000 by "Hard Copy," a television tabloid program, and defendant police officers in the Rodney King case were allegedly paid $40,000 by "A Current Affair," another television program. S.F. Exam'r, Aug. 11, 1995, at A18.

497. One person, who sold her story about O.J. Simpson to "Hard Copy" and supermarket tabloids for $7,600, was dropped as a witness in the criminal case. Egelko, *Ban on Witness Payments Ruled Unconstitutional*, AP Wire, Aug. 8, 1995.

498. Section 132.5 of the California Penal Code made it "a crime for a person to receive any payment or benefit for providing information about what he or she knows or reasonably should know is a crime, or where that person knows or reasonably should know that he or she may be called as a witness in a criminal prosecution." California First Amendment Coalition v. Lungren, 1995 U.S. Dist. LEXIS 11655, at *4 (N.D. Cal. Aug. 9, 1995). Section 1669.7 "render[ed] contracts in violation of § 132.5 void" and authorized the Attorney General or district attorney of the county in which the violation occurred to institute civil action to enjoin enforcement of such contracts. *Id.*

499. *Id.* at *5.

500. The California First Amendment Coalition "is a non-profit organization dedicated to protecting the rights to free expression of California's journalists and citizens." *Id.* at *2.

501. *Id.*

502. *Id.* at *15.

questions.'"[503] In *Machleder v. Diaz*,[504] the case that gave rise to the above-referenced description, a television camera crew approached the plaintiff, with camera rolling, and attempted to interview him about what appeared to be toxic waste stored on property adjacent to his business. The plaintiff alleged that, although he had nothing to do with the adjacent property, or with the materials stored there, the resulting video footage placed him in a false light because it made him appear evasive and defensive in attempting to fend off the reporter and his camera crew.[505] Despite a jury verdict in his favor, however, the Second Circuit concluded that the portrayal of plaintiff as "intemperate and evasive is not false and is not highly offensive to a reasonable person," thereby precluding his claim for false light invasion of privacy.[506]

Similarly, in *Aisenson v. American Broadcasting Co.*,[507] the court rejected plaintiff's claim for false light invasion of privacy and intrusion arising from an "ambush" interview conducted outside his home as he walked to his car. Although plaintiff objected "that the broadcasters chose to freeze the film at the moment he appeared to spot the videocamera" and that he was thereby "unfairly portrayed," the court concluded his "disappointment that a more flattering picture was not broadcast (or that none at all was broadcast) does not rise to the level of a compensable claim for invasion of privacy."[508] In addition, the court held that plaintiff could not maintain a claim for intrusion because, despite his contention that he "could not be seen from the photographer's location unless an enhanced lens was being used," plaintiff "was in full public view from the street at the time he was videotaped."[509] Moreover, the court concluded that the camera crew had neither come "into physical contact with appellant, or endangered the safety of him or his family,"[510] thereby precluding a viable intrusion claim.[511]

---

503. Machleder v. Diaz, 801 F.2d 46, 49 (2d Cir. 1986) (quoting Note, *The Ambush Interview: A False Light Invasion of Privacy?*, 34 CASE W. RES. L. REV. 72, 72 (1983)). In *Wolfson v. Lewis*, 924 F. Supp. 1413, 1424 (E.D. Pa. 1996), another federal court described the "ambush interview" as "a confrontational, surprise interview with an unwilling subject, generally a person who has previously refused to be interviewed. The T.V. journalist approaches the subject surreptitiously with cameras and sound rolling and asks a question calculated to embarrass the subject."
504. 801 F.2d 46 (2d Cir. 1986).
505. *Id.* at 49. For example, the filmed footage depicted the plaintiff ordering the reporter to "[g]et that damn camera out of here" and asserting that "I don't want .... I don't need. ... I don't need any publicity." *Id.* at 50.
506. *Id.* at 59. Previously, the district court had dismissed plaintiff's intrusion-based privacy claim, holding that the reporter's questions, "although aggressive and possibly abrasive, occurred in an encounter with the plaintiff and do not constitute unabated hounding." Machleder v. Diaz, 538 F. Supp. 1364, 1374 (S.D.N.Y. 1982) (citing RESTATEMENT (SECOND) OF TORTS § 652B, cmts. c & d).
507. 269 Cal. Rptr. 379 (Ct. App. 1990).
508. *Id.* at 387.
509. *Id.* at 388.
510. *Id.*
511. See also Marcus Garvey Charter Sch. v. Washington Times Corp., 27 MEDIA L. REP.

One federal court, however, embraced an apparently contrary view in *Wolfson v. Lewis*,[512] where a television camera crew similarly "staked out" plaintiffs' home, as well as that of their parents, in hopes of staging an "ambush interview" in connection with a report on the allegedly high salaries paid to executives in the healthcare industry. Indeed, after an extended evidentiary hearing, the court entered a preliminary injunction prohibiting the defendant camera crew and reporters from "tortious ongoing stalking, harassment, trespass, and invasions of privacy, including Defendants' stalking of Plaintiffs, their three-year-old child, their families, business and social associates."[513]

According to the court, the "use of sophisticated video and recording equipment by T.V. journalists has increased the threat that a person's right to privacy may be violated," while "the television market for scandal and sensationalism has encouraged T.V. journalists to engage in forms of newsgathering that may bring about a clash between the right to privacy and freedom of the press."[514] As a result, the court concluded that "[c]onduct that amounts to a persistent course of hounding, harassment and unreasonable surveillance, even if conducted in a public or semi-public place, may nevertheless rise to the level of invasion of privacy based on intrusion."[515]

The court found such conduct, sufficient to justify a preliminary injunction, during a one week period when a television camera crew "staked out" plaintiffs' residence, followed plaintiffs and their children to work and school in automobiles, and rented a boat equipped with a sophisticated "shot gun" microphone and camera and stationed it in a waterway adjacent to a vacation home owned by plaintiffs' parents.[516] The defendants acted surreptitiously, which plaintiffs claimed placed them in fear of their physical safety and rendered them "prisoners" in the family home.[517] In entering the requested preliminary injunction, the court held that

> the evidence is also sufficient to support a likelihood that a jury could determine that . . . [the journalists] harassed and invaded the Wolfsons' privacy not, as defendants claim, for the legitimate purpose of gathering and

---

(BNA) 1225 (D.C. Super. 1998) (dismissing false light invasion of privacy, intrusion, false imprisonment and assault claims where reporter made no threats of force or harm and did not physically harm or restrain plaintiffs when he photographed them in the main office of a public school).

512. 924 F. Supp. 1413 (E.D. Pa. 1996).
513. *Id.* at 1415-16.
514. *Id.* at 1418.
515. *Id.* at 1420 (citing Galella v. Onassis, 487 F.2d 986 (2d Cir. 1973); RESTATEMENT (SECOND) OF TORTS § 652B, cmt. d)). Plaintiffs were subsequently permitted to amend their complaint to add claims for violation of state and federal wiretap statutes, pursuant to 18 U.S.C. § 2511 and FLA. STAT. § 934.10. See Wolfson v. Lewis, 168 F.R.D. 530 (E.D. Pa. 1996).
516. See 924 F. Supp. at 1422-31.
517. *Id.* at 1431.

broadcasting the news, but to try to obtain entertaining background for their T.V. expose.... A reasonable jury would likely conclude that it is difficult to understand how hounding, harassing, and ambushing the Wolfsons would advance the newsworthy goal of exposing the high salaries paid to U.S. Healthcare executives....[518]

§ 13-4(c). Interference with Contract.

A handful of journalists and media defendants have been faced with claims alleging tortious or other actionable interference with contractual relationships in the course of newsgathering. Typically, such claims have been asserted, not by the interview source herself, but by the person or entity that allegedly stands in a contractual relationship with the source and claims that a journalist, by "inducing" the source to provide information, has violated that contract and/or its confidentiality provisions.[519]

In a series of cases, one plaintiff prosecuted interference with contract claims against a number of media defendants, all of which had broadcast interviews with his former wife in which she allegedly violated the provisions of a confidentiality agreement entered between them in connection with their divorce. In *Huggins v. Povitch*,[520] a New York trial court granted defendants' motion to dismiss the claim, even though they had actual notice of the confidentiality agreement. The court explained that, to recover damages for tortious interference with contract, a plaintiff must demonstrate "1) existence of a valid contract, 2) defendant's knowledge of that contract, 3) defendant's improper interference with that contract, and 4) damages."[521] Thus, the court noted:

> for an action for tortious interference with contract to be sustained, the defendant's actions must be improper and without reasonable justification. The plaintiff must prove that the defendant actively and intentionally procured the breach for the sole purpose of harming the plaintiff through

---

518. *Id.* at 1433.
519. See, e.g., Huggins v. Povitch, 24 MEDIA L. REP. (BNA) 2040 (N.Y. Sup. Ct. 1996); Huggins v. National Broadcasting Co., 1996 WL 763337 (N.Y. Sup. Ct. Feb. 7, 1996); Huggins v. Whitney, 24 MEDIA L. REP. (BNA) 1088 (N.Y. Sup. Ct. 1995). For general discussion of the contours of the tort, see Dobbs, *Tortious Interference with Contractual Relationships*, 34 ARK. L. REV. 335 (1980); Perlman, *Interference with Contract and Other Economic Expectancies: A Clash of Tort and Contract Doctrine*, 49 U. CHI. L. REV. 61 (1982); RESTATEMENT (SECOND) OF TORTS § 766B.
520. 24 MEDIA L. REP. (BNA) 2040 (N.Y. Sup. Ct. 1996).
521. *Id.* at 2047. See also RESTATEMENT (SECOND) OF TORTS § 766 ("One who intentionally and improperly interferes with the performance of a contract (except a contract to marry) between another and a third person by inducing or otherwise causing the third person not to perform the contract, is subject to liability to the other for the pecuniary loss resulting to the other from the failure of the third person to perform the contract.").

wrongful means such as physical violence, fraud, misrepresentation, prosecution of civil or criminal suits or economic pressure. The factors to be considered include the motive of the person who interferes and the societal interest in protecting the freedom of action of the person who interferes.[522]

In dismissing the claim, the court embraced defendants' contention that "the First Amendment freedom of the press to report on newsworthy subjects is an appropriate justification that will preclude a claim of tortious interference."[523] Accordingly, the court held that "a broadcaster whose motive and conduct is intended to foster public awareness or debate cannot be found to have engaged in the wrongful or improper conduct required to sustain a claim for interference with contractual relations."[524] In the case before it, therefore, the court concluded that "the broadcaster's first amendment right to broadcast an issue of public importance, its lack of any motive to harm the plaintiff, and obvious societal interest in encouraging freedom of the press, negate essential elements of the tort."[525]

Although it spawned neither litigation nor legal precedent, one television network's decision temporarily to delay the broadcast of an interview with a former tobacco company executive sparked considerable curiosity about the viability of a tortious interference claim in the newsgathering context.[526] The

---

522. Huggins v. Povitch, 24 MEDIA L. REP. (BNA) at 2047.
523. *Id.*
524. *Id.*
525. *Id.* at 2047-48. The court also noted that, especially given the source's pattern of granting interviews to a number of news media entities, "she needed no inducement from defendant to breach the confidentiality agreement. She initiated an all-out media blitz, including local and international newspapers, radio and television with the assistance of a press agent." *Id.* Indeed, plaintiff instituted analogous actions against other news organizations, which were similarly rejected by New York courts. See, e.g., Huggins v. National Broadcasting Co., 1996 WL 763337, at *4 (N.Y. Sup. Ct. Feb. 7, 1996) ("no facts are alleged to show that defendants intentionally or unjustifiably interfered with the confidentiality agreement" and any "interference that occurred was merely incidental to defendants' exercise of their constitutional right to broadcast newsworthy information," which constitutes a "legitimate" purpose that "did not involve an intent to unjustifiably interfere with the confidentiality agreement"); Huggins v. Whitney, 24 MEDIA L. REP. (BNA) 1088, 1090 (N.Y. Sup. Ct. 1995) ("The United States Supreme Court has held that media organizations cannot be liable or punished (by civil damages or criminal liability) because of the use of 'routine newspaper reporting techniques' to ascertain, and publish, a newsworthy story, . . . no matter how that story was obtained") (quoting Smith v. Daily Mail Publ'g Co., 443 U.S. 97, 103 (1979)).

526. See, e.g., Grossman, *CBS, 60 Minutes and the Unseen Interview*, COLUM. JOURNALISM REV. Jan./Feb. 1996 at 39; Heinke & Bandlow, *Did CBS Choke?* L.A. Daily J., Jan. 11, 1996, at 6; Freeman, Markoff & Sack, *"60 Minutes" and the Law: Can Journalists be Liable for Tortious Interference with Contract?*, N.Y. ST. B.J., July/Aug. 1996 at 24; Kohler, *The CBS Tobacco Story: The Problem Is Not the Lawyers*, 14 COMM. LAW. 11 (Winter 1996); Russomanno & Youm, *The 60 Minutes Controversy: What Lawyers Are Telling the News Media*, COMM. & L., Sept. 1996, at 65.

source had signed a confidentiality agreement with his former employer, which purported to preclude him from publicly disclosing information about the company. In the course of attempting to convince the source to tell his story on camera, the network, *inter alia*, allegedly paid him a consulting fee on another story, paid for him and his wife to come to New York for the purpose of filming the interview, and agreed to indemnify him if the broadcast should result in a defamation action against him. Reportedly, the network declined initially to broadcast the interview based on its concerns that, at the very least, the costs of defending a tortious interference claim in a hostile jurisdiction would be substantial, the risk of an adverse jury verdict in such a venue was palpable, and the law was sufficiently unsettled to create a risk that any such judgment would survive an appeal.[527]

The legal claim was never prosecuted, or tested in court, but some commentators have opined that — for reasons articulated as well by the courts adjudicating the *Huggins* cases — it would likely have been unsuccessful.[528] First, it would appear that a contract that violates public policy — by, for example, prohibiting a party to it from reporting dangers to the public health or safety — would be void and incapable of sustaining an action for inducing its breach.[529] Indeed, in *Branzburg v. Hayes*,[530] the Supreme Court noted that "it is obvious that agreements to conceal information relevant to commission of crime have very little to recommend them from the standpoint of public policy."[531] Second, in the context of newsgathering with respect to matters of public concern, it is unlikely that a court could properly conclude that a journalist's successful efforts to induce a source to provide such information could be deemed "intentional and

---

527. The publicly known facts surrounding the network's initial decision, as well as its subsequent determination to broadcast the interview after the transcript of it was leaked to and published by a newspaper, are recounted by Grossman, *supra*, note 526.

528. See Heinke & Bandlow, *supra* note 526, at 6; Baron, Lane & Schulz, *The Limits of Common Law Liability for Newsgathering*, 4 WM. & MARY BILL RTS. J. 1027 (1996); Chasteen, *In Search of a Smoking Gun: Tortious Interference with Nondisclosure Agreements as an Obstacle to Newsgathering*, 50 FED. COMM. L.J. 483(1998). But see note 537 *infra*.

529. See PROSSER & KEETON, *supra* note 158, § 129, at 194 & n.68; Dr. Miles Med. Co. v. John D. Park & Sons Co., 220 U.S. 373, 406-09 (1911); Gold v. Wolpert, 876 F.2d 1327, 1332 (7th Cir. 1989); Baron, Lane & Schulz, *supra* note 528.

530. 408 U.S. 665, 696 (1972).

531. *Id.* See also Chambers v. Capital Cities/ABC, Inc., 159 F.R.D. 441, 444 (S.D.N.Y. 1995) (confidentiality agreements with employees "can be harmful to the public's ability to rein in improper behavior and in some contexts the ability of the United States to police violations of its laws"); McGrane v. Reader's Digest Ass'n, 822 F. Supp. 1044, 1045 (S.D.N.Y. 1993) ("Courts are increasingly reluctant to enforce secrecy arrangements where matters of substantial concern to the public — as distinct from trade secrets or other legitimately confidential information — may be involved.").

improper interference" with even a valid confidentiality provision.[532] In analogous cases, in which plaintiffs have sought to impose liability for tortious interference with customer relationships arising from the *content* of news media reports, courts have rejected claims of "improper" purpose, finding for example "no indication that the report was broadcast for any reason other than reporting on an issue of public concern."[533]

Finally, substantial First Amendment-based defenses may operate to preclude a tortious interference claim based on "routine newsgathering" in any event.[534] In *Nicholson v. McClatchy Newspapers*,[535] a California Court of Appeal rejected an intrusion claim based on newsgathering conduct alleged to include "soliciting, inquiring, requesting and persuading agents, employees and members of the state

---

532. See RESTATEMENT (SECOND) OF TORTS § 766A, cmt. e ("The interference with the other's performance of his contract is intentional if the actor desires to bring it about or if he knows that the interference is certain or substantially certain to occur as a result of his action."); PROSSER & KEETON, *supra* note 158, § 129, at 983 ("It has always been agreed that a defendant might intentionally interfere with the plaintiff's interests without liability if there were good grounds for the interference, or in other words that some kind of unacceptable purpose was required in addition to intent."). The RESTATEMENT looks to seven factors in assessing whether an alleged interference is "improper":

(1) the nature of the actor's conduct;
(2) the actor's motive;
(3) the interests of the other with which the actor's conduct interferes;
(4) the interests sought to be advanced by the actor;
(5) the societal interests in protecting the freedom of action of the actor and the contractual interests of the other;
(6) the proximity or remoteness of the actor's conduct to the interference and
(7) the relations between the parties.

RESTATEMENT (SECOND) OF TORTS § 767; see Zilg v. Prentice-Hall, Inc., 717 F.2d 671, 677 (2d Cir. 1983), *cert. denied*, 466 U.S. 938 (1984); Italian & French Wine Co. v. Negociants U.S.A., Inc., 842 F. Supp. 693, 700 (W.D.N.Y. 1993); Baron, Lane & Schulz, *supra* note 528, at 1047.

533. Dulgarian v. Stone, 652 N.E.2d 603, 609 (Mass. 1995). Accord Brown & Williamson Tobacco Corp. v. Jacobson, 713 F.2d 262, 272 (7th Cir. 1983), *cert. denied*, 485 U.S. 993 (1988) (purpose of broadcast was "solely to increase the audience ratings of and attract attention to" program); see also Medical Lab. Management Consultants v. American Broadcasting Cos., 30 F. Supp. 2d 1182, 1194 (D. Ariz. 1998) ("Without a showing of falsity, Plaintiffs cannot prevail on an intentional interference with business relationships claim which is based on protected speech."); Ferrara v. Detroit Free Press, Inc., 26 MEDIA L. REP. (BNA) 2355, 2362 (E.D. Mich. 1998) (no tortious interference cause of action where plaintiff failed to allege that statements obtained in violation of federal wiretap act were false).

534. See Smith v. Daily Mail Publ'g Co., 443 U.S. 97, 103-04 (1979); chap.13-3(a) *supra*. See also NAACP v. Claiborne Hardware Co., 458 U.S. 886 (1982) (First Amendment right to petition precludes tortious interference claim); Searle v. Johnson, 709 P.2d 328 (Utah 1985) (First Amendment precludes tortious interference claim based on publicizing conditions at dog pound); Missouri v. NOW, 620 F.2d 1301 (8th Cir.), *cert. denied*, 449 U.S. 842 (1980) (First Amendment right to petition precludes claim for tortious interference arising from boycott).

535. 223 Cal. Rptr. 58, 63 (Ct. App. 1986).

bar to engage in the unauthorized and unlawful disclosure of information," in significant part because it concluded that "the newsgathering component of the freedom of the press — the right to seek out information — is privileged at least to the extent it involves 'routine ... reporting techniques" such as "asking persons questions, including those with confidential or restricted information."[536]

Other commentators have, however, suggested that existing law affords a colorable basis for a tortious interference claim in the newsgathering context, at least when a news source is provided meaningful consideration in exchange for disclosing information in breach of a confidentiality agreement.[537] While "routine reporting techniques" may well shelter under the First Amendment, it can be argued that the Supreme Court's decision in *Cohen v. Cowles Media Co.*[538] — with its admonition that "generally applicable laws do not offend the First Amendment simply because their enforcement against the press has incidental effects on its ability to gather and report the news"[539] — would permit a tortious interference claim to be pursued against the news media in the face of a constitutional challenge.[540]

§ 13-5. Stake Outs.

Watching the comings and goings of sources, chronicling the interactions between the subjects of the news and law enforcement, and simply observing the places that news subjects frequent have long been staples of the newsgathering process. Not surprisingly, therefore, these activities as well have fomented civil litigation against the press.

In one particularly notorious set of circumstances, a federal trial court held that a television station and newspaper were required to go to trial on claims, subsequently settled, brought on behalf of agents of the Bureau of Alcohol, Tobacco and Firearms ("ATF") killed or injured in a raid on facilities maintained by the Branch Davidian religious sect in Waco, Texas.[541] The plaintiffs alleged that the news media's conduct, in staking out the facility in anticipation

---

536. *Id.* See also Wells v. Marton, 794 F. Supp. 1092, 1097-98 (S.D. Fla. 1991) (dismissing tortious interference claim based on interview with source in violation of agreement giving plaintiff exclusive interview rights). But see Jews for Jesus, Inc. v. Jewish Community Relations Council, 968 F.2d 286 (2d Cir. 1992) (First Amendment does not preclude tortious interference claim based on illegal conduct).

537. See Kohler, *supra* note 526, at 11, 24; Russomanno & Youm, *supra* note 526, at 88-89.

538. 501 U.S. 663 (1991).

539. *Id.* at 669 (citing Branzburg v. Hayes, 408 U.S. 665 (1972)).

540. Kohler, *supra* note 526, at 11 ("Absent a clear defense under the First Amendment, the success of such a claim would likely turn on the degree to which the journalists encouraged or induced the source to disregard his agreement.").

541. See Risenhoover v. England, 936 F. Supp. 392 (W.D. Tex. 1996).

of the raid, recklessly endangered the lives of the agents by "tipping off" the Branch Davidians and leading to the subsequent and deadly confrontation between them and the ATF.[542]

At the time of the ATF raid, law enforcement authorities had erected no road blocks near the facility and made no effort to dissuade the news media, including marked vehicles, from moving freely and setting up at locations adjacent to the site of the forthcoming raid.[543] Nevertheless, the court concluded that the First Amendment did not "protect[ ] the media Defendants from liability for any claim for negligence associated with their newsgathering activities on the day of the raid."[544] Relying on the Supreme Court's decision in *Cohen v. Cowles Media Co.*,[545] the court held that the "Texas law of negligence is a law of general applicability," which does not "'target or single out the press'" and is "'generally applicable to the daily transactions of all citizens.'"[546] Accordingly, the court reasoned that defendants were "no more free to cause harm to others while gathering the news than any other individual," just as "it would be ludicrous to assume that the First Amendment would protect a reporter who negligently ran over a pedestrian while speeding merely because the reporter was on the way to cover a news story."[547]

Thus having dispensed with the First Amendment, the court proceeded to conclude that a reasonable jury could find that the defendants had acted negligently in staking out the Branch Davidian facility.[548] The court emphasized that "society," including the press, "has a duty not to interfere with a law enforcement officer during the course of [performing] his responsibilities."[549] In the court's view:

---

542. *Id.* at 401-03.

543. See *id.* at 402 (A journalist "stopped and approached the Trooper and asked if the road ahead were blocked off. The Trooper responded that he had not been assigned to prevent anyone from passing him. [The journalists] then passed the Trooper and parked behind Mulloney's KWTX vehicle. . . . Mulloney was outside of the vehicle filming at a location from which the Compound was visible.") (citations omitted).

544. *Id.* at 403.

545. 501 U.S. 663, 669-70 (1991).

546. Risenhoover v. England, 936 F. Supp. at 404 (quoting Cohen v. Cowles Media Co., 501 U.S. at 670).

547. Risenhoover v. England, 936 F. Supp. at 404.

548. *Id.* at 404-11. The court did note, however, that neither "party has identified any case from any jurisdiction that has held a journalist liable for negligence for actions taken during a law enforcement operation. Nor has the court been able to identify such a case." *Id.* at 405.

549. *Id.* at 407. The court also concluded that media defendants in these circumstances are not protected by the so-called "fireman's rule," which prevents fire and law enforcement officers in many jurisdictions from maintaining tort actions against the owners of property on which they are injured in the course of performing their duties. See *id.* at 405 (citing Carson v. Headrick, 900 S.W.2d 685, 687-88 (Tenn. 1995)).

> The media Defendants equally appreciated the risk of compromising the secrecy of the raid, and the likelihood that agents would be injured if that secrecy were compromised. They were aware that a raid was going to be conducted, and that the timing of the raid would not be disclosed. ATF had consistently refused to confirm a time or date for the raid. . . . Knowing of the violent nature of the Davidians, and the ATF's desire for secrecy, it was entirely foreseeable that a breach of that secrecy would increase the danger attendant upon serving the warrants upon the Davidians. The members of the media recognized that the officers would be harmed if secrecy were not maintained.[550]

Accordingly, the court concluded that the "actions of the Defendants in failing to exercise some degree of caution to avoid warning the Davidians of the impending raid" compounded "the risk that compromising the secrecy of the operation would result in death and injury to a number of law enforcement agents."[551]

Moreover, the court concluded that the defendants' conduct could reasonably be held to constitute a "proximate cause" of plaintiffs' death and injuries. As the court explained:

> The Compound is located in a rural area, with few close neighbors. . . . Across from the Compound are three or four small houses, whose inhabitants and their vehicles are readily visible from the Compound. The presence of strange vehicles on the road would certainly be noticed, particularly when there are a number of them and when they drive aimlessly up and down the road. . . .[552]

Under such circumstances, the court held, a reporter on the scene "should do everything possible to avoid detection when covering what is known to be a secret law enforcement operation."[553]

---

550. 936 F. Supp. at 407.

551. *Id.* at 408. In that regard, the court held that "the social utility of newsgathering in general is not at issue," and should not be weighed against the interest in preventing harm to law enforcement agents. *Id.* See also *id.* at 408 ("Clearly, demanding that the press act responsibly in such a unique situation will not 'chill' first amendment rights, no more so than demanding that any individual citizen act responsibly.").

552. *Id.*

553. *Id.* at 409. See *id.* ("The media arrogantly descended on the Compound as if the First Amendment cloaked them with immunity from acting as reasonable individuals under the circumstances. Their actions are particularly egregious when considered in light of the fact that they knew how dangerous [the Davidians] . . . were. . . ."). But cf. Duran v. Detroit News, Inc., 504 N.W.2d 715, 720 (Mich. App. 1993) (rejecting claim by former Columbian judge living anonymously in Detroit that publication of her name in newspaper, and television report filmed in front of her residence, endangered her life and caused her emotional distress; "defendants' conduct was not so outrageous or extreme to establish liability in tort in light of the fact that plaintiffs used their own names and did not attempt to completely hide their identities while in Detroit").

In *Wolfson v. Lewis*,[554] another federal court held that a television crew's conduct in staking out plaintiffs' residence and the home of their parents warranted preliminary injunctive relief.[555] Once again, the court concluded that the "First Amendment does not . . . shield the press from torts and crimes committed in the pursuit of a story,"[556] Accordingly, the defendants' newsgathering conduct — which consisted in significant part of filming plaintiffs' home from a driveway across the road and photographing and recording activities at plaintiffs' parents home from an adjacent waterway — was actionable as invasion of privacy by intrusion and warranted injunctive relief. Thus, the court held that, although defendants "characterize their activities as 'routine newsgathering' which is protected by the First Amendment . . . , [a] reasonable jury would likely conclude that it is difficult to understand how hounding, harassing, and ambushing the Wolfsons would advance the fundamental policies underlying the First Amendment."[557]

§ 13-6. Communications in the Newsgathering Process.

The law of defamation plays such a ubiquitous role in the legal life of the press, in the context of the content of publications and broadcasts,[558] that it is understandable if the potential for actionable defamation in the newsgathering process is often overlooked. Nevertheless, journalists do routinely talk about the prospective subjects of news reports with other sources in the course of newsgathering, and the statements they make have, on occasion, resulted in litigation wholly apart from anything ultimately published or broadcast to a mass audience. Moreover, other, nondefamatory statements made in the course of newsgathering have been the subject of tort claims as well.

---

554. 924 F. Supp. 1413 (E.D. Pa. 1996).

555. See Chap. 13-4(b) *supra* (discussing underlying facts).

556. Wolfson v. Lewis, 924 F. Supp. at 1417 (citing Galella v. Onassis, 353 F. Supp. 196 (S.D.N.Y. 1972), *aff'd in part*, 487 F.2d 986 (2d Cir. 1973); Dietemann v. Time, Inc., 449 F.2d 245, 249 (9th Cir. 1971)).

557. Wolfson v. Lewis, 924 F. Supp. at 1430-33. In *Wolfson*, the court appeared particularly troubled by the impact of the defendants' newsgathering activities on the plaintiffs' children, who were followed to school in unmarked vehicles and present in the residences that the defendants sought to film and record. See *id.* at 1422-31. In *Cramlet v. Multimedia, Inc.*, 11 MEDIA L. REP. (BNA) 1707 (D. Colo. 1985), another federal court affirmed a $5.9 million verdict, including $4.2 million in punitive damages, in favor of a mother whose child had been unlawfully taken from her by the child's father several months earlier. The defendant, a syndicated television interview program, "baby-sat" while the father appeared on the program, and refused to disclose the child's whereabouts. *Id.* at 1708. The court concluded that the "plaintiff presented sufficient evidence of [defendant's] conspiracy and outrageous conduct to support the jury's conclusions." *Id.* at 1709.

558. See generally R. SACK, LIBEL, SLANDER AND RELATED PROBLEMS (3d ed. 1999).

In *Machleder v. Diaz*,[559] for example, plaintiff alleged, *inter alia*, that a journalist slandered him when she telephoned various public authorities to inquire about what appeared to be barrels of toxic waste stored adjacent to plaintiff's property. Two government officials submitted affidavits indicating that the journalist had asked "something to the effect that 'were you aware that Flexcraft was dumping chemical waste in New Jersey?'"[560] Defendants sought to dismiss the slander claim on the ground that the statements were conditionally privileged at common law as "made in the public interest on an 'occasion when it was [her] duty to speak . . . in protection of some common interest.'"[561] The trial court denied the motion, holding that "the defamatory statements she allegedly made seem to bear no relation to the purpose of her call and may be unprivileged."[562] The jury, however, found in defendants' favor on the issue, a verdict from which the plaintiff did not take an appeal.[563]

In *Rifkin v. Esquire Publishing, Inc.*,[564] plaintiff alleged that a journalist had misrepresented that he had already interviewed the plaintiff and was his friend in an effort to secure an interview with certain third parties, including plaintiff's former wife. The court granted defendant's motion to dismiss his slander claim, which was based on plaintiff's contention that defendant's statements "were slanderous in that they were understood by the persons contacted to mean that plaintiff had broken his long standing policy of not making comments to the media," which allegedly "cast aspersions on his 'integrity, honesty, and lack of capriciousness.'"[565] The court, however, concluded that the statements were not reasonably capable of the asserted defamatory meaning.[566] In addition, the court held that plaintiff had failed to state a claim for invasion of privacy by intrusion. The court concluded that defendant's "attempts to gather information about plaintiff from third parties or elicit the assistance of third parties in contacting plaintiff, even if pursued using subterfuge and fraud, cannot constitute such an intrusion upon *plaintiff's* solitude or seclusion."[567]

In *Davis v. Schucat*,[568] the D.C. Circuit rejected an investigative reporter's claim that slander in the course of newsgathering should be entitled to absolute protection under the First Amendment. The plaintiff had, years earlier, been indicted for, but not convicted of, perjury.[569] The defendant, a freelance journal-

---

559. 538 F. Supp. 1364 (S.D.N.Y. 1982), *rev'd in part*, 801 F.2d 46 (2d Cir. 1986).
560. *Id.* at 1373.
561. *Id.* (quoting Coleman v. Newark Morning Ledger Co., 149 A.2d 193, 202 (N.J. 1959)).
562. 538 F. Supp. at 1374.
563. See Machleder v. Diaz, 801 F.2d 46, 51 (2d Cir. 1986).
564. 8 MEDIA L. REP. (BNA) 1384 (C.D. Cal. 1982).
565. *Id.* at 1387.
566. *Id.*
567. *Id.* at 1386.
568. 510 F.2d 731 (D.C. Cir. 1975).
569. *Id.* at 732.

ist investigating the plaintiff's role in certain insurance programs for the elderly, told two sources — who were business associates of the plaintiff — that plaintiff "'had been convicted of a felony.'"[570] Following a bench trial, the court concluded that the "statements were made maliciously and . . . in reckless disregard of the truth, pursuant to defendant's admitted technique of 'throwing a lot of things out in an interview just to get a response.'"[571]

The D.C. Circuit affirmed the trial court's award of one dollar in nominal compensatory damages and $1,500 in punitive damages; in so doing, it rejected the defendant's contention that "the First Amendment mandates a complete immunity from liability for a slander made to a limited number of people by a reporter in the ordinary course of his preparation of a news story on a subject of general or public interest."[572] Although the court's holding rested primarily on the ground that the defendant had not raised the issue at trial,[573] it also noted that the "fear of a slander action" has no greater "deterrent" effect on an investigative reporter than "fear of a libel action subsequent to publication."[574] Moreover, the court held there was no reason to conclude that "statements made in private cause less harm and are more easily rebutted than public statements."[575] Nevertheless, the court emphasized that its holding should not be read to "imply that a journalists' protection is in any way reduced when he speaks of a pubic figure in private" in the course of newsgathering.[576]

§ 13-7. Audio Recording.

§ 13-7(a). Federal Law.

§ 13-7(a)(1). Fourth Amendment Considerations.

The federal constitutional prohibition against unreasonable searches and seizures[577] renders unlawful the wiretapping of private communications by law

---

570. *Id.* at 733.
571. *Id.* (citing New York Times Co. v. Sullivan, 376 U.S. 254 (1964)).
572. 510 F.2d at 733.
573. *Id.* at 733-34
574. *Id.* at 734.
575. *Id.*
576. *Id.* at 734 n.3. See also American Broadcasting Cos. v. Gill, 1999 Tex. App. LEXIS 4449, at *54-57 (Tex. App. 1999) (granting summary judgment for libel defendants in connection with a number of allegedly defamatory statements made in the context of interviews with several sources for ultimate broadcast); Schermerhorn v. Rosenberg, 426 N.Y.S.2d 274, 284 (App. Div. 1980) (affirming jury verdict for state senator based, *inter alia*, on oral statement by reporter to other state senators alleging that plaintiff had made racially charged remarks to him during interview); Green v. Alton Tel. Printing Co., 438 N.E.2d 203 (Ill. App. 1982) ($9.2 million defamation judgment resulting from reporters' transmission of confidential memorandum, detailing fruits of their own investigation, to law enforcement officers).
577. U.S. CONST., amend. IV.

enforcement or other government employees acting without a valid search warrant.[578] Such unlawful recordings may be excluded from evidence in a criminal trial[579] and may be the basis for a civil action brought against the government and its employees.[580]

Fourth Amendment claims against journalists engaged in surreptitious recordings have not been successful. As a rule, journalists have been found not to have engaged in governmental action, a prerequisite to application of the Fourth Amendment.[581] In addition, several courts have declined to hold journalists liable for conspiring with law enforcement to violate the constitutional rights of a target of unlawful wiretapping.[582] Absent such a conspiracy, courts have concluded there is no basis to impose liability on the press pursuant to the Fourth Amendment.[583] The courts have also rejected Fourth Amendment claims, in media and nonmedia contexts alike, when one of the parties to the communication consents to its interception or recording.[584]

---

578. See Katz v. United States, 389 U.S. 347, 351-52 (1967) ("[T]he Fourth Amendment protects people, not places. What a person knowingly exposes to the public, even in his own home or office, is not a subject of fourth Amendment protection. . . . But what he seeks to preserve as private, even in an area accessible to the public, may be constitutionally protected."); United States v. Mankani, 738 F.2d 538, 542-44 (2d Cir. 1984); United States v. Bunkers, 521 F.2d 1217, 1219-20 (9th Cir.), *cert. denied*, 423 U.S. 989 (1975).

579. See Lee v. Florida, 392 U.S. 378 (1968).

580. See Bivens v. Six Unknown Named Agents, 403 U.S. 388 (1971).

581. See, e.g., Sheppard v. E.W. Scripps Co., 421 F.2d 555, 556 (6th Cir.), *cert. denied*, 400 U.S. 941 (1970); Levitch v. Columbia Broadcasting Sys., 495 F. Supp. 649, 657 (S.D.N.Y. 1980); Mimms v. Philadelphia Newspapers, Inc., 352 F. Supp. 862, 865 (E.D. Pa. 1972); Prahl v. Brosamle, 295 N.W.2d 768, 774 (Wis. App. 1980). But see Berger v. Hanlon, 129 F.3d 505, 515 (9th Cir. 1997), *vacated*, 119 S. Ct. 1706 (1999) ("the 'inextricable' involvement of the media with both the planning and execution of this search, the government's active involvement with the media's newsgathering activities, and the mutually-derived benefits, is more than enough to make the media government actors"). See generally Chap. 12-5 *supra*.

582. See, e.g., Reuber v. United States, 750 F.2d 1039, 1054-56 (D.C. Cir. 1984); Zerilli v. Evening News Ass'n, 628 F.2d 217, 223 n.11 (D.C. Cir. 1980); Benford v. American Broadcasting Cos., 502 F. Supp. 1159, 1161-62 (D. Md. 1980), *aff'd*, 661 F.2d 917 (4th Cir.), *cert. denied*, 454 U.S. 1060 (1981).

583. See In re Providence Journal Co., 820 F.2d 1342, 1350 (1st Cir. 1986), *modified*, 820 F.2d 1354 (1st Cir. 1987), *cert. dismissed*, 485 U.S. 693 (1988) (en banc). See also Dennis v. Sparks, 449 U.S. 24, 27-28 (1980); Adickes v. S.H. Kress & Co., 398 U.S. 144, 150-52 (1970); Phelps v. Wichita Eagle-Beacon, 886 F.2d 1262, 1270-71 (10th Cir. 1989); Cook v. Houston Post, 616 F.2d 791, 794 n.3 (5th Cir. 1980); Manax v. McNamara, 660 F. Supp. 657, 665 (W.D. Tex. 1987), *aff'd*, 842 F.2d 808, 810 (5th Cir. 1988); Pawelek v. Paramount Studios Corp., 571 F. Supp. 1082, 1084 (N.D. Ill. 1983); Baker v. Burlington County Times, 9 MEDIA L. REP. (BNA) 1967, 1967 (D.N.J. 1983).

584. See Osborn v. United States, 385 U.S. 323, 326 (1966); Benford v. American Broadcasting Cos., 502 F. Supp. 1159, 1161 (D. Md. 1980), *aff'd*, 661 F.2d 917 (4th Cir.), *cert. denied*, 454 U.S. 1060 (1981).

§ 13-7(a)(2). Federal Statutes.

Federal statutes prohibit certain forms of wiretapping. In so doing, they provide for both criminal and civil penalties.

§ 13-7(a)(2)(A). Federal Wiretap Act.

Following the Supreme Court's decision in *Katz v. United States*,[585] Congress quickly enacted legislation empowering law enforcement to undertake wiretapping of private communications with judicial authorization.[586] The legislation, popularly known as the Federal Wiretap Act,[587] specifically prohibits certain wiretapping and bugging by private parties, including the press.[588]

§ 13-7(a)(2)(A)(i). Prohibited Conduct.

The Wiretap Act prohibits the intentional interception, disclosure, or use of an oral, wire or electronic communication,[589] or the intentional use of a device to intercept an oral communication.[590] Generally, a violation of the Act may occur when (1) any electronic, mechanical or other device that is affixed,[591] or otherwise transmits a signal through wire,[592] cable or radio, is intentionally used to

---

585. 389 U.S. 347 (1967).

586. The Omnibus Crime Control and Safe Streets Act of 1968, Title III, addresses both wiretaps and bugging. See Pub. L. No. 90-351, 82 Stat. 212 (1968), as amended by Act of Oct. 15, 1970, Pub. L. No. 91-452, 84 Stat. 930 (1970) (codified at 18 U.S.C. §§ 2510-2520 (1976)). The Act was extensively modified by the Electronic Communications Privacy Act of 1986, Pub. L. No. 99-508, 100 Stat. 1848 (1986). That legislation, now titled the Wire and Electronic Communications Interception and Interception of Oral Communications Act, is codified at 18 U.S.C. §§ 2510-2522.

587. See Shubert v. Metrophone, Inc., 898 F.2d 401, 403 (3d Cir. 1990). R. NIMMER, INFORMATION LAW § 8.11 (1997).

588. 18 U.S.C. § 2511. For a discussion of the elements of the offense giving rise to liability under the Act, see Forsyth v. Barr, 19 F.3d 1527 (5th Cir.), *cert. denied*, 513 U.S. 871 (1994); Williams v. Poulos, 11 F.3d 271 (1st Cir. 1993); Stockler v. Garnett, 893 F.2d 856 (6th Cir. 1990).

589. The term "electronic communication" is defined as "any transfer of signs, writing, images, sounds, data, or intelligence of any nature transmitted in whole or in part by a wire, radio, electromagnetic, photo electronic or photo optical system that affects interstate or foreign commerce." 18 U.S.C. § 2510(12). The unintentional or inadvertent interception of a communication is not a violation of the statute. See Shubert v. Metrophone, Inc., 898 F.2d 401, 405 (3d Cir. 1990).

590. 18 U.S.C. § 2511(1).

591. The improper use of implants, or "bugs," is also a violation of the statute. See United States v. Anya, 779 F.2d 532 (9th Cir. 1985).

592. "Wire communication" is defined to include "any aural transfer made in whole or in part through the use of facilities for the transmission of communications by the aid of wire, cable, or other like connection between the point of origin and the point of reception (including the use of such connection in a switching station)." 18 U.S.C. § 2510(1).

intercept[593] an oral communication;[594] (2) the contents[595] of any wire, oral or electronic communication is intentionally disclosed;[596] or (3) the contents of any wire, oral or electronic communication is intentionally used, knowing that such communication was intercepted.[597]

The provisions of the Act prohibiting the intentional disclosure or use of the contents of illegally obtained communications, with knowledge or reason to know they were illegally obtained,[598] have generated increasing litigation implicating the news media. In that regard, courts have recognized that, where a communication has been obtained legally,[599] the publication of its contents does not violate the Act.[600] Application of this provision against a journalist who

---

593. Under the Federal Wiretap Act, "intercept" means "the aural or other acquisition of the contents of any wire, electronic, or oral communication through the use of any electronic, mechanical, or other device." *Id.* § 2510(4). See Steve Jackson Games, Inc. v. United States Secret Serv., 816 F. Supp. 432, 441-42 (W.D. Tex. 1993), *aff'd*, 36 F.3d 457 (5th Cir. 1994) (although the term "interception" should be construed broadly, it does not include the replaying of a recorded communication).

594. 18 U.S.C. § 2511(1)(b). "Oral communications" is defined as "any oral communication uttered by a person exhibiting an expectation that such communication is not subject to interception under circumstances justifying such expectation, but such term does not include any electronic communication." *Id.* § 2510(2). Where an oral communication occurs in the absence of a reasonable expectation of privacy, there is no violation. See Boddie v. American Broadcasting Cos., 731 F.2d 333, 338-39 (6th Cir. 1984), *on remand*, 694 F. Supp. 1304 (N.D. Ohio 1988), *aff'd*, 881 F.2d 267 (6th Cir. 1989), *cert. denied*, 493 U.S. 1028 (1990); Holman v. Central Arkansas Broadcasting Co., 610 F.2d 542, 544-45 (8th Cir. 1979).

595. "Content" is defined as "any information concerning the substance . . . of that communication." 18 U.S.C. § 2510(8).

596. *Id.* § 2511(1)(c). One who endeavors improperly to disclose the contents of any wire, oral or electronic communication to any other person is also in violation of the statute. *Id.*

597. *Id.* § 2511(1)(d). At least one court has held that there is a difference between stored communications and intercepted communications under the Act. See Steve Jackson Games, Inc. v. United States Secret Serv., 816 F. Supp. 432 (W.D. Tex. 1993), *aff'd*, 36 F.3d 457 (5th Cir. 1994) (court found that e-mail is stored electronic communication; therefore, seizure of computer containing e-mail is not unlawful under Federal Wiretap Act).

598. 18 U.S.C. § 2511(1)(c) & (d).

599. See, e.g., Smith v. Cincinnati Post & Times-Star, 475 F.2d 740, 741 (6th Cir. 1973); Peavy v. New Times, Inc., 976 F. Supp. 532 (N.D. Tex. 1997) (obtaining the communication through an open records request for the transcript of a public meeting). Lawful conduct includes obtaining the communication through a proper FOIA request, see, e.g., In re Providence Journal Co., 820 F.2d 1342, 1349-50 (1st Cir. 1986), *modified*, 820 F.2d 1354 (1st Cir. 1987), *cert. dismissed*, 485 U.S. 693 (1988) (en banc), or where the communication occurred prior to the effective date of the Act, see, e.g., Zerilli v. Evening News Ass'n, 628 F.2d 217, 219-22 (D.C. Cir. 1980).

600. See Boettger v. Loverro, 587 A.2d 712 (Pa. 1991) (publication of contents of wiretap transcripts in court files not actionable); Peavy v. New Times, Inc., 976 F. Supp. 532 (N.D. Tex. 1997) (publication of transcript of wiretapped conversations that were read into minutes of public school board meeting not actionable). Cf. Boehner v. McDermott, 1999 U.S. App. LEXIS 23135, *9-21 (D.C. Cir. Sept. 24, 1999) (holding that Congressman's dissemination of tape of illegally

obtained the information lawfully is of doubtful constitutionality in light of the *Cox Broadcasting Corp.–Florida Star* line of cases, in which the Supreme Court has protected the publication of lawfully obtained truthful information.[601]

In *Natoli v. Sullivan*,[602] however, a local daily newspaper and a student university newspaper both received a tape recording of an illegally intercepted private communication. Each of the newspapers, knowing the recording's origins, published its contents. The parties to the illegally recorded conversations sued the newspapers pursuant to the civil remedies provisions of the Wiretap Act.[603] A New York trial court concluded that knowing disclosure of the contents of the illegal interception by the newspapers violated the Wiretap Act, even though the newspapers did not participate in the illegal interception or recordation of the private communication.[604]

The newspapers argued that the First Amendment prohibited an award of damages based on their publication of truthful information contained in the recorded conversations. The court, however, interpreted the *Cox Broadcasting*

---

recorded cellular telephone conversation to news media in violation of federal and state wiretap statutes not protected by First Amendment).

601. See The Florida Star v. B.J.F., 491 U.S. 524 (1989); Smith v. Daily Mail Publ'g Co., 443 U.S. 97 (1979); Landmark Communications, Inc. v. Virginia, 435 U.S. 829 (1978); Oklahoma Publ'g Co. v. District Ct., 430 U.S. 308 (1977); Cox Broadcasting Corp. v. Cohn, 420 U.S. 469 (1975); see also Gardner v. Bradenton Herald, 413 So. 2d 10 (Fla.), *cert. denied*, 459 U.S. 865 (1982) (striking down statute prohibiting publication of name of wiretap subject prior to indictment); Chap. 13-3(a) *supra*. But see Boehner v. McDermott, 1999 U.S. App. LEXIS 23135, *12, *29, *45 (D.C. Cir. Sept. 24, 1999) (court declined to address whether newspapers that published contents of illegally intercepted cellular telephone call could be held liable under federal and state wiretap statutes, but concluded that Congressman who received copy of tape and provided it to newspapers was not protected by First Amendment from civil liability); United States v. Fuller, 202 F. Supp. 356 (N.D. Cal. 1962) (court refused to dismiss indictment for disclosing police and fire department radio messages to radio station, rejecting First Amendment defense).

602. 606 N.Y.S.2d 504 (Sup. Ct. 1993), *aff'd*, 616 N.Y.S.2d 318 (App. Div. 1994). The court reached a different result in a suit based on a state wiretap law in *Boettger v. Loverro*, 502 A.2d 1310 (Pa. Super. 1986), *rev'd*, 555 A.2d 1234 (Pa.), 493 U.S. 885 (1989), *on remand*, 587 A.2d 712 (Pa. 1991). See Chap. 13-3(a) *supra*.

603. See 18 U.S.C. § 2520. In the alternative, the plaintiffs claimed a violation of 47 U.S.C. § 605 arising from the alleged interception of radio communications. See 606 N.Y.S.2d at 507.

604. See 606 N.Y.S.2d at 507 ("The disclosure and use of the contents of intercepted communications where the individual knows or should know of the unauthorized interception is prohibited and is subject to the same sanctions as the interception itself."). See also Bartnicki v. Vopper, No. 3:CV-94-1201, slip. op. at 7, 8 (M.D. Pa. June 17, 1996) (distinguishing *The Florida Star* on ground that Wiretap Act "does not single out the press"). But see Ferrara v. Detroit Free Press, 26 MEDIA L. REP. (BNA) 2355 (E.D. Mich. 1998) (publication of comments made in phone conversation between plaintiff and her husband, and taped by husband, not actionable against reporter who did not know that interception had been made in violation of statute); Mayes v. Lin Television of Texas, Inc., 27 MEDIA L. REP. (BNA) 1214, 1220 (N.D. Tex. 1998) (defendants not liable under federal wiretap statute where plaintiffs "have failed to raise a fact issue as to the requisite knowledge of [defendant] of the tape's illegality").

Corp.–Florida Star line of cases as rejecting a general rule absolving the news media from liability in all such instances. Instead, the court viewed the Supreme Court decisions as limited to occasions where the published information had been part of the public record, albeit placed there in contravention of applicable law.[605] In contrast, the *Natoli* court found the recording at issue was unlawfully made by a private party, was in private hands, and presented "no overriding interest in open government to be protected, nor reliance upon the government's having placed the information in the public domain."[606] As a result, the court struck a balance favoring the individual's interest in privacy protected by the Wiretap Act:

> In permitting the maintenance of these causes of action against the newspapers, the danger of chilling journalism, or generating overdeterrence and an atmosphere of "timidity and self-censorship," is minimal. Here, the newspapers knew they were dealing with recorded conversations between unconsenting parties. The rule prohibiting the publication of the contents of illegal wiretaps or other electronic surveillance with knowledge of the illegality has sufficiently defined parameters to be readily understood and applied.[607]

---

605. 606 N.Y.S.2d at 509.

606. *Id.*

607. *Id.* at 510 (citation omitted). See also Boehner v. McDermott, 1999 U.S. App. LEXIS 23135, *12 (D.C. Cir. Sept. 24, 1999). In *Boehner*, Congressman John Boehner instituted a civil action, under 18 U.S.C. § 511(1)(c), against Congressman James McDermott after McDermott distributed to three newspapers copies of an unlawfully intercepted cellular telephone conversation to which Boehner was a party. The call, which also included several Republican members of the House of Representatives, had been intercepted by a Florida couple who taped it and provided a copy to McDermott, a Democrat. The couple subsequently pled guilty to violating the Federal Wiretap Act and each was fined $500. See 1999 U.S. App. LEXIS 23135, at *6. The district court dismissed Boehner's civil action, holding that, although the tape was unlawfully obtained in the first instance by the Florida couple, neither the federal nor Florida's wiretap statute could constitutionally prohibit McDermott's initial receipt of it. See Boehner v. McDermott, 1998 U.S. Dist. LEXIS 11509, *11 (D.D.C. July 28, 1998) ("information not illegally acquired is lawfully obtained, even though its source may have obtained it illegally," and is therefore protected by the First Amendment).

The District of Columbia Circuit reversed. See Boehner v. McDermott, 1999 U.S. App. LEXIS 23135 (D.C. Cir. Sept. 24, 1999). A divided court concluded that the strict scrutiny contemplated by *The Florida Star v. B.J.F.*, 491 U.S. 524 (1989), was not appropriate, albeit for different reasons. See Boehner v. McDermott, 1999 U.S. App. LEXIS 23135, at *9-21 (opinion of Randolph, J.) (asserting that McDermott's transmission of the tape to the newspapers was not "speech," but rather conduct that included some "'communicative element'") (quoting United States v. O'Brien, 391 U.S. 367, 376 (1968)); 1999 U.S. App. LEXIS, at *49-55 (Ginsburg, J., concurring) (asserting that McDermott had participated in an "illegal transaction" that rendered strict scrutiny under *The Florida Star* inappropriate). Accordingly, the court's majority undertook the "intermediate scrutiny" articulated in *O'Brien* and concluded that the nondisclosure provisions of the Federal Wiretap Act were constitutional as applied to McDermott since (1) the Act's promotion of the

Several federal district courts have, however, reached a different result.[608] In *Peavy v. New Times, Inc.*,[609] for example, a former public school board trustee brought suit against a weekly newspaper and its editor alleging that they violated the federal wiretap statute by publishing a transcript of wiretapped conversations during which Peavy made racial slurs and profane comments. Copies of the audio tape containing the intercepted telephone conversations had been delivered by the anonymous recorder to several fellow school board members. A written transcript of the tape was thereafter read into the minutes of a public meeting of the school board by two trustees. The newspaper obtained a copy of the minutes through a formal request under the state's public records act.

The district court held that the federal wiretap statute could not be constitutionally applied to punish the accurate publication of transcripts of a telephone conversation obtained from school board minutes open to public inspection. The court applied the three-part test articulated by the Supreme Court in *Smith v. Daily Mail Publishing Co.*[610] First, it found that, while the original tape may have been obtained illegally, the newspaper secured the transcript lawfully from school board records open to the public. The court further determined that the racist views of an elected official constitute a matter of public concern:[611]

> The school board meeting embodies the spirit of local government. The public's interest in open government begins at this, the local level. It is in

---

freedom to engage in nonintercepted private speech and the congressional intent "to dry up the market" in illegally intercepted information constitute substantial governmental interests; and (2) whatever incidental restriction on speech is imposed by application of § 2511(1)(c) in this context is no greater than necessary to further these substantial interests. 1999 U.S. App. LEXIS 23135, at *15-20. See *id.* at *21 ("Unless disclosure is prohibited, there will be an incentive for illegal interceptions; and unless disclosure is prohibited, the damage caused by an illegal interception will be compounded. It is not enough to prohibit disclosure only by those who conduct the unlawful eavesdropping.... It was therefore 'essential' for Congress to impose upon ... those not responsible for the interception, a duty of nondisclosure."). The majority affirmatively declined to consider whether § 2511(1)(c) could be constitutionally applied against the press, see 1999 U.S. App. LEXIS 23135, at *12, *29, *45, and Judge Sentelle dissented, on the ground that *The Florida Star* mandated that application of the statute to McDermott be subjected to strict scrutiny under the First Amendment, see *id.* at *56-72 (Sentelle, J., dissenting).

608. See, e.g., Peavy v. New Times, Inc., 976 F. Supp. 532 (N.D. Tex. 1997); Ferrara v. Detroit Free Press, Inc., 26 MEDIA L. REP. (BNA) 2355 (E.D. Mich. 1998); Mayes v. Lin Television of Texas, Inc., 27 MEDIA L. REP. (BNA) 1214, 1220 (N.D. Tex. 1998); Oliver v. WFAA-TV, Inc., 37 F. Supp. 2d 495 (N.D. Tex. 1998); Central Newspapers, Inc. v. Johnson, 722 So. 2d 1224 (La. App. 1998). But see Bartnicki v. Vopper, No. 3:CV-94-1201, slip. op. at 7, 8 (M.D. Pa. June 17, 1996).

609. 976 F. Supp. 532 (N.D. Tex. 1997).

610. 443 U.S. 97 (1979). The district court noted the earlier decision in *Natoli v. Sullivan*, but did not view it as persuasive authority because the case dealt with purely private information, with no public interest served by its revelation, and was decided in a different procedural context. 976 F. Supp. at 538 n.23.

611. 976 F. Supp. at 538.

this arena that citizen participation arguably has the greatest impact. Such participation would not be possible in the absence of the accurate reporting of the proceeding. Public records are, by their very nature, "of interest to those concerned with the administration of government, and a public benefit is performed by the reporting of the true contents of the records by the media. The freedom of the press to publish that information appears to be of critical importance to our type of government in which the citizenry is the final judge of the proper conduct of public business."[612]

Second, the court held that imposing liability on the newspaper would not serve the requisite need to further a state interest of the highest order because the statutory privacy interests of an elected official were less than compelling.[613] Third, the court found that punishing the newspaper for publishing the transcript would result in self-censorship.[614]

The court therefore granted the newspaper's motion for summary judgment, finding that liability could not be constitutionally imposed under the federal wiretap statute on media defendants who publish truthful information obtained from a transcript of a public meeting, even though the media defendants may have known that the information had been illegally obtained by someone else.[615] "Once true information is disclosed in public school board documents open by law to public inspection, the press cannot be sanctioned for publishing that information. Any other conclusion would fly in the face of the First Amendment, which will not 'allow exposing the press to liability for truthfully publishing information released to the public in official . . . records.'"[616]

In a later proceeding,[617] Peavy pursued state and federal wiretap claims against media defendants who received audiotapes of Peavy's phone conversations and used information obtained from them in an investigation into alleged corrupt practices by Peavy in his capacity as a public official. While sustaining the wiretap and privacy claims against Peavy's neighbors, who had recorded the conversations and provided the tapes to the press, the court granted summary judgment for the media defendants. The court held that the wiretap claims were precluded by the First Amendment, even though the reporter knowingly used and disclosed the illegally intercepted communications, because they constituted lawfully obtained, truthful information about a matter of public significance: "[I]t is not incumbent upon the media to determine whether information provided by a source has been derived through legal means," the court concluded, as long

---

612. *Id.* at 539 (quoting Cox Broadcasting Corp. v. Cohn, 420 U.S. 469, 495 (1975)).
613. 976 F. Supp. at 539.
614. *Id.* at 540.
615. *Id.*
616. *Id.* (quoting Cox Broadcasting Corp. v. Cohn, 420 U.S. 469, 496 (1975)).
617. See Oliver v. WFAA-TV, Inc., 37 F. Supp. 2d 495 (N.D. Tex. 1998).

as the media does not participate in the unlawful interception.[618] In this case, the press had done no more than accept the neighbor's offer to provide copies of the tapes, and then suggested, in the interests of authenticity, that the tapes should not be edited. Such conduct, the court found, fell within the bounds of legitimate newsgathering activities, and the information obtained thereby was "lawfully obtained."[619] To require anything more "would undoubtedly result in 'timidity and self-censorship.'"[620] The court acknowledged that the wiretap laws implicate privacy interests, but concluded that they did not rise to the level of state interests of the highest order: "While such statutory rights are certainly important, they fare poorly against the constitutional rights of a free and unfettered press."[621]

§ 13-7(a)(2)(A)(ii). Restricted Equipment.

Use of a conventional extension telephone does not fall within the prohibitions of the Wiretap Act,[622] nor does the use of a video camera.[623] The radio portion of cordless communications[624] and cellular communications, however, are subject to the Act.[625] The Act prohibits the use of devices such as pen registers[626] or trap and trace devices, except for operational management of commu-

---

618. *Id.* at 516.
619. *Id.* at 517.
620. *Id.* (quoting The Florida Star v. B.J.F., 491 U.S. 524, 535 (1989)).
621. 37 F. Supp. 2d at 517.
622. See Williams v. Poulos, 11 F.3d 271, 279-80 (1st Cir. 1993).
623. See United States v. Torres, 751 F.2d 875 (7th Cir. 1984) (video surveillance is not aural, so video cameras do not qualify as a surveillance device under the Wiretap Act). See Chap. 13-8 *infra*; United States v. Koyomejian, 970 F.2d 536 (9th Cir. 1992) (Wiretap Act does not regulate silent video surveillance).
624. See Communications Assistance for Law Enforcement Act, Pub. L. No. 103-414, § 202(a), 108 Stat. 4279 (1994); Askin v. McNulty, 47 F.3d 100, 102-03 (4th Cir.), *cert. denied*, 516 U.S. 944 (1995); McKamey v. Roach, 55 F.3d 1236 (6th Cir. 1995).
625. 18 U.S.C. § 2510(1). See S. REP. NO. 99-541, at 11 (1986). Cellular telephone subscribers, concerned about the ease with which cellular communications can be intercepted, unsuccessfully attempted to invoke the Wiretap Act's prohibition against divulging the contents of such communications as a means of compelling cellular telephone providers to scramble or encrypt their cellular communications. See Shubert v. Metrophone, Inc., 898 F.2d 401 (3d Cir. 1990). The Third Circuit held that, although cellular communications may be easily intercepted, cellular service providers who fail to provide scrambling or encryption have not intentionally divulged the contents of the communications. *Id.* at 405-06. See also Brown v. Waddell, 50 F.3d 285 (4th Cir. 1995) (using pager clones to intercept numeric transmission sent to digital display pager held subject to the Act). See generally Crook, *Sorry, Wrong Number: The Effect of Telephone Technology on Privacy Rights*, 26 WAKE FOREST L. REV. 669 (1991).
626. A pen register is "a mechanical device that records the numbers dialed on a telephone by monitoring the electrical impulses caused when the dial on the telephone is released." Smith v. Maryland, 442 U.S. 735, 736 n.1 (1979). The Supreme Court has determined that the use of a pen register does not implicate a constitutional privacy interest. *Id.* at 742-45.

nications systems,[627] without first obtaining a court order[628] or pursuant to the Foreign Intelligence Surveillance Act.[629] The Wiretap Act also prohibits the unauthorized interception of satellite transmissions.[630]

§ 13-7(a)(2)(A)(iii). The Qualified One-Party Consent Exception.

The Wiretap Act sets forth several exceptions that permit the interception and use of communications.[631] The most important protection, for journalists, is the Act's qualified one-party consent exception. The Act permits the interception or recording of a communication by either the originator or recipient of the communication, or anyone acting with the prior consent of either.[632] Where the person intercepting the communication is either a party to the communication or receives prior consent from such a party, no violation has occurred.[633] This exception permits a journalist to intercept or record her own communications and to work with a source who consents to the interception or recording of the source's communications with third parties.

Nevertheless, the exception is not available if the purpose of the interception is the commission of any criminal or tortious act and the interception otherwise

---

627. See 18 U.S.C. § 3121.

628. Court orders to intercept communications may be obtained pursuant to 18 U.S.C. § 3123.

629. See 50 U.S.C. § 1801. See generally Cinquegrana, *Walls (and Wires) Have Ears: The Background and First Ten Years of the Foreign Intelligence Surveillance Act of 1978*, 137 U. PA. L. REV. 793 (1989).

630. See 28 U.S.C. § 2511(4) & (5).

631. These include exceptions for switchboard operation, providers of communication services, FCC regulators, a person acting under color of law, foreign intelligence activities, electronic communications to the public and prior one-party consent. 18 U.S.C. § 2511(2). See Benford v. American Broadcasting Cos., 502 F. Supp. 1159, 1162 (D. Md. 1980), *aff'd*, 661 F.2d 917 (4th Cir.), *cert. denied*, 454 U.S. 1060 (1981) (statutory exception permitting the interception of a communication while acting under color of law would be available to television network journalist if the only purpose in intercepting a communication was to aid congressional subcommittee investigating practices of the insurance industry); Berger v. Hanlon, 129 F.3d 505 (9th Cir. 1997), *vacated*, 119 S. Ct. 1706 (1999), *aff'd*, 1999 U.S. App. LEXIS 20262 (9th Cir. Aug. 27, 1999) (members of media were acting under color of law, coming within the exception codified at 18 U.S.C. § 2511(2)(c), when they wired federal agent with hidden microphone).

632. 18 U.S.C. § 2511(2)(d). For a discussion of what constitutes "consent" under the Act, see United States v. Lanoue, 71 F.3d 966 (1st Cir. 1995) (consent must be determined under totality of circumstances); United States v. Barone, 913 F.2d 46 (2d. Cir. 1990); United States v. Davanzo, 699 F.2d 1097 (11th Cir. 1983); United States v. Wright, 573 F.2d 681 (1st Cir.), *cert. denied*, 436 U.S. 949 (1978).

633. See Manufacturas Internationale, LTDA v. Manufacturers Hanover Trust Co., 792 F. Supp. 180, 192 (E.D.N.Y. 1992), *aff'd*, 47 F.3d 1159 (2d Cir.), *cert. denied*, 515 U.S. 1132 (1995); Deteresa v. American Broadcasting Co., 121 F.3d 460, 466-67 (9th Cir. 1997), *cert. denied*, 118 S. Ct. 1840 (1998); Berger v. Hanlon, 129 F.3d 505, 516 (9th Cir. 1997), *vacated*, 119 S. Ct. 1706 (1999) *aff'd*, 1999 U.S. App. LEXIS 20262 (9th Cir. Aug. 27, 1999).

violates the Act.[634] Courts have, however, declined to consider subsequent torts associated with the broadcast of information obtained from the interception or recording sufficient to overcome the statutory exception.[635]

---

634. 18 U.S.C. § 2511(2)(d). See Sussman v. American Broadcasting Cos., 1999 U.S. App. LEXIS 19646, at *4-5 (9th Cir. Aug. 18, 1999) ("Where the taping is legal, but is done for the purpose of facilitating some further impropriety, such as blackmail, section 2511 applies. Where the purpose is not illegal or tortious, but the means are, the victims must seek redress elsewhere."); Desnick v. American Broadcasting Cos., 44 F.3d 1345 (7th Cir. 1995) (surreptitious video and audio taping at eye clinic was not a crime or tort); Russell v. American Broadcasting Cos., 23 MEDIA L. REP. (BNA) 2428, 2430-31 (N.D. Ill. 1995) (use of hidden camera and microphone to record journalist's conversations with store manager was not a crime as it did not violate the Illinois eavesdropping statute); Brooks v. American Broadcasting Cos., 737 F. Supp. 431, 437 (N.D. Ohio 1990), *aff'd in part*, 932 F.2d 495 (6th Cir. 1991) (recording of conversation on public street held not to be an interception for the purpose of committing a criminal act because the recording did not violate state surveillance law). Cf. Ferrara v. Detroit Free Press, Inc., 26 MEDIA L. REP. (BNA) 2355 (E.D. Mich. 1998) (taping of phone conversation in order to use recording to blackmail other party to communication negates consent). An earlier version of the Act vitiated the single-party consent defense where the interception was for the purpose of committing "any other injurious act." 18 U.S.C. § 2511(2)(d) (1970). After one court declared the phrase "any other injurious act" to be unconstitutionally vague, see Boddie v. American Broadcasting Cos., 881 F.2d 267 (6th Cir. 1989), *cert. denied*, 493 U.S. 1028 (1990) (journalist who recorded conversation with purpose to embarrass the subject might have engaged in an "injurious act"), and other courts had held that the purpose of the journalist in intercepting a communication was a question of fact, see Benford v. American Broadcasting Cos., 502 F. Supp. 1159 (D. Md. 1980), *aff'd*, 661 F.2d 917 (4th Cir.), *cert. denied*, 454 U.S. 1060 (1981); Brown v. American Broadcasting Cos., 704 F.2d 1296 (4th Cir. 1983), Congress deleted the "injurious act" language from the Act, thereby overruling these cases. See Electronics Communications Privacy Act of 1986, P.L. 99-508, 100 Stat. 825 (1986); S. REP. NO. 99-541, at 15 (1986).

635. See, e.g., Sussman v. American Broadcasting Cos., 1999 U.S. App. LEXIS 19646, at *4 (9th Cir. Aug. 18, 1999) (although tortious use of tape recording could violate section 2511, plaintiffs had "pointed to no state statute or caselaw indicating that it was tortious or illegal for ABC to air the tapings" at issue); Desnick v. American Broadcasting Cos., 44 F.3d 1345, 1353 (7th Cir. 1995) (allegation of defamation by subsequent broadcast); Russell v. American Broadcasting Cos., 23 MEDIA L. REP. (BNA) 2428, 2431 (N.D. Ill. 1995) (allegation of false light invasion of privacy by subsequent broadcast) ("*Desnick* instructs that the critical question under section 2511(2)(d) is *why* the communication was intercepted, not *how* the recording was ultimately used."). Cf. Medical Lab. Management Consultants v. ABC, Inc., 25 MEDIA L. REP. (BNA) 1724 (D. Ariz. 1997) ("[W]hile the *Desnick* court did uphold the trial court's dismissal for failure to state a claim . . . where plaintiffs alleged only invasion of privacy and intentional defamation, Plaintiffs in this action have alleged more relevant facts and causes of action, including an allegation that Defendants intended to steal trade secrets."); Medical Lab. Management Consultants v. American Broadcasting Cos., 30 F. Supp. 2d 1182, 1205 (D. Ariz. (1998) ("Even if Defendants were found liable for fraud, the question is not whether they are ultimately liable for conduct found to be tortious, but whether, at the time the recording took place, they recorded the conversations with the express intent of committing a tort.").

§ 13-7(a)(2)(A)(iv). Sanctions and Remedies.

The Act provides for both criminal[636] and civil[637] penalties.[638] Criminal sanctions include imprisonment,[639] fines,[640] and injunctive relief.[641] In a civil action brought under the Act, a successful plaintiff may recover actual damages, the violator's profits, punitive damages, attorneys fees and litigation costs.[642]

Injunctive relief is also available under the Act.[643] Indeed, in *In re King World Productions, Inc.*,[644] a physician who had been surreptitiously recorded in his office by a nationally syndicated news program obtained an injunction against the broadcast of the resulting videotape from a trial court. The Sixth Circuit, however, directed the district court to vacate its temporary restraining order, holding that the Wiretap Act does not authorize a prior restraint "even if the press's conduct clearly violates § 2511."[645] The court of appeals concluded that "[p]rotection of the right to information that appeals to the public at large and which is disseminated by the media is the cornerstone of the free press clause of the first amendment. No matter how inappropriate the acquisition, or its correctness, the right to disseminate that information is what the Constitution intended to protect."[646]

---

636. 18 U.S.C. § 2511(4)-(5).
637. *Id.* § 2520.
638. See Deal v. Spears, 980 F.2d 1153 (8th Cir. 1992).
639. Violation of the Wiretap Act may result in imprisonment for up to five years. 18 U.S.C. § 2511(4)-(5).
640. *Id.* § 2511 (4)-(5) (authorizing fines up to $250,000 for an individual and $500,000 for an organization).
641. *Id.* §§ 2511(5)(b), 2521.
642. *Id.* § 2520; see Jacobson v. Rose, 592 F.2d 515 (9th Cir. 1978), *cert. denied*, 442 U.S. 930 (1979) (for punitive damages to be awarded, plaintiff must show defendant acted wantonly, recklessly, or maliciously); Deal v. Spears, 980 F.2d 1153 (8th Cir. 1992); Romano v. Terdik, 939 F. Supp. 144 (D. Conn. 1996); Shaver v. Shaver, 799 F. Supp. 576 (E.D.N.C. 1992) (federal courts have discretion as to whether to award damages or attorney fees under the Act); Campiti v. Walonis, 467 F. Supp. 464 (D. Mass. 1979). Damages are available in an amount that is the greater of (1) the sum of the actual damages suffered by the plaintiff and any profits made by the defendant resulting from the violation, or (2) statutory damages of $100 per day for each day of the violation or $10,000, whichever is greater. 18 U.S.C. § 2520(c)(2); see Bess v. Bess, 929 F.2d 1332 (8th Cir. 1991); Rogers v. Wood, 910 F.2d 444, 448 (7th Cir. 1990).
643. 18 U.S.C. § 2520.
644. 898 F.2d 56 (6th Cir. 1990).
645. *Id.* at 59.
646. *Id.* Accord Charter Behavioral Health Sys., L.L.C. v. CBS Inc., No. 3:99-CV-150-MU (W.D.N.C. Apr. 21, 1999) ("prior restraint is all but impossible even where, as in this case, it appears that the press may well have set out to and committed a federal crime in order to obtain the information").

§ 13-7(a)(2)(B). Federal Communications Act.

The Federal Communications Act prohibits the monitoring and divulging of nonpublic[647] radio broadcasts.[648] Violations of Section 605 of the Act, which contains these provisions, may lead to criminal punishment[649] and civil liability.[650] Interceptions authorized under the Wiretap Act are lawful under the Communications Act as well.[651]

The only reported case instituted against the press or its sources under Section 605 of the Communications Act is *United States v. Fuller*,[652] which arose from the unauthorized disclosure of the contents of a nonpublic radio transmission. The prosecution was instituted against a source who regularly intercepted police and fire department radio messages and reported them to an Oakland radio station. The defendant unsuccessfully claimed that the First Amendment protected such disclosure of newsworthy information, particularly when the information was available to anyone listening to the emergency frequencies.[653] The court also rejected the defendant's argument that the anti-censorship provision of the Communications Act[654] prohibited the indictment, limiting that statutory provision to actions initiated by the FCC.[655]

Fuller arose at a time of heightened concerns that the interception of emergency broadcasts by the news media attracted crowds to the scene of emergen-

---

647. Nonpublic broadcasts include emergency transmissions by fire and police, as well as satellite and subscription television transmissions. See United States v. Fuller, 202 F. Supp. 356 (N.D. Cal. 1962); Chartwell Communications Group v. Westbrook, 637 F.2d 459 (6th Cir. 1980).

648. 47 U.S.C. § 605. See generally Bookshester & Gilbert, *Legal Minefield of Electronic Newsgathering*, 13 COMM. LAW. 11 (Spring 1995).

649. Violation of 47 U.S.C. § 605 is punishable by a fine up to $2,000, six months in prison, or both. 47 U.S.C. § 605(e)(1). The punishment may be increased to a $100,000 fine, five years in prison, or both, if the violation was undertaken for "commercial advantage or private financial gain." *Id.* § 605(e)(2).

650. A successful plaintiff may elect to recover actual damages and the profits of the violator, or statutory damages of between $1,000 and $10,000. *Id.* § 605(e)(3)(C)(i). Attorneys fees are also recoverable. *Id.* § 605(e)(3)(C)(iii).

651. *Id.* § 605(a); see Edwards v. State Farm Ins. Co., 833 F.2d 535, 537-38 (5th Cir. 1987); Zerilli v. Evening News Ass'n, 628 F.2d 217, 221 & n.7 (D.C. Cir. 1980); Pub. L. 90-351, 82 Stat. 223 (1968).

652. 202 F. Supp. 356, 356-57 (N.D. Cal. 1962).

653. See *id.* at 357-59 ("It is not unreasonable to conclude that Congress by the inclusion of Section 605 in the Act intended to protect messages of public safety radio services from interception and divulgement by any person, including the press, until the public safety agency using the means of communication authorized the release of the message.").

654. See 47 U.S.C. § 326 ("Nothing in this chapter shall be understood or construed to give the Commission the power of censorship over the radio communications or signals transmitted by any radio station, and no regulation or condition shall be promulgated or fixed by the commission which shall interfere with the right of free speech by means of radio communication.").

655. 202 F. Supp. at 360 ("[T]he Commission is not the charging party, and defendant's possible criminal liability stems from the statute, not any act or regulation of the Commission.").

cies, hampered the movement of emergency vehicles, and assisted the escape of fugitives.[656] The FCC again expressed its concern about press access to and use of nonpublic radio transmissions in the wake of a series of airplane hijackings in the 1970s.[657] At that time, the FCC interpreted Section 605 to prohibit the monitoring and divulging of Federal Aviation Administration communications that had been broadcast to the public on the ground that the dissemination of FAA transmissions created a danger to airline passengers and hampered law enforcement.[658]

§ 13-7(a)(2)(C). Federal Communications Commission Regulations.

The FCC has adopted regulations prohibiting the use of certain licensed transmitting devices,[659] such as wireless microphones,[660] "for the purpose of overhearing or recording the private conversations of the other person unless such use is authorized by all of the parties engaging in the conversation."[661] This all-party consent requirement is not applicable to conversations overheard in public or semi-public places.[662] Whether the FCC has the authority to issue more restrictive regulations than the prohibitions of the Wiretap Act has been questioned.[663]

The FCC has held that the transmissions of amateur radio stations[664] and citizens band radios, may be monitored and divulged.[665] The contents of transmissions of police and fire departments,[666] the Federal Aviation Administra-

---

656. See, e.g., *Monitoring of Police and Fire Radio Transmissions by Broadcast Stations*, 1 RAD. REG. 2d (P&F) 291, 292 (1963) ("Because of their ability to report news instantaneously, broadcast stations, even apart from the prohibitions of Section 605, have a responsibility beyond that of other news media to make sure that their news bulletins do not compromise the public safety.").

657. See *Unauthorized Broadcast of Federal Aviation Communications by Broadcast and Other Federal Communications Commission Licensees*, 74 F.C.C.2d 615 (1972).

658. *Id.*

659. The prohibition applies to any device required to be licensed by 47 U.S.C. § 301. See 47 C.F.R. §§ 15.4(f), 15.104 & 15.154.

660. *Id.* § 15.9.

661. *Id.* §§ 15.4(f), 15.104, 15.154, 2.701(a), 15.11(a) & 73.1206. See Brooks v. American Broadcasting Cos., 737 F. Supp. 431, 437 (N.D. Ohio 1990), *aff'd*, 932 F.2d 495 (6th Cir. 1991) (recorded conversation on a public street is not private under the regulation).

662. 47 C.F.R. §§ 2.701 & 15.11. The exception, however, arguably does not include the transmission of a conversation in which the monitor is a party who is not overhearing the conversation. See Middleton, *Journalists and Tape Recorders: Does Participant Monitoring Invade Privacy?*, 2 COMM/ENT. 287, 314 & n.127 (1979).

663. See Middleton, *supra* note 662, at 315-16 n.190.

664. *Reorganization and Deregulation of Part 97 of the Rules Governing the Amateur Radio Services*, 5 F.C.C.R. 4614.

665. See 47 U.S.C. § 605(a).

666. *Monitoring of Police and Fire Radio Transmissions by Broadcast Stations*, 1 RAD. REG. 2d (P&F) 291 (1963).

tion[667] and taxicab services,[668] however, may not.[669] FCC licensees are also prohibited from broadcasting a recorded telephone conversation without the consent of all parties to the conversation.[670] Notification must be given to all parties that the conversation will be disseminated before any part of it is broadcast live or taped for later broadcast.[671] Violation of these rules may result in substantial fines.[672]

The FCC may impose forfeitures[673] or criminal fines for violations of these regulations.[674] Broadcast licensees are subject to additional fines.[675] Such violations may also affect, at least theoretically, the retention of FCC licenses.[676]

The Commission's interstate telephone tariff regulations also place restrictions on the recording of long distance telephone calls. A call can be recorded if a beep tone is used, all parties to the telephone call consent, or it is announced at the beginning of the call that it is being recorded.[677] The responsibility of enforcing these regulations is placed on the telephone company.[678]

§ 13-7(b). State Law.

§ 13-7(b)(1). Introduction.

Almost every state[679] has enacted legislation to protect its citizens from the unauthorized interception or recording of their private conversations via wire-

---

667. *Unauthorized Broadcast of Federal Aviation Administration Communications by Broadcast and other Federal Communications Commission Licensees*, 74 F.C.C. 2d 615 (1972).
668. In re Dickson, 3 F.C.C.R. 2595 (1988).
669. The mere monitoring of "open" transmissions, such as police dispatchers, is not prohibited. A violation arises when the contents of a transmission are divulged. 47 U.S.C. § 605(a); see United States v. Fuller, 202 F. Supp. 356 (N.D. Cal. 1962).
670. *Amendment of Part 73 of the Commission's Rules and Regulations with Respect to the Broadcast of Telephone Conversations*, 23 F.C.C.2d 1 (1970) (codified at 47 C.F.R. § 73.1206). Express notice is not required if the party "is aware, or may be presumed to be aware from the circumstances of the conversation, that it is being or likely will be broadcast." *Id.* Thus, for example, a caller to a radio call-in program need not receive express notification.
671. Liability of Malrite Guaranteed, 7 F.C.C.R. 5463 (1992).
672. See 8 F.C.C.R. 436 (1993).
673. Non-broadcasters are subject to a forfeiture of up to $10,000 per day. 47 U.S.C. § 503(b)(2)(C). Forfeitures for broadcasters may be set as high as $25,000 per day of violation. *Id.* § 503(b)(2)(A).
674. Criminal fines may be as high as $500 per day. *Id.* § 502.
675. Licensee forfeitures shall not exceed $100,000 per day. *Id.* § 503(b)(2)(B).
676. See *id.* § 312.
677. See Middleton, *supra* note 662, at 320.
678. See *id.* at 319 ("It is the telephone company's responsibility, under penalty of a small fine, to see that its customers are not engaged in illegal tape recordings.").
679. Rhode Island, South Carolina, and Vermont have no wiretap or bugging statute.

tapping[680] or bugging.[681] Traditional eavesdropping[682] is generally not the subject of statutory prohibitions[683] and is permissible in public and semi-public places,[684] so long as amplification equipment is not used.[685] Some states have adopted rules that parallel federal law regarding wiretapping and bugging.[686] Others purport to provide greater privacy protection.[687] Attempts to invalidate these statutes as an unconstitutional interference with a First Amendment right to gather news have been unavailing.[688] Although each state's wiretap and bugging

---

680. Wiretapping is the physical intrusion into a telephone wire, allowing for the interception of a communication between the sender and the receiver. See LaCrone v. Ohio Bell Tel. Co., 182 N.E.2d 15,16-17 (Ohio App. 1961).

681. Bugging is the placement of a recording or transmitting device in a room or other place where the person monitoring is not present. See United States v. Anaya, 779 F.2d 532, 534 (9th Cir. 1985).

682. Eavesdropping is traditionally defined as the listening to, recording or transmitting of a conversation that one can easily overhear with the unaided ear. See Katz v. United States, 389 U.S. 347, 369 (1967).

683. States may prohibit loitering for the purpose of eavesdropping. See, e.g., N.D. CENT. CODE § 12.1-15-02-2; OKLA. STAT. tit. 21, § 1202. Some states have enacted "electronic eavesdropping" statutes that prohibit the use of electronic amplifying or recording devices. See, e.g., CAL. PENAL CODE § 632.

684. See, e.g., United States v. Llanes, 398 F.2d 880, 884 (2d Cir. 1968) ("[C]onversations carried on in a tone of voice quite audible to a person standing outside . . . are conversations knowingly exposed to the public.").

685. See United States v. Carroll, 337 F. Supp. 1260, 1263 (D.D.C. 1971) (salesman was permitted to record competitor's end of telephone conversation because no amplification was used and no contrived position was assumed). Use of an extension telephone to listen in on a telephone conversation surreptitiously has been found actionable as eavesdropping. See Ribas v. Clark, 696 P.2d 637 (Cal. 1985); Florida v. Sarmiento, 397 So. 2d 643, 645 (Fla. 1981). Where a radio device is used to transmit a conversation to a remote recorder, FCC regulations may prohibit the practice without the consent of all parties to the conversation. *1966 Report and Order on the Use of Radio Devices for Eavesdropping*, 2 F.C.C.2d 641 (1966) (codified at 47 C.F.R. §§ 2.701 & 15.11). The FCC does permit the use of such radio devices to record a conversation if a person overhears the conversation within "earshot" and the conversation occurs in "public and semipublic places . . . where persons may reasonably expect their conversation to be overheard." *Id.* at 645. See United States v. Muckenthaler, 584 F.2d 240 (8th Cir. 1978). (holding that plaintiff "did not have a reasonable expectation of privacy" because surveillance was undertaken in a public place without the use of an amplification device).

686. See, e.g., HAW. REV. STAT. § 803-42; MINN. STAT. § 626A.02; N.Y. PENAL LAW § 250.

687. The Federal Wiretap Act is intended as a regulatory minimum, permitting states to impose stricter limitations. See S. REP. NO. 90-1097 (1968); People v. Stevens, 40 Cal. Rptr. 2d 92 (Ct. App. 1995) (California statute prohibiting interception of cordless telephone communications, CAL. PENAL CODE § 632.6(a), not preempted by Federal Communications Act or by federal eavesdropping and wiretapping statutes); Hoskins v. Howard, 971 P.2d 1135, 1138-39 (Idaho 1998) (federal statutes on the subject of electronic surveillance establish a minimum level of protection, and states are free to provide more).

688. See, e.g., Oregon v. Knobel, 777 P.2d 985 (Or App. 1989); Shevin v. Sunbeam Television Corp., 351 So. 2d 723, 726-27 (Fla. 1977), *appeal dismissed*, 435 U.S. 920 (1978); Central Newspapers, Inc. v. Johnson, 722 So. 2d 1224 (La. App. 1998).

statute varies in approach and content, they co-exist with the federal legislation,[689] so long as they remain as stringent as federal law in their protection of privacy.[690]

§ 13-7(b)(2). Consensual Monitoring Jurisdictions.

The majority of states follow the Federal Wiretap Act in permitting the interception or recording of communications by or with the consent of one of the participants.[691] These consensual monitoring jurisdictions prohibit only third-party eavesdropping. Chief among the proponents of the single-party consent rule is New York.[692] Its statute, which is typical of consensual monitoring laws, defines wiretapping as "the intentional overhearing or recording of a telephonic communication by a person other than a sender or receiver thereof, without the consent of either the sender or receiver, by means of any instrument, device, or equipment."[693]

In jurisdictions such as New York, therefore, communications may be intercepted or taped by the originator or recipient or with the permission of either, unless the purpose in doing so is to commit a crime or tort,[694] or "other injurious

---

689. See, e.g., Washington v. Williams, 617 P.2d 1012, 1017-18 (Wash. 1980); Massachusetts v. Vitello, 327 N.E.2d 819, 839 (Mass. 1975); People v. Conklin, 522 P.2d 1049 (Cal.), *appeal dismissed*, 419 U.S. 1064 (1974); People v. Stevens, 40 Cal. Rptr. 2d 92 (Ct. App. 1995); People v. Broady, 158 N.E.2d 817, 823 (N.Y.), *appeal dismissed and cert. denied*, 361 U.S. 8 (1959).

690. See, e.g., Kansas v. Dowdy, 563 P.2d 425 (Kan. 1977); People v. Conklin, 522 P.2d 1049 (Cal.), *appeal dismissed,* 419 U.S. 1064 (1974).

691. Consensual monitoring is the interception or recording of a communication by a participant to the communication or by someone who has obtained the consent of such a participant. Greenawalt, *The Consent Problem in Wiretapping and Eavesdropping: Surreptitious Monitoring with the Consent of a Participant in a Conversation*, 68 COLUM. L. REV. 189 (1968). See, e.g., ALA. CODE § 13A-11-31; ALASKA STAT. § 42.20.310; ARIZ. REV. STAT. § 13-3005 (A); ARK. CODE ANN. § 5-60-120; COLO. REV. STAT. § 18-9-303; D.C. CODE ANN. § 23-542(3); GA. CODE ANN. § 16-11-62; HAW. REV. STAT. § 803-42; IDAHO CODE § 18-6702; IND. CODE § 35-33.5-1-5; IOWA CODE §§ 727.8, 808B.2; KAN. STAT. ANN. § 21-4002; KY. REV. STAT. ANN. §§ 526.010, 526.020; ME. REV. STAT. ANN. tit. 15, §§ 709-10; MINN. STAT. § 626A.02; MISS. CODE ANN. §§ 41-29-531, 41-29-533; MO. REV. STAT. § 542.402; NEB. REV. STAT. §§ 86-702; NEV. REV. STAT. §§ 200.630, 200.650; N.J. STAT. ANN. § 2A:156A-3: N.M. STAT. ANN. § 30-12-1; N.Y. PENAL LAW § 250.05 (intrusion by listening device); N.C. GEN. STAT. §§ 14-155, 15A-287; N.D. CENT. CODE § 12.1-15-02; OHIO REV. CODE ANN. § 2933.52; OKLA. STAT. tit. 13, § 176.3; OR. REV. STAT. § 165.540; S.D. CODIFIED LAWS § 23A-35A-20; TENN. CODE ANN. § 39-13-601; TEX. PENAL CODE ANN. § 16.02; UTAH CODE ANN. § 76-9-403; VA. CODE ANN. § 19.2-62; W. VA. CODE § 62-1D-3: WIS. STAT. ANN. § 968.31; WYO. STAT. ANN. § 7-3-602.

692. See N.Y. PENAL LAW § 250.

693. *Id.* § 250.01.

694. See, e.g., MINN. STAT. § 626A.02(d); Copeland v. Hubbard Broadcasting, Inc., 526 N.W.2d 402, 406 (Minn. App. 1995).

acts."[695] Much of the litigation involving the press in this context concerns the issue of whether a journalist acted with such a purpose.[696]

In *Desnick v. American Broadcasting Cos.*,[697] for example, a television network surreptitiously video and audio taped consultations at an eye clinic. The clinic and two of its surgeons alleged that the network and its employees violated state wiretapping statutes when they recorded conversations at the clinic without authorization. The Seventh Circuit, however, determined that the Illinois and Wisconsin statutes at issue permitted such surreptitious taping by the network's agents because the recording was not done with a purpose to commit a crime, or a tort or "other injurious acts."[698] In the court's view, "[t]elling the world the truth about a Medicare fraud is hardly what the framers of the statute could have had in mind in forbidding a person to record his own conversations if he was trying to commit an 'injurious act.'"[699]

§ 13-7(b)(3). All-Party Consent Jurisdictions.

A minority of states require that all parties to a communication consent before it can be lawfully recorded, thereby prohibiting secret consensual tape recordings.[700] Some courts, however, have construed these statutes to permit consensual recording in certain situations.[701]

The constitutionality of an all-party consent statute was unsuccessfully challenged in *Shevin v. Sunbeam Television Corp.*[702] In that case, a newspaper and

---

695. Similar language in the Federal Wiretap Act was removed after one court deemed the phrase to be unconstitutionally vague. See Boddie v. American Broadcasting Cos., 881 F.2d 267 (6th Cir. 1989), *cert. denied*, 493 U.S. 1028 (1990).

696. See, e.g., Russell v. American Broadcasting Cos., 23 MEDIA L. REP. (BNA) 2428, 2429-31 (N.D. Ill 1995); Copeland v. Hubbard Broadcasting, Inc., 526 N.W.2d 402, 406 (Minn. App. 1995).

697. 44 F.3d 1345 (7th Cir. 1995).

698. *Id.* at 1353 (construing 18 U.S.C. § 2511(2)(d); WIS. STAT. § 968.31(2)(c); 720 ILL. COMP. STAT. 5/14-2).

699. 44 F.3d at 1353-54.

700. See, e.g., CAL. PENAL CODE §§ 631-32; CONN. GEN. STAT. § 52-570d(a); DEL. CODE ANN. tit. 11 § 1335(a); FLA. STAT. § 934.03(2)(a),(3)(d); 720 ILL. COMP. STAT. 5/14-2; LA. REV. STAT. ANN. § 15:1303 (C)(4); MD. CODE ANN., CTS. & JUD. PROC. § 10-402(c)(3); MASS. GEN. LAWS ch. 272, § 99; MICH. COMP. LAWS § 28.807(3); MONT. CODE ANN. § 45-8-213; NEV. REV. STAT. § 200.620 (interception of wire or radio communication); N.H. REV. STAT. ANN. § 570-A:2; 18 PA. CONS. STAT. ANN. § 5703-04; WASH. REV. CODE § 9.73.030. See also Lane v. Allstate Ins. Co., 969 P.2d 938, 940 (Nev. 1998) (recording of telephone conversations without consent of both parties is prohibited unless authorized or ratified by court).

701. See, e.g., Georgia v. Birge, 241 S.E.2d 213, 214 (Ga.), *cert. denied*, 436 U.S. 945 (1978) (interpreting GA. CODE ANN. § 26-3001(1), which makes it unlawful "to intentionally overhear, transmit, or record . . . the private conversation of another," as only prohibiting a situation where all three occurred in a single offense; because a participant cannot "overhear" himself, the court determined that the statute was not intended to prohibit participant recording.).

702. 351 So.2d 723 (Fla. 1977), *appeal dismissed*, 435 U.S. 920 (1978).

television station argued that Florida's wiretap and bugging statute impaired the gathering and dissemination of news to such a degree that it constituted an unconstitutional prior restraint. They asserted that secret recordings not only insure the accuracy of the statements reported,[703] but also that the use of concealed equipment enhances the candor of sources,[704] and the taped statements themselves provide corroboration of the resulting news reports.[705]

The Florida Supreme Court, however, held that the statute does not constitute a prior restraint because it does not prohibit or command what the press may publish.[706] Moreover, the court recognized the legislative policy of protecting the expectation of privacy of each party to a conversation and found that the statute's limitation on the use of secret recordings would result in only a limited impairment of the newsgathering process.[707] Indeed, the court questioned the press's emphasis on such surreptitious recordings and its suggestion that limitations on such a practice would interfere with the exercise of First Amendment freedoms.[708]

---

703. *Id.* at 725.

704. *Id.* at 725 ("Appellees point out that persons engaged in unlawful or undesirable conduct will not speak candidly if they know that their words are being recorded.").

705. *Id.* ("The only effective corroboration of a news story is the recording of the conversation, where the exact words, manner of speech, and inflection can be preserved.").

706. *Id.* at 726.

707. See *id.* at 727:

> [The statute] does not exclude any source from the press, intrude upon the activities of the news media in contacting sources, prevent the parties to the communication from consenting to the recording, or restrict the publication of any information gained from the communication. First Amendment rights do not include a constitutional right to corroborate news gathering activities when the legislature has statutorily recognized the private rights of individuals.

708. *Id.* at 727 (citing Dietemann v. Time, Inc., 449 F.2d 245 (9th Cir. 1971)). See also Central Newspapers, Inc. v. Johnson, 722 So. 2d 1224, 1229 (La. App. 1998) ("[T]he media does not have unfettered rights of access or rights to publicize the contents of any audio and visual event it so desires without the consent of the parties involved just because the First Amendment and Article 1, Section 7 [of the Louisiana Constitution] protect freedom of speech and freedom of the press."); Dickerson v. Raphael, 27 MEDIA L. REP. (BNA) 2215, 2216 (Mich. 1999) (holding that plaintiff entitled to new trial on claim that nonconsensual recording, simultaneous transmission and later broadcast of her conversation with her children in a public park violated MICH. COMP. LAWS § 28.807, because jury should have been instructed that "whether plaintiff's conversation was private depends on whether she intended and reasonably expected it to be private at the time and under the circumstances involved" and not "whether the subject matter" of the conversation "was intended to be private"); Marich v. QRZ Media, Inc., 86 Cal. Rptr. 2d 406 (Ct. App. 1999) (although "plaintiffs could have no reasonable expectation of privacy in connection with a telephone call from a police officer acting on official business, . . . that is not the same as a third person recording the conversation for later use on a commercial television station").

§ 13-7(b)(4). Exceptions.

§ 13-7(b)(4)(A). Inadvertent Interceptions of Communications.

Courts have recognized several exceptions to state wiretap and bugging statutes.[709] As is the case under the Federal Wiretap Act, for example, state wiretap and bugging statutes typically proscribe only intentional, as opposed to inadvertent, interception of communications.[710] The inadvertent interception of communications are common by switchboard operators,[711] and phone systems with extensions or party lines.[712]

§ 13-7(b)(4)(B). Communications in Public Places.

Because the interest underlying most state wiretap and bugging statutes is protection of the participants' reasonable expectation of privacy,[713] the statutes do not typically prohibit the recording or interception of communications made in public places or in circumstances where there is no reasonable expectation of privacy.[714] The courts typically use an objective test to determine whether each of the parties to a communication had a reasonable expectation of privacy.[715]

A non-private communication in a public place includes any communication made in a public gathering, or in any legislative, judicial, executive or adminis-

---

709. See Kersis v. Capital Cities/ABC Inc., 22 MEDIA L. REP. (BNA) 2321, 2324 (Cal. Super. 1994), *rev'd on other grounds sub nom.* Sanders v. American Broadcasting Cos., 60 Cal. Rptr. 2d 595 (Ct. App. 1997), *rev'd*, 978 P.2d 67 (Cal. 1999).
710. See People v. Buchanan, 103 Cal. Rptr. 66 (Ct. App. 1972).
711. See, e.g., People v. Soles, 136 Cal. Rptr. 328 (Ct. App. 1977).
712. See, e.g., Roberts v. Alaska, 453 P.2d 898 (Alaska), *cert. denied*, 396 U.S. 1022 (1969).
713. See Ribas v. Clark, 696 P.2d 637, 640 (Cal. 1985) ("secret monitoring denies the speaker an important aspect of privacy of communications—the right to control the nature and extent of the firsthand dissemination of his statements"); Shevin v. Sunbeam Television Corp., 351 So. 2d 723, 726-27 (Fla. 1977), *appeal dismissed*, 435 U.S. 920 (1978).
714. See, e.g., CAL. PENAL CODE § 632(c); 720 ILL. COMP. STAT. 5/14-3(c) (permits the broadcast of any incidental conversations overheard during a broadcast from a public function). See also Washington v. Forrester, 587 P.2d 179, 184 (Wash. 1978) (extortion demands made to police during telephone call held not to be private conversation).
715. See Coulter v. Bank of Am. Nat'l Trust & Savings Ass'n, 33 Cal. Rptr. 2d 766, 770 (Ct. App. 1994); Deteresa v. American Broadcasting Co., 121 F.3d 460, 465 (9th Cir. 1997), *cert. denied*, 118 S. Ct. 1840 (1998) (affirming summary judgment for defendants on state eavesdropping claim where plaintiff did not have "an objectively reasonable expectation that the conversation would not be divulged to anyone else"); Wilkins v. National Broadcasting Co., 84 Cal. Rptr. 2d 329, 332 (Ct. App. 1999) (dismissing § 632 claim arising from surreptitious recording of conversations that took place in an open patio area of a public restaurant); cf. Sanders v. American Broadcasting Cos., 978 P.2d 67, 78 (Cal. 1999) (jury finding in favor of defendants with respect to claim arising under CAL. PENAL CODE § 632 did not foreclose intrusion claim because fact that "conversations could be overheard" by coworkers does not serve "to negate *all* reasonable expectations of privacy by plaintiff" with respect to surreptitious tape recording of such conversations).

trative proceeding open to the public,[716] or outside "[a] place where one may reasonably expect to be safe from casual or hostile intrusion or surveillance."[717] A non-private communication need not occur in a public place.[718]

---

716. See, e.g., CAL. PENAL CODE § 632(c):

> The term "confidential communication" includes any communication carried on in circumstances as may reasonably indicate that any party to the communication desires it to be confined to the parties thereto, but excludes a communication made in a public gathering or in any legislative, judicial, executive or administrative proceeding open to the public, or in any other circumstance in which the parties to the communication may reasonably expect that the communication may be overheard or recorded.

"Confidentiality" under the California statute "appears to require nothing more than the existence of a reasonable expectation by one of the parties that no one is 'listening in' or overhearing the conversation." Frio v. Superior Ct., 250 Cal. Rptr. 819, 823 (Ct. App. 1988). See Shulman v. Group W Prods., Inc., 955 P.2d 469, 492 (Cal. 1998) ("confidential communication," for purposes of § 632, "includes 'any communication carried on in circumstances as may reasonably indicate that any party to the communication desires it to be confined to the parties thereto, but excludes a communication made in a public gathering . . . or in any other circumstance in which the parties to the communication may reasonably expect that the communication may be overheard or recorded"); Deteresa v. American Broadcasting Co., 121 F.3d 460, 465 (9th Cir. 1997), *cert. denied*, 118 S. Ct. 1840 (1998) ("confidentiality" under California statute requires that one party to the communication have "an objectively reasonable expectation that the conversation would not be divulged to anyone else"); Wilkins v. National Broadcasting Co., 84 Cal. Rptr. 2d 329, 337 (Ct. App. 1999) (rejecting § 632 claim arising from recording of conversations in open patio area of public restaurant because no "trier of fact could find, judged by an objective standard," that plaintiffs "expected that their conversation would not be divulged to anyone else"); cf. Sanders v. American Broadcasting Cos., 978 P.2d 67, 78 (Cal. 1999) (although fact that tape recorded "conversations could be overheard" by co-workers may be sufficient to preclude liability under § 632, that fact "cannot reasonably be construed to negate *all* reasonable expectations of privacy by plaintiff" in such conversations for purposes of intrusion claim).

717. ALA. CODE § 13A-11-30(2). Cf. Dickerson v. Raphael, 27 MEDIA L. REP. (BNA) 2215, 2216 (Mich. 1999) (ordering new trial for plaintiff, who asserted violation of MICH. COMP. LAWS § 28.807, based on nonconsensual recording of conversation between children and their mother in public park).

718. Various situations have been held to constitute non-private communications. See, e.g., Rogers v. Ulrich, 125 Cal. Rptr. 306 (Ct. App. 1976) (city council candidate's private telephone conversation with a public employee concerning public business); People v. Soles, 136 Cal. Rptr. 328 (Ct. App. 1977) (motel guest's telephone conversations concerning illegal activities overheard by the motel switchboard operator); People v. Pedersen, 150 Cal. Rptr. 577 (Ct. App. 1978) (employee's conversation with his employers in company's office concerning the employee's embezzling of company funds). Deteresa v. American Broadcasting Co., 121 F.3d at 464-65 (when "neither party reasonably expects the communication to be confined to the parties, it is not confidential [and] it makes no difference under the statute whether the person reasonably expects that another is listening or not"); Sanders v. American Broadcasting Cos., 978 P.2d 67, 78 (Cal. 1999) (although fact that tape recorded "conversations could be overheard" by co-workers may be sufficient to preclude liability under § 632, that fact "cannot reasonably be construed to negate *all* reasonable expectations of privacy by plaintiff" in such conversations for purposes of intrusion claim).

§ 13-7(b)(4)(C). Communications on Business Premises.

One area of journalistic concern is the issue of whether, for purposes of state wiretap and bugging statutes, a reasonable expectation of privacy inheres in communications that take place on business premises. In *Sanders v. American Broadcasting Cos.*,[719] two telephone psychic counselors sued a television network for, *inter alia*, violation of the California electronic eavesdropping statute. The network journalists had gained access to the interior offices of the Psychic Marketing Group through subterfuge and had used a hidden camera to record the activities and conversations of the plaintiffs.

In response to questions posed as part of a special verdict, the jury found both that the plaintiff carried on his conversations with the undercover reporter "in circumstances which reasonably indicate[d] that [he] desired such communications to be confined to the parties thereto" and that those communications were "made in circumstances in which the parties to the communication may reasonably have expected that the communications may have been overheard."[720] Accordingly, the trial court entered judgment for the defendants with respect to plaintiff's claim under the California electronic eavesdropping statute, and the Court of Appeal held that the jury's finding precluded a common law intrusion claim as well.[721] The California Supreme Court, however, rejected the conclusion that the fact that the tape recorded conversations at issue could be overheard by co-workers served "to negate *all* reasonable expectations of privacy by plaintiff" for purposes of the common law tort of intrusion.[722]

Other courts have taken a comparatively dim view of the expectation of privacy of those engaged in communications in a business context. Thus, courts interpreting the Federal Wiretap Act in the business context have failed to find a protectible privacy interest.[723] In *Russell v. American Broadcasting Cos.*,[724] for example, a television journalist posed as an "undercover" employee at a retail grocery store in Chicago. During this time, she wore a hidden camera and microphone with which she recorded conversations with the store's manager. The manager brought suit under the Federal Wiretap Act, arguing that its single party-consent exemption did not apply because the recording violated the Illinois

---

[719]. 978 P.2d 67 (Cal. 1999).

[720]. *Id.* at 78.

[721]. Sanders v. American Broadcasting Cos., 60 Cal. Rptr. 2d 595, 598 (Ct. App. 1997), *rev'd*, 978 P.2d 67 (Cal. 1999).

[722]. 978 P.2d at 72; see *id.* ("[P]rivacy, for purposes of the intrusion tort, is not a binary, all-or-nothing characteristic. There are degrees and nuances to societal recognition of our expectations of privacy: the fact the privacy one expects in a given setting is not complete or absolute does not render the expectation unreasonable as a matter of law.").

[723]. See, e.g., Desnick v. American Broadcasting Cos., 44 F.3d 1345, 1353 (7th Cir. 1995).

[724]. 23 MEDIA L. REP. (BNA) 2428 (N.D. Ill. 1995).

eavesdropping statute.[725] The court, however, found that, under Illinois law, the parties had no expectation of privacy during the recorded in-store conversations because when "a party to a conversation records it, all he is doing is making a more accurate record of something that he has already heard. This does not violate the declarant's right to privacy."[726]

§ 13-7(b)(4)(D). Unprotected Subject Matter.

In some situations, courts have deemed the subject matter intercepted or recorded outside the protection of the statute and have, therefore, held that it may be recorded without the requisite consent.[727] Communications relating to the commission of a crime are often exempted from state wiretap and bugging statutes and may similarly be intercepted or recorded.[728] In addition, the interception or recording of communications that occur anonymously, repeatedly or at an extremely inconvenient hour, may be permitted.[729]

§ 13-7(b)(4)(E). Use of Unrestricted Equipment.

The types of interception or recording equipment deemed unlawful are generally set forth in state wiretap and bugging statutes. Equipment not identified in the statute or regulations may typically be used.[730] Extension telephones may be employed to intercept a communication in some states if the extension has not been equipped with a device for amplification or recording.[731] In other

---

725. *Id.* at 2430.

726. *Id.* (citations omitted). But cf. Sanders v. American Broadcasting Cos., 978 P.2d 67, 76 n.4 (Cal. 1999) (distinguishing *Russell*).

727. See Washington v. Smith, 540 P.2d 424, 428 (Wash. 1975) (Sounds recorded by a man gunned down in an alley held not to be statutory subject matter: "Gunfire, running, shouting, and [the victim's] screams do not constitute 'conversation' within the term's ordinary connotation of oral exchange, discourse, or discussion.").

728. See, e.g., CAL. PENAL CODE § 633.5 (communications relating to extortion, kidnapping, bribery, violent felony or annoying telephone calls may be recorded without the consent of all parties); GA. CODE ANN. § 26-3006 (permits participant recording where the communication constitutes "the commission of a crime or is directly in the furtherance of a crime."); WASH. REV. CODE § 9.73.030(2)(b) (communications conveying threats of extortion, blackmail, bodily harm and "other unlawful requests or demands.").

729. See WASH. REV. CODE § 9.73.030(2)(c).

730. See, e.g., Cassidy v. American Broadcasting Cos., 377 N.E.2d 126, 129 (Ill. App. 1978) (camera not deemed an "eavesdropping" device under the Illinois wiretapping statute).

731. See People v. Soles, 136 Cal. Rptr. 328 (Ct. App. 1977); Massachusetts v. Vieux, 671 N.E.2d 989 (Mass. App. 1996); Michigan v. Lucas, 470 N.W.2d 460 (Mich. App. 1991); New Hampshire v. Telles, 653 A.2d 554 (N.H. 1995). The California Supreme Court has held that the California Privacy Act prohibits eavesdropping as well as illicit wiretapping, see Ribas v. Clark, 696 P.2d 637 (Cal. 1985) (use of extension telephones for eavesdropping on confidential communications is not exempted), but has indicated a willingness to adopt some form of extension phone exception, see People v. Otto, 831 P.2d 1178, 1190 (Cal.), *cert. denied*, 506 U.S. 956 (1992).

states, where "interception" is broadly defined as the aural acquisition of the content of any wire or oral communication through the use of any electronic, mechanical or other device,[732] extension telephones cannot be used to intercept a communication.[733]

In some states, using a cordless or cellular telephone is the equivalent of broadcasting the conversation to the general public. The cordless or cellular telephone user, therefore, assumes the risk that the conversation will be intercepted.[734] The statutes of other states expressly protect users of cordless or cellular telephones from interception and recording.[735] Many states do not require a warrant for the use of a pen register or a trap and trace device because these devices do not intercept a communication.[736] Video cameras and recorders have been deemed to be a "recording device" within the prohibition of some state wiretap and bugging statutes.[737] Other states, however, follow the federal rule that excludes silent video cameras from coverage under the Federal Wiretap Act.[738]

§ 13-7(b)(4)(F). Law Enforcement Monitoring.

Several states that prohibit consensual monitoring have adopted an exception for law enforcement.[739] In these jurisdictions, the interception or taping of a communication undertaken with the consent of one of the parties involved is lawful when authorized by law enforcement officials.[740]

---

732. See Horm v. Florida, 298 So. 2d 194 (Fla. App. 1974).

733. See Washington v. Corliss, 870 P.2d 317, 320 (Wash. 1994) (where informant tilted telephone receiver so police officer could hear conversation, it was not "intercepted" by a "device" designed to record or transmit as required by state privacy act); Horm v. Florida, 298 So. 2d 194 (Fla. App. 1974).

734. See Chandler v. Alabama, 680 So. 2d 1018 (Ala. Crim. App. 1996); Arizona v. Duran, 901 P.2d 1197 (Ariz. App. 1995); Missouri v. King, 873 S.W.2d 905 (Mo. App. 1994).

735. See, e.g., CAL. PENAL CODE § 632.7; TENN. CODE ANN. § 39-13-604(b)(2); Connecticut v. McVeigh, 620 A.2d 133, 148 (Conn. 1993); Hoskins v. Howard, 971 P.2d 1135, 1139 (Idaho 1998); People v. Fata, 559 N.Y.S.2d 348, 351 (App. Div. 1990); Ohio v. Bidinost, 644 N.E.2d 318, 328 (Ohio 1994); Oregon v. Carston, 913 P.2d 709 (Or. 1996); Washington v. Faford, 910 P.2d 447, 451 (Wash. 1996) ("Whether a [cordless telephone] conversation qualifies as private is a question of fact determined by the intent or reasonable expectations of the parties.").

736. Smith v. Maryland, 398 A.2d 858 (Md. 1978), aff'd, 442 U.S. 735 (1979). But see People v. Bialostok, 610 N.E.2d 374 (N.Y. 1993) (pen register with capacity to monitor telephone conversations treated as eavesdropping device).

737. See, e.g., People v. Gibbons, 263 Cal. Rptr. 905, 907 (Ct. App. 1989).

738. See, e.g., United States v. Torres, 751 F.2d 875 (7th Cir. 1984) (video surveillance is not aural; therefore, video cameras do not qualify as a surveillance device under the Wiretap Act).

739. E.g., CAL. PENAL CODE § 633; MD. CODE ANN., CTS. & JUD. PROC. § 10-402(c)(2); MICH. COMP. LAWS § 750-539g(a).

740. See People v. Fulton, 201 Cal. Rptr. 879 (Ct. App. 1994).

§ 13-7(b)(4)(G). Monitoring of Emergency Communications.

Although federal law limits the use of such communications, several states have addressed the monitoring of broadcasts by emergency agencies somewhat differently.[741] Illinois purports to permit the monitoring and recording of emergency broadcasts by hospitals, clinics, fire departments and other emergency agencies.[742] Florida limits monitoring by emergency agencies to incoming wire communications on published emergency telephone numbers.[743]

§ 13-7(b)(5). Sanctions and Remedies.

State wiretap and bugging statutes provide for a variety of penal and civil remedies.[744] Most statutes provide for various forms of equitable or injunctive relief[745] and for the recovery of actual damages suffered by the injured participant in the intercepted or recorded communication.[746] Some statutes, recognizing the difficulty of proof of actual harm, provide for statutory damages.[747]

§ 13-7(c). Common Law.

The common law of audio recording in the newsgathering context has its genesis, like so much of the law in this area, in the Ninth Circuit's decision in *Dietemann v. Time, Inc.*[748] There, reporters for *Life* magazine, equipped with hidden microphones, entered plaintiff's home under false identities and proceeded to engage him in conversation that was transmitted to a nearby truck, staffed by other *Life* employees and law enforcement officials. Although no California case had addressed the issue, even in the nonmedia context, the court

---

741. See Chap. 13-7(a)(2)(B) *supra*.
742. 720 ILL. COMP. STAT. 5/14-3(d).
743. FLA. STAT. § 934.03(2)(g).
744. See, e.g., ARK. CODE ANN. § 5-60-120 (up to $1,000 fine); CAL. PENAL CODE §§ 631-632 (fines up to $2,500 and jail or imprisonment up to one year); GA. CODE ANN. § 16-11-62 (up to five years, $10,000 fine and restitution); MICH. COMP. LAWS § 28.807(3) & (5) (up to two years and $2,000 fine; in civil action, actual and punitive damages); WIS. STAT. § 968.31 (up to five years and $10,000 fine; in civil action, the greater of actual damages, $100 per day of violation, or $1,000).
745. See, *e.g.*, CAL. PENAL CODE § 637.2(b) MD. CODE ANN., CTS. & JUD. PROC. § 10-402; MO. REV. STAT. § 542.422; 18 PA. CONS. STAT. § 5728.
746. See, e.g., CAL. PENAL CODE § 637.2(a) (injured party may receive the greater of $5,000 or three times the amount of actual damages); CONN. GEN. STAT. § 54-41r; MD. CODE ANN., CTS. & JUD. PROC. § 10-402; TENN. CODE ANN. § 39-13-601(3).
747. See, e.g., CAL. PENAL CODE § 637.2(a)(1) (the greater of $5,000 or three times the actual damages sustained by the plaintiff); DEL. CODE ANN. tit. 11, § 1336(w)(i); FLA. STAT. § 934.01; IDAHO CODE § 18-6709; MO. REV. STAT. § 542.418; N.H. REV. STAT. ANN. § 570-A:11; N.J. STAT. ANN. § 2A:156 A-24; 18 PA. CONS. STAT. § 5725(a)(1); TEX. CRIM. P. CODE ANN. art. 18.20, § 16; W. VA. CODE § 62-1D-12.
748. 449 F.2d 245 (9th Cir. 1971).

recognized that other jurisdictions, in cases not involving the news media, had "consistently held that surreptitious electronic recording of a plaintiff's conversation causing him emotional distress is actionable" at common law.[749] Thus, the court purported to "have little difficulty in concluding that clandestine . . . recordation and transmission of [plaintiff's] conversation without his consent resulting in his emotional distress warrants recovery for invasion of privacy in California."[750] In the court's view:

> One who invites another to his home or office takes a risk that the visitor may not be what he seems, and the visitor may repeat all he hears and observes when he leaves. But he does not and should not be required to take the risk that what is heard and seen will be transmitted by photograph or recording, in our modern world, in full living color and hi-fi to the public at large or to any segment of it that the visitor may select.[751]

In addition, the Ninth Circuit rejected the defendants' suggestion that hidden recording devices "'are indispensable tools of investigative reporting.'"[752] Although it conceded that "[i]nvestigative reporting is an ancient art," the practice of which "long antecedes the invention of miniature cameras and electronic devices," the court held that the "First Amendment has never been construed to accord newsmen immunity from torts or crimes committed during the course of newsgathering."[753]

In *Sanders v. American Broadcasting Cos.*,[754] the California Supreme Court embraced the Ninth Circuit's analysis in *Dietemann*. There, television reporters, equipped with hidden devices, recorded conversations with employees of a "psychic hotline." The plaintiffs, the two employees whose conversations were recorded without their knowledge, secured a jury verdict on their claim of invasion of privacy through intrusion under California law.[755]

The court of appeal reversed the jury's verdict as to one of the plaintiffs, holding that the jury's finding that he "lacked an objectively reasonable expectation

---

749. *Id.* at 247 (citing Nader v. General Motors Corp., 255 N.E.2d 765 (N.Y. 1970) (applying D.C. law); Hamberger v. Eastman, 206 A.2d 239 (N.H. 1964); McDaniel v. Atlanta Coca-Cola Bottling Co., 2 S.E.2d 810 (Ga. App. 1939)).

750. 449 F.2d at 248. But see Ferrara v. Detroit Free Press, Inc., 26 MEDIA L. REP. (BNA) 2355, 2362 (E.D. Mich. 1998) (dismissing invasion of privacy claim that is "indistinguishable" from plaintiff's federal wiretap act claim).

751. 449 F.2d at 249.

752. *Id.* (quoting defendants' brief).

753. *Id.* The Ninth Circuit's discussion of the relevance of the First Amendment to the law of newsgathering generally is discussed at Chap. 12-4(a) *supra*.

754. 978 P.2d 67 (Cal. 1999).

755. *Id.* at 70.

of privacy" precluded a privacy-based cause of action.[756] In that regard, the court concluded that plaintiff's privacy claim "implicates First Amendment freedom of the press issues, resolution of which requires care lest we improperly restrict press freedom."[757]

The California Supreme Court reversed.[758] Although it cautioned that adjudication of any "possible First Amendment defenses" to an intrusion claim based on the surreptitious recording of conversations "must await a later case, as no constitutional issue was decided by the lower courts or presented for our review," it held that the plaintiff in *Sanders* enjoyed "a limited, but legitimate, expectation that [his] conversations and other interactions" would not be "secretly videotaped by undercover television reporters, even though those conversations may not have been completely private from the participants' coworkers."[759] According to the Court's unanimous opinion, written by Justice Werdegar, the facts before the Ninth Circuit in *Dietemann* served to "exemplify the idea of a legitimate expectation of limited privacy":

> [P]rivacy, for purposes of the intrusion tort, is not a binary, all-or-nothing characteristic. There are degrees and nuances to societal recognition of our expectations of privacy: the fact the privacy one expects in a given setting is not complete or absolute does not render the expectation unreasonable as a matter of law. Although the intrusion tort is often defined in terms of "seclusion," the seclusion referred to need not be absolute. "Like 'privacy,' the concept of 'seclusion' is relative. The mere fact that a person can be seen by someone does not automatically mean that he or she can legally be forced to be subject to being seen by everyone."[760]

---

756. See Sanders v. American Broadcasting Cos., 60 Cal. Rptr. 2d 595, 596 (Ct. App. 1997), *rev'd*, 978 P.2d 67 (Cal. 1999). The second plaintiff died during the course of jury deliberations and, as a result, his parents instituted a separate wrongful death action against the same defendants in federal court. See Kersis v. American Broadcasting Cos., No. CV-95-00848-JMJ (9th Cir. June 8, 1999). Shortly after the California Supreme Court's decision in *Sanders,* the Ninth Circuit affirmed a federal district court's dismissal of the wrongful death complaint. *Id.* In the wake of the court of appeals' ruling in *Sanders*, another federal court dismissed other civil actions, brought by other employees videotaped by the same defendants, raising analogous claims. See Sussman v. American Broadcasting Cos., 971 F. Supp. 432 (C.D. Cal. 1997), *aff'd*, 1999 U.S. App. LEXIS 19646 (9th Cir. Aug. 18, 1999) (holding that plaintiffs failed to state claim under 18 U.S.C. § 2511).

757. 60 Cal. Rptr. 2d at 597. See also Medical Lab. Management Consultants v. American Broadcasting Co., 931 F. Supp. 1487 (D. Ariz. 1996); Medical Lab. Management Consultants v. American Broadcasting Cos., 30 F. Supp. 2d 1182, 1190 (D. Ariz. 1998) (rejecting analogous claims).

758. 978 P.2d 67 (Cal. 1999).

759. *Id.* at 69, 72. See also Chap 12-4(c)(3) *supra* (discussing *Sanders*).

760. 978 P.2d at 72 (quoting 1 MCCARTHY, THE RIGHTS OF PUBLICITY AND PRIVACY § 5.10[A][2], at 5-120.1 (1998) and citing Dietemann v. Time, Inc., 449 F.2d 245 (9th Cir. 1971)) (other citations omitted).

By the same token, the Court in *Sanders* emphasized that "investigative journalists" do not "necessarily commit a tort by secretly recording events and conversations in offices, stores or other workplaces."[761] Rather, "[w]hether a reasonable expectation of privacy is violated by such recording depends on the exact nature of the conduct and all of the surrounding circumstances," and liability for intrusion also "requires that the invasion be highly offensive to a reasonable person, considering, among other factors, the motive of the alleged intruder."[762] Thus, the Court explained, "[n]othing we say here prevents a media defendant from attempting to show, in order to negate the offensiveness element of the intrusion tort, that the claimed intrusion, even if it infringed on a reasonable expectation of privacy, was 'justified by the legitimate motive of gathering the news.'"[763]

In adopting this analysis, the California Supreme Court relied on a concept of "limited" privacy drawn both from *Dietemann* and from its own decision in *Shulman v. Group W Productions, Inc.*[764] There, the same court addressed the efficacy of an intrusion claim arising, in part, from the audio recording of an accident victim's statements to a rescue worker, who was equipped with a wireless microphone. In another opinion by Justice Werdegar, the court concluded that whether the victim had a reasonable expectation of privacy in her communications with the worker sufficient to support a cause of action for intrusion constituted a question of fact to be resolved by a jury:

> While one who imparts private information risks the betrayal of his confidence by the other party, a substantial distinction has been recognized between the secondhand repetition of the contents of a conversation and its simultaneous dissemination to an unannounced second auditor, whether that auditor be a person or a mechanical device. . . . [S]uch secret monitor-

---

761. 978 P.2d at 69.

762. *Id.* (citing Shulman v. Group W Prods., Inc., 955 P.2d 469, 490, 496 (Cal. 1998)).

763. 978 P.2d at 77 (quoting Shulman v. Group W Prods., Inc., 955 P.2d at 493). Accord Deteresa v. American Broadcasting Cos., 121 F.3d 460, 465 (9th Cir. 1997), *cert. denied*, 118 S. Ct. 1840 (1998) ("offensiveness" is a function of "the degree of the intrusion, the context, conduct and circumstances surrounding the intrusion as well as the intruder's motives and objectives, the setting into which he intrudes and the expectations of those whose privacy is invaded"); Wilkins v. National Broadcasting Co., 84 Cal. Rptr. 2d 329, 336 (Ct. App. 1999) (finding that recording of business lunch at public restaurant was "not highly offensive to a reasonable person" as a matter of law); Medical Labs. Management Consultants v. American Broadcasting Cos., 30 F. Supp. 2d 1182, 1190 (D. Ariz. 1998) ("the public's interest in the news and the absence of less invasive methods of reporting the story may mitigate the offensiveness of the intrusion") (citing *Shulman*). See also Miller v. National Broadcasting Co., 232 Cal. Rptr. 668, 678 (Ct. App. 1986) ("while what is 'highly offensive to a reasonable person' suggests a standard upon which a jury would properly be instructed, there is a preliminary determination of 'offensiveness' which must be made by the court in discerning the existence of a cause of action for intrusion").

764. 955 P.2d 469 (Cal. 1998).

ing denies the speaker an important aspect of privacy of communication — the right to control the nature and extent of the firsthand dissemination of his statements.[765]

As in *Sanders*, however, Justice Werdegar cautioned in *Shulman* that even an intrusion upon a "reasonable expectation of privacy" is not actionable at common law unless it is "highly offensive."[766] And, "whether a reporter's alleged intrusion into private matters ... is 'offensive' and hence actionable as an invasion of privacy" must be determined by "the extent to which the intrusion was, under the circumstances, justified by the legitimate motive of gathering the news."[767] Thus, although the "mere fact the intruder was in pursuit of a 'story'" will not "justify an otherwise offensive intrusion," Justice Werdegar explained, "[i]nformation collecting techniques that may be highly offensive when done for socially unprotected reasons — for purposes of harassment, blackmail or prurient curiosity, for example — may not be offensive to a reasonable person when employed by journalists in pursuit of a socially or politically important story."[768] In the context of newsgathering, the court suggested, a court must balance the journalistic motive against "the particular method of investigation used"; in other words, while "'routine reporting techniques,' such as asking questions of people with information ('including those with confidential or restricted information') could rarely, if ever, be deemed an actionable intrusion," the same result would not likely obtain in the context of "violation of well-established legal areas of physical or sensory privacy — trespass into a home or tapping a personal telephone line."[769]

The *Dietemann* analysis has, however, been rejected by some courts, at least implicitly. In *McCall v. Courier-Journal*,[770] two newspaper reporters recorded conversations surreptitiously between the plaintiff, a lawyer, and one of his clients, who agreed to wear a hidden recording device to a meeting with the lawyer. The newspaper was investigating the client's allegations that the lawyer

---

765. *Id.* at 492 (quoting Ribas v. Clark, 696 P.2d 637, 640 (Cal. 1985)). The quoted portion of Justice Werdegar's opinion in *Shulman*, which was joined by two other justices, is repeated in her unanimous opinion for the court in *Sanders*. See 978 P.2d at 72.

766. 955 P.2d at 494.

767. *Id.* at 493.

768. *Id.* at 493. Accord Medical Lab. Management Consultants v. American Broadcasting Cos., 30 F. Supp. 2d 1182, 1190 (D. Ariz. 1998) (where it was "undisputed that Defendants were reporting on potential laboratory errors in testing of pap smears, information that was clearly in the public interest because the results of the tests involve vital health issues," court concluded that use of hidden microphone to record conversation with operator of lab "was not highly offensive as a matter of law").

769. 955 P.2d at 494 (citations omitted). See also Miller v. National Broadcasting Co., 232 Cal. Rptr. 668 (Ct. App. 1986).

770. 6 MEDIA L. REP. (BNA) 1112 (Ky. App. 1980), *rev'd on other grounds*, 623 S.W.2d 882 (Ky. 1981), *cert. denied*, 456 U.S. 975 (1982).

had indicated she could "buy her way out" of criminal charges by bribing the judiciary. The plaintiff claimed, *inter alia*, that the reporters "invaded his privacy by concealing a tape recorder" in the client's "purse prior to entering his office."[771] The Kentucky Court of Appeals rejected the claim, reasoning that the plaintiff spoke with his client "at his own risk" since she remained "free to reveal the conversation to anyone."[772] In addition, the court rejected the plaintiff's trespass claim on the ground that when he "suspected," as he conceded he did, that his client had "a recorder on her person, he should have asked her to depart."[773] His conduct in "continuing the conversation" constituted his consent to her presence, which relieved the reporters from liability as well.[774]

The Ninth Circuit has also rejected a plaintiff's claim that the recording of a face-to-face conversation, standing alone, constitutes an actionable invasion of privacy. In *Deteresa v. American Broadcasting Co.*,[775] the trial court concluded that summary judgment for the defendant was appropriate where the plaintiff "submitted no evidence to raise a triable issue of fact that her privacy was invaded by either the audio or video recordation of her *non*-confidential conversation with a person whom she knew was a reporter in a public location."[776] The Court of Appeals affirmed, holding that where the plaintiff "spoke voluntarily and freely with an individual whom she knew was a reporter" and where there was "no dispute that ABC videotaped Deteresa in public view from a public place, broadcast only a five-second clip of the tape, and did not broadcast either her name or her address, no intrusion into seclusion privacy claim lies as a matter of law."[777]

By the same token, in *Wolfson v. Lewis*,[778] a federal trial court entered an injunction prohibiting defendants, a television production crew, "from engaging in conduct, with or without the use of cameras and sound equipment, which invades the privacy" of the plaintiffs.[779] In so holding, the court was particularly disturbed by defendants' use of a "'shotgun mike' in an attempt to intercept and

---

771. 623 S.W.2d at 887.
772. 6 MEDIA L. REP. (BNA) at 1113. Cf. Ex parte State Record Co., 504 S.E.2d 592 (S.C. 1998) (affirming temporary restraining order prohibiting media defendant from disseminating surreptitiously videotaped, privileged communications between criminal suspect and his attorney).
773. 6 MEDIA L. REP. (BNA) at 113.
774. *Id.*; See *id.* (although "[a]ny person who causes another to trespass is also liable therefor," the reporters could not be liable since the client was present with the plaintiff's consent and not a trespasser).
775. 121 F.3d 460 (9th Cir. 1997), *cert. denied*, 118 S. Ct. 1840 (1998).
776. *Id.*
777. *Id.* at 466. Accord Wilkins v. National Broadcasting Co., 84 Cal. Rptr. 2d 329, 336 (Ct. App. 1999) (rejecting common law intrusion claim based on secret taping of business lunch at restaurant open to the public: "NBC photographed the two men in a public place and taped their conversations which were about business, not personal matters").
778. 924 F. Supp. 1413 (E.D. Pa. 1996)
779. *Id.* at 1435.

record, without consent, oral statements and conversations of the occupants" of plaintiffs' family home.[780] The court concluded that such conduct constituted an actionable invasion of privacy by intrusion, even though the plaintiffs' *own* conversations were never actually recorded:

> Both Pennsylvania and Florida[, where the recording occurred,] have recognized a person's right to privacy in oral, wire and electronic communications by enacting statutes making it a crime to intentionally intercept, endeavor to intercept or procure any other person to intercept any wire, oral or electronic or oral communications. . . . The Court finds that there is a likelihood that a jury would find that . . . use of the "shotgun mike" under the circumstances outlined herein was an actionable intrusion.[781]

§ 13-8. Hidden Cameras.

Technology's most visible impact on the law of newsgathering has arguably been in the phenomenon of video recording. The advent of "lipstick" size video cameras, which can be easily and surreptitiously affixed to a lapel or cap, has permitted journalists to record precisely what previously they could only see and report about from memory. Moreover, the availability of such technology, and the vivid images it often yields, has arguably increased the news media's incentive to assume fictitious identities for the purpose of securing access to places where their miniature cameras can record that which was previously shielded from public view.[782]

---

780. *Id.* at 1433-34.

781. *Id.* (citing RESTATEMENT (SECOND) OF TORTS § 652B, cmt. b, Illus. 2, 3). See 18 PA. CONS. STAT. § 5701; FLA. STAT. § 934. See also Marich v. QRZ Media, Inc., 86 Cal. Rptr. 2d 406, 420 (Ct. App. 1999) (parents of victim of drug overdose can maintain intrusion claim for recording of police telephone call notifying them of son's death even if their comments were not recorded since the "fact the actual words spoken by the parents may not be discerned does not preclude the viewer from recognizing the anguish in the response to the phone call"). The court in *Wolfson* subsequently permitted plaintiffs to amend their complaint to allege the interception of communications in violation of state and federal wiretap statutes. See Wolfson v. Lewis, 168 F.R.D. 530 (E.D. Pa. 1996).

782. The use of fictitious identities by journalists is treated in some detail in Chap.13-2 *supra*, and the law surrounding the use of audio recording devices is discussed specifically in Chap. 13-7 *supra*. The Society of Professional Journalists, recognizing the increased use of hidden cameras in newsgathering, promulgated guidelines in 1992 that purport to articulate when hidden cameras are journalistically acceptable, i.e.:

— when information is of "profound importance" or of vital public interest;
— when "all other alternatives" for obtaining the information have been exhausted;
— when reporters "are willing to disclose the nature of the deception and the reason for it;"
— when a news organization demonstrates a "commitment of time and funding necessary to pursue the story fully;"

Once again, the modern law surrounding the use of hidden cameras appears to have its genesis in *Dietemann v. Time, Inc.*[783] The Ninth Circuit's early observations in that case, where magazine reporters equipped with hidden cameras assumed false identities to secure access to plaintiff's home and office, has continued to influence the law even as the available technology has become more sophisticated and its use more ubiquitous: "we have little difficulty," the court in *Dietemann* explained, in "concluding that clandestine photography of the plaintiff in his den and the recordation of his conversation without his consent resulting in emotional distress warrant recovery for invasion of privacy."[784] With respect to the defendants' claim that a First Amendment privilege envelops these "indispensable tools of investigative reporting," the court "strongly disagree[d]" that "hidden mechanical contrivances are 'indispensable tools' of newsgathering'":

> Investigative reporting is an ancient art; its successful practice long antedates the invention of miniature cameras and electronic devices. The First Amendment has never been construed to accord newsmen immunity from torts or crimes committed during the course of newsgathering. The First Amendment is not a license to trespass, to steal, or to intrude by electronic means into the precincts of another's home or office. It does not become such a license simply because the person subjected to the intrusion is reasonably suspected of committing a crime.[785]

Another early case, *Cassidy v. American Broadcasting Cos.*,[786] appeared to limit the broadest reading of *Dietemann* in the hidden camera context. In *Cassidy*, plaintiff, a police officer, was videotaped by a hidden camera from behind a two-way mirror while he was in a massage parlor. The appellate court affirmed summary judgment for defendants on plaintiff's intrusion claim, holding that his status as a public official distinguished the case from *Dietemann*.[787] Specifically, the court held that "the conduct of a policeman on duty is legitimately and necessarily an area upon which the public interest may and should be

---

— when "the harm prevented by the information revealed through deception outweighs any harm caused by the act of deception;" and
— when the news organization has "conducted a meaningful, collaborative and deliberative decision-making process."

See also Logan, *"Stunt Journalism," Professional Norms, and Public Mistrust of the Media*, 9 U. FLA. J.L. & PUB. POL'Y 151, 168 (1998) (proposing several forms of media self-regulation to address "increasingly prevalent" use of deceptive journalistic techniques in order to restore public trust in media).

783. 449 F.2d 245 (9th Cir. 1971).
784. *Id.* at 248.
785. *Id.* at 249.
786. 377 N.E.2d 126 (Ill. App. 1978).
787. See *id.* at 131-32.

focused."[788] Accordingly, "the very status of the policeman as public official . . . is tantamount to an implied consent to informing the general public by all legitimate means regarding his activities in discharge of his public duties."[789]

More recently, appellate courts have focused afresh on the use of hidden cameras as a newsgathering devise in a variety of contexts. In *CBS Inc. v. Davis*,[790] for example, Justice Blackmun — sitting as circuit justice — vacated an injunction entered by a South Dakota court that prohibited a television network from broadcasting videotape footage of operations inside plaintiff's meat packing facility. The footage was obtained through use of a hidden camera worn by one of plaintiff's employees.[791] Justice Blackmun rejected the notion that a prior restraint was justified because surreptitious taping constitutes a "'calculated misdeed,'" explaining that "[s]ubsequent civil or criminal proceedings, rather than prior restraints, ordinarily are the appropriate sanction for calculated defamation or other misdeeds in the First Amendment context."[792] In addition, Justice Blackmun appeared to dismiss the suggestion that the surreptitious taping at issue constituted a "misdeed" in any event.[793]

Similarly, in *In re King World Productions, Inc.*,[794] the Sixth Circuit also vacated an injunction issued by a trial judge prohibiting the broadcast of a videotape of plaintiff, a doctor, allegedly engaging in medical malpractice. Posing as a patient, an employee of the defendant broadcaster surreptitiously videotaped the plaintiff with a hidden camera.[795] The court held that "[p]rotection of the right to information that appeals to the public at large and which is disseminated by the media is the cornerstone of the free press clause of the First Amendment."[796] Accordingly, the court concluded that "[n]o matter how inappropriate the acquisition, or its correctness, the right to disseminate that information is what the Constitution is intended to protect."[797]

Outside the prior restraint context, the most influential appellate treatment of the hidden camera phenomenon is Judge Posner's opinion for the Seventh Circuit in *Desnick v. American Broadcasting Cos.*,[798] another case in which employees of a broadcaster posed as patients and surreptitiously videotaped their interactions with ophthalmologists employed by plaintiff, an eye care clinic. Because

---

[788]. *Id.* at 132.
[789]. *Id.*
[790]. 114 S. Ct. 912 (1994) (Blackmun, J., in chambers).
[791]. *Id.* at 913.
[792]. *Id.* at 914.
[793]. *Id.*
[794]. 898 F.2d 56 (6th Cir. 1990).
[795]. *Id.* at 58.
[796]. *Id.* at 59.
[797]. *Id.* Accord Charter Behavioral Health Sys. L.L.C. v. CBS Inc., No. 3:99-CV-150-MU (W.D.N.C. Apr. 21, 1999).
[798]. 44 F.3d 1345 (7th Cir. 1995).

"no intimate personal facts concerning the two individual plaintiffs . . . were revealed; and the only conversations that were recorded were conversations with" defendant's employees, the court held that there could be no actionable invasion of privacy.[799] The defendants, the court concluded, "did not order the camera-armed testers into the Desnick Eye Center's premises in order to commit a crime or tort."[800] Rather, their purpose "was to see whether the Center's physicians would recommend" unnecessary medical procedures.[801] Thus, the court held, if the "broadcast itself does not contain actionable defamation, and no established rights are invaded in the process of creating it (for the media have no general immunity from tort or contract liability), then the target has no legal remedy even if the investigatory tactics used by the network are surreptitious, confrontational, unscrupulous, and ungentlemanly."[802]

In *Deteresa v. American Broadcasting Co.*,[803] the Ninth Circuit similarly ruled in favor of defendants, a television network and one of its producers, in connection with claims arising from the surreptitious audio and video recording of a conversation between the producer and plaintiff, an American Airlines flight attendant who worked on the flight that O.J. Simpson took from Los Angeles to Chicago the night of the murders of Nicole Simpson and Ron Goldman. Identifying himself as an ABC employee, the producer spoke with the plaintiff outside her front door. When she declined to appear on camera for a live interview, the network instead incorporated approximately five seconds of the videotape with a reporter's voiceover in its broadcast. The district court granted summary judgment to the defendants on all counts, including invasion of privacy in taping the conversation and fraud in failing to inform plaintiff that the encounter was being tape recorded. The Ninth Circuit affirmed, holding that "the intrusion was not sufficiently offensive to state a common law intrusion into privacy claim"[804] because plaintiff was taped in public view from a public place while speaking freely with someone she knew to be a reporter. With respect to the fraud claim,

---

799. *Id.*
800. *Id.*
801. *Id.* at 1355.
802. *Id.* But see Copeland v. Hubbard Broadcasting, Inc., 526 N.W.2d 402, 405 (Minn. App. 1995) (where defendant news organization, accompanying a veterinarian, brought a hidden camera into plaintiff's home, court found that "[n]ewsgathering does not create a license to trespass or to intrude by electronic means into the precincts of another's home or office") (citing Dietemann v. Time, Inc., 449 F.2d 245, 249 (9th Cir. 1971)); Special Force Ministries v. WCCO Television, 584 N.W.2d 789, 793 (Minn. App. 1998) (where television station employee posed as unemployed volunteer and secretly videotaped footage at care facility for mentally retarded persons, court found that "neither the courts nor the legislature has given such representatives carte blanche to commit such torts [as fraud and trespass] in their pursuit of videotape"); Shiffman v. Empire Blue Cross & Blue Shield, 681 N.Y.S.2d 511, 512 (App. Div. 1998) (permitting trespass claim where consent to enter medical office with hidden camera was secured by fraud or misrepresentation).
803. 121 F.3d 460 (9th Cir. 1997), *cert. denied*, 118 S. Ct. 1840 (1998).
804. *Id.* at 466.

the court held that "even if the audiotaping and videotaping were wrongful under tort principles or a statute," the defendants "were not liable for failing to disclose [an] intention to commit those wrongful acts."[805]

Several appellate courts have, however, looked favorably on a variety of civil claims arising from hidden camera investigations by news organizations. In *Sanders v. American Broadcasting Cos.*,[806] the California Supreme Court, in substantial reliance on *Dietemann*, held that plaintiff, who had been secretly videotaped in a largely open work area where co-workers could observe him and listen to his conversations, nevertheless retained a "reasonable expectation of visual or aural privacy against electronic intrusion by a stranger to the workplace." In *Copeland v. Hubbard Broadcasting, Inc.*,[807] one Minnesota appellate court similarly embraced *Dietemann* and held that the use of a hidden camera by a disguised reporter accompanying a veterinarian into plaintiff's home could support an intrusion claim. And, contrary to the Seventh Circuit's reasoning in *Desnick*, some appellate courts have determined that the use of hidden cameras in connection with misrepresentations concerning the identity or purpose of the person "operating" the concealed device can sustain a civil action for fraud or trespass.[808]

The trial courts have also been badly divided concerning the availability of a common law cause of action for injury allegedly resulting from the use of hidden

---

805. *Id.* at 467-68. Accord Willis v. Griffin Television, L.L.C., Case No. 91,812 (Okla. App. Mar. 5, 1999). In *Willis*, an Oklahoma appellate court affirmed dismissal of a host of tort and statutory claims, including trespass, illegal interception of communications, and fraudulent misrepresentation, arising from a television station's hidden camera investigation of local day care centers. Reporters disguised themselves as parents seeking day care for their children and sought a tour of the premises, which they surreptitiously videotaped. The court adopted the *Desnick* analysis, holding that where the "peaceful and non-disruptive news gathering methods [were] not supportive of a claim for trespass," the fraudulent interception and interception of communications claims failed as well. *Id.*, slip op. at 17 (citing Desnick v. American Broadcasting Co., 44 F.3d 1345 (7th Cir. 1995)). The court permitted defamation and false light invasion of privacy claims to proceed, finding that plaintiffs' allegations that the television station disregarded the falsity of its broadcast were sufficient to state claims. Slip op. at 16, 18.

806. 978 P.2d 67, 77 (Cal. 1999) (citing Dietemann v. Time, Inc., 449 F.2d 245, 249 (9th Cir. 1971)); see Chaps. 12-4(c)(3) & 13-7(c) *supra* (discussing *Sanders*). See also Marich v. QRZ Media, Inc., 86 Cal. Rptr. 2d 406 (Ct. App. 1999) (relying on *Sanders* and *Shulman*, appellate court held that plaintiff stated claim for intrusion based on recording of telephone call placed by police to parents of drug-overdose victim). But see Wilkins v. National Broadcasting Co., 84 Cal. Rptr. 2d 329, 336 (Ct. App. 1999) (following *Shulman*, but prior to *Sanders*, California appellate court dismissed intrusion claim based on hidden camera investigation of salesmen secretly videotaped on restaurant patio while meeting with reporters purporting to be potential investors).

807. 526 N.W.2d 402, 405 (Minn. App. 1995) (citing *Dietemann*).

808. See Special Force Ministries v. WCCO Television, 584 N.W.2d 789, 793 (Minn. App. 1998) (fraud and trespass claims in connection with hidden camera investigation of facility for mentally retarded); Shiffman v. Empire Blue Cross & Blue Shield, 681 N.Y.S.2d 511, 512 (App. Div. 1998) (trespass claim arising from hidden camera investigation of doctor).

cameras in newsgathering. In *Food Lion, Inc. v. Capital Cities/ABC Inc.*,[809] a federal court jury returned a verdict for plaintiff, a supermarket chain, for approximately $1,500 in compensatory damages and $5.5 million in punitive damages arising from an undercover investigation involving the use of hidden cameras.[810] In denying defendants' motion for summary judgment, the court concluded that the plaintiff had amassed sufficient evidence to get to a jury on causes of action sounding in fraud, trespass, and breach of fiduciary duty, the latter claim arising from the reporters' decision to infiltrate the plaintiff's operations by applying for and accepting jobs at two of its stores.[811] Thus, although the court did not adjudicate claims concerning the use of hidden cameras per se, it did premise its ruling as to the viability of those causes of action submitted to the jury in part on the fact that (1) defendants had failed to disclose the existence of the cameras or their purpose in having them when they applied for employment in plaintiff's stores and (2) defendants had engaged in surreptitious videotaping at the stores in a manner inconsistent with their duty of loyalty to their putative employer, the supermarket chain.[812] Indeed, in this regard, the court noted that a jury could properly find defendants' "presence in Food Lion to be purely incidental to their jobs with PrimeTime Live and that they hoped to be admitted to areas of the store not open to the general public to 'steal' that which was otherwise not available to them — the images of those areas."[813]

By the same token, other trial courts have held that a television network's use of a hidden camera was not actionable in tort. In *Russell v. American Broadcasting Cos.*,[814] for example, one federal district court rejected plaintiff's in-

---

809. 951 F. Supp. 1224 (M.D.N.C. 1996); 951 F. Supp. 1217 (M.D.N.C. 1996). See Tuley, *Outtakes, Hidden Cameras, and the First Amendment: A Reporter's Privilege*, 38 WM. & MARY L. REV. 1817, 1819 (1997) ("posit[ing] that the courts are biased against television reporter work product, and that this bias arises from a general prejudice against television as a medium"); Borger, *supra* note 6, at 67 (criticizing *Food Lion* court's "excessively narrow analysis [which] fail[s] to recognize that in this context, trespass and other torts are not being used as part of a state's general laws, but are being invoked specifically to deter or punish newsgathering and informing the public").

810. The court subsequently reduced the punitive damage award to $315,000. Food Lion, Inc. v. Capital Cities/ABC, Inc., 984 F. Supp. 923, 940 (M.D.N.C. 1997).

811. 951 F. Supp. at 1227.

812. See 951 F. Supp. 1224, 1229 (M.D.N.C. 1996); 951 F. Supp. 1217, 1219 (M.D.N.C. 1996).

813. *Id.* at 1223. The court distinguished *Desnick* on the ground that, *inter alia*, in that case, the defendants only "entered offices that were open to anyone expressing a desire for ophthalmic services," 44 F.3d at 1352, whereas in *Food Lion*, the defendants were engaged in "the taking of images which would have been unavailable absent misrepresentations which provided entry into restricted portions of Food Lion stores," 951 F. Supp. at 1223.

814. 23 MEDIA L. REP. (BNA) 2428 (N.D. Ill. 1995). See also Russell v. American Broadcasting Cos., 26 MEDIA L. REP. (BNA) 1012 (N.D. Ill. 1997) (rejecting defamation and false light invasion of privacy claims). The court's ruling with respect to statutory claims for violation of federal and state eavesdropping laws is discussed at Chap. 13-7(b)(4) *supra*.

trusion claim on the ground that defendants had done no more than "secretly record[ ] a conversation she willingly had with a co-worker at her place of business."[815] Such conduct, the court held, "is hardly 'offensive prying into the private domain of another,'" and does not state a claim for intrusion.[816] Similarly, in *Frome v. Renner*,[817] another federal trial court dismissed fraud claims arising from a hidden camera investigation in which a reporter posed as a test patient, holding that defendant's "use of a false identity did not affect the basic nature of his relationship with Plaintiff." And, in *Medical Laboratory Management Consultants v. American Broadcasting Cos.*,[818] the court granted summary judgment to a television network on plaintiff's intrusion claim where a journalist wearing a hidden camera and misrepresenting her identity had met with plaintiff in his office conference room and secured a tour of his laboratory for testing pap smears. The court determined that plaintiff had "no reasonable expectation of privacy in the location or contents of the conversations" with the undercover journalist and that "reporting on potential laboratory errors in testing pap smears ... was clearly in the public interest," thereby precluding a finding that the use of hidden cameras in connection with such reporting was "highly offensive."[819] In addition, the court granted summary judgment with respect to plaintiff's trespass claim, finding that he had sustained no damages as a result, but declined to dismiss plaintiff's fraud claim on the ground that, although he could not properly be awarded damages attributable to the resulting broadcast or for emotional distress, plaintiff could potentially recover "'approximately $3,000 in out of pocket costs for medical treatment and psychological counseling.'"[820]

---

815. 23 MEDIA L. REP. (BNA) at 2434.

816. *Id.* Plaintiff's defamation and invasion of privacy claims were subsequently rejected because the broadcast was held to be substantially true or, alternatively, because plaintiff failed to establish actual malice. See Russell v. American Broadcasting Cos., 26 MEDIA L. REP. (BNA) 1012, 1016, 1020 (N.D. Ill. 1997).

817. 26 MEDIA L. REP. (BNA) 1956, 1958 (C.D. Cal. 1997); see *id.* ("'A false representation which cannot possibly affect the intrinsic merits of a business transaction must necessarily be immaterial because reliance upon it could not produce injury in a legal sense.'") (quoting Hill v. Wrather, 323 P.2d 567 (Cal. 1958)).

818. 30 F. Supp. 2d 1182, 1190 (D. Ariz. 1998). The court's dismissal of plaintiff's conspiracy, negligent infliction of emotional distress, trade libel, and unfair business practices claims is addressed in *In re Medical Laboratory Management Consultants*, 931 F. Supp. 1487, 1494 (D. Ariz. 1996).

819. 30 F. Supp. 2d at 1190 (citing Shulman v. Group W Prods., Inc., 955 P.2d 469, 490 (Cal. 1998)). But cf. Sanders v. American Broadcasting Cos., 978 P.2d 67, 77 (Cal. 1999) (finding that employee of telepsychic hotline had "reasonable expectation" of privacy in workplace against electronic recording of his conversations with co-workers).

820. 30 F. Supp. 2d at 1200. See *id.* at 1202-03 (rejecting *Desnick* analysis of trespass claim but finding that plaintiff could not prove any damages caused by the trespass).

§ 13-9. Unauthorized Access to Computer Systems.

§ 13-9(a). Federal Law.

Unauthorized access to a computer may violate federal law. One author has argued that unauthorized use of a password to access a computer bulletin board, or computer network, would constitute a violation of the Wiretap Act.[821] Such unauthorized access may also be a violation of the Computer Fraud and Abuse Act.[822] Accessing any computer, without authorization or by exceeding authorized access, to obtain national security information[823] or information contained in a record of a financial institution,[824] is punishable by fine or imprisonment.[825] Accessing a "Federal interest computer"[826] without authorization or by exceeding authorized access, with the intent to defraud, thereby obtaining anything of value,[827] is also punishable by fine or imprisonment.[828]

§ 13-9(b). State Law.

Many states have reacted to the threat of computer hackers, snoops and thieves by enacting legislation prohibiting unauthorized access to computer sys-

---

821. See H. PERRITT, LAW AND THE INFORMATION SUPERHIGHWAY 111-12 (1996).

822. 18 U.S.C. § 1030. See United States v. Sablan, 92 F.3d 865, 868 (9th Cir. 1996) (Computer Fraud and Abuse Act requires that defendant need only "intentionally" access the computer, the government does not need to prove that defendant intentionally "damaged" computer files); United States v. Morris, 928 F.2d 504 (2d Cir.), *cert. denied*, 502 U.S. 817 (1991); Hotmail Corp. v. Van$ Money Pie, Inc., 47 U.S.P.Q.2d 1020 (N.D. Cal. 1998) (company that attempts to send junk e-mail and in the process falsifies return e-mail addresses, knowingly causing false information to be transmitted to e-mail recipients and causing damage to the e-mail provider's computer system, is likely to be found in violation of the Computer Fraud and Abuse Act). See generally Daly, *The Computer Fraud and Abuse Act — A New Perspective: Let the Punishment Fit the Damage*, 12 J. MARSHALL J. COMPUTER & INFO. L., 445 (1993); Hong, *Hacking Through the Computer Fraud and Abuse Act*, 31 U.C. DAVIS L. REV. 283 (1997).

823. 18 U.S.C. § 1030(a)(1).

824. *Id.* § 1030(a)(2).

825. *Id.* § 1030(c)(1) & (2).

826. "Federal interest computer" means a computer:

(A) exclusively for the use of a financial institution or the United States government, or, in the case of a computer not exclusively for such use, used by or for a financial institution or the United States Government and the conduct constituting the offense affects the use of the financial institution's operation or the government's operation of such computer; or (B) which is one of two or more computers used in committing the offense, not all of which are located in the same State.

Id. § 1030(e)(2).

827. *Id.* § 1030(a)(4). See United States v. Czubinski, 106 F.3d 1069, 1078 (1st Cir. 1997) (accessing files and "merely viewing information" does not constitute obtaining "anything of value").

828. 18 U.S.C. § 1030(c)(3).

tems.[829] These statutes may contain broad prohibitions regarding access to or the use of computerized information. The California statute, for example, applies to any person who "[k]nowingly accesses and without permission takes, copies, or makes use of any data from a computer, computer system, or computer network, or takes or copies any supporting documentation, whether existing or residing internal or external to a computer, computer system, or computer network,"[830] or who "[k]nowingly and without permission accesses or causes to be accessed any computer, computer system, or computer network."[831]

---

829. See, e.g., ALASKA STAT. § 11.46.484; CAL. PENAL CODE § 502; CAL. GOV'T CODE § 11771; CONN. GEN. STAT. §§ 53a-251, 54-142i; DEL CODE ANN. tit. 11, §§ 932, 935, 8606; HAW. REV. STAT. §§ 708-890 to 708-896; IOWA CODE § 716A.2; KY. REV. STAT. ANN. § 434.845; ME. REV. STAT. ANN. tit. 17, § 431; MD ANN. CODE, art. 27, § 146; MASS. GEN. LAWS ch. 266, § 120F; MICH. COMP. LAWS § 752.795; MINN. STAT. § 270B.18; NEV. REV. STAT. § 242.111; N.H. REV. STAT. ANN. § 638:17; N.J. STAT. ANN. § 2A:38A-3; N.M. STAT. ANN. §§ 15-1-9, 30-45-5; N.Y. PENAL LAW § 156.05; OHIO REV. CODE ANN. § 2913.04(B); OKLA. STAT. tit. 21, § 1953; S.C. CODE ANN. § 16-16-20; UTAH CODE ANN. § 76-6-703; WASH. REV. CODE § 9A.52.110; W. VA. CODE § 61-3C-5; WIS. STAT. § 943.70. See also Ohio v. Perry, 697 N.E.2d 624 (Ohio 1998) (Ohio's statute regarding unauthorized computer access preempted by Copyright Act). Some states limit their statutes to the unauthorized access of criminal history records. See, e.g., ARIZ. REV. STAT. § 41-1750; NEB. REV. STAT. § 29-3519; UTAH CODE ANN. § 53-5-214.

830. CAL. PENAL CODE § 502(c)(2).

831. *Id.* § 502(c)(7); see People v. Lawton, 56 Cal. Rptr. 2d 521, 523 (Ct. App. 1996) (defendant violated § 502(c)(7) when he permissibly used a public computer to access information that was not open to the public). See also ACLU v. Miller, 977 F. Supp. 1228, 1232 (N.D. Ga. 1997) (Georgia statute that prohibits internet transactions which "falsely identify" sender is unconstitutional content-based restriction); Briggs v. Maryland, 704 A.2d 904, 910 (Md. 1998); Pennsylvania v. Gerulis, 616 A.2d 686 (Pa. Super. 1992).

Chapter 14

EVOLUTION OF THE JOURNALISTS' PRIVILEGE

§ 14-1. The Privilege at Early Common Law.
§ 14-2. The Constitutional Privilege: The Early Cases.
§ 14-3. *Branzburg v. Hayes*: The Consolidated Cases.
§ 14-4. *Branzburg v. Hayes*.
  § 14-4(a). The Opinion of the Court.
  § 14-4(b). Justice Powell's Concurring Opinion.
  § 14-4(c). Justice Stewart's Dissenting Opinion.
§ 14-5. *Branzburg* in The Supreme Court.
  § 14-5(a). The Prison Access Cases.
  § 14-5(b). The Privilege Cases.
  § 14-5(c). The Incidental Restraint Cases.
  § 14-5(d). The Court Closure Cases.
  § 14-5(e). The *McIntyre* Decision.
  § 14-5(f). The Chambers Opinions.
§ 14-6. *Branzburg* in The Lower Courts.
  § 14-6(a). The Second Circuit Approach.
  § 14-6(b). The Sixth Circuit Approach.

Although it traces its legal force to several alternative sources, journalists and news organizations in the United States today enjoy, in many circumstances, a privilege from compelled disclosure of information not available to most citizens. In some jurisdictions, it is not characterized as a "privilege" at all, though it has much the same force. Most courts, federal and state, have declared that the privilege is grounded in the First Amendment, though the Supreme Court has yet to address the issue squarely. Other courts have developed the privilege as a matter of common law, while most states — though not Congress — have enacted legislation codifying it in some form.

This lack of national uniformity, however, should not obscure the fact that, in one way or another, journalists and news organizations throughout the United States are, more often than not, privileged to refuse to disclose information obtained by them in the course of gathering the news.[1] By the same token, the

---

[1]. See generally REPORTERS COMMITTEE FOR FREEDOM OF THE PRESS, AGENTS OF DISCOVERY: A REPORT ON THE INCIDENCE OF SUBPOENAS SERVED ON THE NEWS MEDIA IN 1997 (1997). Drawing on American precedent, the European Court of Human Rights of the Council of Europe has held that requiring a reporter to disclose confidential sources violates Article 10 of the Convention for the Protection of Human Rights and Fundamental Freedoms, unless justified by an "overriding requirement in the public interest." In re Goodwin v. United Kingdom, No. 16/1994/463/544 (Mar. 27, 1996). The court declared that the protection of a journalist's confidential sources "is one of the basic conditions for press freedom." *Id.* at 17. In so holding, the European Court disapproved a decision of the English House of Lords requiring a journalist to reveal his source. More than 20 European countries are bound by treaty to implement the decision in *Goodwin* in their national law. See also DeHaes & Gijsels v. Belgium, No. 19983/121 (Feb. 24, 1997) (following *Goodwin*). But

privilege's many forms and legal bases do lead to real-world differences in its application and, therefore, call for an understanding of those differences and an appreciation of how they came to develop. Indeed, the truth is that the privilege, in all of its forms, continues to evolve, a phenomenon that renders a sense of how that evolution has progressed thus far essential.

Accordingly, in this chapter, we trace the development of the privilege in the United States, from the earliest shield laws and common law pronouncements at the turn of the last century to the constitutional privilege recognized in different state and federal jurisdictions today. In between, we examine the earliest ruminations about the constitutional privilege, its initial consideration by the Supreme Court in *Branzburg v. Hayes*, and the subsequent (and decidedly infrequent) clues emanating from the Court about its contours and viability.

§ 14-1. The Privilege at Early Common Law.

At common law, courts routinely rejected the occasional suggestion that journalists, like doctors, lawyers, or the clergy, enjoyed a privilege to decline to reveal confidences gained in the course of practicing their professions. In the absence of a statute creating such a privilege, the courts held that the common law admitted of no such exception to the obligation of all citizens to provide testimony pursuant to judicial or other legal process. Indeed, it appears that courts in California,[2] Colorado,[3] New York,[4] Florida,[5] Georgia,[6] Hawaii,[7] New Jersey,[8] Massachusetts,[9] and Missouri[10] all had issued decisions expressly reject-

---

see Camelot Group Plc v. Centaur Communications Ltd., 147 NLJ 1618 (Ct. App. Oct. 23, 1997) ("the public interest in enabling [ ] Plaintiffs to discover a disloyal employee in their midst who leaked [ ] confidential information ... was greater than the public interest in enabling him to escape detection"; journalist ordered to return leaked confidential documents, even though they "contain references, dates and notes which could easily lead to the identification of the source of the information").

2. See People v. Durrant, 48 P. 75, 86 (Cal. 1897); Ex Parte Lawrence, 48 P. 124 (Cal. 1897).
3. See Joslyn v. People, 184 P. 375, 377 (Colo. 1919).
4. See People ex rel. Mooney v. Sheriff of New York County, 199 N.E. 415, 415-16 (N.Y. 1936).
5. See Clein v. Florida, 52 So. 2d 117, 120 (Fla. 1950).
6. See Plunkett v. Hamilton, 70 S.E. 781 (Ga. 1911); Pledger v. Georgia, 3 S.E. 320, 322 (Ga. 1887).
7. See In re Wayne, 4 U.S.D.C. Haw. 475, 476 (1914) ("Though there is a canon of journalistic ethics forbidding the disclosure of a newspaper's source of information — a canon worthy of respect and undoubtedly well-founded, it is subject to a qualification; It must yield when in conflict with the interests of justice — the private interests involved must yield to the interests of the public.").
8. See New Jersey v. Donovan, 30 A.2d 421, 425 (N.J. 1943); In re Grunow, 85 A. 1011 (N.J. 1936).
9. See Brewster v. Boston Herald-Traveler Corp., 20 F.R.D. 416 (D. Mass. 1957).
10. See Ex Parte Holliway, 199 S.W. 412 (Mo. 1917).

ing the notion of a common law-based privilege prior to 1958. Most of these courts emphasized the general rule, applied throughout the law of evidence, "not to extend the classes to whom the privilege from disclosure is granted, but to restrict that privilege."[11]

In *People ex rel. Mooney v. Sheriff of New York County*,[12] for example, the New York Court of Appeals was urged to hold that "the basis for the privilege granted in the cases where it is conceded to be properly granted exists in the case of a reporter."[13] Specifically, the journalists in *Mooney* pointed to "certain common law cases where the privilege is granted, like communications made to a judge, to a district attorney, and to police officers" and argued that the "principle underlying the granting of those privileges exists in the case of the reporter" as well.[14] The court of appeals, however, rejected the suggestion that "the development of the law and changes in social relations require that courts now extend the privilege to a reporter," holding instead that "[i]f that is to be done, it should be done by the Legislature."[15]

This approach, though illustrative of how the common law courts treated claims by journalists that they should not be compelled by courts to reveal the fruits of the newsgathering enterprise, met with at least some early resistance and efforts at legislative reform. In 1896, for example, when a newspaper reporter was jailed after refusing to testify before a grand jury about his sources, the Maryland legislature passed the nation's first "shield law," which granted reporters a broad privilege to decline to provide testimony in judicial proceedings.[16] In all, thirteen states had enacted shield laws by 1968.[17] Nevertheless,

---

11. People ex rel. Mooney v. Sheriff of New York County, 199 N.E. 415, 415-16 (N.Y. 1936). Accord 4 J. WIGMORE, EVIDENCE, § 2192, at 70 (McNaughton rev. ed. 1961) ("We start with the primary assumption that there is a general duty to give what testimony one is capable of giving and that any exemptions which may exist are distinctly exceptional, being so many derogations from a positive general rule."). See generally Ayala & Martyn, *To Tell or Not To Tell: An Analysis of Testimonial Privileges: The Parent-Child and Reporters' Privileges*, 9 ST. JOHN'S J.L. COMM. 163 (1993) (tracing the historical development of the reporters' privilege).

12. 199 N.E. 415 (N.Y. 1936).

13. *Id.* at 415.

14. *Id.*

15. *Id.*

16. See MD. CODE ANN., CTS. & JUD. PROC. § 9-112 (current version). The history of the Maryland shield law's adoption is discussed in *Lightman v. Maryland*, 294 A.2d 149, 152 n.2 (Md. Spec. App.), *aff'd*, 295 A.2d 212 (Md. 1972), *cert. denied*, 411 U.S. 951 (1973).

17. See ALA. CODE tit. 7, § 370 (1958); ARIZ. REV. STAT. § 12-2237 (Cum. Supp. 1966); ARK. STAT. ANN. § 43-917 (1964); CAL. EVID. CODE § 1070 (1966); IND. ANN. STAT. § 2-1733 (Cum. Supp. 1966); KY. REV. STAT. § 421.100 (1963); LA. REV. STAT. § 45:1451 to 45:1454 (Cum. Supp. 1965); MD. CODE ANN. art. 35, § 2 (1965); MICH. STAT. ANN. § 28.945(1) (1954); MONT. REV. CODE, §§ 93-60101, 93-601-2 (1964); N.J. STAT. ANN. §§ 2A:84A-21, 2A:84A-29 (Cum. Supp. 1966); OHIO REV. CODE ANN. §§ 2739.04, 2739.12 (Supp. 1966); PA. STAT. ANN. Tit. 28, § 330 (Cum. Supp. 1965).

courts and commentators appeared to agree that, "[u]nless otherwise specifically provided by statute, communications to newspapers or to newspaper reporters or editors are not privileged."[18]

§ 14-2. The Constitutional Privilege: The Early Cases.

The perceived unresponsiveness of the common law, coupled with the relatively slow pace of legislation and a healthy skepticism of legislative action in this field generally,[19] led journalists and news organizations to look to the Constitution as the principal source of legal authority undergirding the privilege. The first reported decision to address the *bona fides* of a constitutional privilege appears to be the Second Circuit's 1958 opinion in *Garland v. Torre*.[20]

The assertion of a First Amendment-based privilege in *Garland* arose in the context of a defamation action instituted by actress/singer Judy Garland against CBS. Garland claimed that she was defamed as a result of comments about her, attributed to an anonymous CBS executive, that were published in a *New York Herald Tribune* column written by Marie Torre. At deposition, Torre "refused, under repeated questioning, to give the name of this 'network executive,' assert-

---

By 1972, largely in the wake of the outbreak of subpoenas of journalists that spawned, *inter alia*, the Supreme Court's decision in *Branzburg v. Hayes*, 408 U.S. 665 (1972), four additional states had enacted "shield laws." See ALASKA STAT. § 09.25.150 (Supp. 1971); NEV. REV. STAT. § 49.275 (1971); N.M. STAT. ANN. § 20-1-12.1 (1970); N.Y. CIV. RIGHTS LAW, c. 6, § 79-h (McKinney Supp. 1971-1972).

18. 58 AM. JUR. *Witnesses* § 546, at 305; see *id.* ("[A] reporter cannot claim exemption as a witness from answering a question, on the ground that he had received the information under a promise that he would not divulge the name of his informant, and that to do so would subject him to ridicule and contempt, and would cause him to lose his position as a newspaper reporter."); 102 A.L.R. 771 ("It is clearly the general rule that communications made to a journalist do no enjoy any privilege against use as evidence, and newspapermen may be compelled to reveal information given to them in their professional capacity"); 97 C.J.S. *Witnesses* § 259, at 743 ("The rule of privileged communications does not, in the absence of statute, apply to communications to a newspaper editor or reporter, for, although there is a canon of journalistic ethics forbidding the disclosure of a newspaper's source of information, it is subject to qualification and must yield when in conflict with the interests of justice.").

19. Many journalists and news organizations have declined to seek legislative codification of the privilege on the ground that "[s]uch a practice would be potentially destructive of the very freedom that is sought to be preserved." Oregon v. Buchanan, 436 P.2d 729, 731 (Or.), *cert. denied*, 392 U.S. 905 (1968). According to this view, the First Amendment requires government "to resist the normal temptation of rulers to regulate, license, or otherwise pass upon the credentials of those claiming to be authors and publishers," rendering an "invitation to the government to define the membership of that class" suspect. *Id.*

20. 259 F.2d 545 (2d Cir.), *cert. denied*, 358 U.S. 910 (1958). It further appears that, at about the same time, the Supreme Court denied *certiorari* in an unreported Colorado case in which the "constitutional issue was also directly raised." In re Goodfader's Appeal, 367 P.2d 472, 479 (Haw. 1961) (citing Murphy v. Colorado, 365 U.S. 843 (1961)).

ing that to do so would violate a confidence."[21] Torre was subsequently ordered by the trial court to disclose the identity of her source, held in contempt when she continued to decline to do so, and sentenced to ten days' imprisonment (although she was released on her own recognizance pending appeal).[22]

In the court of appeals, Torre's primary argument was "a Constitutional one — to compel newspaper reporters to disclose confidential sources of news would ... encroach upon freedom of the press guaranteed by the First Amendment, because 'it would impose an important practical restraint on the flow of news from news sources to news media and would diminish *pro tanto* the flow of news to the public.'"[23] The Second Circuit, in a unanimous decision by soon-to-be Justice Stewart, embraced Torre's constitutional premise: "we accept at the outset the hypothesis that compulsory disclosure of a journalist's confidential sources of information may entail an abridgment of press freedom by imposing some limitation upon the availability of news."[24] Thus, although the court recognized that "[f]reedom of the press within the historic meaning of the First Amendment meant primarily freedom from previous restraints upon publication and freedom from censorship," it concluded that the "fact that no direct restraint is imposed does not determine the question."[25]

Nevertheless, the *Garland* court further asserted that "freedom of the press, precious and vital though it is to a free society, is not an absolute."[26] Accordingly, the court concluded, a reporter's constitutional privilege to decline to disclose her source's identity can be overcome if "the interest to be served by compelling the testimony of the witness ... justified some impairment of this First Amendment freedom."[27] In the case of Torre's assertion of the privilege, the Second Circuit first noted that, "when the exercise of freedom of the press directly impedes the proper functioning of the judicial process, it must yield."[28] It then determined that the "question asked of the appellant went to the heart of the plaintiff's claim"[29] and that, "[w]hile it is possible that the plaintiff could

---

21. Garland v. Torre, 259 F.2d 545, 547 (2d Cir.), *cert. denied*, 358 U.S. 910 (1958).
22. It is not clear that Torre had expressly promised confidentiality to her source, though she apparently understood such confidentiality to inhere in the reporter-source relationship. *Id.* at 547 n.3.
23. *Id.* at 547-48 (quoting Appellant's Brief).
24. *Id.*
25. *Id.* at 548 (citing NAACP v. Alabama, 357 U.S. 449, 461 (1958) ("[A]bridgment of such rights, even though unintended, may inevitably follow from varied forms of governmental action.")).
26. 259 F.2d at 548.
27. *Id.*
28. *Id.* at 549 n.7.
29. *Id.* at 549-50. In that regard, the court noted that "we are not dealing here with the use of the judicial process to force a wholesale disclosure of a newspaper's confidential sources of news, nor with a case where the identity of the news source is of doubtful relevance or materiality." *Id.*

have learned the identity of the informant by further discovery proceedings directed at CBS, her reasonable efforts in that direction had met with singular lack of success."[30] Accordingly, the court concluded that, under such circumstances, "the Constitution conferred no right to refuse an answer."[31]

Justice Stewart's opinion in *Garland* proved influential, not so much for the result it reached, but for its apparent recognition of some form of privilege and its initial efforts to define the scope of such a constitutional rule. Indeed, much of the judicial debate in the years that followed centered on *Garland* and on Justice Stewart's analysis. Thus, in 1961, although the Hawaii Supreme Court conceded that it had been "unable to find" in other decided cases "any basis for concluding that the denial of a claim under the newsman's code constitutes an impairment of constitutional rights," it "assume[d], for the purposes of this case," on the authority of *Garland*, "that the forced disclosure of a reporter's confidential source of information may, to some extent, constitute an impairment of the freedom of the press."[32]

By the turn of the decade, other courts were more confident. In *In re Grand Jury Witnesses*, for example, a federal district court in California held that professional journalists, employed by a Black Panther Party newspaper, enjoyed a "'journalist's privilege'" to decline to answer grand jury inquiries about their confidential sources, which could be overcome only on a "showing by the government of a compelling and overriding national interest in requiring the testimony" that could not "be served by any alternative means."[33] Similarly, in

---

30. *Id.* at 551. Garland had deposed the two persons she believed might have been the source, both of whom denied the allegation under oath and professed no knowledge of the source's identity. *Id.* at 547.

31. *Id.* at 550.

32. In re Goodfader's Appeal, 367 P.2d 472, 480 (Haw. 1961). As in *Garland*, the Hawaii Supreme Court determined, however, that "such an impairment" was insufficient "to outweigh the necessity of maintaining the court's fundamental authority to compel the attendance of witnesses and to exact their testimony." *Id. Goodfader's Appeal* arose from a civil action instituted by one Gallas against the Civil Service Commission of the City and County of Honolulu, in which she sought reinstatement as the Commission's personnel director. Goodfader, a reporter for a daily newspaper, was present with a photographer at the Commission meeting at which Gallas was discharged. In his deposition in the civil action, Goodfader refused to identify the source of "confidential information" he had received that an attempt to fire Gallas would be made at the meeting. *Id.* at 475. Although the court was not "convinced that there is a First Amendment protection available to deponent," *id.* at 480, it also held, by analogy to the Supreme Court's then-fresh decision in *Hickman v. Taylor*, 329 U.S. 495 (1947) (recognizing protection from discovery for attorney work product), that it was "required to determine whether the inquiry plaintiff desired to make was of enough importance to her case and appeared sufficiently likely to be productive to warrant disregarding or overriding deponent's obligation to the tradition of his calling." 367 P.2d at 483.

33. 322 F. Supp. 573, 574 (N.D. Cal. 1970). Upon applying the aforementioned test, the court concluded that the Government had "clearly and convincingly established a compelling and

Wisconsin v. Knops, the Wisconsin Supreme Court held that a journalist "has a constitutional right to the privilege not to disclose his sources of information received in confidential relationship."[34]

By the same token, other courts considered, and rejected, *Garland*'s recognition of a constitutional privilege. In 1963, the Pennsylvania Supreme Court declined to accept the contention, by a daily newspaper and a host of *amici* representing publishers across the nation, that "the Constitutionally ordained privilege of freedom of the press encompasses and includes the right of nondisclosure of sources of information by newsmen."[35] And, in *Oregon v. Buchanan*, the Oregon Supreme Court held that "there is no constitutional reason for creating a qualified right for some, but not others, to withhold evidence as an aid to newsgathering."[36]

---

overriding interest to which the conflicting constitutional rights of the respondents must give way." *Id.* at 578.

34. 183 N.W.2d 93, 99 (Wis. 1971). The *Knops* case arose, as did many of the reporters' privilege cases of the time, from press reports about violent protest on college campuses. In *Knops*, a newspaper had published an article recounting the reasons for the bombing of Sterling Hall at the University of Wisconsin, based on interviews with the perpetrators. When the student editor declined to identify them to a grand jury, he was held in contempt. In a remarkably candid analysis of the competing interests, as it saw them, the court concluded:

> [I]n a disorderly society such as we are currently experiencing it may well be appropriate to curtail in a very minor way the free flow of information, such curtailment would serve the purpose of restoring an atmosphere in which all of our fundamental freedoms can flourish. One exceedingly fundamental freedom which the public is currently doing without is the freedom to walk into public buildings without having to fear for one's life.

Id. at 98. Accordingly, the court held that "the need for these answers is nothing short of the public's need (and right) to protect itself from physical attack." *Id.* at 98-99. In partial dissent, one justice predicted that, by recognizing that "a journalist may assert a constitutional privilege to protect the confidentiality of his news sources," the court's "opinion will stand as a landmark in legal history." *Id.* at 99 (Heffernan, J., dissenting in part). He parted company with the court, however, on the ground that, in his view, the Government had not sufficiently demonstrated that "no alternative method of getting any of this information is available." *Id.*

35. In re Taylor, 193 A.2d 181, 184 (Pa. 1963). In *Taylor*, the President and City Editor of the *Philadelphia Bulletin* were subpoenaed to testify before a grand jury investigating alleged corruption in the Philadelphia Zoning Board of Adjustment and Department of Licenses and Inspection. The grand jury was apparently interested in unpublished portions of an interview that the *Bulletin* had conducted with a former ward leader. Although the court flatly rejected the constitutional privilege, it upheld the right of the *Bulletin* representatives to withhold the requested information based exclusively on the Pennsylvania Shield Law. See *id.* at 186-87 (citing PA. STAT. ANN. tit. 28, § 330).

36. 436 P.2d 729, 732 (Or.), *cert. denied*, 395 U.S. 905 (1968). In *Buchanan*, as in *In re Taylor*, 193 A.2d 181 (Pa. 1963), national news media representatives urged the court, as *amici curiae*, to recognize a constitutional privilege. The case arose from a grand jury investigation of illegal marijuana usage; a reporter for a student newspaper had written an article based on interviews with seven admitted marijuana users. As discussed in note 19 *supra*, the court concluded that "it would be dangerous business for courts, asserting constitutional grounds, to extend to an employee of a

None of the aforementioned cases, even those that purported to recognize a constitutional privilege, applied it to protect a journalist or news organization from compelled disclosure. That landmark event apparently first took place in *United States v. Caldwell*,[37] one of the several consolidated cases that resulted in the Supreme Court's only direct pronouncement on the subject to date in *Branzburg v. Hayes*.[38]

§ 14-3. *Branzburg v. Hayes*: The Consolidated Cases.

United States v. Caldwell arose, like the other three cases that were ultimately and collectively adjudicated by the Supreme Court in *Branzburg v. Hayes*,[39] from the repeated clashes of the period between government, on the one hand, and allegedly violent, politically dissident groups and the so-called "drug culture," on the other. Fearful that publicity concerning their activities would lead to government identification and prosecution of their members, organizations such as the Black Panther Party and the Weathermen faction of Students for a Democratic Society came to condition the disclosure of information to journalists on promises that their identities would remain confidential. In response, the government turned to the courts to compel journalists to reveal the sources of their information about the allegedly illegal and occasionally violent activity undertaken by these purportedly subversive groups.[40]

'respectable' newspaper a privilege which would be denied to an employee of a disreputable newspaper; or to an episodic newspaper, or to a free-lance writer seeking a story to sell on the open market; or, indeed, to a shaggy nonconformist who wishes only to write out his message and nail it to a tree." 436 P.2d at 732.

37. 434 F.2d 1081 (9th Cir. 1970), *rev'd*, 408 U.S. 665 (1972).

38. 408 U.S. 665 (1972).

39. *Id.* (consolidating for decision Branzburg v. Pound, 461 S.W.2d 345 (Ky. 1970); Branzburg v. Meigs, 503 S.W.2d 748 (Ky. 1971); In re Pappas, 266 N.E.2d 297 (Mass. 1971); United States v. Caldwell, 434 F.2d 1081 (9th Cir. 1970)). See generally Goodale, *Branzburg v. Hayes and the Developing, Qualified Privilege for Newsmen*, 26 HASTINGS L.J. 709 (1975); Monk, *Evidentiary Privilege for Journalists' Sources: Theory and Statutory Protection*, 51 MO. L. REV. 1 (1986); Murasky, *The Journalist's Privilege: Branzburg and its Aftermath*, 52 TEX. L. REV. 829 (1974); Osborn, *The Reporter's Confidentiality Privilege: Updating the Empirical Evidence After a Decade of Subpoenas*, 17 COLUM. HUM. RTS. L. REV. 57 (1985); Comment, *Source Disclosure in Public Figure Defamation Actions: Towards Greater First Amendment Protection*, 33 HASTINGS L.J. 623 (1982); Comment, Branzburg v. Hayes: *A Need for Statutory Protection of News Sources*, 61 KY. L.J. 551 (1973); Note, *Disclosure of Confidential Sources in International Reporting*, 60 S. CAL. L. REV. 1631 (1987); Note, *Circumventing Branzburg: Absolute Protection for Confidential News Sources*, 18 SUFFOLK U.L. REV. 615 (1984). Much of the discussion that follows is adapted from Langley & Levine, *Branzburg Revisited: Confidential Sources and First Amendment Values*, 57 GEO. WASH. L. REV. 13, 16-19 (1988).

40. See, e.g., In re Grand Jury Witnesses, 322 F. Supp. 573, 577 (N.D. Cal. 1970); Wisconsin v. Knops, 183 N.W.2d 93, 94 (Wis. 1971); Osborn, *supra* note 39, at 60 ("Government prosecutors and legislators actively sought the assistance, voluntary or otherwise, of reporters who had established valuable confidential contacts with the leaders and rank-and-file members of these

In *United States v. Caldwell*, a *New York Times* correspondent assigned to report on the Black Panther Party and other militant groups was subpoenaed to testify before a federal grand jury in California. Caldwell moved to quash the subpoena on the ground that such an appearance would destroy his working relationship with his sources.[41] In response, the government contended that the grand jury was investigating possible violations of statutes outlawing, *inter alia*, threats against the President, attempted assassination and conspiracy to assassinate the President, civil disorder, interstate travel to incite a riot, and mail fraud.[42] The government further quoted from a news report, written by Caldwell, which indicated that "'[i]n their role as the vanguard in a revolutionary struggle the Panthers have picked up guns'" and which quoted an officer of the Black Panther Party as saying, "'[w]e advocate the very direct overthrow of the Government by way of force and violence. By picking up guns and moving against it because we recognize it as being oppressive and in recognizing that we know that the only solution to it is armed struggle [sic].'"[43]

Caldwell's motion to quash was denied, although the district court issued two orders protecting Caldwell from having to disclose "confidential associations, sources or information received, developed or maintained by him as a professional journalist in the course of his efforts to gather news for dissemination to the public."[44] When Caldwell refused to appear before the grand jury, he was held in contempt.

On appeal, the Ninth Circuit reversed, asserting that "[t]he need for an untrammeled press takes on special urgency in times of widespread protest and dissent."[45] According to the Ninth Circuit, "the First Amendment protections exist to maintain communication with dissenting groups and to provide the public with a wide range of information about the nature of protest and hetero-

---

'subversive' groups."); Note, *The Newsman's Privilege: Governmental Investigations, Criminal Prosecutions and Private Litigation*, 58 CAL. L. REV. 1198, 1202 (1970) ("There have been dozens, and probably hundreds, of [government] subpoenas in the last two years, most of which were issued in connection with investigations or prosecutions of dissident political groups."); Note, *Reporters and Their Sources: The Constitutional Right to a Confidential Relationship*, 80 YALE L.J. 317, 317 (1970) ("During the past year, federal and state prosecutors across the country have issued subpoenas to newsmen and their employers in order to gain access to confidential information obtained in the process of gathering news about highly controversial topics.").

41. The motion was supported by affidavits, executed by other journalists, that described the impact on news sources of requiring journalists to appear before grand juries. See 434 F.2d at 1084.

42. See 18 U.S.C. §§ 871, 1751, 231, 1341 (1982 & Supp. IV 1986).

43. Branzburg v. Hayes, 408 U.S. 665, 677 (1972) (quoting N.Y. TIMES, Dec. 14, 1969, at 64, cols. 1 & 2).

44. In re Caldwell, 311 F. Supp. 358, 362 (N.D. Cal. 1970), *rev'd*, Caldwell v. United States, 434 F.2d 1081 (9th Cir. 1970), *rev'd sub nom.* Branzburg v. Hayes, 408 U.S. 665 (1972).

45. Caldwell v. United States, 434 F.2d 1081, 1084 (9th Cir. 1970), *rev'd sub nom.* Branzburg v. Hayes, 408 U.S. 665 (1972).

doxy."[46] As a result, the court concluded that the First Amendment requires that the press enjoy a constitutional privilege to decline to appear before a grand jury, lest the "public's First Amendment right to be informed . . . be jeopardized."[47]

Specifically, the Ninth Circuit held that the First Amendment provides a qualified privilege to journalists, defeasible only by a showing of a compelling governmental interest. Absent "some special showing of necessity by the Government," the court held, the privilege further entitled Caldwell to decline to appear before the grand jury at all "because of the potential impact of such an appearance on the flow of news to the public."[48]

In re Pappas, the second of the consolidated cases before the Supreme Court in *Branzburg*, arose when a reporter-photographer, an employee of a New Bedford, Massachusetts television station, refused to answer questions posed by another grand jury.[49] Pappas, assigned to report on civil disorders in New Bedford, attempted to cover a Black Panther news conference at the Panthers' Headquarters in a boarded-up store. As a condition of entry, Pappas agreed not to disclose anything he saw or heard except an anticipated police raid. He remained in the Black Panther headquarters for about three hours; however, he witnessed no raid and wrote no story.[50]

Pappas was summoned before a Bristol County grand jury and refused to answer any questions concerning what had happened inside the Panthers' headquarters. On interlocutory review, the Massachusetts Supreme Judicial Court affirmed the trial court's denial of Pappas' motion to quash.[51] The court took judicial notice that "'in July, 1970, there were serious civil disorders in New Bedford, which involved street barricades, exclusion of the public from certain streets, fires, and similar turmoil,'" and "'that there was gunfire in certain streets.'"[52] Asserting the propriety of the grand jury investigation and the "limited" and "exceptional" nature of testimonial privileges generally, the court concluded that "[a]ny adverse effect upon the free dissemination of news" by virtue of Pappas's being called to testify was only "indirect, theoretical, and uncertain."[53] Accordingly, the court rejected the Ninth Circuit's reasoning in *Caldwell* and "adhere[d] to the view that there exists no constitutional news-

---

46. *Id.* at 1084-85.
47. *Id.* at 1089. See Caldwell, Branzburg v. Hayes: *The Law of Reporter's*, 15 COMM. LAW. 1 (Spring 1997).
48. Branzburg v. Hayes, 408 U.S. at 679.
49. In re Pappas, 266 N.E.2d 297 (Mass. 1971), *aff'd sub nom.* Branzburg v. Hayes, 408 U.S. 665 (1972).
50. See Branzburg v. Hayes, 408 U.S. at 672-75.
51. *Id.* at 673-75.
52. In re Pappas, 266 N.E.2d 297, 299 (Mass. 1971).
53. *Id.* at 302.

man's privilege, either qualified or absolute, to refuse to appear and testify before a court or grand jury."[54]

The remaining two cases that came before the Supreme Court in *Branzburg* involved the aforementioned Mr. Branzburg, a staff reporter for the Louisville, Kentucky *Courier-Journal*.[55] Branzburg had observed several residents of Jefferson County and Frankfort, Kentucky synthesizing hashish from marijuana, as well as using the drugs. He reported his observations in the *Courier-Journal* after promising his "sources" that he would not reveal their identities. When subpoenaed by two Jefferson County grand juries, Branzburg initially appeared but refused to identify the hashish makers. Subsequently, he moved to quash the second subpoena, on the ground that testifying before the grand jury would "'destroy the relationship of trust which he presently enjoys with those in the drug culture'" and would "'driv[e] a wedge of distrust and silence between the news media and the drug culture.'"[56] Although the motion to quash was denied, an order was issued protecting Branzburg from revealing "'confidential associations, sources or information,'"[57] but requiring him to answer questions concerning any criminal acts he observed being committed.

The Kentucky Court of Appeals further rejected Branzburg's argument that appearing before the grand jury at all would damage his effectiveness as a journalist.[58] In so doing, it announced its "misgivings" about the Ninth Circuit's decision in *Caldwell* on the ground that it constituted "a dramatic departure from the generally recognized rule that the sources of information of a newspaper reporter are not privileged under the First Amendment."[59] According to the Kentucky court, Branzburg's concern about jeopardizing his source relationships was "so tenuous that it does not ... present an issue of abridgement of the freedom of the press."[60]

§ 14-4. *Branzburg v. Hayes*.

The Supreme Court entered the debate on June 29, 1972, when it announced its decision in *Branzburg v. Hayes*,[61] a consolidated resolution of the *Caldwell*,

---

54. *Id.* at 302-03.
55. See Branzburg v. Pound, 461 S.W.2d 345 (Ky. 1970), *aff'd sub nom.* Branzburg v. Hayes, 408 U.S. 665 (1972); Branzburg v. Meigs, 503 S.W.2d 748 (Ky. 1971), *aff'd sub nom.* Branzburg v. Hayes, 408 U.S. 665 (1972).
56. Branzburg v. Hayes, 408 U.S. at 669 n.5 (quoting Motion to Quash).
57. *Id.* at 670.
58. See Branzburg v. Meigs, 503 S.W.2d at 751.
59. *Id.*
60. *Id.*
61. 408 U.S. 665 (1972). The consolidated cases attracted *amicus curiae* submissions from most major news organizations and the National District Attorneys Association, as well as briefs and/or argument by a host of leading constitutional scholars and advocates, including Solicitor General

Pappas, and *Branzburg* cases. The Court, however, chose to frame the question before it narrowly, indicating at the outset that the only issue it had undertaken to resolve was "whether requiring newsmen to appear and testify before state or federal grand juries abridges the freedom of speech and press guaranteed by the First Amendment."[62] A bare majority of the Court, formed only with the concurrence of Justice Powell who wrote separately, held "that it does not."[63] Beyond its conclusion that journalists enjoy no privilege to refuse to "appear and testify" before grand juries, therefore, *Branzburg* proved to be less a resolution of the efficacy of a constitutional privilege and more a starting point for additional and ongoing debate.

§ 14-4(a). The Opinion of the Court.

Justice White's opinion for the Court described the "heart" of the claim for constitutional privilege as the assertion that "the burden on newsgathering resulting from compelling reporters to disclose confidential information outweighs any public interest in obtaining the information."[64] In addition, the Court recognized that the "newsmen in these cases do not claim an absolute privilege," but rather that a "reporter should not be forced either to appear or testify before a grand jury or at trial until and unless sufficient grounds are shown for believing that the reporter possesses information relevant to a crime the grand jury is investigating, that the information the reporter has is unavailable from other sources, and the need for the information is sufficiently compelling to override the claimed invasion of First Amendment interests occasioned by the disclosure."[65]

At the outset, the Court dismissed the suggestion that "news gathering does not qualify for First Amendment protection."[66] Rather, the Court emphasized, "without some protection for seeking out the news, freedom of the press could be eviscerated."[67] This principle, which both begins and concludes the Court's analysis, has proven enormously influential in providing the underpinnings of

---

Erwin Griswold, law professors Alexander Bickel and Anthony Amsterdam, and practitioners E. Barrett Prettyman, Jr., Floyd Abrams, and Richard M. Schmidt.

62. *Id.* at 667. The petition for *certiorari* filed in *Caldwell*, the most highly publicized of the four consolidated cases, framed the issue in similar terms: "Whether a newspaper reporter who has published articles about an organization can, under the First Amendment, refuse to appear before a grand jury investigating possible crimes by members of that organization who have been quoted in the published articles." *Id.*

63. *Id.*
64. *Id.* at 681.
65. *Id.* at 680.
66. *Id.* at 681.
67. *Id.*

the First Amendment privilege as well as of constitutional protection for the newsgathering process generally.[68]

In considering a journalist's obligation "to respond to grand jury subpoenas as other citizens do and to answer questions relevant to an investigation into the commission of crime," however, the Court emphasized, first, that the constitutional protection afforded the press must be calibrated to reflect the nature of the governmental action at issue.[69] Thus, the Court distinguished the "incidental burdening of the press that may result from the enforcement of civil or criminal statutes of general applicability" — such as the enforcement of grand jury subpoenas — from "prior restraint or restriction on what the press may publish," "express or implied command[s] that the press publish what it prefers to withhold," "exaction or tax for the privilege of publishing," or "penalty, civil or criminal, related to the content of published material."[70] The Court's emphasis on the nature of the governmental restraint at issue — i.e., whether it constitutes an "incidental" or "direct" burden on the press — has become an important analytical distinction in subsequent cases.[71]

In the context of the case before it, the Court concluded that the burden on newsgathering was "consequential, but uncertain."[72] Justice White noted that, "[f]rom the beginning of our country the press has operated without constitutional protection for press informants, and the press has flourished."[73] Thus, although the record included voluminous affidavits from journalists documenting the deterrent effect of compelled testimony before a grand jury on sources' willingness to provide information for publication, the Court concluded that the "evidence fails to demonstrate that there would be a significant constriction of the flow of news to the public."[74]

---

[68]. See *id.* at 707 ("[A]s we have earlier indicated, news gathering is not without its First Amendment protections. . . .").

[69]. *Id.* at 682.

[70]. *Id.* at 681-82. In this regard, the Court indicated that direct restraints on the newsgathering process — e.g., governmental action that forbids or restricts the "use of confidential sources" or efforts "to require the press to publish its sources of information or indiscriminately to disclose them upon request" — must survive stricter First Amendment scrutiny. *Id.*

[71]. See Chap. 14-5(c) *infra* (discussing Justice White's and the Court's reliance on this theory of "incidental restraints" in other contexts).

[72]. Branzburg v. Hayes, 408 U.S. at 690.

[73]. *Id.* at 697-98. The Court rejected evidence that "press subpoenas ha[d] multiplied, that mutual distrust and tension between press and officialdom ha[d] increased, that reporting styles ha[d] changed, and that there is now more need for confidential sources, particularly where the press seeks news about minority cultural or political groups or dissident organizations suspicious of the law and public officials." *Id.* at 698. According to the Court, such "developments, even if true, are treacherous grounds for a far-reaching interpretation of the First Amendment." *Id.*

[74]. *Id.* at 693-94 (citing Guest & Stanzler, *The Constitutional Argument for Newsmen Concealing Their Sources*, 64 NW. U. L. REV. 18 (1969); V. BLASI, PRESS SUBPOENAS: AN EMPIRICAL AND LEGAL ANALYSIS 6-12); compare 408 U.S. at 736 n.20 (Stewart, J., dissenting) (describing

Second, the Court emphasized that constitutional protection of the newsgathering process may not be fashioned so as to "guarantee the press a constitutional right of special access to information not available to the public generally."[75] According to the Court, the "administration of a constitutional newsman's privilege would present practical and conceptual difficulties of high order," since "[s]ooner or later, it would be necessary to define those categories of newsmen who qualified for the privilege, a questionable procedure in light of the traditional doctrine that liberty of the press is the right of the lonely pamphleteer who uses carbon paper or a mimeograph just as much as of the large metropolitan publisher who uses the latest photocomposition methods."[76] This principle as

---

affidavits submitted by, *inter alia*, Walter Cronkite, Eric Sevareid, Mike Wallace, Dan Rather, and Marvin Kalb) with *id.* at 693 (opinion of the Court) ("we remain unclear how often and to what extent informers are actually deterred from furnishing information when newsmen are forced to testify before a grand jury"). According to the Court:

> The available data indicate that some newsmen rely a great deal on confidential sources and that some informants are particularly sensitive to the threat of exposure and may be silenced if it is held by the Court that, ordinarily, newsmen must testify pursuant to subpoenas, but the evidence fails to demonstrate that there would be a significant constriction of the flow of news to the public if this Court reaffirms the prior common law and constitutional rule regarding the testimonial obligations of newsmen. Estimates of the inhibiting effect of such subpoenas on the willingness of informants to make disclosures to newsmen are widely divergent and to a great extent speculative.

Id. at 693-94. See also REPORTERS COMMITTEE FOR FREEDOM OF THE PRESS, *supra* note 1 (describing newsroom policy changes effected in response to threat or receipt of subpoenas).

75. 408 U.S. at 684 (citing Zemel v. Rusk, 381 U.S. 1 (1965)). In *Zemel v. Rusk*, the Court had upheld the State Department's decision not to issue passports for travel to Cuba, even though such a restriction "render[ed] less than wholly free the flow of information concerning that country." 381 U.S. at 16. In so holding, the Court indicated that the "right to speak and publish does not carry with it the unrestrained right to gather information." *Id.* at 17. The Court in *Zemel* characterized the State Department's ban on travel to Cuba as "an inhibition of action" and noted that there "are few restrictions on action which could not be clothed by ingenious argument in the garb of decreased data flow. For example, the prohibition of unauthorized entry into the White House diminishes the citizen's opportunities to gather information he might find relevant to his opinion of the way the country is being run." *Id.*

Similarly, the Court in *Branzburg* noted that, "[d]espite the fact that news gathering may be hampered, the press is regularly excluded from grand jury proceedings, our own conferences, the meetings of other official bodies gathered in executive session, and the meetings of private organizations. Newsmen have no constitutional right of access to the scenes of crime or disaster when the general public is excluded, and they may be prohibited from attending or publishing information about trials if such restrictions are necessary to assure a defendant a fair trial before an impartial tribunal." 408 U.S. at 684-85. See Chap. 2-3 *supra* (access to judicial proceedings); Chap. 12-3 *infra* (access to crime and disaster scenes).

76. 408 U.S. at 703-04; see Lovell v. City of Griffin, 303 U.S. 444, 450, 452 (1938) (Freedom of the press "is not confined to newspapers and periodicals" and "necessarily embraces pamphlets and leaflets. . . . The press in its historic connotation comprehends every sort of publication which affords a vehicle of information and opinion."). As the Court noted in *Branzburg*:

well has assumed considerable significance in the evolution of constitutional protection for the newsgathering process.[77]

Third, the Court considered the nature of the governmental interest asserted in support of compelled enforcement of grand jury subpoenas issued to journalists. In this regard, the Court acknowledged the "longstanding principle that 'the public . . . has a right to every man's evidence,'" which it deemed "particularly applicable to grand jury proceedings."[78] Indeed, the Court characterized the grand jury as an "'instrument of justice'" that constitutes an important tool in "[f]air and effective law enforcement."[79] Thus, the Court concluded that the "requirement of those cases which hold that a State's interest must be 'compelling' or 'paramount' to justify even an indirect burden on First Amendment rights are also met here."[80]

> The informative function asserted by representatives of the organized press in the present cases is also performed by lecturers, political pollsters, novelists, academic researchers, and dramatists. Almost any author may quite accurately assert that he is contributing to the flow of information to the public, that he relies on confidential sources of information, and that these sources will be silenced if he is forced to make disclosures before a grand jury.

408 U.S. at 705.

77. See, e.g., Pell v. Procunier, 417 U.S. 817 (1974); Saxbe v. Washington Post Co., 417 U.S. 843 (1974); Houchins v. KQED, Inc., 438 U.S. 1 (1978); Richmond Newspapers, Inc. v. Virginia, 448 U.S. 555 (1980); Press-Enter. Co. v. Superior Ct., 478 U.S. 1 (1986).

78. Branzburg v. Hayes, 408 U.S. at 688 (quoting United States v. Bryan, 339 U.S. 323, 331 (1950)).

79. Branzburg v. Hayes, 408 U.S. at 687 (quoting Costello v. United States, 350 U.S. 359, 362 (1965)). See also 408 U.S. at 686-87 (necessity of enforcing grand jury subpoenas "is very much rooted in the ancient role of the grand jury that has the dual function of determining if there is probable cause to believe that a crime has been committed and of protecting citizens against unfounded criminal prosecutions").

The Court's opinion in *Branzburg*, especially as it relates to the competing interests at stake, displays as well an apparent focus on both the confidential sources at issue — i.e., dissident political or cultural groups — and the crimes that they had allegedly committed. See *id.* at 691-92 ("The [First] Amendment does not reach so far as to override the interest of the public in ensuring that neither reporter nor source is invading the rights of other citizens through reprehensible conduct forbidden to all other persons."). Much of the Court's analysis is premised upon the government's interest in "extirpating the traffic in illegal drugs, in forestalling assassination attempts on the President, and in preventing the community from being disrupted by violent disorders endangering both persons and property." *Id.* at 701. In this context, the Court concluded that "[t]he preference for anonymity of those confidential informants involved in actual criminal conduct is presumably a product of their desire to escape criminal prosecution" and that such a "preference . . . is hardly deserving of constitutional protection." *Id.* at 691. See generally Langley & Levine, *supra* note 39, at 20-21.

80. Branzburg v. Hayes, 408 U.S. at 700 (citing NAACP v. Button, 371 U.S. 415, 439 (1963); Thomas v. Collins, 323 U.S. 526, 530 (1945); Bates v. Little Rock, 361 U.S. 516, 524 (1960); NAACP v. Alabama, 357 U.S. 449, 464 (1958)). The Court declined to calibrate the governmental interest according to the magnitude of the criminal conduct being investigated by the grand jury. "By requiring testimony from a reporter in investigations involving some crimes but not in others,"

When the Court applied its analytical framework to the grand jury context, therefore, it had little difficulty in concluding that, in most circumstances, the First Amendment "does not reach so far as to override the interest of the public in ensuring that neither reporter nor source is invading the rights of other citizens through reprehensible conduct forbidden to all other persons."[81] Initially, the Court concluded that "[i]nsofar as any reporter in these cases undertook not to reveal or testify about the crime he witnesses, his claim of privilege under the First Amendment presents no substantial question. The crimes of news sources are no less reprehensible and threatening to the public interest when witnessed by a reporter than when they are not."[82]

In addition, the Court rejected, albeit with somewhat less enthusiasm, the suggestion that the privilege should apply in "those situations where a source is not engaged in criminal conduct but has information suggesting illegal conduct by others."[83] Here, the Court recognized that such "informants presumably desire anonymity in order to avoid being entangled as a witness in a criminal trial or grand jury investigation" and "may fear that disclosure will threaten their job security or personal safety."[84] Nevertheless, the Court concluded that "the relationship of many informants to the press is a symbiotic one which is unlikely to be greatly influenced by the threat of subpoena; quite often, such informants are members of a minority political or cultural group that relies heavily on the media to propagate its views, publicize its aims, and magnify its exposure to the public."[85]

By the same token, the Court explained that, even in the grand jury context, judges must balance the constitutional claim against the asserted governmental interest on the particularized record of each case. "Newsgathering," the Court reemphasized at the conclusion of its constitutional analysis, "is not without its First Amendment protections, and grand jury investigations if instituted or conducted other than in good faith, would pose wholly different issues for resolution under the First Amendment."[86] Not only would "[o]fficial harassment of the press undertaken not for purposes of law enforcement but to disrupt a

---

courts would "be making a value judgment that a legislature had declined to make, since in each case the criminal law involved would represent a considered legislative judgment, not constitutionally suspect, of what conduct is liable to criminal prosecution." Branzburg v. Hayes, 408 U.S. at 706.

81. 408 U.S. at 691-92.
82. *Id.*
83. *Id.* at 693.
84. *Id.*
85. *Id.* at 694-95.
86. *Id.* at 707 (citing Younger v. Harris, 401 U.S. 37, 49, 53-54 (1971)). In *Younger*, the Supreme Court held that a litigant must typically make a "showing of bad faith, harassment, or . . . other unusual circumstance" before a federal court is empowered to enjoin a state court criminal prosecution as based on a constitutionally invalid statute. 401 U.S. at 54.

reporter's relationship with his news sources . . . have no justification," but every grand jury "must operate within the limits of the First Amendment as well as the Fifth."[87]

Finally, the Court applied its constitutional analysis to the consolidated cases before it. It reversed the Ninth Circuit's decision in *Caldwell*, holding that "[i]f there is no First Amendment privilege to refuse to answer the relevant and material questions asked during a good-faith grand jury investigation, then it is *a fortiori* true that there is no privilege to refuse to appear before a grand jury until the Government demonstrates some 'compelling need' for a newsman's testimony."[88] For essentially the same reasons, the Court affirmed the decisions below in the *Pappas* case, asserting that the "only question presented at the present time . . . is whether petitioner Pappas must appear before the grand jury."[89] Lastly, the Court affirmed the decisions in the *Branzburg* cases, on the ground that Branzburg could not "refuse[] to answer questions that directly related to criminal conduct that he had observed and written about."[90]

§ 14-4(b). Justice Powell's Concurring Opinion.

The Court's opinion, written by Justice White, was joined by Chief Justice Burger and Justices Blackmun, Rehnquist, and Powell. Justice Powell, however, wrote a concurring opinion that took pains to "emphasize" what he understood to be "the limited nature of the Court's holding."[91] Because Justice Powell's vote was necessary to create the Court's majority, subsequent analyses of constitutional privilege claims have understandably focused on his brief, three-paragraph opinion in *Branzburg*.

Initially, Justice Powell explained, the Court had not held that "newsmen, subpoenaed to testify before a grand jury, are without constitutional rights with respect to the gathering of news or in safeguarding their sources."[92] Not only would "harassment of newsmen" not be "tolerated," Justice Powell asserted, but "[i]f the newsman is called upon to give information bearing only a remote and tenuous relationship to the subject of the [grand jury] investigation, or if he has some other reason to believe that his testimony implicated confidential source relationships without a legitimate need of law enforcement, he will have access

---

87. Branzburg v. Hayes, 408 U.S. at 707-08.
88. *Id.* at 708.
89. *Id.* at 709. The Court emphasized, however, that Pappas' appearance must be "subject, of course, to the supervision of the presiding judge as to 'the propriety, purposes, and scope of the grand jury inquiry and the pertinence of the probable testimony.'" *Id.* (quoting 266 N.E.2d at 303-04).
90. Branzburg v. Hayes, 408 U.S. at 708.
91. *Id.* at 709 (Powell, J., concurring).
92. *Id.*

to the court on a motion to quash and an appropriate protective order may be entered."[93]

Second, in a passage that has formed the cornerstone of subsequent constitutional law on the subject, Justice Powell indicated that each "claim to privilege should be judged on its facts by the striking of a proper balance between freedom of the press and the obligation of all citizens to give relevant testimony."[94] According to Justice Powell, courts must achieve a "balance of these vital constitutional and societal interests on a case-by-case basis."[95]

Third, Justice Powell distinguished his approach from that adopted by Justice Stewart, joined by Justices Brennan and Marshall, in dissent. Justice Stewart's formulation, Justice Powell explained, would recognize a "constitutional privilege not even to appear before the grand jury unless a court decides that the Government has made" the requisite showing.[96] Although Justice Powell recognized that such an approach "would require a balancing of interests by the court," it would impair the court's ability to "balance the competing interests on their merits in the particular case" and would thereby subordinate too heavily the "societal interest in the detection and prosecution of crime."[97] Instead, Justice Powell asserted, under the Court's rule, the "newsman witness, like all other witnesses, will have to appear" and the court, "when called upon to protect a newsman from improper or prejudicial questioning," would balance the competing governmental and constitutional interests "on their merits in the particular case."[98]

§ 14-4(c). Justice Stewart's Dissenting Opinion.

While acknowledging that "Justice Powell's enigmatic concurring opinion gives some hope of a more flexible view in the future," Justice Stewart, dissenting on behalf of himself and Justices Brennan and Marshall, characterized the Court's opinion as holding that "a newsman has no First Amendment right to protect his sources when called before a grand jury" and thereby "invites state and federal authorities to undermine the historic independence of the press by attempting to annex the journalistic profession as an investigative arm of government."[99]

---

93. *Id.*
94. *Id.*
95. *Id.*
96. *Id.* at 710 n.*.
97. *Id.*
98. *Id.*
99. *Id.* at 710 (Stewart, J., dissenting). Justice Powell disputed this characterization of the Court's holding in his own opinion. See *id.* at 709 (Powell, J., concurring).

Justice Douglas dissented separately, on the ground that, in his view, journalists enjoy an absolute immunity, guaranteed by the First Amendment, "from appearing or testifying before a

Justice Stewart's opinion is noteworthy, and has proven influential, in two substantive respects. First, its explication of the constitutional underpinnings of the privilege constitutes the most elaborate treatment of the subject rendered by any justice, before or since. Second, the constitutional litmus test it championed, though rejected by the Court in the grand jury context, has since become established law in most other circumstances in most American jurisdictions. Thus, although rendered in dissent, Justice Stewart's analysis warrants ongoing consultation in assessing the privilege's validity, application and scope.

Initially, Justice Stewart explained that constitutional protection of the newsgathering process is bottomed on the proposition that "the full flow of information to the public protected by the free-press guarantee would be severely curtailed if no protection whatever were afforded to the process by which news is assembled and disseminated."[100] According to Justice Stewart, "[n]ews must not be unnecessarily cut off at its source, for without freedom to acquire information the right to publish would be impermissibly compromised."[101] Thus, Justice Stewart wrote, the "right to gather news" must include "a right to a confidential relationship between a reporter and his source":

> This proposition follows as a matter of simple logic once three factual predicates are recognized: (1) newsmen require informants to gather news; (2) confidentiality — the promise or understanding that names or certain aspects of communications will be kept off the record — is essential to the creation and maintenance of a news-gathering relationship with informants; and (3) an unbridled subpoena power — the absence of a constitutional right protecting, in *any* way, a confidential relationship from compulsory process — will either deter sources from divulging information or deter reporters from gathering and publishing information.[102]

---

grand jury, unless the reporter himself is implicated in a crime." United States v. Caldwell, 408 U.S. 711, 712 (1972) (Douglas, J., dissenting). Since the Fifth Amendment would apply in the latter situation, Justice Douglas would recognize "no area of inquiry not protected by a privilege" and "the reporter need not appear for the futile purpose of invoking one to each question." *Id.* In that regard, Justice Douglas chastised the *New York Times* for advocating — through Professor Alexander Bickel — "the amazing position that First Amendment rights are to be balanced against other needs or conveniences of government. My belief is that all of the 'balancing' was done by those who wrote the Bill of Rights." *Id.* at 713.

100. *Id.* at 727 (Stewart, J., dissenting). Justice Stewart later expanded on his views concerning the institutional protection afforded by the press clause. See Stewart, *"Or of the Press,"* 26 HASTINGS L.J. 631 (1975). See generally Comegys, *Potter Stewart: An Analysis of His Views on the Press as Fourth Estate*, 59 CHI.-KENT L. REV. 157 (1982).

101. Branzburg v. Hayes, 408 U.S. at 728 (Stewart, J., dissenting).

102. *Id.* at 728. In this regard, Justice Stewart took issue with the majority's alleged insistence that the "impairment of the flow of news . . . be proved with scientific precision." *Id.* at 733. In Justice Stewart's view, the Court had "never before demanded that First Amendment rights rest on elaborate empirical studies demonstrating beyond any reasonable doubt that deterrent effects exist;

Next, Justice Stewart concluded that government may intrude upon the confidential relationship "between a reporter and source" only when it can demonstrate "not only" that "the inquiry is of 'compelling and overriding importance,'" but also that the "investigation is 'substantially related' to the information sought."[103] Moreover, Justice Stewart would also require governmental officials to "show that there is not any means of obtaining the information less destructive of First Amendment liberties" than compelling the disclosure of the identity of a journalist's confidential source.[104] Thus, when a reporter is asked "to appear before a grand jury and reveal confidences," Justice Stewart would require the government:

> (1) [to] show that there is probable cause to believe that the newsman has information that is clearly relevant to a specific probable violation of law; (2) demonstrate that the information sought cannot be obtained by alternative means less destructive of First Amendment rights; and (3) demonstrate a compelling and overriding interest in the information.[105]

In the consolidated cases before the Court, Justice Stewart asserted that the government had not satisfied this standard. Accordingly, he would have affirmed the Ninth Circuit's decision in *Caldwell* and remanded the remaining decisions for further proceedings applying the constitutional standard he had articulated.[106]

§ 14-5. *Branzburg* in The Supreme Court.

Given the uncertainty engendered by the multiple opinions in *Branzburg* and the expressly limited nature of its holding, it appeared virtually certain that the Court would turn its attention to the privilege again in subsequent terms. Despite a host of opportunities, however, the Court has never again accepted for review a case directly raising issues surrounding the constitutional privilege and has

---

we have never before required proof of the exact number of people potentially affected by governmental action, who would actually be dissuaded from engaging in First Amendment activity." *Id.* Rather, Justice Stewart asserted, the Court should ask only "(1) whether there [is] a rational connection between the cause (the governmental action) and the effect (the deterrence or impairment of First Amendment activity), and (2) whether the effect would occur with some regularity, i.e., would not be *de minimis*." *Id.* (citing Grosjean v. American Press Co., 297 U.S. 233, 244-45 (1936); Bates v. City of Little Rock, 361 U.S. 516, 523-24 (1960); Talley v. California, 362 U.S. 60, 64-65 (1960); New York Times Co. v. Sullivan, 376 U.S. 254, 277-78 (1964); NAACP v. Alabama, 357 U.S. 449, 461-66 (1958)). See note 73 *supra* (discussing Court's analysis).

103. 408 U.S. at 739-40 (Stewart, J., dissenting) (quoting Gibson v. Florida Leg. Investigative Comm., 372 U.S. 539, 546 (1963)).

104. Branzburg v. Hayes, 408 U.S. at 740 (Stewart, J., dissenting) (citing Louisiana ex rel. Gremillion v. NAACP, 366 U.S. 293, 296-97 (1961)).

105. 408 U.S. at 743 (Stewart, J., dissenting).

106. *Id.*

appeared content to permit the lower courts to wrestle with the issue unassisted. Indeed, the only guidance emanating from the Supreme Court appears in the form of (1) *dicta* in cases raising different issues and (2) opinions rendered by individual justices in chambers. Perhaps because these infrequent and decidedly nondefinitive clues concerning the contours of the privilege are all that the Court has offered since *Branzburg*, they continue to be consulted and interpreted with something approaching talmudic passion.

§ 14-5(a). The Prison Access Cases.

Shortly after *Branzburg*, the Court considered a trio of cases concerning whether the press enjoys "a constitutional right of access to prisons or their inmates beyond that afforded the general public."[107] In the course of holding that it does not, several justices offered somewhat varying perspectives on the scope of constitutional protection for the newsgathering process first identified in *Branzburg*. In his opinion for the Court in *Pell v. Procunier*, for example, Justice Stewart asserted that, in *Branzburg*, the Court had gone "further" than prior cases and had "acknowledged that 'newsgathering is not without its First Amendment protections,' for 'without some protection for seeking out the news, freedom of the press could be eviscerated.'"[108] The holding in *Branzburg*, Justice Stewart wrote on behalf of the Court in *Pell*, was limited to the conclusion that "the First and Fourteenth Amendments were not abridged by requiring reporters to disclose the identity of their confidential sources to a grand jury when that information was needed in the course of a good-faith criminal investigation."[109] Moreover, in dismissing the news media's claim in *Pell* for "special access to information not shared by members of the public generally," the Court noted that, while "a journalist is free to seek out sources of information not available to the general public" and "that he is *entitled to some constitutional protection of the confidentiality of such sources*," citing *Branzburg*, the government has no "affirmative duty to make available to journalists sources of information not available to members of the public generally."[110]

In *Houchins v. KQED, Inc.*, Chief Justice Burger, writing only for himself and Justices White and Rehnquist, asserted that *Branzburg* offered little support to press claims of a "constitutional right of access to a county jail, over and above

---

107. Pell v. Procunier, 417 U.S. 817, 834 (1974). See also Saxbe v. Washington Post Co., 417 U.S. 843 (1974); Houchins v. KQED, Inc., 438 U.S. 1 (1978). See generally Note, *First Amendment Analysis of State Regulations Prohibiting the Filming of Prisoner Executions*, 60 GEO. WASH. L. REV. 1042 (1992) (discussing *Pell* and *Saxbe* in relation to more recent cases concerning press access to executions).
108. Pell v. Procunier, 417 U.S. at 833 (quoting Branzburg v. Hayes, 408 U.S. at 707, 681).
109. Pell v. Procunier, 417 U.S. at 833.
110. *Id.* at 834 (citing Branzburg v. Hayes, 408 U.S. at 684-85) (emphasis added).

that of other persons, to interview inmates."[111] The Chief Justice characterized *Branzburg*'s acknowledgement that "'newsgathering is not without its First Amendment protections'" as "dictum" that "in no sense implied a constitutional right of access to news sources."[112] According to the Chief Justice, the Court's observation in *Branzburg*

> must be read in context; it was in response to the contention that forcing a reporter to disclose to a grand jury information received in confidence would violate the First Amendment by deterring news sources from communicating information. There is an undoubted right to gather news 'from any source by means within the law,' but that affords no basis for the claim that the First Amendment compels others — private persons or governments — to supply information.[113]

Perhaps the most significant insights concerning *Branzburg* in the prison access cases, however, came from Justice Powell, the author of the "enigmatic" and apparently pivotal concurring opinion in *Branzburg*.[114] In *Saxbe v. Washington Post Co.*, Justice Powell, writing in dissent on behalf of himself and Justices Brennan and Marshall, took the opportunity to explicate further the basis of his views in *Branzburg*. In *Branzburg*, Justice Powell explained, the Court "did not hold that the government is wholly free to restrict press access to newsworthy information. To the contrary, we recognized explicitly that the constitutional guarantee of freedom of the press does extend to some of the antecedent activities that make the right to publish meaningful."[115] In Justice Powell's view, the result in *Branzburg* "hinged on an assessment of the competing societal interests involved in that case rather than on any determination that First Amendment freedoms were not implicated."[116]

Branzburg, according to Justice Powell's opinion in *Saxbe*, stands for two related propositions.[117] First, it holds that government has no constitutional obligation to "justify under the stringent standard of First Amendment review every regulation that might affect in some tangential way the availability of information to the news media."[118] Second, however, *Branzburg* is premised on the Court's recognition that:

---

111. 438 U.S. 1, 3 (1978).
112. *Id.* at 10 (quoting Branzburg v. Hayes, 408 U.S. at 707).
113. Houchins v. KQED, Inc., 438 U.S. at 11 (quoting Branzburg v. Hayes, 408 U.S. at 681-82).
114. 408 U.S. at 725 (Stewart, J., dissenting).
115. Saxbe v. Washington Post Co., 417 U.S. at 859 (Powell, J., dissenting).
116. *Id.* at 859-60.
117. See generally Langley & Levine, *supra* note 39, at 35-38 (reflecting this analysis of Justice Powell's *Saxbe* opinion).
118. Saxbe v. Washington Post Co., 417 U.S. at 860 (Powell, J., dissenting).

> An informed public depends on accurate and effective reporting by the news media. No individual can obtain for himself the information needed for intelligent discharge of his political responsibilities.... [The press] is the means by which the people receive the flow of information and ideas essential to intelligent self-government.[119]

Accordingly, Justice Powell contended, the Court's decision in *Branzburg* rests ultimately on its assessment that inhibition of press and public access to the information at issue in that case had "no palpable impact on the underlying right of the public to the information needed to assert ultimate control over the political process."[120]

Similarly, in a dissenting opinion in *Houchins v. KQED*, joined by Justices Powell and Brennan, Justice Stevens opined that *Branzburg*, at the very least, "impl[ied] that there is a right to acquire knowledge that derives protection from the First Amendment."[121] After *Branzburg*, Justice Stevens wrote, "information gathering is entitled to some measure of constitutional protection," not for the "private benefit of those who might qualify as members of the 'press,' but to insure that the citizens are fully informed regarding matters of public interest and importance."[122]

§ 14-5(b). The Privilege Cases.

In the years since *Branzburg*, the Court has had a handful of occasions to consider other constitutionally based claims of privilege, some emanating from the First Amendment and others from elsewhere in the Constitution. The Court's treatment, in the context of these cases, of its decision in *Branzburg* offers some further clues concerning the contours of the journalists' privilege itself.

Shortly after *Branzburg*, the Court decided *United States v. Nixon*,[123] Richard Nixon's unsuccessful assertion of executive privilege that ultimately toppled his presidency. It is, of course, well known that the President claimed a privilege, inherent in the Constitution's separation of powers between the three branches, to decline to produce, pursuant to a subpoena *duces tecum* issued by a federal court, "certain tape recordings and documents relating to his conversations with aides and advisers."[124] Although the Court rejected the President's claim of absolute privilege, on the ground that "neither the doctrine of separation of powers, nor the need for confidentiality of high-level communications, without more," could sustain it, the Court did recognize a qualified executive privilege

---

119. *Id.* at 863.
120. *Id.* at 872.
121. 438 U.S. at 27 n.15 (Stevens, J., dissenting).
122. *Id.* at 32 (citing Branzburg v. Hayes, 408 U.S. at 681).
123. 418 U.S. 683 (1974).
124. *Id.* at 686.

because the "President's need for complete candor and objectivity from advisers calls for great deference from the courts."[125] In its fullest explication, the Court's assertion of the constitutional necessity for an executive privilege proceeds from many of the same premises that had been offered on behalf of the news media in *Branzburg*:

> The expectation of a President to the confidentiality of his conversations and correspondence, like the claim of confidentiality of judicial deliberations, for example, has all the values to which we accord deference to the privilege of all citizens and, added to those values, is the necessity for protection of the public interest in candid, objective, and even blunt or harsh opinions in Presidential decisionmaking. A President and those who assist him must be free to explore alternatives in the process of shaping policies and making decisions and to do so in a way many would be unwilling to express except privately. These are the circumstances justifying a presumptive privilege for Presidential communications. The privilege is fundamental to the operation of Government and inextricably rooted in the separation of powers under the Constitution.[126]

The Court concluded, however, that "when the ground for asserting privilege as to subpoenaed materials sought for use in a criminal trial is based only on the generalized interest in confidentiality," the executive privilege "must yield to the demonstrated, specific need for evidence in a pending criminal trial."[127] In so holding, Chief Justice Burger's opinion for the unanimous Court "restated" *Branzburg*'s recognition of "the ancient proposition of law, albeit in the context of a grand jury inquiry rather than a trial, that 'the public has a right to every man's evidence.'"[128] Nevertheless, the Court also reiterated *Branzburg*'s recognition that even that interest will often yield to "those persons protected by a constitutional, common law, or statutory privilege."[129] Such privileges, the Court explained, "are designed to protect weighty and legitimate competing interests," but "[w]hatever their origins, these exceptions to the demand for every man's

---

125. *Id.* at 706.

126. *Id.* at 708.

127. *Id.* at 713. Thus, the Court held, "[i]f a President concludes that compliance with a subpoena would be injurious to the public interest he may properly . . . invoke a claim of privilege." *Id.* Once such a claim is made, moreover, it becomes the "duty of the District Court to treat the subpoenaed material as presumptively privileged" and require the party seeking disclosure of presumptively privileged material to "demonstrate" that it is "'essential to the justice of the [pending criminal] case.'" *Id.* (quoting United States v. Burr, 25 Fed. Cas. 187, 192 (C.C. Va. 1807)).

128. United States v. Nixon, 418 U.S. at 709-10 (quoting Branzburg v. Hayes, 408 U.S. 665, 688 (1972)).

129. *Id.*

evidence are not lightly created nor expansively construed, for they are in derogation of the search for truth."[130]

In contrast, the justices largely ignored *Branzburg* five years later when the news media itself returned to the Court in *Herbert v. Lando*,[131] asserting a privilege — similar to that invoked by President Nixon — to shield internal newsroom deliberations from discovery in a defamation action. In his opinion for the Court, Justice White — also the author of the majority opinion in *Branzburg* — neither cites nor discusses that prior decision, even in the context of rejecting the notion that "when a member of the press is alleged to have circulated damaging falsehoods" and is sued for defamation, "the plaintiff is barred from inquiring into the editorial processes of those responsible for the publication."[132] Instead, the Court relied on the constitutional balance struck in *New York Times Co. v. Sullivan*,[133] which obligates a public figure defamation plaintiff to prove that the defendant "in fact entertained serious doubts" about the truth of its publication in order to prevail.[134] Given that standard of liability, the Court concluded in *Herbert*, "[p]ermitting plaintiffs . . . to prove their cases by direct as well as indirect evidence is consistent with the balance struck" in *Sullivan* and its progeny.[135]

Nevertheless, in several separate opinions — including Justice White's for the majority — the justices recognized the existence of at least some First Amendment-based limitations on the scope of such inquiry, even in the context of a defamation action instituted by a public figure. Thus, Justice White rejected the notion that "editorial discussions or exchanges have no constitutional protection from casual inquiry," adding that "[t]here is no law that subjects the editorial process to private or official examination merely to satisfy curiosity or to serve

---

130. *Id.* Chief Justice Burger specifically referenced, as had the Court in *Branzburg*, the Fifth Amendment privilege against self-incrimination, the attorney-client privilege, and the priest-penitent privilege. *Id.* But see Swidler & Berlin v. United States, 118 S. Ct. 2081, 2087-88 (1998) (rejecting narrow construction of attorney-client privilege where client died and information contained in confidential communications was relevant to criminal proceeding, and reasoning that while "both *Nixon* and *Branzburg* dealt with the creation of privileges not recognized by the common law . . . here we deal with one of the oldest recognized privileges in the law").

131. 441 U.S. 153 (1979). The "editorial process" privilege asserted in *Herbert*, as well as the relationship of discovery in civil litigation to the newsgathering process is addressed specifically in Chapter 15-3(c) *infra*.

132. Herbert v. Lando, 441 U.S. at 155. See generally Hunter, *A Reprise on Herbert v. Lando and the Law of Defamation*, 71 KY. L.J. 569 (1983) (discussing relationship between *Herbert* and cases involving the assertion of a confidential source privilege by journalists).

133. 376 U.S. 254 (1964).

134. St. Amant v. Thompson, 390 U.S. 727, 731 (1968).

135. 441 U.S. at 172.

some general end such as the public interest; and if there were, it would not survive constitutional scrutiny."[136]

In a concurring opinion, Justice Powell, much as he had in *Branzburg*, "elaborate[d]" on this aspect of the Court's opinion in a manner he viewed as not "inconsistent" with it.[137] Specifically, Justice Powell "emphasize[d]," as he had in a different context in *Branzburg*, that "in supervising discovery in a libel suit by a public figure, a district court has a duty to consider First Amendment interests."[138] Indeed, according to Justice Powell, the courts must "strik[e] a proper balance" in each case, one that "ensure[s] that the values protected by the First Amendment, though entitled to no constitutional privilege in a case of this kind, are weighed carefully."[139]

More than a decade later, in *University of Pennsylvania v. EEOC*,[140] the Court returned to *Branzburg* in the context of rejecting the claim that "a university enjoys a special privilege grounded in either the common law or the First Amendment, against disclosure of peer review materials that are relevant to charges of racial or sexual discrimination in tenure decisions."[141] Indeed, in rejecting the university-defendant's initial claim of common law privilege, Justice Blackmun's unanimous opinion for the Court relied on *Branzburg* twice, to support its assertions that it "is especially reluctant to recognize a privilege in an area where it appears that Congress has considered the relevant competing concerns but has not provided the privilege itself" and that requiring the EEOC to make a particularized showing of need for peer review materials "would place a substantial litigation-producing obstacle in the way of the Commission's efforts to investigate and remedy alleged discrimination."[142]

---

136. *Id.* at 174.
137. *Id.* at 177-78 (Powell, J., concurring).
138. *Id.*
139. *Id.* at 180. Justice Brennan, dissenting in part from the Court's opinion, would have recognized an explicit, though qualified, "editorial process privilege" applicable to internal discussions between and among journalists. *Id.* at 190-99 (Brennan, J., dissenting in part). In a separate dissenting opinion, Justice Stewart found it unnecessary to address the privilege issue because, in his view, "inquiry into the broad 'editorial process' is simply not relevant in a libel suit brought by a public figure against a publisher." *Id.* at 199 (Stewart, J., dissenting). Finally, Justice Marshall dissented as well, on the ground that "some constraints on pretrial discovery are essential to ensure the 'uninhibited [and] robust' debate on public issues which *Sullivan* contemplated." *Id.* at 202-03 (Marshall, J., dissenting). Justice Marshall further noted, with a citation to Justice Stewart's opinion in *Branzburg*, that "lower courts have displayed sensitivity to First Amendment values in assessing motions to compel disclosure of confidential sources" in defamation actions. *Id.* at 209 n.6 (citing Cervantes v. Time, Inc., 464 F.2d 986, 992-94 (8th Cir. 1972), *cert. denied*, 409 U.S. 1125 (1973); Branzburg v. Hayes, 408 U.S. 665, 741-43 (1972) (Stewart, J., dissenting)).
140. 493 U.S. 182 (1990).
141. *Id.* at 184.
142. *Id.* at 189, 194 (citing Branzburg v. Hayes, 408 U.S. 665, 705-06 (1972)). The Court's reliance on *Branzburg* in these respects is potentially misleading. Although the Court in *Branzburg*

The Court's primary reliance on *Branzburg*, however, came in the context of its discussion of the First Amendment-based, "academic freedom" privilege claimed by the university. In rejecting the existence of such a privilege, the Court in *University of Pennsylvania* asserted that the case "in many respects is similar to *Branzburg*," which it characterized as "reject[ing] the notion that under the First Amendment a reporter could not be required to appear or to testify as to information obtained in confidence without a special showing that the reporter's testimony was necessary."[143] Justice Blackmun specifically reiterated two aspects of the constitutional analysis in *Branzburg*: Justice White's assertions there that "'the First Amendment does not invalidate every incidental burdening of the press that may result from the enforcement of civil or criminal statutes of general applicability'" and that the Court would be reluctant to "recognize a constitutional privilege where it [is] 'unclear how often and to what extent informers are actually deterred from furnishing information when newsmen are forced to testify before a grand jury.'"[144]

Thus, the Court concluded that, as in *Branzburg*, it was "unwilling," in the cause of academic freedom, "'to embark the judiciary on a long and difficult journey to . . . an uncertain destination'"[145] Rather, the Court indicated that it would confine its constitutional analysis, as it had in *Branzburg*, largely to determining whether the governmental authority had exercised its authority in "bad faith," an "abuse" of its "powers [which] might raise First Amendment concerns."[146]

---

noted that "[a]t the federal level, Congress has freedom to determine whether a statutory newsman's privilege is necessary and desirable," 408 U.S. at 705, it did not intimate that "Congress ha[d] considered the relevant competing concerns but ha[d] not provided the privilege itself," 493 U.S. at 189. Similarly, although the Court in *University of Pennsylvania* did preface its citation to *Branzburg* for the latter proposition with an ambiguous "Cf." citation, see *id.* at 194, the referenced discussion in *Branzburg* does not appear to articulate the notion that a specificity requirement "would place a substantial litigation-producing obstacle" in the way of investigation and enforcement, though it does acknowledge that application of a constitutional privilege would require courts to make "preliminary factual and legal determinations with respect to whether the proper predicate had been laid" for the privilege's assertion, 408 U.S. at 705.

143. 493 U.S. at 201.

144. *Id.* at 201 (quoting Branzburg v. Hayes, 408 U.S. at 682, 693, and citing Herbert v. Lando, 441 U.S. 153, 174 (1979)).

145. University of Pennsylvania v. EEOC, 493 U.S. at 201 (quoting Branzburg v. Hayes, 408 U.S. at 703).

146. 493 U.S. at 201 n.8 (citing Branzburg v. Hayes, 408 U.S. at 707). See also Jaffee v. Redmond, 518 U.S. 1 (1996) (holding that "psychotherapist privilege" should be recognized by federal courts pursuant to Fed. R. Evid. 501). In *Jaffee*, the Supreme Court, without citing *Branzburg*, emphasized that federal courts may "define new privileges by interpreting 'common law principles . . . in light of reason and experience.'" 518 U.S. at 11 (quoting Fed. R. Evid. 501). The Court determined that a psychotherapist-patient privilege was necessary because "the mere possibility of disclosure may impede development of the confidential relationship necessary for successful treatment" and was appropriate because every state recognized such a privilege either

§ 14-5(c). The Incidental Restraint Cases.

The Court's constitutional analysis in *University of Pennsylvania v. EEOC*[147] and in *Herbert v. Lando*,[148] although undertaken in the context of asserted claims of privilege, illustrates as well the durability of Justice White's emphasis in *Branzburg* on the distinction between "direct" and "incidental" restrictions on the exercise of First Amendment rights.[149] In addition to those two cases, moreover, the Court has had other occasions, especially in the newsgathering context, to rely upon this aspect of the *Branzburg* analysis in addressing other alleged restraints on First Amendment rights.

In *Zurcher v. Stanford Daily*, for example, the Court rejected an invitation to adopt, in the name of the First Amendment, "a nearly *per se* rule forbidding the search warrant and permitting only the subpoena *duces tecum*" when law enforcement authorities wish to procure materials in possession of a news organization.[150] The First Amendment claim was premised on the assertion that "searches of newspaper offices for evidence of crime reasonably believed to be on the premises will seriously threaten the ability of the press to gather, analyze, and disseminate news."[151]

---

through judicial decision or statute. 518 U.S. at 15-16. It would appear that virtually identical factors support a reporters' privilege, especially since the Court took pains to emphasize that "[i]t is of no consequence that recognition of the privilege in the vast majority of States is the product of legislative action rather than judicial decision" and that, if "the privilege were rejected, confidential conversations . . . would surely be chilled." *Id.* at 21. See generally Boutrous & Strodder, *Retooling the Federal Common-Law Reporter's Privilege*, 17 COMM. LAW. 1 (Spring 1999) (arguing that *Jaffee* warrants recognition of federal common law reporters' privilege pursuant to Fed. R. Evid. 501).

147. 493 U.S. 182 (1990).
148. 441 U.S. 153 (1979).
149. See Branzburg v. Hayes, 408 U.S. at 682. The Court's analytical affinity for the "indirect restraint" concept is discussed and criticized in Barnes, *The Rights of Sources — The Critical Element in the Clash over Reporter's Privilege*, 88 YALE L.J. 1202, 1206 & n. 27 (1979) ("The Court's analysis in *Branzburg* — (1) a strong state interest, (2) given effect through a rule of general applicability, (3) sufficing to overcome an assertion of First Amendment protection not based on pure expression — has been used since in other press cases.") (citing Zurcher v. Stanford Daily, 436 U.S. 547, 563-67 (1978); Saxbe v. Washington Post Co., 417 U.S. 843 (1974); Broadrick v. Oklahoma, 413 U.S. 601, 614-15 (1973)). Indeed, whether a challenged restraint on First Amendment activity is perceived as "direct" or "indirect" is often a function of an arbitrary decision concerning whose First Amendment rights are at stake. See Barnes, *supra,* at 1217 (claiming that compelled disclosure of the identities of confidential sources, if viewed from the perspective of the source's right to engage in anonymous expression, constitutes a direct restraint of that constitutional interest); McIntyre v. Ohio Elections Comm'n, 514 U.S. 334, 345-46 (1995) (invalidating state statute requiring anonymous sources of political speech to reveal their identities).
150. 436 U.S. 547, 563-67 (1978). The subject of newsroom searches is specifically examined in Chapter 15-3(a) *infra.*
151. 436 U.S. at 564.

Although Justice White's opinion for the Court emphasized that, "[w]here the materials sought may be protected by the First Amendment, the requirements of the Fourth Amendment must be applied with 'scrupulous exactitude,'"[152] the majority was "unconvinced" that, absent the imposition of further restrictions on the use of search warrants in the name of the First Amendment, "confidential sources will disappear and that the press will suppress news because of fears of warranted searches."[153] Relying on *Branzburg*, the Court concluded that "[w]hatever incremental effect there may be in this regard if search warrants, as well as subpoenas, are permissible in proper circumstances, it does not make a constitutional difference."[154] In the same vein, the Court discounted the efficacy of the newsroom search as a restraint on First Amendment activity because "the press is not only an important, critical, and valuable asset to society, but it is not easily intimidated."[155]

Once again, as he had in *Branzburg* and would the following term in *Herbert v. Lando*, Justice Powell offered a concurring opinion that purported to amplify the Court's holding. In his separate opinion in *Zurcher*, Justice Powell asserted that, while he agreed with Justice White that "there is no justification for the establishment of a separate Fourth Amendment procedure for the press, a magistrate asked to issue a warrant for the search of press offices can and should take cognizance of the independent values protected by the First Amendment."[156] Moreover, although Justice Powell rejected Justice Stewart's assertion that the former's concurring opinion in *Branzburg* "support[s] the view that the Fourth Amendment contains an implied exception for the press, through the operation of the First Amendment,"[157] he emphasized that his concurrence in *Branzburg*

---

152. *Id.* at 564 (quoting Stanford v. Texas, 379 U.S. 476, 485 (1965)); see 436 U.S. at 566:

> There is no reason to believe, for example, that magistrates cannot guard against searches of the type, scope, and intrusiveness that would actually interfere with the timely publication of a newspaper. Nor, if the requirements of specificity and reasonableness are properly applied, policed, and observed, will there be any occasion or opportunity for officers to rummage at large in newspaper files or to intrude into or deter normal editorial and publication decisions.

153. 436 U.S. at 566.
154. *Id.* (citing Branzburg v. Hayes, 408 U.S. 665 (1972)).
155. 436 U.S. at 566.
156. 436 U.S. at 570 (Powell, J., concurring).
157. *Id.* at 570 n.3 (citing Branzburg v. Hayes, 408 U.S. 665, 709-10 (1972) (Powell, J., concurring)). Justice Stewart dissented in *Zurcher* and asserted that it is "self-evident that police searches of newspaper offices burden the freedom of the press." 436 U.S. at 571 (Stewart, J., dissenting). In so stating, Justice Stewart relied on Justice Powell's observation in *Branzburg* that "'if the newsman is called upon to give information bearing only a remote and tenuous relationship to the subject of the investigation, or if he has some other reason to believe that his testimony implicates confidential source relationships without a legitimate need of law enforcement, he will have access to the court on a motion to quash,'" as support for the contention that "a subpoena would allow a newspaper, through a motion to quash, an opportunity for an adversary hearing." *Id.*

should "properly be read as supporting the view ... that under the warrant requirement of the Fourth Amendment, the magistrate should consider the values of a free press as well as the societal interest in enforcing the criminal laws."[158] *Branzburg*, Justice Powell reiterated in *Zurcher*, stands for the proposition that, "in considering a motion to quash a subpoena directed to a newsman, the court should balance the competing values of a free press and the societal interest in detecting and prosecuting crime."[159]

Justice White returned one last time to the distinction between "direct" and "incidental" restraints in *Cohen v. Cowles Media Co.*[160] There, the Court was asked to invalidate, in the name of the First Amendment, a cause of action for promissory estoppel asserted against a newspaper on the ground that it had abrogated a promise not to reveal the plaintiff-source's identity. According to Justice White, the case did not involve a direct restraint on the news media's ability to publish truthful information — i.e., the identity of the source — but rather was "controlled" by the "well-established line of decisions holding that generally applicable laws do not offend the First Amendment simply because their enforcement has incidental effects on its ability to gather and report the news."[161]

Thus, Justice White held, just as the First Amendment does not "relieve a newspaper reporter of the obligation shared by all citizens to respond to a grand jury subpoena and answer questions relevant to a criminal investigation, even though the reporter might be required to reveal a confidential source,"[162] a state may constitutionally apply its doctrine of promissory estoppel, "a law of general applicability," to the press.[163] Assuming *arguendo* that a "cause of action for promissory estoppel will inhibit truthful reporting because news organizations will have legal incentives not to disclose a confidential source's identity even when that person's identity is itself newsworthy," such an "incidental, and constitutionally insignificant, consequence of applying to the press a generally applicable law" is of no moment.[164]

---

at 476 (Stewart, J., dissenting) (quoting Branzburg v. Hayes, 408 U.S. at 710 (Powell, J., concurring)).

158. Zurcher v. Stanford Daily, 436 U.S. at 570 n.3.

159. *Id.*

160. 501 U.S. 663 (1991). The *Cohen* decision, as well as the law pertaining to breach of promise and related claims against the news media, are addressed in Chapter 13-4(a) *supra*.

161. 501 U.S. at 669.

162. *Id.* (citing Branzburg v. Hayes, 408 U.S. 665 (1972)).

163. 501 U.S. at 670.

164. *Id.* at 670. In dissent, Justice Blackmun, joined by Justices Marshall and Souter, distinguished *Branzburg* on the ground that, while "'the sole issue'" presented by that case was "'the obligation of reporters to respond to grand jury subpoenas as other citizens,'" the application of the law of promissory estoppel "involve[s] the imposition of liability based upon the content of

§ 14-5(d). The Court Closure Cases.

Perhaps most significantly, the Supreme Court has had occasion to revisit *Branzburg* in the context of its watershed explication of the First Amendment-based right of access to judicial proceedings. Although the court closure cases, and the elaborate law of access they have spawned, are treated elsewhere in this volume,[165] their insights concerning the constitutional underpinnings of the journalists' privilege merit separate attention.

In *Richmond Newspapers, Inc. v. Virginia*,[166] where the Court for the first time held that "the right of the public and press to attend criminal trials is guaranteed under the United States Constitution,"[167] but was unable to muster a majority opinion, several justices looked to *Branzburg* as a source of the constitutional right of access.[168] In his opinion announcing the Court's judgment, Chief Justice Burger contended that it "is not crucial whether we describe this right to attend criminal trials to hear, see and communicate observations concerning them as a 'right of access,' or a 'right to gather information.'"[169] In *Branzburg*, the Chief Justice asserted, the Court had already "recognized that 'without some protection for seeking out the news, freedom of the press could be eviscerated.'"[170] Ultimately, the Chief Justice concluded, again invoking *Branzburg*, that "the right to attend criminal trials is implicit in the guarantees of the First Amendment."[171] Justice Stewart also based his concurring conclusion in *Richmond Newspapers, Inc.* — i.e., that "the First and Fourteenth Amendments clearly give the press and the public a right of access to trials themselves" — in

---

speech." *Id.* at 674-75 (Blackmun, J., dissenting) (quoting Branzburg v. Hayes, 408 U.S. at 681-82).

165. See Chaps. 2-3 *supra*.

166. 448 U.S. 555 (1980).

167. *Id.* at 558.

168. Chief Justice Burger announced the Court's judgment, in an opinion joined by Justices White and Stevens. Justice Brennan (joined by Justice Marshall), Justice Stewart, and Justice Blackmun all wrote separate opinions concurring in the judgment, and Justices White and Stevens wrote separately as well. Justice Powell did not participate in the case and Justice Rehnquist dissented.

169. 448 U.S. at 576 (Burger, C.J., announcing judgment) (citing Saxbe v. Washington Post. Co., 417 U.S. 843 (1974); Pell v. Procunier, 417 U.S. 817 (1974)).

170. 448 U.S. at 576 (quoting Branzburg v. Hayes, 408 U.S. 665, 681 (1972)).

171. 448 U.S. at 580 (citing Branzburg v. Hayes, 408 U.S. at 681). The Chief Justice also explored the role of the news media in the newsgathering process. He noted that, "[i]nstead of acquiring information about trials by firsthand observation or by word of mouth from those who attended, people now acquire it chiefly through the print and electronic media." This reality, "[i]n a sense, . . . validates the media claim of functioning as surrogates for the public" and "'contribute[s] to public understanding.'" 448 U.S. at 573 (quoting Nebraska Press Ass'n v. Stuart, 427 U.S. 539, 587 (1976)).

large part on *Branzburg*'s recognition that the "right to publish implies a freedom to gather information."[172]

In his concurring opinion, Justice Stevens recognized that *Richmond Newspapers, Inc.* was indeed a "watershed case," for never before had the Court "squarely held that the acquisition of newsworthy matter is entitled to any constitutional protection whatsoever."[173] Justice Stevens concurred in the view that "the First Amendment protects the public and the press from abridgment of their rights of access to information about the operation of their government," and that "an arbitrary interference with access to important information is an abridgment of the freedoms of speech and of the press protected by the First Amendment."[174] Similarly, Justice Brennan advanced the view that the "First Amendment embodies more than a commitment to free expression and communicative interchange for their own sakes; it has a *structural* role to play in securing and fostering our republican system of self-government."[175] According to Justice Brennan, "[i]mplicit in this structural role" is a constitutional "solicitude" for the "indispensable conditions of meaningful communications."[176] Neither justice, however, premised his analysis on *Branzburg* or the constitutional right to gather news identified there.

In *Globe Newspaper Co. v. Superior Court*,[177] in which Justice Brennan authored the Court's first majority opinion holding that a "right of access is embodied in the First Amendment,"[178] there is similarly no discussion of *Branzburg*. Nevertheless, the Court in *Globe* underscored the need to construe the First Amendment broadly "enough to encompass those rights that, while not unambiguously enumerated in the very terms of the Amendment, are nonetheless necessary to the enjoyment of other First Amendment rights."[179] Thus, the Court held, the "First Amendment embraces a right of access to criminal trials" for the purpose of ensuring that the "constitutionally protected 'discussion of governmental affairs' is an informed one."[180]

Finally, in the two *Press-Enterprise* cases,[181] in which the Court extended the First Amendment right of access to *voir dire* and preliminary hearings in criminal cases, *Branzburg* informed the Court's struggle to define to contours of the constitutional right. Thus, concurring in *Press-Enterprise I*, Justice Stevens once

---

172. 448 U.S. at 599 & n.2 (Stewart, J., concurring in judgment).
173. *Id.* at 582 (Stevens, J., concurring).
174. *Id.*
175. *Id.* at 587 (Brennan, J., concurring in judgment).
176. *Id.*
177. 457 U.S. 596 (1982).
178. *Id.* at 603.
179. *Id.* at 604.
180. *Id.* at 604-05.
181. See Press-Enter. Co. v. Superior Ct., 464 U.S. 501 (1984) ("*Press-Enterprise I*"); Press-Enter. Co. v. Superior Ct., 478 U.S. 1 (1986) ("*Press-Enterprise II*").

again returned to *Branzburg*.[182] According to Justice Stevens, the Court in *Branzburg* "implicitly endorsed" the right of access by "rejecting any suggestion 'that news gathering does not qualify for First Amendment protection.'"[183] The First Amendment privilege identified in *Branzburg* was not, Justice Stevens emphasized, absolute and "did not extend to a reporter's refusal to testify before a grand jury, at least under the facts of that case."[184]

In *Press-Enterprise II*, Justice Stevens dissented from the Court's extension of the presumptive right of access to preliminary hearings, based in significant part on his own analysis of *Branzburg*. In so doing, Justice Stevens again asserted that the right was not absolute, relying in part on the Court's observation in *Branzburg* that "[d]espite the fact that news gathering may be hampered, the press is regularly excluded from grand jury proceedings."[185] Nevertheless, Justice Stevens also reiterated that "'a right to gather news, *of some dimensions*, must exist,'" a principle he asserted had been embraced by the Court in *Branzburg* and undergirds as well the Court's development of the constitutional right of access to judicial proceedings.[186]

§ 14-5(e). The *McIntyre* Decision.

The Court's most recent pronouncement of relevance to the efficacy and contours of the constitutional privilege came in the context of its decision invalidating a provision of the Ohio Election Code that prohibited the distribution of anonymous campaign literature.[187] In *McIntyre v. Ohio Elections Commission*, the Court, relying on its prior decision in *Talley v. California*,[188] held that "an author's decision to remain anonymous, like other decisions concerning omissions or additions to the content of a publication, is an aspect of the freedom of speech protected by the First Amendment."[189] Thus, the Court concluded, a requirement that an author of political expression disclose her identity must be

---

182. *Press-Enterprise I*, 464 U.S. at 519 & n.6 (Stevens, J., concurring).
183. *Id.* (quoting Branzburg v. Hayes, 408 U.S. at 681).
184. *Press-Enterprise I*, 464 U.S. at 519 n.6 (Stevens, J., concurring).
185. 478 U.S. at 27 (Stevens, J., dissenting) (quoting Branzburg v. Hayes, 408 U.S. at 684-85).
186. *Press-Enterprise II*, 478 U.S. at 18 n.3 (Stevens, J., dissenting) (quoting Branzburg v. Hayes, 408 U.S. at 728 (Stewart, J., dissenting)).
187. See McIntyre v. Ohio Elections Comm'n, 514 U.S. 334, 357 (1995) (invalidating OHIO REV. CODE ANN. § 3599.09(A)).
188. 362 U.S. 60 (1960).
189. McIntyre v. Ohio Elections Comm'n, 514 U.S. at 342. See also Rancho Publications v. Superior Ct., 81 Cal. Rptr. 2d 274 (Ct. App. 1999) (newspaper could not be compelled to disclose sources of paid, anonymous "advertorials" with only "speculative" relationship to allegedly defamatory statements; "[c]ompelled source disclosure runs afoul of the First Amendment because some speakers may be chilled into silence without the cover of anonymity").

subject to "'exacting scrutiny,'" and can be upheld "only if it is narrowly tailored to serve an overriding interest."[190]

The act of disseminating information to the public anonymously, the Court emphasized, "is not a pernicious, fraudulent practice, but an honorable tradition of advocacy and of dissent" as well as "a shield from the tyranny of the majority."[191] Accordingly, it "exemplifies the purpose behind the Bill of Rights, and of the First Amendment in particular: to protect unpopular individuals from retaliation — and their ideas from suppression — at the hands of an intolerant society."[192]

Although Justice Stevens' opinion for the Court neither cited *Branzburg* nor referenced the burgeoning case law in the lower courts explicating the constitutional reporters' privilege, the Court's reverence for anonymous speech — and its importance to the values undergirding the First Amendment — echo the press' arguments in *Branzburg* itself and in many of the cases that have followed it.[193] Indeed, Justice Thomas's opinion concurring in the judgment, also bereft of citation to *Branzburg*, adopts an historical analysis of the subject that eloquently fortifies the constitutional foundations of the reporters' privilege.[194]

According to Justice Thomas, the critical inquiry in assessing the validity of the Ohio statute is "whether the phrase 'freedom of speech, or of the press,' as originally understood, protected anonymous political leafletting."[195] In explaining his view that "it did," Justice Thomas canvassed the historical record in some detail and offered several examples of episodes in which the press — populated in those days by the printers themselves — sought to resist governmental efforts to compel them to disclose the identities of the authors whose writings they published. In this context, as Justice Thomas relates it in *McIntyre*, "the Framers' understanding of the relationship between anonymity and freedom of the press became more explicit":[196]

> In 1779, for example, the Continental Congress attempted to discover the identity of an anonymous article in the *Pennsylvania Packet* signed by the name "Leonidas." Leonidas, who actually was Dr. Benjamin Rush, had attacked the members of Congress for causing inflation throughout the States

---

190. 514 U.S. at 347 (quoting First Nat'l Bank of Boston v. Bellotti, 435 U.S. 765, 786 (1978)).
191. 514 U.S. at 357.
192. *Id.*
193. See Chap. 14-4 *supra* (discussing *Branzburg*), and Chap. 14-6 *infra* (discussing lower court cases explicating privilege. See also Langley & Levine, *supra* note 39 (discussing roots of constitutional privilege in protection of unpopular speakers); Barnes, *supra* note 149 (discussing relevance of *Talley v. California*, 362 U.S. 60 (1960), to analysis of *Branzburg* and constitutional privilege).
194. See McIntyre v. Ohio Elections Comm'n, 514 U.S. at 358 (Thomas, J., concurring).
195. *Id.*
196. *Id.* at 359.

and for engaging in embezzlement and fraud. Elbridge Gerry, a delegate from Massachusetts, moved to haul the printer of the newspaper before the Congress to answer questions concerning "Leonidas." Several members of Congress then rose to oppose Gerry's motion on the ground that it invaded the freedom of the press. . . . In the end, these arguments persuaded the assembled delegates, who "sat mute" in response to Gerry's motion. Neither the printer nor Dr. Rush ever appeared before Congress to answer for their publication.[197]

Based on historical evidence such as the foregoing, Justice Thomas concluded that "both Anti-Federalists and Federalists believed that the freedom of the press included the right to publish without revealing the author's name" and that the "Framers shared the belief that such activity was firmly part of the freedom of the press."[198]

§ 14-5(f). The Chambers Opinions.

Although the full Court has not addressed the constitutional privilege directly in the decades since *Branzburg*, individual justices have had the opportunity to consider it in the context of opinions issued in their roles as circuit justices. On rare occasions since *Branzburg*, journalists have taken to a circuit justice orders compelling them to disclose the sources of published or broadcast information.

In the summer and early autumn of 1978, Justices White and Marshall wrote multiple opinions addressing the efficacy of the journalists' privilege in the context of applications filed by the *New York Times* and its reporter, Myron Farber. The *Times* and Farber had been held in contempt of a New Jersey court

---

197. *Id.* (citing 13 LETTERS OF DELEGATES TO CONGRESS 1774-1789 141 n. 1 (G. Gawalt & R. Gephart eds. 1986); Teeter, *Press Freedom and the Public Printing: Pennsylvania, 1775-83*, 45 JOURNALISM Q. 445, 451 (1968)). Apparently, Congress's conception of the freedom of the press was shared in the states as well:

> Also in 1779, the upper house of the New Jersey State Legislature attempted to punish the author of a satirical attack on the Governor . . . who had signed his work "Cincinnatus." Attempting to enforce the crime of seditious libel, the state Legislative Council ordered Isaac Collins — the printer and editor of the newspaper in which the article appeared — to reveal the author's identity. Refusing, Collins declared: "Were I to comply . . . I conceive I should betray the trust reposed in me, and be far from acting as a faithful guardian of the Liberty of the Press." Apparently, the State Assembly agreed that anonymity was protected by the freedom of the press, as it voted to support the editor and publisher by frustrating the Council's orders.

514 U.S. at 362 (citing R. HIXSON, ISAAC COLLINS: A QUAKER PRINTER IN 18TH CENTURY AMERICA 95 (1968)).

198. 514 U.S. at 367. See also Rancho Publications v. Superior Ct., 81 Cal. Rptr. 2d 274, 275 (Ct. App. 1999) ("The anonymous pamphleteer is one of the enduring images of the American revolutionary heritage.").

for refusing to disclose unpublished information obtained by Farber in reporting about the defendant in a murder case. The *Times* was assessed daily fines in the amount of $5,000 and Farber was jailed.

The case first came before a member of the Court in July 1978 when, after Justice Brennan recused himself, Justice White denied the *Times'* and Farber's application to stay enforcement of the criminal defendant's subpoena pending appeal.[199] Justice White concluded that he could not "with confidence predict that four Members of the Court would now vote to grant a petition for certiorari at this stage of the proceedings," in part because "[t]here is no present authority in this Court that a newsman need not produce documents material to the prosecution or defense of a criminal case, or that the obligation to obey an otherwise valid subpoena served on a newsman is conditioned upon the showing of special circumstances."[200] Nevertheless, he left open the possibility that Supreme Court review would become necessary "at a later stage of these proceedings."[201]

The next day, Justice Marshall denied a similar request for a stay pending the filing of a petition for a writ of *certiorari*.[202] The petition, the *Times* and Farber had indicated, would ask the Court to determine whether, "'when a motion to quash a subpoena *duces tecum* issued to the news media is made, the court before which such motion is returnable shall be required to make threshold determinations with respect to the facial validity of the subpoena, as well as preliminary rulings on materiality and privilege, *prior to* compelling the production of all subpoenaed materials.'"[203] Justice Marshall acknowledged "important and unresolved questions regarding the obligation of a newsperson to divulge confidential files and other material sought by the prosecution or defense in connection with criminal proceedings" and indicated "it may well be . . . that forced disclosure of these materials, even to a judge for *in camera* inspection, will have a deleterious effect on the ability of the news media effectively to gather information in the public interest."[204] Nevertheless, Justice Marshall concluded that it was premature for the Court to intervene, especially since if the *Times* and Farber did "refuse to comply with the subpoena, they will have an opportunity in subsequent contempt proceedings to raise the same arguments."[205]

Thereafter, both the *Times* and Farber were held in civil and criminal contempt when they refused to comply with the subpoena.[206] Justice White

---

199. See New York Times Co. v. Jascalevich, 439 U.S. 1301 (1978) (White, J., in chambers).
200. *Id.* at 1302 (citing Branzburg v. Hayes, 408 U.S. 665 (1972)).
201. 439 U.S. at 302.
202. New York Times Co. v. Jascalevich, 439 U.S. 1304 (1978) (Marshall, J., in chambers).
203. *Id.* at 1304 (quoting Application).
204. *Id.*
205. *Id.*
206. On the criminal contempt citation, the *Times* was fined $100,000 and Farber was sentenced

declined to stay enforcement of the civil contempt order, the criminal contempt order already having been stayed pending appeal by the New Jersey courts.[207] Once again, Justice White asserted that there "is no present authority in this Court either that newsmen are constitutionally privileged to withhold duly subpoenaed documents material to the prosecution or defense of a criminal case or that a defendant seeking the subpoena must show extraordinary circumstances before enforcement against newsmen will be had."[208] Even if "four or more members of the Court would hold that a reporter's obligation to comply with the subpoena is subject to some special showing of materiality not applicable in the case of ordinary third-party witnesses," Justice White concluded, the case ought not be accepted for review "at this time" when the order at issue "directs submission of the documents and other materials for only an *in camera* inspection" and "anticipates a full hearing on all issues" in the trial court.[209]

Three days later, the *Times* and Farber unsuccessfully sought the same relief from Justice Marshall.[210] Nevertheless, Justice Marshall disagreed with Justice White, asserting that "[g]iven the likelihood that forced disclosure even for *in camera* review will inhibit the reporter's and newspaper's exercise of First Amendment rights, I believe that some threshold showing of materiality, relevance, and necessity should be required."[211] Justice Marshall could not, however, "conclude in good faith that at least four justices would vote to grant a writ of certiorari with the case in the present posture," and therefore denied the application for stay.[212]

In 1980, Justice Brennan, who had recused himself in *New York Times Co. v. Jascalevich*, granted a similar application in *In re Roche*.[213] Roche, a television reporter in Massachusetts, had participated in preparing news reports about a number of state judges, which led to an investigation of one such judge by the

---

to six months in jail. On the civil contempt citation, the *Times* was fined $5,000 per day and Farber was incarcerated until such time as they complied with the trial court's order. New York Times Co. v. Jascalevich, 439 U.S. 1331, 1333 (1978) (Marshall, J., in chambers).

207. New York Times v. Jascalevich, 439 U.S. 1317 (1978) (White, J., in chambers).
208. *Id.* at 1322.
209. *Id.*
210. New York Times Co. v. Jascalevich, 439 U.S. 1331 (1978) (Marshall, J., in chambers).
211. *Id.* at 1335 (citing Carey v. Hume, 492 F.2d 631 (D.C. Cir.), *cert. dismissed*, 417 U.S. 938 (1974); Baker v. F & F Inv., 470 F.2d 778 (2d Cir. 1972), *cert. denied*, 411 U.S. 966 (1973)).
212. 439 U.S. at 1337. Subsequently, Justice Stewart granted a stay pending consideration of the petition for *certiorari*, which was vacated by the full Court on October 6, 1978. See New York Times Co. v. New Jersey, 439 U.S. 886 (1978). Justice Brennan took no part in the Court's consideration of the motion and Justice Marshall dissented, reaffirming his previously stated view that "the petitioners have raised substantial claims under the First and Fourteenth Amendments." *Id.* at 887 (Marshall, J., dissenting). In all, Farber served more than a month in jail. Ultimately, New Jersey Governor Brendan Byrne pardoned Farber and the *Times* and ordered that all fines paid by the *Times* be refunded.
213. 448 U.S. 1312 (1980) (Brennan, J., in chambers).

Massachusetts Commission on Judicial Conduct. In the course of proceedings before the Commission, it permitted the judge to depose Roche. At his deposition, although Roche testified about his own observations and information furnished to him by identified sources, he refused to disclose the identities of those "whom he had interviewed in confidence, unless they had first been identified by other means."[214] Roche was eventually held in civil contempt by the Massachusetts Supreme Judicial Court.

Although Justice Brennan acknowledged that "[p]redicting the probability of a grant of certiorari and of a reversal of the decision below in this case is an uncertain undertaking," he found "support for the proposition that the First Amendment interposes a threshold barrier to the subpoenaing of confidential information and work product from a newsgatherer."[215] Indeed, while Justice Brennan noted *Branzburg*'s holding that "the First Amendment does not provide newsmen with an absolute or qualified testimonial privilege to be free of relevant questioning about sources by a grand jury," he recognized that "[f]our justices in *Branzburg* discerned at least some protection in the First Amendment for confidences garnered during the course of newsgathering" and that Justice Powell had "emphasize[d] that requests for reporter's documents should be carefully weighed with due deference to the 'vital constitutional and societal interests at stake.'"[216]

Thus, Justice Brennan concluded that "there is at least a limited First Amendment right to resist intrusion into newsgatherers' confidences."[217] Specifically, Justice Brennan asserted that, because "a majority of the Court recognizes at least some degree of constitutional protection for newsgatherers' confidences," there was "a fair prospect that the Court will reverse the decision below."[218]

Finally, in *Roche v. Florida*,[219] a Florida newspaper reporter obtained a copy of a sealed court order in a termination of parental rights proceeding from a confidential source. Subsequently, he wrote an article in which he quoted from

---

214. *Id.* at 1314.
215. *Id.* at 1315.
216. *Id.* (quoting Branzburg v. Hayes, 408 U.S. 665, 710 (1972) (Powell, J., concurring)).
217. 448 U.S. at 1315-16. Justice Brennan distinguished the apparently contrary conclusion reached by Justice White in *New York Times Co. v. Jascalevich* on the ground that it turned "not upon the general meritlessness of a newsman's privilege, but more particularly upon the improbability that such a privilege would be applied to preclude *in camera* inspection of papers by a judge." *Id.* at 1315 n.2.
218. *Id.* at 1316. Two years later, in *Massachusetts v. Corsetti*, 438 N.E.2d 805, 809 (Mass. 1982), the Massachusetts Supreme Judicial Court held that there is no constitutional privilege "where the source is disclosed and the testimony sought from the reporter concerns information already made public." Justice Brennan denied an application for stay in that case, reasoning that there was not a reasonable probability that *certiorari* would be granted.
219. 589 So. 2d 928 (Fla. App. 1991), *review denied*, 599 So. 2d 1279 (Fla. 1992), *cert. denied*, 506 U.S. 1071 (1993).

the order and was subpoenaed to testify as part of an investigation into alleged violations of court rules forbidding public disclosure of the order or its contents. When the reporter refused to identify his source, he was held in contempt, a holding affirmed by the Florida appellate courts on the ground that the State had successfully carried its burden of overcoming the qualified journalists' privilege.[220] Although the Supreme Court granted the reporter's application for stay of enforcement of the contempt order pending the disposition of his petition for a writ of *certiorari*, it ultimately denied that petition and the reporter served eleven days in jail.[221]

§ 14-6. *Branzburg* in The Lower Courts.

Absent further guidance from the Supreme Court, the lower courts have assumed the bulk of judicial responsibility for articulating the scope of the constitutional privilege in the years since *Branzburg*. Although the teachings of the various appellate courts have in no sense been unanimous, it is fair to say that overwhelming numbers of state and federal courts have interpreted *Branzburg*, and the subsequent Supreme Court decisions that have had occasion to revisit it, as recognizing in the First Amendment a qualified journalists' privilege of some dimension applicable in many contexts in which compelled disclosure of unpublished information is sought. Chapter 16 sets forth, in some detail, the lower courts' treatment of the privilege and the host of issues that its application has raised. In this chapter, we limit ourselves to sampling the lower courts' general approach to recognition of the First Amendment-based privilege as well as the reasoning of those courts that have construed *Branzburg* as foreclosing at least some claims of constitutional privilege.

§ 14-6(a). The Second Circuit Approach.

The majority approach to claims of journalists' privilege is, in many ways, exemplified by the Second Circuit. Indeed, within months of the Supreme Court's decision in *Branzburg*, the Second Circuit decided *Baker v. F & F Investment*, an interlocutory appeal of a district judge's decision refusing to compel a journalist to disclose the identity of a confidential source in a civil rights action.[222] In an opinion by Chief Judge Kaufman, the Second Circuit

---

220. *Id.* at 931 ("[T]he purposes served by maintaining the confidentiality of juvenile dependency and termination of parental rights proceedings were contravened by Roche's disclosure of the court order.").

221. *Id.* In prior cases, the Court had refused to grant emergency applications for stays pending disposition of petitions for *certiorari*. See, e.g., Scrivner v. Hargraves, 468 U.S. 1202 (1984); see also Karem v. Priest, 497 U.S. 1042 (1990) (denying application for a stay pending appeal to federal circuit court of petition for writ of habeas corpus on behalf of incarcerated reporter).

222. 470 F.2d 778 (2d Cir. 1972), *cert. denied*, 411 U.S. 966 (1973).

determined that, while "it is safe to conclude, particularly after the Supreme Court's decision in *Branzburg*, ... that federal law does not recognize an absolute or conditional journalist's testimonial 'privilege,' neither does federal law require disclosure of confidential sources in each and every case."[223] According to Chief Judge Kaufman, "courts which must attempt to divine the contours of non-statutory federal law governing the compelled disclosure of confidential journalistic sources must rely on both judicial precedent and a well-informed judgment as to the proper federal public policy to be followed in each case."[224]

In so doing, the Second Circuit looked to the First Amendment and those "values which traditionally have been protected by federal courts applying federal public policy."[225] The Court concluded that:

> [c]ompelled disclosure of confidential sources unquestionably threatens a journalist's ability to secure information that is made available to him only on a confidential basis. . . . The deterrent effect such disclosure is likely to have upon future "undercover" investigative reporting . . . threatens freedom of the press and the public's need to be informed.[226]

Thus, the Second Circuit determined that "[w]hile we recognize that there are cases — few in number to be sure — where First Amendment rights must yield, we are still mindful of the preferred position which the First Amendment occupies in the pantheon of freedoms;" as a result, the court held that "though a journalist's right to protect confidential sources may not take precedence over that rare overriding and compelling interest, . . . there are circumstances, at the very least in civil cases, in which the public interest in non-disclosure of a journalist's confidential sources outweighs the public and private interest in compelled testimony."[227]

Chief Judge Kaufman also took pains to accommodate in his analysis the Second Circuit's prior decision in *Garland v. Torre*[228] and the Supreme Court's in *Branzburg*. In *Garland*, the Court explained, then-judge Stewart "observed that compelled disclosure of a newsman's confidential sources unquestionably raises serious constitutional issues, and that any infringement upon First Amendment rights is justified only in view of an overriding public interest."[229] The result in *Garland* — i.e., that the journalist was ordered to disclose the identity of her source — was appropriate because the libel plaintiff there had

---

223. *Id.* at 781 (citing Branzburg v. Hayes, 408 U.S. 665 (1972)).
224. 470 F.2d at 781.
225. *Id.*
226. *Id.*
227. *Id.* at 683.
228. 259 F.2d 545 (2d Cir.), *cert. denied*, 358 U.S. 910 (1958).
229. Baker v. F & F Inv., 470 F.2d at 784.

exhausted alternative means of acquiring the information and the source's identity "'went to the heart of the plaintiff's claim.'"[230]

Branzburg, the Second Circuit concluded, was "only of tangential relevance" because it had addressed no more than "the right of a journalist to withhold disclosure of confidential sources from a grand jury investigating criminal activities."[231] According to Chief Judge Kaufman, the Court in *Branzburg* had "applied traditional First Amendment doctrine, which teaches that constitutional rights secured by the First Amendment cannot be infringed absent a 'compelling' or 'paramount' state interest."[232] In so doing, the Court in *Branzburg* had "found such an overriding interest in the investigation of crime by the grand jury which '[secures] the safety of the person and property of the citizen.'"[233]

The Second Circuit turned to the journalists' privilege in the context of criminal proceedings in *United States v. Burke*.[234] In that case, a criminal defendant attempted to secure unpublished information from a magazine that had reported about the events underlying the charges against him. Relying on *Baker's* explication of the "'paramount public interest in the maintenance of a vigorous, aggressive and independent press capable of participating in robust, unfettered debate over controversial matters, an interest that has always been a principal concern of the First Amendment,'" the court concluded that there was "no

---

230. *Id.* (quoting Garland v. Torre, 259 F.2d at 550).
231. 470 F.2d at 784 (quoting Branzburg v. Hayes, 408 U.S. at 682) ("'the sole issue before [the Court] is the obligation of reporters to respond to grand jury subpoenas as other citizens do and to answer questions relevant to an investigation into the commission of crime'").
232. 470 F.2d at 784 (quoting NAACP v. Button, 371 U.S. 415 (1963)).
233. 470 F.2d at 784 (quoting Branzburg v. Hayes, 408 U.S. at 682). Chief Judge Kaufman further relied upon Justice Powell's concurring opinion in *Branzburg*, which he said "emphasized the limited nature of the Court's holding":

> If, as Mr. Justice Powell noted . . ., instances will arise in which First Amendment values outweigh the duty of a journalist to testify even in the context of a criminal investigation, surely in civil cases, courts must recognize that the public interest in non-disclosure of journalists' confidential news sources will often be weightier than the private interest in compelled disclosure.

470 F.2d at 784-85 (citing Branzburg v. Hayes, 408 U.S. at 710 (Powell, J., concurring)).

Other appellate courts soon followed the constitutional analysis set forth in *Baker*. In *Carey v. Hume*, 492 F.2d 631 (D.C. Cir.), *cert. dismissed*, 417 U.S. 933 (1974), a case that was held in abeyance by the D.C. Circuit pending the Supreme Court's decision in *Branzburg*, for example, the court similarly applied both *Garland* and *Branzburg* and concluded that the latter decision, "in language if not in holding, left intact, insofar as civil litigation is concerned, the approach taken in *Garland*," an approach that requires a court to "look to the facts on a case-by-case basis in the course of weighing the need for the testimony in question against the claims of the newsman that the public's right to know is impaired." 492 F.2d at 636. See also Zerilli v. Smith, 656 F.2d 705, 712 (D.C. Cir. 1981) (in *Carey*, court had recognized "qualified reporter's privilege"); Cervantes v. Time, Inc., 464 F.2d 986, 992-93 (8th Cir. 1972), *cert. denied*, 409 U.S. 1125 (1973); Silkwood v. Kerr-McGee Corp., 563 F.2d 433, 436-37 (10th Cir. 1977).

234. 700 F.2d 70 (2d Cir.), *cert. denied*, 464 U.S. 816 (1983).

legally-principled reason for drawing a distinction between civil and criminal cases when considering whether the reporter's interest in confidentiality should yield to the moving party's need for probative evidence."[235] Although "a criminal defendant has more at stake than a civil litigant and the evidentiary needs of a criminal defendant may weigh more heavily in the balance," the Second Circuit held that "the standard of review should remain the same" because "the important social interests in the free flow of information that are protected by the reporter's qualified privilege are particularly compelling in criminal cases."[236] In his opinion for the court, Judge Meskill applied in the criminal context the same test for defeating the qualified privilege as the Second Circuit had adopted in the civil context — *i.e.*, the moving party must make "a clear and specific showing that the subpoenaed documents are 'highly material and relevant, necessary or critical to the maintenance of the claim, and not obtainable from other available sources.'"[237]

In *United States v. Cutler*,[238] however, the court ordered journalists and television stations to comply with portions of subpoenas issued to them by the defendant in a contempt proceeding. In so doing, the court concluded that *Burke*'s "articulation of a general test applicable to all phases of a criminal trial was not necessary to the resolution of that case" and the decision "should accordingly be considered as limited to its facts."[239] Judge Mahoney, who wrote the *Cutler* opinion, further advised that it had "been circulated to the active members of this court prior to filing."[240]

The Second Circuit in *Cutler* also revisited the evolution of its case law with respect to the journalists' privilege and indicated that "[w]hatever the doctrinal considerations, we must certainly follow *Branzburg* when fact patterns parallel to *Branzburg* are presented."[241] Nevertheless, the court declined to recognize the "claimed conflict between *Branzburg* and *Burke* that Cutler argues to us," i.e., that the Second Circuit should "no longer follow *Burke* in view of recent Supreme Court statements construing *Branzburg*."[242] Thus, the court noted, although both the majority in *Branzburg* and Justice Powell in his concurring opinion had "explicitly rejected," at least in the grand jury context, the "'three

---

235. *Id.* at 75.
236. *Id.*
237. United States v. Burke, 700 F.2d at 77 (quoting In re Petroleum Prods. Antitrust Litig., 680 F.2d 5, 7 (2d Cir.), *cert. denied*, 459 U.S. 909 (1982)). See also United States v. Cuthbertson, 630 F.2d 139, 147 (3d Cir. 1980), *cert. denied*, 449 U.S. 1126 (1981); United States v. Blanton, 534 F. Supp. 295, 296-97 (S.D. Fla. 1982), *aff'd*, 730 F.2d 1425 (11th Cir. 1984).
238. 6 F.3d 67 (2d Cir. 1993).
239. *Id.* at 73.
240. *Id.* at 73 n.5.
241. *Id.* at 73.
242. *Id.* at 71 (citing University of Pennsylvania v. EEOC, 493 U.S. 182 (1990); Cohen v. Cowles Media Co., 501 U.S. 663 (1991)).

preconditions'" embraced by Justice Stewart in dissent (as well as by the Second Circuit in *Burke*), *Branzburg* requires a balancing of competing interests nonetheless, a balance which led the Second Circuit in *Cutler* to conclude that the defendant there was not entitled to the compelled disclosure of journalists' "testimony and unpublished notes regarding statements by Government Officials."[243]

In *Krase v. Graco Children Products, Inc.*,[244] however, the Second Circuit appeared to retreat from the *Cutler* opinion's appraisal of *Burke* and to reaffirm, as the law of the circuit, the three-part test articulated in *Burke* and prior cases. Unlike *Burke* and *Cutler*, the case arose in the civil context — a third-party subpoena for outtakes in a products liability action — and the court in fact decided the case under the New York Shield Law, not the First Amendment-based privilege.[245] Nevertheless, in the course of its decision ordering the district court to grant a television network's motion to quash, the court expressly rejected the contention that *Cutler* supported the district court's decision enforcing the subpoena. In so doing, the Second Circuit emphasized that it continued to apply a constitutional standard "identical to that embodied in the New York Shield Law," in order to "'protect the important interests of reporters and the public in preserving the confidentiality of journalists' sources.'"[246] The constitutional standard, the court held, requires — in language drawn from *Cutler* itself — that "'disclosure may be ordered only upon a clear and specific showing that the information is: highly material and relevant, necessary or critical to the maintenance of the claim, and not obtainable from other available sources.'"[247]

Shortly after *Krase*, in *Gonzales v. National Broadcasting Co.*,[248] a panel of the court purported to hold that, despite its previous pronouncements in cases such as *Baker*, *Burke*, and *Krase*, the privilege does not apply at all to the compelled disclosure of nonconfidential information such as broadcast "outtakes" or reporters' notes. According to the panel opinion, the circuit's precedent had instead "ground[ed] the journalists' privilege" entirely on the "confidential nature of the information" at issue.[249] After the court vacated the panel opin-

---

243. 6 F.3d at 75.
244. 79 F.3d 346 (2d Cir. 1996).
245. *Id.* at 351 (citing N.Y. CIV. RIGHTS LAW § 79-h(c)).
246. 79 F.3d at 352-53 (citation omitted).
247. *Id.* at 353 (quoting United States v. Cutler, 6 F.3d 67, 71 (2d Cir. 1993)).
248. 155 F.3d 618 (2d Cir. 1998), *vacated*, No. 97-9454 (2d Cir. June 1, 1999).
249. *Id.* at 626. In the wake of the panel's decision, at least two district courts in the Second Circuit felt compelled to follow its holding and to reject claims of privilege asserted by journalists in the context of requests for subpoenas seeking their nonconfidential, but nevertheless unpublished, work product. See In re Ramaekers, 33 F. Supp. 2d 312 (S.D.N.Y. 1999) (seeking tape recording and notes of interview conducted by Reuters reporter); In re Dow Jones & Co., 27 MEDIA L. REP. (BNA) 1307 (S.D.N.Y. 1998), *vacated*, No. 99-7014 (2d Cir. June 8, 1999) (seeking interview notes of *Wall Street Journal* reporter).

ion,[250] however, the panel itself reconsidered its ruling and issued a new decision that "explicitly reaffirm[ed]" the existence of "a qualified privilege for nonconfidential press information,"[251] in both criminal and civil cases.[252] In so holding, the court articulated "broader concerns" than the protection of confidential relationships that "undergird[ ] the qualified privilege for journalists — such as the 'pivotal function of reporters to collect information for public dissemination' and 'the paramount public interest in the maintenance of a vigorous, aggressive and independent press capable of participating in robust, unfettered debate over controversial matters.'"[253]

At the same time, the court "clarif[ied]" its position with respect to the test governing divestiture of the privilege that had been articulated in cases such as *Burke* and *Krase*, explaining that "where nonconfidential information is at stake, the showing needed to overcome the journalists' privilege is less demanding than for material acquired in confidence."[254] Specifically, the court held, to overcome the qualified privilege in the context of nonconfidential information, a litigant seeking to compel disclosure must make a less rigorous showing that "the materials at issue are of likely relevance to a significant issue in the case and are not reasonably obtainable from other available sources."[255] In the case before it, a civil rights action brought by alleged victims of police misconduct, the court concluded that the privilege had been overcome in the context of the plaintiffs'

---

250. See Gonzales v. National Broadcasting Co., No. 97-9454 (2d Cir. June 1, 1999) (vacating 155 F.3d 618 (2d Cir. 1998)).

251. Gonzales v. National Broadcasting Co., 1998 U.S. App. LEXIS 38583, *3 (2d Cir. Aug. 27, 1999). The opinion for the unanimous court was written by Judge Leval, who had not sat on the original panel. Judge Parker — who authored the vacated opinion — had, according to Judge Leval, "disqualified himself from this appeal." *Id.* at *2 n.**. Nevertheless, Judge Leval wrote, "[b]efore learning of the circumstances that led to his disqualification, Judge Parker recognized the need for significant revision of the opinion now withdrawn, and expressed views on the disposition of the appeal substantially similar to those stated herein." *Id.*

252. See *id.* at *11. Indeed, the court in *Gonzalez* explained that, although its opinion in *Cutler* had "included language limiting *Burke*," which had extended the privilege to criminal cases, "to its facts," *id.* at *16 n.3 (citing United States v. Cutler, 6 F.3d at 73), that "language should not be construed to suggest that our *Cutler* opinion challenged the very existence of the privilege for nonconfidential materials." *Id.* Rather, Judge Leval emphasized, the Second Circuit

> understand[s] *Cutler* to limit *Burke* only as to how much of a showing was needed to overcome the privilege when the materials at issue were sought by a criminal defendant. The limitation was meant to lower the bar of the showing required of such a defendant to obtain disclosure of reporters' materials; it resulted from our view in *Cutler* that *Burke* undervalued the needs of criminal defendants in putting on a defense.

Id. (citing United States v. Cutler, 6 F.3d at 73).

253. 1998 U.S. App. LEXIS 38583, at *19 (quoting In re Petroleum Prods. Antitrust Litig., 680 F.2d 5, 8 (2d Cir.), *cert. denied*, 459 U.S. 909 (1982); Baker v. F & F Inv., 470 F.2d at 782).

254. 1998 U.S. App. LEXIS 38583, at *21.

255. *Id.*

subpoena for outtakes of an incident in which a police officer allegedly stopped a vehicle without probable cause.[256]

Finally, the court noted that it had, in prior decisions, "expressed differing views on whether the journalists' privilege is constitutionally required or rooted in federal common law."[257] Nevertheless, Judge Leval indicated that, "[u]ntil Congress legislates to modify the privilege or do away with it," there was no "need" to determine whether it "is founded in the Constitution" or is instead a creature of federal common law.[258]

§ 14-6(b). The Sixth Circuit Approach.

In *In re Grand Jury Proceedings*,[259] the Sixth Circuit rejected a claim of constitutional privilege asserted, like the claims in *Branzburg*, in the context of a grand jury investigation. Indeed, on facts remarkably close to those considered by the Supreme Court in *Branzburg*, the case arose when a journalist was held in contempt for his "failure to comply with a *subpoena duces tecum* issued by the grand jury and directing him to produce video tapes compiled in the course of his reporting on the activities of Detroit youth gangs."[260] The grand jury was investigating the murder of a police officer, "allegedly at the hands of two gang members who may have been present" when the reporter was videotaping.[261]

The Sixth Circuit declined to recognize a "privilege grounded in the First Amendment," because to do so would require it to "restructure the holding of the Supreme Court in *Branzburg*," in which it concluded the Court had "rejected the existence of such a first amendment testimonial privilege."[262] Moreover, the

---

256. See *id.* at *23 (citation omitted):

> The outtakes are clearly relevant to a significant issue in the case. The District Court reasonably found they may assist the trier of fact in assessing whether Deputy Pierce had probable cause to stop the NBC vehicle and might help determine whether he engaged in a pattern or practice of stopping vehicles without probable cause, as the Plaintiffs allege. We are also persuaded that the outtakes contain information that is not reasonably obtainable from other available sources, because they can provide unimpeachably objective evidence of Deputy Pierce's conduct.

257. *Id.* at *22 n.6 (comparing Baker v. F & F Inv., 470 F.2d at 781 ("'absent a federal statute to provide specific instructions, courts which must attempt to divine the contours of non-statutory federal law governing the compelled disclosure of confidential journalistic sources must rely on both judicial precedent and well-informed judgment as to the proper federal public policy to be followed in each case'") with von Bulow v. von Bulow, 811 F.2d 136, 142 (2d Cir. 1987) ("'the process of newsgathering is a protected right under the First Amendment, albeit a qualified one'")).

258. 1998 U.S. App. LEXIS 38583, at *22 n.6.
259. 810 F.2d 580 (6th Cir. 1987).
260. *Id.* at 581.
261. *Id.*
262. *Id.* (citing Branzburg v. Hayes, 408 U.S. 665 (1972)).

Sixth Circuit asserted that Justice Powell's concurring opinion "does not warrant the rewriting of the majority opinion to grant a first amendment testimonial privilege to news reporters;" rather, Judge Norris determined that Justice Powell's concurring opinion "is entirely consistent with the majority opinion, and neither limits nor expands upon its holding."[263] Thus, the Sixth Circuit "decline[d] to join some other circuit courts, to the extent that they have ... adopted the qualified privilege urged by the three Branzburg dissenters and rejected by the majority."[264] Instead, the court held that it was obliged only to

> follow the admonition of the majority in *Branzburg* to make certain that the proper balance is struck between freedom of the press and the obligation of all citizens to give relevant testimony, by determining whether the reporter is being harassed in order to disrupt his relationship with confidential news sources, whether the grand jury's investigation is being conducted in good faith, whether the information sought bears more than a remote and tenuous relationship to the subject of the investigation, and whether a legitimate law enforcement need will be served by the forced disclosure of the confidential source relationship.[265]

---

[263]. 810 F.2d at 584 (citing Branzburg v. Hayes, 408 U.S. at 709-10 (Powell, J., concurring)). According to the Sixth Circuit:

> Perhaps Justice Powell's use of the term "privilege" has provided too great a temptation for those inclined to disagree with the majority opinion. In the sense that the balancing referred to by Justice Powell, when instigated by a reporter seeking to protect a confidential source, may result in the denial to a party of the use of evidence which is reliable, one is reminded of the invocation of a "privilege," as contrasted with an "exclusion" which prohibits the introduction of evidence which is unreliable or calculated to mislead or prejudice. But, this balancing of interests should not then be elevated to the status of a first amendment constitutional privilege.

810 F.2d at 585.

[264]. 810 F.2d at 584 & n.6 (citing Zerilli v. Smith, 656 F.2d 705 (D.C. Cir. 1981); United States v. Burke, 700 F.2d 70 (2d Cir.), *cert. denied*, 464 U.S. 816 (1983); United States v. Cuthbertson, 630 F.2d 139 (3d Cir. 1980), *cert. denied*, 449 U.S. 1126 (1981); LaRouche v. National Broadcasting Co., 780 F.2d 1134 (4th Cir.), *cert. denied*, 479 U.S. 818 (1986); Miller v. Transamerican Press, Inc., 621 F.2d 721 (5th Cir. 1980), *cert. denied*, 450 U.S. 1041 (1981)).

[265]. 810 F.2d at 585. But cf. Southwell v. Southern Poverty Law Center, 949 F. Supp. 1303 (W.D. Mich. 1996) (district court, sitting in Sixth Circuit, applies species of privilege articulated by Eighth Circuit in *Cervantes v. Time, Inc.*, 464 F.2d 986 (8th Cir. 1972), *cert. denied*, 409 U.S. 1125 (1973)). See also United States v. Cutler, 6 F.3d 67 (2d Cir. 1993); United States v. Smith, 135 F.3d 963 (5th Cir. 1998); In re Grand Jury 95-1, 27 MEDIA L. REP. (BNA) 1833 (D.D.C. 1999); In re Grand Jury Subpoena, 947 F. Supp. 1314 (E.D. Ark. 1996). Similarly, in *Texas ex rel. Healey v. McMeans*, 884 S.W.2d 772, 775 (Tex. Crim. App. 1994), the Texas Court of Criminal Appeals, the state's highest court with respect to criminal cases, declared that "in Texas, newsmen have no constitutional privilege, qualified or otherwise, to withhold evidence relevant to a pending criminal prosecution." *Id.* at 1706. The court interpreted *Branzburg* as "rejecting" a claim "of newsman's privilege under the First Amendment." The same Texas court, in *Coleman v. Texas*,

nonetheless subsequently required a "plausible showing to the court that the reporters' testimony would actually be *material* and *favorable* to [the] defensive theories." 966 S.W.2d 525, 528 (Tex. Crim. App. 1998) (emphasis in original). See also In re Owens, 496 S.E.2d 592, 596 (N.C. App. 1998) (relying on *Branzburg* to reject application in criminal proceeding of reporters' privilege to nonconfidential information obtained from nonconfidential source); WTHR-TV v. Cline, 693 N.E.2d 1, 12 (Ind. 1998) ("We cannot read *Branzburg* to find the United States Constitution to require the very test that was rejected in that case").

Chapter 15

STATE SHIELD LAWS AND FEDERAL CODIFICATIONS

§ 15-1. Introduction.
§ 15-2. State Shield Laws.
   § 15-2(a). Constitutionality.
   § 15-2(b). Recipients of Protection.
      § 15-2(b)(1). Definitional Issues.
      § 15-2(b)(2). Standing Issues.
   § 15-2(c). Proceedings Covered.
      § 15-2(c)(1). Criminal Proceedings.
      § 15-2(c)(2). Civil Proceedings.
         § 15-2(c)(2)(A). Third-Party Proceedings.
         § 15-2(c)(2)(B). The Press as a Party.
         § 15-2(c)(2)(C). Non-Judicial Proceedings.
   § 15-2(d). Scope of Protection.
      § 15-2(d)(1). Sources of Information.
      § 15-2(d)(2). Confidential Information.
      § 15-2(d)(3). Nonconfidential Information.
         § 15-2(d)(3)(A). Nonconfidential Sources.
         § 15-2(d)(3)(B). Eyewitness Testimony.
         § 15-2(d)(3)(C). Unpublished Information.
         § 15-2(d)(3)(D). Editorial Process Materials.
         § 15-2(d)(3)(E). Published Information.
   § 15-2(e). Contours of the Privilege.
      § 15-2(e)(1). Absolute Privilege.
      § 15-2(e)(2). Qualified Privilege.
         § 15-2(e)(2)(A). Relevance Requirements.
         § 15-2(e)(2)(B). Exhaustion Requirements.
         § 15-2(e)(2)(C). Other Requirements.
   § 15-2(f). Privilege v. Immunity.
   § 15-2(g). Penalties for Non-Disclosure.
   § 15-2(h). Waiver.
   § 15-2(i). Procedural Requirements.
      § 15-2(i)(1). Procedures Generally.
      § 15-2(i)(2). In Camera Review.
      § 15-2(i)(3). Appellate Review.
      § 15-2(i)(4). Special Broadcast Rules.
      § 15-2(i)(5). Other Requirements.
   § 15-2(j). Choice of Law.
§ 15-3. Federal Codifications.
   § 15-3(a). Search Warrants.
   § 15-3(b). Justice Department and Administrative Regulations.
   § 15-3(c). Federal Rules of Procedure.

§ 15-1. Introduction.

As the preceding chapter suggests, the Constitution has not been the sole source in American law of the journalists' privilege. Indeed, as early as 1896, Maryland became the first state to enact a law that "gives a newspaperman the privilege of not revealing the source of information published by him."[1] Enactment of the Maryland statute followed the imprisonment of John T. Morris, a reporter for the *Baltimore Sun*, who had refused to reveal to a grand jury the source of an article he wrote about the role of public officials and police officers in illegal gambling.[2] The statute, which "served as a model" for many of the thirteen states that had enacted so-called "shield laws" by 1968,[3] protected print journalists from the compelled disclosure of "the source of any news or information procured or obtained by him for and published in the newspaper."[4]

Prior to the late 1960s, case law interpreting the original thirteen shield laws was "sparse."[5] Occasionally, however, a judicial decision prompted a state legislature to amend a shield statute to respond to contemporary events, usually through amendments expanding the law's reach to include electronic media.[6] Some courts, such as the Pennsylvania Supreme Court in *In re Taylor*,[7] construed these laws broadly to protect against the compelled disclosure of any information gathered by a journalist, not simply the identities of confidential sources.[8] Others interpreted the same language more narrowly by distinguishing

---

1. Maryland v. Sheridan, 236 A.2d 18, 19 (Md. 1967). See ch. 249 of the Maryland Acts of 1896 (original version); MD. CODE ANN., CTS. & JUD. PROC. § 9-112 (current version); Bortz & Bortz, *"Pressing Out the Wrinkles" In Maryland's Shield Law for Journalists*, 8 U. BALT. L. REV. 461 (1979).
2. See Tofani v. Maryland, 465 A.2d 413, 415 (Md. 1983).
3. *Id.* at 415. See ALA. CODE tit. 7, § 370 (1958); ARIZ. REV. STAT. ANN. § 12-2237 (Cum. Supp. 1966); ARK. STAT. ANN. § 43-917 (1964); CAL. EVID. CODE § 1070 (1966); IND. ANN. STAT. § 2-1733 (Cum. Supp. 1966); KY. REV. STAT. § 421.100 (1963); LA. REV. STAT. §§ 45:1451 to 45:1454 (Cum. Supp. 1965); MD. CODE ANN., art. 35, § 2 (1965); MICH. STAT. ANN. § 28.945(1) (1954); MONT. REV. CODE, §§ 93-601-1, 93-601-2 (1964); N.J. STAT. ANN. §§ 2A:84A-21, 2A:84A-29 (Cum. Supp. 1966); OHIO REV. CODE ANN. §§ 2739.04, 2739.12 (Supp. 1966); PA. STAT. ANN. tit. 28, § 330 (Cum. Supp. 1965).
4. MD. CODE ANN., art. 35, § 2 (1965); see Tofani v. Maryland, 465 A.2d at 415 & n.1.
5. Tofani v. Maryland, 465 A.2d at 415.
6. The Maryland statute, for example, was amended in 1949 to include "radio or television" reporters within its scope. See *id.* See also OHIO REV. CODE ANN. § 2739.04 (reflecting 1977 amendment of Ohio shield law to include "revelation of news source by broadcasters").
7. 193 A.2d 181 (Pa. 1963).
8. In *Taylor*, a reporter was held in contempt because he refused to comply with a grand jury subpoena ordering the production of unpublished notes and records. Reversing the trial judge, the Pennsylvania Supreme Court held that the reporter's notes and records were protected by the shield law's reference to the "source of any information," which includes "not only the identity of the person, but likewise includes documents, inanimate objects, and all sources of information." *Id.* at 185. Cf. Hatchard v. Westinghouse Broadcasting Co., 532 A.2d 346, 357 (Pa. 1987) (holding that "unpublished documentary information gathered by a television station is discoverable by a

"between the *source* of the information and the *information*" itself.[9]

By 1972, largely in the wake of the outbreak of subpoenas of journalists that spawned, *inter alia*, the Supreme Court's decision in *Branzburg v. Hayes*,[10] four additional states had enacted shield laws.[11] In addition, the Justice Department promulgated guidelines, first issued in 1970, designed to recognize "that compulsory process in some circumstances may have a limiting effect on the exercise of First Amendment rights."[12] In the immediate aftermath of the *Branzburg* decision, several additional states adopted shield legislation.[13] In all, thirty-one states and the District of Columbia[14] have now enacted such statutes.[15] Unlike

---

plaintiff in a libel action" to the extent that "it does not reveal the identity of a personal source of information"). See also Chap. 15-2(d) *infra* (discussing judicial construction of similar statutory language).

9. Maryland v. Sheridan, 236 A.2d 18, 19 n.1 (Md. 1967); see New Jersey v. Donovan, 30 A.2d 421 (N.J. 1943); *Recent Cases*, 77 HARV. L. REV. 556 (1964); Comment, *Newspapermen Not Required to Divulge Confidential Information to Investigating Grand Jury Even After Informant's Identity Has Been Voluntarily Disclosed in Newspaper Article*, 112 U. PA. L. REV. 438 (1964).

10. 408 U.S. 665 (1972).

11. See ALASKA STAT. § 09.25.150 (Supp. 1971); NEV. REV. STAT. § 49.275 (1971); N.M. STAT. ANN. § 20-1-12.1 (1970); N.Y. CIV. RIGHTS LAW, c. 6, § 79-h (McKinney Supp. 1971-1972). The marked increase in the frequency of subpoenas of journalists in the years preceding *Branzburg v. Hayes*, 408 U.S. 665 (1972), is discussed in Chap.14-2 *supra*.

12. United States Dep't of Justice Mem. 692 (Sept. 2, 1970).

13. See, e.g., MINN. STAT. § 595.024; N.D. CENT. CODE § 31-01-06.2; TENN. CODE ANN. § 24-1-208; OKLA. STAT. tit. 12, § 2506; OR. REV. STAT. §§ 44.510-.540. As courts interpreting these statutes have indicated, "enactment of the legislation was in apparent response to the *Branzburg* decision." Grand Forks Herald v. District Ct., 322 N.W.2d 850, 853 (N.D. 1982). See also Austin v. Memphis Publ'g Co., 655 S.W.2d 146, 149 (Tenn. 1983) (noting that Tennessee "Shield Law was enacted nine months after the United States Supreme Court's decision in *Branzburg v. Hayes*").

14. The District of Columbia statute was enacted in 1992. Modeled on the Maryland statute, it was passed by the D.C. Council after the D.C. Court of Appeals indicated that, in its view, the issue of a constitutional privilege remained unresolved. See Wheeler v. Goulart, 593 A.2d 173, 174 (D.C. 1991). The *Wheeler* case arose from the refusal of a *Washington Post* reporter to disclose the source of her published information about a police raid in response to a subpoena in a civil action, even after the trial court had held that she waived whatever constitutional privilege she might assert. The Court of Appeals affirmed, holding that the reporter's nonconditional disclosure of her source to two other persons constituted a waiver of any privilege that might be available. *Id.* at 175.

15. The thirty-two jurisdictions, with parenthetical citation to their respective statutes, are: Alabama (ALA. CODE § 12-21-142); Alaska (ALASKA STAT. §§ 09.25.300-.390); Arizona (ARIZ. REV. STAT. §§ 12-2214, 12-2237); Arkansas (ARK. CODE ANN. § 16-85-510); California (CAL. EVID. CODE § 1070; CAL. CONST. art. I, § 2(b)); Colorado (COLO. REV. STAT. §§ 13-90-119, 24-72.5-101 to 106); Delaware (DEL. CODE ANN. tit. 10, §§ 4320-26); District of Columbia (D.C. CODE ANN. §§ 16-4701 to 4704); Florida (FLA. STAT. § 90.5015); Georgia (GA. CODE ANN. § 24-9-30); Illinois (735 ILL. COMP. STAT. 5/8-901); Indiana (IND. CODE § 34-46-4-1); Kentucky (KY. REV. STAT. ANN. § 421.100); Louisiana (LA. REV. STAT. ANN. §§ 45:1451-1459); Maryland (MD. CODE ANN., CTS. & JUD. PROC. § 9-112); Michigan (MICH. COMP. LAWS § 767.5a); Minnesota (MINN. STAT. § 595.021-.025); Montana (MONT. CODE ANN. §§ 26-1-901 to 903); Nebraska (NEB. REV. STAT. §§ 20-144 to 147); Nevada (NEV. REV. STAT. § 49.275); New Jersey (N.J. STAT. ANN.

the early laws modeled on the Maryland statute, the thirty-one existing shield laws differ in material respects.[16] In addition, several existing statutes have been revised significantly, often in response to judicial interpretation.[17] Efforts to enact uniform federal legislation have failed, although the federal rules of civil and criminal procedure, the aforementioned Justice Department Guidelines, and a federal statute enacted following the Supreme Court's decision in *Zurcher v. Stanford Daily*,[18] all have some relevance to efforts to compel disclosure of a journalist's sources.[19] In this chapter, we explore the contours of the various state statutes as well as those protections against compelled disclosure provided by nonconstitutional sources of federal law.

§§ 2A:84A-21 to 2A:84A-21.8); New Mexico (N.M. R. EVID. 11-514); New York (N.Y. CIV. RIGHTS LAW § 79-h); North Carolina (N.C. GEN. STAT. § 8-53.9); North Dakota (N.D. CENT. CODE § 31-01-06.2); Ohio (OHIO REV. CODE ANN. §§ 2739.04 & 2739.12); Oklahoma (OKLA. STAT. ANN. tit. 12, § 2506); Oregon (OR. REV. STAT. §§ 44.510-.540); Pennsylvania (42 PA. CONS. STAT. § 5942); Rhode Island (R.I. GEN. LAWS § 9-19.1); South Carolina (S.C. CODE ANN. § 19-11-100); Tennessee (TENN. CODE ANN. § 24-1-208).

16. See Chap. 15-2 *infra*. See generally Alexander & Bush, *Shield Laws on Trial: State Court Interpretations of the Journalist's Statutory Privilege*, 23 J. LEGIS. 215 (1997) (analyzing media success under state shield laws in resisting various categories of subpoenas).

17. In both New York and New Jersey, for example, shield laws have been amended on more than one occasion in response to judicial interpretation. In *Maressa v. New Jersey Monthly*, 445 A.2d 376 (N.J.), *cert. denied*, 459 U.S. 907 (1982), for example, the New Jersey Supreme Court recognized that legislative amendment of the shield law had effectively overruled its prior decisions in *Brogan v. Passaic Daily News*, 123 A.2d 473 (N.J. 1956) (pleading fair comment and good faith as affirmative defenses in libel action and testifying as to information received from "reliable" source constitute waiver of privilege), and *In re Bridge*, 295 A.2d 3 (N.J. Super. 1972), *cert. denied*, 410 U.S. 991 (1973) (disclosure of source of information waives privilege as to published and unpublished information). The decision in *Bridge*, and the resulting incarceration of a reporter, prompted 1977 amendments to the shield law creating a statutory privilege protecting unpublished "information," now codified at N.J. STAT. ANN. § 2A:84-21(b), in addition to the statutory privilege protecting "sources."

In New York, the legislature amended the shield law in 1990 to extend the statutory privilege to nonconfidential sources. Before those amendments, the New York Court of Appeals, and most lower courts in New York, had limited the shield law's application to confidential information. See, e.g., Knight-Ridder Broadcasting, Inc. v. Greenberg, 511 N.E.2d 1116, 1117 (N.Y. 1987) (shield law "clearly does not extend its protection to nonconfidential sources or information obtained in the course of gathering or obtaining news for publication"); People v. Korkala, 472 N.Y.S.2d 310 (App. Div. 1984); Hennigan v. Buffalo Courier Express Co., 446 N.Y.S.2d 767 (App. Div. 1981); Dooley v. Boyle, 531 N.Y.S.2d 158 (Sup. Ct. 1988).

Minnesota amended its shield law in 1998 to include expressly unpublished information procured in the course of newsgathering, whether or not the information would tend to identify the source or means through which the information was obtained, within the scope of the privilege. The new law effectively overrules the holding in *Minnesota v. Turner*, 550 N.W.2d 622 (Minn. 1996), which declined to apply the privilege to nonconfidential, unpublished information.

18. 436 U.S. 547 (1978).

19. See Chap. 15-3 *infra*.

§ 15-2. State Shield Laws.

§ 15-2(a). Constitutionality.

Claims that shield laws violate state or federal constitutions have largely, though not uniformly, been unsuccessful. Some early cases dismissed such suggestions without elaboration.[20] In 1980, in the wake of judicial suggestion that its shield law violated the separation of powers,[21] California amended its own Constitution expressly to include the shield law, which had previously been codified only as part of its evidence code.[22] Courts have rejected claims that shield laws violate state constitutional provisions fixing the power of grand juries,[23] that they necessarily conflict with a criminal defendant's right to compulsory process,[24] or that they unconstitutionally restrict a civil plaintiff's ability to vindicate his reputation.[25] At least two courts have declined to embrace claims

---

20. See, e.g., Ex parte Sparrow, 14 F.R.D. 351, 353 (N.D. Ala. 1953) ("There is no merit in plaintiff's contention that such statute is unconstitutional when measured by the test of the Fourteenth Amendment to the Constitution of the United States.").

21. See Farr v. Superior Ct., 99 Cal. Rptr. 342, 348 (Ct. App.), *cert. denied*, 409 U.S. 1011 (1971) (holding that legislature cannot restrict judiciary's "constitutionally compelled duty to control its own officers," i.e., court employee believed to have leaked information to press).

22. Compare CAL. EVID. CODE § 1070 with CAL. CONST. art. I, § 2(b). See generally Delaney v. Superior Ct., 789 P.2d 934, 938-39 (Cal. 1990) (discussing history of California shield law).

23. See Beach v. Shanley, 465 N.E.2d 304, 310 (N.Y. 1984) ("[t]he constitutional provision against impairing a grand jury's power was not intended to prevent the Legislature from creating evidentiary privileges or their equivalent that have an incidental impact on investigations").

24. See Oregon ex rel. Meyers v. Howell, 740 P.2d 792, 794 (Or. App. 1987) (holding that Oregon shield law does not conflict with criminal defendant's right to compulsory process, at least where evidence sought is not "material and favorable" to defendant's case). Other courts have, however, required that the Sixth Amendment rights of criminal defendants be balanced against claims made by journalists pursuant to a shield law, often without apparent regard to the statutory language. See, e.g., In re Farber, 394 A.2d 330, 337 (N.J.), *cert. denied*, 439 U.S. 997 (1978) (declaring facial constitutionality of New Jersey shield law, but recognizing that, at least in some cases, criminal defendant's right to compel witnesses may pose conflict); Miller v. Superior Ct., 77 Cal. Rptr. 2d 827 (Ct. App.), *review granted*, 968 P.2d 462 (Cal. 1998); Chap. 15-2(c)(1) *infra* (citing additional cases).

25. See, e.g., Coughlin v. Westinghouse Broadcasting & Cable Inc., 780 F.2d 340, 342 (3d Cir. 1985), *cert. denied*, 476 U.S. 1187 (1986) ("we are satisfied that the Pennsylvania Shield Law, as applied to public official libel actions, suffers from no state or federal constitutional infirmity"); Jamerson v. Anderson Newspapers, Inc., 469 N.E.2d 1243, 1249-50 (Ind. App. 1984); Maressa v. New Jersey Monthly, 445 A.2d 376, 385 (N.J. 1982); Riley v. Moyed, No. 84C-JA-78 (Del. Super. 1985). In *Coughlin*, although the Third Circuit's *per curium* opinion summarily rejected a constitutional challenge to the Pennsylvania shield law mounted by a public official suing for defamation, Judge Becker submitted a lengthy opinion in which he analyzed each of plaintiff's constitutional claims, including a challenge premised on the Fourteenth Amendment. See, e.g., 780 F.2d at 351 (Becker, J., concurring) (rejecting plaintiff's assertion that the Pennsylvania shield law renders "judicial recourse so difficult as to be meaningless and thus a denial of due process" because statute does not deny plaintiff "his opportunity to bring his case to court and have it heard; victory, while not easy, is also not impossible").

by broadcast journalists that shield laws limited on their face to the print media deny them equal protection of the laws.[26]

The New Mexico Supreme Court, however, did hold that state's shield law unconstitutional, on the ground that, under the state's constitution, "the Legislature lacks power to prescribe by statute rules of evidence and procedure."[27] In New Mexico, "this constitutional power is vested exclusively" in the state Supreme Court "and statutes purporting to regulate practice and procedure in the courts cannot be binding."[28] Other states have declined "to go as far as our sister court in New Mexico and declare the shield statute invalid for that reason."[29] Subsequently, the New Mexico Supreme Court itself promulgated a shield law as part of its rules of evidence.[30]

§ 15-2(b). Recipients of Protection.

§ 15-2(b)(1). Definitional Issues.

The recipients of statutory protection vary, often substantially, from state to state. Some statutes extend their protections to those persons "engaged in newspaper, radio or television journalism,"[31] while others apply to any person "regularly engaged in the business of collecting or writing news for publication, or

---

26. See, e.g., In re Grand Jury Proceedings, 810 F.2d 580, 586 (6th Cir. 1987) (holding that broadcast journalists not deprived of a "basic, fundamental right, in view of the holding of the Supreme Court in *Branzburg* [*v. Hayes*, 408 U.S. 665 (1972)] that the first amendment accords no privilege to news reporters against appearing before a grand jury and answering questions relative to a criminal investigation"); In re Contempt of Stone, 397 N.W.2d 244, 246 (Mich. App. 1986). Given the disagreement of most federal and state appellate courts with the premise of the analysis embraced by the Sixth Circuit and the Michigan Court of Appeals — i.e., that journalists have no constitutional reporters' privilege — see Chap. 14-6(a) *supra*, it is at least arguable that other jurisdictions would be obliged to accept such an equal protection claim, at least in the face of an "as applied" challenge by a broadcast journalist.

27. Ammerman v. Hubbard Broadcasting, Inc., 551 P.2d 1354, 1359 (N.M. 1976), *cert. denied*, 436 U.S. 906 (1978).

28. *Id.*

29. Las Vegas Sun v. Eighth Judicial Dist. Ct., 761 P.2d 849, 853 n.6 (Nev. 1988); see Grand Forks Herald v. District Ct., 322 N.W.2d 850, 853 n.3 (N.D. 1982) (identifying but not deciding the issue because "it was not raised").

30. See N.M. R. EVID. 11-514. California, in contrast, amended its Constitution to include a shield law after one court suggested that, at least as applied to newsgathering about the judiciary, separation-of-powers principles precluded the legislature from restricting the courts' "constitutionally compelled duty to control its own officers." Farr v. Superior Ct., 99 Cal. Rptr. 342, 348 (Ct. App. 1971).

31. ARIZ. REV. STAT. § 12-2237. See KY. REV. STAT. ANN. § 421.100 (statute applies to any "person" who obtains and publishes information "in a newspaper or by a radio or television broadcasting station by which he is engaged or employed, or with which he is connected").

presentation to the public, through a news organization."[32] The Arkansas statute, at least on its face, applies to the editors, reporters, writers, publishers, managers, and owners of "any newspaper, periodical, or radio station," but not to persons in analogous positions in television.[33] In contrast, the Ohio statute was amended in 1977 to extend its protection beyond "newspaper[s]" and "press association[s]" to include radio and television "broadcasting station[s]."[34] The Montana statute specifically applies to "community antenna television service[s],"[35] while the Oregon statute expressly includes "cable television system[s]."[36]

The California shield law now extends its protection to "a publisher, editor, reporter, or other person connected with or employed upon a newspaper, magazine, or other periodical publication, or by a press association or wire service," as well as to a "radio or television station news reporter or other person connected with or employed by a radio or television station."[37] The definitional section of the Indiana statute is particularly exact, specifying that it extends to any:

> person connected with, or any person who has been so connected with or employed by, a newspaper or other periodical issued at regular intervals and having a general circulation, or a recognized press association or wire service, as a bona fide owner, editorial or reportorial employee, who receives or has received income from legitimate gathering, writing, editing

---

32. ALASKA STAT. § 09.25.390(4). The Alaska statute also defines "news organization" to encompass both "an individual, partnership, corporation or other association regularly engaged in the business of (i) publishing a newspaper or other periodical that reports news events, is issued at regular intervals and has a general circulation; (ii) providing newsreels or other motion picture news for public showing; or (iii) broadcasting news to the public by wire, radio, television or facsimile," and "a press association or other association of individuals ... engaged in gathering news and disseminating it to its members for publication." *Id.* § 09.25.390(4). Similarly, the Maryland shield law defines "news media" to include newspapers, magazines, journals, press associations, news agencies, wire services, radio, television, and "[a]ny printed, photographic, mechanical, or electronic means of disseminating news or information to the public." MD. CODE ANN., CTS. & JUD. PROC. § 9-112.

33. ARK. CODE ANN. § 16-85-510. The omission of television appears to be a function of the fact that the statute was first enacted in 1936 and has not been amended since 1949.

34. Compare OHIO REV. CODE ANN. § 2739.12 (original statute enacted in 1953) with *id.* § 2739.04 (1977 enactment applying to "revelation of news source by broadcasters"). Similarly, the Michigan statute was amended in 1986 to include persons "involved in the gathering or preparation of news for broadcast," MICH. COMP. LAWS § 767.5a, after that state's courts had held that "television news reporters" do not "come within the purview of the statute." In re Contempt of Stone, 397 N.W.2d 244, 246 (Mich. App. 1986). See also Tofani v. Maryland, 465 A.2d 413 (Md. 1983) (Maryland amended its statute in 1949 to include radio and television reporters).

35. MONT. CODE ANN. § 26-1-902.

36. OR. REV. STAT. § 44.510(2).

37. CAL. EVID. CODE § 1070 (a) & (b).

and interpretation of news, and any person connected with a licensed radio or television station as owner, official, or as an editorial or reportorial employee who receives or has received income from legitimate gathering, writing, editing, interpreting, announcing or broadcasting of news.[38]

The Tennessee statute, in contrast, applies simply to a "person engaged in gathering information for publication or broadcast," whether "connected with or employed by the news media or press" or "independently engaged in gathering information for publication or broadcast."[39]

Many of these statutory schemes have spawned litigation concerning the ability of various claimants to invoke their protections. Some courts have held that authors unaffiliated with a legislatively defined news organization are not protected by a given jurisdiction's shield law, even when they are concededly gathering information for book-length works of nonfiction.[40] Other decisions, however, have interpreted shield laws to include within their protections "freelance writers" not under contract with a news media entity.[41]

Several courts have grappled with identifying the kinds of journalistic enterprises that qualify for shield law protection. In *Cukier v. American Medical Association*,[42] for example, an Illinois court held that the editors of a leading medical journal may invoke the privilege, even in the context of their evaluation

---

38. IND. CODE § 34-46-4-1. It appears that no Indiana court has yet attempted to distinguish "legitimate" from illegitimate "gathering, writing, editing, interpreting, announcing or broadcasting of news." See generally WTHR-TV v. Cline, 693 N.E.2d 1 (Ind. 1998). See also N.Y. CIV. RIGHTS LAW § 79-h(a)(1)-(8) (containing extensive definitions of "newspaper," "magazine," "news agency," "press association," "wire service," "professional journalist," "newscaster," and "news"); N.M. R. EVID. 11-514(A)(3)-(9) (defining "news," "newspaper," "news agency," "news media," "magazine," "press association," and "wire service"); N.C. GEN. STAT. § 8-53.9 (any "person, company or entity engaged in the business of gathering, compiling, writing, editing, photographing, recording, or processing information for dissemination via any news medium").

39. TENN. CODE ANN. § 24-1-208.

40. See, e.g., Matera v. Superior Ct., 825 P.2d 971, 973 (Ariz. App. 1992) (Arizona statute designed only "to protect members of the media from burdensome subpoenas and broad discovery that would interfere with the ongoing business of gathering and reporting the news to the public"); People v. LeGrand, 415 N.Y.S.2d 252, 255 (App. Div. 1979) (author of book about organized crime not protected by shield law, the provisions of which "evince a clear legislative design to benefit 'professional journalists' and 'newscasters' only. They should not by judicial fiat and strained interpretation be deemed to encompass those engaged in a different field of writing and research."); In re Hadenguest, 5 MEDIA L. REP. (BNA) 2361, 2363-64 (N.Y. Sup. Ct. 1980).

41. See, e.g., Desai v. Hersh, 954 F.2d 1408, 1411 n.3 (7th Cir. 1992), *cert. denied*, 506 U.S. 865 (1992); People v. Villas, 13 Cal. Rptr. 2d 62, 78 (Ct. App. 1992), *cert. denied*, 508 U.S. 975 (1993). But see Northside Sanitary Landfill, Inc. v. Bradley, 462 N.E.2d 1321 (Ind. App. 1984) (finding that person who obtained environmental clean-up report because of personal interest in environmental issues, rather than as freelance journalist, could not invoke statutory privilege); In re Van Ness, 8 MEDIA L. REP. (BNA) 2563, 2564 (Cal. Super. 1982) (holding a freelance writer not protected by shield law).

42. 630 N.E.2d 1198 (Ill. App. 1994).

of manuscripts submitted for publication.[43] The New Jersey Supreme Court has extended the protection of its shield law to employees of a company that issues insurance rating reports.[44] Another New Jersey court has held the shield law applicable to a tabloid publication distributed free of charge, even though the statute, on its face, defines a "newspaper" as a publication having paid circulation.[45] One court, however, concluded that, even though a credit-reporting agency "in a very real sense, is a news-collecting agency," it nevertheless does not fall within the Ohio shield law's definition of "newspaper" or "press association."[46]

§ 15-2(b)(2). Standing Issues.

Several jurisdictions have addressed various standing issues raised by shield laws. A number of courts have held that the statutory "privilege is not that of the informant, but of the newsman."[47] As a result, some courts have concluded that "a promise of confidentiality is not a prerequisite to invoking the protection of the statute. The privilege belongs to the reporter and he cannot be compelled to disclose the source of his news, whether it was given to him in confidence or not."[48]

Courts have reached different conclusions with respect to the standing of nonjournalists affiliated with a news media organization to invoke a given shield law's protections. In *Becnel v. Lucia*,[49] for example, a Louisiana appellate court held that its shield law, which defines a "reporter" as "*any person* regularly engaged in the *business* of collecting, writing or editing news for publication

---

43. *Id.* at 1202. See also In re Grand Jury Investigation, 15 MEDIA L. REP. (BNA) 1469 (Ill. Cir. 1988) (applying privilege to protect anonymous author's identity following publication of essay in medical journal).

44. See In re Burnett, 635 A.2d 1019, 1023-24 (N.J. Super. 1993) ("New Jersey statute . . . broadly defines the term 'news media' to include a publication such as the insurance reports").

45. See In re Avila, 501 A.2d 1018, 1019 (N.J. Super. 1985) ("In determining whether *Avance* is similar enough to a 'newspaper' to qualify as a news medium, we must be sensitive to the legislative momentum that has steadily expanded the scope of the statutory newsperson's privilege since its first enactment . . . .").

46. Deltec, Inc. v. Dun & Bradstreet, Inc., 187 F. Supp. 788, 789-90 (N.D. Ohio 1960).

47. Lightman v. Maryland, 294 A.2d 149, 156 (Md. Spec. App.), *aff'd*, 295 A.2d 212 (Md. 1972), *cert. denied*, 411 U.S. 951 (1973); see Tofani v. Maryland, 465 A.2d 413, 418 n.2 (Md. 1983); New Jersey v. Boiardo, 416 A.2d 793, 798 (N.J. 1980) ("[T]he privilege is that of the newsperson and not the source."); Lipps v. Indiana, 258 N.E.2d 622, 626 (Ind. App. 1970) (Indiana shield law "creates a right personal to the reporter which only he may invoke. . . . [I]t cannot be invoked by the person who communicated with the reporter and now seeks to prevent the reporter from testifying."); Hestand v. Indiana, 273 N.E.2d 282 (Ind. 1971).

48. Tofani v. Maryland, 465 A.2d at 418 n.2. See Gastman v. North Jersey Newspapers Co., 603 A.2d 111, 112 (N.J. Super. 1992) ("we are of the view that a source's expectations of confidentiality are irrelevant in determining the applicability of the privilege").

49. 420 So. 2d 1173 (La. App. 1982).

through the news media,"[50] extends its protections to "an owner-publisher or anyone similarly situated," even if "he was not acting as a 'reporter' in looking over and editing" a publication.[51] A Nevada court, in contrast, has suggested that the statutory privilege may only be invoked by one "who obtained or prepared the requested information in his or her professional capacity in the process of gathering news," although it too purported to be "satisfied that the legislature meant to include newspaper publishers in its definition of 'editorial employees.'"[52]

§ 15-2(c). Proceedings Covered.

Most shield statutes identify, with some degree of specificity, the types of governmental proceedings to which their protections apply. The New Jersey statute, for example, applies on its face to any "legal or quasi-legal proceeding or before any investigative body, including, but not limited to, any court, grand jury, petit jury, administrative agency, the Legislature or legislative committee, or elsewhere."[53] Other shield laws, though less detailed in their statutory language, have also been held to apply broadly. The Arkansas shield law, for example, which applies on its face simply to "any Grand Jury or any other authority,"[54] has been held to apply in all criminal and civil proceedings.[55]

---

50. *Id.* at 1175 (quoting LA. REV. STAT. ANN. § 45:1451) (emphasis supplied by court).
51. Becnel v. Lucia, 420 So. 2d at 1175. See Gastman v. North Jersey Newspapers Co., 603 A.2d 111, 112 (N.J. Super. 1992) ("the protection accorded by the Shield Law is fully applicable to the newspaper itself and to an editor who is not directly involved in the newsgathering activities").
52. Las Vegas Sun, Inc. v. Eighth Judicial Dist. Ct., 761 P.2d 849, 854 & n.7 (Nev. 1988).
53. N.J. STAT. ANN. § 2A:84A-21. See also ALA. CODE § 12-21-142 (statute applicable in "any legal proceeding or trial, before any court or before a grand jury of any court, before the presiding officer of any tribunal or his agent or agents or before any committee of the legislature or elsewhere"); MINN. STAT. § 595.023 (statute applicable to "any court, grand jury, agency, department or branch of the state, or any of its political subdivisions or other public body, or by either house of the legislature or any committee, officer, member or employee thereof"); KY. REV. STAT. ANN. § 421.100 (statute applicable to proceedings before "any grand or petit jury, or before the presiding officer of any tribunal, or his agent or agents, or before the General Assembly, or any committee thereof, or before any city or county legislative body, or any committee thereof, or elsewhere"); N.C. GEN. STAT. § 8-539(a)(2) (statute applies to "[a]ny grand jury proceeding or grand jury investigation; any criminal prosecution, civil suit or related proceeding in any court; and any judicial or quasi-judicial proceeding before any administrative, legislative or regulatory board, agency or tribunal").
54. ARK. CODE ANN. § 16-85-510.
55. See Saxton v. Arkansas Gazette Co., 569 S.W.2d 115, 117 (Ark. 1978). But see In re Grand Jury Subpoena, 947 F. Supp. 1314, 1321 (E.D. Ark. 1996) (Arkansas shield law does not apply to federal grand jury). See also IND. CODE § 34-46-4-2 (shield law applicable, on its face, in "any legal proceedings or elsewhere").

A few statutes are more restrictive. The Colorado shield law, for example, specifically exempts from its coverage any hearing "conducted by, before, or under the general assembly."[56] The Rhode Island statute does not protect against compelled disclosure of the source of any information concerning a grand jury or other "secret proceeding."[57]

Other statutes, either on their face or as construed by the courts, restrict their application in the context of specified categories of proceedings. Indeed, some shield laws do not apply — either expressly or by authoritative construction — to whole categories of governmental proceedings. We examine these restrictions in the sections that follow.

§ 15-2(c)(1). Criminal Proceedings.

Shield laws have been invoked frequently in criminal proceedings in which the news media is not a party but is nevertheless subpoenaed to provide evidence.[58] The protections afforded by the various statutes in the criminal context are, however, far from uniform. The Michigan statute, for example, applies only to grand jury proceedings,[59] while the Rhode Island shield law expressly ex-

---

56. COLO. REV. STAT. § 13-90-119. By the same token, the Colorado statute elsewhere applies its privilege broadly. See *id.* § 24-72.5-101.

57. R.I. GEN. LAWS § 9-19.1-3.

58. See, e.g., In re Burns, 484 So. 2d 658, 659 (La. 1986) (in murder prosecution, LA. REV. STAT. ANN. § 45:1452 held to protect reporter from compelled disclosure of confidential source and "information, such as place of employment, that would tend to identify him"); Nobles v. Georgia, 411 S.E.2d 294, 299 (Ga. App. 1991) (no reversible error in trial court's decision that GA. CODE ANN. § 24-9-30 was not "meant to be used to uncover the source of mere courtroom gossip or speculation" from the press by a criminal defendant convicted of voluntary manslaughter); Stripling v. Georgia, 401 S.E.2d 500, 507 (Ga.), *cert. denied*, 502 U.S. 985 (1991) (in death penalty case, Georgia shield law protected reporter from compelled disclosure of sources because defendant had "failed to show that the information could not have been 'reasonably obtained by alternative means'") (quoting GA. CODE ANN. § 24-9-30); Oregon ex rel. Meyers v. Howell, 740 P.2d 792 (Or. App. 1987) (in misdemeanor prosecution, defendant not entitled to *in camera* review of unpublished newspaper photograph based on OR. REV. STAT. § 44.510). See also REPORTERS COMMITTEE FOR FREEDOM OF THE PRESS, AGENTS OF DISCOVERY: A REPORT ON THE INCIDENCE OF SUBPOENAS SERVED ON THE NEWS MEDIA IN 1997 (1997) (reporting that among media organizations responding to survey, criminal defendants served more subpoenas than prosecutors, law enforcement officials, or parties in civil suits).

59. See MICH. COMP. LAWS § 767.5a; Michigan v. Smith, 4 MEDIA L. REP. (BNA) 1753, 1760 (Mich. Cir. 1978) (holding that governmental "inquiry" referenced in Michigan shield law "plainly speaks" only to "the grand jury's inquiry into criminal activity"). Even in the grand jury context, the Michigan statute's application does not extend to inquiry concerning "a crime punishable by imprisonment for life when it has been established that the information which is sought is essential to the purpose of the proceeding and that other available sources of the information have been exhausted." See also In re Contempt of Stone, 397 N.W.2d 244, 245 (Mich. App. 1986) (holding that, at the time, broadcast journalists were not protected by Michigan statute, even in grand jury context).

cludes from its coverage both the source of any information concerning a grand jury or other secret proceeding and any felony proceeding in which the information sought is deemed necessary to its prosecution.[60] The South Carolina Supreme Court has held that its shield law does not apply where the court, rather than a party to the proceeding, seeks the information.[61]

The broader shield laws of other states are routinely invoked, with mixed results, in the grand jury context.[62] In an oft-cited case, the Pennsylvania Supreme Court invoked its shield law to vacate the contempt conviction of a reporter who refused to comply with a grand jury subpoena ordering the production of his notes and other unpublished information.[63] The New York shield law has withstood a specific constitutional challenge to its applicability in a grand jury proceeding.[64]

Courts have, however, struggled to apply state shield statutes in the face of efforts by criminal defendants to compel testimony or other evidence from journalists. The New Jersey experience, which stems largely from the seminal case of *In re Farber*,[65] is illustrative. In *Farber*, a *New York Times* reporter was held in contempt, fined (along with the newspaper), and imprisoned after refusing to disclose information subpoenaed in the course of a murder trial. The New Jersey

---

60. See R.I. GEN. LAWS § 9-19.1-3.

61. In re Decker, 471 S.E.2d 462 (S.C. 1995).

62. See, e.g., Branzburg v. Pound, 461 S.W.2d 345, 346 (Ky. 1970), *aff'd*, 408 U.S. 665 (1972) (although Kentucky shield law, KY. REV. STAT. ANN. § 421.00, applies to grand jury proceedings, it protects only the disclosure of the identities of sources); In re Grand Jury Proceedings (Ridenhour), 520 So. 2d 372, 374 (La. 1988) (LA. REV. STAT. ANN. § 45:1452 protects against compelled disclosure to grand jury of information that "would indirectly tend to identify" a source, unless "'disclosure is essential to the protection of the public interest'"); Lightman v. Maryland, 294 A.2d 149, 156-57 (Md. Spec. App.), *aff'd*, 295 A.2d 212 (Md. 1972), *cert. denied*, 411 U.S. 951 (1973) (MD. CODE ANN., CTS. & JUD. PROC. § 9-112 applies to grand jury proceedings, but only to compelled disclosure of the identities of sources); Tofani v. Maryland, 465 A.2d 413, 419 (Md. 1983); Tennessee ex rel. Gerbitz v. Curriden, 738 S.W.2d 192 (Tenn. 1987) (government had not offered sufficient "clear and convincing" evidence that information sought by grand jury was unavailable from other sources to compel disclosure from journalist consistent with TENN. CODE ANN. § 24-1-208); In re Grand Jury Subpoena, 947 F. Supp. 1314 (E.D. Ark. 1996) (New York and Arkansas shield laws inapplicable in context of federal grand jury).

63. See In re Taylor, 193 A.2d 181, 185 (Pa. 1963). But see Pennsylvania v. Banner, 17 MEDIA L. REP. (BNA) 1434 (Pa. C.P. 1989) (trial court held that reporter waived shield law privilege by publishing excerpts of an interview with a criminal defendant and by disclosing certain information to a police officer).

64. See Beach v. Shanley, 465 N.E.2d 304, 310 (N.Y. 1984) ("The constitutional provision against impairing a grand jury's power was not intended to prevent the Legislature from creating evidentiary privileges or their equivalent that have an incidental impact on investigations into willful misconduct by public officers."). See also People v. Rand, 519 N.Y.S.2d 606 (Sup. Ct. 1987) (applying three-part constitutional test in grand jury context to order disclosure of nonconfidential information prior to 1990 shield law amendment); People v. Doe, 560 N.Y.S.2d 177 (County Ct. 1990) (ordering appearance of reporter before grand jury).

65. 394 A.2d 330 (N.J.), *cert. denied*, 439 U.S. 997 (1978).

Supreme Court asserted that the state's shield law was intended by the legislature to be broadly construed:

> We read the legislative intent in adopting this statute in its present form as seeking to protect the confidential sources of the press as well as information so obtained by reporters and other news media representatives to the greatest extent permitted by the Constitution of the United States and that of the State of New Jersey.[66]

Nevertheless, the court held that the statute must be applied so as not to conflict with a criminal defendant's constitutional right to confront witnesses.[67] Thus, while journalists are "entitled to a preliminary determination before being compelled to submit the subpoenaed material to a trial judge for [*in camera*] inspection," the criminal defendant had made the requisite showing to compel *in camera* review in Farber's case.[68] Specifically, the defense had demonstrated:

> by a fair preponderance of the evidence, including all reasonable inferences, that there was a reasonable probability or likelihood that the information sought by the subpoena was material and relevant to his defense, that it could not be secured from any less intrusive source, and that the defendant had a legitimate need to see and otherwise use it.[69]

Following *Farber*, the New Jersey legislature amended the shield law to incorporate the balancing test articulated by the state Supreme Court in that case.[70] The revised statute was the subject of extended proceedings in *New Jersey v. Boiardo*,[71] after a criminal defendant attempted to compel disclosure of a letter written to a reporter by a potential prosecution witness. In *Boiardo*, the New Jersey Supreme Court initially reversed the trial court's order requiring *in camera* review, holding that the defense had not met its statutory burden:

> The new law does not require [the reporter] to show that other, less intrusive sources probably contain the same information as that found in the letter; rather, the *defendant* has the burden to prove that it is reasonably probable that this information can *not* be secured from any less intrusive source.[72]

---

66. *Id.* at 335.
67. *Id.* at 337.
68. *Id.* at 339.
69. *Id.* at 338.
70. See N.J. STAT. ANN. §§ 2A:84A-21.3 to 21.4.
71. 414 A.2d 14 (N.J. 1980).
72. *Id.* at 22 (emphasis in original) Indeed, the court emphasized that the "statute declares as clearly as it possibly could the Legislature's belief that disclosure to a trial judge *in camera* represents precisely the same threat to the interests protected by the privilege as disclosure to counsel or to the world." *Id.* at 25.

On remand, the motion to compel was renewed and the trial judge again ordered *in camera* inspection of the letter. Once again, the New Jersey Supreme Court reversed, holding that the defense had not met its burden of proof regarding the availability of alternative sources.[73] The court concluded that it was required to give "effect to the legislative judgment clearly expressed in the new shield law: the need of the press for protection not only from the production of confidential material at trial but also for protection against that limited disclosure that occurs when the court itself examines the material *in camera*."[74]

The California courts have specifically recognized that the state "shield law's protection is overcome in a criminal proceeding on a showing that nondisclosure would deprive the defendant of his federal constitutional right to a fair trial."[75] Thus, in *Delaney v. Superior Court*, the California Supreme Court held that once a journalist makes "a prima facie showing that he is entitled to withhold information under the shield law," the criminal defendant must then make his own threshold demonstration that there is "a reasonable possibility the information will materially assist in his defense," a showing that must be based on something more than "mere speculation."[76]

If such a showing is made, California courts proceed to balance four factors to determine if the criminal defendant's constitutional right to fair trial outweighs the journalist's interest in protecting unpublished information:

- "Whether the unpublished information is confidential or sensitive;"
- "Whether the policies of the shield law will be thwarted by disclosure;"

---

73. New Jersey v. Boiardo, 416 A.2d 793, 796 (N.J. 1980) ("The trial judge . . . held that . . . the alternative sources . . . did not contain a description of what was in the letters. However, this was not the showing required under the statute. Rather, it was defendants' burden to prove that the alternative sources did not contain information substantially similar to the information contained in the letters . . . .").

74. *Id.* at 794. In *In re Schuman*, 552 A.2d 602, 607 (N.J. 1989), the New Jersey Supreme Court held that, although the statutory privilege is qualified with respect to a criminal defendant, it is absolute as applied to the prosecution. Cf. In re Paul, 513 S.E.2d 219, 223 (Ga. 1999) (shield law protects reporter from compelled disclosure of confidential sources and unpublished information sought by prosecution; "this case does not involve a conflict between the defendant's right to a fair trial and the public's right to a free press [but rather, it] presents a conflict between the public's right to evidence at a criminal trial and its competing right to the unencumbered flow of information through the news media"). But see Miller v. Superior Ct., 77 Cal. Rptr. 2d 827 (Ct. App.), *review granted*, 968 P.2d 462 (Cal. 1998) (shield law does not bar prosecution's subpoena but requires balancing of competing interests).

75. Delaney v. Superior Ct., 789 P.2d 934, 946 (Cal. 1990).

76. *Id.* at 948. In *In re Willon*, 55 Cal. Rptr. 2d 245, 248 (Ct. App. 1996), a California appellate court held that, where the court on its own motion, rather than the defendant, seeks to compel a journalist to disclose the identity of a confidential source, the shield law "protects the news media from contempt absent a specific showing that nondisclosure . . . will create a substantial probability of injury to the criminal defendant's right to a fair trial."

- Whether the information sought is important to the criminal defendant's case; and
- "Whether there is an alternative source of the unpublished information."[77]

In *Delaney*, the court held that the criminal defendant had made the requisite showing to overcome the shield law, in part, because he was himself the party seeking disclosure.[78]

Although its shield law admits of no exceptions on its face,[79] courts in Ohio have construed the statute to require a balancing of competing interests when a criminal defendant seeks to compel disclosure of a source of information from a journalist.[80] In *In re McAuley*,[81] a criminal defendant charged with ordering a murder sought to compel a *Cleveland Plain Dealer* reporter to disclose a host of unpublished information concerning an article he had written about the crime, including the identities of his confidential sources. Despite the apparently absolute terms of the privilege codified in the Ohio shield law, an Ohio Court of Appeals declared that "state shield laws do not provide an absolute right not to provide the name of a confidential informant."[82] Rather, the court held, "the privilege of a newsperson is a qualified one in which the newsperson's right to protect that name of the confidential informant must be balanced against the Sixth Amendment right of a defendant in a criminal trial."[83]

By the same token, the *McAuley* court emphasized that "a defendant does not have an absolute right to obtain confidential information from a newsperson" and in fact bears the "burden of proving by relevant evidence that the newsperson or the informant has information or evidence regarding the defendant's

---

77. 789 P.2d at 949-51.

78. *Id.* The *Delaney* court also held that trial judges in California have "discretion in the first instance to determine whether a newsperson's claim of confidentiality or sensitivity is colorable. If the court determines the claim is colorable, it must then receive the newsperson's testimony *in camera*." *Id.* at 952. See People v. DeSoto, 24 MEDIA L. REP. (BNA) 2217, 2220-22 (Cal. Super. 1996) (shield law may yield, at urging of prosecution, in criminal case where prosecution sought outtakes); Miller v. Superior Ct., 77 Cal. Rptr. 2d 827 (Ct. App.), *review granted*, 968 P.2d 462 (Cal. 1998) ("The People have a state due process interest in the disclosure of evidence relevant to a criminal prosecution [which], while not 'trumping' the shield law, is sufficiently compelling to invoke the *Delaney* balancing test.").

79. See OHIO REV. CODE ANN. §§ 2739.04, 2739.12.

80. See, e.g., Ohio v. Geis, 441 N.E.2d 803 (Ohio App. 1981); In re McAuley, 408 N.E.2d 697 (Ohio App. 1979).

81. 408 N.E.2d 697 (Ohio App. 1979).

82. *Id.* at 709.

83. *Id.* See also Weiss v. Thomson Newspapers, Inc., 8 MEDIA L. REP. (BNA) 1258, 1260 (Ohio C.P. 1981) (in a defamation action, court distinguishes *McAuley* on ground that in "a criminal case where a person's liberty or life is in jeopardy and where there is a conflict between a statute (Shield Law) and a constitutional provision, the statute must fall").

guilt or innocence."[84] In addition, the court held that the criminal defendant must

> first demonstrate that there is no other available means of obtaining the confidential information in the reporter's possession, or that he has exhausted all of the available sources. Secondly, the movant must make an effort to obtain the information from the reporter by means other than by obtaining the name of the confidential source. . . . Lastly, the defendant should request an *in camera* inspection by the court of the confidential information. If, after all this is done, there is a reasonable probability that either the newsperson or the informant will provide relevant evidence of the defendant's guilt or innocence, the defendant is entitled to the newsperson's confidential information or the name of the newsperson's informant.[85]

In the case before it, the court held that, although the trial judge had erred in concluding that "as a matter of law" McAuley was "entitled to an absolute privilege," the defendant had not made the requisite showing to compel testimony and other evidence from him.[86]

§ 15-2(c)(2). Civil Proceedings.

§ 15-2(c)(2)(A). Third-Party Proceedings.

Journalists and news organizations have often invoked shield laws when subpoenaed to provide evidence in civil proceedings to which they are not parties.[87] Typically, the courts have construed state shield statutes to provide

---

84. In re McAuley, 408 N.E.2d at 709-10.

85. *Id.* at 709-10.

86. *Id.* at 710. In *Ohio v. Geis*, 441 N.E.2d 803, 810 (Ohio App. 1981), another Ohio appellate court similarly concluded that "before a trial court rules that certain evidence is protected by [the Ohio Shield Law] the trial court must take into account the Sixth Amendment rights of a criminal defendant." The trial court in *Geis* had held a television reporter in civil contempt after he failed to comply with a subpoena issued by a defendant indicted for aggravated drug trafficking. *Id.* at 805-06. The court of appeals held that "the trial court erred by denying [the television station's] motion to quash without making an *in camera* inspection of the [subpoenaed] video tapes, outside of the presence of the parties and counsel, to determine the evidentiary nature of the video tapes." *Id.* at 807. Cf. People v. Royster, 26 MEDIA L. REP. (BNA) 1893, 1896 (N.Y. Sup. Ct. 1997) (quashing subpoena where "the absolute privilege of [N.Y. CIV. RIGHTS LAW § 79-h(b)] applies to the facts of this case and the defense has failed to demonstrate an overriding constitutional interest that would entitle him to the identification of the confidential source or sources").

87. See, e.g., In re Brown & Williamson Tobacco Corp., 24 MEDIA L. REP. (BNA) 1720 (N.Y. Sup. Ct.), *aff'd*, 643 N.Y.S.2d 92 (App. Div. 1996) (New York shield law protects nonparty network from compelled disclosure of outtakes and other unbroadcast information provided by nonconfidential source); Krase v. Graco Children Prods., Inc., 79 F.3d 346 (2d Cir. 1996) (in products liability suit, New York shield law protects nonparty network from compelled disclosure of outtakes); Ex parte Sparrow, 14 F.R.D. 351 (N.D. Ala. 1953) (nonparty newspaper reporter privileged pursuant to Alabama statute to resist subpoena in libel action against magazine); Mar-

greater protection in this context than in criminal cases. In *New York Times Co. v. Superior Court*,[88] the California Supreme Court, in contrast with its application of the shield law in the criminal context in *Delaney v. Superior Court*,[89] held that its protections cannot "be overcome in a *civil* action by a litigant's showing of need for the newsperson's unpublished information."[90] Unlike in *Delaney*, where it held "that a criminal defendant's federal constitutional right to a fair trial may in some cases overcome a claim of immunity under the state shield law," the California Supreme Court concluded that there is no "federal or state constitutional right . . . sufficient to overcome the newsperson's claim of immunity under the state shield law" in civil litigation.[91]

Similarly, in *Austin v. Memphis Publishing Co.*,[92] the Tennessee Supreme Court addressed the applicability of the Tennessee shield law in the context of a wrongful death action arising from a bridge collapse. The plaintiffs sought to compel production from two local newspapers of "any and all correspondence, studies, reports, memoranda, or any other source material used by the newspa-

---

ketos v. American Employers Ins. Co., 460 N.W.2d 272 (Mich. App. 1990) (Michigan shield law does not protect newspaper from order to produce unpublished photographs taken at a fire scene in suit by property owner against insurance carrier); Ryan v. Thoubboron, 26 MEDIA L. REP. (BNA) 1094 (S.D.N.Y. 1998) (nonparty reporter could not be compelled to testify in civil rights suit regarding interview he had conducted with plaintiff, which resulted in publication of article); Davis v. Glanton, 705 A.2d 879 (Pa. Super. 1997) (Pennsylvania shield law requires disclosure by nonparty newspaper in defamation suit of materials which cannot reasonably lead to discovery of identity of confidential source or which can be redacted to protect such information); Grand Forks Herald v. District Ct., 322 N.W.2d 850 (N.D. 1982) (North Dakota shield law does not protect newspaper from subpoena seeking photographs of automobile-motorcycle accident in personal injury action); Fischer v. McGowan, 585 F. Supp. 978 (D.R.I. 1984) (reporter not a party to defamation action may not be compelled to reveal identity of confidential source); Forest Hills Util. Co. v. City of Heath, 302 N.E.2d 593, 596-97 (Ohio C.P. 1973) (in class action against a utility company, newspaper reporter "is not immune from answering questions on discovery depositions because of the fact that she is a newspaper reporter and the information sought has been gleaned by her in the process of gathering news;" reporter is, however, privileged under Ohio shield law not "to identify the sources of information gleaned by her in the process of gathering news"); Dumez v. Houma Mun. Fire & Police Civil Serv. Bd., 341 So. 2d 1206 (La. App. 1976) (in suit by police officer claiming wrongful discharge, Louisiana shield law affords newspaper reporter privilege to refuse to disclose sources of information); CSX Transp., Inc. v. Cox Broadcasting, Inc., 25 MEDIA L. REP. (BNA) 2183 (Ga. Super. 1997) (Georgia shield law protects nonparty reporter from compelled disclosure of videotaped footage of accident scene and interviews).

88. 796 P.2d 811 (Cal. 1990).
89. 789 P.2d 934 (Cal. 1990). See Chap. 15-2(c)(1) *supra* (discussing *Delaney*).
90. New York Times Co. v. Superior Ct., 796 P.2d at 812.
91. *Id.* at 816. Cf. Rancho Publications v. Superior Ct., 81 Cal. Rptr. 2d 274 (Ct. App. 1999) (shield law did not encompass paid advertisements where newspaper was not "engaged in legitimate journalistic purposes" and did not "exercise[] judgmental discretion" in gathering and publishing the advertisements).
92. 655 S.W.2d 146 (Tenn. 1983).

per[s] in preparing various articles dealing with" the bridge collapse.[93] The court rejected the plaintiffs' suggestion that the shield law, enacted in the wake of the Supreme Court's decision in *Branzburg v. Hayes*,[94] "was not intended to apply to civil cases" in the absence of "express language in the statute so limiting the privilege."[95]

§ 15-2(c)(2)(B). The Press as a Party.

A handful of shield laws expressly limit their application to cases in which the press or a journalist is not a party.[96] In addition, several statutes restrict the availability of the privilege in defamation actions. Some of these jurisdictions make the privilege unavailable to protect "the content or source of allegedly defamatory information in a civil action for defamation wherein the defendant asserts a defense based on the content or source of such information."[97] Louisiana's shield law purports to shift the burden of proof of "good faith" to a defendant "with respect to an issue upon which the reporter alleges to have obtained the information from a confidential source."[98] The Minnesota statute limits the availability of the privilege "in any defamation action where the person seeking disclosure can demonstrate that the identity of the source will lead to relevant evidence on the issue of actual malice," but only if "there is probable cause to believe that the source has information clearly relevant to the issue of defamation" and "the information cannot be obtained by any alternative means or remedy less destructive of first amendment rights."[99]

---

93. *Id.* at 147.
94. 408 U.S. 665 (1972).
95. Austin v. Memphis Publ'g Co., 655 S.W.2d at 149. The District of Columbia's shield law has been held to apply in the context of civil litigation to which the press is not a party as well. In *Grunseth v. Marriott Corp.*, 868 F. Supp. 333, 337 (D.D.C. 1994), a Minnesota gubernatorial candidate sued a hotel for breach of implied contract and invasion of privacy in connection with its disclosure of its registration records and receipts to the press. During discovery, the plaintiff sought to subpoena a Minnesota newspaper, its editors and reporters to produce the hotel bill and other unpublished information. *Id.* A federal district court judge quashed the subpoenas, holding that the plaintiff's "efforts are precluded by the First Amendment to the Constitution as well as statutes in both the District of Columbia and the State of Minnesota." *Id.*
96. See GA. CODE ANN. § 24-9-30; S.C. CODE ANN. § 19-11-100; see also ALASKA STAT. § 09.25.340 (providing that, once privilege is conferred, neither reporter nor news organization "may thereafter be permitted to plead or prove the sources of information withheld").
97. OR. REV. STAT. § 44.530(3); see also OKLA. STAT. § 2506(B)(2); R.I. GEN. LAWS § 9-19.1-3; TENN. CODE ANN. § 24-1-208(b).
98. LA. REV. STAT. ANN. § 1454.
99. MINN. STAT. § 595.025. See Bauer v. Gannett Co., 557 N.W.2d 608 (Minn. App. 1997) (reversing blanket order requiring libel defendant to disclose identities of confidential sources). In *McNeilus v. Corporate Report Inc.*, 21 MEDIA L. REP. (BNA) 2171, 2172 (Minn. Dist. 1993), a Minnesota trial court similarly held that the shield law protected media defendants in a defamation action from compelled disclosure of the "identity of newsgathering sources." Nevertheless, "in the

The Illinois shield law was amended in 1985 to include several unique provisions in the defamation context.[100] In all other actions, the Illinois statute requires the party seeking compelled disclosure to articulate a specific public interest that would be harmed if the information is not produced; in the defamation context, however, a plaintiff must identify the necessity of the information sought to the proof of her case and make a prima facie showing of the falsity of the alleged defamation and any harm resulting from it.[101]

Several courts have had occasion to apply the defamation-specific provisions of these shield statutes. In *Capuano v. Outlet Co.*,[102] for example, the Rhode Island Supreme Court held that the state's shield law did not apply in a defamation action: "When the plaintiff is required to show by clear and convincing evidence that the defendant acted with malice, we find it impossible to uphold a discovery ruling that denies the plaintiffs the opportunity to examine the confidential sources on which the defendant relies."[103] In *McNabb v. Oregonian Publishing Co.*,[104] an Oregon appellate court held that the Oregon shield law protected from compelled disclosure to a libel plaintiff "(1) the notes made by the reporter who wrote the article, (2) the names of one or possibly two unnamed persons interviewed by defendant in preparing the article and (3) the substance of defendant's interviews of each of its sources."[105] Because the defense "was not based on the content or source of unpublished information," the court held, the exception contained in the Oregon statute for such circumstances was inapplicable.[106] Moreover, it concluded that, even if application of the statutory privilege limited plaintiff's ability to pursue a defamation claim by depriving him from discovering "matters that are essential to prove actual malice," the state may (and had), by statute, limited his "ability to prove the claim in order to promote other social purposes."[107]

The applicability of state shield laws in the defamation context has also been addressed by courts in jurisdictions in which the relevant statutes are silent on

---

interest of fairness," the court "precluded" defendants from "introducing any evidence at trial regarding such confidential sources that has not been disclosed to Plaintiff." *Id.* at 2172-73.

100. See 735 ILL. COMP. STAT. 5/8-904. Prior to that time, the Illinois shield law did not apply at all in the defamation context. See Desai v. Hersh, 954 F.2d 1408, 1412-13 (7th Cir.), *cert. denied*, 506 U.S. 865 (1992) ("granting an absolute privilege to journalists to maintain the confidentiality of their sources in a libel case is neither required nor authorized").

101. See 735 ILL. COMP. STAT. 5/8-904.

102. 579 A.2d 469 (R.I. 1990).

103. *Id.* at 477.

104. 685 P.2d 458 (Or. App. 1984), *cert. denied*, 469 U.S. 1216 (1985).

105. *Id.* at 462-63.

106. *Id.* at 463.

107. *Id.* See also Taylor v. Miskovsky, 640 P.2d 959, 962-63 (Okla. 1981) (exception for defamation actions in Oklahoma shield law does not apply to libel plaintiff's attempt to compel disclosure of "confidential sources and files obtained" by defendants "nearly two weeks after" defamation action filed).

the issue. In *Weiss v. Thomson Newspapers, Inc.*,[108] for example, an Ohio court held that a defamation plaintiff was not entitled to *in camera* review of materials sought to be withheld from disclosure pursuant to the shield law, precisely because the statute did not expressly authorize such review in the defamation context. The court distinguished *In re McAuley*,[109] a criminal case in which *in camera* review had been required, because in the criminal context "the statute must yield to the Sixth Amendment."[110] In a civil case, the court concluded, "the Legislature has seen fit to enact the Shield Law, which in the opinion of the Court, takes away the Court's authority" to determine whether the documents at issue "are relevant to the Plaintiff's cause of action."[111]

In *Hatchard v. Westinghouse Broadcasting Co.*,[112] the Pennsylvania Supreme Court held that "unpublished documentary information gathered by a television station is discoverable by a plaintiff in a libel action to the extent that the documentary information does not reveal the identity of a personal source of information or may be redacted to eliminate the revelation of a personal source of information." The Court purported to distinguish *In re Taylor*,[113] in which it had previously construed the shield law to protect "inanimate objects such as documents as well as persons," on the ground that materially different interests are implicated in cases alleging defamation.[114] In *Sprague v. Walter*,[115] however, the same court held that a reporter invoking the shield law could nevertheless testify regarding the information received from a source, in defense of a claim of actual malice, and that "no inference either favorable or adverse may be drawn from the act of invoking the privilege as to the reliability of the unidentified source or as to the accuracy of the information supplied."[116]

---

108. 8 MEDIA L. REP. (BNA) 1258 (Ohio C.P. 1981).
109. 408 N.E.2d 697 (Ohio App. 1979).
110. 8 MEDIA L. REP. (BNA) at 1260.
111. *Id.* at 1260-61.
112. 532 A.2d 346, 351 (Pa. 1987).
113. 193 A.2d 181 (Pa. 1963). See Chap. 15-2(d)(1) *infra* (discussing *Taylor*).
114. 532 A.2d at 348. See also Olszewski v. Sinclair Broadcast Group, Inc., 26 MEDIA L. REP. (BNA) 2535, 2536 (Pa. C.P. 1998) (citing *Hatchard*). In *Davis v. Glanton*, 705 A.2d 879 (Pa. Super. 1997), a lower court extended the holding in *Hatchard* to nonparty media entities. See *id.* at 885 ("We can see no reason . . . why the rationale of *Hatchard* is not equally applicable in cases where materials relevant to plaintiff's burden are in the possession of a media entity which is not a party.").
115. 543 A.2d 1078 (Pa. 1988).
116. *Id.* at 1086. Under the Pennsylvania shield law, therefore, invoking the privilege neither raises a presumption of no sources nor any other presumption as to the reliability of the information or its source. "This evidence is simply to be weighed by the fact finder in assessing whether the plaintiff has met the burden of proof." *Id.* at 1083.
In *Sible v. Lee Enterprises, Inc.*, 729 P.2d 1271 (Mont. 1986), *cert. denied*, 483 U.S. 1011 (1987), the Montana Supreme Court applied the general provisions of the Montana statute, which states that "[i]f the person claiming the privilege voluntarily offers to testify or to produce the

Similarly, in *Bilney v. Evening Star Newspaper Co.*,[117] the Maryland Court of Special Appeals held that the Maryland shield law protected newspaper reporters, in the context of a common law intrusion action, from compelled disclosure of the identity of confidential sources who had provided them with allegedly purloined academic transcripts of college athletes. The court rejected the plaintiffs' suggestion that, having invoked the statutory privilege, the reporters should be precluded from relying "upon the defense that this source was a voluntary and gratuitous one."[118]

The court in *Bilney* rejected earlier New Jersey authority holding that "where a reporter testifies about some of his sources, or refers to his unnamed source as a 'reliable' one, he has waived the statutory privilege."[119] New Jersey itself subsequently amended its shield law to address this issue, leading the New Jersey Supreme Court to hold that the law "protects confidential information 'to the greatest extent permitted by the Constitution of the United States."[120] Thus, because there are no countervailing constitutional interests at stake in a defamation action, the New Jersey Supreme Court held in *Maressa v. New Jersey Monthly* that "the newsperson's privilege in a civil action for libel is absolute."[121] Moreover, the court concluded that the doctrine of "waiver" is largely inapplicable in the defamation context:

> Partial disclosure or the assertion of affirmative defenses [such as truth, fair comment, good faith, honest belief, or lack of malice] no longer constitutes a waiver of the Shield Law privilege. Waiver under the Shield Law operates only as to those specific materials that are knowingly and voluntarily disclosed.... We therefore hold that publication of privileged information constitutes a waiver only as to that specific information. The waiver does not operate as to any non-disclosed information.[122]

Indeed, the court in *Maressa* went so far as to extend the shield law privilege in the defamation context to all information gathered or materials created in the

---

source" of his information, he waives it, MONT. CODE ANN. § 26-1-903(2), and held that a reporter in a defamation action "waived his privilege to keep his notes confidential" when he "took the witness stand or testified by way of deposition." 729 P.2d at 1274-75.

117. 406 A.2d 652 (Md. Spec. App. 1979).

118. *Id.* at 657. See Jenoff v. Hearst Corp., 3 MEDIA L. REP. (BNA) 1911, 1911-12 (D. Md. 1978) (plaintiff's motion to compel disclosure of "confidential news sources" in defamation action denied because court "bound by the unequivocal language of the Maryland statute").

119. 406 A.2d at 658 (quoting Brogan v. Passaic Daily News, 123 A.2d 473 (N.J. 1956)). See Jenoff v. Hearst Corp., 3 MEDIA L. REP. (BNA) 1911, 1912 (D. Md. 1978) (distinguishing *Brogan* on ground that New Jersey shield law was "less explicit than the Maryland statute, which precludes compelled disclosure 'in *any* legal proceeding or *trial* . . . *or elsewhere*'") (emphasis in original).

120. Maressa v. New Jersey Monthly, 445 A.2d 376, 379 (N.J.), *cert. denied*, 459 U.S. 907 (1982) (quoting In re Farber, 394 A.2d 330 (N.J. 1978)).

121. 445 A.2d at 379.

122. *Id.* at 386.

editorial process.[123] On the same day, in its decision in *Resorts International, Inc. v. NJM Associates*,[124] the New Jersey Supreme Court applied *Maressa* in holding that "notes, memoranda, rough drafts, editorial comments, sources and other information"[125] are protected from compelled disclosure as well. In contrast, the Kentucky Supreme Court has held that, while the Kentucky statute prohibits the compelled disclosure of the identities of confidential sources in a defamation action and "a fishing expedition will not be tolerated," a defamation plaintiff's "legitimate interest in discovery of information relevant and material" to the defamation action "must be respected."[126] Accordingly, the court affirmed a trial judge's order that a newspaper defendant in a defamation action produce copies of its reporters' notes redacted to delete the names of confidential sources.[127]

New York courts have also held that its shield law "does not establish 'an absolute right' or 'grant journalists complete immunity from all legal consequences of refusing to disclose evidence relating to a news source'" in a defam-

---

123. *Id.* at 383.
124. 445 A.2d 395, 397 (N.J.), *cert. denied*, 459 U.S. 907 (1982).
125. *Id.* at 397. See Gastman v. North Jersey Newspapers Co., 603 A.2d 111, 112 (N.J. Super. 1992) (privilege applies to protect "confidentiality of the author of an unsolicited letter which is published by a newspaper"). A District of Columbia trial court reached the same result in applying that jurisdiction's shield law to preclude defamation plaintiffs from discovering the defendant author's notes, memoranda, and tape recordings of interviews. See Prentice v. McPhilemy, No. 98CA0004309, slip op. at 9 (D.C. Super. May 5, 1999) (statutory exception to qualified privilege when "there is an overriding public interest in the disclosure" does not apply where the asserted "public interest" is the plaintiff's "interest in protecting and defending his or her reputation").
126. Lexington Herald-Leader Co. v. Beard, 690 S.W.2d 374, 379 (Ky. 1984).
127. *Id.* In *Las Vegas Sun, Inc. v. Eighth Judicial District Court*, 761 P.2d 849, 853 (Nev. 1988), however, the Nevada Supreme Court held that the Nevada statute "protects not only sources, but information" so that plaintiffs in a defamation action are "not entitled to the complete notes taken at an interview, even when the source and part of the interview have been disclosed." By the same token, the court was "convinced that the legislature did not intend to allow the use of the news shield law as a sword in libel cases." *Id.* As a result, it held that a news media defendant cannot "rely on the privilege until the day of trial, then renounce the privilege and use previously undisclosed information as a defense." *Id.* Thus, the court announced that:

> [w]hen a plaintiff attempts to discover the basis for a news story which is felt to defame him or her, and the news media defendant relies on the shield law to resist discovery, the defendant will be deemed to have thereby elected to protect the confidentiality of that information. Once the defendant has made such an election, confidentiality may not thereafter be waived whenever it may suit the defendant's convenience; and the defendant may not thereafter rely on it for a defense at trial.

Id.

ation action.[128] In *Sands v. News America Publishing Inc.*,[129] therefore, the appellate division held that news media defendants who invoked the shield law to support their refusal to respond to interrogatories were "precluded from introducing into evidence confidential information or documentation known" to them "unless such information has been disclosed to plaintiffs at least 10 days prior to trial."[130] In addition, the court held that the shield law was inapplicable to materials obtained in preparation for trial, since such information was not "obtained in the course of newsgathering."[131]

§ 15-2(c)(2)(C). Non-Judicial Proceedings.

Most shield statutes, on their face, extend their protections beyond judicial proceedings to include as well legislative and administrative attempts to compel

---

128. Sands v. News America Publ'g Inc., 560 N.Y.S.2d 416, 421 (App. Div. 1990) (quoting Oak Beach Inn Corp. v. Babylon Beacon, Inc., 464 N.E.2d 967, 970 (N.Y. 1984), *cert. denied*, 469 U.S. 1158 (1985)). In *Oak Beach Inn Corp.*, the New York Court of Appeals considered a defamation action arising from publication of an allegedly anonymous letter to the editor. The newspaper declined to reveal voluntarily the identity of the letter writer, and the trial court ordered that its answer be stricken and that it be precluded from presenting a defense. The Court of Appeals affirmed the appellate division's reversal of the trial court's order, holding:

> A newspaper involved in a substantial libel action may well find the threat of contempt less intimidating than the thought of being entirely stripped of its defenses if it continues to preserve the confidentiality of its source. . . . The consequences of nondisclosure imposed . . . should not create new obstacles to newsgathering or undermine the strong legislative policy expressed in the Shield Law. The general rule, that the demanding party should not be granted more relief for nondisclosure than is reasonably necessary to protect legitimate interests, should be applied with special force in cases involving nondisclosure of sources by newspapers and journalists.

464 N.E.2d at 971 (citations omitted). Since the newspaper had determined not to rely on the letter writer in defending against plaintiff's allegations of constitutional malice, the Court of Appeals held that it could proceed with the remainder of its defense. *Id.*

129. 560 N.Y.S.2d 416 (App. Div. 1990).

130. *Id.* at 421. See Collins v. Troy Publ'g Co., 623 N.Y.S.2d 663, 665 (App. Div. 1995) (court refused to consider information gathered from confidential source in adjudicating summary judgment motions to prevent "defendants 'from using as a sword the information which they are shielding from disclosure'"); Greenberg v. CBS Inc., 419 N.Y.S.2d 988, 997 (App. Div. 1979) ("[I]f defendants opt to rely on their statutory privilege, they should be precluded from any use of those sources and information as proof of verification or evidence of responsibility.").

131. 560 N.Y.S.2d at 422. For other New York cases applying its shield law in the defamation context, see Westmoreland v. CBS Inc., 97 F.R.D. 703 (S.D.N.Y. 1983) (holding shield law inapplicable to internal memorandum evaluating allegedly defamatory broadcast and to news release based on that memorandum); Greenleigh Assocs. v. New York Post Corp., 434 N.Y.S.2d 388 (App. Div. 1980) (shield law requires that plaintiff in defamation action attempt to obtain information sought from other sources, before deposing defendant); Mason v. CBS Inc., 15 MEDIA L. REP. (BNA) 2126 (N.Y. Sup. 1988) (precluding pre-complaint discovery of documents, outtakes and photographs pertaining to potential defamation plaintiff); First United Fund Ltd. v. American Banker, Inc., 485 N.Y.S.2d 489 (Sup. Ct. 1985) (holding no privilege to refuse to produce drafts of allegedly defamatory article).

disclosure of the fruits of newsgathering activities.[132] Thus, in *In re Wireman*,[133] the Indiana Supreme Court held that its statute could be invoked in a disciplinary proceeding against an attorney by reporters who declined to testify about assertedly confidential communications.

In New Mexico, where the shield law promulgated by the legislature was held unconstitutional as applied to the judiciary,[134] it nevertheless appears to retain its force in the context of "any proceeding or investigation before, or by, any legislative, . . . executive or administrative body or person."[135] A separate shield provision, enacted as a rule of evidence by the New Mexico Supreme Court, applies only in the context of judicial proceedings.[136]

§ 15-2(d). Scope of Protection.

§ 15-2(d)(1). Sources of Information.

Virtually all shield statutes protect against the compelled disclosure of confidential sources, at least in some circumstances. The Alabama statute, for example, extends its privilege to "the sources of any information procured or obtained" by a journalist that is in fact "published," "broadcast" or "televised."[137] Most other statutes, in contrast, do not appear to require that information received from the source be published or broadcast in order for the source's identity to be protected from compelled disclosure,[138] while the Indiana and Florida statutes expressly disclaim any such requirement.[139] The New York

---

132. See, e.g., TENN. CODE ANN. § 24-1-208(a) (shield law applicable in proceedings before a "court, a grand jury, the general assembly, or any administrative body"); OKLA. STAT. tit. 12, § 2506(A)(1) (defining "State proceeding" covered by shield law to include "any proceeding or investigation before or by any judicial, legislative, executive or administrative body"); MINN. STAT. § 595.023 (statute applies to "any court, grand jury, agency, department or branch of the state, or any of its political subdivisions or other public body, or by either house of the legislature or any committee, officer, member or employee thereof"); LA. REV. STAT. ANN. § 1452 (shield law applicable in "any administrative, judicial or legislative proceeding or anywhere else"); OR. REV. STAT. § 44.250(1) (statute governs any "legislative, executive or judicial officer or body, or any other authority having power to compel testimony or the production of evidence").

133. 367 N.E.2d 1368 (Ind. 1977), *cert. denied*, 436 U.S. 904 (1978).

134. See Ammerman v. Hubbard Broadcasting, Inc., 551 P.2d 1354 (N.M. 1976).

135. N.M. STAT. ANN. § 38-6-7(B)(1). See Ammerman v. Hubbard Broadcasting, Inc., 551 P.2d at 1359 ("We in no way suggest that the privilege may or may not properly be asserted in any proceeding or investigation before, or by any legislative, executive or administrative body or person.").

136. See N.M. R. EVID. 11-514.

137. ALA. CODE § 12-21-142. See KY. REV. STAT. ANN. § 421.100; ARK. CODE ANN. § 16-85-510.

138. See LA. REV. STAT. ANN. § 1452 (statute protects "the identity of any informant or any source of information" obtained by a reporter). See also MONT. CODE ANN. § 26-1-902(1); N.M. R. EVID. 11-514(B)(1); N.D. CENT. CODE § 31-01-06.2; OHIO REV. CODE ANN. § 2739.12; OKLA. STAT. ANN. tit. 12, § 2506(B)(1); OR. REV. STAT. § 44.520(1)(a); TENN. CODE ANN. § 24-1-208(a).

139. See IND. CODE § 34-46-4-2; FLA. STAT. § 90.5015(4).

statute creates a distinction between confidential and nonconfidential sources, providing an absolute privilege with respect to the former and a qualified privilege for the latter.[140]

The Minnesota shield law, which makes explicit that its purpose is to protect "the confidential relationship between the news media and its sources," extends its privilege to the identity of the "person or means from or through which information was obtained," as well as to "any unpublished information" whether or not it "would tend to identify the person or means through which the information was obtained."[141] In Delaware, a reporter seeking to invoke the shield law must state under oath that "disclosure of the information would violate an express or implied understanding with the source ... or would substantially hinder the reporter in the maintenance of existing source relationships or the development of new source relationships."[142]

The courts, in turn, have regularly applied shield statutes to protect journalists against the compelled disclosure of confidential sources.[143] The Rhode Island statute, for example, which applies on its face only to those sources that have provided "confidential" information, has been so construed by the courts.[144] Although not so confined on its face, the Arizona appellate courts have held that its shield law similarly applies only to the compelled disclosure of confidential

---

140. See N.Y. CIV. RIGHTS LAW § 79-h. But see MD. CODE ANN., CTS. & JUD. PROC. § 9-112(c)(1) (absolute privilege applies to the "source of any news or information ... whether or not the source has been promised confidentiality").

141. MINN. STAT. §§ 595.022 & .023.

142. DEL. CODE ANN. tit. 10, § 4322.

143. See, e.g., Bauer v. Gannett Co., 557 N.W.2d 608 (Minn. App. 1997) (Minnesota shield law precludes blanket order requiring disclosure of confidential sources in libel case); Stripling v. Georgia, 401 S.E.2d 500, 507 (Ga.), *cert. denied*, 502 U.S. 985 (1991) (in criminal case, Georgia shield law protects reporter from compelled disclosure of identity of confidential source); In re Paul, 513 S.E.2d 219, 225 (Ga. 1999) (same); Lexington Herald-Leader Co. v. Beard, 690 S.W.2d 374, 375 (Ky. 1984) (in defamation action, news media defendants privileged under Kentucky statute not to disclose "the *names* of informants") (emphasis in original); Dumez v. Houma Mun. Fire & Police Civil Serv. Bd., 341 So. 2d 1206, 1208 (La. App. 1976) (holding that, pursuant to Louisiana shield law, reporter privileged in a civil action to which he was not a party to refuse to disclose identities of confidential informants); In re Grand Jury Proceedings (Ridenhour), 520 So. 2d 372, 374 (La. 1988) (Louisiana statute applies to protect reporter from disclosing identities of confidential sources in grand jury proceedings); Becnel v. Lucia, 420 So. 2d 1173, 1175 (La. App. 1982) (privilege applies to protect identity of author of letter to editor who requested that his name not be published); New York v. Royster, 26 MEDIA L. REP. (BNA) 1893 (N.Y. Sup. Ct. 1997) (New York shield law protects reporter from compelled disclosure of identity of sources in criminal case).

144. See Fischer v. McGowan, 585 F. Supp. 978 (D.R.I. 1984) (a reporter not a party to a defamation action not required to reveal identity of confidential source). See also Pinkard v. Johnson, 118 F.R.D. 517, 521 n.3 (M.D. Ala. 1987) (asserting that ALA. CODE § 12-21-142, "which codifies the reporter privilege, but only as to confidential 'sources of any information,'" reflects a policy of protecting only "confidential 'sources of information' obtained by reporters").

sources.[145] Even when a statute is limited to protection of the identities of confidential sources, courts have typically held that the privilege extends as well to "any disclosure of information, such as place of employment, that would tend to identify" the source.[146] As the Louisiana Supreme Court has recognized, "[o]therwise, through a series of indirect questions, the identity of the informant could be obtained without the need to ask for the informant's name directly, resulting in subversion of the reporter's privilege."[147]

Several courts have been called upon to determine whether a shield law's reference to "sources" of information extends beyond the identities of informants to include, as well, documents, correspondence, tape recordings and other repositories of information that would not otherwise lead to the disclosure of an informant's identity. In *In re Taylor*,[148] the Pennsylvania Supreme Court reversed the contempt conviction of a reporter who had refused to comply with a grand jury subpoena ordering the production of notes, records, and other documents. The court held that, under the Pennsylvania shield law, the term "'[s]ource' means not only the identity of the person, but likewise includes documents, inanimate objects, and all sources of information."[149] In *Hatchard v. Westinghouse Broadcasting Co.*,[150] however, the court appeared to narrow the scope of the *Taylor* holding, determining that "unpublished documentary information gathered by a television station is discoverable by a plaintiff in a libel action to the extent that the documentary information does not reveal the identity of a personal source of information or may be redacted to eliminate the revelation of a personal source of information."[151]

Some jurisdictions have expressly or implicitly rejected the rule in *Taylor*.[152]

---

145. See Matera v. Superior Ct., 825 P.2d 971, 974 (Ariz. App. 1992); Bartlett v. Superior Ct., 722 P.2d 346, 350 (Ariz. App. 1986).

146. In re Burns, 484 So. 2d 658, 659 (La. 1986).

147. *Id.*

148. 193 A.2d 181 (Pa. 1963).

149. *Id.* at 185. See Steaks Unlimited, Inc. v. Deaner, 623 F.2d 264, 279 (3d Cir. 1980) ("Inasmuch as *Taylor* protects all nonpublished portions of a source's statement, we hold that the outtakes of the Mills interview are protected even though the identity of the primary source of information is known."); Lal v. CBS Inc., 726 F.2d 97 (3d Cir. 1984); see also In re Paul, 513 S.E.2d 219, 225 (Ga. 1999) (privilege applies both to identities of sources and to undisclosed information received from sources). But see McMenamin v. Tartaglione, 590 A.2d 802, 811 (Pa. Commw.), *aff'd*, 590 A.2d 753 (Pa. 1991) (in civil case in which non-party journalist asserted statutory and constitutional privilege, court upheld constitutional privilege, but opined that shield law "clearly applies [only] to a reporter protecting his 'confidential sources'").

150. 532 A.2d 346 (Pa. 1987).

151. *Id.* at 351.

152. See, e.g., Ohio v. Geis, 441 N.E.2d 803, 809 (Ohio App. 1981) (rejecting *Taylor* and holding that Ohio legislature's intent "to protect the relationship between an informant, who desires to give information to a . . . news reporter but who fears publicity or . . . possible retribution" was "to be achieved by protecting only the *identity* of the informant"); Forest Hills Util. Co. v. City of

In *People v. Palacio*,[153] an Illinois appellate court held that its shield law does not "constitute a wholesale ban on *ever* calling reporters to testify" and protects only against compelled disclosure of an informant. In *Branzburg v. Pound*,[154] which, of course, became one of the cases consolidated for decision by the Supreme Court in *Branzburg v. Hayes*,[155] the Kentucky Supreme Court held that its shield law's protection of the "source of any information" does not extend to a reporter's eyewitness account of events he observed: "*[i]nformation* as used in the [Kentucky] statute refers to the things or the matters which a reporter learns and *source* refers to the method by which or to the person from whom he learns them."[156] The statute, the court explained, "grants a privilege from disclosing the source of the information but does not grant a privilege against disclosing the information itself."[157]

§ 15-2(d)(2). Confidential Information.

Some shield statutes expressly limit their reach to confidential information. The relevant New Mexico Rule of Evidence, for example, applies on its face only to "the confidential source from or through whom any information was procured" and "any confidential information obtained in the course of pursuing professional activities."[158] Other statutes differentiate between confidential and nonconfidential information, affording broader protection against compelled disclosure to the former.[159] The New York statute, in fact, was amended in 1990 to include expressly such qualified protection for nonconfidential sources and other

---

Heath, 302 N.E.2d 593, 596 (Ohio C.P. 1973) ("it is the name of the informant and not the information itself which is protected"); Williams v. American Broadcasting Cos., 96 F.R.D. 658, 665 (W.D. Ark. 1983) (shield law protects only "sources," which does not include outtakes); cf. Dumez v. Houma Mun. Fire & Police Civil Serv. Bd., 341 So. 2d 1206, 1208 (La. App. 1976) ("while some states have statutorily extended the newsman's privilege to information received, as well as its source and the identity of the informant, our statute grants the privilege only as to the identity of the informant and the source of the information, and not to the information itself"). In *WTHR-TV v. Indiana*, 685 N.E.2d 1091, 1092 n.3 (Ind. App. 1997), an Indiana appellate court "decline[d] to expand the statutory privilege beyond the protection of confidential sources." The state supreme court reversed in *WTHR-TV v. Milam*, 690 N.E.2d 1174 (Ind. 1998), vacating the lower court's order for *in camera* review of outtakes related to a murder story and holding that the request for *in camera* review "fails entirely due to non-compliance with the [Indiana] Trial Rules' requirement of reasonable particularity and materiality," *id.* at 1175.

153. 607 N.E.2d 1375, 1383 (Ill. App. 1993).
154. 461 S.W.2d 345 (Ky. 1970), *aff'd*, 408 U.S. 665 (1972).
155. 408 U.S. 665 (1972). See Chap. 14-4 *supra*.
156. 461 S.W.2d at 347.
157. *Id.*
158. N.M. R. EVID. 11-514(B)(1) & (2).
159. See, e.g., N.Y. CIV. RIGHTS LAW § 79-h (providing absolute immunity to confidential information and sources, and affording qualified immunity to nonconfidential information).

information following a series of judicial decisions holding that the shield law applied only to confidential sources and materials.[160]

Judicial decisions have largely been faithful to such express statutory distinctions. In *Outlet Communications, Inc. v. Rhode Island*,[161] the Rhode Island Supreme Court recognized that its shield law applied, on its face, only to confidential information and therefore held that it did not protect against compelled disclosure of unpublished, but nonconfidential material — i.e., the unbroadcast portion of an interview given, at his invitation, by a person wanted by law enforcement authorities. The court held that "the circumstances surrounding petitioner's acquisition of the information were anything but secret or confidential. The individual here attempted to ensure public exposure by asking 'Channel 10 News' to meet with him on a public sidewalk."[162]

§ 15-2(d)(3). Nonconfidential Information.

§ 15-2(d)(3)(A). Nonconfidential Sources.

Shield statutes typically do not differentiate on their face between the protection afforded confidential and nonconfidential sources.[163] A few statutes expressly state that their protections apply "whether or not the source has been promised confidentiality."[164] As a Maryland appellate court explained in *Lightman v. Maryland*,[165] even before the statute was amended to make that point explicit:

> The statute, on its face, does not purport to protect a newsman from disclosing *only* such sources of news or information published by him that was received in the course of a confidential newsman-informant relationship. On the contrary, while the Legislature may have enacted the statute with the primary purpose in mind of protecting the identity of newsmen's confidential sources, we think the statutory privilege broad enough to encompass

---

160. See, e.g., Knight-Ridder Broadcasting, Inc. v. Greenberg, 511 N.E.2d 1116, 1117 (N.Y. 1987) (shield law "clearly does not extend its protection to nonconfidential sources or information obtained in the course of gathering or obtaining news for publication"); People v. Korkala, 472 N.Y.S.2d 310 (App. Div. 1984); Hennigan v. Buffalo Courier Express Co., 446 N.Y.S.2d 767 (App. Div. 1981); Dooley v. Boyle, 531 N.Y.S.2d 158 (Sup. Ct. 1988). But see Wilkins v. Kalla, 459 N.Y.S.2d 985 (Sup. Ct. 1983); Lawless v. Clay, 9 MEDIA L. REP. (BNA) 1223 (N.Y. Sup. Ct. 1982).

161. 588 A.2d 1050 (R.I. 1991).

162. *Id.* at 1052.

163. See, e.g., ALA. CODE § 12-21-142; FLA. STAT. § 90.5015; KY. REV. STAT. ANN. § 421.100; LA. REV. STAT. ANN. § 1452; MICH. COMP. LAWS § 767.5a; TENN. CODE ANN. § 24-1-208(a).

164. D.C. CODE ANN. § 16-4702(1); MD. CODE ANN., CTS. & JUD. PROC. § 9-112(c)(1).

165. 294 A.2d 149, 156 (Md. Spec. App.), *aff'd*, 295 A.2d 212 (Md. 1972), *cert. denied*, 411 U.S. 951 (1973).

any source of news or information, without regard to whether the source gave his information in confidence or not.

New Jersey courts have reached the same conclusion.[166] By the same token, at least one court has held that, even where a statute does not limit is application to confidential sources, such a limitation is implicit and judicially enforceable.[167]

§ 15-2(d)(3)(B). Eyewitness Testimony.

Both state courts and the statutes that they are called upon to apply are divided concerning the latter's application to the compelled disclosure of events actually observed by a journalist in the course of newsgathering. The California shield law, for example, has been held to apply to a journalist's unpublished, nonconfidential eyewitness observations in a public place.[168] Similarly, in *Henderson v. Colorado*,[169] the Colorado Supreme Court held that a helicopter pilot/reporter who flew police over the home of a suspect could not be compelled to testify regarding the flight path of the helicopter. And, in *Brothers v. Brothers*,[170] an Alabama court applied the state's shield law to protect against compelled testimony about "eyewitness events" in the form of "incidents" witnessed by a reporter "in her reporting capacity and not as an ordinary citizen."

On the other hand, the New Jersey statute expressly removes from its scope "any situation in which a reporter is an eyewitness to, or participant in, any act involving physical violence or property damages."[171] Nevertheless, in *In re*

---

166. See, e.g., Gastman v. North Jersey Newspapers Co., 603 A.2d 111, 112 (N.J. Super. 1992) ("a source's expectations of confidentiality are irrelevant in determining the applicability of the privilege"). See also Florida v. Davis, 720 So. 2d 220, 227-28 (Fla. 1998) (holding under common law, which "is consistent with the recently created 'journalist's privilege,'" that privilege extends to both confidential and nonconfidential communications).

167. See Matera v. Superior Ct., 825 P.2d 971, 974 (Ariz. App. 1992); see also Ohio v. Prade, 26 MEDIA L. REP. (BNA) 2433, 2434 (Ohio C.P. 1998) (holding that Ohio shield law is inapplicable where "[t]here has been no allegation of confidentiality by any party, and the matter of privilege as to a confidential source is not an issue").

168. See Delaney v. Superior Ct., 789 P.2d 934, 941 (Cal. 1990).

169. 879 P.2d 383 (Colo.), *cert. denied*, 513 U.S. 1063 (1994).

170. 16 MEDIA L. REP. (BNA) 1031, 1032 (Ala. Cir. 1989).

171. N.J. STAT. ANN. § 2A:84-21(a); see N.M. R. EVID. 11-514(A)(2) ("'in the course of pursuing professional activities' does not include any situation in which a news media person participates in any act involving physical violence, property damage or criminal conduct"); COLO. REV. STAT. § 13-90-119(2)(c), (d) (privilege does not extend to "information based on a newsperson's personal observation of the commission of a crime if substantially similar news information cannot be obtained by any other means" or to "information based on a newsperson's personal observation of the commission of a class 1, 2 or 3 felony"); FLA. STAT. § 90.5015(2) (privilege "applies only to information or eyewitness observations obtained within the normal scope of employment, and does not apply to eyewitness observations, or video or audio recording, of crimes"); N.C. GEN. STAT. § 8-53.9(d) (statute does not apply to "journalist's eyewitness observations of criminal or tortious conduct").

Woodhaven Lumber & Mill Work,[172] the New Jersey Supreme Court declined to apply the so-called "eyewitness exception" to compel disclosure of photographs of a fire scene in connection with an arson investigation because the photographs captured only the results and not the "act" of arson. In *New Jersey v. Santiago*,[173] the court declined to enforce a criminal defendant's subpoena seeking a reporter's testimony about a shooting because the defendant failed to make a threshold showing that the reporter had witnessed anything. Finally, in *In re Vrazo*,[174] another New Jersey court held that a reporter who observed government workers at their homes, when they were supposed to be on the job, could not be compelled to testify about what he saw:

> The legislative intent, the legislative history, the purpose and design of the act, the spirit of the law, and the breadth of the objective of the legislation — all evidence a desire to create a broad shield law for the news media. The limited "eyewitness" exception must therefore be strictly construed.

Other courts have, however, interpreted their shield statutes not to apply to at least some "eyewitness" testimony. In *Branzburg v. Pound*,[175] the Kentucky Court of Appeals held the state shield law did not apply to "information acquired by the writer's observation during an interview granted to him upon a pledge that the identity of . . . two producers of *hashish* would not be revealed."[176] The court distinguished between "information" — i.e., "the things or the matters which a reporter learns" — and the "source" of such information — i.e., "the method by which or the person from whom he learns them."[177] In the case of Branzburg, the court asserted, the "actual *source* of the information" was both "the reporter's personal observation" and perhaps also an informant "who provided him with information that at a certain time and place he could observe the process of conversion of marijuana into hashish."[178] While the court had "no doubt that the identity of the informant was protected by the statute," it nevertheless concluded that the reporter's actual observations were not:

> In all likelihood the present case is complicated by the fact that the persons who committed the crime were probably the same persons who informed Branzburg that the crime would be, or was being, committed. If so, this is a rare case where informants actually informed against themselves. But in that event the privilege which would have protected disclosure of their identity as *informants* cannot be extended beyond their role as informants

---

172. 589 A.2d 135 (N.J. 1991).
173. 593 A.2d 357 (N.J. Super. 1991).
174. 423 A.2d 695, 700 (N.J. Super. 1980).
175. 461 S.W.2d 345 (Ky. 1970), *aff'd*, 408 U.S. 665 (1972).
176. *Id.* at 346.
177. *Id.* at 347.
178. *Id.*

to protect their identity in the entirely different role as perpetrators of a crime.[179]

Similarly, in *Lightman v. Maryland*,[180] a Maryland appellate court held that the state's shield law did not prevent a grand jury from compelling a reporter to testify, "based on his personal observation," about the location of a "pipe shop" at which he had observed illegal activity. The court concluded that "[w]here a newsman, by dint of his own investigative efforts, personally observes conduct constituting the commission of criminal activities by persons at a particular location, the newsman, and not the persons observed, is the 'source' of the news or information in the sense contemplated by the statute."[181] Accordingly, the court held that the reporter could "lawfully be directed to disclose the location of the pipe shop and describe the identity of all those persons observed by him, including the shopkeeper, who were engaged in the illegal activities."[182]

§ 15-2(d)(3)(C). Unpublished Information.

Many, but by no means all, shield statutes extend some form of protection to the compelled disclosure of unpublished information.[183] The Maryland and Dist-

---

179. *Id.* at 347-48. In explaining its holding, the Kentucky Court of Appeals posited the following scenarios:

> Suppose a newsman or reporter should see the President of the United States or the Governor of the Commonwealth assassinated upon the street; or see a bank robbery in progress; or see a forcible rape committed. Under the construction of the statute sought by petitioner, such a reporter could not be compelled to identify the perpetrator of the crime. We do not think the legislature ever intended such a result.

Id. at 348.

180. 294 A.2d 149 (Md. Spec. App.), *aff'd*, 295 A.2d 212 (Md. 1972), *cert. denied*, 411 U.S. 951 (1973).

181. *Id.* at 156-57.

182. *Id.*

183. See, e.g., CAL. CONST. art. 1, § 2(b) (shield law applies to "any unpublished information obtained or prepared in gathering, receiving or processing of information for communication to the public"); GA. CODE ANN. § 24-9-30 (extending qualified privilege against "disclosure of any information, document, or item obtained or prepared in the gathering or dissemination of news"); MICH. COMP. LAWS § 767.5a(1) (privilege extends to "any unpublished information obtained from an informant, or any unpublished matter or documentation in whatever manner recorded, relating to a communication with an informant"); MINN. STAT. § 595.023 (privilege protects compelled disclosure of "the person or means from or through which information was obtained" and "any unpublished information procured" by a newsperson, including "notes, memoranda, recording tapes, film or other reportorial data whether or not it would tend to identify the person or means through which the information was obtained"); MONT. CODE ANN. § 26-1-902(1) (privilege applies to "any information obtained or prepared or the source of that information"); NEV. REV. STAT. § 49.275 (privilege extends to "any published or unpublished information"); OKLA. STAT. tit. 12, § 2506(A)(5) (defining "unpublished information" protected by statute to include "information not disseminated to the public," such as "notes, outtakes, photographs, tapes or other data of whatever source not

rict of Columbia statutes, for example, contain an elaborate catalogue of privileged, unpublished material, a provision originally added to the Maryland law in 1979; specifically, the privilege applies to "[a]ny news or information procured" by a journalist "for communication to the public but which is not so communicated, in whole or in part, including:"

(i) Notes;
(ii) Outtakes;
(iii) Photographs or photographic negatives;
(iv) Video and sound tapes;
(v) Film; and
(vi) Other data, irrespective of its nature, not itself disseminated in any manner to the public.[184]

Courts have applied such shield legislation according to its terms. In *Grunseth v. Marriott Corp.*,[185] a federal district court applied both the District of Columbia and Minnesota statutes to protect against the compelled disclosure, from a newspaper, its reporters and editors, of a hotel bill that was allegedly shown to them in the course of newsgathering as well as "all notes, records, photographs, and documents either utilized by or in the possession of" the reporters.[186] Similarly, in *Resorts International, Inc. v. NJM Associates*,[187] the New Jersey Supreme Court applied its shield law, in the context of a defamation action, to protect the news media defendant from compelled disclosure of "notes, memoranda, rough drafts, editorial comments, sources and other information sought by plaintiffs."[188]

---

itself disseminated to the public through the medium of communication"); OR. REV. STAT. § 44.510(5); TENN. CODE ANN. § 24-1-208(a) (privilege applies to "any information procured for publication or broadcast").

184. MD. CODE ANN., CTS. & JUD. PROC. § 9-112(c)(2). See D.C. CODE ANN. § 16-4702(2); Bilney v. Evening Star Newspaper Co., 406 A.2d 652, 658 n.2 (Md. Spec. App. 1979) (describing legislative history of 1979 amendment to Maryland shield law).

185. 868 F. Supp. 333, 337 (D.D.C. 1994).

186. *Id.* Accord Prentice v. McPhilemy, No. 98CA0004309, slip op. at 13 (D.C. Super. May 5, 1999) (applying D.C. Shield Law to preclude defamation plaintiff from discovering reporter's notes, memoranda, or tape recordings of interviews).

187. 445 A.2d 395 (N.J.), *cert. denied*, 459 U.S. 907 (1982).

188. *Id.* at 397. See also United States v. Lopez, 14 MEDIA L. REP. (BNA) 2203 (N.D. Ill. 1987) (Illinois statute protects "outtakes"); Las Vegas Sun, Inc. v. Eighth Judicial Dist. Ct., 761 P.2d 849, 852 (Nev. 1988) (Nevada statute extends protection to "a newsman's 'tools,' i.e., notes, tape recordings and photographs"); CSX Transp., Inc. v. Cox Broadcasting, Inc., 25 MEDIA L. REP. (BNA) 2183 (Ga. Super. 1997) (Georgia shield law protects videotaped footage prepared during investigation of train accident); In re Paul, 513 S.E.2d 219 (Ga. 1999) (Georgia shield law protects notes, tapes, and other information relating to reporter's jailhouse interview of criminal defendant); In re Armstrong, 26 MEDIA L. REP. (BNA) 1700 (N.Y. Sup. Ct. 1997) (New York statute extends to taped interviews and related written notes gathered in preparation for potential story that was never broadcast).

Other courts have, however, reached different conclusions based on construction of the language of other shield statutes. The Louisiana Supreme Court, for example, has held that its shield law does not protect a reporter from responding to grand jury questions concerning his knowledge of criminal wrongdoing in a city agency.[189] According to the court, the Louisiana shield statute protects "only the identity of the sources" and "any information that would indirectly tend to identify the source."[190] Similarly, the Ohio Supreme Court has declined to apply that state's shield law to protect against the compelled disclosure of nonbroadcast outtakes, on the ground that the "statute shields the media only from 'disclos[ing] the source of any information procured or obtained.'"[191]

The courts have similarly divided over whether shield legislation protects news organizations from subpoenas seeking the disclosure of unpublished photographs. In *Oregon ex rel. Meyers v. Howell*,[192] an Oregon appellate court held that its statute afforded a privilege to a daily newspaper that resisted the production of unpublished photographs taken at the scene of a political demonstration. The court concluded that the statute "protects absolutely materials that fall within the shield," which "expressly includes photographs 'or other data of whatever sort' within the scope of 'unpublished information' protected from disclosure."[193] Similarly, in *Austin v. Memphis Publishing Co.*,[194] the Tennessee Supreme Court held that its shield law applies to unpublished photographs of a bridge collapse and correctly noted that its "holding is consistent with the decisions of those courts which have reviewed similarly worded shield laws and found them to include protection of non-confidential information."[195] The North

---

189. In re Grand Jury Proceedings (Ridenhour), 520 So. 2d 372, 373 (La. 1988).

190. *Id.* at 374.

191. National Broadcasting Co. v. Court of C.P., 556 N.E.2d 1120, 1127 (Ohio 1990) (quoting OHIO REV. CODE. ANN. § 2739.12). See also Davis v. Glanton, 705 A.2d 879, 882 (Pa. Super. 1997) (Pennsylvania shield law did not protect nonparty newspaper from disclosure of articles or editorials, notes taken in connection with interviews, or documents received in connection with articles or editorials, where "such materials cannot reasonably lead to the identification of sources not revealed in published articles").

192. 740 P.2d 792 (Or. App. 1987).

193. *Id.* at 795 (quoting OR. REV. STAT. § 44.520). See also Reitz v. Gordon, 26 MEDIA L. REP. (BNA) 1447, 1448 (N.D. Ill. 1998) ("There is no question that any visual memorializations of an event, whether photographs, movies, or videotapes, made as part of a newsgathering function by personnel working for a media organization that are not published or otherwise voluntarily disclosed come within the ambit of the Act and the newsgathering privilege.").

194. 655 S.W.2d 146, 150 (Tenn. 1983).

195. *Id.* (citing Lawless v. Clay, 9 MEDIA L. REP. (BNA) 1223 (N.Y. Sup. Ct. 1982); Aerial Burials Inc. v. Minneapolis Star & Tribune Co., 8 MEDIA L. REP. (BNA) 1653 (D. Minn. 1982); In re Vrazo, 423 A.2d 695 (N.J. Super. 1980); Steaks Unlimited, Inc. v. Deaner, 623 F.2d 264 (3d Cir. 1980) (applying Pennsylvania shield law); Hammarly v. Superior Ct., 153 Cal. Rptr. 608 (Ct. App. 1979); Lightman v. Maryland, 294 A.2d 149 (Md. Spec. App.), *aff'd*, 295 A.2d 212 (Md. 1972), *cert. denied*, 411 U.S. 951 (1973)).

Dakota Supreme Court has reached the same conclusion with respect to unpublished photographs of an automobile-motorcycle accident.[196] In *Marketos v. American Employers Insurance Co.*,[197] however, a Michigan appellate court held that its shield law does not protect "nonconfidential materials," including unpublished photographs taken at the scene of an arson investigation.

§ 15-2(d)(3)(D). Editorial Process Materials.

A few shield statutes have also been held to protect the sort of "editorial process" materials before the Supreme Court in *Herbert v. Lando*.[198] Indeed, the express language of many statutes would appear to apply to drafts of published articles and the contents of newsroom discussions with the same force as other unpublished information.[199]

Not surprisingly, therefore, the New Jersey Supreme Court held, in *Maressa v. New Jersey Monthly*,[200] that the statutory privilege in that state is "clearly intended to afford complete and pervasive security against disclosure" of the editorial process. Similarly, in *Resorts International, Inc. v. NJM Associates*,[201] decided the same day as *Maressa*, the court held that the privilege protects "notes, memoranda, rough drafts, editorial comments, sources and other information sought by plaintiffs." And, in *Prentice v. McPhilemy*,[202] a District of Columbia trial court expressly held that, while *Herbert* "may have limited the protections conferred on journalists under the First Amendment, it did not in any way prohibit state legislatures from enacting laws conferring greater protections on journalists."

Courts in other jurisdictions have, however, reached different conclusions. In New York, for example, a federal court held, in the context of General William Westmoreland's celebrated libel action against CBS, that the shield law did not preclude disclosure of an internal memorandum evaluating the broadcast at issue

---

196. See Grand Forks Herald v. District Ct., 322 N.W.2d 850, 854 (N.D. 1982) ("We find nothing ambiguous in the statute. It is not limited to disclosure of confidential sources. It applies, by its own terms, to 'any information or the source of any information' obtained by the news gatherer.") (quoting N.D. CENT. CODE § 1-02-05).
197. 460 N.W.2d 272, 273 (Mich. App. 1990).
198. 441 U.S. 153 (1979).
199. See, e.g., GA. CODE ANN. § 24-9-30 (privilege applies to "any information, document, or item obtained or *prepared* in the gathering or dissemination of news") (emphasis added); S.C. CODE ANN. § 19-11-100; MD. CODE ANN., CTS. & JUD. PROC. § 9-122(c)(2) (privilege applies to any "data, irrespective of its nature, not itself disseminated in any manner to the public"); D.C. CODE ANN. § 16-4702(2); N.C. GEN. STAT. § 8-53.9(c) (statute applies to any "confidential or nonconfidential information, document, or item obtained or prepared while acting as a journalist").
200. 445 A.2d 376, 383 (N.J.), *cert. denied*, 459 U.S. 907 (1982).
201. 445 A.2d 395, 397 (N.J.), *cert. denied*, 459 U.S. 907 (1982).
202. No. 98CA0004309, slip op. at 10 (D.C. Super. May 5, 1999).

prepared by a CBS News executive.[203] Similarly, in *Stokes v. Lorain Journal Co.*,[204] the Ohio shield law was held not to apply to editorial process materials "needed by the Plaintiff's attorney in the preparation of a tort action."

§ 15-2(d)(3)(E). Published Information.

Several shield laws expressly exclude from the scope of their protection material that has been previously published.[205] Other statutes extend their protections to "published or unpublished information" alike.[206] Some courts have applied a waiver theory to hold that published information forfeits its statutory protection.[207]

The Maryland judiciary has addressed this issue on more than one occasion. In *Maryland v. Sheridan*,[208] the Maryland Court of Appeals, in *dicta*, first suggested that the shield law privilege would not apply to prevent a grand jury from asking a reporter about information that "had been disseminated to the world" and did not implicate a confidential source. Fifteen years later, the court returned

---

203. See Westmoreland v. CBS Inc., 97 F.R.D. 703 (S.D.N.Y. 1983); see also First United Fund v. American Banker, 485 N.Y.S.2d 489 (Sup. Ct. 1985) (finding no privilege for drafts of allegedly defamatory article); cf. Sands v. News America Publ'g Inc., 560 N.Y.S.2d 416, 422 (App. Div. 1990) (holding that shield law did not apply to materials obtained in preparation for trial, since they were not "obtained in the course of newsgathering").

204. 266 N.E.2d 857, 863 (Ohio C.P. 1970).

205. See, e.g., R.I. GEN. LAWS § 9-19.1-2; COLO. REV. STAT. § 13-90-119(2)(b) (statute does not apply to "information which has actually been published or broadcast through a medium of mass communication"); LA. REV. STAT. ANN. § 1459(B)(1). The Louisiana statute also contains a somewhat unique provision that expressly authorizes "any custodian of records, photographer, or other representative of a news media organization" subpoenaed to appear at a proceeding and "confirm the publication or broadcast of specific materials" to do so by affidavit instead. *Id.* § 1455.

206. NEV. REV. STAT. § 49.275. See also, e.g., FLA. STAT. § 90.5015(4) (publication or broadcast of information does not waive privilege); N.J. REV. STAT. § 2a:84A-21 (privilege applies "whether or not" the information sought has been "disseminated"); OR. REV. STAT. § 44.530(1) (privilege applies "regardless of whether a person has disclosed elsewhere any of the information or source thereof").

207. See, e.g., Pennsylvania v. Banner, 17 MEDIA L. REP. (BNA) 1434, 1438 (Pa. C.P. 1989) (published quotations and summaries of defendant's statements constituted waiver); People v. Craver, 569 N.Y.S.2d 859, 861 (Sup. Ct. 1990) ("by knowingly publishing excerpts of the interview with the defendant, along with his identity," reporter "waived the statutory privilege with respect to the published portions of that interview"); In re Hadenguest, 5 MEDIA L. REP. (BNA) 2361, 2364 (N.Y. Sup. Ct. 1980) (prior to most recent amendments, New York shield law's protections "may be waived if the information obtained or the identity of its sources is published in any way"); Nulty v. Pennzoil Co., 485 N.Y.S.2d 533 (App. Div. 1985); Stripling v. Georgia, 401 S.E.2d 500, 507 (Ga.), *cert. denied*, 502 U.S. 985 (1991) (trial court properly permitted invocation of Georgia shield law "except as to information already publicly disclosed, in the article or elsewhere"). See also Chap. 15-2(h) *infra*.

208. 236 A.2d 18, 18 (Md. 1967).

to the subject in *Tofani v. Maryland*,[209] when a *Washington Post* reporter declined to testify before a grand jury about information she had already published in the newspaper concerning a series of rapes in a county jail. The court concluded, relying on the *dicta* in *Sheridan*, that where "as here, the reporter voluntarily and intentionally revealed the names of her sources in published news articles, nothing remains to be protected under the statute."[210] Moreover, the court held that "the protection afforded a newsgatherer against compelled 'disclosure' of a news source, in the ordinary and legal signification of that term, and in the sense used in the statute, goes no further than to inhibit the revelation, against the will of the reporter, of those sources not previously disclosed to the public."[211]

§ 15-2(e). Contours of the Privilege.

§ 15-2(e)(1). Absolute Privilege.

The privilege afforded by several shield laws is, at least in some contexts, absolute. The Delaware statute, for example, provides an absolute privilege in non-adjudicative proceedings, including grand jury proceedings, although a less expansive privilege is available in the adjudicative context.[212] Several other statutes, which apply on their face only to the compelled disclosure of the "source of any information," create an absolute privilege as well.[213] Some states, including Pennsylvania, have interpreted similar shield statutes to afford an absolute privilege to unpublished information gathered in the newsgathering process.[214]

A few statutes, on their face, extend an absolute privilege to the compelled disclosure of the identities of sources and other unpublished information.[215] Many statutes, however, calibrate the privilege more precisely, affording an ab-

---

209. 465 A.2d 413 (Md. 1983).

210. *Id.* at 417.

211. *Id.* at 417-18 (emphasis added); see also *id.* at 418 ("It is doubtful that many sources, willing to have their identity publicly disclosed in the media, would withdraw their cooperation unless the reporter could refuse to testify about the source. At most, it is likely that such a source would request anonymity, which would implicate the reporter's statutory privilege.").

212. See DEL. CODE. ANN. tit. 10, §§ 4321-22.

213. See, e.g., IND. CODE § 34-46-4-2; KY. REV. STAT. ANN. § 421.100; ALA. CODE § 12-21-142; Ex parte Sparrow, 14 F.R.D. 351, 353 (N.D. Ala. 1953) (applying Alabama shield law); Jamerson v. Anderson Newspapers, Inc., 469 N.E.2d 1243, 1246 (Ind. App. 1984) (Indiana shield law "confers, without a doubt, an absolute privilege on the news media").

214. See, e.g., 42 PA. CONS. STAT. § 5942; In re Taylor, 193 A.2d 181 (Pa. 1963); Chap. 15-2(d)(3)(C) *supra*.

215. See, e.g., OR. REV. STAT. § 44.520(1)(a)-(b); NEV. REV. STAT. § 49.275.

solute privilege to the "source" of news or information and qualified protection to other unpublished information.[216]

Some courts have declined to apply these statutes as written, at least in the context of criminal proceedings. In *Ohio v. Geis*,[217] an Ohio appellate court held that, although the Ohio shield law "arms radio and television reporters with an absolute privilege to protect the identity of their informants in any judicial proceeding," the statutory privilege must be balanced against the "Sixth Amendment rights of a criminal defendant."[218] As a result, the court concluded, whether or not the shield law will be given effect in a criminal proceeding "must depend on the particular circumstances of each case, the crime charged, the possible defenses, the significance of the informant's testimony, as well as other factors."[219]

Similarly, although the California statute has been held to provide "virtually absolute protection" from contempt to nonparty journalists in civil proceedings,[220] the immunity it creates in the criminal context has been qualified by the courts. The California Supreme Court has asserted that, despite its plain language, the shield law's "protection is overcome in a criminal proceeding on a showing that nondisclosure would deprive the defendant of his federal constitutional right to a fair trial."[221]

The New Jersey shield law, on its face, qualifies its otherwise absolute privilege in the context of criminal proceedings when a defendant seeks to compel disclosure.[222] The statute's absolute privilege, however, applies in any other "legal or quasi-legal proceeding or before any investigative body, including but not limited to, any court, grand jury, petit jury, administrative agency, the Legislature or legislative committee, or elsewhere."[223]

---

216. See, e.g., D.C. CODE ANN. §§ 16-4702(1) & 16-4703(a) (absolute privilege applies "whether or not the source has been promised confidentiality"); MD. CODE ANN., CTS. & JUD. PROC. § 9-112(c) & (d); OKLA. STAT. § 2506(B); N.Y. CIV. RIGHTS LAW § 79-h.

217. 441 N.E.2d 803 (Ohio App. 1981).

218. *Id.* at 809-10 (construing OHIO REV. CODE ANN. § 2739.04).

219. 441 N.E.2d at 810; see also In re McAuley, 408 N.E.2d 697, 709 (Ohio App. 1979) ("a defendant does not have an absolute right to obtain confidential information from a newsperson").

220. Mitchell v. Superior Ct., 690 P.2d 625, 628 (Cal. 1984) (citing CAL. CONST. art. 1, § 2(b)). See New York Times Co. v. Superior Ct., 796 P.2d 811, 812 (Cal. 1990) (shield law's protection cannot "be overcome in a civil action by a litigant's showing of need for the newsperson's unpublished information").

221. Delaney v. Superior Ct., 789 P.2d 934, 946 (Cal. 1990); see also Miller v. Superior Ct., 77 Cal. Rptr. 2d 827 (Ct. App.), *review granted*, 968 P.2d 462 (Cal. 1998) (applying *Delaney* in context of subpoena issued by prosecutor).

222. See N.J. STAT. ANN. §§ 2A:84A-21 & 21.3.

223. *Id.* § 2a:84A-21. See generally In re Farber, 394 A.2d 330 (N.J.), *cert. denied*, 439 U.S. 997 (1978); New Jersey v. Boiardo, 414 A.2d 14 (N.J. 1980).

§ 15-2(e)(2). Qualified Privilege.

The protection afforded by most shield statutes is, at least in some respects, qualified. Many state legislatures have codified a version of the privilege that tracks the formulation articulated by Justice Stewart in his dissenting opinion in *Branzburg v. Hayes*.[224] The Georgia shield law, for example, provides that its privilege applies unless "what is sought: (1) Is material and relevant; (2) Cannot be reasonably obtained by alternative means; and (3) Is necessary to the proper preparation or presentation of the case of a party seeking the information, document, or item."[225] Some shield statutes apply a qualified privilege modeled after Justice Stewart's formulation in all proceedings otherwise subject to their terms.[226]

Other states apply a version of Justice Stewart's formulation of the qualified privilege in some, but not all, proceedings. These statutes typically provide an absolute privilege in some contexts. The District of Columbia shield law, for example, affords an absolute privilege to "the source of any news or information" and a qualified privilege, derived largely from Justice Stewart's *Branzburg* opinion, in all other contexts.[227] The New York statute calibrates its privilege by differentiating between confidential and nonconfidential information — the former receives absolute protection while the latter shelters under the qualified privilege.[228] In New Jersey, criminal defendants seeking to compel disclosure must overcome a qualified privilege, although the privilege is absolute in all other contexts in which the shield law applies.[229]

---

224. 408 U.S. 665, 743 (1972) (Stewart, J., dissenting); see Chap. 14-4(c) *supra*.

225. GA. CODE ANN. § 24-9-30. The Colorado statute reflects a somewhat more elaborate codification of essentially the same qualifications, providing that its privilege does not apply where a subpoenaing party seeking "news information" demonstrates, by a preponderance of the evidence:

(a) That the news information is directly relevant to a substantial issue involved in the proceeding;
(b) That the news information can not be obtained by other reasonable means; and
(c) That a strong interest of the party seeking to subpoena the news persons outweighs the interests under the first amendment . . . of such news person in not responding to a subpoena and of the general public in receiving news information.

COLO. REV. STAT. § 13-90-119(3).

226. See, e.g., *id.*; ARIZ. REV. STAT. § 12-2214; TENN. CODE ANN. § 24-1-208(c); N.M. R. EVID. 11-514(C); GA. CODE ANN. § 24-9-30; N.C. GEN. STAT. § 8-53.9(c).

227. D.C. CODE ANN. § 16-4703(a). See MD. CODE ANN., CTS. & JUD. PROC. § 9-112(d); OKLA. STAT. tit. 12, § 2506(B).

228. See N.Y. CIV. RIGHTS LAW § 79-h.

229. N.J. STAT. ANN. § 2A:84A-21. To overcome the New Jersey privilege in a criminal case, a criminal defendant must demonstrate "by a preponderance of the evidence that there is a reasonable probability that the subpoenaed materials are relevant, material and necessary to the defense, that they could not be secured from any less intrusive source, that the value of the material sought as it

Several states have adopted qualified privileges that differ from Justice Stewart's formulation. The Arkansas privilege, for example, applies unless an article about which information is sought "was written, published, or broadcast in bad faith, with malice, and not in the interest of the public welfare."[230] In Delaware, although an absolute privilege is in force in "non-adjudicative proceedings," the privilege is only applicable in "adjudicative proceedings" if a court determines that "the public interest in having the reporter's testimony" does not "outweigh[] the public interest in keeping the information confidential."[231]

Even where a statute, on its face, sets out an absolute privilege, several state courts have imposed qualifications by judicial construction. The Ohio and California statutes, for example, have both been construed to provide only a qualified privilege in the criminal context when the subpoenaing party is a criminal defendant.[232] The California Supreme Court has held that a criminal defendant can attempt to overcome the shield law privilege by making a threshold showing that there is "a reasonable possibility the information will

---

bears upon the issue of guilt or innocence outweighs the privilege against disclosure, and that the request is not overbroad, oppressive, or unreasonably burdensome." *Id.* § 2A:84A-21.3.

230. ARK. CODE ANN. § 15-85-510. See also COLO. REV. STAT. § 13-90-119(3) (privilege overcome by showing that (a) the information sought is directly relevant to a substantial issue in the case, (b) it cannot be obtained from other sources, and (c) "a strong interest of the party seeking to subpoena the news persons outweighs the interests under the first amendment"); R.I. GEN. LAWS § 9-19.1-3 (privilege overcome, *inter alia*, "if there is substantial evidence that the information sought is necessary (a) for the prosecution of a felony or (b) to prevent a threat to life"); LA. REV. STAT. ANN. § 1453 (privilege will be divested "only when the court, after hearing the parties, shall find the disclosure is essential to the public interest"); MICH. COMP. LAWS § 767.5a (Michigan shield law divested in "an inquiry for a crime punishable by imprisonment for life" when it has been established that the information which is sought is essential to the purpose of the proceeding and that other available sources of the information have been exhausted); MINN. STAT. § 595.024 (subpoenaing party must show, by clear and convincing evidence, that, *inter alia*, "there is probable cause to believe that the source has information clearly relevant to a specific violation of the law other than a misdemeanor" and "that there is a compelling and overriding interest requiring the disclosure of the information where the disclosure is necessary to prevent injustice"); N.D. CENT. CODE § 31-01-06.2 (privilege overcome upon finding that "the failure of disclosure of such evidence will cause a miscarriage of justice").

231. DEL. CODE ANN. tit. 10, § 4323. In making this determination, the court is to consider the importance of the issue involved, the efforts made to obtain information from other sources, the availability of information from other sources, the circumstances under which the reporter received the information and the effect of disclosure on the flow of information. *Id.* See also N.M. R. EVID. 11-514(c) (privilege divested if (1) material sought is "material and relevant," (2) alternative means of securing the material have been exhausted, (3) the information sought "is crucial to the case," and (4) "the need of the party seeking the confidential source or information is of such importance that it clearly outweighs the public interest in protecting the news media's confidential information and sources").

232. See Ohio v. Geis, 441 N.E.2d 803, 810 (Ohio App. 1981); In re McAuley, 408 N.E.2d 697, 709 (Ohio App. 1979); Delaney v. Superior Ct., 789 P.2d 934, 948 (Cal. 1990).

materially assist his defense," a showing that must be based on something more than "mere speculation."[233] Once such a showing is made, the California Supreme Court further requires that a trial judge balance four factors in an effort to determine if the criminal defendant's Sixth Amendment right to a fair trial outweighs the interests protected by the privilege.[234]

§ 15-2(e)(2)(A). Relevance Requirements.

Relatively few courts have had occasion to apply the relevance requirement contained in the qualified privilege afforded by many shield laws. In civil litigation, some courts have held that, for various reasons, subpoenaed information is irrelevant to the case, including because the information sought was gathered by a journalist after the filing of the action or because there is no dispute that a press report accurately quoted protagonists in the litigation.[235] In *Taylor v. Miskovsky*,[236] for example, the Oklahoma Supreme Court held that its shield statute precluded a defamation plaintiff from compelling disclosure of a reporter's notes and other unpublished information relating to an article written two weeks after the filing of his complaint. Because the "state of mind or knowledge required for actual malice must be determined at the time of the writing and publishing of the complained-of material," the court indicated that "confidential sources and files obtained ... nearly two weeks after Appellee filed his lawsuit" could not be "relevant to the issue of actual malice at the time of the publication of such allegedly defamatory articles."[237]

In the criminal context, courts applying shield laws have also rebuffed efforts to compel a journalist's testimony on relevance grounds. In one case, an appellate court held that it was not error for a trial judge to invoke the Georgia

---

233. Delaney v. Superior Ct., 789 P.2d at 948. See also Miller v. Superior Ct., 77 Cal. Rptr. 2d 827 (Ct. App.), *review granted*, 968 P.2d 462 (Cal. 1998) (qualified privilege applies also in criminal proceedings in which information is sought by prosecution); In re Willon, 55 Cal. Rptr. 2d 245, 258 (Ct. App. 1996) (requiring showing of "substantial probability" of injury to fair trial rights where party seeking disclosure of confidential source is not the criminal defendant); People v. Simpson, 23 MEDIA L. REP. (BNA) 2552, 2555-56 (Cal. Super. 1995) (defendant failed to show that knowledge of identity of confidential source would materially assist defense; knowing who leaked information to reporter would only "reveal a police officer in possession of misinformation"); People v. DeSoto, 24 MEDIA L. REP. (BNA) 2217, 2224 (Cal. Super. 1996) (interest of prosecution in securing conviction overrides press interest in maintaining neutrality).

234. 789 P.2d at 949-51. See Chap. 15-2(c)(1) *supra* (discussing factors).

235. See, e.g., Dingman v. Harvell, 814 S.W.2d 362, 369 (Tenn. App. 1991) (where sources do not dispute accuracy of quotations attributed to them in newspaper article, "proof introduced failed to show that there is probable cause to believe that the subpoenaed reporter has information which is relevant"); Taylor v. Miskovsky, 640 P.2d 959, 962 (Okla. 1981) (quashing subpoena for information collected by news reporter after filing of civil action).

236. 640 P.2d 959, 962 (Okla. 1981).

237. *Id.*

shield law to preclude inquiry into the sources of an article reporting on jury deliberations in a manslaughter case.[238] The court concluded that, because the report itself was inaccurate and the jury had not had access to it, "nothing in the language" of the shield law indicates "that it was meant to be used to uncover the source of mere courtroom gossip or speculation."[239] In another criminal case, a Minnesota appellate court rejected a journalist's claim that subpoenaed material about her interviews with participants in a sexual misconduct case was irrelevant, and hence protected by the shield law, on the ground that her "interview notes are 'clearly relevant' to the charges, . . . even though their only potential usefulness . . . may be for impeachment purposes."[240] An Ohio appellate court has, however, reached the opposite conclusion, holding in a criminal case that "the need for evidence that is admissible solely for the purpose of impeaching a witness is insufficient to require its production prior to trial."[241]

§ 15-2(e)(2)(B). Exhaustion Requirements.

Courts applying shield laws that afford a qualified privilege have regularly had occasion to address the requirement, often contained in such legislation, that the party seeking to compel disclosure must first exhaust alternative sources of the information.[242] In *New Jersey v. Boiardo*,[243] where a criminal defendant

---

238. Nobles v. Georgia, 411 S.E.2d 294, 298 (Ga. App. 1991).

239. *Id.* at 299; see also In re Paul, 513 S.E.2d 219, 224 (Ga. 1999) (subpoena requesting information about circumstances surrounding reporter's jailhouse interview in which criminal defendant allegedly confessed sought irrelevant evidence, where "questions all stem from the state's erroneous premise that the statement made to the reporter is analogous to a statement made to a police officer").

240. Minnesota v. Brenner, 488 N.W.2d 339, 341 (Minn. App. 1992).

241. Ohio v. Geis, 441 N.E.2d 803, 807 (Ohio App. 1981); see *id.* ("Absent some showing of prejudice, there is no harm in allowing said evidence to be produced after a witness has testified."); Krase v. Graco Children Prods., Inc., 79 F.3d 346 (2d Cir. 1996) (party seeking material, which can only be used for impeachment purposes, cannot overcome protection of New York shield statute because "[o]rdinarily, impeachment material is not critical or necessary to the maintenance or defense of a claim").

242. See, e.g., Tennessee v. Curriden, 738 S.W.2d 192 (Tenn. 1987); McNeilus v. Corporate Reports, Inc., 21 MEDIA L. REP. (BNA) 2171 (Minn. Dist. 1993); Stripling v. Georgia, 401 S.E.2d 500 (Ga.), *cert. denied*, 502 U.S. 985 (1991); In re Paul, 513 S.E.2d 219 (Ga. 1999); New Jersey v. Boiardo, 414 A.2d 14 (N.J. 1980); New Jersey v. Boiardo, 416 A.2d 793 (N.J. 1980); In re Special Grand Jury Investigation, 472 N.E.2d 450 (Ill. 1984); Cukier v. American Med. Ass'n, 630 N.E.2d 1198, 1202 (Ill. App. 1994); Bartlett v. Superior Ct., 722 P.2d 346 (Ariz. App. 1986); Henderson v. Colorado, 879 P.2d 383 (Colo.), *cert. denied*, 513 U.S. 1063 (1994); Krase v. Graco Children Prods., Inc., 79 F.3d 346 (2d Cir. 1996); In re Brown & Williamson Tobacco Corp., 24 MEDIA L. REP. (BNA) 1720 (N.Y. Sup. Ct.), *aff'd*, 643 N.Y.S.2d 92 (App. Div. 1996); In re CBS Inc., 23 MEDIA L. REP. (BNA) 2311 (N.Y. Sup. Ct. 1995); McCarty v. Bankers Ins. Co., 27 MEDIA L. REP. (BNA) 1051, 1057 (N.D. Fla. 1998) (applying common law, but noting that result would be the same under new Florida shield statute, "as the factors of each are virtually indistinguishable"); In re Armstrong, 26 MEDIA L. REP. (BNA) 1700 (N.Y. Sup. Ct. 1997).

243. 414 A.2d 14 (N.J. 1980); 416 A.2d 793 (N.J. 1980).

attempted to compel the production of a letter written by a potential prosecution witness to a reporter, the New Jersey Supreme Court twice spoke to the efficacy of the exhaustion requirement. First, the court reversed a trial court's order that the letter be produced for *in camera* inspection, holding that the shield law does not require a journalist "to show that other, less intrusive sources probably contain the same information as that found in the letter; rather, the *defendant* has the burden to prove that it is reasonably probable that this information can *not* be secured from any less intrusive source."[244] Since the contents of the letter could be ascertained from the letter writer himself, other letters written by him, or taped phone conversations in which the letter was discussed, the court determined that the defendant had not carried his burden of proof with respect to the exhaustion requirement.

On remand, the defendant renewed his motion to compel and the trial court again ordered an *in camera* review. The New Jersey Supreme Court, however, reversed this order as well, largely on the basis of the defendant's failure to satisfy the exhaustion requirement: "The trial judge . . . held that . . . the alternative sources . . . did not contain a description of what was in the letters. However, this was not the showing required under the statute. Rather, it was defendants' burden to prove that the alternative sources did not contain information substantially similar to the information contained in the letters."[245]

---

244. 414 A.2d at 22. In *In re Arya*, 589 N.E.2d 832, 839 (Ill. App. 1992), an Illinois appellate court held that the party seeking disclosure need not prove that specific alternative *methods* of investigation were unsuccessful. Rather, though the party seeking disclosure must exhaust all available *sources* of information to comply with the shield law, "methods" fall in a different category. The court held that the shield law only requires that the "investigation has been sufficiently thorough and comprehensive that further efforts to obtain the sought-after information would likely be successful," although a mere assertion that an investigation was unsuccessful will not suffice. *Id.* at 840.

245. 416 A.2d at 796. See In re Willon, 55 Cal. Rptr. 2d 245, 258 (Ct. App. 1996) (requiring exhaustion in criminal case). Similarly, in *Tennessee v. Curriden*, 738 S.W.2d 192, 193 (Tenn. 1987), the Tennessee Supreme Court rejected the efforts of a district attorney to divest the qualified privilege embodied in the Tennessee shield law and compel disclosure of the identity of a "'a man who committed a murder but has never been arrested.'" The district attorney's application was supported only by an affidavit sworn by him, which indicated that the reporter had refused "'to give testimony involving information he had regarding a homicide that was being investigated by said grand jury.'" *Id.* The court concluded, based on this showing, that no "investigation or inquiry" appeared to have been made "with officials from surrounding counties," nor has "any check of prison or parole records been shown." *Id.* As a result, the court held that "the State had not offered 'clear and convincing' evidence that the information sought could not reasonably be obtained by alternative means." *Id.* Accord Stripling v. Georgia, 401 S.E.2d 500, 507 (Ga.), *cert. denied*, 502 U.S. 985 (1991) (motion by criminal defendant to compel journalist to disclose identities of confidential sources with information about alleged eavesdropping on his conversations with his lawyers denied on the ground that the "evidence shows that there were fewer than a dozen former employees of the sheriff's office in the relevant time period, and that the defense team made no effort to contact any of them"). But see People v. DeSoto, 24 MEDIA L. REP. (BNA) 2217, 2226

Courts have applied the exhaustion requirement strictly in the civil context as well. In one case, a Minnesota trial court rejected, pursuant to that state's shield statute, a defamation plaintiff's efforts to compel the defendant to disclose the identities of confidential sources for the article at issue.[246] The court rejected the plaintiff's suggestion that interrogatories and document requests directed at the defendant, and questions put to the reporter at deposition, "constitute independent alternative means," and accepted the defendant's contention that such discovery initiatives "are merely repeated attempts at obtaining the desired information from Defendants."[247]

§ 15-2(e)(2)(C). Other Requirements.

The case law surrounding the varied additional requirements that state statutes have included to overcome a qualified privilege is surprisingly sparse, especially given the sheer number of shield laws that include them.[248] The North Dakota Supreme Court, however, has indicated the importance of its statutory requirement that the privilege be overcome only when the failure to do so "'will cause a miscarriage of justice.'"[249] In *Grand Forks Herald v. District Court*, the court noted that, although the statute contains no express requirement that a party seeking compelled disclosure first exhaust alternative sources, "a district court may consider the availability of the evidence from other sources in determining whether or not a miscarriage of justice would occur if disclosure were not ordered."[250]

(Cal. Super. 1996) (whether alternative source requirement applies in criminal cases in California depends on facts of each case).

246. See McNeilus v. Corporate Report, Inc., 21 MEDIA L. REP. (BNA) 2171 (Minn. Dist. 1993).

247. *Id.* at 2174. See Bauer v. Gannett Co., 557 N.W.2d 608 (Minn. App. 1997) (recognizing exhaustion requirement in libel cases); Greenleigh Assocs., Inc. v. New York Post Corp., 434 N.Y.S.2d 388 (App. Div. 1980) (New York shield law requires plaintiff in defamation action attempt to obtain information sought from other sources before deposing defendant); Reitz v. Gordon, 26 MEDIA L. REP. (BNA) 1447, 1448 (N.D. Ill. 1998) ("even though the government's photographs taken at the scene are now missing, the parties have not established that the court can and should find that all non-privileged sources of the information have been exhausted"); In re Armstrong, 26 MEDIA L. REP. (BNA) 1700, 1702 (N.Y. Sup. Ct. 1997) ("Petitioner's showing fails on [two] counts: she does not contend that she has no other evidence . . . and she does not contend that she has sought such evidence elsewhere").

248. See Chap. 15-2(e)(2) *supra* (citing statutory provisions).

249. Grand Forks Herald v. District Ct., 322 N.W.2d 850, 855 (N.D. 1982) (quoting N.D. CENT. CODE § 31-01-06.2).

250. 322 N.W.2d at 855. The court provided additional guidance concerning the contours of the "miscarriage of justice" standard:

> Should parties to a lawsuit abuse the discovery proceedings by requiring disclosure from a news gatherer simply because it is easier or less expensive to acquire evidence in that manner, by conducting a fishing expedition without any firm knowledge that the news gatherer

Similarly, the Louisiana courts have had several occasions to apply the provision of that state's shield statute divesting the privilege only upon a showing that "disclosure is essential to the public interest."[251] Thus, in *Becnel v. Lucia*,[252] a Louisiana appellate court held that the party seeking disclosure of the identity of the author of a letter to the editor had not made the requisite showing and, in *Dumez v. Houma Municipal Fire & Police Civil Service Board*,[253] another court reached the same conclusion with respect to the identities of sources from whom a reporter had solicited opinions about the outcome of a hearing. Indeed, the Louisiana Supreme Court has held that "absent a showing that the identity of [a reporter's] sources is essential to the protection of the public interest," such testimony could not be compelled by a grand jury investigating government corruption.[254]

§ 15-2(f). Privilege v. Immunity.

Shield statutes articulate the nature of the protection they provide in differing and potentially significant ways. Many shield laws purport to create a statutory "privilege" and set forth affirmatively that no person or entity covered by their terms "shall be required to disclose" the sources or information protected by the statute.[255] Other statutes speak directly in the language of privilege, stating for

---

> has information which will be of assistance in a determination of the legal action, or by requiring disclosure of confidential information in instances in which the necessity for a free and unfettered press outweighs the benefits to be obtained from such disclosure, we are confident that our district courts, under the provisions of our shield statute, will be able to weigh the necessary factors, balance the competing interests, and protect the news gatherers from any unwarranted invasion of the news gatherers' privilege provided by the statute.

Id. at 857.
251. LA. REV. STAT. ANN. § 1453.
252. 420 So. 2d 1173, 1176 (La. App. 1982).
253. 341 So. 2d 1206, 1209 (La. App. 1976).
254. In re Grand Jury Proceedings (Ridenhour), 520 So. 2d 372, 374 (La. 1988). In the context of defamation actions, one Minnesota appellate court has suggested that, under the Minnesota shield law, a plaintiff seeking to compel disclosure of the defendant's confidential sources may be required "to make a prima facie showing that the alleged defamatory statements are false." Bauer v. Gannett Co., 557 N.W.2d 608 (Minn. App. 1997). See also Prentice v. McPhilemy, No. 98CA0004309, slip op. at 9 (D.C. Super. May 5, 1999) (holding that exception to D.C. Shield Law permitting compelled disclosure "where there is an overriding public interest" does not apply in context of plaintiff's discovery in a defamation action).
255. OKLA. STAT. tit. 12, § 2506(B). See, e.g., TENN. CODE ANN. § 24-1-208(a) (covered persons "shall not be required . . . to disclose . . . any information or the source of any information procured for publication or broadcast"); LA. REV. STAT. ANN. § 1452 ("no reporter shall be compelled to disclose . . . the identity of any informant or any source of information"); ARIZ. REV. STAT. § 12-2237 (covered persons "shall not be compelled to testify or disclose . . . the source of information procured or obtained"); MONT. CODE ANN. § 26-1-902 (covered persons may not "be examined as to or may be required to disclose any information obtained or prepared or the source of any information"); MINN. STAT. § 595.023 (no covered person "shall be required . . . to disclose"

example that covered persons and entities "shall have a qualified privilege against disclosure."[256] Several shield laws do not expressly reference the concept of privilege but provide essentially the same substantive proscription on the compelled disclosure of information.[257]

The California statute, in contrast, provides that covered persons and entities "cannot be adjudged in contempt" for a refusal to disclose information falling within the law's protection.[258] Construing this formulation, the California Supreme Court has emphasized that the shield law "provides an immunity from being adjudged in contempt; it does not create a privilege."[259] As a result, California courts have considered themselves free to impose sanctions other than contempt against a party journalist who declines to disclose information otherwise protected by the shield law.[260] The California Supreme Court has also held that, because "'the shield law provides only an immunity from contempt, not a privilege,'" an order compelling disclosure may typically not be challenged by writ prior to an adjudication of contempt.[261]

---

protected information). Other statutes make essentially the same point, but do so in the context of asserting a limitation on the power of the state and its instrumentalities. See, e.g., MD. CODE ANN., CTS. & JUD. PROC. § 9-112(c) (a "judicial, legislative, or administrative body, or any body that has the power to issue subpoenas may not compel any person" covered by the statute to disclose protected information); 735 ILL. COMP. STAT. 5/8-901 ("No court may compel any person to disclose the source of any information obtained by a reporter except as provided. . . .").

256. GA. CODE ANN. § 24-9-30. See also N.M. R. EVID. 11-514(B) (covered person "has a privilege to refuse to disclose" confidential sources and information).

257. See, e.g., ALA. CODE § 12-21-142 (no covered person "shall be compelled to disclose . . . the sources of any information"); KY. REV. STAT. ANN. § 421.100 (no covered person "shall be compelled to disclose . . . the source of any information"); OR. REV. STAT. § 44.510 (no covered person "shall be required . . . to disclose" protected information); cf. ARK. CODE ANN. § 16-85-510 ("Before any editor, reporter, or other writer . . . shall be required to disclose . . . the source of information used for the basis of any article," specific showing contemplated by statute must be made).

258. CAL. CONST. art. 1, § 2(b).

259. Delaney v. Superior Ct., 789 P.2d 934, 940 n.6 (Cal. 1990). See also Sci-Sacramento, Inc. v. California Superior Ct., 62 Cal. Rptr. 2d 868, 871 (Ct. App. 1997).

260. See, e.g., Mitchell v. Superior Ct., 690 P.2d 625, 628 (Cal. 1984); Dalitz v. Penthouse Int'l Ltd., 214 Cal. Rptr. 254, 258 (Ct. App. 1985) (court struck defendant's cross-complaint as sanction for failure to disclose confidential sources); New York Times Co. v. Superior Ct., 796 P.2d 811, 816 (Cal. 1990) (although unlikely, nonparty witnesses may be exposed to sanction under California "Code of Civil Procedure section 1992, which states, 'A witness disobeying a subpoena also forfeits to the party aggrieved the sum of five hundred dollars ($500), and all damages which he may sustain by the failure of the witness to attend, which forfeiture and damages may be recovered in a civil action'"); People v. DeSoto, 24 MEDIA L. REP. (BNA) 2217, 2219 (Cal. Super. 1996).

261. New York Times Co. v. Superior Ct., 796 P.2d at 814 (quoting Delaney v. Superior Ct., 789 P.2d at 934). See also Sci-Sacramento, Inc. v. California Superior Ct., 62 Cal. Rptr. 2d at 875-76.

The New York statute contains similar provisions providing an "exemption of professional journalists and newscasters from contempt."[262] It, however, has not been construed as narrowly as the California shield law, largely because the New York statute also contains provisions declaring that "any information obtained in violation" of the statute "shall be inadmissible" and that "no fine or imprisonment may be imposed against a person for any refusal to disclose information privileged" under the shield law.[263] Even in the defamation context, the New York Court of Appeals has held that the shield law precludes a trial court from striking a defendant's answer as a sanction for its refusal to disclose the identity of an anonymous letter writer.[264]

§ 15-2(g). Penalties for Non-Disclosure.

As the foregoing suggests, the most typical, though not the only, sanction under a shield statute for failure to disclose unprotected information is a finding of contempt, especially when a journalist or news organization is not a party to the underlying proceeding.[265] Under the California courts' somewhat unique construction of its shield law, moreover, that state's Supreme Court has suggested that, although unlikely, it is nevertheless possible that a nonparty may be sanctioned under California Code of Civil Procedure section 1992, which provides that "[a] witness disobeying a subpoena also forfeits to the party aggrieved the sum of five hundred dollars ($500), and all damages which he may sustain by the failure of the witness to attend, which forfeiture and damages may be recovered in a civil action."[266]

In those circumstances in which a journalist or news organization is a party to the underlying proceeding, especially in a defamation or related action, some

---

262. N.Y. CIV. RIGHTS LAW § 79-(h)(b) & (c).
263. *Id.* § 79-h(d) & (e). The Louisiana statute also contains a provision holding that no covered person and entity "shall be adjudged in contempt" for the refusal to disclose unpublished, nonconfidential information. LA. REV. STAT. ANN. § 1459(B). It further provides that a covered person or entity "shall not be compelled to disclose" the identity of "any source of information." *Id.* § 1452. The shield law refers to the latter provision as a "conditional privilege from compulsory disclosure of informant or source," and the former as a "qualified protection for nonconfidential news."
264. See Oak Beach Inn Corp. v. Babylon Beacon, Inc., 464 N.E.2d 967, 971 (N.Y. 1984) ("A newspaper involved in a substantial libel action may well find the threat of contempt less intimidating than the thought of being entirely stripped of its defenses if it continues to preserve the confidentiality of its source.").
265. See, e.g., 735 ILL. COMP. STAT. 5/8-909 (contempt appropriate sanction for refusal to comply with final order to disclose information); Newburn v. Howard Hughes Med. Inst., 594 P.2d 1146, 1147 (Nev. 1979) (nonparty reporter held in contempt in civil action for refusal to answer deposition questions); Ohio v. Geis, 441 N.E.2d 803, 806 (Ohio App. 1981) (reporter held in contempt and fined $100 per day by trial court for failure to produce subpoenaed materials; reversed by appellate court).
266. New York Times Co. v. Superior Ct., 796 P.2d 811, 816 (Cal. 1990).

courts have held that additional sanctions, such as in limine orders precluding a defendant from relying on information not produced in discovery pursuant to a shield law, are appropriate.[267] Other courts, however, have held that the statutory language precludes the imposition of any such order or other sanction based on invocation of the statutory privilege in a civil action in which the affected journalist or news organization is a party.[268]

§ 15-2(h). Waiver.

Several shield statutes, on their face, address the issue of waiver. The Montana shield law, for example, provides both that "dissemination in whole or in part does not constitute a waiver" in most circumstances, and that "[i]f the person claiming the privilege testifies, with or without having been subpoenaed or ordered to testify," there is no waiver of the privilege "unless the person voluntarily agrees to waive the privilege or voluntarily discloses the source in the course of his testimony."[269] The Maryland statute, following a 1988 amendment, takes pains to emphasize that "[i]f any person employed by the news media disseminates a source of any news or information, or any portion of the news or information procured while pursuing professional activities, the protection from compelled disclosure . . . is not waived."[270] Other statutes contain similar pro-

---

267. See, e.g., McNeilus v. Corporate Reports, Inc., 21 MEDIA L. REP. (BNA) 2171, 2172-73 (Minn. Dist 1993) ("Defendants are not required to disclose the identities of newsgathering sources. However, in light of Minnesota Rule of Civil Procedure 37.02(b)(2), and in the interest of fairness, Defendants are precluded from introducing any evidence at trial regarding such confidential sources that has not been disclosed to Plaintiff. . . ."); Sands v. News America Publ'g, Inc., 560 N.Y.S.2d 416, 421 (App. Div. 1990) ("defendants should be precluded from introducing into evidence confidential information or documentation known to defendant . . . unless such information has first been disclosed to plaintiffs at least 10 days prior to trial"); Greenberg v. CBS Inc., 419 N.Y.S.2d 988, 997 (App. Div. 1979) ("[I]f defendants opt to rely on their statutory privilege, they should be precluded from any use of those sources and information as proof of verification or evidence of responsibility.").

268. See Chap. 15-2(c)(2)(B) *supra* (citing and discussing cases).

269. MONT. CODE ANN. § 26-1-903. See Sible v. Lee Enters., Inc., 729 P.2d 1271, 1274 (Mont. 1986) (holding, under prior version of shield law, that reporter waived privilege when "he took the witness stand or testified by way of deposition"). The Montana shield law was amended to reverse legislatively the result in *Sible*.

270. MD. CODE ANN., CTS. & JUD. PROC. § 9-112(e). The statute was amended to add this language in response to the decision of the Maryland Court of Appeals in *Tofani v. Maryland*, 465 A.2d 413 (Md. 1983). In *Tofani*, the court of appeals held that a reporter had waived the statutory privilege "by publishing the names of her sources in the newspaper." *Id.* at 415. The court reasoned that "the protection afforded a newsgatherer against compelled 'disclosure' of a news source, in the ordinary and legal signification of that term, goes no further than to inhibit the revelation, against the will of the reporter, of those sources not previously disclosed to the public." *Id.* at 417-18. In so holding, the court in *Tofani* distinguished case law interpreting statutes that "explicitly specify how a waiver may be effected" as "inapposite," which no doubt moved the legislature to add § 9-112(e) to the shield law. *Id.* at 418 (citing People ex rel. Scott v. Silverstein, 412 N.E.2d 692 (Ill. App.

visions.[271]

Some shield laws, however, expressly incorporate the waiver concept in their statutory scheme. The Georgia legislation, for example, provides that covered persons and entities enjoy a qualified privilege "unless it is shown that this privilege has been waived."[272] In Colorado, the shield law provides that the privilege may be waived "only by the voluntary testimony or disclosure of a newsperson that directly addresses the news information or identifies the source of such news information sought."[273] The New Jersey statute provides that the privilege can be overcome in a criminal proceeding by a defendant's showing "by clear and convincing evidence that the privilege has been waived," and that "[p]ublication shall constitute a waiver only as to the specific materials published."[274] The Oregon shield law contains an apparently unique provision declaring that, if "the informant offers the informant as a witness, it is deemed a consent to the examination" also of the journalist claiming the privilege "on the same subject."[275]

Courts have frequently been called upon to determine whether the concept of waiver applies at all, and if so to what extent, in the context of shield statutes that are silent on the issue. In its oft-cited decision in *In re Taylor*,[276] the Pennsylvania Supreme Court became one of the first jurisdictions to address the issue directly. In *Taylor*, a reporter appealed a contempt conviction resulting from his failure to comply with a grand jury subpoena demanding the production of his notes and records. The court rejected a broad concept of waiver under the Pennsylvania shield law, holding instead that "a waiver by a newsman applies only to

---

1980), *rev'd on other grounds*, 429 N.E.2d 483 (Ill. 1981); In re Bridge, 295 A.2d 3 (N.J. Super. 1972), *cert. denied*, 410 U.S. 991 (1973)). See also Bilney v. Evening Star Newspaper Co., 406 A.2d 652, 658 (Md. Spec. App. 1979) (pre-amendment case in which court held that, while "a reporter may, of course, waive the statutory privilege — perhaps unwittingly — in a variety of ways," the reporter's "mere characterization of his source as gratuitous or voluntary is not one of them").

271. See, e.g., S.C. CODE ANN. § 19-11-100 (publication does not constitute waiver); D.C. CODE ANN. § 16-4704 (voluntary disclosure does not constitute waiver); DEL. CODE ANN. tit. 10, § 4325 ("A person does not waive or forfeit the privilege by disclosing all or any part of the information protected by the privilege to any other person."); FLA. STAT. § 90.5015(4) ("a professional journalist does not waive the privilege by publishing or broadcasting information"); OR. REV. STAT. § 44-530(1) (statute applies "regardless of whether a person has disclosed elsewhere any of the information or source thereof").

272. GA. CODE ANN. § 24-9-30.

273. COLO. REV. STAT. § 13-90-119(4).

274. N.J. STAT. ANN. § 2A:84A-21.3. The New Jersey Supreme Court's discussion of the waiver concept in *Maressa v. New Jersey Monthly*, 445 A.2d 376 (N.J.), *cert. denied*, 459 U.S. 907 (1982), in the context of defamation litigation, is discussed in Chap. 15-2(c)(2)(B) *supra*. See also In re Schuman, 552 A.2d 602, 609 (N.J. 1989) (holding that "[t]he language in the [shield law's] 1979 amendment that '[p]ublication shall constitute a waiver as to the specific materials published' applies only to material sought by criminal defendants").

275. OR. REV. STAT. § 44.540.

276. 193 A.2d 181 (Pa. 1963).

the statements made by the informer which are actually published or publicly disclosed and not to other statements made by the informer to the newspaper."[277]

More recently, in *Las Vegas Sun v. Eighth Judicial District Court*,[278] the Nevada Supreme Court applied that state's general waiver statute,[279] and noted as well that the shield law "privilege may be waived even in the absence of a waiver statute."[280] As in *Taylor*, the court in *Las Vegas Sun* concluded that "the disclosure of a source and the attribution of remarks to that source is a clear cut waiver of the shield privilege as to that name and those statements."[281] Applying that principle in the context of defamation litigation, the court held that, "during the discovery process, news media litigants can properly be required to admit and document the precise matters disclosed in their publications or broadcasts."[282]

The New York courts have had several opportunities to address the issue of waiver, a subject on which the state's shield statute is silent. In *Simpson v. Schneiderman*,[283] for example, the court held that the transfer of confidential information from one reporter to another and then to the reporter's attorney did not waive the absolute statutory privilege that applies to confidential information. The court concluded that disclosure to the reporter "did not constitute . . . a

---

277. *Id.* at 186. In a more recent criminal case, the court in *Pennsylvania v. Banner*, 17 MEDIA L. REP. (BNA) 1434 (Pa. C.P. 1989), held that a reporter had waived her statutory privilege by publishing excerpts of an interview with the defendant. The court applied *Taylor*'s waiver concept to find that published quotations and summaries of defendant's statements constituted a waiver as to those statements. *Id.*

278. 761 P.2d 849, 851-52 (Nev. 1988).

279. See NEV. REV. STAT. § 49.385.

280. 761 P.2d at 852 (citing Tofani v. Maryland, 465 A.2d 413, 417 (Md. 1983)).

281. 761 P.2d at 852.

282. *Id.* at 853. Moreover, the Nevada Supreme Court in *Las Vegas Sun* limited, as have other courts, see Chap. 15-2(c)(2) *supra* (citing cases), the application of the waiver principle in the defamation context. Specifically, the court held that, when "a plaintiff attempts to discover the basis of a news story which is felt to defame him or her, and the news media defendant relies on the shield law to resist discovery, the defendant will be deemed to have thereby elected to protect the confidentiality of that information" and "such an election . . . may not thereafter be waived whenever it may suit the defendant's convenience." 761 P.2d at 853. According to the court, such a "dual, selectively self-serving use of the shield privilege would result in excessive prejudice to the plaintiff and waste judicial resources." *Id.* See also Newburn v. Howard Hughes Med. Inst., 594 P.2d 1146, 1148 (Nev. 1979) (Nevada Supreme Court "summarily reject[s]" contention that shield law is absolute and may not be waived "within the intendment of" NEV. REV. STAT. § 49.385 when reporter voluntarily disclosed information to attorney representing litigant and to other parties and witnesses). Cf. Nevada v. Bazile, CR98-0388 (Nev. County Ct. Feb. 19, 1999) (noting that *Las Vegas Sun* and *Newburn* did not address issue before it, court held that Nevada statute shields reporter from testifying regarding jailhouse interview with criminal defendant, where portions of interview were broadcast and others were summarized in broadcast commentary).

283. 21 MEDIA L. REP. (BNA) 1542 (N.Y. Sup. Ct. 1993).

general public disclosure" because the recipient "was not the public; it was a statutorily protected newsgatherer."[284] Moreover, the court held that "is beyond cavil" that the reporter, who was a defendant in a libel action, "could not prepare his defense . . . without providing his attorneys with the relevant documents."[285]

In *People v. Lyons*,[286] another New York court held that, where a confidential source reveals his identity and thereby waives confidentiality, the information he provided to a journalist remains subject to the shield law's protections governing compelled disclosure, from the journalist, of nonconfidential information. Like other jurisdictions, however, New York courts have held that "by knowingly publishing excerpts of the interview with the defendant" in a criminal case, "along with his identity," a journalist has "waived the statutory privilege with respect to the published portions of that interview."[287] Nevertheless, while identification of the source and publication of the information may constitute waiver,

> mere publication of "any such news," would not *per se*, waive the privilege of protecting the identity of the source from disclosure. At the same time, publication solely of the identity of the source, without some reference, at least in part, to "any such news," would be meaningless.[288]

---

284. *Id.* at 1543.
285. *Id.* at 1544. See also People ex rel. Scott v. Silverstein, 412 N.E.2d 692, 696 (Ill. App. 1980), *rev'd on other grounds*, 429 N.E.2d 483 (Ill. 1981) (reporter did not waive shield law privilege in Illinois by divulging information to a third party); People v. Palacio, 607 N.E.2d 1375, 1383 (Ill. App. 1993). See also Sci-Sacramento, Inc. v. California Superior Ct., 62 Cal. Rptr. 2d 868, 872 (Ct. App. 1997) (no waiver where television station submitted outtakes of interview with criminal defendant to trial court for *in camera* review while expressly reserving rights under California shield law).
286. 574 N.Y.S.2d 126 (Sup. Ct. 1991).
287. People v. Craver, 569 N.Y.S.2d 859, 861 (Sup. Ct. 1990). In *Craver*, the court reasoned that once the source was identified, confidentiality was no longer an issue, and the only privilege that might apply was the qualified version codified at N.Y. CIV. RIGHTS LAW § 79-h(c); since that privilege only applies to "unpublished news," however, the court held it did not shield the published portions of an interview. 569 N.Y.S.2d at 861. See also In re Hadenguest, 5 MEDIA L. REP. (BNA) 2361, 2364 (N.Y. Sup. Ct. 1980) (under previous version of shield law, court noted that "[t]he protection afforded" to confidential information "by the statute may be waived if the information obtained or the identity of its source is published in any way"); In re Wolf, 333 N.Y.S.2d 299, 301 (App. Div. 1972) (previous publication and identification of source constituted waiver under previous version of shield law); People v. Zagarino, 411 N.Y.S.2d 494 (Sup. Ct. 1978) (testimony at trial and concomitant identification of confidential source constitute waiver under previous statute); People v. Dupree, 388 N.Y.S.2d 1000 (Sup. Ct. 1976) (publication of material constituted waiver); Nulty v. Pennzoil Co., 485 N.Y.S.2d 533 (App. Div. 1985) (previously published information held discoverable from non-party reporter in civil action).
288. Andrews v. Andreoli, 400 N.Y.S.2d 442, 448 (Sup. Ct. 1977).

Thus, in *People v. Chambers*,[289] the court held that a reporter's identification of confidential sources does not constitute waiver of the confidentiality of the information provided by the source.[290]

§ 15-2(i). Procedural Requirements.

§ 15-2(i)(1). Procedures Generally.

Several shield statutes contain provisions specifying procedural requirements that govern efforts to invoke and/or negate the privilege they afford. The Illinois statute, for example, provides that any person seeking privileged information must apply in writing to the appropriate court for an order divesting the privilege.[291] The application must include the name of the reporter, the relevant news medium, the specific information sought, and its relevance to the proceedings. In most cases, the application must also identify a specific public interest that would be harmed if the information were not made available.[292] The shield law further provides that all proceedings relating to an application for divestiture "shall be as in other civil cases."[293] The Louisiana statute contains similar provisions requiring the person "seeking the information" to apply "for an order to revoke the privilege,"[294] and further provides that a court may order divestiture only after an adversary hearing resulting in "clear and specific findings" that the requesting party has made the requisite statutory showing.[295]

---

289. 15 MEDIA L. REP. (BNA) 1151 (N.Y. Sup. Ct. 1988).

290. *Id.* at 1154. See also People v. Troiano, 486 N.Y.S.2d 991, 994 (Sup. Ct. 1985); In re Guess?, Inc., 17 MEDIA L. REP. (BNA) 1313, 1315 (N.Y. Sup. Ct. 1989) ("It is irrelevant that the source of the information or material is known and not confidential. As long as the information or material itself is cloaked in confidentiality[,] it is privileged."). But cf. Lexington Herald-Leader Co. v. Beard, 690 S.W.2d 374, 375 n.1 (Ky. 1984) ("As to information in the article attributed directly to the former director of the Institute, the statutory privilege against disclosure of the source of the information has been *waived* by publication.").

291. 735 ILL. COMP. STAT. 5/8-903(a). Plaintiffs in defamation actions must also apply for such an order. *Id.* 5/8-903(b).

292. *Id.* 5/8-904. In defamation actions, the plaintiff must address the necessity of the information sought to the proof of her case, and must make a prima facie showing of both the falsity of the allegedly defamatory statement and the actual injury it allegedly caused. *Id.*

293. *Id.* 5/8-905. See In re Arya, 589 N.E.2d 832, 836 (Ill. App. 1992) (civil burden of proof by preponderance of evidence applies to divestiture proceeding in criminal cases).

294. LA. REV. STAT. ANN. § 1453. The Louisiana shield law also contains provisions requiring that any subpoena directed to a journalist, news media organization or its representative "shall be served at least ten days prior to the return date." *Id.* § 1456(A). The statute also empowers news media organizations, journalists, and other covered persons to seek an order with respect to such a subpoena, including a motion to extend the time for response. *Id.* § 1456(B).

295. *Id.* § 1459(B)(2). See also MINN. STAT. § 595.024 (providing that person seeking disclosure may apply for order divesting the privilege, which shall be granted if requisite showing is made by "clear and convincing evidence"); TENN. CODE ANN. § 24-1-208(t)(1), (2); Tennessee v. Curriden, 738 S.W.2d 192, 192 (Tenn. 1987) ("statute provides for a hearing and for a determina-

A few shield statutes require that a subpoena served on a journalist or media entity "shall have attached to it an affidavit of a person with a direct interest in the matters sought."[296] The Delaware statute, in contrast, requires a reporter seeking to invoke the shield law in an adjudicative proceeding to state under oath that "disclosure of the information would violate an express or implied understanding with the source ... or would substantially hinder the reporter in the maintenance of existing source relationships or the development of new source relationships."[297]

§ 15-2(i)(2). In Camera Review.

Shield statutes, and the courts construing them, take varying approaches to the issue of *in camera* review of information putatively protected. In New Mexico, for example, the shield law embodied in the state rules of evidence provides that, "if possible, the determination of whether the exception applies, shall be made, without the court knowing the confidential source or information sought to be protected" but, "if it is not possible for the court to make a determination ... without the court knowing" that information, it "may issue an order requiring disclosure to the court alone, in camera."[298] Following any such *in camera* review, the court is required to enter written findings and conclusions of law, "without disclosing any of the matters for which the privilege is asserted."[299] Although its shield law is silent on the issue, the California Supreme Court has interpreted it to afford a trial court "discretion in the first instance to determine whether a newsperson's claim of confidentiality or sensitivity is colorable. If the court determines the claim is colorable, it must then receive the newsperson's testimony in camera."[300]

In New Jersey, by contrast, the state supreme court has severely restricted the availability of *in camera* review. Although the court did affirm a trial judge's order requiring *in camera* review in *In re Farber*,[301] it twice reversed such orders in *New Jersey v. Boiardo*,[302] emphasizing that the shield law, as amended in the wake of *Farber*, "declares as clearly as it possibly could the Legislature's belief

---

tion that the applicant has established a right to divestiture to override the privilege 'by clear and convincing evidence'").

296. See, e.g., ARIZ. REV. STAT. § 12-2214.
297. DEL. CODE ANN. tit. 10, § 4322.
298. N.M. R. EVID. 11-514(D).
299. *Id.* The Rule further provides that all "counsel and parties shall be permitted to be present at every stage of the proceedings," except at any *in camera* hearing "at which no counsel or party, except the person asserting the privilege, and counsel for that person, shall be permitted to be present." *Id.*
300. Delaney v. Superior Ct., 789 P.2d 934, 952 (Cal. 1990). See also People v. DeSoto, 24 MEDIA L. REP. (BNA) 2217, 2218 (Cal. Super. 1996).
301. 394 A.2d 330 (N.J.), *cert. denied*, 439 U.S. 997 (1978).
302. 414 A.2d 14 (N.J. 1980); 416 A.2d 793 (N.J. 1980).

that disclosure to a trial judge *in camera* represents precisely the same threat to the interests protected by the privilege as disclosure to counsel or to the world."[303] Other jurisdictions, however, have continued to rely upon *Farber* as authorizing *in camera* review.[304]

The Ohio courts have calibrated the propriety of *in camera* review in large measure according to the type of proceeding in which its shield law is invoked. In criminal cases, Ohio appellate courts have instructed criminal defendants to "request an *in camera* inspection by the court of the confidential information. If, after this is done, there is a reasonable probability that either the newsperson or the informant will provide relevant evidence of the defendant's guilt or innocence, the defendant is entitled to the newsperson's confidential information or the name of the newsperson's informant."[305] As the Ohio Court of Appeals explained in *Ohio v. Geis*:[306]

> Such an *in camera* inspection of the evidence serves two purposes. First, it allows the trial court to make an informed decision as to the evidentiary nature of the material in question rather than depending on the representations of counsel. Secondly, the *in camera* inspection allows the trial court to discern that aspect of the evidence, which has evidentiary value from that which does not, as well as to allow the trial court to restrict the availability of that evidence, which has limited evidentiary value.

In civil cases, in contrast, at least one Ohio court has concluded that, because the Sixth Amendment does not require the shield statute to "yield," there is "no

---

303. 414 A.2d at 25. See also 416 A.2d at 794 ("In our first opinion in this case, we gave effect to the legislative judgment clearly expressed in the new shield law: the need of the press for protection not only from the production of confidential material at trial but also for protection against that limited disclosure that occurs when the court itself examines the material *in camera*"). See also Oregon ex rel. Meyers v. Howell, 740 P.2d 792, 798 (Or. App. 1987) (reversing trial court order requiring *in camera* review).

304. "[I]n camera inspections have been permitted where the party requesting disclosure has shown that the information is relevant and material; that it could not be secured from any less intrusive source; and that the party had a legitimate need to see and otherwise use it." Grand Forks Herald v. District Ct., 322 N.W.2d 850, 856-57 n.4 (N.D. 1982) (citing In re Farber, 394 A.2d 330 (N.J.), *cert. denied*, 439 U.S. 997 (1978); New Jersey v. Boiardo, 414 A.2d 14 (N.J. 1980)). See Montana v. District Ct., 546 P.2d 988, 989 (Mont. 1976) ("We are unable to determine the merits of these issues on the record before us. No court is able to determine the relevancy, materiality, necessity, or applicability of the statutes . . . unless that item [of evidence] is first presented to the court for examination").

305. In re McAuley, 408 N.E.2d 697, 710 (Ohio App. 1979). See Ohio v. Geis, 441 N.E.2d 803, 807 (Ohio App. 1981) ("[W]here, as in the case before us, the motion to quash a subpoena duces tecum is supported by a claim that the requested evidence is protected by [the] 'shield law,' the trial court *must* make an *in camera* inspection of the evidence requested to be produced in order to determine the admissibility and relevancy of said evidence.") (emphasis in original).

306. 441 N.E.2d 803, 807 (Ohio App. 1981).

authority for an in-camera inspection."[307] In the court's view, "the Legislature has seen fit to enact the Shield Law which ... takes away the Court's authority to make such a determination."[308]

§ 15-2(i)(3). Appellate Review.

Some shield laws expressly provide for immediate appellate review of a trial court's order compelling disclosure. Several statutes, like Minnesota's, indicate that such orders "may be appealed directly to the court of appeals" and that the "order is stayed and nondisclosure shall remain in full force and effect during the pendency of the appeal."[309] The Tennessee statute not only provides for appellate review of any order requiring disclosure, it obligates the court of appeals to "make an independent determination of the applicability" of the standards set out in the shield law "to the facts in the record and shall not accord a presumption of correctness to the trial court's findings."[310] The Tennessee Supreme Court has interpreted this provision to "contemplate an original hearing and disposition of factual, as well as legal, issues before the Court of Appeals and direct appeal to this Court as a matter of right."[311]

The California Supreme Court has also had occasion to conduct an independent appellate review, although it noted that the state's shield law is silent on the issue.[312] The California law is also silent concerning the availability of appellate review generally, an issue that was addressed by the California Supreme Court in *New York Times Co. v. Superior Court*.[313] There, the court concluded that permitting a newsperson subject to an order compelling disclosure to seek appellate relief via extraordinary writ would be premature. Rather, the court contemplated

---

307. Weiss v. Thomson Newspapers, Inc., 8 MEDIA L. REP. (BNA) 1258, 1260-61 (Ohio C.P. 1981).

308. *Id.*

309. MINN. STAT. § 595.024(3). Either party may request expedited consideration in the court of appeals. *Id.* The Minnesota statute further provides that, where the court "finds that the information sought has been published or broadcast, there shall be no automatic stay unless an appeal is filed within two days after the order is issued." *Id.*; see *id.* § 595.025(3) (applying same rule in defamation context).

Other enactments containing analogous appeal provisions include Louisiana, see LA. REV. STAT. ANN. § 1453; New Mexico, see N.M. R. EVID. 11-514(D); and Alaska, see ALASKA STAT. § 09.25.180. The Illinois shield law provides that the privilege remains "in full force and effect" during the pendency of an appeal, though it does not expressly provide for immediate appellate review. See 735 ILL. COMP. STAT. 5/8-908. Such review, however, appears to be implicit in the divestiture scheme established under the statute. See *id.* 5/8-901 et seq.

310. TENN. CODE ANN. § 24-1-208(3)(A).

311. Tennessee v. Curriden, 738 S.W.2d 192, 193 (Tenn. 1987). The court noted that, while "it is quite unusual for the General Assembly to vest matters of original jurisdiction in the intermediate appellate courts, apparently it has done so in this instance." *Id.*

312. See Delaney v. Superior Ct., 789 P.2d 934, 952 (Cal. 1990).

313. 796 P.2d 811, 816 (Cal. 1990).

that such a newsperson must first suffer an adjudication of contempt, although the entry of a contempt judgment should not lead to incarceration:

> To avoid confinement under a judgment of contempt that may subsequently be set aside, a trial court should stay its judgment of contempt to allow the contemner newsperson sufficient time in which to seek writ relief if the trial court believes there is any colorable argument the newsperson can make against the contempt adjudication. If the trial court nevertheless declines to issue a stay, a reviewing court should do so pending its decision whether to issue an extraordinary writ.[314]

Other courts in states where the shield law does not address the issue of appellate review have permitted the affected journalist or news organization to pursue an extraordinary writ prior to an adjudication of contempt.[315]

§ 15-2(i)(4). Special Broadcast Rules.

A few shield laws impose special procedural requirements on broadcast stations and their employees who seek to invoke the statutory privilege. Typically, these statutes require television and radio stations to "maintain[ ] and keep[ ] open for inspection by a person affected by the broadcast, for a period of at least 180 days from the date of an actual broadcast, an exact recording, transcription, or certified written transcript of the actual broadcast."[316]

---

314. *Id.* at 815. See In re Willon, 55 Cal. Rptr. 2d 245 (Ct. App. 1996) (same). See also Sci-Sacramento, Inc. v. California Superior Ct., 62 Cal. Rptr. 2d 868, 874-75 (Ct. App. 1997) (Where "there was no adjudication of contempt . . . the writ of prohibition is premature insofar as it seeks to litigate the shield law . . . [I]n the further event that the trial court enters a contempt judgment, [the television station] may then pursue its remedy.").

315. See, e.g., In re Paul, 513 S.E.2d 219, 222 (Ga. 1999) (holding "that non-parties engaged in news gathering may file a direct appeal of an order denying them the statutory reporter's privilege under the collateral order exception to the final judgment rule [because] an important right may be lost if review had to await final judgment, and nothing further in the underlying action can affect the issue on appeal"); Lexington Herald-Leader Co. v. Beard, 690 S.W.2d 374, 376 (Ky. 1984) ("Assuming the movant could establish that the lower court, although proceeding within its jurisdiction, was acting incorrectly in circumstances where there is not adequate remedy by appeal and great injustice or irreparable harm will result," a writ is available); Grand Forks Herald v. District Ct., 322 N.W.2d 850, 852, 854 (N.D. 1982) ("Because the order of the District Court is neither appealable nor, apparently, subject to review on appeal from a final judgment," because the newspaper is not a party to the underlying proceeding, "and because it involves a matter of some public interest, we determine to exercise our original jurisdiction" and review the trial court's order compelling disclosure for "an abuse of discretion"). See also In re Grand Jury Proceedings, 810 F.2d 580, 581 (6th Cir. 1987) (federal appellate court reviewed state court order compelling disclosure via writ of habeas corpus sought on the ground that reporter "would be held in custody in violation of the United States Constitution if an order of a Michigan court, holding him in contempt . . . , were enforced as scheduled").

316. N.M. R. EVID. 11-514(B)(2). See also 42 PA. CONS. STAT. § 5942 (requiring transcripts to be kept for one year); OHIO REV. CODE ANN. § 2739.04 (six months).

§ 15-2(i)(5). Other Requirements.

State shield laws occasionally include other procedural requirements, some of which are — at least to the extent included in shield legislation — unique. The Oregon statute, for example, contains a provision safeguarding the "papers, effects or work premises of a person connected with" a news organization from a "search by a legislative, executive or judicial officer or body, ... by search warrant or otherwise."[317] The Louisiana statute includes provisions affording courts discretion to award "reasonable attorneys fees and expenses to the prevailing party,"[318] as well as an elaborate scheme requiring the party issuing a subpoena to a news organization to bear the costs of compliance and pay them into the registry of the court.[319]

§ 15-2(j). Choice of Law.

Shield laws do not typically address issues relating to choice of law.[320] In some early cases, federal courts addressed whether state shield statutes were applicable in that forum. In *Ex parte Sparrow*,[321] a federal court sitting in Alabama applied that state's shield law, "in the absence of any Federal rule on privilege," and in the face of the statute's "clear and unequivocal pronouncement of the public policy of the state in which it sits." In *Baker v. F & F Investment*,[322] decided shortly after the Supreme Court's decision in *Branzburg*, the Second Circuit noted with approval the trial court's reference to the New York and Illinois shield laws in fashioning a privilege based on federal public policy:

> Absent a federal statute to provide specific instructions, courts which must attempt to divine the contours of non-statutory federal law governing the compelled disclosure of confidential journalistic sources must rely on both judicial precedent and a well-informed judgment as to the proper federal public policy to be followed in each case.[323]

Nevertheless, the court relied on federal law and purported to apply neither statutory privilege directly.

---

317. OR. REV. STAT. § 44.520(b)(2). The prohibition does not apply "where probable cause exists to believe" that the newsperson herself "has committed, is committing, or is about to commit a crime." *Id.* See also Chap. 15-3 *infra* (discussing federal search warrant legislation).
318. LA. REV. STAT. ANN. § 1456(C).
319. *Id.* § 1457.
320. But cf. ALASKA STAT. § 09.25.200 (Alaska shield law applies in all judicial proceedings applying Alaska state law).
321. 14 F.R.D. 351, 353 (N.D. Ala. 1953).
322. 470 F.2d 778, 781 (2d Cir. 1972), *cert. denied*, 411 U.S. 966 (1973).
323. *Id.*

In *Mazzella v. Philadelphia Newspapers, Inc.*,[324] however, a federal court sitting in New York applied Pennsylvania law, including the Pennsylvania shield law, in the context of a defamation action against a Pennsylvania-based newspaper. And, a federal court in the District of Columbia has applied the constitutional privilege, as well as the D.C. and Minnesota shield laws, to quash third-party subpoenas directed at reporters for a Minneapolis newspaper, which sought information they gathered in the District of Columbia about a candidate for political office in Minnesota.[325] Because the information was privileged under all three sources of law, the court did not have occasion to determine which privilege in fact applied.[326]

Several state courts have considered conflict of laws issues in applying the Uniform Act to Secure the Attendance of Witnesses from Without a State in Criminal Proceedings (the "Uniform Act"), which has been adopted in most states. In *Codey v. Capital Cities*,[327] for example, a New Jersey grand jury sought to have a New York court issue a subpoena to compel production of videotape outtakes and a reporter's interview notes. The New York trial court held that it was required to defer to the New Jersey court's interpretation of that state's shield law, a conclusion that was ultimately affirmed by the New York Court of Appeals:

> In view of the sensitivity of privilege issues to local policy concerns and particularized legal rules, it would make little sense to construe [the Uniform Act] as authorizing the courts of this State to determine questions of privilege that arise under the law of another jurisdiction and which relate to specific criminal proceedings pending in that other jurisdiction. In these circumstances, the courts of the demanding jurisdiction are better qualified.[328]

Similarly, in *In re Magrino*, another New York appellate court declined to apply New York's shield law in the context of an application under the Uniform

---

324. 479 F. Supp. 523 (E.D.N.Y. 1979).

325. See Grunseth v. Marriott Corp., 868 F. Supp. 333, 337 (D.D.C. 1994). But cf. In re Grand Jury Subpoena, 947 F. Supp. 1314, 1321 (E.D. Ark. 1996) (New York and Arkansas shield laws inapplicable in context of federal grand jury) (citing In re Grand Jury Proceedings, 867 F.2d 562, 564 (9th Cir.), cert. denied, 493 U.S. 906 (1989)).

326. 868 F. Supp. at 337. See also In re American Gen. Life & Accident Ins. Co., 26 MEDIA L. REP. (BNA) 1606 (N.Y. Sup. Ct. 1996) (not deciding whether New York or Alabama law applied because, under either shield law, movants failed to overcome privilege); Prentice v. McPhilemy, No. 98CA0004309, slip op. at 7 (D.C. Super. May 5, 1999) (D.C. Shield Law applies to protect British journalist who gathered information outside the United States because "to impose such limitations would not further the primary purpose of the Act, namely, to encourage the free flow of information to residents of the District").

327. 626 N.E.2d 636, 641-42 (N.Y. 1993).

328. *Id.*

Act to compel a cable television network to appear and produce video outtakes in a Florida criminal proceeding, even though, in contrast to New York, Florida at the time recognized no constitutional privilege governing such nonbroadcast materials.[329] Nevertheless, the New York court rejected the network's contention that compliance with the Florida subpoena would violate New York's public policy.[330]

The Maryland Court of Special Appeals, in adjudicating a California grand jury's efforts to enforce a subpoena issued to a journalist residing in Maryland, similarly rejected the journalist's efforts to invoke the Maryland shield law.[331] The court held that the journalist was required "to look to California law for protection," because the newsgathering at issue "took place in California, not Maryland."[332] In that regard, the court explained:

> The Maryland Press Shield Law was designed to protect newsmen and newswomen in this State; it has no extraterritorial application. The legislature did not enact the Press Shield Law so as to create a sanctuary to which out-of-state newspersons could flee and thereby avoid disclosure of news sources. . . . [The journalist's] attempted utilization of the Maryland Shield Law is disingenuous. We reject it.[333]

In another proceeding instituted by a California court under the Uniform Act, however, an Ohio trial court concluded that the journalist at issue had not been shown to be a "material and necessary witness" within the meaning of the Uniform Act, largely because he was "entitled to privilege under Ohio and California shield laws and under the First Amendment."[334] The Ohio Court of Appeals agreed that, because the California request sought the name of the journalist's confidential source, it must determine whether he "is a material and

---

329. 640 N.Y.S.2d 545 (App. Div. 1996). Compare Gold Coast Publications, Inc. v. Florida, 669 So. 2d 316 (Fla. App. 1996) and Tampa Television, Inc. v. Norman, 647 So. 2d 904 (Fla. App. 1994) (no privilege protecting nonconfidential materials) with Krase v. Graco Children Prods., Inc., 79 F.3d 346 (2d Cir. 1996) (New York shield law protects outtakes). But see FLA. STAT. § 90.5015 (creating statutory newsgathering privilege that protects nonbroadcast materials); Hager v. Culverhouse, 26 MEDIA L. REP. (BNA) 2599, 2600 (Fla. Cir. 1998) (the "new statutory privilege merely codifies the pre-existing common law and constitutional privilege"). See also Florida v. Smith, 27 MEDIA L. REP. (BNA) 1718 (Fla. Cir. 1999) (applying Florida shield law and refusing to extradite Florida journalists to testify in Georgia murder trial).
330. See 640 N.Y.S.2d at 545. Accord In re Robert Grace, 634 N.Y.S.2d 473 (App. Div. 1995) (trial court applies Uniform Act to subpoena for magazine reporter's notes issued in California criminal proceeding).
331. See In re State of California for the County of Los Angeles Grand Jury Investigation, 471 A.2d 1141 (Md. Spec. App.), cert. denied, 467 U.S. 1205 (1984).
332. Id. at 1145.
333. Id.
334. In re McAuley, 408 N.E.2d 697, 703 (Ohio App. 1979).

necessary witness by applying the law concerning the divulgence of confidential news sources by news reporters," specifically the Ohio shield law.[335]

§ 15-3. Federal Codifications.

Although Congress has not enacted federal shield legislation, all three branches of the federal government have promulgated rules that have served to protect journalists from compelled disclosure of the fruits of their newsgathering activities. Thus, Congress has enacted legislation governing searches of news organizations, the executive branch has promulgated its own rules concerning subpoenas directed at journalists and news organizations, and the rules of procedure that govern litigation in the federal courts have been invoked to protect the newsgathering process as well.

§ 15-3(a). Search Warrants.

In *Zurcher v. Stanford Daily*,[336] the Supreme Court held that neither the First nor Fourth Amendments protects news organizations from the issuance or enforcement of search warrants authorizing unannounced searches of their editorial offices. The plaintiffs in *Zurcher*, the student editors of a college newspaper, instituted a civil rights action against local police who had obtained a warrant and searched the newsroom for photographs of a campus demonstration that had turned violent.[337] The Court rejected the plaintiffs' contention, based on the Fourth Amendment, that a warrant could not properly issue to search premises occupied by someone not suspected of a crime:

> The critical element in a reasonable search is not that the owner of the property is suspected of crime but that there is reasonable cause to believe that the specific "things" to be searched and seized are located on the property to which entry is sought.[338]

---

335. *Id.* at 704. The court of appeals went on to conclude that, although the protections of the Ohio shield law are not absolute — as the trial court had held — in criminal cases, "there was not sufficient evidence upon which to demonstrate" that the reporter "was a material and necessary witness" within the meaning of OHIO REV. CODE ANN. § 2939.25-.29, Ohio's codification of the Uniform Act, because the qualified privilege embodied in judicial construction of the Ohio shield law had not been overcome. 408 N.E.2d at 710.

In *Florida v. Smith*, 27 MEDIA L. REP. (BNA) 1718, 1719 (Fla. Cir. 1999), a Florida trial court declined a request by Georgia authorities to extradite two Florida journalists to testify in a murder prosecution there. Because the Florida shield law protects reporters "against compulsion 'to be a witness,'" the court concluded, "the plain meaning of the statutory privilege requires that this qualified privilege be overcome before the Court enters an order compelling the journalists to attend and give testimony in the Georgia trial." *Id.* (citing FLA. STAT. § 90.5015).

336. 436 U.S. 547 (1978).
337. *Id.* at 550-52.
338. *Id.* at 556.

§ 15-3(a) NEWSGATHERING AND THE LAW § 15-3(a)

In addition, the Court held that the First Amendment provides no special protection to newspapers that would require governmental pursuit of such information to be accomplished through issuance of a subpoena *duces tecum* rather than a search warrant.[339] Especially since the Fourth Amendment itself arose from the "long struggle" between the English "Crown and press," the court held there was no historical support for engrafting additional protections in the name of the First Amendment.[340] Nevertheless, the Court did suggest that, in applying the Fourth Amendment's "reasonableness" requirement in the context of a warrant directed at the news media, a magistrate should consider the First Amendment interests at stake by applying the Fourth Amendment with "scrupulous exactitude."[341]

In the wake of *Zurcher*, Congress enacted the Privacy Protection Act of 1980.[342] The Act, which applies to state, local and federal law enforcement officers alike, strictly prohibits the use of searches and seizures to obtain materials from those engaged in designated First Amendment activities.[343] The legislation is designed to require law enforcement authorities to proceed by subpoena rather than search warrant, in the belief that doing so will "lessen greatly the threat that *Stanford Daily* pose[d] to the vigorous exercise of First Amendment rights."[344] With respect to both "work product materials"[345] and "documentary materials"[346] in the press' possession, therefore, the Act provides that "it shall be

---

339. *Id.* at 564 (citing Stanford v. Texas, 379 U.S. 476, 482 (1965); Marcus v. Search Warrant, 367 U.S. 717, 729 (1961)).

340. 436 U.S. at 565.

341. *Id.* at 564 (citations omitted). See *id.* at 569-70 (Powell, J., concurring) ("a magistrate asked to issue a warrant for the search of press offices can and should take cognizance of the independent values protected by the First Amendment"); Roaden v. Kentucky, 413 U.S. 496, 501 (1973) ("A seizure reasonable as to one type of material in one setting may be unreasonable in a different setting or with respect to another kind of material.").

342. 42 U.S.C. §§ 2000aa – 2000aa-12.

343. See S. REP. NO. 94-874, at 4-5 (1980) [hereinafter "Senate Report"].

344. *Id.* at 4-5.

345. 42 U.S.C. § 2000aa-7(b) defines "Work product materials" as

materials, other than contraband or the fruits of a crime or things otherwise criminally possessed, or property designed or intended for use, or which is or has been used, as the means of committing a criminal offense, and

(1) in anticipation of communicating such materials to the public, are prepared, produced, authored, or created, whether by the person in possession of the materials or by any other person;

(2) are possessed for the purposes of communicating such materials to the public; and

(3) include mental impressions, conclusions, opinions, or theories of the person who prepared, produced, authored, or created such material.

346. 42 U.S.C. § 2000aa-7(a) defines "documentary materials" to include

materials upon which information is recorded, and includes, but is not limited to, written or printed materials, photographs, motion picture films, negatives, video tapes, audio tapes, and

unlawful for a government officer or employee, in connection with the investigation or prosecution of a criminal offense, to search for or seize any work product materials possessed by a person *reasonably believed* to have a purpose to disseminate to the public a newspaper, book, broadcast, or other similar form of public communication, in or affecting interstate commerce" or any "documentary materials possessed by a person in connection with" such a purpose.[347]

The Act's prohibition of search warrants against the press is limited somewhat when the warrant seeks "documentary materials," as opposed to journalistic "work product." In the former circumstance, a warrant may issue when "there is reason to believe that the giving of notice pursuant to subpoena *duces tecum* would result in the destruction, alteration, or concealment" of documentary materials or when the materials have not been produced pursuant to court order.[348] In the context of work product materials, although no search may be authorized in such circumstances, a contempt citation to the journalist or news organization may issue.[349] By the same token, any person "aggrieved by a search for or seizure of materials in violation" of the Act may institute a civil action for money damages against either the responsible governmental entity (provided sovereign immunity has, if necessary, been waived) or officer, although evidence seized in violation of the Act cannot be excluded from evidence on that ground.[350]

There has been relatively little case law generated under the Act. In *Lambert v. Polk County*,[351] where police confiscated videotape of a street fight made by a person whose asserted purpose was "to videotape the nighttime street activities" and sell "anything newsworthy that he might videotape,"[352] the court held that

---

other mechanically, magnetically or electronically recorded cards, tapes or discs, but does not include contraband or the fruits of a crime or things otherwise criminally possessed, or property designed or intended for use, or which is or has been used as, the means of committing a criminal offense.

347. *Id.* §§ 2000aa(a) & (b). The Act's prohibitions do not apply when "there is probable cause to believe that the person possessing such materials has committed or is committing the criminal offense to which the materials relate." *Id.* § 2000aa(a)(1) & (b)(1). But see *id.* (searches remain prohibited if "the offense to which the materials relate consists of the receipt, possession, communication, or withholding of such materials," except in the case of certain classified or national security-related materials).
348. *Id.* §§ 2000aa(b)(3), (b)(4).
349. Senate Report *supra* note 343, at 12.
350. 42 U.S.C. §§ 2000aa-6(a), 6(e). See Minneapolis Star & Tribune Co. v. United States, 713 F. Supp. 1308 (D. Minn. 1989) (discussing reasonableness of awards of attorneys fees and costs under the Act). On November 11, 1996, Congress amended 42 U.S.C. § 2000aa(a)(1) to permit searches and seizures where the offense involves child pornography, the sexual exploitation of children, or the sale or purchase of children.
351. 723 F. Supp. 128 (S.D. Iowa 1989).
352. *Id.* at 131.

the videotape constituted "work product materials" under the Act, which are only protected from seizure if "possessed by a person reasonably believed to have a purpose to disseminate to the public" a newspaper, broadcast or similar communication.[353] Thus, because "[t]here was nothing about the way Lambert presented himself" to the police officers "that would have led them to believe that Lambert's purpose was to make a dissemination of the videotape to the public," the court concluded that a claim under the Act was unlikely to succeed.[354]

In *Steve Jackson Games, Inc. v. United States Secret Service*,[355] another court held that federal agents violated the Act when they searched the offices of a computer bulletin board operator and seized computers, computer disks, and other materials. Although the initial search was deemed proper, because the agents' lack of knowledge of the operator's plans to disseminate the seized materials publicly was reasonable, its ongoing possession of the materials after it gained such knowledge violated the Act.[356]

Finally, in *Citicasters v. McCaskill*,[357] the Eighth Circuit held that a search warrant application need not affirmatively set forth the applicability of an exemption to the statute, and that a law enforcement officer may raise an exemption, for the first time, in the context of litigation under the Act.[358] Accordingly, the court permitted a county prosecutor, who had executed a warrant on a television station seeking a videotape of a murder taken by a tourist, to plead that she had "'reason to believe'" that seizure was necessary to "'prevent death . . . or serious bodily injury'" and to prevent "'destruction, alteration or concealment'" of the videotape,[359] even though her application for a warrant was silent on these issues.

---

353. *Id.* at 132 (quoting 42 U.S.C. § 2000aa(a)).

354. 723 F. Supp. at 132. It would appear, however, that the court's conclusion in this regard may be in error, since the Act specifically defines "documentary materials" to include "materials upon which information is recorded" and expressly references videotapes in that regard. 42 U.S.C. § 2000aa-7(a). "Documentary materials" are protected from seizure, regardless of the law enforcement officer's reasonable belief, so long as they are "possessed by a person *in connection with* a purpose to disseminate" it to the public. *Id.* § 2000aa-7(b) (emphasis added).

355. 816 F. Supp. 432 (W.D. Tex. 1993), *aff'd*, 35 F.3d 457 (5th Cir. 1994).

356. *Id.* at 440-41. In a series of cases arising under the Copyright Act, several courts have held improper searches of the homes and offices of defendants in copyright infringement actions arising from their distribution of allegedly copyrighted materials on the Internet. See, e.g., Religious Tech. Center v. Lerma, 908 F. Supp. 1362 (E.D. Va. 1995); Religious Tech. Center v. FACT Net, Inc., 907 F. Supp. 1468 (D. Colo. 1995); Religious Tech. Center v. Netcom, Inc., 907 F. Supp. 1361 (N.D. Cal. 1995).

357. 89 F.3d 1350, 1352 (8th Cir. 1996).

358. *Id.* at 1353 (quoting 42 U.S.C. § 2000aa(b)(2) & (3)). See also 28 C.F.R. §§ 59.1-59.6 (1995) (Attorney General's guidelines for federal agents).

359. 89 F.3d at 1352. See also United States v. Huner, 13 F. Supp. 2d 574 (D. Vt. 1998) (search of offices of publisher of *Vermont Law Week* did not violate Act because he was suspected of a crime); DePugh v. Sutton, 917 F. Supp. 690 (W.D. Mo. 1996) (same).

§ 15-3(b). Justice Department and Administrative Regulations.

The Justice Department has promulgated regulations governing the issuance of subpoenas to journalists and news organizations and the issuance of subpoenas seeking a journalist's telephone toll records. The regulations proceed from the premise that:

> freedom of the press can be no broader than the freedom of reporters to investigate and report the news, [so that] the prosecutorial power of the government should not be used in such a way that it impairs a reporter's responsibility to cover as broadly as possible controversial public issues. This policy statement is thus intended to provide protection for the news media from forms of compulsory process, whether civil or criminal, which might impair the news gathering function.[360]

Although the regulations "shall be adhered to by all members of the [Justice] Department in all cases," they are "not intended to create or recognize any legally enforceable right in any person."[361] Thus, while failure to obtain prior approval of the Attorney General for a subpoena directed at a journalist "may constitute grounds for an administrative reprimand or other appropriate disciplinary action," the regulations do not contain any sanctions for noncompliance.[362]

The regulations require the Justice Department to "strike the proper balance between the public's interest in the free dissemination of ideas and information and the public's interest in effective law enforcement and the fair administration of justice" by undertaking, prior to the issuance of a subpoena to a journalist or for her telephone toll records:

(1) "[a]ll reasonable attempts . . . to obtain information from alternative sources before considering issuing a subpoena;"[363]
(2) negotiations with the media in all cases in which a subpoena is contemplated;[364] and
(3) to secure "the express authorization of the Attorney General."[365]

---

360. 28 C.F.R. § 50.10. The regulations were first promulgated in 1970, see United States Justice Dep't Mem. No. 692 (Sept. 2, 1970), and were amended in 1980 to include provisions relating to telephone toll records. The regulations do not, however, apply to subpoenas seeking commercial or financial information from a news media entity. See 28 C.F.R. § 50.10(m).

361. *Id.* § 50.10 & 10(n).

362. *Id.*

363. *Id.* § 50.10(b).

364. *Id.* § 50.10(c) & (d). With respect to toll records, however, such negotiations may be pursued only if "the responsible Assistant Attorney General determines that such negotiations would not pose a substantial threat to the integrity of the investigation in connection with which the records are sought." *Id.* § 50.10(d).

365. *Id.* § 50.10(e). If a journalist agrees to provide the material at issue and it already has been published or broadcast, a subpoena may issue upon the authorization of the United States Attorney

If the contemplated subpoena is to be issued directly to a journalist, there "should" — in criminal cases — be "reasonable grounds to believe, based on information obtained from nonmedia sources, that a crime has occurred, and that the information sought is essential to a successful investigation."[366] In a civil case, "there should be reasonable grounds, based on nonmedia sources, to believe that the information sought is essential to the successful completion of the litigation in a case of substantial importance."[367] In neither context is a subpoena to be used to "obtain peripheral, nonessential, or speculative information."[368]

If the subpoena under consideration seeks toll records, it may issue solely in criminal cases.[369] Moreover, "there should be reasonable grounds to believe that a crime has been committed and that the information sought is essential to the successful investigation of the crime."[370] The affected journalist must be given timely notice that a subpoena has been authorized and that the government intends to issue it; if such notice is not given in order to protect the integrity of the investigation, it shall be provided as soon as it no longer poses a "clear and substantial threat to the integrity of the investigation."[371]

Federal courts have reached conflicting conclusions with respect to the legal significance of the Justice Department's failure to comply with its own regulations in a given case.[372] In *In re Shain*,[373] for example, the Fourth Circuit held that the regulation provides only an administrative mechanism of enforcement and expressly disclaims any intent "to create or recognize any legally enforceable right in any person." The court concluded, therefore, that the regulation "is of the kind to be enforced internally by a government department, and not by

---

or the responsible Assistant Attorney General, provided that she is personally satisfied that all other requirements are met. *Id.*

366. *Id.* § 50.10(f)(1).

367. *Id.* § 50.10(f)(2).

368. *Id.* § 50.10(f)(1), (2). All subpoenas directed at journalists "should, except in exigent circumstances, be limited to the verification of published information" and any surrounding circumstances that bear on its accuracy. *Id.* § 50.10(f)(4). Moreover, subpoenas "should, wherever possible, be directed at material information regarding a limited subject matter, should cover a reasonably limited period of time, and should avoid requiring production of a large volume of unpublished material." *Id.* § 50.10(f)(6).

369. *Id.* § 50.10(g)(1).

370. *Id.* In addition, the subpoena "should be as narrowly drawn as possible; it should be directed at relevant information regarding a limited subject matter and should cover a reasonably limited time period." *Id.*

371. *Id.* §§ 50.10(g)(2), (3).

372. Some courts have held that the government complied with the guidelines. See In re Lewis, 384 F. Supp. 133, 140 (C.D. Cal. 1974), *aff'd*, 517 F.2d 236, 238-39 (9th Cir. 1975); In re Lewis, 377 F. Supp. 297, 301 (C.D. Cal.), *aff'd*, 501 F.2d 418, 423 (9th Cir. 1974); In re Grand Jury 95-1, 27 MEDIA L. REP. (BNA) 1833 (D.D.C. 1999).

373. 978 F.2d 850, 853-54 (4th Cir. 1992) (citation omitted).

courts through exclusion of evidence."[374] In *In re Williams*,[375] however, the court quashed subpoenas *duces tecum* directed at reporters in part because it was "manifestly clear that the Government ha[d] not discharged the obligation imposed by" the regulations to make all reasonable efforts to obtain the information sought from nonmedia sources prior to considering issuance of a subpoena to reporters.[376]

Some courts have suggested that the Justice Department regulations apply to other federal agencies as well.[377] Others, when called upon to enforce administrative subpoenas,[378] have indicated that enforcement ought not be routine when First Amendment-related activities are implicated.[379] As the D.C. Circuit has emphasized, "[c]urrent first amendment jurisprudence makes clear that before a state or federal body can compel disclosure of information which would trespass upon first amendment freedoms, a 'subordinating interest of the State' must be proffered, and it must be 'compelling.'"[380] Thus, in the context of administrative subpoenas directed against the press, the D.C. Circuit has had occasion to explain that, "while press figures enjoy no special privilege exempting them from laws of general applicability, some balancing or special sensitivity is required in view of the vital function the press serves in a self-governing society."[381] Accordingly, then-Judge Ginsburg wrote for the court, some accommodation of

---

374. *Id.* at 854 (citing United States v. Caceres, 440 U.S. 741 (1979)). See also In re Grand Jury Subpoena, 947 F. Supp. 1314, 1321-22 (E.D. Ark. 1996). See also Goodale, *Special Prosecutor Scalps the Media*, N.Y.L.J., Dec. 5, 1997, at 3 (federal district court's ruling that guidelines do not apply to special prosecutor in Whitewater investigation may have encouraged alleged "secret arrangements" in which special prosecutors "successfully subpoenaed press outlets and apparently required that the matters be kept secret"); Chap. 16-2(c)(1) *infra*.

375. 766 F. Supp. 358, 359-60 (W.D. Pa. 1991), *aff'd by equally divided court*, 963 F.2d 567 (3d Cir. 1992) (en banc).

376. *Id.* See also United States v. Blanton, 534 F. Supp. 295, 297 (S.D. Fla. 1982) (suggesting that government "must" follow 28 C.F.R. § 50.10); Maurice v. NLRB, 7 MEDIA L. REP. (BNA) 2221 (S.D. W. Va. 1981) (holding 28 C.F.R. § 50.10 applicable to National Labor Relations Board and that "[g]overnment agencies must follow their own regulations when important individual constitutional rights are affected, even if such regulations are more strict and rigid than required by law"), *vacated*, 691 F.2d 182 (4th Cir. 1982) (holding that reporter had failed to exhaust administrative remedies).

377. See note 376 *supra* (citing cases).

378. See generally United States v. Morton Salt Co., 338 U.S. 632 (1950); United States v. Powell, 379 U.S. 48 (1964).

379. See FEC v. Machinists Non-Partisan Political League, 655 F.2d 380, 387 (D.C. Cir. 1981); FEC v. Florida for Kennedy Comm., 681 F.2d 1281 (11th Cir. 1982); FEC v. Phillips Publ'g Co., 517 F. Supp. 1308 (D.D.C. 1981); Readers Digest Ass'n v. FEC, 509 F. Supp. 1210 (S.D.N.Y. 1981).

380. FEC v. Machinists Non-Partisan Political League, 655 F.2d at 389 (quoting NAACP v. Alabama, 357 U.S. 449, 463 (1958)). See also FEC v. Florida for Kennedy Comm., 681 F.2d at 1284-85 & n.7 (explaining that "higher degree" of scrutiny must be applied in First Amendment context).

381. SEC v. McGoff, 647 F.2d 185, 191 (D.C. Cir.), *cert. denied*, 452 U.S. 963 (1981).

First Amendment interests is required "to avoid unnecessary encroachment" on the "activities and associations" of a "newspaper publisher and writer."[382] As the following chapter demonstrates, several courts have, therefore, applied the constitutional privilege in the context of administrative subpoenas directed against the press.[383]

§ 15-3(c). Federal Rules of Procedure.

The federal rules of procedure, criminal and civil, contain a number of restrictions on the ability of litigants to compel the disclosure of information from adversaries and third parties alike. Not surprisingly, therefore, such provisions have been invoked by journalists and news organizations to protect information secured in the course of newsgathering.

Rule 17 of the Federal Rules of Criminal Procedure, which governs the issuance of subpoenas in federal criminal proceedings, provides essentially the only means in a criminal case for compelling the testimony or production of materials in the possession of any third party, including a journalist.[384] Rule 17(c), which governs subpoenas *duces tecum*, provides in part that:

> A subpoena may also command the person to whom it is directed to produce the books, papers, documents or other objects designated therein. The court on motion made promptly may quash or modify the subpoena if compliance would be unreasonable or oppressive.[385]

Courts have had numerous occasions to consider whether a subpoena in a criminal case is "unreasonable or oppressive" within the meaning of Rule 17(c) before addressing the potential applicability of a constitutional privilege.[386] In addition, courts have interpreted Rule 17(c) to require that subpoenaed materials

---

382. *Id.* But cf. Oklahoma Press Publ'g Co. v. Walling, 327 U.S. 186, 193 (1946) (rejecting newspaper publisher's challenge to subpoena issued by Administrator of Fair Labor Standards Act on ground that First Amendment "does not forbid this or other regulation which ends in no restraint upon expression or in any other evil outlawed by its terms and purposes").

383. See Chap. 16 *infra*.

384. See United States v. Cuthbertson, 651 F.2d 189, 195 (3d Cir.), *cert. denied*, 454 U.S. 1056 (1981) (explaining that exculpatory evidence in the possession of third parties is retrievable only pursuant to Fed. R. Civ. P. 17(c)).

385. Fed. R. Crim. P. 17(c).

386. See, e.g., United States v. Nixon, 418 U.S. 683, 697-98 (1974) (if Rule 17 is not satisfied, "there would be no occasion to reach the [constitutional] claim of [absolute executive] privilege asserted with respect to the subpoenaed material"); In re Grand Jury 95-1, 27 MEDIA L. REP. (BNA) 1833 (D.D.C. 1999) (finding that compliance with subpoena would not be unreasonable or oppressive under Fed. R. Crim. P. 17(c), before also finding that enforcement of subpoena was not prohibited by common law or First Amendment-based privilege).

be admissible at trial.[387] In *United States v. LaRouche Campaign*,[388] for example, the First Circuit held that certain outtakes of a television network's interview with a key government witness satisfied the relevance and admissibility requirement of Rule 17 because it was likely "the outtakes would reveal inconsistent statements and bias; that is, relevant evidence, admissible at trial."[389] The court, therefore, proceeded to consider the applicability of the constitutional privilege.[390]

Other courts have held that evidence sought from the press only for impeachment purposes does not satisfy the requirements of Rule 17(c).[391] As the Third Circuit explained in *United States v. Cuthbertson*,[392] "because such statements ripen into evidentiary material for purposes of impeachment only if and when the witness testifies at trial, impeachment statements, although subject to subpoena under Rule 17(c), generally are not subject to production and inspection by the moving party prior to trial."[393] Also in *Cuthbertson*, the Third Circuit concluded that Rule 17(c) is not satisfied with respect to "statements by nonwitnesses" based solely on a "general assertion that this material might contain exculpatory information."[394] In this regard, the court emphasized that judges "must be careful that Rule 17(c) is not turned into a broad discovery device, thereby undercutting the strict limitation of discovery in criminal cases found in Fed. R. Crim. P. 16."[395]

The Federal Rules of Civil Procedure, of course, provide for significantly broader discovery than their criminal counterparts and contemplate a range of discovery devices, including interrogatories, requests for production of documents and for admissions, and depositions of parties, as well as subpoenas *duces*

---

387. See, e.g., United States v. Cuthbertson, 630 F.2d 139, 144 (3d Cir. 1980), *cert. denied*, 449 U.S. 1126 (1981). See generally Bowman Dairy Co. v. United States, 341 U.S. 214, 220 (1951); United States v. Nixon, 418 U.S. 683, 699-700 (1974).

388. 841 F.2d 1176 (1st Cir. 1988).

389. *Id.* at 1180. See also United States v. Cutler, 6 F.3d 67, 73 (2d Cir. 1993) (attorney defendant in contempt proceeding entitled to all of his own statements memorialized in reporter's unpublished notes under Rule 17(c) because they "were probably the *only* significant proof regarding his assertedly criminal behavior" in talking to press in violation of gag order).

390. See Chap. 16-2(c)(1) *infra* (discussing application of constitutional privilege in *LaRouche*).

391. See, e.g., United States v. Cuthbertson, 651 F.2d at 192.

392. 630 F.2d at 144.

393. Accord United States v. Cuthbertson, 651 F.2d at 195 ("Neither the government nor the defendants have explained how the CBS materials could be admissible as evidence, unless the interviewees testified and made inconsistent statements."). But cf. United States v. LaRouche Campaign, 841 F.2d at 1180 (whether to enforce subpoena seeking production of impeachment materials "is left to the sound discretion of the district court").

394. 630 F.2d at 145-46.

395. *Id.* at 146.

tecum and *ad testificandum* directed at nonparties.[396] The press has found itself subject to all of these forms of civil discovery.[397]

Rule 26(b)(2) provides that, separate and apart from any applicable privilege, a trial court must limit discovery pursuant to its terms:

> The frequency of extent of use of the discovery methods otherwise permitted under these rules and by any local rule shall be limited by the court if it determines that: (i) the discovery sought is unreasonably cumulative or duplicative, or is obtainable from some other source that is more convenient, less burdensome, or less expensive; (ii) the party seeking discovery has had ample opportunity by discovery in the action to obtain the information sought; or (iii) the burden or expense of the proposed discovery outweighs its likely benefit, taking into account the needs of the case, the amount in controversy, the parties' resources, the importance of the issues at stake in the litigation, and the importance of the proposed discovery in resolving the issue.[398]

Moreover, Rule 26(c) further authorizes a court to grant such protective orders as "justice requires to protect a party or person from annoyance, embarrassment, oppression, or undue burden or expense."[399]

In *Herbert v. Lando*,[400] the Supreme Court suggested that the aforementioned rules grant trial judges "ample power" to protect journalists from "abuse" of the civil discovery process. Indeed, the Court asserted that although

> the deposition-discovery rules are to be accorded a broad and liberal treatment to effect their purpose of adequately informing the litigants in civil trials . . . , the discovery provisions, like all of the Federal Rules of Civil Procedure, are subject to the injunction of Rule 1 that they "be construed to secure the just, *speedy*, and *inexpensive* determination of every action." . . . To this end, the requirements of Rule 26(b)(1) that the material sought in discovery be "relevant" should be firmly applied, and the district courts should not neglect their power to restrict discovery where "justice requires [protection for] a party or person from annoyance, embarrassment, oppression, or undue burden or expense."[401]

---

396. See, e.g., Fed. R. Civ. P. 30(a)(1) (depositions); 33(a) (interrogatories); 34(a) (requests for the production of documents); 36 (requests for admission); 45 (subpoenas).
397. See, e.g., Zerilli v. Smith, 656 F.2d 705, 710 (D.C. Cir. 1981); Baker v. F & F Inv., 470 F.2d 778, 781 (2d Cir. 1972), *cert. denied*, 411 U.S. 966 (1973).
398. Fed. R. Civ. P. 26(b).
399. Fed. R. Civ. P. 26(c).
400. 441 U.S. 153, 177 (1979).
401. *Id.* (emphasis in original) (citations omitted).

In that regard, Justice Powell wrote separately in *Herbert* "to emphasize the additional point that, in supervising discovery in a libel suit by a public figure, a district court has a duty to consider First Amendment interests as well as the private interests of the plaintiff" because, when a "discovery demand arguably impinges on First Amendment rights a district court should measure the degree of relevance required in light of both the private needs of the parties and the public concerns implicated."[402] Especially in libel cases, courts have relied on this language in *Herbert* to call for "the application of Fed. R. Civ. P. 26 . . . with a heightened sensitivity to any First Amendment implication that might result from the compelled disclosure of sources."[403]

---

402. *Id.* at 178-79 (Powell, J., concurring).
403. Bruno & Stillman, Inc. v. Globe Newspaper Co., 633 F.2d 583, 596 (1st Cir. 1980). See also In re Cusumano, 162 F.3d 708 (1st Cir. 1998) (third party subpoena to academic authors in antitrust action quashed pursuant to Rule 26) (citing *Bruno & Stillman, Inc.*).

Chapter 16

THE CONSTITUTIONAL AND COMMON LAW PRIVILEGES

§ 16-1. Introduction.
§ 16-2. The Constitutional Privilege.
   § 16-2(a). Judicial Acceptance.
      § 16-2(a)(1). Federal Courts.
      § 16-2(a)(2). State Courts.
   § 16-2(b). Recipients of Protection.
      § 16-2(b)(1). Definitional Issues.
      § 16-2(b)(2). Standing Issues.
   § 16-2(c). Nature of the Proceedings.
      § 16-2(c)(1). Criminal Proceedings.
      § 16-2(c)(2). Civil Proceedings.
         § 16-2(c)(2)(A). Third-Party Proceedings.
         § 16-2(c)(2)(B). The Press as a Party.
   § 16-2(d). Scope of Protection.
      § 16-2(d)(1). Sources of Information.
      § 16-2(d)(2). Other Confidential Information.
      § 16-2(d)(3). Nonconfidential Information.
         § 16-2(d)(3)(A). Nonconfidential Sources.
         § 16-2(d)(3)(B). Eyewitness Testimony.
         § 16-2(d)(3)(C). Unpublished Information.
         § 16-2(d)(3)(D). Published Information.
   § 16-2(e). Contours of the Privilege.
      § 16-2(e)(1). Generally.
      § 16-2(e)(2). Relevance Requirements.
      § 16-2(e)(3). Exhaustion Requirements.
      § 16-2(e)(4). Other Requirements.
   § 16-2(f). Penalties for Non-Disclosure.
   § 16-2(g). Waiver.
   § 16-2(h). Procedural Requirements.
      § 16-2(h)(1). In Camera Review.
      § 16-2(h)(2). Appellate Review.
   § 16-2(i). Choice of Law.
   § 16-2(j). Avoiding the Privilege.
      § 16-2(j)(1). Third Party Subpoenas.
      § 16-2(j)(2). Other Non-Traditional Subpoenas.
§ 16-3. Common Law Privilege.

§ 16-1. Introduction.

In the decades since the Supreme Court decided *Branzburg v. Hayes*,[1] the lower courts have developed a rich body of decisional law explicating the contours of a constitutional privilege grounded in the First Amendment. In addition,

---

1. 408 U.S. 665 (1972).

a handful of state courts have fashioned common law privileges of similar import to protect the workproduct of journalists. In the pages that follow, we explore case law that, along with the precedent surrounding the shield legislation discussed in the preceding chapter, constitutes the decisional law of reporters' privilege.

§ 16-2. The Constitutional Privilege.

§ 16-2(a). Judicial Acceptance.

§ 16-2(a)(1). Federal Courts.

As discussed in Chapter 14-6, the vast majority of federal and state courts have, in the wake of *Branzburg*, embraced some species of qualified reporters' privilege in the name of the First Amendment. Every federal circuit that has expressly considered the issue, save the Sixth, has recognized the privilege.[2] The

---

2. Those federal circuits that have adopted the qualified privilege, and the appellate case law defining its contours, include:

(1) the District of Columbia Circuit, see Carey v. Hume, 492 F.2d 631 (D.C. Cir.), *cert. dismissed*, 417 U.S. 938 (1974); Zerilli v. Smith, 656 F.2d 705 (D.C. Cir. 1981); Clyburn v. News World Communications, Inc., 903 F.2d 29 (D.C. Cir. 1990);

(2) the First Circuit, see Bruno & Stillman, Inc. v. Globe Newspaper Co., 633 F.2d 583 (1st Cir. 1980); United States v. LaRouche Campaign, 841 F.2d 1176 (1st Cir. 1988); In re Cusumano, 162 F.3d 708 (1st Cir. 1998);

(3) the Second Circuit, see Baker v. F & F Inv., 470 F.2d 778 (2d Cir. 1972), *cert. denied*, 411 U.S. 966 (1973); In re Petroleum Prods. Antitrust Litig., 680 F.2d 5 (2d Cir.), *cert. denied*, 459 U.S. 909 (1982); United States v. Burke, 700 F.2d 70 (2d Cir.), *cert. denied*, 464 U.S. 816 (1983); von Bulow v. von Bulow, 811 F.2d 136 (2d Cir.), *cert. denied*, 481 U.S. 1015 (1987); United States v. Cutler, 6 F.3d 67 (2d Cir. 1993); Krase v. Graco Children Prods., Inc., 79 F.3d 346 (2d Cir. 1996); Gonzales v. National Broadcasting Co., 1998 U.S. App. LEXIS 38583, *22 n.6 (2d Cir. Aug. 27, 1999) (suggesting that privilege may be grounded in federal common law rather than in the Constitution);

(4) the Third Circuit, see Riley v. City of Chester, 612 F.2d 708 (3d Cir. 1979); United States v. Cuthbertson, 630 F.2d 139 (3d Cir. 1980), *cert. denied*, 449 U.S. 1126 (1981); United States v. Cuthbertson, 651 F.2d 189 (3d Cir.), *cert. denied*, 454 U.S. 1056 (1981); United States v. Criden, 633 F.2d 346 (3d Cir. 1980), *cert. denied*, 449 U.S. 1113 (1981); In re Gronowicz, 764 F.2d 983 (3d Cir. 1985), *cert. denied*, 474 U.S. 1055 (1986);

(5) the Fourth Circuit, see United States v. Steelhammer, 539 F.2d 373 (4th Cir. 1976), *modified*, 561 F.2d 539 (4th Cir. 1977) (en banc); LaRouche v. National Broadcasting Co., 780 F.2d 1134 (4th Cir.), *cert. denied*, 479 U.S. 818 (1986); In re Grand Jury Subpoena, 955 F.2d 229 (4th Cir. 1992); In re Shain, 978 F.2d 850 (4th Cir. 1992); Church of Scientology Int'l v. Daniels, 992 F.2d 1329 (4th Cir.), *cert. denied*, 510 U.S. 869 (1993);

(6) the Fifth Circuit, see Miller v. Transamerican Press, Inc., 621 F.2d 721 (5th Cir. 1980), *cert. denied*, 450 U.S. 1041 (1981); In re Selcraig, 705 F.2d 789 (5th Cir. 1983); United States v. Smith, 135 F.3d 963 (5th Cir. 1998);

(7) the Eighth Circuit, see Cervantes v. Time, Inc., 464 F.2d 986 (8th Cir. 1972), *cert. denied*, 409 U.S. 1125 (1973); Gialde v. Time, Inc., 480 F.2d 1295 (8th Cir. 1973);

Sixth Circuit has rejected a claim of constitutional privilege asserted in the grand jury context, though even that decision, in *In re Grand Jury Proceedings*,[3] required courts, in the name of the First Amendment, to determine "whether the reporter is being harassed in order to disrupt his relationship with confidential news sources, whether the grand jury's investigation is being conducted in good faith, whether the information sought bears more than a tenuous relationship to the subject of the investigation, and whether a legitimate law enforcement need will be served by the forced disclosure of the confidential relationship."[4] The Sixth Circuit has not had occasion to consider an assertion of reporters' privilege outside the grand jury context.[5]

The Seventh Circuit has not yet directly addressed a claim of constitutional reporters' privilege in any context. In *Deitchman v. E.R. Squibb & Sons*,[6] however, that court, citing *Branzburg*, held that a scientific researcher enjoyed a qualified privilege to maintain his working files in confidence, a privilege that could be overcome only to prevent a "miscarriage of justice."[7] Moreover, the Seventh Circuit has affirmed a district court order quashing a subpoena directed

---

(8) the Ninth Circuit, see Lewis v. United States, 517 F.2d 236 (9th Cir. 1975); Farr v. Pitchess, 522 F.2d 464 (9th Cir. 1975), *cert. denied*, 427 U.S. 912 (1976); In re Grand Jury Proceedings, 5 F.3d 397 (9th Cir. 1993), *cert. denied*, 510 U.S. 1041 (1994); Star Editorial, Inc. v. United States Dist. Ct., 7 F.3d 856 (9th Cir. 1993); Shoen v. Shoen, 5 F.3d 1289 (9th Cir. 1993); Shoen v. Shoen, 48 F.3d 412 (9th Cir. 1995);

(9) the Tenth Circuit, see Silkwood v. Kerr-McGee Corp., 563 F.2d 433 (10th Cir. 1977); and

(10) the Eleventh Circuit, see United States v. Caporale, 806 F.2d 1487 (11th Cir. 1986), *cert. denied*, 482 U.S. 917 (1987).

3. 810 F.2d 580 (6th Cir. 1987).

4. *Id.* at 585. But cf. Southwell v. Southern Poverty Law Center, 949 F. Supp. 1303 (W.D. Mich. 1996) (recognizing constitutional privilege in defamation context).

5. The Sixth Circuit has held, in the context of lawful commercial speech, that a nonparty newspaper need not comply with a subpoena to disclose the identity of an employer who placed an anonymous job advertisement, where the movant "has failed to convincingly persuade this court that the exercise of the subpoena power . . . is the least extensive means by which the [movant] could reasonably expect to proceed, without unnecessarily burdening [the newspaper]'s constitutional right to free expression." NLRB v. Midland Daily News, 151 F.3d 472, 475 (6th Cir. 1998). Cf. NLRB v. The Bakersfield Californian, 128 F.3d 1339, 1342 (9th Cir. 1997) (newspaper must disclose identity of anonymous advertiser because "[w]ithout this information, the NLRB will almost certainly be unable to identify the anonymous employer, and the investigation [into unfair labor practices] will be unable to proceed").

6. 740 F.2d 556 (7th Cir. 1984).

7. *Id.* at 559 (citing Branzburg v. Hayes, 408 U.S. 665, 709-10 (1972) (Powell, J., concurring)). In *Desai v. Hersh*, 954 F.2d 1408, 1411-12 (7th Cir.), *cert. denied*, 506 U.S. 865 (1992), the Seventh Circuit applied the Illinois Shield Law, 735 ILL. COMP. STAT. 5/8-903, to affirm a lower court decision that a journalist-defendant in a defamation action could testify about the reliability and background of his confidential sources without revealing their identities to the plaintiff. It did not, however, consider the availability of a constitutional privilege. See also United States v. Lloyd, 71 F.3d 1256, 1268-69 (7th Cir. 1995), *cert. denied*, 517 U.S. 1250 (1996) (quashing subpoena of reporter in criminal case on ground that testimony was speculative and not probative in any event).

at a reporter and several other trial courts have expressly recognized the constitutional privilege.[8]

Among those federal circuits that have recognized the privilege, there continues to be significant divergence of analysis. As the discussion in Chapter 14-6 suggests, some circuits that have recognized an expansive constitutional privilege in the civil context have declined to do so in criminal cases. In *In re Shain*,[9] for example, the Fourth Circuit, which has applied a broad constitutional privilege in the civil arena,[10] appeared to limit its reach in criminal cases, holding that Justice White's opinion in *Branzburg*, coupled with Justice Powell's concurring opinion, forecloses assertion of the privilege in "the absence of confidentiality" of the information sought or "vindictiveness" by the subpoenaing party.[11] Similarly, as discussed in Chapter 14-6, in *United States v. Cutler*,[12] the Second Circuit appeared to restrict, albeit in *dicta*, the availability of the broad privilege it had previously recognized in the criminal context in *United States v. Burke*,[13]

---

8. See, e.g., United States v. Lloyd, 71 F.3d 1256, 1268-1269 (7th Cir. 1995); Gulliver's Periodicals, Ltd. v. Chas. Levy Circulating Co., 455 F. Supp. 1197, 1202 (N.D. Ill. 1978) ("Because freedom of the press is implicated, disclosure of confidential sources should not be ordered absent a showing, bordering on a compelling reason, in favor of such disclosure."); United States v. Lopez, 14 MEDIA L. REP. (BNA) 2203, 2204 (N.D. Ill. 1987) ("Although the Seventh Circuit has not yet addressed the question of a reporter's qualified privilege, this court has previously recognized the privilege," and argument that it does not apply in criminal as well as civil cases is "without merit"); United States v. Bingham, 765 F. Supp. 954, 956 (N.D. Ill. 1991) (same); Warzon v. Drew, 155 F.R.D. 183, 186-87 (E.D. Wis. 1994) (recognizing privilege in civil context and granting motion to quash); Neal v. City of Harvey, Illinois, 173 F.R.D. 231 (N.D. Ill. 1997).

9. 978 F.2d 850 (4th Cir. 1992).

10. See, e.g., LaRouche v. National Broadcasting Co., 780 F.2d 1134 (4th Cir.), *cert. denied*, 479 U.S. 818 (1986); Church of Scientology Int'l v. Daniels, 992 F.2d 1329 (4th Cir.), *cert. denied*, 510 U.S. 869 (1993).

11. In re Shain, 978 F.2d at 853. See also United States v. Smith, 135 F.3d 963, 972 (5th Cir. 1998) (declining to recognize privilege not to disclose nonconfidential information in criminal cases).

12. 6 F.3d 67 (2d Cir. 1993).

13. 700 F.2d 70 (2d Cir.), *cert. denied*, 464 U.S. 816 (1983). See United States v. Cutler, 6 F.3d at 73:

[T]he holding in Burke was that the materials sought by the defense, "virtually every document and tape ... that in any way related to the [magazine] article" co-authored by the prosecution witness whom the defense sought to impeach, ... would have been "merely cumulative" in view of "extensive impeachment evidence" concerning the witness that was already in the trial record. ... Burke's articulation of a general test applicable to all phases of a criminal trial was not necessary to the resolution of that case; Burke should accordingly be considered limited to its facts.

Although the panel in *Cutler* indicated, by footnote at this point in the opinion, that it "has been circulated to the active members of this court prior to filing," *id.* at 73 n.5, it proceeded to categorize its own comments as *dicta* as well, see *id.* at 73 ("In any event, as will appear, the

only to disavow such a reading of *Cutler* in *Krase v. Graco Children Products, Inc.*[14] And, in *Gonzales v. National Broadcasting Co.*,[15] a panel of the same court purported to hold that, despite its previous suggestions to the contrary,[16] the privilege does not apply to protect against the compelled disclosure of nonconfidential information at all, a determination that the same panel thereafter repudiated on rehearing, albeit with the suggestion that the privilege may be properly grounded, not in the First Amendment, but in federal common law.[17]

The Eighth Circuit, which has not had occasion to consider the privilege since its early decisions in *Cervantes v. Time, Inc.*[18] and *Gialde v. Time, Inc.*,[19] held in those defamation actions that it could not "routinely grant motions seeking compulsory disclosure of anonymous news sources without first inquiring into the substance of a libel allegation," because to do so would "utterly emasculate the fundamental principles that underlay the line of cases articulating the constitutional restrictions to be engrafted upon the enforcement of State libel laws."[20] Although the court in *Cervantes* held that the libel plaintiff there had not brought forward sufficient evidence either to survive summary judgment or to warrant compelled disclosure of confidential sources, it did not formulate a specific standard against which to measure a claim of constitutional privilege. Lower courts in the Eighth Circuit have, however, adopted such standards borrowed from the decisions of other federal appellate courts.[21]

Some lower federal courts have read their own circuits' precedent narrowly to defeat a claim of constitutional privilege. In *In re Grand Jury Subpoena*, for example, a federal district court in Arkansas found that *Cervantes* "had no

---

resolution of the issues presented by this appeal does not require direct confrontation of the claimed conflict between *Branzburg* and *Burke* that Cutler argues to us.").

14. 79 F.3d 346, 353 (2d Cir. 1996). Although the court's decision in *Krase v. Graco Children Products, Inc.* is premised on the New York Shield Law, N.Y. CIV. RIGHTS LAW § 79-h, its opinion asserted that *Cutler* embraced "a standard identical to that embodied in the New York Shield Law," *id.* at 353, which itself mirrors the standard previously articulated by the Second Circuit in *Burke*. See 700 F.2d at 76-77.

15. 1998 U.S. App. LEXIS 38583 (2d Cir. Aug. 27, 1999); see also Gonzales v. National Broadcasting Co., 155 F.3d 618 (2d Cir. 1998), *vacated*, No. 97-9454 (2d Cir. June 1, 1999).

16. See, e.g., In re Petroleum Prods. Antitrust Litig., 680 F.2d 5 (2d Cir.), *cert. denied*, 459 U.S. 909 (1982).

17. See 1998 U.S. App. LEXIS 38583, at *21 ("the qualified privilege protecting press materials from disclosure applies to nonconfidential as well as to confidential materials"); *id.* at *22 n.6 (noting that "[u]ntil Congress legislates to modify the privilege or do away with it," it is unnecessary to determine whether it "is constitutionally required, or rooted in federal common law").

18. 464 F.2d 986 (8th Cir. 1972), *cert. denied*, 409 U.S. 1125 (1973).

19. 480 F.2d 1295 (8th Cir. 1973).

20. Cervantes v. Time, Inc., 464 F.2d at 993.

21. See, e.g., Lauderback v. American Broadcasting Cos., 8 MEDIA L. REP. (BNA) 2407 (N.D. Iowa 1982); Williams v. American Broadcasting Cos., 96 F.R.D. 658 (W.D. Ark. 1983).

application to grand jury proceedings."[22] The Office of Independent Counsel had issued a grand jury subpoena seeking the transcript and videotape of an ABC interview with Susan McDougal, a central figure in the Whitewater investigation. The court rejected ABC's assertion of privilege, holding that *Branzburg* foreclosed its application in the grand jury context, absent evidence of bad faith by the government or official harassment of the press.[23]

In recent years, several federal circuits have developed a rich, sophisticated body of precedent elucidating the contours of the constitutional privilege. In the space of two years, for example, the Ninth Circuit created a substantial framework surrounding the privilege it had first recognized almost twenty years earlier in *Farr v. Pitchess*.[24] In three separate cases decided in a single year, the court held that (1) the scope of the constitutional privilege is comparatively narrow in the grand jury context;[25] (2) a more expansive privilege, derived from state law, applies to efforts by a libel plaintiff to compel disclosure of the defendant's sources;[26] and (3) that same privilege affords nonparty journalists broad protection from compelled disclosure of unpublished information in civil litigation.[27] Two years later, after further proceedings on remand in the latter case, the Ninth Circuit took pains to emphasize that "routine court-compelled disclosure of research materials poses a serious threat to the vitality of the newsgathering process" and that "compelled disclosure is the exception, not the rule."[28]

---

22. 947 F. Supp. 1314, 1320 (E.D. Ark. 1996).
23. *Id.* at 1318. See also In re Grand Jury 95-1, 27 MEDIA L. REP. (BNA) 1833 (D.D.C. 1999) (privilege does not apply to grand jury subpoena seeking nonconfidential information).
24. 522 F.2d 464 (9th Cir. 1975), *cert. denied*, 427 U.S. 912 (1976).
25. See In re Grand Jury Proceedings, 5 F.3d 397, 401 (9th Cir. 1993), *cert. denied*, 510 U.S. 1041 (1994):

> [W]here a grand jury inquiry is not conducted in good faith, or where the inquiry does not involve a legitimate need of law enforcement, or has only a remote and tenuous relationship to the subject of the investigation, the balance of interests struck by the Branzburg majority may not be controlling.

26. See Star Editorial, Inc. v. United States Dist. Ct., 7 F.3d 856, 861 (9th Cir. 1993) (recognizing privilege, but holding that it can be overcome in a public figure libel case, where plaintiff must "prove actual malice to succeed").
27. See Shoen v. Shoen, 5 F.3d 1289, 1292, 1294 (9th Cir. 1993) ("when facts acquired by a journalist in the course of gathering the news become the target of discovery, a qualified privilege against compelled disclosure comes into play" and "protects a journalist's resource materials regardless of whether these materials contain confidential information").
28. Shoen v. Shoen, 48 F.3d 412, 416 (9th Cir. 1995). But see United States v. Smith, 135 F.3d 963 (5th Cir. 1998) (holding that privilege does not apply to nonconfidential materials).

§ 16-2(a)(2). State Courts.

Like their counterparts in the federal system, the courts of most states have recognized some form of constitutional privilege.[29] In addition, several state courts, sitting in jurisdictions in which the legislature has promulgated a shield law, have looked to the statute as a source of the privilege and have either not had occasion to address the constitutional privilege[30] or have held that the applicable shield law embodies whatever such privilege may otherwise be available.[31] Because of the relatively narrow reach of some shield statutes, however,

---

29. See Norandal, U.S.A., Inc. v. Local Union No. 7468, 13 MEDIA L. REP. (BNA) 2167, 2168 (Ala. Cir. 1986); Nebel v. Mapco Petroleum, Inc., 10 MEDIA L. REP. (BNA) 1871, 1872 (Alaska 1984); Matera v. Superior Ct., 825 P.2d 971, 973 (Ariz. App. 1992); Mitchell v. Superior Ct., 690 P.2d 625, 632 (Cal. 1984); In re Grand Jury Subpoenas, 8 MEDIA L. REP. (BNA) 1418, 1419 (D. Colo. 1982); Connecticut State Bd. of Labor Relations v. Fagin, 370 A.2d 1095, 1097-98 (Conn. Super. 1976); Delaware v. Hall, 16 MEDIA L. REP. (BNA) 1414, 1414-15 (Del. Mun. 1989); Florida v. Davis, 720 So. 2d 220 (Fla. 1998); DeRoburt v. Gannett Co., 507 F. Supp. 880, 886 (D. Haw. 1981); Idaho v. Salsbury, 924 P.2d 208 (Idaho 1996); In re Wright, 700 P.2d 40, 41 (Idaho 1985); Winegard v. Oxberger, 258 N.W.2d 847, 850-52 (Iowa 1977), *cert. denied*, 436 U.S. 905 (1978); Kansas v. Sandstrom, 581 P.2d 812, 814-15 (Kan. 1978), *cert. denied*, 440 U.S. 929 (1979); In re Grand Jury Proceeding (Ridenhour), 520 So. 2d 372, 376 (La. 1988); In re Letellier, 578 A.2d 722, 726 (Me. 1990); Sinnott v. Boston Retirement Bd., 524 N.E.2d 100, 104 (Mass.), *cert. denied*, 488 U.S. 980 (1988); In re Photo Mktg. Ass'n Int'l, 327 N.W.2d 515 (Mich. App. 1982); CBS Inc. v. Campbell, 645 S.W.2d 30, 32-33 (Mo. App. 1982); Missouri ex rel. Classic III, Inc. v. Ely, 954 S.W.2d 650 (Mo. App. 1997); Montana ex rel. Blackberry v. District Ct., 546 P.2d 988 (Mont. 1976); Nevada v. Bazile, CR98-0388 (Nev. County Ct. Feb. 19, 1999); Opinion of the Justices, 373 A.2d 644 (N.H. 1977); New Hampshire v. Siel, 444 A.2d 499, 502-03 (N.H. 1982); O'Neill v. Oakgrove Constr., Inc., 523 N.E.2d 277, 277-78 (N.Y. 1988); North Carolina v. Rogers, 9 MEDIA L. REP. (BNA) 1254, 1255 (N.C. 1983); Taylor v. Miskovsky, 640 P.2d 959, 961-62 (Okla. 1981); Davis v. Glanton, 705 A.2d 879 (Pa. Super. 1997); Hopewell v. Midcontinent Broadcasting Corp., 538 N.W.2d 780, 782 (S.D. 1995), *cert. denied*, 519 U.S. 817 (1996); Dallas Morning News Co. v. Garcia, 822 S.W.2d 675, 678-79 (Tex. App. 1991); Vermont v. St. Peter, 315 A.2d 254, 255 (Vt. 1974); Brown v. Virginia, 204 S.E.2d 429, 430-31 (Va.), *cert. denied*, 419 U.S. 966 (1974); West Virginia ex rel. Hudok v. Henry, 389 S.E.2d 188, 193 (W. Va. 1989) West Virginia ex rel. Charleston Mail Ass'n v. Ranson, 488 S.E.2d 5 (W. Va. 1997); Zelenka v. Wisconsin, 266 N.W.2d 279 (Wis. 1978).

30. These states include Illinois, Minnesota, Nebraska, New Mexico, North Dakota, Tennessee and South Carolina. In Illinois, for example, the state courts have relied on the Illinois shield law in adjudicating privilege claims, although several federal courts sitting in Illinois have recognized the constitutional privilege. See, e.g., Gulliver's Periodicals, Ltd. v. Chas. Levy Circulating Co., 455 F. Supp. 1197 (N.D. Ill. 1978); Alexander v. Chicago Park Dist., 548 F. Supp. 277 (N.D. Ill. 1982); United States v. Bingham, 765 F. Supp. 954 (N.D. Ill. 1991). The North Dakota Supreme Court has affirmatively declined to opine on the validity of the constitutional privilege because of the North Dakota shield law. See Grand Forks Herald v. District Ct., 322 N.W.2d 850, 853 (N.D. 1982) (citing N.D. CENT. CODE § 31-01-06.2).

31. See, e.g., Bartlett v. Superior Ct., 722 P.2d 346, 350-52 (Ariz. App. 1986); Matera v. Superior Ct., 825 P.2d 971, 974 (Ariz. App. 1992) ("[t]he constitutional privilege afforded to reporters in Arizona is codified at [ARIZ. REV. STAT.] § 12-2237"); Lightman v. Maryland, 294 A.2d 149, 157 (Md. Spec. App.), *aff'd*, 295 A.2d 212 (Md. 1972), *cert. denied*, 411 U.S. 951

several state courts have held that the constitution provides protections extending beyond that afforded by the legislatively created privilege.[32]

In *Mitchell v. Superior Court*,[33] for example, the California Supreme Court recognized a broad constitutional privilege arising under both the First Amendment and the analogous provision of the California Constitution. The court reached the issue of constitutional privilege because the immunity from contempt provided by the state shield law did not appear to protect defendant jour-

---

(1973); Marketos v. American Employers Ins. Co., 460 N.W.2d 272, 279 (Mich. App. 1990) ("we are unpersuaded that a journalist's privilege as to nonconfidential materials is compelled by the First Amendment"); WTHR-TV v. Cline, 693 N.E.2d 1, 13 (Ind. 1998) ("[W]e assume without deciding that *Branzburg* did not completely close the door to a qualified reporter's privilege based on the federal constitution. We conclude, however, that the [defendants] have not made the case for recognizing the privilege . . . even if the question is an open one as a general proposition."); Newburn v. Howard Hughes Med. Inst., 594 P.2d 1146, 1148 (Nev. 1979); Capuano v. Outlet Co., 579 A.2d 469, 475 (R.I. 1990); Outlet Communications, Inc. v. Rhode Island, 588 A.2d 1050, 1052 (R.I. 1991). See also Hager v. Culverhouse, 26 MEDIA L. REP. (BNA) 2599, 2600 (Fla. Cir. 1998) (newly created "statutory privilege merely codifies the pre-existing common law and constitutional privilege that protected journalists from compelled testimony"). Cf. In re Taylor, 193 A.2d 181, 184 (Pa. 1963) (prior to *Branzburg*, Pennsylvania Supreme Court applied state shield law, but noted that "the language of [the United States and Pennsylvania] Constitution[s] is clear, and by no stretch of language can it protect or include under 'freedom of the press,' the non-disclosure of sources of information").

32. See Norandal USA, Inc. v. Local Union No. 7468, 13 MEDIA L. REP. (BNA) 2167, 2168 (Ala. Cir. 1986) (although Alabama shield law protects only confidential information, constitutional privilege protects unpublished, nonconfidential material acquired in newsgathering process); Coney v. Alaska, 699 P.2d 899, 902 (Alaska App. 1985); Alaska v. Pruett, 11 MEDIA L. REP. (BNA) 1968 (Alaska Super. 1984); Rancho Publications v. Superior Ct., 81 Cal. Rptr. 2d 274, 279 (Ct. App. 1999) (while California shield law does not encompass paid advertisements not obtained "for journalistic purpose of communicating information to the public," qualified constitutional privilege protected newspaper against compelled disclosure of anonymous sources of advertisement); Delaware v. McBride, 7 MEDIA L. REP. (BNA) 1371, 1371 (Del. Super. 1981); O'Neill v. Oakgrove Constr., Inc., 523 N.E.2d 277, 277-78 (N.Y. 1988); McMenamin v. Tartaglione, 590 A.2d 802, 811 (Pa. Commw.), *aff'd*, 590 A.2d 753 (Pa. 1991). Cf. In re Grand Jury Proceedings (Ridenhour), 520 So. 2d 372, 374-75 (La. 1988) (recognizing constitutional privilege and noting that, at least in some contexts, it is not as broad as privilege afforded by Louisiana shield law).

Before the New York shield law was amended to expand its protections, a number of courts applied the then-broader constitutional privilege recognized by the New York Court of Appeals in *O'Neill v. Oakgrove Construction, Inc.*, 523 N.E.2d 277 (N.Y. 1988). See, e.g., Dooley v. Boyle, 531 N.Y.S.2d 158 (Sup. Ct. 1988); Mason v. CBS Inc., 15 MEDIA L. REP. (BNA) 2126 (N.Y. Sup. Ct. 1988); People v. Cheche, 571 N.Y.S.2d 992 (County Ct. 1991). For cases recognizing a constitutional privilege prior to O'Neill, see People v. Bova, 460 N.Y.S.2d 230 (Sup. Ct. 1983); New York v. Martin, 14 MEDIA L. REP. (BNA) 2349 (N.Y. County Ct. 1988); New York v. Troiano, 486 N.Y.S.2d 991 (County Ct. 1985); CBA Elec. Ltd. v. Ellenberg, 10 MEDIA L. Rep. (BNA) 1095 (N.Y. Civ. Ct. 1983); Wilkins v. Kalla, 459 N.Y.S.2d 985 (Sup. Ct. 1983).

33. 690 P.2d 625, 628 (Cal. 1984).

nalists in civil litigation from "a variety of other sanctions" for the refusal to reveal privileged information.[34] In California, therefore, a journalist enjoys — in addition to the statutory privilege — a constitutional privilege, at least in the civil context, "to withhold disclosure of the identity of a confidential source and of unpublished information supplied by such sources."[35]

The appellate courts in a few jurisdictions have yet to address the viability of the constitutional privilege, even in the absence of a shield statute.[36] A few states have expressly rejected the constitutional privilege, interpreting the Supreme Court's decision in *Branzburg v. Hayes*[37] to have settled the issue, at least in the grand jury and criminal contexts.[38] Texas, for example, has purported to reject the notion of a constitutional privilege in the criminal context, but several appellate courts have embraced it in civil cases.[39] At least one state reached the same conclusion prior to *Branzburg* and has not since had occasion to revisit the issue.[40]

---

34. *Id.*

35. *Id.* at 632.

36. See, e.g., Wheeler v. Goulart, 593 A.2d 173, 174-75 (D.C. 1991) (prior to passage of shield law, D.C. Court of Appeals declined to decide the issue on ground that any privilege had been waived). The courts of Wyoming and Puerto Rico do not appear to have addressed the issue of constitutional privilege in a reported case.

37. 408 U.S. 665 (1972).

38. See Vaughn v. Georgia, 381 S.E.2d 30, 31 (Ga. 1989) (prior to passage of shield law, Georgia Supreme Court declines to recognize privilege under either federal or state constitution); Howard v. Savannah College of Art & Design, Inc., 387 S.E.2d 332 (Ga. 1990); WTHR-TV v. Cline, 693 N.E.2d 1, 13 (Ind. 1998) ("the decisions construing *Branzburg* to recognize a qualified reporter's privilege in our view have misread Supreme Court precedent"); In re Contempt of Stone, 397 N.W.2d 244, 246-48 (Mich. App. 1986); CBS Inc. v. Campbell, 645 S.W.2d 30, 30-32 (Mo. App. 1982) (indicating "a greater willingness to provide protection for the news media in cases involving civil and criminal trials than in grand jury proceedings"); In re Farber, 394 A.2d 330, 333 (N.J.), *cert. denied*, 439 U.S. 997 (1978); Oregon ex rel. Meyers v. Howell, 740 P.2d 792, 795 (Or. App. 1987) ("reporters have no state or federal constitutional right to refuse to testify before grand juries"); Oregon v. Knorr, 8 MEDIA L. REP. (BNA) 2067 (Or. Cir. 1982). Cf. Williams v. American Broadcasting Cos., 96 F.R.D. 658, 665, 667 (W.D. Ark. 1983) (predicting that Arkansas state courts would not recognize constitutional privilege).

39. Compare Texas ex rel. Healey v. McMeans, 884 S.W.2d 772, 775 (Tex. Crim. App. 1994) ("recognition of a 'newsman's privilege' is clearly contrary to well-settled law") and Coleman v. Texas, 966 S.W.2d 525, 526 n.5 (Tex. Crim. App. 1998) ("No such privilege exists.") with Dallas Morning News Co. v. Garcia, 822 S.W.2d 675, 678-79 (Tex. App. 1991) (recognizing privilege in civil context); Channel Two Television Co. v. Dickerson, 725 S.W.2d 470, 471-72 (Tex. App. 1987). But cf. Dolcefino v. Ray, 902 S.W.2d 163, 164 (Tex. App. 1995), *cert. denied*, 517 U.S. 1121 (1996) ("we believe that the unqualified statement in *Channel Two* that the United States Supreme Court has created a qualified privilege for journalists is too broad"). The Texas Court of Criminal Appeals is that state's highest court for criminal proceedings and the Texas Supreme Court is the highest civil court.

40. See In re Goodfader's Appeal, 367 P.2d 472, 480 (Haw. 1961).

Finally, the law of some states is in flux, as appellate courts periodically revisit and modify earlier decisions addressing the privilege. In Colorado, for example, early decisions by the state supreme court purporting to reject the constitutional privilege in the grand jury and civil contexts[41] have been followed by appellate precedent recognizing and applying the privilege.[42] In Massachusetts, the Supreme Judicial Court, acting in the wake of a number of cases declining to recognize a constitutional privilege in the criminal context,[43] refused an invitation to adopt rules providing for an evidentiary privilege on the ground that "while this court has consistently held that there is no constitutionally based privilege under either the First Amendment" or the state constitution, "we have nevertheless held that '[s]ome protection' is provided by the First Amendment for 'any person' who gathers information and prepares it for expression."[44]

---

41. See Pankratz v. District Ct., 609 P.2d 1101, 1103 (Colo. 1980) (court declines to recognize privilege in grand jury context on authority of *Branzburg*); Gagnon v. District Ct., 632 P.2d 567, 569 (Colo. 1981) (reporter could be compelled to disclose identity of confidential source in civil proceeding so long as the information was "relevant or would result in the exposition of other facts and circumstances that would lead to clearly relevant information").

42. See Jones v. Woodward, 15 MEDIA L. REP. (BNA) 2060, 2061 (Colo. App. 1988) (to compel disclosure in civil action, moving party must show that "the information sought is centrally important to the case . . . and is unavailable from any other source").

Similarly, the Idaho Supreme Court declined to recognize a constitutional privilege in *Caldero v. Tribune Publishing Co.*, 562 P.2d 791, 797 (Idaho), *cert. denied*, 434 U.S. 930 (1977), but revisited the issue in *In re Wright*, 700 P.2d 40, 44 (Idaho 1985), holding in the latter case that a qualified privilege arises from both the federal and state constitutions. And, in Kentucky — where the state courts had rejected the notion of a constitutional privilege in the grand jury context in the litigation that became *Branzburg v. Hayes*, see Branzburg v. Meigs, 503 S.W.2d 748, 750 (Ky. App. 1971), *aff'd sub nom.* Branzburg v. Hayes, 408 U.S. 665 (1972) — the state supreme court declined to address the viability of the constitutional privilege in the defamation context on the ground that the trial court had properly held that any such privilege had been overcome, see Lexington Herald-Leader Co. v. Beard, 690 S.W.2d 374, 375 (Ky. 1984). Compare Lightman v. Maryland, 294 A.2d 149, 157 (Md. Spec. App.), *aff'd*, 295 A.2d 212 (Md. 1972), *cert. denied*, 411 U.S. 951 (1973) (holding that *Branzburg* made clear that compelled disclosure of confidential sources involves no "violation of the federal constitution") and Tofani v. Maryland, 465 A.2d 413, 423 (Md. 1983) ("It is clear that *Branzburg* expressly declined to create *any* testimonial privilege, absolute or conditional.") with WBAL-TV v. Maryland, 477 A.2d 776, 782 (Md. 1984) ("we do not decide whether reporters have a qualified privilege not to supply evidence relevant to a civil or criminal trial; nor do we decide whether to adopt the three-part test applied by the trial court to determine whether the need for this evidence has overcome any qualified privilege that might exist").

43. See, e.g., Massachusetts v. Corsetti, 438 N.E.2d 805 (Mass. 1982); In re Pappas, 266 N.E.2d 297 (Mass. 1971), *aff'd sub nom.* Branzburg v. Hayes, 408 U.S. 665 (1972).

44. Petition for the Promulgation of Rules Regarding Protection of Confidential Sources, 479 N.E.2d 154, 158 (Mass. 1985). See also Ayash v. Dana-Farber Cancer Inst., 706 N.E.2d 316, 319 (Mass. App. 1999) (no constitutional privilege or rule of court protecting reporters' sources, but "[n]evertheless, it is well settled that, in supervising discovery, a presiding judge is obliged to consider the effect that compelled discovery would have on the values protected by the First Amendment") (internal quotations omitted).

In Ohio, a state that has long had a shield law, the state supreme court has only had occasion to address the constitutional privilege once, in *Ohio ex rel. National Broadcasting Co. v. Court of Common Pleas*.[45] There, the court appeared to read *Branzburg* to preclude recognition of a privilege, at least in the criminal context: "[A] court may enforce a subpoena over a reporter's claim of privilege, so long as it is persuaded that the subpoena has been requested or issued for a legitimate purpose, rather than for harassment."[46] Subsequent cases, however, have continued to apply the constitutional privilege, even in the criminal context,[47] and there has been no meaningful judicial guidance concerning the efficacy of pre-existing case law recognizing the privilege in the civil context in the wake of *National Broadcasting Co.*[48]

§ 16-2(b). Recipients of Protection.

§ 16-2(b)(1). Definitional Issues.

Several courts have considered the extent to which the constitutional privilege applies to persons other than journalists employed by news organizations and to entities other than the news media. In *Branzburg* itself, the Court observed that the "informative function asserted by representatives of the organized press . . . is also performed by lecturers, political pollsters, novelists, academic researchers, and dramatists."[49] Indeed, the Court emphasized that the "[l]iberty of the press is the right of the lonely pamphleteer who uses carbon paper or a mimeograph as much as the large metropolitan publisher who utilizes the latest photo-composition methods."[50]

In *Silkwood v. Kerr-McGee Corp.*,[51] decided shortly after *Branzburg*, the Tenth Circuit held that a documentary filmmaker was entitled to invoke the

---

45. 556 N.E.2d 1120 (Ohio 1990).
46. *Id.* at 1127. Indeed, in its *National Broadcasting Co.* decision, the Ohio Supreme Court expressly questioned the previously influential decision of an Ohio appellate court in *In re McAuley*, 408 N.E.2d 697, 709 (Ohio App. 1979), which had recognized and applied a qualified constitutional privilege.
47. See, e.g., Ohio v. Daniel, 1990 Ohio App. LEXIS 5877 (Ohio App. Dec. 31, 1990), *cert. denied*, 502 U.S. 1037 (1992); Ohio v. Anaga, 18 MEDIA L. REP. (BNA) 1527, 1528 (Ohio C.P. 1991); Ohio v. Prade, 26 MEDIA L. REP. (BNA) 2433 (Ohio C.P. 1998). But see In re Grand Jury Witness Subpoena of Abraham, 634 N.E.2d 667, 668-69 (Ohio App. 1993) (in grand jury context, "the state does not have to meet the three-pronged test under Ohio law or pursuant to the First Amendment").
48. See, e.g., Fawley v. Quirk, 11 MEDIA L. REP. (BNA) 2336 (Ohio App. 1985); Slage v. Coca Cola, Inc., 507 N.E.2d 794, 795 (Ohio C.P. 1986). But see Ohio ex rel. Nat'l Broadcasting Co. v. Court of C.P., 556 N.E.2d at 1126-27 (suggesting that both these decisions "seem inconsistent with *Branzburg*").
49. Branzburg v. Hayes, 408 U.S. at 705.
50. *Id.* at 704.
51. 563 F.2d 433 (10th Cir. 1977).

privilege. The court concluded that, although the subject of the subpoena was "a film maker rather than a newspaper man,"

> [h]is mission in this case was to carry out investigative reporting for use in the preparation of a documentary film. He is shown to have spent considerable time and effort in obtaining facts and information of the subject matter in this lawsuit, but it cannot be disputed that his intention, at least, was to make use of this in preparation of the film. It strikes us as somewhat anomalous that the appellee would argue that he is not a genuine reporter entitled to the privilege, implying a lack of ability, while at the same time they are making a major legal effort to get hold of his material.[52]

Similarly, in *Solargen Electrical Motor Car Corp. v. American Motors Corp.*,[53] a federal district court held that a television camera operator enjoyed the privilege since, "[i]nsofar as camerapersons in fact gather news, albeit with electric equipment, as well as disseminate information, such individuals reasonably should share the same privilege enjoyed by traditional journalists."[54] And, in *Bell v. City of Des Moines*,[55] the court held that the privilege applies to the news director of a television station.

In *von Bulow v. von Bulow*,[56] the Second Circuit discussed at some length the criteria that should properly guide a court's judgment in determining the privilege's reach. Andrea Reynolds was a companion of the defendant in *von Bulow*, who had been sued by the children of his former wife in connection with his alleged scheme to kill or incapacitate her. Ms. Reynolds invoked the privilege to shield from discovery investigative reports she had commissioned, notes she took at the defendant's criminal trial, and the manuscript of a then-unpublished book she had written about the case.

The Second Circuit held that Ms. Reynolds "is not a member of the class entitled to assert the journalist's privilege."[57] According to the court, "the critical question in determining if a person falls within the class of persons protected by the journalist's privilege is whether the person, at the inception of the investigatory process, had the intent to disseminate to the public the information obtained

---

52. *Id.* at 436-37.
53. 506 F. Supp. 546, 552 (N.D.N.Y. 1981).
54. *Id.* Cf. Tuley, *Outtakes, Hidden Cameras, and the First Amendment: A Reporter's Privilege*, 38 WM. & MARY L. REV. 1817 (1997) (arguing that courts compel disclosure of print media work-product less frequently than they compel disclosure of video outtakes, reflecting bias against medium of television); REPORTERS COMMITTEE FOR FREEDOM OF THE PRESS, AGENTS OF DISCOVERY: A REPORT ON THE INCIDENCE OF SUBPOENAS SERVED ON THE NEWS MEDIA IN 1997 (1997) (survey shows that broadcast media received disproportionate share (71%) of all subpoenas issued to survey respondents).
55. 412 N.W.2d 585, 587-88 (Iowa 1987).
56. 811 F.2d 136 (2d Cir.), *cert. denied*, 481 U.S. 1015 (1987).
57. *Id.* at 138.

through the investigation."[58] In the court's view, a person "who gathers information for personal reasons, unrelated to dissemination of information to the public, will not be deterred from undertaking his search simply by rules which permit discovery of that information in a later civil proceeding."[59] Thus, the court held that an "individual claiming the privilege must demonstrate, through competent evidence, the intent to use material — sought, gathered or received — to disseminate information to the public and that such intent existed at the inception of the newsgathering process."[60]

Not surprisingly, several courts have held that freelance authors are entitled to invoke the privilege. In *Shoen v. Shoen*,[61] the Ninth Circuit applied *von Bulow* and recognized that "[i]nvestigative book authors, like more conventional reporters, have historically played a vital role in bringing to light 'newsworthy' facts on topical and controversial matters of great public importance."[62] The "critical question," the Ninth Circuit affirmed, is whether the person claiming the privilege "is gathering news for dissemination to the public," since "[w]hat makes journalism is not its format but its content."[63] Similarly, in *United States*

---

58. *Id.* at 143.
59. *Id.*
60. *Id.* at 144. The Second Circuit further concluded that courts reviewing a claim of privilege under such circumstances must engage in "an intent-based factual inquiry," one which considers, among other things, (1) the "intended manner of dissemination" — which, the court observed, "may be by newspaper, magazine, book, or private broadcast medium, handbill or the like" and (2) "prior experience as a professional journalist" — though such experience is "not the *sine qua non*" of securing protection. *Id.* See In re Madden, 151 F.3d 125, 130 (3d Cir. 1998) (applying *von Bulow* to find that independent contractor employed as wrestling commentator for 900-number hotline is not a journalist entitled to claim qualified privilege where he was not "engaged in investigative reporting [or] gathering news, and [did not] have the intent at the beginning of the newsgathering process to disseminate this information to the public"). Cf. In re Cusumano, 162 F.3d 708, 714 (1st Cir. 1998) (holding that "academic researchers and commentators" may invoke newsgathering privilege: "[w]hether the creator of the material is a member of the media or of the academy, the courts will make a measure of protection available to him as long as he intended 'at the inception of the newsgathering process' to use the fruits of his research 'to disseminate information to the public'") (quoting von Bulow v. von Bulow, 811 F.2d at 144).
61. 5 F.3d 1289, 1293 (9th Cir. 1993).
62. *Id.* See *id*:

> At the turn of the century, for example, muckraking authors such as Lincoln Steffens and Upton Sinclair exposed widespread corruption and abuse in American life. More recently, social critics such as Rachel Carson, Ralph Nader, Jessica Mitford, and others have written books that have made significant contributions to the public discourse on major issues confronting the American people. Indeed, it would be unthinkable to have a rule that an investigative journalist, such as Bob Woodward, would be protected by the privilege in his capacity as a newspaper reporter writing about Watergate, but not as the author of a book on the same topic.

63. *Id.* (citing von Bulow v. von Bulow, 811 F.2d at 144). In this regard, the Ninth Circuit purported to leave open the question of whether "the journalist's privilege may be invoked by a

§ 16-2(b)(1)　　　　　　NEWSGATHERING AND THE LAW　　　　　　§ 16-2(b)(1)

v. Hubbard,[64] a federal district court rejected the contention that a *Washington Post* reporter was not entitled to the privilege because he had "been subpoenaed regarding a book he is writing for his own personal gain." The court held that "the reporter's privilege must encompass all news gathering efforts, not simply those of newspapers."[65] And, in *Louisiana v. Fontanille*,[66] a Louisiana appellate court held that a book author was protected by the constitutional privilege, even if the state shield law did not apply to him. The court held that the privilege "comprehends every sort of publication which affords a vehicle of information and opinion."[67]

---

person writing a book about a recent historical figure, such as Harry Truman or Albert Einstein, where the intent, arguably, is not the dissemination of 'news,' but the writing of history. We do not rule out the possibility but simply leave the question for another day." 5 F.3d at 1294 n.9. In another case decided by the Ninth Circuit two weeks earlier, the court also avoided deciding whether the First Amendment contemplates a "scholar's privilege" afforded to those engaged in academic research. See In re Grand Jury Proceedings, 5 F.3d 397 (9th Cir. 1993), *cert. denied*, 510 U.S. 1041 (1994). In that case, a Ph.D. candidate in sociology and the author of several publications on the issue of animal rights invoked a "scholar's privilege" to shield him from testimony about a break in at an animal research facility. The court concluded that, because the reporters' constitutional privilege would yield under such circumstances, any "scholar's privilege" would as well. *Id.* at 399-401. See also In re Grand Jury Subpoena, 750 F.2d 223, 224 (2d Cir. 1984) (court considers "record in this case as far too sparse to serve as a vehicle for consideration of whether a scholar's privilege exists").

In *Deitchman v. E.R. Squibb & Sons*, 740 F.2d 556 (7th Cir. 1984), however, the Seventh Circuit recognized a qualified privilege protecting the unpublished fruits of academic research. In *Deitchman*, the defendant in a pharmaceutical products liability case sought to compel disclosure of unpublished research data gathered by the Registry for Hormonal Transplacental Carcinogenesis at the University of Chicago. The court accepted the argument of the Registry's chief researcher that he was presumptively privileged, pursuant to the First Amendment, "to divulge to the public the results of his studies only in his own time and way." *Id.* at 560. Similarly, in *Builders Association of Greater Chicago v. Cook County*, 1998 U.S. Dist. LEXIS 2991 (N.D. Ill. Mar. 10, 1998), a plaintiff challenging the constitutionality of Cook County's Minority and Women Business Enterprise Program sought to discover surveys, interview notes, and other documents from the nonparty Urban League, whose research had been cited by the County in a Predicate Study demonstrating a need for the program. Finding that the Urban League, even if it was a political advocacy group, was entitled to invoke the newsgathering privilege to protect information collected with the intent to disseminate it, the court further held that the plaintiff failed to overcome the privilege, and quashed the subpoena. *Id.* See also Anti-Defamation League v. Superior Ct., 79 Cal. Rptr. 2d 597, 613 (Ct. App. 1998) (private disclosure of non-public information about real parties in interest to foreign governments is outside scope of journalist's privilege).

64. 493 F. Supp. 202, 205 (D.D.C. 1979).

65. *Id.* (quoting Lovell v. City of Griffin, 303 U.S. 444, 452 (1938) ("The press in its historic connotation comprehends every sort of publication which affords a vehicle for information and opinion.")); cf. In re Madden, 151 F.3d 125, 129-30 (3d Cir. 1998) ("As we see it, the privilege is only available to persons whose purposes are those traditionally inherent to the press: persons gathering news for publication.").

66. 1994 La. App. LEXIS 191, at *3-4 (La. App. 1994).

67. *Id.* at *4. See also Rancho Publications v. Superior Ct., 81 Cal. Rptr. 2d 274, 279 (Ct. App. 1999) (state shield law did not protect newspaper from compelled disclosure of anonymous

A number of courts have held that the privilege applies to journalists employed by specialized publications as well as by newspapers and other mass-circulation periodicals. In *Apicella v. McNeil Laboratories, Inc.*,[68] one court held the privilege was available to the chief executive officer of a technical medical journal. Several courts have held that Standard & Poor's, the financial rating service, enjoys the privilege as well.[69] Another has extended the privilege to an investment analyst who researched and wrote a report on a single company and distributed it to potential investors.[70]

Finally, some courts have suggested that the privilege may not be applicable to journalists and publishers who are themselves under investigation for illegal conduct.[71] Even in such circumstances, however, the Fourth Circuit has "caution[ed] district courts to apply with special sensitivity, where values of expres-

---

source of paid advertisements that were not obtained "for the journalistic purpose of communicating information to the public," but compelled disclosure "runs afoul" of constitutional privilege).

68. 66 F.R.D. 78 (E.D.N.Y. 1975).

69. See In re Pan Am Corp., 161 Bankr. 577, 581 (S.D.N.Y. 1993) ("The record allows no other conclusion but that S&P functions as a journalist when gathering information in connection with its rating process and specifically that it was functioning as a journalist, *viz.*, with the intent to use the material to disseminate information to the public, when it gathered the information sought here by Pan Am."); In re Scott Paper Co. Sec. Litig., 145 F.R.D. 366, 370 (E.D. Pa. 1992) (citing Lowe v. SEC, 472 U.S. 181 (1985)):

> S&P's publications have all the attributes identified by the Supreme Court in Lowe as indicative of the press. S&P publishes periodicals with a regular circulation to a general population. Although issuers may pay for its rating services, S&P does not merely publish what the issuer desires as it would with advertisements. In contrast, S&P makes its own analysis, designed not merely for the personal use of rated companies, but for the benefit of all who might read its publications. S&P maintains complete editorial control over the form and content of its publications, and the issuers who pay to be rated have no voice in the decision of which ratings to publish. . . . Regardless of the nature of S&P's sources, the fact remains that S&P publishes information for the benefit of the general public.

70. See Summit Tech. Inc. v. Healthcare Capital Group Inc., 141 F.R.D. 381, 384 (D. Mass. 1992) ("Whether or not Roberts is a member of the 'organized press' *per se*, it appears he is engaged in the dissemination to the investing business community. . . . In short, in this instance, Roberts is entitled to raise the claim of privilege with respect to his confidential source as would any other media reporter.").

71. See, e.g., In re Grand Jury Subpoena, 955 F.2d 229 (4th Cir. 1992) (grand jury investigating allegations of interstate transportation of obscene materials by magazine publisher subpoenaed 2,000 videotapes allegedly depicting sexually explicit conduct); In re Gronowicz, 764 F.2d 983 (3d Cir. 1985), *cert. denied*, 474 U.S. 1055 (1986) (grand jury investigating whether book author committed mail fraud in securing book contract subpoenaed to disclose documents supporting book's claim that he interviewed the Pope). Cf. Anti-Defamation League v. Superior Ct., 79 Cal. Rptr. 2d 597, 608 (Ct. App. 1998) ("We do not believe the alleged unlawfulness of petitioners' information-gathering activities is dispositive of their right to the protection of the First Amendment. Petitioners would be entitled to that protection even if they did violate [a] statute, but only if they obtained, used and disseminated the information at issue as journalists.").

sion are potentially implicated, the traditional rule that 'grand juries are not licensed to engage in arbitrary fishing expeditions, nor may they select targets of investigation out of malice or an intent to harass.'"[72] Indeed, the District of Columbia Circuit has recognized that, even when a journalist or press entity is the subject of a governmental investigation, "some balancing or special sensitivity is required in view of the vital function the press serves in a self-governing society."[73]

§ 16-2(b)(2). Standing Issues.

Surprisingly few courts have considered whether the constitutional privilege is properly invoked by the journalist, the news media entity for which she gathers news, the source of information, or some combination of them. In most cases, courts have addressed the issue only in passing, apparently for the purpose of emphasizing that, whoever holds the privilege, it is designed to protect "an underlying interest of the public."[74] Resolution of the "standing" issue can, however, and occasionally does, have ramifications in litigation.

Thus, in *United States v. Cuthbertson*,[75] the Third Circuit rejected the government's claim that CBS could not invoke the constitutional privilege to protect nonbroadcast outtakes because all of its interview subjects had purported to "waive" the privilege. According to the court, the "privilege belongs to CBS, not the potential witnesses, and it may be waived only by its holder."[76] Similarly, in *Los Angeles Memorial Coliseum Commission v. National Football League*,[77] a federal district court rejected the subpoenaing party's claim that the journalists' sources had waived the privilege by "voluntarily" indicating "that they were the

---

72. In re Grand Jury Subpoena, 955 F.2d at 234 (quoting United States v. R. Enters., 498 U.S. 292, 299 (1991)). See also In re Gronowicz, 764 F.2d at 999 (Higginbotham, J., dissenting) ("I do not think the journalist's privilege, any more than any other evidentiary privilege, can evaporate merely because the person claiming it is the target of the investigation, though undoubtedly it may be somewhat easier for prosecutors to overcome the privilege in this situation.").

73. SEC v. McGoff, 647 F.2d 185, 191 (D.C. Cir.), *cert. denied*, 452 U.S. 963 (1981) (citing Branzburg v. Hayes, 408 U.S. at 709-10 (Powell, J., concurring)). Cf. SEC v. Lowe, 472 U.S. 181 (1985) (discussing the balance between freedom of the press and regulation of investment advice pursuant to the Investment Advisors Act of 1940).

74. Bruno & Stillman, Inc. v. Globe Newspaper Co., 633 F.2d 583, 595 n.12 (1st Cir. 1980) ("'The issue is the public's right to know. That right is the reporter's by virtue of the proxy which the freedom of the press clause of the First Amendment gives to the press in behalf of the public.'") (quoting A. BICKEL, THE MORALITY OF CONSENT 85 (1975)). See also United States v. Steelhammer, 539 F.2d 373, 375 (4th Cir. 1976) ("Actually it is a privilege of the public."). Cf. Anderson v. Nixon, 444 F. Supp. 1195, 1198 (D.D.C. 1978) ("[a]lthough the public interest in a fully informed press provides its basis, the privilege 'is that of the reporter not the informant' or the public") (quoting Branzburg v. Hayes, 408 U.S. at 695).

75. 630 F.2d 139, 147 (3d Cir. 1980), *cert. denied*, 449 U.S. 1126 (1981).

76. *Id.*

77. 89 F.R.D. 489, 494 (C.D. Cal. 1981).

ones who gave information," because the "privilege belongs to the journalist alone and cannot be waived by persons other than the journalist."[78]

In *In re Madden*,[79] the Third Circuit concluded that Madden, a commentator for a wrestling "hotline" operating over a "900" telephone line, was "an entertainer, not a reporter, disseminating hype, not news."[80] Notwithstanding Madden's claim that he had received information from confidential sources for use in his commentary, the court concluded that he was not engaged in investigative reporting, and thus could not invoke the privilege to protect his sources or information.[81]

§ 16-2(c). Nature of the Proceedings.

§ 16-2(c)(1). Criminal Proceedings.

Not surprisingly, given the Supreme Court's decision in *Branzburg*, the constitutional privilege has been embraced by courts most grudgingly in the grand jury context. Several courts have interpreted *Branzburg* to preclude application of the privilege before the grand jury, except in those cases involving harassment of the press, pursuit of a purpose unrelated to the grand jury's proper function, or other evidence of bad faith.[82] The Sixth Circuit, for example, has rejected the contention that the First Amendment-based protection available to journalists in the grand jury context is appropriately described as a privilege at

---

78. *Id.* (citing United States v. Cuthbertson, 630 F.2d at 147).
79. 151 F.3d 125 (3d Cir. 1998).
80. *Id.* at 130.
81. *Id.*
82. See, e.g., In re Grand Jury Proceedings, 810 F.2d 580, 584-86 (6th Cir. 1987); In re Lewis, 517 F.2d 236, 237-38 (9th Cir. 1975); In re Grand Jury Proceedings, 5 F.3d 397, 400-02 (9th Cir. 1993), *cert. denied*, 510 U.S. 1041 (1994); In re Grand Jury Subpoena, 947 F. Supp. 1314, 1318 (E.D. Ark. 1996); In re Grand Jury 95-1, 27 MEDIA L. REP. (BNA) 1833 (D.D.C. 1999); Pankratz v. District Ct., 609 P.2d 1101, 1103 (Colo. 1980); In re Tierney, 328 So. 2d 40, 45 (Fla. App. 1976); Vaughn v. Georgia, 381 S.E.2d 30 (Ga. 1989); Tofani v. Maryland, 465 A.2d 413, 421-22 (Md. 1983); In re Pappas, 266 N.E.2d 297 (Mass. 1971), *aff'd sub nom.* Branzburg v. Hayes, 408 U.S. 665 (1972); New York v. Doe, 560 N.Y.S.2d 177 (County Ct. 1990); In re Contempt of Stone, 397 N.W.2d 244, 248-49 (Mich. App. 1986); In re Grand Jury Witness Subpoena of Abraham, 634 N.E.2d 667, 668 (Ohio App. 1993); West Va. ex rel. Hudok v. Henry, 389 S.E.2d 188, 193 (W. Va. 1989) (dicta); Wisconsin v. Knops, 183 N.W.2d 93, 98 (Wis. 1971). Cf. In re Grand Jury Proceeding, 955 F.2d 229, 233-34 (4th Cir. 1992) (holding, based on *Branzburg*, that First Amendment does not afford magazine and video distributor privilege to refuse to disclose business records to grand jury investigating distributor's alleged transportation of obscene materials); CBS Inc. v. Campbell, 645 S.W.2d 30, 31-33 (Mo. App. 1982) (holding that privilege does not apply in grand jury context where information sought is not confidential, but simply unpublished).

all,[83] although it has held that courts reviewing grand jury subpoenas against the press must

> make certain that the proper balance is struck between the freedom of the press and the obligation of all citizens to give relevant testimony, by determining whether the reporter is being harassed in order to disrupt his relationship with confidential news sources, whether the grand jury's investigation is being conducted in good faith, whether the information sought bears more than a remote and tenuous relationship to the subject of the investigation, and whether a legitimate law enforcement need will be served by forced disclosure of the confidential source relationship.[84]

Similarly, the Ninth Circuit has interpreted *Branzburg* as holding that the "First Amendment does not provide a news gatherer a privilege to refuse to testify before a federal grand jury regarding information received in confidence."[85] Nevertheless, the court held that "where a grand jury inquiry is not conducted in good faith, or where the inquiry does not involve a legitimate need of law enforcement, or has only a remote and tenuous relationship to the subject of the investigation," the balancing of competing interests may yield a different result than in *Branzburg*.[86]

Other courts have, however, recognized a First Amendment-based privilege in the grand jury context.[87] In one such case, the Third Circuit affirmed, through an equally divided en banc court, a district court's express recognition of the

---

83. In re Grand Jury Proceedings, 810 F.2d at 586 (balancing of interests required by *Branzburg* "should not . . . be elevated on the basis of semantical confusion, to the status of a first amendment constitutional privilege").

84. *Id.* at 585.

85. In re Grand Jury Proceedings, 5 F.3d 397, 400 (9th Cir. 1993), *cert. denied*, 510 U.S. 1041 (1994).

86. *Id.* at 401. Accord In re Lewis, 517 F.2d 236, 238 (9th Cir. 1975) (*Branzburg*'s "holding" is that, while "first amendment does not afford a reporter a privilege to refuse to testify before a federal grand jury as to information he received in confidence," reporter "will be protected where a grand jury investigation is 'instituted or conducted other than in good faith'") (quoting Branzburg v. Hayes, 408 U.S. at 707); Nevada v. Bazile, CR98-0388, slip op. at 3 (Nev. County Ct. Feb. 19, 1999) ("While '[t]he question of where Branzburg leaves us . . . seems to depend on which Circuit Court one looks to for guidance,' in the Ninth Circuit, which has resolved the issue, courts balance the interests if the case does not involve a grand jury proceeding, but will only balance in a case involving a grand jury proceeding if the grand jury function has been abused.") (citation omitted).

87. See, e.g., In re Williams, 766 F. Supp. 358, 368 (W.D. Pa. 1991), *aff'd by equally divided court*, 963 F.2d 567 (3d Cir. 1992) (en banc); In re Grand Jury Subpoenas, 8 MEDIA L. REP. (BNA) 1418 (D. Colo. 1982); In re Grand Jury Proceedings (Ridenhour), 520 So. 2d 372, 376 (La. 1988); In re Grand Jury Subpoena, 5 MEDIA L. REP. (BNA) 1153, 1153 (Tex. Dist. 1979); cf. In re Grand Jury Subpoena, 750 F.2d 223, 224 (2d Cir. 1984) (remanding case for further consideration of potential application of First Amendment-based "scholar's privilege").

privilege in the grand jury context.[88] In another, a district court quashed a grand jury subpoena directed at a UPI photographer who had been supplied with a photograph of John Hinckley, apparently taken from his family's home by a secret service agent.[89] The court concluded that the government had invoked the power of the grand jury, which was investigating Hinckley's alleged attempt to assassinate President Reagan, to further an ulterior purpose — i.e., "obtaining the evidence on which to justify and support . . . termination, or other action against" the suspected agent.[90] In quashing the subpoena, the court held that:

> freedom of the press cannot operate without some protection of its sources, and it does no good to say people have a right to publish but not a right to obtain information to publish. . . . [E]very time a court ordered a reporter to testify or go to jail, I think that has a substantial chilling effect on the zeal by which other reporters pursue their sources, and it has a chilling effect on those who have information, often government employees who otherwise might be willing to divulge information that ought to be divulged in the public interest. Therefore, while certainly not an absolute privilege, there is a privilege that needs to be weighed.[91]

Outside the grand jury context, courts have been considerably more expansive in their recognition of a constitutional privilege in criminal proceedings.[92] In a

---

88. See In re Williams, 766 F. Supp. 358 (W.D. Pa. 1991), *aff'd by equally divided court*, 963 F.2d 567 (3d Cir. 1992) (en banc).
89. In re Grand Jury Proceeding, 8 MEDIA L. REP. (BNA) 1418 (D. Colo. 1982).
90. *Id.* at 1419.
91. *Id.* Similarly, in *Morgan v. Florida*, 337 So. 2d 951, 955 (Fla. 1976), the Florida Supreme Court overturned a contempt conviction based on a reporter's refusal to disclose the source of information published in a newspaper article concerning a sealed grand jury presentment. The court concluded that the only governmental interest supporting compelled disclosure was "a generalized interest in the secrecy of governmental operations." *Id.* See also Tribune Co. v. Huffstetler, 489 So. 2d 722, 724 (Fla. 1986) (reporter has qualified privilege against disclosing grand jury materials when competing interest is merely "private" concern for reputation). But see Goodale, *Special Prosecutor Scalps the Media*, N.Y.L.J., Dec. 5, 1997, at 3 (discussing successful subpoenas pursuant to "secret arrangements" between media and special prosecutor in Whitewater investigation following federal district court's determination of inapplicability of both reporters' privilege and Justice Department guidelines "limit[ing] the issuance of subpoenas except in cases of compelling need" (see Chap. 15-3(b) *supra*) to special prosecutor).
92. See, e.g., United States v. Burke, 700 F.2d 70 (2d Cir. 1983), *cert. denied*, 464 U.S. 816 (1983); United States v. Cuthbertson, 651 F.2d 189 (3d Cir.), *cert. denied*, 454 U.S. 1056 (1981); United States v. Cuthbertson, 630 F.2d 139 (3d Cir. 1980), *cert. denied*, 449 U.S. 1126 (1981); United States v. Criden, 633 F.2d 346 (3d Cir. 1980), *cert. denied*, 449 U.S. 1113 (1981); Campbell v. Klevenhagen, 760 F. Supp. 1206 (S.D. Tex. 1991); United States v. Lopez, 14 MEDIA L. REP. (BNA) 2203 (N.D. Ill. 1987); United States v. Bingham, 765 F. Supp. 954 (N.D. Ill. 1991); Farr v. Pitchess, 522 F.2d 464 (9th Cir. 1975); United States v. Buckley, 10 MEDIA L. REP. (BNA) 1336 (W.D. Wash. 1984); United States v. Blanton, 534 F. Supp. 295 (S.D. Fla. 1982); United States v. Meros, 11 MEDIA L. REP. (BNA) 2496 (M.D. Fla. 1985); Florida v. Davis, 720 So. 2d

series of cases, for example, the Third Circuit has held that a broad constitutional privilege applies in criminal cases.[93] In two separate decisions in *United States v. Cuthbertson*,[94] the court held that "the interests of the press that form the foundation for the privilege are not diminished because the nature of the underlying proceeding out of which the request for information arises is a criminal trial."[95] In the court's view, a journalist's "interest in protecting confidential sources, preventing intrusion into the editorial process, and avoiding the possibility of self-censorship created by compelled disclosure of sources and unpublished notes does not change because a case is civil or criminal."[96] Thus, although the court recognized that a defendant's Sixth Amendment rights may be implicated when a journalist seeks to quash a subpoena issued on the defendant's behalf in a criminal case, it held that, "rather than affecting the existence of the qualified privilege, ... these rights are important factors that must be considered in deciding whether, in the circumstances of an individual case, the privilege must yield."[97]

220, 227 (Fla. 1998); Georgia v. Smith, 27 MEDIA L. REP. (BNA) 1718 (Fla. Cir. 1999); Florida v. Overton, 26 MEDIA L. REP. (BNA) 1702 (Fla. Cir. 1998); United States v. Hubbard, 493 F. Supp. 202 (D.D.C. 1979); Coney v. Alaska, 699 P.2d 899, 902 (Alaska App. 1985); McBride v. Delaware, 477 A.2d 174, 180-82 (Del. 1984); Kansas v. Sandstrom, 581 P.2d 812, 815 (Kan. 1978); Nevada v. Bazile, CR98-0388 (Nev. County Ct. Feb. 19, 1999); New Hampshire v. Siel, 444 A.2d 499, 502-03 (N.H. 1982); Vermont v. St. Peter, 315 A.2d 254, 255 (Vt. 1974); Vermont v. Blais, 6 MEDIA L. REP. (BNA) 1537 (Vt. Dist. 1980); Brown v. Virginia, 204 S.E.2d 429, 430-31 (Va. 1974); Zelenka v. Wisconsin, 266 N.W.2d 279 (Wis. 1978); Wisconsin ex rel. Green Bay Newspaper Co. v. Circuit Ct., 335 N.W.2d 367, 373-74 (Wis. 1983); United States v. Caporale, 806 F.2d 1487, 1504 (11th Cir. 1986), *cert. denied*, 482 U.S. 917 (1987). See also Waterman Broadcasting of Florida, Inc. v. Reese, 523 So. 2d 1161, 1162 (Fla. App. 1988) (holding that privilege applicable in criminal cases but that disclosure of information at issue, which involved a confession, satisfied three-part test warranting compelled disclosure).

93. See United States v. Cuthbertson, 630 F.2d 139 (3d Cir.), *cert. denied*, 449 U.S. 1126 (1981); United States v. Cuthbertson, 651 F.2d 189 (3d Cir.), *cert. denied*, 454 U.S. 1056 (1981); United States v. Criden, 633 F.2d 346 (3d Cir. 1980), *cert. denied*, 449 U.S. 1113 (1981).

94. 630 F.2d 139 (3d Cir.), *cert. denied*, 449 U.S. 1126 (1981); 651 F.2d 189 (3d Cir.), *cert. denied*, 454 U.S. 1056 (1981).

95. 630 F.2d at 147.

96. *Id.*

97. *Id.* After affirming the trial court's order that broadcast outtakes be submitted for *in camera* inspection, the court in *Cuthbertson* reversed a subsequent order that they be disclosed to the defendant. See *id.* at 201. After the trial court's second order, the Third Circuit held that it was "persuaded that the defendants failed to meet the test consistently announced in this court's *Riley-Cuthbertson-Criden* trilogy of fair trial-free press cases." *Id.* at 195. "Accordingly, even if the defendants could have met the requirements under rule 17(c), the materials would not be available to defendants in this case because defendants failed to prove an element necessary to overcome the media's qualified privilege: that the only practical access to the information sought is through the media source." *Id.* at 196.

In *United States v. Criden*,[98] the Third Circuit held that, in the criminal context, a claim of reporters' privilege "highlights a tension between the first amendment and the fifth and sixth amendments."[99] While the First Amendment-based privilege may be "absolute" in the absence of "countervailing constitutional concerns," the court asserted that "when constitutional precepts collide, the absolute gives way to the qualified and a balancing process comes into play to determine its limits."[100] Accordingly, the court concluded that the privilege does not apply to protect a journalist from disclosing whether or not she had a conversation with a "self-avowed source."[101]

Other appellate and trial courts have similarly recognized a qualified constitutional privilege in the non-grand jury, criminal context, typically interpreting *Branzburg* "to require that the claimed First Amendment privilege and the opposing need for disclosure be judicially weighed in light of the surrounding facts and a balance struck to determine where lies the paramount interest."[102] Some courts have even suggested that "the important societal interests in the free flow of information that are protected by the reporter's qualified privilege are particularly compelling in criminal cases, since reporters are to be encouraged to investigate and expose evidence of criminal wrongdoing."[103]

---

98. 633 F.2d 346 (3d Cir. 1980), *cert. denied*, 449 U.S. 1113 (1981).
99. *Id.* at 355.
100. *Id.*
101. *Id.* at 358.
102. Farr v. Pitchess, 522 F.2d 464, 468 (9th Cir. 1975). In *Farr*, the Ninth Circuit ultimately determined that, "under the facts presented by this record, the paramount interest to be protected was that of the power of the court to enforce its duty and obligation relative to the guarantee of due process to the defendants in the on-going trial." *Id.* at 469. See In re Grand Jury Proceedings, 5 F.3d 397, 402 (9th Cir. 1993), *cert. denied*, 510 U.S. 1041 (1994) ("In *Farr*, we held that a newspaper reporter did not have a First Amendment privilege to refuse to disclose to a state court the identity of an individual who had disclosed confidential information concerning a criminal trial, in violation of that court's order. . . . [T]he reporter's First Amendment interests were outweighed by the 'paramount interest'" of the criminal defendant.).
103. United States v. Lopez, 14 MEDIA L. REP. (BNA) 2203, 2204 (N.D. Ill. 1987). See also United States v. Bingham, 765 F. Supp. 954, 956 (N.D. Ill. 1991) ("qualified privilege has been held to apply to criminal and civil cases"); United States v. Blanton, 534 F. Supp. 295, 296 (S.D. Fla. 1982) ("The First Amendment . . . requires that a reporter be immune from subpoenas in criminal cases regarding his or her work product unless the party seeking the reporter's testimony first makes a showing of sufficient interest and need"); United States v. Hubbard, 493 F. Supp. 202, 205 (D.D.C. 1979) ("the reporter is protected from the subpoena power of a criminal defendant unless the information is necessary to a fair hearing and there are no alternative avenues for access to the information").

In *Brown v. Virginia*, 204 S.E.2d 429, 431 (Va.), *cert. denied*, 419 U.S. 966 (1974), the Virginia Supreme Court held the privilege will yield in a criminal case only when the reporter's testimony is "essential" to a fair trial, i.e.,

> when there are reasonable grounds to believe that information in the possession of a newsman is material to proof of any element of a criminal offense, or to proof of the defense as-

Other courts, however, have held that the privilege is comparatively narrow in criminal cases and, accordingly, have determined that, on the facts of specific cases, it is outweighed by the "very considerable interests" of criminal defendants.[104] In *United States v. LaRouche Campaign*, for example, the First Circuit rejected a television network's assertion of privilege to prevent its disclosure, for *in camera* review, of outtakes of an interview with a prospective key witness in a criminal case.[105] The court concluded that the defendants' "constitutional rights to a fair trial under the Fifth Amendment and to compulsory process and effective confrontation and cross-examination of adverse witnesses under the Sixth Amendment" overcame the "very light weight" ascribed to the competing First Amendment interests.[106] The Fourth Circuit has indicated that the privilege may similarly be overcome in a criminal case at the instance of the prosecution.[107]

---

serted by the defendant, or to a reduction in the classification or gradation of the offense charged, or to a mitigation of the penalty attached, . . . ; when such information is not otherwise available, the defendant has a due process right to compel disclosure of such information and the identity of the source; and any privilege of confidentiality claimed by the newsman must, upon pain of contempt, yield to that right.

See also Florida v. Davis, 720 So. 2d 220, 227 (Fla. 1998) ("in a criminal case in which the government is seeking information, it would have to establish that the information was relevant to the crime being investigated; that the government could not obtain the information from another source; and that the government has a compelling need to obtain the information").

104. United States v. LaRouche Campaign, 841 F.2d 1176, 1182 (1st Cir. 1988). See also In re Willon, 55 Cal. Rptr. 2d 245, 253 (Ct. App. 1996); Farr v. Superior Ct., 99 Cal. Rptr. 342, 350 (Ct. App. 1971), *cert. denied*, 409 U.S. 1011 (1972) (court balanced defendant's right to a fair trial against First Amendment rights of reporter and concluded that "disclosure of the source of violation may inhibit future violations, the inhibition serves the public purpose declared by the High Court and deprives the public of only that information which that court has declared must be kept from it temporarily if the constitutional right to a fair trial is to be preserved"); West Virginia ex rel. Charleston Mail Ass'n v. Ranson, 488 S.E.2d 5 (W. Va. 1997); WTHR-TV v. Cline, 693 N.E.2d 1, 15 (Ind. 1998) ("It is hardly a novel idea that assertions of privilege must give way to a specific need for evidence in a criminal case.").

105. 841 F.2d at 1182.

106. *Id.* at 1182-83. See also United States v. Sanusi, 813 F. Supp. 149, 155 (E.D.N.Y. 1992) (disclosure of "media workproduct" may be compelled in criminal case "when necessary to ensure fair judicial process").

107. See In re Shain, 978 F.2d 850, 852 (4th Cir. 1992) ("the incidental burden on the freedom of the press in the circumstances of this case does not require the invalidation of the subpoenas issued to the reporters, and absent evidence of governmental harassment or bad faith, the reporters have no privilege different from that of any other citizen not to testify about knowledge relevant to a criminal prosecution"). See also United States v. Markiewicz, 732 F. Supp. 316, 320 (N.D.N.Y. 1990) ("the test to be employed should be flexible and not gauged by the relatively unforgiving test of whether the material sought is highly material, critical, and not available from alternative sources"); Waterman Broadcasting of Florida, Inc. v. Reese, 523 So. 2d 1161, 1162 (Fla. App. 1988); WBAL-TV v. Maryland, 477 A.2d 776, 777-78 (Md. 1984) (assuming existence of qualified privilege, court holds it is overcome in criminal case where prosecution sought outtakes

A few courts have declined to recognize the privilege in the criminal context at all. In *Ohio ex rel. National Broadcasting Co. v. Court of Common Pleas*,[108] for example, the Ohio Supreme Court held that, in the context of a murder trial, news media organizations could be required to preserve "all news and commentary tapes, including outtakes." According to the court, a subpoena may be enforced "over a reporter's claim of privilege," so long as the court "is persuaded that the subpoena has been requested or issued for a legitimate purpose, rather than for harassment."[109]

Similarly, in *United States v. Smith*,[110] the Fifth Circuit expressly rejected the view that Justice Powell's concurring opinion in *Branzburg* constituted a "mandate to construct a broad, qualified newsreporters' privilege in criminal cases," at least when the subpoena at issue seeks nonconfidential information. Rather, the court concluded, in *Branzburg* "Justice Powell meant only to protect newsreporters from intentional harassment by the government," not to erect "a general qualified privilege for newsreporters in criminal cases."[111] And, the Fifth Circuit held, a "single subpoena issued only after considered decision by the Attorney General of the United States to compel production of evidence at a federal trial of a multicount felony indictment is no harassment."[112] In addition, the court determined that the Supreme Court's rejection of the privilege in *Branzburg* could not be limited to a subpoena issued by a grand jury, since there is "little persuasive force" in the distinction between the grand jury and criminal trial in this context: "Surely the public has as great an interest in convicting its criminals as it does in indicting them."[113] Finally, the Fifth Circuit saw no con-

---

of videotaped interview with murder defendant). But see In re Shain, 978 F.2d at 854 (Wilkinson, J., concurring) ("Government subpoenas of news reporters inevitably involve tensions between the needs of law enforcement and those of newsgathering."); Kidwell v. Florida, 720 So. 2d 218, 218 (Fla. 1998) ("extreme care must be taken to ensure that the media is not used as an investigative arm of the government").

108. 556 N.E.2d 1120, 1125 (Ohio 1990).

109. *Id.* at 1127. But see Ohio v. Anaga, 18 MEDIA L. REP. (BNA) 1527, 1528 (Ohio C.P. 1991) (holding in criminal case that "the party seeking information from reporters must meet the three part test of relevance, compelling need and lack of alternate means" and distinguishing *National Broadcasting Co.* on ground that the decision there "was limited to the obligation of the news media to preserve its videotapes until the trial date" and did not "decide the matter now before this court"). See also Minnesota v. Turner, 550 N.W.2d 622, 628 (Minn. 1996) ("In our view, the Supreme Court has declared that no qualified constitutional privilege exists under the First Amendment that would protect reporters from compelled testimony in a criminal case."); WTHR-TV v. Cline, 693 N.E.2d 1, 15 (Ind. 1998) ("the First Amendment does not require in every case a special showing of need and relevance beyond that imposed under discovery procedures when information in a criminal case is demanded from a reporter").

110. 135 F.3d 963, 969 (5th Cir. 1998).

111. *Id.*

112. *Id.*

113. *Id.* at 971.

flict between its holding in *Smith* and its previous decision in *Miller v. Transamerican Press, Inc.*,[114] which recognized the privilege in civil cases, asserting that "[b]ecause the public has much less of an interest in the outcome of civil litigation, in civil cases like *Miller* the interests of the press may weigh far more heavily in favor of some sort of privilege."[115]

These conflicting approaches to application of the privilege in the criminal context have yet to be worked out by the courts in any meaningful fashion. The Second Circuit, for example, initially recognized a broad constitutional privilege in criminal cases in *United States v. Burke*,[116] holding that there was "no legally-principled reason for drawing a distinction between civil and criminal cases when considering whether the reporter's interest in confidentiality should yield to the moving party's need for probative evidence." In that regard, the court reasoned that,

> [t]o be sure, a criminal defendant has more at stake than a civil litigant and the evidentiary needs of a criminal defendant may weigh more heavily in the balance. Nevertheless, the standard of review should be the same. Indeed, the important social interests in the free flow of information that are protected by the reporter's qualified privilege are particularly compelling in criminal cases.[117]

Subsequently, however, in *United States v. Cutler*,[118] the Second Circuit suggested that "*Burke*'s articulation of a general test applicable to all phases of a criminal trial was not necessary to the resolution of that case; *Burke* should accordingly be considered limited to its facts."[119] Nevertheless, the court in *Cutler* quashed a portion of the subpoena before it, holding that a "direct confrontation" of the issues posed by *Burke* was not necessary on the facts of

---

114. 621 F.2d 721 (5th Cir. 1980), *cert. denied*, 450 U.S. 1041 (1981).

115. 135 F.3d at 972. Prior to *Smith*, two federal courts in Texas clashed over the efficacy of the reporters' privilege in criminal cases. In *Karem v. Priest*, 744 F. Supp. 136, 139 (W.D. Tex. 1990), one court held that it could not "concur with the expansive reading given by other courts" to Justice Powell's concurring opinion in *Branzburg*, and specifically rejected the reasoning of "those courts that have permitted a reporter to avoid giving evidence in a criminal case based upon an asserted First Amendment privilege." Subsequently, however, in *Campbell v. Klevenhagen*, 760 F. Supp. 1206, 1208 (S.D. Tex. 1991), another federal court sitting in Texas rejected *Karem* and applied the privilege to quash a subpoena in a criminal case. Compare In re Wright, 700 P.2d 40 (Idaho 1985) (privilege applies to identity of confidential source in criminal case) with Idaho v. Salsbury, 924 P.2d 208, 214 (Idaho 1996) (privilege does not apply to non-confidential material in criminal case).

116. 700 F.2d 70, 77 (2d Cir.), *cert. denied*, 464 U.S. 816 (1983).

117. *Id.* at 77.

118. 6 F.3d 67 (2d Cir. 1993).

119. *Id.* at 73. The court went on to indicate that its opinion "had been circulated to the active members of this court prior to filing." *Id.* at 73 n.5.

record.[120] Most recently, the Second Circuit has reaffirmed that the privilege applies in criminal cases and indicated both that the *Burke* formulation governs subpoenas requesting the disclosure of confidential information and that a less stringent showing is required to compel production of nonconfidential materials.[121] Indeed, in *Gonzales v. National Broadcasting Co.*,[122] the court explained that its "language" in *Cutler* "limiting *Burke* to its facts" should not properly "be construed to suggest that our *Cutler* opinion challenged the very existence of a journalists' privilege," but merely that a "lower" showing is required "to overcome the privilege" when nonconfidential materials are "sought by a criminal defendant."[123]

One federal court has addressed the efficacy of the privilege in the context of a criminal investigation directed *at* a journalist. In *In re Gronowicz*,[124] the Third Circuit considered a claim of constitutional privilege asserted by the author of the book *God's Broker*, in the context of a grand jury subpoena seeking the author's travel records, passports, appointment books, notes and recordings. Gronowicz was the subject of a grand jury inquiry concerning whether he had defrauded his publisher by representing that his book contained the fruits of an actual interview he said he had conducted with Pope John Paul II. A badly divided *en banc* court enforced the subpoena, holding — in six separate opinions — that the subpoena was enforceable because Gronowicz "could constitutionally be prosecuted for misrepresentations about the contents" of his book.[125]

---

120. *Id.*

121. See Gonzales v. National Broadcasting Co., 1998 U.S. App. LEXIS 38583, at *15 (2d Cir. Aug. 27, 1999) (court asserts it is "clear" that, in *Cutler*, it "proceeded on the assumption that, despite the nonconfidential nature of the information sought, a qualified journalists' privilege applied, and the defendant had to show a sufficient need for the information to overcome the privilege"); see also Krase v. Graco Children Prods., Inc., 79 F.3d 346 (2d Cir. 1996) (noting that court in *Cutler* had in fact applied qualified privilege).

122. 1998 U.S. App. LEXIS 38583 (2d Cir. Aug. 27, 1999).

123. *Id.* at *16 n.3. See *id.* at (*Cutler* stands for the proposition that "*Burke* undervalued the needs of criminal defendants in putting on a defense").

124. 764 F.2d 983 (3d Cir. 1985), *cert. denied*, 474 U.S. 1055 (1986).

125. *Id.* at 989. Judge Garth concurred in the court's opinion, emphasizing that "its constitutional holding is limited to answering the precise question: does any first amendment privilege protect the target (Gronowicz) of a grand jury investigation from producing documents sought by a *subpoena duces tecum*" and emphasizing Gronowicz's right to assert a Fifth Amendment privilege at that stage of a criminal proceeding. *Id.* at 989 (Garth, J., concurring). Judge Becker also concurred separately to emphasize that "when a grand jury investigation focuses on the truth of a book," the First Amendment requires that the government "be held to a stronger showing than the 'scant' evidence requirement" typically applied to judge the validity of a subpoena in the grand-jury context. *Id.* at 990 (Becker, J., concurring). Judge Hunter dissented on the ground that a grand jury subpoena to a journalist requires heightened First Amendment scrutiny because the amendment "primarily protects citizens from *government* intrusion into their freedom of expression." *Id.* at 994 (Hunter, J., dissenting). Judge Higginbotham also dissented, asserting that the "compelled disclosure of records, notes and unpublished information compiled in the course of preparing a

§ 16-2(c)(2). Civil Proceedings.

Within a year of the Supreme Court's decision in *Branzburg*, lower courts began to create what has generally proven to be an enduring body of precedent distinguishing the case's result in the civil context. In *Carey v. Hume*,[126] a civil defamation action against journalists Jack Anderson and Brit Hume, the District of Columbia Circuit acknowledged "the emphasis in *Branzburg* upon the public interest in the giving of testimony," but nevertheless concluded that its reasoning does not apply with the same force "in a civil suit rather than a grand jury inquiry into crime."[127] According to the court:

> This difference is of some importance, since the central thrust of Justice White's opinion for the Court concerns the traditional importance of grand juries and the strong public interest in effective enforcement of the criminal law. Justice White also relied on the various procedures available to prosecutors and grand juries to protect informants and on careful use by the Government of the power to compel testimony. Private litigants are not similarly charged with the public interest and may be more prone to seek wholesale and indiscriminate disclosure.[128]

In *Zerilli v. Smith*,[129] a Privacy Act and Fourth Amendment action instituted against the Attorney General by two private plaintiffs, the D.C. Circuit returned to *Carey* and emphasized the broad nature of the constitutional privilege in the civil context. The court recognized that, in less than a decade following *Branzburg*, every federal circuit "that has considered the question has also ruled that a privilege should be readily available in civil cases," and that the Supreme Court's own analysis in *Branzburg* "contains much language suggesting that its holding is confined to the grand jury or criminal context."[130] Accordingly, the court emphasized:

---

work of nonfiction will so inhibit the gathering and recording of facts and intrude upon editorial processes as to chill protected speech." *Id.* at 994 (Higginbotham, J., dissenting). Finally, Judge Slovitar dissented as well, on the ground that the court's failure to recognize a constitutional privilege in this context "opens the way for use of the uniquely powerful weapon of a grand jury investigation to inhibit publication of books because of their content not only by an unscrupulous prosecutor but, what is more dangerous, by one who is imbued with a sense of zealous righteousness." *Id.* at 1000 (Slovitar, J., dissenting). Cf. Marks v. Vehlow, 671 P.2d 473 (Idaho 1983) (no privilege in habeas proceeding concerning reporter's knowledge of whereabouts of missing child).

126. 492 F.2d 631, 636 (D.C. Cir.), *cert. dismissed*, 417 U.S. 938 (1974).
127. *Id.* at 636 n.6.
128. *Id.* at 636.
129. 656 F.2d 705, 711 (D.C. Cir. 1981).
130. *Id.* at 712 & n.42.

In general, when striking the balance between the civil litigant's interest in compelled disclosure and the public interest in protecting a newspaper's confidential sources, we will be mindful of the preferred position of the First Amendment and the importance of a vigorous press. Efforts will be taken to minimize impingement upon reporter's ability to gather news. . . . Thus in the ordinary case the civil litigant's interest in disclosure should yield to the journalist's privilege. Indeed, if the privilege does not prevail in all but the most exceptional cases, its value will be substantially diminished. Unless potential sources are confident that compelled disclosure is unlikely, they will be reluctant to disclose any confidential information to reporters.[131]

As the following discussion illustrates, judicial hospitality to claims of reporters' privilege in the civil context, exemplified by *Carey* and *Zerilli*, has been the rule. By the same token, as *Carey* and *Zerilli* demonstrate as well, courts have applied the privilege somewhat less expansively in the civil context when the journalist from whom compelled disclosure is sought is a party to the litigation.

§ 16-2(c)(2)(A). Third-Party Proceedings.

By and large, the late Judge Skelly Wright's prediction in *Zerilli v. Smith* has proven accurate: in civil cases in which the subpoenaed journalist is not a party, the privilege has prevailed "in all but the most exceptional cases."[132] In *Zerilli* itself, for example, the D.C. Circuit held that, even though the success of the plaintiffs' Privacy Act and Fourth Amendment claims against the government "may depend on the identities of the individuals who leaked wiretap logs" to the subpoenaed journalist, the plaintiffs had not made a sufficient showing that they had "fulfilled their obligation to exhaust possible alternative sources of information" to overcome the constitutional privilege.[133] Similarly, in *Riley v. City of Chester*,[134] the Third Circuit held, in the context of a civil action instituted by a mayoral candidate against city officials alleging violation of his constitutional right to conduct his campaign, that a newspaper reporter was privileged to decline to reveal his sources of published information: "This is simply a situation where a journalist has been called as a witness to a civil suit in which neither she nor her employer has any personal interest."[135]

---

131. *Id.* at 710.
132. *Id.*
133. *Id.* at 714.
134. 612 F.2d 708, 716-17 (3d Cir. 1979).
135. *Id.* at 716. See also Silkwood v. Kerr-McGee Corp., 563 F.2d 433 (10th Cir. 1977) (in civil action alleging violation of constitutional rights by estate of woman exposed to toxic plutonium, court held privilege required balancing of plaintiff's need for information against

Courts have applied the privilege, as in *Zerilli* and *Riley*, to protect nonparty journalists in actions involving alleged infringement of constitutional rights,[136] as well as in actions alleging violations of the antitrust laws,[137] civil rights cases,[138]

---

constitutional interests undergirding privilege); Baker v. F & F Inv., 470 F.2d 778 (2d Cir. 1972), *cert. denied*, 411 U.S. 966 (1973) (privilege applies to protect nonparty journalist from compelled disclosure in civil action).

136. See Silkwood v. Kerr-McGee Corp., 563 F.2d 433 (10th Cir. 1977); Loadholtz v. Fields, 389 F. Supp. 1299, 1300 (M.D. Fla. 1975) ("the paramount interest served by the unrestricted flow of public information protected by the First Amendment outweighs the subordinate interest served by the liberal discovery provisions embodied in the Federal Rules of Civil Procedure"); Builders Ass'n v. Cook County, 1998 U.S. Dist. LEXIS 2991 (N.D. Ill. Mar. 10, 1998).

137. See In re Petroleum Prods. Antitrust Litig., 680 F.2d 5, 9 (2d Cir.), *cert. denied*, 459 U.S. 909 (1982) ("We decline the invitation to hold violations of the antitrust laws to be *sui generis*. Although it is true that the Sherman Act represents Congress's strong commitment to fostering a competitive marketplace, enactment of a statute cannot defeat a constitutional privilege."); Los Angeles Mem'l Coliseum Comm'n v. National Football League, 89 F.R.D. 489, 493 (C.D. Cal. 1981) (in civil antitrust action, court upheld journalist's claim of privilege and "emphasized that the public interest in protecting journalists' confidential sources is even stronger in civil cases than it is in criminal cases"); In re Consumers Union, 495 F. Supp. 582, 585 (S.D.N.Y. 1980) (court quashes subpoena of third-party journalist in Sherman Act litigation); Gulliver's Periodicals, Ltd. v. Chas. Levy Circulating Co., 455 F. Supp. 1197, 1202 (N.D. Ill. 1978) (privilege applied in private antitrust suit since "[d]isclosure of a news source should not be ordered absent some strong and compelling reason in favor of disclosure"); In re Cusumano, 162 F.3d 708, 710 (1st Cir. 1998) ("Mindful that important First Amendment values are at stake, we decline . . . to reverse the district court's denial of [defendant]'s motion to compel production of research materials compiled by two academic investigators [for use] in defending a civil antitrust case."); Solargen Elec. Motor Car Corp. v. American Motors Corp., 506 F. Supp. 546, 553 (N.D.N.Y. 1981) (in civil antitrust suit, privilege protects journalist from compelled disclosure of information regarding meeting with television station owner). But see *id.* at 552 (although court "recognizes that when a non-party journalist is the target of a subpoena in a civil proceeding, as opposed to a criminal action, the First Amendment balance may, in specific situations, shift in favor of non-disclosure," plaintiffs had made showing sufficient to overcome privilege with respect to subpoena for journalists' bank records because they "go[ ] to the very heart of the plaintiffs' conspiracy claim that the defendant automobile manufacturer bribed journalists to disparage the plaintiffs' product").

138. See Baker v. F & F Inv., 470 F.2d 778, 783 (2d Cir. 1972), *cert. denied*, 411 U.S. 966 (1973) ("It would be inappropriate for a court to pick and choose in such gross fashion between different acts of Congressional legislation, labeling one 'exceedingly important' and another less so, without specific directions from the Legislature."); In re Selcraig, 705 F.2d 789, 798-99 (5th Cir. 1983) (privilege applies in civil rights action in which journalist is not a party, but it extends no further than in other civil cases in which press is a party); Doe v. Kohn, Nast & Graf, 853 F. Supp. 147, 152 (E.D. Pa. 1994) (defendants in action under Americans with Disabilities Act cannot make sufficient showing to overcome privilege and secure outtakes of broadcast interviews); Alexander v. Chicago Park Dist., 548 F. Supp. 277, 277-78 (N.D. Ill. 1982) (in civil rights action alleging discrimination against city park system, court "notes" that journalists "are protected from compelled disclosure of 'the sources and source material' which they relied on in writing and publishing the articles concerning the Chicago parks") (citation omitted); Neal v. City of Harvey, Illinois, 173 F.R.D. 231 (N.D. Ill. 1997) (defendant in civil rights action cannot compel reporter's deposition testimony regarding nonconfidential sources or facts surrounding newsgathering activities); Perry v. Keulian, 1997 U.S. Dist. LEXIS 2795 (E.D. Pa. Mar. 11, 1997) (plaintiff in Fair

bankruptcy actions,[139] Lanham Act litigation,[140] invasion of privacy cases,[141] and securities litigation.[142] In addition, courts have vindicated assertions of the constitutional privilege by third-party journalists in wrongful discharge cases,[143] personal injury litigation,[144] products liability actions,[145] administrative proceedings,[146] contract disputes,[147] and defamation actions in which the subpoenaed journalist is not a party.[148] As one trial court summarized the prevailing view,

---

Housing Act suit who failed to overcome qualified media privilege could not subpoena reporter regarding statements defendant made to reporter); Pugh v. Avis Rent A Car Sys., Inc., 26 MEDIA L. REP. (BNA) 1311 (S.D.N.Y. 1997) (civil rights defendant could not compel nonparty television network to produce outtakes and notes of interviews with plaintiffs and plaintiffs' counsel). But see Dillon v. City & County of San Francisco, 748 F. Supp. 722, 727 (N.D. Cal. 1990) (in civil rights action alleging use of excessive force by police officers, court holds that, even if it recognized a privilege protecting a journalist's eyewitness observations from compelled disclosure, "(which in fact it does not), it would find that, on balance, the surrounding facts weigh in favor of enforcement of the subpoena").

139. See In re Pan Am Corp., 161 Bankr. 577, 586 (S.D.N.Y. 1993) (reversing contempt order entered by bankruptcy court against journalists for refusal to produce subpoenaed information).

140. See Re/Max Int'l, Inc. v. Century 21 Real Estate Corp., 846 F. Supp. 910, 911 (D. Colo. 1994) (privilege protects nonparty reporter from compelled deposition in civil action alleging violation of Lanham Act, unfair competition, and deceptive advertising).

141. See, e.g., Sinnott v. Boston Retirement Bd., 524 N.E.2d 100, 102 (Mass.), *cert. denied*, 488 U.S. 980 (1988).

142. See In re Scott Paper Co. Sec. Litig., 145 F.R.D. 366, 372 (E.D. Pa. 1992) (privilege claim upheld in consolidated class action alleging securities fraud). But see In re Dow Jones & Co., 27 MEDIA L. REP. (BNA) 1307 (S.D.N.Y. 1998), *vacated*, No. 99-7014 (2d Cir. June 8, 1999) (en banc) (qualified privilege does not protect nonconfidential, unpublished source materials subpoenaed in federal securities action).

143. See Warzon v. Drew, 155 F.R.D. 183, 186 (E.D. Wis. 1994). Cf. Connecticut State Bd. of Labor Relations v. Fagin, 370 A.2d 1095, 1097-98 (Conn. Super. 1976).

144. See, e.g., O'Neill v. Oakgrove Constr., Inc., 523 N.E.2d 277, 279 (N.Y. 1988) ("[A]ttempts to obtain evidence by subjecting the press to discovery as a nonparty would be widespread if not restricted. The practical burden on time and resources . . . would be particularly inimical to the vigor of a free press."); Johnson v. Bentley, 457 So. 2d 507, 509 (Fla. App. 1984); Zellner v. Mount Nebo Mem'l Gardens, Inc., 26 MEDIA L. REP. (BNA) 1672 (Fla. Cir. 1997). Cf. Farrington v. Crupper Transp. Co., 17 MEDIA L. REP. (BNA) 1781, 1782 (D. Kan. 1990) (court recognizes constitutional privilege, but holds that defendant in personal injury action had made requisite showing to compel disclosure of photographs and negatives of auto accident). But see Carroll Contracting, Inc. v. Edwards, 528 So. 2d 951, 954 (Fla. App. 1988) (newspaper ordered to produce photographs of accident scene); Ko v. Zilog, Inc., 25 MEDIA L. REP. (BNA) 1892 (Idaho 1997).

145. See, e.g., Gilbert v. Allied Chem. Corp., 411 F. Supp. 505, 507 (E.D. Va. 1976).

146. See, e.g., Opinion of the Justices, 373 A.2d 644, 646 (N.H. 1977); West Virginia ex rel. Hudok v. Henry, 389 S.E.2d 188, 193 (W. Va. 1989); Tomblin v. Mayo Clinic, 26 MEDIA L. REP. (BNA) 1351 (Fla. Dep't of Labor & Employment 1997).

147. See Coastline Bldg. Corp. v. Atkins, 26 MEDIA L. REP. (BNA) 1316 (Fla. Cir. 1997).

148. See Shoen v. Shoen, 48 F.3d 412, 415-16 (9th Cir. 1995) (in defamation action, court upholds privilege claim by nonparty journalist because "routine court-compelled disclosure of research materials poses a serious threat to the vitality of the newsgathering process"); Church of

"[i]n civil cases, 'courts must recognize that the public interest in nondisclosure of journalist's news sources will often be weightier than the private interest in compelled disclosure.'"[149]

One possible exception to this rule of thumb may be found in the context of juvenile proceedings. Thus, in *In re Roche*,[150] a Florida court applied the qualified privilege in the context of a confidential juvenile dependency and termination of parental rights proceeding. Asserting the "primary importance" of protecting the rights of children in such proceedings, however, the court of appeals upheld a finding of criminal contempt against a reporter who disseminated information about the closed proceeding.[151]

§ 16-2(c)(2)(B). The Press as a Party.

The privilege has also been applied widely in civil actions in which the press is a party, although its scope has proven somewhat less expansive in that context. Indeed, as early as *Carey v. Hume*, where the D.C. Circuit first recognized the constitutional privilege in civil litigation, it nevertheless held that the party issuing the subpoena, a defamation plaintiff, had made the requisite showing to compel disclosure from the defendant journalist.[152] Thus, Judge Wright has also

---

Scientology, Int'l v. Daniels, 992 F.2d 1329, 1335 (4th Cir.), *cert. denied*, 510 U.S. 869 (1993) (privilege applies to protect nonparty journalist from compelled disclosure of information subpoenaed by plaintiff in defamation action); Dallas Oil & Gas, Inc. v. Mouer, 533 S.W.2d 70, 76 (Tex. App. 1976) (privilege protects nonparty journalist in defamation action against competing newspaper); Davis v. Glanton, 705 A.2d 879, 886 (Pa. Super. 1997) (privilege shields nonparty journalist from disclosure of materials where defamation plaintiff's "speculative justification for release of the subpoenaed information fails to demonstrate that production of the requested material is the only way in which [a] crucial element can be proven"); Rancho Publications v. Superior Ct., 81 Cal. Rptr. 2d 274 (Ct. App. 1999) (privilege protects nonparty newspaper from compelled disclosure of anonymous sources of paid advertisement subpoenaed by plaintiffs in defamation action).

149. Pinkard v. Johnson, 118 F.R.D. 517, 521 (M.D. Ala. 1987) (citation omitted). See also Coastline Bldg. Corp. v. Atkins, 26 MEDIA L. REP. (BNA) 1316, 1318 (Fla. Cir. 1997) ("Plain and simple, newsgathering is the essential precondition of the dissemination of public information. When this process is subverted for the purpose of fostering private litigation, the result has a chilling effect on the function of a free press under the First Amendment.").

150. 589 So. 2d 978 (Fla. App. 1991), *review denied*, 599 So. 2d 1279 (Fla. 1992), *cert. denied*, 506 U.S. 1071 (1993).

151. *Id.* at 981.

152. 492 F.2d 631, 636-39 (D.C. Cir.), *cert. dismissed*, 417 U.S. 938 (1974). In *Carey*, the court held:

> It would be exceedingly difficult for appellee to introduce evidence beyond his own testimony to prove that he did not, at any time of day or night over an indefinite period of several weeks, remove box-fulls of documents from the UMW offices. Even if he did prove that the statements were false, [*New York Times Co. v.*] *Sullivan*[, 376 U.S. 254 (1964)] also requires a showing of malice or reckless disregard of the truth. That further step might be achieved by

proven to be essentially correct when he noted, in *Zerilli v. Smith*, that a "distinction can also be drawn between civil cases in which the reporter is a party, as in a libel action, and cases in which the reporter is not a party. When the journalist is a party, and successful assertion of the privilege will effectively shield him from liability, the equities weigh somewhat more heavily in favor of disclosure."[153]

As Judge Wright anticipated, the issue has arisen most frequently, as it did in *Carey v. Hume*, in the context of defamation litigation "involving public officials or public figures."[154] There, because plaintiffs "must prove both that the allegedly defamatory publication was false, and that it was made with 'actual malice,'" courts have recognized that "[p]roof of actual malice will frequently depend on knowing the identity of the newspaper's informant, since a plaintiff will have to demonstrate the informant was unreliable and that the journalist failed to take adequate steps to verify his story."[155] In such circumstances, some courts have held that the privilege must yield, because "[p]rotecting the source would effectively prevent recovery."[156]

> proof that appellant in fact had no reliable sources, that he misrepresented the reports of his sources, or that reliance upon those particular sources was reckless.
>
> Knowledge of the identity of the alleged sources would logically be an initial element in the proof of any of such circumstances. Although it might be possible to submit the question of malice to the jury simply on the basis of the conflicting allegation of the parties, that procedure would seem to provide the plaintiff little prospect of success in view of his heavy burden of proof. Consequently, we find that the identity of appellant's sources is critical to appellee's claim.

Id. at 636-37 (footnotes omitted).

153. 656 F.2d at 714.
154. *Id.*
155. *Id.*
156. *Id.* See, e.g., Garland v. Torre, 259 F.2d 545, 548-49 (2d Cir.), *cert. denied*, 358 U.S. 910 (1958) (holding that plaintiff in defamation action had made necessary showing to compel disclosure of source's identity prior to *Branzburg* and *New York Times Co. v. Sullivan*, 376 U.S. 254 (1964)); Miller v. Transamerican Press, Inc., 621 F.2d 721, 725 (5th Cir. 1980), *cert. denied*, 450 U.S. 1041 (1981) (in public figure defamation action, plaintiff's motion to compel disclosure of confidential source's identity granted; although "reporter has a First Amendment privilege which protects the refusal to disclose the identity of confidential informants, ... the privilege is not absolute and in a libel case as here presented, the privilege must yield"); Star Editorial, Inc. v. United States Dist. Ct., 7 F.3d 856, 862 (9th Cir. 1993) (trial court "conducted the balancing required by California law in requiring the disclosure of confidential sources" in public figure defamation action); DeRoburt v. Gannett Co., 507 F. Supp. 880, 882 (D. Haw. 1981) (court accepted argument of public figure defamation plaintiff that compelled disclosure of defendants' sources is "relevant and is not privileged" because he would be "severely hampered in meeting his burden of showing 'actual malice' when he is denied critical information from which defendants' state of mind may be inferred"); Laxalt v. McClatchy, 622 F. Supp. 737 (D. Nev. 1985) (newspaper's claim of privilege in public figure defamation action, and counterclaim based on plaintiff's effort to compel disclosure of sources rejected on ground that the "number of and credibility of confidential sources used in preparation of these articles are clearly relevant, ... it appears that the

By the same token, as Judge Wright took "care to point out" in *Zerilli*, "disclosure should by no means be automatic in libel cases. Where other relevant factors suggest disclosure is inappropriate, the privilege should prevail."[157] In *Clyburn v. News World Communications, Inc.*,[158] for example, the D.C. Circuit upheld the district court's finding that a defamation plaintiff had "'utterly failed' to pursue 'obvious alternative sources of information'" and was therefore not entitled to compel disclosure of a source's identity from the defendants. Indeed, several other courts have similarly upheld privilege claims asserted by journalists and other media defendants in defamation actions.[159] Most of these courts

---

only source for this information is [defendant] ... [and] [t]he interest in disclosure ... is compelling"); Tavoulareas v. Piro, 93 F.R.D. 35, 41 (D.D.C. 1981) (court compels disclosure of defendants' internal memoranda, drafts of article at issue, "and other materials related to the editorial and newsgathering processes" because, although "a journalist's first amendment interests are entitled to weight," they are more significant in "nonlibel actions in which the journalist or newspaper protesting discovery has not been a litigant"); Williams v. American Broadcasting Cos., 96 F.R.D. 658 (W.D. Ark. 1983) (ordering disclosure of outtakes in libel action on ground that "with respect to editorial decisions and processes, the test is whether the requested information is a matter of simple 'curiosity' or some nebulous concept such as the 'public interest' or whether it is a genuine matter involving a specific claim of injury resulting from malicious defamation or invasion of privacy"); Goldfeld v. Post Publ'g, 4 MEDIA L. REP. (BNA) 1167, 1169 (Conn. Super. 1978) (identity of confidential source "relevant and goes to the very basis of the plaintiff's case"); Rubera v. Post-Newsweek Stations, 8 MEDIA L. REP. (BNA) 2293 (Conn. Super. 1982); Downing v. Monitor Publ'g Co., 415 A.2d 683, 685 (N.H. 1980) ("'Unless liability is to be completely foreclosed,' the identity of the informer must be available to the plaintiff.") (quoting Herbert v. Lando, 441 U.S. 153, 160 (1979)).

157. 656 F.2d at 714 (citing Cervantes v. Time, Inc., 464 F.2d 986 (8th Cir. 1972), *cert. denied*, 409 U.S. 1125 (1973)).

158. 903 F.2d 29, 35 (D.C. Cir. 1990).

159. See, e.g., LaRouche v. National Broadcasting Co., 780 F.2d 1134, 1139 (4th Cir.), *cert. denied*, 479 U.S. 818 (1986) (in defamation action against television network, trial court did not err in upholding claim of privilege by defendant to prevent compelled disclosure of confidential sources' identities because he "did not exhaust all his non-party depositions before making the motion"); Cervantes v. Time, Inc., 464 F.2d 986, 992 (8th Cir. 1972), *cert. denied*, 409 U.S. 1125 (1983) (privilege claim upheld in public figure defamation action and defendants' summary judgment motion granted on merits because "the depositions and other evidentiary materials comprising this record establish, without room for substantial argument, facts that entitled both defendants to judgment as a matter of law" irrespective of the discovery sought by plaintiff); Lauderback v. American Broadcasting Cos., 8 MEDIA L. REP. (BNA) 2407, 2408 (N.D. Iowa 1982) (privilege applies to prevent libel plaintiff from securing access to broadcast outtakes because "disclosure here constitutes an intrusion into the news gathering and editorial process and impairs the free flow of information so as to implicate the first amendment and plaintiff has not established that this infringement is justified"); Schultz v. Reader's Digest Ass'n, 468 F. Supp. 551, 567 (E.D. Mich. 1979) (relying on *Cervantes*); Mitchell v. Superior Ct., 690 P.2d 625, 634 (Cal. 1984) ("the court may require the plaintiff to make a prima facie showing that the alleged defamatory statements are false before requiring disclosure"); Mason v. CBS Inc., 15 MEDIA L. REP. (BNA) 2126 (N.Y. Sup. Ct. 1988) (denying pre-action discovery of documents, videotapes, and photographs allegedly pertaining to potential defamation plaintiff); Dallas Morning News Co. v. Garcia, 822 S.W.2d 675, 681 (Tex. App. 1991) ("The requirement that substantial falsity must be

seem to concur with the Eighth Circuit's observation, in *Cervantes v. Time, Inc.*,[160] that "to routinely grant motions seeking compulsory disclosure of anonymous sources without first inquiring into the substance of a libel allegation would utterly emasculate the fundamental principles that underlay the line of cases articulating the constitutional restrictions to be engrafted upon the enforcement of State libel laws."[161]

Some courts have attempted to provide an analytical framework for resolving claims of constitutional privilege asserted by defendants in the public figure defamation context. In *Bruno & Stillman, Inc. v. Globe Newspaper Co.*,[162] for example, the First Circuit held that, under such circumstances, "each party has a burden. The plaintiff must establish the relevance of the desired information and the defendant has the burden of establishing the need for preserving confidentiality." Thus, the court concluded:

> As a threshold matter, the court should be satisfied that a claim is not frivolous, a pretense for using discovery powers in a fishing expedition. In this case, plaintiff should show that it can establish jury issues on the essential elements of its case not the subject of contested discovery.... Assuming, however, that the case does not appear frivolous, that falsity appears to be a jury issue, and that the desired information appears more than remotely relevant, the court must assess the extent to which there is a need for confidentiality. Not all information as to sources is equally deserving of confidentiality. An unsolicited letter may be received with no mention of an interest in anonymity; such a letter may casually mention the wish for confidential treatment; it may specifically condition use on the according of

---

shown is designed as a threshold criterion in order to prevent forced disclosure of confidential sources based on a mere pleading that the plaintiff has been injured by an untrue statement."); Philip Morris Cos. v. American Broadcasting Cos., 23 MEDIA L. REP. (BNA) 2438, 2439-40 (Va. Cir. 1995) ("there does exist a qualified reporter's privilege against disclosure in public figure defamation cases"); Missouri ex rel. Classic III, Inc. v. Ely, 954 S.W.2d 650, 657 (Mo. App. 1997) (privilege shields media defendant from compelled disclosure of confidential sources and communications where plaintiffs failed to show that they had exhausted reasonable alternative sources of information, that "the requested information goes to the heart of or is crucial to the plaintiff's claim," and that the defendants "falsely claim[ed] a promise of confidentiality to frustrate prosecution of a legitimate claim").

160. 464 F.2d 986, 993 (8th Cir. 1972), *cert. denied*, 409 U.S. 1125 (1973).

161. *Id.* See also Downing v. Monitor Publ'g Co., 415 A.2d 683, 686 (N.H. 1980) (to compel discovery of otherwise privileged material, libel plaintiff must demonstrate a genuine issue of fact regarding falsity); Dallas Morning News Co. v. Garcia, 822 S.W.2d 675, 682 (Tex. App. 1991) ("If the plaintiff cannot at a minimum produce enough evidence to establish the probable falsity of the defendant's statements, he may not, at the expense of the defendant's constitutional rights, conduct a fishing expedition through its confidential sources in an effort to contrive such a claim."); Southwell v. Southern Poverty Law Center, 949 F. Supp. 1303 (W.D. Mich. 1996) (applying *Cervantes* to grant summary judgment without ordering source disclosure).

162. 633 F.2d 583, 597 (1st Cir. 1980).

such treatment; or it may defer communication of any substance until a commitment to confidentiality is received.[163]

If, after conducting this threshold analysis, the issue remains "in doubt," Judge Coffin suggested in *Bruno & Stillman* that the trial court "may defer consideration of the confidentiality issue and turn to the relevance issue. It may, for example, conduct an *in camera* inspection" and, if that review does not confirm the necessary relevance, "it could refuse disclosure."[164] Moreover, the court may defer disclosure "until more discovery has taken place with the possibility that summary judgment would be appropriate," it may "require that resort to nonconfidential sources first be exhausted," or — where disclosure is otherwise appropriate — it might order that confidential information be sealed or otherwise restrict access to it.[165] In the last analysis, Judge Coffin asserted, the "task is one that demands sensitivity, invites flexibility, and defies formula. While obviously the discretion of the trial judge has wide scope, it is a discretion informed by an awareness of First Amendment values and the precedential effect which decision in any one case would be likely to have."[166]

Some courts have addressed claims of privilege by party journalists or media entities outside the defamation context. In *Williams v. American Broadcasting Cos.*,[167] for example, the court explained that the fate of the privilege in cases alleging other tort claims against the news media does not necessarily mirror judicial consideration of that issue in the defamation context. In cases alleging false light invasion of privacy, the court suggested, "wherein the false light is allegedly the result of selective editing, out-takes of film would be highly

---

163. *Id.*
164. *Id.* at 598.
165. *Id.*
166. *Id.* The Eighth Circuit undertook a similar analysis in *Cervantes v. Time, Inc.*, 464 F.2d 986, 994 (8th Cir. 1972), *cert. denied*, 409 U.S. 1125 (1973):

> Where there is a concrete demonstration that the identity of defense news sources will lead to persuasive evidence on the issue of malice, a District Court should not reach the merits of a defense motion for summary judgment until and unless the plaintiff is first given a meaningful opportunity to cross-examine those sources, whether they be anonymous or known. . . . The point of principal importance is that there must be a showing of cognizable prejudice before the failure to permit examination of anonymous news sources can rise to the level of error. Mere speculation or conjecture about the fruits of such examination simply will not suffice.

Accord Tavoulareas v. Piro, 93 F.R.D. 35, 39 (D.D.C. 1981) (court first postpones consideration of public figure libel plaintiff's motion to compel disclosure of confidential sources and later, following additional discovery, orders defendants to produce requested documents redacted to "withhold information regarding any confidential source whose identity has not yet been established through other independent means"); Bauer v. Gannett Co., 557 N.W.2d 608 (Minn. App. 1997) (applying five-factor test to ascertain viability of source privilege in libel action).

167. 96 F.R.D. 669 (W.D. Ark. 1983).

probative and in many cases the only proof of selective editing."[168] By the same token, in "intrusion cases, out-takes could be relevant, but not crucial, necessarily, to proof of the fact of invasion and the extent of it."[169] Finally, in disclosure and appropriation cases, where "the gist of the tort is defendant's use for his or her benefit or actual disclosure," out-takes would "not necessarily be particularly relevant."[170]

In *Anderson v. Nixon*,[171] syndicated columnist Jack Anderson instituted a civil action against nineteen government officials, including President Nixon. The defendants, in turn, sought the compelled disclosure of the identities of sources who provided Anderson with the information upon which he based his claim. The court rejected Anderson's claim of privilege on the ground that he was "not being obliged to disclose his sources. Plaintiff's pledge of confidentiality would have remained unchallenged had he not invoked the aid of the Court seeking compensatory and punitive damages based on his claim of conspiracy."[172] Thus, the court held that Anderson could not "have it both ways. Plaintiff is not a bystander in the process but a principal. He cannot ask for justice and deny it to those he accuses."[173]

Finally, courts have applied the privilege in the context of administrative proceedings in which the media or a journalist is a party. Thus, in *SEC v. McGoff*,[174] the SEC instituted a formal, non-public investigation centering on a controversial newspaper publisher. In the course of that proceeding, the agency sought to enforce subpoenas, issued to the publisher, which sought records of two companies he controlled. The court concluded that "an accommodation was required to avoid unnecessary encroachment" on the publisher's "activities and associations as a newspaper publisher and writer" and therefore foreclosed the agency from seeking documents "relating solely to 'editorial policy' or news gathering."[175] By the same token, the court noted that, with respect to any additional

---

168. *Id.* at 669.
169. *Id.*
170. *Id.* But see Cape Publications, Inc. v. Bridges, 387 So. 2d 436, 439-40 (Fla. App. 1980) (in invasion of privacy action based on publication of plaintiff's photograph, court held privilege overcome with respect to photographs, negatives, notes, and memoranda relating to published article because claim for punitive damages required plaintiff to prove "actual malice").
171. 444 F. Supp. 1195 (D.D.C. 1978).
172. *Id.* at 1199.
173. *Id.* See also Driscoll v. Morris, 111 F.R.D. 459, 463 (D. Conn. 1986) (reporter who brought action alleging actionable interference with his relationship with confidential source has "placed at issue the identity of his sources" and had thereby "waived the privilege against disclosure"); Campus Communications, Inc. v. Freedman, 374 So. 2d 1169, 1171 (Fla. App. 1979) (news organization, which sued for lost business due to stolen newspapers, could not assert constitutional privilege).
174. 647 F.2d 185 (D.C. Cir. 1981).
175. *Id.* at 191.

documents, a media entity "enjoy[s] no special privilege ... to withhold information others must furnish to the investing public."[176]

§ 16-2(d). Scope of Protection.

§ 16-2(d)(1). Sources of Information.

Virtually every jurisdiction that has recognized a constitutional privilege at all has held that it protects a journalist, at least as a threshold matter, against the compelled disclosure of confidential sources.[177] These courts have proceeded from the premise that "[c]ompelling a reporter to disclose the identity of a source may significantly interfere with [the press'] news gathering ability; journalists frequently depend on informants to gather news, and confidentiality is often essential to establishing a relationship with an informant."[178]

In *In re Selcraig*,[179] for example, a discharged school official sought to compel the disclosure of a reporter's confidential sources in the context of his civil action against his former employer for "publicizing false and stigmatizing

---

176. *Id.* at 190.
177. See, e.g., Carey v. Hume, 492 F.2d 631 (D.C. Cir.), *cert. dismissed*, 417 U.S. 938 (1974); Zerilli v. Smith, 656 F.2d 705 (D.C. Cir. 1981); Clyburn v. News World Communications, Inc., 903 F.2d 29 (D.C. Cir. 1990); Tavoulareas v. Piro, 93 F.R.D. 35 (D.D.C. 1981); Bruno & Stillman, Inc. v. Globe Newspaper Co., 633 F.2d 583 (1st Cir. 1980); In re Cusumano, 162 F.3d 708 (1st Cir. 1998); Summit Tech., Inc. v. Healthcare Capital Group, Inc., 141 F.R.D. 381 (D. Mass. 1992); Garland v. Torre, 259 F.2d 545 (2d Cir.), *cert. denied*, 358 U.S. 910 (1958); Baker v. F & F Inv., 470 F.2d 778 (2d Cir. 1972), *cert. denied*, 411 U.S. 966 (1973); In re Petroleum Prods. Antitrust Litig., 680 F.2d 5 (2d Cir.), *cert. denied*, 459 U.S. 909 (1982); Gonzales v. National Broadcasting Co., 1998 U.S. App. LEXIS 38583 (2d Cir. Aug. 27, 1999); Aequitron Med. Inc. v. CBS Inc., 24 MEDIA L. REP. (BNA) 1025, 1027 (S.D.N.Y. 1995); United States v. Sanusi, 813 F. Supp. 149 (E.D.N.Y. 1992); Riley v. City of Chester, 612 F.2d 708 (3d Cir. 1979); United States v. Morrison, 622 F. Supp. 1009 (D. Md. 1985); Miller v. Transamerican Press, Inc., 621 F.2d 721 (5th Cir. 1980), *cert. denied*, 450 U.S. 1041 (1981); In re Selcraig, 705 F.2d 789 (5th Cir. 1983); Campbell v. Klevenhagen, 760 F. Supp. 1206 (S.D. Tex. 1991); Cervantes v. Time, Inc., 464 F.2d 986 (8th Cir. 1972); Farr v. Pitchess, 522 F.2d 464 (9th Cir. 1975); Star Editorial, Inc. v. United States Dist. Ct., 7 F.3d 856 (9th Cir. 1993); Laxalt v. McClatchy, 622 F. Supp. 737 (D. Nev. 1985); Los Angeles Mem'l Coliseum Comm'n v. National Football League, 89 F.R.D. 489 (C.D. Cal. 1981); Silkwood v. Kerr-McGee Corp., 563 F.2d 433 (10th Cir. 1977); Mitchell v. Superior Ct., 690 P.2d 625, 632 (Cal. 1984); Kansas v. Sandstrom, 581 P.2d 812, 814 (Kan. 1978); Dallas Morning News Co. v. Garcia, 822 S.W.2d 675, 677 (Tex. App. 1991); West Virginia ex rel. Hudok v. Henry, 389 S.E.2d 188, 193 (W. Va. 1989). Compare In re Roche, 411 N.E.2d 466 (Mass. 1980) (affirming contempt order against reporter who refused to disclose confidential sources in deposition in misconduct proceeding against judge by Commission on Judicial Conduct) with Sinnott v. Boston Retirement Bd., 524 N.E.2d 100, 102 (Mass.), *cert. denied*, 488 U.S. 980 (1988) (denying motion to compel identity of confidential sources in civil action eight years after *Roche*).
178. Zerilli v. Smith, 656 F.2d 705, 711 (D.C. Cir. 1981) (citing Note, *Reporters and Their Sources: The Constitutional Right to a Confidential Relationship*, 80 YALE L.J. 317 (1970)).
179. 705 F.2d 789 (5th Cir. 1983).

charges against him."[180] The district court had held its own proceedings designed "to assure that whether the school district's officers were the source of the reporter's information was central to the claim; that circumstantial evidence pointed to a school district officer or employee as the communicant; and that alternative ways of confirming that hypothesis had been exhausted."[181] At their conclusion, the trial judge ordered the reporter to testify *in camera* for the limited purpose of establishing "whether a school district officer was the source of his information."[182] When the reporter declined, he was held in contempt.

The Fifth Circuit reversed, holding the "necessity of obtaining the information was not yet established and the reporter's qualified privilege, therefore, not yet overcome."[183] According to the court, a plaintiff seeking to compel disclosure of a journalist's confidential source should, beyond a showing of relevance and exhaustion of alternative sources, also be "required at least to demonstrate by affidavits or depositions, and not by mere allegation, a prima facie case" of liability.[184]

Similarly, in *In re Petroleum Products Antitrust Litigation*,[185] the Second Circuit reversed an order holding a publisher in civil contempt for its failure to produce a document containing the names of several confidential sources. The document was requested by subpoena issued to the publisher in a multidistrict antitrust action in which it was not a party. The court emphasized that the "law in this Circuit is clear that to protect the important interests of reporters and the public in preserving the confidentiality of journalists' sources, disclosure may be ordered only upon a clear and specific showing that the information is: highly material and relevant, necessary or critical to the maintenance of the claim, and not obtainable from other available sources."[186] Upon its own application of the privilege, the court concluded that the "names of the sources sought in this instance bear at most a tenuous and speculative relationship" to the plaintiff's claims; it held, therefore, that the "necessity of confidentiality, essential to fulfillment of the pivotal function of reporters to collect information for public dissemination, cannot be overcome simply by suggesting — with no basis to support the assertion — that the reporter may unknowingly have been used by those sources in their illegal activities."[187]

---

180. *Id.* at 791.
181. *Id.* at 792.
182. *Id.*
183. *Id.*
184. *Id.* at 798.
185. 680 F.2d 5 (2d Cir.), *cert. denied*, 459 U.S. 909 (1982).
186. *Id.* at 7.
187. *Id.* at 8. For other cases applying the privilege in the confidential source context when the press is not a party to the litigation, see, e.g., Riley v. City of Chester, 612 F.2d 708, 716-17 (3d Cir. 1979); Silkwood v. Kerr-McGee Corp., 563 F.2d 433, 438 (10th Cir. 1977); Baker v. F & F Inv., 470 F.2d 778, 785 (2d Cir. 1972), *cert. denied*, 411 U.S. 988 (1973); Zerilli v. Smith, 656

The identities of confidential sources have also received presumptive constitutional protection from compelled disclosure in civil actions in which the press is a party, most notably defamation actions.[188] In such cases, some courts have held that the defamation plaintiff has made the requisite showing to overcome the privilege,[189] and others have concluded that the privilege prevents such compelled source disclosure.[190] Even those courts that have rejected specific assertions of the constitutional privilege to protect confidential sources in the defamation context have emphasized that "courts must always be alert to the possibilities of limiting impingements upon press freedoms to the minimum; and one way of doing so is to make compelled disclosure by a journalist a last resort after pursuit of other opportunities have failed."[191]

F.2d 705, 711 (D.C. Cir. 1981); Los Angeles Mem'l Coliseum Comm'n v. National Football League, 89 F.R.D. 489, 496 (C.D. Cal. 1981); Summit Tech., Inc. v. Healthcare Capital Group, Inc., 141 F.R.D. 381, 385 (D. Mass. 1992); Ko v. Zilog, Inc., 25 MEDIA L. REP. (BNA) 1892 (Idaho 1997).

188. In one nondefamation action, in which a journalist instituted litigation against several governmental officials, the court held that, if he wished to pursue his case, he would be required to reveal the identities of certain confidential sources to the defendants. See Anderson v. Nixon, 444 F. Supp. 1195, 1199 (D.D.C. 1978) ("Here, the newsman is not being obliged to disclose his sources. Plaintiff's pledge of confidentiality would have remained unchallenged had he not invoked the aid of the Court seeking compensatory and punitive damages based on his claim of conspiracy. Plaintiff is attempting to use the First Amendment simultaneously as a sword and a shield.").

189. See, e.g., Garland v. Torre, 259 F.2d 545, 550 (2d Cir.), cert. denied, 358 U.S. 910 (1958); Carey v. Hume, 492 F.2d 631, 638-39 (D.C. Cir.), cert. dismissed, 417 U.S. 938 (1974); Miller v. Transamerican Press, Inc., 621 F.2d 721, 725 (5th Cir. 1980), cert. denied, 450 U.S. 1041 (1981); Star Editorial, Inc. v. United States Dist. Ct., 7 F.3d 856, 861-62 (9th Cir. 1993); Laxalt v. McClatchy, 622 F. Supp. 737 (D. Nev. 1985).

190. See, e.g., Cervantes v. Time, Inc., 464 F.2d 986, 993 (8th Cir. 1972), cert. denied, 409 U.S. 1125 (1973); Clyburn v. News World Communications, Inc., 903 F.2d 29, 35 (D.C. Cir. 1990); Dallas Morning News Co. v. Garcia, 822 S.W.2d 675, 677 (Tex. App. 1991); Philip Morris Cos. v. American Broadcasting Cos., 23 MEDIA L. REP. (BNA) 2438, 2440 (Va. Cir. 1995); Missouri ex rel. Classic III, Inc. v. Ely, 954 S.W.2d 650 (Mo. App. 1997).

191. Carey v. Hume, 492 F.2d at 639. Accord Miller v. Transamerican Press, Inc., 621 F.2d at 725 ("[T]here is a more apparent interest in protecting the confidentiality of journalists' sources in libel cases than in grand jury proceedings. . . . In a libel case, the plaintiff and the press are on opposite sides. And a defamed plaintiff might relish an opportunity to retaliate against the informant."); Star Editorial, Inc. v. United States Dist. Ct., 7 F.3d at 860 (quoting Mitchell v. Superior Ct., 690 P.2d 625, 632 (Cal. 1984)) ("We conclude that in a civil action a reporter, editor, or publisher has a qualified privilege to withhold disclosure of the identity of confidential sources and of unpublished information supplied by such sources. The scope of that privilege in each particular case will depend upon the consideration and weighing of a number of interrelated factors."); Dallas Morning News Co. v. Garcia, 822 S.W.2d 675, 683 (Tex. App. 1991) ("Every plaintiff in every libel case will testify that he or she believes the published statements are false. If this were the only requirement, the qualified privilege would be no privilege at all; anyone could overcome it merely by filing a libel suit and expressing the opinion that the defendant's statements were false.").

Two cases illustrate the diligence with which trial judges have approached the protection of confidential sources in the defamation context. In *Tavoulareas v. Piro*, a trial judge rejected efforts by a defamation plaintiff to compel the disclosure of "'any expense vouchers, reimbursement requests, travel logs, diaries, or telephone bills relating to or generated in the course of'" the defendant newspaper's investigation of the article at issue in the litigation.[192] The court accepted the defendant's argument that, by "requesting materials that might be used to piece together the identities of off-the-record sources, . . . plaintiffs are attempting to obtain indirectly information that this Court has ruled they are not yet entitled to through direct discovery," given their failure to exhaust alternative sources of such information.[193] In that same case, the trial judge also took care to permit the defendants to redact from other documents responsive to plaintiff's discovery "information regarding any confidential source whose identity has not yet been established through other independent means."[194]

In *DeRoburt v. Gannett Co.*,[195] a trial judge in a defamation action revisited and reversed his imposition of sanctions against the defendants for their refusal to disclose the identities of confidential sources. Originally, the court had held that a "media defendant cannot have it both ways: he cannot enjoy the protection afforded by the heavy burden imposed upon a public official . . . and at the same time enjoy a privilege that prevents the plaintiff from obtaining the evidence necessary to carry that burden."[196] Accordingly, the court held that, should the defendants continue to refuse to reveal their sources, it would instruct the jury that "there shall arise a presumption that the defendant had no source."[197] Prior to trial, however, one of the defendants' sources died, leading to their voluntary disclosure of his identity, and the name of the other was discovered by the plaintiff independently. Thus, the court reconsidered its earlier ruling and held that it was no longer necessary to indulge in a no-source presumption. The Ninth Circuit affirmed, holding that, under the circumstances, "[f]or the district judge to then instruct the jury that it should conclusively presume that there were no sources would have been contrary to the evidence presented at trial by both parties and contrary to the truth."[198]

Confidential sources have also received presumptive protection in many criminal proceedings in which the press is not a party. One federal trial judge held, for example, that a television network's assertion of privilege in a criminal

---

192. 93 F.R.D. 35, 38 (D.D.C. 1981).
193. *Id.* at 38.
194. *Id.* at 39.
195. 859 F.2d 714 (9th Cir. 1987), *cert. denied*, 493 U.S. 846 (1989).
196. DeRoburt v. Gannett Co., 6 MEDIA L. REP. (BNA) 2473, 2475 (D. Haw. 1981).
197. *Id.* at 2478 (quoting Downing v. Monitor Publ'g Co., 415 A.2d 683, 686 (N.H. 1980)).
198. 859 F.2d at 715.

case had been overcome with respect to "outtakes" of a police search that had not been broadcast, but took pains to emphasize that the network could "obscure the identity of a confidential source whose identity it agreed, at the government's request, to protect."[199] The body of precedent in criminal cases is less consistent than in the civil context, however, because of the failure of some courts to recognize any privilege at all in at least some criminal cases.[200]

Finally, courts have touched upon the relevance of a precise promise of confidentiality to the privilege's protection of a source's identity. In some cases, where a promise of confidentiality is either undisputed or established by record evidence, courts have accorded that fact considerable weight.[201] The absence of an express promise of confidentiality is not, however, necessarily fatal to a claim of privilege. In *Bruno & Stillman, Inc. v. Globe Newspaper Co.*,[202] for example, the First Circuit suggested that even the identity of the source of an unsolicited letter to the editor may, under some circumstances, shelter under the privilege; ultimately, "[w]hether and to what extent such a *nunc pro tunc* undertaking" to shield the "source's" identity after the fact "merits protection by the court is a matter for its discriminating judgment," a judgment that should properly focus on the source's "reasonable expectation of confidentiality."[203]

---

199. United States v. Sanusi, 813 F. Supp. 149, 161 (E.D.N.Y. 1992).

200. See Chap. 16-2(c)(1) *supra* (citing cases).

201. See, e.g., Silkwood v. Kerr-McGee Corp., 563 F.2d 433, 434 (10th Cir. 1977) ("In an affidavit which is in the record," documentary filmmaker stated that he had "assured the interviewees, who demanded confidentiality, that the information would be kept confidential. He also assured those interviewees who requested that their identities be not revealed that he would respect their requests.").

202. 633 F.2d 583, 597 (1st Cir. 1980).

203. In *Bruno & Stillman*, the reporter testified concerning his practice with respect to source confidentiality:

> Q. Do you have a policy as to when you consider sources confidential and when you don't?
> A. Yes, sir.
> Q. Can you explain to me what that is?
> A. It's when I tell them I don't so treat them.
> Q. Fair enough. When you tell someone that you will treat them confidentially, that is when it is confidential to you?
> A. Yes, sir.
> Q. But when a witness says to you this is confidential, and you don't say it back to them, it's not confidential? You don't treat it as confidential?
> A. Not necessarily.
> Q. Not necessarily? That is up to you to decide?
> A. Yes, sir.

Id. at 593-94.

§ 16-2(d)(2). Other Confidential Information.

The constitutional privilege has also been held to protect other information received by journalists in confidence, beyond the identities of their sources. In *Los Angeles Memorial Coliseum Commission v. National Football League*,[204] for example, the court sustained an assertion of privilege by journalists who claimed that "to require them to disclose unpublished materials regarding their reporting would necessarily force disclosure of information given to them in confidence as well as the identities of their sources." The court concluded that to permit the defendant in a civil action "to rummage through" a journalist's "notes of confidential conversations would subvert the guarantee of freedom of the press embodied in the First Amendment."[205] In the defamation case of *Tavoulareas v. Piro*,[206] the court appeared to adopt a slightly different approach, one which permitted the defendant-journalists and their newspaper to invoke the privilege as to any confidential information the disclosure of which "may expose a source to whom the defendants have extended an assurance of confidentiality."

In *In re Cusumano*,[207] the court upheld an assertion of the privilege by academic investigators who sought protection for notes, transcripts, and tape recordings of interviews, as well as correspondence with interview subjects, when these materials were subpoenaed by the defendant, Microsoft Corporation, in a civil antitrust action. After finding that the research materials "fall along the continuum of confidentiality at a point sufficient to justify significant protection,"[208] the First Circuit concluded that compelling disclosure not only would "hamstring" future research efforts but would impede "the free flow of information to the public, thus denigrating a fundamental First Amendment value."[209]

§ 16-2(d)(3). Nonconfidential Information.

Most information gathered by journalists is not received pursuant to an express or implied promise of confidentiality. Such information can include the identities of nonconfidential, but otherwise unidentified sources; a journalist's eyewitness observations; notes, drafts and other workproduct; unpublished infor-

---

204. 89 F.R.D. 489, 491 (C.D. Cal. 1981).
205. *Id.* at 496. See Silkwood v. Kerr-McGee Corp., 563 F.2d 433, 434, 438 (10th Cir. 1977) (indicating that district court should consider "the nature of the evidence sought" in evaluating claim of privilege encompassing compelled disclosure of "confidential information" gathered "in the course of making a factual investigation of events surrounding the death" of plaintiff's decedent).
206. 93 F.R.D. 35, 39-40 (D.D.C. 1981).
207. 162 F.3d 708 (1st Cir. 1998).
208. *Id.* at 715.
209. *Id.* at 717.

mation received in source interviews or from nonconfidential documents; and even the journalist's published works.

The courts have been called upon to resolve assertions of the constitutional privilege in the context of such nonconfidential information with increasing frequency. Generally, although there are some notable exceptions,[210] they have rejected the contention that a promise of confidentiality is a prerequisite to the privilege's invocation. As one trial court suggested, the "contention that discovery is outside of First Amendment concern because it does not seek the identity of confidential sources is a total misconception of the scope of the free press interest."[211]

Several courts have adopted a "flexible" approach to the privilege's application outside the realm of confidential information.[212] As the following discussion suggests, the cases — though by no means unanimous — appear to recognize something of "a continuum," at one end of which is that information that is actually published or broadcast, such as testimony verifying "'whether [an article] was truly published on the date asserted and whether [the reporter] did in fact interview'" the sources identified in the article.[213] Such information is typically held to fall outside the scope of the privilege.[214] Further along the continuum is "'[a] reporter's observations of a public place or event'"[215] which,

---

210. See, e.g., Marketos v. American Employers Ins. Co., 460 N.W.2d 272, 273 (Mich. App. 1990); Dolcefino v. Ray, 902 S.W.2d 163 (Tex. App. 1995), *cert. denied*, 517 U.S. 1121 (1996); United States v. Smith, 135 F.3d 963, 972 (5th Cir. 1998) ("this court has theorized that confidentiality is a prerequisite for the news reporters' privilege"); In re Owens, 496 S.E.2d 592, 596 (N.C. App. 1998) ("we hold that the trial court . . . properly declined to recognize a news reporter's privilege to refuse to testify in a criminal proceeding regarding non-confidential information obtained from a non-confidential source").

211. In re Consumers Union, 495 F. Supp. 582, 585 (S.D.N.Y. 1980) See von Bulow v. von Bulow, 811 F.2d 136, 142 (2d Cir.), *cert. denied*, 481 U.S. 1015 (1987) ("the relationship between the journalist and his source may be confidential or nonconfidential for purposes of the privilege" and "unpublished resource material likewise may be protected"); Mitchell v. Superior Ct., 690 P.2d 625, 632 (Cal. 1984) ("in a civil action a reporter, editor, or publisher has a qualified privilege to withhold disclosure of the identity of a confidential source and of unpublished information supplied by such sources"); Neal v. City of Harvey, Illinois, 173 F.R.D. 231, 234 (N.D. Ill. 1997) (while confidentiality "'is an important element in balancing the defendants' need for the material against the interests of the journalist in preventing production,' . . . the court engage[s] in the balancing inquiry only after concluding that the sought information [is] highly material, relevant, and 'critical to the maintenance of the defense,' a showing that the defendants in this case have not made") (citations omitted); Florida v. Davis, 720 So. 2d 220 (Fla. 1998) (recognizing qualified privilege extending to both confidential and nonconfidential information).

212. See Gonzales v. National Broadcasting Co., 1998 U.S. App. LEXIS 38583 (2d Cir. Aug. 27, 1999); United States v. Markiewicz, 732 F. Supp. 316, 320 (N.D.N.Y. 1990).

213. 732 F. Supp. at 319 (quoting Maughan v. NL Indus., 524 F. Supp. 93, 95 (D.D.C. 1981)).

214. See Chap. 16-2(d)(3)(D) *infra*.

215. Alexander v. Chicago Park Dist., 548 F. Supp. 277, 278 (N.D. Ill. 1982), *quoted in* United States v. Markiewicz, 732 F. Supp. at 319.

at least in some circumstances, will be treated "no different than that of other individuals."[216] Other species of nonconfidential information are typically afforded relatively broad protection from compelled disclosure, although the resulting privilege may be somewhat "diminished when the subpoenaing party does not seek testimony of a confidential nature."[217]

The above-referenced analysis of the range of existing precedent notwithstanding, however, some courts have rejected the notion that the privilege protects against the compelled disclosure of nonconfidential information entirely. Most notably, in *United States v. Smith*,[218] the Fifth Circuit held that "newsreporters enjoy no qualified privilege not to disclose nonconfidential information in criminal cases."[219] The court asserted that, unlike the compelled disclosure of confidential sources, "there is little reason to fear that on-the-record sources will avoid the press simply because the media might turn over nonconfidential statements" since, "[p]resumably, on-the-record sources expect beforehand that the government, along with the rest of the public, will view their nonconfidential statements when they are aired by the media."[220] In addition, the Fifth Circuit expressed little sympathy for the media's contention that "[r]esponding to discovery may well take valuable time, decreasing to that extent resources available for news reporting."[221] In the court's view, "the press here is not differently situated from any other business that may find itself possessing evidence relevant to a criminal trial."[222] Finally, the court noted the absence of an "empirical basis for assertions that the media will avoid important stories or destroy its archives in response to rare requests for criminal discovery."[223]

---

216. 548 F. Supp. at 278.
217. United States v. Markiewicz, 732 F. Supp. at 319 (citing Bruno & Stillman, Inc. v. Globe Newspaper Co., 633 F.2d 583, 597 (1st Cir. 1980); In re Petroleum Prods. Antitrust Litig., 680 F.2d 5 (2d Cir.), *cert. denied*, 459 U.S. 909 (1982)). See Chap. 16-2(c)(1) & (2) *supra* (citing cases).
218. 135 F.3d 963 (5th Cir. 1998).
219. *Id.* at 972.
220. *Id.* at 970.
221. *Id.*
222. *Id.* at 971.
223. *Id.* (citing Zurcher v. Stanford Daily, 436 U.S. 547, 563-67 (1978)). A panel of the Second Circuit embraced the Fifth Circuit's reasoning in *Smith* in Gonzales v. National Broadcasting Co., 155 F.3d 618, 625 (2d Cir. 1998), *vacated*, No. 97-9454 (2d Cir. June 1, 1999), in an opinion in which it purported to distinguish prior authority in that circuit that had appeared to extend the privilege to nonconfidential information. See 155 F.3d at 622 (distinguishing von Bulow v. von Bulow, 811 F.2d 136, 142 (2d Cir.), *cert. denied*, 481 U.S. 1015 (1987); In re Petroleum Prods. Antitrust Litig., 680 F.2d 5, (2d Cir.), *cert. denied*, 459 U.S. 909 (1982)). Subsequently, the court vacated that opinion and the panel itself thereafter issued a revised decision that sought to "explicitly reaffirm" the circuit's recognition of a "qualified privilege for nonconfidential press information." Gonzales v. National Broadcasting Co., 1998 U.S. App. LEXIS 38583, at *4 (2d Cir. Aug. 27, 1999). In the interim, however, several district courts in the Second Circuit had felt bound by the initial opinion in *Gonzales* to hold that the privilege was unavailable in the context of

§ 16-2(d)(3)(A). Nonconfidential Sources.

Most courts have indicated that, for the privilege to apply, at least as a threshold matter, "the relationship between the journalist and his source may be confidential or nonconfidential."[224] Often, the issue of confidentiality of the journalist-source relationship arises in the context of efforts to compel the journalist's testimony concerning published and/or unpublished portions of the source's statements. In *United States v. Cuthbertson*,[225] for example, the Third Circuit upheld CBS's assertion of privilege even though the government, the subpoenaing party, had "obtained waivers from all of its witnesses permitting disclosure of their statements held by CBS." The court concluded that the privilege could not be limited "solely" to the protection of confidential sources:

> The compelled production of a reporter's resource materials can constitute a significant intrusion into the newsgathering and editorial processes. Like the compelled disclosure of confidential sources, it may substantially undercut the public policy favoring the free flow of information to the public that is the foundation for the privilege. . . . Of course, the lack of a confidential source may be an important element in balancing the defendant's need for the material sought against the interest of the journalist in preventing production in a particular case.[226]

In *United States v. Criden*,[227] however, the Third Circuit rejected a reporter's effort to assert the privilege to forestall "the threshold question of whether" she had a conversation with a self-avowed source. The court concluded that, under the circumstances of the criminal case before it, the defendants had "established a record sufficient to demonstrate their entitlement to the limited information sought."[228] In so doing, the court noted that, in the typical case, a criminal defendant "probably should be required to prove less to obtain the reporters' version of a conversation already voluntarily disclosed by the self-confessed source than to obtain the identity of the source itself."[229]

---

nonconfidential information. See, e.g., In re Dow Jones & Co., 27 MEDIA L. REP. (BNA) 1307 (S.D.N.Y. 1998), *vacated*, No. 99-7014 (2d Cir. June 8, 1999); In re Ramaekers, 33 F. Supp. 2d 312 (S.D.N.Y. 1999).

224. von Bulow v. von Bulow, 811 F.2d 136, 142 (2d Cir.), *cert. denied*, 481 U.S. 1015 (1987). But see Dolcefino v. Ray, 902 S.W.2d 163, 165 (Tex. App. 1995), *cert. denied*, 517 U.S. 1121 (1996) ("The reason for having a reporter's privilege is so that informants will know that if they speak to the press, courts will not force the press to disclose their identity. Plainly, there is no danger of that" where the source has voluntarily come forward).

225. 630 F.2d 139, 147 (3d Cir. 1980), *cert. denied*, 449 U.S. 1126 (1981).
226. *Id.* (citations omitted).
227. 633 F.2d 346, 357, 361 (3d Cir. 1980), *cert. denied*, 449 U.S. 1113 (1981).
228. *Id.* at 358.
229. *Id.*

In *Shain v. United States*,[230] the Fourth Circuit rejected a similar assertion of privilege by two reporters who had interviewed a state senator and published portions of his comments in their newspapers. The reporters did not claim that the interview "was confidential or that information obtained was given in confidence."[231] The court, therefore, concluded that "the absence of confidentiality or vindictiveness in the facts of this case fatally undermines the reporters' claim to a First Amendment privilege," and required them to "testify for no more than five minutes each to confirm that [their source] had in fact made the statements they had reported."[232]

§ 16-2(d)(3)(B). Eyewitness Testimony.

The personal observations of journalists, especially in public places, have typically been held by the trial courts to fall outside the scope of the constitutional privilege. In *Alexander v. Chicago Park District*,[233] a federal district court enforced a subpoena seeking "reporters' testimony as to their personal observations" of certain city parks during their investigation for a published newspaper series entitled "Our Squandered Legacy." The court held that a "reporter's observations of a public place or event are no different in kind than that of other individuals; and as to this, they are not entitled to constitutional protection."[234]

---

230. 978 F.2d 850 (4th Cir. 1992).
231. *Id.* at 851.
232. *Id.* at 852, 853. See also In re Gronowicz, 764 F.2d 983 (3d Cir. 1985), *cert. denied*, 474 U.S. 1055 (1986) (in grand jury context, Third Circuit holds that author may be questioned concerning whether he fabricated quotations attributed to assertedly nonconfidential sources in his book); United States v. LaRouche Campaign, 841 F.2d 1176, 1181 (1st Cir. 1988) ("We have been referred to no authoritative sources demonstrating how any chilling effect could result from the disclosure of statements made for publication without any expectation of confidentiality."); In re Owens, 496 S.E.2d 592 (N.C. App. 1998) (no constitutional privilege to refuse to testify in criminal proceeding regarding nonconfidential information obtained from nonconfidential source). But see Penland v. Long, 922 F. Supp. 1080, 1084 (W.D.N.C. 1995) ("the journalists' qualified privilege under the First Amendment encompasses nonconfidential information from non-confidential sources.").

In *Kaiyala v. City of Seattle*, 20 MEDIA L. REP. (BNA) 1740 (W.D. Wash. 1992), a federal trial court confronted a journalist's claim that she was privileged not to testify concerning her personal observations of her source's demeanor during a nonconfidential interview. Although the court noted that "it is unclear whether the qualified privilege extends to a case in which the information sought to be discovered consists of a reporter's personal impressions of an interviewee — impressions she has already confided to the party seeking discovery," it held that the subpoenaing party had not demonstrated that such testimony was relevant to the case. *Id.* at 1742.

233. 548 F. Supp. 277 (N.D. Ill. 1982).
234. *Id.* at 278 (citing Gilbert v. Allied Chem. Corp., 411 F. Supp. 505, 511 (E.D. Va. 1976); Branzburg v. Pound, 461 S.W.2d 345 (Ky. 1970), *aff'd*, 408 U.S. 665 (1972); Lightman v. Maryland, 294 A.2d 149 (Md. Spec. App. 1972), *aff'd*, 295 A.2d 212 (Md.), *cert. denied*, 411 U.S. 951 (1973); Rosato v. Superior Ct., 124 Cal. Rptr. 427 (Ct. App. 1975), *cert. denied*, 427 U.S. 912

Similarly, in *Dillon v. City of San Francisco*,[235] the court compelled a reporter to testify concerning his eyewitness observations, made while "on assignment," of an "alleged beating of the plaintiff by defendant police officers." The court found dispositive the fact that the reporter had "not been asked to reveal any confidential sources or information, nor has he been requested to produce or discuss any resource materials" and rejected the "proposition that such personal observations are privileged simply because the eyewitness is a journalist."[236]

The *Dillon* court found unpersuasive the reporter's argument that requiring him to testify "will seriously damage the news gathering process by causing sources to mistrust him and refuse to cooperate with him."[237] In this regard, the court "doubt[ed]" whether compelling the reporter to testify "as to his personal observations, which did not come from sources, could in any way limit his ability to obtain information from sources in the future."[238] Indeed, more than one court has held that the constitutional privilege is inapplicable to videotaped outtakes on the ground that there is no difference between a journalist's eyewitness testimony of an event and an electronic recording of it, which does not implicate any confidential sources of information.[239]

In *United States v. Steelhammer*,[240] however, the Fourth Circuit divided sharply on the issue, in the context of a subpoena to require journalists to testify concerning what they had observed at a union meeting. A panel of the court first credited the argument that, "if a reporter is compelled to testify to what he has observed or heard while present at a rally or meeting of persons assembled to discuss problems peculiar to their interests, but also of general concern, then

---

(1976)). See also Minnesota v. Turner, 550 N.W.2d 622 (Minn. 1996) (no privilege with respect to reporter's eyewitness observations in criminal case).

235. 748 F. Supp. 722, 724 (N.D. Cal. 1990).

236. *Id.* at 726. See also Pinkard v. Johnson, 118 F.R.D. 517, 521 (M.D. Ala. 1987); Miller v. Mecklenburg County, 602 F. Supp. 675, 679 (W.D.N.C. 1985); In re Ziegler, 550 F. Supp. 530, 532 (W.D.N.Y. 1982). In *Kaiyala v. City of Seattle*, 20 MEDIA L. REP. (BNA) 1740, 1742 n.3 (W.D. Wash. 1992), one federal trial court explained that the "rationale behind these cases is that a reporter should not be immunized from testifying about events which any other person might have observed, and about which that person could be compelled to testify."

237. 748 F. Supp. at 726 n.5.

238. *Id.*

239. See Bartlett v. Superior Ct., 722 P.2d 346 (Ariz. App. 1986); CBS Inc. v. Jackson, 578 So. 2d 698, 700 (Fla. 1991); Ex parte Grothe, 687 S.W.2d 736, 737 (Tex. Crim. App. 1984), *cert. denied*, 474 U.S. 944 (1985); Idaho v. Salsbury, 924 P.2d 208 (Idaho 1996). See also Miami Herald Publ'g Co. v. Morejon, 561 So. 2d 577, 580 (Fla. 1990) (journalist had no First Amendment privilege to refuse to testify about eyewitness observations of a relevant event in a criminal case, even though journalist was engaged in newsgathering); Kidwell v. Florida, 720 So. 2d 218, 218 (Fla. 1998) ("Like an eyewitness-observation, a direct confession to a reporter is direct evidence of a crime that would not fall within the information protected under the qualified privilege.").

240. 539 F.2d 373 (1976), *modified*, 561 F.2d 539 (4th Cir. 1977) (en banc).

thereafter, in retaliation, the sponsors of the occasion will in all probability bar them from later gatherings."[241] Thus, the panel held that the "privilege of the public" to receive such information "calls . . . for judicial restraint in the judicial laying on of sanctions."[242] The *en banc* court, however, affirmed the district court's judgment holding the reporters in civil contempt by a vote of 4-3, but vacated their sentences on the ground that the underlying litigation had concluded in the interim.[243] The majority adopted the reasoning of Judge Winter, who had dissented from the panel opinion because "the absence of a claim of confidentiality and the lack of evidence of vindictiveness tip the scale to the conclusion that the district court was correct."[244]

§ 16-2(d)(3)(C). Unpublished Information.

The constitutional privilege has been applied by most, though by no means all, courts that have had occasion to consider efforts to compel the disclosure of unpublished, but nonconfidential materials gathered or created in the prepublication process. The Ninth Circuit canvassed this body of precedent in *Shoen v. Shoen*,[245] and concluded that "when facts acquired by a journalist in the course of gathering the news become the target of discovery, a qualified privilege against compelled disclosure comes into play."[246] In *Shoen*, the court considered whether, in the context of a defamation action instituted against the founder of the U-Haul Company by two of his sons, a journalist "may be compelled to testify and produce notes and tape recordings of interviews he conducted" with the defendant.[247] Although the court recognized that the information at issue "was not obtained under promise of confidentiality," it nevertheless found the argument in favor of extending the privilege to nonconfidential, but unpublished material "so persuasive" as to require only the following elaboration:

---

241. 539 F.2d at 374.
242. *Id.*
243. 561 F.2d at 540.
244. 539 F.2d at 376 (Winter, J., dissenting).
245. 5 F.3d 1289, 1292 (9th Cir. 1993); see also Shoen v. Shoen, 48 F.3d 412 (9th Cir. 1995).
246. 5 F.3d at 1292. Indeed, the Ninth Circuit asserted that "[e]ight of the other nine circuits that have decided the question" have recognized such a privilege protecting the "facts acquired by a journalist in the course of gathering the news." *Id.* (citing Bruno & Stillman, Inc. v. Globe Newspaper Co., 633 F.2d 583, 595-96 (1st Cir. 1980); United States v. Burke, 700 F.2d 70, 77 (2d Cir.), *cert. denied*, 464 U.S. 816 (1983); United States v. Cuthbertson, 630 F.2d 139, 147 (3d Cir. 1980), *cert. denied*, 449 U.S. 1126 (1981); LaRouche v. National Broadcasting Co., 780 F.2d 1134, 1139 (4th Cir.), *cert. denied*, 479 U.S. 818 (1986); Miller v. Transamerican Press, 621 F.2d 721, 725 (5th Cir. 1980), *cert. denied*, 450 U.S. 1041 (1981); Cervantes v. Time, Inc., 464 F.2d 986, 992-93 & n.9 (8th Cir. 1972), *cert. denied*, 409 U.S. 1125 (1973); Silkwood v. Kerr-McGee Corp., 563 F.2d 433, 436-37 (10th Cir. 1977); Zerilli v. Smith, 656 F.2d 705, 714 (D.C. Cir. 1981)). As the discussion that follows suggests, not all courts would embrace the same construction of the breadth of this body of precedent.
247. 5 F.3d at 1290.

[T]he compelled disclosure of non-confidential information harms the press' ability to gather information by "damaging confidential sources' trust in the press' capacity to keep secret and, in a broader sense, by converting the press in the public's mind into an investigative arm of prosecutors and the courts. It is their independent status that often enables reporters to gain access, without a pledge of confidentiality, to meetings or places where a policeman or a politician would not be welcome. If perceived as an adjunct of the police or of the courts, journalists might well be shunned by persons who might otherwise give them information without a promise of confidentiality, barred from meetings which they would otherwise be free to attend and describe, or even physically harassed if, for example, observed taking notes or photographs at a public rally."[248]

The Ninth Circuit emphasized that "the absence of confidentiality may be considered in the balance of competing interests as a factor that diminishes the journalist's, and the public's, interest in non-disclosure."[249] Ultimately, however, the court held that compelled disclosure must be "the exception, not the rule."[250]

The Ninth Circuit's approach has been embraced as well by other appellate courts. In *United States v. Cuthbertson*,[251] for example, the Third Circuit held that criminal defendants were not entitled to compel the disclosure of a television network's "outtakes" of videotaped interviews, even though the interviewees had all consented to production of their nonbroadcast statements. The court concluded that the "compelled production of a reporter's resource materials can constitute a significant intrusion into the newsgathering and editorial processes" which, "like the compelled disclosure of confidential sources . . . may substantially undercut the public policy favoring the free flow of information to the public that is the foundation for the privilege."[252] Perhaps the leading trial court

---

248. *Id.* at 1294-95 (quoting Morse & Zucker, *The Journalist's Privilege*, in TESTIMONIAL PRIVILEGES 474-75 (S. Stone & R. Liebman eds. 1983)). See also Miller v. Mecklenburg County, 602 F. Supp. 675, 678 (W.D.N.C. 1985) (the "majority view clearly is that non-confidential material received by a reporter from an investigative source is protected by qualified privilege"). But see United States v. Smith, 135 F.3d 963, 972 (5th Cir. 1998); In re Owens, 496 S.E.2d 592, 596 (N.C. App. 1998).

249. 5 F.3d at 1295. See In re Letellier, 578 A.2d 722, 727 (Me. 1990) ("[W]hen there is no confidential source or information at stake, the identification of First Amendment interests is a more elusive task."); Maine v. Hohler, 543 A.2d 364, 365 (Me. 1988) ("nothing in the Constitution compels us to recognize a qualified privilege" where the information at issue is nonconfidential).

250. 48 F.3d at 416.

251. 630 F.2d 139, 147 (3d Cir. 1980), *cert. denied*, 449 U.S. 1126 (1981).

252. *Id.* at 147. See also In re Gronowicz, 764 F.2d 983, 994 (3d Cir. 1985), *cert. denied*, 474 U.S. 1055 (1986) (Higginbotham, J., dissenting) ("compelled disclosure of records, notes and unpublished information compiled in the course of preparing a work of nonfiction will so inhibit the gathering and recording of facts and intrude upon editorial process as to chill protected speech"). In *Gronowicz*, in which the Third Circuit held that the privilege did not apply in the context of a legitimate grand jury investigation of a journalist himself, Judge Higginbotham, in dissent, dis-

decision on the subject is *Loadholtz v. Fields*,[253] in which, shortly after *Branzburg*, the court declared the "distinction" between confidential and unpublished information "utterly irrelevant to the 'chilling effect' that the enforcement of these subpoenas," which sought unpublished notes of and testimony concerning a journalist's interview with the defendant, "would have on the flow of information to the press and to the public. The compelled production of a reporter's resource materials is equally as invidious as the compelled disclosure of his confidential informants."

In *United States v. LaRouche Campaign*,[254] the First Circuit appeared more circumspect in its application of the privilege in the context of unpublished information. The district court in *LaRouche* had held NBC in civil contempt for its failure to produce, for *in camera* review, outtakes of its interview with a prospective prosecution witness, only a small portion of which was broadcast.[255] Writing for a panel that included then-Judge Breyer, Judge Coffin recognized that, when "there is no confidential source or information at stake, the identification of First Amendment interests is a more elusive task."[256] And, while "some courts have stated in conclusory fashion that any distinction between subpoenas seeking confidential and nonconfidential materials is 'irrelevant as to the chilling effect' that results when the materials are disclosed," the First Circuit concluded that "no illuminating examples or reasoning are produced to support the conclusion."[257]

Judge Coffin then proceeded to identify five "asserted First Amendment interests" potentially affected by a subpoena seeking nonbroadcast information: specifically, he noted that compelled disclosure may (1) "increase the chances of harassment of the interviewee-witness;" (2) pose a "'threat of administrative and

---

cussed the premise of the court's recognition of "a privilege against disclosure of a reporter's 'unpublished notes'" in *Cuthbertson*; the privilege, he noted,

> is necessary for "protecting confidential sources, preventing intrusion into the editorial process, and avoiding the possibility of self-censorship created by compelled disclosure...." The "hassle" and exposure that complying with subpoenas such as this one may entail, it has been observed, may lead journalists to suppress writings that could pique a prosecutor's curiosity.

Id. at 998 (quoting United States v. Cuthbertson, 630 F.2d at 147); see 630 F.2d at 998 (quoting Blasi, *The Newsman's Privilege: An Empirical Study*, 70 MICH. L. REV. 229, 271 (1971) (empirical study finding that "reporters most hindered by the possibility of being subpoenaed are those who seek a composite picture, who check and cross-check their information with numerous sources ... and who keep extensive files and tapes for future verification reference")).

253. 389 F. Supp. 1299, 1303 (M.D. Fla. 1975).
254. 841 F.2d 1176 (1st Cir. 1988).
255. See *id.* at 1177.
256. *Id.* at 1181.
257. *Id.* (quoting United States v. Blanton, 534 F. Supp. 295, 297 (S.D. Fla. 1982) and citing Loadholtz v. Fields, 389 F. Supp. at 1303; United States v. Cuthbertson, 630 F.2d at 139).

judicial intrusion' into the newsgathering and editorial process;" (3) create the "disadvantage of a journalist appearing to be 'an investigative arm of the judicial system' or a research tool of government or of a private party;" (4) engender a "disincentive to 'compile and preserve nonbroadcast material;'" and (5) "burden" a journalist's "time and resources in responding to subpoenas."[258] The court discounted the first asserted interest, at least in the context of the case before it, on the ground that it "seems to be tied to confidentiality," which was not at issue because the interviewee "not only appeared in the broadcast" but had already "given substantial testimony" against his putative harassers.[259] The remaining asserted interests, however, raised "legitimate" constitutional concerns, which the court held must be balanced, at least in a criminal case, against the defendants' countervailing Fifth Amendment interests:

> We discern a lurking and subtle threat to journalists and their employers if disclosure of outtakes, notes, and other unused information, even if non-confidential, becomes routine and casually, if not cavalierly, compelled. To the extent that compelled disclosure becomes commonplace, it seems likely indeed that internal policies of destruction of materials may be devised and choices as to subject matter made, which could be keyed to avoiding disclosure requests or compliance therewith rather than to the basic function of providing news and comment. In addition, frequency of subpoenas would not only preempt the otherwise productive time of journalists and other employees but measurably increase expenditures for legal fees. Finally, observing Justice Powell's essential concurring opinion in Branzburg, "certainly we do not hold . . . that state and federal authorities are free to annex the news media as an investigative arm of government."[260]

Other appellate courts have similarly scrutinized claims of constitutional privilege in the context of unpublished information. In *United States v. Cutler*,[261] for example, the Second Circuit rejected an assertion that the defendant in a criminal contempt proceeding — which was based on his alleged improper statements to the news media — was not entitled to production of unpublished reporters' notes and outtakes "to defend against the charge that his statements were criminally contemptuous." According to the court, other than the defen-

---

258. 841 F.2d at 1181-82.
259. *Id.* at 1181.
260. *Id.* at 1182 (quoting Branzburg v. Hayes, 408 U.S. at 709 (Powell, J., concurring)). In the case before it, the First Circuit concluded that *in camera* review of the unpublished outtakes at issue was appropriate in light of the following factors: "this is a criminal case; the materials sought concern a major witness who was closely connected with the defendants in activities that are the subject of their indictment; the witness is predictably — from his past testimony — hostile; and the material sought is an extensive interview likely to offer the basis for impeachment." 841 F.2d at 1182.
261. 6 F.3d 67, 73 (2d Cir. 1993).

dant's own testimony, "which of course cannot be compelled, the evidence ... from the Reporters and the TV Stations is probably the *only* significant proof regarding his assertedly criminal behavior."[262] By the same token, however, the court rejected the defendant's effort to compel disclosure of unpublished notes of the reporters' interviews with a variety of government officials.[263]

In *Gonzales v. National Broadcasting Co.*,[264] the Second Circuit sought to come to grips with its prior case law concerning the privilege's efficacy in the context of nonconfidential, unpublished information, ultimately concluding both that the privilege extends to protect such material and that the showing required to overcome its assertion is less rigorous than in the context of confidential

---

262. *Id.* The court added that,

> even if Cutler [the defendant in the contempt proceeding] should choose to testify, we see no justification for consigning him to his unassisted memory when clearly relevant evidence is readily available from the Reporters and TV Stations. Finally, one of Cutler's major lines of defense is that the statements alleged to be contemptuous were in fact "repl[ies] to charges of misconduct" that are expressly precluded from the purview of Rule 7. That defense would be undercut if Cutler could not obtain relevant evidence regarding the context of his statements that is available only from the Reporters and the TV Stations.

Id. See also CBS Inc. v. Cobb, 536 So. 2d 1067, 1069 (Fla. App. 1988) (in criminal case, where defendant was "literally, fighting for his life," outtakes of interview with defendant should be disclosed to him).

263. See 6 F.3d at 74-75 (citations omitted):

> The comparative impact of Cutler's public statements and other publicity regarding the *Gotti* case manifestly depends upon what was published on that subject, not upon what is in the Reporters' unpublished notes. Similarly, the unpublished notes will cast no light on what Cutler was entitled to say "in response to *public allegations* that Mr. Cutler had engaged in misconduct ... ," and will provide no assistance to Cutler in establishing that his statements "concerned matters other than the pending *Gotti* case." Finally, the content of the unpublished notes, by definition unknown to Cutler at the time that he made the statements upon which the contempt charges are premised, can hardly have affected his intent in making those statements.

See also In re Ramaekers, 33 F. Supp. 2d 312, 315-16 (S.D.N.Y. 1999) (holding that, even if privilege applied to nonbroadcast audiotape, movant had satisfied constitutional standard).

Anticipating the Fifth Circuit's decision in *United States v. Smith*, 135 F.3d 963, 972 (5th Cir. 1998) (no privilege not to disclose nonconfidential outtakes in criminal proceeding), in *Cinel v. Connick*, 792 F. Supp. 492, 499 (E.D. La. 1992), a federal trial court noted that, "although some courts have recognized a federal common law qualified privilege in all source materials used by a reporter, the Fifth Circuit has never extended this protection beyond the compelled disclosure of confidential informants." Accordingly, because the media defendants in the case before it did not "contend that the compelled disclosure of an inventory of 'unpublished material in their possession' would require them to disclose the identity of a confidential informant," the court held that it "was bound to interpret the federal common law reporter's privilege narrowly." *Id.* See also CBS Inc. v. Campbell, 645 S.W.2d 30, 31 (Mo. App. 1982) (no privilege to protect against compelled disclosure of outtakes in grand jury context); WTHR-TV v. Cline, 693 N.E.2d 1 (Ind. 1998) (no constitutional privilege against disclosure of unaired footage for *in camera* review).

264. 1998 U.S. App. LEXIS 38583 (2d Cir., Aug. 27, 1999).

sources and workproduct. After initially purporting to conclude that *no* privilege protects against the compelled disclosure of nonconfidential, unpublished information,[265] the court changed course and "explicitly" held that the qualified privilege protecting press materials from disclosure applies to nonconfidential as well as to confidential materials.[266] The privilege, the court determined, protects interests "broader" than the need to ensure that confidential sources are not inhibited from providing information to the press:

> If the parties to any lawsuit were free to subpoena the press at will, it would likely become standard operating procedure for those litigating against an entity that had been the subject of press attention to sift through press files in search of information supporting their claims. The resulting wholesale exposure of press files to litigant scrutiny would burden the press with heavy costs of subpoena compliance, and could otherwise impair its ability to perform its duties — particularly if potential sources were deterred from speaking to the press, or insisted on remaining anonymous, because of the likelihood that they would be sucked into litigation. Incentives would also arise for press entities to clean out files containing potentially valuable information lest they incur substantial costs in the event of future subpoenas. And permitting litigants unrestricted, court-enforced access to journalistic resources would risk the symbolic harm of making journalists appear to be an investigative arm of the judicial system, the government, or private parties.[267]

But, the court emphasized, "where the protection of confidential sources is not involved, the nature of the press interest protected by the privilege is narrower" and "the showing needed to over overcome the privilege is less demanding."[268] Thus, the Second Circuit concluded in *Gonzales*, "[w]here a civil litigant seeks nonconfidential materials from a nonparty press entity, the litigant is entitled to the requested discovery notwithstanding a valid assertion of the journalists' privilege if he can show that the materials at issue are of likely relevance to a significant issue in the case, and are not reasonably obtainable from other available sources."[269]

---

265. See Gonzales v. National Broadcasting Co., 155 F.3d 618, 625 (2d Cir. 1998), *vacated*, No. 97-9454 (2d Cir. June 1, 1999).
266. 1998 U.S. App. LEXIS 38583, at *4.
267. *Id.* at *20.
268. *Id.* at *21 (citing Shoen v. Shoen, 5 F.3d 1289, 1295-96 (9th Cir. 1993)).
269. 1998 U.S. App. LEXIS 38583, at *22. In *Gonzales* itself, the court concluded that the privilege had been overcome because the outtakes at issue — depicting a police officer allegedly stopping a motorist without probable cause — were both likely relevant to the plaintiffs' civil rights claims of police misconduct and "not reasonably obtainable from other available sources, because they can provide unimpeachably objective evidence" of the defendant's conduct. *Id.* at *24.

§ 16-2(d)(3)(C)   CONSTITUTIONAL AND COMMON LAW PRIVILEGES   § 16-2(d)(3)(C)

Regardless of the nature of the showing required to divest the privilege, courts have upheld its assertion in a wide variety of contexts to preclude the compelled disclosure of broadcast outtakes,[270] unpublished photographs and negatives,[271] reporter's notes, drafts and other written workproduct,[272] letters received by

---

270. See, e.g., United States v. Lopez, 14 MEDIA L. REP. (BNA) 2203, 2204 (N.D. Ill. 1987) (privilege "extends to all underlying, unpublished material gathered in preparation for a news story or broadcast *regardless of whether the source of the material is confidential*") (emphasis in original); United States ex rel. Vuitton et Fils, S.A. v. Karen Bags, Inc., 600 F. Supp. 667, 670 (S.D.N.Y. 1985); United States v. Bingham, 765 F. Supp. 954, 960 (N.D. Ill. 1991) (ordering disclosure of transcript of outtakes but quashing subpoena for outtakes themselves); Lauderback v. American Broadcasting Cos., 8 MEDIA L. REP. (BNA) 2407, 2408 (N.D. Iowa 1982) ("The privilege has been recognized to apply to production of outtake material as well, even where the sources themselves are known."); Doe v. Kohn, Nast & Graf, 853 F. Supp. 147, 152 (E.D. Pa. 1994) ("The mere fact that some of plaintiff's videotaped remarks would be admissible does not alone warrant compelled production of unbroadcast outtakes. Otherwise, the qualified reporter's privilege would be a mirage."); Williams v. American Broadcasting Cos., 96 F.R.D. 658, 666-67 (W.D. Ark. 1983); New York v. Griffin, 21 MEDIA L. REP. (BNA) 1030, 1031-32 (N.Y. Sup. Ct. 1992); Channel Two Television Co. v. Dickerson, 725 S.W.2d 470, 471 (Tex. App. 1987). But see CBS Inc. v. Jackson, 578 So. 2d 698, 700 (Fla. 1991) (privilege does not apply to videotaped outtakes recording reporter's eyewitness observation of arrest of criminal defendant); cf. United States v. Sanusi, 813 F. Supp. 149, 160 (E.D.N.Y. 1992) (privilege overcome on showing, *inter alia*, that it "operates weakly, if at all" in case in which television network "entered defendant's home without the consent of defendant or his family," and as "a participant in the execution of a search warrant . . . under color of official right").

271. See, e.g., O'Neill v. Oakgrove Constr., Inc., 523 N.E.2d 277, 277-78 (N.Y. 1988) (rejecting effort of automobile accident victim to compel disclosure of nonconfidential photographs because constitutional privilege "extends to confidential and non-confidential materials" and is "triggered where the material sought for disclosure . . . was prepared or collected in the course of newsgathering"); Johnson v. Bentley, 457 So. 2d 507, 509 (Fla. App. 1984). Cf. West Virginia ex rel. Charleston Mail Ass'n v. Ranson, 488 S.E.2d 5 (W. Va. 1997) (privilege overcome after criminal defendant shows with particularity that unpublished, nonconfidential photos are "highly material and relevant; . . . necessary and critical to the . . . defense; and . . . not obtainable from other available sources," followed by *in camera* review). But see Carroll Contracting, Inc. v. Edwards, 528 So. 2d 951, 954 (Fla. App. 1988) (newspaper required to produce photographs of accident scene where, even if qualified privilege applied, petitioner made showing sufficient to overcome privilege); Weathers v. American Family Mut. Ins. Co., 17 MEDIA L. REP. (BNA) 1846, 1848 (D. Kan. 1990) (court compels disclosure of 247 unpublished photographs of plaintiff because, *inter alia*, a "lesser showing of need and materiality is required if the information is not confidential"); Farrington v. Crupper Transp. Co., 17 MEDIA L. REP. (BNA) 1781, 1782 (D. Kan. 1990); Medlin v. Bettis, 17 MEDIA L. REP. (BNA) 1783 (Kan. Dist. 1990); Marketos v. American Employers Ins. Co., 460 N.W.2d 272, 273 (Mich. App. 1990).

272. See, e.g., Gulliver's Periodicals, Ltd. v. Chas. Levy Circulating Co., 455 F. Supp. 1197, 1200 (N.D. Ill. 1978) (quashing subpoena seeking documents "which constitute, relate or refer to any interview, conversation, communication or other contact" with source "in the preparation of or otherwise concerning" published article); In re Scott Paper Co. Sec. Litig., 145 F.R.D. 366, 367 (E.D. Pa. 1992) (quashing subpoena for "notes and other unpublished documents reflecting communications between" Standard & Poor's ("S&P") and company it rated, as well as information about S&P's "internal procedures and deliberative processes"); In re Pan Am Corp., 161 Bankr. 577, 582 (S.D.N.Y. 1993) ("journalist's privilege does not cover only that information which a

reporters and their publications,[273] deposition testimony from journalists,[274] and even a reporter's personal, educational and employment background.[275] In defamation cases, however, courts have typically held — especially in the wake of the Supreme Court's rejection of an "editorial process" privilege in *Herbert v. Lando*[276] — that unpublished materials relating to the publication or broadcast at issue cannot be withheld from a plaintiff, at least if the case proceeds to trial.[277] Even in the context of defamation litigation, however, several courts have held that "the first amendment extends a degree of protection to journalists subject to discovery demands that impinge upon editorial and newsgathering activities" and that judges must therefore "not only weigh the litigant's need for discovery, . . .

---

journalist actually intends to publish" but also "unpublished resource material"); Solargen Elec. Motor Car Corp. v. American Motors Corp., 506 F. Supp. 546, 553 (N.D.N.Y. 1981) (privilege applies to "papers relating to meetings" with journalists, which "directly implicate[] legitimate First Amendment interests, specifically the news editorial process"); Gilbert v. Allied Chem. Corp., 411 F. Supp. 505, 507 (E.D. Va. 1976).

273. See, e.g., Delaware v. McBride, 7 MEDIA L. REP. (BNA) 1371, 1371 (Del. Super. 1981).

274. See, e.g., Re/Max Int'l, Inc. v. Century 21 Real Estate Corp., 846 F. Supp. 910, 912 (D. Colo. 1994) (privilege applied to prevent deposition of reporter about his interview with a non-confidential source). But see Kidwell v. Florida, 720 So. 2d 218, 218 (Fla. 1998) ("Like an eyewitness-observation, a direct confession to a reporter is direct evidence of a crime that would not fall within the information protected under the qualified privilege.").

275. See, e.g., In re Consumers Union, 495 F. Supp. 582, 587 (S.D.N.Y. 1980) (litigant had sought background information to qualify nonparty journalist as an "expert"). See generally Norandal USA, Inc. v. Local Union No. 7468, 13 MEDIA L. REP. (BNA) 2167, 2168 (Ala. Cir. 1986) (constitutional privilege protects unpublished, nonconfidential information acquired in the newsgathering process).

276. 441 U.S. 153, 169-70 (1979); see Chap. 14-5(c) *supra* (discussing *Herbert*).

277. See, e.g., First United Fund v. American Banker, 485 N.Y.S.2d 489 (Sup. Ct. 1985) (finding no privilege for previous drafts of allegedly libelous article); Williams v. American Broadcasting Cos., 96 F.R.D. 658, 669 (W.D. Ark. 1983) (compelling production of outtakes in defamation action on ground that such evidence "would be highly probative and in some cases the only proof of selective editing"). The court in *Williams* added that, while the same analysis applied to a "false light" invasion of privacy claim, a different outcome might obtain in an "intrusion" case, where "out-takes could be relevant, but not crucial, necessarily, to proof of the fact of invasion and the extent of it," or in a publication of private facts or "appropriation" claim, where "the gist of the tort is defendant's use for his or her benefit or actual disclosure" and "out-takes would not necessarily be particularly relevant." *Id.* See also Food Lion Inc. v. Capital Cities/ABC Inc., 951 F. Supp. 1211 (M.D.N.C. 1996) (in suit for trespass and fraud arising from television network's use of hidden cameras, court held privilege did not preclude limited discovery concerning other hidden camera investigations by network); Cape Publications, Inc. v. Bridges, 387 So. 2d 436, 439-40 (Fla. App. 1980) (in invasion of privacy action based on newspaper's distribution of photograph of plaintiff, court compelled disclosure of photographs, negatives, notes, and memoranda relating to story); Florida v. Searles, 24 MEDIA L. REP. (BNA) 2470, 2471 (Fla. Cir. 1996).

but also must carefully consider the seriousness of the intrusion on the editorial and newsgathering processes."[278]

§ 16-2(d)(3)(D). Published Information.

Most subpoenas received by the news media seek not the compelled disclosure of the identities of confidential sources, nor even unpublished information, but rather, copies of published or broadcast materials and appropriate authentication of their contents.[279] Typically, news organizations comply with such subpoenas following negotiations designed to eliminate the need for live testimony and to secure appropriate compensation for the retrieval, copying and sale of published or broadcast materials.[280]

On occasion, however, subpoenas seeking the production of published or broadcast information become the subject of litigation. In these cases, most courts have recognized that the constitutional privilege is implicated, though the First Amendment interests at stake may be attenuated.[281] In *United States v. Markiewicz*,[282] for example, one federal trial court denied, albeit without prejudice, a motion to quash a subpoena seeking testimony from three reporters that "the defendants made the statements reported in the newspapers" and attributed to them. The court concluded that "a qualified first amendment privilege applies to the present situation" because

> [c]ompelling the reporters to testify in court will arguably obstruct, in some fashion, the free flow of information to the public because the reporters will be in court testifying and not gathering information or writing articles. Although the testimony sought may be short in nature, this court is only too well aware of the fact that gauging when a witness will be called is not, and

---

278. Tavoulareas v. Piro, 93 F.R.D. 35, 41 (D.D.C. 1981). Accordingly, some courts have required that a defamation plaintiff demonstrate that he has stated a prima facie case by, for example, surviving a motion to dismiss or for summary judgment based on issues such as defamatory meaning, falsity, or common law privilege — to which unpublished information concerning the editorial process is not relevant — before permitting discovery of unpublished information. See, e.g., Foretich v. Chung, 22 MEDIA L. REP. (BNA) 2472, 2474-75 (D.D.C. 1994).

279. See REPORTERS COMMITTEE FOR FREEDOM OF THE PRESS, *supra* note 54, at 7-8. Of subpoenas issued to broadcast journalists responding to the survey in 1997, 80% requested material already broadcast, whereas only 1.4% sought confidential material. *Id.* Of subpoenas issued to newspapers responding to the survey in 1997, 42% requested published material, whereas 8.16% sought confidential material. *Id.*

280. *Id.* at 6-7.

281. See, e.g., United States v. Markiewicz, 732 F. Supp. 316, 317 (N.D.N.Y. 1990); United States v. Blanton, 534 F. Supp. 295, 296 (S.D. Fla. 1982); United States v. Meros, 11 MEDIA L. REP. (BNA) 2496, 2496 (M.D. Fla. 1985); In re Consumers Union, 495 F. Supp. 582, 587 (S.D.N.Y. 1980); Nevada v. Bazile, CR98-0388 (Nev. County Ct. Feb. 19, 1999).

282. 732 F. Supp. 316, 317 (N.D.N.Y. 1990).

cannot be, an exact science.... In the end, the interest of being free to conduct the business of a reporter weighs in favor of permitting the movants to assert their first amendment privileges.[283]

Nevertheless, the court held that the subpoenas should not be quashed, subject to the reporters' right to "raise the issue anew if they in good faith believe, after testimony has been given in the case, that their testimony will be unduly cumulative."[284]

Other courts have quashed subpoenas in analogous circumstances in which testimony is sought "verifying that ... quotations and statements" contained in a published article "were in fact made."[285] By the same token, most courts have concluded that requiring a reporter to testify "whether [an article] was truly published on the date asserted and whether [the reporter] did in fact interview [the defendants] ... before writing the article,"[286] will not "set off many first amendment alarms and bells."[287]

§ 16-2(e). Contours of the Privilege.

§ 16-2(e)(1). Generally.

Unlike several shield statutes, which create an absolute privilege at least in some contexts,[288] the constitutional privilege is universally held to be qualified. The lion's share of jurisdictions have adopted some variant of the privilege derived initially from the Second Circuit's watershed decision in *Garland v. Torre*.[289] In *Garland*, the court held that a reporter's First Amendment interest yielded to a libel plaintiff's motion to compel disclosure of a confidential source where that information "went to the heart of the plaintiff's claim" and where plaintiff's "reasonable efforts" to learn "the identity of the informant by further discovery proceedings ... had met with singular lack of success."[290]

Subsequent cases built upon the Second Circuit's comments in *Garland* and conducted pointed inquiries designed to ascertain whether, in the face of an

---

283. *Id.* at 320-21.
284. *Id.* at 322.
285. United States v. Blanton, 534 F. Supp. 295, 296 (S.D. Fla. 1982). See also United States v. Meros, 11 MEDIA L. REP. (BNA) 2496, 2496 (M.D. Fla. 1985) (defendant demonstrated "no compelling reason why" court should order testimony authenticating news stories).
286. Maughan v. NL Indus., 524 F. Supp. 93, 95 (D.D.C. 1981).
287. United States v. Markiewicz, 732 F. Supp. at 319. See also In re Consumers Union, 495 F. Supp. 582, 587 (S.D.N.Y. 1980) ("burden of responding" to discovery request seeking reprints of published articles does not "represent an incursion on First Amendment interests substantial enough to warrant quashing" subpoena).
288. See Chap. 15-2(e)(1) *supra*.
289. 259 F.2d 545 (2d Cir.), *cert. denied*, 358 U.S. 910 (1958).
290. *Id.* at 550-51.

assertion of constitutional privilege, the party seeking compelled disclosure had made a showing that "the information sought" is not merely relevant, but "goes to the heart" of its claim and is unavailable "from someone other than" the journalist.[291] And, although the Supreme Court rejected a claim of privilege in the grand jury context in *Branzburg v. Hayes*, Justice Stewart's dissenting opinion looked to *Garland* as well and articulated a constitutional test that would require the party seeking to overcome the constitutional privilege to

> (1) show that there is probable cause to believe that the newsman has information that is clearly relevant to a specific probable violation of law; (2) demonstrate that the information sought cannot be obtained by alternative means less destructive of First Amendment rights; and (3) demonstrate a compelling and overriding interest in the information.[292]

This formulation, although rendered in dissent, has become, along with *Garland*, the basis upon which most appellate courts have embraced a relatively precise, multi-factor test governing whether the privilege must yield in the context of a specific case. In *Zerilli v. Smith*,[293] for example, the D.C. Circuit interpreted its earlier decision in *Carey v. Hume*[294] to require a party seeking compelled disclosure to show (1) that the information sought is more than "marginally relevant" to the claim; (2) that it in fact "goes to 'the heart of the matter'"; and (3) that the party has "exhausted every reasonable alternative source of information."[295] Similarly, in *In re Petroleum Products Antitrust Litigation*,[296] the Second Circuit interpreted its own post-*Garland* and post-*Branzburg* decision in *Baker v. F & F Investment*[297] to require, in order "to protect the important interests of reporters and the public in preserving the confidentiality of journalists' sources," that disclosure "be ordered only upon a clear and specific showing that the information is: highly material and relevant, necessary or critical to the maintenance of the claim, and not obtainable from other

---

291. Carey v. Hume, 492 F.2d 631, 636-38 (D.C. Cir.), *cert. dismissed*, 417 U.S. 938 (1974) (citing Garland v. Torre, 259 F.2d 545 (2d Cir.), *cert. denied*, 358 U.S. 910 (1958)). See also Baker v. F & F Inv., 470 F.2d 778, 784 (2d Cir. 1972), *cert. denied*, 411 U.S. 966 (1973) (citing *Garland*).
292. 408 U.S. 665, 743 (1972) (Stewart, J., dissenting).
293. 656 F.2d 705, 713 (D.C. Cir. 1981).
294. 492 F.2d 631 (D.C. Cir.), *cert. dismissed*, 417 U.S. 938 (1974).
295. Zerilli v. Smith, 656 F.2d at 713 (quoting Carey v. Hume, 492 F.2d at 636).
296. 680 F.2d 5, 7 (2d Cir.), *cert. denied*, 459 U.S. 909 (1982).
297. 470 F.2d 778, 783-85 (2d Cir. 1972), *cert. denied*, 411 U.S. 966 (1973).

sources."[298] Most other federal and state appellate courts have embraced similar formulations.[299]

In the context of nonconfidential information, however, the Second Circuit has modified the applicable standard, holding that "when protection of confidentiality is not at stake, the privilege should be more easily overcome."[300] Accordingly, at least in that circuit, "[w]here a civil litigant seeks nonconfidential materials from a nonparty press entity, the litigant is entitled to the requested discovery notwithstanding a valid assertion of the journalists' privilege if he can

---

298. In re Petroleum Prods. Antitrust Litig., 680 F.2d at 7 (citing Baker v. F & F Inv., 470 F.2d at 783-85).

299. See, e.g., Riley v. City of Chester, 612 F.2d 708, 716-17 (3d Cir. 1979) (requiring showing of "relevance and necessity," that "other means of obtaining the information" have been "exhausted," and that "material sought . . . provide[s] a source of crucial information going to the heart of" the claim) (citations omitted); LaRouche v. National Broadcasting Co., 780 F.2d 1134, 1139 (4th Cir.), *cert. denied*, 479 U.S. 818 (1986) (applying "three part test: (1) whether the information is relevant, (2) whether the information can be obtained by alternative means, and (3) whether there is a compelling interest in the information"); Miller v. Transamerican Press, Inc., 621 F.2d 721, 726 (5th Cir. 1980), *cert. denied*, 450 U.S. 1041 (1981) (applying "three part test first outlined in *Garland*: (1) is the information relevant, (2) can the information be obtained by alternative means, and (3) is there a compelling interest in the information?"); Shoen v. Shoen, 5 F.3d 1289, 1296 & n.14 (9th Cir. 1993) ("Once the privilege is properly invoked, the burden shifts to the requesting party to demonstrate a sufficiently compelling need for the journalist's material to overcome the privilege," specifically (1) "that the information sought is not obtainable from another source," (2) "the information sought is relevant, material and non-cumulative," and (3) the information "is crucial to the maintenance of plaintiffs' claims"); Silkwood v. Kerr-McGee Corp., 563 F.2d 433, 438 (10th Cir. 1977) (requiring courts to weigh the "type of controversy" as well as "1. Whether the party seeking information has independently attempted to obtain the information elsewhere and has been unsuccessful. 2. Whether the information goes to the heart of the matter. [and] 3. Whether the information is of certain relevance"); United States v. Caporale, 806 F.2d 1487, 1504 (11th Cir. 1986) ("information may only be compelled from a reporter claiming privilege if it is highly relevant, necessary to the proper presentation of the case, and unavailable from other sources").

The state courts have also largely embraced the *Garland* formulation. See, e.g., Norandal USA, Inc. v. Local Union No. 7468, 13 MEDIA L. REP. (BNA) 2167, 2168 (Ala. Cir. 1986); Alaska v. Pruett, 11 MEDIA L. REP. (BNA) 1968 (Alaska Sup. 1984); Mitchell v. Superior Ct., 690 P.2d 625, 632-33 (Cal. 1984); Connecticut State Bd. of Labor Relations v. Fagin, 370 A.2d 1095, 1097-98 (Conn. Super. 1976); Delaware v. McBride, 7 MEDIA L. REP. (BNA) 1371, 1371 (Del. Super. 1981); Florida v. Davis, 720 So. 2d 220, 227 (Fla. 1998); In re Wright, 700 P.2d 40, 44 (Idaho 1985); Winegard v. Oxberger, 258 N.W.2d 847, 852 (Iowa 1977), *cert. denied*, 436 U.S. 905 (1978); King v. Photo Marketing Ass'n Int'l, 327 N.W.2d 515 (Mich. App. 1982); Missouri ex rel. Classic III, Inc. v. Ely, 954 S.W.2d 650 (Mo. App. 1997); New Hampshire v. Siel, 444 A.2d 499, 502-03 (N.H. 1982); O'Neill v. Oakgrove Constr., Inc., 523 N.E.2d 277, 279 (N.Y. 1988); Davis v. Glanton, 705 A.2d 879 (Pa. Super. 1997); Channel Two Television Co. v. Dickerson, 725 S.W.2d 470, 471-72 (Tex. App. 1987); West Virginia ex rel. Hudok v. Henry, 389 S.E.2d 188, 193 (W. Va. 1989); Wisconsin ex rel. Green Bay Newspaper Co. v. Circuit Ct., 335 N.W.2d 367, 373-74 (Wis. 1983); Kurzynski v. Spaeth, 538 N.W.554, 559-60 (Wis. App. 1995).

300. Gonzales v. National Broadcasting Co., 1998 U.S. App. LEXIS 38583, at *21 (2d Cir. Aug. 27, 1999).

show that the materials at issue are of likely relevance to a significant issue in the case, and are not reasonably obtainable from other available sources."[301]

A few courts have either refrained from articulating precise multi-factor tests or rejected them. In *Cervantes v. Time, Inc.*,[302] the Eighth Circuit upheld a journalist's refusal to identify his confidential source in a defamation action, but did so without reference to a multi-factor test by determining that the plaintiff had not come forward with sufficient evidence to state a prima facie case. In *Bruno & Stillman, Inc. v. Globe Newspaper Co.*,[303] the First Circuit opined that "[w]hether or not the process of taking First Amendment concerns into consideration can be said to represent recognition by the Court of a 'conditional', or 'limited' privilege is, we think, largely a question of semantics. The important point . . . is that courts faced with enforcing requests for the discovery of materials used in the preparation of journalistic reports should be aware of the possibility that the unlimited or unthinking allowance of such requests will impinge upon First Amendment rights."

Thus, the court in *Bruno & Stillman* eschewed a "black letter pronouncement" and proceeded instead to "balance the potential harm to the free flow of information that might result against the asserted need for the requested information."[304] In so doing, it suggested that, "[a]s a threshold matter, the trial court should be satisfied that a claim is not frivolous, a pretense for using discovery powers in a fishing expedition;" should consider "the extent to which there is a need for confidentiality;" and should assess whether to "require that resort to nonconfidential sources first be exhausted."[305] Ultimately, however, the First Circuit emphasized that it had "refrain[ed] from further categorizing with any precision what inquiries should be made by the court or in what sequence. The task is one that demands sensitivity, invites flexibility, and defies formula."[306]

Finally, as discussed elsewhere in this chapter,[307] a few appellate courts have held that a constitutional privilege, at least as articulated in Justice Stewart's dissenting opinion in *Branzburg*,[308] does not apply in the criminal context or to nonconfidential information. Instead, these courts have suggested that First Amendment considerations are relevant to the issue of compelled disclosure only

---

301. *Id.* at *22.
302. 464 F.2d 986, 994-95 (8th Cir. 1972).
303. 633 F.2d 583, 595 (1st Cir. 1980).
304. *Id.* at 596.
305. *Id.*
306. *Id.* See also In re Cusumano, 162 F.3d 708, 716 (1st Cir. 1998) (court should "place those factors that relate to the movants' need for information on one pan of the scales and those that reflect the objector's interest in confidentiality and the potential injury to free flow of information that disclosure portends on the opposite pan").
307. See Chaps. 16-2(c)(1) & (d)(3) *supra*.
308. 408 U.S. at 723 (Stewart, J., dissenting).

to the extent specifically referenced by Justice Powell in his concurring opinion in *Branzburg*.[309] As the Sixth Circuit has asserted, in "the sense that the balancing referred to by Justice Powell, when instigated by a reporter seeking to protect a confidential source, may result in the denial to a party of the use of evidence that is reliable, one is reminded of the invocation of a 'privilege,' as contrasted with an 'exclusion.'"[310] This "semantical confusion," the court concluded, should not obscure the obligation of the trial courts to strike a balance between the First Amendment and the citizen's obligation to give relevant testimony by determining

> whether the grand jury's investigation is being conducted in good faith, whether the information sought bears more than a remote and tenuous relationship to the subject of the investigation, and whether a legitimate law enforcement need will be served by forced disclosure of the confidential source relationship.[311]

In the discussion that follows, we address both the application of the multi-factor test in the context of specific cases and the use of alternative formulations or more "flexible" standards to balance the competing interests.

§ 16-2(e)(2). Relevance Requirements.

As the preceding discussion indicates, most formulations of the constitutional privilege require the party seeking compelled disclosure to demonstrate not simply that the information it seeks is relevant, but that it "is crucial to the claim."[312] Not surprisingly, courts have had occasion to assess the significance of putatively privileged information across the spectrum of judicial proceedings.

---

309. *Id.* at 710 (Powell, J., concurring).

310. In re Grand Jury Proceedings, 810 F.2d 580, 585 (6th Cir. 1987).

311. *Id.* at 586. See also United States v. Smith, 135 F.3d 963, 970 (5th Cir. 1998) (relying on Justice Powell's formulation in *Branzburg*); United States v. Markiewicz, 732 F. Supp. 316, 321 (N.D.N.Y. 1990) (holding that "the appropriate standard for reviewing the claimed privilege" in the context of a criminal case in which the government seeks nonconfidential information "is whether the testimony sought is relevant, not unduly cumulative, and not available from other sources," but "the requirement of a high level of materiality should be diminished to one of relevancy").

312. United States v. Criden, 633 F.2d 346, 359 (3d Cir. 1980), *cert. denied*, 449 U.S. 1113 (1981). In *Dallas Morning News Co. v. Garcia*, 822 S.W.2d 675, 680 (Tex. App. 1991) (citation omitted), a Texas appellate court noted, but found insignificant, the fact that most courts have required a showing of both "relevance" and "necessity."

> The deletion of "relevancy" as a separate requirement does not significantly alter the plaintiff's burden of proof. "Relevancy" is no more than the standard established . . . that the sources' identities must "go to the heart" of the plaintiff's libel claim. In other words, the information sought must be "critical" to the plaintiff's case. The relevancy requirement adds nothing to the test that is not already encompassed in the "necessary or critical" element. If

In the criminal context, courts have found the requisite "relevance and importance" in a number of different contexts, from testimony tending to confirm charges of prosecutorial misconduct,[313] to outtakes tending to rebut charges of criminal contempt against defense counsel.[314] In other circumstances, courts have held that the testimony sought to be compelled from journalists in criminal cases, especially when offered for purposes of impeachment, is cumulative or speculative and therefore not "crucial" to the defense.[315]

---

the information is necessary or critical to the plaintiff's case, it follows that it is also highly material and relevant.

Id. Cf. Coastal Transp. Inc. v. WAWS Fox 30, 25 MEDIA L. REP. (BNA) 2247, 2248 (Fla. Cir. 1997) ("absent the existence of pending lawsuit, the Court has little to no authority" to enjoin media "to preserve certain video tapes and photographs alleged to have evidentiary value").

313. See United States v. Criden, 633 F.2d at 359 (holding that testimony by reporter, confirming that she spoke with prosecutor — a nonconfidential source — had requisite "relevance and importance to the particular proceeding"); United States v. Sanusi, 813 F. Supp. 149, 159 (E.D.N.Y. 1992) (although outtakes of government raid on defendant's home not relevant to motion to suppress, they "bear upon defendant's constitutional right to a jury trial" because they contained "exculpatory evidence," i.e., "an exhaustive search of defendant's apartment failed to reveal a shred of evidence of credit-card fraud").

314. See, e.g., United States v. Cutler, 6 F.3d 67, 73 (2d Cir. 1993) (other than the lawyer's own testimony, "which of course cannot be compelled," evidence in outtakes of his interviews with the press "is probably the *only* significant proof regarding his assertedly criminal behavior").

315. See, e.g., United States v. Burke, 700 F.2d 70, 77-78 (2d Cir.), *cert. denied*, 464 U.S. 816 (1983) (where witness "had been impeached thoroughly during trial" and immunity agreement had been read to jury, "any further impeachment evidence introduced against him would serve a solely cumulative purpose"); United States v. Hubbard, 493 F. Supp. 202, 205 (D.D.C. 1979) (testimony by reporter concerning FBI briefing "would be merely hearsay testimony provided by one of the participants to the reporter" and court had "already heard testimony from numerous eyewitnesses to the briefing"); Campbell v. Klevenhagen, 760 F. Supp. 1206, 1214 (S.D. Tex. 1991) (reporters' testimony concerning identity of sources not sufficiently relevant because defendant's argument in support of disclosure was "based on a number of contingencies," including whether, if "sources were called to testify, and if those sources were to give testimony which was otherwise inconsistent with the defense's theory of self defense then the [reporters] would be called to impeach that testimony"); United States v. Cutler, 6 F.3d 67, 74 (2d Cir. 1993) (reporters' notes regarding statements by government officials concerning defendant not relevant); United States v. Marcos, 17 MEDIA L. REP. (BNA) 2005 (S.D.N.Y. 1990) (outtakes not necessary for impeachment); United States ex rel. Vuitton et Fils, S.A. v. Karen Bags, Inc., 600 F. Supp. 667 (S.D.N.Y. 1985) (impeachment evidence sought from press cumulative); Coney v. Alaska, 699 P.2d 899, 902 (Alaska App. 1985) ("possibility of this information helping the defense was remote"); Brown v. Virginia, 204 S.E.2d 429, 431 (Va.), *cert. denied*, 419 U.S. 966 (1974); Zelenka v. Wisconsin, 266 N.W.2d 279 (Wis. 1978). But see United States v. Cuthbertson, 651 F.2d 189, 196 (3d Cir.), *cert. denied*, 454 U.S. 1056 (1981) (court orders *in camera* review of broadcast outtakes and holds that, if sources' "testimony at trial differs from their statements to CBS, the defendants will have the opportunity to obtain the materials for impeachment purposes" because "prior statements of prospective witnesses are 'unique bits of evidence that are frozen at a particular place and time'") (citations omitted); United States v. LaRouche, 841 F.2d 1176, 1182 (1st Cir. 1988) (affirming order requiring *in camera* review of outtakes where "the materials sought concern a major witness who was closely connected with the defendants in activities that are the subject of their indictment" and witness is

The testimony of journalists or the introduction in evidence of their work product has typically failed to clear the heightened burden of "crucial" relevance in civil litigation in which the journalist (or the media entity with which he or she is affiliated) is not a party. Courts have held compelled disclosure to be inappropriate on this ground in antitrust,[316] civil rights,[317] discrimination,[318] bankruptcy,[319] invasion of privacy,[320] workers' compensa-

---

hostile); United States v. Bingham, 765 F. Supp. 954, 957 (N.D. Ill. 1991) (where witness's testimony is "directly contradicted" by outtakes, defendants "are seeking highly relevant prior inconsistent statements" through subpoena for outtakes); United States v. Markiewicz, 732 F. Supp. 316, 322 (N.D.N.Y. 1990) ("Given the high burden of proof which the government must meet at a criminal trial, proof of phone conversations plus proof of the use of newspapers as facilities of interstate commerce is not unduly cumulative.").

316. See, e.g., In re Petroleum Prods. Antitrust Litig., 680 F.2d 5, 8 (2d Cir.), *cert. denied*, 459 U.S. 909 (1982) ("The necessity for confidentiality, essential to fulfillment of the pivotal function of reporters to collect information for public dissemination, cannot be overcome simply by suggesting — with no basis to support the assertion — that the reporter may unknowingly have been used by those sources in their illegal activities."); Los Angeles Mem'l Coliseum Comm'n v. National Football League, 89 F.R.D. 489, 494 (C.D. Cal. 1981) (information about media leaks, sought by defendants in support of change of venue motion, does not go "to the heart of any element of the underlying claims"); Re/Max Int'l, Inc. v. Century 21 Real Estate Corp., 846 F. Supp. 910, 912 (D. Colo. 1994) (impeachment evidence sought from journalist in unfair competition action had only *de minimis* value).

317. See, e.g., Riley v. City of Chester, 612 F.2d 708, 718 (3d Cir. 1979) (where multiple witnesses had testified that mayor supplied information about plaintiff to the media, there was insufficient showing that testimony of reporter on same subject was necessary, especially since information "appears to have only marginal relevance to plaintiff's case"); Neal v. City of Harvey, Illinois, 173 F.R.D. 231 (N.D. Ill. 1997) (civil rights defendant failed to make showing of "actual relevance" of reporter's deposition testimony); Perry v. Keulian, 1997 U.S. Dist. LEXIS 2795, at *3 (E.D. Pa. Mar. 11, 1997) (quashing subpoena of nonparty reporter where plaintiff in Fair Housing Act suit "made no showing whatsoever as to the . . . cruciality of the information"); Pugh v. Avis Rent A Car Sys., Inc., 26 MEDIA L. REP. (BNA) 1311, 1315 (S.D.N.Y. 1997) ("because Defendant offers only unsupported speculation as to what information the outtakes might contain, Defendant . . . fails to make a clear and specific showing that the information sought is necessary or critical to its claim"); but see Gonzales v. National Broadcasting Co., 1998 U.S. App. LEXIS 38583, at *23-24 (2d Cir. Aug. 27, 1999) (plaintiffs entitled to compel disclosure of videotape outtakes allegedly depicting defendant police officer in civil rights action stopping vehicle without probable cause).

318. See, e.g., Doe v. Kohn, Nast & Graf, 853 F. Supp. 147, 152 (E.D. Pa. 1994) (in suit under Americans with Disabilities Act, production of outtakes of broadcast interviews not compelled because, although plaintiff discussed relevant matters in outtakes, "his statements were consistent with each other and with his deposition testimony"); see *id.* ("The mere fact that some of plaintiff's videotaped remarks would be admissible does not alone warrant compelled production of unbroadcast outtakes. Otherwise, the qualified reporter's privilege would be a mirage.").

319. See, e.g., In re Pan Am Corp., 161 Bankr. 577, 585 (S.D.N.Y. 1993) (in adversary bankruptcy proceeding concerning party's alleged failure to honor commitment to fund reorganization, testimony concerning what media entity "believed" about that party's "intentions" is not "highly material or relevant, necessary or critical" to claim).

320. See, e.g., Sinnott v. Boston Retirement Bd., 524 N.E.2d 100, 102 (Mass.), *cert. denied*,

tion,[321] contract,[322] and defamation actions.[323] In those defamation actions in which the media entity or journalist is a party, however, courts have been more likely to hold that the unpublished information — especially concerning the defendant's pre-publication state of mind — is "crucial" to plaintiff's ability to demonstrate constitutional "malice" by the requisite clear and convincing evidence,[324] although some courts have insisted both that constitutional malice

---

488 U.S. 980 (1988); Lamberto v. Bown, 326 N.W.2d 305, 308 (Iowa 1982). In *Lamberto*, the plaintiff, a lawyer, had filed a complaint against a banker alleging claims for invasion of privacy and defamation. Because the plaintiff had voluntarily dismissed his slander claim, leaving only a cause of action for invasion of privacy sounding in intrusion upon seclusion, the court held that the reporter's information — which went only to the defamation-related issue of publication — was no longer relevant. *Id.* at 307. In addition, the court noted that "[t]estimony to be used solely for testing credibility can scarcely be said to go to the 'heart' of the case." *Id.*

321. Tomblin v. Mayo Clinic, 26 MEDIA L. REP. (BNA) 1351, 1352 (Fla. Dep't of Labor & Employment 1997) (subpoena seeking irrelevant information "will serve only to burden a member of the media and is therefore unreasonable").

322. Coastline Bldg. Corp. v. Atkins, 26 MEDIA L. REP. (BNA) 1316, 1317 (Fla. Cir. 1997) (quashing subpoena directed at gathering information to rebut damage claim, because reporter's information "has no conceivable relevance to this contract dispute . . . and the record in this proceeding does not reflect that [the reporter] can add anything regarding the alleged breach or damages flowing from it").

323. See, e.g., Church of Scientology Int'l v. Daniels, 992 F.2d 1329, 1335 (4th Cir.), *cert. denied*, 510 U.S. 869 (1993) (court did not abuse its discretion in denying plaintiff's request for discovery from *USA Today* in defamation action against corporate executive, especially since newspaper "offered to stipulate to the accuracy of the quotation" of executive that appeared in print); Shoen v. Shoen, 48 F.3d 412, 417 (9th Cir. 1995) (reporter's interviews with defendant, which post-dated alleged defamation, were not sufficiently relevant to overcome privilege since a showing that defendant "harbored ill will toward" plaintiffs "at a time after the alleged libels — even only one month later — cannot, without more, establish actual malice"); Summit Tech., Inc. v. Healthcare Capital Group, Inc., 141 F.R.D. 381, 385 (D. Mass. 1992) (identity of person that provided information to defendant's primary source "is relevant for discovery purposes," but "is more tangential than primary"); In re Consumers Union, 495 F. Supp. 582, 588 (S.D.N.Y. 1980) (where plaintiff already had evidence that defendant in case alleging conspiracy to defame had provided information to reporter, his "acknowledgment is not needed to prove his receipt of such materials" and his "state of mind is of no relevance"); cf. Solargen Elec. Motor Car Corp. v. American Motors Corp., 506 F. Supp. 546, 553 (N.D.N.Y. 1981) (in case alleging antitrust conspiracy to disseminate false information about plaintiffs, reporter's bank records "relevant and material" to claim that defendants had paid journalists to write unfavorable articles about plaintiffs).

324. See, e.g., Star Editorial, Inc. v. United States Dist. Ct., 7 F.3d 856, 861 (9th Cir. 1993) ("Actual malice would be extremely difficult to prove without knowing whether the confidential sources existed and, if so, what they said and whether they were credible."); Carey v. Hume, 492 F.2d 631, 638 (D.C. Cir.), *cert. dismissed*, 417 U.S. 938 (1974) ("the facts disclosed by the record before us at this time are inadequate to support a conclusion that appellee is so unlikely to meet the admittedly heavy *Sullivan* burden that no purpose would be served by disclosure of the identity of the sources"); Miller v. Transamerican Press, Inc., 621 F.2d 721, 726 (5th Cir. 1980), *cert. denied*, 450 U.S. 1041 (1981) (where "only source for the allegedly libelous statement" is the defendant's confidential informant, the "only way" that plaintiff can prove constitutional malice "is to show that [defendant] knew the story was false or that it was reckless to rely on the informant");

necessarily be at issue[325] and that plaintiff otherwise has made a sufficient showing that it can — with the assistance of compelled disclosure — satisfy its heavy burden of proof.[326] In non-defamation actions in which the press is a party, courts have similarly tended to find the requisite relevance to satisfy the constitutional standard.[327]

§ 16-2(e)(3). Exhaustion Requirements.

Perhaps the most significant hurdle imposed by the qualified privilege is the requirement that a party seeking to overcome it first exhaust, without success, alternative sources of the same information. In a broad range of cases — civil and criminal — courts have viewed particularized enforcement of the exhaustion requirement as a means of avoiding the need to resolve what might otherwise become a clash of competing interests. In *Zerilli v. Smith*,[328] for example, the plaintiffs in an action under the federal privacy act propounded interrogatories to the government, seeking the identity of public officials who allegedly leaked material to the news media. The government responded by denying that any official had leaked information, but provided the names of all those public officials who had access to it.[329] The plaintiffs did not seek further discovery from the government; instead, they noticed the depositions of reporters in an

---

DeRoburt v. Gannett Co., 6 MEDIA L. REP. (BNA) 2473, 2477 (D. Haw. 1981) (in case where plaintiff has already survived motion for summary judgment, because "'actual malice' is a crucial element" of plaintiff's claim, evidence "that defendants had no sources or unreliable sources would be evidence of reckless disregard of the truth"); Dow Jones & Co. v. Superior Ct., 303 N.E.2d 847, 849 (Mass. 1973); Williams v. American Broadcasting Cos., 96 F.R.D. 661 (W.D. Ark. 1983) (where claim of constitutional malice is bottomed on allegations of "selective editing," it can "hardly be seriously argued that the out-takes are not 'relevant'"). But cf. *id.* at 669 (although outtakes held relevant to defamation claim, they would likely be "relevant, but not crucial" to intrusion claim).

325. See, e.g., Foretich v. Chung, 22 MEDIA L. REP. (BNA) 2472 (D.D.C. 1994).
326. See, e.g., Cervantes v. Time, Inc., 464 F.2d 986, 994 (8th Cir. 1972), *cert. denied*, 409 U.S. 1125 (1973) (absent "a concrete demonstration that the identity of defense news sources will lead to persuasive evidence on the issue of malice," trial court should not compel disclosure of source's identity before reaching "the merits of a defense motion for summary judgment"); Dallas Morning News Co. v. Garcia, 822 S.W.2d 675, 677 (Tex. App. 1991).
327. See, e.g., SEC v. McGoff, 647 F.2d 185, 192 (D.C. Cir.), *cert. denied*, 452 U.S. 963 (1981) (in enforcement proceeding, agency demonstrated "'a substantial relationship' between the information sought and an important government interest"); Anderson v. Nixon, 444 F. Supp. 1195, 1199 n.4 (D.D.C. 1978) (in civil rights action brought by journalist, court held that plaintiff's sources of information relevant to his claim that he had been "intimidated and injured"); Food Lion, Inc. v. Capital Cities/ABC Inc., 951 F. Supp. 1211 (M.D.N.C. 1996) (in trespass and fraud action against television network for use of hidden cameras, network's use of hidden cameras in other investigations deemed relevant).
328. 656 F.2d 705 (D.C. Cir. 1981).
329. *Id.* at 708.

effort to ascertain the source of the leaks.[330] The D.C. Circuit upheld the reporters' invocation of the privilege, in significant part because "[e]ven when the information [sought] is crucial to a litigant's case, reporters should be compelled to disclose their sources only after the litigant has shown that he has exhausted every reasonable alternative source of information."[331]

Speaking through Judge Wright, the court emphasized that, although "there are some limits to the obligation to pursue alternative sources," the obligation is "clearly very substantial" and may require "the taking of as many as 60 depositions" as a "reasonable prerequisite to compelled disclosure."[332] A host of other courts have reached the same conclusion, especially in civil litigation in which the press is not a party.[333]

---

330. *Id.* at 709.

331. *Id.* at 713.

332. *Id.* at 714. See also In re Petroleum Prods. Antitrust Litig., 680 F.2d 5, 8-9 (2d Cir.), *cert. denied*, 459 U.S. 909 (1982) ("While hundreds of depositions have already been taken, there is no indication that anyone has been asked" whether they were a source of information provided to a newsletter; "[a]dditional depositions may be necessary to uncover" whether and how newsletter received information.).

The court in *Zerilli* also rejected the plaintiffs' argument that "deposing Justice Department employees would be time-consuming, costly, and unproductive;" in the court's view, "[a]t the very least," the plaintiffs could have deposed the four employees who had access to the information. 656 F.2d at 715. See also In re Roche, 448 U.S. 1312, 1316 (1980) (Brennan, J., in chambers) (suggesting harm caused by requiring taking of 65 depositions would not "outweigh the unpalatable choice that civil contempt would impose upon" reporter); In re Pan Am Corp., 161 Bankr. 577, 585 (S.D.N.Y. 1993) (rejecting argument that "additional depositions would be a burden" on the bankrupt's estate on ground that there is "no authority . . . for the proposition that the requirement of unavailability is obviated by such hardship, even if proven").

333. See, e.g., In re Petroleum Prods. Antitrust Litig., 680 F.2d 5, 8 (2d Cir.), *cert. denied*, 459 U.S. 909 (1982) (in civil antitrust action, court held that plaintiffs "failed to explore any alternative means of discovering whether the oil companies used" newsletter "as part of their purported price fixing conspiracy"); Riley v. City of Chester, 612 F.2d 708, 717 (3d Cir. 1979) (civil litigant had not overcome privilege because it had not shown that "'his only practical access to crucial information necessary for the development of the case is through the newsman's sources'") (quoting Gilbert v. Allied Chem. Corp., 411 F. Supp. 505, 510 (E.D. Va. 1976)); In re Pan Am Corp., 161 Bankr. 577, 585 (S.D.N.Y. 1993) (in bankruptcy action, court held that unsecured creditors had "failed to clearly and specifically demonstrate the unavailability of the information from other sources;" according to the court, the creditors "had not even worked up a sweat, much less exhausted itself"); Connecticut State Bd. of Labor Relations v. Fagin, 370 A.2d 1095, 1098 (Conn. Super. 1976); Sinnott v. Boston Retirement Bd., 524 N.E.2d 100, 102 (Mass.), *cert. denied*, 488 U.S. 980 (1988); McMenamin v. Tartaglione, 590 A.2d 802, 811 (Pa. Commw.), *aff'd*, 590 A.2d 753 (Pa. 1991); Solargen Elec. Motor Car Corp. v. American Motors Corp., 506 F. Supp. 546, 553 (N.D.N.Y. 1981) (plaintiff failed to exhaust alternative sources of information relating to meetings between broadcaster and defendant); Farhat v. Farhat, 25 MEDIA L. REP. (BNA) 2151, 2152 (Fla. Cir. 1997) ("The plaintiff has had, and still has, ample opportunity to depose other persons believed to have relevant information. Also, past newspaper articles and television broadcasts . . . provide the evidence relevant to the motion."); Ko v. Zilog, Inc., 25 MEDIA L. REP. (BNA) 1892 (Idaho 1997) (defendant must depose each plaintiff in attempt to discover source of violation of

In *Ashcraft v. Conoco, Inc.*,[334] for example, a federal district court denied Conoco's motion to compel disclosure of confidential sources who revealed to a reporter the terms of a sealed settlement agreement in a toxic tort action, because Conoco had not yet questioned all potential sources of the leak. "Although this task would be cumbersome and possibly fruitless, until such efforts have been pursued, it cannot be said that all *reasonable* non-media outlets have been exhausted."[335] Later that year, however, Conoco renewed its motion to compel. Finding that the company had unsuccessfully exhausted all reasonable means of discovering the information, by gathering sworn interrogatory testimony from 139 individuals, and after the court had questioned all court employees with knowledge of the terms of the settlement, the court granted the motion to compel.[336]

In *Gonzales v. National Broadcasting Co.*,[337] the Second Circuit held that the exhaustion requirement operates with less force when a subpoena requests only nonconfidential material. In such circumstances, the party seeking to compel disclosure must demonstrate only that the information is "not reasonably obtainable from other available sources."[338] Indeed, in *Gonzales*, the court concluded that there were no "other available sources" for the information contained in the broadcast outtakes at issue — which allegedly depicted the defendant police officer in a civil rights action stopping a vehicle without probable cause — because the video promised to "provide unimpeachably objective evidence" of the officer's conduct.[339]

Even in the criminal context, however, some courts have been vigilant in their application of the exhaustion requirement. In *United States v. Cuthbertson*,[340] for

---

court's protective order before court will consider compelling nonparty reporter to disclose his source); Neal v. City of Harvey, Illinois, 173 F.R.D. 231, 233 (N.D. Ill. 1997) (civil defendant's claim that reporter's knowledge of statements made by defendant, co-defendant and plaintiff "is hers alone and would not be obtainable through any other sources is frivolous" since defendant "knows what he himself said [and] [h]e can, if necessary, depose his co-defendant . . . [and] plaintiff"); Perry v. Keulian, 1997 U.S. Dist. LEXIS 2795, at *1-2 (E.D. Pa. Mar. 11, 1997) (plaintiffs in Fair Housing Act suit who "have not asked the Defendant herself" if she made actionable statements, and who "have failed to show that they have made an effort to obtain this information from her or any other sources . . . have failed to sustain their burden in overcoming [the nonparty reporter's] First Amendment privilege"); McCarty v. Bankers Ins. Co., 27 MEDIA L. REP. (BNA) 1051, 1058 (N.D. Fla. 1998) (plaintiff "has failed to overcome the heavy burden of showing by clear and convincing evidence that he has been unable to identify and obtain the information which it seeks from [the reporter] from the other sources").

334. 26 MEDIA L. REP. (BNA) 1620 (E.D.N.C. 1998).
335. *Id.* at 1628 (emphasis in original).
336. 1998 U.S. Dist. LEXIS 16371, at *2-3 (E.D.N.C. Sept. 3, 1998).
337. 1998 U.S. App. LEXIS 38583 (2d Cir. Aug. 27, 1999).
338. *Id.* at *22.
339. *Id.* at *24.
340. 651 F.2d 189 (3d Cir.), *cert. denied*, 454 U.S. 1056 (1981).

example, the Third Circuit applied the requirement to preclude a criminal defendant from securing access to broadcast outtakes. The court held that "to overcome the media's federal common law qualified privilege the seeker of information must demonstrate that his only practical means of access to the information sought is through the media."[341] The outtakes, according to the court, contained the identities of no potential witnesses of whom defendants were not already aware. Moreover, none of these witnesses had yet testified, so there was no basis to suspect that their testimony, if given, would conflict with statements contained in the outtakes or that the same or similar impeachment evidence could not be secured from other sources.[342] Other courts have also applied the exhaustion requirement in the criminal context, with the same result,[343] even in cases in which there was reason to believe that alternative sources might invoke a privilege as well.[344]

By the same token, some courts have held that the burden of exhaustion has been carried in criminal cases. In another Third Circuit case, *United States v. Criden*,[345] before subpoenaing a journalist, the defendants sought testimony from

---

341. *Id.* at 195.

342. See *id.* at 196. In *United States v. Markiewicz*, 732 F. Supp. 316, 321 (N.D.N.Y. 1990), the court correctly noted that, as was the case in *Cuthbertson*, the exhaustion and relevance "factors may overlap" but are "distinct," especially in the criminal context. As the court in *Markiewicz* explained, "some testimony may not be available from other sources, for example only a subpoenaed reporter may be able to testify that a defendant made a certain statement. Yet, such testimony may be overly cumulative because the defendant's statement may only be relevant to one point which has been demonstrated by several other statements of different content which were already attributed to the defendant." *Id.*

343. See, e.g., United States v. Burke, 700 F.2d 70, 77 n.8 (2d Cir.), *cert. denied*, 464 U.S. 816 (1983) (appellant failed to make requisite "clear and specific showing that the materials could not be obtained from another source," especially since it had not sought testimony from third party present during defendants' interview with journalist); United States v. Blanton, 534 F. Supp. 295, 296 (S.D. Fla. 1982) (government failed to overcome privilege when it had "literally made only a few incomplete telephone inquiries" to locate alternative sources "and failed to negotiate in good faith with the reporter's counsel"); United States v. Hubbard, 493 F. Supp. 202, 205 (D.D.C. 1979) (in face of defendants' claim that "their attempts to obtain information" from the government about a FBI briefing had been "frustrated" because agents "have been uniformly vague in recalling particulars of the briefing, only one agent took notes, no recording of the briefing was made, and the Court had quashed the subpoenas of two of the participants," court held that "the reporter's information is available from alternative sources" since approximately 100 agents attended meeting); United States v. Caporale, 806 F.2d 1487, 1504 (11th Cir. 1986) (where "FBI agents . . . testified themselves" at an "evidentiary hearing as to the origination of the rumor" published by subpoenaed journalist, criminal defendant "failed to show" that reporter "had information that was unavailable from other sources"); Alaska v. Pruett, 11 MEDIA L. REP. (BNA) 1968 (Alaska Super. 1984); New Hampshire v. Siel, 444 A.2d 499, 503 (N.H. 1982).

344. See, e.g., United States v. Burke, 700 F.2d 70, 78 (2d Cir.), *cert. denied*, 464 U.S. 816 (1983) ("'prediction'" that alternative source would "claim attorney-client privilege" did not "insulate defense counsel from his duty to exhaust all reasonable alternatives").

345. 633 F.2d 346 (3d Cir. 1980), *cert. denied*, 449 U.S. 1113 (1981).

a prosecutor concerning alleged leaks from his office as well as the fruits of an internal Justice Department investigation of the same leaks. The court concluded that the reporter who received the leak, allegedly from the prosecutor, then became "the most logical source of information about the conversation . . . because she was the other participant in it."[346] Having interrogated the prosecutor, "and having noted the unresolved questions regarding his testimony, defendants' next step was to call" the reporter.[347] Other courts resolving claims of reporters' privilege in the criminal context have reached similar conclusions.[348]

The exhaustion requirement has proven least imposing in defamation actions in which compelled disclosure is sought from a journalist or media defendant. In *Carey v. Hume*,[349] for example, the plaintiff sought to compel the defendant-reporter's testimony concerning the identity of his sources, who had allegedly been eyewitnesses to the plaintiff's alleged wrongdoing. The court emphasized that the "values resident in the protection of confidential sources . . . point towards compelled disclosure from the newsman himself as normally the end, and not the beginning, of the inquiry."[350] Nevertheless, it concluded that the plaintiff should not be required to depose the "very substantial number of employees" that worked in the plaintiff's office building, especially since the eyewitness "observations in question could have been made by anyone from an office boy to a top officer, and in any part of the building."[351] Under these circumstances, the court determined, "the concept of exhaustion of remedies" is not "invoked by guideposts as vague as these," which afford a plaintiff "no reasonable basis to know where to begin."[352]

Nevertheless, the court closed its discussion of the exhaustion requirement with an admonition:

---

346. *Id.* at 359.

347. *Id.* The Third Circuit noted that only the reporter would "be able to testify" to the prosecutor's "credibility with respect to the conversation. Her recollection . . . is also a valuable source of information about his motives for disclosing, and particularly for initiating the dialogue with her. Defendants quite clearly have no other source from which they can acquire this insight." *Id.* at 359.

348. See, e.g., United States v. Markiewicz, 732 F. Supp. 316, 322 (N.D.N.Y. 1990) (attempts to "contact people who may have heard any of the statements referred to in the overt acts" relating to conspiracy claim unsuccessful "mainly because these statements were made in front of the co-conspirators of the speaking parties who either are fugitives, unidentified or co-defendants"); United States v. Sanusi, 813 F. Supp. 149, 160 (E.D.N.Y. 1992) (in context of subpoena by criminal defendant seeking broadcast outtakes of search of his home, court concluded it was "plain" that "the material — the tape itself — is not obtainable from any other source").

349. 492 F.2d 631 (D.C. Cir.), *cert. dismissed*, 417 U.S. 938 (1974).

350. *Id.* at 638.

351. *Id.*

352. *Id.* at 638-39.

The courts must always be alert to the possibilities of limiting impingements upon press freedom to the minimum; and one way of doing so is to make compelled disclosure by a journalist a last resort after pursuit of other opportunities has failed. But neither must litigants be made to carry wide-ranging and onerous burdens where the path is as ill-lighted as that emerging from appellant's deposition.[353]

Several other courts, in the context of defamation litigation against the media, have found the lightposts as dim as did the D.C. Circuit in *Carey v. Hume* and have ultimately held that the libel plaintiff before them had indeed exhausted alternative sources of the privileged information.[354]

Many other courts, however, have held that defamation plaintiffs have failed to exhaust alternative sources and have not therefore made a showing sufficient to overcome the constitutional privilege. In a more recent case emanating from the D.C. Circuit, *Clyburn v. News World Communications, Inc.*,[355] the court applied the admonition of *Carey v. Hume* and affirmed the trial court's finding that the plaintiff had "'utterly failed' to pursue 'obvious alternative sources of information.'" Similarly, in *LaRouche v. National Broadcasting Co.*,[356] the Fourth Circuit held that the plaintiff's failure to depose either a "revealed" non-confidential source or a second "confidential source who had come forward during the litigation" undercut his claim that he had exhausted alternative means of acquiring the information he sought to compel from the defendant.[357] Finally,

---

353. *Id.*
354. See, e.g., Miller v. Transamerican Press, Inc., 621 F.2d 721, 726 (5th Cir. 1980), *cert. denied*, 450 U.S. 1041 (1981) (court held that libel plaintiff had finally exhausted alternative sources after three previous motions to compel testimony from defendant-journalist had been denied); Star Editorial, Inc. v. United States Dist. Ct., 7 F.3d 856, 858 (9th Cir. 1993) (although court considered it a "last resort," disclosure from defendant compelled after plaintiff had "deposed all of the available twenty non-confidential sources for the article"); DeRoburt v. Gannett Co., 6 MEDIA L. REP. (BNA) 2473, 2477 (D. Haw. 1981) ("plaintiff has amply demonstrated that information regarding defendants' sources is not otherwise available to him" since "depositions of defendant's employees have met with refusal to disclose and he has no independent avenues of obtaining the information").
355. 903 F.2d 29, 35 (D.C. Cir. 1990).
356. 780 F.2d 1134, 1137 (4th Cir.), *cert. denied*, 479 U.S. 818 (1986).
357. See also Bruno & Stillman, Inc. v. Globe Newspaper Co., 633 F.2d 583, 598 n.16 (1st Cir. 1980) (case remanded for, *inter alia*, further inquiry concerning whether other "avenues" of securing information "should first be explored, or that circumstances did not justify such further effort"); Lauderback v. American Broadcasting Cos., 8 MEDIA L. REP. (BNA) 2407, 2408 (N.D. Iowa 1982) (plaintiff's motion to compel disclosure of outtakes in defamation action denied because plaintiff "has made no showing that he has exhausted alternate sources of information, that alternate methods of discovery of this information, particularly deposition testimony, are inadequate, or that he believes the outtakes contain information not otherwise available through discovery"); Dallas Morning News Co. v. Garcia, 822 S.W.2d 675, 683 (Tex. App. 1991) (exhaustion requirement not satisfied where only reporter deposed before filing motion to compel); Philip Morris Cos. v. American Broadcasting Cos., 23 MEDIA L. REP. (BNA) 2438, 2440 (Va. Cir. 1995)

courts have typically sustained claims of privilege, based on a defamation plaintiff's failure to exhaust alternative sources, in cases in which the news media or journalist is not a party.[358]

§ 16-2(e)(4). Other Requirements.

In assessing the applicability of the qualified privilege in a given case, courts have — for a variety of reasons — often ventured beyond the more familiar "relevance" and "exhaustion" requirements. Those courts that have expressed skepticism about the privilege's constitutional pedigree, for example, have nevertheless scrutinized efforts to compel disclosure from journalists to determine whether "the reporter is being harassed in order to disrupt his relationship with confidential news sources," whether the party seeking the journalist's testimony is acting "in good faith," whether the information sought "bears more than a remote and tenuous relationship" to the matters at issue, and whether a "legitimate" need will be furthered by compelled disclosure.[359] Relying on the Supreme Court's decision in *Branzburg*, several courts that expressly recognize the privilege have inquired as well whether a subpoena to a journalist has been issued for purposes of "harassment" in order to "disrupt a reporter's relationship with his news sources."[360]

In addition, in assessing the heightened relevance that is typically deemed necessary to overcome the qualified privilege, some courts have held that the party seeking to compel disclosure must make a showing of "necessity."[361] Such a showing, several courts have suggested, requires that plaintiffs in civil litigation establish a prima facie case on the merits — often by surviving a defendant's motion for summary judgment — before compelled disclosure from a journalist will be considered.[362]

("Philip Morris needs to show that it has exhausted other reasonably available sources of the information likely to be held by the confidential sources").

358. See, e.g., Shoen v. Shoen, 5 F.3d 1289, 1297 (9th Cir. 1993) (plaintiff's "failure to depose" defendant "before pursuing" journalist indicated it was "too early in the discovery process for . . . journalist privilege to yield"); Summit Tech., Inc. v. Healthcare Capital Group, Inc., 141 F.R.D. 381, 385 (D. Mass. 1992) (plaintiff "may well be able to learn the source's identity from a person other than" reporter); Davis v. Glanton, 705 A.2d 879, 885-86 (Pa. Super. 1997) (affirming order compelling production of reporter's notes upon finding that "it would be futile to seek [the information] elsewhere," but quashing order to produce notes and documents containing information not shown to be unavailable from any other source).

359. In re Grand Jury Proceedings, 810 F.2d 580, 586 (6th Cir. 1987). See also United States v. Smith, 135 F.3d 963, 969 (5th Cir. 1998); United States v. Cutler, 6 F.3d 67 (2d Cir. 1993).

360. Anderson v. Nixon, 444 F. Supp. 1195, 1198 (D.D.C. 1978) (quoting Branzburg v. Hayes, 408 U.S. 665, 707 (1972)).

361. See, e.g., Riley v. City of Chester, 612 F.2d 708, 717 (3d Cir. 1979); Weathers v. American Family Mut. Ins. Co., 17 MEDIA L. REP. (BNA) 1846, 1847 (D. Kan. 1990).

362. See, e.g., In re Selcraig, 705 F.2d 789, 797 (5th Cir. 1983) ("At this stage, the record does not establish even prima facie, by affidavit or deposition, the elements of a claim for liability.");

§ 16-2(e)(4) CONSTITUTIONAL AND COMMON LAW PRIVILEGES § 16-2(e)(4)

Moreover, some courts have adopted a "totality of the circumstances" approach, which assesses — beyond the "relevance" and "exhaustion" requirements — a host of other factors, including the need for preserving confidentiality in the given case,[363] whether the litigation is "a pretense for using discovery powers in a fishing expedition,"[364] and the extent to which a decision upholding an assertion of privilege would jeopardize a criminal defendant's Sixth Amendment rights.[365] In California, for example, that state's Supreme Court has

---

Bruno & Stillman, Inc. v. Globe Newspaper Co., 633 F.2d 583, 597 (1st Cir. 1980) ("plaintiff should show that it can establish jury issues on the essential elements of its case not the subject of the contested discovery"); Cervantes v. Time, Inc., 464 F.2d 986, 994 (8th Cir. 1972) (defamation plaintiff had not "produced a scintilla of proof supporting a finding that either defendant in fact entertained serious doubts about the truth of a single sentence in the article"); Foretich v. Chung, 22 MEDIA L. REP. (BNA) 2472 (D.D.C. 1994) (compelled disclosure inappropriate at least until motion for summary judgment adjudicated); DeRoburt v. Gannett Co., 6 MEDIA L. REP. (BNA) 2473, 2477 (D. Haw. 1981) (compelled disclosure appropriate because "plaintiff's claim is not without merit" since plaintiff "withstood defendants' summary judgment motion based on the *New York Times* 'actual malice' standard").

Initially, the Iowa Supreme Court supplemented its version of the qualified privilege by requiring that the party seeking disclosure also make a showing that "a claim or defense is not patently frivolous." Winegard v. Oxberger, 258 N.W.2d 847, 852 (Iowa 1977), *cert. denied*, 436 U.S. 905 (1978). Subsequently, however, that same court determined that such a requirement "is duplicative and unnecessary in view of the other elements" of the qualified privilege. Lamberto v. Bown, 326 N.W.2d 305, 308 (Iowa 1982).

363. See, e.g., Star Editorial, Inc. v. United States Dist. Court, 7 F.3d 856, 861 (9th Cir. 1993) (judge must assess "importance of protecting confidentiality in the case before the court"); Bruno & Stillman, Inc. v. Globe Newspaper Co., 633 F.2d 583, 597 (1st Cir. 1980) ("court must assess the extent to which there is a need for confidentiality" since not "all information as to sources is equally deserving of confidentiality"); United States v. Cuthbertson, 630 F.2d 139, 147 (3d Cir. 1980), *cert. denied*, 449 U.S. 1126 (1981) ("Of course, the lack of a confidential source may be an important element in balancing the defendant's need for the material sought against the interest of the journalist in preventing production in a particular case."); Weathers v. American Family Mut. Ins. Co., 17 MEDIA L. REP. (BNA) 1846, 1848 (D. Colo. 1990) (court must "examine the nature of the information" sought since a lesser showing of need and materiality is required if the information is not confidential) (citing Continental Cablevision Inc. v. Storer Broadcasting Co., 583 F. Supp. 427 (E.D. Mo. 1984)).

364. Bruno & Stillman, Inc. v. Globe Newspaper Co., 633 F.2d 583, 597 (1st Cir. 1980).

365. See, e.g., United States v. Cuthbertson, 630 F.2d 139, 147 (3d Cir. 1980), *cert. denied*, 449 U.S. 1126 (1981) ("A defendant's sixth amendment and due process rights certainly are not irrelevant when a journalist's privilege is asserted.").

One trial judge has indicated that, in addition to the other factors traditionally consulted in determining the privilege's applicability in the criminal context, "the court must be confident that the person asserting the privilege does not do so as a means of justifying otherwise illegal conduct." United States v. Sanusi, 813 F. Supp. 149, 156 (E.D.N.Y. 1992). In *Sanusi*, a television camera crew had accompanied federal law enforcement authorities on a search of defendant's home. Holding the privilege inapplicable to a demand by the defendant for the television network's outtakes, the court asserted:

> It is not only defendant's ability to meet the necessary three-part test that allows him to overcome CBS's qualified privilege. It is also the fact that the privilege operates weakly, if at all,

supplemented the familiar multi-factor test by asking courts to consider "the nature of the litigation and whether the reporter is a party," as well as "the importance of protecting confidentiality in the case at hand."[366]

§ 16-2(f). Penalties for Non-Disclosure.

In those cases in which an assertion of constitutional privilege has been rejected, courts have proceeded to consider and impose a variety of penalties upon those journalists and media entities that thereupon continue to decline to comply with the court's order. When the journalist or media entity is not a party to the underlying litigation, courts are typically restricted to holding the recalcitrant in contempt, either criminal or civil.[367] In *United States v. Steelhammer*,[368] for example, a trial judge ordered two reporters incarcerated for six months following their refusal to identify their sources in a civil contempt trial. Although the Fourth Circuit declined to determine whether the reporters had been held in civil or criminal contempt, it nevertheless suggested that a civil contempt finding may be "favored" in such situations because it affords the journalist an ongoing "opportunity" to "absolve" himself.[369]

---

in this case. CBS entered defendant's home without the consent of defendant or his family. As a participant in the execution of a search warrant, it did so, in effect, under color of official right.

Id. at 160. Under these circumstances, the court concluded that the "First Amendment is a shield, not a sword. Even a reporter must accept limits on how far upon another person's privacy he or she may intrude." *Id.* See also Food Lion, Inc. v. Capital Cities/ABC Inc., 951 F. Supp. 1211, 1216 (M.D.N.C. 1996) (in fraud and trespass case arising from television network's use of hidden cameras, court relied on *Sanusi* and held that, "[t]o allow ABC to hide behind a qualified First Amendment privilege in order to camouflage tortious behavior on the part of its agents is unacceptable").

366. Mitchell v. Superior Ct., 690 P.2d 625, 632-33 (Cal. 1984). Accord Missouri ex rel. Classic III, Inc. v. Ely, 954 S.W.2d 650 (Mo. App. 1997).

367. See, e.g., In re Shain, 978 F.2d 850, 851 (4th Cir. 1992) (holding noncomplying journalists in contempt and ordering them incarcerated for two days during criminal trial); United States v. Criden, 633 F.2d 346, 348 (3d Cir. 1980), *cert. denied*, 449 U.S. 1113 (1981) (holding reporter in civil contempt and ordering incarceration for failure to testify in criminal case); In re Owens, 496 S.E.2d 592 (N.C. App. 1998) (affirming criminal contempt finding against noncompliant reporter during criminal trial); Ashcraft v. Conoco, Inc., 1998 U.S. Dist. LEXIS 16371 (E.D.N.C. Sept. 3, 1998).

368. 539 F.2d 373, 374 (4th Cir. 1976), *modified*, 561 F.2d 539 (4th Cir. 1977) (en banc).

369. *Id.* at 376. On subsequent *en banc* review, three members of the full court determined that "the reporters were held in civil contempt and they may not now legally be punished since the underlying proceeding has terminated." 561 F.2d at 540. Accordingly, although a majority of the *en banc* court concluded that the reporters' contempt convictions should be affirmed, it held that, "for differing reasons, the reporters may not now be further punished for their refusals to answer." *Id.* See In re Pan Am Corp., 161 Bankr. 577, 586 (S.D.N.Y. 1993) ("Where the underlying order that resulted in a finding of civil contempt is invalidated, a contempt order must also be reversed.") (citing United States v. Mine Workers of Am., 330 U.S. 258, 294-95 (1947)).

In *United States v. Criden*,[370] the Third Circuit rejected a journalist's contention that a civil contempt proceeding instituted against her was moot because the pretrial phase of the underlying criminal case had ended. Specifically, the journalist argued that only a criminal contempt proceeding could properly be invoked to vindicate the court's authority, "whereas civil contempt is reserved solely to compel action or testimony for the benefit of the litigant" seeking it.[371] The court of appeals disagreed. Although it acknowledged that it "may not always be easy to classify a particular act as belonging to either one of these two classes," the court's exercise of its power "may partake of the characteristics of both."[372] Accordingly, "[s]anctions for civil contempt may be used either to compensate the complainant for losses sustained, or to coerce the defendant into compliance with the court's order, thereby vindicating the court's institutional authority."[373] In the last analysis, the court of appeals concluded, a trial judge "must retain authority to impose sanctions when its rules are deliberately flouted. Otherwise, the court's effectiveness would be blunted and public respect and esteem for the judicial institution seriously dissipated."[374]

Based on such judicial authority, a number of courts have ordered nonparty journalists incarcerated in the wake of a contempt citation,[375] although it appears

---

370. 633 F.2d 346 (3d Cir. 1980), *cert. denied*, 449 U.S. 1113 (1981).
371. *Id.* at 351.
372. *Id.*
373. *Id.*; see *id.* ("[A]lthough 'civil contempt is *primarily* coercive in nature,' no bright line separates civil and criminal contempt. . . . We do not perceive the role of the district court in this important case as a hired umpire dragged in from the street to preside over a dispute between private litigants.") (quoting In re Grand Jury Investigation, 600 F.2d 420, 423 & n.6 (3d Cir. 1979)).
374. 633 F.2d at 353.
375. See, e.g., Shoen v. Shoen, 48 F.3d 412, 414 (9th Cir. 1995) (court of appeals stayed trial court order of "immediate incarceration" for civil contempt pending appeal); In re Selcraig, 705 F.2d 789, 795 (5th Cir. 1983); Farr v. Pitchess, 522 F.2d 464, 466 (9th Cir. 1975) (reporter held in contempt and "sent to jail" until he disclosed name of confidential source); Campbell v. Klevenhagen, 760 F. Supp. 1206, 1208 (S.D. Tex. 1991) (reporter held in criminal contempt and ordered incarcerated for thirty days by state trial court successfully sought writ of habeas corpus in federal court); In re Tierney, 328 So. 2d 40, 45 (Fla. App. 1976) (reporter incarcerated until she agreed to respond to grand jury inquiries); Wisconsin v. Knops, 183 N.W.2d 93 (Wis. 1971) (reporter sentenced to prison for five months, seven days, "or until appellant purges himself of the contempt").

In *Massachusetts v. Corsetti*, 438 N.E.2d 805, 810 (Mass. 1982), the Massachusetts Supreme Judicial Court affirmed the use of summary contempt proceedings as a vehicle to incarcerate a reporter who disobeyed a court order requiring disclosure of the identity of his confidential source, "because refusal of the witness to answer a question could delay interminably the trial of a case." See also Massachusetts v. McDonald, 6 MEDIA L. REP. (BNA) 2230 (Mass. Super. 1980) (upholding finding of contempt where reporter refused to testify concerning identity of confidential source in murder trial).

that such orders are more often than not stayed pending appeal.[376] Most courts have, however, confined their exercise of the contempt power to the imposition of monetary fines, ranging from one to several thousand dollars per day until the contempt is purged, in both criminal[377] and civil[378] cases.

In those cases in which a journalist or media entity is a defendant, the range of sanctions available to a trial judge has expanded beyond exercise of the contempt power. In defamation actions, most notably, several courts have imposed a variety of creative sanctions, from the entry of default judgments against a media defendant, to an order striking the recalcitrant party's affirmative defenses, to a directed verdict of liability, to an instruction to the jury that the defendant had no source at all for the allegedly defamatory statements.[379] Most courts, however, have simply precluded a defendant who declines to reveal the identity of a confidential source from relying on that source — by name or otherwise — in its efforts to demonstrate that it exercised due care or to rebut a plaintiff's claim that it harbored a reckless disregard for the truth.

---

376. See Chap. 16-2(h)(2) *infra* (discussing availability of appellate review). In some cases, bail has been available to prevent immediate incarceration following a contempt order. See, e.g., Ex parte Grothe, 687 S.W.2d 736, 738 n.2 (Tex. Crim. App. 1984), *cert. denied*, 474 U.S. 944 (1985).

377. See, e.g., United States v. Cutler, 6 F.3d 67, 70 (2d Cir. 1993) ($1.00 per day); United States v. LaRouche Campaign, 841 F.2d 1176, 1177 (1st Cir. 1988) ($500 per day); In re Gronowicz, 764 F.2d 983, 984 (3d Cir. 1985), *cert. denied*, 474 U.S. 1055 (1986) ($500 per day); In re Farber, 394 A.2d 330, 332 (N.J. 1978) ($5,000 per day).

378. See, e.g., In re Petroleum Prods. Antitrust Litig., 680 F.2d 5, 7 (2d Cir.), *cert. denied*, 459 U.S. 909 (1982) ($100 per day); von Bulow v. von Bulow, 811 F.2d 136, 138 (2d Cir.), *cert. denied*, 481 U.S. 1015 (1987) ($500 per day); In re Pan Am Corp., 161 Bankr. 577, 579 (S.D.N.Y. 1993) ($1,000 per day). In one case, the Vermont Supreme Court reversed a lower court's order that a reporter held in contempt pay prospective fines and attorneys' fees since the criminal defendant's "right to compel a newsreporter's testimony ha[d] not [yet] been clearly defined." Vermont v. Gundlah, 624 A.2d 368, 370 (Vt. 1993).

379. See Downing v. Monitor Publ'g Co., 415 A.2d 683, 686 (N.H. 1980):

> Of course, the trial court is free to exercise its contempt power to enforce its order. We are aware, however, that most media personnel have refused to obey court orders to disclose, electing to go to jail instead. Confining newsmen to jail in no way aids the plaintiff in proving his case. Although we do not say that the contempt power should not be exercised, we do say that something more is required to protect the rights of a libel plaintiff. Therefore, we hold that when a defendant in a libel action, brought by a plaintiff who is required to prove actual malice under *New York Times [v. Sullivan]*, refuses to declare his sources of information upon a valid order of the court, there shall arise a presumption that the defendant had no source. This presumption may be removed by a disclosure of the sources a reasonable time before trial.

Accord Woodcock v. Journal Publ'g Co., 1990 Conn. Super. LEXIS 59, at *8-9 (Conn. Super. June 25, 1990); Turner v. Dolcefino, No. 92-32914 (Tex. Dist., July 3, 1996) (jury instruction that refusal to disclose source constitutes presumptive evidence of constitutional malice).

In *DeRoburt v. Gannett Co.*,[380] for example, the defendant newspaper refused to reveal the identities of its confidential sources in the face of a libel plaintiff's motion to compel such information. As a sanction, the trial court initially determined to instruct the jury "that the defendant had no source."[381] Subsequently, however, one of the sources died, freeing the defendant to reveal his identity, and the plaintiff ascertained the identity of the other source through independent means. Accordingly, the trial court withdrew its proposed "no source" instruction and instead advised the jury that it could consider the defendant's "long delay in revealing his claimed sources" in assessing his "credibility as a witness."[382]

§ 16-2(g). Waiver.

Although it is generally recognized that the waiver of a constitutional right will not be inferred lightly,[383] several courts have considered assertions that the constitutional privilege has been waived either by the journalist or by the source. Some courts, for example, have indicated that the privilege may be waived if a journalist "submits to an interview or files an affidavit detailing the substance of the conversation with respect to which he is asked to testify."[384] Others have concluded that a reporter waives the privilege when he affirmatively institutes litigation to which the identity of his confidential sources is relevant.[385]

Several courts have held, however, that a source's decision to shed its anonymity does not constitute a waiver of the privilege invoked by a journalist. In *Los Angeles Memorial Coliseum Commission v. National Football League*,[386] for example, the court held that, because the "privilege belongs to the journalist alone," it cannot "be waived by persons other than the journalist." Similarly, in

---

380. 507 F. Supp. 880, 883 (D. Haw. 1981), *subsequent proceeding*, 859 F.2d 714 (9th Cir. 1987).
381. 507 F. Supp. at 887 (quoting Downing v. Monitor Publ'g Co., 415 A.2d 683, 686 (N.H. 1980)).
382. 859 F.2d at 716 (quoting jury instruction).
383. See Curtis Publ'g Co. v. Butts, 388 U.S. 130, 145 (1967) ("where the ultimate effect of sustaining a claim of waiver might be an imposition on [freedom of speech and the press], we are unwilling to find waiver in circumstances which fall short of being clear and compelling").
384. United States v. Markiewicz, 732 F. Supp. 316, 320 (N.D.N.Y. 1990) (citing Pinkard v. Johnson, 118 F.R.D. 517, 523 (M.D. Ala. 1987)).
In *Wheeler v. Goulart*, 593 A.2d 173, 174-75 (D.C. 1991), the District of Columbia Court of Appeals held that a journalist's disclosure of the identity of a confidential source to two persons constituted a waiver of any constitutional privilege.
385. See, e.g., Driscoll v. Morris, 111 F.R.D. 459 (D. Conn. 1986); Anderson v. Nixon, 444 F. Supp. 1195, 1199-1200 (D.D.C. 1978) ("there is strong precedent in analogous situations suggesting that in initiating and maintaining a lawsuit such as the one in this case the newsman waives his qualified privilege of silence where his sources have information that go to the heart of the defense").
386. 89 F.R.D. 489, 494 (C.D. Cal. 1981).

United States v. Cuthbertson,[387] the Third Circuit held that "the fact that the government has obtained waivers from its witnesses" does not operate to vitiate the journalist's privilege to decline to testify about communications with those sources: "The privilege belongs to" the journalist, "not the potential witnesses, and it may be waived only by its holder."[388]

Nevertheless, at least one court has held that the constitutional privilege may be abrogated when the source itself admits to providing information to a journalist. In *United States v. Criden*,[389] the Third Circuit distinguished *Cuthbertson* and concluded that, although the source's admission "did not constitute a waiver" of the reporter's "own qualified privilege not to reveal her unpublished recollections as to the contents of her discussions with" him, the source's self-identification operated to tip the "balance" of the "'defendant's need for the material against the interests underlying the privilege'" in favor of compelled disclosure.[390]

§ 16-2(h). Procedural Requirements.

The litigation of claims of constitutional privilege is often intertwined with noteworthy but unsettled issues of procedure. The two most frequently encountered — the court's authority to order *in camera* review to resolve an assertion of privilege, and the availability of appellate review of a court order compelling disclosure — are treated in the discussion that follows. Several other procedural issues are implicated by the constitutional privilege as well.

First, in those cases in which disclosure is sought from a nonparty journalist, a court may not have jurisdiction to compel the nonparty to appear or to testify.[391] Second, although a trial court's decision abrogating a claim of constitutional privilege is typically subject to searching review on appeal,[392] it would appear

---

[387]. 630 F.2d 139, 147 (3d Cir. 1980), *cert. denied*, 449 U.S. 1126 (1981).

[388]. *Id.* at 147 (citing Republic Gear Co. v. Borg-Warner Corp., 381 F.2d 551 (2d Cir. 1967) (attorney-client privilege may be waived only by client)).

[389]. 633 F.2d 346 (3d Cir. 1980), *cert. denied*, 449 U.S. 1113 (1981).

[390]. *Id.* at 360 (quoting United States v. Cuthbertson, 630 F.2d at 148); cf. Pugh v. Avis Rent A Car Sys., Inc., 26 MEDIA L. REP. (BNA) 1311, 1316 (S.D.N.Y. 1997) ("In light of the important interests beyond confidentiality that are served by the reporter's qualified privilege, coupled with the fact that the party seeking disclosure has made no showing that the nonpublished information is relevant or necessary to its claim or that the nonpublished information at issue cannot be obtained from other available sources, this Court concludes that CBS has not waived the qualified privilege by interviewing six individuals in a group or by interviewing one individual in the presence of Plaintiffs' counsel.").

[391]. See, e.g., Gialde v. Time, Inc., 480 F.2d 1295, 1299 n.2 (8th Cir. 1973); Coastal Transp. Inc. v. WAWS Fox 30, 25 MEDIA L. REP. (BNA) 2247, 2248 (Fla. Cir. 1997).

[392]. Cf. Bose Corp. v. Consumers Union, 466 U.S. 485, 499 (1984) ("in cases raising First Amendment issues . . . an appellate court has an obligation to 'make an independent examination of the whole record' in order to make sure that 'the judgment does not constitute a forbidden intrusion

that a decision upholding the assertion of privilege is reviewable only for an abuse of discretion.[393]

Third, it appears reasonably well settled — at least in civil cases in federal court — that a journalist seeking to assert the constitutional privilege may either move for a protective order or for an order quashing the subpoena entirely before appearing for deposition (or at trial) or producing documents.[394] As one court has observed, there would appear to be "no purpose in arbitrarily postponing a decision" on such motions "until after the reporters have been forced to appear."[395] Nevertheless, courts have occasionally required a journalist to "appear for his deposition and then raise any objection to the testimony or documents sought" so as to permit the court to "balance the need for confidentiality against the need for disclosure."[396]

In Wisconsin, the state supreme court has endorsed a specific procedure for invocation of the privilege, at least in criminal cases. A claimant must first show that he or she is a journalist seeking to protect confidential sources.[397] Then, the criminal defendant seeking disclosure "must offer some proof, beyond mere speculation, that there is a reasonable probability that the subpoenaed witness's testimony will be competent, relevant, material and favorable to the defense," and that he has exhausted alternative sources.[398]

---

on the field of free expression'") (quoting New York Times Co. v. Sullivan, 376 U.S. 254, 284-86 (1964)).

393. See, e.g., Zerilli v. Smith, 656 F.2d 705, 710 (D.C. Cir. 1981); In re Cusumano, 162 F.3d 708, 713 (1st Cir. 1998).

394. See, e.g., Deitchman v. E.R. Squibb & Sons, Inc., 740 F.2d 556, 558 (7th Cir. 1984) (citing Fed. R. Civ. P. 26(c) (protective orders) and Fed. R. Civ. P. 45(b) & (d)(1) (motion to quash or modify)); Los Angeles Mem'l Coliseum Comm'n v. National Football League, 89 F.R.D. 489, 496 (C.D. Cal. 1981) ("Although it may make sense for a journalist who is an actual party in a civil suit to appear and claim the privilege with regard to particular questions and documents, such a procedure should not be imposed on non-party journalists.") (citing Fed. R. Civ. P. 45(b) and Fed. R. Civ. P. 26(c)).

395. Los Angeles Mem'l Coliseum Comm'n v. National Football League, 89 F.R.D. at 496.

396. Weathers v. American Family Mut. Ins. Co., 17 MEDIA L. REP. (BNA) 1534, 1535 (D. Kan. 1989). See Solargen Elec. Motor Car Corp. v. American Motors Corp., 506 F. Supp. 546, 552 (N.D.N.Y. 1981) ("reporters cannot refuse to appear, and must instead respond to the subpoenas and assert whatever privilege they may properly invoke in response to particular questions"); United States v. Criden, 633 F.2d 346, 350 (3d Cir. 1980), *cert. denied*, 449 U.S. 1113 (1981); Silkwood v. Kerr-McGee Corp., 563 F.2d 433, 436-37 (10th Cir. 1977); Rosario v. New York Times Co., 84 F.R.D. 626, 631 (S.D.N.Y. 1979).

397. Wisconsin ex rel. Green Bay Newspaper Co. v. Circuit Ct., 335 N.W.2d 367, 373 (Wis. 1983).

398. *Id.* at 373. The Iowa Supreme Court has adopted similar procedures. See Lamberto v. Bown, 326 N.W.2d 305, 308 (Iowa 1982) (court must first determine if party resisting disclosure is in "class" of persons entitled to invoke the privilege; if so, "the material is to be treated as presumptively privileged, and the burden falls on the requesting party to satisfy the court by a preponderance of the evidence, including all reasonable inferences," that privilege has been overcome); Bell v. City of Des Moines, 412 N.W.2d 585 (Iowa 1987). See also Dallas Morning

Fourth, some courts have required the parties to a dispute over the constitutional privilege to assist its decisionmaking process without requiring the journalist either to testify or to produce the documents at issue for *in camera* review. As the Tenth Circuit noted in *Silkwood v. Kerr-McGee Corp.*:[399]

> The trial court is empowered to compel the parties to catalogue: in the case of [the party moving to compel disclosure], the evidence that it is seeking to the extent of its knowledge plus a showing of its efforts to obtain the information from other sources; in the case of appellant, a description which does not reveal information which is claimed to be privileged of the various documents and a description of the witnesses interviewed sufficient to permit the court to carry out a weighing process. . . . Once the parties have done their work, the trial court can come to grips with the merits.

At least one court has ordered a media entity to prepare an inventory of relevant materials in its possession, to be filed *in camera* and under seal for the court's information.[400]

Some courts have sought to impose restrictions on the use of assertedly privileged information, even when compelled disclosure is ordered. Thus, courts have limited compelled disclosure to the transcripts of outtakes (rather than the film footage itself),[401] have restricted the disclosure of confidential information to counsel,[402] and have suggested that attendance at a deposition in which such information would be disclosed be limited accordingly.[403] One court has ordered a criminal defendant, whose service of a subpoena on a reporter was "unwarranted" and interposed for purposes of harassment, to pay the reporter's attorneys fees.[404]

§ 16-2(h)(1). In Camera Review.

As a general matter, courts considering claims of reporters' privilege have recognized that even compelled disclosure of assertedly privileged material for *in camera* inspection raises constitutional concerns and have, accordingly, declined to order such review absent a showing that the privilege is likely to

---

News Co. v. Garcia, 822 S.W.2d 675, 679 (Tex. App. 1991) (party asserting privilege must first adduce evidence, by affidavit or live testimony, showing that privilege presumptively applies; burden then shifts to party seeking disclosure).

399. 563 F.2d 433, 438 (10th Cir. 1977).
400. See Cinel v. Connick, 792 F. Supp. 492, 498 (E.D. La. 1992).
401. See United States v. Bingham, 765 F. Supp. 954, 960 (N.D. Ill. 1991).
402. See Miller v. Transamerican Press, Inc., 621 F.2d 721, 727 (5th Cir. 1980), *cert. denied*, 450 U.S. 1041 (1981).
403. Bruno & Stillman, Inc. v. Globe Newspaper Co., 633 F.2d 583, 598 (1st Cir. 1980).
404. See Florida v. Selinger, 13 MEDIA L. REP. (BNA) 1055, 1057 (Fla. Cir. 1986).

yield. In *In re Selcraig*,[405] for example, the trial court had ordered an *in camera* hearing expressly designed to protect the reporter's "qualified first amendment privilege as far as possible" by limiting the scope of permissible questioning even by the court itself. When the reporter refused to testify, even *in camera*, he was held in contempt. The Fifth Circuit vacated the contempt citation and remanded for additional proceedings, holding that the trial court had failed to require a showing of the necessity of the reporter's testimony before requiring that it be received *in camera*.[406]

Similarly, in *United States v. Burke*,[407] the Second Circuit held that a trial court had properly declined to order *in camera* review of documents in the possession of a magazine before concluding that they were privileged from compelled disclosure. By the same token, the court of appeals emphasized that its holding should not "be read as an indictment or criticism of *in camera* review."[408] Indeed, the Second Circuit expressly "encourage[d] the courts to inspect potentially sensitive documents, especially in situations where, as here, the record reveals that the . . . papers were not sufficiently voluminous to render *in camera* review impracticable."[409] Nevertheless, the court concluded that such review is not necessary where there is no "reasonable grounds to believe that inspection . . . would yield any probative evidence."[410] Pursuant to these standards, courts have often had occasion to order *in camera* review for the purpose of determining whether compelled disclosure is warranted.[411] In *United States v.*

---

405. 705 F.2d 789, 792 (5th Cir. 1983).

406. *Id.* at 798. See Doe v. Kohn, Nast & Graf, 853 F. Supp. 147, 149 (E.D. Pa. 1994) (court "cannot compel the production" of outtakes, "even for in camera inspection, unless the moving party has satisfied certain threshold requirements," including making a showing "that the information sought is unavailable elsewhere and consists of 'relevant evidentiary material'"); Missouri ex rel. Classic III, Inc. v. Ely, 954 S.W.2d 650, 656 (Mo. App. 1997) ("[A] court should not conduct an *in camera* review simply because a party requests privileged information. Rather, '[the movant must] first show[] that he is unable to acquire the information from another source.'") (quoting United States v. Cuthbertson, 630 F.2d 139, 148 (3d Cir. 1980), *cert. denied*, 449 U.S. 1126 (1981)). But see Note, *Outtakes, Hidden Cameras, and the First Amendment: A Reporter's Privilege*, 38 WM. & MARY L. REV. 1817 (1997) (arguing that *Cuthbertson* and *Kohn, Nast & Graf* together imply that videotaped outtakes, if understood as "unique bits of evidence that are frozen at a particular place and time," will always be unobtainable from other sources and therefore will be available for *in camera* review on a mere showing of "evidentiary relevance and good faith").

407. 700 F.2d 70 (2d Cir.), *cert. denied*, 464 U.S. 816 (1983).

408. *Id.* at 78 n.9.

409. *Id.*

410. *Id.* Accord Dallas Morning News Co. v. Garcia, 822 S.W.2d 675, 679 (Tex. App. 1991) (rejecting notion that *in camera* inspection is always necessary before claim of privilege is sustained).

411. See, e.g., Bruno & Stillman, Inc. v. Globe Newspaper Co., 633 F.2d 583, 598 (1st Cir. 1980); United States v. LaRouche Campaign, 841 F.2d 1176, 1183 (1st Cir. 1988) ("An *in camera* proceeding seems especially suited to the needs of all parties in cases like this — where there is a very likely need for the materials by the defense, a very real if generalized concern about excessive

Cuthbertson,[412] for example, the Third Circuit initially considered, but ultimately rejected, a television network's claim that its transcripts of outtakes and related audiotapes were privileged even from *in camera* inspection.[413]

Some courts have held, however, that *in camera* review is not a necessary condition precedent to compelled disclosure. In *United States v. Cutler*,[414] for example, the Second Circuit rejected the contention that a trial court had "erred

---

disclosure on the part of the media, a judicial economy interest in avoiding delay during trial, and the possibility that by the time a decision must be made on disclosure to a party the need for disclosure will have disappeared or diminished."); United States v. Sanusi, 813 F. Supp. 149, 159 (E.D.N.Y. 1992); United States v. Gambino, 741 F. Supp. 412, 414 (S.D.N.Y. 1990); United States v. Buckley, 10 MEDIA L. REP. (BNA) 1336, 1337 (W.D. Wash. 1984); Karem v. Priest, 744 F. Supp. 136, 137 (W.D. Tex. 1990); Denk v. Iowa Dist. Ct., 20 MEDIA L. REP. (BNA) 1454, 1455 (Iowa 1992) ("If the trial court finds a threshold showing of compelling need for subordination of the privilege, the court *must* then order an in camera examination of the evidence sought. The purpose of the in-camera inspection is to determin[e] if the evidence is necessary to the claim or defense, and whether it would probably be admissible at trial."); New Hampshire v. Siel, 444 A.2d 499, 503 (N.H. 1982); Wisconsin ex rel. Green Bay Newspaper Co. v. Circuit Ct., 335 N.W.2d 367, 373-74 (Wis. 1983); Montana ex rel. Blackberry v. District Ct., 546 P.2d 988 (Mont. 1976); West Virginia ex rel. Charleston Mail Ass'n v. Ranson, 488 S.E.2d 5 (W. Va. 1997) ("Once a criminal defendant has shown with particularity that the unpublished, nonconfidential information requested from a news source satisfies the three-part threshold balancing test, the circuit court shall conduct an *in camera* review of the requested material.").

412. 630 F.2d 139, 148-49 (3d Cir. 1980), *cert. denied*, 449 U.S. 1126 (1981).

413. Although the trial court subsequently held, based on that review, that the privilege should yield, the court of appeals reversed, holding that the defendants had failed to prove "an element necessary to overcome the media's qualified privilege: that the only practical access to the information sought is through the media source." United States v. Cuthbertson, 651 F.2d 189, 196 (3d Cir.), *cert. denied*, 454 U.S. 1056 (1981). In a concurring opinion, Chief Judge Seitz offered additional guidance concerning the utility of, and appropriate limitations on, the use of *in camera* review:

> By employing this protective device, the person opposing disclosure can obtain an impartial determination of whether the documents contain material that is producible under the subpoena and, in the case of a qualified privilege, whether such material is subject to disclosure under an appropriate balancing test. *In camera* inspection provides for this determination without causing the documents to lose their confidential status.
>
> * * * *
>
> Given the kinds of material that a district court may view *in camera*, and the deeply held privacy interest or privilege of the person opposing disclosure, I believe that a district court should consider *in camera* material to be in its possession for a limited purpose only. Therefore, ordinarily a district court should not consider the merits of the asserted privilege, much less decide to disclose the material, until after it has determined that the party seeking disclosure would have the right to compel production of the material if it were still in the hands of the person opposing disclosure. Otherwise, a device intended to protect the person opposing disclosure could be converted into a device by which that person must disclose material that could not have been obtained by it directly.

Id. at 198-99 (Seitz, C.J., concurring).

414. 6 F.3d 67, 74 (2d Cir. 1993).

in denying [a] . . . motion to quash the subpoenas rather than first reviewing the outtakes *in camera*." The court concluded that trial judges are not "mandate[d to] exercise . . . [their] discretion to review" materials *in camera* "before ordering their disclosure," especially when the media's "suggestion of *in camera* review was conditioned upon their right to appeal any ruling that ordered disclosure."[415]

§ 16-2(h)(2). Appellate Review.

Those journalists and media entities that have unsuccessfully asserted the constitutional privilege in a trial court have explored a variety of avenues of appellate relief. Especially when the journalist is not a party to the proceeding, an adjudication of contempt has typically permitted prompt appellate review.[416] In federal courts, for example, appellate jurisdiction to review a contempt order rests on 28 U.S.C. § 1291.[417] Of course, a contempt order typically carries with it a penalty, which can range from continuing fines to incarceration,[418] although the imposition of such penalties is often — though not always — stayed by the trial court pending appeal.[419]

When a state court in fact imposes the penalty of incarceration, one avenue of further review has been by petition for writ of habeas corpus to a federal district court.[420] Federal courts of appeals have, in turn, been held to have jurisdiction to

---

415. *Id.*

416. See, e.g., In re Roche, 411 N.E.2d 466, 468 n.1 (Mass. 1980) ("[a]n adjudication of civil contempt against a nonparty constitutes a final judgment appealable pursuant to Mass. R. App. P. 1(c)"). See also In re Madden, 151 F.3d 125, 127 (3d Cir. 1998) (deeming final an order issued by district court sitting in Pennsylvania that granted journalists' privilege to nonparty commentator subpoenaed for evidence in action pending in Connecticut, and granting review because, "[w]ere we to reject jurisdiction, appellate review of this order would be impossible").

417. See, e.g., Shoen v. Shoen, 5 F.3d 1289, 1291 (9th Cir. 1993); Newton v. National Broadcasting Co., 726 F.2d 591, 592 (9th Cir. 1984). As the Second Circuit recognized in *von Bulow v. von Bulow*, 811 F.2d 136, 138 (2d Cir.), *cert. denied*, 481 U.S. 1013 (1987), a "contempt order, being a final appealable order," can secure appellate review of orders compelling production or other discovery which, "standing alone, of course would not be appealable since they are interlocutory orders." See also United States v. Smith, 135 F.3d 963, 967 (5th Cir. 1998) (holding that government in criminal case may properly appeal from district court order quashing subpoena to television station pursuant to 18 U.S.C. § 3731, whether or not appeal could be pursued pursuant to 28 U.S.C. § 1291).

418. See Chap. 16-2(f) *supra*.

419. See, e.g., United States v. Cutler, 6 F.3d 67, 70 (2d Cir. 1993); United States v. LaRouche Campaign, 841 F.2d 1176, 1177 (1st Cir. 1988); von Bulow v. von Bulow, 811 F.2d 136, 138 (2d Cir.), *cert. denied*, 481 U.S. 1015 (1987); Riley v. City of Chester, 612 F.2d 708, 713 (3d Cir. 1979); In re Pan Am Corp., 161 Bankr. 577, 579 (S.D.N.Y. 1993).

420. See, e.g., Farr v. Pitchess, 522 F.2d 464, 466 (9th Cir. 1975) (incarcerated reporter, "[u]nsuccessful in obtaining relief in the state courts," sought writ of habeas corpus pursuant to 28 U.S.C. § 2254); In re Grand Jury Proceedings, 810 F.2d 580, 582 (6th Cir. 1987) (court of appeals found that absent petition for writ of habeas corpus "there was no avenue for review of the federal

consider a district court's decision denying habeas relief.[421] At least one judge, however, has expressed "considerable doubt" about the propriety of "federal habeas review," on the ground that the constitutional privilege is not "clearly established."[422]

Because of the risk inherent in an adjudication of contempt, most journalists and media entities faced with an order compelling disclosure have sought other routes of interlocutory appellate relief. Although some trial courts have declined to certify such interlocutory appeals,[423] many others have done so, especially in civil cases in which the journalist is a party and prompt adjudication of the interlocutory issue of privilege would facilitate the efficient resolution of the underlying litigation.[424] When courts have declined to certify an interlocutory appeal, some journalists have attempted to secure appellate review, without an adjudication of contempt, via petition for writ of mandamus.[425] In California especially, appellate review via an extraordinary writ has not been unusual in civil cases.[426] Finally, some courts routinely permit interlocutory appeals in cases where an order requires compelled disclosure of a confidential source.[427]

Several such issues were addressed in the criminal context by the Third Circuit in *United States v. Cuthbertson*,[428] in which a district court ordered that broadcast outtakes submitted for *in camera* review "be turned over to the defendants after commencement of trial but *before* the witnesses testified because they qualified as exculpatory evidence." CBS sought appellate review both by filing a notice of appeal and a petition for writ of mandamus. The court explained that the distinction between appeal and mandamus "is one *with* a difference":

---

constitutional contentions" regarding reporters' privilege); Karem v. Priest, 744 F. Supp. 136, 137 (W.D. Tex. 1990); Campbell v. Klevenhagen, 760 F. Supp. 1206, 1208 (S.D. Tex. 1991).

421. See Farr v. Pitchess, 522 F.2d 464, 466 (9th Cir. 1975) (appellate jurisdiction based on 28 U.S.C. § 1291).

422. In re Grand Jury Proceedings, 810 F.2d 580, 589 (6th Cir. 1987) (Guy, J., concurring).

423. See, e.g., von Bulow v. von Bulow, 811 F.2d 136, 140 (2d Cir.), *cert. denied*, 481 U.S. 1015 (1987) (district court declined to certify interlocutory appeal pursuant to 28 U.S.C. § 1292(b) on ground that litigant claiming privilege was "toying with the court" and engaging in "reprehensible" "eleventh-hour move").

424. See, e.g., Carey v. Hume, 492 F.2d 631, 632 (D.C. Cir.), *cert. dismissed*, 417 U.S. 938 (1974) (interlocutory appeal pursuant to 28 U.S.C. § 1292(b) in defamation action in which defendant journalist had been ordered to disclose identity of confidential source); Bruno & Stillman, Inc. v. Globe Newspaper Co., 633 F.2d 583, 586 (1st Cir. 1980); Miller v. Transamerican Press, Inc., 621 F.2d 721, 722 (5th Cir. 1980), *cert. denied*, 450 U.S. 1041 (1981); Downing v. Monitor Publ'g Co., 415 A.2d 683, 686 (N.H. 1980).

425. See, e.g., Star Editorial, Inc. v. United States Dist. Ct., 7 F.3d 856, 858 (9th Cir. 1993); Dallas Morning News Co. v. Garcia, 822 S.W.2d 675, 679 (Tex. App. 1991).

426. See, e.g., Mitchell v. Superior Ct., 690 P.2d 625, 628 (Cal. 1984).

427. See, e.g., Gadsden County Times, Inc. v. Horne, 426 So. 2d 1234, 1240 (Fla. App. 1983).

428. 651 F.2d 189, 192 (3d Cir.), *cert. denied*, 454 U.S. 1056 (1981).

On appeal, our scope of review is plenary: we review the court's choice, interpretation, and application of a legal precept. If an exercise of discretion by the district court is challenged, we determine whether the discretion was abused. If facts found by the trial court are controverted, we apply the "clearly erroneous" rule. By contrast, the peremptory writ of mandamus has generally been used to confine an inferior court to a lawful exercise of its prescribed jurisdiction or to compel it to exercise its authority when it has a duty to do so. An arbitrary and technical definition of "jurisdiction" has been avoided and, for present purposes, we note that mandamus is proper to confine a lower court to the terms of an appellate tribunal's mandate. In each case the petitioner has the burden of showing that its right to mandamus relief is "clear and indisputable."[429]

In the case before it, the Third Circuit determined that CBS could properly seek review via appeal, asserting that "contempt citations are not the exclusive means by which a third party may appeal from trial court discovery orders."[430] Rather, the court recognized a "distinction between a person named in a subpoena who must withstand contempt proceedings before lodging an appeal, and a person not named in a subpoena but who nevertheless asserts privilege in materials subject to court order."[431] Because CBS, having relinquished custody of its outtakes by producing them for *in camera* review, was "neither a recipient of an outstanding subpoena nor a witness," it was "not subject to the contempt requirement" before seeking appellate review of the district court's orders.[432] As the court explained:

> In the absence of the more lenient method of appealing interlocutory orders available to civil litigants under 28 U.S.C. § 1292(b) and Fed. R. Civ. P. 54(b), a steadfast requirement that CBS incur contempt before appealing would foreclose it from obtaining review of important issues likely to arise after it submits the documents to the district court. Such a rule would be disadvantageous both to CBS and to the development of this uncertain area of the law.[433]

Not all courts have, however, accommodated the press' attempts to secure appellate review. In *Gialde v. Time, Inc.*,[434] for example, a news media defendant

---

429. *Id.* at 193 (quoting Will v. United States, 389 U.S. 90, 95-98 (1967); Bankers Life & Cas. Co. v. Holland, 346 U.S. 379, 384 (1953)).
430. 651 F.2d at 193.
431. *Id.*
432. *Id.* See United States v. RMI Co., 599 F.2d 1183, 1186 (3d Cir. 1979) ("persons affected by the disclosure of allegedly privileged materials may intervene in pending criminal proceedings and seek protective orders, and if protection is denied, seek immediate appellate review").
433. 651 F.2d at 194.
434. 480 F.2d 1295, 1297 (8th Cir. 1973).

in a defamation action sought to appeal a trial court's order that its reporter "disclose the source of his information verifying the truth of certain portions of the published article." The Eighth Circuit asserted that the "general rule appears to be that a preliminary order such as here involved is not an appealable order," because it "applies no sanctions" and there "is no certainty that the defendant will ultimately refuse to answer questions propounded by the court, nor is it established what sanctions, if any, may be applied by the court in event" the reporter "persists in his refusal."[435] Before the reporter could be held in contempt, the court continued, "due process" requires that he "be afforded an opportunity to show cause why he should not be" so adjudged.[436] Thus, the Eighth Circuit concluded that the case "illustrates the wisdom of the general rule limiting appeals to final orders. The appeal attempted here will greatly delay disposition of the case and likely substantially increase the cost of litigation."[437]

Some appellate courts have refused to adjudicate claims of privilege under the doctrine of mootness. In *Morgan v. Roberts*,[438] for example, two television stations complied with a trial court's order to produce outtakes but also sought to appeal their claim of privilege. The Eleventh Circuit held that the appeal was moot due to the lack "of an actual present case or controversy because there is no issue still in litigation on which the district court could act."[439] The court rejected the contention that the issue was one "capable of repetition yet evading review," because the appellants "could have preserved the issue by applying for a stay until an appeal could be heard" and a "theoretical possibility of recurrence" of a similar subpoena was "not sufficient" to warrant review in the moot case.[440]

The standard of review applied by appellate courts has varied as well, sometimes with the vehicle by which appellate review is secured and sometimes

---

435. *Id.* at 1300.

436. *Id.* The Eighth Circuit further noted that an interlocutory appeal pursuant to 28 U.S.C. § 1292(b) was not available because "the District Court refused to make the required certification and, on the contrary, stated that an immediate appeal would not advance the ultimate termination of the litigation." 480 F.2d at 1297. In addition, the court rejected defendants' petition for writ of mandamus pursuant to 28 U.S.C. § 1651 on the ground that "[m]andamus is an extraordinary remedy reserved for extraordinary situations" and should not be used "as a substitute for an interlocutory appeal." 480 F.2d at 1302. But see *id.* at 1302-04 (Heaney, J., dissenting) (asserting that mandamus relief was appropriate in part because "appeal after disclosure would not be an adequate remedy to protect the asserted privilege" and case "involves interests protected by the First Amendment which deserved permanent protection").

437. 480 F.2d at 1301.

438. 702 F.2d 945, 946 (11th Cir. 1983).

439. *Id.*

440. *Id.* at 947. But cf. United States v. Steelhammer, 539 F.2d 373, 376 (4th Cir. 1976) (en banc) (regardless of whether contempt citation is classified as civil or criminal it is not moot because "a like kind of difficulty is altogether likely to arise from time to time with some frequency and, indeed, even among the same or similar actors").

with the reviewing court's perception of the First Amendment interests at stake. For example, some courts have held that, because a contempt order for failure to disclose unpublished information "is intimately connected" to the preceding denial of a motion to quash, the order is reviewed for an abuse of discretion.[441] Other courts, however, have concluded that, because such orders "implicate First Amendment issues," they are "subject to a heightened level of scrutiny" on appeal.[442]

§ 16-2(i). Choice of Law.

Claims of constitutional privilege can raise complicated choice of law issues, especially in the federal courts.[443] By the same token, because the constitutional privilege is, by definition, grounded in the overriding command of the First Amendment, it should — and typically has been held — to apply in all cases in federal and state courts.[444]

Indeed, in federal court litigation, where jurisdiction is grounded in federal law, it has been generally recognized that "the court must apply federal law and

---

441. See United States v. LaRouche Campaign, 841 F.2d 1176, 1178 (1st Cir. 1988).

442. In re Pan Am Corp., 161 Bankr. 577, 580 n. 1 (S.D.N.Y. 1993) (citing Bose Corp. v. Consumers Union, 466 U.S. 485, 499 (1984)). Similarly, in *Hurley v. Irish-American Gay, Lesbian & Bisexual Group of Boston*, 515 U.S. 557 (1995), the Supreme Court, holding that a parade constitutes expression for purposes of the First Amendment, stated that "review of petitioners' claim that their activity is indeed in the nature of protected speech carries with it a constitutional duty to conduct an independent examination of the record as a whole, without deference to the trial court." *Id.* at 567 (citing Bose Corp. v. Consumers Union, 466 U.S. 485, 499 (1984)).

443. See, e.g., Cervantes v. Time, Inc., 464 F.2d 986, 989 n.5 (8th Cir. 1972), *cert. denied*, 409 U.S. 1125 (1973) (in case presenting "somewhat unusual situation where a deposition is being taken in New York for use in an action based on diversity of citizenship pending" in Missouri, court concluded that witness, a citizen of New York, could not claim New York shield law privilege not recognized in Missouri because Missouri choice-of-law rules dictate that "the admissibility of evidence is governed by the law of the State where the testimony is to be heard"); Williams v. American Broadcasting Cos., 96 F.R.D. 662-66 (W.D. Ark. 1983) (court resolves conflict between law of New York, where defendants prepared broadcast, and Arkansas, where action was instituted and plaintiff resides, by holding that Arkansas law applies and its shield law does not protect nonconfidential outtakes, unlike Pennsylvania shield law, which contains similar language).

444. See, e.g., Miller v. Transamerican Press, Inc., 621 F.2d 721, 724-25 (5th Cir. 1980), *cert. denied*, 450 U.S. 1041 (1981) (court concludes it unnecessary to resolve potential conflicts between California, Virginia, Texas, and D.C. law of privilege, since "each jurisdiction with an interest in having its law applied limits the reporter's privilege to the protections afforded by the First Amendment"); In re Ramaekers, 33 F. Supp. 2d 312, 315 (S.D.N.Y. 1999) ("'Federal courts comprise a single system applying a single body of law, and no litigant has a right to have the interpretation of one federal court rather than that of another determine his case'") (quoting Menowitz v. Brown, 991 F.2d 36, 40 (2d Cir. 1998)).

will not ordinarily recognize state-created privileges."[445] As a practical matter, however, federal courts have looked to state law, even in federal question cases, for guidance in defining the contours of the constitutional privilege.[446] And, in those cases "in which state law provides the rule of decision," federal courts will typically look to state law-based privileges, pursuant to Federal Rule of Evidence 501,[447] before considering application of the constitutional privilege.[448] In either instance, however, any potential conflict between federal and state law would

---

445. Dillon v. City & County of San Francisco, 748 F. Supp. 722, 724 (N.D. Cal. 1990); accord Lewis v. United States, 517 F.2d 236, 237 (9th Cir. 1975); Gulliver's Periodicals, Ltd. v. Chas. Levy Circulating Co., 455 F. Supp. 1197, 1200 (N.D. Ill. 1978); In re Ramaekers, 33 F. Supp. 2d 312, 315 (S.D.N.Y. 1999). Indeed, in *Doe v. Kohn, Nast & Graf*, 853 F. Supp. 147, 148 n.4 (E.D. Pa. 1994), the court not only noted that, "because jurisdiction over this case is not based on diversity of citizenship," a state shield law was not applicable, it further indicated that this result was not altered by the "presence of supplemental state causes of action." See Titan Sports Inc. v. Turner Broadcasting Sys. Inc., 967 F. Supp. 142, 144-45 (W.D. Pa. 1997), *rev'd on other grounds sub nom.* In re Madden, 151 F.3d 125 (3d Cir. 1998).

446. See, e.g., von Bulow v. von Bulow, 811 F.2d 136, 144 (2d Cir.), *cert. denied*, 481 U.S. 1015 (1987) ("In examining the boundaries of the journalist's privilege, we may consider also the applicable state law, in this case, New York's so-called 'Shield Law'.... Although we are not bound to follow New York law, neither should we ignore New York's policy of giving protection to professional journalists."); Baker v. F & F Inv., 470 F.2d 778, 781-82 (2d Cir. 1972), *cert. denied*, 411 U.S. 966 (1973); Riley v. City of Chester, 612 F.2d 708, 715 (3d Cir. 1979) ("Although we are not bound to follow the Pennsylvania [shield] law, neither should we ignore Pennsylvania's public policy giving newspaper reporters protection from divulging their sources."); Los Angeles Mem'l Coliseum Comm'n v. National Football League, 89 F.R.D. 489, 492 (C.D. Cal. 1981) ("even in cases in which all claims are based exclusively on federal law, federal courts in 'moulding federal privileges under the common law development approach of Rule 501,' have traditionally sought guidance from existing state law") (quoting 10 J. MOORE, MOORE'S FEDERAL PRACTICE § 501.08 (2d ed. 1976)); Gulliver's Periodicals, Ltd. v. Chas. Levy Circulating Co., 455 F. Supp. 1197, 1200 (N.D. Ill. 1978) ("where, as in this case, there is no controlling federal statute on the asserted privilege, the district court for its guidance may consider existing state law concerning the privilege"). But see Dillon v. City & County of San Francisco, 748 F. Supp. 722, 725 n.2 (N.D. Cal. 1990) (suggesting that reference to state law is only appropriate where state "law and federal common law claims were present and federal and state law coincided").

447. See FED. R. EVID. 501 ("in civil actions and proceedings, with respect to an element of a claim or defense as to which State law supplies the rule of decision, the privilege of a witness, person, government, State, or political subdivision thereof shall be determined in accordance with State law").

448. See Lewis v. United States, 517 F.2d 236, 237 n.2 (9th Cir. 1975); Star Editorial, Inc. v. United States Dist. Ct., 7 F.3d 856, 859 (9th Cir. 1993):

> This defamation action was brought by Dangerfield against the Star in California Superior Court. Then, based on diversity of citizenship, it was removed to federal court. State law will clearly provide the rule of decision. Thus, it is clear that the existence and the extent of the claimed privilege is controlled by California law.

appear to be of little moment since, in the end, "both look to the First Amendment . . . to define and determine the newsman's privilege."[449]

One court, however, has held that differences between the scope of the constitutional privilege as interpreted by the courts of Florida and Georgia required a Florida trial court to decline to extradite two Florida journalists to testify in a criminal trial in Georgia where, the court concluded, the privilege has been construed too narrowly.[450] The court asserted that "the constitutional and statutory law of Florida is of primary importance" in determining whether to compel the journalists to subject themselves to the jurisdiction of the Georgia courts, especially since the "journalists gathered the information within the State of Florida while acting as professional journalists for a Florida media organization," and their interests would not necessarily be protected in Georgia, which "will not protect the journalist to the same extent as Florida would."[451]

§ 16-2(j). Avoiding the Privilege.

§ 16-2(j)(1). Third Party Subpoenas.

As the foregoing discussion illustrates, the constitutional privilege — as well as state shield legislation — often places a formidable obstacle in the path of those seeking to compel the disclosure of the fruits of newsgathering directly from journalists and news organizations. As a result, creative litigants have experimented with a variety of techniques for circumventing the privilege and securing the same information through other means. On occasion, the press has argued that these alternative measures violate the privilege as well.

In *Reporters Committee for Freedom of the Press v. American Telephone & Telegraph Co.*,[452] for example, a host of journalists and news organizations sought to enjoin AT&T's policy of releasing their toll call records in response to subpoenas issued by governmental officials. The D.C. Circuit rejected the contention that the First Amendment requires, at least in the criminal context, that journalists receive prior notice of such subpoenas so that the constitutional privi-

---

449. Weathers v. American Family Mut. Ins. Co., 17 MEDIA L. REP. (BNA) 1534, 1535 (D. Kan. 1989).

450. See Georgia v. Smith, 27 MEDIA L. REP. (BNA) 1718, 1719-23 (Fla. Cir. 1999).

451. *Id.* at 1722-23 (comparing Florida v. Davis, 720 So. 2d 220, 227 (Fla. 1998) with Vaughn v. Georgia, 381 S.E.2d 30, 31 (Ga. 1989)). The court recognized that its decision conflicted with analogous determinations made by other courts in circumstances in which state law, as opposed to the First Amendment, governed. See 27 MEDIA L. REP. (BNA) at 1722 (citing In re McAuley, 408 N.E.2d 697, 709 (Ohio App. 1979); In re Codey, 626 N.E.2d 636, 641 (N.Y. 1993)); see also Chap. 15-2(j) *supra*.

452. 593 F.2d 1030 (D.C. Cir. 1978), *cert. denied*, 440 U.S. 949 (1979).

lege could be invoked.[453] Moreover, the court suggested that the same reasoning may apply to third party subpoenas seeking a journalist's hotel, airline and taxi records.[454]

Nevertheless, several courts and individual judges have since rejected the majority's reasoning in *Reporters Committee*. Dissenting in *Smith v. Maryland*,[455] in which the full Court held that there is no general Fourth Amendment right to privacy in business records, Justice Marshall cautioned that the ruling could not constitutionally be applied to subpoenas seeking the toll records of journalists.[456] Several state courts have reached the same result.[457] In *Reporters Committee* itself, Judge Wright dissented on the ground that enforcing such subpoenas would effectively "restrain or foreclose" journalists from "making use of their telephone for long distance calls," which places a burden "squarely and directly — and exclusively — on First Amendment rights."[458]

In the civil context, moreover, courts have applied the privilege to foreclose third party discovery aimed at securing access to journalists' hotel, airline, credit card and rental car records. In *Philip Morris Co. v. American Broadcasting Cos.*,[459] for example, a Virginia trial court held that the privilege applied to a libel plaintiff's efforts to subpoena such information from the companies that the defendants had patronized in the course of newsgathering. Initially, the court extended the constitutional privilege to "all documentary or electronically compiled evidence that is the product of the reporter's news gathering activities," which are the "fruits, if not the alter ego, of the journalist's news gathering activities and warrant the same protection under the First Amendment as is afforded to the journalist."[460]

---

453. *Id.* at 1056; see *id.* at 1053 ("The First Amendment does not guarantee journalists the right to preserve the secrecy of their sources in the face of good faith criminal investigation. Moreover, Government inspection of third-party records, while it may inhibit plaintiffs' news-gathering activity, does not impermissibly abridge such activity.").

454. *Id.* at 1046; see *id.* at 1043-44 (rejecting argument that such subpoenas violate Fourth Amendment in face of "well-settled rule that a person has no expectation of privacy in the business records of a third party") (citing SEC v. Jerry T. O'Brien, Inc., 467 U.S. 735 (1984); United States v. Miller, 425 U.S. 435 (1976)).

455. 442 U.S. 735 (1979).

456. *Id.* at 751 (Marshall, J., dissenting) (enforcement of subpoenas for a journalist's toll records "impedes . . . journalistic endeavor[s] that are the hallmark of a truly free society").

457. See, e.g., New Jersey v. Hunt, 450 A.2d 952, 955-57 (N.J. 1982); Idaho v. Thompson, 760 P.2d 1162, 1167 (Idaho 1988) (citing Justice Marshall's dissenting opinion in *Smith v. Maryland*).

458. 593 F.2d at 1090 (Wright, J., dissenting).

459. 23 MEDIA L. REP. (BNA) 1434 (Va. Cir. 1995).

460. *Id.* at 1437. See *id.* ("True, it is possible for a reporter to employ alternative means of research in order to evade creating a paper trail, but these alternative means, in today's society, are unreasonable and would unduly burden and infringe on First Amendment freedoms."). Although the court in *Philip Morris Co.* initially held that the plaintiff had made the requisite showing to overcome the qualified privilege, it subsequently reconsidered its decision, largely on the ground

The United States Senate has similarly declined to enforce subpoenas seeking the phone records of journalists. In proceedings arising from an internal Senate investigation of leaks concerning the confirmation hearings of Justice Clarence Thomas, a special independent prosecutor sought to subpoena the phone records of journalists who disseminated allegedly confidential FBI materials.[461] The Senate Rules Committee, however, refused to enforce the subpoenas on the ground that doing so "would send the wrong message to the American public" and would "have a chilling effect on the media and could close a door where more doors need opening."[462]

In at least one case, civil litigants have attempted to avoid application of the qualified privilege by seeking testimony from a journalist's spouse. In *Goulart v. Barry*,[463] plaintiffs in a civil rights action sought to compel disclosure of the identity of a reporter's confidential source from his then-wife. The court rejected a claim of constitutional privilege as well as a separate claim of spousal privilege since neither the journalist nor his wife had an interest in the proceeding.[464]

§ 16-2(j)(2). Other Non-Traditional Subpoenas.

Other attempts to exhaust alternative avenues of securing substantive information in the possession of journalists have led litigants to seek the disclosure of telephone records, expense vouchers, travel logs, and the like directly from the news organizations for which they work. In *Tavoulareas v. Piro*,[465] for example,

---

that "[t]here may yet occur, during the course of discovery, the revelation of sufficient information from other sources that it will not be necessary to impinge on the qualified privilege." Philip Morris Co. v. American Broadcasting Co., 23 MEDIA L. REP. (BNA) 1434 (Va. Cir. 1995). In the interim, however, one credit card company released the journalists' records to the plaintiff. See Wall St. J., Feb. 24, 1995, at A1.

A federal district court reached the same result in *Food Lion Inc. v. Capital Cities/ABC Inc.*, 24 MEDIA L. REP. (BNA) 2431, 2432-33 (M.D.N.C.), *aff'd*, 951 F. Supp. 1211 (M.D.N.C. 1996), holding that a plaintiff in an action alleging fraud, trespass and other torts against a news media defendant could not evade the privilege by serving subpoenas on "hotels, letter carriers, and telecommunications companies." *Id.* at 2432. According to the court, such discovery "improperly infringes upon a protected First Amendment interest of ABC, namely the protection of confidential sources." *Id.* at 2433.

461. See, e.g., Newsday, Mar. 26, 1992, at 5; USA Today, Feb. 25, 1992, at 2A; L.A. Times, Mar. 18, 1992, at B6.

462. Newsday, Mar. 26, 1992, at 5 (quoting Senate Rules Committee Chairman Wendell Ford). For other examples of efforts to secure phone records, see N.Y. Times, Oct. 27, 1991, § 4, at 16 (efforts by Procter & Gamble Co. to enlist police to search phone records of 800,000 business and home phones to identify leak of allegedly confidential information to *Wall Street Journal*); Christian Sci. Monitor, Aug. 24 1989, at U.S. 8 (efforts by Bush Administration to identify leak of Justice Department investigatory information to television network).

463. 18 MEDIA L. REP. (BNA) 2001 (D.C. Super. 1991).

464. *Id.* at 2004-06.

465. 93 F.R.D. 35, 39 (D.D.C. 1981).

a defamation plaintiff sought such information in order to piece together the identity of a confidential source. The court granted the defendants' motion for a protective order, holding that the source's identity was itself protected by the qualified privilege and the records were of "minimal relevance to any factual issue other than to the discovery of the confidential source."[466]

Similarly, in *Grunseth v. Marriott Corp.*,[467] a candidate for political office instituted a civil action for breach of contract and invasion of privacy against a hotel that had disclosed billing records concerning the plaintiff to a newspaper. In the course of the litigation, the candidate sought to subpoena copies of the records from the newspaper and its reporters.[468] The court declined to enforce the subpoenas, holding that doing so would be tantamount to "compelling a reporter to disclose the identity of his source."[469]

In *Solargen v. American Motors Corp.*,[470] however, another court enforced a subpoena for a journalist's bank records in a civil antitrust action. The plaintiff claimed that the defendants had bribed certain journalists to publish and broadcast defamatory information about it.[471] Although the court quashed subpoenas seeking various unpublished materials concerning the editorial process, it held that disclosure of the journalists' bank records would not interfere with newsgathering and were therefore not privileged.[472]

§ 16-3. Common Law Privilege.

Although most states — both before and after the Supreme Court's decision in *Branzburg v. Hayes*[473] — have rejected the notion of a common law reporters' privilege,[474] a few state courts, most notably the Supreme Court of Washington,

---

466. *Id.*
467. 868 F. Supp. 333 (D.D.C. 1994).
468. *Id.* at 335.
469. *Id.*
470. 506 F. Supp. 546 (N.D.N.Y. 1981).
471. *Id.* at 548.
472. *Id.* at 552-53.
473. 408 U.S. 665 (1972).
474. See, e.g., In re Dow Jones & Co., 27 MEDIA L. REP. (BNA) 1307, 1310 (S.D.N.Y. 1998), *vacated*, No. 99-7014 (2d Cir. June 8, 1999); Williams v. American Broadcasting Cos., 96 F.R.D. 658, 667 (W.D. Ark. 1983); Hurst v. Georgia, 287 S.E.2d 677, 678 (Ga. App. 1982); Georgia Communications, Inc. v. Horne, 294 S.E.2d 725, 726 (Ga. App. 1982) (citing Plunkett v. Hamilton, 70 S.E. 781 (Ga. 1911); In re Goodfader's Appeal, 367 P.2d 472, 480 (Haw. 1961)). But see Boutrous & Stodder, *Retooling the Federal Common-Law Reporter's Privilege*, 17 COMM. LAW. 1, 22 (Spring 1999) (arguing in favor of federal common law privilege pursuant to Fed. R. Evid. 501); Riley v. City of Chester, 612 F.2d 708, 713-18 (3d Cir. 1979) (arguably grounding privilege in common law); cf. Gonzales v. National Broadcasting Co., 1998 U.S. App. LEXIS 38583, at *22 n.6 (2d Cir. 1999) (suggesting that, although previous decisions had "expressed differing views on whether the journalists' privilege is constitutionally required, or rooted in federal common law," there is no need to resolve the issue "[u]ntil Congress legislates to modify the privilege or do away

have grounded their state's privilege firmly in the common law.[475] In *Senear v. Daily Journal-American*,[476] a public figure libel action against a newspaper, the court refused to consider the validity of a federal constitutional privilege, declining to "ventur[e] on the uncertain terrain of federal constitutional interpretation if it is not necessary to do so."[477] Nevertheless, the court embraced a qualified, common law privilege that applies to journalists and news organizations when the interest of the journalist in nondisclosure is supported by a need to maintain confidentiality.[478] The privilege can be overcome only by a showing that (1) the claim of the party seeking disclosure is not frivolous or interposed "for the purpose of harassing the reporter;" (2) the information sought is necessary or critical to the cause of action or defense; and (3) a reasonable effort has been made to acquire the information by other means.[479] In a subsequent case, the court explained that:

> A party seeking to defeat a claim of reporter's privilege must do more than state a cause of action. The party must show further that he or she can "establish jury issues on the essential elements of [his or her] case not the subject of the contested discovery."[480]

The Washington Supreme Court extended the common law privilege to criminal cases in *Washington v. Rinaldo*.[481] There, a criminal defendant subpoenaed newspaper records for information designed to impeach a prosecution witness. The trial court ordered the material to be produced for *in camera* inspection, but the court of appeals reversed, finding an absolute privilege under the state constitution. The Washington Supreme Court disagreed, holding instead that the qualified privilege in *Senear* applied but cautioning that the balancing of competing interests may be a closer question in criminal cases where the defendant's

---

with it"); Jaffee v. Redmond, 518 U.S. 1, 8 (1996) (recognizing federal common law privilege governing psychotherapist-patient communications).

475. See Thompson v. Minnesota, 170 N.W.2d 101, 103 (Minn. 1969).
476. 641 P.2d 1180 (Wash. 1982).
477. *Id.* at 1182.
478. *Id.* at 1184.
479. *Id.* at 1183. In *Senear* itself, the trial court, on remand, denied the plaintiff's motion to compel disclosure on the ground that the actual identity of the source, as opposed to the information itself, was neither necessary nor critical to the plaintiff's claim, and the plaintiff had not exhausted alternative sources. Senear v. Daily Journal-Am., 8 MEDIA L. REP. (BNA) 2489, 2490-91 (Wash. Super. 1982). See also Clampitt v. Thurston County, 658 P.2d 641 (Wash. 1983) (applying *Senear* privilege in an outrage case); Olsen v. Allen, 710 P.2d 822, 823 (Wash. App. 1985) (remanding trial court order denying book author's claim of privilege because trial court did not make "a record sufficient to allow meaningful appellate review"); National Union Fire Ins. Co. v. Seafirst Co., 14 MEDIA L. REP. (BNA) 1190 (W.D. Wash. 1987).
480. Clampitt v. Thurston County, 658 P.2d at 646 (quoting Bruno & Stillman, Inc. v. Globe Newspaper Co., 633 F.2d 583, 597 (1st Cir. 1980)).
481. 689 P.2d 392 (Wash. 1984).

right to a fair trial presents a more compelling case for disclosure than in the civil context.[482]

The Massachusetts Supreme Judicial Court has also indicated that "common law principles may justify" vindicating an assertion of privilege, even in the grand jury context.[483] Indeed, the court held that the common law requires a judicial "weighing" of "(a) the public interest in having every person's evidence available against (b) the public interest in the free flow of information."[484] In the case before it, the court considered a number of factors, including that (1) the sources at issue had probably already been questioned by the grand jury; (2) the reporter's testimony would be inadmissible as hearsay; and (3) compelled disclosure would likely lead sources to shy away from providing information to the press. Thus, the court held that "the low likelihood of benefit to the grand jury from the revelation of the sources balanced against the public interest in encouraging the dissemination of information leads us to conclude that the grand jury had no right to insist on the reporter's testimony."[485]

---

482. *Id.* at 394-95. See also Washington v. Terwilliger, 11 MEDIA L. REP. (BNA) 2463, 2464 (Wash. Super. 1985) (even where source is not confidential, when reporter's notes are unpublished, the requesting party must demonstrate a reasonable probability that the information sought is relevant and material and that his claim is meritorious to overcome privilege).

483. In re John Doe Grand Jury Investigation, 574 N.E.2d 373, 375 (Mass. 1991).

484. *Id.*

485. *Id.* at 377. The court's decision in *In re John Doe Grand Jury Investigation* had been presaged by its earlier suggestion in *In re Roche*, 411 N.E.2d 466, 477 (Mass. 1980):

> [W]e note our willingness to consider, in future cases, whether the central role a free discussion of public affairs plays in a self-governing society requires, as a matter of Massachusetts practice, that persons addressing such issues be afforded more clearly defined protection.... [T]he development of initially narrow common law rules, subject to modification by the Legislature or this court in light of future experience, might represent an appropriately cautious initial step toward developing a set of coherent guidelines capable of governing the complex and troubling conflict between the public interest in free and informed expression and the equally compelling public interest in securing all evidence necessary to fair and accurate adjudication.

See also Ayash v. Dana-Farber Cancer Inst., 1999 Mass. App. LEXIS 244 (Mass. App. Feb. 26, 1999). In *Ayash*, a Massachusetts appellate court vacated both an order compelling the disclosure of confidential sources and an order imposing civil contempt sanctions, in the context of a civil suit against a news reporter and publisher based on a series of articles discussing an accidental chemotherapy overdose administered to two patients. Applying the "[d]eveloping common law protection for news reporters' confidential sources," *id.* at *9, the court found that the defendants had made a threshold showing "that disclosure of [the reporter's] confidential sources presents a danger to the free flow of information that is more than speculative or theoretical," *id.* at *19. Accordingly, the court remanded for a determination "whether, as to the libel claim against the ... defendants, [the] disclosure of additional confidential sources would achieve more than the 'needless disclosure of confidential relationships.'" *Id.* at *20 (citation omitted).

Appendix A

FEDERAL STATUTES

FREEDOM OF INFORMATION ACT

5 U.S.C. § 552. Public information; agency rules, opinions, orders, records, and proceedings.

§ 552(a).

(a) Each agency shall make available to the public information as follows:

(1) Each agency shall separately state and currently publish in the Federal Register for the guidance of the public—

(A) descriptions of its central and field organization and the established places at which, the employees (and in the case of a uniformed service, the members) from whom, and the methods whereby, the public may obtain information, make submittals or requests, or obtain decisions;

(B) statements of the general course and method by which its functions are channeled and determined, including the nature and requirements of all formal and informal procedures available;

(C) rules of procedure, descriptions of forms available or the places at which forms may be obtained, and instructions as to the scope and contents of all papers, reports, or examinations;

(D) substantive rules of general applicability adopted as authorized by law, and statements of general policy or interpretations of general applicability formulated and adopted by the agency; and

(E) each amendment, revision, or repeal of the foregoing.

Except to the extent that a person has actual and timely notice of the terms thereof, a person may not in any manner be required to resort to, or be adversely affected by, a matter required to be published in the Federal Register and not so published. For the purpose of this paragraph, matter reasonably available to the class of persons affected thereby is deemed published in the Federal Register when incorporated by reference therein with the approval of the Director of the Federal Register.

(2) Each agency, in accordance with published rules, shall make available for public inspection and copying—

(A) final opinions, including concurring and dissenting opinions, as well as orders, made in the adjudication of cases;

(B) those statements of policy and interpretations which have been adopted by the agency and are not published in the Federal Register;

(C) administrative staff manuals and instructions to staff that affect a member of the public;

(D) copies of all records, regardless of form or format, which have been released to any person under paragraph (3) and which, because of the nature of their subject matter, the agency determines have become or are likely to become the subject of subsequent requests for substantially the same records; and

(E) a general index of the records referred to under subparagraph (D); unless the materials are promptly published and copies offered for sale. For records created on

APPENDIX A — FEDERAL STATUTES

or after November 1, 1996, within one year after such date, each agency shall make such records available, including by computer telecommunications or, if computer telecommunications means have not been established by the agency, by other electronic means. To the extent required to prevent a clearly unwarranted invasion of personal privacy, an agency may delete identifying details when it makes available or publishes an opinion, statement of policy, interpretation, staff manual, instruction, or copies of records referred to in subparagraph (D). However, in each case the justification for the deletion shall be explained fully in writing, and the extent of such deletion shall be indicated on the portion of the record which is made available or published, unless including that indication would harm an interest protected by the exemption in subsection (b) under which the deletion is made. If technically feasible, the extent of the deletion shall be indicated at the place in the record where the deletion was made. Each agency shall also maintain and make available for public inspection and copying current indexes providing identifying information for the public as to any matter issued, adopted, or promulgated after July 4, 1967, and required by this paragraph to be made available or published. Each agency shall promptly publish, quarterly or more frequently, and distribute (by sale or otherwise) copies of each index or supplements thereto unless it determines by order published in the Federal Register that the publication would be unnecessary and impracticable, in which case the agency shall nonetheless provide copies of such index on request at a cost not to exceed the direct cost of duplication. Each agency shall make the index referred to in subparagraph (E) available by computer telecommunications by December 31, 1999. A final order, opinion, statement of policy, interpretation, or staff manual or instruction that affects a member of the public may be relied on, used, or cited as precedent by an agency against a party other than an agency only if—

    (i) it has been indexed and either made available or published as provided by this paragraph; or

    (ii) the party has actual and timely notice of the terms thereof.

(3)(A) Except with respect to the records made available under paragraphs (1) and (2) of this subsection, each agency, upon any request for records which (i) reasonably describes such records and (ii) is made in accordance with published rules stating the time, place, fees (if any), and procedures to be followed, shall make the records promptly available to any person.

(B) In making any record available to a person under this paragraph, an agency shall provide the record in any form or format requested by the person if the record is readily reproducible by the agency in that form or format. Each agency shall make reasonable efforts to maintain its records in forms or formats that are reproducible for purposes of this section.

(C) In responding under this paragraph to a request for records, an agency shall make reasonable efforts to search for the records in electronic form or format, except when such efforts would significantly interfere with the operation of the agency's automated information system.

(D) For purposes of this paragraph, the term "search" means to review, manually or by automated means, agency records for the purpose of locating those records which are responsive to a request.

(4)(A)(i) In order to carry out the provisions of this section, each agency shall promulgate regulations, pursuant to notice and receipt of public comment, specifying the schedule of fees applicable to the processing of requests under this section and establishing procedures and guidelines for determining when such fees should be waived or reduced. Such schedule shall conform to the guidelines which shall be promulgated, pursuant to notice and receipt of public comment, by the Director of the Office of Management and Budget and which shall provide for a uniform schedule of fees for all agencies.

(ii) Such agency regulations shall provide that—

(I) fees shall be limited to reasonable standard charges for document search, duplication, and review, when records are requested for commercial use;

(II) fees shall be limited to reasonable standard charges for document duplication when records are not sought for commercial use and the request is made by an educational or noncommercial scientific institution, whose purpose is scholarly or scientific research; or a representative of the news media; and

(III) for any request not described in (I) or (II), fees shall be limited to reasonable standard charges for document search and duplication.

(iii) Documents shall be furnished without any charge or at a charge reduced below the fees established under clause (ii) if disclosure of the information is in the public interest because it is likely to contribute significantly to public understanding of the operations or activities of the government and is not primarily in the commercial interest of the requester.

(iv) Fee schedules shall provide for the recovery of only the direct costs of search, duplication, or review. Review costs shall include only the direct costs incurred during the initial examination of a document for the purposes of determining whether the documents must be disclosed under this section and for the purposes of withholding any portions exempt from disclosure under this section. Review costs may not include any costs incurred in resolving issues of law or policy that may be raised in the course of processing a request under this section. No fee may be charged by any agency under this section—

(I) if the costs of routine collection and processing of the fee are likely to equal or exceed the amount of the fee; or

(II) for any request described in clause (ii)(II) or (III) of this subparagraph for the first two hours of search time or for the first one hundred pages of duplication.

(v) No agency may require advance payment of any fee unless the requester has previously failed to pay fees in a timely fashion, or the agency has determined that the fee will exceed $250.

(vi) Nothing in this subparagraph shall supersede fees chargeable under a statute specifically providing for setting the level of fees for particular types of records.

(vii) In any action by a requester regarding the waiver of fees under this section, the court shall determine the matter de novo: Provided, That the court's review of the matter shall be limited to the record before the agency.

APPENDIX A — FEDERAL STATUTES

(B) On complaint, the district court of the United States in the district in which the complainant resides, or has his principal place of business, or in which the agency records are situated, or in the District of Columbia, has jurisdiction to enjoin the agency from withholding agency records and to order the production of any agency records improperly withheld from the complainant. In such a case the court shall determine the matter de novo, and may examine the contents of such agency records in camera to determine whether such records or any part thereof shall be withheld under any of the exemptions set forth in subsection (b) of this section, and the burden is on the agency to sustain its action. In addition to any other matters to which a court accords substantial weight, a court shall accord substantial weight to an affidavit of an agency concerning the agency's determination as to technical feasibility under paragraph (2)(C) and subsection (b) and reproducibility under paragraph (3)(B).

(C) Notwithstanding any other provision of law, the defendant shall serve an answer or otherwise plead to any complaint made under this subsection within thirty days after service upon the defendant of the pleading in which such complaint is made, unless the court otherwise directs for good cause shown.

(D) Repealed. Pub.L. 98-620, Title IV, § 402(2), Nov. 8, 1984, 98 Stat. 3357.

(E) The court may assess against the United States reasonable attorney fees and other litigation costs reasonably incurred in any case under this section in which the complainant has substantially prevailed.

(F) Whenever the court orders the production of any agency records improperly withheld from the complainant and assesses against the United States reasonable attorney fees and other litigation costs, and the court additionally issues a written finding that the circumstances surrounding the withholding raise questions whether agency personnel acted arbitrarily or capriciously with respect to the withholding, the Special Counsel shall promptly initiate a proceeding to determine whether disciplinary action is warranted against the officer or employee who was primarily responsible for the withholding. The Special Counsel, after investigation and consideration of the evidence submitted, shall submit his findings and recommendations to the administrative authority of the agency concerned and shall send copies of the findings and recommendations to the officer or employee or his representative. The administrative authority shall take the corrective action that the Special Counsel recommends.

(G) In the event of noncompliance with the order of the court, the district court may punish for contempt the responsible employee, and in the case of a uniformed service, the responsible member.

(5) Each agency having more than one member shall maintain and make available for public inspection a record of the final votes of each member in every agency proceeding.

(6)(A) Each agency, upon any request for records made under paragraph (1), (2), or (3) of this subsection, shall—

> (i) determine within 20 days (excepting Saturdays, Sundays, and legal public holidays) after the receipt of any such request whether to comply with such request and shall immediately notify the person making such request of such determination and the reasons therefor, and of the right of such person to appeal to the head of the agency any adverse determination; and

(ii) make a determination with respect to any appeal within twenty days (excepting Saturdays, Sundays, and legal public holidays) after the receipt of such appeal. If on appeal the denial of the request for records is in whole or in part upheld, the agency shall notify the person making such request of the provisions for judicial review of that determination under paragraph (4) of this subsection.

(B)(i) In unusual circumstances as specified in this subparagraph, the time limits prescribed in either clause (i) or clause (ii) of subparagraph (A) may be extended by written notice to the person making such request setting forth the unusual circumstances for such extension and the date on which a determination is expected to be dispatched. No such notice shall specify a date that would result in an extension for more than ten working days, except as provided in clause (ii) of this subparagraph.

(ii) With respect to a request for which a written notice under clause (i) extends the time limits prescribed under clause (i) of subparagraph (A), the agency shall notify the person making the request if the request cannot be processed within the time limit specified in that clause and shall provide the person an opportunity to limit the scope of the request so that it may be processed within that time limit or an opportunity to arrange with the agency an alternative time frame for processing the request or a modified request. Refusal by the person to reasonably modify the request or arrange such an alternative time frame shall be considered as a factor in determining whether exceptional circumstances exist for purposes of subparagraph (C).

(iii) As used in this subparagraph, "unusual circumstances" means, but only to the extent reasonably necessary to the proper processing of the particular requests—

(I) the need to search for and collect the requested records from field facilities or other establishments that are separate from the office processing the request;

(II) the need to search for, collect, and appropriately examine a voluminous amount of separate and distinct records which are demanded in a single request; or

(III) the need for consultation, which shall be conducted with all practicable speed, with another agency having a substantial interest in the determination of the request or among two or more components of the agency having substantial subject-matter interest therein.

(iv) Each agency may promulgate regulations, pursuant to notice and receipt of public comment, providing for the aggregation of certain requests by the same requestor, or by a group of requestors acting in concert, if the agency reasonably believes that such requests actually constitute a single request, which would otherwise satisfy the unusual circumstances specified in this subparagraph, and the requests involve clearly related matters. Multiple requests involving unrelated matters shall not be aggregated.

(C)(i) Any person making a request to any agency for records under paragraph (1), (2), or (3) of this subsection shall be deemed to have exhausted his administrative remedies with respect to such request if the agency fails to comply with the applicable time limit provisions of this paragraph. If the Government can show exceptional circumstances exist and that the agency is exercising due diligence in responding to the request, the court may retain jurisdiction and allow the agency ad-

APPENDIX A — FEDERAL STATUTES

ditional time to complete its review of the records. Upon any determination by an agency to comply with a request for records, the records shall be made promptly available to such person making such request. Any notification of denial of any request for records under this subsection shall set forth the names and titles or positions of each person responsible for the denial of such request.

(ii) For purposes of this subparagraph, the term "exceptional circumstances" does not include a delay that results from a predictable agency workload of requests under this section, unless the agency demonstrates reasonable progress in reducing its backlog of pending requests.

(iii) Refusal by a person to reasonably modify the scope of a request or arrange an alternative time frame for processing a request (or a modified request) under clause (ii) after being given an opportunity to do so by the agency to whom the person made the request shall be considered as a factor in determining whether exceptional circumstances exist for purposes of this subparagraph.

(D)(i) Each agency may promulgate regulations, pursuant to notice and receipt of public comment, providing for multitrack processing of requests for records based on the amount of work or time (or both) involved in processing requests.

(ii) Regulations under this subparagraph may provide a person making a request that does not qualify for the fastest multitrack processing an opportunity to limit the scope of the request in order to qualify for faster processing.

(iii) This subparagraph shall not be considered to affect the requirement under subparagraph (C) to exercise due diligence.

(E)(i) Each agency shall promulgate regulations, pursuant to notice and receipt of public comment, providing for expedited processing of requests for records—

(I) in cases in which the person requesting the records demonstrates a compelling need; and

(II) in other cases determined by the agency.

(ii) Notwithstanding clause (i), regulations under this subparagraph must ensure—

(I) that a determination of whether to provide expedited processing shall be made, and notice of the determination shall be provided to the person making the request, within 10 days after the date of the request; and

(II) expeditious consideration of administrative appeals of such determinations of whether to provide expedited processing.

(iii) An agency shall process as soon as practicable any request for records to which the agency has granted expedited processing under this subparagraph. Agency action to deny or affirm denial of a request for expedited processing pursuant to this subparagraph, and failure by an agency to respond in a timely manner to such a request shall be subject to judicial review under paragraph (4), except that the judicial review shall be based on the record before the agency at the time of the determination.

(iv) A district court of the United States shall not have jurisdiction to review an agency denial of expedited processing of a request for records after the agency has provided a complete response to the request.

(v) For purposes of this subparagraph, the term "compelling need" means—

FREEDOM OF INFORMATION ACT

(I) that a failure to obtain requested records on an expedited basis under this paragraph could reasonably be expected to pose an imminent threat to the life or physical safety of an individual; or

(II) with respect to a request made by a person primarily engaged in disseminating information, urgency to inform the public concerning actual or alleged Federal Government activity.

(vi) A demonstration of a compelling need by a person making a request for expedited processing shall be made by a statement certified by such person to be true and correct to the best of such person's knowledge and belief.

(F) In denying a request for records, in whole or in part, an agency shall make a reasonable effort to estimate the volume of any requested matter the provision of which is denied, and shall provide any such estimate to the person making the request, unless providing such estimate would harm an interest protected by the exemption in subsection (b) pursuant to which the denial is made.

(b) This section does not apply to matters that are—

(1) (A) specifically authorized under criteria established by an Executive order to be kept secret in the interest of national defense or foreign policy and (B) are in fact properly classified pursuant to such Executive order;

(2) related solely to the internal personnel rules and practices of an agency;

(3) specifically exempted from disclosure by statute (other than section 552b of this title), provided that such statute (A) requires that the matters be withheld from the public in such a manner as to leave no discretion on the issue, or (B) establishes particular criteria for withholding or refers to particular types of matters to be withheld;

(4) trade secrets and commercial or financial information obtained from a person and privileged or confidential;

(5) inter-agency or intra-agency memorandums or letters which would not be available by law to a party other than an agency in litigation with the agency;

(6) personnel and medical files and similar files the disclosure of which would constitute a clearly unwarranted invasion of personal privacy;

(7) records or information compiled for law enforcement purposes, but only to the extent that the production of such law enforcement records or information (A) could reasonably be expected to interfere with enforcement proceedings, (B) would deprive a person of a right to a fair trial or an impartial adjudication, (C) could reasonably be expected to constitute an unwarranted invasion of personal privacy, (D) could reasonably be expected to disclose the identity of a confidential source, including a State, local, or foreign agency or authority or any private institution which furnished information on a confidential basis, and, in the case of a record or information compiled by criminal law enforcement authority in the course of a criminal investigation or by an agency conducting a lawful national security intelligence investigation, information furnished by a confidential source, (E) would disclose techniques and procedures for law enforcement investigations or prosecutions, or would disclose guidelines for law enforcement investigations or prosecutions if such disclosure could reasonably be expected to risk circumvention of the law, or (F) could reasonably be expected to endanger the life or physical safety of any individual;

(8) contained in or related to examination, operating, or condition reports prepared by, on behalf of, or for the use of an agency responsible for the regulation or supervision of financial institutions; or

(9) geological and geophysical information and data, including maps, concerning wells.

Any reasonably segregable portion of a record shall be provided to any person requesting such record after deletion of the portions which are exempt under this subsection. The amount of information deleted shall be indicated on the released portion of the record, unless including that indication would harm an interest protected by the exemption in this subsection under which the deletion is made. If technically feasible, the amount of the information shall be indicated at the place in the record where such deletion is made.

(c)(1) Whenever a request is made which involves access to records described in subsection (b)(7)(A) and—

    (A) the investigation or proceeding involves a possible violation of criminal law; and

    (B) there is reason to believe that

        (i) the subject of the investigation or proceeding is not aware of its pendency, and

        (ii) disclosure of the existence of the records could reasonably be expected to interfere with enforcement proceedings, the agency may, during only such time as that circumstance continues, treat the records as not subject to the requirements of this section.

(2) Whenever informant records maintained by a criminal law enforcement agency under an informant's name or personal identifier are requested by a third party according to the informant's name or personal identifier, the agency may treat the records as not subject to the requirements of this section unless the informant's status as an informant has been officially confirmed.

(3) Whenever a request is made which involves access to records maintained by the Federal Bureau of Investigation pertaining to foreign intelligence or counterintelligence, or international terrorism, and the existence of the records is classified information as provided in subsection (b)(1), the Bureau may, as long as the existence of the records remains classified information, treat the records as not subject to the requirements of this section.

(d) This section does not authorize withholding of information or limit the availability of records to the public, except as specifically stated in this section. This section is not authority to withhold information from Congress.

(e)(1) On or before February 1 of each year, each agency shall submit to the Attorney General of the United States a report which shall cover the preceding fiscal year and which shall include—

    (A) the number of determinations made by the agency not to comply with requests for records made to such agency under subsection (a) and the reasons for each such determination;

    (B)(i) the number of appeals made by persons under subsection (a)(6), the result of such appeals, and the reason for the action upon each appeal that results in a denial of information; and

        (ii) a complete list of all statutes that the agency relies upon to authorize the agency to withhold information under subsection (b)(3), a description of whether a court has upheld the decision of the agency to withhold information under each such statute, and a concise description of the scope of any information withheld;

(C) the number of requests for records pending before the agency as of September 30 of the preceding year, and the median number of days that such requests had been pending before the agency as of that date;

(D) the number of requests for records received by the agency and the number of requests which the agency processed;

(E) the median number of days taken by the agency to process different types of requests;

(F) the total amount of fees collected by the agency for processing requests; and

(G) the number of full-time staff of the agency devoted to processing requests for records under this section, and the total amount expended by the agency for processing such requests.

(2) Each agency shall make each such report available to the public including by computer telecommunications, or if computer telecommunications means have not been established by the agency, by other electronic means.

(3) The Attorney General of the United States shall make each report which has been made available by electronic means available at a single electronic access point. The Attorney General of the United States shall notify the Chairman and ranking minority member of the Committee on Government Reform and Oversight of the House of Representatives and the Chairman and ranking minority member of the Committees on Governmental Affairs and the Judiciary of the Senate, no later than April 1 of the year in which each such report is issued, that such reports are available by electronic means.

(4) The Attorney General of the United States, in consultation with the Director of the Office of Management and Budget, shall develop reporting and performance guidelines in connection with reports required by this subsection by October 1, 1997, and may establish additional requirements for such reports as the Attorney General determines may be useful.

(5) The Attorney General of the United States shall submit an annual report on or before April 1 of each calendar year which shall include for the prior calendar year a listing of the number of cases arising under this section, the exemption involved in each case, the disposition of such case, and the cost, fees, and penalties assessed under subparagraphs (E), (F), and (G) of subsection (a)(4). Such report shall also include a description of the efforts undertaken by the Department of Justice to encourage agency compliance with this section.

(f) For purposes of this section, the term—

(1) "agency" as defined in section 551(1) of this title includes any executive department, military department, Government corporation, Government controlled corporation, or other establishment in the executive branch of the Government (including the Executive Office of the President), or any independent regulatory agency; and

(2) "record" and any other term used in this section in reference to information includes any information that would be an agency record subject to the requirements of this section when maintained by an agency in any format, including an electronic format.

APPENDIX A — FEDERAL STATUTES

(g) The head of each agency shall prepare and make publicly available upon request, reference material or a guide for requesting records or information from the agency, subject to the exemptions in subsection (b), including—

(1) an index of all major information systems of the agency;

(2) a description of major information and record locator systems maintained by the agency; and

(3) a handbook for obtaining various types and categories of public information from the agency pursuant to chapter 35 of title 44, and under this section.

GOVERNMENT IN THE SUNSHINE ACT

§ 552(b).

(a) For purposes of this section —

(1) the term "agency" means any agency, as defined in section 552(e) of this title, headed by a collegial body composed of two or more individual members, a majority of whom are appointed to such position by the President with the advice and consent of the Senate, and any subdivision thereof authorized to act on behalf of the agency;

(2) the term "meeting" means the deliberations of at least the number of individual agency members required to take action on behalf of the agency where such deliberations determine or result in the joint conduct or disposition of official agency business, but does not include deliberations required or permitted by subsection (d) or (e); and

(3) the term "member" means an individual who belongs to a collegial body heading an agency.

(b) Members shall not jointly conduct or dispose of agency business other than in accordance with this section. Except as provided in subsection (c), every portion of every meeting of an agency shall be open to public observation.

(c) Except in a case where the agency finds that the public interest requires otherwise, the second sentence of subsection (b) shall not apply to any portion of an agency meeting, and the requirements of subsections (d) and (e) shall not apply to any information pertaining to such meeting otherwise required by this section to be disclosed to the public, where the agency properly determines that such portion or portions of its meeting or the disclosure of such information is likely to —

(1) disclose matters that are

(A) specifically authorized under criteria established by an Executive order to be kept secret in the interests of national defense or foreign policy and

(B) in fact properly classified pursuant to such Executive order;

(2) relate solely to the internal personnel rules and practices of an agency;

(3) disclose matters specifically exempted from disclosure by statute (other than section 552 of this title), provided that such statute

(A) requires that the matters be withheld from the public in such a manner as to leave no discretion on the issue, or

(B) establishes particular criteria for withholding or refers to particular types of matters to be withheld;

(4) disclose trade secrets and commercial or financial information obtained from a person and privileged or confidential;

(5) involve accusing any person of a crime, or formally censuring any person;

(6) disclose information of a personal nature where disclosure would constitute a clearly unwarranted invasion of personal privacy;

(7) disclose investigatory records compiled for law enforcement purposes, or information which if written would be contained in such records, but only to the extent that the production of such records or information would

(A) interfere with enforcement proceedings,

(B) deprive a person of a right to a fair trial or an impartial adjudication,

(C) constitute an unwarranted invasion of personal privacy,

(D) disclose the identity of a confidential source and, in the case of a record compiled by a criminal law enforcement authority in the course of a criminal investigation, or by an agency conducting a lawful national security intelligence investigation, confidential information furnished only by the confidential source,

(E) disclose investigative techniques and procedures, or

(F) endanger the life or physical safety of law enforcement personnel;

(8) disclose information contained in or related to examination, operating, or condition reports prepared by, on behalf of, or for the use of an agency responsible for the regulation or supervision of financial institutions;

(9) disclose information the premature disclosure of which would —

(A) in the case of an agency which regulates currencies, securities, commodities, or financial institutions, be likely to (i) lead to significant financial speculation in currencies, securities, or commodities, or (ii) significantly endanger the stability of any financial institution; or

(B) in the case of any agency, be likely to significantly frustrate implementation of a proposed agency action, except that subparagraph (B) shall not apply in any instance where the agency has already disclosed to the public the content or nature of its proposed action, or where the agency is required by law to make such disclosure on its own initiative prior to taking final agency action on such proposal; or

(10) specifically concern the agency's issuance of a subpoena, or the agency's participation in a civil action or proceeding, an action in a foreign court or international tribunal, or an arbitration, or the initiation, conduct, or disposition by the agency of a particular case of formal agency adjudication pursuant to the procedures in section 554 of this title or otherwise involving a determination on the record after opportunity for a hearing.

(d)(1) Action under subsection (c) shall be taken only when a majority of the entire membership of the agency (as defined in subsection (a)(1)) votes to take such action. A separate vote of the agency members shall be taken with respect to each agency meeting a portion or portions of which are proposed to be closed to the public pursuant to subsection (c), or with respect to any information which is proposed to be withheld under subsection (c). A single vote may be taken with respect to a series of meetings, a portion or portions of which are proposed to be closed to the public, or with respect to any information concerning such series of meetings, so long as each meeting in such series involves the same particular matters and is scheduled to be held no more than thirty days after the initial meeting in such series. The vote of each agency member participating in such vote shall be recorded and no proxies shall be allowed.

* * * * *

APPENDIX A — FEDERAL STATUTES

(3) Within one day of any vote taken pursuant to paragraph (1) or (2), the agency shall make publicly available a written copy of such vote reflecting the vote of each member on the question. If a portion of a meeting is to be closed to the public, the agency shall, within one day of the vote taken pursuant to paragraph (1) or (2) of this subsection, make publicly available a full written explanation of its action closing the portion together with a list of all persons expected to attend the meeting and their affiliation.

(4) Any agency, a majority of whose meetings may properly be closed to the public pursuant to paragraph (4), (8), (9)(A), or (10) of subsection (c), or any combination thereof, may provide by regulation for the closing of such meetings or portions thereof in the event that a majority of the members of the agency votes by recorded vote at the beginning of such meeting, or portion thereof, to close the exempt portion or portions of the meeting, and a copy of such vote, reflecting the vote of each member on the question, is made available to the public. The provisions of paragraphs (1), (2), and (3) of this subsection and subsection (e) shall not apply to any portion of a meeting to which such regulations apply: Provided, that the agency shall, except to the extent that such information is exempt from disclosure under the provisions of subsection (c), provide the public with public announcement of the time, place, and subject matter of the meeting and of each portion thereof at the earliest practicable time.

(e)(1) In the case of each meeting, the agency shall make public announcement, at least one week before the meeting, of the time, place, and subject matter of the meeting, whether it is to be open or closed to the public, and the name and phone number of the official designated by the agency to respond to requests for information about the meeting. Such announcement shall be made unless a majority of the members of the agency determines by a recorded vote that agency business requires that such meeting be called at an earlier date, in which case the agency shall make public announcement of the time, place, and subject matter of such meeting, and whether open or closed to the public, at the earliest practicable time.

(2) The time or place of a meeting may be changed following the public announcement required by paragraph (1) only if the agency publicly announces such change at the earliest practicable time. The subject matter of a meeting, or the determination of the agency to open or close a meeting, or portion of a meeting, to the public, may be changed following the public announcement required by this subsection only if (A) a majority of the entire membership of the agency determines by a recorded vote that agency business so requires and that no earlier announcement of the change was possible, and (B) the agency publicly announces such change and the vote of each member upon such change at the earliest practicable time.

(3) Immediately following each public announcement required by this subsection, notice of the time, place, and subject matter of a meeting, whether the meeting is open or closed, any change in one of the preceding, and the name and phone number of the official designated by the agency to respond to requests for information about the meeting, shall also be submitted for publication in the Federal Register.

(f)(1) For every meeting closed pursuant to paragraphs (1) through (10) of subsection (c), the General Counsel or chief legal officer of the agency shall publicly certify that, in his or her opinion, the meeting may be closed to the public and shall state each relevant exemptive provision. A copy of such certification, together with a statement from the presiding officer of the meeting setting forth the time and place of the meeting, and the persons present, shall be retained by the agency. The agency shall maintain a complete transcript or electronic recording adequate to record fully the proceedings of each meeting, or portion of a meeting, closed to the public, except that in the case of a meeting, or portion of a meeting, closed to the public pursuant to paragraph (8), (9)(A), or (10) of subsection (c), the agency shall maintain either such a transcript or recording, or a set of minutes. Such minutes shall fully and clearly describe all matters discussed and shall provide a full and accurate summary of any actions taken, and the reasons therefor, including a description of each of the views expressed on any item and the record of any rollcall vote (reflecting the vote of each member on the question). All documents considered in connection with any action shall be identified in such minutes.

(2) The agency shall make promptly available to the public, in a place easily accessible to the public, the transcript, electronic recording, or minutes (as required by paragraph (1)) of the discussion of any item on the agenda, or of any item of the testimony of any witness received at the meeting, except for such item or items of such discussion or testimony as the agency determines to contain information which may be withheld under subsection (c). Copies of such transcript, or minutes, or a transcription of such recording disclosing the identity of each speaker, shall be furnished to any person at the actual cost of duplication or transcription. The agency shall maintain a complete verbatim copy of the transcript, a complete copy of the minutes, or a complete electronic recording of each meeting, or portion of a meeting, closed to the public, for a period of at least two years after such meeting, or until one year after the conclusion of any agency proceeding with respect to which the meeting or portion was held, whichever occurs later.

* * * * *

(h)(1) The district courts of the United States shall have jurisdiction to enforce the requirements of subsections (b) through (f) of this section by declaratory judgment, injunctive relief, or other relief as may be appropriate. Such actions may be brought by any person against an agency prior to, or within sixty days after, the meeting out of which the violation of this section arises, except that if public announcement of such meeting is not initially provided by the agency in accordance with the requirements of this section, such action may be instituted pursuant to this section at any time prior to sixty days after any public announcement of such meeting. Such actions may be brought in the district court of the United States for the district in which the agency meeting is held or in which the agency in question has its headquarters, or in the District Court for the District of Columbia. In such actions a defendant shall serve his answer within thirty days after the service of the complaint. The burden is on the defendant to sustain his action. In deciding such cases the court may examine in camera any portion of the transcript, electronic recording, or minutes of a meeting closed to the public, and may take such additional evidence as it deems necessary. The court, having due regard for orderly administration and the public interest, as well as the interests of the parties, may grant such equitable relief as it deems appropriate, including granting an injunction against future violations of this section or ordering the agency to make available to the public such portion of the transcript, recording, or minutes of a meeting as is not authorized to be withheld under subsection (c) of this section.

(2) Any Federal court otherwise authorized by law to review agency action may, at the application of any person properly participating in the proceeding pursuant to other

APPENDIX A — FEDERAL STATUTES

applicable law, inquire into violations by the agency of the requirements of this section and afford such relief as it deems appropriate. Nothing in this section authorizes any Federal court having jurisdiction solely on the basis of paragraph (1) to set aside, enjoin, or invalidate any agency action (other than an action to close a meeting or to withhold information under this section) taken or discussed at any agency meeting out of which the violation of this section arose.

* * * * *

(k) Nothing herein expands or limits the present rights of any person under section 552 of this title, except that the exemptions set forth in subsection (c) of this section shall govern in the case of any request made pursuant to section 552 to copy or inspect the transcripts, recordings, or minutes described in subsection (f) of this section. The requirements of chapter 33 of title 44, United States Code, shall not apply to the transcripts, recordings, and minutes described in subsection (f) of this section.

(l) This section does not constitute authority to withhold any information from Congress, and does not authorize the closing of any agency meeting or portion thereof required by any other provision of law to be open.

FEDERAL WIRETAP ACT

18 U.S.C. §§ 2510-2511, 2520

§ 2510. Definitions.

As used in this chapter —

(1) "wire communication" means any aural transfer made in whole or in part through the use of facilities for the transmission of communications by the aid of wire, cable, or other like connection between the point of origin and the point of reception (including the use of such connection in a switching station) furnished or operated by any person engaged in providing or operating such facilities for the transmission of interstate or foreign communications or communications affecting interstate or foreign commerce and such term includes any electronic storage of such communication;

(2) "oral communication" means any oral communication uttered by a person exhibiting an expectation that such communication is not subject to interception under circumstances justifying such expectation, but such term does not include any electronic communication;

(3) "State" means any State of the United States, the District of Columbia, the Commonwealth of Puerto Rico, and any territory or possession of the United States;

(4) "intercept" means the aural or other acquisition of the contents of any wire, electronic, or oral communication through the use of any electronic, mechanical, or other device.

(5) "electronic, mechanical, or other device" means any device or apparatus which can be used to intercept a wire, oral, or electronic communication other than —

(a) any telephone or telegraph instrument, equipment or facility, or any component thereof, (i) furnished to the subscriber or user by a provider of wire or electronic communication service in the ordinary course of its business and being used by the subscriber or user in the ordinary course of its business or furnished by such subscriber or user for connection to the facilities of such service and used in the ordinary course of its business; or (ii) being used by a provider of wire or electronic communication service in the ordinary course of its business, or by an investigative or law enforcement officer in the ordinary course of his duties;

(b) a hearing aid or similar device being used to correct subnormal hearing to not better than normal;

(6) "person" means any employee, or agent of the United States or any State or political subdivision thereof, and any individual, partnership, association, joint stock company, trust, or corporation;

(7) "Investigative or law enforcement officer" means any officer of the United States or of a State or political subdivision thereof, who is empowered by law to conduct investigations of or to make arrests for offenses enumerated in this chapter, and any attorney authorized by law to prosecute or participate in the prosecution of such offenses;

(8) "contents", when used with respect to any wire, oral, or electronic communication, includes any information concerning the substance, purport, or meaning of that communication;

(9) "Judge of competent jurisdiction" means —

(a) a judge of a United States district court or a United States court of appeals; and

(b) a judge of any court of general criminal jurisdiction of a State who is authorized by a statute of that State to enter orders authorizing interceptions of wire, oral, or electronic communications;

(10) "communication common carrier" shall have the same meaning which is given the term "common carrier" by section 153(h) of title 47 of the United States Code;

(11) "aggrieved person" means a person who was a party to any intercepted wire, oral, or electronic communication or a person against whom the interception was directed;

(12) "electronic communication" means any transfer of signs, signals, writing, images, sounds, data, or intelligence of any nature transmitted in whole or in part by a wire, radio, electromagnetic, photoelectronic or photo-optical system that affects interstate or foreign commerce, but does not include —

(A) any wire or oral communication;

(B) any communication made through a tone — only paging device; or

(C) any communication from a tracking device (as defined in section 3117 of this title);

(13) "user" means any person or entity who —

(A) uses an electronic communication service; and

(B) is duly authorized by the provider of such service to engage in such use;

(14) "electronic communications system" means any wire, radio, electromagnetic, photo-optical or photoelectronic facilities for the transmission of electronic communications, and any computer facilities or related electronic equipment for the electronic storage of such communications;

(15) "electronic communication service" means any service which provides to users thereof the ability to send or receive wire or electronic communications;

(16) "readily accessible to the general public" means, with respect to a radio communication, that such communication is not —

(A) scrambled or encrypted;

(B) transmitted using modulation techniques whose essential parameters have been withheld from the public with the intention of preserving the privacy of such communication;

(C) carried on a subcarrier or other signal subsidiary to a radio transmission;

(D) transmitted over a communication system provided by a common carrier, unless the communication is a tone only paging system communication;

(E) transmitted on frequencies allocated under part 25, subpart D, E, or F of part 74, or part 94 of the Rules of the Federal Communications Commission, unless, in the case of a communication transmitted on a frequency allocated under part 74 that is not exclusively allocated to broadcast auxiliary services, the communication is a two-way voice communication by radio; or

(F) an electronic communication;

(17) "electronic storage" means —

(A) any temporary, intermediate storage of a wire or electronic communication incidental to the electronic transmission thereof; and

(B) any storage of such communication by an electronic communication service for purposes of backup protection of such communication; and

(18) "aural transfer" means a transfer containing the human voice at any point between and including the point of origin and the point of reception.

§ 2511. Interception and disclosure of wire, oral, or electronic com-munications prohibited.

(1) Except as otherwise specifically provided in this chapter any person who —

(a) intentionally intercepts, endeavors to intercept, or procures any other person to intercept or endeavor to intercept, any wire, oral, or electronic communication;

(b) intentionally uses, endeavors to use, or procures any other person to use or endeavor to use any electronic, mechanical, or other device to intercept any oral communication when —

(i) such device is affixed to, or otherwise transmits a signal through, a wire, cable, or other like connection used in wire communication; or

(ii) such device transmits communications by radio, or interferes with the transmission of such communication; or

(iii) such person knows, or has reason to know, that such device or any component thereof has been sent through the mail or transported in interstate or foreign commerce; or

(iv) such use or endeavor to use

(A) takes place on the premises of any business or other commercial establishment the operations of which affect interstate or foreign commerce; or

(B) obtains or is for the purpose of obtaining information relating to the operations of any business or other commercial establishment the operations of which affect interstate or foreign commerce; or

(v) such person acts in the District of Columbia, the Commonwealth of Puerto Rico, or any territory or possession of the United States;

(c) intentionally discloses, or endeavors to disclose, to any other person the contents of any wire, oral, or electronic communication, knowing or having reason to know that the information was obtained through the interception of a wire, oral, or electronic communication in violation of this subsection;

(d) intentionally uses, or endeavors to use, the contents of any wire, oral, or electronic communication, knowing or having reason to know that the information was obtained through the interception of a wire, oral, or electronic communication in violation of this subsection; or

(e)(i) intentionally discloses, or endeavors to disclose, to any other person the contents of any wire, oral, or electronic communication, intercepted by means authorized by sections 2511(2)(A)(ii), 2511(b)-(c), 2511(e), 2516, and 2518 of this subchapter, (ii) knowing or having reason to know that the information was obtained through the interception of such a communication in connection with a criminal investigation, (iii) having obtained or received the information in connection with a criminal investigation, and (iv) with intent to improperly obstruct, impede, or interfere with a duly authorized criminal investigation,

(2)(a)(i) It shall not be unlawful under this chapter for an operator of a switchboard, or an officer, employee, or agent of a provider of wire or electronic communication service, whose facilities are used in the transmission of a wire or electronic communication, to intercept, disclose, or use that communication in the normal course of his employment while engaged in any activity which is a necessary incident to the rendition of his service or to the protection of the rights or property of the provider of that service, except that a provider of wire communication service to the public shall not utilize service observing or random monitoring except for mechanical or service quality control checks.

(ii) Notwithstanding any other law, providers of wire or electronic communication service, their officers, employees, and agents, landlords, custodians, or other persons, are authorized to provide information, facilities, or technical assistance to persons authorized by law to intercept wire, oral, or electronic communications or to conduct electronic surveillance, as defined in section 101 of the Foreign Intelligence Surveillance Act of 1978, if such provider, its officers, employees, or agents, landlord, custodian, or other specified person, has been provided with —

(A) a court order directing such assistance signed by the authorizing judge, or

(B) a certification in writing by a person specified in section 2518(7) of this title or the Attorney General of the United States that no warrant or court order is required by law, that all statutory requirements have been met, and that the specified assistance is required, setting forth the period of time during which the provision of the information, facilities, or technical assistance is authorized and specifying the information, facilities, or technical assistance required. No provider of wire or electronic communication service, officer, employee, or agent thereof, or landlord, custodian, or other specified person shall disclose the existence of any interception or surveillance or the device used to accomplish the interception or surveillance with respect to which the person has been furnished a court order or certification under this chapter, except as may otherwise be required by legal process and then only after prior notification to the Attorney General or to the principal prosecuting attorney of a State or any political subdivision of a State, as may be appropriate. Any such disclosure, shall render such person liable for the civil damages provided for in section 2520. No cause of action shall lie in any court against any provider of wire or electronic communication service, its officers, employees, or agents, landlord, custodian, or other specified person for provid-

APPENDIX A — FEDERAL STATUTES

ing information, facilities, or assistance in accordance with the terms of a court order or certification under this chapter.

(b) It shall not be unlawful under this chapter for an officer, employee, or agent of the Federal Communications Commission, in the normal course of his employment and in discharge of the monitoring responsibilities exercised by the Commission in the enforcement of chapter 5 of title 47 of the United States Code, to intercept a wire or electronic communication, or oral communication transmitted by radio, or to disclose or use the information thereby obtained.

(c) It shall not be unlawful under this chapter for a person acting under color of law to intercept a wire, oral, or electronic communication, where such person is a party to the communication or one of the parties to the communication has given prior consent to such interception.

(d) It shall not be unlawful under this chapter for a person not acting under color of law to intercept a wire, oral, or electronic communication where such person is a party to the communication or where one of the parties to the communication has given prior consent to such interception unless such communication is intercepted for the purpose of committing any criminal or tortious act in violation of the Constitution or laws of the United States or of any State.

(e) Notwithstanding any other provision of this title or section 705 or 706 of the Communications Act of 1934, it shall not be unlawful for an officer, employee, or agent of the United States in the normal course of his official duty to conduct electronic surveillance, as defined in section 101 of the Foreign Intelligence Surveillance Act of 1978, as authorized by that Act.

(f) Nothing contained in this chapter or chapter 121, or section 705 of the Communications Act of 1934, shall be deemed to affect the acquisition by the United States Government of foreign intelligence information from international or foreign communications, or foreign intelligence activities conducted in accordance with otherwise applicable Federal law involving a foreign electronic communications system, utilizing a means other than electronic surveillance as defined in section 101 of the Foreign Intelligence Surveillance Act of 1978, and procedures in this chapter or chapter 121 and the Foreign Intelligence Surveillance Act of 1978 shall be the exclusive means by which electronic surveillance, as defined in section 101 of such Act, and the interception of domestic wire and oral communications may be conducted.

(g) It shall not be unlawful under this chapter or chapter 121 of this title for any person —

    (i) to intercept or access an electronic communication made through an electronic communication system that is configured so that such electronic communication is readily accessible to the general public;

    (ii) to intercept any radio communication which is transmitted —

        (I) by any station for the use of the general public, or that relates to ships, aircraft, vehicles, or persons in distress;

        (II) by any governmental, law enforcement, civil defense, private land mobile, or public safety communications system, including police and fire, readily accessible to the general public;

        (III) by a station operating on an authorized frequency within the bands allocated to the amateur, citizens band, or general mobile radio services; or

        (IV) by any marine or aeronautical communications system;

(iii) to engage in any conduct which —

(I) is prohibited by section 633 of the Communications Act of 1934; or

(II) is excepted from the application of section 705(a) of the Communications Act of 1934 by section 705(b) of that Act;

(iv) to intercept any wire or electronic communication the transmission of which is causing harmful interference to any lawfully operating station or consumer electronic equipment, to the extent necessary to identify the source of such interference; or

(v) for other users of the same frequency to intercept any radio communication made through a system that utilizes frequencies monitored by individuals engaged in the provision or the use of such system, if such communication is not scrambled or encrypted.

(h) It shall not be unlawful under this chapter —

(i) to use a pen register or a trap and trace device (as those terms are defined for the purposes of chapter 206 (relating to pen registers and trap and trace devices) of this title); or

(ii) for a provider of electronic communication service to record the fact that a wire or electronic communication was initiated or completed in order to protect such provider, another provider furnishing service toward the completion of the wire or electronic communication, or a user of that service, from fraudulent, unlawful or abusive use of such service.

(3)(a) Except as provided in paragraph (b) of this subsection, a person or entity providing an electronic communication service to the public shall not intentionally divulge the contents of any communication (other than one to such person or entity, or an agent thereof) while in transmission on that service to any person or entity other than an addressee or intended recipient of such communication or an agent of such addressee or intended recipient.

(b) A person or entity providing electronic communication service to the public may divulge the contents of any such communication —

(i) as otherwise authorized in section 2511(2)(a) or 2517 of this title;

(ii) with the lawful consent of the originator or any addressee or intended recipient of such communication;

(iii) to a person employed or authorized, or whose facilities are used, to forward such communication to its destination; or

(iv) which were inadvertently obtained by the service provider and which appear to pertain to the commission of a crime, if such divulgence is made to a law enforcement agency.

(4)(a) Except as provided in paragraph (b) of this subsection or in subsection (5), whoever violates subsection (1) of this section shall be fined under this title or imprisoned not more than five years, or both.

(b) If the offense is a first offense under paragraph (a) of this subsection and is not for a tortious or illegal purpose or for purposes of direct or indirect commercial advantage or private commercial gain, and the wire or electronic communication with respect to which the offense under paragraph (a) is a radio communication that is not scrambled, encrypted, or transmitted using modulation techniques the essential parameters of which have been withheld from the public with the intention of preserving the privacy of such communication, then —

APPENDIX A — FEDERAL STATUTES

(i) if the communication is not the radio portion of a cellular telephone communication, a cordless telephone communication that is transmitted between the cordless telephone handset and the base unit, a public land mobile radio service communication or a paging service communication, and the conduct is not that described in subsection (5), the offender shall be fined under this title or imprisoned not more than one year, or both; and

(ii) if the communication is the radio portion of a cellular telephone communication, a cordless telephone communication that is transmitted between the cordless telephone handset and the base unit, a public land mobile radio service communication or a paging service communication, the offender shall be fined under this title.

(c) Conduct otherwise an offense under this subsection that consists of or relates to the interception of a satellite transmission that is not encrypted or scrambled and that is transmitted —

(i) to a broadcasting station for purposes of retransmission to the general public; or

(ii) as an audio subcarrier intended for redistribution to facilities open to the public, but not including data transmissions or telephone calls, is not an offense under this subsection unless the conduct is for the purposes of direct or indirect commercial advantage or private financial gain.

(5)(a)(i) If the communication is —

(A) a private satellite video communication that is not scrambled or encrypted and the conduct in violation of this chapter is the private viewing of that communication and is not for a tortious or illegal purpose or for purposes of direct or indirect commercial advantage or private commercial gain; or

(B) a radio communication that is transmitted on frequencies allocated under subpart D of part 74 of the rules of the Federal Communications Commission that is not scrambled or encrypted and the conduct in violation of this chapter is not for a tortious or illegal purpose or for purposes of direct or indirect commercial advantage or private commercial gain, then the person who engages in such conduct shall be subject to suit by the Federal Government in a court of competent jurisdiction.

(ii) In an action under this subsection —

(A) if the violation of this chapter is a first offense for the person under paragraph (a) of subsection (4) and such person has not been found liable in a civil action under section 2520 of this title, the Federal Government shall be entitled to appropriate injunctive relief; and

(B) if the violation of this chapter is a second or subsequent offense under paragraph (a) of subsection (4) or such person has been found liable in any prior civil action under section 2520, the person shall be subject to a mandatory $500 civil fine.

(b) The court may use any means within its authority to enforce an injunction issued under paragraph (ii)(A), and shall impose a civil fine of not less than $500 for each violation of such an injunction.

FEDERAL WIRETAP ACT

§ 2520. Recovery of civil damages authorized.

(a) In General. — Except as provided in section 2511(2)(a)(ii), any person whose wire, oral, or electronic communication is intercepted, disclosed, or intentionally used in violation of this chapter may in a civil action recover from the person or entity which engaged in that violation such relief as may be appropriate.

(b) Relief. — In an action under this section, appropriate relief includes —
   (1) such preliminary and other equitable or declaratory relief as may be appropriate;
   (2) damages under subsection (c) and punitive damages in appropriate cases; and
   (3) a reasonable attorney's fee and other litigation costs reasonably incurred.

(c) Computation of Damages. — (1) In an action under this section, if the conduct in violation of this chapter is the private viewing of a private satellite video communication that is not scrambled or encrypted or if the communication is a radio communication that is transmitted on frequencies allocated under subpart D of part 74 of the rules of the Federal Communications Commission that is not scrambled or encrypted and the conduct is not for a tortious or illegal purpose or for purposes of direct or indirect commercial advantage or private commercial gain, then the court shall assess damages as follows:
   (A) If the person who engaged in that conduct has not previously been enjoined under section 2511(5) and has not been found liable in a prior civil action under this section, the court shall assess the greater of the sum of actual damages suffered by the plaintiff, or statutory damages of not less than $50 and not more than $500.
   (B) If, on one prior occasion, the person who engaged in that conduct has been enjoined under section 2511(5) or has been found liable in a civil action under this section, the court shall assess the greater of the sum of actual damages suffered by the plaintiff, or statutory damages of not less than $100 and not more than $1000.

(2) In any other action under this section, the court may assess as damages whichever is the greater of —
   (A) the sum of the actual damages suffered by the plaintiff and any profits made by the violator as a result of the violation; or
   (B) statutory damages of whichever is the greater of $100 a day for each day of violation or $10,000.

(d) Defense. — A good faith reliance on —
   (1) a court warrant or order, a grand jury subpoena, a legislative authorization, or a statutory authorization;
   (2) a request of an investigative or law enforcement officer under section 2518(7) of this title; or
   (3) a good faith determination that section 2511(3) of this title permitted the conduct complained of; is a complete defense against any civil or criminal action brought under this chapter or any other law.

(e) Limitation. — A civil action under this section may not be commenced later than two years after the date upon which the claimant first has a reasonable opportunity to discover the violation.

APPENDIX A — FEDERAL STATUTES

PRIVACY PROTECTION ACT OF 1980

42 U.S.C. §§ 2000aa, 2000aa-5–2000aa-7 and 2000aa-11–2000aa-12

§ 2000aa. Searches and seizures by government officers and employees in connection with investigation or prosecution of criminal offenses.

(a) Work product materials

Notwithstanding any other law, it shall be unlawful for a government officer or employee, in connection with the investigation or prosecution of a criminal offense, to search for or seize any work product materials possessed by a person reasonably believed to have a purpose to disseminate to the public a newspaper, book, broadcast, or other similar form of public communication, in or affecting interstate or foreign commerce; but this provision shall not impair or affect the ability of any government officer or employee, pursuant to otherwise applicable law, to search for or seize such materials, if —

    (1) there is probable cause to believe that the person possessing such materials has committed or is committing the criminal offense to which the materials relate: Provided, however, that a government officer or employee may not search for or seize such materials under the provisions of this paragraph if the offense to which the materials relate consists of the receipt, possession, communication, or withholding of such materials or the information contained therein (but such a search or seizure may be conducted under the provisions of this paragraph if the offense consists of the receipt, possession, or communication of information relating to the national defense, classified information, or restricted data under the provisions of section 793, 794, 797, or 798 of title 18, or section 2274, 2275, or 2277 of this title, or section 783 of title 50; or

    (2) there is reason to believe that the immediate seizure of such materials is necessary to prevent the death of, or serious bodily injury to, a human being.

(b) Other documents

Notwithstanding any other law, it shall be unlawful for a government officer or employee, in connection with the investigation or prosecution of a criminal offense, to search for or seize documentary materials, other than work product materials, possessed by a person in connection with a purpose to disseminate to the public a newspaper, book, broadcast, or other similar form of public communication, in or affecting interstate or foreign commerce; but this provision shall not impair or affect the ability of any government officer or employee, pursuant to otherwise applicable law, to search for or seize such materials, if —

    (1) there is probable cause to believe that the person possessing such materials has committed or is committing the criminal offense to which the materials relate: Provided, however, that a government officer or employee may not search for or seize such materials under the provisions of this paragraph if the offense to which the materials relate consists of the receipt, possession, communication, or withholding of such materials or the information contained therein (but such a search or seizure may be conducted under the provisions of this paragraph if the offense consists of the receipt, possession, or communication of information relating to the national defense, classified information, or restricted data under the provisions of section 793, 794, 797, or 798 of title 18, or section 2274, 2275, or 2277 of this title, or section 783 of title 50;

    (2) there is reason to believe that the immediate seizure of such materials is necessary to prevent the death of, or serious bodily injury to, a human being;

(3) there is reason to believe that the giving of notice pursuant to a subpoena duces tecum would result in the destruction, alteration, or concealment of such materials; or

(4) such materials have not been produced in response to a court order directing compliance with a subpoena duces tecum, and

(A) all appellate remedies have been exhausted; or

(B) there is reason to believe that the delay in an investigation or trial occasioned by further proceedings relating to the subpoena would threaten the interests of justice.

(c) Objections to court ordered subpoenas; affidavits

In the event a search warrant is sought pursuant to paragraph (4)(B) of subsection (b) of this section, the person possessing the materials shall be afforded adequate opportunity to submit an affidavit setting forth the basis for any contention that the materials sought are not subject to seizure.

§ 2000aa-5. Border and customs searches.

This chapter shall not impair or affect the ability of a government officer or employee, pursuant to otherwise applicable law, to conduct searches and seizures at the borders of, or at international points of, entry into the United States in order to enforce the customs laws of the United States.

§ 2000aa-6. Civil actions by aggrieved persons.

(a) Right of action

A person aggrieved by a search for or seizure of materials in violation of this chapter shall have a civil cause of action for damages for such search or seizure —

(1) against the United States, against a State which has waived its sovereign immunity under the Constitution to a claim for damages resulting from a violation of this chapter, or against any other governmental unit, all of which shall be liable for violations of this chapter by their officers or employees while acting within the scope or under color of their office or employment; and

(2) against an officer or employee of a State who has violated this chapter while acting within the scope or under color of his office or employment, if such State has not waived its sovereign immunity as provided in paragraph (1).

(b) Good faith defense

It shall be a complete defense to a civil action brought under paragraph (2) of subsection (a) of this section that the officer or employee had a reasonable good faith belief in the lawfulness of his conduct.

(c) Official immunity

The United States, a State, or any other governmental unit liable for violations of this chapter under subsection (a)(1) of this section, may not assert as a defense to a claim arising under this chapter the immunity of the officer or employee whose violation is complained of or his reasonable good faith belief in the lawfulness of his conduct, except that such a defense may be asserted if the violation complained of is that of a judicial officer.

(d) Exclusive nature of remedy

The remedy provided by subsection (a)(1) of this section against the United States, a State, or any other governmental unit is exclusive of any other civil action or proceeding

APPENDIX A — FEDERAL STATUTES

for conduct constituting a violation of this chapter, against the officer or employee whose violation gave rise to the claim, or against the estate of such officer or employee.

(e) Admissibility of evidence

Evidence otherwise admissible in a proceeding shall not be excluded on the basis of a violation of this chapter.

(f) Damages; costs and attorneys' fees

A person having a cause of action under this section shall be entitled to recover actual damages but not less than liquidated damages of $1,000, and such reasonable attorneys' fees and other litigation costs reasonably incurred as the court, in its discretion, may award: Provided, however, that the United States, a State, or any other governmental unit shall not be liable for interest prior to judgment.

(g) Attorney General; claims settlement; regulations

The Attorney General may settle a claim for damages brought against the United States under this section, and shall promulgate regulations to provide for the commencement of an administrative inquiry following a determination of a violation of this chapter by an officer or employee of the United States and for the imposition of administrative sanctions against such officer or employee, if warranted.

(h) Jurisdiction

The district courts shall have original jurisdiction of all civil actions arising under this section.

§ 2000aa-7. Definitions.

(a) "Documentary materials", as used in this chapter, means materials upon which information is recorded, and includes, but is not limited to, written or printed materials, photographs, motion picture films, negatives, video tapes, audio tapes, and other mechanically, magentically or electronically recorded cards, tapes, or discs, but does not include contraband or the fruits of a crime or things otherwise criminally possessed, or property designed or intended for use, or which is or has been used as, the means of committing a criminal offense.

(b) "Work product materials", as used in this chapter, means materials, other than contraband or the fruits of a crime or things otherwise criminally possessed, or property designed or intended for use, or which is or has been used, as the means of committing a criminal offense, and —

(1) in anticipation of communicating such materials to the public, are prepared, produced, authored, or created, whether by the person in possession of the materials or by any other person;

(2) are possessed for the purposes of communicating such materials to the public; and

(3) include mental impressions, conclusions, opinions, or theories of the person who prepared, produced, authored, or created such material.

(c) "Any other governmental unit", as used in this chapter, includes the District of Columbia, the Commonwealth of Puerto Rico, any territory or possession of the United States, and any local government, unit of local government, or any unit of State government.

PRIVACY PROTECTION ACT OF 1980

§ 2000aa-11. Guidelines for Federal officers and employees.

(a) Procedures to obtain documentary evidence; protection of certain privacy interests

The Attorney General shall, within six months of October 13, 1980, issue guidelines for the procedures to be employed by any Federal officer or employee, in connection with the investigation or prosecution of an offense, to obtain documentary materials in the private possession of a person when the person is not reasonably believed to be a suspect in such offense or related by blood or marriage to such a suspect, and when the materials sought are not contraband or the fruits or instrumentalities of an offense. The Attorney General shall incorporate in such guidelines —

(1) a recognition of the personal privacy interests of the person in possession of such documentary materials;

(2) a requirement that the least intrusive method or means of obtaining such materials be used which do not substantially jeopardize the availability or usefulness of the materials sought to be obtained;

(3) a recognition of special concern for privacy interests in cases in which a search or seizure for such documents would intrude upon a known confidential relationship such as that which may exist between clergyman and parishioner; lawyer and client; or doctor and patient; and

(4) a requirement that an application for a warrant to conduct a search governed by this subchapter be approved by an attorney for the government, except that in an emergency situation the application may be approved by another appropriate supervisory official if within 24 hours of such emergency the appropriate United States Attorney is notified.

(b) Use of search warrants; reports to Congress

The Attorney General shall collect and compile information on, and report annually to the Committees on the Judiciary of the Senate and the House of Representatives on the use of search warrants by Federal officers and employees for documentary materials described in subsection (a)(3) of this section.

§ 2000aa-12. Binding nature of guidelines; disciplinary actions for violations; legal proceedings for non-compliance prohibited.

Guidelines issued by the Attorney General under this subchapter shall have the full force and effect of Department of Justice regulations and any violation of these guidelines shall make the employee or officer involved subject to appropriate administrative disciplinary action. However, an issue relating to the compliance, or the failure to comply, with guidelines issued pursuant to this subchapter may not be litigated, and a court may not entertain such an issue as the basis for the suppression or exclusion of evidence.

Appendix B
STATE STATUTES

Part One:
NEWSPERSON SHIELD LAWS

Alabama

§ 12-21-142. Journalist source privilege.

No person engaged in, connected with or employed on any newspaper, radio broadcasting station or television station, while engaged in a news gathering capacity, shall be compelled to disclose in any legal proceeding or trial, before any court or before a grand jury of any court, before the presiding officer of any tribunal or his agent or agents or before any committee of the Legislature or elsewhere the sources of any information procured or obtained by him and published in the newspaper, broadcast by any broadcasting station, or televised by any television station on which he is engaged, connected with or employed.

Alaska

§ 09.25.300. Claiming of privilege by public official or reporter.

Except as provided in AS 09.25.300-09.25.390, a public official or reporter may not be compelled to disclose the source of information procured or obtained while acting in the course of duties as a public official or reporter.

§ 09.25.310. Challenge of privilege before superior or supreme court.

(a) When a public official or reporter claims the privilege in a cause being heard before the supreme court or a superior court of this state, a person who has the right to question the public official or reporter in that proceeding, or the court on its own motion, may challenge the claim of privilege. The court shall make or cause to be made whatever inquiry the court thinks necessary to a determination of the issue. The inquiry may be made instanter by way of questions put to the witness claiming the privilege and a decision then rendered, or the court may require the presence of other witnesses or documentary showing or may order a special hearing for the determination of the issue of privilege.

(b) The court may deny the privilege and may order the public official or the reporter to testify, imposing whatever limits upon the testimony and upon the right of cross-examination of the witness as may be in the public interest or in the interest of a fair trial, if it finds the withholding of the testimony would

  (1) result in a miscarriage of justice or the denial of a fair trial to those who challenge the privilege; or
  (2) be contrary to the public interest.

§ 09.25.320. Challenge of privilege before other bodies.

(a) This section is applicable to a hearing held under the laws of this state

APPENDIX B — STATE STATUTES

(1) before a court other than the supreme or a superior court;

(2) before a court commissioner, referee, or other court appointee;

(3) in the course of legislative proceedings or before a commission, agency, or committee created by the legislature;

(4) before an agency or representative of an agency of the state, borough, city or other municipal corporation, or other body; or

(5) before any other forum of this state.

(b) If, in a hearing, a public official or a reporter should refuse to divulge the source of information, the agency body, person, official, or party seeking the information may apply to the superior court for an order divesting the official or reporter of the privilege. When the issue is raised before the supreme or a superior court, the application must be made to that court.

(c) Application for an order shall be made by verified petition setting out the reasons why the disclosure is essential to the administration of justice, a fair trial in the instant proceeding, or the protection of the public interest. Upon application, the court shall determine the notice to be given to the public official or reporter and fix the time and place of hearing. The court shall make or cause to be made whatever inquiry the court thinks necessary, and make a determination of the issue as provided for in AS 09.25.310.

§ 09.25.330. Order subject to review.

An order of the superior court entered under AS 09.25.300–09.25.390 shall be subject to review by the supreme court, by appeal or by certiorari, as the rules of that court may provide. During the pendency of the appeal, the privilege shall remain in full force and effect.

§ 09.25.340. Extent of privilege.

When a public official or reporter claims the privilege conferred by AS 09.25.300–09.25.390 and the public official or reporter has not been divested of the privilege by order of the supreme or superior court, neither the public official or reporter nor the news organization with which the reporter was associated may thereafter be permitted to plead or prove the sources of information withheld, unless the informant consents in writing or in open court.

§ 09.25.350. Application of privilege in other courts.

AS 09.25.300–09.25.390 also apply to proceedings held under the laws of the United States or any other state where the law of this state is being applied.

§ 09.25.360. AS 09.25.300–09.25.390 do not abridge other privileges.

AS 09.25.300–09.25.390 may not be construed to abridge any of the privileges recognized under the laws of this state, whether at common law or by statute.

§ 09.25.390. Definitions for AS 09.25.300–09.25.390.

In AS 09.25.300–09.25.390, unless the context otherwise requires,

(1) "news organization" means

(A) an individual, partnership, corporation, or other association regularly engaged in the business of

    (i) publishing a newspaper or other periodical that reports news events, is issued at regular intervals, and has a general circulation;

    (ii) providing newsreels or other motion picture news for public showing; or

    (iii) broadcasting news to the public by wire, radio, television, or facsimile;

(B) a press association or other association of individuals, partnerships, corporations, or other associations described in (A)(i), (ii), or (iii) of this paragraph engaged in gathering news and disseminating it to its members for publication;

(2) "privilege" means the conditional privilege granted to public officials and reporters to refuse to testify as to a source of information;

(3) "public official" means a person elected to a public office created by the Constitution or laws of this state, whether executive, legislative, or judicial, and who was holding that office at the time of the communication for which privilege is claimed;

(4) "reporter" means a person regularly engaged in the business of collecting or writing news for publication, or presentation to the public, through a news organization; it includes persons who were reporters at the time of the communication, though not at the time of the claim of privilege.

Arizona

§ 12-2214. Requirements for subpoena of media witnesses.

A. A subpoena for the attendance of a witness or for production of documentary evidence issued in a civil or criminal proceeding and directed to a person engaged in gathering, reporting, writing, editing, publishing or broadcasting news to the public, and which relates to matters within these news activities, shall have attached to it an affidavit of a person with a direct interest in the matters sought which states all of the following:

    1. Each item of documentary and evidentiary information sought from the person subpoenaed.

    2. That the affiant or his representative has attempted to obtain each item of information from all other available sources, specifying which items the affiant has been unable to obtain.

    3. The identity of the other sources from which the affiant or his representative has attempted to obtain the information.

    4. That the information sought is relevant and material to the affiant's cause of action or defense.

    5. That the information sought is not protected by any lawful privilege.

    6. That the subpoena is not intended to interfere with the gathering, writing, editing, publishing, broadcasting and disseminating of news to the public as protected by the first amendment, Constitution of the United States, or by article II, section 6, Constitution of Arizona.

B. A subpoena served on a person described in subsection A without the required affidavit attached to it has no effect.

C. If the affidavit is controverted or a motion to quash the subpoena or for a protective order is filed by the person subpoenaed, the command of the subpoena shall be postponed until a hearing is held and an order is entered by the court. After the hearing the command of the subpoena shall be carried out in accordance with the order of the court.

APPENDIX B — STATE STATUTES

D. This section does not apply to a subpoena for the attendance of a witness or the production of documentary evidence issued by or on behalf of a grand jury or a magistrate during an investigative criminal proceeding.

§ 12-2237. Reporter and informant.

A person engaged in newspaper, radio, television or reportorial work, or connected with or employed by a newspaper, radio or television station, shall not be compelled to testify or disclose in a legal proceeding or trial or any proceeding whatever, or before any jury, inquisitorial body or commission, or before a committee of the legislature, or elsewhere, the source of information procured or obtained by him for publication in a newspaper or for broadcasting over a radio or television station with which he was associated or by which he is employed.

Arkansas

§ 16-85-510. Disclosure of newspaper, periodical, or radio station sources.

Before any editor, reporter, or other writer for any newspaper, periodical, or radio station, or publisher of any newspaper or periodical, or manager or owner of any radio station shall be required to disclose to any grand jury or to any other authority the source of information used as the basis for any article he may have written, published, or broadcast, it must be shown that the article was written, published, or broadcast in bad faith, with malice, and not in the interest of the public welfare.

California

Cal. Const. art. I, § 2(b).

(b) A publisher, editor, reporter, or other person connected with or employed upon a newspaper, magazine, or other periodical publication, or by a press association or wire service, or any person who has been so connected or employed, shall not be adjudged in contempt by a judicial, legislative, or administrative body, or any other body having the power to issue subpoenas, for refusing to disclose the source of any information procured while so connected or employed for publication in a newspaper, magazine or other periodical publication, or for refusing to disclose any unpublished information obtained or prepared in gathering, receiving or processing of information for communication to the public.

Nor shall a radio or television news reporter or other person connected with or employed by a radio or television station, or any person who has been so connected or employed, be so adjudged in contempt for refusing to disclose the source of any information procured while so connected or employed for news or news commentary purposes on radio or television, or for refusing to disclose any unpublished information obtained or prepared in gathering, receiving or processing of information for communication to the public.

As used in this subdivision, "unpublished information" includes information not disseminated to the public by the person from whom disclosure is sought, whether or not related information has been disseminated and includes, but is not limited to, all notes, outtakes, photographs, tapes or other data of whatever sort not itself disseminated to the public through a medium of communication, whether or not published information based upon or related to such material has been disseminated.

California Evidence Code

§ 1070. Newsman's refusal to disclose news source.

(a) A publisher, editor, reporter, or other person connected with or employed upon a newspaper, magazine, or other periodical publication, or by a press association or wire service, or any person who has been so connected or employed, cannot be adjudged in contempt by a judicial, legislative, administrative body, or any other body having the power to issue subpoenas, for refusing to disclose, in any proceeding as defined in Section 901, the source of any information procured while so connected or employed for publication in a newspaper, magazine or other periodical publication, or for refusing to disclose any unpublished information obtained or prepared in gathering, receiving or processing of information for communication to the public.

(b) Nor can a radio or television news reporter or other person connected with or employed by a radio or television station, or any person who has been so connected or employed, be so adjudged in contempt for refusing to disclose the source of any information procured while so connected or employed for news or news commentary purposes on radio or television, or for refusing to disclose any unpublished information obtained or prepared in gathering, receiving or processing of information for communication to the public.

(c) As used in this section, "unpublished information" includes information not disseminated to the public by the person from whom disclosure is sought, whether or not related information has been disseminated and includes, but is not limited to, all notes, outtakes, photographs, tapes or other data of whatever sort not itself disseminated to the public through a medium of communication, whether or not published information based upon or related to such material has been disseminated.

Colorado

§ 13-90-119. Privilege for newsperson.

(1) As used in this section, unless the context otherwise requires:

(a) "Mass medium" means any publisher of a newspaper or periodical; wire service; radio or television station or network; news or feature syndicate; or cable television system.

(b) "News information" means any knowledge, observation, notes, documents, photographs, films, recordings, videotapes, audiotapes, and reports, and the contents and sources thereof, obtained by a newsperson while engaged as such, regardless of whether such items have been provided to or obtained by such newsperson in confidence.

(c) "Newsperson" means any member of the mass media and any employee or independent contractor of a member of the mass media who is engaged to gather, receive, observe, process, prepare, write, or edit news information for dissemination to the public through the mass media.

APPENDIX B — STATE STATUTES

(d) "Press conference" means any meeting or event called for the purpose of issuing a public statement to members of the mass media, and to which members of the mass media are invited in advance.

(e) "Proceeding" means any civil or criminal investigation, discovery procedure, hearing, trial, or other process for obtaining information conducted by, before, or under the authority of any judicial body of the state of Colorado. Such term shall not include any investigation, hearing, or other process for obtaining information conducted by, before, or under the authority of the general assembly.

(f) "Source" means any person from whom or any means by or through which news information is received or procured by a newsperson, while engaged as such, regardless of whether such newsperson was requested to hold confidential the identity of such person or means.

(2) Notwithstanding any other provision of law to the contrary and except as provided in subsection (3) of this section, no newsperson shall, without such newsperson's express consent, be compelled to disclose, be examined concerning refusal to disclose, be subjected to any legal presumption of any kind, or be cited, held in contempt, punished, or subjected to any sanction in any judicial proceedings for refusal to disclose any news information received, observed, procured, processed, prepared, written, or edited by a newsperson, while acting in the capacity of a newsperson; except that the privilege of nondisclosure shall not apply to the following:

    (a) News information received at a press conference;

    (b) News information which has actually been published or broadcast through a medium of mass communication;

    (c) News information based on a newsperson's personal observation of the commission of a crime if substantially similar news information cannot reasonably be obtained by any other means;

    (d) News information based on a newsperson's personal observation of the commission of a class 1, 2, or 3 felony.

(3) Notwithstanding the privilege of nondisclosure granted in subsection (2) of this section, any party to a proceeding who is otherwise authorized by law to issue or obtain subpoenas may subpoena a newsperson in order to obtain news information by establishing by a preponderance of the evidence, in opposition to a newsperson's motion to quash such subpoena:

    (a) That the news information is directly relevant to a substantial issue involved in the proceeding;

    (b) That the news information cannot be obtained by any other reasonable means; and

    (c) That a strong interest of the party seeking to subpoena the newsperson outweighs the interests under the first amendment to the United States constitution of such newsperson in not responding to a subpoena and of the general public in receiving news information.

(4) The privilege of nondisclosure established by subsection (2) of this section may be waived only by the voluntary testimony or disclosure of a newsperson that directly addresses the news information or identifies the source of such news information sought. A publication or broadcast of a news report through the mass media concerning the subject area of the news information sought, but which does not directly address the specific

news information sought, shall not be deemed a waiver of the privilege of nondisclosure as to such specific news information.

(5) In any trial to a jury in an action in which a newsperson is a party as a result of such person's activities as a newsperson and in which the newsperson has invoked the privilege created by subsection (2) of this section, the jury shall be neither informed nor allowed to learn that such newsperson invoked such privilege or has thereby declined to disclose any news information.

(6) Nothing in this section shall preclude the issuance of a search warrant in compliance with the federal "Privacy Protection Act of 1980", 42 U.S.C. § 2000aa.

§ 24-72.5-101. Legislative declaration.

The general assembly finds that an informed citizenry, which results from the free flow of information between citizens and the mass media, and the preservation of news information sources for the mass media is of vital concern to all people of the state of Colorado and that the interest of the state in such area is so great that the state shall retain jurisdiction over the use of any subpoena power or the exercise of any other authority by any governmental entity to obtain news information or the identification of the source of such information within the knowledge or possession of newspersons, which is hereby declared to be a matter of statewide concern.

§ 24-72.5-102. Definitions.

As used in this article, unless the context otherwise requires:

(1) "Governmental entity" means the state and any state agency or institution, county, city and county, incorporated city or town, school district, special improvement district, authority, and every other kind of district, instrumentality, or political subdivision of the state organized pursuant to law. "Governmental entity" shall include entities governed by home rule charters.

(2) "Mass medium" means any publisher of a newspaper or periodical; wire service; radio or television station or network; news or feature syndicate; or cable television system.

(3) "News information" means any knowledge, observation, notes, documents, photographs, films, recordings, videotapes, audiotapes, and reports, and the contents and sources thereof, obtained by a newsperson while engaged as such, regardless of whether such items have been provided to or obtained by such newsperson in confidence.

(4) "Newsperson" means any member of the mass media and any employee or independent contractor of a member of the mass media who is engaged to gather, receive, observe, process, prepare, write, or edit news information for dissemination to the public through the mass media.

(5) "Press conference" means any meeting or event called for the purpose of issuing a public statement to members of the mass media, and to which members of the mass media are invited in advance.

(6) "Proceeding" means any investigation, hearing, or other process for obtaining information conducted by, before, or under the authority of any executive or administrative body, panel, or officer of the state of Colorado or any city, county, city and county, or other political subdivision of the state. Such term shall not include any investigation,

hearing, or other process for obtaining information conducted by, before, or under the authority of the general assembly.

(7) "Source" means any person from whom or any means by or through which news information is received or procured by a newsperson, regardless of whether such newsperson was requested to hold confidential the identity of such person or means.

§ 24-72.5-103. Compelled disclosure of news information — privilege.

(1) Notwithstanding any other provision of law to the contrary, and except as otherwise provided by section 24-72.5-104, no newsperson shall, without the express consent of such newsperson, be compelled to disclose, be examined concerning refusal to disclose, or be subject to any process to compel disclosure or to impose any sanction for nondisclosure in connection with any proceeding of a governmental entity for refusal to disclose any news information received, observed, procured, processed, prepared, written, or edited by a newsperson, while acting in the capacity of a newsperson; except that the privilege of nondisclosure shall not apply to the following:

(a) News information received at a press conference;

(b) News information that has actually been published or broadcasted through the mass media;

(c) News information based on a newsperson's personal observation of the commission of an act which, under any statute, law, or ordinance, is deemed to be a criminal offense if substantially similar news information cannot reasonably be obtained by any other means;

(d) News information based on a newsperson's personal observation of the commission of a class 1, 2, or 3 felony.

§ 24-72.5-104. Limit of nondisclosure privilege for newsperson.

(1) Notwithstanding the privilege of nondisclosure established in section 24-72.5-103, a governmental entity otherwise authorized by law to issue or obtain subpoenas may subpoena a newsperson in order to obtain news information by establishing, by a preponderance of the evidence:

(a) That the news information is directly relevant to a substantial issue involved in the proceeding;

(b) That the news information cannot be obtained by any other reasonable means; and

(c) That a strong interest of the party seeking to subpoena the newsperson outweighs the interests under the first amendment to the United States constitution of such newsperson in not responding to a subpoena and of the general public in receiving news information.

§ 24-72.5-105. Waiver of privilege.

The privilege of nondisclosure established in section 24-72.5-103 may be waived only by the voluntary testimony or disclosure of a newsperson that directly addresses the news information or identifies the source of such news information sought by a governmental entity. A publication or broadcast of a news report through the mass media concerning the subject area of the news information sought, but which does not directly address the news information sought by such governmental entity, shall not be deemed a waiver of the privilege of nondisclosure as to such specific news information.

§ 24-72.5-106. Ability to obtain search warrant not affected.

Nothing in this article shall preclude the issuance of a search warrant pursuant to the federal "Privacy Protection Act of 1980", 42 U.S.C. § 2000aa.

Delaware

Title 10

§ 4320. Definitions.

As used in this subchapter:

(1) "Adjudicative proceeding" means any judicial or quasi-judicial proceeding in which the rights of parties are determined but does not include any proceeding of a grand jury.

(2) "Information" means any oral, written or pictorial material and includes, but is not limited to, documents, electronic impulses, expressions of opinion, films, photographs, sound records, and statistical data.

(3) "Reporter" means any journalist, scholar, educator, polemicist, or other individual who either:

    a. At the time he obtained the information that is sought was earning his principal livelihood by, or in each of the preceding 3 weeks or 4 of the preceding 8 weeks had spent at least 20 hours engaged in the practice of, obtaining or preparing information for dissemination with the aid of facilities for the mass reproduction of words, sounds, or images in a form available to the general public; or

    b. Obtained the information that is sought while serving in the capacity of an agent, assistant, employee, or supervisor of an individual who qualifies as a reporter under subparagraph a.

(4) "Person" means individual, corporation, business trust, estate, trust, partnership or association, governmental body, or any other legal entity.

(5) "Source" means a person from whom a reporter obtained information by means of written or spoken communication or the transfer of physical objects, but does not include a person from whom a reporter obtained information by means of personal observation unaccompanied by any other form of communication and does not include a person from whom another person who is not a reporter obtained information, even if the information was ultimately obtained by a reporter.

(6) "Testify" means give testimony, provide tangible evidence, submit to a deposition, or answer interrogatories.

(7) "Within the scope of his professional activities" means any situation, including a social gathering, in which the reporter obtains information for the purpose of disseminating it to the public, but does not include any situation in which the reporter intentionally conceals from the source the fact that he is a reporter and does not include any situation in which the reporter is an eyewitness to or participant in an act involving physical violence or property damage.

APPENDIX B — STATE STATUTES

§ 4321. Privilege in nonadjudicative proceedings.

A reporter is privileged in a nonadjudicative proceeding to decline to testify concerning either the source or content of information that he obtained within the scope of his professional activities.

§ 4322. Privilege in adjudicative proceedings.

A reporter is privileged in an adjudicative proceeding to decline to testify concerning the source or content of information that he obtained within the scope of his professional activities if he states under oath that the disclosure of the information would violate an express or implied understanding with the source under which the information was originally obtained or would substantially hinder the reporter in the maintenance of existing source relationships or the development of new source relationships.

§ 4323. Exceptions to the privilege in adjudicative proceedings.

(a) Unless the disclosure of the content of the information would substantially increase the likelihood that the source of the information will be discovered, the privilege provided by § 4322 shall not prevent a reporter from being required in an adjudicative proceeding to testify concerning the content, but not the source, of information that he obtained within the scope of his professional activities if the judge determines that the public interest in having the reporter's testimony outweighs the public interest in keeping the information confidential. In making this determination, the judge shall take into account the importance of the issue on which the information is relevant, the efforts that have been made by the subpoenaing party to acquire evidence on the issue from alternative sources, the sufficiency of the evidence available from alternative sources, the circumstances under which the reporter obtained the information, and the likely effect that disclosure of the information will have on the future flow of information to the public.

(b) The privilege provided by § 4322 shall not prevent a reporter from being required in an adjudicative proceeding to testify concerning either the source or the content of information that he obtained within the scope of his professional activities if the party seeking to have the reporter testify proves by a preponderance of the evidence that the sworn statement submitted by the reporter as required by § 4322 is untruthful.

§ 4324. Determination of privilege claim.

A person who invokes the privilege provided by this subchapter may not be required to testify in any proceeding except by court order. If a person invokes the privilege in any proceeding other than a court proceeding, the body or party seeking to have the person testify may apply to the Superior Court for an order requiring the claimant of the privilege to testify. If the Court determines that the claimant does not qualify for the privilege under the provisions of this subchapter, it shall order him to testify.

§ 4325. Waiver.

If a reporter waives the privilege provided by this subchapter with respect to certain facts, he may be cross-examined on the testimony or other evidence he gives concerning those facts but not on other facts with respect to which he claims the privilege. A reporter does not waive or forfeit the privilege by disclosing all or any part of the information protected by the privilege to any other person.

§ 4326. Short title.

This subchapter may be cited as the "Reporters' Privilege Act."

District of Columbia

§ 16-4701. Definitions.

For the purpose of this chapter, the term "news media" means:
(1) Newspapers;
(2) Magazines;
(3) Journals;
(4) Press associations;
(5) News agencies;
(6) Wire services;
(7) Radio;
(8) Television; or
(9) Any printed, photographic, mechanical, or electronic means of disseminating news and information to the public.

§ 16-4702. Compelled disclosure prohibited.

Except as provided in section 16-4703, no judicial, legislative, administrative, or other body with the power to issue a subpoena shall compel any person who is or has been employed by the news media in a news gathering or news disseminating capacity to disclose:

(1) The source of any news or information procured by the person while employed by the news media and acting in an official news gathering capacity, whether or not the source has been promised confidentiality; or

(2) Any news or information procured by the person while employed by the news media in the course of pursuing professional activities that is not itself communicated in the news media, including any:
(A) Notes;
(B) Outtakes;
(C) Photographs or photographic negatives;
(D) Video or sound tapes;
(E) Film; or
(F) Other data, irrespective of its nature, not itself communicated in the news media.

§ 16-4703. Compelled disclosure permitted.

(a) A court may compel disclosure of news or information otherwise protected from disclosure under section 16-4702(2) if the court finds that the party seeking the news or information established by clear and convincing evidence that:

(1) The news or information is relevant to a significant legal issue before a judicial, legislative, administrative, or other body that has the power to issue a subpoena;

(2) The news or information could not, with due diligence, be obtained by any alternative means; and

(3) There is an overriding public interest in the disclosure.

(b) A court may not compel disclosure of the source of any information protected under section 16-4702.

§ 16-4704. Activities not constituting a waiver.

The publication by the news media or the dissemination by a person employed by the news media of a source of news or information, or a portion of the news or information, procured while pursuing professional activities shall not constitute a waiver of the protection from compelled disclosure that is contained in section 16-4702.

Florida

§ 90.5015. Journalist's privilege.

(1) Definitions. — For purposes of this section, the term:

(a) "Professional journalist" means a person regularly engaged in collecting, photographing, recording, writing, editing, reporting, or publishing news, for gain or livelihood, who obtained the information sought while working as a salaried employee of, or independent contractor for, a newspaper, news journal, news agency, press association, wire service, radio or television station, network, or news magazine. Book authors and others who are not professional journalists, as defined in this paragraph, are not included in the provisions of this section.

(b) "News" means information of public concern relating to local, statewide, national, or worldwide issues or events.

(2) Privilege. — A professional journalist has a qualified privilege not to be a witness concerning, and not to disclose the information, including the identity of any source, that the professional journalist has obtained while actively gathering news. This privilege applies only to information or eyewitness observations obtained within the normal scope of employment and does not apply to physical evidence, eyewitness observations, or visual or audio recording of crimes. A party seeking to overcome this privilege must make a clear and specific showing that:

(a) The information is relevant and material to unresolved issues that have been raised in the proceeding for which the information is sought;

(b) The information cannot be obtained from alternative sources; and

(c) A compelling interest exists for requiring disclosure of the information.

(3) Disclosure. — A court shall order disclosure pursuant to subsection (2) only of that portion of the information for which the showing under subsection (2) has been made and shall support such order with clear and specific findings made after a hearing.

(4) Waiver. — A professional journalist does not waive the privilege by publishing or broadcasting information.

(5) Construction. — This section must not be construed to limit any privilege or right provided to a professional journalist under law.

(6) Authentication. — Photographs, diagrams, video recordings, audio recordings, computer records, or other business records maintained, disclosed, provided, or produced by a professional journalist, or by the employer or principal of a professional journalist, may be authenticated for admission in evidence upon a showing, by affidavit of the professional journalist, or other individual with personal knowledge, that the photograph, diagram, video recording, audio recording, computer record, or other business record is a true and accurate copy of the original, and that the copy truly and accurately reflects the observations and facts contained therein.

(7) Accuracy of evidence. — If the affidavit of authenticity and accuracy, or other relevant factual circumstance, causes the court to have clear and convincing doubts as to the authenticity or accuracy of the proferred evidence, the court may decline to admit such evidence.

(8) Severability. — If any provision of this section or its application to any particular person or circumstance is held invalid, that provision or its application is severable and does not affect the validity of other provisions or applications of this section.

Georgia

§ 24-9-30. Persons, companies, or other entities engaged in gathering or dissemination of news.

Any person, company, or other entity engaged in the gathering and dissemination of news for the public through a newspaper, book, magazine, or radio or television broadcast shall have a qualified privilege against disclosure of any information, document, or item obtained or prepared in the gathering or dissemination of news in any proceeding where the one asserting the privilege is not a party, unless it is shown that this privilege has been waived or that what is sought:

(1) Is material and relevant;
(2) Cannot be reasonably obtained by alternative means; and
(3) Is necessary to the proper preparation or presentation of the case of a party seeking the information, document, or item.

Illinois

735 ILCS 5/8-901. Source of information.

Source of information. No court may compel any person to disclose the source of any information obtained by a reporter except as provided in Part 9 of Article VIII of this Act [735 ILCS 5/8-901 et seq.].

735 ILCS 5/8-902. Definitions.

As used in this Act:

(a) "reporter" means any person regularly engaged in the business of collecting, writing or editing news for publication through a news medium on a full-time or part-time basis; and includes any person who was a reporter at the time the information sought was procured or obtained.

(b) "news medium" means any newspaper or other periodical issued at regular intervals and having a general circulation; a news service; a radio station; a television station;

a community antenna television service; and any person or corporation engaged in the making of news reels or other motion picture news for public showing.

(c) "source" means the person or means from or through which the news or information was obtained.

735 ILCS 5/8-903. Application to court.

(a) In any case, except a libel or slander case, where a person claims the privilege conferred by Part 9 of Article VIII of this Act, the person or party, body or officer seeking the information so privileged may apply in writing to the circuit court serving the county where the hearing, action or proceeding in which the information is sought for an order divesting the person named therein of such privilege and ordering him or her to disclose his or her source of the information.

(b) In libel or slander cases where a person claims the privilege conferred by Part 9 of Article VIII of this Act, the plaintiff may apply in writing to the court for an order divesting the person named therein of such privilege and ordering him or her to disclose his or her source of information.

735 ILCS 5/8-904. Contents of application.

The application provided in Section 8-903 of this Act shall allege: the name of the reporter and of the news medium with which he or she was connected at the time the information sought was obtained; the specific information sought and its relevancy to the proceedings; and, either, a specific public interest which would be adversely affected if the factual information sought were not disclosed, or, in libel or slander cases, the necessity of disclosure of the information sought to the proof of plaintiff's case. Additionally, in libel or slander cases, the plaintiff must include in the application provided in Section 8-903 a prima facie showing of falsity of the alleged defamation and actual harm or injury due to the alleged defamation.

735 ILCS 5/8-905. Civil proceeding.

All proceedings in connection with obtaining an adjudication upon the application not otherwise provided in Part 9 of Article VIII of this Act shall be as in other civil cases.

735 ILCS 5/8-906. Consideration by court.

In granting or denying divestiture of the privilege provided in Part 9 of Article VIII of this Act the court shall have due regard to the nature of the proceedings, the merits of the claim or defense, the adequacy of the remedy otherwise available, if any, the relevancy of the source, and the possibility of establishing by other means that which it is alleged the source requested will tend to prove.

735 ILCS 5/8-907. Court's findings.

An order granting divestiture of the privilege provided in Part 9 of Article VIII of this Act shall be granted only if the court, after hearing the parties, finds:

(1) that the information sought does not concern matters, or details in any proceeding, required to be kept secret under the laws of this State or of the Federal government; and

(2) that all other available sources of information have been exhausted and, either, disclosure of the information sought is essential to the protection of the public interest involved or, in libel or slander cases, the plaintiff's need for disclosure of the information sought outweighs the public interest in protecting the confidentiality of sources of information used by a reporter as part of the news gathering process under the particular facts and circumstances of each particular case.

If the court enters an order divesting the person of the privilege granted in Part 9 of Article VIII of this Act it shall also order the person to disclose the information it has determined should be disclosed, subject to any protective conditions as the court may deem necessary or appropriate.

735 ILCS 5/8-908. Privilege continues during pendency of appeal.

Privilege continues during pendency of appeal. In case of an appeal the privilege conferred by Part 9 of Article VIII of this Act remains in full force and effect during the pendency of such appeal.

735 ILCS 5/8-909. Contempt.

A person refusing to testify or otherwise comply with the order to disclose the source of the information as specified in such order, after such order becomes final, may be adjudged in contempt of court and punished accordingly.

Indiana

§ 34-46-4-1. Applicability of Chapter.

This chapter applies to the following persons:
(1) any person connected with, or any person who has been connected with or employed by:
    (A) a newspaper or other periodical issued at regular intervals and having a general circulation; or
    (B) a recognized press association or wire service;
as a bona fide owner, editorial or reportorial employee, who receives or has received income from legitimate gathering, writing, editing and interpretation of news; and
(2) any person connected with a licensed radio or television station as owner, official, or as an editorial or reportorial employee who receives or has received income from legitimate gathering, writing, editing, interpreting, announcing or broadcasting of news.

§ 34-46-4-2. Privilege against disclosure of source of information.

A person described in section 1 of this chapter shall not be compelled to disclose in any legal proceedings or elsewhere the source of any information procured or obtained in the course of the person's employment or representation of a newspaper, periodical, press association, radio station, television station, or wire service, whether:
(1) published or not published:

APPENDIX B — STATE STATUTES

    (A) in the newspaper or periodical; or
    (B) by the press association or wire service; or
(2) broadcast or not broadcast by the radio station or television station; by which the person is employed.

Kentucky

§ 421.100. Newspaper, radio or television broadcasting station personnel need not disclose source of information.

No person shall be compelled to disclose in any legal proceeding or trial before any court, or before any grand or petit jury, or before the presiding officer of any tribunal, or his agent or agents, or before the general assembly, or any committee thereof, or before any city or county legislative body, or any committee thereof, or elsewhere, the source of any information procured or obtained by him, and published in a newspaper or by a radio or television broadcasting station by which he is engaged or employed, or with which he is connected.

Louisiana

§ 45:1451. Definitions.

"Reporter" shall mean any person regularly engaged in the business of collecting, writing or editing news for publication through a news media. The term reporter shall include all persons who were previously connected with any news media as aforesaid as to the information obtained while so connected.

"News Media" shall include
(a) Any newspaper or other periodical issued at regular intervals and having a paid general circulation;
(b) Press associations;
(c) Wire service;
(d) Radio;
(e) Television; and
(f) Persons or corporations engaged in the making of news reels or other motion picture news for public showing.

§ 45:1452. Conditional privilege from compulsory disclosure of informant or source.

Except as hereinafter provided, no reporter shall be compelled to disclose in any administrative, judicial or legislative proceedings or anywhere else the identity of any informant or any source of information obtained by him from another person while acting as a reporter.

§ 45:1453. Revocation of privilege; procedure.

In any case where the reporter claims the privilege conferred by this Part, the persons or parties seeking the information may apply to the district court of the parish in which the reporter resides for an order to revoke the privilege. In the event the reporter does not reside within the state, the application shall be made to the district court of the parish where the hearing, action or proceeding in which the information is sought is pending. The application for such an order shall set forth in writing the reason why the disclosure is essential to the protection of the public interest and service of such application shall be made upon the reporter. The order shall be granted only when the court, after hearing the parties, shall find the disclosure is essential to the public interest. Any such order shall be appealable under Article 2083 of the Louisiana Code of Civil Procedure. In case of any such appeal, the privilege set forth in R.S. 45:1452 shall remain in full force and effect during pendency of such appeal.

§ 45:1454. Defamation; burden of proof.

If the privilege granted herein is claimed and if, in a suit for damages for defamation, a legal defense of good faith has been asserted by a reporter or by a news media with respect to an issue upon which the reporter alleges to have obtained information from a confidential source, the burden of proof shall be on the reporter or news media to sustain this defense.

§ 45:1455. Substitution of affidavit for appearance and return; effect.

A. When a subpoena is served on a news media organization or reporter as those terms are defined in R.S. 45:1451 or on any custodian of records, photographer, or other representative of a news media organization, in any judicial or administrative proceeding to which neither the news media organization nor any reporter, custodian of records, photographer, or other representative is a party, or in any legislative proceeding, it shall not be necessary for the news media organization, the reporter, the custodian of records, the photographer, or the representative thus subpoenaed to appear or to testify in response to the subpoena: (1) to confirm the circulation or the broadcast audience of the news media organization, or (2) to confirm the publication or broadcast of specified materials, if the reporter, custodian of records, photographer, or other representative of the news media organization delivers by registered mail or by hand, before or at the time specified in the subpoena, an affidavit in conformity with Subsection B of this Section together with any documents or records described in the subpoena to the clerk of the court or other tribunal, or, if there is no clerk, then to the court or other tribunal, or, with respect to a deposition subpoena, to the party requesting the issuance of the subpoena.

B. An affidavit delivered pursuant to Subsection A of this Section shall state in substance each of the following:

(1) The name of the proceeding and any docket number assigned to such proceeding as shown on the subpoena itself.

(2) The name of the affiant and his business title or other description indicating his position or relationship to the party to whom the subpoena was issued if he is not the person to whom it was directed.

(3) The dates of publication or broadcast records searched and the dates of publication or broadcast of the documents or records actually produced.

(4) A statement that the documents or records produced were published or broadcast by the news media organization.

(5) If requested, a statement summarizing the circulation or broadcast audience of the news media organization.

APPENDIX B — STATE STATUTES

(6) If requested, a statement describing the placement of an article within a publication.

(7) An itemization of the costs of complying with the subpoena.

C. An affidavit conforming to the requirements of Subsection B of this Section shall be received in evidence and shall be prima facie proof of its contents. A copy of any document, or the text thereof, or of any record, including, without limitation, any article, photograph, or sound or video recording, identified in the affidavit and stated in the affidavit to have been published or broadcast shall be received in evidence and shall be prima facie proof of publication or broadcast as stated in the affidavit.

D. This Section shall not affect the rights of parties to production of documents pursuant to the laws governing discovery or other laws pertaining thereto.

§ 45:1456. Service of subpoenas; motion to quash or obtain additional time; award of costs.

A. Unless otherwise ordered by the court, upon a showing of good cause therefor, a subpoena issued to any news media organization, reporter, custodian of records, photographer, or other representative of any news media organization, which is governed by R.S. 45:1455 through 1458, shall be served at least ten days prior to the return date specified in the subpoena.

B. Nothing contained herein shall be construed to preclude or limit the right of the news media organization, reporter, photographer, custodian of records, or other representative of any news media organization to seek an order with respect to a subpoena pursuant to Article 1354 or Article 1426 of the Code of Civil Procedure, including, without limitation, an order continuing the return date specified in the subpoena or quashing the subpoena on the ground that additional time is reasonably necessary for compliance with the subpoena.

C. In a proceeding to quash any subpoena governed by R.S. 45:1455 through 1458, the court may, after contradictory hearing, grant reasonable attorney fees and expenses to the prevailing party in the contradictory hearing.

§ 45:1457. Payment of cost of compliance; deposit into registry of court.

A. Upon receipt of a subpoena governed by R.S. 45:1455 through 1458, the news media organization, reporter, custodian of records, photographer, or other representative of any news media organization shall notify the party requesting the issuance of the subpoena of the reasonable cost of compliance with the subpoena and the method of calculating the cost.

B. Upon receipt of notification of the cost of compliance as provided in Subsection A of this Section, the party requesting the issuance of the subpoena shall deposit into the registry of the court money or other security in the amount of such cost not less than two days prior to the return date specified in the subpoena. If this amount is not timely deposited, the subpoenaed party may file an affidavit with the court or tribunal setting forth that fact and no further compliance with the subpoena shall be necessary.

The cost of compliance calculated by the subpoenaed party shall be presumed to be reasonable unless the party requesting issuance of the subpoena requests a hearing, and the court finds, after such hearing, that the cost of compliance calculated by the subpoenaed party is not reasonable, in which case the court shall make an adjustment of the amount deposited into the registry of the court. The court may, after contradictory hearing, grant reasonable attorney fees and expenses to the prevailing party in that contradictory hearing.

Any amount deposited into the registry of the court pursuant to this Section shall be taxed as court costs pursuant to the rules governing the proceeding.

§ 45:1458. Application to other proceedings and discovery.

The provisions of R.S. 45:1455 through 1458 shall apply to subpoenas issued in connection with all legislative hearings, administrative proceedings, grand jury hearings and proceedings conducted under Article 66 of the Code of Criminal Procedure. The provisions of this Chapter shall also govern all subpoenas issued in connection with depositions or other discovery authorized by law.

§ 45:1459. Qualified protection for nonconfidential news.

A. "News" shall mean any written, oral, pictorial, photographic, electronic, or other information or communication, whether or not recorded, concerning local, national, or worldwide events or other matters of public concern or public interest or affecting the public welfare.

B. (1) Notwithstanding the provisions of any law to the contrary, no reporter or news media organization, as those terms are defined in R.S. 45:1451, nor any photographer, custodian of records, or other representative of any news media organization shall be adjudged in contempt by any court in connection with any civil or criminal proceeding, or by the legislature or other body having contempt powers, nor shall a grand jury seek to have such person held in contempt by any court, legislature, or other body having contempt powers for refusing or failing to disclose any news which was not published or broadcast but was obtained or prepared by such person in the course of gathering or obtaining news, or the source of any such news, even if such news was not obtained or received in confidence, unless a court has found that the party seeking such news has made a clear and specific showing that the news:

    (a) Is highly material and relevant;

    (b) Is critical or necessary to the maintenance of a party's claim, defense, or proof of an issue material thereto; and

    (c) Is not obtainable from any alternative source.

(2) A court shall order disclosure only of such portion, or portions, of the news sought as to which the above-described showing has been made and shall support such order with clear and specific findings made after a contradictory hearing.

(3) In any proceeding brought pursuant to this Subsection, the court may, after a contradictory hearing, grant reasonable attorney fees and expenses to the prevailing party in such hearing.

C. Notwithstanding the provisions of any law to the contrary, a person entitled to claim the qualified protection provided under the provisions of Subsection B of this Section to whom a subpoena is directed may, within ten days after the service thereof, or, on or before the time specified in the subpoena for compliance, if such time is less than ten days after service, serve upon the attorney designated in the subpoena written objection specifying the grounds for his objection. Once objection is made, the party serving the subpoena shall not be entitled to compliance except pursuant to an order of the court from which the subpoena was issued. The party serving the subpoena may, if objection has been made, move upon notice to the person who served the objection for an order compelling compliance with such subpoena after a hearing in conformity with the provisions of Subsection B of this Section and based upon the findings required therein.

D. (1) In addition to the provisions of Subsections B and C of this Section, and notwithstanding the provisions of any law to the contrary, no grand jury, or official body, acting on behalf or under the authority of the attorney general or a district attorney, shall request, make arrangement for, or otherwise cause the service of a subpoena upon any person entitled to claim the exemption provided under Subsection B of this Section unless the attorney general or a district attorney, acting either alone or upon the direction of a grand jury, has certified in writing that the information sought by such subpoena:

(a) Is highly material and relevant;

(b) Bears directly on the guilt or innocence of the accused; and

(c) Is not obtainable from any alternative source.

(2) The written certification shall be made available to the subpoenaed person upon that person's request. If the certification required by this subsection is made, the provisions of Subsection C of this Section shall not apply.

E. Any order ordering disclosure pursuant to Subsection C of this Section or compelling compliance with a subpoena pursuant to Subsection D of this Section shall be appealable under Code of Civil Procedure Article 2083. In case of any such appeal, the qualified protection set forth in Subsection B of this Section shall remain in full force and effect during the pendency of such appeal.

Maryland

Maryland Code, Courts and Judicial Proceedings

§ 9-112. Privileged communications — News media.

(a) Definitions. — In this section "news media" means:

(1) Newspapers;

(2) Magazines;

(3) Journals;

(4) Press associations;

(5) News agencies;

(6) Wire services;

(7) Radio;

(8) Television; and

(9) Any printed, photographic, mechanical, or electronic means of disseminating news and information to the public.

(b) Persons affected. — The provisions of this section apply to any person who is, or has been, employed by the news media in any news gathering or news disseminating capacity.

(c) Scope of privilege. — Except as provided in subsection (d) of this section, any judicial, legislative, or administrative body, or any body that has the power to issue subpoenas may not compel any person described in subsection (b) of this section to disclose:

(1) The source of any news or information procured by the person while employed by the news media, whether or not the source has been promised confidentiality; or

(2) Any news or information procured by the person while employed by the news media, in the course of pursuing professional activities, for communication to the public but which is not so communicated, in whole or in part, including:

    (i) Notes;

    (ii) Outtakes;

    (iii) Photographs or photographic negatives;

    (iv) Video and sound tapes;

    (v) Film; and

    (vi) Other data, irrespective of its nature, not itself disseminated in any manner to the public.

(d) Court may compel disclosure. —

(1) A court may compel disclosure of news or information, if the court finds that the party seeking news or information protected under subsection (c)(2) of this section has established by clear and convincing evidence that:

    (i) The news or information is relevant to a significant legal issue before any judicial, legislative, or administrative body, or any body that has the power to issue subpoenas;

    (ii) The news or information could not, with due diligence, be obtained by any alternate means; and

    (iii) There is an overriding public interest in disclosure.

(2) A court may not compel disclosure under this subsection of the source of any news or information protected under subsection (c)(1) of this section.

(e) Waiver. — If any person employed by the news media disseminates a source of any news or information, or any portion of the news or information procured while pursuing professional activities, the protection from compelled disclosure under this section is not waived by the individual.

Michigan

§ 767.5a. Privileged communications of news reporter; exception.

(1) A reporter or other person who is involved in the gathering or preparation of news for broadcast or publication shall not be required to disclose the identity of an informant, any unpublished information obtained from an informant, or any unpublished matter or documentation, in whatever manner recorded, relating to a communication with an informant, in any inquiry authorized by this act, except an inquiry for a crime punishable by imprisonment for life when it has been established that the information which is sought is essential to the purpose of the proceeding and that other available sources of the information have been exhausted.

Minnesota

§ 595.021. News media; protection of sources; citation.

Sections 595.021 to 595.025 may be cited as the "Minnesota free flow of information act."

APPENDIX B — STATE STATUTES

§ 595.022. Public policy.

In order to protect the public interest and the free flow of information, the news media should have the benefit of a substantial privilege not to reveal sources of information or to disclose unpublished information. To this end, the freedom of press requires protection of the confidential relationship between the news gatherer and the source of information. The purpose of sections 595.021 to 595.025 is to insure and perpetuate, consistent with the public interest, the confidential relationship between the news media and its sources.

§ 595.023. Disclosure prohibited.

Except as provided in section 595.024, no person who is or has been directly engaged in the gathering, procuring, compiling, editing, or publishing of information for the purpose of transmission, dissemination or publication to the public shall be required by any court, grand jury, agency, department or branch of the state, or any of its political subdivisions or other public body, or by either house of the legislature or any committee, officer, member, or employee thereof, to disclose in any proceeding the person or means from or through which information was obtained, or to disclose any unpublished information procured by the person in the course of work or any of the person's notes, memoranda, recording tapes, film or other reportorial data whether or not it would tend to identify the person or means through which the information was obtained.

§ 595.024. Exception and procedure.

Subdivision 1. A person seeking disclosure may apply to the district court of the county where the person employed by or associated with a news media resides, has a principal place of business or where the proceeding in which the information sought is pending.

Subd. 2. Disclosure allowed; conditions. The application shall be granted only if the court determines after hearing the parties that the person making application, by clear and convincing evidence, has met all three of the following conditions:

(1) that there is probable cause to believe that the specific information sought (i) is clearly relevant to a gross misdemeanor or felony, or (ii) is clearly relevant to a misdemeanor so long as the information would not tend to identify the source of the information or the means through which it was obtained,

(2) that the information cannot be obtained by alternative means or remedies less destructive of first amendment rights, and

(3) that there is a compelling and overriding interest requiring the disclosure of the information where the disclosure is necessary to prevent injustice.

Subd. 3. Determination; appeal. The district court shall consider the nature of the proceedings, the merits of the claims and defenses, the adequacies of alternative remedies, the relevancy of the information sought, and the possibility of establishing by other means that which the source is expected or may tend to prove. The court shall make its appropriate order after making findings of fact. The order may be appealed directly to the court of appeals according to the rules of appellate procedure. The order is stayed and nondisclosure shall remain in full force and effect during the pendency of the appeal. Where the court finds that the information sought has been published or broadcast, there shall be no automatic stay unless an appeal is filed within two days after the order is issued. Either party may request expedited consideration.

§ 595.025. Defamation.

Subdivision 1. The prohibition of disclosure provided in section 595.023 shall not apply in any defamation action where the person seeking disclosure can demonstrate that the identity of the source will lead to relevant evidence on the issue of actual malice.

Subdivision 2. Notwithstanding the provisions of subdivision 1, the identity of the source of information shall not be ordered disclosed unless the following conditions are met:

 (a) that there is probable cause to believe that the source has information clearly relevant to the issue of defamation;

 (b) that the information cannot be obtained by any alternative means or remedy less destructive of first amendment rights.

Subdivision 3. The court shall make its order on the issue of disclosure after making findings of fact, which order may be appealed to the court of appeals according to the rules of appellate procedure. During the appeal the order is stayed and nondisclosure shall remain in full force and effect.

Montana

§ 26-1-901. Short title.

This part shall be known and may be cited as the "Media Confidentiality Act".

§ 26-1-902. Extent of privilege.

(1) Without his or its consent no person, including any newspaper, magazine, press association, news agency, news service, radio station, television station, or community antenna television service or any person connected with or employed by any of these for the purpose of gathering, writing, editing, or disseminating news may be examined as to or may be required to disclose any information obtained or prepared or the source of that information in any legal proceeding if the information was gathered, received, or processed in the course of his employment or its business.

(2) A person described in subsection (1) may not be adjudged in contempt by a judicial, legislative, administrative, or any other body having the power to issue subpoenas for refusing to disclose or produce the source of any information or for refusing to disclose any information obtained or prepared in gathering, receiving, or processing information in the course of his or its business.

§ 26-1-903. Waiver of privilege.

(1) Except as provided in subsection (2), dissemination in whole or in part does not constitute a waiver of provisions of 26-1-902.

(2) If the person claiming the privilege testifies, with or without having been subpoenaed or ordered to testify or produce the source, before a judicial, legislative, administrative, or other body having the power to issue subpoenas or judicially enforceable orders, he does not waive the provisions of 26-1-902 unless the person voluntarily agrees to waive the privilege or voluntarily discloses the source in the course of his testimony. Except as provided in this subsection, the provisions of 26-1-902 may not be waived.

APPENDIX B — STATE STATUTES

Nebraska

§ 20-144. Finding by Legislature.

The Legislature finds:

(1) That the policy of the State of Nebraska is to insure the free flow of news and other information to the public, and that those who gather, write, or edit information for the public or disseminate information to the public may perform these vital functions only in a free and unfettered atmosphere;

(2) That such persons shall not be inhibited, directly or indirectly, by governmental restraint or sanction imposed by governmental process, but rather that they shall be encouraged to gather, write, edit, or disseminate news or other information vigorously so that the public may be fully informed;

(3) That compelling such persons to disclose a source of information or disclose unpublished information is contrary to the public interest and inhibits the free flow of information to the public;

(4) That there is an urgent need to provide effective measures to halt and prevent this inhibition;

(5) That the obstruction of the free flow of information through any medium of communication to the public affects interstate commerce; and

(6) That sections 20-144 to 20-147 are necessary to insure the free flow of information and to implement the first and fourteenth amendments and Article I, section 5, of the United States Constitution, and the Nebraska Constitution.

§ 20-145. Terms, defined.

For purposes of the Free Flow of Information Act, unless the context otherwise requires:

(1) Federal or state proceeding shall include any proceeding or investigation before or by any federal or state judicial, legislative, executive, or administrative body;

(2) Medium of communication shall include, but not be limited to, any newspaper, magazine, other periodical, book, pamphlet, news service, wire service, news or feature syndicate, broadcast station or network, or cable television system;

(3) Information shall include any written, audio, oral, or pictorial news or other material;

(4) Published or broadcast information shall mean any information disseminated to the public by the person from whom disclosure is sought;

(5) Unpublished or nonbroadcast information shall include information not disseminated to the public by the person from whom disclosure is sought, whether or not related information has been disseminated and shall include, but not be limited to, all notes, outtakes, photographs, film, tapes, or other data of whatever sort not itself disseminated to the public through a medium of communication, whether or not published or broadcast information based upon or related to such material has been disseminated;

(6) Processing shall include compiling, storing, transferring, handling, and editing of information; and

(7) Person shall mean any individual, partnership, limited liability company, corporation, association, or other legal entity existing under or authorized by the law of the United States, any state or possession of the United States, the District of Columbia, the Commonwealth of Puerto Rico, or any foreign country.

§ 20-146. Procuring, gathering, writing, editing, or disseminating news or other information; not required to disclose to courts or public.

No person engaged in procuring, gathering, writing, editing, or disseminating news or other information to the public shall be required to disclose in any federal or state proceeding:

(1) The source of any published or unpublished, broadcast or nonbroadcast information obtained in the gathering, receiving, or processing of information for any medium of communication to the public; or

(2) Any unpublished or nonbroadcast information obtained or prepared in gathering, receiving, or processing of information for any medium of communication to the public.

§ 20-147. Act, how cited.

Sections 20-144 to 20-147 shall be known and may be cited as the Free Flow of Information Act.

Nevada

§ 49.275. News media.

No reporter, former reporter or editorial employee of any newspaper, periodical or press association or employee of any radio or television station may be required to disclose any published or unpublished information obtained or prepared by such person in such person's professional capacity in gathering, receiving or processing information for communication to the public, or the source of any information procured or obtained by such person, in any legal proceedings, trial or investigation:

1. Before any court, grand jury, coroner's inquest, jury or any officer thereof.
2. Before the legislature or any committee thereof.
3. Before any department, agency or commission of the state.
4. Before any local governing body or committee thereof, or any officer of a local government.

§ 49.385. Waiver of privilege by voluntary disclosure.

1. A person upon whom these rules confer a privilege against disclosure of a confidential matter waives the privilege if he or his predecessor while holder of the privilege voluntarily discloses or consents to disclosure of any significant part of the matter.

2. This section does not apply if the disclosure is:
    (a) Itself a privileged communication; or
    (b) Made to an interpreter employed merely to facilitate communications.

New Jersey

§ 2A:84A-21. Newspaperman's privilege.

Rule 27.

Subject to Rule 37, a person engaged on, engaged in, connected with, or employed by news media for the purpose of gathering, procuring, transmitting, compiling, editing or disseminating news for the general public or on whose behalf news is so gathered, pro-

APPENDIX B — STATE STATUTES

cured, transmitted, compiled, edited or disseminated has a privilege to refuse to disclose, in any legal or quasi-legal proceeding or before any investigative body, including, but not limited to, any court, grand jury, petit jury, administrative agency, the Legislature or legislative committee, or elsewhere.

a. The source, author, means, agency or person from or through whom any information was procured, obtained, supplied, furnished, gathered, transmitted, compiled, edited, disseminated, or delivered; and

b. Any news or information obtained in the course of pursuing his professional activities whether or not it is disseminated.

The provisions of this rule insofar as it relates to radio or television stations shall not apply unless the radio or television station maintains and keeps open for inspection, for a period of at least 1 year from the date of an actual broadcast or telecast, an exact recording, transcription, kinescopic film or certified written transcript of the actual broadcast or telecast.

§ 2A:84A-21a. Definitions.

Unless a different meaning clearly appears from the context of this act, as used in this act:

a. "News media" means newspapers, magazines, press associations, news agencies, wire services, radio, television or other similar printed, photographic, mechanical or electronic means of disseminating news to the general public.

b. "News" means any written, oral or pictorial information gathered, procured, transmitted, compiled, edited or disseminated by, or on behalf of any person engaged in, engaged on, connected with or employed by a news media and so procured or obtained while such required relationship is in effect.

c. "Newspaper" means a paper that is printed and distributed ordinarily not less frequently than once a week and that contains news, articles of opinion, editorials, features, advertising, or other matter regarded as of current interest, has a paid circulation and has been entered at a United States post office as second class matter.

d. "Magazine" means a publication containing news which is published and distributed periodically, has a paid circulation and has been entered at a United States post office as second class matter.

e. "News agency" means a commercial organization that collects and supplies news to subscribing newspapers, magazines, periodicals and news broadcasters.

f. "Press association" means an association of newspapers or magazines formed to gather and distribute news to its members.

g. "Wire service" means a news agency that sends out syndicated news copy by wire to subscribing newspapers, magazines, periodicals or news broadcasters.

h. "In the course of pursuing his professional activities" means any situation, including a social gathering, in which a reporter obtains information for the purpose of disseminating it to the public, but does not include any situation in which a reporter intentionally conceals from the source the fact that he is a reporter, and does not include any situation in which a reporter is an eyewitness to, or participant in, any act involving physical violence or property damage.

§ 2A:84A-21.1. Criminal proceeding; subpoena; disclosure of information; application of act.

Where a newsperson is required to disclose information pursuant to a subpoena issued by or on behalf of a defendant in a criminal proceeding, not including proceedings before administrative or investigative bodies, grand juries, or legislative committees or commissions, the provisions and procedures in this act are applicable to the claim and exercise of the newsperson's privilege under Rule 27 (C. 2A:84A-21).

§ 2A:84A-21.2. Time of proceedings.

Proceedings pursuant to this act shall take place before the trial, except that the court may allow a motion to institute proceedings pursuant to this act to be made during trial if the court determines that the evidence sought is newly discovered and could not have been discovered earlier through the exercise of due diligence.

§ 2A:84A-21.3. Prima facie showing subpoenaed materials obtained during professional activities; waiver of privilege or other grounds for disclosure; hearing.

a. To sustain a claim of the newsperson's privilege under Rule 27 the claimant shall make a prima facie showing that he is engaged in, connected with, or employed by a news media for the purpose of gathering, procuring, transmitting, compiling, editing or disseminating news for the general public or on whose behalf news is so gathered, procured, transmitted, compiled, edited or disseminated, and that the subpoenaed materials were obtained in the course of pursuing his professional activities.

b. To overcome a finding by the court that the claimant has made a prima facie showing under a. above, the party seeking enforcement of the subpoena shall show by clear and convincing evidence that the privilege has been waived under Rule 37 (C. 2A:84A-29) or by a preponderance of the evidence that there is a reasonable probability that the subpoenaed materials are relevant, material and necessary to the defense, that they could not be secured from any less intrusive source, that the value of the material sought as it bears upon the issue of guilt or innocence outweighs the privilege against disclosure, and that the request is not overbroad, oppressive, or unreasonably burdensome which may be overcome by evidence that all or part of the information sought is irrelevant, immaterial, unnecessary to the defense, or that it can be secured from another source. Publication shall constitute a waiver only as to the specific materials published.

c. The determinations to be made by the court pursuant to this section shall be made only after a hearing in which the party claiming the privilege and the party seeking enforcement of the subpoena shall have a full opportunity to present evidence and argument with respect to each of the materials or items sought to be subpoenaed.

§ 2A:84A-21.4. In camera inspection; hearing; determination of admissibility; order for production.

Upon a finding by the court that there has been a waiver as to any of the materials sought or that any of the materials sought meet the criteria set forth in subsection 3.b., the court shall order the production of such materials, and such materials only, for in camera inspection and determination as to its probable admissibility in the trial. The party claiming the privilege and the party seeking enforcement of the subpoena shall be entitled

APPENDIX B — STATE STATUTES

to a hearing in connection with the in camera inspection of such materials by the court, during which hearing each party shall have a full opportunity to be heard. If the court, after its in camera review of the materials, determines that such materials are admissible according to the standards set forth in subsection 3.b., the court shall direct production of such materials, and such materials only.

§ 2A:84A-21.5. Hearings; findings of fact and conclusions of law.

After any hearing conducted by the court pursuant to section 3 or 4 hereof, the court shall make specific findings of fact and conclusions of law with respect to its rulings, which findings shall be in writing or set forth on the record.

§ 2A:84A-21.6. Appeals; stay of penalty; sealing of record; return of privileged material.

An interlocutory appeal taken from a decision to uphold or quash a subpoena shall act as a stay of all penalties which may have been imposed for failure to comply with the court's order. The record on appeal shall be kept under seal until such time as appeals are exhausted. In the event that all material or any part thereof is found to be privileged, the record as to that privileged material shall remain permanently sealed. Any subpoenaed materials which shall, upon exhaustion and determination of such appeals, be found to be privileged, shall be returned to the party claiming the privilege.

§ 2A:84A-21.7. Co-defendants; notice of proceedings; right to intervene.

Where proceedings are instituted hereunder by one of several co-defendants in a criminal trial, notice shall be provided to all of the co-defendants. Any co-defendant shall have the right to intervene if the co-defendant can demonstrate, pursuant to section 3, that the materials sought by the issuance of the subpoena bear upon his guilt or innocence. Where such intervention is sought by a co-defendant, that co-defendant shall be required, prior to being permitted to participate in any in camera proceeding, to make that showing required of a defendant in section 3.

§ 2A:84A-21.8. Assessment of costs or counsel fee.

If the court finds no reasonable basis for requesting the information has been shown, costs, including counsel fee, may be assessed against the party seeking enforcement of the subpoena. Where an application for costs or counsel fee is made, the judge shall set forth his reasons for awarding or denying same.

§ 2A:84A-21.9. News media person or entity; freedom from searches and seizures of documentary materials; exceptions.

Any person, corporation, partnership, proprietorship or other entity engaged on, engaged in, connected with, or otherwise employed in gathering, procuring, transmitting, compiling, editing, publishing, or disseminating news for the public, or on whose behalf news is so gathered, procured, transmitted, compiled, edited, published or disseminated shall be free from searches and seizures, by State, county and local law enforcement officers with respect to any documentary materials obtained in the course of pursuing the aforesaid activities whether or not such material has been or will be disseminated or published.

This section shall not restrict or impair the ability of any law enforcement officer, pursuant to otherwise applicable law, to search for or seize such materials, if there is probable cause to believe that:

    a. The person, corporation, partnership, proprietorship or other entity possessing the materials has committed or is committing the criminal offense for which the materials are sought; or

    b. The immediate seizure of the materials is necessary to prevent the death of or serious bodily injury to a human being; or

    c. The giving of notice pursuant to a subpoena duces tecum would result in the destruction, alteration or deliberate concealment of the documentary materials other than work product; or

    d. The documentary materials, other than work product, have not been produced in response to a court order directing compliance with a subpoena duces tecum, and

        (1) All appellate remedies have been exhausted by the party seeking to quash the subpoena duces tecum; or

        (2) There is a probability that the delay in an investigation or trial occasioned by further proceedings relating to the subpoena would threaten the interests of justice. In the event a search warrant is sought pursuant to this subparagraph, the person, corporation, partnership, proprietorship or other entity possessing the materials shall be afforded adequate opportunity to submit an affidavit to the court setting forth the basis for any contention that the materials sought are not subject to seizure.

§ 2A:84A-29. Waiver of privilege by contract or previous disclosure; lim-itations.

Rule 37.

A person waives his right or privilege to refuse to disclose or to prevent another from disclosing a specified matter if he or any other person while the holder thereof has (a) contracted with anyone not to claim the right or privilege or, (b) without coercion and with knowledge of his right or privilege, made disclosure of any part of the privileged matter or consented to such a disclosure made by anyone.

A disclosure which is itself privileged or otherwise protected by the common law, statutes or rules of court of this State, or by lawful contract, shall not constitute a waiver under this section. The failure of a witness to claim a right or privilege with respect to 1 question shall not operate as a waiver with respect to any other question.

§ 2A:84A-30. Admissibility of disclosure wrongfully compelled.

Rule 38.

Evidence of a statement or other disclosure is inadmissible against the holder of the privilege if the disclosure was wrongfully made or erroneously required.

§ 2A:84A-31. Reference to exercise of privileges.

Rule 39.

APPENDIX B — STATE STATUTES

If a privilege is exercised not to testify or to prevent another from testifying, either in the action or with respect to particular matters, or to refuse to disclose or to prevent another from disclosing any matter, the judge and counsel may not comment thereon, no presumption shall arise with respect to the exercise of the privilege, and the trier of fact may not draw any adverse inference therefrom. In those jury cases wherein the right to exercise a privilege, as herein provided, may be misunderstood and unfavorable inferences drawn by the trier of the fact, or be impaired in the particular case, the court, at the request of the party exercising the privilege, may instruct the jury in support of such privilege.

§ 2A:84A-32. Effect of error in overruling claim of privilege.

Rule 40.

(1) A party may predicate error on a ruling disallowing a claim of privilege only if he is the holder of the privilege.

(2) If a witness refuses to answer a question, under color of a privilege claimed pursuant to Rules 23 through 38, after the judge has ordered the witness to answer, and a contempt proceeding is brought against the witness, the court hearing the same shall order it dismissed if it appears that the order directing the witness to answer was erroneous.

New Mexico

New Mexico Rules of Evidence

§ 11-514. News media-confidential source or information privilege.

A. Definitions. Unless a different meaning clearly appears from the context of this rule, as used in this rule:

(1) a communication is "confidential" if not intended to be disclosed to third persons other than those to whom disclosure is in furtherance of the rendition of professional news media services or those reasonably necessary for the transmission of the communication;

(2) "in the course of pursuing professional activities" does not include any situation in which a news media person participates in any act involving physical violence, property damage or criminal conduct;

(3) "news" means any written, oral or pictorial information gathered, procured, transmitted, compiled, edited or disseminated by, or on behalf of any person engaged or employed by a news media and so procured or obtained while such required relationship is in effect;

(4) "newspaper" means a news service that is printed or distributed electronically and distributed ordinarily not less frequently than once a week and that contains news, articles of opinion, editorials, features, advertising, or other matter regarded as of current interest;

(5) "news agency" means a commercial organization that collects and supplies news to subscribing newspapers, magazines, periodicals and news broadcasters;

(6) "news media" means newspapers, magazines, press associations, news agencies, wire services, radio, television or other similar printed, photographic, mechanical or electronic means of disseminating news to the general public;

(7) "magazine" means a publication containing news which is published and distributed periodically;

(8) "press association" means an association of newspapers or magazines formed to gather and distribute news to its members;

(9) "wire service" means a news agency that sends out syndicated news copy by wire to subscribing newspapers, magazines, periodicals or news broadcasters.

B. General rule of privilege. A person engaged or employed by news media for the purpose of gathering, procuring, transmitting, compiling, editing or disseminating news for the general public or on whose behalf news is so gathered, procured, transmitted, compiled, edited or disseminated has a privilege to refuse to disclose:

(1) the confidential source from or through whom any information was procured, obtained, supplied, furnished, gathered, transmitted, compiled, edited, disseminated, or delivered in the course of pursuing professional activities; and

(2) any confidential information obtained in the course of pursuing professional activities.

The provisions of this rule insofar as it relates to radio stations shall not apply unless the radio station maintains and keeps open for inspection by a person affected by the broadcast, for a period of at least one hundred eighty (180) days from the date of an actual broadcast, an exact recording, transcription, or certified written transcript of the actual broadcast.

The provisions of this rule insofar as it relates to television stations shall not apply unless the television station maintains and keeps open for inspection by a person affected by the broadcast, for a period of at least one year from the date of an actual telecast, an exact recording, transcription, kinescope film or certified written transcript of the actual telecast.

C. Exception. There is no privilege under this rule in any action in which the party seeking the evidence shows by a preponderance of evidence, including all reasonable inferences, that:

(1) a reasonable probability exists that a news media person has confidential information or sources that are material and relevant to the action;

(2) the party seeking disclosure has reasonably exhausted alternative means of discovering the confidential information or sources sought to be disclosed;

(3) the confidential information or source is crucial to the case of the party seeking disclosure; and

(4) the need of the party seeking the confidential source or information is of such importance that it clearly outweighs the public interest in protecting the news media's confidential information and sources.

D. Procedure. If a person defined in Paragraph B claims the privilege granted, and the court is asked to determine whether the exception applies, a hearing shall be held in open court, to consider all information, evidence or argument deemed relevant by the court. If possible, the determination of whether the exception applies, shall be made, without requiring disclosure of the confidential source or information sought to be protected by the privilege.

If it is not possible for the court to make a determination of whether the exception applies, without the court knowing the confidential source or information sought to be protected, the court may issue an order requiring disclosure to the court alone, in camera.

APPENDIX B — STATE STATUTES

Following the in camera hearing the court shall enter written findings of fact and conclusions of law, without disclosing any of the matters for which the privilege is asserted, and a written order directing that disclosure either shall or shall not be made to the party seeking disclosure.

Evidence submitted to the court in camera, and any record of the in camera proceedings, shall be sealed and preserved to be made available to an appellate court, in the event of an appeal, and the contents shall not otherwise be revealed without the consent of the person asserting the privilege.

All counsel and parties shall be permitted to be present at every stage of the proceedings under this rule, except at the in camera hearing, at which no counsel or party, except the person asserting the privilege, and counsel for that person, shall be permitted to be present.

Any order requiring an in camera disclosure or ordering or denying disclosure may be appealed by any party or by the person asserting the privilege, if not a party, in the procedural manner provided by the Rules of Appellate Procedure.

New Mexico Statutes Annotated

§ 38-6-7. News sources and information.

A. Unless disclosure be essential to prevent injustice, no journalist or newscaster, or working associates of a journalist or newscaster, shall be required to disclose before any proceeding or authority, either:

(1) the source of any published or unpublished information obtained in the gathering, receiving or processing of information for any medium of communication to the public; or

(2) any unpublished information obtained or prepared in gathering, receiving or processing of information for any medium of communication to the public.

B. For the purpose of this act [this section]:

(1) "proceeding or authority" includes any proceeding or investigation before, or by, any legislative, judicial, executive or administrative body or person;

(2) "medium of communication" means any newspaper, magazine, press association, news service, wire service, news or feature syndicate, broadcast or television station or network, or cable television system;

(3) "information" means any written, oral or pictorial news or other material;

(4) "published information" means any information disseminated to the public by the person from whom disclosure is sought;

(5) "unpublished information" includes information not disseminated to the public by the person from whom disclosure is sought, whether or not related information has been disseminated, and includes but is not limited to, all notes, news copy, outtakes, photographs, films, recording tapes or other data of whatever sort not disseminated to the public through a medium of communication;

(6) "processing" includes compiling, storing and editing of information;

(7) "journalist" means any person who, for gain is engaged in gathering, preparing, editing, analyzing or commenting on news for a newspaper, magazine, news agency, news or feature syndicate, press association or wire service, or who was so engaged at the time a source or information was procured;

(8) "newscaster" means any person who, for gain is engaged in gathering, preparing, editing, analyzing, commenting on or broadcasting news for radio or television transmission, or who was so engaged at the time a source or information was procured; and

(9) "working associates [associate]" means any person who works for the person, in his capacity as a journalist or newscaster, from whom a source or information is sought and who was so engaged at the time a source or information was procured, or any person employed by the same individual or entity that employs the person, in his capacity as a journalist or newscaster, from whom a source or information is sought, and who was so engaged at the time a source or information was procured.

C. If the proceeding in which disclosure is sought is in the district court, that court will determine whether disclosure is essential to prevent injustice. In all other proceedings, application shall be made to the district court of the county in which the proceeding is being held for an order for disclosure. Disclosure shall, in no event, be ordered except upon written order of the district court stating the reasons why disclosure is essential to prevent injustice. Such an order is appealable to the supreme court if the appeal is docketed in that court within ten days after its entry. The matter shall be considered as an extraordinary proceeding and shall be heard de novo and within twenty days from date of docketing. The taking of an appeal shall operate to stay proceedings as to the prevention of injustice issue only in the district court.

New York

New York Civil Rights Law

§ 79-h. Special provisions relating to persons employed by, or connected with, news media.

(a) Definitions. As used in this section, the following definitions shall apply:

(1) "Newspaper" shall mean a paper that is printed and distributed ordinarily not less frequently than once a week, and has done so for at least one year, and that contains news, articles of opinion (as editorials), features, advertising, or other matter regarded as of current interest, has a paid circulation and has been entered at United States post-office as second-class matter.

(2) "Magazine" shall mean a publication containing news which is published and distributed periodically, and has done so for at least one year, has a paid circulation and has been entered at a United States post-office as second-class matter.

(3) "News agency" shall mean a commercial organization that collects and supplies news to subscribing newspapers, magazines, periodicals and news broadcasters.

(4) "Press association" shall mean an association of newspapers and/or magazines formed to gather and distribute news to its members.

(5) "Wire service" shall mean a news agency that sends out syndicated news copy by wire to subscribing newspapers, magazines, periodicals or news broadcasters.

(6) "Professional journalist" shall mean one who, for gain or livelihood, is engaged in gathering, preparing, collecting, writing, editing, filming, taping or photographing of news intended for a newspaper, magazine, news agency, press association or wire service or other professional medium or agency which has as one of its regular functions the processing and researching of news intended for dissemination to the public; such person shall be someone performing said function either as a regular employee or

APPENDIX B — STATE STATUTES

as one otherwise professionally affiliated for gain or livelihood with such medium of communication.

(7) "Newscaster" shall mean a person who, for gain or livelihood, is engaged in analyzing, commenting on or broadcasting, news by radio or television transmission.

(8) "News" shall mean written, oral, pictorial, photographic, or electronically recorded information or communication concerning local, national or worldwide events or other matters of public concern or public interest or affecting the public welfare.

(b) Exemption of professional journalists and newscasters from contempt: Absolute protection for confidential news. Notwithstanding the provisions of any general or specific law to the contrary, no professional journalist or newscaster presently or having previously been employed or otherwise associated with any newspaper, magazine, news agency, press association, wire service, radio or television transmission station or network or other professional medium of communicating news or information to the public shall be adjudged in contempt by any court in connection with any civil or criminal proceeding, or by the legislature or other body having contempt powers, nor shall a grand jury seek to have a journalist or newscaster held in contempt by any court, legislature or other body having contempt powers for refusing or failing to disclose any news obtained or received in confidence or the identity of the source of any such news coming into such person's possession in the course of gathering or obtaining news for publication or to be published in a newspaper, magazine, or for broadcast by a radio or television transmission station or network or for public dissemination by any other professional medium or agency which has as one of its main functions the dissemination of news to the public, by which such person is professionally employed or otherwise associated in a news gathering capacity notwithstanding that the material or identity of a source of such material or related material gathered by a person described above performing a function described above is or is not highly relevant to a particular inquiry of government and notwithstanding that the information was not solicited by the journalist or newscaster prior to disclosure to such person.

(c) Exemption of professional journalists and newscasters from contempt: Qualified protection for nonconfidential news. Notwithstanding the provisions of any general or specific law to the contrary, no professional journalist or newscaster presently or having previously been employed or otherwise associated with any newspaper, magazine, news agency, press association, wire service, radio or television transmission station or network or other professional medium of communicating news to the public shall be adjudged in contempt by any court in connection with any civil or criminal proceeding, or by the legislature or other body having contempt powers, nor shall a grand jury seek to have a journalist or newscaster held in contempt by any court, legislature, or other body having contempt powers for refusing or failing to disclose any unpublished news obtained or prepared by a journalist or newscaster in the course of gathering or obtaining news as provided in subdivision (b) of this section, or the source of any such news, where such news was not obtained or received in confidence, unless the party seeking such news has made a clear and specific showing that the news: (i) is highly material and relevant; (ii) is critical or necessary to the maintenance of a party's claim, defense or proof of an issue material thereto; and (iii) is not obtainable from any alternative source. A court shall order disclosure only of such portion, or portions, of the news sought as to which the above-described showing has been made and shall support such order with clear and specific findings made after a hearing. The provisions of this subdivision shall not affect the availability, under appropriate circumstances, of sanctions under section thirty-one hundred twenty-six of the civil practice law and rules.

(d) Any information obtained in violation of the provisions of this section shall be inadmissible in any action or proceeding or hearing before any agency.

(e) No fine or imprisonment may be imposed against a person for any refusal to disclose information privileged by the provisions of this section.

(f) The privilege contained within this section shall apply to supervisory or employer third person or organization having authority over the person described in this section.

(g) Notwithstanding the provisions of this section, a person entitled to claim the exemption provided under subdivision (b) or (c) of this section waives such exemption if such person voluntarily discloses or consents to disclosure of the specific information sought to be disclosed to any person not otherwise entitled to claim the exemptions provided by this section.

North Carolina

§ 8-53.9. Persons, companies, or other entities engaged in gathering or dissemination of news

(a) Definitions. The following definitions apply in this section:

(1) Journalist. — Any person, company, or entity, or the employees, independent contractors, or agents of that person, company, or entity, engaged in the business of gathering, compiling, writing, editing, photographing, recording, or processing information for dissemination via any news medium.

(2) Legal proceeding. — Any grand jury proceeding or grand jury investigation; any criminal prosecution, civil suit, or related proceeding in any court; and any judicial or quasi-judicial proceeding before any administrative, legislative, or regulatory board, agency, or tribunal.

(3) News medium. — Any entity regularly engaged in the business of publication or distribution of news via print, broadcast, or other electronic means accessible to the general public.

(b) A journalist has a qualified privilege against disclosure in any legal proceeding of any confidential or nonconfidential information, document, or item obtained or prepared while acting as a journalist.

(c) In order to overcome the qualified privilege provided by subsection (b) of this section, any person seeking to compel a journalist to testify or produce information must establish by the greater weight of the evidence that the testimony or production sought:

(1) Is relevant and material to the proper administration of the legal proceeding for which the testimony or production is sought;

(2) Cannot be obtained from alternate sources; and

(3) Is essential to the maintenance of a claim or defense of the person on whose behalf the testimony or production is sought.

Any order to compel any testimony or production as to which the qualified privilege has been asserted shall be issued only after notice to the journalist and a hearing and shall include clear and specific findings as to the showing made by the person seeking the testimony or production.

(d) Notwithstanding subsections (b) and (c) of this section, a journalist has no privilege against disclosure of any information, document, or item obtained as the result of the

APPENDIX B — STATE STATUTES

journalist's eyewitness observations of criminal or tortious conduct, including any physical evidence or visual or audio recording of the observed conduct.

North Dakota

§ 31-01-06.2. Disclosure of news sources and information required only on court order.

No person shall be required in any proceeding or hearing to disclose any information or the source of any information procured or obtained while the person was engaged in gathering, writing, photographing, or editing news and was employed by or acting for any organization engaged in publishing or broadcasting news, unless directed by an order of a district court of this state which, after hearing, finds that the failure of disclosure of such evidence will cause a miscarriage of justice.

Ohio

§ 2739.04. Revelation of news source by broadcasters.

No person engaged in the work of, or connected with, or employed by any noncommercial educational or commercial radio broadcasting station, or any noncommercial educational or commercial television broadcasting station, or network of such stations, for the purpose of gathering, procuring, compiling, editing, disseminating, publishing, or broadcasting news shall be required to disclose the source of any information procured or obtained by such person in the course of his employment, in any legal proceeding, trial, or investigation before any court, grand jury, petit jury, or any officer thereof, before the presiding officer of any tribunal, or his agent, or before any commission, department, division, or bureau of this state, or before any county or municipal body, officer, or committee thereof.

Every noncommercial educational or commercial radio broadcasting station, and every noncommercial educational or commercial television broadcasting station shall maintain for a period of six months from the date of its broadcast thereof, a record of those statements of information the source of which was procured or obtained by persons employed by the station in gathering, procuring, compiling, editing, disseminating, publishing, or broadcasting news.

As used in this section:

(A) "Record" includes a tape, disc, script, or any other item or document that sets forth the content of the statements that are required by this section to be recorded.

(B) "Noncommercial educational television or radio broadcasting station" means a television or radio broadcast station that is licensed by the federal communications commission as a noncommercial educational radio or television broadcast station, transmits only noncommercial programs for educational purposes, and is owned and operated by:

(1) A public agency or institution or nonprofit private foundation, corporation, or association;

(2) A municipal corporation.

§ 2739.12. Newspaper reporters not required to reveal source of information.

No person engaged in the work of, or connected with, or employed by any newspaper or any press association for the purpose of gathering, procuring, compiling, editing, disseminating, or publishing news shall be required to disclose the source of any information procured or obtained by such person in the course of his employment, in any legal proceeding, trial, or investigation before any court, grand jury, petit jury, or any officer thereof, before the presiding officer of any tribunal, or his agent, or before any commission, department, division, or bureau of this state, or before any county or municipal body, officer or committee thereof.

Oklahoma

§ 2506. Newsman's Privilege.

A. As used in this section:
  1. "State proceeding" includes any proceeding or investigation before or by any judicial, legislative, executive or administrative body in this state;
  2. "Medium of communication" includes any newspaper, magazine, other periodical, book, pamphlet, news service, wire service, news or feature syndicate, broadcast station or network, or cable television system;
  3. "Information" includes any written, oral or pictorial news or other material;
  4. "Published information" means any information disseminated to the public by the person from whom disclosure is sought;
  5. "Unpublished information" includes information not disseminated to the public by the person from whom disclosure is sought, whether or not related information has been disseminated, and includes, but is not limited to, all notes, outtakes, photographs, tapes or other data of whatever sort not itself disseminated to the public through a medium of communication, whether or not published information based upon or related to such material has been disseminated;
  6. "Processing" includes compiling, storing and editing of information; and
  7. "Newsman" means any man or woman who is a reporter, photographer, editor, commentator, journalist, correspondent, announcer, or other individual regularly engaged in obtaining, writing, reviewing, editing, or otherwise preparing news for any newspaper, periodical, press association, newspaper syndicate, wire service, radio or television station, or other news service. Any individual employed by any such news service in the performance of any of the above-mentioned activities shall be deemed to be regularly engaged in such activities. However, "newsman" shall not include any governmental entity or individual employed thereby engaged in official governmental information activities.

B. No newsman shall be required to disclose in a state proceeding either:
  1. The source of any published or unpublished information obtained in the gathering, receiving or processing of information for any medium of communication to the public; or
  2. Any unpublished information obtained or prepared in gathering, receiving or processing of information for any medium of communication to the public; unless the court finds that the party seeking the information or identity has established by clear and convincing evidence that such information or identity is relevant to a significant issue in the action and could not with due diligence be obtained by alternate means.

APPENDIX B — STATE STATUTES

This subsection does not apply with respect to the content or source of allegedly defamatory information, in a civil action for defamation wherein the defendant asserts a defense based on the content or source of such information.

Oregon

§ 44.510. Definitions for ORS 44.510 to 44.540.

As used in ORS 44.510 to 44.540, unless the context requires otherwise:

(1) "Information" has its ordinary meaning and includes, but is not limited to, any written, oral, pictorial or electronically recorded news or other data.

(2) "Medium of communication" has its ordinary meaning and includes, but is not limited to, any newspaper, magazine or other periodical, book, pamphlet, news service, wire service, news or feature syndicate, broadcast station or network, or cable television system. Any information which is a portion of a governmental utterance made by an official or employee of government within the scope of his or her governmental function, or any political publication subject to ORS 260.512, 260.522 and 260.532, is not included within the meaning of "medium of communication."

(3) "Processing" has its ordinary meaning and includes, but is not limited to, the compiling, storing and editing of information.

(4) "Published information" means any information disseminated to the public.

(5) "Unpublished information" means any information not disseminated to the public, whether or not related information has been disseminated. "Unpublished information" includes, but is not limited to, all notes, out-takes, photographs, tapes or other data of whatever sort not themselves disseminated to the public through a medium of communication, whether or not published information based upon or related to such material has been disseminated.

§ 44.520. Limitation on compellable testimony from media persons; search of media persons' papers, effects or work premises prohibited; exception.

(1) No person connected with, employed by or engaged in any medium of communication to the public shall be required by a legislative, executive or judicial officer or body, or any other authority having power to compel testimony or the production of evidence, to disclose, by subpoena or otherwise:

(a) The source of any published or unpublished information obtained by the person in the course of gathering, receiving or processing information for any medium of communication to the public; or

(b) Any unpublished information obtained or prepared by the person in the course of gathering, receiving or processing information for any medium of communication to the public.

(2) No papers, effects or work premises of a person connected with, employed by or engaged in any medium of communication to the public shall be subject to a search by a legislative, executive or judicial officer or body, or any other authority having power to compel the production of evidence, by search warrant or otherwise. The provisions of this subsection, however, shall not apply where probable cause exists to believe that the person has committed, is committing or is about to commit a crime.

§ 44.530. Application of ORS 44.520.

(1) ORS 44.520 applies regardless of whether a person has disclosed elsewhere any of the information or source thereof, or any of the related information.

(2) ORS 44.520 continues to apply in relation to any of the information, or source thereof, or any related information, even in the event of subsequent termination of a person's connection with, employment by or engagement in any medium of communication to the public.

(3) The provisions of ORS 44.520(1) do not apply with respect to the content or source of allegedly defamatory information, in civil action for defamation wherein the defendant asserts a defense based on the content or source of such information.

§ 44.540. Effect of informant as witness.

If the informant offers the informant as a witness, it is deemed a consent to the examination also of a person described in ORS 44.520 on the same subject.

Pennsylvania

§ 42:5942. Confidential communications to news reporters.

(A) GENERAL RULE. — No person engaged on, connected with, or employed by any newspaper of general circulation or any press association or any radio or television station, or any magazine of general circulation, for the purpose of gathering, procuring, compiling, editing or publishing news, shall be required to disclose the source of any information procured or obtained by such person, in any legal proceeding, trial or investigation before any government unit.

(B) EXCEPTION. — The provisions of subsection (a) insofar as they relate to radio or television stations shall not apply unless the radio or television station maintains and keeps open for inspection, for a period of at least one year from the date of the actual broadcast or telecast, an exact recording, transcription, kinescopic film or certified written transcript of the actual broadcast or telecast.

Rhode Island

§ 9-19.1-1. Newspaper defined.

A newspaper or periodical as described in this chapter must be issued at regular intervals and have a paid circulation.

§ 9-19.1-2. Nondisclosure of confidential information.

Except as provided in § 9-19.1-3, no person shall be required by any court, grand jury, agency, department, or commission of the state of Rhode Island to reveal confidential association, to disclose any confidential information or to disclose the source of any confidential information received or obtained by him in his capacity as a reporter, editor, commentator, journalist, writer, correspondent, news photographer, or other person directly engaged in the gathering or presentation of news for any accredited newspaper, periodical, press association, newspaper syndicate, wire service, or radio or television station.

APPENDIX B — STATE STATUTES

§ 9-19.1-3. Qualifications.

(a) The privilege conferred by § 9-19.1-2 shall not apply to any information which has at any time been published, broadcast, or otherwise made public by the person claiming the privilege.

(b) The privilege conferred by § 9-19.1-2 shall not apply:

(1) To the source of any allegedly defamatory information in any case where the defendant, in a civil action for defamation, asserts a defense based on the source of such information; or

(2) To the source of any information concerning the details of any grand jury or other proceeding which was required to be secret under the laws of the state.

(c) In any case where a person claims a privilege conferred by this statute, the person seeking the information or the source of the information may apply to the superior court for an order divesting the privilege. If the court, after hearing the parties, shall find that there is substantial evidence that disclosure of the information or of the source of the information is necessary to permit a criminal prosecution for the commission of a specific felony, or to prevent a threat to human life, and that such information or the source of such information is not available from other prospective witnesses, the court may make such order as may be proper under the circumstance. Any such order shall be appealable under the provisions of chapter 24 of title 9.

South Carolina

§ 19-11-100. Qualified privilege against disclosure for news media; waiver.

(A) A person, company, or entity engaged in or that has been engaged in the gathering and dissemination of news for the public through a newspaper, book, magazine, radio, television, news or wire service, or other medium has a qualified privilege against disclosure of any information, document, or item obtained or prepared in the gathering or dissemination of news in any judicial, legislative, or administrative proceeding in which the compelled disclosure is sought and where the one asserting the privilege is not a party in interest to the proceeding.

(B) The person, company, or other entity may not be compelled to disclose any information or document or produce any item obtained or prepared in the gathering or dissemination of news unless the party seeking to compel the production or testimony establishes by clear and convincing evidence that this privilege has been knowingly waived or that the testimony or production sought:

(1) is material and relevant to the controversy for which the testimony or production is sought;

(2) cannot be reasonably obtained by alternative means; and

(3) is necessary to the proper preparation or presentation of the case of a party seeking the information, document, or item.

(C) Publication of any information, document, or item obtained in the gathering and dissemination of news does not constitute a waiver of the qualified privilege against compelled disclosure provided for in this section.

Tennessee

§ 24-1-208. Persons gathering information for publication or broadcast — Disclosure.

(a) A person engaged in gathering information for publication or broadcast connected with or employed by the news media or press, or who is independently engaged in gathering information for publication or broadcast, shall not be required by a court, a grand jury, the general assembly, or any administrative body, to disclose before the general assembly or any Tennessee court, grand jury, agency, department, or commission any information or the source of any information procured for publication or broadcast.

(b) Subsection (a) shall not apply with respect to the source of any allegedly defamatory information in any case where the defendant in a civil action for defamation asserts a defense based on the source of such information.

(c)(1) Any person seeking information or the source thereof protected under this section may apply for an order divesting such protection. Such application shall be made to the judge of the court having jurisdiction over the hearing, action or other proceeding in which the information sought is pending.

(2) The application shall be granted only if the court after hearing the parties determines that the person seeking the information has shown by clear and convincing evidence that:

(A) There is probable cause to believe that the person from whom the information is sought has information which is clearly relevant to a specific probable violation of law;

(B) The person has demonstrated that the information sought cannot reasonably be obtained by alternative means; and

(C) The person has demonstrated a compelling and overriding public interest of the people of the state of Tennessee in the information.

(3)(A) Any order of the trial court may be appealed to the court of appeals in the same manner as other civil cases. The court of appeals shall make an independent determination of the applicability of the standards in this subsection to the facts in the record and shall not accord a presumption of correctness to the trial court's findings.

(B) The execution of or any proceeding to enforce a judgment divesting the protection of this section shall be stayed pending appeal upon the timely filing of a notice of appeal in accordance with Rule 3 of the Tennessee Rules of Appellate Procedure, and the appeal shall be expedited upon the docket of the court of appeals upon the application of either party.

(C) Any order of the court of appeals may be appealed to the supreme court of Tennessee as provided by law.

APPENDIX B — STATE STATUTES

Part Two:

WIRETAP AND EAVESDROPPING LAWS
(selected provisions)

Alabama

§ 13A-11-30. Definitions.

The following definitions apply to this article:

(1) Eavesdrop. To overhear, record, amplify or transmit any part of the private communication of others without the consent of at least one of the persons engaged in the communication, except as otherwise provided by law.

(2) Private place. A place where one may reasonably expect to be safe from casual or hostile intrusion or surveillance, but such term does not include a place to which the public or a substantial group of the public has access.

(3) Surveillance. Secret observation of the activities of another person for the purpose of spying upon and invading the privacy of the person observed.

§ 13A-11-31. Criminal eavesdropping.

(a) A person commits the crime of criminal eavesdropping if he intentionally uses any device to eavesdrop, whether or not he is present at the time.

(b) Criminal eavesdropping is a Class A misdemeanor.

§ 13A-11-32. Criminal surveillance.

(a) A person commits the crime of criminal surveillance if he intentionally engages in surveillance while trespassing in a private place.

(b) Criminal surveillance is a Class B misdemeanor.

§ 13A-11-33. Installing an eavesdropping device.

(a) A person commits the crime of installing an eavesdropping device if he intentionally installs or places a device in a private place with knowledge it is to be used for eavesdropping and without permission of the owner and any lessee or tenant or guest for hire of the private place.

(b) Installing an eavesdropping device in a private place is prima facie evidence of knowledge that the device is to be used for eavesdropping.

(c) Installing an eavesdropping device is a Class C felony.

§ 13A-11-35. Divulging illegally-obtained information.

(a) A person commits the crime of divulging illegally-obtained information if he knowingly or recklessly uses or divulges information obtained through criminal eavesdropping or criminal surveillance.

(b) Divulging illegally-obtained information is a Class B misdemeanor.

Alaska

§ 42.20.300. Unauthorized publication or use of communications.

(a) Except for a party to a private conversation, a person who receives or assists in receiving, or who transmits or assists in transmitting a private communication may not divulge or publish the existence, contents, substance, purport, effect, or meaning of the communication, except through authorized channels of transmission or reception

(1) to the addressee or the agent or attorney of the addressee;

(2) to a person employed or authorized to forward a communication to its destination;

(3) to proper accounting or distributing officers of the various communicating centers over which the communication may be passed;

(4) to the master of a ship under whom the person is serving;

(5) to another on demand of lawful authority; or

(6) in response to a subpoena issued or order entered by a court of competent jurisdiction.

(b) Except as provided in AS 12.37, a person not authorized by a party to the communication may not intentionally intercept a private communication or divulge or publish the existence, contents, substance, purport, effect, or meaning of the intercepted communication to any person.

(c) A person who is not entitled to a communication but who has received the communication may not use it or any information contained in it for personal benefit or another's benefit.

(d) A person who has received a communication and who knows or reasonably should know that the communication and the information contained in it was obtained in violation of this section may not divulge or publish the existence, contents, substance, purport, effect, or meaning of the communication or any part of the communication.

(e) A person who has become acquainted with a communication or the information contained in it, and who is not entitled to the communication, may not use the same for personal benefit or another's benefit, or divulge or publish the existence, contents, substance, purport, effect, or meaning of the communication or any part of the communication.

§ 42.20.310. Eavesdropping.

(a) A person may not

(1) use an eavesdropping device to hear or record all or any part of an oral conversation without the consent of a party to the conversation;

(2) use or divulge any information which the person knows or reasonably should know was obtained through the illegal use of an eavesdropping device for personal benefit or another's benefit;

(3) publish the existence, contents, substance, purport, effect or meaning of any conversation the person has heard through the illegal use of an eavesdropping device;

(4) divulge, or publish the existence, contents, substance, purport, effect
or meaning of any conversation the person has become acquainted with after the person knows or reasonably should know that the conversation and the information contained in the conversation was obtained through the illegal use of an eavesdropping device.

(b) In this section "eavesdropping device" means any device capable of being used to hear or record oral conversation whether the conversation is conducted in person, by telephone, or by any other means; provided that this definition does not include devices used for the restoration of the deaf or hard-of-hearing to normal or partial hearing.

§ 42.20.320. Exemptions.

(a) The following activities are exempt from the provisions of AS 42.20.300 and 42.20.310:

(1) listening to a radio or wireless communications of any sort where the same are publicly made;

(2) hearing conversation when heard by employees of a common carrier by wire incidental to the normal course of their employment in the operation, maintenance, or repair of the equipment of the common carrier by wire, provided the information obtained is not used or divulged in any manner by the hearer;

(3) a broadcast by radio or other means whether it is a live broadcast or recorded for the purpose of later broadcasts of any function where the public
is in attendance and the conversations that are overheard are incidental to the main purpose for which the broadcast is then being made;

(4) recording or listening with the aid of any device to an emergency communication made in the normal course of operations by a federal, state, or local law enforcement agency or institutions dealing in emergency services, including hospitals, clinics, ambulance services, fire fighting agencies, a public utility emergency repair facility, civilian defense establishment, or military installations;

(5) inadvertent interception of telephone conversations over party lines;

(6) a peace officer, or a person acting at the direction or request of a peace officer, engaging in conduct authorized by or under AS 12.37;

(7) interception, listening, or recording of communications by a peace officer, or a person acting under the direction or request of a peace officer, in an emergency where the communications are received from a device that intercepts the communications of a person

    (A) barricaded and not exiting or surrendering at the direction or request of a peace officer, in circumstances where there is an imminent risk of harm to life or property;

    (B) holding another person hostage; or

    (C) threatening the imminent illegal use of an explosive.

(b) Notwithstanding any other provision of law, a person who inadvertently intercepts a private communication that appears to pertain to the commission of a crime may report the information to a law enforcement agency.

(c) In this section, "explosive" has the meaning given in AS 11.81.900.

§ 42.20.330. Penalty.

A person who violates any of the provisions of AS 42.20.300 and 42.20.310 is guilty of a class A misdemeanor.

§ 42.20.390. Definitions.

In AS 42.20.300–42.20.390,

(1) "communications common carrier" means a business or person engaged as a common carrier for hire in the transmission of communications by wire, cable, satellite, electromagnetic waves, or radio, not including radio broadcasting;

(2) "contents" includes information obtained from a private communication concerning the existence, substance, purport, or meaning of the communication, or the identity of a party of the communication;

(3) "eavesdropping device" means a device or apparatus, including an induction coil, that can be used to intercept an oral, wire, or electronic communication, other than

   (A) a hearing aid or similar device used for the restoration of subnormal hearing to not better than normal; or

   (B) a telephone or telegraph instrument, equipment, or facility, or any component of such an instrument, equipment, or facility

      (i) being used by a provider of wire or electronic communication service in the ordinary course of its business; or

      (ii) furnished to a subscriber or user by a provider of wire or electronic communication service in the ordinary course of its business and being used by the subscriber or user in the ordinary course of its business;

(4) "electronic communication" means any transfer of signs, signals, writing, images, sounds, data, or intelligence of any nature transmitted in whole or in part by a wire, radio, electromagnetic, photoelectronic or photo-optical system, including a cellular or cordless telephone communication, but does not include

   (A) wire or oral communications;

   (B) communications made through a tone-only paging device;

   (C) communications made through a tracking device consisting of an electronic or mechanical device that permits the tracking of the movement of a person or object; or

   (D) communications that are disseminated by the sender with the intent or

expectation, or through a method of transmission that is so configured, that the communication is readily accessible to the general public;

(5) "electronic communication service" means a service that provides to users of the service the ability to send or receive wire or electronic communications;

(6) "employee" includes a person who is an officer, agent, or employee of, or a person under contract with, a business or a government entity;

(7) "intercept" means the aural or other acquisition of the contents of an oral, wire, or electronic communication through the use of any electronic, mechanical, or other device, including the acquisition of the contents by simultaneous transmission or by recording;

(8) "oral communication" means human speech used to communicate information from one party to another;

(9) "private communication" means an oral, wire, or electronic communication uttered or transmitted by a person who has a reasonable expectation that the communication is not subject to interception;

(10) "wire communication" means human speech used to communicate information from one party to another in whole or in part through the use of facilities for the transmission of communications by wire, cable, or other similar connection between the point of origin and the point of reception furnished or operated by a telephone, telegraph, or radio company for hire as a communications common carrier, but does not include the radio

portion of a cordless telephone communication that is transmitted between the cordless telephone handset and the base unit.

Arizona

§ 13-3004. Definitions.

In this chapter, unless the context otherwise requires:

1. "Aural transfer" means a communication containing the human voice at any point between and including the point of origin and the point of reception.

2. "Communication service provider" means any person engaged in providing a service which allows its users to send or receive wire or electronic communications.

3. "Electronic communication" means any transfer of signs, signals, writing, images, sounds, data or intelligence of any nature transmitted in whole or in part by a wire, radio, electromagnetic, photoelectronic or photooptical system but does not include any of the following:

   (a) Any wire or oral communication.
   (b) Any communication made through a tone-only paging device.
   (c) Any communication from a tracking device.

4. "Electronic communication system" means any communication or computer facilities or related electronic equipment for the transmission, processing or electronic storage of electronic communications.

5. "Electronic storage" means either of the following:

   (a) Any temporary, intermediate storage of a wire or electronic communication incidental to the electronic transmission.
   (b) Any storage of the communication by an electronic communication service provider for purposes of backup protection of the communication.

6. "Intercept" means the aural or other acquisition of the contents of any wire, electronic or oral communication through the use of any electronic, mechanical or other device.

7. "Oral communication" means a spoken communication uttered by a person exhibiting an expectation that such communication is not subject to interception under circumstances justifying such expectation, but does not include any electronic communication.

8. "Pen register" means a device which records or decodes electronic or other impulses which identify the numbers dialed or otherwise transmitted on the telephone line or communication facility to which the device is attached.

9. "Person" means any individual, enterprise, public or private corporation, unincorporated association, partnership, firm, society, governmental authority or entity, including the subscriber to the communication service involved, and any law enforcement officer.

10. "Readily accessible to the general public" means a radio communication that is not:

    (a) Scrambled or encrypted.
    (b) Transmitted using modulation techniques with essential parameters that have been withheld from the public to preserve the privacy of the communication.
    (c) Carried on a subcarrier or other signal subsidiary to a radio transmission.
    (d) Transmitted over a communication system provided by a common carrier, unless the communication is a tone-only paging system communication.

(e) Transmitted on frequencies allocated under part 25, subpart D, E or F or part 74 or part 94 of the rules of the federal communications commission. If a communication transmitted on a frequency allocated under part 74 is not exclusively allocated to broadcast auxiliary services, the communication is a two-way voice communication system by radio.

11. "Remote computing service" means providing to the public any computer storage or processing services by means of an electronic communication system.

12. "Trap and trace device" means a device which captures the incoming electronic or other impulses which identify the originating number of an instrument or device from which a wire or electronic communication was transmitted.

13. "Wire communication" means any aural transfer which is made in whole or in part through the use of facilities for the transmission of communications by the aid of wire, cable or other like connection between the point of origin and the point of reception, including the use of a connection in a switching station, and that is furnished or operated by any person engaged in providing or operating the facilities for the transmission of communications. Wire communication also includes any electronic storage of the communication.

§ 13-3005. Interception of wire, electronic and oral communications.

A. Except as provided in this section and § 13-3012, a person is guilty of a class 5 felony who either:

1. Intentionally intercepts a wire or electronic communication to which he is not a party, or aids, authorizes, employs, procures or permits another to so do, without the consent of either a sender or receiver thereof.

2. Intentionally intercepts a conversation or discussion at which he is not present, or aids, authorizes, employs, procures or permits another to so do, without the consent of a party to such conversation or discussion.

3. Intentionally intercepts the deliberations of a jury or aids, authorizes, employs, procures or permits another to so do.

B. Except as provided in §§ 13-3012 and 13-3017, a person who intentionally and without lawful authority installs or uses a pen register or trap and trace device on the telephone lines or communications facilities of another person which are utilized for wire or electronic communication is guilty of a class 6 felony.

§ 13-3012. Exemptions.

The following are exempt from the provisions of this chapter:

* * * * *

6. The interception of any radio communication that is transmitted:

(a) By any station for the use of the general public or if the transmission relates to ships, aircraft, vehicles or persons in distress.

(b) By any government, law enforcement, civil defense, private land mobile or public safety communication system, including police and fire systems, that are readily accessible to the general public.

(c) By any station that operates on an authorized frequency within the bands that are allocated to the amateur, citizens band or general mobile radio services.

APPENDIX B — STATE STATUTES

(d) By any marine or aeronautical communications system.

(e) Through a system using frequencies that are monitored by persons who are engaged in the provision or the use of the system or by other persons using the same frequency if the communication is not scrambled or encrypted.

* * * * *

9. The interception of any wire, electronic or oral communication by any person, if the interception is effected with the consent of a party to the communication or a person present during the communication.

* * * * *

11. The interception or access of electronic communication made through an electronic communication system that is configured so that the electronic communication is readily accessible to the general public.

12. The interception of radio communication that is transmitted:

(a) By a station for the use of the general public or ships, aircraft, vehicles or persons in distress.

(b) By a governmental, law enforcement, civil defense, private land, mobile or public safety communications system, including police and fire.

(c) By a station operating on an authorized frequency within the bands allocated to the amateur, citizens band or general mobile radio services.

(d) By a marine or aeronautical communications system.

* * * * *

Arkansas

§ 5-60-120. Interception and recording.

(a) It shall be unlawful for a person to intercept a wire, oral, or telephonic communication, defined as communications that utilize the electromagnetic spectrum frequencies of forty-six to forty-nine megahertz (46-49 mghz.) generally used by cordless telephone technology and eight hundred forty to eight hundred eighty megahertz (840-880 mghz.) generally used by cellular telephone technology, and to record or possess a recording of such communication unless such a person is a party to the communication or one (1) of the parties to the communication has given prior consent to such interception and recording.

(b) Any violation of this section shall be a Class A misdemeanor.

(c)(1) It shall not be unlawful for such an act to be committed by a person acting under the color of law.

(2) It is an exception to the application of subsection (a) of this section that an officer, employee, or agent of a public telephone utility provides information, facilities, or technical assistance to a person acting under the color of law to intercept a wire, oral, or telephonic communication.

(3) It shall not be unlawful under this section for an operator of a switchboard, or an officer, employee, or agent of any public telephone utility whose facilities are used in the transmission of a wire communication to intercept, disclose, or use that communication in the normal course of his employment while engaged in any activity which is a necessary incident to the rendition of his service or to the protection of the rights or property of the public telephone utility of such communication.

(d) The provisions of this section do not apply to telecommunication services offered by public telephone utilities.

California

Cal. Penal Code § 631. Wiretapping.

(a) Prohibited acts; punishment; recidivists. Any person who, by means of any machine, instrument, or contrivance, or in any other manner, intentionally taps, or makes any unauthorized connection, whether physically, electrically, acoustically, inductively, or otherwise, with any telegraph or telephone wire, line, cable, or instrument, including the wire, line, cable, or instrument of any internal telephonic communication system, or who willfully and without the consent of all parties to the communication, or in any unauthorized manner, reads, or attempts to read, or to learn the contents or meaning of any message, report, or communication while the same is in transit or passing over any wire, line, or cable, or is being sent from, or received at any place within this state; or who uses, or attempts to use, in any manner, or for any purpose, or to communicate in any way, any information so obtained, or who aids, agrees with, employs, or conspires with any person or persons to unlawfully do, or permit, or cause to be done any of the acts or things mentioned above in this section, is punishable by a fine not exceeding two thousand five hundred dollars ($2,500), or by imprisonment in the county jail not exceeding one year, or by imprisonment in the state prison, or by both a fine and imprisonment in the county jail or in the state prison. If the person has previously been convicted of a violation of this section or Section 632, 632.5, 632.6, 632.7, or 636, he or she is punishable by a fine not exceeding ten thousand dollars ($10,000), or by imprisonment in the county jail not exceeding one year, or by imprisonment in the state prison, or by both a fine and imprisonment in the county jail or in the state prison.

(b) Exceptions. This section shall not apply (1) to any public utility engaged in the business of providing communications services and facilities, or to the officers, employees or agents thereof, where the acts otherwise prohibited herein are for the purpose of construction, maintenance, conduct or operation of the services and facilities of the public utility, or (2) to the use of any instrument, equipment, facility, or service furnished and used pursuant to the tariffs of a public utility, or (3) to any telephonic communication system used for communication exclusively within a state, county, city and county, or city correctional facility.

(c) Evidence. Except as proof in an action or prosecution for violation of this section, no evidence obtained in violation of this section shall be admissible in any judicial, administrative, legislative, or other proceeding.

(d) Operative date of section. This section shall become operative on January 1, 1994.

§ 632. Eavesdropping.

(a) Every person who, intentionally and without the consent of all parties to a confidential communication, by means of any electronic amplifying or recording device, eavesdrops upon or records the confidential communication, whether the communication is carried on among the parties in the presence of one another or by means of a telegraph, telephone, or other device, except a radio, shall be punished by a fine not exceeding two thousand five hundred dollars ($2,500), or imprisonment in the county jail not exceeding one year, or in the state prison, or by both that fine and imprisonment. If the person has previously been convicted of a violation of this section or Section 631, 632.5, 632.6, 632.7, or 636, the person shall be punished by a fine not exceeding ten thousand dollars ($10,000), by imprisonment in the county jail not exceeding one year, or in the state prison, or by both that fine and imprisonment.

(b) The term "person" includes an individual, business association, partnership, corporation, limited liability company, or other legal entity, and an individual acting or purporting to act for or on behalf of any government or subdivision thereof, whether federal, state, or local, but excludes an individual known by all parties to a confidential communication to be overhearing or recording the communication.

(c) The term "confidential communication" includes any communication carried on in circumstances as may reasonably indicate that any party to the communication desires it to be confined to the parties thereto, but excludes a communication made in a public gathering or in any legislative, judicial, executive or administrative proceeding open to the public, or in any other circumstance in which the parties to the communication may reasonably expect that the communication may be overheard or recorded.

* * * * *

§ 632.5. Cellular radio telephone interceptions.

(a) Every person who, maliciously and without the consent of all parties to the communication, intercepts, receives or assists in intercepting or receiving a communication transmitted between cellular radio telephones or between any cellular radio telephone and a landline telephone shall be punished by a fine not exceeding two thousand five hundred dollars ($2,500), by imprisonment in the county jail not exceeding one year or in the state prison, or by both that fine and imprisonment. If the person has been previously convicted of a violation of this section or Section 631, 632, 632.6, 632.7, or 636, the person shall be punished by a fine not exceeding ten thousand dollars ($10,000), by imprisonment in the county jail not exceeding one year or in the state prison, or by both that fine and imprisonment.

* * * * *

(c) As used in this section and Section 635, "cellular radio telephone" means a wireless telephone authorized by the Federal Communications Commission to operate in the frequency bandwidth reserved for cellular radio telephones.

§ 632.6. Cordless or cellular telephones interceptions.

(a) Every person who, maliciously and without the consent of all parties to the communication, intercepts, receives or assists in intercepting or receiving a communication transmitted between cordless telephones as defined in subdivision (c), between any cordless telephone and a landline telephone, or between a cordless telephone and a cellular telephone shall be punished by a fine not exceeding two thousand five hundred dollars ($2,500), by imprisonment in the county jail not exceeding one year, or in the state prison, or by both that fine and imprisonment. If the person has been convicted previously of a violation of Section 631, 632, 632.5, 632.7, or 636, the person shall be punished by a fine not exceeding ten thousand dollars ($10,000), or by imprisonment in the county jail not exceeding one year, or in the state prison, or by both that fine and imprisonment.

WIRETAP AND EAVESDROPPING LAWS

* * * * *

(c) As used in this section and in Section 635, "cordless telephone" means a two-way low power communication system consisting of two parts–a "base" unit which connects to the public switched telephone network and a handset or "remote" unit–which are connected by a radio link and authorized by the Federal Communications Commission to operate in the frequency bandwidths reserved for cordless telephones.

§ 632.7. Cordless or cellular radio telephones; intentional recordation.

(a) Every person who, without the consent of all parties to a communication, intercepts or receives and intentionally records, or assists in the interception or reception and intentional recordation of, a communication transmitted between two cellular radio telephones, a cellular radio telephone and a landline telephone, two cordless telephones, a cordless telephone and a landline telephone, or a cordless telephone and a cellular radio telephone, shall be punished by a fine not exceeding two thousand five hundred dollars ($2,500), or by imprisonment in a county jail not exceeding one year, or in the state prison, or by both that fine and imprisonment. If the person has been convicted previously of a violation of this section or of Section 631, 632, 632.5, 632.6, or 636, the person shall be punished by a fine not exceeding ten thousand dollars ($10,000), by imprisonment in a county jail not exceeding one year, or in the state prison, or by both that fine and imprisonment.

* * * * *

(c) As used in this section, each of the following terms have the following meaning:

(1) "Cellular radio telephone" means a wireless telephone authorized by the Federal Communications Commission to operate in the frequency bandwidth reserved for cellular radio telephones.

(2) "Cordless telephone" means a two-way, low power communication system consisting of two parts, a "base" unit which connects to the public switched telephone network and a handset or "remote" unit, that are connected by a radio link and authorized by the Federal Communications Commission to operate in the frequency bandwidths reserved for cordless telephones.

(3) "Communication" includes, but is not limited to, communications transmitted by voice, data, or image, including facsimile.

§ 633.5. Recording communications relating to commission of specified crimes.

Nothing in Section 631, 632, 632.5, 632.6, or 632.7 prohibits one party to a confidential communication from recording the communication for the purpose of obtaining evidence reasonably believed to relate to the commission by another party to the communication of the crime of extortion, kidnapping, bribery, any felony involving violence against the person, or a violation of Section 653m. Nothing in Section 631, 632, 632.5, 632.6, or 632.7 renders any evidence so obtained inadmissible in a prosecution for extortion, kidnapping, bribery, any felony involving violence against the person, a violation of Section 653m, or any crime in connection therewith.

APPENDIX B — STATE STATUTES

§ 634. Trespass for the purpose of committing prohibited acts.

Any person who trespasses on property for the purpose of committing any act, or attempting to commit any act, in violation of Section 631, 632, 632.5, 632.6, 632.7, or 636 shall be punished by a fine not exceeding two thousand five hundred dollars ($2,500), by imprisonment in the county jail not exceeding one year or in the state prison, or by both that fine and imprisonment. If the person has previously been convicted of a violation of this section or Section 631, 632, 632.5, 632.6, 632.7, or 636, the person shall be punished by a fine not exceeding ten thousand dollars ($10,000), by imprisonment in the county jail not exceeding one year or in the state prison, or by both that fine and imprisonment.

§ 637. Disclosure of telegraphic or telephonic message.

Every person not a party to a telegraphic or telephonic communication who willfully discloses the contents of a telegraphic or telephonic message, or any part thereof, addressed to another person, without the permission of such person, unless directed so to do by the lawful order of a court, is punishable by imprisonment in the state prison, or in the county jail not exceeding one year, or by fine not exceeding five thousand dollars ($5,000), or by both fine and imprisonment.

§ 637.2. Civil action by person injured.

(a) Any person who has been injured by a violation of this chapter may bring an action against the person who committed the violation for the greater of the following amounts:
   (1) Five thousand dollars ($5,000).
   (2) Three times the amount of actual damages, if any, sustained by the plaintiff.
(b) Any person may, in accordance with Chapter 3 (commencing with Section 525) of Title 7 of Part 2 of the Code of Civil Procedure, bring an action to enjoin and restrain any violation of this chapter, and may in the same action seek damages as provided by subdivision (a).
(c) It is not a necessary prerequisite to an action pursuant to this section that the plaintiff has suffered, or be threatened with, actual damages.

Colorado

§ 18-9-301. Definitions.

As used in sections 18-9-301 to 18-9-305, unless the context otherwise requires:
(1) "Aggrieved person" means a person who was a party to any intercepted wire, oral, or electronic communication or a person against whom the interception was directed.
(1.5) "Aural transfer" means a transfer containing the human voice at any point between and including the point of origin and the point of reception.
(2) "Common carrier" means any person engaged as a common carrier for hire in intrastate, interstate, or foreign communication by wire or radio or in intrastate, interstate, or foreign radio transmission of energy.
(3) "Contents" when used with respect to any wire, oral, or electronic communication, includes any information concerning the substance, purport, or meaning of that communication.

(3.3) "Electronic communication" means any transfer of signs, signals, writing, images, sounds, data, or intelligence of any nature transmitted in whole or in part by a wire, radio, electromagnetic, photoelectronic, or photo-optical system that affects interstate or foreign commerce but does not include:

    (a) Deleted by Laws 1997, H.B. 97-1268, S 2.
    (b) Any wire or oral communication;
    (c) Any communication made through a tone-only paging device; or
    (d) Any communication from a tracking device.

(3.5) "Electronic communication service" means any service which provides to users thereof the ability to send or receive wire or electronic communications.

(3.7) "Electronic communications system" means any wire, radio, electromagnetic, photo-optical, or photoelectronic facilities for the transmission of electronic communications and any computer facilities or related electronic equipment for the electronic storage of such communications.

(4) "Electronic, mechanical, or other device" means any device or apparatus which can be used to intercept a wire, oral, or electronic communication, other than:

    (a) Any telephone or telegraph instrument, equipment, or facility, or any component thereof, furnished to the subscriber or user by a provider of wire or electronic communication service in the ordinary course of its business and being used by the subscriber or user in the ordinary course of its business, or furnished by such subscriber or user for connection to the facilities of such service and being used in the ordinary course of its business, or being used by a provider of wire or electronic communication service in the ordinary course of its business or by an investigative or law enforcement officer in the ordinary course of his duties;

    (b) A hearing aid or similar device being used to correct subnormal hearing to not better than normal hearing.

(4.5) "Electronic storage" means:

    (a) Any temporary, intermediate storage of a wire or electronic communication incidental to the electronic transmission thereof; and

    (b) Any storage of such communication by an electronic communication service for purposes of backup protection of such communication.

(5) "Intercept" means the aural or other acquisition of the contents of any wire, electronic, or oral communication through the use of any electronic, mechanical, or other device.

* * * * *

(8) "Oral communication" means any oral communication uttered by any person believing that such communication is not subject to interception, under circumstances justifying such belief, but does not include any electronic communication.

* * * * *

(8.5) "Readily accessible to the general public" means, with respect to a radio communication, that such communication is not:

    (a) Scrambled or encrypted;
    (b) Transmitted using modulation techniques having essential parameters withheld from the public with the intention of preserving the privacy of such communication;
    (c) Carried on a subcarrier or other signal subsidiary to a radio transmission;

APPENDIX B — STATE STATUTES

(d) Transmitted over a communication system provided by a common carrier, unless the communication is a tone-only paging system communication; or

(e) Transmitted on frequencies allocated under part 25, subpart D, E or F of part 74 or part 94 of the rules of the federal communications commission, unless, in the case of a communication transmitted on a frequency allocated under part 74 that is not exclusively allocated to broadcast auxiliary services, the communication is a two-way voice communication by radio.

* * * * *

(8.9) "User" means any person or entity which uses an electronic communication service and is duly authorized by the provider of such service to engage in such use.

(9) "Wire communication" means any aural transfer made in whole or in part through the use of facilities for the transmission of communications by the aid of wire, cable, or other like connection, including the use of such connection in a switching station, between the point of origin and the point of reception, furnished or operated by any person engaged in providing or operating such facilities for the transmission of communications and includes any electronic storage of such communication.

§ 18-9-303. Wiretapping prohibited.

(1) Any person not a sender or intended receiver of a telephone or telegraph communication commits wiretapping if he:

(a) Knowingly overhears, reads, takes, copies, or records a telephone, telegraph, or electronic communication without the consent of either a sender or a receiver thereof or attempts to do so; or

(b) Intentionally overhears, reads, takes, copies, or records a telephone, telegraph, or electronic communication for the purpose of committing or aiding or abetting the commission of an unlawful act; or

(c) Knowingly uses for any purpose or discloses to any person the contents of any such communication, or attempts to do so, while knowing or having reason to know the information was obtained in violation of this section; or

(d) Knowingly taps or makes any connection with any telephone or telegraph line, wire, cable, or instrument belonging to another or with any electronic, mechanical, or other device belonging to another or installs any device whether connected or not which permits the interception of messages; or

(e) Knowingly prevents, obstructs, or delays, by any means whatsoever, the sending, transmission, conveyance, or delivery in this state of any message, communication, or report by or through any telegraph or telephone line, wire, cable, or other facility or any electronic, mechanical, or other device; or

(f) Knowingly uses any apparatus to unlawfully do, or cause to be done, any act prohibited by this section or aids, authorizes, agrees with, employs, permits, or intentionally conspires with any person to violate the provisions of this section.

(2) Wiretapping is a class 6 felony; except that, if the wiretapping involves a cordless telephone, it is a class 1 misdemeanor.

§ 18-9-304. Eavesdropping prohibited.

(1) Any person not visibly present during a conversation or discussion commits eavesdropping if he:

    (a) Knowingly overhears or records such conversation or discussion without the consent of at least one of the principal parties thereto, or attempts to do so; or

    (b) Intentionally overhears or records such conversation or discussion for the purpose of committing, aiding, or abetting the commission of an unlawful act; or

    (c) Knowingly uses for any purpose, discloses, or attempts to use or disclose to any other person the contents of any such conversation or discussion while knowing or having reason to know the information was obtained in violation of this section; or

    (d) Knowingly aids, authorizes, agrees with, employs, permits, or intentionally conspires with any person to violate the provisions of this section.

(2) Eavesdropping is a class 6 felony.

§ 18-9-305. Exceptions.

(1) Nothing in sections 18-9-302 to 18-9-304 shall be interpreted to prevent a news agency, or an employee thereof, from using the accepted tools and equipment of that news medium in the course of reporting or investigating a public and newsworthy event; nor shall said sections prevent any person from using wiretapping or eavesdropping devices on his own premises for security or business purposes if reasonable notice of the use of such devices is given to the public.

* * * * *

(4.3) It shall not be unlawful under sections 18-9-302 to 18-9-304 for any person:

    (a) To intercept or access an electronic communication made through an electronic communications system that is configured so that such electronic communication is readily accessible to the general public;

    (b) To intercept any radio communication which is transmitted by:

        (I) Any station for the use of the general public or that relates to ships, aircraft, vehicles, or persons in distress;

        (II) Any governmental, law enforcement, civil defense, private land mobile, or public safety communications system, including police and fire, readily accessible to the general public;

        (III) A station operating on an authorized frequency within the bands allocated to the amateur, citizens band, or general mobile radio services; or

        (IV) Any marine or aeronautical communications system;

    (c) To engage in any conduct which is:

        (I) Prohibited by section 633 of the federal "Communications Act of 1934", as amended; or

        (II) Excepted from the application of section 705(a) of the federal "Communications Act of 1934", as amended, by section 705(b) of said act;

* * * * *

(4.7) A person or entity providing an electronic communication service to the public shall not intentionally divulge the contents of any communication other than a communication to such person or entity, or an agent thereof, while in transmission on that service to any person or entity other than an addressee or intended recipient of such communica-

APPENDIX B — STATE STATUTES

tion or an agent of such addressee or intended recipient; except that a person or entity providing electronic communication service to the public may divulge the contents of any such communication:

(a) As otherwise authorized in section 16-15-102(12), (13), (14), and (16), C.R.S., and section 18-9-305(2) and (3);

(b) With the lawful consent of the originator or any addressee or intended recipient of such communication;

(c) To a person employed or authorized, or whose facilities are used, to forward such communication to its destination; or

(d) Which were inadvertently obtained by the service provider and which appear to pertain to the commission of a crime, if such divulgence is made to a law enforcement agency.

* * * * *

(5) The exceptions in this section shall be affirmative defenses.

Connecticut

§ 52-570d. Illegal recording of private telephonic communications.

(a) No person shall use any instrument, device or equipment to record an oral private telephonic communication unless the use of such instrument, device or equipment (1) is preceded by consent of all parties to the communication and such prior consent either is obtained in writing or is part of, and obtained at the start of, the recording, or (2) is preceded by verbal notification which is recorded at the beginning and is part of the communication by the recording party, or (3) is accompanied by an automatic tone warning device which automatically produces a distinct signal that is repeated at intervals of approximately fifteen seconds during the communication while such instrument, device or equipment is in use.

(b) The provisions of subsection (a) of this section shall not apply to:

* * * * *

(3) Any person who, as the recipient of a telephonic communication which conveys threats of extortion, bodily harm or other unlawful requests or demands, records such telephonic communication;

* * * * *

(6) Any officer, employee or agent of a Federal Communications Commission licensed broadcast station who records a telephonic communication solely for broadcast over the air;

* * * * *

(8) Any officer, employee or agent of a Federal Communications Commission broadcast licensee who records a telephonic communication as part of a broadcast network or cooperative programming effort solely for broadcast over the air by a licensed broadcast station.

(c) Any person aggrieved by a violation of subsection (a) of this section may bring a civil action in the superior court to recover damages, together with costs and a reasonable attorney's fee.

Delaware

Title 11, § 1335. Violation of privacy.

(a) A person is guilty of violation of privacy when, except as authorized by law, the person:

(1) Trespasses on property intending to subject anyone to eavesdropping or other surveillance in a private place; or

(2) Installs in any private place, without consent of the person or persons entitled to privacy there, any device for observing, photographing, recording, amplifying or broadcasting sounds or events in that place or uses any such unauthorized installation; or

(3) Installs or uses outside a private place any device for hearing, recording, amplifying or broadcasting sounds originating in that place which would not ordinarily be audible or comprehensible outside, without the consent of the person or persons entitled to privacy there; or

(4) Intercepts without the consent of all parties thereto a message by telephone, telegraph, letter or other means of communicating privately, including private conversation; or

(5) Divulges without the consent of the sender and the receiver the existence or contents of any message by telephone, telegraph, letter or other means of communicating privately if the accused knows that the message was unlawfully intercepted or if the accused learned of the message in the course of employment with an agency engaged in transmitting it.

(b) This section does not apply to:

(1) Overhearing of messages through a regularly installed instrument on a telephone party line or an extension or any other regularly installed instrument or equipment;

* * * * *

(c) Violation of privacy is a class A misdemeanor.

§ 1336. Wiretapping and electronic surveillance.

(a) As used in this section:

(1) "Aggrieved person" means a person who was a party to any intercepted wire or oral communication or a person against whom the interception was directed.

(2) "Communication common carrier" means any person engaged as a common carrier for hire, in intrastate, interstate or foreign communication by wire or radio or in intrastate, interstate or foreign radio transmission of energy; but a person engaged in radio broadcasting shall not, while so engaged, be deemed a common carrier.

(3) "Contents" when used with respect to any wire or oral communication, includes any information concerning the identity of the parties to such communication or the existence, substance, purport or meaning of that communication.

(4) "Court of competent jurisdiction" means the Superior Court of this State.

(5) "Intercept" means the aural acquisition of the contents of any wire or oral communication through the use of any electronic, mechanical or other device.

(6) "Intercepting device" means any electronic, mechanical or other device or apparatus that can be used to intercept a wire or oral communication other than:

APPENDIX B — STATE STATUTES

a. Any telephone or telegraph instrument, equipment or facility, or any component thereof, furnished to the subscriber or user by a communication common carrier in the ordinary course of its business and being used by the subscriber or user in the ordinary course of its business, or being used by a communication common carrier in the ordinary course of its business or by an investigative or law-enforcement officer in the ordinary course of duties;

b. A hearing aid or similar device being used to correct subnormal hearing to not better than normal.

* * * * *

(9) "Oral communication" means any oral communication uttered by a person exhibiting an expectation that such communication is not subject to interception under circumstances justifying such expectation.

(10) "Person" means a human being who has been born and is alive, and, where appropriate, a public or private corporation, an unincorporated association, a partnership, a government or a governmental instrumentality and includes any officer or employee of the State or a political subdivision thereof.

(11) "Wire communication" means any communication made in whole or in part through the use of facilities for the transmission of communications by wire, cable or other like connection between the point of origin and the point of reception furnished or operated by a telephone, telegraph or radio company for hire as a communication common carrier.

(b)(1) Except as otherwise specifically provided in this section or otherwise by law, any person who: (i) Willfully intercepts, endeavors to intercept or procures any other person to intercept or endeavor to intercept any wire or oral communication; or (ii) willfully discloses or endeavors to disclose to any other person the contents of any wire or oral communication, or evidence derived therefrom, knowing or having reason to know that the information was obtained through the interception of a wire or oral communication in violation of this section; or (iii) willfully uses or endeavors to use the contents of any wire or oral communication, or evidence derived therefrom, knowing or having reason to know that the information was obtained through the interception of a wire or oral communication in violation of this section; shall be guilty of a class G felony.

* * * * *

(c) It shall not be unlawful under this section for:

(1) An operator of a switchboard or an officer, agent or employee of a communication common carrier, whose facilities are used in the transmission of a wire communication, to intercept, disclose or use that communication in the normal course of employment while engaged in any activity which is a necessary incident to the rendition of service or to the protection of the rights or property of the carrier of such communication. No communication common carrier shall utilize service observing or random monitoring except for mechanical or service quality control checks. It shall not be unlawful under this section for an officer, employee or agent of any communication common carrier to provide information, facilities or technical assistance to an investigative or law-enforcement officer who, pursuant to this section, is authorized, by the Superior Court, to intercept a wire or oral communication.

(2) A person acting under color of law to intercept a wire or oral communication, where such person is a party to the communication or 1 of the parties to the communi-

cation has given prior consent to such interception, unless such communication is intercepted for the purpose of committing any criminal or tortious act in violation of the Constitution or laws of the United States or of this State or for the purpose of committing any other injurious act.

* * * * *

(w)(1) Any person whose wire or oral communication is intercepted, disclosed or used in violation of this section shall have a civil cause of action against any person who intercepts, discloses or uses or procures any other person to intercept, disclose or use such communication, and shall be entitled to recover from any such person:

 (i) Actual damages, but not less than liquidated damages computed at the rate of $100 a day for each day of violation, or $1,000, whichever is higher;

 (ii) Punitive damages; and

 (iii) A reasonable attorney's fee and other litigation costs reasonably incurred.

* * * * *

District of Columbia

§ 23-541. Definitions.

As used in this subchapter —

(1) the term "wire communication" means any communication made in whole or in part through the use of facilities for the transmission of communications by the aid of wire, cable, or other like connection between the point of origin and the point of reception furnished or operated by any person engaged as a common carrier in providing or operating such facilities;

(2) the term "oral communication" means any oral communication uttered by a person exhibiting an expectation that the communication is not subject to interception under circumstances justifying the expectation;

(3) the term "intercept" means the aural acquisition of the contents of any wire or oral communication through the use of any intercepting device;

(4) the term "intercepting device" means any electronic, mechanical, or other device or apparatus which can be used to intercept a wire or oral communication other than —

 (A) any telephone or telegraph instrument, equipment, or facility, or any component thereof, (i) furnished to the subscriber or user by a communications common carrier in the ordinary course of its business and being used by the subscriber or user in the ordinary course of its business; or (ii) being used by a communications common carrier in the ordinary course of its business, or by an investigative or law enforcement officer in the ordinary course of his duties; or

 (B) a hearing aid or similar device being used to correct subnormal hearing to not better than normal;

* * * * *

(6) the term "contents", when used with respect to any wire or oral communication, includes any information concerning the identity of the parties to the communication or the existence, substance, purport, or meaning of that communication;

* * * * *

APPENDIX B — STATE STATUTES

(9) the term "aggrieved person" means a person who was a party to any intercepted wire or oral communication or a person against whom the interception was directed;

(10) the term "communication common carrier" has the same meaning which is given the term "common carrier" by section 3(h) of the Communications Act of 1934 (47 U.S.C. 153(h));

* * * * *

§ 23-542. Interception or disclosure of wire or oral communication.

(a) Except as otherwise specifically provided in this subchapter, any person who in the District of Columbia —

(1) willfully intercepts, endeavors to intercept, or procures any other person to intercept or endeavor to intercept any wire or oral communication;

(2) willfully discloses or endeavors to disclose to any other person the contents of any wire or oral communication, or evidence derived therefrom, knowing or having reason to know that the information was obtained through the interception of a wire or oral communication; or

(3) willfully uses or endeavors to use the contents of any wire or oral communication, or evidence derived therefrom, knowing or having reason to know, that the information was obtained through the interception of a wire or oral communication; shall be fined not more than $10,000 or imprisoned not more than five years, or both; except that paragraphs (2) and (3) of this subsection shall not apply to the contents of any wire or oral communication, or evidence derived therefrom, that has become common knowledge or public information.

(b) It shall not be unlawful under this section for —

* * * * *

(3) a person not acting under color of law to intercept a wire or oral communication, where such person is a party to the communication, or where one of the parties to the communication has given prior consent to such interception, unless such communication is intercepted for the purpose of committing any criminal or tortious act in violation of the Constitution or laws of the United States, any State, or the District of Columbia, or for the purpose of committing any other injurious act.

§ 23-554. Recovery of civil damages.

(a) Any person whose wire or oral communication is intercepted, disclosed, or used in violation of this subchapter shall —

(1) have a civil cause of action against any person who intercepts, discloses, or uses, or procures any other person to intercept, disclose, or use, such communications; and

(2) be entitled to recover from any such person —

(A) actual damages, but not less than liquidated damages computed at the rate of $100 a day for each day of violation, or $1,000 whichever is higher;

(B) punitive damages; and

(C) a reasonable attorney's fee and other litigation costs reasonably incurred.

* * * * *

Florida

§ 934.02. Definitions.

As used in this chapter:

(1) "Wire communication" means any aural transfer made in whole or in part through the use of facilities for the transmission of communications by the aid of wire, cable, or other like connection between the point of origin and the point of reception including the use of such connection in a switching station furnished or operated by any person engaged in providing or operating such facilities for the transmission of intrastate, interstate, or foreign communications or communications affecting intrastate, interstate, or foreign commerce. Such term includes any electronic storage of such communication but does not include the radio portion of a cordless telephone communication that is transmitted between the cordless telephone handset and the base unit.

(2) "Oral communication" means any oral communication uttered by a person exhibiting an expectation that such communication is not subject to interception under circumstances justifying such expectation and does not mean any public oral communication uttered at a public meeting or any electronic communication.

(3) "Intercept" means the aural or other acquisition of the contents of any wire, electronic, or oral communication through the use of any electronic, mechanical, or other device.

(4) "Electronic, mechanical, or other device" means any device or apparatus which can be used to intercept a wire, electronic, or oral communication other than:

  (a) Any telephone or telegraph instrument, equipment, or facility, or any component thereof:

    1. Furnished to the subscriber or user by a provider of wire or electronic communication service in the ordinary course of its business and being used by the subscriber or user in the ordinary course of its business or furnished by such subscriber or user for connection to the facilities of such service and used in the ordinary course of its business; or

    2. Being used by a communications common carrier in the ordinary course of its business or by an investigative or law enforcement officer in the ordinary course of her or his duties.

  (b) A hearing aid or similar device being used to correct subnormal hearing to not better than normal.

(5) "Person" means any employee or agent of the State of Florida or political subdivision thereof, of the United States, or of any other state or political subdivision thereof, and any individual, partnership, association, joint stock company, trust, or corporation.

* * * * *

(7) "Contents," when used with respect to any wire, oral, or electronic communication, includes any information concerning the substance, purport, or meaning of that communication.

* * * * *

(9) "Aggrieved person" means a person who was a party to any intercepted wire, oral, or electronic communication or a person against whom the interception was directed.

* * * * *

APPENDIX B — STATE STATUTES

(11) "Communication common carrier" shall have the same meaning which is given the term "common carrier" in 47 U.S.C. § 153(h).

(12) "Electronic communication" means any transfer of signs, signals, writing, images, sounds, data, or intelligence of any nature transmitted in whole or in part by a wire, radio, electromagnetic, photoelectronic, or photo-optical system that affects intrastate, interstate, or foreign commerce, but does not include:

(a) The radio portion of a cordless telephone communication that is transmitted between the cordless telephone handset and the base unit;

(b) Any wire or oral communication;

(c) Any communication made through a tone-only paging device; or

(d) Any communication from an electronic or mechanical device which permits the tracking of the movement of a person or an object.

(13) "User" means any person or entity who:

(a) Uses an electronic communication service, and

(b) Is duly authorized by the provider of such service to engage in such use.

(14) "Electronic communications system" means any wire, radio, electromagnetic, photo-optical, or photoelectronic facilities for the transmission of electronic communications, and any computer facilities or related electronic equipment for the electronic storage of such communications.

(15) "Electronic communication service" means any service which provides to users thereof the ability to send or receive wire or electronic communications.

(16) "Readily accessible to the general public" means, with respect to a radio communication, that such communication is not:

(a) Scrambled or encrypted;

(b) Transmitted using modulation techniques whose essential parameters have been withheld from the public with the intention of preserving the privacy of such communication;

(c) Carried on a subcarrier or other signal subsidiary to a radio transmission;

(d) Transmitted over a communications system provided by a common carrier, unless the communication is a tone-only paging system communication; or

(e) Transmitted on frequencies allocated under part 25; subpart D, subpart E or subpart F of part 74; or part 94 of the Rules of the Federal Communications Commission, unless, in the case of a communication transmitted on a frequency allocated under part 74 that is not exclusively allocated to broadcast auxiliary services, the communication is a two-way voice communication by radio.

(17) "Electronic storage" means:

(a) Any temporary intermediate storage of a wire or electronic communication incidental to the electronic transmission thereof.

(b) Any storage of a wire or electronic communication by an electronic communication service for purposes of backup protection of such communication.

(18) "Aural transfer" means a transfer containing the human voice at any point between and including the point of origin and the point of reception.

(19) "Remote computing service" means the provision to the public of computer storage or processing services by means of an electronic communications system.

* * * * *

§ 934.03. Interception and disclosure of wire, oral, or electronic communications.

(1) Except as otherwise specifically provided in this chapter, any person who:

(a) Intentionally intercepts, endeavors to intercept, or procures any other person to intercept or endeavor to intercept any wire, oral, or electronic communication;

(b) Intentionally uses, endeavors to use, or procures any other person to use or endeavor to use any electronic, mechanical, or other device to intercept any oral communication when:

1. Such device is affixed to, or otherwise transmits a signal through, a wire, cable, or other like connection used in wire communication; or

2. Such device transmits communications by radio or interferes with the transmission of such communication;

(c) Intentionally discloses, or endeavors to disclose, to any other person the contents of any wire, oral, or electronic communication, knowing or having reason to know that the information was obtained through the interception of a wire, oral, or electronic communication in violation of this subsection; or

(d) Intentionally uses, or endeavors to use, the contents of any wire, oral, or electronic communication, knowing or having reason to know that the information was obtained through the interception of a wire, oral, or electronic communication in violation of this subsection; shall be punished as provided in subsection (4).

* * * * *

(2)(d) It is lawful under §§ 934.03-934.09 for a person to intercept a wire, oral, or electronic communication when all of the parties to the communication have given prior consent to such interception.

* * * * *

(h) It shall not be unlawful under §§ 934.03-934.09 for any person:

1. To intercept or access an electronic communication made through an electronic communication system that is configured so that such electronic communication is readily accessible to the general public.

2. To intercept any radio communication which is transmitted:

a. By any station for the use of the general public, or that relates to ships, aircraft, vehicles, or persons in distress;

b. By any governmental, law enforcement, civil defense, private land mobile, or public safety communications system, including any police or fire communications system, readily accessible to the general public;

c. By a station operating on an authorized frequency within the bands allocated to the amateur, citizens band, or general mobile radio services; or

d. By any marine or aeronautical communications system.

3. To engage in any conduct which:

a. Is prohibited by § 633 of the Communications Act of 1934; or

b. Is excepted from the application of § 705(a) of the Communications Act of 1934 by § 705(b) of that act.

* * * * *

(4)(a) Except as provided in paragraph (b), whoever violates subsection (1) is

APPENDIX B — STATE STATUTES

guilty of a felony of the third degree, punishable as provided in § 775.082, § 775.083, § 775.084 or § 934.41.

(b) If the offense is a first offense under paragraph (a) and is not for any tortious or illegal purpose or for purposes of direct or indirect commercial advantage or private commercial gain, and the wire or electronic communication with respect to which the offense under paragraph (a) was committed is a radio communication that is not scrambled or encrypted:

1. If the communication is not the radio portion of a cellular telephone communication, a public land mobile radio service communication, or a paging service communication, and the conduct is not that described in subparagraph (2)(h)7., the person committing the offense is guilty of a misdemeanor of the first degree, punishable as provided in § 775.082 or § 775.083.

2. If the communication is the radio portion of a cellular telephone communication, a public land mobile radio service communication, or a paging service communication, the person committing the offense is guilty of a misdemeanor of the second degree, punishable as provided in § 775.082 or § 775.083.

§ 934.10. Civil remedies.

(1) Any person whose wire, oral, or electronic communication is intercepted, disclosed, or used in violation of §§ 934.03-934.09 shall have a civil cause of action against any person or entity who intercepts, discloses, or uses, or procures any other person or entity to intercept, disclose, or use, such communications and shall be entitled to recover from any such person or entity which engaged in that violation such relief as may be appropriate, including:

(a) Preliminary or equitable or declaratory relief as may be appropriate;

(b) Actual damages, but not less than liquidated damages computed at the rate of $100 a day for each day of violation or $1,000, whichever is higher;

(c) Punitive damages; and

(d) A reasonable attorney's fee and other litigation costs reasonably incurred.

(2) A good faith reliance on:

(a) A court order, subpoena, or legislative authorization as provided in §§ 934.03-934.09, or

(b) A good faith determination that federal or Florida law permitted the conduct complained of shall constitute a complete defense to any civil or criminal, or administrative action arising out of such conduct under the laws of this state.

(3) A civil action under this section may not be commenced later than 2 years after the date upon which the claimant first has a reasonable opportunity to discover the violation.

Georgia

§ 16-11-60. Definitions.

As used within this part, the term:

(1) "Device" means an instrument or apparatus used for overhearing, recording, intercepting, or transmitting sounds or for observing, photographing, recording, or transmitting visual images and which involves in its operation electricity, electronics, infrared, laser or similar beams, but not including merely focusing, lighting, illuminating equipment, optical magnifying equipment, or a device commonly referred to as an "individual

hearing aid," and not including a "pen register" or "trap and trace device" as defined in this Code section.

* * * * *

(3) "Private place" means a place where one is entitled reasonably to expect to be safe from casual or hostile intrusion or surveillance.

* * * * *

§ 16-11-62. Eavesdropping.

It shall be unlawful for:

(1) Any person in a clandestine manner intentionally to overhear, transmit, or record or attempt to overhear, transmit, or record the private conversation of another which shall originate in any private place;

(2) Any person, through the use of any instrument or apparatus, without the consent of all persons observed, to observe, photograph, or record the activities of another which occur in any private place and out of public view; provided, however, that it shall not be unlawful to use any camera, photographic equipment, videotape equipment, or other devices to observe, photograph, or record the activities of persons incarcerated in any jail, correctional institution, or any other facility in which persons who are charged with or who have been convicted of the commission of a crime are incarcerated, provided that such equipment shall not be used while the prisoner is discussing his case with his attorney;

(3) Any person to go on or about the premises of another or any private place for the purpose of invading the privacy of others by eavesdropping upon their conversations or secretly observing their activities;

(4) Any person intentionally and secretly to intercept by the use of any device, instrument, or apparatus the contents of a message sent by telephone, telegraph, letter, or by any other means of private communication;

(5) Any person to divulge to any unauthorized person or authority the content or substance of any private message intercepted lawfully in the manner provided for in Code Section 16-11-65; or

(6) Any person to commit any other acts of a nature similar to those set out in paragraphs (1) through (5) of this Code section which invade the privacy of another.

§ 16-11-66. Interception of wire, oral, or electronic communication by party thereto.

(a) Nothing in Code Section 16-11-62 shall prohibit a person from intercepting a wire, oral, or electronic communication where such person is a party to the communication or one of the parties to the communication has given prior consent to such interception.

* * * * *

§ 16-11-66.1. Interception of cellular radio telephone communications.

(a) As used in this Code section, the term "cellular radio telephone" means a wireless telephone authorized by the Federal Communications Commission to operate in the frequency bandwidth reserved for cellular radio telephones.

APPENDIX B — STATE STATUTES

(b)(1) It shall be unlawful for any person, without the consent of at least one of the parties to the communication, intentionally to intercept, receive, or assist in intercepting or receiving a communication transmitted between cellular radio telephones or between any cellular radio telephone and a landline telephone.

(2) It shall be unlawful for any person to broadcast, print, or publish the contents of any communication transmitted between cellular radio telephones or between any cellular radio telephone and a landline telephone if the communication has been intercepted in violation of paragraph (1) of this subsection.

* * * * *

(d) Any person convicted of violating paragraph (1) or paragraph (2) of subsection (b) of this Code section shall be guilty of a misdemeanor of a high and aggravated nature.

§ 16-11-69. Penalty.

Except as otherwise provided in subsection (d) of Code Section 16-11-66.1, any person violating any of the provisions of this part shall be guilty of a felony and, upon conviction thereof, shall be punished by imprisonment for not less than one nor more than five years or a fine not to exceed $10,000.00, or both.

Hawaii

§ 803-41. Definitions.

In this part:

"Aggrieved person" means a person who was party to any intercepted wire, oral, or electronic communication or a person against whom the interception was directed.

"Aural transfer" means a transfer containing the human voice at any point between and including the point of origin and the point of reception.

"Contents" when used with respect to any wire, oral, or electronic communication, includes any information concerning the substance, purport, or meaning of that communication.

"Electronic communication" means any transfer of signs, signals, writing, images, sounds, data, or intelligence of any nature transmitted in whole or in part by a wire, radio, electromagnetic, photoelectronic, or photo-optical system that affects intrastate, interstate, or foreign commerce. The term "electronic communication" includes, but is not limited to, "display pagers" which can display visual message as part of the paging process, but does not include:

(1) The radio portion of a cordless telephone communication that is transmitted between the cordless telephone handset and the base unit;

(2) Any wire or oral communication;

(3) Any communication made through a tone-only paging device; or

(4) Any communication from a tracking device.

"Electronic communication system" means any wire, radio, electromagnetic, photo-optical, or photoelectronic facilities for the transmission of electronic communications, and any computer facilities or related electronic equipment for the electronic storage of such communications.

"Electronic, mechanical, or other device" means any device or apparatus which can be used to intercept a wire, oral, or electronic communication other than:

(1) Any telephone or telegraph instrument, equipment or facility, or any component thereof, (A) furnished to the subscriber or user by a provider of wire or electronic communication service in the ordinary course of its business and being used by the subscriber or user in the ordinary course of its business or furnished by such subscriber or user for connection to the facilities of such services and used in the ordinary course of its business; or (B) being used by a provider of wire or electronic communication service in the ordinary course of its business, or by an investigative or law enforcement officer in the ordinary course of the officer's duties; or

(2) A hearing aid or similar device being used to correct subnormal hearing to not better than normal.

"Electronic storage" means:

(1) Any temporary, intermediate storage of a wire or electronic communication incidental to the electronic transmission thereof; and

(2) Any storage of such communication by an electronic communication service for purposes of backup protection of such communication.

"Intercept" means the aural or other acquisition of the contents of any wire, electronic, or oral communication through the use of any electronic, mechanical, or other device.

"Investigative or law enforcement officer" means any officer of the State or political subdivision thereof, who is empowered by the law of this State to conduct investigations of or to make arrests for offenses enumerated in this part.

"Oral communication" means any oral communication uttered by a person exhibiting an expectation that such communication is not subject to interception under circumstances justifying such expectation, but such term does not include any electronic communication.

* * * * *

"Person" means any official, employee, or agent of the United States or this State or political subdivision thereof, and any individual, partnership, association, joint stock company, trust, or corporation.

"Readily accessible to the general public" means, with respect to radio communication, that such communication is not:

(1) Scrambled or encrypted;

(2) Transmitted using modulation techniques whose essential parameters have been withheld from the public with the intention of preserving the privacy of such communication;

(3) Carried on a subcarrier or other signal subsidiary to a radio transmission;

(4) Transmitted over a communication system provided by a common carrier, unless the communication is a tone-only paging system communication; or

(5) Transmitted on frequencies allocated under part 25, subpart D, E, or F of part 74 or part 94 of the Rules of the Federal Communications Commission, unless in the case of a communication transmitted on a frequency allocated to broadcast auxiliary services, the communication is a two-way voice communication by radio.

"Tracking device" means an electronic or mechanical device which permits the tracking of the movement of a person or object.

* * * * *

"User" means any person or entity who:

(1) Uses an electronic communication service; and

APPENDIX B — STATE STATUTES

(2) Is duly authorized by the provider of such service to engage in such use.

"Wire communication" means any aural transfer made in whole or in part through the use of facilities for the transmission of communications by the aid of wire, cable, or other like connection between the point of origin and the point of reception (including the use of such connection in a switching station) furnished or operated by any person engaged in providing or operating such facilities for the transmission of intrastate, interstate, or foreign communications. The term "wire communication" includes, but is not limited to, cellular telephones, cordless telephones, except for the radio portion of a cordless telephone communication that is transmitted between the cordless telephone handset and the base unit, "tone and voice" pagers which transmit a voice message along with a paging signal, and any electronic storage of a wire communication.

§ 803-42. Interception, use or disclosure of wire, oral, or electronic communications.

(a) Except as otherwise specifically provided in this part any person who:

(1) Intentionally intercepts, endeavors to intercept, or procures any other person to intercept or endeavor to intercept, any wire, oral, or electronic communication;

(2) Intentionally uses, endeavors to use, or procures any other person to use or endeavor to use any electronic, mechanical, or other device to intercept any wire, oral, or electronic communication;

(3) Intentionally discloses, or endeavors to disclose, to any other person the contents of any wire, oral, or electronic communication, knowing or having reason to know that the information was obtained through the interception of a wire, oral, or electronic communication in violation of this part;

(4) Intentionally uses, or endeavors to use, the contents of any wire, oral, or electronic communication, knowing or having reason to know that the information was obtained through the interception of a wire, oral, or electronic communication in violation of this part;

(5)(A) Intentionally accesses without authorization a facility through which an electronic communication service is provided; or

(B) Intentionally exceeds an authorization to access that facility; and thereby obtains, alters, or prevents authorized access to a wire or electronic communication while it is in electronic storage;

(6) Intentionally installs or uses a pen register or a trap and trace device without first obtaining a court order; or

(7) Intentionally installs or uses a mobile tracking device without first obtaining a search warrant or other order authorizing the installation and use of such device; shall be guilty of a class C felony.

* * * * *

(b)(3) It shall not be unlawful under this part for a person not acting under color of law to intercept a wire, oral, or electronic communication where such person is a party to the communication or where one of the parties to the communication has given prior consent to such interception unless such communication is intercepted for the purpose of committing any criminal or tortious act in violation of the Constitution or laws of the United States or of this State; provided that installation in any private place, without consent of the person or persons entitled to privacy therein, of any device for recording, amplifying, or broadcasting sounds or events in that place, or use of any such unauthorized installation, or installation or use outside a private place of such device to intercept sounds originating in that place which would not ordinarily be audible or comprehensible outside, without the consent of the person or persons entitled to privacy therein is prohibited.

(4) It shall not be unlawful under this part for a person acting under color of law to intercept a wire, oral, or electronic communication, when such person is a party to the communication or one of the parties to the communication has given prior consent to such interception.

* * * * *

(7) It shall not be unlawful under this part for any person:

(A) To intercept or access an electronic communication made through an electronic communication system configured so that such electronic communication is readily accessible to the general public.

(B) To intercept any radio communication which is transmitted:

(i) By any station for the use of the general public, or that relates to ships, aircraft, vehicles, or persons in distress;

(ii) By any governmental, law enforcement, civil defense, private land mobile, or public safety communications system, including police and fire, readily accessible to the general public;

(iii) By a station operating on an authorized frequency within the bands allocated to the amateur, citizens band, or general mobile radio services; or

(iv) By any marine or aeronautical communications system.

(C) To engage in any conduct which:

(i) Is prohibited by section 633 of the Communications Act of 1934; or

(ii) Is excepted from the application of section 705(a) of the Communications Act of 1934 by section 705(b) of that Act.

* * * * *

§ 803-48. Recovery of civil damages.

Any person whose wire, oral, or electronic communication is accessed, intercepted, disclosed, or used in violation of this part shall (1) have a civil cause of action against any person who accesses, intercepts, discloses, or uses, or procures any other person to access, intercept, disclose, or use such communications, and (2) be entitled to recover from any such person:

(A) The greater of (i) the sum of the actual damages suffered by the plaintiff and any profits made by the violator as a result of the violation, or (ii) statutory damages of whichever is the greater of $100 day for each day of violation or $10,000;

(B) Punitive damages, where appropriate; and

(C) A reasonable attorney's fee and other litigation costs reasonably incurred.

The aggrieved person may also seek and be awarded such preliminary, and other equitable or declaratory relief as may be appropriate. A good faith reliance on a court order shall constitute a complete defense to any civil action brought under this part.

APPENDIX B — STATE STATUTES

Idaho

§ 18-6701. Definitions.

Definitions as used in this chapter:

(1) "Wire communication" means any communication made in whole or in part through the use of facilities for the transmission of communications by the aid of wire, cable, or other like connection between the point of origin and the point of reception, furnished or operated by any person engaged as a common carrier in providing or operating such facilities for the transmission of intrastate, interstate or foreign communications.

(2) "Oral communication" means any oral communication uttered by a person under circumstances justifying an expectation that said communication is not subject to interception.

(3) "Intercept" means the aural acquisition of the contents of any wire or oral communication through the use of any electronic, mechanical, or other device.

(4) "Electronic, mechanical, or other device" means any device or apparatus which can be used to intercept a wire or oral communication other than:

(a) Any telephone or telegraph instrument, equipment or facility or any component thereof furnished to the subscriber or user by a communications common carrier in the ordinary course of its business and being used by the subscriber or user in the ordinary course of its business, or being used by a communications common carrier in the ordinary course of its business, or by an investigative or law enforcement officer in the ordinary course of his duties;

(b) A hearing aid or similar device being used to correct subnormal hearing to not better than normal;

(5) "Person" means any employee or agent of the state or political subdivision thereof and any individual, partnership, association, joint stock company, trust, cooperative, or corporation.

* * * * *

(7) "Contents" when used with respect to any wire or oral communication include any information concerning the identity of the parties to such communication or the existence, substance, purport, or meaning of that communication.

* * * * *

(9) "Aggrieved person" means a person who was a party to any illegally intercepted wire or oral communication or a person against whom the interception was illegally directed.

(10) "Communications common carrier" means any person engaged as a common carrier for hire, in intrastate, interstate or foreign communication by wire or radio, or in intrastate, interstate, or foreign radio transmission of energy.

§ 18-6702. Interception and disclosure of wire or oral communications prohibited.

(1) Except as otherwise specifically provided in this chapter, any person who:

(a) Willfully intercepts, endeavors to intercept, or procures any other person to intercept or endeavor to intercept any wire or oral communication; or

(b) Willfully uses, endeavors to use, or procures any other person to use or endeavor to use any electronic, mechanical, or other device to intercept any oral communication when:

   1. Such device is affixed to, or otherwise transmits a signal through, a wire, cable, or other like connection used in wire communication; or

   2. Such device transmits communications by radio or interferes with the transmission of such communication; or

(c) Willfully discloses, or endeavors to disclose, to any other person the contents of any wire or oral communication, knowing or having reason to know that the information was obtained through the interception of a wire or oral communication in violation of this subsection; or

(d) Willfully uses, or endeavors to use, the contents of any wire or oral communication, knowing or having reason to know that the information was obtained through the interception of a wire or oral communication in violation of this subsection shall be guilty of a felony and is punishable by imprisonment in the state prison for a term not to exceed five (5) years or by a fine not to exceed five thousand dollars ($5,000), or by both fine and imprisonment.

* * * * *

(2)(d) It is lawful under this chapter for a person to intercept a wire or oral communication when one of the parties to the communication have given prior consent to such interception.

* * * * *

§ 18-6709. Recovery of civil damages.

Any person whose wire or oral communication is intercepted, disclosed, or used in violation of this chapter shall have a civil cause of action against any person who intercepts, discloses, uses, or procures any other person to intercept, disclose, or use such communications, and shall be entitled to recover from any such person:

(a) Actual damages, but not less than liquidated damages computed at the rate of one hundred dollars ($100) a day for each day of violation or one thousand dollars ($1,000), whichever is higher;

(b) Punitive damages; and

(c) A reasonable attorney's fee and other litigation costs reasonably incurred.

* * * * *

Illinois

5/14-1. Definition.

(a) Eavesdropping device.

An eavesdropping device is any device capable of being used to hear or record oral conversation whether such conversation is conducted in person, by telephone, or by any other means; Provided, however, that this definition shall not include devices used for the restoration of the deaf or hard-of-hearing to normal or partial hearing.

(b) Eavesdropper.

APPENDIX B — STATE STATUTES

An eavesdropper is any person, including law enforcement officers, who operates or participates in the operation of any eavesdropping device contrary to the provisions of this Article.

(c) Principal.

A principal is any person who:

(1) Knowingly employs another who illegally uses an eavesdropping device in the course of such employment; or

(2) Knowingly derives any benefit or information from the illegal use of an eavesdropping device by another; or

(3) Directs another to use an eavesdropping device illegally on his behalf.

(d) Conversation.

For the purposes of this Article, the term conversation means any oral communication between 2 or more persons regardless of whether one or more of the parties intended their communication to be of a private nature under circumstances justifying that expectation.

5/14-2. Elements of the offense.

A person commits eavesdropping when he:

(a) Uses an eavesdropping device to hear or record all or any part of any conversation unless he does so (1) with the consent of all of the parties to such conversation or (2) in accordance with Article 108A or Article 108B of the "Code of Criminal Procedure of 1963", approved August 14, 1963, as amended; or

(b) Uses or divulges, except as authorized by this Article or by Article 108A or 108B of the "Code of Criminal Procedure of 1963", approved August 14, 1963, as amended, any information which he knows or reasonably should know was obtained through the use of an eavesdropping device.

* * * * *

5/14-3. Exemptions.

The following activities shall be exempt from the provisions of this Article:

(a) Listening to radio, wireless and television communications of any sort where the same are publicly made;

* * * * *

(c) Any broadcast by radio, television or otherwise whether it be a broadcast or recorded for the purpose of later broadcasts of any function where the public is in attendance and the conversations are overheard incidental to the main purpose for which such broadcasts are then being made;

(d) Recording or listening with the aid of any device to any emergency communication made in the normal course of operations by any federal, state or local law enforcement agency or institutions dealing in emergency services, including, but not limited to, hospitals, clinics, ambulance services, fire fighting agencies, any public utility, emergency repair facility, civilian defense establishment or military installation;

(e) Recording the proceedings of any meeting required to be open by the Open Meetings Act, as amended;

* * * * *

(i) Recording of a conversation made by or at the request of a person, not a law enforcement officer or agent of a law enforcement officer, who is a party to the conversation, under reasonable suspicion that another party to the conversation is committing, is about to commit, or has committed a criminal offense against the person or a member of his or her immediate household, and there is reason to believe that evidence of the criminal offense may be obtained by the recording.

* * * * *

5/14-4. Sentence.

Eavesdropping, for a first offense, is a Class 4 felony, and, for a second or subsequent offense, is a Class 3 felony.

5/14-6. Civil remedies.

(1) Any or all parties to any conversation upon which eavesdropping is practiced contrary to this Article shall be entitled to the following remedies:

   (a) To an injunction by the circuit court prohibiting further eavesdropping by the eavesdropper and by or on behalf of his principal, or either;

   (b) To all actual damages against the eavesdropper or his principal or both;

   (c) To any punitive damages which may be awarded by the court or by a jury;

   (d) To all actual damages against any landlord, owner or building operator, or any common carrier by wire who aids, abets, or knowingly permits the eavesdropping concerned;

   (e) To any punitive damages which may be awarded by the court or by a jury against any landlord, owner or building operator, or common carrier by wire who aids, abets, or knowingly permits the eavesdropping concerned.

* * * * *

Indiana

§ 35-33.5-1-2. Applicability of definitions.

The definitions in this chapter apply throughout this article.

§ 35-33.5-1-3. "Designated offense" defined.

"Designated offense" means the following:

(1) A Class A, Class B, or Class C felony that is a controlled substance offense (IC 35-48-4).

(2) Murder (IC 35-42-1-1), while committing or attempting to commit a controlled substance offense under IC 35-48-4-1 through IC 35-48-4-4.

§ 35-33.5-1-4. "Extension" defined.

"Extension" means an extension of the duration for which a warrant remains effective under this article.

APPENDIX B — STATE STATUTES

§ 35-33.5-1-5. "Interception" defined.

"Interception" means the intentional:
(1) recording of; or
(2) acquisition of the contents of;
a telephonic or telegraphic communication by a person other than a sender or receiver of that communication, without the consent of the sender or receiver, by means of any instrument, device, or equipment under this article. This term includes the intentional recording of communication through the use of a computer or a FAX (facsimile transmission) machine.

§ 35-33.5-1-6. "Warrant" defined.

"Warrant" means a warrant authorizing the interception of telephonic or telegraphic communication under this article.

§ 35-33.5-5-4. Civil cause of action.

(a) A person whose communications are intercepted, disclosed, or used in violation of this article:
    (1) has a civil cause of action against a person who intercepts, discloses, uses, or procures another person to intercept, disclose, or use a communication in violation of this article; and
    (2) is entitled to recover from that person the following:
        (A) The greater of:
            (i) actual damages;
            (ii) liquidated damages computed at a rate of one hundred dollars ($100) each day for each day of violation; or
            (iii) one thousand dollars ($1,000).
        (B) Court costs.
        (C) Punitive damages, when determined to be appropriate by the court.
        (D) Reasonable attorney's fees.

(b) A good faith reliance on a warrant or an extension issued under this article constitutes a complete defense to a civil action brought under this section.

(c) A person described in IC 34-46-4-1 has an affirmative defense under this section if the person was unaware that the communication was intercepted in violation of this article and:
    (1) has not intercepted the communication;
    (2) has not procured another person to intercept or disclose the communication; and
    (3) has used a communication for the purpose of assisting the person to independently confirm information contained in a communication.

(d) An action under this section must be brought within two (2) years after the date that the interception, disclosure, or use of a communication in violation of this article initially occurs whichever is later.

Iowa

§ 727.8. Electronic and mechanical eavesdropping.

Any person, having no right or authority to do so, who taps into or connects a listening or recording device to any telephone or other communication wire, or who by any electronic or mechanical means listens to, records, or otherwise intercepts a conversation or communication of any kind, commits a serious misdemeanor; provided, that the sender or recipient of a message or one who is openly present and participating in or listening to a communication shall not be prohibited hereby from recording such message or communication; and further provided, that nothing herein shall restrict the use of any radio or television receiver to receive any communication transmitted by radio or wireless signal.

§ 808B.1. Definitions.

As used in this chapter, unless the context otherwise requires:

1. "Aggrieved person" means a person who was a party to an intercepted wire communication or oral communication or a person against whom the interception was directed.

2. "Contents" when used with respect to a wire communication or oral communication, includes any information concerning the identity of the parties to the communication or the existence, substance, purpose, or meaning of that communication.

3. "Court" means a district court in this state.

4. "Electronic, mechanical, or other device" means a device or apparatus which can be used to intercept a wire communication or oral communication other than either of the following:

    a. A telephone or telegraph instrument, equipment, or facility, or any component of it which is either of the following:

        (1) Furnished to the subscriber or user by a communications common carrier in the ordinary course of its business and being used by the subscriber or user in the ordinary course of the subscriber's or user's business.

        (2) Being used by a communications common carrier in the ordinary course of its business, or by an investigative or law enforcement officer in the ordinary course of the officer's duties.

    b. A hearing aid or similar device being used to correct subnormal hearing to not better than normal hearing.

5. "Intercept" or "interception" means the aural acquisition of the contents of a wire communication or oral communication through the use of an electronic, mechanical, or other device.

* * * * *

7. "Oral communication" means an oral communication uttered by a person exhibiting an expectation that the communication is not subject to interception, under circumstances justifying that expectation.

* * * * *

9. "Wire communication" means a communication made in whole or in part through the use of facilities for the transmission of communications by the aid of wire, cable, or other like connection between the point of origin and the point of reception, furnished or

operated by a person engaged as a common carrier in providing or operating the facilities for the transmission of communications.

§ 808B.2. Unlawful acts.

1. Except as otherwise specifically provided in this chapter, a person who does any of the following commits a class "D" felony:

    a. Willfully intercepts, endeavors to intercept, or procures any other person to intercept or endeavor to intercept, a wire communication or oral communication.

    b. Willfully uses, endeavors to use, or procures any other person to use or endeavor to use an electronic, mechanical, or other device to intercept any oral communication when either of the following applies:

        (1) The device is affixed to, or otherwise transmits a signal through, a wire, cable, or other like connection used in wire communication.

        (2) The device transmits communications by radio, or interferes with the transmission of radio communications.

    c. Willfully discloses, or endeavors to disclose, to any other person the contents of a wire communication or oral communication, knowing or having reason to know that the information was obtained through the interception of a wire communication or oral communication in violation of this subsection.

    d. Willfully uses, or endeavors to use, the contents of a wire communication or oral communication, knowing or having reason to know that the information was obtained through the interception of a wire communication or oral communication in violation of this subsection.

* * * * *

2. c. It is not unlawful under this chapter for a person not acting under color of law to intercept a wire communication or oral communication if the person is a party to the communication or if one of the parties to the communication has given prior consent to the interception, unless the communication is intercepted for the purpose of committing a criminal or tortious act in violation of the Constitution or laws of the United States or of any state or for the purpose of committing any other injurious act.

* * * * *

§ 808B.8. Civil damages.

1. A person whose wire communication or oral communication is intercepted, disclosed, or used in violation of this chapter shall:

    a. Have a civil cause of action against any person who intercepts, discloses, or uses or procures any other person to intercept, disclose, or use such communications.

    b. Be entitled to recover from any such person all of the following:

        (1) Actual damages, but not less than liquidated damages computed at the rate of one hundred dollars a day for each day of violation, or one thousand dollars, whichever is higher.

        (2) Punitive damages upon a finding of a willful, malicious, or reckless violation of this chapter.

        (3) A reasonable attorney's fee and other litigation costs reasonably incurred.

* * * * *

3. A person whose wire communication or oral communication is intercepted, disclosed, or used in violation of this chapter may seek an injunction, either temporary or permanent, against any person who violates this chapter.

Kansas

§ 21-4001. Eavesdropping.

(a) Eavesdropping is knowingly and without lawful authority:

(1) Entering into a private place with intent to listen surreptitiously to private conversations or to observe the personal conduct of any other person or persons therein;

(2) Installing or using outside a private place any device for hearing, recording, amplifying or broadcasting sounds originating in such place, which sounds would not ordinarily be audible or comprehensible outside, without the consent of the person or persons entitled to privacy therein; or

(3) Installing or using any device or equipment for the interception of any telephone, telegraph or other wire communication without the consent of the person in possession or control of the facilities for such wire communication.

(b) A "private place" within the meaning of this section is a place where one may reasonably expect to be safe from uninvited intrusion or surveillance, but does not include a place to which the public has lawful access.

* * * * *

(d) Eavesdropping is a class A nonperson misdemeanor.

§ 21-4002. Breach of privacy.

(a) Breach of privacy is knowingly and without lawful authority:

(1) Intercepting, without the consent of the sender or receiver, a message by telephone, telegraph, letter or other means of private communication; or

(2) Divulging, without the consent of the sender or receiver, the existence or contents of such message if such person knows that the message was illegally intercepted, or if such person illegally learned of the message in the course of employment with an agency in transmitting it.

(b) Subsection (a)(1) shall not apply to messages overheard through a regularly installed instrument on a telephone party line or on an extension.

(c) Breach of privacy is a class A nonperson misdemeanor.

Kentucky

§ 526.010. Definition.

The following definition applies in this chapter, unless the context otherwise requires:

"Eavesdrop" means to overhear, record, amplify or transmit any part of a wire or oral communication of others without the consent of at least one (1) party thereto by means of any electronic, mechanical or other device.

§ 526.020. Eavesdropping.

(1) A person is guilty of eavesdropping when he intentionally uses any device to eavesdrop, whether or not he is present at the time.
(2) Eavesdropping is a Class D felony.

§ 526.030. Installing Eavesdropping Device.

(1) A person is guilty of installing an eavesdropping device when he intentionally installs or places such a device in any place with the knowledge that it is to be used for eavesdropping.
(2) Installing an eavesdropping device is a Class D felony.

§ 526.070. Exceptions.

A person is not guilty under this chapter when he:
(1) Inadvertently overhears the communication through a regularly installed telephone party line or on a telephone extension but does not divulge it;

* * * * *

Louisiana

§ 322. Wire-tapping prohibited.

No person shall tap or attach any devices for the purpose of listening in on wires, cables, or property owned and used by any person, for the transmission of intelligence by magnetic telephone or telegraph, without the consent of the owner.

Whoever violates this Section shall be fined not less than ten dollars nor more than three hundred dollars, or imprisoned for not more than three months.

This Section shall not be construed to prevent officers of the law, while in the actual discharge of their duties, from tapping in on wires or cables for the purpose of obtaining information to detect crime.

§ 1301. Short title.

This Chapter may be cited and referred to as the "Electronic Surveillance Act".

§ 1302. Definitions.

As used in this Chapter:
(1) "Aggrieved person" means a person who was party to any intercepted wire or oral communication or a person against whom the interception was directed.

* * * * *

(3) "Aural transfer" means a transfer containing the human voice at any point between and including the point of origin and the point of reception.
(4) "Communications common carrier" means any person engaged as a common carrier for hire in communication by wire or radio; however, a person engaged in commercial radio broadcasting which is supervised by the Federal Communications Commission shall not, insofar as such person is so engaged, be deemed a common carrier.

(5) "Contents" when used with respect to any wire, electronic, or oral communication includes any information concerning the substance, purport, or meaning of that communication.

* * * * *

(7)(a) "Electronic communication" means any transfer of signs, signals, writings, images, sounds, data, or intelligence of any nature transmitted in whole or in part by a wire, radio, electromagnetic, photoelectronic, or photo-optical system, but does not include any of the following:

(i) Any oral communication.

(ii) Any communication made through a tone-only paging device.

(iii) Any communication from a tracking device used to locate a mobile object by emission of a sound signal.

(b) "Electronic communication" specifically includes the radio portion of a cordless, portable, or cellular telephone communication that is transmitted between the cordless, portable, or cellular handset and the base or transmitting tower or unit.

(8) "Electronic communications service" means any service which provides to users thereof the ability to send or receive wire or electronic communications.

(9) "Electronic communications system" means any wire, radio, electromagnetic, photo-optical, or photoelectronic facilities used for the transmission of wire or electronic communications, and any computer facilities or related electronic equipment for the electronic storage of such communication.

(10) "Electronic, mechanical, or other device or means" denotes any device or apparatus which can be used to intercept a wire, electronic, or oral communication other than:

(a) Any telephone or telegraph instrument, equipment, or facility, or any component thereof, either:

(i) Furnished to the subscriber or user by a communications common carrier in the ordinary course of its business and being used by the subscriber or user in the ordinary course of its business, or

(ii) Being used by a communications common carrier in the ordinary course of its business, or by an investigative or law enforcement officer in the ordinary course of his duties.

(b) A hearing aid or similar device being used to correct subnormal hearing to not better than normal.

(11) "Intercept" means the aural acquisition of the contents of any wire or oral communication through the use of any electronic, mechanical, or other device.

* * * * *

(14) "Oral communication" means any oral communication uttered by a person exhibiting an expectation that such communication is not subject to interception under circumstances justifying such expectation, but such term does not include any electronic communication.

* * * * *

(16) "Person" means any employee or agent of the state or a political subdivision thereof, and any individual, partnership, association, joint stock company, trust, or corporation.

APPENDIX B — STATE STATUTES

* * * * *

(18) "Wire communication" or "communication by wire" means any aural transfer made in whole or in part through the use of facilities used for the transmission of communications by aid of wire, cable, or other like connection between the points of origin and reception, including the use of such connection in a switching station, furnished or operated by any person licensed to engage in providing or operating such facilities for the transmission of communications and such term includes any electronic storage of such communication, and such term includes the radio portion of a cordless, portable, or cellular telephone communication that is transmitted between the cordless, portable, or cellular handset and the base or transmitting tower or unit.

§ 1303. Interception use and disclosure of wire, electronic, or oral communications.

A. Except as otherwise specifically provided in this Chapter, it shall be unlawful for any person to:

(1) Willfully intercept, endeavor to intercept, or procure any other person to intercept or endeavor to intercept, any wire or oral communication;

(2) Willfully use, endeavor to use, or procure any other person to use or endeavor to use, any electronic, mechanical, or other device to intercept any oral communication when:

    (a) Such device is affixed to, or otherwise transmits a signal through, a wire, cable, or other like connection used in wire communication; or

    (b) Such device transmits communications by radio or interferes with the transmission of such communication;

(3) Willfully disclose, or endeavor to disclose, to any other person the contents of any wire or oral communication, knowing or having reason to know that the information was obtained through the interception of a wire or oral communication in violation of this Subsection; or

(4) Willfully use, or endeavor to use, the contents of any wire or oral communication, knowing or having reason to know that the information was obtained through the interception of a wire or oral communication in violation of this Subsection.

B. Any person who violates the provisions of this Section shall be fined not more than ten thousand dollars and imprisoned for not less than two years nor more than ten years at hard labor, without benefit of probation, parole, or suspension of sentence.

* * * * *

C. (4) It shall not be unlawful under this Chapter for a person not acting under color of law to intercept a wire or oral communication where such person is a party to the communication or where one of the parties to the communication has given prior consent to such interception, unless such communication is intercepted for the purpose of committing any criminal or tortious act in violation of the constitution or laws of the United States or of the state or for the purpose of committing any other injurious act.

* * * * *

§ 1312. Recovery of civil damages.

A. Any person whose wire or oral communication is intercepted, disclosed, or used in violation of this Chapter shall have a civil cause of action against any person who intercepts, discloses, or uses, or procures any other person to intercept, disclose, or use such communications, and be entitled to recover from any such person:

(1) Actual damages, but not less than liquidated damages computed at the rate of one hundred dollars a day for each day of violation or one thousand dollars, whichever is greater.

(2) A reasonable attorney's fee and other litigation costs reasonably incurred.

(3) Punitive damages.

* * * * *

Maine

Title 15, § 709. Definitions

The following words and phrases as used in this chapter, unless the context otherwise indicates, shall have the following meanings.

1. Communication common carrier. "Communication common carrier" means any telephone or telegraph company.

* * * * *

2. Contents. "Contents," when used with respect to any wire or oral communication, means any information concerning the identity of the parties to such communication or the existence, contents, substance, purport or meaning of that communication.

3. Intercepting device. "Intercepting device" means any device or apparatus which can be used to intercept a wire or oral communication other than:

A. Any telephone or telegraph instrument, equipment or facility or any component thereof being used by a communication common carrier in the ordinary course of its business or extension telephones used by a subscriber to telephone service; or

B. A hearing aid or similar device being used to correct subnormal hearing to not better than normal.

4. Intercept. "Intercept" means to hear, record or aid another to hear or record the contents of any wire or oral communication through the use of any intercepting device by any person other than:

A. The sender or receiver of that communication;

B. A person within the range of normal unaided hearing or subnormal hearing corrected to not better than normal; or

C. A person given prior authority by the sender or receiver.

* * * * *

5. Oral communications. "Oral communications" means any oral communications uttered by a person exhibiting an expectation that such communication is not subject to interception under circumstances justifying such expectation.

6. Person. "Person" means any individual, partnership, association, joint stock company, trust or corporation, or any other legal entity, whether or not any of the foregoing is

APPENDIX B — STATE STATUTES

an officer, agent or employee of the United States, a state or a political subdivision of a state.

7. Wire communication. "Wire communication" means any communication made in whole or in part through the use of facilities for transmission of communications by the aid of wire, cable or other like connection between the point of origin and the point of reception.

§ 710. Offenses.

1. Interception, oral communications prohibited. Any person, other than an employee of a common carrier as defined in this chapter, a law enforcement officer or an investigative officer as defined in this chapter, carrying out practices otherwise permitted by this chapter, who intentionally or knowingly intercepts, attempts to intercept or procures any other person to intercept or attempt to intercept, any wire or oral communication is guilty of a Class C crime.

* * * * *

3. Disclosure, or use of wire or oral communications prohibited. A person is guilty of a Class C crime if he:

    A. Intentionally or knowingly discloses or attempts to disclose to any person the contents of any wire or oral communication, knowing that the information was obtained through interception; or

    B. Intentionally or knowingly uses or attempts to use the contents of any wire or oral communication, knowing that the information was obtained through interception.

* * * * *

5. Possession of interception devices prohibited. A person, other than an employee of a common carrier as defined in this chapter, a law enforcement officer or an investigative officer as defined in this chapter, carrying out practices otherwise permitted by this chapter, who has in his possession any device, contrivance, machine or apparatus designed or commonly used for intercepting wire or oral communications defined in this chapter, is guilty of a Class C crime.

* * * * *

§ 711. Civil remedy.

Any party to a conversation intercepted, disclosed or used in violation of this chapter shall have a civil cause of action against any person who intercepts, discloses or uses such communications and shall be entitled to recover from any such persons:

1. Damages. Actual damages, but not less than liquidated damages, computed at the rate of $100 per day for each day of violation; and

2. Attorney's fee. A reasonable attorney's fee and other litigation disbursements reasonably incurred.

§ 712. Exceptions.

1. Switchboard operators, communication common carrier agent. It is not a violation of this chapter for an operator of a switchboard or an officer, employee or agent of any communication common carrier, as defined in this chapter, to intercept, disclose or use

that communication in the normal course of employment while engaged in any activity which is a necessary incident to the rendition of service or to the protection of the rights or property of the carrier of the communication, provided that the communication common carriers shall not utilize service for observing or random monitoring, except for mechanical or service quality control checks, nor shall any such officer, employee or agent use or disclose to another the contents as defined in this chapter of the communication so intercepted.

* * * * *

Maryland

Maryland Code, Courts and Judicial Proceedings

§ 10-401. Definitions.

As used in this subtitle, the following terms have the meanings indicated:

(1)(i) "Wire communication" means any aural transfer made in whole or in part through the use of facilities for the transmission of communications by the aid of wire, cable, or other like connection between the point of origin and the point of reception (including the use of a connection in a switching station) furnished or operated by any person licensed to engage in providing or operating such facilities for the transmission of communications.

(ii) "Wire communication" includes any electronic storage of a communication described in this paragraph.

(iii) "Wire communication" does not include the radio portion of a cordless telephone communication that is transmitted between the cordless telephone handset and the base unit.

(2)(i) "Oral communication" means any conversation or words spoken to or by any person in private conversation.

(ii) "Oral communication" does not include any electronic communication.

(3) "Intercept" means the aural or other acquisition of the contents of any wire, electronic, or oral communication through the use of any electronic, mechanical, or other device.

(4) "Electronic, mechanical, or other device" means any device or electronic communication other than:

(i) Any telephone or telegraph instrument, equipment or other facility for the transmission of electronic communications, or any component thereof, (a) furnished to the subscriber or user by a provider of wire or electronic communication service in the ordinary course of its business and being used by the subscriber or user in the ordinary course of its business or furnished by the subscriber or user for connection to the facilities of the service and used in the ordinary course of its business; or (b) being used by a communications common carrier in the ordinary course of its business, or by an investigative or law enforcement officer in the ordinary course of his duties; or

(ii) A hearing aid or similar device being used to correct subnormal hearing to not better than normal.

(5) "Person" means any employee or agent of this State or a political subdivision thereof, and any individual, partnership, association, joint stock company, trust, or corporation.

APPENDIX B — STATE STATUTES

* * * * *

(7) "Contents" when used with respect to any wire, oral, or electronic communication, includes any information concerning the identity of the parties to the communication or the existence, substance, purport, or meaning of that communication.

(8) "Judge of competent jurisdiction" means a judge of a circuit court.

(9) "Communications common carrier" means any person engaged as a common carrier for hire in the transmission of wire or electronic communications.

(10) "Aggrieved person" means a person who was a party to any intercepted wire, oral, or electronic communication or a person against whom the interception was directed.

(11)(i) "Electronic communication" means any transfer of signs, signals, writing, images, sounds, data, or intelligence of any nature transmitted in whole or in part by a wire, radio, electromagnetic, photoelectronic, or photo-optical system.

(ii) "Electronic communication" does not include:

1. The radio portion of a cordless telephone communication that is transmitted between the cordless telephone handset and the base unit;
2. Any wire or oral communication;
3. Any communication made through a tone-only paging device; or
4. Any communication from a tracking device.

(12) "User" means any person or entity that:

(i) Uses an electronic communication service; and

(ii) Is duly authorized by the provider of the service to engage in that use.

(13) "Electronic communications system" means any wire, radio, electromagnetic, photo-optical, or photoelectronic facilities for the transmission of electronic communications, and any computer facilities or related electronic equipment for the electronic storage of electronic communications.

(14) "Electronic communication service" means any service that provides to users of the service the ability to send or receive wire or electronic communications.

(15) "Readily accessible to the general public" means, with respect to a radio communication, that the communication is not:

(i) Scrambled or encrypted;

(ii) Transmitted using modulation techniques the essential parameters of which have been withheld from the public with the intention of preserving the privacy of the communication; or

(iii) Except for tone-only paging device communications, transmitted over frequencies reserved for private use and licensed for private use under federal or State law.

(16) "Electronic storage" means:

(i) Any temporary, intermediate storage of a wire or electronic communication incidental to the electronic transmission of the communication; and

(ii) Any storage of a wire or electronic communication by an electronic communication service for purposes of backup protection of the communication.

(17) "Aural transfer" means a transfer containing the human voice at any point between and including the point of origin and the point of reception.

§ 10-402. Interception of communications.

(a) Unlawful acts. — Except as otherwise specifically provided in this subtitle it is unlawful for any person to:

(1) Willfully intercept, endeavor to intercept, or procure any other person to intercept or endeavor to intercept, any wire, oral, or electronic communication;

(2) Willfully disclose, or endeavor to disclose, to any other person the contents of any wire, oral, or electronic communication, knowing or having reason to know that the information was obtained through the interception of a wire, oral, or electronic communication in violation of this subtitle; or

(3) Willfully use, or endeavor to use, the contents of any wire, oral, or electronic communication, knowing or having reason to know that the information was obtained through the interception of a wire, oral, or electronic communication in violation of this subtitle.

(b) Penalty. — Any person who violates subsection (a) of this section is guilty of a felony and is subject to imprisonment for not more than 5 years or a fine of not more than $10,000, or both.

(c) Lawful acts. — (3) It is lawful under this subtitle for a person to intercept a wire, oral, or electronic communication where the person is a party to the communication and where all of the parties to the communication have given prior consent to the interception unless the communication is intercepted for the purpose of committing any criminal or tortious act in violation of the Constitution or laws of the United States or of this State.

* * * * *

(7) It is lawful under this subtitle for a person:

(i) To intercept or access an electronic communication made through an electronic communication system that is configured so that the electronic communication is readily accessible to the general public;

(ii) To intercept any radio communication that is transmitted:

1. By any station for the use of the general public, or that relates to ships, aircraft, vehicles, or persons in distress;

2. By any governmental, law enforcement, civil defense, private land mobile, or public safety communications system, including police and fire, readily accessible to the general public;

3. By a station operating on an authorized frequency within the bands allocated to the amateur, citizens band, or general mobile radio services; or

4. By any marine or aeronautical communications system;

(iii) To intercept any wire or electronic communication the transmission of which is causing harmful interference to any lawfully operating station or consumer electronic equipment, to the extent necessary to identify the source of the interference; or

(iv) For other users of the same frequency to intercept any radio communication made through a system that utilizes frequencies monitored by individuals engaged in the provision or the use of the system, if the communication is not scrambled or encrypted.

* * * * *

APPENDIX B — STATE STATUTES

§ 10-410. Civil liability.

(a) Civil liability. — Any person whose wire, oral, or electronic communication is intercepted, disclosed, or used in violation of this subtitle shall have a civil cause of action against any person who intercepts, discloses, or uses, or procures any other person to intercept, disclose, or use the communications, and be entitled to recover from any person:

(1) Actual damages but not less than liquidated damages computed at the rate of $100 a day for each day of violation or $1,000, whichever is higher;

(2) Punitive damages; and

(3) A reasonable attorney's fee and other litigation costs reasonably incurred.

* * * * *

Massachusetts

§ 99. Interception of wire and oral communications.

Interception of wire and oral communications.—

A. Preamble.

The general court finds that organized crime exists within the commonwealth and that the increasing activities of organized crime constitute a grave danger to the public welfare and safety. Organized crime, as it exists in the commonwealth today, consists of a continuing conspiracy among highly organized and disciplined groups to engage in supplying illegal goods and services. In supplying these goods and services organized crime commits unlawful acts and employs brutal and violent tactics. Organized crime is infiltrating legitimate business activities and depriving honest businessmen of the right to make a living.

The general court further finds that because organized crime carries on its activities through layers of insulation and behind a wall of secrecy, government has been unsuccessful in curtailing and eliminating it. Normal investigative procedures are not effective in the investigation of illegal acts committed by organized crime. Therefore, law enforcement officials must be permitted to use modern methods of electronic surveillance, under strict judicial supervision, when investigating these organized criminal activities.

The general court further finds that the uncontrolled development and unrestricted use of modern electronic surveillance devices pose grave dangers to the privacy of all citizens of the commonwealth. Therefore, the secret use of such devices by private individuals must be prohibited. The use of such devices by law enforcement officials must be conducted under strict judicial supervision and should be limited to the investigation of organized crime.

B. Definitions. As used in this section—

1. The term "wire communication" means any communication made in whole or in part through the use of facilities for the transmission of communications by the aid of wire, cable, or other like connection between the point of origin and the point of reception.

2. The term "oral communication" means speech, except such speech as is transmitted over the public air waves by radio or other similar device.

3. The term "intercepting device" means any device or apparatus which is capable of transmitting, receiving, amplifying, or recording a wire or oral communication other than a hearing aid or similar device which is being used to correct subnormal hearing to normal and other than any telephone or telegraph instrument, equipment,

facility, or a component thereof, (a) furnished to a subscriber or user by a communications common carrier in the ordinary course of its business under its tariff and being used by the subscriber or user in the ordinary course of its business; or (b) being used by a communications common carrier in the ordinary course of its business.

4. The term "interception" means to secretly hear, secretly record, or aid another to secretly hear or secretly record the contents of any wire or oral communication through the use of any intercepting device by any person other than a person given prior authority by all parties to such communication; provided that it shall not constitute an interception for an investigative or law enforcement officer, as defined in this section, to record or transmit a wire or oral communication if the officer is a party to such communication or has been given prior authorization to record or transmit the communication by such a party and if recorded or transmitted in the course of an investigation of a designated offense as defined herein.

5. The term "contents", when used with respect to any wire or oral communication, means any information concerning the identity of the parties to such communication or the existence, contents, substance, purport, or meaning of that communication.

6. The term "aggrieved person" means any individual who was a party to an intercepted wire or oral communication or who was named in the warrant authorizing the interception, or who would otherwise have standing to complain that his personal or property interest or privacy was invaded in the course of an interception.

7. The term "designated offense" shall include the following offenses in connection with organized crime as defined in the preamble: arson, assault and battery with a dangerous weapon, extortion, bribery, burglary, embezzlement, forgery, gaming in violation of section seventeen of chapter two hundred and seventy-one of the general laws, intimidation of a witness or juror, kidnapping, larceny, lending of money or things of value in violation of the general laws, mayhem, murder, any offense involving the possession or sale of a narcotic or harmful drug, perjury, prostitution, robbery, subornation of perjury, any violation of this section, being an accessory to any of the foregoing offenses and conspiracy or attempt or solicitation to commit any of the foregoing offenses.

8. The term "investigative or law enforcement officer" means any officer of the United States, a state or a political subdivision of a state, who is empowered by law to conduct investigations of, or to make arrests for, the designated offenses, and any attorney authorized by law to participate in the prosecution of such offenses.

9. The term "judge of competent jurisdiction" means any justice of the superior court of the commonwealth.

10. The term "chief justice" means the chief justice of the superior court of the commonwealth.

11. The term "issuing judge" means any justice of the superior court who shall issue a warrant as provided herein or in the event of his disability or unavailability any other judge of competent jurisdiction designated by the chief justice.

12. The term "communication common carrier" means any person engaged as a common carrier in providing or operating wire communication facilities.

13. The term "person" means any individual, partnership, association, joint stock company, trust, or corporation, whether or not any of the foregoing is an officer, agent or employee of the United States, a state, or a political subdivision of a state.

APPENDIX B — STATE STATUTES

14. The terms "sworn" or "under oath" as they appear in this section shall mean an oath or affirmation or a statement subscribed to under the pains and penalties of perjury.

15. The terms "applicant attorney general" or "applicant district attorney" shall mean the attorney general of the commonwealth or a district attorney of the commonwealth who has made application for a warrant pursuant to this section.

16. The term "exigent circumstances" shall mean the showing of special facts to the issuing judge as to the nature of the investigation for which a warrant is sought pursuant to this section which require secrecy in order to obtain the information desired from the interception sought to be authorized.

C. Offenses.

1. Interception, oral communications prohibited.

Except as otherwise specifically provided in this section any person who—willfully commits an interception, attempts to commit an interception, or procures any other person to commit an interception or to attempt to commit an interception of any wire or oral communication shall be fined not more than ten thousand dollars, or imprisoned in the state prison for not more than five years, or imprisoned in a jail or house of correction for not more than two and one half years, or both so fined and given one such imprisonment.

Proof of the installation of any intercepting device by any person under circumstances evincing an intent to commit an interception, which is not authorized or permitted by this section, shall be prima facie evidence of a violation of this subparagraph.

* * * * *

3. Disclosure or use of wire or oral communications prohibited.

Except as otherwise specifically provided in this section any person who—

    a. willfully discloses or attempts to disclose to any person the contents of any wire or oral communication, knowing that the information was obtained through interception; or

    b. willfully uses or attempts to use the contents of any wire or oral communication, knowing that the information was obtained through interception, shall be guilty of a misdemeanor punishable by imprisonment in a jail or a house of correction for not more than two years or by a fine of not more than five thousand dollars or both.

* * * * *

6. Any person who permits or on behalf of any other person commits or attempts to commit, or any person who participates in a conspiracy to commit or to attempt to commit, or any accessory to a person who commits a violation of subparagraphs 1 through 5 of paragraph C of this section shall be punished in the same manner as is provided for the respective offenses as described in subparagraphs 1 through 5 of paragraph C.

D. Exemptions.

1. Permitted interception of wire or oral communications.

It shall not be a violation of this section—

    a. for an operator of a switchboard, or an officer, employee, or agent of any communication common carrier, whose facilities are used in the transmission of a wire communication, to intercept, disclose, or use that communication in the normal course of his employment while engaged in any activity which is a necessary incident to the rendition of service or to the protection of the rights or property of the carrier of such communication, or which is necessary to prevent the use of such facilities in violation of section fourteen A of chapter two hundred and sixty-nine of the general laws; provided, that said communication common carriers shall not utilize service observing or random monitoring except for mechanical or service quality control checks.

b. for persons to possess an office intercommunication system which is used in the ordinary course of their business or to use such office intercommunication system in the ordinary course of their business.

c. for investigative and law enforcement officers of the United States of America to violate the provisions of this section if acting pursuant to authority of the laws of the United States and within the scope of their authority.

d. for any person duly authorized to make specified interceptions by a warrant issued pursuant to this section.

e. for investigative or law enforcement officers to violate the provisions of this section for the purposes of ensuring the safety of any law enforcement officer or agent thereof who is acting in an undercover capacity, or as a witness for the commonwealth; provided, however, that any such interception which is not otherwise permitted by this section shall be deemed unlawful for purposes of paragraph P.

2. Permitted disclosure and use of intercepted wire or oral communications.

a. Any investigative or law enforcement officer, who, by any means authorized by this section, has obtained knowledge of the contents of any wire or oral communication, or evidence derived therefrom, may disclose such contents or evidence in the proper performance of his official duties.

b. Any investigative or law enforcement officer, who, by any means authorized by this section has obtained knowledge of the contents of any wire or oral communication, or evidence derived therefrom, may use such contents or evidence in the proper performance of his official duties.

c. Any person who has obtained, by any means authorized by this section, knowledge of the contents of any wire or oral communication, or evidence derived therefrom, may disclose such contents while giving testimony under oath or affirmation in any criminal proceeding in any court of the United States or of any state or in any federal or state grand jury proceeding.

d. The contents of any wire or oral communication intercepted pursuant to a warrant in accordance with the provisions of this section, or evidence derived therefrom, may otherwise be disclosed only upon a showing of good cause before a judge of competent jurisdiction.

e. No otherwise privileged wire or oral communication intercepted in accordance with, or in violation of, the provisions of this section shall lose its privileged character.

* * * * *

Q. Civil remedy.

Any aggrieved person whose oral or wire communications were intercepted, disclosed or used except as permitted or authorized by this section or whose personal or property interests or privacy were violated by means of an interception except as permitted or authorized by this section shall have a civil cause of action against any person who so intercepts, discloses or uses such communications or who so violates his personal, property or privacy interest, and shall be entitled to recover from any such person—

    1. actual damages but not less than liquidated damages computed at the rate of $100 per day for each day of violation or $1000, whichever is higher;

    2. punitive damages; and

    3. a reasonable attorney's fee and other litigation disbursements reasonably incurred. Good faith reliance on a warrant issued under this section shall constitute a complete defense to an action brought under this paragraph.

*****

Michigan

§ 750.539a. Definitions.

As used in sections 539a to 539i:

(1) "Private place" means a place where one may reasonably expect to be safe from casual or hostile intrusion or surveillance but does not include a place to which the public or substantial group of the public has access.

(2) "Eavesdrop" or "eavesdropping" means to overhear, record, amplify or transmit any part of the private discourse of others without the permission of all persons engaged in the discourse. Neither this definition or any other provision of this act shall modify or affect any law or regulation concerning interception, divulgence or recording of messages transmitted by communications common carriers.

(3) "Surveillance" means to secretly observe the activities of another person for the purpose of spying upon and invading the privacy of the person observed.

(4) "Person" means any individual, partnership, corporation or association.

§ 750.539b. Trespassing for purpose of eavesdropping or surveillance.

A person who trespasses on property owned or under the control of any other person, to subject that person to eavesdropping or surveillance is guilty of a misdemeanor.

§ 750.539c. Eavesdropping upon private conversation.

Any person who is present or who is not present during a private conversation and who willfully uses any device to eavesdrop upon the conversation without the consent of all parties thereto, or who knowingly aids, employs or procures another person to do the same in violation of this section, is guilty of a felony punishable by imprisonment in a state prison for not more than 2 years or by a fine of not more than $2,000.00, or both.

§ 750.539d. Installation of device for observing, photographing or eavesdropping in private place.

Any person who installs in any private place, without the consent of the person or persons entitled to privacy there, any device for observing, photographing, or eavesdropping upon the sounds or events in such place, or uses any such unauthorized installation, is guilty of a felony punishable by imprisonment in a state prison for not more than 2 years or by a fine of not more than $2,000.00, or both.

§ 750.539e. Use or divulgence of information.

Any person who uses or divulges any information which he knows or reasonably should know was obtained in violation of sections 539b, 539c or 539d is guilty of a felony, punishable by imprisonment in a state prison not more than 2 years, or by a fine of not more than $2,000.00.

§ 750.539h. Civil remedies.

Any parties to any conversation upon which eavesdropping is practiced contrary to this act shall be entitled to the following civil remedies:
- (a) An injunction by a court of record prohibiting further eavesdropping.
- (b) All actual damages against the person who eavesdrops.
- (c) Punitive damages as determined by the court or by a jury.

Minnesota

§ 626A.01. Definitions.

Subdivision 1. Terms. As used in sections 626A.01 to 626A.23, the terms defined in this section have the meanings given them.

Subdivision 2. Person. "Person" means any individual, partnership, corporation, joint stock company, trust, or association, including but not limited to, the subscriber to the telephone or telegraph service involved and any law enforcement officer.

Subdivision 3. Wire communications. "Wire communication" means any aural transfer made in whole or in part through the use of facilities for the transmission of communications by the aid of wire, cable, or other like connection between the point of origin and the point of reception, including the use of such connection in a switching station. "Wire communication" includes any electronic storage of the communication.

Subdivision 4. Oral communication. "Oral communication" means any oral communication uttered by a person exhibiting an expectation that such communication is not subject to interception under circumstances justifying such expectation, but the term does not include any electronic communication.

Subdivision 5. Intercept. "Intercept" means the aural or other acquisition of the contents of any wire, electronic, or oral communication through the use of any electronic, mechanical, or other device.

Subdivision 6. Electronic, mechanical or other device. "Electronic, mechanical, or other device" means any device or apparatus which can be used to intercept a wire, electronic, or oral communication other than

(a) any telephone or telegraph instrument, equipment or facility, or any component thereof, (i) furnished to the subscriber or user by a provider or wire or electronic communications service in the ordinary course of its business and being used by the subscriber or user in the ordinary course of its business or furnished by a subscriber or user for connection to the facilities of service and used in the ordinary course of its business; or (ii) being used by a communications common carrier in the ordinary

APPENDIX B — STATE STATUTES

course of its business, or by an investigative or law enforcement officer in the ordinary course of duties;

(b) a hearing aid or similar device being used to correct subnormal hearing to not better than normal;

(c) that which is specifically designed to only record conversations to which the operator of the device is a party;

(d) that which is used in the normal course of broadcasting by radio or television; or

(e) that which is otherwise commonly used for a purpose or purposes other than overhearing or recording conversations.

In determining whether a device which is alleged to be an electronic, mechanical, or other device is, in fact, such a device there shall be taken into account, among other things, the size, appearance, directivity, range, sensitivity, frequency, power, or intensity, and the representations of the maker or manufacturer as to its performance and use.

Subdivision 7. Investigative or law enforcement officer. "Investigative or law enforcement officer" means any officer of the United States or of a state or political subdivision thereof, or a university of Minnesota peace officer who is empowered by law to conduct investigations of or to make arrests for offenses enumerated in this chapter, or any attorney authorized by law to prosecute or participate in the prosecution of such offenses.

Subdivision 8. Contents. "Contents," when used with respect to any wire, electronic, or oral communication, includes any information concerning the substance, purport, or meaning of that communication.

Subdivision 9. Aggrieved person. "Aggrieved person" means a person who was a party to any intercepted wire, electronic, or oral communication or a person against whom the interception was directed.

Subdivision 10. Manufacturer. "Manufacturer" means any person who is engaged in the business of manufacturing electronic, mechanical or other devices, or who otherwise produces any such device for sale or distribution.

Subdivision 11. Dealer. "Dealer" means any person not a manufacturer who is engaged in the business of selling electronic, mechanical or other devices. The term "dealer" shall include wholesalers, retailers and dealers in used intercepting devices.

Subdivision 12. Bureau. "Bureau" means the bureau of criminal apprehension.

Subdivision 13. Communications common carrier. "Communications common carrier" means any individual, partnership, corporation, or association which provides telephone or telegraph service to subscribers or users pursuant to tariffs on file with the Minnesota Public Utilities Commission or the Federal Communications Commission.

Subdivision 14. Electronic communication. "Electronic communication" means transfer of signs, signals, writing, images, sounds, data, or intelligence of any nature transmitted in whole or in part by a wire, radio, electromagnetic, photoelectronic, or photo-optical system but does not include:

(1) a wire or oral communication;

(2) a communication made through a tone-only paging device; or

(3) a communication from a tracking device, defined as an electronic or mechanical device which permits the tracking of the movement of a person or object.

Subdivision 15. User. "User" means a person or entity who:

(1) uses an electronic communication service; and

(2) is duly authorized by the provider of the service to engage in the use.

Subdivision 16. Electronic communications system. "Electronic communications system" means a wire, radio, electromagnetic, photo-optical, or photoelectronic facility for the transmission of electronic communications, and a computer facility or related electronic equipment for the electronic storage of communications.

Subdivision 17. Electronic communication service. "Electronic communication service" means a service that provides to users of the service the ability to send or receive wire or electronic communications.

Subdivision 18. Readily accessible to the general public. "Readily accessible to the general public" means, with respect to a radio communication, that the communication is not:

(1) scrambled or encrypted;

(2) transmitted using modulation techniques whose essential parameters have been withheld from the public with the intention of preserving the privacy of the communication;

(3) carried on a subcarrier or other signal subsidiary to a radio transmission;

(4) transmitted over a communication system provided by a common carrier, unless the communication is a tone-only paging system communication; or

(5) transmitted on frequencies allocated under part 25, subpart D, E, or F of part 74, or part 94 of title 47 of the Code of Federal Regulations, unless in the case of a communication transmitted on a frequency allocated under part 74 of title 47 of the Code of Federal Regulations that is not exclusively allocated to broadcast auxiliary services, the communication is a two-way voice communication by radio.

Subdivision 19. Electronic storage. "Electronic storage" means:

(1) a temporary, intermediate storage of a wire or electronic communication incidental to the electronic transmission of the communication; and

(2) a storage of communication described in clause (1) by an electronic communication service for purposes of backup protection of the communication.

Subdivision 20. Aural transfer. "Aural transfer" means a transfer containing the human voice at any point between and including the point of origin and the point of reception.

§ 626A.02. Interception and disclosure of wire or oral communications.

Subdivision 1. Offenses. Except as otherwise specifically provided in this chapter any person who

(a) intentionally intercepts, endeavors to intercept, or procures any other person to intercept or endeavor to intercept, any wire, electronic, or oral communication;

(b) intentionally uses, endeavors to use, or procures any other person to use or endeavor to use any electronic, mechanical, or other device to intercept any oral communication when

(i) such device is affixed to, or otherwise transmits a signal through, a wire, cable, or other like connection used in wire communication; or

(ii) such device transmits communications by radio, or interferes with the transmission of such communication;

(c) intentionally discloses, or endeavors to disclose, to any other person the contents of any wire, electronic, or oral communication, knowing or having reason to know that the information was obtained through the interception of a wire, electronic, or oral communication in violation of this subdivision; or

APPENDIX B — STATE STATUTES

(d) intentionally uses, or endeavors to use, the contents of any wire, electronic, or oral communication, knowing or having reason to know that the information was obtained through the interception of a wire, electronic, or oral communication in violation of this subdivision; shall be punished as provided in subdivision 4, or shall be subject to suit as provided in subdivision 5.
Subdivision 2. Exemptions.

* * * * *

(d) It is not unlawful under this chapter for a person not acting under color of law to intercept a wire, electronic, or oral communication where such person is a party to the communication or where one of the parties to the communication has given prior consent to such interception unless such communication is intercepted for the purpose of committing any criminal or tortious act in violation of the constitution or laws of the United States or of any state.

(e) It is not a violation of this chapter for a person:

(1) to intercept or access an electronic communication made through an electronic communication system that is configured so that the electronic communication is readily accessible to the general public;

(2) to intercept any radio communication that is transmitted:

(i) by a station for the use of the general public, or that relates to ships, aircraft, vehicles, or persons in distress;

(ii) by a governmental, law enforcement, civil defense, private land mobile, or public safety communications system, including police and fire, readily accessible to the general public;

(iii) by a station operating on an authorized frequency within the bands allocated to the amateur, citizens band, or general mobile radio services; or

(iv) by a marine or aeronautical communications system;

(3) to engage in any conduct which:

(i) is prohibited by section 553 of title 47 of the United States Code; or

(ii) is excepted from the application of section 605(a) of title 47 of the United States Code by section 605(b) of that title;

(4) to intercept a wire or electronic communication the transmission of which is causing harmful interference to any lawfully operating station or consumer electronic equipment, to the extent necessary to identify the source of such interference; or

(5) for other users of the same frequency to intercept any radio communication made through a system that utilizes frequencies monitored by individuals engaged in the provision or the use of such system, if the communication is not scrambled or encrypted.

* * * * *

(g) It is not unlawful under this chapter for a person not acting under color of law to intercept the radio portion of a cordless telephone communication that is transmitted between the cordless telephone handset and the base unit if the initial interception of the communication was obtained inadvertently.
Subdivision 3. Disclosing communications.

(a) Except as provided in paragraph (b), a person or entity providing an electronic communications service to the public must not intentionally divulge the contents of any communication other than one to the person or entity, or an agent of the person or entity, while in transmission on that service to a person or entity other than an addressee or intended recipient of the communication or an agent of the addressee or intended recipient.

(b) A person or entity providing electronic communication service to the public may divulge the contents of a communication:

(1) as otherwise authorized in subdivision 2, paragraph (a), and section 626A.09;

(2) with the lawful consent of the originator or any addressee or intended recipient of the communication;

(3) to a person employed or authorized, or whose facilities are used, to forward the communication to its destination; or

(4) that were inadvertently obtained by the service provider in the normal course of business if there is reason to believe that the communication pertains to the commission of a crime, if divulgence is made to a law enforcement agency.

Subdivision 4. Penalties.

(a) Except as provided in paragraph (b) or in subdivision 5, whoever violates subdivision 1 shall be fined not more than $20,000 or imprisoned not more than five years, or both.

(b) If the offense is a first offense under paragraph (a) and is not for a tortious or illegal purpose or for purposes of direct or indirect commercial advantage or private commercial gain, and the wire or electronic communication with respect to which the offense under paragraph (a) is a radio communication that is not scrambled or encrypted, then:

(1) if the communication is not the radio portion of a cellular telephone communication, a public land mobile radio service communication, a cordless telephone communication transmitted between the cordless telephone handset and the base unit, or a paging service communication, and the conduct is not that described in subdivision 5, the offender shall be fined not more than $3,000 or imprisoned not more than one year, or both; and

(2) if the communication is the radio portion of a cellular telephone communication, a public land mobile radio service communication, a cordless telephone communication transmitted between the cordless telephone handset and the base unit, or a paging service communication, the offender shall be fined not more than $500.

(c) Conduct otherwise an offense under this subdivision that consists of or relates to the interception of a satellite transmission that is not encrypted or scrambled and that is transmitted:

(1) to a broadcasting station for purposes of retransmission to the general public; or

(2) as an audio subcarrier intended for redistribution to facilities open to the public, but not including data transmissions or telephone calls, is not an offense under this subdivision unless the conduct is for the purposes of direct or indirect commercial advantage or private financial gain.

Subdivision 5. Civil action. (a)(1) If the communication is:

(i) a private satellite video communication that is not scrambled or encrypted and the conduct in violation of this chapter is the private viewing of that com-

APPENDIX B — STATE STATUTES

munication and is not for a tortious or illegal purpose or for purposes of direct or indirect commercial advantage or private commercial gain; or

(ii) a radio communication that is transmitted on frequencies allocated under subpart D of part 74 of title 47 of the Code of Federal Regulations and that is not scrambled or encrypted and the conduct in violation of this chapter is not for a tortious or illegal purpose or for purposes of direct or indirect commercial advantage or private commercial gain, then the person who engages in such conduct is subject to suit by the county or city attorney in whose jurisdiction the violation occurs.

(2) In an action under this subdivision:

(i) if the violation of this chapter is a first offense for the person under subdivision 4, paragraph (a), and the person has not been found liable in a civil action under section 626A.13, the city or county attorney is entitled to seek appropriate injunctive relief; and

(ii) if the violation of this chapter is a second or subsequent offense under subdivision 4, paragraph (a), or the person has been found liable in a prior civil action under section 626A.13, the person is subject to a mandatory $500 civil fine.

(b) The court may use any means within its authority to enforce an injunction issued under paragraph (a), clause (2)(i), and shall impose a civil fine of not less than $500 for each violation of such an injunction.

§ 626A.13. Civil remedies.

Subdivision 1. In general. Except as provided in section 2511(2)(a)(ii) of title 18 of the United States Code, a person whose wire, oral, or electronic communication is intercepted, disclosed, or intentionally used in violation of this chapter may in a civil action recover from the person or entity that engaged in that violation relief as may be appropriate.

Subdivision 2. Relief. In an action under this section, appropriate relief includes:

(1) temporary and other equitable or declaratory relief as may be appropriate;

(2) damages under subdivision 3 and punitive damages in appropriate cases; and

(3) a reasonable attorney's fee and other litigation costs reasonably incurred.

Subdivision 3. Computation of damages.

(a) In an action under this section, if the conduct in violation of this chapter is the private viewing of a private satellite video communication that is not scrambled or encrypted or if the communication is a radio communication that is transmitted on frequencies allocated under subpart D of part 74 of title 47 of the Code of Federal Regulations that is not scrambled or encrypted and the conduct is not for a tortious or illegal purpose or for purposes of direct or indirect commercial advantage or private commercial gain, then the court shall assess damages as follows:

(1) If the person who engaged in that conduct has not previously been enjoined under section 626A.02, subdivision 5, and has not been found liable in a prior civil action under this section, the court shall assess the greater of the sum of actual damages suffered by the plaintiff, or statutory damages of not less than $50 and not more than $500.

(2) If, on one prior occasion, the person who engaged in that conduct has been enjoined under section 626A.02, subdivision 5, or has been found liable in a civil

action under this section, the court shall assess the greater of the sum of actual damages suffered by the plaintiff, or statutory damages of not less than $100 and not more than $1,000.

(b) In any other action under this section, the court may assess as damages whichever is the greater of:

(1) the sum of three times the actual damages suffered by the plaintiff and any profits made by the violator as a result of the violation; or

(2) statutory damages of whichever is the greater of $100 a day for each day of violation or $10,000.

Subdivision 4. Defense. A good faith reliance on:

(1) a court warrant or order, a grand jury subpoena, a legislative authorization, or a statutory authorization;

(2) a request of an investigative or law enforcement officer under United States Code, title 18, section 2518(7); or

(3) a good faith determination that section 626A.02, subdivision 3, permitted the conduct complained of; is a complete defense against any civil or criminal action brought under this chapter or any other law.

Subdivision 5. Limitation. A civil action under this section may not be begun later than two years after the date upon which the claimant first has a reasonable opportunity to discover the violation.

§ 626A.32. Civil cause of action.

Subdivision 1. Cause of action. Except as provided in section 626A.28, subdivision 5, a provider of electronic communication service, subscriber, or customer aggrieved by a violation of this chapter in which the conduct constituting the violation is engaged in with a knowing or intentional state of mind may, in a civil action, recover from the person or entity which engaged in that violation relief as may be appropriate.

Subdivision 2. Relief. In a civil action under this section, appropriate relief includes:

(1) temporary and other equitable or declaratory relief as may be appropriate;

(2) damages under subdivision 3; and

(3) a reasonable attorney's fee and other litigation costs reasonably incurred.

Subdivision 3. Damages. The court may assess as damages in a civil action under this section the sum of the actual damages suffered by the plaintiff and any profits made by the violator as a result of the violation, but in no case is a person entitled to recover to receive less than the sum of $1,000.

Subdivision 4. Defense. A good faith reliance on:

(1) a court warrant or order, a grand jury subpoena, a legislative authorization, or a statutory authorization; or

(2) a good faith determination that section 626A.02, subdivision 3, permitted the conduct complained of; is a complete defense to a civil or criminal action brought under sections 626A.26 to 626A.34 or any other law.

Subdivision 5. Limitation. A civil action under this section may not be commenced later than two years after the date upon which the claimant first discovered or had a reasonable opportunity to discover the violation.

APPENDIX B — STATE STATUTES

Mississippi

§ 41-29-501. Definitions.

As used in this article, the following terms shall have the meaning ascribed to them herein unless the context requires otherwise:

(a) "Aggrieved person" means a person who was a party to an intercepted wire, oral or other communication or a person against whom the interception was directed.

(b) "Communication common carrier" has the meaning given the term "common carrier" by 47 U.S.C. § 153(h) and shall also mean a provider of communication services.

(c) "Contents," when used with respect to a wire, oral or other communication, includes any information concerning the identity of the parties to the communication or the existence, substance, purport or meaning of that communication.

(d) "Covert entry" means any entry into or onto premises which if made without a court order allowing such an entry under this article would be a violation of criminal law.

(e) "Director" means the Director of the Bureau of Narcotics or, if the director is absent or unable to serve, the Assistant Director of the Bureau of Narcotics.

(f) "Electronic, mechanical or other device" means a device or apparatus primarily designed or used for the nonconsensual interception of wire, oral or other communications.

(g) "Intercept" means the aural or other acquisition of the contents of a wire, oral or other communication through the use of an electronic, mechanical or other device.

(h) "Investigative or law enforcement officer" means an officer of this state or of a political subdivision of this state who is empowered by law to conduct investigations of, or to make arrests for, offenses enumerated in Section 41-29-505, or an attorney authorized by law to prosecute or participate in the prosecution of such offenses.

(i) "Judge of competent jurisdiction" means a justice of the Supreme Court or a circuit court judge.

(j) "Oral communication" means an oral communication uttered by a person exhibiting an expectation that the communication is not subject to interception under circumstances justifying that expectation.

(k) "Other communication" means any transfer of an electronic or other signal, including fax signals, computer generated signals, other similar signals, or any scrambled or encrypted signal transferred via wire, radio, electromagnetic, photoelectric or photo-optical system from one party to another in which the involved parties may reasonably expect the communication to be private.

(l) "Prosecutor" means a district attorney with jurisdiction in the county in which the facility or place where the communication to be intercepted is located or a legal assistant to the district attorney if designated in writing by the district attorney on a case by case basis.

(m) "Residence" means a structure or the portion of a structure used as a person's home or fixed place of habitation to which the person indicates an intent to return after any temporary absence.

(n) "Wire communication" means a communication made in whole or in part through the use of facilities for the transmission of communications by the aid of wire, cable or other like connection between the point of origin and the point of reception furnished or operated by a person engaged as a common carrier in providing or operating the facilities for the transmission of communications and includes cordless telephones, voice pagers, cellular telephones, any mobile telephone, or any communication conducted through the facilities of a provider of communication services.

§ 41-29-529. Civil cause of action.

(1) A person whose wire, oral or other communication is intercepted, disclosed or used in violation of this article shall have a civil cause of action against any person who intercepts, discloses or uses or procures another person to intercept, disclose or use the communication, and is entitled to recover from the person:

    (a) Actual damages but not less than liquidated damages computed at a rate of One Hundred Dollars ($100.00) a day for each day of violation or One Thousand Dollars ($1,000.00), whichever is higher;

    (b) Punitive damages; and

    (c) A reasonable attorney's fee and other litigation costs reasonably incurred.

(2) A good faith reliance on a court order is a complete defense to any civil or criminal action brought under this article.

§ 41-29-531. Exceptions to civil liability.

It is an exception to the application of Section 41-29-529(1) that:

* * * * *

(e) A person not acting under color of law intercepts a wire, oral or other communication if the person is a party to the communication, or if one of the parties to the communication has given prior consent to the interception unless the communication is intercepted for the purpose of committing any criminal or tortious act in violation of the Constitution or laws of the United States or of this state, or for the purpose of committing any other injurious act.

§ 41-29-533. Penalties.

(1) Any person who knowingly and intentionally possesses, installs, operates or monitors an electronic, mechanical or other device in violation of this article shall be guilty of a misdemeanor and, upon conviction thereof, shall be sentenced to not more than one (1) year in the county jail or fined not more than Ten Thousand Dollars ($10,000.00), or both.

(2) Any person who violates the provisions of Section 41-29-511 shall be guilty of a felony and, upon conviction thereof, shall be sentenced to not more than five (5) years in the State Penitentiary and fined not more than Ten Thousand Dollars ($10,000.00).

Missouri

§ 542.400. Definitions.

As used in sections 542.400 to 542.424, the following words and phrases mean:

(1) "Aggrieved person", a person who was a party to any intercepted wire communication or a person against whom the interception was directed;

(2) "Communication common carrier", an individual or corporation undertaking to transport messages for compensation;

APPENDIX B — STATE STATUTES

(3) "Contents", when used with respect to any wire communication, includes any information concerning the identity of the parties, the substance, purport, or meaning of that communication;

(4) "Court of competent jurisdiction", any circuit court having general criminal jurisdiction within the territorial jurisdiction where the communication is to be intercepted including any circuit judge specially assigned by the supreme court of Missouri pursuant to section 542.404;

(5) "Electronic, mechanical, or other device", any device or apparatus which can be used to intercept a wire communication other than:

> (a) Any telephone or telegraph instrument, equipment or facility, or any component thereof, owned by the user or furnished to the subscriber or user by a communications common carrier in the ordinary course of its business and being used by the subscriber or user in the ordinary course of its business or being used by a communications common carrier in the ordinary course of its business or by an investigative office or law enforcement officer in the ordinary course of his duties; or
>
> (b) A hearing aid or similar device being used to correct subnormal hearing to not better than normal;

(6) "Intercept", the aural acquisition of the contents of any wire communication through the use of any electronic or mechanical device, including but not limited to interception by one spouse of another spouse;

(7) "Investigative officer" or "law enforcement officer or agency", any officer or agency of this state or a political subdivision of this state, who is empowered by law to conduct investigations of or to make arrests for offenses enumerated in sections 542.400 to 542.542, and any attorney authorized by law to prosecute or participate in the prosecution of such offenses;

(8) "Oral communication", any communication uttered by a person exhibiting an expectation that such communication is not subject to interception under circumstances justifying such expectation;

(9) "Person", any employee, or agent of this state or political subdivision of this state, and any individual, partnership, association, joint stock company, trust, or corporation;

(10) "Prosecuting attorney", the elected prosecuting attorney of the county or the circuit attorney of any city not contained within a county;

(11) "State", state of Missouri and political subdivisions of the state;

(12) "Wire communication", any communication made in whole or in part through the use of facilities for the transmission of communications by the aid of wire, cable, or other like connection between the point of origin and the point of reception including the use of such connection in a switching station furnished or operated by any person engaged as a common carrier in providing or operating such facilities for the transmission of local, state or interstate communications.

§ 542.402. Penalty; defenses.

1. Except as otherwise specifically provided in sections 542.400 to 542.424, a person is guilty of a class D felony and upon conviction shall be punished as provided by law, if such person:

> (1) Knowingly intercepts, endeavors to intercept, or procures any other person to intercept or endeavor to intercept, any wire communication;

(2) Knowingly uses, endeavors to use, or procures any other person to use or endeavor to use any electronic, mechanical, or other device to intercept any oral communication when such device transmits communications by radio or interferes with the transmission of such communication; provided, however, that nothing in sections 542.400 to 542.424 shall be construed to prohibit the use by law enforcement officers of body microphones and transmitters in undercover investigations for the acquisition of evidence and the protection of law enforcement officers and others working under their direction in such investigations;

(3) Knowingly discloses, or endeavors to disclose, to any other person the contents of any wire communication, when he knows or has reason to know that the information was obtained through the interception of a wire communication in violation of this subsection; or

(4) Knowingly uses, or endeavors to use, the contents of any wire communication, when he knows or has reason to know that the information was obtained through the interception of a wire communication in violation of this subsection.

2. It is not unlawful under the provisions of sections 542.400 to 542.424:

* * * * *

(3) For a person not acting under law to intercept a wire communication where such person is a party to the communication or where one of the parties to the communication has given prior consent to such interception unless such communication is intercepted for the purpose of committing any criminal or tortious act.

Montana

§ 45-8-213. Privacy in communications.

(1) Except as provided in 69-6-104, a person commits the offense of violating privacy in communications if he knowingly or purposely:

* * * * *

(c) records or causes to be recorded any conversation by use of a hidden electronic or mechanical device which reproduces a human conversation without the knowledge of all parties to the conversation. Subsection (c) does not apply to duly elected or appointed public officials or employees when the transcription or recording is done in the performance of official duty, to persons speaking at public meetings, or to persons given warning of the recording.

* * * * *

(2) (a) A person convicted of the offense of violating privacy in communications shall be fined not to exceed $500 or imprisoned in the county jail for a term not to exceed 6 months, or both.

(b) On a second conviction of subsection (1)(a) or (1)(b), a person shall be imprisoned in the county jail for a term not to exceed 1 year or be fined an amount not to exceed $1,000, or both.

(c) On a third or subsequent conviction of subsection (1)(a) or (1)(b), a person shall be imprisoned in the state prison for a term not to exceed 5 years or be fined an amount not to exceed $10,000, or both.

APPENDIX B — STATE STATUTES

Nebraska

§ 86-701. Terms, defined.

As used in sections 86-701 to 86-707.15, unless the context otherwise requires:

(1) Aggrieved person shall mean a person who was a party to any intercepted wire, electronic, or oral communication or a person against whom the interception was directed;

(2) Aural transfer shall mean a transfer containing the human voice at any point between and including the point of origin and the point of reception;

(3) Contents, when used with respect to any wire, electronic, or oral communication, shall include any information concerning the substance, purport, or meaning of that communication;

(4) Electronic, mechanical, or other device shall mean any device or apparatus which can be used to intercept a wire, electronic, or oral communication other than (a) any telephone or telegraph instrument, equipment, or facility, or any component thereof, (i) furnished to the subscriber or user by a provider in the ordinary course of its business and being used by the subscriber or user in the ordinary course of its business or furnished by such subscriber or user for connection to the facilities of such service and used by the subscriber or user in the ordinary course of its business or (ii) being used by a provider in the ordinary course of its business or by an investigative or law enforcement officer in the ordinary course of his or her duties or (b) a hearing aid or similar device being used to correct subnormal hearing to not better than normal;

(5) Electronic communication shall mean any transfer of signs, signals, writing, images, sounds, data, or intelligence of any nature transmitted in whole or in part by a wire, radio, electromagnetic, photoelectronic, or photo-optical system but shall not include:

(a) The radio portion of a cordless telephone communication that is transmitted between the cordless telephone handset and the base unit;

(b) Any wire or oral communication;

(c) Any communication made through a tone-only mobile paging device; or

(d) Any communication from a mobile tracking device as defined in section 86-707.08;

(6) Electronic communication service shall mean any service which provides to users thereof the ability to send or receive wire or electronic communications;

(7) Electronic communications system shall mean any wire, radio, electromagnetic, photo-optical, or photoelectronic facilities for the transmission of electronic communications and any computer facilities or related electronic equipment for the electronic storage of such communications;

(8) Electronic storage shall mean:

(a) Any temporary, intermediate storage of a wire or electronic communication incidental to the electronic transmission thereof; and

(b) Any storage of such communication by an electronic communication service for purposes of backup protection of such communication;

(9) Intercept shall mean the aural or other acquisition of the contents of any wire, electronic, or oral communication through the use of any electronic, mechanical, or other device;

(10) Investigative or law enforcement officer shall mean a law enforcement officer as defined in section 81-1401 and shall include the Attorney General and his or her deputies

or assistants, a county attorney and his or her deputies, and agents of the United States Federal Bureau of Investigation, Drug Enforcement Administration, Marshals Service, Secret Service, Bureau of Alcohol, Tobacco, and Firearms, Treasury Department, Customs Service, Justice Department, and Internal Revenue Service;

(11) Mobile phone communication shall mean a radio communication that is transmitted on frequencies allocated under the rules of the Federal Communications Commission;

(12) Oral communication shall mean any oral communication uttered by a person exhibiting an expectation that such communication is not subject to interception under circumstances justifying such expectation but shall not include any electronic communication;

(13) Pen register shall mean a device which records or decodes electronic or other impulses which identify the numbers dialed or otherwise transmitted on the telephone line to which such device is attached but shall not include any device used by a provider or customer of an electronic communication service for billing or recording as an incident to billing for communications services provided by such provider or any device used by a provider or customer of an electronic communication service for cost accounting or other like purposes in the ordinary course of its business;

(14) Provider shall mean any person who provides an electronic communication service and who has authorized access to or possession or control of the facilities or equipment necessary to implement the order to intercept a wire or electronic communication or the order to install a pen register or a trap-and-trace device;

(15) Readily accessible to the general public shall mean, with respect to a radio communication, that such communication is not:

(a) Scrambled or encrypted;

(b) Transmitted using modulation techniques the essential parameters of which have been withheld from the public with the intention of preserving the privacy of such communication;

(c) Carried on a subcarrier or other signal subsidiary to a radio transmission;

(d) Transmitted over an electronic communications system by a provider unless the communication is a tone-only paging system communication; or

(e) Transmitted on frequencies allocated under part 25, subpart D, E or F of part 74 or part 94 of the rules of the Federal Communications Commission unless, in the case of a communication transmitted on a frequency allocated under part 74 that is not exclusively allocated to broadcast auxiliary services, the communication is a two-way voice communication by radio;

(16) Trap-and-trace device shall mean a device which captures the incoming electronic or other impulses which identify the originating number of an instrument or device from which a wire or electronic communication was transmitted;

(17) User shall mean any person or entity who:

(a) Uses an electronic communication service; and

(b) Is duly authorized by the provider of such service to engage in such use; and

(18) Wire communication shall mean any aural transfer made in whole or in part through the use of facilities for the transmission of communications by the aid of wire, cable, or other like connection, including the use of such connection in a switching station, between the point of origin and the point of reception furnished or operated by any person engaged in providing or operating such facilities for the transmission of commu-

nications. Wire communication shall include any electronic storage of such communication but shall not include the radio portion of a cordless telephone communication that is transmitted between the cordless telephone handset and the base unit.

§ 86-702. Unlawful acts.

(1) Except as otherwise specifically provided in sections 86-701 to 86-707, it shall be unlawful to:

(a) Intentionally intercept, endeavor to intercept, or procure any other person to intercept or endeavor to intercept any wire, electronic, or oral communication;

(b) intentionally use, endeavor to use, or procure any other person to use or endeavor to use any electronic, mechanical, or other device to intercept any oral communication when (i) such device is affixed to, or otherwise transmits a signal through, a wire, cable, or other like connection used in wire communication or (ii) such device transmits communications by radio or interferes with the transmission of such communication;

(c) intentionally disclose or endeavor to disclose to any other person the contents of any wire, electronic, or oral communication, knowing or having reason to know that the information was obtained through the interception of a wire, electronic, or oral communication in violation of this subsection;

(d) intentionally use or endeavor to use the contents of any wire, electronic, or oral communication, knowing or having reason to know that the information was obtained through the interception of a wire, electronic, or oral communication in violation of this subsection; or

(e) having knowledge that an investigative or law enforcement officer has been authorized or has applied for authorization under sections 86-701 to 86-712 to intercept a wire, oral, or electronic communication, give notice or attempt to give notice of the possible interception to any person in order to obstruct, impede, or prevent such interception. Except as provided in subdivisions (4)(a) and (5)(b) of this section, any person who violates this subsection shall be guilty of a Class IV felony.

(2)(a) It shall not be unlawful under sections 86-701 to 86-707 for an employer on his, her, or its business premises, for an operator of a switchboard, or for an officer, employee, or agent of any provider, the facilities of which are used in the transmission of a wire communication, to intercept, disclose, or use that communication in the normal course of his, her, or its employment while engaged in any activity which is a necessary incident to the rendition of his, her, or its service or to the protection of the rights or property of the carrier or provider of such communication services. Such employers and providers shall not utilize service observing or random monitoring except for mechanical, service quality, or performance control checks as long as reasonable notice of the policy of random monitoring is provided to their employees.

(b) It shall not be unlawful under sections 86-701 to 86-707 for a person acting under color of law to intercept a wire, electronic, or oral communication when such person is a party to the communication or one of the parties to the communication has given prior consent to such interception.

(c) It shall not be unlawful under sections 86-701 to 86-707 for a person not acting under color of law to intercept a wire, electronic, or oral communication when such person is a party to the communication or when one of the parties to the communication has given prior consent to such interception unless such communication is intercepted for the purpose of committing any criminal or tortious act in violation of the Constitution or laws of the United States or of any state.

(d) It shall not be unlawful under sections 86-701 to 86-707:

(i) To intercept or access an electronic communication made through an electronic communications system that is configured so that such electronic communication is readily accessible to the general public;

(ii) To intercept any radio communication which is transmitted:

(A) By any station for the use of the general public or that relates to ships, aircraft, vehicles, or persons in distress;

(B) By any governmental, law enforcement, emergency management, private land mobile, or public safety communications system, including police and fire, readily accessible to the general public;

(C) By a station operating on an authorized frequency within the bands allocated to the amateur, citizens band, or general mobile radio services; or

(D) By any marine or aeronautical communications system;

(iii) To engage in any conduct which:

(A) Is prohibited by section 633 of the federal Communications Act of 1934, 47 U.S.C. § 151 et seq.; or

(B) Is excepted from the application of section 705(a) of the federal Communications Act of 1934, 47 U.S.C. § 151 et seq., by section 705(b) of such act;

(iv) To intercept any wire or electronic communication the transmission of which is causing harmful interference to any lawfully operating station or consumer electronic equipment to the extent necessary to identify the source of such interference; or

(v) For other users of the same frequency to intercept any radio communication made through a system that utilizes frequencies monitored by individuals engaged in the provision or the use of such system if such communication is not scrambled or encrypted.

* * * * *

(4)(a) If the offense is a first offense under subsection (1) of this section and is not for a tortious or illegal purpose or for purposes of direct or indirect commercial advantage or private commercial gain and the wire or electronic communication with respect to the offense under subsection (1) of this section is a radio communication that is not scrambled or encrypted, then:

(i) If the communication is not the radio portion of a cellular telephone communication, a public land mobile radio service communication, or a paging service communication and the conduct is not that described in subsection (5) of this section, the offender shall be guilty of a Class I misdemeanor; or

(ii) If the communication is the radio portion of a cellular telephone communication, a public land mobile radio service communication, or a paging service communication, the offender shall be guilty of a Class III misdemeanor.

(b) Conduct, otherwise an offense under this subsection that consists of or relates to the interception of a satellite transmission that is not encrypted or scrambled and that is transmitted: (i) To a broadcasting station for purposes of retransmission to the general public; or (ii) as an audio subcarrier intended for redistribution to facilities open to the public but not including data transmissions or telephone calls, shall not be an offense under this subsection unless the conduct is for the purposes of direct or indirect commercial advantage or private financial gain.

(5)(a) If the communication is:

(i) A private satellite video communication that is not scrambled or encrypted and the conduct in violation of sections 86-701 to 86-707 is the private viewing of that communication and is not for a tortious or illegal purpose or for purposes of direct or indirect commercial advantage or private commercial gain; or

(ii) a radio communication that is transmitted on frequencies allocated under subpart D of part 74 of the rules of the Federal Communications Commission and that is not scrambled or encrypted and the conduct in violation of sections 86-701 to 86-707 is not for a tortious or illegal purpose or for purposes of direct or indirect commercial advantage or private commercial gain, then the person who engages in such conduct shall be subject to suit by the state in a court of competent jurisdiction.

(b) In an action under this subsection:

(i) If the violation is a first offense by the person under subsection (1) of this section and such person has not been found liable in a civil action under section 86-707.02, the state shall be entitled to appropriate injunctive relief; and

(ii) If the violation is a second or subsequent offense under subsection (1) of this section or such person has been found liable in any prior civil action under section 86-707.02, the person shall be subject to a mandatory five hundred dollar civil fine.

(c) The court may use any means within its authority to enforce an injunction issued under this subsection and shall impose a civil fine of not less than five hundred dollars for each violation of such an injunction.

§ 86-707. Violations.

It shall be unlawful for any person to (1) intentionally and without lawful authority cut, break, tap, or make connection with any telegraph or telephone line, wire, cable, or instrument or electronic, mechanical, or other device or read or copy in any unauthorized manner any message, communication, or report passing over it, in this state, (2) intentionally and without lawful authority prevent, obstruct, or delay, by any means or contrivance whatsoever, the sending, transmission, conveyance, or delivery in this state of any authorized message, communication, or report by or through any telegraph or telephone line, wire, or cable under the control of any telegraph or telephone company doing business in this state, (3) aid, agree with, employ, or conspire with any person or persons to unlawfully do or perform, or cause to be done, any of the acts described in subdivisions (1) and (2) of this section, or (4) occupy, use a line, or knowingly permit another to occupy, use a line, room, table, establishment, or apparatus to unlawfully do or cause to be done any of the acts described in this section. Any person who violates this section shall be guilty of a Class IV felony.

§ 86-707.02. Wire, electronic, or oral communication; intercepted.

(1) Any person whose wire, electronic, or oral communication is intercepted, disclosed, or intentionally used in violation of sections 86-701 to 86-707 and 86-707.03 to 86-707.08 may in a civil action recover from the person or entity which engaged in that violation such relief as may be appropriate.

(2) In an action under this section, appropriate relief shall include:

(a) Such preliminary and other equitable or declaratory relief as may be appropriate;

(b) Damages under subsection (3) of this section; and

(c) Reasonable attorney's fees and other litigation costs reasonably incurred.

(3)(a) In an action under this section, if the conduct in violation of sections 86-701 to 86-707 and 86-707.03 to 86-707.08 is the private viewing of a private satellite video communication that is not scrambled or encrypted or if the communication is a radio communication that is transmitted on frequencies allocated under subpart D of part 74 of the rules of the Federal Communications Commission that is not scrambled or encrypted and the conduct is not for a tortious or illegal purpose or for purposes of direct or indirect commercial advantage or private commercial gain, then the court shall assess damages as follows:

(i) If the person who engaged in such conduct has not previously been enjoined under subsection (5) of section 86-702 and has not been found liable in a prior civil action under this section, the court shall assess the greater of the sum of actual damages suffered by the plaintiff or statutory damages of not less than fifty dollars and not more than five hundred dollars; or

(ii) If on one prior occasion the person who engaged in such conduct has been enjoined under subsection (5) of section 86-702 or has been found liable in a civil action under this section, the court shall assess the greater of the sum of actual damages suffered by the plaintiff or statutory damages of not less than one hundred dollars and not more than one thousand dollars.

(b) In any other action under this section, the court may assess as damages whichever is the greater of:

(i) The sum of the actual damages suffered by the plaintiff and any profits made by the violator as a result of the violation; or

(ii) Statutory damages of whichever is the greater of one hundred dollars a day for each day of violation or ten thousand dollars.

(4) A good faith reliance on (a) a court warrant or order, a grand jury subpoena, a legislative authorization, or a statutory authorization, (b) a request of an investigative or law enforcement officer under section 86-705, or (c) a good faith determination that section 86-702 permitted the conduct complained of shall be a complete defense against any civil or criminal action brought under sections 86-701 to 86-707 and 86-707.03 to 86-707.08 or any other law.

(5) A civil action under this section may not be commenced later than two years after the date upon which the claimant first discovered or had a reasonable opportunity to discover the violation.

Nevada

§ 200.610. Definitions.

As used in 200.610 to 200.690, inclusive:

1. "Person" includes public officials and law enforcement officers of the state and of a county or municipality or other political subdivision of the state.

2. "Wire communication" means the transmission of writing, signs, signals, pictures and sounds of all kinds by wire, cable, or other similar connection between the points of

origin and reception of such transmission, including all facilities and services incidental to such transmission, which facilities and services include, among other things, the receipt, forwarding and delivering of communications.

3. "Radio communication" means the transmission of writing, signs, signals, pictures, and sounds of all kinds by radio or other wireless methods, including all facilities and services incidental to such transmission, which facilities and services include, among other things, the receipt, forwarding and delivering of communications. The term does not include the transmission of writing, signs, signals, pictures and sounds broadcast by amateurs or public or municipal agencies of the State of Nevada, or by others for the use of the general public.

§ 200.620. Interception and attempted interception of wire or radio communication.

1. Except as otherwise provided in NRS 179.410 to 179.515, inclusive, 209.419 and 704.195, it is unlawful for any person to intercept or attempt to intercept any wire communication unless:

   (a) The interception or attempted interception is made with the prior consent of one of the parties to the communication; and

   (b) An emergency situation exists and it is impractical to obtain a court order as required by NRS 179.410 to 179.515, inclusive, before the interception, in which event the interception is subject to the requirements of subsection 3. If the application for ratification is denied, any use or disclosure of the information so intercepted is unlawful, and the person who made the interception shall notify the sender and the receiver of the communication that:

   (1) The communication was intercepted; and

   (2) Upon application to the court, ratification of the interception was denied.

2. This section does not apply to any person, or to the officers, employees or agents of any person, engaged in the business of providing service and facilities for wire communication where the interception or attempted interception is to construct, maintain, conduct or operate the service or facilities of that person.

3. Any person who has made an interception in an emergency situation as provided in paragraph (b) of subsection 1 shall, within 72 hours of the interception, make a written application to a justice of the supreme court or district judge for ratification of the interception. The interception must not be ratified unless the applicant shows that:

   (a) An emergency situation existed and it was impractical to obtain a court order before the interception; and

   (b) Except for the absence of a court order, the interception met the requirements of NRS 179.410 to 179.515, inclusive.

4. NRS 200.610 to 200.690, inclusive, do not prohibit the recording, and NRS 179.410 to 179.515, inclusive, do not prohibit the reception in evidence, of conversations on wire communications installed in the office of an official law enforcement or fire-fighting agency, or a public utility, if the equipment used for the recording is installed in a facility for wire communications or on a telephone with a number listed in a directory, on which emergency calls or requests by a person for response by the law enforcement or fire-fighting agency or public utility are likely to be received. In addition, those sections do not prohibit the recording or reception in evidence of conversations initiated by the law enforcement or fire-fighting agency or public utility from such a facility or telephone in

connection with responding to the original call or request, if the agency or public utility informs the other party that the conversation is being recorded.

§ 200.650. Unauthorized, surreptitious intrusion of privacy by listening device.

Except as otherwise provided in 179.410 to 179.515, inclusive, and 704.195, a person shall not intrude upon the privacy of other persons by surreptitiously listening to, monitoring or recording, or attempting to listen to, monitor or record, by means of any mechanical, electronic or other listening device, any private conversation engaged in by the other persons, or disclose the existence, content, substance, purport, effect or meaning of any conversation so listened to, monitored or recorded, unless authorized to do so by one of the persons engaging in the conversation.

§ 200.690. Penalties.

1. A person who willfully and knowingly violates NRS 200.620 to 200.650, inclusive:
   (a) Shall be punished for a category D felony as provided in NRS 193.130.
   (b) Is liable to a person whose wire or oral communication is intercepted without his consent for:
   (1) Actual damages or liquidated damages of $100 per day of violation but not less than $1,000, whichever is greater;
   (2) Punitive damages; and
   (3) His costs reasonably incurred in the action, including a reasonable attorney's fee, all of which may be recovered by civil action.
2. A good faith reliance by a public utility on a written request for interception by one party to a conversation is a complete defense to any civil or criminal action brought against the public utility on account of the interception.

New Jersey

2A:156A-1. Short title.

This act shall be known and may be cited as the "New Jersey Wiretapping and Electronic Surveillance Control Act."

2A:156A-2. Definitions.

As used in this act:

a. "Wire communication" means any aural transfer made in whole or in part through the use of facilities for the transmission of communications by the aid of wire, cable or other like connection between the point of origin and the point of reception, including the use of such connection in a switching station, furnished or operated by any person engaged in providing or operating such facilities for the transmission of intrastate, interstate or foreign communication. "Wire communication" includes any electronic storage of such communication, and the radio portion of a cordless telephone communication that is transmitted between the cordless telephone handset and the base unit;

b. "Oral communication" means any oral communication uttered by a person exhibiting an expectation that such communication is not subject to interception under circumstances justifying such expectation, but does not include any electronic communication;

APPENDIX B — STATE STATUTES

c. "Intercept" means the aural or other acquisition of the contents of any wire, electronic or oral communication through the use of any electronic, mechanical, or other device;

d. "Electronic, mechanical or other device" means any device or apparatus, including an induction coil, that can be used to intercept a wire, electronic or oral communication other than:

(1) Any telephone or telegraph instrument, equipment or facility, or any component thereof, furnished to the subscriber or user by a provider of wire or electronic communication service in the ordinary course of its business and being used by the subscriber or user in the ordinary course of its business; or furnished by such subscriber or user for connection to the facilities of such service and used in the ordinary course of its business; or being used by a provider of wire or electronic communication service in the ordinary course of its business, or by an investigative or law enforcement officer in the ordinary course of his duties; or

2) A hearing aid or similar device being used to correct subnormal hearing to not better than normal;

e. "Person" means that term as defined in R.S. 1:1-2 and includes any officer or employee of the State or of a political subdivision thereof;

f. "Investigative or law enforcement officer" means any officer of the State of New Jersey or of a political subdivision thereof who is empowered by law to conduct investigations of, or to make arrests for, any offense enumerated in section 8 of P.L.1968, c. 409 (2A:156A-8) and any attorney authorized by law to prosecute or participate in the prosecution of any such offense;

g. "Contents," when used with respect to any wire, electronic or oral communication, includes any information concerning the identity of the parties to such communication or the existence, substance, purport, or meaning of that communication, except that for purposes of sections 22, 23, 24 and 26 of P.L.1993, c. 29 (2A:156A-28, 2A:156A-29, and 2A:156A-30) contents, when used with respect to any wire, electronic, or oral communication means any information concerning the substance, purport or meaning of that communication;

h. "Court of competent jurisdiction" means the Superior Court;

i. "Judge," when referring to a judge authorized to receive applications for, and to enter, orders authorizing interceptions of wire, electronic or oral communications, means one of the several judges of the Superior Court to be designated from time to time by the Chief Justice of the Supreme Court to receive applications for, and to enter, orders authorizing interceptions of wire, electronic or oral communications pursuant to this act;

j. "Communication common carrier" means any person engaged as a common carrier for hire, in intrastate, interstate or foreign communication by wire or radio or in intrastate, interstate or foreign radio transmission of energy; but a person engaged in radio broadcasting shall not, while so engaged, be deemed a common carrier;

k. "Aggrieved person" means a person who was a party to any intercepted wire, electronic or oral communication or a person against whom the interception was directed;

l. "In-progress trace" means the determination of the origin of a telephonic communication to a known telephone during the communication;

m. "Electronic communication" means any transfer of signs, signals, writing, images, sounds, data, or intelligence of any nature transmitted in whole or in part by a wire, radio, electromagnetic, photoelectric or photo-optical system that affects interstate, intrastate or foreign commerce, but does not include:

(1) Any wire or oral communication;

(2) Any communication made through a tone-only paging device; or

(3) Any communication from a tracking device;

n. "User" means any person or entity who:

(1) Uses an electronic communication service; and

(2) Is duly authorized by the provider of such service to engage in such use;

o. "Electronic communication system" means any wire, radio, electromagnetic, photo-optical or photoelectronic facilities for the transmission of electronic communications, and any computer facilities or related electronic equipment for the electronic storage of such communications;

p. "Electronic communication service" means any service which provides to the users thereof the ability to send or receive wire or electronic communications;

q. "Electronic storage" means:

(1) Any temporary, intermediate storage of a wire or electronic communication incidental to the electronic transmission thereof; and

(2) Any storage of such communication by an electronic communication service for purpose of backup protection of the communication;

r. "Readily accessible to the general public" means, with respect to a radio communication, that such communication is not:

(1) Scrambled or encrypted;

(2) Transmitted using modulation techniques whose essential parameters have been withheld from the public with the intention of preserving the privacy of such communication;

(3) Carried on a subcarrier or other signal subsidiary to a radio transmission;

(4) Transmitted over a communication system provided by a common carrier, unless the communication is a tone-only paging system communication; or

(5) Transmitted on frequencies allocated under part 25, subpart D, E or F of part 74 or part 94 of the Rules of the Federal Communications Commission, unless, in the case of a communication transmitted on a frequency allocated under part 74 that is not exclusively allocated to broadcast auxiliary services, the communication is a two-way voice communication by radio;

s. "Remote computing service" means the provision to the public of computer storage or processing services by means of an electronic communication system;

t. "Aural transfer" means a transfer containing the human voice at any point between and including the point of origin and the point of reception;

u. "Tracking device" means an electronic or mechanical device which permits the tracking of the movement of a person or device.

2A:156A-3. Interception, disclosure or use of wire or oral communications.

Except as otherwise specifically provided in this act, any person who:

a. Purposely intercepts, endeavors to intercept, or procures any other person to intercept or endeavor to intercept any wire, electronic or oral communication; or

b. Purposely discloses or endeavors to disclose to any other person the contents of any wire, electronic or oral communication, or evidence derived therefrom, knowing or hav-

APPENDIX B — STATE STATUTES

ing reason to know that the information was obtained through the interception of a wire, electronic or oral communication; or

c. Purposely uses or endeavors to use the contents of any wire, electronic or oral communication, or evidence derived therefrom, knowing or having reason to know, that the information was obtained through the interception of a wire, electronic or oral communication; shall be guilty of a crime of the third degree. Subsections b. and c. of this section shall not apply to the contents of any wire, electronic or oral communication, or evidence derived therefrom, that has become common knowledge or public information.

2A:156A-4. Exceptions.

It shall not be unlawful under this act for:

* * * * *

c. Any person acting at the direction of an investigative or law enforcement officer to intercept a wire, electronic or oral communication, where such person is a party to the communication or one of the parties to the communication has given prior consent to such interception; provided, however, that no such interception shall be made unless the Attorney General or his designee or a county prosecutor within his authority determines that there exists a reasonable suspicion that evidence of criminal conduct will be derived from such interception;

d. A person not acting under color of law to intercept a wire, electronic or oral communication, where such person is a party to the communication or one of the parties to the communication has given prior consent to such interception unless such communication is intercepted or used for the purpose of committing any criminal or tortious act in violation of the Constitution or laws of the United States or of this State or for the purpose of committing any other injurious act. The fact that such person is the subscriber to a particular telephone does not constitute consent effective to authorize interception of communications among parties not including such person on that telephone. Any person who unlawfully intercepts or uses such communication as provided in this paragraph shall be subject to the civil liability established in section 24 of P.L.1968, c. 409 (C. 2A:156A-24), in addition to any other criminal or civil liability imposed by law;

e. Any person to intercept or access an electronic communication made through an electronic communication system that is configured so that such electronic communication is readily accessible to the general public;

f. Any person to intercept any radio communication which is transmitted:

(1) by any station for the use of the general public, or that relates to ships, aircraft, vehicles, or persons in distress;

(2) by any governmental, law enforcement, civil defense, private land mobile, or public safety communication system, including police and fire, readily accessible to the general public;

(3) by a station operating on an authorized frequency within the bands allocated to the amateur, citizens band, or general mobile radio services; or

(4) by any marine or aeronautical communications system;

g. Any person to engage in any conduct which:

(1) is prohibited by section 633 of the Communications Act of 1934; or

(2) is excepted from the application of section 705(a) of the Communications Act of 1934 by section 705(b) of that Act;

* * * * *

2A:156A-24. Civil action for unlawful interception, disclosure or use of wire or oral communication.

Any person whose wire, electronic or oral communication is intercepted, disclosed or used in violation of this act shall have a civil cause of action against any person who intercepts, discloses or uses or procures any other person to intercept, disclose or use, such communication; and shall be entitled to recover from any such person:
    a. Actual damages, but not less than liquidated damages computed at the rate of $100.00 a day for each day of violation, or $1,000.00, whichever is higher;
    b. Punitive damages; and
    c. A reasonable attorney's fee and other litigation costs reasonably incurred.

2A:156A-32. Civil action.

a. Except as provided in subsection d. of section 23 of P.L.1993, c. 29 (2A:156A-29), any service provider, subscriber or customer aggrieved by any violation of sections 21, 22, 23, or 24 of P.L.1993, c. 29 (2A:156A-27, 2A:156A-28, 2A:156A-29, or 2A:156A-30) may recover, in a civil action, such relief as may be appropriate from the person or entity which knowingly or purposefully engaged in the conduct constituting the violation.
    b. In a civil action under this section, appropriate relief may include:
        (1) such preliminary and other equitable or declaratory relief as may be appropriate;
        (2) damages under subsection c. of this section; and
        (3) reasonable attorney fees and other litigation costs reasonably incurred.
    c. The court may assess as damages in a civil action under this section the sum of the actual damages suffered by the plaintiff and any profits made by the violator as a result of the violation, but in no case shall a person entitled to recover receive less than the sum of $1,000.
    d. A civil action under this section may not be commenced later than two years after the date upon which the claimant first discovered or had a reasonable opportunity to discover the violation.

New Mexico

§ 30-12-1. Interference with communications.

Interference with communications consists of knowingly and without lawful authority:
    A. displacing, removing, injuring or destroying any radio station, television tower, antenna or cable, telegraph or telephone line, wire, cable, pole or conduit belonging to another, or the material or property appurtenant thereto;
    B. cutting, breaking, tapping or making any connection with any telegraph or telephone line, wire, cable or instrument belonging to or in the lawful possession or control of another, without the consent of such person owning, possessing or controlling such property;
    C. reading, interrupting, taking or copying any message, communication or report intended for another by telegraph or telephone without the consent of a sender or intended recipient thereof;

D. preventing, obstructing or delaying the sending, transmitting, conveying or delivering in this state of any message, communication or report by or through telegraph or telephone; or

E. using any apparatus to do or cause to be done any of the acts hereinbefore mentioned or to aid, agree with, comply or conspire with any person to do or permit or cause to be done any of the acts hereinbefore mentioned.

Whoever commits interference with communications is guilty of a misdemeanor, unless such interference with communications is done:

(1) under a court order as provided in Sections 30-12-2 through 30-12-11 NMSA 1978; or

(2) by an operator of a switchboard or an officer, employee or agent of any communication common carrier in the normal course of his employment while engaged in any activity which is a necessary incident to the rendition of his services or to the protection of rights or property of the carrier of such communication; or

(3) by a person acting under color of law in the investigation of a crime, where such person is a party to the communication, or one of the parties to the communication has given prior consent to such interception, monitoring or recording of such communication.

§ 30-12-11. Right of privacy.

A. Any person whose wire or oral communication is intercepted, disclosed or used in violation of this act shall:

(1) have a civil cause of action against any person who intercepts, discloses or uses, or procures any other person to intercept, disclose or use such communications; and

(2) be entitled to recover from any such person actual damages, but not less than liquidated damages computed at the rate of one hundred dollars ($100) for each day of violation or one thousand dollars ($1,000), whichever is higher; punitive damages; and a reasonable attorney's fee and other litigation costs reasonably incurred.

B. A good faith reliance on a court order or on the provisions of this act shall constitute a complete defense to any civil or criminal action.

C. Any communications common carrier which in good faith acts in reliance upon a court order or in compliance with any of the provisions of this act shall not be liable for any civil or criminal action.

New York

New York Penal Code

§ 250.00. Eavesdropping; definitions of terms.

The following definitions are applicable to this article:

1. "Wiretapping" means the intentional overhearing or recording of a telephonic or telegraphic communication by a person other than a sender or receiver thereof, without the consent of either the sender or receiver, by means of any instrument, device or equipment. The normal operation of a telephone or telegraph corporation and the normal use of the services and facilities furnished by such corporation pursuant to its tariffs or necessary to protect the rights or property of said corporation shall not be deemed "wiretapping."

2. "Mechanical overhearing of a conversation" means the intentional overhearing or recording of a conversation or discussion, without the consent of at least one party thereto, by a person not present thereat, by means of any instrument, device or equipment.

3. "Telephonic communication" means any aural transfer made in whole or in part through the use of facilities for the transmission of communications by the aid of wire, cable or other like connection between the point of origin and the point of reception (including the use of such connection in a switching station) furnished or operated by any person engaged in providing or operating such facilities for the transmission of communications and such term includes any electronic storage of such communications.

4. "Aural transfer" means a transfer containing the human voice at any point between and including the point of origin and the point of reception.

5. "Electronic communication" means any transfer of signs, signals, writing, images, sounds, data, or intelligence of any nature transmitted in whole or in part by a wire, radio, electromagnetic, photoelectronic or photo-optical system, but does not include:

(a) any telephonic or telegraphic communication; or

(b) any communication made through a tone only paging device; or

(c) any communication made through a tracking device consisting of an electronic or mechanical device which permits the tracking of the movement of a person or object; or

(d) any communication that is disseminated by the sender through a method of transmission that is configured so that such communication is readily accessible to the general public.

6. "Intercepting or accessing of an electronic communication" and "intentionally intercepted or accessed" mean the intentional acquiring, receiving, collecting, overhearing, or recording of an electronic communication, without the consent of the sender or intended receiver thereof, by means of any instrument, device or equipment, except when used by a telephone company in the ordinary course of its business or when necessary to protect the rights or property of such company.

7. "Electronic communication service" means any service which provides to users thereof the ability to send or receive wire or electronic communications.

8. "Unlawfully" means not specifically authorized pursuant to article seven hundred or seven hundred five of the criminal procedure law.

§ 250.05. Eavesdropping.

A person is guilty of eavesdropping when he unlawfully engages in wiretapping, mechanical overhearing of a conversation, or intercepting or accessing of an electronic communication.

Eavesdropping is a class E felony.

§ 250.25. Tampering with private communications.

A person is guilty of tampering with private communications when:

1. Knowing that he does not have the consent of the sender or receiver, he opens or reads a sealed letter or other sealed private communication; or

2. Knowing that a sealed letter or other sealed private communication has been opened or read in violation of subdivision one of this section, he divulges without the consent of

APPENDIX B — STATE STATUTES

the sender or receiver, the contents of such letter or communication, in whole or in part, or a resume of any portion of the contents thereof; or

3. Knowing that he does not have the consent of the sender or receiver, he obtains or attempts to obtain from an employee, officer or representative of a telephone or telegraph corporation, by connivance, deception, intimidation or in any other manner, information with respect to the contents or nature thereof of a telephonic or telegraphic communication; except that the provisions of this subdivision do not apply to a law enforcement officer who obtains information from a telephone or telegraph corporation pursuant to section 250.35; or

4. Knowing that he does not have the consent of the sender or receiver, and being an employee, officer or representative of a telephone or telegraph corporation, he knowingly divulges to another person the contents or nature thereof of a telephonic or telegraphic communication; except that the provisions of this subdivision do not apply to such person when he acts pursuant to section 250.35.

Tampering with private communications is a class B misdemeanor.

North Carolina

§ 14-155. Unauthorized connections with telephone or telegraph.

It shall be unlawful for any person to tap or make any connection with any wire or apparatus of any telephone or telegraph company operating in this State, except such connection as may be authorized by the person or corporation operating such wire or apparatus. Any person violating this section shall be guilty of a Class 3 misdemeanor. Each day's continuance of such unlawful connection shall be a separate offense. No connection approved by the Federal Communications Commission or the North Carolina Utilities Commission shall be a violation of this section.

§ 15A-286. Definitions.

As used in this Article, unless the context requires otherwise:

(1) "Aggrieved person" means a person who was a party to any intercepted wire, oral, or electronic communication or a person against whom the interception was directed.

(2) "Attorney General" means the Attorney General of the State of North Carolina, unless otherwise specified.

(3) "Aural transfer" means a transfer containing the human voice at any point between and including the point of origin and the point of reception.

(4) "Chapter 119 of the United States Code" means Chapter 119 of Part I of Title 18, United States Code, being Public Law 90-351, the Omnibus Crime Control and Safe Streets Act of 1968, as amended by the Electronic Communications Privacy Act of 1986.

(5) "Communications common carrier" shall have the same meaning which is given the term "common carrier" by section 153(h) of Title 47 of the United States Code.

(6) "Contents" when used with respect to any wire, oral, or electronic communication means and includes any information concerning the substance, purport, or meaning of that communication.

(7) "Electronic, mechanical, or other device" means any device or apparatus which can be used to intercept a wire, oral, or electronic communication other than:

    a. Any telephone or telegraph instrument, equipment, or facility, or any component thereof:

1. Furnished to the subscriber or user by a provider of wire or electronic communication service in the ordinary course of its business and being used by the subscriber or user in the ordinary course of its business or furnished by the subscriber or user for connection to the facilities of such service and used in the ordinary course of its business; or

2. Being used by a provider of wire or electronic communication service in the ordinary course of its business or by an investigative or law enforcement officer in the ordinary course of the officer's duties.

  b. A hearing aid or similar device being used to correct subnormal hearing to not better than normal.

(8) "Electronic communication" means any transfer of signs, signals, writing, images, sounds, data, or intelligence of any nature transmitted in whole or in part by a wire, radio, electromagnetic, photoelectronic, or photooptical system that affects interstate or foreign commerce but does not include:

  a. Any wire or oral communication;
  b. Any communication made through a tone-only paging device; or
  c. Any communication from a tracking device (as defined in section 3117 of Title 18 of the United States Code).

(9) "Electronic communication service" means any service which provides to users thereof the ability to send or receive wire or electronic communications.

(10) "Electronic communication system" means any wire, radio, electronic, magnetic, photo-optical, or photoelectronic facilities for the transmission of electronic communications, and any computer facilities or related electronic equipment for the storage of such communications.

(11) "Electronic surveillance" means the interception of wire, oral, or electronic communications as provided by this Article.

(12) "Electronic storage" means:

  a. Any temporary, intermediate storage of a wire or electronic communication incidental to the electronic transmission thereof; and
  b. Any storage of such communication by an electronic communication service for the purposes of backup protection of the communication.

(13) "Intercept" means the aural or other acquisition of the contents of any wire, oral, or electronic communication through the use of any electronic, mechanical, or other device.

(14) "Investigative or law enforcement officer" means any officer of the State of North Carolina or any political subdivision thereof, who is empowered by the laws of this State to conduct investigations of or to make arrests for offenses enumerated in G.S. 15A-290, and any attorney authorized by the laws of this State to prosecute or participate in the prosecution of those offenses, including the Attorney General of North Carolina.

(15) "Judge" means any judge of the trial divisions of the General Court of Justice.

(16) "Judicial review panel" means a three-judge body, composed of such judges as may be assigned by the Chief Justice of the Supreme Court of North Carolina, which shall review applications for electronic surveillance orders and may issue orders valid throughout the State authorizing such surveillance as provided by this Article, and which shall submit a report of its decision to the Chief Justice.

(17) "Oral communication" means any oral communication uttered by a person exhibiting an expectation that such communication is not subject to interception under circum-

stances justifying such expectation, but the term does not include any electronic communication.

(18) "Person" means any employee or agent of the United States or any state or any political subdivision thereof, and any individual, partnership, association, joint stock company, trust, or corporation.

(19) "Readily accessible to the general public" means, with respect to a radio communication, that the communication is not:

    a. Scrambled or encrypted;

    b. Transmitted using modulation techniques whose essential parameters have been withheld from the public with the intention of preserving the privacy of the communication;

    c. Carried on a subcarrier or other signal subsidiary to a radio transmission;

    d. Transmitted over a communications system provided by a common carrier, unless the communication is a tone-only paging system communication; or

    e. Transmitted on frequencies allocated under Part 25, Subpart D, E or F or Part 94 of the Rules of the Federal Communications Commission as provided by 18 U.S.C. § 2510(16)(E).

(20) "User" means any person or entity who:

    a. Uses an electronic communications service; and

    b. Is duly authorized by the provider of the service to engage in the use.

(21) "Wire communication" means any aural transfer made in whole or in part through the use of facilities for the transmission of communications by the aid of wire, cable, or other like connection between the point of origin and the point of reception (including the use of such connection in a switching station) furnished or operated by any person engaged in providing or operating such facilities for the transmission of interstate or foreign communications or communications affecting interstate or foreign commerce and the term includes any electronic storage of such communication.

§ 15A-287. Interception and disclosure of wire, oral, or electronic com-munications.

(a) Except as otherwise specifically provided in this Article, a person is guilty of a Class H felony if, without the consent of at least one party to the communication, the person:

    (1) Willfully intercepts, endeavors to intercept, or procures any other person to intercept or endeavor to intercept, any wire, oral, or electronic communication.

    (2) Willfully uses, endeavors to use, or procures any other person to use or endeavor to use any electronic, mechanical, or other device to intercept any oral communication when:

        a. The device is affixed to, or otherwise transmits a signal through, a wire, cable, or other like connection used in wire communications; or

        b. The device transmits communications by radio, or interferes with the transmission of such communications.

    (3) Willfully discloses, or endeavors to disclose, to any other person the contents of any wire, oral, or electronic communication, knowing or having reason to know that the information was obtained through violation of this Article; or

(4) Willfully uses, or endeavors to use, the contents of any wire or oral communication, knowing or having reason to know that the information was obtained through the interception of a wire or oral communication in violation of this Article.

(b) It is not unlawful under this Article for any person to:

(1) Intercept or access an electronic communication made through an electronic communication system that is configured so that the electronic communication is readily accessible to the general public;

(2) Intercept any radio communication which is transmitted:

   a. For use by the general public, or that relates to ships, aircraft, vehicles, or persons in distress;

   b. By any governmental, law enforcement, civil defense, private land mobile, or public safety communication system, including police and fire, readily available to the general public;

   c. By a station operating on any authorized band within the bands allocated to the amateur, citizens band, or general mobile radio services; or

   d. By any marine or aeronautical communication system; or

(3) Intercept any communication in a manner otherwise allowed by Chapter 119 of the United States Code.

(c) It is not unlawful under this Article for an operator of a switchboard, or an officer, employee, or agent of a provider of electronic communication service, whose facilities are used in the transmission of a wire or electronic communication, to intercept, disclose, or use that communication in the normal course of employment while engaged in any activity that is a necessary incident to the rendition of his or her service or to the protection of the rights or property of the provider of that service, provided that a provider of wire or electronic communication service may not utilize service observing or random monitoring except for mechanical or service quality control checks.

(d) It is not unlawful under this Article for an officer, employee, or agent of the Federal Communications Commission, in the normal course of his employment and in discharge of the monitoring responsibilities exercised by the Commission in the enforcement of Chapter 5 of Title 47 of the United States Code, to intercept a wire or electronic communication, or oral communication transmitted by radio, or to disclose or use the information thereby obtained.

(e) Any person who, as a result of the person's official position or employment, has obtained knowledge of the contents of any wire, oral, or electronic communication lawfully intercepted pursuant to an electronic surveillance order or of the pendency or existence of or implementation of an electronic surveillance order who shall knowingly and willfully disclose such information for the purpose of hindering or thwarting any investigation or prosecution relating to the subject matter of the electronic surveillance order, except as is necessary for the proper and lawful performance of the duties of his position or employment or as shall be required or allowed by law, shall be guilty of a Class G felony.

(f) Any person who shall, knowingly or with gross negligence, divulge the existence of or contents of any electronic surveillance order in a way likely to hinder or thwart any investigation or prosecution relating to the subject matter of the electronic surveillance order or anyone who shall, knowingly or with gross negligence, release the contents of any wire, oral, or electronic communication intercepted under an electronic surveillance order, except as is necessary for the proper and lawful performance of the duties of his

APPENDIX B — STATE STATUTES

position or employment or as is required or allowed by law, shall be guilty of a Class 1 misdemeanor.

(g) Any public officer who shall violate subsection (a) or (d) of this section or who shall knowingly violate subsection (e) of this section shall be removed from any public office he may hold and shall thereafter be ineligible to hold any public office, whether elective or appointed.

§ 15A-296. Recovery of civil damages.

(a) Any person whose wire, oral, or electronic communication is intercepted, disclosed, or used in violation of this Article, has a civil cause of action against any person who intercepts, discloses, uses, or procures any other person to intercept, disclose, or use such communications, and is entitled to recover from any other person:

  (1) Actual damages, but not less than liquidated damages, computed at the rate of one hundred dollars ($100) a day for each day of violation or one thousand dollars ($1,000), whichever is higher;
  (2) Punitive damages; and
  (3) A reasonable attorneys' fee and other litigation costs reasonably incurred.

(b) Good faith reliance on a court order or on a representation made by the Attorney General or a district attorney is a complete defense to any civil or criminal action brought under this Article.

North Dakota

§ 12.1-15-02. Interception of wire or oral communications — Eavesdropping.

1. A person is guilty of a class C felony if he:
  a. Intentionally intercepts any wire or oral communication by use of any electronic, mechanical, or other device; or
  b. Intentionally discloses to any other person or intentionally uses the contents of any wire or oral communication, knowing that the information was obtained through the interception of a wire or oral communication.

2. A person is guilty of a class A misdemeanor if he secretly loiters about any building with intent to overhear discourse or conversation therein and to repeat or publish the same with intent to vex, annoy, or injure others.

3. It is a defense to a prosecution under subsection 1 that:
  a. The actor was authorized by law to intercept, disclose, or use, as the case may be, the wire or oral communication.
  b. The actor was (1) a person acting under color of law to intercept a wire or oral communication, and (2) he was a party to the communication or one of the parties to the communication had given prior consent to such interception.
  c. (1) The actor was a party to the communication or one of the parties to the communication had given prior consent to such interception, and (2) such communication was not intercepted for the purpose of committing a crime or other unlawful harm.

§ 12.1-15-04. Definitions.

In sections 12.1-15-02 through 12.1-15-04:

WIRETAP AND EAVESDROPPING LAWS

1. "Communications common carrier" shall have the meaning prescribed for the term "common carrier" by section 8-07-01.

2. "Contents", when used with respect to any wire or oral communication, includes any information concerning the identity of the parties to such communication or the existence, substance, purport, or meaning of that communication.

3. "Electronic, mechanical, or other device" means any device or apparatus which can be used to intercept a wire or oral communication other than:

 a. Any telephone or telegraph instrument, equipment, or facility, or any component thereof, (1) furnished to the subscriber or user by a communications common carrier in the ordinary course of its business and being used by subscriber or user in the ordinary course of its business; or (2) being used by a communications common carrier in the ordinary course of its business, or by an investigative or law enforcement officer in the ordinary course of his duties.

 b. A hearing aid or similar device being used to correct subnormal hearing to not better than normal.

4. "Intercept" means the aural acquisition of the contents of any wire or oral communication through the use of an electronic, mechanical, or other device, or by secretly overhearing the communication.

5. "Oral communication" means any oral communication uttered by a person exhibiting an expectation that such communication is not subject to interception under circumstances justifying such expectation.

6. "Wire communication" means any communication made in whole or in part through the use of facilities for the transmission of communications by the aid of wire, cable, or other like connection between the point of origin and the point of reception furnished or operated by any person engaged as a common carrier in providing or operating such facilities for the transmission of communications.

Ohio

§ 2933.51. Definitions.

As used in sections 2933.51 to 2933.66 of the Revised Code:

(A) "Wire communication" means an aural transfer that is made in whole or in part through the use of facilities for the transmission of communications by the aid of wires or similar methods of connecting the point of origin of the communication and the point of reception of the communication, including the use of a method of connecting the point of origin and the point of reception of the communication in a switching station, if the facilities are furnished or operated by a person engaged in providing or operating the facilities for the transmission of communications. "Wire communication" includes an electronic storage of a wire communication.

(B) "Oral communication" means an oral communication uttered by a person exhibiting an expectation that the communication is not subject to interception under circumstances justifying that expectation. "Oral communication" does not include an electronic communication.

(C) "Intercept" means the aural or other acquisition of the contents of any wire, oral, or electronic communication through the use of an interception device.

APPENDIX B — STATE STATUTES

(D) "Interception device" means an electronic, mechanical, or other device or apparatus that can be used to intercept a wire, oral, or electronic communication. "Interception device" does not mean any of the following:

(1) A telephone or telegraph instrument, equipment, or facility, or any of its components, if the instrument, equipment, facility, or component is any of the following:

(a) Furnished to the subscriber or user by a provider of wire or electronic communication service in the ordinary course of its business and being used by the subscriber or user in the ordinary course of its business;

(b) Furnished by a subscriber or user for connection to the facilities of a provider of wire or electronic communication service and used in the ordinary course of that subscriber's or user's business;

(c) Being used by a provider of wire or electronic communication service in the ordinary course of its business or by an investigative or law enforcement officer in the ordinary course of the officer's duties that do not involve the interception of wire, oral, or electronic communications.

(2) A hearing aid or similar device being used to correct subnormal hearing to not better than normal.

(E) "Investigative officer" means any of the following:

(1) An officer of this state or a political subdivision of this state, who is empowered by law to conduct investigations or to make arrests for a designated offense;

(2) A person described in divisions (A)(11)(a) and (b) of section 2901.01 of the Revised Code;

(3) An attorney authorized by law to prosecute or participate in the prosecution of a designated offense;

(4) A secret service officer appointed pursuant to section 309.07 of the Revised Code;

(5) An officer of the United States, a state, or a political subdivision of a state who is authorized to conduct investigations pursuant to the "Electronic Communications Privacy Act of 1986," 100 Stat. 1848-1857, 18 U.S.C. 2510-2521 (1986), as amended.

(F) "Interception warrant" means a court order that authorizes the interception of wire, oral, or electronic communications and that is issued pursuant to sections 2933.53 to 2933.56 of the Revised Code.

(G) "Contents," when used with respect to a wire, oral, or electronic communication, includes any information concerning the substance, purport, or meaning of the communication.

(H) "Communications common carrier" means a person who is engaged as a common carrier for hire in intrastate, interstate, or foreign communications by wire, radio, or radio transmission of energy. "Communications common carrier" does not include, to the extent that the person is engaged in radio broadcasting, a person engaged in radio broadcasting.

(I) "Designated offense" means any of the following:

(1) A felony violation of section 1315.53, 1315.55, 2903.01, 2903.02, 2903.11, 2905.01, 2905.02, 2905.11, 2905.22, 2907.02, 2907.21, 2907.22, 2909.02, 2909.03, 2909.04, 2911.01, 2911.02, 2911.11, 2911.12, 2913.02, 2913.04, 2913.42, 2913.51, 2915.02, 2915.03, 2917.01, 2917.02, 2921.02, 2921.03, 2921.04, 2921.32, 2921.34,

WIRETAP AND EAVESDROPPING LAWS

2923.20, 2923.32, 2925.03, 2925.04, 2925.05, or 2925.06 or of division (B) of section 2915.05 of the Revised Code;

(2) A violation of section 2919.23 of the Revised Code that, had it occurred prior to the effective date of this amendment, would have been a violation of section 2905.04 of the Revised Code as it existed prior to that date;

(3) A felony violation of section 2925.11 of the Revised Code that is not a minor drug possession offense, as defined in section 2925.01 of the Revised Code;

(4) Complicity in the commission of a felony violation of a section listed in division (I)(1), (2), or (3) of this section;

(5) An attempt to commit, or conspiracy in the commission of, a felony violation of a section listed in division (I)(1), (2), or (3) of this section, if the attempt or conspiracy is punishable by a term of imprisonment of more than one year.

(J) "Aggrieved person" means a person who was a party to an intercepted wire, oral, or electronic communication or a person against whom the interception of the communication was directed.

(K) "Person" means a person, as defined in section 1.59 of the Revised Code, or a governmental officer, employee, or entity.

(L) "Special need" means a showing that a licensed physician, licensed practicing psychologist, attorney, practicing clergyman, journalist, or either spouse is personally engaging in continuing criminal activity, was engaged in continuing criminal activity over a period of time, or is committing, has committed, or is about to commit, a designated offense, or a showing that specified public facilities are being regularly used by someone who is personally engaging in continuing criminal activity, was engaged in continuing criminal activity over a period of time, or is committing, has committed, or is about to commit, a designated offense.

(M) "Journalist" means a person engaged in, connected with, or employed by, any news media, including a newspaper, magazine, press association, news agency, or wire service, a radio or television station, or a similar media, for the purpose of gathering, processing, transmitting, compiling, editing, or disseminating news for the general public.

(N) "Electronic communication" means a transfer of a sign, signal, writing, image, sound, datum, or intelligence of any nature that is transmitted in whole or in part by a wire, radio, electromagnetic, photoelectronic, or photo-optical system. "Electronic communication" does not mean any of the following:

(1) A wire or oral communication;

(2) A communication made through a tone-only paging device;

(3) A communication from an electronic or mechanical tracking device that permits the tracking of the movement of a person or object.

(O) "User" means a person or entity that uses an electronic communication service and is duly authorized by the provider of the service to engage in the use of the electronic communication service.

(P) "Electronic communications system" means a wire, radio, electromagnetic, photoelectronic, or photo-optical facility for the transmission of electronic communications, and a computer facility or related electronic equipment for the electronic storage of electronic communications.

(Q) "Electronic communication service" means a service that provides to users of the service the ability to send or receive wire or electronic communications.

APPENDIX B — STATE STATUTES

(R) "Readily accessible to the general public" means, with respect to a radio communication, that the communication is none of the following:

(1) Scrambled or encrypted;

(2) Transmitted using a modulation technique, the essential parameters of which have been withheld from the public with the intention of preserving the privacy of the communication;

(3) Carried on a subcarrier or other signal subsidiary to a radio transmission;

(4) Transmitted over a communications system provided by a communications common carrier, unless the communication is a tone-only paging system communication;

(5) Transmitted on a frequency allocated under part 25, subpart D, E or F of part 74 or part 94 of the Rules of the Federal Communications Commission, as those provisions existed on the effective date of this amendment, unless, in the case of a communication transmitted on a frequency allocated under part 74 that is not exclusively allocated to broadcast auxiliary services, the communication is a two-way voice communication by radio.

(S) "Electronic storage" means a temporary, intermediate storage of a wire or electronic communication that is incidental to the electronic transmission of the communication, and a storage of a wire or electronic communication by an electronic communication service for the purpose of backup protection of the communication.

(T) "Aural transfer" means a transfer containing the human voice at a point between and including the point of origin and the point of reception.

(U) "Pen register" means a device that records or decodes electronic impulses that identify the numbers dialed, pulsed, or otherwise transmitted on telephone lines to which the device is attached.

(V) "Trap and trace device" means a device or apparatus that connects to a telephone or telegraph instrument, equipment, or facility and determines the origin of a wire communication to a telephone or telegraph instrument, equipment, or facility but does not intercept the contents of a wire communication.

§ 2933.52. Prohibition against interception of communications.

(A) No person purposely shall do any of the following:

(1) Intercept, attempt to intercept, or procure another person to intercept or attempt to intercept a wire, oral, or electronic communication;

(2) Use, attempt to use, or procure another person to use or attempt to use an interception device to intercept a wire, oral, or electronic communication, if either of the following applies:

(a) The interception device is affixed to, or otherwise transmits a signal through, a wire, cable, satellite, microwave, or other similar method of connection used in wire communications;

(b) The interception device transmits communications by radio, or interferes with the transmission of communications by radio.

(3) Use, or attempt to use, the contents of a wire, oral, or electronic communication, knowing or having reason to know that the contents were obtained through the interception of a wire, oral, or electronic communication in violation of sections 2933.51 to 2933.66 of the Revised Code.

(B) This section does not apply to any of the following:

* * * * *

(4) A person who is not a law enforcement officer and who intercepts a wire, oral, or electronic communication, if the person is a party to the communication or if one of the parties to the communication has given the person prior consent to the interception, and if the communication is not intercepted for the purpose of committing a criminal offense or tortious act in violation of the laws or Constitution of the United States or this state or for the purpose of committing any other injurious act;

* * * * *

(9) The interception or accessing of an electronic communication made through an electronic communication system that is configured so that the electronic communication is readily accessible to the general public.

(10) The interception of a radio communication that is transmitted by any of the following:

    (a) A station for the use of the general public;

    (b) Governmental, law enforcement, civil defense, private land mobile, or public safety communications system, including a police or fire system, that is readily accessible to the general public;

    (c) A station operating on an authorized frequency within the bands allocated to the amateur, citizen band, or general mobile radio services;

    (d) A marine or aeronautical communications system.

(11) The interception of a radio communication that relates to a ship, aircraft, vehicle, or person in distress.

(12) The interception of a wire or electronic communication the transmission of which is causing harmful interference to a lawfully operating station or consumer electronic equipment, to the extent necessary to identify the source of that interference.

(13) Other users of the same frequency to intercept a radio communication made through a system that utilizes frequencies monitored by individuals engaged in the provision or the use of that system, if the communication is not scrambled or encrypted.

(C) Whoever violates this section is guilty of interception of wire, oral, or electronic communications, a felony of the fourth degree.

§ 2933.65. Civil action.

(A) A person whose wire, oral, or electronic communications are intercepted, disclosed, or intentionally used in violation of sections 2933.51 to 2933.66 of the Revised Code may bring a civil action to recover from the person or entity that engaged in the violation any relief that may be appropriate and that includes, but is not limited to, the following:

    (1) The preliminary and other equitable or declaratory relief that is appropriate;

    (2) Whichever of the following is greater:

        (a) Liquidated damages computed at a rate of two hundred dollars per day for each day of violation or liquidated damages of ten thousand dollars, whichever is greater;

APPENDIX B — STATE STATUTES

(b) The sum of actual damages suffered by the plaintiff and the profits, if any, made as a result of the violation by the person or entity that engaged in the violation.

(3) Punitive damages, if appropriate;

(4) Reasonable attorney's fees and other litigation expenses that are reasonably incurred in bringing the civil action.

(B) Good faith reliance on an interception warrant, extension of an interception warrant, other court order, a grant of an oral order for an interception, a grand jury subpoena, a legislative or statutory authorization, or a good faith determination that divisions (A) and (B) of section 2933.521 of the Revised Code permitted the conduct that is the subject of a complaint is a complete defense to a civil action or criminal action that is brought under the laws of this state and that arises out of the execution of the warrant or the oral order.

(C) A claimant who brings a civil action under division (A) of this section shall commence the civil action within two years after the date on which the claimant first has a reasonable opportunity to discover the violation.

(D) The remedies and sanctions described in sections 2933.51 to 2933.66.

Oklahoma

Title 13

§ 176.1. Short title.

Sections 1 through 14 of this act shall be known and may be cited as the "Security of Communications Act".

§ 176.2. Definitions.

As used in the Security of Communications Act:

1. "Aggrieved person" means a person who was a party to any intercepted wire, oral or electronic communication or a person against whom the interception was directed;

2. "Aural acquisition" means obtaining knowledge of a communication through the sense of hearing which is contemporaneous with the communication;

3. "Communication common carrier" means, for the purposes of the Security of Communications Act only, any telephone or telegraph company, rural telephone cooperative, communications transmission company or other public communications company under the laws of this state;

4. "Communication facility" means any and all public and private instrumentalities used or useful in the transmission of writing, signs, signals, pictures, or sounds of all kinds and includes mail, telephone, wire, radio, and all other means of communication;

5. "Contents", when used with respect to any wire, oral or electronic communication, includes any information concerning the substance, purport or meaning of that communication;

6. "Electronic communication" means any transfer of signs, signals, writing, images, sounds, data, or intelligence of any nature transmitted in whole or in part by a wire, radio, electromagnetic, photoelectronic or photo-optical system, but does not include:

a. the radio portion of a cordless telephone communication that is transmitted between the cordless telephone headset and the base unit,

b. any wire or oral communication,

c. any communication made through a tone-only paging device, or

d. any communication from a tracking device;

7. "Electronic, mechanical or other device" means any device or apparatus which can be used to intercept a wire, oral or electronic communication other than:

a. any telephone or telegraph instrument, equipment or facility or any component thereof furnished to the subscriber or user by a communication common carrier or other lawful supplier in the ordinary course of its business which is being used by the subscriber or user in the ordinary course of its business, or being used by a communication common carrier in the ordinary course of business or being used by a law enforcement officer in the ordinary course of his duties,

b. a hearing aid or similar device being used to correct subnormal hearing to not better than normal;

8. "Intercept" means the aural acquisition of the contents of any wire, oral or electronic communication through the use of any electronic, mechanical or other device;

9. "Judge of competent jurisdiction" means the Presiding Judge of the Court of Criminal Appeals;

10. "Law enforcement officer" means any person who is employed by the United States, this state or political subdivision thereof and is empowered by law to conduct investigations of, or to make arrests for, offenses enumerated in the Security of Communications Act or similar federal offenses and any attorney authorized by law to prosecute or participate in the prosecution of such offenses;

11. "Oral communication" means any communication uttered by a person exhibiting an expectation that such communication is not subject to interception under circumstance justifying such expectation;

12. "Person" means any individual, partnership, association, joint-stock company, trust, corporation or political subdivision including an employee or agent thereof; and

13. "Wire communication" means any communication made in whole or in part through the use of facilities for the transmission of communications by the aid of wire, cable or other like connection between the point of origin and the point of reception furnished or operated by any person engaged as a communication common carrier in providing or operating such facilities for the transmission of intrastate, interstate or foreign communications.

§ 176.3. Prohibited acts.

Except as otherwise specifically provided in this act, any person is guilty of a felony and upon conviction shall be punished by a fine of not less than Five Thousand Dollars ($5,000), or by imprisonment of not more than five (5) years, or by both who:

1. Willfully intercepts, endeavors to intercept or procures any other person to intercept or endeavor to intercept any wire, oral or electronic communication;

2. Willfully uses, endeavors to use or procures any other person to use or endeavor to use any electronic, mechanical or other device to intercept any oral communication;

3. Willfully discloses or endeavors to disclose to any other person the contents of any wire, oral or electronic communication, knowing or having reason to know that the in-

APPENDIX B — STATE STATUTES

formation was obtained in violation of the provisions of the Security of Communications Act;

4. Willfully uses or endeavors to use the contents of any wire, oral or electronic communication, knowing or having reason to know that the information was obtained in violation of the provisions of the Security of Communications Act;

5. Willfully and maliciously, without legal authority, removes, injures or obstructs any telephone or telegraph line, or any part or appurtenances or apparatus connected thereto, or severs any wires thereof;

* * * * *

§ 176.4. Acts not prohibited.

It is not unlawful pursuant to the Security of Communications Act for:

* * * * *

5. a person not acting under color of law to intercept a wire, oral or electronic communication when such person is a party to the communication or when one of the parties to the communication has given prior consent to such interception unless the communication is intercepted for the purpose of committing any criminal act;

* * * * *

Oregon

§ 165.535. Definitions.

As used in ORS 41.910, 133.723, 133.724, 165.540 and 165.545:

(1) "Conversation" means the transmission between two or more persons of an oral communication which is not a telecommunication or a radio communication.

(2) "Person" means any person as defined in ORS 174.100 and includes public officials and law enforcement officers of the state, county, municipal corporation or any other political subdivision of the state.

(3) "Radio communication" means the transmission by radio or other wireless methods of writing, signs, signals, pictures and sounds of all kinds, including all instrumentalities, facilities, equipment and services (including, among other things, the receipt, forwarding and delivering of communications) incidental to such transmission.

(4) "Telecommunication" means the transmission of writing, signs, signals, pictures and sounds of all kinds by aid of wire, cable or other similar connection between the points of origin and reception of such transmission, including all instrumentalities, facilities, equipment and services (including, among other things, the receipt, forwarding and delivering of communications) incidental to such transmission.

§ 165.540. Obtaining contents of communications.

(1) Except as otherwise provided in ORS 133.724 or subsections (2) to (7) of this section, no person shall:

(a) Obtain or attempt to obtain the whole or any part of a telecommunication or a radio communication to which such person is not a participant, by means of any device, contrivance, machine or apparatus, whether electrical, mechanical, manual or otherwise, unless consent is given by at least one participant.

(b) Tamper with the wires, connections, boxes, fuses, circuits, lines or any other equipment or facilities of a telecommunication or radio communication company over which messages are transmitted, with the intent to obtain unlawfully the contents of a telecommunication or radio communication to which such person is not a participant.

(c) Obtain or attempt to obtain the whole or any part of a conversation by means of any device, contrivance, machine or apparatus, whether electrical, mechanical, manual or otherwise, if all participants in the conversation are not specifically informed that their conversation is being obtained.

(d) Obtain the whole or any part of a conversation, telecommunication or radio communication from any person, while knowing or having good reason to believe that such conversation, telecommunication or radio communication was initially obtained in a manner prohibited by this section.

(e) Use or attempt to use, or divulge to others any conversation, telecommunication or radio communication obtained by any means prohibited by this section.

* * * * *

(3) The prohibitions in subsection (1)(a), (b) or (c) of this section shall not apply to subscribers or members of their family who perform the acts prohibited in subsection (1) of this section in their homes.

(4) The prohibitions in subsection (1)(a) of this section do not apply to the receiving or obtaining of the contents of any radio or television broadcast transmitted for the use of the general public.

* * * * *

(6) The provisions in subsection (1)(c) of this section do not apply to a person who records a conversation during a felony that endangers human life.

(7) The prohibition in subsection (1)(c) of this section shall not apply to persons who intercept or attempt to intercept with an unconcealed recording device the oral communications that are part of any of the following proceedings:

(a) Public or semipublic meetings such as hearings before governmental or quasi-governmental bodies, trials, press conferences, public speeches, rallys and sporting or other events;

(b) Regularly scheduled classes or similar educational activities in public or private institutions; or

(c) Private meetings or conferences if all others involved knew or reasonably should have known that the recording was being made.

(8) The prohibitions in subsection (1)(a), (c), (d) and (e) of this section do not apply to any:

(a) Radio communication which is transmitted by a station operating on an authorized frequency within the amateur or citizens bands; or

(b) Person who intercepts a radio communication which is transmitted by any governmental, law enforcement, civil defense or public safety communications system, including police and fire, readily accessible to the general public provided that the interception is not for purposes of illegal activity.

(9) Violation of subsection (1) of this section, subsection (2)(b) or subsection (5)(b) or (c) of this section is a Class A misdemeanor.

APPENDIX B — STATE STATUTES

§ 165.543. Interception of communications.

(1) Except as provided in ORS 133.724 or as provided in ORS 165.540(2)(a), any person who willfully intercepts, attempts to intercept or procures any other person to intercept or attempt to intercept any wire or oral communication where such person is not a party to the communication and where none of the parties to the communication has given prior consent to the interception, is guilty of a Class A misdemeanor.

(2) As used in this section, the terms "intercept" and "wire or oral communication" have the meanings provided under ORS 133.721.

Pennsylvania

§ 5701. Short title.

This chapter shall be known and may be cited as the "Wiretapping and Electronic Surveillance Control Act."

§ 5702. Definitions.

As used in this chapter, the following words and phrases shall have the meanings given to them in this section unless the context clearly indicates otherwise:

"Aggrieved person." A person who was a party to any intercepted wire, electronic or oral communication or a person against whom the interception was directed.

"Aural transfer." A transfer containing the human voice at any point between and including the point of origin and the point of reception.

"Communication common carrier." Any person engaged as a common carrier for hire, in intrastate, interstate or foreign communication by wire or radio or in intrastate, interstate or foreign radio transmission of energy; however, a person engaged in radio broadcasting shall not, while so engaged, be deemed a common carrier.

"Contents." As used with respect to any wire, electronic or oral communication, is any information concerning the substance, purport, or meaning of that communication.

"Court." The Superior Court. For the purposes of Subchapter C only, the term shall mean the court of common pleas.

"Electronic communication." Any transfer of signs, signals, writing, images, sounds, data or intelligence of any nature transmitted in whole or in part by a wire, radio, electromagnetic, photoelectronic or photo-optical system, except:

(1) The radio portion of a cordless telephone communication that is transmitted between the cordless telephone handset and the base unit.

(2) Any wire or oral communication.

(3) Any communication made through a tone-only paging device.

(4) Any communication from a tracking device (as defined in this section).

"Electronic communication service." Any service which provides to users the ability to send or receive wire or electronic communications.

"Electronic communication system." Any wire, radio, electromagnetic, photo-optical or photoelectronic facilities for the transmission of electronic communications, and any computer facilities or related electronic equipment for the electronic storage of such communications.

"Electronic, mechanical or other device." Any device or apparatus, including, but not limited to, an induction coil or a telecommunication identification interception device, that can be used to intercept a wire, electronic or oral communication other than:

(1) Any telephone or telegraph instrument, equipment or facility, or any component thereof, furnished to the subscriber or user by a provider of wire or electronic communication service in the ordinary course of its business, or furnished by such subscriber or user for connection to the facilities of such service and used in the ordinary course of its business, or being used by a communication common carrier in the ordinary course of its business, or by an investigative or law enforcement officer in the ordinary course of his duties.

(2) A hearing aid or similar device being used to correct subnormal hearing to not better than normal.

(3) Equipment or devices used to conduct interceptions under section 5704(15) (relating to exceptions to prohibition of interception and disclosure of communications).

"Electronic storage."

(1) Any temporary, intermediate storage of a wire or electronic communication incidental to the electronic transmission thereof.

(2) Any storage of such a communication by an electronic communication service for purpose of backup protection of the communication.

"Home." The residence of a nonconsenting party to an interception, provided that access to the residence is not generally permitted to members of the public and the party has a reasonable expectation of privacy in the residence under the circumstances.

"In-progress trace." The determination of the origin of a telephonic communication to a known telephone during an interception.

"Intercept." Aural or other acquisition of the contents of any wire, electronic or oral communication through the use of any electronic, mechanical or other device. The term shall include the point at which the contents of the communication are monitored by investigative or law enforcement officers.

"Investigative or law enforcement officer." Any officer of the United States, of another state or political subdivision thereof, or of the Commonwealth or political subdivision thereof, who is empowered by law to conduct investigations of or to make arrests for offenses enumerated in this chapter or an equivalent crime in another jurisdiction, and any attorney authorized by law to prosecute or participate in the prosecution of such offense. The term shall include, but not be limited to, employees of the Pennsylvania Crime Commission, authorized to investigate crimes enumerated in section 5708 (relating to order authorizing interception of wire or oral communications).

"Judge." When referring to a judge authorized to receive applications for, and to enter, orders authorizing interceptions of wire, electronic or oral communications pursuant to Subchapter B (relating to wire, electronic or oral communication), any judge of the Superior Court.

"One call system." A communication system established by users to provide a single telephone number for contractors or designers or any other person to call notifying users of the caller's intent to engage in demolition or excavation work.

"Oral communication." Any oral communication uttered by a person possessing an expectation that such communication is not subject to interception under circumstances justifying such expectation. The term does not include any electronic communication.

APPENDIX B — STATE STATUTES

"Organized crime."

(1) The unlawful activity of an association trafficking in illegal goods or services, including but not limited to, gambling, prostitution, loan sharking, controlled substances, labor racketeering, or other unlawful activities; or

(2) any continuing criminal conspiracy or other unlawful practice which has as its objective:

(i) large economic gain through fraudulent or coercive practices; or

(ii) improper governmental influence.

"Pen register." A device which is used to capture, record or decode electronic or other impulses which identify the numbers dialed or otherwise transmitted, with respect to wire or electronic communications, on the targeted telephone. The term includes a device which is used to record or decode electronic or other impulses which identify the existence of incoming and outgoing wire or electronic communications on the targeted telephone. The term does not include a device used by a provider or customer of a wire or electronic communication service for billing, or recording as an incident to billing, for communication service provided by the provider, or any device used by a provider, or customer of a wire communication service for cost accounting or other like purposes in the ordinary course of business.

"Person." Any employee, or agent of the United States or any state or political subdivision thereof, and any individual, partnership, association, joint stock company, trust or corporation.

"Readily accessible to the general public." As used with respect to a radio communication, that such communication is not:

(1) scrambled or encrypted;

(2) transmitted using modulation techniques of which the essential parameters have been withheld from the public with the intention of preserving the privacy of the communication;

(3) carried on a subscriber or other signal subsidiary to a radio transmission;

(4) transmitted over a communication system provided by a common carrier, unless the communication is a tone-only paging system communication; or

(5) transmitted on frequencies allocated under 47 CFR Parts 25, 74D, E, F or 94, unless, in the case of a communication transmitted on a frequency allocated under Part 74 which is not exclusively allocated to broadcast auxiliary services, the communication is a two-way voice communication by radio.

"Remote computing service." The provision to the public of computer storage or processing services by means of an electronic communications system.

"State." Any state of the United States, the District of Columbia, the Commonwealth of Puerto Rico and any territory or possession of the United States.

"Telecommunication identification interception device." Any equipment or device capable of intercepting any electronic communication which contains any electronic serial number, mobile identification number, personal identification number or other identification number assigned by a telecommunication service provider for activation or operation of a telecommunication device.

"Tracking device." An electronic or mechanical device which permits only the tracking of the movement of a person or object.

"Trap and trace device." A device which captures the incoming electronic or other impulses which identify the originating number of an instrument or device from which a wire or electronic communication was transmitted.

"User." Any person or entity who:

(1) uses an electronic communication service; and

(2) is duly authorized by the provider of the service to engage in the use.

"Wire communication." Any aural transfer made in whole or in part through the use of facilities for the transmission of communication by wire, cable or other like connection between the point of origin and the point of reception, including the use of such a connection in a switching station, furnished or operated by a telephone, telegraph or radio company for hire as a communication common carrier. The term includes any electronic storage of such communication.

§ 5703. Interception, disclosure or use of wire, electronic or oral communications.

Except as otherwise provided in this chapter, a person is guilty of a felony of the third degree if he:

(1) intentionally intercepts, endeavors to intercept, or procures any other person to intercept or endeavor to intercept any wire, electronic or oral communication;

(2) intentionally discloses or endeavors to disclose to any other person the contents of any wire, electronic or oral communication, or evidence derived therefrom, knowing or having reason to know that the information was obtained through the interception of a wire, electronic or oral communication; or

(3) intentionally uses or endeavors to use the contents of any wire, electronic or oral communication, or evidence derived therefrom, knowing or having reason to know, that the information was obtained through the interception of a wire, electronic or oral communication.

§ 5704. Exceptions.

It shall not be unlawful under this chapter for:

* * * * *

(4) A person, to intercept a wire, electronic or oral communication, where all parties to the communication have given prior consent to such interception.

* * * * *

(10) Any person:

(i) to intercept or access an electronic communication made through an electronic communication system configured so that the electronic communication is readily accessible to the general public;

(ii) to intercept any radio communication which is transmitted:

(A) by a station for the use of the general public, or which relates to ships, aircraft, vehicles or persons in distress;

(B) by any governmental, law enforcement, civil defense, private land mobile or public safety communication system, including police and fire systems, readily accessible to the general public;

(C) by a station operating on an authorized frequency within the bands allocated to the amateur, citizens band or general mobile radio services; or

(D) by any marine or aeronautical communication system;

(iii) to engage in any conduct which:

(a) is prohibited by section 633 of the Communications Act of 1934 (48 Stat. 1105, 47 U.S.C. § 553); or

(b) is excepted from the application of section 705(a) of the Communications Act of 1934 (47 U.S.C. § 605(a)) by section 705(b) of that act (47 U.S.C. § 605(b)); or

(iv) to intercept any wire or electronic communication the transmission of which is causing harmful interference to any lawfully operating station, to the extent necessary to identify the source of the interference.

* * * * *

§ 5725. Civil cause of action.

(a) Cause of action.—Any person whose wire, electronic or oral communication is intercepted, disclosed or used in violation of this chapter shall have a civil cause of action against any person who intercepts, discloses or uses or procures any other person to intercept, disclose or use, such communication; and shall be entitled to recover from any such person:

(1) Actual damages, but not less than liquidated damages computed at the rate of $100 a day for each day of violation, or $1,000, whichever is higher.

(2) Punitive damages.

(3) A reasonable attorney's fee and other litigation costs reasonably incurred.

(b) Waiver of sovereign immunity.—To the extent that the Commonwealth and any of its officers, officials or employees would be shielded from liability under this section by the doctrine of sovereign immunity, such immunity is hereby waived for the purposes of this section.

(c) Defense.—It is a defense to an action brought pursuant to subsection (a) that the actor acted in good faith reliance on a court order or the provisions of this chapter.

Rhode Island

§ 12-5.1-1. Definitions.

As used in this chapter:

(1) The term "aggrieved person" means an individual who was a party to any intercepted wire or oral communication or against whom the interception was directed.

(2) The term "communications common carrier" means any person engaged as a common carrier for hire in the transmission of communications by wire or radio.

(3) The term "contents", when used with respect to any wire or oral communication, includes any information concerning the identity of the parties to that communication or the existence, substance, purport, or meaning of that communication.

(4) The term "designated offense" shall mean the offenses of murder, robbery, kidnapping, extortion, assault with a dangerous weapon, and assault with intent to rob or murder; arson in the first degree, arson in the second degree, or arson in the third degree; bribery or larceny involving the receipt of stolen property of a value of more than five

hundred dollars ($500); any violation of chapter 28 of title 21 where the offense is punishable by imprisonment for more than one year; any violation of chapters 19, 47, or 51 of title 11, where the offense is punishable by imprisonment for more than one year; the lending of money at a rate of interest in violation of law; and conspiracy to commit any of the foregoing offenses.

(5) The term "intercept" means to acquire aurally the contents of any wire or oral communication through the use of any intercepting device.

(6) The term "intercepting device" means any device or apparatus which can be used to intercept wire or oral communications other than:

(A) Any telephone or telegraph instrument, equipment, or facility or any component thereof, furnished to the subscriber or user by a communications common carrier in the ordinary course of its business, used by a subscriber or user of facilities of a communications common carrier, or by a communications common carrier in the ordinary course of its business, or by an investigative or law enforcement officer in the ordinary course of his duties; or

(B) A hearing aid or similar device which is being used to correct subnormal hearing to normal.

(7) The term "investigative or law enforcement officer" means any officer of the United States, this state, or a political subdivision of this state, who is empowered by law to conduct investigations of, or to make arrests for, the designated offenses, the attorney general, and his or her assistants.

(8) The term "oral communications" means any oral communication uttered by a person exhibiting an expectation that such communication is not subject to interception under circumstances justifying such expectation.

(9) The term "person" means any individual, partnership, association, joint stock company, trust, or corporation, whether or not any of the foregoing is an officer, agent, or employee of the United States, a state, or a political subdivision of a state.

(10) The term "wire communications" means any communication made in whole or in part through the use of facilities for the transmission of communications by the aid of wire, cable, or other like connection between the point of origin and the point of reception, furnished or operated by any person engaged as a common carrier in providing or operating such facilities for the transmission of communications.

§ 12-5.1-13. Civil cause of action.

(a) Any person whose wire or oral communication is intercepted, disclosed, or used in violation of this chapter shall have a civil cause of action against any person who intercepts, discloses, or uses the communications, and shall be entitled to recover from that person:

(1) Actual damages, but not less than liquidated damages, computed at the rate of one hundred dollars ($100) per day for each day of violation, or one thousand dollars ($1,000), whichever is higher;

(2) Punitive damages; and

(3) Reasonable attorneys' fees and other litigation disbursements reasonably incurred.

(b) Good faith reliance on a court order issued under this chapter shall constitute a complete defense to any civil or criminal action brought under this section or any other law. Any communications common carrier and its employees shall be deemed to have

APPENDIX B — STATE STATUTES

acted in good faith upon receipt of a certified copy of the court order issued under this chapter and the representations of the attorney general or an assistant attorney general specially designated by the attorney general.

South Carolina

§ 16-17-470. Eavesdropping or peeping.

It is unlawful for a person to be an eavesdropper or a Peeping Tom on or about the premises of another or to go upon the premises of another for the purpose of becoming an eavesdropper or a Peeping Tom. The term "Peeping Tom", as used in this section, is defined as a person who peeps through windows, doors, or other like places, on or about the premises of another, for the purpose of spying upon or invading the privacy of the persons spied upon and any other conduct of a similar nature, that tends to invade the privacy of others. A person who violates the provisions of this section is guilty of a misdemeanor and, upon conviction, must be fined not more than five hundred dollars or imprisoned not more than three years, or both.

South Dakota

§ 22-21-1. Trespassing with intent to eavesdrop.

Any person who, except as authorized by law:
(1) Trespasses on property with intent to subject anyone to eavesdropping or other surveillance in a private place; or
(2) Installs in any private place, without the consent of the person or persons entitled to privacy there, any device for observing, photographing, recording, amplifying or broadcasting sounds or events in such place, or uses any such unauthorized installation; is guilty of a Class 1 misdemeanor. Subdivision (2) shall not apply to law enforcement officers, or to those acting under their direction, while engaged in the performance of their lawful duties.

§ 23A-35A-1. Definition of terms.

Terms used in this chapter mean:
(1) "Aggrieved person," a person who was a party to any intercepted wire or oral communication or a person against whom the interception was directed;
(2) "Attorney general," the attorney general of the State of South Dakota, unless otherwise specified;
(3) "Chapter 119 of the United States Code," Chapter 119 of Part I of Title 18, United States Code, being Public Law 90-351, the Omnibus Crime Control and Safe Streets Act of 1968;
(4) "Communications common carrier," the meaning which is given the term "common carrier" by section 153(h) of Title 47 of the United States Code;
(5) "Contents," when used with respect to any wire or oral communication, any information concerning the identity of the parties to such communication or the existence, substance, purport, or meaning of that communication;
(6) "Electronic, mechanical or other device," any device or apparatus which can be used to intercept a wire or oral communication other than:

(a) any telephone or telegraph instrument, equipment or facility, or any component thereof, (i) furnished to the subscriber or user by a communications common carrier in the ordinary course of its business and being used by the subscriber or user in the ordinary course of its business; or (ii) being used by a communications common carrier in the ordinary course of its business, or by an investigative or law enforcement officer in the ordinary course of his duties;

(b) a hearing aid or similar device being used to correct subnormal hearing to not better than normal;

(7) "Intercept," the aural acquisition of the contents of any wire or oral communication through the use of any electronic, mechanical or other device;

(8) "Investigative or law enforcement officer," any officer of the State of South Dakota or any political subdivision thereof who is empowered by the laws of this state to conduct investigations of or to make arrests for offenses designated and enumerated in this chapter, any law enforcement officer of the United States and any attorney authorized by the laws of this state to prosecute or participate in the prosecution of offenses designated and enumerated in this chapter;

(9) "Judge," or "judge of competent jurisdiction," the judge of any circuit court of the State of South Dakota;

(10) "Oral communication," any oral communication uttered by a person exhibiting an expectation that such communication is not subject to interception under circumstances justifying such expectation;

(11) "Pen register," a device which records or decodes electronic or other impulses which identify the numbers dialed or otherwise transmitted on the telephone line to which the device is attached, but the term does not include any device used by a provider or customer of a wire communication service for billing, or recording as an incident to billing, for communications services provided by the provider or customer of a wire communication service for cost accounting or other like purposes in the ordinary course of its business;

(12) "Person," any employee, or agent of the United States or any state or political subdivision thereof, and any individual, partnership, limited liability company, association, joint stock company, trust or corporation;

(13) "State's attorney," the qualified state's attorney of any county of the State of South Dakota;

(14) "Trap and trace device," a device which captures the incoming electronic or other impulses which identify the originating number of an instrument or device from which a wire communication was transmitted; and

(15) "Wire communication," any communication made in whole or in part through the use of facilities for the transmission of communications by the aid of wire, cable or other like connection between the point of origin and the point of reception furnished or operated by any person engaged as a common carrier in providing or operating such facilities for the transmission of interstate or foreign communications.

§ 23A-35A-20 Unlawful interception or recording.

Except as provided in s 23A-35A-21, a person is guilty of a Class 5 felony who being:

(1) Not a sender or receiver of a telephone or telegraph communication, knowingly and by means of an instrument or device overhears or records a telephone or telegraph

communication, or aids, authorizes, employs, procures or permits another to so do, without the consent of either a sender or receiver thereof;

(2) Not present during a conversation or discussion, knowingly and by means of an instrument or device overhears or records such conversation or discussion, or aids, authorizes, employs, procures or permits another to so do, without the consent of a party to such conversation or discussion; or

(3) Not a member of a jury, knowingly records or listens to by means of an instrument or device the deliberations of such jury or aids, authorizes, employs, procures or permits another to so do.

Tennessee

§ 39-13-601. Wiretapping and electronic surveillance.

(a)(1) Except as otherwise specifically provided in § 39-13-601–39-13-603 and title 40, chapter 6, part 3, a person commits an offense who:

(A) Intentionally intercepts, endeavors to intercept, or procures any other person to intercept or endeavor to intercept, any wire, oral, or electronic communication;

(B) Intentionally uses, endeavors to use, or procures any other person to use or endeavor to use any electronic, mechanical, or other device to intercept any oral communication when:

(i) Such device is affixed to, or otherwise transmits a signal through, a wire, cable, or other like connection used in wire communication; or

(ii) Such device transmits communications by radio, or interferes with the transmission of such communication;

(C) Intentionally discloses, or endeavors to disclose, to any other person the contents of any wire, oral or electronic communication, knowing or having reason to know that the information was obtained through the interception of a wire, oral, or electronic communication in violation of this subsection; or

(D) Intentionally uses, or endeavors to use, the contents of any wire, oral or electronic communication, knowing or having reason to know, that the information was obtained through the interception of a wire, oral or electronic communication in violation of this subsection.

(2) A violation of subdivision (a)(1) shall be punished as provided in § 39-13-602 and shall be subject to suit as provided in § 39-13-603.

(b)(1) It is lawful under § 39-13-601–39-13-603 and title 40, chapter 6, part 3 for an officer, employee, or agent of a provider of wire or electronic communications service, or a telecommunications company, whose facilities are used in the transmission of a wire communication, to intercept, disclose or use that communication in the normal course of employment while engaged in any activity which is necessary to the rendition of service or to the protection of the rights or property of the provider of that service. Nothing in § 39-13-601–39-13-603 and title 40, chapter 6, part 3 shall be construed to prohibit a telecommunications or other company from engaging in service observing for the purpose of maintaining service quality standards for the benefit of consumers.

* * * * *

(5) It is lawful under § 39-13-601–39-13-603 and title 40, chapter 6, part 3 for a person not acting under color of law to intercept a wire, oral, or electronic communi-

cation where the person is a party to the communication or where one of the parties to the communication has given prior consent to the interception unless the communication is intercepted for the purpose of committing any criminal or tortious act in violation of the constitution or laws of the state of Tennessee.

(6) It is unlawful to intercept any wire, oral, or electronic communication for the purpose of committing a criminal act.

(7) It is lawful, unless otherwise prohibited by state or federal law, for any person:

(A) To intercept or access an electronic communication made through an electronic communication system that is configured so that the electronic communication is readily accessible to the general public;

(B) To intercept any radio communication which is transmitted by:

(i) Any station for the use of the general public, or that relates to ships, aircraft, vehicles, or persons in distress;

(ii) Any governmental, law enforcement, civil defense, private land mobile, or public safety communications system, including police and fire, readily accessible to the general public;

(iii) Any station operating on an authorized frequency within the bands allocated to the amateur, citizens band, or general mobile radio services; or

(iv) Any marine or aeronautical communications system;

(C) To intercept any wire or electronic communication, the transmission of which is causing harmful interference with any lawfully operating station or consumer electronic equipment, to the extent necessary to identify the source of such interference; or

(D) For other users of the same frequency to intercept any radio communication made through a system that utilizes frequencies monitored by individuals engaged in the provision or the use of such system, if such communication is not scrambled or encrypted.

(c)(1) Except as provided in subdivision (c)(2), a person or entity providing an electronic communication service to the public shall not intentionally divulge the contents of any communication (other than one to such person or entity, or an agent thereof) while in transmission on that service to any person or entity other than an addressee or intended recipient of such communication or an agent of such addressee or intended recipient.

(2) A person or entity providing electronic communication service to the public may divulge the contents of any such communication:

(A) As otherwise authorized in subdivisions (b)(1)-(3) or § 40-6-306;

(B) With the lawful consent of the originator or any addressee or intended recipient of such communication;

(C) To a person employed or authorized, or whose facilities are used, to forward such communication to its destination; or

(D) Which were inadvertently obtained by the service provider and which appear to pertain to the commission of a crime, if such divulgence is made to a law enforcement agency.

§ 39-13-602. Penalty.

A person who violates § 39-13-601(a) commits a Class D felony.

APPENDIX B — STATE STATUTES

§ 39-13-603. Civil actions.

(a) Except as provided in § 39-13-601(b)(4), any aggrieved person whose wire, oral or electronic communication is intentionally intercepted, disclosed, or used in violation of § 39-13-601 or title 40, chapter 6, part 3 may in a civil action recover from the person or entity which engaged in that violation the following relief:
    (1) The greater of:
        (A) The sum of the actual damages, including any damage to personal or business reputation or relationships, suffered by the plaintiff and any profits made by the violator as a result of the violation; or
        (B) Statutory damages of one hundred dollars ($100) a day for each day of violation or ten thousand dollars ($10,000), whichever is greater; and
    (2) Punitive damages; and
    (3) A reasonable attorney's fee and other litigation costs reasonably incurred.
(b) Any person whose wire, oral, or electronic communication is or is about to be intercepted, disclosed, or used in violation of § 39-13-601 or title 40, chapter 6, part 3 may seek to enjoin and restrain such violation and may in the same action seek damages as provided by subsection (a).
(c) It is a complete defense against any civil or criminal action brought under § 39-13-601 or title 40, chapter 6, part 3 that there was good faith reliance on a court warrant or order, a grand jury subpoena, a legislative authorization, or a statutory authorization, or if there was a good faith determination that § 39-13-601(c) permitted the conduct complained of.
(d) A civil action under this section or title 40, chapter 6, part 3 may not be commenced later than two (2) years after the date upon which the claimant first discovered or had a reasonable opportunity to discover the violation.

§ 39-13-604. Interception of cellular or cordless telephone transmissions.

(a) As used in this section, unless the context otherwise requires:
    (1) "Cellular radio telephone" means a wireless telephone authorized by the federal communications commission to operate in the frequency bandwidth reserved for cellular radio telephones;
    (2) "Communication" includes, but is not limited to, communications transmitted by voice, data, or image, including facsimile;
    (3) "Cordless telephone" means a two-way, low power communication system consisting of two (2) parts, a "base" unit which connects to the public switched telephone network and a handset or "remote" unit, that are connected by a radio link and authorized by the federal communications commission to operate in the frequency bandwidths reserved for cordless telephones;
    (4) "Disseminating," as used in this section and § 39-13-605, means the playing or duplicating of the recording in a manner other than authorized herein; and
    (5) "Party" means only those individuals who participate in a conversation and whose presence as participants is known to all other participants.
(b)(1) A person commits an offense who, without the consent of at least one (1) party to a communication, intentionally records or disseminates a communication transmitted between two (2) cellular radio telephones, a cellular radio telephone and a landline telephone, or a cordless telephone and a cellular radio telephone.

(2) A person commits an offense who intentionally disseminates a communication transmitted between two (2) cordless telephones or a cordless telephone and a landline telephone if such dissemination is not authorized by a court order.

(c)(1) A violation of subsection (b) is a Class A misdemeanor.

(2) A violation of subsection (b) is a Class E felony if the defendant knowingly publishes, distributes or otherwise disseminates to another the intercepted or recorded communication.

* * * * *

Texas

§ 16.02. Unlawful Interception, Use, or Disclosure of Wire, Oral, or Electronic Communications.

(a) In this section, "covert entry," "communication common carrier," "contents," "electronic, mechanical, or other device," "intercept," "investigative or law enforcement officer," "oral communication," "electronic communication," "readily accessible to the general public," and "wire communication" have the meanings given those terms in Article 18.20, Code of Criminal Procedure.

(b) A person commits an offense if he:

(1) intentionally intercepts, endeavors to intercept, or procures another person to intercept or endeavor to intercept a wire, oral, or electronic communication;

(2) intentionally discloses or endeavors to disclose to another person the contents of a wire, oral, or electronic communication if he knows or has reason to know the information was obtained through the interception of a wire, oral, or electronic communication in violation of this subsection;

(3) intentionally uses or endeavors to use the contents of a wire, oral, or electronic communication if he knows or is reckless about whether the information was obtained through the interception of a wire, oral, or electronic communication in violation of this subsection;

(4) knowingly or intentionally effects a covert entry for the purpose of intercepting wire, oral, or electronic communications without court order or authorization; or

(5) intentionally uses, endeavors to use, or procures any other person to use or endeavor to use any electronic, mechanical, or other device to intercept any oral communication when the device:

(A) is affixed to, or otherwise transmits a signal through a wire, cable, or other connection used in wire communications; or

(B) transmits communications by radio or interferes with the transmission of communications by radio.

(c) It is an affirmative defense to prosecution under Subsection (b) that:

* * * * *

(4) a person not acting under color of law intercepts a wire, oral, or electronic communication if the person is a party to the communication or if one of the parties to the communication has given prior consent to the interception unless the communication is intercepted for the purpose of committing any criminal or tortious act in violation of the constitution or laws of the United States or of this state or for the purpose of committing any other injurious act;

APPENDIX B — STATE STATUTES

* * * * *

(7) a person intercepts or obtains access to an electronic communication that was made through an electronic communication system that is configured to permit the communication to be readily accessible to the general public;

(8) a person intercepts radio communication, other than a cordless telephone communication that is transmitted between a cordless telephone handset and a base unit, that is transmitted:

(A) by a station for the use of the general public;

(B) to ships, aircraft, vehicles, or persons in distress;

(C) by a governmental, law enforcement, civil defense, private land mobile, or public safety communications system that is readily accessible to the general public, unless the radio communication is transmitted by a law enforcement representative to or from a mobile data terminal;

(D) by a station operating on an authorized frequency within the bands allocated to the amateur, citizens band, or general mobile radio services; or

(E) by a marine or aeronautical communications system;

* * * * *

(f) Except as provided by Subsections (d) and (h), an offense under this section is a felony of the second degree.

(g) For purposes of this section:

(1) An immediate life-threatening situation exists when human life is directly threatened in either a hostage or barricade situation.

(2) "Member of a law enforcement unit specially trained to respond to and deal with life-threatening situations" means a peace officer who has received a minimum of 40 hours a year of training in hostage and barricade suspect situations. This training must be evidenced by the submission of appropriate documentation to the Commission on Law Enforcement Officer Standards and Education.

(h)(1) A person commits an offense if, knowing that a government attorney or an investigative or law enforcement officer has been authorized or has applied for authorization to intercept wire, electronic, or oral communications, the person obstructs, impedes, prevents, gives notice to another of, or attempts to give notice to another of the interception.

(2) An offense under this subsection is a state jail felony.

Utah

§ 76-9-401. Definitions.

For purposes of this part:

(1) "Private place" means a place where one may reasonably expect to be safe from casual or hostile intrusion or surveillance.

(2) "Eavesdrop" means to overhear, record, amplify, or transmit any part of a wire or oral communication of others without the consent of at least one party thereto by means of any electronic, mechanical, or other device.

(3) "Public" includes any professional or social group of which the victim of a defamation is a member.

§ 76-9-402. Privacy violation.

(1) A person is guilty of privacy violation if, except as authorized by law, he:

(a) Trespasses on property with intent to subject anyone to eavesdropping or other surveillance in a private place; or

(b) Installs in any private place, without the consent of the person or persons entitled to privacy there, any device for observing, photographing, recording, amplifying, or broadcasting sounds or events in the place or uses any such unauthorized installation; or

(c) Installs or uses outside of a private place any device for hearing, recording, amplifying, or broadcasting sounds originating in the place which would not ordinarily be audible or comprehensible outside, without the consent of the person or persons entitled to privacy there.

(2) Privacy violation is a class B misdemeanor.

§ 76-9-403. Communication abuse.

(1) A person commits communication abuse if, except as authorized by law, he:

(a) Intercepts, without the consent of the sender or receiver, a message by telephone, telegraph, letter, or other means of communicating privately; this paragraph does not extend to:

(i) Overhearing of messages through a regularly installed instrument on a telephone party line or on an extension; or

(ii) Interception by the telephone company or subscriber incident to enforcement of regulations limiting use of the facilities or to other normal operation and use; or

(b) Divulges without consent of the sender or receiver the existence or contents of any such message if the actor knows that the message was illegally intercepted or if he learned of the message in the course of employment with an agency engaged in transmitting it.

(2) Communication abuse is a class B misdemeanor.

Vermont

[NO STATUTES]

Virginia

§ 19.2-61. Definitions.

As used in this chapter:

"Wire communication" means any aural transfer made in whole or in part through the use of facilities for the transmission of communications by the aid of wire, cable, or other like connection, including the use of such connection in a switching station, furnished or operated by any person engaged in providing or operating such facilities for the transmission of communications and includes electronic storage of such communication;

"Oral communication" means any oral communication uttered by a person exhibiting an expectation that such communication is not subject to interception under circumstances justifying such expectations but does not include any electronic communication;

APPENDIX B — STATE STATUTES

"Intercept" means any aural or other means of acquisition of the contents of any wire, electronic or oral communication through the use of any electronic, mechanical or other device;

"Electronic, mechanical or other device" means any device or apparatus which can be used to intercept a wire, electronic or oral communication other than:

(a) Any telephone or telegraph instrument, equipment or facility, or any component thereof, (i) furnished to the subscriber or user by a provider of wire or electronic communication service in the ordinary course of its business and being used by the subscriber or user in the ordinary course of its business or furnished by the subscriber or user for connection to the facilities of such service and used in the ordinary course of the subscriber's or user's business; or (ii) being used by a communications common carrier in the ordinary course of its business, or by an investigative or law-enforcement officer in the ordinary course of his duties;

(b) A hearing aid or similar device being used to correct subnormal hearing to not better than normal;

"Person" means any employee or agent of the Commonwealth or a political subdivision thereof, and any individual, partnership, association, joint stock company, trust or corporation;

"Investigative or law-enforcement officer" means any officer of the United States or of a state or political subdivision thereof, who is empowered by law to conduct investigations of or to make arrests for offenses enumerated in this chapter, and any attorney authorized by law to prosecute or participate in the prosecution of such offenses;

"Contents" when used with respect to any wire, electronic or oral communication, includes any information concerning the substance, purport or meaning of that communication;

"Judge of competent jurisdiction" means a judge of any circuit court of the Commonwealth with general criminal jurisdiction;

"Communications common carrier" means any person engaged as a common carrier for hire in communication by wire or radio or in radio transmission of energy;

"Aggrieved person" means a person who was a party to any intercepted wire, electronic or oral communication or a person against whom the interception was directed;

"Electronic communication" means any transfer of signs, signals, writing, images, sounds, data, or intelligence of any nature transmitted in whole or in part by a wire, radio, electromagnetic, photoelectronic or photo-optical system. The term does not include:

    1. Any wire communication or oral communication as defined herein;

    2. Any communication made through a tone-only paging device; or

    3. Any communication from an electronic or mechanical device which permits the tracking of the movement of a person or object;

"User" means any person or entity who uses an electronic communication service and is duly authorized by the provider of such service to engage in such use;

"Electronic communication system" means any wire, radio, electromagnetic, photo-optical or photoelectronic facilities for the transmission of electronic communications, and any computer facilities or related electronic equipment for the electronic storage of such communications;

"Electronic communication service" means any service which provides to users thereof the ability to send or receive wire or electronic communications;

"Readily accessible to the general public" means, with respect to a radio communication, that such communication is not (i) scrambled or encrypted, (ii) transmitted using modulation techniques whose essential parameters have been withheld from the public with the intention of preserving the privacy of such communication; (iii) carried on a subcarrier or other signal subsidiary to a radio transmission, (iv) transmitted over a communication system provided by a communications common carrier, unless the communication is a tone-only paging system communication; or (v) transmitted on frequencies allocated under Part 25, subpart D, E or F of Part 74 or Part 94 of the Rules of the Federal Communications Commission, unless, in the case of a communication transmitted on a frequency allocated under Part 74 that is not exclusively allocated to broadcast auxiliary services, the communication is a two-way voice communication by radio;

"Electronic storage" means any temporary, intermediate storage of a wire or electronic communication incidental to the electronic transmission thereof and any storage of such communication by an electronic communication service for purposes of backup protection of such communication;

"Aural transfer" means a transfer containing the human voice at any point between and including the point of origin and the point of reception;

"Pen register" means a device which records or decodes electronic or other impulses which identify the numbers dialed or otherwise transmitted on the telephone line to which such device is attached. The term does not include any device used by a provider or customer of a wire or electronic communication service for billing, or recording as an incident to billing, for communications services provided by such provider or any device used by a provider or customer of a wire communication service for cost accounting or other like purposes in the ordinary course of the provider's or customer's business;

"Trap and trace device" means a device which captures the incoming electronic or other impulses identifying the originating number of an instrument or device from which a wire or electronic communication was transmitted; and

"Remote computing service" means the provision to the public of computer storage or processing services by means of an electronic communications system.

§ 19.2-62. Interception, disclosure or use of wire, electronic or oral communications.

A. Except as otherwise specifically provided in this chapter any person who:

1. Intentionally intercepts, endeavors to intercept or procures any other person to intercept or endeavor to intercept, any wire, electronic or oral communication;

2. Intentionally uses, endeavors to use, or procures any other person to use or endeavor to use any electronic, mechanical or other device to intercept any oral communication;

3. Intentionally discloses, or endeavors to disclose, to any other person the contents of any wire, electronic or oral communication knowing or having reason to know that the information was obtained through the interception of a wire, electronic or oral communication; or

4. Intentionally uses, or endeavors to use, the contents of any wire, electronic or oral communication, knowing or having reason to know that the information was obtained through the interception of a wire or oral communication; shall be guilty of a Class 6 felony.

APPENDIX B — STATE STATUTES

B. 1. It shall not be unlawful under this chapter for an operator of a switchboard, or an officer, employee or agent of a provider of wire or electronic communications service, whose facilities are used in the transmission of a wire communication, to intercept, disclose or use that communication in the normal course of his employment while engaged in any activity which is a necessary incident to the rendition of his service or to the protection of the rights or property of the provider of that service. However, a provider of wire communication service to the public shall not utilize service observing or random monitoring except for mechanical or service quality control checks. It shall not be a criminal offense under this chapter for providers of wire or electronic communications service, their officers, employees and agents, landlords, custodians, or other persons pursuant to a court order under this chapter, to provide information facilities or technical assistance to an investigative or law-enforcement officer, who, pursuant to this chapter, is authorized to intercept a wire, electronic or oral communication.

2. It shall not be a criminal offense under this chapter for a person to intercept a wire, electronic or oral communication, where such person is a party to the communication or one of the parties to the communication has given prior consent to such interception.

3. It shall not be a criminal offense under this chapter for any person:

(a) To intercept or access an electronic communication made through an electronic communication system that is configured so that such electronic communication is readily accessible to the general public;

(b) To intercept any radio communication which is transmitted (i) by any station for the use of the general public, or that relates to ships, aircraft, vehicles, or persons in distress, (ii) by any governmental, law-enforcement, civil defense, private land mobile, or public safety communications system, including police and fire, readily accessible to the general public, (iii) by a station operating on an authorized frequency within the bands allocated to the amateur, citizens band, or general mobile radio services; or (iv) by any marine or aeronautical communications system;

* * * * *

§ 19.2-69. Civil cause of action.

Any person whose wire, electronic or oral communication is intercepted, disclosed or used in violation of this chapter shall (i) have a civil cause of action against any person who intercepts, discloses or uses, or procures any other person to intercept, disclose or use such communications, and (ii) be entitled to recover from any such person:

1. Actual damages but not less than liquidated damages computed at the rate of $100 a day for each day of violation or $1,000, whichever is higher;

2. Punitive damages; and

3. A reasonable attorney's fee and other litigation costs reasonably incurred.

A good faith reliance on a court order or legislative authorization shall constitute a complete defense to any civil or criminal action brought under this chapter or under any other law.

Washington

§ 9.73.030. Intercepting, recording or divulging private communication.

(1) Except as otherwise provided in this chapter, it shall be unlawful for any individual, partnership, corporation, association, or the state of Washington, its agencies, and political subdivisions to intercept, or record any:

    (a) Private communication transmitted by telephone, telegraph, radio, or other device between two or more individuals between points within or without the state by any device electronic or otherwise designed to record and/or transmit said communication regardless how such device is powered or actuated, without first obtaining the consent of all the participants in the communication;

    (b) Private conversation, by any device electronic or otherwise designed to record or transmit such conversation regardless how the device is powered or actuated without first obtaining the consent of all the persons engaged in the conversation.

(2) Notwithstanding subsection (1) of this section, wire communications or conversations (a) of an emergency nature, such as the reporting of a fire, medical emergency, crime, or disaster, or (b) which convey threats of extortion, blackmail, bodily harm, or other unlawful requests or demands, or (c) which occur anonymously or repeatedly or at an extremely inconvenient hour, or (d) which relate to communications by a hostage holder or barricaded person as defined in RCW 70.85.100, whether or not conversation ensues, may be recorded with the consent of one party to the conversation.

(3) Where consent by all parties is needed pursuant to this chapter, consent shall be considered obtained whenever one party has announced to all other parties engaged in the communication or conversation, in any reasonably effective manner, that such communication or conversation is about to be recorded or transmitted: Provided, that if the conversation is to be recorded that said announcement shall also be recorded.

(4) An employee of any regularly published newspaper, magazine, wire service, radio station, or television station acting in the course of bona fide news gathering duties on a full time or contractual or part time basis, shall be deemed to have consent to record and divulge communications or conversations otherwise prohibited by this chapter if the consent is expressly given or if the recording or transmitting device is readily apparent or obvious to the speakers. Withdrawal of the consent after the communication has been made shall not prohibit any such employee of a newspaper, magazine, wire service, or radio or television station from divulging the communication or conversation.

§ 9.73.060. Civil action.

Any person who, directly or by means of a detective agency or any other agent, violates the provisions of this chapter shall be subject to legal action for damages, to be brought by any other person claiming that a violation of this statute has injured his business, his person, or his reputation. A person so injured shall be entitled to actual damages, including mental pain and suffering endured by him on account of violation of the provisions of this chapter, or liquidated damages computed at the rate of one hundred dollars a day for each day of violation, not to exceed one thousand dollars, and a reasonable attorney's fee and other costs of litigation.

APPENDIX B — STATE STATUTES

§ 9.73.080. Penalty.

Except as otherwise provided in this chapter, any person who violates RCW 9.73.030 is guilty of a gross misdemeanor.

West Virginia

§ 62-1D-1. Short title.

This act shall be known and may be cited as the "West Virginia Wiretapping and Electronic Surveillance Act."

§ 62-1D-2. Definitions.

As used in this article, unless the context in which used clearly requires otherwise, the following terms have the meanings indicated:

(a) "Aggrieved person" means a person who was a party to any intercepted wire, oral or electronic communication or a person against whom the interception was directed.

(b) "Communications common carrier" means any telegraph company or telephone company and any radio common carrier.

(c) "Contents," when used with respect to any wire, oral or electronic communication, includes any information concerning the substance, purport or meaning of that communication.

(d) "Electronic, mechanical or other device" means any device or apparatus

   (i) which can be used to intercept a wire, oral or electronic communication or

   (ii) the design of which render it primarily useful for the surreptitious interception of any such communication. There is excepted from this definition:

   (1) Any telephone or telegraph instrument, equipment or facility or any component thereof:

   (a) Furnished to the subscriber or user by a provider of wire or electronic communication service in the ordinary course of its business and being used by the subscriber or user in the ordinary course of its business; or furnished by such subscriber or user for connection to the facilities of such service and used in the ordinary course of its business; or

   (b) being used by a communications common carrier in the ordinary course of its business or by an investigative or law-enforcement officer in the ordinary course of his duties; or

   (2) A hearing aid or similar device being used to correct subnormal hearing to not better than normal; or

   (3) Any device used in a lawful consensual monitoring including, but not limited to, tape recorders, telephone induction coils, answering machines, body transmitters and pen registers.

(e) "Intercept" means the aural or other acquisition of the contents of any wire, electronic or oral communication through the use of any electronic, mechanical or other device.

(f) "Designated judge" means a circuit court judge designated by the chief justice of the West Virginia supreme court of appeals to hear and rule on applications for the interception of wire, oral or electronic communications.

(g) "Investigative or law-enforcement officer" means a member or members of the department of public safety [West Virginia state police] who is or are empowered by law to conduct investigations of or to make arrest for offenses enumerated in this chapter.

(h) "Oral communication" means any oral communication uttered by a person exhibiting an expectation that such communication is not subject to interception under circumstances justifying such expectation, but such term does not include any electronic communication.

(i) "Pen register" means a device which records or decodes electronic or other impulses which identify the numbers dialed or otherwise transmitted on the telephone line to which such device is attached, but such term does not include any device used by a provider or customer of a wire or electronic communication service for billing, or recording as an incident to billing, for communications services provided by such provider or any device used by a provider or customer of a wire communication service for cost accounting or other like purposes in the ordinary course of its business.

(j) "Person" means any person, individual, partnership, association, joint stock company, trust or corporation and includes any police officer, employee or agent of this state or of a political subdivision thereof.

(k) "Wire communication" means any aural transfer made in whole or in part through the use of facilities for the transmission of communications by the aid of wire, cable or other like connection between the point of origin and the point of reception (including the use of such connection in a switching station) furnished or operated by any person engaged in providing or operating such facilities for the transmission of interstate or foreign communications or communications affecting interstate or foreign commerce and such term includes any electronic storage of such communication, but such term does not include the radio portion of a cordless telephone communication that is transmitted between the cordless telephone handset and the base unit.

(l) "Electronic communication" means any transfer of signs, signals, writing, images, sounds, data or intelligence of any nature transmitted in whole or in part by a wire, radio, electromagnetic, photoelectronic or photo-optical system but does not include:

(1) The radio portion of a cordless telephone communication that is transmitted between the cordless telephone handset and the base unit;

(2) Any wire or oral communication;

(3) Any combination made through a tone-only paging device.

(m) "User" means any person or entity who or which uses an electronic communication service and is duly authorized by the provider of such service to engage in such use.

(n) "Electronic communications system" means any wire, radio, electromagnetic, photo-optical or photoelectronic facilities for the transmission of electronic communications, and any computer facilities or related electronic equipment for the electronic storage of such communications.

(o) "Electronic communication service" means any service which provides to users thereof the ability to send or receive wire or electronic communications.

(p) "Aural transfer" means a transfer containing the human voice at any point between and including the point of origin and the point of reception.

(q) "Trap and trace device" means a device which captures the incoming electronic or other impulses which identify the originating number of an instrument or device from which a wire or electronic communication was transmitted.

§ 62-1D-3. Interception of communications.

(a) Except as otherwise specifically provided in this article, it is unlawful for any person to:

(1) Intentionally intercept, attempt to intercept or procure any other person to intercept or attempt to intercept, any wire, oral or electronic communication; or

(2) Intentionally disclose or intentionally attempt to disclose to any other person the contents of any wire, oral or electronic communication, knowing or having reason to know that the information was obtained through the interception of a wire, oral or electronic communication in violation of this article; and

(3) Intentionally use or disclose or intentionally attempt to use or disclose the contents of any wire, oral or electronic communication or the identity of any party thereto, knowing or having reason to know that such information was obtained through the interception of a wire, oral or electronic communication in violation of this article.

(b) Any person who violates subsection (a) of this section is guilty of a felony, and, upon conviction thereof, shall be imprisoned in the penitentiary for not more than five years or fined not more than ten thousand dollars or both fined and imprisoned.

(c) It is lawful under this article for an operator of a switchboard or an officer, employee, or provider of any wire or electronic communication service whose facilities are used in the transmission of a wire communication to intercept, disclose or use that communication or the identity of any party to that communication in the normal course of his or her employment while engaged in any activity which is a necessary incident to the rendition of his or her service or to the protection of the rights or property of the carrier of the communication. Providers of wire or electronic communication services may not utilize service observing or random monitoring except for mechanical or service quality control checks.

(1) Notwithstanding any other law, any provider of wire or electronic communications services, or the directors, officers, employees, agents, landlords or custodians of any such provider, are authorized to provide information, facilities or technical assistance to persons authorized by this article to intercept wire, oral or electronic communication if such provider or its directors, officers, employees, agents, landlords or custodians has been provided with a duly certified copy of a court order directing such assistance and setting forth the period of time during which the provision of the information, facilities, or technical assistance is authorized and specifying the information, facilities or assistance required. No cause of action shall lie in any court against any such provider of wire or electronic communication services, its directors, officers, agents, landlords or custodians for providing information facilities or assistance in accordance with the terms of any such order.

(2) It is lawful under this article for a person to intercept a wire, oral or electronic communication where the person is a party to the communication or where one of the parties to the communication has given prior consent to the interception unless the communication is intercepted for the purpose of committing any criminal or tortious act in violation of the constitution or laws of the United States or the constitution or laws of this state.

§ 62-1D-12. Civil cause of action.

(a) Any person whose wire, oral or electronic communication is intercepted, disclosed, used or whose identity is disclosed in violation of this article shall have a civil cause of action against any person who so intercepts, discloses, or uses, or procures any other person to intercept, disclose, or use the communications, and shall be entitled to recover from any such person or persons:

(1) Actual damages, but not less than one hundred dollars for each day of violation;

(2) Punitive damages, if found to be proper; and

(3) Reasonable attorney fees and reasonable costs of litigation incurred.

(b) A good faith reliance by a provider of electronic or wire communication services on a court order or legislative authorization constitutes a complete defense to any civil or criminal action brought under this article or any other law.

§ 62-1D-14. Trespassing to place or remove equipment.

Any person who trespasses upon any premises with the intent to place, adjust or remove wiretapping or electronic surveillance or eavesdropping equipment without an order from the designated judge authorizing the same is guilty of a felony, and, upon conviction thereof, shall be imprisoned in the penitentiary for not more than five years.

Wisconsin

§ 968.27. Definitions.

In §§ 968.28 to 968.37:

(1) "Aggrieved person" means a person who was a party to any intercepted wire, electronic or oral communication or a person against whom the interception was directed.

(2) "Aural transfer" means a transfer containing the human voice at any point from the point of origin to the point of reception.

(3) "Contents" when used with respect to any wire, electronic or oral communication, includes any information concerning the substance, purport or meaning of that communication.

(4) "Electronic communication" means any transfer of signs, signals, writing, images, sounds, data or intelligence of any nature wholly or partially transmitted by a wire, radio, electromagnetic, photoelectronic or photo-optical system. "Electronic communication" does not include any of the following:

(a) The radio portion of a cordless telephone communication that is transmitted between the cordless telephone handset and the base unit.

(b) Any wire or oral communication.

(c) Any communication made through a tone-only paging device.

(d) Any communication from a tracking device.

(5) "Electronic communication service" means any service that provides its users with the ability to send or receive wire or electronic communications.

(6) "Electronic communications system" means any wire, radio, electromagnetic, photo-optical or photoelectronic facilities for the transmission of electronic communications, and any computer facilities or related electronic equipment for the electronic storage of those communications.

APPENDIX B — STATE STATUTES

(7) "Electronic, mechanical or other device" means any device or apparatus which can be used to intercept a wire, electronic or oral communication other than:

(a) Any telephone or telegraph instrument, equipment or facilities, or any component thereof, which is:

1. Furnished to the subscriber or user by a provider of electronic or wire communication service in the ordinary course of its business and being used by the subscriber or user in the ordinary course of its business or furnished by the subscriber or user for connection to the facilities of the service and used in the ordinary course of its business; or

2. Being used by a provider of electronic or wire communication service in the ordinary course of its business, or by a law enforcement officer in the ordinary course of his or her duties.

(b) A hearing aid or similar device being used to correct subnormal hearing to not better than normal.

(8) "Electronic storage" means any of the following:

(a) Any temporary, intermediate storage of a wire or electronic communication incidental to the electronic transmission thereof.

(b) Any storage of a wire or electronic communication by an electronic communication service for purposes of backup protection of the communication.

(9) "Intercept" means the aural or other acquisition of the contents of any wire, electronic or oral communication through the use of any electronic, mechanical or other device.

(10) "Investigative or law enforcement officer" means any officer of this state or political subdivision thereof, who is empowered by the laws of this state to conduct investigations of or to make arrests for offenses enumerated in §§ 968.28 to 968.37, and any attorney authorized by law to prosecute or participate in the prosecution of those offenses.

(11) "Judge" means the judge sitting at the time an application is made under § 968.30 or his or her successor.

(12) "Oral communication" means any oral communication uttered by a person exhibiting an expectation that the communication is not subject to interception under circumstances justifying the expectation. "Oral communication" does not include any electronic communication.

(13) "Pen register" means a device that records or decodes electronic or other impulses that identify the numbers dialed or otherwise transmitted on the telephone line to which the device is attached. "Pen register" does not include any device used by a provider or customer of a wire or electronic communication service for billing, or recording as an incident to billing, for communications services provided by the provider or any device used by a provider or customer of a wire communication service for cost accounting or other like purposes in the ordinary course of its business.

(14) "Readily accessible to the general public" means, with respect to a radio communication, that the communication is not any of the following:

(a) Scrambled or encrypted.

(b) Transmitted using modulation techniques whose essential parameters have been withheld from the public with the intention of preserving the privacy of the communication.

(c) Carried on a subcarrier or other signal subsidiary to a radio transmission.

(d) Transmitted over a communication system provided by a common carrier, including a cellular mobile radio telecommunications utility, as defined in § 196.202(1), unless the communication is a tone-only paging system communication.

(e) Transmitted on frequencies allocated under 47 CFR part 25, subpart D, E or F of part 74 or part 94, unless in the case of a communication transmitted on a frequency allocated under 47 CFR part 74 that is not exclusively allocated to broadcast auxiliary services, the communication is a 2-way voice communication by radio.

(15) "Trap and trace device" means a device that captures the incoming electronic or other impulses that identify the originating number of an instrument or device from which a wire or electronic communication was transmitted.

(16) "User" means any person who or entity that:

(a) Uses an electronic communication service; and

(b) Is duly authorized by the provider of the service to engage in that use.

(17) "Wire communication" means any aural transfer made in whole or in part through the use of facilities for the transmission of communications by the aid of wire, cable, microwave or other like connection between the point of origin and the point of reception, including the use of the connection in any switching station, furnished or operated by any person engaged as a public utility in providing or operating the facilities for the transmission of intrastate, interstate or foreign communications. "Wire communication" includes the electronic storage of any such aural transfer, but does not include the radio portion of a cordless telephone communication that is transmitted between the cordless telephone handset and the base unit.

§ 968.31. Interception, use and disclosure of wire, electronic or oral communications.

(1) Except as otherwise specifically provided in §§ 196.63 or 968.28 to 968.30, whoever commits any of the acts enumerated in this section may be fined not more than $10,000 or imprisoned for not more than 5 years or both:

(a) Intentionally intercepts, attempts to intercept or procures any other person to intercept or attempt to intercept, any wire, electronic or oral communication.

(b) Intentionally uses, attempts to use or procures any other person to use or attempt to use any electronic, mechanical or other device to intercept any oral communication.

(c) Discloses, or attempts to disclose, to any other person the contents of any wire, electronic or oral communication, knowing or having reason to know that the information was obtained through the interception of a wire, electronic or oral communication in violation of this section or under circumstances constituting violation of this section.

(d) Uses, or attempts to use, the contents of any wire, electronic or oral communication, knowing or having reason to know that the information was obtained through the interception of a wire, electronic or oral communication in violation of this section or under circumstances constituting violation of this section.

(e) Intentionally discloses the contents of any oral, electronic or wire communication obtained by authority of §§ 968.28, 968.29 and 968.30, except as therein provided.

(f) Intentionally alters any wire, electronic or oral communication intercepted on tape, wire or other device.

(2) It is not unlawful under §§ 968.28 to 968.37:

* * * * *

(c) For a person not acting under color of law to intercept a wire, electronic or oral communication where the person is a party to the communication or where one of the parties to the communication has given prior consent to the interception unless the communication is intercepted for the purpose of committing any criminal or tortious act in violation of the constitution or laws of the United States or of any state or for the purpose of committing any other injurious act.

(d) For any person to intercept or access an electronic communication made through an electronic communication system that is configured so that the electronic communication is readily accessible to the general public.

(e) For any person to intercept any radio communication that is transmitted:

1. By any station for the use of the general public, or that relates to ships, aircraft, vehicles or persons in distress;

2. By any governmental, law enforcement, civil defense, private land mobile or public safety communications system, including police and fire, readily accessible to the general public;

3. By a station operating on an authorized frequency within the bands allocated to the amateur, citizens band or general mobile radio services; or

4. By any marine or aeronautical communications system.

(f) For any person to engage in any conduct that:

1. Is prohibited by section 633 of the communications act of 1934; or

2. Is excepted from the application of section 705(a) of the communications act of 1934 by section 705(b) of that act.

* * * * *

Wyoming

§ 7-3-601. Definitions.

(a) As used in this act:

(i) "Aggrieved person" means any person who participated in an oral, wire or electronic communication intercepted as defined in this act, or a person against whom the interception was directed;

(ii) "Contents of an oral, wire or electronic communication" includes information concerning the identity of the parties participating in the communication and the existence, meaning, substance or purport of the communication;

(iii) "Electronic communication" means any transfer of signs, signals, writing, images, sounds, data or intelligence of any nature transmitted in whole or in part by a wire, radio, electromagnetic, photoelectronic or photo-optical system that affects interstate or foreign commerce but does not include:

(A) The radio portion of a cordless telephone communication that is transmitted between the cordless telephone handset and the base unit;

(B) Any wire or oral communication;

(C) Any communication made through a tone-only paging device; or

(D) Any communication made through a tracking device.

(iv) "Electronic, mechanical or other device" means any device or apparatus which can be used to intercept a wire, oral or electronic communication, other than:

    (A) Any telephone, telex or telegraph equipment, or component thereof, used in the ordinary course of business; or

    (B) A hearing aid or similar device used solely to correct subnormal hearing.

(v) "Intercept" means the aural or other acquisition of the contents of any oral, wire or electronic communication by use of an electronic, mechanical or other device;

(vi) "Judge" means a judge of a district court;

(vii) "Oral communication" means any oral communication uttered by a person who reasonably expects and circumstances justify the expectation that the communication is not subject to interception but does not include any electronic communication;

(viii) "Peace officer" means as defined in W.S. 7-2-101 and includes any law enforcement officer with federal criminal enforcement jurisdiction;

(ix) "Provider of wire or electronic communication service" means any person who provides a service which consists of communications by wire, radio, electronic, laser or other transmission of energy;

(x) "Wire communication" means any aural transfer made in whole or in part through the use of facilities for the transmission of communications by the aid of wire, cable or other like connection, including the use of such connection in a switching station, between the point of origin and the point of reception, furnished or operated by any person engaged in providing or operating such facilities for the transmission of intrastate, interstate or foreign communications, and includes any electronic storage of such communication, but the term does not include the radio portion of a cordless telephone communication that is transmitted between the cordless telephone handset and the base unit;

(xi) "This act" means W.S. 7-3-601 through 7-3-611.

§ 7-3-602. Prohibition against interception or disclosure of wire, oral or electronic communications.

(a) Except as provided in subsection (b) of this section, no person shall willfully:

(i) Intercept any wire, oral or electronic communication;

(ii) Disclose to another person the contents of any wire, oral or electronic communication, knowing or having reason to know that the information was obtained through the interception of a wire, oral or electronic communication in violation of this section;

(iii) Use the contents of any wire, oral or electronic communication knowing or having reason to know that the information was obtained through the interception of a wire, oral or electronic communication in violation of this section.

(b) Nothing in subsection (a) of this section prohibits:

* * * * *

(iv) Any person from intercepting an oral, wire or electronic communication where the person is a party to the communication or where one (1) of the parties to the communication has given prior consent to the interception unless the communication is intercepted for the purpose of committing any criminal or tortious act;

APPENDIX B — STATE STATUTES

* * * * *

§ 7-3-609. Recovery of civil damages.

(a) Any person whose wire, oral or electronic communication is intercepted, disclosed or used in violation of this act may recover damages against any person who intercepts, discloses, uses or procures any other person to intercept, disclose or use the communications as follows:

    (i) Actual damages but not less than one thousand dollars ($1,000) a day for each day of violation;

    (ii) Punitive damages; and

    (iii) Reasonable attorney's fees and other litigation costs reasonably incurred.

(b) A good faith reliance on a court order constitutes a complete defense to any civil or criminal action brought under this act.

TABLE OF CASES

A

A & T Consultants, Inc. v. Sharp, 904 S.W.2d 668 (Tex. 1995) — § 11-2, nn. 23, 29; § 11-7(f)(2), n. 273

ABC, Inc. v. Powell, 47 M.J. 363 (C.A.A.F. 1997) — § 3-1(e), n. 330

Abrams v. United States, 250 U.S. 616 (1919) — § 1-2(a), n. 17

Abu-Jamal v. Price, 23 Media L. Rep. (BNA) 2406 (W.D. Pa. 1995) — § 7-1, n. 5; § 8-1, n. 52

ACLU v. Miller, 977 F. Supp. 1228 (N.D. Ga. 1997) — § 13-9(b), n. 831

Acumenics Research & Tech. v. Department of Justice, 843 F.2d 800 (4th Cir. 1988) — § 10-2(c)(5), n. 127

Adams County Record v. Greater North Dakota Ass'n, 529 N.W.2d 830 (N.D. 1995) — § 9-1, n. 15; § 11-3(e), n. 51

Adderly v. Florida, 385 U.S. 39 (1966) — § 13-3(c)(1), n. 180

Adickes v. S.H. Kress & Co., 398 U.S. 144 (1970) — § 13-7(a)(1), n. 583

Aequitron Medical, Inc. v. CBS Inc., 24 Media L. Rep. (BNA) 1025 (S.D.N.Y. 1995) — § 16-2(d)(1), n. 177

Aequitron Medical, Inc. v. CBS Inc., 964 F. Supp. 704 (S.D.N.Y. 1997) — § 12-4(c)(3), n. 332

Aerial Burials Inc. v. Minneapolis Star & Tribune Co., 8 Media L. Rep. (BNA) 1653 (D. Minn. 1982) — § 15-2(d)(3)(C), n. 195

Affiliated Constr. Trades Found. v. Regional Jail & Correctional Facility Auth., 490 S.E.2d 708 (W. Va. 1997) — § 11-2, nn. 13, 29; § 11-3(e), n. 53

AFSCME v. County of Cook, 555 N.E.2d 361 (Ill. 1990) — § 11-2, n. 22

A.G. Becker, Inc. v. Board of Governors, 502 F. Supp. 378 (D.D.C. 1980) — § 9-5(a)(8)(J), n. 180

Aisenson v. American Broadcasting Cos., 269 Cal. Rptr. 379 (Ct. App. 1990) — § 12-2(a), nn. 8-10; § 13-4(b), nn. 507-10

Alabama-Tombigbee Rivers Coalition v. Department of Interior, 26 F.3d 1103 (11th Cir. 1994) — § 10-3(c), n. 302

Alaska v. Pruett, 11 Media L. Rep. (BNA) 1968 (Alaska Super. 1984) — § 16-2(a)(2), n. 32; § 16-2(e)(1), n. 299; § 16-2(e)(3), n. 343

Alaska Wildlife Alliance v. Rue, 948 P.2d 976 (Alaska 1997) — § 11-7(a), n. 179

Alberghini v. Tizes, 328 N.Y.S.2d 272 (Sup. Ct. 1972) — § 11-5(a)(3), n. 91

Albia Publ'g Co. v. Klobnak, 434 N.W.2d 636 (Iowa 1989) — § 9-6(d), n. 305

Albuquerque Publ'g Co. v. Department of Justice, 726 F. Supp. 851 (D.D.C. 1989) — § 10-2(c)(8)(E), nn. 210, 211, 215

Alexander v. Chicago Park Dist., 548 F. Supp. 277 (N.D. Ill. 1982) — § 16-2(a)(2), n. 30; § 16-2(c)(2)(A), n. 138; § 16-2(d)(3), n. 215; § 16-2(d)(3)(B), nn. 233, 234

Allen v. Combined Communications Corp., 7 Media L. Rep. (BNA) 2417 (Colo. Dist. 1981) — § 12-4(c)(3), nn. 268-76

Allied Daily Newspapers of Washington v. Eikenberry, 848 P.2d 1258 (Wash. 1993) — § 2-3, n. 301

Althaus v. Evansville Courier Co., 615 N.E.2d 441 (Ind. App. 1993) — § 11-7(d), n. 260

Aluminum Co. of Am. v. National Marine Fisheries Serv., 92 F.3d 902 (9th Cir. 1996) — § 9-5(b)(2), n. 198

Alvarez v. Gersten, 450 So. 2d 861 (Fla. App. 1983) — § 5-2(a)(5), n. 223

Amato v. Richmond, 157 F.R.D. 26 (E.D. Va. 1994) — § 3-2(e), nn. 421, 422

TABLE OF CASES

American Broadcasting Cos. v. Cuomo, 570 F.2d 1080 (2d Cir. 1977) — § 9-2(b), n. 42

American Broadcasting Cos. v. Gill, 1999 Tex. App. LEXIS 4449 (Tex. App. 1999) — § 13-6, n. 576

American Broadcasting Cos. v. Siebert, 442 N.Y.S.2d 855 (Sup. Ct. 1981) — § 11-1, n. 5

American Centennial Ins. Co. v. EEOC, 722 F. Supp. 180 (D.N.J. 1989) — § 10-2(c)(4), n. 114

American Civil Liberties Union Found. v. Deukmejian, 651 P.2d 822 (Cal. 1982) — § 11-5(a), n. 82; § 11-5(c), n. 169; § 11-6, n. 178

American Fed'n of Gov't Employees v. Department of Commerce, 632 F. Supp. 1272 (D.D.C. 1986) — § 10-2(b)(3), n. 39

American Soc'y of Dermatology v. Shalala, 962 F. Supp. 144 (D.C. Cir. 1996) — § 9-5(b)(2), n. 218

Ammerman v. Hubbard Broadcasting, Inc., 551 P.2d 1354 (N.M. 1976) — § 15-2(a), nn. 27, 28; § 15-2(c)(2)(C), nn. 134, 135

Amoco Prod. Co. v. Landry, 426 So. 2d 220 (La. App. 1982) — § 9-1, n. 15; § 11-1, n. 7

Amrep Corp. v. FTC, 768 F.2d 1171 (10th Cir. 1985) — § 9-5(a)(8)(J), n. 181

Anaya v. United States, 815 F.2d 1373 (10th Cir. 1987) — § 5-2(a)(3), n. 137

Anderson v. Cryovac, Inc., 805 F.2d 1 (1st Cir. 1986) — § 5-2(c), n. 370; § 6-1(a)(3), nn. 50-52; § 6-1(a)(4), nn. 62, 64, 73; § 6-1(a)(5), n. 108

Anderson v. Home Ins. Co., 924 P.2d 1123 (Colo. App. 1996) — § 6-1(b), nn. 163, 186

Anderson v. Nixon, 444 F. Supp. 1195 (D.D.C. 1978) — § 16-2(b)(2), n. 74; § 16-2(c)(2)(B), nn. 171-73; § 16-2(d)(1), n. 188; § 16-2(e)(2), n. 327; § 16-2(e)(4), n. 360; § 16-2(g), n. 385

Anderson v. Secretary of Health & Human Servs., 80 F.3d 1500 (10th Cir. 1996) — § 10-2(h), nn. 288, 289

Anderson v. Strong Memorial Hosp., 573 N.Y.S.2d 828 (Sup. Ct. 1991) — § 13-4(a)(3)(A)(i), nn. 437-44

Anderson v. WROC-TV, 441 N.Y.S.2d 220 (Sup. Ct. 1981) — § 12-4(a), nn. 148, 172, 188

Andrade v. United States Sentencing Comm'n, 989 F.2d 308 (9th Cir. 1993) — § 10-2(b)(2), n. 27

Andrews v. Andreoli, 400 N.Y.S.2d 442 (Sup. Ct. 1977) — § 15-2(h), n. 288

Andrews v. Department of Justice, 769 F. Supp. 314 (E.D. Mo. 1991) — § 10-2(c)(7), n. 167

Andrews v. Independent Sch. Dist. No. 29, 737 P.2d 929 (Okla. 1987) — § 9-6(b), n. 258

Animal Legal Defense Fund v. Shalala, 104 F.3d 424 (D.C. Cir. 1997) — § 9-5(b)(2), nn. 198, 218

Anonymous v. Anonymous, 550 N.Y.S.2d 704 (App. Div. 1990) — § 3-3(b), n. 513

Anonymous v. Board of Educ., 616 N.Y.S.2d 867 (Sup. Ct. 1994) — § 11-7(m), n. 352

Anti-Defamation League v. Superior Ct., 79 Cal. Rptr. 2d 597 (Ct. App. 1998) — § 13-3(b), n. 134; § 16-2(b)(1), nn. 63, 71

Apicella v. McNeil Laboratories, Inc., 66 F.R.D. 78 (E.D.N.Y. 1975) — § 16-2(b)(1), n. 68

Application of National Broadcasting Co., 828 F.2d 340 (6th Cir. 1987) — § 3-1(a), nn. 15-24

Appman v. Worthington, 746 S.W.2d 165 (Tenn. 1987) — § 11-7(b)(3)(A), n. 220

Arieff v. Department of Navy, 712 F.2d 1462 (D.C. Cir. 1983) — § 10-2(c)(7), nn. 156, 166

Arizona v. Duran, 901 P.2d 1197 (Ariz. App. 1995) — § 13-7(b)(4)(E), n. 734

TABLE OF CASES

Arizona v. Hicks, 480 U.S. 321 (1987) — § 12-4(a), n. 128
Arizona Bd. of Regents v. Phoenix Newspapers, Inc., 806 P.2d 348 (Ariz. 1991) — § 11-7(a)(1), n. 186
Arizona Press Club, Inc. v. Arizona Bd. of Tax Appeals, 558 P.2d 697 (Ariz. 1976) — § 9-6(b), n. 271
Arkansas Best Corp. v. General Elec. Capital Corp., 878 S.W.2d 708 (Ark. 1994) — § 6-1(b), nn. 163, 187
Arkansas Dep't of Fin. & Admin. v. Pharmacy Ass'n, Inc., 970 S.W.2d 217 (Ark. 1998) — § 11-5(a)(3), n. 95
Arkansas Dep't of Health v. Westark Christian Action Council, 910 S.W.2d 199 (Ark. 1995) — § 11-7(j), n. 309
Arkansas Educ. Television Comm'n v. Forbes, 523 U.S. 666 (1998) — § 1-1, n. 11
Arkansas Gazette Co. v. Pickens, 522 S.W.2d 350 (Ark. 1975) — § 9-6(j), n. 411
Arkansas Television Co. v. Tedder, 662 S.W.2d 174 (Ark. 1983) — § 3-1(a), n. 10
Arkansas Writers' Project, Inc. v. Ragland, 481 U.S. 221 (1987) — § 1-1, n. 5
Armstead v. Lima City Bd. of Educ., 600 N.E.2d 1085 (Ohio App. 1991) — § 9-6(i)(4), n. 395
Armstrong v. Executive Office of the President, 877 F. Supp. 690 (D.D.C. 1995) — § 10-2(b)(2), n. 22
Armstrong v. Executive Office of the President, 90 F.3d 553 (D.C. Cir. 1996) — § 10-2(b)(2), n. 29
Arney v. Director, Kansas State Penitentiary, 671 P.2d 559 (Kan. 1983) — § 8-1, n. 54
Aronson v. HUD, 866 F.2d 1 (1st Cir. 1989) — § 10-2(h), n. 285
Arrington v. New York Times Co., 434 N.E.2d 1319 (N.Y. 1982) — § 12-1, n. 2; § 12-2(a), nn. 13, 14; § 12-4(c)(3), n. 283
Artway v. Attorney Gen., 81 F.3d 1235 (3d Cir. 1996) — § 11-7(c), n. 256
A.S. Abell Publ'g Co. v. Board of Regents, 514 A.2d 25 (Md. App. 1986) — § 9-6(b), n. 259
Asbury Park Press, Inc. v. Borough of Seaside Heights, 586 A.2d 870 (N.J. Super. 1990) — § 11-7(b)(1), n. 210
Ashcraft v. Conoco, Inc., 1998 U.S. Dist. LEXIS 16371 (E.D.N.C. Sept. 3, 1998) — § 16-2(e)(3), n. 336; § 16-2(f), n. 367
Ashcraft v. Conoco, Inc., 26 Media L. Rep. (BNA) 1620 (E.D.N.C. 1998) — § 13-3(a), n. 116; § 13-3(b), n. 134; § 16-2(e)(3), nn. 334, 335
Ashland Publ'g Co. v. Asbury, 612 S.W.2d 749 (Ky. App. 1980) — § 3-1(a), nn. 9, 12
Ashley v. Public Disclosure Comm'n, 560 P.2d 1156 (Wash. App. 1977) — § 11-7(b)(3)(A), n. 220
Ashley v. Washington State Pub. Disclosure Comm'n, 560 P.2d 1156 (Wash. App. 1977) — § 11-7(f)(2), n. 275
Askin v. McNulty, 47 F.3d 100 (4th Cir. 1995) — § 13-7(a)(2)(A)(ii), n. 624
Associated Press v. Bell, 510 N.E.2d 313 (N.Y. 1987) — § 3-1(a)(4), nn. 170, 175
Associated Press v. Board of Pub. Educ., 804 P.2d 376 (Mont. 1991) — § 9-1, n. 17
Associated Press v. Bost, 656 So. 2d 113 (Miss. 1995) — § 4-3, n. 87
Associated Press v. Bradshaw, 410 N.W.2d 577 (S.D. 1987) — § 3-3(a), nn. 437, 484-86
Associated Press v. District Ct., 705 F.2d 1143 (9th Cir. 1983) — § 5-2(b), n. 296
Associated Press v. NLRB, 301 U.S. 103 (1937) — § 13-3(b), n. 130
Associated Press v. United States Dist. Ct., 705 F.2d 1143 (9th Cir. 1983) — § 5-1, n. 24; § 5-2(a), nn. 41-53; § 5-2(a)(3), n. 177; § 5-2(a)(7), n. 252

TABLE OF CASES

Association of Am. Physicians & Surgeons v. Clinton, 989 F. Supp. 8 (D.D.C. 1997) — § 9-5(b)(7), n. 249

Association of Am. Physicians & Surgeons v. Clinton, 997 F.2d 898 (D.C. Cir. 1993) — § 9-5(b)(2), n. 219; § 9-5(b)(3), n. 225

Association of Retired R.R. Workers v. United States Retirement Bd., 830 F.2d 331 (D.C. Cir. 1987) — § 10-2(c)(4), n. 117

AT&T Communications of West Virginia v. Public Serv. Comm'n, 423 S.E.2d 859 (W. Va. 1992) — § 11-5(a)(3), n. 95

Atkinson v. FDIC, 1 Gov't Disclosure Serv. (P-H) 80,034 (D.D.C. 1980) — § 10-2(c)(9), n. 222

Atlanta Journal v. Long, 369 S.E.2d 755 (Ga. 1988) — § 6-1(c)(1), n. 210

Atlantic City Convention Center Auth. v. South Jersey Publ'g Co., 637 A.2d 1261 (N.J. 1994) — § 9-3, n. 58; § 11-2, n. 13

Attorney Gen. v. School Comm., 375 N.E.2d 1188 (Mass. 1978) — § 9-6(i)(1)(A), n. 372

Audubon Soc'y v. United States Forest Serv., 104 F.3d 1201 (10th Cir. 1997) — § 10-2(c)(3), n. 104

Ault v. Hustler Magazine, Inc., 13 Media L. Rep. (BNA) 2232 (D. Or. 1987) — § 13-2(a), nn. 25, 26

Ault v. Hustler Magazine, Inc., 860 F.2d 877 (9th Cir. 1988) — § 13-3(b), nn. 145, 146, 149

Austin Daily Herald v. Mork, 507 N.W.2d 854 (Minn. App. 1993) — § 2-1(d), n. 98; § 3-1(c), nn. 266-68

Austin v. Memphis Publ'g Co., 655 S.W.2d 146 (Tenn. 1983) — § 15-1, n. 13; § 15-2(c)(2)(A), nn. 92, 93, 95; § 15-2(d)(3)(C), nn. 194, 195

Aviation Consumer Action Project v. Washburn, 535 F.2d 101 (D.C. Cir. 1976) — § 9-5(b)(5), n. 232

Avirgan v. Hull, 118 F.R.D. 252 (D.D.C. 1987) — § 3-2(e), n. 423

Ayala v. Speckard, 102 F.2d 649 (2d Cir. 1996) (Ayala I) — § 3-1(c), nn. 285, 286, 290

Ayala v. Speckard, 131 F.3d 62 (2d Cir. 1997) — § 3-1(b), n. 247; § 3-1(c), nn. 289-96

Ayash v. Dana-Farber Cancer Inst., 1999 Mass. App. LEXIS 244 (Mass. App. Feb. 26, 1999) — § 16-3, n. 485

Ayash v. Dana-Farber Cancer Inst., 706 N.E.2d 316 (Mass. App. 1999) — § 16-2(a)(2), n. 44

Ayeni v. CBS Inc., 848 F. Supp. 362 (E.D.N.Y. 1994) — § 12-4(a), nn. 149, 150, 172; § 12-5, nn. 368-71; § 12-6(a), n. 373

Ayeni v. Mottola, 35 F.3d 680 (2d Cir. 1994) — § 12-4(a), nn. 150, 151; § 12-5, n. 371

B

Babets v. Secretary of Executive Office, 526 N.E.2d 1261 (Mass. 1988) — § 11-3(a), n. 36; § 11-5(a)(4), n. 103

Badhwar v. Department of Air Force, 829 F.2d 182 (D.C. Cir. 1987) — § 10-2(c)(6), n. 133

Baez v. Department of Justice, 647 F.2d 1328 (D.C. Cir. 1980) — § 10-2(c)(2), nn. 55, 97; § 10-2(c)(8)(C), n. 191

Bagby v. School Dist., 528 P.2d 1299 (Colo. 1974) — § 9-6(c), nn. 288, 289

Baggs v. Eagle-Picher Indus., 957 F.2d 268 (6th Cir. 1992) — § 12-4(c)(3), n. 291

Bailey v. Systems Innovation, Inc., 852 F.2d 93 (3d Cir. 1988) — § 7-1, nn. 72, 73

Baker v. Burlington County Times, 9 Media L. Rep. (BNA) 1967 (D.N.J. 1983) — § 13-7(a)(1), n. 583

TABLE OF CASES

Baker v. F & F Inv., 470 F.2d 778 (2d Cir. 1972) — § 14-5(f), n. 211; § 14-6(a), nn. 222-33, 253; § 15-2(j), nn. 322, 323; § 15-3(c), n. 397; § 16-2(a)(1), n. 2; § 16-2(c)(2)(A), nn. 135, 138; § 16-2(d)(1), nn. 177, 187; § 16-2(e)(1), nn. 291, 297, 298; § 16-2(i), n. 446

Ballard v. Herzke, 924 S.W.2d 652 (Tenn. 1996) — § 6-1(a)(3), n. 59; § 11-7(m), n. 347

Baltimore Sun Co. v. Colbert, 593 A.2d 224 (Md. 1991) — § 2-3, nn. 296, 298; § 3-1(a), nn. 44, 46, 47; § 3-1(a)(6), n. 197

Baltimore Sun Co. v. Maryland, 667 A.2d 166 (Md. 1995) — § 3-3(b), n. 549

Baltimore Sun Co. v. Thanos, 607 A.2d 565 (Md. Spec. App. 1992) — § 5-2(b), n. 343

Banco Popular de Puerto Rico v. Greenblatt, 964 F.2d 1227 (1st Cir. 1992) — § 6-1(b), n. 188

Bangor Publ'g Co. v. Bangor, 544 A.2d 733 (Me. 1988) — § 11-7(a)(1), n. 185

Bank of Am. Nat'l Trust & Sav. Ass'n v. Hotel Rittenhouse Assocs., 800 F.2d 339 (3d Cir. 1986) — § 6-1(a)(4), n. 68; § 6-1(a)(5), n. 105; § 6-1(b), nn. 158-63; § 6-1(c)(1), n. 216

Bankers Life & Cas. Co. v. Holland, 346 U.S. 379 (1953) — § 16-2(h)(2), n. 429

Bantam Books, Inc. v. Sullivan, 372 U.S. 58 (1963) — § 2-1(d), n. 70

Barger v. Courier-Journal, 20 Media L. Rep. (BNA) 1189 (Ky. App. 1991) — § 12-3, n. 102

Barile v. City Comptroller, 288 N.Y.S.2d 191 (Sup. Ct. 1968) — § 9-6(d), n. 297

Barker v. City of Portland, 767 P.2d 460 (Or. App. 1989) — § 9-6(j), n. 407

Barney v. IRS, 618 F.2d 1268 (8th Cir. 1980) — § 10-2(c)(8)(A), n. 180

Barr v. Arco Chem. Corp., 529 F. Supp. 1275 (S.D. Tex. 1982) — § 12-4(b), n. 208

Barron v. Florida Freedom Newspapers, Inc., 531 So. 2d 113 (Fla. 1988) — § 3-2(a), nn. 372, 374; § 3-2(b), nn. 375-80; § 6-1(a)(5), n. 109; § 6-1(c), nn. 205-09

Barry v. Seigle, 422 So. 2d 63 (Fla. App. 1982) — § 11-2, n. 30

Barry v. United States, 865 F.2d 1317 (D.C. Cir. 1989) — § 3-1(a)(3), n. 139; § 5-2(a)(3), n. 186

Barry v. Washington Post Co., 529 A.2d 319 (D.C. 1987) — § 11-5(a)(6), n. 143

Bartlett v. Superior Ct., 722 P.2d 346 (Ariz. App. 1986) — § 15-2(d)(1), n. 145; § 15-2(e)(2)(B), n. 242; § 16-2(a)(2), n. 31; § 16-2(d)(3)(B), n. 239

Bartnicki v. Vopper, No. 3:CV-94-1201, slip. op. (M.D. Pa. June 17, 1996) — § 13-7(a)(2)(A)(i), nn. 604, 608

Barton v. Shupe, 525 N.E.2d 812 (Ohio 1988) — § 11-7(a)(3), n. 192

Barvick v. Cisneros, 941 F. Supp. 1015 (D. Kan. 1996) — § 11-7(j), n. 309

Bates v. City of Little Rock, 361 U.S. 516 (1960) — § 14-4(c), n. 102

Bates v. Little Rock, 361 U.S. 516 (1960) — § 14-4(a), n. 80

Bauer v. Gannett Co., 557 N.W.2d 608 (Minn. App. 1997) — § 15-2(c)(2)(B), n. 99; § 15-2(d)(1), n. 143; § 15-2(e)(2)(B), n. 247; § 15-2(e)(2)(C), n. 254; § 16-2(c)(2)(B), n. 166

Baugh v. CBS Inc., 828 F. Supp. 745 (N.D. Cal. 1993) — § 12-4(a), nn. 189-99; § 12-4(c)(2), n. 243; § 13-2(b), nn. 45-49

Beach v. Shanley, 465 N.E.2d 304 (N.Y. 1984) — § 15-2(a), n. 23; § 15-2(c)(1), n. 64

Beard v. Department of Justice, 917 F. Supp. 61 (D.D.C. 1996) — § 10-2(b)(2), n. 30

Beckham v. Board of Educ., 873 S.W.2d 575 (Ky. 1994) — § 11-7(a)(3), n. 193

Beckman Indus. v. International Ins. Co., 966 F.2d 470 (9th Cir. 1992) — § 6-1(a)(1), n. 17

Becnel v. Lucia, 420 So. 2d 1173 (La. App. 1982) — § 15-2(b)(2), nn. 49-51; § 15-2(d)(1), n. 143; § 15-2(e)(2)(C), n. 252

TABLE OF CASES

Bedingfield v. Birmingham News Co., 595 So. 2d 1379 (Ala. 1992) — § 11-7(f)(6), n. 294

Belcher v. Mansi, 569 F. Supp. 379 (D.R.I. 1983) — § 9-6(e), n. 321

Bell v. City of Des Moines, 412 N.W.2d 585 (Iowa 1987) — § 16-2(b)(1), n. 55; § 16-2(h), n. 398

Bello v. South Shore Hosp., 429 N.E.2d 1011 (Mass. 1981) — § 11-3(e), n. 51

Belluomo v. KAKE TV & Radio, Inc., 596 P.2d 832 (Kan. App. 1979) — § 12-4(a), nn. 164, 188; § 12-4(c)(1), nn. 228-33; § 12-4(c)(2), n. 243; § 12-4(c)(3), n. 260

Belo Broadcasting Corp. v. Clark, 654 F.2d 423 (5th Cir. 1981) — § 4-2(a), n. 44; § 5-2(b), nn. 322, 327-37

Benavides v. Bureau of Prisons, 993 F.2d 257 (D.C. Cir. 1993) — § 10-2(h), n. 285

Benford v. American Broadcasting Cos., 502 F. Supp. 1159 (D. Md. 1980) — § 13-7(a)(1), nn. 582, 584; § 13-7(a)(2)(A)(iii), nn. 631, 634

Benis v. Department of State, 801 F.2d 1386 (D.C. Cir. 1986) — § 10-2(c)(8), n. 175

Berger v. Cable News Network, 24 Media L. Rep. (BNA) 1757 (D. Mont. 1996), *vacated on other grounds*, 119 S. Ct. 1706 (1999) — § 13-3(b), nn. 147-49

Berger v. Hanlon, 129 F.3d 505 (9th Cir. 1997), *vacated*, 119 S. Ct. 1706 (1999) — § 12-4(a), nn. 122, 137, 188; § 12-5, nn. 343-48; § 13-7(a)(1), n. 581; § 13-7(a)(2)(A)(iii), nn. 631, 633

Berger v. Hanlon, 1999 U.S. App. LEXIS 20262 (9th Cir. Aug. 27, 1999) — § 12-4(a), nn. 122, 137, 173; § 12-5, n. 349

Berry v. Department of Justice, 733 F.2d 1343 (9th Cir. 1984) — § 5-2(d), n. 438

Berry v. Peoples Broadcasting Corp., 547 N.E.2d 231 (Ind. 1989) — § 9-6(e), n. 321

Berry County Sheriff's Merit Bd. v. Peoples Broadcasting Corp., 547 N.E.2d 231 (Ind. 1989) — § 9-6(h), n. 345

Bess v. Bess, 929 F.2d 1332 (8th Cir. 1991) — § 13-7(a)(2)(A)(iv), n. 642

Beth v. Garamendi, 283 Cal. Rptr. 829 (Ct. App. 1991) — § 11-9, n. 371

Bethel Sch. Dist. v. Fraser, 478 U.S. 675 (1986) — § 1-1, n. 16

Bethiaume's Estate v. Pratt, 365 A.2d 792 (Me. 1976) — § 12-4(c)(3), n. 294

B.H. v. Ryder, 856 F. Supp. 1285 (N.D. Ill. 1994) — § 3-2(d), nn. 415-17

Bilder v. Township of Delavan, 334 N.W.2d 252, 255 (Wis. 1983) — § 6-1(c)(1), n. 222

Billings Gazette v. Justice Ct., 771 F. Supp. 1062 (D. Mont. 1987) — § 3-1(a)(2), n. 102

Bilney v. Evening Star Newspaper Co., 406 A.2d 652 (Md. Spec. App. 1979) — § 13-3(b), n. 137; § 15-2(c)(2)(B), nn. 117-19; § 15-2(d)(3)(C), n. 184; § 15-2(h), n. 270

Bindrim v. Mitchell, 155 Cal. Rptr. 29 (Ct. App. 1979) — § 13-4(a)(1)(A), nn. 340-44

Binghamton Press Co. v. Board of Educ., 412 N.Y.S.2d 492 (App. Div. 1979) — § 9-6(c), n. 288

Birch v. United States Postal Serv., 803 F.2d 1206 (D.C. Cir. 1986) — § 10-2(c)(8), n. 176

Birmingham News Co. v. Hunt, 624 So. 2d 1117 (Ala. Crim. App. 1993) — § 5-2(a)(3), nn. 135, 181, 186, 190

Birmingham News Co. v. Peevy, 21 Media L. Rep. (BNA) 2125 (Ala. Cir. 1993) — § 11-2, n. 17

Birmingham News Co. v. Roper, 4 Media L. Rep. (BNA) 1075 (N.D. Ala. 1978) — § 9-4, n. 70

Bishop v. Craft-Jones, 2 F. Supp. 2d 1317 (D. Or. 1998) — § 3-3(a), n. 436; § 6-2(a), n. 268

Bivens v. Six Unknown Named Agents, 403 U.S. 388 (1971) — § 12-4(a), n. 150; § 13-7(a)(1), n. 580

TABLE OF CASES

Black v. Georgia Dep't of Transp., 417 S.E.2d 655 (Ga. 1992) — § 11-7(f)(5), n. 292
Black v. United States, 24 Cl. Ct. 461 (1991) — § 6-1(c)(2), n. 228
Black Hills Alliance v. United States Forest Serv., 603 F. Supp. 117 (D.S.D. 1984) — § 10-2(c)(10), n. 225
Black Panther Party v. Kehoe, 117 Cal. Rptr. 106 (Ct. App. 1974) — § 11-1, n. 8; § 11-5(a), n. 81
Blackford ex rel. Cherokee Junior High Sch. PTA v. School Bd., 375 So. 2d 578 (Fla. App. 1979) — § 9-6(c), n. 287
Blackston v. Alabama, 30 F.3d 117 (11th Cir. 1994) — § 9-6(e), n. 322
Blackwood v. Cates, 297 N.C. 163 (1979) — § 12-4(c)(3), n. 324
Blair v. City of Winchester, 743 S.W.2d 28 (Ky. App. 1987) — § 9-6(i)(1)(C), n. 380
Blalock v. United States, 844 F.2d 1546 (11th Cir. 1988) — § 3-1(a)(3), n. 143
Blankenship v. City of Hoover, 590 So. 2d 245 (Ala. 1991) — § 11-7(a)(2), n. 191
Blaylock v. Staley, 732 S.W.2d 152 (Ark. 1987) — § 11-2, n. 20; § 11-7(h), n. 302
Bludworth v. Palm Beach Newspapers, Inc., 476 So. 2d 775 (Fla. App. 1985) — § 5-2(a)(5), n. 226
Blue v. Bureau of Prisons, 570 F.2d 529 (5th Cir. 1988) — § 10-2(h), n. 287
Board of Airport Comm'rs v. Jews for Jesus, Inc., 482 U.S. 569 (1987) — § 1-1, n. 7
Board of Educ. v. Pico, 457 U.S. 853 (1982) — § 1-2(b), n. 28
Board of Pardons v. Freedom of Info. Comm., 563 A.2d 314 (Conn. App. 1989) — § 11-5(a)(5), n. 119
Board of Pub. Instruction v. Doran, 224 So. 2d 693 (Fla. 1969) — § 9-6(h), n. 343
Board of Regents v. Atlanta Journal, 378 S.E.2d 305 (Ga. 1989) — § 11-7(a), n. 183
Board of Trustees v. Board of County Comm'rs, 606 P.2d 1069 (Mont. 1980) — § 9-6(c), n. 287
Board of Trustees v. Cox Enters., 679 S.W.2d 86 (Tex. App. 1984) — § 9-6(a), n. 253; § 9-6(j), n. 407
Boddie v. American Broadcasting Cos., 731 F.2d 333 (6th Cir. 1984) — § 13-7(a)(2)(A)(i), n. 594
Boddie v. American Broadcasting Cos., 881 F.2d 267 (6th Cir. 1989) — § 12-2(a), n. 24; § 13-2(a), n. 17; § 13-7(a)(2)(A)(iii), n. 634; § 13-7(b)(2), n. 695
Boehner v. McDermott, 1998 U.S. Dist. LEXIS 11509 (D.D.C. July 28, 1998) — § 13-7(a)(2)(A)(i), n. 607
Boehner v. McDermott, 1999 U.S. App. LEXIS 23135 (D.C. Cir. Sept. 24, 1999) — Preface, n. 4; § 13-3(a), nn. 102, 105; § 13-3(b), n. 137; § 13-3(c)(8)(A), n. 262; § 13-7(a)(2)(A)(i), nn. 600, 601, 607
Boettger v. Loverro, 502 A.2d 1310 (Pa. Super. 1986), *rev'd*, 555 A.2d 1234 (Pa.), *vacated*, 493 U.S. 885 (1989), *on remand*, 587 A.2d 712 (Pa. 1991) — § 13-7(a)(2)(A)(i), n. 602
Boettger v. Loverro, 555 A.2d 1234 (Pa. 1989), *vacated*, 493 U.S. 885 (1989) — § 13-3(b), n. 129
Boettger v. Loverro, 587 A.2d 712 (Pa. 1991) — § 13-3(b), n. 129; § 13-7(a)(2)(A)(i), n. 600
Bollinger v. San Diego Civil Serv. Comm'n, 84 Cal. Rptr. 2d 27 (Ct. App. 1999) — § 9-6(i)(1)(C), n. 381
Boos v. Barry, 485 U.S. 312 (1988) — § 1-1, n. 3
Booth Newspapers, Inc. v. Midland Circuit Judge, 377 N.W.2d 868 (Mich. App. 1985) — § 6-1(a)(1), n. 15

TABLE OF CASES

Booth Newspapers, Inc. v. Twelfth Dist. Ct. Judge, 432 N.W.2d 400 (Mich. App. 1988) — § 3-1(a), n. 47; § 3-1(a)(2), nn. 101, 102

Booth Newspapers, Inc. v. University of Michigan Bd. of Regents, 507 N.W.2d 422 (Mich. 1993) — § 11-7(g), n. 299

Booth Newspapers, Inc. v. Wyoming City Council, 425 N.W.2d 695 (Mich. App. 1988) — § 9-6(c), n. 287

Borreca v. Fasi, 369 F. Supp. 906 (D. Haw. 1974) — § 9-2(a), n. 33; § 9-2(b), n. 42

Bose Corp. v. Consumers Union, 466 U.S. 485 (1984) — § 16-2(h), n. 392; § 16-2(h)(2), n. 442

Bougas v. Chief of Police of Lexington, 354 N.E.2d 872 (Mass. 1976) — § 11-5(a), n. 78; § 11-7(b)(3)(B), nn. 228, 229

Bowen v. New York Comm'n of Correction, 484 N.Y.S.2d 210 (App. Div. 1984) — § 9-6(d), n. 290

Bowers v. Hardwick, 478 U.S. 186 (1986) — § 2-2(a), n. 121

Bowers v. Shelton, 453 S.E.2d 741 (Ga. 1995) — § 11-7(f)(2), nn. 273, 274

Bowman Dairy Co. v. United States, 341 U.S. 214 (1951) — § 15-3(c), n. 387

Bradshaw v. Shaw, 360 A.2d 123 (N.H. 1976) — § 9-6(j), n. 416

Branch v. FBI, 658 F. Supp. 204 (D.D.C. 1987) — § 10-2(c)(8)(C), n. 190

Brandenburg v. Ohio, 395 U.S. 444 (1969) — § 13-3(c)(7), n. 254

Branzburg v. Hayes, 408 U.S. 665 (1972) — § 1-4(a), n. 60; § 1-5, nn. 76-78; § 2-2(c), nn. 180, 185; § 3-1(a)(3), n. 122; § 7-1, n. 13; § 7-3, n. 146; § 8-1, nn. 11, 16; § 8-3, nn. 90, 91; § 12-2(a), nn. 34, 41; § 12-4(a), nn. 170, 175; § 13-3(a), n. 98; § 13-3(b), n. 134; § 13-3(c), nn. 163, 164; § 13-3(c)(9)(B), n. 320; § 13-4(a)(2)(A), n. 373; § 13-4(a)(2)(B), n. 380; § 13-4(a)(2)(C), n. 404; § 13-4(c), nn. 530, 531, 539; § 14-1, n. 17; § 14-2, n. 38; § 14-3, nn. 39, 43-45, 48-50, 55-57; § 14-4, nn. 61-63; § 14-4(a), nn. 78-90; § 14-4(b), nn. 91-98; § 14-4(c), nn. 99-106; § 14-5(a), nn. 108, 110-13, 122; § 14-5(b), nn. 128, 139, 142, 144-46; § 14-5(c), nn. 149, 154, 157, 162, 164; § 14-5(d), nn. 170, 171, 183, 185, 186; § 14-5(f), nn. 200, 216; § 14-6(a), nn. 223, 231, 233; § 14-6(b), nn. 262, 263; § 15-1, nn. 10, 11; § 15-2(a), n. 26; § 15-2(c)(2)(A), n. 94; § 15-2(d)(1), n. 155; § 15-2(e)(2), n. 224; § 16-1, n. 1; § 16-2(a)(1), n. 7; § 16-2(a)(2), nn. 37, 42, 43; § 16-2(b)(1), nn. 49, 50, 73; § 16-2(b)(2), n. 74; § 16-2(c)(1), nn. 82, 86; § 16-2(d)(3)(C), n. 260; § 16-2(e)(1), nn. 308, 309; § 16-2(e)(4), n. 360; § 16-3, n. 473

Branzburg v. Meigs, 503 S.W.2d 748 (Ky. 1971) — § 14-3, nn. 39, 55, 58-60; § 16-2(a)(2), n. 42

Branzburg v. Pound, 461 S.W.2d 345 (Ky. 1970) — § 14-3, n. 55; § 15-2(c)(1), n. 62; § 15-2(d)(1), nn. 154-57; § 15-2(d)(3)(B), nn. 175-79, 234

Braun v. Taft, 201 Cal. Rptr. 654 (Ct. App. 1984) — § 11-9, n. 364; § 11-7(a)(2), n. 189

Breiner v. Takao, 835 P.2d 637 (Haw. 1992) — § 7-2, n. 140

Brent v. Paquette, 567 A.2d 976 (N.H. 1989) — § 9-6(f), n. 330

Brewster v. Boston Herald-Traveler Corp., 20 F.R.D. 416 (D. Mass. 1957) — § 14-1, n. 9

Brian W. v. Superior Ct., 574 P.2d 788 (Cal. 1978) — § 3-3(a), nn. 480-83; § 5-2(a)(3), n. 198

Bridges v. California, 314 U.S. 252 (1941) — § 2-1(a), n. 11; § 2-1(c), nn. 37-42; § 7-4, n. 221

Briggs v. Maryland, 704 A.2d 904 (Md. 1998) — § 13-9(b), n. 831

Briscoe v. Reader's Digest Ass'n, 483 P.2d 34 (Cal. 1971) — § 12-4(a), n. 156

Broadrick v. Oklahoma, 413 U.S. 601 (1973) — § 1-1, n. 7; § 14-5(c), n. 149

Brogan v. Passaic Daily News, 123 A.2d 473 (N.J. 1956) — § 15-2(c)(2)(B), n. 119

TABLE OF CASES

Brooks v. American Broadcasting Cos., 737 F. Supp. 431 (N.D. Ohio 1990) — § 12-2(a), nn. 20-26; § 13-7(a)(2)(A)(iii), n. 634; § 13-7(a)(2)(C), n. 661

Brothers v. Brothers, 16 Media L. Rep. (BNA) 1031 (Ala. Cir. 1989) — § 15-2(d)(3)(B), n. 170

Brouillet v. Cowles Publ'g Co., 791 P.2d 526 (Wash. 1990) — § 11-5(a)(5), n. 125

Brown & Williamson Tobacco Corp. v. FTC, 710 F.2d 1165 (6th Cir. 1983) — § 3-2(a), nn. 351, 356; § 6-1(a)(4), n. 61; § 6-1(a)(5), n. 116; § 6-1(c), nn. 197-99

Brown & Williamson Tobacco Corp. v. Jacobson, 713 F.2d 262 (7th Cir. 1983) — § 13-4(c), n. 533

Brown v. Advantage Eng'g Inc., 960 F.2d 1013 (11th Cir. 1992) — § 6-1(b), nn. 157, 159, 187; § 6-1(c), nn. 200-03; § 6-1(c)(2), n. 233

Brown v. American Broadcasting Cos., 704 F.2d 1296 (4th Cir. 1983) — § 13-7(a)(2)(A)(iii), n. 634

Brown v. East Baton Rouge Parish Sch. Bd., 405 So. 2d 1148 (La. App. 1981) — § 9-6(i)(1)(A), n. 370

Brown v. Iowa Legislative Council, 490 N.W.2d 551 (Iowa 1992) — § 11-2, n. 26

Brown v. Palmer, 944 F.2d 732 (10th Cir. 1991) — § 8-5, nn. 142, 144

Brown v. Stackler, 612 F.2d 1057 (7th Cir. 1980) — § 10-2(h), n. 289

Brown v. Virginia, 204 S.E.2d 429 (Va. 1974) — § 16-2(a)(2), n. 29; § 16-2(c)(1), nn. 92, 103; § 16-2(e)(2), n. 315

Brown v. Waddell, 50 F.3d 285 (4th Cir. 1995) — § 13-7(a)(2)(A)(ii), n. 625

Bruno & Stillman, Inc. v. Globe Newspaper Co., 633 F.2d 583 (1st Cir. 1980) — § 15-3(c), n. 403; § 16-2(a)(1), n. 2; § 16-2(b)(2), n. 74; § 16-2(c)(2)(B), nn. 162-66; § 16-2(d)(1), nn. 177, 202, 203; § 16-2(d)(3), n. 217; § 16-2(d)(3)(C), n. 246; § 16-2(e)(1), nn. 303-06; § 16-2(e)(3), n. 357; § 16-2(e)(4), nn. 362-64; § 16-2(h), n. 403; § 16-2(h)(1), n. 411; § 16-2(h)(2), n. 424; § 16-3, n. 480

Bryant v. Mars, 830 S.W.2d 869 (Ark. 1992) — § 11-5(a)(4), nn. 98, 115

Bryant v. Secretary of the Army, 862 F. Supp. 574 (D.D.C. 1994) — § 8-5, n. 141

Buffalo Broadcasting Co. v. City of Buffalo, 511 N.Y.S.2d 759 (App. Div. 1987) — § 11-7(b)(8), n. 247

Buffalo Broadcasting Co. v. New York Dep't of Correctional Servs., 578 N.Y.S.2d 928 (App. Div. 1992) — § 8-1, n. 52

Buffalo News v. Buffalo Enter. Dev. Corp., 578 N.Y.S.2d 945 (App. Div. 1991) — § 11-3(e), n. 50

Buffalo News v. Buffalo Enter. Dev. Corp., 644 N.E.2d 277 (N.Y. 1994) — § 11-8, n. 355

Buffalo News v. Buffalo Mun. Hous. Auth., 558 N.Y.S.2d 364 (App. Div. 1990) — § 11-7(a)(2), n. 189

Builders Ass'n of Greater Chicago v. Cook County, 1998 U.S. Dist. LEXIS 2991 (N.D. Ill. Mar. 10, 1998) — § 16-2(b)(1), n. 63; § 16-2(c)(2)(A), n. 136

Bundren v. Peters, 732 F. Supp. 1486 (E.D. Tenn. 1989) — § 9-6(c), n. 289

Bureau of Nat'l Affairs, Inc. v. Department of Justice, 742 F.2d 1484 (D.C. Cir. 1984) — § 10-2(b)(1), nn. 5, 6

Burka v. Department of Health & Human Servs., 87 F.3d 508 (D.C. Cir. 1996) — § 10-2(b)(1), n. 10

Burkes v. Klausner, 24 Media L. Rep. (BNA) 2276 (Wis. Cir. 1996) — § 6-1(a)(4), n. 75

Burson v. Freeman, 504 U.S. 191 (1992) — § 1-1, n. 5; § 8-4, nn. 124-29

Burtis v. New York Police Dep't, 659 N.Y.S.2d 875 (App. Div. 1997) — § 11-7(b)(9), n. 250

TABLE OF CASES

Butterworth v. Smith, 494 U.S. 624 (1990) — § 7-1, n. 46; § 7-3, n. 188; § 3-1(a)(3), n. 113; § 5-2(a)(3), nn. 153, 191
Buzbee v. Journal Newspapers, Inc., 465 A.2d 426 (Md. 1983) — § 3-1(a), n. 11

C

Cable News Network, Inc. v. American Broadcasting Cos., 518 F. Supp. 1238 (N.D. Ga. 1981) — § 9-1, n. 4, 6; § 9-2, n. 19-29; § 9-2(b), n. 47
Cable News Network, Inc. v. United States, 824 F.2d 1046 (D.C. Cir. 1987) — § 3-1(b), nn. 217-19
Cable News v. Superior Ct., 1994 WL 315850 (D. Guam 1994) — § 2-3, n. 308
Cafeteria Workers v. McElroy, 367 U.S. 886 (1961) — § 8-5, n. 142
Cain v. Hearst Corp., 878 S.W.2d 577 (Tex. 1994) — § 12-1, n. 2
Cal-Almond, Inc. v. Department of Agric., 960 F.2d 105 (9th Cir. 1992) — § 10-2(c)(4), n. 113
Calder v. IRS, 890 F.2d 781 (5th Cir. 1989) (IRS records) — § 9-4, n. 71
Caldero v. Tribune Publ'g Co., 562 P.2d 791 (Idaho 1977) — § 16-2(a)(2), n. 42
Caldwell v. Lambrou, 391 A.2d 590 (N.J. Super. 1978) — § 9-6(g), n. 339
Caldwell & Gregory, Inc. v. University of S. Mississippi, 716 So. 2d 1120 (Miss. App. 1998) — § 11-5(a)(3), n. 93
California v. Steiner, 26 Media L. Rep. (BNA) 1575 (Cal. Super. 1998) — § 5-2(a)(3), nn. 189, 194
California First Amendment Coalition v. Calderon, 150 F.3d 976 (9th Cir. 1998) — § 2-3, n. 311; § 8-2, nn. 83-89
California First Amendment Coalition v. Lungren, 1995 U.S. Dist. LEXIS 11655 (N.D. Cal. Aug. 9, 1995) — § 13-4(a), n. 325; § 13-4(a)(4), nn. 498-502
California First Amendment Coalition v. Lungren, 1995 WL 482066 (N.D. Cal. Aug. 10, 1995) — § 7-4, nn. 213-21
California Forestry Ass'n v. U.S. Forest Serv., 102 F.3d 609 (D.C. Cir. 1996) — § 9-5(b)(2), n. 201; § 9-5(b)(7), n. 248
Camelot Group Plc v. Centaur Communications Ltd., 147 NLJ 1618 (Ct. App. Oct. 23, 1997) — § 14-1, n. 1
Campbell v. Department of Justice, 164 F.3d 20 (D.C. Cir. 1998) — § 10-2(b)(3), nn. 40, 41; § 10-2(b)(5), n. 51; § 10-2(c)(2), nn. 95, 96; § 10-2(c)(8), n. 176; § 10-2(c)(8)(C), n. 190
Campbell v. Klevenhagen, 760 F. Supp. 1206 (S.D. Tex. 1991) — § 16-2(c)(1), nn. 92, 115; § 16-2(d)(1), n. 177; § 16-2(e)(2), n. 315; § 16-2(f), n. 375; § 16-2(h)(2), n. 420
Campbell v. Town of Machias, 661 A.2d 1133 (Me. 1995) — § 11-1, n. 8; § 11-8, nn. 354, 358; § 11-5(a)(6), n. 132
Campiti v. Walonis, 467 F. Supp. 464 (D. Mass. 1979) — § 13-7(a)(2)(A)(iv), n. 642
Campus Communications, Inc. v. Freedman, 374 So. 2d 1169 (Fla. App. 1979) — § 16-2(c)(2)(B), n. 173
Cape Publications, Inc. v. Bridges, 387 So. 2d 436 (Fla. App. 1980) — § 16-2(c)(2)(B), n. 170; § 16-2(d)(3)(C), n. 277
Cape Publications, Inc. v. Bridges, 423 So. 2d 426 (Fla. App. 1982) — § 12-2(a), nn. 11, 12; § 12-4(a), n. 179
Cape Publications, Inc. v. Hitchner, 549 So. 2d 1374 (Fla. 1989) — § 13-3(a), n. 107
Capeletti Bros. v. Department of Transp., 499 So. 2d 855 (Fla. App. 1986) — § 9-6(h), n. 344

TABLE OF CASES

Capital City Press v. East Baton Rouge Parish Metro. Council, 696 So. 2d 562 (La. 1997) — § 11-7(a)(1), nn. 185, 186

Capital Newspapers Div. of Hearst Corp. v. Burns, 496 N.E.2d 665 (N.Y. 1986) — § 11-4, nn. 58, 66; § 11-5(a)(2), n. 89

Capital Newspapers Div. of Hearst Corp. v. Lee, 530 N.Y.S.2d 872 (App. Div. 1988) — § 3-1(a)(2), nn. 90, 98, 100, 102

Capital Newspapers Div. of Hearst Corp. v. Whalen, 505 N.E.2d 932 (N.Y. 1987) — § 11-3(a), n. 33

Capital Newspapers v. Moynihan, 519 N.E.2d 825 (N.Y. 1988) — § 3-3(a), nn. 497-99

Cappabianca v. Commissioner, 847 F. Supp. 1558 (M.D. Fla. 1994) — § 10-2(c)(8), n. 174

Capuano v. Outlet Co., 579 A.2d 469 (R.I. 1990) — § 15-2(c)(2)(B), n. 102; § 16-2(a)(2), n. 31

Carbondale Township v. Murray, 440 A.2d 1273 (Pa. Commw. 1982) — § 11-7(f)(3), n. 286

Care & Protection of Edith, 659 N.E.2d 1174 (Mass. 1996) — § 3-3(a), n. 506

Carey v. Hume, 492 F.2d 631 (D.C. Cir. 1974) — § 14-5(f), n. 211; § 14-6(a), n. 233; § 16-2(a)(1), n. 2; § 16-2(c)(2), n. 126; § 16-2(c)(2)(B), n. 152; § 16-2(d)(1), nn. 177, 189, 191; § 16-2(e)(1), nn. 291, 294, 295; § 16-2(e)(2), n. 324; § 16-2(e)(3), nn. 349-53; § 16-2(h)(2), n. 424

Carl v. Board of Regents, 577 P.2d 912 (Okla. 1978) — § 9-6(b), n. 269

Carpenter v. United States, 484 U.S. 19 (1987) — § 6-1(a)(5), n. 111; § 13-3(c)(5), nn. 234, 235; § 13-3(c)(6), nn. 238, 239-42; § 13-3(c)(7), nn. 244, 245; § 13-3(c)(8)(A), nn. 271-73

Carroll Contracting, Inc. v. Edwards, 528 So. 2d 951 (Fla. App. 1988) — § 16-2(c)(2)(A), n. 144; § 16-2(d)(3)(C), n. 271

Carroll v. Princess Anne, 393 U.S. 175 (1968) — § 2-1(d), n. 109

Carson v. Headrick, 900 S.W.2d 685 (Tenn. 1995) — § 13-5, n. 549

Carter v. City of Nashua, 308 A.2d 847 (N.H. 1973) — § 9-6(d), n. 291

Carter v. Department of Commerce, 830 F.2d 388 (D.C. Cir. 1987) — § 10-2(h), nn. 276, 278

Cashel v. Regents of Univ. of Mich., 367 N.W.2d 841 (Mich. App. 1982) — § 11-5(c), n. 169

Cassidy v. American Broadcasting Cos., 377 N.E.2d 126 (Ill. App. 1978) — § 13-7(b)(4)(E), n. 730; § 13-8, nn. 786-89

Cazalas v. Department of Justice, 709 F.2d 1051 (5th Cir. 1983) — § 10-2(h), n. 285

CBA Elec. Ltd. v. Ellenberg, 10 MEDIA L. Rep. (BNA) 1095 (N.Y. Civ. Ct. 1983) — § 16-2(a)(2), n. 32

CBS Inc. v. Campbell, 645 S.W.2d 30 (Mo. App. 1982) — § 16-2(a)(2), nn. 29, 38; § 16-2(c)(1), n. 82; § 16-2(d)(3)(C), n. 263

CBS Inc. v. Cobb, 536 So. 2d 1067 (Fla. App. 1988) — § 16-2(d)(3)(C), n. 262

CBS Inc. v. Davis, 510 U.S. 1315, 114 S. Ct. 912 (1994) — § 2-1(d), nn. 74, 98, 106; § 12-4(c)(3), nn. 261-67; § 13-3(a), n. 80; § 13-8, nn. 790-93

CBS Inc. v. Jackson, 578 So. 2d 698 (Fla. 1991) — § 16-2(d)(3)(B), n. 239; § 16-2(d)(3)(C), n. 270

CBS Inc. v. Partee, 556 N.E.2d 648 (Ill. App. 1990) — § 11-5(a)(5), n. 126

CBS Inc. v. Smith, 681 F. Supp. 794 (S.D. Fla. 1988) — § 8-4, nn. 130, 133, 136, 138

CBS Inc., v. United States Dist. Ct., 729 F.2d 1174 (9th Cir. 1983) (John DeLorean) — § 3-1(a), n. 54

TABLE OF CASES

CBS Inc. v. United States Dist. Ct., 765 F.2d 823 (9th Cir. 1985) — § 3-1(d), nn. 308, 320, 323; § 5-2(d), nn. 417-19, 423

CBS Inc. v. Young, 522 F.2d 234 (6th Cir. 1975) — § 2-3, n. 308; § 7-1, nn. 7-14; § 7-3, n. 161

Cefalu v. Globe Newspaper Co., 391 N.E.2d 935 (Mass. App. 1979) — § 12-2(b), n. 83

Center for Auto Safety v. EPA, 731 F.2d 16 (D.C. Cir. 1984) — § 10-2(h), nn. 277, 279

Center for Auto Safety v. Tiemann, 414 F. Supp. 215 (D.D.C. 1976) — § 9-5(b)(7), n. 246

Central Hudson Gas & Elec. Corp. v. Public Serv. Comm'n, 447 U.S. 557 (1980) — § 1-1, n. 12

Central Michigan Univ. Supervisory-Tech. Ass'n, MEA/NEA v. Board of Trustees of Cent. Michigan Univ., 567 N.W.2d 696 (Mich. App. 1997) — § 11-7(m), n. 345

Central Newspapers, Inc. v. Johnson, 722 So. 2d 1224 (La. App. 1998) — § 13-7(a)(2)(A)(i), n. 608; § 13-7(b)(1), n. 688; § 13-7(b)(3), n. 708

Central South Carolina Chapter v. Martin, 431 F. Supp. 1182 (D.S.C. 1977) — § 7-1, n. 6

Certain Interested Individuals v. Pulitzer Publ'g Co., 895 F.2d 460 (8th Cir. 1990) — § 5-2(a)(1), nn. 100, 103; § 5-2(a)(2), n. 118

Cervantes v. J.C. Penney Co., 595 P.2d 975 (Cal. 1979) — § 12-4(a), n. 167

Cervantes v. Time, Inc., 464 F.2d 986 (8th Cir. 1972) — § 14-5(b), n. 139; § 14-6(a), n. 233; § 16-2(a)(1), nn. 2, 18, 20; § 16-2(c)(2)(B), nn. 157, 159-61, 166; § 16-2(d)(1), nn. 177, 190; § 16-2(d)(3)(C), n. 246; § 16-2(e)(1), n. 302; § 16-2(e)(2), n. 326; § 16-2(e)(4), n. 362; § 16-2(i), n. 443

Chambers v. Birmingham News Co., 552 So. 2d 854 (Ala. 1989) — § 11-1, n. 5

Chambers v. Capital Cities/ABC, Inc., 159 F.R.D. 441 (S.D.N.Y. 1995) — § 13-4(c), n. 531

Chandler v. Alabama, 680 So. 2d 1018 (Ala. Crim. App. 1996) — § 13-7(b)(4)(E), n. 734

Chandler v. Florida, 449 U.S. 560 (1981) — § 2-1(a), n. 4; § 4-1, nn. 29-36

Channel 10, Inc. v. Gunnarson, 337 F. Supp. 634 (D. Minn. 1972) — § 8-3, n. 103

Channel 10, Inc. v. Independent Sch. Dist., 215 N.W.2d 814 (Minn. 1974) — § 9-6(i)(1)(A), n. 369; § 9-6(j), n. 407

Channel Two Television Co. v. Dickerson, 725 S.W.2d 470 (Tex. App. 1987) — § 16-2(a)(2), n. 39; § 16-2(d)(3)(C), n. 270; § 16-2(e)(1), n. 299

Chapadeau v. Utica Observer-Dispatch, 341 N.E.2d 569 (N.Y. 1975) — § 13-4(a)(3)(A)(i), n. 431

Charlottesville Newspapers, Inc. v. Berry, 206 S.E.2d 267 (Va. 1974) — § 6-1(c)(1), n. 222

Charter Behavioral Health Sys. v. CBS Inc., No. 3:99-CV-150-MU (W.D.N.C. Apr. 21, 1999) — § 2-1(d), n. 99; § 12-4(b), n. 202; § 13-2(b), n. 44; § 13-7(a)(2)(A)(iv), n. 646; § 13-8, n. 797

Chartwell Communications Group v. Westbrook, 637 F.2d 459 (6th Cir. 1980) — § 13-7(a)(2)(B), n. 647

Chase v. Robson, 435 F.2d 1059 (7th Cir. 1970) — § 7-1, nn. 10, 45; § 7-2, n. 140

Chesapeake Bay Found. v. Department of Agric., 11 F.3d 211 (D.C. Cir. 1993) — § 10-2(h), nn. 286, 287

Cheyenne K. v. Superior Ct., 256 Cal. Rptr. 68 (Ct. App. 1989) — § 3-3(a), n. 495

Chicago Council of Lawyers v. Bauer, 522 F.2d 242 (7th Cir. 1975) — § 7-1, nn. 52-56, 71; § 7-2, n. 87

Child Protection Group v. Cline, 350 S.E.2d 541 (W. Va. 1986) — § 11-5(a), n. 83; § 11-5(a)(5), n. 126

TABLE OF CASES

Christiansen v. Missouri State Bd. of Accountancy, 764 S.W.2d 943 (Mo. App. 1988) — § 9-6(i)(6), n. 402

Chrysler Corp. v. Brown, 441 U.S. 281 (1979) — § 10-2(a), n. 1; § 10-2(c)(4), n. 110; § 10-2(f), nn. 251-59

Church of Scientology Int'l v. Daniels, 992 F.2d 1329 (4th Cir. 1993) — § 16-2(a)(1), nn. 2, 10; § 16-2(c)(2)(A), n. 148; § 16-2(e)(2), n. 323

Church of Scientology Int'l v. Department of Justice, 30 F.3d 224 (1st Cir. 1994) — § 10-2(a), n. 2; § 10-2(h), n. 277

Church of Scientology Int'l v. IRS, 995 F.2d 916 (9th Cir. 1993) — § 10-2(c)(8), n. 176

Church of Scientology v. Department of Army, 611 F.2d 738 (9th Cir. 1979) — § 10-2(c)(7), n. 169

Church of Scientology v. IRS, 816 F. Supp. 1138 (W.D. Tex. 1993) — § 10-2(c)(8)(D), n. 200

Church of Scientology v. United States Postal Serv., 700 F.2d 486 (9th Cir. 1983) — § 10-2(h), nn. 286, 287

CIA v. Sims, 471 U.S. 159 (1984) — § 10-2(c)(4), nn. 109, 111, 112, 117

Cianci v. New Times Publ'g Co., 88 F.R.D. 562 (S.D.N.Y. 1980) — § 6-1(c)(1), n. 210

Cincinnati Gas & Electric Co. v. General Electric Co., 854 F.2d 900 (6th Cir. 1988) — § 3-2(d), n. 406

Cinel v. Connick, 792 F. Supp. 492 (E.D. La. 1992) — § 16-2(d)(3)(C), n. 263; § 16-2(h), n. 400

Cipollone v. Liggett Group, Inc., 785 F.2d 1108 (3d Cir. 1986) — § 6-1(a)(3), nn. 47-49; § 6-1(a)(5), nn. 103, 113, 115, 116

Citicasters v. McCaskill, 89 F.3d 1350 (8th Cir. 1996) — § 15-3(a), nn. 357-59

Citizens Comm'n on Human Rights v. FDA, 45 F.3d 1325 (9th Cir. 1995) — § 10-2(b)(3), n. 40

Citizens for Alternatives to Animal Labs, Inc. v. Board of Trustees, 703 N.E.2d 1218 (N.Y. 1998) — § 11-3(a), n. 35

Citizens for Envtl. Quality v. Department of Agric., 602 F. Supp. 534 (D.D.C. 1984) — § 10-2(c)(7), n. 156

Citizens to Preserve Overton Park, Inc. v. Volpe, 401 U.S. 402 (1971) — § 10-2(f), n. 260

Citizens to Recall Mayor James Whitlock v. Whitlock, 844 P.2d 74 (Mont. 1992) — § 9-1, n. 18

Citizens to Recall Mayor Whitlock v. Whitlock, 844 P.2d 74 (Mont. 1992) — § 11-7(a)(3), n. 192

City Council v. Cooper, 358 So. 2d 440 (Ala. 1978) — § 9-6(c), n. 287

City Council v. Reno Newspapers, Inc., 784 P.2d 974 (Nev. 1989) — § 9-6(j), n. 416

City of Chester v. Getek, 572 A.2d 1319 (Pa. Commw. 1990) — § 11-7(f)(5), n. 290

City of College Park v. Cotter, 525 A.2d 1059 (Md. 1987) — § 9-6(d), n. 295

City of Columbia v. ACLU of South Carolina, 475 S.E.2d 747 (S.C. 1996) — § 11-7(a)(3), n. 195

City of Dubuque v. Telegraph Herald, Inc., 297 N.W.2d 523 (Iowa 1980) — § 11-5(a)(5), n. 119

City of Fayetteville v. Edmark, 801 S.W.2d 275 (Ark. 1990) — § 11-5(a)(4), n. 108

City of Fayetteville v. Rose, 743 S.W.2d 817 (Ark. 1988) — § 11-7(b)(3)(A), n. 220

City of Flagstaff v. Bleeker, 600 P.2d 49 (Ariz. App. 1979) — § 9-6(b), n. 271

City of Gainesville v. Florida ex rel. Int'l Ass'n of Fire Fighters, 298 So. 2d 478 (Fla. App. 1974) — § 11-7(a)(4), n. 196

TABLE OF CASES

City of Grand Forks v. Grand Forks Herald, 307 N.W.2d 572 (N.D. 1981) — § 12-1, n. 2

City of Hartford v. Chase, 942 F.2d 130 (2d Cir. 1991) — § 6-1(b), nn. 169, 187; § 6-1(a)(1), n. 8

City of Helen v. White County News, 25 Media L. Rep. (BNA) 1123 (Ga. Super. 1996) — § 6-1(b), n. 186

City of Kenai v. Kenai Peninsula Newspapers, 642 P.2d 1316 (Alaska 1982) — § 11-7(a)(1), n. 185

City of Kingston v. Surles, 582 N.Y.S.2d 844 (App. Div. 1992) — § 11-8, n. 356

City of Lakewood v. Plain Dealer Publ'g Co., 486 U.S. 750 (1988) — § 1-1, n. 7

City of Las Cruces v. Public Employee Labor Relations Bd., 917 P.2d 451 (N.M. 1996) — § 11-7(a)(4), n. 196

City of Los Angeles v. Superior Ct., 49 Cal. Rptr. 2d 35 (Ct. App. 1996) — § 11-7(m), n. 344

City of Miami v. Metropolitan Dade County, 745 F. Supp. 683 (S.D. Fla. 1990) — § 5-2(a)(5), n. 226

City of Monmouth v. Galesburg Printing & Publ'g Co., 494 N.E.2d 896 (Ill. App. 1986) — § 11-5(a)(5), n. 122

City of New Carrollton v. Rogers, 410 A.2d 1070 (Md. 1980) — § 9-6(d), n. 304

City of Oak Creek v. King, 436 N.W.2d 285 (Wis. 1989) — § 8-3, nn. 94-101; § 13-3(c)(3), nn. 210-16

City of Prescott v. Town of Chino Valley, 803 P.2d 891 (Ariz. 1990) — § 9-6(h)(6), n. 365

City of Santa Rosa v. Press Democrat, 232 Cal. Rptr. 445 (Ct. App. 1986) — § 11-7(b), n. 204

City of Springfield v. Events Publ'g Co., 951 S.W.2d 366 (Mo. App. 1997) — § 11-7(*l*), n. 341; § 11-9, n. 371

City of St. Matthews v. Voice of St. Matthews, 519 S.W.2d 811 (Ky. 1974) — § 11-1, n. 2

City of Stamford v. Freedom of Info. Comm'n, 696 A.2d 321 (Conn. 1997) — § 11-7(m), n. 348

City of Virginia Beach v. Department of Commerce, 995 F.2d 1247 (4th Cir. 1993) — § 10-2(c)(6), n. 134

City of Westminster v. Dogan Constr. Co., 930 P.2d 585 (Colo. 1997) — § 11-7(a)(1), n. 188

Civic W. Corp. v. Zila Indus., Inc. 135 Cal. Rptr. 915 (Ct. App. 1977) — § 12-4(a), n. 162

Civil Serv. Comm'n v. Pinder, 812 P.2d 645 (Colo. 1991) — § 11-5(c), n. 169

C.L. v. Edson, 409 N.W.2d 417 (Wis. App. 1987) — § 6-1(b), n. 187

Clampitt v. Thurston County, 658 P.2d 641 (Wash. 1983) — § 16-3, n. 479

Clark-Cowlitz Joint Operating Agency v. FERC, 798 F.2d 499 (D.C. Cir. 1986) — § 9-5(a)(8)(J), n. 179

Claybrook v. Slater, 111 F.3d 904 (D.C. Cir. 1997) — § 9-5(b)(4), n. 229

Clein v. Florida, 52 So. 2d 117 (Fla. 1950) — § 14-1, n. 5

Cleveland Bd. of Educ. v. Loudermill, 470 U.S. 532 (1985) — § 9-6(i)(1)(C), n. 381

Cliff v. Narragansett Television, L.P., 688 A.2d 805 (R.I. 1996) — § 12-4(a), n. 175

Cline v. Board of Trustees, 351 N.Y.S.2d 81 (Sup. Ct. 1973) — § 9-6(f), n. 330

Clinton v. Association of Am. Physicians & Surgeons, 997 F.2d 898 (D.C. Cir. 1993) — § 10-2(b)(2), n. 29

TABLE OF CASES

Clyburn v. News World Communications, Inc., 903 F.2d 29 (D.C. Cir. 1990) — § 16-2(a)(1), n. 2; § 16-2(c)(2)(B), n. 158; § 16-2(d)(1), nn. 177, 190; § 16-2(e)(3), n. 355

CNA Fin. Corp. v. Brown, 830 F.2d 1132 (D.C. Cir. 1987) — § 10-2(c)(4), n. 110

CNA Fin. Corp. v. Donovan, 830 F.2d 1132 (D.C. Cir. 1987) — § 10-2(c)(4), n. 109; § 10-2(h), n. 270

Coalition Against Police Abuse v. Superior Ct., 216 Cal. Rptr. 614 (Ct. App. 1985) — § 6-1(a)(3), n. 46

Coastal States Gas Corp. v. Department of Energy, 617 F.2d 854 (D.C. Cir. 1980) — § 10-2(c)(6), nn. 141-45, 149, 153

Coastal Transp. Inc. v. WAWS Fox 30, 25 Media L. Rep. (BNA) 2247 (Fla. Cir. 1997) — § 16-2(e)(2), n. 312; § 16-2(h), n. 391

Coastline Bldg. Corp. v. Atkins, 26 Media L. Rep. (BNA) 1316 (Fla. Cir. 1997) — § 16-2(c)(2)(A), nn. 147, 149; § 16-2(e)(2), n. 322

Coates v. Cincinnati, 402 U.S. 611 (1971) — § 1-1, n. 7

Codey v. Capital Cities, 626 N.E.2d 636 (N.Y. 1993) — § 15-2(j), nn. 327, 328

Cohan v. City of Thousand Oaks, 35 Cal. Rptr. 2d 782 (Ct. App. 1994) — § 9-6(a), n. 252

Cohen v. Beneficial Indus. Loan Corp., 337 U.S. 541 (1949) — § 2-3, n. 306

Cohen v. Cowles Media Co., 14 Media L. Rep. (BNA) 1460 (Minn. Dist. 1987) — § 13-4(a)(2)(A), nn. 370-73

Cohen v. Cowles Media Co., 15 Media L. Rep. (BNA) 2288 (Minn. Dist. 1988) — § 13-4(a)(2)(A), nn. 374-77

Cohen v. Cowles Media Co., 445 N.W.2d 248 (Minn. App. 1989) — § 13-4(a)(2), nn. 366, 367, 369; § 13-4(a)(2)(B), nn. 378-85; § 13-4(a)(3)(A)(ii), nn. 454, 455

Cohen v. Cowles Media Co., 457 N.W.2d 199 (Minn. 1990), rev'd, 501 U.S. 663 (1991) — § 13-4(a)(2), n. 368; § 13-4(a)(2)(B), nn. 386-97; § 13-4(a)(3)(A)(ii), n. 458

Cohen v. Cowles Media Co., 479 N.W.2d 387 (Minn. 1992) — § 13-4(a)(2)(D), nn. 418-20; § 13-4(a)(3), n. 421; § 13-4(a)(3)(A)(ii), n. 460

Cohen v. Cowles Media Co., 501 U.S. 663 (1991) — § 1-5, n. 79; § 12-4(c)(2), n. 249; § 12-4(c)(3), n. 326; § 13-2(a), n. 14; § 13-2(b), nn. 73, 76; § 13-4(a), n. 328; § 13-4(a)(1)(A), nn. 350, 351; § 13-4(a)(2)(C), nn. 398-417; § 13-4(a)(3), n. 422; § 13-4(a)(3)(B), nn. 479, 485, 495; § 13-4(c), nn. 538, 539; § 13-5, nn. 545, 546; § 14-5(c), nn. 160-64; § 14-6(a), n. 242

Cole v. Colorado, 673 P.2d 345 (Colo. 1983) — § 9-6(b), n. 273

Coleman v. Newark Morning Ledger Co., 149 A.2d 193 (N.J. 1959) — § 13-6, n. 561

Coleman v. Texas, 966 S.W.2d 525 (Tex. Crim. App. 1998) — § 14-6(b), n. 265; § 16-2(a)(2), n. 39

College Entrance Examination Bd. v. Pataki, 889 F. Supp. 554 (N.D.N.Y. 1995) — § 11-7(a)(5), n. 200

Collins v. Camden County Dep't of Health, 491 A.2d 66 (N.J. Super. 1984) — § 11-2, n. 13

Collins v. New York State Div. of Parole, 674 N.Y.S.2d 145 (App. Div. 1998) — § 11-7(c), n. 255

Collins v. Troy Publ'g Co., 623 N.Y.S.2d 663 (App. Div. 1995) — § 15-2(c)(2)(B), n. 130

Colorado v. Denver Publ'g Co., 597 P.2d 1038 (Colo. 1979) — § 2-1(c), n. 61

Colten v. Kentucky, 407 U.S. 104 (1972) — § 13-3(c)(3), n. 209

Combined Communications Corp. v. Finesilver, 672 F.2d 818 (10th Cir. 1982) — § 9-2, n. 29; § 9-2(b), n. 46; § 9-3, n. 59; § 9-6(e), n. 322

TABLE OF CASES

Commercial Printing Co. v. Rush, 549 S.W.2d 790 (Ark. 1977) — § 9-6(i)(1)(C), n. 383

Common Cause v. NRC, 674 F.2d 921 (D.C. Cir. 1982) — § 9-5(a)(3), n. 99; § 9-5(a)(7), n. 130; § 9-5(a)(8), nn. 137, 139-41; § 9-5(a)(8)(B), nn. 149, 150; § 9-5(a)(8)(F), nn. 164-66; § 9-5(a)(8)(I), nn. 175, 176; § 9-5(a)(9)(A), nn. 184, 185; § 9-5(a)(9)(B), n. 189

Common Council v. Peru Daily Tribune, Inc., 440 N.E.2d 726 (Ind. App. 1982) — § 9-6(j), n. 407

Commonwealth v. Wiseman, 249 N.E.2d 610 (Mass. 1969) — § 12-4(b), n. 200; § 12-6(a), nn. 377-79

Communications Sys. v. FCC, 595 F.2d 797 (D.C. 1978) — § 9-5(a)(3), n. 99

Computer Prof'ls for Social Responsibility v. United States Secret Serv., 72 F.3d 897 (D.C. Cir. 1996) — § 10-2(c)(8)(D), n. 199

Concerned Ratepayers Ass'n v. Public Utility Dist. No. 1, 960 P.2d 466 (Wash. App. 1998) — § 11-7(*l*), n. 341

Condon v. Reno, 155 F.3d 453 (4th Cir. 1998) — § 11-7(k), n. 336

Coney v. Alaska, 699 P.2d 899 (Alaska App. 1985) — § 16-2(a)(2), n. 32; § 16-2(c)(1), n. 92; § 16-2(e)(2), n. 315

Connecticut v. Burak, 431 A.2d 1246 (Conn. Super. 1981) — § 3-1(a)(4), n. 168

Connecticut v. Clein, 1996 Conn. Super. LEXIS 1292 (Conn. Super. 1996) — § 5-2(a)(2), n. 131

Connecticut v. Kelly, 695 A.2d 1 (Conn. App. 1997) — § 2-1(d), n. 98; § 3-1(a), nn. 44, 52

Connecticut v. McVeigh, 620 A.2d 133 (Conn. 1993) — § 13-7(b)(4)(E), n. 735

Connecticut v. Ross, 543 A.2d 284 (Conn. 1988) — § 5-2(b), n. 342

Connecticut Magazine v. Moraghan, 676 F. Supp. 38 (D. Conn. 1987) — § 7-1, n. 36

Connecticut State Bd. of Labor Relations v. Fagin, 370 A.2d 1095 (Conn. Super. 1976) — § 16-2(a)(2), n. 29; § 16-2(c)(2)(A), n. 143; § 16-2(e)(1), n. 299; § 16-2(e)(3), n. 333

Connell v. Town of Hudson, 733 F. Supp. 465 (D.N.H. 1990) — § 8-3, nn. 102-05

Connick v. Myers, 461 U.S. 138 (1983) — § 1-1, n. 14

Consolidated Edison Co. v. Public Serv. Comm'n, 447 U.S. 530 (1980) — § 1-1, n. 3

Consumer Prod. Safety Comm'n v. GTE Sylvania, Inc., 447 U.S. 102 (1980) — § 10-2(c)(4), n. 115

Consumers Union v. Heimann, 589 F.2d 531 (D.C. Cir. 1978) — § 10-2(c)(9), n. 218

Consumers Union v. Periodical Correspondents' Ass'n, 515 F.2d 1341 (D.C. Cir. 1975) — § 9-3, nn. 49, 50, 57

Consumers Union v. Veterans Admin., 301 F. Supp. 796 (S.D.N.Y. 1969) — § 10-2(c)(5), n. 124

Continental Cablevision Inc. v. Storer Broadcasting Co., 583 F. Supp. 427 (E.D. Mo. 1984) — § 16-2(e)(4), n. 363

Continental Oil Co. v. FPC, 519 F.2d 31 (5th Cir. 1975) — § 10-2(c)(5), n. 127

Contra Costa Newspapers Inc. v. Superior Ct., 72 Cal. Rptr. 2d 69 (Ct. App. 1998) — § 7-3, nn. 146, 160, 163

Conway v. United States, 852 F.2d 187 (6th Cir. 1988) — § 4-2(a), n. 40

Cook v. Craig, 127 Cal. Rptr. 712 (Ct. App. 1976) — § 11-1, nn. 5, 7

Cook v. First Morris Bank, 719 A.2d 724 (N.J. Super. 1998) — § 3-2(a), n. 350; § 4-3, nn. 91, 92

Cook v. Houston Post, 616 F.2d 791 (5th Cir. 1980) — § 13-7(a)(1), n. 583

Cooner v. Board of Educ., 663 P.2d 1002 (Ariz. App. 1982) — § 9-6(i)(1)(B), n. 377

TABLE OF CASES

Cooper v. Bales, 233 S.E.2d 306 (S.C. 1977) — § 9-6(f), n. 330

Cooper v. Department of Lottery, 640 N.E.2d 1299 (Ill. App., 1994) — § 11-1, nn. 6, 7; § 11-5(a)(3), n. 96

Cooper Hosp. Univ. Med. Center v. Sullivan, 183 F.R.D. 135 (D.N.J. 1998) — § 6-1(a)(2), n. 39; § 6-1(a)(5), nn. 104, 118

Coopersmith v. Gold, 594 N.Y.S.2d 521 (Sup. Ct. 1992) — § 6-1(c)(2), n. 228

Copeland v. Hubbard Broadcasting, Inc., 526 N.W.2d 402 (Minn. App. 1995) — § 12-4(a), nn. 172, 175; § 12-4(c)(3), n. 325; § 13-2(b), nn. 49, 57; § 13-7(b)(2), nn. 694, 696; § 13-8, nn. 802, 807

Copeland v. Marshall, 641 F.2d 880 (D.C. Cir. 1980) — § 10-2(h), n. 289

Copely Press, Inc. v. City of Springfield, 493 N.E.2d 127 (Ill. App. 1986) — § 11-5(a)(5), n. 122

Copley Press, Inc. v. Administrative Office of Cts., 648 N.E.2d 324 (Ill. App. 1995) — § 5-2(d), n. 434; § 11-3(c), n. 45

Copley Press, Inc. v. San Diego County Super. Ct., 7 Cal. Rptr. 2d 841 (Ct. App. 1992) — § 6-1(d), n. 257

Copley Press, Inc. v. Superior Ct., 278 Cal. Rptr. 443 (Ct. App. 1991) — § 5-2(c), nn. 397, 399, 400

Copley Press, Inc. v. Superior Ct., 74 Cal. Rptr. 2d 69 (Ct. App. 1998) — § 6-1(b), nn. 159-61, 163

Core v. United States Postal Serv., 730 F.2d 946 (4th Cir. 1984) — § 10-2(c)(7), n. 165

Cornelius v. NAACP Legal Defense & Educ. Fund, Inc., 473 U.S. 788 (1985) — § 1-1, n. 11

Costello v. United States, 350 U.S. 359 (1965) — § 14-4(a), n. 79

Costlow v. Cusimano, 311 N.Y.S.2d 92 (App. Div. 1970) — § 12-4(a), n. 183

Coughlin v. Westinghouse Broadcasting & Cable Inc., 780 F.2d 340 (3d Cir. 1985) — § 15-2(a), n. 25

Coulter v. Bank of Am. Nat'l Trust & Savings Ass'n, 33 Cal. Rptr. 2d 766 (Ct. App. 1994) — § 12-2(a), n. 65; § 13-7(b)(4)(B), n. 715

County Council v. SHL Systemhouse Corp., 182 F.R.D. 161 (E.D. Pa. 1998) — § 6-1(a)(5), nn. 104, 111, 113

County of Saratoga v. Newman, 476 N.Y.S.2d 1020 (Sup. Ct. 1984) — § 9-6(i)(1)(D), n. 386

Courier-Journal & Louisville Times Co. v. Peers, 747 S.W.2d 125 (Ky. 1988) — § 6-1(b), n. 188; § 6-1(c), n. 204

Courier-Journal v. Gash, 9 Media L. Rep. (BNA) 1735 (Ky. Cir. 1983) — § 9-4, n. 65

Courier-Journal v. Marshall, 828 F.2d 361 (6th Cir. 1987) — § 6-1(a)(5), nn. 104, 120

Cowles Publ'g Co. v. City of Spokane, 849 P.2d 1271 (Wash. App. 1993) — § 11-7(b)(3), n. 216

Cowles Publ'g Co. v. Magistrate Ct., 800 P.2d 640 (Idaho 1990) — § 2-3, n. 313; § 3-1(a)(2), nn. 92, 95, 102, 104; § 5-2(a)(6), n. 239

Cox Arizona Publications, Inc. v. Collins, 852 P.2d 1194 (Ariz. 1993) — § 11-5(a)(6), n. 141

Cox Broadcasting Corp. v. Cohn, 420 U.S. 469 (1975) — § 2-1(c), n. 59; § 12-4(a), nn. 130, 170; § 13-3(a), nn. 83-90; § 13-4(a)(2)(A), n. 373; § 13-7(a)(2)(A)(i), nn. 601, 612, 616

Cox Communications, Inc. v. Lowe, 328 S.E.2d 394 (Ga. App. 1985) — § 12-6(b), nn. 392-94

Cozzolino v. City of Fontana, 289 P.2d 248 (Cal. App. 1955) — § 9-6(i)(1)(B), n. 376

TABLE OF CASES

Craemer v. Superior Ct., 71 Cal. Rptr. 193 (Ct. App. 1968) — § 5-2(a)(3), n. 169
Craig v. Harney, 331 U.S. 367 (1947) — § 2-1(c), nn. 45-47; § 2-2(b), n. 153; § 2-2(c), n. 195
Crain Communications, Inc. v. Hughes, 539 N.E.2d 1099 (N.Y. 1989) — § 6-1(b), n. 188
Cramlet v. Multimedia, Inc., 11 Media L. Rep. (BNA) 1707 (D. Colo. 1985) — § 13-5, n. 557
Cranford v. Montgomery County, 481 A.2d 221 (Md. 1984) — § 11-9, n. 363
Critical Mass Energy Project v. NRC, 975 F.2d 871 (D.C. Cir. 1992) — § 10-2(c)(5), nn. 126, 128-30
Cromer v. Superior Ct., 167 Cal. Rptr. 671 (Ct. App. 1980) — § 5-2(a)(6), n. 248
Crooker v. Bureau of Alcohol, Tobacco & Firearms, 670 F.2d 1051 (D.C. Cir. 1981) — § 10-2(c)(3), nn. 102-05
Cruickshank v. Ellis, 226 N.W.2d 192 (Minn. 1929) — § 13-4(a)(2)(B), n. 390
Crumpton v. Stone, 59 F.3d 1400 (D.C. Cir. 1995) — § 10-2(c)(1), n. 54
Cruz v. Beto, 405 U.S. 319 (1972) — § 8-1, n. 7
Crystal Grower's Corp. v. Dobbins, 616 F.2d 458 (10th Cir. 1980) — § 6-1(c)(1), n. 216; § 6-1(d), n. 256
CSX Transp., Inc. v. Cox Broadcasting, Inc., 25 Media L. Rep. (BNA) 2183 (Ga. Super. 1997) — § 15-2(c)(2)(A), n. 87; § 15-2(d)(3)(C), n. 188
Cuban Am. Bar Ass'n, Inc. v. Christopher, 43 F.3d 1412 (11th Cir. 1995) — § 9-1, n. 5
Cuccaro v. Secretary of Labor, 770 F.2d 355 (3d Cir. 1985) — § 10-2(c)(8)(D), n. 199
Cukier v. American Med. Ass'n, 630 N.E.2d 1198 (Ill. App. 1994) — § 15-2(b)(1), nn. 42, 43; § 15-2(e)(2)(B), n. 242
Cullen v. Grove Press, Inc., 276 F. Supp. 727 (S.D.N.Y. 1967) — § 12-4(b), n. 200; § 12-6(a), n. 379; § 13-4(a)(1)(A), nn. 329-34, 339; § 13-4(a)(3)(A)(i), n. 430
Cullen v. Margiotta, 811 F.2d 698 (2d Cir. 1987) — § 5-2(a)(3), n. 150
Cunningham v. Oregon Dep't of Corrections, 166 F.3d 342 (9th Cir. 1998) — § 8-1, n. 54
Curran v. Department of Justice, 813 F.2d 473 (D.C. Cir. 1987) — § 10-2(c)(8)(A), n. 183
Curtis Publ'g Co. v. Butts, 388 U.S. 130 (1967) — § 16-2(g), n. 383

D

Dabney v. Reagan, 559 F. Supp. 861 (S.D.N.Y. 1982) — § 9-5(b)(4), n. 229
Dacosta v. Department of Justice, 782 F. Supp. 147 (D.D.C. 1992) — § 10-2(b)(4), n. 43
Daily Gazette Co. v. Caryl, 380 S.E.2d 209 (W. Va. 1989) — § 11-7(f)(2), n. 273
Daily Gazette Co. v. Committee on Legal Ethics, 326 S.E.2d 705 (W. Va. 1984) — § 9-4, n. 67
Daily Gazette Co. v. Harrigan, 618 N.Y.S.2d 469 (App. Div. 1994) — § 3-3(a), n. 499
Daily Gazette Co. v. North Colonie Bd. of Educ., 412 N.Y.S.2d 494 (App. Div. 1979) — § 9-6(b), n. 266
Daily Gazette Co. v. Schenectady, 673 N.Y.S.2d 783 (App. Div. 1998) — § 11-7(a)(3), n. 195
Daily Gazette Co. v. Town of Cobleskill, 444 N.Y.S.2d 44 (Sup. Ct. 1981) — § 9-6(g), n. 338
Daily Gazette Co. v. West Virginia Bd. of Med., 352 S.E.2d 66 (W. Va. 1986) — § 9-4, n. 68
Daily Gazette Co. v. West Virginia Dev. Office, 482 S.E.2d 180 (W. Va. 1996) — § 11-5(a)(4), n. 98

TABLE OF CASES

Daily Gazette Co. v. Withrow, 350 S.E.2d 738 (W. Va. 1986) — § 11-5(a)(4), n. 109; § 11-7(m), nn. 344, 346, 349, 351

Daily Herald Co. v. Munro, 838 F.2d 380 (9th Cir. 1988) — § 8-4, nn. 130-39

Daily Journal Corp. v. Superior Ct., 979 P.2d 982 (Cal. 1999) — Preface, n. 3; § 5-2(a)(3), nn. 174, 177, 178, 194

Daily Times Democrat v. Graham, 162 So.2d 474 (Ala. 1964) — § 12-4(c)(2), n. 251

Dale v. Birmingham News Co., 452 So. 2d 1321 (Ala. 1984) — § 9-6(i)(1)(A), n. 370

Dalitz v. Penthouse Int'l Ltd., 214 Cal. Rptr. 254 (Ct. App. 1985) — § 15-2(f), n. 260

Dallas Morning News Co. v. Garcia, 822 S.W.2d 675 (Tex. App. 1991) — § 16-2(a)(2), nn. 29, 39; § 16-2(c)(2)(B), nn. 159, 161; § 16-2(d)(1), nn. 177, 190, 191; § 16-2(e)(2), nn. 312, 326; § 16-2(e)(3), n. 357; § 16-2(h), n. 398; § 16-2(h)(1), n. 410; § 16-2(h)(2), n. 425

Dallas Oil & Gas, Inc. v. Mouer, 533 S.W.2d 70 (Tex. App. 1976) — § 16-2(c)(2)(A), n. 148

Dalton v. Idaho Dairy Prods. Comm'n, 684 P.2d 983 (Idaho 1984) — § 11-7(i), n. 308

Davenport v. Garcia, 834 S.W.2d 4 (Tex. 1992) — § 7-1, n. 82

Davidson v. City of Westminster, 649 P.2d 894 (Cal. 1982) — § 12-4(a), n. 167

Davin v. Department of Justice, 60 F.3d 1043 (3d Cir. 1995) — § 10-2(h), n. 283

Davis v. East Baton Rouge Parish School Dist., 78 F.3d 920 (5th Cir. 1996) — § 6-1(a)(5), nn. 121, 122; § 9-6(d), n. 290

Davis v. Glanton, 705 A.2d 879 (Pa. Super. 1997) — § 15-2(c)(2)(A), n. 87; § 15-2(c)(2)(B), n. 114; § 15-2(d)(3)(C), n. 191; § 16-2(a)(2), n. 29; § 16-2(c)(2)(A), n. 148; § 16-2(e)(1), n. 299; § 16-2(e)(3), n. 358

Davis v. Municipal Ct., 22 Media L. Rep. (BNA) 2466 (Cal. Super. 1994) — § 3-1(a)(2), n. 102

Davis v. Schucat, 510 F.2d 731 (D.C. Cir. 1975) — § 13-6, nn. 568-76

Davis v. United States, 641 A.2d 484 (D.C. 1994) — § 5-2(a)(3), nn. 143, 168

Day v. Shalala, 23 F.3d 1052 (6th Cir. 1994) — § 10-2(b)(2), n. 28

Dayton Newspapers v. Rauch, 465 N.E.2d 458 (Ohio 1984) — § 11-7(d), n. 257

Deal v. Spears, 980 F.2d 1153 (8th Cir. 1992) — § 13-7(a)(2)(A)(iv), nn. 638, 642

Deatherage v. State Examining Bd., 932 P.2d 1267 (Wash. App.), *rev'd on other grounds*, 948 P.2d 828 (Wash. 1997) — § 4-1, n. 36

De Corse v. City of Buffalo, 659 N.Y.S.2d 604 (App. Div. 1997) — § 11-8, n. 354

DeHaes & Gijsels v. Belgium, No. 19983/121 (Feb. 24, 1997) — § 14-1, n. 1

Deitchman v. E.R. Squibb & Sons, 740 F.2d 556 (7th Cir. 1984) — § 16-2(a)(1), nn. 6, 7; § 16-2(b)(1), n. 63; § 16-2(h), n. 394

Del Papa v. Board of Regents, 956 P.2d 770 (Nev. 1998) — § 9-6(c), nn. 286, 287

Del Papa v. Steffen, 915 P.2d 245 (Nev. 1996) — § 2-1(c), n. 52

Del Papa v. Steffen, 920 P.2d 489 (Nev. 1996) — § 2-1(c), n. 52

DeLaMater v. Marion Civil Serv. Comm., 554 N.W.2d 875 (Iowa 1996) — § 11-7(a)(5), nn. 198, 202, 203

Delan v. CBS Inc., 458 N.Y.S.2d 608 (App. Div. 1983) — § 12-6(a), nn. 380-84

Delaney v. Superior Ct., 789 P.2d 934 (Cal. 1990) — § 15-2(a), n. 22; § 15-2(c)(1), nn. 75-78; § 15-2(c)(2)(A), n. 89; § 15-2(d)(3)(B), n. 168; § 15-2(e)(1), n. 221; § 15-2(e)(2), nn. 232, 233; § 15-2(f), nn. 259, 261; § 15-2(i)(2), n. 300; § 15-2(i)(3), n. 312

Delaware v. Hall, 16 Media L. Rep. (BNA) 1414 (Del. Mun. 1989) — § 16-2(a)(2), n. 29

Delaware v. McBride, 7 Media L. Rep. (BNA) 1371 (Del. Super. 1981) — § 16-2(a)(2), n. 32; § 16-2(d)(3)(C), n. 273; § 16-2(e)(1), n. 299

Delaware v. Shipley, 497 A.2d 1052 (Del. Super. 1985) — § 3-1(a)(1), n. 73

TABLE OF CASES

Delaware Solid Waste Auth. v. News Journal Co., 480 A.2d 628 (Del. 1984) — § 11-5(a), n: 77
DeLisle v. Rivers, 161 F.3d 370 (6th Cir. 1998) — § 2-1(a), n. 15
Della Serra v. Borough of Mountainside, 481 A.2d 547 (N.J. Super. 1984) — § 9-6(i)(6), n. 403
Delome Publ'g Co. v. National Oceanic & Atmospheric Admin., 917 F. Supp. 867 (D. Me. 1996) — § 10-2(c)(3), n. 102
Deltec, Inc. v. Dun & Bradstreet, Inc., 187 F. Supp. 788 (N.D. Ohio 1960) — § 15-2(b)(1), n. 46
Demers v. City of Minneapolis, 468 N.W.2d 71 (Minn. 1991) — § 11-7(a)(3), n. 192
Dempsey v. National Enquirer, Inc., 702 F. Supp. 927 (D. Me. 1988) — § 12-2(a), n. 12; § 12-4(a), n. 179; § 12-4(c)(1), nn. 220, 221
Denk v. Iowa Dist. Ct., 20 Media L. Rep. (BNA) 1454 (Iowa 1992) — § 16-2(h)(1), n. 411
Dennis v. Sparks, 449 U.S. 24 (1980) — § 13-7(a)(1), n. 583
Dennis v. United States, 183 F.2d 201 (2d Cir. 1950) — § 2-1(d), n. 75
Denoux v. Bertel, 682 So. 2d 300 (La. App. 1996) — § 11-3(c), n. 46
Denver Post Corp. v. University of Colorado, 739 P.2d 874 (Colo. App. 1987) — § 11-5(a)(4), n. 113
Denver Publ'g Co. v. Dreyfus, 520 P.2d 104 (Colo. 1974) — § 11-7(d), n. 258
Denver Publ'g Co. v. University of Colorado, 812 P.2d 682 (Colo. App. 1990) — § 11-7(a), n. 184
Department of Air Force v. Rose, 425 U.S. 352 (1976) — § 10-2(a), n. 3; § 10-2(c)(1), nn. 52, 53; § 10-2(c)(3), n. 100; § 10-2(c)(7), nn. 157, 166
Department of Defense v. FLRA, 510 U.S. 487 (1994) — § 10-2(b)(3), n. 34; § 10-2(c)(7), n. 167
Department of Highway Safety & Motor Vehicles v. Krejci Co., 570 So. 2d 1322 (Fla. App. 1990) — § 11-7(k), n. 317
Department of Justice v. Julian, 486 U.S. 1 (1988) — § 10-2(c)(6), n. 133
Department of Justice v. Landano, 508 U.S. 165 (1993) — § 10-2(c)(8)(D), nn. 198, 203-05
Department of Justice v. Provensano, 469 U.S. 14 (1989) — § 10-2(c)(4), n. 110
Department of Justice v. Reporters Comm. for Freedom of the Press, 489 U.S. 749 (1989) — § 10-2(b)(3), n. 33; § 10-2(c)(1), n. 52; § 10-2(c)(7), nn. 167, 169; § 10-2(c)(8)(A), n. 182; § 10-2(c)(8)(C), n. 195
Department of Justice v. Tax Analysts, 492 U.S. 136 (1989) — § 10-2(b)(1), nn. 5, 14; § 10-2(b)(3), n. 32
Department of Navy v. FLRA, 840 F.2d 1131 (3d Cir. 1988) — § 10-2(c)(7), n. 163
Department of State v. Ray, 502 U.S. 164 (1991) — § 10-2(c)(1), n. 52; § 10-2(c)(7), nn. 156, 167, 169
Department of State v. Washington Post Co., 456 U.S. 595 (1982) — § 10-2(c)(7), nn. 156, 164
DePugh v. Sutton, 917 F. Supp. 690 (W.D. Mo. 1996) (same) — § 15-3(a), n. 359
DeRoburt v. Gannett Co., 507 F. Supp. 880 (D. Haw. 1981) — § 16-2(a)(2), n. 29; § 16-2(c)(2)(B), n. 156; § 16-2(f), nn. 380-82
DeRoburt v. Gannett Co., 6 Media L. Rep. (BNA) 2473 (D. Haw. 1981) — § 16-2(d)(1), nn. 196, 197; § 16-2(e)(2), n. 324; § 16-2(e)(3), n. 354; § 16-2(e)(4), n. 362
DeRoburt v. Gannett Co., 859 F.2d 714 (9th Cir. 1987) — § 16-2(d)(1), nn. 195, 198

TABLE OF CASES

Des Moines Indep. Community Sch. Dist. Pub. Records v. Des Moines Register & Tribune Co., 487 N.W.2d 666 (Iowa 1992) — § 6-1(b), n. 187; § 11-7(m), n. 351

Des Moines Register & Tribune Co. v. Iowa District Ct., 426 N.W.2d 142 (Iowa 1988) — § 3-1(a)(2), nn. 90, 95, 102

Desai v. Hersh, 954 F.2d 1408 (7th Cir. 1992) — § 15-2(b)(1), n. 41; § 15-2(c)(2)(B), n. 100; § 16-2(a)(1), n. 7

Desnick v. American Broadcasting Cos., 44 F.3d 1345 (7th Cir. 1995) —§ 12-4(c)(2), nn. 234-49; § 12-4(c)(3), nn. 314, 324; § 13-2(a), nn. 2-6; § 13-2(b), nn. 30-38; § 13-7(a)(2)(A)(iii), nn. 634, 635; § 13-7(b)(2), nn. 697-99; § 13-7(b)(4)(C), n. 723; § 13-8, nn. 798-802, 805

Desnick v. Capital Cities/ABC Inc., 851 F. Supp. 303 (N.D. Ill. 1994) — § 12-4(c)(2), nn. 234, 243

Deteresa v. American Broadcasting Co., 121 F.3d 460 (9th Cir. 1997) — § 12-2(a), n. 65; § 12-2(b), n. 75; § 13-2(a), nn. 4, 5; § 13-2(b), n. 53; § 13-7(a)(2)(A)(iii), n. 633; § 13-7(b)(4)(B), nn. 715, 716, 718; § 13-7(c), nn. 763, 775-77, 803-05;

Detroit Free Press, Inc. v. 36th Dist. Judge, 24 Media L. Rep. (BNA) 1886 (Mich. App. 1996) — § 4-3, n. 100

Detroit Free Press, Inc. v. Department of Justice, 73 F.3d 93 (6th Cir. 1996) — § 10-2(c)(8)(C), n. 196; § 10-2(h), n. 287

Detroit Free Press, Inc. v. Oakland County Sheriff, 418 N.W.2d 124 (Mich. App. 1987) — § 11-7(b)(1), n. 208

Detroit Free Press, Inc. v. Recorder's Ct. Judge, 294 N.W.2d 827 (Mich. 1980) — § 2-2(b), n. 136

Detroit News, Inc. v. City of Detroit, 460 N.W.2d 312 (Mich. App. 1990) — § 9-6(j), n. 410

Detroit News, Inc. v. City of Detroit, 516 N.W.2d 151 (Mich. App. 1994) — § 11-7(*l*), n. 341

Detroit News, Inc. v. Recorder's Ct. Judge, 514 N.W.2d 148 (Mich. 1994) — § 5-2(a), n. 59

DeZimm v. Connelie, 476 N.E.2d 646 (N.Y. 1985) — § 11-7(b)(9), n. 249

DeZimm v. Connelie, 479 N.Y.S.2d 871 (App. Div. 1984) — § 11-7(b), n. 204

Diaz v. Lukash, 624 N.E.2d 156 (N.Y. 1993) — § 11-7(d), n. 257

Dickerson v. Hayes, 543 So. 2d 836 (Fla. App. 1989) — § 11-7(e), n. 268

Dickerson v. Raphael, 27 Media L. Rep. (BNA) 2215 (Mich. 1999) — § 12-2(a), n. 26; § 13-7(b)(3), n. 708; § 13-7(b)(4)(B), n. 717

Diehl v. Virginia, 384 S.E.2d 801 (Va. 1989), *vacated*, 390 S.E.2d 550 (Va. 1990) — § 2-1(a), n. 4

Dietemann v. Time, Inc., 284 F. Supp. 925 (C.D. Cal. 1968) — § 12-4(a), n. 155; § 12-5, n. 354

Dietemann v. Time, Inc., 449 F.2d 245 (9th Cir. 1971) — § 12-2(a), n. 34; § 12-4(a), nn. 152-59, 171; § 12-4(c)(1), n. 227; § 12-4(c)(3), nn. 252-55, 260, 304, 312; § 12-5, nn. 350-56; § 13-2(b), nn. 27-29, 57; § 13-3(c), n. 165; § 13-4(a)(2)(A), nn. 373, 377; § 13-5, n. 556; § 13-7(b)(3), n. 708; § 13-7(c), nn. 748-53, 760; § 13-8, nn. 783-85, 802, 806

Dillon v. City & County of San Francisco, 748 F. Supp. 722 (N.D. Cal. 1990) — § 16-2(c)(2)(A), n. 138; § 16-2(d)(3)(B), nn. 235-38; § 16-2(i), nn. 445, 446

Dingman v. Harvell, 814 S.W.2d 362 (Tenn. App. 1991) — § 15-2(e)(2)(A), n. 235

Direct Mail Serv., Inc. v. Registrar of Motor Vehicles, 5 N.E.2d 545 (Mass. 1937) — § 11-7(k), n. 315

TABLE OF CASES

Dirksen v. Department of Health & Human Servs., 803 F.2d 1456 (9th Cir. 1986) — § 10-2(c)(3), n. 105

Dobronski v. FCC, 17 F.3d 275 (9th Cir. 1994) — § 10-2(b)(2), n. 24

Doe by Doe v. B.P.S. Guard Servs., Inc., 945 F.2d 1422 (8th Cir. 1991) — § 12-4(c)(3), n. 294

Doe v. American Broadcasting Cos., 543 N.Y.S.2d 455 (App. Div. 1989) — § 13-4(a)(3)(A)(i), nn. 433-36

Doe v. Board of Regents, 452 S.E.2d 776 (Ga. App. 1994) — § 11-5(a)(2), n. 88; § 11-7(b)(5), n. 238

Doe v. Department of Justice, 790 F. Supp. 17 (D.D.C. 1992) — § 10-2(c)(8)(D), n. 200

Doe v. Kohn, Nast & Graf, 853 F. Supp. 147 (E.D. Pa. 1994) — § 16-2(c)(2)(A), n. 138; § 16-2(d)(3)(C), n. 270; § 16-2(e)(2), n. 318; § 16-2(h)(1), n. 406; § 16-2(i), n. 445

Doe v. Methodist Hosp., 690 N.E.2d 281 (Ind. 1997) — § 12-1, n. 2

Doe v. Museum of Science & History, 22 Media L. Rep. (BNA) 2497 (Fla. Cir. 1994) — § 3-2(b), nn. 381-84

Doe v. Registrar of Motor Vehicles, 528 N.E.2d 880 (Mass. App. 1988) — § 11-7(k), nn. 316, 318

Doe v. Roe, 495 A.2d 1235 (Me. 1985) — § 6-1(b), n. 188

Doe v. Santa Fe Indep. Sch. Dist., 933 F. Supp. 647 (S.D. Tex. 1996) — § 3-2(a), n. 357; § 3-2(b), n. 386

Doe v. Shapiro, 852 F. Supp. 1256 (E.D. Pa. 1994) — § 6-1(b), n. 188; § 6-1(c)(1), nn. 218, 219

Doe v. Superior Ct., 721 P.2d 617 (Alaska 1986) — § 11-7(a)(1), n. 188

Doe v. Univision Television Group, Inc., 717 So. 2d 63 (Fla. App. 1998) — § 13-4(a)(3)(B), nn. 486-89

Doe v. Walker, 15 Media L. Rep. (BNA) 1333 (Fla. Cir. 1988) — § 6-1(c)(2), n. 229

Does I-III v. Archdiocese of Santa Fe, Inc., 924 P.2d 273 (N.M. App. 1996) — § 6-1(c)(1), n. 227

Doherty v. Department of Justice, 775 F.2d 49 (2d Cir. 1985) — § 10-2(e), n. 249

Dolcefino v. Ray, 902 S.W.2d 163 (Tex. App. 1995) — § 16-2(a)(2), n. 39; § 16-2(d)(3), n. 210; § 16-2(d)(3)(A), n. 224

Dong v. Smithsonian Inst., 125 F.3d 877 (D.C. Cir. 1997) — § 10-2(b)(2), n. 30

Donrey Media Group v. Ikeda, 959 F. Supp. 1280 (D. Haw. 1996) — § 11-7(h), n. 302

Donrey of Nevada v. Bradshaw, 798 P.2d 144 (Nev. 1990) — § 11-7(b)(1), n. 212

Doolan v. BOCES, 398 N.E.2d 533 (N.Y. 1979) — § 11-5(c), n. 167; § 11-7(a)(2), n. 189

Dooley v. Boyle, 531 N.Y.S.2d 158 (Sup. Ct. 1988) — § 15-1, n. 17; § 15-2(d)(2), n. 160; § 16-2(a)(2), n. 32

Douglas Oil Co. v. Petrol Stops Northwest, 441 U.S. 211 (1979) — § 3-1(a), n. 2; § 3-1(a)(3), nn. 106, 137; § 5-2(a)(3), nn. 135, 150, 152, 154, 159, 194

Douglass v. Hustler Magazine, Inc., 769 F.2d 1128 (7th Cir. 1985) — § 12-4(c)(3), n. 283

Dove Audio, Inc. v. Lungren, 1995 WL 432631 (C.D. Cal. June 14, 1995) — § 7-3, n. 158; § 7-4, nn. 198-204

Dow Jones & Co. v. Department of Justice, 917 F.2d 571 (D.C. Cir. 1990) — § 10-2(b)(2), n. 26; § 10-2(c)(6), n. 138

Dow Jones & Co. v. Superior Ct., 303 N.E.2d 847 (Mass. 1973) — § 16-2(e)(2), n. 324

Dowling v. United States, 473 U.S. 207 (1985) — § 13-3(c)(8)(B), n. 278

Downing v. Monitor Publ'g Co., 415 A.2d 683 (N.H. 1980) —§ 16-2(c)(2)(B), nn. 156, 161; § 16-2(d)(1), n. 197; § 16-2(f), nn. 379, 381; § 16-2(h)(2), n. 424

TABLE OF CASES

Downs v. Austin, 522 So. 2d 931 (Fla. App. 1988) — § 11-7(b)(3)(B), n. 229
Dr. Miles Med. Co. v. John D. Park & Sons Co., 220 U.S. 373 (1911) — § 13-4(c), n. 529
Driscoll v. Morris, 111 F.R.D. 459 (D. Conn. 1986) — § 16-2(c)(2)(B), n. 173; § 16-2(g), n. 385
DTH Publ'g Corp. v. University of North Carolina at Chapel Hill, 496 S.E.2d 8 (N.C. App. 1998) — § 3-2(a), nn. 335, 336, 358
Dubuque v. Telegraph Herald, Inc., 297 N.W.2d 523 (Iowa 1980) — § 11-7(a)(1), n. 185
Duff v. Basilica of Saint John, 26 Media L. Rep. (BNA) 1156 (Iowa Dist. 1997) — § 4-3, nn. 92 101
Dulgarian v. Stone, 652 N.E.2d 603 (Mass. 1995) — § 13-4(c), n. 533
Dumez v. Houma Mun. Fire & Police Civil Serv. Bd., 341 So. 2d 1206 (La. App. 1976) — § 15-2(c)(2)(A), n. 87; § 15-2(d)(1), nn. 143, 152; § 15-2(e)(2)(C), n. 253
Duncan v. Louisiana, 391 U.S. 145 (1968) — § 2-1(a), n. 2
Dunn v. Alabama State Univ. Bd. of Trustees, 628 So. 2d 519 (Ala. 1993), *overruled on other grounds*, Watkins v. Board of Trustees of Alabama State Univ., 703 So. 2d 335 (Ala. 1997) — § 9-6(h)(6), n. 366
Dunn v. Town of Emerald Isle, 722 F. Supp. 1309 (M.D.N.C. 1989) — § 12-1, n. 2
Duran v. Detroit News, Inc., 504 N.W.2d 715 (Mich. App. 1993) — § 13-5, n. 553
Durns v. Bureau of Prisons, 804 F.2d 701 (D.C. Cir. 1986) — § 10-2(c)(6), n. 138
Dusky v. United States, 362 U.S. 402 (1960) — § 3-1(a)(5), n. 181
Dutton v. Guste, 395 So. 2d 683 (La. 1981) — § 11-7(m), n. 350

E

Early v. The Toledo Blade, 26 Media L. Rep. (BNA) 2569 (Ohio App. 1998) — § 13-3(a), nn. 90, 102
Early v. The Toledo Blade, No. 90-3434, slip op. (Ohio C.P. July 9, 1997) — § 12-2(b), n. 75; § 12-4(c)(1), n. 220; § 13-3(b), n. 137
East Baton Rouge Parish School Bd. v. Capital City Press, 78 F.3d 920 (5th Cir. 1996) — § 7-1, nn. 74-80
Eastman Kodak Co. v. Worden, 25 Media L. Rep. (BNA) 1485 (W.D.N.Y. 1996) — § 6-1(a)(1), n. 6
Easton Area Joint Sewer Auth. v. Morning Call, Inc., 581 A.2d 684 (Pa. Commw. 1990) — § 9-6(i)(1)(B), n. 376
Edward A. Sherman Publ'g Co. v. Goldberg, 443 A.2d 1252 (R.I. 1982) — § 3-3(a), nn. 444, 506
Edwards v. State Farm Ins. Co., 833 F.2d 535 (5th Cir. 1987) — § 13-7(a)(2)(B), n. 651
EEOC v. Erection Co., 900 F.2d 168 (9th Cir. 1990) — § 6-1(b), n. 187; § 6-1(c), n. 196
EEOC v. National Children's Center, Inc., 98 F.3d 1406 (D.C. Cir. 1996) — § 6-1(a)(3), n. 56
El Dia, Inc. v. Rossello, 165 F.3d 106 (1st Cir. 1999) — § 9-2(b), n. 42
El Vocero de Puerto Rico v. Puerto Rico, 508 U.S. 147 (1993) — § 2-2(g), nn. 272-77; § 3-1(a)(2), n. 89; § 5-2(a)(6), n. 237
Ellerbe v. Andrews, 623 So. 2d 41 (La. App. 1993) — § 11-7(b)(4), n. 236
Elrod v. Burns, 427 U.S. 347 (1976) — § 2-1(d), n. 74; § 7-4, n. 221
Emery v. City of Rawlins, 596 P.2d 675 (Wyo. 1979) — § 9-6(c), nn. 285, 289
Empire Blue Cross & Blue Shield v. Janet Greeson's A Place for Us, Inc., 62 F.3d 1217 (9th Cir. 1995) — § 6-1(b), n. 188

TABLE OF CASES

Empire Realty Corp. v. New York State Div. of Lottery, 657 N.Y.S.2d 504 (App. Div. 1997) — § 11-7(i), n. 307

Energy Research Found. v. Defense Nuclear Facilities Safety Bd., 917 F.2d 581 (D.C. Cir. 1990) — § 9-5(a)(2), n. 89

Enprotech Corp. v. Renda, 983 F.2d 17 (3d Cir. 1993) — § 6-1(a)(4), n. 69; § 6-1(b), nn. 165, 188

Environmental Tech., Inc. v. EPA, 822 F. Supp. 1226 (E.D. Va. 1993) — § 10-2(f), n. 257

EPA v. Mink, 410 U.S. 73 (1973) —§ 10-2(b)(3), n. 35; § 10-2(c)(2), nn. 89, 91-93; § 10-2(c)(6), n. 146

Epps v. Department of Justice, 801 F. Supp. 787 (D.D.C. 1992), *modified*, 995 F.2d 305 (D.C. Cir. 1993) — § 10-2(c)(8)(C), n. 192

Ericson v. University of Alaska, 23 Media L. Rep. (BNA) 1724 (Alaska Super. 1994) — § 11-7(a), n. 180

Essential Info., Inc. v. United States Info. Agency, 134 F.3d 1165 (D.C. Cir. 1998) — § 10-2(c)(4), n. 114

Estate of Hearst, 136 Cal. Rptr. 821 (Ct. App. 1977) — § 6-1(b), n. 159

Estate of Rosenbaum v. New York City, 21 Media L. Rep. (BNA) 1987 (E.D.N.Y. 1993) — § 3-2(e), n. 424

Estes v. Texas, 381 U.S. 532 (1965) — § 2-1(a), n. 4; § 2-2(b), n. 135; § 4-1, nn. 3-28

Ettlinger v. FBI, 596 F. Supp. 867 (D. Mass. 1984) — § 10-2(b)(5), n. 51

Eudaly v. City of Colleyville, 642 S.W.2d 75 (Tex. App. 1982) — § 9-6(e), n. 315

Eugene Cervi & Co. v. Russell, 519 P.2d 1189 (Colo. 1974) — § 11-7(j), n. 309

Evening News Ass'n v. City of Troy, 339 N.W.2d 421 (Mich. 1983) — § 11-5(a), n. 79; § 11-5(a)(6), n. 132; § 11-7(b)(3)(A), n. 222

Ex parte Birmingham News Co., 624 So. 2d 1117 (Ala. Crim. App. 1993) — § 2-3, nn. 291, 294, 296, 298; § 3-1(a), nn. 30, 31, 64; § 3-1(a)(3), n. 126; § 5-2(a)(6), n. 239

Ex parte Consolidated Publ'g Co., 601 So. 2d 423 (Ala. 1992) — § 3-1(a), nn. 13, 14, 4-11

Ex parte First Charleston Corp., 495 S.E.2d 423 (S.C. 1998) — § 3-1(a)(1), n. 67; § 3-1(a)(4), n. 171

Ex parte Greenville News, 482 S.E.2d 556 (S.C. 1997) — § 3-1(d), n. 303; § 5-2(d), n. 415

Ex parte Grothe, 687 S.W.2d 736 (Tex. Crim. App. 1984) — § 16-2(d)(3)(B), n. 239; § 16-2(f), n. 376

Ex parte Holliway, 199 S.W. 412 (Mo. 1917) — § 14-1, n. 10

Ex parte Island Packet, 417 S.E.2d 575 (S.C. 1992) — § 3-3(a), n. 473

Ex parte Lawrence, 48 P. 124 (Cal. 1897) — § 14-1, n. 2

Ex parte Lexington County, 442 S.E.2d 589 (S.C. 1994) — § 3-1(a), n. 55

Ex parte Sparrow, 14 F.R.D. 351 (N.D. Ala. 1953) — § 15-2(a), n. 20; § 15-2(c)(2)(A), n. 87; § 15-2(e)(1), n. 213; § 15-2(j), n. 321

Ex parte State Record Co., 504 S.E.2d 592 (S.C. 1998) — § 13-3(a), n. 122; § 13-7(c), n. 772

Ex parte Strum, 136 A. 312 (Md. Spec. App. 1927) — § 4-1, n. 4

Ex parte The Island Packet, 417 S.E.2d 575 (S.C. 1992) — § 3-1(a), n. 33; § 6-2(a), nn. 278-80

Express News Corp. v. MacRae, 787 S.W.2d 451 (Tex. Crim. App. 1990) — § 5-2(a), n. 59

F

FAA v. Robertson, 422 U.S. 255 (1974) — § 10-2(c)(4), n. 109
Fairfield v. American Photocopy Equip. Co., 291 P.2d 194 (Cal. App. 1955) — § 12-4(a), n. 166
Falcone v. IRS, 714 F.2d 646 (6th Cir. 1983) — § 10-2(h), n. 285
Falwell v. Penthouse Int'l, 521 F. Supp. 1204 (W.D. Va. 1981) — § 12-1, n. 2
Farbman & Sons v. New York City Health & Hosp. Corp., 464 N.E.2d 437 (N.Y. 1984) — § 11-9, n. 363
Farese v. Department of Justice, 683 F. Supp. 273 (D.D.C. 1987) — § 10-2(c)(8)(C), n. 194
Farhat v. Farhat, 25 Media L. Rep. (BNA) 2151 (Fla. Cir. 1997) — § 16-2(e)(3), n. 333
Farr v. Pitchess, 522 F.2d 464 (9th Cir. 1975) — § 16-2(a)(1), nn. 2, 24; § 16-2(c)(1), nn. 92, 102; § 16-2(d)(1), n. 177; § 16-2(f), n. 375; § 16-2(h)(2), nn. 420, 421
Farr v. Superior Ct., 99 Cal. Rptr. 342 (Ct. App. 1971) — § 15-2(a), nn. 21, 30; § 16-2(c)(1), n. 104
Farrell v. City of Detroit, 530 N.W.2d 105 (Mich. App. 1995) — § 11-2, n. 22
Farrington v. Crupper Transp. Co., 17 Media L. Rep. (BNA) 1781 (D. Kan. 1990) — § 16-2(c)(2)(A), n. 144; § 16-2(d)(3)(C), n. 271
Farron v. City of San Francisco, 265 Cal. Rptr. 317 (Ct. App. 1989) — § 9-6(b), n. 267
Fathers Are Parents Too, Inc. v. Hunstein, 415 S.E.2d 322 (Ga. App. 1992) — § 9-6(b), n. 271
Faulk v. State's Attorney for Harford County, 474 A.2d 880 (Md. 1984) — — § 11-1, n. 8; § 11-5(a), n. 81
Fawley v. Quirk, 11 Media L. Rep. (BNA) 2336 (Ohio App. 1985) — § 16-2(a)(2), n. 48
FBI v. Abramson, 456 U.S. 615 (1982) — § 10-2(c)(8), n. 172
FCC v. ITT World Communications, 466 U.S. 463 (1984) — § 9-5(a)(2), n. 92; § 9-5(a)(3), n. 94
FEC v. Florida for Kennedy Comm., 681 F.2d 1281 (11th Cir. 1982) — § 15-3(b), nn. 379, 380
FEC v. Machinists Non-Partisan Political League, 655 F.2d 380 (D.C. Cir. 1981) — § 15-3(b), nn. 379, 380
FEC v. Phillips Publ'g Co., 517 F. Supp. 1308 (D.D.C. 1981) — § 15-3(b), n. 379
Federal Open Market Comm. v. Merrill, 443 U.S. 340 (1979) — § 10-2(c)(6), nn. 135, 136, 151
Federated Publications, Inc. v. Boise City, 915 P.2d 21 (Idaho 1996) — § 11-7(a)(1), n. 185; § 11-7(a)(3), n. 195
Federated Publications, Inc. v. Kurtz, 615 P.2d 440 (Wash. 1980) — § 5-2(a), n. 79; § 5-2(a)(7), n. 250
Federated Publications, Inc. v. Swedberg, 633 P.2d 74 (Wash. 1981) — § 2-1(d), n. 66
Ferguson v. FBI, 957 F.2d 1059 (2d Cir. 1992) — § 10-2(c)(8), n. 176; § 10-2(c)(8)(D), n. 201
Ferguson v. Stephens, 623 So. 2d 711 (La. App. 1993) — § 11-7(f)(6), n. 296
Ferrara v. Detroit Free Press, Inc., 1997 U.S. Dist. LEXIS 22624 (E.D. Mich. Dec. 30, 1997) — § 6-1(a)(3), n. 54; § 6-1(a)(4), n. 85
Ferrara v. Detroit Free Press, Inc., 26 Media L. Rep. (BNA) 2355 (E.D. Mich. 1998) — Preface, n. 4; § 13-4(c), n. 533; § 13-7(a)(2)(A)(i), nn. 604, 608; § 13-7(a)(2)(A)(iii), n. 634; § 13-7(c), n. 750
Fidelity Fin. Servs. v. Hicks, 642 N.E.2d 759 (Ill. App. 1994) — § 6-1(b), n. 185

TABLE OF CASES

Fincher v. Georgia, 497 S.E.2d 632 (Ga. App. 1998) — § 11-7(a), n. 179; § 11-7(a)(3), n. 192

Finger v. Omni Publications, Int'l, 566 N.E.2d 141 (N.Y. 1990) — § 12-4(b), n. 213

Fink v. Lefkowitz, 393 N.E.2d 463 (N.Y. 1979) — § 11-5(a), n. 79; § 11-7(b)(9), n. 252

Finn v. Shiller, 72 F.3d 1182 (4th Cir. 1996) — § 3-1(a)(3), n. 139; § 5-2(a)(3), n. 186

Firestone v. News-Press Publ'g Co., 538 So. 2d 457 (Fla. 1989) — § 8-4, nn. 130, 133, 136

First Amendment Coalition v. Judicial Inquiry & Review Bd., 784 F.2d 467 (3d Cir. 1986) — § 9-4, n. 68

First Nat'l Bank of Boston v. Bellotti, 435 U.S. 765 (1978) — § 1-3, n. 49; § 1-4(a), n. 53; § 2-1(c), n. 60; § 14-5(e), n. 190

First United Fund v. American Banker, 485 N.Y.S.2d 489 (Sup. Ct. 1985) — § 15-2(c)(2)(B), n. 131; § 15-2(d)(3)(D), n. 203; § 16-2(d)(3)(C), n. 277

Fischer v. Los Angeles Unified Sch. Dist., 82 Cal. Rptr. 2d 452 (Ct. App. 1999) — § 9-6(i)(1)(B), n. 377

Fischer v. McGowan, 585 F. Supp. 978 (D.R.I. 1984) — § 15-2(c)(2)(A), n. 87; § 15-2(d)(1), n. 144

Fiumara v. Higgins, 572 F. Supp. 1093 (D.N.H. 1983) — § 10-2(c)(3), n. 105

Florida v. Bennett, 19 Media L. Rep. (BNA) 1383 (Fla. Cir. 1991) — § 5-2(a)(5), n. 223

Florida v. Black, 24 Media L. Rep. (BNA) 2117 (Fla. Cir. 1996) — § 5-2(a)(5), n. 224

Florida v. D.H.W., 686 So. 2d 1331 (Fla. 1996) — § 5-2(a)(9), n. 281

Florida v. Davis, 720 So. 2d 220 (Fla. 1998) — § 15-2(d)(3)(A), n. 166; § 16-2(a)(2), n. 29; § 16-2(c)(1), nn. 92, 103; § 16-2(d)(3), n. 211; § 16-2(e)(1), n. 299; § 16-2(i), n. 451

Florida v. Eyrich, 22 Media L. Rep. (BNA) 1863 (Fla. Cir. 1993) — § 7-1, n. 82

Florida v. Globe Communications Corp., 622 So. 2d 1066 (Fla. App. 1993) — § 2-1(c), n. 62

Florida v. Globe Communications Corp., 648 So. 2d 110 (Fla. 1994) — § 2-1(c), n. 61

Florida v. Kozma, 22 Media L. Rep. (BNA) 1539 (Fla. Cir. 1994) — § 3-1(a), n. 62

Florida v. Olson, 586 So. 2d 1239 (Fla. App. 1991) — § 8-1, n. 55

Florida v. Overton, 26 Media L. Rep. (BNA) 1702 (Fla. Cir. 1998) — § 16-2(c)(1), n. 92

Florida v. Sarmiento, 397 So. 2d 643 (Fla. 1981) — § 13-7(b)(1), n. 685

Florida v. Searles, 24 Media L. Rep. (BNA) 2470 (Fla. Cir. 1996) — § 16-2(d)(3)(C), n. 277

Florida v. Selinger, 13 Media L. Rep. (BNA) 1055 (Fla. Cir. 1986) — § 16-2(h), n. 404

Florida v. Smith, 27 Media L. Rep. (BNA) 1718 (Fla. Cir. 1999) — § 15-2(j), nn. 329, 334

Florida v. Tillett, 111 So. 2d 716 (Fla. App. 1959) — § 5-2(a)(3), n. 171

Florida ex rel. Cummer v. Pace, 159 So. 679 (Fla. 1935) — § 11-4, n. 65

Florida ex rel. Miami Herald Publ'g Co. v. McIntosh, 340 So. 2d 904 (Fla. 1977) — § 7-1, n. 82

Florida Freedom Newspapers, Inc. v. McCrary, 497 So. 2d 652 (Fla. App. 1986) — § 5-2(a)(5), nn. 223, 224

Florida Freedom Newspapers, Inc. v. McCrary, 520 So. 2d 32 (Fla. 1988) — § 7-2, n. 139

Florida Publ'g Co. v. Fletcher, 340 So. 2d 914 (Fla. 1976) — § 12-3, nn. 95-102; § 12-4(a), nn. 175, 185-87

Florida Publ'g Co. v. Morgan, 322 S.E.2d 233 (Ga. 1984) — § 3-3(a), nn. 437, 475-77; § 3-3(b), n. 525

TABLE OF CASES

Florida Soc'y of Newspaper Editors v. Florida Pub. Serv. Comm'n, 543 So. 2d 1262 (Fla. App. 1989) — § 11-9, n. 368

Florida Star, The v. B.J.F., 491 U.S. 524 (1989) — § 2-1(c), n. 59; § 7-1, n. 46; § 13-3(a), nn. 99-107; § 13-3(b), n. 129; § 13-4(a)(2)(C), n. 403; § 13-4(a)(3)(B), n. 475; § 13-7(a)(2)(A)(i), nn. 601, 607, 620

Florida State Univ. v. Hatton, 672 So. 2d 576 (Fla. App. 1996) — § 11-7(g), n. 297

Floyd County Bd. of Educ. v. Ratliff, 955 S.W.2d 921 (Ky. 1997) — § 9-6(g), n. 338

FLRA v. Department of Defense, 977 F.2d 545 (11th Cir. 1992) — § 10-2(c)(7), n. 158

FLRA v. Department of Treasury, 884 F.2d 1446 (D.C. Cir. 1989) — § 10-2(c)(7), n. 163

FLRA v. Department of Veterans Affairs, 958 F.2d 503 (2d Cir. 1992) — § 10-2(c)(7), n. 158

Flynt v. Weinberger, 762 F.2d 134 (D.C. Cir. 1985) — § 8-5, n. 160

FMC Corp. v. Capital Cities/ABC, Inc., 915 F.2d 300 (7th Cir. 1990) — § 13-3(b), nn. 150-61

Fogel v. Forbes, Inc., 500 F. Supp. 1081 (E.D. Pa. 1980) — § 12-2(b), n. 81

Food Chem. News, Inc. v. Advisory Comm. on Food & Drug Admin., 760 F. Supp. 220 (D.D.C. 1991) — § 10-3(c), n. 300

Food Chem. News, Inc. v. Davis, 378 F. Supp. 1048 (D.D.C. 1974) — § 9-5(b)(2), n. 211

Food Chem. News, Inc. v. Department of Health & Human Servs., 980 F.2d 1468 (D.C. Cir. 1992) — § 10-3(c), nn. 295, 297, 300

Food Chem. News, Inc. v. Young, 900 F.2d 328 (D.C. Cir. 1990) — § 9-5(b)(2), nn. 201, 211, 216

Food Lion Inc. v. Capital Cities/ABC Inc., 24 Media L. Rep. (BNA) 2431 (M.D.N.C. 1996) — § 16-2(j)(1), n. 460

Food Lion Inc. v. Capital Cities/ABC Inc., 951 F. Supp. 1211 (M.D.N.C. 1996) — § 16-2(d)(3)(C), n. 277; § 16-2(e)(2), n. 327; § 16-2(e)(4), n. 365

Food Lion, Inc. v. Capital Cities/ABC Inc., 951 F. Supp. 1224 (M.D.N.C. 1996); 951 F. Supp. 1217 (M.D.N.C. 1996) — Preface, n. 6; § 13-8, nn. 809-13

Food Lion, Inc. v. Capital Cities/ABC, Inc., 20 Media L. Rep. (BNA) 2263 (M.D.N.C. 1992) — § 13-3(a), n. 122

Food Lion, Inc. v. Capital Cities/ABC, Inc., 887 F. Supp. 811 (M.D.N.C. 1995) — § 12-4(c)(3), nn. 319-35; § 13-2(b), nn. 58-60, 70-73, 76; § 13-3(c)(7), n. 245; § 13-4(a)(3)(A)(i), n. 430; § 13-4(a)(3)(B), n. 471

Food Lion, Inc. v. Capital Cities/ABC, Inc., 946 F. Supp. 420 (M.D.N.C. 1996) — § 13-2(b), n. 67

Food Lion, Inc. v. Capital Cities/ABC, Inc., 951 F. Supp. 1217 (M.D.N.C. 1996) — § 12-4(c)(3), n. 322; § 13-2(b), nn. 58, 65-69

Food Lion, Inc. v. Capital Cities/ABC, Inc., 964 F. Supp. 956 (M.D.N.C. 1997) — § 12-4(c)(3), n. 327

Food Lion, Inc. v. Capital Cities/ABC, Inc., 984 F. Supp. 923 (M.D.N.C. 1997) — § 12-4(c)(3), n. 321; § 13-2(b), nn. 65, 76; § 13-8, n. 810

Food Lion, Inc. v. Capital Cities/ABC, Inc., No. 6:92-CV-00592, slip op. (M.D.N.C. Aug. 22, 1994) — § 12-4(c)(3), n. 323; § 13-2(b), n. 69

Food Lion, Inc. v. Capital Cities/ABC, Inc., No. 6:92CV00592, slip op. (M.D.N.C. Apr. 26, 1994) — § 13-2(b), nn. 63, 64

Fordyce v. City of Seattle, 55 F.3d 436 (9th Cir. 1995) — § 12-2(a), nn. 15-19

Forest Hills Util. Co. v. City of Heath, 302 N.E.2d 593 (Ohio C.P. 1973) — § 15-2(c)(2)(A), n. 87; § 15-2(d)(1), n. 152

TABLE OF CASES

Foretich v. Chung, 22 Media L. Rep. (BNA) 2472 (D.D.C. 1994) — § 16-2(d)(3)(C), n. 278; § 16-2(e)(2), n. 325; § 16-2(e)(4), n. 362
Foretich v. Lifetime Cable, 777 F. Supp. 47 (D.D.C. 1991) — § 12-6(a), n. 376
Forsham v. Califano, 587 F.2d 1128 (D.C. Cir. 1978) — § 10-2(b)(3), n. 34
Forsham v. Harris, 445 U.S. 169 (1980) — § 10-2(b)(1), n. 13
Forster v. Manchester, 189 A.2d 147 (Pa. 1963) — § 12-2(a), nn. 3, 4
Forsyth v. Barr, 19 F.3d 1527 (5th Cir. 1994) — § 13-7(a)(2)(A), n. 588
Fort Wayne Journal-Gazette v. Baker, 788 F. Supp. 379 (N.D. Ind. 1992) — § 2-1(d), n. 70
Founding Church of Scientology of Washington, D.C. v. Levi, 579 F. Supp. 1060 (D.D.C. 1982) — § 10-2(c)(8)(D), n. 201
Founding Church of Scientology v. Bell, 603 F.2d 945 (D.C. Cir. 1979) — § 10-2(c)(4), n. 112; § 10-2(h), nn. 280, 283
Founding Church of Scientology v. Smith, 721 F.2d 828 (D.C. Cir. 1983) — § 10-2(c)(3), n. 103
Frazee v. United States Forest Serv., 97 F.3d 367 (9th Cir. 1996) — § 10-2(c)(5), n. 125
Freedom Newspapers, Inc. v. Bowerman, 739 P.2d 881 (Colo. App. 1987) — § 11-7(d), n. 259
Freedom Newspapers, Inc. v. Denver & Rio Grande W. R.R., 731 P.2d 740 (Colo. App. 1986) — § 11-7(f)(1), n. 270; § 11-7(f)(4), n. 287
Freedom Newspapers, Inc. v. Tollefson, 961 P.2d 1150 (Colo. App. 1998) — § 11-7(a)(2), n. 189
Freeman v. Department of Justice, 822 F. Supp. 1064 (S.D.N.Y. 1993) — § 10-2(b)(4), n. 43
Friedman v. FBI, 605 F. Supp. 306 (N.D. Ga. 1981) — § 10-2(c)(8)(C), n. 194
Frio v. Superior Ct., 250 Cal. Rptr. 819 (Ct. App. 1988) — § 13-7(b)(4)(B), n. 716
Frome v. Renner, 26 Media L. Rep. (BNA) 1956 (C.D. Cal. 1997) — § 12-4(c)(2), n. 249; § 12-4(c)(3), n. 327; § 13-2(b), n. 57; § 13-8, n. 817
FTC v. Freecom Communications, Inc., 966 F. Supp. 1066 (D. Utah 1997) — § 2-1(d), n. 99
FTC v. Grolier Inc., 462 U.S. 19 (1983) — § 10-2(c)(6), nn. 132, 147-50
FTC v. Standard Fin. Management Corp., 830 F.2d 404 (1st Cir. 1987) — § 6-1(a)(4), nn. 60, 73; § 6-1(b), nn. 167, 183; § 6-1(c)(1), n. 216
Fulani v. League of Women Voters Educ. Fund, 684 F. Supp. 1185 (S.D.N.Y. 1988) — § 9-2(b), n. 45
Fund for Constitutional Gov't v. National Archives & Records Serv., 656 F.2d 856 (D.C. Cir. 1981) — § 5-2(a)(3), nn. 144, 175; § 10-2(c)(4), n. 112; § 10-2(c)(7), n. 157
Furtado v. Sierra Community College, 80 Cal. Rptr. 2d 589 (Ct. App. 1998) — § 9-6(i)(1)(B), n. 378

G

Gadsden County Times, Inc. v. Horne, 426 So. 2d 1234 (Fla. App. 1983) — § 16-2(h)(2), n. 427
Gagnon v. District Ct., 632 P.2d 567 (Colo. 1981) — § 16-2(a)(2), n. 41
Galella v. Onassis, 353 F. Supp. 196 (S.D.N.Y. 1972) — § 13-5, n. 556
Galella v. Onassis, 487 F.2d 986 (2d Cir. 1973) — § 12-2(a), nn. 27-37, 45; § 12-4(b), n. 214; § 12-4(c)(1), n. 227; § 12-6(a), n. 373; § 13-3(b), n. 130; § 13-3(c), n. 165; § 13-3(c)(2), nn. 190-92; § 13-4(a)(2)(A), n. 373; § 13-4(a)(2)(B), n. 380; § 13-4(b), n. 515

TABLE OF CASES

Gallant v. NLRB, 26 F.3d 168 (D.C. Cir. 1994) — § 10-2(b)(1), n. 6
Galvin v. FOIC, 518 A.2d 64 (Conn. 1986) — § 11-7(d), n. 257
Gannett Co. v. City Clerk's Office, 596 N.Y.S.2d 968 (Sup. Ct.) — § 11-7(j), n. 313
Gannett Co. v. Delaware, 571 A.2d 735 (Del. 1989) — § 5-2(c), nn. 414, 415
Gannett Co. v. DePasquale, 443 U.S. 368 (1979) — § 2-2(a), nn. 110, 111; § 2-2(b), nn. 125-41, 144-60; § 2-2(f), n. 256; § 2-3, nn. 290, 312; § 3-1(a), n. 42; § 3-1(a)(4), nn. 149-51, 155-57, 159, 165; § 3-1(a)(5), n. 187; § 3-2(a), nn. 337, 338; § 6-1(a)(3), n. 54
Gannett Co. v. Falvey, 582 N.Y.S.2d 580 (App. Div. 1992) — § 3-1(a)(2), nn. 98-101
Gannett Co. v. Mark, 387 N.Y.S.2d 336 (App. Div. 1976) — § 3-1(d), n. 324
Gannett Pac. Corp. v. Richardson, 580 P.2d 49 (Haw. 1978) — § 3-1(a), n. 10; § 3-1(a)(2), n. 96
Gardner v. Bradenton Herald, 413 So. 2d 10 (Fla. 1982) — § 13-7(a)(2)(A)(i), n. 601
Garland v. Georgia, 325 S.E.2d 131 (Ga. 1985) — § 2-1(c), n. 40
Garland v. Torre, 259 F.2d 545 (2d Cir. 1958) — § 14-2, nn. 20-31; § 14-6(a), nn. 228, 230; § 16-2(c)(2)(B), n. 156; § 16-2(d)(1), nn. 177, 189; § 16-2(e)(1), nn. 289-91
Garrett v. Estelle, 424 F. Supp. 468 (N.D. Tex.), *rev'd*, 556 F.2d 1274 (5th Cir. 1977) — § 8-2, nn. 67, 69-73
Gastman v. North Jersey Newspapers Co., 603 A.2d 111 (N.J. Super. 1992) — § 15-2(b)(2), nn. 48, 51; § 15-2(c)(2)(B), n. 125; § 15-2(d)(3)(A), n. 166
Gates v. Schlesinger, 366 F. Supp. 797 (D.D.C. 1973) — § 9-5(b)(3), n. 225; § 9-5(b)(5), nn. 232, 238; § 9-5(b)(6), n. 243
Gautier v. Pro-Football, Inc., 107 N.E.2d 485 (N.Y. 1952) — § 12-2(b), n. 84
Gelbard v. United States, 408 U.S. 41 (1972) — § 3-1(a)(1), n. 78; § 5-2(a)(1), n. 84
General Tire, Inc. v. Kepple, 970 S.W.2d 520 (Tex. 1998) — § 6-1(a)(6), n. 128
Gentile v. State Bar, 501 U.S. 1030 (1991) — § 7-1, n. 3; § 7-2, nn. 94-119
George v. Record Custodian, 485 N.W.2d 460 (Wis. App. 1992) — § 11-5(a)(4), n. 110
George W. Prescott Publ'g Co. v. Register of Probate, 479 N.E.2d 658 (Mass. 1985) — § 6-1(c), n. 204
George W. Prescott Publ'g Co. v. Stoughton Div., Dist. Ct., 701 N.E.2d 307 (Mass. 1998) — § 2-1(d), n. 98; § 3-3(a), n. 506
Georgia v. Birge, 241 S.E.2d 213 (Ga. 1978) — § 13-7(b)(3), n. 701
Georgia v. Smith, 27 Media L. Rep. (BNA) 1718 (Fla. Cir. 1999) — § 16-2(c)(1), n. 92; § 16-2(i), nn. 450, 451
Georgia v. Williams, 7 Media L. Rep. (BNA) 1852 (Ga. Super. 1981) — § 7-1, n. 82
Georgia Communications, Inc. v. Horne, 294 S.E.2d 725 (Ga. App. 1982) — § 16-3, n. 474
Gerstein v. Superintendent Search Screening Comm., 541 N.E.2d 984 (Mass. 1989) — § 9-6(g), n. 338; § 9-6(i)(1)(A), nn. 371, 372
Gertz v. Robert Welch, Inc., 418 U.S. 323 (1974) — § 13-4(a)(2)(C), n. 410
Ghiglione v. School Comm., 378 N.E.2d 984 (Mass. 1978) — § 9-6(g), n. 337
Gialde v. Time, Inc., 480 F.2d 1295 (8th Cir. 1973) — § 16-2(a)(1), nn. 2, 19; § 16-2(h), n. 391; § 16-2(h)(2), nn. 434-37
Giboney v. Empire Storage & Ice Co., 336 U.S. 490 (1949) — § 13-3(c), n. 162
Gibson v. Florida Leg. Investigative Comm., 372 U.S. 539 (1963) — § 14-4(c), n. 103
Gibson v. Illinois State Bd. of Educ., 683 N.E.2d 894 (Ill. App. 1997) — § 11-7(g), n. 297
Gifford v. FOIC, 631 A.2d 252 (Conn. 1993) — § 11-7(b)(1), n. 209

TABLE OF CASES

Gilbert v. Allied Chem. Corp., 411 F. Supp. 505 (E.D. Va. 1976) — § 16-2(c)(2)(A), n. 145; § 16-2(d)(3)(B), n. 234; § 16-2(d)(3)(C), n. 272; § 16-2(e)(3), n. 333
Gill v. Hearst Publ'g Co., 253 P.2d 441 (Cal. 1953) — § 12-2(b), nn. 76-79; § 12-4(c)(1), n. 220
Gintert v. Howard Publications, Inc., 565 F. Supp. 829 (N.D. Ind. 1983) — § 13-4(a)(3)(A)(ii), n. 467
Glenmede Trust Co. v. Thompson, 56 F.3d 476 (3d Cir. 1995) — § 6-1(a)(5), nn. 104, 117, 118; § 6-1(b), n. 187; § 6-1(c), nn. 190-93
Globe Newspaper Co. v. Boston Retirement Bd., 446 N.E.2d 1051 (Mass. 1983) — § 11-1, n. 9; § 11-5(a), n. 83
Globe Newspaper Co. v. Chief Med. Exmr., 533 N.E.2d 1356 (Mass. 1989) — § 11-7(d), n. 257
Globe Newspaper Co. v. Fenton, 819 F. Supp. 89 (D. Mass. 1993) — § 5-1, n. 36
Globe Newspaper Co. v. Massachusetts, 556 N.E.2d 356 (Mass. 1990) — § 3-1(d), n. 324
Globe Newspaper Co. v. Pokaski, 868 F.2d 497 (1st Cir. 1989) — § 5-1, nn. 22-35
Globe Newspaper Co. v. Police Comm'r, 648 N.E.2d 419 (Mass., 1995) — § 11-1, n. 6
Globe Newspaper Co. v. Superior Ct., 457 U.S. 596 (1982) — § 1-5, n. 74; § 2-2(a), n. 122; § 2-2(d), nn. 202-24; § 2-3, nn. 290, 294, 312; § 3-1(c), nn. 255-58; § 3-1(e), n. 330; § 3-2(a), nn. 344, 352; § 5-1, n. 31; § 5-2(a)(8), n. 275; § 6-1(a)(4), n. 84; § 6-1(c), n. 203; § 14-5(d), nn. 177-80
Goland v. CIA, 607 F.2d 339 (D.C. Cir. 1978) — § 10-2(b)(1), n. 5; § 10-2(b)(2), n. 26
Gold Coast Publications, Inc. v. Florida, 669 So. 2d 316 (Fla. App. 1996) — § 15-2(j), n. 329
Gold v. Wolpert, 876 F.2d 1327 (7th Cir. 1989) — § 13-4(c), n. 529
Goldberg v. Johnson, 485 So. 2d 1386 (Fla. App. 1986) — § 6-1(c), n. 204
Goldfeld v. Post Publ'g, 4 Media L. Rep. (BNA) 1167 (Conn. Super. 1978) — § 16-2(c)(2)(B), n. 156
Goldman v. Weinberger, 475 U.S. 503 (1986) — § 8-5, nn. 140, 141
Goldstein v. Levi, 415 F. Supp. 303 (D.D.C. 1976) — § 10-2(h), n. 287
Gonzales v. National Broadcasting Co., 155 F.3d 618 (2d Cir. 1998), *vacated*, No. 97-9454 (2d Cir. June 1, 1999) — § 14-6(a), nn. 248-50; § 16-2(a)(1), n. 15; § 16-2(d)(3), n. 223; § 16-2(d)(3)(C), n. 265
Gonzales v. National Broadcasting Co., 1998 U.S. App. LEXIS 38583 (2d Cir. Aug. 27, 1999) — Preface, n. 5; § 14-6(a), nn. 251-58; § 16-2(a)(1), nn. 2, 15, 17; § 16-2(c)(1), nn. 121, 122; § 16-2(d)(1), n. 177; § 16-2(d)(3), nn. 212, 223; § 16-2(d)(3)(C), nn. 264-69; § 16-2(e)(1), nn. 300, 301; § 16-2(e)(2), n. 317; § 16-2(e)(3), nn. 337-39; § 16-3, n. 474
Gooding v. Wilson, 405 U.S. 518 (1972) — § 1-1, n. 12
Goodman v. Fuller, 960 F.2d 149 (6th Cir. 1992) — § 6-1(b), n. 187; § 6-1(c), n. 196
Goodson Todman Enters. v. Town Bd. of Milan, 542 N.Y.S.2d 373 (App. Div. 1989) — § 9-6(b), n. 268
Gordon v. Thornberg, 790 F. Supp. 374 (D.R.I. 1992) — § 10-2(c)(8)(D), n. 206
Gorman v. University of Rhode Island, 646 F. Supp. 799 (D.R.I. 1986), *modified*, 837 F.2d 7 (1st Cir. 1988) — § 9-6(e), n. 322
Goulart v. Barry, 18 Media L. Rep. (BNA) 2001 (D.C. Super. 1991) — § 16-2(j)(1), nn. 463, 464
Government Land Bank v. GSA, 671 F.2d 663 (1st Cir. 1982) — § 10-2(c)(6), n. 135
Grand Central Partnership, Inc. v. Cuomo, 166 F.3d 473 (2d Cir. 1999) — § 10-2(b)(1), n. 5; § 10-2(b)(2), n. 28; § 10-2(c)(8)(D), n. 205

TABLE OF CASES

Grand Forks Herald v. District Ct., 322 N.W.2d 850 (N.D. 1982) — § 15-1, n. 13; § 15-2(a), n. 29; § 15-2(c)(2)(A), n. 87; § 15-2(d)(3)(C), n. 196; § 15-2(e)(2)(C), nn. 249, 250; § 15-2(i)(2), n. 304; § 15-2(i)(3), n. 315; § 16-2(a)(2), n. 30
Grant v. Smith, 574 F.2d 252 (5th Cir. 1978) — § 13-2(a), n. 20
Great Falls Tribune Co. v. Cascade County Sheriff, 775 P.2d 1267 (Mont. 1989) — § 9-1, n. 18
Great Falls Tribune Co. v. Day, 959 P.2d 508 (Mont. 1998) — § 9-1, nn. 16, 18
Great Falls Tribune Co. v. District Ct., 608 P.2d 116 (Mont. 1980) — § 3-1(a), n. 12
Great Falls Tribune Co. v. Great Falls Pub. Schs., 841 P.2d 502 (Mont. 1992) — § 9-1, n. 17
Greater Miami Baseball Club Ltd. Partnership v. Selig, 955 F. Supp. 37 (S.D.N.Y. 1997) — § 6-1(a)(1), nn. 14, 15; § 6-1(a)(4), n. 75
Green v. Alton Tel. Printing Co., 438 N.E.2d 203 (Ill. App. 1982) — § 13-6, n. 576
Green v. Chicago Tribune Co., 675 N.E.2d 249 (Ill. App. 1996) — § 12-2(b), n. 87; § 12-4(b), n. 204
Green Valley Sch., Inc. v. Cowles Florida Broadcasting, Inc., 327 So. 2d 810 (Fla. App. 1976) — § 12-3, n. 102; § 12-4(a), nn. 151, 188; § 12-4(b), n. 206; § 12-6(a), n. 373
Greenberg v. CBS Inc., 419 N.Y.S.2d 988 (App. Div. 1979) — § 15-2(c)(2)(B), n. 130; § 15-2(g), n. 267
Greenleigh Assocs., Inc. v. New York Post Corp., 434 N.Y.S.2d 388 (App. Div. 1980) — § 15-2(c)(2)(B), n. 131; § 15-2(e)(2)(B), n. 247
Greenwood v. Wolchik, 544 A.2d 1156 (Vt. 1988) — § 3-1(a)(4), n. 174; § 5-2(a)(6), n. 239
Greer v. Spock, 424 U.S. 828 (1976) — § 8-5, nn. 143, 144; § 13-3(c)(1), n. 180
Gregory v. FDIC, 631 F.2d 896 (D.C. Cir. 1980) — § 10-2(c)(9), n. 221
Griffin v. S.W. Devanney & Co., 775 P.2d 555 (Colo. 1989) — § 11-5(a)(3), n. 97
Griswold v. Connecticut, 381 U.S. 479 (1965) — § 1-3, n. 49; § 2-2(a), n. 121
Griswold v. Mt. Diablo Unified Sch. Dist., 134 Cal. Rptr. 3 (Ct. App. 1976) — § 9-6(j), n. 409
Grosjean v. American Press Co., 297 U.S. 233 (1936) — § 1-3, nn. 44-47; § 14-4(c), n. 102
Grossnickle v. Grossnickle, 935 S.W.2d 830 (Tex. App. 1996) — § 7-1, n. 78
Group W Television, Inc. v. Maryland, 626 A.2d 1032 (Md. Spec. App. 1993) — § 5-2(b), nn. 296, 338
Grove Fresh Distribs. Inc. v. Everfresh Juice Co., 134 F.3d 374 (7th Cir. 1998) — § 6-1(c), n. 196
Grove Fresh Distribs. Inc. v. Everfresh Juice Co., 1998 U.S. App. LEXIS 1836 (7th Cir. Nov. 19, 1997) — § 6-1(a)(4), n. 85
Grove Fresh Distribs. Inc. v. Everfresh Juice Co., 24 F.3d 893 (7th Cir. 1994) — § 3-2(c), n. 403; § 6-1(a)(4), n. 85; § 6-1(c), n. 196
Grumman Aircraft Eng'g Corp. v. Renegotiation Bd., 425 F.2d 578 (D.C. Cir. 1970) — § 10-2(c)(5), n. 124
Grunseth v. Marriott Corp., 868 F. Supp. 333 (D.D.C. 1994) — § 15-2(c)(2)(A), n. 95; § 15-2(d)(3)(C), nn. 185, 186; § 15-2(j), nn. 325, 326; § 16-2(j)(2), nn. 467-69
GTE Sylvania, Inc. v. Consumers Union, 445 U.S. 375 (1980) — § 10-2(f), n. 259
Gulf & W. Indus. v. United States, 615 F.2d 527 (D.C. Cir. 1979) — § 10-2(c)(5), n. 127
Gulliver's Periodicals, Ltd. v. Chas. Levy Circulating Co., 455 F. Supp. 1197 (N.D. Ill. 1978) — § 16-2(a)(1), n. 8; § 16-2(a)(2), n. 30; § 16-2(c)(2)(A), n. 137; § 16-2(d)(3)(C), n. 272; § 16-2(i), nn. 445, 446

TABLE OF CASES

Guy Gannett Publ'g Co. v. University of Maine, 555 A.2d 470 (Me. 1989) — § 11-7(e), n. 266

H

Hackworth v. Board of Educ., 447 S.E.2d 78 (Ga. App. 1994) — § 11-7(a), n. 184
Haeberle v. Texas Int'l Airlines, 739 F.2d 1019 (5th Cir. 1984) — § 7-3, n. 160
Hager v. Culverhouse, 26 Media L. Rep. (BNA) 2599 (Fla. Cir. 1998) — § 15-2(j), n. 329; § 16-2(a)(2), n. 31
Hagestad v. Tragesser, 49 F.3d 1430 (9th Cir. 1995) — § 6-1(b), n. 187; § 6-1(c), nn. 194-96
Haggerty v. Bloomington Bd. Pub. Safety, 474 N.E.2d 114 (Ind. App. 1985) — § 9-2(a), n. 36
Hagin v. Department of Motor Vehicles, 588 N.E.2d 750 (N.Y. 1992) — § 11-7(e), n. 266
Hagler v. Philadelphia Newspapers, Inc., 24 Media L. Rep. (BNA) 2332 (E.D. Pa. 1996) — § 12-5, n. 371
Hain v. Board of Sch. Directors, 641 A.2d 661 (Pa. Commw. 1994) — § 9-6(e), n. 317; § 9-6(j), n. 411
Halifax Hosp. Med. Center v. News-Journal Corp., 724 So. 2d 567 (Fla. 1999) — § 9-6(h)(3), n. 356
Halperin v. CIA, 629 F.2d 144 (D.C. Cir. 1980) — § 10-2(c)(2), n. 90
Halquist v. Department of Corrections, 783 P.2d 1065 (Wash. 1989) — § 8-2, n. 73
Hamberger v. Eastman, 206 A.2d 239 (N.H. 1964) — § 13-7(c), n. 749
Hamilton v. Accu-Tek, 942 F. Supp. 136 (E.D.N.Y. 1996) — § 4-2(a), n. 73; § 4-3, n. 112
Hammarly v. Superior Ct., 153 Cal. Rptr. 608 (Ct. App. 1979) — § 15-2(d)(3)(C), n. 195
Hammock v. Hoffmann-LaRoche, Inc., 662 A.2d 546 (N.J. 1995) — § 6-1(a)(1), nn. 18-30; § 6-1(a)(6), nn. 124, 150; § 6-1(c)(1), n. 210
Hancock Bros. v. Jones, 293 F. Supp. 1229 (N.D. Cal. 1968) — § 5-2(d), n. 434
Hanig v. Department of Motor Vehicles, 588 N.E.2d 750 (N.Y. 1992) — § 11-7(k), nn. 314, 318
Hanlon v. Berger, 119 S. Ct. 1706 (1999) — Preface, n. 2; § 12-4(a), nn. 135-37; § 12-5, nn. 339, 342
Hanson Bros. Meat Packing Co. v. Department of Agric., 640 F. Supp. 402 (D. Pa. 1986) — § 10-2(c)(3), n. 102
Harbolt v. Department of State, 616 F.2d 772 (5th Cir. 1980) — § 10-2(c)(7), n. 169
Hardaway Co. v. Rives, 422 S.E.2d 854 (Ga. 1992) — § 11-5(a), n. 77
Harkey v. Abate, 346 N.W.2d 74 (Mich. App. 1983) — § 12-4(c)(3), nn. 252, 294
Harman v. City of New York, 140 F.3d 111 (2d Cir. 1998) — § 9-2(b), n. 44
Harris v. Easton Publ'g Co., 483 A.2d 1377 (Pa. Super. 1984) — § 13-3(b), n. 140
Hartzel v. United States, 322 U.S. 680 (1944) — § 13-3(c)(9)(B), nn. 310-13
Harvey v. Department of Justice, 747 F. Supp. 29 (D.D.C. 1990) — § 10-2(c)(8)(D), n. 206
Hastings & Sons Publ'g Co. v. City Treasurer of Lynn, 375 N.E.2d 299 (Mass. 1978) — § 11-7(a)(2), n. 189
Hatchard v. Westinghouse Broadcasting Co., 532 A.2d 346 (Pa. 1987) — § 15-1, n. 8; § 15-2(c)(2)(B), nn. 112-14; § 15-2(d)(1), nn. 150, 151
Hathaway v. Joint Sch. Dist. No. 1, 342 N.W.2d 682 (Wis. 1984) — § 11-7(i), n. 308

TABLE OF CASES

Hawaii Org. of Police Officers v. Society of Prof'l Journalists, 927 P.2d 386 (Haw. 1996) — § 11-4, n. 67; § 11-7(a)(3), nn. 192, 195

Hawk Eye v. Jackson, 521 N.W.2d 750 (Iowa 1994) — § 11-7(b)(10), n. 254

Hayden v. National Sec. Agency/Central Sec. Serv., 608 F.2d 1381 (D.C. Cir. 1979) — § 10-2(c)(2), nn. 88, 94

Haynik v. Zimlich, 508 N.E.2d 195 (Ohio C.P. 1986) — § 12-3, n. 93

Hays v. Marano, 493 N.Y.S.2d 904 (App. Div. 1985) — § 5-2(a)(3), n. 172

Hazelwood Sch. Dist. v. Kuhlmeier, 484 U.S. 260 (1988) — § 1-1, n. 16

Hearst Corp. v. Hoppe, 580 P.2d 246 (Wash. 1978) — § 11-5(a)(4), n. 100

Hearst Corp. v. Justices of Super. Ct., 24 Media L. Rep. (BNA) 1478 (Mass. 1996) — § 4-3, n. 100

Hearst v. Estate of Hearst, 27 Media L. Rep. (BNA) 1223 (Cal. App. 1998) — § 6-1(c), nn. 204, 208

Hechler v. Casey, 333 S.E.2d 799 (W. Va. 1985) — § 11-5(a), n. 77

Heffron v. International Soc'y for Krishna Consciousness, 452 U.S. 640 (1981) — § 1-1, nn. 6, 10

Hemenway v. Hughes, 601 F. Supp. 1002 (D.D.C. 1985) — § 10-2(b)(3), n. 41; § 10-2(c)(7), n. 169

Henderson v. Colorado, 879 P.2d 383 (Colo. 1994) — § 15-2(d)(3)(B), n. 169; § 15-2(e)(2)(B), n. 242

Hengel v. City of Pine Bluff, 821 S.W.2d 761 (Ark. 1991) — § 11-7(b)(1), n. 210; § 11-7(b)(2), n. 215

Hennigan v. Buffalo Courier Express Co., 446 N.Y.S.2d 767 (App. Div. 1981) — § 15-1, n. 17; § 15-2(d)(2), n. 160

Hensley v. Eckerhart, 461 U.S. 424 (1983) — § 10-2(h), n. 289

Herald Ass'n v. Ellison, 419 A.2d 323 (Vt. 1980) — § 5-2(a)(7), n. 250

Herald Co. v. Ann Arbor Pub. Schs., 568 N.W.2d 411 (Mich. App. 1997) — § 11-5(a)(4), n. 105; § 11-5(a)(5), n. 124; § 11-6, n. 175

Herald Co. v. Bay City, 577 N.W.2d 696 (Mich. App. 1998) — § 9-6(b), n. 258; § 9-6(i)(1)(A), n. 369

Herald Co. v. City of Kalamazoo, 581 N.W.2d 295 (Mich. App. 1997) — § 11-5(a)(6), n. 132

Herald Co. v. Mariani, 487 N.Y.S.2d 413 (App. Div. 1985) — § 5-2(a)(6), n. 239

Herald Co. v. McNeal, 511 F. Supp. 269 (E.D. Miss. 1981) — § 2-3, n. 310

Herald Co. v. Murray, 524 N.Y.S. 2d 949 (App. Div. 1988) — § 11-7(d), n. 257

Herald Co. v. Weisenberg, 452 N.E.2d 1190 (N.Y. 1983) — § 9-4, n. 64

Herald Publ'g Co. v. Barnwell, 351 S.E.2d 878 (S.C. App. 1986) — § 9-6(g), n. 338

Herbert v. Lando, 441 U.S. 153 (1979) — § 14-5(b), nn. 131, 132, 135-39, 144; § 14-5(c), n. 148; § 15-2(d)(3)(D), n. 198; § 15-3(c), nn. 400-02; § 16-2(c)(2)(B), n. 156; § 16-2(d)(3)(C), n. 276

Herring v. Meachum, 11 F.3d 374 (2d Cir. 1993) — § 3-1(a), n. 25

Hestand v. Indiana, 273 N.E.2d 282 (Ind. 1971) — § 15-2(b)(2), n. 47

Hewitt v. Webster, 118 So. 2d 688 (La. App. 1960) — § 5-2(a)(3), n. 176

Hickman v. Taylor, 329 U.S. 495 (1947) — § 10-2(c)(6), n. 148; § 14-2, n. 32

Hill v. Wrather, 323 P.2d 567 (Cal. 1958) — § 13-8, n. 817

Hinds County Bd. of Supervisors v. Common Cause of Mississippi, 551 So. 2d 107 (Miss. 1989) — § 9-6(e), n. 316

HIP of New Jersey v. New Jersey Dep't of Banking & Ins., 707 A.2d 1044 (N.J. Super. 1998) — § 11-7(f)(2), n. 277

TABLE OF CASES

Hirschkop v. Snead, 594 F.2d 356 (4th Cir. 1979) — § 7-1, nn. 54, 71

Hitchcock v. Florida, 578 So. 2d 685 (Fla. 1990), *vacated*, 505 U.S. 1215 (1992) — § 2-1(b), n. 32

Hitt v. Mabry, 687 S.W.2d 791 (Tex. App. 1985) — § 9-6(c), n. 287

HLI Lordship Indus. v. Committee for Purchase from the Blind & Other Severely Handicapped, 615 F. Supp. 970 (E.D. Va. 1985), *rev'd on other grounds*, 791 F.2d 1136 (4th Cir. 1986) — § 9-5(b)(7), n. 246

Hogan v. Hearst Corp., 945 S.W.2d 246 (Tex. App. 1997) — § 13-3(a), nn. 90, 104

Hokanson v. High Sch. Dist., 589 P.2d 907 (Ariz. 1978) — § 9-6(f), n. 324

Holden v. Minnesota, 137 U.S. 483 (1890) — § 8-2, n. 80

Holland v. Eads, 614 So. 2d 1012 (Ala. 1993) — § 6-1(a)(5), n. 109

Holman v. Central Arkansas Broadcasting Co., 610 F.2d 542 (8th Cir. 1979) — § 12-6(b), nn. 389-91; § 13-7(a)(2)(A)(i), n. 594

Holmes v. Elias, 27 Media L. Rep. (BNA) 1031 (E.D. Pa. 1998) — § 6-1(b), nn. 166, 168, 171

Holmes v. Morales, 924 S.W.2d 920 (Tex. 1996) — § 11-3(a), n. 33; § 11-7(b)(3)(B), nn. 229, 230

Holmes v. Underwood & Underwood, 233 N.Y.S. 153 (App. Div. 1929) — § 12-2(a), n. 14

Home News Publ'g Co. v. New Jersey, 570 A.2d 1267 (N.J. Super. 1990) — § 11-4, n. 72

Home News v. New Jersey Dep't of Health, 677 A.2d 195 (N.J. 1996) — § 11-7(j), n. 309

Homsy v. King World Entertainment, Inc., 1997 Tex. App. LEXIS 761 (Tex. App. Feb. 6, 1997) — § 13-2(a), n. 6

Hone v. Cortland City Sch. Dist., 985 F. Supp. 262 (N.D.N.Y. 1997) — § 13-3(c)(2), nn. 196, 201

Honolulu Advertiser, Inc. v. Takao, 580 P.2d 58 (Haw. 1978) — § 5-2(a)(6), nn. 242, 248

Hoover v. Department of Interior, 611 F.2d 1132 (5th Cir. 1980) — § 10-2(c)(6), nn. 135, 138

Hopewell v. Midcontinent Broadcasting Corp., 538 N.W.2d 780 (S.D. 1995) — § 16-2(a)(2), n. 29

Hopkins v. HUD, 929 F.2d 81 (2d Cir. 1991) — § 10-2(c)(6), nn. 142, 143

Hopkinson v. Shillinger, 866 F.2d 1185 (10th Cir. 1989) — § 10-2(c)(8), n. 173; § 10-2(c)(8)(D), n. 206

Horm v. Florida, 298 So. 2d 194 (Fla. App. 1974) — § 13-7(b)(4)(E), nn. 732, 733

Horne v. Patton, 287 So. 2d 824 (Ala. 1973) — § 11-7(e), n. 266

Horton v. California, 496 U.S. 128 (1990) — § 12-4(a), n. 128

Hoskins v. Howard, 971 P.2d 1135 (Idaho 1998) — § 13-7(b)(1), n. 687; § 13-7(b)(4)(E), n. 735

Houchins v. KQED, Inc., 438 U.S. 1 (1978) — § 1-3, n. 43; § 1-4(b), n. 63; § 2-2(f), n. 267; § 8-1, nn. 31-51; § 8-3, n. 92; § 11-7(k), n. 338; § 12-2(a), n. 41; § 13-3(a), n. 98; § 14-4(a), n. 77; § 14-5(a), nn. 107, 111-14, 121, 122

Houghton v. Franscell, 870 P.2d 1050 (Wyo. 1994) — § 11-7(e), n. 266

Houman v. Mayor & Council, 382 A.2d 413 (N.J. Super. 1977) — § 9-6(g), nn. 338, 342

Houston Chronicle Publ'g Co. v. City of Houston, 531 S.W.2d 177 (Tex. App. 1975) — § 11-1, n. 2; § 11-7(b)(1), nn. 210-12; § 11-7(b)(2), n. 215; § 11-7(b)(7), n. 243

Houston Chronicle Publ'g Co. v. Crapitto, 907 S.W.2d 99 (Tex. App. 1995) — § 3-1(b), n. 221

TABLE OF CASES

Houston Chronicle Publ'g Co. v. McMaster, 598 S.W.2d 864 (Tex. Crim. App. 1980) — § 3-1(d), n. 324

Houston Chronicle Publ'g Co. v. Woods, 949 S.W.2d 492 (Tex. App. 1997) — § 5-2(a)(2), n. 126

Howard Publications, Inc. v. Lake Michigan Charters, Ltd., 649 N.E.2d 129 (Ind. App. 1995) — § 13-3(a), n. 122

Howard Publications, Inc. v. Lake Michigan Charters, Ltd., 658 N.E.2d 582 (Ind. 1995) — § 2-1(d), n. 86

Howard v. Savannah College of Art & Design, Inc., 387 S.E.2d 332 (Ga. 1990) — § 16-2(a)(2), n. 38

Howell v. New York Post Co., 612 N.E.2d 699 (N.Y. 1993) — § 12-4(b), nn. 202, 211-15; § 12-6(a), n. 384

Howell v. Tribune Entertainment Co., 106 F.3d 215 (7th Cir. 1997) — § 12-6(a), n. 376; § 13-3(b), n. 140

H.S. Gere & Sons v. Frey, 509 N.E.2d 271 (Mass. 1987) — § 6-1(b), n. 188

Hudson v. School Dist., 578 S.W.2d 301 (Mo. App. 1979) — § 9-6(h)(1), n. 346; § 9-6(i)(1)(C), n. 384

Huggins v. National Broadcasting Co., 1996 WL 763337 (N.Y. Sup. Ct. Feb. 7, 1996) — § 13-4(c), nn. 519, 525

Huggins v. Povitch, 24 Media L. Rep. (BNA) 2040 (N.Y. Sup. Ct. 1996) — § 13-4(c), nn. 519-25

Huggins v. Whitney, 24 Media L. Rep. (BNA) 1088 (N.Y. Sup. Ct. 1995) — § 13-4(c), nn. 519, 525

Humiston v. Universal Film Mfg. Co., 178 N.Y.S. 752 (App. Div. 1919) — § 12-2(b), n. 84

Hunerjager v. Dixie Elec. Membership Corp., 434 So. 2d 590 (La. App. 1983) — § 11-7(*l*), n. 340

Hunt v. CIA, 981 F.2d 1116 (9th Cir. 1992) — § 10-2(c)(4), n. 110

Hunt v. NRC, 611 F.2d 332 (10th Cir. 1979) — § 9-5(a)(2), nn. 84, 91; § 9-5(a)(3), n. 100

Hurley v. Irish-American Gay, Lesbian & Bisexual Group of Boston, 515 U.S. 557 (1995) — § 16-2(h)(2), n. 442

Huron Envtl. Activist League v. EPA, 917 F. Supp. 34 (D.D.C. 1996) — § 9-5(b)(2), n. 209

Hurst v. Georgia, 287 S.E.2d 677 (Ga. App. 1982) — § 16-3, n. 474

Huskey v. Dallas Chronicle, Inc., 13 Media L. Rep. (BNA) 1057 (D. Or. 1986) — § 12-6(b), n. 391

Huskey v. National Broadcasting Co., 632 F. Supp. 1282 (N.D. Ill. 1986) — § 12-6(b), nn. 387, 388; § 13-4(a)(1)(A), nn. 345-50; § 13-4(a)(2)(B), n. 382; § 13-4(a)(3)(A)(i), n. 444

Hustler Magazine, Inc. v. Falwell, 485 U.S. 46 (1988) — § 13-2(b), nn. 37, 73, 76; § 12-4(c)(2), n. 248; § 12-4(c)(3), n. 333; § 13-4(a)(2)(C), n. 412; § 13-4(a)(3)(A)(i), n. 430; § 13-4(a)(3)(B), n. 471

Hutchinson v. Luddy, 581 A.2d 578 (Pa. Super. 1990) — § 3-2(a), nn. 343, 358; § 6-1(c)(1), nn. 225-27

I

IBEW, Local 3 v. NLRB, 845 F.2d 1177 (2d Cir. 1988) — § 10-2(c)(7), n. 163

TABLE OF CASES

Idaho v. Salsbury, 924 P.2d 208 (Idaho 1996) — § 16-2(a)(2), n. 29; § 16-2(c)(1), n. 115; § 16-2(d)(3)(B), n. 239

Idaho v. Thompson, 760 P.2d 1162 (Idaho 1988) — § 16-2(j)(1), n. 457

Iglesias v. CIA, 525 F. Supp. 547 (D.D.C. 1981) — § 10-2(c)(4), n. 108

Illinois v. Abbott & Assocs., Inc., 460 U.S. 557 (1983) — § 3-1(a)(3), nn. 106, 111; § 5-2(a)(3), n. 153

Illinois Inst. for Continuing Legal Educ. v. Department of Labor, 545 F. Supp. 1229 (N.D. Ill. 1982) — § 10-2(b)(2), n. 30

In re a Minor, 537 N.E.2d 292 (Ill. 1989) — § 2-1(c), nn. 56, 64; § 3-3(b), n. 549

In re a Minor, 595 N.E.2d 1052 (Ill. 1992) — § 3-3(b), nn. 521, 547-56

In re ABC, Inc. (Hinckley), 537 F. Supp. 1168 (D.D.C. 1982) — § 5-2(b), n. 345

In re Access to Certain Records of Rhode Island Advisory Comm. on Code of Judicial Conduct, 637 A.2d 1063 (R.I. 1994) — § 6-1(d), n. 259

In re Agent Orange Prod. Liab. Litig., 821 F.2d 139 (2d Cir. 1987) — § 6-1(a)(1), n. 16; § 6-1(a)(3), nn. 55-57

In re Agent Orange Prod. Liab. Litig., 98 F.R.D. 539 (E.D.N.Y. 1983) — § 6-1(a)(4), n. 81; § 6-1(c)(1), n. 216

In re Alexander Grant & Co. Litig., 820 F.2d 352 (11th Cir. 1987) — § 6-1(a)(3), n. 46; § 6-1(a)(5), n. 119

In re Alvarez, 351 F. Supp. 1089 (S.D. Cal. 1972) — § 3-1(a)(3), n. 113

In re Am. Continental Corp. Litig., 18 Media L. Rep. (BNA) 2303 (D. Ariz. 1991) — § 6-1(a)(5), n. 120

In re Am. Gen. Life & Accident Ins. Co., 26 Media L. Rep. (BNA) 1606 (N.Y. Sup. Ct. 1996) — § 15-2(j), n. 326

In re Am. Tobacco Co., 880 F.2d 1520 (2d Cir. 1989) — § 6-1(a)(5), n. 119

In re Analytical Sys., 83 B.R. 833 (N.D. Ga. 1987) — § 6-1(b), n. 187

In re Application & Affidavit for a Search Warrant (Hughes), 923 F.2d 324 (4th Cir. 1991) — § 5-2(a)(2), nn. 120, 127, 132

In re Application for News Media Coverage in the Matter of M.S., 662 N.Y.S.2d 207 (Fam. Ct. 1997) — § 3-3(a), n. 499; § 3-3(b), n. 518

In re Application of Dow Jones & Co., 842 F.2d 603 (2d Cir. 1988) — § 2-1(a), n. 2

In re Application of NBC, Inc., 828 F.2d 340 (6th Cir. 1987) — § 5-2(a), nn. 55, 56

In re Application of New York 1 News & CBS Inc., 22 Media L. Rep. (BNA) 1406 (S.D.N.Y. 1994) — § 5-2(a)(5), n. 223

In re Armstrong, 26 Media L. Rep. (BNA) 1700 (N.Y. Sup. Ct. 1997) — § 15-2(d)(3)(C), n. 188; § 15-2(e)(2)(B), nn. 242, 247

In re Arya, 589 N.E.2d 832 (Ill. App. 1992) — § 15-2(e)(2)(B), n. 244; § 15-2(i)(1), n. 293

In re Asbestos Prods. Liab. Litig., 19 Media L. Rep. (BNA) 1220 (E.D. Pa. 1991) — § 3-2(d), nn. 412-14

In re Associated Press, 162 F.3d 503 (7th Cir. 1998) — § 2-3, nn. 304, 312; § 5-1, n. 35; § 5-2(a)(5), nn. 223, 227; § 5-2(b), n. 358

In re Avila, 501 A.2d 1018 (N.J. Super. 1985) — § 15-2(b)(1), n. 45

In re Baldwin-United Corp., 770 F.2d 328 (2d Cir. 1985) — § 6-1(b), n. 169

In re Baltimore Sun Co. (Goetz), 886 F.2d 60 (4th Cir. 1989) — § 5-2(a)(2), nn. 119-26

In re Baltimore Sun Co., 841 F.2d 74 (4th Cir. 1988) — § 5-2(c), nn. 375-80

In re Biaggi, 478 F.2d 489 (2d Cir. 1973) — § 5-2(a)(3), nn. 136, 157, 162

In re Brand Name Prescription Drug Antitrust Litig., 1996 U.S. Dist. LEXIS 9838 (N.D. Ill. July 9, 1996) — § 6-1(a)(4), n. 81

TABLE OF CASES

In re Bridge, 295 A.2d 3 (N.J. Super. 1972) — § 15-1, n. 17; § 15-2(h), n. 270

In re Brown & Williamson Tobacco Corp., 24 Media L. Rep. (BNA) 1720 (N.Y. Sup. Ct. 1996) — § 15-2(c)(2)(A), n. 87; § 15-2(e)(2)(B), n. 242

In re Brown, 18 Media L. Rep. (BNA) 1460 (Fla. County Ct. 1990) — § 3-3(a), n. 459; § 3-3(b), n. 514

In re Buentipo, 26 Media L. Rep. (BNA) 1888 (Haw. Fam. Ct. 1997) — § 6-2(b), nn. 298-303

In re Buffalo News, 969 F. Supp. 869 (W.D.N.Y. 1997) — § 5-2(a)(2), n. 129

In re Burnett, 635 A.2d 1019 (N.J. Super. 1993) — § 15-2(b)(1), n. 44

In re Burns, 484 So. 2d 658 (La. 1986) — § 15-2(c)(1), n. 58; § 15-2(d)(1), nn. 146, 147

In re Caldwell, 311 F. Supp. 358 (N.D. Cal. 1970), rev'd, Caldwell v. United States, 434 F.2d 1081 (9th Cir. 1970), rev'd sub nom. Branzburg v. Hayes, 408 U.S. 665 (1972) — § 14-3, n. 44

In re Capital Cities/ABC, Inc.'s Application for Access to Sealed Transcripts, 913 F.2d 89 (3d Cir. 1990) — § 5-2(a)(3), nn. 166, 172, 179, 187

In re CBS Inc., 23 Media L. Rep. (BNA) 2311 (N.Y. Sup. Ct. 1995) — § 15-2(e)(2)(B), n. 242

In re CBS Inc. (Salerno), 828 F.2d 958 (2d Cir. 1987) — § 5-2(b), nn. 324, 344

In re CBS Inc. (Shannon), 540 F. Supp. 769 (N.D. Ill. 1982) — § 5-2(a)(8), n. 273; § 5-2(b), n. 319

In re Charlotte Observer, 882 F.2d 850 (4th Cir. 1989) — § 3-1(a), nn. 49-53, 55-57, 61; § 3-1(d), n. 314; § 5-2(a), n. 52

In re Charlotte Observer, 921 F.2d 47 (4th Cir. 1990) — § 2-1(d), n. 98; § 3-1(a)(3), n. 116

In re Cincinnati Enquirer, 94 F.3d 198 (6th Cir. 1996) — § 3-2(d), nn. 406-11

In re Closure of Jury Voir Dire, 516 N.W.2d 514 (Mich. App. 1994) — § 3-1(b), n. 252

In re Closure of Preliminary Examination, 505 N.W.2d 24 (Mich. App. 1993) — § 3-1(a), nn. 58, 60; § 3-1(a)(2), n. 103

In re Codey, 626 N.E.2d 636 (N.Y. 1993) — § 16-2(i), n. 451

In re Consumers Power Co. Sec. Litig., 109 F.R.D. 45 (E.D. Mich. 1985) — § 3-1(a), n. 10

In re Consumers Union, 495 F. Supp. 582 (S.D.N.Y. 1980) — § 16-2(c)(2)(A), n. 137; § 16-2(d)(3), n. 211; § 16-2(d)(3)(C), n. 275; § 16-2(d)(3)(D), nn. 281, 287; § 16-2(e)(2), n. 323

In re Contempt of Stone, 397 N.W.2d 244 (Mich. App. 1986) — § 15-2(a), n. 26; § 15-2(b)(1), n. 34; § 15-2(c)(1), n. 59; § 16-2(a)(2), n. 38; § 16-2(c)(1), n. 82

In re Continental Illinois Sec. Litig., 732 F.2d 1302 (7th Cir. 1984) — § 3-1(a), n. 31; § 3-2(c), n. 403; § 6-1(a)(4), nn. 61, 88; § 6-1(a)(5), n. 120; § 6-1(c)(1), n. 211; § 6-1(c)(2), nn. 228, 235-38

In re Coordinated Pretrial Proceedings in Petroleum Prods. Antitrust Litig., 101 F.R.D. 34 (C.D. Cal. 1984) — § 6-1(a)(1), n. 15; § 6-1(c)(1), nn. 211, 220, 221; § 6-1(c)(2), n. 228

In re Cusumano, 162 F.3d 708 (1st Cir. 1998) — § 15-3(c), n. 403; § 16-2(a)(1), n. 2; § 16-2(b)(1), n. 60; § 16-2(c)(2)(A), n. 137; § 16-2(d)(1), n. 177; § 16-2(d)(2), nn. 207-09; § 16-2(e)(1), n. 306; § 16-2(h), n. 393

In re D.R., 624 N.E.2d 1120 (Ohio County Ct. 1993) — § 3-3(a), n. 490

In re Daily Item, 456 A.2d 580 (Pa. Super. 1983) — § 3-1(c), n. 300

In re Dallas Morning News Co., 916 F.2d 205 (5th Cir. 1990) — § 3-1(b), nn. 220, 221; § 5-2(c), n. 373

TABLE OF CASES

In re Decker, 471 S.E.2d 462 (S.C. 1995) — § 15-2(c)(1), n. 61

In re Detention of D.A.H., 924 P.2d 49 (Wash. App. 1996) — § 3-1(a)(2), n. 96; § 3-2(b), n. 374

In re Detention of Hendrickson, 25 Media L. Rep. (BNA) 1543 (Wash. Super. 1996) — § 3-2(b), n. 374

In re Detroit Free Press, 11 Media L. Rep. (BNA) 1368 (Mich. App. 1985) — § 7-3, n. 187

In re Dickson, 3 F.C.C.R. 2595 (1988) — § 13-7(a)(2)(C), n. 668

In re Disclosure of Juror Names & Addresses, 592 N.W.2d 798 (Mich. App. 1999) — § 5-2(c), nn. 388, 394; § 7-3, n. 187

In re Donovan, 801 F.2d 409 (D.C. Cir. 1986) — § 5-2(a)(3), n. 136

In re Dow Jones & Co. v. Simon, 488 U.S. 946 (1988) — § 7-1, n. 81

In re Dow Jones & Co., 142 F.3d 496 (D.C. Cir. 1998) — § 3-1(a)(3), nn. 119-21, 124, 125, 128, 130, 131, 133, 134, 142, 144-47; § 5-2(a)(3), nn. 177, 180, 181, 184, 187, 192, 199, 200

In re Dow Jones & Co., 27 Media L. Rep. (BNA) 1307 (S.D.N.Y. 1998), *vacated*, No. 99-7014 (2d Cir. June 8, 1999) — § 14-6(a), n. 249; § 16-2(c)(2)(A), n. 142; § 16-2(d)(3), n. 223; § 16-3, n. 474

In re Dow Jones & Co., 842 F.2d 603 (2d Cir. 1988) — § 2-3, n. 310; § 7-1, nn. 20, 27-36, 78

In re du Pont, 25 Media L. Rep. (BNA) 2436 (Del. Ch. 1997) — § 6-1(c), nn. 204, 208, 209

In re Eisenberg, 654 F.2d 1107 (5th Cir. 1981) — § 3-1(a)(3), n. 113

In re Estate of Zimmer, 442 N.W.2d 578 (Wis. App. 1989) — § 6-1(b), nn. 163, 186

In re Express-News Corp., 695 F.2d 807 (5th Cir. 1982) — § 7-3, nn. 153-58

In re Farber, 394 A.2d 330 (N.J. 1978) — § 15-2(a), n. 24; § 15-2(c)(1), nn. 65-69; § 15-2(c)(2)(B), n. 120; § 15-2(e)(1), n. 223; § 15-2(i)(2), nn. 301, 304; § 16-2(a)(2), n. 38; § 16-2(f), n. 377

In re Ford Motor Co. Bronco II Prods. Liab. Litig. (Ford I), 1995 U.S. Dist. LEXIS 15867 (E.D. La. Oct. 28, 1994) — § 6-1(b), n. 182

In re Ford Motor Co. Bronco II Prods. Liab. Litig. (Ford II), 1995 U.S. Dist. LEXIS 5672 (E.D. La. Apr. 12, 1995) — § 6-1(b), nn. 182-84

In re Ford Motor Co. Bronco II Prods. Liab. Litig. (Ford III), 1995 U.S. Dist. LEXIS 8298 (E.D. La. June 9, 1995) — § 6-1(b), nn. 182-84

In re Four Search Warrants, 945 F. Supp. 1563 (N.D. Ga. 1996) — § 5-2(a)(2), nn. 109, 122

In re Gannett News Serv., 772 F.2d 113 (5th Cir. 1985) — § 5-2(a)(5), n. 223

In re Gannett River States Publ'g Corp., 27 Media L. Rep. (BNA) 1096 (Miss. 1998) — § 2-3, n. 301

In re Gannett River States Publ'g Corp., 630 So. 2d 351 (Miss. 1994) — § 2-3, nn. 291, 296; § 3-1(b), n. 253

In re Gault, 387 U.S. 1 (1967) — § 3-3(a), nn. 432, 433

In re Glens Falls Newspapers, Inc., 614 N.Y.S.2d 628 (App. Div. 1994) — § 2-3, n. 291

In re Globe Newspaper Co. (Hurley), 920 F.2d 88 (1st Cir. 1990) — § 5-2(c), nn. 381-92; § 7-3, n. 160

In re Globe Newspaper Co., 729 F.2d 47 (1st Cir. 1984) — § 2-3, nn. 293, 308; § 3-1(a)(1), nn. 67, 71-83; § 5-1, n. 24; § 5-2(a)(1), nn. 85, 92-95; § 5-2(a)(7), nn. 257, 259; § 5-2(a)(8), nn. 268, 269; § 5-2(b), n. 296

TABLE OF CASES

In re Goodfader's Appeal, 367 P.2d 472 (Haw. 1961) — § 14-2, nn. 20, 32; § 16-2(a)(2), n. 40; § 16-3, n. 474

In re Goodwin v. United Kingdom, No. 16/1994/463/544 (Mar. 27, 1996) — § 14-1, n. 1

In re Grand Jury, 103 F.3d 1140 (3d Cir. 1997) — § 5-2(a)(3), n. 195

In re Grand Jury 95-1, 27 Media L. Rep. (BNA) 1833 (D.D.C. 1999) — § 14-6(b), n. 265; § 15-3(b), n. 372; § 15-3(c), n. 386; § 16-2(a)(1), n. 23; § 16-2(c)(1), n. 82

In re Grand Jury Empaneled March 8, 1983, 579 F. Supp. 189 (E.D. Tenn. 1984) — § 3-1(a)(3), n. 130; § 5-2(a)(3), n. 181

In re Grand Jury Investigation, 600 F.2d 420 (3d Cir. 1979) — § 16-2(f), n. 373

In re Grand Jury Investigation, 610 F.2d 202 (5th Cir. 1980) — § 3-1(a)(3), nn. 119, 120, 139; § 5-2(a)(3), n. 137

In re Grand Jury Investigation, 15 Media L. Rep. (BNA) 1469 (Ill. Cir. 1988) — § 15-2(b)(1), n. 43

In re Grand Jury Investigation (90-3-2), 748 F. Supp. 1188 (E.D. Mich. 1990) — § 3-1(a)(3), nn. 113, 139; § 5-2(a)(3), n. 186

In re Grand Jury Investigation, 580 N.E.2d 868 (Ohio C.P. 1991) — § 5-2(a)(3), n. 164

In re Grand Jury Investigation (Lance v. Dep't of Justice), 610 F.2d 202 (5th Cir. 1980) — § 5-2(a)(3), n. 186

In re Grand Jury Investigation (New Jersey State Comm'n), 630 F.2d 996 (3d Cir. 1980) — § 5-2(a)(3), n. 151

In re Grand Jury Investigation of Cerro Maravilla Events, 783 F.2d 20 (1st Cir. 1986) — § 5-2(a)(3), n. 151

In re Grand Jury Matter (Catania), 682 F.2d 61 (3d Cir. 1982) — § 5-2(a)(3), nn. 137, 155

In re Grand Jury Proceeding, 955 F.2d 229 (4th Cir. 1992) — § 16-2(c)(1), n. 82

In re Grand Jury Proceedings (Freeman), 708 F.2d 1571 (11th Cir. 1983) — § 2-3, n. 304

In re Grand Jury Proceedings (Kluger), 827 F.2d 868 (2d Cir. 1987) — § 5-2(a)(3), n. 151

In re Grand Jury Proceedings (Ridenhour), 520 So. 2d 372 (La. 1988) — § 15-2(c)(1), n. 62; § 15-2(d)(1), n. 143; § 15-2(d)(3)(C), nn. 189, 190; § 15-2(e)(2)(C), n. 254; § 16-2(a)(2), nn. 29, 32; § 16-2(c)(1), n. 87

In re Grand Jury Proceedings, 5 F.3d 397 (9th Cir. 1993) — § 16-2(a)(1), nn. 2, 25; § 16-2(b)(1), n. 63; § 16-2(c)(1), nn. 82, 85, 86, 102

In re Grand Jury Proceedings, 800 F.2d 1293 (4th Cir. 1986) — § 5-2(a)(3), n. 165

In re Grand Jury Proceedings, 810 F.2d 580 (6th Cir. 1987) — § 14-6(b), nn. 259-65; § 15-2(a), n. 26; § 15-2(i)(3), n. 315; § 16-2(a)(1), nn. 3, 4; § 16-2(c)(1), nn. 82-84; § 16-2(e)(1), nn. 310, 311; § 16-2(e)(4), n. 359; § 16-2(h)(2), nn. 420, 422

In re Grand Jury Proceedings, 851 F.2d 860 (6th Cir. 1988) — § 5-2(a)(3), n. 137

In re Grand Jury Proceedings, 867 F.2d 562 (9th Cir. 1989) — § 15-2(j), n. 325

In re Grand Jury Proceedings, 914 F.2d 1372 (9th Cir. 1990) — § 3-1(a)(3), n. 120

In re Grand Jury Proceedings, 942 F.2d 1195 (7th Cir. 1991) — § 5-2(a)(3), n. 135

In re Grand Jury Subpoena, 5 Media L. Rep. (BNA) 1153 (Tex. Dist. 1979) — § 16-2(c)(1), n. 87

In re Grand Jury Subpoena, 750 F.2d 223 (2d Cir. 1984) — § 16-2(b)(1), n. 63; § 16-2(c)(1), n. 87

In re Grand Jury Subpoena, 955 F.2d 229 (4th Cir. 1992) — § 16-2(a)(1), n. 2; § 16-2(b)(1), n. 71

TABLE OF CASES

In re Grand Jury Subpoena, 947 F. Supp. 1314 (E.D. Ark. 1996) — § 14-6(b), n. 265; § 15-2(c), n. 55; § 15-2(j), n. 325; § 15-3(b), n. 374; § 15-2(c)(1), n. 62; § 16-2(a)(1), nn. 22, 23; § 16-2(c)(1), n. 82

In re Grand Jury Subpoena, 103 F.3d 234 (2d Cir. 1996) — § 5-2(a)(1), n. 100

In re Grand Jury Subpoena (Doe No. 4 v. Doe No. 1), 103 F.3d 234 (2d Cir. 1996) — § 3-1(a)(3), nn. 114, 129, 130, 132, 143, 134-36, 138-41; § 5-2(a)(3), nn. 181, 186, 188, 193, 194

In re Grand Jury Subpoena Duces Tecum, 797 F.2d 676 (8th Cir. 1986) — § 3-1(a)(3), n. 114

In re Grand Jury Subpoena (Under Seal), 920 F.2d 235 (4th Cir. 1990) — § 5-2(a)(3), n. 137

In re Grand Jury Subpoenas, 8 Media L. Rep. (BNA) 1418 (D. Colo. 1982) — § 16-2(a)(2), n. 29; § 16-2(c)(1), nn. 87, 89, 90

In re Grand Jury Summoned Oct. 12, 1970, 321 F. Supp. 238 (N.D. Ohio 1970) — § 3-1(a)(3), nn. 113, 114

In re Grand Jury Testimony, 832 F.2d 60 (5th Cir. 1987) — § 5-2(a)(3), n. 150

In re Grand Jury Witness Subpoena of Abraham, 634 N.E.2d 667 (Ohio App. 1993) — § 16-2(a)(2), n. 47; § 16-2(c)(1), n. 82

In re Grand Jury Witnesses, 322 F. Supp. 573 (N.D. Cal. 1970) — § 14-2, n. 33; § 14-3, n. 40

In re Greensboro News Co., 727 F.2d 1320 (4th Cir. 1984) — § 3-1(b), nn. 231, 232, 237

In re Greenville News Co., 505 S.E.2d 340 (S.C. 1998) — § 3-1(a)(4), n. 171

In re Gronowicz, 764 F.2d 983 (3d Cir. 1985) — § 16-2(a)(1), n. 2; § 16-2(b)(1), nn. 71, 72; § 16-2(c)(1), nn. 124, 125; § 16-2(d)(3)(A), n. 232; § 16-2(d)(3)(C), n. 252; § 16-2(f), n. 377

In re Grunow, 85 A. 1011 (N.J. 1936) — § 14-1, n. 8

In re Guess?, Inc., 17 Media L. Rep. (BNA) 1313 (N.Y. Sup. Ct. 1989) — § 15-2(h), n. 290

In re Guidelines for Experimental Use of Cameras in Utah S. Ct., 911 P.2d 978 (Utah 1995) — § 4-3, n. 99

In re Hadenguest, 5 Media L. Rep. (BNA) 2361 (N.Y. Sup. Ct. 1980) — § 15-2(b)(1), n. 40; § 15-2(d)(3)(E), n. 207; § 15-2(h), n. 287

In re Halkin, 598 F.2d 176 (D.C. Cir. 1979) — § 6-1(a)(2), n. 31

In re Hattiesburg Am., 26 Media L. Rep. (BNA) 2183 (Miss. 1998) — § 7-1, n. 82

In re Hearst Estate, 136 Cal. Rptr. 821 (Ct. App. 1977) — § 11-1, n. 2; § 11-3(c), n. 47

In re Herald Co. (Klepfer), 734 F.2d 93 (2d Cir. 1984) — § 2-3, nn. 293, 297; § 3-1(a), nn. 28, 36, 40; § 3-1(a)(4), nn. 160, 166, 167

In re Hinds, 449 A.2d 483 (N.J. 1982) — § 2-1(c), nn. 40, 41; § 7-2, n. 103

In re Hughes County Action, 452 N.W.2d 128 (S.D. 1990) — § 3-3(a), n. 486

In re Indianapolis Newspapers Inc., 837 F. Supp. 956 (S.D. Ind. 1992) — § 5-2(c), n. 394

In re Investigation Before April 1975 Grand Jury, 531 F.2d 600 (D.C. Cir. 1976) — § 3-1(a)(3), n. 113

In re Iowa Freedom of Info. Council, 724 F.2d 658 (8th Cir. 1983) — § 2-2(d), n. 220; § 3-1(d), n. 314; § 3-2(c), nn. 392-401; § 6-1(c)(2), n. 229

In re J.D.C, 594 A.2d 70 (D.C. 1991) — § 3-3(a), nn. 507-11

In re J.S., 438 A.2d 1125 (Vt. 1981) — § 3-3(a), nn. 434, 436, 437, 444, 472-74

In re J.S., 640 N.E.2d 1379 (Ill. App. 1994) — § 7-1, n. 82

In re Joanne M., 659 N.E.2d 864 (Ohio App. 1995) — § 3-3(b), n. 536

TABLE OF CASES

In re John Doe Grand Jury Investigation, 574 N.E.2d 373 (Mass. 1991) — § 16-3, nn. 483-85
In re Johnson, 461 N.W.2d 767 (S.D. 1990) — § 6-1(b), n. 185
In re Johnson, 598 N.E.2d 406 (Ill. App. 1992) — § 6-1(a)(4), n. 67; § 6-1(c)(1), n. 216; § 6-1(c)(2), n. 228
In re Johnson, 632 A.2d 539 (N.J. App. 1993) — § 2-1(d), n. 86
In re K.F., 559 A.2d 663 (Vt. 1989) — § 3-3(a), n. 473
In re Kaczynski, 24 Media L. Rep. (BNA) 1700 (D. Mont. 1996) — § 5-2(a)(2), nn. 128, 129, 132
In re Kansas City Star Co., 143 F.R.D. 223 (W.D. Mo. 1992) — § 5-2(a)(4), n. 201
In re Kansas City Star Co., 666 F.2d 1168 (8th Cir. 1981) — § 5-2(a)(1), n. 91
In re Katherine B., 596 N.Y.S.2d 847 (App. Div. 1993) — § 3-3(b), n. 513
In re King World Productions, Inc., 898 F.2d 56 (6th Cir. 1990) — § 2-1(d), n. 98; § 13-2(b), nn. 39-44; § 13-3(a), n. 122; § 13-7(a)(2)(A)(iv), nn. 644-46; § 13-8, nn. 794-97
In re Knight Publ'g Co., 743 F.2d 231 (4th Cir. 1984) — § 2-3, nn. 295, 299, 312; § 3-1(a)(6), n. 206; § 5-2(a)(2), nn. 124, 125; § 6-1(a)(4), n. 84
In re Knoxville News-Sentinel Co., 723 F.2d 470 (6th Cir. 1983) — § 6-1(c), n. 189
In re Letellier, 578 A.2d 722 (Me. 1990) — § 16-2(a)(2), n. 29; § 16-2(d)(3)(C), n. 249
In re Lewis, 25 Media L. Rep. (BNA) 2179 (Fla. Cir. 1997) — § 6-2(a), nn. 272, 273
In re Lewis, 377 F. Supp. 297 (C.D. Cal. 1974) — § 15-3(b), n. 372
In re Lewis, 384 F. Supp. 133 (C.D. Cal. 1974) — § 15-3(b), n. 372
In re Lewis, 517 F.2d 236 (9th Cir. 1975) — § 16-2(c)(1), nn. 82, 86
In re Lifetime Cable, 17 Media L. Rep. (BNA) 1648 (D.C. Cir. 1990) — § 2-1(d), n. 98
In re M.C., 527 N.W.2d 290 (S.D. 1995) — § 3-3(a), nn. 488, 489
In re Macon Tel. Publ'g Co., 900 F. Supp. 489 (M.D. Ga. 1995) — § 5-2(a)(2), n. 122
In re Madden, 151 F.3d 125 (3d Cir. 1998) — § 16-2(b)(1), nn. 60, 65; § 16-2(b)(2), nn. 79-81; § 16-2(h)(2), n. 416; § 16-2(i), n. 445
In re Magrino, 640 N.Y.S.2d 545 (App. Div. 1996) — § 15-2(j), nn. 329, 330
In re Marcovitz Children, 22 Media L. Rep. (BNA) 1031 (N.Y. County Ct. 1992) — § 3-3(b), n. 513
In re Marriage of Johnson, 598 N.E.2d 406 (Ill. App. 1992) — § 6-1(b), nn. 185, 187
In re Marriage of Lechowick, 77 Cal. Rptr. 2d 395 (Ct. App. 1998) — § 3-2(b), n. 374; § 6-1(c), nn. 204, 207
In re Marriage of Purcell, 879 P.2d 468 (Colo. App. 1994) — § 6-1(b), n. 187
In re Maxfield, 945 P.2d 196 (Wash. 1997) — § 11-7(*l*), n. 340
In re McAuley, 408 N.E.2d 697 (Ohio App. 1979) — § 15-2(c)(1), nn. 80-86; § 15-2(c)(2)(B), n. 109; § 15-2(e)(1), n. 219; § 15-2(e)(2), n. 232; § 15-2(i)(2), n. 305; § 15-2(j), nn. 334, 335; § 16-2(a)(2), n. 46; § 16-2(i), n. 451
In re Medical Laboratory Management Consultants, 931 F. Supp. 1487 (D. Ariz. 1996) — § 13-8, n. 818
In re Memphis Publ'g Co., 887 F.2d 646 (6th Cir. 1989) — § 7-3, n. 186
In re Meyer, 25 Media L. Rep. (BNA) 2244 (Colo. Dist. 1997) — § 11-7(d), n. 260
In re Modification of the Code of Judicial Conduct Relating to Broadcasting and Photographing Ct. Proceedings, 628 S.W.2d 573 (Ark. 1982) — § 4-3, n. 92
In re Morrissey, 168 F.3d 134 (4th Cir. 1999) — § 7-2, n. 130
In re Motion of Atlanta Journal-Constitution, 502 S.E.2d 720 (Ga. 1998) — § 2-3, n. 305
In re Multicounty Grand Jury Proceedings, 847 P.2d 812 (Okla. Crim. App. 1993) — § 7-3, n. 188
In re Murphy, 560 F.2d 326 (8th Cir. 1977) — § 10-2(c)(6), n. 151

TABLE OF CASES

In re NASDAQ Market-Makers Antitrust Litig., 164 F.R.D. 346 (S.D.N.Y. 1996) — § 6-1(a)(5), n. 107

In re National Broadcasting Co. (Criden), 648 F.2d 814 (3d Cir. 1981) — § 5-2(b), nn. 306, 311-18; § 5-2(c), n. 369; § 6-1(a)(4), n. 74; § 6-1(b), n. 161; § 6-1(c)(2), n. 240

In re National Broadcasting Co. (Jenrette), 653 F.2d 609 (D.C. Cir 1981) — § 5-2(a)(8), n. 273; § 5-2(b), nn. 305, 307-10

In re National Broadcasting Co., (Myers) 635 F.2d 945 (2d Cir. 1980) — § 3-1(a), n. 54; § 5-2(a)(8), n. 273; § 5-2(b), nn. 300-04

In re National Broadcasting Co., 681 F.2d 919 (3d Cir. 1982) — § 5-2(b), n. 318

In re NBC Subsidiary (NBC-TV), Inc. v. Superior Ct., 980 P.2d 337 (Cal. 1999) - Preface, n. 3

In re New York Times Co., 828 F.2d 110 (2d Cir. 1987) — § 2-3, n. 299; § 3-1(a)(1), n. 85; § 5-1, n. 24; § 5-2(a)(1), nn. 82, 96-99; § 5-2(a)(7), nn. 251-54

In re New York Times Co., 834 F.2d 1152 (2d Cir. 1987) — § 5-2(a)(1), n. 99; § 5-2(a)(2), n. 129; § 5-2(a)(7), nn. 255, 257

In re New York Times Co., 878 F.2d 67 (2d Cir. 1989) — § 7-1, n. 36

In re New York Times Co., 9 Media L. Rep. (BNA) 2077 (N.D. Ga. 1983) — § 5-2(a)(4), n. 203

In re Newsday, Inc., 895 F.2d 74 (2d Cir. 1990) — § 5-2(a)(1), n. 102; § 5-2(a)(2), nn. 108, 121, 131

In re N.H., 626 N.E.2d 697 (Ohio C.P. 1992) — § 3-3(a), nn. 440, 490

In re N.H.B., 769 P.2d 844 (Utah App. 1989) — § 3-3(a), nn. 437, 444, 459; § 3-3(b), n. 526

In re Nogues, 22 Media L. Rep. (BNA) 1932 (Fla. County Ct. 1994) — § 3-3(b), n. 514

In re North, 16 F.3d 1234 (D.C. Cir. 1994) — § 6-1(d), n. 260; § 3-1(a)(3), nn. 109, 118; § 5-2(a)(3), nn. 137, 166, 197

In re Office Suites for World & Islam Studies Enter., 925 F. Supp. 738 (M.D. Fla. 1996) — § 5-2(a)(2), n. 122

In re Oliver, 333 U.S. 257 (1948) — § 2-2(a), n. 110; § 2-2(b), n. 135

In re Oliver, 452 F.2d 111 (7th Cir. 1971) — § 7-1, n. 54

In re Oneonta Star Div. of Ottaway Newspapers, Inc. v. Mogavero, 434 N.Y.S.2d 781 (App. Div. 1980) — § 2-3, n. 313

In re Orion Pictures Corp., 21 F.3d 24 (2d Cir. 1994) — § 6-1(a)(5), n. 112

In re Owens, 496 S.E.2d 592 (N.C. App. 1998) — § 14-6(b), n. 265; § 16-2(d)(3), n. 210; § 16-2(d)(3)(A), n. 232; § 16-2(d)(3)(C), n. 248; § 16-2(f), n. 367

In re Pac. & S. Co., 361 S.E.2d 159 (Ga. 1987) — § 5-2(b), n. 338

In re Pan Am Corp., 161 Bankr. 577 (S.D.N.Y. 1993) —§ 16-2(b)(1), n. 69; § 16-2(c)(2)(A), n. 139; § 16-2(d)(3)(C), n. 272; § 16-2(e)(2), n. 319; § 16-2(e)(3), nn. 332, 333; § 16-2(f), nn. 369, 378; § 16-2(h)(2), nn. 419, 442

In re Pappas, 266 N.E.2d 297 (Mass. 1971) — § 14-3, nn. 39, 49-54; § 16-2(a)(2), n. 43; § 16-2(c)(1), n. 82

In re Paul, 513 S.E.2d 219 (Ga. 1999) — § 15-2(c)(1), n. 74; § 15-2(d)(1), nn. 143, 149; § 15-2(d)(3)(C), n. 188; § 15-2(e)(2)(A), n. 239; § 15-2(e)(2)(B), n. 242; § 15-2(i)(3), n. 315

In re Permitting of Media Coverage for an Indefinite Period, 539 A.2d 976 (R.I. 1988) — § 4-2(b), n. 83; § 4-3, n. 98

In re Perrigo Co., 128 F.3d 430 (6th Cir. 1997) — § 6-1(a)(4), n. 62

TABLE OF CASES

In re Petition of Am. Historical Assoc., 49 F. Supp. 2d 274 (S.D.N.Y. 1999) — § 5-2(a)(3), n. 163

In re Petition of Arkansas Bar Ass'n, 609 S.W.2d 28 (Ark. 1980) — § 4-3, nn. 99, 109

In re Petition of Craig, 131 F.3d 99 (2d Cir. 1997) — § 5-2(a)(3), nn. 158, 160, 163

In re Petition of Post-Newsweek Stations, Fla., Inc., 370 So. 2d 764 (Fla. 1979) — § 4-1, n. 30; § 4-3, nn. 92, 101, 109, 111

In re Petroleum Prods. Antitrust Litig., 680 F.2d 5 (2d Cir. 1982) — § 14-6(a), nn. 237, 253; § 16-2(a)(1), nn. 2, 16; § 16-2(c)(2)(A), n. 137; § 16-2(d)(1), nn. 177, 185-87; § 16-2(d)(3), nn. 217, 223; § 16-2(e)(1), nn. 296, 298; § 16-2(e)(2), n. 316; § 16-2(e)(3), nn. 332, 333; § 16-2(f), n. 378

In re Philadelphia Newspapers, Inc. (Martin), 746 F.2d 964 (3d Cir. 1984) — § 5-2(b), nn. 340-42

In re Photo Mktg. Ass'n Int'l, 327 N.W.2d 515 (Mich. App. 1982) — § 16-2(a)(2), n. 29

In re Policy Management Sys. Corp., 67 F.3d 296, 23 Media L. Rep. (BNA) 2486 (4th Cir. 1995) — § 6-1(a)(4), nn. 62, 71, 81, 89-93

In re Polypropylene Carpet Antitrust Litig., 181 F.R.D. 680 (N.D. Ga. 1998) — § 5-2(a)(3), n. 173

In re Presha, 677 A.2d 806 (N.J. Super. 1996) — § 3-3(a), n. 478

In re Providence Journal Co., 820 F.2d 1342 (1st Cir. 1986), *modified*, 820 F.2d 1354 (1st Cir. 1987) — § 2-1(d), n. 109; § 13-7(a)(1), n. 583; § 13-7(a)(2)(A)(i), n. 599

In re Quinn, 517 N.W.2d 895 (Minn. 1994) — § 11-7(b)(3)(B), n. 229

In re Ramaekers, 33 F. Supp. 2d 312 (S.D.N.Y. 1999) — § 14-6(a), n. 249; § 16-2(d)(3), n. 223; § 16-2(d)(3)(C), n. 263; § 16-2(i), nn. 444, 445

In re Reporters Comm. for Freedom of the Press, 773 F.2d 1325 (D.C. Cir. 1985) — § 3-2(e), n. 419; § 6-1(a)(3), nn. 46, 54; § 6-1(c)(1), n. 211

In re Reuben R., 641 N.Y.S.2d 621 (Sup. Ct. 1996) — § 3-3(b), n. 513

In re Richmond Newspapers, Inc., 16 Media L. Rep. (BNA) 1049 (Va. App. 1988) — § 6-2(a), n. 280; § 6-2(b), nn. 290, 294, 295

In re Robert Grace, 634 N.Y.S.2d 473 (App. Div. 1995) — § 15-2(j), n. 330

In re Roche, 411 N.E.2d 466 (Mass. 1980) — § 16-2(d)(1), n. 177; § 16-2(h)(2), n. 416; § 16-3, n. 485

In re Roche, 448 U.S. 1312 (1980) — § 14-5(f), nn. 213-18; § 16-2(e)(3), n. 332

In re Roche, 589 So. 2d 978 (Fla. App. 1991) — § 16-2(c)(2)(A), nn. 150, 151

In re Russell, 726 F.2d 1007 (4th Cir. 1984) — § 7-1, nn. 68-70; § 7-2, n. 139

In re Russo, 53 F.R.D. 564 (C.D. Cal. 1971) — § 3-1(a)(3), nn. 113, 115; § 5-2(a)(3), n. 143

In re San Juan Star Co., 662 F.2d 108 (1st Cir. 1981) — § 6-1(a)(2), n. 31; § 7-2, n. 139

In re Savitt/Adler Litig., 1997 WL 797511 (N.D.N.Y. Dec. 23, 1997), *modified*, 26 Media L. Rep. (BNA) 1882 (N.D.N.Y. 1998) — § 6-1(a)(4), n. 85; § 6-1(a)(5), nn. 104, 107, 108, 119; § 6-1(c)(1), n. 218

In re Sawyer, 360 U.S. 622 (1959) — § 7-2, n. 88

In re Schuman, 552 A.2d 602 (N.J. 1989) — § 15-2(c)(1), n. 74; § 15-2(h), n. 274

In re Scott Paper Co. Sec. Litig., 145 F.R.D. 366 (E.D. Pa. 1992) — § 16-2(b)(1), n. 69; § 16-2(c)(2)(A), n. 142; § 16-2(d)(3)(C), n. 272

In re Sealed Case (Juvenile Transfer), 893 F.2d 363 (D.C. Cir. 1990) — § 3-3(a), n. 468

In re Sealed Case, 151 F.3d 1059 (D.C. Cir. 1998) — § 3-1(a)(3), nn. 109, 128; § 5-2(a)(3), n. 180

In re Sealed Case, 20 Media L. Rep. (BNA) 2231 (D.D.C. 1993) — § 5-2(a)(4), n. 202

In re Sealed Case, 26 Media L. Rep. (BNA) 1319 (D.C. Cir. 1997) — § 5-2(a)(3), n. 197

TABLE OF CASES

In re Search of 1993 Jeep Grand Cherokee, 958 F. Supp. 205 (D. Del. 1996) — § 5-2(a)(2), n. 129

In re Search of Flower Aviation of Kansas, Inc., 789 F. Supp. 366 (D. Kan. 1992) — § 5-2(a)(2), n. 120

In re Search Warrant for Secretarial Area Outside Office of Gunn, 855 F.2d 569, 570 (8th Cir. 1988) — § 5-2(a)(1), n. 103; § 5-2(a)(2), nn. 111-18

In re Search Warrants in Connection with Investigation of Columbus/HCA Health Care Corp., 971 F. Supp. 251 (W.D. Tex. 1997) — § 5-2(a)(2), n. 110

In re Search Warrants Issued on June 11, 1988, for the Premises of Three Bldgs. at UNISYS, Inc., 710 F. Supp. 701 (D. Minn. 1989) — § 5-2(a)(2), nn. 112, 128, 131

In re Search Warrants, 26 Media L. Rep. (BNA) 1127 (Colo. County Ct. 1997) — § 5-2(a)(2), n. 129

In re Search Warrants, 26 Media L. Rep. (BNA) 2564 (M.D.N.C. 1998) — § 5-2(a)(2), nn. 120, 128, 130

In re Selcraig, 705 F.2d 789 (5th Cir. 1983) —§ 16-2(a)(1), n. 2; § 16-2(c)(2)(A), n. 138; § 16-2(d)(1), nn. 177, 179-84; § 16-2(e)(4), n. 362; § 16-2(f), n. 375; § 16-2(h)(1), nn. 405, 406

In re Shain, 978 F.2d 850 (4th Cir. 1992) — § 15-3(b), nn. 373, 374; § 16-2(a)(1), nn. 2, 9, 11; § 16-2(c)(1), n. 107; § 16-2(f), n. 367

In re South Carolina Press Ass'n, 946 F.2d 1037 (4th Cir. 1991) — § 2-3, n. 312; § 3-1(b), nn. 233-38, 242

In re Special Grand Jury 89-2, 143 F.3d 565 (10th Cir. 1998) — § 5-2(a)(3), nn. 152, 154-56, 182, 195, 200

In re Special Grand Jury Investigation, 472 N.E.2d 450 (Ill. 1984) — § 15-2(e)(2)(B), n. 242

In re State of California for the County of Los Angeles Grand Jury Investigation, 471 A.2d 1141 (Md. Spec. App. 1984) — § 15-2(j), nn. 331-33

In re State Record Co., 504 S.E.2d 592 (S.C. 1998) — § 2-1(d), nn. 97, 98

In re Stone, 703 P.2d 1319 (Colo. App. 1985) — § 7-3, n. 187

In re Storer Communications, Inc., 828 F.2d 330 (6th Cir. 1987) — § 2-3, n. 294; § 5-2(a), n. 55

In re Subpoena to Nixon, 360 F. Supp. 1 (D.D.C. 1973) — § 3-1(a)(3), n. 146

In re Subpoena to Testify Before Grand Jury, 864 F.2d 1559 (11th Cir. 1989) — § 2-3, nn. 305, 306; § 3-1(a)(3), nn. 108, 114, 122, 124, 143; § 5-2(a)(3), n. 151; § 7-1, n. 38; § 7-3, n. 188

In re Swearingen Aviation Corp., 486 F. Supp. 9 (D. Md. 1979) — § 3-1(a)(3), n. 114

In re Symington, 209 B.R. 678 (D. Md. 1997) — § 2-3, n. 310; § 6-1(d), nn. 263-66

In re Taylor, 193 A.2d 181 (Pa. 1963) — § 14-2, nn. 35, 36; § 15-1, nn. 7, 8; § 15-2(c)(1), n. 63; § 15-2(c)(2)(B), n. 113; § 15-2(d)(1), nn. 148, 149, 152; § 15-2(e)(1), n. 214; § 15-2(h), nn. 276, 277; § 16-2(a)(2), n. 31

In re Thomas Chase, 446 N.Y.S.2d 1000 (Fam. Ct. 1982) — § 3-3(a), n. 499

In re Tierney, 328 So. 2d 40 (Fla. App. 1976) — § 16-2(c)(1), n. 82; § 16-2(f), n. 375

In re Times-World Corp., 488 S.E.2d 677 (Va. App. 1997) —§ 3-1(a)(5), nn. 194, 196; § 5-2(a), n. 59

In re T.R., 556 N.E.2d 439 (Ohio 1990) — § 3-3(a), nn. 490, 490; § 3-3(b), nn. 519-30; § 7-1, n. 82

In re Tribune Co. (Sierra), 784 F.2d 1518 (11th Cir. 1986) — § 2-3, n. 305; § 3-1(a), nn. 28, 32; § 5-2(b), n. 347

TABLE OF CASES

In re Two Sealed Search Warrants, 710 A.2d 202 (Del. Super. 1997) — § 5-2(a)(2), nn. 107, 123, 129
In re Van Ness, 8 Media L. Rep. (BNA) 2563 (Cal. Super. 1982) — § 15-2(b)(1), n. 41
In re Vericker, 446 F.2d 244 (2d Cir. 1971) — § 13-3(c)(8)(A), n. 270; § 13-3(c)(8)(B), n. 275
In re Vescovo Special Grand Jury, 473 F. Supp. 1335 (C.D. Cal. 1979) — § 3-1(a)(3), n. 113; § 5-2(a)(3), n. 142
In re Video-Indiana, Inc. (Edwards), 672 F.2d 1289 (7th Cir. 1982) — § 5-2(b), nn. 319, 321-24, 326
In re Vrazo, 423 A.2d 695 (N.J. Super. 1980) — § 15-2(d)(3)(B), n. 174; § 15-2(d)(3)(C), n. 195
In re Wade, 969 F.2d 241 (7th Cir. 1992) — § 10-2(h), n. 275
In re Washington Post Co., 807 F.2d 383 (4th Cir. 1986) — § 2-3, nn. 297, 300, 302, 303, 308, 310; § 3-1(a)(6), nn. 197-208; § 3-1(d), nn. 315-21, 325; § 5-1, n. 24; § 5-2(a)(2), nn. 123-25; § 5-2(a)(7), n. 252; § 5-2(a)(9), n. 283
In re Wayne, 4 U.S.D.C. Haw. 475 (1914) — § 14-1, n. 7
In re WFMJ Broadcasting Co., 566 F. Supp. 1036 (N.D. Ohio 1983) — § 5-2(a)(7), n. 264; § 5-2(a)(8), n. 273
In re Williams, 766 F. Supp. 358 (W.D. Pa. 1991) — § 15-3(b), nn. 375, 376; § 16-2(c)(1), nn. 87, 88
In re Willon, 55 Cal. Rptr. 2d 245 (Ct. App. 1996) — § 15-2(c)(1), n. 76; § 15-2(e)(2), n. 233; § 15-2(e)(2)(B), n. 245; § 15-2(i)(3), n. 314; § 16-2(c)(1), n. 104
In re Wolf, 333 N.Y.S.2d 299 (App. Div. 1972) — § 15-2(h), n. 287
In re Woodhaven Lumber & Mill Work, 589 A.2d 135 (N.J. 1991) — § 15-2(d)(3)(B), n. 172
In re Worrell Enters., 419 S.E.2d 271 (Va. App. 1992) — § 5-2(a)(5), n. 225
In re Wright, 700 P.2d 40 (Idaho 1985) — § 16-2(a)(2), nn. 29, 42; § 16-2(c)(1), n. 115; § 16-2(e)(1), n. 299
In re Ziegler, 550 F. Supp. 530 (W.D.N.Y. 1982) — § 16-2(d)(3)(B), n. 236
Independent State Store Union v. Pennsylvania Liquor Control Bd., 432 A.2d 1375 (Pa. 1981) — § 9-6(b), n. 257
Indiana ex rel. Post-Tribune Publ'g Co. v. Porter Super. Ct., 412 N.E.2d 748 (Ind. 1980) — § 3-1(a)(1), n. 73
Indiana State Bd. of Health v. Journal-Gazette Co., 608 N.E.2d 989 (Ind. App. 1993) — § 9-6(i)(1)(A), n. 368
Indianapolis Convention & Visitors Ass'n v. Indianapolis Newspapers, Inc., 577 N.E.2d 208 (Ind. App. 1991) — § 11-3(e), n. 52
Industrial Found. of South v. Texas Indus. Accounting Bd., 540 S.W.2d 668 (Tex. 1976) — § 11-5(c), n. 167
Interception of Wire & Oral Communications (Kattar), 682 F. Supp. 669 (D.N.H. 1988) — § 5-2(a)(1), n. 91
International Bhd. of Elec. Workers Local 68 v. Denver Metro. Major League Baseball Stadium Dist., 880 P.2d 160 (Colo. App. 1994) — § 11-7(f)(1), n. 272
International Bhd. of Elec. Workers Local No. 5 v. HUD, 852 F.2d 87 (3d Cir. 1988) — § 10-2(c)(7), n. 162
International Longshoremen's & Warehousemen's Union v. Los Angeles Export Terminal, Inc., 81 Cal. Rptr. 2d 456 (Ct. App. 1999) — § 9-6(b), n. 257; § 9-6(j), n. 416
International Soc'y for Krishna Consciousness, Inc. v. Lee, 505 U.S. 672 (1992) — § 1-1, nn. 6, 10

TABLE OF CASES

Iowa Freedom of Info. Council v. Wifvat, 328 N.W.2d 920 (Iowa 1983) — § 3-1(a), n. 12; § 5-2(a)(7), n. 252
Ippolito v. Lennon, 542 N.Y.S.2d 3 (App. Div. 1989) — § 13-3(b), n. 149
Irons & Sears v. Dann, 606 F.2d 1215 (D.C. Cir. 1979) — § 10-2(c)(4), n. 108
Irons v. FBI, 880 F.2d 1446 (1st Cir. 1989) — § 10-2(c)(8)(D), n. 202; § 10-2(c)(8)(F), n. 216
Irval Realty, Inc. v. Board of Pub. Util. Comm'rs, 294 A.2d 425 (N.J. 1972) — § 11-5(c), n. 170
Irwin v. Dowd, 366 U.S. 717 (1961) — § 2-1(a), nn. 13, 15
Italian & French Wine Co. v. Negociants U.S.A., Inc., 842 F. Supp. 693 (W.D.N.Y. 1993) — § 13-4(c), n. 532
Ivanhoe Citrus Ass'n v. Handley, 612 F. Supp. 1560 (D.D.C. 1985) — § 10-2(c)(7), n. 157

J

Jackson v. Playboy Enterprises, Inc., 574 F. Supp. 10 (S.D. Ohio 1983) — § 12-2(a), nn. 6, 7
Jacobson v. Rose, 592 F.2d 515 (9th Cir. 1978) — § 13-7(a)(2)(A)(iv), n. 642
Jacova v. Southern Radio & Television Co., 83 So. 2d 34 (Fla. 1955) — § 12-3, n. 102; § 12-4(c)(2), n. 250
Jaffe v. CIA, 573 F. Supp. 377 (D.D.C. 1983) — § 10-2(c)(8)(E), nn. 210, 211
Jaffee v. Redmond, 518 U.S. 1 (1996) — § 14-5(b), n. 146; § 16-3, n. 474
Jamerson v. Anderson Newspapers, Inc., 469 N.E.2d 1243 (Ind. App. 1984) — § 15-2(a), n. 25; § 15-2(e)(1), n. 213
James v. Hines, 1998 WL 720735 (Ky. App. Oct. 16, 1998) — § 7-1, n. 82
Jaubert v. Crowley Post-Signal, Inc., 375 So. 2d 1386 (La. 1979) — § 12-2(b), nn. 74, 75
J.B. Pictures, Inc. v. Department of Defense, 86 F.3d 236 (D.C. Cir. 1996) — § 8-5, nn. 145-50; § 9-2, n. 24; § 9-2(b), n. 44
Jefferson County Bd. of Educ. v. Courier-Journal, 551 S.W.2d 25 (Ky. App. 1977) — § 9-6(i)(1)(D), n. 386
Jeffries v. Mississippi, 724 So. 2d 897 (Miss. 1998) — § 2-1(c), n. 61; § 2-1(d), n. 99
Jenkins v. Winchester Star, 8 Media L. Rep. (BNA) 1403 (W.D. Va. 1981) — § 12-6(b), n. 391
Jenoff v. Hearst Corp., 3 Media L. Rep. (BNA) 1911 (D. Md. 1978) — § 15-2(c)(2)(B), nn. 118, 119
Jepson, Inc. v. Makita Elec. Works, Ltd., 30 F.3d 854 (7th Cir. 1996) — § 6-1(a)(5), n. 103
Jersawitz v. Hanberry, 783 F.2d 1532 (11th Cir. 1986) — § 8-1, n. 52
Jews for Jesus, Inc. v. Jewish Community Relations Council, 968 F.2d 286 (2d Cir. 1992) — § 13-4(c), n. 536
Jochims v. Isuzu Motors, Ltd., 151 F.R.D. 338 (S.D. Iowa 1993) — § 6-1(a)(5), n. 120; § 6-1(c)(2), n. 237
John Doe Agency v. John Doe Corp., 493 U.S. 146 (1989) — § 10-2(c)(1), n. 52; § 10-2(c)(8), n. 173
John P. v. Whalen, 429 N.E.2d 117 (N.Y. 1981) — § 11-8, n. 355
Johnson v. Adams, 629 F. Supp. 1563 (E.D. Tex. 1986) — § 9-3, n. 59; § 9-6(e), n. 321
Johnson v. Bentley, 457 So. 2d 507 (Fla. App. 1984) — § 16-2(c)(2)(A), n. 144; § 16-2(d)(3)(C), n. 271

TABLE OF CASES

Johnson v. Greater Southeast Community Hosp. Corp., 951 F.2d 1268 (D.C. Cir. 1991) — § 6-1(a)(5), n. 105
Johnson v. Mississippi, 476 So. 2d 1195 (Miss. 1985) — § 2-1(a), n. 2
Johnson v. Nash, 608 A.2d 200 (N.H. 1992) — § 9-6(i)(1)(C), n. 381
Johnson v. NRC, 766 F.2d 1182 (7th Cir. 1985) — § 9-5(a)(8)(J), n. 182; § 9-5(a)(9)(A), n. 183
Johnson v. Stephan, 6 F.3d 691 (10th Cir. 1993) — § 8-1, n. 53
Johnson v. Wells, 566 F.2d 1016 (5th Cir. 1978) — § 10-2(b)(2), n. 28
Johnson Newspaper Corp. v. Hamblin, 499 N.Y.S.2d 341 (Sup. Ct. 1986) — § 5-2(a)(6), n. 242
Johnson Newspaper Corp. v. Melino, 563 N.Y.S.2d 380 (App. Div. 1990) — § 9-1, n. 4
Johnson Newspaper Corp. v. Melino, 564 N.E.2d 1046 (N.Y. 1990) — § 9-1, n. 8; § 9-4, n. 67
Johnson Newspaper Corp. v. Morton, 862 F.2d 25 (2d Cir. 1988) — § 3-1(a)(4), nn. 169, 171
Johnson Newspaper Corp. v. Stainkamp, 463 N.Y.S.2d 122 (App. Div. 1983) — § 11-8, n. 356
Jones v. Clinton, 12 F. Supp. 2d 931 (E.D. Ark. 1998) — § 6-1(a)(3), n. 54; § 6-1(a)(4), nn. 94, 95, 98-102; § 6-1(a)(5), n. 119
Jones v. Clinton, 138 F.3d 758 (8th Cir. 1998) — § 6-1(a)(4), n. 97
Jones v. Clinton, 990 F. Supp. 657 (E.D. Ark. 1998) — § 6-1(a)(4), n. 96
Jones v. FBI, 41 F.3d 238 (6th Cir. 1994) — § 10-2(c)(8), n. 176; § 10-2(c)(8)(C), n. 191
Jones v. Woodward, 15 Media L. Rep. (BNA) 2060 (Colo. App. 1988) — § 16-2(a)(2), n. 42
Jones/Seymour v. LeFebvre, 19 Media L. Rep. (BNA) 2064 (E.D. Pa. 1992) — § 12-6(b), n. 391
Jordan v. Department of Justice, 591 F.2d 753 (D.C. Cir. 1978) — § 10-2(c)(3), n. 103; § 10-2(c)(6), n. 139
Jordan v. Department of Justice, 691 F.2d 514 (D.C. Cir. 1982) — § 10-2(h), n. 289
Joslyn v. People, 184 P. 375 (Colo. 1919) — § 14-1, n. 3
Journal Publ'g Co. of Rockville, Inc. v. Town of Enfield, 373 A.2d 193 (Conn. Super. 1974) — § 9-6(c), n. 288
Journal Publ'g Co. v. Mechem, 801 F.2d 1233 (10th Cir. 1986) — § 7-3, nn. 159-63
Journal/Sentinel, Inc. v. Aagerup, 429 N.W.2d 772 (Wis. App. 1988) — § 11-7(d), n. 260
Joy v. North, 692 F.2d 880 (2d Cir. 1982) — § 6-1(a)(4), n. 85; § 6-1(a)(5), n. 116; § 6-1(c)(1), n. 210; § 6-1(c)(2), n. 238
Judicial Watch, Inc. v. Clinton, 76 F.3d 1232 (D.C. Cir. 1996) — § 9-5(b)(2), nn. 210, 211

K

Kaganove v. EPA, 856 F.2d 884 (7th Cir. 1988) — § 10-2(c)(3), n. 105
Kaiyala v. City of Seattle, 20 Media L. Rep. (BNA) 1740 (W.D. Wash. 1992) — § 16-2(d)(3)(A), n. 232; § 16-2(d)(3)(B), n. 236
Kamasinski v. United States, No. 98-1427 (1st Cir. Mar. 19, 1999) — § 2-3, n. 310
Kamman v. IRS, 56 F.3d 46 (9th Cir. 1995) — § 10-2(c)(1), n. 53
Kamyr A.B. v. Kamyr, Inc., 20 Media L. Rep. (BNA) 1969 (N.D.N.Y. 1992) — § 6-1(a)(5), n. 110
Kansas v. Aikens, 932 P.2d 408 (Kan. 1997) — § 3-1(b), n. 230
Kansas v. Dowdy, 563 P.2d 425 (Kan. 1977) — § 13-7(b)(1), n. 690

TABLE OF CASES

Kansas v. Sandstrom, 581 P.2d 812 (Kan. 1978) — § 16-2(a)(2), n. 29; § 16-2(c)(1), n. 92; § 16-2(d)(1), n. 177

Kansas ex rel. Murray v. Palmgren, 646 P.2d 1091 (Kan. 1982) — § 9-6(b), n. 269

Kansas ex rel. Stephan v. Board of County Comm'rs, 770 P.2d 455 (Kan. 1989) — § 9-6(c), n. 279

Kansas City Star Co. v. Lewellen, 15 Media L. Rep. 2345 (Mo. Cir. 1988) — § 9-6(j), n. 410

Kansas City Star Co. v. Shields, 771 S.W.2d 101 (Mo. App. 1989) — § 9-6(j), n. 407

Karem v. Priest, 497 U.S. 1042 (1990) — § 14-5(f), n. 221

Karem v. Priest, 744 F. Supp. 136 (W.D. Tex. 1990) — § 16-2(c)(1), n. 115; § 16-2(h)(1), n. 411; § 16-2(h)(2), n. 420

Katz v. National Archives & Records Admin., 68 F.3d 1438 (D.C. Cir. 1995) — § 10-2(b)(2), n. 29

Katz v. Scott, 653 N.Y.S.2d 346 (App. Div. 1997) — § 11-7(j), n. 309

Katz v. United States, 389 U.S. 347 (1967) — § 13-7(a)(1), n. 578; § 13-7(a)(2)(A), n. 585; § 13-7(b)(1), n. 682

Katzman v. Victoria's Secret Catalogues, 923 F. Supp. 580 (S.D.N.Y. 1996) — § 4-2(a), nn. 69-73

Kay v. Ehrler, 499 U.S. 432 (1991) — § 10-2(h), n. 285

Kay v. FCC, 867 F. Supp. 11 (D.D.C. 1994) — § 10-2(c)(8), n. 174

KCOB/KLVN, Inc. v. Jasper County Bd. of Supervisors, 473 N.W.2d 171 (Iowa 1991) — § 9-6(d), n. 295; § 9-6(g), n. 339

Kearney v. Department of Mental Health, 425 N.W.2d 161 (Mich. App. 1988) — § 11-4, n. 73

Kearns-Tribune Corp. v. Hornak, 917 P.2d 79 (Utah App. 1996) — § 3-3(a), n. 478

Kearns-Tribune Corp. v. Lewis, 685 P.2d 515 (Utah 1984) — § 3-1(a), n. 12; § 3-1(a)(2), nn. 92, 96; § 5-2(a)(6), n. 239

Kearns-Tribune Corp. v. Utah Bd. of Corrections, 2 Media L. Rep. (BNA) 1353 (D. Utah 1977) — § 8-2, nn. 80, 81

Keddie v. Rutgers Univ., 689 A.2d 702 (N.J. 1997) — § 9-6(f), n. 331; § 11-2, n. 13; § 11-4, n. 56; § 11-5(c), n. 170; § 11-7(m), n. 348

Keene Publ'g Corp. v. Cheshire County Super. Ct., 406 A.2d 137 (N.H. 1979) — § 2-3, n. 309

Kemner v. Monsanto Co., 492 N.E.2d 1327 (Ill. 1986) — § 7-1, n. 82; § 7-2, n. 140

Kennedy v. Powell, 401 So. 2d 453 (La. App. 1981) — § 9-6(j), n. 415

Kent v. United States, 383 U.S. 541 (1966) — § 3-3(a), n. 433

Kentucky Bd. of Exmrs. v. Courier-Journal, 826 S.W.2d 324 (Ky. 1992) — § 11-5(a)(5), nn. 123, 127-30

Kersis v. American Broadcasting Cos., 1999 U.S. App. LEXIS 15222 (9th Cir. June 8, 1999) — § 12-4(c)(3), n. 302

Kersis v. American Broadcasting Cos., No. CV-95-00848-JMJ (9th Cir. June 8, 1999) — § 13-7(c), n. 756

Kersis v. Capital Cities/ABC Inc., 22 Media L. Rep. (BNA) 2321 (Cal. Super. 1994), *rev'd on other grounds sub nom.* Sanders v. American Broadcasting Cos., 60 Cal. Rptr. 2d 595 (Ct. App. 1997), *rev'd*, 978 P.2d 67 (Cal. 1999) — § 12-4(c)(3), n. 305; § 13-7(b)(4)(A), n. 709

Kestenbaum v. Michigan State Univ., 294 N.W.2d 228 (Mich. App. 1980) — § 11-5(a)(5), n. 127

Keys v. Department of Justice, 830 F.2d 337 (D.C. Cir. 1987) — § 10-2(h), n. 283

TABLE OF CASES

KGTV Channel 10 v. Superior Ct., 32 Cal. Rptr. 2d 181 (Ct. App. 1994) — § 3-3(a), nn. 494, 495

Kheel v. Ravitch, 464 N.E.2d 118 (N.Y. 1984) — § 11-5(a)(4), n. 98

Kidwell v. Florida, 720 So. 2d 218 (Fla. 1998) — § 16-2(c)(1), n. 107; § 16-2(d)(3)(B), n. 239; § 16-2(d)(3)(C), n. 274

Kilgore v. R.W. Page Corp., 385 S.E.2d 406 (Ga. 1989) — § 11-7(d), n. 258

Kimberlin v. Department of Justice, 139 F.3d 944 (D.C. Cir. 1998) — § 10-2(c)(8), n. 172; § 10-2(e), n. 246

Kimberlin v. Department of Treasury, 774 F.2d 204 (7th Cir. 1985) — § 10-2(c)(8)(F), n. 216

Kimberlin v. Quinlan, 145 F.R.D. 1 (D.D.C. 1992) — § 3-2(e), nn. 420, 422

Kimes v. Stone, 84 F.3d 1121 (9th Cir. 1996) — § 12-4(a), n. 137; § 12-5, n. 349

King v. Photo Marketing Ass'n Int'l, 327 N.W.2d 515 (Mich. App. 1982) — § 16-2(e)(1), n. 299

Kirwan v. Diamondback, 721 A.2d 196 (Md. 1998) — § 11-7(g), n. 300

Kissinger v. Reporters Comm. for Freedom of the Press, 445 U.S. 136 (1980) — § 10-2(b)(1), nn. 5, 6; § 10-2(b)(3), n. 32; § 10-2(h), n. 272

Kleindienst v. Mandel, 408 U.S. 753 (1972) — § 1-3, nn. 49, 50; § 2-2(c), n. 185

Kline & Sons v. Fallows, 478 N.Y.S.2d 524 (Sup. Ct. 1984) — § 11-9, n. 374

Kloepfer v. Commissioner of Educ., 440 N.Y.S.2d 785 (App. Div. 1981) — § 9-6(g), n. 341

KMOV-TV v. Kirksey, 26 MEDIA L. REP. (BNA) 2435 (Mo. Cir. 1998) — § 4-3, n. 101

Kneeland v. National Collegiate Athletic Ass'n, 850 F.2d 224 (5th Cir. 1988) — § 11-3(e), n. 53

Knight Publ'g Co. v. University of South Carolina, 367 S.E.2d 20 (S.C. 1988) — § 9-6(b), n. 259

Knight-Ridder Broadcasting, Inc. v. Greenberg, 511 N.E.2d 1116 (N.Y. 1987) — § 15-1, n. 17; § 15-2(d)(2), n. 160

Knoxville News-Sentinel v. Huskey, 982 S.W.2d 359 (Tenn. Crim. App. 1998) — § 5-2(e), nn. 469-72

KNSD Channels 7/39 v. Superior Ct. of San Diego County, 74 Cal. Rptr. 2d 595 (Ct. App. 1998) — § 5-2(b), nn. 297, 302, 320, 326

Ko v. Zilog, Inc., 25 Media L. Rep. (BNA) 1892 (Idaho 1997) — § 16-2(c)(2)(A), n. 144; § 16-2(d)(1), n. 187; § 16-2(e)(3), n. 333

Koch v. Koch Indus., Inc., 6 F. Supp. 2d 1185 (D. Kan. 1998) — § 7-1, nn. 4, 30

Konigsberg v. Coughlin, 501 N.E.2d 1 (N.Y. 1986) — § 11-4, n. 66; § 11-7(c), n. 255

Konigsberg v. State Bar of California, 366 U.S. 36 (1961) — § 13-4(a)(2)(C), n. 415

Kovach v. Maddux, 238 F. Supp. 835 (M.D. Tenn. 1965) — § 9-3, n. 55

KOVR-TV Inc. v. Superior Ct., 37 Cal. Rptr. 2d 431 (Ct. App. 1995) — § 12-4(a), nn. 169, 171; § 12-6(a), nn. 374-76

Kowalczyk v. Department of Justice, 73 F.3d 386 (D.C. Cir. 1996) — § 10-2(b)(3), n. 41

KPNX Broadcasting Co. v. Maricopa County Super. Ct., 678 P.2d 431 (Ariz. 1984) — § 7-1, nn. 25, 44

KPNX Broadcasting Co. v. Superior Ct., 459 U.S. 1302 (1982) — § 7-1, nn. 41-44

KQED, Inc. v. Vasquez, 1991 U.S. Dist. LEXIS 1971 (N.D. Cal. 1991) — § 8-2, nn. 74-77

TABLE OF CASES

Krase v. Graco Children Prods., Inc., 79 F.3d 346 (2d Cir. 1996) — § 14-6(a), nn. 244-47; § 15-2(c)(2)(A), n. 87; § 15-2(e)(2)(A), n. 241; § 15-2(e)(2)(B), n. 242; § 15-2(j), n. 329; § 16-2(a)(1), nn. 2, 14; § 16-2(c)(1), n. 121

Krause v. Rhodes, 535 F. Supp. 338 (N.D. Ohio 1979) — § 3-1(a)(3), n. 122

Krikorian v. Department of State, 984 F.2d 461 (D.C. Cir. 1993) — § 10-2(e), n. 248; § 10-2(h), n. 278

KTVY-TV v. United States, 919 F.2d 1465 (10th Cir. 1990) — § 10-2(c)(8), n. 173; § 10-2(c)(8)(C), n. 193

Kuhn v. City of Detroit, 610 F. Supp. 364 (E.D. Mich. 1984) — § 5-2(a)(1), n. 101

Kureczka v. FOIC, 636 A.2d 777 (Conn. 1994) — § 11-7(a)(1), n. 186

Kurland v. McLaughlin, 505 N.Y.S.2d 967 (App. Div. 1986) — § 11-8, n. 356

Kurlander v. Sch. Comm., 451 N.E.2d 138 (Mass. App. 1983) — § 9-6(h), n. 345

Kurtzman v. Hankin, 714 A.2d 450 (Pa. Super. 1998) — § 6-1(a)(3), n. 54; § 6-1(c)(1), n. 227

Kurzynski v. Spaeth, 538 N.W.554 (Wis. App. 1995) — § 16-2(e)(1), n. 299

L

Laborers Int'l Union v. City of Aberdeen, 642 P.2d 418 (Wash. App. 1982) — § 11-1, n. 7

Lac Courte Oreilles Band v. Wisconsin, 17 Media L. Rep. (BNA) 1381 (W.D. Wis. 1990) — § 4-2(a), nn. 62-65

LaCrone v. Ohio Bell Tel. Co., 182 N.E.2d 15 (Ohio App. 1961) — § 13-7(b)(1), n. 680

Lake v. Walmart Stores, Inc., 582 N.W.2d 231 (Minn. 1998) — § 12-1, n. 2

Lakeland Ledger Publ'g Co. v. Prison Health Servs. Inc., 718 So. 2d 204 (Fla. Cir. 1997) — § 6-1(b), n. 186

Lal v. CBS Inc., 551 F. Supp. 356 (E.D. Pa. 1982) — § 12-4(a), n. 180

Lal v. CBS Inc., 726 F.2d 97 (3d Cir. 1984) — § 15-2(d)(1), n. 149

Laman v. McCord, 432 S.W.2d 753 (Ark. 1968) — § 11-5(c), n. 167

Lambert v. Judicial Nominating Council, 681 N.E.2d 285 (Mass. 1997) — § 11-7(a)(1), n. 185

Lambert v. Polk County, 723 F. Supp. 128 (S.D. Iowa 1989) — § 15-3(a), nn. 351-54

Lamberto v. Bown, 326 N.W.2d 305 (Iowa 1982) — § 16-2(e)(2), n. 320; § 16-2(e)(4), n. 362; § 16-2(h), n. 398

Lamont v. Postmaster General, 381 U.S. 301 (1965) — § 1-3, nn. 39, 48

Landmark Communications, Inc. v. Virginia, 435 U.S. 829 (1978) — § 2-1(c), nn. 51-56; § 5-2(a)(3), n. 173; § 9-4, n. 67; § 13-3(a), nn. 91-94, 105; § 13-3(b), n. 129; § 13-3(c)(7), nn. 247, 249; § 13-4(a)(2)(C), n. 403; § 13-7(a)(2)(A)(i), n. 601

Lane City Sch. Dist. v. Parks, 637 P.2d 1383 (Or. App. 1981) — § 11-5(a)(4), n. 109

Lane v. Allstate Ins. Co., 969 P.2d 938 (Nev. 1998) — § 13-7(b)(3), n. 700

Lanphere & Urbaniak v. Colorado, 21 F.3d 1508 (10th Cir. 1994) — § 5-2(e), n. 461

Laramie River Conservation Council v. Dinger, 567 P.2d 731 (Wyo. 1977) — § 9-6(f), n. 330; § 11-9, n. 364

LaRocca v. Board of Educ., 602 N.Y.S.2d 1009 (Sup. Ct. 1993) — § 11-7(a)(1), n. 185; § 11-7(m), n. 352

LaRouche v. National Broadcasting Co., 780 F.2d 1134 (4th Cir. 1986) — § 14-6(b), n. 264; § 16-2(a)(1), nn. 2, 10; § 16-2(c)(2)(B), n. 159; § 16-2(d)(3)(C), n. 246; § 16-2(e)(1), n. 299; § 16-2(e)(3), n. 356

Larson v. Philadelphia Newspapers, Inc., 543 A.2d 1181 (Pa. Super. 1988) — § 13-3(b), nn. 127-31

TABLE OF CASES

Las Vegas Sun, Inc. v. Eighth Judicial Dist. Ct., 761 P.2d 849 (Nev. 1988) — § 15-2(a), n. 29; § 15-2(b)(2), n. 52; § 15-2(c)(2)(B), n. 127; § 15-2(d)(3)(C), n. 188; § 15-2(h), nn. 278-82

Lauderback v. American Broadcasting Cos., 8 Media L. Rep. (BNA) 2407 (N.D. Iowa 1982) — § 16-2(a)(1), n. 21; § 16-2(c)(2)(B), n. 159; § 16-2(d)(3)(C), n. 270; § 16-2(e)(3), n. 357

Laudig v. Board of Voter Registration, 585 N.E.2d 700 (Ind. App. 1992) — § 11-7(h), n. 303

Lauro v. City of New York, 39 F. Supp. 2d 351 (S.D.N.Y. 1999) — § 12-3, nn. 93, 102; § 12-5, n. 356

Lawless v. Clay, 9 Media L. Rep. (BNA) 1223 (N.Y. Sup. Ct. 1982) — § 15-2(d)(2), n. 160; § 15-2(d)(3)(C), n. 195

Lawson v. Dixon, 25 F.3d 1040 (4th Cir. 1994) — § 8-2, nn. 57-60

Lawson v. Dixon, 446 S.E.2d 799 (N.C. 1994) — § 8-2, n. 58

Laxalt v. McClatchy, 622 F. Supp. 737 (D. Nev. 1985) — § 16-2(c)(2)(B), n. 156; § 16-2(d)(1), nn. 177, 189

Le Mistral, Inc. v. Columbia Broadcasting Sys., 402 N.Y.S.2d 815 (App. Div. 1978) — § 12-3, n. 112; § 12-4(a), n. 164; § 12-4(c)(1), nn. 224-27; § 12-4(c)(2), nn. 239, 249

Lead Indus. Ass'n v. OSHA, 610 F.2d 70 (2d Cir. 1979) — § 10-2(e), n. 249

Lee v. Florida, 392 U.S. 378 (1968) — § 13-7(a)(1), n. 579

Lee v. Penthouse Int'l Ltd., 25 Media L. Rep. (BNA) 1651 (C.D. Cal. 1997) — § 13-3(b), n. 140

Lee v. The Columbian, Inc., 16 Media L. Rep. (BNA) 1261 (Wash. Super. 1989) — § 13-3(c)(2), nn. 193-96

Lee v. The Columbian, Inc., 826 P.2d 217 (Wash. App. 1991) — § 12-2(b), n. 82

Legislative Joint Auditing Comm. v. Woosley, 722 S.W.2d 581 (Ark. 1987) — § 11-5(a), n. 77

Leham v. San Francisco, 145 Cal. Rptr. 493 (Ct. App. 1978) — § 11-4, n. 58

Lehrhaupt v. Flynn, 356 A.2d 35 (N.J. Super. 1976) — § 9-6(h)(1), n. 348

Leiserson v. City of San Diego, 229 Cal. Rptr. 22 (Ct. App. 1986) — § 8-3, nn. 113-18

Lence v. Hagadone Investment Co., 853 P.2d 1230 (Mont. 1993) — § 13-3(b), nn. 123-26

Lepelletier v. FDIC, 164 F.3d 37 (D.C. Cir. 1999) — § 10-2(c)(7), nn. 162, 167

Lesar v. Department of Justice, 636 F.2d 472 (D.C. Cir. 1980) — § 10-2(c)(2), n. 97; § 10-2(c)(3), n. 101

Lesher Communications, Inc. v. Superior Ct., 274 Cal. Rptr. 154 (Ct. App. 1990) — § 5-2(c), nn. 397, 398

Leucadia, Inc. v. Applied Extrusion Techs., Inc., 998 F.2d 157 (3d Cir. 1993) — § 6-1(a)(4), n. 66; § 6-1(a)(5), nn. 111, 113; § 6-1(c)(1), nn. 213-17

Levine v. United States Dist. Ct., 764 F.2d 590 (9th Cir. 1985) — § 7-1, nn. 58-62; § 7-2, n. 139

Levitch v. Columbia Broadcasting Sys., 495 F. Supp. 649 (S.D.N.Y. 1980) — § 13-7(a)(1), n. 581

Lewis v. Baxley, 368 F. Supp. 768 (M.D. Ala. 1973) — § 9-3, n. 56

Lewis v. Spurney, 456 So. 2d 206 (La. App. 1984) — § 11-7(f)(2), n. 278

Lewis v. United States, 517 F.2d 236 (9th Cir. 1975) — § 16-2(a)(1), n. 2; § 16-2(i), nn. 445, 448

Lewiston Daily Sun, Inc. v. City of Auburn, 544 A.2d 335 (Me. 1988) — § 9-6(j), n. 410

TABLE OF CASES

Lexington Herald-Leader Co. v. Beard, 690 S.W.2d 374 (Ky. 1984) — § 15-2(c)(2)(B), nn. 126, 127; § 15-2(d)(1), n. 143; § 15-2(h), n. 290; § 15-2(i)(3), n. 315; § 16-2(a)(2), n. 42

Lexington Herald-Leader Co. v. University of Kentucky Presidential Search Comm., 732 S.W.2d 884 (Ky. 1987) — § 9-6(b), n. 267

Lexington-Fayette Urban County Gov't v. Lexington Herald-Leader Co., 941 S.W.2d 469 (W. Va. 1997) — § 11-7(m), n. 352

Libertarian Party of Indiana v. Board of Voter Registration, 778 F. Supp. 1458 (S.D. Ind. 1991) — § 11-7(h), n. 302

Librach v. Cooper, 778 S.W.2d 351 (Mo. App. 1989) — § 9-6(i)(1)(C), n. 383; § 11-7(m), n. 350

Lieber v. Board of Trustees, 680 N.E.2d 374 (Ill. 1997) — § 11-7(g), n. 297

Liebreich v. Church of Scientology, 25 Media L. Rep. (BNA) 2215 (Fla. Cir. 1997) — § 2-3, n. 310

Lightman v. Maryland, 294 A.2d 149 (Md. Spec. App. 1972) — § 14-1, n. 16; § 15-2(b)(2), n. 47; § 15-2(c)(1), n. 62; § 15-2(d)(3)(A), n. 165; § 15-2(d)(3)(B), nn. 180-82; § 15-2(d)(3)(C), n. 195; § 16-2(a)(2), nn. 31, 42; § 16-2(d)(3)(B), n. 234

LiMandri v. Judkins, 60 Cal. Rptr. 2d 539 (Ct. App. 1997) — § 13-2(b), n. 53

Line v. Ronkainen, 37 N.W.2d 237 (Minn. 1949) — § 13-4(a)(2)(B), n. 388

Lipps v. Indiana, 258 N.E.2d 622 (Ind. App. 1970) — § 15-2(b)(2), n. 47

Littlejohn v. BIC Corp., 851 F.2d 673 (3d Cir. 1988) — § 3-2(c), n. 398; § 6-1(a)(4), nn. 70, 74, 75; § 6-1(a)(5), nn. 112, 120; § 6-1(c)(1), n. 216; § 6-1(c)(2), nn. 228, 239-44

Livingston v. Isuzu Motors, Ltd., 910 F. Supp. 1473 (D. Mont. 1995) — § 6-1(c)(2), n. 237

Livingston v. Kentucky Post, 14 Media L. Rep. (BNA) 2076 (Ky. Cir. 1987) — § 12-2(b), n. 80

Loadholtz v. Fields, 389 F. Supp. 1299 (M.D. Fla. 1975) — § 16-2(c)(2)(A), n. 136; § 16-2(d)(3)(C), nn. 253, 257

Lodge v. Knowlton, 391 A.2d 893 (N.H. 1978) — § 11-3(a), n. 34

Logsdon v. Graham Ford Co., 376 N.E.2d 1333 (Ohio 1978) — § 13-2(a), n. 19

Loigman v. Kimmelman, 505 A.2d 958 (N.J. 1986) — § 11-5(c), n. 170

Lombardo v. Handler, 397 F. Supp. 792 (D.D.C. 1975) — § 9-5(b)(2), nn. 203, 205

Long v. IRS, 596 F.2d 362 (9th Cir. 1979) — § 10-2(b)(1), n. 10

Long v. IRS, 932 F.2d 1309 (9th Cir. 1991) — § 10-2(h), n. 289

Los Angeles City Council v. Taxpayers for Vincent, 466 U.S. 789 (1984) — § 1-1, n. 7

Los Angeles Free Press, Inc. v. City of Los Angeles, 88 Cal. Rptr. 605 (Ct. App. 1970) — § 8-3, n. 121; § 9-2(a), n. 36; § 9-2(b), nn. 41, 46

Los Angeles Mem'l Coliseum Comm'n v. National Football League, 89 F.R.D. 489 (C.D. Cal. 1981) — § 16-2(b)(2), nn. 77, 78; § 16-2(c)(2)(A), n. 137; § 16-2(d)(1), nn. 177, 187; § 16-2(d)(2), nn. 204, 205; § 16-2(e)(2), n. 316; § 16-2(g), n. 386; § 16-2(h), nn. 394, 395; § 16-2(i), n. 446

Los Angeles Police Dep't v. Superior Ct., 135 Cal. Rptr. 575 (Ct. App. 1977) — § 11-4, n. 58

Los Angeles Times v. County of Los Angeles, 956 F. Supp. 1530 (C.D. Cal. 1996) — § 6-1(c), n. 189; § 6-1(d), n. 262

Louisiana v. Campbell, 566 So. 2d 1038 (La. App. 1990) — § 11-7(b)(3)(B), n. 227

Louisiana v. Eaton, 483 So. 2d 651 (La. App. 1986) — § 5-2(a), n. 59; § 3-1(a)(5), nn. 189-92

TABLE OF CASES

Louisiana v. Fletcher, 537 So. 2d 805 (La. App. 1989) — § 5-2(a)(6), n. 239
Louisiana v. Fontanille, 1994 La. App. LEXIS 191 (La. App. 1994) — § 16-2(b)(1), nn. 66, 67
Louisiana v. Guidry, 364 So. 2d 589 (La. 1978) — § 9-6(c), n. 289
Louisiana v. Mart, 697 So. 2d 1055 (La. App. 1997) — § 5-2(b), nn. 297, 312, 317, 360
Louisiana v. McDaniel, 504 So. 2d 160 (La. 1987) — § 11-7(b)(1), n. 210
Louisiana v. Widenhouse, 556 So. 2d 187 (La. App. 1990) — § 5-2(a)(5), n. 224
Louisiana v. Womack, 551 So. 2d 855 (La. App.1989) — § 2-3, n. 291
Louisiana ex rel. Gremillion v. NAACP, 366 U.S. 293 (1961) — § 14-4(c), n. 104
Lovell v. Alderete, 630 F.2d 428 (5th Cir. 1980) — § 10-2(h), n. 286
Lovell v. City of Griffin, 303 U.S. 444 (1938) — § 14-4(a), n. 76; § 16-2(b)(1), n. 65
Lowe v. SEC, 472 U.S. 181 (1985) — § 16-2(b)(1), n. 69
Lowndes Prods., Inc. v. Brower, 191 S.E.2d 761 (S.C. 1972) — § 13-2(b), n. 66
Luban, Settlements and the Erosion of the Public Realm, 83 Geo. L.J. 2619 (1995) — § 6-1(b), n. 156
Lugar v. Edmondson Oil Co., 457 U.S. 922 (1982) — § 12-5, n. 362
Lurie v. Department of Army, 970 F. Supp. 19 (D.D.C. 1997) — § 10-2(c)(8)(C), n. 196
Lutz v. Lutz, 20 MEDIA L. REP. (BNA) 2029 (Mich. Cir. 1992) — § 6-1(c), n. 204
Lykins v. Department of Justice, 725 F.2d 1455 (D.C. Cir. 1984) — § 10-2(h), n. 283
Lyon v. Dunne, 580 N.Y.S.2d 803 (App. Div. 1992) — § 11-5(a)(5), n. 127; § 11-7(a)(3), n. 195

M

Maas v. United States, 371 F.2d 348 (D.C. Cir. 1966) — § 13-4(a)(1)(B), n. 361
MacEwan v. Holm, 359 P.2d 413 (Or. 1961) — § 11-7(i), n. 308
Machleder v. Diaz, 538 F. Supp. 1364 (S.D.N.Y. 1982), *rev'd in part*, 801 F.2d 46 (2d Cir. 1986) — § 12-4(c)(3), n. 278; § 13-4(b), n. 506; § 13-6, nn. 559-63
Machleder v. Diaz, 801 F.2d 46 (2d Cir. 1986) — § 12-4(c)(3), nn. 277-85; § 13-4(b), nn. 503-06
Madsen v. Women's Health Center, Inc., 512 U.S. 1277 (1994) — § 13-3(c)(2), n. 200
Magenis v. Fisher Broadcasting, Inc., 798 P.2d 1106 (Or. App. 1990) — § 12-4(a), nn. 176-78
Maine v. Hohler, 543 A.2d 364 (Me. 1988) — § 16-2(d)(3)(C), n. 249
Malone v. Meekins, 650 P.2d 351 (Alaska 1982) — § 9-6(b), n. 273
Manax v. McNamara, 660 F. Supp. 657 (W.D. Tex. 1987) — § 13-7(a)(1), n. 583
Mankato Free Press v. Dempsey, 581 N.W.2d 311 (Minn. 1998) — § 3-1(d), n. 324; § 5-2(d), n. 419
Mann v. State's Attorney, 468 A.2d 124 (Md. Spec. App. 1983) — § 8-1, n. 52
Mannon v. Frick, 295 S.W.2d 158 (Mont. 1956) — § 5-2(a)(3), n. 171
Manos v. Department of Air Force, 829 F. Supp. 1191 (N.D. Cal. 1993) — § 10-2(h), n. 285
Manufacturas Internationale, LTDA v. Manufacturers Hanover Trust Co., 792 F. Supp. 180 (E.D.N.Y. 1992) — § 13-7(a)(2)(A)(iii), n. 633
Mapother v. Department of Justice, 3 F.3d 1533 (D.C. Cir. 1993) — § 10-2(c)(6), n. 146
Marcus v. Search Warrant, 367 U.S. 717 (1961) — § 15-3(a), n. 339
Marcus v. St. Tammany Parish Sch. Bd., 1997 U.S. Dist. LEXIS 8380 (E.D. La. 1997) — § 6-1(b), n. 175; § 6-1(c), n. 189; § 6-1(a)(5), n. 122

TABLE OF CASES

Marcus Garvey Charter Sch. v. Washington Times Corp., 27 Media L. Rep. (BNA) 1225 (D.C. Super. 1998) — § 12-2(b), nn. 75, 84; § 12-4(b), n. 206; § 13-4(b), n. 511; § 12-4(c)(2), n. 249

Maressa v. New Jersey Monthly, 445 A.2d 376 (N.J. 1982) — § 15-1, n. 17; § 15-2(a), n. 25; § 15-2(c)(2)(B), nn. 120-23; § 15-2(d)(3)(D), n. 200; § 15-2(h), n. 274

Margoulis v. City of Cleveland, 584 N.E.2d 665 (Ohio 1992) — § 11-2, n. 20

Marich v. QRZ Media, Inc., 86 Cal. Rptr. 2d 406 (Ct. App. 1999) — § 12-4(a), n. 169; § 13-7(c), n. 781; § 13-8, n. 806; § 13-7(b)(3), n. 708

Maricopa Audubon Soc'y v. United States Forest Serv., 108 F.3d 1082 (9th Cir. 1997) — § 10-2(a), n. 3

Marin Indep. Journal v. Municipal Ct., 16 Cal. Rptr. 2d 550 (Ct. App. 1993) — § 2-1(c), n. 54; § 13-3(a), n. 122

Marina Management Serv. v. Kentucky Cabinet for Tourism, 906 S.W.2d 318 (Ky. 1995) — § 11-7(f)(2), n. 274

Marion County Sheriff's Merit Bd. v. People Broadcasting Corp., 547 N.E.2d 235 (Ind. 1989) — § 9-4, n. 67

Marisol A. v. Giuliani, 929 F. Supp. 660 (S.D.N.Y. 1996) — § 4-2(a), nn. 66-68

Marisol A. v. Giuliani, 26 Media L. Rep. (BNA) 1151 (S.D.N.Y. 1997) — § 5-1, n. 17; § 6-1(d), n. 250; § 6-1(a)(3), n. 54; § 6-1(a)(4), n. 60; § 6-1(a)(5), n. 118

Mark v. King Broadcasting Co., 618 P.2d 512 (Wash. App. 1980) — § 12-2(b), n. 73

Marketos v. American Employers Ins. Co., 460 N.W.2d 272 (Mich. App. 1990) — § 15-2(c)(2)(A), n. 87; § 15-2(d)(3)(C), n. 197; § 16-2(a)(2), n. 31; § 16-2(d)(3), n. 210; § 16-2(d)(3)(C), n. 271

Marks v. Department of Justice, 578 F.2d 261 (9th Cir. 1978) — § 10-2(b)(3), n. 39

Marks v. Vehlow, 671 P.2d 473 (Idaho 1983) — § 16-2(c)(1), n. 125

Maroscia v. Levi, 569 F.2d 1000 (7th Cir. 1977) — § 10-2(c)(3), n. 101

M.A. Schapiro & Co. v. SEC, 339 F. Supp. 467 (D.D.C. 1972) — § 10-2(c)(9), nn. 219, 220

Marsh v. Richmond Newspapers, Inc., 288 S.E.2d 415 (Va. 1982) — § 9-6(g), nn. 340, 341

Marshall v. Egan, No. C1-94-13844 (Minn. Dist. July 7, 1994) — § 13-3(c)(2), n. 200

Marshall v. Egan, No. C6-94-1390 (Minn. App. July 1, 1994) — § 13-3(c)(2), n. 200

Marston v. Gainesville Sun Publ'g Co., 341 So. 2d 783 (Fla. App. 1976) — § 9-6(b), n. 259

Martin v. City of Struthers, 319 U.S. 141 (1943) — § 1-3, n. 49

Martin v. Consultants & Adm'rs, Inc., 966 F.2d 1078 (7th Cir. 1992) — § 5-2(a)(3), n. 137

Martin v. Musteen, 799 S.W.2d 540 (Ark. 1990) — § 11-7(b)(3)(A), n. 223

Martin v. Office of Special Counsel, 819 F.2d 1181 (D.C. Cir. 1987) — § 10-2(c)(6), n. 132

Martin v. Struthers, 319 U.S. 141 (1943) — § 12-4(c)(3), n. 284

Martindell v. International Tel. & Tel. Corp., 594 F.2d 291 (2d Cir. 1979) — § 6-1(a)(1), n. 16

Maryland v. Cottman Transmission Sys., Inc., 542 A.2d 859 (Md. Spec. App. 1988) — § 3-2(a), nn. 356, 358; § 6-1(c)(2), n. 229

Maryland v. Sheridan, 236 A.2d 18 (Md. 1967) — § 15-1, nn. 1, 9; § 15-2(d)(3)(E), n. 208

Marzen v. Department of Health & Human Servs., 632 F. Supp. 785 (N.D. Ill. 1985) — § 10-2(c)(8)(A), n. 180

TABLE OF CASES

Mason v. CBS Inc., 15 Media L. Rep. (BNA) 2126 (N.Y. Sup. 1988) — § 15-2(c)(2)(B), n. 131; § 16-2(a)(2), n. 32; § 16-2(c)(2)(B), n. 159
Mason v. Schriver, 14 F. Supp. 2d 321 (S.D.N.Y. 1998) — § 3-1(c), n. 297
Masonite Corp. v. County of Mendocino Air Quality Management Dist., 49 Cal. Rptr. 2d 639 (Ct. App. 1996) — § 11-5(d), n. 173; § 11-5(a)(3), n. 91
Massachusetts v. Corsetti, 438 N.E.2d 805 (Mass. 1982) — § 14-5(f), n. 218; § 16-2(a)(2), n. 43; § 16-2(f), n. 375
Massachusetts v. Marshall, 253 N.E.2d 333 (Mass. 1969) — § 3-1(c), n. 262
Massachusetts v. Martin, 629 N.E.2d 297 (Mass. 1994) — § 3-1(c), nn. 260-65
Massachusetts v. McDonald, 6 MEDIA L. REP. (BNA) 2230 (Mass. Super. 1980) — § 16-2(f), n. 375
Massachusetts v. Salvi, 24 Media L. Rep. (BNA) 1734 (Mass. Super. 1996) — § 4-3, n. 100
Massachusetts v. Vieux, 671 N.E.2d 989 (Mass. App. 1996) — § 13-7(b)(4)(E), n. 731
Massachusetts v. Vitello, 327 N.E.2d 819 (Mass. 1975) — § 13-7(b)(1), n. 689
Massachusetts v. Wiseman, 249 N.E.2d 610 (Mass. 1969) — § 13-4(a)(1)(A), nn. 335-39
Massey v. FBI, 3 F.3d 620 (2d Cir. 1993) — § 10-2(c)(3), n. 101; § 10-2(c)(8)(D), n. 205
Matera v. Superior Ct., 825 P.2d 971 (Ariz. App. 1992) — § 15-2(b)(1), n. 40; § 15-2(d)(1), n. 145; § 15-2(d)(3)(A), n. 167; § 16-2(a)(2), nn. 29, 31
Matlack, Inc. v. EPA, 868 F. Supp. 627 (D. Del. 1994) — § 10-2(h), n. 287
Matthews v. Forrest, 69 S.E.2d 553 (N.C. 1952) — § 12-4(c)(3), n. 322
Maughan v. NL Indus., 524 F. Supp. 93 (D.D.C. 1981) — § 16-2(d)(3), n. 213; § 16-2(d)(3)(D), n. 286
Maurice v. NLRB, 7 Media L. Rep. (BNA) 2221 (S.D. W. Va. 1981), *vacated*, 691 F.2d 182 (4th Cir. 1982) — § 15-3(b), n. 376
Maurice River Township Bd. of Educ. v. Maurice River Township Teachers Ass'n, 475 A. 2d 59 (N.J. Super. 1984) — § 9-6(e), n. 321
Mayes v. Lin Television of Texas, Inc., 27 Media L. Rep. (BNA) 1214 (N.D. Tex. 1998) — § 13-3(b), n. 133; § 13-7(a)(2)(A)(i), nn. 604, 608
Mayfair Chrysler Plymouth, Inc. v. Baldarotta, 453 N.W.2d 922 (Wis. App. 1990) — § 11-7(b)(3)(B), n. 228
Mayo v. United States Gov't Printing Office, 9 F.3d 1450 (9th Cir. 1994) — § 10-2(b)(2), n. 26
Mayor of Baltimore v. Burke, 506 A.2d 683 (Md. Spec. App. 1985) — § 11-4, n. 74
Mazzella v. Philadelphia Newspapers, Inc., 479 F. Supp. 523 (E.D.N.Y. 1979) — § 15-2(j), n. 324
McBride v. Delaware, 477 A.2d 174 (Del. 1984) — § 16-2(c)(1), n. 92
McBride v. Village of Michiana, 100 F.3d 457 (6th Cir. 1996) — § 9-2(b), n. 42
McBride v. Village of Michiana, 26 Media L. Rep. (BNA) 1833 (W.D. Mich. 1998) — § 9-2(b), n. 44
McCall v. Courier-Journal, 6 Media L. Rep. (BNA) 1112 (Ky. App. 1980), *rev'd on other grounds*, 623 S.W.2d 882 (Ky. 1981) — § 13-7(c), nn. 770-74
McCambridge v. City of Little Rock, 766 S.W.2d 909 (Ark. 1989) — § 11-5(a)(4), n. 108; § 11-7(b)(3)(B), n. 229
McCarty v. Bankers Ins. Co., 27 Media L. Rep. (BNA) 1051 (N.D. Fla. 1998) — § 15-2(e)(2)(B), n. 242; § 16-2(e)(3), n. 333
McClain v. College Hosp., 492 A.2d 991 (N.J. 1985) — § 11-5(c), n. 170
McClatchy Newspapers v. Superior Ct., 245 Cal. Rptr. 774 (Cal. 1988) — § 11-3(c), n. 47

TABLE OF CASES

McClatchy Newspapers v. Superior Ct., 751 P.2d 1329 (Cal. 1988) — § 3-1(a)(3), n. 127; § 5-2(a)(3), nn. 136, 176

McClatchy Newspapers, Inc. v. Fresno County Superior Ct., 19 Media L. Rep. (BNA) 1555 (Cal. App. 1991) — § 2-1(d), n. 98

McClellan Ecological Seepage Situation v. Carlucci, 835 F.2d 1282 (9th Cir. 1987) — § 10-2(b)(5), nn. 47, 51

McComas v. Board of Educ., 475 S.E.2d 280 (W. Va. 1996) — § 9-6(c), n. 284; § 9-6(j), n. 415

McCoy Restaurants, Inc. v. City of Orlando, 392 So. 2d 252 (Fla. 1980) — § 9-6(b), n. 274

McCraig v. Talladega Publ'g Co., 544 So. 2d 875 (Ala. 1989) — § 12-4(a), n. 182

McCullough v. FDIC, 1 Gov't Disclosure Serv. (P-H) 80,194 (D.C. Cir. 1980) — § 10-2(c)(9), n. 221

McCutchen v. Department of Health & Human Servs., 30 F.3d 183 (D.C. Cir. 1994) — § 10-2(c)(7), n. 157

McDaniel v. Atlanta Coca-Cola Bottling Co., 2 S.E.2d 810 (Ga. App. 1939) — § 13-7(c), n. 749

McDonnell v. United States, 4 F.3d 1227 (3d Cir. 1993) — § 10-2(b)(3), n. 37; § 10-2(c)(7), n. 169; § 10-2(c)(8), n. 174; § 10-2(c)(8)(D), n. 205

McDonnell v. United States, 870 F. Supp. 576 (D.N.J. 1994) — § 10-2(h), n. 289

McGehee v. Casey, 718 F.2d 1137 (D.C. Cir. 1983) — § 13-3(c)(9)(B), n. 315

McGrane v. Reader's Digest Ass'n, 822 F. Supp. 1044 (S.D.N.Y. 1993) — § 13-4(c), n. 531

McGraw-Hill Cos. v. Procter & Gamble Co., 515 U.S. 1309, 116 S. Ct. 6 (1995) — § 2-1(d), n. 102; § 13-3(a), nn. 82, 113, 115

McIntyre v. Ohio Elections Comm'n, 514 U.S. 334 (1995) — § 14-5(c), n. 149; § 14-5(e), nn. 187-98

McKamey v. Roach, 55 F.3d 1236 (6th Cir. 1995) — § 13-7(a)(2)(A)(ii), n. 624

McKeiver v. Pennsylvania, 403 U.S. 528 (1971) — § 3-3(a), n. 442

McKnight v. Simpson's Beauty Supply, Inc., 358 S.E.2d 107 (N.C. App. 1987) — § 13-2(b), n. 66

McLaughlin v. Philadelphia Newspapers, Inc., 348 A.2d 376 (Pa. 1975) — § 11-1, n. 2

McMenamin v. Tartaglione, 590 A.2d 802 (Pa. Commw. 1991) — § 15-2(d)(1), n. 149; § 16-2(a)(2), n. 32; § 16-2(e)(3), n. 333

McMullan v. Wohlgemuth, 308 A.2d 888 (Pa. 1973) — § 11-7(i), n. 307

McNabb v. Oregonian Publ'g Co., 685 P.2d 458 (Or. App. 1984) — § 15-2(c)(2)(B), nn. 104-07

McNally v. United States, 483 U.S. 350 (1987) — § 13-3(c)(6), n. 238

McNamara v. Department of Justice, 949 F. Supp. 478 (W.D. Tex. 1996) — § 10-2(h), n. 282

McNeilus v. Corporate Reports, Inc., 21 Media L. Rep. (BNA) 2171 (Minn. Dist. 1993) — § 15-2(c)(2)(B), n. 99; § 15-2(e)(2)(B), nn. 242, 246, 247; § 15-2(g), n. 267

Mead Data Cent., Inc. v. Department of Air Force, 566 F.2d 242 (D.C. Cir. 1977) — § 10-2(c)(6), n. 152

Medical Lab. Management Consultants v. American Broadcasting Cos., 931 F. Supp. 1487 (D. Ariz. 1996) — § 12-4(c)(3), n. 295; § 13-2(b), n. 57; § 13-7(c), n. 757

Medical Lab. Management Consultants v. American Broadcasting Cos., 25 Media L. Rep. (BNA) 1724 (D. Ariz. 1997) — § 13-7(a)(2)(A)(iii), n. 635

TABLE OF CASES

Medical Lab. Management Consultants v. American Broadcasting Cos., 30 F. Supp. 2d 1182 (D. Ariz. 1998) — § 12-4(c)(2), nn. 241, 246, 248; § 12-4(c)(3), nn. 295, 317, 327; § 13-2(b), nn. 57, 69, 71; § 13-4(c), n. 533; § 13-7(a)(2)(A)(iii), n. 635; § 13-7(c), nn. 757, 763, 768; § 13-8, nn. 818-20

Medlin v. Bettis, 17 Media L. Rep. (BNA) 1783 (Kan. Dist. 1990) — § 16-2(d)(3)(C), n. 271

Meeropol v. Meese, 790 F.2d 942 (D.C. Cir. 1986) — § 10-2(b)(3), n. 40

Memphis Publ'g Co. v. Burnett, 871 S.W.2d 359 (Ark. 1994) — § 3-1(b), n. 251

Memphis Publ'g Co. v. City of Memphis, 871 S.W.2d 681 (Tenn. 1994) — § 11-5(a)(4), n. 115

Memphis Publ'g Co. v. Holt, 710 S.W.2d 513 (Tenn. 1986) — § 5-2(a)(5), n. 226

Menowitz v. Brown, 991 F.2d 36 (2d Cir. 1998) — § 16-2(i), n. 444

Mermelstein v. SEC, 629 F. Supp. 672 (D.D.C. 1986) — § 9-5(a)(8)(H), n. 171; § 10-2(c)(9), n. 220

Methodist Hosp., Inc. v. Sullivan, 91 F.3d 1026 (7th Cir. 1996) — § 6-1(d), n. 261

Metter v. Los Angeles Examiner, 95 P.2d 491 (Cal. App. 1939) — § 12-4(a), n. 152; § 13-3(b), n. 144

Meyer v. ABC, Inc., 25 Media L. Rep. (BNA) 1605 (Colo. Dist. 1997) — § 11-7(d), n. 260

Meyer v. Bush, 981 F.2d 1288 (D.C. Cir. 1993) — § 10-2(b)(2), nn. 22, 29

Meyerhoff v. EPA, 958 F.2d 1498 (9th Cir. 1992) — § 10-3(c), n. 300

Miami Herald Publ'g Co. v. Chappell, 403 So. 2d 1342 (Fla. App. 1981) — § 5-2(a), n. 59; § 3-1(a)(5), nn. 185, 193-96

Miami Herald Publ'g Co. v. City of N. Miami, 452 So. 2d 572 (Fla. App. 1984) — § 11-5(c), n. 167

Miami Herald Publ'g Co. v. Collazo, 329 So. 2d 333 (Fla. App. 1976) — § 6-1(b), n. 187; § 11-7(m), n. 351

Miami Herald Publ'g Co. v. Florida, 363 So. 2d 603 (Fla. App. 1978) — § 3-1(d), nn. 315, 321, 322, 325

Miami Herald Publ'g Co. v. Lewis, 426 So. 2d 1 (Fla. 1982) — § 2-3, nn. 296, 309

Miami Herald Publ'g Co. v. Morejon, 561 So. 2d 577 (Fla. 1990) — § 16-2(d)(3)(B), n. 239

Michael H. v. Gerald D., 491 U.S. 110 (1989) — § 2-2(h), n. 281

Michigan v. Lucas, 470 N.W.2d 460 (Mich. App. 1991) — § 13-7(b)(4)(E), n. 731

Michigan v. Smith, 4 Media L. Rep. (BNA) 1753 (Mich. Cir. 1978) — § 15-2(c)(1), n. 59

Michigan United Conservation Club v. CBS News, 485 F. Supp. 893 (W.D. Mich. 1980) — § 13-4(a)(3)(A)(ii), n. 467

Miglionico v. Birmingham News Co., 378 So. 2d 677 (Ala. 1979) — § 9-6(h), n. 345; § 9-6(h)(4), nn. 359, 360; § 9-6(j), nn. 407, 410

Military Audit Project v. Casey, 656 F.2d 724 (D.C. Cir. 1981) — § 10-2(b)(3), n. 32; § 10-2(c)(2), nn. 94, 98

Miller v. California, 413 U.S. 15 (1973) — § 1-1, n. 12

Miller v. Casey, 730 F.2d 773 (D.C. Cir. 1984) — § 10-2(c)(2), n. 97

Miller v. Department of Agric., 13 F.3d 260 (8th Cir. 1993) — § 10-2(c)(8)(A), n. 181

Miller v. Department of State, 779 F.2d 1378 (8th Cir. 1985) — § 10-2(h), nn. 275, 286, 287

Miller v. Mecklenburg County, 602 F. Supp. 675 (W.D.N.C. 1985) — § 16-2(d)(3)(B), n. 236; § 16-2(d)(3)(C), n. 248

TABLE OF CASES

Miller v. National Broadcasting Co., 232 Cal. Rptr. 668 (Ct. App. 1986) — § 12-2(a), n. 7; § 12-4(a), nn. 160-72, 178, 188, 196, 199; § 12-4(c)(2), n. 243; § 12-4(c)(3), nn. 292-94, 310; § 13-7(c), nn. 763, 769

Miller v. Superior Ct., 77 Cal. Rptr. 2d 827 (Ct. App. 1998) — § 15-2(a), n. 24; § 15-2(c)(1), nn. 74, 78; § 15-2(e)(1), n. 221; § 15-2(e)(2), n. 233

Miller v. Transamerican Press, Inc., 621 F.2d 721 (5th Cir. 1980) — § 14-6(b), n. 264; § 16-2(a)(1), n. 2; § 16-2(c)(1), n. 114; § 16-2(c)(2)(B), n. 156; § 16-2(d)(1), nn. 177, 189, 191; § 16-2(d)(3)(C), n. 246; § 16-2(e)(1), n. 299; § 16-2(e)(2), n. 324; § 16-2(e)(3), n. 354; § 16-2(h), n. 402; § 16-2(h)(2), n. 424; § 16-2(i), n. 444

Mills v. Alabama, 384 U.S. 214 (1966) — § 1-4(b), n. 64; § 8-4, n. 123

Milton v. Hayes, 770 P.2d 14 (Okla. 1989) — § 11-7(h), n. 302

Mimms v. Philadelphia Newspapers, Inc., 352 F. Supp. 862 (E.D. Pa. 1972) — § 13-7(a)(1), n. 581

Minier v. CIA, 88 F.3d 796 (9th Cir. 1996) — § 10-2(c)(4), n. 111

Minneapolis Star & Tribune Co. v. Kammeyer, 341 N.W.2d 550 (Minn. 1983) — § 3-1(a), nn. 7, 9

Minneapolis Star & Tribune Co. v. Minnesota Comm'r of Revenue, 460 U.S. 575 (1983) — § 1-1, n. 3

Minneapolis Star & Tribune Co. v. Schumacher, 392 N.W.2d 197 (Minn. 1986) — § 6-1(b), n. 188; § 6-1(c)(2), n. 228

Minneapolis Star & Tribune Co. v. United States, 713 F. Supp. 1308 (D. Minn. 1989) — § 15-3(a), n. 350

Minnesota v. Bowles, 530 N.W.2d 521 (Minn. 1995) — § 7-3, nn. 189, 193

Minnesota v. Brenner, 488 N.W.2d 339 (Minn. App. 1992) — § 15-2(e)(2)(A), n. 240

Minnesota v. Hennepin County, 505 N.W.2d 294 (Minn. 1993) — § 6-1(b), n. 188

Minnesota v. Swart, 20 Media L. Rep. (BNA) 1703 (Minn. App. 1992) — § 5-2(c), n. 384

Minnesota v. Turner, 550 N.W.2d 622 (Minn. 1996) — § 15-1, n. 17; § 16-2(c)(1), n. 109; § 16-2(d)(3)(B), n. 234

Minot Daily News v. Holum, 380 N.W.2d 347 (N.D. 1986) — § 3-1(a), n. 48; § 3-1(a)(2), nn. 96, 99

Mintz v. Director, Dep't of Motor Vehicles, 691 F.2d 507 (9th Cir. 1982) — § 8-3, n. 121

Miscavige v. IRS, 2 F.3d 366 (11th Cir. 1993) — § 10-2(h), n. 269

Mississippi Comm'n on Judicial Performance v. Emmanuel, 688 So. 2d 222 (Miss. 1996) — § 4-3, n. 87

Mississippi Publishers Corp. v. Circuit Ct., 12 Media L. Rep. (BNA) 1342 (Miss. 1985) — § 7-1, n. 82

Missoulian v. Board of Regents, 675 P.2d 962 (Mont. 1984) — § 9-1, n. 16; § 9-6(i)(1)(B), n. 375

Missouri ex rel. Classic III, Inc. v. Ely, 954 S.W.2d 650 (Mo. App. 1997) — § 16-2(a)(2), n. 29; § 16-2(c)(2)(B), n. 159; § 16-2(d)(1), n. 190; § 16-2(e)(1), n. 299; § 16-2(e)(4), n. 366; § 16-2(h)(1), n. 406

Missouri v. King, 873 S.W.2d 905 (Mo. App. 1994) — § 13-7(b)(4)(E), n. 734

Missouri v. NOW, 620 F.2d 1301 (8th Cir. 1980) — § 13-4(c), n. 534

Missouri v. Simmons, 944 S.W.2d 165 (Mo. 1997) — § 4-1, n. 36

Missouri ex rel. Missouri Local Gov't Retirement Sys. v. Bill, 935 S.W.2d 659 (Mo. App. 1996) — § 11-7(a)(2), n. 189

Mitchell v. Board of Educ., 493 N.Y.S.2d 826 (App. Div. 1985) — § 9-6(e), n. 321

Mitchell v. Borakove, 639 N.Y.S.2d 791 (App. Div. 1996) — § 11-7(d), n. 257

TABLE OF CASES

Mitchell v. Greenburg, 640 So. 2d 1367 (La. App. 1994) — § 11-7(e), n. 266
Mitchell v. Superior Ct., 690 P.2d 51 (Ariz. 1984) — § 5-2(d), n. 435
Mitchell v. Superior Ct., 690 P.2d 625 (Cal. 1984) — § 15-2(e)(1), n. 220; § 15-2(f), n. 260; § 16-2(a)(2), nn. 29, 33-35; § 16-2(c)(2)(B), n. 159; § 16-2(d)(1), nn. 177, 191; § 16-2(d)(3), n. 211; § 16-2(e)(1), n. 299; § 16-2(e)(4), n. 366; § 16-2(h)(2), n. 426
Mitzner v. Sobol, 570 N.Y.S.2d 402 (Sup. Ct. 1991) — § 11-5(d), n. 173
Moffit v. Willis, 459 So. 2d 1018 (Fla. 1984) — § 9-3, n. 57
Mokhiber v. Davis, 537 A.2d 1100 (D.C. 1988) — § 3-2(a), n. 340; § 6-1(a)(1), n. 17; § 6-1(a)(3), nn. 46, 54, 59; § 6-1(a)(4), n. 63; § 6-1(c)(1), n. 216
Moncrief v. Hanton, 10 Media L. Rep. (BNA) 1620 (N.D. Ohio 1984) — § 12-5, n. 358
Monson v. Oklahoma ex rel. Oklahoma Corp. Comm'n, 673 P.2d 839 (Okla. 1983) — § 9-6(b), n. 271
Montana v. District Ct., 546 P.2d 988 (Mont. 1976) — § 15-2(i)(2), n. 304
Montana ex rel. Blackberry v. District Ct., 546 P.2d 988 (Mont. 1976) — § 16-2(a)(2), n. 29; § 16-2(h)(1), n. 411
Montana ex rel. Great Falls Tribune Co v. Montana Eighth Judicial Dist. Ct., 777 P.2d 345 (Mont. 1989) — § 3-1(d), n. 324
Montana ex rel. Missoulian v. Montana Twenty-First Judicial Dist. Ct., 933 P.2d 829 (Mont. 1997) — § 1-3, n. 49; § 2-1(d), n. 98; § 5-2(a), n. 79; § 7-1, nn. 31, 35, 56
Montana Human Rights Div. v. City of Billings, 649 P.2d 1283 (Mont. 1982) — § 11-7(e), n. 266
Montoya v. Texas, 1998 Tex. App. LEXIS 7377 (Tex. App. Nov. 25, 1998) — § 4-3, nn. 92, 100
Moore v. Alaska, 553 P.2d 8, 21 (Alaska 1976) — § 9-6(d), n. 305
Moore v. City of East Cleveland, 431 U.S. 494 (1977) — § 2-2(a), n. 121
Moore v. Collins, 897 S.W.2d 496 (Tex. App. 1995) — § 11-9, n. 375
Moore v. Regents of Univ. of California, 249 Cal. Rptr. 494 (Ct. App. 1988) — § 13-3(b), n. 154
Moore v. Santucci, 543 N.Y.S.2d 103 (App. Div. 1989) — § 11-7(b)(3)(B), n. 231; § 11-7(b)(9), n. 252
Morgan v. Celender, 780 F. Supp. 307 (W.D. Pa. 1992) — § 12-6(a), n. 373; § 13-2(a), n. 6; § 13-4(a)(3)(B), nn. 473-76
Morgan v. Florida, 337 So. 2d 951 (Fla. 1976) — § 16-2(c)(1), n. 91
Morgan v. Roberts, 702 F.2d 945 (11th Cir. 1983) — § 16-2(h)(2), nn. 438-40
Morning Call, Inc. v. Lower Saucon Township, 627 A.2d 297 (Pa. Commw. 1993) — § 11-7(m), n. 351
Morris v. Martin, 434 N.E.2d 1079 (N.Y. 1982) — § 11-5(a)(2), n. 88
Mothers on the Move, Inc. v. Messer, 652 N.Y.S.2d 773 (App. Div. 1997) — § 11-7(a)(1), n. 185
M.P. v. Schwartz, 853 F. Supp. 164 (D. Md. 1994) — § 6-1(c)(1), n. 222
Mudge Rose Guthrie Alexander & Ferdon v. United States Int'l Trade Comm'n, 846 F.2d 1527 (D.C. Cir. 1988) — § 10-2(c)(4), n. 116
Muhammad v. United States Bureau of Prisons, 789 F. Supp. 449 (D.D.C. 1992) — § 10-2(g), n. 262
Mullins v. City of Griffin, 886 F. Supp. 21 (N.D. Ga. 1995) — § 6-1(b), n. 175
Mulqueeny v. National Comm'n on the Observance of Int'l Women's Year, 549 F.2d 1115 (7th Cir. 1975) — § 9-5(b)(7), n. 246
Multimedia WMAZ, Inc. v. Georgia, 353 S.E.2d 173 (Ga. 1987) — § 4-3, n. 99

TABLE OF CASES

Multimedia WMAZ, Inc. v. Kubach, 443 S.E.2d 491 (Ga. App. 1994) — § 13-4(a)(3)(B), nn. 481-85
Municipality of Anchorage v. Anchorage Daily News, 794 P.2d 584 (Alaska 1990) — § 11-7(a), n. 183
Munroe v. Braatz, 549 N.W.2d 451 (Wis. App. 1996) — § 11-9, n. 376
Muratore v. M/S Scotia Prince, 656 F. Supp. 471 (D. Me. 1987), *modified on other grounds*, 845 F.2d 347 (1st Cir. 1988) — § 12-2(b), n. 75
Murphy v. Colorado, 365 U.S. 843 (1961) — § 14-2, n. 20
Murphy v. Florida, 421 U.S. 794 (1975) — § 2-1(a), n. 15
Murray v. New York Magazine Co., 267 N.E.2d 256 (N.Y. 1971) — § 12-2(b), n. 84
Musicom Int'l, Inc. v. Serubo, 22 Media L. Rep. (BNA) 2507 (E.D. Pa. 1994) — § 6-1(a)(5), n. 110
Myers & Chapman, Inc. v. Thomas G. Evans, Inc., 374 S.E.2d 385 (N.C. 1988) — § 13-2(b), n. 68

N

NAACP v. Alabama, 357 U.S. 449 (1958) — § 14-2, n. 25; § 14-4(a), n. 80; § 14-4(c), n. 102; § 15-3(b), n. 380
NAACP v. Button, 371 U.S. 415 (1963) — § 14-4(a), n. 80; § 14-6(a), n. 232
NAACP v. Claiborne Hardware Co., 458 U.S. 886 (1982) — § 13-4(c), n. 534; § 13-4(a)(2)(C), n. 401
Nader v. Baroody, 396 F. Supp. 1231 (D.D.C. 1975) — § 9-5(b)(2), n. 211
Nader v. Dunlop, 370 F. Supp. 177 (D.D.C. 1973) — § 9-5(b)(3), n. 224; § 9-5(b)(5), nn. 232, 236, 238; § 9-5(b)(6), n. 242
Nader v. General Motors Corp., 255 N.E.2d 765 (N.Y. 1970) — § 13-7(c), n. 749
Nadler v. Department of Justice, 955 F.2d 1479 (11th Cir. 1992) — § 10-2(c)(8)(C), n. 192
Nasrallah v. Missouri State Bd. of Chiropractic Exm'rs, 1996 Mo. App. LEXIS 1994 (Mo. App. Nov. 26, 1996) — § 9-6(i)(1)(C), n. 380
Nation Magazine v. Department of Defense, 762 F. Supp. 1558 (S.D.N.Y. 1991) — § 8-5, nn. 151, 156-59, 161-69
Nation Magazine v. United States Customs Serv., 71 F.3d 885 (D.C. Cir. 1995) — § 10-2(b)(3), n. 40
National Anti-Hunger Coalition v. President's Private Sector Survey on Cost Control, 557 F. Supp. 524 (D.D.C. 1983) — § 9-5(b)(7), n. 246
National Anti-Hunger Coalition v. President's Private Sector Survey on Cost Control, 566 F. Supp. 1515 (D.D.C. 1983) — § 9-5(b)(7), n. 248
National Anti-Hunger Coalition v. President's Private Sector Survey on Cost Control, 711 F.2d 1071 (D.C. Cir. 1983) — § 9-5(b)(1), n. 196
National Ass'n of Concerned Vets v. Secretary of Defense, 675 F.2d 1319 (D.C. Cir. 1982) — § 10-2(h), n. 289
National Ass'n of Retired Fed. Employees v. Horner, 879 F.2d 873 (D.C. Cir. 1989) — § 10-2(c)(7), nn. 159, 160, 162, 164
National Broadcasting Co. v. Association of State Democratic Chairs, 14 Media L. Rep. (BNA) 1383 (N.D. Ohio 1987) — § 9-2(b), n. 45
National Broadcasting Co. v. Cleland, 697 F. Supp. 1204 (N.D. Ga. 1988) — § 8-4, nn. 130, 136
National Broadcasting Co. v. Cleveland, 526 N.E.2d 786 (Ohio 1988) — § 11-1, n. 6

TABLE OF CASES

National Broadcasting Co. v. Colburg, 699 F. Supp. 241 (D. Mont. 1988) — § 8-4, nn. 130, 136

National Broadcasting Co. v. Communications Workers of Am., 860 F.2d 1022 (11th Cir. 1988) — § 9-2(b), n. 45

National Broadcasting Co. v. Cooperman, 501 N.Y.S.2d 405 (App. Div. 1986) — § 7-1, n. 36; § 7-2, n. 125

National Broadcasting Co. v. Court of C.P., 556 N.E.2d 1120 (Ohio 1990) — § 15-2(d)(3)(C), n. 191

National Broadcasting Co. v. SBA, 836 F. Supp. 121 (S.D.N.Y. 1993) — § 10-2(c)(10), n. 226

National Indep. Bus. Alliance v. City of Beverly Hills, 180 Cal. Rptr. 59 (Ct. App. 1982) — § 9-6(d), n. 290

National Nutritional Foods Ass'n v. Califano, 603 F.2d 327 (2d Cir. 1979) — § 9-5(b)(2), n. 211

National Org. for Women v. Department of Health & Human Servs., 736 F.2d 727 (D.C. Cir. 1984) — § 10-2(f), nn. 259, 260

National Parks & Conservation Ass'n v. Kleppe, 547 F.2d 673 (D.C. Cir. 1976) — § 10-2(c)(5), n. 127

National Parks & Conservation Ass'n v. Morton, 498 F.2d 765 (D.C. Cir. 1974) — § 10-2(c)(5), nn. 119, 125-27

National Sec. Archive v. Department of Defense, 880 F.2d 1381 (D.C. Cir. 1989) — § 10-2(b)(5), n. 48

National Treasury Employees Union v. United States Customs Serv., 802 F.2d 525 (D.C. Cir. 1986) — § 10-2(c)(3), n. 105

National Union Fire Ins. Co. v. Seafirst Co., 14 Media L. Rep. (BNA) 1190 (W.D. Wash. 1987) — § 16-3, n. 479

National W. Life Ins. Co. v. United States, 512 F. Supp. 454 (N.D. Tex. 1980) — § 10-2(c)(7), n. 165

National Wildlife Fed'n v. United States Forest Serv., 861 F.2d 1114 (9th Cir. 1988) — § 10-2(c)(6), n. 140

Nationwide Bldg. Maintenance v. Sampson, 559 F.2d 704 (D.C. Cir. 1976) — § 10-2(h), n. 287

Natoli v. Sullivan, 606 N.Y.S.2d 504 (Sup. Ct. 1993) — § 13-7(a)(2)(A)(i), nn. 602-07

Natural Resource Defense Council v. Defense Nuclear Facilities Safety Bd., 969 F.2d 1248 (D.C. Cir. 1992) — § 9-5(a)(8)(C), nn. 153, 155

Natural Resources Defense Council v. Pena, 147 F.3d 1012 (D.C. Cir. 1998) — § 9-5(b)(7), nn. 244, 248

NBC, Inc. v. Santa Clara County Super. Ct., 27 Media L. Rep. (BNA) 1160 (Cal. Super. 1998) — § 5-2(b), nn. 297, 314

NBC Subsidiary (NBC-TV), Inc. v. Superior Ct., 980 P.2d 337 (Cal. 1999) — § 3-2(a), nn. 359-71

Neal v. City of Harvey, Illinois, 173 F.R.D. 231 (N.D. Ill. 1997) — § 16-2(a)(1), n. 8; § 16-2(c)(2)(A), n. 138; § 16-2(d)(3), n. 211; § 16-2(e)(2), n. 317; § 16-2(e)(3), n. 333

Nebel v. Mapco Petroleum, Inc., 10 Media L. Rep. (BNA) 1871 (Alaska 1984) — § 16-2(a)(2), n. 29

Nebraska Press Ass'n v. Stuart, 427 U.S. 539 (1976) — § 2-1(d), nn. 65-91, 99; § 7-1, nn. 3, 57; § 7-2, nn. 87, 88; § 14-5(d), n. 171

Neese v. Paris Special Sch. Dist., 813 S.W.2d 432 (Tenn. App. 1990) — § 9-6(c), n. 288

Neff v. Time, Inc., 406 F. Supp. 858 (W.D. Pa. 1976) — § 12-2(b), n. 84

TABLE OF CASES

Nelson v. Boundary County, 706 P.2d 94 ((Idaho App. 1985) — § 9-4, n. 67
Nero v. Hyland, 386 A.2d 846 (N.J. 1978) — § 9-4, n. 66
Neufeld v. IRS, 646 F.2d 661 (D.C. Cir. 1981) — § 10-2(e), n. 248
Nevada v. Bazile, CR98-0388 (Nev. County Ct. Feb. 19, 1999) — § 15-2(h), n. 282; § 16-2(a)(2), n. 29; § 16-2(c)(1), nn. 86, 92; § 16-2(d)(3)(D), n. 281
Nevens v. City of Chino, 44 Cal. Rptr. 50 (Ct. App. 1965) — § 9-6(e), n. 321
New England Coalition for Energy Efficiency & Env't v. Office of Governor, 670 A.2d 815 (Vt. 1995) — § 11-3(a), n. 36
New Group Boston, Inc. v. Massachusetts, 568 N.E.2d 600 (Mass. 1991) — § 3-3(a), nn. 500-04
New Hampshire v. Guajardo, 605 A.2d 217 (N.H. 1992) — § 3-1(a), n. 58
New Hampshire v. Siel, 444 A.2d 499 (N.H. 1982) — § 16-2(a)(2), n. 29; § 16-2(c)(1), n. 92; § 16-2(e)(1), n. 299; § 16-2(e)(3), n. 343; § 16-2(h)(1), n. 411
New Hampshire v. Telles, 653 A.2d 554 (N.H. 1995) — § 13-7(b)(4)(E), n. 731
New Hampshire v. Weber, 624 A.2d 967 (N.H. 1993) — § 3-1(a), n. 59
New Jersey v. Boiardo, 414 A.2d 14 (N.J. 1980) — § 15-2(c)(1), nn. 71, 72; § 15-2(e)(1), n. 223; § 15-2(e)(2)(B), nn. 242-45; § 15-2(i)(2), nn. 303, 304
New Jersey v. Boiardo, 416 A.2d 793 (N.J. 1980) — § 15-2(b)(2), n. 47; § 15-2(c)(1), nn. 73, 74; § 15-2(e)(2)(B), n. 242; § 15-2(i)(2), nn. 302, 303
New Jersey v. Cantor, 534 A.2d 83 (N.J. Super. 1987) — § 13-3(c), n. 162; § 13-3(c)(4), nn. 222-24, 226-29
New Jersey v. Donovan, 30 A.2d 421 (N.J. 1943) — § 14-1, n. 8; § 15-1, n. 9
New Jersey v. Grecco, 455 A.2d 485 (N.J. Super. 1982) — § 5-2(a), n. 78; § 5-2(a)(7), n. 263
New Jersey v. Hauptmann, 180 A. 809 (N.J. 1935) — § 2-1(a), n. 3; § 4-1, n. 2
New Jersey v. Hunt, 450 A.2d 952 (N.J. 1982) — § 16-2(j)(1), n. 457
New Jersey v. Lashinsky, 404 A.2d 1121 (N.J. 1979) — § 9-2(a), nn. 30, 31; § 13-3(c)(3), nn. 204-09; § 13-3(c)(4), n. 225
New Jersey v. Santiago, 593 A.2d 357 (N.J. Super. 1991) — § 15-2(d)(3)(B), n. 173
New Jersey v. Williams, 459 A.2d 641 (N.J. 1983) — § 3-1(a), nn. 6, 10, 12, 46; § 3-1(a)(1), n. 73; § 3-1(a)(4), n. 169
New Jersey Div. of Youth & Family Servs. v. J.B., 576 A.2d 261 (N.J. 1990) — § 3-1(a), n. 33; § 3-3(b), nn. 513, 514, 534
New Jersey ex rel. K.P., 709 A.2d 315 (N.J. Super. 1997) — § 3-2(b), n. 388; § 3-3(a), nn. 436, 478
New Mexico v. McCormack, 682 P.2d 742 (N.M. App. 1984) — § 13-3(c)(1), nn. 185-89
New Mexico ex rel. Blanchard v. City Comm'rs of Clovis, 750 P.2d 469 (N.M. App. 1988) — § 11-7(a)(1), n. 185
New Mexico Mun. League, Inc. v. New Mexico Envtl. Impact Bd., 539 P.2d 221 (N.M. App. 1975) — § 9-6(d), n. 295
New State Ice Co. v. Liebmann, 285 U.S. 262 (1932) — § 4-1, n. 35
New York v. Arroyo, 675 N.Y.S.2d 272 (County Ct. 1998) — § 3-1(a), n. 44; § 3-1(a)(4), nn. 163, 171
New York v. Doe, 560 N.Y.S.2d 177 (County Ct. 1990) — § 16-2(c)(1), n. 82
New York v. Ferber, 458 U.S. 747 (1982) — § 1-1, nn. 7, 12; § 13-3(c), n. 162
New York v. Georgia M., 22 Media L. Rep. (BNA) 2252 (N.Y. Fam. Ct. 1994) — § 4-3, n. 103
New York v. Griffin, 21 Media L. Rep. (BNA) 1030 (N.Y. Sup. Ct. 1992) — § 16-2(d)(3)(C), n. 270

TABLE OF CASES

New York v. Martin, 14 MEDIA L. REP. (BNA) 2349 (N.Y. County Ct. 1988) — § 16-2(a)(2), n. 32

New York v. Royster, 26 Media L. Rep. (BNA) 1893 (N.Y. Sup. Ct. 1997) — § 15-2(d)(1), n. 143

New York v. Troiano, 486 N.Y.S.2d 991 (County Ct. 1985) — § 16-2(a)(2), n. 32

New York 1 News v. Office of President of Borough of Staten Island, 631 N.Y.S.2d 479 (App. Div. 1995) — § 11-7(a)(3), n. 192

New York News, Inc. v. Grinker, 537 N.Y.S.2d 770 (Sup. Ct. 1989) — § 11-8, n. 356

New York News, Inc. v. Office of Special State Prosecutor, 544 N.Y.S.2d 151 (App. Div. 1989) — § 11-7(b)(3)(A), n. 226

New York Times Co. v. Demakos, 529 N.Y.S.2d 97 (App. Div. 1988) — § 3-1(a)(6), n. 212

New York Times Co. v. Jascalevich, 439 U.S. 1301 (1978) — § 14-5(f), nn. 199-212

New York Times Co. v. NASA, 920 F.2d 1002 (D.C. Cir. 1990) — § 10-2(c)(7), n. 156

New York Times Co. v. New Jersey, 439 U.S. 886 (1978) — § 14-5(f), n. 212

New York Times Co. v. New York State Dep't of Health, 660 N.Y.S.2d 810 (Sup. Ct. 1997) — § 11-7(e), n. 267

New York Times Co. v. Rothwax, 533 N.Y.S.2d 73 (App. Div. 1988) — § 7-1, n. 36; § 7-2, n. 125

New York Times Co. v. Sullivan, 376 U.S. 254 (1964) — § 1-1, n. 12; § 1-2(b), n. 27; § 1-3, n. 42; § 13-4(a)(2)(A), n. 373; § 13-4(a)(2)(B), nn. 379, 394; § 13-4(a)(2)(C), nn. 401, 410; § 13-4(a)(3)(A)(i), n. 430; § 13-4(a)(3)(A)(ii), n. 467; § 13-6, n. 571; § 14-4(c), n. 102; § 14-5(b), n. 133; § 16-2(c)(2)(B), n. 156; § 16-2(h), n. 392

New York Times Co. v. Superior Ct., 60 Cal. Rptr. 2d 410 (Ct. App. 1997) — § 11-7(a), n. 182

New York Times Co. v. Superior Ct., 796 P.2d 811 (Cal. 1990) —§ 15-2(c)(2)(A), nn. 88, 90; § 15-2(e)(1), n. 220; § 15-2(f), nn. 260, 261; § 15-2(g), n. 266; § 15-2(i)(3), nn. 313, 314

New York Times Co. v. United States, 403 U.S. 713 (1971) — § 12-4(c)(3), n. 265; § 13-3(a), nn. 78-80, 105; § 13-3(c)(9), n. 284; § 13-3(c)(9)(A), nn. 294-97

Newark Morning Ledger Co. v. Saginaw County Sheriff, 514 N.W.2d 214 (Mich. App. 1994) — § 11-1, n. 8

Newberry Publ'g Co. v. Newberry County Comm'n, 417 S.E.2d 870 (S.C. 1992) — § 11-5(a), n. 83

Newburn v. Howard Hughes Med. Inst., 594 P.2d 1146 (Nev. 1979) — § 15-2(g), n. 265; § 15-2(h), n. 282; § 16-2(a)(2), n. 31

Newman v. Graddick, 696 F.2d 796 (11th Cir. 1983) — § 3-1(d), n. 324; § 3-2(a), nn. 341-45; § 5-2(a)(2), n. 122

News & Observer Publ'g Co. v. Interim Bd. of Educ., 223 S.E.2d 580 (N.C. App. 1976) — § 9-6(d), n. 298

News & Observer Publ'g Co. v. North Carolina ex rel. Starling, 322 S.E.2d 133 (N.C. 1984) — § 5-2(a)(5), n. 226; § 9-4, n. 71

News & Observer Publ'g Co. v. Poole, 412 S.E.2d 7 (N.C. 1992) — § 9-6(f), n. 330

News & Observer Publ'g Co. v. Wake County Hosp. Sys., 284 S.E.2d 542 (N.C. App. 1981) — § 11-5(a)(4), n. 109; § 11-7(m), n. 344

News & Sun-Sentinel Co. v. Schwab, Twitty & Hanser Architect Group, 596 So. 2d 1029 (Fla. 1992) — § 11-3(e), n. 53

News Group Boston, Inc. v. Massachusetts, 568 N.E.2d 600 (Mass. 1991) — § 6-2(a), nn. 283-85

TABLE OF CASES

Newsday, Inc. v. Sise, 518 N.E.2d 930 (N.Y. 1987) — § 5-2(c), n. 413

News-Journal Co. v. Billingsley, 1980 Del. Ch. LEXIS 553 (Del. Ch. Oct. 7, 1980) — § 11-5(a)(7), n. 148; § 11-7(a)(3), n. 193

News-Journal Corp. v. Foxman, 939 F.2d 1499 (11th Cir. 1991) — § 7-1, nn. 37-40

Newspapers of New England, Inc. v. Clerk-Magistrate, 531 N.E.2d 1261 (Mass. 1988) — § 5-2(a)(2), nn. 115121, 127

Newspapers of New Hampshire, Inc. v. City of Concord, 13 Media L. Rep. (BNA) 1685 (N.H. Super. 1986) — § 9-6(b), n. 258

Newspapers, Inc. v. Breier, 279 N.W.2d 179 (Wis. 1979) — § 11-7(b)(2), n. 215

News-Press & Gazette Co. v. Cathcart, 974 S.W.2d 576 (Mo. App. 1998) — § 11-7(d), n. 260

News-Press Publ'g Co. v. Florida, 345 So. 2d 865 (Fla. App. 1977) — § 5-2(a)(5), n. 223

News-Press Publ'g Co. v. Gadd, 388 So. 2d 276 (Fla. App. 1980) — § 11-5(a), n. 77

Newton v. National Broadcasting Co., 726 F.2d 591 (9th Cir. 1984) — § 16-2(h)(2), n. 417

Nichols v. Bennett, 544 N.W.2d 428 (Wis. 1996) — § 11-7(b)(3)(A), n. 220

Nichols v. Gamso, 315 N.E.2d 770 (N.Y. 1974) — § 11-6, n. 175

Nichols v. Hendrix, 27 Media L. Rep. (BNA) 1503 (N.D. Ga. 1999) — § 12-4(a), n. 151; § 12-5, nn. 365-67

Nichols v. Reno, 931 F. Supp. 748 (D. Colo. 1996) — § 9-5(a)(2), n. 86

Nichols v. United States, 325 F. Supp. 130 (D. Kan. 1971) — § 10-2(b)(1), n. 7

Nicholson v. McClatchy Newspapers, 223 Cal. Rptr. 58 (Ct. App. 1986) — § 12-4(a), n. 170; § 13-3(b), nn. 131-34; § 13-4(c), nn. 535, 536

Nicita v. City of Detroit, 487 N.W.2d 814 (Mich. App. 1992) — § 11-7(f)(4), n. 287

9 to 5 Org. for Women Office Workers v. Board of Governors of Fed. Reserve Sys., 721 F.2d 1 (1st Cir. 1983) — § 10-2(c)(5), n. 128

Nix v. United States, 572 F.2d 998 (4th Cir. 1978) — § 10-2(c)(3), n. 101

Nixon v. Warner Communications, Inc., 435 U.S. 589 (1978) — § 4-2(a), n. 44; § 5-1, nn. 5, 6, 29, 7-14; § 5-2(b), nn. 295, 298, 308; § 6-1(c), n. 189; § 6-1(a)(3), n. 53; § 6-1(a)(5), nn. 106, 111

NLRB v. Midland Daily News, 151 F.3d 472 (6th Cir. 1998) — § 16-2(a)(1), n. 5

NLRB v. Robbins Tire & Rubber Co., 437 U.S. 214 (1978) — § 10-2(a), n. 1; § 10-2(c)(8)(A), nn. 178, 182, 183; § 10-2(h), n. 277

NLRB v. Sears, Roebuck & Co., 421 U.S. 132 (1975) — § 10-2(b)(3), n. 34; § 10-2(c)(6), nn. 132, 134, 139, 142, 144, 151

NLRB v. The Bakersfield Californian, 128 F.3d 1339 (9th Cir. 1997) — § 16-2(a)(1), n. 5

Nobles v. Georgia, 411 S.E.2d 294 (Ga. App. 1991) — § 15-2(c)(1), n. 58; § 15-2(e)(2)(A), nn. 238, 239

Norandal, U.S.A., Inc. v. Local Union No. 7468, 13 Media L. Rep. (BNA) 2167 (Ala. Cir. 1986) — § 16-2(a)(2), nn. 29, 32; § 16-2(d)(3)(C), n. 275; § 16-2(e)(1), n. 299

Norris v. Monroe City Sch. Bd., 580 So. 2d 425 (La. App. 1991) — § 9-6(g), n. 339

North Carolina v. Demery, 22 Media L. Rep. (BNA) 2383 (N.C. Super. 1994) — § 3-1(a)(4), n. 171

North Carolina v. Rogers, 9 Media L. Rep. (BNA) 1254 (N.C. 1983) — § 16-2(a)(2), n. 29

North Dakota v. Ash, 22 Media L. Rep. (BNA) 1607 (N.D. County Ct. 1993) — § 3-1(a)(2), n. 99

TABLE OF CASES

North Mississippi Communications, Inc. v. Jones, 792 F.2d 1330 (5th Cir. 1986) — § 9-2(b), n. 42
North v. Walsh, 881 F.2d 1088 (D.C. Cir. 1989) — § 10-2(b)(3), n. 34
Northern California Police Practices Project v. Craig, 153 Cal. Rptr. 173 (Ct. App. 1979) — § 11-6, n. 178
Northside Realty Assocs. v. United States, 605 F.2d 1348 (5th Cir. 1979) — § 13-2(a), n. 20
Northside Sanitary Landfill, Inc. v. Bradley, 462 N.E.2d 1321 (Ind. App. 1984) — § 15-2(b)(1), n. 41
Northwest Coalition for Alternatives to Pesticides v. Browner, 941 F. Supp. 197 (D.D.C. 1996) — § 10-2(c)(5), n. 127
Northwest Publications, Inc. v. Anderson, 259 N.W.2d 254 (Minn. 1977) — § 5-2(a)(4), n. 201
Norwood v. FAA, 993 F.2d 570 (6th Cir. 1993) — § 10-2(c)(7), n. 169
Nulty v. Pennzoil Co., 485 N.Y.S.2d 533 (App. Div. 1985) — § 15-2(d)(3)(E), n. 207; § 15-2(h), n. 287
Nye v. United States, 313 U.S. 33 (1941) — § 2-1(c), n. 36

O

Oak Beach Inn Corp. v. Babylon Beacon, Inc., 464 N.E.2d 967 (N.Y. 1984) — § 15-2(c)(2)(B), n. 128; § 15-2(f), n. 260
Obiajulu v. City of Rochester, 625 N.Y.S.2d 779 (App. Div. 1995) — § 11-7(a), n. 183
Observer Publ'g Co. v. Poole, 412 S.E.2d 7 (N.C. 1992) — § 11-3(d), n. 48
Occidental Chem. Co. v. Mayo, 351 So. 2d 336 (Fla. 1977) — § 9-6(b), n. 271
O'Connell v. CBS Inc., 782 F.2d 1414 (7th Cir. 1986) — § 13-3(b), n. 140
O'Connell v. Housatonic Valley Publ'g Co., 1991 Conn. Super. LEXIS 2749 (1991) — § 13-4(a)(3)(B), nn. 469-71
Ogden Newspapers, Inc. v. City of Williamstown, 453 S.E.2d 631 (W. Va. 1994) — § 11-7(b), n. 205; § 11-7(b)(1), nn. 210-12
Oglesby v. Department of Army, 920 F.2d 57 (D.C. Cir. 1990) — § 10-2(b)(4), n. 42; § 10-2(g), n. 263; § 10-2(h), n. 275
Ohio v. Anaga, 18 Media L. Rep. (BNA) 1527 (Ohio C.P. 1991) — § 16-2(a)(2), n. 47; § 16-2(c)(1), n. 109
Ohio v. Barker, 23 Media L. Rep. (BNA) 1124 (Ohio C.P. 1994) — § 7-1, n. 5; § 8-1, n. 52
Ohio v. Bidinost, 644 N.E.2d 318 (Ohio 1994) — § 13-7(b)(4)(E), n. 735
Ohio v. Daniel, 1990 Ohio App. LEXIS 5877 (Ohio App. Dec. 31, 1990) — § 16-2(a)(2), n. 47
Ohio v. Evans, 26 Media L. Rep. (BNA) 1735 (Ohio C.P. 1997) — § 3-3(a), nn. 439, 478, 490
Ohio v. Geis, 441 N.E.2d 803 (Ohio App. 1981) — § 15-2(c)(1), nn. 80, 86; § 15-2(d)(1), n. 152; § 15-2(e)(1), nn. 217-19; § 15-2(e)(2), n. 232; § 15-2(e)(2)(A), n. 241; § 15-2(g), n. 265; § 15-2(i)(2), nn. 305, 306
Ohio v. Nobles, 21 Media L. Rep. (BNA) 1501 (Ohio C.P. 1993) — § 3-1(a)(4), nn. 169, 171
Ohio v. Perry, 697 N.E.2d 624 (Ohio 1998) — § 13-9(b), n. 829
Ohio v. Prade, 26 Media L. Rep. (BNA) 2433 (Ohio C.P. 1998) — § 15-2(d)(3)(A), n. 167; § 16-2(a)(2), n. 47

TABLE OF CASES

Ohio ex rel. Allright Parking v. Cleveland, 591 N.E.2d 708 (Ohio 1992) — § 11-5(a)(3), n. 91

Ohio ex rel. Beacon Journal Publ'g Co. v. City of Akron, 640 N.E.2d 164 (Ohio 1994) — § 11-7(a), n. 184

Ohio ex rel. Beacon Journal Publ'g Co. v. McMonagle, 8 Media L. Rep. (BNA) 1927 (Ohio App. 1982) — § 7-3, n. 158

Ohio ex rel. Beacon Journal Publ'g Co. v. Waters, 617 N.E.2d 1110 (Ohio 1993) — § 5-2(a)(3), nn. 136, 176

Ohio ex rel. Cater v. City of N. Olmsted, 631 N.E.2d 1048 (Ohio 1994) — § 11-7(a)(5), n. 203

Ohio ex rel. Cincinnati Enquirer v. Hamilton County, 662 N.E.2d 334 (Ohio 1996) — § 11-2, n. 11; § 11-7(b)(8), n. 244

Ohio ex rel. Cincinnati Post v. Court of C.P., 570 N.E.2d 1101 (Ohio 1991) — § 2-1(d), n. 98; § 7-3, n. 187

Ohio ex rel. Clark v. Toledo, 584 N.E.2d 662 (Ohio 1992) — § 11-9, n. 367

Ohio ex rel. Dayton Newspapers, Inc. v. Rauch, 465 N.E.2d 458 (Ohio 1984) — § 11-7(d), n. 260

Ohio ex rel. Dispatch Printing Co. v. Lias, 628 N.E.2d 1368 (Ohio 1994) — § 3-3(b), nn. 531-35

Ohio ex rel. E.W. Scripps Co. v. Stillwell, 10 Media L. Rep. (BNA) 1380 (Ohio App. 1993) — § 7-1, n. 82

Ohio ex rel. Fant v. Enright, 610 N.E.2d 997 (Ohio 1993) — § 11-4, n. 58

Ohio ex rel. Findlay Publ'g Co. v. Hancock County Bd. of Comm'rs, 684 N.E.2d 1222 (Ohio 1997) — § 11-2, n. 14; § 11-7(m), nn. 344, 346, 349

Ohio ex rel. Findlay Publ'g Co. v. Schroeder, 669 N.E.2d 835 (Ohio 1996) — § 11-7(d), nn. 261, 262; § 11-7(j), n. 309

Ohio ex rel. Gannett Satellite Info. Network v. Petro, 685 N.E.2d 1223 (Ohio 1997) — § 11-5(d), n. 171; § 11-5(a)(6), n. 139; § 11-7(b)(3)(A), n. 219; § 11-7(f)(6), n. 294

Ohio ex rel. Gannett Satellite Info. Network v. Shirley, 678 N.E.2d 557 (Ohio 1997) — § 11-7(a)(1), n. 185

Ohio ex rel. Johnson v. City of Cleveland, 603 N.E.2d 1011 (Ohio 1992) — § 11-7(b)(5), n. 239

Ohio ex rel. Jones v. Myers, 581 N.E.2d 629 (Ohio C.P. 1991) — § 11-7(a)(2), n. 191

Ohio ex rel. Kinsley v. Berea Bd. of Educ., 582 N.E.2d 653 (Ohio App. 1990) — § 11-5(a)(4), n. 109

Ohio ex rel. Lippitt v. Kovacic, 591 N.E.2d 422 (Ohio App. 1991) — § 11-5(a)(2), n. 88

Ohio ex rel. Lorain Journal Co. v. Lorain, 621 N.E.2d 894 (Ohio App. 1993) — § 11-7(a)(1), n. 187

Ohio ex rel. MADD v. Gosser, 485 N.E.2d 706 (Ohio 1985) — § 11-5(c), n. 167

Ohio ex rel. Master v. Cleveland, 667 N.E.2d 974 (Ohio 1996) — § 11-5(d), n. 172; § 11-7(b), n. 204

Ohio ex rel. Mazzaro v. Ferguson, 550 N.E.2d 464 (Ohio 1990) — § 11-7(f)(6), n. 295

Ohio ex rel. McGee v. Ohio State Bd. of Psychiatry, 550 N.E.2d 945 (Ohio 1990) — § 11-7(b)(3)(B), n. 229

Ohio ex rel. McGowan v. Cuyahoga Metro. Hous. Auth., 678 N.E.2d 1388 (Ohio 1997) — § 11-9, n. 372

Ohio ex rel. Miami Student v. Miami Univ., 680 N.E.2d 956 (Ohio 1997) — § 11-7(g), nn. 297, 301

TABLE OF CASES

Ohio ex rel. Milo's Beauty Supply Co. v. Ohio Bd. of Cosmetology, 361 N.E.2d 444 (Ohio 1977) — § 11-7(i), n. 308

Ohio ex rel. Multimedia, Inc. v. Snowden, 647 N.E.2d 1374 (Ohio 1995) — § 11-7(a)(1), n. 188; § 11-7(b)(4), n. 234

Ohio ex rel. Multimedia, Inc. v. Whalen, 549 N.E.2d 167 (Ohio 1990) — § 11-7(b)(8), n. 247

Ohio ex rel. Nat'l Broadcasting Co. v. Court of C.P., 556 N.E.2d 1120 (Ohio 1990) — § 7-2, n. 125; § 16-2(a)(2), nn. 45, 46, 48; § 16-2(c)(1), nn. 108, 109

Ohio ex rel. News Herald v. Ottawa County Ct. of C.P., 671 N.E.2d 5 (Ohio 1996) — § 2-1(d), n. 99; § 2-3, n. 308; § 3-3(a), nn. 504, 506; § 6-2(a), n. 277

Ohio ex rel. Olander v. French, 680 N.E.2d 962 (Ohio 1997) — § 11-9, n. 372

Ohio ex rel. Outlet Communications, Inc. v. Lancaster Police Dep't, 528 N.E.2d 175 (Ohio 1988) — § 11-7(b)(1), n. 209

Ohio ex rel. Patterson v. Ayers, 171 N.E.2d 508 (Ohio 1960) — § 11-7(k), n. 314

Ohio ex rel. Petty v. Whalen, 549 N.E.2d 167 (Ohio App. 1989) — § 11-7(a)(2), n. 189

Ohio ex rel. Plain Dealer Publ'g Co. v. Lesak, 457 N.E.2d 821 (Ohio 1984) — § 11-7(f)(3), n. 286

Ohio ex rel. Plain Dealer v. Ohio Dep't of Ins., 687 N.E.2d 661 (Ohio 1997) — § 11-7(f)(2), n. 274

Ohio ex rel. Polovischak v. Mayfield, 552 N.E.2d 635 (Ohio 1990) — § 11-6, n. 178

Ohio ex rel. Scripps Howard Broadcasting Co. v. Cuyahoga County Court of C.P., 652 N.E.2d 179 (Ohio 1995) — § 6-2(a), nn. 276, 277

Ohio ex rel. Steckman v. Jackson, 639 N.E.2d 83 (Ohio 1994) — § 11-7(b), n. 206

Ohio ex rel. Strothers v. Wertheim, 684 N.E.2d 1239 (Ohio 1997) — § 11-3(e), n. 51

Ohio ex rel. The Repository v. Unger, 504 N.E.2d 37 (Ohio 1986) — § 3-1(a), n. 1; § 3-1(a)(4), n. 175

Ohio ex rel. Thompson Newspapers, Inc. v. Martin, 546 N.E.2d 939 (Ohio 1989) — § 11-6, n. 178; § 11-7(b)(3)(B), n. 229

Ohio ex rel. WHIO-TV-7 v. Lowe, 673 N.E.2d 1360 (Ohio 1997) — § 11-1, n. 3; § 5-2(a)(5), n. 224

Ohio ex rel. Wilson-Simmons v. Lake County Sherriff's Dep't, 693 N.E.2d 789 (Ohio 1998) — § 11-2, n. 14

Ohio ex rel. WLWT-TV5 v. Leis, 673 N.E.2d 1365 (Ohio 1997) — § 11-5(d), n. 172

Ohio ex rel. Zauderer v. Joseph, 577 N.E.2d 444 (Ohio App. 1989) — § 11-4, n. 66

O'Kane v. United States Customs Serv., 169 F.3d 1308 (11th Cir. 1999) — § 10-2(c)(7), nn. 160, 167

Oklahoma v. Bernstein, 5 Media L. Rep. (BNA) 2313 (Okla. Dist. 1980) — § 13-3(c)(1), n. 175

Oklahoma v. Patton, 837 P.2d 483 (Okla. 1992) — § 9-6(e), n. 317

Oklahoma v. United States, 161 F.3d 1266 (10th Cir. 1998) — § 11-7(k), n. 336

Oklahoma Hosp. Ass'n v. Oklahoma Publ'g Co., 748 F.2d 1421 (10th Cir. 1984) — § 6-1(a)(1), n. 15

Oklahoma Press Publ'g Co. v. Walling, 327 U.S. 186 (1946) — § 15-3(b), n. 382

Oklahoma Publ'g Co. v. District Ct., 430 U.S. 308 (1977) — § 2-1(c), n. 59; § 3-3(b), n. 553; § 13-3(a), nn. 81, 82; § 13-7(a)(2)(A)(i), n. 601

Oklahoma State Bd. of Med. Licensure & Supervision v. Migliaccio, 917 P.2d 483 (Okla. App. 1996) — § 11-7(a)(3), n. 192

Okonkwo v. Lacy, 104 F.3d 21 (2d Cir. 1997) — § 3-1(c), nn. 288, 290

O'Laskey v. Sortino, 273 Cal. Rptr. 674 (Ct. App. 1990) — § 12-2(a), n. 65

TABLE OF CASES

Oliva v. Department of Justice, 996 F.2d 1475 (2d Cir. 1993) — § 10-2(c)(8)(D), n. 204

Oliver v. WFAA-TV, Inc., 37 F. Supp. 2d 495 (N.D. Tex. 1998) — Preface, n. 4; § 13-3(a), n. 105; § 13-3(b), n. 137; § 13-7(a)(2)(A)(i), nn. 608, 617-21

O'Lone v. Estate of Shabazz, 482 U.S. 342 (1987) — § 8-1, n. 2

Olsen v. Allen, 710 P.2d 822 (Wash. App. 1985) — § 16-3, nn. 479, 480

Olszewski v. Sinclair Broadcast Group, Inc., 26 Media L. Rep. (BNA) 2535 (Pa. C.P. 1998) — § 15-2(c)(2)(B), n. 114

O'Neill v. Oakgrove Constr., Inc., 523 N.E.2d 277 (N.Y. 1988) — § 16-2(a)(2), nn. 29, 32; § 16-2(c)(2)(A), n. 144; § 16-2(d)(3)(C), n. 271; § 16-2(e)(1), n. 299

Oneonta Star v. County of Schoharie, 492 N.Y.S.2d 145 (App. Div. 1985) — § 9-6(b), n. 273

Open America v. Watergate Special Prosecution Force, 547 F.2d 605 (D.C. Cir. 1976) — § 10-2(b)(4), n. 43

Opinion of the Justices, 373 A.2d 644 (N.H. 1977) — § 16-2(a)(2), n. 29; § 16-2(c)(2)(A), n. 146

Orange County Publications v. Sawyer, 14 Media L. Rep. (BNA) 1766 (N.Y. Sup. Ct. 1987) — § 5-2(a)(4), n. 201

Oregon v. Buchanan, 436 P.2d 729 (Or. 1968) — § 14-2, nn. 19, 36

Oregon v. Carston, 913 P.2d 709 (Or. 1996) — § 13-7(b)(4)(E), n. 735

Oregon v. Hartfield, 624 P.2d 588 (Or. 1981) — § 5-2(a)(3), n. 167

Oregon v. Knobel, 777 P.2d 985 (Or App. 1989) — § 13-7(b)(1), n. 688

Oregon v. Knorr, 8 Media L. Rep. (BNA) 2067 (Or. Cir. 1982) — § 16-2(a)(2), n. 38

Oregon County R-IV Sch. Dist. v. LeMon, 739 S.W.2d 553 (Mo. App. 1987) — § 11-7(g), n. 297

Oregon ex rel. Meyers v. Howell, 740 P.2d 792 (Or. App. 1987) — § 15-2(a), n. 24; § 15-2(c)(1), n. 58; § 15-2(d)(3)(C), nn. 192, 193; § 15-2(i)(2), n. 303; § 16-2(a)(2), n. 38

Oregon ex rel. Sports Management News, Inc. v. Nachtigal, 921 P.2d 1304 (Or. 1996) — § 6-1(a)(5), n. 110

Oregon Newspaper Publishers Ass'n v. Department of Corrections, 966 P.2d 819 (Or. App. 1998) — § 8-2, n. 89

Oregonian Publ'g Co. v. United States Dist. Ct., 19 Media L. Rep. (BNA) 1704 (9th Cir. 1991) — § 6-1(b), n. 187

Oregonian Publ'g Co. v. United States Dist. Ct., 920 F.2d 1462 (9th Cir. 1990) — § 2-3, n. 295; § 3-1(a)(6), nn. 197, 203, 211; § 5-2(a)(9), nn. 283, 289-94

Orford Teachers Ass'n v. Watson, 427 A.2d 21 (N.H. 1981) — § 9-1, n. 15; § 9-6(f), nn. 325, 330

Organization for a Better Austin v. Keefe, 402 U.S. 415 (1971) — § 2-1(d), n. 70; § 12-4(b), n. 203

Osborn v. United States, 385 U.S. 323 (1966) — § 13-7(a)(1), n. 584

Oshkosh Northwestern Co. v. Oshkosh Library Bd., 373 N.W.2d 459 (Wis. App. 1985) — § 9-6(f), n. 330

Ottoway Newspapers v. Appeals Ct., 362 N.E.2d 1189 (Mass. 1977) — § 11-7(f)(3), n. 281

Outlet Communications, Inc. v. Rhode Island, 588 A.2d 1050 (R.I. 1991) — § 16-2(a)(2), n. 31

P

Pacific Legal Found. v. Council on Envtl. Quality, 636 F.2d 1259 (D.C. Cir. 1980) — § 9-5(a)(3), nn. 96, 99; § 9-5(a)(5), n. 109

TABLE OF CASES

Painting & Drywall Work Preservation Fund, Inc. v. HUD, 936 F.2d 1300 (D.C. Cir. 1991) — § 10-2(c)(7), nn. 159, 160
Palko v. Connecticut, 302 U.S. 319 (1937) — § 2-2(a), n. 121
Palm Beach Newspapers, Inc. v. Burk, 471 So. 2d 571 (Fla. App. 1985) — § 5-2(a)(5), n. 225
Palm Beach Newspapers, Inc. v. Burk, 504 So. 2d 378 (Fla. 1987) — § 5-2(a)(5), n. 224
Palm Beach Newspapers, Inc. v. Cook, 434 So. 2d 355 (Fla. App. 1983) — § 3-1(d), nn. 316, 321, 322, 325
Palm Beach v. Gradison, 296 So. 2d 473 (Fla. 1974) — § 9-6(a), n. 252
Palmieri v. New York, 779 F.2d 861 (2d Cir. 1985) — § 3-2(d), n. 408; § 6-1(a)(1), n. 16
Pan Am. World Airways, Inc. v. CAB, 684 F.2d 31 (D.C. Cir. 1982) — § 9-5(a)(5), n. 110
Pankratz v. District Ct., 609 P.2d 1101 (Colo. 1980) — § 16-2(a)(2), n. 41; § 16-2(c)(1), n. 82
Pansy v. Borough of Stroudsburg, 23 F.3d 772 (3d Cir. 1994) — § 6-1(a)(1), nn. 8, 15, 17; § 6-1(a)(4), n. 69; § 6-1(b), nn. 157, 164-75; § 6-1(c), n. 191
Pantos v. City & County of San Francisco, 198 Cal. Rptr. 489 (Ct. App. 1984) — § 6-1(d), n. 258
Parker v. Boyer, 93 F.3d 445 (8th Cir. 1996) — § 12-4(a), n. 151
Parker v. Clarke, 905 F. Supp. 638 (E.D. Mo. 1995) — § 12-4(a), n. 151; § 12-5, nn. 359-64
Parker v. Lee, 378 S.E.2d 677 (Ga. 1989) — § 11-7(b)(3)(B), n. 229
Patterson v. Colorado, 205 U.S. 454 (1907) — § 2-1(a), n. 11
Patton v. Yount, 467 U.S. 1025 (1984) — § 2-1(a), n. 13; § 2-1(b), n. 32
Paul v. Davis, 424 U.S. 693 (1976) — § 12-5, n. 358
Pawelek v. Paramount Studios Corp., 571 F. Supp. 1082 (N.D. Ill. 1983) — § 13-7(a)(1), n. 583
Pawtucket Teachers Alliance v. Brady, 556 A.2d 556 (R.I. 1989) — § 11-7(a), n. 183; § 11-5(a)(5), n. 119
Payne v. Department of Justice, 722 F. Supp. 229 (E.D. Pa. 1989) — § 10-2(c)(8)(D), n. 206
Payne v. Grand Rapids Police Chief, 443 N.W.2d 481 (Mich. App. 1988) — § 11-7(b)(3)(A), n. 222
P.B. v. C.C., 647 N.Y.S.2d 732 (App. Div. 1996) — § 3-3(b), n. 513
Pearson v. Board of Health, 525 N.E.2d 400 (Mass. 1988) — § 9-6(c), n. 288
Pearson v. Dodd, 410 F.2d 701 (D.C. Cir. 1970) — § 13-3(b), nn. 138-43
Pearson v. James, 105 F.3d 828 (2d Cir. 1997) — § 3-1(c), nn. 288, 290
Peavy v. New Times, Inc., 976 F. Supp. 532 (N.D. Tex. 1997) — Preface, n. 4; § 13-3(b), n. 137; § 13-7(a)(2)(A)(i), nn. 599, 600, 608, 609-16
Pedini v. Bowles, 940 F. Supp. 1020 (N.D. Tex. 1996) — § 7-1, n. 70
Pell v. Procunier, 417 U.S. 817 (1974) — § 1-4(a), n. 58; § 8-1, nn. 3-10, 12-30; § 14-4(a), n. 77; § 14-5(a), nn. 107-10; § 14-5(d), n. 169
Peloquin v. Arsenault, 616 N.Y.S.2d 716 (Sup. Ct. 1994) — § 9-6(e), n. 317
Penland v. Long, 922 F. Supp. 1080 (W.D.N.C. 1995) — § 16-2(d)(3)(A), n. 232
Pennekamp v. Florida, 328 U.S. 331 (1946) — § 2-1(c), nn. 43, 44
Pennington v. Washtenaw County Sheriff, 336 N.W.2d 828 (Mich. App. 1983) — § 11-7(b)(5), n. 239
Pennsylvania v. Banner, 17 Media L. Rep. (BNA) 1434 (Pa. C.P. 1989) — § 15-2(c)(1), n. 63; § 15-2(d)(3)(E), n. 207; § 15-2(h), n. 277

TABLE OF CASES

Pennsylvania v. Bercaw, 20 Media L. Rep. (BNA) 1518 (Pa. C.P. 1992) — § 3-1(a)(4), n. 171

Pennsylvania v. Chini, 18 Media L. Rep. (BNA) 1335 (Pa. C.P. 1990) — § 13-3(c)(3), nn. 217-20

Pennsylvania v. Frattarola, 485 A.2d 1147 (Pa. Super. 1984) — § 5-2(a)(1), n. 93; § 5-2(a)(6), n. 243

Pennsylvania v. Freeman, 25 Media L. Rep. (BNA) 1225 (Pa. C.P. 1996) — § 5-2(b), n. 312; § 5-2(a)(6), n. 248

Pennsylvania v. Gerulis, 616 A.2d 686 (Pa. Super. 1992) — § 13-9(b), n. 831

Pennsylvania v. Lambert, 723 A.2d 684 (Pa. 1998) — § 7-2, n. 97

Pennsylvania v. Mines, 680 A.2d 1227 (Pa. Commw. 1996) — § 11-7(b)(2), n. 215

Pennsylvania v. Sartin, 708 A.2d 121 (Pa. Super. 1998) — § 2-3, n. 306

Pennzoil Co. v. FPC, 534 F.2d 627 (5th Cir. 1976) — § 10-2(c)(10), n. 226

Penwell v. Taft Broadcasting Co., 469 N.E.2d 1025 (Ohio App. 1984) — § 12-3, nn. 92, 93; § 12-4(c)(1), n. 220

People v. Ayala, 685 N.E.2d 492 (N.Y. 1997) — § 3-1(c), n. 287

People v. Berliner, 3 Media L. Rep. (BNA) 1942 (N.Y. Sup. Ct. 1978) — § 13-3(c), n. 172

People v. Board of Educ., 353 N.E.2d 147 (Ill. App. 1976) — § 9-6(i)(1)(A), n. 373

People v. Bova, 460 N.Y.S.2d 230 (Sup. Ct. 1983) — § 16-2(a)(2), n. 32

People v. Broady, 158 N.E.2d 817 (N.Y. 1959) — § 13-7(b)(1), n. 689

People v. Brown, 653 N.Y.S.2d 544 (App. Div. 1997) — § 3-1(c), n. 287

People v. Buchanan, 103 Cal. Rptr. 66 (Ct. App. 1972) — § 13-7(b)(4)(A), n. 710

People v. Chambers, 15 Media L. Rep. (BNA) 1151 (N.Y. Sup. Ct. 1988) — § 15-2(h), nn. 289, 290

People v. Cheche, 571 N.Y.S.2d 992 (County Ct. 1991) — § 16-2(a)(2), n. 32

People v. C.M., 614 N.Y.S.2d 491 (Sup. Ct. 1994) — § 3-1(a), n. 29; § 3-1(c), n. 283

People v. Conklin, 522 P.2d 1049 (Cal. 1974) — § 13-7(b)(1), nn. 689, 690

People v. Cordero, 541 N.Y.S.2d 417 (App. Div. 1989) — § 3-1(a), n. 29

People v. Craver, 569 N.Y.S.2d 859 (Sup. Ct. 1990) — § 15-2(d)(3)(E), n. 207; § 15-2(h), n. 287

People v. Davis, 22 Media L. Rep. (BNA) 2465 (Cal. Mun. 1994) — § 2-2(f), n. 264

People v. DeSoto, 24 Media L. Rep. (BNA) 2217 (Cal. Super. 1996) — § 15-2(c)(1), n. 78; § 15-2(e)(2), n. 233; § 15-2(e)(2)(B), n. 245; § 15-2(f), n. 260; § 15-2(i)(2), n. 300

People v. Doe, 560 N.Y.S.2d 177 (County Ct. 1990) — § 15-2(c)(1), n. 64

People v. Dolbeer, 29 Cal. Rptr. 573 (Ct. App. 1963) — § 13-3(c)(8)(A), n. 266

People v. Dupree, 388 N.Y.S.2d 1000 (Sup. Ct. 1976) — § 15-2(h), n. 287

People v. Durrant, 48 P. 75 (Cal. 1897) — § 14-1, n. 2

People v. Fata, 559 N.Y.S.2d 348 (App. Div. 1990) — § 13-7(b)(4)(E), n. 735

People v. Ford, 654 N.Y.S.2d 2 (App. Div. 1997) — § 3-1(c), n. 287

People v. Franklin, 22 Media L. Rep. (BNA) 1255 (N.Y. Crim. 1993) — § 3-1(a)(4), n. 171

People v. Fulton, 201 Cal. Rptr. 879 (Ct. App. 1994) — § 13-7(b)(4)(F), n. 740

People v. Garrett, 637 N.E.2d 615 (Ill. App. 1994) — § 3-1(c), n. 264

People v. Gibbons, 263 Cal. Rptr. 905 (Ct. App. 1989) — § 13-7(b)(4)(E), n. 737

People v. Glogowski, 517 N.Y.S.2d 403 (County Ct. 1987) — § 5-2(a)(7), nn. 262, 265

People v. Hinton, 286 N.E.2d 265 (N.Y. 1972) — § 3-1(c), n. 283

People v. Hodges, 657 N.Y.S.2d 857 (Sup. Ct. 1997) — § 5-2(a)(4), n. 201

TABLE OF CASES

People v. Holveck, 565 N.E.2d 919 (Ill. 1990) — § 3-1(a), n. 59
People v. Korkala, 472 N.Y.S.2d 310 (App. Div. 1984) — § 15-1, n. 17; § 15-2(d)(2), n. 160
People v. Kunkin, 100 Cal. Rptr. 845 (Ct. App. 1972), *rev'd on other grounds*, 507 P.2d 1392 (Cal. 1973) — § 13-3(c)(8)(A), nn. 264, 265, 270
People v. Kunkin, 507 P.2d 1392 (Cal. 1973) — § 13-3(c)(8)(A), nn. 257-70
People v. Lawton, 56 Cal. Rptr. 2d 521 (Ct. App. 1996) — § 13-9(b), n. 831
People v. Leggans, 625 N.E.2d 1133 (Ill. App. 1993) — § 3-1(c), n. 269
People v. LeGrand, 415 N.Y.S.2d 252 (App. Div. 1979) — § 15-2(b)(1), n. 40
People v. Lyons, 574 N.Y.S.2d 126 (Sup. Ct. 1991) — § 15-2(h), n. 286
People v. Manson, 71 Cal. App. 3d 1, 139 Cal. Rptr. 275 (2d Dist.(Ct. App. 1977) — § 2-1(a), n. 5
People v. Martin, 22 Media L. Rep. (BNA) 2312 (Cal. Mun. 1994) — § 3-1(a)(2), n. 102
People v. Martinez, 624 N.E.2d 1027 (N.Y. 1993) — § 3-1(c), n. 278
People v. McCloud, 194 Cal. Rptr. 75 (Ct. App. 1983) — § 11-7(b)(1), n. 208
People v. McIntosh, 26 Media L. Rep. (BNA) 1891 (N.Y. County Ct. 1997) — § 3-1(a)(4), n. 171; § 5-2(a)(7), n. 249
People v. McLoughlin, 473 N.Y.S.2d 904 (Sup. Ct. 1983) — § 5-1, nn. 12, 13
People v. Munday, 117 N.E. 286 (Ill. 1917) — § 4-1, n. 4
People v. Otto, 831 P.2d 1178 (Cal. 1992) — § 13-7(b)(4)(E), n. 731
People v. Palacio, 607 N.E.2d 1375 (Ill. App. 1993) — § 15-2(d)(1), n. 153; § 15-2(h), n. 285
People v. Parker, 31 Cal. Rptr. 716 (Ct. App. 1963) — § 13-3(c)(8)(A), n. 266
People v. Parkison, 25 Media L. Rep. (BNA) 2503 (Cal. Super. 1997) — § 5-2(a), n. 59
People v. Pearson, 624 N.E.2d 1027 (N.Y. 1993) — § 3-1(c), nn. 282-84
People v. Pedersen, 150 Cal. Rptr. 577 (Ct. App. 1978) — § 13-7(b)(4)(B), n. 718
People v. Pepe, 653 N.Y.S.2d 101 (App. Div. 1997) — § 3-1(c), n. 287
People v. Private Sanitation Indus. Ass'n, 519 N.Y.S.2d 106 (County Ct. 1987) — § 5-2(a)(3), n. 179; § 5-2(d), n. 435
People v. Rand, 519 N.Y.S.2d 606 (Sup. Ct. 1987) — § 15-2(c)(1), n. 64
People v. Rivera, 654 N.Y.S.2d 771 (App. Div. 1997) — § 3-1(c), n. 287
People v. Rollins, 24 Media L. Rep. (BNA) 2569 (Cal. Super. 1996) — § 2-2(f), n. 264; § 3-1(a), n. 34
People v. Rowe, 18 Media L. Rep. (BNA) 1980 (N.Y. County Ct. 1991) — § 3-1(a)(4), n. 171
People v. Royster, 26 Media L. Rep. (BNA) 1893 (N.Y. Sup. Ct. 1997) — § 15-2(c)(1), n. 86
People v. Schmitz, 24 Media L. Rep. (BNA) 2535 (Mich. App. 1996) — § 7-1, n. 70
People v. Simpson, 23 Media L. Rep. (BNA) 2552 (Cal. Super. 1995) — § 15-2(e)(2), n. 233
People v. Soles, 136 Cal. Rptr. 328 (Ct. App. 1977) — § 13-7(b)(4)(A), n. 711; § 13-7(b)(4)(B), n. 718; § 13-7(b)(4)(E), n. 731
People v. Speck, 242 N.E.2d 208 (Ill. 1965), *vacated in part*, 403 U.S. 946 (1971) — § 2-1(a), n. 6
People v. Stevens, 40 Cal. Rptr. 2d 92 (Ct. App. 1995) — § 13-7(b)(1), nn. 687, 689
People v. Superior Ct. (1973 Grand Jury), 531 P.2d 761 (Cal. 1975) — § 5-2(a)(3), n. 178
People v. Troiano, 486 N.Y.S.2d 991 (Sup. Ct. 1985) — § 15-2(h), n. 290
People v. Villas, 13 Cal. Rptr. 2d 62 (Ct. App. 1992) — § 15-2(b)(1), n. 41
People v. Ystueta, 418 N.Y.S.2d 508 (Dist. Ct. 1979) — § 9-6(e), n. 317

TABLE OF CASES

People v. Zagarino, 411 N.Y.S.2d 494 (Sup. Ct. 1978) — § 15-2(h), n. 287

People ex rel. Better Broadcasting Council, Inc. v. Keane, 309 N.E.2d 362 (Ill. App. 1974) — § 11-7(f)(2), n. 278

People ex rel. Byron v. Board of Trustees, 412 N.E.2d 1188 (Ill. App. 1980) — § 9-6(b), n. 259

People ex rel. Cooper v. Carlson, 328 N.E.2d 675 (Ill. App. 1975) — § 9-6(i)(1)(A), n. 368

People ex rel. Difanis v. Barr, 414 N.E.2d 731 (Ill. 1980) — § 9-6(b), n. 273

People ex rel. Mooney v. Sheriff of New York County, 199 N.E. 415 (N.Y. 1936) — § 14-1, nn. 4, 11-15

People ex rel. Scott v. Silverstein, 412 N.E.2d 692 (Ill. App. 1980), *rev'd on other grounds*, 429 N.E.2d 483 (Ill. 1981) — § 15-2(h), nn. 270, 285

People for Ethical Treatment of Animals v. Barshefsky, 925 F. Supp. 844 (D.D.C. 1996) — § 9-5(b)(2), n. 209

People for Ethical Treatment of Animals v. Berosini, 895 P.2d 1269 (Nev. 1995) — § 12-4(c)(3), nn. 286-95

Pepsico, Inc. v. Redmond, 46 F.3d 29 (7th Cir. 1995) — § 3-2(c), nn. 402-04; § 6-1(b), n. 187; § 6-1(d), n. 254; § 6-1(c)(2), n. 236

Peralta v. United States Attorney's Office, 136 F.3d 169 (D.C. Cir. 1998) — § 10-2(b)(1), n. 5

Perkey v. Department of Motor Vehicles, 721 P.2d 50 (1986) — § 11-7(k), n. 316

Perkins v. Freedom of Info. Comm'n, 635 A.2d 783 (Conn. 1993) — § 11-5(a)(5), n. 123

Perlongo v. Iron River Co-operative TV Antenna Corp., 332 N.W.2d 502 (Mich. App. 1983) — § 9-6(b), n. 274

Perry v. Keulian, 1997 U.S. Dist. LEXIS 2795 (E.D. Pa. Mar. 11, 1997) — § 16-2(c)(2)(A), n. 138; § 16-2(e)(2), n. 317; § 16-2(e)(3), n. 333

Person-Wolinsky Assocs. v. Nyquist, 377 N.Y.S.2d 897 (Sup. Ct. 1975) — § 11-7(i), n. 307

Persons for Free Speech at SAC v. United States Air Force, 675 F.2d 1010 (8th Cir. 1982) — § 8-5, n. 142

Petition for the Promulgation of Rules Regarding Protection of Confidential Sources, 479 N.E.2d 154 (Mass. 1985) — § 16-2(a)(2), n. 44

Petroleum Info. Corp. v. Department of Interior, 976 F.2d 1429 (D.C. Cir. 1992) — § 10-2(c)(6), n. 139

Petty v. Wurst, 550 N.E.2d 214 (Ohio App. 1989) — § 11-1, n. 7

PG Publ'g Co. v. County of Washington, 638 A.2d 422 (Pa. Commw. 1994) — § 11-7(*l*), n. 341

PG Publ'g Co. v. Pennsylvania, 614 A.2d 1106 (Pa. 1992) — § 5-2(a)(2), n. 120

Phelps v. Wichita Eagle-Beacon, 886 F.2d 1262 (10th Cir. 1989) — § 13-7(a)(1), n. 583

Philadelphia Newspapers, Inc. v. Hepps, 475 U.S. 767 (1986) — § 13-4(a)(2)(C), n. 401

Philadelphia Newspapers, Inc. v. NRC, 727 F.2d 1195 (D.C. Cir. 1984) — § 9-5(a)(8)(J), n. 181

Philip Morris Cos. v. American Broadcasting Cos., 23 Media L. Rep. (BNA) 1434 (Va. Cir. 1995) — § 16-2(j)(1), nn. 459, 460

Philip Morris Cos. v. American Broadcasting Cos., 23 Media L. Rep. (BNA) 2438 (Va. Cir. 1995) — § 16-2(c)(2)(B), n. 159; § 16-2(d)(1), n. 190; § 16-2(e)(3), n. 357

Philip Morris, Inc. v. Harshbarger, 122 F.3d 58 (1st Cir. 1997) — § 10-2(b)(2), n. 28

Phillippi v. CIA, 546 F.2d 1009 (D.C. Cir. 1976) — § 10-2(d), n. 228

TABLE OF CASES

Phoenix Newspapers, Inc. v. Arizona, 927 P.2d 340 (Ariz. App. 1996) — § 11-7(h), n. 305

Phoenix Newspapers, Inc. v. Department of Corrections, 934 P.2d 801 (Ariz. App. 1997) — § 8-1, n. 52

Phoenix Newspapers, Inc. v. Superior Ct., 680 P.2d 166 (Ariz. App. 1983) — § 5-2(d), n. 416

Phoenix Newspapers, Inc. v. United States Dist. Ct., 156 F.3d 940 (9th Cir. 1998) — § 2-3, nn. 291, 312; § 5-2(c), nn. 401-09

Pickering v. Board of Educ., 391 U.S. 563 (1968) — § 1-1, n. 14

Piedmont v. Winston-Salem, 434 S.E.2d 176 (N.C. 1993) — § 5-2(a)(5), n. 226

Pierce v. School Comm., 322 F. Supp. 957 (D. Mass. 1971) — § 9-6(e), n. 321; § 9-6(i)(4), n. 396

Pierce v. St. Vrain Valley Sch. Dist., 944 P.2d 646 (Colo. App. 1997) — § 11-7(m), n. 350

Pigman v. Evansville Press, 537 N.E.2d 547 (Ind. App. 1989) — § 5-2(a)(3), n. 176

Pine v. McGreavy, 687 A.2d 1244 (R.I. 1997) — § 9-6(b), n. 254

Pinkard v. Johnson, 118 F.R.D. 517 (M.D. Ala. 1987) — § 15-2(d)(1), n. 144; § 16-2(c)(2)(A), n. 149; § 16-2(d)(3)(B), n. 236; § 16-2(g), n. 384

Pinkava v. Corrigan, 581 N.E.2d 1181 (Ohio 1990) — § 11-7(b)(5), n. 238

Pittsburgh Press Co. v. Pittsburgh Comm'n on Human Relations, 413 U.S. 376 (1973) — § 13-4(a)(2)(C), n. 410

Pledger v. Georgia, 3 S.E. 320 (Ga. 1887) — § 14-1, n. 6

Plunkett v. Hamilton, 70 S.E. 781 (Ga. 1911) — § 14-1, n. 6; § 16-3, n. 474

Pokorny v. City of Schuyler, 275 N.W.2d 281 (Neb. 1979) — § 9-6(d), n. 295

Police Department of Chicago v. Mosley, 408 U.S. 92 (1975) — § 1-1, n. 4

Poliquin v. Garden Way, Inc., 989 F.2d 527 (1st Cir. 1993) — § 6-1(a)(4), nn. 76-79

Pollack v. Department of Justice, 49 F.3d 115 (4th Cir. 1995) — § 10-2(g), nn. 267, 268

Pollard v. FBI, 705 F.2d 1151 (9th Cir. 1983) — § 10-2(c)(8)(D), n. 200

Pooler v. Nyquist, 392 N.Y.S.2d 948 (Sup. Ct. 1976) — § 11-1, n. 7

Port Townsend Publ'g Co. v. Brown, 567 P.2d 664 (Wash. App. 1977) — § 9-6(i)(1)(A), n. 373

Poss v. NLRB, 654 F.2d 659 (10th Cir. 1977) — § 10-2(c)(6), n. 138

Post-Newsweek Stations, Fla., Inc. v. Doe, 612 So. 2d 549 (Fla. 1992) — § 5-2(a)(5), n. 226

Post-Newsweek Stations, Fla., Inc. v. Florida, 474 So. 2d 344 (Fla. App. 1985) — § 5-2(a)(5), n. 223

Post-Tribune v. Police Dep't, 643 N.E.2d 307 (Ind. 1994) — § 11-7(b)(2), n. 215; § 11-7(b)(5), n. 238

Pottle v. School Comm. of Braintree, 482 N.E.2d 813 (Mass. 1985) — § 11-7(a), n. 184

Poughkeepsie Newspapers, Inc. v. Rosenblatt, 459 N.Y.S.2d 857 (App. Div. 1983) — § 3-1(c), n. 301

Poway v. Superior Ct., 73 Cal. Rptr. 2d 777 (Ct. App. 1998) — § 11-7(m), n. 344

Prahl v. Brosamle, 295 N.W.2d 768 (Wis. App. 1980) — § 12-3, nn. 103-12; § 12-4(a), nn. 164, 185, 188; § 12-4(c)(2), nn. 239, 243; § 12-4(c)(3), nn. 256-60; § 12-5, nn. 357, 358; § 13-7(a)(1), n. 581

Pratt v. Webster, 673 F.2d 408 (D.C. Cir. 1982) — § 10-2(c)(8), n. 176; § 10-2(c)(8)(D), n. 207

Pratt & Whitney Canada, Inc. v. United States, 14 Cl. Ct. 268 (1988) — § 6-1(a)(4), n. 60; § 6-1(c)(1), n. 216

TABLE OF CASES

Pratt & Whitney Canada, Inc. v. United States, 15 Media L. Rep. (BNA) 1033 (Cl. Ct. 1988) — § 6-1(c)(2), n. 228

Prentice v. McPhilemy, No. 98CA0004309, slip op. (D.C. Super. May 5, 1999) —§ 15-2(c)(2)(B), n. 125; § 15-2(d)(3)(C), n. 186; § 15-2(d)(3)(D), n. 202; § 15-2(e)(2)(C), n. 254; § 15-2(j), n. 326

Prescott v. Newsday, Inc., 541 N.Y.S.2d 501 (App. Div. 1989) — § 12-6(a), n. 376

Press-Enterprise Co. v. Superior Ct. (Press-Enterprise I), 464 U.S. 501 (1984) — § 2-2(a), n. 123; § 2-2(e), nn. 225-46; § 2-3, n. 300; § 3-1(a), nn. 26, 43; § 3-1(a)(6), n. 205; § 3-1(b), nn. 213-16, 222, 228; § 3-1(c), nn. 279, 298; § 5-1, nn. 1, 2; § 5-2(a)(2), nn. 124, 125; § 5-2(a)(4), n. 210; § 5-2(a)(7), n. 258; § 5-2(a)(9), n. 286; § 5-2(c), n. 364; § 7-3, n. 144; § 9-1, n. 3; § 14-5(d), nn. 181-84

Press-Enterprise Co. v. Superior Ct. (Press-Enterprise II), 478 U.S. 1 (1986) — § 2-2(a), nn. 119, 120, 123, 124; § 2-2(f), nn. 248-70; § 2-2(g), n. 271; § 2-3, n. 299; § 3-1(a), nn. 1, 2, 26, 43, 44; § 3-1(a)(2), nn. 88, 90-92, 97; § 3-1(a)(3), nn. 105, 122, 123; § 3-1(a)(5), nn. 188, 194; § 3-1(c), n. 299; § 3-2(b), n. 373; § 3-3(a), n. 495; § 5-1, nn. 3, 25, 31, 35; § 5-2(a)(3), nn. 178, 186, 190; § 5-2(a)(5), n. 232; § 5-2(a)(6), n. 236; § 5-2(a)(7), nn. 254, 258; § 9-1, nn. 3, 5; § 14-4(a), n. 77; § 14-5(d), nn. 181, 185, 186

Press-Enterprise Co. v. Superior Ct., 27 Cal. Rptr. 2d 708 (Ct. App. 1994) — § 5-2(a)(3), nn. 169, 190

Press-Enterprise, Inc. v. Benton Area School Dist., 604 A.2d 1221 (Pa. Commw. 1992) — § 9-6(j), n. 407

Pretash v. City of Leadville, 715 P.2d 1272 (Colo. App. 1985) — § 11-7(b)(7), n. 243

Pring v. Penthouse Int'l, Ltd., 695 F.2d 438 (10th Cir. 1982) — § 13-4(a)(3)(A)(ii), n. 467

Procter & Gamble Co. v. Bankers Trust Co., 900 F. Supp. 186 (S.D. Ohio 1995) — § 13-3(a), nn. 115-19

Procter & Gamble Co. v. Bankers Trust Co., 23 Media L. Rep. (BNA) 2535 (6th Cir. 1995) — § 13-3(a), n. 113

Procter & Gamble Co. v. Bankers Trust Co., 78 F.3d 219 (6th Cir. 1996) — § 2-1(d), nn. 98, 100-09; § 6-1(a)(1), nn. 7, 8; § 13-3(a), nn. 108-12, 114, 120-22

Procunier v. Martinez, 416 U.S. 396 (1974) — § 8-1, n. 29; § 6-1(a)(2), n. 40

Progressive Animal Welfare Soc'y v. University of Washington, 884 P.2d 592 (Wash. 1994) — § 11-5(a), n. 77; § 11-5(a)(3), n. 94; § 11-5(b), n. 161; § 11-7(i), n. 307

Providence Journal Co. v. Clerk of Family Ct., 643 A.2d 210 (R.I. 1994) — § 6-1(b), n. 187; § 6-1(c), n. 204

Providence Journal Co. v. Cresto, 716 A.2d 726 (R.I. 1998) — § 5-2(b), n. 361

Providence Journal Co. v. Department of Army, 981 F.2d 552 (1st Cir. 1992) — § 10-2(c)(6), nn. 142, 143; § 10-2(c)(8)(D), n. 208

Providence Journal Co. v. FBI, 602 F.2d 1010 (1st Cir. 1979) — § 3-1(a)(1), n. 79; § 5-2(a)(1), n. 100

Providence Journal Co. v. Rodgers, 711 A.2d 1131 (R.I. 1998) — § 5-1, n. 14; § 5-2(b), nn. 359-63

Providence Journal Co. v. Sundlun, 616 A.2d 1131 (R.I. 1992) — § 11-7(a)(1), n. 186

Providence Journal Co. v. Superior Ct., 593 A.2d 446 (R.I. 1991) — § 3-1(b), n. 221

Pryor v. Reno, 171 F.3d 1281 (11th Cir. 1999) — § 11-7(k), n. 336

Public Citizen v. Barshefsky, 939 F. Supp. 31 (D.C. Cir. 1996) — § 9-5(b)(5), n. 232

Public Citizen v. Committee on the Bicentennial of the U.S. Const., 622 F. Supp. 753 (D.D.C. 1985) — § 9-5(b)(2), n. 210

TABLE OF CASES

Public Citizen v. Department of Justice, 491 U.S. 440 (1989) — § 9-5(b)(1), n. 196; § 9-5(b)(2), nn. 212-17; § 9-5(b)(7), nn. 246, 247; § 10-3(c), n. 301

Public Citizen v. Farm Credit Ass'n, 938 F.2d 290 (D.C. Cir. 1991) — § 10-2(c)(9), n. 223

Public Citizen v. Liggett Group, Inc., 858 F.2d 775 (1st Cir. 1988) — § 6-1(a)(1), n. 17; § 6-1(a)(3), nn. 51, 54, 59; § 6-1(a)(5), n. 103

Public Citizen v. National Advisory Comm. on Microbiological Criteria for Foods, 886 F.2d 419 (D.C. Cir. 1989) — § 9-5(b)(2), n. 198

Public Citizen v. National Econ. Comm., 703 F. Supp. 113 (D.D.C. 1989) — § 9-5(b)(5), n. 238; § 9-5(b)(7), n. 248

Public Citizen Health Research Group v. FDA, 704 F.2d 1280 (D.C. Cir. 1983) — § 10-2(c)(5), n. 122

Public Citizen Health Research Group v. HEW, 668 F.2d 537 (D.C. Cir. 1981) — § 9-5(a)(2), n. 84

Publicker Indus. v. Cohen, 733 F.2d 1059 (3d Cir. 1984) — § 3-1(d), n. 314; § 3-2(a), nn. 346-56; § 6-1(a)(4), n. 84; § 6-1(a)(5), n. 103; § 6-1(c)(1), n. 216; § 6-1(c)(2), nn. 229-32

Pugh v. Avis Rent A Car Sys., Inc., 26 Media L. Rep. (BNA) 1311 (S.D.N.Y. 1997) — § 16-2(c)(2)(A), n. 138; § 16-2(e)(2), n. 317; § 16-2(g), n. 390

Pulitzer Publ'g Co. v. Missouri State Employees' Retirement Sys., 927 S.W.2d 477 (Mo. App. 1996) — § 11-7(a)(2), n. 191

Q

Quad-City Community News Serv. v. Jebens, 334 F. Supp. 8 (S.D. Iowa 1971) — § 9-2(a), n. 33; § 9-2(b), n. 39

Quinn v. Johnson, 381 N.Y.S.2d 875 (App. Div. 1976) — § 12-4(b), n. 203; § 12-6(a), n. 376

Quinon v. FBI, 86 F.3d 1222 (D.C. Cir. 1996) — § 10-2(h), n. 277

R

Rabin v. Department of State, 980 F. Supp. 116 (E.D.N.Y. 1997) — § 10-2(b)(4), n. 43; § 10-2(h), n. 273

Radio & Television News Ass'n v. United States Dist. Ct., 781 F.2d 1443 (9th Cir. 1986) — § 7-1, nn. 15-19, 21-26

Rafferty v. Hartford Courant Co., 416 A.2d 1215 (Conn. Super. 1980) — § 12-2(b), n. 88

Railroad Comm'n of Texas v. United States, 765 F.2d 221 (D.C. Cir. 1985) — § 9-5(a)(3), nn. 98, 99

Rainey v. Levitt, 525 N.Y.S.2d 551 (Sup. Ct. 1988) — § 11-7(a)(5), n. 202

Ramirez v. Time, Inc., 12 Media L. Rep. (BNA) 2230 (N.Y. Sup. Ct. 1986) — § 13-2(a), nn. 7, 8

Ramsey v. City of Sand Point, 936 P.2d 126 (Alaska 1997) — § 9-6(i)(1)(B), n. 378

Ramsey v. Georgia Gazette Publ'g Co., 297 S.E.2d 94 (Ga. App. 1982) — § 13-4(a)(3)(B), n. 484

Rancho Publications v. Superior Ct., 81 Cal. Rptr. 2d 274 (Ct. App. 1999) — § 14-5(e), nn. 189, 198; § 15-2(c)(2)(A), n. 91; § 16-2(a)(2), n. 32; § 16-2(b)(1), n. 67; § 16-2(c)(2)(A), n. 148

Rand v. National Broadcasting Co., N.Y. L.J. April 19, 1989 (N.Y. Sup. Ct. 1989) — § 12-4(a), n. 184

Rankin v. McPherson, 483 U.S. 378 (1987) — § 1-1, n. 14

TABLE OF CASES

R.A.V. v. City of St. Paul, 505 U.S. 377 (1992) — § 1-1, n. 12
Rawls v. Conde Nast Publications, Inc., 446 F.2d 313 (5th Cir. 1971) — § 12-4(a), n. 181
Ray v. Department of Justice, 856 F. Supp. 1576 (1994) — § 10-2(h), n. 285
Ray v. Turner, 587 F.2d 1187 (D.C. Cir. 1978) — § 10-2(c)(2), nn. 95-97; § 10-2(h), n. 276
RCA Global Communications, Inc. v. FCC, 524 F. Supp. 579 (D. Del. 1981) — § 10-2(b)(1), n. 5
Readers Digest Ass'n v. FEC, 509 F. Supp. 1210 (S.D.N.Y. 1981) — § 15-3(b), n. 379
Red & Black Publ'g Co. v. Board of Regents, 427 S.E.2d 257 (Ga. 1993) — § 11-7(g), nn. 299, 300
Red Lion Broadcasting Co. v. FCC, 395 U.S. 367 (1969) — § 1-2(b), n. 27; § 1-3, n. 49
Redding v. Brady, 606 P.2d 1193 (Utah 1980) — § 9-6(h)(1), n. 348
Reed v. Zizka, 1998 Conn. Super. LEXIS 1522 (Conn. Super. May 28, 1998) — § 6-1(a)(1), n. 10; § 6-1(a)(3), n. 46; § 6-1(a)(5), n. 116
Reeves v. Fox Television Network, 983 F. Supp. 703 (N.D. Ohio 1997) — § 12-3, n. 107; § 12-4(a), n. 188
Regents of Univ. of California v. Superior Ct., 976 P.2d 808 (Cal. 1999) — § 9-6(b), n. 259; § 9-6(c), n. 286; § 9-6(j), nn. 411, 415
Register Div. of Freedom Newspapers v. County of Orange, 205 Cal. Rptr. 92 (Ct. App. 1984) — § 9-4, n. 71; § 11-5(a)(4), n. 109; § 11-5(a)(6), n. 138; § 11-7(m), n. 350
Rehabilitation Hosp. Serv. Corp. v. Delta-Hills Health Sys. Agency, Inc., 687 S.W.2d 840 (Ark. 1985) — § 9-6(b), n. 275
Reilly v. McKnight, 439 N.Y.S.2d 727 (App. Div. 1981) — § 5-2(a)(6), n. 246
Reitz v. Gordon, 26 Media L. Rep. (BNA) 1447 (N.D. Ill. 1998) — § 15-2(d)(3)(C), n. 193; § 15-2(e)(2)(B), n. 247
Reliance Ins. Co. v. Barron's, 428 F. Supp. 200 (S.D.N.Y. 1977) — § 6-1(a)(2), n. 31
Religious Tech. Center v. FACT Net, Inc., 907 F. Supp. 1468 (D. Colo. 1995) — § 15-3(a), n. 356
Religious Tech. Center v. Lerma, 908 F. Supp. 1362 (E.D. Va. 1995) — § 15-3(a), n. 356
Religious Tech. Center v. Netcom, Inc., 907 F. Supp. 1361 (N.D. Cal. 1995) — § 15-3(a), n. 356
Re/Max Int'l, Inc. v. Century 21 Real Estate Corp., 846 F. Supp. 910 (D. Colo. 1994) — § 16-2(c)(2)(A), n. 140; § 16-2(d)(3)(C), n. 274; § 16-2(e)(2), n. 316
Reno v. ACLU, 521 U.S. 844 (1997) — § 1-1, nn. 5, 7
Rentz v. City of Moultrie, 203 S.E.2d 216 (Ga. 1974) — § 11-7(h), n. 302
Reporters Committee for Freedom of the Press v. American Telephone & Telegraph Co., 593 F.2d 1030 (D.C. Cir. 1978) — § 16-2(j)(1), nn. 452-54, 458
Republic Airlines v. CAB, 756 F.2d 1304 (10th Cir. 1995) — § 9-5(a)(3), n. 99
Republic Gear Co. v. Borg-Warner Corp., 381 F.2d 551 (2d Cir. 1967) — § 16-2(g), n. 388
Republic of Philippines v. Westinghouse Elec. Corp., 949 F.2d 653 (3d Cir. 1991) — § 6-1(a)(4), nn. 66, 86, 87; § 6-1(a)(5), nn. 111, 123; § 6-1(c)(1), nn. 212, 216
Resorts Int'l, Inc. v. NJM Assocs., 445 A.2d 395 (N.J. 1982) — § 15-2(c)(2)(B), nn. 124, 125; § 15-2(d)(3)(C), nn. 187, 188; § 15-2(d)(3)(D), n. 201
Reuber v. Food Chemical News, Inc., 925 F.2d 703 (4th Cir. 1991) — § 13-3(b), nn. 135-37
Reuber v. United States, 750 F.2d 1039 (D.C. Cir. 1984) — § 13-7(a)(1), n. 582
Reynolds v. Guiliani, 27 Media L. Rep. (BNA) 1383 (S.D.N.Y. 1999) — § 4-3, n. 104
Rhode Island v. Cianci, 496 A.2d 139 (R.I. 1985) — § 5-2(b), n. 361; § 5-2(a)(5), n. 223

TABLE OF CASES

Ribas v. Clark, 696 P.2d 637 (Cal. 1985) — § 13-7(c), n. 765; § 12-4(c)(3), n. 312; § 13-7(b)(1), n. 685; § 13-7(b)(4)(B), n. 713; § 13-7(b)(4)(E), n. 731
Richmond Newspapers, Inc. v. Virginia, 281 S.E.2d 915 (Va. 1981) — § 2-3, n. 296; § 3-1(a), nn. 10, 12
Richmond Newspapers, Inc. v. Virginia, 448 U.S. 555 (1980) — § 1-4(b), nn. 62, 63; § 1-5, nn. 73, 75, 83, 84; § 2-2(a), n. 110; § 2-2(b), n. 162; § 2-2(c), nn. 163-74, 177-200; § 2-2(d), n. 220; § 2-3, n. 312; § 3-1(c), nn. 254, 256; § 3-2(a), nn. 337, 338; § 5-1, n. 21; § 5-2(a), n. 53; § 5-2(b), n. 346; § 8-5, n. 166; § 9-2, n. 23; § 12-4(a), n. 130; § 13-3(c)(1), n. 187; § 13-3(c)(9)(B), n. 320; § 14-4(a), n. 77; § 14-5(d), nn. 166-76
Rideau v. Louisiana, 373 U.S. 723 (1963) — § 2-1(a), n. 14
Rifkin v. Esquire Publ'g, Inc., 8 Media L. Rep. (BNA) 1384 (C.D. Cal. 1982) — § 13-2(a), nn. 22-24; § 13-6, nn. 564-67
Riley v. City of Chester, 612 F.2d 708 (3d Cir. 1979) —§ 16-2(a)(1), n. 2; § 16-2(c)(2)(A), nn. 134, 135; § 16-2(d)(1), nn. 177, 187; § 16-2(e)(1), n. 299; § 16-2(e)(2), n. 317; § 16-2(e)(3), n. 333; § 16-2(e)(4), n. 361; § 16-2(h)(2), n. 419; § 16-2(i), n. 446; § 16-3, n. 474
Riley v. Moyed, No. 84C-JA-78 (Del. Super. 1985) — § 15-2(a), n. 25
Ripskis v. HUD, 746 F.2d 1 (D.C. Cir. 1984) — § 10-2(c)(7), nn. 161, 162, 168, 169
Risenhoover v. England, 936 F. Supp. 392 (W.D. Tex. 1996) — § 12-3, nn. 113-18; § 13-5, nn. 541-53
Ristau v. Casey, 647 A.2d 642 (Pa. Commw. 1994) — § 9-6(b), n. 267
Rivera-Puig v. Garcia-Rosario, 785 F. Supp. 278 (D.P.R. 1992) — § 3-1(a)(2), nn. 93, 94
Rivera-Puig v. Garcia-Rosario, 983 F.2d 311 (1st Cir. 1992) — § 2-2(g), n. 274
Rivero v. Superior Ct., 63 Cal. Rptr. 2d 213 (Ct. App. 1997) — § 11-5(a)(6), n. 137
R.L. Polk & Co. v. Ryan, 694 N.E.2d 1027 (Ill. App. 1998) — § 11-7(k), n. 334
Roaden v. Kentucky, 413 U.S. 496 (1973) — § 15-3(a), n. 341
Robert v. Mississippi Republican Party, 465 So. 2d 1050 (Miss. 1985) — § 11-7(k), nn. 314, 315
Roberts v. Alaska, 453 P.2d 898 (Alaska 1969) — § 13-7(b)(4)(A), n. 712
Roberts v. City of Cranston Zoning Bd., 448 A.2d 779 (R.I. 1982) — § 9-6(b), n. 271
Roberts v. City of Palmdale, 20 Cal. Rptr. 2d 330, 853 P.2d 496 (Cal. 1993) — § 11-5(a)(4), nn. 110, 113; § 11-7(m), n. 345
Robinson v. City of Denver, Civ. No. 94 N 0771, slip op. (D. Colo. Feb. 26, 1999) — § 12-4(a), nn. 150, 151, 185, 188
Robinson v. Merritt, 375 S.E.2d 204 (W. Va. 1988) — § 11-7(e), n. 267
Rocap v. Indiek, 539 F.2d 174 (D.C. Cir. 1976) — § 10-2(b)(2), n. 25
Roche v. Florida, 589 So. 2d 928 (Fla. App. 1991) — § 14-5(f), nn. 219-21
Rockdale Citizen Publ'g Co. v. Georgia, 463 S.E.2d 864 (Ga. 1995) — § 2-1(d), n. 98; § 3-1(a), n. 44
Rockdale Citizen Publ'g Co. v. Georgia, 468 S.E.2d 764 (Ga. 1996) — § 3-1(a), n. 44
Rogers v. City of Burbank, 23 Cal. Rptr. 2d 412 (Ct. App. 1993) — § 11-7(l), n. 343
Rogers v. Ulrich, 125 Cal. Rptr. 306 (Ct. App. 1976) — § 13-7(b)(4)(B), n. 718
Rogers v. Wood, 910 F.2d 444 (7th Cir. 1990) — § 13-7(a)(2)(A)(iv), n. 642
Rojem v. Department of Justice, 775 F. Supp. 6 (D.D.C. 1991) — § 10-2(c)(8), n. 175
Romano v. Terdik, 939 F. Supp. 144 (D. Conn. 1996) — § 13-7(a)(2)(A)(iv), n. 642
Rosales-Lopez v. United States, 451 U.S. 182 (1981) — § 2-1(a), n. 2
Rosario v. New York Times Co., 84 F.R.D. 626 (S.D.N.Y. 1979) — § 16-2(h), n. 396
Rosato v. Superior Ct., 124 Cal. Rptr. 427 (Ct. App. 1975) — § 16-2(d)(3)(B), n. 234
Rose v. Freedom of Info. Comm'n, 602 A.2d 1019 (Conn. 1992) — § 9-6(g), n. 342

TABLE OF CASES

Rosenfeld v. Department of Justice, 57 F.3d 803 (9th Cir. 1995) — § 10-2(c)(8), n. 176
Roulette v. Department of Cent. Management Servs., 490 N.E.2d 60 (Ill. App. 1986) — § 11-5(a), n. 82
Rovinsky v. McKaskle, 722 F.2d 197 (5th Cir. 1984) — § 5-2(b), n. 346
Rubera v. Post-Newsweek Stations, 8 Media L. Rep. (BNA) 2293 (Conn. Super. 1982) — § 16-2(c)(2)(B), n. 156
Ruberti, Girvin & Ferlazzo v. New York State Div. of State Police, 641 N.Y.S.2d 411 (App. Div. 1996) — § 11-7(a)(5), n. 201
Ruggieri v. Johns-Manville Prods. Corp., 503 F. Supp. 1036 (D.R.I. 1980) — § 7-1, n. 71
Ruotolo v. Department of Transp., 53 F.3d 4 (2d Cir. 1995) — § 10-2(b)(3), n. 39
Rural Hous. Alliance v. Department of Agric., 498 F.2d 73 (D.C. Cir. 1974) — § 10-2(c)(7), n. 169
Rushford v. New Yorker Magazine, 846 F.2d 249 (4th Cir. 1988) — § 6-1(a)(4), nn. 80-84; § 6-1(c)(1), nn. 210, 212
Rushforth v. Council of Econ. Advisors, 762 F.2d 1038 (D.C. Cir. 1985) — § 9-5(a)(2), nn. 84, 85
Russell v. American Broadcasting Cos., 23 Media L. Rep. (BNA) 2428 (N.D. Ill. 1995) —§ 12-4(c)(2), n. 249; § 12-4(c)(3), n. 317; § 13-7(a)(2)(A)(iii), nn. 634, 635; § 13-7(b)(2), n. 696; § 13-7(b)(4)(C), nn. 724-26; § 13-8, nn. 814-16
Russell v. American Broadcasting Cos., 26 Media L. Rep. (BNA) 1012 (N.D. Ill. 1997) — § 13-8, nn. 814, 816
Russell v. Gregoire, 124 F.3d 1079 (9th Cir. 1997) — § 11-7(c), n. 256
Ruzicka v. Conde Nast Publications, Inc., 733 F. Supp. 1289 (D. Minn. 1990) — § 13-4(a)(3)(A)(ii), nn. 446-52, 455, 456
Ruzicka v. Conde Nast Publications, Inc., 794 F. Supp. 303 (D. Minn. 1992) — § 13-4(a)(3)(A)(ii), nn. 460-63
Ruzicka v. Conde Nast Publications, Inc., 939 F.2d 578 (8th Cir. 1991) — § 13-4(a)(3)(A)(ii), nn. 453, 457-59
Ruzicka v. Conde Nast Publications, Inc., 999 F.2d 1319 (8th Cir. 1993) — § 13-4(a)(3)(A)(ii), nn. 445, 464-68
Ryan v. Department of Justice, 617 F.2d 781 (D.C. Cir. 1980) — § 10-2(c)(6), n. 137
Ryan v. Thoubboron, 26 Media L. Rep. (BNA) 1094 (S.D.N.Y. 1998) — § 15-2(c)(2)(A), n. 87

S

Sabanosh v. Durant, 1997 WL 804871 (Conn. Super. Dec. 17, 1997) — § 6-1(a)(6), n. 137
Sacramento Bee v. United States Dist. Ct., 656 F.2d 477 (9th Cir. 1981) — § 2-3, nn. 291, 308, 310, 312
Sacramento Newspaper Guild v. Sacramento County Bd. of Supervisors, 69 Cal. Rptr. 480 (Ct. App. 1968) — § 9-6(c), nn. 280, 288, 289; § 9-6(j), n. 410
SafeCard Servs., Inc. v. SEC, 926 F.2d 1197 (D.C. Cir. 1991) — § 10-2(b)(3), n. 40; § 10-2(c)(8)(C), n. 196
Salcines v. Tampa Television, 454 So. 2d 639 (Fla. App. 1984) — § 11-7(b)(7), n. 243
Samuel v. Curtis Publ'g Co., 122 F. Supp. 327 (N.D. Cal. 1954) — § 12-2(b), n. 84
San Antonio Express-News v. Morrow, 44 M.J. 706 (Air Force Crim. App. 1996) — § 3-1(e), n. 330
San Antonio Express-News v. Roman, 861 S.W.2d 265 (Tex. App. 1993) — § 2-1(d), n. 98

TABLE OF CASES

San Bernardino County Dep't of Soc. Servs. v. Superior Ct., 283 Cal. Rptr. 332 (Ct. App. 1991) — § 3-3(a), nn. 435, 440; § 3-3(b), nn. 522, 537-46, 549

San Diego Union v. City Council, 196 Cal. Rptr. 45 (Ct. App. 1983) — § 9-6(h)(1), n. 347; § 9-6(i)(1)(B), n. 375

San Francisco Examiner v. Plummer, 19 Media L. Rep. (BNA) 1319 (Cal. Super. 1991) — § 11-7(d), n. 258

San Francisco Examiner v. Vasquez, 20 Media L. Rep. (BNA) 1328 (Cal. Super. 1992) — § 8-2, n. 77

San Gabriel Valley Tribune v. Superior Ct., 192 Cal. Rptr. 415 (Ct. App. 1983) — § 11-7(f)(1), n. 270; § 11-7(f)(2), n. 276

San Jose Mercury-News v. Municipal Ct., 638 P.2d 655 (Cal. 1982) — § 2-2(f), n. 250

Sanchez v. Pena, 17 F. Supp. 2d 1235 (D.N.M. 1998) — § 9-5(b)(2), n. 198

Sanders v. American Broadcasting Cos., 60 Cal. Rptr. 2d 595 (Ct. App. 1997), *rev'd*, 978 P.2d 67 (Cal. 1999) — § 12-4(c)(3), n. 306; § 13-7(b)(4)(A), n. 709; § 13-7(b)(4)(C), n. 721; § 13-7(c), nn. 756, 757

Sanders v. American Broadcasting Cos., 978 P.2d 67 (Cal. 1999) — Preface, n. 3; § 12-2(a), nn. 57, 59, 65; § 12-4(c)(3), nn. 296-318; § 13-1, n. 1; § 13-7(b)(4)(B), nn. 715, 716; § 13-7(b)(4)(C), nn. 718-22, 726; § 13-7(c), nn. 754-63; § 13-8, nn. 806, 819

Sanders v. Benton, 579 P.2d 815 (Okla. 1978) — § 9-6(b), nn. 257, 266

Sanders v. City of Fort Smith, 473 S.W.2d 182 (Ark. 1971) — § 9-6(g), n. 335

Sands v. News America Publ'g, Inc., 560 N.Y.S.2d 416 (App. Div. 1990) —§ 15-2(c)(2)(B), nn. 128-31; § 15-2(d)(3)(D), n. 203; § 15-2(g), n. 267

Sarasota Herald Tribune v. Holtzendorf, 507 So. 2d 667 (Fla. App. 1987) — § 5-2(d), nn. 416, 423

Savannah College of Art & Design v. School of Visual Arts, Inc., 515 S.E.2d 370 (Ga. 1999) — § 6-1(b), nn. 159, 188

Save the Dolphins v. Department of Commerce, 404 F. Supp. 407 (N.D. Cal. 1975) — § 10-2(b)(1), n. 12

Savitt v. Vacco, 1996 U.S. Dist. LEXIS 16875 (N.D.N.Y. Nov. 8, 1996) — § 6-1(a)(3), n. 59

Saxbe v. Washington Post Co., 417 U.S. 843 (1974) — § 1-3, n. 38; § 1-4(a), n. 59; § 1-4(b), nn. 61, 64; § 8-1, n. 4; § 14-4(a), n. 77; § 14-5(a), nn. 107, 115-20; § 14-5(c), n. 149; § 14-5(d), n. 169

Saxton v. Arkansas Gazette Co., 569 S.W.2d 115 (Ark. 1978) — § 15-2(c), n. 55

Scheetz v. Morning Call, Inc., 747 F. Supp. 1515 (E.D. Pa. 1990) — § 13-3(b), n. 137

Scheetz v. Morning Call, Inc., 946 F.2d 202 (3d Cir. 1991) — § 12-5, n. 358

Schell v. Department of Health & Human Servs., 843 F.2d 933 (6th Cir. 1988) — § 10-2(c)(6), n. 140

Schermerhorn v. Rosenberg, 426 N.Y.S.2d 274 (App. Div. 1980) — § 13-6, n. 576

Schiller v. NLRB, 964 F.2d 1205 (D.C. Cir. 1992) — § 10-2(c)(3), nn. 100, 101; § 10-2(h), n. 283

Schmiedicke v. Clare Sch. Bd., 577 N.W.2d 706 (Mich. App. 1998) — § 9-6(i)(1)(B), n. 377

Schnell v. Farmers Ins. Exch., 23 Media L. Rep. (BNA) 1542 (Wis. Cir. 1994) — § 6-1(b), n. 187

Schultz v. Reader's Digest Ass'n, 468 F. Supp. 551 (E.D. Mich. 1979) — § 16-2(c)(2)(B), n. 159

Schumacher v. Lisbon Sch. Bd., 582 N.W.2d 183 (Iowa 1998) — § 9-6(i)(4), n. 395; § 9-6(j), n. 416

TABLE OF CASES

Sci-Sacramento, Inc. v. California Superior Ct., 62 Cal. Rptr. 2d 868 (Ct. App. 1997) — § 15-2(f), n. 259; § 15-2(h), n. 285; § 15-2(i)(3), n. 314

Scott v. Records Access Officer, 480 N.E.2d 1071 (N.Y. 1985) — § 11-7(b)(10), n. 253

Scott v. Smith, 728 S.W.2d 515 (Ark. 1987) — § 11-5(a)(4), n. 108

Scottsdale Unified Sch. Dist. No. 48 v. KPNX Broadcasting Co., 955 P.2d 534 (Ariz. 1998) — § 11-7(j), n. 309

Scrivner v. Hargraves, 468 U.S. 1202 (1984) — § 14-5(f), n. 221

Searle v. Johnson, 709 P.2d 328 (Utah 1985) — § 13-4(c), n. 534

Seattle Times Co. v. Ishikawa, 640 P.2d 716 (Wash. 1982) — § 3-1(a), n. 27; § 5-2(a), n. 79

Seattle Times Co. v. Rhinehart, 467 U.S. 20 (1984) — § 3-2(e), nn. 418, 419; § 6-1(a)(2), nn. 32-46; § 6-1(a)(4), n. 74; § 6-1(a)(5), n. 119

Seattle Times Co. v. United States Dist. Ct., 845 F.2d 1513 (9th Cir. 1988) — § 3-1(a)(1), nn. 65, 67, 69, 71, 86; § 5-2(a)(8), nn. 267-71

SEC v. Jerry T. O'Brien, Inc., 467 U.S. 735 (1984) — § 16-2(j)(1), n. 454

SEC v. Kaufman, 835 F. Supp. 157 (S.D.N.Y. 1993) — § 10-2(h), n. 285

SEC v. Lowe, 472 U.S. 181 (1985) — § 16-2(b)(1), n. 73

SEC v. McGoff, 647 F.2d 185 (D.C. Cir. 1981) — § 15-3(b), nn. 381, 382; § 16-2(b)(1), n. 73; § 16-2(c)(2)(B), nn. 174-76; § 16-2(e)(2), n. 327

SEC v. Stratton Oakmont, Inc., 24 Media L. Rep. (BNA) 2179 (D.C. Cir. 1996) — § 6-1(d), n. 260; § 6-1(a)(1), n. 17

SEC v. Van Waeyenberghe, 990 F.2d 845 (5th Cir. 1993) — § 6-1(b), nn. 183, 187

Secretary of State of Maryland v. Joseph H. Munson Co., 467 U.S. 947 (1984) — § 1-1, n. 7

Seghers v. Community Advancement, Inc., 357 So. 2d 626 (La. App. 1978) — § 9-6(b), n. 275

Semayne's Case, 77 Eng. Rep. 194, 5 Co. Rep. 91a, 91b, 195 (K.B. 1604) — § 12-4(a), n. 129

Senear v. Daily Journal-Am., 8 Media L. Rep. (BNA) 2489 (Wash. Super. 1982) — § 16-3, n. 479

Senear v. Daily Journal-Am., 641 P.2d 1180 (Wash. 1982) — § 16-3, nn. 476-79

Senk v. Board of Pardons, 521 A.2d 532 (Pa. Commw. 1987) — § 11-7(c), n. 255

Sentinel Communications Co. v. School Bd., 20 Media L. Rep. 1103 (Fla. Cir. 1992) — § 9-6(j), n. 410

Sentinel Communications Co. v. Watson, 615 So. 2d 768 (Fla. App. 1993) — § 7-3, n. 185

Sentinel Star Co. v. Booth, 372 So. 2d 100 (Fla. App. 1979) — § 5-2(a)(5), n. 223

Sentinel Star Co. v. Edwards, 387 So. 2d 367 (Fla. App. 1980) — § 3-2(a), n. 335

Shackelford v. City of Abilene, 585 S.W.2d 665 (Tex. 1979) — § 9-6(f), n. 330

Shain v. United States, 978 F.2d 850 (4th Cir. 1992) — § 16-2(d)(3)(A), nn. 230-32

Shannon v. Hansen, 469 N.W.2d 412 (Iowa 1991) — § 11-7(b)(10), n. 254

Shaver v. Shaver, 799 F. Supp. 576 (E.D.N.C. 1992) — § 13-7(a)(2)(A)(iv), n. 642

Shaw v. FBI, 749 F.2d 58 (D.C. Cir. 1984) — § 10-2(c)(8)(D), nn. 202, 206

Sheehan v. City of Binghamton, 398 N.Y.S.2d 905 (App. Div. 1977) — § 11-7(b)(2), n. 214

Shelley v. Kraemer, 334 U.S. 1 (1948) — § 13-4(a)(2)(B), n. 379

Shenandoah Publ'g House, Inc. v. Fanning, 368 S.E.2d 253 (Va. 1988) — § 6-1(c), n. 209; § 6-1(c)(1), n. 222

Sheppard v. E.W. Scripps Co., 421 F.2d 555 (6th Cir. 1970) — § 13-7(a)(1), n. 581

TABLE OF CASES

Sheppard v. Maxwell, 384 U.S. 333 (1966) — § 2-1(b), nn. 16-31, 33, 34; § 3-1(a), n. 45; § 7-1, nn. 1, 2, 44; § 7-2, n. 84

Sherrill v. Amerada Hess Corp., 504 S.E.2d 802 (N.C. App. 1998) — § 7-1, nn. 73, 82

Sherrill v. Knight, 569 F.2d 124 (D.C. Cir. 1977) — § 8-5, n. 169; § 9-2(a), nn. 32-37; § 9-2(b), n. 44

Shevin v. Byron, Harless, Schaffer, Reid & Assocs., 379 So. 2d 633 (Fla. 1980) — § 11-5(a)(4), n. 101

Shevin v. Sunbeam Television Corp., 351 So. 2d 723 (Fla. 1977) — § 13-7(b)(1), n. 688; § 13-7(b)(3), nn. 702-08; § 13-7(b)(4)(B), n. 713

Shew v. Freedom of Info. Comm'n, 714 A.2d 664 (Conn. 1998) — § 11-5(a)(4), n. 108

Shiffman v. Empire Blue Cross & Blue Shield, 681 N.Y.S.2d 511 (App. Div. 1998) — § 13-2(b), n. 48; § 13-8, nn. 802, 808; § 12-4(c)(2), n. 243; § 12-4(c)(3), nn. 325, 327

Shoen v. Shoen, 5 F.3d 1289 (9th Cir. 1993) — § 16-2(a)(1), nn. 2, 27; § 16-2(b)(1), nn. 61-63; § 16-2(d)(3)(C), nn. 245-49, 268; § 16-2(e)(1), n. 299; § 16-2(e)(3), n. 358; § 16-2(h)(2), n. 417

Shoen v. Shoen, 48 F.3d 412 (9th Cir. 1995) —§ 16-2(a)(1), nn. 2, 28; § 16-2(c)(2)(A), n. 148; § 16-2(d)(3)(C), nn. 245, 250; § 16-2(e)(2), n. 323; § 16-2(f), n. 375

Short v. Board of Managers, 442 N.E.2d 1235 (N.Y. 1982) — § 11-7(e), n. 266

Short v. Western Elec. Co., 566 F. Supp. 932 (D.N.J. 1982) — § 6-1(b), n. 188

Shubert v. Metrophone, Inc., 898 F.2d 401 (3d Cir. 1990) — § 13-7(a)(2)(A), n. 587; § 13-7(a)(2)(A)(i), n. 589; § 13-7(a)(2)(A)(ii), n. 625

Shulman v. Group W Prods., Inc., 59 Cal. Rptr. 2d 434 (Ct. App. 1996) — § 12-2(b), n. 75

Shulman v. Group W Prods., Inc., 955 P.2d 469 (Cal. 1998) — Preface, n. 3; § 12-2(a), nn. 48-65; § 12-3, n. 102; § 12-4(b), nn. 204, 216-18; § 12-4(c)(3), nn. 310-12, 317, 327; § 13-7(b)(4)(B), n. 716; § 13-7(c), nn. 762-69; § 13-8, n. 819

Shurberg Broadcasting of Hartford, Inc. v. FCC, 617 F. Supp. 825 (D.D.C. 1985) — § 9-5(a)(8)(J), n. 181

Shuttlesworth v. City of Birmingham, 382 U.S. 87 (1965) — § 13-3(c)(3), n. 209

Sible v. Lee Enters., Inc., 729 P.2d 1271 (Mont. 1986) — § 15-2(c)(2)(B), n. 116; § 15-2(h), n. 269

Sidebottom v. Schiriro, 927 F. Supp. 1221 (E.D. Mo. 1996) — § 8-1, n. 52

Siedle v. Putnam Inv., Inc., 147 F.3d 7 (1st Cir. 1998) — § 6-1(c), nn. 196, 203

Sigma Delta Chi v. Speaker, Md. House of Delegates, 310 A.2d 156 (Md. 1973) — § 9-3, n. 59; § 9-6(e), n. 322

Silkwood v. Kerr-McGee Corp., 563 F.2d 433 (10th Cir. 1977) — § 14-6(a), n. 233; § 16-2(a)(1), n. 2; § 16-2(b)(1), nn. 51, 52; § 16-2(c)(2)(A), nn. 135, 136; § 16-2(d)(1), nn. 177, 187, 201; § 16-2(d)(2), n. 205; § 16-2(d)(3)(C), n. 246; § 16-2(e)(1), n. 299; § 16-2(h), nn. 396, 399

Simmons v. Conger, 86 F.3d 1080 (11th Cir. 1996) — § 3-2(a), n. 357

Simon v. City of Auburn, 519 N.E.2d 205 (Ind. App. 1988) — § 9-6(c), n. 289

Simon & Schuster, Inc. v. New York State Crime Victims Bd., 502 U.S. 105 (1991) — § 1-1, nn. 3-5; § 7-4, nn. 200, 201; § 13-4(a)(1)(B), n. 361

Simpson v. Schneiderman, 21 Media L. Rep. (BNA) 1542 (N.Y. Sup. Ct. 1993) — § 15-2(h), nn. 283-85

Sims v. CIA, 642 F.2d 562 (D.C. Cir. 1980) — § 10-2(c)(7), n. 157

Singer v. United States, 380 U.S. 24 (1965) — § 2-2(b), n. 136

Sinnott v. Boston Retirement Bd., 524 N.E.2d 100 (Mass. 1988) — § 16-2(a)(2), n. 29; § 16-2(c)(2)(A), n. 141; § 16-2(d)(1), n. 177; § 16-2(e)(2), n. 320; § 16-2(e)(3), n. 333

TABLE OF CASES

Skelton v. United States Postal Serv., 678 F.2d 35 (5th Cir. 1982) — § 10-2(c)(6), n. 145

Slage v. Coca Cola, Inc., 507 N.E.2d 794 (Ohio C.P. 1986) — § 16-2(a)(2), n. 48

Smith v. Cincinnati Post & Times-Star, 475 F.2d 740 (6th Cir. 1973) — § 13-7(a)(2)(A)(i), n. 599

Smith v. Daily Mail Publ'g Co., 435 U.S. 829 (1978) — § 13-4(a)(2)(A), n. 373

Smith v. Daily Mail Publ'g Co., 443 U.S. 97 (1979) — § 2-1(c), nn. 57-64; § 3-3(a), nn. 438, 445, 506; § 3-3(b), n. 555; § 7-1, n. 46; § 12-2(a), n. 41; § 13-2(a), n. 15; § 13-3(a), nn. 95-98, 102, 103, 107; § 13-3(b), n. 134; § 13-3(c)(7), nn. 247, 248; § 13-4(a)(2)(C), nn. 403, 406, 410; § 13-4(a)(3)(A)(i), n. 430; § 13-4(c), nn. 525, 534; § 13-7(a)(2)(A)(i), nn. 601, 610

Smith v. Fairman, 98 F.R.D. 445 (C.D. Ill. 1982) — § 12-6(b), nn. 385, 386

Smith v. Goguen, 415 U.S. 566 (1974) — § 1-1, n. 7

Smith v. Maryland, 398 A.2d 858 (Md. 1978) — § 13-7(b)(4)(E), n. 736

Smith v. Maryland, 442 U.S. 735 (1979) — § 13-7(a)(2)(A)(ii), n. 626; § 16-2(j)(1), nn. 455-57

Smith v. United States Dist. Ct., 956 F.2d 647 (7th Cir. 1992) — § 5-2(b), n. 324; § 6-1(d), n. 255; § 6-1(c)(2), n. 234

Snepp v. United States, 444 U.S. 507 (1980) — § 13-3(c)(8)(A), n. 273; § 13-4(a)(1)(B), nn. 352, 354, 363-65; § 13-4(a)(3)(A)(i), n. 444

Snyder v. Ringgold, 26 Media L. Rep. (BNA) 1249 (4th Cir. 1998) — § 9-2(b), nn. 42, 44

Soares v. Connecticut, 8 F.3d 917 (2d Cir. 1993) — § 12-4(a), n. 150

Society of Prof'l Journalists v. Briggs, 675 F. Supp. 1308 (D. Utah 1987) — § 6-1(b), n. 185

Society of Prof'l Journalists v. Bullock, 743 P.2d 1166 (Utah 1987) — § 2-3, n. 311; § 5-2(a), n. 59; § 3-1(a)(5), n. 188; § 5-2(a)(6), n. 241

Society of Prof'l Journalists v. Secretary of Labor, 616 F. Supp. 569 (D. Utah 1985) — § 9-4, n. 61

Sofamor Danek Group, Inc. v. Gaus, 61 F.3d 929 (D.C. Cir. 1995) — § 9-5(b)(2), n. 211

Solargen Elec. Motor Car Corp. v. American Motors Corp., 506 F. Supp. 546 (N.D.N.Y. 1981) — § 16-2(b)(1), nn. 53, 54; § 16-2(c)(2)(A), n. 137; § 16-2(d)(3)(C), n. 272; § 16-2(e)(2), n. 323; § 16-2(e)(3), n. 333; § 16-2(h), n. 396; § 16-2(j)(2), nn. 470-72

Solomon v. National Enquirer Inc., 24 Media L. Rep. (BNA) 2269 (D. Md. 1996) — § 12-2(b), n. 73

Soucie v. David, 448 F.2d 1067 (D.C. Cir. 1971) — § 10-2(b)(1), n. 8; § 10-2(c)(6), n. 138

South Bend Tribune v. Elkhart Circuit Ct., 691 N.E.2d 200 (Ind. App. 1998) — § 7-1, nn. 33, 35

South Carolina v. Byram, 485 S.E.2d 360 (S.C. 1997) — § 4-1, n. 36; § 4-3, nn. 99, 109

South Carolina v. Hill, 501 S.E.2d 122 (S.C. 1998) — § 4-3, n. 100

South Coast Newspapers, Inc. v. City of Oceanside, 206 Cal. Rptr. 527 (Ct. App. 1984) — § 11-7(b), n. 204; § 11-7(b)(1), n. 210

Southam News v. INS, 674 F. Supp. 881 (D.D.C. 1987) — § 10-2(b)(5), n. 48

Southeastern Newspapers Corp. v. Georgia, 454 S.E.2d 452 (Ga. 1995) — § 3-1(a), n. 34

Southwell v. Southern Poverty Law Center, 949 F. Supp. 1303 (W.D. Mich. 1996) — § 14-6(b), n. 265; § 16-2(a)(1), n. 4; § 16-2(c)(2)(B), n. 161

Southwestern Bell Tel. Co. v. State Corp. Comm'n, 629 P.2d 1174 (Kan. App. 1981) — § 9-6(b), n. 256

TABLE OF CASES

Southwestern Newspapers Corp. v. Curtis, 584 S.W.2d 362 (Tex. App. 1979) — § 9-2(b), nn. 38-40, 43

Southwestern Oregon Publ'g Co., v. Southwestern Oregon Community College Dist., 559 P.2d 1289 (Or. App. 1977) — § 9-6(i)(1)(D), n. 388

Sovereign v. Dunn, 498 N.W.2d 62 (Minn. App. 1993) — § 9-6(b), n. 265

Spannaus v. Department of Justice, 942 F. Supp. 656 (D.D.C. 1996) — § 10-2(b)(1), n. 6

Special Force Ministries v. WCCO Television, 584 N.W.2d 789 (Minn. App. 1998) — § 12-4(b), n. 203; § 12-4(c)(3), n. 327; § 13-2(b), nn. 49, 57, 76; § 13-8, nn. 802, 808; § 12-4(c)(2), n. 243; § 12-4(c)(3), nn. 259, 324, 325

Sports Management News, Inc. v. Nachtigal, 921 P.2d 1304 (Or. 1996) — § 3-2(c), n. 403

Spradlin v. Fulton, 982 S.W.2d 255 (Mo. 1998) — § 9-6(h), n. 343; § 9-6(h)(3), n. 356

Sprague v. Walter, 543 A.2d 1078 (Pa. 1988) — § 15-2(c)(2)(B), nn. 115, 116

St. Amant v. Thompson, 390 U.S. 727 (1968) — § 14-5(b), n. 134

St. Cloud Newspapers, Inc. v. District 742 Community Schs., 332 N.W.2d 1 (Minn. 1983) — § 9-6(c), n. 288

St. Michael's Convalescent Hosp. v. California, 643 F.2d 1369 (9th Cir. 1981) — § 10-2(b)(2), n. 28

St. Paul's Benevolent Educ. & Missionary Inst. v. United States, 506 F. Supp. 822 (N.D. Ga. 1980) — § 10-2(c)(5), n. 120

Stahl v. Oklahoma, 665 P.2d 839 (Okla. Crim. App. 1983) — § 13-3(c)(1), nn. 174, 177-84

Stamy v. Packer, 138 F.R.D. 412 (D.N.J. 1990) — § 6-1(c), n. 189

Standard & Poor's Corp. v. Commodity Exch., Inc., 541 F. Supp. 1273 (S.D.N.Y. 1982) — § 6-1(c)(2), n. 229

Stanfield v. Florida Dep't of Children & Families, 698 So. 2d 321 (Fla. App. 1997) — § 7-1, n. 65

Stanfield v. Salvation Army, 695 So. 2d 501 (Fla. App. 1997) — § 11-3(e), n. 50

Stanford v. Texas, 379 U.S. 476 (1965) — § 14-5(c), n. 152; § 15-3(a), n. 339

Stanley v. Georgia, 394 U.S. 557 (1969) — § 1-3, n. 49

Stapp v. Overnite Transp. Co., 1998 U.S. Dist. LEXIS 6412 (D. Kan. Apr. 9, 1998) — § 6-1(c), n. 202; § 6-1(c)(1), n. 226

Star Editorial, Inc. v. United States Dist. Ct., 7 F.3d 856 (9th Cir. 1993) — § 16-2(a)(1), nn. 2, 26; § 16-2(c)(2)(B), n. 156; § 16-2(d)(1), nn. 177, 189, 191; § 16-2(e)(2), n. 324; § 16-2(e)(3), n. 354; § 16-2(e)(4), n. 363; § 16-2(h)(2), n. 425; § 16-2(i), n. 448

Star Publ'g Co. v. Parks, 875 P.2d 837 (Ariz. App. 1993) — § 11-7(d), n. 259

State Employees Ass'n v. Department of Management & Budget, 404 N.W.2d 606 (Mich. 1987) — § 11-4, n. 58

Steaks Unlimited, Inc. v. Deaner, 623 F.2d 264 (3d Cir. 1980) — § 15-2(d)(1), n. 149; § 15-2(d)(3)(C), n. 195

Stein v. Department of Justice, 662 F.2d 1245 (7th Cir. 1981) — § 10-2(c)(2), nn. 88, 90, 94

Steinberg v. Department of Justice, 23 F.3d 548 (D.C. Cir. 1994) — § 10-2(c)(8)(D), n. 205

Stephano v. News Group Publications, Inc., 474 N.E.2d 580 (N.Y. 1984) — § 13-4(a)(3)(A)(i), n. 427

Sterling Drug, Inc. v. FTC, 450 F.2d 698 (D.C. Cir. 1971) — § 10-2(c)(5), n. 127

Stern v. FBI, 737 F.2d 84 (D.C. Cir. 1984) — § 10-2(c)(8), n. 172

TABLE OF CASES

Steve Jackson Games, Inc. v. United States Secret Serv., 816 F. Supp. 432 (W.D. Tex. 1993) — § 13-7(a)(2)(A)(i), nn. 593, 597; § 15-3(a), nn. 355, 356
Stevens v. New York Racing Ass'n, 665 F. Supp. 164 (E.D.N.Y. 1987) — § 9-2(a), n. 36; § 9-2(b), n. 42
Stewart v. Maybury, 3 P.2d 138 (Wash. 1931) — § 11-7(k), n. 315
Stockler v. Garnett, 893 F.2d 856 (6th Cir. 1990) — § 13-7(a)(2)(A), n. 588
Stockton Newspapers, Inc. v. Members of Redevelopment Agency, 214 Cal. Rptr. 561 (Ct. App. 1985) — § 9-6(c), n. 287
Stokes v. Lorain Journal Co., 266 N.E.2d 857 (Ohio C.P. 1970) — § 15-2(d)(3)(D), n. 204
Stone v. Consolidated Publ'g Co., 404 So. 2d 678 (Ala. 1981) — § 11-5(c), n. 168; § 11-7(b)(3)(A), n. 220
Stone v. University of Md. Med. Sys. Corp., 855 F.2d 178 (4th Cir. 1988) — § 6-1(c), n. 196
Stone v. University of Md. Med. Sys. Corp., 948 F.2d 128 (4th Cir. 1991) — § 6-1(a)(4), n. 83; § 6-1(c)(1), n. 210
Stressman v. American Black Hawk Broadcasting Co., 416 N.W.2d 685 (Iowa 1987) — § 12-4(c)(1), nn. 222, 223
Stripling v. Georgia, 401 S.E.2d 500 (Ga. 1991) — § 15-2(c)(1), n. 58; § 15-2(d)(1), n. 143; § 15-2(d)(3)(E), n. 207; § 15-2(e)(2)(B), nn. 242, 245
Strout v. United States Parole Comm'n, 842 F. Supp. 948 (E.D. Mich. 1994) — § 10-2(b)(5), n. 50
Sublette County Rural Health Care Dist. v. Miley, 942 P.2d 1101 (Wyo. 1997) — § 11-7(f)(2), n. 274
Sudol v. Borough of North Arlington, 348 A.2d 216 (N.J. Super. 1975) — § 9-6(e), n. 321
Sullivan v. City of Pittsburgh, 561 A.2d 863 (Pa. Commw. 1989) — § 11-7(b)(1), n. 209
Sullivan v. National Football League, 839 F. Supp. 6 (D. Mass. 1993) — § 7-3, n. 186
Summers v. Department of Justice, 140 F.3d 1077 (D.C. Cir. 1998) — § 10-2(c)(2), n. 57
Summit Tech. Inc. v. Healthcare Capital Group Inc., 141 F.R.D. 381 (D. Mass. 1992) — § 16-2(b)(1), n. 70; § 16-2(d)(1), nn. 177, 187; § 16-2(e)(2), n. 323; § 16-2(e)(3), n. 358
Sunbeam Television Corp. v. Florida, 723 So. 2d 275 (Fla. App. 1998) — § 4-3, nn. 93, 101
Sussman v. American Broadcasting Cos., 971 F. Supp. 432 (C.D. Cal. 1997) — § 13-7(c), n. 756; § 12-4(c)(3), n. 302
Sussman v. American Broadcasting Cos., 1999 U.S. App. LEXIS 19646 (9th Cir. Aug. 18, 1999) — § 13-7(a)(2)(A)(iii), nn. 634, 635
Suttleworth v. City of Camden, 610 A.2d 985 (N.J. Super. 1992) — § 11-7(b)(7), n. 243
Swaney v. Tilford, 898 S.W.2d 462 (Ark. 1995) — § 11-7(f)(6), n. 295
Swate v. Taylor, 12 F. Supp. 2d 591 (S.D. Tex. 1998) — § 12-4(a), n. 151; § 12-5, n. 371
Swickard v. Wayne County Med. Exmr., 475 N.W.2d 304 (Mich. 1991) — § 11-7(d), n. 261
Swidler & Berlin v. United States, 118 S. Ct. 2081 (1998) — § 14-5(b), n. 130; § 10-2(c)(8)(C), n. 190
Symons v. Chrysler Corp. Loan Guar. Bd., 670 F.2d 238 (D.C. Cir. 1981) — § 9-5(a)(2), n. 84

TABLE OF CASES

T

Tacoma Pub. Library v. Woessner, 951 P.2d 357 (Wash. App. 1998) — § 11-7(a)(2), n. 189

Talbot v. Concord Union Sch. Dist., 323 A.2d 912 (N.H. 1974) — § 9-6(i)(1)(D), n. 386

Tallahassee Democrat, Inc. v. Willis, 370 So. 2d 867 (Fla. App. 1979) — § 5-2(a)(5), n. 223

Talley v. California, 362 U.S. 60 (1960) — § 14-4(c), n. 102; § 14-5(e), nn. 188, 193

Tampa Television, Inc. v. Norman, 647 So. 2d 904 (Fla. App. 1994) — § 15-2(j), n. 329

Tartan Oil Corp. v. New York Dep't of Tax. & Fin., 668 N.Y.S.2d 76 (App. Div. 1998) — § 11-7(f)(2), n. 273

Tasin v. SIFCO Indus., 553 N.E.2d 257 (Ohio 1990) — § 7-3, n. 187

Tate v. Canonica, 5 Cal. Rptr. 28 (Ct. App. 1960) — § 12-4(a), n. 175

Tavoulareas v. Piro, 93 F.R.D. 35 (D.D.C. 1981) — § 16-2(c)(2)(B), nn. 156, 166; § 16-2(d)(1), n. 177; § 16-2(d)(2), n. 206; § 16-2(d)(3)(C), n. 278; § 16-2(j)(2), nn. 465, 466

Tavoulareas v. Washington Post Co., 724 F.2d 1010 (D.C. Cir. 1984) — § 6-1(a)(3), nn. 56, 57

Tavoulareas v. Washington Post Co., 737 F.2d 1170 (D.C. Cir. 1984) — § 6-1(a)(3), n. 48

Tax Analysts v. Department of Justice, 913 F. Supp. 599 (D.D.C. 1996) — § 10-2(b)(1), n. 10

Tax Data Corp. v. Hutt, 826 P.2d 353 (Colo. App. 1991) — § 11-2, n. 21

Taylor v. Appleton, 30 F.3d 1365 (11th Cir. 1994) — § 10-2(g), n. 265

Taylor v. Miskovsky, 640 P.2d 959 (Okla. 1981) — § 15-2(c)(2)(B), n. 107; § 15-2(e)(2)(A), nn. 235, 236, 237; § 16-2(a)(2), n. 29

Television Wisconsin, Inc. v. NLRB, 410 F. Supp. 999 (W.D. Wis. 1976) — § 10-2(b)(3), n. 37

Tennessee v. Cooper, 1998 Tenn. Crim. App. LEXIS 923 (Tenn. Crim. App. Sept. 9, 1998) — § 4-3, n. 100

Tennessee v. Curriden, 738 S.W.2d 192 (Tenn. 1987) — § 15-2(e)(2)(B), nn. 242, 245; § 15-2(i)(1), n. 295; § 15-2(i)(3), n. 311

Tennessee v. Drake, 701 S.W.2d 604 (Tenn. 1985) — § 5-2(a), n. 42

Tennessee v. Huskey, 1999 Tenn. Crim. App. LEXIS 76 (Tenn. Crim. App. Jan. 29, 1999) — § 5-2(e), n. 472

Tennessee v. James, 902 S.W.2d 911 (Tenn. 1995) — § 3-3(b), n. 557

Tennessee v. James, 1996 WL 22631 (Tenn. 1996) — § 3-3(a), n. 490; § 3-3(b), n. 557

Tennessee v. Pike, 1997 Tenn. Crim. App. LEXIS 1186 (Tenn. Crim. App. Nov. 26, 1997) — § 4-3, nn. 99, 100, 101

Tennessee v. The Tennessean, 902 S.W.2d 911 (Tenn. 1995) — § 3-3(a), n. 490

Tennessee ex rel. Gerbitz v. Curriden, 738 S.W.2d 192 (Tenn. 1987) — § 15-2(c)(1), n. 62

Tennesssean v. Electric Power Bd. of Nashville, 979 S.W.2d 297 (Tenn. 1998) — § 11-7(*l*), n. 341

Texaco, Inc. v. Louisiana Land & Exploration Co., 805 F. Supp. 385 (M.D. La. 1992) — § 11-5(a)(4), n. 108

Texas ex rel. Healey v. McMeans, 884 S.W.2d 772 (Tex. Crim. App. 1994) — § 14-6(b), n. 265; § 16-2(a)(2), n. 39

Themo v. New England Newspaper Publ'g Co., 27 N.E.2d 753 (Mass. 1940) — § 12-2(b), nn. 83, 84

Thomas v. Board of Trustees, 215 N.E.2d 434 (Ohio App. 1966) — § 9-6(g), n. 335

TABLE OF CASES

Thomas v. Collins, 323 U.S. 526 (1945) — § 14-4(a), n. 80
Thomas v. Pearl, 998 F.2d 447 (7th Cir. 1993) — § 12-4(c)(2), n. 246
Thompson v. City of Clio, 765 F. Supp. 1066 (M.D. Ala. 1991) — § 9-6(e), n. 322
Thompson v. Minnesota, 170 N.W.2d 101 (Minn. 1969) — § 16-3, n. 475
Thornburgh v. Abbott, 490 U.S. 401 (1989) — § 8-1, n. 2
Thurner Heat Treating Corp. v. NLRB, 839 F.2d 1256 (7th Cir. 1988) — § 10-2(c)(6), n. 138
Time, Inc. v. Hill, 385 U.S. 374 (1967) — § 12-4(c)(3), n. 283; § 13-4(a)(1)(A), nn. 332, 339; § 13-4(a)(3)(A)(i), n. 430
Time, Inc. v. U.S. Postal Serv., 667 F.2d 329 (2d Cir. 1981) — § 9-5(a)(2), nn. 89, 90; § 9-5(a)(8)(J), n. 181
Times Herald Printing Co. v. Jones, 717 S.W.2d 933 (Tex. App. 1986), *vacated*, 730 S.W.2d 648 (Tex. 1987) — § 6-1(c)(1), n. 222
Times Newspapers, Ltd. v. McDonnell Douglas Corp., 387 F. Supp. 189 (C.D. Cal. 1974) — § 3-2(e), n. 420
Times Publ'g Co. v. Florida, 632 So. 2d 1072 (Fla. App. 1994) — § 2-1(d), n. 86
Times Publ'g Co. v. Florida, 718 So. 2d 1246 (Fla. App. 1998) — § 3-1(d), n. 314
Times Publ'g Co. v. Florida Dep't of Corrections, 375 So. 2d 307 (Fla. App. 1979) — § 8-1, n. 56
Times-Mirror Co. v. Superior Ct., 813 P.2d 240 (Cal. 1991) — § 11-9, n. 378; § 11-5(a)(4), n. 100
Times-Mirror Co. v. United States, 873 F.2d 1210 (9th Cir. 1989) — § 5-2(a)(2), nn. 105-10; § 5-2(a)(3), n. 178
Times-News Publ'g Co. v. North Carolina, 476 S.E.2d 450 (N.C. App. 1996) — § 5-2(b), nn. 297, 326, 360; § 11-7(b)(3)(A), nn. 224-26; § 11-7(m), n. 348
Times-Picayune Publ'g Corp. v. Lee, 15 Media L. Rep. (BNA) 1713 (E.D. La. 1988) — § 9-2(b), n. 42
Tinker v. Des Moines Indep. Community Sch. Dist., 393 U.S. 503 (1969) — § 1-1, n. 16
Titan Sports Inc. v. Turner Broadcasting Sys. Inc., 967 F. Supp. 142 (W.D. Pa. 1997), *rev'd on other grounds sub nom.* In re Madden, 151 F.3d 125 (3d Cir. 1998) — § 16-2(i), n. 445
Tofani v. Maryland, 465 A.2d 413 (Md. 1983) — § 15-1, nn. 2-5; § 15-2(b)(1), n. 34; § 15-2(b)(2), nn. 47, 48; § 15-2(c)(1), n. 62; § 15-2(d)(3)(E), nn. 209-11; § 15-2(h), nn. 270, 280; § 16-2(a)(2), n. 42; § 16-2(c)(1), n. 82
Tolar v. School Bd. of Liberty County, 398 So. 2d 427 (Fla. 1981) — § 9-6(j), n. 414
Tomblin v. Mayo Clinic, 26 Media L. Rep. (BNA) 1351 (Fla. Dep't of Labor & Employment 1997) — § 16-2(c)(2)(A), n. 146; § 16-2(e)(2), n. 321
Toth v. Disciplinary Bd., 562 N.W.2d 744 (N.D. 1997) — § 11-7(m), n. 350
Totten v. Time, Inc., 14 Media L. Rep. (BNA) 1027 (Mass. Super. 1987), *rev'd on other grounds*, 532 N.E.2d 1211 (Mass. 1989) — § 12-6(a), n. 384
Tovar v. Texas, 949 S.W.2d 370 (Tex. Crim. App. 1997) — § 9-6(j), n. 409
Trauernicht v. Board of Coop. Educ. Serv., 407 N.Y.S.2d 398 (Sup. Ct. 1978) — § 11-7(a)(4), n. 197
Traverse City Record Eagle v. Traverse City Area Pub. Schs., 459 N.W.2d 284 (Mich. App. 1990) — § 11-7(a)(4), n. 197
Travis v. Reno, 163 F.3d 1000 (7th Cir. 1998) — § 11-7(k), nn. 335-39
Tribune Co. v. Cannella, 458 So. 2d 1075 (Fla. 1984) — § 11-4, n. 67; § 11-8, n. 354
Tribune Co. v. Hardee Mem. Hosp., 19 Media L. Rep. (BNA) 1318 (Fla. Cir. 1991) — § 6-1(b), n. 186

TABLE OF CASES

Tribune Co. v. Huffstetler, 489 So. 2d 722 (Fla. 1986) — § 16-2(c)(1), n. 91
Tribune Co. v. School Bd., 367 So. 2d 627 (Fla. 1979) — § 9-6(i)(1)(B), n. 376
Tribune Newspapers West, Inc. v. Superior Ct., 218 Cal. Rptr. 505 (Ct. App. 1985) — § 3-3(a), nn. 439, 493-95
Tribune-Review Publ'g Co. v. Allegheny County Hous. Auth., 662 A.2d 677 (Pa. Commw. 1995) — § 11-7(j), n. 312
Triestman v. Department of Justice, 878 F. Supp. 667 (S.D.N.Y. 1995) — § 10-2(b)(3), n. 35
Troutt Brothers v. Emison, 841 S.W.2d 604 (Ark. 1992) — § 11-5(a), n. 77
Trustees v. Mississippi Publishers Corp., 478 So. 2d 269 (Miss. 1985) — § 9-6(c), n. 287
Tsokalas v. Purtill, 756 F. Supp. 89 (D. Conn. 1991) — § 3-1(a), n. 25
Tuft v. City of St. Louis, 936 S.W.2d 113 (Mo. App. 1997) — § 11-7(m), nn. 350, 353
Tull v. Brown, 494 S.E.2d 855 (Va. 1988) — § 11-7(b)(8), n. 245
Tunley v. Municipality of Anchorage Sch. Dist., 631 P.2d 67 (Alaska 1980) — § 9-6(d), n. 295
Turner v. Dolcefino, No. 92-32914 (Tex. Dist., July 3, 1996) — § 16-2(f), n. 379
Turner v. North Charleston Police Dep't, 351 S.E.2d 583 (S.C. App. 1984) — § 11-7(b)(3)(A), n. 219
Turner v. Safley, 482 U.S. 78 (1987) — § 8-1, n. 2
Turner Broadcasting Sys., Inc. v. FCC, 512 U.S. 622 (1994) — § 1-1, nn. 3-6, 9
Twohig v. Blackmer, 918 P.2d 332 (N.M. 1996) — § 7-2, nn. 136-42

U

Ukiah Daily Journal v. Superior Ct., 211 Cal. Rptr. 673 (Ct. App. 1985) — § 3-1(b), nn. 226-30
Under Seal v. Under Seal, 27 F.3d 564, 22 Media L. Rep. (BNA) 1922 (4th Cir. 1994) — § 6-1(c)(1), nn. 223, 224
Union Leader Corp. v. City of Nashua, 686 A.2d 310 (N.H. 1996) — § 11-7(b)(1), n. 209
Union Leader Corp. v. Fenniman, 620 A.2d 1039 (N.H. 1993) — § 11-7(a)(3), n. 194
Union Leader Corp. v. New Hampshire Hous. Fin. Auth., 705 A.2d 725 (N.H. 1997) — § 11-1, n. 7; § 11-5(a)(3), n. 97; § 11-7(f)(2), n. 274
Union Oil Co. v. FPC, 542 F.2d 1036 (9th Cir. 1976) — § 10-2(c)(5), n. 120
United Nuclear Corp. v. Cranford Ins. Co., 905 F.2d 1424 (10th Cir. 1990) — § 6-1(b), n. 187; § 6-1(c), n. 203; § 6-1(a)(1), n. 16
United States v. A.D., 28 F.3d 1353 (3d Cir. 1994) — § 3-2(a), n. 357; § 3-3(a), nn. 434, 450-59, 461; § 6-2(a), n. 269; § 6-1(c)(2), n. 229
United States v. Albertini, 472 U.S. 675 (1985) — § 8-5, nn. 142, 144
United States v. Alexander, 428 A.2d 42 (D.C. 1981) — § 5-2(a)(3), n. 150
United States v. Amodeo, 44 F.3d 141 (2d Cir. 1995) (Amodeo I) — § 6-1(a)(4), nn. 62, 71, 72; § 6-1(d), nn. 245-47
United States v. Amodeo, 71 F.3d 1044 (2d Cir. 1995) (Amodeo II) — § 3-2(d), n. 411; § 5-1, nn. 15-20; § 5-2(a), n. 53; § 6-1(a)(5), n. 107; § 6-1(b), n. 177; § 6-1(d), nn. 245, 248-53
United States v. Anaya, 779 F.2d 532 (9th Cir. 1985) — § 13-7(b)(1), n. 681
United States v. Anderson, 799 F.2d 1438 (11th Cir. 1986) — § 5-2(a)(3), n. 137; § 5-2(a)(4), nn. 203, 212-20; § 5-2(a)(5), n. 225
United States v. Anderson, 46 M.J. 728 (Army Crim. App. 1997) — § 3-1(e), nn. 329-33
United States v. Andreas, 1998 U.S. Dist. LEXIS 11347 (N.D. Ill. July 16, 1998) — § 5-2(b), nn. 323, 343

TABLE OF CASES

United States v. Andreas, 150 F.3d 766 (7th Cir. 1998) — § 5-1, n. 16; § 5-2(a), nn. 53, 54

United States v. Ansaldo N. Am., Inc. 26 Media L. Rep. (BNA) 1285 (S.D.N.Y. 1997) — § 5-2(a)(9), nn. 284, 287

United States v. Antar, 38 F.3d 1348 (3d Cir. 1994) — § 2-3, nn. 292, 299; § 3-1(a), n. 63; § 5-2(c), nn. 365-73; § 6-2(a), n. 277; § 7-3, nn. 176-85

United States v. Anya, 779 F.2d 532 (9th Cir. 1985) — § 13-7(a)(2)(A)(i), n. 591

United States v. Appelquist, 145 F.3d 976 (8th Cir. 1998) — § 12-4(a), n. 151; § 12-5, n. 364

United States v. Barone, 913 F.2d 46 (2d. Cir. 1990) — § 13-7(a)(2)(A)(iii), n. 632

United States v. Beckham, 789 F.2d 401 (6th Cir. 1986) — § 5-2(b), nn. 296, 337; § 5-2(a)(7), n. 264

United States v. Bingham, 765 F. Supp. 954 (N.D. Ill. 1991) —§ 16-2(a)(1), n. 8; § 16-2(a)(2), n. 30; § 16-2(c)(1), nn. 92, 103; § 16-2(d)(3)(C), n. 270; § 16-2(h), n. 401

United States v. Blanton, 534 F. Supp. 295 (S.D. Fla. 1982) — § 14-6(a), n. 237; § 15-3(b), n. 376; § 16-2(c)(1), nn. 92, 103; § 16-2(d)(3)(C), n. 257; § 16-2(d)(3)(D), nn. 281, 285; § 16-2(e)(3), n. 343

United States v. Boesky, 674 F. Supp. 1128 (S.D.N.Y. 1987) — § 5-2(d), n. 434

United States v. Bottone, 365 F.2d 389 (2d Cir. 1966) — § 13-3(c)(8)(A), n. 268; § 13-3(c)(8)(B), n. 275

United States v. Boyce, 594 F.2d 1246 (9th Cir. 1979) — § 13-3(c)(9), n. 282

United States v. Brooklier, 685 F.2d 1162 (9th Cir. 1982) — § 2-3, nn. 291, 295, 297; § 3-1(a), nn. 1, 42; § 3-1(b), nn. 213, 230; § 5-2(a), nn. 45, 47, 58; § 5-2(b), n. 342; § 3-1(a)(4), nn. 153, 160, 164, 165; § 5-2(a)(7), nn. 252, 254

United States v. Brown, 925 F.2d 1301 (10th Cir. 1991) — § 13-3(c)(8)(B), n. 276

United States v. Bryan, 339 U.S. 323 (1950) — § 14-4(a), n. 78

United States v. Buckley, 10 Media L. Rep. (BNA) 1336 (W.D. Wash. 1984) — § 16-2(c)(1), n. 92; § 16-2(h)(1), n. 411

United States v. Bunkers, 521 F.2d 1217 (9th Cir. 1975) — § 13-7(a)(1), n. 578

United States v. Burke, 700 F.2d 70 (2d Cir. 1983) — § 14-6(a), nn. 234-37; § 14-6(b), n. 264; § 16-2(a)(1), nn. 2, 13; § 16-2(c)(1), nn. 92, 116, 117; § 16-2(d)(3)(C), n. 246; § 16-2(e)(2), n. 315; § 16-2(e)(3), nn. 343, 344; § 16-2(h)(1), nn. 407-10

United States v. Burr, 25 Fed. Cas. 187 (C.C. Va. 1807) — § 14-5(b), n. 127

United States v. Byrd, 812 F. Supp. 76 (D.S.C. 1993) — § 3-1(d), n. 318

United States v. Cable News Network Inc., 865 F. Supp. 1549 (S.D. Fla. 1994) — § 2-1(d), n. 96

United States v. Caceres, 440 U.S. 741 (1979) — § 15-3(b), n. 374

United States v. Caldwell, 408 U.S. 711 (1972) — § 14-4(c), n. 99

United States v. Caldwell, 434·F.2d 1081 (9th Cir. 1970), *rev'd sub nom.* Branzburg v. Hayes, 408 U.S. 665 (1972) — § 14-3, n. 39

United States v. Camacho, 22 Media L. Rep. (BNA) 1845 (S.D. Fla. 1994) — § 5-2(b), n. 339

United States v. Caporale, 806 F.2d 1487 (11th Cir. 1986) — § 16-2(a)(1), n. 2; § 16-2(c)(1), n. 92; § 16-2(e)(1), n. 299; § 16-2(e)(3), n. 343

United States v. Carpentier, 526 F. Supp. 292 (E.D.N.Y. 1981) — § 5-2(d), n. 416; § 5-2(a)(8), n. 273

United States v. Carroll, 337 F. Supp. 1260 (D.D.C. 1971) — § 13-7(b)(1), n. 685

United States v. Castellano, 610 F. Supp. 1151 (S.D.N.Y. 1985) — § 5-2(a), n. 57

TABLE OF CASES

United States v. Centennial Builders, Inc., 747 F.2d 678 (11th Cir. 1984) — § 13-2(a), n. 20

United States v. Certain Real Property, 977 F. Supp. 833 (E.D. Mich. 1997) — § 5-2(a)(2), n. 110

United States v. Chagra, 701 F.2d 354 (5th Cir. 1983) — § 2-3, nn. 306, 309, 312; § 3-1(a), nn. 1, 19, 42, 44, 48; § 3-1(a)(1), nn. 65-67, 70, 71

United States v. Charmer Indus., 711 F.2d 1164 (2d Cir. 1983) — § 5-2(d), n. 434

United States v. Childress, 58 F.3d 693 (D.C. Cir. 1995) — § 7-3, n. 190

United States v. Cianfrani, 573 F.2d 835 (3d Cir. 1978) — § 5-2(a)(1), nn. 93, 101

United States v. Cleveland, 128 F.3d 267 (5th Cir. 1997) — § 7-3, nn. 168-75

United States v. Cojab, 996 F.2d 1404 (2d Cir. 1993) — § 2-3, nn. 297, 299, 306; § 3-1(a), nn. 35-41; § 5-2(a), n. 52

United States v. Colson, 662 F.2d 1389 (11th Cir. 1981) — § 5-2(a)(4), n. 219

United States v. Corbitt, 879 F.2d 224 (7th Cir. 1989) — § 5-2(d), nn. 426-34

United States v. Corces, 1997 U.S. Dist. LEXIS 11139 (M.D. Fla. 1997) — § 5-1, n. 37

United States v. Corrigan, 144 F.3d 763 (11th Cir. 1998) — § 8-5, n. 142

United States v. Criden, 633 F.2d 346 (3d Cir. 1980) — § 16-2(a)(1), n. 2; § 16-2(c)(1), nn. 92, 93, 98-101; § 16-2(d)(3)(A), nn. 227-29; § 16-2(e)(2), nn. 312, 313; § 16-2(e)(3), nn. 345-47; § 16-2(f), nn. 367, 370-74; § 16-2(g), nn. 389, 390; § 16-2(h), n. 396

United States v. Criden, 675 F.2d 550 (3d Cir. 1982) — § 2-3, nn. 295-97, 309; § 3-1(a), n. 1; § 3-1(a)(4), nn. 153, 160-63; § 5-2(a)(7), n. 257; § 6-1(a)(3), n. 59

United States v. Criden, 681 F.2d 919 (3d Cir. 1982) — § 6-1(b), n. 161

United States v. Cuthbertson, 630 F.2d 139 (3d Cir. 1980) — § 14-6(a), n. 237; § 14-6(b), n. 264; § 15-3(c), nn. 387, 392, 394, 395; § 16-2(a)(1), n. 2; § 16-2(b)(2), nn. 75, 76, 78; § 16-2(c)(1), nn. 92-97; § 16-2(d)(3)(A), nn. 225, 226; § 16-2(d)(3)(C), nn. 246, 251, 252, 257; § 16-2(e)(4), nn. 363, 365; § 16-2(g), nn. 387, 388, 390; § 16-2(h)(1), nn. 406, 412, 413

United States v. Cuthbertson, 651 F.2d 189 (3d Cir. 1981) — § 15-3(c), nn. 384, 391, 393; § 16-2(a)(1), n. 2; § 16-2(c)(1), nn. 92, 93; § 16-2(e)(3), nn. 340-42; § 16-2(h)(1), n. 413; § 16-2(h)(2), nn. 428-33

United States v. Cutler, 6 F.3d 67 (2d Cir. 1993) — § 14-6(a), nn. 238-43, 247, 252; § 14-6(b), n. 265; § 15-3(c), n. 389; § 16-2(a)(1), nn. 2, 12; § 16-2(c)(1), nn. 118-20; § 16-2(d)(3)(C), nn. 261-63; § 16-2(e)(2), nn. 314, 315; § 16-2(e)(4), n. 359; § 16-2(f), n. 377; § 16-2(h)(1), nn. 414, 415; § 16-2(h)(2), n. 419

United States v. Cutler, 58 F.3d 825 (2d Cir. 1995) — § 7-2, nn. 126-30

United States v. Czubinski, 106 F.3d 1069 (1st Cir. 1997) — § 13-9(a), n. 827

United States v. Danovaro, 877 F.2d 583 (7th Cir. 1989) — § 3-1(a)(6), nn. 197, 201

United States v. Davanzo, 699 F.2d 1097 (11th Cir. 1983) — § 13-7(a)(2)(A)(iii), n. 632

United States v. Davis, 904 F. Supp. 564 (E.D. La. 1995) — § 7-1, nn. 33, 34

United States v. De Los Santos, 810 F.2d 1326 (5th Cir. 1987) — § 3-1(a), n. 29

United States v. DeLorean, 729 F.2d 1174 (9th Cir. 1990) — § 2-1(d), n. 70

United States v. DiGilio, 538 F.2d 972 (3d Cir. 1976) — § 13-3(c)(5), n. 235

United States v. Doherty, 675 F. Supp. 719 (D. Mass. 1987) — § 5-2(c), nn. 393-96; § 7-3, n. 144

United States v. Dorfman, 690 F.2d 1230 (7th Cir. 1982) — § 5-2(b), n. 348; § 5-2(a)(1), nn. 101, 87-90

United States v. Duran, 884 F. Supp. 526 (D.D.C. 1995) — § 5-2(a)(7), n. 264

United States v. Eaves, 685 F. Supp. 1243 (N.D. Ga. 1988) — § 5-2(b), n. 338

TABLE OF CASES

United States v. Edmond, 730 F. Supp. 1144 (D.D.C. 1990) — § 7-3, n. 190
United States v. Edwards, 430 A.2d 1321 (D.C. 1981) — § 3-1(a)(1), nn. 67, 73
United States v. Edwards, 672 F.2d 1289 (7th Cir. 1982) — § 5-1, n. 14; § 5-2(a)(1), n. 101
United States v. Edwards, 785 F.2d 1293 (5th Cir. 1986) — § 4-2(a), n. 40
United States v. Edwards, 823 F.2d 111 (5th Cir. 1987) — § 3-1(c), n. 256; § 3-1(d), n. 309; § 5-2(c), nn. 410-12
United States v. Eisenberg, 711 F.2d 959 (11th Cir. 1983) — § 3-1(a)(3), n. 139; § 5-2(a)(3), n. 186
United States v. Ellis, 90 F.3d 447 (11th Cir. 1996) — § 5-2(a), n. 80; § 5-2(d), nn. 446-48; § 5-2(e), nn. 476-79
United States v. El-Sayegh, 131 F.3d 158 (D.C. Cir. 1997) — § 5-2(a)(9), nn. 283, 291; § 6-1(a)(4), n. 71
United States v. Espy, 31 F. Supp. 2d 1 (D.D.C. 1998) — § 5-2(c), n. 394; § 7-3, nn. 144, 186
United States v. Farmer, 32 F.3d 369 (8th Cir. 1994) — § 3-1(a), n. 27
United States v. Ferle, 563 F. Supp. 252 (D.R.I. 1983) — § 5-2(a)(1), n. 91
United States v. Fierer, 26 Media L. Rep. (BNA) 1090 (N.D. Ga. 1997) — § 5-1, n. 37
United States v. Ford, 830 F.2d 596 (6th Cir. 1987) — § 7-1, nn. 63-67
United States v. Fort, 14 Media L. Rep. (BNA) 1942 (N.D. Ill. 1987) — § 7-1, n. 5; § 8-1, n. 52
United States v. Foster, 469 F.2d 1 (1st Cir. 1972) — § 3-1(a), n. 21
United States v. Fowler, 932 F.2d 306 (4th Cir. 1991) — § 13-3(c)(5), n. 235
United States v. Franklin, 546 F. Supp. 1133 (N.D. Ind. 1982) — § 7-3, n. 186
United States v. Fuller, 202 F. Supp. 356 (N.D. Cal. 1962) — § 13-7(a)(2)(A)(i), n. 601; § 13-7(a)(2)(B), nn. 647, 652-55; § 13-7(a)(2)(C), n. 669
United States v. Gambino, 741 F. Supp. 412 (S.D.N.Y. 1990) — § 16-2(h)(1), n. 411
United States v. Gangi, 1998 U.S. Dist. LEXIS 6308 (S.D.N.Y. May 4, 1998) — § 5-2(a)(5), nn. 223, 227, 232
United States v. Gerena, 869 F.2d 82 (2d Cir. 1989) — § 5-2(a)(1), n. 100
United States v. Giraldi, 858 F. Supp. 85 (S.D. Tex. 1994) — § 5-2(c), n. 389
United States v. Girard, 601 F.2d 69 (2d Cir. 1979) — § 13-3(c)(5), n. 235; § 13-3(c)(9)(B), n. 315
United States v. Glens Falls Newspapers Inc., 160 F.3d 853 (2d Cir. 1998) — § 6-1(b), nn. 163, 165, 169, 176-81
United States v. Gonzales, 150 F.3d 1246 (10th Cir. 1998) — § 5-2(e), nn. 451, 453, 455-63
United States v. Gonzalez, 927 F. Supp. 768 (D. Del. 1996) — § 5-2(d), n. 416
United States v. Gotti, 753 F. Supp. 443 (E.D.N.Y. 1990) — § 3-1(a)(1), nn. 74, 84
United States v. Gotti, 771 F. Supp. 567 (E.D.N.Y. 1991) — § 5-2(a)(1), n. 100
United States v. Grace, 461 U.S. 171 (1983) — § 1-1, n. 6
United States v. Greenwald, 479 F.2d 320 (6th Cir. 1973) — § 13-3(c)(8)(B), n. 275
United States v. Gurney, 558 F.2d 1202 (5th Cir. 1977) — § 3-1(c), n. 256; § 5-2(b), n. 346; § 5-2(c), nn. 378, 412; § 7-3, n. 167; § 5-2(a)(3), nn. 179, 196
United States v. Guzzino, 766 F.2d 302 (7th Cir. 1985) — § 5-2(b), n. 319
United States v. Haller, 837 F.2d 84 (2d Cir. 1988) — § 2-3, nn. 299, 306; § 3-1(a), nn. 30, 36; § 3-1(a)(3), n. 126; § 3-1(a)(6), nn. 197, 202, 203, 209, 210; § 5-2(a)(3), n. 193; § 5-2(a)(9), n. 283
United States v. Harrelson, 713 F.2d 1114 (5th Cir. 1983) — § 7-3, nn. 164-67, 185

TABLE OF CASES

United States v. Hastings, 9 Media L. Rep. (BNA) 1488 (S.D. Fla. 1983) — § 5-2(a)(8), n. 273

United States v. Hastings, 695 F.2d 1278 (11th Cir. 1983) — § 3-1(a), n. 25; § 4-2(a), nn. 38, 40-48

United States v. Hill, 893 F. Supp. 1039 (N.D. Fla. 1994) — § 7-1, n. 4

United States v. Hood, ARMY 9401841 (Army Crim. App. Feb. 20, 1996) — § 3-1(e), n. 330

United States v. Hood, Appx. to United States v. Anderson, 46 M.J. 728 (Army Crim. App. 1997) — § 3-1(e), n. 331

United States v. Hubbard, 493 F. Supp. 202 (D.D.C. 1979) — § 16-2(b)(1), nn. 64, 65; § 16-2(c)(1), nn. 92, 103; § 16-2(e)(2), n. 315; § 16-2(e)(3), n. 343

United States v. Huner, 13 F. Supp. 2d 574 (D. Vt. 1998) — § 15-3(a), n. 359

United States v. Hung, 629 F.2d 908 (4th Cir. 1980) — § 13-3(c)(9), n. 282

United States v. Jackson, 969 F. Supp. 881 (S.D.N.Y. 1997) — § 5-2(c), n. 373

United States v. Jacobson, 785 F. Supp. 563 (E.D. Va. 1992) — § 3-1(c), nn. 270-72

United States v. Jeter, 775 F.2d 670 (6th Cir. 1985) — § 13-3(c)(5), n. 235

United States v. John Doe, Inc. I, 481 U.S. 102, 104 (1987) — § 5-2(a)(3), nn. 152, 153

United States v. Kaczynski, No. CRS-96-259 GEB (E.D. Cal. 1997) — § 7-3, n. 194

United States v. Kaczynski, 154 F.3d 930 (9th Cir. 1998) — § 2-1(a), n. 9; § 5-2(a), nn. 60-72

United States v. Kampiles, 609 F.2d 1233 (7th Cir. 1979) — § 13-3(c)(9), n. 282

United States v. Kentucky Util. Co., 927 F.2d 252 (6th Cir. 1991) — § 6-1(a)(1), n. 16

United States v. Kerley, 753 F.2d 617 (7th Cir. 1985) — § 4-2(a), n. 40

United States v. King, 911 F. Supp. 113 (S.D.N.Y. 1995) (King I) — § 3-1(b), n. 239

United States v. King, 140 F.3d 76 (2d Cir. 1998) (King II) — § 3-1(b), nn. 239-50

United States v. King, 26 Media L. Rep. (BNA) 1464 (S.D.N.Y. 1998) — § 3-1(b), n. 243

United States v. Kooistra, 796 F.2d 1390 (11th Cir. 1986) — § 3-1(a)(6), n. 197

United States v. Koyomejian, 970 F.2d 536 (9th Cir. 1992) — § 13-7(a)(2)(A)(ii), n. 623

United States v. Lacayo, 572 F. Supp. 1222 (S.D. Fla. 1983) — § 5-2(a)(8), n. 273

United States v. Lanoue, 71 F.3d 966 (1st Cir. 1995) — § 13-7(a)(2)(A)(iii), n. 632

United States v. LaRouche Campaign, 841 F.2d 1176 (1st Cir. 1988) — § 15-3(c), nn. 388-90, 393; § 16-2(a)(1), n. 2; § 16-2(c)(1), nn. 104-06; § 16-2(d)(3)(A), n. 232; § 16-2(d)(3)(C), nn. 254-60; § 16-2(f), n. 377; § 16-2(h)(1), n. 411; § 16-2(h)(2), nn. 419, 441

United States v. LaValley, 957 F.2d 1309 (6th Cir. 1992) — § 8-5, n. 142

United States v. Lester, 282 F.2d 750 (3d Cir. 1960) — § 13-3(c)(8)(A), n. 267; § 13-3(c)(8)(B), n. 277

United States v. Llanes, 398 F.2d 880 (2d Cir. 1968) — § 13-7(b)(1), n. 684

United States v. Lloyd, 71 F.3d 1256 (7th Cir. 1995) — § 16-2(a)(1), nn. 7, 8

United States v. Lopez, 14 Media L. Rep. (BNA) 2203 (N.D. Ill. 1987) — § 15-2(d)(3)(C), n. 188; § 16-2(a)(1), n. 8; § 16-2(c)(1), nn. 92, 103; § 16-2(d)(3)(C), n. 270

United States v. Lovecchio, 561 F. Supp. 221 (M.D. Pa. 1983) — § 3-1(a)(3), nn. 110, 115; § 5-2(a)(3), n. 141

United States v. Maddox, 7 Media L. Rep. (BNA) 2600 (S.D. Fla. 1982) — § 5-2(a)(8), n. 273

United States v. Manglitz, 773 F.2d 1463 (4th Cir. 1985) — § 5-2(a)(3), n. 145

United States v. Mankani, 738 F.2d 538 (2d Cir. 1984) — § 13-7(a)(1), n. 578

TABLE OF CASES

United States v. Marchetti, 466 F.2d 1309 (4th Cir. 1972) — § 13-4(a)(1)(B), nn. 353, 355-62

United States v. Marcos, 17 Media L. Rep. (BNA) 2005 (S.D.N.Y. 1990) — § 16-2(e)(2), n. 315

United States v. Markiewicz, 732 F. Supp. 316 (N.D.N.Y. 1990) — § 16-2(c)(1), n. 107; § 16-2(d)(3), nn. 212, 213, 215, 217; § 16-2(d)(3)(D), nn. 281-84, 287; § 16-2(e)(1), n. 311; § 16-2(e)(3), nn. 342, 348; § 16-2(g), n. 384

United States v. Martin, 684 F. Supp. 341 (D. Mass. 1988) — § 3-1(a)(1), n. 84; § 5-2(a)(1), n. 95; § 5-2(a)(8), n. 268

United States v. Martin, 746 F.2d 964 (3d Cir. 1984) — § 5-2(a)(8), n. 273; § 6-1(c)(2), n. 234

United States v. Masselli, 638 F. Supp. 206 (S.D.N.Y. 1986) — § 5-2(a)(1), n. 101

United States v. Matthews, 11 F. Supp. 2d 656 (D. Md. 1998) — § 13-3(c), nn. 162, 165, 167-71

United States v. McAusland, 979 F.2d 970 (4th Cir. 1992) — § 13-3(c)(5), n. 235

United States v. McDougal, 940 F. Supp. 224 (E.D. Ark. 1996) — § 5-2(a)(5), n. 233

United States v. McDougal, 103 F.3d 651 (8th Cir. 1996) — § 5-2(a)(5), n. 227; § 5-2(b), nn. 349-58; § 6-1(a)(4), n. 101

United States v. McKnight, 771 F.2d 388 (8th Cir. 1985) — § 5-2(b), n. 343; § 5-2(d), n. 434

United States v. McVeigh, 918 F. Supp. 1452 (W.D. Okla. 1996) — § 5-2(a), n. 80; § 5-2(e), nn. 460, 473-75

United States v. McVeigh, 931 F. Supp. 753 (D. Colo. 1996) — § 4-2(a), n. 38

United States v. McVeigh, 106 F.3d 325 (10th Cir. 1996) — § 3-1(c), n. 257

United States v. McVeigh, 964 F. Supp. 313 (D. Colo. 1997) — § 7-2, nn. 131, 132

United States v. McVeigh, 97-X-29, April 26, 1997, at 1997 WL 202233 — § 7-3, nn. 194, 195

United States v. McVeigh, 119 F.3d 806 (10th Cir. 1997) — § 2-3, n. 308; § 5-1, nn. 14, 22; § 5-2(a), nn. 73-77; § 5-2(a)(7), n. 249

United States v. McVeigh, 153 F.3d 1166 (10th Cir. 1998) — § 2-1(a), n. 10

United States v. McVeigh, 157 F.3d 809 (10th Cir. 1998) — § 7-2, nn. 133-35

United States v. Meros, 11 Media L. Rep. (BNA) 2496 (M.D. Fla. 1985) — § 16-2(c)(1), n. 92; § 16-2(d)(3)(D), nn. 281, 285

United States v. Microsoft Corp., 165 F.3d 952 (D.C. Cir. 1999) — § 3-2(e), nn. 426-31; § 6-1(a)(3), nn. 51, 57

United States v. Milken, 780 F. Supp. 123 (S.D.N.Y. 1991) — § 5-2(d), nn. 441-45

United States v. Miller, 425 U.S. 435 (1976) — § 16-2(j)(1), n. 454

United States v. Miller, 579 F. Supp. 862 (S.D. Fla. 1984) — § 5-2(a)(8), nn. 273, 277-79

United States v. Mine Workers of Am., 330 U.S. 258 (1947) — § 16-2(f), n. 369

United States v. Mitchell, 551 F.2d 1252 (D.C. Cir. 1976), *rev'd sub nom.* Nixon v. Warner Communications, Inc., 435 U.S. 589 (1978) — § 5-1, n. 7; § 5-2(b), nn. 308, 310

United States v. Moody, 746 F. Supp. 1090 (M.D. Ga. 1990) — § 3-1(c), n. 256

United States v. Morison, 844 F.2d 1057 (4th Cir. 1988) — § 13-3(c)(5), nn. 232, 235; § 13-3(c)(9), n. 285; § 13-3(c)(9)(B), nn. 301-10, 314-23

United States v. Morris, 928 F.2d 504 (2d Cir. 1991) — § 13-9(a), n. 822

United States v. Morrison, 622 F. Supp. 1009 (D. Md. 1985) — § 16-2(d)(1), n. 177

United States v. Morton Salt Co., 338 U.S. 632 (1950) — § 15-3(b), n. 378

United States v. Mouzin, 559 F. Supp. 463 (C.D. Cal. 1983) — § 5-2(a)(8), n. 273

TABLE OF CASES

United States v. Muckenthaler, 584 F.2d 240 (8th Cir. 1978) — § 13-7(b)(1), n. 685
United States v. Myers, 635 F.2d 945 (2d Cir. 1980) — § 6-1(c)(2), n. 238
United States v. New York Times Co., 328 F. Supp. 324 (S.D.N.Y.), *remanded*, 444 F.2d 544 (2d Cir.), *rev'd*, 403 U.S. 713 (1971) — § 13-3(c)(9)(A), nn. 290-93
United States v. Nichols, 169 F.3d 1255 (10th Cir. 1999) — § 2-1(a), n. 10
United States v. $9,041,598.68, 976 F. Supp. 654 (S.D. Tex. 1997) — § 6-1(a)(3), n. 46; § 6-1(a)(4), n. 64; § 6-1(a)(5), n. 104
United States v. Nix, 976 F. Supp. 417 (S.D. Miss. 1997) — § 5-2(a), nn. 47, 53
United States v. Nixon, 418 U.S. 683 (1974) — § 14-5(b), nn. 123-30; § 15-3(c), nn. 386, 387
United States v. Noriega, 917 F.2d 1543 (11th Cir. 1990) — § 2-1(d), nn. 92-95
United States v. Northrop Corp., 746 F. Supp. 1002 (C.D. Cal. 1990) — § 3-1(a)(6), nn. 197, 210; § 5-2(a)(3), nn. 183, 186, 190
United States v. O'Brien, 391 U.S. 367 (1968) — § 1-1, n. 6; § 13-7(a)(2)(A)(i), n. 607
United States v. Oregon, 19 Media L. Rep. (BNA) 1506 (D. Or. 1991) — § 6-1(b), n. 187
United States v. Pageau, 535 F. Supp. 1031 (N.D.N.Y. 1982) — § 5-2(a)(8), n. 273
United States v. Peters, 754 F.2d 753 (7th Cir. 1985) — § 3-1(b), nn. 223-25, 232; § 5-1, n. 24; § 5-2(b), n. 339
United States v. Poindexter, 732 F. Supp. 170 (D.D.C. 1990) — § 5-2(b), n. 357; § 5-2(a)(5), nn. 233-35
United States v. Porter, 988 F. Supp. 519 (M.D. Pa. 1997) — § 5-2(a), nn. 47, 49, 54; § 5-2(d), n. 448
United States v. Posner, 594 F. Supp. 930 (S.D. Fla. 1984) — § 5-2(b), nn. 296, 339
United States v. Powell, 379 U.S. 48 (1964) — § 15-3(b), n. 378
United States v. Preate, 927 F. Supp. 163 (M.D. Pa. 1996) — § 5-2(d), nn. 423, 440
United States v. Preate, 91 F.3d 10 (3d Cir. 1996) — § 2-3, n. 304; § 5-2(d), n. 423
United States v. Procter & Gamble Co., 356 U.S. 677 (1958) — § 3-1(a)(3), n. 127; § 5-2(a)(3), n. 136
United States v. Providence Tribune Co., 241 F. 524 (D.R.I. 1917) — § 3-1(a)(3), n. 110
United States v. R. Enters., 498 U.S. 292 (1991) — § 16-2(b)(1), n. 72
United States v. Raffoul, 826 F.2d 218 (3d Cir. 1987) — § 2-3, nn. 291-98; § 3-1(c), nn. 273-77; § 5-2(b), n. 342; § 5-2(c), n. 371
United States v. Rahman, 22 Media L. Rep. (BNA) 1063 (S.D.N.Y. 1993) — § 5-2(a)(5), n. 223
United States v. Riggs, 739 F. Supp. 414 (N.D. Ill. 1990) — § 13-3(c)(8)(B), nn. 276, 278
United States v. Riggs, 743 F. Supp. 556 (N.D. Ill. 1990) — § 13-3(c), n. 166; § 13-3(c)(7), nn. 246-56; § 13-3(c)(8)(B), n. 274
United States v. RMI Co., 599 F.2d 1183 (3d Cir. 1979) — § 16-2(h)(2), n. 432
United States v. Rosenthal, 763 F.2d 1291 (11th Cir. 1985) — § 5-2(b), n. 348; § 5-2(a)(1), n. 101
United States v. Rosner, 352 F. Supp. 915 (S.D.N.Y. 1972) — § 13-3(c)(5), n. 237
United States v. Ross, 33 F.3d 1507 (11th Cir. 1994) — § 7-3, n. 191
United States v. Rowlee, 899 F.2d 1275 (2d Cir. 1990) — § 13-3(c)(7), n. 256
United States v. Russo, No. 9373-(WMB)-(1) (filed Dec. 29, 1971), *dismissed* (C.D. Cal. May 11, 1973) — § 13-3(c)(9)(B), n. 299
United States v. Sablan, 92 F.3d 865 (9th Cir. 1996) — § 13-9(a), n. 822
United States v. Salameh, 992 F.2d 445 (2d Cir. 1993) — § 7-2, nn. 120-25
United States v. Salemme, 985 F. Supp. 193 (D. Mass. 1997) — § 5-1, nn. 14, 20; § 5-2(a), nn. 52, 54

TABLE OF CASES

United States v. Salemme, 985 F. Supp. 197 (D. Mass. 1997) — § 5-2(a)(5), n. 232

United States v. Salerno, 481 U.S. 739 (1987) — § 3-1(a)(1), n. 69

United States v. Sanders, 17 F. Supp. 2d 141 (E.D.N.Y. 1998) — § 13-3(c), n. 165; § 13-3(c)(5), n. 237

United States v. Sanusi, 813 F. Supp. 149 (E.D.N.Y. 1992) — § 12-4(a), nn. 138-48; § 16-2(c)(1), n. 106; § 16-2(d)(1), nn. 177, 199; § 16-2(d)(3)(C), n. 270; § 16-2(e)(2), n. 313; § 16-2(e)(3), n. 348; § 16-2(e)(4), n. 365; § 16-2(h)(1), n. 411

United States v. Saunders, 611 F. Supp. 45 (S.D. Fla. 1985) — § 5-2(a)(8), nn. 272-76

United States v. Schlette, 842 F.2d 1574 (9th Cir. 1988) — § 5-2(a), nn. 68, 70; § 5-2(b), nn. 324, 337; § 5-2(d), nn. 436-40

United States v. Scott, 48 M.J. 663 (Army Crim. App. 1998) — § 3-1(e), n. 326; § 5-2(f), nn. 480-84

United States v. Seagraves, 265 F.2d 876 (3d Cir. 1959) — § 13-3(c)(8)(A), n. 267

United States v. Sells Eng'g, Inc., 463 U.S. 418 (1983) — § 5-2(a)(3), nn. 151, 153, 173

United States v. Shenberg, 791 F. Supp. 292 (S.D. Fla. 1991) — § 5-2(a)(2), n. 131

United States v. Shenberg, 817 F. Supp. 118 (S.D. Fla. 1993) — § 5-2(b), nn. 296, 338

United States v. Sherman, 581 F.2d 1358 (9th Cir. 1978) — § 7-3, nn. 145-52

United States v. Simone, 14 F.3d 833 (3d Cir. 1994) — § 3-1(d), nn. 302-14; § 5-2(c), n. 368

United States v. Smith, 123 F.3d 140 (3d Cir. 1997) — § 2-3, nn. 309, 312; § 3-1(a)(3), nn. 116, 117, 124, 125, 128, 134, 142; § 3-1(d), n. 324; § 5-2(a)(3), nn. 172, 173, 177, 180, 195, 197; § 5-2(d), nn. 422, 424, 440

United States v. Smith, 602 F. Supp. 388 (M.D. Pa. 1985) — § 5-2(a)(5), n. 225

United States v. Smith, 776 F.2d 1104 (3d Cir. 1985) — § 5-1, n. 24; § 5-2(a)(3), nn. 179, 185, 190; § 5-2(a)(4), nn. 203-11

United States v. Smith, 787 F.2d 111 (3d Cir. 1986) — § 3-1(c), n. 256; § 5-2(b), nn. 319, 347; § 5-2(c), n. 368; § 6-1(b), n. 160; § 5-2(a)(3), n. 137

United States v. Smith, 992 F. Supp. 743 (D.N.J. 1998) — § 5-2(d), nn. 422, 424; § 3-1(a)(3), n. 118; § 5-2(a)(3), n. 137

United States v. Smith, 135 F.3d 963 (5th Cir. 1998) — § 14-6(b), n. 265; § 16-2(a)(1), nn. 2, 11, 28; § 16-2(c)(1), nn. 110-15; § 16-2(d)(3), nn. 210, 218-23; § 16-2(d)(3)(C), nn. 248, 263; § 16-2(e)(1), n. 311; § 16-2(e)(4), n. 359; § 16-2(h)(2), n. 417

United States v. Steelhammer, 539 F.2d 373 (4th Cir. 1976), *modified*, 561 F.2d 539 (4th Cir. 1977) — § 16-2(a)(1), n. 2; § 16-2(b)(2), n. 74; § 16-2(d)(3)(B), nn. 240-44; § 16-2(f), nn. 368, 369; § 16-2(h)(2), n. 440

United States v. Suarez, 880 F.2d 626 (2d Cir. 1989) — § 5-2(e), nn. 463-68

United States v. Thaw, 353 F.2d 581 (4th Cir. 1965) — § 13-3(c)(6), n. 242

United States v. Thomas, 25 Media L. Rep. (BNA) 2116 (E.D. Pa. 1997) — § 5-2(a)(2), n. 129

United States v. Three Juveniles, 862 F. Supp. 651 (D. Mass. 1994) — § 3-3(a), nn. 460-63

United States v. Three Juveniles, 61 F.3d 86 (1st Cir. 1995) — § 3-3(a), nn. 445, 464-71

United States v. Tijerina, 412 F.2d 661 (10th Cir. 1969) — § 7-1, nn. 48-51; § 7-2, n. 139

United States v. Tomison, 969 F. Supp. 587 (E.D. Cal. 1997) — § 5-2(a)(5), n. 223

United States v. Torres, 751 F.2d 875 (7th Cir. 1984) — § 13-7(a)(2)(A)(ii), n. 623; § 13-7(b)(4)(E), n. 738

United States v. Town of Moreau, 979 F. Supp. 129 (N.D.N.Y. 1997) — § 3-2(d), n. 411; § 6-1(b), n. 187

United States v. Travers, 25 M.J. 61 (C.M.A. 1987) — § 3-1(e), n. 331

TABLE OF CASES

United States v. Truong Dinh Hung, 629 F.2d 908 (4th Cir. 1981) — § 13-3(c)(9)(B), nn. 309, 315
United States v. Valenti, 987 F.2d 708 (9th Cir. 1993) — § 2-3, nn. 290, 309; § 3-1(c), n. 256
United States v. Varani, 435 F.2d 758 (6th Cir. 1970) — § 13-3(c), n. 162
United States v. Vazquez, 31 F. Supp. 2d 85 (D. Conn. 1998) — § 5-1, n. 17; § 5-2(b), nn. 302, 319; § 5-2(a)(5), n. 225
United States v. Walczak, 783 F.2d 852 (9th Cir. 1986) — § 5-2(a)(3), n. 151
United States v. Wang, 898 F. Supp. 758 (D. Colo. 1995) — § 13-3(c)(6), n. 238
United States v. Washington Post Co., 446 F.2d 1322 (D.C. Cir. 1971) — § 13-3(c)(9)(A), nn. 286-89, 294
United States v. Webbe, 791 F.2d 103 (8th Cir. 1986) — § 5-1, n. 20; § 5-2(b), nn. 296, 337, 353
United States v. Weber Aircraft Corp., 465 U.S. 792 (1984) — § 10-2(c)(6), nn. 133, 135
United States v. White, 855 F. Supp. 13 (D. Mass. 1994) — § 5-2(b), n. 348; § 3-1(a)(1), n. 85; § 5-2(a)(1), n. 95; § 5-2(a)(7), nn. 256-58, 260, 261
United States v. Wolfson, 55 F.3d 58 (2d Cir. 1995) — § 5-2(a)(5), nn. 228-32
United States v. Wright, 573 F.2d 681 (1st Cir. 1978) — § 13-7(a)(2)(A)(iii), n. 632
United States v. Yonkers Bd. of Educ., 587 F. Supp. 51 (S.D.N.Y. 1984) — § 4-2(a), n. 40
United States ex rel. Bennett v. Rundle, 419 F.2d 599 (3d Cir. 1969) — § 3-1(a)(4), n. 158
United States ex rel. Pulitzer Publ'g Co., 635 F.2d 676 (8th Cir. 1980) — § 3-1(b), n. 213
United States ex rel. Vuitton et Fils, S.A. v. Karen Bags, Inc., 600 F. Supp. 667 (S.D.N.Y. 1985) — § 16-2(d)(3)(C), n. 270; § 16-2(e)(2), n. 315
United States Postal Serv. v. Council of Greenburgh Civic Ass'ns, 453 U.S. 114 (1981) — § 13-3(c)(1), n. 180
United Techs. Corp. v. FAA, 102 F.3d 688 (2d Cir. 1996) — § 10-2(c)(5), n. 127
United Techs. Corp. v. NLRB, 777 F.2d 90 (2d Cir. 1985) — § 10-2(c)(8)(D), n. 201
University of Alaska v. Geistauts, 666 P.2d 424 (Alaska 1983) — § 9-6(i)(1)(B), n. 377
University of Conn. v. Freedom of Info. Comm'n, 585 A.2d 690 (Conn. 1991) — § 11-7(b)(7), n. 243
University of Pa. v. EEOC, 493 U.S. 182 (1990) — § 14-5(b), nn. 140-46; § 14-5(c), n. 147; § 14-6(a), n. 242
Upjohn Co. v. Freeman, 906 S.W.2d 92 (Tex. App. 1995) — § 6-1(a)(6), n. 127
Upjohn Co. v. United States, 449 U.S. 383 (1981) — § 10-2(c)(6), n. 154
US W. Communications, Inc. v. Office of Consumer Advocate, 498 N.W.2d 711 (Iowa 1993) — § 11-7(i), n. 307
Utah v. Archuleta, 857 P.2d 234 (Utah 1993) — § 5-2(a)(6), nn. 240-48
Utah v. Krueger, 975 P.2d 489 (Utah App. 1999) — § 13-3(c), nn. 162, 165

V

Valco Cincinnati v. N & D Machining Serv., 492 N.E.2d 814 (Ohio 1986) — § 11-5(a)(3), n. 91
Vallejos v. California Highway Patrol, 152 Cal. Rptr. 846 (Ct. App. 1979) — § 11-1, n. 6; § 11-5(a), n. 78
Valley Broadcasting Co. v. United States Dist. Ct., 798 F.2d 1289 (9th Cir. 1986) — § 5-2(a), n. 68; § 5-2(b), nn. 319, 321-26; § 6-1(c), n. 196

TABLE OF CASES

Van Bourg, Allen, Weinberg & Roger v. NLRB, 751 F.2d 982 (9th Cir. 1985) — § 10-2(c)(6), n. 138
Vandiver v. Star-Telegram, Inc., 756 S.W.2d 103 (Tex. App. 1988) — § 11-5(a)(5), n. 124
Vaughn v. Georgia, 381 S.E.2d 30 (Ga. 1989) —§ 16-2(a)(2), n. 38; § 16-2(c)(1), n. 82; § 16-2(i), n. 451
Vaughn v. Rosen, 484 F.2d 820 (D.C. Cir. 1973) — § 10-2(h), nn. 280-83
Vaughn v. Rosen, 523 F.2d 1136 (D.C. Cir. 1975) — § 10-2(c)(3), n. 100
Veilleux v. National Broadcasting Co., 8 F. Supp. 2d 23 (D. Me. 1998) — § 13-2(a), n. 6; § 13-4(a)(3)(B), nn. 490-95
Veltri v. Charleston Urban Renewal Auth., 363 S.E.2d 746 (W. Va. 1987) — § 9-6(f), n. 330
Vermont v. Blais, 6 Media L. Rep. (BNA) 1537 (Vt. Dist. 1980) — § 16-2(c)(1), n. 92
Vermont v. Densmore, 624 A.2d 1138 (Vt. 1993) — § 5-2(d), nn. 418, 420-23
Vermont v. Gundlah, 624 A.2d 368 (Vt. 1993) — § 16-2(f), n. 378
Vermont v. Koch, 730 A.2d 577 (Vt. 1999) — § 3-2(b), n. 374
Vermont v. LaBounty, 702 A.2d 82 (Vt. 1997) — § 5-2(d), n. 425
Vermont v. Schaefer, 599 A.2d 337 (Vt. 1991) — § 2-3, n. 305; § 3-1(a)(4), nn. 172-80; § 5-2(a)(6), n. 239
Vermont v. St. Peter, 315 A.2d 254 (Vt. 1974) — § 16-2(a)(2), n. 29; § 16-2(c)(1), n. 92
Vermont v. Tallman, 537 A.2d 422 (Vt. 1987) — § 3-1(a)(4), n. 174
Vermont Low Income Advocacy Council, Inc. v. Usery, 546 F.2d 509 (2d Cir. 1976) — § 10-2(h), n. 286
Virelli v. Goodson-Todman Enterprises, 536 N.Y.S.2d 571 (App. Div. 1989) — § 13-4(a)(3)(A)(i), nn. 424-32
Virgil v. Sports Illustrated, 424 F. Supp. 1286 (S.D. Cal. 1976) — § 12-4(c)(3), n. 283
Virmani v. Presbyterian Health Servs. Corp., 515 S.E.2d 675 (N.C. 1999) — § 3-2(a), nn. 335, 358; § 6-1(c), n. 207; § 6-1(c)(2), n. 233
von Bulow v. von Bulow, 811 F.2d 136 (2d Cir. 1987) — § 14-6(a), n. 257; § 16-2(a)(1), n. 2; § 16-2(b)(1), nn. 56-60, 63; § 16-2(d)(3), nn. 211, 223; § 16-2(d)(3)(A), n. 224; § 16-2(f), n. 378; § 16-2(h)(2), nn. 417, 419, 423; § 16-2(i), n. 446

W

Wagar v. United States Dep't of Justice, 846 F.2d 1040 (6th Cir. 1988) — § 6-1(b), n. 188
Wait v. Florida Power & Light Co., 372 So. 2d 420 (Fla. 1979) — § 11-5(c), n. 167; § 11-9, n. 376
WALB-TV, Inc. v. Gibson, 501 S.E.2d 281 (Ga. 1998) — § 4-3, n. 108
Wallace v. Guzman, 687 So. 2d 1351 (Fla. App. 1997) — § 11-7(f)(2), nn. 273, 279
Waller v. Georgia, 467 U.S. 39 (1984) — § 2-2(b), n. 143; § 2-2(f), n. 247; § 3-1(a)(4), nn. 154, 155, 157, 158; § 3-1(c), nn. 280, 281
Warth v. Department of Justice, 595 F.2d 521 (9th Cir. 1979) — § 10-2(b)(2), n. 27
Warth v. Seldin, 422 U.S. 490 (1975) — § 2-3, n. 310
Warzon v. Drew, 155 F.R.D. 183 (E.D. Wis. 1994) — § 16-2(a)(1), n. 8; § 16-2(c)(2)(A), n. 143
Washington v. Corliss, 870 P.2d 317 (Wash. 1994) — § 13-7(b)(4)(E), n. 733
Washington v. Faford, 910 P.2d 447 (Wash. 1996) — § 13-7(b)(4)(E), n. 735
Washington v. Forrester, 587 P.2d 179 (Wash. 1978) — § 13-7(b)(4)(B), n. 714
Washington v. Glucksberg, 521 U.S. 702 (1997) — § 2-2(a), n. 121

TABLE OF CASES

Washington v. Lee, 957 P.2d 741 (Wash. 1998) — § 13-3(c)(2), n. 202
Washington v. Loukaitis, 918 P.2d 535 (Wash. App. 1996) — § 3-3(a), n. 490
Washington v. Rinaldo, 689 P.2d 392 (Wash. 1984) — § 16-3, nn. 481, 482
Washington v. Smith, 540 P.2d 424 (Wash. 1975) — § 13-7(b)(4)(D), n. 727
Washington v. Terwilliger, 11 Media L. Rep. (BNA) 2463 (Wash. Super. 1985) — § 16-3, n. 482
Washington v. Williams, 617 P.2d 1012 (Wash. 1980) — § 13-7(b)(1), n. 689
Washington Ass'n for Television & Children v. FCC, 665 F.2d 1264 (D.C. Cir. 1981) — § 9-5(a)(3), n. 97
Washington Legal Found. v. United States Sentencing Comm'n, 17 F.3d 1446 (D.C. Cir. 1994) — § 9-5(b)(2), n. 218
Washington Legal Found. v. American Bar Ass'n, 648 F. Supp. 1353 (D.D.C. 1986) — § 9-5(b)(7), nn. 245, 247
Washington Legal Found. v. United States Sentencing Comm'n, 21 Media L. Rep. (BNA) 2110 (D.D.C. 1993) — § 9-5(b)(2), n. 200
Washington Post Co. v. Department of Health & Human Servs., 690 F.2d 252 (D.C. Cir. 1982) — § 10-2(c)(5), nn. 123, 126
Washington Post Co. v. Department of Justice, 863 F.2d 96 (D.C. Cir. 1988) — § 10-2(c)(8)(B), nn. 185, 186
Washington Post Co. v. Minority Bus. Opportunity Comm'n, 560 A.2d 517 (D.C. 1989) — § 11-5(a)(3), n. 91
Washington Post Co. v. New York State Ins. Dep't, 463 N.E.2d 604 (N.Y. 1984) — § 11-5(a), n. 77
Washington Post Co. v. Robinson, 935 F.2d 282 (D.C. Cir. 1991) — § 3-1(a)(6), nn. 197, 203, 209; § 5-2(a)(9), nn. 282-88
Waterbury Teachers Ass'n v. Freedom of Info. Comm'n, 694 A.2d 1241 (Conn. 1997) — § 9-6(i)(1)(D), n. 389
Waterman Broadcasting of Florida, Inc. v. Reese, 523 So. 2d 1161 (Fla. App. 1988) — § 16-2(c)(1), nn. 92, 107
Watkins v. Board of Trustees of Alabama State Univ., 703 So. 2d 335 (Ala. 1997) — § 9-6(h)(6), n. 366
Watson v. Cronin, 384 F. Supp. 652 (D. Colo. 1974) — § 8-3, n. 121; § 9-2(a), n. 36
W.B. v. R.K., 18 Media L. Rep. (BNA) 2207 (Minn. Dist. 1991) — § 6-1(c)(1), n. 222
WBAL-TV v. Maryland, 477 A.2d 776 (Md. 1984) — § 16-2(a)(2), n. 42; § 16-2(c)(1), n. 107
WBZ-TV4 v. District Attorney, 562 N.E.2d 817 (Mass. 1990) — § 5-2(a)(3), nn. 137, 190
WBZ-TV4 v. Executive Office of Labor, 610 N.E.2d 923 (Mass. 1993) — § 9-4, n. 69
W.C.H. of Waverly, Missouri., Inc. v. Meredith Corp., 13 Media L. Rep. (BNA) 1648 (W.D. Mo. 1986) — § 12-4(b), nn. 201, 207-10; § 13-2(b), nn. 54-57
W.D.I.A. Corp. v. McGraw-Hill, Inc., No. C-1-93-448 (W.D. Ohio Apr. 4, 1995) — § 13-2(a), n. 17
W.D.I.A. Corp. v. McGraw-Hill, Inc., 34 F. Supp. 2d 612 (S.D. Ohio 1998) — § 13-2(a), nn. 9-13, 16-20; § 13-2(b), n. 76; § 13-4(a)(3)(B), n. 495
We The People, Inc. v. NRC, 746 F. Supp. 213 (D.D.C. 1990) — § 9-5(a)(5), n. 114
Weatherhead v. United States, 157 F.3d 735 (9th Cir. 1998) — § 10-2(c)(2), nn. 67, 89, 96
Weathers v. American Family Mut. Ins. Co., 17 Media L. Rep. (BNA) 1534 (D. Kan. 1989) — § 16-2(h), n. 396; § 16-2(i), n. 449

TABLE OF CASES

Weathers v. American Family Mut. Ins. Co., 17 Media L. Rep. (BNA) 1846 (D. Kan. 1990) — § 16-2(d)(3)(C), n. 271; § 16-2(e)(4), nn. 361, 363

Weber v. Multimedia Entertainment, Inc., 26 Media L. Rep. (BNA) 1376 (S.D.N.Y. 1998) — § 12-6(a), n. 373

Webster Groves School Dist. v. Pulitzer Publ'g Co., 898 F.2d 1371 (8th Cir. 1990) — § 3-2(b), nn. 385-89; § 5-1, n. 20; § 5-2(b), n. 353; § 6-2(b), nn. 296, 297

Wehling v. Columbia Broadcasting Sys., 721 F.2d 506 (5th Cir. 1983) — § 12-2(b), nn. 71, 72

Weisberg v. Department of Justice, 631 F.2d 824 (D.C. Cir. 1980) — § 10-2(b)(1), n. 11

Weisberg v. Department of Justice, 848 F.2d 1265 (D.C. Cir. 1988) — § 10-2(h), n. 286

Weiss v. Thomson Newspapers, Inc., 8 Media L. Rep. (BNA) 1258 (Ohio C.P. 1981) — § 15-2(c)(1), n. 83; § 15-2(c)(2)(B), nn. 108-11; § 15-2(i)(2), nn. 307, 308

Wells v. Marton, 794 F. Supp. 1092 (S.D. Fla. 1991) — § 13-4(c), n. 536

Wells v. Sarasota Herald Tribune Co., 546 So. 2d 1105 (Fla. App. 1989) — § 11-7(b)(3)(A), n. 220

WESH Television, Inc. v. Freeman, 691 So. 2d 532 (Fla. App. 1997) — § 5-2(a)(5), n. 226

West Virginia v. Hanna, 378 S.E.2d 640 (W. Va. 1987) — § 2-1(a), n. 4

West Virginia v. Moore, 902 F. Supp. 715 (S.D. W. Va. 1995) — § 6-1(a)(3), n. 54

West Virginia ex rel. Charleston Mail Ass'n v. Ranson, 488 S.E.2d 5 (W. Va. 1997) — § 16-2(a)(2), n. 29; § 16-2(c)(1), n. 104; § 16-2(d)(3)(C), n. 271; § 16-2(h)(1), n. 411

West Virginia ex rel. Herald Mail Co. v. Hamilton, 267 S.E.2d 544 (W. Va. 1980) — § 3-1(a), n. 1

West Virginia ex rel. Hudok v. Henry, 389 S.E.2d 188 (W. Va. 1989) — § 16-2(a)(2), n. 29; § 16-2(c)(1), n. 82; § 16-2(c)(2)(A), n. 146; § 16-2(d)(1), n. 177; § 16-2(e)(1), n. 299

Westchester Radiological v. Blue Cross/Blue Shield, 138 F.R.D. 33 (S.D.N.Y. 1991) — § 6-1(a)(1), n. 16

Westchester Rockland Newspapers, Inc. v. Leggett, 399 N.E.2d 518 (N.Y. 1979) — § 3-1(a), n. 11; § 3-1(a)(4), n. 170; § 3-1(a)(5), nn. 182-86

Westinghouse Broadcasting Co. v. Dukakis, 409 F. Supp. 895 (D. Mass. 1976) — § 9-2(b), n. 42; § 9-6(e), n. 319

Westinghouse Broadcasting Co. v. Sergeant-at-Arms of Gen. Ct., 375 N.E.2d 1205 (Mass. 1978) — § 11-3(b), n. 41

Westinghouse Broadcasting Corp. v. National Transp. Safety Bd., 8 Media L. Rep. (BNA) 1177 (D. Mass. 1982) — § 8-3, nn. 106-10

Westinghouse Elec. Corp. v. Schlesinger, 542 F.2d 1190 (4th Cir. 1976) — § 10-2(f), n. 256

Westmoreland v. CBS Inc., 97 F.R.D. 703 (S.D.N.Y. 1983) — § 15-2(c)(2)(B), n. 131; § 15-2(d)(3)(D), n. 203

Westmoreland v. CBS Inc., 596 F. Supp. 1166 (S.D.N.Y. 1984) — § 4-2(a), nn. 50-56

Westmoreland v. CBS Inc., 752 F.2d 16 (2d Cir. 1985) — § 3-2(a), n. 357; § 4-2(a), nn. 49, 50, 57-61

WFTV, Inc. v. Florida, 704 So. 2d 188 (Fla. App. 1997) — § 4-3, n. 101

Wheeler v. Goulart, 593 A.2d 173 (D.C. 1991) — § 15-1, n. 14; § 16-2(a)(2), n. 36; § 16-2(g), n. 384

White v. Battaglia, 434 N.Y.S.2d 537 (App. Div. 1980) — § 9-6(d), n. 309

White v. City of Norwalk, 900 F.2d 1421 (9th Cir. 1990) — § 9-6(e), n. 315

White v. Regan, 575 N.Y.S.2d 375 (App. Div. 1991) — § 11-2, n. 31

TABLE OF CASES

Whitehead v. Nevada Comm'n on Judicial Discipline, 893 P.2d 866 (Nev. 1995) — § 9-4, n. 68

Whitehurst v. Kavanaugh, 636 N.Y.S.2d 591 (Sup. Ct. 1995) — § 3-1(a), n. 52

Whitney v. California, 274 U.S. 357 (1927) — § 1-2(c), nn. 33, 34

Wiggins v. Burge, 173 F.R.D. 226 (N.D. Ill. 1997) — § 6-1(a)(5), nn. 103, 104, 122

Wiggins v. McDevitt, 473 A.2d 420 (Me. 1984) — § 11-7(f)(2), n. 273; § 11-9, n. 365

Wilder v. Commissioner of Internal Revenue, 601 F. Supp. 241 (N.D. Ala. 1984) — § 10-2(c)(3), n. 105

Wildmon v. Berwick Universal Pictures, 803 F. Supp. 1167 (N.D. Miss. 1992) — § 13-4(a)(3)(B), nn. 477-80

Wilk v. American Med. Ass'n, 635 F.2d 1295 (7th Cir. 1980) — § 6-1(a)(4), n. 73

Wilkins v. Kalla, 459 N.Y.S.2d 985 (Sup. Ct. 1983) — § 15-2(d)(2), n. 160; § 16-2(a)(2), n. 32

Wilkins v. National Broadcasting Co., 84 Cal. Rptr. 2d 329 (Ct. App. 1999) — § 12-4(c)(1), n. 221; § 13-2(b), nn. 50-53; § 13-7(b)(4)(B), nn. 715, 716; § 13-7(c), nn. 763, 777; § 13-8, n. 806

Wilkinson v. Legal Servs. Corp., 865 F. Supp. 891 (D.D.C. 1994), *rev'd on other grounds*, 80 F.3d 535 (D.C. Cir. 1996) — § 9-5(a)(8)(B), n. 149; § 9-5(a)(8)(I), n. 174; § 9-5(a)(8)(J), n. 180

Wilkinson v. Wiegand, 1997 Conn. Super. LEXIS 1699 (Conn. Super. June 17, 1997) — § 3-2(b), n. 374; § 6-1(c), n. 204

Will v. United States, 389 U.S. 90 (1967) — § 16-2(h)(2), n. 429

Williams v. American Broadcasting Cos., 96 F.R.D. 658 (W.D. Ark. 1983) — § 15-2(d)(1), n. 152; § 16-2(a)(1), n. 21; § 16-2(a)(2), n. 38; § 16-2(c)(2)(B), nn. 156, 167-70; § 16-2(d)(3)(C), nn. 270, 277; § 16-2(e)(2), n. 324; § 16-2(i), n. 443; § 16-3, n. 474

Williams v. City of Mineola, 575 So. 2d 683 (Fla. App. 1991) — § 11-7(d), nn. 258, 263

Williams v. FBI, 822 F. Supp. 808 (D.D.C. 1993) — § 10-2(c)(8)(D), n. 200

Williams v. Florida, 736 So. 2d 699 (Fla. App. 1999) — § 3-1(b), n. 252

Williams v. Indiana, 690 N.E.2d 162 (Ind. 1997) — § 3-1(c), n. 277

Williams v. KCMO Broadcasting, 472 S.W.2d 1 (Mo. App. 1971) — § 12-3, nn. 89-92

Williams v. Poulos, 11 F.3d 271 (1st Cir. 1993) — § 13-7(a)(2)(A), n. 588; § 13-7(a)(2)(A)(ii), n. 622

Williams v. Stafford, 589 P.2d 322 (Wyo. 1979) — § 3-1(a)(1), n. 86

Williams v. Superior Ct., 19 Cal. Rptr. 2d 882 (Ct. App. 1993) — § 11-1, n. 8

Williams v. Superior Ct., 852 P.2d 377 (Cal. 1993) — § 11-7(b)(3)(B), n. 231

Willie Nelson Music Co. v. Commissioner, 12 Media L. Rep. (BNA) 1657 (U.S. Tax Ct. 1985) — § 6-1(c)(1), n. 222

Willis v. Griffin Television, L.L.C., Case No. 91,812 (Okla. App. Mar. 5, 1999) — § 12-4(b), n. 205; § 12-4(c)(2), nn. 241, 246; § 13-2(b), nn. 34, 47; § 13-7(c), n. 805

Wilson v. American Motors Corp., 759 F.2d 1568 (11th Cir. 1985) — § 3-2(a), n. 345; § 6-1(b), n. 160; § 6-1(c), n. 203; § 6-1(c)(1), n. 216; § 6-1(c)(2), n. 233

Wilson v. Freedom of Info. Comm'n, 435 A.2d 353 (Conn. 1980) — § 11-1, n. 5

Wilson v. Layne, 119 S. Ct. 1692 (1999) — Preface, n. 1; § 12-4(a), nn. 119-34; § 12-5, nn. 340, 348, 371

Wilson v. Science Applications Int'l Corp., 60 Cal. Rptr. 2d 883 (Ct. App. 1997) — § 6-1(a)(1), n. 1; § 6-1(c), n. 204

Winegard v. Oxberger, 258 N.W.2d 847 (Iowa 1977) — § 16-2(a)(2), n. 29; § 16-2(e)(1), n. 299; § 16-2(e)(4), n. 362

TABLE OF CASES

Wings v. Dunlap, 527 N.W.2d 407 (Iowa App. 1994) — § 11-7(a)(1), n. 185
Wisconsin v. Cummings, 546 N.W.2d 406 (Wis. 1996) — § 5-2(a)(2), n. 107
Wisconsin v. Gilmore, 535 N.W.2d 21 (Wis. App. 1995) — § 5-2(a)(1), n. 86
Wisconsin v. Knops, 183 N.W.2d 93 (Wis. 1971) — § 14-2, n. 34; § 14-3, n. 40; § 16-2(c)(1), n. 82; § 16-2(f), n. 375
Wisconsin v. Swanson, 284 N.W.2d 655 (Wis. 1979) — § 9-6(b), n. 256; § 9-6(c), n. 288
Wisconsin ex rel. Blum v. Board of Educ., 565 N.W.2d 140 (Wis. App. 1997) — § 11-7(g), n. 297
Wisconsin ex rel. Green Bay Newspaper Co. v. Circuit Ct., 335 N.W.2d 367 (Wis. 1983) — § 16-2(c)(1), n. 92; § 16-2(e)(1), n. 299; § 16-2(h), nn. 397, 398; § 16-2(h)(1), n. 411
Wisconsin ex rel. Herget v. Waukesha County Cir. Ct., 267 N.W.2d 309 (Wis. 1978) — § 3-3(a), n. 435
Wisconsin ex rel. Journal/Sentinel, Inc. v. Pleva, 456 N.W.2d 359 (Wis. 1990) — § 9-6(b), n. 276
Wisconsin ex rel. Newspapers, Inc. v. Showers, 398 N.W.2d 154 (Wis. 1987) — § 9-6(c), n. 289
Wisconsin ex rel. Richards v. Foust, 477 N.W.2d 608 (Wis. 1991) — § 11-7(b)(3)(B), n. 232
Wisconsin ex rel. Schaeve v. Van Lare, 370 N.W.2d 271 (Wis. App. 1985) — § 9-6(g), n. 340; § 9-6(i)(1)(B), n. 377
Wisconsin ex rel. Young v. Shaw, 477 N.W.2d 340 (Wis. App. 1991) — § 11-7(b)(10), n. 253
Wisconsin Family Counseling Servs. v. Wisconsin, 291 N.W.2d 631 (Wis. App. 1980) — § 11-5(a), n. 83
Wisconsin Freedom of Info. Council v. Hill, 7 Media L. Rep. (BNA) 2061 (Wis. Cir. 1981) — § 9-2(b), n. 40
Witherspoon v. Illinois, 391 U.S. 510 (1968) — § 3-1(b), n. 227
Wittek v. Cirigliano, 576 N.Y.S.2d 527 (App. Div. 1991) — § 2-1(d), n. 98
WJW-TV v. City of Cleveland, 686 F. Supp. 177 (N.D. Ohio 1988), *vacated as moot*, 878 F.2d 906 (6th Cir. 1989) — § 9-3, n. 58
Wm. J. Kline & Sons, Inc. v. County of Hamilton, 663 N.Y.S.2d 339 (App. Div. 1997) — § 9-6(f), nn. 325, 330; § 9-6(h), n. 344
Wojtczak v. Department of Justice, 548 F. Supp. 143 (E.D. Pa. 1982) — § 10-2(c)(8), n. 175
Wolf v. Zoning Bd. of Adjustment, 192 A.2d 305 (N.J. Super. 1963) — § 9-6(b), n. 257
Wolfe v. Department of Health & Human Servs., 711 F.2d 1077 (D.C. Cir. 1983) — § 10-2(b)(1), n. 5
Wolfe v. Department of Health & Human Servs., 839 F.2d 768 (D.C. Cir. 1988) — § 10-2(c)(6), nn. 140, 146
Wolfinger v. Sentinel Communications Co., 538 So. 2d 1276 (Fla. App. 1989) — § 5-2(a)(5), n. 226
Wolfskill v. Henderson, 823 S.W.2d 112 (Mo. App. 1991) — § 11-7(a)(3), n. 194
Wolfson v. Lewis, 168 F.R.D. 530 (E.D. Pa. 1996) — § 13-4(b), n. 515; § 13-7(c), n. 781
Wolfson v. Lewis, 924 F. Supp. 1413 (E.D. Pa. 1996) — § 12-2(a), nn. 38-47; § 12-2(b), n. 75; § 13-4(b), nn. 503, 512-18; § 13-5, nn. 554-57; § 13-7(c), nn. 778-81
Wolhar v. General Motors Corp., 712 A.2d 464 (Del. Super. 1997) — § 6-1(a)(1), n. 17; § 6-1(a)(5), n. 111; § 6-1(a)(6), n. 146

TABLE OF CASES

Wood v. Fort Dodge Messenger, 13 Media L. Rep. (BNA) 1610 (Iowa Dist. 1986) — § 12-4(a), n. 187
Wood v. Georgia, 370 U.S. 375 (1962) — § 2-1(c), nn. 48-50; § 7-3, n. 148
Wood v. Marston, 442 So. 2d 934 (Fla. 1983) — § 9-6(e), n. 316
Woodcock v. Journal Publ'g Co., 1990 Conn. Super. LEXIS 59 (Conn. Super. June 25, 1990) — § 16-2(f), n. 379
Word of Faith World Outreach Center Church, Inc. v. Sawyer, 90 F.3d 118 (5th Cir. 1996) — § 13-2(b), n. 72
Worrell Newspapers of Indiana, Inc. v. Westhafer, 739 F.2d 1219 (7th Cir. 1984) — § 2-1(c), nn. 53, 55; § 13-3(a), n. 122; § 5-2(a)(3), n. 173; § 6-1(a)(3), n. 48
Woznicki v. Erickson, 531 N.W.2d 465 (Wis. App. 1995) — § 11-7(a), n. 179
Woznicki v. Erickson, 549 N.W.2d 699 (Wis. 1996) — § 11-7(*l*), n. 341; § 11-5(a)(5), n. 127
WPIX, Inc. v. League of Women Voters, 595 F. Supp. 1484 (S.D.N.Y. 1984) — § 9-2, n. 21; § 9-2(b), nn. 45, 47
WTHR-TV v. Cline, 693 N.E.2d 1 (Ind. 1998) — § 14-6(b), n. 265; § 15-2(b)(1), n. 38; § 16-2(a)(2), nn. 31, 38; § 16-2(c)(1), nn. 104, 109; § 16-2(d)(3)(C), n. 263
WTHR-TV v. Indiana, 685 N.E.2d 1091 (Ind. App. 1997) — § 15-2(d)(1), n. 152
WTHR-TV v. Milam, 690 N.E.2d 1174 (Ind. 1998) — § 15-2(d)(1), n. 152
Wyatt v. Cole, 504 U.S. 158 (1992) — § 12-4(a), n. 137; § 12-5, n. 349
Wyoming ex rel. Feeney v. District Ct., 607 P.2d 1259 (Wyo. 1980) — § 5-2(a)(6), n. 239

Y

Yakima Newspapers, Inc. v. City of Yakima, 890 P.2d 544 (Wash. App. 1995) — § 11-7(m), nn. 350, 352; § 11-9, n. 367
Yarbray v. Southern Bell Tel. & Tel. Co., 409 S.E.2d 835 (Ga. 1991) — § 12-4(c)(3), n. 291
Yarbrough v. Young, 462 So. 2d 515 (Fla. App. 1985) — § 9-6(d), n. 298
Yaro v. Board of Appeals, 410 N.E.2d 725 (Mass. App. 1980) — § 9-6(e), n. 316
Yeager v. DEA, 678 F.2d 315 (D.C. Cir. 1982) — § 10-2(e), n. 246; § 10-2(b)(1), n. 10
Yeste v. Miami Herald Publ'g Co., 451 So. 2d 491 (Fla. App. 1984) — § 9-4, n. 70; § 11-7(j), n. 309
Y.G. v. Jewish Hosp., 795 S.W.2d 488 (Mo. App. 1990) — § 12-2(b), nn. 85-97; § 12-6(a), n. 373
York v. Story, 324 F.2d 450 (9th Cir. 1963) — § 12-5, n. 354
Young v. Rice, 826 S.W.2d 252 (Ark. 1992) — § 11-7(a), n. 184; § 11-5(a)(5), n. 119; § 11-7(a)(5), nn. 201, 203
Younger v. Harris, 401 U.S. 37, 49 (1971) — § 14-4(a), n. 86

Z

Zacchini v. Scripps-Howard Broadcasting Co., 351 N.E.2d 454 (Ohio 1976), *rev'd on other grounds*, 433 U.S. 562 (1977) — § 13-3(b), n. 149
Zacchini v. Scripps-Howard Broadcasting Co., 433 U.S. 562 (1977) — § 13-4(a)(2)(C), n. 404
Zamora v. Adams, 25 Media L. Rep. (BNA) 1638 (Tex. Dist. 1997) — § 2-1(d), n. 99
Zelenka v. Wisconsin, 266 N.W.2d 279 (Wis. 1978) — § 16-2(a)(2), n. 29; § 16-2(c)(1), n. 92; § 16-2(e)(2), n. 315

TABLE OF CASES

Zellner v. Mount Nebo Mem'l Gardens, Inc., 26 Media L. Rep. (BNA) 1672 (Fla. Cir. 1997) — § 16-2(c)(2)(A), n. 144

Zemel v. Rusk, 381 U.S. 1 (1965) — § 1-3, n. 50; § 2-2(c), n. 191; § 9-2, n. 27; § 14-4(a), n. 75

Zenith Radio Corp. v. Matsushita Elec. Indus. Co., 529 F. Supp. 866 (E.D. Pa. 1981) — § 6-1(a)(1), n. 9; § 6-1(a)(4), nn. 60, 73; § 6-1(c)(2), n. 228

Zerilli v. Evening News Ass'n, 628 F.2d 217 (D.C. Cir. 1980) — § 13-7(a)(1), n. 582; § 13-7(a)(2)(A)(i), n. 599; § 13-7(a)(2)(B), n. 651

Zerilli v. Smith, 656 F.2d 705 (D.C. Cir. 1981) — § 14-6(a), n. 233; § 14-6(b), n. 264; § 15-3(c), n. 397; § 16-2(a)(1), n. 2; § 16-2(c)(2), nn. 129-33; § 16-2(c)(2)(B), nn. 153-57; § 16-2(d)(1), nn. 177, 178, 187; § 16-2(d)(3)(C), n. 246; § 16-2(e)(1), nn. 293, 295; § 16-2(e)(3), nn. 328-32; § 16-2(h), n. 393

Zielke v. Wagner, 684 N.E.2d 1095 (Ill. App. 1997) — § 6-1(b), n. 157

Zilg v. Prentice-Hall, Inc., 717 F.2d 671 (2d Cir. 1983) — § 13-4(c), n. 532

Zinda v. Louisiana Pacific Corp., 440 N.W.2d 548 (Wis. 1989) — § 12-1, n. 2

Zorc v. Vero Beach, 722 So. 2d 891 (Fla. App. 1998) — § 9-6(h)(6), n. 364; § 9-6(j), nn. 414, 415

Zubeck v. El Paso County Retirement Plan, 961 P.2d 597 (Colo. App. 1998) — § 11-7(a)(2), n. 191; § 11-7(f)(2), n. 274

Zurcher v. Stanford Daily, 436 U.S. 547 (1978) — § 13-3(c)(9)(B), n. 320; § 14-5(c), nn. 149-59; § 15-1, n. 18; § 15-3(a), nn. 336-41; § 16-2(d)(3), n. 223

TABLE OF STATUTES

Text of the following available in Lexstat Service of Lexis-Nexis.™

United States Constitution

U.S. Const., preamble — § 1-2(b), n. 26
U.S. Const. art. I, § 5, cl. 2 — § 9-3, n. 48
U.S. Const., amend. IV — § 13-7(a)(1), n. 577
U.S. Const., amend. V — § 2-1(a), n. 2
U.S. Const., amend. VI — § 2-1(a), n. 2; § 2-2(a), n. 112

United States Code

5 U.S.C. § 10(a)(3) — § 9-5(b)(6), n. 241
5 U.S.C. § 3(2) — § 9-5(b)(2), n. 199
5 U.S.C. § 552 — § 9-5(a)(1), nn. 78, 80; § 11-1, n. 4
5 U.S.C. § 552(a)(2) — § 10-2(b)(1), n. 18
5 U.S.C. § 552(a)(2)(C) — § 10-2(b)(1), n. 9
5 U.S.C. § 552(a)(2)(D) — § 10-2(b)(1), n. 16
5 U.S.C. § 552(a)(2)(E) — § 10-2(b)(1), n. 17
5 U.S.C. § 552(a)(3) — § 10-2(b)(3), n. 31; § 10-2(g), n. 261
5 U.S.C. § 552(a)(3)(A) — § 10-2(b)(3), n. 38
5 U.S.C. § 552(a)(3)(B) — § 10-2(b)(1), nn. 19, 20; § 10-2(b)(3), n. 37
5 U.S.C. § 552(a)(3)(C) — § 10-2(b)(4), n. 40
5 U.S.C. § 552(a)(4)(A) — § 10-2(g), n. 261
5 U.S.C. § 552(a)(4)(A)(ii) — § 10-2(b)(5), n. 46
5 U.S.C. § 552(a)(4)(A)(ii)(I) — § 10-2(b)(5), n. 47
5 U.S.C. § 552(a)(4)(A)(ii)(II) — § 10-2(b)(5), n. 48
5 U.S.C. § 552(a)(4)(A)(ii)(III) — § 10-2(b)(5), n. 49
5 U.S.C. § 552(a)(4)(B) — § 10-2(b)(3), n. 32; § 10-2(c)(2), n. 89; §10-2(h), nn. 270-72, 276
5 U.S.C. § 552(a)(4)(E) — § 10-2(h), nn. 284, 286, 288, 291
5 U.S.C. § 552(a)(4)(F) — § 10-2(h), nn. 274, 291
5 U.S.C. § 552(a)(6)(A) — § 10-2(b)(4), n. 42
5 U.S.C. § 552(a)(6)(A)(i) — § 10-2(g), nn. 264, 265; § 10-2(b)(4), n. 42
5 U.S.C. § 552(a)(6)(A)(ii) — § 10-2(g), n. 266-68
5 U.S.C. § 552(a)(6)(B) — § 10-2(b)(4), nn. 42, 44
5 U.S.C. § 552(a)(6)(B)(i) — § 10-2(b)(4), n. 45
5 U.S.C. § 552(a)(6)(B)(ii) — § 10-2(b)(4), n. 44
5 U.S.C. § 552(a)(6)(C) — § 10-2(b)(4), n. 42; § 10-2(h), n. 273
5 U.S.C. § 552(a)(6)(D) — § 10-2(b)(4), n. 43
5 U.S.C. § 552(a)(6)(E) — § 10-2(b)(4), n. 43
5 U.S.C. § 552(b) — § 10-2(e), nn. 245, 247
5 U.S.C. § 552(b)(1) — § 10-2(c)(2), n. 55; § 11-5(a), n. 84
5 U.S.C. § 552(b)(2) — § 10-2(c)(3), n. 99; § 11-5(a)(1), n. 85
5 U.S.C. § 552(b)(3) — § 10-2(c)(4), n. 106
5 U.S.C. § 552(b)(3)(A) — § 10-2(c)(1), n. 54; § 10-2(c)(4), n. 114
5 U.S.C. § 552(b)(3)(B) — § 10-2(c)(4), nn. 115, 116
5 U.S.C. § 552(b)(4) — § 10-2(c)(5), n. 118
5 U.S.C. § 552(b)(5) — § 10-2(c)(6), n. 131

TABLE OF STATUTES

5 U.S.C. § 552(b)(6) — § 10-2(c)(7), n. 155; § 10-2(c)(8)(C), n. 188
5 U.S.C. § 552(b)(7) — § 10-2(c)(8), n. 170
5 U.S.C. § 552(b)(7)(A) — § 10-2(c)(8)(A), n. 177
5 U.S.C. § 552(b)(7)(B) — § 10-2(c)(8)(B), n. 184
5 U.S.C. § 552(b)(7)(C) — § 10-2(c)(8)(C), n. 187
5 U.S.C. § 552(b)(7)(D) — § 10-2(c)(8)(D), n. 197
5 U.S.C. § 552(b)(7)(E) — § 10-2(c)(8)(E), nn. 209, 212-14
5 U.S.C. § 552(b)(7)(F) — § 10-2(c)(8)(F), n. 214
5 U.S.C. § 552(b)(8) — § 10-2(c)(9), n. 217
5 U.S.C. § 552(b)(9) — § 10-2(c)(10), n. 224
5 U.S.C. § 552(c)(1) — § 10-2(d), n. 227; § 10-2(d)(1), nn. 229, 231, 235
5 U.S.C. § 552(c)(1)(A) — § 10-2(d)(1), n. 232
5 U.S.C. § 552(c)(1)(B)(i) — § 10-2(d)(1), n. 233
5 U.S.C. § 552(c)(1)(B)(ii) — § 10-2(d)(1), n. 234
5 U.S.C. § 552(c)(2) — § 10-2(d), n. 227; § 10-2(d)(2), nn. 236, 239, 241
5 U.S.C. § 552(c)(3) — § 10-2(d), n. 227; § 10-2(d)(3), nn. 243, 244
5 U.S.C. § 552(e) — § 9-5(a)(2), n. 86
5 U.S.C. § 552(f) — § 9-5(a)(2), n. 86; § 10-2(b)(2), n. 21
5 U.S.C. § 552(f)(2) — § 10-2(b)(1), n. 13
5 U.S.C. § 552a — § 9-5(a)(1), n. 80
5 U.S.C. § 552b — § 9-5(a)(1), nn. 77, 81, 83
5 U.S.C. § 552b(a) — § 9-5(a)(2), nn. 86, 89
5 U.S.C. § 552b(a)(2) — § 9-5(a)(3), n. 94
5 U.S.C. § 552b(a)(3) — § 9-5(a)(3), n. 93
5 U.S.C. § 552b(b) — § 9-5(a)(5), nn. 109, 112
5 U.S.C. § 552b(c) — § 9-5(a)(8), nn. 138, 142, 144
5 U.S.C. § 552b(c)(1) — § 9-5(a)(8)(A), n. 145
5 U.S.C. § 552b(c)(10) — § 9-5(a)(6), n. 117; § 9-5(a)(8)(J), n. 177
5 U.S.C. § 552b(c)(2) — § 9-5(a)(8)(B), n. 147
5 U.S.C. § 552b(c)(3) — § 9-5(a)(8)(C), n. 151
5 U.S.C. § 552b(c)(4) — § 9-5(a)(7), n. 134; § 9-5(a)(8)(D), n. 156
5 U.S.C. § 552b(c)(5) — § 9-5(a)(8)(E), n. 159
5 U.S.C. § 552b(c)(6) — § 9-5(a)(8)(F), n. 162; § 9-6(h)(4), n. 358
5 U.S.C. § 552b(c)(7) — § 9-5(a)(8)(G), n. 167
5 U.S.C. § 552b(c)(8) — § 9-5(a)(6), n. 116; § 9-5(a)(7), n. 134; § 9-5(a)(8)(H), n. 169
5 U.S.C. § 552b(c)(9) — § 9-5(a)(7), n. 134; § 9-5(a)(8)(I), n. 172
5 U.S.C. § 552b(c)(9)(A) — § 9-5(a)(6), n. 116; § 9-5(a)(8)(I), n. 173
5 U.S.C. § 552b(c)(9)(B) — § 9-5(a)(8)(I), n. 174
5 U.S.C. § 552b(c)(10) — § 9-5(a)(7), n. 134
5 U.S.C. § 552b(d)(1) — § 9-5(a)(7), nn. 124, 125
5 U.S.C. § 552b(d)(2) — § 9-5(a)(7), n. 133
5 U.S.C. § 552b(d)(3) — § 9-5(a)(7), nn. 126-28
5 U.S.C. § 552b(d)(4) — § 9-5(a)(7), nn. 135, 136
5 U.S.C. § 552b(e)(1) — § 9-5(a)(4), nn. 101-03
5 U.S.C. § 552b(e)(2) — § 9-5(a)(4), nn. 104, 106-08
5 U.S.C. § 552b(e)(3) — § 9-5(a)(4), n. 105
5 U.S.C. § 552b(f)(1) — § 9-5(a)(6), nn. 115, 118-20; § 9-5(a)(7), nn. 129, 131
5 U.S.C. § 552b(f)(2) — § 9-5(a)(6), nn. 121, 122; § 9-5(a)(7), n. 132
5 U.S.C. § 552b(h)(1) — § 9-5(a)(9)(A), nn. 182, 184; § 9-5(a)(9)(B), nn. 187, 188, 189

TABLE OF STATUTES

5 U.S.C. § 552b(h)(2)(i) — § 9-5(a)(9)(B), nn. 191, 192
5 U.S.C. § 552b(i) — § 9-5(a)(9)(A), n. 186
5 U.S.C. § 552b(k) — § 9-5(a)(6), n. 123
5 U.S.C. §§ 701 to 706 — § 10-2(f), n. 257
5 U.S.C. App. II §§ 1-15 — § 9-5(a)(1), n. 80; § 9-5(b)(1), n. 194
5 U.S.C. App. II § 2(a) — § 9-5(b)(1), n. 195
5 U.S.C. App. II § 2(b) — § 9-5(b)(1), n. 196
5 U.S.C. App. II § 3(2) — § 9-5(b)(2), nn. 200, 208
5 U.S.C. App. II § 3(2)(C)(i)-(iii) — § 9-5(b)(2), n. 219
5 U.S.C. App. II § 4(a) — § 9-5(b)(2), n. 221
5 U.S.C. App. II § 4(b) — § 9-5(b)(2), n. 222
5 U.S.C. App. II § 5(b)(2) — § 9-5(b)(2), n. 198
5 U.S.C. App. II § 8(b)(3) — § 10-3(c), n. 300
5 U.S.C. App. II § 9(a) — § 9-5(b)(2), n. 200
5 U.S.C. App. II § 10(a)(1) — § 9-5(b)(4), n. 226
5 U.S.C. App. II § 10(a)(2) — § 9-5(b)(4), n. 230
5 U.S.C. App. II § 10(a)(3) — § 9-5(b)(6), n. 239
5 U.S.C. App. II § 10(b) — § 10-3(b), n. 293; § 10-3(c), n. 296
5 U.S.C. App. II § 10(c) — § 10-3(b), n. 294
5 U.S.C. App. II § 10(d) — § 9-5(b)(4), n. 227; § 9-5(b)(5), n. 237
5 U.S.C. App. II § 10(e) — § 9-5(b)(4), n. 228
5 U.S.C. App. II § 10(f) — § 9-5(b)(4), n. 229
5 U.S.C. App. II § 11(a) — § 10-3(c), n. 298
5 U.S.C. App. II § 13 — § 10-3(c), n. 299
15 U.S.C. § 30 — § 3-2(e), n. 420; § 6-1(a)(3), n. 57
18 U.S.C. §§ 1 to 16 — § 3-1(a)(6), n. 208
18 U.S.C. § 231 — § 14-3, n. 42
18 U.S.C. § 1030 — § 13-9(a), n. 822
18 U.S.C. § 1030(a)(1) — § 13-9(a), n. 823
18 U.S.C. § 1030(a)(2) — § 13-9(a), n. 824
18 U.S.C. § 1030(a)(4) — § 13-9(a), n. 827
18 U.S.C. § 1030(c)(1) — § 13-9(a), n. 825
18 U.S.C. § 1030(c)(2) — § 13-9(a), n. 825
18 U.S.C. § 1030(c)(3) — § 13-9(a), n. 828
18 U.S.C. § 1030(e)(2) — § 13-9(a), n. 826
18 U.S.C. § 1341 — § 13-3(c)(6), n. 238; § 14-3, n. 42
18 U.S.C. § 1343 — § 13-3(c)(7), n. 243
18 U.S.C. § 1346 — § 13-3(c)(6), n. 238
18 U.S.C. § 1751 — § 14-3, n. 42
18 U.S.C. § 1905 — § 10-2(f), n. 253
18 U.S.C. § 1961 — § 13-3(c)(7), n. 245
18 U.S.C. § 1961 et seq. — § 12-4(c)(3), n. 320; § 13-2(b), n. 62
18 U.S.C. § 2071(a) — § 13-3(c)(5), n. 236
18 U.S.C. § 2252 — § 13-3(c), n. 168
18 U.S.C. § 2314 — § 13-3(c)(8)(A), n. 269; § 13-3(c)(8)(B), nn. 274, 278, 279
18 U.S.C. § 2315 — § 13-3(c)(8)(B), n. 280
18 U.S.C. § 2510 — § 12-2(a), n. 21
18 U.S.C. § 2510(1) — § 13-7(a)(2)(A)(ii), n. 625
18 U.S.C. § 2510(2) — § 13-7(a)(2)(A)(i), n. 594

TABLE OF STATUTES

18 U.S.C. § 2510(4) — § 13-7(a)(2)(A)(i), n. 593
18 U.S.C. § 2510(8) — § 13-7(a)(2)(A)(i), n. 595
18 U.S.C. § 2510(12) — § 13-7(a)(2)(A)(i), n. 589
18 U.S.C. § 2511 — § 13-3(a), n. 122; § 13-4(b), n. 515; § 13-7(a)(2)(A), n. 588
18 U.S.C. § 2511(1) — § 3-1(a)(1), n. 79; § 13-7(a)(2)(A)(i), nn. 590, 592
18 U.S.C. § 2511(1)(b) — § 13-7(a)(2)(A)(i), n. 594
18 U.S.C. § 2511(1)(c) — § 13-7(a)(2)(A)(i), nn. 596, 598, 607
18 U.S.C. § 2511(1)(d) — § 13-2(b), n. 71; § 13-7(a)(2)(A)(i), nn. 597, 598
18 U.S.C. § 2511(2) — § 13-7(a)(2)(A)(iii), n. 631
18 U.S.C. § 2511(2)(c) — § 13-7(a)(2)(A)(iii), n. 631
18 U.S.C. § 2511(2)(d) — § 12-2(a), n. 24; § 13-7(a)(2)(A)(iii), nn. 632, 634, 635; § 13-7(b)(2), n. 698
18 U.S.C. § 2511(4)-(5) — § 13-7(a)(2)(A)(iv), nn. 636, 639, 640
18 U.S.C. § 2515 — § 3-1(a)(1), n. 79; § 5-2(a)(1), n. 85
18 U.S.C. § 2517(1) & (3) — § 5-2(a)(1), n. 86
18 U.S.C. § 2520 — § 3-1(a)(1), n. 79; § 13-7(a)(2)(A)(i), n. 603; § 13-7(a)(2)(A)(iv), nn. 637, 642, 643
18 U.S.C. § 2520(c)(2) — § 13-7(a)(2)(A)(iv), n. 642
18 U.S.C. § 2710 — § 11-5(b), n. 164
18 U.S.C. § 2721(a) — § 11-7(k), n. 322
18 U.S.C. § 2721(b) — § 11-7(k), n. 323
18 U.S.C. § 2721(b)(11) — § 11-7(k), n. 324
18 U.S.C. § 2721(b)(12) — § 11-7(k), n. 325
18 U.S.C. § 2721(c) — § 11-7(k), n. 326
18 U.S.C. § 2723(a) — § 11-7(k), n. 328
18 U.S.C. § 2723(b) — § 11-7(k), n. 327
18 U.S.C. § 2724(b) — § 11-7(k), n. 330
18 U.S.C. § 2725(1) — § 11-7(k), n. 322
18 U.S.C. § 2725(2) — § 11-7(k), n. 329
18 U.S.C. § 2725(3) — § 11-7(k), n. 321
18 U.S.C. § 3006A — § 5-2(e), n. 449
18 U.S.C. § 3006A(d)(4)(A) — § 5-2(e), n. 454
18 U.S.C. § 3006A(d)(4)(B) — § 5-2(e), n. 455
18 U.S.C. § 3006A(d)(4)(C)-(E) — § 5-2(e), n. 456
18 U.S.C. § 3006A(d)(5) — § 5-2(e), n. 452
18 U.S.C. § 3006A(e) — § 5-2(e), n. 450
18 U.S.C. § 3121 — § 13-7(a)(2)(A)(ii), n. 627
18 U.S.C. § 3123 — § 13-7(a)(2)(A)(ii), n. 628
18 U.S.C. § 401(1) — § 2-1(c), n. 36
18 U.S.C. § 641 — § 13-3(c)(5), nn. 231, 233
18 U.S.C. § 793 — § 13-3(c)(9), n. 281; § 13-3(c)(9)(A), nn. 288, 291
18 U.S.C. § 794 — § 13-3(c)(9), n. 281
18 U.S.C. § 795 — § 13-3(c)(9), n. 281
18 U.S.C. § 796 — § 13-3(c)(9), n. 281
18 U.S.C. § 797 — § 13-3(c)(9), n. 281
18 U.S.C. § 798 — § 13-3(c)(9), n. 281
18 U.S.C. § 799 — § 13-3(c)(9), n. 281
18 U.S.C. § 871 — § 14-3, n. 42
18 U.S.C. § 952 — § 13-3(c)(9), n. 281

TABLE OF STATUTES

18 U.S.C. §§ 2510-2520 — § 5-2(a)(1), n. 81; § 13-7(a)(2)(A), n. 586
18 U.S.C. § 2511(5)(b) — § 13-7(a)(2)(A)(iv), n. 641
18 U.S.C. §§ 2512(9) & (10)(a) — § 5-2(a)(1), n. 83
18 U.S.C. § 2521 — § 13-7(a)(2)(A)(iv), n. 641
18 U.S.C. §§ 2721-2725 — § 11-7(k), n. 320
18 U.S.C. §§ 4001, 4002 — § 13-4(a)(1)(B), n. 361
18 U.S.C. § 4241(a) — § 3-1(a)(5), n. 181
18 U.S.C. §§ 5031-5042 — § 3-3(a), n. 451
18 U.S.C. § 5038(e) — § 3-3(a), n. 461
20 U.S.C. § 1232g(b) — § 3-2(b), n. 387
20 U.S.C. § 1232g-i — § 11-7(g), n. 300
21 U.S.C. § 848(q)(9) — § 5-2(e), n. 450
28 U.S.C. § 1292(b) — § 16-2(h)(2), nn. 423, 424
28 U.S.C. § 1651 — § 7-1, n. 8
28 U.S.C. § 1863(b)(7) — § 5-2(c), n. 382
28 U.S.C. § 1920 — § 10-2(h), n. 290
28 U.S.C. § 2511(4) & (5) — § 13-7(a)(2)(A)(ii), n. 630
42 U.S.C. § 405 — § 11-7(j), n. 311
42 U.S.C. § 1983 — § 12-2(a), n. 16; § 12-5, nn. 354, 356, 358
42 U.S.C. § 2000aa(a) — § 15-3(a), nn. 347, 353
42 U.S.C. § 2000aa(a)(1) — § 15-3(a), nn. 347, 350
42 U.S.C. § 2000aa(b) — § 15-3(a), n. 347
42 U.S.C. § 2000aa(b)(1) — § 15-3(a), n. 347
42 U.S.C. § 2000aa(b)(2) — § 15-3(a), n. 358
42 U.S.C. § 2000aa(b)(3) — § 15-3(a), nn. 348, 358
42 U.S.C. § 2000aa(b)(4) — § 15-3(a), n. 348
42 U.S.C. § 2000aa-7(a) — § 15-3(a), nn. 346, 354
42 U.S.C. § 2000aa-7(b) — § 15-3(a), nn. 345, 354
42 U.S.C. §§ 2000aa - 2000aa-12 — § 15-3(a), n. 342
42 U.S.C. §§ 2000aa-6(a), 6(e) — § 15-3(a), n. 350
42 U.S.C. §§ 2161-2166 — § 13-3(c)(9), n. 281
42 U.S.C. §§ 2274-2277 — § 13-3(c)(9), n. 281
42 U.S.C. §§ 2286-2286i — § 9-5(a)(8)(C), n. 154
42 U.S.C. § 10608(a) — § 4-2(a), n. 38
44 U.S.C. § 2107 — § 5-1, n. 11
44 U.S.C. §§ 2201-2207 — § 10-2(b)(2), n. 29
47 U.S.C. § 301 — § 13-7(a)(2)(C), n. 659
47 U.S.C. § 312 — § 13-7(a)(2)(C), n. 676
47 U.S.C. § 326 — § 13-7(a)(2)(B), n. 654
47 U.S.C. § 502 — § 13-7(a)(2)(C), n. 674
47 U.S.C. § 503(b)(2)(A) — § 13-7(a)(2)(C), n. 673
47 U.S.C. § 503(b)(2)(B) — § 13-7(a)(2)(C), n. 675
47 U.S.C. § 503(b)(2)(C) — § 13-7(a)(2)(C), n. 673
47 U.S.C. § 605 — § 13-7(a)(2)(A)(i), n. 603; § 13-7(a)(2)(B), nn. 648, 649
47 U.S.C. § 605(a) — § 13-7(a)(2)(B), n. 651; § 13-7(a)(2)(C), nn. 665, 669
47 U.S.C. § 605(e)(1) — § 13-7(a)(2)(B), n. 649
47 U.S.C. § 605(e)(2) — § 13-7(a)(2)(B), n. 649
47 U.S.C. § 605(e)(3)(C)(i) — § 13-7(a)(2)(B), n. 650
47 U.S.C. § 605(e)(3)(C)(iii) — § 13-7(a)(2)(B), n. 650

TABLE OF STATUTES

50 U.S.C. § 421(a) & (b) — § 13-3(c)(9), n. 281
50 U.S.C. § 783(b) — § 13-3(c)(9), n. 281
50 U.S.C. § 1801 — § 13-7(a)(2)(A)(ii), n. 629
50 U.S.C. App. II § 781 — § 13-3(c)(9), n. 281

Code of Federal Regulations

3 C.F.R. § 167 — § 10-2(c)(2), n. 57
3 C.F.R. § 190 — § 10-2(c)(2), n. 57
3 C.F.R. § 191 — § 10-2(c)(2), n. 57
3 C.F.R. § 333 — § 10-2(c)(2), nn. 57, 58
3 C.F.R. §§ 166-178 — § 10-2(c)(2), n. 57
5 C.F.R. §§ 1303.1-1303.70 — § 10-2(b)(2), n. 23
16 C.F.R. §§ 4.8-4.11 — § 10-2(b)(2), n. 24
16 C.F.R. § 4.11 — § 10-2(g), n. 265
16 C.F.R. §§ 1015.1-1015.20 — § 10-2(b)(2), n. 24
16 C.F.R. § 1015.3 — § 10-2(b)(3), n. 36
28 C.F.R. § 16.3(b) — § 10-2(b)(3), n. 38
28 C.F.R. § 26.4 — § 8-2, n. 66
28 C.F.R. § 50.9 — § 2-4, nn. 314, 315
28 C.F.R. § 50.9(b) — § 2-4, n. 314
28 C.F.R. § 50.9(c)(1-6) — § 2-4, nn. 316, 317
28 C.F.R. § 50.9(e) — § 2-4, n. 318
28 C.F.R. § 50.9(f) — § 2-4, n. 319
28 C.F.R. § 50.10 — § 15-3(b), nn. 361, 376, 360-62
28 C.F.R. § 50.10(b) — § 15-3(b), n. 363
28 C.F.R. § 50.10(c) — § 15-3(b), n. 364
28 C.F.R. § 50.10(d) — § 15-3(b), n. 364
28 C.F.R. § 50.10(e) — § 15-3(b), n. 365
28 C.F.R. § 50.10(f)(1) — § 15-3(b), nn. 366, 368
28 C.F.R. § 50.10(f)(2) — § 15-3(b), nn. 367, 368
28 C.F.R. § 50.10(f)(4) — § 15-3(b), n. 368
28 C.F.R. § 50.10(f)(6) — § 15-3(b), n. 368
28 C.F.R. § 50.10(g)(1) — § 15-3(b), nn. 369, 370
28 C.F.R. § 50.10(g)(2), (3) — § 15-3(b), n. 371
28 C.F.R. § 50.10(m) — § 15-3(b), n. 360
28 C.F.R. § 50.10(n) — § 15-3(b), nn. 361, 362
28 C.F.R. §§ 59.1-59.6 — § 15-3(a), n. 358
28 C.F.R. § 540.62(b) — § 13-4(a)(1)(A), n. 346
31 C.F.R. § 409.1 — § 9-2(a), n. 34
34 C.F.R. § 99.30 — § 3-2(b), n. 387
39 C.F.R. §§ 7.1-7.8 (1993) — § 9-5(a)(4), n. 108
41 C.F.R. §§ 101-6.1001 to 101-6.1035 — § 9-5(b)(1), n. 194
41 C.F.R. § 101-6.1002(a) — § 9-5(b)(2), n. 202
41 C.F.R. § 101-6.1003 — § 9-5(b)(2), n. 209
41 C.F.R. § 101-6.1004 — § 9-5(b)(2), n. 220
41 C.F.R. § 101-6.1005 — § 9-5(b)(2), n. 206
41 C.F.R. § 101-6.1005(d) — § 9-5(b)(2), n. 201
41 C.F.R. § 101-6.1009 — § 9-5(b)(2), n. 202
41 C.F.R. § 101-6.1011 — § 9-5(b)(2), n. 207

TABLE OF STATUTES

41 C.F.R. § 101-6.1013(a) — § 9-5(b)(2), nn. 202, 204
41 C.F.R. § 101-6.1013(c) — § 9-5(b)(2), n. 207
41 C.F.R. § 101-6.1015(a) — § 9-5(b)(2), nn. 202, 204
41 C.F.R. § 101-6.1015(a)(1) — § 9-5(b)(2), n. 202
41 C.F.R. § 101-6.1015(b) — § 9-5(b)(2), n. 204
41 C.F.R. § 101-6.1015(b)(1) — § 9-5(b)(4), n. 230
41 C.F.R. § 101-6.1015(b)(2) — § 9-5(b)(4), n. 231
41 C.F.R. § 101-6.1021 — § 9-5(b)(6), n. 240
41 C.F.R. § 101-6.1023(a) — § 9-5(b)(5), nn. 233, 234
41 C.F.R. § 101-6.1023(c) — § 9-5(b)(5), n. 235
41 C.F.R. § 101-6.1023(d) — § 9-5(b)(5), n. 237
41 C.F.R. § 101-6.1025 — § 10-3(b), n. 294
47 C.F.R. § 2.701 — § 13-7(a)(2)(C), n. 662
47 C.F.R. § 2.701(a) — § 12-2(a), n. 25; § 13-7(a)(2)(C), n. 661
47 C.F.R. § 15.4(f) — § 13-7(a)(2)(C), nn. 659, 661
47 C.F.R. § 15.9 — § 13-7(a)(2)(C), n. 660
47 C.F.R. § 15.11 — § 13-7(a)(2)(C), n. 662
47 C.F.R. § 15.11(a) — § 13-7(a)(2)(C), n. 661
47 C.F.R. § 15.104 — § 13-7(a)(2)(C), n. 659
47 C.F.R. § 15.154 — § 13-7(a)(2)(C), n. 659
47 C.F.R. § 73.1206 — § 13-7(a)(2)(C), nn. 661, 670

Federal Rules of Civil Procedure

Fed. R. Civ. P. 15(g) — § 5-2(b), n. 358; § 5-2(a)(5), n. 227
Fed. R. Civ. P. 17(c) — § 15-3(c), nn. 389, 384-86
Fed. R. Civ. P. 26(b)(2) — § 15-3(c), n. 398
Fed. R. Civ. P. 26(b)(3) — § 10-2(c)(6), n. 147
Fed. R. Civ. P. 26(c) — § 6-1(a)(1), nn. 6, 7; § 6-1(a)(2), n. 31; § 6-1(a)(3), n. 51; § 6-1(a)(5), nn. 110, 114, 119; § 15-3(c), n. 399; § 16-2(h), n. 394
Fed. R. Civ. P. 26(c) —
Fed. R. Civ. P. 30(a)(1) — § 15-3(c), n. 396
Fed. R. Civ. P. 33(a) — § 15-3(c), n. 396
Fed. R. Civ. P. 34(a) — § 15-3(c), n. 396
Fed. R. Civ. P. 36 — § 15-3(c), n. 396
Fed. R. Civ. P. 43(a) — § 3-2(a), n. 334
Fed. R. Civ. P. 45 — § 15-3(c), n. 396
Fed. R. Civ. P. 45(b) — § 16-2(h), n. 394
Fed. R. Civ. P. 45(d)(1) — § 16-2(h), n. 394
Fed. R. Civ. P. 77(b) — § 3-2(a), n. 334

Federal Rules of Criminal Procedure

Fed. R. Crim. P. 6 — § 3-1(a)(3), n. 135
Fed. R. Crim. P. 6(d) — § 3-1(a)(3), n. 107
Fed. R. Crim. P. 6(e) — § 3-1(d), n. 324; § 5-2(a)(3), nn. 137, 141, 166; § 5-2(d), n. 424; § 10-2(c)(4), nn. 108, 112
Fed. R. Crim. P. 6(e)(2) — § 3-1(a)(3), nn. 109, 110, 139; § 5-2(a)(3), nn. 138, 173
Fed. R. Crim. P. 6(e)(3) — § 3-1(a)(3), n. 109
Fed. R. Crim. P. 6(e)(3)(A)(i) — § 5-2(a)(3), n. 147
Fed. R. Crim. P. 6(e)(3)(A)(ii) — § 5-2(a)(3), n. 148

TABLE OF STATUTES

Fed. R. Crim. P. 6(e)(3)(C) — § 5-2(a)(3), nn. 144, 159
Fed. R. Crim. P. 6(e)(3)(C)(ii) — § 5-2(a)(3), n. 146
Fed. R. Crim. P. 6(e)(3)(C)(iii) — § 5-2(a)(3), n. 149
Fed. R. Crim. P. 6(e)(3)(C)(iv) — § 7-2, n. 135
Fed. R. Crim. P. 6(e)(4) — § 5-2(a)(3), n. 139
Fed. R. Crim. P. 6(e)(5) — § 3-1(a)(3), nn. 108, 125, 133, 134
Fed. R. Crim. P. 6(e)(6) — § 5-2(a)(3), nn. 140, 177
Fed. R. Crim. P. 7(f) — § 5-2(a)(4), n. 209
Fed. R. Crim. P. 16(d) — § 5-2(a)(5), n. 221
Fed. R. Crim. P. 17(b) — § 5-2(a), n. 54
Fed. R. Crim. P. 17(c) — § 15-3(c), n. 385
Fed. R. Crim. P. 32(c)(4) — § 5-2(d), n. 424
Fed. R. Crim. P. 41(g) — § 5-2(a)(2), n. 110
Fed. R. Crim. P. 53 — § 4-2(a), n. 38

Federal Rules of Evidence

Fed. R. Evid. 404(b) — § 5-2(a)(4), n. 214
Fed. R. Evid. 501 — § 14-5(b), n. 146; § 16-2(i), n. 447

Alabama Constitution

Ala. Const. art. I, § 13 — § 3-1(a), n. 1
Ala. Const. art. IV, § 57 — § 9-3, n. 52

Alabama Code

Ala. Code § 5-3A-11 — § 11-5(a)(7), n. 145
Ala. Code § 12-15-65 — § 3-3(a), n. 447
Ala. Code § 12-21-142 — § 15-1, n. 15; § 15-2(c), n. 53; § 15-2(d)(1), nn. 137, 144; § 15-2(d)(3)(A), n. 163; § 15-2(e)(1), n. 213; § 15-2(f), n. 257
Ala. Code § 13A-11-30(2) — § 13-7(b)(4)(B), n. 717
Ala. Code § 13A-14-2 — § 9-6(e), n. 311
Ala. Code § 15-18-83(a)(6) — § 8-2, n. 64
Ala. Code § 22-9A-21(e) — § 11-7(j), n. 313
Ala. Code § 26-14-8(c) — § 11-7(b)(5), n. 238
Ala. Code § 36-12-40 — § 11-4, n. 67; § 11-8, n. 357; § 11-5(a)(3), n. 90
Ala. Code § 40-1-33 — § 11-7(f), n. 269
Ala. Code tit. 7, § 370 — § 14-1, n. 17; § 15-1, n. 3

Alaska Statutes

Alaska Stat. § 09.25.115(a)(h) — § 11-2, n. 19
Alaska Stat. § 09.25.120 — § 11-2, n. 18
Alaska Stat. § 09.25.120(6) — § 11-7(b)(9), n. 248
Alaska Stat. § 09.25.120(6)(D), (E) — § 11-7(b)(7), n. 243
Alaska Stat. § 09.25.150 — § 14-1, n. 17; § 15-1, n. 11
Alaska Stat. § 09.25.180 — § 15-2(i)(3), n. 309
Alaska Stat. § 09.25.200 — § 15-2(j), n. 320
Alaska Stat. § 09.25.220(3) — § 11-2, nn. 18, 28
Alaska Stat. §§ 09.25.300-.390 — § 15-1, n. 15

TABLE OF STATUTES

Alaska Stat. § 09.25.340 — § 15-2(c)(2)(B), n. 96
Alaska Stat. § 09.25.390(4) — § 15-2(b)(1), n. 32
Alaska Stat. § 11.46.484 — § 13-9(b), n. 829
Alaska Stat. §§ 12.61.100 to 12.61.150 — § 11-7(b)(5), n. 237
Alaska Stat. § 26.23.200(1) — § 8-3, n. 112
Alaska Stat. § 28.10.505(e) — § 11-7(k), n. 331
Alaska Stat. § 31.05.035 — § 11-5(a)(8), n. 154
Alaska Stat. § 38.06.060 — § 11-5(a)(8), n. 150
Alaska Stat. § 42.20.310 — § 13-7(b)(2), n. 691
Alaska Stat. § 44.62.310(a) — § 9-6(b), n. 255
Alaska Stat. § 44.62.310(a) — § 9-6(b), nn. 263, 269; § 9-6(h)(2), n. 351
Alaska Stat. § 44.62.310(b) — § 9-6(g), n. 340
Alaska Stat. § 44.62.310(c)(1) — § 9-6(h)(3), n. 353
Alaska Stat. § 44.62.310(c)(2) — § 9-6(h)(4), n. 359; § 9-6(i)(1)(B), n. 378
Alaska Stat. § 44.62.310(c)(3) — § 9-6(h)(2), n. 349
Alaska Stat. § 44.62.310(d) — § 9-6(i)(2), n. 390
Alaska Stat. § 44.62.310(e) — § 9-6(d), n. 295
Alaska Stat. § 44.62.310(f) — § 9-6(j), n. 415

Arizona Revised Statutes

Ariz. Rev. Stat. § 12-2214 — § 15-1, n. 15; § 15-2(e)(2), n. 226; § 15-2(i)(1), n. 296
Ariz. Rev. Stat. § 12-2237 — § 14-1, n. 17; § 15-1, nn. 3; § 15-2(b)(1), n. 31; § 15-2(f), n. 255
Ariz. Rev. Stat. § 13-705 — § 8-2, n. 63
Ariz. Rev. Stat. § 13-3005 (A) — § 13-7(b)(2), n. 691
Ariz. Rev. Stat. § 15-721F(2) — § 9-6(b), n. 270
Ariz. Rev. Stat. § 27-152.01 — § 11-5(a)(8), nn. 156, 157
Ariz. Rev. Stat. § 28-450 — § 11-7(k), n. 332
Ariz. Rev. Stat. § 38-431(3) — § 9-6(c), n. 284
Ariz. Rev. Stat. § 38-431(5) — § 9-6(b), n. 261
Ariz. Rev. Stat. § 38-431.01(D) — § 9-6(f), n. 327
Ariz. Rev. Stat. § 38-431.02(C) — § 9-6(d), nn. 294, 298
Ariz. Rev. Stat. § 38-431.03A — § 9-6(g), n. 339
Ariz. Rev. Stat. § 38-431.03(A)(3), (4) — § 9-6(h)(6), n. 364
Ariz. Rev. Stat. § 38-431.03(D) — § 9-6(g), n. 342
Ariz. Rev. Stat. § 38-431.07(A) — § 9-6(j), nn. 408, 413
Ariz. Rev. Stat. § 38-431.08(A)(1) — § 9-6(b), n. 271
Ariz. Rev. Stat. § 39-121 — § 11-5(a)(6), n. 140
Ariz. Rev. Stat. § 39-121.03(A) & (D) — § 11-4, n. 59
Ariz. Rev. Stat. § 39-122 — § 11-5(a)(6), n. 140
Ariz. Rev. Stat. § 41-1750 — § 13-9(b), n. 829

Arkansas Code Annotated

Ark. Code Ann. §§ 5-28-213, 12-12-506 — § 11-7(b)(5), n. 238
Ark. Code Ann. § 5-60-120 — § 13-7(b)(2), n. 691; § 13-7(b)(5), n. 744
Ark. Code Ann. § 6-18-507(c) — § 9-6(i)(4), n. 395
Ark. Code Ann. § 9-27-309 — § 6-2(a), n. 274
Ark. Code Ann. § 9-27-352 — § 11-7(b)(1), n. 209

TABLE OF STATUTES

Ark. Code Ann. § 12-12-211 — § 11-5(a)(6), n. 134; § 11-7(b)(4), n. 234
Ark. Code Ann. § 12-12-1003(e) — § 11-7(b)(4), n. 234
Ark. Code Ann. § 15-85-510 — § 15-2(e)(2), n. 230
Ark. Code Ann. § 16-55-122 — § 6-1(a)(6), n. 136
Ark. Code Ann. § 16-85-510 — § 15-1, n. 15; § 15-2(b)(1), n. 33; § 15-2(c), n. 54; § 15-2(d)(1), n. 137; § 15-2(f), n. 257
Ark. Code Ann. § 16-90-502(d)(2) — § 8-2, n. 63
Ark. Code Ann. §§ 20-18-102, 20-18-304 — § 11-7(j), n. 313
Ark. Code Ann. §§ 25-18-401-25-18-403 — § 6-1(a)(6), n. 136
Ark. Code Ann. § 25-19-103(2) — § 9-6(b), nn. 255, 261, 275
Ark. Code Ann. § 25-19-104 — § 9-6(j), n. 409
Ark. Code Ann. § 25-19-105(b)(9)(A) — § 11-5(a)(3), n. 95; § 11-7(f)(5), n. 290
Ark. Code Ann. § 25-19-106(a) — § 9-6(h)(2), n. 350
Ark. Code Ann. § 25-19-106(b)(2) — § 9-6(d), n. 300
Ark. Code Ann. § 25-19-106(c) — § 9-6(g), n. 332
Ark. Code Ann. § 25-19-107(d) — § 9-6(j), n. 417
Ark. Code Ann. § 25-27-102(5) — § 11-2, n. 17
Ark. Code Ann. § 43-917 — § 14-1, n. 17; § 15-1, n. 3
Ark. Code Ann. § 55-301 — § 11-5(a)(8), n. 158

California Constitution

Cal. Const. art. I, § 2(a) — § 7-4, n. 214
Cal. Const. art. I, § 2(b) — § 15-1, n. 15; § 15-2(a), n. 22; § 15-2(d)(3)(C), n. 183; § 15-2(e)(1), n. 220; § 15-2(f), n. 258
Cal. Const. art. IV, § 7(c) — § 9-3, n. 54
Cal. Const. art. IX § 9(g) — § 9-4, n. 63

California Code

Cal. Bus. & Prof. Code § 827 — § 9-6(i)(6), n. 400
Cal. Civ. Code § 56-10 — § 11-7(e), n. 265
Cal. Civ. Code § 1669.7 — § 7-4, nn. 205, 212
Cal. Civ. Code § 1708.8 — § 12-2(a), n. 66
Cal. Civ. Code § 1708.8(a) — § 12-2(a), n. 67
Cal. Civ. Code § 1708.8(b) — § 12-2(a), n. 68
Cal. Civ. Code § 1708.8(d) — § 12-2(a), n. 69
Cal. Civ. Code § 1799.3(a) — § 11-5(b), n. 164
Cal. Civ. Code § 1899.5(d) — § 11-5(b), n. 161
Cal. Civ. Code § 3344(a) — § 12-4(a), n. 192
Cal. Civ. Code § 3425.3 — § 12-4(a), n. 193
Cal. Civ. Proc. Code § 124 — § 3-2(a), n. 360
Cal. Civ. Proc. Code § 129 — § 11-7(d), n. 264
Cal. Civ. Proc. Code § 237 — § 7-3, n. 192
Cal. Educ. Code § 48912(b) & (c) — § 9-6(i)(4), n. 398
Cal. Educ. Code § 48918 — § 9-6(i)(4), n. 398
Cal. Educ. Code § 49076 — § 11-7(g), n. 297
Cal. Elec. Code § 606 — § 11-7(h), n. 302
Cal. Elec. Code §§ 17120, 17122 — § 11-7(h), n. 302
Cal. Evid. Code § 761 — § 7-4, n. 219

TABLE OF STATUTES

Cal. Evid. Code §§ 1043-1047 — § 11-7(a)(3), n. 195
Cal. Evid. Code § 1070 — § 14-1, n. 17; § 15-1, nn. 3, 15; § 15-2(a), n. 22
Cal. Evid. Code § 1070(a) & (b) — § 15-2(b)(1), n. 37
Cal. Gov't Code §§ 6090, 6091 — § 9-6(e), n. 317
Cal. Gov't Code §§ 6254(h), 54956.8 — § 11-7(f)(5), n. 290
Cal. Gov't Code §§ 6254.7(d), 6254.15 — § 11-7(i), n. 306
Cal. Gov't Code § 6252 — § 11-2, n. 18
Cal. Gov't Code § 6252(a) — § 11-3(a), n. 33; § 11-3(b), n. 43; § 11-3(d), n. 49
Cal. Gov't Code § 6253(a) — § 11-1, n. 5
Cal. Gov't Code § 6254(a) — § 11-5(a)(4), n. 102
Cal. Gov't Code § 6254(a), (d)(3) — § 11-5(a)(4), n. 98
Cal. Gov't Code § 6254(b) — § 11-5(a)(4), n. 113
Cal. Gov't Code § 6254(c) — § 11-7(e), n. 267
Cal. Gov't Code § 6254(d) — § 11-5(a)(7), n. 145; § 11-7(f)(3), n. 280
Cal. Gov't Code § 6254(e) — § 11-5(a)(8), n. 150
Cal. Gov't Code § 6254(f) — § 11-7(c), n. 255; § 11-5(a)(6), nn. 132, 137; § 11-7(b)(1), n. 207; § 11-7(b)(7), n. 243; § 11-7(b)(8), n. 244; § 11-7(b)(9), n. 248; § 11-7(b)(10), n. 254
Cal. Gov't Code § 6254(f)(1) — § 11-7(b)(1), n. 213
Cal. Gov't Code § 6254(f)(2) — § 11-7(b)(5), n. 238
Cal. Gov't Code § 6254(i) — § 11-7(f), n. 269; § 11-7(f)(2), n. 273
Cal. Gov't Code § 6254(n) — § 11-7(f), n. 269; § 11-7(f)(2), n. 275
Cal. Gov't Code § 6254(p) — § 11-5(a)(1), n. 86
Cal. Gov't Code § 6254(u) — § 11-5(b), n. 165
Cal. Gov't Code § 6254.5 — § 11-5(d), n. 171
Cal. Gov't Code § 6254.8 — § 11-7(a)(2), n. 189
Cal. Gov't Code § 6254.9 — § 11-2, n. 27
Cal. Gov't Code § 6254.9(a-e) — § 11-2, n. 24
Cal. Gov't Code § 6255 — § 11-5(c), n. 169
Cal. Gov't Code § 6256 — § 11-2, n. 19; § 11-4, n. 67
Cal. Gov't Code § 6256.1 — § 11-4, n. 68
Cal. Gov't Code § 6257 — § 11-4, nn. 60, 65, 69; § 11-6, nn. 175, 178
Cal. Gov't Code § 6258 — § 11-9, nn. 362, 368
Cal. Gov't Code § 6259 — § 11-9, nn. 361, 378
Cal. Gov't Code § 6259(a) — § 11-9, n. 369
Cal. Gov't Code § 6259(d) — § 11-9, n. 371
Cal. Gov't Code § 6267 — § 11-5(b), n. 163
Cal. Gov't Code § 11121 — § 9-6(b), n. 260
Cal. Gov't Code § 11121(a) — § 9-6(b), n. 271
Cal. Gov't Code § 11123 — § 9-6(e), nn. 311, 313
Cal. Gov't Code § 11123(a) — § 9-6(h)(2), n. 351
Cal. Gov't Code § 11125(a) — § 9-6(d), n. 294
Cal. Gov't Code § 11125(e) — § 9-6(d), n. 308
Cal. Gov't Code § 11125.1 — § 9-6(f), n. 330
Cal. Gov't Code §§ 11126 — § 9-6(g), n. 332
Cal. Gov't Code § 11126(a) — § 9-6(i)(1)(B), n. 377; § 9-6(i)(1)(C), n. 380
Cal. Gov't Code § 11126(i) — § 9-6(h)(3), n. 353
Cal. Gov't Code § 11126(y) — § 9-6(h)(5), n. 363
Cal. Gov't Code § 11126.3(b) — § 9-6(g), n. 340

TABLE OF STATUTES

Cal. Gov't Code § 11127 — § 9-6(b), n. 261
Cal. Gov't Code § 11130 — § 9-6(j), n. 411
Cal. Gov't Code § 11130.3 — § 9-6(j), n. 411
Cal. Gov't Code § 11130.5 — § 9-6(j), nn. 416, 417
Cal. Gov't Code § 11130.7 — § 9-6(j), n. 409
Cal. Gov't Code § 11132 — § 9-6(e), n. 311
Cal. Gov't Code § 11771 — § 13-9(b), n. 829
Cal. Gov't Code § 54952.2 — § 9-6(c), n. 287
Cal. Gov't Code § 54952.2(c)(5) — § 9-6(c), n. 282
Cal. Gov't Code § 54953(a) — § 9-6(h)(2), n. 351
Cal. Gov't Code § 54953.5 — § 9-6(e), n. 317
Cal. Gov't Code § 54953.5(b) — § 9-6(f), n. 331
Cal. Gov't Code § 54953.6 — § 9-6(e), n. 319
Cal. Gov't Code § 54954.1 — § 9-6(d), n. 310
Cal. Gov't Code § 54954.3(a) — § 9-6(e), n. 315
Cal. Gov't Code § 54954.5 — § 9-6(g), n. 338
Cal. Gov't Code § 54956 — § 9-6(d), nn. 298, 299; § 9-6(g), n. 332
Cal. Gov't Code § 54956.5 — § 9-6(d), n. 301
Cal. Gov't Code § 54957 — § 9-6(i)(1)(B), nn. 375, 377; § 9-6(i)(1)(C), n. 382
Cal. Gov't Code § 54957.7 — § 9-6(g), nn. 338, 340
Cal. Gov't Code § 54960(b) — § 9-6(f), n. 331
Cal. Gov't Code § 54960.1 — § 9-6(j), n. 415
Cal. Gov't Code § 54960.5 — § 9-6(j), nn. 415-17
Cal. Health & Safety Code § 32155 — § 9-6(i)(6), n. 400
Cal. Penal Code § 116.5 — § 7-4, n. 197
Cal. Penal Code § 118 — § 7-4, n. 219
Cal. Penal Code § 127 — § 7-4, n. 219
Cal. Penal Code § 132.5 — § 7-4, n. 205
Cal. Penal Code § 132.5(a) — § 7-4, n. 209
Cal. Penal Code § 132.5(b-c) — § 7-4, n. 207
Cal. Penal Code § 132.5(d)-(e) — § 7-4, n. 208
Cal. Penal Code § 132.5(f) — § 7-4, n. 210
Cal. Penal Code § 132.5(g) — § 7-4, n. 211
Cal. Penal Code § 138 — § 7-4, n. 219
Cal. Penal Code § 146e(a) — § 13-3(c)(8)(A), n. 263
Cal. Penal Code § 409.5(a), (d) — § 8-3, n. 111
Cal. Penal Code § 496 — § 13-3(c)(8)(A), n. 259
Cal. Penal Code § 502 — § 13-9(b), n. 829
Cal. Penal Code § 502(c)(2) — § 13-9(b), n. 830
Cal. Penal Code § 502(c)(7) — § 13-9(b), n. 831
Cal. Penal Code § 631 — § 13-7(b)(3), n. 700; § 13-7(b)(5), n. 744
Cal. Penal Code § 632 — § 12-4(c)(3), n. 302; § 13-7(b)(1), n. 683; § 13-7(b)(3), n. 700; § 13-7(b)(4)(B), n. 715; § 13-7(b)(5), n. 744
Cal. Penal Code § 632(c) — § 13-7(b)(4)(B), nn. 714, 716
Cal. Penal Code § 632.6(a) — § 13-7(b)(1), n. 687
Cal. Penal Code § 632.7 — § 13-7(b)(4)(E), n. 735
Cal. Penal Code § 633 — § 13-7(b)(4)(F), n. 739
Cal. Penal Code § 633.5 — § 13-7(b)(4)(D), n. 728
Cal. Penal Code § 637.2(a) — § 13-7(b)(5), n. 746

TABLE OF STATUTES

Cal. Penal Code § 637.2(a)(1) — § 13-7(b)(5), n. 747
Cal. Penal Code § 637.2(b) — § 13-7(b)(5), n. 745
Cal. Penal Code § 646.9(a) — § 13-3(c)(2), n. 198
Cal. Penal Code § 646.9(e) — § 13-3(c)(2), n. 199
Cal. Penal Code § 924.2 — § 5-2(a)(3), n. 167
Cal. Penal Code § 924.4 — § 5-2(a)(3), n. 170
Cal. Penal Code § 938.1 — § 5-2(a)(3), n. 168
Cal. Penal Code § 938.1(b) — § 5-2(a)(3), n. 169
Cal. Penal Code § 939 — § 3-1(a)(3), n. 107
Cal. Penal Code § 939.1 — § 3-1(a)(3), n. 112
Cal. Penal Code § 3605 — § 8-2, n. 63
Cal. Penal Code § 13300 — § 11-7(b)(4), n. 234
Cal. Veh. Code § 1808.21 — § 11-7(k), n. 319
Cal. Veh. Code §§ 1808.21-1808.47 — § 11-7(k), n. 332
Cal. Welf. & Inst. Code § 389 — § 6-2(a), n. 274
Cal. Welf. & Inst. Code § 676(a) — § 3-3(a), nn. 449, 479, 492

Colorado Constitution

Colo. Const. art. II, § 6 — § 3-1(a), n. 1
Colo. Const. art. V, § 14 — § 9-3, n. 52

Colorado Revised Statutes

Colo. Rev. Stat. § 8-1-115 — § 11-7(i), n. 306
Colo. Rev. Stat. § 13-90-119 — § 15-1, n. 15; § 15-2(c), n. 56
Colo. Rev. Stat. § 13-90-119(2)(b) — § 15-2(d)(3)(E), n. 205
Colo. Rev. Stat. § 13-90-119(2)(c), (d) — § 15-2(d)(3)(B), n. 171
Colo. Rev. Stat. § 13-90-119(3) — § 15-2(e)(2), nn. 225, 230
Colo. Rev. Stat. § 13-90-119(4) — § 15-2(h), n. 273
Colo. Rev. Stat. § 16-11-404 — § 8-2, n. 63
Colo. Rev. Stat. § 18-9-303 — § 13-7(b)(2), n. 691
Colo. Rev. Stat. § 24-6-402(1)(a) — § 9-6(i)(1)(A), n. 368
Colo. Rev. Stat. § 24-6-402(1)(c) — § 9-6(d), n. 298
Colo. Rev. Stat. § 24-6-402(1)(d) — § 9-6(b), nn. 255, 261; § 9-6(i)(1)(A), n. 368
Colo. Rev. Stat. § 24-6-402(2)(d) — § 9-6(f), nn. 323, 325, 328
Colo. Rev. Stat. § 24-6-402(2)(e) — § 9-6(c), n. 281
Colo. Rev. Stat. § 24-6-402(3) — § 9-6(g), n. 332
Colo. Rev. Stat. § 24-6-402(3)(a) — § 9-6(g), n. 340
Colo. Rev. Stat. § 24-6-402(3)(a)(II) — § 9-6(h)(6), nn. 364, 365
Colo. Rev. Stat. § 24-6-402(3)(a)(IV) — § 9-6(h)(5), n. 362
Colo. Rev. Stat. § 24-6-402(3)(c) — § 9-6(i)(2), n. 391
Colo. Rev. Stat. § 24-6-402(4) — § 9-6(g), n. 340
Colo. Rev. Stat. § 24-6-402(4)(a) — § 9-6(h)(3), n. 353
Colo. Rev. Stat. § 24-6-402(4)(b) — § 9-6(h)(6), n. 365
Colo. Rev. Stat. § 24-6-402(4)(c) — § 9-6(h)(2), n. 352
Colo. Rev. Stat. § 24-6-402(4)(d) — § 9-6(h)(5), n. 362
Colo. Rev. Stat. § 24-6-402(4)(g) — § 9-6(h), n. 344
Colo. Rev. Stat. § 24-6-402(4)(h) — § 9-6(i)(4), n. 394
Colo. Rev. Stat. § 24-6-402(6) — § 9-6(b), n. 272

TABLE OF STATUTES

Colo. Rev. Stat. § 24-6-402(8) — § 9-6(j), n. 415
Colo. Rev. Stat. § 24-72-202(7) — § 11-2, n. 17
Colo. Rev. Stat. § 24-72-204(1)(a) — § 11-5(b), n. 161
Colo. Rev. Stat. § 24-72-204(2)(a)(IV) — § 11-7(f)(5), n. 291
Colo. Rev. Stat. § 24-72-204(3.5) — § 11-7(k), n. 331
Colo. Rev. Stat. § 24-72-204(3.5)(d) — § 11-7(k), n. 333
Colo. Rev. Stat. § 24-72-303 — § 11-7(b)(4), n. 235
Colo. Rev. Stat. § 24-72.5-101 — § 15-2(c), n. 56
Colo. Rev. Stat. § 24-72.5-101 to 106 — § 15-1, n. 15
Colo. Rev. Stat. § 25-8-405 — § 11-7(i), n. 306
Colo. Rev. Stat. § 39-21-113(4)(a) — § 11-7(f)(2), n. 273

Connecticut Constitution

Conn. Const. art. I, § 10 — § 3-1(a), n. 1
Conn. Const. art. III, § 16 — § 9-3, n. 52

Connecticut General Statutes

Conn. Gen. Stat. § 1-18a(a) — § 9-6(b), n. 261
Conn. Gen. Stat. § 1-18a(b) — § 9-6(c), n. 281
Conn. Gen. Stat. § 1-18a(e)(1) — § 9-6(i)(1)(B), n. 375
Conn. Gen. Stat. § 1-18a(e)(3) — § 9-6(h)(5), n. 362
Conn. Gen. Stat. § 1-18a(e)(5) — § 9-6(h)(3), n. 355; § 9-6(h)(4), n. 357; § 9-6(h)(6), n. 366; § 9-6(i)(3), n. 392; § 9-6(i)(4), n. 394; § 9-6(i)(6), n. 401
Conn. Gen. Stat. § 1-19(a) — § 11-2, n. 31
Conn. Gen. Stat. § 1-19(b)(2) — § 9-6(h)(4), n. 357; § 9-6(i)(3), n. 392
Conn. Gen. Stat. § 1-19(b)(3) — § 11-5(a)(6), nn. 133, 135; § 11-7(b)(9), n. 248
Conn. Gen. Stat. § 1-19(b)(4) — § 11-7(m), n. 348
Conn. Gen. Stat. § 1-19(b)(5) — § 9-6(h)(3), n. 355; § 11-7(i), n. 306
Conn. Gen. Stat. § 1-19(b)(7) — § 11-7(f)(5), n. 290
Conn. Gen. Stat. § 1-19(b)(8) — § 9-6(i)(6), n. 401
Conn. Gen. Stat. § 1-19(b)(10) — § 11-7(f)(2), n. 273
Conn. Gen. Stat. § 1-19(b)(11) — § 9-6(i)(4), n. 394
Conn. Gen. Stat. § 1-21f — § 9-6(d), n. 296; § 9-6(j), n. 417
Conn. Gen. Stat. § 1-21(a) — § 9-6(d), nn. 294, 299; § 9-6(f), n. 327; § 9-6(g), n. 338
Conn. Gen. Stat. § 1-21a(a) — § 9-6(e), n. 317
Conn. Gen. Stat. § 14-10 — § 11-7(k), n. 331
Conn. Gen. Stat. § 46b-122 — § 3-3(a), n. 448
Conn. Gen. Stat. § 52-570d(a) — § 13-7(b)(3), n. 700
Conn. Gen. Stat. § 53-450(a) — § 11-5(b), n. 164
Conn. Gen. Stat. § 53a-251 — § 13-9(b), n. 829
Conn. Gen. Stat. § 54-41r — § 13-7(b)(5), n. 746
Conn. Gen. Stat. § 54-100 — § 8-2, n. 64
Conn. Gen. Stat. § 54-142i — § 13-9(b), n. 829

Delaware Constitution

Del. Const. art. I, § 9 — § 3-1(a), n. 1
Del. Const. art. II, § 11 — § 9-3, n. 52

TABLE OF STATUTES

Delaware Code Annotated

Del. Code Ann. tit. 7, § 5505 — § 11-5(a)(8), nn. 156, 158
Del. Code Ann. tit. 10, §§ 4320-26 — § 15-1, n. 15
Del. Code Ann. tit. 10, §§ 4321-22 — § 15-2(e)(1), n. 212
Del. Code Ann. tit. 10, § 4322 — § 15-2(d)(1), n. 142; § 15-2(i)(1), n. 297
Del. Code Ann. tit. 10, § 4323 — § 15-2(e)(2), n. 231
Del. Code Ann. tit. 10, § 4325 — § 15-2(h), n. 271
Del. Code Ann. tit. 11, §§ 932, 935 — § 13-9(b), n. 829
Del. Code Ann. tit. 11, § 1335(a) — § 13-7(b)(3), n. 700
Del. Code Ann. tit. 11, § 1336(w)(i) — § 13-7(b)(5), n. 747
Del. Code Ann. tit. 11, § 4209(f) — § 8-2, n. 79
Del. Code Ann. tit. 11, § 8606 — § 13-9(b), n. 829
Del. Code Ann. tit. 16, § 3110, tit. 29, § 10002(d)(6) — § 11-7(j), n. 309
Del. Code Ann. tit. 21, § 305 — § 11-7(k), n. 332
Del. Code Ann. tit. 29, § 10002(a) — § 9-6(b), n. 272; § 11-3(b), n. 42
Del. Code Ann. tit. 29, § 10002(a)(3) — § 11-3(d), n. 49
Del. Code Ann. tit. 29, § 10002(d) — § 11-2, n. 18; § 11-5(a)(6), n. 134
Del. Code Ann. tit. 29, §10002(d)(2) — § 11-7(f)(2), n. 277
Del. Code Ann. tit. 29, § 10002(d)(3) —§ 11-5(a)(6), n. 139; § 11-5(a)(7), n. 147; § 11-7(b), n. 206; § 11-7(b)(6), n. 240; § 11-7(j), n. 310
Del. Code Ann. tit. 29, § 10002(d)(4) — § 11-7(b)(1), n. 209; § 11-7(b)(6), n. 240
Del. Code Ann. tit. 29, § 10002(d)(6) — § 11-5(c), n. 169
Del. Code Ann. tit. 29, § 10002(d)(8) — § 11-7(a)(4), n. 196
Del. Code Ann. tit. 29, § 10002(d)(12) — § 11-5(b), n. 163
Del. Code Ann. tit. 29, § 10002(g) — § 11-7(g), n. 298
Del. Code Ann. tit. 29, § 10003 — § 11-4, n. 56
Del. Code Ann. tit. 29, § 10004(b)(1) — § 9-6(i)(1)(B), n. 376; § 9-6(i)(6), n. 401
Del. Code Ann. tit. 29, § 10004(b)(4) — § 9-6(i)(1)(D), n. 387
Del. Code Ann. tit. 29, § 10004(b)(6) — § 9-6(h), n. 344
Del. Code Ann. tit. 29, § 10004(b)(7) — § 9-6(i)(4), n. 397
Del. Code Ann. tit. 29, § 10004(b)(8) — § 9-6(i)(1)(B), n. 376
Del. Code Ann. tit. 29, § 10004(b)(9) — § 9-6(i)(1)(B), n. 376; § 9-6(i)(4), n. 397
Del. Code Ann. tit. 29, § 10004(b)(11) — § 9-6(h)(5), n. 363
Del. Code Ann. tit. 29, § 10004(b)(12) — § 9-6(h)(6), n. 365
Del. Code Ann. tit. 29, § 10004(c) — § 9-6(g), n. 342
Del. Code Ann. tit. 29, § 10004(e)(1) — § 9-6(d), n. 300
Del. Code Ann. tit. 29, § 10004(h)(5) — § 9-6(i)(2), n. 390
Del. Code Ann. tit. 29, § 10005(d) — § 11-9, n. 372
Del. Code Ann. tit. 29, § 10112(b)(5) — § 11-4, n. 70

District of Columbia Code Annotated

D.C. Code Ann. § 1-1524(a)(1) — § 11-5(a)(3), n. 95; § 11-7(i), n. 306; § 11-7(f)(1), n. 271
D.C. Code Ann. § 1-1524(a)(2) — § 11-5(a)(5), n. 120
D.C. Code Ann. § 1-1524(a)(3) — § 11-5(a)(6), nn. 133, 135, 136, 142
D.C. Code Ann. § 16-2316(e) — § 3-3(a), nn. 447, 507
D.C. Code Ann. §§ 16-4701 to 4704 — § 15-1, n. 15
D.C. Code Ann. § 16-4702(1) — § 15-2(d)(3)(A), n. 164; § 15-2(e)(1), n. 216

TABLE OF STATUTES

D.C. Code Ann. § 16-4702(2) — § 15-2(d)(3)(C), n. 184; § 15-2(d)(3)(D), n. 199
D.C. Code Ann. § 16-4703(a) — § 15-2(e)(1), n. 216; § 15-2(e)(2), n. 227
D.C. Code Ann. § 16-4704 — § 15-2(h), n. 271
D.C. Code Ann. § 23-542(3) — § 13-7(b)(2), n. 691

Florida Administrative Code

Fla. Admin. Code Ann. r. 33-15.001 — § 8-2, n. 64
Fla. Admin. Code Ann. r. 33-15.002 — § 8-2, n. 65

Florida Constitution

Fla. Const. art. I, § 4 — § 3-1(a), n. 1
Fla. Const. art. V, § 11(d) — § 9-4, n. 66

Florida Statutes

Fla. Stat. § 1.01(3) — § 11-4, n. 55
Fla. Stat. § 63.162(2) — § 11-7(j), n. 309
Fla. Stat. § 69.081 — § 6-1(a)(6), n. 132
Fla. Stat. § 69.081(4) — § 6-1(a)(6), n. 133
Fla. Stat. § 69.081(6) — § 6-1(a)(6), n. 134
Fla. Stat. § 90.5015 — § 15-1, n. 15; § 15-2(j), nn. 329, 334; § 15-2(d)(3)(A), n. 163
Fla. Stat. § 90.5015(2) — § 15-2(d)(3)(B), n. 171
Fla. Stat. § 90.5015(4) — § 15-2(h), n. 271; § 15-2(d)(1), n. 139; § 15-2(d)(3)(E), n. 206
Fla. Stat. § 98.211 — § 11-7(h), n. 304
Fla. Stat. § 106.25(5) — § 11-7(h), n. 303
Fla. Stat. § 112.21(1) — § 11-7(f), n. 269
Fla. Stat. § 112.215(7) — § 11-7(f), n. 269
Fla. Stat. § 119 — § 11-7(b)(8), n. 246
Fla. Stat. §§ 119.01-119.16 — § 11-5(b), n. 166; § 11-8, n. 357
Fla. Stat. § 119.01(a) — § 11-4, n. 54
Fla. Stat. § 119.011(1) — § 11-2, n. 17
Fla. Stat. § 119.011(2) — § 11-3(e), n. 50
Fla. Stat. § 119.011(3)(c)(2) — § 11-7(b)(1), n. 209
Fla. Stat. § 119.011(3)(d)(2) — § 11-7(b)(3)(A), n. 219
Fla. Stat. § 119.07(1)(a) — § 11-4, nn. 63, 70
Fla. Stat. § 119.07(1)(m) — § 11-7(b)(6), nn. 241, 242
Fla. Stat. § 119.07(3)(a) — § 11-7(f)(5), n. 290
Fla. Stat. § 119.07(3)(c) — § 11-7(e), n. 268
Fla. Stat. § 119.07(3)(d) — § 11-7(b), n. 206; § 11-7(b)(3), n. 217; § 11-7(b)(3)(A), n. 220
Fla. Stat. § 119.07(3)(f) — § 11-7(b)(9), n. 249
Fla. Stat. § 119.07(3)(k) — § 11-7(a)(1), n. 186
Fla. Stat. § 119.07(3)(o) — § 11-2, nn. 24, 27; § 11-7(f)(4), n. 287
Fla. Stat. § 119.07(3)(w) — § 11-7(l), n. 341
Fla. Stat. § 119.07(3)(z) — § 11-7(b)(5), n. 237
Fla. Stat. § 119.085 — § 11-2, n. 19
Fla. Stat. § 119.11(1) — § 11-9, n. 362
Fla. Stat. § 119.12(2) — § 11-9, n. 368
Fla. Stat. § 119.14(2) — § 11-3(a), n. 32

TABLE OF STATUTES

Fla. Stat. § 199.07(3)(q) — § 11-7(i), n. 306
Fla. Stat. § 228.093(3)(d) — § 11-7(g), n. 297
Fla. Stat. § 230.23(4)(m) — § 9-6(i)(4), n. 397
Fla. Stat. § 286.011 — § 9-5(a)(1), n. 80
Fla. Stat. § 286.011(1) — § 9-6(g), n. 342; § 9-6(h)(2), n. 352; § 9-6(j), n. 415
Fla. Stat. § 286.011(2) — § 9-6(f), n. 328; § 9-6(j), n. 406
Fla. Stat. § 286.011(7) — § 9-6(j), n. 417
Fla. Stat. § 286.011(8) — § 9-6(h)(6), n. 366
Fla. Stat. § 286.0105 — § 9-6(b), n. 255
Fla. Stat. § 377.075 — § 11-5(a)(8), nn. 156, 157
Fla. Stat. § 382.025(4) — § 11-7(j), n. 313
Fla. Stat. § 494.0012(3)-(5) — § 11-5(a)(7), n. 145
Fla. Stat. § 655.057 — § 11-7(f)(3), n. 281
Fla. Stat. § 794.03 — § 13-3(a), n. 100
Fla. Stat. § 905.24 — § 3-1(a)(3), n. 109
Fla. Stat. § 905.27 — § 3-1(a)(3), n. 113
Fla. Stat. § 922.11(2) — § 8-2, n. 64
Fla. Stat. § 934 — § 13-7(c), n. 781
Fla. Stat. § 934.01 — § 13-7(b)(5), n. 747
Fla. Stat. § 934.03(2)(a) — § 13-7(b)(3), n. 700
Fla. Stat. § 934.03(2)(g) — § 13-7(b)(4)(G), n. 743
Fla. Stat. § 934.03(3)(d) — § 13-7(b)(3), n. 700
Fla. Stat. § 934.10 — § 13-4(b), n. 515
Fla. Stat. § 945.10(1) — § 11-7(c), n. 255
Fla. Stat. § 985.05 — § 6-2(a), n. 282
Fla. Stat. § 985.205 — § 6-2(a), n. 281

Georgia Constitution

Ga. Const. art. III, § 4, para. 11 — § 9-3, n. 54

Georgia Code Annotated

Ga. Code Ann. § 7-1-70 — § 11-7(f)(3), n. 285
Ga. Code Ann. § 15-11-28(c) — § 3-3(a), n. 447
Ga. Code Ann. § 15-11-58 — § 6-2(a), n. 274
Ga. Code Ann. § 16-11-62 — § 13-7(b)(2), n. 691; § 13-7(b)(5), n. 744
Ga. Code Ann. § 16-5-92 — § 13-3(c)(2), n. 202
Ga. Code Ann. § 21-5-50 — § 11-7(f)(2), n. 279
Ga. Code Ann. § 24-9-30 — § 15-1, n. 15; § 15-2(c)(1), n. 58; § 15-2(c)(2)(B), n. 96; § 15-2(d)(3)(C), n. 183; § 15-2(d)(3)(D), n. 199; § 15-2(e)(2), nn. 225, 226; § 15-2(f), n. 256; § 15-2(h), n. 272
Ga. Code Ann. § 26-3001(1) — § 13-7(b)(3), n. 701
Ga. Code Ann. § 26-3006 — § 13-7(b)(4)(D), n. 728
Ga. Code Ann. § 26-9901 — § 13-3(a), n. 84
Ga. Code Ann. §§ 35-3-34, 35-3-35 — § 11-7(b)(4), n. 235
Ga. Code Ann. § 40-5-2 — § 11-7(k), n. 332
Ga. Code Ann. § 50-5A-11 — § 11-7(f)(3), n. 282
Ga. Code Ann. § 50-14-4 — § 9-6(g), n. 339
Ga. Code Ann. § 50-14-1(a)(2) — § 9-6(c), n. 282

TABLE OF STATUTES

Ga. Code Ann. § 50-14-1(b) — § 9-6(h)(2), n. 350; § 9-6(j), n. 415
Ga. Code Ann. § 50-14-1(c) — § 9-6(e), n. 317
Ga. Code Ann. § 50-14-1(d) — § 9-6(d), nn. 298, 305
Ga. Code Ann. § 50-14-3(5) — § 9-6(i)(3), n. 392
Ga. Code Ann. § 50-18-70(a) — § 11-2, n. 17
Ga. Code Ann. § 50-18-72(a)(3) — § 11-7(b)(7), n. 243
Ga. Code Ann. § 50-18-72(a)(6) — § 11-7(f)(5), n. 290

Hawaii Revised Statutes

Haw. Rev. Stat. § 92-2(1) — § 9-6(b), n. 255
Haw. Rev. Stat. § 92-5(a)(3) — § 9-6(i)(1)(D), n. 388
Haw. Rev. Stat. § 92-5(a)(4) — § 9-6(h)(6), n. 365
Haw. Rev. Stat. § 92-5(a)(5), (6) — § 9-6(h)(5), n. 362
Haw. Rev. Stat. § 92-5(b) — § 9-6(c), nn. 281, 284, 287
Haw. Rev. Stat. § 92-7 — § 9-6(d), n. 293
Haw. Rev. Stat. § 92-9(c) — § 9-6(e), nn. 317, 320
Haw. Rev. Stat. § 92-13 — § 9-6(j), n. 413
Haw. Rev. Stat. § 92-41 — § 9-6(d), n. 305
Haw. Rev. Stat. § 92F-3 — § 11-2, n. 17
Haw. Rev. Stat. § 92F-11(c) — § 11-2, n. 30
Haw. Rev. Stat. § 92F-13(5) — § 11-3(b), n. 40
Haw. Rev. Stat. § 571-41 — § 3-3(a), n. 448
Haw. Rev. Stat. §§ 708-890 to 708-896 — § 13-9(b), n. 829
Haw. Rev. Stat. § 803-42 — § 13-7(b)(1), n. 686; § 13-7(b)(2), n. 691
Haw. Rev. Stat. § 831-1 — § 11-7(b)(1), n. 209

Idaho Constitution

Idaho Const. art. 3, § 12 — § 9-3, n. 51
Idaho Const. art. I, § 18 — § 3-1(a), n. 1

Idaho Code

Idaho Code § 9-337 — § 11-2, n. 17
Idaho Code § 9-340 — § 11-5(a)(6), n. 140
Idaho Code § 9-340(2) — § 11-2, n. 26
Idaho Code § 9-340(4)(a)(i) & (ii) — § 11-7(i), n. 306
Idaho Code § 9-340(7) — § 11-7(f)(4), n. 287
Idaho Code § 9-340(11) — § 11-5(a)(5), n. 121; § 11-7(f)(3), n. 280
Idaho Code § 9-340(16) — § 11-2, nn. 27, 28
Idaho Code § 9-340(21) — § 11-7(f)(3), n. 280
Idaho Code § 9-340(36) — § 11-5(a)(5), n. 122
Idaho Code § 16-1608(b), 20-519 — § 3-3(a), n. 448
Idaho Code § 18-6702 — § 13-7(b)(2), n. 691; § 13-7(b)(5), n. 747
Idaho Code § 19-2716 — § 8-2, n. 79
Idaho Code § 26-1112 — § 11-7(f)(3), n. 285
Idaho Code § 67-2341(3) — § 9-6(g), n. 334
Idaho Code § 67-2341(6)(b) — § 9-6(d), nn. 297, 299
Idaho Code § 67-2342(1) — § 9-6(h)(2), n. 351
Idaho Code § 67-2343(2) — § 9-6(d), n. 300

TABLE OF STATUTES

Idaho Code § 67-2344(1) — § 9-6(f), n. 326
Idaho Code § 67-2345(1) — § 9-6(g), nn. 332, 339
Idaho Code § 67-2345(1)(b) — § 9-6(i)(1)(B), n. 375; § 9-6(i)(1)(C), n. 380; § 9-6(i)(4), n. 395
Idaho Code § 67-2345(1)(g) — § 9-6(i)(2), n. 391
Idaho Code § 67-2347(2) — § 9-6(j), n. 412
Idaho Code § 67-2347(3) — § 9-6(j), n. 408

Illinois Constitution

Ill. Const. art. IV, § 5(c) — § 9-3, n. 54

Illinois Compiled Statutes

5 Ill. Comp. Stat. 140/2(a) — § 11-3(a), n. 33; § 11-3(b), n. 38; § 11-7(g), n. 299
5 Ill. Comp. Stat. 140/2(c) — § 11-2, nn. 11, 17, 18
5 Ill. Comp. Stat. 140/2(d) — § 11-2, n. 18
5 Ill. Comp. Stat. 140/3 — § 11-1, n. 5; § 11-2, n. 15
5 Ill. Comp. Stat. 140/6(a) — § 11-4, n. 69
5 Ill. Comp. Stat. 140/6(b) — § 11-4, nn. 70, 73
5 Ill. Comp. Stat. 140/7 — § 11-5(b), n. 160
5 Ill. Comp. Stat. 140/7(1)(a) — § 11-5(a)(2), n. 88
5 Ill. Comp. Stat. 140/7(1)(b) — § 11-7(b)(10), n. 253
5 Ill. Comp. Stat. 140/7(1)(b)(i-v) — § 11-5(a)(5), n. 122
5 Ill. Comp. Stat. 140/7(1)(b)(ii) & (iii) — § 11-7(a)(1), n. 186
5 Ill. Comp. Stat. 140/7(1)(b)(v) — § 11-7(b)(5), n. 237
5 Ill. Comp. Stat. 140/7(1)(c) — § 11-5(a)(6), nn. 133, 135
5 Ill. Comp. Stat. 140/7(1)(c)(i) — § 11-7(b)(3), n. 218
5 Ill. Comp. Stat. 140/7(1)(c)(v) — § 11-7(b)(9), nn. 248, 251
5 Ill. Comp. Stat. 140/7(1)(d) — § 11-7(c), n. 255; § 11-7(b)(4), n. 234
5 Ill. Comp. Stat. 140/7(1)(d)(i) — § 11-7(b)(1), n. 209; § 11-7(b)(2), n. 215
5 Ill. Comp. Stat. 140/7(1)(f) — § 11-3(b), n. 40; § 11-5(a)(4), n. 104
5 Ill. Comp. Stat. 140/7(1)(g) — § 11-5(a)(3), nn. 91, 92, 97; § 11-7(f)(1), n. 271
5 Ill. Comp. Stat. 140/7(1)(h) — § 11-7(f)(1), n. 271; § 11-7(f)(4), n. 288
5 Ill. Comp. Stat. 140/7(1)(i) — § 11-7(f)(1), n. 271
5 Ill. Comp. Stat. 140/7(1)(k) — § 11-7(f)(1), n. 271
5 Ill. Comp. Stat. 140/7(1)(n) — § 11-5(a)(4), nn. 111, 114
5 Ill. Comp. Stat. 140/7(1)(p) — § 11-2, n. 24; § 11-7(f)(1), n. 271
5 Ill. Comp. Stat. 140/7(1)(r) — § 11-7(f)(1), n. 271
5 Ill. Comp. Stat. 140/7(1)(q) — § 11-7(a)(4), n. 196
5 Ill. Comp. Stat. 140/7(1)(x) — § 11-5(a)(7), n. 145; § 11-7(f)(3), n. 284
5 Ill. Comp. Stat. 140/7(aa), (b)(i) — § 11-7(e), n. 267
5 Ill. Comp. Stat. 140/7(w) — § 11-5(a)(1), n. 86
5 Ill. Comp. Stat. 140/7(y) — § 11-7(l), n. 342
5 Ill. Comp. Stat. 140/8 — § 11-6, n. 176
5 Ill. Comp. Stat. 140/11(a) — § 11-9, n. 359
5 Ill. Comp. Stat. 140/11(b) — § 11-9, n. 360
5 Ill. Comp. Stat. 140/11(h) — § 11-9, n. 362
116 Ill. Comp. Stat. 203(d) — § 11-4, n. 68
705 Ill. Comp. Stat. 405/1-5(6) — § 3-3(b), n. 548

TABLE OF STATUTES

705 Ill. Comp. Stat. 405/1-6 — § 3-3(a), n. 447
720 Ill. Comp. Stat. 5/14-2 — § 13-7(b)(2), n. 698; § 13-7(b)(3), n. 700
720 Ill. Comp. Stat. 5/14-3(c) — § 13-7(b)(4)(B), n. 714
720 Ill. Comp. Stat. 5/14-3(d) — § 13-7(b)(4)(G), n. 742
725 Ill. Comp. Stat. 5/119-5(d) — § 8-2, n. 63
735 Ill. Comp. Stat. 5/8-901 — § 15-1, n. 15; § 15-2(c)(2)(B), nn. 100, 101; § 15-2(f), n. 255; § 15-2(g), n. 265; § 15-2(i)(1), nn. 292, 293; § 15-2(i)(3), n. 309
735 Ill. Comp. Stat. 5/8-901 et seq. — § 15-2(i)(3), n. 309
735 Ill. Comp. Stat. 5/8-903 — § 16-2(a)(1), n. 7
735 Ill. Comp. Stat. 5/8-903(a) & (b) — § 15-2(i)(1), n. 291

Indiana Constitution

Ind. Const. art. I, § 12 — § 3-1(a), n. 1
Ind. Const. art. IV, § 13 — § 9-3, n. 52

Indiana Code

Ind. Ann. Stat. § 2-1733 (Cum. Supp. 1966) — § 14-1, n. 17
Ind. Ann. Stat. § 2-1733 (Cum. Supp. 1966) — § 15-1, n. 3
Ind. Code §§ 4-13.4-2-7, 4-13.4-5-2(b) — § 11-7(f)(4), n. 287
Ind. Code § 5-2-12-11 — § 11-7(c), n. 256
Ind. Code § 5-14-1.5-2(a)(1) — § 9-6(b), n. 255
Ind. Code § 5-14-1.5-3(a) — § 9-6(e), n. 311; § 9-6(h)(2), n. 351
Ind. Code § 5-14-1.5-4(c) — § 9-6(f), n. 326
Ind. Code § 5-14-1.5-6.1(4) — § 9-6(i)(1)(B), n. 379
Ind. Code § 5-14-1.5-6.1(8) — § 9-6(i)(1)(B), n. 379
Ind. Code § 5-14-1.5-6.1(9) — § 9-6(i)(1)(A), n. 371; § 9-6(i)(1)(B), n. 379
Ind. Code § 5-14-1.5-6.1(b)(1), (6) — § 9-6(h), n. 344
Ind. Code § 5-14-1.5-6.1(b)(2) — § 9-6(h)(6), n. 366
Ind. Code § 5-14-1.5-6.1(b)(7) — § 9-6(i)(4), n. 397
Ind. Code § 5-14-1.5-7(a) — § 9-6(j), n. 410
Ind. Code § 5-14-3-2 — § 11-2, n. 31
Ind. Code § 5-14-3-4(a)(4) — § 11-7(i), n. 306
Ind. Code § 5-14-3-4(b)(11) — § 11-2, n. 23
Ind. Code § 5-14-3-5(c)(3)(B) — § 11-7(b)(5), n. 238
Ind. Code §§ 9-14-3.5-1 to 9-14-3.5-15 — § 11-7(k), n. 331
Ind. Code § 20-8.1-5-10 — § 9-6(i)(4), n. 395
Ind. Code § 34-46-4-1 — § 15-1, n. 15; § 15-2(b)(1), n. 38; § 15-2(c), n. 55; § 15-2(d)(1), n. 139; § 15-2(e)(1), n. 213
Ind. Code § 35-33.5-1-5 — § 13-7(b)(2), n. 691
Ind. Code § 35-38-6-6 — § 8-2, n. 62
Ind. Code § 36-2-2-8 — § 9-6(d), n. 299

Iowa Code

Iowa Code § 21.2 — § 9-6(b), n. 276
Iowa Code § 21.2(1)(a) — § 9-6(b), n. 260
Iowa Code § 21.2(2) — § 9-6(c), n. 284
Iowa Code § 21.4(1) — § 9-6(d), n. 295
Iowa Code § 21.5 — § 9-6(g), n. 332; § 9-6(i)(4), n. 395

TABLE OF STATUTES

Iowa Code § 21.5(1)(c) — § 9-6(h)(6), n. 366
Iowa Code § 21.5(1)(d) — § 9-6(i)(6), n. 405
Iowa Code § 21.5(1)(e) — § 9-6(i)(4), n. 398
Iowa Code § 21.5(1)(g) — § 9-6(h)(5), n. 362; § 11-7(b)(9), n. 248
Iowa Code § 21.5(1)(h) — § 9-6(h)(5), n. 362; § 11-7(b)(9), n. 248
Iowa Code § 21.5(2) — § 9-6(g), n. 341
Iowa Code § 21.5(5) — § 9-6(h), n. 345
Iowa Code § 21.6(3) — § 9-6(j), n. 417
Iowa Code § 21.6(3)(a) — § 9-6(j), n. 412
Iowa Code § 21.6(3)(d) — § 9-6(j), n. 413
Iowa Code § 21.7 — § 9-6(e), n. 317
Iowa Code § 21.11 — § 9-6(b), n. 276
Iowa Code § 22.1 — § 11-2, n. 18
Iowa Code § 22.3(A) — § 11-2, n. 23
Iowa Code § 22.3(A)(3) — § 11-2, n. 25
Iowa Code § 22.7(4) — § 11-5(a)(4), n. 111
Iowa Code § 22.7(6) — § 11-5(a)(3), n. 95
Iowa Code § 22.7(9) — § 11-7(b)(1), n. 209
Iowa Code § 22.7(19) — § 11-7(a)(5), n. 199
Iowa Code § 22.13 — § 11-7(m), n. 350
Iowa Code § 321.11 — § 11-7(k), n. 331
Iowa Code § 45-221(16) — § 11-2, n. 27
Iowa Code § 68A.7(11) — § 11-7(a), n. 184
Iowa Code § 144.43 — § 11-7(j), n. 313
Iowa Code § 692.19 — § 11-7(b)(4), n. 234
Iowa Code § 716A.2 — § 13-9(b), n. 829
Iowa Code § 727.11(1) — § 11-5(b), n. 164
Iowa Code § 749B — § 11-5(b), n. 162
Iowa Code § 727.8 — § 13-7(b)(2), n. 691
Iowa Code § 808B.2 — § 13-7(b)(2), n. 691

Kansas Statutes Annotated

Kan. Stat. Ann. § 9-1712 — § 11-7(f)(3), nn. 281, 285
Kan. Stat. Ann. § 21-3914 — § 11-7(i), n. 307
Kan. Stat. Ann. § 21-4002 — § 13-7(b)(2), n. 691
Kan. Stat. Ann. § 38-1607 — § 6-2(a), n. 286
Kan. Stat. Ann. § 38-1652 — § 6-2(a), n. 287
Kan. Stat. Ann. tit. 42, § 5(A) — § 9-6(e), n. 311
Kan. Stat. Ann. § 45-217(e)(1) — § 11-3(e), n. 51
Kan. Stat. Ann. § 45-217(f)(1) — § 11-2, n. 18
Kan. Stat. Ann. § 45-221 — § 11-5(a)(3), n. 90
Kan. Stat. Ann. § 45-221(a)(10) — § 11-7(b)(3), n. 218
Kan. Stat. Ann. § 45-221(a)(17) — § 11-7(f)(2), n. 278
Kan. Stat. Ann. § 45-221(a)(26) — § 11-7(l), n. 340
Kan. Stat. Ann. § 74-2012 — § 11-7(k), n. 332
Kan. Stat. Ann. § 75-4317(a) — § 9-6(c), nn. 279, 287
Kan. Stat. Ann. § 75-4318(a) — § 9-6(b), n. 275
Kan. Stat. Ann. § 75-4318(c) — § 9-6(d), n. 292
Kan. Stat. Ann. § 75-4318(e) — § 9-6(e), n. 317

TABLE OF STATUTES

Kan. Stat. Ann. § 75-4319(a) — § 9-6(g), nn. 332, 338
Kan. Stat. Ann. § 75-4319(b)(2) — § 9-6(h)(6), n. 364
Kan. Stat. Ann. § 75-4319(b)(3) — § 9-6(i)(1)(D), n. 386
Kan. Stat. Ann. § 75-4319(b)(4) — § 9-6(h)(3), n. 355
Kan. Stat. Ann. § 75-4319(b)(5) — § 9-6(i)(3), n. 393; § 9-6(i)(4), n. 398
Kan. Stat. Ann. § 75-4320(a) — § 9-6(j), nn. 406, 412
Kan. Stat. Ann. § 75-4320(c) — § 9-6(j), n. 417

Kentucky Constitution

Ky. Const. § 14 — § 3-1(a), n. 1

Kentucky Revised Statutes Annotated

Ky. Rev. Stat. Ann. § 17-150(2) — § 11-5(a)(6), n. 133
Ky. Rev. Stat. Ann. § 61.800 — § 9-6(h)(2), n. 350
Ky. Rev. Stat. Ann. § 61.805(2) — § 9-6(b), n. 260
Ky. Rev. Stat. Ann. § 61.810(1) — § 9-6(c), nn. 282, 284
Ky. Rev. Stat. Ann. § 61.810(1)(c) — § 9-6(h)(6), n. 364
Ky. Rev. Stat. Ann. § 61.810(1)(e) — § 9-6(i)(1)(D), n. 388
Ky. Rev. Stat. Ann. § 61.810(1)(f) — § 9-6(i)(1)(C), nn. 380, 382, 384
Ky. Rev. Stat. Ann. § 61.810(1)(j) — § 9-6(b), n. 271
Ky. Rev. Stat. Ann. § 61.810(2) — § 9-6(c), n. 287
Ky. Rev. Stat. Ann. § 61.810(6) — § 9-6(i)(4), n. 394
Ky. Rev. Stat. Ann. § 61.815 — § 9-6(g), n. 333
Ky. Rev. Stat. Ann. § 61.815(1) — § 9-6(g), n. 338
Ky. Rev. Stat. Ann. § 61.815(4) — § 9-6(g), n. 340
Ky. Rev. Stat. Ann. § 61.840 — § 9-6(e), n. 317
Ky. Rev. Stat. Ann. § 61.846 — § 9-6(j), n. 408
Ky. Rev. Stat. Ann. § 61.848 — § 9-6(j), n. 408
Ky. Rev. Stat. Ann. § 61.870(1) — § 11-3(b), n. 38
Ky. Rev. Stat. Ann. § 61.870(1)(h) — § 11-3(e), n. 51
Ky. Rev. Stat. Ann. § 61.870(1)(j) — § 11-3(d), n. 49
Ky. Rev. Stat. Ann. § 61.870(2) — § 11-2, nn. 11, 17, 18
Ky. Rev. Stat. Ann. § 61.870(3) — § 11-4, n. 64
Ky. Rev. Stat. Ann. § 61.872 — § 11-4, n. 54
Ky. Rev. Stat. Ann. § 61.872(2) — § 11-4, nn. 62, 63
Ky. Rev. Stat. Ann. § 61.874(2) — § 11-2, n. 29
Ky. Rev. Stat. Ann. § 61.878(1)(c) — § 11-5(a)(8), n. 151
Ky. Rev. Stat. Ann. § 61.878(1)(f) — § 11-7(f)(5), n. 290
Ky. Rev. Stat. Ann. § 61.878(1)(g) — § 11-7(b)(3), n. 217; § 11-7(b)(3)(A), n. 220
Ky. Rev. Stat. Ann. § 61.878(4) — § 11-6, nn. 175, 176
Ky. Rev. Stat. Ann. § 61.880(1) — § 11-4, n. 67
Ky. Rev. Stat. Ann. § 61.880(2) — § 11-8, n. 358
Ky. Rev. Stat. Ann. § 61.882(1) — § 11-9, nn. 359, 361
Ky. Rev. Stat. Ann. § 61-882(4) — § 11-9, n. 362
Ky. Rev. Stat. Ann. § 61-920 — § 9-6(d), n. 296
Ky. Rev. Stat. Ann. § 224.10-210 — § 6-1(a)(6), n. 138

TABLE OF STATUTES

Ky. Rev. Stat. Ann. § 421.100 — § 14-1, n. 17; § 15-1, nn. 3, 15; § 15-2(b)(1), n. 31; § 15-2(c), n. 53; § 15-2(d)(1), n. 137; § 15-2(d)(3)(A), n. 163; § 15-2(e)(1), n. 213; § 15-2(f), n. 257
Ky. Rev. Stat. Ann. § 431.250 — § 8-2, nn. 64, 65
Ky. Rev. Stat. Ann. § 434.845 — § 13-9(b), n. 829
Ky. Rev. Stat. Ann. § 446.010(26) — § 11-4, n. 55
Ky. Rev. Stat. Ann. § 526.010 — § 13-7(b)(2), n. 691
Ky. Rev. Stat. Ann. § 526.020 — § 13-7(b)(2), n. 691

Louisiana Constitution

La. Const. art. I, § 6 — § 3-1(a), n. 1
La. Const. art. XII, § 3 — § 9-1, nn. 11, 14

Louisiana Revised Statutes Annotated

La. Code Civ. Proc. Ann. art. 1426(D) — § 6-1(a)(6), n. 135
La. Code Juv. Proc. Ann. art. 407 — § 3-3(a), nn. 448, 449
La. Rev. Stat. Ann. § 15:570 — § 8-2, n. 63
La. Rev. Stat. Ann. § 15:1303(C)(4) — § 13-7(b)(3), n. 700
La. Rev. Stat. Ann. tit. 42, §§ 6.1(A)(2), 6.2(A)(3) — § 9-6(i)(1)(D), n. 386
La. Rev. Stat. Ann. tit. 42, §§ 6.1(A)(5), 6.2(A)(6) — § 9-6(h)(5), n. 363
La. Rev. Stat. Ann. tit. 42, § 7.1(B) — § 9-6(f), n. 326
La. Rev. Stat. Ann. tit. 42, § 8(A), (B) — § 9-6(e), n. 317
La. Rev. Stat. Ann. tit. 42, § 13 — § 9-6(j), n. 412
La. Rev. Stat. Ann. § 42:6.1(A)(1) — § 9-6(i)(1)(B), nn. 375, 377
La. Rev. Stat. Ann. § 42:6.1(B) — § 9-6(b), n. 271
La. Rev. Stat. Ann. § 44:1 — § 11-2, n. 17
La. Rev. Stat. Ann. § 44:3 — § 11-7(b)(8), n. 246
La. Rev. Stat. Ann. § 44:3.A(1) — § 11-7(b)(6), nn. 241, 242
La. Rev. Stat. Ann. § 44:3.A(3) — § 11-7(b)(9), n. 248
La. Rev. Stat. Ann. § 44:4(4) — § 11-7(f)(3), n. 280
La. Rev. Stat. Ann. § 44:33(B) — § 11-7(f)(6), n. 296
La. Rev. Stat. Ann. § 44:35(D) — § 11-9, n. 371
La. Rev. Stat. Ann. § 44:35(E) — § 11-9, n. 370
La. Rev. Stat. Ann. § 45:1451 — § 15-2(b)(2), n. 50
La. Rev. Stat. Ann. §§ 45:1451 to 45:1454 (Cum. Supp. 1965) — § 14-1, n. 17; § 15-1, n. 3
La. Rev. Stat. Ann. §§ 45:1451 to 45:1459 — § 15-1, n. 15
La. Rev. Stat. Ann. § 45:1452 — § 15-2(c)(1), nn. 58, 62
La. Rev. Stat. Ann. §§ 540-544 — § 11-7(c), n. 256
La. Rev. Stat. Ann. § 1452 —§ 15-2(c)(2)(C), n. 132; § 15-2(d)(1), n. 138; § 15-2(d)(3)(A), n. 163; § 15-2(f), nn. 255, 263
La. Rev. Stat. Ann. § 1453 — § 15-2(e)(2), n. 230; § 15-2(e)(2)(C), n. 251; § 15-2(i)(1), n. 294; § 15-2(i)(3), n. 309
La. Rev. Stat. Ann. § 1454 — § 15-2(c)(2)(B), n. 98
La. Rev. Stat. Ann. § 1455 — § 15-2(d)(3)(E), n. 205
La. Rev. Stat. Ann. § 1456(A) — § 15-2(i)(1), n. 294
La. Rev. Stat. Ann. § 1456(B) — § 15-2(i)(1), n. 294
La. Rev. Stat. Ann. § 1456(B)(2) — § 15-2(i)(1), n. 294

La. Rev. Stat. Ann. § 1456(C) — § 15-2(i)(5), n. 318
La. Rev. Stat. Ann. § 1457 — § 15-2(i)(5), n. 319
La. Rev. Stat. Ann. § 1459(B) — § 15-2(f), n. 263
La. Rev. Stat. Ann. § 1459(B)(1) — § 15-2(d)(3)(E), n. 205

Maine Revised Statutes Annotated

Me. Rev. Stat. Ann. tit. 1, § 402(2)(B) — § 9-6(b), n. 255
Me. Rev. Stat. Ann. tit. 1, § 402(3) — § 11-2, n. 17
Me. Rev. Stat. Ann. tit. 1, § 403 — § 9-6(e), n. 311; § 9-6(f), n. 328
Me. Rev. Stat. Ann. tit. 1, § 405(6)(B) — § 9-6(i)(4), n. 395
Me. Rev. Stat. Ann. tit. 1, § 405(6)(D) — § 9-6(i)(1)(D), n. 386
Me. Rev. Stat. Ann. tit. 1, § 409(2) — § 9-6(j), nn. 406, 415
Me. Rev. Stat. Ann. tit. 1, § 410 — § 9-6(j), n. 412
Me. Rev. Stat. Ann. tit. 15, § 709 — § 13-7(b)(2), n. 691
Me. Rev. Stat. Ann. tit. 15, § 710 — § 13-7(b)(2), n. 691
Me. Rev. Stat. Ann. tit. 15, § 3308 — § 6-2(a), n. 274
Me. Rev. Stat. Ann. tit. 16, §§ 611-622 — § 11-7(b)(6), n. 240
Me. Rev. Stat. Ann. tit. 16, § 614(1)(A) — § 11-7(b)(3), n. 218; § 11-7(b)(3)(A), n. 219
Me. Rev. Stat. Ann. tit. 17, § 431 — § 13-9(b), n. 829
Me. Rev. Stat. Ann. tit. 29-A, §§ 255-256, 2102 — § 11-7(k), n. 331

Maryland Constitution

Md. Const. art. III, § 21 — § 9-3, n. 52

Maryland Code Annotated

Md. Code Ann., art. 27, § 146 — § 13-9(b), n. 829
Md. Code Ann., art. 27, § 583 — § 11-5(b), n. 164
Md. Code Ann., art. 35, § 2 — § 14-1, n. 17; § 15-1, nn. 3, 4
Md. Code Ann., Cts. & Jud. Proc. § 9-112 — § 14-1, n. 16; § 15-1, nn. 1, 15; § 15-2(b)(1), n. 32; § 15-2(c)(1), n. 62
Md. Code Ann., Cts. & Jud. Proc. § 9-112(c) — § 15-2(e)(1), n. 216; § 15-2(f), n. 255
Md. Code Ann., Cts. & Jud. Proc. § 9-112(c)(1) — § 15-2(d)(1), n. 140; § 15-2(d)(3)(A), n. 164
Md. Code Ann., Cts. & Jud. Proc. § 9-112(c)(2) — § 15-2(d)(3)(C), n. 184
Md. Code Ann., Cts. & Jud. Proc. § 9-112(d) — § 15-2(e)(1), n. 216; § 15-2(e)(2), n. 227
Md. Code Ann., Cts. & Jud. Proc. § 9-112(e) — § 15-2(h), n. 270
Md. Code Ann., Cts. & Jud. Proc. § 9-122(c)(2) — § 15-2(d)(3)(D), n. 199
Md. Code Ann., Cts. & Jud. Proc. § 10-402 — § 13-7(b)(5), nn. 745, 746
Md. Code Ann., Cts. & Jud. Proc. § 10-402(c)(2) — § 13-7(b)(4)(F), n. 739
Md. Code Ann., Cts. & Jud. Proc. § 10-402(c)(3) — § 13-7(b)(3), n. 700
Md. Code Ann., State Gov't § 10-502(h) — § 9-6(b), n. 260
Md. Code Ann., State Gov't § 10-503(a)(2) — § 9-6(c), nn. 281, 284
Md. Code Ann., State Gov't § 10-506(a) — § 9-6(d), n. 295
Md. Code Ann., State Gov't § 10-507(b) — § 9-6(e), n. 317
Md. Code Ann., State Gov't § 10-508 — § 9-6(g), n. 332
Md. Code Ann., State Gov't § 10-508(a)(2) — § 9-6(h)(4), n. 359
Md. Code Ann., State Gov't § 10-508(a)(9) — § 9-6(i)(1)(D), n. 386
Md. Code Ann., State Gov't § 10-508(a)(10) — § 9-6(h)(5), n. 363

TABLE OF STATUTES

Md. Code Ann., State Gov't § 10-509(d) — § 9-6(f), n. 330; § 9-6(g), nn. 338, 340
Md. Code Ann., State Gov't § 10-510(d) — § 9-6(j), n. 416
Md. Code Ann., State Gov't § 10-510(d)(3) — § 9-6(j), n. 411
Md. Code Ann., State Gov't § 10-510(d)(5) — § 9-6(j), n. 417
Md. Code Ann., State Gov't § 10-611 — § 11-2, n. 17; § 11-4, n. 63; § 11-6, n. 175
Md. Code Ann., State Gov't § 10-614(a) — § 11-4, n. 62
Md. Code Ann., State Gov't § 10-614(b)(1) — § 11-4, n. 67
Md. Code Ann., State Gov't § 10-616(a) — § 11-5(b), n. 163
Md. Code Ann., State Gov't § 10-616(p) — § 11-7(k), n. 331
Md. Code Ann., State Gov't § 10-617(d) — § 11-5(a)(8), nn. 150, 151
Md. Code Ann., State Gov't § 10-617(f) — § 11-7(f), n. 269
Md. Code Ann., State Gov't § 10-618(a) — § 11-5(c), n. 169
Md. Code Ann., State Gov't § 10-618(e) — § 11-7(f)(5), n. 291
Md. Code Ann., State Gov't § 10-618(f)(2) — § 11-5(a)(6), n. 133
Md. Code Ann., State Gov't § 10-622 — § 11-8, n. 358
Md. Code Ann., State Gov't § 10-623(a)(1) — § 11-9, n. 361
Md. Code Ann., State Gov't § 10-623(b)(3) — § 11-9, n. 368
Md. Code Ann., State Gov't § 10-623(c) — § 11-9, n. 377
Md. Code Ann., State Gov't § 10-623(d) — § 11-9, n. 370
Md. Code Ann., State Gov't § 10-623(f) — § 11-9, n. 372
Md. Code Ann., State Gov't § 15-823 — § 11-7(f)(2), n. 279

Massachusetts General Laws

Mass. Gen. Laws ch. 4, § 7 — § 11-2, n. 12
Mass. Gen. Laws ch. 4, § 7, cl. 26 — § 11-2, n. 18; § 11-3(c), n. 45
Mass. Gen. Laws ch. 4, § 7, cl. 26(a) — § 11-5(a)(2), n. 87
Mass. Gen. Laws ch. 4, § 7, cl. 26(d) — § 11-5(a)(4), n. 103
Mass. Gen. Laws ch. 4, § 7, cl. 26(g) — § 11-7(f)(2), n. 277
Mass. Gen. Laws ch. 4, § 7, cl. 26(i)(2) & (3) — § 11-7(f)(5), n. 292
Mass. Gen. Laws ch. 30A, § 11A — § 9-6(b), n. 271; § 9-6(h)(3), n. 354
Mass. Gen. Laws ch. 30A, § 11A1/2 — § 9-6(c), n. 281; § 9-6(d), nn. 292, 298; § 9-6(e), n. 317; § 9-6(g), n. 338; § 9-6(h)(2), n. 351
Mass. Gen. Laws ch. 30A, § 11A1/2(1) — § 9-6(h)(4), n. 359
Mass. Gen. Laws ch. 34, § 9G — § 9-6(d), n. 292; § 9-6(h)(4), n. 359; § 9-6(j), n. 408
Mass. Gen. Laws ch. 39, § 23B — § 9-6(d), n. 292; § 9-6(e), n. 317; § 9-6(i)(1)(A), n. 371
Mass. Gen. Laws ch. 39, § 23B(1) — § 9-6(h)(4), n. 359
Mass. Gen. Laws ch. 39, § 23C — § 9-6(e), n. 314
Mass. Gen. Laws ch. 41, § 97D — § 11-7(b)(5), n. 238
Mass. Gen. Laws ch. 41, § 98F — § 11-7(b)(2), n. 215
Mass. Gen. Laws ch. 66, § 10(a) — § 11-2, n. 15; § 11-4, n. 54; § 11-6, n. 177
Mass. Gen. Laws ch. 66, § 10(b) — § 11-4, nn. 61, 67; § 11-8, n. 354
Mass. Gen. Laws ch. 66, § 10(c) — § 11-5(a), n. 77; § 11-5(b), n. 165
Mass. Gen. Laws ch. 66, § 18 — § 11-3(b), n. 41
Mass. Gen. Laws ch. 93, § 106(2) — § 11-5(b), n. 164
Mass. Gen. Laws ch. 111, § 70E(b) — § 11-7(e), n. 265
Mass. Gen. Laws ch. 119, § 65 — § 3-3(a), nn. 448, 501
Mass. Gen. Laws ch. 266, § 120F — § 13-9(b), n. 829
Mass. Gen. Laws ch. 272, § 99 — § 13-7(b)(3), n. 700

TABLE OF STATUTES

Mass. Gen. Laws ch. 276, § 100 — § 11-7(c), n. 255
Mass. Gen. Laws ch. 279, § 65 — § 8-2, n. 63

Michigan Constitution

Mich. Const. art. IV, § 20 — § 9-3, n. 52
Mich. Const. art. VIII, § 4 — § 9-4, n. 63

Michigan Compiled Laws

Mich. Comp. Laws §§ 15.231-15.246 — § 11-8, n. 357
Mich. Comp. Laws § 15.232(b)(i) — § 11-3(a), n. 37
Mich. Comp. Laws § 15.232(b)(ii) — § 11-3(b), n. 38
Mich. Comp. Laws § 15.232(b)(iii) — § 11-7(g), n. 299
Mich. Comp. Laws § 15.232(b)(iv) — § 11-3(e), n. 51
Mich. Comp. Laws § 15.232(b)(v) — § 11-3(c), n. 45
Mich. Comp. Laws § 15.232(e)(2) — § 11-2, nn. 17, 28
Mich. Comp. Laws § 15.233(1) — § 11-4, nn. 55, 65
Mich. Comp. Laws § 15.233(2) — § 11-5(c), n. 169
Mich. Comp. Laws § 15.233(3) — § 11-2, n. 29
Mich. Comp. Laws § 15.234(1) — § 11-4, n. 73
Mich. Comp. Laws § 15.234(3) — § 11-4, n. 71
Mich. Comp. Laws § 15.235(1) — § 11-4, n. 60
Mich. Comp. Laws § 15.235(2) — § 11-4, nn. 67, 68
Mich. Comp. Laws § 15.240(2) — § 11-4, n. 61
Mich. Comp. Laws § 15.240(5) — § 11-9, n. 370
Mich. Comp. Laws § 15.243 — § 11-5(a), n. 80
Mich. Comp. Laws § 15.243(1)(b) — § 11-7(b)(3), n. 218; § 11-7(b)(3)(A), n. 221
Mich. Comp. Laws § 15.243(1)(f) — § 11-5(a)(6), n. 136
Mich. Comp. Laws § 15.243(1)(g) — § 11-5(a)(3), n. 91; § 11-7(i), n. 306
Mich. Comp. Laws § 15.243(1)(k) — § 11-7(f)(4), n. 289
Mich. Comp. Laws § 15.243(1)(k)(ii) — § 11-7(f)(5), n. 293
Mich. Comp. Laws § 15.243(1)(m) — § 11-7(e), n. 267
Mich. Comp. Laws § 15.243(1)(n) — § 11-5(a)(4), nn. 101, 105, 106
Mich. Comp. Laws § 15.243(1)(t) — § 11-5(a)(6), n. 135
Mich. Comp. Laws § 15.244(1) — § 11-6, n. 176
Mich. Comp. Laws § 15.263 — § 9-6(h)(2), n. 352
Mich. Comp. Laws § 15.263(1) — § 9-6(e), nn. 317, 318
Mich. Comp. Laws § 15.263(11) — § 9-6(i)(5), n. 399
Mich. Comp. Laws § 15.264(b) — § 9-6(d), n. 307
Mich. Comp. Laws § 15.265(4) — § 9-6(d), n. 298
Mich. Comp. Laws § 15.266(1) — § 9-6(d), n. 308
Mich. Comp. Laws § 15.267 — § 9-6(g), n. 339
Mich. Comp. Laws § 15.268(e) — § 9-6(h)(6), n. 366
Mich. Comp. Laws § 15.268(f) — § 9-6(i)(1)(A), n. 369
Mich. Comp. Laws § 15.269(1) — § 9-6(f), n. 324
Mich. Comp. Laws § 15.270 — § 9-6(j), n. 408
Mich. Comp. Laws § 15.271 — § 9-6(j), n. 408
Mich. Comp. Laws § 15.272 — § 9-6(j), n. 409
Mich. Comp. Laws § 28.807 — § 13-7(b)(4)(B), n. 717

TABLE OF STATUTES

Mich. Comp. Laws § 28.807(3) — § 13-7(b)(3), n. 700; § 13-7(b)(5), n. 744
Mich. Comp. Laws § 28.807(5) — § 13-7(b)(5), n. 744
Mich. Comp. Laws § 28.945(1) — § 14-1, n. 17; § 15-1, n. 3
Mich. Comp. Laws § 243(1)(t)(ix) — § 11-7(a), n. 182
Mich. Comp. Laws §§ 445.1712 to 445.1714 — § 11-5(b), n. 164
Mich. Comp. Laws § 750.160a — § 8-3, n. 112
Mich. Comp. Laws § 750-539g(a) — § 13-7(b)(4)(F), n. 739
Mich. Comp. Laws § 752.795 — § 13-9(b), n. 829
Mich. Comp. Laws § 767.5a — § 15-1, n. 15; § 15-2(b)(1), n. 34; § 15-2(c)(1), n. 59; § 15-2(d)(3)(A), n. 163; § 15-2(e)(2), n. 230
Mich. Comp. Laws § 767.5a(1) — § 15-2(d)(3)(C), n. 183

Minnesota Constitution

Minn. Const. art. IV, § 14 — § 9-3, n. 52

Minnesota Statutes

Minn. Stat. § 13.01, Subd. 7 — § 11-2, n. 18
Minn. Stat. § 13.03, Subd. 5 — § 11-2, n. 25
Minn. Stat. § 13.30 — § 11-5(a)(4), n. 116
Minn. Stat. § 13.82(5) — § 11-7(b)(3)(B), n. 229
Minn. Stat. § 13.82(16) — § 11-7(b)(9), n. 248
Minn. Stat. § 13.82(17) — § 11-7(b)(1), n. 208
Minn. Stat. § 15.17 — § 5-2(a)(4), n. 201
Minn. Stat. § 15.162 — § 11-5(b), n. 162
Minn. Stat. § 260.155(c) — § 3-3(a), n. 448
Minn. Stat. § 270B.18 — § 13-9(b), n. 829
Minn. Stat. § 325I.02, subd. 1 — § 11-5(b), n. 164
Minn. Stat. § 471.705.1 — § 9-6(j), n. 416
Minn. Stat. § 471.705.1d — § 9-6(g), n. 332
Minn. Stat. § 471.705.1d(b)(3) — § 9-6(i)(3), n. 392; § 9-6(i)(5), n. 399
Minn. Stat. § 471.705.1d(c) — § 9-6(i)(1)(C), n. 383
Minn. Stat. § 471.705.1d(e) — § 9-6(h)(6), n. 364
Minn. Stat. § 471.705.2 — § 9-6(j), nn. 406, 412, 413
Minn. Stat. § 559.125 — § 11-7(c), n. 255
Minn. Stat. § 595.021 — § 15-1, n. 15
Minn. Stat. § 595.022 — § 15-1, n. 15; § 15-2(d)(1), n. 141
Minn. Stat. § 595.023 — § 15-1, n. 15; § 15-2(c), n. 53; § 15-2(c)(2)(C), n. 132; § 15-2(d)(1), n. 141; § 15-2(d)(3)(C), n. 183; § 15-2(f), n. 255
Minn. Stat. § 595.024 — § 15-1, nn. 13, 15; § 15-2(e)(2), n. 230; § 15-2(i)(1), n. 295
Minn. Stat. § 595.024(3) — § 15-2(i)(3), n. 309
Minn. Stat. § 595.025 — § 15-1, n. 15; § 15-2(c)(2)(B), n. 99
Minn. Stat. § 595.025(3) — § 15-2(i)(3), n. 309
Minn. Stat. § 609.748 — § 13-3(c)(2), n. 200
Minn. Stat. § 609.749 — § 13-3(c)(2), nn. 200, 202
Minn. Stat. § 626A.02 — § 13-7(b)(1), n. 686; § 13-7(b)(2), n. 691
Minn. Stat. § 626A.02(d) — § 13-7(b)(2), n. 694

TABLE OF STATUTES

Mississippi Constitution

Miss. Const. art. III, § 24 — § 3-1(a), n. 1
Miss. Const. art. IV, § 58 — § 9-3, n. 52

Mississippi Code Annotated

Miss. Code Ann. § 25-41-3(a) — § 9-6(i)(2), n. 390
Miss. Code Ann. § 25-41-7(4)(e) — § 9-6(b), n. 272
Miss. Code Ann. § 25-41-7(4)(g) — § 9-6(h)(3), n. 353
Miss. Code Ann. § 25-41-11 — § 9-6(f), n. 326
Miss. Code Ann. § 25-41-13(1) — § 9-6(d), n. 298
Miss. Code Ann. §§ 25-61-1 to 25-61-17 — § 9-6(f), n. 330
Miss. Code Ann. § 25-61-3 — § 11-3(d), n. 48
Miss. Code Ann. § 25-61-3(b) — § 11-2, n. 18
Miss. Code Ann. § 25-61-9(4) — § 11-5(a)(3), n. 93
Miss. Code Ann. § 25-61-10 — § 11-2, nn. 25, 31; § 11-3(b), n. 39
Miss. Code Ann. § 41-29-531 — § 13-7(b)(2), n. 691
Miss. Code Ann. § 41-29-533 — § 13-7(b)(2), n. 691
Miss. Code Ann. § 43-21-203(6) — § 3-3(a), n. 448
Miss. Code Ann. § 53-5-11 — § 11-5(a)(8), n. 158
Miss. Code Ann. § 81-14-167 — § 11-7(f)(3), n. 281
Miss. Code Ann. § 99-19-55(2) — § 8-2, nn. 64, 65

Missouri Constitution

Mo. Const. art. I, § 35 — § 3-1(a), n. 1
Mo. Const. art. III, § 20 — § 9-3, n. 52

Missouri Revised Statutes

Mo. Rev. Stat. § 109.80 — § 11-4, n. 56
Mo. Rev. Stat. § 256.050 — § 11-5(a)(8), nn. 156, 158
Mo. Rev. Stat. § 369.099(2) — § 11-7(f)(3), n. 281
Mo. Rev. Stat. § 542.402 — § 13-7(b)(2), n. 691
Mo. Rev. Stat. § 542.418 — § 13-7(b)(5), n. 747
Mo. Rev. Stat. § 542.422 — § 13-7(b)(5), n. 745
Mo. Rev. Stat. § 546.740 — § 8-2, n. 63
Mo. Rev. Stat. § 610.010(2) — § 9-6(b), n. 260
Mo. Rev. Stat. § 610.010(3) — § 9-6(c), n. 281
Mo. Rev. Stat. § 610.010(6) — § 11-2, n. 17
Mo. Rev. Stat. § 610.011(2) — § 9-6(e), n. 311; § 9-6(h)(2), n. 350
Mo. Rev. Stat. § 610.015 — § 9-6(e), n. 311
Mo. Rev. Stat. § 610.020 — § 9-6(d), n. 295
Mo. Rev. Stat. § 610.021 — § 9-6(g), n. 332
Mo. Rev. Stat. § 610.021(1) — § 9-6(h)(6), n. 364; § 11-7(m), n. 348
Mo. Rev. Stat. § 610.021(2) — § 9-6(h)(3), n. 356
Mo. Rev. Stat. § 610.021(3) — § 11-7(a)(3), n. 192
Mo. Rev. Stat. § 610.021(5) — § 9-6(i)(3), n. 392
Mo. Rev. Stat. § 610.021(6) — § 9-6(i)(4), n. 395
Mo. Rev. Stat. § 610.021(7) — § 9-6(i)(3), n. 392

TABLE OF STATUTES

Mo. Rev. Stat. § 610.021(8) — § 9-6(i)(3), n. 392
Mo. Rev. Stat. § 610.021(10) — § 11-2, n. 27
Mo. Rev. Stat. § 610.021(11) — § 9-6(i)(3), n. 392
Mo. Rev. Stat. § 610.021(12) — § 9-6(i)(3), n. 392
Mo. Rev. Stat. § 610.021(14) — § 9-6(h), n. 344
Mo. Rev. Stat. § 610.021(15) — § 9-6(i)(3), n. 392
Mo. Rev. Stat. § 610.022(3) — § 9-6(g), n. 340
Mo. Rev. Stat. § 610.027.3 — § 9-6(j), nn. 412, 416, 417
Mo. Rev. Stat. § 610.100.2 — § 11-7(b)(1), n. 209
Mo. Rev. Stat. § 610.100.3 — § 11-7(b)(5), n. 238
Mo. Rev. Stat. § 610.150 — § 11-7(b)(8), n. 244

Montana Constitution

Mont. Const. art. II, § 9 — § 9-1, n. 12
Mont. Const. art. II, § 9 — § 9-1, n. 16
Mont. Const. art. III, § 6 — § 3-1(a), n. 1
Mont. Const. art. V, § 10 — § 9-3, n. 51

Montana Code Annotated

Mont. Code Ann. § 2-3-101 — § 9-6(e), n. 315
Mont. Code Ann. § 2-3-102(1)(a) — § 9-6(b), n. 272
Mont. Code Ann. § 2-3-104(4) — § 9-6(d), n. 305
Mont. Code Ann. § 2-3-112(1) — § 9-6(d), n. 300; § 9-6(h)(5), n. 363
Mont. Code Ann. § 2-3-203(1) — § 9-6(b), nn. 255, 275
Mont. Code Ann. § 2-3-203(3) — § 9-6(h)(4), n. 357
Mont. Code Ann. § 2-3-211 — § 9-6(e), n. 319
Mont. Code Ann. § 2-3-212(2)(c) — § 9-6(f), n. 324
Mont. Code Ann. § 2-3-221 — § 9-6(j), n. 417
Mont. Code Ann. § 2-6-101 — § 11-5(a)(3), n. 90
Mont. Code Ann. §§ 2-6-101 to 2-6-103 — § 11-5(a)(6), n. 140
Mont. Code Ann. § 2-6-110(1) — § 11-2, n. 25
Mont. Code Ann. § 2-6-202(1) — § 11-2, n. 18
Mont. Code Ann. §§ 26-1-901 to 903 — § 15-1, n. 15
Mont. Code Ann. § 26-1-902 — § 15-2(f), n. 255; § 15-2(h), n. 269; § 15-2(b)(1), n. 35
Mont. Code Ann. § 26-1-902(1) — § 15-2(d)(1), n. 138; § 15-2(d)(3)(C), n. 183
Mont. Code Ann. § 26-1-903(2) — § 15-2(c)(2)(B), n. 116
Mont. Code Ann. § 45-5 — § 13-3(c)(2), n. 202
Mont. Code Ann. § 45-7-401 — § 9-6(j), n. 409
Mont. Code Ann. § 45-8-213 — § 13-7(b)(3), n. 700
Mont. Code Ann. § 46-11-701 — § 5-2(a), n. 79
Mont. Code Ann. § 46-19-103(6) — § 8-2, n. 63
Mont. Code Ann. § 50-16-501 et seq. — § 9-6(i)(3), n. 392
Mont. Code Ann. § 50-16-601 et seq. — § 9-6(i)(3), n. 392
Mont. Rev. Code, §§ 93-601-1, 93-601-2 (1964) — § 14-1, n. 17; § 15-1, n. 3

Nebraska Constitution

Neb. Const. art. I, § 13 — § 3-1(a), n. 1
Neb. Const. art. III, § 11 — § 9-3, n. 52

TABLE OF STATUTES

Nebraska Revised Statutes

Neb. Rev. Stat. §§ 20-144 to 20-147 — § 15-1, n. 15
Neb. Rev. Stat. § 29-2534 — § 8-2, n. 63
Neb. Rev. Stat. § 29-3519 — § 13-9(b), n. 829
Neb. Rev. Stat. § 29-3520 — § 11-7(b)(4), n. 235
Neb. Rev. Stat. § 29-3521(1) — § 11-7(b)(1), n. 208
Neb. Rev. Stat. § 84-1408 — § 9-6(h)(2), n. 352
Neb. Rev. Stat. § 84-1409(1) — § 9-6(b), n. 260
Neb. Rev. Stat. § 84-1410(1)(a) — § 9-6(h)(6), n. 366; § 9-6(i)(1)(D), n. 387
Neb. Rev. Stat. § 84-1410(3) — § 9-6(g), n. 341
Neb. Rev. Stat. § 84-1410(4) — § 9-6(c), n. 284; § 9-6(h), n. 345
Neb. Rev. Stat. § 84-1411(1) — § 9-6(d), n. 295
Neb. Rev. Stat. § 84-1411(2) — § 9-6(e), n. 315
Neb. Rev. Stat. § 84-1412(1) — § 9-6(e), n. 317
Neb. Rev. Stat. § 84-1412(2) — § 9-6(e), nn. 314, 317
Neb. Rev. Stat. § 84-1413(5) — § 9-6(f), n. 327
Neb. Rev. Stat. § 84-1414(2) — § 9-6(j), n. 408
Neb. Rev. Stat. § 84-1414(3) — § 9-6(j), n. 406
Neb. Rev. Stat. § 84-712.01(1) — § 11-2, n. 18
Neb. Rev. Stat. § 84-712.01(2) — § 11-2, n. 30
Neb. Rev. Stat. § 84-712.09 — § 11-9, n. 375
Neb. Rev. Stat. § 86-702 — § 13-7(b)(2), n. 691

Nevada Constitution

Nev. Const. art. IV, § 15 — § 9-3, n. 53

Nevada Revised Statutes

Nev. Rev. Stat. § 41.0385 — § 6-1(a)(6), n. 139
Nev. Rev. Stat. § 49.275 — § 14-1, n. 17; § 15-1, n. 11; § 15-1, n. 15; § 15-2(d)(3)(C), n. 183; § 15-2(d)(3)(E), n. 206; § 15-2(e)(1), n. 215
Nev. Rev. Stat. § 49.385 — § 15-2(h), nn. 279, 282
Nev. Rev. Stat. § 62.193(1) — § 3-3(a), n. 448
Nev. Rev. Stat. § 122.040(6) — § 11-7(j), n. 313
Nev. Rev. Stat. § 176.355 — § 8-2, n. 63
Nev. Rev. Stat. § 179A.100(5)(I) — § 11-7(b)(4), n. 234
Nev. Rev. Stat. § 200(5)(b)(2) — § 13-3(c)(2), n. 202
Nev. Rev. Stat. § 200.620 — § 13-7(b)(3), n. 700
Nev. Rev. Stat. § 200.630 — § 13-7(b)(2), n. 691
Nev. Rev. Stat. § 200.650 — § 13-7(b)(2), n. 691
Nev. Rev. Stat. § 241.015(3) — § 9-6(b), n. 272
Nev. Rev. Stat. § 241.020(1) — § 9-6(e), n. 311
Nev. Rev. Stat. § 241.020(2) — § 9-6(d), n. 294
Nev. Rev. Stat. § 241.030 — § 9-6(g), n. 332
Nev. Rev. Stat. § 241.030(1) — § 9-6(i)(3), n. 392
Nev. Rev. Stat. § 241.030(3) — § 9-6(h), n. 345
Nev. Rev. Stat. § 241.030(3)(a) — § 9-6(b), n. 271
Nev. Rev. Stat. § 241.035 — § 9-6(f), n. 330
Nev. Rev. Stat. § 241.035(2) — § 9-6(f), n. 326

Nev. Rev. Stat. § 241.035(3) — § 9-6(e), n. 317
Nev. Rev. Stat. § 241.036 — § 9-6(j), n. 415
Nev. Rev. Stat. § 242.111 — § 13-9(b), n. 829
Nev. Rev. Stat. § 481.063 — § 11-7(k), n. 332
Nev. Rev. Stat. § 481.063(5)(h) — § 11-7(k), n. 333
Nev. Stat. Ann. § 10:4-14 — § 9-6(f), n. 324

New Hampshire Constitution

N.H. Const. part I, art. 8 — § 9-1, n. 13
N.H. Const. part I, art. 8 — § 9-1, n. 9
N.H. Const. part II, art. 8 — § 9-3, n. 52

New Hampshire Revised Statutes Annotated

N.H. Rev. Stat. Ann. § 91-A:1-a — § 9-6(b), n. 255
N.H. Rev. Stat. Ann. § 91-A:1-a — § 9-6(b), n. 261
N.H. Rev. Stat. Ann. § 91-A:2II — § 9-6(e), n. 317; § 9-6(f), n. 327
N.H. Rev. Stat. Ann. § 91-A:3I(a) — § 9-6(h)(2), n. 351
N.H. Rev. Stat. Ann. § 91-A:3I(c) — § 9-6(g), n. 341
N.H. Rev. Stat. Ann. § 91-A:3II — § 9-6(i)(1)(C), n. 382
N.H. Rev. Stat. Ann. § 91-A:3II(c) — § 9-6(h)(4), n. 359
N.H. Rev. Stat. Ann. § 91-A:4II — § 9-6(f), n. 331
N.H. Rev. Stat. Ann. § 91-A:5 — § 9-6(i)(2), n. 390
N.H. Rev. Stat. Ann. § 169-C:14 — § 3-3(a), n. 446
N.H. Rev. Stat. Ann. § 260:14 — § 11-7(k), n. 332
N.H. Rev. Stat. Ann. § 351-A:1(I) — § 11-5(b), n. 164
N.H. Rev. Stat. Ann. § 570-A:2 — § 13-7(b)(3), n. 700
N.H. Rev. Stat. Ann. § 570-A:11 — § 13-7(b)(5), n. 747
N.H. Rev. Stat. Ann. § 630:6 — § 8-2, n. 63
N.H. Rev. Stat. Ann. § 638:17 — § 13-9(b), n. 829

New Jersey Constitution

N.J. Const., art. I, § 22 — § 3-3(a), n. 478

New Jersey Statutes Annotated

N.J. Stat. Ann. § 2A:4A-60(i) — § 3-3(a), n. 478
N.J. Stat. Ann. § 2A:38A-3 — § 13-9(b), n. 829
N.J. Stat. Ann. § 2A:84-21(a) — § 15-2(d)(3)(B), n. 171
N.J. Stat. Ann. § 2A:84-21(b) — § 15-1, n. 17
N.J. Stat. Ann. § 2A:84A-21 — § 14-1, n. 17; § 15-1, n. 3; § 15-2(c), n. 53; § 15-2(d)(3)(E), n. 206; § 15-2(e)(1), nn. 222, 223; § 15-2(e)(2), n. 229
N.J. Stat. Ann. §§ 2A:84A-21 to 2A:84A-21.8 — § 15-1, n. 15
N.J. Stat. Ann. § 2A:84A-21.3 — § 15-2(c)(1), n. 70; § 15-2(e)(1), n. 222; § 15-2(e)(2), n. 229; § 15-2(h), n. 274
N.J. Stat. Ann. § 2A:84A-21.4 — § 15-2(c)(1), n. 70
N.J. Stat. Ann. § 2A:84A-29 — § 14-1, n. 17; § 15-1, n. 3
N.J. Stat. Ann. § 2A:156A-3— § 13-7(b)(2), n. 691

TABLE OF STATUTES

N.J. Stat. Ann. § 2A:156A-24 — § 13-7(b)(5), n. 747
N.J. Stat. Ann. § 2A:170-29(2)(b) — § 13-3(c)(3), n. 205
N.J. Stat. Ann. § 2C:7-6 — § 11-7(c), n. 256
N.J. Stat. Ann. § 2C:28-8 — § 13-3(c)(4), n. 223
N.J. Stat. Ann. § 2C:29-8.1 — § 7-4, n. 221
N.J. Stat. Ann. § 2C:49-7(c) — § 8-2, n. 64
N.J. Stat. Ann. § 10:4-7 — § 9-6(h)(4), n. 357
N.J. Stat. Ann. § 10:4-8(a) — § 9-6(b), nn. 271, 273; § 9-6(i)(2), n. 390
N.J. Stat. Ann. § 10:4-8(b) — § 9-6(c), n. 282
N.J. Stat. Ann. § 10:4-8(d) — § 9-6(d), n. 305
N.J. Stat. Ann. § 10:4-12 — § 9-6(g), n. 332
N.J. Stat. Ann. § 10:4-12(b)(1) — § 9-6(h)(2), n. 352
N.J. Stat. Ann. § 10:4-12(b)(2) — § 9-6(h)(2), n. 352
N.J. Stat. Ann. § 10:4-12(b)(4) — § 9-6(i)(1)(D), n. 386
N.J. Stat. Ann. § 10:4-12(b)(5) — § 9-6(h)(3), n. 354
N.J. Stat. Ann. § 10:4-12(b)(7) — § 9-6(h)(6), n. 364
N.J. Stat. Ann. § 10:4-12(b)(9) — § 9-6(i)(6), n. 403
N.J. Stat. Ann. § 10:4-14 — § 9-6(f), n. 328
N.J. Stat. Ann. § 10:4-17 — § 9-6(j), n. 412
N.J. Stat. Ann. § 19:44B-2 — § 11-7(f)(2), n. 279
N.J. Stat. Ann. § 47:1A-2 — § 11-3(d), n. 48
N.J. Stat. Ann. § 47:1A-2.1 — § 11-2, n. 21
N.J. Stat. Ann. § 47:1A-3 — § 11-7(b)(3)(A), n. 220

New Mexico Constitution

N.M. Const. art. IV, § 12 — § 9-3, n. 51

New Mexico Statutes Annotated

N.M. Stat. Ann. § 10-15-1(A) — § 9-6(b), nn. 262, 271; § 9-6(e), n. 319; § 9-6(g), n. 342
N.M. Stat. Ann. § 10-15-1(B) — § 9-6(b), n. 255
N.M. Stat. Ann. § 10-15-1(C) — § 9-6(d), n. 306
N.M. Stat. Ann. § 10-15-1(D) — § 9-6(d), n. 295
N.M. Stat. Ann. § 10-15-1(H)(1) — § 9-6(i)(6), n. 403
N.M. Stat. Ann. § 10-15-1(H)(2) — § 9-6(i)(1)(B), n. 376
N.M. Stat. Ann. § 10-15-1(H)(4) — § 9-6(i)(4), n. 398
N.M. Stat. Ann. § 10-15-1(H)(6) — § 9-6(h)(3), n. 353
N.M. Stat. Ann. § 10-15-1(H)(7) — § 9-6(h)(6), n. 366
N.M. Stat. Ann. § 10-15-1(I) — § 9-6(g), n. 340
N.M. Stat. Ann. § 10-15-3(A) — § 9-6(j), n. 415
N.M. Stat. Ann. § 10-15-3(B) — § 9-6(j), n. 408
N.M. Stat. Ann. § 10-15-3(C) — § 9-6(j), n. 406
N.M. Stat. Ann. § 15-1-9 — § 13-9(b), n. 829
N.M. Stat. Ann. § 20-1-12.1 — § 14-1, n. 17; § 15-1, n. 11
N.M. Stat. Ann. § 29-10-3 — § 11-7(b)(1), nn. 207, 208
N.M. Stat. Ann. § 30-11-1 — § 13-7(b)(2), n. 691
N.M. Stat. Ann. § 30-45-5 — § 13-9(b), n. 829
N.M. Stat. Ann. § 31-14-15 — § 8-2, n. 63
N.M. Stat. Ann. § 32A-2-16(B) — § 3-3(a), n. 447

TABLE OF STATUTES

N.M. Stat. Ann. § 38-6-7(B)(1) — § 15-2(c)(2)(C), n. 135
N.M. Stat. Ann. § 66-2-7.1 — § 11-7(k), n. 332

New York Constitution

N.Y. Const. art. III, § 10 — § 9-3, n. 52

New York Laws

N.Y. Banking Law § 36(10) — § 11-7(f)(3), n. 286
N.Y. Civ. Rights Law § 50 — § 12-2(a), n. 14; § 12-4(a), n. 184; § 13-4(a)(3)(A)(i), n. 427
N.Y. Civ. Rights Law § 51 — § 12-2(a), n. 14; § 12-4(a), n. 184; § 13-4(a)(1)(A), n. 331; § 13-4(a)(3)(A)(i), n. 427
N.Y. Civ. Rights Law § 79-h — § 14-1, n. 17; § 15-1, nn. 11, 15; § 15-2(d)(1), n. 140; § 15-2(d)(2), n. 159; § 15-2(e)(1), n. 216; § 15-2(e)(2), n. 228
N.Y. Civ. Rights Law § 79-h(a)(1)-(8) — § 15-2(b)(1), n. 38
N.Y. Civ. Rights Law § 79-h(b) — § 15-2(c)(1), n. 86; § 15-2(f), n. 262
N.Y. Civ. Rights Law § 79-h(c) — § 14-6(a), n. 245; § 15-2(f), n. 262; § 15-2(h), n. 287
N.Y. Civ. Rights Law § 79-h(d) & (e) — § 15-2(f), n. 263
N.Y. Crim. Proc. Law § 390.50 — § 5-2(d), n. 425
N.Y. Crim. Proc. Law § 720.15(3) — § 3-3(a), n. 496
N.Y. Fam. Ct. Act § 741(b) — § 3-3(a), n. 447
N.Y. Gen. Bus. Law §§ 671-674 — § 11-5(b), n. 164
N.Y. Jud. L. § 4 — § 3-2(b), n. 374
N.Y. Penal Law § 156.05 — § 13-9(b), n. 829
N.Y. Penal Law § 215.28 — § 7-4, n. 221
N.Y. Penal Law § 240.25 — § 13-3(c)(2), n. 191
N.Y. Penal Law § 250 — § 13-7(b)(1), n. 686; § 13-7(b)(2), n. 692
N.Y. Penal Law § 250.01 — § 13-7(b)(2), n. 693
N.Y. Penal Law § 250.05 — § 13-7(b)(2), n. 691
N.Y. Pub. Off. Law § 84 — § 11-1, n. 5
N.Y. Pub. Off. Law § 86(1) — § 11-3(c), n. 45
N.Y. Pub. Off. Law § 86(3) — § 11-3(c), n. 45; § 11-3(d), n. 49
N.Y. Pub. Off. Law § 86(4) — § 11-2, n. 17
N.Y. Pub. Off. Law § 87(1)(b)(iii) — § 11-4, n. 70
N.Y. Pub. Off. Law § 87(1)(h) — § 11-4, n. 70
N.Y. Pub. Off. Law § 87(2) — § 11-1, n. 5; § 11-2, n. 15; § 11-5(a), nn. 77, 80
N.Y. Pub. Off. Law § 87(2)(c) — § 11-7(a)(4), n. 196; § 11-7(f)(4), n. 287
N.Y. Pub. Off. Law § 87(2)(d) — § 11-5(a)(3), nn. 95, 97; § 11-5(a)(7), n. 149; § 11-7(f)(1), n. 271
N.Y. Pub. Off. Law § 87(2)(e) — § 11-5(a)(6), nn. 132, 135, 136
N.Y. Pub. Off. Law § 87(2)(e)(iii) — § 11-7(b)(7), n. 243
N.Y. Pub. Off. Law § 87(2)(e)(iv) — § 11-7(b)(9), nn. 248, 250
N.Y. Pub. Off. Law § 87(2)(g) — § 11-5(a)(4), n. 98
N.Y. Pub. Off. Law § 87(3)(b) — § 11-7(a)(2), n. 189
N.Y. Pub. Off. Law § 89(2)(b)(i) — § 11-7(a), n. 184
N.Y. Pub. Off. Law § 89(2)(b)(ii) — § 11-7(e), n. 267
N.Y. Pub. Off. Law § 89(2)(b)(iii) — § 11-7(i), n. 307
N.Y. Pub. Off. Law § 89(3) — § 11-2, n. 29; § 11-4, nn. 54, 65, 67, 69

TABLE OF STATUTES

N.Y. Pub. Off. Law § 89(4) — § 11-9, n. 373
N.Y. Pub. Off. Law § 89(4)(a) — § 11-8, n. 356
N.Y. Pub. Off. Law § 89(4)(b) — § 11-9, n. 359
N.Y. Pub. Off. Law § 89.3 — § 11-4, n. 62
N.Y. Pub. Off. Law § 102(1) — § 9-6(c), n. 278
N.Y. Pub. Off. Law § 103(a) — § 9-6(e), n. 311
N.Y. Pub. Off. Law § 104(1) — § 9-6(d), nn. 294, 309
N.Y. Pub. Off. Law § 104(2) — § 9-6(d), n. 309
N.Y. Pub. Off. Law § 105 — § 9-6(g), n. 332
N.Y. Pub. Off. Law § 105(1) — § 9-6(g), n. 339
N.Y. Pub. Off. Law § 105(1)(a)-(c) — § 9-6(h)(5), n. 362
N.Y. Pub. Off. Law § 105(1)(d) — § 9-6(h)(6), n. 366
N.Y. Pub. Off. Law § 105(1)(h) — § 9-6(h)(3), n. 353
N.Y. Pub. Off. Law § 106(3) — § 9-6(f), n. 327
N.Y. Pub. Off. Law § 107(1) — § 9-6(j), nn. 410, 411
N.Y. Pub. Off. Law § 107(2) — § 9-6(j), nn. 416, 417
N.Y. Pub. Off. Law § 108(1) — § 9-6(b), n. 271
N.Y. Pub. Off. Law § 108(2) — § 9-6(b), n. 273

North Carolina Constitution

N.C. Const. art. I, § 35 — § 3-1(a), n. 1

North Carolina General Statutes

N.C. Gen. Stat. § 8-53.9 — § 15-1, n. 15; § 15-2(b)(1), n. 38
N.C. Gen. Stat. § 8-53.9(a)(2) — § 15-2(c), n. 53
N.C. Gen. Stat. § 8-53.9(c) — § 15-2(d)(3)(D), n. 199; § 15-2(e)(2), n. 226
N.C. Gen. Stat. § 8-53.9(d) — § 15-2(d)(3)(B), n. 171
N.C. Gen. Stat. § 14-155 — § 13-7(b)(2), n. 691
N.C. Gen. Stat. § 15-190 — § 8-2, n. 63
N.C. Gen. Stat. § 15A-287 — § 13-7(b)(2), n. 691
N.C. Gen. Stat. § 54-109.105 — § 11-5(a)(7), n. 146
N.C. Gen. Stat. § 75-1 — § 13-2(b), n. 68
N.C. Gen. Stat. § 89E-14(c) — § 11-5(a)(8), n. 150
N.C. Gen. Stat. § 95-36 — § 11-7(a)(4), n. 196
N.C. Gen. Stat. § 132-1 — § 11-2, nn. 13, 18
N.C. Gen. Stat. §§ 132-1 to 132-9 — § 11-4, n. 67
N.C. Gen. Stat. § 132-1.1 — § 11-5(a)(4), nn. 111, 117
N.C. Gen. Stat. § 132-1.2(1) & (4) — § 11-7(i), n. 306
N.C. Gen. Stat. § 132-1.3 — § 6-1(a)(6), n. 140
N.C. Gen. Stat. § 132-1.4(b) — § 11-7(b)(7), n. 243
N.C. Gen. Stat. § 132-1.4(c)(1)-(3) — § 11-7(b)(1), n. 213
N.C. Gen. Stat. § 132-1.4(c)(4) — § 11-7(b)(8), n. 244
N.C. Gen. Stat. § 132-1.4(c)(5) — § 11-7(b)(8), n. 247
N.C. Gen. Stat. § 132-1.4(c)(6) — § 11-7(b)(5), n. 238
N.C. Gen. Stat. § 143-318.10(a) — § 9-6(h)(2), n. 351
N.C. Gen. Stat. § 143-318.10(d) — § 9-6(c), n. 284
N.C. Gen. Stat. § 143-318.10(e) — § 9-6(f), n. 330
N.C. Gen. Stat. § 143-318.11(a)(5) — § 9-6(h)(6), n. 364

N.C. Gen. Stat. § 143-318.11(a)(7) — § 9-6(i)(3), n. 392
N.C. Gen. Stat. § 143-318.11(a)(8) — § 9-6(i)(1)(A), n. 374
N.C. Gen. Stat. § 143-318.11(a)(10) — § 9-6(i)(4), nn. 395, 397
N.C. Gen. Stat. § 143-318.11(a)(12) — § 9-6(h)(2), n. 352
N.C. Gen. Stat. § 143-318.11(c) — § 9-6(g), n. 337
N.C. Gen. Stat. § 143-318.18(6) — § 9-6(i)(6), n. 401

North Dakota Constitution

N.D. Const. art. I, § 22 — § 3-1(a), n. 1
N.D. Const. art. IV, § 14 — § 9-3, n. 51
N.D. Const. art. XI, § 5 — § 9-1, n. 14
N.D. Const. art. XI, § 6 — § 9-1, n. 14

North Dakota Century Code

N.D. Cent. Code § 1-02-05 — § 15-2(d)(3)(C), n. 196
N.D. Cent. Code § 12.1-15-02 — § 13-7(b)(2), n. 691
N.D. Cent. Code § 12.1-15-02-2 — § 13-7(b)(1), n. 683
N.D. Cent. Code § 27-20-24(5) — § 3-3(a), n. 448
N.D. Cent. Code § 31-01-06.2 — § 15-1, nn. 13, 15; § 15-2(d)(1), n. 138; § 15-2(e)(2), n. 230; § 15-2(e)(2)(C), n. 249; § 16-2(a)(2), n. 30
N.D. Cent. Code § 39-33-05(12) — § 11-7(k), n. 331
N.D. Cent. Code § 44-04-18.5 — § 11-2, n. 25
N.D. Cent. Code § 44-04-19 — § 9-6(b), nn. 255, 275
N.D. Cent. Code § 44-04-20 — § 9-6(d), n. 292

Ohio Constitution

Ohio Const. art. I, § 16 — § 3-1(a), n. 1
Ohio Const. art. II, § 13 — § 9-3, n. 52

Ohio Administrative Code

Ohio Admin. Code § 5120-9-54 — § 8-2, n. 64
Ohio Admin. Code § 5120-9-54(B) — § 8-2, n. 65

Ohio Revised Code Annotated

Ohio Rev. Code Ann. § 121.22(B)(1) — § 9-6(b), n. 261
Ohio Rev. Code Ann. § 121.22(B)(2) — § 9-6(c), n. 279
Ohio Rev. Code Ann. § 121.22(C) — § 9-6(e), n. 311; § 9-6(f), n. 328
Ohio Rev. Code Ann. § 121.22(D) — § 9-6(i)(6), n. 401
Ohio Rev. Code Ann. § 121.22(F) — § 9-6(d), n. 296
Ohio Rev. Code Ann. § 121.22(G) — § 9-6(g), n. 332
Ohio Rev. Code Ann. § 121.22(G)(1) — § 9-6(i)(6), n. 405
Ohio Rev. Code Ann. § 121.22(G)(3) — § 9-6(h)(6), n. 366
Ohio Rev. Code Ann. § 121.22(G)(5) — § 9-6(h)(2), n. 352
Ohio Rev. Code Ann. § 121.22(H) — § 9-6(g), n. 342
Ohio Rev. Code Ann. § 121.22(I)(2) — § 9-6(j), n. 412; § 9-6(j), n. 417
Ohio Rev. Code Ann. § 121.22(I)(4) — § 9-6(j), n. 413
Ohio Rev. Code Ann. § 149.43(A) — § 11-2, n. 14

TABLE OF STATUTES

Ohio Rev. Code Ann. § 149.43(A)(1) — § 11-5(a)(2), n. 88
Ohio Rev. Code Ann. § 149.43(A)(1)(d) — § 11-7(j), n. 310
Ohio Rev. Code Ann. § 149.43(A)(1)(g) — § 11-5(a)(4), n. 112
Ohio Rev. Code Ann. § 149.43(A)(2) — § 11-7(b)(3), n. 218
Ohio Rev. Code Ann. § 149.43(A)(2)(a) — § 11-7(b), n. 204
Ohio Rev. Code Ann. § 149.43(A)(2)(c) — § 11-7(b)(3)(A), n. 219; § 11-7(b)(9), n. 248
Ohio Rev. Code Ann. § 149.43(B) — § 11-4, n. 54
Ohio Rev. Code Ann. § 149.431 — § 11-7(f)(2), n. 278
Ohio Rev. Code Ann. § 315.21(c)(3) — § 13-2(a), n. 19
Ohio Rev. Code Ann. § 2739.04 — § 14-1, n. 17; § 15-1, nn. 3, 6, 15; § 15-2(b)(1), n. 34; § 15-2(c)(1), n. 79; § 15-2(i)(4), n. 316
Ohio Rev. Code Ann. § 2739.12 — § 14-1, n. 17; § 15-1, nn. 3, 15; § 15-2(b)(1), n. 34; § 15-2(c)(1), n. 79; § 15-2(d)(1), n. 138; § 15-2(d)(3)(C), n. 191
Ohio Rev. Code Ann. § 2913.04(B) — § 13-9(b), n. 829
Ohio Rev. Code Ann. § 2917.13(B) — § 8-3, n. 112
Ohio Rev. Code Ann. § 2933.52 — § 13-7(b)(2), n. 691
Ohio Rev. Code Ann. §§ 2939.25 to 2939.29 — § 15-2(j), n. 335
Ohio Rev. Code Ann. § 2949.25 — § 8-2, n. 64
Ohio Rev. Code Ann. § 4501.27 — § 11-7(k), n. 331
Ohio Rev. Code Ann. §§ 5703.21, 718.07 — § 11-7(f), n. 269

Oklahoma Constitution

Okla. Const. art. II, § 22 — § 13-3(c)(1), n. 183
Okla. Const. art. II, § 6 — § 3-1(a), n. 1

Oklahoma Statutes

Okla. Stat. tit. 6, § 207 — § 11-7(f)(3), n. 285
Okla. Stat. tit. 6, § 208 — § 11-7(f)(3), n. 283
Okla. Stat. tit. 12, § 2506 — § 15-1, nn. 13, 15
Okla. Stat. tit. 12, § 2506(A)(1) — § 15-2(c)(2)(C), n. 132
Okla. Stat. tit. 12, § 2506(A)(5) — § 15-2(d)(3)(C), n. 183
Okla. Stat. tit. 12, § 2506(B) — § 15-2(e)(1), n. 216; § 15-2(e)(2), n. 227; § 15-2(f), n. 255
Okla. Stat. tit. 12, § 2506(B)(1) — § 15-2(d)(1), n. 138
Okla. Stat. tit. 12, § 2506(B)(2) — § 15-2(c)(2)(B), n. 97
Okla. Stat. tit. 13, § 176.3 — § 13-7(b)(2), n. 691
Okla. Stat. tit. 21, § 1202 — § 13-7(b)(1), n. 683
Okla. Stat. tit. 21, § 1835(a) — § 13-3(c)(1), n. 176
Okla. Stat. tit. 21, § 1953 — § 13-9(b), n. 829
Okla. Stat. tit. 22, § 1015 — § 8-2, n. 64
Okla. Stat. tit. 25, § 304(1) — § 9-6(b), nn. 261, 275
Okla. Stat. tit. 25, § 306 — § 9-6(c), n. 287
Okla. Stat. tit. 25, § 307(B)(5) — § 9-6(i)(4), n. 397
Okla. Stat. tit. 25, § 307(C) — § 9-6(h)(3), n. 354
Okla. Stat. tit. 25, § 311(A)(11) — § 9-6(d), n. 299
Okla. Stat. tit. 25, § 312(C) — § 9-6(e), n. 317
Okla. Stat. tit. 25, § 314 — § 9-6(j), n. 409
Okla. Stat. tit. 51, § 24A.1 — § 11-5(a)(3), n. 90

TABLE OF STATUTES

Okla. Stat. tit. 51, § 24A.3.2 — § 11-3(e), n. 51
Okla. Stat. tit. 51, § 24A.5 — § 11-7(k), n. 332
Okla. Stat. tit. 51, § 24A.8 — § 11-7(b)(2), n. 215
Okla. Stat. tit. 51, § 24A.10 — § 11-7(f)(2), n. 278
Okla. Stat. tit. 63, § 1-323(a) — § 11-7(j), n. 309

Oregon Constitution

Or. Const. art. I, § 16 — § 3-1(a), n. 1
Or. Const. art. IV, § 14 — § 9-3, n. 51

Oregon Revised Statutes

Or. Rev. Stat. § 30.402 — § 6-1(a)(6), n. 141
Or. Rev. Stat. § 44.250(1) — § 15-2(c)(2)(C), n. 132
Or. Rev. Stat. § 44.510 — § 15-2(f), n. 257; § 15-2(c)(1), n. 58
Or. Rev. Stat. §§ 44.510 to 44.540 — § 15-1, nn. 13, 15
Or. Rev. Stat. § 44.510(2) — § 15-2(b)(1), n. 36
Or. Rev. Stat. § 44.510(5) — § 15-2(d)(3)(C), n. 183
Or. Rev. Stat. § 44.520 — § 15-2(d)(3)(C), n. 193
Or. Rev. Stat. § 44.520(1)(a) — § 15-2(d)(1), n. 138
Or. Rev. Stat. § 44.520(1)(a)-(b) — § 15-2(e)(1), n. 215
Or. Rev. Stat. § 44.520(2)(b) — § 15-2(i)(5), n. 317
Or. Rev. Stat. § 44.530(1) — § 15-2(d)(3)(E), n. 206; § 15-2(h), n. 271
Or. Rev. Stat. § 44.530(3) — § 15-2(c)(2)(B), n. 97
Or. Rev. Stat. § 44.540 — § 15-2(h), n. 275
Or. Rev. Stat. § 137.473 — § 8-2, n. 62
Or. Rev. Stat. § 165.540 — § 13-7(b)(2), n. 691
Or. Rev. Stat. § 192.501(1) — § 11-5(a)(4), n. 112
Or. Rev. Stat. § 192.501(2) — § 11-5(a)(3), n. 92
Or. Rev. Stat. § 192.640(1) — § 9-6(d), nn. 293, 295; § 9-6(f), n. 326
Or. Rev. Stat. § 192.660(1)(a) — § 9-6(i)(1)(A), n. 373
Or. Rev. Stat. § 192.660(1)(j) — § 9-6(h)(3), n. 353
Or. Rev. Stat. § 192.660(3) & (4) — § 9-6(i)(1)(D), n. 386
Or. Rev. Stat. § 192.690 — § 9-6(i)(2), n. 390
Or. Rev. Stat. § 192.690(1) — § 9-6(h)(3), n. 354
Or. Rev. Stat. § 295.018 — § 11-7(f)(3), n. 282
Or. Rev. Stat. § 419B.310(1) — § 3-3(a), n. 448
Or. Rev. Stat. § 469.090 — § 11-5(a)(8), n. 155
Or. Rev. Stat. §§ 586 to 589 — § 11-7(c), n. 256

Pennsylvania Constitution

Pa. Const. art. I, § 11 — § 3-1(a), n. 1
Pa. Const. art. V, § 18(h) — § 13-3(b), n. 128

Pennsylvania Consolidated Statutes

18 Pa. Cons. Stat. § 5503(a)(4) — § 13-3(c)(3), n. 218
18 Pa. Cons. Stat. § 5701 — § 13-7(c), n. 781
18 Pa. Cons. Stat. § 5703-04 — § 13-7(b)(3), n. 700

TABLE OF STATUTES

18 Pa. Cons. Stat. § 5725(a)(1) — § 13-7(b)(5), n. 747
18 Pa. Cons. Stat. § 5728 — § 13-7(b)(5), n. 745
42 Pa. Cons. Stat. § 3334 — § 13-3(b), n. 128
42 Pa. Cons. Stat. § 5942 — § 15-1, n. 15; § 15-2(e)(1), n. 214; § 15-2(i)(4), n. 316
42 Pa. Cons. Stat. § 6336(d) — § 3-3(a), n. 448
42 Pa. Cons. Stat. § 9711(1) — § 8-2, n. 64

Pennsylvania Statutes Annotated

Pa. Stat. Ann. tit. 28, § 330 — § 14-1, n. 17; § 14-2, n. 35; § 15-1, n. 3
Pa. Stat. Ann. tit. 65, § 66.2 — § 11-4, n. 56
Pa. Stat. Ann. tit. 65, § 273 — § 9-6(c), n. 279; § 9-6(d), n. 305
Pa. Stat. Ann. tit. 65, § 277 — § 9-6(g), n. 332
Pa. Stat. Ann. tit. 65, § 277(c) — § 9-6(h), n. 345
Pa. Stat. Ann. tit. 65, § 278 — § 9-6(g), n. 332
Pa. Stat. Ann. tit. 65, § 278(b) — § 9-6(g), n. 338
Pa. Stat. Ann. tit. 65, § 279(a) — § 9-6(d), nn. 298, 300
Pa. Stat. Ann. tit. 65, § 281 — § 9-6(e), n. 317
Pa. Stat. Ann. tit. 65, § 284 — § 9-6(j), n. 409
Pa. Stat. Ann. tit. 65, § 285 — § 9-6(j), n. 411

Rhode Island General Laws

R.I. Gen. Laws § 9-19.1 — § 15-1, n. 15
R.I. Gen. Laws § 9-19.1-3 — § 15-2(c), n. 57; § 15-2(c)(1), n. 60; § 15-2(c)(2)(B), n. 97; § 15-2(d)(3)(E), n. 205; § 15-2(e)(2), n. 230
R.I. Gen. Laws § 11-18-32(a) — § 11-5(b), n. 164
R.I. Gen. Laws § 38-2-2(4)(N) — § 11-7(f)(5), n. 290
R.I. Gen. Laws § 38-2-2(16) — § 11-7(b)(7), n. 243
R.I. Gen. Laws § 38-2-2(d)(1) — § 11-7(a), n. 184; § 11-7(a)(2), n. 189
R.I. Gen. Laws § 38-2-2(d)(4) — § 11-7(b)(1), n. 209
R.I. Gen. Laws § 39-21.1-17 — § 11-7(b)(8), n. 244
R.I. Gen. Laws § 42-46-2(a) — § 9-6(c), n. 288
R.I. Gen. Laws § 42-46-2(b) — § 9-6(b), nn. 255, 273
R.I. Gen. Laws § 42-46-4 — § 9-6(g), nn. 338, 340
R.I. Gen. Laws § 42-46-5(a)(2) — § 9-6(i)(1)(D), n. 388
R.I. Gen. Laws § 42-46-5(c) — § 9-6(b), n. 271
R.I. Gen. Laws § 42-46-7(b) — § 9-6(f), n. 327
R.I. Gen. Laws § 42-46-8(d) — § 9-6(j), n. 415

South Carolina Constitution

S.C. Const. art. III, § 23 — § 9-3, n. 52

South Carolina Code Annotated

S.C. Code Ann. § 1-20 — § 11-5(c), n. 169
S.C. Code Ann. § 16-16-20 — § 13-9(b), n. 829
S.C. Code Ann. § 19-11-100 — § 15-1, n. 15; § 15-2(c)(2)(B), n. 96; § 15-2(d)(3)(D), n. 199; § 15-2(h), n. 271
S.C. Code Ann. § 24-3-550 — § 8-2, nn. 64, 65

TABLE OF STATUTES

S.C. Code Ann. § 30-4-10 — § 11-5(c), n. 169
S.C. Code Ann. § 30-4-40(1) — § 11-7(i), n. 306
S.C. Code Ann. § 30-4-40(3) — § 11-5(a)(6), n. 135
S.C. Code Ann. § 30-4-40(a)(1) — § 9-6(h)(3), n. 355
S.C. Code Ann. § 30-4-40(a)(3) — § 11-7(b)(9), n. 248
S.C. Code Ann. § 30-4-60 — § 9-6(e), n. 311
S.C. Code Ann. § 30-4-70(a)(1) — § 9-6(i)(1)(C), n. 382
S.C. Code Ann. § 30-4-70(b) — § 9-6(c), n. 284
S.C. Code Ann. § 30-4-90(c) — § 9-6(e), n. 317
S.C. Code Ann. § 30-4-100(a) — § 9-6(j), n. 406
S.C. Code Ann. § 30-4-110 — § 9-6(j), n. 409
S.C. Code Ann. § 56-3-540 — § 11-7(k), n. 331

South Dakota Constitution

S.D. Const. art. III, § 15 — § 9-3, n. 52
S.D. Const. art. VI, § 20 — § 3-1(a), n. 1

South Dakota Codified Laws

S.D. Codified Laws § 1-25-1 — § 9-6(j), n. 409
S.D. Codified Laws § 1-25-2 — § 9-6(g), n. 341
S.D. Codified Laws § 1-25-2(2) — § 9-6(i)(4), n. 395
S.D. Codified Laws § 1-25-2(3) — § 9-6(h)(6), n. 366
S.D. Codified Laws § 22-22-40 — § 11-7(b)(4), n. 234
S.D. Codified Laws § 23A-27A-34 — § 8-2, n. 64
S.D. Codified Laws § 23A-35A-20 — § 13-7(b)(2), n. 691
S.D. Codified Laws § 26-7A-36 — § 3-3(a), nn. 449, 487
S.D. Codified Laws § 26-8-32 — § 3-3(a), n. 484
S.D. Codified Laws § 34-25-1 — § 11-7(j), n. 313
S.D. Codified Laws § 37-29-1 et seq. — § 12-4(c)(3), n. 263

Tennessee Constitution

Tenn. Const. art. I, § 17 — § 3-1(a), n. 1
Tenn. Const. art. II, § 22 — § 9-3, n. 52

Tennessee Code Annotated

Tenn. Code Ann. § 8-44-102(a) — § 9-6(e), n. 311; § 9-6(h)(2), n. 352
Tenn. Code Ann. § 8-44-102(d) — § 9-6(c), n. 287
Tenn. Code Ann. § 8-44-104(a) — § 9-6(f), n. 328
Tenn. Code Ann. § 8-44-106(a) — § 9-6(j), n. 406
Tenn. Code Ann. § 8-44-201 — § 9-6(i)(1)(D), n. 387
Tenn. Code Ann. § 10-7-301(6) — § 11-2, n. 17
Tenn. Code Ann. § 10-7-504(a)(5)(A)(iii) — § 11-5(a)(4), n. 111
Tenn. Code Ann. § 24-1-208 — § 15-1, nn. 13, 15; § 15-2(b)(1), n. 39; § 15-2(c)(1), n. 62
Tenn. Code Ann. § 24-1-208(3)(A) — § 15-2(i)(3), n. 310
Tenn. Code Ann. § 24-1-208(a) — §15-2(c)(2)(C), n. 132; § 15-2(d)(1), n. 138; § 15-2(d)(3)(A), n. 163; § 15-2(d)(3)(C), n. 183; § 15-2(f), n. 255
Tenn. Code Ann. § 24-1-208(b) — § 15-2(c)(2)(B), n. 97

TABLE OF STATUTES

Tenn. Code Ann. § 24-1-208(c) — § 15-2(e)(2), n. 226
Tenn. Code Ann. § 24-1-208(t)(1), (2) — § 15-2(i)(1), n. 295
Tenn. Code Ann. § 37-1-124(d) — § 6-2(a), n. 289
Tenn. Code Ann. § 37-1-153 — § 6-2(a), n. 288
Tenn. Code Ann. § 39-13-601 — § 13-7(b)(2), n. 691
Tenn. Code Ann. § 39-13-601(3) — § 13-7(b)(5), n. 746
Tenn. Code Ann. § 39-13-604(b)(2) — § 13-7(b)(4)(E), n. 735
Tenn. Code Ann. § 39-17-315(c) — § 13-3(c)(2), n. 202
Tenn. Code Ann. § 40-23-116 — § 8-2, nn. 64, 65
Tenn. Code Ann. §§ 55-25-101 to 55-25-112 — § 11-7(k), n. 331

Texas Constitution

Tex. Const. art. I, § 13 — § 3-1(a), n. 1
Tex. Const. art. III, § 16 — § 9-3, n. 53

Texas Code

Tex. Crim. P. Code Ann. art. 18.20 § 16 — § 13-7(b)(5), n. 747
Tex. Crim. P. Code Ann. § 35.29 — § 7-3, n. 192
Tex. Crim. P. Code Ann. § 43.20 — § 8-2, n. 62
Tex. Crim. P. Code Ann. § 43.20 (804) — § 8-2, n. 63
Tex. Gov't Code Ann. § 522.116 — § 11-7(f)(6), n. 294
Tex. Gov't Code Ann. § 552.002 — § 11-2, n. 17
Tex. Gov't Code Ann. § 552.003(a)(1) — § 11-3(a), n. 33
Tex. Gov't Code Ann. § 552.108 — § 11-5(a)(6), n. 134
Tex. Gov't Code Ann. § 552.110 — § 11-7(i), n. 306
Tex. Gov't Code Ann. § 552.113 — § 11-5(a)(8), n. 154
Tex. Gov't Code Ann. § 552.301(a) — § 11-8, n. 355
Tex. Gov't Code Ann. § 552.302 — § 11-8, n. 355
Tex. Gov't Code Ann. § 552.353 — § 11-9, n. 375
Tex. Penal Code Ann. § 16.02 — § 13-7(b)(2), n. 691
Tex. Rev. Civ. Stat. Ann. art. 350, § 20 — § 11-7(f)(3), n. 281
Tex. Rev. Civ. Stat. Ann. art. 6252-17, § 1(a) — § 9-6(c), n. 282
Tex. Rev. Civ. Stat. Ann. art. 6252-17, § 1(c) — § 9-6(b), n. 255
Tex. Rev. Civ. Stat. Ann. art. 6252-17, § 2(a) — § 9-6(g), n. 338
Tex. Rev. Civ. Stat. Ann. art. 6252-17, § 2(g) — § 9-6(i)(1)(C), n. 380
Tex. Rev. Civ. Stat. Ann. art. 6252-17, § 2(q) — § 9-6(h)(3), n. 354
Tex. Rev. Civ. Stat. Ann. art. 6252-17, § 3 — § 9-6(j), n. 407
Tex. Rev. Civ. Stat. Ann. art. 6252-17, § 3A — § 9-6(d), n. 303
Tex. Transp. Code Ann. §§ 731.001-731.009 — § 11-7(k), n. 331

Utah Constitution

Utah Const. art. I, § 11 — § 3-1(a), n. 1
Utah Const. art. VI, § 15 — § 9-3, n. 53

Utah Code Annotated

Utah Code Ann. § 52-4-2(2) — § 9-6(b), n. 273
Utah Code Ann. § 52-4-5(1) — § 9-6(i)(1)(D), n. 387

TABLE OF STATUTES

Utah Code Ann. § 52-4-5(1)(a) — § 9-6(i)(3), n. 392
Utah Code Ann. § 52-4-5(2) — § 9-6(h)(6), n. 366
Utah Code Ann. § 52-4-6(3) — § 9-6(d), n. 305
Utah Code Ann. § 52-4-7 — § 9-6(e), n. 317; § 9-6(f), n. 324
Utah Code Ann. § 52-4-9 — § 9-6(j), n. 416
Utah Code Ann. § 52-4-9(1) — § 9-6(j), n. 408
Utah Code Ann. § 53-5-214 — § 13-9(b), n. 829
Utah Code Ann. § 63-2-103(12)(a)(ii) — § 11-7(b)(5), n. 238
Utah Code Ann. § 63-2-301(2)(g) — § 11-7(b)(5), n. 238
Utah Code Ann. § 63-2-302(2)(d) — § 11-7(b)(5), n. 238
Utah Code Ann. § 63-2-304(8)(e) — § 11-7(b)(9), n. 248
Utah Code Ann. § 63-2-307 — § 11-6, n. 175
Utah Code Ann. § 76-6-703 — § 13-9(b), n. 829
Utah Code Ann. § 76-9-403 — § 13-7(b)(2), n. 691
Utah Code Ann. § 77-19-11(4) — § 8-2, n. 64
Utah Code Ann. § 77-19-11(4)(a) — § 8-2, n. 65
Utah Code Ann. §§ 78-74 — § 3-2(b), n. 374

Virginia Constitution

Va. Const. art. I, § 12 — § 3-1(a)(5), n. 194

Virginia Code Annotated

Va. Code Ann. § 2.1-37.13 — § 13-3(a), n. 92
Va. Code Ann. § 2.1-341 — § 9-6(b), nn. 255, 261, 275; § 9-6(c), n. 279
Va. Code Ann. § 2.1-342(A)(4), para. 4 — § 11-2, n. 19
Va. Code Ann. § 2.1-342(B)(3) — § 11-7(f)(2), n. 273
Va. Code Ann. § 2.1-342(B)(29) — § 11-7(l), n. 340
Va. Code Ann. § 2.1-343 — § 9-6(e), nn. 311, 317
Va. Code Ann. § 2.1-344 — § 9-6(g), n. 332
Va. Code Ann. § 2.1-344(A)(1) — § 9-6(i)(1)(C), n. 380
Va. Code Ann. § 2.1-344(A)(4) — § 9-6(h)(4), n. 357
Va. Code Ann. § 2.1-344(A)(6) — § 9-6(h)(3), n. 353
Va. Code Ann. § 2.1-344(A)(7) — § 9-6(h)(6), n. 365
Va. Code Ann. § 2.1-344(A)(14) — § 9-6(h)(3), n. 354
Va. Code Ann. § 2.1-344(A)(17) — § 9-6(h)(5), n. 362
Va. Code Ann. § 2.1-344(A)(20) — § 9-6(h)(5), n. 362
Va. Code Ann. § 2.1-344(A)(21) — § 9-6(h)(5), n. 362
Va. Code Ann. § 2.1-346 — § 9-6(j), n. 406
Va. Code Ann. § 8.01-420.01 — § 6-1(a)(6), n. 142
Va. Code Ann. § 15.1-135.1 — § 11-7(b)(4), n. 234
Va. Code Ann. § 16.1-300 — § 6-2(b), nn. 291, 292, 293
Va. Code Ann. § 16.1-302 — § 3-3(a), n. 448
Va. Code Ann. § 19.2-62 — § 13-7(b)(2), n. 691
Va. Code Ann. § 46.2-208 — § 11-7(k), nn. 319, 332
Va. Code Ann. § 53.1-234 — § 8-2, n. 63

Vermont Constitution

Vt. Const. ch. II, § 8 — § 9-3, n. 52

Vermont Statutes Annotated

Vt. Stat. Ann. tit. 1, § 310(2) — § 9-6(c), n. 284
Vt. Stat. Ann. tit. 1, § 312(b) — § 9-6(f), nn. 324, 327
Vt. Stat. Ann. tit. 1, § 312(e) — § 9-6(b), n. 271
Vt. Stat. Ann. tit. 1, § 312(h) — § 9-6(e), n. 315
Vt. Stat. Ann. tit. 1, § 313 — § 9-6(h)(2), n. 351
Vt. Stat. Ann. tit. 1, § 313(a) — § 9-6(g), n. 339
Vt. Stat. Ann. tit. 1, § 313(a)(7) — § 9-6(i)(4), n. 395
Vt. Stat. Ann. tit. 1, § 317 — § 11-7(f)(3), n. 280
Vt. Stat. Ann. tit. 10, § 101 — § 11-5(a)(8), n. 159
Vt. Stat. Ann. tit. 29 § 542 — § 11-5(a)(8), n. 152
Vt. Stat. Ann. tit. 33, § 651(c) — § 3-3(a), n. 446

Washington Constitution

Wash. Const. art. II, § 11 — § 9-3, n. 52

Washington Revised Code

Wash. Rev. Code § 4.24.601 — § 6-1(a)(6), n. 143
Wash. Rev. Code § 4.24.611 — § 6-1(a)(6), n. 143
Wash. Rev. Code § 9.61.230 — § 13-3(c)(2), n. 194
Wash. Rev. Code § 9.73.030 — § 12-2(a), n. 17; § 13-7(b)(3), n. 700
Wash. Rev. Code § 9.73.030(2)(b) — § 13-7(b)(4)(D), n. 728
Wash. Rev. Code § 9.73.030(2)(c) — § 13-7(b)(4)(D), n. 729
Wash. Rev. Code § 9A.52.110 — § 13-9(b), n. 829
Wash. Rev. Code § 10.95.180 — § 8-2, n. 79
Wash. Rev. Code § 10.95.185 — § 8-2, n. 64
Wash. Rev. Code § 13.34.110 — § 3-3(a), n. 448
Wash. Rev. Code § 42.17.260(5) — § 11-7(i), n. 307
Wash. Rev. Code § 42.17.301(1)(h) — § 11-7(i), n. 307
Wash. Rev. Code § 42.17.310(1)(d) — § 11-7(b)(3), n. 217; § 11-7(b)(8), n. 246
Wash. Rev. Code § 42.17.310(1)(g) — § 11-7(f)(5), n. 293
Wash. Rev. Code § 42.17.310(1)(h) — § 11-5(a)(3), n. 93
Wash. Rev. Code § 42.17.310(1)(v) — § 11-7(l), n. 342
Wash. Rev. Code § 42.17.440 — § 11-7(f)(2), n. 279
Wash. Rev. Code § 42.30.020(1)(a) — § 9-6(b), nn. 260, 271
Wash. Rev. Code § 42.30.070 — § 9-6(d), nn. 296, 300
Wash. Rev. Code § 42.30.110 — § 9-6(g), n. 332
Wash. Rev. Code § 42.30.110(1)(g) — § 9-6(i)(1)(A), n. 374
Wash. Rev. Code § 42.30.110(1)(h) — § 9-6(i)(1)(A), n. 370
Wash. Rev. Code § 42.30.110(1)(i) — § 9-6(h)(6), n. 366
Wash. Rev. Code § 42.30.110(1)(k) — § 9-6(h)(3), n. 354
Wash. Rev. Code § 42.30.120(1) — § 9-6(j), n. 412
Wash. Rev. Code § 42.30.130 — § 9-6(h)(2), n. 351
Wash. Rev. Code § 42.30.140(1) — § 9-6(i)(6), n. 401
Wash. Rev. Code § 42.30.140(4)(a) — § 9-6(i)(1)(D), n. 386
Wash. Rev. Code § 42.32.030 — § 9-6(f), n. 328
Wash. Rev. Code § 68.50.300 — § 11-7(d), n. 259

West Virginia Constitution

W. Va. Const. art. III, § 17 — § 3-1(a), n. 1

West Virginia Code

W. Va. Code § 6-9A-2(4) — § 9-6(i)(6), n. 404
W. Va. Code § 6-9A-3 — § 9-6(d), n. 294
W. Va. Code § 6-9A-4 — § 9-6(g), n. 342
W. Va. Code § 6-9A-4(3) — § 9-6(i)(4), n. 398
W. Va. Code § 6-9A-4(5) — § 9-6(i)(3), n. 393
W. Va. Code § 6-9A-4(9) — § 9-6(h)(3), n. 353
W. Va. Code § 6-9A-5 — § 9-6(f), n. 326
W. Va. Code § 11-1C-14 — § 11-5(a)(8), n. 153
W. Va. Code § 11-10-5(d) — § 11-7(f)(2), n. 273
W. Va. Code §§ 17A-2A-1 to 17A-2A-14 — § 11-7(k), n. 331
W. Va. Code § 29B-1-4 — § 11-5(a)(3), n. 92
W. Va. Code § 29B-1-4(1) — § 11-5(a)(3), n. 91
W. Va. Code § 29B-1-4(4) — § 11-5(a)(6), n. 134
W. Va. Code § 29B-1-4(5) — § 11-5(b), n. 161
W. Va. Code § 49-5-2 — § 3-3(a), n. 448
W. Va. Code § 49-7-3 — § 13-3(a), n. 96
W. Va. Code § 61-3C-5 — § 13-9(b), n. 829
W. Va. Code § 62-1D-3 — § 13-7(b)(2), n. 691
W. Va. Code § 62-1D-12 — § 13-7(b)(5), n. 747

Wisconsin Constitution

Wis. Const. art. IV, § 10 — § 9-3, n. 52

Wisconsin Statutes

Wis. Stat. § 19.32(2) — § 11-2, n. 17; § 11-5(a)(4), n. 98
Wis. Stat. § 19.37(3) — § 11-9, n. 370
Wis. Stat. § 19.82(1) — § 9-6(b), nn. 255, 260, 270
Wis. Stat. § 19.84(3) — § 9-6(d), n. 298
Wis. Stat. § 19.85(1) — § 9-6(g), n. 340
Wis. Stat. § 19.85(1)(b) — § 9-6(i)(1)(C), n. 383; § 9-6(i)(6), n. 405
Wis. Stat. § 19.85(1)(e) — § 9-6(h)(3), n. 353
Wis. Stat. § 19.85(1)(f) — § 9-6(i)(3), n. 392
Wis. Stat. § 19.90 — § 9-6(e), n. 317
Wis. Stat. § 19.96 — § 9-6(j), nn. 409, 412
Wis. Stat. § 19.97 — § 9-6(j), nn. 406, 417
Wis. Stat. § 938.299(1)(a) — § 3-3(a), n. 447
Wis. Stat. § 938.396 — § 6-2(a), n. 272
Wis. Stat. § 943.70 — § 13-9(b), n. 829
Wis. Stat. § 968.31 — § 13-7(b)(5), n. 744
Wis. Stat. § 968.31(2)(c) — § 13-7(b)(2), n. 698

Wyoming Constitution

Wyo. Const. art. I, § 8 — § 3-1(a), n. 1
Wyo. Const. art. III, § 14 — § 9-3, n. 52

TABLE OF STATUTES

Wyoming Statutes Annotated

Wyo. Stat. Ann. § 7-3-602 — § 13-7(b)(2), n. 691
Wyo. Stat. Ann. § 7-13-409 — § 11-7(c), n. 255
Wyo. Stat. Ann. § 7-13-908 — § 8-2, n. 62
Wyo. Stat. Ann. § 9-2-803 — § 11-5(a)(8), n. 158
Wyo. Stat. Ann. § 9-692.1 — § 11-8, n. 355
Wyo. Stat. Ann. § 14-6-224(b) — § 3-3(a), n. 448
Wyo. Stat. Ann. § 16-4-402(a) — § 9-6(c), n. 285
Wyo. Stat. Ann. § 16-4-402(a)(ii) — § 9-6(b), n. 272
Wyo. Stat. Ann. § 16-4-403(a) — § 9-6(j), n. 415
Wyo. Stat. Ann. § 16-4-403(b) — § 9-6(e), n. 315
Wyo. Stat. Ann. § 16-4-404(d) — § 9-6(d), n. 302
Wyo. Stat. Ann. § 16-4-405(a)(iii) — § 9-6(h)(6), n. 366
Wyo. Stat. Ann. § 16-4-405(a)(xi) — § 9-6(i)(4), n. 395
Wyo. Stat. Ann. § 16-4-203((b)(iv) — § 11-7(f)(5), n. 291

INDEX

A

"ABSCAM."
Trial records, §5-2(b).

ABSOLUTE PRIVILEGE.
State Shield laws, §15-2(e)(1).

ABSTENTION DOCTRINE.
Participants in judicial process, access to, §7-1.

ABUSE, NEGLECT, DEPENDENCY, AND CUSTODY PROCEEDINGS. (*See also* CHILDREN).
Judicial proceedings, access to, §3-3(b).
Settlement proceedings, §3-2(d).

ACCESS.
Attorneys, §7-2.
Executive and legislative branches, access to, §§9-1 to 9-6. (*See* EXECUTIVE AND LEGISLATIVE BRANCHES, ACCESS TO).
Federal Advisory Committee Act, access to records under, §10-3.
Federal government records, §§10-1 to 10-3. (*See* FEDERAL GOVERNMENT RECORDS, ACCESS TO).
Judicial proceedings, §§2-1 to 2-4, 3-1 to 3-3. (*See* JUDICIAL PROCEEDINGS, ACCESS TO).
Judicial records, §§5-1, 5-2, 6-1, 6-2. (*See* JUDICIAL RECORDS, ACCESS TO).
Jurors, §7-3.
Newsgathering and right of, §1-5.
Police records, §11-7(b).
Public places and events, §§8-1 to 8-5. (*See* PUBLIC PLACES AND EVENTS, ACCESS TO).
State government records, §§11-1 to 11-9. (*See* STATE GOVERNMENT RECORDS, ACCESS TO).

ACCIDENT REPORTS.
Police records, access to, §11-7(b)(10).

ACCIDENT SCENES.
Public places and events, access to, §8-3.

ACCOMPANYING AUTHORIZED INDIVIDUALS.
Nongovernmental places, newsgathering in, §12-5.

ACCUSATION OF CRIME OR FORMAL CENSURE, EXEMPTIONS.
Government in the Sunshine Act, §9-5(a)(8)(E).

ACTIVE FILES, INVESTIGATORY RECORDS.
Police records, access to, §11-7(b)(3)(A).

ADMINISTRATIVE APPEALS.
Freedom of Information Act, §10-2(g).
State government records, access to, §11-8.

ADMINISTRATIVE PROCEEDINGS.
Executive and legislative branches, access to, §9-4.
Judicial records, access to, §5-1.
Vouchers, Criminal Justice Act, §5-2(e).

ADMINISTRATIVE REGULATIONS.
Federal codifications, §15-3(b).

ADMISSIBILITY OF EVIDENCE.
Suppression hearings, §3-1(a)(4).

ADOPTION.
Cameras in the courtroom, §4-3.
Privacy interests, §3-2(b).

"ADVISORY COMMITTEE" DEFINED.
Federal Advisory Committee Act, §9-5(b)(2).

ADVISORY COMMITTEES.
State government records, access to, §11-3(d).

AFFIDAVITS.
Bail and detention, §5-2(a)(8).
Suppression hearings, probable cause, §3-1(a)(4).

1257

INDEX

AGENCY PARTICIPATION IN CIVIL ACTIONS OR PROCEEDINGS, EXEMPTIONS.
Government in the Sunshine Act, §9-5(a)(8)(J).

AGENCY PERSONNEL RULES, EXEMPTIONS.
Freedom of Information Act, §10-2(c)(3).

AGENCY RESPONSE TIME, LIMITATIONS ON.
Freedom of Information Act, §10-2(b)(4).

AGENT OR SURROGATE, PRESS AS, §1-4(b).

AIDS CASE.
Pretrial motions, records, and pleadings, §6-1(c)(1).

AIRPLANE CRASH SCENE, §8-3.

ALABAMA.
Prison overcrowding, §3-2.

ALL-PARTY CONSENT JURISDICTIONS.
Audio recording, §13-7(b)(3).

AMBUSH INTERVIEW.
Sources and interview subjects, §13-4(b).

AMERICAN BAR ASSOCIATION.
Cameras in the courtroom, §4-1.
Gag orders, §7-2.
Judicial records, access to, §5-1.

ANCILLARY PROCEEDINGS.
Grand jury, §§3-1(a)(2), 3-1(a)(3), 5-2(a)(3).

ANONYMITY.
Juvenile offenders, §2-1(c).

ANTITRUST LAWSUIT.
Depositions, §3-2(e).
Pretrial motions, records, and pleadings, §6-1(c)(1).

ANTIWAR SENTIMENT.
Military operations, §8-5.

APPEALS, ADMINISTRATIVE.
Freedom of Information Act, §10-2(g).
State government records, access to, §11-8.

APPEALS BY NON-PARTY.
Supreme Court, constitutional right of access in, §2-3.

APPELLATE REVIEW.
Cameras in the courtroom, §§4-2(b), 4-3.
Constitutional privilege, procedural requirements, §16-2(h)(2).
State Shield laws, §15-2(i)(3).

APPLICATIONS FOR EMPLOYMENT.
State government records, access to, §11-7(a)(1).

APPOINTMENT OF COUNSEL.
Vouchers, Criminal Justice Act, §5-2(e).

APPRAISALS, REAL ESTATE.
State government records, access to, §11-7(f)(5).

AQUARIAN FOUNDATION.
Discovery, §6-1(a)(2).

ARIZONA, GOVERNOR OF.
Court records, §6-1(d).

ARMED ROBBERY.
Juvenile proceedings, §3-3(a).

ARMY COURT OF CRIMINAL APPEALS, §3-1(e).

ARREST AND INCIDENT REPORTS.
Police records, access to, §11-7(b)(1).

ARTIFICIAL INSEMINATION.
Criminal trials, §3-1(c).

ASBESTOS LITIGATION.
Settlement proceedings, §3-2(d).

ASSOCIATION OF NEWSPAPERS OR BROADCASTERS.
Challenge of closure order, §2-3.

ATTORNEY-CLIENT PRIVILEGE.
Pretrial hearings, access to, §3-1(a).

ATTORNEYS.
Access to, §7-2.
Conflicts of interest, §§3-1(a), 5-2(a).
Trade secrets, §3-2(c).

ATTORNEY'S FEES.
Vouchers, Criminal Justice Act, §5-2(e).

INDEX

AUDIO RECORDING, §13-7.
All-party consent jurisdictions,
§13-7(b)(3).
Business premises, communications on,
§13-7(b)(4)(C).
Common law, §13-7(c).
Consensual monitoring jurisdictions,
§13-7(b)(2).
Consent, all-party, §13-7(b)(3).
Consent, qualified one-party,
§13-7(a)(2)(A)(iii).
Emergency communications, monitoring
of, §13-7(b)(4)(G).
Exception, qualified one-party consent,
§13-7(a)(2)(A)(iii).
Exceptions, §13-7(b)(4).
FCC Regulations, §13-7(a)(2)(C).
Federal Communications Act,
§13-7(a)(2)(B).
Federal Communications Commission
Regulations, §13-7(a)(2)(C).
Federal law, §13-7(a).
Federal Wiretap Act, §13-7(a)(2)(A).
Fourth Amendment considerations,
§13-7(a)(1).
Inadvertent interceptions of
communications, §13-7(b)(4)(A).
Interceptions of communications,
inadvertent, §13-7(b)(4)(A).
Law enforcement monitoring,
§13-7(b)(4)(F).
Means of newsgathering, §13-7.
Monitoring of emergency communications,
§13-7(b)(4)(G).
One-party consent exception,
§13-7(a)(2)(A)(iii).
Prohibited conduct, §13-7(a)(2)(A)(i).
Public places, communications in,
§13-7(b)(4)(B).
Qualified one-party consent exception,
§13-7(a)(2)(A)(iii).
Remedies, §§13-7(a)(2)(A)(iv), 13-7(b)(5).
Restricted equipment, §13-7(a)(2)(A)(ii).
Sanctions and remedies,
§§13-7(a)(2)(A)(iv), 13-7(b)(5).
State law, §13-7(b).
Trial records, §5-2(b).
Unprotected subject matter,
§13-7(b)(4)(D).
Unrestricted equipment, use of,
§13-7(b)(4)(E).
Wiretap Act, §13-7(a)(2)(A).

AUDITS OF PUBLIC OFFICES.
State government records, access to,
§11-7(f)(6).

AUTHORIZED INDIVIDUALS, ACCOMPANYING.
Nongovernmental places, newsgathering
in, §12-5.

AUTOMATIC SEALING PROVISIONS.
Judicial records, access to, §§5-1, 5-2(a).

AUTOMOBILE ACCIDENT SCENE, §8-3.

AUTOPSY REPORTS.
State government records, access to,
§11-7(d).

AVOIDANCE OF CONSTITUTIONAL PRIVILEGE, §16-2(j).

B

BAIL AND DETENTION.
Access to hearings, §3-1(a).
Judicial proceedings, access to, §3-1(a)(1).
Judicial records, access to, §5-2(a)(8).
Reduction hearing, §5-2(a)(8).
Suppression hearings, §5-2(a)(7).

BALANCING STANDARDS.
Abuse, neglect, dependency, and custody
proceedings, §3-3(b).

BANKRUPTCY PROCEEDINGS.
Court records, §6-1(d).

BANKS.
Freedom of Information Act (FOIA)
exemptions, §10-2(c)(9).
Government in the Sunshine Act
exemptions, §9-5(a)(8)(H).
State government records, access to,
§§11-5(a)(7), 11-7(f)(3).

BARRY, MARION.
Plea agreements, §5-2(a)(9).

BARS AND RESTAURANTS.
Nongovernmental places, newsgathering
in, §12-4(c)(1).

INDEX

BENCH CONFERENCES.
Cameras in the courtroom, §4-3.
Criminal trials, §3-1(c).

BIDS AND PROPOSALS.
State government records, access to, §11-7(f)(4).

BIFURCATED GRAND JURY PROCEEDINGS, §3-1(a)(3).

BILLS OF PARTICULARS.
Information and indictment, §5-2(a)(4).

BLANKET SEALING ORDERS.
Judicial records, access to, §5-2(a).

BOMBINGS.
Gag orders, §7-2.
Judicial records, access to, §5-2(a).
Oklahoma City bombing, §§5-2(e), 7-2.
Unabomber trial, §5-2(a).
Vouchers, Criminal Justice Act, §5-2(e).
World Trade Center bombing case, §7-2.

BOND HEARINGS. (*See* BAIL AND DETENTION).

BRADSHAW **BALANCING TEST.**
Juvenile proceedings, §3-3(a).

BRANZBURG V. HAYES, §§14-4 to 14-6.
Chambers opinions, §14-5(f).
Closure of court cases, §14-5(d).
Concurring opinion, §14-4(b).
Consolidated cases, §14-3.
Court closure cases, §14-5(d).
Dissenting opinion, §14-4(c).
Evolution of journalists' privilege, §§14-4 to 14-6.
Incidental restraint cases, §14-5(c).
Justice Powell's concurring opinion, §14-4(b).
Justice Stewart's dissenting opinion, §14-4(c).
Lower courts, §14-6.
McIntyre decision, §14-5(e).
Opinion of court, §14-4(a).
Prison access cases, §14-5(a).
Privilege cases, §14-5(b).
Restraint cases, §14-5(c).
Second Circuit approach, §14-6(a).
Sixth Circuit approach, §14-6(b).

Supreme Court, §14-5.

BREACH OF CONTRACT.
Settlement agreements, §6-1(b).
Sources and interview subjects, §§13-4(a), 13-4(c).

BRIBERY.
Information and indictment, §5-2(a)(4).
Search warrants, §5-2(a)(2).
Trial records, §5-2(b).

"BRILAB."
Trial records, §5-2(b).

BROADCAST RULES.
State Shield laws, §15-2(i)(4).
Trial records, §5-2(b).

BURGLARY TRIAL.
Cameras in the courtroom, §4-1.

BUSINESSES, PRIVATE.
Nongovernmental places, newsgathering in, §12-4(c).

BUSINESS INFORMATION.
Depositions, §3-2(e).
Pretrial motions, records, and pleadings, §6-1(c)(1).

BUSINESS PREMISES.
Communications on, audio recording, §13-7(b)(4)(C).

BUSINESS RECORDS.
State government records, access to, §11-7(f)(1).

BUSINESS WEEK.
Restraining publication, §2-1(d).

C

CALIFORNIA.
Abuse, neglect, dependency, and custody proceedings, §3-3(b).
Cameras in the courtroom, §4-3.
Checkbook journalism, §7-4.
Disaster, accident and crime scenes, §8-3.
Executions, §8-2.
Juvenile proceedings, §3-3(a).
Voir dire questionnaire, §5-2(c).

CAMERAS, HIDDEN.
Means of newsgathering, §13-8.

1260

INDEX

CAMERAS IN THE COURTROOM,
§§4-1 to 4-3.
Challenges, constitutional, §4-2(a).
Changing rules, §4-2(b).
Constitutional challenges and waiver, §4-2(a).
Federal Court proceedings, §4-2.
Judicial proceedings, access to, §2-1(a).
State Court proceedings, §4-3.
Supreme Court precedent, §4-1.
Waiver, §4-2(a).

CATEGORIES OF MEETINGS.
State and local government, statutory access to meetings of, §9-6(i).

CATEGORIES OF RECORDS.
State government records, access to, §11-7.

CENSURE, FORMAL.
Government in the Sunshine Act exemptions, §9-5(a)(8)(E).

CHALLENGES, CONSTITUTIONAL.
Cameras in the courtroom, §4-2(a).

CHALLENGES TO CLOSED MEETINGS.
Federal Advisory Committee Act, §9-5(b)(7).
Government in the Sunshine Act, §9-5(a)(9).
Grand jury records, §5-2(a)(3).
State and local government, statutory access to meetings of, §9-6(j).

CHAMBERS CONFERENCES AND OPINIONS.
Branzburg v. Hayes, §14-5(f).
Criminal trials, §3-1(c).
Pretrial hearings, access to, §3-1(a).

CHANGE OF VENUE.
Judicial proceedings, access to, §2-1(a).
Pretrial hearings, access to, §3-1(a).
Sheppard Mandate, §2-1(b).

CHECKBOOK JOURNALISM, §7-4.
Sources and interview subjects, §13-4(a)(4).

CHECKS AND BALANCES.
Agent or surrogate, press as, §1-4(b).
Freedom of the press, §1-4(a).

Supreme Court, constitutional right of access in, §2-2(c).

CHILDREN. *(See also* JUVENILES AND JUVENILE PROCEEDINGS; MINOR'S TESTIMONY).
Abuse and neglect, juvenile court records, §6-2(b).
Cameras in the courtroom, §4-3.
Consent, §12-6(a).
Neglected children, §3-2(d).
Settlement proceedings, §3-2(d).

CHOICE OF LAW.
Constitutional privilege, §16-2(i).
State Shield laws, §15-2(j).

CIVIL COMMITMENT.
Privacy interests, §3-2(b).

CIVIL LIABILITY.
Means of newsgathering, §13-3(b).

CIVIL PROCEEDINGS.
Cameras in the courtroom, §§4-2(a), 4-3.
Constitutional privilege, §16-2(c)(2).
Government in the Sunshine Act exemptions, §9-5(a)(8)(J).
Judicial proceedings, access to, §3-2.
Judicial records, access to, §§6-1, 6-2.
State and local government, statutory access to meetings of, §9-6(h)(6).
State Shield laws, §15-2(c)(2).

CIVIL RIGHTS MARCHERS.
Voir dire, §3-1(b).

CLASS ACTIONS, §3-2.

CLEAR AND PRESENT DANGER DOCTRINE.
Gag orders, §7-2.

CLEAR AND PRESENT DANGER STANDARD.
Restraining publication, §2-1(d).

CLINTON, BILL.
Grand jury proceedings, §3-1(a)(3).
Presidential Deputy Chief of Staff, §6-1(d).

CLOSED FILES, INVESTIGATORY RECORDS.
Police records, access to, §11-7(b)(3)(B).

INDEX

CLOSED MEETINGS AND PROCEEDINGS, §2-1(a).
Bail and detention hearings, §3-1(a)(1).
Branzburg v. Hayes, §14-5(d).
Challenges to, §§9-5(a)(9), 9-5(b)(7), 9-6(j).
Civil proceedings, §3-2(a).
Criminal trials, §3-1(c).
Evolution of journalists' privilege, §14-5(d).
Federal Advisory Committee Act, §§9-5(b)(5), 9-5(b)(7).
Findings, §2-2(h).
Government in the Sunshine Act, §§9-5(a)(7), 9-5(a)(9).
Post-trial matters, §3-1(c).
Procedures, §9-5(a)(9).
State and local government, statutory access to meetings of, §9-6(j).
Supreme Court, constitutional right of access in, §§2-2(a), 2-2(b), 2-2(c), 2-2(f).

CLOSURE, PARTIAL.
Criminal trials, §3-1(c).
Pretrial hearings, access to, §3-1(a).

CLOSURE HEARINGS, §2-3.

CLOSURE MOTION.
Justice Department guidelines, §2-3.

CLOSURE ORDERS.
Supreme Court, constitutional right of access in, §2-2(a).

CLOSURE RULE, MANDATORY.
Juvenile proceedings, §3-3(a).

CNN (CABLE NEWS NETWORK).
Tape recordings, restraining publication, §2-1(d).

CO-CONSPIRATORS.
Information and indictment, §5-2(a)(4).

COHEN V. COWLES MEDIA CO.
Sources and interview subjects, §§13-4(a)(2), 13-4(a)(3).

COLLATERAL ORDER DOCTRINE, §2-3.

COLLECTIVE BARGAINING.
State and local government, statutory access to meetings of, §9-6(i)(1)(D).

COMMENCEMENT OF MEETING, CHALLENGES PRIOR TO.
Government in the Sunshine Act, §9-5(a)(9)(A).

COMMERCIAL INFORMATION, EXEMPTIONS.
Freedom of Information Act, §10-2(c)(5).
Government in the Sunshine Act, §9-5(a)(8)(D).
State and local government, statutory access to meetings of, §9-6(h)(3).

COMMITMENT, CIVIL.
Privacy interests, §3-2(b).

COMMITTEE ON COURT ADMINISTRATION AND CASE MANAGEMENT, JUDICIAL CONFERENCE'S.
Cameras in the courtroom, §4-2(b).

COMMITTEES, ADVISORY.
State government records, access to, §11-3(d).

COMMON LAW.
Audio recording, §13-7(c).
Contempt, §2-1(c).
Discovery documents, §5-2(a)(5).
Evolution of journalists' privilege, §14-1.
Exemptions, access to state government records, §11-5(c).
Grand jury records, §5-2(a)(3).
Judicial records, access to, §5-2(a).
Presumption of access to judicial records, §5-1.
Privileges, §16-3.

COMMON LAW PRIVILEGES, §16-3.

COMMUNICATIONS. (*See also* INTERCEPTED COMMUNICATIONS).
Disclosure of illegally seized communications, §3-1(a)(1).
In newsgathering process, §13-6.

COMPETENCY HEARINGS.
Access to, §3-1(a).
Judicial proceedings, access to, §3-1(a)(5).

1262

INDEX

COMPETENCY HEARINGS—Cont'd
Judicial records, access to, §5-2(a).

COMPETING INTERESTS, DISCOVERY MATERIALS.
Judicial records, access to, §6-1(a)(5).

COMPILATIONS OF CRIMINAL HISTORIES.
Police records, access to, §11-7(b)(4).

COMPUTER SYSTEMS.
Federal law, §13-9(a).
State law, §13-9(b).
Unauthorized access to, §13-9.

CONDITIONAL ACCESS.
Abuse, neglect, dependency, and custody proceedings, §3-3(b).
Criminal trials, §3-1(c).

CONFESSIONS.
Judicial proceedings, access to, §2-1(a).
Police records, access to, §11-7(b)(6).

CONFIDENTIAL INFORMATION.
Commercial information, exemptions, §§9-5(a)(8)(D), 9-6(h)(3), 10-2(c)(5).
Constitutional privilege, scope of protection, §16-2(d)(2).
Depositions, §3-2(e).
Freedom of Information Act, §10-2(c)(5).
Government in the Sunshine Act, §9-5(a)(8)(D).
State and local government, statutory access to meetings of, §9-6(h)(3).
State Shield laws, §15-2(d)(2).

CONFIDENTIALITY AGREEMENT.
Court files, §6-1(c).

CONFIDENTIALITY ORDERS.
Depositions, §3-2(e).
Participants in judicial process, access to, §7-1.

CONFIDENTIALITY PROVISION.
Settlement agreements, §6-1(b).

CONFLICTS OF INTEREST.
Attorneys, §3-1(a).
Judicial records, access to, §5-2(a).

CONSENSUAL MONITORING JURISDICTIONS.
Audio recording, §13-7(b)(2).

CONSENT.
Audio recording, §§13-7(a)(2)(A)(iii), 13-7(b)(3).
Cameras in the courtroom, §4-3.
Federal Wiretap Act, qualified one-party consent, §13-7(a)(2)(A)(iii).
Settlement proceedings, §3-2(d).
Special issues, newsgathering in nongovernmental places, §12-6.

CONSPIRACY ACTION.
Pretrial motions, records, and pleadings, §6-1(c)(1).

CONSTITUTIONAL CHALLENGES AND WAIVER.
Cameras in the courtroom, §4-2(a).

CONSTITUTIONAL FOUNDATIONS.
Judicial proceedings, access to, §§2-1 to 2-4.

CONSTITUTIONALITY.
Cameras in the courtroom, §4-1.
State Shield laws, §15-2(a).

CONSTITUTIONAL OVERVIEW.
Executive and legislative branches, access to, §9-1.
Means of newsgathering, §13-3(a).

CONSTITUTIONAL PRIVILEGE, §§1-4(a), 16-2.
Appellate review, procedural requirements, §16-2(h)(2).
Avoidance of privilege, §16-2(j).
In camera review, procedural requirements, §16-2(h)(1).
Choice of law, §16-2(i).
Civil proceedings, §16-2(c)(2).
Confidential information, scope of protection, §16-2(d)(2).
Contours of privilege, §16-2(e).
Criminal proceedings, §16-2(c)(1).
Definitional issues, recipients of protection, §16-2(b)(1).
Early cases, §14-2.
Evolution of journalists' privilege, §14-2.
Exhaustion requirements, §16-2(e)(3).
Eyewitness testimony, §16-2(d)(3)(B).

1263

INDEX

CONSTITUTIONAL PRIVILEGE—
Cont'd
Federal courts, judicial acceptance, §16-2(a)(1).
Judicial acceptance, §16-2(a).
Nature of proceedings, §16-2(c).
Nonconfidential information, scope of protection, §16-2(d)(3).
Nonconfidential sources, §16-2(d)(3)(A).
Non-disclosure penalties, §16-2(f).
Non-traditional subpoenas, avoidance of privilege, §16-2(j)(2).
Party, press as, §16-2(c)(2)(B).
Penalties for non-disclosure, §16-2(f).
Procedural requirements, §16-2(h).
Published information, §16-2(d)(3)(D).
Recipients of protection, §16-2(b).
Relevance requirements, §16-2(e)(2).
Review, procedural requirements, §§16-2(h)(1), 16-2(h)(2).
Scope of protection, §16-2(d).
Sources of information, scope of protection, §16-2(d)(1).
Standing issues, recipients of protection, §16-2(b)(2).
State courts, judicial acceptance, §16-2(a)(2).
Subpoenas, avoidance of privilege, §§16-2(j)(1), 16-2(j)(2).
Third-party proceedings, §16-2(c)(2)(A).
Third party subpoenas, avoidance of privilege, §16-2(j)(1).
Unpublished information, §16-2(d)(3)(C).
Waiver, §16-2(g).

CONTEMPT.
Common law, §2-1(c).
Criminal, §§2-1(c), 2-1(d).
Grand jury proceedings, §3-1(a)(2).
Grand jury records, §5-2(a)(3).
Participants in judicial process, access to, §7-1.
Settlement agreements, §6-1(b).
Tape recordings, restraining publication, §2-1(d).

CONTINUANCE.
Judicial proceedings, access to, §2-1(a).
Pretrial hearings, access to, §3-1(a).

CONTRACTS. (*See also* BREACH OF CONTRACT).

Interference with, §13-4(c).
Proposals and bids, access to state government records, §11-7(f)(4).

CONVERSION.
Means of newsgathering, §13-3.

CORONER REPORTS.
State government records, access to, §11-7(d).

CORPORATE PROXY BATTLE.
Civil proceedings, §3-2.

CORRECTIONAL FACILITIES.
Public places and events, access to, §§8-1, 8-2.

COURT CLERKS.
Memorandum addressed to, §6-1(d).
Minute books, §6-1(d).

COURT FILES.
Judicial records, access to, §6-1(c).

COURTS MARTIAL.
Judicial proceedings, access to, §3-1(e).
Judicial records, access to, §5-2(f).

COURT TV.
Cameras in the courtroom, §4-2(a).

CREDENTIALS, PRESS.
Executive and legislative branches, access to, §9-2(a).

CRIME, ACCUSATION OF.
Government in the Sunshine Act exemptions, §9-5(a)(8)(E).

CRIME SCENES.
Nongovernmental places, newsgathering in, §12-3.
Public places and events, access to, §8-3.

CRIMINAL CONDUCT.
Means of newsgathering, §13-3. (*See* MEANS OF NEWSGATHERING).

CRIMINAL CONTEMPT, §§2-1(c), 2-1(d).

CRIMINAL HARASSMENT.
Means of newsgathering, §13-3(c)(2).

CRIMINAL HISTORIES.
Judicial proceedings, access to, §2-1(a).
Police records, access to, §11-7(b)(4).

INDEX

CRIMINAL JUSTICE ACT VOUCHERS.
Judicial records, access to, §5-2(e).

CRIMINAL LIABILITY.
Means of newsgathering, §13-3(c).

CRIMINAL PROCEEDINGS.
Agent or surrogate, press as, §1-4(b).
Cameras in the courtroom, §4-3.
Constitutional privilege, §16-2(c)(1).
Grand jury records, §5-2(a)(3).
Information and indictment, §5-2(a)(4).
Judicial proceedings, access to, §3-1.
Judicial records, access to, §§5-1, 5-2.
Juvenile proceedings, §3-3(a).
Nebraska bar-press guidelines, restraining publication, §2-1(d).
Right of access, §1-5.
State Shield laws, §15-2(c)(1).
Suppression hearings, §5-2(a)(7).
Supreme Court, constitutional right of access in, §§2-2(a), 2-2(c), 2-2(f), 2-2(h), 2-3.
Trespass, means of newsgathering, §13-3(c)(1).

CRIMINAL SANCTIONS AGAINST MEDIA.
Judicial proceedings, access to, §2-1(c).

CRIMINAL TRESPASS.
Means of newsgathering, §13-3(c)(1).

CRITICISM OF GRAND JURY INSTRUCTIONS, SHERIFF'S, §2-1(c).

CUSTODY.
Cameras in the courtroom, §4-3.
Privacy interests, §3-2(b).

D

DANGER, FINDINGS OF.
Criminal trials, §3-1(c).

DEATH PENALTY.
Executions, access to public places and events, §8-2.
Voir dire, §3-1(b).

DEFAMATION.
Discovery, §6-1(a)(2).

Sources and interview subjects, §13-4(a)(1)(A).

DEFENSE CONTRACTING INDUSTRY.
Search warrants, §5-2(a)(2).

DEFINED TERMS.
"Advisory Committee," Federal Advisory Committee Act, §9-5(b)(2).
"Meeting," Government in the Sunshine Act, §9-5(a)(3).
Recipients of protection, constitutional privilege, §16-2(b)(1).
State Shield laws, §15-2(b)(1).

DELAY.
Supreme Court, constitutional right of access in, §2-3.

DELINQUENCY PROCEEDINGS.
Transcripts and records, access to, §6-2(a).

DEMOCRATIC MODEL.
Rationale of preference, §1-2(b).

DEPARTMENT OF JUSTICE. (*See* JUSTICE DEPARTMENT).

DEPOSITIONS.
Judicial proceedings, access to, §3-2(e).

DETENTION. (*See* BAIL AND DETENTION).

DISASTER SCENES.
Nongovernmental places, newsgathering in, §12-3.
Public places and events, access to, §8-3.

DISCIPLINARY MATTERS.
Criminal sanctions against media, §2-1(c).
Gag orders, §7-2.
State and local government, statutory access to meetings of, §§9-6(i)(1)(C), 9-6(i)(6).
State government records, access to, §11-7(a)(3).

DISCLOSURE, EXEMPTIONS.
Freedom of Information Act, §10-2(c)(4).
Government in the Sunshine Act, §§9-5(a)(8)(C), 9-5(a)(8)(I).
State and local government, statutory access to meetings of, §9-6(h)(2).
State government records, access to, §11-5.

INDEX

DISCOVERY.
Judicial records, access to, §§5-2(a)(5), 6-1(a).

DISCRIMINATORY ACCESS.
Executive and legislative branches, access to, §9-2(b).

DISMISSAL OF CHARGES.
Judicial records, access to, §5-1.

DISORDERLY CONDUCT.
Disaster, accident and crime scenes, §8-3.
Means of newsgathering, §13-3(c)(3).

DISQUALIFICATION OF JUDGE.
Access to pretrial hearings, §3-1(a).
Judicial records, access to, §5-2(a).

DISTRICT OF COLUMBIA.
Plea agreements, §5-2(a)(9).

DIVORCE.
Cameras in the courtroom, §4-3.
Privacy interests, §3-2(b).

DOCKET.
Pretrial hearings, access to, §3-1(a).
Search warrants, §5-2(a)(2).

DOCTORS.
Court records, §6-1(d).
Criminal trials, §3-1(c).

DOCUMENTARY EVIDENCE.
Grand jury records, §5-2(a)(3).

DONAHUE, PHIL.
Executions, access to, §8-2.

DOVER AIR FORCE BASE.
Military operations, §8-5.

DRUG-RELATED CASES.
Bail and detention, §5-2(a)(8).
Criminal trials, §3-1(c).
Plea agreements, §5-2(a)(9).
Pretrial hearings, access to, §3-1(a).
Voir dire, §3-1(b).
Vouchers, Criminal Justice Act, §5-2(e).

DUE PROCESS.
Cameras in the courtroom, §4-1.
Judicial proceedings, access to, §2-1(a).

E

EDITORIAL PROCESS MATERIALS.
State Shield laws, §15-2(d)(3)(D).

EDUCATIONAL RECORDS.
State government records, access to, §11-7(g).

ELECTIONS.
Public places and events, access to, §8-4.
State government records, access to, §11-7(h).

ELECTRONIC MEDIA. (*See also* CAMERAS IN THE COURTROOM; COMPUTER SYSTEMS; ELECTRONIC SURVEILLANCE).
Tapes. (*See* AUDIO RECORDING; VIDEOTAPES AND RECORDINGS).
Wiretap Act, §13-7(a)(2)(A). (*See* FEDERAL WIRETAP ACT).

ELECTRONIC SURVEILLANCE. (*See also* WIRETAPPING).
Bail and detention hearings, §3-1(a)(1).
Judicial records, access to, §5-2(a)(1).
Suppression hearings, §5-2(a)(7).

EL VOCERO DE PUERTO RICO V. PUERTO RICO.
Supreme Court, constitutional right of access in, §2-2(g).

EMBARRASSMENT.
Court files, §6-1(c).

EMERGENCY COMMUNICATIONS.
Audio recording, §13-7(b)(4)(G).
Police records, access to, §11-7(b)(8).

EMOTIONAL TRAUMA.
Juvenile proceedings, §3-3(a).
Pretrial hearings, access to, §3-1(a).

EMPLOYER AND EMPLOYEE. (*See also* PERSONNEL MATTERS).
Negotiations, statutory access to meetings of state and local government, §9-6(i)(1)(D).

ESPIONAGE.
Means of newsgathering, §13-3(c)(9).
Plea hearings, §3-1(a)(6).

INDEX

ESTABLISHING RIGHT OF ACCESS.
Judicial proceedings, access to, §3-2(a).

ESTOPPEL, PROMISSORY.
Sources and interview subjects, §13-4(a).

EVOLUTION OF JOURNALISTS' PRIVILEGE, §§14-1 to 14-6.
Branzburg v. Hayes, §§14-4 to 14-6.
Chambers opinions, §14-5(f).
Closure of court cases, §14-5(d).
Common law, early, §14-1.
Concurring opinion, §14-4(b).
Consolidated cases, *Branzburg v. Hayes,* §14-3.
Constitutional privilege, early cases, §14-2.
Court closure cases, §14-5(d).
Dissenting opinion, §14-4(c).
Early cases, constitutional privilege, §14-2.
Early common law, §14-1.
Incidental restraint cases, §14-5(c).
Justice Powell's concurring opinion, *Branzburg v. Hayes,* §14-4(b).
Justice Stewart's dissenting opinion, *Branzburg v. Hayes,* §14-4(c).
Lower courts, §14-6.
McIntyre decision, §14-5(e).
Opinion of court, §14-4(a).
Prison access cases, §14-5(a).
Privilege cases, §14-5(b).
Restraint cases, §14-5(c).
Second Circuit approach, §14-6(a).
Sixth Circuit approach, §14-6(b).
Supreme Court, §14-5.

EXAMINATIONS, PROMOTIONAL.
State government records, access to, §11-7(a)(5).

EXCEPTIONS.
Audio recording, §13-7(b)(4).
Federal Wiretap Act, qualified one-party consent, §13-7(a)(2)(A)(iii).
Supreme Court, constitutional right of access in, §2-2(c).

EXCLUSION (C)(1), FREEDOM OF INFORMATION ACT,
§10-2(d)(1).

EXCLUSION (C)(2), FREEDOM OF INFORMATION ACT,
§10-2(d)(2).

EXCLUSION (C)(3), FREEDOM OF INFORMATION ACT,
§10-2(d)(3).

EXCLUSIONS.
Challenge of closure order, excluded party, §2-3.
Freedom of Information Act, §10-2(d).
Juvenile proceedings, mandatory rule of exclusion, §3-3(a).
Suppression hearings, exclusionary rule, §3-1(a)(4).

EXECUTIONS.
Public places and events, access to, §8-2.

EXECUTIVE AND LEGISLATIVE BRANCHES, ACCESS TO, §§9-1 to 9-6.
Administrative proceedings, non-statutory access to, §9-4.
Constitutional overview, §9-1.
Credentials, press, §9-2(a).
Discriminatory access, §9-2(b).
Executive events, non-statutory access to, §9-2.
Federal Advisory Committee Act, §9-5(b). (*See* FEDERAL ADVISORY COMMITTEE ACT).
Federal government meetings, statutory access to, §9-5.
Government in the Sunshine Act, §9-5(a). (*See* GOVERNMENT IN THE SUNSHINE ACT).
Issuance of press credentials, §9-2(a).
Legislative proceedings, non-statutory access to, §9-3.
Non-statutory access.
   Administrative proceedings, §9-4.
   Executive events, §9-2.
   Legislative proceedings, §9-3.
Press credentials, issuance of, §9-2(a).
State and local government, §9-6. (*See* STATE AND LOCAL GOVERNMENT, STATUTORY ACCESS TO MEETINGS OF).
State government records, access to, §§11-3(a), 11-3(b).

INDEX

EXECUTIVE PRIVILEGE.
Grand jury proceedings, §3-1(a)(3).

EXEMPTION 1: NATIONAL SECURITY.
Freedom of Information Act, §10-2(c)(2).
Government in the Sunshine Act, §9-5(a)(8)(A).

EXEMPTION 2: INTERNAL AGENCY PERSONNEL RULES.
Freedom of Information Act, §10-2(c)(3).
Government in the Sunshine Act, §9-5(a)(8)(B).

EXEMPTION 3: DISCLOSURE PROHIBITED BY OTHER FEDERAL STATUTES.
Freedom of Information Act, §10-2(c)(4).
Government in the Sunshine Act, §9-5(a)(8)(C).

EXEMPTION 4: TRADE SECRETS AND CONFIDENTIAL COMMERCIAL INFORMATION.
Freedom of Information Act, §10-2(c)(5).
Government in the Sunshine Act, §9-5(a)(8)(D).

EXEMPTION 5: ACCUSATION OF CRIME OR FORMAL CENSURE.
Government in the Sunshine Act, §9-5(a)(8)(E).

EXEMPTION 5: INTERNAL AGENCY MEMORANDA AND POLICY DISCUSSIONS.
Freedom of Information Act, §10-2(c)(6).

EXEMPTION 6: PERSONAL PRIVACY.
Freedom of Information Act, §10-2(c)(7).
Government in the Sunshine Act, §9-5(a)(8)(F).

EXEMPTION 7: LAW ENFORCEMENT INVESTIGATIONS.
Freedom of Information Act, §10-2(c)(8).
Government in the Sunshine Act, §9-5(a)(8)(G).

EXEMPTION 7A, FREEDOM OF INFORMATION ACT,
§10-2(c)(8)(A).

EXEMPTION 7B, FREEDOM OF INFORMATION ACT,
§10-2(c)(8)(B).

EXEMPTION 7C, FREEDOM OF INFORMATION ACT,
§10-2(c)(8)(C).

EXEMPTION 7D, FREEDOM OF INFORMATION ACT,
§10-2(c)(8)(D).

EXEMPTION 7E, FREEDOM OF INFORMATION ACT,
§10-2(c)(8)(E).

EXEMPTION 7F, FREEDOM OF INFORMATION ACT,
§10-2(c)(8)(F).

EXEMPTION 8: FINANCIAL INSTITUTIONS.
Freedom of Information Act, §10-2(c)(9).
Government in the Sunshine Act, §9-5(a)(8)(H).

EXEMPTION 9: OIL AND GAS WELLS.
Freedom of Information Act, §10-2(c)(10).

EXEMPTION 9: PREMATURE DISCLOSURE OF INFORMATION.
Government in the Sunshine Act, §9-5(a)(8)(I).

EXEMPTION 10: AGENCY PARTICIPATION IN CIVIL ACTIONS OR PROCEEDINGS.
Government in the Sunshine Act, §9-5(a)(8)(J).

EXEMPTIONS.
Disclosure. (*See* DISCLOSURE, EXEMPTIONS).
Freedom of Information Act, §10-2(c).
Government in the Sunshine Act, §9-5(a)(8).
State and local government, statutory access to meetings of, §9-6(h).

INDEX

EXEMPTIONS—Cont'd
State government records, §11-5. (*See* STATE GOVERNMENT RECORDS, ACCESS TO).
State government records, access to, §11-5(a).

EXEMPT MATERIAL, SEGREGATION OF.
Freedom of Information Act, §10-2(e).
State government records, access to, §11-6.

EXHAUSTION REQUIREMENTS.
Constitutional privilege, §16-2(e)(3).
State Shield laws, §15-2(e)(2)(B).

EXHIBITS, TRIAL.
Discovery materials, filed, §6-1(a)(4).
Preliminary hearings, §5-2(a)(6).
Trade secrets, §3-2(c).

EXIT POLLING.
Voters and polling places, §8-4.

***EX PARTE* TEMPORARY RESTRAINING ORDER,** §2-1(d).

EXPERIMENTAL AUDIOVISUAL COVERAGE.
Cameras in the courtroom, §4-3.

EXPERT WITNESSES.
Vouchers, Criminal Justice Act, §5-2(e).

EXTORTION.
Post-trial matters, §3-1(c).
Voir dire, §3-1(b).

EYEWITNESS TESTIMONY.
Constitutional privilege, §16-2(d)(3)(B).
State Shield laws, §15-2(d)(3)(B).

F

FACA (FEDERAL ADVISORY COMMITTEE ACT), ACCESS TO RECORDS UNDER, §10-3.

"FAILURE OF THE MARKETPLACE," §1-2(a).

FAIR TRIAL/FREE PRESS, CONSTITUTIONAL LAW OF.
Judicial proceedings, access to, §2-1.

FBI (FEDERAL BUREAU OF INVESTIGATION).
Agent misconduct, suppression hearings, §3-1(a)(4).
Sting operation, trial records, §5-2(b).

FCC REGULATIONS.
Audio recording, §13-7(a)(2)(C).

FEDERAL ADVISORY COMMITTEE ACT, §9-5(b).
"Advisory Committee" defined, §9-5(b)(2).
Challenges to closed meetings, §9-5(b)(7).
Closed meetings, challenges to, §9-5(b)(7).
Closure of meetings, §9-5(b)(5).
Definition of "Advisory Committee," §9-5(b)(2).
Federal government records, access to, §10-3.
Meetings, §§9-5(b)(3), 9-5(b)(4), 9-5(b)(5), 9-5(b)(6), 9-5(b)(7).
Notice of meetings, §9-5(b)(4).
Procedures to close meetings, §9-5(b)(5).
Public access to meetings, §9-5(b)(6).

FEDERAL BUREAU OF INVESTIGATION (FBI).
Agent misconduct, suppression hearings, §3-1(a)(4).
Sting operation, trial records, §5-2(b).

FEDERAL CODIFICATION, §15-3.
Administrative regulations, §15-3(b).
Audio recording, §13-7(a).
Computer systems, unauthorized access to, §13-9(a).
Federal Rules of Procedure, §15-3(c).
Federal Wiretap Act, §13-7(a)(2)(A). (*See* FEDERAL WIRETAP ACT).
Freedom of Information Act. (*See* FREEDOM OF INFORMATION ACT (FOIA)).
Freedom of Information Act (FOIA), §10-2.
Government in the Sunshine Act, §9-5(a). (*See* GOVERNMENT IN THE SUNSHINE ACT).
Justice department regulations, §15-3(b).
Search warrants, §15-3(a).

FEDERAL COMMUNICATIONS ACT.
Audio recording, §13-7(a)(2)(B).

FEDERAL COMMUNICATIONS COMMISSION REGULATIONS.
Audio recording, §13-7(a)(2)(C).

FEDERAL COURT PROCEEDINGS.
Cameras in the courtroom, §4-2.
Constitutional privilege, judicial acceptance, §16-2(a)(1).

FEDERAL GOVERNMENT MEETINGS, STATUTORY ACCESS TO, §9-5.

FEDERAL GOVERNMENT RECORDS, ACCESS TO, §§10-1 to 10-3.
Federal Advisory Committee Act, access to records under, §10-3.
Freedom of Information Act, §10-2. (*See* FREEDOM OF INFORMATION ACT (FOIA)).

FEDERAL GOVERNMENT SECRETS AND ESPIONAGE STATUTES.
Means of newsgathering, §13-3(c)(9).

FEDERAL JUDICIAL CENTER.
Cameras in the courtroom, §4-3.

FEDERAL LAW. (*See* FEDERAL CODIFICATION).

FEDERAL RULES OF PROCEDURE.
Federal codifications, §15-3(c).

FEDERAL SYSTEM.
Grand jury proceedings, §3-1(a)(3).

FEDERAL WIRETAP ACT, §13-7(a)(2)(A).
Audio recording, §13-7(a)(2)(A).
Bail and detention hearings, §3-1(a)(1).
Consent, qualified one-party, §13-7(a)(2)(A)(iii).
Exception, qualified one-party consent, §13-7(a)(2)(A)(iii).
One-party consent exception, §13-7(a)(2)(A)(iii).
Prohibited conduct, §13-7(a)(2)(A)(i).
Qualified one-party consent exception, §13-7(a)(2)(A)(iii).

Remedies, §13-7(a)(2)(A)(iv).
Restricted equipment, §13-7(a)(2)(A)(ii).
Sanctions and remedies, §13-7(a)(2)(A)(iv).

FEES AND EXPENSES.
Freedom of Information Act, §10-2(b)(5).
Vouchers, Criminal Justice Act, §5-2(e).

FELONIES.
Juvenile proceedings, §3-3(a).

FINANCIAL INFORMATION.
Discovery, §6-1(a)(2).
State and local government, statutory access to meetings of, §9-6(h)(3).
State government records, access to, §§11-5(a)(3), 11-7(f).

FINANCIAL INSTITUTIONS.
Freedom of Information Act exemptions, §10-2(c)(9).
Government in the Sunshine Act exemptions, §9-5(a)(8)(H).
State government records, access to, §11-5(a)(7).

FINDINGS OF FACT.
Bail and detention hearings, §3-1(a)(2).
Civil proceedings, §3-2.
Closure hearings, §2-3.
Criminal trials, §3-1(c).
Dependency proceedings, §3-3(b).
Judicial records, access to, §5-2(a).
Juvenile proceedings, §3-3(a).
Military courts, §5-2(f).
Plea hearings, §3-1(a)(6).
Pretrial hearings, access to, §3-1(a).
Probable cause, §3-1(a)(2).
Search warrants, §5-2(a)(2).
Supreme Court, constitutional right of access in, §2-2(a).
Trial records, §5-2(b).
United States Army Court of Criminal Appeals, §3-1(e).
Voir dire, §3-1(b).

FIRST AMENDMENT.
Free speech model, §1-5.
Structural model, §1-5.
Supreme Court, constitutional right of access in, §2-2(a).

INDEX

FITNESS HEARINGS.
Juvenile proceedings, §3-3(a).

FLORIDA.
Cameras in the courtroom, §4-3.
Juvenile court records, §6-2(a).

FOIA (FREEDOM OF INFORMATION ACT), §10-2.
(*See* FREEDOM OF INFORMATION ACT (FOIA)).

FORMER JURORS, §7-3.

FOURTEENTH AMENDMENT.
Supreme Court, constitutional right of access in, §2-2(b).

FOURTH AMENDMENT.
Audio recording, §13-7(a)(1).

FRAUD.
Means of newsgathering, §13-2.
Search warrants, §5-2(a)(2).
Voters and polling places, §8-4.

FREEDOM OF EXPRESSION, PRINCIPLE OF, §1-1.

FREEDOM OF INFORMATION ACT (FOIA), §10-2.
Administrative appeals, §10-2(g).
Agency personnel rules, exemptions, §10-2(c)(3).
Agency response time, limitations on, §10-2(b)(4).
Appeals, administrative, §10-2(g).
Banks, exemptions, §10-2(c)(9).
Commercial information, exemptions, §10-2(c)(5).
Confidential commercial information, exemptions, §10-2(c)(5).
Disclosure forbidden by other federal statutes, exemptions, §10-2(c)(4).
Exclusion (c)(1), §10-2(d)(1).
Exclusion (c)(2), §10-2(d)(2).
Exclusion (c)(3), §10-2(d)(3).
Exclusions, §10-2(d).
Exemption 1: national security, §10-2(c)(2).
Exemption 2: internal agency personnel rules, §10-2(c)(3).
Exemption 3: disclosure forbidden by other federal statutes, §10-2(c)(4).
Exemption 4: trade secrets and confidential commercial information, §10-2(c)(5).
Exemption 5: internal agency memoranda and policy discussions, §10-2(c)(6).
Exemption 6: personal privacy, §10-2(c)(7).
Exemption 7: law enforcement investigations, §10-2(c)(8).
Exemption 7A, §10-2(c)(8)(A).
Exemption 7B, §10-2(c)(8)(B).
Exemption 7C, §10-2(c)(8)(C).
Exemption 7D, §10-2(c)(8)(D).
Exemption 7E, §10-2(c)(8)(E).
Exemption 7F, §10-2(c)(8)(F).
Exemption 8: financial institutions, §10-2(c)(9).
Exemption 9: oil and gas wells, §10-2(c)(10).
Exemptions in general, §10-2(c).
Exempt material, segregation of, §10-2(e).
Fees, §10-2(b)(5).
Financial institutions, exemptions, §10-2(c)(9).
Gas and oil wells, exemptions, §10-2(c)(10).
Internal agency memoranda and policy discussions, exemptions, §10-2(c)(6).
Internal agency personnel rules, exemptions, §10-2(c)(3).
Investigations, exemptions, §10-2(c)(8).
Law enforcement investigations, exemptions, §10-2(c)(8).
Limitations on agency response time, §10-2(b)(4).
Litigation, §10-2(h).
Memoranda, exemptions, §10-2(c)(6).
National security, exemptions, §10-2(c)(2).
Obtaining information, §10-2(b).
Oil and gas wells, exemptions, §10-2(c)(10).
Organizations, §10-2(b)(2).
Other federal statutes, disclosure forbidden by, exemptions, §10-2(c)(4).
Personal privacy, exemptions, §10-2(c)(7).
Personnel rules, exemptions, §10-2(c)(3).
Policy discussions, exemptions, §10-2(c)(6).
Procedures, §10-2(b)(3).

INDEX

FREEDOM OF INFORMATION ACT (FOIA)—Cont'd
Records, §10-2(b)(1).
Response time, limitations on, §10-2(b)(4).
Reverse FOIA suits, §10-2(f).
Segregation of exempt material, §10-2(e).
Time, limitations on, §10-2(b)(4).
Trade secrets and confidential commercial information, exemptions, §10-2(c)(5).
Wells, exemptions, §10-2(c)(10).

FREEDOM OF SPEECH. (*See also* FIRST AMENDMENT).
Supreme Court, constitutional right of access in, §2-2(c).

FREEDOM OF THE PRESS. (*See also* FIRST AMENDMENT).
In general, §1-4.
Judicial proceedings, access to, §2-1.
Press clause, §1-4(a).
Supreme Court, constitutional right of access in, §2-2(c).

FREEDOM TO LISTEN.
Supreme Court, constitutional right of access in, §2-2(c).

FREE SPEECH MODEL.
First Amendment, §1-5.

FUNCTIONAL CONSIDERATIONS.
Access to pretrial hearings, §3-1(a).
Civil proceedings, §3-2.
Grand jury proceedings, §3-1(a)(3).
Grand jury records, §5-2(a)(3).
Information and indictment, §5-2(a)(4).
Judicial records, access to, §5-1.
Juvenile proceedings, §3-3(a).
Post-trial matters, §3-1(c).
Pretrial hearings, access to, §3-1(a).
Settlement proceedings, §3-2(d).
Supreme Court, constitutional right of access in, §§2-2(a), 2-2(c), 2-2(h).

G

GAG ORDERS, §2-1(d).
Attorneys, §7-2.
Judicial proceedings, access to, §2-1(a).
Participants in judicial process, access to, §7-1.

GANG-RELATED ARMED ROBBERY.
Juvenile proceedings, §3-3(a).

GANNETT CO. V. DEPASQUALE.
Supreme Court, constitutional right of access in, §2-2(b).

GAS AND OIL WELLS.
Freedom of Information Act exemptions, §10-2(c)(10).
State government records, access to, §11-5(a)(8).

GENERAL RULE OF SECRECY.
Grand jury proceedings, §3-1(a)(2).

GEOLOGICAL INFORMATION.
Freedom of Information Act exemptions, §10-2(c)(10).
State government records, access to, §11-5(a)(8).

GHANA.
Plea hearings, §3-1(a)(6).

GLOBE NEWSPAPER CO. V. SUPERIOR COURT.
Supreme Court, constitutional right of access in, §2-2(d).

GOOD CAUSE.
Competing interests, discovery materials, §6-1(a)(5).

GOVERNMENT IN THE SUNSHINE ACT, §9-5(a).
Accusation of crime or formal censure, exemptions, §9-5(a)(8)(E).
Agencies subject to the Act, §9-5(a)(2).
Agency participation in civil actions or proceedings, exemptions, §9-5(a)(8)(J).
Banks, exemptions, §9-5(a)(8)(H).
Censure, formal, exemptions, §9-5(a)(8)(E).
Challenges to closed meetings, §9-5(a)(9).
Civil actions or proceedings, agency participation in, exemptions, §9-5(a)(8)(J).
Closed meetings, challenges to, §9-5(a)(9).
Closed meetings procedures, §9-5(a)(7).
Commencement of meeting, challenges prior to, §9-5(a)(9)(A).

INDEX

GOVERNMENT IN THE SUNSHINE ACT—Cont'd
Commercial information, confidential, exemptions, §9-5(a)(8)(D).
Confidential commercial information, exemptions, §9-5(a)(8)(D).
Crime, accusation of, exemptions, §9-5(a)(8)(E).
Definition of "meeting," §9-5(a)(3).
Disclosure of information, premature, exemptions, §9-5(a)(8)(I).
Disclosure prohibited by other federal statutes, exemptions, §9-5(a)(8)(C).
Exemption 1: national security, §9-5(a)(8)(A).
Exemption 2: internal agency personnel rules, §9-5(a)(8)(B).
Exemption 3: disclosure prohibited by other federal statutes, §9-5(a)(8)(C).
Exemption 4: trade secrets and confidential commercial information, §9-5(a)(8)(D).
Exemption 5: accusation of crime or formal censure, §9-5(a)(8)(E).
Exemption 6: personal privacy, §9-5(a)(8)(F).
Exemption 7: law enforcement investigations, §9-5(a)(8)(G).
Exemption 8: financial institutions, §9-5(a)(8)(H).
Exemption 9: premature disclosure of information, §9-5(a)(8)(I).
Exemption 10: agency participation in civil actions or proceedings, §9-5(a)(8)(J).
Exemptions, §9-5(a)(8).
Financial institutions, exemptions, §9-5(a)(8)(H).
Internal agency personnel rules, exemptions, §9-5(a)(8)(B).
Investigations, law enforcement, exemptions, §9-5(a)(8)(G).
Law enforcement investigations, exemptions, §9-5(a)(8)(G).
"Meeting," defined, §9-5(a)(3).
National security, exemptions, §9-5(a)(8)(A).
Notice of meetings, §9-5(a)(4).
Other federal statutes, disclosure prohibited by, exemptions, §9-5(a)(8)(C).
Participation by agency in civil actions or proceedings, exemptions, §9-5(a)(8)(J).
Personal privacy, exemptions, §9-5(a)(8)(F).
Personnel rules, internal agency, exemptions, §9-5(a)(8)(B).
Post-meeting challenges, §9-5(a)(9)(B).
Premature disclosure of information, exemptions, §9-5(a)(8)(I).
Prior to commencement of meeting, §9-5(a)(9)(A).
Procedures to close meetings, §9-5(a)(7).
Time of challenges to closed meetings, §9-5(a)(9).
Trade secrets and confidential commercial information, exemptions, §9-5(a)(8)(D).
Transcripts and tapes, access to meeting, §9-5(a)(6).

GOVERNMENT OFFICIALS. (*See* PUBLIC OFFICIALS).

GOVERNMENT PROPERTY, THEFT OF.
Means of newsgathering, §13-3(c)(5).

GOVERNMENT RECORDS.
Federal government records, access to, §§10-1 to 10-3.
Freedom of Information Act, §10-2. (*See* FREEDOM OF INFORMATION ACT (FOIA)).
State government records, §§11-1 to 11-9. (*See* STATE GOVERNMENT RECORDS, ACCESS TO).

GOVERNMENT SECRETS.
Means of newsgathering, §13-3(c)(9).

GRAND JURY.
Access to proceedings, §3-1(a).
Instructions, sheriff's criticism of, §2-1(c).
Judicial proceedings, access to, §3-1(a)(3).
Judicial records, access to, §5-2(a).
Plea hearings, §3-1(a)(6).
Post-trial records, §5-2(d).
Review, §3-1(a)(2).

GRENADA.
Military operations, §8-5.

1273

INDEX

GUARDIANSHIP.
Cameras in the courtroom, §4-3.

GUIDELINES, JUSTICE DEPARTMENT.
Supreme Court, constitutional right of access in, §2-4.

GUILTY PLEA.
Plea hearings, §3-1(a)(6).

H

HANDICAPPED STUDENT.
Privacy interests, §3-2(b).

HARASSMENT.
Cameras in the courtroom, §4-1.
Means of newsgathering, §13-3(c)(2).

HEARINGS. (*See also* SUPPRESSION HEARINGS).
Voir dire, §3-1(b).

HEARSAY.
Court records, §6-1(d).
Judicial proceedings, access to, §2-1(a).

HIDDEN CAMERAS.
Means of newsgathering, §13-8.

HISTORICAL CONSIDERATIONS.
Access to pretrial hearings, §3-1(a).
Civil proceedings, §3-2.
Grand jury.
   Proceedings, §§3-1(a)(2), 3-1(a)(3).
   Records, §5-2(a)(3).
Information and indictment, §5-2(a)(4).
Judicial records, access to, §5-2(a).
Juvenile proceedings, §3-3(a).
Post-trial matters, §3-1(c).
Search warrants, §5-2(a)(2).
Supreme Court, constitutional right of access in, §§2-2(a), 2-2(c), 2-2(d), 2-2(e), 2-2(f), 2-2(h).

I

ILLINOIS DEPARTMENT OF CHILDREN AND FAMILY SERVICES.
Settlement proceedings, §3-2(d).

IMMUNITY DISTINGUISHED FROM PRIVILEGE.
State Shield laws, §15-2(f).

IMPEACHMENT, PRESIDENTIAL.
Grand jury proceedings, §3-1(a)(3).

IMPERSONATION.
Means of newsgathering, §§13-2(b), 13-3(c)(4).

INADMISSIBLE EVIDENCE.
Judicial proceedings, access to, §2-1(a).
Judicial records, access to, §5-2(a).

INADVERTENT INTERCEPTIONS OF COMMUNICATIONS.
Audio recording, §13-7(b)(4)(A).

***IN CAMERA* EXAMINATION.**
Civil proceedings, §3-2.
Constitutional privilege, §16-2(h)(1).
Grand jury records, §5-2(a)(3).
Post-trial matters, §3-1(c).
Pretrial hearings, access to, §3-1(a).
State Shield laws, §15-2(i)(2).
Voir dire proceedings, §3-1(b).

INCARCERATION AND INCARCERATED PERSONS.
(*See* PRISONS AND PRISONERS).

INCIDENTAL RESTRAINT CASES.
Evolution of journalists' privilege, §14-5(c).

INCIDENT REPORTS.
Police records, access to, §11-7(b)(1).

INDICTMENTS.
Grand jury records, §5-2(a)(3).

INFORMANTS.
Police records, access to, §11-7(b)(7).
Supreme Court, constitutional right of access in, §2-3.

INFORMATION, RIGHT TO ACQUIRE AND RIGHT TO KNOW, §1-3.

INFORMATION ACCESS PROVIDER, §6-1(d).

INFORMATION AND INDICTMENT.
Judicial records, access to, §5-2(a)(4).

INJUNCTIVE RELIEF.
Restraining publication, §2-1(d).

INDEX

INJURY TO REPUTATION.
State and local government, statutory access to meetings of, §9-6(h)(4).

INMATES. (*See also* PRISONS AND PRISONERS).
Nongovernmental places, newsgathering in, §12-6(b).
Public places and events, access to, §§8-1, 8-2.

INSTRUCTIONS TO GRAND JURY, SHERIFF'S CRITICISM OF, §2-1(c).

INTER-AGENCY AND INTRA-AGENCY MEMORANDA.
State government records, access to, §11-5(a)(4).

INTERCEPTED COMMUNICATIONS.
Audio recording, §13-7(b)(4)(A).
Judicial records, access to, §5-2(a)(1).
Suppression hearings, §5-2(a)(7).

INTERFERENCE WITH CONTRACT.
Sources and interview subjects, §13-4(c).

INTERNAL AGENCY MEMORANDA AND POLICY DISCUSSIONS.
Freedom of Information Act exemptions, §10-2(c)(6).

INTERNAL AGENCY PERSONNEL RULES AND PRACTICES.
Freedom of Information Act exemptions, §10-2(c)(3).
Government in the Sunshine Act exemptions, §9-5(a)(8)(B).
State government records, access to, §11-5(a)(1).

INTERNET DISCLOSURE.
Grand jury proceedings, §3-1(a)(3).

INTERROGATORIES, §3-2(e).

INTERSTATE TRANSPORTATION OF STOLEN PROPERTY.
Means of newsgathering, §13-3(c)(8)(B).

INTERVIEWS FOR EMPLOYMENT.
State and local government, statutory access to meetings of, §9-6(i)(1)(A).

INTERVIEW SUBJECTS, §13-4. (*See* SOURCES AND INTERVIEW SUBJECTS).

INTIMIDATION.
Voters and polling places, §8-4.

INVASION OF PRIVACY.
State and local government, statutory access to meetings of, §9-6(h)(4).
State government records, access to, §11-5(a)(5).

INVESTIGATIONS.
Freedom of Information Act exemptions, §10-2(c)(8).
Government in the Sunshine Act exemptions, §9-5(a)(8)(G).
Records, access to police records, §11-7(b)(3).
Search warrants, ongoing investigations, §5-2(a)(2).

INVESTIGATORY TECHNIQUES.
Police records, access to, §11-7(b)(9).

IRAN-CONTRA INVESTIGATION, COURT RECORDS, §6-1(d).

ISSUANCE OF PRESS CREDENTIALS.
Executive and legislative branches, access to, §9-2(a).

J

JOINT REPRESENTATION.
Pretrial hearings, access to, §3-1(a).

JOURNALISTS' PRIVILEGE. (*See* PRIVILEGES).

JUDICIAL ACCEPTANCE.
Constitutional privilege, §16-2(a).

JUDICIAL CONFERENCE.
Cameras in the courtroom, §§4-2(a), 4-2(b).

JUDICIAL DISCIPLINARY PROCEEDINGS.
Criminal sanctions against media, §2-1(c).

JUDICIAL DISQUALIFICATION, §5-2(a).
Access to pretrial hearings, §3-1(a).

INDEX

JUDICIAL PROCEEDINGS, ACCESS TO, §§2-1 to 2-4, 3-1 to 3-3.
Abuse, neglect, dependency, and custody proceedings, §3-3(b).
Bail and detention hearings, §3-1(a)(1).
Civil proceedings, §3-2.
Competency hearings, §3-1(a)(5).
Constitutional foundations, §§2-1 to 2-4.
Courts martial, §3-1(e).
Criminal proceedings, §3-1.
Criminal sanctions against media, §2-1(c).
Depositions, §3-2(e).
El Vocero de Puerto Rico v. Puerto Rico, §2-2(g).
Establishing right of access, §3-2(a).
Fair trial/free press, constitutional law of, §2-1.
Free press, constitutional law of, §2-1.
Gannett Co. v. DePasquale, §2-2(b).
Globe Newspaper Co. v. Superior Court, §2-2(d).
Grand jury proceedings, §3-1(a)(3).
Guidelines, Justice Department, §2-4.
Judicial records, access to, §5-2(b).
Justice Department guidelines, §2-4.
Juvenile delinquency, §3-3(a).
Juvenile proceedings, §3-3.
Lower courts, §§3-1, 3-2.
Lower courts in general, §§3-1 to 3-3.
Military courts, §3-1(e).
Perspectives on constitutional right of access, §2-2(a).
Plea hearings, §3-1(a)(6).
Post-trial proceedings, §3-1(d).
Preliminary hearings, §3-1(a)(2).
Press-Enterprise Co. v. Superior Court (Press-Enterprise I), §§2-2(e), 2-2(h).
Press-Enterprise Co. v. Superior Court (Press-Enterprise II), §§2-2(f), 2-2(h).
Pretrial proceedings, §3-1(a).
Privacy interests, §3-2(b).
Procedural requirements, §2-3.
Publication, restraining, §2-1(d).
Restraining publication, §2-1(d).
Richmond Newspapers, Inc. v. Virginia, §2-2(c).
Right of access, establishing, §3-2(a).

Right of access in Supreme Court, constitutional, §2-2.
Sanctions against media, criminal, §2-1(c).
Settlement proceedings, §3-2(d).
Sheppard Mandate, §2-1(b).
Sources and interview subjects, §13-4(a)(2)(A).
Sources and interview subjects, judicial pronouncements prior to, §13-4(a)(1).
State government records, access to, §11-3(c).
Suppression hearings, §3-1(a)(4).
Supreme Court, constitutional right of access in, §2-2.
Trade secrets, §3-2(c).
Trial proceedings, §3-1(c).
Voir dire proceedings, §3-1(b).

JUDICIAL RECORDS, ACCESS TO, §§5-1, 5-2, 6-1, 6-2.
Bail and detention records, §5-2(a)(8).
Civil proceedings, §§6-1, 6-2.
Competing interests, discovery materials, §6-1(a)(5).
Court files, §6-1(c).
Courts martial, §5-2(f).
Criminal Justice Act vouchers, §5-2(e).
Criminal proceedings, §§5-1, 5-2.
Delinquency proceedings, transcripts and records of, §6-2(a).
Detention records, §5-2(a)(8).
Discovery documents, §5-2(a)(5).
Discovery materials, §6-1(a).
Filed discovery materials, §6-1(a)(4).
Grand jury records, §5-2(a)(3).
Information and indictment, §5-2(a)(4).
Jury records, §5-2(c).
Juvenile records, §6-2.
Law reform, discovery materials, §6-1(a)(6).
Military courts, §5-2(f).
Motions, pretrial, §6-1(c)(1).
Plea agreements, §5-2(a)(9).
Pleadings, pretrial, §6-1(c)(1).
Post-trial records, §5-2(d).
Preliminary hearings, §5-2(a)(6).
Pretrial motions, records, and pleadings, §6-1(c)(1).
Pretrial records, §5-2(a).
Records, §§5-2, 6-1, 6-2.

JUDICIAL RECORDS, ACCESS TO—Cont'd
Right of access, sources of, §5-1.
Search warrants, §5-2(a)(2).
Seattle Times Co. v. Rhinehart, discovery materials, §6-1(a)(2).
Settlement agreements, §6-1(b).
Sources of access right, §5-1.
Suppression hearing records, §5-2(a)(7).
Transcripts and records of delinquency proceedings, §6-2(a).
Transcripts of judicial proceedings, §6-1(c)(2).
Trial records, §5-2(b).
Unfiled discovery materials, §6-1(a)(3).
Vouchers, Criminal Justice Act, §5-2(e).
Wiretap records, §5-2(a)(1).

JUDICIAL REVIEW STANDARDS.
Supreme Court, constitutional right of access in, §§2-2(c), 2-2(d).

JURY AND JURORS. (*See also* GRAND JURY; *VOIR DIRE*).
Access to, §7-3.
Cameras in the courtroom, §§4-1, 4-2(b), 4-3.
Checkbook journalism, §7-4.
Judicial proceedings, access to, §2-1(a).
Judicial records, access to, §5-2(c).
Master list, §6-1(d).
Misconduct, post-trial matters, §3-1(c).
Privacy interests, access to pretrial hearings, §3-1(a).
Sequestration, §§2-1(a), 2-1(b).
Sheppard Mandate, §2-1(b).
Suppression hearings, §3-1(a)(4).
Tampering, §7-4.
Testimony, post-trial matters, §3-1(c).

JURY SELECTION. (*See VOIR DIRE*).

JUSTICE DEPARTMENT.
Challenge of closure order, §2-3.
Guidelines, constitutional right of access in Supreme Court, §2-4.
Regulations, federal codifications, §15-3(b).
Supreme Court, constitutional right of access in, §2-2(c).

JUVENILES AND JUVENILE PROCEEDINGS.
Access to judicial proceedings, §3-3.
Access to juvenile records, §6-2.
Cameras in the courtroom, §4-3.
Criminal sanctions against media, §2-1(c).
Delinquency, access to judicial proceedings, §3-3(a).
Pretrial hearings, access to, §3-1(a).
Privacy interests, §3-2(b).

K

KACZYNSKI, THEODORE.
Judicial records, access to, §5-2(a).

KANSAS.
Juvenile court records, §6-2(a).

KIDNAPPING.
Juvenile proceedings, §3-3(a).

KNOWLEDGE, RIGHT TO, §1-3.

L

LABOR NEGOTIATIONS RECORDS.
State government records, access to, §11-7(a)(4).

LAW ENFORCEMENT AND LAW ENFORCEMENT PERSONNEL.
Audio recording, law enforcement monitoring, §13-7(b)(4)(F).
Cameras in the courtroom, §4-1.
Depositions, §3-2(e).
Disaster, accident and crime scenes, §8-3.
Freedom of Information Act exemptions, §10-2(c)(8).
Government in the Sunshine Act exemptions, §9-5(a)(8)(G).
Investigations, §§9-5(a)(8)(G), 10-2(c)(8).
Judicial records, access to, §5-2(a)(1).
Participants in judicial process, access to, §7-1.
Pretrial hearings, access to, §3-1(a).
Records, §11-7(b). (*See* POLICE RECORDS, ACCESS TO).
Safety of personnel, criminal trials, §3-1(c).
Search warrants, §5-2(a)(2).
State government records, access to, §§11-5(a)(6), 11-7(b).

INDEX

LAW ENFORCEMENT AND LAW ENFORCEMENT PERSONNEL—Cont'd
Statutory access to meetings of state and local government, exemptions, §9-6(h)(5).
Suppression hearings, §3-1(a)(4).

LEGISLATIVE BRANCH, §§9-1 to 9-6.
(*See* EXECUTIVE AND LEGISLATIVE BRANCHES, ACCESS TO).

LIBEL TRIAL.
Cameras in the courtroom, §4-2(a).

LIBERTY MODEL.
Rationale of preference, §1-2(c).

LICENSING, PROFESSIONAL.
State and local government, statutory access to meetings of, §9-6(i)(6).

LIMITATIONS ON AGENCY RESPONSE TIME.
Freedom of Information Act, §10-2(b)(4).

LIMITED CLOSURE.
Supreme Court, constitutional right of access in, §2-2(e).

LITIGATION.
Freedom of Information Act, §10-2(h).
State government records, access to, §§11-7(m), 11-9.

"LITTLE GREYSTONE."
Prisons and prisoners, §8-1.

LOCAL COURT RULES.
Cameras in the courtroom, §4-2(a).

LOCAL GOVERNMENT, §9-6. (*See* STATE AND LOCAL GOVERNMENT, STATUTORY ACCESS TO MEETINGS OF).

LOWER COURTS.
Access to judicial proceedings, §§3-1 to 3-3.
Evolution of journalists' privilege, §14-6.

M

MAILS AND MAILING.
Information, right to acquire, §1-3.

Means of newsgathering, mail fraud, §13-3(c)(6).

MARITAL DISSOLUTION PROCEEDING.
Court files, §6-1(c).

MARKETPLACE MODEL.
Rationale of preference, §1-2(a).

MASSACHUSETTS.
Juvenile proceedings, §3-3(a).
Minor sex victims, §2-2(c).

***MCINTYRE* DECISION.**
Evolution of journalists' privilege, §14-5(e).

MCVEIGH, TIMOTHY.
Gag orders, §7-2.
Juror identification, §7-3.
Vouchers, Criminal Justice Act, Oklahoma City bombing, §5-2(e).

MEANS OF NEWSGATHERING, §§13-1 to 13-9.
Audio recording, §13-7. (*See* AUDIO RECORDING).
Cameras, hidden, §13-8.
Civil liability, §13-3(b).
Communications in newsgathering process, §13-6.
Computer systems, unauthorized access to, §13-9.
Constitutional overview, §13-3(a).
Conversion, §13-3.
Criminal conduct, §13-3.
    Civil liability, §13-3(b).
    Constitutional overview, §13-3(a).
    Criminal harassment, §13-3(c)(2).
    Criminal liability, §13-3(c).
    Criminal trespass, §13-3(c)(1).
    Disorderly conduct, §13-3(c)(3).
    Espionage statutes, §13-3(c)(9).
    Federal government secrets and espionage statutes, §13-3(c)(9).
    Government property, theft of, §13-3(c)(5).
    Government secrets, §13-3(c)(9).
    Harassment, §13-3(c)(2).
    Impersonation of public official, §13-3(c)(4).

MEANS OF NEWSGATHERING—
Cont'd
Criminal conduct—Cont'd
  Interstate transportation of stolen
    property, §13-3(c)(8)(B).
  Mail fraud, §13-3(c)(6).
  Pentagon Papers case, §13-3(c)(9)(A).
  Public official, impersonation of,
    §13-3(c)(4).
  Purloined documents, receiving,
    §13-3(c)(8).
  Receiving purloined documents or other
    property, §13-3(c)(8).
  Stolen property, §13-3(c)(8).
  Theft of government property,
    §13-3(c)(5).
  Trespass, §13-3(c)(1).
  Wire fraud, §13-3(c)(7).
Criminal harassment, §13-3(c)(2).
Criminal liability, §13-3(c).
Criminal trespass, §13-3(c)(1).
Disorderly conduct, §13-3(c)(3).
Espionage statutes, §13-3(c)(9).
Federal government secrets and espionage
  statutes, §13-3(c)(9).
Fraud, §13-2.
Government property, theft of,
  §13-3(c)(5).
Government secrets, §13-3(c)(9).
Harassment, §13-3(c)(2).
Hidden cameras, §13-8.
Impersonation in newsgathering, §13-2(b).
Impersonation of public official,
  §13-3(c)(4).
Interstate transportation of stolen property,
  §13-3(c)(8)(B).
Interview subjects, §13-4. (*See* SOURCES
  AND INTERVIEW SUBJECTS).
Mail fraud, §13-3(c)(6).
Misrepresentation in newsgathering,
  §13-2(a).
Pentagon Papers case, §13-3(c)(9)(A).
Public official, impersonation of,
  §13-3(c)(4).
Purloined documents, receiving,
  §13-3(c)(8).
Receiving purloined documents or other
  property, §13-3(c)(8).
Recording, audio, §13-7.

Sources and interview subjects, §13-4.
  (*See* SOURCES AND INTERVIEW
  SUBJECTS).
Stake outs, §13-5.
Stolen documents, §13-3.
Stolen property, §13-3(c)(8).
Theft, §13-3.
Theft of government property, §13-3(c)(5).
Trespass, §13-3(c)(1).
Unauthorized access to computer systems,
  §13-9.
Wire fraud, §13-3(c)(7).

MEDICAL MATTERS.
Court records, §6-1(d).
Criminal trials, §3-1(c).
Physicians, §§3-1(c), 6-1(d).
State and local government, statutory
  access to meetings of, §9-6(i)(3).
State government records, access to,
  §11-7(e).

MEETINGS.
Federal Advisory Committee Act,
  §§9-5(b)(3) to 9-5(b)(7).
Government in the Sunshine Act,
  definitions, §9-5(a)(3).
State and local government, §9-6. (*See*
  STATE AND LOCAL
  GOVERNMENT, STATUTORY
  ACCESS TO MEETINGS OF).
State and local government, statutory
  access to meetings of, §§9-6(c),
  9-6(e).

MEMORANDA.
Freedom of Information Act exemptions,
  §10-2(c)(6).
State government records, access to,
  §11-5(a)(4).

MENTAL CONDITIONS.
Competency hearings, §3-1(a)(5).
Consent, §12-6(a).
Privacy interests, §3-2(b).

MENTAL ILLNESS DEFENSE.
Judicial records, access to, §5-2(a).

MICROSOFT CORP.
Depositions, §3-2(e).

MILITARY COURTS.
Judicial proceedings, access to, §3-1(e).

INDEX

MILITARY COURTS—Cont'd
Judicial records, access to, §5-2(f).

MILITARY OPERATIONS.
Public places and events, access to, §8-5.

MINNESOTA.
Sources and interview subjects, §§13-4(a)(2)(B), 13-4(a)(2)(D), 13-4(a)(3)(A).

MINOR'S TESTIMONY.
Abuse, neglect, dependency, and custody proceedings, §3-3(b).
Criminal trials, §3-1(c).
Juvenile proceedings, §3-3(a).
Pretrial hearings, access to, §3-1(a).
Privacy interests, §3-2(b).
Supreme Court, constitutional right of access in, §2-2(c).
Trial records, §5-2(b).

MINUTE BOOKS, §6-1(d).

MINUTES.
Minute books, §6-1(d).
State and local government, statutory access to meetings of, §9-6(f).

MISREPRESENTATION. (*See also* FRAUD).
Means of newsgathering, §13-2(a).

MONITORING OF EMERGENCY COMMUNICATIONS.
Audio recording, §13-7(b)(4)(G).

MOOTNESS.
Challenge of closure order, §2-3.

MOTIONS, PRETRIAL.
Judicial records, access to, §6-1(c)(1).

MOTOR VEHICLE RECORDS.
State government records, access to, §11-7(k).

MURDER CASES.
Juvenile proceedings, §3-3(a).
Pretrial hearings, access to, §3-1(a).
Suppression hearings, §3-1(a)(4).
Supreme Court, constitutional right of access in, §§2-2(e), 2-2(f).
Voir dire, §3-1(b).

N

NATIONAL SECURITY.
Freedom of Information Act exemptions, §10-2(c)(2).
Government in the Sunshine Act exemptions, §9-5(a)(8)(A).
Plea hearings, §3-1(a)(6).
Sources and interview subjects, §13-4(a)(1)(B).
Supreme Court, constitutional right of access in, §2-3.

NATIONWIDE PUBLICITY.
Restraining publication, §2-1(d).

NEBRASKA BAR-PRESS GUIDELINES.
Criminal cases, restraining publication, §2-1(d).

NEGOTIATIONS.
Employer-employee, statutory access to meetings of state and local government, §9-6(i)(1)(D).
Settlement proceedings, §3-2(d).

NEW YORK STATE.
Abuse, neglect, dependency, and custody proceedings, §3-3(b).
Cameras in the courtroom, §4-3.
Juvenile proceedings, §3-3(a).
Sources and interview subjects, §13-4(a)(3)(A).

NICHOLS, TERRY.
Gag orders, §7-2.
Vouchers, Criminal Justice Act, Oklahoma City bombing, §5-2(e).

911 TAPES.
Police records, access to, §11-7(b)(8).

NIXON, RICHARD M.
Watergate scandal, §5-1.

NOLO CONTENDERE PLEA.
Plea hearings, §3-1(a)(6).

NONCONFIDENTIAL INFORMATION.
Constitutional privilege, scope of protection, §16-2(d)(3).
State Shield laws, §15-2(d)(3).

INDEX

NONCONFIDENTIAL SOURCES.
Constitutional privilege, §16-2(d)(3)(A).
State Shield laws, §15-2(d)(3)(A).

NON-DISCLOSURE PENALTIES.
Constitutional privilege, §16-2(f).
State Shield laws, §15-2(g).

NONGOVERNMENTAL ORGANIZATIONS.
State government records, access to, §11-3(e).

NONGOVERNMENTAL PLACES, NEWSGATHERING IN, §§12-1 to 12-6.
Accompanying authorized individuals, §12-5.
Authorized individuals, accompanying, §12-5.
Bars, §12-4(c)(1).
Businesses, private, §12-4(c).
Children and mentally impaired individuals, consent, §12-6(a).
Consent, special issues, §12-6.
Crime and disaster scenes, §12-3.
Disaster scenes, §12-3.
The home, §12-4(a).
Inmates, consent, §12-6(b).
Prisoners, consent, §12-6(b).
Private areas in general, §12-4(c)(3).
Private businesses, §12-4(c).
Private property, §12-4.
Public areas in general, §12-4(c)(2).
Public institutions, §12-4(b).
Public places, §12-2.
Public street, §12-2(a).
Public view, §12-2(b).
Restaurants and bars, §12-4(c)(1).
Street, public, §12-2(a).
View, public, §12-2(b).

NON-JUDICIAL PROCEEDINGS.
State Shield laws, §15-2(c)(2)(C).

NON-STATUTORY ACCESS.
Executive and legislative branches, access to, §§9-2 to 9-4.

NON-TRADITIONAL SUBPOENAS, AVOIDANCE OF PRIVILEGE.
Constitutional privilege, §16-2(j)(2).

NORIEGA, MANUEL ANTONIA.
Tape recordings, restraining publication, §2-1(d).

NOTICE.
Cameras in the courtroom, §§4-2(b), 4-3.
Closure hearings, §2-3.
Criminal trials, §3-1(c).
Federal Advisory Committee Act, §9-5(b)(4).
Government in the Sunshine Act, §9-5(a)(4).
Plea hearings, §3-1(a)(6).
Pretrial hearings, access to, §3-1(a).
Search warrants, §5-2(a)(2).
State and local government, statutory access to meetings of, §§9-6(d), 9-6(j).
Voir dire, §3-1(b).

NUCLEAR POWER.
Settlement proceedings, §3-2(d).

O

OBJECTIONS.
Cameras in the courtroom, §§4-2(a), 4-3.
Court files, §6-1(c).
Trade secrets, §3-2(c).

OBTAINING INFORMATION.
Freedom of Information Act, §10-2(b).

OHIO.
Disaster, accident and crime scenes, §8-3.

OIL AND GAS WELLS.
Freedom of Information Act exemptions, §10-2(c)(10).
State government records, access to, §11-5(a)(8).

OIL COMPANIES.
Pretrial motions, records, and pleadings, §6-1(c)(1).

OKLAHOMA CITY BOMBING.
Gag orders, §7-2.
Vouchers, Criminal Justice Act, §5-2(e).

ONE-PARTY CONSENT EXCEPTION.
Federal Wiretap Act, §13-7(a)(2)(A)(iii).

OPERATION DESERT STORM, §8-5.

OPERATION ILL-WIND.
Search warrants, §5-2(a)(2).

OPINION OF COURT.
Evolution of journalists' privilege, §14-4(a).

ORDERS.
Grand jury records, §5-2(a)(3).

ORGANIZATIONS.
Freedom of Information Act, §10-2(b)(2).
State government records, access to, §11-3.

OTHER STATUTES, DISCLOSURE PROHIBITED BY, EXEMPTIONS.
Freedom of Information Act, §10-2(c)(4).
Government in the Sunshine Act, §9-5(a)(8)(C).
State and local government, statutory access to meetings of, §9-6(h)(2).
State government records, access to, §11-5(a)(2).

OVERRIDING INTERESTS.
Grand jury records, §5-2(a)(3).
Pretrial hearings, access to, §3-1(a).

P

PARTICIPANTS IN JUDICIAL PROCESS, ACCESS TO, §§7-1 to 7-4.
Restraining publication, §2-1(d).

PARTIES. (*See also* STANDING).
State Shield laws, press as party, §15-2(c)(2)(B).

PATERNITY.
Privacy interests, §3-2(b).

PAYING FOR NEWS.
Checkbook journalism, §7-4.
Sources and interview subjects, §13-4(a)(4).

PENALTIES FOR NON-DISCLOSURE.
Constitutional privilege, §16-2(f).
State Shield laws, §15-2(g).

PENDING CASES, COMMENTARY ON.
Criminal sanctions against media, §2-1(c).

PENTAGON PAPERS CASE.
Means of newsgathering, §13-3(c)(9)(A).

PERFORMANCE REVIEWS, PERSONNEL.
State and local government, statutory access to meetings of, §9-6(i)(1)(B).

PER SE **RULE.**
Restraining publication, §2-1(d).

PERSIAN GULF WAR.
Military operations, §8-5.

PERSONAL PRIVACY.
Freedom of Information Act exemptions, §10-2(c)(7).
Government in the Sunshine Act exemptions, §9-5(a)(8)(F).
Invasion of, §§9-6(h)(4), 11-5(a)(5).
State and local government, statutory access to meetings, §9-6(h)(4).
State government records, access to, §11-5(a)(5).

PERSONNEL MATTERS.
Freedom of Information Act exemptions, personnel rules, §10-2(c)(3).
Government in the Sunshine Act exemptions, internal agency rules, §9-5(a)(8)(B).
State and local government, statutory access to meetings of, §§9-6(h)(1), 9-6(i)(1).
State government records, access to, §§11-5(a)(1), 11-7(a).

PERSPECTIVES ON CONSTITUTIONAL RIGHT OF ACCESS.
Judicial proceedings, access to, §2-2(a).

PHOTOGRAPHS.
State government records, access to, §11-7(d).

PHYSICIANS.
Court records, §6-1(d).
Criminal trials, §3-1(c).

PLEA AGREEMENTS.
Judicial records, access to, §5-2(a)(9).

PLEADINGS.
Information and indictment, §5-2(a)(4).

INDEX

PLEADINGS—Cont'd
Judicial records, access to, §6-1(c)(1).

PLEA HEARINGS.
Access to, §3-1(a).
Grand jury records, §5-2(a)(3).
Judicial proceedings, access to, §3-1(a)(6).

POLICE. (*See* LAW ENFORCEMENT AND LAW ENFORCEMENT PERSONNEL).

POLICE BLOTTER.
Police records, access to, §11-7(b)(2).

POLICE MISCONDUCT.
Suppression hearings, §3-1(a)(4).

POLICE RECORDS, ACCESS TO,
§11-7(b).
Accident reports, §11-7(b)(10).
Active files, investigatory records, §11-7(b)(3)(A).
Arrest and incident reports, §11-7(b)(1).
Closed files, investigatory records, §11-7(b)(3)(B).
Compilations of criminal histories, §11-7(b)(4).
Confessions, §11-7(b)(6).
Criminal histories, rap sheets and other compilations of, §11-7(b)(4).
Emergency 911 tapes, §11-7(b)(8).
Incident reports, §11-7(b)(1).
Informants, confidential, §11-7(b)(7).
Investigatory records, §11-7(b)(3).
Investigatory techniques, §11-7(b)(9).
Police blotter, §11-7(b)(2).
Rap sheets and other compilations of criminal histories, §11-7(b)(4).
911 tapes, §11-7(b)(8).
Victim information, §11-7(b)(5).

POLICY DISCUSSIONS.
Freedom of Information Act exemptions, §10-2(c)(6).

POLITICAL CANDIDATES.
Voters and polling places, §8-4.

POLLING PLACES.
Public places and events, access to, §8-4.

POLYGRAPH EXAMINATIONS.
Prisons and prisoners, §8-1.

POOL REPORTERS.
Depositions, §3-2(e).

POST-MEETING CHALLENGES.
Government in the Sunshine Act, §9-5(a)(9)(B).

POST-TRIAL MATTERS.
Judicial proceedings, access to, §3-1(d).
Judicial records, access to, §5-2(d).

PREFERENCE, RATIONALE OF,
§1-2.

PRELIMINARY HEARINGS.
Access to, §3-1(a).
Judicial proceedings, access to, §3-1(a)(2).
Judicial records, access to, §§5-1, 5-2(a)(6).
Supreme Court, constitutional right of access in, §§2-2(a), 2-2(c), 2-2(g).

PRELIMINARY INJUNCTIONS.
Transcripts of judicial proceedings, §6-1(c)(2).

PREMATURE DISCLOSURE OF INFORMATION.
Government in the Sunshine Act exemptions, §9-5(a)(8)(I).

PRESENTENCE REPORTS.
Post-trial records, §5-2(d).

PRESIDENTIAL AIDES.
Grand jury proceedings, §3-1(a)(3).

PRESIDENTIAL DEPUTY CHIEF OF STAFF, §6-1(d).

PRESIDENTIAL IMPEACHMENT.
Grand jury proceedings, §3-1(a)(3).

PRESIDENTIAL TESTIMONY.
Discovery materials, filed, §6-1(a)(4).

PRESS CLAUSE.
Freedom of the press, §1-4(a).

PRESS CREDENTIALS.
Executive and legislative branches, access to, §9-2(a).

1283

INDEX

PRESS-ENTERPRISE CO. V. SUPERIOR COURT (PRESS-ENTERPRISE I).
Supreme Court, constitutional right of access in, §§2-2(e), 2-2(h).

PRESS-ENTERPRISE CO. V. SUPERIOR COURT (PRESS-ENTERPRISE II).
Supreme Court, constitutional right of access in, §§2-2(f), 2-2(h).

PRESUMPTION OF OPENNESS.
Abuse, neglect, dependency, and custody proceedings, §3-3(b).
Grand jury proceedings, §3-1(a)(2).
Grand jury records, §5-2(a)(3).
Suppression hearings, §3-1(a)(4).

PRESUMPTION OF SECRECY.
Grand jury proceedings, §3-1(a)(3).

PRESUMPTIVE RIGHT OF ACCESS.
Abuse, neglect, dependency, and custody proceedings, §3-3(b).
Judicial records, access to, §5-1.
Supreme Court, constitutional right of access in, §2-2(c).

PRETRIAL MATTERS.
Bail and detention hearings, §3-1(a)(1).
Cameras in the courtroom, §4-1.
Criminal trials, §3-1(c).
Depositions, §3-2(e).
Discovery documents, §5-2(a)(5).
Judicial proceedings, access to, §§2-1(a), 3-1(a).
Judicial records, access to, §§5-2(a), 6-1(c)(1).
Military courts, §5-2(f).
Supreme Court, constitutional right of access in, §§2-2(b), 2-2(f), 2-2(h).
Transcripts of judicial proceedings, §6-1(c)(2).

PRETRIAL PUBLICITY.
Suppression hearings, §3-1(a)(4).

PRIOR RESTRAINT DOCTRINE.
Jurors, §7-3.
Juvenile proceedings, §3-3(a).
Participants in judicial process, access to, §7-1.
Restraining publication, §2-1(d).

PRISONS AND PRISONERS.
Consent of prisoners, newsgathering in nongovernmental places, §12-6(b).
Evolution of journalists' privilege, prison access cases, §14-5(a).
Information, right to acquire, §1-3.
Overcrowding, §3-2.
Public places and events, access to, §§8-1, 8-2.
Right of access to prisons, §1-4(a).

PRIVACY INTERESTS.
Invasion of privacy, §§9-6(h)(4), 11-5(a)(5).
Judicial proceedings, access to, §3-2(b).
Jurors', §§2-2(e), 3-1(a), 3-1(b).
Pretrial hearings, access to, §3-1(a).
Search warrants, §5-2(a)(2).
Sources and interview subjects, §13-4(a)(1)(A).
State and local government, statutory access to meetings, §9-6(h)(4).
State government records, access to, §11-5(a)(5).
Voir dire, §3-1(b).

PRIVATE BUSINESSES.
Nongovernmental places, newsgathering in, §12-4(c).

PRIVATE PROPERTY.
Nongovernmental places, newsgathering in, §12-4.

PRIVILEGE CASES.
Evolution of journalists' privilege, §14-5(b).

PRIVILEGE DISTINGUISHED FROM IMMUNITY.
State Shield laws, §15-2(f).

PRIVILEGES.
Common law, §16-3.
Constitutional, §16-2. (*See* CONSTITUTIONAL PRIVILEGE).
Evolution, §§14-1 to 14-6. (*See* EVOLUTION OF JOURNALISTS' PRIVILEGE).

PROBABLE CAUSE.
Hearings, §3-1(a)(2).
Preliminary hearings, §5-2(a)(6).
Suppression hearings, §3-1(a)(4).

INDEX

PROBATION AND PAROLE.
State and local government, statutory access to meetings of, §9-6(i)(2).
State government records, access to, §11-7(c).

PROFESSIONAL LICENSING.
State and local government, statutory access to meetings of, §9-6(i)(6).

PROMISSORY ESTOPPEL.
Sources and interview subjects, §13-4(a).

PROMOTIONAL EXAMINATIONS.
State government records, access to, §11-7(a)(5).

PROPOSALS AND BIDS.
State government records, access to, §11-7(f)(4).

PROPRIETARY INFORMATION.
State government records, access to, §11-7(i).

PROTECTIVE ORDERS.
Competing interests, discovery materials, §6-1(a)(5).
Discovery, §6-1(a)(2).
Discovery materials, unfiled, §6-1(a)(3).
Trade secrets, §3-2(c).

PSEUDONYMS.
Criminal trials, §3-1(c).

PSYCHIATRISTS AND PSYCHIATRIC MATTERS.
Privacy interests, §3-2(b).
State and local government, statutory access to meetings of, §9-6(i)(3).

PSYCHOLOGICAL HARM.
Abuse, neglect, dependency, and custody proceedings, §3-3(b).
Criminal trials, victims, §3-1(c).

PSYCHOLOGISTS.
Privacy interests, §3-2(b).

PSYCHOSEXUAL EVALUATION.
Post-trial records, §5-2(d).

PUBLIC AFFAIRS.
Agent or surrogate, press as, §1-4(b).

PUBLIC AREAS.
Nongovernmental places, newsgathering in, §12-4(c)(2).

PUBLIC ASSISTANCE.
State and local government, statutory access to meetings of, §9-6(i)(5).

PUBLICATION, RESTRAINING.
Judicial proceedings, §2-1(d).
Juvenile proceedings, §3-3(a).

PUBLICATIONS, RIGHT TO RECEIVE, §1-3.

PUBLIC DOCKET.
Pretrial hearings, access to, §3-1(a).

PUBLIC FIGURES.
Depositions, §3-2(e).

PUBLIC FORUM.
Disaster, accident and crime scenes, §8-3.
Military operations, §8-5.
Supreme Court, constitutional right of access in, §2-2(c).
Voters and polling places, §8-4.

PUBLIC INSTITUTIONS.
Newsgathering in nongovernmental places, §12-4(b).

PUBLIC INTEREST MATTERS.
Depositions, §3-2(e).
Grand jury records, §5-2(a)(3).
Juvenile proceedings, §3-3(a).
Search warrants, §5-2(a)(2).
Settlement proceedings, §3-2(d).

PUBLICITY.
Juvenile proceedings, §3-3(a).
Pretrial hearings, access to, §3-1(a).
Sheppard Mandate, §2-1(b).
Supreme Court, constitutional right of access in, §§2-2(b), 2-2(f).
Voir dire, §3-1(b).

PUBLIC OFFICES.
Audits, access to state government records, §11-7(f)(6).

PUBLIC OFFICIALS.
Agent or surrogate, press as, §1-4(b).
Bribery of, §5-2(a)(4).
Impersonation, means of newsgathering, §13-3(c)(4).

1285

INDEX

PUBLIC OFFICIALS—Cont'd
Information, right to acquire, §1-3.
Information and indictment, §5-2(a)(4).
Suppression hearings, §3-1(a)(4).

PUBLIC PLACES AND EVENTS, ACCESS TO, §§8-1 to 8-5.
Accident scenes, §8-3.
Audio recording, §13-7(b)(4)(B).
Correctional facilities, §§8-1, 8-2.
Crime scenes, §8-3.
Disaster scenes, §8-3.
Elections, §8-4.
Executions, §8-2.
Inmates, §§8-1, 8-2.
Military operations, §8-5.
Nongovernmental places, newsgathering in, §12-2.
Polling places, §8-4.
Prisons and prisoners, §§8-1, 8-2.
Voters, §8-4.

PUBLIC POLICY.
Settlement proceedings, §3-2(d).

PUBLIC SAFETY MATTERS.
State and local government, statutory access to meetings of, §9-6(h)(5).

PUBLIC SCHOOL.
Privacy interests, §3-2(b).

PUBLIC STREET.
Nongovernmental places, newsgathering in, §12-2(a).

PUBLIC UTILITY RECORDS.
State government records, access to, §11-7*(l)*.

PUBLIC VIEW.
Nongovernmental places, newsgathering in, §12-2(b).

PUBLISHED INFORMATION.
Constitutional privilege, §16-2(d)(3)(D).
State Shield laws, §15-2(d)(3)(E).

PUERTO RICO.
Bail and detention hearings, §3-1(a)(2).
Closure of preliminary hearings, §2-2(g).

PURLOINED DOCUMENTS, RECEIVING.
Means of newsgathering, §13-3(c)(8).

Q

QUALIFIED ONE-PARTY CONSENT EXCEPTION.
Federal Wiretap Act, §13-7(a)(2)(A)(iii).

QUALIFIED PRIVILEGE.
State Shield laws, §15-2(e)(2).

QUASHAL OF SUBPOENAS.
Grand jury records, §5-2(a)(3).

QUESTIONNAIRE.
Transcripts of *voir dire,* §5-2(c).
Voir dire, §3-1(b).

QUI TAM **ACTIONS.**
Grand jury records, §5-2(a)(3).

R

RACIST KILLINGS.
Plea hearings, §3-1(a)(6).

RACKETEERING.
Post-trial matters, §3-1(c).

RAPE CASES.
Supreme Court, constitutional right of access in, §§2-2(c), 2-2(e).

RAP SHEETS AND OTHER COMPILATIONS OF CRIMINAL HISTORIES.
Police records, access to, §11-7(b)(4).

RATIONALE OF PREFERENCE, §1-2.
Democratic model, §1-2(b).
Liberty model, §1-2(c).
Marketplace model, §1-2(a).

REAGAN, RONALD.
Discovery documents, §5-2(a)(5).

REAL ESTATE APPRAISALS.
State government records, access to, §11-7(f)(5).

REASONABLENESS STANDARD.
Supreme Court, constitutional right of access in, §2-2(d).

RECEIVING PURLOINED DOCUMENTS OR OTHER PROPERTY.
Means of newsgathering, §13-3(c)(8).

INDEX

RECIPIENTS OF PROTECTION.
Constitutional privilege, §16-2(b).
State Shield laws, §15-2(b).

RECORD FINDINGS. (*See* FINDINGS OF FACT).

RECORDING. (*See also* AUDIO RECORDING).
Audio recording, §13-7. (*See* AUDIO RECORDING).
Cameras in the courtroom, §§4-1 to 4-3. (*See* CAMERAS IN THE COURTROOM).

RECORDS.
Freedom of Information Act, §10-2(b)(1).
Grand jury records, §5-2(a)(3).
Judicial records, §§5-1, 5-2, 6-1, 6-2. (*See* JUDICIAL RECORDS, ACCESS TO).
Police records, §11-7(b). (*See* POLICE RECORDS, ACCESS TO).
Search warrants, §5-2(a)(2).
State government records, §§11-1 to 11-9. (*See* STATE GOVERNMENT RECORDS, ACCESS TO).
Supreme Court, constitutional right of access in, §2-2(f).

REDACTED MATERIAL.
Grand jury records, §5-2(a)(3).

REHABILITATIVE IDEAL.
Juvenile proceedings, §3-3(a).

RELEVANCE REQUIREMENTS.
Constitutional privilege, §16-2(e)(2).
State Shield laws, §15-2(e)(2)(A).

REMEDIES.
Audio recording, §§13-7(a)(2)(A)(iv), 13-7(b)(5).
Federal Wiretap Act, §13-7(a)(2)(A)(iv).

REPRESENTATIVE OF THE PRESS.
Supreme Court, constitutional right of access in, §2-3.

REPUTATION.
Court files, §6-1(c).
State and local government, statutory access to meetings of, §9-6(h)(4).
Trade secrets, §3-2(c).

RESPONSE TIME LIMITATIONS.
Freedom of Information Act, §10-2(b)(4).

RESTAURANTS AND BARS.
Nongovernmental places, newsgathering in, §12-4(c)(1).

RESTRAINING PUBLICATION.
Judicial proceedings, access to, §2-1(d).

RESTRAINT CASES.
Evolution of journalists' privilege, §14-5(c).

RESTRICTED EQUIPMENT.
Federal Wiretap Act, §13-7(a)(2)(A)(ii).

RETAINED COUNSEL.
Vouchers, Criminal Justice Act, §5-2(e).

REVERSE FREEDOM OF INFORMATION ACT SUITS, §10-2(f).

REVIEW. (*See also* APPELLATE REVIEW).
Constitutional privilege, procedural requirements, §§16-2(h)(1), 16-2(h)(2).

RHODE ISLAND.
Cameras in the courtroom, §4-3.

RICHMOND NEWSPAPERS, INC. V. VIRGINIA.
Supreme Court, constitutional right of access in, §2-2(c).

RIGHT OF ACCESS.
Judicial proceedings, access to, §§2-2, 3-2(a).
Judicial records, access to, §5-1.
Supreme Court, constitutional, §2-2.

RIGHTS OF THE PUBLIC.
As interchangeable with rights of press, §2-2(h).

RIGHT TO ACQUIRE INFORMATION AND THE RIGHT TO KNOW, §1-3.

RIGHT TO KNOW, §1-3.

RIGHT TO PUBLISH.
Supreme Court, constitutional right of access in, §2-2(f).

INDEX

RIGHT TO RECEIVE PUBLICATIONS, §1-3.

ROBBERY.
Juvenile proceedings, §3-3(a).

ROBING ROOM, JUDGE'S. (*See* CHAMBERS CONFERENCES AND OPINIONS).

RUZICKA V. CONDE NAST PUBLICATIONS.
Sources and interview subjects, §13-4(a)(3)(A)(ii).

S

SAFE HARBOR PROVISIONS.
Gag orders, §7-2.

SAFETY INTERESTS.
Disaster, accident and crime scenes, §8-3.
Search warrants, §5-2(a)(2).

SALARY INFORMATION.
State government records, access to, §11-7(a)(2).

SANCTIONS AND REMEDIES.
Audio recording, §§13-7(a)(2)(A)(iv), 13-7(b)(5).
Federal Wiretap Act, §13-7(a)(2)(A)(iv).
Judicial proceedings access, criminal sanctions against media, §2-1(c).

SCHOOL DISTRICT.
Privacy interests, §3-2(b).

SEALED RECORDS AND TRANSCRIPTS. (*See also* CLOSED MEETINGS AND PROCEEDINGS).
Judicial records, access to, §5-1.
Justice Department guidelines, §2-3.
Supreme Court, constitutional right of access in, §§2-2(f), 2-3.
Trade secrets, §3-2(c).
Trade secrets, sealed opinion, §3-2(c).

SEARCH WARRANTS.
Federal codifications, §15-3(a).
Judicial records, access to, §§5-2(a)(1), 5-2(a)(2).

SEATTLE TIMES CO. V. RHINEHART, **DISCOVERY MATERIALS.**
Judicial records, access to, §6-1(a)(2).

SECOND CIRCUIT APPROACH.
Evolution of journalists' privilege, §14-6(a).

SECRECY PRESUMPTION.
Grand jury proceedings, §3-1(a)(3).

SECRECY RULE.
Grand jury records, §5-2(a)(3).

SECURITIES LAWS.
Discovery documents, §5-2(a)(5).

SEGREGATION OF EXEMPT MATERIAL.
Freedom of Information Act, §10-2(e).
State government records, access to, §11-6.

SEIZURE OF EVIDENCE.
Suppression hearings, §3-1(a)(4).

SELECTIVE ACCESS.
Criminal trials, §3-1(c).

SENSATIONALIZED CASES.
Cameras in the courtroom, §4-1.
Judicial proceedings, access to, §2-1(a).
Participants in judicial process, access to, §7-1.

SENTENCE REDUCTION HEARING, §3-1(c).

SENTENCING HEARINGS.
Post-trial matters, §3-1(c).
Post-trial records, §5-2(d).

SEQUESTRATION OF JURY.
Criminal trials, §3-1(c).
Judicial proceedings, access to, §2-1(a).
Sheppard Mandate, §2-1(b).

SETTLEMENT AND SETTLEMENT AGREEMENTS.
Access to judicial records, §6-1(b).
Discovery materials, filed, §6-1(a)(4).
Proceedings, access to judicial proceedings, §3-2(d).

SEXUAL OFFENSE VICTIMS.
Cameras in the courtroom, §4-3.
Criminal trials, §3-1(c).
Pretrial hearings, access to, §3-1(a).

1288

SEXUAL OFFENSE VICTIMS—Cont'd
Pretrial motions, records, and pleadings, §6-1(c)(1).
Privacy interests, §3-2(b).
Supreme Court, constitutional right of access in, §2-2(c).

SHEPPARD **MANDATE.**
Judicial proceedings, access to, §2-1(b).

SHERIFF.
Criticism of grand jury instructions, §2-1(c).
Vouchers, Criminal Justice Act, §5-2(e).

SHERMAN ACT.
Depositions, §3-2(e).

SHIELD LAWS, §15-2. (*See* STATE SHIELD LAWS).

SIMPSON, O.J., TRIAL OF.
Cameras in the courtroom, §4-3.
Checkbook journalism, §7-4.

SIXTH AMENDMENT.
Suppression hearings, §3-1(a)(4).
Supreme Court, constitutional right of access in, §2-2(a).

SIXTH CIRCUIT APPROACH.
Evolution of journalists' privilege, §14-6(b).

SKETCH ARTISTS.
Criminal trials, §3-1(c).

SOURCES AND INTERVIEW SUBJECTS, §13-4.
Ambush interview, §13-4(b).
Breach of contract and promissory estoppel, §13-4(a).
Checkbook journalism, §§7-4, 13-4(a)(4).
Cohen-inspired and related causes of action, §13-4(a)(3).
Cohen v. Cowles Media Co., §13-4(a)(2).
Constitutional privilege, scope of protection, §16-2(d)(1).
Contract, interference with, §13-4(c).
Contract breach, §13-4(a).
Defamation and privacy context, §13-4(a)(1)(A).
Interference with contract, §13-4(c).
Judicial pronouncements prior to, §13-4(a)(1).
Minnesota, §§13-4(a)(2)(B), 13-4(a)(2)(D), 13-4(a)(3)(A).
Minnesota Appellate Courts, §§13-4(a)(2)(B), 13-4(a)(2)(D).
National security context, §13-4(a)(1)(B).
New York experiences, §13-4(a)(3)(A).
Paying for news, §13-4(a)(4).
Prisons and prisoners, §8-1.
Privacy context, §13-4(a)(1)(A).
Promissory estoppel and breach of contract, §13-4(a).
Ruzicka v. Conde Nast Publications, §13-4(a)(3)(A)(ii).
State Shield laws, §15-2(d)(1).
Supreme Court, §13-4(a)(2)(C).
Trial court proceedings, §13-4(a)(2)(A).
Voters and polling places, §8-4.

SOURCES OF ACCESS RIGHT.
Judicial records, access to, §5-1.

SPECIAL BROADCAST RULES.
State Shield laws, §15-2(i)(4).

SPECIAL INTERESTS.
Juvenile proceedings, §3-3(a).

STAKE OUTS.
Means of newsgathering, §13-5.

STANDARDS.
Criminal trials, §3-1(c).

STANDARDS FOR CRIMINAL JUSTICE, AMERICAN BAR ASSOCIATION'S.
Cameras in the courtroom, §4-1.

STANDARDS OF JUDICIAL REVIEW.
Supreme Court, constitutional right of access in, §§2-2(c), 2-2(d).

STANDING.
Challenge of closure order, §2-3.
Constitutional privilege, recipients of protection, §16-2(b)(2).
State Shield laws, §15-2(b)(2).

STARR, KENNETH.
Grand jury proceedings, §3-1(a)(3).

INDEX

STATE AND LOCAL GOVERNMENT, STATUTORY ACCESS TO MEETINGS OF, §9-6.
Categories of meetings, §9-6(i).
Challenges to improperly noticed or closed meetings, §9-6(j).
Civil litigation matters, exemptions, §9-6(h)(6).
Closed meetings, challenges to, §9-6(j).
Collective bargaining, §9-6(i)(1)(D).
Commercial information, exemptions, §9-6(h)(3).
Confidential financial and commercial information, exemptions, §9-6(h)(3).
Disciplinary matters, personnel, §9-6(i)(1)(C).
Disciplinary proceedings, professional, §9-6(i)(6).
Disclosure prohibited by other laws, exemptions, §9-6(h)(2).
Employer-employee negotiations and collective bargaining, §9-6(i)(1)(D).
Entities subject to open meeting laws, §9-6(b).
Exemptions, §9-6(h).
Financial information, exemptions, §9-6(h)(3).
Improperly noticed or closed meetings, challenges to, §9-6(j).
Injury to reputation, exemptions, §9-6(h)(4).
Interviews for employment, §9-6(i)(1)(A).
Invasion of personal privacy, exemptions, §9-6(h)(4).
Law enforcement matters, exemptions, §9-6(h)(5).
Licensing, professional, §9-6(i)(6).
Medical or psychiatric matters, §9-6(i)(3).
Meetings, access to, §9-6(e).
Meetings subject to open meeting laws, §9-6(c).
Minutes, access to, §9-6(f).
Negotiations, employer-employee, §9-6(i)(1)(D).
Notice, challenges to improperly noticed meetings, §9-6(j).
Notice requirements, §9-6(d).
Other laws, disclosure prohibited by, exemptions, §9-6(h)(2).
Performance reviews, personnel, §9-6(i)(1)(B).
Personal privacy, exemptions, §9-6(h)(4).
Personnel matters, §§9-6(h)(1), 9-6(i)(1).
Probation and parole boards, §9-6(i)(2).
Procedures, §9-6(g).
Professional licensing and disciplinary proceedings, §9-6(i)(6).
Psychiatric matters, §9-6(i)(3).
Public assistance, matters involving, §9-6(i)(5).
Public safety matters, exemptions, §9-6(h)(5).
Reputation, exemptions, §9-6(h)(4).
Student information, §9-6(i)(4).
Tapes, access to, §9-6(f).
Transcripts, access to, §9-6(f).

STATE CONSTITUTIONS.
Privacy interests, §3-2(b).

STATE COURTS.
Cameras in the courtroom, §4-3.
Constitutional privilege, judicial acceptance, §16-2(a)(2).

STATE GOVERNMENT.
Meetings, §9-6. (*See* STATE AND LOCAL GOVERNMENT, STATUTORY ACCESS TO MEETINGS OF).
Records, §§11-1 to 11-9. (*See* STATE GOVERNMENT RECORDS, ACCESS TO).

STATE GOVERNMENT RECORDS, ACCESS TO, §§11-1 to 11-9.
Accident reports, §11-7(b)(10).
Active files, investigatory records, §11-7(b)(3)(A).
Administrative appeals, §11-8.
Advisory committees, §11-3(d).
Appeals, administrative, §11-8.
Applications for employment, §11-7(a)(1).
Appraisals, real estate, §11-7(f)(5).
Arrest and incident reports, §11-7(b)(1).
Audits of public offices, §11-7(f)(6).
Autopsy reports, §11-7(d).
Bank records, §11-7(f)(3).
Banks, §11-5(a)(7).
Bids and proposals, contract, §11-7(f)(4).
Business records, §11-7(f)(1).

INDEX

STATE GOVERNMENT RECORDS, ACCESS TO—Cont'd
Categories of records, §11-7.
Closed files, investigatory records, §11-7(b)(3)(B).
Committees, advisory, §11-3(d).
Common law exemptions, §11-5(c).
Compilations of criminal histories, §11-7(b)(4).
Confessions, §11-7(b)(6).
Contract proposals and bids, §11-7(f)(4).
Coroner reports, autopsy reports, and photographs, §11-7(d).
Criminal histories, rap sheets and other compilations of, §11-7(b)(4).
Disciplinary records, §11-7(a)(3).
Disclosure, exemptions from, §11-5.
Educational records, §11-7(g).
Election records, §11-7(h).
Emergency 911 tapes, §11-7(b)(8).
Examinations, promotional, §11-7(a)(5).
Executive branch, §11-3(a).
Exemptions from disclosure, §11-5.
  Banks, §11-5(a)(7).
  Common law exemptions, §11-5(c).
  Financial information, §11-5(a)(3).
  Financial institution records, §11-5(a)(7).
  Gas wells, geological information relating to, §11-5(a)(8).
  Geological information relating to oil and gas wells, §11-5(a)(8).
  Inter-agency and intra-agency memoranda, §11-5(a)(4).
  Internal agency personnel rules and practices, §11-5(a)(1).
  Invasion of privacy, disclosures constituting an, §11-5(a)(5).
  Law enforcement records, §11-5(a)(6).
  Memoranda, inter-agency and intra-agency, §11-5(a)(4).
  Oil and gas wells, geological information relating to, §11-5(a)(8).
  Other statutes, disclosures forbidden by, §11-5(a)(2).
  Personnel rules and practices, internal, §11-5(a)(1).
  Privacy, disclosures constituting an invasion of, §11-5(a)(5).
  Statutory exemptions, §11-5(a).
  Trade secrets and certain financial information, §11-5(a)(3).
  Unwarranted invasion of privacy, disclosures constituting an, §11-5(a)(5).
  Waiver of exemptions, §11-5(d).
  Wells, oil and gas, §11-5(a)(8).
Exempt material, segregation of, §11-6.
Financial data, §11-7(f)(2).
Financial information, §§11-5(a)(3), 11-7(f).
Financial institution records, §11-5(a)(7).
Gas wells, geological information relating to, §11-5(a)(8).
Geological information relating to oil and gas wells, §11-5(a)(8).
Incident reports, §11-7(b)(1).
Informants, confidential, §11-7(b)(7).
Inter-agency and intra-agency memoranda, §11-5(a)(4).
Internal agency personnel rules and practices, §11-5(a)(1).
Invasion of privacy, disclosures constituting an, §11-5(a)(5).
Investigatory records, §11-7(b)(3).
Investigatory techniques, §11-7(b)(9).
Judicial branch, §11-3(c).
Labor negotiations, records of, §11-7(a)(4).
Law enforcement records, §§11-5(a)(6), 11-7(b).
Legislative branch, §11-3(b).
Litigation, §11-9.
Litigation records, §11-7(m).
Medical records, §11-7(e).
Memoranda, inter-agency and intra-agency, §11-5(a)(4).
Motor vehicle records, §11-7(k).
911 tapes, §11-7(b)(8).
Nongovernmental organizations, §11-3(e).
Oil and gas wells, geological information relating to, §11-5(a)(8).
Organizations, §11-3.
Other statutes, disclosures forbidden by, §11-5(a)(2).
Personnel records, §11-7(a).
Personnel rules and practices, internal, §11-5(a)(1).

INDEX

STATE GOVERNMENT RECORDS, ACCESS TO—Cont'd
Photographs, coroner reports, autopsy reports, §11-7(d).
Police blotter, §11-7(b)(2).
Police records, §11-7(b).
Privacy, disclosures constituting an invasion of, §11-5(a)(5).
Probation and parole reports, §11-7(c).
Procedures in general, §11-4.
Promotional examinations, §11-7(a)(5).
Proposals and bids, contract, §11-7(f)(4).
Proprietary information, §11-7(i).
Public offices, audits of, §11-7(f)(6).
Public utility records, §11-7*(l)*.
Rap sheets and other compilations of criminal histories, §11-7(b)(4).
Real estate appraisals, §11-7(f)(5).
Records in general, §11-2.
Salary information, §11-7(a)(2).
School records, §11-7(g).
Segregation of exempt material, §11-6.
Statutory exemptions, §11-5(a).
Trade secrets and certain financial information, §11-5(a)(3).
Trade secrets and proprietary information, §11-7(i).
Unwarranted invasion of privacy, disclosures constituting an, §11-5(a)(5).
Victim information, §11-7(b)(5).
Vital statistics, §11-7(j).
Voting records, §11-7(h).
Waiver of exemptions, §11-5(d).
Wells, oil and gas, §11-5(a)(8).

STATE SHIELD LAWS, §15-2.
Absolute privilege, §15-2(e)(1).
Appellate review, §15-2(i)(3).
Broadcast rules, special, §15-2(i)(4).
In camera review, §15-2(i)(2).
Choice of law, §15-2(j).
Civil proceedings, §15-2(c)(2).
Confidential information, §15-2(d)(2).
Constitutionality, §15-2(a).
Contours of the privilege, §15-2(e).
Criminal proceedings, §15-2(c)(1).
Definitional issues, §15-2(b)(1).
Editorial process materials, §15-2(d)(3)(D).
Exhaustion requirements, §15-2(e)(2)(B).

Eyewitness testimony, §15-2(d)(3)(B).
Immunity distinguished from privilege, §15-2(f).
Juvenile confidentiality, §3-3(a).
Nonconfidential.
   Information, §15-2(d)(3).
   Sources, §15-2(d)(3)(A).
Non-disclosure penalties, §15-2(g).
Non-judicial proceedings, §15-2(c)(2)(C).
Party, press as, §15-2(c)(2)(B).
Penalties for non-disclosure, §15-2(g).
Privilege distinguished from immunity, §15-2(f).
Procedural requirements, §15-2(i).
Procedures in general, §15-2(i)(1).
Proceedings covered in general, §15-2(c).
Published information, §15-2(d)(3)(E).
Qualified privilege, §15-2(e)(2).
Recipients of protection, §15-2(b).
Relevance requirements, §15-2(e)(2)(A).
Scope of protection in general, §15-2(d).
Sources of information, §15-2(d)(1).
Special broadcast rules, §15-2(i)(4).
Standing issues, §15-2(b)(2).
Third-party proceedings, §15-2(c)(2)(A).
Unpublished information, §15-2(d)(3)(C).
Waiver, §15-2(h).

STATE STATUTES.
Audio recording, §13-7(b).
Computer systems, unauthorized access to, §13-9(b).

STENOGRAPHIC TRANSCRIPTS.
Discovery documents, §5-2(a)(5).

STIGMA.
Juvenile proceedings, §3-3(a).

STIPULATION OF THE PARTIES.
Military courts, §5-2(f).
Restraining publication, §2-1(d).

STOLEN PROPERTY.
Means of newsgathering, §13-3.

STRATEGY OF INVESTIGATION.
Grand jury proceedings, §3-1(a)(3).

STREETS, PUBLIC.
Newsgathering in nongovernmental places, §12-2(a).

INDEX

STRUCTURAL ROLE OF THE FIRST AMENDMENT, §1-5.
Supreme Court, constitutional right of access in, §2-2(c).

STUDENT INFORMATION.
State and local government, statutory access to meetings of, §9-6(i)(4).

SUBPOENAS.
Constitutional privilege, avoidance of privilege, §§16-2(j)(1), 16-2(j)(2).
Grand jury records, §5-2(a)(3).

SUNSHINE ACT, §9-5(a). (*See* GOVERNMENT IN THE SUNSHINE ACT).

SUPPRESSION HEARINGS.
Access to, §3-1(a).
Judicial proceedings, access to, §3-1(a)(4).
Judicial records, access to, §5-2(a).
Supreme Court, constitutional right of access in, §§2-2(b), 2-2(f).

SUPREME COURT.
Cameras in the courtroom, §§4-1, 4-2(b).
Constitutional right of access in, §2-2.
El Vocero de Puerto Rico v. Puerto Rico, §2-2(g).
Evolution of journalists' privilege, §14-5.
Gannett Co. v. DePasquale, §2-2(b).
Globe Newspaper Co. v. Superior Court, §2-2(d).
Guidelines, Justice Department, §2-4.
Justice Department guidelines, §2-4.
Perspectives on constitutional right of access, §2-2(a).
Press-Enterprise Co. v. Superior Court (Press-Enterprise I), §§2-2(e), 2-2(h).
Press-Enterprise Co. v. Superior Court (Press-Enterprise II), §§2-2(f), 2-2(h).
Procedural requirements, §2-3.
Richmond Newspapers, Inc. v. Virginia, §2-2(c).
Sources and interview subjects, §13-4(a)(2)(C).
Supreme Court doctrine, §2-2(h).

SUPREME COURT DOCTRINE.
Constitutional right of access in Supreme Court, §2-2(h).

SURROGATE OR AGENT, PRESS AS, §1-4(b).

SURVEILLANCE. (*See also* ELECTRONIC SURVEILLANCE).
Stake outs, §13-5.

T

TABLOID JOURNALISM. (*See* SENSATIONALIZED CASES).

TAPES. (*See* AUDIO RECORDING; VIDEOTAPES AND RECORDINGS).

TAX ON PUBLICATIONS.
Information, right to acquire, §1-3.

TECHNOLOGY. (*See also* ELECTRONIC MEDIA).
Future, cameras in the courtroom, §4-1.

TEXAS.
Executions, §8-2.

THEFT.
Means of newsgathering, §13-3.

THIRD PARTIES.
Discovery documents, §5-2(a)(5).
Discovery materials, §§6-1(a)(3), 6-1(a)(4).
Judicial records, access to, §5-2(a)(1).
Participants in judicial process, access to, §7-1.
State Shield laws, §15-2(c)(2)(A).
Subpoenas, avoidance of constitutional privilege, §16-2(j)(1).

THIRD PARTIES STANDING DOCTRINE, §7-1.

THREATS.
Criminal trials, §3-1(c).

TIME AND TIME LIMITATIONS.
Checkbook journalism, §7-4.
Freedom of Information Act, time limitations, §10-2(b)(4).
Government in the Sunshine Act, challenges to closed meetings, §9-5(a)(9).

INDEX

TIME AND TIME LIMITATIONS— Cont'd
Supreme Court, constitutional right of access in, §2-3.

TOBACCO-RELATED LITIGATION.
Court files, §6-1(c).

TRADE SECRETS.
Cameras in the courtroom, §4-3.
Competing interests, discovery materials, §6-1(a)(5).
Depositions, §3-2(e).
Freedom of Information Act exemptions, §10-2(c)(5).
Government in the Sunshine Act exemptions, §9-5(a)(8)(D).
Judicial proceedings, access to, §3-2(c).
Pretrial motions, records, and pleadings, §6-1(c)(1).
State government records, access to, §§11-5(a)(3), 11-7(i).

TRADITION.
Judicial records, access to, §5-1.
Juvenile proceedings, §3-3(a).
Post-trial matters, §3-1(c).
Pretrial hearings, access to, §3-1(a).
Supreme Court, constitutional right of access in, §2-2(c).

TRANSCRIPTS. (*See also* SEALED RECORDS AND TRANSCRIPTS).
Civil proceedings, §3-2(a).
Closed proceedings, §3-1(b).
Delinquency proceedings, access to judicial records, §6-2(a).
Discovery documents, §5-2(a)(5).
Government in the Sunshine Act, §9-5(a)(6).
Grand jury records, §5-2(a)(3).
Judicial records, access to, §§5-1, 6-1(c)(2).
Pretrial hearings, access to, §3-1(a).
State and local government, statutory access to meetings of, §9-6(f).
Suppression hearings, §5-2(a)(7).
Trade secrets, §3-2(c).
Trial records, §5-2(b).
Videotapes, §5-2(b).
Voir dire, §§3-1(b), 5-1.

TRANSFER HEARINGS.
Court records, §6-2(a).

TRESPASS.
Means of newsgathering, §13-3(c)(1).

TRIAL JUDGES.
Sheppard Mandate, §2-1(b).

TRIAL PROCEEDINGS. (*See* JUDICIAL PROCEEDINGS, ACCESS TO).

U

UMBRELLA ORDERS.
Competing interests, discovery materials, §6-1(a)(5).
Discovery materials, unfiled, §6-1(a)(3).

UNABOMBER TRIAL.
Judicial records, access to, §5-2(a).

UNDERCOVER POLICE.
Criminal trials, §3-1(c).
Pretrial hearings, access to, §3-1(a).

UNITED STATES ARMY COURT OF CRIMINAL APPEALS, §3-1(e).

UNPROTECTED SUBJECT MATTER.
Audio recording, §13-7(b)(4)(D).

UNPUBLISHED INFORMATION.
Constitutional privilege, §16-2(d)(3)(C).

UNRESTRICTED EQUIPMENT, USE OF.
Audio recording, §13-7(b)(4)(E).

UNWARRANTED INVASION OF PRIVACY.
State and local government, statutory access to meetings of, §9-6(h)(4).
State government records, access to, §11-5(a)(5).

UTILITY RATES.
Settlement proceedings, §3-2(d).

V

VENUE CHANGE. (*See* CHANGE OF VENUE).

INDEX

VICTIMS. (*See also* MINOR'S TESTIMONY; SEXUAL OFFENSE VICTIMS).
Police records, access to, §11-7(b)(5).
Supreme Court, constitutional right of access in, §2-2(c).

VIDEOTAPES AND RECORDINGS.
Bail and detention, §5-2(a)(8).
Depositions, §5-2(a)(5).
State and local government, statutory access to meetings of, §9-6(f).
Trial records, transcripts of videotapes, §5-2(b).

VIEW, PUBLIC.
Nongovernmental places, newsgathering in, §12-2(b).

VIOLENCE, PROTECTION OF PARTIES OR WITNESSES FROM.
Pretrial hearings, access to, §3-1(a).

VIOLENT CRIMES.
Juvenile proceedings, §3-3(a).

VIRGINIA.
Criminal sanctions against media, §2-1(c).
Supreme Court, constitutional right of access in, §2-2(c).

VITAL STATISTICS.
State government records, access to, §11-7(j).

VOIR DIRE.
Access to judicial proceedings, §3-1(b).
Cameras in the courtroom, §4-3.
Judicial records, access to, §5-1.
Pretrial hearings, access to, §3-1(a).
Sheppard Mandate, §2-1(b).
Supreme Court, constitutional right of access in, §§2-2(a), 2-2(e).
Transcripts, §5-2(c).

VOTERS AND VOTING.
Public places and events, access to, §8-4.
State government records, access to, §11-7(h).

VOUCHERS, CRIMINAL JUSTICE ACT.
Judicial records, access to, §5-2(e).

W

WAIVER.
Cameras in the courtroom, §4-2(a).
Constitutional privilege, §16-2(g).
State government records access, exemptions, §11-5(d).
State Shield laws, §15-2(h).

WALL STREET JOURNAL.
Juvenile proceedings, §3-3(a).

WARREN COMMISSION, §7-2.

WASHINGTON STATE.
Voters and polling places, §8-4.

WATERGATE SCANDAL.
Judicial records, access to, §5-1.
Trial records, §5-2(b).

WELLS, OIL AND GAS.
Freedom of Information Act exemptions, §10-2(c)(10).
State government records, access to, §11-5(a)(8).

WEST VIRGINIA.
Juvenile offenders, criminal sanctions against media, §2-1(c).

WIRE FRAUD.
Means of newsgathering, §13-3(c)(7).
Voir dire, §3-1(b).

WIRETAPPING.
Judicial records, access to, §5-2(a)(1).
Search warrants, transcripts, §5-2(a)(2).
Suppression hearings, court-ordered wiretaps, §5-2(a)(7).
Wiretap Act, §13-7(a)(2)(A). (*See* FEDERAL WIRETAP ACT).

***WITHERSPOON*-RELATED *VOIR DIRE*,** §3-1(b).

WITNESSES. (*See also* MINOR'S TESTIMONY).
Cameras in the courtroom, §§4-1, 4-3.
Checkbook journalism, §7-4.
Discovery materials, filed, §6-1(a)(4).
Executions, §8-2.
Grand jury proceedings, §§3-1(a)(2), 3-1(a)(3).
Grand jury records, §5-2(a)(3).

INDEX

WITNESSES—Cont'd
Transcripts of *voir dire*, §5-2(c).

WORLD TRADE CENTER BOMBING CASE, §7-2.

REF KF 2750 .D54 1999

For Reference

Not to be taken from this room

Poynter Institute
93008361